Collins Chinese Dictionary

www.collins.co.uk

Collins® and Bank of English® are registered trademarks of HarperCollins Publishers Limited

Collins is an imprint of HarperCollins Publishers

ISBN 0-00-716329-0

HarperCollins Publishers, Inc.
10 East 53rd Street, New York, NY 10022

ISBN 0-06-059532-9

CIP information available on request

HarperCollins books may be purchased for educational, business, or sales promotional use. For information, please write to: Special Markets Department,
HarperCollins Publishers Inc., 10 East 53rd Street
New York, NY 10022

www.harpercollins.com

Typeset by Lexus Ltd and Wordcraft

A catalogue record for this book is available from the British Library

Printed and bound in Italy by Legoprint S.P.A.

EDITORI

吴

Marianne Davidson, Julie Kleeman, Sarah Waldram

顾凌志　顾越施　李欣　梅榕　申丕
吴乐军　於斌　赵立光

Julie Le Boulanger, Anthony Coogan, Kellie Dunn, Raphaëlle Frappin, Bob Grossmith, Jane Goldie, Julie Helmert, Derek Hird, Cordelia Lilly, Toby Lincoln, Duncan Marshall, Tom Mitford, Peter Offord, Rachel Stein, Peter Terrell, Esther Tyldesley

English-Chinese translation in collaboration with Lexus Ltd

SPECIAL CONSULTANTS/ **特邀顾问**

董琨教授，中国社会科学院语言研究所
Professor Dong Kun, Institute of Linguistics, Chinese Academy of Social Sciences

王立弟教授，北京外国语大学高级翻译学院院长
Professor Wang Lidi, Graduate School of Translation and Interpretation, Beijing Foreign Studies University

Dr David Pattinson, Department of East Asian Studies, Leeds University

Jack Halpern, The CJK Dictionary Institute, Inc.

FOR THE PUBLISHERS/ **出版经理人**

Jeremy Butterfield
Lorna Knight
Helen Newstead

TYPESETTING/ **排版**

Wordcraft
Elfreda Crehan for Lexus Ltd

Special thanks to Jim Kell of the Bell Educational Trust for access to the linguistic queries sent to the China Daily 21st Century Bell Language Column between 1998 and 2002.

William Collins' dream of knowledge for all began with the publication of his first book in 1819. A self-educated mill worker, he not only enriched millions of lives, but also founded a flourishing publishing house. Today, staying true to this spirit, Collins books are packed with inspiration, innovation and practical expertise. They place you at the centre of a world of possibility and give you exactly what you need to explore it.

Language is the key to this exploration, and at the heart of Collins Dictionaries is language as it is really used. New words, phrases and meanings spring up every day, and all of them are captured and analysed by the Collins Word Web. Constantly updated, and with over 2.5 billion entries, this living language resource is unique to our dictionaries.

Words are tools for life. And a Collins Dictionary makes them work for you.

Collins. Do more.

出版前言

《外研社－柯林斯英汉汉英词典》由外语教学与研究出版社和英国柯林斯出版公司共同合作出版。柯林斯出版公司是一家以出版词典见长的出版社。自1824年出版第一部英语词典起，她出版词典的历史至今已将近有200年，属于世界上几大词典出版社之一，我国英语学习者所熟知的Collins Cobuild词典系列即是其旗下的品牌。

《外研社－柯林斯英汉汉英词典》就是同样以出版词典为强项的外研社联合柯林斯出版公司共同推出的一部专门针对中国英国英语学习者编写的词典。为什么这样说？

一、由中英两国词典专家共同编纂。本词典的英语词条是由以英语为母语的英国词典专家编写完成；中文词条则由中国社会科学院语言研究所专家在计算机词频统计的基础上编辑遴选出来。这样编纂出来的词典才能保证是真实的和可靠的，而且为了保证译文规范、准确、地道，中英双方的词典编纂专家密切协作，对翻译和词义进行了深入的探讨、磋商。丰富翔实的例证突出表现了典型的真实语境。

二、基于世界上最大的语料库一柯林斯Word Web语料库。这个收词25亿的数字化英语宝库不仅包含了多种英式英语和美式英语的语篇，而且每日更新，保证了语料的真实、自然和时代感。

三、注重搭配。本词典不仅标出了动词、名词、形容词同介词的搭配，也提供了动词与副词，动词与名词，形容词与名词的搭配用法。

四、特设“词义提示”专栏。本词典的另一大特色是在多义项词条的每一义项之首提供了“词义提示”，方便了读者对释义的检索。

另外各项语言知识专栏不仅诠释语法、用法难点，而且对有典型文化内涵的词，提供了详细的背景知识和介绍。附录涵盖大量日常交际用语、多种书信范例及公文写作指南，进一步增加了这部词典的实用价值。

综上所述，《外研社－柯林斯英汉汉英词典》在设计上充分考虑到读者的实际需求，从独特的英语视角将许多新信息纳入该词典，相信必然会对广大的英语学习者带来裨益。

学术与辞书部
外语教学与研究出版社

林戊荪先生序

这本词典的出版是个创举。本来，英汉汉英词典在我国就极少见，由中英两家以出词典见长的出版社联手编辑外语词典，更是出版观念上的突破。那么，英汉汉英双向词典以及两国出版社联手编词典的优势究竟在哪里？

年轻时在美国学法语时曾用过法英英法词典。我的切身体会是，这类词典对于初学者来说，不仅使用便捷，而且会有助于他们重视两种语言之间的相互转换，并逐步学会用自己母语以外的另一种语言思考问题。初学翻译者，则更需要使用这类词典。

两国出版社和语言专家联手编纂词典的最大优势在于：为使用者提供了地道的中英文解释和例句，这是两国专家经过共同讨论取得的成果。这里，不妨举几个例子加以说明。斜体处皆为地道的中英文。

踩：
解释：贬低（别人）puts down
例句：He never praises people – he only *puts them down.*

睬：
解释：take notice of
例句：他太没人缘，晚会上没人睬他。He is *not very good with people* and no one *takes any notice of* him at parties.

再看英汉部分，也颇有特色。这里因篇幅所限，只能提到在我看来是最可取的一点。英语中的“暗礁”往往是那些常见的、源于Anglo-Saxon语、拼写起来很简单的“小字”。这些多义词有许多习惯用法，初学者遇到了要加倍小心，切不可自以为是。有的字和短语，看来面熟，但用你已知的意思上下文无法加以解释，此时就要查阅词典，直到使“暗礁”浮出水面为止。如back的不同用法:

to break the back of a job 度过最艰难的时刻
to do sth behind sb's back 背着某人做某事
to have one's back to the wall 陷入绝境
to take the back seat（退居二线）把权力让与他人
to turn one's back on sb 不理睬某人

又如brain 和break:

to pick sb's brains 问某人的意见
to break the news to sb 委婉地向某人透露消息
to take a break 休息一下
a lucky break 好运气

现代人编词典，不再靠个人或少数人奋斗，而依托庞大的语料库。如柯林斯的Cobuild语料库，就从报刊图书和广播电视中搜集了25亿的资料，并在此基础上编纂词典。这一做法，绝非任何个人或集体靠手工操作能力所能达到的。使用这类英语语料库编纂的词典可以保证我们学到最常用、最地道的英语。无论你是学生还是商业人士，你都可从中找到你所需要的英语知识。

人们喜欢用活字典来形容一位博学的老师。其实，词典就是位随叫随到、百问不厌的老师，是人们学外语、做翻译须臾不可或缺的良师益友。目前，市场上词典种类繁多，令人眼花缭乱，选好和用好词典是门学问，但愿这篇简短的介绍能多少有助于你做出正确的选择。

前外文局局长
中国翻译工作者协会常务副会长
全国高级翻译专业职称评委会主任
《中国翻译》主编
林戊荪
2004年4月20日

▼ 目录/Contents

如何使用本词典

英汉部分

以下是词典中出现的主要内容的提纲。我们旨在尽可能清晰、有效地为你提供最详尽的说明。

1 顺序

1.1 在英语部分，除了短语动词外(见1.3)，所有词条都严格按照字母顺序排列。例如，开头字母为大写的词条位于拼写相同但以小写字母开头的词条前面。

1.2 词条的排列顺序如下：

大写字母
小写字母
大写+句点
小写+句点
大写+数字
小写+数字

B
b.
B4
BA

1.3 短语动词出现在所属的词条末尾，其他同根词条之前。例如，**buy back**, **buy in**, **buy into**, **buy off**, **buy out** 和 **buy up** 都出现在 **buyer** 之前。

1.4 除了短语动词，两个或两个以上单词构成的复合词按照字母顺序以词条的形式出现：

pedestrian
pedestrian crossing
pedestrianized
pedestrian precinct

2 同音异义词

2.1 书写相同但发音完全不同的单词作为单独的词条出现，并且用数字上标加以区分：

bow[1] [bəu] *n* [c] **1** (*knot*) 蝴蝶结 **2** (*weapon*) 弓 **3** [音] 琴弓
bow[2] [bau] **I** *n* [c] **1** (*of head, body*) 鞠躬 **2** [航海] (*also:* ***bows***) 船首 **II** *vi* (*with head, body*) 鞠躬 **III** *vt* [+ *head*]

如上所示，数字上标明确表明该单词的发音完全不同。

2.2 书写和发音都相同的单词视作同一词条：

bear [bɛə(r)] (*pt* **bore,** *pp* **borne**) **I** *n* [c] (*animal*) 熊 **II** *vt* **1** [文] (*carry*) [+ *object*] 携带 **2** (*support*) [+ *weight*] 支撑 **3** [+ *responsibility*] 承担 **4** [+ *cost*] 负担 **5** (*tolerate*) [+ *person*]

2.3 如果单词的重音随词性的变化而变化，不同的词性及相应的音标列在同一词条下：

escort [*n* ˈɛskɔːt, *vb* ɪsˈkɔːt]

3 词条的变化形式

3.1 词条的某些部分可置于圆括号中，表明两种书写形式均可：

among(st) [əˈmʌŋ(st)] *prep*

3.2 单词的拼写变化也作为单独的词条录入，并参见首先出现的拼写形式：

maneuver [məˈnuːvə(r)] [美] *vt, vi, n* **= manoeuvre**

3.3 单词的美式拼写总是在括号中给出：

axe (美 **ax**) [æks]

3.4 不规则动词的时态变化和不规则名词的复数形式作为单独的词条出现，并且指示参照原形：

went [wɛnt] *pt of* **go**

children [ˈtʃɪldrən] *n* [*pl*] *of* **child**

4 词目构成

本词典中的词目通常由下列要素构成：

4.1 词条

本词典收录了500个最常用的英语单词，并且加注特别的标志，以帮助读者明确学习和理解的先后次序。在这些单词中，列举了大量真实地道的例句，有助于了解单词在真实语言环境中的用法。

✪**decision** [dɪˈsɪʒən] *n* **1** [c] (*choice*) 决定 ◊ *The government has announced its decision.* 政府已经宣布了决定。**2** [u] (*act of choosing*) 决心 ◊ *The moment of decision can't be delayed.* 下决心的时刻不能拖了。**3** [u] (*decisiveness*) 决断力 ♦ **to make a decision** 作出决定

4.2 音标

英语单词的注音采用国际音标(IPA)，用方括号标识。完整的音标表参见第31页。注音以英式发音为主，当美式发音与英式发音完全不同时，加注美式发音，例如 *schedule*, *vase*。

vase [vɑːz, (美) veɪs]

4.3 语法结构

4.3.1 词性

词性用小写斜体字母表注在单词的音标后。如果一个单词有一个以上的词性，用罗马数字标识：

key [kiː] **I** *n* [C] **1** (*for lock, mechanism*) 钥匙 **2** [*of computer, typewriter, piano*] 键 **3** [音] 调 **4** ♦**the key (to sth)** (*to*

词性列表参见第29页。

4.3.2 名词

C, U, S 和 PL 等符号表示名词的各种形式。

C表示可数名词，并具有复数形式(例如：*I'm reading a book; she's bought several books*)。

U表示不可数名词，不具有复数形式(例如：*Lesley refused to give me more information*)。

S(用于单数名词)是指该名词总是用作单数，而且通常跟在 *a*, *an* 或 *the* 之后(例如：*We need to persuade people to respect the environment.*)。

PL 是指该名词总是用作复数形式，并且相关的动词或代词也相应地使用复数形式(例如：*These clothes are ready to wear.*)。

hairdryer [ˈhɛədraɪə(r)] *n* [C] 吹风机
hair gel *n* [U] 发胶
kick-off [ˈkɪkɔf] [体育] *n* [S] 开场时间

4.3.3 短语动词的词性

VI — 用作不及物动词，动词及其小品词不可分开：

❑**melt away** *vi* **1** [*people* +] 逐渐散去 **2** [*doubts* +] 消除

VT — 用作及物动词，动词及其小品词可用宾语隔开。

VT [不可拆分] — 用作及物动词，动词及其小品词不能分开的：

❑**laugh at** *vt* [不可拆分] **1** [字] 对…发笑 **2** [喻] (*mock*) 嘲笑
❑**laugh off** *vt* [+ *criticism, problem*] 对…一笑置之

4.3.4 动词和名词的变体

动词和名词的不规则变化直接列在相关的词条后, 便于查阅:

✪**child** [tʃaɪld] (*pl* **children**) *n* [c]

✪**fly** [flaɪ] (*pt* **flew**, *pp* **flown**) **I** *vt*

4.4 词义划分

4.4.1 如果一个单词有一个以上的词义, 则归入不同的意类, 用阿拉伯数字标出:

challenging [ˈtʃælɪndʒɪŋ] *adj*
1 [+ *job, task*] 具有挑战性的
2 [+ *tone, look etc*] 挑衅的

4.4.2 进一步的词义区分在括号中用斜体表示, 包括下列几种情况:

同义词置于在圆括号中，有助于拓展英语知识。

definitive [dɪˈfɪnɪtɪv] *adj*
1 (*conclusive*) [+ *answer*] 确定的
2 (*authoritative*) [+ *version, account*] 权

使用词条的主要语境也置于括号中, 例如:

— 用作及物动词的名词宾语:

tighten [ˈtaɪtn] **I** *vt* **1** [+ *rope, strap*] 拉紧 **2** [+ *screw, bolt*] 弄紧 **3** [+ *grip, security, rules etc*] 加紧 **II** *vi* **1** [*grip* +]

— 用作不及物动词的名词主语:

circulate [ˈsəːkjuleɪt] **I** *vi* [*traffic, blood* +] 循环; [*news, rumour* +] 散播; [*person* +] (*at party*) 交际 **II** *vt* [+ *report*] 传阅

— 用作形容词的名词补足语:

tasteless [ˈteɪstlɪs] *adj* **1** [+ *food*] 无味的 **2** [+ *remark, joke*] 不雅的 **3** [+ *furniture, decor etc*] 低俗的

— 其他用于界定或限制该词条的单词：

believer [bɪ'liːvə(r)] *n* [c] **1** (*in idea, activity*) 笃信者 **2** [宗] 信徒

用汉语标注词条的专业学科领域：

bishop ['bɪʃəp] *n* [c] **1** [宗] 主教 **2** [国际象棋] 象

本词典中所使用的所有专业学科领域缩略词参见第29页。

4.5 短语

短语用黑体表示，并跟在实心黑体菱形标志后。短语包括不同种类的固定结构，感叹语和其他语法结构：

to do something behind sb's back
back and forth
too bad!
on balance
to begin to do *or* doing sth

4.6 例子

例子用斜体表示。英语中最常用的500个单词，都给出了大量的例子及在相应语境中的翻译，有助于读者在具体的语境中正确使用单词。

✪**large** [lɑːdʒ] *adj* **1** (*big*) [+ *house, person etc*] 大的；[+ *number, amount*] 大量的 ◊ *a large number of people* 许多人 ◊ *We are facing a large number of problems.* 我们面临大量的问题。**2** (*serious*) [+ *problem, question*] 重大的 ♦**at large** (*as a whole*) 整个 ◊ *their attitude to the* …

4.7 翻译

一般情况下，作为最精确、有效的方法，每个意义只提供一个翻译。

在某些情况下，如果根本没有相应的翻译对等语，则提供该词的解释，而不是翻译。

au pair ['əu'pɛə(r)] *n* [c] 为学习语言而住在当地人家里并提供家政服务的外国年轻人

5 语体形式

使用正确的语体与人交流是十分重要的。给公司同事写信和给朋友写信需要使用两种不同的语体。为了帮助使用者选择正确恰当的语体，本词典在英汉和汉英两部分都对单词和表达方式作了标注。

修辞色彩缩略语列表见第30页。

6 关键词

标注了KEYWORD的单词，例如 **have** 和 **do**，都是英语中使用最频繁的单词。因为它们是构成英语的基本要素，并且具有多种不同的词义和用法，故对其进行尤为详细深入的注释。本词典对关键词作了特别的设计，便于读者查找词义及用法搭配。

✪ have

KEYWORD

[hæv] (*pt, pp* **had**)

I *vt*

1 (*possess*) 有 ♦**he has** *or* **he has got blue eyes/dark hair** 他长着蓝眼睛/黑头发 ♦**do you have** *or* **have you got a car/phone?** 你有车/电话吗？♦**I have** *or* **I have got an idea** 我有个主意 ♦**to have** *or* **have got sth to do** 有必须得做的事 ♦**she had her eyes closed** 她闭上了眼睛

2 (*with meals, drinks*) ♦**to have breakfast** 吃早饭 ♦**to have a**

...

7 语言注释

为了帮助读者更加准确、熟巧地掌握并运用英语，我们对一些易混淆词进行了详细的比较说明。

📖 用**fat**形容某人胖，显得过于直接，甚至有些粗鲁。比较礼貌而又含蓄的说法是**plump**或**chubby**，后者更为正式。**overweight**和**obese**暗示某人因为肥胖而有健康问题。**obese**是医学术语，表示某人极度肥胖或超重。一般而言，应尽量避免当面使用任何表示肥胖的词语。

7 文化注释

对于英语国家中特有的文化现象，我们都加注了说明及解释。

> **MISS, MRS, MS**
> 在说英语的国家中，**Mrs**（夫人）用于已婚女士的姓名前。**Miss**（小姐）用于未婚女士的姓名前。有些女士认为，让人们知道她是否结婚并不重要，所以往往用**Ms**（女士）称呼自己。与**Mr**（先生）类似，**Ms**不表明任何婚姻状况。

如何使用本词典

汉英部分

以下是词典中出现的主要内容的提纲。本词典旨在尽可能清晰、有效地为你提供最详尽的说明。

1 顺序

1.1 在汉语部分, 词目按传统顺序排列, 即单字词条下嵌入以相同汉字开头的多字词条。

这 zhè
这个 zhège
这里 zhèlǐ
这么 zhème
这些 zhèxiē
蔗 zhè
蔗糖 zhètáng

1.2 单字词条按拼音字母顺序排序, 再按声调顺序排序。注意, 轻声排在四声之后。同音字按笔画的多寡排列, 笔画少的在前, 笔画多的在后。

召 zhào
兆 zhào
照 zhào

笔画相同的同音字按起笔笔画排列, 顺序为: 一 丨 丿 丶 乛

1.3 单字词条下的多字词条也先按照拼音(包括声调), 再按照笔画数进行排序。

蒸 zhēng
蒸馏 zhēngliú
蒸气 zhēngqì
蒸汽 zhēngqì

2 部首和汉字索引

如果使用者不知道所使用汉字的发音, 部首目录和检字表位于汉英部分之前。有关如何使用部首索引, 参见部首和汉字索引的第一部分。

3 交叉索引

多音字,即有一个以上发音的汉字,会标明“另见”，后接另一个发音。

> 供 gōng [动] **1** (供应) supply **2** (提供) provide
> ▷另见 gòng
>
> 供 gòng **I** [动] **1** (供奉) lay (*pt, pp* laid) ◊供奉祭品 lay offerings **2** (招
> …
> ▷另见 gōng

4 词目构成

汉语部分的词条有两个层次,单字词条和多字词条,但它们的构成方式基本相同:

4.1 拼音

所有词条都标注汉语拼音。

4.2 语法结构

4.2.1 词性在方括号中用中文标注，紧随拼音之后。如果有一个以上的词性,用罗马数字标识:

> 早 zǎo **I** [名] morning **II** [副] a long time ago ◊这事我早就知道了。I knew about this a long time ago. **III** [形] early ♦早餐 breakfast ◊你早点来。Come early.

词性列表参见第29页。

4.2.2 惯用语，包括成语和其他惯用语，作为单独的条目列出，但不标词性。

4.3 词义划分

4.3.1 如果一个词条有一个以上的词义,则归入不同的意类,用阿拉伯数字标出。

> 震 zhèn **I** [动] **1** (震动) shake (*pt* shook, *pp* shaken) **2** (激动) be excited **II** [名] earthquake ◊余震 after-shock

4.3.2 当一个词条有多种含义时，读者可以根据阿拉伯数字后圆括号中的信息找到相关的语境，进而查到正确的翻译。圆括号中的信息起到“路标”的功能，指向恰当的翻译。圆括号有如下几种功用:

主词条的同义词或近义词:

> 症候 zhènghòu [名] **1** (症状) symptom **2** (疾病) disease

典型语境:在括号中显示使用主词条的典型情境,例如:

— 动词的名词宾语或主语:

> 旺 wàng [形] **1** (火) roaring **2** (人、生意) flourishing **3** (花) blooming ◇十月菊花开得正旺。In October the chrysanthemums are in full bloom.

— 形容词的名词补足语:

> 细 xì **I** [形] **1** (绳、线等) thin **2** (沙、粮等) fine **3** (声、语等) gentle **4** (节、则等) detailed ♦细节 details (*pl*) **II** [副] minutely ♦细看 scrutinize ◇细问 ask in detail ◇细想 consider carefully

— 定义或用于限制主词条的其他词:

> 蒸 zhēng [动] **1** (指烹饪方法) steam **2** (蒸发) evaporate

— 该词使用的专业领域:

> 硬件 yìngjiàn [名] **1** (计算机) hardware **2** (设备) equipment

用修辞色彩缩略语标注语体色彩:

> 治学 zhìxué [动] (书) study

修辞色彩缩略语列表见第29页。

4.4 例子

4.4.1 以词的形式出现的例子,包括少数的四字习语(成语等),作为该汉字的核心意义出现在解释之后,前面用实心的菱形♦标出。

4.4.2 更完整的例子,前面用空心的菱形◇标出。

4.5 翻译

4.5.1 一般情况下,作为最精确、有效的方法,每个意义只提供一个翻译。

4.5.2 在某些情况下,如果根本没有相应的翻译对等语,则提供该词的解释，而不是翻译，用斜体表示。

> 压岁钱 yāsuìqián [名] *traditional gifts of money given to children during the Spring Festival*

4.5.3 不规则动词的过去式和过去分词和名词的复数形式出现在英语翻译之后，便于查阅。不规则动词的过去式和过去分词形式的完整列表见第32页。

> 包涵 bāohán [动] forgive (*pt* forgave, *pp* forgiven) ◇招待不周，请多包涵！ Please forgive me for giving you such a poor reception.

4.5.4 以-s 结尾的名词，若用作复数，则标注为pl，若用作单数，则标注为sg

> 鬓发 bìnfà [名] sideburns (*pl*)

> 丛书 cóngshū [名] series (*sg*)

4.5.5 必要时，同时给出美式英语和英式英语两种翻译。

> 棒子 bàngzi [名] **1** (棍子) club **2** (玉米) corn (英), maize (美)

4.5.6 可供选择的部分前标有“或”：

> 摄影 shèyǐng [动] **1** (照相) take a photo (*pt* took, *pp* taken) **2** (拍电影) shoot a film (英) 或 movie (美) (*pt*, *pp* shot)

5 语言注释

为了帮助读者更加准确、熟巧地掌握并运用英语，我们对一些易混淆词进行了详细的比较说明。

> 📖 **person** 的复数形式通常为 **people**。 *At least fifty-four people have been killed.* **persons** 通常只用于非常正式的场合，或作为法律用语。

How to use the Dictionary

ENGLISH-CHINESE SIDE

Below you will find an outline of how information is presented in your dictionary. Our aim is to give you the maximum amount of detail in the clearest and most helpful way.

1 Alphabetical order

1.1 On the English side, strict alphabetical order applies for all headwords except for phrasal verbs (see 1.3 below). For instance, a headword with an initial capital comes before the same word with a lower-case initial.

1.2 Alphabetical order for headwords is as follows:

upper case
lower case
upper case + full stop
lower case + full stop
upper case + numeral
lower case + numeral

B
b.
B4
BA *etc.*

1.3 Phrasal verbs appear in alphabetical order at the end of the entry they belong with and before any other headwords. Thus, **buy back**, **buy in**, **buy into**, **buy off**, **buy out** and **buy up** all appear before **buyer**.

1.4 Except for phrasal verbs, all other compounds consisting of two or more words are shown as headwords in alphabetical order:

pedestrian
pedestrian crossing
pedestrianized
pedestrian precinct

2 Homonyms

2.1 Words which are written in the same way but have different pronunciations are shown as separate headwords and differentiated by the use of numbers:

bow[1] [bəu] *n* [c] **1** (*knot*) 蝴蝶结 **2** (*weapon*) 弓 **3** (音) 琴弓
bow[2] [bau] **I** *n* [c] **1** (*of head, body*) 鞠躬 **2** (航海) (*also:* ***bows***) 船首 **II** *vi* (*with head, body*) 鞠躬 **III** *vt* [+ *head*]

2.2 Words which are written in the same way and have the same pronunciation are treated at the same headword:

bear [bɛə(r)] (*pt* **bore,** *pp* **borne**) **I** *n* [c] (*animal*) 熊 **II** *vt* **1** [文](*carry*) [+ *object*] 携带 **2** (*support*) [+ *weight*] 支撑 **3** [+ *responsibility*] 承担 **4** [+ *cost*] 负担 **5** (*tolerate*) [+ *person*]

2.3 Where the stress in a word changes according to which part of speech it is being used in, the different parts of speech are treated under the same headword, and the change of stress is indicated in the phonetic transcription:

escort [*n* ˈɛskɔːt, *vb* ɪsˈkɔːt]

3 Alternative forms of headwords

3.1 Part of a headword may be placed within round brackets to indicate that it is optional:

among(st) [əˈmʌŋ(st)] *prep*

3.2 Spelling variants of headwords are entered as headwords and cross-referred to the primary form thus:

maneuver [məˈnuːvə(r)] [美] *vt, vi, n* = **manoeuvre**

3.3 American spellings of words are always shown, at the headword which is spelled in the British way:

axe (美 **ax**) [æks]

3.4 Past tenses of irregular verbs, and inflections of irregular nouns are shown as headwords in their own right and cross-referred to the base form:

went [wɛnt] *pt of* **go**

children [ˈtʃɪldrən] *n* [*pl*] *of* **child**

4 The structure of entries

A typical English entry in your dictionary will be made up of the following elements:

4.1 The headword

As noted above, a part of the headword may be placed in brackets to show that it is optional, or a spelling variant of the headword may also be shown directly after the headword.

4.2 **Phonetic transcription**

Phonetics for English words appear in square brackets immediately after the headword. They are shown using the International Phonetic Alphabet (IPA), and a complete list of the symbols used in this system can be found on page 31. The pronunciation given is for British English, but the American pronunciation is also shown where the pronunciation differs significantly from the British form, eg schedule, vase.

vase [vɑːz, (美) veɪs]

4.3 **Grammatical information**

4.3.1 Parts of speech appear in italic, lower case after the phonetic spelling of the headword. Where a word has more than one part of speech, Roman numerals are used:

key [kiː] **I** *n* [c] **1** *(for lock, mechanism)* 钥匙 **2** *[of computer, typewriter, piano]* 键 **3** [音] 调 **4** ♦**the key (to sth)** *(to*

For a full list of parts of speech used, see page 29.

4.3.2 We have used the notation C, U and S and PL to show whether nouns are countable, uncountable, singular or plural. C means that the noun is countable, and has a plural form (eg *I'm reading a book; she's bought several books*). U means that the noun is not normally counted, and is not used in the plural (eg *Lesley refused to give me more information*). S (for singular noun) means the noun is always singular, and is usually preceded by *a*, *an* or *the* (eg *We need to persuade people to respect the environment*). PL means the noun is always plural, and is used with plural verbs or pronouns (eg *These clothes are ready to wear*).

hairdryer ['hɛədraɪə(r)] *n* [c] 吹风机
hair gel *n* [u] 发胶
kick-off ['kɪkɔf] [体育] *n* [s] 开场时间

4.3.3 For phrasal verbs, the parts of speech we have used are explained below:
VI – the verb and its particle are never separated, and the meaning is intransitive:

❑ **melt away** *vi* **1** *[people +]* 逐渐散去 **2** *[doubts +]* 消除

VT – the verb and its particle can be separated by the object and the meaning is transitive.
VT [不可拆分] – the verb and its particle cannot be separated, and the overall meaning is transitive :

❑**laugh at** *vt* [不可拆分] **1** [字] 对…发笑 **2** [喻] (*mock*) 嘲笑
❑**laugh off** *vt* [+ *criticism, problem*] 对…一笑置之

4.3.4 Information on irregular inflections of verbs and nouns is shown after the headword to enable you to use the word correctly:

✪**child** [tʃaɪld] (*pl* **children**) *n* [c]

✪**fly** [flaɪ] (*pt* **flew**, *pp* **flown**) **I** *vt*

4.4 **Meaning divisions**

4.4.1 Where a word or a grammatical category has more than one meaning, it is divided into categories which are shown by an Arabic numeral:

challenging ['tʃælɪndʒɪŋ] *adj*
1 [+ *job, task*] 具有挑战性的
2 [+ *tone, look etc*] 挑衅的

4.4.2 Distinctions of meaning are shown by the use of bracketed information in italics, which can be of the following kinds:

– a synonym of the headword, which is placed in round brackets.

definitive [dɪ'fɪnɪtɪv] *adj*
1 (*conclusive*) [+ *answer*] 确定的
2 (*authoritative*) [+ *version, account*] 权

– a typical context for the headword, shown in square brackets, such as:

– noun objects for transitive verbs:

tighten ['taɪtn] **I** *vt* **1** [+ *rope, strap*] 拉紧 **2** [+ *screw, bolt*] 弄紧 **3** [+ *grip, security, rules etc*] 加紧 **II** *vi* **1** [*grip* +]

– noun subjects for intransitive verbs:

circulate ['səːkjuleɪt] **I** *vi* [*traffic, blood* +] 循环; [*news, rumour* +] 散播; [*person* +] (*at party*) 交际 **II** *vt* [+ *report*] 传阅

– noun complements for adjectives:

tasteless ['teɪstlɪs] *adj* **1** [+ *food*] 无味的 **2** [+ *remark, joke*] 不雅的
3 [+ *furniture, decor etc*] 低俗的

– other words defining or restricting the headword:

believer [bɪ'liːvə(r)] *n* [c] **1** *(in idea, activity)* 笃信者 **2** [宗] 信徒

– a label in Chinese indicating the field in which the word is used:

bishop ['bɪʃəp] *n* [c] **1** [宗] 主教 **2** [国际象棋] 象

You will find a complete list of labels used in the dictionary on page 29.

4.5 Phrases

These are shown in bold preceded by a solid black lozenge. Phrases include set constructions of many different kinds, as well as exclamations and grammatical structures:

to do something behind sb's back
back and forth
too bad!
on balance
to begin to do *or* doing sth

4.6 Examples

Examples are shown in italics preceded by an empty lozenge. The most common 500 words in English have all been given a significant number of examples to help you to use the translations in context.

✪ **large** [lɑːdʒ] *adj* **1** *(big)* [+ *house, person etc*] 大的; [+ *number, amount*] 大量的 ◊ *a large number of people* 许多人 ◊ *We are facing a large number of problems.* 我们面临大量的问题。**2** *(serious)* [+ *problem, question*] 重大的 ♦ **at large** *(as a whole)* 整个 ◊ *their attitude to the* ...

4.7 Translations

In general, we have only given one translation per meaning, since we believe this is the most accurate and helpful approach. In a few cases, there is no equivalent at all, and an explanation rather than a translation has to be given.

au pair ['əu'pɛə(r)] *n* [c] 为学习语言而住在当地人家里并提供家政服务的外国年轻人

5 Levels of formality and familiarity

It is very important to communicate with the person you are talking or writing to in a way which is appropriate to the nature of the relationship between you. You would write very differently to a business colleague and to a friend. In order to help you choose which forms of expression to use and which to avoid, we have labelled words and expressions on both sides. The full list of these labels in on page 30.

6 **Keywords**

Words given the heading KEYWORD, such as **have** and **do**, are among the most widely used in English. They have been treated in special depth because they constitute the basic elements of English and have very many uses and meanings. We have given them a special design to make it easier to find the meaning or construction you are looking for.

✪ **have**
KEYWORD
[hæv] (*pt, pp* **had**)
I *vt*
1 (*possess*) 有 ♦**he has** *or* **he has got blue eyes/dark hair** 他长着蓝眼睛/黑头发 ♦**do you have** *or* **have you got a car/phone?** 你有车/电话吗? ♦**I have** *or* **I have got an idea** 我有个主意 ♦**to have** *or* **have got sth to do** 有必须得做的事 ♦**she had her eyes closed** 她闭上了眼睛
2 (*with meals, drinks*) ♦**to have breakfast** 吃早饭 ♦**to have a**

...

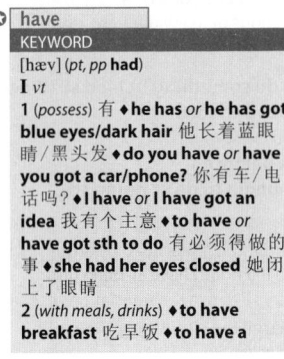

CHINESE-ENGLISH SIDE

1 **Order**

1.1 On the Chinese side, head entries are ordered traditionally, that is by single-character entries with multiple-character entries beginning with the same character nested below them.

这	zhè
这个	zhège
这里	zhèlǐ
这么	zhème
这些	zhèxiē
这样	zhèyàng
这种	zhèzhǒng
蔗	zhè
蔗糖	zhètáng
贞	zhēn
贞操	zhēncāo

1.2 Single character entries are ordered by pinyin, that is alphabetically and then by tone. In Chinese, there are four tones, each represented by a different mark above the relevant vowel:

¯	first tone	(flat tone)	mā
ˊ	second tone	(rising tone)	má
ˇ	third tone	(falling rising tone)	mǎ
ˋ	fourth tone	(falling tone)	mà
	light or no tone		ma

Where characters have the same pinyin and tone, they are ordered by the number of strokes in the characters, with the smallest number of strokes first.

召 zhào
兆 zhào
照 zhào

Where characters have the same pinyin, tone, and number of strokes, they are ordered by the first stroke in the character, as follows:

一丨丿丶乛

1.3 The multiple-character entries nested below single-character entries are similarly ordered by pinyin (including tone), and then by number of strokes.

蒸 zhēng
蒸馏 zhēngliú
蒸气 zhēngqì
蒸汽 zhēngqì

2 **Radical and character index**

If you do not know the pronunciation for the Chinese character you are looking for, you can use the index before the start of the Chinese-English side. For further information on how to use the radical index, see the introduction to that section.

3 **Cross-references**

Polyphones, that is characters with more than one pronunciation, are cross-referred to the alternative pinyin.

供 gōng [动] **1** (供应) supply **2** (提供) provide
▷另见 gòng

供 gòng **I** [动] **1** (供奉) lay (*pt, pp* laid) ◇供奉祭品 lay offerings **2** (招
...
▷另见 gōng

4 The structure of entries

On the Chinese side there are two levels of entry (single-character entries and multiple-character entries), but these are essentially structured the same way:

4.1 Pinyin

Pinyin romanization is given for all single-character and multiple-character entries.

4.2 Grammatical Information

4.2.1 Parts of speech appear in square brackets after the pinyin. Where a word has more than one part of speech, Roman numerals are used:

> 早 zǎo **I** [名] morning **II** [副] a long time ago ◊这事我早就知道了。 I knew about this a long time ago. **III** [形] early ♦早餐 breakfast ◊你早点来。 Come early.

For a full list of parts of speech used, see page 29.

4.2.2 Parts of speech are not given for head idioms (chengyu and other idioms), since these are often phrasal.

4.3 Meaning divisions

4.3.1 Where a word or grammatical category has more than one meaning, it is divided into categories which are shown by an Arabic numeral.

> 震 zhèn **I** [动] **1** (震动) shake (*pt* shook, *pp* shaken) **2** (激动) be excited **II** [名] earthquake ◊余震 after-shock

4.3.2 Further distinctions of meaning are shown by the use of information in round brackets after the meaning category number. This information functions as a 'signpost' to help the user select the right translation when there are many different possible translations to choose from. This indicating material can be of the following kinds:

– a synonym of the headword, or superordinate:

> 症候 zhènghòu [名] **1** (症状) symptom **2** (疾病) disease

– a typical context for the headword, shown in brackets, such as:

– noun objects and subjects for verbs:

旺 wàng [形] **1** (火) roaring **2** (人、生意) flourishing **3** (花) blooming ◇十月菊花开得正旺。In October the chrysanthemums are in full bloom.

– noun complements for adjectives:

细 xì **I** [形] **1** (绳、线等) thin **2** (沙、粮等) fine **3** (声、语等) gentle **4** (节、则等) detailed ♦细节 details (*pl*) **II** [副] minutely ♦细看 scrutinize ◇细问 ask in detail ◇细想 consider carefully

– other words defining or restricting the headword:

蒸 zhēng [动] **1** (指烹饪方法) steam **2** (蒸发) evaporate

– a label indicating the field in which the word is used:

硬件 yìngjiàn [名] **1** (计算机) hardware **2** (设备) equipment

– a style label, which is used to mark non-neutral words and expressions as a warning to the user:

治学 zhìxué [动] (书) study

You will find a complete list of labels used in the dictionary on page 29.

4.4 **Examples**

4.4.1 Word examples, as well as a few 4-character idioms (chengyu etc.), appear under meanings which function as core senses of single characters, and are preceded by a solid lozenge ♦.

4.4.2 Fuller examples are preceded by an empty lozenge ◇.

4.5 **Translations**

4.5.1 In general, we have only given one translation per meaning, since we believe this is the most accurate and helpful approach.

4.5.2 In a few cases, there is no equivalent at all, and an explanation rather than a translation has to be given. In such cases it is shown in italics.

压岁钱 yāsuìqián [名] *traditional gifts of money given to children during the Spring Festival*

4.5.3 British and American English variants are shown where appropriate:

棒子 bàngzi [名] **1** (棍子) club **2** (玉米) corn (英), maize (美)

4.5.4 Alternative parts of translations are preceded by “或” ('or'):

摄影 shèyǐng [动] **1** (照相) take a photo (*pt* took, *pp* taken) **2** (拍电影) shoot a film (英) 或 movie (美) (*pt*, *pp* shot)

略语表 / Reference list

▼ 词性 / PARTS OF SPEECH

abbreviation	*abbr*	简
adjective	*adj*	形
adverb	*adv*	副
auxiliary verb	*aux vb*	助动
conjunction	*conj*	连
compound	*cpd* [复合词]	复合词
definite article	*def art*	定冠词
indefinite article	*indef art*	不定冠词
interjection	*int*	叹
noun	*n*	名
noun abbreviation	*n abbr*	名词缩写
singular noun	*n sing*	单数名词
noun (plural)	*n(pl)*	名词(复数)
noun plural	*npl*	复数名词
numeral	*num*	数
plural	*pl*	复数
plural adjective	*pl adj*	复数形容词
plural pronoun	*pl pron*	复数代词
past participle	*pp*	过去分词
prefix	*prefix*	前缀
preposition	*prep*	介
pres part	*pres part*	现在分词
pronoun	*pron*	代
past tense	*pt*	过去时
suffix	*suffix*	后缀
verb	*vb*	动
intransitive verb	*vi*	不及物动词
transitive verb	*vt*	及物动词
indicates that particle cannot be separated from the main verb	*vt* [不可拆分]	及物动词[不可拆分]

▼ 专业学科领域 / SUBJECT FIELD LABELS

ADMINISTRATION	行政
AGRICULTURE	农
ANATOMY	解剖
ARCHITECTURE	建筑
ART	艺术
ASTROLOGY	占星术
ASTRONOMY	天文
MOTORING	汽车
AVIATION	航空
BASEBALL	棒球
BIOLOGY	生物
BOTANY	植
BOXING	拳击
CARDS	纸牌
CHEMISTRY	化
CHESS	国际象棋
CINEMA	电影
COMMERCE	商
COMPUTING	计算机
CRICKET	板球
COOKING	烹饪
DRAWING	绘画

略语表 / Reference list

ELECTRICITY	电子	POLITICS	政治
FINANCE	经济	POLICE	警察
FOOTBALL	足球	POST OFFICE	邮政
GEOGRAPHY	地理	PSYCHOLOGY	心理
GEOLOGY	地质	PUBLISHING	出版
GEOMETRY	几何	RADIO	广播
GOLF	高尔夫	RAILWAYS	铁路
GRAMMAR	语法	RELIGION	宗
HISTORY	历史	RUGBY	橄榄球
INDUSTRY	工业	SCIENCE	科学
LAW	法	SCHOOL	教育
LINGUISTICS	语言	SOCIOLOGY	社会
LITERATURE	文学	SPACE	宇航
MATHEMATICS	数	SPORT	体育
MEDICINE	医	TECHNICAL USAGE	术语
METEOROLOGY	气象	TELECOMMUNICATIONS	电信
MILITARY	军	TENNIS	网球
MINING	矿	TEXT MESSAGING	手机短信
MUSIC	音	THEATRE	戏剧
MYTHOLOGY	神	TELEVISION	电视
NAUTICAL	航海	PUBLISHING	排版
PARLIAMENT	议会	UNIVERSITY	大学
PHILOSOPHY	哲	ZOOLOGY	动
PHOTOGRAPHY	摄影		
PHYSICS	物		
PHYSIOLOGY	生理		

▼ 修辞色彩缩略语 / REGISTER LABELS

dialect	方	pejorative	贬
euphemism	婉	humble	谦
formal	正式	respectful	敬
formerly	旧	slang	俚
humorous	诙谐	spoken language	口
informal	非正式	written	书
literary	文	polite	客套
offensive	侮辱	literal	字
old-fashioned	过时	figurative	喻
very offensive	疑讳 / 讳		

发音简表 / Guide to English phonetics

▼ 辅音 / CONSONANTS

[p]	puppy	[f]	farm raffle
[b]	baby	[v]	very rev
[t]	tent	[θ]	thin maths
[d]	daddy	[ð]	that other
[k]	cork kiss chord	[l]	little ball
[g]	gag guess	[r]	rat rare
[s]	so rice kiss	[m]	mummy comb
[z]	cousin buzz	[n]	no ran
[ʃ]	sheep sugar	[ŋ]	singing bank
[ʒ]	pleasure beige	[h]	hat reheat
[tʃ]	church	[x]	loch
[dʒ]	judge general		

▼ 半元音 / SEMIVOWELS

[j]	yet	[w]	wet

▼ 元音 / VOWELS

[iː]	heel	[ə]	over above
[ɪ]	hit pity	[əː]	urn fern work
[ɛ]	set tent	[ɔ]	wash pot
[æ]	bat apple	[ɔː]	born cork
[ɑː]	after car calm	[u]	full soot
[ʌ]	fun cousin	[uː]	pool lewd

▼ 双元音 / DIPHTHONGS

[ɪə]	beer tier	[au]	owl foul now
[ɛə]	tear fair there	[əu]	low no
[eɪ]	date plaice day	[ɔɪ]	boil boy oily
[aɪ]	life buy cry	[uə]	poor tour

不规则动词 / English irregular verbs

Present	Past tense	Past participle
arise	arose	arisen
awake	awoke	awoken
be (am, is, are; being)	was, were	been
bear	bore	born(e)
beat	beat	beaten
become	became	become
begin	began	begun
bend	bent	bent
bet	bet, betted	bet, betted
bid (*at auction, cards*)	bid	bid
bid (*say*)	bade	bidden
bind	bound	bound
bite	bit	bitten
bleed	bled	bled
blow	blew	blown
break	broke	broken
breed	bred	bred
bring	brought	brought
build	built	built
burn	burnt, burned	burnt, burned
burst	burst	burst
buy	bought	bought
can	could	(been able)
cast	cast	cast
catch	caught	caught
choose	chose	chosen
cling	clung	clung
come	came	come
cost	cost	cost
cost (*work out price of*)	costed	costed
creep	crept	crept
cut	cut	cut
deal	dealt	dealt
dig	dug	dug
do (does)	did	done
draw	drew	drawn
dream	dreamed, dreamt	dreamed, dreamt
drink	drank	drunk
drive	drove	driven
dwell	dwelt	dwelt
eat	ate	eaten

Present	Past tense	Past participle
fall	fell	fallen
feed	fed	fed
feel	felt	felt
fight	fought	fought
find	found	found
flee	fled	fled
fling	flung	flung
fly	flew	flown
forbid	forbad(e)	forbidden
forecast	forecast	forecast
forget	forgot	forgotten
forgive	forgave	forgiven
forsake	forsook	forsaken
freeze	froze	frozen
get	got	got, (美) gotten
give	gave	given
go (goes)	went	gone
grind	ground	ground
grow	grew	grown
hang	hung	hung
hang (*execute*)	hanged	hanged
have	had	had
hear	heard	heard
hide	hid	hidden
hit	hit	hit
hold	held	held
hurt	hurt	hurt
keep	kept	kept
kneel	knelt, kneeled	knelt, kneeled
know	knew	known
lay	laid	laid
lead	led	led
lean	leant, leaned	leant, leaned
leap	leapt, leaped	leapt, leaped
learn	learnt, learned	learnt, learned
leave	left	left
lend	lent	lent
let	let	let
lie (lying)	lay	lain
light	lit, lighted	lit, lighted
lose	lost	lost

不规则动词 / English irregular verbs

Present	Past tense	Past participle
make	made	made
may	might	—
mean	meant	meant
meet	met	met
mistake	mistook	mistaken
mow	mowed	mown, mowed
must	(had to)	(had to)
pay	paid	paid
put	put	put
quit	quit, quitted	quit, quitted
read	read	read
rid	rid	rid
ride	rode	ridden
ring	rang	rung
rise	rose	risen
run	ran	run
say	said	said
see	saw	seen
seek	sought	sought
sell	sold	sold
send	sent	sent
set	set	set
sew	sewed	sewn
shake	shook	shaken
shear	sheared	shorn, sheared
shed	shed	shed
shine	shone	shone
shoot	shot	shot
show	showed	shown
shrink	shrank	shrunk
shut	shut	shut
sing	sang	sung
sink	sank	sunk
sit	sat	sat
slay	slew	slain
sleep	slept	slept
slide	slid	slid
sling	slung	slung
slit	slit	slit
smell	smelt, smelled	smelt, smelled
sow	sowed	sown, sowed
speak	spoke	spoken

Present	Past tense	Past participle
speed	sped, speeded	sped, speeded
spell	spelt, spelled	spelt, spelled
spend	spent	spent
spill	spilt, spilled	spilt, spilled
spin	spun	spun
spit	spat	spat
spoil	spoiled, spoilt	spoiled, spoilt
spread	spread	spread
spring	sprang	sprung
stand	stood	stood
steal	stole	stolen
stick	stuck	stuck
sting	stung	stung
stink	stank	stunk
stride	strode	stridden
strike	struck	struck
strive	strove	striven
swear	swore	sworn
sweep	swept	swept
swell	swelled	swollen, swelled
swim	swam	swum
swing	swung	swung
take	took	taken
teach	taught	taught
tear	tore	torn
tell	told	told
think	thought	thought
throw	threw	thrown
thrust	thrust	thrust
tread	trod	trodden
wake	woke, waked	woken, waked
wear	wore	worn
weave	wove	woven
weave *(wind)*	weaved	weaved
wed	wedded, wed	wedded, wed
weep	wept	wept
win	won	won
wind	wound	wound
wring	wrung	wrung
write	wrote	written

Aa

A¹, a [eɪ, ə] *n* [c/u] (*letter*) 英语的第一个字母 ♦**A shares** [英:经济] A股 ♦**from A to B** 从一地到另一地

A² [eɪ] *n* [c/u] **1** [音] C大调音阶中的第六音 **2** [教育, 大学] 优

✪ **a**

KEYWORD

[eɪ, ə] (*before vowel or silent h:* **an**) *indef art*

1 (*article*) 一个 ♦**a man** 一个男人 ♦**a girl** 一个女孩 ♦**a mirror** 一面镜子 ♦**an elephant** 一只大象 ♦**she's a doctor** 她是一名医生 ♦**what a beautiful baby!** 多么漂亮的一个小宝宝啊! ♦**have you got a dishwasher?** 你有洗碗机吗? ♦**they haven't got a television** 他们没有电视 ♦**a Mrs Blair telephoned** 一位布莱尔夫人打电话了

2 (*one*) 一 ♦**a year ago** 一年前 ♦**a hundred/thousand/million pounds** 100 / 1000 / 100 万英镑 ♦**a third of the population** 三分之一的人口

3 (*expressing ratios, prices etc*) ♦**five hours a day/week** 一天/一周5个小时 ♦**five times a day** 一天5次 ♦**100 km an hour** 每小时100公里 ♦**it costs £5 a person** 每人付5镑 ♦**30p a kilo** 每公斤30便士

A & E [英] *n abbr* (= ***accident and emergency***) 急诊室 [美=**ER**]

aback [ə'bæk] *adv* ♦**to be taken aback** 大吃一惊

abandon [ə'bændən] **I** *vt* **1** (*leave*) [+ *person, family*] 抛弃 **2** [+ *car*] 丢弃 **3** (*give up*) [+ *search, idea, research*] 放弃 **II** *n* ♦**with abandon** 尽情地 ♦**to abandon o.s. to sth** 使自己沉溺于某事 ♦**to abandon ship** 弃船

abandoned [ə'bændənd] *adj* **1** [+ *building, vehicle*] 废弃的 **2** [+ *child*] 被遗弃的

abate [ə'beɪt] *vi* [*storm, violence* +] 减弱

abattoir ['æbətwɑː(r)] [英] *n* [c] 屠宰场 [美=**slaughterhouse**]

abbey ['æbɪ] *n* [c] 大修道院

abbreviation [əbriːvɪ'eɪʃən] *n* [c] 缩写 ♦**CD is an** *or* **the abbreviation for compact disc** CD是compact disc 的缩写

abdomen ['æbdəmɛn] *n* [c] 腹部

abdominal [æb'dɔmɪnl] *adj* [+ *pain*] 腹部的

abduct [æb'dʌkt] *vt* 绑架

abduction [æb'dʌkʃən] *n* [c/u] 诱拐

abide [ə'baɪd] *vt* ♦**I can't abide it/him** 我无法忍受这事/他 ♦**I can't abide living here** 住在这儿让我受不了

❑**abide by** *vt* [不可拆分] [+ *rule, decision*] 遵守

ability [ə'bɪlɪtɪ] *n* **1** [s] (*capacity*) ♦**ability (to do sth)** (做某事的)能力 **2** [c/u] (*talent, skill*) 才能 ♦**to the best of my ability/abilities** 尽我最大的努力

✪**able** ['eɪbl] *adj* **1** ♦**to be able to do sth** (*have skill, ability*) 能够做某事 ◊ *The giant frog is able to jump three metres.* 大青蛙能够跳3米远。; (*have opportunity*) 可以做某事 ◊ *You'll be able to read in peace here.* 你可以在这里安静地看书。 **2** (*clever*) [+ *pupil, player*] 有才能的 📖 用法参见 **can**

abnormal [æb'nɔːməl] *adj* [+ *behaviour, child, situation*] 反常的

abnormality [æbnɔː'mælɪtɪ] *n* **1** [u] (*abnormal nature*) 变态 **2** [c] (*abnormal feature*) 异常

aboard [ə'bɔːd] **I** *prep* [+ *ship, plane*] 在…上 **II** *adv* 在飞机/船/火车上

abolish [ə'bɔlɪʃ] *vt* [+ *system, practice*] 废止

abolition [æbə'lɪʃən] *n* [u] 废除

abort [ə'bɔːt] *vt* **1** [+ *child, foetus*] 使流产 **2** [+ *plan, mission*] 使中止

abortion [ə'bɔːʃən] [医] *n* [c/u] 流产 ♦**to have an abortion** 流产

abortive [ə'bɔːtɪv] [正式] *adj* [+ *attempt, coup*] 夭折的

about
KEYWORD
[ə'baut]
I *prep*
1 (*relating to*) 关于 ♦**a book about London** 关于伦敦的一本书 ♦**what's it about?** 这是关于什么的？♦**she knows a lot about art** 她对艺术懂得很多 ♦**we talked about it** 我们谈到了这事 ♦**management is about motivating people** 管理就是要激发大家的热情 ♦**to be sorry/pleased/angry about sth** 对某事感到抱歉/开心/生气 ♦**there's something odd about this** 这有点怪怪的 ♦**we'll have to do something about this** 我们对此要采取点儿措施 ♦**what or how about eating out?** 出去吃怎么样？
2 (*place*) 在…各处 ♦**he was wandering about the garden** 他在花园里到处闲逛 ♦**clothes scattered about the room** 扔得满屋各处都是的衣服 ♦**it must be about here somewhere** 一定在这周围的某个地方
3 [正式](*around*) 围绕 ♦**a chain hung about her neck** 环绕在她脖子上的一条项链
II *adv*
1 (*approximately*) 大约 ♦**about a hundred/thousand people** 大约100 / 1000 人 ♦**at about two o'clock** 在两点钟左右
2 (*place*) 在 ♦**to leave things lying about** 把东西到处乱放 ♦**to run/walk about** 到处跑/到处走 ♦**is Paul about?** 保罗在吗？♦**there's a lot of flu/money about** 正在流行流感/资金充足 ♦**to be about to do sth** 正要做某事 ♦**he was about to leave** 他正要离开

above [ə'bʌv] **I** *prep* 1 (*higher than*) 在…上面 2 (*greater than, more than*) (*in number*) 超过 3 (*in rank, authority*) 级别高于 4 ♦**to be above sth** (*better, superior*) 不屑于某事 5 ♦**to be above suspicion/criticism** (*beyond*) 无法猜疑/指责的 6 (*in loudness*) (*over*) 高过 ◊ *I couldn't hear her above all the noise.* 太吵了，我听不见她在说什么。7 (*in importance*) (*before*) 胜过 **II** *adv* 1 (*in position*) (*higher up, overhead*) 在上面 2 (*in amount, number*) (*greater, more*) 以上 3 (*in authority, power*) 上级 4 (*in writing*) 在上文 **III** *adj* ♦**the above address** 上述地址 ♦**above all** 首先 ♦**from above** 从上面 ♦**any/none of the above** 上述中任一/无一

abrasive [ə'breɪzɪv] **I** *adj* 1 [+ *substance*] 磨砂的 2 [+ *person, manner*] 粗暴的 **II** *n* 磨砂材料

abroad [ə'brɔːd] *adv* 1 [*be* +] 在国外 2 [*go* +] 到国外 ♦**there is a feeling/rumour abroad that ...** 一种情绪/谣言在到处流传…

abrupt [ə'brʌpt] *adj* 1 (*sudden*) [+ *action, ending etc*] 突然的 2 (*curt*) [+ *person, manner*] 鲁莽的

abruptly [ə'brʌptlɪ] *adv* 1 (*suddenly*) [*leave, end* +] 突然地 2 (*curtly*) [*speak* +] 生硬地

abscess ['æbsɪs] *n* [c] 脓肿

absence ['æbsəns] *n* 1 [c/u] [*of person*] 缺席 2 [s] [*of thing*] 缺乏 ♦**in sb's absence** 在某人不在场时 ♦**in the absence of sth** 在缺乏某物的情况下

absent [*adj* 'æbsənt, *vb* æb'sɛnt] **I** *adj* 1 (*from work, school*) 缺席的；(*at home*) [+ *parent*] 不同住的 2 (*inattentive*) 心不在焉的 **II** *vt* [正式] ♦**to absent o.s. from sth** 未出席某事 ♦**to be absent** 不在 ♦**to be absent from sth** 不存在于某事 ♦**absent without leave** [军] 擅离职守

absentee [æbsən'tiː] *n* [c] 缺席者

absent-minded ['æbsənt'maɪndɪd] *adj* 心不在焉的

absolute ['æbsəluːt] **I** *adj* 1 (*complete*) [+ *beginner, confidence*] 完全的 2 (*utter*) (*used for emphasis*) 绝对的 3 [+ *power, monarchy*] 专制的 4 (*definite*) 确凿的 5 (*universal*) [+ *truth, rule*] 绝对的 **II** *n* [c] 绝对 ♦**the absolute minimum/maximum** 绝对最小/最大值

absolutely [æbsə'luːtlɪ] *adv* 1 (*utterly*) (*used for emphasis*) 绝对地 2 ♦**absolutely (not)** (*certainly*) (*used *for emphasis*) 绝对（不是）地

absorb [əb'zɔːb] *vt* **1**（字）[+ *liquid, light*] 吸收 **2**（喻）[+ *shock, impact, sound*] 消减；(*assimilate*) [+ *group, business*] 并入；(*cope with*) [+ *effects, losses*] 承受；[+ *information, facts*] 理解 ♦ **to be absorbed in a book** 专心致志地读一本书

absorbent cotton [əb'zɔːbənt-]［美］*n* [U] 脱脂棉［英 = **cotton wool**］

absorbing [əb'zɔːbɪŋ] *adj* [+ *book, film etc*] 引人入胜的

abstain [əb'steɪn] *vi* **1** (*in vote*) 弃权 **2** ♦ **to abstain from eating/drinking** 节制饮食/戒酒

abstract [*n, adj* 'æbstrækt, *vb* æb'strækt] **I** *adj* **1** [+ *idea, quality*] 抽象的 **2**［艺术］抽象派的 **3**［语言］[+ *noun*] 抽象的 **II** *n* [C] (*summary*) 摘要 **III** *vt*［正式］♦ **to abstract sth (from)**（从…中）抽取某物 ♦ **in the abstract** 抽象地

absurd [əb'səːd] **I** *adj* (*ridiculous*) 荒谬的 ◊ *That's absurd.* 岂有此理。 **II** *n* ♦ **the absurd**［正式］荒诞的事

abundance [ə'bʌndəns] *n* [S] 丰富 ♦ **an abundance of** 大量的 ♦ **in abundance** 充足的

abundant [ə'bʌndənt] *adj* 丰富的

abuse [*n* ə'bjuːs, *vb* ə'bjuːz] **I** *n* **1** [U] (*insults*) 辱骂 **2** [U] (*ill-treatment*) (*physical*) 虐待；(*sexual*) 猥亵 **3** [C/U] (*misuse*) [*of power, alcohol, drug*] 滥用 **II** *vt* **1** (*insult*) 辱骂 **2** (*ill-treat*) (*physically*) 虐待 **3** (*sexually*) [+ *child*] 摧残 **4** (*misuse*) [+ *power, alcohol, drug*] 滥用 ♦ **to be open to abuse** 易产生弊病的

abusive [ə'bjuːsɪv] *adj* **1** (*insulting*) [+ *person, language*] 谩骂的 **2** (*violent*) [+ *person*] 残暴的；[+ *relationship*] 暴虐的

abysmal [ə'bɪzməl] *adj* [+ *conditions, wages, performance*] 糟糕的 ♦ **an abysmal failure** 彻底的失败

abyss [ə'bɪs]［文］*n* [C] **1** (*deep hole*) 无底洞 **2** (*disaster*) 深渊 **3** (*gap, gulf*) 鸿沟

academic [ækə'dɛmɪk] **I** *adj* **1** [+ *system, books, freedom*] 学术的 **2** [+ *person*] 学究的 **3**［贬］(*irrelevant*) 空谈的 **II** *n* 大学教师

academic year *n* [C] 学年

academy [ə'kædəmɪ] *n* [C] **1** (*organisation*) 学会 **2** (*school, college*) 学院

accelerate [æk'sɛləreɪt] **I** *vi* **1** [*process* +] 加快 **2**［汽车］加速 **II** *vt* [+ *process*] 使加快

acceleration [æksɛlə'reɪʃən] *n* [U] **1** [*of process, change*] 加快 **2**［汽车］加速 **3**［物］加速度

accelerator [æk'sɛləreɪtə(r)]［汽车］*n* [C] 加速器

accent ['æksɛnt] *n* [C] **1** (*pronunciation*) 口音 **2** (*written mark*) 重音符号 ♦ **to speak with an (Irish/French) accent** 讲话带（爱尔兰/法国）口音 ♦ **to have a strong/German accent** 带有浓重的/德国口音 ♦ **the accent is on ...** (*emphasis, stress*) 重点在… ♦ **to put the accent on sth** 将着重点放在某事上

accentuate [æk'sɛntjueɪt] *vt* (*emphasise*) 使突出

✪ **accept** [ək'sɛpt] *vt* **1** [+ *invitation, advice, responsibility, credit cards etc*] 接受 **2** (*as true, valid*) [+ *fact, view*] 接受；(*as inevitable*) [+ *change, sb's death*] 接受 **3** [+ *person*] 接纳 ◊ *Stephen was finally accepted into the family.* 斯蒂芬最终被这个家庭所接纳。 ♦ **to accept that ...** (*acknowledge*) 承认…

acceptable [ək'sɛptəbl] *adj* **1** (*permissible*) 可接受的 **2** (*suitable*) 合意的 **3** (*adequate*) 令人满意的 ♦ **acceptable to sb** 某人可以接受的 ♦ **it is acceptable for sb to do sth** 某人做某事是可以接受的

acceptance [ək'sɛptəns] *n* **1** [C/U] [*of an offer*] 接受 **2** [U] [*of an idea*] 赞同 **3** [U] [*of a situation*] 容忍 **4** [U] [*of something new*] 认可 **5** [U] [*of a person*] 接纳

access ['æksɛs] **I** *n* [U] ♦ **access (to sth)** (*to building, room*) 进入（某物）；(*to information, papers*)（某物的）使用权 ♦ **access (to sb)** (*to person*) 接近（某人） **II** *vt*［计算机］存取 ♦ **to have access to sb** [+ *child*] 有见某人的机会 ♦ **to have access to sth** [+ *information, library, phone*] 有享用某物的机会 ♦ **to gain access (to sth)** 得以进入（某物）

accessible [æk'sɛsəbl] *adj*

♦ **accessible (to sb)** [*place, object* +] 易于(某人)接近的; [*knowledge, service, commodity* +] (对某人)易得到的; [*art, culture* +] (对某人)易理解的

accessory [æk'sɛsərɪ] *n* [c] **1** (*for room, car*) 附件 **2** [服饰] 饰品 **3** [法] ♦ **an accessory to the crime** 犯罪同谋

accident ['æksɪdənt] *n* [c] **1** (*involving vehicle*) 事故 **2** (*mishap*) 意外 **3** (*chance event*) 偶然事件 ♦ **to have an accident** 出事故 ♦ **to meet with an accident** 出事故 ♦ **by accident** (*unintentionally*) 无意中; (*by chance*) 偶然

accidental [æksɪ'dɛntl] *adj* 意外的

accidentally [æksɪ'dɛntəlɪ] *adv* (*unintentionally*) 意外地

accident and emergency [英] *n* [c] 急诊室

acclaim [ə'kleɪm] [正式] **I** *vt* ♦ **to be acclaimed (for/as sth)** (因某事/作为某事而)受赞扬 **II** *n* ♦ **to win** *or* **receive acclaim** 受到赞扬

accolade ['ækəleɪd] [正式] *n* [c] 荣誉

accommodate [ə'kɔmədeɪt] *vt* **1** (*hold*) [*car, hotel etc* +] 容纳 **2** (*put up*) 为…提供住宿 **3** (*satisfy*) 使满意 ♦ **to accommodate o.s. to sth** 使自己适应某事

accommodation [əkɔmə'deɪʃən] **I** *n* **1** [U] (*place to stay*) 住处 **2** [U] [正式] (*space*) 空位 **3** [c] [正式] (*agreement*) 和解 **II accommodations** [美] *n* [*pl*] = **accommodation**

accompaniment [ə'kʌmpənɪmənt] *n* [c] **1** (*complement*) 伴随物 **2** [音] 伴奏 ♦ **to the accompaniment of sth** [+ *cheers, shouting etc*] 在某物的伴随下

accompany [ə'kʌmpənɪ] *vt* **1** [正式] (*escort*) 陪伴 **2** (*complement*) 与…相配合 **3** [音] 为…伴奏

accomplice [ə'kʌmplɪs] *n* [c] 同谋

accomplish [ə'kʌmplɪʃ] *vt* 完成

accomplished [ə'kʌmplɪʃt] *adj* [+ *cook, musician etc*] 有造诣的; [+ *performance*] 精湛的

accomplishment [ə'kʌmplɪʃmənt] *n* **1** [c] (*achievement*) 成就 **2** [c] [正式] (*skill*) 技能 **3** [U] (*completion*) 完成

✪ **accord** [ə'kɔːd] **I** *n* [c] (*agreement, treaty*) 协议 ◊ *the 1991 peace accord* 1991年和平协议 **II** *vt* [正式] (*grant*) 授予 **III** *vi* ♦ **to accord with sth** [正式] (*correspond*) 和某事相符 ♦ **of its own accord** (*by itself*) 自行地 ♦ **of one's own accord** (*voluntarily*) 自愿地 ♦ **in accord (with)** [正式] (与…)一致 ♦ **with one accord** [文] 一致地

accordance [ə'kɔːdəns] *n* ♦ **in accordance with sth** [+ *sb's wishes, the law etc*] 根据某事

according [ə'kɔːdɪŋ] ♦ **according to** *prep* [+ *person*] 据…所说; [+ *account, information*] 根据 ♦ **to go/work out according to plan** 按计划进行/发展 ♦ **the gospel according to (St) Matthew/Luke** 马太/路加福音

accordingly [ə'kɔːdɪŋlɪ] *adv* **1** (*appropriately*) 相应地 **2** (*consequently*) 因此

accordion [ə'kɔːdɪən] *n* [c] 手风琴; (*also: **piano accordion***) 键盘式手风琴

✪ **account** [ə'kaunt] **I** *n* [c] **1** (*with bank, at shop*) 账户 ◊ *I have an account with Barclays.* 我在巴克莱银行有一个账户。 **2** [商] (*client, customer*) 客户 ◊ *The agency has won two important new accounts.* 代理公司赢得了两个重要的新客户。 **3** (*report*) 描述 ◊ *He gave an account of what happened.* 他对发生的事情做了一番描述。 **II accounts** *n* [*pl*] [商] 账 ◊ *He kept the accounts.* 他记账。 **III** *vt* ♦ **to be accounted sth** [正式] 被视为某事 ♦ **to buy/pay for sth on account** 分期付款购买某物 ♦ **to give a good account of o.s.** 使自己表现不错 ♦ **to be brought** *or* **called** *or* **held to account for sth** 被要求就某事作出解释 ♦ **to be of no/little account** [正式] 完全不/不大重要 ♦ **on no account** 绝对不 ♦ **on account of** 因为 ♦ **to take sth into account, take account of sth** 考虑到某事 ♦ **by** *or* **from all accounts** 根据大家所说

❑ **account for** *vt* [不可拆分] **1** (*explain*) 解释 ◊ *How do you account for the company's high staff* *turnover?* 你如何解释公司如此频繁的人事变动？**2** (*represent*) 占 ◊ *Software accounts for over half of our product range.* 软件产品占我们产品系列的一半以上。♦ **to be not accounted for** 未解释的

accountable [ə'kauntəbl] *adj* ♦ **to be accountable (to sb/for sth)** (向某人/就某事) 负责 ♦ **to be held accountable for sth** 被认为应对某事负责

accountant [ə'kauntənt] *n* [c] 会计师

accumulate [ə'kjuːmjuleɪt] **I** *vt* 积累 **II** *vi* 累积

accumulation [əkjuːmju'leɪʃən] *n* [c/u] [*of debts, evidence*] 积累

accuracy ['ækjurəsɪ] *n* [u] **1** [*of information, measurements*] 准确 **2** [*of person, device*] 精确

accurate ['ækjurɪt] *adj* **1** [+ *information, measurement, instrument*] 精确的；[+ *description, account, person, aim*] 准确的；[+ *person, work*] 正确的 **2** [+ *weapon, throw*] 精确的

accurately ['ækjurɪtlɪ] *adv* **1** [*measure, predict* +] 精确地 **2** [*describe, assess, report, aim* +] 准确地

accusation [ækju'eɪzʃən] *n* **1** [c/u] (*criticism*) 谴责 **2** [c] (*allegation*) 控告

accuse [ə'kjuːz] *vt* **1** ♦ **to accuse sb of (doing) sth** [*of dishonesty, immorality*] 指责某人(做)某事 **2** ♦ **to be accused of sth** [*of crime*] 被指控某事

accused [ə'kjuːzd] [法] *n* ♦ **the accused** 被告

accustomed [ə'kʌstəmd] *adj* **1** ♦ **to be/become accustomed to (doing) sth** 习惯于/开始习惯于(做)某事 **2** ♦ **to become/be accustomed to sth** [*eyes* +] 开始适应/适应某事 **3** (*usual*) ♦ **his/her accustomed response** 他/她的惯常反应

ace [eɪs] *n* [c] **1** A纸牌 **2** [网球] 发球得分 ♦ **the ace of spades** 黑桃A

ache [eɪk] **I** *vi* **1** [*part of body* +] 痛 **2** ♦ **to ache for sth/to do sth** (*yearn*) 渴望某事/做某事 **II** *n* [c] 疼痛 ♦ **I've got (a) stomach/toothache** 我胃/牙痛 ♦ **I'm aching all over** 我浑身疼痛 ♦ **aches and pains** 周身不适

achieve [ə'tʃiːv] *vt* **1** [+ *aim*] 实现 **2** [+ *victory, success, result*] 取得

achievement [ə'tʃiːvmənt] *n* **1** [c] (*accomplishment*) [*of person, organization*] 成就 **2** [u] (*fulfilment*) 实现 ♦ **it was quite an achievement** 这是个了不起的成就

acid ['æsɪd] **I** *n* **1** [c/u] [化] 酸 **2** [u] [非正式] (*LSD*) 迷幻药 **II** *adj* **1** [化] [+ *soil*] 酸性的 **2** (*sharp*) [+ *taste*] 酸的；[+ *remark, humour*] 尖刻的 ♦ **citric/hydrochloric acid** 柠檬/盐酸

acidic [ə'sɪdɪk] *adj* **1** (*containing acid*) [+ *substance*] 酸性的 **2** (*sharp*) [+ *taste, smell*] 酸的

acknowledge [ək'nɔlɪdʒ] *vt* **1** [正式] [+ *fact, situation, problem*] 承认 **2** [+ *person met*] 对…打招呼 **3** [+ *letter, parcel*] (*by replying*) 告知收到 **4** (*recognize value of*) [+ *achievement, status*] 认可 ♦ **to acknowledge that ...** 承认…

acknowledgement [ək'nɔlɪdʒmənt] **I** *n* **1** [s] (*acceptance*) 承认 **2** [c] [*of letter, parcel*] 收到通知 **3** [u] (*gesture of recognition*) 反应 **II acknowledgements** *n* [*pl*] (*in book*) 致谢

acne ['æknɪ] *n* [u] 痤疮

acorn ['eɪkɔːn] *n* [c] 橡果

acoustic [ə'kuːstɪk] *adj* **1** [+ *guitar, instrument*] 非电传音的 **2** [+ *signal*] 声音的

acquaint [ə'kweɪnt] [正式] *vt* ♦ **to acquaint sb with sth** (*inform*) 把某事通知某人 ♦ **to acquaint o.s. with sth** 开始知道某事 ♦ **to be acquainted with sb/sth** [+ *person*] 认识某人；[+ *fact*] 了解某事

acquaintance [ə'kweɪntəns] *n* **1** [c] (*person*) 熟人 **2** [u] (*familiarity*) (*with person*) 结识；(*with subject*) 了解 ♦ **to make sb's acquaintance** [正式] 结识某人

acquainted [ə'kweɪntɪd] *adj* **1** [正式] ♦ **to be/get acquainted with sth** 了解/开始了解某事 **2** [正式] ♦ **to be acquainted (with sb)** (和某人) 相识 **3** ♦ **to get** *or* **become**

acquainted (with sb) 开始了解(某人)

acquire [ə'kwaɪə(r)] *vt* **1** (*obtain, buy*) 获得 **2** (*learn, develop*) [+ *skill, habit*] 学到 **3** (*gain*) [+ *reputation*] 取得

acquisition [ækwɪ'zɪʃən] *n* **1** [c] (*thing obtained*) 获得物 **2** [u] (*getting*) [*of property, goods*] 获得; [*of habit*] 形成; [*of skill*] 习得

acquit [ə'kwɪt] *vt* (*clear*) ♦**to acquit sb (of sth)** [法] 宣判某人(无罪) ♦**to acquit o.s. well/badly** [正式] 表现良好/不好

acre ['eɪkə(r)] *n* [c] 英亩

acrobatic [ækrə'bætɪk] *adj* [+ *movement, display*] 杂技的

acronym ['ækrənɪm] *n* [c] 首字母缩略词

> **acronym**(首字母缩略词)是一种特殊的缩写形式,它可以像一个普通单词那样读出。例如,**NATO**(北约)和**AIDS**(艾滋病)。**acronym** 是由组成这个名称的每个词的第一个字母构成。**NATO** 代表 **North Atlantic Treaty Organization**(北大西洋公约组织); **AIDS** 代表 **acquired immune deficiency syndrome**(获得性免疫缺损综合征); **DOS** 代表 **disk operating system**(磁盘操作系统)。首字母缩略词比全称更常用,因为它们说起来更方便。

✪**across** [ə'krɔs] **I** *prep* **1** (*moving from one side to the other of*) 穿过 ◊ *He walked across the room.* 他穿过这个房间。**2** (*situated on the other side of*) [*of street, river, room etc*] 在…对面 ◊ *the houses across the street* 在街对面的房子 **3** (*extending from one side to the other of*) 跨越 ◊ *the bridge across Lake Washington* 跨越华盛顿湖的桥 **4** (*over*) 搭在…上 ◊ *Her clothes were lying across the chair.* 她的衣服正搭在椅子上。**5** (*involving different groups*) 跨越 ◊ *parties from across the political spectrum* 跨越政治派别的党派 **II** *adv* **1** (*to/from a particular place/person*) 从/向对面 ◊ *Richard walked across to the window.* 理查德向对面的窗户走去。**2** (*from one side to the other*) 从一边到另一边 **3** ♦**across from** (*opposite*) 在…对面 ◊ *They parked across from the theatre.* 他们把车停在剧院的对面。**4** ♦**across at/to** (*towards*) 朝向 ◊ *He glanced across at his wife.* 他朝他的妻子瞥了一眼。**5** (*in width*) 宽 ◊ *a hole 200 metres across* 200米宽的洞 ♦**to get** *or* **put sth across to sb** 让某人明白某事

acrylic [ə'krɪlɪk] **I** *adj* [+ *material, paint*] 丙烯酸的 **II** *n* [u] (*textile*) 丙烯酸 **III acrylics** *n* [*pl*] (*paint*) 丙烯酸

ACT *n abbr* (= ***American College Test***) 美国大学入学测试

✪**act** [ækt] **I** *vi* **1** (*take action*) 行动 ◊ *We have to act quickly.* 我们得立即行动起来。**2** (*behave*) 举止 ◊ *They were acting suspiciously.* 他们举止可疑。**3** ♦**to act for** *or* **on behalf of sb** [*lawyer* +] 代表某人行事 **4** ♦**to act as sb/sth** 担任某职务/充当某物 ◊ *Mr. Thang acted as interpreter.* 唐先生担当口译工作。**5** (*work*) [*drug, chemical* +] 见效 ◊ *The drug acts swiftly, preventing liver damage.* 药物很快见效,保护肝脏免受伤害。**6** (*in play, film*) 演戏 ◊ *I was acting in a play in Edinburgh.* 我在爱丁堡演过一出戏。**7** (*pretend*) 假装 ◊ *Ignore her, she's just acting.* 别理她,她只是假装的。**II** *vt* (*in play, film*) [+ *part, role*] 扮演 ◊ *I acted the part of Malvolio.* 我扮演了马尔瓦里奥这个角色。**III** *n* [c] **1** (*action*) 行动 ◊ *the act of reading* 阅读 ◊ *acts of sabotage* 破坏行动 **2** ♦**it's (just** *or* **all) an act** (*pretence*) 这(只)是做做样子 ◊ *His anger was real. It wasn't an act.* 他真的生气了,并不是做做样子。**3** [戏剧] [*of play, opera*] 幕; [*of performer*] 节目 ◊ *a show consisting of songs and comedy acts* 一场由演唱和喜剧节目组成的演出 **4** [法] 法令 ◊ *the 1944 Education Act* 1944 年教育法令 ♦**to act surprised/act the innocent** 装出惊讶/无辜的样子 ♦**act of God** [法] 不可抗力 ♦**in the act of doing sth** 正在做某事时 ♦**to catch sb in the act (of doing sth)** 当场捉住某人(做某

事）♦**to get one's act together** [非正式] 有条理地筹划

❑**act on** *vt* [不可拆分] [+ *advice, information*] 根据…行动 ◊ *The police are acting on information received last night.* 警察正根据昨晚收到的情报采取行动。

❑**act out** *vt* **1** (*in play*) [+ *event*] 将…表演出来 ◊ *The students act out events from history.* 学生们将历史事件表演出来。**2** (*in behaviour*) [+ *fantasy, desire*] 用行动表达

❑**act up** [非正式] *vi* **1** [*car, TV etc* +] 出故障 ◊ *The TV is acting up again.* 电视机又出故障了。**2** [*child* +] 捣乱

acting [ˈæktɪŋ] **I** *n* [U] **1** (*profession*) 表演 **2** (*art*) 演技 **II** *adj* [+ *manager, director etc*] 代理的

✪**action** [ˈækʃən] **I** *n* **1** [U] (*steps, measures*) 行动 ◊ *We need government action to prevent these crimes.* 我们需要政府采取行动阻止这些罪行。**2** [C] (*deed*) 行为 ◊ *He could not be held responsible for his actions.* 他不应被认为要对他的行为负责。**3** [C] (*movement*) 动作 ◊ *Their every action was recorded.* 他们的每个动作都被录了下来。**4** [C] (*in court*) 诉讼 ◊ *a libel action* 诽谤诉讼 **5** ♦**the action** [非正式] 精彩的活动 ◊ *Hollywood is where the action is now.* 现今精彩的活动都在好莱坞。**6** [U] [军] 行动 ◊ *military action* 军事行动 **II** *adj* [+ *movie, hero*] 动作的 ♦**to take action** 采取行动 ♦**to put a plan/policy into action** 将计划/政策付诸实施 ♦**to bring an action against sb** [法] 对某人提出起诉 ♦**killed/missing/wounded in action** [军] 在战斗中阵亡/失踪/受伤 ♦**out of action** [*person* +] 不能活动; [*machine* +] 出故障

action replay [英] *n* [C] 慢镜头回放

activate [ˈæktɪveɪt] *vt* [+ *mechanism*] 使活动

active [ˈæktɪv] **I** *adj* **1** [+ *person, life*] 活跃的 **2** (*in organisation or campaign*) 积极的 **3** (*concrete, positive*) [+ *step, support*] 积极的 **4** (*operative*) 活跃的 **5** [+ *ingredient*] 速效的 **6** [+ *volcano*] 活的 **II** *n* ♦**the active** [语言] 主动语态 ♦**to play an active part** *or* **role (in sth)** 积极参加(某事)

actively [ˈæktɪvlɪ] *adv* **1** (*directly*) [+ *involved*] 积极地 **2** (*positively*) [+ *encourage, discourage*] 积极地

activist [ˈæktɪvɪst] *n* [C] 积极分子

activity [ækˈtɪvɪtɪ] **I** *n* **1** [U] (*being active*) 活跃 **2** [C] (*pastime*) 活动 **II activities** *n* [*pl*] (*actions*) 活动

actor [ˈæktə(r)] *n* [C] 演员

actress [ˈæktrɪs] *n* [C] 女演员

actual [ˈæktjuəl] *adj* **1** (*real, genuine*) 真实的 **2** (*for emphasis*) 实际上的

✪**actually** [ˈæktjuəlɪ] *adv* **1** (*indicating or emphasising truth*) 实际地 ◊ *I was so bored I actually fell asleep.* 我闷透了，竟然睡着了。◊ *Actually, we have the same opinion.* 实际上我们有同样的观点。**2** (*in fact*) 事实上 ◊ *I'm not a student, I'm a doctor, actually.* 我不是个学生，事实上，我是位医生。

> **actually** 和 **really** 都用于强调陈述的内容。**actually** 用于强调某个情形下的确存在的事实，通常该事实出人意料，或者跟刚刚提及的事情形成对比。*All the characters in the novel actually existed... He actually began to cry.* 它还可以用来强调叙述的精确性或者表示对他人的更正。*No one was actually drunk... We couldn't actually see the garden.* 在谈话中使用 **really** 是为了强调正在谈论的内容。*I really think he's sick.* **really** 用于形容词或者副词前，与 **very** 含义相似。*This is really serious.*

acupuncture [ˈækjupʌŋktʃə(r)] *n* [U] 针刺疗法

acupuncturist [ˈækjupʌŋktʃərɪst] *n* [C] 针灸医生

acute [əˈkjuːt] *adj* **1** (*severe*) [+ *embarrassment, shortage*] 严重的 **2** [医] [+ *illness, infection*] 急性的 **3** (*keen, sharp*) [+ *mind, senses, observer*] 敏锐的 **4** [数] ♦**acute angle** 锐角 **5** [语言] [+ *accent*] 带重音符号的 ♦**e acute** 尖重音 e

acutely [ə'kjuːtlɪ] *adv* (*intensely*) [+ *aware, conscious*] 敏锐地; [+ *embarrassing, sensitive*] 剧烈地

AD *adv abbr* (= **Anno Domini**) 公元

ad [æd] [非正式] *n* (*advertisement*) 广告

adamant ['ædəmənt] *adj* ♦**to be adamant about sth/that ...** 对某事/…抱坚决态度

adapt [ə'dæpt] **I** *vt* **1** (*alter, change*) 使适合 **2** (*for television, cinema*) [+ *novel, play*] 改编 **II** *vi* ♦**to adapt (to)** 适应 ♦**to adapt o.s.** 使自己适应

adaptable [ə'dæptəbl] *adj* [+ *person, object, material*] 适应性强的

adaptor [ə'dæptə(r)] [电子] *n* [c] 转接器

✪ **add** [æd] **I** *vt* **1** (*put in, put on*) 加入 ◊ *Add the grated cheese to the sauce.* 把磨碎的奶酪加入酱汁中。 **2** ♦**to add (together)** (*calculate total of*) 加(起来) ◊ *Add three and fourteen.* 3 加14 。 ◊ *Add all the interest and other charges together.* 把所有的收益和其他收费加起来。 **3** (*say*) 补充 **4** (*give*) 增添 ◊ *The herbs add flavour.* 香料增添特殊风味。 **II** *vi* **1** (*calulate*) 做加法 **2** ♦**to add to** (*increase*) 增加 ◊ *This all adds to the cost.* 这都增加了成本。 ♦**he added that ...** 他接着说…

❑**add on** *vt* 附加 ◊ *They add on 9 per cent for service.* 他们附加9% 的服务费。

❑**add up I** *vi* **1** (*calulate*) 做加法 ◊ *Many young children cannot add up.* 许多幼龄儿童不会做加法。 **2** (*accumulate*) 累积 **3** (*appear consistent*) 合情合理 **II** *vt* (*calculate total of*) 把…加起来 ♦**it doesn't add up** 这说不通

❑**add up to** *vt* [不可拆分] (*amount to*) 合计达

added ['ædɪd] *adj* (*extra*) 额外的

addict ['ædɪkt] *n* [c] **1** ♦**drug/heroin addict** 吸毒/海洛因成瘾的人 **2** ♦**TV/football addict** 电视/足球迷

addicted [ə'dɪktɪd] *adj* ♦**to be addicted to sth** [+ *drugs, drink*] 对某事上瘾; [+ *TV, chocolate etc*] 对某事入迷

addiction [ə'dɪkʃən] *n* [c/u] **1** (*to drugs, alcohol*) 瘾 **2** (*to gambling, boxing*) 入迷

addictive [ə'dɪktɪv] *adj* **1** [+ *drug*] 易上瘾的 **2** [+ *activity*] 使人入迷的

addition [ə'dɪʃən] *n* **1** [u] [数] 加法 **2** ♦**(with/by) the addition of** (通过)添加… **3** [c] ♦**addition (to)** (*thing added*) 增添物 ♦**in addition** 另外 ♦**in addition to** 除…之外

additional [ə'dɪʃənl] *adj* 附加的

additive ['ædɪtɪv] *n* [c] 添加剂

address [ə'drɛs] **I** *n* [c] **1** (*postal address*) 地址 **2** (*speech*) 演说 **II** *vt* **1** [+ *letter, parcel*] 在…上写收件人姓名地址 **2** [正式] (*speak to*) [+ *person*] 对…说话; [+ *meeting, conference etc*] 向…讲话 ♦**to give an address (to sb/at sth)** (*speech*) (对某人/在某场合)做演讲 ♦**form of address** 称呼 ♦**to be addressed to sb** [*letter, parcel* +] 是写给某人的 ♦**to address a remark to sb** [正式] 对某人进行评论 ♦**to address sb as ...** 称某人为… ♦**to address (o.s. to) a problem** 致力于处理某个问题

address book *n* [c] 通讯录

adept ['ædɛpt] *adj* ♦**adept (at)** 熟练的

adequate ['ædɪkwɪt] *adj* **1** (*sufficient*) 足够的 **2** (*satisfactory*) 符合要求的 **3** (*appropriate*) [+ *response, reply etc*] 恰当的

adequately ['ædɪkwɪtlɪ] *adv* **1** (*sufficiently*) 足够地 **2** (*satisfactorily*) 恰当地

adhere [əd'hɪə(r)] *vi* **1** ♦**adhere to** [正式] (*stick to*) 黏附 **2** (喻) (*abide by*) [+ *rule, decision, treaty*] 遵守 **3** (*hold to*) [+ *opinion, belief*] 坚持

adhesive [əd'hiːzɪv] **I** *n* [c/u] 黏合剂 **II** *adj* 有黏性的

adhesive tape *n* [u] **1** [英] 胶带 **2** [美: 医] 绊创膏

adjacent [ə'dʒeɪsənt] *adj* 邻近的 ♦**adjacent to** 邻近

adjective ['ædʒɛktɪv] *n* [c] 形容词

adjoining [ə'dʒɔɪnɪŋ] *adj* [+ *room, office etc*] 相邻的

adjourn [ə'dʒəːn] **I** *vt* (*break off*) [+ *meeting, trial*] 休 **II** *vi* (*break off*) [*meeting* +] 休会; [*trial* +] 休庭

♦**they adjourned to the pub** [英:非正式]他们转移到酒吧去了

adjudicate [ə'dʒuːdɪkeɪt] [正式] **I** *vt* [+ *claim, dispute, contest*] 裁决 **II** *vi* ♦**to adjudicate (on sth)** (就某事)做出裁定

adjust [ə'dʒʌst] **I** *vt* **1** (*change*) [+ *approach, policy etc*] 调整 **2** (*rearrange*) [+ *clothing*] 整理 **3** [+ *device, position, setting*] 校准 **4** [+ *eyes, vision*] 使适应 **II** *vi* **1** (*adapt*) 适应 **2** ♦**to adjust to** 适应 ♦**to adjust** *or* **become adjusted (to sth)** [*eyes, vision* +] 适应(某事)

adjustable [ə'dʒʌstəbl] *adj* 可调节的

adjustment [ə'dʒʌstmənt] *n* [c] **1** (*to machine*) 校正 **2** [*of prices, wages*] 调整 **3** (*in behaviour, thinking*) 改变 ♦**to make an adjustment to sth** 对某物作调整

admin ['ædmɪn] [非正式] *n* 管理 ♦**to do the admin** 做杂事

administer [əd'mɪnɪstə(r)] *vt* **1** [+ *country, department*] 掌管 **2** [+ *test*] 监管 **3** [正式] [+ *drug*] 使用 ♦**to administer justice** 执法

administration [ədmɪnɪs'treɪʃən] *n* **1** [u] (*organizing, supervising*) 管理 **2** [c] (*managing body*) 管理部门 ♦**the (Reagan/Clinton) Administration** [美] (里根/克林顿)政府

administrative [əd'mɪnɪstrətɪv] *adj* [+ *costs, staff, system*] 行政的

administrator [əd'mɪnɪstreɪtə(r)] *n* [c] 行政人员

admiral ['ædmərəl] *n* [c] 海军上将

admiration [ædmə'reɪʃən] *n* [u] 钦佩 ♦**in admiration** [*stare, gasp etc* +] 满怀钦佩 ♦**to have great admiration for sth/sb** 对某物/某人无限钦佩

admire [əd'maɪə(r)] *vt* **1** (*like, respect*) [+ *person*] 钦佩 **2** (*look at*) [+ *something beautiful*] 欣赏 ♦**I admire your courage/honesty** 我钦佩你的勇气/诚实

admirer [əd'maɪərə(r)] *n* [c] **1** ♦**an admirer of sth/sb** (*fan*) 某物/某人的赞赏者 **2** (*suitor*) 爱慕者

admission [əd'mɪʃən] *n* **1** [c/u] (*admittance*) 进入许可 **2** [c/u] (*of country to organization*) 加入许可 **3** [c/u] (*to hospital*) 住院 **4** [u] (*to exhibition, night club etc*) 进入 **5** [u] (*also:* ***admission charge, admission fee***) 入场费 **6** [c/u] (*confession*) 承认 ♦**admission free/£2.50** 免费入场/入场费2.50英镑 ♦**to gain admission (to)** [正式]获准进入 ♦**by his/her own admission** 据他/她自己承认 ♦**an admission of guilt/failure** 承认罪责/失败

admit [əd'mɪt] *vt* **1** (*confess*) 承认 **2** (*accept*) [+ *defeat, responsibility*] 接受 **3** (*permit to enter*) (*to club, organization*) 接纳; (*to place, area*) 准许…进入 ♦**he admits that ...** 他承认… ♦**I must admit that ...** 我不得不承认… ♦**to be admitted to hospital** 住进医院 ♦**"children not admitted"** "儿童不得入内" ♦**this ticket admits two** 这张票可让两人入场

❑**admit to** *vt* [不可拆分] (*confess*) [+ *murder etc*] 承认 ♦**to admit to doing sth** *or* **having done sth** 承认做过某事

admittance [əd'mɪtəns] *n* [u] (*to building, hospital*) 准许进入; (*as member, student etc*) 进入权 ♦**"no admittance"** "禁止入内" ♦**to gain admittance (to sth)** (*cross threshold*) 有权进入(某处); (*as member, student, employee etc*) 被(某处)录取

admittedly [əd'mɪtɪdlɪ] *adv* 公认地

adolescence [ædəu'lɛsns] *n* [u] 青春期

adolescent [ædəu'lɛsnt] **I** *adj* 青春期的 **II** *n* [c] (*teenager*) 青少年

adopt [ə'dɔpt] *vt* **1** [+ *plan, approach, attitude*] 采用 **2** [+ *child*] 收养

adopted [ə'dɔptɪd] *adj* **1** [+ *child*] 被收养的 **2** [+ *country, home*] 移居的

adoption [ə'dɔpʃən] *n* **1** [c/u] [*of child*] 收养 **2** [u] [*of policy*] 采用

adoptive [ə'dɔptɪv] *adj* **1** [+ *parent, mother, father*] 收养的 **2** [+ *country, town, city etc*] 移居的

adore [ə'dɔː(r)] *vt* **1** [+ *person*] 敬慕 **2** [非正式] [+ *film, activity, food etc*] 喜爱

adorn [ə'dɔːn] *vt* (*decorate*) 装饰 ♦**adorned with** 用…装饰的

Adriatic [eɪdrɪ'ætɪk] *n* ♦**the Adriatic (Sea)** 亚得里亚（海）

adrift [ə'drɪft] *adj* **1** [*boat, crew* +] 漂浮的 **2**（喻）[*person* +] 漂泊无依的 ♦**to come adrift** [英] [*wire, rope, fastening etc* +] 脱落 ♦**to set adrift** [+ *boat, crew*] 使漂流

ADT [美] *abbr* (= ***Atlantic Daylight Time***) 大西洋夏令时

adult ['ædʌlt] **I** *n* [c] **1** (*person*) 成年人 **2** (*animal, bird, insect*) 成体 **II** *adj* **1** (*grown-up*) [+ *life*] 成年的 **2** [+ *animal, bird, insect*] 成熟的 **3** (*for adults*) 成人的 **4** (*explicit*) [+ *literature, film*] 色情的; (*mature*) 成熟的

adultery [ə'dʌltərɪ] *n* [u] 通奸 ♦**to commit adultery** 有通奸行为

adulthood ['ædʌlthud] *n* [u] 成年

advance [əd'vɑːns] **I** *vi* **1** (*move forward*) 前进 **2** (*make progress*) 进展 **II** *n* **1** [c/u] (*development*) 发展 **2** [c/u] (*movement forward*) 挺进 **3** [c] (*money*) 预付款 **III** *adj* [+ *notice, warning*] 预先的 **IV** *vt* **1** [+ *money*] 预付 **2** (*propose*) [+ *theory, idea*] 提出 **3** (*bring forward*) 提前 **V advances** *n* [*pl*] ♦**to make advances to sb** [过时] (*amorously*) 向某人献殷勤 ♦**troops are advancing on the capital** 部队正朝首都挺进 ♦**in advance** [*book, prepare, plan* +] 提前 ♦**in advance of** (*before*) 在…之前 ♦**(to pay sb) an advance on sth** 预付（某人）某事的费用 ♦**advance booking** [戏剧] 提前预订

advanced [əd'vɑːnst] *adj* **1** (*highly developed*) [+ *system, device*] 先进的; [+ *country*] 发达的 **2** [教育] [+ *student, pupil*] 高年级的; [+ *course, work*] 高等的 **3** [+ *stage, level*] ♦**to be at/reach an advanced stage/level** 到晚期 **4** [正式] [+ *years, age*] 老的

advantage [əd'vɑːntɪdʒ] *n* [c] **1** (*benefit*) 好处 **2** (*favourable factor*) 有利因素 **3** (*superiority*) 优势; [网球] 优势分 ♦**to have the advantage of being/doing sth** 由于某事/做某事而占据优势 ♦**to take advantage of** [+ *person*] 利用; [+ *opportunity*] 利用 ♦**to use** *or* **turn sth to one's advantage** 使某事转化为对自己有利 ♦**the advantage of x over y** x胜过y的优势 ♦**to have an advantage over sb** 胜过某人 ♦**to (best/good) advantage** 达到（最佳/很好的）效果

advantageous [ædvən'teɪdʒəs] *adj* 有利的 ♦**advantageous to sb** 对某人有利的

advent ['ædvənt] *n* **1** ♦**the advent of** (*arrival*) …的出现 **2** [宗] ♦**Advent** 降临节

adventure [əd'vɛntʃə(r)] *n* **1** [c] (*exciting event*) 冒险活动 **2** [u] (*excitement*) 冒险

adventurous [əd'vɛntʃərəs] *adj* **1** (*bold*) [+ *person*] 喜欢冒险的 **2** (*innovative*) [+ *thing*] 冒险的

adverb ['ædvəːb] *n* [c] 副词

adversary ['ædvəsərɪ] *n* [c] 对手

adverse ['ædvəːs] *adj* [+ *effect, conditions*] 不利的; [+ *reaction, publicity*] 敌对的

adversity [əd'vəːsɪtɪ] *n* [u/c] 逆境 ♦**in the face of adversity** 面临逆境

advert ['ædvəːt] [英] *n* 广告 [美 = **ad**]

advertise ['ædvətaɪz] **I** *vi* (*in newspaper, on television etc*) 做广告 **II** *vt* **1** [+ *product, event*] 为…做广告 **2** [+ *job*] 刊登 ♦**to advertise for sth/sb** [+ *staff, accommodation*] 登广告征求某物/某人

advertisement [əd'vəːtɪsmənt] [商] *n* [c] (*in newspaper, classified ads, on television*) 广告 ♦**to be an advertisement for sth** [尤英] 为某事做宣传

advertiser ['ædvətaɪzə(r)] *n* [c] (*in newspaper, on television etc*) 广告人

advertising ['ædvətaɪzɪŋ] *n* [u] **1** (*advertisements*) 广告 **2** (*industry*) 广告业

advertising agency *n* [c] 广告公司

advertising campaign *n* [c] 宣传活动

advice [əd'vaɪs] *n* [u] 忠告 ♦**a piece of advice** 一条建议 ♦**to ask (sb) for advice (about/on sth)** 征求（某人）（关于某事的）意见 ♦**to take (legal) advice** [正式] 征求（律师的）意见 ♦**take my advice** [非正式] 听我的劝告

> 📖 请勿将**advice**和**advise**混淆。**advice**含有字母**c**，是名词。*She gave me some useful advice…Let me give you a piece of advice.* **advise**含有字母**s**，是动词。*The teacher advised him to study harder if he wanted to do well in his exams.*

advisable [əd'vaɪzəbl] [正式] *adj* ♦**it is/would be advisable to …** …是可取的

advise [əd'vaɪz] *vt* **1** (*tell*) ♦**to advise sb to do sth** 劝某人做某事 **2** (*help*) ♦**to advise sb on sth** 在某事上劝某人 **3** [正式] (*inform*) ♦**to advise sb of sth** 将某事通知某人 ♦**to advise sb against sth/doing sth** 劝某人不要接受某事/做某事

📖 用法参见 **advice**

adviser [əd'vaɪzə(r)] *n* [c] 顾问

advisory [əd'vaɪzərɪ] [正式] *adj* [+ *role, capacity, body etc*] 咨询的 ♦**in an advisory capacity** 以顾问身份

advocate [*n* 'ædvəkɪt, *vb* 'ædvəkeɪt] **I** [正式] *vt* (*support, recommend*) 拥护 **II** *n* [c] **1** (*barrister*) 辩护人 **2** [正式] (*supporter, proponent*) 拥护者

Aegean [iː'dʒiːən] *n* ♦**the Aegean (Sea)** 爱琴海

aerial ['ɛərɪəl] **I** [英] *n* [c] 天线 [美=**antenna**] **II** *adj* [+ *attack, photograph*] 空中的

aerobics [ɛə'rəubɪks] **I** *n* [U] 有氧健身操 **II** *cpd* [复合词] [+ *class, instructor*] 健身操

aeroplane ['ɛərəpleɪn] [英] *n* [c] 飞机 [美=**airplane**]

aerosol ['ɛərəsɔl] *n* [c] (*can, spray*) 按钮式喷雾器

aesthetic [iːs'θɛtɪk] *adj* 审美的

affable ['æfəbl] *adj* [+ *person, nature*] 和蔼可亲的

affair [ə'fɛə(r)] **I** *n* **1** [s] (*matter, business*) 事情 **2** [c] (*romance*) 风流韵事 **II affairs** *n* [*pl*] **1** (*matters*) 事务 **2** (*personal concerns*) 私事 ♦**to have an affair (with sb)** (和某人)发生暧昧关系 ♦**that's your/my affair** 那是你/我的私事

affect [ə'fɛkt] *vt* **1** (*influence*) [+ *person, object*] 影响 **2** [*disease* +] 侵袭 **3** (*emotionally*) 感动 **4** [文] (*feign*) ♦**to affect interest/concern** 佯装感兴趣/关心

> 📖 请勿将**affect**和**effect**混淆。如果某事物**affects**某人或某事，则它影响了该人或该事，或者使他们发生改变。*Fitness affects you mentally and physically, and how you feel affects your relationships and your ability to cope...Noise affects different people in different ways.* **affect**的名词形式是**effect**。如果某事物**affect**你，它对你有**effect**。*…the effect of noise on people in factories… the effect of the anaesthetic…* **effect**也可以用作动词。如果你**effect**某事，例如某个变化或修理某物，你促使该事发生或做了这件事。**effect**作为动词时，是一个比较正式的词汇，而且比作为名词时的用法少见得多。*She had effected a few rather hasty repairs.*

affected [ə'fɛktɪd] *adj* [+ *behaviour, person*] 做作的

affection [ə'fɛkʃən] **I** *n* [U] (*fondness*) 喜爱 **II affections** *n* [*pl*] 爱慕 ♦**to feel affection for sb** 喜欢某人 ♦**to win sb's affection** 赢得某人的爱慕

affectionate [ə'fɛkʃənɪt] *adj* [+ *person, kiss, animal*] 有感情的 ♦**to be affectionate towards sb** 钟爱某人

affinity [ə'fɪnɪtɪ] *n* **1** [s] (*bond*) ♦**to have an affinity with sb/sth** 和某人/某物有亲近感 **2** [c] (*resemblance*) 相似

afflict [ə'flɪkt] *vt* ♦**to be afflicted with** *or* **by sth** 被某事所折磨

affluent ['æfluənt] *adj* (*wealthy*) [+ *person, surroundings*] 富裕的

afford [ə'fɔːd] *vt* **1** ♦**to be able to afford (to buy/pay) sth** 买/支付得起某物 **2** ♦**to be able to afford (to do) sth** (*permit o.s.*) 担负得起(做)某事 **3** [正式] (*provide*) [+ *opportunity, protection*] 提供

affordable [ə'fɔːdəbl] *adj* 买得起的

Afghanistan [æf'gænɪstæn] *n* 阿富汗

afield [ə'fiːld] *adv* ♦**(from) far afield**（来自）远方 ♦**(from) further** *or* **farther afield**（来自）更远的地方

afloat [ə'fləut] *adv* ♦**to keep sth afloat** 使某物浮在水面上; (*financially*) 使某物维持下去

afoot [ə'fut] *adv* ♦**there is something afoot** 某事正在进行中 ♦**plans/moves are afoot to ...** 正有计划/行动…

afraid [ə'freɪd] *adj* (*frightened*) 害怕的 ♦**to be afraid of sb/sth** 害怕某人/某物 ♦**to be afraid to do sth/ of doing sth** 怕做某事 ♦**to be afraid for sb** 担心某人 ♦**to be afraid that ...** (*worry, fear*) 担心…; (*expressing apology, disagreement*) 恐怕… ♦**don't be afraid to ...** (*expressing reassurance*) 不要有顾虑… ♦**I'm afraid so/not** 恐怕是/不是的

afresh [ə'frɛʃ] *adv* [*start* +] 重新

Africa ['æfrɪkə] *n* 非洲

African ['æfrɪkən] **I** *adj* 非洲的 **II** *n* [c] (*person*) 非洲人

African-American I *n* [c] 美国黑人 **II** *adj* 美国黑人的

✪**after** ['ɑːftə(r)] **I** *prep* **1** (*in time*) 在…以后 ◊ *She arrived just after breakfast.* 她刚好在早饭后到。**2** (*in place, order*) 在…后面 ◊ *I wrote my signature after Penny's.* 我把名字签在潘妮的后面。**II** *adv* (*afterwards*) 以后 ◊ *Soon after, he began preparing the meal.* 不久以后，他开始准备饭菜。**III** *conj* (*once*) 在…以后 ◊ *They felt ill after they had eaten.* 他们吃完后感到不舒服。♦**the day after tomorrow** 后天 ♦**it's ten after eight** [美] 现在是8 点过10分 [英=**past**] ♦**day after day/year after year** 日复一日/年复一年 ♦**to call/shout/stare after sb** 在某人身后叫/喊/瞪眼 ♦**the second biggest, after Germany** 紧随德国之后的第二大 ♦**to clean/tidy/ clear up after sb** (*for*) 替某人打扫/整理/清理 ♦**to be after sb** (*chasing, following*) 追逐某人 ◊ *The police are after him.* 警察在追缉他。♦**to be after sth** (*trying to get*) 想得到某物 ♦**to ask after sb** 询问某人的情况 ♦**to be named after sb/sth** [英] 以某人/某物的名字命名 ♦**after all** 毕竟 ♦**after you!** 您先请！♦**after doing sth** 做完某事后 ◊ *after flying to London* 飞抵伦敦后

> **after, afterwards** 和 **later** 用于表示某事发生在说话的时间，或者某个特定事情之后。**after** 可以和 **not long**、**shortly** 等连用。*After dinner she spoke to him…I returned to England after visiting India…Shortly after, she called me.* 在无须指明某个特定时间或事件时，可以用 **afterwards**。*Afterwards we went to a night club…You'd better come and see me later.* **afterwards** 可以和 **soon**、**shortly** 等连用。*Soon afterwards, he came to the clinic.* **later** 表示某事发生在说话之后，可以和 **a little**、**much** 或 **not much** 等连用。*I'll go and see her later…A little later, the lights went out...I learned all this much later.* 可以用 **after**、**afterwards** 和 **later** 后跟表示时间段的词语，表示某事发生的时间。*...five years after his death…She wrote about it six years later/afterwards.*

aftermath ['ɑːftəmɑːθ] *n* ♦**(in) the aftermath (of)** 在…结束后的一个时期里

afternoon ['ɑːftə'nuːn] *n* [c/u] 下午 ♦**this afternoon** 今天下午 ♦**tomorrow/yesterday afternoon** 明天/昨天下午 ♦**(good) afternoon!** (*goodbye*) 再见！; (*hello*) 下午好！

after-shave (lotion) ['ɑːftəʃeɪv-] *n* [u] 须后（润肤）水

aftersun ['ɑːftə(r)'sʌn] *n* [u] 晒后修复霜

afterwards ['ɑːftəwədz] (美 **afterward** ['ɑːftəwəd]) *adv* 以后 用法参见 **after**

✪**again** [ə'gɛn] *adv* **1** (*a second or another time*) 又一次地 ◊ *He kissed her again.* 他又一次吻了她。

2 (*returning to previous state*) 又 ◊ *She opened the door and then closed it again.* 她打开门，随着又关上了。**♦again and again/time and again** 一再 **♦now and again** 时而 **♦(but) then** *or* **there again** （但）另一方面

✪ **against** [ə'gɛnst] **I** *prep* **1** (*leaning on, touching*) 紧靠在 ◊ *He stood the ladder against the wall.* 他把梯子紧靠在墙上。◊ *She pressed her nose against the window.* 她把鼻子紧贴在窗户上。**2** (*opposed to*) 反对 ◊ *He is against privatization.* 他反对私有化。**3** (*towards*) (*expressing hostility*) 针对 ◊ *violence against women* 针对妇女的暴力 **4** (*in game or competition*) 同…对抗 ◊ *They'll be playing against Australia.* 他们将在比赛中同澳大利亚队对抗。**5 ♦to protect against sth** 保护免受某种伤害 ◊ *The cream protects against sunburn.* 这种润肤霜保护皮肤免受晒伤。**6** (*compared to*) 和…对比 ◊ *The pound has fallen against the dollar.* 英镑和美元的比值有所下跌。**II** *adv* (*in opposition*) 反对 ◊ *283 votes in favour and 29 against* 283 票赞成，29 票反对 **♦against the law/rules** 违反法律/规则 **♦against sb's wishes/advice** 违背某人的意愿/忠告 **♦against one's will** 违背自己的意愿 **♦to have sth against sb** 讨厌某人 **♦to have nothing against sb** 并不讨厌某人 **♦against a background of ...** 在…的背景下 **♦against a blue background** 衬着蓝色的背景 **♦(as) against** (*compared to*) 和…相比

✪ **age** [eɪdʒ] **I** *n* **1** [c/u] [*of person, object*] 年龄 ◊ *I'm the same age as you.* 我和你同龄。**2** [u] (*being old*) 老年 ◊ *He is showing signs of age.* 他开始显老了。**3** [c] (*period in history*) 时代 ◊ *We live in an age of uncertainty.* 我们生活在一个动乱的时代。**II** *vi* [*person* +] 变老 ◊ *He has aged a lot.* 他变老了许多。**III** *vt* [+ *person*] 使…见老 ◊ *The worry had aged him.* 忧愁使他见老了。**♦what age is he?** 他多大了？**♦you don't look your age** 你看起来与你年纪不相符 **♦20 years of age** 20 岁 **♦at the age of 20** 20 岁时 **♦to be under age** [*person* +] 未成年 **♦under age smoking/drinking/sex** 未成年抽烟/喝酒/性行为 **♦to come of age** [*person* +] 达到法定年龄 **♦an age, ages** [非正式] 很长时间 ◊ *I haven't seen you for ages!* 我很长时间没见到你了！**♦the Stone/Bronze/Iron Age** 石器/铜器/铁器时代 **♦the age of steam/television/chivalry** 蒸汽/电视/骑士时代 **♦through the ages** 历代

aged[1] [eɪdʒd] *adj* **♦aged 10** 10 岁

aged[2] ['eɪdʒɪd] **I** *adj* (*elderly*) 老年的 **II** *n* [*pl*] **♦the aged** 老人

age group *n* [c] 同一年龄的人们 **♦the 40 to 50 age group** 年龄在 40 岁到 50 岁的人们

age limit *n* [c] 年龄限制

agency ['eɪdʒənsɪ] *n* [c] **1** [商] 代理处 **2** [尤美] (*government body*) 机构

agenda [ə'dʒɛndə] *n* [c] **1** [*of meeting*] 议程 **2** (*political*) 议事日程 **♦on the/sb's agenda** (*for meeting*) 在（某人的）议事日程中 **♦high on the agenda** (*political*) 首要事件 **♦to set the agenda** 设定议程 **♦to have one's own agenda** 有自己的专门议题 **♦a hidden agenda** 秘密议程

agent ['eɪdʒənt] *n* [c] **1** (*representative*) 代理人 **2** (*for actor, writer, musician*) 经纪人 **3** (*spy*) 间谍 **4** (*chemical*) 剂 **5 ♦the/an agent of sth** (*instrument*) 某事的催化物

age of consent *n* **♦the age of consent** 承诺年龄 **♦under/over the age of consent** 未满/超过承诺年龄

aggravate ['ægrəveɪt] *vt* **1** (*make worse*) [+ *situation*] 使恶化 **2** [非正式] (*annoy*) [+ *person*] 激怒

aggression [ə'grɛʃən] *n* [u] 侵略 **♦an act of aggression** 侵犯行为

aggressive [ə'grɛsɪv] *adj* **1** (*belligerent*) 好战的 **2** (*forceful*) [+ *salesman, campaign*] 有闯劲的

aghast [ə'gɑːst] [正式] *adj* **♦aghast (at)** [+ *behaviour, situation*] （被…）吓呆

agile ['ædʒaɪl] *adj* **1** (*physically*) 灵活的 **2** (*mentally*) 敏捷的

agitate ['ædʒɪteɪt] **I** *vi* ♦**to agitate for/against sth** (*campaign*) 鼓吹某事/鼓吹反对某事 **II** *vt* **1** (*upset*) [+ *person*] 使焦虑 **2** [正式] (*shake*) [+ *liquid*] 搅动

agitated ['ædʒɪteɪtɪd] *adj* [+ *person*] 焦虑的

AGM *n abbr* (= ***annual general meeting***) 年度会议

✪ **ago** [ə'gəu] *adv* ♦**2 days ago** 两天前 ♦**long ago/a long time ago** 很久以前 ♦**how long ago?** 多久以前？♦**as long ago as 1925** 早在1925年

agonizing ['ægənaɪzɪŋ] *adj* **1** [+ *pain, death*] 令人痛苦的 **2** [+ *wait*] 烦人的 **3** [+ *decision, choice*] 折磨人的

agony ['ægənɪ] *n* [C/U] 痛苦 ♦**to be in agony** 在极度痛苦中

✪ **agree** [ə'griː] **I** *vi* **1** (*have same opinion*) 同意 ◊ *They find it hard to agree about this.* 他们觉得很难同意这一点。**2** ♦**to agree to sth/to do sth** 同意某事/做某事 ◊ *He has agreed to our proposal.* 他已经同意了我们的建议。**3** ♦**to agree with sth** (*approve of*) 对某事表示赞同 ◊ *I don't agree with children smoking.* 我不赞同儿童吸烟。**4** ♦**to agree (with sth)** [*figures, total* +] (*tally*) (和某事) 相符 ◊ *This bill doesn't agree with my calculations.* 这账单和我算的结果不相符。**5** ♦**to agree (with sth)** [*account, story* +] (*be consistent*) (和某事) 一致 ◊ *His statement agrees with those of other witnesses.* 他的陈述和其他证人的完全一致。**6** ♦**to agree (with sth)** (*according to grammar*) [*word* +] (和某事) 一致 ◊ *The subject must agree with the verb.* 主语必须和动词保持数的一致。**II** *vt* ♦**to agree sth** [英] (*decide*) 商定 ◊ *We have agreed a price.* 我们商定了价格。♦**to agree with sb about sth** [*person* +] 关于某事赞成某人的看法 ♦**I agree with what you say** 我同意你说的观点 ♦**milk doesn't agree with me** 我喝不惯牛奶 ♦**to agree on sth** [+ *price, arrangement*] 商定某事 ♦**to be agreed on sth** 就某事达成协议 ♦**to agree that ...** 同意…

agreeable [ə'griːəbl] *adj* **1** (*pleasant*) [+ *sensation*] 令人愉快的；[+ *person*] 容易相处的 **2** (*willing*) ♦**to be agreeable (to sth/to doing sth)** 欣然同意 (某事/做某事)

agreed [ə'griːd] *adj* [+ *time, place, price*] 约定的

agreement [ə'griːmənt] *n* **1** [C] ♦**an agreement (on sth)** (*decision, arrangement*) (关于某事的) 协议 **2** [U] ♦**agreement (on sth)** (*concurrence*) (关于某事的) 一致意见 **3** [U] (*consent*) 同意 **4** [U] (*in grammar*) 一致 ♦**to be in agreement (with sb/sth)** (与某人) 意见一致/同意 (某事) ♦**to nod one's head in agreement** 点头表示同意 ♦**to reach an agreement** 达成共识

agricultural [ægrɪ'kʌltʃərəl] *adj* [+ *land, worker*] 农业的

agriculture ['ægrɪkʌltʃə(r)] *n* [U] 农业

ahead [ə'hɛd] *adv* **1** (*in front*) (*of place*) 在前地 **2** (*in work, achievements*) 提前地 **3** (*in competition*) 领先地 **4** (*in the future*) 在未来 ♦**the days/months ahead** 今后几天/几个月 ♦**to think/plan ahead** 事先考虑/计划 ♦**ahead of** (*in front of*) 在…之前；(*before in time*) 在…面前；(*in advance of*) [+ *event*] 预先；(*in ranking, progress*) 领先 ♦**ahead of time/schedule** 提前 ♦**to get ahead of sb** (*in front of*) 超过某人；(*in progress*) 超越 ♦**a year ahead** (*in advance*) 提前一年 ♦**to send sb (on) ahead** 送某人先走 ♦**to go (on) ahead** 先走 ♦**right** *or* **straight ahead** (*direction*) 笔直向前；(*location*) 正前方 ♦**go ahead!** (*giving permission*) 干吧！

✪ **aid** [eɪd] **I** *n* **1** [U] (*support*) (*to country, people*) 援助 **2** [U] [正式] (*assistance*) 帮助 **3** [C] (*device*) 辅助 ◊ *teaching aids* 教学辅助设备 **II** *vt* **1** (*support*) [+ *country, people*] 援助 **2** (*help*) [+ *person, organization*] 协助 **3** (*facilitate*) [+ *process*] 促进 ♦**with the aid of sb/sth** 在某人/某物的帮助下 ♦**in aid of** [尤英] [+ *charity*] 用以援助 ♦**to come/go to sb's aid** 前来/往援助某人 ♦**to aid and**

abet [法] 同谋
aide [eɪd] *n* [c] 助手
AIDS [eɪdz] *n abbr* (= ***acquired immune deficiency syndrome***) 艾滋病
ailing ['eɪlɪŋ] *adj* **1** [+ *person*] 久病不起的 **2** [+ *economy, industry*] 每况愈下的
ailment ['eɪlmənt] *n* [c] 小病
aim [eɪm] **I** *vt* ♦**to aim sth (at sb/sth)** [+ *gun, camera*] 将某物瞄准（某人/某物）; [+ *punch, kick*] 将某物对准（某人/某物）**II** *vi* (*with weapon*) 瞄准 **III** *n* **1** [c] (*objective*) 目标 **2** [s] (*in shooting*) 瞄准 ♦**to be aimed at sb** [*remarks, campaign* +] 针对某人 ♦**to be aimed at achieving sth** 意在获取某物 ♦**to aim at sth** (*with weapon*) 瞄准某物 ♦**to aim to do sth** [非正式] 打算做某事 ♦**to take aim (at sth/sb)** 向（某物/某人）瞄准
ain't [eɪnt] [非正式] = **am not, aren't, isn't**
✪**air** [ɛə(r)] **I** *n* **1** [u] (*atmosphere*) 空气 ◊ *He breathed in the cold night air.* 他呼吸了夜晚清凉的空气。**2** [c] [过时] (*tune*) 曲调 **3** [s] (*appearance*) 神情 ◊ *with an air of superiority* 摆出高人一等的神情 **II** *vt* **1** [+ *room*] 使通气 **2** [+ *clothes*] 晾干 **3** [+ *opinions, grievances*] 发表 **4** (*broadcast*) [+ *programme*] 播放 **III** *cpd* [复合词] [+ *travel*] 乘飞机; [+ *fare*] 飞机 ♦**in/into/through the air** 在/进入/穿过天空 ◊ *He threw the ball (up) into the air.* 他把球抛向天空。♦**by air** (*flying*) 乘飞机 ♦**to clear the air** 澄清事实 ♦**in the air** 在空中 ♦**up in the air** (*undecided*) 悬而未决 ♦**to be/come off (the) air** [*programme, station* +] 停止播放 ♦**to be/go on (the) air** [*programme, station* +] 正在/开始播放
airbag ['ɛəbæg] *n* [c] (*in car*) 安全气袋
airbed ['ɛəbɛd] [英] *n* [c] 充气床垫
air-conditioned ['ɛəkən'dɪʃənd] *adj* 装有空调的
air conditioner *n* [c] 空调
air conditioning [-kən'dɪʃənɪŋ] *n* [u] 空气调节
aircraft ['ɛəkrɑːft] (*pl* **aircraft**) *n* [c] 飞行器
airfield ['ɛəfiːld] *n* [c] 停机坪
air force I *n* [c] 空军 **II** *cpd* [复合词] [+ *pilot, base*] 空军 ♦**the air force** 空军
air hostess [英] *n* [c] 空中小姐 [美 = **stewardess**]
airlift ['ɛəlɪft] **I** *n* [c] 空运 **II** *vt* 空运
airline ['ɛəlaɪn] *n* [c] 航空公司
airliner ['ɛəlaɪnə(r)] *n* [c] 班机
airmail ['ɛəmeɪl] *n* [u] ♦**by airmail** 航空邮寄
airplane ['ɛəpleɪn] [美] *n* [c] 飞机 [英 = **aeroplane**]
airport ['ɛəpɔːt] *n* [c] 飞机场
air raid *n* [c] 空袭
air terminal [尤英] *n* [c] 航空集散站
airtight ['ɛətaɪt] *adj* **1** [+ *container*] 密封的 **2** [美] [+ *case, alibi*] 无懈可击的
airy ['ɛərɪ] *adj* **1** [+ *room, building*] 通风的 **2** (*casual*) [+ *manner*] 没头脑的
aisle [aɪl] *n* [c] (*in church, theatre, supermarket, on plane*) 过道 ♦**to walk down the aisle** (*get married*) 结婚 ♦**aisle seat** (*on plane*) 靠过道的座位
ajar [ə'dʒɑː(r)] *adj* [*door* +] 微开的
akin [ə'kɪn] *adj* ♦**akin to** (*similar to*) 相似的
à la carte [ɑːlɑː'kɑːt] *adj, adv* 照菜单点
alarm [ə'lɑːm] **I** *n* **1** [u] (*anxiety*) 惊慌 **2** [c] (*warning device*) (*in house, car etc*) 警报 **3** [c] (*on clock*) 闹钟 **II** *vt* [+ *person*] 使惊慌 ♦**to raise/sound the alarm** 拉响警报 ♦**to view** *or* **regard sth with alarm** 警觉地看待某事物
alarm call *n* [c] 唤醒电话
alarm clock *n* [c] 闹钟
alarmed [ə'lɑːmd] *adj* **1** [+ *person*] 惊恐的 **2** [+ *house, car etc*] 装有警报器的
alarming [ə'lɑːmɪŋ] *adj* 令人惊恐的
Albania [æl'beɪnɪə] *n* 阿尔巴尼亚
albeit [ɔːl'biːɪt] *conj* (*although*) 尽管
album ['ælbəm] *n* [c] **1** (*for stamps, photos etc*) 册子 **2** (*LP*) 唱片
alcohol ['ælkəhɔl] *n* [u] **1** 酒 **2** 酒精

alcohol-free ['ælkəhɔl'fri:] *adj* [+ *beer, wine*] 无酒精的

alcoholic [ælkə'hɔlɪk] I *n* [c] 酒鬼 II *adj* [+ *drink*] 含酒精的 ♦**his alcoholic father** 他那嗜酒成瘾的父亲

alcoholism ['ælkəhɔlɪzəm] *n* [u] 酒精中毒

ale [eɪl] *n* [c/u] 麦酒

alert [ə'lə:t] I *adj* 1 (*wide awake*) 警觉的 2 ♦**alert to sth** [+ *danger, opportunity*] 对某事警觉 II *n* [c] (*situation*) ♦**a security alert** 安全警戒 III *vt* [+ *authorities, police*] 使警觉 ♦**to alert sb to sth** 使某人对某事警觉 ♦**on the alert (for sth)** (对某事)警觉 ♦**on alert** 警惕着 ♦**to give the alert** 发出警报

A level [英] *n* [c/u] 中学中高级考试

algebra ['ældʒɪbrə] *n* [u] 代数

Algeria [æl'dʒɪərɪə] *n* 阿尔及利亚

alias ['eɪlɪəs] I *n* [c] [*of criminal*] 化名 II *prep* ♦**Peter Lewis, alias John Lord** 比得·路易斯，化名约翰·洛德

alibi ['ælɪbaɪ] *n* [c] 不在场证据

alien ['eɪlɪən] I *n* [c] 1 (*foreigner*) 外侨 2 (*extra-terrestrial*) 外星人 II *adj* 1 (*foreign*) 异己的 2 (*from outer space*) 外星的 3 [正式] ♦**alien (to)** 与…截然不同的

alienate ['eɪlɪəneɪt] *vt* [+ *person*] 使疏远 ♦**to alienate sb from sb/sth** 使某人疏远某人/某物

alight [ə'laɪt] I *adj* 1 [*fire* +] 燃着的 2 [*eyes, face* +] 闪耀的 II *vi* 1 [正式] [*bird* +] 飞落 2 [*passenger* +] 下来 ♦**to set sth alight** 点着某物

align [ə'laɪn] *vt* [+ *objects*] 对齐 ♦**to align o.s. with sb** 与某人结盟

alike [ə'laɪk] I *adj* ♦**to be/look alike** 是/看起来相似的 II *adv* (*similarly*) 相似地 ♦**winter and summer alike** 无论冬夏

alive [ə'laɪv] *adj* 1 (*living*) ♦**to be alive** 活着的 2 (*lively*) [+ *place, person*] ♦**to be/feel alive** 充满活力的 3 (*thriving*) ♦**to be alive** 活跃的 ♦**to be burned/buried alive** 活活烧死/活埋 ♦**to keep sb alive** 维持某人的生命 ♦**alive with** 充满… ♦**alive to** 意识到 ♦**to bring sth alive** [+ *story, description*] 使某物活灵活现; [+ *person, place, event*] 使某物活跃起来 ♦**to come alive** [*story, description* +] 使某物活灵活现; [*person, place, event* +] 使活跃起来 ♦**alive and kicking** 生龙活虎的 ♦**alive and well** 安然无恙的

✪ **all**

KEYWORD

[ɔ:l]

I *adj* 所有的 ♦**all day/night** 整日/夜 ♦**all big cities** 所有的大城市 ♦**all five books** 所有的5本书 ♦**all the time/his life** 始终/他的整个一生 ♦**all the books** 所有的书

II *pron*

1 全部 ♦**it's all settled** 全都安顿好了 ♦**all I could do was apologize** 我所能做的全部就是道歉 ♦**all that remains is to ...** 所有剩下的就是要… ♦**I ate it all, I ate all of it** 我把它全都吃了 ♦**have you got it all?** 你全都有了吗? ♦**all of us** 我们中的所有人 ♦**all of the time** 每时每刻 ♦**all of the boys** 所有的男孩子 ♦**we all sat down** 我们都坐下了 ♦**is that all?** (*anything else?*) 那就是全部吗? ; (*in shop*) 就这些吗? ; (*not more expensive?*) 就这个价吗?

2 (*in expressions*) ♦**after all** (*considering*) 毕竟; (*regardless*) 终究 ♦**all but the strongest/smallest** *etc* (*all except for*) 只有最强壮的/最小的{等} ♦**to have seen/done it all** 全都看了/做了 ♦**all in** [非正式] (*exhausted*) 筋疲力尽的; [英:非正式] (*inclusive*) 全都包括在内 ♦**all in all** 总之 ♦**for all I know/care** 我一无所知/不关我事 ♦**in all** 总共 ♦**best of all** 最好不过的是

III *adv*

1 (*emphatic*) 完全 ♦**he was doing it all by himself** 他完全是自己做的 ♦**all alone** 孤零零的 ♦**all around** 周围 ♦**it's not as hard as all that** 不算太难 ♦**all the more/the better** 更加/更好 ♦**she all but died** (*almost*) 她几乎要死掉了

2 (*in scores*) ♦**the score is 2 all** 比分2比2平

Allah ['ælə] *n* 安拉
allay [ə'leɪ] *vt* [+ *fears*] 减轻
allegation [ælɪ'geɪʃən] *n* [C] 指控 ♦**allegations of brutality/corruption** 对暴行/腐败的指控
allege [ə'lɛdʒ] [正式] *vt* ♦**to allege that ...** (*claim*) 宣称… ♦**he is alleged to have killed her** 据称他杀了她
alleged [ə'lɛdʒd] [正式] *adj* 据称的
allegedly [ə'lɛdʒɪdlɪ] *adv* 据说地
allegiance [ə'liːdʒəns] *n* [C/U] ♦**allegiance (to)** 忠诚
allergic [ə'ləːdʒɪk] *adj* [+ *reaction, response*] 过敏的 ♦**to be allergic to sth** [+ *peanuts, cats etc*] 对某物过敏; [非正式] [+ *work, mornings, etc*] 对某物反感
allergy ['ælədʒɪ] [医] *n* [C/U] 过敏症 ♦**to have an allergy to sth** 对某物有过敏症
alleviate [ə'liːvɪeɪt] *vt* **1** [+ *pain*] 减轻 **2** [+ *poverty, misery*] 缓和
alley ['ælɪ] *n* [C] (*street*) 小巷
alliance [ə'laɪəns] *n* [C] **1** (*group*) 联盟 **2** ♦**alliance (with)** (*relationship*) (与…) 联盟
allied ['ælaɪd] *adj* **1** [+ *nation*] 同盟的 **2** [+ *forces, troops*] 同盟国的 **3** (*related*) [+ *industries, disciplines*] 相关的 ♦**allied to** 与…相关的
alligator ['ælɪgeɪtə(r)] *n* [C] 短吻鳄
allocate ['æləkeɪt] *vt* [+ *time, money, tasks, rooms*] 分配
allot [ə'lɔt] *vt* (*allocate*) ♦**to allot sth (to sb)** [+ *time*] 拨给 (某人) 某物; [+ *money, seats*] 分配给 (某人) 某物 ♦**in/within the alloted time** 在规定时间内

> **ALLOTMENT**
> 花园和园艺是英国文化的重要方面。如果城镇和城市居民只有一个小花园或根本没有园地, 他们可以向当地政府租一块公地。这些小块土地通常用来种植蔬菜和水果, 但也可以种植其他植物花草。

all-out ['ɔːlaut] **I** *adj* [+ *effort, attack*] 竭尽全力的 **II** *adv* ♦**to go all out for sth/to do sth** 为某事竭尽全力/竭尽全力做某事 ♦**all-out strike** 全体罢工
✪**allow** [ə'lau] *vt* **1** (*permit*) [+ *practice, behaviour*] 允许 ◊ *Henry doesn't allow smoking in his office.* 亨利不允许在他的办公室吸烟。**2** (*set aside*) [+ *sum, time, amount*] 留出 ◊ *Please allow 28 days for delivery.* 请留出28天的发货期。**3** ♦**to allow sth to happen** (*by failing to prevent sth*) 容许某事发生 ◊ *Don't allow the soil to dry out.* 不要让土壤干透。◊ *We cannot allow the situation to deteriorate.* 我们不容许情况恶化。**4** ♦**to allow sb to do sth** (*make sth possible*) 允许某人做某事 ◊ *The extra money allows them to distribute more aid.* 额外的款项使他们能够提供更多援助。◊ *The mother allowed her children to go to the park.* 母亲允许孩子们去公园。**5** [+ *claim, goal*] 认可 ◊ *After an appeal, the goal was allowed.* 经过申诉, 这一入球得到认可。♦**to allow sb to do sth** (*give permission for sth*) 允许某人做某事 ◊ *They allow their children to stay up late.* 他们允许自己的孩子们晚睡。♦**to be allowed to do sth** 被允许做某事 ◊ *The children are not allowed to watch too much TV.* 孩子们不被允许看太多电视。♦**smoking is not allowed** 禁止吸烟 ♦**to allow that ...** [正式] (*concede*) 承认…
❑**allow for** *vt* [不可拆分] [+ *delay, inflation, possibility*] 考虑到 ◊ *Allow for long delays on all routes north.* 要考虑到所有向北路线的长时间阻塞。
❑**allow of** *vt* [不可拆分] (*permit*) 容许
allowance [ə'lauəns] *n* [C] **1** (*welfare payment*) 津贴 **2** (*allocation*) 限额 **3** (*for expenses*) 补助 **4** [美] 零用钱 [英=**pocket money**] **5** ♦**tax allowance** 免税额 ♦**to make allowances for** [+ *thing, situation*] 顾及到; [+ *person*] 考虑到
alloy ['ælɔɪ] *n* [C/U] 合金 ♦**an alloy of ...** …的合金
all right I *adj* ♦**to be all right** (*satisfactory*) 还不错的; (*well, safe*) 安然无恙的 **II** *adv* **1** (*well*) [*go, work out* +] 顺利地 **2** (*properly*) [*see, hear,*

work +] 没问题地 **3** (*as answer*) (*okay*) 可以 ♦**it's** *or* **that's all right by me** 对我来说没问题

ally [*n* 'ælaɪ, *vb* ə'laɪ] **I** *n* [C] **1** [*of country*] 同盟国 **2** ♦**the Allies** (*during World War I*) 协约国; (*during World War II*) 同盟国 **3** (*friend, supporter*) 死党 **II** *vt* ♦**to ally o.s. with sth/sb** 和某组织/某人结盟

almighty [ɔːl'maɪtɪ] **I** [非正式] *adj* (*tremendous*) [+ *row, problem etc*] 巨大的 **II** *n* ♦**the Almighty** 上帝 ♦**Almighty God** 全能的上帝

almond ['ɑːmənd] *n* [C/U] **1** (*nut*) 杏仁 **2** (*tree*) 杏树

✪**almost** ['ɔːlməust] *adv* 差不多 ◊ *I spent almost a month in China.* 我在中国待了差不多一个月。 ♦**almost certainly** 几乎肯定

alone [ə'ləun] **I** *adj* **1** (*not with other people*) 独自的 **2** (*having no family or friends*) 孤独的 **3** ♦**to be alone together** (*with no other people*) 单独在一起 **II** *adv* **1** (*unaided*) 独自地 **2** ♦**in Florida/France alone** (*merely*) (*used for emphasis*) 仅仅在佛罗里达/法国 ♦**to leave sb/sth alone** (*undisturbed*) 不要打扰某人/某物 ♦**to be alone with sb** 与某人独处 ♦**let alone ...** 更谈不上… ♦**I alone survived** 只有我幸存下来

✪**along** [ə'lɔŋ] **I** *prep* **1** (*towards one end of*) 沿着 ◊ *He drove his car along East Street.* 他沿着东大街开车。 **2** (*on, beside*) [+ *road, corridor, river*] 沿着 ◊ *the houses built along the river* 沿着河建造的房屋 **II** *adv* 沿着 ◊ *Halfway along, turn right into Hope St.* 沿着路往前走到一半，往右拐到希望街。 ♦**to be coming along (fine** *or* **nicely)** 进行(顺利) ♦**to take/bring sb** 带某人一同前往 ♦**he was hopping/limping along** 他跳跃/蹒跚着前行 ♦**along with** (*together with*) 与…一起 ♦**all along** (*all the time*) 自始至终

alongside [ə'lɔŋ'saɪd] **I** *prep* **1** (*next to*) 在…旁边 **2** (*together with*) 与…并肩 **II** *adv* [*come, stop* +] 并排地

aloof [ə'luːf] *adj* (*distant*) 冷淡的 ♦**to stay** *or* **keep aloof from sth** 远离某事

aloud [ə'laud] *adv* [*read, speak* +] 大声地

alphabet ['ælfəbɛt] *n* ♦**the alphabet** 字母表

Alps [ælps] *n* [*pl*] ♦**the Alps** 阿尔卑斯山脉

✪**already** [ɔːl'rɛdɪ] *adv* 已经 ◊ *I have already started making dinner.* 我已经开始做晚餐了。◊ *They've spent nearly a million dollars on it already.* 他们在这上面已经花了近百万美金。◊ *He was already late for his appointment.* 他约会已经迟到了。 ♦**is it five o'clock already?** (*expressing surprise*) 已经到5点了吗？

alright ['ɔːl'raɪt] *adv* = **all right**

✪**also** ['ɔːlsəu] *adv* **1** (*too*) 也 ◊ *a pianist who also plays guitar* 一个也会弹吉他的钢琴家 **2** (*moreover*) 同样 ◊ *Six other passengers were also injured.* 其他六个乘客同样受了伤。

> 📖 **also** 和 **too** 在语意上很接近，但是，**also** 从不用在句末，而 **too** 却常用于句末。*He was also an artist and lived at Compton...He's a singer and an actor too...I've been to Beijing and to Shanghai too...I've been to Beijing and also to Shanghai.*

altar ['ɔltə(r)] [宗] *n* [C] 祭坛

alter ['ɔltə(r)] **I** *vt* [+ *plans, policy, situation*] 更改 **II** *vi* 改变

alteration [ɔltə'reɪʃən] *n* [C] 改动

alternate [*adj* ɔl'təːnɪt, *vb* 'ɔltəːneɪt] **I** *adj* **1** (*successive*) [+ *actions, events*] 交替的 **2** [美] (*alternative*) [+ *plan, method, solution*] 供替换的 [英 = **alternative**] **II** *vi* **1** ♦**to alternate (with)** 轮流 **2** ♦**to alternate (between)** 交替 ♦**on alternate days/weeks** 隔天/周

alternative [ɔl'təːnətɪv] **I** *adj* **1** [英] [+ *plan, method, solution*] 另外的 [美 = **alternate**] **2** (*non-conventional*) [+ *technology, energy*] 非常规的; [+ *comedy, comedian*] 另类的 **II** *n* [C] ♦**(an) alternative (to)** …的替代 ♦**to have no alternative (but to)** (除…外) 别无选择

alternatively [ɔl'təːnətɪvlɪ] *adv* 或者

✪**although** [ɔːlˈðəu] *conj* **1** (*despite the fact that*) 尽管◊*Although he was late he stopped for a sandwich.* 尽管已经晚了，他还是停下来吃了一个三明治。**2** (*but*) 但是◊*Something was wrong, although I couldn't work out what.* 有些不对头，但我不知道是什么。
📖 用法参见 **though**

altitude [ˈæltɪtjuːd] *n* [C/U] [*of place, plane*] 高度 ♦**at an altitude of 30,000 ft** 在海拔3万英尺的高度 ♦**at high/low altitude** 在高/低海拔处 ♦**to gain/lose altitude** 升高/降低海拔

altogether [ɔːltəˈgɛðə(r)] *adv* **1** (*completely*) 完全 **2** (*far*) (*used for emphasis*) ♦**altogether different/stronger/better** *etc* 全然不同/更强/更好{等} **3** (*in total*) 总共 **4** (*on the whole, in all*) 总之 ♦**how much is that altogether?** 总共多少钱？

aluminium [æljuˈmɪnɪəm] (美 **aluminum** [əˈluːmɪnəm]) *n* [U] 铝

✪**always** [ˈɔːlweɪz] *adv* **1** (*at all times*) 总是◊*He's always late.* 他总是迟到。**2** (*continuously*) 一直◊*He has always been the family solicitor.* 他一直做家庭事务律师。♦**you can/could always try again** 你总是可以重新开始

Alzheimer's (disease) [ˈæltshaɪməz-] *n* [U] 阿尔茨海默(病)

AM [广播] *abbr* (= ***amplitude modulation***) 调幅

am [æm] *vb see* **be**

a.m. *adv abbr* (= ***ante meridiem***) 上午

amalgamate [əˈmælgəmeɪt] *vi, vt* [*organizations, companies* +] 合并

amass [əˈmæs] *vt* [+ *fortune, information*] 积累

amateur [ˈæmətə(r)] **I** *n* [C] (*non-professional*) 业余爱好者 **II** *adj* **1** [+ *boxing, athletics*] 非职业的 **2** [+ *player, person*] 业余的 ♦**amateur dramatics** 业余演出

amaze [əˈmeɪz] *vt* 使惊讶 ♦**to be amazed (at/by/that ...)** (对/被…)惊讶

amazement [əˈmeɪzmənt] *n* [U] 惊异

amazing [əˈmeɪzɪŋ] *adj* (*surprising, fantastic*) 令人惊讶的

Amazon [ˈæməzən] *n* **1** ♦**the Amazon** (*river*) 亚马孙河 **2** [C] (*woman*) (*in mythology*) 亚马孙族女战士 **3** [C] (*woman*) (*resembling mythological woman*) 魁梧而有男子气概的女子 ♦**the Amazon jungle** 亚马孙丛林

ambassador [æmˈbæsədə(r)] *n* [C] 大使

amber [ˈæmbə(r)] **I** *n* [U] (*substance*) 琥珀 **II** *adj* (*in colour*) 琥珀色的 **III** *cpd* [复合词] [+ *jewellery, earrings*] 琥珀 ♦**the lights are on amber** [英] 琥珀色交通灯亮起

ambiguous [æmˈbɪgjuəs] *adj* **1** (*unclear, confusing*) [+ *word, phrase, reply*] 意义不明确的 **2** (*conflicting*) [+ *feelings*] 模棱两可的

ambition [æmˈbɪʃən] *n* **1** [C] ♦**an ambition (to do sth)** (做某事的)志向 **2** [U] (*desire*) 抱负 ♦**to achieve one's ambition** 实现自己的抱负

ambitious [æmˈbɪʃəs] *adj* **1** [+ *person*] 雄心勃勃的 **2** [+ *idea, project*] 宏大的

ambulance [ˈæmbjuləns] *n* [C] 救护车

ambush [ˈæmbuʃ] **I** *n* [C/U] 伏击 **II** *vt* 埋伏 ♦**to lie in ambush (for sb)** 埋伏着等候(某人)

amend [əˈmɛnd] **I** *vt* [+ *law, text*] 修正 **II** *n* ♦**to make amends (for sth)** (因某事)赔偿

amendment [əˈmɛndmənt] *n* [C/U] **1** (*to law*) 修正 **2** [美] ♦**the First/Second Amendment** (*to US Constitution*) 第一/二修正案 **3** (*to letter, essay etc*) 修改

amenities [əˈmiːnɪtɪz] *n* [*pl*] (*features, facilities*) 便民设施 ♦**"close to all amenities"** "毗邻便民设施"

America [əˈmɛrɪkə] *n* 美洲

American [əˈmɛrɪkən] **I** *adj* 美国的 **II** *n* [C] (*person*) 美国人

American football [英] *n* **1** [U] (*sport*) 美式足球 [美=**football**] **2** [C] (*ball*) 橄榄球 [美=**football**]

Amex [ˈæmɛks] *n abbr* (= ***American Stock Exchange***) 美国证券交易所

amiable [ˈeɪmɪəbl] *adj* [+ *person*] 亲

切的

amicable ['æmɪkəbl] *adj* 1 [+ *relationship*] 和睦的 2 [+ *parting, divorce, settlement*] 友好的

amid(st) [ə'mɪd(st)] *prep* 1 [文] (*at the same time as*) 在…当中 2 (*surrounded by*) 在…中间

amiss [ə'mɪs] I *adj* ♦**something is amiss** 出问题了 II [英] *adv* ♦**it would not go** *or* **come amiss** 不会出岔子的

ammunition [æmju'nɪʃən] *n* [U] 1 (*for weapon*) 弹药 2 (*in argument*) 进攻手段

amnesty ['æmnɪstɪ] *n* 1 [C/U] (*to political prisoners*) 大赦 2 [C] (*by police for weapons etc*) 特赦 ♦**to grant amnesty to sb** 特赦某人

among(st) [ə'mʌŋ(st)] *prep* 1 (*surrounded by, included in*) 在…当中 2 [+ *group of people*] 在…当中 3 [*share, distribute* +] (*between*) 在…当中 ♦**talking/arguing among themselves/yourselves** 他们/你们自己彼此交谈/争论

> 如果指两个以上的人或物，用 **among** 或 **amongst**。如果只指两个人或物，用 **between**。 *…an area between Mars and Jupiter…an argument between his mother and another woman…an opportunity to discuss these issues amongst themselves.* **amongst** 是有些过时的表达方式。注意，如果你 **between** 某些东西或某些人，他们在你的两侧。如果你 **among** 或 **amongst** 某些东西或某些人，他们在你的周围。*…the bag standing on the floor between us…the sound of a pigeon among the trees…*

amount [ə'maunt] I *n* [C/U] (*quantity*) 数量; [*of money*] 数额; [*of work*] 总量 II *vi* ♦**to amount to sth** (*total*) 总共达到某数; (*be same as*) 相当于某事 ♦**any amount of** 许多

amp [æmp] *n* [C] 安培 ♦**a 13 amp plug** 一个13安培的插头

ample ['æmpl] *adj* 1 (*sufficient*) [+ *supplies, space, opportunity*] 充足的 2 (*large*) [+ *stomach, bosom*] 宽阔的 ♦**this is ample** 这绰绰有余

amplifier ['æmplɪfaɪə(r)] *n* [C] 扬声器

amplify ['æmplɪfaɪ] *vt* 1 [+ *sound*] 放大 2 [+ *feeling, fear*] 增加 3 [+ *idea, statement*] 详述

amputate ['æmpjuteɪt] *vt* 截去

amuse [ə'mjuːz] *vt* 1 (*make laugh*) 使发笑 2 (*distract, entertain*) 给…消遣 ♦**to amuse o.s.** 自娱自乐 ♦**to keep sb amused** 给某人提供消遣 ♦**to be amused at/by sth** 被某事逗乐 ♦**he was not amused (by)** 他对…不为所动

amusement [ə'mjuːzmənt] I *n* 1 [U] (*mirth*) 愉悦 2 [U] (*entertainment*) 娱乐 3 [C] (*pastime*) 消遣 II **amusements** *n* [*pl*] 娱乐活动 ♦**much to my amusement** 令我十分开心的是

amusement arcade *n* [C] 游乐场

amusement park [尤美] *n* [C] 游乐场

amusing [ə'mjuːzɪŋ] *adj* [+ *story, person*] 有趣的

an [æn, ən] *def art see* **a**

anaemia (美 **anemia**) [ə'niːmɪə] *n* [U] 贫血症

anaemic (美 **anemic**) [ə'niːmɪk] *adj* 1 [医] 贫血的 2 (喻) 索然无味的

anaesthetic (美 **anesthetic**) [ænɪs'θɛtɪk] *n* [C/U] 麻醉剂 ♦**local anaesthetic** 局部麻醉 ♦**general anaesthetic** 全身麻醉 ♦**under anaesthetic** 处于麻醉状态

analog(ue) ['ænəlɔg] I *adj* 1 [+ *watch, display*] 指针式的 2 [+ *computer, signal*] 模拟的 II [正式] *n* [C] ♦**an analogue of** …的模拟

analogy [ə'nælədʒɪ] *n* [C/U] 相似 ♦**to draw an analogy between** 找出…之间的相似之处 ♦**by analogy** 用类推法

analyse (美 **analyze**) ['ænəlaɪz] *vt* 1 [+ *situation, information*] 分析 2 [化, 医] 解析 3 (*psychoanalyse*) 精神分析

analyses [ə'næləsiːz] *n* [*pl*] *of* **analysis**

analysis [ə'næləsɪs] (*pl* **analyses**) *n* 1 [C/U] [*of situation, statistics*] 分析 2 [C/U] [化, 医] 解析 3 [U] (*psychoanalysis*) 精神分析 ♦**in the last** *or* **final analysis** 归根结底

analyst ['ænəlɪst] *n* [c] **1** (*political, industrial*) 分析者 **2** (*psychoanalyst*) 心理分析师

analytic(al) [ænə'lɪtɪk(l)] *adj* **1** (*logical*) [+ *mind, approach*] 分析的 **2** (*scientific*) 解析的

analyze ['ænəlaɪz] [美] *vt* = **analyse**

anarchy ['ænəkɪ] *n* [U] (*chaos, disorder*) 混乱

anatomy [ə'nætəmɪ] *n* **1** [U] (*science*) 解剖学 **2** [c] ♦**my/his anatomy** (*body*) 我/他的身体

ancestor ['ænsɪstə(r)] *n* [c] 祖先

ancestral [æn'sɛstrəl] *adj* 祖传的

anchor ['æŋkə(r)] **I** *n* [c] 锚 **II** *vi* 抛锚 **III** *vt* **1** (*fix*) ♦**to anchor sth (to sth)** 把某物固定(在某物上) **2** [+ *boat*] 停泊 ♦**to drop anchor** 抛锚 ♦**to weigh anchor** 起锚

anchovy ['æntʃəvɪ] *n* [C/U] 鳀鱼

ancient ['eɪnʃənt] *adj* **1** [+ *Greece, Rome, monument*] 古代的 **2** (*very old*) 古老的 **3** [非正式] (*aged, antiquated*) [+ *person*] 老的; [+ *car*] 老式的

✪ **and** [ænd] *conj* 和 ♦**men and women** 男人和女人 ♦**we walked for hours and hours** 我们几个小时几个小时接连地走 ♦**he talked and talked** 他说啊说啊 ♦**better and better** 越来越好 ♦**to try and do sth** 试着做某事

Andes ['ændiːz] *n* [*pl*] ♦**the Andes** 安第斯山脉

Andorra [æn'dɔːrə] *n* 安道尔

anemia *etc* [ə'niːmɪə] [美] = **anaemia** *etc*

anesthetic *etc* [ænɪs'θɛtɪk] [美] = **anaesthetic** *etc*

anew [ə'njuː] *adv* [*start* +] 重新

angel ['eɪndʒəl] *n* [c] **1** (*spirit*) 天使 **2** (*kind person*) 可爱的人

anger ['æŋgə(r)] **I** *n* [U] 生气 **II** *vt* 使生气 ♦**words spoken in anger** 气话

angina [æn'dʒaɪnə] *n* [U] 心绞痛

angle ['æŋgl] **I** *n* [c] **1** [数] 角 **2** (*position, direction*) 角度 **3** (*approach*) 视角 **II** *vi* **1** (*face, point*) 指向 **2** ♦**to angle for sth** [+ *compliments*] 转弯抹角地得到某物 **III** *vt* (*position*) 转换角度 ♦**at an angle** 倾斜地 ♦**an angle of ninety/sixty degrees** 90度/60度角

angler ['æŋglə(r)] *n* [c] 钓鱼的人

Anglican ['æŋglɪkən] **I** *adj* [+ *church, priest, service*] 英国圣公会的 **II** *n* [c] 英国圣公会教徒 ♦**the Anglican Church** 英国圣公会教堂

angling ['æŋglɪŋ] *n* [U] 钓鱼

Angola [æŋ'gəulə] *n* 安哥拉

angrily ['æŋgrɪlɪ] *adv* [*react, deny* +] 气愤地

angry ['æŋgrɪ] *adj* **1** [+ *person, response*] 生气的 **2** [+ *wound, rash*] 发炎的 ♦**to be angry with sb/about sth** 对某人/某事生气 ♦**to get angry** 发怒 ♦**to make sb angry** 使某人生气

> 📖 **angry** 指某人在特定时间或场合的情绪或感觉。如果某人经常生气，可以说他是 **bad-tempered**。*She's a bad-tempered young lady.* 可以用 **furious** 描述某人非常生气。*Senior police officers are furious at the mistake.* **annoyed** 或 **irritated** 表示某人生气的程度不是很重。*The Prime Minister looked annoyed but calm…a man irritated by the barking of his neighbour's dog…* 如果一件事情经常或不断发生，它会使人感到 **irritated**。如果某个人经常感到恼火，可以用 **irritable** 形容他。

anguish ['æŋgwɪʃ] *n* [U] **1** (*mental*) 极度痛苦 **2** (*physical*) 剧痛

animal ['ænɪməl] **I** *n* [c] **1** (*creature*) 动物 **2** (*type of person*) 与众不同的人 **3** [贬] (*brute*) 禽兽 **II** *adj* [+ *fats, products, instinct, attraction*] 动物的

animate [*vb* 'ænɪmeɪt, *adj* 'ænɪmɪt] **I** *adj* (*living*) 有生命的 **II** *vt* (*enliven*) [+ *person, face*] 使有生气

animated ['ænɪmeɪtɪd] *adj* **1** [+ *person, expression, conversation*] 生气勃勃的 **2** [+ *film, feature*] 动画的

animation [ænɪ'meɪʃən] *n* **1** [C/U] (*computer, cartoon*) 动画片制作 **2** [U] (*liveliness*) 生气

animosity [ænɪˈmɔsɪtɪ] *n* [c/u] 憎恨
aniseed [ˈænɪsiːd] *n* [u] 茴香子
ankle [ˈæŋkl] [解剖] *n* [c] 踝
annex [ˈænɛks] **I** *n* [c] **1** (*joined to main building*) 群房 **2** (*separate building*) 附属建筑 **II** *vt* (*take over*) [+ *land, territory*] 兼并
annexe [ˈænɛks] [英] *n* = **annex**
annihilate [əˈnaɪəleɪt] *vt* **1** (*destroy*) [+ *people*] 消灭 **2** (*defeat*) [+ *enemy, opponent*] 歼灭
anniversary [ænɪˈvəːsərɪ] *n* [c] **1** ♦**anniversary (of sth)** (某事的) 周年纪念 **2** (*also:* ***wedding anniversary***) 结婚周年纪念
✪ **announce** [əˈnauns] **I** *vt* **1** (*declare*) [+ *decision, engagement etc*] 宣布 ◊ *The TV presenter announced the grave news.* 电视解说员宣布了这条重大消息。**2** (*at station or airport*) 通告 **II** *vi* (*say*) 说 ◊ *"I'm going to bed," she announced.* "我要睡觉了，" 她说道。♦**to announce that ...** (*in official statement, in a clear way*) 宣布…; (*at airport or station*) 通告 ♦**the government has announced that ...** 政府宣称…
announcement [əˈnaunsmənt] *n* [c] **1** (*statement*) 宣布 **2** (*notice*) (*in newspaper*) 通知 **3** (*at airport or station*) 通告 ♦**the anouncement of his resignation/death/engagement** 他的退休/死亡/订婚的通告 ♦**to make an announcement** 发表声明
announcer [əˈnaunsə(r)] *n* [c] (*on radio, TV*) (*male*) 男播音员; (*female*) 女播音员
annoy [əˈnɔɪ] *vt* 使烦恼
annoyance [əˈnɔɪəns] *n* **1** [u] (*feeling*) 厌烦 **2** [c] (*annoying thing*) 使人厌烦的东西 ♦**to his/my annoyance ...** 让他/我烦恼的是…
annoyed [əˈnɔɪd] *adj* 厌烦的 ♦**to be annoyed at sth/with sb** 对某事/某人感到厌烦 ♦**to be annoyed about sth** 对某事厌烦 ♦**to get annoyed (about sth)** (对某事)感到厌烦
📖 用法参见 **angry**

> 📖 请勿将 **annoyed** 和 **annoying** 混淆。如果你感到 **annoyed**，表示你相当生气。*David could see Jane waiting for him outside the cinema. She looked annoyed...I was annoyed by his selfish behaviour.* 某人或某事物 **annoying**，则表示该人或该事物令人感到非常生气或令人无法容忍。*You must have found my attitude annoying...Does he have any annoying habits I should know about?*

annoying [əˈnɔɪɪŋ] *adj* [+ *noise, habit, person*] 讨厌的 ♦**how annoying!** 真是讨厌!
📖 用法参见 **annoyed**
annual [ˈænjuəl] **I** *adj* **1** (*once every year*) [+ *meeting, report*] 每年的 **2** (*during a year*) [+ *sales, income, rate*] 年度的 **II** *n* [c] **1** (*book*) 年刊 **2** (*plant*) 一年生植物
annually [ˈænjuəlɪ] *adv* **1** (*once a year*) 每年地 **2** (*during a year*) 一年地
annum [ˈænəm] *n see* **per**
anonymous [əˈnɔnɪməs] *adj* **1** [+ *letter, gift, phone call*] 匿名的 **2** [+ *person*] 不知名的 **3** (*boring*) [+ *place, clothing*] 无特色的 ♦**to remain anonymous** 不留名的
anorak [ˈænəræk] *n* [c] **1** (*jacket*) 连帽防风夹克 **2** [英:贬] (*person*) 迷
anorexia [ænəˈrɛksɪə] (*also:* ***anorexia nervosa***) [医] *n* [u] 厌食症
anorexic [ænəˈrɛksɪk] **I** *adj* 患厌食症的 **II** *n* [c] 厌食症患者
✪ **another** [əˈnʌðə(r)] **I** *adj* **1** ♦**another book** (*one more*) 再一本书 ◊ *I need another book, I've finished this one.* 我再需要一本书，这本已经读完了。**2** (*a different one*) 另外的 ◊ *Can I have another book, this one's torn.* 能不能给我另外一本书，这本书撕坏了。**3** ♦**another 5 years/miles/kilos** 再有5年/英里/公斤 ◊ *Continue down the road for another 2 kilometres.* 沿着这条路再走两公里。**II** *pron* **1** (*one more*) 再一个 ◊ *He had a drink, then poured another.* 他喝了一杯，随后又倒

了一杯。**2** (*a different one*) 不同的一个 ◊ *a civil war, with one community against another* 不同群体间进行的一场内战 ♦**one another** 相互 ♦**one (shop) after another** 一个（商店）挨着一个（商店） ♦**another drink?** 再来一杯？

✪**answer** ['ɑːnsə(r)] **I** *n* [c] **1** (*reply*) (*to question*) 回答; (*to letter*) 回信 **2** (*solution*) (*to problem, in exam or quiz*) 答案 **II** *vi* (*reply*) (*to question*) 回答; (*to telephone ringing, knock at door*) 应答 **III** *vt* **1** (*reply to*) [+ *person*] 答复; [+ *question*] (*asked by person, in exam or quiz*) 回答; [+ *letter*] 回复; [+ *advertisement, prayers*] 回应 ◊ *She answered an advert for a job as a cook.* 她应聘了厨师的招聘广告。**2** (*satisfy*) [+ *need*] 满足 **3** = **answer to** ♦**there was no answer** (*on telephone*) 无人接听; (*at door*) 无人应答 ♦**in answer to ...** 回应… ♦**to answer the phone** 接听电话 ♦**to answer the door** 应声开门

❑**answer back I** *vi* 顶嘴 **II** *vt* 跟…顶嘴

❑**answer for** *vt* [不可拆分] [+ *crimes, actions*] 承受…的后果 ◊ *One of these days you will answer for your crimes.* 总有一天你要为你的罪责承担后果。

❑**answer to** *vt* [不可拆分] [+ *description*] 符合 ◊ *A man answering to his description was seen in Glasgow.* 一个和他的描述相符的男人出现在格拉斯哥。

answering machine ['ɑːnsərɪŋ-] *n* [c] 电话答录机

answerphone ['ɑːnsə(r)fəun] *n* [c] = **answering machine**

ant [ænt] *n* 蚂蚁

antagonism [æn'tægənɪzəm] *n* [u] 敌对

Antarctic [ænt'ɑːktɪk] *n* ♦**the Antarctic** 南极

Antarctica [ænt'ɑːktɪkə] *n* 南极洲

antelope ['æntɪləup] (*pl* **antelope** *or* **antelopes**) *n* [c] 羚羊

antenatal ['æntɪ'neɪtl] *adj* [+ *care, treatment*] 产前的

antenna [æn'tɛnə] *n* [c] **1** (*pl* **antennae** [æn'tɛniː]) [*of insect*] 触角 **2** (*pl* **antennas**) [*of radio, TV*] (*aerial*) 天线

anthem ['ænθəm] *n* [c] 赞美诗

anthology [æn'θɔlədʒɪ] *n* [c] [*of poetry, stories etc*] 选集

anthropology [ænθrə'pɔlədʒɪ] *n* [u] 人类学

anti... ['æntɪ] *prefix* **1** (*expressing opposition*) 反 **2** (*intended to destroy or prevent sth*) 抗

antibiotic ['æntɪbaɪ'ɔtɪk] *n* [c] 抗生素

antibody ['æntɪbɔdɪ] *n* [c] 抗体

anticipate [æn'tɪsɪpeɪt] *vt* **1** (*expect, foresee*) 预期 **2** (*be prepared for*) 提前行动 **3** (*look forward to*) 期望 ♦**this is worse/better than I anticipated** 这比我原先期望的要坏/好

anticipation [æntɪsɪ'peɪʃən] *n* [u] **1** ♦**in anticipation of sth** (*preparation for*) 预期某事 **2** (*excitement*) 期待某事 ♦**thanking you in anticipation** [正式] 预致谢意

anticlimax ['æntɪ'klaɪmæks] *n* [c/u] 虎头蛇尾

anticlockwise ['æntɪ'klɔkwaɪz] [英] *adv* 逆时针方向地

antics ['æntɪks] *n* [*pl*] **1** [*of animals, children*] 滑稽动作 **2** [*of politicians, celebrities*] 丑态

anti-depressant [æntɪdɪ'prɛsənt] *n* [c] (*medicine*) 抗抑郁症药; (*activity, substance*) 兴奋剂

antidote ['æntɪdəut] *n* [c] **1** (*to poison*) 解毒剂 **2** ♦**an antidote to sth** [+ *unpleasant situation*] 解决某事的良方

antifreeze ['æntɪfriːz] [汽车] *n* [u] 防冻剂

antihistamine ['æntɪ'hɪstəmɪn] *n* [c/u] 抗组织胺

antiquated ['æntɪkweɪtɪd] *adj* (*outdated*) 过时的

antique [æn'tiːk] **I** *n* [c] (*valuable old object*) 古董 **II** *cpd* [复合词] [+ *furniture, jewellery*] 古式

antiquity [æn'tɪkwɪtɪ] *n* **1** [u] (*the past*) 古代 **2** [c] (*old object*) 古物

antiseptic [æntɪ'sɛptɪk] **I** *n* [c/u] 杀菌剂 **II** *adj* 杀菌的

antisocial ['æntɪ'səuʃəl] *adj*

1 (*unsociable*) 不喜社交的
2 (*offensive*) 冒犯他人的

antlers ['æntləz] *n* [*pl*] 鹿角

anxiety [æŋ'zaɪətɪ] *n* **1** [c/u] (*concern*) 焦虑 **2** [u] [医] 焦虑症 ♦**anxiety over** *or* **about sth** 对某事感到焦虑 ♦**his anxiety to please/to do well** (*eagerness*) 他急于取悦他人/好好表现的愿望

anxious ['æŋkʃəs] *adj* **1** (*worried*) [+ *expression, person*] 忧虑的
2 (*worrying*) [+ *situation, time*] 不安的 ♦**to be anxious to do sth** (*keen*) 渴望做某事 ♦**to be anxious that ...** (*keen*) 极力希望… ♦**to get** *or* **grow anxious** 感到忧虑 ♦**anxious for sth** 热切渴望某事

any
KEYWORD
['ɛnɪ]
I *adj*
1 (*in negatives, in questions*) 一些的 ♦**I haven't any chocolate/sweets** 我没有巧克力/糖果了 ♦**without any help** 没有任何帮助 ♦**there was hardly any food** 几乎没有食物了 ♦**there were hardly any potatoes** 几乎没有土豆了 ♦**have you got any chocolate/sweets?** 你有巧克力/糖果吗？♦**are there any others?** 还有其他人吗？
2 (*in 'if' clauses*) 任何的 ♦**if there are any tickets left** 如果有票剩下的话
3 (*no matter which*) 任何的 ♦**take any card you like** 你喜欢哪张卡就拿哪张 ♦**any excuse will do** 任何一个理由都行 ♦**any teacher will tell you that ...** 任何一个老师都会告诉你…
4 (*in expressions*) ♦**any day now** 从现在起的任何一天 ♦**(at) any moment** (在)任何时候 ♦**any time** (*whenever*) 不论何时；(*also:* ***at any time***) 在任何时候 ◊ *He could be sent for (at) any time.* 他可以随叫随到。♦**any time you feel like a chat, just call me** 任何时候你想聊天，就给我打电话 ♦**the bomb could go off (at) any time** 炸弹任何时候都可能爆炸 ♦**at any rate** (*more precisely*) 至少；(*whatever the case*) 无论如何 ♦**she wanted to buy a dress but not just any dress** 她想买件礼服，但要有点特别的那种
II *pron*
1 (*in negatives*) 一些 ♦**I didn't eat any (of it)** 我一点东西也没吃 ♦**I haven't any (of them)** 我一个也没有 ♦**there was nothing any of us could do to help** 我们没有一个人能帮得上忙
2 (*in questions*) 一些 ♦**have you got any?** 你有吗？♦**can any of you sing?** 你们中间有谁会唱歌？
3 (*in 'if' clauses*) 任何一 ♦**if any of you would like to take part, ...** 如果你们中任何人想参加的话，…
4 (*no matter which one(s)*) 无论哪一个 ♦**help yourself to any of the books** 无论哪本书你随便拿
III *adv*
1 (*with negative*) 丝毫 ♦**I can't see things getting any better** 我看不出事情有丝毫好转 ♦**I don't play tennis any more** 我不再打网球了 ♦**don't wait any longer** 不再等了
2 (*in questions*) …一点 ♦**are you feeling any better?** 你感觉稍好一点吗？♦**do you want any more soup/sandwiches?** 你还想再要点汤/三明治吗？
3 (*in 'if' clauses*) 再…一点 ♦**if it had been any colder we would have frozen to death** 如果再冷一点，我们就要被冻死了

anybody ['ɛnɪbɔdɪ] *pron* = **anyone**

anyhow ['ɛnɪhau] *adv* **1** = **anyway**
2 [英：非正式](*haphazardly*) 随随便便地 ♦**do it anyhow** 随随便便地做 ♦**she leaves things just anyhow** 她就是随随便便地乱放东西

anymore [ɛnɪ'mɔː(r)] *adv* = **any more** *see* **any**

anyone ['ɛnɪwʌn] *pron* **1** (*in negatives, 'if' clauses*) 任何人 **2** (*in questions*) 任何一个人 **3** (*no matter who*) 不论什么人 ♦**I can't see anyone** 我见不到任何人 ♦**did anyone see you?** 有人看到你

吗？♦**did you speak to anyone?** 你对任何人说起过吗？♦**does anyone want a cake?** 有人想要块蛋糕吗？♦**if anyone should phone ...** 如果有人打电话… ♦**anyone could do it** 任何人都能做到 ♦**anyone who is anyone** 重要人物

✪**anything** [ˈɛnɪθɪŋ] *pron* **1** (*in negatives, questions, 'if' clauses*) 任何事 **2** (*no matter what*) 无论何事物 ♦**I can't see anything** 我什么也看不见 ♦**hardly anything** 几乎没有任何东西 ♦**can you see anything?** 你能看到些什么吗？♦**did you find anything?** 你找到些什么吗？♦**if anything happens to me ...** 如果任何事情发生在我身上… ♦**he'll eat anything** 他什么东西都会吃 ♦**you can say anything you like** 你可以畅所欲言 ♦**anything will do** 什么都行 ♦**anything between ... and...** 在…和…之间的样子 ♦**the lecture was anything but boring** 讲座绝对不无聊 ♦**anything but!** 绝对不！♦**I wouldn't do that for anything** [非正式] 我决不会那样做的 ♦**he's as clever as anything** [非正式] 他极其聪明 ♦**if anything** 如果有什么不同的话 ♦**the painting didn't fetch anything like that much** 这副画根本没卖到那么高的价钱

anytime [ˈɛnɪtaɪm] *adv* 任何时候

anyway [ˈɛnɪweɪ] *adv* **1** (*besides*) 无论如何 **2** (*all the same*) 还是 **3** (*at least*) 至少 **4** (*in short*) 总之 **5** (*well*) 不管怎样 ♦**I shall go anyway** 不论如何我要走了 ♦**why are you phoning, anyway?** 你到底为什么打电话？

anywhere [ˈɛnɪwɛə(r)] *adv* **1** (*in negatives, questions, 'if' clauses*) 任何地方 **2** (*no matter where*) 无论哪里 ♦**I can't see him anywhere** 我哪里都见不到他 ♦**have you seen the scissors anywhere?** 你在哪儿见过剪刀吗？♦**put your case down anywhere** 把箱子放在哪儿都行 ♦**anywhere in the world** 世界的任何地方 ♦**I would have known him anywhere** 到哪儿我都认得他

apart [əˈpɑːt] *adv* **1** [*move, pull* +] 分开 **2** ♦**sit apart from the others** 不和其他人坐在一起 ♦**to be apart** [*couple, family* +] 分开 ♦**to live apart** 分居 ♦**10 miles apart** 相距10英里 ♦**a long way apart** 意见迥异 ♦**with one's legs/feet apart** 某人的腿/脚分开 ♦**to take sth apart** 拆卸某物 ♦**to come** *or* **fall apart** 崩溃 ♦**apart from** (*excepting*) 除去; (*in addition to*) 除了…以外 ♦**I can't tell them apart** 我不能分辨二者 ♦**set apart (from)** 位于…的远处

apartment [əˈpɑːtmənt] **I** *n* [c] [美] 公寓 [英=**flat**] **II apartments** *n* [*pl*] [英] 房间

apartment building, apartment house [美] *n* [c] 公寓楼 [英=**block of flats**]

apathy [ˈæpəθɪ] *n* [u] 冷漠

ape [eɪp] **I** *n* [c] 猿 **II** *vt* (*imitate*) 模仿

aperitif [əˈpɛrɪtiːf] *n* [c] 开胃酒

aperture [ˈæpətʃjuə(r)] *n* [c] **1** [正式] (*hole, gap*) 孔 **2** [摄影] 孔径

apiece [əˈpiːs] *adv* (*in number*) 每人; (*in cost*) 每个

apologetic [əpɔləˈdʒɛtɪk] *adj* [+ *tone, letter, person*] 道歉的 ♦**to be apologetic about ...** 为…感到抱歉

apologize [əˈpɔlədʒaɪz] *vi* 道歉 ♦**I apologize (for...)** [正式] 我（为…而）道歉 ♦**to apologize to sb (for sth)** 向某人（为某事）道歉

apology [əˈpɔlədʒɪ] *n* [c/u] 道歉 ♦**to make (sb) an apology** 向（某人）道歉 ♦**to send one's apologies** [正式] (*for one's absence*) 致歉 ♦**to offer** *or* **make one's apologies** [正式] 表达某人的歉意 ♦**please accept my apologies** [正式] 请接受我的道歉 ♦**I make no apologies for what I said** 我不为我所说的话感到抱歉

apostrophe [əˈpɔstrəfɪ] *n* [c] 撇号

appal (美 **appall**) [əˈpɔːl] *vt* (*shock*) 使惊骇

appalled [əˈpɔːld] *adj* (*horrified*) 惊骇的 ♦**to be appalled by/at sth** 对某事物感到惊骇 ♦**to be appalled that ...** …使人惊骇

appalling [ə'pɔːlɪŋ] *adj* **1** (*shocking*) [+ *destruction, conditions, behaviour*] 骇人听闻的 **2** (*great, intense*) [+ *headache, ignorance*] 严重的 ♦ **she's an appalling cook** (*bad, poor*) 她是个差劲的厨师

apparatus [æpə'reɪtəs] *n* [C/U] **1** (*equipment*) 装置 **2** [*of organization, system*] 机构 ♦ **a piece of apparatus** 一件仪器

apparel [ə'pærəl] [尤美：正式] *n* [U] 衣服

apparent [ə'pærənt] *adj* **1** (*seeming*) 表面上的 **2** (*obvious*) 明显的 ♦ **it is apparent that ...** 显然… ♦ **for no apparent reason** 原因不明地

apparently [ə'pærəntlɪ] *adv* 表面看来

appeal [ə'piːl] **I** *vi* **1** ♦ **to appeal (to sb)** (*be attractive*) 吸引（某人）**2** [法] 上诉 **II** *vt* [美] [+ *decision, verdict*] 上诉 **III** *n* **1** [C] (*request*) 请求 **2** [C] (*for good cause*) 呼吁 **3** [C/U] [法] 上诉 **4** [U] (*attraction, charm*) 吸引力 ♦ **to appeal (to sb) for sth** 为某事（向某人）呼吁 ♦ **he appealed for calm/silence** 他请求大家平静下来/安静下来 ♦ **it doesn't appeal to me** 这一点也引不起我的兴趣 ♦ **to appeal against a decision/verdict** [英] 对决定/判决进行上诉 ♦ **to appeal to the Supreme Court** 上诉最高法庭 ♦ **right of appeal** [法] 上诉权

appealing [ə'piːlɪŋ] *adj* **1** (*attractive*) [+ *idea, person*] 吸引人的 **2** (*pleading*) [+ *look, tone*] 恳求的

✪ **appear** [ə'pɪə(r)] *vi* **1** (*seem*) 看起来 ◊ *He appears confident.* 他看起来很有信心。**2** (*come into view, begin to develop*) 出现 ◊ *Two men suddenly appeared at the door.* 两个男人突然出现在门口。◊ *The flowers appear in early summer.* 这种花开在初夏。**3** (*become available*) 问世 ◊ *New diet books appear every week.* 每周都有新的减肥食谱出售。**4** (*in court*) 出庭 ♦ **to appear to be/have** 看起来是/有 ◊ *The aircraft appears to have crashed.* 这架飞机看起来是已经坠毁了。♦ **it appears/it would appear that ...** 看起来似乎是… ♦ **to appear in a play/film** 出演电视剧/电影

appearance [ə'pɪərəns] *n* **1** [S] (*arrival*) 出现 **2** [S] (*look, aspect*) 外表 **3** [C] (*in public, on TV*) 露面 ♦ **to put in an appearance** (*show your face*) 露一下面 ♦ **to keep up appearances** 装门面 ♦ **to/by/from all appearances** 显然 ♦ **to make an appearance** (*on TV, in public*) 露面 ♦ **in order of appearance** (*in film, play*) 按出场顺序

appease [ə'piːz] *vt* 安抚

appendices [ə'pɛndɪsiːz] *n* [*pl*] *of* **appendix**

appendicitis [əpɛndɪ'saɪtɪs] *n* [U] 阑尾炎

appendix [ə'pɛndɪks] (*pl* **appendices** *or* **appendixes**) [尤美=**appendixes**] *n* [C] **1** [解剖] 阑尾 **2** (*to publication*) 附录 ♦ **to have one's appendix out** 切除阑尾

appetite ['æpɪtaɪt] *n* [C/U] **1** (*desire to eat*) 食欲 **2** ♦ **an appetite for sth** (*desire*) 对某事的爱好 ♦ **the walk has given me an appetite** 散步增进了我的食欲

appetizer ['æpɪtaɪzə(r)] *n* [C] (*first course*) 开胃食品

applaud [ə'plɔːd] **I** *vi* (*clap*) 鼓掌欢迎 **II** *vt* **1** (*praise*) [+ *person, behaviour*] 称赞 **2** (*cheer*) [+ *actor, singer etc*] 鼓掌

applause [ə'plɔːz] *n* [U] (*clapping*) 掌声

apple ['æpl] *n* [C] 苹果 ♦ **she is the apple of her father's eye** 她是父亲的掌上明珠

appliance [ə'plaɪəns] [正式] *n* [C] (*device*) 器具

applicable [ə'plɪkəbl] *adj* (*relevant*) ♦ **applicable (to)** 适用于 ♦ **if/where applicable** 如果适用

applicant ['æplɪkənt] *n* [C] (*for job, place at college*) 申请人

application [æplɪ'keɪʃən] *n* **1** [C] (*for job, grant etc*) 申请 **2** [U] (*hard work*) 专心 **3** [C/U] (*use*) [*of knowledge, theory etc*] 应用 **4** [C/U] (*applying*) [*of cream, paint etc*] 敷用 **5** [C] [计算机] (*program*) 应用程序 ♦ **on application** 申请之时 ♦ **the application of sth to sth** 某物对某物的应用

application form *n* [C] 申请表格

apply [ə'plaɪ] **I** *vi* **1** ♦**to apply (to sb)** (*be relevant*) （对某人）适用 **2** (*make application*) （向某处）提出申请 **II** *vt* **1** (*use*) [+ *principle, technique*] 应用 **2** [+ *paint, polish etc*] 涂 ♦**to apply for sth** [+ *job, grant, membership*] 申请某事 ♦**to apply to sb** [+ *council, governing body*] 向某人提出申请 ♦**to apply to do sth** 申请做某事 ♦**to apply the brakes** [正式] 刹车 ♦**to apply o.s. (to sth)** 致力于（某事）

appoint [ə'pɔɪnt] *vt* ♦**to appoint sb (to sth)** (*to post*) 任命某人为（某职）; (*to political position, post of honour*) 委任某人为（某职） ♦**to appoint sb manager** 任命某人为经理

appointed [ə'pɔɪntɪd] *adj* ♦**(at) the appointed time/hour** （在）约定时间/钟点

appointment [ə'pɔɪntmənt] *n* **1** [c] (*arranged meeting*) (*in business, politics*) 约会; (*with hairdresser, dentist, doctor*) 预约 **2** [c/u] (*selection*) 任命 **3** [c] (*post*) 职务 ♦**to make an appointment (with sb)** (*in business, politics*) （和某人）订一个约会; (*to see hairdresser, dentist, doctor*) （和某人）预约 ♦**by appointment** 根据预约

appraisal [ə'preɪzl] *n* ♦**an appraisal (of)** （…的）评估

appreciate [ə'priːʃɪeɪt] **I** *vt* **1** (*like, value*) 欣赏 **2** (*be grateful for*) 感谢 **3** (*understand, be aware of*) 理解 **II** *vi* (*increase in value*) [*currency, shares, property etc* +] 涨价 ♦**I (really) appreciate your help** 我（十分）感谢你的帮助 ♦**I appreciate that ...** 我意识到… ♦**I'd appreciate it if ...** 如蒙…我将不胜感激

appreciation [əpriːʃɪ'eɪʃən] *n* **1** [u] (*enjoyment*) 欣赏 **2** [u] (*gratitude*) 感激 **3** [s/u] (*understanding*) ♦**appreciation (of)** （对…的）了解 **4** [s/u] (*in value*) 涨价

appreciative [ə'priːʃɪətɪv] *adj* **1** (*praising*) 赞赏的 **2** ♦**appreciative of** (*grateful*) 感激的

apprehend [æprɪ'hɛnd] *vt* **1** [正式] (*catch*) 逮捕 **2** [文] (*understand*) 领会

apprehension [æprɪ'hɛnʃən] *n* **1** [c/u] [正式] (*fear*) 忧虑 **2** [u] [正式] (*arrest*) 逮捕 ♦**in** *or* **with apprehension** 在恐惧中

apprehensive [æprɪ'hɛnsɪv] *adj* ♦**apprehensive about** *or* **of** (*fearful*) 担心…的

apprentice [ə'prɛntɪs] **I** *n* [c] 学徒 **II** *vt* ♦**to be apprenticed to sb** 给某人当学徒 ♦**an apprentice plumber/carpenter** *etc* 管子工/木匠｛等｝学徒

approach [ə'prəutʃ] **I** *vi* (*draw near*) [*person, car* +] 走近; [*event, time* +] 临近 **II** *vt* **1** (*draw near to*) [+ *place, person*] 向…靠近; [+ *event*] 临近 **2** (*consult, speak to*) [+ *person*] 接洽 **3** (*deal with*) [+ *situation, problem*] 处理 **III** *n* [c] **1** (*advance*) [*of person*] 靠近 **2** (*to a problem, situation*) 方式 **3** ♦**approach to sth** (*access, path*) 通往某地的途径 **4** (*proposal*) 对某事的提议 ♦**to approach sb about sth** 就某事同某人接触 ♦**the approach of Christmas/winter** 圣诞节/冬天的临近

appropriate [*adj* ə'prəuprɪɪt, *vb* ə'prəuprɪeɪt] **I** *adj* (*suitable*) [+ *remarks, behaviour, clothing*] 恰当的; [+ *person, authority*] 相关的 **II** *vt* [正式] (*steal*) [+ *property, materials, funds*] 盗用; [+ *idea*] 剽窃 ♦**it is/seems appropriate to ...** …是/似乎是恰当的 ♦**it is appropriate that ...** …是恰当的 ♦**to take appropriate action** 采取适当的行动 ♦**appropriate to sth** 与某物相称 ♦**appropriate for sth/sb** 适合于某物/某人

appropriately [ə'prəuprɪɪtlɪ] *adv* **1** (*sensibly*) [*dress, act* +] 恰当地 **2** (*acceptably*) 合适地 ♦**appropriately enough ...** (*emphasizing suitability*) 再合适不过地…

approval [ə'pruːvəl] *n* [u] **1** (*permission*) 批准 **2** (*liking*) 赞成 ♦**to meet with sb's approval** [*proposal etc* +] 获得某人的赞同 ♦**to give one's approval to sth** 对某事表示同意 ♦**approval for sth** 对某事的批准 ♦**on approval** 包退包换的 ♦**seal** *or* **stamp of approval** 批准

approve [ə'pruːv] **I** *vt* **1** (*authorize*) [+ *publication, product, action*] 批准 **2** (*pass*) [+ *motion, decision*] 通过 **II** *vi* 赞成 ♦ **to be approved by sb** (*authorized*) 被某人批准

> 📖 如果某当权者**approve**某个计划或者行动，他正式表示认可并且同意此事可以进行。例如，某委员会**approve**一个决议，即允许执行该决议。*At least the idea is now accepted and has even been approved by Parliament.* 若某当权者**approve**某物，比如某个建筑或产品，表示他们对它感到满意并允许投入使用或销售。如果某一药品被**approved**，医生可以将它应用于临床治疗。*...premises which have been approved by the local authority...*
> 如果你**approve of**某种行为或事情，则表示你很乐意看到它已经发生或者即将发生。*I don't like the whole idea, I didn't approve of this meeting...His return to the office was widely approved of.*
> 如果你**approve of**某人或者某物，例如某本书或某部电影，则表示你喜欢他或对他赞赏有加。*Do you think your father will approve of me?...He did not approve of my taste in pictures.*

❑ **approve of** *vt* [不可拆分] **1** (*be pleased about*) [+ *action, event, idea*] 赞成 **2** (*like, admire*) [+ *person, thing*] 称许

approved [ə'pruːvd] *adj* 被认可的

approx. [ə'prɔks] *abbr* (= ***approximately***) 大约地

approximate [*adj* ə'prɔksɪmɪt, *vb* ə'prɔksɪmeɪt] **I** *adj* [+ *amount, number, age*] 近似的 **II** *vi* ♦ **to approximate to** (*resemble*) 接近于

approximately [ə'prɔksɪmɪtlɪ] *adv* 大约地

APR *n abbr* (= ***annual percentage rate***) 年度百分率

Apr. *abbr* (= ***April***) 四月

apricot ['eɪprɪkɔt] *n* [C/U] (*fruit*) 杏子

April ['eɪprəl] *n* [C/U] 四月 ♦ *see also* **July**

April Fool's Day *n* [C/U] 愚人节

> **April Fool's Day**
> 4月1是**April Fool's Day**（愚人节），英国人互相开各种各样的玩笑，搞恶作剧。谁要是上当，就称之为**April Fools**。有时甚至连媒体也跟着凑热闹，编造新闻故事，发出骗人的报导。例如，在意大利，曾有报道说意大利面条长在树上。

apron ['eɪprən] *n* [C] **1** (*clothing*) 围裙 **2** (*at airport*) ♦ **the apron** 停机坪

apt [æpt] *adj* **1** (*suitable*) [+ *comment, description etc*] 恰当的 **2** (*likely*) ♦ **to be apt to do sth** 易于做某事的

aptitude ['æptɪtjuːd] *n* [C/U] (*capability, talent*) 天资 ♦ **to have an aptitude for sth** 有做某事的天分

aquarium [ə'kwɛərɪəm] (*pl* **aquariums** *or* **aquaria**) *n* [C] **1** (*fish tank*) 养鱼缸 **2** (*building*) 水族馆

Aquarius [ə'kwɛərɪəs] *n* **1** [U] (*sign*) 宝瓶座 **2** [C] (*person*) 属宝瓶座的人 ♦ **I'm (an) Aquarius** 我是宝瓶座的

aquatic [ə'kwætɪk] *adj* **1** (*living in water*) [+ *plant, animal*] 水生的 **2** (*relating to water*) [+ *sports, studies*] 水上的

Arab ['ærəb] **I** *adj* 阿拉伯的 **II** *n* [C] 阿拉伯人

Arabia [ə'reɪbɪə] *n* 阿拉伯半岛

Arabian [ə'reɪbɪən] *adj* 阿拉伯的

Arabic ['ærəbɪk] **I** *adj* [+ *language, script etc*] 阿拉伯的 **II** *n* [U] (*language*) 阿拉伯语 ♦ **Arabic numeral** 阿拉伯数字

arable ['ærəbl] *adj* **1** [+ *crop, farming*] 垦殖的 **2** [+ *land*] 可耕的

arbitrary ['ɑːbɪtrərɪ] *adj* (*random*) [+ *attack, decision*] 任意的

arbitration [ɑːbɪ'treɪʃən] *n* [U] [*of dispute, quarrel*] 仲裁 ♦ **the dispute went to arbitration** 争论交付仲裁

arc [ɑːk] *n* [C] **1** (*curve*) 弧形 **2** (*in geometry*) 弧

arcade [ɑː'keɪd] *n* [C] **1** (*shopping centre*) 拱廊式街道 **2** (*also:* ***amusement arcade***) 游乐场

arch [ɑːtʃ] **I** *n* [C] **1** (*curved structure*) 拱 **2** [*of foot*] 足弓 **II** *vt* [+ *one's back*]

使成弓形 **III** *vi* 拱起 **IV** *adj* **1** [+ *expression, look*] 调皮的 **2** (*superior*) [+ *tone, behaviour*] 高人一等的

archaeology [ɑːkɪ'ɔlədʒɪ] *n* [U] 考古学

archaic [ɑː'keɪɪk] *adj* 过时的

archbishop [ɑːtʃ'bɪʃəp] *n* [C] 大主教

archeology *etc* [ɑːkɪ'ɔlədʒɪ] [美] = **archaeology** *etc*

archetypal ['ɑːkɪtaɪpəl] *adj* 典型的

architect ['ɑːkɪtɛkt] *n* [C] **1** [*of building*] 建筑师 **2** [正式] [*of idea, event*] 设计师

architectural [ɑːkɪ'tɛktʃərəl] *adj* 建筑的

architecture ['ɑːkɪtɛktʃə(r)] *n* [U] **1** (*design of buildings*) 建筑学 **2** (*style of building*) 建筑风格

archive ['ɑːkaɪv] **I** *n* [C] **1** (*collection*) [*of papers, records, films etc*] 档案 **2** (*place*) 档案馆 **II** *adj* [+ *material, film*] 档案的 **III** *vt* 把…存档 **IV archives** *n* [*pl*] **1** (*collection*) [*of papers, records, films etc*] 档案 **2** (*place*) 档案室 ♦**archive file** [计算机] 档案文件

Arctic ['ɑːktɪk] **I** *n* ♦**the Arctic** 北极区 **II** *adj* **1** [+ *ice, explorer etc*] 北极的 **2** [非正式] (*freezing*) 极冷的

ardent ['ɑːdənt] *adj* [+ *admirer, supporter*] 热烈的

arduous ['ɑːdjuəs] *adj* (*difficult and tiring*) [+ *task*] 艰巨的; [+ *journey*] 艰苦的

are [ɑː(r)] *vb see* **be**

✪**area** ['ɛərɪə] *n* **1** [C] (*region, zone*) 地区 ◊ *people who live in rural areas* 住在乡村地区的人 **2** [C] [*of room, building etc*] (*used for particular activity*) 区 ◊ *a picnic area* 野餐区 **3** [C/U] [数, 几何] 面积 **4** [C] (*part*) [*of surface*] 部分 ◊ *Apply cream to the affected area.* 把药膏涂在患部。**5** [C] (*subject, topic*) 领域 **6** [C] (*aspect*) 方面 ◊ *She controls every area of his life.* 她控制着他生活的各个方面。**7** ♦**the area** [非正式: 足球] 罚球区 ♦**in the London area** 在伦敦周边地区 ♦**in my/your area** 在我/你住的地区 ◊ *The schools in our area are terrible.* 我们所住地区的学校很糟糕。♦**to cover/occupy an area of 50 sq km** 占地面积50平方公里 ♦**50 sq km in area** 面积50平方公里

area code [尤美] *n* [C] 区号 [英 = **dialling code**]

arena [ə'riːnə] *n* [C] **1** (*for sport, entertainment*) 竞技场 **2** ♦**the political/economic arena** 政治/经济舞台

aren't [ɑːnt] = **are not**

Argentina [ɑːdʒən'tiːnə] *n* 阿根廷

Argentine ['ɑːdʒəntaɪn] *adj* 阿根廷的

Argentinian [ɑːdʒən'tɪnɪən] **I** *adj* 阿根廷的 **II** *n* [C] (*person*) 阿根廷人

arguably ['ɑːgjuəblɪ] *adv* 可证明地 ♦**it is arguably ...** 这可以认为…

argue ['ɑːgjuː] **I** *vi* **1** (*quarrel*) ♦**to argue (with sb) (about sth)** (为某事) (和某人) 争吵 **2** (*claim*) ♦**to argue that ...** 论证… **II** *vt* (*debate*) [+ *case, point*] 辩论 ♦**to argue for/against sth** 据理赞成/反对某事

argument ['ɑːgjumənt] *n* [C/U] **1** (*quarrel*) 争吵 **2** (*reason*) 论点 ♦**to get into an argument (with sb)** (和某人) 开始一场争论 ♦**an argument for/against sth** 赞成/反对某事的论据

Aries ['ɛərɪz] *n* **1** [U] (*sign*) 白羊座 **2** [C] (*person*) 属白羊座的人 ♦**I'm (an) Aries** 我是白羊座的

arise [ə'raɪz] (*pt* **arose**, *pp* **arisen**) *vi* **1** (*emerge*) [*problem, difficulty etc* +] 出现 **2** ♦**to arise from/out of sth** (*result from*) 由某事引起 **3** ♦**to arise from sth** [正式] (*from sitting, kneeling*) 从某处站起来; (*from bed*) 起床 ♦**if the need/opportunity arises** 一旦有需要/机会

arisen [ə'rɪzn] *pp of* **arise**

arithmetic [ə'rɪθmətɪk] *n* [U] **1** [数] 算术 **2** (*in particular calculation*) 计算 **3** ♦**the arithmetic** (*of particular situation*) 数字

✪**arm** [ɑːm] **I** *n* [C] **1** [*of person*] 胳膊 **2** [*of jacket, shirt etc*] 袖子 **3** [*of chair*] 扶手 **4** [*of organization etc*] 部门 ◊ *the political arm of the movement* 该运动的政治部门 **II** *vt* [+ *person, nation*] 武装 **III arms** *n* [*pl*] (*weapons*) 武器 **IV** *cpd* [复合词]

♦**arms** [+ *dealer, trade*] 军火 ♦**arm in arm** 臂挽臂地 ♦**to cost an arm and a leg** [非正式] 要价过高 ♦**at arm's length** 距离一臂远的 ♦**to keep sb at arm's length** 同某人保持一定距离 ♦**to welcome sb/sth with open arms** 热烈欢迎某人/某事 ♦**to twist sb's arm** [非正式] 对某人施加压力 ♦**a shot in the arm** 兴奋剂

armchair ['ɑːmtʃɛə(r)] *n* [c] 扶手椅

armed [ɑːmd] *adj* **1** [+ *robber, policeman etc*] 武装的 **2** [+ *conflict, attack etc*] 武力的 ♦**the armed forces** 武装部队 ♦**armed with a knife** 携带小刀的

armed robbery *n* [c/u] 持枪抢劫

Armenia [ɑː'miːnɪə] *n* 亚美尼亚

armour (美 **armor**) ['ɑːmə(r)] *n* [u] **1** [*of knight, soldier*] 盔甲 **2** [军] (*also:* ***armour-plating***) [*of tank*] 装甲钢板; (*tanks*) 装甲部队

armpit ['ɑːmpɪt] *n* [c] 腋窝

armrest ['ɑːmrɛst] *n* [c] 扶手

✪ **army** ['ɑːmɪ] **I** *n* **1** ♦**the army** 军队 ◊ *He joined the army.* 他参军了。 **2** (*host*) ♦**an army of sth** 一大群某物 ◊ *an army of volunteers* 一大群志愿者 **II** *cpd* [复合词] [+ *officer, unit, uniform*] 军队

A road [英] *n* [c] 主干公路

aroma [ə'rəumə] *n* [c] [*of food, coffee*] 香味; [*of flower*] 芳香 ♦**the aroma of ...** …的香味

aromatherapy [ərəumə'θɛrəpɪ] *n* [u] 芳香疗法

arose [ə'rəuz] *pt of* **arise**

✪ **around** [ə'raund] **I** *adv* (*about*) 到处 ◊ *They wandered around.* 他们到处闲逛。 **II** *prep* **1** (*encircling*) 围绕 ◊ *We were sitting around a table.* 我们正围绕桌子坐着。 ◊ *It measures fifteen feet around the trunk.* 树干合抱有15英尺。 **2** (*near*) 在附近 ◊ *We don't live around here.* 我们不住在附近。 **3** (*about, roughly*) (*with numbers, weights, times, dates*) 大约 ◊ *There were around 200 people.* 大约有200人。 ◊ *It was around 5 o'clock.* 那时大约5点钟。 ♦**is he around?** 他在吗?

arouse [ə'rauz] *vt* **1** [+ *anger, interest, passion*] 激起 **2** ♦**to be aroused** (*sexually*) 被激起情欲 **3** [正式] (*from sleep*) 唤醒

arrange [ə'reɪndʒ] **I** *vt* **1** (*organize*) [+ *meeting, tour, appointment etc*] 安排 **2** (*put in order*) [+ *books, objects*] 整理; [+ *flowers*] 布置 **3** ♦**to be arranged by sb** [*piece of music* +] 由某人改编 **II** *vi* ♦**to arrange to do sth** 安排做某事 ♦**it was arranged that ...** 已安排好… ♦**to arrange for sth to be done** 就做某事做好安排

arrangement [ə'reɪndʒmənt] **I** *n* [c] **1** (*agreement*) 约定 **2** (*grouping, layout*) [*of books, furniture*] 布置 **3** (*display*) [*of flowers*] 插花 **4** [*of piece of music*] 改编的乐曲 **II arrangements** *n* [*pl*] (*plans, preparations*) 安排 ♦**to make an arrangement to do sth** 为做某事做好安排 ♦**to come to an arrangement with sb** 和某人达成协议 ♦**by arrangement** 根据约定 ♦**to make arrangements (for sth)** (为某事)做好准备工作

array [ə'reɪ] *n* [c] **1** (*display*) ♦**an array of things** 一排东西 **2** (*range*) ♦**an array of people/things** 一大批人/物 **3** (*network*) 阵列

arrears [ə'rɪəz] *n* [*pl*] (*money owed*) 欠款 ♦**to be in/get into arrears (with rent)** 拖欠(租金) ♦**to be paid in arrears** 事后结算 ♦**rent arrears** 欠租

arrest [ə'rɛst] **I** *vt* **1** (*detain*) 逮捕 **2** [正式] (*stop*) [+ *process, development*] 抑制 **II** *n* [c/u] (*detention*) 拘捕 ♦**to make an arrest** 逮捕 ♦**to place sb under arrest** 将某人逮捕 ♦**to be under arrest** 被逮捕 ♦**to arrest sb's attention** [正式] 吸引某人的注意力

arrival [ə'raɪvl] *n* **1** [c/u] [*of person, vehicle, letter*] 到达 **2** [s] [*of invention, idea, product*] 出现 **3** [c] (*newcomer*) (*in job, at place*) 新到者

arrive [ə'raɪv] *vi* **1** [*person, vehicle* +] 到 **2** [*letter, meal* +] 来

❏ **arrive at** *vt* [不可拆分] [+ *idea, decision*] 达到

📖 用法参见 **reach**

arrogance ['ærəgəns] *n* [u] 傲慢

arrogant ['ærəgənt] *adj* 傲慢的
arrow ['ærəu] *n* [c] **1** (*weapon*) 箭 **2** (*sign*) 箭头标志
arse [ɑːs] [英:非正式,疑讳] *n* [c] 屁股 [美=**ass**]
arsenal ['ɑːsɪnl] *n* [c] **1** (*stockpile, supply*) 军火储备 **2** (*building*) 军火库
arson ['ɑːsn] **I** *n* [u] 纵火 **II** *cpd* [复合词] [+ *attack*] 纵火
✪ **art** [ɑːt] **I** *n* **1** [u] (*paintings, sculpture etc*) 艺术 ◊ *an exhibition of modern art* 一场现代艺术展 **2** [u] (*activity of drawing, painting etc*) 美术 ◊ *I've never been any good at art.* 我一向对美术不在行。**3** [c] (*skill*) 技艺 **II** *cpd* [复合词] [+ *exhibition, collection, student*] 艺术 **III arts** *n* [*pl*] **1** ♦**the arts** (*creative activities*) 艺术活动 ◊ *a patron of the arts* 一位艺术活动赞助人 **2** (*in education*) 文科 **IV** *cpd* [复合词] ♦**arts** [+ *graduate, student, course*] 文科 ♦**work of art** 艺术品 ♦**the art of survival** 生存的技巧
art college *n* [c] 美术学院
artery ['ɑːtərɪ] *n* [c] **1** (*blood vessel*) 动脉 **2** (*route*) 要道
art gallery *n* [c] **1** (*large, national*) 美术馆 **2** (*small, private*) 画廊
arthritis [ɑː'θraɪtɪs] *n* [u] 关节炎
artichoke ['ɑːtɪtʃəuk] *n* [c/u] **1** (*also: **globe artichoke***) 洋蓟 **2** (*also: **Jerusalem artichoke***) 菊芋
article ['ɑːtɪkl] **I** *n* [c] **1** [正式] (*object, item*) 物品 **2** (*in newspaper*) 文章 **3** (*in document*) 条款 **4** [语言] 冠词 **II articles** [英] *n* [*pl*] (*training*) (*in law, accountancy*) 契约 ♦**articles of clothing** 服装
articulate [*adj* ɑː'tɪkjulɪt, *vb* ɑː'tɪkjuleɪt] **I** *adj* **1** [+ *person*] 表达能力强的 **2** [+ *speech, writing*] 表达清楚的 **II** *vt* **1** [正式] (*express*) [+ *feelings, ideas*] 明确表达 **2** (*pronounce*) 清晰地发音
artificial [ɑːtɪ'fɪʃəl] *adj* **1** (*man-made*) [+ *flowers, leg, lake*] 人造的 **2** (*false*) [+ *conditions, situation*] 人为的 **3** (*affected*) [+ *manner, person*] 矫揉造作的
artist ['ɑːtɪst] *n* [c] **1** (*painter, sculptor*) 画家 **2** (*writer, composer etc*) 艺术家 **3** (*musician, actor etc*) 表演艺术家
artistic [ɑː'tɪstɪk] *adj* **1** [+ *person*] 艺术性强的 **2** [+ *tradition, freedom*] 艺术的 **3** [+ *design, arrangement*] 精美的
art school *n* = **art college**
artwork ['ɑːtwəːk] *n* **1** [u] (*for advert, book etc*) 插图 **2** [c] (*work of art*) 艺术作品

✪ **as**
KEYWORD
[æz, əz]
I *conj*
1 (*referring to time*) 当…时 ♦**he came in as I was leaving** 我离开时他进来了 ♦**as the years went by** 随着时间的推移
2 (*since, because*) 因为 ♦**as you can't come, I'll go on my own** 既然你不能来，我就自己去
3 (*referring to manner, way*) 像…一样 ♦**as you can see** 如你所见到的 ♦**as she said** 如她所说 ♦**do as you wish** 按你的愿望去做 ♦**it's on the left as you go in** 在你进入时的左侧
II *prep*
1 (*in the capacity of*) 作为 ♦**he works as a salesman** 他做推销员的工作 ♦**as a teacher, I am very aware that ...** 作为老师，我非常清楚… ♦**she was dressed as a nun** 她穿得像个修女 ♦**he gave it to me as a present** 他把它作为礼物送给我 ♦**to come as a surprise/shock** 出人意料/令人震惊地来了
2 (*when*) 在…时 ♦**he was very energetic as a child** 他小时候精力很旺盛
III *adv*
1 (*in comparisons*) ♦**as big/good/easy** *etc* **as...** 像…一样大/好/容易{等} ♦**you're as tall as he is** *or* **as him** 你和他一样高 ♦**twice as big/good** *etc* **as...** …的两倍大/比…好得多 ♦**as much money/many books as...** 同…一样多的钱/书 ♦**as much/many as...** 和…一样 ♦**as soon as** 一…就…
2 (*in expressions*) ♦**as if** *or* **though** 好像 ♦**you think I'm lying to you? as if (I would)!** 你认为我在向你撒

谎吗？(我)才不会呢！♦ **as from** *or* **of tomorrow** 从明天起 ♦ **as for** *or* **to that** 至于那一点 ♦ **he inquired as to what the problem was** 有关存在什么问题，他进行了了解

asap, ASAP *adv abbr* (= ***as soon as possible***) 尽快

asbestos [æz'bɛstəs] *n* [U] 石棉

ascend [ə'sɛnd] **I** *vt* **1** [*+ hill, stairs*] 登 **2** ♦ **to ascend the throne** 登上王位 **II** *vi* **1** (*lead*) [*staircase, path +*] 上升 **2** (*travel*) [*lift, vehicle etc +*] 上升 **3** ♦ **to ascend to power** 掌权 ♦ **in ascending order** 按由小到大的次序

ascent [ə'sɛnt] *n* [C] **1** (*slope, path*) 斜坡 **2** (*climb*) (*by vehicle, elevator*) 上升；(*by person*) [*of mountain*] 攀登

ascertain [æsə'teɪn] *vt* [正式] (*establish*) [*+ details, facts*] 查明 ♦ **to ascertain who/what ...** 查明谁/什么… ♦ **to ascertain that ...** 查明…

ASEAN ['æsɪæn] *n abbr* (= ***Association of South-East Asian Nations***) 东盟

ash [æʃ] **I** *n* **1** [U] [*from fire, cigarette*] 灰末 **2** [C/U] (*tree*) 白蜡树 **II ashes** *n* [*pl*] **1** [*of fire*] 灰烬 **2** (*remains*) 骨灰 ♦ **to burn sth to ashes** 将某物烧为灰烬

ashamed [ə'ʃeɪmd] *adj* ♦ **to be/feel ashamed** (*embarrassed, guilty*) 感到羞愧 ♦ **to be ashamed of sb/sth** 对某人/某事感到羞愧 ♦ **to be ashamed of o.s. (for having done sth)** 因自己(做了某事)而感到惭愧 ♦ **to be ashamed to admit sth** 耻于承认某事

ashore [ə'ʃɔː(r)] *adv* **1** [*be +*] 在岸上 **2** [*swim, go +*] 向岸地

ashtray ['æʃtreɪ] *n* [C] 烟灰缸

Ash Wednesday *n* [C/U] 圣灰星期三

Asia ['eɪʃə] *n* 亚洲

Asian ['eɪʃən] **I** *adj* 亚洲的 **II** *n* [C] (*person*) 亚洲人

aside [ə'saɪd] **I** *adv* **1** ♦ **to put** *or* **lay sth aside** 把某物放到一边 **2** ♦ **to stand/step/move aside** 站/走/挪到一边 **3** ♦ **to take** *or* **draw sb aside** 把某人拉到一边 **4** ♦ **to set** *or* **put sth aside** 存储某物 **II** *n* [C] **1** (*to audience, camera*) 旁白 **2** (*digression*) 题外话 ♦ **to brush** *or* **sweep objections aside** 对反对意见置之不理 {或} 不顾反对意见

aside from [尤美] *prep* 除了…之外

✪ **ask** [ɑːsk] **I** *vt* **1** ♦ **to ask (sb) a question** 问(某人)一个问题 **2** (*invite*) 邀请 ◊ *I asked her to the party.* 我邀请她参加聚会。 **II** *vi* 问 ♦ **to ask (sb) whether/why ...** 问(某人)是否/为什么… ♦ **to ask sb to do sth** 请求某人做某事 ♦ **to ask to do sth** 要求做某事 ♦ **to ask sb the time** 向某人询问时间 ♦ **to ask sb about sth** 向某人打听某事 ♦ **I asked him his name** 我问他叫什么 ♦ **to ask (for/sb's) permission/forgiveness** 请求(某人的)许可/原谅 ♦ **to ask sb's opinion** 征询某人意见 ♦ **if you ask me** 据我看 ♦ **to ask (about) the price** 询问价钱 ♦ **to ask sb out to dinner** 请某人出去吃饭

❑ **ask after** *vt* [不可拆分] [*+ person*] 问候

❑ **ask for** *vt* [不可拆分] **1** (*ask to have*) [*+ thing*] 要 **2** (*ask to see*) [*+ person*] 找 ♦ **you're asking for trouble!** 你在自找麻烦！♦ **you asked for it!** 你自讨苦吃！

asking price ['ɑːskɪŋ-] *n* ♦ **the asking price** 索价

asleep [ə'sliːp] *adj* 睡着的 ♦ **to be asleep** 睡着了 ♦ **to fall asleep** 入睡

AS level [英:教育] *n* 介于GCSE 和A level之间的等级考试

asparagus [əs'pærəgəs] *n* [U] 芦笋

aspect ['æspɛkt] *n* [C] **1** (*element*) [*of subject*] 方面 **2** (*quality, appearance*) 面貌 **3** [正式] (*outlook*) ♦ **a south-west aspect** 朝西南方向

aspirations [æspə'reɪʃənz] *n* [*pl*] 志向 ♦ **her aspirations to a movie career** 她从事电影工作的志向

aspire [əs'paɪə(r)] *vi* ♦ **to aspire to** 有志于

aspirin ['æsprɪn] *n* **1** [U] (*drug*) 阿司匹林 **2** [C] (*tablet*) 阿司匹林药片

ass [æs] *n* [C] **1** (*animal*) 驴 **2** [非正式] (*idiot*) 傻瓜 **3** [美:非正式，疑讳]

(bottom) 屁股 [英=**arse**]

assassin [ə'sæsɪn] *n* [c] 刺客

assassinate [ə'sæsɪneɪt] *vt* 暗杀 📖 用法参见 **kill**

assault [ə'sɔːlt] **I** *n* [c/u] *(attack) (on individual, by army)* 攻击; *(on belief, idea)* 抨击 **II** *vt (attack)* 袭击; *(sexually)* 强奸 ♦**assault and battery** [法] 人身攻击 ♦**to be charged with assault** 被指控侵犯人身 ♦**an assault on sb/sth** 对某人/某事的攻击

assemble [ə'sɛmbl] **I** *vt* **1** *(gather together) [+ people, group]* 集合 **2** *(fit together) [+ machinery, object]* 装配 **II** *vi (gather) [people, crowd +]* 聚集

assembly [ə'sɛmblɪ] *n* **1** [c] *(meeting)* 集会 **2** [c] *(institution)* 议会 **3** [u] *(construction) [of vehicles etc]* 装配 **4** [c/u] *(in school)* 集合

assert [ə'səːt] *vt* **1** *[+ opinion, innocence]* 宣称 **2** *[+ authority]* 维护 ♦**to assert o.s.** 坚持己见

assertion [ə'səːʃən] *n* [c/u] *(statement, claim)* 断言

assess [ə'sɛs] *vt* **1** *(gauge) [+ problem, situation, abilities]* 估量 **2** *(calculate) [+ tax, value]* 估价 **3** *[+ student, work]* 评估

assessment [ə'sɛsmənt] *n* [c/u] **1** *(evaluation) [of problem, situation, abilities]* 评估 **2** *(calculation) [of tax, value]* 估价 **3** *[of student, work]* 评价

asset ['æsɛt] **I** *n* [c] *(useful quality, person etc)* 宝贵财富 **II assets** *n [pl]* [商] *(property, funds)* 资产 ♦**to be an asset to sb/sth** 为某人/某物的难得之材

assign [ə'saɪn] *vt* **1** ♦**to assign sth to sb** *[+ task]* 把某物分配给某人 **2** *[+ cause, meaning, value]* 将某物赋予某处 ♦**to be assigned to sth** *[+ place, group]* 被指派到某处 ♦**to be assigned sb/sth** 被分配了某人/某物

assignment [ə'saɪnmənt] *n* [c] *(task)* 任务; *(for student)* 作业

assimilate [ə'sɪmɪleɪt] **I** *vt* **1** *(learn) [+ ideas, methods etc]* 吸收 **2** ♦**to be assimilated** *[immigrants +]* 同化 **II** *vi [immigrants +]* 同化

assist [ə'sɪst] *vt [+ person]* 帮助; *[+ injured person]* 扶助

assistance [ə'sɪstəns] *n* [u] 帮助 ♦**to be of assistance** 有帮助

assistant [ə'sɪstənt] **I** *n* [c] **1** *(helper)* 助手 **2** [英] *(in shop)* 营业员 **II** *adj* ♦**assistant secretary/professor** 副部长/教授

associate [*adj, n* ə'səuʃɪɪt, *vb* ə'səuʃɪeɪt] **I** *vt* **1** *(in your thoughts)* 联想 **2** ♦**to be associated with sth** 和某事有关 **II** *vi* ♦**to associate with sb** 和某人交往 **III** *n* [c] *(at work)* 同事 ♦**to associate o.s. with sth** 与某物有联系 ♦**associate member** 准成员 ♦**associate director** 副主管

association [əsəusɪ'eɪʃən] *n* **1** [c] *(group)* 协会 **2** ♦**to have associations (with sth/for sb)** *(mental connection)* 有(对某事/某人的)联想 **3** [c/u] *(involvement, link)* ♦**association (with sb/sth)** (同某人/某物的)联系 ♦**in association with** *(in collaboration with)* 与…联合

assorted [ə'sɔːtɪd] *adj (various, mixed)* 各种各样的 ♦**in assorted sizes** 不同尺寸

assortment [ə'sɔːtmənt] *n* [c] ♦**an assortment of sth** *[of shapes, colours]* 一批花色齐全的某物; *[of objects, people]* 各种各样的某物

assume [ə'sjuːm] *vt* **1** *(suppose)* 假设 **2** *[+ responsibility, power]* 承担 **3** *(adopt) [+ appearance, attitude]* 呈现; *[+ name]* 采用 ♦**let us assume that ...** 让我们假设…

assumption [ə'sʌmpʃən] *n* **1** [c] *(supposition)* 假定 **2** [u] *[of responsibility, power]* 承担 ◊ *the assumption of total responsibility* 承担全部责任 ♦**on the assumption that** *(on condition that)* 根据…这一假设

assurance [ə'ʃuərəns] *n* **1** [c/u] *(assertion, promise)* 保证 **2** [u] ♦**with assurance** *(confidence)* 有把握 **3** [u] [英] *(insurance)* 保险

assure [ə'ʃuə(r)] *vt* **1** *(reassure)* 使确信 **2** *(guarantee) [+ happiness, success etc]* 保证 ♦**the series is assured of success** 这部连续剧保证能获得成功

AST [美] *abbr* (= ***Atlantic Standard Time***) 大西洋标准时间

asterisk ['æstərɪsk] *n* [c] 星号

asthma ['æsmə] *n* [U] 哮喘
astonish [ə'stɔnɪʃ] *vt* 使惊讶
astonishing [ə'stɔnɪʃɪŋ] *adj* 惊人的 ♦**I find it astonishing that ...** 我对…感到惊讶
astonishment [ə'stɔnɪʃmənt] *n* [U] 惊讶 ♦**in astonishment** 惊讶地 ♦**to my astonishment** 令我吃惊的是
astound [ə'staund] *vt* 使震惊
astray [ə'streɪ] *adv* ♦**to go astray** [*letter* +] 丢失 ♦**to lead sb astray** 将某人引入歧途
astride [ə'straɪd] *prep* 骑跨
astrology [əs'trɔlədʒɪ] *n* [U] 占星术
astronaut ['æstrənɔːt] *n* [C] 宇航员
astronomer [əs'trɔnəmə(r)] *n* [C] 天文学家
astronomical [æstrə'nɔmɪkl] *adj* **1** (*enormous*) [+ *odds, price*] 极巨大的 **2** [+ *science*] 天文学的
astronomy [əs'trɔnəmɪ] *n* [U] 天文学
astute [əs'tjuːt] *adj* [+ *person, decision*] 精明的
asylum [ə'saɪləm] *n* **1** [U] [政治] (*refuge*) 避难 **2** [C] (*mental hospital*) 精神病院 ♦**to seek (political) asylum** 寻求(政治)避难 ♦**to grant** *or* **give sb (political) asylum** 授予{或}给予某人(政治)避难权 ♦**to claim (political) asylum** 要求(政治)避难

✪ **at**

KEYWORD

[æt] *prep*

1 (*position, time, age*) 在 ♦**we had dinner at a restaurant** 我们在一家饭店吃了饭 ♦**at home** 在家 ♦**at school** 在学校 ♦**at work** (*not at home*) 在工作 ♦**at my brother's** 在我哥哥家 ♦**at the baker's** 在面包房 ♦**at the bus stop** 在公交车站 ♦**what time will you arrive at the hotel?** 你几点到宾馆? ♦**to be sitting at a table/desk** 坐在桌边/书桌边 ♦**there's someone at the door** 门口有人; (*towards*) ♦**to throw sth at sb** 向某人扔某物 ♦**the question was directed at me** 问题是直接针对我的 ♦**to wave/frown at sb** 冲某人招手/皱眉 ♦**at four o'clock** 在4点钟 ♦**at night** 在晚上 ♦**at Christmas** 在圣诞节 ♦**at the weekend** 在周末 ♦**she died at the age of 76** 她在76岁时去世了

2 (*referring to price, speed etc*) 以 ♦**apples at £2 a kilo** 苹果每公斤两镑 ♦**at 50 km/h** 以每小时50公里的速度 ♦**two at a time** 每次2个

3 (*in measurements*) 达 ♦**at 110 kilos, she's very overweight** 达到110公斤，她严重超重了

4 (*referring to activity*) 在…方面 ♦**he's at work on a novel** 他正在写一本小说 ♦**to play at cowboys** 扮演牛仔 ♦**to be good at sth/at doing sth** 擅长某事/做某事

5 (*referring to cause*) 由于 ♦**shocked/surprised/annoyed at sth** 由于某事而震惊/吃惊/恼怒

6 (*in expressions*) ♦**not at all** (*in answer to question*) 一点也不; (*in answer to thanks*) 别客气 ♦**I'm not at all tired** 我一点儿也不累 ♦**there's nothing at all to see** 没有任何值得看的

ate [eɪt] *pt of* **eat**
atheist ['eɪθɪɪst] *n* [C] 无神论者
Athens ['æθɪnz] *n* 雅典
athlete ['æθliːt] *n* [C] 运动员
athletic [æθ'lɛtɪk] *adj* **1** [+ *tradition, excellence etc*] 体育的 **2** (*sporty*) [+ *person*] 运动的 **3** (*muscular*) [+ *build, frame*] 健壮的
athletics [æθ'lɛtɪks] *n* [U] 田径运动
Atlantic [ət'læntɪk] **I** *adj* 大西洋的 **II** *n* ♦**the Atlantic (Ocean)** 大西洋
atlas ['ætləs] *n* [C] 地图册
ATM *n abbr* (= ***Automated Telling Machine***) 自动取款机
atmosphere ['ætməsfɪə(r)] *n* **1** [C] [*of planet*] 大气层 **2** [S] (*feel*) [*of place*] 气氛 **3** [C] (*air*) 空气
atom ['ætəm] [物] *n* [C] 原子
atomic [ə'tɔmɪk] *adj* 原子的
atom(ic) bomb *n* [C] 原子弹
atrocious [ə'trəuʃəs] *adj* 糟透的
atrocity [ə'trɔsɪtɪ] *n* [C] (*act of cruelty*) 暴行
attach [ə'tætʃ] *vt* **1** (*fasten, join*) 附上 **2** [+ *importance, significance etc*] 把…

放在 ♦**to be attached to sb/sth** *(emotionally)* 喜爱某人/某物

attachment [ə'tætʃmənt] *n* **1** [c/u] *(affection)* ♦**attachment (to sb)** (对某人的)爱慕之情 **2** [c] *[of tool, computer file]* 附件

✪ **attack** [ə'tæk] **I** *vt* **1** *(assault)* [+ *person*] 袭击 **2** [+ *place, troops*] 攻击 **3** *(criticise)* [+ *person, idea*] 抨击 ◊ *He attacked the press for misleading the public.* 他抨击新闻界误导公众。**4** *(tackle)* [+ *task, problem etc*] 着手 **5** *(in sport)* 进攻 **II** *vi* [军, 体育] 进攻 **III** *n* **1** [c/u] *(on person)* 袭击 **2** [c/u] *(military assault)* 攻击 **3** [c] *(criticism)* 抨击 **4** [c/u] *[of illness]* 发作 ◊ *an attack of asthma, an asthma attack* 哮喘发作 **5** [c] *(in sport)* 进攻 ♦**to come under attack** *(assault)* 遭到袭击; *(criticism)* 遭到抨击 ♦**to launch an attack** *(assault)* 发动进攻; *(criticism)* 发起抨击 ♦**an attack on sb** *(assault)* 袭击某人; *(criticism)* 抨击某人

attacker [ə'tækə(r)] *n* [c] 攻击者

attain [ə'teɪn] *vt* **1** [+ *state, condition*] 达到 **2** [+ *ambition, rank*] 获得 **3** [+ *age*] 到达

✪ **attempt** [ə'tɛmpt] **I** *n* [c] *(try)* 尝试 **II** *vt* *(try)* 试图 **III** *vi* ♦**to attempt to do sth** 试图做某事 ♦**an attempt to do sth** 做某事的企图 ♦ **an attempt on sb's life** 企图杀害某人 ♦**he made no attempt to help** 他并未试着帮忙 ♦**at** *or* **on the first attempt** 首次尝试 ♦**he attempted a smile** 他试图挤出一丝微笑 ♦**an attempt at humour** 试图表示幽默

attend [ə'tɛnd] *vt* **1** *(be member of)* [+ *school, church, course*] 上 **2** *(take part in)* [+ *lecture, conference*] 参加

❑ **attend to** *vt* [不可拆分] **1** [+ *needs, affairs*] 处理 **2** [+ *patient, customer*] 照料

attendance [ə'tɛndəns] *n* **1** [u] *(presence)* 出席 **2** [c/u] *(people present)* 出席者

attendant [ə'tɛndənt] **I** *n* [c] *(person)* 服务员 **II** *adj* [+ *dangers, risks, publicity*] 伴随的

attention [ə'tɛnʃən] **I** *n* [u] **1** *(concentration)* 注意 **2** *(care)* 照料 **II** *int* [军] 立正 ♦**for the attention of ...** 收件人为… ♦**it has come to my attention that ...** 我已开始注意到… ♦**to draw sb's attention to sth** 把某人的注意力引向某事 ♦**to stand to/at attention** [军] 立正站着 ♦**to pay attention (to sth/sb)** 关注(某事/某人) ♦**to attract sb's attention** 吸引某人的注意

attentive [ə'tɛntɪv] *adj* **1** *(intent)* [+ *audience*] 聚精会神的 **2** *(polite, helpful)* [+ *person*] 体贴的; [+ *service*] 周到的 ♦**he is attentive to his wife** 他对妻子很体贴

attic ['ætɪk] *n* [c] 阁楼

attitude ['ætɪtjuːd] *n* [c/u] **1** *(mental view)* 看法 **2** *(behaviour)* 态度 **3** *(posture)* 姿势 **4** ♦**kids/women with attitude** *(aggressive style)* 争强好胜的孩子/女人

attorney [ə'təːnɪ] [美] *n* [c] *(lawyer)* 律师 ♦**power of attorney** 代理权

Attorney General *n* [c] **1** [英] 检察总长 **2** [美] 司法部长

attract [ə'trækt] *vt* **1** [+ *people, animals, metal*] 吸引 **2** *(gain)* [+ *support, publicity*] 获得; [+ *sb's interest, attention*] 引起

attraction [ə'trækʃən] **I** *n* [u] *(charm, appeal)* *[of person]* 吸引力 **II attractions** *n* [*pl*] *(also:* ***tourist attractions****)* *(amusements)* 游览胜地 ♦**the attraction of sth** *[of place, activity etc]* 某物的诱人之处

attractive [ə'træktɪv] *adj* **1** [+ *man, woman*] 有魅力的; [+ *thing, place*] 吸引人的 **2** *(interesting)* [+ *price, idea, offer*] 令人感兴趣的 ♦**he was very attractive to women** 他对女人很有吸引力

attribute [*n* 'ætrɪbjuːt, *vb* ə'trɪbjuːt] **I** *n* [c] 特性 **II** *vt* ♦**to attribute sth to sb** [+ *poem, painting, remark*] 认为某物出自某人; [+ *quality, motive*] 认为某人具有某物 ♦**to attribute sth to sth** [+ *situation, cause*] 把某事归因于某事

aubergine ['əubəʒiːn] [英] *n* **1** [c/u] *(vegetable)* 茄子 [美=**eggplant**] **2** [u] *(colour)* 紫红色

auburn ['ɔːbən] *adj* [+ *hair*] 赤褐色的

auction ['ɔːkʃən] **I** *n* [c] 拍卖 **II** *vt*

拍卖
❑**auction off** *vt* 拍卖掉
auctioneer [ɔːkʃə'nɪə(r)] *n* [c] 拍卖师
audible ['ɔːdɪbl] *adj* 听得见的
audience ['ɔːdɪəns] *n* [c] **1** (*in theatre etc*) 观众 **2** [广播, 电视] 听众 **3** (*public*) 读者 **4** (*interview*) (*with Queen, Pope etc*) 接见
audio ['ɔːdɪəu] *adj* [+ *cassette, tape*] 音响的
audio-visual ['ɔːdɪəu'vɪzjuəl] *adj* [+ *materials, equipment*] 视听的
audit ['ɔːdɪt] [商] **I** *vt* [+ *accounts*] 审计 **II** *n* [c] 查账
audition [ɔː'dɪʃən] **I** *n* [c] [电影, 戏剧] 试演 **II** *vi* ♦**to audition (for sth)** 试演(某剧) **III** *vt* 让…试演
auditor ['ɔːdɪtə(r)] *n* [c] (*accountant*) 审计员
auditorium [ɔːdɪ'tɔːrɪəm] *n* [c] (*pl* **auditoria** [ɔːdɪ'tɔːrɪə]) **1** (*in theatre, concert hall*) 观众席 **2** [美] (*for concerts, lectures*) 礼堂
Aug. *abbr* (= ***August***) 八月
augment [ɔːg'ment] *vt* [+ *income, salary etc*] 增加
August ['ɔːgəst] *n* [c/u] 八月 *see also* **July**
aunt [ɑːnt] *n* [c] (*father's sister*) 姑母; (*father's older brother's wife*) 伯母; (*father's younger brother's wife*) 婶母; (*mother's sister*) 姨母; (*mother's brother's wife*) 舅母
auntie, aunty ['ɑːntɪ] [非正式] *n* = **aunt**
au pair ['əu'pɛə(r)] *n* [c] 为学习语言而住在当地人家里并提供家政服务的外国年轻人
aura ['ɔːrə] *n* ♦**an aura of sth** 某物的一种氛围
auspicious [ɔːs'pɪʃəs] [正式] *adj* [+ *opening, start, occasion*] 吉利的
austerity [ɔs'tɛrɪtɪ] *n* [u] **1** (*hardship*) ♦**time/period of austerity** 经济紧缩年代/时期 **2** [正式] (*simplicity*) 朴素
Australia [ɔs'treɪlɪə] *n* 澳大利亚
Australian [ɔs'treɪlɪən] **I** *adj* 澳大利亚的 **II** *n* [c] (*person*) 澳大利亚人
Austria ['ɔstrɪə] *n* 奥地利
Austrian ['ɔstrɪən] **I** *adj* 奥地利的 **II** *n* [c] (*person*) 奥地利人
authentic [ɔː'θɛntɪk] *adj* **1** (*genuine*) [+ *cuisine*] 正宗的; [+ *painting*] 真的; [+ *document*] 真实的 **2** (*reliable*) [+ *account*] 可靠的
author ['ɔːθə(r)] *n* [c] **1** (*writer*) [*of novel*] 作家; [*of text*] 作者 **2** (*originator*) [*of plan, scheme*] 发起人
authoritarian [ɔːθɔrɪ'tɛərɪən] [贬] **I** *adj* [+ *attitudes, government*] 独裁主义的 **II** *n* [c] 独裁主义者
authoritative [ɔː'θɔrɪtətɪv] *adj* **1** [+ *person, manner*] 命令式的 **2** [+ *account, study*] 权威的
✪**authority** [ɔː'θɔrɪtɪ] *n* **1** [u] (*power*) 权威 ◊ *He had an air of authority.* 他有一种权威的姿态。**2** [u] (*right, permission*) 许可 ◊ *The bank closed my account without my authority.* 银行未经我的许可就结了我的账户。**3** ♦**an authority on sth** (*expert*) 某方面的权威 ◊ *She's a world authority on heart disease.* 她是位心脏病方面的世界级权威 。**4** [c] (*government body, ruling body*) 当局 ◊ *the local authority* 地方当局 ♦**to have the authority to do sth** 具有做某事的权力
authorize ['ɔːθəraɪz] *vt* 授权 ♦**to authorize sb/to be authorized to do sth** 授权某人/被授权做某事
autobiography [ɔːtəbaɪ'ɔgrəfɪ] *n* [c] 自传
autograph ['ɔːtəgrɑːf] **I** *n* [c] 亲笔签名 **II** *vt* 亲笔签名于
automatic [ɔːtə'mætɪk] **I** *adj* **1** [+ *process, machine*] 自动的 **2** [+ *reaction*] 无意识的 **3** [+ *action, punishment*] 必然发生的 **II** *n* [c] **1** (*rifle, pistol*) 自动枪 **2** (*car*) 自动挡
automatically [ɔːtə'mætɪklɪ] *adv* **1** (*by itself*) 自动地 **2** (*without thinking*) 无意识地 **3** (*as a matter of course*) 自然而然地
automobile ['ɔːtəməbiːl] [美] *n* [c] 汽车
autonomous [ɔː'tɔnəməs] *adj* **1** (*self-governing*) [+ *country*] 自治的; [+ *organization, group*] 独立自主的 **2** (*independent*) [+ *individual, person*] 独立的
autonomy [ɔː'tɔnəmɪ] *n* [u] **1** (*self-government*) [*of country*] 自治; [*of organization*] 独立自主 **2** [正式]

(*independence*) [*of person*] 自主权
autumn ['ɔːtəm] [英] *n* [c/u] 秋季 [美=**fall**] ♦**in (the) autumn** 在秋季
auxiliary [ɔːg'zɪlɪərɪ] I *adj* 1 [+ *staff, service, force*] 辅助的 2 [+ *equipment*] 备用的 II *n* [c] 1 (*person*) 助手 2 (*in grammar*) 助动词 ♦**auxiliary verb** 助动词
Av. *abbr* = **Ave.**
avail [ə'veɪl] [正式] I *vt* ♦**to avail o.s. of sth** [+ *offer, opportunity, service*] 利用某物 II *n* ♦**to** *or* **of little avail** 没多大效果 ♦**to** *or* **of no avail** 没有效果
availability [əveɪlə'bɪlɪtɪ] *n* [u] [*of goods, staff etc*] 获得的可能性
✪**available** [ə'veɪləbl] *adj* 1 (*obtainable*) [+ *article, service*] 可用的 ◊ *Breakfast is available from 6 a.m.* 从早晨6点起可用早餐。 ◊ *the best available information* 可享用的最佳资讯 2 [+ *person*] (*unoccupied*) 有空的 ◊ *The minister was not available.* 部长没空。; (*unattached*) 单身的 3 [+ *time*] 空闲的 ◊ *I have very few days available at the moment.* 我目前没几天是空闲的。 ♦**every available means** 每个可利用的方法 ♦**is the manager available?** 经理有空吗? ♦**he is not available for comment** 他现在无法发表意见 ♦**to make sth available to sb** 使某人可以享用某物 ♦**available for hire/rent/sale** 可供雇用/出租/出售
avalanche ['ævəlɑːnʃ] *n* 1 [c] 雪崩 2 [s] [*of people, mail, events*] 涌现
Ave. *abbr* (= ***avenue***) 大街
avenge [ə'vɛndʒ] *vt* [+ *death*] 替…报仇
avenue ['ævənjuː] *n* [c] 1 (*lined with shops, houses*) 大街; (*tree-lined*) 林阴道 2 (*means, solution*) 途径
average ['ævərɪdʒ] I *n* [c] 1 [数] (*mean*) 平均数 2 ♦**the average (for sth/sb)** (某物/某人的)平均水平 II *adj* 1 [数] 平均的 2 (*ordinary*) 普通的 3 (*mediocre*) 平庸的 III *vt* 平均为 ♦**on average** 平均 ♦**an average of ten days** 平均10天左右 ♦**above/below (the) average** 高于/低于平均水平
❑**average out** I *vi* ♦**to average out at/to sth** 平均为某数值 II *vt* 得出…的平均数
averse [ə'vəːs] *adj* [正式] ♦**I'm/he's not averse to sth/doing sth** 我/他不反对某事/做某事
avert [ə'vəːt] *vt* 1 (*prevent*) [+ *accident, war*] 避免 2 (*turn away*) ♦**to avert one's eyes/gaze from sth** 将目光/注视从某物上移开
avid ['ævɪd] *adj* [+ *supporter, reader*] 热切的
avocado [ævə'kɑːdəu] [英] *n* [c/u] (*also:* ***avocado pear***) 鳄梨
avoid [ə'vɔɪd] *vt* 1 (*dodge*) [+ *person, obstacle*] 避免 2 (*prevent*) [+ *trouble, danger*] 防止 3 (*evade, shun*) 躲避 ♦**to avoid doing sth** 避免做某事
await [ə'weɪt] [正式] *vt* 1 (*wait for*) 等待 2 (*be in store for*) 等待着 ♦**long awaited** [+ *event, opportunity*] 期待已久的
awake [ə'weɪk] (*pt* **awoke,** *pp* **awoken** *or* **awakened**) I *adj* ♦**to be awake** 醒着的 II *vt* [文] 唤醒 III *vi* [文] 醒来 ♦**wide awake** 完全清醒 ♦**he lay awake all night worrying** 他整晚忧心忡忡地睡不着觉
awakening [ə'weɪknɪŋ] *n* [c] 觉醒 ♦**a rude awakening** 猛然醒悟
award [ə'wɔːd] I *n* [c] 1 (*prize*) 奖 2 [法] (*damages*) 赔偿金 II *vt* 1 [+ *prize*] 授予 2 [法] [+ *damages*] 判给 3 [+ *penalty, free kick*] 判罚
aware [ə'wɛə(r)] *adj* ♦**politically/socially aware** 有政治/社会意识的 ♦**to be aware of sth** (*know about*) 意识到某事; (*be conscious of*) 觉察到某事 ♦**to be aware that ...** 知道… ♦**I am fully** *or* **well aware that ...** 我充分意识到…
awareness [ə'wɛənɪs] *n* [u/s] (*knowledge*) 意识 ♦**to develop** *or* **raise people's awareness of sth** 增强人们对某事的意识
awash [ə'wɔʃ] *adj* 1 ♦**awash (with)** [+ *with water*] (被…)淹没的 2 ♦**awash with** (*knee-deep in*) 充斥的
✪**away** [ə'weɪ] I *adv* 1 [*move, walk* +] …开 ◊ *He rose and walked slowly away.* 他站起身,慢慢地走开。 2 (*not present*) 不在 ◊ *Jason is away in*

Germany. 杰森现在在德国。◊ *She was away at the time of the accident.* 发生意外时她不在。**3** ♦ **to put sth away** 妥善保存某物 ♦ **to hide sth away** 藏起某物 **4** [*melt, fade, fall* +] …掉 ◊ *The snow has already melted away.* 雪已经融化掉了。**II** *adj* [+ *match, game*] 客场的 ♦ **a week/month away** 还有一个星期/月 ♦ **two kilometres away** 离这里两公里远 ♦ **to play away** 在对方球场比赛 ♦ **it's two hours away by car** 有两小时车程 ♦ **away from** 远离 ◊ *a pleasant spot away from the city* 一个远离城市的宜人之地 ♦ **to work/pedal/scrub away** 连续不断地工作/蹬车/擦洗

awe [ɔː] **I** *n* [U] (*respect*) 敬畏 **II** *vt* ♦ **to be awed by sth/sb** 对某事/某人肃然起敬 ♦ **to be in awe of** *or* **awed by sb/sth** 敬畏某人/某事

awesome [ˈɔːsəm] *adj* **1** (*impressive*) 使人敬畏的 **2** [非正式] (*amazing*) 令人惊叹的

awful [ˈɔːfəl] **I** *adj* **1** (*frightful*) 糟糕的 **2** (*dreadful*) [+ *shock, crime etc*] 可怕的 **3** ♦ **to look/feel awful** (*ill*) 看起来/感觉很糟糕的 **II** *adv* [美:非正式] (*very*) 十分地 ♦ **an awful lot (of)** (*amount*) 大量的; (*number*) 非常多的

awfully [ˈɔːfəlɪ] *adv* (*very*) (*used for emphasis*) 非常 ♦ **would you mind awfully if ...?** 你非常介意…吗?

awkward [ˈɔːkwəd] *adj* **1** (*clumsy*) [+ *movement*] 笨拙的 **2** (*inconvenient*) [+ *time, question*] 令人尴尬的 **3** (*difficult to use, do, or carry*) 不方便的 **4** (*deliberately difficult*) [+ *person*] 不合作的 ♦ **he's at an awkward age** 他正处于爱找别扭的年龄

awoke [əˈwəuk] *pt of* **awake**

awoken [əˈwəukən] *pp of* **awake**

axe (美 **ax**) [æks] **I** *n* [C] 斧 **II** *vt* 大刀阔斧地削减 ♦ **to have an axe to grind** [非正式] 另有企图

axes[1] [ˈæksɪz] *n* [*pl*] *of* **ax(e)**

axes[2] [ˈæksiːz] *npl of* **axis**

axle [ˈæksl] [汽车] *n* [C] 轴

aye [aɪ] [英] **I** *int* (*yes*) 是 ♦ **to vote aye** 投赞成票 **II** *n* ♦ **the ayes** 投赞成票者

azalea [əˈeɪzlɪə] *n* [C] 杜鹃花

Azerbaijan [æzəbaɪˈdʒɑːn] *n* 阿塞拜疆

Bb

B¹, b [biː] *n* [c/u] (*letter*) 英语的第二个字母

B² [biː] *n* **1** [c/u] [音] C 大调音阶中的第七音 **2** [c] [教育, 大学] (*mark*) 良

B³ [手机短信] *abbr* = **be**

b. *abbr* (= **born**) 出生

B4 [手机短信] *abbr* = **before**

BA *n abbr* (= ***Bachelor of Arts***) (*qualification*) 文科学士学位; (*person*) 文科学士

baby ['beɪbɪ] **I** *n* [c] **1** (*infant*) 婴儿 **2** [尤美:非正式] (*darling*) 宝贝 **II** *cpd* [复合词] **1** [+ *seal, elephant*] 幼小动物 **2** [+ *vegetable*] 嫩菜 ◊ *baby sweetcorn* 嫩的甜玉米 ♦**to have a baby** 生孩子 ♦**to be a baby** [非正式] 真是个小孩儿

baby carriage [美] *n* [c] 婴儿车 [英 = **pram**]

baby food *n* [c/u] 婴儿食品

babysit ['beɪbɪsɪt] (*pt, pp* **babysat**) *vi* 代人照看孩子

babysitter ['beɪbɪsɪtə(r)] *n* [c] 代人照看孩子的人

baby wipe *n* [c] 婴儿卫生纸

bachelor ['bætʃələ(r)] *n* [c] **1** (*unmarried man*) 单身汉 **2** ♦**Bachelor of Arts/Science** (*degree*) 文/理科学士学位; [英] (*person*) 文/理科学士

✪ **back** [bæk] **I** *n* [c] **1** [*of person, animal*] 背部 **2** (*not front*) [*of hand, neck, legs*] 背面; [*of house, door, book*] 后面; [*of car*] 后部; [*of train*] 尾部; [*of chair*] 靠背 **3** [足球] (*defender*) 后卫 **II** *vt* **1** (*support*) [+ *candidate, plan*] 支持 ◊ *The union will back Mr Green.* 工会将支持格林先生。; (*financially*) 资助 ◊ *The group is backed by big multinationals.* 该团体由大型的跨国公司资助。 **2** (*bet on*) [+ *horse, team*] 下赌注于 ◊ *Did you back the winner?* 你是否赌赢家? **3** (*reverse*) [+ *car*] 倒 ◊ *She backed the car a few feet.* 她把车向后倒了几英尺。 **III** *vi* (*reverse*) [*person, car etc* +] 倒着行驶 ◊ *She backed out of the drive.* 她倒着行驶出车道。 **IV** *adj* **1** [+ *garden, door, room, wheels*] 后面的 **2** [+ *payment, rent*] 拖欠的 **V** *adv* **1** (*not forward*) 向后 ◊ *Charlie glanced back.* 查理向后扫了一眼。 **2** (*returned*) ♦**to be back** 回来 ◊ *He's back.* 他回来了。 **3** (*when returning sth*) 还 ◊ *She handed the knife back.* 她把刀还回来了。 ◊ *Can I have it back?* 我能要回它吗? **4** (*repetition*) 回 ◊ *She stared back at me.* 她回瞪着我。 **5** (*in the past*) 以前 ◊ *The story starts back in 1950.* 故事开始于1950年。 **6** (*away*) 远离 ◊ *Keep back from the edge of the platform.* 站在远离站台边缘的地方。 ♦**to do sth behind sb's back** 背着某人做某事 ♦**to turn one's back on sb/sth** (喻) 不理睬某人/某事 ♦**to have one's back to the wall** (喻) 陷入绝境 ♦**to break the back of a job** 度过最艰难的时刻 ♦**to take a back seat** (喻) 把权利让与他人 ♦**back and forth** 来回 ♦**at the back (of)** (*of crowd, building*) 在(…的)后面 ♦**back to front** [尤英] 前后倒置 ◊ *You've got your T-shirt on back to front.* 你把T恤衫前后穿反了。

❑**back away** *vi* 向后退

❑**back down** *vi* 做出让步

❑**back off** *vi* (*draw back*) 退避

❑**back onto** *vt* [不可拆分] 背靠

❑**back out** *vi* (*withdraw*) 退出 ♦**to back out of sth** [+ *deal, agreement etc*] 退出某事

❑**back up I** *vt* **1** (*support*) [+ *statement, theory etc*] 证实 ◊ *Her views are backed up by an official report on crime.* 她的观点被一份官方犯罪报告证实了。 **2** (*provide alibi for*) [+ *friend, accomplice*] 为…作证 ◊ *The girl denied being there, and the man backed her up.* 女孩否定当时在那里,男子为她作了证。 **3** (*help*) [+ *person*] 支持 ◊ *His employers backed him up.* 他的雇主支持他。 **4** [计算机] [+ *disk*] 备份 **5** (*reverse*) [+ *car*] 倒 **II** *vi* (*reverse*) [*person, car* +] 倒行

backache ['bækeɪk] *n* [c/u] 背痛

backbone ['bækbəun] *n* **1** [c] 脊椎骨 **2** [u] (*courage*) 骨气 **3** [s] (*key person*) 中坚

backfire [bæk'faɪə(r)] *vi* **1** [*plan* +] 事与愿违 **2** [*car, engine* +] 回火

backgammon ['bækgæmən] *n* [u] 十五子棋

background ['bækgraund] **I** *n* **1** [c] [*of picture, scene, events*] 背景 **2** [c/u] [*of person*] (*origins*) 出身; (*experience*) 经验 **II** *cpd* [复合词] [+ *noise, music, information*] 背景 ♦**in the background** 在背后 ♦**family background** 家庭出身 ♦**background reading** 辅助材料阅读

backing ['bækɪŋ] *n* **1** [u] (*support*) 支持; (*financial*) 资助 **2** [c] (*layer*) 背衬 **3** [c] [音] 伴奏音乐

backlog ['bæklɔg] *n* [c] 积压

backpack ['bækpæk] *n* [c] 双肩背包

backpacker ['bækpækə(r)] *n* [c] 背包旅行者

> **BACKPACKER**
> **Backpacker** 一词指预算紧张的青年旅行者。他们把全部的随身物品放在一个背包里，尽可能地节俭开支，为的是能延长旅行时间多了解一个地区，多看一些地方。

backside ['bæksaɪd] [非正式] *n* [c] 屁股

backslash ['bækslæʃ] *n* [c] 后斜线

backstage [bæk'steɪdʒ] *adv* 后台

backstroke ['bækstrəuk] *n* [u] (*also: **the backstroke***) 仰泳

backup ['bækʌp] **I** *adj* **1** [+ *staff, services*] 备用的 **2** [计算机] [+ *copy, file, disk*] 备份的 **II** *n* **1** [u] (*support*) 支持 **2** [c] (*reserve*) 备份

backward ['bækwəd] **I** *adj* **1** [+ *glance, movement*] 向后的 **2** [贬] [+ *country*] 落后的; [+ *person*] 迟钝的 **II** *adv* [尤美] = **backwards** ♦**a backward step** (喻) 倒退

backwards ['bækwədz] *adv* **1** [*move, look* +] 向后地 **2** (*in reverse*) [*count, work* +] 倒着地 **3** (喻) 倒退地 ◊ *Technologically, this is a step backwards.* 技术上这是个退步。 **4** (*in time*) 向后地 ♦**to move backwards and forwards** 来回移动 ♦**to know sth backwards** *or* [美] **backward and forward** 极熟悉某事

backyard [bæk'jɑːd] *n* [c] [*of house*] 后院

bacon ['beɪkən] *n* [u] 腌猪肉

bacteria [bæk'tɪərɪə] *n* [*pl*] 细菌

✪ **bad** [bæd] *adj* **1** (*not good*) [+ *weather, health, conditions, temper*] 坏的; [+ *actor, driver*] 不胜任的; [+ *behaviour, habit*] 不良的 **2** (*wicked*) [+ *person*] 恶的 **3** (*naughty*) [+ *child*] 不听话的 **4** (*serious*) [+ *mistake, accident, headache*] 严重的 **5** (*injured*) [+ *back, arm*] 有病的 **6** (*rotten*) [+ *fruit, meat etc*] 腐烂的 ♦**to be bad for sth/sb** 对某事/某物有害 ♦**to be bad at sth/at doing sth** 不擅长某事/做某事 ♦**to feel bad about sth** (*guilty*) 对某事感到愧疚 ♦**to feel bad that ...** (*guilty*) 因…而感到愧疚 ♦**to go bad** [*food, milk* +] 变质 ♦**to go from bad to worse** 每况愈下 ♦**not bad** 不错 ◊ *The wine wasn't bad.* 这葡萄酒不错。 ♦**too bad!** 那没办法！

bade [bæd] *pt of* **bid**

badge [bædʒ] *n* [c] **1** [英] (*metal, cloth*) 徽章 [美 = **button**] **2** (喻) [*of power etc*] 象征

badger ['bædʒə(r)] **I** *n* [c] 獾 **II** *vt* 纠缠

bad language *n* [u] 粗话

badly ['bædlɪ] *adv* **1** (*poorly*) [*work, play* +] 不令人满意地; [+ *dressed*] 不得体地 **2** (*seriously*) [+ *damaged, injured*] 严重地 ♦**to think badly of sb/sth** 认为某人/某事不好 ♦**to reflect badly on sb/sth** 对某人/某事有坏影响 ♦**to want/need sth badly** 非常想要/需要某物 ♦**to be badly off** (*in a bad situation*) 境况不好; (*financially*) 穷困

badminton ['bædmɪntən] *n* [u] 羽毛球

bad-tempered ['bæd'tɛmpəd] *adj* (*by nature*) 脾气坏的; (*on one occasion*) 发脾气的
📖 用法参见 **angry**

baffle ['bæfl] *vt* (*puzzle*) 使困惑

baffled ['bæfld] *adj* [+ *expression*] 困惑的 ♦**to be baffled (by sth)** (被某事) 困惑

bag [bæg] **I** *n* [c] **1** (*made of paper, plastic, with handle*) 袋 **2** (*suitcase*) 行李箱 **3** (*handbag*) 手袋 **4** [贬, 非正式] (*woman*) 讨厌的女人 **II** *vt* [英: 非正式] (*claim*) 抢占 ♦**bags of** [英: 非正式] (*lots of*) 许多 ♦**to pack one's bags** 准备离开 ♦**to have bags under one's eyes** 有眼袋 ♦**it's in the bag** [非正式] 稳操胜券

baggage ['bægɪdʒ] *n* [u] **1** (*luggage*) 行李 **2** (喻) 累赘

baggage allowance *n* [c] (*at airport*) 行李限重

baggage (re)claim *n* [u] (*at airport*) 行李领取

baggy ['bægɪ] *adj* [+ *suit, trousers, sweater*] 宽松的

bagpipes ['bægpaɪps] *n* [*pl*] 风笛

> **BAGPIPES**
> **bagpipes**，风笛，是一种总能让人联想起苏格兰的古老乐器。演奏者，即**pipers**，通过一根管子把气吹到一个袋子里，然后挤压袋子把气送出其他管子，使发出嗡嗡的响声。风笛能制造出浓郁的结婚和官方庆典活动的气氛。乐手们盛装起来，身着代表苏格兰不同家族图案的传统褶皱短裙。现场观看这样的风笛军乐队演奏蔚为壮观。

bail [beɪl] **I** *n* [u] [法] (*payment*) 保释金; (*release*) 保释 **II** *vt* [+ *prisoner*] 准许保释 **III** *vi* (*also: **bail out***) (*on boat*) 舀出 ♦**grant bail (to)** [+ *prisoner*] 准许保释 ♦**on bail** [+ *prisoner*] 保释中 ♦**to be released on bail** 被保释
❑**bail out** *vt* **1** [+ *prisoner*] 保释 **2** (喻) [+ *firm, industry*] 使摆脱困境; [+ *friend*] 帮助摆脱困境

bait [beɪt] **I** *n* [u/s] **1** (*for fish*) 鱼饵 **2** (*for animal*) 诱饵 **3** (喻) (*for criminal etc*) 引诱物 **II** *vt* **1** [+ *hook, trap*] 放上诱饵 **2** (*tease*) [+ *person*] 侮弄

bake [beɪk] **I** *vt* **1** [+ *potatoes, cake, bread*] 烤 **2** [+ *clay*] 烤硬 **II** *vi* **1** [*bread, cake etc* +] 烤 **2** (*make cakes etc*) [*person* +] 烘烤食品
📖 用法参见 **cook**

baked beans [beɪkt-] *n* [*pl*] [英] (*beans*) 烘豆; [美] (*with pork*) 有肉的烘豆

baked potato [beɪkt-] *n* [c] 烤土豆

baker ['beɪkə(r)] *n* [c] **1** (*person*) 面包师 **2** (*shop*) (*also: **baker's***) 面包店

bakery ['beɪkərɪ] *n* [c] 面包房

baking ['beɪkɪŋ] **I** *n* [u] **1** (*activity*) 烤食品 **2** (*cakes, bread*) 烘烤的面食 **II** *adj* [非正式] (*hot*) 灼热的 ♦**baking hot** 炎热

baking powder *n* [u] 发酵粉

balance ['bæləns] **I** *n* **1** [u] (*equilibrium*) [*of person, object*] 平衡 **2** [u/s] (喻) (*in situation*) 平衡 **3** [c] (*in bank account*) 余额 **4** [s] (*remainder to be paid*) 余欠之数 **II** *vt* **1** [+ *object*] 使平衡 **2** [+ *budget, account*] 使收支平衡 **3** [+ *pros and cons*] 权衡 **4** (*compensate for*) 弥补 **5** (*make equal*) 等量齐观 **III** *vi* [*person, object* +] 保持平衡 ♦**to keep/lose one's balance** 保持/失去平衡 ♦**off balance** 失去平衡 ♦**to hang in the balance** 悬而未决 ♦**on balance** 总的来看 ♦**balance of payments** 国际收支差额 ♦**balance of trade** 进出口贸易差额 ♦**balance carried forward** 余额转下页 ♦**balance brought forward** 余额承前页 ♦**to balance the books** 平衡收支

balanced ['bælənst] *adj* **1** (*unbiased*) [+ *report*] 不偏不倚的 **2** [+ *diet*] 均衡的 **3** (*calm*) [+ *person*] 平和的

balance sheet *n* [c] 资产负债表

balcony ['bælkənɪ] *n* [c] **1** [*of building*] (*open*) 露台; (*covered*) 阳台 **2** (*in cinema, theatre*) 楼座

bald [bɔːld] *adj* **1** [+ *head, person*] 秃的 **2** [+ *tyre*] 严重磨损的 **3** [+ *statement*] 直截了当的 ♦**to go bald** 变秃

ball [bɔːl] **I** *n* [c] **1** (*football, golf ball etc*) 球 **2** [*of wool, string*] 团 **3** (*sphere*) 球状 **4** (*dance*) 舞会 **5** [*of foot, thumb*] 球形部分 **II** *vt* (*also: **ball up***) [+ *paper, cloth*] 把…抟成团 ♦**to start** *or* **get** *or* **set the ball rolling** 开始 ♦**to play ball (with sb)** [非正式: 喻] (与某人) 协作 ♦**to be on the ball** 敏锐 ♦**the ball is in your**

court 轮到你了 ♦**to have a ball** [非正式] 过得愉快
ballerina [bælə'riːnə] *n* [c] 芭蕾舞女演员
ballet ['bæleɪ, (美) bæ'leɪ] *n* **1** [u] (*art form*) 芭蕾舞 **2** [c] (*particular work*) 芭蕾舞剧
ballet dancer *n* [c] 芭蕾舞演员
balloon [bə'luːn] **I** *n* [c] **1** (*child's*) 气球 **2** (*also:* ***hot-air balloon***) 热气球 **II** *vi* (*increase in size*) 膨胀
ballot ['bælət] **I** *n* [c] (*vote*) 无记名投票 **II** *vt* [+ *group*] 使投票表决
ballpoint (pen) ['bɔːlpɔɪnt(-)] *n* [c] 圆珠笔
ballroom ['bɔːlrum] *n* [c] 舞厅
ballroom dancing *n* [u] 交际舞
Baltic ['bɔːltɪk] *n* ♦**the Baltic (Sea)** 波罗的海
bamboo [bæm'buː] *n* [u] **1** (*plant*) 竹子 **2** (*material*) 竹
bamboo shoots *n* [*pl*] 竹笋
ban [bæn] **I** *n* [c] (*prohibition*) 禁止 **II** *vt* (*prohibit*) 禁止 ♦**to be banned from driving** 被禁止开车
banana [bə'nɑːnə] *n* [c] 香蕉
band [bænd] **I** *n* [c] **1** (*group*) [*of supporters, helpers, rebels etc*] 群 **2** [音] (*jazz, rock etc*) 乐队; (*military*) 军乐队 **3** (*strip*) [*of cloth*] 带子; [*of light, land*] 条纹 **4** (*loop*) [*of metal, material*] 箍 **5** (*range*) 幅度 **II** *vt* [英] [+ *tax*] 划分级别 [美 = **bracket**]
❑**band together** *vi* 联合
bandage ['bændɪdʒ] **I** *n* [c] 绷带 **II** *vt* [+ *wound, leg*] 用绷带包扎
Band-Aid® ['bændeɪd] [美] *n* [c] 邦迪创可贴 [英 = **plaster**]
B&B *n abbr* = **bed and breakfast**
bandit ['bændɪt] *n* [c] 强盗
bang [bæŋ] **I** *n* [c] **1** (*noise*) [*of door*] 砰的一声; [*of gun, exhaust*] 爆炸声 **2** (*blow*) 撞击 **II** *int* 砰 **III** *vt* **1** [+ *door*] 砰地一声关上 **2** (*also:* ***bang on***) [+ *wall, drum etc*] 大声撞击 **3** [+ *one's head, elbow etc*] 撞 **IV** *vi* **1** [*door* +] 砰地关上 **2** [*firework, engine* +] 砰砰作响 **V** *adv* ♦**to be bang on time/in the middle** [非正式] 正准时/当中 **VI bangs** *n* [*pl*] [美] (*fringe*) 刘海 [英 = **fringe**] ♦**to bang into sth/sb** 猛撞某物/某人
Bangladesh [bæŋglə'dɛʃ] *n* 孟加拉国
bangle ['bæŋgl] *n* [c] (*bracelet*) 镯
banish ['bænɪʃ] *vt* (*exile*) 放逐
banister(s) ['bænɪstə(z)] *n* [*pl*] 楼梯扶手
banjo ['bændʒəu] (*pl* **banjoes** *or* **banjos**) *n* [c] 班卓琴
✪**bank** [bæŋk] **I** *n* [c] **1** [经济] (*building, institution*) 银行 **2** [*of data*] 库 **3** [*of river, lake*] 岸 **4** [*of earth*] 斜坡 **5** [*of fog*] 一堆 **6** [*of switches, dials*] 排 **II** *vi* **1** [*plane* +] 倾斜飞行 **2** [商] ♦**to bank with** 在…有银行账户
❑**bank on** *vt* [不可拆分] (*rely on*) 指望
bank account *n* [c] 银行账户
bank balance *n* [c] 银行存款余额
bank card *n* [c] **1** [英] (*for cash machine*) 银行卡 [美 = **ATM card**] **2** [美] (*credit card*) 银行信用卡 [英 = **banker's card**]
banker ['bæŋkə(r)] *n* [c] 银行家
bank holiday [英] *n* [c] 法定假期 [美 = **national holiday**]
banking ['bæŋkɪŋ] *n* [u] 银行业
banknote ['bæŋknəut] *n* [c] 纸币
bankrupt ['bæŋkrʌpt] **I** *adj* **1** [+ *person, company*] 破产的 **2** (喻) ♦**morally bankrupt** 道德沦丧 **II** *n* [c] [*person*] 破产者 **III** *vt* [+ *person, organization*] 使破产 ♦**to go bankrupt** 破产 ♦**to be made bankrupt** 宣告破产
bankruptcy ['bæŋkrʌptsɪ] *n* **1** [u] (字) 破产 **2** [c] (*particular instance*) 破产 **3** [u] (喻) 完全缺乏
bank statement *n* [c] 银行结单
banner ['bænə(r)] *n* [c] **1** (*for decoration, advertising*) 横幅 **2** (*carried in a demonstration*) 横幅标语
bannister(s) ['bænɪstə(z)] *n* [*pl*] = **banister(s)**
banquet ['bæŋkwɪt] *n* [c] 盛宴
baptism ['bæptɪzəm] *n* [c/u] 洗礼

BAPTISM

baptism，洗礼，是一种基督教仪式。牧师把水浇在受洗人额头上，或把受洗人浸在水中，以示其罪已得到原谅，或已成为该教堂的一员。实际上，这种仪式与新生儿正式命名（**christened**）同时进行。

baptize [bæp'taɪz] *vt* 给…施行洗礼
bar [bɑː(r)] **I** *n* [c] **1** (*place for drinking*) 酒吧 **2** (*counter*) (*in pub*) 吧台 **3** (*rod*) [*of metal etc*] 条 **4** (*on window, in prison*) 铁栏杆 **5** (*tablet*) [*of soap, chocolate*] 块 **6** (喻) (*obstacle*) 障碍 **7** [尤英:音] 小节线 [美= **measure**] **8** [法] ♦**the Bar** (*profession*) 律师业 **II** *vt* **1** [+ *way, road*] 阻挡 **2** [+ *door, window*] 闩上 **3** [+ *person, activity*] 禁止 ♦**to be behind bars** [*prisoner* +] 坐牢 ♦**no holds barred** 竭尽全力 ♦**bar none** 无例外
barbaric [bɑː'bærɪk] *adj* 野蛮的
barbecue ['bɑːbɪkjuː] **I** *n* [c] **1** (*cooking device*) 烤肉架 **2** (*meal, party*) 烧烤聚会 **II** *vt* 烧烤
barbed wire ['bɑːbd-] *n* [u] 有刺铁丝
barber ['bɑːbə(r)] *n* [c] **1** (*person*) 男理发师 **2** [英] (*shop*) ♦**barber's** 男子理发店 [美= **barber shop**]
barber shop *n* [c] 男子理发店
bar code *n* [c] 条形码
bare [bɛə(r)] **I** *adj* **1** (*naked*) [+ *body, feet*] 裸露的 **2** (*not covered*) [+ *rock, floor*] 光秃的 **3** (*empty*) [+ *cupboard, shelf, room*] 空的 **4** [+ *minimum, essentials*] 基本的 **II** *vt* (*reveal*) [+ *one's body, teeth*] 露出 ♦**with one's bare hands** 赤手空拳 ♦**to bare one's soul** 诉说衷肠
barefoot(ed) ['bɛəfut(ɪd)] **I** *adj* 赤脚的 **II** *adv* 赤脚地
barely ['bɛəlɪ] *adv* (*scarcely*) 几乎不
bargain ['bɑːgɪn] **I** *n* [c] **1** (*good buy*) 廉价品 **2** (*deal, agreement*) 协议 **II** *vi* **1** (*negotiate*) ♦**to bargain (with sb)** (与某人)谈判 **2** (*haggle*) (与某人)讨价还价 ♦**to drive a hard bargain** 极力讨价还价 ♦**into the bargain** 此外
❑**bargain for, bargain on** *vt* [不可拆分] 预料
barge [bɑːdʒ] *n* [c] (*boat*) 驳船
❑**barge in** [非正式] *vi* **1** (*enter*) 闯进 **2** (*interrupt*) 打断
❑**barge into** [非正式] *vt* [不可拆分] **1** [+ *room*] 闯入 **2** (*bump into*) [+ *person*] 碰撞
bark [bɑːk] **I** *n* **1** [u] [*of tree*] 树皮 **2** [c] [*of dog*] 犬吠声 **II** *vi* [*dog* +] 叫 ♦**she's barking up the wrong tree** [非正式] 她搞错了对象
barley ['bɑːlɪ] *n* [u] 大麦
barmaid ['bɑːmeɪd] [尤英] *n* [c] 酒吧女侍 [美= **bartender**]
barman ['bɑːmən] (*pl* **barmen**) [尤英] *n* [c] 酒吧男侍 [美= **bartender**]
barn [bɑːn] *n* [c] 仓房
barometer [bə'rɔmɪtə(r)] *n* [c] 晴雨表
baron ['bærən] *n* [c] 男爵 ♦**press/drug baron** 报业/毒品大王
baroness ['bærənɪs] *n* [c] (*wife of baron*) 男爵夫人; (*in own right*) 女男爵
barracks ['bærəks] (*pl* **barracks**) *n* [c] 营房
barrage ['bærɑːʒ, (美) bə'rɑːʒ] *n* [c] **1** [军] 火力网 **2** (*dam*) 拦河坝 **3** (喻) [*of criticism, questions etc*] 连珠炮
barrel ['bærəl] *n* [c] **1** (*cask*) [*of wine, beer*] 桶; [*of oil*] 琵琶桶 **2** [*of gun*] 枪管
barren ['bærən] *adj* **1** (*infertile*) [+ *land*] 不毛的 **2** (*bare*) [+ *landscape*] 贫瘠的 **3** (喻) [+ *spell, patch*] 无成效的
barricade [bærɪ'keɪd] **I** *n* [c] 路障 **II** *vt* [+ *road, entrance*] 在…设路障 ♦**to barricade oneself in** 把自己关在里面
barrier ['bærɪə(r)] *n* [c] **1** (*at frontier, entrance*) 关口 **2** [英] (*also:* ***crash barrier***) 护栏 **3** (*to progress, communication etc*) 障碍
barring ['bɑːrɪŋ] *prep* 除非
barrister ['bærɪstə(r)] [英] *n* [c] 律师
barrow ['bærəu] *n* [c] **1** (*also:* ***wheelbarrow***) 手推车 **2** [英] (*for selling fruit, vegetables etc*) 手推双轮车
bartender ['bɑːtɛndə(r)] [美] *n* [c] 酒吧侍者 [英= **barman, barmaid**]
✪**base** [beɪs] **I** *n* [c] **1** (*bottom*) [*of post, tree*] 底部 ◊ *the base of the cliffs* 悬崖的底部; [*of cup, vase*] 底座 **2** (*layer*) [*of paint, make up*] 底 ◊ *Use this paint as a base before you varnish.* 在你上清漆前，先用这种漆作为底漆。 **3** [棒球] 垒 **4** (*basis*) 根基 **5** (*centre*) (*military*) 基地 ◊ *an army base* 军事基地; (*for individual, organization*) 总部 ◊ *The company has its base in*

London. 该公司的总部设在伦敦。**II** *vt* ♦**to base sth on** *or* **upon sth** 以某物作为某物的根据 **III** *adj* [文][+ *mind, thoughts*] 卑鄙的 ♦**to be based on sth** 以某物为根据 ♦**to be based at** [*troops, employee* +] 以…为基地 ♦**I'm based in London** 我长驻伦敦

baseball ['beɪsbɔːl] *n* **1** [U] (*sport*) 棒球◊ *He likes baseball.* 他喜欢棒球。**2** [C] (*ball*) 棒球◊ *Each box contains five baseballs.* 每个盒子里装有5个棒球。

basement ['beɪsmənt] **I** *n* [C] 地下室 **II** *adj* [+ *flat, apartment, kitchen etc*] 地下室的

bases[1] ['beɪsɪz] *n* [*pl*] *of* **base**

bases[2] ['beɪsiːz] *n* [*pl*] *of* **basis**

bash [bæʃ] [非正式] **I** *vt* (*hit*) 猛击 **II** *vi* (*crash*) ♦**to bash into/against sth/sb** 猛撞某物/某人 **III** *n* [C] **1** (*party*) 聚会 **2** [英](*try*) ♦**to have a bash (at sth/at doing sth)** 尝试(某事/做某事)

❑**bash up** *vt* [英](*beat up*) 痛打

basic ['beɪsɪk] *adj* **1** [+ *principle, rule, right*] 基本的 **2** (*primitive*) [+ *facilities*] 根本的 *see also* **basics**

basically ['beɪsɪklɪ] *adv* **1** (*fundamentally*) 基本上 **2** (*in fact, put simply*) 简而言之

basics ['beɪsɪks] *n* [*pl*] ♦**the basics** 基本点

basil ['bæzl] *n* [U] 罗勒属植物

basin ['beɪsn] *n* [C] **1** (*bowl*) 盆 **2** (*also: **wash basin***) 洗脸盆 **3** [*of river, lake*] 流域

basis ['beɪsɪs] (*pl* **bases**) *n* [C] **1** (*starting point*) 基础 **2** (*foundation*) 根据 ♦**on a voluntary basis** 基于自愿 ♦**on a regular basis** 定期 ♦**on the basis of what you've said** 根据你所说的话

basket ['bɑːskɪt] *n* [C] **1** (*container*) 筐 **2** (*in basketball*) 球篮

basketball ['bɑːskɪtbɔːl] *n* **1** [U] (*sport*) 篮球 **2** [C] (*ball*) 篮球

bass [beɪs] [音] *n* **1** [C] (*singer*) 男低音 **2** [U] (*part*) 低音部 **3** [C/U] (*also: **bass guitar***) 低音吉他 **4** [U] (*on radio, music system etc*) 低音

bastard ['bɑːstəd] *n* [C] **1** [非正式,疑讳] 王八蛋 **2** [过时](*illegitimate offspring*) 私生子

bat [bæt] **I** *n* [C] **1** (*animal*) 蝙蝠 **2** (*for cricket, baseball*) 球板 **3** [英](*for table tennis*) 球拍 [美=**paddle**] **II** *vi* [板球,棒球] 用板/棒击球 **III** *vt* ♦**he didn't bat an eyelid** *or* [美] **eye** 他未露声色 ♦**off one's own bat** [英] 独立地做某事

batch [bætʃ] *n* [C] [*of letters, papers, applicants, goods*] 批

bath [bɑːθ] **I** *n* [C] **1** [英](*bathtub*) 浴缸 [美=**bathtub**] **2** (*act of bathing*) 洗澡 **II** *vt* [英][+ *baby, patient*] 给…洗澡 [美=**bathe**] **III baths** *n* [*pl*] (*swimming pool*) 室内公共游泳池 ♦**to have** *or* **take a bath** 洗澡

bathe [beɪð] **I** *vi* **1** [尤英:正式](*swim*) 戏水 **2** [尤美](*have a bath*) 洗澡 **II** *vt* **1** [+ *wound*] 清洗 **2** [美][+ *baby, patient*] 给…洗澡 [英=**bath**] **3** (喻)(*in light, warmth*) 笼罩

bathing ['beɪðɪŋ] [尤英:正式] *n* [U] 游泳

bathing costume [英] *n* = **bathing suit**

bathing suit *n* [C] 游泳衣

bathrobe ['bɑːθrəub] *n* [C] 浴衣

bathroom ['bɑːθrum] *n* [C] **1** (*in house*) 卫生间 **2** [美](*toilet*) 厕所 [英=**toilet**] ♦**to go to the bathroom** [美] 去卫生间

bath towel *n* [C] 浴巾

bathtub ['bɑːθtʌb] [美] *n* [C] 浴缸 [英=**bath**]

baton ['bætən, (美) bə'tɑːn] *n* [C] **1** [音] 指挥棒 **2** (*in athletics*) 接力棒 **3** [英](*truncheon*) 警棍

batter ['bætə(r)] **I** *vt* **1** [+ *child, wife*] 连续猛打 **2** [*wind, rain* +] 吹打 **II** *n* [U] [烹饪] 奶蛋面糊

battered ['bætəd] *adj* **1** [+ *wife, child*] 受虐的 **2** [+ *suitcase, car*] 破旧不堪的

battery ['bætərɪ] *n* [C] **1** (*for torch, radio etc*) 电池 **2** (*in car*) 电瓶 **3** [*of tests*] 一连串 **4** [*of cameras, lights*] 电池组

battle ['bætl] **I** *n* [C] **1** [军] 战役 **2** (喻)(*struggle*) 斗争 **II** *vi* **1** (*fight*) 交战 **2** (*struggle*) ♦**to battle for sth/to do sth** 力争某事/做某事 **3** (*compete*) ♦**to battle (with sb) for sth/to do sth** (与某人)争夺某

物/争做某事 ♦ **that's half the battle** 那是成功的一半 ♦ **it's a** *or* **we're fighting a losing battle** 这/我们注定要失败 ♦ **to do battle (with sb)** (*fight*) (与某人) 交战; (*compete*) (与某人) 争高下

battlefield ['bætlfi:ld] *n* [c] 战场

bay [beɪ] **I** *n* [c] **1** [地理] 湾 **2** (*for loading, parking etc*) 隔间 **II** *adj* [+ *horse*] 红棕色的 ♦ **to hold** *or* **keep sb/sth at bay** 不让某人/某物接近

bazaar [bə'zɑ:(r)] *n* [c] **1** (*market*) 市场 **2** (*fete*) 义卖市场

BBC *n abbr* (= ***British Broadcasting Corporation***) ♦ **the BBC** 英国广播公司

BC *adv abbr* (= ***before Christ***) 公元前

be

KEYWORD

[bi:] (*pt* **was, were**, *pp* **been**)

I *vi*

1 (*with complement*) 是 ♦ **I'm English/Chinese** 我是英国人/中国人 ♦ **she's tall/pretty** 她长得高/漂亮 ♦ **I'm tired/hot** 我累了/很热 ♦ **she's hungry/thirsty** 她饿了/渴了 ♦ **your hair's wet** 你的头发湿了 ♦ **he's a doctor** 他是医生 ♦ **this is my mother** 这是我妈妈 ♦ **who is it?** 这是谁? ♦ **it's only me/the postman** 是我/邮递员啊 ♦ **it was Diana who paid the bill** 是黛安娜付的账单 ♦ **2 and 2 are 4** 2加2等于4 ♦ **be careful/quiet!** 当心/安静!

2 (*referring to time, date*) 是 ♦ **it's 5 o'clock** 现在是5点钟 ♦ **it's the 28th of April, it's April 28th** 今天是4月28日

3 (*describing weather*) ♦ **it's hot/cold** 天热/冷 ♦ **it's foggy/wet** 天有雾/天气潮湿 ♦ **it's windy today** 今天有风

4 (*talking about health*) ♦ **how are you?** 你身体怎么样? ♦ **I'm fine, thanks** 我很好，谢谢 ♦ **I'm better now** 我现在好多了

5 (*talking about age*) 有 ♦ **how old are you?** 你多大了? ♦ **I'm 16 (years old)** 我16 (岁) ♦ **I'll be 18 on Friday** 星期五我就18岁了

6 (*talking about place*) 在 ♦ **Madrid is in Spain** 马德里在西班牙 ♦ **it's on the table** 在桌上 ♦ **the supermarket isn't far from here** 超市离这儿不远 ♦ **I won't be here tomorrow** 我明天不在这儿 ♦ **have you been to Beijing?** 你去过北京吗? ♦ **we've been here for ages** 我们已经在这里好久了 ♦ **where have you been?** 你去哪儿了? ♦ **has the postman been yet?** 邮递员来过了吗? ♦ **the meeting will be in the canteen** 会议将在食堂举行

7 (*referring to distance*) 有 ♦ **it's 10 km to the village** 这儿离村庄有10公里 ♦ **it's 20 miles from here to London** 从这儿到伦敦有20英里

8 (*cost*) 花 ♦ **how much was the meal?** 这顿饭花了多少钱? ♦ **that'll be £5 please** 请付5英镑 ♦ **these trousers are only £30** 这条裤子仅仅30英镑

9 (*linking clauses*) 是 ♦ **the problem is that ...** 问题是… ♦ **the fact is that ...** 事实是…

10 (*exist, occur etc*) 存在 ♦ **the best singer that ever was** 曾经有过的最好的歌手 ♦ **is there a God?** 存在上帝吗? ♦ **be that as it may** 即使如此

11 (*assessing a situation*) ♦ **it is likely that he'll resign** 很可能他将辞职 ♦ **it is difficult for me to complain** 我很难抱怨

II *aux vb*

1 (*forming continuous tenses*) ♦ **what are you doing?** 你在干什么? ♦ **it is raining** 天下着雨 ♦ **people are using their cars too much** 人们正在过多地使用汽车 ♦ **they're coming tomorrow** 他们明天来

2 (*forming passives*) ♦ **to be murdered** 被谋杀 ♦ **he was killed in a car crash** 他在一场车祸中丧生 ♦ **the building was designed by a famous architect** 这座建筑由一位著名的建筑师设计 ♦ **the box had been opened**

盒子已被打开了
3 (*with "to" infinitive*) ♦**the house is to be sold** 房子将要出售 ♦**what is to be done?** 我们该怎么办？ ♦**these flowers are to be found all over the country** 这些花在全国都能看得到 ♦**the thief was nowhere to be seen** 小偷不知去向
4 (*in tag questions*) ♦**it was fun, wasn't it?** 有意思，是不是？♦**it wasn't good timing, was it?** 时间选得不太好，是不是？♦**he's good-looking, isn't he?** 他长得不错，是不是？♦**so you're back again, are you?** 所以你又回来了，是不是？
5 (*in short answers*) ♦**"was it where I said?" – "yes, it was/no, it wasn't"** "就在我说的地方吗？" "是/不是" ♦**"you're all right, aren't you?" – "yes, I am/no, I'm not"** "你还好，是不是？" "是的，我还好/不，我不好"

beach [biːtʃ] **I** *n* [c] 海滩 **II** *vt* [+ *boat*] 使靠岸
beacon ['biːkən] *n* [c] **1** (*signal*) 信号灯 **2** (喻) 指路明灯
bead [biːd] **I** *n* [c] **1** (*glass, plastic etc*) 小珠子 **2** [*of sweat*] 滴 **II beads** *n* [*pl*] (*necklace*) 项链
beak [biːk] *n* [c] 鸟喙
beam [biːm] **I** *n* [c] **1** [*of wood, metal*] 梁 **2** [*of light*] 束 **3** [广播, 物] 射线 **II** *vi* **1** (*smile*) 喜形于色 **2** (*shine*) 发光 **III** *vt* (*send*) [+ *signals, pictures*] 播送 ♦**to drive on full** *or* **main** *or* [美] **high beam** 驾车时，前大灯都开着
bean [biːn] *n* [c] 豆 ♦**coffee/cocoa beans** 咖啡/可可豆
bean sprouts *n* [*pl*] 豆芽
bear [bɛə(r)] (*pt* **bore,** *pp* **borne**) **I** *n* [c] (*animal*) 熊 **II** *vt* **1** [文] (*carry*) [+ *object*] 携带 **2** (*support*) [+ *weight*] 支撑 **3** [+ *responsibility*] 承担 **4** [+ *cost*] 负担 **5** (*tolerate*) [+ *person*] 容忍 **6** (*endure*) 忍受 **7** (*show*) [+ *traces, signs*] 留有 **8** (*stand up to*) [+ *examination, scrutiny*] 经得起 **9** [正式] [+ *malice, ill will*] 心怀 **10** [商] [+ *interest, dividend*] 产生 **11** [过时] [*woman* +] [+ *children*] 生育 **12** [*plant* +] [+ *fruit*] 结出 **III** *vi* ♦**to bear right/left** [汽车] 向右/左转 ♦**to bear no resemblance/relation to** 与…无相似之处/没有关联 ♦**to bring pressure/influence to bear on sb** 对某人施加压力/影响
❏**bear down on** *vt* [不可拆分] **1** (*move towards*) 冲向 ◊ *The girl flashed a smile at the television crew and cameras bearing down on her.* 女孩冲着涌过来的电视工作人员和相机镜头微笑。**2** (*press*) 压
❏**bear out** *vt* [+ *person, suspicions, claims*] 证实
❏**bear up** *vi* [*person* +] 挺得住 ◊ *He bore up well.* 他咬紧牙关坚持下来。
❏**bear with** *vt* [不可拆分] [+ *person*] 容忍
beard [bɪəd] *n* [c] 胡须
bearded ['bɪədɪd] *adj* 有胡须的
bearer ['bɛərə(r)] *n* [c] **1** [*of letter, news*] 送信人 **2** [正式] [*of cheque, passport*] 持有人
bearing ['bɛərɪŋ] *n* **1** [U] [正式] (*posture*) 举止 **2** (*connection*) ♦**to have a bearing on sth** 与某事有关系 **3** [c] [术语] 轴承 ♦**to get** *or* **find one's bearings** 确定自己的位置; (喻) 确定自己的方向 ♦**to take a bearing** 判明位置
beast [biːst] *n* [c] **1** [文] (*animal*) 野兽 **2** [过时, 非正式] (*person*) 野蛮的人
✪**beat** [biːt] (*pt* **beat,** *pp* **beaten**) **I** *n* [c] **1** [*of heart*] 跳动 **2** [音] (*rhythm*) 节拍 **3** [*of policeman*] 巡逻区域 ◊ *on the beat* 在巡逻 **II** *vt* **1** (*strike*) [+ *wife, child*] 打 ◊ *She was beaten to death.* 她被打死了。**2** [+ *eggs, cream*] 搅 **3** (*defeat*) [+ *opponent, record*] 击败 ◊ *Arsenal beat Oxford United 5-1.* 阿森纳队以5比1击败了牛津联合队。**III** *vi* **1** [*heart* +] 跳动 **2** (*strike*) 拍打 ◊ *The rain beat against the window.* 雨水打在窗户上。◊ *Somebody was beating at the door.* 有人在用力敲门。♦**to beat time** [音] 打拍子 ♦**beat it!** [非正式] 走开！ ♦**you can't beat it** 什么也比不上它 ♦**off the beaten track** 在人迹罕至之处

❑**beat down** I *vi* 1 [*rain* +] 瓢泼而下 2 [*sun* +] 曝晒 II *vt* [+ *seller*] 迫使…压低价格
❑**beat off** *vt* [+ *attack, attacker*] 打退
❑**beat up** *vt* [+ *person*] 狠打 ♦**to beat oneself up about sth** [非正式] 因某事而折磨自己

beaten ['biːtn] *pp of* **beat**

beating ['biːtɪŋ] *n* [c] (*physical*) 痛打 ♦**to take a beating** (*in contest*) 惨败 ♦**that will take some beating** [非正式] 难以超越

beautiful ['bjuːtɪful] *adj* 1 [+ *woman, day, place, weather*] 美丽的 2 [+ *shot, performance*] 精彩的

> 当描写人的外表时，女人、女孩和婴儿用 **beautiful** 和 **pretty** *one of the most beautiful women in the world... She's a very pretty little girl.*，**beautiful** 比 **pretty** 程度更深。与之相对，描写男人的词是 **handsome**。*He is still very handsome.* **good-looking** 和 **attractive** 可用于两性。

beautifully ['bjuːtɪflɪ] *adv* 1 [*play, sing etc* +] 极好地 2 [+ *quiet, written etc*] 令人满意地

beauty ['bjuːtɪ] I *n* 1 [u] (*quality*) 美 2 [c] (*beautiful woman*) 美人 3 [c] (喻) (*attraction*) ♦**the beauty of it is that ...** 好处在于… II **beauties** *n* [*pl*] [文] 魅力

beauty parlour (美 **beauty parlor**) *n* [c] 美容院

beauty salon *n* = **beauty parlour**

beaver ['biːvə(r)] *n* [c] 海狸
❑**beaver away** *vi* 勤奋工作 ♦**to beaver away at sth** 孜孜不倦地做某事

became [bɪ'keɪm] *pt of* **become**

✪**because** [bɪ'kɔz] *conj* 因为 ◊ *He did it because he was angry.* 他因为生气才那么做的。♦**because of** 因为

> 我们在解释一件事发生的原因时，可以使用 **because**、**as** 或 **since**。**because** 最为常用，并且是唯一可以回答以 **why** 提出的问题。*"Why can't you come?" – "Because I'm too busy."* 在引出含有原因的从句时，尤其是在书面语中，我们可以用 **as** 或 **since** 代替 **because**。*I was rather nervous, as I hadn't seen her for a long time... Since the juice is quite strong, you should always dilute it.*

beckon ['bɛkən] I *vt* [+ *person*] 招手 II *vi* 1 (*signal*) ♦**to beckon (to sb)** (向某人) 招手 2 (喻) 吸引

✪**become** [bɪ'kʌm] (*pt* **became**, *pp* **become**) *vi* 1 (+ *noun*) 成为 ◊ *He became a professional footballer.* 他成了一名职业足球运动员。 2 (+*adj*) 变 ◊ *The smell became stronger.* 气味变浓了。♦**what has become of him?** 他的情况怎么样了？

BEd *n abbr* (= ***Bachelor of Education***) (*qualification*) 教育学学士学位; (*person*) 教育学学士

bed [bɛd] *n* [c] 1 (*piece of furniture*) 床 2 (*bottom*) [*of river, sea*] 底部 3 [*of flowers*] 坛 ◊ *beds of strawberries and rhubarb* 一小片一小片的草莓和大黄 4 [*of coal, clay*] 层 ♦**to go to bed** 去睡觉 ♦**to go to bed with sb** 与某人发生性关系
❑**bed down** *vi* [*person* +] 过夜

bed and breakfast *n* 1 [u] (*service*) 住宿加早餐 2 [c] (*guest house*) 兼包早餐的旅馆

bedclothes ['bɛdkləuðz] *n* [*pl*] 床上用品

bedding ['bɛdɪŋ] *n* [u] 床上用品

bed linen *n* [u] 床单和枕套

bedroom ['bɛdrum] *n* [c] 卧室

bedside ['bɛdsaɪd] *n* ♦**at sb's bedside** 在床前护理某人

bedside lamp *n* [c] 床头灯

bedside table *n* [c] 床头柜

bedsit(ter) ['bɛdsɪt(ə(r))] [英] *n* [c] 卧室兼起居室

bedspread ['bɛdsprɛd] *n* [c] 床罩

bedtime ['bɛdtaɪm] *n* [u] 就寝时间 ♦**at bedtime** 睡前 ♦**it's past my bedtime** 已经过了我的就寝时间 ♦**a bedtime story** 睡前讲的故事

bee [biː] *n* [c] 蜜蜂 ♦**to have a bee in one's bonnet (about sth)** 总想着（某事）

beech [biːtʃ] *n* 1 [c] (*tree*) 山毛榉 2 [u] (*wood*) 山毛榉木

beef [biːf] *n* [u] 牛肉 ♦**roast beef** 烤牛肉

❑**beef up** *vt* [非正式] [+ *security etc*] 加强

beefburger ['biːfbəːgə(r)] [英] *n* [c] 牛肉汉堡包

Beefeater ['biːfiːtə(r)] *n* [c] 伦敦塔守卫

beehive ['biːhaɪv] *n* [c] 蜂房

been [biːn] *pp of* **be**

beer [bɪə(r)] *n* [u] (*substance*) 啤酒 ♦**would you like a beer?** 你想喝一瓶啤酒吗?

beet [biːt] *n* 1 [u] (*crop*) 甜菜 2 [c] [美] (*red vegetable*) 甜菜根 [英 = **beetroot**]

beetle ['biːtl] *n* [c] 甲虫

beetroot ['biːtruːt] [英] *n* [c/u] 甜菜根 [美 = **beet**]

✪**before** [bɪ'fɔː(r)] **I** *prep* 1 (*in time*) 之前 ◊ *just before Christmas* 就在圣诞节前 2 [正式] (*in front of, ahead of*) 在…前面 ◊ *They stopped before a large white house.* 他们在一座大白房子前面停了下来。◊ *the duty which lay before me* 摆在我面前的职责 **II** *conj* (*in time*) 在…之前 ◊ *Can I see you before you leave?* 你走之前，我去看你，好吗? **III** *adv* (*time*) 以前 ◊ *Have you been to Greece before?* 你以前去过希腊吗? ♦**before doing sth** 在做某事之前 ♦**the day/week before** 前一天/上一个星期 ♦**I've never seen it before** 我以前从没见过

beforehand [bɪ'fɔːhænd] *adv* 事先

beg [bɛg] **I** *vi* [*beggar* +] 乞讨 **II** *vt* 1 [+ *food, money*] 讨 2 [+ *favour*] 请求 3 [+ *forgiveness, mercy etc*] 乞求 ♦**to beg for sth** 乞求某物 ♦**to beg sb to do sth** 恳求某人做某事 ♦**I beg your pardon** (*apologizing*) 对不起; (*not hearing*) 请再说一遍 ♦**to beg the question (as to) whether** 令人质疑

❑**beg off** *vi* 请求免除

began [bɪ'gæn] *pt of* **begin**

beggar ['bɛgə(r)] **I** *n* [c] 乞丐 **II** *vt* (*impoverish*) 使贫穷

✪**begin** [bɪ'gɪn] (*pt* **began**, *pp* **begun**) **I** *vt* 开始 ◊ *He had begun his career as a painter.* 他开始了他的画家生涯。**II** *vi* 开始 ◊ *The concert begins at 5 p.m.* 音乐会下午5点开始。♦**to begin doing** *or* **to do sth** 开始做某事 ♦**I can't begin to thank you** 我真不知道怎样感谢你 ♦**beginning (from) Monday** (从)星期一开始 ♦**to begin with ...** 首先… ◊ *To begin with, I was sceptical, but I was soon convinced.* 起初我持怀疑态度，但很快就相信了。◊ *You should invite your closest friends to begin with, and then see if there's room for anybody else.* 你首先应该邀请最亲近的朋友，然后再看是否有位置给其他人。

> **begin**、**start** 和 **commence** 的意思相同，但 **begin** 比 **start** 稍正式一些，而 **commence** 则很正式，并且通常不用于口语。*The meeting is about to begin...He tore the list up and started a fresh one...The academic year commences at the beginning of October.* 当谈及起动车辆和机器时用 **start**。*I couldn't start the car.* 当谈及创办一项业务或其他组织时，也要用 **start**。*He's started his own printing business.* 注意 **begin**，**start** 和 **commence** 后面都可以跟动词的 **-ing** 形式或名词，但只有 **begin** 和 **start** 可以跟由 **to** 引导的不定式。

beginner [bɪ'gɪnə(r)] *n* [c] 初学者

beginning [bɪ'gɪnɪŋ] **I** *n* [c] [*of event, period, book*] 开始 **II** **beginnings** *n* [*pl*] 征兆 ♦**at the beginning** 开始时 ♦**right from the beginning** *or* **from the very beginning** 从一开始

begun [bɪ'gʌn] *pp of* **begin**

behalf [bɪ'hɑːf] *n* ♦**on behalf of,** [美] **in behalf of** (*as representative of*) 代表; (*for benefit of*) 为…的利益 ♦**on my/his behalf** 代表我/他

behave [bɪ'heɪv] *vi* 1 [*person* +] 表现 2 [*object* +] 运转 3 (*behave well*) 行为得体 ♦**to behave oneself** 守规矩

behaviour (美 **behavior**)

[bɪ'heɪvjə(r)] *n* **1** [U] 举止 **2** [C/U] [心理, 社会] 行为

✪ **behind** [bɪ'haɪnd] **I** *prep* **1** (*at the back of*) 在…后面 ◊ *Behind the cottage was a shed.* 在小屋的后面是一个棚子。**2** (*supporting*) 支持 ◊ *The country is behind the President.* 整个国家都支持总统。**3** (*in race, career etc*) 落后于 **4** (*responsible for*) 对…负责 ◊ *It is not clear who is behind the killing.* 谁是这次谋杀的幕后策划者，目前尚不清楚。**II** *adv* **1** (*at/towards the back*) 在/向后面 ◊ *I sat in the front row and Mick sat behind.* 我坐在前排，米克坐在后面。**2** [*stay, wait* +] 留在原处 *Afterwards Ian asked me to stay behind.* 后来，伊恩叫我留在原处。**III** *n* [非正式] (*buttocks*) 屁股 ♦**to be behind (schedule)** 落后于(计划) ♦**we're behind (them) in technology** 在技术方面，我们没有(他们)那么好 ♦**to get behind** 落后 ♦**to leave sth behind** (*forget*) 落下 ♦**to get left behind** [*person* +] 被甩掉

beige [beɪʒ] *adj* 灰棕色的

Beijing ['beɪ'dʒɪŋ] *n* 北京

being ['biːɪŋ] *n* **1** [U] (*existence*) 存在 **2** [C] (*creature*) 生物 ♦**to come into being** 形成 ♦**to bring sth into being** 使某事物出现

belated [bɪ'leɪtɪd] *adj* [+ *thanks, welcome*] 来迟的

belch [bɛltʃ] **I** *vi* **1** [*person* +] 打嗝 **2** (*also:* ***belch out***) [*smoke, steam etc* +] 喷出 **II** *vt* (*also:* ***belch out***) [+ *smoke, steam etc*] 喷出 **III** *n* [C] 打嗝

Belgian ['bɛldʒən] **I** *adj* 比利时的 **II** *n* [C] (*person*) 比利时人

Belgium ['bɛldʒəm] *n* 比利时

belief [bɪ'liːf] *n* **1** [U/S] (*opinion*) 看法 **2** [C/U] (*trust, faith*) 信仰 ♦**contrary to popular belief** 与普遍观点相反的是 ♦**beyond belief** 难以置信 ♦**in the belief that** 相信

✪ **believe** [bɪ'liːv] **I** *vt* [+ *person, story*] 相信 ◊ *I didn't believe him.* 我不相信他。**II** *vi* ♦**to believe in** [+ *God, ghosts*] 信; [+ *honesty, discipline*] 坚信 ◊ *I believe in being truthful.* 我相信诚实是好的。♦**to believe that …** 认为… ◊ *Experts believe that the drought will be extensive.* 专家们认为干旱的波及面会很广。♦**he is believed to be abroad** 人们认为他在国外 ♦**I don't believe in corporal punishment** 我不相信体罚有益处 ♦**to believe in sb/oneself** 对某人/自己有信心

> 📖 如果你**believe**某事，你认为那是真的，即使你不能合理地证明。你可以**believe a claim**，**believe that**某事将要发生，或者**believe that**某事应该被完成。*No one ever believes the official answer…I believed that I was at the beginning of a great adventure…The government believes that such powers are essential.* 如果你**believe in**上帝，你认为上帝是存在的。如果你**believe in**鬼，你认为世上有鬼。如果你**believe in**某事，诸如一个系统，你认为它能正常运转。如果你**believe in**做某事，你觉得这么做是对的。*Elaine believes in love…The Kirks are a modern couple, and believe in dividing all tasks equally between them.*

believer [bɪ'liːvə(r)] *n* [C] **1** (*in idea, activity*) 笃信者 **2** [宗] 信徒

bell [bɛl] *n* [C] **1** [*of church*] 钟 **2** (*also:* ***handbell***) 摇铃 **3** (*on door*) 门铃 ♦**that rings a bell** [非正式] 那使人想起某事

bellow ['bɛləu] **I** *vi* **1** [*person* +] 大声叫喊 **2** [*bull* +] 吼叫 **II** *vt* [+ *orders*] 大声叫 **III** *n* [C] (*sound*) 大吼

belly ['bɛlɪ] *n* [C] [*of person, animal*] 腹部

belly button [非正式] *n* [C] 肚脐

belong [bɪ'lɔŋ] *vi* ♦**to belong to** [+ *person*] 属于; [+ *club, society etc*] 是…的成员 ♦**this book belongs here** 这本书应该在这里 ♦**which category does it belong in?** 它是属于哪个范畴的？

belongings [bɪ'lɔŋɪŋz] *n* [*pl*] 所有物

beloved [bɪ'lʌvɪd] **I** *adj* [+ *person, thing, place*] 心爱的 **II** *n* [C] [过时] 心爱的人

below [bɪ'ləu] **I** *prep* **1** (*beneath*) 在…之下 **2** (*less than*) [+ *level, rate*] 低于 **II** *adv* **1** (*beneath*) 下面 **2** (*less*) 以下 ♦**below zero** 零度以下 ♦**below sea level** 在海平面以下 ♦**temperatures below normal** *or* **average** 低于正常{或}平均温度 ♦**see below** (*in piece of writing*) 见下

belt [bɛlt] **I** *n* [c] **1** (*clothing*) 腰带 **2** [*of land, sea, air*] 地带 **3** [术语] 传动带 **II** *vt* [非正式] (*hit*) 抽打 **III** *vi* [非正式] ♦**to belt along/down/into** *etc* 迅速去/下/入{等} ♦**to tighten one's belt** (喻) 节衣缩食 ♦**to have sth under one's belt** 完成某事

❑**belt out** *vt* [非正式] [+ *song*] 大声唱

❑**belt up** [英:非正式] *vi* 住口

beltway ['bɛltweɪ] [美] *n* [c] (*ring road*) 环城公路 [英=**ring road**]

bemused [bɪ'mjuːzd] *adj* [+ *person, expression*] 迷惑的

bench [bɛntʃ] *n* [c] **1** (*seat*) 长椅 **2** (*table*) (*in factory, laboratory etc*) 工作台 **3** [英:政治] 议员席 **4** [法] ♦**the Bench** 法官席 ♦**to be on the bench** [体育] (*substitute*) 候补

bend [bɛnd] (*pt, pp* **bent**) **I** *vt* [+ *leg, arm, bar, wire*] 使弯曲 **II** *vi* **1** [*person* +] 屈身 **2** [*leg, arm, bar, wire* +] 弯曲 **3** [*road, river* +] 转弯 **III** *n* [c] **1** (*in road, river*) 弯 **2** (*in pipe*) 弯曲部分 **IV bends** *n* [*pl*] ♦**the bends** 潜水员病 ♦**to bend the rules** 变通

❑**bend down** *vi* 弯腰

❑**bend over I** *vi* 俯身 ♦**to bend over backwards (to do sth)** (喻) 竭力(做某事) **II** *vt* [+ *table, wall*] 弯腰靠近

beneath [bɪ'niːθ] **I** *prep* **1** (*in position*) 在…之下 **2** (*in status*) ♦**beneath him/her** 有失他/她的身份 **II** *adv* 在下面

beneficial [bɛnɪ'fɪʃəl] *adj* [+ *effect, influence*] 有益的 ♦**beneficial to** 有益于

benefit ['bɛnɪfɪt] **I** *n* **1** [c/u] (*advantage*) 好处 **2** [c/u] (*money*) 救济金 **3** [c] (*also:* ***benefit concert/dinner***) 募捐 **II** *vt* 有益于 **III** *vi* ♦**to benefit from sth** 从某事中获益 ♦**to have the benefit of sth** 受益于某事 ♦**to be of benefit (to sb)** (对某人)有益 ♦**to give sb the benefit of the doubt** 在证据不足的情况下，假定某人无辜

benevolent [bɪ'nɛvələnt] *adj* **1** [+ *person*] 仁慈的 **2** [英] [+ *organization, fund*] 慈善的

benign [bɪ'naɪn] *adj* **1** [+ *person, attitude*] 仁慈的 **2** [医] 良性的

bent [bɛnt] **I** *pt, pp of* **bend II** *n* (*inclination*) 天赋 **III** *adj* **1** [+ *wire, pipe*] 弯曲的 **2** [英:非正式] (*dishonest*) 贪污受贿的 ♦**to be bent on (doing) sth** 决心做某事

bereaved [bɪ'riːvd] **I** *adj* 丧失亲友的 **II** *n* [*pl*] ♦**the bereaved** 丧失亲人的人

beret ['bɛreɪ] *n* [c] 贝雷帽

berry ['bɛrɪ] *n* [c] 浆果

berth [bəːθ] **I** *n* [c] **1** (*bed*) (*on boat, train*) 卧铺 **2** [航海] (*mooring*) 泊位 **II** *vi* [*ship* +] 停泊 ♦**to give sb/sth a wide berth** 躲开某人/某物

beside [bɪ'saɪd] *prep* (*next to*) 在…旁边 ♦**to be beside oneself with rage/excitement** 愤怒/兴奋得发狂 ♦**that's beside the point** 那是离题了 *see also* **besides**

besides [bɪ'saɪdz] **I** *adv* **1** (*also:* ***beside***) (*in addition*) 另外 **2** (*in any case*) 而且 **II** *prep* (*also:* ***beside***) (*in addition to, as well as*) 除…之外

> **besides** 引出的事物包括在我们所谈及的事情之内。*She is very intelligent besides being very beautiful.* 不过，当我们说 **the only person besides** 另外某人时，或 **the only thing besides** 另外某物时，我们指在某一特定场合或上下文中的惟一其他人或物。*There was only one person besides me who knew where the money was hidden.* 介词 **except** 后面通常跟我们的陈述中惟独不包括的那些物、人、事的名词或代词形式。*She spoke to everyone except me... I never take any drugs, except aspirin for colds.* **except** 也可作连词，引导从句或副词短语。*There was nothing more to do now*

except wait…Travelling was impossible except in the cool of the morning. **except** 还可以引出由连词 **that**、**when** 或 **if** 引导的从句。*The house stayed empty, except when we came for the holidays.* **except for** 是用在名词前的介词短语，用来引出某人或某物，说明要不是有某人或某物，所陈述的便为全部事实。*Everyone was late except for Richard.* **unless** 是连词，后面的从句表示某事不会发生或不会成为事实。*Unless you really want to lose weight, it will be hard to stick to a diet.*

✪ **best** [bɛst] **I** *adj* (*in quality, suitability, extent*) 最好的 ◊ *It's one of the best films I've seen.* 这是我看过的最好的电影之一。**II** *adv* 最 ◊ *He is best known as an actor.* 他是位家喻户晓的演员。◊ *What music do you like best?* 你最喜欢什么样的音乐？ **III** *n* ♦**the best 1** (*in quality etc*) 最好的事物 ◊ *We offer only the best to our clients.* 我们只为客户提供最上乘的产品。**2** (*in achievement*) 最大努力 ◊ *He knows how to get the best out of his students.* 他懂得如何发挥学生的最大潜力。♦**the best thing to do is …** 最好是… ♦**the best part of** (*most of*) 大部分 ♦**you'd best leave early** 你最好早点离开 ♦**at best** 至多 ♦**to be at one's best** 处于最佳状态 ♦**to make the best of sth** 既来之则安之 ♦**to do** *or* **try one's best** 尽某人最大的努力 ♦**to the best of my knowledge** 尽我所知 ♦**to the best of my ability** 尽我能力所及 ♦**it's for the best** 是一件好事 ♦**he's not exactly patient at the best of times** 即使在最好的情况下，他也不怎么耐心 ♦**to have the best of both worlds** 两全其美

best-before date ['bɛstbɪ'fɔː(r)-] *n* [c] (*on food etc*) 保质日期

best man *n* [c] 男傧相

bestow [bɪ'stəu] [正式] *vt* ♦**to bestow sth on sb** [+ *honour, title*] 赠与某人某物

bestseller ['bɛst'sɛlə(r)] *n* [c] (*book*) 畅销书

bet [bɛt] (*pt, pp* **bet** *or* **betted**) **I** *n* [c] (*wager*) 赌注 **II** *vt* **1** (*wager*) ♦**to bet sb 100 pounds that …** 就…和某人赌100英镑 **2** (*expect, guess*) ♦**to bet (that)** 断定 **III** *vi* (*wager*) ♦**to bet on** [+ *horse, result*] 下赌注于 ♦**it's a good** *or* **safe bet that …** 非常有可能… ♦**I wouldn't bet on it** [非正式] 我不敢打包票 ♦**you bet** *or* **you bet your life** [非正式] 那还用说

betray [bɪ'treɪ] *vt* **1** [+ *friend, country, comrade*] 背叛 **2** [+ *sb's trust, confidence*] 辜负 **3** (*reveal*) [+ *emotion*] 流露

✪ **better** ['bɛtə(r)] **I** *adj* **1** (*comparative of good*) 更好的 ◊ *The results were better than expected.* 结果比预期的更好。**2** (*after an illness or injury*) 好转的 ◊ *Are you better now?* 你现在好点了吗？**II** *adv* **1** (*comparative of well*) 更好地 ◊ *Some people can ski better than others.* 一些人比其他人滑雪滑得好。**2** (*more*) [*like* +] 更 ◊ *I always liked you better than Sandra.* 与桑德拉相比，我总是更喜欢你。**III** *vt* [+ *score, record*] 提高 ◊ *We have bettered last year's figures.* 我们比去年的数字又有了提高。**IV** *n* ♦**to get the better of** [*curiosity etc* +] 占…的上风 ◊ *My curiosity got the better of me.* 我的好奇心占了上风。♦**to get better** (*improve*) 变得更好; [*sick person* +] 渐愈 ♦**to feel better** 感觉好一些 ♦**that's better!** 那就好多了！♦**it would be better to …** 不如… ♦**you're better waiting till tomorrow** 你最好等到明天 ♦**I'd better go** *or* **I had better go** 我得走了 ♦**you'd better do it** *or* **you had better do it** 你最好做这件事 ♦**he thought better of it** 他重新考虑后决定不做 ♦**to better oneself** 提高自己 ♦**to change for the better** 有好转

better off *adj* **1** ♦**to be better off** (*wealthier*) 较富裕的 **2** (*more comfortable etc*) 情况更好的 ♦**you'd be better off without him** 不和他在一起，你会过得更好

betting ['bɛtɪŋ] *n* [U] **1** (*gambling*) 赌

博 **2** (*odds*) 差距

betting shop [英] *n* [c] 彩票经营店

✪ **between** [bɪ'twiːn] **I** *prep* **1** (*in space*) 在…中间 ◊ *He was sitting between two old ladies.* 他坐在两个老妇人中间。**2** (*in time*) 介于…之间 ◊ *between 9 and 10 tomorrow* 在明天9点至10点之间 **3** (*in amount, age etc*) 介于…之间 ◊ *people aged between 18 and 30* 年龄在18至30之间的人们 ◊ *It weighs between 30 and 40 kilos.* 它重约30至40公斤。**4** (*among*) 之间 ◊ *the relationship between doctors and patients* 医生与患者之间的关系 **5** (喻) 之间 ◊ *the obstacles that lay between him and success* 摆在他和成功之间的障碍 **II** *adv* ♦ **in between** (*in space*) 在…中间 ◊ *Court Road and all the little side streets in between* 考特路与所有那些夹在中间的小街道; (*in time*) 期间 ◊ *He had to make two flights, with a 5-hour wait in between.* 他得坐两次航班，期间要等5个小时。♦ **to choose between** [+ *two things*] 从中选一个 ♦ **to be shared/divided between people** 由大家一起分享/分用 ♦ **the road between here and London** 这里和伦敦之间的道路 ♦ **we only had 5 pounds between us** 我们俩一共只有5英镑 ♦ **between you and me, between ourselves** 私下 📖 用法参见 **among**

beverage ['bɛvərɪdʒ] [正式] *n* [c] 饮料

beware [bɪ'wɛə(r)] *vi* ♦ **beware!** 注意！♦ **to beware of (doing) sth** 留神(做)某事 ♦ **"beware of the dog"** “当心狗”

bewildered [bɪ'wɪldəd] *adj* (*stunned, confused*) 困惑的

beyond [bɪ'jɔnd] **I** *prep* **1** (*on the other side of*) [+ *house, line*] 在…的另一边 **2** (喻) 超出…的范围 **3** (*after*) [+ *time, date, age*] 迟于 **4** (*past*) [+ *understanding, recognition*] 超过 **5** (*exceeding*) 超出 **II** *adv* **1** (*in space*) 在另一边 **2** (*in time*) 在…之后 ♦ **beyond doubt** 毫无疑问 ♦ **to be beyond repair** 无法修理 ♦ **it's beyond me** 我不能理解

Bhutan [buː'tɑːn] *n* 不丹

bias ['baɪəs] *n* **1** [u] (*prejudice*) 成见 **2** [c] (*preference*) 偏向

bias(s)ed ['baɪəst] *adj* [+ *jury, judgement, reporting*] 有偏见的 ♦ **to be bias(s)ed against** 对…有偏见 ♦ **to be bias(s)ed towards** 偏向于

bib [bɪb] *n* (*for baby*) 围嘴

Bible ['baɪbl] [宗] *n* [c] ♦ **the Bible** 圣经

bibliography [bɪblɪ'ɔgrəfɪ] *n* [c] (*in text*) 参考书目

bicarbonate of soda [baɪ'kɑːbənɪt-] *n* [u] **1** (*for baking*) 小苏打 **2** (*medicinal*) 碳酸氢钠

biceps ['baɪsɛps] (*pl* **biceps**) *n* [c] 二头肌

bicker ['bɪkə(r)] *vi* (*squabble*) 口角 ♦ **to bicker with sb** 与某人口角

bicycle ['baɪsɪkl] *n* [c] 自行车 ♦ **to ride a bicycle** 骑自行车

bicycle pump *n* [c] 自行车打气筒

bid [bɪd] (*pt* **bade** *or* **bid,** *pp* **bid** *or* **bidden**) **I** *n* [c] **1** (*attempt*) 尝试 **2** (*at auction*) 出价 **3** (*to buy a company*) 投标 **II** *vi* (*at auction*) 出价竞买 **III** *vt* (*offer*) 出价 ♦ **to bid sb farewell/goodnight** [正式] 向某人道别/说晚安

bidder ['bɪdə(r)] *n* [c] 投标人 ♦ **the highest bidder** 出价最高的人

bidet ['biːdeɪ] *n* [c] 坐浴盆

✪ **big** [bɪg] *adj* **1** (*in size*) [+ *man, country, object*] 大的 **2** [非正式] [+ *person*] (*important*) 有影响的 ◊ *Their father was very big in the army.* 他们的父亲在军中很有影响。**3** [+ *ideas*] 远大的 ◊ *He's got a lot of big ideas about how to change the system.* 就如何改变体制，他有一些远大的想法。**4** (*major*) [+ *change, increase, problem*] 大的 ◊ *The biggest problem is unemployment.* 最大的问题是失业问题。♦ **big brother/sister** 哥哥/姐姐 ♦ **big words** [非正式] 深奥的词语 ♦ **in a big way** [非正式] 大张旗鼓

bigheaded ['bɪg'hɛdɪd] [非正式] *adj* 自大的

big toe *n* [c] 大脚趾

bike [baɪk] *n* [c] **1** (*bicycle*) 自行车 **2** (*motorcycle*) 摩托车

bikini [bɪ'kiːnɪ] *n* [c] 比基尼

bilingual [baɪˈlɪŋɡwəl] *adj* [+ *dictionary, secretary*] 双语的 ♦ **to be bilingual** 能讲两国语言的

bill [bɪl] **I** *n* [c] **1** (*requesting payment*) 账单 **2** [英] (*in restaurant*) 账单 [美 = **check**] **3** [政治] 法案 **4** [美] (*banknote*) 钞票 [英 = **note**] **5** [*of bird*] 鸟喙 **6** [戏剧] 节目单 **II** *vt* **1** [+ *customer*] 给…开账单 **2** (*advertise*) 宣传 ♦ **to fit** *or* **fill the bill** 合乎要求 ♦ **bill of fare** [过时] 菜单 ♦ **"post no bills"** "禁止张贴" ♦ **bill of exchange** 汇票 ♦ **bill of lading** 提单 ♦ **bill of sale** 卖据

billboard [ˈbɪlbɔːd] *n* [c] 广告牌

billfold [ˈbɪlfəuld] [美] *n* [c] 钱夹 [英 = **wallet**]

billiards [ˈbɪljədz] *n* [u] 台球

✪ **billion** [ˈbɪljən] *n* [c] 十亿

bin [bɪn] **I** *n* [c] **1** [英] (*for rubbish*) 垃圾箱 [美 = **garbage can or trash can**] **2** (*container*) 箱 **II** *vt* [英: 非正式] (*throw away*) 扔掉

bind [baɪnd] (*pt, pp* **bound**) **I** *vt* **1** (*tie*) 捆 **2** (*tie together*) [+ *hands, feet*] 绑 **3** (*connect*) 使联合 **4** (*oblige*) 约束 **5** [+ *book*] 装订 **II** *n* [英: 非正式] (*nuisance*) 麻烦

❑ **bind over** *vt* [法] ♦ **to bind sb over (to keep the peace)** 保证某人遵守法纪

binder [ˈbaɪndə(r)] *n* [c] (*file*) 文件夹

binding [ˈbaɪndɪŋ] **I** *adj* [+ *agreement, contract*] 具有约束力的 **II** *n* [c] [*of book*] 装订

binge [bɪndʒ] [非正式] **I** *n* ♦ **to go on a binge** 狂欢作乐 **II** *vi* ♦ **to binge on chocolate/whisky** 无节制地吃巧克力/喝威士忌酒

bingo [ˈbɪŋɡəu] *n* [u] 宾戈(一种赌博游戏)

binoculars [bɪˈnɔkjuləz] *n* [*pl*] 双筒望远镜

biochemistry [baɪəˈkɛmɪstrɪ] *n* [u] 生物化学

biodegradable [ˈbaɪəudɪˈɡreɪdəbl] *adj* 可由生物降解的

biography [baɪˈɔɡrəfɪ] *n* [c] 传记 ♦ **a biography of Dylan Thomas** 迪兰•托马斯传

biological [baɪəˈlɔdʒɪkl] *adj* **1** [+ *process, weapon, warfare, washing powder*] 生物的 **2** [+ *research, science*] 生物学的

biology [baɪˈɔlədʒɪ] *n* [u] 生物学

birch [bəːtʃ] *n* **1** [c] (*tree*) 桦树 **2** [u] (*wood*) 桦木

bird [bəːd] *n* [c] **1** [动] 鸟 **2** [英: 非正式] (*woman*) 姑娘 ♦ **a bird in the hand** 已到手的东西 ♦ **to kill two birds with one stone** 一举两得

bird of prey *n* [c] 猛禽

bird-watching [ˈbəːdwɔtʃɪŋ] *n* [u] 野鸟习性观察

Biro® [ˈbaɪərəu] [英] *n* [c] 圆珠笔

birth [bəːθ] *n* **1** [c/u] [*of baby, animal*] 出生 **2** [s] (喻) 开始 ♦ **to give birth (to)** [+ *child, animal*] 分娩; [+ *idea*] 促成

birth certificate *n* [c] 出生证明

birth control *n* [u] 节育

birthday [ˈbəːθdeɪ] **I** *n* [c] 生日 **II** *cpd* [复合词] [+ *cake, card, present etc*] 生日

birthplace [ˈbəːθpleɪs] *n* [c] **1** 出生地 **2** (喻) 发祥地

biscuit [ˈbɪskɪt] *n* [c] **1** [英] (*cookie*) 饼干 [美 = **cookie**] **2** [美] (*cake*) 小圆饼

bishop [ˈbɪʃəp] *n* [c] **1** [宗] 主教 **2** [国际象棋] 象

bistro [ˈbiːstrəu] *n* [c] 小餐馆

✪ **bit** [bɪt] **I** *pt of* **bite** **II** *n* [c] **1** [尤英] (*piece*) 少许 ◊ *a bit of string* 一小段绳子 **2** [尤英] (*part*) 部分 ◊ *Now comes the really important bit.* 现在要说的是最重要的部分。 **3** (*tool*) 钻头 **4** [计算机] 比特 **5** [*of horse*] 嚼子 **6** [美] (*coin*) 12.5 美分的硬币 ♦ **to come** *or* **fall to bits** (*break*) 破碎 ♦ **bits and pieces** *or* **bits and bobs** [非正式] 零碎儿 ♦ **a bit of** 有点 ◊ *I'm sorry, the room's in a bit of a mess.* 对不起，房间有点乱。 ♦ **a bit mad/dangerous** 有点疯狂/危险 ♦ **it's/that's a bit much** [非正式] 有点过分 ♦ **bit by bit** 一点一点 ♦ **to do one's bit** 尽自己的一份力量 ♦ **every bit as good/interesting as** 与…同样好/有趣 ♦ **for a bit** [非正式] 一会儿 ♦ **quite a bit** 不少

bitch [bɪtʃ] **I** *n* [c] **1** (*dog*) 母狗 **2** [非正式，疑讳] (*woman*) 恶毒的女人 **II** *vi* [非正式] (*complain*) 埋怨

✪ **bite** [baɪt] (*pt* **bit**, *pp* **bitten**) **I** *vt* [*person, dog, snake, mosquito* +] 咬 **II** *vi* **1** [*dog etc* +] 咬人 **2** (喻) (*take effect*) [*action, policy* +] 生效 **III** *n* [c] **1** (*act of biting*) ◊ *He took another bite of his apple.* 他又咬了一口苹果。**2** (*mouthful*) 口 ◊ *I enjoyed every bite.* 我每一口吃得都很香。**3** (*from dog*) 咬伤 **4** (*from snake, mosquito*) 咬痕 ♦ **to bite one's nails** 咬指甲 ♦ **to bite one's lip** *or* **tongue** [非正式] 保持沉默 ♦ **to have a bite to eat** [非正式] 吃点东西

bitter ['bɪtə(r)] **I** *adj* **1** [+ *person, experience*] 充满怨恨的 **2** [+ *taste*] 苦的 **3** [+ *disappointment, blow*] 难以忍受的 **4** [+ *wind, weather*] 严寒的 **5** [+ *argument, fighting*] 激烈的 **II** *n* [u] [英] (*beer*) 苦啤酒 ♦ **to the bitter end** 坚持到底

bitterly ['bɪtəlɪ] *adv* [*say, laugh* +] 怨恨地; [*regret* +] 惨痛地; [*resent* +] 十分; [*weep, complain* +] 强烈地; [+ *jealous, disappointed, ashamed*] 非常地; [*oppose, criticize* +] 刻薄地 ♦ **it's bitterly cold** 天气寒冷刺骨

bitterness ['bɪtənɪs] *n* [u] **1** [*of person*] 怨恨 **2** [*of conflict, dispute*] 怀恨

bizarre [bɪ'zɑː(r)] *adj* [+ *story, contraption*] 稀奇古怪的

✪**black** [blæk] **I** *adj* **1** (*in colour*) [+ *paint, jacket, cat*] 黑色的 **2** [+ *person*] 黑人的 **3** [+ *tea, coffee*] 不加牛奶的 **4** [+ *humour*] 黑色的 ◊ *a black comedy* 黑色喜剧 **5** (*grim*) 暗淡的 ◊ *one of the blackest days of his political career* 他政治生涯中最暗淡的一个日子 **II** *n* **1** [u] (*colour*) 黑色 **2** [c] (*person*) 黑人 ◊ *the first black to be elected to Congress* 第一个被选入国会的黑人 **III** *vt* [英] 抵制 ◊ *The Union blacked incoming goods at the docks.* 工会抵制了进入码头的货物。♦ **to give sb/to have a black eye** 把某人眼睛打青/眼睛青了 ♦ **black and blue** (*bruised*) 青一块，紫一块的 ♦ **there it is in black and white** 白纸黑字清清楚楚地写着 ♦ **to be in the black** (*in credit*) 有赢余 ❑ **black out** *vi* (*faint*) 暂时失去知觉

blackberry ['blækbərɪ] *n* [c] 黑莓

blackbird ['blækbɜːd] *n* [c] 乌鸫

blackboard ['blækbɔːd] *n* [c] 黑板

blackcurrant ['blæk'kʌrənt] [英] *n* [c] 黑醋栗

blacken ['blækn] *vt* **1** (字) 使变黑 **2** (喻) [+ *sb's name, reputation*] 败坏

black ice *n* [u] 薄冰

blackmail ['blækmeɪl] **I** *n* [u] 敲诈 **II** *vt* 敲诈

black market *n* [c] 黑市 ♦ **on the black market** 在黑市上

blackout ['blækaut] *n* [c] **1** (*in wartime*) 灯火管制 **2** (*power cut*) 停电 **3** [电视, 广播] 封锁 **4** [医] 暂时性昏迷 ♦ **to have a blackout** [医] 暂时性昏迷

black pepper *n* [u] 黑胡椒

black pudding [英] *n* [c/u] 黑香肠

> **BLACK PUDDING**
> **black pudding**，黑香肠，是英国传统早餐中的一种食品，因表皮颜色而得名。成分主要为猪油和猪血，切成厚圆片，炸食。

Black Sea *n* ♦ **the Black Sea** 黑海

bladder ['blædə(r)] [解剖] *n* [c] 膀胱

blade [bleɪd] *n* [c] **1** [*of knife, sword*] 刃 **2** [*of oar*] 桨叶 **3** [*of propeller*] 螺旋桨翼 ♦ **a blade of grass** 一片草叶

blame [bleɪm] **I** *n* [u] (*for mistake, crime*) 责备 **II** *vt* ♦ **to blame sb for sth** 为某事责备某人 ♦ **to take the blame (for sth)** (对某事) 负责 ♦ **to be to blame (for sth)** 该 (为某事) 负责任 ♦ **to blame sth on sb** 把某事归咎于某人 ♦ **you can't blame him for trying** 你不能怪他去尝试 ♦ **who's to blame?** 是谁的责任？♦ **I'm not to blame** 责任不在我

bland [blænd] *adj* **1** [+ *personality, building, film*] 枯燥乏味的 **2** [+ *taste, food*] 平淡无味的

blank [blæŋk] **I** *adj* **1** [+ *paper, cassette*] 空白的 **2** [+ *expression*] 茫然的 **II** *n* [c] **1** (*on form*) 空白处 **2** (*cartridge*) 空弹 ♦ **my mind went blank** *or* **was a blank** 我的大脑一片空白 ♦ **we drew a blank** [非正式] 我们白费心机了

blanket ['blæŋkɪt] **I** *n* [c] **1** (*for bed*) 毛毯 **2** [*of snow, fog*] 层 **II** *adj* (*comprehensive*) [+ *ban, coverage*] 全面的 **III** *vt* [*snow* +] 覆盖

blast [blɑːst] **I** *n* [c] **1** [*of wind, air, whistle, horn*] 一阵 **2** (*explosion*) 爆炸 **II** *vt* **1** (*blow up*) 炸掉 **2** (*shoot*) 枪击 **III** *int* [非正式] 该死 ♦ **(at) full blast** [*play music etc* +] 最大限度地 ❑ **blast off** *vi* [航天] 发射上天

blatant ['bleɪtənt] *adj* [+ *discrimination, attempt*] 公然的

blatantly ['bleɪtəntlɪ] *adv* [*lie* +] 极明显地; [+ *untrue*] 显然地; [+ *sexist*] 明显地 ♦ **it's blatantly obvious** 显而易见

blaze [bleɪz] **I** *n* [c] **1** (*fire*) 大火 **2** [*of colour, light*] 强烈 **3** [*of glory, publicity*] 大量 **II** *vi* **1** [*fire* +] 熊熊燃烧 **2** (*also: **blaze away***) [*guns* +] 连连开枪 **3** [文] [*eyes* +] 放光彩 **III** *vt* ♦ **to blaze a trail** 开辟新路 ♦ **in a blaze of publicity** 在公众瞩目之下 ♦ **to blaze with colour** [*garden etc* +] 鲜艳夺目

blazer ['bleɪzə(r)] *n* [c] [*of school, team etc*] 上装

bleach [bliːtʃ] **I** *n* [U] (*chemical*) 漂白剂 **II** *vt* **1** [+ *fabric, foodstuff etc*] 漂白 **2** [+ *hair*] 漂淡颜色

bleachers ['bliːtʃəz] [美: 体育] *n* [*pl*] 露天看台

bleak [bliːk] *adj* **1** [+ *place*] 凄凉的 **2** [+ *weather*] 阴冷的 **3** [+ *future, outlook*] 暗淡的 **4** [+ *expression, voice*] 冷酷的

bleed [bliːd] (*pt, pp* **bled**) **I** *vi* **1** [医] [*person, arm, wound etc* +] 流血 **2** (*run*) [*colour* +] 渗色 **II** *vt* [+ *brakes, radiator*] 抽出…的液体/气体 ♦ **my nose is bleeding** 我流鼻血了 ♦ **to bleed to death** 流血而死

blemish ['blɛmɪʃ] **I** *n* [c] **1** (*on skin, fruit*) 瑕疵 **2** (喻) 缺陷 **II** *vt* (喻) [+ *reputation*] 损害

blend [blɛnd] **I** *n* [c] [*of tea, whisky*] 混合物 **II** *vt* **1** [+ *ingredients*] 混合 **2** [+ *ideas, styles, policies etc*] 融合 **III** *vi* (*also: **blend in***) [*colours, sounds* +] 调和 ♦ **to blend in with sth** 与某物融为一体

blender ['blɛndə(r)] *n* [c] 搅拌器

bless [blɛs] *vt* [宗] 赐福 ♦ **to be blessed with** 具有 ♦ **bless you!** (*after sneeze*) 上帝保佑!; [非正式] (*expressing affection*) 愿上帝保佑你

> 14 世纪时，黑死病席卷欧洲。人们相信打喷嚏是得病的前兆，不久就会死。当一个人打喷嚏后，身旁的人就会说 **Bless you!** 希望上帝能保佑这个人的灵魂。

blessing ['blɛsɪŋ] *n* [c] **1** (*approval*) 应允 **2** (*godsend*) 幸事 **3** [宗] 赐福 ♦ **to count one's blessings** 看自己有多幸运 ♦ **it was a blessing in disguise** 因祸得福 ♦ **a mixed blessing** 优劣参半

blew [bluː] *pt of* **blow**

blight [blaɪt] **I** *vt* [+ *career, life etc*] 损害 **II** *n* **1** [c] (喻) 损害 **2** [U] [*of plants*] 枯萎病

blind [blaɪnd] **I** *adj* **1** [医] 失明的 **2** [+ *faith, panic, obedience*] 盲目的 **3** [+ *corner*] 看不见另一头的 **II** *n* (*for window*) 向上卷的帘子 **III** *vt* **1** [医] 使…失明 **2** (*dazzle*) 使晕眩 **3** (喻) (*make insensitive*) 使意识不到 **IV the blind** *n* [*pl*] (*blind people*) 盲人 ♦ **to go blind** 失明 ♦ **to be blind to sth** 对某事意识不到 ♦ **blind in one eye** 一只眼睛失明 ♦ **to turn a blind eye (to sth)** (对某事) 视而不见

blind alley *n* [c] **1** [美] (*without exit*) 死胡同 [英 = **cul-de-sac**] **2** (喻) 无出路

blindfold ['blaɪndfəuld] **I** *n* [c] 蒙眼的布 **II** *adj* (*also: **blindfolded***) 蒙住眼睛的 **III** *vt* 蒙住眼睛 ♦ **I could do it blindfold** 我闭着眼睛都能做

blindly ['blaɪndlɪ] *adv* **1** (*without seeing*) 看不见地 **2** (*without thinking*) 盲目地

blindness ['blaɪndnɪs] *n* [U] **1** (*disability*) 失明 **2** (喻) 意识不到

blink [blɪŋk] **I** *vi* **1** [*person, animal* +] 眨眼睛 **2** [*light* +] 闪烁 **II** *vt* ♦ **to blink one's eyes** 眨眼睛 **III** *n* [c] [*of eyes*] 一眨 ♦ **in the blink of an eye** 转眼之间 ♦ **the TV's on the blink** [非正式] 电视出毛病了

bliss [blɪs] *n* [U] 巨大的幸福

blister ['blɪstə(r)] **I** *n* [C] **1** (*on skin*) 水泡 **2** (*in paint, rubber*) 气泡 **II** *vi* **1** [*skin* +] 起泡 **2** [*paint* +] 呈气泡状

blizzard ['blɪzəd] *n* [C] 暴风雪

bloated ['bləutɪd] *adj* **1** (*swollen*) [+ *face, stomach, body*] 肿胀的 **2** (*full*) ♦ **to feel bloated** 觉得饱

blob [blɔb] [非正式] *n* [C] **1** [*of glue, paint*] 一滴 **2** (*something indistinct*) 模糊不清的东西

block [blɔk] **I** *n* [C] **1** (*group of buildings*) 街区 **2** (*toy*) 积木 **3** [*of stone, wood, ice*] 块 **II** *vt* **1** [+ *entrance, road*] 堵塞 **2** [+ *view*] 挡住 **3** [+ *activity, agreement*] 阻止 ♦ **block of flats** *or* [美] **apartment block** 公寓楼 ♦ **3 blocks from here** 离这里有3个街区那么远 ♦ **to have a (mental) block about sth** 对某事感到(脑子)一片空白 ♦ **block and tackle** [术语] 滑轮组
❑ **block off** *vt* [+ *door, window*] 堵住
❑ **block out** *vt* [+ *thought, memory*] 尽可能不想
❑ **block up I** *vt* [+ *sink, pipe etc*] 堵塞 **II** *vi* [*sink, pipe* +] 堵

blockade [blɔ'keɪd] **I** *n* [C] 封锁 **II** *vt* 封锁

blockage ['blɔkɪdʒ] *n* [C] (*in pipe, tube*) 堵塞

blockbuster ['blɔkbʌstə(r)] [非正式] *n* [C] (*film, book*) 风靡一时的事物

block capitals *n* [*pl*] 大写字母 ♦ **in block capitals** 用大写字母

block letters *n* [*pl*] = **block capitals**

bloke [bləuk] [英: 非正式] *n* [C] 家伙

blond(e) [blɔnd] **I** *adj* **1** [+ *hair*] 金色的 **2** [+ *person*] 金发的人 **II** *n* [C] ♦ **blonde** (*woman*) 金发女子

blood [blʌd] *n* [U] **1** [生物] 血液 **2** (*referring to person's ancestry*) 血统 ♦ **in cold blood** 残忍地 ♦ **new** *or* **fresh** *or* **young blood** (喻) 新生力量

blood donor *n* [C] 献血者

blood group *n* [C] 血型

blood poisoning *n* [U] 血中毒

blood pressure *n* [U] 血压 ♦ **to have high/low blood pressure** 有高/低血压 ♦ **to take sb's blood pressure** 量某人的血压

bloodshed ['blʌdʃɛd] *n* [U] 流血

bloodshot ['blʌdʃɔt] *adj* [+ *eyes*] 充血的

bloodstream ['blʌdstriːm] *n* [C] 血流

blood test *n* [C] 验血 ♦ **to have a blood test** 验血

blood transfusion *n* [C] 输血

blood type *n* = **blood group**

blood vessel *n* [C] 血管

bloody ['blʌdɪ] **I** *adj* **1** [+ *battle, riot*] 血腥的 **2** [+ *knife, nose etc*] 血淋淋的 **3** [英: 非正式, 疑讳] ♦ **this bloody ...** 这个该死的… **II** *vt* [+ *nose, hands*] 使流血 ♦ **bloody heavy/good** [英: 非正式, 疑讳] 重/好极了

bloom [bluːm] **I** *n* [C] (*flower*) 花 **II** *vi* **1** [*tree, flower* +] 开花 **2** (喻) [*talent etc* +] 得以发展 ♦ **to be in bloom** [*plant* +] 盛开

blossom ['blɔsəm] **I** *n* [C/U] 花 **II** *vi* 开花 ♦ **to blossom (into sth)** (喻) 成长(为某事)

blot [blɔt] **I** *n* [C] **1** (*on text*) 污迹 **2** (喻) (*on name etc*) 损坏 **II** *vt* **1** (*with blotting paper*) 吸干 **2** (*with towel*) 吸干 ♦ **a blot on the landscape** 有碍观瞻的物体 ♦ **to blot one's copybook** 损坏自己的名誉
❑ **blot out** *vt* **1** [+ *view*] 遮挡 **2** [+ *memory*] 清除

blotchy ['blɔtʃɪ] *adj* [+ *complexion*] 斑斑点点的

blouse [blauz, (美) blaus] *n* [C] (*woman's garment*) 女士衬衫

> **shirts**男女都可以穿，但**blouses**只是女装。

blow [bləu] (*pt* **blew**, *pp* **blown**) **I** *n* [C] **1** (*punch*) 拳打 **2** (喻) (*setback*) 打击 **II** *vi* **1** [*wind, sand, dust etc* +] 吹 **2** [*person* +] 吹气 **3** [*whistle, horn* +] 响 **III** *vt* **1** [*wind* +] 吹 **2** [+ *whistle, horn*] 吹 **3** (*destroy*) (*by explosion*) 炸毁 **4** [非正式] [+ *chance*] 失去 **5** [非正式] (*spend*) [+ *money*] 挥霍 ♦ **to come to blows** 互相殴打 ♦ **a fuse has blown** 保险丝烧断了 ♦ **to blow one's nose** 擤鼻子 ♦ **you've blown it!** 你把事情弄糟了!
❑ **blow away I** *vt* 吹走 **II** *vi* 刮跑
❑ **blow down** *vt* [+ *tree, house*] 刮倒

❑**blow off** I *vt* [+ *hat etc*] 刮走 II *vi* [*hat etc* +] 刮跑 ♦**to be blown off course** [*ship* +] 被吹得偏离了航向
❑**blow out** *vt* [+ *flame, candle*] 吹灭
❑**blow over** *vi* [*trouble, crisis* +] 平息
❑**blow up** I *vi* (*explode*) 爆炸 II *vt* **1** (*destroy*) [+ *bridge etc*] 使爆炸 **2** (*inflate*) [+ *balloon, tyre*] 冲气 **3** [摄影] (*enlarge*) 放大

blow-dry [ˈbləudraɪ] I *vt* [+ *hair*] 吹干 II *n* [c] (*hairstyle*) 吹风定型

blown [bləun] *pp of* **blow**

✪**blue** [bluː] I *adj* **1** (*in colour*) 蓝色的 **2** [非正式] (*depressed*) 抑郁的 ◊ *There's no reason for me to feel so blue.* 我不知道为什么感到这么抑郁。II *n* [U] 蓝色 III **blues** *n* [*pl*] **1** [音] ♦**the blues** 蓝调 **2** [非正式] (*depression*) ♦**to have the blues** 感到抑郁 ♦**blue movie/joke** 色情电影/笑话 ♦**(only) once in a blue moon** (仅是)难得的一次 ♦**out of the blue** 意料之外

bluebell [ˈbluːbɛl] *n* [c] 风铃草

blueberry [ˈbluːbərɪ] *n* [c] 越橘

blue cheese *n* [c/U] 蓝奶酪

blueprint [ˈbluːprɪnt] *n* **1** ♦**a blueprint (for)** (喻)(…的)蓝图 **2** [c] [建筑] (…的)设计图

blue tit *n* [c] 蓝山雀

bluff [blʌf] I *vi* (*pretend, threaten*) 虚张声势 II *n* **1** [c/U] (*deception*) 虚张声势 **2** [c] [地理] (*steep cliff or bank*) 峭壁 III *adj* [+ *man*] 直截了当的 ♦**to call sb's bluff** 叫某人摊牌

blunder [ˈblʌndə(r)] I *n* [c] (*mistake*) 失策 II *vi* (*bungle*) 犯愚蠢的错误 ♦**to blunder into sb/sth** 笨手笨脚地撞倒人/某物

blunt [blʌnt] I *adj* **1** (*not sharp*) [+ *pencil, knife*] 钝的 **2** [+ *person, remark*] 直率的 II *vt* **1** [+ *scissors, chisel etc*] 弄钝 **2** [+ *appetite, emotion*] 使减弱 ♦**blunt instrument** [法] 钝器 ♦**to be blunt ...** 坦率地说…

blur [bləː(r)] I *n* [c] (*in vision, memory*) 模糊不清 II *vt* **1** [+ *vision, image*] 模糊 **2** [+ *distinction*] 使模糊不清 III *vi* [*image* +] 变模糊

blush [blʌʃ] I *vi* (*with shame, embarrassment*) 脸红 II *n* [c] 脸红 ♦**to spare** *or* **save sb's blushes** 不让某人感到脸红

blusher [ˈblʌʃə(r)] *n* [c/U] 胭脂

Blvd. *abbr* (= **boulevard**) 大街

B.O. *n abbr* [英:非正式] (= ***body odour***) 狐臭

board [bɔːd] I *n* **1** [c] (*piece of wood*) 木板 **2** [c] (*also:* ***noticeboard***) 公告板 **3** [c] (*also:* ***blackboard***) 黑板 **4** [c] (*for chess etc*) 盘 **5** [c] (*committee*) 委员会 **6** [c] (*in firm*) 董事会 **7** [U] (*at hotel*) 膳食 II *vt* [正式] [+ *ship, train, plane*] 上 III *vi* [正式] (*on ship, train, plane*) 登上 ♦**full/half board** [英] 全日/部分膳食供应 ♦**board and lodging** 食宿 ♦**on board** 在船/车/飞机上 ♦**to take sth on board** [+ *idea, suggestion*] 接受某事物 ♦**above board** 光明正大 ♦**across the board** (*as adv*) 全面地; (*as adj*) 全面的 ♦**to go by the board** 被忽略
❑**board up** *vt* [+ *door, window*] 用板覆盖

board game *n* [c] 棋盘游戏

boarding card [ˈbɔːdɪŋ-] *n* [c] 登机卡

boarding pass [ˈbɔːdɪŋ-] *n* = **boarding card**

boarding school [ˈbɔːdɪŋ-] *n* [c/U] 寄宿学校

boardroom [ˈbɔːdruːm] *n* [c] 董事会议室

boast [bəust] I *vi* ♦**to boast (about** *or* **of)** 说(关于某事的)大话 II *vt* (*possess, have*) 夸耀 III *n* 自夸 ♦**to boast that ...** 夸耀说…

boat [bəut] *n* [c] **1** (*small vessel*) 船 **2** (*ship*) 轮船 ♦**to go by boat** 乘船去 ♦**to be in the same boat** 处境相同 ♦**to rock the boat** 捣乱

bob [bɔb] *vi* (*also:* ***bob up and down***) [*boat, cork* +] 上下浮动
❑**bob up** *vi* 浮现

bode [bəud] *vi* ♦**to bode well/ill (for)** (为…)预示着好运/厄运

✪**body** [ˈbɔdɪ] *n* **1** [c] [解剖] 身体 ◊ *My whole body hurt.* 我的整个身体都在痛。**2** [c] (*torso, trunk*) 躯干 **3** [c] (*corpse*) 尸体 ◊ *Police later found a body.* 警方后来找到了一具尸体。**4** [s] (*main part*) [*of building*] 主体 ◊ *the main body of the church* 教堂的主体; [*of speech, document*] 正文 **5** [c] [*of car*] 身 **6** [c] (*organization*)

团体 ◊ *public bodies such as local authorities* 像地方当局这样的公共团体 **7** [c] (*quantity*) [*of evidence*] 许多 ◊ *There is a growing body of evidence pointing to these effects.* 越来越多的证据表明了这些后果。**8** [u] [*of wine etc*] 黏稠

bodybuilding ['bɔdɪ'bɪldɪŋ] *n* [u] 健身

bodyguard ['bɔdɪgɑːd] *n* [c] (*of statesman, celebrity*) 保镖

bodywork ['bɔdɪwəːk] [汽车] *n* [u] 车身

bog [bɔg] **I** *n* [c] (*marsh*) 沼泽 **II** *vt* ♦ **to get bogged down** 被缠住

bogus ['bəugəs] *adj* [+ *claim, evidence etc*] 伪造的

bohemian [bəu'hiːmɪən] **I** *adj* (*writer, lifestyle*) 放荡不羁的 **II** *n* [c] (*unconventional person*) 放荡不羁的人

boil [bɔɪl] **I** *vt* **1** [+ *water*] 烧开 **2** [+ *eggs, potatoes etc*] 煮 **II** *vi* [*liquid* +] 沸腾 **III** *n* [医] 疖子 ♦ **to boil a kettle** 烧开水 ♦ **to be boiling with anger** *or* **rage** 气愤至极 ♦ **to come to the** *or* [美] **a boil** 开始沸腾 ♦ **to bring a liquid to the boil** 把液体烧至沸腾
📖 用法参见 **cook**
❑ **boil down to** *vt* [不可拆分] 归根结底
❑ **boil over** *vi* [*kettle, milk* +] 沸腾至溢出

boiled egg ['bɔɪld-] *n* [c] 煮鸡蛋

boiled potatoes ['bɔɪld-] *n* [*pl*] 煮土豆

boiler ['bɔɪlə(r)] *n* [c] (*device*) 锅炉

boiling (hot) ['bɔɪlɪŋ-] [非正式] *adj* ♦ **I'm boiling (hot)** 我太热了 ♦ **it's boiling (hot)** 太热了
📖 用法参见 **hot**

boiling point ['bɔɪlɪŋ-] *n* [u] [*of liquid*] 沸点

boisterous ['bɔɪstərəs] *adj* (*noisy, excitable*) [+ *person, crowd*] 喧闹的

bold [bəuld] **I** *adj* **1** (*brave*) [+ *person, action*] 大胆的 **2** [+ *pattern, colours*] 突出的 **II** *n* [u] [排版] 粗体字 ♦ **in bold** [排版] 用粗体字 ♦ **if I may be so bold** 恕我冒昧

bollard ['bɔləd] *n* [c] **1** [英:汽车] 护柱 **2** [航海] 系缆柱

bolt [bəult] **I** *n* [c] **1** (*to lock door*) 插销 **2** (*used with nut*) 螺钉 **II** *vt* **1** [+ *door*] 闩 **2** (*fasten*) ♦ **to bolt sth to sth** 把某物栓在某物上 **3** [+ *food*] 囫囵吞下 **III** *vi* (*run very fast*) [*horse* +] 迅速跑开; [*person* +] 跑开 **IV** *adv* ♦ **bolt upright** 笔直 ♦ **a bolt of lightning** 一道闪电 ♦ **a bolt from the blue** 晴天霹雳

bomb [bɔm] **I** *n* [c] 炸弹 **II** *vt* 轰炸

bombard [bɔm'bɑːd] *vt* [军] 连续炮击 ♦ **to bombard sb with questions/requests** 连珠炮似地向某人提问题/要求

bomber ['bɔmə(r)] *n* [c] **1** [航空] 轰炸机 **2** (*terrorist*) 恐怖分子

bombing ['bɔmɪŋ] *n* [c/u] 轰炸

bombshell ['bɔmʃɛl] *n* [c] (*revelation*) 爆炸性事件

bond [bɔnd] **I** *n* [c] **1** (*link*) [*of affection etc*] 纽带 **2** [经济] 公债 **II** *vi* **1** ♦ **to bond (with)** [*mother* +] [+ *child*] (与)…联结 **2** [*material* +] 黏合 **III bonds** [文] *n* [*pl*] (*ties*) 约束

bone [bəun] **I** *n* **1** [c/u] (*in body of human, animal*) [解剖] 骨头 **2** [c] (*in fish*) 刺 **II** *vt* [+ *meat, fish*] 剔除骨刺 ♦ **I've got a bone to pick with you** 我对你有怨言 ♦ **to make no bones about sth** 公开承认某事

bone marrow *n* [u] 骨髓

bonfire ['bɔnfaɪə(r)] *n* [c] **1** (*as part of a celebration*) 篝火 **2** (*to burn rubbish*) 火堆

Bonfire Night [英] *n* [u] 篝火之夜
用法参见 **Guy Fawkes Night**

bonnet ['bɔnɪt] *n* [c] **1** [英] [*of car*] 引擎罩 [美 = **hood**] **2** (*hat*) 在颌下系带的帽子

bonus ['bəunəs] *n* [c] **1** (*extra payment*) (*on wages*) 红利 **2** (*additional benefit*) 额外收获

bony ['bəunɪ] *adj* **1** [+ *arm, face, fingers, person*] 瘦的 **2** [解剖] 骨的 **3** [+ *fish*] 多刺的

boo [buː] **I** *int* **1** (*as joke*) 在吓唬别人时发出的声音: 呔 **2** (*as criticism*) 在表示批评时发出的声音: 呸 **II** *vt* 为…喝倒彩 **III** *vi* 发嘘声表示不满 **IV** *n* [c] 嘘声

✪ **book** [buk] **I** *n* [c] **1** (*novel etc*) 书 **2** [*of stamps, tickets*] 册 **II** *vt* **1** [+ *ticket, table, seat, room*] 预订 **2** [*traffic*

warden, police officer +] 登记◊ *I was booked for speeding.* 我因超速驾车而被记名。**3** [足球] 记名警告
III books *n* [*pl*] [商] (*accounts*) 账目 ♦**by the book** 照章办事 ♦**to throw the book at sb** 重罚某人 ♦**fully booked** 预订一空 ♦**to keep the books** 作簿记
❑**book in** [英] *vi* (*at hotel*) 登记入住 [美 = **check in**]
❑**book into** [英] *vt* [不可拆分] [+ *hotel*] 登记入住 [美 = **check into**]
❑**book up** *vi* 预订 ♦**all seats are booked up** 所有座位都被预订了 ♦**the hotel is booked up** 这个宾馆已经订满了

bookcase ['bukkeɪs] *n* [c] 书橱

booking ['bukɪŋ] *n* [c] 预订

booking office [英: 铁路, 戏剧] *n* [c] 售票处 [美 = **ticket office**]

bookkeeping ['buk'kiːpɪŋ] *n* [u] 簿记

booklet ['buklɪt] *n* [c] 小册子

bookmaker ['bukmeɪkə(r)] *n* [c] 赌注登记人

bookmark ['bukmɑːk] **I** *n* [c] 书签 **II** *vt* [计算机] 放书签

bookseller ['bukselə(r)] *n* [c] 书商

bookshelf ['bukʃelf] *n* [c] 书架

bookshop ['bukʃɔp] [英] *n* [c] 书店 [美 = **bookstore**]

bookstore ['bukstɔː(r)] [尤美] *n* = **bookshop**

boom [buːm] **I** *n* [c] **1** (*noise*) 轰轰声 **2** [经济] 繁荣 **3** (*in prices, popularity*) 兴盛 **II** *vi* **1** (*also:* ***boom out***) [*guns, thunder* +] 发出隆隆的响声; [*voice* +] 发出低沉有力的声音 **2** [*sales, business, economy* +] 繁荣

boost [buːst] **I** *n* [c] **1** (*to sales, economy etc*) 促进 **2** (*to confidence, morale*) 增强 **II** *vt* **1** [+ *sales, economy etc*] 促进 **2** [+ *confidence, morale*] 增强

boot [buːt] **I** *n* [c] **1** (*footwear*) (*for winter*) 靴子; (*for football, walking etc*) 鞋 **2** [英] [*of car*] 车后行李箱 [美 = **trunk**] **II** *vt* [非正式] (*kick*) 猛踢 ♦**... to boot** (*in addition*) 再者… ♦**to get** *or* **be given the boot** [非正式] 被解雇
❑**boot up** [计算机] **I** *vt* 使运行 **II** *vi* 开始运行

booth [buːð] *n* [c] **1** (*for telephoning*) 隔开的小间 **2** (*for voting*) 投票站 **3** (*at fair*) 摊子

booze [buːz] [非正式] **I** *n* [u] 酒 **II** *vi* 饮酒

border ['bɔːdə(r)] **I** *n* [c] **1** [*of country*] 边界 **2** (*in garden*) 花坛 **3** (*band, edge*) (*on cloth etc*) 饰边 **II** *vt* **1** [+ *road*] 环绕 **2** [+ *another country*] 与…接壤 **III Borders** *n* [英: 地理] ♦**the Borders** 英格兰与苏格兰交界区
❑**border on** *vt* [不可拆分] (喻) [+ *insanity, brutality*] 近于

borderline ['bɔːdəlaɪn] *n* [c] 边境线 ♦**to be on the borderline** (*in exam etc*) 两可之间

bore [bɔː(r)] **I** *pt of* **bear II** *vt* **1** [+ *hole*] 钻 **2** [+ *oil well, tunnel*] 开凿 **3** [+ *person*] 使厌烦 **III** *n* **1** ♦**12-bore shotgun** 12膛径的猎枪 **2** ♦**to be a bore** [*person* +] 令人讨厌的人; [*situation* +] 令人厌烦的事 ♦**it's a bore** 令人讨厌 ♦**it/he bores me to tears** *or* **to death** *or* **stiff** 它/他把我烦死了 ♦**to be bored (with sth)** (对某事) 不感兴趣 ♦**to be bored to tears** *or* **bored to death** *or* **bored stiff** [非正式] 厌烦得要死

> 如果你感觉**bored**，是因为你对所做的事情不感兴趣，或没有你所感兴趣的事情去做。*If you're bored, we could go for a walk.* 当你觉得某人、某地或某物没意思而使你感觉乏味时，就可以用**boring**来形容。*a boring job…a boring little mining town…He can be a bit boring sometimes.*

boredom ['bɔːdəm] *n* [u] **1** (*state of being bored*) 厌烦 **2** (*boring quality*) 乏味

boring ['bɔːrɪŋ] *adj* (*tedious*) [+ *person, job, film*] 乏味的

born [bɔːn] *adj* ♦**to be born** [*baby* +] 出生 ♦**to be born of** *or* **to sb** [正式] 是某人的孩子 ♦**a born comedian** 天生的喜剧演员 ♦**born and bred** 土生土长

borne [bɔːn] *pp of* **bear**

borough ['bʌrə, (美) 'bʌrəu] *n* [c] 自治城市

borrow ['bɔrəu] *vt* (*from sb, from library*) 借 ♦ **can I borrow a pen please?** 我能不能借枝笔？

bosom ['buzəm] **I** *n* **1** [c] [过时] (*also:* ***bosoms***) [*of woman*] 乳房 **2** [s] [文] [*of family, community*] 中间 **II** *adj* [+ *friend*] 亲密的

boss [bɔs] **I** *n* [c] **1** (*employer*) 老板 **2** [非正式] (*leader*) 领导 **II** *vt* 支配 ♦ **to be one's own boss** 一切由自己作主
❑ **boss around, boss about** *vt* 对某人呼来唤去

bossy ['bɔsɪ] *adj* 霸道的

botany ['bɔtənɪ] *n* [u] 植物学

✪ **both** [bəuθ] **I** *adj* 两者都 ◊ *Both policies make good sense.* 两项政策都很有道理。**II** *pron* **1** (*things*) 两者 ◊ *Most of them speak English or German or both.* 他们大都会说英语或者德语，或者两种语言都会。**2** (*people*) 两个 ◊ *He's fond of you both.* 你们两个他都喜欢。**III** *conj* ♦ **both A and B** A和B两者都 ♦ **both (of them)** (他们) 两个都 ♦ **both of us went** *or* **we both went** 我们两个都去了 ♦ **they saw both of us** 我们两个他们都见了

bother ['bɔðə(r)] **I** *vt* **1** (*worry*) 烦扰 **2** (*disturb*) 打扰 **II** *vi* 在乎 **III** *n* **1** [u] (*trouble*) 麻烦 **2** [u] (*difficulty*) 费力 **3** [s] (*nuisance*) 麻烦事 **IV** *int* (*also:* ***bother it***) [尤英：过时] 真讨厌 ♦ **to bother doing sth** *or* **to do sth** 费心做某事 ♦ **I can't be bothered to go** (*it's unnecessary*) 我没必要去; (*I'm too lazy*) 我没劲去 ♦ **don't bother** 不用了 ♦ **it's no bother** 不麻烦 ♦ **it's a bother** 是件麻烦事

bottle ['bɔtl] **I** *n* **1** [c] (*glass etc container*) (*for milk, wine, perfume*) 瓶子 **2** [c] (*amount contained*) 瓶 **3** [c] [*baby's* +] 奶瓶 **4** [u] [英：非正式] (*courage*) 胆量 **II** *vt* **1** [+ *beer, wine*] 装瓶 **2** [+ *fruit*] 装罐储藏 ♦ **a bottle of wine/milk** 一瓶葡萄酒/牛奶 ♦ **a wine/milk bottle** 葡萄酒/牛奶瓶 ♦ **bottled beer** 瓶装啤酒 ♦ **bottled water** 瓶装水
❑ **bottle up** *vt* [+ *emotion*] 抑制

bottle bank [英] *n* [c] 旧瓶回收处

bottle opener *n* [c] 开瓶器

bottom ['bɔtəm] **I** *n* **1** [c] [*of container, sea*] 底部 **2** [c] [*of page, list*] 下端 **3** [u/s] [*of class, league*] 最后一名 **4** [s] [*of organization, company*] 最底层 **5** [c] [*of hill, tree, stairs*] 最底部 **6** [c] (*buttocks*) 臀部 **7** [c] (*also:* ***bottoms***) [*of bikini, tracksuit*] 下装 **II** *adj* **1** (*lowest*) 最下面的 **2** (*least important*) [+ *rung, position*] 最低的 ♦ **at the bottom of** 在…的底部 ♦ **to get to the bottom of sth** 彻底查明某事
❑ **bottom out** *vi* [*recession etc* +] 降到最低点

bought [bɔːt] *pt, pp of* **buy**

boulder ['bəuldə(r)] *n* [c] 巨石

bounce [bauns] **I** *vi* **1** [*ball* +] 弹起 **2** [*hair* +] 跳动 **3** [*cheque* +] 退回 **II** *vt* **1** [+ *ball*] 拍 **2** [+ *cheque*] 拒付 **III** *n* [c/u] [*of ball*] 弹起 ♦ **to bounce on** [+ *bed etc*] 蹦跳上 ♦ **to bounce up and down** 上下跳动 ♦ **to bounce in/out** *etc* [*person* +] 蹦跳地进来/出去 {等}

bouncer ['baunsə(r)] [非正式] *n* [c] (*at dance, club*) 保安

bound [baund] **I** *pt, pp of* **bind II** *n* [c] [文] (*leap*) 跳 **III** *vi* (*leap*) 大步快走 **IV** *vt* (*border*) 接壤 **V** *adj* ♦ **bound by** [+ *law, regulation*] 被…约束 **VI bounds** *n* [*pl*] (*limit*) 限制 ♦ **to be bound to do sth** (*certain*) 一定做某事; (*obliged*) 有义务做某事 ♦ **bound for** [航海，汽车，铁路] 开往 ♦ **to be bound up in sth** 忙于某事 ♦ **to be bound up with sth** 与某事密切相关 ♦ **out of bounds** [+ *place*] 不准进入 ♦ **to know no bounds** 无可限量

boundary ['baundrɪ] *n* [c] (*border, limit*) 边界

bouquet ['bukeɪ] *n* **1** [c] [*of flowers*] 束 **2** [c/u] [*of wine*] 芳香

bourbon ['buəbən] [美] *n* [u] 波旁威士忌

bourgeois ['buəʒwɑː] *adj* [贬] 资产阶级的

bout [baut] *n* [c] **1** [*of illness*] 发作 **2** [*of activity*] 次 **3** [拳击等] 场

boutique [buː'tiːk] *n* [c] 小型精品店

bow[1] [bəu] *n* [c] **1** (*knot*) 蝴蝶结

2 (*weapon*) 弓 3 [音] 琴弓
bow² [bau] **I** *n* [c] **1** (*of head, body*) 鞠躬 **2** [航海] (*also:* **bows**) 船首 **II** *vi* (*with head, body*) 鞠躬 **III** *vt* [+ *head*] 低头 ♦ **to bow to** [+ *pressure, sb's wishes*] 服从 ♦ **to bow to the inevitable** 向命运低头
❑ **bow out** *vi* ♦ **to bow out (of sth)** 退出(某事)
bowels ['bauəlz] *n* [*pl*] **1** [解剖] 肠 **2** [文] [*of the earth etc*] 深处
bowl [bəul] **I** *n* [c] **1** (*container for eating*) 碗 **2** (*contents*) 一碗的量 **3** (*for washing clothes/dishes*) 盆 **4** [*of toilet*] 马桶 **5** [体育] (*ball*) 木球 *see also* **bowls** **6** [*of pipe*] 烟斗 **7** [尤美] (*stadium*) 体育场 **II** *vi* [板球] 投球
❑ **bowl over** *vt* **1** (*knock over*) 撞倒 **2** (*impress*) 使大吃一惊
bowler ['bəulə(r)] *n* [c] **1** [板球] 投球员 **2** [英] = **bowler hat**
bowler hat [英] *n* [c] 圆顶硬礼帽
bowling ['bəulɪŋ] *n* [u] (*game*) 保龄球 ♦ **to go bowling** 打保龄球
bowling alley *n* [c] (*building*) 保龄球球道
bowling green *n* [c] 地滚球草地球场
bowls [bəulz] [英] *n* [u] (*game*) 地滚球戏 [美 = **lawn bowling**]
bow tie [bəu-] *n* [c] 蝶形领结
box [bɔks] **I** *n* [c] **1** (*container*) 盒子 **2** (*contents*) 盒 ◊ *a box of chocolates/tissues* 一盒巧克力/纸巾 **3** (*also:* ***cardboard box***) 纸箱 **4** (*crate*) 箱 **5** [戏剧, 体育] 包厢 **6** ♦ **the box** [英: 非正式] (*television*) 电视 **7** ♦ **the box** [足球] (*penalty area*) 罚球区 **8** [英] (*road marking*) 十字路口路面的方格标记 **9** (*on form*) 方框 **II** *vt* (*put in a box*) 装箱 **III** *vi* [体育] 拳击
❑ **box in** *vt* [+ *car, person*] 围困
boxer ['bɔksə(r)] *n* [c] **1** (*person*) 拳击运动员 **2** (*dog*) 斗拳狗
boxer shorts, boxers *n* [*pl*] 平角裤
boxing ['bɔksɪŋ] [体育] *n* [u] 拳击
Boxing Day [英] *n* [c/u] 圣诞节后的第一天，是公共假日
boxing gloves *n* [*pl*] 拳击手套
boxing ring *n* [c] 拳击台
box office *n* **1** [c] (*in theatre/cinema*) 售票处 **2** [s] (喻) 票房 ♦ **a box office success** 非常卖座
✪ **boy** [bɔɪ] *n* [c] **1** (*male child*) 男孩 **2** (*young man*) 男青年 ◊ *the age when girls get interested in boys* 女孩子开始对男青年感兴趣的年龄 **3** [非正式] (*son*) 儿子
boycott ['bɔɪkɔt] **I** *n* [c] 联合抵制 **II** *vt* [+ *product, place, event*] 联合抵制
boyfriend ['bɔɪfrɛnd] *n* [c] 男朋友
boyish ['bɔɪɪʃ] *adj* **1** [+ *man, looks, smile*] 男孩子气的 **2** [+ *woman*] 男孩式的
bra [brɑː] *n* [c] 胸罩
brace [breɪs] **I** *n* [c] **1** (*on teeth*) 牙箍 **2** (*on leg, neck*) 支架 **II braces** *n* [*pl*] **1** [英] 背带 [美 = **suspenders**] **2** [美: 排版] (*also:* ***curly braces***) 大括弧 [英 = **curly brackets**] **III** *vt* [+ *knees, shoulders*] 绷紧 ♦ **to brace oneself** (*in order to steady oneself*) 使自己紧靠; (喻) (*for shock*) 稳定情绪
bracelet ['breɪslɪt] *n* [c] 手镯
bracing ['breɪsɪŋ] *adj* [+ *air, climate, walk, swim*] 令人振奋的
bracket ['brækɪt] **I** *n* [c] **1** (*group, range*) 类别 **2** [术语] 托架 **3** (*also:* ***round bracket***) 圆括号 **4** (*also:* ***square bracket***) 方括号 **II** *vt* **1** (*also:* ***bracket together***) (喻) 把…归入同类 **2** [+ *word, phrase*] 把…括在括号内 ♦ **income bracket** 收入阶层 ♦ **in brackets** 括号内
brag [bræg] *vi* ♦ **to brag (about)** 吹嘘
braid [breɪd] **I** *n* **1** [u] (*on clothes, curtains*) 穗带 **2** [c] [美] (*plait*) 辫子 [英 = **plait**] **II** *vt* [美] [+ *hair*] 把…编成辫子 [英 = **plait**]
Braille [breɪl] *n* [u] 布莱叶盲文
brain [breɪn] **I** *n* **1** [c] [解剖] 脑 **2** [u] (喻) 大脑 **II brains** *n* [*pl*] **1** [烹饪] 脑髓 **2** (*intelligence*) 智力 ♦ **he's got brains** 他很聪慧 ♦ **he's the brains of the organization** [非正式] 他是该组织的中枢人物 ♦ **to pick sb's brains** [非正式] 问某人的意见 ♦ **to rack one's brains** 绞尽脑汁
brainwash ['breɪnwɔʃ] *vt* 给…洗脑
brainy ['breɪnɪ] *adj* [非正式] [+ *child, person*] 聪明的
braise [breɪz] *vt* 炖
brake [breɪk] **I** *n* [c] **1** [汽车] 刹车

2（喻）阻碍 II *vi* [*driver, vehicle* +] 刹车 III *vt* [+ *vehicle*] 刹

brake light *n* [c] 刹车灯

bran [bræn] *n* [u] 麸

branch [brɑːntʃ] *n* [c] **1** [*of tree*] 树枝 **2** [*of shop*] 分店; [*of bank, company etc*] 分支机构 **3** [*of family, organization*] 支系 **4** [*of subject*] 分科

❑ **branch off** *vi* **1** [*road, path* +] 分叉 **2** [*person* +] 转向

❑ **branch out** *vi* ♦ **to branch out into** 向新的方向发展

brand [brænd] I *n* [c] **1** (*make*) 牌子 **2**（喻）(*type*) 模式 II *vt* **1**（喻）♦ **to brand sb a racist** *etc* 给某人栽上种族主义者{等}的恶名 **2** [+ *cattle*] 打烙印于

brand-new ['brænd'njuː] *adj* 全新的

brandy ['brændɪ] *n* [c/u] 白兰地酒

brash [bræʃ] *adj* (*forward, cheeky*) 莽撞的

brass [brɑːs] *n* [u] (*metal*) 铜 ♦ **the brass (section)** [音] 铜管乐器

brass band *n* [c] 铜管乐队

brassiere ['bræsɪə(r)] [过时] *n* [c] 胸罩

brat [bræt] [贬] *n* [c] (*child*) 臭小孩儿

brave [breɪv] I *adj* **1** [+ *person*] 勇敢的 **2** [+ *attempt, smile, action*] 英勇的 II *n* [c] [过时] (*warrior*) 北美印第安勇士 III *vt* (*face up to*) 勇敢面对 ♦ **to put a brave face on sth** 面对某事时显示出勇气

bravery ['breɪvərɪ] *n* [u] 英勇

brawl [brɔːl] I *n* [c] (*in pub, street*) 打闹 II *vi* 打架

Brazil [brə'zɪl] *n* 巴西

breach [briːtʃ] I *vt* **1** [+ *agreement, law*] 违反 **2** [+ *security, defences*] 突破 **3** [正式] [+ *wall, barrier*] 冲破 II *n* [c] **1** [*of agreement, law*] 违反 **2** (*gap*) (*in wall, barrier*) 缺口 **3** [正式] (*rupture*) (*between people, groups*) 破裂 ♦ **breach of the peace** [法] 扰乱治安罪 ♦ **breach of security** 冲破重围 ♦ **breach of contract** 违背合同

bread [brɛd] *n* [u] 面包

breadbin ['brɛdbɪn] [英] *n* [c] 面包箱 [美 = **breadbox**]

breadbox ['brɛdbɔks] [美] *n* = **breadbin**

breadcrumbs ['brɛdkrʌmz] *n* [*pl*] 面包屑

breadth [brɛtθ] *n* [u] **1** (*width*) 宽度 **2**（喻）[*of experience, knowledge*] 丰富

✪ **break** [breɪk] (*pt* **broke**, *pp* **broken**) I *vt* **1** [+ *cup, window etc*] 打碎 **2** [+ *leg, arm*] 弄断 **3** [+ *equipment*] 损坏 **4** [+ *promise, contract*] 违背 **5** [+ *law, rule*] 违反 **6** [+ *record*] 打破 **7** [+ *habit, pattern etc*] 改变 **8** [+ *person*] 毁掉 ◊ *He never let his jailers break him.* 他是永远不会让他的监狱看守弄垮的。**9** [+ *fall, impact*] 减弱 ◊ *The trees broke his fall.* 树丛使他下落的坠势稍缓。**10** [+ *news*] 透露 ◊ *Then Louise broke the news that she was leaving me.* 然后路易丝向我透露她要和我分手。**11** [+ *code*] 破译 **12** [网球] [+ *sb's serve*] 破发成功 II *vi* **1** [*cup, window etc* +] 破碎 **2** [*storm, weather* +] 突然发生 **3** [*dawn, day* +] 破晓 **4** [*story, news* +] 传开 **5** (*pause, rest*) 暂停 ◊ *They broke for lunch.* 他们暂停去吃午餐了。**6** [*wave* +] 冲击 **7** [*voice* +] (*of boy*) 变声 III *n* **1** [c] (*rest*) 休息 ◊ *I'm going to have a break.* 我要休息一下。**2** [c] (*pause, interval*) 间歇 ◊ *There was a break in the middle of the day's events.* 那天的活动中有一次间歇。**3** [c] (*fracture*) 骨折 **4** [u] [英:教育] 课间休息 [美 = **recess**] **5** [c] [非正式] (*chance*) 运气 ◊ *Her big break came when she appeared on TV.* 上电视的机会给她带来了好运气。**6** [c] (*holiday*) 休假 ♦ **to break the news to sb** 委婉地向某人透露消息 ♦ **to break even** [商] 收支持平 ♦ **to break with sb/sth** 与某人绝交/放弃某事 ♦ **to break free** *or* **loose (of sb/sth)** [*person, animal* +] 摆脱（某人/某事）♦ **to take a break** (*for a few minutes*) 休息一下; (*have a holiday*) 休假 ♦ **without a break** 连续不断 ♦ **a lucky break** 好运气

❑ **break away** *vi* (*from pursuer etc*) 逃脱

❑ **break down** I *vi* **1** [*machine, car* +] 坏掉 **2** [化] 分解 **3** [*person* +] 情绪失控 **4** [*talks* +] 破裂 II *vt* **1** [+ *figures, data*] 把…分类 **2** [+ *door etc*] 捣毁 **3** [化] 分解 **4**（喻）[+ *barriers, prejudices*] 解除

❑**break in** I *vi* 1 [*burglar* +] 破门而入 2 (*interrupt*) 打断 II *vt* [+ *new shoes, engine etc*] 使合用
❑**break into** *vt* [不可拆分] 1 [+ *house*] 强行进入 2 [+ *new activity*] 开始进入 ◊ *She finally broke into films after an acclaimed stage career.* 继一段成功的舞台生涯之后她最终投身电影业。♦**to break into song/a run** 突然唱起来/跑了起来
❑**break off** I *vi* 1 [*branch* +] 折断 2 [*speaker* +] 突然打住 II *vt* 1 [+ *branch, piece of chocolate*] 折断 2 [+ *talks*] 突然终止 3 [+ *engagement, relationship*] 断绝 ♦**to break it off with sb** 同某人分手
❑**break open** *vt* [+ *door, window etc*] 用力打开
❑**break out** *vi* 1 (*begin*) [*war, fight* +] 爆发 2 (*escape*) [*prisoner* +] 逃脱 ♦**to break out in spots/a rash/a sweat** 突然出了一身红点/疹子/汗
❑**break through** I *vi* [*sun* +] 显现 II *vt* [不可拆分] [+ *defences, barrier*] 突破
❑**break up** I *vi* 1 [*ship* +] 碎裂 2 [*couple, marriage* +] 破裂 3 [*meeting, party* +] 纷纷离去 4 [英] 学期结束 II *vt* 1 [+ *rocks, biscuit etc*] 弄碎 2 [+ *journey, day*] 使有间歇 3 [+ *fight etc*] 调停 4 [+ *meeting, demonstration*] 驱散 5 [+ *marriage*] 使破裂 ♦**to break up with sb** 同某人分手

breakdown ['breɪkdaun] *n* [c] 1 [汽车] 故障 2 [*of system, talks*] 中断 3 [*of marriage*] 破裂 4 [医] (*also:* ***nervous breakdown***) 精神崩溃 5 [*of costs, figures*] 分类细目 ♦**to have a breakdown** 精神崩溃

breakfast ['brɛkfəst] I *n* [c/u] 早餐 II *vi* [正式] 吃早餐
📖 用法参见 **meal**

break-in ['breɪkɪn] *n* [c] 闯入

breakthrough ['breɪkθruː] *n* [c] 1 (*achievement*) 重要成果 2 (*progress*) 突破性进展

breast [brɛst] *n* 1 [c] [*of woman*] 乳房 2 [c] [文] (*chest*) 胸部 3 [c/u] [烹饪] (*of chicken, lamb*) 胸脯肉 4 [c] [*of bird*] 前胸 ♦**to make a clean breast of sth** 坦白承认某事

breast-feed ['brɛstfiːd] (*pt, pp* **breast-fed**) I *vt* 母乳哺养 II *vi* 母乳哺养

breaststroke ['brɛststrəuk] *n* [u] (*also:* ***the breaststroke***) 蛙泳

breath [brɛθ] *n* 1 [c/u] (*intake of air*) 呼吸 2 [u] (*air from mouth*) 口气 ♦**out of breath** 上气不接下气 ♦**under one's breath** 低声说 ♦**bad breath** 口臭 ♦**to get one's breath back** [英] 恢复正常呼吸 ♦**to go out for a breath of (fresh) air** 出去呼吸(新鲜)空气 ♦**a breath of fresh air** (喻) 新意 ♦**there wasn't a breath of wind** 一丝风都没有 ♦**to catch one's breath** 喘口气 ♦**to hold one's breath** 屏住呼吸 ♦**don't hold your breath!** (喻) [非正式] 别太指望了！ ♦**to be short of breath** 呼吸短促 ♦**to take a deep breath** 深呼一口气 ♦**it takes your breath away** 使人心醉神迷

Breathalyzer®, Breathalyser® ['brɛθəlaɪzə(r)] *n* [c] 测醉器

breathe [briːð] I *vt* 1 [+ *air*] 呼吸 2 [文] (*whisper*) 低语 II *vi* 呼吸 ♦**I won't breathe a word about it** 我不会透露一点儿风声的 ♦**to breathe life into sth** 给某事带来活力
❑**breathe in** I *vi* 吸入 II *vt* [+ *air, smoke*] 吸入
❑**breathe out** *vi* 呼出

breathing ['briːðɪŋ] *n* [u] 呼吸

breathless ['brɛθlɪs] *adj* (*from exertion*) 气喘吁吁的 ♦**breathless with excitement** 激动地透不过气来

breathtaking ['brɛθteɪkɪŋ] *adj* [+ *speed, view*] 惊人的

breath test *n* [c] 呼吸测醉分析

breed [briːd] (*pt, pp* **bred**) I *vt* 1 [+ *animals*] 繁殖 2 [+ *plants*] 培植 3 (喻) (*give rise to*) [+ *situation, quality, hate, suspicion*] 引起 II *vi* [动] 繁殖 III *n* [c] 1 [动] 品种 2 (*type, class*) 类型

breeze [briːz] I *n* [c] 微风 II *vi* ♦**to breeze in/out** 飘然而至/去 ♦**it was a breeze** [非正式] 这是小事一桩

breezy ['bri:zɪ] *adj* **1** [*+ manner, tone*] 轻松活泼的 **2** [*+ weather*] 惠风和畅的

brew [bru:] **I** *vt* **1** [*+ tea, coffee*] 冲泡 **2** [*+ beer*] 酿造 **II** *vi* **1** [*crisis +*] 酝酿 **2** [*storm +*] 即将来临 **3** [*tea, coffee +*] 煮 **4** [*beer +*] 酿制 **III** *n* [c] [*of tea, coffee*] (*drink*) 饮料; (*type*) 茶或咖啡的种类

brewery ['bru:ərɪ] *n* [c] 啤酒厂

bribe [braɪb] **I** *n* [c] 贿赂 **II** *vt* [*+ person, witness*] 行贿 ♦ **to bribe sb to do sth** 贿赂某人去做某事

bribery ['braɪbərɪ] *n* [U] (*with money, favours*) 行贿

bric-a-brac ['brɪkəbræk] *n* [U] 小摆设

brick [brɪk] *n* [C/U] (*for building*) 砖 ❑ **brick up** *vt* [*+ door, window*] 用砖填砌

bricklayer ['brɪkleɪə(r)] *n* [c] 砌砖工

bride [braɪd] *n* [c] 新娘

bridegroom ['braɪdgru:m] *n* [c] 新郎

bridesmaid ['braɪdzmeɪd] *n* [c] 伴娘

bridge [brɪdʒ] **I** *n* **1** [c] [建筑] 桥 **2** [c] [航海] 舰桥 **3** [c] [*of nose*] 鼻梁 **4** [U] [纸牌] 桥牌 **5** [c] (喻) 桥梁作用 **II** *vt* (喻) [*+ gap, gulf*] 跨越

bridle ['braɪdl] **I** *n* [c] 马笼头 **II** *vt* [*+ horse*] 给…套笼头 **III** *vi* ♦ **to bridle (at)** [文] [*+ memory, comment etc*] 表示愤怒

brief [bri:f] **I** *adj* **1** [*+ period, visit, appearance*] 短暂的 **2** [*+ description, speech*] 简短的 **II** *n* [c] [尤英: 正式] (*task*) 任务 **III** *vt* (*inform*) 对…作任务指示 **IV briefs** *n* [*pl*] **1** (*for men*) 男式三角内裤 **2** (*for women*) 女式三角内裤 ♦ **in brief …** 简而言之… ♦ **I'll try to be brief** 我尽量简单地说

briefcase ['bri:fkeɪs] *n* [c] 公事包

briefing ['bri:fɪŋ] *n* [C/U] 发布会

briefly ['bri:flɪ] *adv* [*smile, talk, explain, say +*] 简短地

brigadier [brɪgə'dɪə(r)] *n* [c] 准将

bright [braɪt] *adj* **1** [*+ light*] 亮的 **2** [*+ weather, day*] 晴朗的 **3** [*+ room*] 明亮的 **4** (*clever*) [*+ person*] 聪明的; [*+ idea*] 巧妙的 **5** (*lively*) [*+ person*] 愉快的 **6** [*+ colour*] 鲜亮的 **7** [*+ clothes*] 鲜艳的 **8** [*+ outlook, future*] 光明的 ♦ **to look on the bright side** 抱着乐观的态度

brilliance ['brɪljəns] *n* [U] **1** [*of light, sun*] 光辉 **2** [*of person, talent*] 才华横溢

brilliant ['brɪljənt] *adj* **1** [*+ person, mind*] 才华横溢的 **2** [*+ idea, performance*] 出色的 **3** [*+ sunshine, light, colour*] 光彩夺目的 **4** (*successful*) [*+ career, future*] 辉煌的 **5** [尤英: 非正式] (*wonderful*) 棒极了的

brim [brɪm] **I** *n* [c] [*of hat*] 帽边 **II** *vi* ♦ **to be brimming with** [*+ confidence, love*] 洋溢 ♦ **her eyes were brimming with tears** 她的眼里溢满了泪水 ♦ **to be full to the brim** 满到边

brine [braɪn] *n* [U] 盐水

✪ **bring** [brɪŋ] (*pt, pp* **brought**) *vt* **1** [*+ thing, person*] (*with you*) 带来 ◊ *He brought Judy with him.* 他把朱迪带来了。; (*to sb*) 拿来 ◊ *Would you bring me a glass of water?* 请给我拿杯水来，好吗？ **2** (*move*) 移 ◊ *She brought her hands up to her face.* 她将手移到脸上。 **3** [*+ satisfaction, trouble*] 带来 ◊ *Her three children brought her joy.* 她的3个孩子给她带来欢乐。 **4** (*cause to come*) 使来到 ◊ *What brought you to this town in the first place?* 究竟是什么使你来到这个城市的呢？ ♦ **to bring sth to a stop/an end** 使某事停止/结束 ♦ **I can't bring myself to fire him** 我不忍心解雇他

❑ **bring about** *vt* (*cause*) 造成

❑ **bring along** *vt* 随身携带

❑ **bring around** *vt* = **bring round**

❑ **bring back** *vt* **1** (*return*) 带回来 ◊ *She brought my book back.* 她把我的书带回来了。 **2** (*restore*) [*+ hanging etc*] 恢复 ◊ *Some people want to bring back the death penalty.* 一些人想恢复死刑。 **3** [*+ memory*] 使人回忆起 ◊ *Your article brought back sad memories for me.* 你的文章使我回忆起一些难过的往事。

❑ **bring down** *vt* **1** [*+ government*] 使…倒台 **2** [*+ price*] [*competition, circumstances +*] 降低 ◊ *The discovery of new oilfields brought the price* *down.* 新油田的发现使油价有所降低。; [*company, government* +] 调低◊ *They brought down income taxes.* 他们调低了所得税。

❑**bring forth** *vt* [正式] 取出

❑**bring forward** *vt* **1** [+ *meeting*] 提前 **2** [+ *argument, proposal*] 提出 **3** [簿记] 承前

❑**bring in** *vt* **1** [+ *law, system, object, person*] 引进◊ *It would be a mistake to bring in an outsider.* 引一个局外人进来会是一个错误。 **2** [+ *money*] 挣得 **3** [法] [+ *verdict*] 宣判

❑**bring off** *vt* [+ *attempt, plan*] 完成

❑**bring on** *vt* [+ *illness, pain*] 导致

❑**bring out** *vt* (*publish, produce*) [+ *book, album*] 出版 ♦**to bring out the best/worst in sb** 使某人最好/最坏的一面显现出来

❑**bring round** *vt* [+ *unconscious person*] 使苏醒

❑**bring up** *vt* **1** (*rear*) [+ *child*] 抚养 **2** [+ *question, subject*] 提出 **3** [非正式] (*vomit*) [+ *food*] 呕出

brink [brɪŋk] *n* ♦**to be on the brink of** [+ *disaster, war etc*] 在…的边缘

brisk [brɪsk] *adj* **1** (*abrupt*) [+ *tone, person*] 简捷直接的 **2** [+ *pace*] 轻快的 **3** [+ *trade, business*] 兴旺的 **4** [+ *breeze, weather*] 清新的 ♦**to go for a brisk walk** 快步走路

bristle ['brɪsl] **I** *n* [c] **1** (*animal hair, hair of beard*) 毛发楂儿 **2** [*of brush*] 硬毛 **II** *vi* **1** [*person* +] (*in anger*) 愤怒 **2** [*hairs* +] 竖起 ♦**to bristle with sth** 布满某物

Brit [brɪt] [非正式] *n* [c] 英国人

Britain ['brɪtən] *n* (*also:* ***Great Britain***) 英国 ♦**in Britain** 在英国

> **BRITAIN**
>
> **Britain** 或 **Great Britain** 由英格兰、威尔士、苏格兰和北爱尔兰组成。如指整个不列颠，应慎用 **England** 和 **English**，以免引起苏格兰和北爱尔兰人的不满。**United Kingdom** 作为王国的官方称谓，常简略为 **the UK**，覆盖大不列颠及北爱尔兰。**British Isles** 包括大不列颠、北爱尔兰、爱尔兰共和国（不隶属 **the UK**）和四周岛屿。

British ['brɪtɪʃ] **I** *adj* 英国的 **II** *n* [*pl*] ♦**the British** 英国人

British Isles [-aɪlz] *n* [*pl*] ♦**the British Isles** 不列颠群岛

brittle ['brɪtl] *adj* (*fragile*) [+ *glass, bones etc*] 脆弱的

B-road ['biːrəud] [英] *n* [c] 辅路

broad [brɔːd] **I** *adj* **1** [+ *street, shoulders*] 宽的 **2** [+ *smile*] 明显的 **3** [+ *range*] 广泛的 **4** (*general*) [+ *outlines, distinction etc*] 概略的; [+ *sense*] 广义的 **5** [+ *accent*] 浓重的 **II** *n* [c] [美: 非正式] (*woman*) 女人 ♦**in broad daylight** 光天化日之下 ♦**a broad hint** 明显的暗示

broadband ['brɔːdbænd] [计算机] **I** *adj* 宽带的 **II** *n* 宽带

broad bean [尤英] *n* [c] 蚕豆 [美 = **fava bean**]

broadcast ['brɔːdkɑːst] (*pt, pp* **broadcast**) **I** *n* [c] 广播 **II** *vt* 播送 **III** *vi* 广播

broaden ['brɔːdn] **I** *vt* [+ *scope, appeal*] 扩大 **II** *vi* **1** [*river, smile* +] 变宽 **2** [*scope, appeal* +] 扩大影响 ♦**to broaden the/sb's mind** 拓宽思想/拓宽某人的思想

broadly ['brɔːdlɪ] *adv* **1** (*in general terms*) 大体上 **2** [*smile* +] ♦**to smile broadly** 咧嘴笑 ♦**broadly speaking** 广义地说

broadminded ['brɔːd'maɪndɪd] *adj* 宽宏大量的

broccoli ['brɔkəlɪ] *n* [U] 花椰菜

brochure ['brəuʃjuə(r), (美) brəu'ʃur] *n* [c] (*booklet*) 小册子

broil [brɔɪl] [美] *vt* 烤 [英 = **grill**] 📖 用法参见 **cook**

broke [brəuk] **I** *pt of* **break** **II** *adj* [非正式] (*penniless*) 身无分文的 ♦**to go broke** [非正式] [*company, person* +] 破产

broken ['brəukn] **I** *pp of* **break** **II** *adj* **1** [+ *window, cup etc*] 破碎的 **2** [+ *machine*] 坏损的 **3** [+ *promise, vow*] 背弃的 **4** [+ *line*] ♦**broken line** 虚线 ♦**a broken leg** 折断的腿 ♦**a broken marriage** 破裂的婚姻 ♦**a broken home** 破裂的家庭 ♦**in broken English/French** 用蹩脚的英语/法语

broker ['brəukə(r)] **I** *n* [c] (*in shares etc*) 经纪人 **II** *vt* [政治] [+ *agreement,* *ceasefire*] 斡旋

bronchitis [brɔŋˈkaɪtɪs] *n* [U] 支气管炎

bronze [brɔnz] **I** *n* **1** [U] (*metal*) 青铜 **2** [C] (*sculpture*) 青铜像 **3** [C] [体育] (*also:* ***bronze medal***) 铜牌 **II** *adj* (*in colour*) 古铜色的

brooch [brəutʃ] *n* [C] 胸针

brood [bruːd] **I** *n* [C] **1** (*baby birds*) 同窝幼鸟 **2** [*of children*] 同个家庭的一群孩子 **II** *vi* ♦ **to brood on** *or* **over** *or* **about sth** 沉思某事

broom [brum] *n* [C] (*for cleaning*) 扫帚

Bros. [商] *abbr* (= ***brothers***) 兄弟

broth [brɔθ] *n* [C/U] 清汤

brothel [ˈbrɔθl] *n* [C] 妓院

✪ **brother** [ˈbrʌðə(r)] *n* [C] **1** (*in family*) 兄弟; (*elder*) 哥哥; (*younger*) 弟弟 **2** [宗] 教友 **3** (喻) 哥们儿

brother-in-law [ˈbrʌðərɪnlɔː] *n* [C] (*older sister's husband*) 姐夫; (*younger sister's husband*) 妹夫; (*husband's older brother*) 大伯子; (*husband's younger brother*) 小叔子; (*wife's older brother*) 内兄; (*wife's younger brother*) 内弟

brought [brɔːt] *pt, pp of* **bring**

brow [brau] *n* [C] **1** (*forehead*) 额 **2** (*eyebrow*) 眉毛 **3** ♦ **brow of a hill** 山顶

✪ **brown** [braun] **I** *adj* **1** (*in colour*) [+ *object*] 褐色的; [+ *hair, eyes*] 棕色的 **2** (*tanned*) [+ *skin, person*] 晒黑的 **II** *n* [U] (*colour*) 褐色 **III** *vi* [烹饪] 变成褐色 **IV** *vt* [烹饪] 烧至金黄

brown bread *n* [U] 黑面包

Brownie [ˈbraunɪ] **I** *n* [C] 幼年女童军队员 **II Brownies** *n* [*pl*] ♦ **the Brownies** 幼年女童军

> **Brownies**
>
> **Brownies** 是英国的 **Girlguiding UK** 和美国的 **Girl Scouts** 组织的少年部，7到10岁的英国女孩和6到8岁的美国女孩可自愿加入。**Brownies** 的成员要学习一些实际的东西：独立、帮助别人、保护环境和了解其他文化。大家以赢得被称作 **badges** 的各项特别兴趣奖为荣，奖项包括：运动、园艺、烹饪、户外技巧、世界大事、阅读等。

brown rice *n* [U] 糙米

brown sugar *n* [U] 红糖

browse [brauz] **I** *vi* **1** 浏览 **2** (*in shop*) 随意翻阅 **3** [*cow etc* +] 吃草 **II** *n* ♦ **to have a browse (around)** 随意逛逛

browser [ˈbrauzə(r)] [计算机] *n* [C] 浏览器

bruise [bruːz] **I** *n* [C] **1** (*on face etc*) 青瘀 **2** (*on fruit*) 伤处 **II** *vt* **1** [+ *person, fruit*] 碰伤 **2** [+ *arm, leg etc*] (*one's own*) 挫伤; (*other person's*) 弄伤 **III** *vi* **1** [*person* +] 显出瘀痕 **2** [*fruit* +] 被碰伤

Brunei [ˈbruːnaɪ] *n* 文莱

brunette [bruːˈnɛt] *n* [C] 棕发女子

brush [brʌʃ] **I** *n* [C] **1** (*tool*) (*for cleaning, for decorating*) 刷子; (*for hair*) 发刷; [*artist's* +] 画笔 **2** (*unpleasant encounter*) 遭遇 **II** *vt* **1** (*sweep*) [+ *carpet etc*] 刷 (*with hands*) 拂拭 **2** (*groom*) [+ *hair*] 梳 **3** (*also:* ***brush against***) [+ *person, object*] 轻拂 ♦ **a brush with death** 差点丢命的遭遇 ♦ **a brush with the police** 与警察的小摩擦 ♦ **to brush one's teeth** 刷牙

❑ **brush aside, brush away** *vt* [+ *protest, criticism*] 漠视

❑ **brush off** *vt* [+ *person*] 怠慢

❑ **brush past** *vt* [+ *person, object*] 擦过

❑ **brush up (on)** *vt* [+ *subject, language*] 复习

Brussels sprout [ˈbrʌslz-] *n* [C] 芽甘蓝

brutal [ˈbruːtl] *adj* **1** [+ *person, killing*] 残忍的 **2** [+ *honesty, frankness*] 直率的

brute [bruːt] **I** *n* [C] (*person*) 畜牲 **II** *adj* [+ *strength, force*] 蛮力的 ♦ **by brute force** 凭蛮力

BS [美] *n abbr* = **BSc**

BSc *n abbr* (= ***Bachelor of Science***) (*qualification*) 理科学士学位; (*person*) 理科学士

BST *abbr* (= ***British Summer Time***) 英国夏令时

BTW *abbr* (= ***by the way***) 顺便说一句

bubble [ˈbʌbl] **I** *n* [C] **1** (*in liquid*) 泡 **2** (*also:* ***soap bubble***) 肥皂泡 **II** *vi* [*liquid* +] 起泡 ♦ **to be bubbling**

(over) with confidence/ideas 充满信心/想法
bubble bath *n* [U] (*liquid*) 泡泡浴液
bubble gum *n* [U] 泡泡糖
buck [bʌk] **I** *n* [C] **1** [美：非正式] (*dollar*) 元 **2** (*rabbit*) 雄兔 **3** (*deer*) 雄鹿 **II** *vi* [*horse* +] 弓背跳跃 ♦**to make a fast** *or* **quick buck** [非正式] 很快地捞一笔 ♦**to pass the buck** [非正式] 推卸责任
❏**buck up** [英：非正式] **I** *vi* 振作精神 **II** *vt* (*cheer up*) [+ *person, sb's spirits*] 使振奋精神 ♦**to buck one's ideas up** 振奋某人的精神
bucket ['bʌkɪt] **I** *n* [C] **1** (*pail*) 桶 **2** (*contents*) 一桶 **II** *vi* [英：非正式] ♦**it** *or* **the rain is bucketing down** 大雨倾盆而下
buckle ['bʌkl] **I** *n* [C] (*on shoe, belt*) 扣环 **II** *vt* **1** [+ *shoe, belt*] 扣住 **2** (*distort*) [+ *object*] 使变形 **III** *vi* **1** [*object* +] 变形 **2** [*legs, knees* +] 腿软
❏**buckle down** *vi* ♦**to buckle down (to sth)** [非正式] 开始认真地做(某事)
bud [bʌd] **I** *n* [C] (*on tree, plant*) (*leaf bud*) 芽; (*flower bud*) 蓓蕾 **II** *vi* **1** (*produce leaves*) 萌芽 **2** (*produce flowers*) 出花苞 ♦**to nip sth in the bud** [非正式] 把某事消灭在萌芽状态
Buddhism ['budɪzəm] *n* [U] 佛教
Buddhist ['budɪst] **I** *adj* 佛教的 **II** *n* [C] 佛教徒
budding ['bʌdɪŋ] *adj* **1** [+ *actor, writer*] 初露头角的 **2** [+ *romance, democracy*] 开始发展的
buddy ['bʌdɪ] [非正式] *n* [C] **1** [尤美] (*friend*) 朋友 **2** [美] (*form of address*) 老兄
budge [bʌdʒ] **I** *vt* **1** [+ *object*] 稍微移动 **2** (喻) [+ *person*] 动摇 **II** *vi* **1** [*object* +] 移动 **2** (喻) [*person* +] 改变立场
budgerigar ['bʌdʒərɪgɑː(r)] *n* [C] 小长尾鹦鹉
budget ['bʌdʒɪt] **I** *n* [C] [*of person, government*] 预算 **II** *vt* [+ *sum of money*] 预算出 **III** *vi* ♦**to budget for sth** 为某事做预算 **IV** *adj* (*economy*) [+ *travel agents etc*] 廉价的 ♦**I'm on a tight budget** 我经济拮据
budgie ['bʌdʒɪ] [非正式] *n* = **budgerigar**
buff [bʌf] **I** *n* [C] [非正式] (*enthusiast*) 爱好者 **II** *adj* (*in colour*) 暗黄色的 **III** *vt* (*polish*) 擦亮
buffalo ['bʌfələu] (*pl* **buffalo** *or* **buffaloes**) *n* [C] **1** [英] 水牛 **2** [美] (*bison*) 野牛
buffer ['bʌfə(r)] **I** *n* [C] **1** [尤英：铁路] 缓冲器 **2** [计算机] 缓冲存储器 **3** (喻) (*against harm, shortage etc*) 缓冲储备 **II** *vt* (*protect*) 保护
buffet[1] ['bufeɪ, (美) bu'feɪ] *n* [C] **1** (*in station*) 餐厅 **2** (*food*) 自助餐 **3** [英：铁路] (*also:* ***buffet car***) 餐车 [美 = **dining car**]
buffet[2] ['bʌfɪt] *vt* [*wind, sea* +] 冲击
bug [bʌg] **I** *n* [C] **1** [尤美] (*insect*) 虫子 **2** [计算机] (*in program*) 病毒 **3** [非正式] (*virus*) 病菌 **4** (*hidden microphone*) 窃听器 **II** *vt* **1** [非正式] (*annoy*) 烦扰 **2** [+ *room, telephone etc*] 窃听 ♦**I've got** *or* **been bitten by the travel bug** [非正式] 我迷上了旅游
buggy ['bʌgɪ] [英] *n* [C] (*for baby*) 婴儿车 [美 = **stroller**]
✪**build** [bɪld] (*pt, pp* **built**) **I** *n* [C/U] [*of person*] 体格 ◊ *He is of medium build.* 他中等体格。**II** *vt* **1** [+ *house, machine*] 建造 **2** (喻) [+ *organization, relationship*] 建立 ◊ *I wanted to build a relationship with my team.* 我想同我的团队建立起关系。**III** *vi* 建设
❏**build into** *vt* **1** [+ *wall, ceiling*] 固定在 ◊ *The TV was built into the ceiling.* 电视被固定在天花板上。**2** (喻) [+ *policy, system, product*] 纳入 ◊ *We have to build computers into the school curriculum.* 我们必须将计算机纳入学校课程安排中。
❏**build on, build upon** *vt* [不可拆分] (喻) [+ *success etc*] 建基于 ◊ *We must build on the success of these industries.* 我们必须依靠这些企业的成功。
❏**build up I** *vt* **1** [+ *business, collection*] 发展起来 **2** [+ *confidence, morale*] 激励 **II** *vi* (*accumulate*) 积聚 ♦**don't build your hopes up (too soon)** 不要(这么早)期望这么高

builder ['bɪldə(r)] *n* [c] (*worker*) 建筑工人

✪**building** ['bɪldɪŋ] *n* **1** [c] (*house, office etc*) 建筑物 **2** [u] (*industry, construction*) 建设 ◊ *Building has stopped while the dispute is being resolved.* 在解决分歧期间建设工作暂停。

building site *n* [c] 建筑工地

building society [英] *n* [c] 建屋互助会 [美= **savings and loan association**]

built [bɪlt] **I** *pt, pp of* **build II** *adj* ♦**well-/heavily-built** [+ *person*] 体态优美/粗笨的

built-in ['bɪltɪn] *adj* **1** [+ *device*] 内置式的 **2** [+ *safeguards*] 内在的

built-up ['bɪltʌp] *adj* [+ *area*] 被建筑物覆盖的

bulb [bʌlb] *n* [c] **1** [电子] 电灯泡 **2** [植] 球茎

Bulgaria [bʌl'gɛərɪə] *n* 保加利亚

bulge [bʌldʒ] **I** *n* [c] **1** (*bump*) 凸起 **2** (*in birth rate, sales*) 激增 **II** *vi* [*eyes, muscles, stomach etc* +] 凸出 ♦**to be bulging with** 塞满

bulimia [bə'lɪmɪə] *n* [u] (*also:* ***bulimia nervosa***) 暴食症

bulimic [bə'lɪmɪk] *adj* 患有暴食症的

bulk [bʌlk] *n* **1** [s/u] [*of person*] 肥硕的身躯 **2** [s] [*of object*] 庞然大物 ♦**to buy/sell in bulk** [商] 批量购买/销售 ♦**the bulk of** (*most of*) 大部分的

bulky ['bʌlkɪ] *adj* [+ *equipment, parcel*] 笨重的

bull [bul] *n* [c] **1** [动] 公牛 **2** (*male elephant/whale*) 雄兽 **3** [宗] 教皇诏书

bulldozer ['buldəuzə(r)] *n* [c] 推土机

bullet ['bulɪt] *n* [c] 子弹

bulletin ['bulɪtɪn] *n* [c] **1** [电视等] (*news update*) 公告 **2** (*journal*) 会刊

bulletin board *n* [c] **1** [计算机] 公共留言板 **2** [美] (*noticeboard*) 布告栏 [英= **noticeboard**]

bullfighting ['bulfaɪtɪŋ] *n* [u] 斗牛

bully ['bulɪ] **I** *n* [c] 恃强凌弱者 **II** *vt* 欺侮 ♦**to bully sb into (doing) sth** 胁迫某人(做)某事

bum [bʌm] [非正式] *n* [c] **1** [英] (*backside*) 屁股 **2** [尤美] (*tramp*) 流浪汉

❑**bum around** [非正式] *vi* 闲荡

bumblebee ['bʌmblbiː] *n* [c] 大黄蜂

bump [bʌmp] **I** *n* [c] **1** (*swelling*) (*on head*) 肿包 **2** (*jolt*) 重击 **3** [非正式] (*in car*) (*minor accident*) 碰撞 **4** (*on road*) 隆起物 **II** *vt* (*strike*) 碰 **III** *vi* (*jolt*) [*car* +] 颠簸

❑**bump into** *vt* [不可拆分] **1** (*strike*) [+ *obstacle, person*] 撞到 **2** [非正式] (*meet*) [+ *person*] 碰见

bumper ['bʌmpə(r)] **I** *n* [c] [汽车] 保险杠 **II** *adj* ♦**bumper crop/harvest** 大丰收

bumpy ['bʌmpɪ] *adj* **1** [+ *road*] 崎岖不平的 **2** [+ *flight, ride*] 颠簸的

bun [bʌn] *n* [c] **1** [烹饪] 小圆面包 **2** (*hair style*) 圆髻

bunch [bʌntʃ] **I** *n* [c] **1** [*of flowers*] 束 **2** [*of keys, bananas, grapes*] 串 **3** [非正式] [*of people*] 群 **II bunches** *n* [*pl*] [英] (*in hair*) 双辫

❑**bunch up, bunch together I** *vi* 挤在一起 **II** *vt* 聚集

bundle ['bʌndl] **I** *n* [c] (*parcel*) [*of clothes*] 包裹; [*of papers*] 捆 **II** *vt* (*put*) ♦**to bundle sth/sb into** 匆匆忙忙地把某事/某人塞进 ♦**a bundle of fun/laughs** 非常好玩/风趣 ♦**he was a bundle of nerves** 他感到非常紧张

❑**bundle off** *vt* [+ *person*] 匆忙送走

❑**bundle up** *vt* 捆扎

bungalow ['bʌŋgələu] *n* [c] 平房

bungee jumping ['bʌndʒiː'dʒʌmpɪŋ] *n* [u] 蹦极跳

bungle ['bʌŋgl] *vt* 搞糟

bunion ['bʌnjən] *n* [c] 拇囊炎肿

bunk [bʌŋk] *n* [c] (*bed*) 铺位 ♦**to do a bunk** [英:非正式] 逃走

❑**bunk off** [英:非正式] **I** *vi* (*from school, work*) 擅自走掉 **II** *vt* [+ *school, work*] 擅自离开

bunk beds *n* [*pl*] 双层床

bunker ['bʌŋkə(r)] *n* [c] **1** [军] 掩体 **2** [高尔夫] 沙坑 **3** (*coal store*) 煤箱

bunny ['bʌnɪ] [非正式] *n* [c] (*also:* ***bunny rabbit***) 小兔子

buoy [bɔɪ, (美) buːɪ] *n* [c] 浮标

❑**buoy up** *vt* [+ *person*] 鼓舞

buoyant ['bɔɪənt] *adj* **1** (*able to float*) 有浮力的 **2** [商] [+ *economy, market*]

繁荣的; [+ *prices, currency*] 上涨的 **3** [+ *person, mood*] 愉快的

burden ['bəːdn] **I** *n* [c] **1** (*responsibility, worry*) 负担 **2** [正式] (*load*) 负荷 **II** *vt* ♦**to burden sb with** [+ *problem, news*] 使某人负担某事 ♦**to be a burden on sb** 成为某人的累赘

bureau ['bjuərəu] (*pl* **bureaux** *or* **bureaus**) *n* [c] **1** (*office*) (*for travel, information etc*) 办事处 **2** [英] (*writing desk*) 书桌 **3** [美] (*chest of drawers*) 五斗橱

bureaucracy [bjuə'rɔkrəsɪ] *n* [c] **1** [通常贬] 官僚作风 **2** (*system*) 官僚体系

bureaucrat ['bjuərəkræt] [通常贬] *n* [c] 官僚

bureaux ['bjuərəuz] *n* [*pl*] *of* **bureau**

burger ['bəːgə(r)] *n* [c] 汉堡包

burglar ['bəːglə(r)] *n* [c] 窃贼 📖 用法参见 **thief**

burglar alarm *n* [c] 防盗铃

burglary ['bəːglərɪ] *n* **1** [c] (*act*) 盗窃 **2** [u] (*crime*) 盗窃罪

burial ['bɛrɪəl] *n* [c/u] 葬礼

burn [bəːn] (*pt, pp* **burned** *or* [英] **burnt**) **I** *vt* **1** [+ *papers etc*] 焚烧 **2** [+ *fuel*] 燃烧 **3** [+ *toast, rice*] 烧焦 **II** *vi* **1** [*fire, flame* +] 燃烧 **2** [*house, car* +] 烧着 **3** [*food* +] 烧煳了 **4** [*person, skin* +] (*in sun*) 晒伤 **5** (*sting*) [*eyes, throat* +] 灼痛 **III** *n* [c] 烧伤 ♦**I've burnt myself!** 我把自己烫伤了！ ♦**the cigarette burnt a hole in her dress** 香烟在她的连衣裙上烫了个洞 ♦**to be burning with impatience/ambition** 充满极度的不耐烦/野心

❑**burn down I** *vt* [+ *house etc*] 烧毁 **II** *vi* [*house etc* +] 烧毁

❑**burn out** *vi* [*writer etc* +] 精疲力竭 ♦**to burn oneself out** 累垮自己

❑**burn up I** *vi* [*spacecraft* +] 烧毁 **II** *vt* [+ *fuel, energy*] 消耗

burning ['bəːnɪŋ] *adj* **1** [+ *house, car*] 着火的 **2** (*also:* **burning hot**) [+ *sand, desert*] 灼热的 **3** [+ *ambition, desire*] 强烈的 **4** [+ *issue, question*] 激烈的

burnt [bəːnt] *pt, pp of* **burn**

burp [bəːp] [非正式] **I** *n* [c] 打嗝声 **II** *vi* 打嗝

burrow ['bʌrəu] **I** *n* [c] [*of rabbit etc*] 地洞 **II** *vi* **1** (*dig*) 打洞 **2** (*rummage*) 搜寻

burst [bəːst] (*pt, pp* **burst**) **I** *vt* **1** [+ *bag, balloon etc*] 爆炸 **2** [*river* + *banks etc*] 溃决 **II** *vi* [*pipe, tyre* +] 爆裂 **III** *n* [c] [*of gunfire, applause, laughter*] 一阵 ♦**to burst into flames** 突然着火 ♦**to burst into tears** 突然大哭起来 ♦**to burst out laughing** 突然大笑起来 ♦**to be bursting with** (*full of*) 挤满; [+ *pride, curiosity*] 充满 ♦**to be bursting to do sth** [非正式] 急于做某事 ♦**to burst open** [*door etc* +] 猛然打开 ♦**a burst of energy/activity** 一股劲/一阵行动 ♦**a burst pipe** 破裂的水管 ♦**a burst blood vessel** 爆裂的血管

❑**burst in on** *vt* [不可拆分] [+ *person*] 突然出现

❑**burst into** *vt* [不可拆分] [+ *room etc*] 闯入

❑**burst out of** *vt* [不可拆分] [+ *room etc*] 冲出

bury ['bɛrɪ] *vt* **1** (*in ground*) 掩埋 **2** [+ *dead person*] 埋葬 **3** (喻) (*under rubble, debris*) 埋 ♦**to bury oneself in one's work** 埋头工作 ♦**to bury one's face in one's hands** 双手掩面 ♦**to bury one's head in the sand** 逃避现实 ♦**to bury the hatchet** 言归于好

bus [bʌs] *n* [c] 公共汽车

bus driver *n* [c] 公共汽车司机

bush [buʃ] *n* **1** [c] (*plant*) 灌木 **2** [u] (*scrubland*) 荒野 ♦**to beat about the bush** 拐弯抹角

bushy ['buʃɪ] *adj* **1** [+ *tail, hair, eyebrows*] 浓密的 **2** [+ *plant*] 茂密的

busily ['bɪzɪlɪ] *adv* 忙碌地

✪**business** ['bɪznɪs] *n* **1** [u/s] (*matter, question*) 事情 ◊ *I've some important business to discuss.* 我有重要事情要进行讨论。**2** [c] (*firm*) 公司 ◊ *a small business* 一家小公司 **3** [u] (*occupation*) 商业 ◊ *a career in business* 从商生涯 **4** [u] (*trade*) 生意 ◊ *Companies would lose business.* 公司生意将下滑。♦**to be away on business** 出差 ♦**he's in the insurance/transport business** 他在做保险/运输业务 ♦**to do business with sb** 和某人做生意

♦ **to go out of business** 破产 ♦ **to get down to business** 开始干正事 ♦ **to make it one's business to do sth** 主动承担办某事 ♦ **he means business** [非正式] 他是认真的 ♦ **to have no business doing sth** 无权做某事 ♦ **it's none of your business** 别多管闲事 ♦ **that's my business** 那是我自己的事

business class (*on aircraft*) **I** *n* [U] 公务舱 **II** *adv* 乘公务舱

businesslike ['bɪznɪslaɪk] *adj* 高效率的

businessman ['bɪznɪsmən] (*pl* **businessmen**) *n* [C] 商人

business trip *n* [C] 出差

businesswoman ['bɪznɪswumən] (*pl* **businesswomen**) *n* [C] 女商人

busker ['bʌskə(r)] [英] *n* [C] **1** (*singer*) 街头艺人 **2** (*musician*) 街头音乐家

> **BUSKER**
> **buskers** 指在街上或其他公共场所演奏乐器或歌唱的街头艺人。住在英美城市里的人可以经常得到来自他们的娱乐。过路人可以停下来听，然后在他们放在身边地上的帽子或琴盒里放上些零钱。**buskers** 还有可能跳上你所乘坐的火车或公共汽车，为你演奏几站地。

bus pass *n* [C] 公交车通票

bus shelter *n* [C] 公交车候车亭

bus station *n* [C] 公共汽车车站

bus stop *n* [C] 公共汽车站

bust [bʌst] **I** *vt* **1** [非正式] (*break*) 打破 **2** [非正式] (*arrest*) 逮捕 **II** *n* [C] **1** (*breasts*) 胸部 **2** (*sculpture*) 胸像 **III** *adj* [非正式] (*broken*) 坏 ♦ **to go bust** [非正式] [*company* +] 破产

bustle ['bʌsl] **I** *vi* [*person* +] 忙碌 **II** *n* [U] (*activity*) 繁忙

bustling ['bʌslɪŋ] *adj* [+ *town, place*] 喧嚷的 ♦ **to be bustling with people/activity** 到处是人群/活动

busy ['bɪzɪ] **I** *adj* **1** [+ *person*] 忙的 **2** [+ *shop, street*] 繁忙的 **3** [+ *schedule, time, day*] 忙碌的 **4** [尤美：通信] [+ *line*] 占线的 [英 = **engaged**] **II** *vt* ♦ **to busy oneself (with sth)** 忙于做（某事）♦ **he's a very busy man** 他是个大忙人 ♦ **I'm busy** 我正忙着呢

busy signal [美] *n* [C] 忙音 [英 = **engaged tone**]

✪ **but**

KEYWORD

[bʌt]

I

1 *conj* (*yet, however*) 但是 ♦ **I'd love to come, but I'm busy** 我想来，但是有事 ♦ **he may not be very bright, but he is hard-working** 他可能不是很聪明，但很努力 ♦ **but then** 不过 ♦ **she isn't English but American** 她不是英国人而是美国人 ♦ **enjoyable but tiring** 很开心但也很累 ♦ **not only ... but also** 不但…而且

2 (*showing disagreement, surprise etc*) ♦ **but that's far too expensive!** 但是那太贵了！ ♦ **but it does work!** 但那确实奏效！

II *prep* (*apart from, except*) 除了 ♦ **nothing but** 仅仅 ♦ **anything but** 决不 ♦ **they've got no-one but themselves to blame** 他们只有责备自己 ♦ **who but ...?** 除了…还有谁？

III *adv*

1 (*just, only*) 只 ♦ **to name but two** 只提两个 ♦ **had I but known** 要是我知道的话 ♦ **I can but try** 我只能试一下 ♦ **you cannot (help) but be impressed** 你不能不产生深刻印象 ♦ **she's but a child** 她只不过是个孩子

2 ♦ **but for** (*without*) 若不是；(*except for*) 除了 ♦ **but for his help/him, we wouldn't have finished the job** 没有他的帮助/他，我们还没有完成工作呢 ♦ **the box was empty but for a small piece of paper** 除了一张小纸片外，盒子里空空如也

> **but** 主要用作连词。*I was going to stay till tomorrow but I've changed my mind.* **however** 主要用作副词，多用于书面语。*Most of the crops failed. The cotton did quite well, however.*

butcher ['butʃə(r)] **I** *n* [c] **1** (*person*) 肉商 **2** (*tyrant, murderer*) 刽子手 **3** (*shop*) (*also:* ***butcher's***) 肉铺 **II** *vt* **1** [+ *prisoners, children*] 屠杀 **2** [+ *meat, animal*] 屠宰

butler ['bʌtlə(r)] *n* [c] 男管家

butt [bʌt] **I** *n* [c] **1** [*of gun, tool*] 柄 **2** [*of cigarette*] 烟蒂 **3** [英](喻)(*target*) [*of teasing, criticism etc*] 对象 **4** (*barrel*) 大桶 **5** [美:非正式](*backside*) 屁股 **II** *vt* [*goat, person* +] 顶撞

❑**butt in** *vi* (*interrupt*) 插嘴

butter ['bʌtə(r)] **I** *n* [U] 黄油 **II** *vt* [+ *bread*] 涂黄油于

buttercup ['bʌtəkʌp] *n* [c] 金凤花

butterfly ['bʌtəflaɪ] *n* **1** [c] (*insect*) 蝴蝶 **2** [U] (*also:* ***the butterfly***) (*in swimming*) 蝶泳

buttocks ['bʌtəks] *n* [*pl*] 臀部

button ['bʌtn] **I** *n* [c] **1** (*on clothes*) 钮扣 **2** (*on machine*) 按钮 **3** [美](*badge*) 徽章 [英=**badge**] ♦**on the button** [非正式] 准确 **II** *vt* (*also:* ***button up***) 扣钮扣

✪**buy** [baɪ] (*pt, pp* **bought**) **I** *vt* **1** 买 **2** [商][+ *company*] 收购 **3** (喻)[+ *time, freedom*] 赢得 ◊ *It was a risky operation, but might buy more time.* 这样做有风险，但可能会赢得更多的时间。**II** *n* [c] (*purchase*) 所买之物 ◊ *Other good buys include cameras and toys.* 其他买来的好东西还包括相机和玩具。♦**to buy sb sth** 给某人买某物 ♦**to buy sb a drink** 请某人喝一杯 ♦**to buy sth from a shop** 从店里购买某物 ♦**to buy sth off** *or* **from sb** 从某人处购买某物

❑**buy back** *vt* 回买

❑**buy in** [英] *vt* [+ *goods*] 买进

❑**buy into** [英:商] *vt* [不可拆分] 入股

❑**buy off** *vt* (*bribe*) 贿赂

❑**buy out** *vt* [+ *business partner*] 全部通吃

❑**buy up** *vt* [+ *land, property*] 全部买进

buyer ['baɪə(r)] *n* [c] **1** (*purchaser*) 买主 **2** (*for store*) 采购员

buzz [bʌz] **I** *n* **1** [c] (*noise*) 嗡嗡声 **2** [非正式](*phone call*) ♦**to give sb a buzz** 给某人打电话 **II** *vi* [*insect, machine* +] 发出嗡嗡声 **III** *vt* [非正式](*call on intercom etc*) 用蜂音器传呼 ♦**to be buzzing with activity/conversation** 充斥着活动/谈论

❑**buzz off** [尤英:非正式] *vi* 走开

buzzer ['bʌzə(r)] *n* [c] 蜂鸣器

✪ **by**

KEYWORD

[baɪ]

I *prep*

1 (*referring to cause, agent*) 被 ♦**he was struck by a football** 他被足球打中了 ♦**a painting by Picasso** 毕加索的画 ♦**surrounded by a fence** 由篱笆围着

2 (*referring to method, manner, means*) ♦**by bus/car/train** 乘公共汽车/汽车/火车 ♦**to pay by cheque** 以支票支付 ♦**she grabbed him by the arm** 她抓住了他的胳膊 ♦**by moonlight/candlelight** 借助月光/烛光 ♦**by saving hard, you can …** 通过使劲攒钱，你能…

3 (*via, through*) 经由 ♦**he came in by the back door** 他从后门进来

4 (*close to, beside*) 靠近 ♦**he was standing by the door** 他正站在门边 ♦**the house by the river** 河边的房子

5 (*past*) 经过 ♦**she rushed by me** 她急匆匆地从我身边过去

6 (*with times, dates, years*) 以前 ♦**by 4 o'clock** 4点以前 ♦**by April 7** 4月7号以前 ♦**by 2005** 2005年以前 ♦**by this time tomorrow** 到明天这个时候 ♦**by the time I got here** 到我到这儿的时候 ♦**by now/then** 到如今/那时

7 (*during*) ♦**by day/night** 在白天/晚上

8 (*specifying number, quantity, rate*) 按 ♦**sold by the kilo/metre** 按公斤/米卖 ♦**paid by the hour** 按小时付酬 ♦**parcels arrived by the dozen** 按打发来的包裹 ♦**little by little, bit by bit** 一点一点地

9 (*specifying degree of change*) 相差 ♦**crime has increased by 10 per cent** 犯罪率上升了10%

10 (*in measurements*) ♦**a room 3 metres by 4** 一间长3米宽4米的房间 ♦**it's broader by a metre**

宽了1米
11 [数] ♦**to divide/multiply by 3** 被3除/乘
12 *(according to)* ♦**by law** 按照法律 ♦**to play by the rules** 按规则玩游戏 ♦**it's all right by me** 对我来说没问题 ♦**by profession/birth/nature** 就职业/祖籍/天性而言
13 ♦**by myself/himself** *etc* *(unaided)* 我/他等自己; *(alone)* 我/他等单独
II *adv*
1 *see* **go by, pass by** *etc*
2 ♦**by and by** *(in the past)* 不久以后; *(in the future)* 不久
3 ♦**by and large** 大体说来

> 如果你说*I'll be home by ten o'clock*，你的意思是你要在10点或10点以前到家，但绝不会晚于10点。如果你说*I'll be home before ten o'clock*，你的意思是10点是你到家的最晚时间，你可能9点以前就到家了。如果你说*I'll be at home until 10 o'clock*，你的意思是10点以前你会在家里，但10点以后就不在了。当我们谈论某人写了一本书或剧本、导演了一部电影、作了一部乐曲或画了一幅画时，我们说一部作品是**by**那个人或是**written by**那个人。*...three books by Jane Austen...a collection of piano pieces by Mozart...a painting by Picasso* 当我们谈到某人给你写信或留言时，我们说信或留言是**from**那个人。*He received a letter from his brother...It's a message from your boss.*

bye(-bye) ['baɪ('baɪ)] [非正式] *int* 再见
by-election ['baɪɪlɛkʃən] [英] *n* [c] 补缺选举
bypass ['baɪpɑːs] **I** *n* [c] **1** [汽车] 旁道 **2** [医] *(operation)* 分流术 **II** *vt*
1 [+ *town*] [*road, driver* +] 绕过
2 *(ignore)* [+ *person, problem etc*] 避开
by-product ['baɪprɔdʌkt] *n* [c] **1** [*of industrial process*] 副产品 **2** [*of situation*] 附带结果
byte [baɪt] [计算机] *n* [c] 字节

Cc

C¹, c [siː] *n* [c/u] **1** (*letter*) 英语的第三个字母 **2** [教育, 大学] (*mark*) 中等
C² [siː] **I** *n* [c/u] [音] C大调音阶中的第一音 **II** *abbr* (= ***Celsius, centigrade***) 摄氏
c. *abbr* **1** (= ***circa***) 大约 **2** (= ***cent(s)***) 分
cab [kæb] *n* [c] **1** (*taxi*) 出租车 **2** [*of truck, tractor, train*] 驾驶室 **3** (*horse-drawn*) 轻便两轮马车
cabaret ['kæbəreɪ] **I** *n* **1** [u] (*live entertainment*) 餐馆、夜总会里的歌舞表演 **2** [c] (*show*) 餐馆、夜总会里的歌舞表演 **II** *cpd* [复合词] [+ *act, singer*] 餐馆、夜总会里的歌舞表演的
cabbage ['kæbɪdʒ] *n* [c/u] 卷心菜
cabin ['kæbɪn] *n* [c] **1** (*on ship*) 船舱 **2** (*on plane*) 机舱 **3** (*house*) 小木屋
cabin crew *n* [c] 机组人员
cabinet ['kæbɪnɪt] *n* [c] **1** (*cupboard*) 贮藏橱; (*display cabinet*) 陈列柜 **2** [政治] 内阁
cabinet minister *n* [c] 内阁大臣
cable ['keɪbl] **I** *n* **1** [c/u] (*rope*) 缆绳 **2** [c/u] [电子] 电缆 **3** [u] (*also: **cable television***) 有线电视 **II** *vt* **1** [+ *person*] 发电报; [+ *message, money*] 用电报拍发 **2** [+ *city, building*] (*for cable TV*) 配备电缆
cable car ['keɪblkɑː(r)] *n* [c] 缆车
cable television *n* [u] 有线电视
cactus ['kæktəs] (*pl* **cactuses** *or* **cacti** ['kæktaɪ]) *n* [c] 仙人掌
café ['kæfeɪ] *n* [c] 咖啡店
cafeteria [kæfɪ'tɪərɪə] *n* [c] 自助餐厅
caffeine ['kæfiːn] *n* [u] 咖啡因
cage [keɪdʒ] *n* [c] 笼子
cagoule [kə'guːl] *n* [c] 连帽防雨长夹克衫
cake [keɪk] *n* **1** [c/u] (*sponge, fruitcake etc*) (*large*) 蛋糕; (*small*) 糕点 **2** [c] [*of soap*] 块 **3** [c] (*savoury*) ♦ **crab/rice/potato cake** 蟹/米/土豆饼 ♦ **it's a piece of cake** [非正式] 太容易了 ♦ **he wants to have his cake and eat it** 他想两者兼得
calcium ['kælsɪəm] *n* [u] 钙
calculate ['kælkjuleɪt] *vt* **1** (*work out*) [+ *number, amount*] 计算 **2** (*estimate*) [+ *effect*] 预测 ♦ **to calculate (that) ...** (*using maths*) 计算…; (*judge*) 判断 **3** ♦ **to be calculated to do sth** 使适合某种目的
calculation [kælkju'leɪʃən] *n* **1** [c/u] [数] 计算 **2** [c/u] (*estimate*) 预测 **3** [u] (*selfishness*) 自私的打算
calculator ['kælkjuleɪtə(r)] *n* [c] 计算器
calendar ['kæləndə(r)] *n* [c] **1** (*showing date*) 日历 **2** (*schedule*) (*for organization*) 日程表; (*for person*) 日程安排 **3** (*system*) 历法
calf [kɑːf] (*pl* **calves**) *n* [c] **1** 小牛 **2** [动] (*elephant*) 幼兽; (*whale*) 崽 **3** [解剖] 腿肚
caliber ['kælɪbə(r)] [美] *n* = **calibre**
calibre (美 **caliber**) ['kælɪbə(r)] *n* **1** [u] [*of person, skill, work*] 质量 **2** [c] [*of gun*] 口径
✪ **call** [kɔːl] **I** *vt* **1** (*name*) 为…取名 ◊ *We called our son Ian.* 我们为儿子取名为伊恩。 **2** (*address as*) 称呼 ◊ *What did you call him?* 你称呼他什么? ◊ *Her name's Elizabeth but everyone calls her Liz.* 她名叫伊丽莎白，但每个人都称呼她莉兹。 **3** (*describe as*) 说成是 ◊ *They called him a traitor.* 他们把他说成是叛徒。 **4** (*shout*) 喊 ◊ *I heard someone calling my name.* 我听见有人大声喊我的名字。 **5** [通信] 打电话 ◊ *Call me when you get home.* 你回家后打电话给我。 **6** (*summon*) [+ *person*] 召唤; [+ *witness*] 传唤 ◊ *I think we should call the doctor.* 我认为我们应该请医生。 ◊ *I was called as an expert witness.* 我被作为专家证人传唤。 **7** (*arrange*) [+ *meeting*] 召集; [+ *strike*] 下令举行 ◊ *He called a press conference.* 他召集了一场记者招待会。 **8** (*announce*) [+ *flight*] 广播 ◊ *They've just called our flight.* 他们刚刚广播我们的班机即将起飞。 **II** *vi* **1** (*shout*) 喊 **2** (*telephone*) 打电话 ◊ *May I ask*

who's calling? 请问您是哪位？ **3** (*also:* ***call in, call round***) 访问 ◊ *Good night. Do call again.* 晚安。请再次光临。◊ *Do call round the college again.* 欢迎再次访问我校。**4** (*stop*) [*ship, train, bus* +] 停靠 **III** *n* **1** [c] (*shout*) [*of person*] 大喊 ◊ *a call for help* 求救声 ◊ *He gave a loud call.* 他大喊了一声。**2** [c] [通信] 电话 ◊ *Were there any calls while I was out?* 我不在时有人打电话来吗？ **3** [c] (*demand*) ♦**call for sth** 对某事的要求 ◊ *MPs renewed their call for electoral reform.* 议员们重申他们对选举改革的要求。**4** [c] [*of bird, animal*] 鸟兽的叫声 **5** [c] (*visit*) 探访 ◊ *The doctor made three calls to sick patients.* 医生3次探访病人。 **6** [c] (*summons*) [*for flight*] 呼叫 ◊ *That's the call for our flight.* 刚刚广播我们的飞机要起飞。**7** [s] (喻) (*lure*) 召唤 ◊ *All his life he had felt the call of the sea.* 他一生中都感到大海的召唤。♦**to be called sth** [*person* +] 被叫某名; [*object* +] 被称为某物 ◊ *She's called Susan.* 她叫苏姗。◊ *A dictionary of synonyms is called a thesaurus.* 同义词字典称为类属词典。♦**who's calling?** [通信] 请问是谁？ ♦**to be on call** [*nurse, doctor* +] 值班 ♦**to make a phone call** 打电话 ♦**a long-distance call** 长途电话 ♦**a local call** 本地电话 ♦**to give sb a call** 打电话给某人 ♦**to pay a call on sb** 拜访某人 ♦**there's not much call for these items** 对这些东西没什么需求 ♦**a call for sb to do sth** 要求某人做某事

❑**call back I** *vi* **1** (*return*) 回来 **2** [通信] 再打电话 **II** *vt* [通信] 给…回电话

❑**call for** *vt* [不可拆分] **1** (*fetch*) [+ *person*] 去接; [+ *parcel*] 去取 ◊ *I'll call for you at seven o'clock.* 我7点来接你。**2** (*demand*) 要求 ◊ *They are calling for your resignation.* 他们要求你辞职。**3** (*require*) 需要 ◊ *Does the situation call for military intervention?* 当前的形势是否需要军事干涉？ ♦**to call for sb to do sth** 要求某人做某事

❑**call in I** *vt* **1** [+ *doctor, expert, police*] 召来 **2** (*request return of*) [+ *loan*] 下令收回; [+ *books*] 要求退回 **II** *vi* 访问

❑**call off** *vt* [+ *deal, event*] 取消

❑**call on** *vt* [不可拆分] (*visit*) 拜访 ♦**to call on sb to do sth** 呼吁某人做某事

❑**call out I** *vi* 叫喊 **II** *vt* **1** (*shout*) 喊 ◊ *He called out my name.* 他喊出我的名字。**2** (*summon*) [+ *police, doctor, fire service*] 召唤 **3** (*order out*) [+ *troops*] 命令

❑**call up** *vt* **1** [军] 征召…入伍 **2** [通信] 给…打电话

❑**call upon** *vt* [不可拆分] = **call on**

callbox ['kɔːlbɔks] [英: 通信] *n* [c] 电话亭

call centre (美 **call center**) *n* [c] [通信] 电话中心

caller ['kɔːlə(r)] *n* [c] **1** (*visitor*) 来访者 **2** [通信] 打电话者 ♦**hold the line, caller!** 请别挂线！

callous ['kæləs] *adj* [+ *person*] 麻木不仁的; [+ *act, attitude*] 冷酷无情的

calm [kɑːm] **I** *adj* **1** [+ *person*] 冷静的; [+ *voice*] 镇静的; [+ *place*] 安宁的 **2** (*not stormy*) [+ *sea*] 平静的; [+ *weather*] 平静无风的 **II** *n* [U/s] (*tranquillity*) 平静 **III** *vt* [+ *person, child, animal*] 使平静; [+ *nerves, fears*] 平息

❑**calm down I** *vt* [+ *person, animal*] 使平静 **II** *vi* [*person* +]平静下来

calmly ['kɑːmlɪ] *adv* [*say, react* +] 平静地

Calor gas® ['kælə(r)-] *n* [U] 罐装煤气

calorie ['kælərɪ] *n* [c] 卡路里

calves [kɑːvz] *n* [*pl*] *of* **calf**

Cambodia [kæm'bəudɪə] *n* 柬埔寨

Cambodian [kæm'bəudɪən] **I** *adj* 柬埔寨的 **II** *n* [c] (*person*) 柬埔寨人

camcorder ['kæmkɔːdə(r)] *n* [c] 摄像放像机

came [keɪm] *pt of* **come**

camel ['kæməl] *n* [c] 骆驼

camera ['kæmərə] *n* [c] **1** [摄影] 照相机 **2** [电影, 电视] 摄影机 ♦**on camera** 在电视摄像机前 ♦**in camera** [法] 在法官的私室里

cameraman ['kæmərəmæn] (*pl* **cameramen**) *n* [c] 摄影师

Cameroon [kæmə'ruːn] *n* 喀麦隆

camomile ['kæməumaɪl] *n* [U] 黄春菊

camouflage ['kæməflɑːʒ] **I** *n* **1** [U] [军] 伪装 **2** [U/S] [动] 保护色 **II** *vt* [军] 伪装

camp [kæmp] **I** *n* **1** [C] (*for refugees, prisoners, soldiers*) 营 **2** [C/U] (*encampment*) 临时居住的帐篷 **3** [C] (*faction*) 阵营 **II** *vi* 扎营 **III** *adj* [非正式] 娘娘腔的 ♦**to go camping** 外出露营

✪ **campaign** [kæm'peɪn] **I** *n* [C] **1** (*for change*) 运动 **2** [军] 战役 **II** *vi* [*pressure group* +] 发起运动 ♦**to campaign for/against sth** 为/反对某事参加运动

campaigner [kæm'peɪnə(r)] *n* [C] 参加活动的人 ♦**campaigner for/against sth** 为提倡/反对某事而参加某事的人

camp bed [英] *n* [C] 折叠床 [美= **cot**]

camper ['kæmpə(r)] *n* [C] **1** (*person*) 野营者 **2** (*also:* ***camper van***) 野营车

campfire ['kæmp'faɪə(r)] *n* [C] 营火

camping ['kæmpɪŋ] *n* [U] 野营

campsite ['kæmpsaɪt] *n* [C] 营地

campus ['kæmpəs] *n* [C] 校园 ♦**to live on campus** 住校

✪ **can**[1] [kæn] **I** *n* [C] **1** (*for food, drinks*) 罐头; (*with lid*) 容器; (*for petrol, oil*) 罐 ◊ *I had to take a can to the garage to get some petrol.* 我不得不带个罐去加油站买汽油。**2** (*contents*) 一听所装的量 **3** (*contents and container*) 一罐 **II** *vt* [+ *food, drink*] 罐装 ♦**to carry the can** [英:非正式] 承担责任

✪ **can**[2]

KEYWORD

[kæn] (*negative* **cannot, can't;** *conditional, pt* **could**) *aux vb*

1 (*be able to*) 能 ♦**can I help you?** (*in shop*) 您要买点儿什么?; (*in general*) 我能帮你吗? ♦**you can do it if you try** 如果试试的话你是能做的 ♦**I can't hear/see anything** 我什么也听/看不见 ♦**I can't remember** 我不记得了 ♦**she can't sleep** 她不能入睡 ♦**you can always try telephoning him at home** 你可以试着往他家里打电话 ♦**as you can imagine ...** 就如你能想像的那样… ♦**how can I ever thank you?** 我该怎么谢你才好呢? ♦**I can't understand why ...** 我不能理解为什么…

2 (*know how to*) 会 ♦**I can swim/drive** 我会游泳/开车 ♦**can you play a musical instrument?** 你会一种乐器吗?

3 (*permission, requests*) 可以 ♦**can I use your phone?** 我可以用你的电话吗? ♦**can you help me?** 你可以帮我一下吗? ♦**can't you leave me alone?** 你就不能让我单独呆一会儿吗? ♦**this cannot be allowed to continue** 不能再这样下去了

4 (*disbelief, puzzlement*) ♦**it can't be true!** 这不可能是真的! ♦**you can't be serious!** 你不是认真的吧! ♦**it can't have been them!** 不可能是他们! ♦**what can he want?** 他究竟想要什么?

5 (*possibility*) 可能 ♦**the illness can last for up to six months** 病情可能持续近6个月 ♦**he can be very unpleasant** 他有时会非常不高兴 ♦**can she have finished already?** 她有可能已经完成了吗? ♦**how can millions of dollars disappear?** 成百万的美金怎么可能消失呢?

can，could 和 **be able to** 都是用来表示某人有能力做某事，后接原形动词。**can** 或 **be able to** 的现在式都可以指现在，但 **can** 更为常用。*They can all read and write... The snake is able to catch small mammals.* **could** 或 **be able to** 的过去式可用来指过去。**will** 或 **shall** 加 **be able to** 则用于表示将来。指在某一特定时间能够做某事，用 **be able to**。*After treatment he was able to return to work.* **can** 和 **could** 用于表示可能性。**could** 指的是某个特定情况下的可能性，而 **can** 则表示一般情况下的可能性。*Many jobs could be lost...Too much salt can be harmful.* 在谈论过去的时候，使用 **could have** 加过去分词形式。*It could have been* *much worse.* 在谈论规则或表示许可的时候，用**can** 表示现在，用**could** 表示过去。*They can leave at any time.* 注意，当表示请求时，**can** 和**could** 两者都可。*Can I have a drink?... Could we put the fire on?* 但表示建议时只能使用**could**。*You could phone her and ask.*

Canada ['kænədə] *n* 加拿大
Canadian [kə'neɪdɪən] **I** *adj* 加拿大的 **II** *n* [c] (*person*) 加拿大人
canal [kə'næl] *n* [c] **1** (*for ships, barges*) 运河 **2** (*for irrigation*) 水渠 **3** [解剖] 管
Canaries [kə'nɛərɪz] *n* [*pl*] ♦**the Canaries** 加那利群岛
canary [kə'nɛərɪ] *n* [c] 金丝雀
Canary Islands *n* [*pl*] ♦**the Canary Islands** 加那利群岛
cancel ['kænsəl] *vt* [+ *meeting, visit, reservation, flight*] 取消; [+ *contract, order*] 撤销; [+ *document*] 废除; [+ *debt*] 注销; [+ *cheque, stamp etc*] 盖销
❑**cancel out** *vt* 抵消 ♦**they cancel each other out** 他们相互抵消
cancellation [kænsə'leɪʃən] *n* **1** [c/u] [*of meeting, visit, flight*] 取消; [*of debt*] 注销 **2** [c] (*cancelled seat, holiday*) 退票
cancer ['kænsə(r)] *n* **1** [c/u] [医] 癌症 **2** [占星术] ♦**Cancer** [u] (*sign*) 巨蟹座 [c] (*person*) 巨蟹座的人 ♦**to be (a) Cancer** 是巨蟹座的人
candidate ['kændɪdeɪt] *n* [c] **1** (*for job*) 候选人 **2** (*in exam*) 报考者 **3** [政治] 候选人 ♦**he's a prime candidate for a heart attack** 他很容易患心脏病
candle ['kændl] *n* [c] 蜡烛 ♦**to burn the candle at both ends** 操劳过度 ♦**he can't hold a candle to you** 他比不上你
candlestick ['kændlstɪk] *n* [c] 烛台
candy ['kændɪ] [美] *n* [c/u] 糖果 ♦**piece of candy** 一块糖果 [英 = **sweet**]
candy bar [美] *n* [c] 条形巧克力
candyfloss ['kændɪflɔs] [英] *n* [u] 棉花糖 [美 = **cotton candy**]
cane [keɪn] **I** *n* **1** [c/u] [植] 茎 **2** [u] (*for furniture, baskets*) 藤条 **3** [c] (*stick*) 手杖 **II** *vt* [教育] 用笞杖打 ♦**to get or be given the cane** [教育] 被笞
canister ['kænɪstə(r)] *n* [c] [*of gas, chemicals*] 霰弹筒; (*for tea, sugar*) 罐; [电影, 摄影] 匣子
cannabis ['kænəbɪs] *n* [u] 大麻
canned [kænd] *adj* **1** [+ *fruit, vegetables*] 罐装的 **2** [非正式] [+ *music, laughter*] 预先录制的
cannon ['kænən] (*pl* **cannon** *or* **cannons**) *n* [c] **1** (*artillery piece*) 大炮 **2** (*automatic gun*) 机关炮
cannot ['kænɔt] = **can not**
canoe [kə'nuː] **I** *n* [c] 独木船 **II** *vi* ♦**to go canoeing** 去划独木船
canoeing [kə'nuːɪŋ] *n* [u] 划独木船
canon ['kænən] *n* [c] **1** (*clergyman*) 大教堂教士 **2** [正式] (*rule*) 准则
can opener [-'əupnə(r)] *n* [c] 开罐器
can't [kɑːnt] = **can not**
canteen [kæn'tiːn] *n* [c] **1** (*in workplace, school*) 食堂 **2** [英] [*for cutlery*] 餐具柜 **3** (*flask*) 水壶
canter ['kæntə(r)] **I** *vi* [*horse* +] 慢跑 **II** *n* [c] 慢跑
Cantonese [kæntɔ'niːz] **I** *adj* 广东的 **II** *n* **1** [c] (*person*) 广东人 **2** [u] (*language*) 广东话
canvas ['kænvəs] *n* **1** [u] (*fabric*) 帆布 **2** [c] (*painting*) 油画 ♦**under canvas** (*in a tent*) 在帐篷里
canvass ['kænvəs] **I** *vi* (*seeking support*) 游说 **II** *vt* **1** (*for research*) [+ *opinions, views, people*] 征求意见 **2** (*seeking support*) [+ *electorate*] 拉选票 ♦**to canvass for sb** 为某人拉选票 ♦**to canvass opinion** 征求意见
canyon ['kænjən] *n* [c] 峡谷
cap [kæp] **I** *n* [c] **1** (*hat*) 帽 **2** (*top*) [*of pen*] 套子; [*of bottle*] 盖 **3** (*for toy gun*) 火药帽 **4** (*for swimming*) 游泳帽 **5** [英: 足球, 板球] 国家运动队队员 **II** *vt* **1** (*complete*) 达到顶峰 **2** [政治] (*put limit on*) 给…定限额 **3** [英: 足球, 板球] 选…入国家队 **4** [+ *tooth*] 包 ♦**capped with sth** 被某物覆盖 ♦**and to cap it all, he said ...** 更有甚者，他说… ♦**to have a tooth capped** 包牙
capability [keɪpə'bɪlɪtɪ] *n* [c/u] **1** (*competence*) 能力 **2** (*military, nuclear etc*) 能力 ♦**to be beyond**

sb's capabilities 超出某人的能力范围 ♦**to have the capability to do sth** 有做某事的能力;［军］有做某事的能力

capable ['keɪpəbl] *adj* (*able*) [+ *person*] 有能力的 ♦**to be capable of sth** [+ *speed, output*] 有做某事的能力 ♦**to be capable of doing sth** 有做某事的能力

capacity [kə'pæsɪtɪ] *n* **1** [s] [*of container, ship*] 容量; [*of stadium, theatre*] 可容纳人数; [*of lift*] 可装载人数 **2** [U] [*of factory*] 产量 **3** [C/U] (*capability*) 能力 **4** [s] (*role*) 职位 ♦**filled to capacity** 没有位置 ♦**a capacity crowd** 座无虚席 ♦**to work at full capacity** 以最大限度工作 ♦**capacity for sth/to do sth** 某事/做某事的能力 ♦**in his capacity as** 以他作为…的身份 ♦**in an advisory capacity** 以顾问的身份

cape [keɪp] *n* [C] **1** (*headland*) 海角 **2** (*cloak*) 斗篷 **3** ♦**the Cape** 好望角

caper ['keɪpə(r)] *n* [C] **1**［烹饪］续随子花蕾 **2**［非正式］(*frolic*) 恶作剧;［贬］胡闹

✪ **capital** ['kæpɪtl] **I** *n* **1** [C] (*city*) 首都 ◊ *the Danish capital, Copenhagen* 丹麦的首都，哥本哈根 **2** [U] (*money*) 资本 ◊ *He provided most of the capital.* 他提供了大部分的资本。 **3** [C] (*also: **capital letter***) 大写字母 **II** *adj*［法］[+ *offence, crime*] 死刑 ♦**in capitals** 用大写字母 ◊ *The name was written in capitals.* 名字是用大写的。♦**capital R/L** *etc* 大写字母 R / L{等}

capitalism ['kæpɪtəlɪzəm] *n* [U] 资本主义

capitalist ['kæpɪtəlɪst] **I** *adj* [+ *system, society*] 资本主义的 **II** *n* [C] 资本家

capitalize ['kæpɪtəlaɪz] **I** *vi* ♦**to capitalize on sth** 利用某事 **II** *vt*［商］为…提供资本

capital punishment *n* [U] 死刑

Capricorn ['kæprɪkɔːn] *n* **1** [U] (*sign*) 摩羯座 **2** [C] (*person*) 摩羯座的人 ♦**I'm (a) Capricorn** 我是摩羯座的

caps [kæps] *n* [*pl*] *abbr* (= ***capital letters***) 大写字母

capsize [kæp'saɪz] **I** *vt* 使倾覆 **II** *vi* 倾覆

capsule ['kæpsjuːl] *n* [C] **1** [*of medicine*] 胶囊 **2** (*spacecraft*) 太空舱

captain ['kæptɪn] **I** *n* [C] **1** [*of ship*] 船长 **2** [*of plane*] 机长 **3** [*of team*] 队长 **4** (*in army*) 上尉 **5** (*in navy*) 上校 **6**［美:警察］副巡官 **II** *vt* **1** [+ *ship*] 当船长 **2** [+ *team*] 当队长

caption ['kæpʃən] *n* [C] 标题

captivity [kæp'tɪvɪtɪ] *n* [U] 监禁 ♦**in captivity** 被监禁

capture ['kæptʃə(r)] **I** *vt* **1** (*catch*) [+ *animal*] 捕获; [+ *person*] 俘虏 **2** [+ *town, country*] 攻占 **3**［商］[+ *share of market*] 占有 **4** (*reflect*) [+ *mood, atmosphere, spirit*] 反映 **II** *n* [U] **1** [*of person*] 被捕 **2** [*of town*] 占领 ♦**to capture sb's imagination** 使某人为之神往

✪ **car** [kɑː(r)] *n* [C] **1**［汽车］汽车 **2**［美:铁路］车厢［英 = **carriage, coach**］♦**by car** 乘汽车 ♦**the dining/buffet car**［英:铁路］餐车

carafe [kə'ræf] *n* [C] [*of wine, water*] 精美的盛葡萄酒或水的玻璃容器

caramel ['kærəməl]［烹饪］*n* **1** [C] (*piece of confectionery*) 太妃糖 **2** [U] (*burnt sugar*) 焦糖

carat ['kærət] *n* [C] **1** [*of diamond*] 克拉 **2** [*of gold*] 开 ♦**18-carat gold** 18开金

caravan ['kærəvæn] *n* [C] **1**［英］(*vehicle*) 活动住房［美 = **trailer**］**2** (*in desert*) 旅行队

caravan site［英］*n* [C] 活动住房停放处

carbohydrate [kɑːbəu'haɪdreɪt] *n* [C/U] 碳水化合物

carbon ['kɑːbən] *n* [U] 碳

carbonated ['kɑːbəneɪtɪd] *adj* [+ *drink*] 带气的

carbon dioxide [-daɪ'ɔksaɪd] *n* [U] 二氧化碳

carbon monoxide [-mɔ'nɔksaɪd] *n* [U] 一氧化碳

car boot sale［英］*n* [C] 将不要的物品放在汽车行李箱中出售

carburettor (美 **carburetor**) [kɑːbju'rɛtə(r)] *n* [C] 汽化器

card [kɑːd] *n* **1** [C] (*record card, index card etc*) 卡片 **2** [C] (*also: **playing***

card) 扑克牌 3 [c] (*greetings card*) 贺卡 4 [c] (*also:* **business card**) 名片 5 [c] (*bank card, credit card etc*) 信用卡 6 [c] (*membership card*) 会员卡 7 [u] (*material*) 厚纸板 ♦**to play cards** 打牌

cardboard ['kɑːdbɔːd] *n* [u] 硬纸板

card game *n* [c] 纸牌游戏

cardigan ['kɑːdɪgən] *n* [c] 开襟毛衣

cardinal ['kɑːdɪnl] **I** *adj* [+ *rule, principle*] 基本的 **II** *n* [c] [宗] 红衣主教

✪**care** [kɛə(r)] **I** *n* 1 [u] (*attention*) 照顾 ◊ *She needed a lot of care at home.* 她在家需要不少照顾。2 [c] (*worry*) 烦恼 **II** *vi* 关心 ♦**with care** 小心 ♦**in sb's care** 由某人照顾 ♦**take care!** (*saying goodbye*) 慢走！ ♦**to take care to do sth** 确保做某事 ♦**to take care of sb** 照顾某人 ♦**to take care of sth** [+ *possession, clothes*] 保管某物; [+ *problem, situation*] 处理某物 ♦**to be in care** [英] 由福利院抚养 ♦**the child has been taken into care** 这个孩子被送入福利院抚养 ♦**not to have a care in the world** 无忧无虑 ♦**would you care to join us?** [正式] 你想和我们一起去吗？ ♦**would you care for some tea?** 你想喝点茶吗？ ♦**I don't care for it/him** [过时] 我不喜欢它/他 ♦**I don't care to remember** (*choose*) 我不想去记住 ♦**"care of ...", "in care of"** [美] (*on letter*) "由…转交" ♦**I don't care** 我不在乎 ♦**who cares!** [非正式] 谁管呢！ ♦**I couldn't care less,** [美: 非正式] **I could care less** 我才不在乎呢

❑**care about** *vt* [不可拆分] [+ *person, thing, idea*] 关心

❑**care for** *vt* [不可拆分] 1 (*look after*) 照顾 2 (*like*) 喜欢

career [kə'rɪə(r)] **I** *n* [c] 1 (*job, profession*) 事业 2 (*working life*) 生涯 **II** *vi* ♦**to career off a road/into a tree** 冲出路面/撞到树上 ♦**his school/university career** 他的学校/大学生涯

carefree ['kɛəfriː] *adj* [+ *person*] 无忧无虑的; [+ *period*] 轻松愉快的

careful ['kɛəful] *adj* 1 (*cautious*) 小心的 2 (*thorough*) [+ *work, thought, analysis*] 仔细的 ♦**(be) careful!** 小心！ ♦**to be careful with sth** [+ *money*] 谨慎地使用某物; [+ *fragile object*] 小心对待某物 ♦**to be careful (not) to do sth** 小心（别）做某事

carefully ['kɛəfəlɪ] *adv* 1 (*cautiously*) 小心地 2 (*methodically*) 用心地

caregiver ['kɛə'gɪvə(r)] [美] *n* [c] 照顾者 [英 = **carer**]

careless ['kɛəlɪs] *adj* (*negligent*) [+ *person, worker*] 粗心的; [+ *driving*] 疏忽的; [+ *mistake*] 疏忽造成的 ♦**how careless of me!** 我真是太不小心了！ ♦**it was careless of him to let the dog out** 他真不当心，把狗放了出去 ♦**to be careless with sth** [+ *money, resources*] 对某物很随便 ♦**to be careless of sth** [正式] (*heedless*) 不顾某物

carelessness ['kɛəlɪsnɪs] *n* [u] (*negligence*) 粗心大意

carer ['kɛərə(r)] [英] *n* [c] 照顾者 [美 = **caregiver, caretaker**]

caress [kə'rɛs] **I** *vt* 爱抚 **II** *n* [c] 爱抚

caretaker ['kɛəteɪkə(r)] *n* [c] 1 [英] [*of building*] 看门人 [美 = **janitor**] 2 [美] [*of person*] 照顾者 [英 = **carer**]

car ferry ['kɑːfɛrɪ] *n* [c] 汽车渡轮

cargo ['kɑːgəu] (*pl* **cargoes**) *n* [c/u] 货物

car hire [英] *n* [u] 汽车出租 [美 = **car rental**]

Caribbean [kærɪ'biːən] **I** *n* ♦**the Caribbean (Sea)** 加勒比海 **II** *adj* 加勒比海的

caring ['kɛərɪŋ] *adj* [+ *person, society, organization*] 有爱心的

car keys *n* [*pl*] 车钥匙

carnation [kɑː'neɪʃən] *n* [c] 康乃馨

carnival ['kɑːnɪvl] *n* 1 [c/u] (*festival*) 狂欢节 2 [c] [美] 游艺团 [英 = **fair, funfair**]

carol ['kærəl] *n* [c] ♦**(Christmas) carol** 圣诞颂歌

car park [英] *n* [c] 停车场 [美 = **parking lot**]

carpenter ['kɑːpɪntə(r)] *n* [c] 木匠

carpentry ['kɑːpɪntrɪ] *n* [u] 1 木工业 2 (*at school, college etc*) 木工手艺

carpet ['kɑːpɪt] **I** *n* [c] 1 (*fitted*) 地毯; (*rug*) 小地毯 2 [文] [*of leaves, snow*]

厚厚的一层 **II** *vt* [+ *room, stairs*] 铺地毯于

car rental *n* [U] 汽车出租

carriage ['kærɪdʒ] *n* **1** [C] [英:铁路] 车厢 [美 = **car**] **2** [C] (*horse-drawn*) 马车 **3** [U] [商] (*delivery*) 运费 ♦**carriage free** [商] 运费免付 ♦**carriage paid** [商] 运费已付

carriageway ['kærɪdʒweɪ] [英] *n* [C] 车道

carrier ['kærɪə(r)] *n* [C] **1** (*airline*) 航空公司 **2** (*freight company*) 运输公司 **3** [医] 带菌者

carrier bag [英] *n* [C] 购物袋 [美 = **shopping bag**]

carrot ['kærət] *n* **1** [C/U] 胡萝卜 **2** [C] (*incentive*) 诱饵 ♦**a carrot and stick approach** 软硬兼施的做法

✪ **carry** ['kærɪ] **I** *vt* **1** [+ *person*] 抱; (*by hand with the arm down*) 提; (*on one's back*) 背; (*by hand*) 拿 ◊ *She carried her son to the car.* 她把儿子抱到车上。 **2** (*take*) [+ *message*] 传递 ◊ *He was carrying a message of thanks to the President.* 他代人向总统表达了谢意。 **3** (*have on person*) 带着 ◊ *He always carried a gun.* 他总是带着枪。 **4** (*transport*) [*ship, plane* +] 运载 ◊ *The ship could carry seventy passengers.* 这只船能载70名乘客。 **5** (*pass*) [+ *motion, bill*] 通过 ◊ *The motion was carried by 259 votes to 162.* 这项提案以259对162票通过。 **6** (*involve*) [+ *risk, responsibility, penalty*] 带来 **7** [医] [+ *disease, virus*] 传染 ◊ *Rats carry nasty diseases.* 老鼠传染严重的疾病。 **8** (*have*) [+ *picture, slogan*] 刊登 **II** *vi* [*sound* +] 传播 ◊ *Sound seems to carry better in the evening air.* 声音好像在傍晚空气中传播得远些。 ♦**to get carried away** (*by enthusiasm, idea*) 失去自制力 ♦**to carry sth further/to extremes** 进一步做某事/把某事做到极至

❑**carry forward** *vt* (*in book-keeping*) [+ *balance*] 结转

❑**carry off** *vt* ♦**to carry it off** (*succeed*) 顺利完成

❑**carry on I** *vi* **1** (*continue*) 继续 **2** [非正式] (*make a fuss*) 吵吵闹闹 **II** *vt* **1** (*conduct*) [+ *conversation, research*] 继续进行 **2** (*continue*) [+ *work, tradition*] ♦**to carry on with sth** 继续做某事 ♦**to carry on doing sth** 继续做某事

❑**carry out** *vt* [+ *order, instruction*] 执行; [+ *investigation, attack*] 进行; [+ *plan, threat*] 实行

❑**carry over** *vt* 延续

❑**carry through** *vt* 成功地完成

cart [kɑːt] **I** *n* [C] **1** (*for people, goods*) 大车 **2** [美] (*motorized*) 轻便小车 **3** [美] (*also:* ***shopping cart***) 手推车 [英 = **trolley**] **4** (*handcart*) 手推车 **II** *vt* [非正式] ♦**to cart sb/sth away/around** 费力地运送/随身携带某人/某物

carton ['kɑːtən] *n* [C] **1** [尤美] (*cardboard box*) 纸箱 **2** [*of milk, juice, yoghurt*] 容器 **3** [*of cigarettes*] 一条

cartoon [kɑː'tuːn] *n* [C] **1** (*drawing*) 漫画 **2** [英] (*comic strip*) 系列幽默画 **3** (*animated*) 卡通片

cartridge ['kɑːtrɪdʒ] *n* [C] **1** (*for gun*) 弹壳 **2** [*of ink*] (*for pen*) 笔芯; (*for printer*) 墨盒 **3** (*for camera*) 胶卷盒 **4** [术语] 匣子

carve [kɑːv] *vt* **1** [烹饪] [+ *meat*] 把…切片 **2** [+ *wood, stone, figure*] 雕刻; [+ *initials, design*] 刻 ♦**to carve (out) a career for o.s.** 为自己创业

❑**carve up** *vt* [+ *land, property*] 划分

carving ['kɑːvɪŋ] *n* **1** [C] (*object*) 雕刻品 **2** [C/U] (*design*) 雕刻 **3** [U] (*technique*) 雕刻术

car wash *n* [C] 汽车擦洗

✪ **case** [keɪs] *n* **1** [C] (*instance*) 情况 ◊ *This causes problems in some cases.* 这在某些情况下引起了问题。 **2** [C] [*of doctor, social worker, solicitor etc*] 个案 **3** [C] (*before judge, tribunal etc, for investigation*) 案件 ◊ *a murder case* 一桩谋杀案 ◊ *one of Sherlock Holmes's most famous cases* 夏洛克·福尔摩斯最出名的案件之一 **4** [C] (*container*) 盒子 **5** [C] [英] (*also:* ***suitcase***) 行李箱 **6** [C] (*quantity*) [*of wine, whisky*] 一箱 ◊ *a case of champagne* 一箱香槟酒 **7** [C/U] [语言] 格 ♦**lower/upper case** 小/大写 ♦**to have a good case** (*argument*) 有充足的论证 ♦**there's a strong case for/against reform** 有强烈支持/反对改革的理由 ♦**it's a case of trying to get fit** 需

要保持健康 ♦ **in case of** [+ *fire, emergency*] 如果发生 ♦ **in case he comes** 以防万一他会来 ♦ **in case you hadn't noticed** 如果你还没注意到的话 ♦ **in any case** 无论如何 ♦ **just in case** 以防万一 ♦ **in that case** 既然是那样 ♦ **if that is the case** 如果是这样的话 ♦ **a case in point** 恰当的例子

cash [kæʃ] **I** *n* [U] **1** (*notes and coins*) 现金 **2** (*money*) 现款 **II** *vt* [+ *cheque, money order*] 兑现 ♦ **to pay (in) cash** 付现金 ♦ **cash on delivery** 货到交款 ♦ **cash down** 即刻付款

❑ **cash in** *vt* [+ *insurance policy, shares*] 把…兑为现金

❑ **cash in on** *vt* [不可拆分] 从…中获利

cashback ['kæʃbæk] *n* [U] **1** (*discount*) 现金折扣 **2** (*with debit card*) 取现金; (*system*) 现金支取,即在用银行卡付款时要求提取一定数额现金

cash card [英] *n* [C] 提款卡

cash desk [英] *n* [C] 收款台

cash dispenser [英] *n* [C] 自动取款机 [美 = **ATM**]

cashew [kæ'ʃuː] *n* [C] (*also:* ***cashew nut***) 腰果

cashier [kæ'ʃɪə(r)] *n* [C] (*in bank*) 出纳员; (*in shop, restaurant*) 收银员

cashmere ['kæʃmɪə(r)] **I** *n* [U] 山羊绒 **II** *adj* 山羊绒的

cashpoint ['kæʃpɔɪnt] [英] *n* [C] 自动取款机 [美 = **ATM**]

cash register *n* [C] 出纳机

casino [kə'siːnəu] *n* [C] 赌场

casket ['kɑːskɪt] *n* [C] **1** [美] (*coffin*) 棺材 **2** [文] (*for jewellery*) 小盒

casserole ['kæsərəul] **I** *n* [C] **1** (*food*) 沙锅 **2** (*container*) (*also:* ***casserole dish***) 炖锅 **II** *vt* 炖

cassette [kæ'sɛt] *n* [C] 磁带

cassette player *n* [C] 放音机

cassette recorder *n* [C] 录音机

cast [kɑːst] (*pt, pp* **cast**) **I** *vt* **1** (*throw*) [+ *light, shadow*] 投射; [+ *net, fishing line*] 投 **2** [+ *statue*] 铸造 **3** [戏剧] ♦ **to cast sb as sth** 分配某人扮演某个角色 **II** *vi* (*in fishing*) 抛 **III** *n* [C] **1** [戏剧] 演员表 **2** (*mould*) 模子 **3** (*also:* ***plaster cast***) 石膏 ♦ **to cast one's vote** 投票 ♦ **to cast doubt on sth** 对某事产生怀疑 ♦ **to cast a glance** 瞧一瞧 ♦ **to cast an eye** *or* **one's eye(s) over sth** 看一眼某物 ♦ **to cast a spell on sb** [*witch, fairy etc* +] 施咒于某人; (喻) 迷住某人 ♦ **to cast sb/sth into sth** [文] 将某人/某物扔入某处

❑ **cast about, cast around** *vi* ♦ **to cast about for sth** 想方设法寻找

❑ **cast aside** *vt* (*reject*) 抛弃

❑ **cast off I** *vt* [文] (*get rid of*) 抛弃 **II** *vi* **1** [航海] 解船缆 **2** (*in knitting*) 收针

❑ **cast on** (*in knitting*) **I** *vi* 起针 **II** *vt* [+ *stitch*] 开始编织

❑ **cast out** *vt* (*get rid of*) 驱除

caster sugar ['kɑːstə-] (英 **castor sugar**) *n* [U] 精白砂糖

cast-iron ['kɑːstaɪən] *adj* **1** (*metal*) 铸铁制的 **2** (*certain*) [+ *guarantee, alibi*] 无可质疑的

castle ['kɑːsl] *n* [C] **1** 城堡 **2** [国际象棋] 车

castor sugar *n* = **caster sugar**

casual ['kæʒjul] *adj* **1** (*chance*) [+ *remark*] 漫不经心的; [+ *observer*] 偶然的 **2** (*non-permanent*) [+ *work, workers*] 临时的 **3** (*unconcerned*) 随便的 **4** (*informal*) [+ *clothes*] 非正式的 ♦ **casual wear** 便服 ♦ **casual sex** 随便的性行为

casually ['kæʒjulɪ] *adv* **1** (*in a relaxed way*) 漫不经心地 **2** [*dress, say, mention* +] 随便地 **3** (*by chance*) 偶然地

casualty ['kæʒjultɪ] *n* **1** [C] [*of war, accident*] (*injured*) 伤病员; (*dead*) 伤亡人员 **2** [C] [*of situation, event*] 牺牲品 **3** [U] [英] (*in hospital*) 急诊室 [美 = **emergency room, ER**] ♦ **heavy casualties** [军] 伤亡惨重

cat [kæt] *n* [C] **1** 猫 **2** (*lion, tiger etc*) 猫科动物 ♦ **(a game of) cat and mouse** 猫捉老鼠(的游戏)

catalogue (美 **catalog**) ['kætəlɔg] **I** *n* [C] **1** (*for mail order*) 目录 **2** [*of exhibition*] 目录 **3** [*of library*] 书目 **4** (*series*) [*of events, faults*] 一系列 **II** *vt* **1** [+ *objects*] 把…编入目录 **2** [+ *events, faults*] 列举

catalytic converter [kætə'lɪtɪk kən'vəːtə(r)] [汽车] *n* [C] 催化转化器

cataract ['kætərækt] [医] *n* [C] 白内

障

catarrh [kə'tɑː(r)] *n* [U] 黏膜炎

catastrophe [kə'tæstrəfɪ] *n* [C] 大灾难

catch [kætʃ] (*pt, pp* **caught**) **I** *vt* **1** [+ *animal, fish*] 捕获; [+ *thief, criminal*] 抓获 **2** [+ *ball*] 接 **3** [+ *bus, train, plane*] 赶上 **4** (*discover*) [+ *person*] 发现 **5** (*causing damage*) (*strike*) 打; (*snag*) 钩住 **6** (*hear*) 听清楚 **7** [+ *flu, illness*] 染上 ◊ *I caught a cold.* 我感冒了。**II** *vi* (*on branches, door etc*) 被钩住 **III** *n* [C] **1** [*of ball etc*] 接住 **2** [*of fish*] 捕获量 **3** (*downside*) 蹊跷 **4** (*on door, window, bag*) 闩 **5** (*game*) ♦ **to play catch** 玩掷球游戏 ♦ **to catch sb doing sth** 撞见某人做某事 ♦ **to catch sb's attention** *or* **eye** 引起某人的注意 ♦ **to catch the light** 反光 ♦ **to be** *or* **get caught in sth** [+ *storm*] 遇到某事; [+ *traffic jam*] 不巧碰到某事; [+ *crossfire*] 遭到某事

❑ **catch on** *vi* **1** (*understand*) 理解 **2** (*become popular*) 流行起来 ♦ **to catch on to sth** 理解某事

❑ **catch out** [英] *vt* 证明有错

❑ **catch up** *vi* **1** (*walking, driving*) 追上 **2** (*in standard*) 赶上 ♦ **to be caught up in sth** 被卷入某事

❑ **catch up on** *vt* [不可拆分] [+ *work, sleep*] 弥补

❑ **catch up with** *vt* [不可拆分] (*walking, driving, in standard*) 赶上 ♦ **the law caught up with him yesterday** 昨天警方发现他做了违法的事 ♦ **his past caught up with him** 他的过去阴影不散

catching ['kætʃɪŋ] *adj* [非正式] (*infectious*) 传染性的

categorize ['kætɪgəraɪz] *vt* 把…分类 ♦ **to categorize sb/sth as** 认定某人/某事为

category ['kætɪgərɪ] *n* [C] 种类

cater ['keɪtə(r)] *vi* **1** ♦ **to cater for** (*supply food for*) [+ *occasion, wedding, party*] 承办 **2** ♦ **to cater for** *or* (美) **to sth** [+ *sb's needs, tastes*] 迎合某事 **3** ♦ **to cater for** *or* (美) **to sb** [+ *readers, consumers*] 迎合某人

caterer ['keɪtərə(r)] *n* [C] 酒席承办人

catering ['keɪtərɪŋ] *n* [U] **1** (*industry*) 饮食业 **2** (*for specific occasion*) 酒席承办 ♦ **to do the catering** 承办饮食

caterpillar ['kætəpɪlə(r)] *n* [C] 毛虫

cathedral [kə'θiːdrəl] *n* [C] 大教堂

Catholic ['kæθəlɪk] **I** *adj* 天主教的 **II** *n* [C] 天主教徒

Catseye® ['kæts'aɪ] [英:汽车] *n* [C] 反光灯

cattle ['kætl] *n* [*pl*] 牛

catwalk ['kætwɔːk] *n* [C] **1** (*for models*) T 型台 **2** (*bridge*) 狭窄通道

caught [kɔːt] *pt, pp of* **catch**

cauliflower ['kɔlɪflauə(r)] *n* [C/U] 菜花

✪ **cause** [kɔːz] **I** *n* **1** [C] [*of event*] 起因 ◊ *Nobody knew the cause of the explosion.* 没有人知道这次爆炸的起因。**2** [U] (*reason*) 理由 **3** [C] (*aim, principle*) 事业 ◊ *He is sympathetic to our cause.* 他支持我们的事业。**II** *vt* (*produce, lead to*) 导致 ◊ *Does smoking cause cancer?* 吸烟是否导致癌症? ♦ **to have cause for sth/to do sth** 某事/做某事有原因 ♦ **there is no cause for concern** 没有理由担心 ♦ **to cause sb to do sth** 促使某人做某事 ♦ **to cause sth to happen** 导致某事发生

caution ['kɔːʃən] **I** *n* **1** [U] (*prudence*) 谨慎 **2** [C] [英:警察] 警告 **II** *vt* [英:警察] 警告 ♦ **to caution sb that ...** 警告某人… ♦ **to caution sb against sth / against doing sth** 警告某人某事/防止某人做某事

cautious ['kɔːʃəs] *adj* 谨慎的 ♦ **to be cautious about doing sth** 对做某事持谨慎的态度

cave [keɪv] **I** *n* [C] 山洞 **II** *vi* ♦ **to go caving** 探察洞穴

❑ **cave in** *vi* **1** [*roof, wall* +] 倒塌 **2** [*person* +] (*to demands, pressure*) 屈服 ♦ **to cave in to sth/sb** 屈服于某事/某人

caviar(e) ['kævɪɑː(r)] *n* [U] 鱼子酱

cavity ['kævɪtɪ] *n* [C] [正式] (*in wall, tooth*) 洞; (*in body*) 腔

cc *abbr* **1** (= ***cubic centimetre(s)***) 立方厘米 **2** (= ***carbon copy***) 抄送

CD *n abbr* (= ***compact disc***) 激光唱片

CDC [美] *n abbr* (= ***Center for Disease Control***) 疾病控制中心

CD player *n* [c] 激光唱机
CD-ROM [siːdiːˈrɔm] *n abbr* (= ***compact disc read-only memory***) 光盘只读存储器 ♦**on CD-ROM** 光盘版
CDT [美] *abbr* (= ***Central Daylight Time***) 中部夏令时
cease [siːs] [正式] **I** *vi* 停止 **II** *vt* [+ *production, operations, work*] 停止 ♦**to cease doing sth** 停止做某事 ♦**to cease trading** 停止营业 ♦**to cease to do sth** 停止做某事 ♦**he never ceases to amaze me** 他不停地使我惊讶
ceasefire [ˈsiːsfaɪə(r)] *n* [c] 停火
cedar [ˈsiːdə(r)] *n* **1** [c] (*tree*) 雪松 **2** [u] (*wood*) 雪松木材
ceiling [ˈsiːlɪŋ] *n* [c] **1** (*in room*) 天花板 **2** (*limit*) (*on amount, salaries etc*) 最高限度 ♦**to put a ceiling on sth** 给某物制定上限
celebrate [ˈsɛlɪbreɪt] **I** *vt* **1** [+ *success, birthday*] 庆祝 **2** [宗] [+ *mass*] 主持 **II** *vi* 庆祝
celebrated [ˈsɛlɪbreɪtɪd] *adj* [+ *author, film*] 著名的
celebration [sɛlɪˈbreɪʃən] *n* [c/u] 庆祝
celebrity [sɪˈlɛbrɪtɪ] *n* **1** [c] (*person*) 名人 **2** [u] (*fame*) 名望
celery [ˈsɛlərɪ] *n* [u] 芹菜 ♦**a stick of celery** 一根芹菜
cell [sɛl] *n* [c] **1** [生物] 细胞 **2** (*in prison*) 牢房; (*in monastery*) 单人小室 **3** (*group*) 小组
cellar [ˈsɛlə(r)] *n* [c] 地下室; (*for wine*) 酒窖
cellist [ˈtʃɛlɪst] *n* [c] 大提琴手
cello [ˈtʃɛləu] *n* [c] 大提琴
cellophane® [ˈsɛləfeɪn] *n* [u] 玻璃纸
cellphone [ˈsɛlfəun] *n* [c] 手机
cellular phone *n* = **cellphone**
Celsius [ˈsɛlsɪəs] *adj* 摄氏的
Celt [kɛlt, sɛlt] *n* [c] 凯尔特人
Celtic [ˈkɛltɪk, ˈsɛltɪk] *adj* 凯尔特的
cement [səˈmɛnt] **I** *n* [u] **1** (*powder*) 黏固剂 **2** (*concrete*) 水泥 **3** (*glue*) 胶接剂 **II** *vt* **1** (*stick, glue*) 胶合 **2** [+ *relationship, agreement*] 巩固 ◊ *Nothing cements a friendship between countries so much as trade.* 没有什么能像贸易一样如此这般地巩固两国之间的友谊。 **3** [+ *path, floor*] 铺水泥于
cemetery [ˈsɛmɪtrɪ] *n* [c] 墓地
censor [ˈsɛnsə(r)] **I** *vt* [+ *newspaper report, book, play etc*] 审查 **II** *n* [c] 审查员
censorship [ˈsɛnsəʃɪp] *n* [u] [*of book, play etc*] 审查制度; [*of news*] 审查
census [ˈsɛnsəs] *n* [c] 人口调查
cent [sɛnt] *n* [c] 分
centenary [sɛnˈtiːnərɪ] [英] *n* [c] 一百周年 [美 = **centennial**]
centennial [sɛnˈtɛnɪəl] [美] *n* [c] 一百周年 [英 = **centenary**]
center [ˈsɛntə(r)] [美] *n* = **centre**
centigrade [ˈsɛntɪgreɪd] *adj* 摄氏的
centimetre (美 **centimeter**) [ˈsɛntɪmiːtə(r)] *n* [c] 厘米
centipede [ˈsɛntɪpiːd] *n* [c] 蜈蚣
✪ **central** [ˈsɛntrəl] *adj* **1** (*in the centre*) 中心的 ◊ *central London* 伦敦中心 ◊ *The cafe was near Oxford Street, very central for her.* 这家咖啡店靠近牛津街，对她来说很近。 **2** [+ *committee, government*] 中央的 ◊ *the central committee of the Cuban communist party* 古巴共产党中央委员会 **3** (*most important*) [+ *idea, figure*] 最关键的 ◊ *the central character in the film* 电影主角 ◊ *She is the central person in this project.* 她是这个工程中最关键的人物。
Central America *n* 中美洲
central heating *n* [u] 中央供暖系统
central reservation [英: 汽车] *n* [c] 中央分车带 [美 = **median strip**]
✪ **centre** (美 **center**) [ˈsɛntə(r)] **I** *n* **1** [c] [*of circle, line, town, activity*] 中心 ◊ *the centre of the room* 房间当中 ◊ *the city centre* 市中心 ◊ *London is the major international insurance centre.* 伦敦是重要的国际保险中心。 **2** [c] (*building*) 中心 **3** [s] [政治] 中间派 **II** *vt* [排版] (*on page*) 使…居中; [+ *object*] 把…放在中央; [摄影] 将…放在中心位置 ◊ *It's a lovely shot - just a pity it isn't a bit better centred.* 照得很好，可惜有点偏了。; [足球] [+ *ball*] 将…传至球场中央 ♦**to be at the centre of sth** 是某事的关键 ♦**to be the centre of attention** *or* **interest** 注

意{或}兴趣的焦点 ♦**to centre** or **be centred on** (*focus on*) 集中于 ♦**to be centred in London/Rome** 集中于伦敦/罗马

✪**century** ['sɛntjurɪ] *n* [C] **1** (*period*) 世纪 **2** [板球] 百分 ♦**the 21st century** 21 世纪 ♦**in the twenty-first century** 在21 世纪

CEO *n abbr* (= ***chief executive officer***) 首席执行官

ceramic [sɪ'ræmɪk] *adj* 陶瓷的

cereal ['siːrɪəl] *n* **1** [C] (*plant, crop*) 谷类植物 **2** [C/U] (*also:* ***breakfast cereal***) 谷类食品

ceremonial [sɛrɪ'məunɪəl] **I** *adj* 礼节性的 **II** *n* [U] 礼仪

ceremony ['sɛrɪmənɪ] *n* **1** [C] (*event*) 典礼; (*ritual*) 礼仪 **2** [U] (*formality*) 仪式 ♦**to stand on ceremony** 拘于礼节

certain ['səːtən] *adj* **1** (*sure*) [*person* +] 肯定的 **2** [+ *defeat, success, victory, death*] 一定的 **3** (*some*) [+ *times, people, days*] 某些 ♦**to be certain that ...** [*person* +] 肯定… ♦**it is certain that ...** 肯定… ♦**he is certain to be there** 他肯定在那儿 ♦**to make certain that ...** 证实… ♦**to be certain of** 肯定 ♦**a certain coldness/pleasure** 有点冷淡/高兴 ♦**a certain amount of sth** 一定量的某物 ♦**to know sth for certain** 确定某事

certainly ['səːtənlɪ] *adv* **1** (*undoubtedly*) 无疑地 **2** (*of course*) 当然 ♦**certainly not** 绝对不行

certainty ['səːtəntɪ] *n* **1** [U] (*assurance*) 确定 **2** [C/U] (*inevitability*) 必然的事 ♦**all that can be said with certainty is that ...** 惟一确定无疑的是… ♦**there is no certainty that ...** 不能肯定… ♦**there are never any certainties** 从来都没有必然的事

certificate [sə'tɪfɪkɪt] *n* [C] **1** [*of birth, marriage etc*] 证 **2** (*diploma*) 结业证书

certified mail ['səːtɪfaɪd-] [美] *n* [U] 挂号信

certify ['səːtɪfaɪ] *vt* **1** (*attest to*) 证实 ◊ *The National Election Council is supposed to certify the results.* 国家选举委员会应该证实这些结果。**2** (*award diploma to*) 发证书给 **3** (*declare insane*) 确诊为精神失常 ♦**to certify that ...** 证明… ♦**to certify sb dead** 确证某人死亡

cf. *abbr* (= ***confer***) 比较

CFC *n abbr* (= ***chlorofluorocarbon***) 氟氯化炭

ch. *abbr* (= ***chapter***) 章

Chad [tʃæd] *n* 乍得

chain [tʃeɪn] **I** *n* **1** [C/U] 链条 **2** [C] (*piece of jewellery*) 链子 **3** [C] [*of islands, mountains*] 一系列 **4** [C] [*of shops, hotels*] 连锁 **5** [C] [*of events, circumstances*] 一连串 **II** *vt* ♦**to chain sb/sth to sth** 用链条将某人/某物拴在某物上 ♦**in chains** 用枷锁锁着 ♦**to pull the chain** 冲厕所

❑**chain up** *vt* [+ *prisoner, dog*] 用链条拴住

chair [tʃɛə(r)] **I** *n* [C] **1** 椅子; (*armchair*) 扶手椅 **2** [英: 大学] 大学教授职位 **3** (*chairperson*) 主席 **II** *vt* [+ *meeting*] 主持 ♦**the chair** [美] (*electric chair*) 电椅

chair lift ['tʃɛəlɪft] *n* [C] 架空吊椅

chairman ['tʃɛəmən] (*pl* **chairmen**) *n* [C] [*of committee, company, meeting*] 主席

chairperson ['tʃɛəpəːsn] *n* [C] 主席

chairwoman ['tʃɛəwumən] (*pl* **chairwomen**) *n* [C] 女主席

chalet ['ʃæleɪ] *n* [C] 小木屋

chalk [tʃɔːk] **I** *n* **1** [U] 白垩 **2** [C/U] (*for writing*) 粉笔 **II** *vt* 用粉笔写 ♦**a piece of chalk** (*for blackboard*) 一支粉笔

❑**chalk up** *vt* [+ *success, victory*] 取得

challenge ['tʃælɪndʒ] **I** *n* [C/U] **1** (*hard task*) 挑战 **2** (*to authority, ideas*) 异议; (*to rival, competitor*) 挑战 **II** *vt* [+ *authority, right, idea*] 质疑; [+ *rival, competitor*] 向…挑战 ♦**to rise to the challenge** 迎接挑战 ♦**to challenge sb to do sth** 向某人提出挑战做某事 ♦**to challenge sb to a fight/game** 挑战某人打架/比赛

challenging ['tʃælɪndʒɪŋ] *adj* **1** [+ *job, task*] 具有挑战性的 **2** [+ *tone, look etc*] 挑衅的

chamber ['tʃeɪmbə(r)] **I** *n* [C] **1** (*meeting room*) 会议室; (*room for*

particular purpose) 房间 **2** ［政治］(*section of parliament*) 议院
II chambers *n* [*pl*] ［法］(*for judges*) 法官办公室；(*for barristers*) 律师事务所 ♦**chamber of commerce** 商会 ♦**the Upper/Lower Chamber** ［政治］上/下议院

chambermaid ['tʃeɪmbəmeɪd] *n* [c] (*in hotel*) 旅馆女服务员

champagne [ʃæm'peɪn] *n* [c/u] 香槟酒

champion ['tʃæmpɪən] **I** *n* [c] **1** [*of league, contest*] 冠军 **2** [*of cause, person, underdog*] 拥护者 **II** *vt* [+ *cause, principle, person*] (*support*) 支持; (*defend*) 捍卫

championship ['tʃæmpɪənʃɪp] *n* **1** [c] (*contest*) 锦标赛 **2** [s] (*title*) 冠军称号

✪**chance** [tʃɑːns] **I** *n* **1** [c/u] (*likelihood, possibility*) 可能性 **2** [s] (*opportunity*) 机会 **3** [u] (*luck*) 运气 ◊ *It all depends on chance.* 全靠运气。**II** *vt* **1** (*risk*) ♦**to chance it** 碰碰运气 **2** ♦**to chance to do sth** ［正式］碰巧做某事 **III** *adj* [+ *meeting, discovery*] 偶然的 ♦**he hasn't much chance of winning** 他赢的机会不大 ♦**to stand a chance of (doing) sth** 有（做）某事的希望 ♦**there is little chance of his coming** 他来的机会很小 ♦**the chances are that ...** 很可能… ♦**the chance to do sth** 做某事的机会 ◊ *She left before I had the chance to reply.* 她在我有机会回答前就离开了。♦**to give sb the chance to do sth** 给某人做某事的机会 ♦**it's the chance of a lifetime** 一生难得的机会 ♦**to take a chance (on sth)** 冒险（做某事）♦**by chance** 偶然 ♦**by any chance** 有没有可能 ◊ *Are they by any chance related?* 他们是否有可能有联系？
❑**chance (up)on** ［正式］*vt* ［不可拆分］[+ *person, thing*] 偶然遇到

chancellor ['tʃɑːnsələ(r)] *n* [c] **1** (*head of government*) 总理 **2** ［英］[*of university*] 校长 **3** ［英］= **Chancellor of the Exchequer**

Chancellor of the Exchequer ［英］*n* [c] 财政大臣

chandelier [ʃændə'lɪə(r)] *n* [c] 枝形吊灯

✪**change** [tʃeɪndʒ] **I** *vt* **1** (*alter*) 改变 ◊ *You can't change human nature.* 你不可能改变人的本性。**2** (*replace*) [+ *wheel, battery etc*] 换 ◊ *Try changing the battery.* 试试换电池。**3** [+ *trains, buses etc*] 换 ◊ *At Glasgow I changed trains for Greenock.* 我在格拉斯哥换火车去格林诺克。**4** [+ *clothes*] 换 ◊ *I'll just change my shirt.* 我要换衬衫。**5** [+ *bed, sheets*] 更换 **6** [+ *job, address*] 更改 ◊ *His doctor advised him to change his job.* 他的医生建议他换工作。◊ *He has changed his address.* 他更改了他的地址。**7** (*put fresh nappy on*) [+ *baby*] 更换 **8** (*replace*) [+ *nappy*] 换 ◊ *She fed the baby and changed its nappy.* 她给婴儿喂了饭，换了尿布。**9** (*exchange*) [+ *money*] 兑换 ◊ *These places charge exorbitant rates for changing money.* 这些地方对换汇收取极高的手续费。**9** (*transform*) ♦**to change sb/sth into sth** 将某人/某物变成某物; (*by magic*) 将某人/某物变成某物 ◊ *The witch changed him into a frog.* 女巫把他变成了一只青蛙。
II *vi* **1** (*alter*) 变化 ◊ *Little has changed since then.* 从那时至今没什么变化。**2** (*change clothes*) 换衣 ◊ *They allowed her to shower and change.* 他们允许她冲澡和换衣服。**3** [*traffic lights* +] 变色 ◊ *The lights changed to green.* 交通灯变绿了。**4** (*on bus, train etc*) 换车 **5** (*be transformed*) ♦**to change into sth** 变成某物 **III** *n* **1** [c/u] (*alteration*) 转变 ◊ *I dislike change of any kind.* 我不喜欢任何方式的转变。**2** [s] (*novelty*) 变化 ◊ *It's a change to finally win a match.* 最后赢一场也是个变化。**3** [c] [*of government, climate, job*] 更换 ◊ *A change of leadership alone will not be enough.* 更换领导本身是不够的。**4** [u] (*referring to money*) (*coins*) 零钱 ◊ *I haven't got any change.* 我没零钱。; (*money returned*) 找头 ◊ *The shopkeeper handed Hooper his change.* 店主递给了胡珀他的找头。♦**to change sth for sth** 将某物换成某物 ♦**to change one's mind** 改变主意 ♦**to**

change gear [英：汽车] 换挡 [美=**to shift gear**] ♦**to change hands** (*be sold*) 转手买卖 ♦**she changed into an old skirt** 她换上了一条旧裙子 ♦**it makes a change** 换换花样 ♦**for a change** 为了改变一下 ♦**a change of clothes/underwear** 一套换洗的衣服/内衣 ♦**a change of scene** 换换环境 ♦**small change** 零钱 ♦**to give sb change for** *or* **of 10 pounds** 给某人10英镑的零钱 ♦**keep the change!** 不用找了！

❑**change over** *vi* ♦**to change over to sth** 改变成某事

changeable ['tʃeɪndʒəbl] *adj* [+ *weather*] 多变的; [+ *person*] 变化无常的

change machine *n* [C] 零钱兑换机

changing ['tʃeɪndʒɪŋ] *adj* [+ *world, attitudes, role*] 日新月异的

changing room [英] *n* [C] **1** (*in shop*) 试衣室 **2** [体育] 更衣室

channel ['tʃænl] **I** *n* [C] **1** [电视] 频道 **2** (*for water*) 沟渠 **3** (*for shipping*) 水道 **4** (*groove*) 凹槽 **5** (喻) (*means*) 途径 **II** *vt* ♦**to channel sth into** [+ *money, resources*] 调拨某物于; [+ *energies*] 引导某物于 ♦**through the usual/normal channels** 经过通常的/一般的渠道 ♦**the (English) Channel** 英吉利海峡

Channel Tunnel *n* ♦**the Channel Tunnel** 英法海底隧道

chant [tʃɑːnt] **I** *n* [C] **1** (*from crowd*) 反复喊叫 **2** [宗] 赞美诗 **II** *vt* **1** [+ *word, name, slogan*] 反复喊 **2** [宗] 唱 **III** *vi* **1** [*supporters, demonstrators* +] 反复喊 **2** [宗] 唱歌 ♦**the demonstrators chanted their disapproval** 示威者反复抗议

chaos ['keɪɔs] *n* [U] 混乱

chaotic [keɪ'ɔtɪk] *adj* [+ *mess, jumble etc*] 紊乱的; [+ *situation, life etc*] 混乱的

chap [tʃæp] [英：非正式] *n* [C] **1** (*man*) 家伙 **2** ♦**old chap** [过时] (*term of address*) 老兄

chapel ['tʃæpl] *n* **1** [C] (*in church*) 小教堂 **2** [C] (*in hospital, prison, school*) 附属教堂 **3** [C/U] (*non-conformist chapel*) 非国教教堂 **4** [C] [*of union*] 职工会

chapped [tʃæpt] *adj* [+ *skin, lips*] 皲裂的

chapter ['tʃæptə(r)] *n* [C] **1** [*of book*] 章 **2** (*in life, history*) 时期 ◊ *a new chapter in the history of international relations* 国际关系史上新的一页 **3** [宗] 大教堂的全体教士

character ['kærɪktə(r)] *n* **1** [C] (*nature*) [*of person, place*] 特性; [*of object, idea*] 性质 **2** [C/U] (*reputation*) 名誉 **3** [C] (*in novel, film*) 角色 **4** [U] (*moral strength*) 毅力 **5** [C] [非正式] (*eccentric*) 怪人 **6** [C] (*letter, symbol etc*) 字母 ♦**a strange/sad character** [非正式] 一个古怪/可悲的人 ♦**a person of good character** 道德高尚的人 ♦**to behave in/out of character** 行为与自身特性相符/不相符

characteristic [kærɪktə'rɪstɪk] **I** *adj* 特有的 **II** *n* [C] 特征 ♦**to be characteristic of sb/sth** 反映某人/某物的特性

characterize ['kærɪktəraɪz] [正式] *vt* **1** (*typify*) 以…为特征 **2** (*describe the character of*) 描绘 ♦**to characterize sb/sth as** 把某人/某物描绘成

charcoal ['tʃɑːkəul] *n* [U] (*for fuel*) 木炭; (*for drawing*) 炭笔 ♦**a piece of charcoal** 一块木炭

✪**charge** [tʃɑːdʒ] **I** *n* [C] **1** (*fee*) 费用 ◊ *No charge is made for repairs.* 免费修理。**2** (*accusation*) 指控 ◊ *a murder charge* 一项谋杀指控 **3** (*attack*) 猛攻 **4** (*explosive*) (*in cartridge*) 炸药量 **5** [电子] 电荷 ◊ *an electrical charge* 一个电荷 **II** *vt* **1** [+ *sum of money*] 要价; [+ *customer, client*] 收费 ◊ *They charged fifty cents admission.* 他们收了50美分的入场费。**2** [警察] ♦**to charge sb (with sth)** 控告某人（犯某罪） **3** (*attack*) [+ *enemy*] 猛攻 ◊ *an order to charge enemy positions* 猛攻敌人阵地的命令 **4** (*also:* ***charge up***) [+ *battery*] 使充电 **III** *vi* **1** [*animal* +] 向前冲 **2** [军] (*attack*) 冲锋 **IV charges** *n* [*pl*] (*bank charges, telephone charges etc*) 费 ♦**is there a charge?** 要收费吗？♦**there's no charge** 免费 ♦**at no extra charge**

不额外收费 ♦ **free of charge** 免费 ♦ **in/under sb's charge** (*responsibility*) 在某人照管下 ◊ *My first concern is for the people under my charge.* 我首先考虑的是由我照管的人。♦ **to take charge of sb** 管理某人 ♦ **to take charge of sth** 掌管某物 ♦ **to be in charge (of sth/sb)** (*of person, machine*) 主管(某事/某人); (*of business*) 负责(某事/某人) ♦ **how much do you charge?** 你收费多少? ♦ **to charge sb £20 for sth** 因某物收某人20英镑 ♦ **to charge an expense to sb's account** 将某项消费记到某人账上 ♦ **to charge in/out/off** *etc* 急速进来/出去/离开{等} ♦ **to charge into a room/down the road** *etc* 跑进房间/跑上马路{等}

charge card *n* [c] **1** [英](*for particular shop*) 记账卡 **2** [美](*credit card*) 信用卡

charger ['tʃɑːdʒə(r)] *n* [c] **1** (*also: **battery charger***) 充电器 **2** [过时](*warhorse*) 战马

charismatic [kærɪs'mætɪk] *adj* 极有性格魅力的

charity ['tʃærɪtɪ] *n* **1** [c] (*organization*) 慈善机构 **2** [U] (*money, gifts*) 赈济 **3** [U] (*kindness, generosity*) 仁慈 ♦ **to give money to charity** 把钱捐给慈善团体 ♦ **to raise money for charity** 为慈善团体募捐

charity shop [英] *n* [c] 慈善商店 [美= **thrift shop**]

> **CHARITY SHOP**
> **charity shops**(美国称之为**thrift shops**)是廉价品追求者的快乐之源。人们把闲置的衣服、书籍、玩具和其他物品送到慈善商店,慈善商店的存在离不开人们的捐赠。慈善商店的全部收入归特定的慈善机构所有,比如,**Oxfam**(救济发展中国家人民的机构)或**Barnados**(帮助英国贫困儿童的机构)。

charm [tʃɑːm] **I** *n* **1** [c/U] [*of place, thing*] 魅力; [*of person*] 迷人的特性 **2** [c] (*for good luck*) 护身符 **3** [c] (*spell*) 符咒 **4** [c] (*on bracelet, necklace*) 坠儿 **II** *vt* 迷住

charming ['tʃɑːmɪŋ] *adj* [+ *person*] 迷人的; [+ *place, custom*] 吸引人的

chart [tʃɑːt] **I** *n* [c] **1** (*graph, diagram*) 图表 **2** (*map*) 海图 **II** *vt* **1** [+ *progress, development*] 详述 **2** [+ *land, sea, stars*] 绘制 **III the charts** *n* [*pl*] [音] 流行音乐排行榜 ♦ **to be in the charts** [*record, pop group* +] 在排行榜上

charter ['tʃɑːtə(r)] **I** *vt* 包租 **II** *n* [c] 宪章

charter flight *n* [c] 包机

chase [tʃeɪs] **I** *vt* **1** (*pursue*) 追赶 **2** ♦ **to chase sb off one's land/away from a place** 将某人赶出某人的土地/从某处赶走 **3** (*seek*) [+ *job, money, opportunity*] 寻找 **II** *n* [c] (*pursuit*) 追逐

❑ **chase down** *vt* **1** [美](*run after*) 追上 **2** (*track down*) [+ *person*] 寻觅到; [+ *information*] 设法寻找

❑ **chase up** *vt* [+ *person*] 催; [+ *information*] 寻找

chat [tʃæt] **I** *vi* (*also: **have a chat***) 聊天 **II** *n* [c] (*conversation*) 聊天

❑ **chat up** [英:非正式] *vt* 与…调情

chat room [计算机] *n* [c] 聊天室

chat show [英] *n* [c] 访谈节目 [美= **talk show**]

chatter ['tʃætə(r)] **I** *vi* **1** [*person* +] 喋喋不休 **2** [文][*bird, animal* +] 唧唧叫 **3** [*teeth* +] 打战 **II** *n* [U] **1** [*of people*] 喋喋不休 **2** [文][*of birds, animals*] 唧唧声

chauffeur ['ʃəufə(r)] **I** *n* [c] 司机 **II** *vt* ♦ **to chauffeur sb around** 开车载某人到处转

chauvinist ['ʃəuvɪnɪst] *n* [c] **1** 沙文主义者 **2** (*also: **male chauvinist***) 大男子主义者

cheap [tʃiːp] **I** *adj* **1** (*inexpensive*) 便宜的 **2** (*reduced*) [+ *ticket*] 降价的; [+ *fare, rate*] 廉价的 **3** (*poor quality*) 劣质的 **4** [+ *remark, joke*] 粗鄙的 **II** *adv* ♦ **to buy/sell sth cheap** 廉价买/卖某物 ♦ **that was a cheap shot** 那可真够低级的

cheaply ['tʃiːplɪ] *adv* 便宜地

cheat [tʃiːt] **I** *vi* (*in game, exam*) 作弊 **II** *vt* 欺骗 **III** *n* [c] (*in games, exams*) 作弊者; (*in business*) 骗子; (*sexually*)

不忠的人 ♦**to feel cheated** 感到受骗上当 ♦**to cheat sb out of sth** 骗取某人的某物

❑**cheat on** [非正式] *vt* [不可拆分] [+ *husband, girlfriend, etc*] 不忠实于

check [tʃɛk] **I** *vt* **1** (*examine, verify*) [+ *bill, progress, facts, figures*] 核对; [+ *passport, ticket*] 检查 **2** (*also:* ***check in***) [+ *luggage*] (*at airport*) 托运 **3** (*halt*) [+ *advance, disease*] 制止 **4** (*restrain*) [+ *impulse*] 抑制; [+ *person*] 使突然停止 **II** *vi* **1** (*investigate*) 检查 **2** (*tally*) 符合 **III** *n* [c] **1** (*inspection*) 检查 **2** (*curb*) 制止 **3** [美] (*in restaurant etc*) 账单 [英 = **bill**] **4** [美 : 经济] = **cheque 5** (*pattern*) (*gen pl*) 方格图案 **6** [美] (*mark*) 勾号 [英 = **tick**] **IV** *adj* (*also:* ***checked***) [+ *pattern, cloth*] 方格图案的 ♦**to check that ...** 检查… ♦**to check sth against sth** 将某物与某物相比较 ♦**to check on sb/sth** 察看某人/某物 ♦**to check with sb** 向某人证实 ♦**to keep a check on sb/sth** (*watch*) 监视某人/某物 ♦**to hold** *or* **keep sb/sth in check** 控制某人/某物 ♦**"check"** [国际象棋] "将军"

❑**check in I** *vi* (*at hotel, clinic*) 登记; (*at airport*) 办理登机手续 **II** *vt* 托运

❑**check into** *vt* [+ *hotel, clinic*] 登记入住

❑**check off** *vt* 核对

❑**check out I** *vi* (*of hotel*) 结账离开 **II** *vt* (*investigate*) [+ *story*] 证实; [+ *person*] 查对

❑**check up** *vi* 检查

❑**check up on** *vt* [不可拆分] (*investigate*) 追查

checkbook ['tʃɛkbuk] [美] *n* = **cheque book**

checked [tʃɛkt] *adj see* **check**

checkers ['tʃɛkəz] [美] *n* [*pl*] 西洋跳棋 [英 = **draughts**]

check-in ['tʃɛkɪn-] (*also:* ***check-in desk***) *n* [c] (*at airport*) 旅客验票台

checking account ['tʃɛkɪŋ-] [美] *n* [c] [经济] 活期存款账户 [英 = **current account**]

checklist ['tʃɛklɪst] *n* [c] 一览表

checkout ['tʃɛkaut] *n* [c] (*in shop*) 付款台

checkpoint ['tʃɛkpɔɪnt] *n* [c] (*on border*) 边防检查站

checkroom ['tʃɛkruːm] [美] *n* [c] (*left-luggage office*) 行李寄存处

check-up ['tʃɛkʌp] *n* [c] (*by doctor*) 体检; (*by dentist*) 牙科检查 ♦**to have a check-up** (*by doctor*) 进行体检; (*by dentist*) 进行牙科检查

cheddar ['tʃɛdə(r)] *n* [u] 切达干酪

cheek [tʃiːk] *n* **1** [c] (*on face*) 面颊 **2** [u] [非正式] (*impudence*) 厚颜无耻 ♦**to have the cheek to do sth** 居然有脸做某事

cheekbone ['tʃiːkbəun] *n* [c] 颧骨

cheeky ['tʃiːkɪ] [尤英] *adj* 恬不知耻的

cheer [tʃɪə(r)] **I** *vt* **1** [+ *team, speaker*] 用欢呼声激励 **2** (*gladden*) 使高兴 **II** *vi* 欢呼 **III** *n* [c] **1** 喝彩 ♦**cheers!** [尤英] (*toast*) 干杯!; [英 : 非正式] (*thanks*) 多谢

❑**cheer on** *vt* 为…鼓气

❑**cheer up I** *vi* [*person* +] 振作起来 **II** *vt* [+ *person*] 使…高兴起来

cheerful ['tʃɪəful] *adj* **1** [+ *wave, smile, person*] 兴高采烈的 **2** [+ *place, object*] 使人感到愉快的

cheerio [tʃɪərɪ'əu] [英 : 过时, 非正式] *int* 再见

cheerleader ['tʃɪəliːdə(r)] *n* [c] 拉拉队长

cheese [tʃiːz] *n* [c/u] 干酪

cheeseburger ['tʃiːzbəːgə(r)] *n* [c] 干酪汉堡包

cheesecake ['tʃiːzkeɪk] *n* [c/u] 干酪饼

chef [ʃɛf] *n* [c] 厨师

chemical ['kɛmɪkl] **I** *adj* **1** [+ *reaction, composition*] 化学的 **2** [军] [+ *warfare, weapon*] 化学的 **II** *n* [c] 化学剂

chemist ['kɛmɪst] *n* [c] **1** [英] (*also:* ***chemist's***) 药商 [美 = **pharmacy**] **2** [英] (*in shop*) 药剂师 [美 = **druggist, pharmacist**] **3** (*scientist*) 化学家

> 在英式英语中，售药或者配药的商店通常叫做 **chemist** 或者 **chemist's**。*She went into a chemist's and bought some aspirin.* **pharmacy** 也表示同样的意思，但不常用。在美式英语中，也使用 **pharmacy**。另一个

同义词是**druggist**。**drugstore** 也表示同样意思，但通常是指除了药品以外还兼售饮料、小吃和其他小商品的商店。*At the drugstore I bought a can of Coke and the local papers.*

chemistry ['kɛmɪstrɪ] *n* [U] 化学
cheque (美 **check**) [tʃɛk] *n* [C] 支票 ♦ **to pay by cheque** 用支票付款
cheque book (美 **checkbook**) ['tʃɛkbuk] *n* [C] 支票簿
cheque card [英] *n* [C] (*also:* ***cheque guarantee card***) 支票保付卡
cherish ['tʃɛrɪʃ] *vt* [+ *person, object*] 爱护; [+ *right, freedom*] 珍惜; [+ *hope*] 抱有; [+ *memory*] 怀念
cherry ['tʃɛrɪ] *n* [C] **1** (*fruit*) 樱桃 **2** (*also:* ***cherry tree***) 樱桃树
chess [tʃɛs] *n* [U] 象棋
chest [tʃɛst] *n* [C] **1** (*part of body*) 胸部 **2** (*box*) 箱子 ♦ **to get sth off one's chest** [非正式] 倾诉积存已久的话
chestnut ['tʃɛsnʌt] **I** *n* [C] **1** (*nut*) 栗子 **2** (*also:* ***chestnut tree***) 栗子树 **II** *adj* [+ *hair*] 栗色的 ♦ **old chestnut** 老掉牙的论调
chest of drawers *n* [C] 五斗橱
chew [tʃuː] **I** *vt* [+ *food, gum*] 嚼; [+ *pen, fingernails*] 咬 **II** *vi* 咀嚼
chewing gum ['tʃuːɪŋ-] *n* [U] 口香糖
chic [ʃiːk] *adj* [+ *clothes*] 雅致的; [+ *person, place*] 时髦的
chick [tʃɪk] *n* [C] **1** (*young bird*) 小鸟 **2** [非正式] (*girl*) 妞
chicken ['tʃɪkɪn] *n* **1** [C] (*bird*) (*young*) 小鸡; (*grown*) 鸡 **2** [C/U] (*meat*) 鸡肉 **3** [C] [非正式] (*coward*) 胆小鬼
❑ **chicken out** [非正式] *vi* 因胆怯而放弃 ♦ **to chicken out of (doing) sth** 因胆怯而放弃（做）某事
chickenpox ['tʃɪkɪnpɔks] *n* [U] 水痘
chick pea *n* [C] 鹰嘴豆
✪ **chief** [tʃiːf] **I** *n* [C] [*of organization, department*] 首领 ◊ *the police chief* 警长; [*of tribe*] 酋长 **II** *adj* 首要的 ◊ *one of his chief rivals* 他的首要竞争对手之一
chief executive (officer) *n* [C] 总经理
chiefly ['tʃiːflɪ] *adv* 主要

✪ **child** [tʃaɪld] (*pl* **children**) *n* [C] **1** 儿童 **2** (*son, daughter*) 孩子 ◊ *Their children are all married.* 他们的孩子都结婚了。◊ *a father and his two teenage children* 一位父亲和他的两个十几岁的孩子 ♦ **she's just had her second child** 她刚生了第二个孩子
childbirth ['tʃaɪldbəːθ] *n* [U] 分娩
childcare ['tʃaɪldkɛə] *n* [U] 儿童托管服务
childhood ['tʃaɪldhud] **I** *n* [U] 童年 **II** *cpd* [复合词] [+ *disease, memory, friend*] 童年期
childish ['tʃaɪldɪʃ] *adj* **1** [贬] [+ *person, behaviour*] 幼稚的 **2** [+ *games, enthusiasm*] 孩子般的
child minder [英] *n* [C] 保姆
children ['tʃɪldrən] *n* [*pl*] *of* **child**
child seat [汽车] *n* [C] 儿童座
Chile ['tʃɪlɪ] *n* 智利
Chilean ['tʃɪlɪən] **I** *adj* 智利的 **II** *n* [C] (*person*) 智利人
chill [tʃɪl] **I** *n* [C] **1** (*in air, water*) 寒气 **2** (*illness*) 着凉 **II** *adj* [+ *wind, air*] 凉飕飕的 **III** *vt* **1** (*cool*) [+ *food, drinks*] 使冷冻 **2** [文] (*frighten*) 使…害怕 ♦ **to catch a chill** 着凉 ♦ **it sent a chill down my spine** 这使我胆战心惊 ♦ **I'm chilled to the bone** *or* **marrow** 我感到寒气刺骨 ♦ **"serve chilled"** "冰镇食用"
❑ **chill out** [非正式] *vi* 放松一下
chilli (美 **chili**) ['tʃɪlɪ] *n* [C/U] 辣椒
chilly ['tʃɪlɪ] *adj* **1** [+ *weather, day*] 相当冷的 **2** [+ *response, welcome*] 冷淡的 ♦ **to feel** *or* **be chilly** [*person* +] 感到寒冷 ♦ **it's a bit chilly today** 今天有点冷
📖 用法参见 **cold**
chimney ['tʃɪmnɪ] *n* [C] 烟囱
chimpanzee [tʃɪmpæn'ziː] *n* [C] 黑猩猩
chin [tʃɪn] *n* [C] 下巴 ♦ **(keep your) chin up!** 振作精神！♦ **to take sth on the chin** 勇敢地忍受某事
China ['tʃaɪnə] *n* 中国
china ['tʃaɪnə] **I** *n* [U] **1** (*also:* ***china clay***) 陶瓷 **2** (*crockery*) 瓷器 **II** *cpd* [复合词] [+ *cup, plate*] 瓷
Chinese [tʃaɪ'niːz] (*pl* **Chinese**) **I** *adj* 中国的 **II** *n* **1** [C] (*person*) 中国人 **2** [U] (*language*) 汉语

chip [tʃɪp] **I** *n* [c] **1** [英] 薯条 [美= **(French) fry**] **2** [美] (*snack*) 薯片 [英 = **crisp**] **3** [*of wood*] 屑片 **4** [*of glass, stone*] 碎片 **5** (*in glass, cup etc*) 缺口 **6** (*for gambling*) 筹码 **7** [计算机] (*also: **microchip***) 集成电路片 **II** *vt* [+ *cup, plate*] 碰出缺口 ♦**to have a chip on one's shoulder** [非正式] 持寻衅的态度 ♦**he's a chip off the old block** [非正式] 他和他老子一样 ♦**when the chips are down** [非正式] 当危急关头
❑**chip in** [非正式] *vi* **1** (*financially*) 捐助 **2** (*interrupt*) 插嘴

chip shop [英] *n* [c] 薯条店

> **CHIP SHOP**
> chip shop，也叫 fish and chip shops 或俗称 chippies，是专卖外卖食品的小店，不仅出售炸鱼排和薯条（另见 fish and chips），还出售肉饼、香肠和其他英国传统食品。如果要带回家吃，你可以让店员打包；如果你要在街上吃，也可以不包。为了保温，店员还会用纸包好。

chiropodist [kɪ'rɔpədɪst] [英] *n* [c] 足医

chisel ['tʃɪzl] **I** *n* [c] 凿子 **II** *vt* [+ *wood, stone*] 凿

chives [tʃaɪvz] *n* [*pl*] 细香葱

chlorine ['klɔːriːn] *n* [U] 氯气

chocolate ['tʃɔklɪt] **I** *n* **1** [U] 巧克力 **2** [C/U] (*drinking chocolate*) 巧克力饮料 **3** [C] (*piece of confectionery*) 巧克力糖 **II** *cpd* [复合词] [+ *cake, pudding, mousse*] 巧克力 ♦**bar of chocolate** 巧克力条 ♦**piece of chocolate** 一块巧克力

choice [tʃɔɪs] **I** *n* **1** [C/U] (*between items*) 选择 **2** [C] (*option*) 选择 **3** [C] (*item chosen, preference*) 被选中的东西 **II** *adj* [正式] (*quality*) 优质的 ♦**a wide choice** 多种多样 ♦**it's available in a choice of colours** 有各种颜色供选择 ♦**to make a choice** 作出选择 ♦**to have no/little choice** 没有/没有太多选择 ♦**the book/film of your choice** 你所选择的书/电影

choir ['kwaɪə(r)] *n* [C] **1** 合唱团 **2** (*area of church*) 唱诗班的席位

choke [tʃəuk] **I** *vi* (*on food, drink etc*) 噎住; (*with smoke, dust*) 呛 **II** *vt* **1** (*strangle*) [*rope etc* +] 使窒息 ♦**to choke sb** 掐某人的脖子 **2** (*block*) ♦**to be choked with sth** 塞满某物 **III** *n* [C] [汽车] 阻塞门 ♦**to choke on sth** 被某物噎了 ♦**to choke to death** 呛死
❑**choke back** *vt* [+ *tears*] 忍住

cholesterol [kə'lɛstərɔl] *n* [U] 胆固醇

choose [tʃuːz] (*pt* **chose**, *pp* **chosen**) **I** *vt* [+ *clothes, profession, candidate etc*] 挑选 **II** *vi* ♦**to choose between** 在…之间作出选择 ♦**to choose from** 从…中选择 ♦**to choose to do sth** 选择做某事

chop [tʃɔp] **I** *vt* **1** [+ *wood*] 劈 **2** (*also: **chop up***) [+ *vegetables, fruit, meat*] 切 **II** *n* [C] [烹饪] 排骨 ♦**to get the chop** [英: 非正式] [*project* +] 被终止; [*person* +] 被解雇
❑**chop down** *vt* [+ *tree*] 砍倒
❑**chop off** *vt* [+ *arm, leg*] 砍
❑**chop up** *vt* 切

chopsticks ['tʃɔpstɪks] *n* [*pl*] 筷子

chord [kɔːd] *n* [C] **1** [音] 和弦 **2** [数] 弦

chore [tʃɔː(r)] **I** *n* [C] (*unpleasant task*) 琐碎烦人的杂务 **II the chores** *n* [*pl*] 家庭杂务 ♦**household chores** 家务

chorus ['kɔːrəs] **I** *n* [C] **1** (*refrain*) 齐唱 **2** (*song*) 合唱曲 **3** (*choir, not soloists*) 合唱队 **4** [*of complaints, criticism*] 异口同声 **II** *vt* 异口同声地说 ♦**in chorus** 一齐

chose [tʃəuz] *pt of* **choose**

chosen ['tʃəuzn] *pp of* **choose**

Christ [kraɪst] **I** *n* 耶稣 **II** *int* [非正式, 疑讳] 耶稣

christen ['krɪsn] *vt* **1** [+ *baby*] 洗礼时给…命名 **2** (*with nickname*) 取绰号为

christening ['krɪsnɪŋ] *n* [C] 洗礼

Christian ['krɪstɪən] **I** *adj* 基督教的 **II** *n* [C] 基督徒

Christianity [krɪstɪ'ænɪtɪ] *n* [U] 基督教

Christian name *n* [C] 教名

Christmas ['krɪsməs] *n* [C/U] **1** [宗] (*festival*) 圣诞节 **2** (*period*) 圣诞节

期间 ♦**Happy** *or* **Merry Christmas!** 圣诞快乐！♦**at Christmas** 在圣诞节 ♦**for Christmas** 为了圣诞节

Christmas card *n* [c] 圣诞卡

Christmas Day *n* [c/u] 圣诞日

Christmas Eve *n* [c/u] 圣诞夜

Christmas tree *n* [c] 圣诞树

chrome [krəum] *n* [u] 铬黄

chronic ['krɔnɪk] *adj* **1** [医][+ *illness*] 慢性的 **2** [+ *liar, smoker, etc*] 积习难改的 **3** (*serious*) [+ *problem, shortage*] 严重的

chrysanthemum [krɪ'sænθəməm] [植] *n* [c] 菊花

chubby ['tʃʌbɪ] *adj* [+ *cheeks, child*] 肥胖的

📖 用法参见 **fat**

chuck [tʃʌk] [非正式] *vt* **1** (*throw*) [+ *object*] 扔 **2** [+ *job, hobby*] 放弃 **3** [+ *boyfriend, girlfriend*] 抛弃

❑ **chuck away** *vt see* **chuck out**

❑ **chuck out** *vt* **1** [+ *person*] 撵走 **2** (*also:* ***chuck away***) [+ *rubbish*] 扔掉

chuckle ['tʃʌkl] **I** *vi* 暗笑 **II** *n* [c] 轻声笑 ♦**to have a chuckle about sth** 因某事发笑

chunk [tʃʌŋk] *n* [c] **1** [*of ice, food etc*] 大块 **2** [非正式][*of land, income*] 相当大的部分

church [tʃəːtʃ] *n* **1** [c/u] (*building*) 教堂 **2** [c] (*denomination*) 教会 ♦**the Church of England** 英国国教会

churchyard ['tʃəːtʃjɑːd] *n* [c] 教堂墓地

churn [tʃəːn] **I** *n* [c] **1** (*for butter*) 搅拌器 **2** (*also:* ***milk churn***) 大桶 **II** *vt* (*also:* ***churn up***) [+ *mud, water, dust*] 剧烈搅动 **III** *vi* [*stomach* +] 翻腾

❑ **churn out I** *vt* [+ *objects, books*] 粗制滥造

chute [ʃuːt] *n* [c] **1** (*slide*) 滑道 **2** (*for rubbish, coal, parcels, laundry*) 倾卸槽 **3** [非正式](*parachute*) 降落伞

chutney ['tʃʌtnɪ] *n* [c/u] 酸辣酱

CID [英] *n abbr* (= ***Criminal Investigation Department***) ♦**the CID** 刑事调查部

cider ['saɪdə(r)] *n* [c/u] **1** [英](*alcoholic*) 苹果酒 **2** [美](*non-alcoholic*) 苹果汁

cigar [sɪ'gɑː(r)] *n* [c] 雪茄烟

cigarette [sɪgə'rɛt] *n* [c] 香烟

cinema ['sɪnəmə] *n* **1** [c] [英](*place*) 电影院 [美=**movie theater**] **2** [u] (*film-making*) 电影业

cinnamon ['sɪnəmən] *n* [u] 肉桂

circle ['səːkl] **I** *n* **1** [c] 圆圈 **2** [c] [*of friends*] 圈子 ◊ *He has a small circle of friends.* 他有一小圈朋友。**3** [s] (*in cinema, theatre*) 楼厅 **II** *vi* [*bird, plane* +] 盘旋 **III** *vt* (*move round, surround*) 环绕

circuit ['səːkɪt] *n* [c] **1** [电子] 电路 **2** [英](*track*) 赛车道 **3** (*lap*) 环道 ♦**the lecture circuit** 巡回讲学

circular ['səːkjulə(r)] **I** *adj* **1** [+ *shape*] 圆形的; [+ *movement, motion*] 环形的 **2** [+ *argument*] 循环论证的 **3** [+ *journey, route*] 绕圈的 **II** *n* [c] **1** (*letter*) 供传阅的函件 **2** (*advertisement*) 传单

circulate ['səːkjuleɪt] **I** *vi* [*traffic, blood* +] 循环; [*news, rumour* +] 散播; [*person* +] (*at party*) 交际 **II** *vt* [+ *report*] 传阅

circulation [səːkju'leɪʃən] *n* **1** [u] [*of air*] 流通; [*of blood*] 循环; [*of document*] 传阅 **2** [c] [*of newspaper, magazine*] 发行量 ♦**in circulation** 在流通中

circumstances ['səːkəmstənsɪz] *n* [*pl*] **1** (*conditions, state of affairs*) 情况 **2** [*of accident, death*] 事实 **3** (*financial condition*) 状况 ♦**in** *or* **under the circumstances** 在这种情况下 ♦**under no circumstances** 决不

circus ['səːkəs] *n* **1** [c] (*show*) 马戏团 **2** [c] (喻) 乱哄哄 **3** [英](*in street names*) ♦**Circus** 广场

cite [saɪt] *vt* **1** (*quote*) [+ *example*] 引用 **2** [法][+ *person*] 传讯; [+ *fact*] 引证

citizen ['sɪtɪzn] *n* [c] [*of country*] 公民; [*of town, area*] 居民

citizenship ['sɪtɪznʃɪp] *n* [u] 公民身份

citrus fruit ['sɪtrəs-] *n* [c/u] 柑橘属果实

✪ **city** ['sɪtɪ] *n* [c] 城市 ♦**the City** [英:经济] 英国伦敦商业区

> **THE CITY**
> **the City**（伦敦商业区）是伦敦的一部分，位于市中心的东部。很多重要的金融机构都将总部设在这里，譬如英格兰银

行、伦敦证券交易所和其他几个主要银行。这些金融机构的所在地通常统称为**the City**。在历史上，这个地区是伦敦的心脏，有自己的市长和警力。

city centre [尤英] *n* [c] 市中心 [美= **downtown**]

civic ['sɪvɪk] *adj* **1** [+ *leader, authorities*] 城市的 **2** [+ *duties, pride*] 公民的

civil ['sɪvɪl] *adj* **1** [+ *unrest*] 国内的 **2** (*not military*) 民用的 **3** (*not religious*) [+ *ceremony*] 非宗教的 **4** (*not criminal*) [+ *case*] 民事的 **5** (*polite*) ♦ **to be civil (to sb)** 礼貌地(对某人)

civilian [sɪ'vɪlɪən] **I** *n* [c] 平民 **II** *adj* [+ *population, casualties, life*] 平民的

civilization [sɪvɪlaɪ'zeɪʃən] *n* [c/u] (*society*) 文明

civilized ['sɪvɪlaɪzd] *adj* **1** (*socially advanced*) [+ *society, people*] 文明的 **2** (*polite*) [+ *person, behaviour*] 有教养的

civil law *n* [u] 民法

civil rights *n* [*pl*] 公民权

civil servant *n* [c] 公务员

Civil Service *n* ♦ **the Civil Service** 行政机关

civil war *n* [c/u] 内战

cl *abbr* (= ***centilitre***(***s***)) 厘升

✪**claim** [kleɪm] **I** *vt* **1** (*allege*) 声称 **2** (*for o.s.*) [+ *responsibility, credit*] 声称; [+ *success rate*] 自称 ◊ *The terrorists claimed responsibility for the bombing.* 恐怖分子声称对这起爆炸事件负责。 **3** (*demand*) [+ *expenses, rights, inheritance*] 要求 ◊ *Voluntary workers can claim travelling expenses.* 义工可以申请回交通费。 **4** [+ *compensation, damages, benefit*] 索取 **5** [正式] (*take*) ♦ **the disease claimed millions of lives** 此病使上百万人丧生 **II** *vi* (*for insurance*) 提出索赔 **III** *n* [c] **1** (*assertion*) 声称 **2** (*application*) (*for pension, wage rise, compensation*) 索赔 **3** (*to inheritance, land*) 要求 **4** (*right to demand*) 权利 ♦ **to claim that ...** 声称… ♦ **to claim to be/have sth** 声称是/有某物 ◊ *a man claiming to be a journalist* 一位声称是记者的人 ♦ **to claim** *or* **make a claim on one's insurance** 提出保险索赔的要求 ♦ **insurance claim** 保险索赔要求 ♦ **to put in a claim for** [+ *expenses*] 就…提出索赔要求 ♦ **to have a claim on sb** 对某人有要求权 ♦ **his claim to fame** 他出名的来由 ♦ **to lay claim to sth** 对某物提出所有权要求

clam [klæm] [动，烹饪] *n* [c] 蛤蜊
❑ **clam up** [非正式] *vi* 沉默不语

clamber ['klæmbə(r)] *vi* ♦ **to clamber up a hill/over a wall** 攀登山坡/费劲地爬墙

clamp [klæmp] **I** *n* [c] **1** (*device*) 夹具 **2** [英] (*also:* ***wheel clamp***) 车轮固定夹 [美= **Denver boot**] **II** *vt* **1** (*attach*) ♦ **to clamp sth to sth** 将某物与某物紧夹在一起 **2** (*put*) ♦ **to clamp sth on/round sth** 将某物固定在某物上 **3** [英] [+ *wheel, car*] 锁 [美= **boot**]
❑ **clamp down** *vi* 强行限制
❑ **clamp down on** *vt* [不可拆分] [+ *people, activities*] 压制

clan [klæn] *n* [c] (*family*) 家族

clap [klæp] **I** *vi* [*audience* +] 鼓掌 **II** *vt* ♦ **to clap one's hands** 拍手 **III** *n* **1** ♦ **to give sb a clap** 向某人鼓掌 **2** ♦ **a clap of thunder** 一声霹雳 ♦ **to clap a hand over sth** 突然用手将某物捂住 ♦ **to clap sb on the back** 拍某人的背

claret ['klærət] *n* [c/u] (*wine*) 波尔多红葡萄酒

clarify ['klærɪfaɪ] *vt* 澄清

clarinet [klærɪ'nɛt] [音] *n* [c] 单簧管

clarity ['klærɪtɪ] *n* [u] 清晰度

clash [klæʃ] **I** *n* [c] **1** (*fight, disagreement*) 冲突; [*of personalities*] 矛盾 **2** [文] (*metallic noise*) 撞击声 **II** *vi* **1** (*fight*) [*rival gangs* +] 发生冲突 **2** (*disagree*) [*political opponents etc* +] 有重大分歧 **3** (*be in conflict*) [*beliefs, ideas, views* +] 不一致 **4** [*colours, styles* +] 不协调 **5** [*events, dates, appointments* +] 有冲突 **6** [文] [*weapons, pans etc* +] 撞击

clasp [klɑːsp] **I** *n* [c] **1** [*of necklace, bag*] 扣子 **2** (*hold, embrace*) 紧握 **II** *vt* (*hold, embrace*) 紧抱 ♦ **he clasped her to him** 他紧紧地

抱住她

✪**class** [klɑːs] **I** *n* **1** [c] [教育] *(group of pupils)* 班级; *(lesson)* 课 **2** [c/u] *(social)* 阶级 **3** [c] *(type, group)* 种类 ◊ *We can identify several classes of fern.* 我们可以识别几种蕨类植物。 **4** [u] *(sophistication)* 风度 ◊ *His performance showed enormous class.* 他的表现显示出极好的风度。 **II** *cpd* [复合词] [+ *structure, conflict, struggle*] 阶级 **III** *vt* *(categorize)* ♦ **to class sb/sth as** 将某人/某物分类为 ◊ *At nineteen you're still classed as a teenager.* 即使十九岁，你仍被定为十几岁的青少年。 ♦ **in class** [教育] 上课时 ♦ **to be in a class of one's own** 独一无二

classic ['klæsɪk] **I** *adj* **1** [+ *example*] 典型的 **2** [+ *film, work etc*] 经典的 **3** [+ *style, dress etc*] 传统式样的 **II** *n* [c] *(film, novel etc)* 经典 ♦ **to be a classic** 典范

classical ['klæsɪkl] *adj* **1** *(traditional)* 传统的 **2** [音] 古典的 **3** *(Greek, Roman)* 古希腊或古罗马文明的

Classics ['klæsɪks] *n* [u] 古典学

classification [klæsɪfɪ'keɪʃən] *n* **1** [u] *(process)* 分类 **2** [c] *(category)* 类别

classified ad ['klæsɪfaɪd] *(also: **classified advertisement**)* *n* [c] 分类广告栏

classify ['klæsɪfaɪ] *vt* [+ *books, fossils etc*] 分类 ♦ **to classify sb/sth as sth** 将某人/某物归类为某物

classmate ['klɑːsmeɪt] *n* [c] 同学

classroom ['klɑːsruːm] *n* [c] 教室

classy ['klɑːsɪ] [非正式] *adj* [+ *person*] 时髦的; [+ *restaurant, hotel*] 奢华的; [+ *neighbourhood*] 高级的; [+ *performance*] 出色的

clatter ['klætə(r)] **I** *vi* [文] [*dishes, pots etc* +] 发出喀嗒声 **II** *n* [s] [文] 喀嗒声 ♦ **to clatter around** 乒乒乓乓地乱动 ♦ **he clattered down the stairs** 他乒乒乓乓地下了楼梯

clause [klɔːz] *n* [c] **1** [法] 条款 **2** [语言] 从句 ♦ **main/subordinate clause** [语言] 主/从句

claustrophobic [klɔːstrə'fəubɪk] *adj* **1** [+ *place, situation*] 导致幽闭恐怖的 **2** ♦ **to be/feel claustrophobic** 患/感到幽闭恐怖

claw [klɔː] *n* [c] [*of cat, tiger, bird*] 爪子; [*of lobster, crab*] 钳子
❑ **claw at** *vt* [不可拆分] **1** *(scratch)* 挠 **2** *(grab)* 抓 ♦ **to claw at the air** 抓空

clay [kleɪ] *n* [u] 黏土

clean [kliːn] **I** *adj* **1** [+ *place, surface, clothes etc*] 干净的; [+ *water*] 清洁的 **2** *(in habits)* [+ *person, animal*] 爱清洁的 **3** *(fair)* [+ *fight, contest*] 公正的 **4** *(not offensive)* [+ *joke, story*] 纯净的 **5** *(spotless)* [+ *record, reputation*] 清白的 **6** *(well-defined)* [+ *edge, line*] 平整的 **7** [医] [+ *fracture*] 边缘整齐的 **II** *vt* [+ *car, cooker etc*] 弄干净; [+ *room*] 打扫 **III** *adv* [非正式] ♦ **he clean forgot** 他忘得一干二净 **IV** *n* ♦ **to give sth a clean** 把某物清理干净 ♦ **to come clean about sth** [非正式] 全盘招供某事 ♦ **a clean driving licence** *or* (美) **record** 未有违章记录的驾照 ♦ **a clean sheet of paper** 一张白纸 ♦ **to make a clean break** *or* **start** 重新开始 ♦ **to clean one's teeth** [英] 刷牙 ♦ **the thief got clean away** [非正式] 小偷逃得无影无踪
❑ **clean out** *vt* **1** [+ *cupboard, drawer*] 清理干净 **2** [非正式] [+ *person*] 耗尽…的钱财
❑ **clean up** **I** *vt* **1** [+ *room, place*] 打扫干净; [+ *mess*] 整理 **2** (喻) *(remove crime from)* 整治 **II** *vi* **1** 打扫干净 **2** [非正式] *(make profit)* 发大财

cleaner ['kliːnə(r)] *n* **1** [c] *(person)* 清洁工 **2** [c/u] *(substance)* 清洁剂

cleaning ['kliːnɪŋ] *n* [u] [*of house etc*] 扫除 ♦ **to do the cleaning** 做扫除

cleanse [klɛnz] *vt* **1** [+ *face, cut*] 清洗 **2** [+ *mind, organization*] 净化 ♦ **to cleanse sth of sth** 使某物不再受某物的污染

cleanser ['klɛnzə(r)] *n* [c/u] *(for face)* 洁肤霜

✪**clear** [klɪə(r)] **I** *adj* **1** *(understandable)* [+ *explanation, account*] 明确的 **2** *(visible)* [+ *footprint, photograph*] 清晰的 ◊ *television which transmits far clearer pictures* 传送更加清晰图像的电视 **3** *(audible)* [+ *voice, echo*] 清晰的 ◊ *He called out my name in a clear voice.* 他清楚地叫出我的名

字。◊ *His voice was very clear.* 他的声音非常清晰。**4** (*obvious*) 无疑的 ◊ *a clear case of homicide* 确信无疑的谋杀案 **5** (*definite*) [+ *choice, commitment*] 明确的 ◊ *The letter contained a clear commitment to reopen talks.* 这封信明确承诺要重新开始谈判。**6** [+ *profit, majority*] 绝对的 ◊ *They won the vote by a clear majority.* 他们赢得绝对多数选票。**7** (*transparent*) [+ *glass, plastic, water*] 透明的 ◊ *a clear glass panel* 一张透明玻璃板
8 (*unobstructed*) [+ *road, way, floor etc*] 畅通的 ◊ *The runway is clear, go ahead and land.* 跑道畅通无阻，可以降落。**9** (*untroubled*) [+ *conscience*] 清白的 **10** (*cloudless*) [+ *day, sky*] 晴朗的 **11** (*healthy*) [+ *skin, eyes*] 明亮的 **II** *vt* **1** [+ *place, room*] 清空 ◊ *The police cleared the building following a bomb alert.* 收到炸弹警告后，警察清空了那幢建筑。**2** ♦ **to clear sth from sth** [+ *rubbish, weeds*] 从某处清理出某物 ◊ *Firemen were still clearing rubble from apartments.* 消防队员还在从单元房里清理出瓦砾。
3 [+ *slums*] 拆除 **4** [法] [+ *suspect*] 宣告无罪 **5** (*jump*) [+ *fence, wall*] 跳过 **6** (*authorize*) 允许 ◊ *The helicopter was cleared for take-off.* 直升飞机被允许起飞。**7** [+ *cheque*] 兑现 ◊ *The bank cleared the cheque in three days.* 银行在3天内兑现了支票。
8 [商] ♦ **"half price to clear"** "半价清仓" **III** *vi* **1** [*weather, sky* +] 变晴; [*fog, smoke* +] 消散 ◊ *We're expecting this weather to clear soon.* 我们期望很快就会天晴。◊ *The fog had cleared a little.* 雾已经散开一点了。**2** [*cheque* +] 兑现 ◊ *Allow time for the cheque to clear.* 要等支票兑现。**IV** *adv* ♦ **clear of sth** [+ *place, ground*] 不接触某物
V *n* ♦ **to be in the clear** (*free of suspicion*) 不被怀疑; (*free of danger*) 安然无事 ♦ **to be clear about sth** 很明确某事 ♦ **to make o.s. clear** 表达清楚 ♦ **to make sth clear to sb** 使某人理解某事 ♦ **to keep** *or* **stay** *or* **steer clear of sb/sth** 避开某人/某物 ♦ **to have a clear head** 头脑清醒 ♦ **to clear the table** 收拾饭桌 ♦ **to clear one's throat** 清喉咙 ♦ **to clear sb of doing sth** [+ *suspect*] 洗刷某人某罪 ♦ **to clear a profit** 获得一笔净利 ♦ **to be in the clear** (*out of danger*) 无危险
❑ **clear away I** *vt* [+ *plates etc*] 清除 **II** *vi* (*remove plates etc*) 收拾
❑ **clear off** [非正式] *vi* (*leave*) 走开 ◊ *Clear off and leave me alone.* 快走开，别烦我。
❑ **clear out I** *vi* (*leave*) 走开 **II** *vt* [+ *cupboard, room*] 清除
❑ **clear up I** *vt* **1** [+ *room, mess*] 清理 **2** [+ *mystery, problem*] 澄清 **II** *vi* **1** (*tidy up*) 清理 **2** [*illness* +] 痊愈 **3** [*rain* +] 转晴

clearance ['klɪərəns] *n* [c/u] **1** (*removal*) [*of trees, mines etc*] 清除; [*of slums*] 拆除 **2** [*of place*] 清理 **3** (*authorization*) 许可 **4** [*of bridge*] 净空 ♦ **to get** *or* **be given clearance to land** 得到降落许可

clear-cut ['klɪə'kʌt] *adj* [+ *case, issue*] 黑白分明的

clearing ['klɪərɪŋ] *n* [c] (*in wood*) 林中空地

clearly ['klɪəlɪ] *adv* **1** (*with vb*) [*explain* +] 明确地; [*think* +] 清醒地; [*see* +] 清楚地; [*speak, hear* +] 清晰地 **2** (*with adj*) [+ *visible, audible*] 清楚地 **3** (*obviously*) 显然

clench [klɛntʃ] *vt* [+ *fist*] 捏紧; [+ *teeth*] 咬紧

clergy ['klə:dʒɪ] *n* [*pl*] 神职人员

clerk [klɑ:k, (美) klə:rk] *n* [c] **1** (*office worker*) 职员 **2** [美] (*sales person*) 售货员

clever ['klɛvə(r)] *adj* **1** (*intelligent*) 聪明的 **2** (*sly, crafty*) 要小聪明的 **3** (*ingenious*) [+ *device, arrangement*] 巧妙的

cliché ['kli:ʃeɪ] *n* [c] 陈词滥调

click [klɪk] **I** *vi* **1** [*device, switch, camera* +] 发出喀嗒声 **2** [计算机] 按 **3** [非正式] (*get on*) ♦ **to click (with sb)** (和某人) 一见如故 **4** [非正式] (*become clear*) 豁然开朗 **II** *vt* (*make sound with*) 使…发出喀嗒声 **III** *n* [c] **1** (*sound*) 喀嗒声 **2** [计算机] ♦ **with a click of one's mouse** 按一下鼠标 ♦ **to click on sth** [计算机] 点击某处 ♦ **to click one's tongue**

咂咂舌头 ♦**to click one's heels** 咯嚓一声立正

client ['klaɪənt] *n* [c] [*of lawyer*] 委托人; [*of company, restaurant, shop*] 顾客

cliff [klɪf] *n* [c] 悬崖

climate ['klaɪmɪt] *n* **1** [c/u] (*weather*) 气候 **2** [c] [*of opinion etc*] 气候

climax ['klaɪmæks] **I** *n* **1** [c] [*of event, career*] 高峰 **2** [c/u] (*sexual*) 高潮 **II** *vi* 达到高潮

climb [klaɪm] **I** *vt* (*also:* ***climb up***) [+ *tree etc*] 爬; [+ *mountain, hill*] 攀登; [+ *ladder*] 登; [+ *stairs, steps*] 上 **II** *vi* **1** [*sun* +] 徐徐上升 **2** [*plane* +] 爬升 **3** [*prices, shares* +] 上涨 **4** [*person* +] (*on frame, up mountain etc*) 攀爬 **5** (*move with effort*) ♦**to climb into/onto/over sth** 爬入/上/过某物 **III** *n* [c] [*of mountain, hill*] 攀登 ♦**to go climbing** 去爬山

❑**climb down** *vi* (*in argument, dispute*) 退让

climber ['klaɪmə(r)] *n* [c] **1** (*mountaineer*) 登山者 **2** (*plant*) 攀缘植物

climbing ['klaɪmɪŋ] *n* [u] 攀登

clinch [klɪntʃ] *vt* [+ *argument, contest*] 拿下; [+ *deal*] 达成

cling [klɪŋ] (*pt, pp* **clung**) *vi* **1** ♦**to cling (on)to** [+ *person, object*] 紧紧抓住; [+ *idea, belief*] 坚持 **2** ♦**to cling to sb's body** [*clothes, dress* +] 紧紧地贴在身上

clingfilm ['klɪŋfɪlm] [英] *n* [u] 保鲜纸 [美 = **plastic wrap**]

clinic ['klɪnɪk] [医] *n* [c] (*place*) 诊所; (*session*) 门诊

clinical ['klɪnɪkl] *adj* **1** [医] [+ *tests, trials*] 临床的 **2** (喻) (*dispassionate*) 客观的

clip [klɪp] **I** *n* [c] **1** (*for papers etc*) 回形针; (*for hair*) 发夹 **2** [电视, 电影] 剪辑 **II** *vt* **1** (*fasten*) 夹住 **2** (*cut*) [+ *hedge*] 修剪; [+ *nails*] ♦**to clip papers together** 将纸张夹在一起

clipping ['klɪpɪŋ] *n* [c] (*from newspaper*) 剪报

cloak [kləuk] **I** *n* [c] (*cape*) 斗篷 **II** *vt* [文] (*in mist, secrecy*) 掩藏

cloakroom ['kləukruːm] *n* [c] **1** (*for coats*) 衣帽间 **2** [英] (*bathroom*) 厕所

clock [klɔk] *n* [c] 钟 ♦**around the clock** [*work, guard* +] 日夜不停 ♦**to turn** *or* **put the clock back** (喻) 回到过去 ♦**to work against the clock** 争分夺秒地工作 ♦**30,000 miles on the clock** [英: 汽车] 里程计上记有3万英里行程

❑**clock in** *vi* (*for work*) 打卡上班

❑**clock off** *vi* (*from work*) 打卡下班

❑**clock on** *vi* = **clock in**

❑**clock out** *vi* = **clock off**

❑**clock up** [英] *vt* [+ *hours, miles*] 达到

clockwise ['klɔkwaɪz] **I** *adv* 顺时针地 **II** *adj* [+ *direction*] 顺时针的

clockwork ['klɔkwəːk] **I** *n* ♦**to go like clockwork** 顺利地进行 **II** *adj* [+ *model, toy*] 机械的

clog [klɔg] **I** *n* [c] (*shoe*) 木屐 **II** *vt* (*also:* ***clog up***) [+ *drain, pipe, skin, pores*] 堵塞; [+ *roads*] 阻塞 **III** *vi* (*also:* ***clog up***) [*drain, pipe* +] 堵塞

clone [kləun] **I** *n* [c] **1** [*of animal, plant*] 克隆 **2** (喻) (*object*) 复制品; (*person*) 几乎一模一样的人 **II** *vt* [+ *animal, plant*] 无性繁殖

✪**close**[1] [kləus] **I** *adj* **1** (*near*) 近的 **2** (*devoted*) 亲密的 ◊ *She and Linda were very close.* 她和琳达很亲密。 **3** [+ *relative*] 直系的 ◊ *the death of a close relative* 一位直系亲属的死亡 **4** [+ *contact, ties*] 密切的; [+ *connection, resemblance*] 严密的 ◊ *He keeps in close contact with his sons.* 他和儿子们保持密切的联系。◊ *There is a close connection between pain and tension.* 疼痛与紧张是息息相关的。 **5** [+ *examination, look*] 彻底的 ◊ *She took a closer look at the car.* 她更彻底地检查了那辆车。 **6** [+ *contest*] 势均力敌的 ◊ *It is close but we are going to win.* 双方势均力敌但我们会赢的。 **7** (*oppressive*) [+ *weather, atmosphere*] 闷热的 ◊ *It's very close today, isn't it?* 今天很闷热，是不是？ **II** *adv* (*near*) 紧紧地 ◊ *The children followed close behind them.* 孩子们紧紧地跟着他们。♦**close to** (*near*) 近 ◊ *The museum is quite close to the port.* 博物馆距离港口相当近。♦**how close is Edinburgh to Glasgow?** 爱丁堡距离格拉斯哥有多近？♦**a close friend** 一位密友 ♦**she's very close**

to her brother 她和她兄弟很亲近 ♦ **it was a close shave** *or* **call** *or* **thing** 这真是死里逃生 ♦ **at close quarters** 很接近 ♦ **to see sth close up** *or* **to** 从近处看某事 ♦ **close by, close at hand** 在近旁 ♦ **close to** *or* **on 30 years** 近30年 ♦ **she was close to tears** 她几乎要哭了

✪ **close**[2] [kləuz] **I** *vt* **1** [+ *door, window, lid*] 关 ◊ *He closed the door behind him.* 他走前把门关上了。 **2** [+ *shop, factory*] 关闭 ◊ *They closed the local college.* 他们关闭了当地的学院 **3** (*finalize*) [+ *sale, deal*] 结束 ◊ *He needs another $30,000 to close the deal.* 他还需要3万美元来完结这个交易。 **4** (*end*) [+ *case, conversation*] 结束 **II** *vi* **1** [*door, window, lid* +] 关 ◊ *She heard the door close.* 她听见门关了。 **2** [*shop, library* +] 关门 ◊ *Many libraries close on Saturdays at 1 p.m.* 很多图书馆星期六下午一点关门。 **3** (*end*) [*film, book* +] 收尾 ◊ *The film closes with a scene of sickening violence.*这部电影以一个令人作呕的暴力镜头收尾。 **III** *n* [s] (*end*) 结束 ◊ *the close of the day* 黄昏时分 ♦ **to bring sth to a close** 结束某事 ♦ **to draw to a close** 接近尾声

❑ **close down I** *vi* [*factory, business* +] 关闭 **II** *vt* [+ *factory, business*] 使关闭

❑ **close in** *vi* **1** [*hunters, police* +] 包围 **2** [*winter, darkness* +] 渐渐缩短 ♦ **the days are closing in** 白天渐渐变短

❑ **close off** *vt* [+ *area*] 封锁

❑ **close on** *vt* [不可拆分] (*in race, pursuit*) 渐渐赶上

closed [kləuzd] *adj* **1** (字) [+ *door, window*] 关着的; [+ *shop, library*] 关着门的; [+ *road*] 封锁着的 **2** (喻) [+ *society, community*] 闭关自守的

closely ['kləuslɪ] *adv* **1** [*examine, watch* +] 仔细地 **2** [*connected*] 密切地 **3** [*resemble* +] 非常 **4** [*follow* +] 紧紧地 **5** [*work* +] 密切地 ♦ **we are closely related** 我们是近亲 ♦ **a closely guarded secret** 一个严格保守的秘密

closet ['klɔzɪt] **I** *n* [c] [美] 壁橱 [英= **cupboard**] **II** *adj* 隐蔽的 ♦ **to come out of the closet** (喻) 从隐蔽状态转为公开

close-up ['kləusʌp] [摄影] *n* [c] 特写

closing time *n* [c/u] (*in shop, pub*) 关门时间

closure ['kləuʒə(r)] *n* **1** [c/u] [*of factory, business*] 倒闭 **2** [c] [*of road, border*] 封锁

clot [klɔt] **I** *n* [c] (*blood*) (*also:* ***blood clot***) 凝块 **II** *vi* [*blood* +] 凝固

cloth [klɔθ] *n* **1** [c/u] (*fabric*) 布料 **2** [c] (*for cleaning, dusting*) 布 **3** [c] (*tablecloth*) 桌布 ♦ **piece of cloth** 一块布

clothe [kləuð] *vt* (*provide with clothes*) 供给…衣服 ♦ **clothed in green** 穿绿色衣服

clothes [kləuðz] *n* [*pl*] 衣服 ♦ **to put one's clothes on** 穿衣服 ♦ **to take one's clothes off** 脱衣服

clothesline ['kləuðzlaɪn] *n* [c] 晾衣绳

clothes peg [英] *n* [c] 晾衣夹 [美= **clothespin**]

clothespin ['kləuðzpɪn] [美] *n* [c] 晾衣夹 [英= **clothes peg**]

clothing ['kləuðɪŋ] *n* [u] 衣服 ♦ **an item** *or* **a piece of clothing** 一件衣服

> 📖 **clothing** 是不可数名词。不能用clothings 或a clothing。*He took off his wet clothing.* 可以说 **an item of clothing**，**a piece of clothing** 或者 **an article of clothing**。

clotted cream ['klɔtɪd-] [英] *n* [u] 浓缩奶油

cloud [klaud] **I** *n* **1** [c/u] (*in sky*) 云 **2** [c] [*of smoke, dust*] 雾 **II** *vt* [+ *sb's judgement, view*] 使模糊; [+ *outlook, atmosphere*] 使暗淡 ♦ **every cloud has a silver lining** 黑暗中总有一线光明

❑ **cloud over** *vi* **1** [*sky* +] 阴云密布 **2** [*face, eyes* +] 阴沉下来 ♦ **it's clouding over** 天阴了

cloudy ['klaudɪ] *adj* **1** [+ *day, sky, weather*] 多云的 **2** [+ *liquid*] 混浊的 ♦ **it's cloudy** 天阴

clove [kləuv] *n* [c] **1** (*spice*) 丁香 **2** [*of garlic*] 瓣

clown [klaun] **I** *n* [c] (*in circus*) 小丑 **II** *vi* (*also:* ***clown about, clown around***) 胡闹

✪ **club** [klʌb] **I** *n* [c] **1** (*society, place*) 俱乐部 ◊ *a chess club* 象棋俱乐部 ◊ *I'll see you at the club.* 我在俱乐部见你。**2** [体育] 俱乐部 ◊ *Liverpool football club* 利物浦足球俱乐部 **3** (*nightclub*) 夜总会 **4** (*weapon*) 大头棒 **5** (*stick*) (*also:* ***golf club***) 球棒 **II** *vt* (*hit*) 用棒棍打 **III** *vi* ♦ **to club together** [英] (*for gift, card*) 凑钱 **IV clubs** *n* [*pl*] [纸牌] 梅花 ♦ **to club sb to death** 用棍棒将某人打死

club class *n* [u] 会员级

clue [kluː] *n* [c] **1** (*in investigation*) 线索 **2** (*in crossword, game*) 提示 **3** (喻) (*indication*) 线索 ♦ **I haven't a clue** [非正式] 我一无所知

clump [klʌmp] *n* [c] [*of trees, grass*] 丛; [*of hair*] 绺

clumsy ['klʌmzɪ] *adj* **1** [+ *person*] 笨手笨脚的 **2** [+ *effort, attempt*] 笨拙的 **3** [+ *object*] 不好使用的

clung [klʌŋ] *pt, pp of* **cling**

cluster ['klʌstə(r)] **I** *n* [c] [*of people*] 群; [*of things, cases*] 组 **II** *vt* ♦ **to be clustered around sth** 聚集在某物的周围

❑ **cluster around** *vt* [不可拆分] 聚集

❑ **cluster together** *vi* [*people* +] 成群; [*things* +] 成簇

clutch [klʌtʃ] **I** *vt* 紧抓 **II** *n* [c] [汽车] 离合器 **III clutches** *n* [*pl*] ♦ **to fall into sb's clutches** 陷入某人的控制中

❑ **clutch at** *vt* [不可拆分] (字) 抓住

clutter ['klʌtə(r)] **I** *vt* (*also:* ***clutter up***) 使凌乱 **II** *n* [u] 杂乱的东西

cm *abbr* (= ***centimetre(s)***) 厘米

Co. *abbr* **1** (= ***company***) 公司 **2** (= ***county***) 郡

c/o *abbr* (= ***care of***) 由…转交

coach [kəutʃ] **I** *n* [c] **1** [英] 长途汽车 [美 = **bus**] **2** (*horse-drawn*) 大马车 **3** [英] [*of train*] 车厢 [美 = **car**] **4** [体育] (*trainer*) 教练 **5** (*tutor*) 私人教师 **II** *vt* **1** [体育] 训练 **2** [教育] 辅导

coach trip [英] *n* [c] 长途汽车旅行团 ♦ **to go on a coach trip** 参加长途汽车旅行团

coal [kəul] *n* **1** [u] (*substance*) 煤 **2** [c] (*piece of coal*) 煤块

coalition [kəuə'lɪʃən] *n* [c/u] **1** (*government*) 联合 **2** (*with same aim*) 联盟

coal mine ['kəulmaɪn] *n* [c] 煤矿

coarse [kɔːs] *adj* **1** [+ *cloth, salt, sand*] 粗的 **2** (*vulgar*) [+ *person, remark*] 粗俗的

coast [kəust] **I** *n* [c] 海岸 **II** *vi* **1** [*car, bicycle* +] 滑行 **2** (*in school, competition*) 毫不费力地进行 ♦ **to coast to success/to a victory** 轻松取胜

coastal ['kəustl] *adj* [+ *area, town, waters*] 沿海的

coastguard ['kəustgɑːd] [尤英] *n* **1** [c] (*person*) 海岸警卫队队员 **2** ♦ **the coastguard** (*service*) 海岸警卫队

coastline ['kəustlaɪn] *n* [c] 海岸线

coat [kəut] **I** *n* [c] **1** (*overcoat*) 外套 **2** [*of animal*] 皮毛 **3** [*of paint, varnish*] 层 **II** *vt* 撒满

coat hanger *n* [c] 衣架

coating ['kəutɪŋ] *n* [c] [*of chocolate, sugar, oil*] 一层; [*of dust*] 外层

coax [kəuks] *vt* ♦ **to coax sb into doing sth** 哄某人做某事

cob [kɔb] *n see* **corn**

cobbled ['kɔbld] *adj* [+ *street*] 用大卵石铺的

cobweb ['kɔbwɛb] *n* [c] 蜘蛛网

cocaine [kə'keɪn] *n* [u] 可卡因

cock [kɔk] **I** *n* [c] **1** [英] 公鸡 [美 = **rooster**] **2** [英] (*male bird*) 雄禽 **3** [非正式, 疑讳] (*penis*) 阴茎 **II** *vt* **1** [+ *head, ear*] 翘起 **2** [+ *gun*] 扳起…的扳机

cockerel ['kɔkərəl] [尤英] *n* [c] 小公鸡

cockpit ['kɔkpɪt] *n* [c] (*in aircraft*) 驾驶舱; (*in racing car*) 驾驶座

cockroach ['kɔkrəutʃ] *n* [c] 蟑螂

cocktail ['kɔkteɪl] *n* [c] **1** (*drink*) 鸡尾酒 **2** (喻) 合成物

cocoa ['kəukəu] *n* [u] 可可

coconut ['kəukənʌt] *n* **1** [c] (*nut*) 椰子 **2** [u] (*flesh*) 椰肉

COD *abbr* (= ***cash on delivery,*** [美] ***collect on delivery***) 货到付款

cod [kɔd] (*pl* **cod** *or* **cods**) *n* **1** [c] (*fish*) 鳕鱼 **2** [u] (*as food*) 鳕鱼

code [kəud] *n* 1 [c] [*of practice, behaviour*] 准则 2 [c] (*cipher*) 密码 3 [c] (*as reference*) 标记 4 [c] [通信] 区号 5 [c/U] [计算机, 科学] 编码 ♦ **code of conduct** 行为准则 ♦ **code of practice** 实践准则 ♦ **in code** 用密码

co-ed ['kəu'ɛd] **I** *adj abbr* [教育] (= ***coeducational***) 男女同校的 **II** *n abbr* [美] (*female student*) 男女同校的女生

coffee ['kɔfɪ] *n* 1 [U] 咖啡 2 [c] (*cup of coffee*) 一杯咖啡 ♦ **black coffee** 黑咖啡 ♦ **white coffee** 牛奶咖啡 ♦ **coffee with cream** 加奶油的咖啡

coffee bar *n* [c] 咖啡馆

coffee bean *n* [c] 咖啡豆

coffee break *n* [c] 工间休息时间

coffee pot *n* [c] 咖啡壶

coffee shop *n* [c] 咖啡店

coffee table *n* [c] 咖啡桌

coffin ['kɔfɪn] *n* [c] 棺材

cog [kɔg] [术语] *n* [c] 轮齿

cognac ['kɔnjæk] *n* 1 [c/U] (*liquid*) 法国白兰地 2 [c] (*glass of cognac*) 一杯法国白兰地

cognitive ['kɔgnɪtɪv] [正式] *adj* 认识的

coherent [kəu'hɪərənt] *adj* 1 [+ *strategy, policy*] 连贯的 2 [+ *person*] 条理清楚的

coil [kɔɪl] **I** *n* [c] 1 [*of rope, wire*] 卷 2 (*loop*) 圈 3 [汽车, 电子] 线圈 4 (*contraceptive*) 子宫节育环 **II** *vt* (*also:* ***coil up***) [+ *rope etc*] 卷 **III** *vi* [*rope etc* +] 盘绕

coin [kɔɪn] **I** *n* [c] 硬币 **II** *vt* [+ *word, slogan*] 创造

coincide [kəuɪn'saɪd] *vi* 1 [*events* +] 同时发生 2 [*ideas, views* +] 相一致 ♦ **to coincide with sth** [*event* +] 和某事同时发生

coincidence [kəu'ɪnsɪdəns] *n* [c/U] 巧合

Coke® [kəuk] *n* [U] (*drink*) 可口可乐

coke [kəuk] *n* [U] 1 (*fuel*) 焦炭 2 [非正式] (*cocaine*) 可卡因

cola ['kəulə] *n* [c/U] 可乐

colander ['kɔləndə(r)] *n* [c] 滤器

cold [kəuld] **I** *adj* 1 [+ *water, object*] 凉的; [+ *weather, room, meat*] 冷的 2 [+ *person*] (*unemotional*) 冷淡的; (*unfriendly*) 不友好的 **II** *n* 1 [U] (*weather*) ♦ **the cold** 寒冷天气 2 [c] (*illness*) 感冒 ◊ *I've got a cold.* 我感冒了。♦ **it's cold** 天气寒冷 ♦ **to be** *or* **feel cold** [*person* +] 感到冷 ♦ **to catch (a) cold** 患感冒 ♦ **in cold blood** [*kill etc* +] 残忍地 ♦ **to have/get cold feet (about sth)** (在某事上)临阵畏缩

> 📖 **freezing** 可用于强调天气很冷，尤其是有霜冻的严冬。夏季如果气温低于平均温度，可以用 **cool**。通常，**cold** 表示的温度比 **cool** 低。**cool** 表示温度适宜、凉爽。*A cool breeze swept off the sea; it was pleasant out there.* 如果非常 **cool**，或太 **cool**，可以用 **chilly**。

coldly ['kəuldlɪ] *adv* [*speak, behave* +] 冷漠地

cold sore [英:医] *n* [c] 唇疱疹 [美= **fever blister**]

coleslaw ['kəulslɔː] [烹饪] *n* [U] 酸卷心菜丝

colic ['kɔlɪk] [医] *n* [U] 急腹痛

collaborate [kə'læbəreɪt] *vi* 1 (*on book, research*) 合作 2 (*with enemy*) 勾结 ♦ **to collaborate (with sb) on sth** (与某人)合作做某事

collaboration [kəlæbə'reɪʃən] *n* 1 [c/U] (*on book, research*) 合作 2 [U] (*with enemy*) 勾结 ♦ **in collaboration with** 与…合作

collapse [kə'læps] **I** *vi* [*building, table* +] 倒坍; [*system, company* +] 瓦解; (*from hunger, weakness etc*) [*person* +] 倒下 **II** *n* [S/U] [*of building, table*] 倒坍; [*of system, company*] 瓦解; (*from hunger, weakness etc*) 垮掉

collar ['kɔlə(r)] **I** *n* [c] 1 [*of coat, shirt*] 领子 2 [*of dog, cat*] 颈圈 **II** *vt* [非正式] [+ *person*] 抓住

collarbone ['kɔləbəun] *n* [c] 锁骨

colleague ['kɔliːg] *n* [c] 同事

collect [kə'lɛkt] **I** *vt* 1 [+ *wood, litter etc*] 采集 2 (*as hobby*) 收集 3 [英] (*fetch*) [+ *person*] 接; [+ *object*] 取 4 [+ *money, donations*] 募捐 5 [+ *debts, taxes etc*] 收 6 [+ *mail*] 取 **II** *vi* 1 [*dust, dirt* +] 积聚 2 (*for charity, gift*) 募捐 ♦ **to call collect, make a**

collect call [美:通信] 打对方付款的电话 [英 = **to reverse the charges**] ♦**to collect o.s.** *or* **one's thoughts** 使自己镇定下来 ♦**collect on delivery** [美:商] 货到付款

collection [kəˈlɛkʃən] *n* **1** [c] [*of art, stamps etc*] 收藏品 **2** [c] [*of poems, stories etc*] 文集 **3** [u] (*picking up*) [*of goods, mail*] 收取; [*of data*] 收集 **4** [c] (*for charity, gift*) 募捐

collective [kəˈlɛktɪv] **I** *adj* 集体的 **II** *n* [c] 合作社

collector [kəˈlɛktə(r)] *n* [c] **1** [*of art, stamps etc*] 收藏家 **2** ♦**tax/debt collector** 收税/讨债员 ♦**a collector's item** 一件收藏品

college [ˈkɔlɪdʒ] *n* **1** [c/u] (*for further education*) 学院 **2** [c] [*of university*] 学院 ♦**to go to college** 上大学 ♦**college of education** [英] 师范学院

collide [kəˈlaɪd] *vi* [*cars, people* +] 碰撞 ♦**to collide with sth/sb** 与某物/某人碰撞

collision [kəˈlɪʒən] *n* [c/u] (*of vehicles*) 碰撞 ♦**to be on a collision course** (字) 必然相撞; (喻) 必然发生冲突

cologne [kəˈləun] *n* [c/u] (*also:* ***eau de cologne***) 科隆香水

Colombia [kəˈlɔmbɪə] *n* 哥伦比亚

Colombian [kəˈlɔmbɪən] **I** *adj* 哥伦比亚的 **II** *n* [c] (*person*) 哥伦比亚人

colon [ˈkəulən] *n* [c] **1** (*punctuation mark*) 冒号 **2** [解剖] 结肠

colonel [ˈkə:nl] *n* [c] 上校

colonial [kəˈləunɪəl] *adj* 殖民地的

colony [ˈkɔlənɪ] *n* [c] **1** (*country*) 殖民地 **2** [*of animals*] 群体

color *etc* [ˈkʌlə(r)] [美] = **colour** *etc*

✪ **colour** (美 **color**) [ˈkʌlə(r)] **I** *n* **1** [c] 颜色 **2** [c] (*skin colour*) 肤色 ◊ *South Africans of all colours* 各种肤色的南非人 **3** [u] (*interest*) 生动 **II** *vt* **1** (*with paint, crayons, dye*) 给…着色 ◊ *Does she colour her hair?* 她染头发吗? **2** (*affect*) [+ *judgement, account*] 影响 **III** *vi* (*blush*) 脸红 **IV** *cpd* [复合词] [+ *film, photograph, television*] 彩色 ♦**in colour** [+ *film, illustrations*] 彩色

❑ **colour in** *vt* [+ *picture*] 给…着色

colour-blind (美 **color-blind**) [ˈkʌləblaɪnd] *adj* 色盲的

coloured (美 **colored**) [ˈkʌləd] *adj* **1** [+ *illustration etc*] 有色的 **2** [过时] [+ *person*] 有色的 ♦**brightly coloured** 色泽鲜艳

colour film (美 **color film**) *n* [c/u] 彩色胶卷

colourful (美 **colorful**) [ˈkʌləful] *adj* **1** (*brightly coloured*) 色泽鲜艳的 **2** [+ *account, history*] 丰富多彩的 **3** [+ *personality*] 引人注目的

colouring (美 **coloring**) [ˈkʌlərɪŋ] *n* **1** [u] (*complexion*) 面色 **2** [c/u] (*in food*) 色素

colour television (美 **color television**) *n* [c/u] 彩色电视

column [ˈkɔləm] *n* [c] **1** [建筑] 支柱 **2** [*of smoke*] 柱形物 **3** [*of people, tanks*] 纵队 **4** (*in newspaper etc*) 专栏

coma [ˈkəumə] [医] *n* [c/u] 昏迷 ♦**to be in a coma** 处于昏迷状态

comb [kəum] **I** *n* [c] 梳子 **II** *vt* **1** [+ *hair*] 梳理 **2** (*search*) [+ *area*] 彻底搜寻

combat I *n* [军] [u/c] 战斗 **II** *vt* (*oppose*) [+ *drugs, crime etc*] 与…斗争

combination [kɔmbɪˈneɪʃən] *n* [c] **1** (*mixture*) 混合 **2** (*for lock, safe etc*) 密码

combine [*vb* kəmˈbaɪn, *n* ˈkɔmbaɪn] **I** *vt* ♦**to combine sth with sth** 将某物与某物结合起来 **II** *vi* [*qualities, situations* +] 结合; [*people, groups* +] 组合; [化] 化合 **III** *n* [经济] 联合公司 ♦**a combined effort** 协力

✪ **come**

KEYWORD

[kʌm] (*pt* **came**, *pp* **come**) *vi*

1 (*move towards, arrive*) 来 ♦**come here!** 到这儿来! ♦**I'm just coming!** 我这就来! ♦**can I come too?** 我也能来吗? ♦**come with me** 跟我来 ♦**a girl came into the room** 一个女孩进了房间 ♦**he came to a door** 他到了门口 ♦**why don't you come to lunch on Saturday?** 何不星期六过来吃午饭呢? ♦**to come to/and do sth** 来做某事 ♦**he's come here to work** 他已经到了这儿工作

2 ♦**to come to** (*reach*) 到达;

(*amount to*) 达到 ♦ **her hair came to her waist** 她的头发长到腰的位置了 ♦ **to come to a decision** 做出决定 ♦ **the bill came to £40** 账单共计40英镑
3 (*occur*) ♦ **an idea came to me** 我想到了一个主意 ♦ **it suddenly came to me that ...** 我突然想到…
4 (*in inheritance, as payment etc*) ♦ **to come to sb** 留给某人
5 (*be, become*) ♦ **to come first/second/last** *etc* (*in series*) 排在第一/第二/最后{等}; (*in competition, race*) 位居第一/第二/最后{等} ♦ **to come loose/undone** *etc* 松了/解开了{等} ♦ **I've come to like him** 我开始喜欢上他了 ♦ **how did you come to meet him?** 你是怎么遇到他的？
6 (*be available*) ♦ **it comes in blue or green** 蓝色或绿色的有现货
7 (*in expressions*) ♦ **when you come down to it, when it comes down to it** 归根结底 ♦ **come to think of it** 再想想 ◊ *You know, when you come to think of it, this is very odd.* 再想想的话，这是很奇怪的。 ♦ **when it comes to ...** 当谈到…

❑ **come about** *vi* [*discovery, solution* +] 发生

❑ **come across I** *vt* [不可拆分] (*find*) 偶然发现 **II** *vi* ♦ **to come across well/badly** [*person* +] 留下好/坏印象; [*idea, meaning* +] 表达清楚/不清楚

❑ **come along** *vi* **1** 来 **2** (*arrive*) 不期而至 ♦ **it was lucky you came along** 真幸运你来了 **3** (*come on the scene*) 出现 ♦ **when an exciting new author comes along ...** 当一个令人兴奋的新作家出现时… **4** (*make progress*) 进展 ♦ **come along!** (*encouraging*) 快一点！

❑ **come apart** *vi* 裂成碎片

❑ **come around** *vi* **1** (*visit*) 来访 **2** (*agree*) 改变态度 **3** (*reoccur*) 来到 ◊ *I can't believe Christmas has come around again so fast!* 我不能相信这么快又是圣诞节了！ **4** (*regain consciousness*) 苏醒过来

❑ **come at** *vt* [不可拆分] 扑向 ♦ **he came at me with a knife** 他拿着刀扑向我

❑ **come away** *vi* **1** (*depart*) 离开 **2** (*become detached*) 脱落

❑ **come back** *vi* **1** (*return*) 回来 ♦ **I'm coming back to that** (*in discussion etc*) 我过会儿再回到那个问题 ♦ **can I come back to you on that one?** 我能过会儿再跟你讨论那个问题吗？ ♦ **to come back into fashion** 重新又流行起来 **2** (*come to mind*) ♦ **it will come back to you** 你会回想起来的 ♦ **it all came back** 全都想起来了

❑ **come between** *vt* [不可拆分] 离间

❑ **come by** *vt* [不可拆分] (*acquire*) 得到 ♦ **jobs were hard to come by** 很难找到工作

❑ **come down** *vi* **1** [*price* +] 降低 **2** (*fall to ground*) [*plane* +] 坠落; [*tree* +] 倒下; [*building* +] 倒塌 **3** (*descend*) 降下

❑ **come down on** *vt* [不可拆分] (*declare support for*) ♦ **to come down on the side of sth** 声明支持某事的一方

❑ **come down to** *vt* [不可拆分] 归结为

❑ **come down with** *vt* [不可拆分] [+ *illness*] 染上

❑ **come forward** *vi* (*volunteer*) 自告奋勇

❑ **come from** *vt* [不可拆分] [+ *place, source*] 来自 ♦ **I come from London** 我来自伦敦 ♦ **where do you come from?** 你是哪里人？ ♦ **the feeling of elation that comes from winning** 来自胜利的得意感

❑ **come in** *vi* **1** (*to room, house etc*) 进入 ♦ **come in!** 进来！ ♦ **the tide is coming in** 潮水正在上涨 **2** [*report, mail, phone call* +] 收到 **3** [*money, salary* +] 进账 **4** (*on deal etc*) 参与 **5** (*become common*) [*system* +] 普遍起来; [*idea, fashion* +] 流行起来 **6** (*fit in*) 起作用

❑ **come in for** *vt* [不可拆分] [+ *criticism*] 受到

❑ **come into** *vt* [不可拆分] **1** (*inherit*) 继承 **2** (*be involved in*) 起作用 **3** (*play a role*) ♦ **money doesn't come into it** 钱不是问题 **4** (*enter*) ♦ **to come into operation/force** 开始运行/生效 ♦ **to come**

into fashion 开始流行

❑**come of** *vt* [不可拆分] (*result from*) 是…的结果 ♦**nothing came of it** 没有任何结果 ♦**no good will come of it** 这不会产生任何好处

❑**come off I** *vi* **1** [*button, handle* +] 脱落 **2** (*succeed*) [*event, attempt, plan* +] 成功 ♦**to come off best/worst** *etc* 表现最佳/最差{等} **II** *vt* [不可拆分] **1** [+ *drug, medicine*] 戒掉 **2** [非正式] ♦**come off it!** 别胡扯了!

❑**come on** *vi* **1** (*progress*) [*pupil, work, project* +] 进展 ♦**come on!** (*giving encouragement*) 来!; (*hurry up*) 快一点! **2** [*lights, heating, electricity* +] 接通

❑**come on to** *vt* [不可拆分] 开始讨论

❑**come out** *vi* **1** [*person* +] (*out of house, for evening etc*) 出去 **2** (*appear*) [*sun* +] 出现 **3** (*become known*) 为人所知 **4** (*become available*) [*book* +] 出版; [*film* +] 上映 **5** (*be printable*) [*photograph* +] 冲洗得出 **6** (*as homosexual*) 公开承认是同性恋 **7** (喻) (*emerge*) 显得 **8** (*be erased*) [*stain* +] 除去 **9** [*workers* +] ♦**to come out (on strike)** 罢工 **10** (*declare o.s.*) ♦**to come out against/in favour of sth** 宣布反对/支持某事

❑**come out in** *vt* [不可拆分] ♦**to come out in spots/in a rash** 起满小包/疹子

❑**come out with** *vt* [不可拆分] [+ *remark*] 说出

❑**come over I** *vt* [不可拆分] [*feeling* +] 牢牢控制 ♦**I don't know what's come over him!** 我不知道他是怎么了! **II** *vi* **1** (*appear*) 表现 ♦**to come over as** 表现为 **2** (*visit*) 顺便拜访 ♦**I'll come over later** 我一会儿过来

❑**come round** *vi* = **come around**

❑**come through I** *vt* [不可拆分] (*survive*) [+ *crisis, illness*] 经历…而幸存 **II** *vi* **1** (*be obvious*) 清晰可辨 **2** (*arrive*) [*call, news, money* +] 传来

❑**come to** *vi* (*regain consciousness*) 苏醒

❑**come under** *vt* [不可拆分] **1** [+ *criticism, pressure, attack*] 受到 **2** [+ *heading*] 归入 **3** [+ *authority*] 受…支配

❑**come up** *vi* **1** (*approach*) 走近 **2** (*arise*) [*problem, opportunity* +] 突然出现 **3** (*be about to happen*) 即将发生 **4** (*be mentioned*) 被提到 **5** (*rise*) [*sun* +] 升起

❑**come up against** *vt* [不可拆分] [+ *resistance, difficulties*] 碰到

❑**come upon** *vt* [不可拆分] (*find*) 偶然碰到

❑**come up to** *vt* [不可拆分] **1** (*get on for*) 接近 ♦**it's coming up to 11 o'clock** 快到11点钟了 **2** (*approach*) 走近 **3** (*meet*) ♦**the film didn't come up to our expectations** 电影没有我们预期的那么好

❑**come up with** *vt* [不可拆分] [+ *idea, suggestion*] 提出; [+ *money*] 设法弄到

comeback ['kʌmbæk] *n* **1** ♦**to make a comeback** [*pop star, sportsperson* +] 东山再起; [*fashion* +] 重新流行 **2** ♦**to have no comeback** 得不到补偿

comedian [kə'miːdɪən] [戏剧, 电视] *n* [c] 喜剧演员

comedy ['kɔmɪdɪ] *n* **1** [u] (*humour*) 幽默 **2** [c] (*play, film*) 喜剧

comet ['kɔmɪt] *n* [c] 彗星

comfort ['kʌmfət] **I** *n* **1** [u] (*physical, material*) 舒适 **2** [c/u] (*solace, relief*) 安慰 **II** *vt* (*console*) 安慰 **III comforts** *n* [*pl*] 使生活舒适的东西 ♦**to live in comfort** 过着舒适的生活

comfortable ['kʌmfətəbl] *adj* **1** [*person* +] ♦**to be comfortable** (*physically*) 舒服的; (*financially*) 富足的 **2** [+ *furniture, room, clothes*] 使人舒服的 **3** [医] [+ *sick person*] 情况良好的 **4** [+ *life, job etc*] 轻松的 **5** [+ *victory, majority*] 不费力的 ♦**to make o.s. comfortable** 自在点 ♦**I don't feel very comfortable about it** 我对这件事感到不自在 ♦**to be/feel comfortable with sth/sb** 对某事/某人感到舒坦

comfortably ['kʌmfətəblɪ] *adv* **1** [*sit, settle* +] 舒服地 **2** [*live* +] 宽裕地

3 ♦**to be comfortably off** 生活宽裕

comfort station [美] *n* [c] 公共厕所

comic ['kɔmɪk] **I** *adj* **1** (*also: **comical***) 滑稽的 **2** [+ *actor, opera*] 喜剧的 **II** *n* [c] **1** (*comedian*) 喜剧演员 **2** [英] (*magazine*) 连环漫画 [美 = **comic book**]

comic book [美] *n* [c] 连环漫画 [英 = **comic**]

✪**coming** ['kʌmɪŋ] *adj* [+ *event, attraction*] 即将到来的 ◊ *the coming election* 即将到来的选举 ♦**in the coming months** 下几个月

comma ['kɔmə] *n* [c] 逗号

command [kə'mɑːnd] **I** *n* **1** [c] (*order*) 命令 **2** [U] [军] (*authority*) 指挥 **3** [U] (*mastery*) [*of subject*] 运用能力 **4** [c] [计算机] 指令 **II** *vt* **1** [文] ♦**to command sb to do sth** 命令某人做某事 **2** [+ *troops*] 指挥 **3** [+ *respect, attention, obedience*] 博得 ♦**to be in command** [*person, government* +] 处于指挥地位 ♦**to be in command of sth** [军] 指挥某事 ♦**to have/take command of sth** [+ *situation*] 控制/取得控制某事; [军] [+ *squadron etc*] 指挥某事 ♦**at sb's command** [正式] [+ *money, resources etc*] 可自由支配

commander [kə'mɑːndə(r)] [军] *n* [c] 指挥官

commemorate [kə'mɛməreɪt] *vt* [+ *person, event*] 纪念

commence [kə'mɛns] [正式] *vt, vi* 开始

commencement [kə'mɛnsmənt] *n* **1** [U] [正式] 开始 **2** [c/U] [美:大学] 学位授予典礼 [英 = **graduation**]

commend [kə'mɛnd] [正式] *vt* (*praise*) 表扬 ♦**to commend sb for sth/for doing sth** 表扬某人某事/做某事 ♦**to commend sth/sb to sb** (*recommend*) 向某人推荐某物/某人

comment ['kɔmɛnt] **I** *n* **1** [c/U] (*written, spoken*) 评论 **2** [s] (*reflection*) (*on situation, development etc*) 写照 **II** *vi* ♦**to comment (on sth)** (对某事)发表意见 ♦**"no comment"** "无可奉告" ♦**to comment that ...** 评论…

> **comment on** 或 **make a comment about** 某个情形，即对该情形发表意见。*Mr Cook has not commented on these reports... I was wondering whether you had any comments.* **mention** 某事，表示简要地提及未谈到的话题。*He mentioned that he might go to New York.* **remark on** 或 **make a remark about** 某事，表示把你的想法或所见到的事情说出来，通常是以一种比较随意的方式。*Visitors have remarked on how well the children look...General Smith's remarks about the conflict.*

commentary ['kɔməntərɪ] *n* **1** [c/U] (*on match, proceedings*) 实况报道 **2** [c] (*book, article*) 集注

commentator ['kɔmənteɪtə(r)] *n* [c] **1** (*describing match, proceedings*) 解说员 **2** (*expert*) 评论者

commerce ['kɔməːs] *n* [U] 贸易

commercial [kə'məːʃəl] **I** *adj* [+ *organization, activity*] 商业的; [+ *success, failure*] 从盈利角度出发; [+ *television, radio*] 商业性的 **II** *n* [c] (*advertisement*) 广告 ♦**Christmas has become too commercial** 圣诞节已经变得太商业化了

commission [kə'mɪʃən] **I** *n* **1** [c/U] (*to artist, musician etc*) 委托 **2** [c] (*piece of work*) 委托项目 **3** [c/U] (*money*) 佣金 **4** [c] (*committee*) 委员会 **5** [c] [军] 授衔令 **II** *vt* **1** [+ *study, book, painting etc*] 委托人做 **2** [军] 任命 ♦**out of commission** (*not working*) 不能使用 ◊ *His car is out of commission.* 他的车坏了。♦**I get 10% commission** 我得到10%的佣金 ♦**to commission sb to do sth** 委托某人做某事 ♦**to commission sth from sb** 委托某人做某事

commissioner [kə'mɪʃənə(r)] *n* [c] **1** (*in organization, government*) 长官 **2** (*also: **police commissioner***) 警察局长

commit [kə'mɪt] *vt* **1** [+ *crime, offence*] 犯; [+ *sin, adultery*] 做 **2** (*pledge*) [+ *money, resources*] 调配 **3** ♦**to commit sb to** [+ *hospital,* *prison*] 把某人关进 ♦ **to commit suicide** 自杀 ♦ **to commit sth to sth** (*pledge*) 调配某物用于某事 ♦ **to commit o.s. (to doing sth)** 承诺(做某事) ♦ **to commit sth to writing** 书面记录某事 ♦ **to commit sb for trial** [英] 将某人送交刑事法庭受审

commitment [kə'mɪtmənt] *n* **1** [U] (*to ideology, system*) ♦ **commitment (to sth)** 献身(于某事) **2** [C] (*obligation*) 义务 ♦ **to make a commitment (to do sth)** 作出承诺(做某事)

committed [kə'mɪtɪd] *adj* [+ *writer, politician*] 忠诚的; [+ *Christian*] 虔诚的 ♦ **to be committed to sth/doing sth** 尽忠于某事/做某事

✪ **committee** [kə'mɪtɪ] *n* [C] 委员会 ♦ **to be on a committee** 任委员会委员

commodity [kə'mɔdɪtɪ] *n* [C] 商品

✪ **common** ['kɔmən] **I** *adj* **1** (*usual*) 常见的 ◊ *Jones is a common name there.* 琼斯在那儿是个常见的名字。 **2** (*shared*) 共同的 ◊ *Our countries share a common frontier.* 我们的国家有共同的边界线。 **3** (*not special*) 普通的 ◊ *the common man* 普通人 **4** (*vulgar*) [+ *person, manners*] 粗俗的 ◊ *She's a little common at times.* 她有时有点俗气。 **II** *n* [C] (*area*) 公用地 ♦ **common to** 常见于 ♦ **in common use** 常用 ♦ **it's common knowledge that ...** 大家都知道… ♦ **for the common good** 为了大家的利益 ♦ **the idea has become common currency** 这观点已是众所周知的了 ♦ **common ground** 共同点 ♦ **to have sth in common** [*people* +] 有某些共同点; [*things* +] 有共同的某特征 ♦ **to have sth in common with sb/sth** 与某人/某物有某共同点 ♦ **not to have anything in common (with sb/sth)** (与某人/某物)没有任何共同点

commonly ['kɔmənlɪ] *adv* 通常地

commonplace ['kɔmənpleɪs] **I** *adj* 普通的 **II** *n* [C] 寻常的事

Commons ['kɔmənz] [英] *n* ♦ **the Commons** (*also: **House of Commons***) 下议院

common sense *n* [U] 常识

Commonwealth ['kɔmənwɛlθ] *n* ♦ **the Commonwealth** 英联邦

commotion [kə'məuʃən] *n* [C/U] 混乱

communal ['kɔmju:nl] *adj* **1** (*shared*) [+ *area, room, kitchen*] 公用的 **2** (*between communities*) [+ *tension, violence*] 小群体间的

commune [*n* 'kɔmju:n, *vb* kə'mju:n] **I** *n* [C] (*group*) 公社 **II** *vi* [文] ♦ **to commune with sth** 与某物沟通 ◊ *to commune with nature* 与大自然交融

communicate [kə'mju:nɪkeɪt] **I** *vi* **1** (*by writing, speaking etc*) 联络 **2** (*talk openly*) 沟通 **II** *vt* [+ *idea, decision, feeling*] 表达 ♦ **to communicate with sb** (*by writing, speaking etc*) 与某人联络; (*talk openly to*) 与某人沟通

communication [kəmju:nɪ'keɪʃən] **I** *n* **1** [U] 交流 **2** [C] [正式] (*message*) 信息 **II communications** *n* [*pl*] 通讯

communion [kə'mju:nɪən] *n* [U] (*also: **Holy Communion***) 圣餐仪式 ♦ **to take communion** 领圣餐 ♦ **communion with nature** 与大自然的交融

communism ['kɔmjunɪzəm] *n* [U] 共产主义

communist ['kɔmjunɪst] **I** *adj* 共产主义的 **II** *n* [C] 共产主义者

✪ **community** [kə'mju:nɪtɪ] *n* [C] **1** (*neighbourhood*) 社区 **2** ♦ **the business/black/Jewish community** 商业界/黑人/犹太人 ♦ **a sense of community** 社区感

community centre (美 **community center**) *n* [C] 社区活动中心

community service [法] *n* [U] 社区服务

commute [kə'mju:t] **I** *vi* 乘车上下班 **II** *vt* ♦ **to be commuted (to life imprisonment)** 减刑(为终生监禁) **III** *n* [C] (*journey*) 乘车上下班的路程 ♦ **to commute to/from London/Brighton** 去/从伦敦/布赖顿乘车上下班 ♦ **to commute between Oxford and Birmingham**

乘车上下班往返于牛津与伯明翰之间

commuter [kə'mjuːtə(r)] *n* [c] 乘车上下班的人

compact [*adj*, *vb* kəm'pækt, *n* 'kɔmpækt] **I** *adj* **1** [+ *camera, cassette, car*] 袖珍的; [+ *size, design, shape*] 小巧的 **II** *vt* 将…压紧在一起 **III** *n* [c] (*also:* ***powder compact***) 粉盒

compact disc *n* [c] 激光唱片 [美 = *also* **compact disk**]

compact disc player *n* [c] 激光唱机 [美 = *also* **compact disk player**]

companion [kəm'pænjən] *n* [c] 同伴

companionship [kəm'pænjənʃɪp] *n* [u] 陪伴

✪ **company** ['kʌmpənɪ] *n* **1** [c] (*firm*) 公司 **2** [c] [戏剧] 剧团 **3** [c] [军] 连 **4** [u] (*companionship*) 交往 ♦ **Smith and Company** 史密斯公司 ♦ **he's good company** 他是个好伙伴 ♦ **we have company** 我们有客人 ♦ **to keep sb company** 陪伴某人 ♦ **to part company (with sb)** (*when walking etc*) (与某人) 分手; (*in work, relationship*) (与某人) 断绝联系

company car *n* [c] 单位公车

company director *n* [c] 公司董事

comparable ['kɔmpərəbl] *adj* [+ *size, quality*] 类似的; [+ *place, situation, job*] 可比较的 ♦ **comparable to** 比得上

comparative [kəm'pærətɪv] **I** *adj* **1** (*relative*) [+ *ease, safety, freedom, peace*] 比较而言的 **2** [+ *study*] 用比较方法的 **3** [+ *adjective, adverb, literature, religion*] 比较的 **II** *n* ♦ **the comparative** 比较级

comparatively [kəm'pærətɪvlɪ] *adv* (*relatively*) [+ *easy, safe, peaceful*] 相对地

compare [kəm'pɛə(r)] **I** *vt* 比较 **II** *vi* ♦ **to compare favourably/unfavourably (with sth/sb)** 比得上/比不上 (某物/某人) **III** *n* ♦ **beyond** *or* **without compare** [文] 无与伦比 ♦ **to compare sb/sth with** *or* **to sth** (*contrast*) 将某人/某物与某物相比较 ♦ **to compare sb/sth to** (*liken to*) 把某人/某物比作 ♦ **compared with** *or* **to** 与…相比 ♦ **you can't compare ...** 你不能将…相比 ♦ **how does he compare with his predecessor?** 和他前任比起来他怎么样? ♦ **her garden can't compare with ours** 她的花园没法和我们的相比

comparison [kəm'pærɪsn] *n* [c/u] 比较 ♦ **it is an unfair comparison** 这样比较是不公平的 ♦ **for comparison** 以作比较 ♦ **in** *or* **by comparison (with)** (与…) 比较起来 ♦ **(there's) no comparison** 不能相提并论

compartment [kəm'pɑːtmənt] *n* [c] **1** [铁路] 隔间 **2** [*of wallet, fridge etc*] 格

compass ['kʌmpəs] *n* [c] **1** (*for finding direction*) 指南针 **2** (*also:* ***pair of compasses***) (*for drawing circles*) 圆规 ♦ **beyond/within the compass of** [正式] 超出/在…的范围

compassion [kəm'pæʃən] *n* [u] 同情 ♦ **sb's compassion for sb** 某人对某人的同情

compassionate [kəm'pæʃənɪt] *adj* [+ *person, look*] 有同情心的 ♦ **on compassionate grounds** 出于特殊照顾

compatible [kəm'pætɪbl] *adj* [+ *people*] 意气相投的; [+ *ideas, activities*] 协调的; [计算机] 兼容的 ♦ **to be compatible with sb** 与某人意气相投 ♦ **to be compatible with sth** [*activity, idea* +] 与某物一致; [计算机] 与某物兼容

compel [kəm'pɛl] *vt* ♦ **to compel sb to do sth** 强制某人做某事 ♦ **to feel compelled to do sth** 感到不得不做某事

compelling [kəm'pɛlɪŋ] *adj* [+ *evidence, reason*] 令人信服的

compensate ['kɔmpənseɪt] **I** *vt* ♦ **to compensate sb (for sth)** (由于某事) 赔偿某人 **II** *vi* ♦ **to compensate (for sth)** 弥补 (某事)

compensation [kɔmpən'seɪʃən] *n* **1** [u] (*money*) 赔偿金 **2** [c/u] (喻) (*for disappointment etc*) 补偿 **3** [c/u] (*adjustment*) 补偿 ♦ **compensation for sth** (*money*) 因某事而获得的赔偿金; (喻) (*for disappointment etc*) 因某事而得到的补偿 ♦ **in compensation (for sth)** (*money*) 作

为(某事的)赔偿金

compete [kəm'piːt] *vi* [*companies, rivals* +] 竞争; (*in contest, game*) 比赛 ♦ **to compete for sth** [*companies, rivals* +] 争夺某物; (*in contest, game*) 争夺某物 ♦ **to compete with sb/sth (for sth)** [*companies, rivals* +] 与某人/某物竞争(以得到某物); (*in contest, game*) 与某人/某物竞争(以获得某奖项)

competence ['kɔmpɪtəns] *n* [U] 能力

competent ['kɔmpɪtənt] *adj* [+ *person*] 称职的; [+ *piece of work*] 合格的

competition [kɔmpɪ'tɪʃən] *n* **1** [U] (*rivalry*) (*for job, position, between companies*) 竞争 **2** [C] (*contest*) 竞赛 ♦ **in competition with** 与…竞争

competitive [kəm'pɛtɪtɪv] *adj* **1** [+ *industry, society*] 竞争性的 **2** [+ *person*] 求胜心切的 **3** [+ *price, product*] 有竞争力的 **4** [+ *sport*] 竞技性的

competitor [kəm'pɛtɪtə(r)] *n* [C] **1** (*in business*) 竞争对手 **2** (*participant*) 参赛者

complacent [kəm'pleɪsnt] *adj* 自满的 ♦ **to be complacent about sth** 对某事疏忽大意

complain [kəm'pleɪn] *vi* **1** ♦ **to complain (about sth)** (*to relevant person*) (就某事)投诉; (*grumble*) (就某事)诉苦 **2** [医] ♦ **to complain of sth** 诉说某病痛 ♦ **to complain to sb (about sth)** (就某事)向某人投诉 ♦ **to complain that ...** 抱怨…

complaint [kəm'pleɪnt] *n* **1** [C] (*criticism*) 抱怨 **2** [U] (*complaining*) 投诉 **3** [C] (*reason for complaining*) 抱怨的原因 **4** [C] (*illness*) 疾病 ♦ **to make a complaint (to sb)** (向某人)投诉

complement [*n* 'kɔmplɪmənt, *vb* 'kɔmplɪmɛnt] **I** *n* [C] **1** ♦ **a complement (to sth)** (*enhancement*) (与某物)互补的东西; (*supplement*) (某物的)补充 **2** [*of staff, things*] 需要/允许的数额 **3** [语言] 补语 **II** *vt* **1** (*enhance*) 与…相辅相成 **2** (*supplement*) 与…配套 **3** (*combine well with*) 互补 ♦ **to have a full complement of** …都齐全了

> 请勿将 **complement** 和 **compliment** 混淆。**complement** 指使某事物变得完整、良好或者有效。例如，如果一种食物 **complement** 另一种食物，或是另一种食物的 **complement**，表示这两种食物搭配得很好。如果两个人彼此 **complement**，表示他们的个性相符。*Rice is a good complement to curry...He complements his wife perfectly.* 如果你 **compliment** 某人，或者 **pay them a compliment**，表示你欣赏他们或对他们赞赏有加。*I always compliment her cooking skills...She blushed every time he paid her a compliment.*

complementary [kɔmplɪ'mɛntərɪ] *adj* [+ *approaches, skills*] 互补的; [+ *medicine, therapies*] 非传统的

✪ **complete** [kəm'pliːt] **I** *adj* **1** (*total*) 完全的 **2** (*whole*) 完整的 **3** (*finished*) 完成的 **II** *vt* **1** (*finish*) [+ *piece of work, building*] 完成 **2** (*make whole*) [+ *collection, set etc*] [*person* +] 使完整; [*thing* +] 使完美 **3** (*fill in*) [+ *form, coupon*] 填写 ♦ **complete with** 附带

completely [kəm'pliːtlɪ] *adv* [+ *different, satisfied, untrue etc*] 完全; [*forget, destroy etc* +] 彻底

completion [kəm'pliːʃən] *n* [U] [*of project, piece of work, building*] 完成; [*of sale*] 正式完成 ♦ **to be nearing completion** 接近尾声 ♦ **on completion of sth** 某物完成后

complex ['kɔmplɛks] **I** *adj* 复杂的 **II** *n* [C] **1** (*group of buildings*) 综合性建筑 **2** [心理] 情结 ♦ **to have a complex about sth** 对某事有强烈的情绪反应

complexion [kəm'plɛkʃən] *n* [C] **1** (*colouring*) 面色 **2** [正式] [*of event etc*] 性质

compliance [kəm'plaɪəns] *n* [U] 遵从 ♦ **compliance with sth** 遵守某事 ♦ **in compliance with** 服从…

complicate ['kɔmplɪkeɪt] *vt* 使复杂化 ♦ **to complicate matters** *or* **things further, ...** 更加复杂的是…

complicated ['kɔmplɪkeɪtɪd] *adj* 复杂的

complication [kɔmplɪ'keɪʃən] *n* 1 [C/U] (*problem*) 问题 2 [C] [医] 并发症

compliment [*n* 'kɔmplɪmənt, *vb* 'kɔmplɪmɛnt] I *n* [C] 1 (*remark*) 赞美 2 (*action*) 荣幸 II *vt* 赞美 ♦ **to pay sb a compliment** 赞美某人 ♦ **to take sth as a compliment** 把某事当作是对自己的肯定 ♦ **(my) compliments to the chef!** 向厨师致意！ ♦ **to compliment sb on sth** 为某事赞美某人 ♦ **to compliment sb for doing sth** 因为做某事赞美某人

📖 用法参见 **complement**

complimentary [kɔmplɪ'mɛntərɪ] *adj* 1 (*approving*) [+ *remark*] 赞美的; [+ *person*] 赞不绝口的 2 (*free*) [+ *ticket, seat, copy*] 赠送的 ♦ **to be complimentary about sb/sth** 对某人/某事赞不绝口

comply [kəm'plaɪ] *vi* ♦ **to comply (with sth)** [*person* +] 遵从(某事); [*thing* +] 遵守(某事)

component [kəm'pəunənt] I *n* [C] [*of plan*] 组成部分; [*of weapon, body, substance*] 成分; [工业, 商] (*for machinery etc*) 部件 II *adj* [+ *parts, elements*] 组成的

compose [kəm'pəuz] *vt* 1 ♦ **to be composed of** 由…组成 2 (*write*) [+ *music*] 创作; [正式] [+ *poem, letter*] 写 ♦ **to compose o.s.** 使自己镇定下来

composed [kəm'pəuzd] *adj* (*calm*) 沉着的

composer [kəm'pəuzə(r)] *n* [C] 作曲家

composition [kɔmpə'zɪʃən] *n* 1 [U] (*make-up*) [*of thing*] 组成; [*of substance*] 构成成分; [*of group*] 结构 2 [C] (*essay*) 作文 3 [C/U] [音] 作品

composure [kəm'pəuʒə(r)] *n* [U] [*of person*] 镇静 ♦ **to keep/lose one's composure** 保持/不再镇静 ♦ **to regain one's composure** 恢复镇静

compound [*n, adj* 'kɔmpaund, *vb* kəm'paund] I *n* [C] 1 [化] 化合物 2 (*enclosure*) 场地 3 [语言] 复合词 II *adj* 1 [+ *structure, eye, leaf etc*] 复合的 2 [语言] 复合的 III *vt* [正式] [+ *problem, tragedy*] 使…更糟

comprehend [kɔmprɪ'hɛnd] [正式] *vt* 理解

comprehension [kɔmprɪ'hɛnʃən] *n* 1 [U] (*understanding*) 理解 2 [C/U] [教育] 理解力练习 ♦ **it's beyond my comprehension** 我无法理解

comprehensive [kɔmprɪ'hɛnsɪv] I *adj* 1 [+ *review, list*] 全面的 2 (*of insurance*) 综合的 II *n* [C] [英] (*also: **comprehensive school***) 综合性中学

compress [*vb* kəm'prɛs, *n* 'kɔmprɛs] I *vt* 1 [+ *gas, material etc*] 压缩 ◊ *Moira compressed her lips and looked away.* 莫伊拉紧抿着嘴，朝别处看。2 (*summarize*) [+ *text, information*] 概括 3 [计算机] [+ *data, file*] 压缩 II *n* [C] [医] 敷布

comprise [kəm'praɪz] [正式] *vt* 1 (*consist of*) (*also: **be comprised of***) 包括 2 (*constitute*) 构成

compromise ['kɔmprəmaɪz] I *n* [C/U] 妥协 II *vi* 妥协 III *vt* [+ *beliefs, principles*] 损害 IV *cpd* [复合词] [+ *decision, solution*] 折中 ♦ **to compromise with sb** 与某人妥协

compulsion [kəm'pʌlʃən] *n* 1 [C] (*desire, impulse*) 强烈的欲望 2 [U] (*pressure*) 强制

compulsive [kəm'pʌlsɪv] *adj* [+ *liar, gambler*] 强迫性的 ♦ **it's compulsive reading/viewing** 这是本/部令人着迷的书/片子

compulsory [kəm'pʌlsərɪ] *adj* 必须的; [+ *course*] 必修的 ◊ *compulsory military service* 义务兵役 ♦ **to make sth compulsory** 使某事强制化 ♦ **it is compulsory to wear a seat belt** 必须系安全带

computer [kəm'pjuːtə(r)] I *n* [C] 计算机 II *cpd* [复合词] [+ *language, program, system, technology etc*] 电脑 ♦ **it was designed by computer** 这是由电脑设计的

computer game *n* [C] 电脑游戏

computer programmer *n* [C] 电脑编程员

computer programming *n* [U] 电脑编程

computer science *n* [U] 计算机科学

computer studies *n* [U] 计算机学

computing [kəm'pjuːtɪŋ] I *n* [U] 计算机运用; (*also: **computing studies***) 计算机学 II *cpd* [复合词] [+ *course,* *skills*] 电脑

con [kɔn] [非正式] **I** *vt* **1** (*deceive*) 欺骗 **2** (*cheat*) ♦ **to con sb (out of sth)** 骗取某人(某物) **II** *n* [c] (*trick*) 骗局 ♦ **to con sb into doing sth** 骗某人去做某事

conceal [kən'siːl] *vt* [+ *object*] 隐藏; [+ *secret, emotion*] 掩饰 ♦ **to conceal sth from sb** 对某人隐瞒某事

concede [kən'siːd] **I** *vt* (*admit*) 承认 **II** *vi* 让步 ♦ **to concede that ...** 承认…

conceited [kən'siːtɪd] *adj* 自高自大的

conceive [kən'siːv] **I** *vt* **1** [+ *child*] 怀上 **2** [+ *idea, plan*] 构想出 **II** *vi* **1** [*woman, female animal* +] 怀孕 **2** (*imagine*) ♦ **I cannot conceive of ...** 我不能想象… ♦ **I cannot conceive how/why ...** 我不能想像怎么/为什么…

concentrate ['kɔnsəntreɪt] **I** *vi* 集中精力 **II** *vt* **1** ♦ **to be concentrated in** [+ *place*] 集中在 **2** ♦ **to concentrate one's energies/attention on sth** 集中精力/注意力于某事 ♦ **to concentrate on sth** (*keep attention on*) 全神贯注于某事; (*focus on*) 集中注意力于某事 ♦ **to concentrate on doing sth** 集中精力于做某事

concentrated ['kɔnsəntreɪtɪd] *adj* **1** [+ *juice, solution*] 浓缩的 **2** [+ *effort, attempt*] 集中的

concentration [kɔnsən'treɪʃən] *n* **1** [U] (*ability to concentrate*) 专心 **2** [U] (*focus*) ♦ **concentration on sth/on doing sth** 集中于某事/做某事 **3** [C/U] (*in one area, space*) 集中 **4** [C/U] [化] 浓度

concept ['kɔnsɛpt] *n* [C] 概念

✪ **concern** [kən'səːn] **I** *n* **1** [U] (*anxiety*) 担忧 ◊ *There is no cause for concern.* 没必要担忧。 **2** [C] (*cause of anxiety*) 关切的事 ◊ *Unemployment was the electorate's main concern.* 失业是选民们最关切的问题。 **3** [U/S] (*care*) 关心 **4** [S] (*affair*) 事务 ◊ *That's your concern.* 那是你的事。 **5** [C] (*firm*) 公司 ◊ *It's a family concern.* 这是个家族公司。 **II** *vt* **1** (*worry*) 使担忧 ◊ *One of the things that concerns me is the rise in vandalism.* 令我担忧的问题之一是蓄意破坏案件的上升。 **2** (*be about*) 关于 ◊ *The book concerns two middle-aged men.* 这本书是有关两位中年男性的。 **3** (*involve*) 关系到 ◊ *That doesn't concern you.* 这跟你没关系。 ♦ **that's none of your concern** 这不关你事儿 ♦ **concern for sb** 为某人担心 ♦ **it concerns me that ...** 令我担心的是… ♦ **to concern o.s. with** 关心 ♦ **as far as I'm concerned** 据我看来 ♦ **as far as his career is concerned** 就他的事业来说 ♦ **"to whom it may concern"** "致有关人士" ♦ **the people concerned** (*in question*) 有关人士; (*involved*) 相关人士

concerned [kən'səːnd] *adj* (*worried*) 担心的 ♦ **to be concerned about sb/sth** 担心某人/某事 ♦ **to be concerned that ...** 担心… ♦ **we're concerned for her** 我们为她担忧 ♦ **to be concerned with sth** (*be worried about*) 关心某事; (*be about*) 关于某事

concerning [kən'səːnɪŋ] *prep* 关于

concert ['kɔnsət] *n* [C] 音乐会 ♦ **in concert 1** [音] 现场表演 **2** [正式] (*together*) 合作

concerted [kən'səːtɪd] *adj* [+ *effort, action*] 一致的

concert hall *n* [C] 音乐厅

concession [kən'sɛʃən] *n* [C] **1** (*compromise*) 让步 **2** (*right*) 特许权 **3** [英] (*reduced price*) 减价 [美 = **reduction**]

concise [kən'saɪs] *adj* [+ *description, text*] 简洁的

conclude [kən'kluːd] **I** *vt* **1** (*finish*) 结束 **2** [正式] [+ *treaty, deal, agreement*] 缔结 **II** *vi* ♦ **to conclude with sth** [*event* +] 以某物而告终; [*speaker* +] 以某物收尾 ♦ **I'd like to conclude by saying ...** 我想讲的最后一句话是… ♦ **to conclude that ...** 断定… ♦ **"that," he concluded, "is why we did it"** "那," 他断定说, "就是我们这样做的原因"

conclusion [kən'kluːʒən] *n* **1** [S] (*end*) [*of speech, chapter*] 结尾 **2** [S] [正式] [*of treaty, deal, agreement*] 缔

结 3 [c] (*deduction*) 结论 ♦ **to come to the conclusion that ...** 得出的结论是… ♦ **in conclusion** 总之

conclusive [kən'kluːsɪv] *adj* [+ *evidence, proof*] 确凿的

concrete ['kɔŋkriːt] **I** *n* [U] 混凝土 **II** *adj* **1** (字) [+ *block, floor*] 混凝土的 **2** (喻) [+ *proposal, evidence*] 确实的

concussion [kən'kʌʃən] *n* [U] 脑震荡

condemn [kən'dɛm] *vt* **1** (*denounce*) 谴责 **2** (*sentence*) ♦ **to condemn sb to death/life imprisonment** *etc* 判处某人死刑/无期徒刑{等} **3** (*declare unsafe*) [+ *building*] 宣告…不适于居住

condemnation [kɔndɛm'neɪʃən] *n* [C/U] 谴责

condensation [kɔndɛn'seɪʃən] *n* [U] 凝结的小水珠

condense [kən'dɛns] **I** *vt* [+ *report, book*] 使简缩 **II** *vi* [*vapour* +] 凝结

✪ **condition** [kən'dɪʃən] **I** *n* **1** [S] (*state*) 状态 ◊ *You can't go home in that condition.* 在那种状态下你不能回家。**2** [C] (*stipulation*) 条件 ◊ *the conditions of our release* 我们释放的条件 **3** [C] (*illness*) 疾病 ◊ *Hypothermia is an extremely complex condition.* 体温过低是种非常复杂的疾病。**II** *vt* **1** ♦ **to condition sb (to do sth)** 训练某人 (做某事) ◊ *We are conditioned to think that way.* 我们被训练成那样思考。**2** [+ *hair, skin*] 使状况良好 **III conditions** *n* [*pl*] 环境 ◊ *People are living in appalling conditions.* 人们的居住环境糟糕透了。♦ **in good/poor condition** 状况良好/不好 ♦ **out of condition** 健康状况欠佳 ♦ **a heart condition** 心脏病 ♦ **weather conditions** 天气形势 ♦ **on condition that** 在…条件下

conditional [kən'dɪʃənl] **I** *adj* 有条件的 **II** *n* [语言] ♦ **the conditional** 条件从句 ♦ **to be conditional on** *or* **upon sth** 视某事而定

conditioner [kən'dɪʃənə(r)] *n* [C/U] **1** (*for hair*) 护发素 **2** (*for fabric*) 柔顺剂

condo ['kɔndəu] [美:非正式] *n* [C] **1** (*apartment*) 产权归住房者所有的公寓套房 **2** (*building*) 产权归住房者所有的公寓楼

condom ['kɔndəm] *n* [C] 安全套

condominium [kɔndə'mɪnɪəm] [美] *n* [C] **1** (*apartment*) 产权归住房者所有的公寓套房 **2** (*building*) 产权归住房者所有的公寓楼

condone [kən'dəun] *vt* [+ *misbehaviour, crime*] 容忍

conduct [*n* 'kɔndʌkt, *vb* kən'dʌkt] **I** *n* **1** [U] [*of person*] 行为 **2** [S] [*of task, activity*] 方式 **II** *vt* **1** [+ *survey, research, experiment etc*] 进行 **2** [+ *life*] 表现 **3** [+ *orchestra, choir etc*] 指挥 **4** [+ *heat, electricity*] 传导 ♦ **to conduct o.s.** (*behave*) 表现

conducted tour [kən'dʌktɪd-] *n* [C] **1** [*of area*] 有导游解说的旅游 **2** [*of building*] 有导游解说的参观

conductor [kən'dʌktə(r)] *n* [C] **1** [*of orchestra*] 指挥家 **2** [美] (*on train*) 列车员 [英 = **guard**] **3** (*on bus*) 售票员 **4** [电子] 导体

cone [kəun] *n* [C] **1** (*shape*) 圆锥体 **2** (*also: **traffic cone***) 锥形路标 **3** (*on tree*) 球果 **4** (*also: **ice cream cone***) 锥形蛋卷冰淇淋 **5** (*ice cream*) 蛋筒

confectioner's sugar [美] *n* [U] 糖粉 [英 = **icing sugar**]

confectionery [kən'fɛkʃənrɪ] [正式] *n* [U] 甜食

confer [kən'fəː(r)] **I** *vt* [正式] ♦ **to confer sth (on sb)** [+ *power, authority, status*] 授予(某人)某物; [+ *advantage, benefit*] (给某人)带来某物; [+ *degree*] 授予(某人)某物 **II** *vi* ♦ **to confer (with sb about sth)** (就某事和某人)商议

✪ **conference** ['kɔnfərəns] *n* [C] (*meeting*) 会议 ♦ **to be in conference** 在开会

confess [kən'fɛs] **I** *vi* (*to sin, crime*) 坦白 **II** *vt* [+ *sin, guilt, crime*] 坦白; [+ *weakness, ignorance*] 承认 ♦ **to confess to sth/to doing sth** 承认某事/做了某事 ♦ **to confess sth to sb** 向某人坦白某事 ♦ **I must confess that ...** 我得承认…

confession [kən'fɛʃən] *n* **1** [C/U] (*admission*) 坦白 **2** [C] (*written*) 供认状 **3** [C/U] [宗] 忏悔 ♦ **to make a confession** 坦白 ♦ **to go to confession** [宗] 作忏悔

confide [kən'faɪd] I *vi* ♦**to confide in sb** 向某人吐露秘密 II *vt* ♦**to confide sth to sb** 向某人倾吐某事 ♦**to confide to sb that ...** 向某人吐露…

confidence ['kɔnfɪdns] *n* **1** [U] (*faith*) 信赖 **2** [U] (*self-assurance*) 自信 **3** [C] (*secret*) 秘密 ♦**to have (every) confidence in sb/sth** 对某人/某事（很）有信心 ♦**to have (every) confidence that ...** 对…（很）有信心 ♦**to take sb into one's confidence** 把某人作为知心人 ♦**in confidence** [*speak, say, write etc* +] 秘密地

confident ['kɔnfɪdənt] *adj* (*self-assured*) 自信的 ♦**to be confident that ...** 有信心… ♦**to be confident of sth/of doing sth** 对某事/做某事充满信心 ♦**to be confident about sth** 对某事充满信心

confidential [kɔnfɪ'dɛnʃəl] *adj* [+ *report, information*] 机密的; [+ *tone*] 表示信任的

confine [kən'faɪn] *vt* **1** (*imprison*) ♦**to confine sb to sth** 将某人限制在某处 **2** (*limit*) ♦**to confine sth (to sth)** 控制某物（在某物之内）♦**to confine o.s. to sth/to doing sth** 只局限于某事/做某事

confined [kən'faɪnd] *adj* [+ *space, area*] 狭小的 ♦**to be confined to** [+ *place, group*] 仅限于…

confines ['kɔnfaɪnz] *n* [*pl*] (*boundaries*) [*of area*] 范围; (*limitations*) [*of situation*] 界限

confirm [kən'fəːm] *vt* **1** (*verify*) [+ *statement, report, story etc*] 肯定; [+ *appointment, date*] 确认 **2** (*bear out*) [+ *suspicion, fear*] 证实 **3** [宗] 给…施坚信礼 ♦**to confirm that ...** [*person, data* +] 证实…

confirmation [kɔnfə'meɪʃən] *n* [C/U] **1** (*verification*) [*of belief, statement, report etc*] 证实 **2** [*of appointment, date*] 确认 **3** [宗] 坚信礼

confiscate ['kɔnfɪskeɪt] *vt* 没收 ♦**to confiscate sth from sb** 没收某人的某物

conflict [*n* 'kɔnflɪkt, *vb* kən'flɪkt] I *n* **1** [U] (*disagreement, fighting*) 冲突 **2** [C/U] (*difference*) [*of interests, loyalties etc*] 矛盾 II *vi* **1** ♦**to conflict with sth** [*opinions, research etc* +] 与某事截然不同 III *n* ♦**to be in conflict (with sb)** （与某人）发生冲突

conform [kən'fɔːm] *vi* 循规蹈矩 ♦**to conform to sth** [+ *expectations, regulations etc*] 与某事物相符

confront [kən'frʌnt] *vt* **1** [+ *opponent, enemy*] 面对 **2** （喻）[*problem, task* +] 面对 ♦**to be confronted with sth** [+ *problem, task*] 面临某事

confrontation [kɔnfrən'teɪʃən] *n* [C/U] (*dispute*) 对抗; (*fight*) 冲突

confuse [kən'fjuːz] *vt* **1** (*perplex*) 把…弄糊涂 **2** (*mix up*) 混淆 **3** (*complicate*) 搞乱 ♦**to confuse sb/sth with sb/sth** 把某人/某物与某人/某物搞混

confused [kən'fjuːzd] *adj* **1** (*bewildered*) 困惑的 **2** (*disordered*) 混乱的 ♦**to get confused** [*person* +] 糊涂

confusing [kən'fjuːzɪŋ] *adj* 含混不清的

confusion [kən'fjuːʒən] *n* **1** [C/U] (*uncertainty*) 惶惑 **2** [U] (*mix-up*) 混淆 **3** [C/U] (*perplexity*) 困惑 **4** [U] (*disorder*) 混乱

congested [kən'dʒɛstɪd] *adj* **1** [+ *road, area*] 拥挤不堪的 **2** [正式] [+ *nose, arteries*] 不通的

congestion [kən'dʒɛstʃən] *n* [U] **1** (*of road*) 堵塞 **2** (*in nose, throat*) 堵塞; (*in lungs*) 充血

Congo ['kɔŋgəu] *n* 刚果

congratulate [kən'grætjuleɪt] *vt* 祝贺 ♦**to congratulate sb on sth/on doing sth** 祝贺某人某事/做某事

congratulations [kəngrætju'leɪʃənz] *n* [*pl*] 祝贺 ♦**congratulations!** 恭喜！ ♦**congratulations on your engagement!** 祝贺你订婚了！

congregation [kɔŋgrɪ'geɪʃən] *n* [C] 教堂会众

congress ['kɔŋgrɛs] *n* [C] **1** (*conference*) 代表大会 **2** [美] ♦**Congress** 国会

congressman ['kɔŋgrɛsmən] (*pl* **congressmen**) [美] *n* [C] 国会议员

congresswoman ['kɔŋgrɛswumən] (*pl* **congresswomen**) [美] *n* [C] 女国会议员

conifer [ˈkɔnɪfə(r)] *n* [c] 针叶树
conjunction [kənˈdʒʌŋkʃən] [语言] *n* [c] 连词 ♦**in conjunction with** 与…一道
conjure [ˈkʌndʒə(r)] *vi* [*magician* +] 变魔术
❑**conjure up** *vt* [+ *memory, image*] 使…浮现于脑际
connect [kəˈnɛkt] **I** *vt* **1** (*join*) 连接 **2** [通信] [+ *caller*] 给…接通; [+ *telephone, subscriber*] 接通 **3** (喻) (*associate*) 将…联系起来 **II** *vi* ♦**to connect with** [+ *train, plane etc*] 与…联运 ♦**to connect sth to sth** (*join*) 将某物与某物连接起来; (*to electricity supply etc*) 将某物与某物接通 ♦**to connect sth with sth** (*join*) 将某物与某物连接起来 ♦**to connect sb/sth with sb/sth** (*associate*) 将某人/某物与某人/某物联系起来 ♦**to be connected with sth** (*associated*) 与某事有关系
connection [kəˈnɛkʃən] **I** *n* **1** [c/u] (*link*) 联系 **2** [c] [电子] 接头 **3** [c] (*train, plane etc*) 联运 **4** [c] [通信] (*for caller, new subscriber*) 接通 **II connections** *n* [*pl*] (*people*) 熟人 ♦**what is the connection between them?** 他们之间有什么关系? ♦**to have a connection with** *or* **to sb/sth** 与某人/某物有联系 ♦**in connection with** 与…有关 ♦**to miss/get one's connection** 误了/赶上要换的交通工具
conquer [ˈkɔŋkə(r)] *vt* **1** [+ *country, enemy*] 征服 **2** [+ *fear, feelings, problem*] 克服
conquest [ˈkɔŋkwɛst] *n* **1** [c/u] [*of country, space etc*] 征服 **2** [c] (*sexual*) 俘虏
cons [kɔnz] *n* [*pl*] **1** = **conveniences** *see* **mod cons 2** *see* **pro**
conscience [ˈkɔnʃəns] *n* **1** [c] (*sense of morality*) 是非感 **2** [u] (*belief*) 良心 ♦**to have a guilty/clear conscience** 感到内疚/问心无愧 ♦**to have sth on one's conscience** 因某事而感到内疚 ♦**in all** *or* **good conscience** [正式] 凭良心
conscientious [kɔnʃɪˈɛnʃəs] *adj* 认真的 ♦**to be conscientious about sth/about doing sth** 认真地对待某事/做某事
conscious [ˈkɔnʃəs] *adj* **1** (*awake*) 清醒的 **2** (*deliberate*) [+ *decision, effort*] 蓄意的 ♦**to be conscious of sth** 意识到某事 ♦**to be conscious that ...** 意识到… ♦**to be politically conscious/health-conscious** 有政治/健康意识 ♦**to become conscious of/that** 意识到
consciousness [ˈkɔnʃəsnɪs] *n* **1** [u] [医] 知觉 **2** [c/u] (*mind*) 脑海 **3** [u] (*mentality*) [*of group, society etc*] 意识 ♦**to lose consciousness** 失去知觉 ♦**to regain consciousness** 恢复知觉
consecutive [kənˈsɛkjutɪv] *adj* 连续的
consensus [kənˈsɛnsəs] *n* [s] 一致 ♦**the consensus (of opinion) is that ...** 一致的(意见)是…
consent [kənˈsɛnt] **I** *n* [u] 许可 **II** *vi* ♦**to consent (to do sth)** 同意(做某事) ♦**to consent to sth** 同意(某事) ♦**to give one's consent** 同意 ♦**by common** *or* **mutual consent** 经一致同意
consequence [ˈkɔnsɪkwəns] *n* **1** [c] (*result*) 后果 **2** (*importance*) ♦**of consequence** 重要性 ♦**in consequence** 因而 ♦**it's of little/no consequence** 这是无关紧要的
consequently [ˈkɔnsɪkwəntlɪ] *adv* 所以
conservation [kɔnsəˈveɪʃən] *n* [u] [*of environment*] 环保; [*of energy etc*] 节约; [*of paintings, books, buildings, species*] 保护
conservative [kənˈsəːvətɪv] **I** *adj* **1** (*traditional*) [+ *person, attitude*] 保守的 **2** (*cautious*) [+ *estimate*] 保守的 **3** (*right-wing*) 右派的 **4** [英:政治] ♦**Conservative** 保守党 **II** *n* [c] **1** (*right-wing*) 保守主义者 **2** [英:政治] ♦**Conservative** 保守党人士
Conservative Party [英] *n* ♦**the Conservative Party** 保守党
conservatory [kənˈsəːvətrɪ] *n* [c] **1** (*on house*) 暖房 **2** [音] 音乐学院
conserve [*vt* kənˈsəːv, *n* ˈkɔnsəːv] **I** *vt* [+ *resources, supplies, energy*] 保存; [+ *forest, building, species*] 保护 **II** *n* [c/u] (*jam*) 果酱
✪**consider** [kənˈsɪdə(r)] *vt* **1** (*think about*) 考虑 ◊ *They are having a*

meeting to consider the report. 他们在开会考虑这份报告。**2** (*take into account*) 考虑到◊ *You have to consider the feelings of others.* 你需要考虑到其他人的感觉。
3 (*believe*) ♦**to consider sb (to be) an idiot/a coward** *etc* 认为某人是傻子/胆小鬼{等} ♦**to consider doing sth** 考虑做某事 ♦**all things considered** 考虑到各个方面 ♦**they consider themselves (to be) superior/happy** 他们认为自己高人一等/开心 ♦**she considered it a disaster** 她认为这是个灾难

considerable [kən'sɪdərəbl] *adj* 相当的

considerably [kən'sɪdərəblɪ] *adv* [*improve, vary* +] 在很大程度上; [+ *bigger, smaller etc*] 相当地

considerate [kən'sɪdərɪt] *adj* 体贴的

consideration [kənsɪdə'reɪʃən] *n* **1** [U] (*deliberation*) 考虑 **2** [C] (*factor*) 要考虑的因素 **3** [U] (*thoughtfulness*) ♦**consideration (for)** (对…的) 顾及 ♦**to take sth into consideration** 考虑到某事 ♦**under consideration** 在考虑中 ♦**out of consideration for sb/sth** 顾及到某人/某事

considering [kən'sɪdərɪŋ] **I** *prep* 考虑到 **II** *conj* ♦**considering (that) ...** 考虑到…

consignment [kən'saɪnmənt] *n* [C] 托运

consist [kən'sɪst] *vi* ♦**to consist of** 由…组成

consistency [kən'sɪstənsɪ] *n* [U] **1** [*in actions, policies etc*] 连贯性 **2** [*of yoghurt, cream etc*] 粘稠度

consistent [kən'sɪstənt] *adj* [+ *person*] 一贯的; [+ *argument, theory, ideas*] 一致的 ♦**to be consistent with** 与…相符

consolation [kɔnsə'leɪʃən] *n* [C/U] 安慰

consolation prize *n* [C] **1** (*in competition*) 安慰奖 **2** (喻) 安慰表示

console [*vb* kən'səul, *n* 'kɔnsəul] **I** *vt* 安慰 **II** *n* [C] 操纵台

consolidate [kən'sɔlɪdeɪt] *vt* [+ *position, power, success*] 巩固

consommé [kən'sɔmeɪ] *n* [C/U] 清炖肉汤

consonant ['kɔnsənənt] *n* [C] 辅音

conspicuous [kən'spɪkjuəs] *adj* [+ *person, feature*] 惹人注目的 ♦**to make o.s. conspicuous** 引人注目 ♦**he was conspicuous by his absence** 他因缺席而引人注目

conspiracy [kən'spɪrəsɪ] *n* [C/U] ♦**conspiracy (to do sth)** (做某事的) 阴谋

constable ['kʌnstəbl] [英] *n* [C] (最低等级的) 警员

constant ['kɔnstənt] *adj* **1** (*ever-present*) [+ *threat, pressure, pain, reminder etc*] 不断的 **2** (*repeated*) [+ *interruptions, demands etc*] 重复的 **3** (*fixed*) [+ *temperature, speed etc*] 恒定的

> **constant**，**continual** 和 **continuous** 都可以表示某事持续发生或一直存在。**constant** 表示某种事情总是发生或从未消失过。*He was in constant pain...Jane's constant criticism…* **continual** 表示某事在一段时间内经常发生，尤其指人们不愿看到的情况。*...his continual drinking...continual demands to cut costs…* **continuous** 表示某事一直延续而不停止或毫无停止的迹象。*...days of continuous rain...a continuous background noise…*

constantly ['kɔnstəntlɪ] *adv* **1** (*repeatedly*) 不断地 **2** (*uninterruptedly*) 持续地

constipated ['kɔnstɪpeɪtɪd] *adj* 便秘的

constipation [kɔnstɪ'peɪʃən] *n* [U] 便秘

constituency [kən'stɪtjuənsɪ] *n* [C] **1** (*area*) 选区 **2** (*people*) 选民

constitute ['kɔnstɪtju:t] *vt* **1** (*represent*) [+ *challenge, emergency*] 是 **2** (*comprise*) 组成

constitution [kɔnstɪ'tju:ʃən] *n* [C] **1** [*of country*] 宪法; [*of club, organization*] 章程 **2** (*health*) 体质 **3** (*formation*) 组成 ♦**she's got the**

constitution of an ox 她健壮得像头公牛

constitutional [kɔnstɪ'tjuːʃənl] *adj* [+ *right, crisis, reform*] 宪法的

constraint [kən'streɪnt] *n* **1** [c] (*restriction*) 限制 **2** [u] (*restraint*) 约束 **3** [u] (*strain*) 约束感 ♦**to do sth under constraint** 受逼迫而做某事

construct [*vt* kən'strʌkt, *n* 'kɔnstrʌkt] **I** *vt* **1** [+ *building, road, machine*] 建造 **2** [+ *theory, argument*] 构思 **II** *n* [c] (*idea*) 观念

construction [kən'strʌkʃən] *n* **1** [u] [*of building, road, machine*] 建造 **2** [c] (*structure*) 建筑 **3** [c] (*interpretation*) 解释 ♦**to be under construction** [*building, road etc* +] 建造中

constructive [kən'strʌktɪv] *adj* [+ *criticism, suggestion, discussion etc*] 建设性的; [+ *person*] 有助益的

consul ['kɔnsl] *n* [c] 领事

consulate ['kɔnsjulɪt] *n* [c] 领事馆

consult [kən'sʌlt] *vt* [+ *doctor, lawyer, friend*] 咨询; [+ *book, map*] 查阅 ♦**to consult sb about sth** 就某事向某人咨询

consultant [kən'sʌltənt] **I** *n* [c] **1** [尤英] (*doctor*) 会诊医师 [美 = **specialist**] **2** (*adviser*) 顾问 **II** *cpd* [复合词] [+ *paediatrician, surgeon, psychiatrist*] 顾问 ♦**a consultant to sb** 某人的顾问

consultation [kɔnsəl'teɪʃən] *n* **1** [c] (*meeting*) 磋商会议 **2** [c] [尤英] (*session*) (*with doctor*) 会诊; (*with lawyer*) 咨询 **3** [u] (*discussion*) 磋商 **4** [u] [尤英] (*obtaining advice*) (*with doctor*) 会诊; (*with lawyer*) 咨询 ♦**in consultation with** 与…磋商

consulting room [kən'sʌltɪŋ-] [英: 医] *n* [c] 诊察室 [美 = **doctor's office**]

consume [kən'sjuːm] *vt* **1** [+ *food*] 吃; [+ *drink*] 喝 **2** [+ *fuel, energy, time*] 消耗 **3** [*fire* +] 烧毁 **4** [文] [*emotion, idea* +] 充满 ◊ *He was consumed by rage.* 他生气得不得了。

consumer [kən'sjuːmə(r)] *n* [c] [*of goods, services*] 消费者; [*of resources*] 使用者

consumption [kən'sʌmpʃən] *n* [u] **1** (*act of consuming*) [*of food*] 进食; [*of drink*] 饮用; [*of fuel, energy etc*] 消耗 **2** (*amount consumed*) [*of food, drink, fuel, energy, etc*] 消耗量 **3** (*buying*) 消费 **4** [过时] (*tuberculosis*) 肺结核 ♦**unfit for human consumption** 不适于人类使用

cont. *abbr* (= ***continued***) 转至

contact ['kɔntækt] **I** *n* **1** [c/u] (*communication*) 联络 **2** [u] (*touch*) 接触 **3** [c] (*person*) 熟人 **II** *vt* 联系 ♦**to be in contact with sb** 与某人有联络 ♦**to come into contact with sb/sth** 与某人/某事有接触 ♦**to make contact (with sb)** (和某人) 取得联络 ♦**to lose contact (with sb)** (与某人) 失去联系

contact lenses *n* [*pl*] 隐形眼镜

contagious [kən'teɪdʒəs] *adj* **1** [+ *disease*] 接触传染的 **2** [+ *laughter, enthusiasm*] 感染性的

contain [kən'teɪn] *vt* **1** (*hold*) [+ *objects*] 装有; [+ *component, ingredient etc*] 含有; [*letter, report, film* +] 包含 **2** (*control*) [+ *growth, spread*] 控制; [+ *fire, violence*] 阻止…的蔓延; [+ *curiosity, delight*] 抑制 ♦**I could hardly contain myself** 我几乎不能控制自己

container [kən'teɪnə(r)] *n* [c] **1** (*box, jar etc*) 容器 **2** (*for transport*) 集装箱

contaminate [kən'tæmɪneɪt] *vt* [+ *water, food, soil etc*] 污染

cont'd *abbr* (= ***continued***) 转至

contemplate ['kɔntəmpleɪt] *vt* **1** (*consider*) [+ *course of action*] 仔细考虑 **2** (*think about*) [+ *idea, subject*] 慎重考虑 **3** (*regard*) [+ *person, painting etc*] 凝视 ♦**to contemplate doing sth** 想做某事

contemporary [kən'tɛmpərərɪ] **I** *adj* **1** (*present-day*) [+ *art, music, society, artist etc*] 当代的 **2** (*of the same time*) [+ *account, writer, artist etc*] 同一时代的 **II** *n* [c] (*person*) 同代人 ♦**Shakespeare and his contemporaries** 莎士比亚和他的同代人

contempt [kən'tɛmpt] *n* [u] 轻视 ♦**to have contempt for sb/sth** 瞧不起某人/某物 ♦**to hold sb in contempt** 藐视某人 ♦**to be beneath contempt** 实在是不值一顾 ♦**contempt of court** 蔑视法庭

contend [kən'tɛnd] **I** *vi* **1** ♦**to contend with** [+ *problem, difficulty*] 对付 **2** ♦**to contend for** [+ *power, title, medal, prize*] 争夺 **II** *vt* ♦**to contend that ...** 争辩道… ♦**he has a lot to contend with** 他有许多问题要处理

content[1] ['kɔntɛnt] **I** *n* [U] **1** [*of speech, book, film*] 内容 **2** ♦**fat/moisture content** 脂肪/水分含量 **II contents** *n* [*pl*] [*of bottle, packet*] 所含之物; [*of letter, speech*] 内容 ♦**(table of) contents** 目录

content[2] [kən'tɛnt] **I** *adj* (*satisfied*) 满足的 **II** *vt* (*satisfy*) ♦**to content o.s. with sth/with doing sth** 满足于某事/做某事 ♦**to be content with sth** 满足于某事 ♦**to be content to do sth** 乐于做某事

contented [kən'tɛntɪd] *adj* 心满意足的

contentment [kən'tɛntmənt] *n* [U] 心满意足

contest [*n* 'kɔntɛst, *vt* kən'tɛst] **I** *n* [C] **1** (*competition*) 比赛 **2** (*for control, power etc*) 竞争 **II** *vt* **1** [+ *statement, decision*] 反驳 **2** [尤英] [+ *election, competition*] 角逐 **3** ♦**to contest sb's will** 对某人的遗嘱提出质疑

contestant [kən'tɛstənt] *n* [C] 参赛者

context ['kɔntɛkst] *n* [C/U] **1** [*of events, ideas etc*] 环境 **2** [*of word, phrase*] 上下文 ♦**in context** 纵观全局 ♦**out of context** 断章取义

continent ['kɔntɪnənt] *n* [C] 大陆 ♦**the Continent** [英] (*mainland Europe*) 欧洲大陆 ♦**on the Continent** [英] 在欧洲大陆

continental [kɔntɪ'nɛntl] **I** *adj* **1** [英] (*of the European continent*) [+ *country, Europe*] 欧洲大陆的; (*typical of European continent*) [+ *person, place, thing*] 欧式的 **2** [美] (*on mainland*) 北美大陆的 **II** *n* [C] [英] [非正式] 欧洲大陆人

continental breakfast *n* [C] 欧洲大陆式早餐

continual [kən'tɪnjuəl] *adj* **1** (*repeated*) [+ *harassment, demands, changes etc*] 频频的 **2** (*ceaseless*) [+ *pressure, pain, struggle etc*] 连续不断的

📖 用法参见 **constant**

continually [kən'tɪnjuəlɪ] *adv* **1** (*repeatedly*) [*change, interrupt, try etc* +] 一再地 **2** (*ceaselessly*) [*evolve, grow, sob etc* +] 不停地

continuation [kəntɪnju'eɪʃən] *n* **1** [U] [*of war, situation etc*] 持续 **2** [C] (*extension*) 继续 **3** [C] [*of story*] 续篇

✪ **continue** [kən'tɪnjuː] **I** *vi* **1** (*carry on uninterrupted*) [*situation, event etc* +] 继续 **2** (*after interruption*) [*event* +] 继续; [*speaker* +] 继续说 **II** *vt* **1** (*carry on uninterrupted*) 继续 **2** (*after interruption*) 继续; [*speaker* +] 继续说 ◊ *He arrived in Norway, where he continued his campaign.* 他到达了挪威，继续进行他的运动。 ◊ *"OK," she continued after a pause.* "好"，她停了一下后继续说。 ♦**to continue to do sth** *or* **doing sth** 持续做某事 ♦**to continue with sth** 继续某事 ♦**to continue up/along/through sth** 继续上/沿着/走过某处 ♦**"to be continued"** "未完待续" ♦**"continued on page 10"** "转至第10页"

continuity [kɔntɪ'njuːɪtɪ] *n* **1** [C/U] (*in policy, management etc*) 连贯性 **2** [U] [电视, 电影] 各场景的串联

continuous [kən'tɪnjuəs] *adj* **1** [+ *process, growth etc*] 连续不停的 **2** [+ *line, surface*] 不断延伸的 **3** [语言] [+ *tense*] 进行时的

📖 用法参见 **constant**

continuous assessment [英] *n* [U] 连续性评估

continuously [kən'tɪnjuəslɪ] *adv* 持续不断地

contour ['kɔntuə(r)] *n* [C] **1** (*shape, outline*) 轮廓 **2** (*also:* ***contour line***) (*on map*) 地形线

contraception [kɔntrə'sɛpʃən] *n* [U] 避孕

contraceptive [kɔntrə'sɛptɪv] **I** *n* [C] (*drug*) 避孕药; (*device*) 避孕工具 **II** *adj* [+ *device, method, pill*] 避孕的

contract [*n* 'kɔntrækt, *vb* kən'trækt] **I** *n* [C] 合同 **II** *vi* **1** (*become smaller*) [*metal, muscle* +] 收缩 **2** ♦**to contract (with sb) to do sth** (和某人)订做某事的合同 **III** *vt* [+ *illness*] 感染 **IV** *cpd* [复合词]

[+ *work*] 合同 ♦**contract of employment** 工作合同
❑**contract out** [英] **I** *vt* [+ *work*] 把…包出去 **II** *vi* 退出和约
contractor [kən'træktə(r)] *n* [c] 承包商
contradict [kɔntrə'dɪkt] *vt* **1** (*challenge*) [+ *person, statement etc*] 驳斥 **2** (*be contrary to*) 与…相悖
contradiction [kɔntrə'dɪkʃən] *n* [c/u] 矛盾 ♦**a contradiction in terms** 措辞矛盾
contrary[1] ['kɔntrərɪ] **I** *adj* (*opposite, different*) 相反的 **II** *n* [c/u] ♦**the contrary** 相反 ♦**on the contrary** 正相反 ♦**contrary to popular opinion** 与公众看法相反 ♦**to the contrary** 相反的

> 📖 请勿将 **on the contrary** 和 **in contrast** 混淆。**on the contrary** 用于驳斥某人或某事，指出他们是错误的。*'People just don't do things like that.' – 'On the contrary, they do them all the time.'* **in contrast** 用来表示你现在谈论的内容与先前所说的内容是截然不同的。*The company said yesterday that in contrast with much of the rest of the industry, it is currently enjoying rapid growth.*

contrary[2] [kən'trɛərɪ] *adj* (*argumentative*) 好与人作对的
contrast [*n* 'kɔntrɑːst, *vb* kən'trɑːst] **I** *n* [c/u] **1** 明显的差异 **2** ♦**to be a contrast to sth** 与某物截然不同 **II** *vt* 对比 **III** *vi* ♦**to contrast with sth** 与某事形成对照 ♦**by** *or* **in contrast** 对比之下 ♦**in contrast to ...** 与…形成对比 ♦**to contrast sth with sth** 将某物与某物进行对比 📖 用法参见 **contrary**
contribute [kən'trɪbjuːt] **I** *vi* ♦**to contribute (to sth)** (*help*) (为某事) 做贡献; (*with money*) (给某事) 捐助; (*write articles*) (为某刊) 撰稿; (*be a cause*) 造成 (某事) **II** *vt* ♦**to contribute 10 pounds (to sth)** (给某事) 捐献10英镑 ♦**to contribute an article to sth** 给某刊投稿
contribution [kɔntrɪ'bjuːʃən] **I** *n* [c] **1** (*donation*) 捐献 **2** (*help*) 贡献 **3** (*article*) 稿件 **II contributions** *n* [*pl*] [英] 定期扣缴
contributor [kən'trɪbjutə(r)] *n* [c] **1** (*to appeal, fund*) 捐献者 **2** (*to magazine*) 投稿人
✪**control** [kən'trəul] **I** *vt* [+ *country, organization*] 统治; [+ *person, emotion, disease, fire*] 控制; [+ *machine, process*] 操纵; [+ *wages, prices*] 管制 **II** *n* [u] [*of country, organization*] 控制权; [*of people*] 指挥能力; [*of vehicle, machine*] 控制 **III controls** *n* [*pl*] **1** [*of vehicle, machine, TV*] 操纵装置 **2** ♦**price/planning** *etc* **controls** 价格/规划管制 ♦**to control o.s.** 克制自己 ♦**to take control (of sth)** 控制住 (某事) ♦**to lose control (of sth)** (*emotionally*) 克制不住 (某事); (*in vehicle, on machine*) 失去 (对某物的) 控制 ♦**to keep control (of sth)** 保持 (对某物的) 控制 ♦**to keep control of o.s.** 控制自己 ♦**to be in control (of sth)** (*of situation, car etc*) 控制着 (某事) ♦**to be under control** [*fire, situation* +] 处于控制之下 ♦**to be out of control** [*fire, situation* +] 失去控制 ♦**the car went out of control** 那辆车失控了 ♦**circumstances beyond our control** 不在我们控制之中的情况 ♦**to be at the controls** 操纵
control tower *n* [c] 指挥调度台
controversial [kɔntrə'vəːʃl] *adj* [+ *decision, issue, person*] 有争议的; [+ *book, film*] 引起争论的
controversy ['kɔntrəvəːsɪ] *n* [c/u] 辩论
convene [kən'viːn] [正式] **I** *vt* [+ *meeting, conference*] 召集 **II** *vi* [*parliament, inquiry* +] 正式开始; [*people* +] 开会
convenience [kən'viːnɪəns] **I** *n* **1** [u] (*ease, suitability*) 方便 **2** [c] (*useful thing*) 便利设施 **II conveniences** *n* [*pl*] 方便的用具 ♦**at sb's convenience** 在某人方便的时候 ♦**at your earliest convenience** 在你方便时尽早
convenient [kən'viːnɪənt] *adj* [+ *method, system, time*] 方便的; [+ *place*] 近便的 ♦**to be convenient**

for [+*person*] 适合于; [+*place*] 容易到达

convent ['kɔnvənt] *n* [c] 女修道院

convention [kən'vɛnʃən] *n* **1** [c/u] (*custom*) 社会习俗 **2** [c] (*conference*) [*of organization, group*] 大会; (*political*) 代表大会 **3** [c] (*agreement*) 协定

conventional [kən'vɛnʃənl] *adj* [+*person, behaviour*] 符合习俗的; [+*method, product*] 传统的; [+*war, weapons*] 常规的

conversation [kɔnvə'seɪʃən] *n* [c/u] 交谈 ♦**to have a conversation (about sth/with sb)** (和某人)谈(某事) ♦**to make conversation** 说应酬话

conversely [kɔn'vəːslɪ] *adv* 正相反

conversion [kən'vəːʃən] *n* **1** [c/u] (*transformation*) [*of substance*] 转化; [*of building*] 改建 **2** [c/u] [*of quantity, money*] 换算 **3** [c/u] [*of person*] (*to belief*) 改变信仰; (*to religion*) 皈依 **4** [c] [橄榄球] 触地得分后再射门得的分 ♦**the conversion of sth into sth** 从某物到某物的转变 ♦**sb's conversion to sth** [+*Islam, Christianity*] 某人对某教的皈依; [+*belief*] 某人转而对某事的信仰

convert [*vb* kən'vəːt, *n* 'kɔnvəːt] **I** *vt* **1** (*transform*) [+*substance*] 使转化; [+*building*] 改建; [+*vehicle, equipment*] 改装 **2** [+*person*] (*to belief*) 使…改变信仰; (*to religion*) 使…皈依 **3** [+*quantity, money*] 把…折合 **4** [橄榄球] 触地得分后再射中球门获得附加分 **II** *vi* [宗] 皈依 **III** *n* [c] (*to belief*) 改变信仰的人; (*to religion*) 皈依者 ♦**to convert sth into sth** [+*substance*] 将某物转化成某物; [+*building*] 将某建筑改建成某建筑 ♦**to convert sth to sth** [+*equipment*] 将某物改装成某物 ♦**to convert to sth** [*person* +] (*to belief*) 改为信仰某物; (*to religion*) 皈依某教

convertible [kən'vəːtəbl] **I** *n* [c] (*car*) 折篷汽车 **II** *adj* [+*currency*] 可兑换的

convey [kən'veɪ] [正式] *vt* **1** ♦**to convey sth (to sb)** [+*information, idea, thanks*] (向某人)传达某事 **2** ♦**to convey sb/sth to sth** [+*cargo, traveller*] 将某人/某物运送至某处

conveyor belt [kən'veɪə-] *n* [c] 传送带

convict [*vt* kən'vɪkt, *n* 'kɔnvɪkt] **I** *vt* ♦**to convict sb (of sth)** 宣判某人有(…)罪 **II** *n* [c] (*person*) 囚犯

conviction [kən'vɪkʃən] *n* **1** [c] (*belief*) 坚定的信仰 **2** [u] (*certainty*) 坚信 **3** [c/u] [法] 定罪

convince [kən'vɪns] *vt* **1** (*cause to believe*) 使信服 **2** [尤美] (*persuade*) 说服 ♦**to convince sb of sth** 使某人相信某事 ♦**to convince sb that ...** 说服某人… ♦**to convince sb to do sth** [尤美] 说服某人去做某事

convinced [kən'vɪnst] *adj* ♦**to be convinced that ...** 坚信… ♦**to be/become convinced of sth** 确信/开始相信某事

convincing [kən'vɪnsɪŋ] *adj* 令人信服的

convoy ['kɔnvɔɪ] *n* [c] 车/船队 ♦**in convoy** 由…护送

COO *n abbr* (= ***chief operating officer***) 首席营运官

cook [kuk] **I** *vt* [+*food, meat, vegetables*] 烹调; [+*meal*] 做 **II** *vi* **1** [*person* +] 做饭 **2** [*food* +] 烧 **III** *n* [c] 厨师 ♦**a good cook** 会做饭的人

> 📖 表示烹调的具体方法时，通常会使用比**cook**更具体的词。比如，用烤箱烤肉用**roast**，烤面包或蛋糕则用**bake**。用水煮蔬菜用**boil**，隔水蒸食物则用**steam**。用油炒肉类或蔬菜用**fry**。用火烤食物可以用**grill**，或在美式英语中用**broil**。烤面包一般不用**grill**，而用**toast**。

❑**cook up** [非正式] *vt* [+*scheme*] 策划; [+*excuse, story*] 捏造

cookbook ['kukbuk] *n* [c] 菜谱

cooker ['kukə(r)] [英] *n* [c] 厨灶 [美 = **stove**]

cookery ['kukərɪ] *n* [u] 烹饪

cookery book [英] *n* = **cookbook**

cookie ['kukɪ] [美] *n* [c] **1** (*for eating*) 小甜饼 [英 = **biscuit**] **2** [计算机] 记忆块

cooking ['kukɪŋ] **I** *n* [U] **1** (*activity*) 烹调 **2** (*food*) 饭菜 **II** *cpd* [复合词] [+ *apples, chocolate, cheese*] 烹调用; [+ *utensils*] 用于烹饪

cool [ku:l] **I** *adj* **1** [+ *water, breeze, evening, place*] 凉的 **2** (*light*) [+ *clothes*] 凉爽的 **3** (*calm, unemotional*) 冷静的 **4** (*unfriendly*) 冷淡的 **5** [非正式] (*good*) 顶呱呱的; (*fashionable*) 酷的 **II** *vt* 使变凉 **III** *vi* 冷下来 **IV** *n* ♦ **to keep/lose one's cool** [非正式] 保持冷静/失去自制而激动起来 ♦ **it's quite cool today** 今天挺凉 ♦ **to keep sth cool** 保持某物的凉度 ♦ **(that's) cool!** [非正式] (*fine*) 再好不过! ♦ **a cool two million dollars** [非正式] 整整两百万美元
❑ **cool down I** *vi* **1** (*become colder*) 变凉 **2** (喻) [*person, situation* +] 平息; **II** *vt* **1** (*decrease heat of*) 冷却 **2** (喻) [+ *person, situation*] 使冷静下来
❑ **cool off I** *vi* (*after heat*) 变凉 **II** *vt* 使变凉
📖 用法参见 **cold**

co-operate [kəu'ɔpəreɪt] *vi* **1** (*collaborate*) 合作 **2** (*be helpful*) 配合 ♦ **to co-operate with sb** (*collaborate with*) 与某人合作; (*be helpful to*) 配合某人

co-operation [kəuɔpə'reɪʃən] *n* [U] **1** (*collaboration*) 合作 **2** (*help*) 配合

co-operative [kəu'ɔpərətɪv] **I** *adj* [+ *person, attitude*] 乐意合作的; [+ *effort*] 合作的 **II** *n* [C] (*factory, business*) 合作社

co-ordinate [*vt* kəu'ɔ:dɪneɪt, *n* kəu'ɔ:dɪnət] **I** *vt* [+ *activity, work, effort, limbs, movement*] 协调 **II** *n* [C] [数, 地理] 坐标

co-ordination [kəuɔ:dɪ'neɪʃən] *n* [U] **1** [*of activity, work, efforts*] 协作 **2** [*of movements*] 协调

cop [kɔp] [非正式] *n* [C] 警察

cope [kəup] *vi* 对付 ♦ **to cope with sth/with doing sth** [+ *problem, situation, task*] 妥善地处理某事/做某事

copper ['kɔpə(r)] **I** *n* **1** [U] (*metal*) 铜 **2** [C] [英: 非正式] (*policeman/woman*) 警察 **II coppers** *n* [*pl*] (*small change, coins*) 铜板 **III** *cpd* [复合词] [+ *pipe, bracelet etc*] 铜

copy ['kɔpɪ] **I** *n* **1** [C] (*duplicate*) 复制品 **2** [C] (*issue*) [*of book, record, newspaper*] 本/张/份 **3** [U] [出版] (*text*) 文字稿 **II** *vt* **1** (*imitate*) [+ *person, idea etc*] 模仿 **2** (*also:* ***copy out***) 抄写 ♦ **to make a copy of sth** 复印某物 ♦ **to make good copy** [出版] 成为好材料 ♦ **to copy sth into a notebook** 将某事写在笔记本里
❑ **copy down** *vt* 记下来

copyright ['kɔpɪraɪt] *n* [U] 版权

coral ['kɔrəl] *n* [U] (*substance*) 珊瑚

cord [kɔ:d] **I** *n* [C/U] **1** (*string*) 绳 **2** [电子] 电线 **II** *cpd* [复合词] (*corduroy*) 灯心绒的 **III cords** *n* [*pl*] (*trousers*) 灯心绒裤子

cordial ['kɔ:dɪəl] **I** *adj* 热烈诚挚的 **II** *n* [C/U] **1** [英] (*fruit drink*) 甜饮料 **2** [美] (*alcoholic drink*) 香甜酒 [英 = **liqueur**]

cordless ['kɔ:dlɪs] *adj* [+ *phone, kettle etc*] 无绳的

cordon ['kɔ:dn] *n* [C] [军, 警察] 警戒线
❑ **cordon off** *vt* [+ *area*] 封锁

corduroy ['kɔ:dərɔɪ] **I** *n* [U] 灯心绒 **II** *cpd* [复合词] [+ *jacket, trousers etc*] 灯心绒

core [kɔ:(r)] **I** *n* [C] [*of fruit*] 核; [*of building, place*] 中心; [*of earth*] 地核; [*of nuclear reactor*] 活性区; [*of problem, issue*] 核心 **II** *vt* [+ *apple, pear etc*] 去掉…的果核 ♦ **to be a Republican/royalist to the core** 是个十足的共和主义者/保皇主义者

coriander [kɔrɪ'ændə(r)] *n* [U] 香菜

cork [kɔ:k] **I** *n* **1** [C] (*stopper*) 瓶塞 **2** [U] (*material*) 软木 **II** *cpd* [复合词] [+ *mat, tile etc*] 软木制

corkscrew ['kɔ:kskru:] *n* [C] 瓶塞钻

corn [kɔ:n] *n* **1** [U] [英] (*cereal crop*) 谷物 [美 = **grain**] **2** [U] [美] (*maize*) 玉米 [英 = **maize**] **3** [C] (*on foot*) 鸡眼 ♦ **corn on the cob** 玉米(棒子)

corned beef ['kɔ:nd-] *n* [U] 腌牛肉

corner ['kɔ:nə(r)] **I** *n* [C] **1** 角落 **2** [*of road*] 街角 **3** [足球] (*also:* ***corner kick***) 角球 **4** [拳击] 场角 **II** *vt* [+ *person, animal*] 使走投无路 **III** *vi* [*car, driver* +] 拐弯 ♦ **to cut corners** (喻) 走捷径 ♦ **to be (just) round** *or*

around the corner（喻）即将发生 ♦**to turn the corner**（喻）渡过难关 ♦**to corner the market** 垄断市场

cornflakes ['kɔːnfleɪks] *n* [*pl*] 玉米片

cornflour ['kɔːnflauə(r)]［英］*n* [U] 玉米面［美=**cornstarch**］

cornstarch ['kɔːnstɑːtʃ]［美］*n* [U] 玉米面［英=**cornflour**］

coronary ['kɔrənərɪ]［医］**I** *n* [C] (*also: **coronary thrombosis***) 冠心病 **II** *adj* [+ *artery*] 冠状动脉的 ♦**to have a coronary** 患冠心病

coronation [kɔrə'neɪʃən] *n* [C] 加冕典礼

coroner ['kɔrənə(r)] *n* [C] 验尸官

Corp. *abbr* (= ***corporation***) 股份有限公司

corporal ['kɔːprəl] *n* [C] 下士

corporal punishment *n* [U] 体罚

corporate ['kɔːpərɪt] *adj* [+ *executive, culture, earnings, image*] 公司的; [+ *client*] 集团的; [+ *responsibility*] 共同的

corporation [kɔːpə'reɪʃən] *n* [C] **1**［商］股份有限公司 **2**［英］[*of town*] 市政当局

corps [kɔː(r)] (*pl* **corps**) *n* [C] **1**［军］特种部队 **2** [*of diplomats, journalists*] 团

corpse [kɔːps] *n* [C] 死尸

correct [kə'rɛkt] **I** *adj* **1** [+ *answer, details, amount, spelling*] 正确的; [+ *decision, means, procedure*] 适当的 **2** (*socially*) [+ *person, behaviour*] 得体的 **II** *vt* **1** (*put right*) [+ *mistake, fault, person*] 纠正 **2** (*mark*) [+ *exam*] 批改 ♦**you are correct** 你是对的

correction [kə'rɛkʃən] *n* **1** [C] 修改 **2** [U] (*correcting*) 改正

correspond [kɔrɪs'pɔnd] *vi* **1** (*be equivalent*) ♦**to correspond (to sth)**（与某物）相符合 **2** (*write*) ♦**to correspond (with sb)**（和某人）通信

correspondence [kɔrɪs'pɔndəns] *n* **1** [U] (*letter-writing*) 通信 **2** [U] (*letters*) 信件 **3** [C] (*relationship*) 一致

correspondent [kɔrɪs'pɔndənt] *n* [C] (*reporter*) 记者

corresponding [kɔrɪs'pɔndɪŋ] *adj* 相应的

corridor ['kɔrɪdɔː(r)] *n* [C] (*in house, building*) 走廊; (*on train*) 车厢过道

corrode [kə'rəud] **I** *vi* [*metal* +] 受腐蚀 **II** *vt* [+ *metal*] 腐蚀

corrupt [kə'rʌpt] **I** *adj* **1** [+ *person*] 腐败的 **2** [+ *data*] 破坏的 **II** *vt* **1** [+ *person*] 使堕落 **2** [+ *data*] 破坏 ♦**corrupt practices** 贪赃舞弊的行为

corruption [kə'rʌpʃən] *n* [U] 贪赃舞弊

'cos [kɔz]［英:非正式］*conj* 因为

cosmetic [kɔz'mɛtɪk] **I** *n* [C] (*beauty product*) 化妆品 **II** *adj* [+ *measure, improvement*] 表面的

cosmetic surgery *n* [U] 整容手术

cosmic ['kɔzmɪk] *adj* 宇宙的

cosmopolitan [kɔzmə'pɔlɪtn] *adj* [+ *place, person, outlook*] 世界性的

✪**cost** [kɔst] (*pt, pp* **cost**) **I** *n* **1** [C] 价格 ◊ *the cost of a loaf of bread* 一条面包的价格 **2** [C/U]（喻）(*loss, damage etc*) 代价 ◊ *The cost in human life was enormous.* 付出了巨大的生命代价。**II** *vt* **1** (*be priced at*) 价格为 ◊ *It cost five thousand dollars.* 价格为5000美元。**2**［商］(*work out cost of*) [+ *project, purchase etc*] (*pt, pp* *costed*) 估价 **III costs** *n* [*pl*] **1** (*overheads*) 成本 **2**［法］诉讼费用 ♦**how much does it cost?** 这多少钱？♦**it cost me fifty pounds** 这花了我50英镑 ♦**it costs 5 pounds/too much** 价格为5英镑/太高 ♦**what will it cost to have it repaired?** 修理它要多少钱？♦**it cost him his life/job** 这让他付出了生命/失去工作的代价 ♦**the cost of living** 生活费用 ♦**at all costs** 不惜一切代价

co-star ['kəustɑː(r)]［电视，电影］**I** *n* [C] 合演者 **II** *vi* ♦**to co-star (with sb)**（与某人）联袂主演

Costa Rica ['kɔstə'riːkə] *n* 哥斯达黎加

costly ['kɔstlɪ] *adj* **1** (*expensive*) 昂贵的 **2**（喻）代价惨重的

costume ['kɔstjuːm] *n* **1** [C/U] [*of actor, artist*] 戏装 **2** [U] (*style of dress*) 服装式样

cosy（美 **cozy**）['kəuzɪ] *adj* **1** [+ *room, house*] 温暖舒适的 **2** [+ *person*] ♦**to be/feel cosy** 感到舒适安逸 **3** [+ *chat, evening, atmosphere*] 亲切友好的

cot ['kɔt] *n* [c] **1** [英](*child's*) 幼儿床 [美= **crib**] **2** [美](*bed*) 帆布床 [英= **camp bed**]

cottage ['kɔtɪdʒ] *n* [c] 村舍

cottage cheese *n* [u] 农家鲜干酪

cottage pie [英] *n* [c/u] 农家馅饼

cotton ['kɔtn] **I** *n* [u] **1** (*fabric*) 棉布 **2** (*plant*) 棉树 **3** (*thread*) 棉线 **II** *cpd* [复合词][+ *dress, sheets etc*] 棉布

❑ **cotton on** [英:非正式] *vi* ♦ **to cotton on (to sth)** 明白(某事)

cotton candy [美] *n* [u] 棉花糖 [英 = **candy floss**]

cotton wool [英] *n* [u] 脱脂棉 [美= **absorbent cotton**]

couch [kautʃ] **I** *n* [c] **1** 长沙发 **2** (*doctor's, psychiatrist's*) 诊察台 **II** *vt* ♦ **to be couched in polite language/legal terms** 以礼貌的语言/法律措辞表达

cough [kɔf] **I** *vi* **1** [*person* +] 咳嗽 **2** [*engine* +] 喀喀作响 **II** *n* [c] (*noise, illness*) 咳嗽 **III** *vt* [+ *blood*] 咳 ♦ **to have a cough** 咳嗽

❑ **cough up I** *vt* **1** [+ *blood*] 咳出 **2** [非正式][+ *money*] 不情愿地支付 **II** *vi* [非正式] 出钱

cough mixture [英] *n* [u] 咳嗽糖浆

✪ **could**

KEYWORD

[kud] *aux vb* → 另见 **can**

1 (*referring to past*) ♦ **we couldn't go to the party** 我们没能去参加聚会 ♦ **last year we couldn't afford a holiday** 去年我们度不起假 ♦ **he could be very unkind** 他可能会很刻薄 ♦ **he couldn't read or write** 他不会读也不会写 ♦ **we could hear him whistling** 我们能听到他正在吹口哨 ♦ **she said she couldn't hear me** 她说听不见我说的话

2 (*possibility*) ♦ **he could be in the library** 他可能在图书馆 ♦ **I couldn't be happier** 我再高兴不过了 ♦ **he could be released next year** 他明年可能被释放 ♦ **you could have been killed!** 可能你连命都没了! ♦ **the accident could have been caused by an oil leak** 事故可能是由石油泄漏引起的

3 (*in conditionals*) (*with "if"*) ♦ **if we had more time, I could finish this** 如果有更多时间,我能够完成的 ♦ **we'd have a holiday, if we could afford it** 如果能支付得起的话,我们就去度假了 ♦ **I couldn't have done this without you** 若没有你,我是做不成这事的

4 (*in offers, suggestions, requests*) 可以 ♦ **I could call a doctor** 我可以叫个医生 ♦ **we could always go to the cinema** 我们还是可以去看电影 ♦ **couldn't you give him a call?** 你可不可以给他打个电话? ♦ **could I borrow the car?** 我可以借一下车吗? ♦ **if I could just interrupt you for a minute** 我是否可以打扰你一小会儿 ♦ **he asked if he could make a phone call** 他问是否可以打个电话

5 (*emphatic*) ♦ **you could at least be polite!** 你至少可以礼貌点儿! ♦ **you could have told me!** 你早该告诉我! ♦ **I could scream!** 我真想大叫! ♦ **how could you have lied to me?** 你怎么能向我撒谎呢?

couldn't ['kudnt] = **could not**

✪ **council** ['kaunsl] *n* [c] **1** [*of city, county*] 议会 **2** (*in names*) 理事会 ◊ *the Arts Council* 艺术理事会

council estate [英] *n* [c] 由市政经营的房产

council house [英] *n* [c] 地方当局建造的简易住宅

councillor ['kaunslə(r)] *n* [c] 地方议员

council tax [英] *n* [u] 市政税,由英国地方政府根据房屋价值而征收并自由支配的税种

counsel ['kaunsl] **I** *n* **1** [u] (*advice*) 劝告 **2** [c] (*lawyer*) 诉务律师 **II** *vt* **1** (*advise*) [+ *person*] 给…提建议 **2** [+ *caution, patience*] 建议 ♦ **to keep one's own counsel** 将自己的意见保密 ♦ **counsel for the defence, defence counsel** 辩护律师 ♦ **counsel for the prosecution, prosecuting counsel** 公诉律师 ♦ **to counsel sb to do sth** [正式] 劝告某人做某事

counselling (美 **counseling**) ['kaunsəlɪŋ] *n* [u] 辅导

counsellor (美 **counselor**) ['kaunslə(r)] *n* [c] **1** (*advisor*) 顾问 **2** [美](*lawyer*) 律师

count [kaunt] **I** *vt* **1** (*also:* ***count up***) 数 **2** (*include*) 把…计算在内 **II** *vi* **1** (*add*) 数 **2** (*enter into consideration*) 认可 **3** (*matter*) 有价值 **III** *n* [c] **1** (*total*) [*of things, people, votes*] 数目 **2** (*level*) [*of pollen, alcohol etc*] 计数 **3** (*nobleman*) 伯爵 ♦ **to count (up) to 10** 数到10 ♦ **to count the cost of sth** 计算某事的成本 ♦ **not counting the children** 儿童不算在内 ♦ **10 counting him** 算上他10个 ♦ **count yourself lucky** 你应该感到幸运 ♦ **to count as sth** 算得上某事 ♦ **it counts for little/a lot** 没用/有用 ♦ **to keep/lose count of sth** 知道/不知道某事的数目

❑ **count against** *vt* [不可拆分] 对…不利

❑ **count down** *vt* [不可拆分] [+ *seconds, minutes*] 倒着数 ♦ **to be counting down the days to sth** 迫切期待着某事的到来

❑ **count down to** *vt* [不可拆分] **1** (字) [+ *midnight, blast-off*] 倒读数至 **2** (喻) [+ *Christmas, anniversary, etc*] 迫切期待着

❑ **count in** *vt* [+ *person*] 把…算在内

❑ **count on, count upon** *vt* [不可拆分] [+ *support, help*] 指望; [+ *person*] 依靠 ♦ **to count on doing sth** 指望做某事

❑ **count out** *vt* [不可拆分] **1** [+ *coins, notes*] 清点 **2** (*exclude*) [+ *person*] 不把…算入

countdown ['kauntdaun] *n* [c] (*to launch*) 倒计时

counter ['kauntə(r)] **I** *n* [c] **1** (*desk*) (*in shop, café, bank, post office*) 柜台 **2** (*in game*) 筹码 **3** (*for keeping count*) 计数器 **4** ♦ **a counter to sth** 对某事物的反作用 **II** *vt* **1** (*offset*) 反击 **2** (*respond to*) 反驳 **III** *adv* ♦ **to run** *or* **be counter to sth** 违背某事 ♦ **to buy/sell sth under the counter** 私下买/卖某物 ♦ **to counter with sth/by doing sth** 用某事/通过做某事来反对

counteract ['kauntər'ækt] *vt* [+ *effect, tendency*] 对抗

counterclockwise ['kauntə'klɔkwaɪz] [美] **I** *adv* 逆时针方向地 [英 = **anticlockwise**] **II** *adj* 逆时针方向的 [英 = **anticlockwise**]

counterfeit ['kauntəfɪt] **I** *adj* [+ *money, goods, document*] 伪造的 **II** *n* [c] 仿制品 **III** *vt* 伪造

counterpart ['kauntəpɑːt] *n* [c] [*of person, company etc*] 相对应的人/物

countertop ['kauntətɔp] [美] *n* [c] 厨房里做饭的平台 [英 = **worktop**]

countess ['kauntɪs] *n* [c] (*in own right*) 女伯爵; (*wife of count/earl*) 伯爵夫人

countless ['kauntlɪs] *adj* 无数的

✪ **country** ['kʌntrɪ] **I** *n* **1** [c] (*nation*) 国家 **2** [s] (*population*) 全国人民 **3** [c] (*native land*) 家乡 ◊ *He loved his country.* 他热爱自己的家乡。 **4** [u] (*area*) 地区 ◊ *mountainous country* 山区 **5** (*countryside*) ♦ **the country** 乡下 ◊ *a healthy life in the country* 乡下的健康生活 **II** *cpd* [复合词] (*also:* ***country and western***) [+ *music, singer*] 西部乡村 ♦ **in the country** 在乡下

country house [英] *n* [c] 乡间别墅

countryside ['kʌntrɪsaɪd] *n* [u] 农村

county ['kauntɪ] *n* [c] 郡

coup [kuː] *n* [c] **1** (*also:* ***coup d'état***) 政变 **2** (*achievement*) 意外而成功的行动

couple ['kʌpl] **I** *n* [c] **1** (*married*) 夫妻; (*living together*) 情侣 **2** (*twosome*) 对 **3** ♦ **a couple of** (*two*) 两个; (*a few*) 几个 **II** *vt* ♦ **coupled with sth** 配上某物 ♦ **to couple sth to sth** [+ *machinery*] 将某物与某物连接起来

coupon ['kuːpɔn] *n* [c] **1** (*voucher*) 折价券 **2** (*form*) 索取单

courage ['kʌrɪdʒ] *n* [u] 勇气 ♦ **to have the courage to do sth** 有勇气做某事

courageous [kə'reɪdʒəs] *adj* 勇敢的

courgette [kuə'ʒɛt] [英] *n* [c/u] 密生西葫芦 [美 = **zucchini**]

courier ['kurɪə(r)] *n* [c] **1** (*messenger*)

信使 **2** (*rep*) 旅游团的服务员

✪ **course** [kɔːs] **I** *n* **1** [c] (*educational*) 课程 **2** [c] [*of injections, antibiotics*] 疗程 **3** [c] (*direction*) [*of life, events, time etc*] 进程; [*of ship, aircraft*] 航向; [*of river*] 流向 **4** [c] (*also:* ***course of action***) 做法 **5** [*of meal*] ♦ **first/next/last course** 第一/下一/最后一道菜 **6** [c] (*for golf, horse-racing*) 场; (*for cycling*) 道 **II** *vi* [文] ♦ **to course down/through sth** 在某物上/中迅速流动 ♦ **of course** (*naturally*) 自然; (*certainly*) 当然 ◊ *That is of course true.* 自然是真的。◊ *Of course you should accept.* 你当然应该接受。♦ **of course!** 没问题！ ♦ **of course not!** 当然不行！ ♦ **in the course of the next few days** 在今后几天期间 ♦ **to be on course for ...** 在迈向…的正确方向上 ♦ **to run** *or* **take its course** 听其自然发展 ♦ **a course of action** 做法 ♦ **a course of treatment** 一个疗程 ♦ **a course of lectures** 系列讲座

✪ **court** [kɔːt] **I** *n* [c] **1** [法] (*place*) 法庭; (*people*) 全体审判员 **2** (*for tennis, badminton etc*) 球场 **3** (*royal*) 宫廷 **II** *vt* **1** (*seek*) [+ *publicity, popularity*] 试图获得 **2** (*risk*) [+ *disaster, unpopularity*] 招致 **3** [过时] [+ *man, woman*] 与…谈恋爱 **III** *vi* [*couple* +] 恋爱 ♦ **to take sb to court** 起诉某人 ♦ **to settle sth out of court** 庭外和解 ♦ **to go to court** [法] 起诉 ♦ **to hold court** 接待仰慕者

courteous ['kəːtɪəs] *adj* 谦恭有礼的

courtesy ['kəːtəsɪ] **I** *n* [U] (*politeness*) 谦恭有礼 **II** *cpd* [复合词] [+ *bus, car etc*] 免费 ♦ **(by) courtesy of ...** (*thanks to*) 承蒙…

courthouse ['kɔːthaus] [美] *n* [c] 法院 [英 = **court**]

courtroom ['kɔːtruːm] *n* [c] 法庭

courtyard ['kɔːtjɑːd] *n* [c] 庭院

cousin ['kʌzn] *n* [c] (*older male on father's side*) 堂兄; (*younger male on father's side*) 堂弟; (*older female on father's side*) 堂姐; (*younger female on father's side*) 堂妹; (*older male on mother's side*) 表兄; (*younger male on mother's side*) 表弟 (*older female on mother's side*) 表姐; (*younger female on mother's side*) 表妹 ♦ **first cousin** 嫡堂或表兄弟姐妹 ♦ **second cousin** 远房堂或表兄弟姐妹

✪ **cover** ['kʌvə(r)] **I** *vt* **1** ♦ **to cover sth (with sth)** (用某物)盖着某物 ◊ *She covered her face with her hands.* 她用手蒙着自己的脸。**2** (*travel*) [+ *distance*] 行 ◊ *We covered twenty kilometres a day.* 我们每天行20公里。**3** (*in insurance*) ♦ **to cover sb (against sth)** 给某人保(某事的)险 ◊ *We're not covered against accidental damage.* 我们没有保意外损害险。**4** (*deal with*) [*law, regulation* +] 适用于; [*speaker, writer, course* +] 讨论; [*journalist, reporter* +] 报道 ◊ *The law covers four categories of experiments.* 这条法则适用于4种试验。◊ *We've covered a wide range of subjects today.* 我们今天讨论了一系列广泛的课题。◊ *My editor asked me to cover the elections.* 编辑叫我报道这些选举。**5** (*be sufficient money for*) 足够支付 ◊ *£1.50 to cover postage* 1英镑50便士用来支付邮资 **II** *n* **1** [c] (*for furniture, machinery etc*) 套子 **2** [c] (*jacket*) [*of book, magazine*] 封面 **3** [U] (*insurance*) 保险 **4** [U] (*shelter*) 掩蔽物 ◊ *They ran for cover.* 他们向可以躲避的地方跑去。**5** [c] (*for illegal activities*) 幌子 **III covers** *n* [*pl*] (*on bed*) 铺盖 ♦ **to be covered in** *or* **with sth** [+ *mud, blood, dust etc*] 被某物覆盖 ♦ **to take cover** 隐蔽 ♦ **under cover** 躲起来 ♦ **under cover of darkness** 在黑夜的掩护下 ♦ **under separate cover** 在另函内

❑ **cover for** *vt* [不可拆分] **1** [+ *wrongdoer*] 为…隐瞒 **2** [+ *absent colleague*] 代替

❑ **cover up I** *vt* **1** ♦ **to cover sth up (with sth)** [+ *person, object*] (用某物)将某物盖住 **2** [+ *facts, feelings, mistakes*] (用某事)掩饰某事 **II** *vi* ♦ **to cover up for sb** 替某人掩饰

coverage ['kʌvərɪdʒ] *n* [U] [电视, 出版] 报道 ♦ **television coverage of the conference** 大会的电视报道 ♦ **to give full coverage of** 全面报道

covering ['kʌvərɪŋ] *n* [c] (*layer,*

around sth) 层 ♦**floor/wall covering** 地板/墙壁覆盖物

covert ['kəuvət] *adj* [+ *operation, action, support*] 秘密的

cover-up ['kʌvərʌp] *n* [c] 掩盖

cow [kau] **I** *n* [c] **1** (*farm animal*) 奶牛 **2** [动] [*of elephant, whale*] 雌兽 **3** [非正式, 疑讳] (*woman*) 婆娘 **II** *vt* (*intimidate*) 胁迫

coward ['kauəd] *n* [c] 胆小鬼

cowardly ['kauədlɪ] *adj* [+ *act*] 怯懦的; [+ *person*] 胆小的

cowboy ['kaubɔɪ] *n* [c] **1** (*in US*) 牛仔 **2** [英] [非正式] (*tradesman*) 奸滑之辈

cozy ['kəuzɪ] [美] *adj* = **cosy**

CPA [美] *n abbr* (= ***certified public accountant***) 会计师

crab [kræb] *n* **1** [c] (*creature*) 螃蟹 **2** [u] (*meat*) 蟹肉

crack [kræk] **I** *n* **1** [c] (*in bone, dish, glass, wall*) 裂缝 **2** [s] (*gap*) 缝隙 **3** [c] (*noise*) 噼啪声; [+ *of whip*] 噼啪声 **4** [c] [非正式] (*joke*) 挖苦话 **5** [非正式] (*attempt*) ♦**to have a crack (at sth)** 尝试(某事) **6** [u] (*drug*) 纯可卡因 **II** *vt* **1** (*break*) [+ *dish, glass, mirror*] 使开裂; [+ *bone*] 使骨折; [+ *nut, egg*] 打破 **2** (*noisily*) [+ *whip, twig*] 使噼啪作响 **3** (*solve*) [+ *problem, code*] 解决 **III** *vi* **1** [*dish, mirror, pipe* +] 开裂 **2** [非正式] [*person* +] (*lose control*) 垮掉 **IV** *adj* [+ *soldier, athlete*] 技艺高超的 ♦**to crack one's head/knee on sth** 头/膝盖在某物上撞了一下 ♦**to crack an egg into a bowl** 打一个鸡蛋在碗里 ♦**to crack a joke** 讲笑话 ♦**to get cracking** [英: 非正式] 开始大干起来

❑**crack down on** *vt* [不可拆分] [+ *drug dealers, crime etc*] 对…严惩不贷

❑**crack up** *vi* [非正式] (*mentally*) 精神崩溃

cracked [krækt] *adj* **1** [+ *dish, glass, mirror*] 破裂的 **2** [非正式] (*mad*) 疯狂的

cracker ['krækə(r)] *n* [c] **1** (*biscuit*) 薄脆饼干 **2** (*also:* ***Christmas cracker***) 圣诞爆竹 ♦**she's a cracker** [英: 非正式] 她棒极了 ♦**it was a cracker of a match** [英: 非正式] 那场比赛棒极了 ♦**he's crackers** [英: 非正式] 他疯了

crackle ['krækl] **I** *vi* [*fire, radio, telephone* +] 发噼啪声 **II** *n* [c] [*of fire, radio, telephone*] 噼啪声

cradle ['kreɪdl] **I** *n* [c] (*baby's*) 摇篮 **II** *vt* [+ *child, object*] 抱 ♦**the cradle of civilization** 文明的发源地

craft [krɑːft] (*pl* **craft**) **I** *n* [c] **1** (*boat*) 船舶; (*plane*) 飞机 **2** (*weaving, pottery etc*) 工艺 **3** (*trade*) 行业 **II** *vt* 精工制作

craftsman ['krɑːftsmən] (*pl* **craftsmen**) *n* [c] 手艺人

craftsmanship ['krɑːftsmənʃɪp] *n* [u] 工艺技巧

cram [kræm] **I** *vt* **1** ♦**to cram sth into sth** 将某物塞入某物 ♦**to cram sb into sth** 将某人挤入某物 **2** (*fill*) [+ *place*] 挤满 **II** *vi* **1** ♦**to cram into sth** [+ *building, vehicle*] 挤进某处 **2** (*for exam*) 临时抱佛脚 ♦**to cram sth with** *or* **full of sth** 用某物将某物塞得满满的

cramp [kræmp] **I** *n* [c/u] 抽筋 **II** *vt* ♦**to cramp sb's style** [非正式] 使某人不能放开手脚 ♦**to have cramp (in one's leg)** (腿)抽筋

cramped [kræmpt] *adj* [+ *room, building*] 狭小的; [+ *conditions*] 受限制的

cranberry ['krænbərɪ] **I** *n* [c] 越橘 **II** *cpd* [复合词] [+ *juice*] 越橘

crane [kreɪn] **I** *n* [c] **1** (*machine*) 起重机 **2** (*bird*) 鹤 **II** *vt* ♦**to crane one's neck** 伸长脖子 **III** *vi* ♦**to crane forward** 向前伸长脖子

cranefly ['kreɪnflaɪ] *n* [c] 大蚊

crap [kræp] [非正式, 疑讳] **I** *adj* 糟糕的 **II** *n* [u] **1** (*faeces*) 屎 **2** (*nonsense*) 胡扯 **III** *vi* 拉屎 ♦**to have a crap** 拉屎

crash [kræʃ] **I** *n* [c] **1** [*of car*] 撞击; [*of plane*] 坠机 **2** [*of stock market, business*] 暴跌 **3** (*noise*) 哗啦声 **II** *vt* [+ *car, plane etc*] 使撞毁 **III** *vi* **1** [*car, driver* +] 撞击; [*plane* +] 坠毁 **2** [*market, firm* +] 突然倒台 **3** [计算机] 死机 **4** (*clatter*) 轰然猛撞 ♦**a car/plane crash** 撞车/飞机失事 ♦**to crash into sth** 猛地撞上某物 ♦**he crashed the car into a wall** 他把车撞到了墙上

crash helmet *n* [c] 安全帽

crate [kreɪt] *n* [c] (*box*) 装货箱; (*for bottles*) 装瓶箱 ♦**a crate of oranges/beer** 一箱桔子/啤酒

cravat [krə'væt] *n* [c] 男用领结

crave [kreɪv] *vt* (*also:* ***crave for***) [+ *attention, affection*] 渴望得到; [+ *food, drink*] 渴求

crawfish ['krɔːfɪʃ] (*pl* **crawfish**) [美] *n* [c/u] 淡水螯虾 [英 = **crayfish**]

crawl [krɔːl] **I** *vi* **1** [*adult, child, insect* +] 爬; [*vehicle* +] 徐缓而行 **2** [非正式] (*grovel*) ♦**to crawl (to sb)** 拍(某人的)马屁 **II** *n* [u] (*also:* ***the crawl***) (*in swimming*) 自由泳 ♦**to do the crawl** 游自由泳 ♦**to be crawling with** [非正式] [+ *people, things*] 充满了 ♦**to drive along at a crawl** 缓慢地行进

crayfish ['kreɪfɪʃ] (*pl* **crayfish**) *n* [c/u] 淡水螯虾

crayon ['kreɪən] *n* [c] **1** (*coloured pencil*) 彩色铅笔 **2** (*wax crayon*) 彩色蜡笔

craze [kreɪz] *n* [c] (*fashion*) 一时的狂热 ♦**a craze for sth** 狂热地爱好某物

crazy ['kreɪzɪ] [非正式] *adj* (*mad*) 发疯的 ♦**to be crazy about sth/doing sth** 对某事/做某事着迷 ♦**to be crazy about sb** 为某人神魂颠倒 ♦**to go crazy** 发疯 ♦**to make** *or* **drive sb crazy** 使某人心烦意乱 ♦**like crazy** 拼命

creak [kriːk] **I** *vi* [*floorboard, door* +] 嘎吱嘎吱作响 **II** *n* [c] (*sound*) 嘎吱嘎吱声

cream [kriːm] **I** *n* **1** [u] (*dairy cream*) 奶油 **2** [c/u] (*for skin*) 乳霜 **3** (*élite*) ♦**the cream** 精华 **II** *adj* (*in colour*) 乳白色的

❑ **cream off** *vt* [+ *people*] 选拔; [+ *money, profits*] 提取并挪为私用

cream cheese *n* [u] 奶油干酪

creamy ['kriːmɪ] *adj* **1** (*containing cream*) 含大量奶油的 **2** (*smooth*) 光滑细腻的

crease [kriːs] **I** *n* [c] (*in cloth, paper*) (*fold*) 折痕; (*wrinkle*) 皱纹; (*in trousers*) 折缝 **II** *vt* (*wrinkle*) 使起皱 **III** *vi* [*cloth, paper* +] 起皱; [*face* +] 皱起来

✪ **create** [kriː'eɪt] *vt* [+ *job, situation, wealth, problem etc*] 创造; [+ *feeling*] 引起

creation [kriː'eɪʃən] *n* **1** [u] (*act*) 创造 **2** [c] (*work*) 作品 **3** [u] [宗] (*also:* ***the creation***) 创世

creative [kriː'eɪtɪv] *adj* **1** [+ *person*] 有创造力的 **2** [+ *use, manner*] 创造性的

creator [kriː'eɪtə(r)] *n* [c] 创造者

creature ['kriːtʃə(r)] *n* [c] **1** (*animal*) 动物 **2** (*person*) 人

crèche [krɛʃ] [英] *n* [c] 托儿所

credentials [krɪ'dɛnʃlz] *n* [*pl*] **1** (*qualifications*) 资格 **2** (*references*) 证明书 **3** (*identifying papers*) 证件

credibility [krɛdɪ'bɪlɪtɪ] *n* [u] [*of person, organization*] 信誉; [*of candidate, policy, idea*] 可靠性; [*of statement, claim*] 可信性 ♦**to lose one's credibility** 失去信誉

credible ['krɛdɪbl] *adj* [+ *person, organization*] 可靠的; [+ *candidate, policy, idea*] 有希望的; [+ *statement, claim*] 可信的

credit ['krɛdɪt] **I** *n* **1** [u] (*financial*) 贷款 **2** [u] (*recognition*) 赞扬 **3** [c] [教育, 大学] 学分 **II** *vt* **1** ♦**the money will be credited to you/your account** 钱会记入你的账户 **2** (*believe*) 相信 **III credits** *n* [*pl*] 片尾字幕 ♦**to be in credit** [尤英] [*person, bank account* +] 有余额 ♦**on credit** 赊账 ♦**it's to his credit that ...** 他值得赞扬的是… ♦**to have sth to one's credit** 完成某事 ♦**to take the credit for sth** 把某事归功于自己 ♦**it does you credit** 你值得为此受到称赞 ♦**he's a credit to his family** 他是他家庭的骄傲 ♦**would you** *or* **can you credit it!** 难以置信! ♦**to credit sb with sth** 将某事归功于某人 ◊ *I used to credit you with a bit of common sense.* 我曾认为你有点常识。

credit card *n* [c] 信用卡

creek [kriːk] *n* [c] **1** [英] (*inlet*) 小海湾 **2** [美] (*stream*) 小溪 ♦**to be up the creek (without a paddle)** [非正式] 处于困境

creep [kriːp] (*pt, pp* **crept**) **I** *vi* **1** [*person, animal* +] ♦**to creep up/down/into sth** 蹑手蹑脚地走上/下/进某处 **2** [*mist* +] ♦**to creep in**

不知不觉地到来 **3** [*inflation, rate, price* +] ♦**to creep up** 渐渐上升 **4** [*mistakes, complacency, doubts* +] ♦**to creep in** 渐渐产生 **II** *n* [c] [非正式] (*person*) 马屁精 ♦**it makes my flesh creep** 使我毛骨悚然 ♦**to creep up on sb** [*person* +] 悄悄靠近某人; [*feeling* +] 不知不觉地降临到某人身上 ♦**it gives me the creeps** [非正式] 这使我毛骨悚然

creepy ['kri:pɪ] [非正式] *adj* [+ *story, place, person*] 令人毛骨悚然的

cremate [krɪ'meɪt] *vt* 火化

crematorium [krɛmə'tɔ:rɪəm] (*pl* **crematoria**) *n* [c] 火化场

crepe [kreɪp] **I** *n* **1** [u] (*fabric*) 绉织物 **2** [c] (*pancake*) 薄煎饼 **3** [u] (*rubber*) 绉胶 **II** *cpd* [复合词] [+ *dress, jacket etc*] 绉织的

crept [krɛpt] *pt, pp of* **creep**

crescent ['krɛsnt] *n* [c] **1** (*shape*) 月牙形 **2** [尤英] (*in street names*) 新月形街道

cress [krɛs] *n* [u] 水芹

crest [krɛst] *n* [c] **1** (*top*) [*of hill*] 峰; [*of wave*] 波峰 **2** [*of bird*] 羽冠 **3** (*coat of arms*) 饰章

crew [kru:] *n* **1** [c] [*of ship, aircraft, spacecraft*] 全体工作人员 **2** [c] [电视, 电影等] 组 **3** [s] [非正式] (*gang*) 一帮

crew neck ['kru:nɛk] *n* [c] (*also: **crew neck sweater***) 圆式紧衣领

crib [krɪb] **I** *n* [c] **1** [美] (*for baby*) 有围栏的童床 [英 = **cot**] **2** (*nativity scene*) 耶稣诞生的情景雕像 **II** *vi* [非正式, 过时] (*copy*) 抄袭

cricket ['krɪkɪt] *n* **1** [u] (*sport*) 板球 **2** [c] (*insect*) 蟋蟀

> **CRICKET**
> 在大英帝国时代，**cricket**（板球）做为一种夏季运动引入印度、巴基斯坦和澳大利亚等国。如今，板球在这些国家依然十分盛行。两队各11名队员，通常为男性。队员通常穿传统的白色运动服。板球的规则以复杂著称。两队轮流击球。击球的队尽力争取最多次数的**run**（跑垒），其打击手在两组称为**stump**（三门柱）的柱子间跑。另一队争取在击球手跑到门柱前用球击中门柱，还可以在球触地前接住球将该击球手淘汰出局。

cricketer ['krɪkɪtə(r)] *n* [c] 板球运动员

crime [kraɪm] *n* **1** [c] (*illegal act*) 罪行 **2** [u] (*illegal activities*) 犯罪活动 **3** [c] (喻) 罪过

criminal ['krɪmɪnl] **I** *n* [c] 罪犯 **II** *adj* **1** [法] [+ *offence, activity, record*] 犯罪的; [+ *law, court*] 刑事的 **2** (喻) (*wrong*) 应受责备的

crimson ['krɪmzn] *adj* 深红色的

cringe [krɪndʒ] *vi* (*in embarrassment*) 畏缩 ♦**to cringe with embarrassment/horror** 由于尴尬/恐惧而畏缩

cripple ['krɪpl] **I** *vt* **1** [+ *person*] 使…变跛 **2** [+ *ship, plane*] 严重损坏 **3** [+ *organization, system*] 使陷于瘫痪 **II** *n* [c] [过时] 残废 ♦**crippled with arthritis** 因关节炎而残疾

crises ['kraɪsi:z] *n* [*pl*] *of* **crisis**

crisis ['kraɪsɪs] (*pl* **crises**) *n* [c/u] 危机

crisp [krɪsp] **I** *adj* **1** [+ *bacon, biscuit*] 松脆的; [+ *lettuce, apple*] 新鲜而脆生的 **2** [+ *weather, day*] 清新凉爽的 **3** [+ *tone, manner*] 干脆的 **4** [+ *cotton, shirt, paper*] 挺括的 **II** *n* [c] [英] (*potato crisp*) 薯片 [美 = **chip, potato chip**]

crispy ['krɪspɪ] *adj* 松脆的

criteria [kraɪ'tɪərɪə] *n* [*pl*] *of* **criterion**

criterion [kraɪ'tɪərɪən] (*pl* **criteria**) *n* [c] 标准

critic ['krɪtɪk] *n* [c] **1** [*of person, system, policy*] 批评家 **2** (*reviewer*) 评论员

critical ['krɪtɪkl] *adj* **1** (*crucial*) 关键的 **2** (*serious*) 危急的 **3** (*seriously ill*) 病危的 **4** (*negative*) [+ *person, remark*] 吹毛求疵的 **5** (*analytical*) [+ *examination, analysis, study etc*] 一丝不苟的 **6** (*from critics*) [+ *acclaim, success*] 评论的 ♦**in a critical condition** 情况危急 ♦**to be critical of sb/sth** 批评某人/某事

critically ['krɪtɪklɪ] *adv* **1** (*crucially*) [+ *important*] 极其 **2** (*seriously*) [+ *low, ill, injured*] 严重地 **3** (*negatively*) [*speak, say* +] 以批评的态度 **4** (*analytically*) [*examine, think, study* +] 一丝不苟地 **5** (*by critics*) [+ *acclaimed, successful*] 根据评论家判断

criticism ['krɪtɪsɪzəm] *n* **1** [U] (*censure*) 批评 **2** [C] (*complaint*) 指责 **3** [U] [*of book, play etc*] 评论

criticize ['krɪtɪsaɪz] *vt* 批评 ♦ **to criticize sb for (doing) sth** 批评某人(做)某事

Croat ['krəuæt] *n* **1** [C] (*person*) 克罗地亚人 **2** [U] (*language*) 克罗地亚语

Croatia [krəu'eɪʃə] *n* 克罗地亚

Croatian [krəu'eɪʃən] **I** *adj* 克罗地亚的 **II** *n* = **Croat**

crochet ['krəuʃeɪ] **I** *n* [U] 钩针编织 **II** *vi, vt* 用钩针编织

crockery ['krɔkərɪ] *n* [U] 陶器

crocodile ['krɔkədaɪl] *n* [C] 鳄鱼

crocus ['krəukəs] *n* [C] 番红花

croissant ['kwæsnt] *n* [C] 羊角面包

crook [kruk] *n* [C] **1** [非正式] (*criminal*) 坏蛋 **2** (*stick*) [*of shepherd, bishop*] 手杖 ♦ **the crook of one's arm/leg** 臂弯/膝弯

crooked ['krukɪd] *adj* **1** (*twisted*) [+ *nose, teeth*] 变形的; [+ *line*] 弯曲的 **2** (*off-centre*) [+ *picture, tie*] 歪的 **3** [非正式] (*dishonest*) 不老实的

crop [krɔp] **I** *n* **1** [C] (*plants*) 庄稼 **2** [C] (*amount produced*) 收成 **3** [S] (喻) (*batch*) 一批 **4** [C] (*hairstyle*) 平头 **5** [C] (*also: **riding crop***) 短马鞭 **II** *vt* **1** [+ *hair*] 剪短 **2** [*animal* +] [+ *grass*] 啃吃

❑ **crop up** *vi* **1** (*appear unexpectedly*) 意外地出现 **2** (*appear*) 被提到

cross [krɔs] **I** *n* [C] **1** (*x shape*) 交叉符号; (*showing disagreement*) 叉号 **2** (*crucifix shape*) 十字 **3** [宗] 十字架 **4** (*mixture*) ♦ **a cross between sth and sth** 某物和某物的混合物 **5** (*crossbreed*) 杂交品种 **6** [足球] 横传 **II** *vt* **1** [*person* +] [+ *street, room etc*] 横穿 **2** [*road, railway, bridge* +] [+ *river, land etc*] 横跨 **3** [+ *arms, legs, fingers*] 交叉 **4** [*smile, expression* +] [+ *face*] 显露在 **5** [英] [+ *cheque*] 在支票上画两条平行线,只可转账无法兑现 **6** (*crossbreed*) ♦ **to cross sth with sth** 将某物与某物交配 **7** [足球] [+ *ball*] 横传 **8** (*oppose*) [+ *person*] 阻挠 **III** *vi* **1** [*roads, lines* +] 相交 **2** ♦ **to cross from ... to ...** (*walking*) 从…走到…; (*on ferry*) 从…横渡到… **IV** *adj* (*angry*) 生气的 ♦ **the thought never crossed my mind** 我从来都没这么想过 ♦ **to cross o.s.** [宗] 划十字祈求上帝保佑 ♦ **we have a crossed line** [英] (*on telephone*) 我们的电话串线了 ♦ **they've got their lines** *or* **wires crossed** (喻) 他们相互误会了 ♦ **to be/get cross with sb** 生某人的气 ♦ **to be/get cross about sth** 因为某事生气 ♦ **it makes me very cross** 这令我很生气

❑ **cross off** *vt* (*delete*) 取消

❑ **cross out** *vt* (*delete*) 取消

❑ **cross over** *vi* (*cross the street*) 过马路 ♦ **to cross over from ... to ...** 从…到…去

cross-country [krɔs'kʌntrɪ] **I** *n* [U] (*running*) 越野赛跑 **II** *adj* [+ *running, race, skier, journey etc*] 越野的 **III** *adv* ♦ **to go cross-country** 走小路

crossing ['krɔsɪŋ] *n* [C] **1** (*voyage*) 横渡 **2** [英] (*also: **pedestrian crossing***) 人行横道 [美 = **crosswalk**]

crossing guard [美] *n* [C] 为保证儿童安全过马路手持暂停指挥牌的交通管理员 [英 = **lollipop man, lollipop lady**]

crossroads ['krɔsrəudz] (*pl* **crossroads**) *n* [C] (*junction, decisive point*) 十字路口

cross section *n* [C] **1** [*of population*] 典型 **2** [*of object*] 横截面

crosswalk ['krɔswɔːk] [美] *n* [C] 人行横道 [英 = **(pedestrian) crossing**]

crossword ['krɔswəːd] *n* [C] (*also: **crossword puzzle***) 填字游戏

crotch [krɔtʃ], **crutch** [krʌtʃ] *n* [C] **1** (*groin*) 胯部 **2** [*of garment*] 裤裆

crouch [krautʃ] *vi* (*also: **crouch down***) 蹲 ♦ **to be crouching** 蹲着 ♦ **to crouch over sth** 蹲在某物上

crouton ['kruːtɔn] *n* [C] 烤的/炸的面包丁

crow [krəu] **I** *n* [C] (*bird*) 乌鸦 **II** *vi* **1** [*cockerel* +] 啼叫 **2** (*boast*) ♦ **to crow about** *or* **over sth** 因某事得意洋洋

crowd [kraud] **I** *n* [c] [*of people, fans etc*] 人群 **II** *vt* (*cram*) 挤满 **III** *vi* **1** (*gather*) ♦ **to crowd around sb/sth** 聚集在某人/某处周围 **2** (*cram*) ♦ **to crowd into sth** 大批涌入某处 ♦ **the/our crowd** [*of friends etc*] 一伙人/我们这伙人 ♦ **crowds of people** 大批人群 ♦ **don't crowd me** 别挤我
❑ **crowd in** *vi* 大批涌入

crowded ['kraudɪd] *adj* **1** (*full*) [+ *room, ship, train*] 拥挤的 **2** (*densely populated*) [+ *area*] 人口众多的; [+ *conditions*] 拥挤的 ♦ **to be crowded with** [+ *people*] 挤满了; [+ *things*] 满是

crown [kraun] **I** *n* [c] **1** [*of monarch*] 皇冠 **2** ♦ **the Crown** (*monarchy*) 君主立宪政府 **3** (*top*) [*of head*] 头顶; [*of hat*] 帽顶 **4** (*on tooth*) 假齿冠 **II** *vt* **1** [+ *monarch*] 为…加冕 **2** [文] [+ *hill, cliff*] 覆盖…的顶端 **3** (喻) [+ *event, career*] 圆满地结束 ♦ **to crown sb king** 加冕某人为国王

crown jewels *n* [*pl*] ♦ **the Crown Jewels** 御宝

crucial ['kruːʃl] *adj* 关键性的 ♦ **to be crucial to sth** 对某事是至关重要的

crucifix ['kruːsɪfɪks] *n* [c] 耶稣十字架

crude [kruːd] *adj* **1** (*simple*) 简陋的 **2** (*vulgar*) 粗俗的 **3** (*not processed*) 未加工的

crude oil *n* [u] 原油

cruel ['kruəl] *adj* **1** (*unkind*) [+ *person*] 残忍的; [+ *treatment, behaviour*] 恶毒的 **2** (*tough*) [+ *situation, action, world*] 残酷的 ♦ **to be cruel to sb** 残酷地对待某人

cruelty ['kruəltɪ] *n* [u] [*of person*] 残忍; [*of situation, action*] 残酷性 ♦ **cruelty to animals** 对动物的虐待

cruise [kruːz] **I** *n* [c] 游船 **II** *vi* **1** (*go on cruise*) 坐游船 **2** [*car, ship, aircraft* +] 以中等速度航行 **3** [*taxi* +] 漫无目的地行驶 ♦ **to be/go on a cruise** 乘游船旅行 ♦ **world cruise** 环球游船旅行 ♦ **to cruise up** *or* **along a road** 在路上缓慢行驶

crumb [krʌm] *n* [c] **1** [*of bread, cake*] 碎屑 **2** [*of information, comfort*] 一点点

crumble ['krʌmbl] **I** *vi* **1** [*plaster, earth etc* +] 破碎 **2** (*also:* ***crumble away***) [*building, cliff etc* +] 碎裂 **3** [*system, relationship, hope* +] 崩溃 **II** *vt* [+ *bread, biscuit etc*] 弄碎

crumpet ['krʌmpɪt] *n* **1** [c] [尤英:烹饪] 烤面饼 **2** [u] [英:非正式,疑讳] (*attractive women*) 性感女人

crumple ['krʌmpl] **I** *vt* (*also:* ***crumple up***) [+ *paper, clothes*] 弄皱 **II** *vi* [*face* +] 皱起来

crunch [krʌntʃ] **I** *vt* **1** (*with teeth*) 嘎吱嘎吱地咬嚼 **2** (*underfoot*) 使发出刺耳的碎裂声 **II** *vi* [*gravel, wheels* +] 发出嘎吱声 **III** *n* **1** [c] (*sound*) 嘎吱声 **2** (*moment of truth*) ♦ **the crunch** 关键时刻 ♦ **if/when it comes to the crunch** 如果/当必须得做点什么的时候

crunchy ['krʌntʃɪ] *adj* [+ *salad, vegetables, cornflakes, nuts*] 脆的

crush [krʌʃ] **I** *vt* **1** [+ *tin, box*] 压坏 **2** (*break up*) [+ *garlic*] 压碎; [+ *ice*] 碾碎 **3** (*squeeze*) [+ *person*] 使挤在一起 **4** (*defeat*) [+ *army, opposition*] 镇压 **5** (*devastate*) [+ *hopes, person*] 使意气消沉 **II** *n* [c] **1** (*crowd*) 拥挤的人群 **2** [非正式] ♦ **to have a crush on sb** 迷恋某人 ♦ **to be crushed to death** 被压死

crust [krʌst] *n* [c] (*on bread, pastry*) 皮; (*on snow, ice*) 硬表层 ♦ **the earth's crust** 地壳

crusty ['krʌstɪ] *adj* [+ *loaf, bread*] 有脆皮的

crutch [krʌtʃ] *n* [c] **1** (*stick*) 拐杖 **2** (喻) (*support*) 支持 **3** [尤英] = **crotch** ♦ **on crutches** 拄拐杖

cry [kraɪ] **I** *vi* (*weep*) 哭 **II** *vt* (*also:* ***cry out***) 叫喊 **III** *n* [c] **1** (*shriek*) (*human*) 尖叫; [*of bird, animal*] 大叫 **2** (*shout*) 叫喊 ♦ **what are you crying about?** 你哭什么? ♦ **to cry for help** 呼救 ♦ **a cry for help** 呼救声 ♦ **to have a good cry** 痛哭一场 ♦ **it's a far cry from ...** 和…大相径庭
❑ **cry off** *vi* 打退堂鼓
❑ **cry out** *vi, vt* 叫喊

❑ **cry out for** *vt* [不可拆分] (*need*) 迫切需要

cryptic ['krɪptɪk] *adj* [+ *remark, clue*] 有隐义的

crystal ['krɪstl] **I** *n* **1** [c] (*mineral*) 结晶体 **2** [c/u] (*in jewellery*) 水晶 **3** [u] (*glass*) 晶质玻璃制品 **II** *cpd* [复合词] [+ *glass, vase*] 水晶

CTC [英] *n abbr* (= ***city technology college***) 城市科技学院

CU [手机短信] *abbr* (= ***see you***) 再见！

cub [kʌb] **I** *n* [c] **1** (*young lion, wolf, fox, bear*) 幼兽 **2** (*also:* ***cub scout***) 幼童军 **II the Cubs** *n* [*pl*] (*also:* ***the Cub Scouts***) 幼童军

Cuba ['kjuːbə] *n* 古巴

Cuban ['kjuːbən] **I** *adj* 古巴的 **II** *n* [c] (*person*) 古巴人

cube [kjuːb] **I** *n* [c] **1** (*shape*) 立方体 **2** [数] [*of number*] 立方 **II** *vt* [数] 使自乘两次

cubicle ['kjuːbɪkl] *n* [c] 小室

cuckoo ['kukuː] *n* [c] 杜鹃

cucumber ['kjuːkʌmbə(r)] *n* [c/u] 黄瓜

cuddle ['kʌdl] **I** *vt, vi* 搂抱 **II** *n* [c] 拥抱 ♦ **to have a cuddle** 拥抱 ♦ **to give sb a cuddle** 拥抱某人

cue [kjuː] *n* [c] **1** (*in theatre*) 提示 **2** (*stick*) 球杆 **3** (喻) ♦ **a cue for sth/to do sth** 某事/做某事的暗示 ♦ **to take one's cue from sb** (喻) 以某人为榜样 ♦ **on cue** (*at the expected time*) 就在这时

cuff [kʌf] **I** *n* [c] **1** [*of sleeve*] 袖口 **2** [美] [*of trousers*] 翻边 [英 = **turn-up**] **3** (*blow*) 轻轻的一拍 **II** *vt* (*hit*) 用掌轻拍 ♦ **off the cuff** 未经准备

cufflinks ['kʌflɪŋks] *n* [*pl*] 袖扣

cuisine [kwɪ'ziːn] *n* [u] [*of country, region*] 烹饪

CUL8R [手机短信] *abbr* (= ***see you later***) 一会儿见

cul-de-sac ['kʌldəsæk] [尤英] *n* [c] (*road*) 死胡同 [美 = **dead end**]

culinary ['kʌlɪnərɪ] [正式] *adj* 烹饪的

cull [kʌl] **I** *vt* **1** [+ *animals*] 杀掉…中的一部分以减少其数量 **2** ♦ **to cull sth from sth** [+ *story, idea*] 从某物中精选出某物 **II** *n* [c] [*of animals*] 剔除

culminate ['kʌlmɪneɪt] *vi* ♦ **to culminate in** *or* **with sth** 终于获得某物

culprit ['kʌlprɪt] *n* [c] **1** (*perpetrator*) 罪犯 **2** (*cause*) 原因

cult [kʌlt] **I** *n* [c] **1** [宗] 异教 **2** (*fashion*) 时尚 **II** *cpd* [复合词] [+ *status*] 狂热崇拜的; [+ *film*] 风靡一时的 ♦ **cult figure** 崇拜偶像

cultivate ['kʌltɪveɪt] *vt* **1** [+ *land*] 耕作; [+ *crop*] 种植 **2** (喻) [+ *attitude, image, skill*] 培养; [+ *person*] 结交; [+ *relationship*] 建立

cultivation [kʌltɪ'veɪʃən] *n* [u] **1** [*of land*] 耕种; [*of crop*] 种植 **2** (喻) [*of attitude, image, skill*] 培养

cultural ['kʌltʃərəl] *adj* [+ *heritage, tradition, exchange*] 文化的

culture ['kʌltʃə(r)] *n* **1** [c/u] 文化 **2** [c] [生物] 培养的细菌

cultured ['kʌltʃəd] *adj* **1** [+ *person*] 有修养的 **2** [+ *pearl*] 人工养殖的

cumin ['kʌmɪn] *n* [u] 小茴香

cunning ['kʌnɪŋ] **I** *adj* [+ *person, plan, idea*] 狡猾的 **II** *n* [u] 狡诈

✪ **cup** [kʌp] **I** *n* [c] **1** (*for drinking*) 杯子 **2** (*trophy*) 奖杯 **3** (*quantity*) 杯 **4** [*of bra*] 罩杯 **II** *vt* ♦ **to cup sth in one's hands** 用手屈拢着某物 ♦ **a cup of tea** 一杯茶 ♦ **to cup one's hands** 捧起手

cupboard ['kʌbəd] *n* [c] **1** (*piece of furniture*) 柜子 **2** [英] (*room*) 小储藏室 [美 = **closet**]

cup final *n* [c] 优胜杯决赛

curate ['kjuərɪt] *n* [c] 助理牧师

curator [kjuə'reɪtə(r)] *n* [c] [*of museum, gallery*] 馆长

curb [kəːb] **I** *vt* [+ *powers, expenditure*] 约束; [+ *emotion, behaviour*] 抑制 **II** *n* [c] **1** (*restraint*) ♦ **curb on sth** 对某事的管制 **2** [美] = **kerb**

curdle ['kəːdl] **I** *vi* 凝结 **II** *vt* 使凝结

cure [kjuə(r)] **I** *vt* **1** [医] [+ *illness*] 治好; [+ *patient*] 治愈 **2** (*solve*) [+ *problem*] 解决 **3** (*preserve*) [+ *meat, fish*] 熏; [+ *skin, hide*] 腌 **II** *n* [c] **1** [医] 疗法 **2** (*solution*) 对策 ♦ **to be cured**

of sth 被治好了某病

curfew [ˈkəːfjuː] *n* [C/U] 宵禁令 ♦**to put** *or* **place sth/sb under curfew** 对某处/某人实行宵禁 ♦**to impose a curfew on sth/sb** 对某处/某人实行宵禁

curiosity [kjuərɪˈɔsɪtɪ] *n* **1** [U] (*inquisitiveness*) 好奇心 **2** [C] (*unusual thing*) 奇物

curious [ˈkjuərɪəs] *adj* **1** (*inquisitive*) 好奇的 **2** (*strange*) 奇特的 ♦**to be curious about sb/sth** 对某人/某物感到好奇 ♦**to be curious to know/see ...** 好奇地想知道/看…

curl [kəːl] **I** *n* [C] [*of hair*] 卷发; [*of smoke*] 缕 **II** *vt* [+ *hair*] 使变卷 **III** *vi* **1** [*hair* +] 卷曲 **2** [*smoke* +] 盘绕
❑**curl up** *vi* [*person, animal* +] 蜷作一团

curler [ˈkəːlə(r)] *n* [C] 卷发夹

curly [ˈkəːlɪ] *adj* [+ *hair, leaves, tail*] 拳曲的

currant [ˈkʌrnt] *n* [C] **1** (*dried grape*) 无子葡萄干; (*also:* ***blackcurrant***) 黑加仑; (*also:* ***redcurrant***) 红加仑 **2** (*bush*) (*also:* ***blackcurrant***) 黑加仑灌木; (*also:* ***redcurrant***) 红加仑灌木

currency [ˈkʌrnsɪ] *n* [C/U] **1** 货币 **2** ♦**to gain currency** 流行起来 ♦**to have currency** 流行

✪**current** [ˈkʌrnt] **I** *n* [C] **1** [*of air, water*] 流 **2** [电子] 电流 **3** [*of opinion, thought etc*] 趋势 **II** *adj* **1** (*present*) [+ *situation, tendency, policy etc*] 目前的 ◊ *The current situation is very different.* 目前的情况很不同。 **2** (*accepted*) [+ *idea, thought, custom*] 流行的 ◊ *This custom was still current in the 1960s.* 这个习俗在20世纪60年代还是很流行。 ♦**the current issue** [*of magazine*] 最近一期

current account [英] *n* [C] 活期存款账户 [美 = **checking account**]

current affairs *n* [*pl*] 时事 ♦**a current affairs programme** 时事讨论节目

currently [ˈkʌrntlɪ] *adv* 现在

curriculum [kəˈrɪkjuləm] (*pl* **curriculums** *or* **curricula**) *n* [C] **1** (*for all subjects*) 全部课程 **2** (*for particular subject*) 课程

curriculum vitae [-ˈviːtaɪ] [尤英] *n* [C] 简历 [美 = **résumé**]

curry [ˈkʌrɪ] **I** *n* [C/U] (*dish*) 咖哩 **II** *vt* ♦**to curry favour with sb** 拍某人的马屁

curry powder *n* [U] 咖哩粉

curse [kəːs] **I** *vi* (*swear*) 诅咒 **II** *vt* **1** (*swear at*) 诅咒 **2** (*complain about*) 咒骂 **III** *n* [C] **1** (*spell*) 诅咒 **2** (*swearword*) 咒骂的话 **3** (*scourge*) 灾祸 ♦**to curse sb for sth/for doing sth** 因某事/做某事而咒骂某人

cursor [ˈkəːsə(r)] [计算机] *n* [C] 光标

curt [kəːt] *adj* [+ *reply, tone, person*] 唐突无礼的

curtain [ˈkəːtn] *n* [C] **1** [尤英] (*at window*) 窗帘 [美 = **drape**] **2** (*in theatre*) 帷幕 ♦**to draw the curtains** (*together*) 拉上窗帘; (*apart*) 拉开窗帘

curve [kəːv] **I** *n* [C] 曲线; (*in road*) 弯曲部分 **II** *vi* [*road, line* +] 弯曲; [*structure, spine etc* +] 成曲线形

curved [kəːvd] *adj* 弯曲的

cushion [ˈkuʃən] **I** *n* [C] **1** (*on sofa, chair*) 靠垫 **2** (喻) [*of air*] 垫状物 **II** *vt* **1** [+ *impact, fall*] 对…起缓冲作用 **2** [+ *shock, effect*] 缓和…的影响

custard [ˈkʌstəd] *n* [U] (*for pouring*) 蛋奶沙司; (*set*) 蛋奶糕

custody [ˈkʌstədɪ] *n* [U] **1** [*of child*] 监护权 **2** (*for offenders*) 拘留 ♦**to be remanded in custody** 拘留候审 ♦**to take sb into custody** 拘捕某人

custom [ˈkʌstəm] **I** *n* **1** [C/U] (*tradition*) 传统 **2** [C/U] (*convention*) 惯例 **3** [C] (*habit*) 习惯 **4** [U] [英] [*of shop*] 光顾 **II customs** *n* [*pl*] 海关 ♦**to go through customs** 过海关

customer [ˈkʌstəmə(r)] *n* [C] (*in shop*) 顾客 ♦**he's a cool customer** [非正式] 他是个很酷的家伙

customize [ˈkʌstəmaɪz] *vt* [+ *product, car, software etc*] 按顾客的具体要求制造

customs officer *n* [C] 海关官员

✪**cut** [kʌt] (*pt, pp* **cut**) **I** *vt* **1** [+ *bread, meat*] 切 **2** (*injure*) ♦**to cut one's**

hand/knee 割破手/膝盖 **3** (*shorten*) [+ *grass, hair, nails*] 修剪 **4** (*remove*) [+ *scene, episode, paragraph*] 删剪 **5** (*reduce*) [+ *prices, spending*] 削减 **6** (*stop*) [+ *supply*] 中断 **7** (*shape*) [+ *clothes*] 剪裁 **8** [尤美:非正式] (*miss*) [+ *class, school*] 逃避 **II** *vi* (*take shortcut*) ♦ **to cut across** *or* **through a place** 穿过某处抄近路 **III** *n* **1** [c] (*injury*) 伤口 **2** [c] (*reduction*) (*in salary, spending etc*) 削减 **3** [c] (*interruption*) (*in supply*) 中断 **4** [c] [*of meat*] 切下的肉块 **5** [s] [*of garment*] 款式 ♦ **to cut sth in half** [+ *food, object*] 将某物切成两半; [+ *line, path*] 将某物分成两部分 ♦ **to cut o.s.** 割破自己 ♦ **to cut a hole in sth** 在某物上打个洞 ♦ **to cut a tooth** 长牙 ♦ **to get** *or* **have one's hair cut** 剪发 ♦ **to cut a visit short** 缩短访问时间 ♦ **to make a cut in sth** 在某物上划一下 ♦ **a cut and blow-dry** 剪发吹干 ♦ **to be a cut above ...** 比…高一等

❑ **cut across** *vt* [不可拆分] [*issue, problem* +] [+ *groups, generations*] 影响到

❑ **cut back** *vt* **1** [+ *plants, foliage*] 修剪 **2** (*also:* ***cut back on***) [+ *production, expenditure*] 削减

❑ **cut down** *vt* **1** [+ *tree*] 砍倒 **2** (*reduce*) [+ *consumption etc*] 减少 ♦ **to cut sb down to size** [非正式] 使某人摆正自己的位置

❑ **cut down on** *vt* [不可拆分] [+ *alcohol, coffee, cigarettes etc*] 减少

❑ **cut in** *vi* **1** (*interrupt*) ♦ **to cut in (on sb)** 打断(某人) **2** [*car, driver* +] 超车抢道

❑ **cut off I** *vt* [+ *part of sth*] 切掉 **2** [+ *person, village*] 使隔绝 **3** [+ *supply*] 停止供应 **4** [通信] (*during conversation*) 中断…的通话 ♦ **to get cut off** [通信] 通话中断

❑ **cut out I** *vt* **1** [+ *coupon, newspaper article*] 剪下 **2** (*stop*) [+ *activity*] 停止 **3** (*remove*) [+ *scene, episode, paragraph*] 删去 **4** (*keep out*) [+ *light*] 遮蔽 **II** *vi* [*engine* +] 不再起作用

❑ **cut up** *vt* **1** [+ *paper, food*] 切碎 **2** [+ *driver, car*] 超车抢道 ♦ **to be cut up about sth** [尤英:非正式] 因某事伤心

cutback ['kʌtbæk] *n* [c] ♦ **cutback (in sth)** 减少(某物)

cute [kjuːt] *adj* **1** [非正式] (*sweet*) [+ *child, dog, house*] 可爱的 **2** [尤美:非正式] (*attractive*) 迷人的 **3** [美:尤贬] (*clever*) 小聪明的

cutlery ['kʌtlərɪ] [英] *n* [u] 餐具

cutlet ['kʌtlɪt] *n* [c] 炸肉饼 ♦ **vegetable/nut cutlet** 蔬菜/坚果炸饼

cut-price ['kʌt'praɪs] [英] *adj* 削价的 [美 = **cut-rate**]

cut-rate ['kʌt'reɪt] [美] *adj* 削价的 [英 = **cut-price**]

cutting ['kʌtɪŋ] **I** *n* [c] **1** [英] (*from newspaper*) 剪报 [美 = **clipping**] **2** [英:铁路] 路基 [美 = **cut**] **3** (*from plant*) 插条 **II** *adj* [+ *remark*] 尖刻的 ♦ **at the cutting edge of sth** 在某事的前沿

CV *n abbr* (= ***curriculum vitae***) 简历

cyanide ['saɪənaɪd] *n* [u] 氰化物

cybercafé ['saɪbəkæfeɪ] *n* [c] 网吧

cyberspace ['saɪbəspeɪs] *n* [u] 电脑空间

cycle ['saɪkl] **I** *n* [c] **1** [*of events, seasons etc*] 周期; [*of songs, poems*] 组 **2** (*bicycle*) 自行车 **3** [术语] (*movement*) 循环 **II** *vi* 骑自行车 **III** *cpd* [复合词] [+ *shop, helmet, ride*] 自行车 ♦ **to go cycling** 骑自行车

cycle hire *n* [u] 自行车出租

cycle lane *n* [c] 自行车道

cycle path *n* [c] 自行车道

cycling ['saɪklɪŋ] *n* [u] 骑自行车 ♦ **to go on a cycling holiday** [英] 骑自行车旅行度假

cyclist ['saɪklɪst] *n* [c] 骑自行车的人

cyclone ['saɪkləun] *n* [c] 龙卷风

cylinder ['sɪlɪndə(r)] *n* [c] **1** (*shape*) 圆柱体 **2** [*of gas*] 罐 **3** (*in engine, machine etc*) 汽缸

cymbal ['sɪmbl] *n* [c] 钹

cynic ['sɪnɪk] *n* [c] 愤世嫉俗者

cynical ['sɪnɪkl] *adj* [+ *person, attitude*] 愤世嫉俗的 ♦ **to be cynical about sth** 不信任某事

cynicism ['sɪnɪsɪzəm] *n* [u] 愤世嫉俗 ♦ **cynicism (about sth/sb)** (对某事/某人的)不信任感

Cypriot ['sɪprɪət] **I** *adj* 塞浦路斯的 **II** *n* [c] (*person*) 塞浦路斯人
Cyprus ['saɪprəs] *n* 塞浦路斯
cyst [sɪst] *n* [c] 囊肿
cystitis [sɪs'taɪtɪs] *n* [u] 膀胱炎
Czech [tʃɛk] **I** *adj* 捷克的 **II** *n* **1** [c] (*person*) 捷克人 **2** [u] (*language*) 捷克语
Czech Republic *n* ♦ **the Czech Republic** 捷克共和国

Dd

D¹, d [diː] *n* [c/u] (*letter*) 英语的第四个字母
D² [diː] **I** *n* **1** [c/u] [音]C大调音阶中的第二音 **2** [c] [教育, 大学] (*mark*) 差 **II** [美:政治] *abbr* = **democrat(ic)**
d. *abbr* (= ***died***) 死亡
D.A. [美] *n abbr* (= ***district attorney***) 地方检察官
dab [dæb] **I** *vt* **1** [+ *eyes, lips*] 轻擦 **2** [+ *paint, cream*] 轻而快地涂 **II** *n* [c] [非正式] ♦**a dab (of sth)** [*of paint, glue*] 少量(的某物) ♦**to dab a wound with sth** 用某物轻搽伤口 ♦**to be a dab hand at sth/doing sth** [英:非正式] 是某方面的能手/擅长做某事
❑**dab at** *vt* [不可拆分] [+ *mouth, eyes, paper*] 轻轻地按
dabble ['dæbl] *vi* ♦**to dabble in sth** [+ *politics, antiques etc*] 涉猎某事 ♦**she dabbled with drugs** 她染上了毒品
dad [dæd] [非正式] *n* [c] 爸爸
daddy ['dædɪ] [非正式] *n* = **dad**
daffodil ['dæfədɪl] *n* [c] 黄水仙
daft [dɑːft] [英:非正式] *adj* (*silly*) 傻的 ♦**to be daft about sb/sth** 酷爱某人/某事
dagger ['dægə(r)] *n* [c] 匕首 ♦**to be at daggers drawn with sb** [英] 与某人势不两立 ♦**to look daggers at sb** 对某人怒目而视
daily ['deɪlɪ] **I** *adj* 每日的 **II** *n* [c] (*newspaper*) 日报 **III** *adv* 每日 ♦**twice daily** 每天两次 ♦**daily life** 日常生活
dairy ['dɛərɪ] **I** *n* [c] **1** (*company*) 牛奶及乳品店 **2** (*on farm*) 牛奶场 **II** *adj* **1** (*made from milk*) [+ *products, produce*] 乳制品的 **2** (*producing milk*) [+ *cattle, cow, herd*] 产乳的; [+ *industry, farming*] 生产乳品的
daisy ['deɪzɪ] *n* [c] 雏菊
dam [dæm] **I** *n* [c] (*on river*) 水坝 **II** *vt* [+ *river*] 建水坝于
damage ['dæmɪdʒ] **I** *n* [u] **1** (*harm*) 损坏 **2** (*dents, scratches etc*) 损伤 **3** (*to sb's reputation etc*) 损害 **II** *vt* **1** (*spoil, break*) [+ *object, building*] 毁坏 **2** (*harm*) [+ *reputation, economy*] 破坏 **III damages** *n* [*pl*] [法] 损害赔偿金 ♦**to pay 5,000 pounds in damages** 支付5,000英镑赔偿金 ♦**to cause/inflict damage** (*physically*) 造成损失; (喻) 造成破坏
damn [dæm] **I** *adj* [非正式] (*also* ***damned***) 该死的 **II** *adv* [非正式] (*also* ***damned***) 非常地 **III** *n* [非正式] ♦**I don't give a damn** 我根本不在乎 **IV** *vt* (*condemn*) 指责 ♦**damn (it)!** [非正式, 疑讳] 该死!
damned [dæmd] **I** *adj* = **damn** **II** *adv* = **damn**
damning ['dæmɪŋ] *adj* [+ *evidence, report*] 非常不利的
damp [dæmp] **I** *adj* [+ *building, air, cloth*] 潮湿的 **II** *n* [u] (*in air, in walls*) 湿气 **III** *vt* **1** (*also* ***dampen***) [+ *cloth*] 使潮湿; [+ *enthusiasm, spirits etc*] 打击
❑**damp down** *vt* [不可拆分] (*calm*) 减轻
dampen [dæmpn] *vt* **1** [+ *enthusiasm, spirits*] 使减弱 **2** (*make wet*) 弄湿
dance [dɑːns] **I** *n* **1** [c] (*e.g. waltz, tango*) 舞蹈 **2** [c] (*social event*) 舞会 **3** [u] (*dancing*) 舞蹈 **II** *vi* 跳舞 ♦**to dance the tango** 跳探戈 ♦**to dance with sb** 和某人跳舞 ♦**to dance about/off** [文] 欢呼雀跃
dance floor *n* [c] 舞池
dancer ['dɑːnsə(r)] *n* [c] **1** (*professional*) 舞蹈演员 **2** (*person who is dancing*) 跳舞者 ♦**to be a good/bad dancer** 舞跳得好/不好
dancing ['dɑːnsɪŋ] *n* [u] 跳舞 ♦**to go dancing** 去跳舞
dandelion ['dændɪlaɪən] *n* [c] 蒲公英
dandruff ['dændrəf] *n* [u] 头皮屑
Dane [deɪn] *n* [c] 丹麦人
danger ['deɪndʒə(r)] *n* **1** [u] (*unsafe situation*) 危险 **2** [c] (*hazard, risk*) 威胁 ♦**there is a danger of/that ...** 有…的危险 ♦**"danger!"** (*on*

sign) "危险！" ♦ **your life is/you are in danger** 你有生命危险/你有危险 ♦ **to put sb/sb's life in danger** 危及某人/某人的生命 ♦ **to be in danger of doing sth** 有…的危险 ♦ **out of danger** [+ *patient*] 脱离危险 ♦ **to be a danger to sb/sth** 是对某人/某物的威胁

dangerous ['deɪndʒrəs] *adj* 危险的 ♦ **it's dangerous to ...** …是危险的

dangle ['dæŋgl] **I** *vi* ♦ **to dangle from sth** [*earrings, keys* +] 某处悬吊着 **II** *vt* (*swing*) [+ *keys, toy*] 摇晃; [+ *arms, legs*] 晃荡

Danish ['deɪnɪʃ] **I** *adj* 丹麦的 **II** *n* [U] (*language*) 丹麦语

dare [dɛə(r)] **I** *vt* ♦ **to dare sb to do sth** 激某人做某事 **II** *vi* ♦ **to dare (to) do sth** 敢做某事 **III** *n* [c] 激将 ♦ **I daren't tell him** [英] 我不敢告诉他 ♦ **I dare say** (*I suppose*) 我相信 ♦ **don't you dare** 你竟敢 ♦ **how dare you!** 你怎敢！♦ **to do sth for a dare** 因为受到激将而做某事

daring ['dɛərɪŋ] **I** *adj* **1** (*audacious*) [+ *escape, rescue, person*] 勇敢的 **2** (*bold*) [+ *film, question, artist*] 大胆的 **II** *n* [U] (*courage*) 勇敢

dark [dɑːk] **I** *adj* **1** (*in brightness*) [+ *room, night*] 黑暗的 **2** (*in complexion*) [+ *eyes, hair, skin*] 黑色的; [+ *person*] 头发和皮肤深色的 **3** (*in colour*) [+ *suit, fabric etc*] 深色的 **4** (*unpleasant*) [+ *time*] 黑暗的; [+ *look*] 阴郁的; [+ *remark*] 悲观的; [+ *rumour*] 恶毒的 **II** *n* ♦ **the dark** 黑暗 ♦ **dark blue/green** 深蓝色/绿色 ♦ **dark chocolate** (*plain chocolate*) 黑巧克力 ♦ **it is/is getting dark** 天黑了 ♦ **after dark** 天黑以后 ♦ **to be in the dark about sth** 对某事一无所知

darken [dɑːkn] **I** *vt* 使变黑 **II** *vi* **1** (*become darker*) [*sky, clouds* +] 变黑 **2** [文][*face* +] 阴沉

darkness ['dɑːknɪs] *n* [U] 黑暗

darkroom ['dɑːkrum] *n* [c] 暗房

darling ['dɑːlɪŋ] **I** *n* **1** (*as address*) (*dear*) 亲爱的 **2** [c] (*kind, helpful person*) 好人 **II** *adj* 心爱的 ♦ **to be the darling of sb, to be sb's darling** (*favourite*) 受到某人的宠爱

dart [dɑːt] **I** *vi* **1** [*person, animal* +] 急冲 **2** [文][*eyes* +] 飞快地瞥一眼 **II** *vt* [文][+ *look, glance*] 瞥 **III** *n* [c] **1** (*in game*) 飞镖 **2** (*weapon*) 镖 **IV darts** *n* [*pl*] 投镖游戏

dartboard ['dɑːtbɔːd] *n* [c] 镖靶

dash [dæʃ] **I** *n* **1** [c] (*in punctuation*) 破折号 **2** ♦ **a dash of sth** [*of lemon juice, milk etc*] 少量的某物 **3** ♦ **to make a dash for somewhere** (*rush*) 冲向某地 **4** [c] (*dashboard*) 仪表板 **5** [c] [美](*race*) 短跑 **II** *vi* ♦ **to dash in/out/upstairs** 猛冲进来/出去/上楼 **III** *vt* **1** [文](*throw*) 扔向 **2** [+ *hopes*] 使破灭 ♦ **a dash of soda** 少量苏打 ♦ **to make a dash for it** 得赶紧走了 ♦ **I must dash** [非正式] 我得赶紧走了

❑ **dash away** *vi* = **dash off**

❑ **dash off I** *vi* 赶 **II** *vt* (*write, compose*) 匆忙完成

dashboard ['dæʃbɔːd] *n* [c] 仪表板

data ['deɪtə] *n* [*pl*] 数据

database ['deɪtəbeɪs] *n* [c] 数据库

data processing [-'prəusɛsɪŋ] *n* [U] 数据处理

date [deɪt] **I** *n* [c] **1** (*particular day*) 日期 **2** (*meeting with friend*) 约会 **3** (*friend*) 约会对象 **4** (*fruit*) 海枣 **II** *vt* **1** (*establish date of*) [+ *event, object*] 确定…的年代 **2** (*write date on*) [+ *letter, cheque*] 给…注明日期 **3** (*go out with*) [+ *person*] 和…约会 **III** *vi* **1** (*go out with sb*) 约会 **2** (*become old-fashioned*) 过时 ♦ **what's the date today?, what's today's date?** 今天几号？♦ **date of birth** 出生日期 ♦ **to date** (*until now*) 迄今 ♦ **to be out of date** (*old-fashioned*) 落伍; (*expired*) 过期 ♦ **to be up to date** (*modern*) 时新 ♦ **to bring sth up to date** [+ *correspondence, information*] 更新某物 ♦ **to bring sb up to date** 告知某人最新动态 ♦ **to keep up to date** 紧随形势 ♦ **to keep sb up to date (with sth)** 告知某人（某事的）最新动态 ♦ **it was dated 5th July** [+ *letter*] 信上的日期是7月5日

❑ **date back** *vi* ♦ **date back (to)** 回溯（至…）

❑ **date from** *vi*（自…）存在至今

dated ['deɪtɪd] *adj* [+ *expression, style*]

过时的

✪ **daughter** [ˈdɔːtə(r)] *n* [c] 女儿

daughter-in-law [ˈdɔːtərɪnlɔː] (*pl* **daughters-in-law**) *n* [c] 媳妇

daunting [ˈdɔːntɪŋ] *adj* [+ *task, prospect*] 吓人的

dawdle [ˈdɔːdl] *vi* 磨蹭 ♦ **to dawdle over (doing) sth** 慢吞吞做某事

dawn [dɔːn] **I** *n* **1** [c/u] [*of day*] 黎明 **2** ♦ **the dawn of sth** 某事的开端 **II** *vi* **1** [*day* +] 开始 **2** [文] [*period, age* +] 开始 ♦ **from dawn to dusk** 从早到晚

❑ **dawn on, dawn upon** *vt* [不可拆分] ♦ **it dawned on me/him that ...** 我/他逐渐意识到…

✪ **day** [deɪ] *n* **1** [c] (*period of 24 hours*) 天 ◊ *three days ago* 3 天前 **2** [c/u] (*daylight hours*) 白天 ◊ *during the day* 在白天 **3** [c/u] (*working day*) 工作日 ◊ *The office is only open during the day.* 办公室只在工作日开放。 **4** [c] (*heyday*) 时代 ◊ *The days of the silent film are long gone.* 无声电影的时代早已过去。 ♦ **the day before/after** 前/后一天 ♦ **the day after tomorrow** 后天 ♦ **the day before yesterday** 前天 ♦ **these days** (*nowadays*) 现在 ♦ **day in, day out** 日复一日 ♦ **to the day** 一天也不差 ♦ **the following day** 第二天 ♦ **the day that I ...** 我…的那一天 ♦ **day by day/from day to day** 一天天地 ♦ **one day a week** 每周一天 ♦ **one day/some day/one of these days** 有一天 ♦ **the other day** 在不久前某天 ♦ **by day** 在白天 ♦ **all day (long)** 一天到晚 ♦ **day and night** 日日夜夜地 ♦ **to work an 8 hour day** 每天工作8小时 ♦ **to call it a day** 停工

daybreak [ˈdeɪbreɪk] *n* [u] 黎明 ♦ **at daybreak** 拂晓时

day-care centre (美 **day-care center**) [ˈdeɪkɛə-] *n* [c] **1** (*for children*) 日托托儿所 **2** (*for old people*) 日间看护中心

daydream [ˈdeɪdriːm] **I** *vi* 做白日梦 **II** *n* [c] 白日梦

daylight [ˈdeɪlaɪt] *n* [u] 白昼

day nursery *n* [c] 托儿所

day return [英] *n* [c] (*ticket*) 当天来回的车票 [美 = **round trip ticket**]

daytime [ˈdeɪtaɪm] **I** *n* ♦ **in the daytime** 在白天 **II** *adj* [+ *television*] 日间的; [+ *telephone number*] 白天的

day-to-day [ˈdeɪtəˈdeɪ] *adj* [+ *life, routine*] 日常的 ♦ **on a day-to-day basis** 一天天地

day trip *n* [c] 当天来回的旅行

daze [deɪz] *n* ♦ **in a daze** (*confused*) 茫然地

dazed [deɪzd] *adj* (*confused*) 头晕眼花的

dazzle [ˈdæzl] **I** *vt* **1** (*blind*) 使目眩 **2** (*impress*) 使惊奇 **II** *n* **1** ♦ **the dazzle of sth** (*attraction*) 某物的魅力 **2** [u] (*glare*) 强光

dazzling [ˈdæzlɪŋ] *adj* **1** [+ *light, sun*] 耀眼的 **2** [+ *smile*] 迷人的 **3** [+ *display, performance*] 精彩的

D/D *abbr* (= ***direct debit***) 直接借记

dead [dɛd] **I** *adj* **1** (*not alive*) [+ *person, animal, plant*] 死的 **2** (*not working*) [+ *phone, line*] 坏的; [*battery*] 不能再用的 **3** (*finished*) [+ *cigarette, drink*] 用完了的 **4** (*total, absolute*) [+ *centre*] 正; [+ *silence*] 完全的 **II** *adv* **1** [非正式] (*very*) 非常地 **2** ♦ **dead against** (*completely*) 绝对反对 **III** *n* [*pl*] ♦ **the dead** 死者 ♦ **to drop (down) dead** 暴毙 ♦ **to stop dead** 突然停止 ♦ **dead tired** 精疲力竭 ♦ **dead on time** 完全准时 ♦ **dead ahead** 正前方 ♦ **dead on target** 正中目标 ♦ **dead centre/in the middle** 正中央 ♦ **over my dead body!** [非正式] 绝对不行！ ♦ **the line has gone dead** [通信] (*interrupted conversation*) 通话断了; (*on picking up the receiver*) 线路不通 ♦ **my leg/arm has gone dead** (*numb*) 我的腿/胳膊麻了 ♦ **at/in the dead of night** 夜深人静时 ♦ **at/in the dead of winter** [文] 在隆冬

> 📖 请勿将 **dead** 与 **died** 混淆。**died** 是动词 **die** 的过去式和过去分词，表示动作。*She died in 1934...Two men have died since the rioting broke out.* **died** 不能用作形容词，要表达形容词词性时应该使用 **dead**。*More than 2,200 dead birds have been found…My parents are dead. They died a long time ago.*

dead end *n* [c] **1** (*street*) 死路 **2** (*impasse*) 僵局

deadline ['dɛdlaɪn] *n* [c] 截止日期 ♦ **to work to a deadline** 根据截止日期工作 ♦ **to meet a deadline** 如期

deadly ['dɛdlɪ] **I** *adj* **1** [+ *poison, disease, dose, weapon*] 致命的 **2** (*devastating*) [+ *logic, insult*] 恶毒的 **II** *adv* **1** ♦ **deadly dull** 极其枯燥 **2** ♦ **deadly serious** 极其严肃

Dead Sea *n* ♦ **the Dead Sea** 死海

deaf [dɛf] **I** *adj* **1** (*totally*) 聋的; (*partially*) 耳背的 **2** ♦ **deaf to sth** 不听某事 **II** *n* [*pl*] ♦ **the deaf** 耳聋者 ♦ **to turn a deaf ear to sth** 对某事充耳不闻

deafen ['dɛfn] *vt* 使聋

deafening ['dɛfnɪŋ] *adj* [+ *noise*] 震耳欲聋的

deafness ['dɛfnɪs] *n* [U] 耳聋

✪ **deal** [diːl] (*pt, pp* **dealt**) **I** *n* [c] (*agreement*) 协议 ◊ *a business deal* 买卖协议 **II** *vt* **1** ♦ **to deal (out)** [+ *card*] 发给 ◊ *He dealt each player a card.* 他发给每个打牌的人一张牌。**2** (*sell*) [+ *drugs*] 出售 ♦ **to do/make/strike a deal with sb** 和某人做买卖 ♦ **it's a deal!** [非正式] 成交! ♦ **a good/fair/bad deal** 好的/公平的/不公的待遇 ♦ **a good** *or* **great deal (of)** 大量(的…) ♦ **to deal a (severe/heavy) blow to sb/sth** (严重/沉重地)打击某人/某事

❑ **deal in** [商] *vt* [不可拆分] 经营

❑ **deal out** *vt* [+ *punishment, criticism*] 使遭受

❑ **deal with** *vt* [不可拆分] **1** [+ *criminal, wrongdoer etc*] 惩处 ◊ *Criminals should be dealt with severely.* 罪犯应该被严厉惩处。 **2** [+ *company*] 和…有往来 **3** [+ *problem*] 处理 **4** [*book, film* +] [+ *subject*] 论述

dealer ['diːlə(r)] *n* [c] **1** (*in goods, services*) 商人 **2** (*in drugs*) 毒品贩子 **3** (*in card game*) 发牌人

dealings ['diːlɪŋz] *n* [*pl*] **1** (*transactions*) 往来 **2** (*relations*) 交往

dealt [dɛlt] *pt, pp of* **deal**

dean [diːn] *n* [c] **1** [*of church, cathedral*] 教长 **2** [英] [*of university, college*] 系主任 **3** [美] [*of school, college*] 教务长

dear [dɪə(r)] **I** *adj* **1** [+ *friend, house, car*] 亲爱的 **2** ♦ **to be dear to sb** 对某人很珍贵 **3** [尤英] (*expensive*) 昂贵的 **II** *n* ♦ **(my) dear** 亲爱的 **III** *int* ♦ **oh dear/dear dear/dear me!** 呵/哎呀! ♦ **Dear Sir/Madam** (*in letter*) 亲爱的先生/女士 ♦ **Dear Mr/Mrs X** 亲爱的X先生/夫人 ♦ **Dear Peter/Jane** 亲爱的彼得/简 ♦ **to be dear to sb's heart** 在某人心目中非常重要

dearly ['dɪəlɪ] *adv* **1** ♦ **to love sb dearly** 深爱某人 **2** ♦ **I would dearly love to ...** 我很想… **3** ♦ **to pay dearly (for sth)** (为某事)付出沉重代价

death [dɛθ] *n* **1** [C/U] [*of person, animal*] 死亡 **2** [s] (*end*) [*of way of life, tradition*] 消亡 **3** [c] (*fatality*) 死亡 ♦ **(to die) a horrible/lonely death** 恐怖地/孤独地死去 ♦ **(a matter of) life and death** 生死攸关(的事情) ♦ **to put sb to death** 处死某人 ♦ **to be stabbed/beaten to death** 被刺死/打死 ♦ **to scare/bore sb to death** 吓死某人/使某人感到无聊之极

death penalty *n* ♦ **the death penalty** 死刑

death sentence [法] *n* [c] 死刑判决

debatable [dɪ'beɪtəbl] *adj* 可争辩的 ♦ **it is debatable whether...** 是否…尚未决定

debate [dɪ'beɪt] **I** *n* **1** [C/U] (*discussion*) 讨论 **2** [c] (*formal discussion*) 辩论 **II** *vt* **1** [+ *topic, issue, motion*] 讨论 **2** [+ *course of action*] 考虑 ♦ **to debate whether ...** 盘算是否…

debit ['dɛbɪt] **I** *n* [c] 记入借方的款项 **II** *vt* 将…记入某人的借方

debit card *n* [c] 借记卡

debris ['dɛbriː] *n* [U] **1** (*rubble*) 碎片 **2** (*mess*) (*after meal, party etc*) 杯盘狼藉 **3** (*things lying about*) 废物

debt [dɛt] *n* **1** [c] (*sum of money owed*) 债务 **2** [U] (*state of owing money*) 欠债 ♦ **to be in/get into debt** 负债 ♦ **to be/get out of debt** 不欠债

♦ **bad debt** 坏账 ♦ **to be in sb's debt/owe sb a debt** [正式] 欠某人的人情债

debtor ['dɛtə(r)] *n* [c] 债务人

debut ['deɪbjuː] **I** *n* [c] 首次亮相 **II** *cpd* [复合词] [+ *album, match, performance*] 首次问世

Dec. *abbr* (= ***December***) 十二月

decade ['dɛkeɪd] *n* [c] 十年

decaffeinated [dɪ'kæfɪneɪtɪd] *adj* [+ *coffee*] 不含咖啡因的

decay [dɪ'keɪ] **I** *vi* **1** (*rot*) [*body, leaves, teeth* +] 腐烂 **2** [*society, system etc* +] 腐朽 **II** *n* [u] **1** [*of body, tooth*] 腐烂 **2** [*of society, system etc*] 腐朽

deceased [dɪ'siːst] [正式] **I** *adj* 已故的 **II** *n* ♦ **the deceased** 死者

deceit [dɪ'siːt] *n* [c/u] 欺骗

deceitful [dɪ'siːtful] *adj* 骗人的

deceive [dɪ'siːv] *vt* (*fool*) 欺骗 ♦ **to deceive sb into doing sth** 骗某人去做某事 ♦ **to deceive o.s.** 自欺

December [dɪ'sɛmbə(r)] *n* [c/u] 十二月 *see also* **July**

decency ['diːsənsɪ] *n* [u] 正派 ♦ **he didn't have the decency to ...** 他没有…的礼数

decent ['diːsənt] *adj* **1** (*proper*) [+ *education, wages, English etc*] 体面的; [+ *interval, behaviour*] 适当的 **2** (*honest*) [+ *person*] 受尊重的 ♦ **to do the decent thing** 识时务 ♦ **they were very decent about it** 他们对此很公正 ♦ **that was very decent of him** 他那么做真是个好人 ♦ **are you decent?** [非正式] (*dressed*) 你穿戴像样吗?

deception [dɪ'sɛpʃən] *n* **1** [u] (*deceiving*) 欺骗 **2** [c] (*deceitful act*) 诡计

deceptive [dɪ'sɛptɪv] *adj* [+ *appearance, impression*] 骗人的

✪ **decide** [dɪ'saɪd] **I** *vt* **1** (*settle*) [+ *question, argument*] 解决 **2** (*persuade*) [+ *person*] 使下决心 ◊ *I don't know what decided me to come.* 我不知道什么使我下决心来这儿。**II** *vi* 决定 ♦ **to decide to do sth** 决定做某事 ♦ **to decide on** *or* **upon sth** (*choose*) 决定某事 ♦ **to decide in favour of/against (doing) sth** 决定(做)某事/反对(做)某事 ♦ **to decide that ...** 决定… ♦ **I can't decide whether ...** 我无法决定是否…

decidedly [dɪ'saɪdɪdlɪ] *adv* 明显地

decimal ['dɛsɪməl] **I** *adj* [+ *system, currency*] 十进位的 **II** *n* [c] 小数 ♦ **to three decimal places** 保留到小数点后3位

✪ **decision** [dɪ'sɪʒən] *n* **1** [c] (*choice*) 决定 ◊ *The government has announced its decision.* 政府已经宣布了决定。**2** [u] (*act of choosing*) 决心 ◊ *The moment of decision can't be delayed.* 下决心的时刻不能拖了。**3** [u] (*decisiveness*) 决断力 ♦ **to make a decision** 作出决定

decisive [dɪ'saɪsɪv] *adj* **1** [+ *battle, phase*] 决定性的 **2** [+ *person*] 果断的 **3** [+ *manner, reply*] 坚定果断的

deck [dɛk] *n* [c] **1** (*on ship*) (*floor*) 舱面; (*top deck*) 甲板 **2** [*of bus*] 层面 **3** (*also* ***tape deck, record deck, cassette deck***) 磁带录音机的走带装置 **4** [尤美] [*of cards*] 一副 [英 = **pack**] ♦ **(to go up) on deck** (上到)在甲板上 ♦ **below deck(s)** 甲板下 ❑ **deck out** *vt* 用…装扮

deckchair ['dɛktʃɛə(r)] *n* [c] 折叠式躺椅

declaration [dɛklə'reɪʃən] *n* [c] **1** (*statement*) 宣布 **2** (*public announcement*) 宣言

declare [dɪ'klɛə(r)] **I** *vt* **1** (*state*) [+ *intention, attitude*] 宣布; [+ *support*] 表明; [+ *income*] 申报 **2** (*at customs*) [+ *goods*] 报关 **II** *vi* 宣称 ♦ **to declare sb innocent/insane** 宣布某人无罪/精神失常 ♦ **to declare war (on sb)** (向某人)宣战

decline [dɪ'klaɪn] **I** *n* ♦ **a decline in sth** 某物的下降 **II** *vt* (*turn down*) [+ *invitation, offer*] 谢绝 **III** *vi* [*strength, health* +] 衰退; [*business, population* +] 萎缩 ♦ **to be on the decline/in decline** 正在衰落 ♦ **to fall into decline** 衰弱 ♦ **to decline to do sth** 婉言拒绝做某事

decor ['deɪkɔː(r)] *n* [u] [*of house, room*] 装饰

decorate ['dɛkəreɪt] *vt* **1** (*adorn*) ♦ **to decorate (with)** (用…)装饰 **2** (*paint etc*) [+ *room, house*] 装潢 ♦ **to be decorated** (*awarded medal*) 被授

予勋章

decoration [dɛkəˈreɪʃən] *n* **1** [c/u] *(adornment)* 装饰 **2** [u] *[of room, building]* 装饰 **3** [c] *(medal)* 勋章 ♦**for decoration** 用于装饰

decorator [ˈdɛkəreɪtə(r)] *n* [c] **1** [英] *(painter)* 粉刷工 **2** [美] 室内装饰家 [英 = **interior decorator**]

decrease [*n* ˈdiːkriːs, *vb* diːˈkriːs] **I** *n* [c] *(reduction, drop)* ♦**decrease (in sth)** (某物的)减少 **II** *vt, vi* 减少 ♦**to be on the decrease** 正在减少

decree [dɪˈkriː] **I** *n* [c] **1** *(by ruler)* 法令 **2** [美] *(in law court)* 判决 **II** *vt* 颁布 ♦**to decree that ...** 下令…

dedicate [ˈdɛdɪkeɪt] *vt* **1** ♦**to dedicate one's time/life to (doing) sth** 把时间/一生奉献给(做)某事 **2** [+ *book, song*] 把…献给 ♦**to dedicate o.s. to sth** 致力于某事

dedicated [ˈdɛdɪkeɪtɪd] *adj* **1** [+ *person*] 专心致志的 **2** *(specialized)* [+ *word processor, software*] 专门的 ♦**to be dedicated to sth/doing sth** [+ *person*] 专心致志于/做某事; [+ *book, museum*] 专门关于某物/做某事的

dedication [dɛdɪˈkeɪʃən] *n* **1** [u] *(devotion)* 献身 **2** [c] *(in book)* 题献; *(on radio)* 献辞

deduce [dɪˈdjuːs] *vt* 推断 ♦**to deduce that ...** 推断…

deduct [dɪˈdʌkt] *vt* ♦**to deduct sth (from sth)** (从某物)中减去某物

deduction [dɪˈdʌkʃən] *n* **1** [c] *(conclusion)* 推论 **2** [u] *(deductive reasoning)* 演绎 **3** [u] *(subtraction)* 扣除 **4** [c] *(amount deducted)* 扣除额

deed [diːd] *n* [c] **1** [文] *(feat)* 行为 **2** *(document)* 契约

deem [diːm] [正式] *vt (judge, consider)* 认为 ♦**to deem it wise/unnecessary** 认为是明智的/没必要的

deep [diːp] **I** *adj* **1** [+ *water, hole, cut, breath*] 深的 **2** [+ *voice, sound*] 低沉的 **3** [+ *sleep*] 酣睡的 **4** *(profound)* [+ *person*] 高深莫测的; [+ *thoughts, ideas*] 深刻的; [+ *love, sympathy etc*] 深厚的 **5** *(serious)* [+ *trouble, concern*] 严重的 **6** [+ *colour*] 浓重的 **II** *adv* 深 ♦**it is 1 m deep** [+ *water, pool*] 它有1米深; [+ *shelf*] 它有1米厚 ♦**to be deep in thought/conversation** 沉思/深谈 ♦**to take a deep breath** 深呼吸 ♦**in deepest sympathy** 最深切的同情 ♦**ankle-/knee-deep (in water)** (水深)及脚踝/及膝 ♦**deep down/inside** 在内心深处 ♦**to go/run deep** 加重 ♦**to stand three deep** 围了3层

deepen [ˈdiːpn] **I** *vt* **1** [+ *hole*] 加深 **2** *(extend)* [+ *knowledge, awareness etc*] 加深 **3** [+ *gloom, recession*] 使强烈 **II** *vi* **1** [*crisis, feelings* +] 深化 **2** [*sound, voice* +] 变低沉 **3** [*river, sea etc* +] 变深

deep end *n* ♦**the deep end** [*of swimming pool*] 深水区 ♦**to be thrown in at the deep end** 被勉为其难

deep freeze *n* [c] 冷藏箱

deep-fried [ˈdiːpˈfraɪd] *adj* 油炸的

deep-fry [ˈdiːpˈfraɪ] *vt* 油炸

deeply [ˈdiːplɪ] *adv* **1** [*breathe, sigh* +] 深深地 **2** *(profoundly)* [*depressed, moved, religious*] 非常地 **3** [*sleep* +] 沉沉地

deer [dɪə(r)] (*pl* **deer**) *n* [c] 鹿 ♦**red deer** 赤鹿 ♦**roe deer** 牝鹿

default [dɪˈfɔːlt] **I** *n* [c] **1** *(in computing)* ♦**default (value/setting)** 默认(值/设置) **2** ♦**to be in default (on/of sth)** [+ *loan, debt*] 拖欠(某物) **II** *vi* ♦**to default on a debt** 拖欠借款 ♦**to win by default** 因对手未出场而赢得比赛

defeat [dɪˈfiːt] **I** *n* [c/u] **1** *[of army]* 战败 **2** *[of team]* 击败 **3** *(failure)* 失败 **II** *vt* **1** [+ *enemy, opposition*] 战胜 **2** [+ *team*] 击败 **3** [+ *plan, proposal etc*] 否决 **4** *(be too difficult for)* [*task, challenge* +] 难住

defect [*n* ˈdiːfɛkt, *vb* dɪˈfɛkt] **I** *n* [c] *(flaw)* 缺点 **II** *vi* ♦**to defect (to/from)** 背叛(投奔于/了) ♦**hearing defect** 听觉缺陷

defective [dɪˈfɛktɪv] *adj* 有缺点的

defence (美 **defense**) [dɪˈfɛns] **I** *n* **1** [u] *(protection)* 防御 **2** [u] [军] 国防措施 **3** [c] ♦**defence (of sth)** *(justification)* (为某事的)辩护 **4** [c] *(in court)* 辩护 **5** ♦**the defence** *(in court)* 被告方 **6** [s/pl] *(in sport)* 守方

II *cpd* [复合词] [+ *spending, cuts, minister*] 国防开支 **III defences** *n* [*pl*] **1** [军] 军事能力 **2** [*of body*] 抵抗力 ♦ **to come to sb's defence** 上前为某人辩护 ♦ **in defence of sth/sb** 为某事/某人辩护 ♦ **to use a knife in defence** 用匕首防身 ♦ **a defence against sth** 对某物的抵抗力 ♦ **the Ministry of Defence,** [美] **the Department of Defense** 国防部 ♦ **witness for the defence** 被告方证人

defenceless [dɪ'fɛnslɪs] *adj* 无自卫能力的

defend [dɪ'fɛnd] *vt* **1** (*protect*) 防御 **2** (*justify*) 为…辩护 **3** (*in court*) 为…辩护 **4** (*in sport*) [+ *goal, record, title*] 防守 ♦ **to defend o.s.** 自卫

defendant [dɪ'fɛndənt] *n* [c] 被告

defender [dɪ'fɛndə(r)] *n* [c] **1** [*of view, policy*] 拥护者 **2** (*in team*) 防守队员

defense [dɪ'fɛns] [美] *n* = **defence**

defensive [dɪ'fɛnsɪv] **I** *adj* **1** [+ *weapons, measures*] 防御的 **2** [+ *behaviour, manner*] 防卫的 **II** *n* ♦ **on the defensive** 采取守势

defer [dɪ'fəː(r)] **I** *vt* (*postpone*) 推迟 **II** *vi* ♦ **to defer to sb** 遵从某人的意见

defiance [dɪ'faɪəns] *n* [u] 藐视 ♦ **in defiance of sth** [+ *the rules, sb's orders etc*] 无视某事

defiant [dɪ'faɪənt] *adj* [+ *tone, reply, person*] 藐视的

deficiency [dɪ'fɪʃənsɪ] *n* **1** [c/u] (*lack*) 缺乏 **2** [c/u] (*inadequacy*) 缺陷

deficient [dɪ'fɪʃənt] [正式] *adj* (*inadequate*) 缺乏的 ♦ **to be deficient in sth** (*lacking*) 缺乏某物

deficit ['dɛfɪsɪt] *n* [c] 赤字

define [dɪ'faɪn] *vt* **1** [+ *limits, boundaries, role*] 限定 **2** [+ *expression, word*] 解释

definite ['dɛfɪnɪt] *adj* **1** (*fixed*) [+ *plan, answer, views*] 明确的 **2** (*distinct*) [+ *improvement, possibility, advantage*] 肯定的 **3** (*certain*) [+ *proof, evidence, information*] 确切的 ♦ **is that definite?** 肯定吗？♦ **he was definite about it** 他对此很肯定

definitely ['dɛfɪnɪtlɪ] *adv* 确定地

definition [dɛfɪ'nɪʃən] *n* **1** [c] [*of word*] 定义 **2** [u] (*clarity*) [*of thought, expression*] 明确性 **3** [u] [*of photograph, features*] 清晰度 ♦ **by definition** 就本身而言

definitive [dɪ'fɪnɪtɪv] *adj* **1** (*conclusive*) [+ *answer*] 确定的 **2** (*authoritative*) [+ *version, account*] 权威性的

deflate [diː'fleɪt] **I** *vt* **1** [+ *tyre, balloon*] 放出…的气 **2** [+ *person, hopes*] 使泄气 **II** *vi* [*tyre, dinghy* +] 放气

deflect [dɪ'flɛkt] *vt* [+ *attention, criticism, shot, blow*] 使转向 ♦ **to deflect sb (from ...)** 使某人转变（…）

defraud [dɪ'frɔːd] *vt* ♦ **to defraud sb (of sth)** 从某人处骗取（某物）

defrost [diː'frɔst] **I** *vt* **1** [+ *fridge, freezer*] 除去…的冰霜 **2** [+ *food*] 使解冻 **II** *vi* **1** [*fridge, freezer* +] 除霜 **2** [*food* +] 解冻

defuse [diː'fjuːz] *vt* **1** [+ *bomb*] 拆除…的引信 **2** [+ *crisis, situation*] 使缓和

defy [dɪ'faɪ] *vt* **1** (*refuse to obey*) [+ *person*] 公然反抗；[+ *law, ban*] 蔑视 **2** [+ *description, comprehension*] 使不能 **3** ♦ **to defy sb to do sth** (*dare*) 看某人敢不敢做某事

degree [dɪ'griː] *n* [c] **1** ♦ **degree (of sth)** (*level*) （某事的）程度 **2** (*measure of temperature, angle, latitude*) 度 **3** (*at university*) 学位 ♦ **with varying degrees of success** 不同程度的成功 ♦ **to some degree/a certain degree** 从某种/一定程度上来说 ♦ **10 degrees below (zero)** 零下10度 ♦ **a degree in maths** 数学学位 ♦ **by degrees** (*gradually*) 逐渐地

dehydrated [diːhaɪ'dreɪtɪd] *adj* 脱水的

delay [dɪ'leɪ] **I** *vt* **1** (*postpone*) [+ *decision, ceremony*] 推迟 **2** (*make late*) [+ *person*] 耽搁；[+ *plane, train*] 延误 **II** *vi* 耽搁 **III** *n* [c/u] 延误 ♦ **to be delayed** [*person, flight, departure etc* +] 被耽搁了 ♦ **without delay** 立即

delegate [*n* 'dɛlɪgɪt, *vb* 'dɛlɪgeɪt] **I** *n* [c] 代表 **II** *vt* **1** ♦ **to delegate sb to do sth** 委派某人做某事 **2** ♦ **to delegate sth (to sb)** [+ *task*] 委托某

事（给某人）

delete [dɪˈliːt] *vt* **1** (*cross out*) 删除 **2**［计算机］(*remove*) [+ *file, folder, message*] 删除

deli [ˈdɛlɪ] *n* [c] 熟食店

deliberate [*adj* dɪˈlɪbərɪt, *vb* dɪˈlɪbəreɪt] **I** *adj* **1** (*intentional*) 故意的 **2** (*careful*) 审慎的 **II** *vi* (*think*) 仔细考虑 ♦ **it wasn't deliberate** 那不是故意的

deliberately [dɪˈlɪbərɪtlɪ] *adv* **1** (*intentionally*) 故意地 **2** (*carefully*) 审慎地

delicacy [ˈdɛlɪkəsɪ] *n* **1** [u] (*fragility*) [*of material*] 娇嫩 **2** [c] (*choice food*) 珍馐美味 **3** [u] (*sensitivity*) [*of problem, situation*] 微妙

delicate [ˈdɛlɪkɪt] *adj* **1** (*fine*) [+ *features, hands, flower*] 柔软的 **2** (*fragile*) [+ *object, material*] 易碎的 **3** (*sensitive*) [+ *problem, situation, issue etc*] 微妙的 **4** (*frail*) [+ *person, health*] 脆弱的 **5** (*subtle*) [+ *colour, flavour, smell*] 清淡可口的

delicatessen [dɛlɪkəˈtɛsn] *n* [c] 熟食店

delicious [dɪˈlɪʃəs] *adj* **1** [+ *food, smell*] 美味的 **2** [+ *feeling*] 美妙的

delight [dɪˈlaɪt] **I** *n* **1** [u] (*feeling*) 快乐 **2** [c] (*person, experience*) 令人开心的人/事 **II** *vt* (*please*) 使快乐 **III** *vi* ♦ **to delight in sth** 以某事为乐 ♦ **to my delight ...** 令我高兴的是… ♦ **to take (a) delight in sth/doing sth** 以某事/做某事为乐 ♦ **she was a delight to interview** 采访她是一件乐事

delighted [dɪˈlaɪtɪd] *adj* ♦ **delighted (at** *or* **with sth)** （对某事）感到高兴 ♦ **to be delighted to do sth** 乐意做某事 ♦ **I'd be delighted** 我十分乐意

delightful [dɪˈlaɪtful] *adj* 使人快乐的

delinquent [dɪˈlɪŋkwənt] **I** *adj* [+ *teenager, child*] 违法的 **II** *n* [c] 违法者

deliver [dɪˈlɪvə(r)] *vt* **1** (*bring*) [+ *letter, parcel etc*] 传送 **2**［正式］♦ **to be delivered into sb's hands/care** (*handed over*) 移交到某人手中/给某人照看 **3** [+ *baby*] 接生 **4** [+ *speech, lecture etc*] 发表 **5** (*come up with*) 履行诺言 **6**［正式］[+ *verdict, judgement*] 宣告 **7**［正式］[+ *warning, ultimatum*] 发出 **8**［正式］[+ *blow*] 给予 **9**［正式］♦ **to deliver sb from sth** (*release*) 将某人从某事中解救出来

delivery [dɪˈlɪvərɪ] **I** *n* **1** [u] (*distribution*) [*of goods, mail*] 传送 **2** [c] (*consignment*) 递送的货物 **3** [u] [*of speaker*] 讲演 **4** [c/u]［医］分娩 **II** *cpd*［复合词］[+ *man, service*] 送货 ♦ **to take delivery of sth** 收到某物 ♦ **allow 28 days for delivery** 交货期为28天

delusion [dɪˈluːʒən] *n* 错觉 ♦ **to be under a/the delusion that ...** 有…的错觉 ♦ **to have delusions of grandeur** 自大狂想症

deluxe [dəˈlʌks] *adj* 豪华的

delve [dɛlv] *vi* ♦ **to delve into sth** [+ *subject, past*] 探究某事; [+ *cupboard, handbag*] 翻找某物

Dem.［政治］*abbr* = **democrat(ic)**

✪ **demand** [dɪˈmɑːnd] **I** *vt* **1** (*ask for*) [+ *apology, explanation, pay rise*] 要求 **2** (*require*) [+ *patience, attention*] 需要 **II** *n* **1** [c] (*request*) 要求 ◊ *There have been demands for improved services.* 一直以来都有改进服务的要求。**2** [u] (*for product*) 需求量 ◊ *Demand for this product is increasing.* 对这种产品的需求量越来越大。**III demands** *n* [*pl*] (*requirements*) 要求 ◊ *the demands of a new job* 新工作的要求 ♦ **to demand to do sth** 要求做某事 ♦ **to demand sth from** *or* **of sb** 要求某人某事 ♦ **I have many demands on my time** 我有许多工作要花时间去做 ♦ **to make demands on sb/sth** 对某人/某事提出要求 ♦ **to be in demand** 受欢迎 ♦ **on demand** 随时地

demanding [dɪˈmɑːndɪŋ] *adj* **1** [+ *work*] 高要求的 **2** [+ *boss, child*] 苛求的

demented [dɪˈmɛntɪd] *adj* **1**［正式］(*ill*) 发狂的 **2**［非正式］(*crazed*) 发狂的

demise [dɪˈmaɪz]［正式］*n* [u] **1** (*end*) 结束 **2** (*death*) 死亡

demo [ˈdɛməu]［英］［非正式］*n abbr* [c] (= ***demonstration***) 示威

democracy [dɪ'mɔkrəsɪ] *n* **1** [U] (*system*) 民主 **2** [C] (*country*) 民主国
democrat ['dɛməkræt] *n* [C] **1** (*believer in democracy*) 民主主义者 **2** ♦**Democrat** 民主党人
democratic [dɛmə'krætɪk] *adj* 民主的 ♦**Democratic** 民主党的
Democratic Party [美] *n* ♦**the Democratic Party** 民主党
demolish [dɪ'mɔlɪʃ] *vt* **1** [+ *building*] 拆毁 **2** [+ *argument*] 推翻
demolition [dɛmə'lɪʃən] *n* [C/U] [*of building*] 拆毁
demon ['diːmən] **I** *n* [C] (*evil spirit*) 恶魔 **II** *adj* (*skilled, enthusiastic*) 胜人一筹的
demonstrate ['dɛmənstreɪt] **I** *vt* **1** (*make clear*) [+ *theory*] 表明 **2** (*show*) [+ *skill, appliance*] 演示 **3** (*prove*) 证实 **II** *vi* ♦**to demonstrate (for/against sth)** 示威（支持/反对某事）♦**to demonstrate that ...** 证实… ♦**to demonstrate how to do sth** 演示如何做某事
demonstration [dɛmən'streɪʃən] *n* [C] **1** (*protest march*) 示威 **2** (*proof*) 证实 **3** [*of appliance, cooking etc*] 演示 ♦**to hold/stage a demonstration** 举行示威
demonstrator ['dɛmənstreɪtə(r)] *n* [C] **1** (*protester*) 示威者 **2** (*sales person*) 向顾客演示产品的推销员
demote [dɪ'məut] *vt* **1** [+ *employee*] 使降级 **2** [英] (*relegate*) [+ *team*] 使降级
den [dɛn] *n* [C] **1** [*of fox, lion*] 兽穴 **2** [尤美] (*room*) 私室 **3** ♦**drinking/gambling den** 饮酒/赌博秘室 ♦**a den of iniquity/vice** 藏污纳垢之处
denial [dɪ'naɪəl] *n* **1** [C/U] (*refutation*) 否定 **2** [U] (*refusal*) 拒绝 **3** ♦**to be in denial** 拒绝接受
denim ['dɛnɪm] **I** *n* [U] (*fabric*) 斜纹粗棉布 **II denims** *n* [*pl*] (*jeans*) 工装裤
Denmark ['dɛnmɑːk] *n* 丹麦
denomination [dɪnɔmɪ'neɪʃən] *n* [C] **1** (*religious*) 宗派 **2** [*of money*] 货币单位
denounce [dɪ'nauns] *vt* [+ *person, action*] 谴责 ♦**to denounce sb as a traitor/impostor** 痛斥某人是叛徒/骗子
dense [dɛns] *adj* **1** [+ *crowd, forest*] 稠密的 **2** [+ *smoke, fog*] 浓厚的 **3** [非正式] (*stupid*) 愚钝的
densely ['dɛnslɪ] *adv* ♦**densely populated** 人口稠密的 ♦**densely wooded** 丛林密布的
density ['dɛnsɪtɪ] *n* [C/U] 密度
dent [dɛnt] **I** *n* [C] (*in metal, box*) 凹部 **II** *vt* **1** [+ *metal, box*] 使…凹陷 **2** [+ *pride, ego, confidence*] 削弱 ♦**to make a dent in sth** [+ *car*] 在某物上弄个小凹痕; [+ *savings*] 削弱某物
dental ['dɛntl] *adj* [+ *treatment, hygiene etc*] 牙齿的
dentist ['dɛntɪst] *n* [C] **1** (*person*) 牙医 **2** ♦**the dentist('s)** 牙医诊所
dentures ['dɛntʃəz] *n* [*pl*] 假牙
Denver boot ['dɛnvə(r)-] [美] 车轮固定夹 [英 = **clamp, wheel clamp**]
deny [dɪ'naɪ] *vt* **1** [+ *charge, allegation, accusation*] 否定 **2** ♦**to deny sb sth** [+ *permission, chance, access*] 拒绝某人某事 **3** [正式] (*disown*) [+ *country, religion, person*] 否认…与己有关 ♦**he denies having said it** 他否认这样说过 ♦**to deny that ...** 否认…
deodorant [diː'əudərənt] *n* [C/U] 除臭剂
depart [dɪ'pɑːt] *vi* **1** ♦**to depart (from/for somewhere)** [*traveller, visitor* +] (从某地) 出发/出发 (赶往某地); [*bus, plane, train* +] 出发 **2** ♦**to depart from sth** (*stray from*) 不合某事
✪**department** [dɪ'pɑːtmənt] *n* [C] **1** (*in shop*) 部 **2** (*in school or college*) 系 **3** (*in government*) 部 ♦**that's not my department** 那不是我的专责 ♦**Department of State** [美] 国务院 ♦**Department of Health/the Environment** [英] 卫生/环境部
department store *n* [C] 百货商店
departure [dɪ'pɑːtʃə(r)] *n* **1** [C/U] [*of visitor, traveller, plane etc*] 出发 **2** [C] (*scheduled journey*) 离去 **3** [C/U] [正式] [*of employee, colleague*] 离去 **4** ♦**a departure from sth** 背离某事 ♦**a new departure** 新起点
departure lounge *n* [C] 候机厅
depend [dɪ'pɛnd] *vi* **1** ♦**to depend on sth** (*be decided by*) 依某物而定

2 ♦**you can depend on me/him** *(rely on, trust)* 你可以信赖我/他 3 ♦**to depend on sb/sth** *(for survival)* 依靠某人/某物为生 ♦**it (all) depends** 要看情况而定 ♦**depending on the result ...** 根据结果…

dependable [dɪˈpɛndəbl] *adj* 可靠的

dependant, dependent [dɪˈpɛndənt] *n* [C] *(person)* 受赡养者

dependence [dɪˈpɛndəns] *n* [U] 依赖

dependent [dɪˈpɛndənt] **I** *adj* ♦**to be dependent on sb/sth** [+ *person, decision*] 依赖某人/某物 **II** *n* = **dependant**

depict [dɪˈpɪkt] *vt* **1** *(in picture)* 描绘 **2** *(describe)* 描述

deplete [dɪˈpliːt] *vt* [正式] 大量消耗

deport [dɪˈpɔːt] *vt* ♦**to deport sb (from somewhere)** [+ *criminal, illegal immigrant*] 将某人(从某地)逐出

deposit [dɪˈpɔzɪt] **I** *n* [C] **1** *(money)* *(in account)* 储蓄; *(on goods)* 保证金; *(on house, bottle, when hiring)* 押金 **2** *(residue)* *(from chemical process)* 沉淀物 **3** [*of ore, oil, minerals etc*] 沉积 **II** *vt* **1** [+ *money*] 把…存入… **2** *(put, leave)* 寄存 **3** *(from chemical or geological process)* 沉积 ♦**to put down a deposit of 50 pounds** 支付50英镑的保证金

depot [ˈdɛpəu] *n* [C] **1** *(storehouse)* 仓库 **2** *(for vehicles)* 车库 **3** [美] *(station)* 车站 [英 = **station**]

depreciate [dɪˈpriːʃɪeɪt] *vi* [*currency, property, value etc* +] 贬值

depress [dɪˈprɛs] *vt* **1** [+ *person*] 使沮丧 **2** [+ *price, wages*] 使跌价 **3** *(press down)* [+ *accelerator, lever*] 压下

depressed [dɪˈprɛst] *adj* **1** [+ *person*] 沮丧的 **2** [+ *prices*] 降低的 **3** [+ *industry*] 萧条的 **4** [+ *area*] 不景气的 ♦**to feel depressed** 感到沮丧 ♦**to get depressed** 心情沮丧

depressing [dɪˈprɛsɪŋ] *adj* [+ *place, situation etc*] 令人沮丧的

depression [dɪˈprɛʃən] *n* **1** [U] [*of person*] 抑郁症 **2** [C] *(slump)* *(in economy)* 萧条 **3** [C] *(weather system)* 低气压 **4** [C] *(hollow)* 凹陷

deprivation [dɛprɪˈveɪʃən] *n* [C/U] **1** *(poverty)* 穷困 **2** *(loss)* 丧失 ♦**sleep deprivation** 失眠

deprive [dɪˈpraɪv] *vt* ♦**to deprive sb of sth** 剥夺某人某物 ♦**to deprive o.s. (of sth)** (对某物)自我克制

deprived [dɪˈpraɪvd] *adj* [+ *area, background, child, family*] 贫困的

dept. *abbr* (= ***department***) 部系

depth [dɛpθ] *n* **1** [C/U] *(from top to bottom)* [*of hole, water*] 深 **2** [C/U] *(from front to back)* [*of cupboard, shelf etc*] 厚度 **3** [U] [*of emotion, feeling*] 深厚 **4** [U] [*of knowledge*] 渊博; [*of understanding etc*] 深刻 **5** ♦**the depths** [文] [*of ocean, earth*] 深处 ♦**at/to/from a depth of 3 metres** 在/到/从3米深处 ♦**18 metres in depth** 深18米 ♦**to be/go out of one's depth** *(in water)* 水深没顶处 ♦**to be/feel out of one's depth** *(in situation)* 力所不及 ♦**to study/analyse sth in depth** 深入研究/分析某事 ♦**an in-depth investigation/analysis** 深入的调查/分析 ♦**the depths of the forest/countryside** 森林深处/乡郊野外 ♦**in the depths of despair/recession/winter** 深深陷入绝望/衰退中/在隆冬

deputy [ˈdɛpjutɪ] **I** *n* [C] **1** *(second in command)* 副 **2** *(elected member)* 下院议员 **3** [美] *(also **deputy sheriff**)* 县助理司法行政长官 **II** *adj* ♦**deputy chairman/director** 副主席/总监 ♦**deputy head** [英] *(in school)* 学监

derail [dɪˈreɪl] *vt* **1** ♦**to be derailed** [*train* +] 出轨 **2** [+ *plan, negotiations*] 使离开原定进程

derelict [ˈdɛrɪlɪkt] **I** *adj* [+ *building*] 弃置的 **II** *n* [C] [正式] *(vagrant)* 无家可归者

derive [dɪˈraɪv] **I** *vt* ♦**to derive sth (from sth)** [+ *pleasure, benefit*] (从某事中)取得某事 **II** *vi* ♦**to derive from/be derived from sth** *(originate in)* [*word* +] 从某物中派生出; [*situation* +] 来自某物

derogatory [dɪˈrɔgətərɪ] *adj* [+ *remark, comment*] 贬低的

descend [dɪˈsɛnd] **I** *vt* [正式] [+ *stairs, hill*] 下 **II** *vi* **1** [正式] *(go down)* 下来 **2** ♦**to descend (on/upon sb/sth)**

[*calm, hush, gloom* +] 向（某人/某物）袭来；[*visitors, tourists* +] 突然涌向（某人/某地）♦ **to be descended from** [*person* +] 是…的后裔；[*animal* +] 由…演变而来 ♦ **to descend to sth/to doing sth** [+ *lying, begging etc*] 屈尊于某事/做某事 ♦ **in descending order** 按递减的顺序

descendant [dɪˈsɛndənt] *n* [C] 后裔

descent [dɪˈsɛnt] *n* **1** [C/U] [*of mountain, hill etc*] 下坡 **2** [C/U] (*by aircraft*) 下降 **3** [U] (*origin*) 血统 **4** [C] (*slope*) 斜坡 ♦ **of African/European descent** 非洲/欧洲血统

✪ **describe** [dɪsˈkraɪb] *vt* 描述 ♦ **to describe sth/sb/o.s. as ...** 把某事/某人/自己描述成… ◊ *a man described by the police as extremely dangerous* 一个被警察描述为极为危险的人 ♦ **to describe sb/sth to sb** 向某人描述某人/某事

description [dɪsˈkrɪpʃən] *n* [C/U] 描述 ♦ **of some/any description** 某/任何一种

desert [*n* ˈdɛzət, *vb* dɪˈzəːt] **I** *n* **1** [C/U] [地理] 沙漠 **2** [C]（喻）(*wasteland*) 荒地 **II** *vt* (*leave*) [+ *place*] 离弃；[+ *person*] 遗弃 **III** *vi* [军] 逃跑

deserted [dɪˈzəːtɪd]] *adj* 被舍弃的

deserve [dɪˈzəːv] *vt* 应受 ♦ **to deserve to do sth** 应该获得某事

deserving [dɪˈzəːvɪŋ] *adj* 应得的

✪ **design** [dɪˈzaɪn] **I** *n* **1** [U] (*art, process, layout, shape*) 设计 **2** [C] (*drawing*) 图样 ◊ *a design for a new office block* 新办公楼区的图样 **3** [C] (*pattern*) 图案 **II** *vt* [+ *kitchen, product, test, system*] 设计 ♦ **to be designed for sb/to do sth** 专门为某人/做某事设计 ♦ **by design** (*on purpose*) 故意地 ♦ **to have designs on sb/sth** 对某人/某事抱不良企图

designate [*vb* ˈdɛzɪgneɪt, *adj* ˈdɛzɪgnɪt] **I** *vt* **1** (*nominate*) 指定 **2** ♦ **to be designated for/as sth** 专门用于某事 **II** *adj* ♦ **chairman/prime minister designate** 已受委任的主席/首相 ♦ **in designated areas** 在指定区域

designer [dɪˈzaɪnə(r)] **I** *n* [C] 设计者 **II** *cpd* [复合词] [+ *clothes, label, jeans etc*] 名师设计的

desirable [dɪˈzaɪərəbl] *adj* **1** (*attractive*) 称心如意的 **2** (*sexually attractive*) 性感的 **3** (*proper*) 值得想望的 ♦ **it is desirable that ...** …是合乎要求的

desire [dɪˈzaɪə(r)] **I** *n* **1** [C] [正式] (*urge*) 愿望 **2** [U] (*sexual*) 情欲 **II** *vt* **1** [正式] (*want*) 想望 **2** (*sexually*) 想要 ♦ **to desire to do sth** 想望做某事 ♦ **the desired effect/result** 期望的效果/结果

desk [dɛsk] *n* [C] **1** (*in office*) 办公桌 **2** (*for pupil*) 书桌 **3** (*in hotel, at airport, hospital etc*) 服务台 **4** ♦ **news/fashion desk** (*department*) 新闻/时装部

desk clerk [美] *n* [C] 接待员 [英= **receptionist**]

desktop publishing [ˈdɛsktɔp-] *n* [U] 桌面出版

desolate [ˈdɛsəlɪt] *adj* **1** [+ *place*] 荒凉的 **2** [+ *person*] 孤寂的

despair [dɪsˈpɛə(r)] **I** *n* [U] 绝望 **II** *vi* 绝望 ♦ **in despair** 绝望地 ♦ **to despair of doing sth** 丧失做某事的信心 ♦ **to despair at sb/sth** 对某人/某事绝望

despatch [dɪsˈpætʃ] *n, vt* = **dispatch**

desperate [ˈdɛspərɪt] *adj* **1** [+ *person*] 绝望的 **2** [+ *attempt, effort*] 铤而走险的 **3** [+ *situation*] 危急的 **4** [+ *criminal, person*] 不顾死活的 ♦ **to be desperate for sth/to do sth** 极想某事/做某事

desperately [ˈdɛspərɪtlɪ] *adv* **1** (*frantically*) [*struggle, shout etc* +] 拼命地 **2** (*terribly, awfully*) [+ *ill, unhappy etc*] 极度地 ♦ **desperately trying to escape** 拼命逃窜 ♦ **he desperately needs help** 他极度需要帮助

desperation [dɛspəˈreɪʃən] *n* [U] 绝望 ♦ **in** *or* **out of (sheer) desperation** 处于/出于（完全的）绝望

despise [dɪsˈpaɪz] *vt* 鄙视

despite [dɪsˈpaɪt] *prep* 尽管

dessert [dɪˈzəːt] *n* [C/U] 饭后甜点

dessert spoon *n* [C] **1** (*object*) 点心匙 **2** (*quantity*) 一点心匙的量

destination [dɛstɪˈneɪʃən] *n* [C] [*of traveller, mail, supplies etc*] 目的地

destined [ˈdɛstɪnd] *adj* **1** (*bound*) ♦**to be destined to do sth/for sth** 注定做某事/做某事 **2** ♦**to be destined for sth** [*goods* +] 指定送到某地; [*person* +] 指定送到某地

destiny [ˈdɛstɪnɪ] *n* **1** [C] (*future*) 命运 **2** [U] (*fate*) 缘分

destroy [dɪsˈtrɔɪ] *vt* **1** [+ *building, object*] 破坏 **2** [+ *faith, confidence*] 打破 **3** [+ *animal*] 杀死

destruction [dɪsˈtrʌkʃən] *n* [U] **1** (*act of destroying*) 破坏 **2** (*state of being destroyed*) 毁灭

destructive [dɪsˈtrʌktɪv] *adj* **1** [+ *capacity, force*] 破坏性的 **2** [+ *child, person*] 有危害的

detach [dɪˈtætʃ] [正式] **I** *vt* 分开 **II** *vi* 分离

detached [dɪˈtætʃt] *adj* [+ *person, attitude*] 客观的 ♦**detached house** 独立式住房

detail [ˈdiːteɪl] **I** *n* **1** [C] (*individual feature, minor point*) 细节 **2** [U] (*in picture, work etc*) 细节 **II** *vt* [正式] (*list*) 详述 **III details** *n* [*pl*] 详情 ♦**in detail** 详细地 ♦**to (not) go into details** (*usually negative*) (没有)详细叙述

detailed [ˈdiːteɪld] *adj* [+ *account, description*] 详细的

detain [dɪˈteɪn] *vt* **1** [正式] (*keep, delay*) 耽搁 **2** [*police* +] 扣留 **3** (*in hospital*) 留下

detect [dɪˈtɛkt] *vt* **1** (*sense*) 察觉 **2** [+ *illness, disease*] 发现 **3** [+ *enemy, pollution*] 侦查

detection [dɪˈtɛkʃən] *n* [U] **1** [*of illness, disease*] 发现 **2** [*of criminal, secret*] 侦查 ♦**to escape/avoid detection** [*criminal* +] 逃之夭夭; [*mistake* +] 未被察觉

detective [dɪˈtɛktɪv] *n* [C] **1** (*in police*) 侦探 **2** [英] ♦**detective inspector/constable/sergeant** 刑侦警察 **3** [美] 侦探 ♦**(private) detective** 私家侦探

detective story, detective novel *n* [C] 侦探小说

detention [dɪˈtɛnʃən] *n* **1** [U] (*arrest*) 扣留 **2** [C/U] (*at school*) 课后留校 ♦**to be in detention** 被课后留校

deter [dɪˈtəː(r)] *vt* (*discourage*) [+ *person*] 吓住; [+ *crime*] 威慑 ♦**to deter sb from doing sth** 威慑某人不做某事

detergent [dɪˈtəːdʒənt] *n* [C/U] 清洁剂

deteriorate [dɪˈtɪərɪəreɪt] *vi* 恶化

determination [dɪtəːmɪˈneɪʃən] *n* **1** [U] (*resolve*) 决心 **2** [C/U] (*establishment*) 确定

determine [dɪˈtəːmɪn] *vt* **1** [正式] (*discover*) [+ *facts*] 确定 **2** (*decide on*) [+ *budget, amount*] 决定 **3** [正式] (*dictate*) 决定 ♦**to determine that ...** [正式] (*decide*) 决定…; (*establish*) 确定… ♦**to determine to do sth** [正式] 决定做某事

determined [dɪˈtəːmɪnd] *adj* **1** [+ *person*] 坚定的 **2** [+ *effort, attempt*] 坚决的 ♦**to be determined to do sth** 决心做某事

deterrent [dɪˈtɛrənt] **I** *n* [C] **1** (*nuclear*) 威慑因素 **2** [法] 威慑手段 **II** *adj* [+ *effect*] 威慑的 ♦**to act as a deterrent** 发挥威慑作用

detest [dɪˈtɛst] *vt* 嫌恶

detour [ˈdiːtuə(r)] *n* [C] **1** ♦**to make a detour** 绕道 **2** [美] (*on road*) 绕行道路 [英 = **diversion**]

detract [dɪˈtrækt] *vi* ♦**to detract from sth** [+ *effect, achievement, pleasure etc*] 减损某物

detrimental [dɛtrɪˈmɛntl] *adj* ♦**detrimental (to sth)** (对某事)不利的 ♦**to have a detrimental effect (on sb/sth)** (对某人/某事)有不利影响

devastate [ˈdɛvəsteɪt] *vt* **1** (*destroy*) 破坏 **2** (*shock*) ♦**to be devastated (by sth)** (被某事)震惊

devastating [ˈdɛvəsteɪtɪŋ] *adj* **1** [+ *weapon, storm*] 破坏性的 **2** [+ *news, effect*] 惊人的

✪**develop** [dɪˈvɛləp] **I** *vt* **1** (*change and improve*) [+ *business, idea, relationship*] 发展; [+ *land, resource*] 开发 **2** (*produce*) [+ *product, weapon*] 开发 **3** [摄影] 冲洗 **4** (*begin to have*) [+ *fault, engine trouble*] 逐步显现; [+ *disease*] 显现…的症状 **II** *vi* **1** (*evolve*) [*person* +] 成长; [*country, situation, friendship, skill* +] 发展 **2** (*appear*) [*facts, symptoms* +] 逐步产生; [*problem, difficulty* +] 逐步显现 ♦**to develop a taste for sth** 逐步

形成对某物的喜好 ♦ **to develop into sth** 发展成某物

developing country [dɪˈvɛləpɪŋ-] *n* [c] 发展中国家

✪ **development** [dɪˈvɛləpmənt] *n* **1** [u] (*growth*) 成长 ◊ *the development of the embryo* 胚胎的成长; (*political, economic*) 发展 **2** [c] (*event*) 新形势 ◊ *the latest developments in Moscow* 莫斯科最近的形势 **3** [u] [*of land, area*] 开发 **4** [c] (*building complex*) 新开发地 ◊ *an industrial development* 新开发的工业园区 ♦ **an unexpected development** 出乎意料的新事件

device [dɪˈvaɪs] *n* [c] **1** (*apparatus*) 设备 **2** (*ploy, stratagem*) 手法 ♦ **explosive device** (*bomb*) 引爆装置 ♦ **to leave sb to their own devices** 听任某人自行其是

devil [ˈdɛvl] *n* **1** [c] (*evil spirit*) 魔鬼 **2** [c] ♦ **poor/lucky devil** 可怜/幸运的家伙 **3** ♦ **the Devil** 撒旦 ♦ **go on, be a devil!** [非正式] 来，怕什么！ ♦ **talk of the devil!** 说到某人，某人就到！ ♦ **what/how/why the devil ..?** [非正式] (*used for emphasis*) 究竟什么/如何/为什么…？

devious [ˈdiːvɪəs] *adj* **1** [+ *person, mind*] 不光明正大的 **2** [+ *route, path*] 迂回的

devise [dɪˈvaɪz] *vt* **1** [+ *plan, scheme*] 想出 **2** [+ *machine*] 设计

devoid [dɪˈvɔɪd] *adj* ♦ **devoid of sth** (*lacking*) 毫无某物

devote [dɪˈvəut] *vt* ♦ **to devote time/energy to sth** 为某事付出时间/精力 ♦ **to devote o.s. to sth** 致力于某事

devoted [dɪˈvəutɪd] *adj* **1** (*enthusiastic*) 热中的 **2** (*loving*) [+ *husband, daughter etc*] 忠诚的 **3** ♦ **devoted to sth** (*specialising in*) 致力于某事的 ♦ **to be devoted to sb** 深爱某人 ♦ **Horace is devoted to his garden** 霍勒斯热中于园艺

devotion [dɪˈvəuʃən] *n* [u] **1** (*to person*) 热爱 **2** (*to duty, job etc*) 献身

devour [dɪˈvauə(r)] *vt* **1** (*eat*) 狼吞虎咽似地吃 **2** (*read*) 贪婪地读

devout [dɪˈvaut] *adj* [+ *person*] 虔诚的 ♦ **a devout Catholic/Muslim** *etc* 虔诚的天主教徒/穆斯林{等}

dew [djuː] *n* [u] 露水

diabetes [daɪəˈbiːtiːz] *n* [u] 糖尿病

diabetic [daɪəˈbɛtɪk] **I** *adj* **1** [+ *person, patient*] 患糖尿病的 **2** [+ *coma*] 糖尿病的 **3** [+ *chocolate, jam*] 糖尿病患者食用的 **II** *n* [c] 糖尿病患者

diagnose [daɪəgˈnəuz] *vt* [+ *illness, problem*] 诊断 ♦ **to be diagnosed as ...** [*person* +] 被诊断为患了…; [*illness* +] 被诊断为… ♦ **to be diagnosed as suffering from/having ...** 被诊断为患有…

diagnosis [daɪəgˈnəusɪs] (*pl* **diagnoses**) *n* [c/u] 诊断

diagonal [daɪˈægənl] **I** *adj* [+ *line*] 斜的 **II** *n* [c] **1** (*in geometry*) 对角线 **2** (*in pattern or design*) 斜纹

diagonally [daɪˈægənəlɪ] *adv* 倾斜地

diagram [ˈdaɪəgræm] *n* [c] 图解

dial [ˈdaɪəl] **I** *n* [c] **1** (*on clock or meter*) 标度盘 **2** (*on radio*) 调谐度盘 **3** (*on telephone*) 拨号盘 **II** *vt* [+ *number*] 拨 **III** *vi* 拨号 ♦ **can I dial London direct?** 我可以直接往伦敦打电话吗？

dialect [ˈdaɪəlɛkt] *n* [c/u] 方言

dialling code [ˈdaɪəlɪŋ-] [英] *n* [c] 电话区号 [美 = **area code**]

dialling tone [ˈdaɪəlɪŋ-] [英] *n* [c] 拨号音 [美 = **dial tone**]

dialogue (美 **dialog**) [ˈdaɪəlɔg] *n* [c/u] **1** (*conversation*) 对话 **2** (*discussions*) 交换意见 **3** (*in play, film, novel etc*) 对白

dial tone [美] *n* = **dialling tone**

diameter [daɪˈæmɪtə(r)] *n* [c] 直径 ♦ **15 cm in diameter** 直径为15厘米

diamond [ˈdaɪəmənd] **I** *n* [c] **1** (*gem*) 钻石 **2** (*shape*) 菱形 **II diamonds** *n* [*pl*] (*on playing cards*) 方块 ♦ **the six/king of diamonds** 方块6/K

diaper [ˈdaɪəpə(r)] [美] *n* [c] 尿布 [英 = **nappy**]

diarrhoea (美 **diarrhea**) [daɪəˈriːə] *n* [u] 腹泻 ♦ **to have diarrhoea** 腹泻

diary [ˈdaɪərɪ] *n* [c] **1** (*engagements book*) 日记簿 **2** (*daily account*) 日记 ♦ **to keep a diary** 记日记 ♦ **video/tape diary** 录像带/磁带日记

dice [daɪs] (*pl* **dice**) **I** *n* **1** [C] (*in game*) 骰子 **2** [U] (*game*) 掷骰赌博 **II** *vt* (*in cooking*) 将…切成丁

dictate [*vb* dɪk'teɪt, *n* 'dɪkteɪt] **I** *vt* **1** [+ *letter, memo etc*] 口述 **2** (*determine*) [+ *conditions*] 规定 **II** *vi* ♦**to dictate to sb** (*order about*) 命令某人 **III** *n* [C] (*order*) 命令 ♦**the dictates of one's conscience** 某人的做人原则 ♦**common sense dictates that ...** 依据常识…

dictation [dɪk'teɪʃən] *n* **1** [U] [*of letter*] 口述 **2** [C/U] (*at school, college*) 听写

dictator [dɪk'teɪtə(r)] [贬] *n* [C] **1** (*ruler*) 独裁者 **2** (*overbearing person*) 霸道的人

dictatorship [dɪk'teɪtəʃɪp] *n* **1** [C/U] (*government*) 独裁政府 **2** [C] (*country*) 独裁国家

dictionary ['dɪkʃənrɪ] *n* [C] 词典

did [dɪd] *pt of* **do**

didn't ['dɪdnt] = **did not**

✪ **die** [daɪ] **I** *vi* **1** [*person, animal, plant* +] 死 **2** [*love, hope* +] 消失 **3** [*engine* +] 熄灭 **II** *n* [C] (*pl* **dice**) (*for games*) 骰子 ♦**to die of** *or* **from sth** 死于某事 ♦**to die a natural/violent death** 自然死亡/惨死 ♦**to be dying** [*person, plant, animal* +] 奄奄一息 ♦**old habits die hard** 积习难改 ♦**I'm dying of thirst/boredom** 我渴死了/无聊死了 ♦**to be dying for sth/to do sth** 渴望某事/做某事

❑ **die away** *vi* [*sound, light* +] 逐渐消失

❑ **die down** *vi* **1** [*wind* +] 停止 **2** [*fire* +] 熄灭 **3** [*excitement, controversy, laughter* +] 平息

❑ **die out** *vi* **1** [*custom, way of life* +] 灭亡 **2** [*species* +] 灭绝

📖 用法参见 **dead**

> 📖 在需要解释某人的死亡原因时，可以说他们**die of**或**die from**某个具体原因。*Both he and my mother died of cancer... He died from brain injuries five days later.* 还可以用**be dying of thirst, hunger, boredom**或者**curiosity**来强调非常口渴、饥饿、厌倦或好奇的状态。这是非正式用法。*Order a pot of tea, I'm dying of thirst.*

diesel ['diːzl] *n* **1** [U] (*also* ***diesel oil***) 柴油 **2** [C] (*vehicle*) 柴油机驱动的车辆

diet ['daɪət] **I** *n* **1** [C/U] (*food intake*) 饮食 **2** [C] (*restricted food*) (*medical*) 特种饮食；(*slimming*) 减肥饮食 **3** ♦**a diet of mindless pop songs/soap operas** 多得令人腻烦的无聊的流行歌曲/肥皂剧 **II** *vi* 节食 **III** *cpd* [复合词] 特制的 ♦**to be on a diet** 实行减肥节食 ♦**to go on a diet** 开始减肥节食 ♦**to live on a diet of fish and rice** 以鱼和米为主食

differ ['dɪfə(r)] *vi* **1** (*be different*) ♦**to differ (from sth)** （与某物）不同 **2** (*disagree*) ♦**to differ (on sth)** （就某事）意见不同 ♦**to agree to differ** 同意保留各自不同意见

difference ['dɪfrəns] *n* **1** [C] (*between things, people*) 差异 **2** [S] (*between two quantities*) 差 **3** [C] (*disagreement*) 分歧 ♦**the difference in size/colour** 尺寸/颜色上的差异 ♦**to make a/no difference (to sb/sth)** （对某人/某事）有/无影响 ♦**I can't tell the difference between them** 我看不出他们的区别 ♦**to settle/resolve one's differences** 消除分歧

✪ **different** ['dɪfrənt] *adj* **1** (*not the same*) 不同的 **2** (*unusual*) 不同寻常的 ♦**different from** 与…不同 ♦**different to** *or* [美] **than** 与…不同

differentiate [dɪfə'rɛnʃɪeɪt] **I** *vi* ♦**to differentiate between one thing and another** 区分一事与另一事 **II** *vt* ♦**to differentiate sth from sth** (*distinguish*) 把某物与某物区分开；(*set apart*) 使某物与某物有区别

differently ['dɪfrəntlɪ] *adv* **1** [*feel, think etc* +] 不同地 **2** [*treat, regard* +] 有差异地 **3** [*shaped, designed* +] 不同地

✪ **difficult** ['dɪfɪkəlt] *adj* **1** [+ *task, problem, decision*] 困难的 **2** [+ *person, child*] 执拗的 ◊ *Don't be difficult!* 别那么执拗！♦**I found it difficult to ...** 我认为…很难 ♦**it is difficult being a parent** 为人父母很难 ♦**it is difficult for us to understand**

her 我们很难理解她 ♦ **it is difficult to save** 省钱是件难事

difficulty ['dɪfɪkəltɪ] *n* **1** [c] (*problem*) 困难 **2** [u] [*of question, exam*] 难度 ♦ **to have difficulty/difficulties** 有困难 ♦ **to be in difficulty** 陷入困境 ♦ **he stood up with difficulty** 他艰难地站了起来

dig [dɪg] (*pt, pp* **dug**) **I** *vt* **1** [+ *hole*] 挖 **2** [+ *garden*] 掘土 **3** ♦ **to dig sth into sth** (*sink*) 将某物伸进某物 **II** *vi* **1** (*with spade*) 挖掘 **2** ♦ **to dig into sth** (*sink*) 戳进 **III** *n* **1** (*prod*) ♦ **to give sb a dig in the ribs** 戳了某人肋部一下 **2** [c] (*also* ***archaeological dig***) (*excavation*) 考古挖掘 **3** [非正式] ♦ **to have/take a dig at sb** (*criticism*) 挖苦某人

❑ **dig in** (*also* ***dig o.s. in***) **I** *vi* [*soldiers* +] 挖壕固守 **II** *vt* [+ *compost*] 翻土时把…混入泥土中 ♦ **to dig one's heels in** (喻)坚持自己的立场

❑ **dig into** *vt* [不可拆分] [+ *savings*] 动用

❑ **dig out** *vt* **1** [+ *survivors, car*] 发掘出 **2** [非正式] (*find*) 找寻到

❑ **dig up** *vt* **1** [+ *plant, body*] 挖出 **2** [+ *land, area*] 掘起 **3** (*discover*) [+ *information, evidence*] 搜集

digest [*vb* daɪ'dʒɛst, *n* 'daɪdʒɛst] **I** *vt* **1** [+ *food, meal*] 消化 **2** [+ *facts, information etc*] 领会 **II** *vi* [*food, meal* +] 消化 **III** *n* [c] (*book*) 摘要

digestion [dɪ'dʒɛstʃən] *n* **1** [u] (*process*) 消化 **2** [c] (*system*) 消化能力

digit ['dɪdʒɪt] *n* [c] **1** (*number*) 0到9之间的任何一个数字 **2** [正式] (*finger*) 手指; (*toe*) 足趾

digital ['dɪdʒɪtl] *adj* **1** [+ *clock, watch etc*] 数字的 **2** [+ *recording, technology*] 数码的

digital camera *n* [c] 数码相机

digital television *n* [u] 数字电视

dignified ['dɪgnɪfaɪd] *adj* [+ *person, manner*] 高贵的

dignity ['dɪgnɪtɪ] *n* [u] **1** (*composure*) 庄严 **2** (*worth*) 尊严 **3** (*self-respect*) 高贵

digs [dɪgz] [英:非正式,过时] *n* [*pl*] (*lodgings*) 住宿处

dilemma [daɪ'lɛmə] *n* [c] (*political, moral*) 进退两难 ♦ **to be in a dilemma** 处在进退两难的境地

diligent ['dɪlɪdʒənt] *adj* **1** [+ *worker*] 勤奋的 **2** [+ *research, work*] 细致的

dilute [daɪ'lu:t] **I** *vt* **1** [+ *liquid*] 冲淡 **2** [+ *belief, principle*] 削弱 **II** *adj* [+ *liquid, solution*] 稀释的

dim [dɪm] **I** *adj* **1** (*not bright*) [+ *light*] 暗淡的; [+ *room, place*] 昏暗的 **2** (*unclear*) [+ *outline, figure*] 模糊的 **3** (*faint*) [+ *memory, sight*] 模糊的 **4** [+ *future, prospects*] 暗淡的 **5** [非正式] (*stupid*) 迟钝的 **II** *vt* **1** [+ *light*] 使变淡 **2** [美:汽车] ♦ **to dim one's lights** 打近光灯 [英 = **dip**] **III** *vi* [*light* +] 变暗 ♦ **to take a dim view of sth** 对某事持不赞成的态度

dime [daɪm] [美] *n* [c] 一角银币 ♦ **a dime a dozen** 多得很

dimension [daɪ'mɛnʃən] **I** *n* [c] **1** (*aspect*) 方面 **2** (*in maths, science*) 维 **II dimensions** *n* [*pl*] **1** (*measurements*) 面积 **2** (*scale, size*) 尺寸

diminish [dɪ'mɪnɪʃ] *vi, vt* 减小

dimple ['dɪmpl] *n* [c] 酒窝

din [dɪn] *n* [s] [+ *row, racket*] 喧闹声

dine [daɪn] [正式] *vi* 进餐

❑ **dine out** *vi* 外出吃饭

diner ['daɪnə(r)] *n* [c] **1** (*person*) 就餐者 **2** [美] (*restaurant*) 廉价餐馆

dinghy ['dɪŋgɪ] *n* [c] **1** (*inflatable*) (*also* ***rubber dinghy***) 橡皮筏 **2** (*also* ***sailing dinghy***) 小船

dingy ['dɪndʒɪ] *adj* **1** [+ *street, room*] 阴暗的 **2** [+ *clothes, curtains etc*] 邋遢的

dining car ['daɪnɪŋ-] [英] *n* [c] 餐车

dining room ['daɪnɪŋ-] *n* [c] **1** (*in house*) 饭厅 **2** (*in hotel*) 餐厅

dining table ['daɪnɪŋ-] *n* [c] 餐桌

dinner ['dɪnə(r)] *n* **1** [c/u] (*evening meal*) 晚餐 **2** [c/u] (*lunch*) 午餐 **3** [c] (*formal meal*) 正餐

📖 用法参见 **meal**

dinner jacket [英] *n* [c] 男用晚礼服 [美 = **tuxedo**]

dinner party *n* [c] 宴会

dinner time *n* [c/u] **1** (*in evening*) 晚饭时间 **2** (*at midday*) 午饭时间

dinosaur ['daɪnəsɔ:(r)] *n* [c] **1** 恐龙 **2** [贬] 庞然大物

dip [dɪp] **I** *vt* **1** (*into liquid*) [+ *bread, spoon, finger*] 蘸 **2** (*into container*) [+ *hand*] 伸进 **3** [英] [+ *headlights*] 使…变暗 [美 = **dim**] **II** *vi* **1** [*ground, road* +] 倾斜 **2** [*boat* +] 下降 **3** ♦ **to dip into sth** [+ *container*] 伸进某物; [+ *book*] 翻阅某物; [+ *savings*] 动用某物 **4** (*decrease, fall*) 下降 **III** *n* **1** [c] (*slope*) 斜坡 **2** (*swim*) ♦ **to take a dip/go for a dip** 下下水 **3** [c/u] (*sauce*) 奶油沙司 **4** [c] (*decrease*) 下降

diploma [dɪ'pləumə] *n* [c] 毕业文凭

diplomacy [dɪ'pləuməsɪ] *n* [u] **1** (*between governments*) 外交 **2** (*tact*) 外交手腕

diplomat ['dɪpləmæt] *n* [c] 外交官

diplomatic [dɪplə'mætɪk] *adj* **1** [+ *mission, solution etc*] 外交上的 **2** (*tactful*) [+ *person*] 老练的; [+ *answer, letter*] 圆滑的 ♦ **to break off/resume diplomatic relations (with sb)** (与某人) 断绝/恢复外交关系)

dipstick ['dɪpstɪk] [英] *n* [c] 量油尺

dire [daɪə(r)] *adj* **1** [+ *consequences, poverty*] 极端的 **2** [非正式] (*terrible*) 可怕的 ♦ **to be in dire straits** (*financially*) 捉襟见肘 ♦ **to be in dire need of sth** 极需某物

✪ **direct** [daɪ'rɛkt] **I** *adj* **1** [+ *route, flight*] 直达的 **2** [+ *sunlight, contact, experience, challenge*] 直接的 ◊ *"keep out of direct sunlight"* "避免阳光直接照射" ◊ *She died as a direct result of this injection.* 注射这支针剂是导致她死亡的直接原因。◊ *He avoided giving a direct answer.* 他避免作出直截了当的回答。**3** [+ *descendant*] 直系的 **II** *vt* **1** (*show*) 给…指路 ◊ *Could you direct them to my office, please?* 请您告诉他们如何到我的办公室，好吗？◊ *I directed the way for the stranger.* 我给那个陌生人指路。**2** (*send*) [+ *letter*] 寄往 ◊ *His mail is being directed to his new address.* 他的信件正寄往他的新住处。**3** (*focus*) [+ *attention, remark*] 集中于 **4** (*manage*) [+ *company, project etc*] 管理 **5** [+ *play, film, programme*] 导演 **6** [正式] (*order*) ♦ **to direct sb to do sth** 指引某人做某事 **III** *adv* (*directly*) [*go, write, fly* +] 直接地 ◊ *You can fly direct to Amsterdam from Liverpool.* 你可以从利物浦直接飞往阿姆斯特丹。♦ **to direct one's attention to sth** 把注意力集中于某物

direct debit [英] *n* [c/u] 直接借记

direction [dɪ'rɛkʃən] **I** *n* **1** [c] (*way*) (*for travelling*) 方向; (*of development*) 趋势 **2** [u] [*of film, play etc*] 导演 **II directions** *n* [*pl*] **1** (*to get somewhere*) 指路说明 **2** (*for doing something*) 用法说明 ♦ **sense of direction** 方向感 ♦ **in the direction of** (*towards*) 朝 ♦ **in all directions** (*everywhere*) 向四面八方 ♦ **to ask for directions** 问路 ♦ **directions for use** 使用说明

directly [dɪ'rɛktlɪ] *adv* **1** ♦ **directly above/below/in front** *etc* 正上/下/前方 {等} **2** (*straight*) [*go, fly* +] 径直地 **3** (*at once*) 立即 **4** (*as a direct result*) 直接地

✪ **director** [dɪ'rɛktə(r)] *n* [c] **1** [*of company*] 经理 **2** [*of organization, public authority*] 主任 **3** [*of play, film etc*] 导演

directory [dɪ'rɛktərɪ] *n* [c] **1** (*also **telephone directory***) 电话号码簿 **2** (*list of names, addresses etc*) 姓名地址录 **3** (*on computer*) 文件名录

directory enquiries [-ɪn'kwaɪərɪz] [英] *n* [u] 查号台 [美 = **information, directory assistance**]

dirt [də:t] *n* [u] **1** 污物 **2** (*earth*) 泥土 ♦ **to treat sb like dirt** 视某人如草芥

dirty ['də:tɪ] **I** *adj* **1** [+ *clothes, face etc*] 脏的 **2** [+ *joke, magazine*] 黄色的 **II** *vt* [+ *clothes, face etc*] 弄脏

dirty trick *n* [c] 卑鄙伎俩 ♦ **a dirty tricks campaign** 大骗局

disability [dɪsə'bɪlɪtɪ] *n* **1** [c] (*physical*) 伤残 **2** [c] (*mental*) 残疾 **3** [u] (*state of being disabled*) 残废

disabled [dɪs'eɪbld] **I** *adj* **1** (*physically*) 伤残的 **2** (*mentally*) 残疾的 **II** *n* [*pl*] ♦ **the disabled** 残疾人

disadvantage [dɪsəd'vɑ:ntɪdʒ] *n* [c/u] (*drawback*) 不利 ♦ **to be** *or* **work to sb's disadvantage** 对某人不利 ♦ **to be at a disadvantage** 处

于不利地位

disagree [dɪsə'griː] *vi* **1** ♦**to disagree (with sb)** 不同意（某人的观点）♦**to disagree (with sth)** （对某事表示）不同意 **2** [尤英] ♦**to disagree with sth** (*oppose*) 反对某事 ♦**I disagree with you** 我不同意你的看法 ♦**garlic disagrees with me** 大蒜不对我的口味

disagreeable [dɪsə'griːəbl] *adj* **1** [+ *encounter, experience, smell*] 令人不快的 **2** [+ *person*] 难相处的

disagreement [dɪsə'griːmənt] *n* **1** [U] (*objection*) 反对 **2** [C] (*argument*) 争执 ♦**to have a disagreement (with sb)** （与某人）意见不统一

disappear [dɪsə'pɪə(r)] *vi* **1** (*from view*) [*person, vehicle, object* +] 消失 **2** (*go missing*) 失踪 **3** (*cease to exist*) 消失 ♦**to disappear from view** 不见

disappearance [dɪsə'pɪərəns] *n* **1** [C/U] [*of person*] 失踪 **2** [C] (*loss, theft*) [*of vehicle, object*] 失窃 **3** [U] [*of custom, species*] 消失

disappoint [dɪsə'pɔɪnt] *vt* [+ *person*] 使失望

disappointed [dɪsə'pɔɪntɪd] *adj* 失望的 ♦**to be disappointed in sb** 对某人失望 ♦**to be disappointed that ...** 令人失望的是…

> 📖 请勿将 **disappointed** 与 **disappointing** 混淆。如果你 **disappointed**，表示你由于某事没有发生或某事不如期望的那么好而感到沮丧。*Helen was disappointed that he hadn't called...I know that my dad will be very disappointed when he hears my exam results.* 某事物 **disappointing** 表示该事物没有达到你的期望值，令你感到失望。*The food at the restaurant was disappointing.*

disappointing [dɪsə'pɔɪntɪŋ] *adj* [+ *result, book, performance*] 使人失望的

📖 用法参见 **disappointed**

disappointment [dɪsə'pɔɪntmənt] *n* **1** [U] (*emotion*) 失望 **2** [C] (*cause*) 令人失望的人/事 ♦**to my disappointment** 令我失望的是

disapproval [dɪsə'pruːvəl] *n* [U] 不赞成

disapprove [dɪsə'pruːv] *vi* ♦**to disapprove (of sb/sth)** 不同意（某人/某事）

disarm [dɪs'ɑːm] **I** *vt* **1** [+ *soldier, terrorist*] 解除…的武装 **2** (*win over*) 消除 **II** *vi* (*give up weapons*) 放下武器

disarmament [dɪs'ɑːməmənt] *n* [U] 裁军

disaster [dɪ'zɑːstə(r)] *n* [C/U] **1** (*earthquake, flood etc*) 灾难 **2** (*accident, crash etc*) 灾祸 **3** (*fiasco*) 惨败 **4** (*serious situation*) 灾难

disastrous [dɪ'zɑːstrəs] *adj* **1** (*catastrophic*) 灾难性的 **2** (*unsuccessful*) 惨败的

disbelief ['dɪsbə'liːf] *n* [U] 怀疑 ♦**in disbelief** 怀疑地

disc [dɪsk] *n* [C] **1** (*round, flat object*) 圆盘 **2** (*in backbone*) 椎间盘 **3** [过时] (*record*) 唱片 **4** [计算机] = **disk**

discard [dɪs'kɑːd] *vt* [+ *unwanted object*] 丢弃；[+ *idea, plan, system*] 抛弃

discern [dɪ'səːn] [正式] *vt* **1** (*see*) 隐约看见 **2** (*identify*) 看出

discharge [*vb* dɪs'tʃɑːdʒ, *n* 'dɪstʃɑːdʒ] **I** *vt* **1** [+ *waste, water, blood*] 排出 **2** (*from hospital*) 允许…离开 **3** (*from armed services*) 使…离开 **4** (*from court/prison*) 释放 **5** [+ *duties*] 使免除 **6** [正式] (*settle*) [+ *debt*] 清偿 **7** [过时] (*fire*) [+ *gun, weapon*] 射出 **II** *n* **1** [C/U] [正式] [*of waste, gas*] 排放 **2** [C/U] [正式] (*from eye, wound*) 分泌物 **3** [U] (*dismissal*) [*of patient*] 出院证明；[*of soldier*] 退役；[*of defendant*] 释放

discipline ['dɪsɪplɪn] **I** *n* **1** [U] [*of children, pupils*] 纪律 **2** [U] (*self-control*) 约束 **3** [C] (*branch of knowledge*) 学科 **II** *vt* **1** (*train*) ♦**to discipline o.s. (to do sth)** 训练自己（做某事）**2** (*punish*) 惩处

disc jockey *n* [C] 简称为DJ，意为广播电台或迪斯科舞厅流行音乐唱片播放及介绍人

disclose [dɪs'kləuz] *vt* [+ *information*] 透露 ♦**to disclose that ...** (*reveal*) 透露…

disco ['dɪskəu] *n* **1** (*nightclub*) 迪斯科舞厅 **2** (*event*) 迪斯科

discoloured (美 **discolored**) [dɪs'kʌləd] *adj* 褪色的

discomfort [dɪs'kʌmfət] **I** *n* [U] **1** (*in body*) 不舒服 **2** (*unease*) 不安 **II discomforts** *n* [*pl*] 不舒服的事

disconnect [dɪskə'nɛkt] *vt* **1** [+ *pipe, tap, hose etc*] 拆开 **2** [+ *computer, cooker, TV etc*] 断开 **3** ♦**to be disconnected** (*for non-payment of bill*) 被切断; (*during telephone conversation*) 被中断

discontent [dɪskən'tɛnt] *n* [C] 不满意

discontented [dɪskən'tɛntɪd] *adj* 不满的

discontinue [dɪskən'tɪnju:] *vt* **1** [正式] [+ *visits, treatment*] 停止 **2** [正式] [+ *payments*] 中止 **3** ♦**to be discontinued** [*product* +] 停产

discount [*n* 'dɪskaunt, *vb* dɪs'kaunt] **I** *n* [C/U] 折扣 **II** *vt* **1** [+ *goods*] 打折扣 **2** (*ignore, reject*) 不理会 ♦**to give sb a discount on sth** 给予某人某物的折扣 ♦**at a discount** (*cheaply*) 在打折出售

discourage [dɪs'kʌrɪdʒ] *vt* **1** (*dishearten*) [+ *person*] 使泄气 **2** (*dissuade*) ♦**to discourage sb from doing sth** 劝某人不做某事 **3** [+ *activity*] 设法阻止 ♦**to be discouraged** 感到气馁

discover [dɪs'kʌvə(r)] *vt* 发现 ♦**to discover that ...** (*find out*) 发现… ♦**to discover how to do sth** 发现如何做某事

> **discover, find** 和 **find out** 都可以表示"发现"。*He discovered the whole school knew about it...The young child finds that noise attracts attention...We found out that she was wrong.* **discover** 比 **find** 更正式，多用于科研文章或正式的调查报告中，比如，**discover** 某种疾病的治疗方法。还可以用 **discover** 表示意外地发现某物。*This well-known flower was discovered in 1903.* 如果你看不到你想找的东西，可以说你无法 **find** 它，而不能用 **discover** 或 **find out**。*I'm lost – I can't find the bridge.* 可以说某人 **find out** 某个事实，而不能用 **find** 和 **discover**。*I found out the train times.*

discovery [dɪs'kʌvərɪ] *n* **1** [C/U] [*of treasure, cure*] 发现 **2** [C] (*thing found*) 被发现的事物 ♦**to make a discovery** 发现 ♦**the discovery that ...** …的发现

discredit [dɪs'krɛdɪt] *vt* **1** [+ *person, group*] 使丧失名誉 **2** [+ *claim, idea*] 使不可信

discreet [dɪs'kri:t] *adj* **1** (*diplomatic*) [+ *person, remark*] 谨慎的 **2** (*quiet, secretive*) 悄声的 **3** [+ *decor, appearance, place*] 精巧的 ♦**at a discreet distance** 保持一定恭敬的距离

discrepancy [dɪs'krɛpənsɪ] *n* [C/U] ♦**discrepancy (between two things)** (*inconsistency*) （两者间的）差异 ♦**a discrepancy in sth** 在某事上存在的差异

discretion [dɪs'krɛʃən] *n* [U] (*tact*) 谨慎 ♦**at the discretion of sb** [正式] 由某人自行处理 ♦**to have the discretion to do sth** [正式] 有做某事的决定权 ♦**to use one's discretion** [正式] 由某人自行决定

discriminate [dɪs'krɪmɪneɪt] *vi* **1** ♦**to discriminate between two things** 区别两种事物 **2** ♦**to discriminate against/in favour of sb** 歧视/特别优待某人

discrimination [dɪskrɪmɪ'neɪʃən] *n* [U] **1** (*bias*) 歧视 **2** (*discernment*) 辨别力 ♦**racial/sexual discrimination** 种族/性别歧视

discuss [dɪs'kʌs] *vt* **1** (*talk over*) 讨论 **2** (*analyse*) 论述 ♦**to discuss what/how/who ...** 讨论做什么/如何/谁做…

discussion [dɪs'kʌʃən] *n* [C/U] **1** (*talk*) 讨论 **2** (*debate*) (*in article, lecture etc*) 论述 ♦**under discussion** 正在讨论中

disdain [dɪs'deɪn] **I** *n* [U] 蔑视 **II** *vt* 蔑视 **III** *vi* ♦**to disdain to do sth** 不屑做某事

disease [dɪ'zi:z] *n* **1** [C/U] (*illness*) 病 **2** [C] [文] (*affliction*) 弊病

disembark [dɪsɪm'bɑ:k] [正式] *vi*

[*passengers* +] 离船/下飞机/下车

disgrace [dɪs'greɪs] **I** *n* [U] (*shame, dishonour*) 耻辱 **II** *vt* [+ *one's family, country*] 使受耻辱 ♦ **it's a disgrace!** 这是件丢人的事! ♦ **to be a disgrace to sb** (*cause of shame*) 是某人的耻辱

disgraceful [dɪs'greɪsful] *adj* [+ *behaviour, condition, state*] 可耻的

disgruntled [dɪs'grʌntld] *adj* [+ *person, tone*] 不满的

disguise [dɪs'gaɪz] **I** *n* **1** [C] (*make-up, costume*) 伪装品 **2** [U] (*art*) 乔装打扮 **II** *vt* **1** ♦ **(to be) disguised (as sth/sb)** [*person* +] 假扮成(某物/某人) **2** [+ *fact, emotions*] 掩饰 **3** [+ *voice*] 伪装 ♦ **in disguise** 乔装着 ♦ **there's no disguising the fact that ...** 毫不隐瞒事实真相… ♦ **to disguise o.s. (as sb)** 把自己假扮(成某人)

disgust [dɪs'gʌst] **I** *n* [U] 厌恶 **II** *vt* 使厌恶 ♦ **she walked off in disgust** 她厌恶地走开了

disgusted [dɪs'gʌstɪd] *adj* 感到厌恶的

disgusting [dɪs'gʌstɪŋ] *adj* **1** (*revolting*) [+ *food, habit*] 令人作呕的 **2** (*disgraceful*) [+ *behaviour, situation*] 讨厌的

dish [dɪʃ] **I** *n* [C] **1** (*piece of crockery*) (*for serving*) 盘;(*for eating*) 碟 **2** (*contents*) 盘 **3** (*recipe, food*) 一道菜 **4** (*also* ***satellite dish***) 盘形物 **II dishes** *n* [*pl*] 碗碟 ♦ **to do** *or* **wash the dishes** 刷洗碗碟
❑ **dish out** *vt* **1** (*serve*) [+ *food*] 分配 **2** (*give out*) [+ *money, books, drugs*] 分发;[+ *advice, criticism*] 施加
❑ **dish up** [非正式] **I** *vt* [+ *food*] 把…盛在盘中端上 **II** *vi* 装盘上菜

dishcloth ['dɪʃklɔθ] *n* [C] (*for drying dishes*) 擦碗布;(*for washing dishes*) 洗碗布

dishonest [dɪs'ɔnɪst] *adj* **1** [+ *person*] 不诚实的 **2** [+ *behaviour*] 不正直的

dishonourable (美 **dishonorable**) [dɪs'ɔnərəbl] *adj* [+ *person, behaviour*] 不光彩的

dish soap [美] *n* [U] 洗洁剂 [英 = **washing-up liquid**]

dishtowel ['dɪʃtauəl] [美] *n* [C] 擦碗布 [英 = **tea towel**]

dishwasher ['dɪʃwɔʃə(r)] *n* [C] 洗碗机

dishwashing liquid ['dɪʃwɔʃɪŋ-] [美] *n* [U] 洗洁剂 [英 = **washing-up liquid**]

disillusioned [dɪsɪ'luːʒənd] ♦ **(to become) disillusioned (with sth)** (变得)(对某事)不抱幻想

disinfect [dɪsɪn'fɛkt] *vt* [+ *object, wound, water*] 给…消毒

disinfectant [dɪsɪn'fɛktənt] *n* [C/U] 消毒剂

disintegrate [dɪs'ɪntɪgreɪt] *vi* **1** [*object* +] 支离破碎 **2** [*marriage, partnership* +] 崩溃 **3** [*organization* +] 瓦解

disk [dɪsk] *n* [C] [计算机] (*hard*) 硬盘; (*floppy*) 软盘

disk drive *n* [C] 磁盘驱动器

diskette [dɪs'kɛt] *n* [计算机] = **disk**

dislike [dɪs'laɪk] **I** *n* **1** [U] (*feeling*) ♦ **dislike (of sb/sth)** 讨厌(某人/某物) **2** [C] (*object of dislike*) 不喜欢的东西 **II** *vt* 不喜欢 ♦ **to take a dislike to sb/sth** 厌恶某人/某事 ♦ **one's likes and dislikes** 某人的爱好和厌恶 ♦ **I dislike the idea** 我不喜欢这个主意 ♦ **to dislike doing sth** 不喜欢做某事

dislocate ['dɪsləkeɪt] [+ *finger, shoulder, jaw etc*] 使…脱臼 ♦ **he has dislocated his shoulder** 他的肩膀脱臼了

disloyal [dɪs'lɔɪəl] *adj* (*to country, family, friend*) 不忠诚的

dismal ['dɪzml] *adj* **1** (*depressing*) [+ *weather, place, mood*] 阴沉的 **2** (*very bad*) [+ *prospects, record, failure*] 令人忧郁的

dismantle [dɪs'mæntl] *vt* **1** [+ *machine, structure*] 拆除 **2** [+ *organisation, system*] 废除

dismay [dɪs'meɪ] **I** *n* [U] 气馁 **II** *vt* 使气馁 ♦ **much to my dismay** 颇令我失望

dismiss [dɪs'mɪs] *vt* **1** [+ *worker*] 解雇 **2** (*send away*) 让…离开 **3** [+ *case, charge*] 驳回 **4** [+ *possibility, problem, idea*] 不考虑

dismissal [dɪs'mɪsl] *n* **1** [C/U] (*sacking*) 解雇 **2** [U] (*disregard*) 不予考虑

disobedience [dɪsə'biːdɪəns] *n* [U] 不服从

disobedient [dɪsə'biːdɪənt] *adj* 不服从的

disobey [dɪsə'beɪ] *vt* **1** [+ *person*] 不顺从 **2** [+ *order*] 不服从

disorder [dɪs'ɔːdə(r)] *n* **1** [U] (*untidiness*) 杂乱 **2** [U] (*rioting*) 动乱 **3** [C] (*illness*) 失调 ♦**civil/public disorder** 市民动乱

disorganized [dɪs'ɔːgənaɪzd] *adj* **1** [+ *person*] 缺乏条理的 **2** [+ *event*] 无序的

disown [dɪs'əun] *vt* **1** [+ *action, comment*] 否认同…有关系 **2** [+ *child*] 不认

dispatch, despatch [dɪs'pætʃ] **I** *vt* **1** (*send*) [+ *message, goods, mail*] 发送; [+ *messenger, soldiers*] 派遣 **2** [过时] (*deal with*) [+ *business*] 迅速办理 **3** [过时] (*kill*) [+ *person, animal*] 杀死 **II** *n* **1** [U] (*sending*) 派遣 **2** [C] (*report*) 报告

dispel [dɪs'pɛl] *vt* [+ *idea, fear*] 消除

dispense [dɪs'pɛns] *vt* **1** [+ *medicines*] 配 **2** [+ *advice, justice*] 施与 **3** [*machine* +] [+ *product*] 售出 ❑**dispense with** *vt* [不可拆分] **1** (*get rid of*) 摆脱 **2** (*do without*) 用不着

dispenser [dɪs'pɛnsə(r)] *n* [C] (*machine*) 自动售货机

disperse [dɪs'pəːs] **I** *vt* **1** [+ *smoke, leaflets, crowd*] 驱散 **II** *vi* **1** [*oil, smoke, fog, cloud* +] 散去 **2** [*crowd* +] 散开

displace [dɪs'pleɪs] *vt* **1** (*supplant*) 取代 **2** ♦**to be displaced** [*people* +] 背井离乡

display [dɪs'pleɪ] **I** *n* **1** [C] (*in shop, at exhibition*) 陈列 **2** [C] (*exhibition*) 展览 **3** [C/U] (*show*) [*of feeling*] 表现 **4** [C] (*information on screen*) 显示 **5** [C] (*screen*) 显示屏 **II** *vt* **1** (*show*) [+ *exhibits*] 陈列; [+ *feelings, courage*] 表现; (*proudly*) 炫耀 **2** [+ *results, information*] 显示 ♦**on display** [+ *exhibits, goods, work*] 正在展览的

displease [dɪs'pliːz] *vt* (*offend, annoy*) 使不高兴

disposable [dɪs'pəuzəbl] *adj* [+ *lighter, nappy, razor*] 一次性的 ♦**disposable income** 可支配的收入

disposal [dɪs'pəuzl] *n* [U] 清理 ♦**to have sth at one's disposal** 手边有某物 ♦**to put sth at sb's disposal** 把某事交某人自由处理

dispose [dɪs'pəuz] ♦**to dispose of** *vt* [不可拆分] **1** (*get rid of*) [+ *body, unwanted goods*] 把…处理掉 **2** (*deal with*) [+ *problem, task*] 处理 **3** [正式] (*kill*) 干掉

disposed [dɪs'pəuzd] *adj* [正式] (*inclined, willing*) ♦**to be disposed to do sth** 倾向于做某事 ♦**to be well/favourably/ill disposed towards sb** 认为…很好/不好

disposition [dɪspə'zɪʃən] *n* **1** [C] (*nature*) 性情 **2** [正式] ♦**a disposition to do sth** (*inclination*) 做某事的倾向 ♦**of a nervous disposition** 生性紧张的

disproportionate [dɪsprə'pɔːʃənət] *adj* [+ *amount, effect*] 不相称的 ♦**disproportionate to sth** 与某事不相称的

disprove [dɪs'pruːv] *vt* [+ *belief, theory*] 证明…不成立

dispute [dɪs'pjuːt] **I** *n* [C/U] **1** (*between people*) 争论 **2** (*industrial*) 争执 **3** (*between countries, organizations*) 争端 **II** *vt* [+ *fact, statement*] 对…提出质疑; [+ *ownership, rights*] 争夺 ♦**to be in dispute** [*people, countries* +] 有纠纷; [+ *issue*] 有争论 ♦**I don't dispute that ...** 我毫不怀疑…

disqualify [dɪs'kwɔlɪfaɪ] *vt* [+ *team, competitor*] 取消…的资格 ♦**to disqualify sb from (doing) sth** 取消某人(做)某事的资格 ♦**to be disqualified from driving** [英] 被取消驾驶的资格

disregard [dɪsrɪ'gɑːd] **I** *vt* (*ignore*) 不理 **II** *n* [U] ♦**disregard (for sth)** 忽视(某事)

disrupt [dɪs'rʌpt] *vt* **1** (*interrupt*) [+ *conversation, meeting*] 扰乱 **2** (*disturb*) [+ *plan, process*] 妨碍

disruption [dɪs'rʌpʃən] *n* [C/U] **1** (*interruption*) 扰乱 **2** (*disturbance*) 混乱

dissatisfaction [dɪssætɪs'fækʃən] *n* [U] 不满

dissatisfied [dɪs'sætɪsfaɪd] *adj* ♦**dissatisfied (with sth)** (对某事)

不满

dissect [dɪ'sɛkt] *vt* **1** [+ *animal, body*] 解剖 **2** (*scrutinize*) [+ *theory, work*] 仔细分析

dissent [dɪ'sɛnt] **I** *n* [U] (*disagreement*) 异议 **II** *vi* (*disagree*) 不同意

dissertation [dɪsə'teɪʃən] *n* [C] 学位论文

dissolve [dɪ'zɔlv] **I** *vt* **1** (*in liquid*) 溶解 **2** ♦ **to be dissolved** [*organization, marriage* +] 终结; [*parliament* +] 被解散 **II** *vi* [*material* +] 溶解 ♦ **to dissolve in(to) tears/laughter** 情不自禁地流泪/大笑起来

distance ['dɪstns] **I** *n* **1** [C/U] (*between two places*) 距离 **2** [U] (*remoteness*) 遥远 **3** [U] [正式] (*reserve*) 冷淡 **II** *vt* ♦ **to distance o.s. (from sb/sth)** 逐渐疏远(某人/某物) ♦ **in the distance** 在远处 ♦ **from a distance** 从远处 ♦ **what's the distance to London?** 到伦敦的距离有多远? ♦ **to be some distance/quite a distance/a fair distance from sth** (*far*) 距离某物相当远 ♦ **within walking distance** 步行可到 ♦ **(at) a distance of 2 metres** 相距两米的距离 ♦ **keep your distance!** 保持距离!

distant ['dɪstnt] *adj* **1** [+ *place*] 远的 **2** [+ *future, past*] 久远的 **3** [+ *relative, cousin*] 远房的 **4** (*aloof*) [+ *person, manner*] 冷淡的 **5** (*absent*) [+ *person, look*] 茫然的

distil (美 **distill**) [dɪs'tɪl] *vt* **1** [+ *water, whisky*] 蒸馏 **2** (*extract*) [+ *information, ideas etc*] ♦ **distilled from sth** 提取某物的精华

distillery [dɪs'tɪlərɪ] *n* [C] 酒厂

distinct [dɪs'tɪŋkt] *adj* **1** (*different*) 截然不同的 **2** (*clear*) [+ *smell, flavour etc*] 明显的 **3** (*unmistakable*) [+ *advantage, change*] 明确的 ♦ **as distinct from** (*in contrast to*) 不同于

distinction [dɪs'tɪŋkʃən] *n* **1** [C] (*difference*) 区别 **2** (*honour*) ♦ **to have the distinction of being sth** 具有成就某事的杰出表现 **3** [C] (*in exam*) (*honour, award*) 优秀 ♦ **to draw** *or* **make a distinction (between two things)** 区分(两事物) ♦ **a writer/wine of distinction** 知名作家/葡萄酒

distinctive [dɪs'tɪŋktɪv] *adj* 与众不同的

distinguish [dɪs'tɪŋgwɪʃ] **I** *vt* **1** [正式] (*identify*) [+ *details, sounds*] 辨别 **2** ♦ **to distinguish one thing from another** (*differentiate*) 将一事物于另一事物区别开来 **3** ♦ **to distinguish sb/sth from others** (*set apart*) 使某人/某物显得与众不同 **II** *vi* ♦ **to distinguish between truth and fiction** 分清事实和虚构 ♦ **to distinguish o.s.** 出名

distinguished [dɪs'tɪŋgwɪʃt] *adj* **1** (*eminent*) 杰出的 **2** (*in appearance*) 高贵的

distinguishing [dɪs'tɪŋgwɪʃɪŋ] *adj* ♦ **distinguishing feature/characteristic** 明显的特征

distort [dɪs'tɔːt] *vt* **1** [+ *statement, fact, idea*] 歪曲 **2** [+ *sound, shape, image*] 使失真

distract [dɪs'trækt] *vt* [+ *person*] 使分心 ♦ **to distract sb's attention** 分散某人的注意力

distracted [dɪs'træktɪd] *adj* 心烦意乱的

distraction [dɪs'trækʃən] *n* **1** [C/U] (*diversion*) 精神涣散 **2** [C] (*amusement*) 消遣 ♦ **to drive sb to distraction** 使某人发狂

distraught [dɪs'trɔːt] *adj* 心烦意乱的

distress [dɪs'trɛs] **I** *n* [U] 极度忧伤 **II** *vt* (*cause anguish to*) 使忧伤 ♦ **in distress** [*ship, aircraft etc* +] 遭难的; [*person* +] 处于危难中

distressing [dɪs'trɛsɪŋ] *adj* [+ *experience, time*] 使人痛苦的

distribute [dɪs'trɪbjuːt] *vt* **1** (*hand out*) [+ *food, leaflets*] 分发 **2** (*share out*) [+ *resources, profits, work etc*] 分配 **3** (*supply*) [+ *goods*] (*to shops*) 配送

distribution [dɪstrɪ'bjuːʃən] *n* **1** [U] [*of food, supplies, newspaper*] 分发 **2** [C/U] [*of resources, wealth, power*] 分布 **3** [U] [*of films*] 发行

distributor [dɪs'trɪbjutə(r)] *n* [C] **1** (*in business*) 批发商 **2** (*in car engine*) 配电盘

district ['dɪstrɪkt] *n* [C] **1** [*of country, town*] 地区 **2** (*official area*) 行政区 **3** (*in titles*) 区

district attorney [美] *n* [c]地方检察官

distrust [dɪs'trʌst] **I** *n* [U] 怀疑 **II** *vt* 不信任

disturb [dɪs'tɜːb] *vt* **1** (*interrupt*) 打扰 **2** (*upset*) 使心烦 **3** (*rearrange*) [+ *belongings, papers etc*] 弄乱 ♦**sorry to disturb you** 对不起，打扰您了

> 请勿将**interrupt**与**disturb**混淆。如果你**interrupt**某个正在讲话的人，表示你说或做某事打断他们讲话。*He tried to speak, but she interrupted him.* 如果想要跟某个正在讲话或开会的人谈话，正确的表达是*Sorry to interrupt.* 如果**interrupt**某个过程或者活动，就意味着使它中断一段时间。*The match took nearly three hours and was interrupted at times by rain.* 如果**disturb**某人，就是使他们停止了正在做的事情并且令他们感到不快。*Find a quiet, warm, comfortable room where you won't be disturbed.*

disturbance [dɪs'tɜːbəns] *n* **1** [c/U] (*upheaval, upset*) 干扰 **2** [c] (*violent incident*) 骚乱 **3** [c/U] (*emotional, psychological*) 失调 ♦**to cause a disturbance** 引起混乱

disturbed [dɪs'tɜːbd] *adj* **1** (*worried, anxious*) 不安的 **2** (*unhappy*) [+ *childhood, relationship etc*] 有问题的 **3** (*traumatised, damaged*) 精神失常的 ♦**mentally disturbed** 精神受困扰的 ♦**emotionally disturbed** 情绪失常的

disturbing [dɪs'tɜːbɪŋ] *adj* [+ *experience, situation, aspect*] 令人不安的

disused [dɪs'juːzd] *adj* [+ *building*] 废弃的

ditch [dɪtʃ] **I** *n* [c] **1** (*at roadside, in field*) 沟 **2** (*also* ***irrigation ditch***) 沟渠 **II** *vt* [非正式][+ *partner*] 同…断绝关系；[+ *car, sofa etc*] 丢弃；[+ *plan, policy*] 抛弃

dither ['dɪðə(r)] [贬] *vi* 犹豫不决

ditto ['dɪtəu] *adv* 同样地

dive [daɪv] **I** *vi* **1** [*swimmer* +] (*into water*) 跳水；(*under water*) 潜水 **2** [*bird* +] 俯冲 **3** [*fish, submarine* +] 潜入水中 **4** ♦**to dive into/under sth** (*leap*) 钻入某物中/下 **5** ♦**to dive into sth** [+ *bag, drawer etc*] 把手伸进某物 **II** *n* [c] **1** (*into water*) 跳水 **2** (*underwater*) 潜水 **3** [非正式，贬] (*place*) 下等娱乐场所 **4** (*in football*) ♦**to take a dive** 假摔

diver ['daɪvə(r)] *n* [c] 潜水员

diverse [daɪ'vɜːs] *adj* 多种多样的

diversion [daɪ'vɜːʃən] *n* **1** [c] [英] (*for traffic*) 临时改道 [美=**detour**] **2** [c/U] (*distraction*) 注意力的转移 **3** [c/U] [*of profits, funds*] 转移 **4** [c/U] [*of ship*] 转向 ♦**to create a diversion** 转移注意力

diversity [daɪ'vɜːsɪtɪ] *n* **1** [U] (*variety*) 多样性 **2** (*range*) ♦**a diversity of** 各种各样的

divert [daɪ'vɜːt] *vt* **1** (*re-route*) [+ *traffic, plane*] 使绕道行驶 **2** [+ *money, resources*] 转移 **3** (*amuse*) 使欢娱 ♦**to divert (sb's) attention from sth** 转移(某人)对某事的注意力

divide [dɪ'vaɪd] **I** *vt* **1** ♦**to divide (up)** (*separate*) (*into groups, areas*) 划分 **2** (*in maths*) 除 **3** ♦**to divide sth between/among sb/sth** (*share*) 在两个/3个以上的人/物之间分配某物 **4** ♦**to divide sth (from sth)** (*keep separate*) [*road, frontier* +] 将某物(与某物)分隔 **5** (*split*) 使有分歧 **II** *vi* **1** [*people* +] (*into groups*) 分开 **2** [*cells* +] 分裂 **III** *n* [c] (*gulf, rift*) 分水岭 ♦**to divide sth in half** 将某物一分为二 ♦**40 divided by 5** 40除以5 ♦**divide 7 into 35** 7除35

divided highway [dɪ'vaɪdɪd-] [美] *n* [c] 有隔离带的高速公路 [英=**dual carriageway**]

divine [dɪ'vaɪn] **I** *adj* **1** (*from God*) [+ *inspiration, punishment*] 神的 **2** [过时](*wonderful*) 极好的 **II** *vi* ♦**to divine for sth** [+ *water, metal*] 勘探某物

diving ['daɪvɪŋ] *n* [U] **1** (*underwater*) 潜水 **2** (*from board*) 跳水

diving board *n* [c] 跳水板

divinity [dɪ'vɪnɪtɪ] *n* **1** [U] (*quality of being divine*) 神性 **2** [c] (*god, goddess*) 神 **3** [U] (*theology*) 神学

division [dɪ'vɪʒən] *n* **1** [U] (*splitting*

up) 分开 **2** [u] [数] 除法 **3** [u] (*sharing out*) [*of labour, resources*] 分配 **4** [c/u] (*gulf*) 分歧 **5** [c] (*department*) 部门 **6** [c] (*military unit*) 师 **7** [c] (*in sport, especially football*) 级 **8** [c] [英] (*in parliament*) 分组表决

divorce [dɪ'vɔːs] **I** *n* [c/u] 离婚 **II** *vt* **1** [+ *spouse*] 与…离婚 **2** [正式] (*dissociate*) ♦ **to divorce sth from sth** 将某事与某事脱离 **III** *vi* 离婚

divorced [dɪ'vɔːst] *adj* 离异的 ♦ **to be divorced from sb** 与某人离婚 ♦ **to get divorced** 离婚

divorcee [dɪvɔː'siː] *n* [c] 离了婚的人

DIY [英] *n abbr* (= ***do-it-yourself***) 自己动手的活计 ♦ **to do DIY** 自己动手做

> **DIY**
> 英国人对**DIY**很上瘾，有时幽默地称其为一种全民性消遣。**DIY**意为**do-it-yourself**，是指自己动手制作和修理东西，尤其是在家里。房主不雇佣专业的建筑工人、木匠或油漆匠，这样不仅省钱，还能从自己动手改进家里的设备、环境中得到莫大的满足感。专门的**DIY**商店销售工具、油漆和其他能满足**DIY**爱好者嗜好的用品。

dizzy ['dɪzɪ] *adj* **1** ♦ **to feel dizzy** 感到头晕 **2** [+ *turn, spell*] 头晕的 **3** [+ *woman, blonde*] 傻乎乎的 ♦ **the dizzy heights of ...** 使人晕乎乎的…高度 ♦ **to make sb dizzy** 使人头晕目眩

DJ *n abbr* **1** (= ***disc jockey***) 简称为DJ，意为广播电台或迪斯科舞厅流行音乐唱片播放及介绍人 **2** [英] (= ***dinner jacket***) 男用晚礼服 [美 = **tuxedo**]

DNA *n abbr* (= ***deoxyribonucleic acid***) 脱氧核糖核酸

✪ **do**

KEYWORD

[duː] (*pt* **did**, *pp* **done**)

I *vt*

1 (*be engaged in, achieve*) 做 ♦ **what are you doing?** 你在做什么呢？ ♦ **what is he doing here?** 他怎么在这儿？ ♦ **are you doing anything tomorrow evening?** 你明晚有什么打算？ ♦ **what you should do is ...** 你应该做的是… ♦ **we must do everything possible to help them** 我们必须想尽一切办法帮助他们 ♦ **what did you do with the money?** (*how did you spend it*) 你怎么用这笔钱的？; (*where did you put it*) 你把钱放哪儿了？ ♦ **what are you going to do about this?** 你打算对此怎么办？

2 (*for a living*) ♦ **what do you do?** 你做什么工作？

3 (*with noun*) ♦ **to do the cooking** 做饭 ♦ **to do one's teeth/hair** 刷牙/做头发 ♦ **we're doing "Othello" at school** (*studying it*) 我们正在学校里学习«奥赛罗»; (*performing it*) 我们正在学校里排演«奥赛罗»

4 (*referring to speed, distance*) ♦ **the car was doing 100** 汽车以100英里的时速行进 ♦ **we've done 200 km already** 我们的时速已达到了200公里

5 (*cause*) ♦ **the explosion did a lot of damage** 爆炸造成了很大损失 ♦ **a holiday will do you good** 休次假会对你有好处

II *vi*

1 (*act, behave*) 做 ♦ **do as I do** 跟我做 ♦ **do as I tell you** 按我告诉你的做

2 (*get on*) 进展 ♦ **he's doing well/badly at school** 他的学习成绩很好/很差 ♦ **the firm is doing well** 这个公司业绩良好 ♦ **"how do you do?" – "how do you do?"** "你好" "你好"

3 (*suit*) 行 ♦ **will it do?** 行吗？ ♦ **it doesn't do to upset her** 不可以让她心烦意乱

4 (*be sufficient*) 足够 ♦ **will £15 do?** 15镑够吗？ ♦ **that'll do** 足够了 ♦ **that'll do!** (*in annoyance*) 够了！

III *aux vb*

1 (*in negative constructions*) ♦ **I don't understand** 我不懂 ♦ **she doesn't want it** 她不想要这个 ♦ **he didn't seem to care** 他看起来并不在乎 ♦ **don't be silly!** 别傻了！

2 (*to form questions*) ♦ **do you like jazz?** 你喜欢爵士乐吗？ ♦ **what do you think?** 你怎么想？ ♦ **where does she live?** 她住在哪里？ ♦ **didn't you know?** 你难道不知道吗？ ♦ **why didn't you come?** 你为什么没来？
3 (*for emphasis, in polite expressions*) ♦ **people do make mistakes sometimes** 有时人们的确犯一些错误 ♦ **she does seem rather late** 看来她的确是晚了 ♦ **do sit down/help yourself** 赶快坐啊/千万别客气 ♦ **do take care!** 千万保重！ ♦ **oh do shut up!** 噢，赶快闭嘴吧！
4 (*used to avoid repeating vb*) 用于避免动词的重复 ♦ **I make more money than he does** 我比他挣得钱多 ♦ **they say they don't care, but they do** 他们说不在乎，但实际是在乎的 ♦ **he asked me to help him and I did** 他让我帮一下忙，我照做了 ♦ **(and) so do I** 我也是 ♦ **and neither did we** 我们也不 ♦ **better than I do** 比我做得好 ♦ **"who made this mess?" – "I did"** "是谁弄得乱七八糟的？" "是我" ♦ **"do you have a metal detector?" – "no, I don't"** "你有金属检测器吗？" "不，我没有"
5 (*in question tags*) ♦ **I don't know him, do I?** 我不认识他，是吗？ ♦ **you like him, don't you?** 你喜欢他，不是吗？ ♦ **she lives in London, doesn't she?** 她住在伦敦，不是吗？
IV *n* [英：非正式] (*party etc*) 聚会 ♦ **we're having a little do on Saturday** 我们星期六有个小型聚会 ♦ **it was quite a do** 那是个相当大型的聚会
❑ **do away with** *vt* [不可拆分] (*get rid of*) 处理掉
❑ **do for** [非正式] *vt* [不可拆分] ♦ **to be done for** 完蛋 ♦ **if I can't finish this report, I'm done for** 如果完不成这份报告，我就完蛋了
❑ **do in** [非正式] *vt* (*kill*) 干掉
❑ **do out of** [非正式] *vt* (*deprive of*) 夺去 ♦ **he did me out of my share** 他把我那份儿夺去了
❑ **do up** *vt* [不可拆分] **1** (*fasten*) [+ *laces*] 系紧；[+ *dress, coat, buttons*] 扣上 **2** [尤英] (*renovate*) [+ *room, house*] 装修
❑ **do with** *vt* [不可拆分] **1** (*need*) ♦ **I could do with a drink/some help** 我想喝一杯/需要帮助 **2** (*be connected*) ♦ **to have to do with** 与…有关 ♦ **what has it got to do with you?** 这跟你有什么关系？ ♦ **I won't have anything to do with it** 我跟这事毫不相干 ♦ **it has to do with money** 这跟钱有关 ♦ **it was something to do with football** 这是与足球有关的
❑ **do without I** *vt* [不可拆分] 没有…也行 **II** *vi* 不用也行

d.o.b. *abbr* (= ***date of birth***) 出生日期

dock [dɔk] **I** *n* **1** [C] [航海] 船坞 **2** ♦ **the dock** (*in law court*) 刑事法庭的被告席 **3** [C/U] [植] 一种阔叶野草，名为酸模 **II** *vi* **1** [*ship* +] 入船坞 **2** [*spacecraft* +] 对接 **III** *vt* **1** [+ *salary, wages*] 扣减 **2** [+ *ship*] 靠码头 **3** [+ *spacecraft*] 使对接 **IV docks** *n* [*pl*] [航海] 港区

dockyard [ˈdɔkjɑːd] *n* [C] 船舶修造厂

doctor [ˈdɔktə(r)] **I** *n* [C] **1** (*medic*) 医生 **2** ♦ **the doctor's** 诊所 **3** (*PhD etc*) 博士 **II** *vt* [+ *food, drink*] 下药；[+ *figures, photograph*] 窜改 ♦ **doctor's office** [美] 诊所 [英 = **surgery**]

document [*n* ˈdɔkjumənt, *vb* ˈdɔkjumɛnt] **I** *n* [C] **1** (*gen*) 文件 **2** [计算机] 文档 **II** *vt* 记录…事实

documentary [dɔkjuˈmɛntərɪ] **I** *n* [C] 纪录片 **II** *adj* [+ *evidence*] 书面的

documentation [dɔkjumənˈteɪʃən] *n* [U] 证件

dodge [dɔdʒ] **I** *vt* **1** [+ *blow, ball, car*] 躲开 **2** [+ *tax, military service*] 逃避 **3** [+ *question, issue etc*] 搪塞 **II** *vi* 躲闪 **III** *n* [C] (*trick*) 诡计 ♦ **to dodge out of the way** 躲开

dodgy [ˈdɔdʒɪ] [非正式] *adj* **1** (*suspect*) [+ *person, deal*] 狡猾的 **2** (*risky, unsafe*) 冒险的

does [dʌz] *vb see* **do**

doesn't ['dʌznt] = **does not**
dog [dɔg] **I** *n* [c] **1** 狗 **2** (*male*) 雄兽 **II** *vt* [*problems, injuries* +] 缠住 ♦**to go to the dogs** 大不如前
do-it-yourself ['duːɪtjɔː'sɛlf] **I** *n* [ʊ] 自己动手的活计 **II** *adj* [+ *store*] 出售供购买者自行装配物品的
dole [dəul] [非正式] *n* [ʊ] [英] ♦**(the) dole** (*payment*) 失业救济金 [美 = **welfare**] ♦**(to be) on the dole** [英] 靠失业救济金生活 [美 = **on welfare**]
❑**dole out** *vt* **1** [+ *food*] 发放 **2** [+ *money*] 施舍
doll [dɔl] *n* [c] (*toy*) 娃娃
✪**dollar** ['dɔlə(r)] *n* [c] (货币单位) 元
dolphin ['dɔlfɪn] *n* [c] 海豚
dome [dəum] *n* [c] 圆屋顶
domestic [də'mɛstɪk] *adj* **1** [+ *flight, politics, news*] 国内的 **2** [+ *appliances*] 家用的 **3** [+ *chores, violence*] 家庭的 **4** [+ *animal*] 驯养的
domesticated [də'mɛstɪkeɪtɪd] *adj* **1** [+ *animal*] 驯化的 **2** [+ *person*] 居家型的
dominant ['dɔmɪnənt] *adj* [+ *position, role, figure*] 占主导地位的
dominate ['dɔmɪneɪt] *vt* **1** [+ *discussion, place*] 在…中占首要地位 **2** [+ *person*] 支配
Dominican Republic [də'mɪnɪkən-] *n* ♦**the Dominican Republic** 多米尼加共和国
domino ['dɔmɪnəu] (*pl* **dominoes**) *n* [c] 多米诺骨牌 ♦**domino effect** 多米诺效应
dominoes ['dɔmɪnəuz] *n* [ʊ] 多米诺骨牌游戏
donate [də'neɪt] *vt* **1** ♦**to donate (to sb)** [+ *money, clothes*] 捐赠(给某人) **2** [+ *blood, organs*] 捐献
donation [də'neɪʃən] *n* **1** [ʊ] (*act of giving*) 捐赠 **2** [c] (*contribution*) 捐赠物 **3** [c/ʊ] [*of blood, organs*] 捐献
done [dʌn] *pp of* **do**
donkey ['dɔŋkɪ] *n* [c] 驴
donor ['dəunə(r)] *n* [c] **1** [*of blood, heart, kidney etc*] 捐献者 **2** (*to charity*) 捐赠者
donor card *n* [c] 器官捐献卡
don't [dəunt] = **do not**
donut ['dəunʌt] [美] *n* = **doughnut**
doodle ['duːdl] **I** *n* [c] 涂鸦 **II** *vi* 涂鸦
doom [duːm] **I** *n* [ʊ] **1** (*ruin*) 毁灭 **2** (*fate*) 厄运 **3** (*feeling of depression*) 悲观 **II** *vt* ♦**to be doomed to failure** 注定要失败
✪**door** [dɔː(r)] *n* [c] **1** [*of house, room, railway carriage*] 门 **2** (*doorway*) 门口 ♦**to answer the door** 应门 ♦**out of doors** 在门外 ♦**from door to door** 挨家挨户地
doorbell ['dɔːbɛl] *n* [c] 门铃
door handle *n* [c] 门把手
doorknob ['dɔːnɔb] *n* [c] 门上的球形把手
doorstep ['dɔːstɛp] *n* [c] 门前台阶 ♦**on one's doorstep** 很近
doorway ['dɔːweɪ] *n* [c] 门口 ♦**in the doorway** 在门口
dope [dəup] **I** *n* [非正式] **1** [ʊ] (*cannabis*) 麻醉品 **2** [ʊ] (*illegal drug*) 毒品 **3** [c] (*person*) 呆子 **4** [ʊ] (*information*) 内部消息 **II** *vt* [+ *horse, person*] 给…服麻醉品
dormitory ['dɔːmɪtrɪ] *n* [c] **1** (*room*) 宿舍 **2** [美] (*building*) 宿舍楼 [英 = **hall of residence**]
dosage ['dəusɪdʒ] *n* [c] 用药计量; (*on label*) 用量
dose [dəus] **I** *n* [c] **1** [*of medicine*] 一剂 **2** [英] (*bout*) [*of flu*] 一次 **II** *vt* ♦**to dose sb/o.s. (up) with aspirin** *etc* 给某人/自己服阿斯匹林{等}
dot [dɔt] **I** *n* [c] **1** (*small round mark*) 圆点 **2** (*speck, spot*) (*in the distance*) 小点 **II** *vt* [+ *area, landscape*] 星罗棋布于 ♦**on the dot** (*punctually*) 准时地 ♦**dotted with** 密布着
dot-com [dɔt'kɔm] *n* [c] 网络公司
dotted line ['dɔtɪd-] *n* [c] 虚线 ♦**to sign on the dotted line** 签字画押
double ['dʌbl] **I** *adj* **1** [+ *doors, tracks*] 双的 **2** [+ *murder, wedding*] 成双的 **3** [+ *helping, share, whisky, garage*] 双份的 **4** (*for two*) [+ *room, sheet*] 双人的 **II** *n* **1** ♦**to be sb's double** 酷似某人 **2** [c] (*drink*) 双份 **III** *vt* [+ *offer, size*] 使…增至两倍 **IV** *vi* [*population, size* +] 变成两倍 ♦**double five two six** [英] (*5526*) 五五二六 ♦**it's spelt with a double "M"** 它的拼写中有两个"M" ♦**double the size/number (of**

sth) (是某物) 大小/数量的两倍 ◆**double in size/weight** 两倍大/重 ◆**to double as sth** 兼做某事 ◆**at** *or* **on the double** [非正式] (*immediately*) 迅速地
❑**double back** *vi* [*person* +] 原路折回
❑**double up** **I** *vi* **1** (*bend over*) 直不起腰 **2** (*share room*) 共用 **II** *vt* 使…身体弯曲 ◆**to be doubled up with pain/laughter** 痛得/笑得弯下了身

double bass *n* [c/u] 低音提琴

double bed *n* [c] 双人床

double-check ['dʌbl'tʃɛk] **I** *vt* 再检查 **II** *vi* 复查

double-click ['dʌbl'klɪk] *vi* 双击

double-decker ['dʌbl'dɛkə(r)] [尤英] *n* [c] (*bus*) 双层公共汽车

double glazing [-'gleɪzɪŋ] [英] *n* [u] 双层玻璃

double room *n* [c] 双人房

doubles ['dʌblz] [网球] *n* [u] 双打

doubly ['dʌblɪ] *adv* 加倍地

doubt [daut] **I** *n* [c/u] (*uncertainty*) 怀疑 **II** *vt* **1** (*disbelieve*) [+ *person*] 怀疑; [+ *person's word*] 不信 **2** (*mistrust, suspect*) 怀疑 ◆**without (a) doubt** 无疑地 ◆**to be in doubt** 不确定 ◆**beyond doubt** 毫无疑问地 ◆**no doubt** 无疑地 ◆**to doubt if** *or* **whether ...** 拿不准是否… ◆**I doubt it (very much)** 我(很)怀疑 ◆**I don't doubt that ...** 我毫不怀疑…

doubtful ['dautful] *adj* **1** (*questionable*) ◆**it is doubtful that/whether ...** 不能确定…/是否… **2** (*unconvinced*) [+ *person*] ◆**to be doubtful that/whether ...** 怀疑…/是否… ◆**to be doubtful about sth** 对某事有怀疑 ◆**I'm a bit doubtful** 我有点怀疑

doubtless ['dautlɪs] *adv* 无疑地

dough [dəu] *n* [u] **1** 生面团 **2** [非正式] (*money*) 钱

doughnut (美 **donut**) ['dəunʌt] *n* [c] 炸面饼圈

dove [dʌv] *n* [c] (*bird*) 鸽子

✪**down** [daun] **I** *n* [u] (*soft feathers*) 绒毛 **II** *adv* **1** (*downwards*) 向下 ◊ *She looked down.* 她向下看。**2** (*in a lower place*) 在下面 ◊ *They're down on the ground floor.* 他们在下面底层。**3** (*in or towards the south*) 在南方 ◊ *They live down in London.* 他们住在伦敦。◊ *They've gone down south to London.* 他们南下去伦敦。**III** *prep* **1** (*towards lower level*) 沿着…往下 ◊ *They walked down the steps.* 他们沿着台阶往下走。**2** (*at lower part of*) 在下面 ◊ *She lives down the street.* 她住在街那边。◊ *a ledge 40ft down the rock face* 在岩石表面以下40英尺处的岩石架 **3** (*along*) 沿着 ◊ *He walked down the road.* 他沿街走去。**IV** *vt* [非正式] [+ *drink*] 喝下 ◆**down there** 在那儿 ◆**down here** 在这儿 ◆**the price of meat is down** (*lower*) 肉的价格下降了 ◆**I've got it down in my diary** (*written*) 我已把它写进了日记里 ◆**to pay 5 pounds down** [尤美] 现付5英镑 ◆**England are two goals down** (*behind*) 英格兰落后两球 ◆**I'm down to my last five pounds** 我就剩最后5英镑了 ◆**five down, two to go** 完成了5项，还剩两项 ◆**to be down for sth** 被安排做某事 ◆**down with X!** 打倒X! ◆**it's all down to hard work** 都是由于工作太辛苦的缘故 ◆**to down tools** [英] 停工

down-and-out ['daunəndaut] *n* [c] (*tramp*) 穷困潦倒的人

downfall ['daunfɔːl] *n* [c] **1** (*failure*) 垮台 **2** (*cause of failure*) ◆**to be sb's downfall** 是某人垮台的原因

downhill ['daun'hɪl] **I** *adv* **1** [*go, drive, walk* +] 向坡下 **2** [*face, look* +] 往山下 **II** *n* [c] (*also* ***downhill race***) (*in skiing*) 下坡滑雪比赛 ◆**to go downhill** (喻) [*business, person* +] 每况愈下

Downing Street ['daunɪŋ-] [英] *n* ◆**10 Downing Street** 唐宁街10号

> **DOWNING STREET**
> **Downing Street** 在伦敦威斯敏斯特区，是英国首相和财政部大臣的官邸所在(分别为10号和11号)。媒体常用唐宁街来指首相或政府。

download ['daunləud] *vt* 下载

downright ['daunraɪt] **I** *adj* (*used for*

emphasis) 彻头彻尾的 **II** *adv* (*used for emphasis*) 十分地

Down's syndrome [daunz-] *n* [U] 唐氏综合征

downstairs ['daun'stɛəz] **I** *adv* **1** (*on or to floor below*) 楼下 **2** (*on or to ground level*) 在一层 **II** *adj* 楼下的

down-to-earth ['dauntu'ə:θ] *adj* [*+ person, manner*] 务实的

downtown ['daun'taun] [美] **I** *adv* **1** [*be, work +*] 在市中心 **2** [*go +*] 去市中心 **II** *adj* ♦ **downtown Chicago** 芝加哥的市中心

down under [英: 非正式] *adv* (*in Australia or New Zealand*) 澳大利亚和新西兰

downward ['daunwəd] **I** *adj* 向下的 **II** *adv* = **downwards** ♦ **a downward trend** 没落的趋势

downwards ['daunwədz] *adv* 向下

doz. *abbr* (= ***dozen***) 一打

doze [dəuz] **I** *vi* 打瞌睡 **II** *n* [S] 瞌睡 ♦ **to have a doze** 打个瞌睡

❑ **doze off** *vi* 打盹

dozen ['dʌzn] *n* [C] 一打 ♦ **a dozen books** 一打书 ♦ **two dozen eggs** 两打鸡蛋 ♦ **dozens of** 许多

Dr (尤美 **Dr.**) *abbr* **1** (= ***doctor***) 医生 **2** (= ***Drive***) 私家车道

drab [dræb] *adj* [*+ building, clothes*] 单调的

draft [drɑ:ft] **I** *n* **1** [C] (*first version*) 草稿 **2** [C] [*of bill*] 草案 **3** [C] (*bank draft*) 汇票 **4** ♦ **the draft** [美: 军] 征兵 **II** *vt* **1** [*+ letter, book, speech*] 起草 **2** [军] ♦ **to be drafted** 应征入伍 **3** ♦ **to draft sb in** (*to do a job*) 选派某人 *see also* **draught**

drag [dræg] **I** *vt* **1** (*pull*) [*+ large object, body*] 拖 **2** (*force*) ♦ **to drag sb out of a car/upstairs** 把某人从车里拖出来/拖到楼上 **3** (喻) ♦ **it's impossible to drag him out of bed/out of the house** 让他下床/离开房子是不可能的 **4** (*search*) [*+ river, lake*] 打捞 **II** *vi* [*time, film +*] 拖沓 **III** *n* **1** [非正式] ♦ **a drag** 累赘 **2** (*women's clothing*) ♦ **in drag** 男人穿着女子服装 **3** [U] [航海, 航空] 阻力 ♦ **to drag your feet** *or* **heels** 故意拖沓 ♦ **to drag sth out of sb** 逼某人交待某事

❑ **drag away** *vt* ♦ **to drag sb away (from sth)** 迫使某人离开(某物) ♦ **to drag o.s. away (from sth)** 迫使自己离开(某物)

❑ **drag on** *vi* [*meeting, concert, war +*] 拖延

❑ **drag out** *vt* (*prolong*) 拖长

dragon ['drægn] *n* [C] 龙

dragonfly ['drægənflaɪ] *n* [C] 蜻蜓

drain [dreɪn] **I** *n* **1** [C] (*in street*) 排水沟 **2** ♦ **to be a drain on sth** [*+ resources, funds*] 某物的大量的消耗 **II** *vt* **1** [*+ land, marsh, pond*] 排去…的水 **2** [*+ vegetables*] 使…流干 **3** [*+ liquid*] 排掉 **4** [*+ glass, cup*] 喝干 **5** (*exhaust*) [*+ person*] 使…精疲力竭 **III** *vi* [*liquid +*] 流入 ♦ **to feel drained (of energy** *or* **emotion)** 感到(精力{或}感情)耗尽 ♦ **(to go) down the drain)** [非正式] 白费

drainage ['dreɪnɪdʒ] **I** *n* [U] 排水 **II** *cpd* [复合词] [*+ ditch, system*] 排水系统

drainpipe ['dreɪnpaɪp] *n* [C] 排水管

drama ['drɑ:mə] *n* **1** [U] (*theatre*) 戏剧 **2** [C] (*play*) 一出戏剧 **3** [C/U] (*excitement*) 戏剧性

dramatic [drə'mætɪk] **I** *adj* **1** (*marked, sudden*) 戏剧性的 **2** (*exciting, impressive*) 激动人心的 **3** (*theatrical*) 戏剧的 **II** *cpd* [复合词] [*+ society, group*] 戏剧的

dramatics [drə'mætɪks] *n* [U] 业余的戏剧活动

drank [dræŋk] *pt of* **drink**

drape [dreɪp] *vt* [*+ cloth, flag, clothing*] 披上

drapes [dreɪps] [美] *n* [*pl*] 窗帘 [英 = **curtains**]

drastic ['dræstɪk] *adj* **1** [*+ measure, step etc*] 严厉的 **2** [*+ change, reduction*] 剧烈的

draught (美 **draft**) [drɑ:ft] **I** *n* [C] [*of air*] 气流 **II** *adj* [*+ beer, bitter etc*] 散装的 ♦ **on draught** [*+ beer*] 散装的

draughts [drɑ:fts] [英] *n* [U] 西洋跳棋 [美 = **checkers**]

✪ **draw** [drɔ:] (*pt* **drew**, *pp* **drawn**) **I** *vt* **1** [*+ picture, map*] 画 **2** (*pull*) [*+ cart*] 拖 **3** [*+ curtains, blinds*] (*close*) 拉上; (*open*) 拉开 **4** ♦ **to draw sth/sb somewhere** (*move*) 把某人/某物拉到某地 ◊ *He drew his chair nearer the fire.* 他把椅子拉到炉火旁。

5 (*take out*) [+ *gun, knife, sword*] 拔出
6 (*attract*) [+ *response*] 引起
7 [+ *breath*] 吸 8 ♦**to draw (out) money from a bank/an account** 从银行/帐户上取钱◊ *He drew fifty pounds from his savings account.* 他从活期帐户上取走了50英镑。
9 [+ *wages, salary*] 领取 10 [+ *water*] 汲取 11 ♦**to draw a conclusion (from sth)** (从某事中)得出结论
12 ♦**to draw a comparison/distinction (between two things)** (在两事物之间)作一比较 **II** *vi*
1 (*with pen, pencil etc*) 画画 2 ♦**to draw near/close/away** (*move*) 走近/开 3 ♦**to draw (with/against sb)** [尤英:体育] (与某人)打成平局 ◊ *Brazil drew against Spain.* 巴西队与西班牙队战平。[美=**tie**]
III *n* [c] 1 [尤英:体育] 平局◊ *The match ended in a draw.* 比赛以平局告终。[美=**tie**] 2 (*lottery*) 抽奖 ◊ *She won 200 pounds in a prize draw.* 她在一次抽奖中赢了200英镑。
♦**to draw (sb's) attention (to sth)** 吸引(某人的)注意力(到某物)
♦**to draw near** *or* **close** (*approach*) [*person, event* +] 临近 ♦**to draw level/alongside** 慢慢接近 ♦**to draw to a close** 结束

❑**draw in I** *vi* [英][*nights* +] 变长 ◊ *The nights draw in and the mornings get darker.* 黑夜变长，早晨天色变得昏暗。**II** *vt* (*also* ***draw into***) (*involve*) 使参与◊ *She's the perfect hostess, drawing everyone into the conversation.* 她是位出色的主持人，能使每个人都参与到谈话中来。

❑**draw on I** *vt* [不可拆分] (*also* ***draw upon***) [+ *resources*] 凭借◊ *The company drew on its vast resources to fund the project.* 公司凭借其大量的资源为这个项目提供资金。; [+ *imagination, knowledge*] 靠◊ *He drew on his imagination to write about Moscow.* 他靠想像力描写莫斯科。**II** *vi* (*pass*) 临近◊ *As the afternoon drew on, we got impatient.* 随着下午的临近，我们变得不耐烦起来。

❑**draw out** *vi* ♦**draw out (of)** [*train, bus* +] (*leave*) 离开◊ *The train drew out of the station.* 火车驶离车站。

❑**draw up I** *vi* (*stop*) [*car, bus etc* +] 停下来◊ *Just before eleven a bus drew up.* 就在11点前，一辆公共汽车停了下来。**II** *vt*
1 [+ *document, plan*] 草拟◊ *I drew up plans for the new course.* 我为新课程草拟了计划。2 [+ *chair etc*] 拉近 ◊ *He drew up a chair and sat down.* 他把椅子拉近坐了下来。

drawback ['drɔːbæk] *n* [c] 欠缺

drawer [drɔː(r)] *n* [c] 1 [*of desk etc*] 抽屉 **II drawers** *n* [*pl*] [过时] (*knickers*) 内裤

drawing ['drɔːɪŋ] *n* 1 [c] (*picture*) 素描 2 [u] (*skill, discipline*) 绘画

drawing pin [英] *n* [c] 图钉 [美= **thumbtack**]

drawing room [过时] *n* [c] 客厅

drawn [drɔːn] **I** *pp of* **draw** **II** *adj* (*haggard*) 憔悴的

dread [drɛd] **I** *n* [u] ♦**dread (of)** (对…的)畏惧 **II** *vt* (*fear*) 惧怕

dreadful ['drɛdful] *adj* [+ *weather, day, person etc*] 糟透的 ♦**I feel dreadful!** (*ill*) 我觉得很不舒服!; (*ashamed*) 我感到心里不好受!

dream [driːm] (*pt, pp* **dreamed** *or* **dreamt**) **I** *n* [c] 1 (*when asleep*) 梦
2 (*ambition*) 梦想 **II** *vi* ♦**to dream about** (*when asleep*) 梦到 ♦**to have a dream about sb/sth** (*when asleep*) 梦到某人/某事 ♦**sweet dreams!** (*sleep well!*) 睡个好觉! ♦**to dream that ...** (*when asleep*) 梦见…; (*when wishing for sth*) 渴望… ♦**to dream of doing sth** (*fantasize*) 梦想着做某事 ♦**I wouldn't dream of...** 我永远不…

❑**dream up** *vt* [+ *plan, idea etc*] 凭空想出

dreamer ['driːmə(r)] *n* [c] 空想家

dreamt [drɛmt] *pt, pp of* **dream**

dreamy ['driːmɪ] *adj* 1 (*faraway*) [+ *expression*] 心不在焉的
2 (*gorgeous*) [+ *music, picture*] 梦幻般的

dreary ['drɪərɪ] *adj* [+ *place, time etc*] 沉闷的

drench [drɛntʃ] *vt* (*soak*) 使湿透 ♦**drenched to the skin** (*used for* *emphasis)* 浑身湿透

dress [drɛs] **I** *n* **1** [c] *(frock)* 连衣裙 **2** [u] *(clothing)* 服装 **II** *vt* **1** [+ *child*] 给…穿衣 **2** [+ *wound*] 敷裹 **3** [+ *salad*] 拌 **III** *vi* 穿衣 ♦ **to dress o.s., get dressed** 穿好衣服 ♦ **she dresses in jeans** 她身穿牛仔服 ❑ **dress down** *vi* 穿上便装 ❑ **dress up** *vi* **1** *(wear best clothes)* 穿上盛装 **2** ♦ **to dress up as** *(in fancy dress)* 化装成

dress circle [英] *n* [c] *(in theatre)* 二楼正座

dresser ['drɛsə(r)] *n* [c] **1** [英] *(cupboard)* 碗橱 **2** [美] *(chest of drawers)* 梳妆台 **3** ♦ **a smart dresser** 穿着利索的人

dressing ['drɛsɪŋ] *n* **1** [c] *(on a wound)* 敷料 **2** [c/u] ♦ **(salad) dressing** 调料

dressing gown *n* [c] 晨衣

dressing room *n* [c] **1** *(in a theatre)* 化装室 **2** *(in a sports stadium)* 更衣室

dressing table *n* [c] 梳妆台

dressmaker ['drɛsmeɪkə(r)] *n* [c] 做女服童装的裁缝

drew [druː] *pt of* **draw**

dribble ['drɪbl] **I** *vi* **1** *(trickle)* [*liquid* +] 一滴滴地流 **2** [*baby, person* +] 流口水 **3** *(in football, basketball)* 运球 **II** *vt* **1** *(in football, basketball)* [+ *ball*] 运 **2** [+ *liquid*] 使一滴滴地流

dried [draɪd] *adj* [+ *fruit, herbs*] 干的; [+ *eggs, milk*] 粉状的

drier ['draɪə(r)] *n* = **dryer**

drift [drɪft] **I** *vi* **1** [*boat* +] 漂流 **2** [*sand, snow, mist* +] 飘散 **II** *n* **1** [c] [*snow*] 吹积物 **2** [s/u] *(movement) (of people)* 迁移 **3** [s] *(meaning)* 大意 ♦ **to drift away** [*crowd, people* +] 散去 ♦ **to drift apart** [*friends, couple* +] 疏远 ♦ **to drift into** [+ *crime, prostitution*] 不知不觉地陷入 ♦ **to get** *or* **follow sb's drift** 明白某人的大意 ♦ **to get** *or* **follow the drift of sth** 明白某事的大意 ❑ **drift off** *vi* ♦ **to drift off (to sleep)** 慢慢睡着

drill [drɪl] **I** *n* **1** [c] *(tool, machine) (for DIY etc)* 钻; [*of dentist*] 钻头; *(for mining etc)* 钻孔器 **2** [u] *(fabric)* 斜纹布 **3** [c] *(for fire, air raid)* 演习 **II** *vt* **1** [+ *hole*] 在…上钻孔 **2** *(train)* [+ *troops*] 训练 **3** [+ *pupils*] *(in grammar, maths, singing etc)* 训练 **III** *vi* **1** ♦ **to drill (into)** [*wall, floor etc* +] (在…)钻孔 **2** ♦ **to drill (for)** [*oil, water, gas* +] 钻(探某物)

drink [drɪŋk] *(pt* **drank,** *pp* **drunk)** **I** *n* **1** [c] *(tea, water etc)* 饮料 **2** [c] *(alcoholic)* 酒 **3** [u] *(alcohol)* 饮酒 **II** *vt* [+ *tea, water etc*] 喝 **III** *vi* *(drink alcohol)* 喝酒 ♦ **to have a drink** 喝一杯; *(alcoholic)* 喝酒 ♦ **to take** *or* **have a drink of ...** 喝… ♦ **a drink of water** 一杯水 ♦ **would you like something to drink?** 你想喝点什么吗? ❑ **drink in** *vt* [+ *sight*] 陶醉于; [+ *words*] 听…听得出神 ❑ **drink to** *vt* [不可拆分] 为…干杯 ❑ **drink up** *vt, vi* 喝光

drink-driving ['drɪŋk'draɪvɪŋ] [英] *n* [u] 酒后驾车 [美 = **drunk driving**]

drinker ['drɪŋkə(r)] *n* [c] **1** ♦ **tea/coffee/beer drinker** 喝茶/咖啡/啤酒的人 **2** *(of alcohol)* 酗酒者 ♦ **a heavy/moderate/habitual drinker** *(of alcohol)* 过度/适度/习惯性饮酒者

drinking water ['drɪŋkɪŋ-] *n* [u] 饮用水

drip [drɪp] **I** *n* [c] **1** *(drop)* 一滴 **2** *(sound)* 水滴声 **3** [医] 滴液 **4** [非正式] *(person)* 讨厌鬼 **II** *vi* **1** [*water, rain* +] 滴下 **2** [*tap* +] 漏水 **3** [*washing, clothes etc* +] 滴水 **III** *vt* *(spill, trail)* 使滴下

✪ **drive** [draɪv] *(pt* **drove,** *pp* **driven)** **I** *n* **1** [c] *(journey)* 车程 ◊ *It's a thirty mile drive.* 有30英里的车程。**2** [c] *(also* ***driveway****)* 私家车道 ◊ *A private drive leads up to the palace.* 一条私家车道通往宫殿。**3** *(in road names)* ♦ **15 Alexander Drive** 亚历山大大道15号 **4** [u] *(energy)* 干劲 **5** [c] *(campaign)* 运动 ◊ *a drive to recruit more staff* 征召更多成员的运动 **6** [c] *(in golf)* 猛击 **7** [c] *(also* ***CD ROM/disk drive****)* 驱动器 **II** *vt* **1** [+ *vehicle*] 驾驶 ◊ *It's her turn to drive the car.* 该她驾车了。**2** ♦ **to drive sb to the station/airport** 驱车送某人去车站/飞机场 **3** *(run)* [+ *machine, motor, wheel*] 推动 **4** [+ *nail, stake etc*] ♦ **to**

drive sth into sth 把某物钉入某物 5 [*+ animal*] 驱赶 6 [*+ people*] 迫使 ◊ *The war drove thousands of people into Thailand.* 战争迫使成千上万的人进入泰国。7 [*+ ball*] 猛击 ◊ *Tom drove the ball into the net.* 汤姆将球击入网内。8 (*incite, encourage*) 驱使 ◊ *a man driven by greed and envy* 受到贪欲和嫉妒驱使的男人 **III** *vi* 1 (*at controls of vehicle*) 开车 ◊ *They have never learned to drive.* 他们从未学过开车。2 (*travel*) 开车 ♦ **to go for a drive** 开车兜风 ♦ **it's a 3-hour drive from London** 到伦敦要3个小时的车程 ♦ **left-/right-hand drive** 左/右手座驾驶 ♦ **front-/rear-wheel drive** 前/后轮驱动 ♦ **he drives a taxi/lorry** 他开出租车/卡车 ♦ **to drive sb mad/to desperation** 逼得某人发疯/绝望 ♦ **to drive sb to (do) sth** 迫使某人做某事 ♦ **to drive at 50 km an hour** 以每小时50公里的速度驾车 ♦ **what are you driving at?** 你是什么意思？

❑ **drive away** *vt* 赶走 ◊ *Increased crime is driving away customers.* 不断增长的犯罪赶走了顾客。

❑ **drive off I** *vt* (*repel*) 击退 ◊ *The government drove the guerrillas off using infantry.* 政府出动步兵团击退了游击队员。**II** *vi* [*car, driver +*] 驱车离开 ◊ *He drove off without saying goodbye.* 他没道别就驱车离开了。

❑ **drive on** *vi* 一直不停地开 ◊ *We drove on for a few miles.* 我们一直不停地开了几英里。

❑ **drive out** *vt* (*force to leave*) 逐出 ◊ *He cut his prices to drive out rivals.* 为了逐出竞争对手，他降低了价格。

drive-in ['draɪvɪn] [美] **I** *n* [c] (*restaurant*) 免下车餐馆；(*movie theater*) 免下车电影院 **II** *adj* [*+ restaurant, movie theater*] 免下车的

driven ['drɪvn] *pp of* **drive**

driver ['draɪvə(r)] *n* [c] 1 [*of own car*] 驾驶员 2 [*of taxi, bus, lorry, train*] 司机 3 (*chauffeur*) 司机

driver's license ['draɪvəz-] [美] *n* [c] 驾驶执照 [英 = **driving licence**]

driveway ['draɪvweɪ] *n* [c] 车道

driving ['draɪvɪŋ] **I** *n* [U] (*motoring*) 驾驶 **II** *adj* ♦ **driving rain/snow/wind** 瓢泼大雨/暴雪/暴风

driving instructor *n* [c] 驾驶教练

driving lesson *n* [c] 驾驶课

driving licence [英] *n* [c] 驾驶执照 [美 = **driver's license**]

driving test *n* [c] 驾驶执照考试

drizzle ['drɪzl] **I** *n* [s/U] 蒙蒙细雨 **II** *vi* ♦ **it is drizzling** 下着毛毛雨

droop [druːp] *vi* 1 [*flower +*] 发蔫 2 [*shoulders, head +*] 垂下

drop [drɔp] **I** *n* 1 [c] [*of liquid*] 滴 2 (*reduction*) ♦ **a drop in sth** 某物的下降 3 (*vertical distance*) ♦ **a 300m drop/a drop of 300m** 300米的落差 4 [c] (*also* ***air drop***) (*delivery*) (*by parachute etc*) 空投 **II** *vt* 1 (*accidentally*) 失手落下；(*deliberately*) 放 2 (*lower*) [*+ arm, leg, hand etc*] 垂下 3 [*+ voice*] 降低 4 (*reduce*) [*+ price*] 降低 5 (*drop off*) (*set down from car*) 将…送到 6 (*abandon*) [*+ idea, case etc*] 丢弃 7 (*from team*) 解雇 **III** *vi* 1 (*fall*) [*amount, level +*] 下降；[*object +*] 落下 2 (*flop*) 倒下 3 (*die down*) [*wind +*] 减弱 4 (*fall*) [*voice +*] 压低 **IV drops** *n* [*pl*] (*medicine*) 滴剂 ♦ **a drop of 10%** 10%的下降 ♦ **chocolate/fruit drops** 巧克力/水果球形糖 ♦ **to drop sb a line** 给某人留言 ♦ **to drop a hint** 随便暗示一下

❑ **drop by** *vi* 顺便拜访

❑ **drop in** [非正式] *vi* (*visit*) ♦ **to drop in (on sb)** 顺便拜访（某人）

❑ **drop off I** *vi* (*fall asleep*) 睡着 **II** *vt* [*+ passenger*] 将…送到

❑ **drop out** *vi* 1 (*withdraw*) 退出 2 (*of college, university etc*) 辍学

drought [draut] *n* [c/U] 旱灾

drove [drəuv] **I** *pt of* **drive II** *n* ♦ **droves of people** 一群群的人 ♦ **they came in (their) droves** 他们成群结队地进来

drown [draun] **I** *vt* 1 (*deliberately*) [*+ person, animal*] 使淹死 2 ♦ **to be drowned** 被淹死 3 (*also* ***drown out***) [*+ sound, voice*] 淹没 **II** *vi* [*person, animal +*] 溺死

drowsy ['drauzɪ] *adj* 昏昏欲睡的

✪ **drug** [drʌg] **I** *n* [c] **1** (*prescribed*) 药 ◊ *This drug is prescribed to treat hay fever.* 开的这种药是用来治疗花粉热的。**2** (*recreational*) 毒品 ◊ *Cocaine is a highly addictive drug.* 可卡因是一种极为容易上瘾的毒品。**II** *vt* (*sedate*) [+ *person, animal*] 使麻醉 ♦ **to be on drugs** 吸毒 ♦ **to take drugs** 吸毒 ♦ **hard/soft drugs** 硬/软毒品

drug addict *n* [c] 吸毒成瘾者

drug dealer *n* [c] 毒品贩子

druggist ['drʌgɪst] [美] *n* [c] **1** (*pharmacist*) (*person*) 药剂师 [英 = **chemist**] **2** ♦ **druggist('s)** (*shop*) 药店
📖 用法参见 **chemist**

drugstore ['drʌgstɔː(r)] [美] *n* [c] 杂货店 [英 = **chemist**]
📖 用法参见 **chemist**

drum [drʌm] **I** *n* [c] **1** (*instrument*) 鼓 **2** (*container*) 圆桶 **II** *vi* **1** [*rain* +] 发出敲击声 **2** (*with fingers*) 敲击 **III** *vt* [+ *fingers*] 敲打 **IV drums** *n* [*pl*] (*kit*) 鼓
❑ **drum into** *vt* 反复灌输
❑ **drum up** *vt* [+ *enthusiasm, support*] 竭力争取

drummer ['drʌmə(r)] *n* [c] 鼓手

drunk [drʌŋk] **I** *pp of* **drink II** *adj* 醉的 **III** *n* [c] (*drunkard*) 醉汉 ♦ **to get drunk** 喝醉了

drunk driving ['drʌŋk'draɪvɪŋ] [美] *n* [U] 酒后驾车 [英 = **drink-driving**]

drunken ['drʌŋkən] *adj* [+ *laughter, party, sleep*] 酒醉引起的; [+ *person*] 醉的

dry [draɪ] **I** *adj* **1** [+ *ground, clothes, paint*] 干的 **2** [+ *climate, weather, day*] 干燥的 **3** [+ *skin, hair*] 干枯的 **4** (*empty*) [+ *lake, riverbed, well*] 干涸的 **5** [+ *wine, sherry*] 不甜的 **6** [+ *humour, account*] 装成正经的 **7** (*uninteresting*) [+ *lecture, subject, style*] 枯燥无味的 **II** *vt* [+ *clothes, hair*] 把…弄干 **III** *vi* [*paint, washing* +] 变干 ♦ **on dry land** 在陆地上 ♦ **to dry (up) the dishes** 擦干碗碟 ♦ **to dry one's hands/hair** 擦干手/头发 ♦ **to dry one's eyes** 擦干眼泪
❑ **dry off I** *vi* 变干 **II** *vt* 把…弄干
❑ **dry out** *vi* 干透
❑ **dry up** *vi* **1** [*river, well* +] 干涸 **2** (*stop*) [*supply, flow etc* +] 停滞 **3** (*during speech*) 忘词

dry-clean ['draɪ'kliːn] *vt* 干洗

dry-cleaner ['draɪ'kliːnə(r)] *n* [c] **1** (*also* ***dry cleaner's***) 干洗店 **2** (*person*) 干洗商

dryer ['draɪə(r)] *n* [c] **1** (= *tumble dryer, spin-dryer*) 干衣机 **2** (*hair dryer*) 吹风机

dryness ['draɪnɪs] *n* [U] **1** [*of ground*] 干涸 **2** [*of climate, weather*] 干燥 **3** [*of skin*] 干枯

DST [美] *n abbr* (= ***Daylight Saving Time***) 夏令时

DTP *n abbr* (= ***desktop publishing***) 桌面出版系统

dual ['djuəl] *adj* 双的

dual carriageway [英] *n* [c] 双行道 [美 = **divided highway**]

dub [dʌb] *vt* **1** [+ *film, TV programme*] 为…配音 **2** (*nickname*) ♦ **a man dubbed 'the terminator'** 被冠以"终结者"绰号的人 ♦ **dubbed into Spanish/French** 用西班牙语/法语译配

dubious ['djuːbɪəs] *adj* [+ *claim, reputation, company*] 可疑的 ♦ **to have the dubious honour/pleasure/distinction of ...** 令人怀疑的…的荣誉/愉快/区别 ♦ **to be dubious about sth** 对某事半信半疑

duck [dʌk] **I** *n* **1** [c] (*bird*) 鸭 **2** [U] (*as food*) 鸭肉 **II** *vi* (*also* ***duck down***) 急忙弯下身子 **III** *vt* **1** [+ *blow*] 急忙避开 **2** [+ *duty, responsibility*] 逃避

due [djuː] **I** *adj* **1** ♦ **to be due** [*person, train, bus* +] 应到; [*baby* +] 预期; [*rent, payment* +] 应支付 **2** ♦ **to be due (to sb)** (*owed*) [+ *money, holidays*] 应给（某人）**3** (*proper*) [+ *consideration*] 适当的 **II** *n* ♦ **to give sb his (*or* her) due** 公平对待他/她 **III** *adv* ♦ **due north/south** 正北方/南方 **IV dues** *n* [*pl*] (*for club, union*) 应付款 ♦ **due to ...** (*because of*) 由于… ♦ **to be due to sth/sb** 由于某事/某人 ♦ **to be due for sth** 应得某物 ♦ **I am due 6 days' leave** 我应有6天的休假 ♦ **I am due 5 pounds** 我应得5英镑 ♦ **she's due next week** [非正式] (*to* *give birth*) 她下星期临产 ♦**in due course** (*eventually*) 在适当的时候

duel ['djuəl] *n* [c] **1** (*formal fight*) 决斗 **2** (*ongoing dispute*) 争辩

duet [djuː'ɛt] *n* [c] 二重唱曲/奏曲

dug [dʌg] *pt, pp of* **dig**

duke [djuːk] *n* [c]公爵 ♦**the Duke of Edinburgh** 爱丁堡公爵

dull [dʌl] **I** *adj* **1** (*not bright*) [+ *weather, day*] 阴沉的; [+ *light, colour*] 暗淡的 **2** (*boring*) [+ *event, place, person, book*] 单调乏味的 **3** (*sluggish*) 迟钝的 **4** [+ *sound, pain*] 隐约的 **II** *vt* **1** [+ *pain, grief*] 减轻 **2** [+ *mind, senses*] 使迟钝 **III** *vi* [*eyes, expression etc* +] 变得呆滞

duly ['djuːlɪ] *adv* **1** (*as expected*) 如期地 **2** (*correctly*) 适当地

dumb [dʌm] *adj* **1** (*mute, silent*) 哑的 **2** [贬] (*stupid, foolish*) 愚蠢的 **3** [美:非正式] (*silly, annoying*) [+ *idea*] 傻的 ♦**to be struck dumb** 哑口无言

dummy ['dʌmɪ] **I** *n* [c] **1** [英] (*for baby*) 橡皮奶头 [美 = **pacifier**] **2** (*mannekin*) 人体模型 **3** [非正式] (*idiot*) 笨蛋 **4** (*in cards*) (*also* ***dummy hand***) 明手牌 **II** *adj* (*false*) 假的 ♦**a dummy run** [英] (*test run*) 试演

dump [dʌmp] **I** *n* [c] **1** (*tip*) (*for rubbish*) 垃圾场 **2** [非正式] (*pigsty, tip*) 脏乱的地方 **3** (*store*) (*for ammunition, arms*) 临时存放处 **II** *vt* **1** (*put down*) 丢下 **2** (*get rid of*) 倾倒 **3** [+ *computer data*] 转储 ♦**to be down in the dumps** [非正式] 神情沮丧 ♦**"no dumping"** "严禁乱倒垃圾"

dumpling ['dʌmplɪŋ] *n* [c] 饺子

Dumpster® [美] ['dʌmpstə(r)] *n* [c] (用以装运工地废料的无盖)废料筒 [英 = **skip**]

dune [djuːn] *n* [c] (*also* ***sand dune***) 沙丘

dung [dʌŋ] *n* [U] 粪

dungarees [dʌŋgə'riːz] *n* [*pl*] (*for work*) 工装裤; (*for child, woman*) 背带裤

dungeon ['dʌndʒən] *n* [c] 地牢

dunk [dʌŋk] *vt* 把…浸一浸

duplex ['djuːplɛks] [美] *n* [c] **1** (*house*) 供两家居住的房屋 **2** (*apartment*) 跨两层楼的公寓套房

duplicate [*n, adj* 'djuːplɪkət, *vb* 'djuːplɪkeɪt] **I** *n* [c] [*of document, key*] 复制品 **II** *adj* [+ *key, copy*] 复制的 **III** *vt* **1** (*repeat*) [+ *success, result*] 重复 **2** (*copy*) [+ *document, tape*] 复制 **3** (*reuse, rehash*) 重做

durable ['djuərəbl] *adj* [+ *goods, materials*] 耐用的

duration [djuə'reɪʃən] *n* [U] [*of process, course, film*] 持续时间 ♦**for the duration of the holiday/his stay** 假期/他停留期间 ♦**for the duration** 在接下去的时期内 ♦**of 8 months' duration** 长达8个月

✪**during** ['djuərɪŋ] *prep* **1** (*throughout*) 在…期间 ◊ *Snowstorms are common during winter.* 暴风雪在冬天是常见的。◊ *Many soldiers died during the war.* 在战争期间许多战士阵亡了。**2** (*at some point in*) 在…时候 ◊ *During the night the fence blew down.* 在夜里的时候篱笆给吹倒了。

dusk [dʌsk] *n* [U] 黄昏 ♦**at dusk** 黄昏时刻

dust [dʌst] **I** *n* [U] (*dirt*) (*outdoors*) 尘土; (*indoors*) 灰尘 **II** *vt* **1** [+ *furniture*] 拭去…上的灰尘 **2** ♦**to dust sth with sth** [+ *cake*] (*with flour, sugar*) 把某物撒在某物上

❑**dust off, dust down** *vt* **1** ♦**to dust o.s. off** 重新振作起来 **2** (*reuse*) 重新使用

dustbin ['dʌstbɪn] [英] *n* [c] 垃圾箱 [美 = **garbage can**]

duster ['dʌstə(r)] *n* [c] (*cloth*) 抹布

dustman ['dʌstmən] [英] (*pl* **dustmen**) *n* [c] 清洁工 [美 = **garbage man**]

dusty ['dʌstɪ] *adj* 满是尘土的

Dutch [dʌtʃ] **I** *adj* 荷兰的 **II** *n* [U] (*language*) 荷兰语 **III** *adv* ♦**to go Dutch (on sth)** [非正式] 各人自己付(某物的)钱 **IV the Dutch** *n* [*pl*] (*people*) 荷兰人

Dutchman ['dʌtʃmən] (*pl* **Dutchmen**) *n* [c] 荷兰人

Dutchwoman ['dʌtʃwumən] (*pl* **Dutchwomen**) *n* [c] 荷兰妇女

duty ['djuːtɪ] **I** *n* [C/U] **1** (*responsibility*) 责任 **2** (*tax*) 税 **II duties** *n* [*pl*] (*tasks*) 任务 ♦**it is my duty to ...** …是我的职责 ♦**to**

pay duty on sth 支付某物的税 ♦**to report for duty** 述职 ♦**to be on/off duty** [+ *policeman, nurse*] 上/下班 ♦**duty chemist/officer/doctor** 值班药剂师/官员/医生

duty-free ['dju:tɪ'fri:] *adj* [+ *drink, cigarettes*] 免税的 ♦**duty-free shop** 免税商店

duvet ['du:veɪ] [英] *n* [c] 羽绒被

DVD player *n* [c] DVD播放器

dwarf [dwɔ:f] (*pl* **dwarves**) **I** *n* [c] **1** (*in stories*) 小矮人 **2** [过时, 讳] (*small person*) 矮子 **II** *adj* [+ *shrub, plant etc*] 矮小的 **III** *vt* 使相形见绌

dwell [dwɛl] (*pt, pp* **dwelt**) *vi* [正式] 住

❑ **dwell on** *vt* [不可拆分] 详述

dwelt [dwɛlt] *pt, pp of* **dwell**

dwindle ['dwɪndl] *vi* [*resources, supplies, strength* +] 缩小

dye [daɪ] **I** *n* [c/u] (*for hair, cloth*) 染料 **II** *vt* 染色 ♦**to dye sth red/black** 把某物染成红色/黑色

dying ['daɪɪŋ] **I** *adj* **1** [+ *person, animal*] 垂死的 **2** (*final*) [+ *wishes, words, breath*] 临终的; [+ *days, moments etc*] 行将完结的 **3** (*fading*) [+ *tradition, industry*] 行将消失的 **II** *n* [*pl*] ♦**the dying** 垂死的人

dynamic [daɪ'næmɪk] *adj* 生气勃勃的

dynamite ['daɪnəmaɪt] **I** *n* [u] **1** (*explosive*) 甘油炸药 **2** (*something controversial*) 具有爆炸性的事/物 **3** [非正式] (*sensational*) 轰动的事/物 **II** *vt* 炸毁

dyslexia [dɪs'lɛksɪə] *n* [u] 诵读困难

dyslexic [dɪs'lɛksɪk] *adj* 诵读有困难的

Ee

E¹, e [iː] [c/u] *(letter)* 英语的第五个字母

E² [iː] **I** *n* [c/u] ［音］C大调音阶中的第三音 **II** *abbr* **1** *(direction)* = **east** **2** ［非正式］*(drug)* = **ecstasy**

✪ **each** [iːtʃ] **I** *adj* [+ *thing, person, idea*] 每 **II** *pron* *(each one)* 每个 ◊ *two bedrooms, each with three beds* 两间卧室，每间有3张床 ♦ **each one of them** 他们中的每一个 ♦ **each other** 互相 ♦ **they have 2 books each** 他们每人有两本书 ♦ **they cost 5 pounds each** 每个售价5镑 ♦ **each of us** 我们每个人

> 📖 **each** 表示一个群体中的每一个人或物，强调的是每一个个体。**every** 指由两个以上的个体组成的群体中的所有的人或物，强调的是整体。*He listened to every news bulletin ... an equal chance for every child ...* 注意，**each** 指两个当中的任何一个。*Each apartment has two bedrooms ... We each carried a suitcase.* **each** 和 **every** 后面都只能跟名词单数形式。

eager [ˈiːɡə(r)] *adj* *(keen)* 热切的 ♦ **eager to do** 急于做 ♦ **eager for** 渴望

eagle [ˈiːɡl] *n* [c] 鹰

ear [ɪə(r)] *n* [c] **1** ［解剖］耳朵 **2** [*of wheat*] 穗 ♦ **to have an ear for language/music** 有语言/音乐欣赏能力 ♦ **to be up to one's ears in debt/work** 深陷入债务/工作 ♦ **we'll play it by ear** （喻）我们会见机行事

earache [ˈɪəreɪk] *n* [c/u] 耳朵痛

eardrum [ˈɪədrʌm] *n* [c] 鼓膜

earl [əːl] ［英］*n* [c] 伯爵

earlier [ˈəːlɪə(r)] **I** *adj* **1** [+ *date, time etc*] 较早的 **2** [+ *edition, idea*] 以前的 **II** *adv* [*leave, go etc* +] 提早 ♦ **earlier this year** 本年初 ♦ **she left earlier than us** 她比我们早离开 ♦ **I can't come any earlier** 我不能来得再早了

✪ **early** [ˈəːlɪ] **I** *adv* **1** *(in day, month etc)* 在初期 ◊ *early this morning* 今天一大早 ◊ *early last week* 上星期初 **2** *(before usual time)* [*get up, go to bed, arrive, leave* +] 早 ◊ *I usually get up early.* 我通常早起床。**II** *adj* **1** *(near the beginning)* [+ *stage, career*] 早期的 ◊ *the early stages of pregnancy* 怀孕早期 ◊ *Shakespeare's early works* 莎士比亚的早期著作 **2** *(in history)* [+ *Christians, settlers*] 早期的 **3** *(premature)* [+ *death, departure*] 提早的 **4** *(quick)* [+ *reply*] 很快的 ◊ *We look forward to your early reply.* 我们期待您及早的答复。♦ **early on** 在初期 ♦ **early in the morning** 清早 ♦ **in the early** *or* **early in the spring/19th century** 早春/19世纪初期 ♦ **she's in her early forties** 她40出头 ♦ **in the early hours of the morning** 凌晨 ♦ **you're early!** 你怎么这么早！ ♦ **to take the early train** 坐早班火车 ♦ **to have an early night** 早上床 ♦ **at your earliest convenience** ［商，行政］在您尽早方便时

early retirement *n* ♦ **to take early retirement** 提前退休

earmark [ˈɪəmɑːk] *vt* ♦ **to earmark (for)** [+ *funds, site etc*] 指定…用途

earn [əːn] *vt* **1** [+ *salary, money*] 挣得 **2** ［商］[+ *interest*] 生利 **3** [+ *praise, hatred, reputation*] 博得 ♦ **to earn one's** *or* **a living** 谋生 ♦ **he's earned a rest/reward** 他应得休息/奖励

earnest [ˈəːnɪst] *adj* **1** [+ *person, manner*] 认真的 **2** [+ *wish, effort*] 诚挚的 ♦ **to do sth in earnest** 认真地做某事 ♦ **to be in earnest** ［正式］认真地

earnings [ˈəːnɪŋz] *n* [*pl*] 收入

earphones [ˈɪəfəunz] *n* [*pl*] 耳机

earplugs [ˈɪəplʌɡz] *n* [*pl*] *(to keep out sound, water)* 耳塞

earring [ˈɪərɪŋ] *n* [c] 耳环

earshot [ˈɪəʃɔt] *n* ♦ **within earshot**

(of sb/sth) 在（某人/某物）的听力所及范围内 ♦**out of earshot (of sb/sth)** 不在（某人某物的）听力范围之内

earth [əːθ] **I** *n* **1** [U/S] (*also:* ***the Earth***) (*planet*) 地球 **2** [U] (*land surface*) 陆地 **3** [U] (*soil*) 泥土 **4** [C] [英: 电子] 接地 [美=**ground**] **5** [C] [*of fox*] 穴 **II** *vt* [英: 电子] 把…接地 [美=**ground**] ♦**what/where/why on earth ...?** 究竟什么/在哪/为什么…？♦**to bring sb/come down to earth** 使某人回到现实中来

earthquake [ˈəːθkweɪk] *n* [C] 地震

ease [iːz] **I** *n* [U] **1** (*easiness*) 容易 **2** (*comfort*) 安适 **II** *vt* (*reduce*) [+ *pain, problem*] 减轻; [+ *tension*] 缓和 **III** *vi* **1** (*lessen*) [*tension* +] 缓和 **2** [*pain, grief* +] 减轻 **3** [*rain, snow* +] 减弱 ♦**to be/feel at ease** 放松 ♦**(stand) at ease!** [军] 稍息！♦**with ease** 不费吹灰之力 ♦**to ease sth in/out** 将某物慢慢挪入/挪出

❑**ease off, ease up** *vi* (*lessen*) [*wind, rain* +] 减弱; [*pressure, tension* +] 缓和

❑**ease up** *vi* **1** = **ease off** **2** (*reduce one's effort*) 放松

easily [ˈiːzɪlɪ] *adv* **1** (*without difficulty*) 不费力地 **2** (*for emphasis*) 很可能 **3** (*quickly*) 容易地 **4** (*in a relaxed way*) 从容自在地

✪**east** [iːst] **I** *n* **1** [S/U] 东方 ◊ *The sun rises in the east.* 太阳从东方升起。**2** ♦**the East** (*the Orient*) 东方国家; [过时: 政治] (*Iron Curtain*) 东方集团 **II** *adj* 东部的 **III** *adv* 向东方 ♦**the east of Spain** 西班牙东部 ♦**to the east** 以东 ♦**the east wind** 东风 ♦**east of** … 以东 ◊ *It's 15 miles or so east of Manchester.* 它位于曼彻斯特以东15英里左右。

Easter [ˈiːstə(r)] *n* [U] 复活节 ♦**the Easter holidays** 复活节假期 ♦**Happy Easter!** 复活节快乐！

Easter egg *n* [C] 复活节彩蛋

eastern [ˈiːstən] *adj* **1** [地理] 东部的 **2** ♦**Eastern** (*oriental*) 东方的 ♦**Eastern Europe** 东欧

Easter Sunday *n* [C/U] 复活主日

✪**easy** [ˈiːzɪ] **I** *adj* **1** (*simple*) 容易的 **2** (*relaxed*) 自在的 ◊ *an easy conversation* 畅谈 ◊ *Everyone wants a free and easy life.* 每个人都想过自由自在的生活。**3** (*comfortable*) [+ *life, time*] 安逸的 **4** [+ *target, prey*] 易上当的 ◊ *Tourists have become easy prey.* 旅客成了容易受害的人。**II** *adv* ♦**to take it** *or* **things easy** (*relax*) 放松一点; (*go slowly*) 不慌不忙; (*not worry*) 不急 ♦**dogs are easy to train** 狗很容易训练 ◊ *The shower is easy to install.* 这个淋浴很容易安装。♦**it's easy to train dogs** 训狗是容易的 ◊ *It's easy to get lost in this part of town.* 在镇子的这边容易迷路。♦**it's easy for sb to do sth** 对于某人来说，做某事是容易的 ◊ *That's easy for you to say!* 你说得轻松！♦**to make life easier** 使生活更方便 ♦**to feel** *or* **be easy about sth** 对某事感到安心 ♦**I'm easy** [非正式] 我随便 ♦**payment on easy terms** [商] 分期付款 ♦**that's easier said than done** 说时容易做时难

easy-going [ˈiːzɪˈɡəuɪŋ] *adj* 脾气随和的

eat [iːt] (*pt* **ate**, *pp* **eaten**) **I** *vt* **1** [+ *food, breakfast, lunch, etc*] 吃 **II** *vi* **1** (*consume food*) 吃 **2** (*have a meal*) 吃饭

❑**eat away** (*also:* ***eat away at***) *vt* **1** [*sea, rust* +] 侵蚀 **2** = **eat into**

❑**eat into** *vt* [不可拆分] [+ *time, savings, resources*] 吞噬

❑**eat out** *vi* 下馆子吃饭

❑**eat up** **I** *vt* **1** [+ *food*] 把…吃光 **2**（喻）[+ *money, time*] 消耗 **II** *vi* 吃光

eavesdrop [ˈiːvzdrɔp] *vi* ♦**to eavesdrop (on sb/sth)** 偷听（某人/某事）

ebony [ˈɛbənɪ] *n* [U] (*wood*) 乌木

e-business [ˈiːbɪznɪs] *n* **1** [C] (*company*) 电子商务公司 **2** [U] (*commerce*) 电子商务

EC *n abbr* (= ***European Community***) ♦**the EC** 欧洲共同市场

eccentric [ɪkˈsɛntrɪk] **I** *adj* **1** [+ *person*] 怪僻的 **2** [+ *behaviour, views, ideas*] 古怪的 **II** *n* [C] 古怪的人

ECG *n abbr* (= ***electrocardiogram***) 心电图 [美=**EKG**]

echo ['ɛkəu] (*pl* **echoes**) **I** *n* [c] **1** [*of sound*] 回音 **2** [*of opinion, attitude*] 共鸣 **II** *vt* (喻) (*repeat*) 重复 **III** *vi* **1** [*sound* +] 发出回声 **2** [*cave, room* +] 产生回响

eclipse [ɪ'klɪps] **I** *n* [c] [*of sun, moon*] 食 **II** *vt* [+ *achievement*] 使失色

eco-friendly ['i:kəu'frɛndlɪ] *adj* 有益于生态的

ecological [i:kə'lɔdʒɪkəl] *adj* [+ *damage, disaster*] 生态的; [+ *group, movement*] 主张生态保护的

ecology [ɪ'kɔlədʒɪ] *n* [u] **1** (*environment*) 生态 **2** (*subject*) 生态学

e-commerce ['i:kɔmə:s] *n* = **e-business**

✪ **economic** [i:kə'nɔmɪk] *adj* **1** [+ *system, history, reform*] 经济的 **2** (*profitable*) [+ *business etc*] 有利可图的

economical [i:kə'nɔmɪkl] *adj* **1** [+ *system, car, machine*] 节约的 **2** [+ *person*] 省俭的

economics [i:kə'nɔmɪks] *n* **1** [u] [教育, 大学] 经济学 **2** [PL] [*of project, situation*] 经济意义

economist [ɪ'kɔnəmɪst] *n* [c] 经济学家

economize [ɪ'kɔnəmaɪz] *vi* (*make savings*) 节约 ♦ **to economize on sth** 节约用某物

✪ **economy** [ɪ'kɔnəmɪ] *n* **1** [c] [*of country*] 经济 **2** [u] (*thrift*) 节约 ♦ **economies of scale** 规模经济

economy class I *adj* 经济舱的 **II** *adv* 经济舱地 **III** *n* [u] 经济舱

ecstasy ['ɛkstəsɪ] *n* **1** [c/u] (*rapture*) 狂喜 **2** [u] (*drug*) 迷幻药 ♦ **to be in ecstasy** 兴奋极了 ♦ **to go into ecstasies over** 对…发狂

ecstatic [ɪk'stætɪk] *adj* [+ *welcome, reaction, person*] 欣喜若狂的

Ecuador ['ɛkwədɔ:(r)] *n* 厄瓜多尔

eczema ['ɛksɪmə] *n* [u] 湿疹

edge [ɛdʒ] **I** *n* [c] **1** (*border*) [*of road, town*] 边缘; [*of lake*] 边 ◊ *She was standing at the water's edge.* 她站在水边。 **2** [*of table, chair etc*] 棱 **3** [*of knife, sword etc*] 刃 **II** *vi* ♦ **to edge forward** 一点一点地向前移动 ♦ **on edge** 紧张不安 ♦ **to have the** *or* **an edge (over sb)** 胜过(某人) ♦ **to edge past** 缓缓通过 ♦ **to edge away from** 悄悄离开 ❏ **edge out** *vt* (*in contest*) 小胜

edgy ['ɛdʒɪ] [非正式] *adj* (*nervous, agitated*) 紧张的

edible ['ɛdɪbl] *adj* [+ *mushroom, plant*] 可食用的

edit ['ɛdɪt] *vt* **1** [+ *text, report*] 校订 **2** [+ *book*] 编辑 **3** [+ *film, broadcast*] 剪辑 **4** [+ *newspaper, magazine*] 主编 ❏ **edit out** *vt* (*of book, film*) 删去

edition [ɪ'dɪʃən] *n* [c] **1** [*of book, newspaper, magazine*] 版 **2** [电视, 广播] 集

editor ['ɛdɪtə(r)] *n* [c] **1** [*of newspaper, magazine, book*] 编辑 **2** [*of text, report*] 校订者 **3** 剪辑者 **4** [电视, 广播] 编辑 ♦ **foreign/literary editor** 外文/文学编辑

editorial [ɛdɪ'tɔ:rɪəl] **I** *adj* [+ *staff, meeting, policy*] 编辑的 **II** *n* [c] [*of newspaper*] 社论

EDT [美] *abbr* (= ***Eastern Daylight Time***) 东部夏令时

educate ['ɛdjukeɪt] *vt* **1** (*teach*) 教育 **2** (*instruct*) 使懂得 ♦ **she was educated at ...** 她在…受的教育

educated ['ɛdjukeɪtɪd] *adj* [+ *person*] 受过教育的

education [ɛdju'keɪʃən] *n* [u/s] (*schooling, teaching*) 教育

educational [ɛdju'keɪʃənl] *adj* **1** [+ *institution, policy, needs*] 教育的 **2** (*instructive*) [+ *experience*] 有教育意义的

eel [i:l] *n* [c/u] 鳗鱼

eerie ['ɪərɪ] *adj* (*strange*) [+ *feeling, light, silence*] 令人恐惧的

✪ **effect** [ɪ'fɛkt] **I** *n* **1** [c/u] (*result, consequence*) 影响 ◊ *the effect of divorce on children* 离婚对儿童产生的影响 **2** [c] (*impression*) [*of speech, picture etc*] 效果 ◊ *Don't move, or you'll destroy the effect.* 别动，不然你会破坏效果的。 **II** *vt* [正式] [+ *repairs, savings etc*] 完成 ◊ *Production was halted until repairs could be effected.* 在修理完成之前停止生产。 **III effects** *n* [*pl*] **1** [正式] (*belongings*) 财物 **2** [电影] 特别效果 ♦ **to come into** *or* **take effect** [*law* +] 生效 ♦ **to take effect**

[*drug* +] 见效 ♦**to put** *or* **bring** *or* **carry sth into effect** 实施某事 ♦**to have an effect on sb/sth** 对某人/某事产生影响 ♦**in effect** 实际上 ♦**his letter is to the effect that ...** 他信的大意是… ♦**to good/no effect** 有/无效
📖 用法参见 **affect**

effective [ɪ'fɛktɪv] *adj* **1** (*successful*) 有效的 **2** (*actual*) [+ *leader, command*] 事实上的 ♦**to become effective** [法] 生效

effectively [ɪ'fɛktɪvlɪ] *adv* **1** (*successfully*) 有效地 **2** (*in reality*) 事实上

efficiency [ɪ'fɪʃənsɪ] *n* [U] [*of person, organization*] 效率

efficient [ɪ'fɪʃənt] *adj* [+ *person, organization, system*] 效率高的

efficiently [ɪ'fɪʃəntlɪ] *adv* 效率高地

✪**effort** ['ɛfət] *n* **1** [U] (*energy*) 努力 ◊ *a waste of effort* 白费力 **2** [C] (*attempt*) 尝试 ◊ *It was a good effort.* 这是个很好的尝试。**3** [U/S] (*physical/mental exertion*) 费力 ◊ *It was an effort to concentrate.* 费劲地集中精力。♦**to make an effort to do sth** 努力做某事 ♦**with an effort** 费力地

effortless ['ɛfətlɪs] *adj* [+ *movement, style*] 不费劲的

e.g. *adv abbr* (= ***exempli gratia***) (*for example*) 举例来说

egg [ɛg] *n* **1** [C] [*of bird, turtle etc*] 蛋 **2** [C/U] (*for eating*) 蛋 **3** [C] [生物] 卵子
❑**egg on** *vt* (*in fight etc*) 怂恿

eggcup ['ɛgkʌp] *n* [C] 蛋杯

eggplant ['ɛgplɑːnt] [美] *n* [C/U] 茄子 [英=**aubergine**]

eggshell ['ɛgʃɛl] **I** *n* [C/U] 蛋壳 **II** *adj* [+ *paint*] 淡黄褐色的

egg white *n* [C/U] 蛋白

egg yolk *n* [C/U] 蛋黄

ego ['iːgəu] *n* [C] (*self-esteem*) 自尊

Egypt ['iːdʒɪpt] *n* 埃及

Egyptian [ɪ'dʒɪpʃən] **I** *adj* 埃及的 **II** *n* [C] (*person*) 埃及人

✪**eight** [eɪt] *num* 八 *see also* **five**

✪**eighteen** [eɪ'tiːn] *num* 十八 *see also* **fifteen**

eighteenth [eɪ'tiːnθ] *num* 第十八 *see also* **fifth**

eighth [eɪtθ] *num* **1** 第八 **2** (*fraction*) 八分之一 *see also* **fifth**

eightieth ['eɪtɪɪθ] *num* 第八十

✪**eighty** ['eɪtɪ] *num* 八十 *see also* **fifty**

Eire ['ɛərə] *n* 爱尔兰共和国

✪**either** ['aɪðə(r)] **I** *adj* **1** (*one or other*) 两者任一的 ◊ *Either bus will take you there.* 两路公共汽车之中任一辆都会把你带到那儿。**2** (*both, each*) 两者中每一方的 ◊ *In either case the answer is the same.* 两者答案是一样的。**II** *pron* **1** (*after negative*) 两者之中任何一个 ◊ *There was no sound from either of the flats.* 两个单元都没声音。**2** (*after interrogative*) 两者之中任何一个 ◊ *"Which one?" – "Either of them."* "哪一个？" "哪个都行。" **III** *adv* (*in negative statements*) 也 ◊ *His singing is hopeless and he can't act either.* 他唱歌不行，表演也不行。**IV** *conj* ♦**either ... or ...** 要么…要么… ♦**on either side** 在两边 ♦**I don't like either of them** 两个我都不喜欢 ♦**no, I don't either** 不，我也不 ♦**I haven't seen either one or the other** 我两个都没看见

eject [ɪ'dʒɛkt] **I** *vt* **1** [+ *object*] 喷射 ◊ *He fired a shot, then ejected the spent cartridge.* 他开了一枪，然后倒出了用过的弹夹。**2** [+ *tenant, gatecrasher*] 驱逐 **II** *vi* [*pilot* +] 弹射出来

EKG [美] *n abbr* = **ECG**

elaborate [*adj* ɪ'læbərɪt, *vb* ɪ'læbəreɪt] **I** *adj* (*complex*) [+ *network, plan*] 复杂的; [+ *ritual, ceremony*] 精心制作的 **II** *vt* (*develop*) [+ *plan, policy*] 仔细制订 **III** *vi* ♦**to elaborate (on sth)** [+ *idea, plan etc*] 详述(某事)

elastic [ɪ'læstɪk] **I** *n* [U] (*material*) 橡皮 **II** *adj* **1** (*stretchy*) 有弹性的 **2** (喻) (*adaptable*) 灵活的

elastic band [英] *n* [C] 橡皮筋 [美=**rubber band**]

elbow ['ɛlbəu] **I** *n* [C] **1** [解剖] 肘 **2** [*of sleeve*] 肘部 **II** *vt* [+ *person*] 用肘打 ♦**to elbow one's way through the crowd** 挤过人群 ♦**to elbow sb aside** 把某人挤到一旁

elder ['ɛldə(r)] **I** *adj* [+ *brother, sister etc*] 年龄较大的 ◊ *He had none of* *his elder brother's charm.* 他没有他哥哥的魅力。**II** *n* [c] **1** [正式] (*older person*) 长者; (*in tribe etc*) 头人 **2** (*tree*) 接骨木

elderly ['ɛldəlɪ] **I** *adj* (*old*) 年长的 **II** *n* [*pl*] ♦**the elderly** 老人家

eldest ['ɛldɪst] **I** *adj* [+ *child, daughter*] 年龄最大的 **II** *n* [s]/PL 年龄最大的孩子

elect [ɪ'lɛkt] **I** *vt* [+ *government, councillor, spokesman etc*] 选举 **II** *adj* ♦**the president elect** [正式] 当选的总统 ♦**to elect to do sth** [正式] (*choose*) 选择做某事

✪**election** [ɪ'lɛkʃən] *n* **1** [c] (*ballot*) 选举 **2** [s] [*of person, government*] 当选 ♦**to hold an election** 举行选举

electoral [ɪ'lɛktərəl] *adj* [+ *system*] 选举的

electorate [ɪ'lɛktərɪt] *n* [c] 选民

electric [ɪ'lɛktrɪk] *adj* **1** [+ *lawnmower, toothbrush*] 电动的 **2** [+ *current, charge, socket*] 电的 **3** (喻) [+ *mood, atmosphere*] 高度刺激的

electrical [ɪ'lɛktrɪkl] *adj* **1** [+ *appliance, equipment*] 电动的 **2** [+ *system*] 电的 **3** [+ *industry, failure*] 电力的 ◊ *a blackout resulting from an electrical failure* 断电造成的黑暗

electric blanket *n* [c] 电热毯

electric fire [英] *n* [c] 电热炉

electric guitar *n* [c/u] 电吉他

electrician [ɪlɛk'trɪʃən] *n* [c] 电工

electricity [ɪlɛk'trɪsɪtɪ] **I** *n* [u] **1** (*energy*) 电 **2** (*supply*) 供电 **II** *cpd* [复合词] **1** [+ *company*] 电力 **2** [+ *bill, meter*] 电

electric razor *n* [c] 电动剃须刀

electric shock *n* [c] 触电

electrify [ɪ'lɛktrɪfaɪ] *vt* **1** [+ *rail network*] 使电气化 **2** (喻) (*thrill*) 使震惊

electrocute [ɪ'lɛktrəkjuːt] *vt* 使触电死亡 ♦**to electrocute o.s.** 电死自己

electronic [ɪlɛk'trɔnɪk] *adj* 电子的

electronics [ɪlɛk'trɔnɪks] **I** *n* [u] (*technology*) 电子学 **II** *n* [*pl*] [*of machine*] 电子仪器

elegance ['ɛlɪgəns] *n* [u] **1** [*of person, building*] 雅致 **2** [*of piece of writing*] 典雅

elegant ['ɛlɪgənt] *adj* **1** [+ *person, building*] 优雅的 **2** [+ *idea, prose*] 上乘的

element ['ɛlɪmənt] **I** *n* [c] **1** (*part*) [*of job, process, plan*] 要素 **2** [化] 元素 **3** [*of heater, kettle etc*] 电热丝 **II elements** *n* [*pl*] ♦**the elements** (*weather*) 自然力 ♦**the story contains an element of truth** 这个故事有真实的成分 ♦**criminal elements** 为非作歹的人 ♦**to be in one's element** 各得其所

elementary [ɛlɪ'mɛntərɪ] *adj* 初级的

elementary school [ɛlɪ'mɛntərɪskuːl] [美] *n* [c/u] 小学 [英=**primary school**]

elephant ['ɛlɪfənt] *n* [c] 大象

elevate ['ɛlɪveɪt] [正式] *vt* **1** (*in rank*) 提升…的职位 **2** (*in amount, intensity*) 提高 **3** (*physically*) 使上升

elevator ['ɛlɪveɪtə(r)] *n* [c] [美] 电梯 [英=**lift**]

✪**eleven** [ɪ'lɛvn] *num* 十一 *see also* **five**

eleventh [ɪ'lɛvnθ] *num* 第十一 ♦**at the eleventh hour** 在最后时刻 *see also* **fifth**

elicit [ɪ'lɪsɪt] *vt* **1** [+ *response, reaction*] 引导出 **2** [正式] [+ *information*] 推导出

eligible ['ɛlɪdʒəbl] *adj* [+ *man, woman*] 合意的 ♦**to be eligible for sth** 符合某事的条件 ♦**to be eligible to do sth** 合格做某事

eliminate [ɪ'lɪmɪneɪt] *vt* **1** [+ *poverty*] 消除; [+ *smoking*] 戒除 **2** [+ *team, contestant, candidate*] 淘汰

élite [eɪ'liːt] **I** *n* [c] 精英 **II** *adj* 精锐的

elm [ɛlm] *n* **1** [c] (*also: **elm tree***) 榆树 **2** [u] (*wood*) 榆木

eloquent ['ɛləkwənt] *adj* **1** [+ *speech, description*] 有说服力的 **2** [+ *person*] 能言善辩的

El Salvador [ɛl'sælvədɔː(r)] *n* 萨尔瓦多

✪**else** [ɛls] *adv* ♦**or else** (*otherwise*) 否则; (*threatening*) 要不然 ◊ *Don't talk to me like that again, or else!* 别这么跟我说话，要不够你受的！ ♦**something else, anything else** 其他东西，任何其他东西 ♦**where else?** 别的什么地方？

♦**what else?** 其他什么？ ♦**somewhere else** 其他地方 ♦**everywhere else** 其他任何地方 ♦**everyone else** 其他人 ♦**nobody else** 没有其他人 ♦**little else** 其他什么都没有 ♦**if nothing else** 起码

elsewhere [ɛls'wɛə(r)] *adv* **1** [*be* +] 在别处 **2** [*go* +] 到别处

elusive [ɪ'luːsɪv] *adj* **1** [+ *person, animal*] 不易找到的 **2** [+ *quality*] 难以捉摸的

e-mail ['iːmeɪl] **I** *n* [c/u] 电子邮件 **II** *vt* **1** [+ *person*] 给…发电子邮件 **2** [+ *file, document*] 用电子邮件寄

e-mail account *n* [c] 电子邮件账号

e-mail address *n* [c] 电子邮件地址

embankment [ɪm'bæŋkmənt] *n* [c] [*of road, railway, river*] 堤

embargo [ɪm'bɑːgəu] (*pl* **embargoes**) **I** *n* [c] 限制贸易令 **II** *vt* [+ *goods*] 禁运 ♦**to impose** *or* **place an embargo on sth** 对某物实行禁运 ♦**to lift an embargo** 解禁

embark [ɪm'bɑːk] *vi* [航海] ♦**to embark (on)** 登上
❑**embark on** *vt* [不可拆分] [+ *task, course of action*] 着手

embarrass [ɪm'bærəs] *vt* **1** (*emotionally*) 使不好意思 **2** [+ *politician, government*] 使陷入困境

embarrassed [ɪm'bærəst] *adj* [+ *laugh, silence*] 尴尬的 ♦**to be embarrassed** 不好意思的

embarrassing [ɪm'bærəsɪŋ] *adj* **1** [+ *statement, situation*] 令人尴尬的 **2** (*to politician, government*) 令人难堪的

embarrassment [ɪm'bærəsmənt] *n* **1** [u] (*feeling*) 难堪 **2** [c] (*situation, problem*) 令人为难的事情 **3** [c] (*person*) 使人为难的人 ♦**to be an embarrassment to sb** 是令某人困窘的人/事

embassy ['ɛmbəsɪ] *n* [c] 大使馆

embody [ɪm'bɔdɪ] *vt* **1** [+ *idea, quality*] 体现 **2** (*include, contain*) 包含

embrace [ɪm'breɪs] **I** *vt* **1** (*hug*) 拥抱 **2** (喻) (*welcome*) [+ *new idea, system etc*] 欣然接受 **3** (*include*) [+ *group of people, things*] 包括 **II** *vi* (*hug*) 拥抱 **III** *n* [c] (*hug*) 拥抱

embroider [ɪm'brɔɪdə(r)] *vt* **1** [+ *cloth*] 在…上刺绣 **2** (喻) [+ *a story, the truth*] 渲染

embroidery [ɪm'brɔɪdərɪ] *n* **1** [c/u] (*cloth*) 绣制品 **2** [u] (*activity*) 刺绣

embryo ['ɛmbrɪəu] *n* [c] [生物] 胚胎 ♦**in embryo** (喻) 在酝酿中

emerald ['ɛmərəld] *n* [c] (*gem*) 祖母绿

emerge [ɪ'məːdʒ] *vi* **1** (*come out*) [*person* +] 出来 **2** (*become known*) [*evidence, facts* +] 暴露 **3** (*come into existence*) [*new idea, movement, society* +] 兴起 ♦**to emerge from sth** (*from room, building*) 从某物中出现; (*from crisis, recession*) 摆脱某种状况; (*from discussion, investigation*) 从某物中暴露出 ♦**it emerged that ...** 事实显现…

emergence [ɪ'məːdʒəns] *n* [u] [*of new idea, nation*] 出现

emergency [ɪ'məːdʒənsɪ] **I** *n* [c] (*crisis*) 紧急情况 **II** *cpd* [复合词] [+ *repair, talks, supplies, aid*] 紧急 ♦**in an emergency** 在紧急情况下 ♦**a state of emergency** [政治] 紧急状况

emergency brake [美:汽车] *n* [c] 紧急刹车 [英=**handbrake**]

emergency exit *n* [c] 安全出口

emergency landing *n* [c] 紧急着陆 ♦**to make an emergency landing** 进行紧急着陆

emergency room [美] *n* [c] 急诊室 [英=**accident and emergency**]

emergency services *n* [*pl*] ♦**the emergency services** (*fire, police, ambulance*) 紧急服务

emigrate ['ɛmɪgreɪt] *vi* 移居外国

emigration [ɛmɪ'greɪʃən] *n* [u] 移居外国

eminent ['ɛmɪnənt] *adj* [+ *scientist, writer*] 卓越的

emission [ɪ'mɪʃən] [正式] **I** *n* [c/u] [*of radiation, gas*] 散发 **II emissions** *n* [*pl*] 废物

emit [ɪ'mɪt] *vt* [+ *heat, light, smell, sound*] 发出

emotion [ɪ'məuʃən] *n* **1** [c/u] (*feeling*) 感情 **2** [u] (*as opposed to reason*) 情感

emotional [ɪ'məuʃənl] *adj* 1 [+ *support, problems*] 感情的; [+ *stress*] 情绪的 2 [+ *person*] 易动感情的 3 [+ *scene, issue*] 令人情绪激动的 4 [+ *speech, plea*] 动人的 ♦ **to get emotional** 动感情的

emperor ['ɛmpərə(r)] *n* [C] 皇帝

emphasis ['ɛmfəsɪs] (*pl* **emphases** ['ɛmfəsiːz]) *n* [C/U] 1 (*on word, syllable*) 重音 2 (喻) 重点 ♦ **to put** *or* **place emphasis on sth** (喻) 把重点放在某事上 ♦ **the emphasis is on reading** 着重于阅读

emphasize ['ɛmfəsaɪz] *vt* 1 [+ *word, point*] 强调 2 (*make conspicuous*) 使明显 ♦ **I must emphasize that ...** 我必须强调…

emphatic [ɛm'fætɪk] *adj* 1 [+ *statement, denial*] 断然的 2 [+ *person, manner*] 强硬的 3 [+ *victory*] 令人瞩目的

empire ['ɛmpaɪə(r)] *n* [C] 1 (*group of countries*) 帝国 2 (喻) (*group of companies*) 王国 ♦ **a business/publishing empire** 商业/出版王国

employ [ɪm'plɔɪ] **I** *vt* 1 [+ *person, workforce*] 雇用 2 (*use*) [+ *methods, materials*] 使用 **II** *n* ♦ **to be in sb's employ** [正式] 受雇于某人 ♦ **he was employed as a technician** 他受雇做技师

employee [ɪmplɔɪ'iː] *n* [C] 雇员

employer [ɪm'plɔɪə(r)] *n* [C] 雇主

employment [ɪm'plɔɪmənt] *n* [U] (*work*) 工作 ♦ **to find employment** 找到工作 ♦ **to be in employment** 有工作 ♦ **place of employment** 工作地点

employment agency *n* [C] 职业介绍所

empower [ɪm'pauə(r)] *vt* 1 ♦ **to empower sb to do sth** [正式] 授权某人做某事 2 [+ *women, minority*] 授予…权利

empress ['ɛmprɪs] *n* [C] (*woman ruling empire*) 女皇; (*wife of emperor*) 皇后

emptiness ['ɛmptɪnɪs] *n* [U] 1 [*of area, region etc*] 空旷 2 [*of life etc*] 空虚

empty ['ɛmptɪ] **I** *adj* 1 [+ *glass, container*] 空的 2 [+ *place, street*] 无人的 3 [+ *house, room*] 空的 4 [+ *threat, gesture*] 虚张声势的 **II** *vt* 1 [+ *bin, ashtray*] 倒空 2 [+ *room, house etc*] 使空 **III** *vi* [*room, building* +] 成为空的 ♦ **on an empty stomach** 空着肚子 ♦ **to empty sth into sth** (*pour out*) 将某物全部倒入某物中 ♦ **to empty into** [*river* +] 流入

empty-handed ['ɛmptɪ'hændɪd] *adj* ♦ **to go away empty-handed** 一无所获地离开 ♦ **he returned empty-handed** 他空手回来

emulsion [ɪ'mʌlʃən] *n* [C/U] 1 (*also:* ***emulsion paint***) 乳状油漆 2 [摄影] 感光乳剂

enable [ɪ'neɪbl] *vt* 1 ♦ **to enable sb to do sth** (*make possible*) 使某人能够做某事 2 (*permit, allow*) [*law* +] 批准

enamel [ɪ'næməl] *n* 1 [C/U] (*for decoration*) 搪瓷 2 [C/U] (*also:* ***enamel paint***) 瓷漆 3 [U] (*on tooth*) 珐琅质

enc. *abbr* (= ***enclosed, enclosure***) 附

enchant [ɪn'tʃɑːnt] *vt* (*delight*) 使入迷

enchanting [ɪn'tʃɑːntɪŋ] *adj* [+ *place, child*] 迷人的

encl. *abbr* (= ***enclosed, enclosure***) = **enc.**

enclose [ɪn'kləuz] *vt* 1 [+ *garden, space*] 围住 2 [+ *object in wrapping etc*] 包住 3 (*in letter*) [+ *cheque*] 附入 ♦ **enclosed by sth** 被某物围住 ♦ **please find enclosed** 兹附上

enclosure [ɪn'kləuʒə(r)] *n* [C] 1 (*area of land*) 围场 2 (*in letter*) 附件

encompass [ɪn'kʌmpəs] *vt* (*include*) 包含

encore [ɔŋ'kɔː(r)] [戏剧] **I** *n* [C] 加演的节目 ◊ *The Stone Roses have never played an encore.* Stone Roses 乐队从不应观众要求而加演节目。 **II** *int* 再来一个

encounter [ɪn'kauntə(r)] **I** *n* [C] 1 (*meeting*) 相遇 2 (*experience*) 遭遇 **II** *vt* 1 [正式] [+ *person*] 意外遇见 2 [+ *difficulty, problem*] 遭到

encourage [ɪn'kʌrɪdʒ] *vt* 1 [+ *person*] 鼓励 2 [+ *activity, attitude*] 支持 3 [+ *growth, industry*] 助长 ♦ **to encourage sb to do sth** 鼓励某人去做某事 ♦ **to be**

encouraged by sth 由于某事受到鼓励

encouragement [ɪn'kʌrɪdʒmənt] *n* [U] (*support*) 鼓励

encouraging [ɪn'kʌrɪdʒɪŋ] *adj* [+ *meeting, news*] 令人鼓舞的

encyclop(a)edia [ɛnsaɪkləu'piːdɪə] *n* [C] 百科全书

✪ **end** [ɛnd] **I** *n* **1** [S] [*of period, event*] 末期 ◊ *at the end of August* 在8月末 **2** [S] [*of film, book*] 末尾 **3** [C] [*of street, queue, rope, table*] 尽头 **4** [C] [*of town*] 端 **5** [C] [*of pencil, finger etc*] 末梢 **6** [C] (*purpose*) 目的 ◊ *for political ends* 为了政治目的 **II** *vt* (*finish, stop*) [+ *fighting, strike*] 终止 **III** *vi* **1** [*meeting, film, book* +] 结束 **2** [*journey, road, river* +] 终结 ♦ **at the end of the day** (喻) 到头来 ♦ **to come to an end** 完结 ♦ **to be at an end** 结束 ♦ **in the end** 最终 ♦ **at the end of the street** 在街的尽头 ♦ **from end to end** 从头到尾 ♦ **to make sb's hair stand on end** 使某人毛骨悚然 ♦ **no end** [非正式] (*a lot*) 许多 ♦ **for hours on end** 连续几个小时 ♦ **to bring sth to an end, put an end to sth** 使某事终止 ♦ **to this end, with this end in view** 为了达到这个目的 ♦ **to make ends meet** 勉强维持生活 ♦ **to end in tragedy/disaster** 以悲剧/大祸收尾

❑ **end up** *vi* ♦ **to end up in/at** [+ *place*] 最终到了; [+ *trouble, a mess etc*] 结束于 ♦ **to end up doing sth** 以做某事告终

endanger [ɪn'deɪndʒə(r)] *vt* [+ *lives, prospects*] 危害 ♦ **an endangered species** 一个濒于灭绝的物种

endearing [ɪn'dɪərɪŋ] *adj* [+ *personality, smile*] 使人喜爱的

endeavour (美 **endeavor**) [ɪn'dɛvə(r)] [正式] **I** *n* **1** [C] (*attempt*) 尝试 **2** [U] (*effort*) 努力 **II** *vi* ♦ **to endeavour to do sth** 尝试做某事

ending ['ɛndɪŋ] *n* [C] **1** [*of book, film, play etc*] 结局 **2** [语言] 词尾 ♦ **a happy ending** 美满结局

endless ['ɛndlɪs] *adj* **1** (*very lengthy*) [+ *drought, war, speech*] 没完没了的 **2** (*interminable*) [+ *arguments, meetings*] 无休止的 **3** (*very long, very large*) [+ *forest, beach*] 无穷尽的 **4** [+ *possibilities*] 无限的

endorse [ɪn'dɔːs] *vt* **1** (*approve*) [+ *proposal, plan, candidate*] 赞同 **2** [商] [+ *product, company*] 为…做广告 **3** [+ *cheque*] 在…背后签字 ♦ **to have one's driving licence endorsed** [英] 执照被注上违章记录

endorsement [ɪn'dɔːsmənt] *n* **1** [C/U] (*approval*) 赞同 **2** [C] [英] (*on driving licence*) 违章记录 **3** [C] [商] (*for product, company*) 商业广告

endurance [ɪn'djuərəns] *n* [U] 忍耐

endure [ɪn'djuə(r)] **I** *vt* (*bear*) [+ *pain, suffering*] 忍耐 **II** *vi* (*last*) [*relationship, work of art* +] 持续

enemy ['ɛnəmɪ] **I** *n* **1** [C] (*opponent*) 敌人 **2** ♦ **the enemy** [军] 敌军 **II** *cpd* [复合词] [+ *forces, strategy, aircraft*] 敌方的 ♦ **to make an enemy of sb** 使某人与自己为敌

energetic [ɛnə'dʒɛtɪk] *adj* **1** [+ *person*] 精力充沛的 **2** [+ *activity*] 生机勃勃的

energy ['ɛnədʒɪ] **I** *n* [U] **1** (*strength*) 力量 **2** (*power*) 能源 **II energies** *n* [*pl*] 精力

enforce [ɪn'fɔːs] *vt* [+ *law, rule*] 执行

engage [ɪn'geɪdʒ] **I** *vt* **1** [正式] [+ *attention, interest*] 吸引 **2** [正式] (*employ*) [+ *consultant, lawyer, sb's services*] 雇用 **3** [汽车] [+ *clutch*] 接合 **4** [军] [+ *enemy*] 与…交战 **II** *vi* [术语] 啮合 ♦ **to engage in** [+ *commerce, research etc*] 从事于 ♦ **to engage sb in conversation** 使某人参加谈话

engaged [ɪn'geɪdʒd] *adj* **1** (*to be married*) 已订婚的 **2** [英: 通信] 被占用的 [美 = **busy**] **3** [英] [+ *toilet*] 被占用的 [美 = **occupied**] ♦ **to get engaged (to)** (与…) 订婚 ♦ **he is engaged in research** [正式] 他正从事研究

engaged tone [英: 通信] *n* [C] 忙音

engagement [ɪn'geɪdʒmənt] *n* **1** [C] [正式] (*appointment*) 约会 **2** [C] (*to marry*) 婚约 **3** [C/U] [军] (*battle*) 交战 **4** [C] (*employment*) 受聘期 ♦ **I have a previous engagement** 我有个前约

engagement ring *n* [C] 订婚戒指

engaging [ɪnˈgeɪdʒɪŋ] *adj* [+ *personality, smile*] 有吸引力的

engine [ˈɛndʒɪn] *n* [c] **1** [汽车] 发动机 **2** [铁路] 机车

engineer [ɛndʒɪˈnɪə(r)] **I** *n* [c] **1** (*who designs machines, bridges etc*) 工程师 **2** (*who repairs machines, phones etc*) 机械师 **3** [美] (*train driver*) 火车司机 **4** (*on ship*) 轮机员 **II** *vt* **1** [+ *bridge, building etc*] 设计 **2** (喻) [+ *situation, event*] 策划

engineering [ɛndʒɪˈnɪərɪŋ] *n* [u] **1** (*design, construction*) [*of roads, bridges, machinery*] 工程 **2** (*science*) 工程学 ♦**engineering works** *or* **factory** 机械工厂

England [ˈɪŋglənd] *n* 英格兰

English [ˈɪŋglɪʃ] **I** *adj* 英国的 **II** *n* (*language*) 英语 **III the English** *n* [*pl*] (*people*) 英国人 ♦**an English speaker** 一个讲英语的人

English Channel *n* ♦**the English Channel** 英吉利海峡

Englishman [ˈɪŋglɪʃmən] (*pl* **Englishmen**) *n* [c] 英格兰男人

Englishwoman [ˈɪŋglɪʃwumən] (*pl* **Englishwomen**) *n* [c] 英格兰女人

engrave [ɪnˈgreɪv] *vt* 雕刻

engraving [ɪnˈgreɪvɪŋ] *n* [c] (*picture, print*) 雕刻品

engrossed [ɪnˈgrəust] *adj* ♦**engrossed in** [+ *book, programme*] 全神贯注于

enhance [ɪnˈhɑːns] *vt* **1** [+ *enjoyment, beauty, value*] 增加 **2** [+ *reputation*] 提高

enjoy [ɪnˈdʒɔɪ] *vt* **1** (*take pleasure in*) [+ *life, marriage*] 享受…的乐趣 **2** [正式] (*have benefit of*) [+ *good health, privilege*] 享有 ♦**to enjoy doing sth** (*like doing*) 喜欢做某事 ♦**to enjoy o.s.** 过得快活 ♦**enjoy your meal!** 吃好！

enjoyable [ɪnˈdʒɔɪəbl] *adj* 有乐趣的

enjoyment [ɪnˈdʒɔɪmənt] *n* [u] 乐趣

enlarge [ɪnˈlɑːdʒ] **I** *vt* **1** (*make bigger*) 扩大 **2** [摄影] 放大 **II** *vi* 增大 ♦**to enlarge on** *or* **upon** [正式] [+ *subject*] 详述

enlargement [ɪnˈlɑːdʒmənt] *n* **1** [u] (*expansion*) 扩大 **2** [c] [摄影] 放大的照片

enlightened [ɪnˈlaɪtnd] *adj* [+ *person, policy, system*] 开明的

enlist [ɪnˈlɪst] **I** *vi* [军] 应募 **II** *vt* **1** [军] 征募 **2** [+ *support, help*] 赢得 ♦**enlisted man** [美：军] 士兵

enormous [ɪˈnɔːməs] *adj* **1** (*in size or amount*) [+ *room, dog*] 庞大的 **2** (*in degree or extent*) [+ *pleasure, success, disappointment*] 巨大的

✪**enough** [ɪˈnʌf] **I** *adj* [+ *time, books, people*] 足够的 ◊ *They had enough cash for a one-way ticket.* 他们有足够的现金支付单程票。 **II** *pron* (*sufficient, more than desired*) 足够的东西 ◊ *I've got five thousand dollars, I hope it's enough.* 我有5000美金，希望足够了。◊ *I only met him once, and that was enough.* 我只见过他一次，足已了。**III** *adv* **1** ♦**big/old/tall enough** 足够大/到年龄了/足够高 **2** (*reasonably*) ♦**it's nice/interesting enough** 相当好/相当有趣 ♦**enough time/money to do sth** 有足够的时间/金钱去做某事 ♦**he has not worked enough** 他工作不够努力 ♦**have you got enough?** 你够吗？♦**enough to eat** 够吃 ♦**will 5 be enough?** 5个够吗？♦**I've had enough!** 我受够了！♦**it's hot/difficult enough as it is** 已经够热/难的了 ♦**he was kind enough to lend me the money** 他很仁慈，借钱给我 ♦**(that's) enough!** 够了！♦**I've had enough of him** 我已经受够他了 ♦**that's enough, thanks** 足已，谢谢 ♦**funnily/interestingly enough ...** 说来也奇怪/有趣…

enquire [ɪnˈkwaɪə(r)] *vt, vi* = **inquire**

enquiry [ɪnˈkwaɪərɪ] *n* = **inquiry**

enrage [ɪnˈreɪdʒ] *vt* 激怒

enrich [ɪnˈrɪtʃ] *vt* **1** (*improve*) 使丰富 **2** (*financially*) 使富裕

enrol (美 **enroll**) [ɪnˈrəul] **I** *vt* **1** (*at school, university*) 招…入学 **2** (*on course, in club*) 注册 **II** *vi* (*at school, university, on course, in club*) 注册

enrolment (美 **enrollment**) [ɪnˈrəulmənt] *n* [u] (*registration*) 注册

en route [ɔnˈruːt] *adv* (*on the way*) 在途中 ♦**en route to/from** 在去/从…来的途中

en suite [ɔn'swiːt] [英] *adj* 1 [+ *bathroom*] 接连的 2 [+ *bedroom*] 带浴室的

ensure [ɪn'ʃuə(r)] [正式] *vt* [+ *success, safety*] 保证 ♦**to ensure that ...** 保证…

entail [ɪn'teɪl] *vt* (*involve*) 牵涉

enter ['ɛntə(r)] **I** *vt* 1 [正式][+ *room, building*] 进入 2 [+ *army, profession, Parliament*] 入 3 [+ *race, competition*] 参加 4 [+ *new phase, period*] 开始进入 5 (*write down*) (*in book*) 登录 6 [计算机] [+ *data*] 输入 **II** *vi* 1 [正式] (*come or go in*) 进来 ♦**to enter sb for sth** (*for competition, race*) 给某人报名参加某事 ♦**as the war enters its second month** 当战争进入第2个月时

❑**enter for** *vt* [不可拆分] [+ *race, competition*] 报名参加

❑**enter into** [正式] *vt* [不可拆分] 1 [+ *agreement, talks*] 开始进入 2 (*be relevant to*) 构成…的一部分

enterprise ['ɛntəpraɪz] *n* 1 [c] (*company, business*) 企业 2 [c] (*venture*) 事业 3 [u] (*initiative*) 事业心 ♦**free enterprise** 自由企业 ♦**private enterprise** 私营企业

enterprising ['ɛntəpraɪzɪŋ] *adj* 有进取心的

entertain [ɛntə'teɪn] **I** *vt* 1 (*amuse*) 给…娱乐 2 (*invite*) [+ *guest*] 招待 3 [正式] (*consider*) [+ *idea, suggestion*] 考虑 **II** *vi* 款待

entertainer [ɛntə'teɪnə(r)] *n* [c] 表演者

entertaining [ɛntə'teɪnɪŋ] **I** *adj* 引人入胜的 **II** *n* [u] 招待

entertainment [ɛntə'teɪnmənt] *n* 1 [u] (*amusement*) 娱乐活动 2 [c] (*show*) 表演会

enthusiasm [ɪn'θuːzɪæzəm] *n* 1 [u] (*eagerness*) 热情 2 [c] (*interest*) 兴趣 ♦**enthusiasm for sth** 对某事的热情

enthusiast [ɪn'θuːzɪæst] *n* [c] (*fan*) 爱好者 ♦**a jazz enthusiast** 爵士乐爱好者

enthusiastic [ɪnθuːzɪ'æstɪk] *adj* (*excited, eager*) [+ *person*] 极感兴趣的; [+ *response, reception*] 热情的 ♦**to be enthusiastic about sth** 对某事满怀热情

entire [ɪn'taɪə(r)] *adj* 整个的

entirely [ɪn'taɪəlɪ] *adv* 完全地

entitle [ɪn'taɪtl] *vt* ♦**to entitle sb to sth** 给某人获得某物的资格 ♦**to entitle sb to do sth** 给某人做某事的权利 ♦**to be entitled to sth** 有资格获得某物 ♦**to be entitled to do sth** 有资格做某事

entitled [ɪn'taɪtld] *adj* [+ *book, film etc*] ♦**entitled "The Next Generation"** 题为"下一代"

entity ['ɛntɪtɪ] [正式] *n* [c] 实体

entrance[1] ['ɛntrns] *n* [c] 1 (*way in*) 入口 2 (*arrival*) 到场 ♦**the entrance to sth** 某处的入口 ♦**to gain entrance to** [+ *university, profession etc*] 加入; [正式] [+ *place*] 能够进入 ♦**to deny sb entrance** 拒绝让某人入场

entrance[2] [ɪn'trɑːns] *vt* (*enchant*) 使入迷

entrance examination *n* [c] 入学考试

entrance fee *n* [c] 入场费

entrance ramp [美:汽车] *n* [c] 通向高速公路的岔道 [英=**slip road**]

entrant ['ɛntrnt] *n* [c] 1 (*in competition*) 参赛者 2 [英:教育,大学] 新学员

entrepreneur ['ɔntrəprə'nəː(r)] *n* [c] 企业家

entrust [ɪn'trʌst] *vt* ♦**to entrust sth to sb** 交托某事给某人 ♦**to entrust sb with sth** 把某事委托给某人

entry ['ɛntrɪ] *n* 1 [c] (*way in*) 入口 2 [c] (*in competition*) 登记 3 [c] (*item*) (*in diary*) 项目; [计算机] 输入; (*in reference book*) 条目 4 [u] (*arrival*) (*in country*) 进入权; (*in room*) 入场; (*in institution*) 加入 ♦**"no entry"** (*to land, room*) "禁止入内"; [汽车] "禁止通行" ♦**single/double entry book-keeping** [商] 单/复式记账

envelope ['ɛnvələup] *n* [c] 信封

envious ['ɛnvɪəs] *adj* [+ *person, glance*] 羡慕的 ♦**to be envious of sth/sb** 羡慕某物/某人

environment [ɪn'vaɪərnmənt] *n* [c/u] (*surroundings*) 环境 ♦**the environment** (*natural world*) 自然环境

environmental [ɪnvaɪərn'mɛntl] *adj* **1** (*of the natural world*) 环境保护的 **2** (*of surroundings*) 有关环境的 ♦**environmental studies** [教育] 环境学
environmentalist [ɪnvaɪərn-'mɛntlɪst] *n* [c] 环境保护论者
environmentally [ɪnvaɪərn'mɛntlɪ] *adv* ♦**environmentally sound/harmful** *etc* 环境上有利/有害{等}的
environmentally friendly *adj* 不污染环境的
envisage [ɪn'vɪzɪdʒ] *vt* (*foresee*) 设想 ♦**I envisage that ...** 我设想…
envision [ɪn'vɪʒən] [美] *vt* = **envisage**
envoy ['ɛnvɔɪ] *n* [c] (*diplomat*) 使者
envy ['ɛnvɪ] **I** *n* [U] (*jealousy*) 羡慕 **II** *vt* (*be jealous of*) 羡慕 ♦**to envy sb sth** 羡慕某人的某物
epic ['ɛpɪk] **I** *n* [c] (*book, film, poem*) 史诗 **II** *adj* [+ *journey*] 英雄的
epidemic [ɛpɪ'dɛmɪk] **I** *n* [c] [*of disease*] 流行 **II** *adj* 流行性的
epilepsy ['ɛpɪlɛpsɪ] *n* [U] 癫痫
epileptic fit [ɛpɪ'lɛptɪk-] *n* [c] 癫痫发作
episode ['ɛpɪsəud] *n* [c] **1** (*period, event*) 插曲 **2** [电视, 广播] (*instalment*) 集
epitomize [ɪ'pɪtəmaɪz] *vt* 集中体现
equal ['iːkwl] **I** *adj* **1** [+ *size, number, amount*] 相等的 **2** [+ *intensity, importance*] 同样的 **II** *n* [c] (*peer*) 相仿的人 **III** *vt* **1** [+ *number, amount*] 等于 **2** (*match, rival*) 比得上 ♦**they are roughly equal in size** 它们大小差不多 ♦**to be equal to** (*the same as*) 与…相同 ♦**to be equal to a task/demand** 胜任一项任务/要求 ♦**79 minus 14 equals 65** 79 减 14 等于 65
equality [iː'kwɔlɪtɪ] *n* [U] 平等 ♦**equality of opportunity** 机会均等
equalize ['iːkwəlaɪz] **I** *vi* [英: 足球等] 拉平比分 **II** *vt* (*balance*) [+ *society, opportunities*] 使平等
equally ['iːkwəlɪ] *adv* **1** [*share, divide etc* +] 平等地 **2** [+ *good, important etc*] 同样地 ♦**they are equally clever** 他们同样聪明 ♦**equally, ...** (*introducing clause*) 同时，…
equation [ɪ'kweɪʃən] [数] *n* [c] 等式
equator [ɪ'kweɪtə(r)] *n* ♦**the equator** 赤道
Equatorial Guinea *n* 赤道几内亚
equilibrium [iːkwɪ'lɪbrɪəm] *n* **1** [C/U] (*balance*) 平衡 **2** [U] (*composure*) 心境的安宁
equip [ɪ'kwɪp] *vt* **1** ♦**to equip (with)** [+ *person, army*] 装备 **2** [+ *room, car etc*] 配备 ♦**to equip sb for sth/to do sth** (*prepare*) 为某事/做某事使某人做好准备 ♦**to be well equipped** 装备充分的
equipment [ɪ'kwɪpmənt] *n* [U] 设备
equivalent [ɪ'kwɪvələnt] **I** *adj* 相同的 **II** *n* [c] (*equal*) 相当的人/物 ♦**the equivalent of** (*amount etc*) …的等值物 ♦**to be equivalent to** 与…相等
ER I *n abbr* [美: 医] (= ***emergency room***) 急诊室 [英 = **A & E** *or* **casualty**] **II** *abbr* [英] (= ***Elizabeth Regina***) 伊丽莎白女王
era ['ɪərə] *n* [c] 时代 ♦**the post-war era** 战后年代
erase [ɪ'reɪz] *vt* **1** [+ *words, mark*] 擦掉 **2** [+ *sound from tape etc*] 抹掉 **3** (喻) [+ *thought, memory*] 消除
eraser [ɪ'reɪzə(r)] [尤美] *n* [c] 橡皮 [英 = **rubber**]
erect [ɪ'rɛkt] **I** *adj* **1** [+ *person, posture*] 挺直的 **2** [+ *tail, ears*] 竖起的 **3** [+ *penis*] 勃起的 **II** *vt* [正式] (*build*) [+ *building, bridge*] 架设; (*assemble*) [+ *barrier*] 设置 ♦**to hold o.s. erect** 把身子挺直
erection [ɪ'rɛkʃən] *n* **1** [U] [*of building, statue*] 建造 **2** [U] [*of tent, fence etc*] 架设 **3** [c] [生理] 勃起
Eritrea [ɛrɪ'treɪə] *n* 厄立特里亚
erode [ɪ'rəud] **I** *vt* **1** [+ *soil, rock*] 侵蚀 **2** [正式] [+ *confidence, authority*] 削弱 **II** *vi* **1** [*soil, rock* +] 遭侵蚀 **2** [正式] [*confidence, authority* +] 削弱
erosion [ɪ'rəuʒən] *n* [U] **1** [*of soil, rock*] 侵蚀 **2** [正式] [*of confidence, authority, freedom*] 削弱
erotic [ɪ'rɔtɪk] *adj* **1** [+ *experience, dream*] 引起性欲的 **2** [+ *books, films*] 色情的
errand ['ɛrənd] *n* [c] 差事 ♦**to run errands** 跑腿 ♦**to go on an**

errand 跑腿 ♦**an errand of mercy** 仁慈之行

erratic [ɪ'rætɪk] *adj* [+ *behaviour, progress*] 不规则的

error ['ɛrə(r)] *n* [c/u] 差错 ♦**to make an error** 犯错误 ♦**typing/mathematical error** 打字/算术差错 ♦**in error** 错误地

erupt [ɪ'rʌpt] *vi* **1** [*volcano* +] 喷发 **2** [*war, crisis* +] 爆发

eruption [ɪ'rʌpʃən] *n* **1** [c/u] [*of volcano*] 喷发 **2** [c] [*of conflict, violence*] 爆发

escalate ['ɛskəleɪt] **I** *vi* [*conflict, crisis* +] 逐步升级 **II** *vt* [+ *conflict, crisis*] 使逐步升级

escalator ['ɛskəleɪtə(r)] *n* [c] 自动扶梯

escape [ɪs'keɪp] **I** *n* **1** [c/u] (*from prison*) 逃跑 **2** (*from accident*) ♦**a narrow/lucky escape** 九死一生 **3** [c/u] (*from person*) 逃脱 **4** [c] (喻) 逃避 **II** *vi* **1** (*get away*) 逃走 **2** (*from jail*) 逃跑 **3** (*from accident*) ♦**to escape unhurt** 安然逃脱 **4** (*leak*) [*gas, liquid, heat* +] 漏出 **III** *vt* [+ *injury*] 避免 ♦**to escape from** [+ *place*] 从…逃跑；[+ *person*] 避开 ♦**to escape to (another place)** 逃往(某处) ♦**to escape to safety** 安全逃走 ♦**his name escapes me** 我想不起他的名字 ♦**to escape sb's attention** 避开某人的注意

escort [*n* 'ɛskɔːt, *vb* ɪs'kɔːt] **I** *n* [c] **1** [警, 军] 护卫 **2** (*companion*) 陪同 **II** *vt* [+ *person*] 护送 ♦**under escort** 被护送 ♦**to escort sb to the door** 送某人到门口

Eskimo ['ɛskɪməu] *n* [c] (*person*) 爱斯基摩人

esp. *abbr* (= ***especially***) 尤其

especially [ɪs'pɛʃlɪ] *adv* **1** (*particularly*) 尤其 **2** (*more than usually*) [+ *happy, gifted, fond of sb*] 特别

espionage ['ɛspɪənɑːʒ] [政治, 军, 商] *n* [u] 间谍活动

essay ['ɛseɪ] *n* **1** [教育] 论文 **2** (*paper, discussion*) 散文

essence ['ɛsns] *n* **1** [u] (*true nature*) 本质 **2** [c/u] [烹饪] 香精 ♦**in essence** [正式] 基本上 ♦**speed is of the essence** [正式] 速度是至关重要的

essential [ɪ'sɛnʃl] **I** *adj* **1** (*necessary, vital*) 必要的 **2** (*basic*) 基本的 **II** **essentials** *n*[*pl*] (*necessities*) 必需品 ♦**it is essential that ...** …是必要的 ♦**it is essential to ...** 必须…

essentially [ɪ'sɛnʃəlɪ] [正式] *adv* **1** (*basically*) 基本来说 **2** (*mainly*) 大致上

EST [美] *abbr* (= ***Eastern Standard Time***) 东部标准时间

establish [ɪs'tæblɪʃ] *vt* **1** (*set up*) [+ *company, relations, contact*] 建立 **2** (*find out*) [+ *facts, cause*] 证实 **3** (*acquire*) [+ *reputation*] 确立 ♦**to establish that ...** [正式] 证实…

established [ɪs'tæblɪʃt] *adj* **1** [+ *organization*] 已被确认的 ◊ *the established church* 国教 **2** [+ *custom, practice*] 历时已久的

establishment [ɪs'tæblɪʃmənt] *n* **1** [u] [正式] [*of organization, company etc*] 建立 **2** [c] [正式] (*shop, restaurant etc*) 机构 **3** ♦**the Establishment** 领导集团

estate [ɪs'teɪt] *n* [c] **1** (*land*) 庄园 **2** [英] (*also:* ***housing estate***) 住宅区 **3** [法] (*money and property*) 遗产

estate agent [英] *n* [c] 房地产经纪人 [美 = **realtor** *or* **real estate agent**]

estate car [英] *n* [c] 旅行车 [美 = **station wagon**]

esthetic [ɪs'θɛtɪk] [美] *adj* = **aesthetic**

estimate [*n* 'ɛstɪmət, *vb* 'ɛstɪmeɪt] **I** *n* [c] **1** (*calculation*) 估计 **2** (*assessment*) 评估 **3** [商] [*of price*] 估价 **II** *vt* (*reckon, calculate*) 估计 ♦**the damage was estimated at 300 million pounds** 估计损失为3亿英镑 ♦**I estimate that ...** 我估计…

Estonia [ɛs'təunɪə] *n* 爱沙尼亚

Estonian [ɛs'təunɪən] **I** *adj* 爱沙尼亚的 **II** *n* **1** [c] (*person*) 爱沙尼亚人 **2** [u] (*language*) 爱沙尼亚语

ETA *n abbr* (= ***estimated time of arrival***) 估计到达时间

etc (尤美 **etc.**) *abbr* (= ***et cetera***) 等等

eternal [ɪ'təːnl] *adj* **1** (*everlasting*) [+ *youth, life*] 永久的 **2** (*unchanging*) [+ *truths, questions, values*] 永恒的

eternity [ɪ'tə:nɪtɪ] [宗] *n* [U] 永生 ♦**it seemed to last for an eternity** [非正式] 时间长得似乎无穷无尽

ethical ['ɛθɪkl] *adj* **1** (*relating to ethics*) [+ *question, problem*] 伦理的 **2** (*morally right*) 合乎道德的

ethics ['ɛθɪks] **I** *n* [U] (*study of moral philosophy*) 伦理学 **II** *n* [*pl*] (*morality*) 道德准则

Ethiopia [i:θɪ'əupɪə] *n* 埃塞俄比亚

Ethiopian [i:θɪ'əupɪən] **I** *adj* 埃塞俄比亚的 **II** *n* [C] (*person*) 埃塞俄比亚人

ethnic ['ɛθnɪk] *adj* **1** [+ *population*] 种族的 **2** [+ *music, culture etc*] 具有民族特色的

ethnic minority *n* [C] 少数民族

etiquette ['ɛtɪkɛt] *n* [U] 礼节

EU *n abbr* (= ***European Union***) ♦**the EU** 欧洲共同体

euro ['juərəu] (*pl* **euros**) *n* [C] 欧元

Europe ['juərəp] *n* 欧洲

European [juərə'pi:ən] **I** *adj* 欧洲的 **II** *n* [C] (*person*) 欧洲人

European Community [旧] *n* ♦**the European Community** 欧洲共同市场

European Union *n* ♦**the European Union** 欧洲共同体

evacuate [ɪ'vækjueɪt] *vt* **1** [+ *people*] 疏散 **2** [+ *place*] 撤离

evade [ɪ'veɪd] *vt* **1** [+ *tax*] 逃避 **2** [+ *question, issue*] 回避 **3** [+ *duty, responsibility*] 规避 **4** (*elude*) [+ *person*] 逃脱；[文] [*happiness, love* +] 回避 ♦**to evade capture** 逃脱擒拿

evaluate [ɪ'væljueɪt] *vt* [+ *situation, importance*] 评估

evaporate [ɪ'væpəreɪt] *vi* **1** [*liquid* +] 挥发 **2**（喻）[*anger, fear, hopes* +] 消失

eve [i:v] *n* ♦ **on the eve of** 在…的前夕

✪**even** ['i:vn] **I** *adv* 甚至 ◊ *He didn't even hear what I said.* 他甚至根本没听见我的话。**II** *adj* **1** (*flat*) 平坦的 ◊ *The road isn't very even.* 路不很平坦。**2** (*constant*) [+ *temperature, rate*] 平稳的 **3** (*equal*) [+ *contest, score*] 势均力敌的 ◊ *It was an even contest.* 这是一场势均力敌的较量。; [+ *distribution*] 均等的 ◊ *a more even distribution of wealth* 更加均等的财富分配 **4** [+ *number*] 偶数的 ◊ *houses with even numbers* 带偶数门牌号的房子 ♦**even more** 甚至更多 ♦**even better/faster** 甚至更好/快 ♦**even if** 即使 ♦**even though** 尽管 ♦**even so** 虽然如此 ♦**not even** 连…也不 ♦**even as** [文] 正当 ♦**even he was there** 连他都在那儿 ♦**even on Sundays** 甚至星期天 ♦**to break even** 不盈不亏 ♦**now we're even** [非正式] 现在我们两清了 ♦**to get even with sb** [非正式] 报复某人

❑**even out I** *vi* 拉平 **II** *vt* 使均匀

evening ['i:vnɪŋ] *n* [C/U] **1** (*early*) 傍晚 **2** (*late*) 晚上 **3** (*whole period, event*) 晚上 ♦**in the evening** 在晚上 ♦**this evening** 今晚 ♦**tomorrow/yesterday evening** 明/昨晚

evening class *n* [C] 夜校

evening dress *n* **1** [C] (*gown*) 女装晚礼服 **2** [U] (*formal clothing*) 晚礼服

evenly ['i:vnlɪ] *adv* [*distribute, spread, breathe* +] 均匀地；[*divide* +] 均等地

✪**event** [ɪ'vɛnt] *n* [C] **1** (*occurrence*) 事件 **2** [体育] 比赛项目 ♦**in the normal course of events** 按照事情自然发展的进程 ♦**in the event of/that ...** 如果…发生 ♦**in the event** [英] 到头来 ♦**in any event** 不管怎样

eventful [ɪ'vɛntful] *adj* [+ *day, life, game, journey*] 丰富多彩的

eventual [ɪ'vɛntʃuəl] *adj* [+ *outcome, aim*] 最终的

eventually [ɪ'vɛntʃuəlɪ] *adv* **1** (*finally*) 终于 **2** (*ultimately*) 最终

> 📖 请勿将**eventually**和**finally**混淆。如果某事拖延了很久，或者经历了相当复杂的过程后终于发生了，可以说它**eventually**发生了 *Eventually, they got to the hospital... I found Victoria Avenue eventually.* **eventually**还可以表示发生的一系列事情中的最后一件事，通常这最后的一件事是前面一系列事情的结果。*Eventually, they were forced to return to England.* 在经历了长期等待或期盼后，某事终于发

生了，可以说它**finally**发生了。*Finally, I went to bed... The heat of the sun finally became too much for me.* **finally**还可以表示发生的一系列事情当中最后的一件事。*The sky turned red, then purple, and finally black.*

✪ **ever** ['ɛvə(r)] *adv* **1** (*at any time*) 从来 ◊ *Neither of us has ever been to Japan.* 我们俩都从来没去过日本。◊ *I forbid you ever to use that word!* 我不允许你在任何时候用那个字眼！**2** (*always*) 总是 ◊ *Ever hopeful, he continued to apply for jobs.* 他总是满怀希望，又继续申请工作了。♦**have you ever seen it/been there** *etc*? 你曾经见过它/去过那儿{等}吗？♦**ever since** (*adv*) 从…以来 ◊ *We have been friends ever since.* 我们从那时以来一直是朋友。; (*conj*) 自从 ◊ *Jack has loved trains ever since he was a boy.* 杰克自小就喜爱火车。♦**why ever not?** 究竟为什么不呢？♦**who ever would do such a thing?** 究竟谁会做这样的事？♦**the best ever** 迄今最佳 ♦**hardly ever** 几乎从不 ♦**better than ever** 前所未有的好 ♦**she's ever so pretty** [英:非正式] 她非常漂亮 ♦**I like him ever so much.** [英:非正式] 我很喜欢他。♦**he's ever such a good dancer** [英:非正式] 他跳舞跳得很好 ♦**thank you ever so much** 非常感谢你 ♦**yours ever** [英:过时] (*in letters*) 你永久的朋友 ♦**as ever** 照常

evergreen ['ɛvəgri:n] **I** *n* [c] 常绿植物 **II** *adj* 常绿的

everlasting [ɛvə'lɑ:stɪŋ] *adj* [+ *love, life*] 永恒的

✪ **every**
KEYWORD
['ɛvrɪ] *adj*
1 (*each*) 每个 ♦**every village should have a post office** 每个村庄都应该有一个邮局 ♦**every one of them** (*people*) 他们中的每个人; (*objects*) 每个
2 (*all possible*) 一切可能的 ♦**there is every chance that ...** 很有可能… ♦**recipes for every occasion** 各个场合均适用的菜谱 ♦**I have every confidence in him** 我对他有十足的信心 ♦**I gave you every assistance** 我给你各种可能的援助
3 (*with time words*) 每 ♦**every day/week** 每天/周 ♦**every Sunday** 每个星期天 ♦**every other week** 每隔一周 ♦**every other/third day** 每隔一天/每三天 ♦**every few days/minutes** 每隔几天/分钟 ♦**every now and then** *or* **again** 不时地
4 (*statistics*) ♦**one in every five people** 每五人中有一人
📖 用法参见 **each**

everybody ['ɛvrɪbɔdɪ] *pron* 每人 ♦**everybody knows about it** 谁都知道 ♦**everybody else** 其他所有人

everyday ['ɛvrɪdeɪ] *adj* **1** (*daily*) [+ *life, routine*] 日常的 **2** (*usual, common*) [+ *problem, occurrence*] 平常的

everyone ['ɛvrɪwʌn] *pron* = **everybody**

📖 请勿将**everyone**和**every one**混淆。**everyone**总是指人，并且用作单数名词。*Everyone likes him...On behalf of everyone in the school, I'd like to thank you...* 在短语**every one**中，**one**是代词，在不同的上下文当中，它能够指代任何人或事物。其后经常紧随单词**of**，*We've saved seeds from every one of our plants...Every one of them phoned me.* 在这些例子当中，**every one**是表达**all**的含义，而且语气更强烈。

✪ **everything** ['ɛvrɪθɪŋ] *pron* 所有事物 ♦**is everything OK?** 都还好吧？♦**everything is ready** 所有都准备就绪 ♦**he did everything possible** 他尽了最大努力

everywhere ['ɛvrɪwɛə(r)] **I** *adv* 各处 **II** *pron* 所有地方 ♦**there's rubbish everywhere** 到处都是垃圾 ♦**everywhere you go** 无论你去哪里

evict [ɪ'vɪkt] *vt* [+ *squatter, tenant*] 逐出

evidence ['ɛvɪdns] *n* [U] **1** (*proof*) 根据 **2** [法] (*information*) 证据; (*objects*) 物证; (*testimony*) 证言 **3** (*signs, indications*) 迹象 ♦ **to produce sth as evidence** [法] 提供某物作为证据 ♦ **to give evidence** [法] 作证 ♦ **to show evidence of sth** 表明某事 ♦ **to be in evidence** [*quality* +] 明显的; [*soldiers, tourists etc* +] 可看见的

evident ['ɛvɪdnt] *adj* 明显的 ♦ **to be evident (to sb/that ...)** (对某人来说/…) 显而易见

evidently ['ɛvɪdntlɪ] *adv* **1** (*obviously*) 明显地 **2** (*apparently*) 显然地

evil ['i:vl] **I** *adj* [+ *person, system*] 邪恶的 **II** *n* **1** [U] (*wickedness*) 邪恶 **2** [C] (*curse, scourge*) 祸害 ♦ **the evils of alcohol** 酗酒的害处 ♦ **a necessary evil** 不可避免的邪恶

evoke [ɪ'vəuk] [正式] *vt* [+ *feeling, memory*] 引起

evolution [i:və'lu:ʃən] *n* [U] **1** [生物] 进化 **2** (*development*) 演变

evolve [ɪ'vɔlv] **I** *vi* **1** [*animal, plant etc* +] 演化 **2** [*plan, style, organization* +] 逐步形成 **II** *vt* [+ *scheme, style*] 发展 ♦ **to evolve from sth** 从某物演化而来 ♦ **to evolve into sth** 演化成某物

ewe [ju:] *n* [C] 母羊

ex- [ɛks] *prefix* (*former*) [+ *husband, president etc*] 前 ♦ **my ex-wife** 我的前妻

exact [ɪg'zækt] **I** *adj* **1** (*precise*) [+ *time, number, word etc*] 确切的 **2** [+ *person, worker*] 严谨的 **3** (*used for emphasis*) 恰恰 **II** *vt* ♦ **to exact sth (from sb)** [正式] (向某人) 索取某物 ♦ **astrology is not an exact science** 占星术并不是一门精确的科学 ♦ **to be exact** 准确来说

exactly [ɪg'zæktlɪ] *adv* **1** (*precisely*) 确切地 ◊ *a tower exactly ten metres in height.* 一座正好10米高的塔。 **2** (*indicating emphasis*) 正是 **3** (*indicating agreement*) 一点不错 ♦ **at 5 o'clock exactly** 在5点整时 ♦ **not exactly** (*indicating disagreement*) 不完全是 ♦ **he's not exactly rich/poor** 他一点也算不上富/穷

exaggerate [ɪg'zædʒəreɪt] **I** *vi* 夸张 **II** *vt* **1** (*overemphasize*) [+ *situation, effects*] 夸大 **2** (*draw attention to*) [*feature, quality* +] 使扩大

exaggeration [ɪgzædʒə'reɪʃən] *n* [C/U] 夸张

exam [ɪg'zæm] *n* 测验

examination [ɪgzæmɪ'neɪʃən] *n* **1** [C/U] (*inspection*) [*of object, plan, accounts*] 检查 **2** [C] [正式: 教育, 大学] (*exam*) 考试 **3** [C/U] [医] 体检 ♦ **the matter is under examination** 这件事尚在审查中

examine [ɪg'zæmɪn] *vt* **1** (*inspect*) [+ *object, plan, accounts*] 检查 **2** [教育, 大学] 对…进行测验 **3** [医] 检查

examiner [ɪg'zæmɪnə(r)] [教育, 大学] *n* [C] **1** (*setting exam*) 主考官 **2** (*marking exam*) 判卷官

✪**example** [ɪg'zɑ:mpl] *n* [C] **1** (*typical illustration*) 例子 **2** (*model*) [*of good behaviour etc*] 榜样 ◊ *Their example shows us what we are all capable of.* 他们树立的榜样显示出我们也都能做到些什么。 ♦ **for example** 例如 ♦ **an example of sth** 某物的例子 ♦ **to set an example** 树立榜样 ♦ **to follow sb's example** 学习某人的榜样 ♦ **he is an example to us all** 他是我们每一个人的楷模 ♦ **to make an example of sb** 惩罚某人以儆戒他人

exasperated [ɪg'zɑ:spəreɪtɪd] *adj* ♦ **exasperated (at** *or* **by** *or* **with sth)** (被某事) 搞得恼火

excavate ['ɛkskəveɪt] *vt* **1** [*archaeologist* +] 发掘 **2** [正式] (*dig*) 挖掘

exceed [ɪk'si:d] [正式] *vt* **1** (*be greater than*) [+ *number, amount, expectations*] 超出 **2** (*go beyond*) [+ *speed limit, budget*] 超过; [+ *powers, duties*] 超越

exceedingly [ɪk'si:dɪŋlɪ] [过时] *adv* 极其

excel [ɪk'sɛl] **I** *vi* ♦ **to excel (in/at)** [+ *sports, business etc*] 擅长 **II** *vt* ♦ **to excel o.s.** 出类拔萃

excellence ['ɛksələns] *n* [U] 卓越

excellent ['ɛksələnt] **I** *adj* 极好的 **II** *int* ♦ **excellent!** 太好了!

except [ɪk'sɛpt] *prep* (*apart from*) 除

了 ♦**except for** 除了…外 ♦**except that ...** 除了… ♦**except if/when** …时例外

exception [ɪk'sɛpʃən] *n* [c] (*special, case*) 例外 ♦**to make an exception** 破例 ♦**with the exception of** 除…外 ♦**to take exception (to sth)** (对某事)不悦

exceptional [ɪk'sɛpʃənl] *adj* **1** (*outstanding*) [+ *person, talent*] 杰出的 **2** [正式] (*unusual*) [+ *situation, circumstances*] 独特的

exceptionally [ɪk'sɛpʃənlɪ] *adv* 格外

excerpt ['ɛksəːpt] *n* [c] (*from text, film*) 选录

excess [*n* ɪk'sɛs, 'ɛksɛs, *adj* 'ɛksɛs] **I** *n* **1** ♦**an excess of** 过多◊ *Inflation results from an excess of demand over supply.* 通货膨胀是供过于求的结果。**2** [c] [英:保险] 保险押金 **II** *adj* [+ *water, fat*] 过多的 **III excesses** *n* [*pl*] [*of person, war*] 过分的行为 ♦**in excess of** 超过 ♦**to do sth to excess** 过度做某事

excess baggage *n* [u] 超重行李

excessive [ɪk'sɛsɪv] *adj* [+ *amount, force*] 过分的

exchange [ɪks'tʃeɪndʒ] **I** *vt* **1** [+ *gifts, addresses*] 交换 **2** [+ *greetings, glances*] 互换 **3** ♦**to exchange sth (for sth)** [+ *goods*] 用某物交换(某物) **II** *n* **1** [c/u] (*giving and receiving*) [*of information, views, gifts, prisoners*] 交换; [*of students, sportspeople etc*] 交流 **2** [c] [正式] (*conversation*) 交锋 **3** [c] (*also: **telephone exchange***) 电话局 ♦**in exchange (for)** 作为(对…的)交换

exchange rate *n* [c] 汇率

Exchequer [ɪks'tʃɛkə(r)] [英] *n* ♦**the Exchequer** 财政部

excite [ɪk'saɪt] *vt* **1** [+ *person*] 刺激 **2** [+ *enthusiasm, curiosity*] 引起 **3** (*sexually*) 使兴奋

excited [ɪk'saɪtɪd] *adj* 兴奋的 ♦**to be excited about sth/about doing sth** 对某事/做某事感到激动 ♦**to get excited** 激动兴奋

excitement [ɪk'saɪtmənt] *n* [u] (*exhilaration*) 兴奋

exciting [ɪk'saɪtɪŋ] *adj* [+ *time, event, place*] 令人兴奋的

excl. *abbr* (= ***excluding, exclusive (of)***) 不含

exclaim [ɪks'kleɪm] **I** *vi* 大声叫嚷 **II** *vt* ♦**to exclaim that ...** 叫喊…

exclamation [ɛksklə'meɪʃən] *n* [c] 惊叫

exclamation mark [英], **exclamation point** [美] *n* [c] 感叹号

exclude [ɪks'kluːd] *vt* **1** (*leave out*) [+ *person*] 把…排斥在外; [+ *substance, fact*] 不包括 **2** (*rule out*) [+ *possibility*] 排除 **3** [+ *child*] (*from school*) 开除 ♦**to exclude sb from sth** [+ *place, activity*] 拒绝某人做某事 ♦**to exclude sth from sth** 将某物排除于某物之外

excluding [ɪks'kluːdɪŋ] *prep* 不包括

exclusion [ɪks'kluːʒən] *n* [c/u] **1** [*of person, fact, possibility*] 排除在外 **2** [*of child*] (*from school*) 开除 ♦**to the exclusion of sth** 把某事除外

exclusive [ɪks'kluːsɪv] **I** *adj* **1** [+ *club, district*] 高级的 **2** [出版] [+ *story, interview*] 独家的 **II** *n* [c] [出版] 独家报道 ♦**have exclusive use of sth** 有使用某物的专有权 ♦**to be exclusive to sth** 只有某处才有的 ♦**mutually exclusive** 互不相容 ♦**exclusive of postage/tax** 不含邮费/税

exclusively [ɪks'kluːsɪvlɪ] *adv* (*only*) 仅仅; (*entirely*) 完全

excruciating [ɪks'kruːʃɪeɪtɪŋ] *adj* **1** [+ *pain*] 极其的 **2** [+ *boredom, embarrassment*] 难以忍受的

excursion [ɪks'kəːʃən] *n* [c] (*trip*) (*by tourists*) 游览; (*shopping etc*) 短途旅行 ♦**to go on an excursion** 去旅行 ♦**an excursion into** (喻) (*venture*) 涉猎于

excuse [*n* ɪks'kjuːs, *vb* ɪks'kjuːz] **I** *n* [c/u] (*justification*) 借口 **II** *vt* **1** (*justify*) [+ *person, behaviour*] 是…的正当理由 **2** (*forgive*) [+ *person, behaviour*] 原谅 ♦**an excuse to do/not to do sth** 做/不做某事的借口 ♦**to make an excuse** 找借口 ♦**to make excuses for sb** 给某人找借口 ♦**there's no excuse for such behaviour** 没有理由这样表现 ♦**to be excused from (doing) sth**

被免除(做)某事 ♦ **to excuse sb for sth/for doing sth** 原谅某人某事/做某事 ♦ **excuse me!** (*attracting attention*) 劳驾！; (*as apology*) 对不起！ ♦ **excuse me, please** 请原谅 ♦ **excuse me?** [美] 对不起，你说什么？[英=**pardon?** *or* **sorry?**] ♦ **he excused himself and left the room** 他说了声"请原谅"就离开了房间 ♦ **if you'll excuse me** 请见谅

ex-directory [ˈɛksdɪˈrɛktərɪ] [英:通信] *adj* [+ *number*] 未列入电话簿的 [美=**unlisted**] ♦ **she's ex-directory** 她的电话未列入电话簿

execute [ˈɛksɪkjuːt] *vt* **1** [+ *person*] 将…处死 **2** [正式][+ *plan, order*] 实行 **3** [+ *manoeuvre*] 完成

execution [ɛksɪˈkjuːʃən] *n* **1** [C/U] [*of person*] 处死刑 **2** [U] [正式][*of plan, order*] 实施 **3** [U] [*of manoeuvre*] 完成

executive [ɪgˈzɛkjutɪv] **I** *n* **1** [C] (*person*) 主管人员 **2** [C] (*committee*) 执行委员会 **3** [政治] ♦ **the executive** 政府行政部门 **II** *adj* **1** [+ *committee*] 执行的; [+ *role, decision*] 行政的 **2** (*for executives*) [+ *car*] 豪华的; [+ *plane*] 专用的 ♦ **executive briefcase** 密码公文箱 ♦ **executive toy** 办公室的小玩意儿

exempt [ɪgˈzɛmpt] **I** *adj* ♦ **exempt from** [+ *duty, obligation*] 免除的 **II** *vt* ♦ **to exempt sb from sth** [+ *duty, obligation*] 免除某人某事

exercise [ˈɛksəsaɪz] **I** *n* **1** [U] (*physical exertion*) 运动 **2** [C] (*series of movements*) 练习 **3** [C] [教育, 音] 练习 **4** [C] [军] 演习 **5** [S] [正式][*of authority etc*] 行使 **II** *vt* **1** (*use*) [+ *right, authority etc*] 行使; [+ *patience, restraint, care etc*] 运用 **2** [+ *muscles*] 锻炼; [+ *mind*] 运用 **3** [+ *dog*] 遛 **III** *vi* [*person* +] 锻炼 ♦ **to take** *or* **get exercise** 做健身活动 ♦ **to do exercises** [体育] 锻炼身体

exercise book [英:教育] *n* [C] 练习本 [美=**notebook**]

exert [ɪgˈzəːt] *vt* [正式][+ *influence, pressure*] 施加 ♦ **to exert o.s.** 尽力

exertion [ɪgˈzəːʃən] *n* [U] 尽力

exhale [ɛksˈheɪl] [正式] **I** *vi* (*breathe out*) 呼气 **II** *vt* [+ *air, smoke*] 呼出

exhaust [ɪgˈzɔːst] **I** *n* [尤英] **1** [C] (*also:* ***exhaust pipe***) 排气管 **2** [U] (*fumes*) 废气 **II** *vt* **1** [+ *person*] 使精疲力竭 **2** [+ *money, resources etc*] 耗尽 **3** [+ *topic*] 详尽无遗地论述 ♦ **to exhaust o.s.** 精疲力竭

exhausted [ɪgˈzɔːstɪd] *adj* (*tired*) 精疲力竭的

exhaustion [ɪgˈzɔːstʃən] *n* [U] (*tiredness*) 精疲力竭

exhibit [ɪgˈzɪbɪt] **I** *n* [C] **1** [艺术] 展览品 **2** [法] 物证 **II** *vt* **1** [+ *quality, ability, emotion*] 显示 **2** [+ *paintings*] 展出 **III** *vi* [艺术] 展出作品

exhibition [ɛksɪˈbɪʃən] *n* **1** [C] [*of paintings etc*] 展览会 **2** [S] (*display*) [*of skill, talent etc*] 表演 ♦ **to make an exhibition of o.s.** 出洋相

exhilarating [ɪgˈzɪləreɪtɪŋ] *adj* [+ *experience, feeling*] 使人兴奋的

exile [ˈɛksaɪl] **I** *n* **1** [U] (*condition, state*) 流亡 **2** [C] (*person*) 流亡者 **II** *vt* 使流亡 ♦ **in exile** 在流亡中

exist [ɪgˈzɪst] *vi* **1** (*be present*) 存在 **2** (*live, subsist*) 生存 ♦ **to exist on sth** 靠某物生存

existence [ɪgˈzɪstəns] *n* **1** [U] (*reality*) 存在 **2** [C] (*life*) 生活 ♦ **to be in existence** 存在的

existing [ɪgˈzɪstɪŋ] *adj* (*present, actual*) 现有的

exit [ˈɛksɪt] **I** *n* [C] **1** (*from room, building, motorway etc*) 出口 **2** (*departure*) ♦ **to make a hasty/quick exit** 急速离去 **II** *vt* **1** [正式][+ *room, building*] 离开 **2** [计算机] 退出 **III** *vi* [戏剧] 退场 ♦ **to exit from sth** [正式][+ *room, motorway etc*] 离开某处

exit ramp [美:汽车] *n* [C] 离开高速公路的岔道 [英=**slip road**]

exotic [ɪgˈzɔtɪk] *adj* [+ *food, place*] 有异国情调的

expand [ɪksˈpænd] **I** *vt* **1** [+ *business, staff, numbers*] 扩展 **2** [+ *area*] 拓展 **II** *vi* **1** [*business* +] 扩展 **2** [*gas, metal* +] 膨胀 ♦ **to expand on sth** [+ *notes, story, comments*] 详述某事

expanse [ɪksˈpæns] *n* [C] [*of sea, sky, land*] 广阔

expansion [ɪksˈpænʃən] *n* **1** [C/U] [*of business, population, economy*] 扩展

2 [U] [*of gas, metal*] 膨胀

✪ **expect** [ɪks'pɛkt] **I** *vt* **1** (*anticipate*) 预料◊ *I expect it will rain.* 我预计会下雨。**2** (*await*) 期待◊ *I am expecting an important letter.* 我正在等一封重要的信。**3** [+ *baby*] 怀有◊ *She was expecting her second child.* 她正怀着她的第2个孩子。**4** (*require*) 期望◊ *They expect a good tip.* 他们期望得到不少小费。**5** (*suppose*) 料想◊ *I expect you're tired.* 我想你一定累了吧。**II** *vi* ♦ **to be expecting** (*be pregnant*) 怀孕 ♦ **to expect sth to happen** 预期某事将发生 ♦ **to expect sb to do sth** (*anticipate*) 期望某人做某事◊ *I expected him to turn down the invitation.* 我想他会谢绝这个邀请。; (*require*) 指望某人做某事◊ *I wasn't expecting you to help.* 我并没有指望你帮忙。♦ **to expect to do sth** 预计要做某事 ♦ **I expect so** 我想会的 ♦ **as expected** 如所预料的

expectation [ɛkspɛk'teɪʃən] *n* [C/U] **1** (*hope*) 期望 **2** (*belief*) 预计 ♦ **against** *or* **contrary to all expectation(s)** 出乎意料 ♦ **to live up to sb's expectations** 不负人望 ♦ **in the expectation that ...** 预计…

expedition [ɛkspə'dɪʃən] *n* [C] **1** (*to explore*) 探险 **2** (*to go shopping, fishing*) 出行

expel [ɪks'pɛl] *vt* **1** [+ *child*] (*from school*) 把…开除 **2** [+ *person*] (*from place*) 赶走 **3** [+ *gas, liquid*] 排出

expend [ɪks'pɛnd] [正式] *vt* [+ *money, time, energy*] 花费

expenditure [ɪks'pɛndɪtʃə(r)] *n* **1** [C/U] [*of money*] 开支 **2** [U] [*of energy, time*] 消耗

expense [ɪks'pɛns] **I** *n* [C/U] (*cost*) 费用 **II expenses** *n* [*pl*] 经费 ♦ **to go to the expense of doing sth** 花钱于做某事 ♦ **at great expense** 以很大代价 ♦ **to do sth at one's own expense** 自己花钱做某事 ♦ **at the expense of** 以…为代价 ♦ **to make a joke at sb's expense** 说笑话让某人出丑

expense account *n* [C] 支出账

expensive [ɪks'pɛnsɪv] *adj* **1** [+ *article*] 昂贵的 **2** [+ *mistake*] 代价高的; [+ *tastes*] 奢华的

✪ **experience** [ɪks'pɪərɪəns] **I** *n* **1** [U] (*in job*) 经验◊ *He has managerial experience.* 他有管理经验。**2** [U] [*of life*] 阅历 **3** [C] (*individual event*) 经历◊ *The funeral was a painful experience.* 那次追悼会是个痛苦的经历。**II** *vt* [+ *feeling, problem*] 体验 ♦ **to know from experience** 根据经验知道 ♦ **to learn from experience** 从经验中学到

experienced [ɪks'pɪərɪənst] *adj* 有经验的

experiment [*n* ɪks'pɛrɪmənt, *vb* ɪks'pɛrɪmɛnt] **I** *n* [C] **1** [科学] 实验 **2** (*trial*) 试用 **II** *vi* **1** ♦ **to experiment (with/on)** [科学] (用…) 做实验 **2** (喻) 试验 ♦ **to perform** *or* **conduct** *or* **carry out an experiment** 做实验 ♦ **as an experiment** 作为实验 ♦ **an experiment in sth** 在某事上的试点

experimental [ɪkspɛrɪ'mɛntl] *adj* **1** (*innovative*) [+ *methods, ideas, art forms*] 实验性的 **2** [科学] [+ *tests, results*] 根据实验的 ♦ **at the experimental stage** 处于试验阶段

expert ['ɛkspə:t] **I** *n* [C] (*specialist*) 专家 **II** *adj* [+ *opinion, help, advice*] 专家的 ♦ **an expert on sth** 某事的专家 ♦ **expert in** *or* **at doing sth** 做某事的高手 ♦ **expert witness** [法] 专家证人

expertise [ɛkspə:'ti:z] *n* [U] 专门知识

expire [ɪks'paɪə(r)] *vi* **1** [*passport, licence etc* +] 过期 **2** [文] (*die*) 逝世

expiry date *n* [C] [*of credit card, passport, visa, contract etc*] 到期日; (*on drug, medicine*) 有效期

explain [ɪks'pleɪn] **I** *vt* **1** (*make understandable*) [+ *situation, contract*] 解释 **2** (*give reasons for*) [+ *decision, actions*] 阐明 ♦ **to explain why/how** *etc* 解释为什么/如何{等} ♦ **to explain sth to sb** 向某人解释某事 ♦ **to explain that ...** 解释…
❑ **explain away** *vt* [+ *mistake, situation*] 把…解释过去

explanation [ɛksplə'neɪʃən] *n* **1**

[c/u] *(reason)* ♦ **explanation (for)** (对…的)解释 **2** [c] *(description)* ♦ **explanation (of)** (…的)说明

explanatory [ɪks'plænətrɪ] [正式] *adj* [+ *statement, comment*] 说明的

explicit [ɪks'plɪsɪt] *adj* **1** *(clear)* [+ *support, permission*] 明确的 **2** *(blatant)* [+ *sex, violence*] 显然可见的 ♦ **to be explicit about sth** *(frank)* 对某事直言不讳

explode [ɪks'pləud] **I** *vi* **1** [*bomb* +] 爆炸 **2** [*population* +] 猛增 **3** [*person* +] *(with rage etc)* 迸发 ◊ *Simon exploded with anger.* 西蒙勃然大怒。**II** *vt* **1** [+ *bomb, tank*] 使爆炸 **2** [+ *myth, theory*] 戳穿

exploit [*n* 'ɛksplɔɪt, *vb* ɪks'plɔɪt] **I** *n* *(deed, feat)* 英勇业绩 **II** *vt* **1** *(make use of)* [+ *opportunity, talent*] 利用; [+ *resources*] 开发; *(unfairly)* [+ *person, idea*] 剥削

exploitation [ɛksplɔɪ'teɪʃən] *n* [u] **1** [*of person, idea*] 剥削 **2** [*of resources*] 开发

explore [ɪks'plɔː(r)] **I** *vt* **1** [+ *place, space*] 探索 **2** *(with hands)* 探察 **3** [+ *idea, suggestion*] 探究 **II** *vi* **1** *(look around)* 探险 **2** ♦ **to explore for oil** 勘探石油

explorer [ɪks'plɔːrə(r)] *n* [c] 探险者

explosion [ɪks'pləuʒən] *n* [c] **1** [*of bomb*] 爆炸 **2** *(increase)* [*of population*] 激增 **3** *(outburst)* [*of rage, laughter etc*] 迸发

explosive [ɪks'pləusɪv] **I** *adj* **1** [+ *device, effect*] 爆炸的 **2** (喻) [+ *situation, issue*] 爆炸性的; [+ *person, temper*] 暴躁的 **II** *n* [c/u] *(substance, device)* 炸药

export [*vb* ɛks'pɔːt, *n, cpd* 'ɛkspɔːt] **I** *vt* [+ *goods, ideas, problems, file*] 输出 **II** *n* **1** [u] *(process)* 出口 **2** [c] *(product)* 出口物 **III** *cpd* [复合词] [+ *duty, permit, licence*] 出口

exporter [ɛks'pɔːtə(r)] *n* [c] 出口商

expose [ɪks'pəuz] *vt* *(reveal)* [+ *object*] 显露; [+ *impostor, scandal*] 揭穿 ♦ **to expose sb to sth** [+ *radiation, virus etc*] 使某人接触某物 ♦ **to expose o.s.** [法] 性暴露

exposed [ɪks'pəuzd] *adj* **1** [+ *house, place etc*] 无遮蔽的 **2** [电子] [+ *wire*] 裸露的

exposure [ɪks'pəuʒə(r)] *n* **1** [u] *(to poison, radiation)* ♦ **exposure (to)** 暴露(在…中) **2** [u] [医] 冻伤 **3** [u] *(publicity)* 公开露面 **4** [u] [*of wrongdoing, impostor*] 揭露 **5** [c] [摄影] *(shot)* 软片 ◊ *a camera capable of taking a hundred exposures* 能拍100张照片的照相机; *(amount of light)* [c/u] 曝光量 ♦ **to die from** *or* **of exposure** [医] 死于冻馁

express [ɪks'prɛs] **I** *vt* **1** [+ *idea, view, concern*] 表达 **2** [正式] [+ *quantity, number*] ♦ **expressed as a percentage/fraction** *etc* 用百分比/分数{等}表示的 **II** *adj* **1** [正式] *(clear)* [+ *command, wishes etc*] 明确的 **2** *(deliberate)* [+ *purpose, intention*] 专门的 **3** [+ *service, mail*] 特快的 **III** *n* [c] *(train, coach)* 快车 **IV** *adv* [*send* +] 用快递 ♦ **to express o.s.** 表达自己的意思 ♦ **how does this attitude express itself?** 这个态度如何体现出?

expression [ɪks'prɛʃən] *n* **1** [c] *(word, phrase)* 言辞 **2** [c/u] *(on face)* 表情 **3** [c/u] [*of idea, emotion*] 表达 **4** [u] *(feeling)* [*of actor, singer etc*] 感情

expressive [ɪks'prɛsɪv] *adj* [+ *face*] 富于表情的 ♦ **expressive of** [正式] 表达…的

expressway [ɪks'prɛsweɪ] [汽车] *n* [c] 高速公路

exquisite [ɛks'kwɪzɪt] *adj* **1** *(beautiful)* [+ *lace, workmanship*] 精致的; [+ *taste*] 高雅的 **2** [文] *(keenly felt)* [+ *pleasure, relief*] 极其的

ext. [通信] *abbr* (= ***extension***) 分机

extend [ɪks'tɛnd] **I** *vt* **1** [+ *visit*] 延长 **2** [+ *building*] 扩展 **3** [+ *contract, deadline*] 给…延期 **4** [+ *arm, hand*] 伸出 **5** [+ *welcome, invitation*] 发出 **6** [商] [+ *credit*] 提供 **II** *vi* **1** [*land, road* +] 延伸 **2** [*period* +] 延续 **3** [*influence, power etc* +] 延及 ◊ *His influence extends beyond the TV viewing audience.* 他的影响超出了电视观众的范围。♦ **to extend from** *(protrude)* 从…中伸出 ♦ **to extend to** *(include)* 涉及

extension [ɪks'tɛnʃən] *n* [c] **1** [*of building*] 扩建部分 **2** [*of contract, visa*] 延期 **3** [*of rights, campaign, idea*] 扩展 **4** [电子] 延长部分 **5** [*of road,* *railway*] 附加部分 **6** (*to wire, table*) 延伸部分 **7** [通信] 分机 ♦**extension 3718** [通信] 3718 分机

extensive [ɪks'tɛnsɪv] *adj* **1** [+ *area, grounds*] 广阔的 **2** [+ *damage*] 巨大的 **3** [+ *inquiries, discussion*] 广泛的 **4** [+ *use*] 大量的

extent [ɪks'tɛnt] *n* [U/S] **1** [*of area, land etc*] 大小 **2** [*of problem, damage etc*] 程度 ♦**to a certain extent** 在一定程度上 ♦**to a large extent** 在很大程度上 ♦**to the extent of ...** 到了…地步 ♦**to some extent** 在某种程度上 ♦**to such an extent that ...** 到这样的程度，以至于… ♦**to what extent?** 到什么程度？

exterior [ɛks'tɪərɪə(r)] **I** *adj* (*external*) [+ *drain, wall*] 外部的 **II** *n* [C] **1** (*outside*) [*of building, vehicle*] 外部 **2** (*appearance*) [*of person*] 外表

external [ɛks'təːnl] **I** *adj* **1** [+ *wall, surface*] 外部的 **2** [尤英] [+ *examiner, auditor*] 外界的 **II externals** *n* [*pl*] 外表 ♦**for external use only** [医] 只供外用 ♦**external affairs** [政治] 外交事务

extinct [ɪks'tɪŋkt] *adj* **1** [+ *animal, plant*] 灭绝的 **2** [+ *volcano*] 熄灭的

extinction [ɪks'tɪŋkʃən] *n* [U] [*of species*] 灭绝 ♦**to face extinction** 面临灭绝

extinguish [ɪks'tɪŋgwɪʃ] *vt* **1** [正式] [+ *fire*] 扑灭；[+ *light, cigarette*] 熄灭 **2** [文] [+ *hope, memory*] 使破灭

extra ['ɛkstrə] **I** *adj* [+ *thing, person, amount*] 额外的 **II** *adv* **1** (*in addition*) 额外地 **2** [非正式] (*particularly*) 特别地 **III** *n* [C] **1** (*luxury*) 额外的事物 **2** (*surcharge*) 另外的收费 **3** [电影, 戏剧] 配角 ♦**wine will cost extra** 酒另外收钱 ♦**there are no hidden extras** (*on bill*) 没有隐含的额外费用

extract [*vb* ɪks'trækt, *n* 'ɛkstrækt] **I** *vt* **1** [文] (*take out*) [+ *object*] 取出 **2** [+ *money, promise, information*] 逼取 **3** [+ *tooth*] 拔出 **4** [+ *substance, mineral etc*] 提取 **II** *n* **1** [C] (*from novel, recording*) 摘录 **2** [C/U] [*of substance*] 提出物 ♦**lemon extract, extract of lemon** 柠檬精

extradite ['ɛkstrədaɪt] [正式] *vt* 引渡 ♦**to be extradited to Britain** 被引渡到英国

extraordinary [ɪks'trɔːdnrɪ] *adj* **1** (*exceptional*) 非凡的 **2** [正式] [+ *meeting*] 特别的 ♦**the extraordinary thing is that ...** 令人惊奇的是…

extravagance [ɪks'trævəgəns] *n* **1** [U] (*spending*) 奢侈 **2** [C] (*luxury*) 奢侈品

extravagant [ɪks'trævəgənt] *adj* **1** (*lavish*) [+ *person, tastes*] 奢侈的 **2** (*wasteful*) 浪费的 **3** (*exaggerated*) [+ *praise, generosity*] 过度的 **4** (*unrealistic*) [+ *ideas, claim*] 过分的

extreme [ɪks'triːm] **I** *adj* **1** [+ *poverty, caution*] 极度的 **2** [+ *opinions, methods etc*] 极端的 **3** [+ *point, edge*] 末端的 **II** *n* [C] 极端 ♦**the extreme right/left** [政治] 极右/左 ♦**extremes of temperature** 冷热气温悬殊 ♦**in the extreme** [正式] 极度 ♦**to go to extremes** 走极端 ♦**to go from one extreme to the other** 从一个极端到另一个极端

extremely [ɪks'triːmlɪ] *adv* **1** (*with adj*) [+ *useful, hot, heavy*] 非常 **2** (*with adv*) [+ *carefully, well, hard*] 非常

extremist [ɪks'triːmɪst] **I** *n* [C] 过激分子 **II** *adj* [+ *views, group*] 极端主义的

extrovert ['ɛkstrəvəːt] **I** *adj* [尤英] 外向的 [美=**extroverted**] **II** *n* [C] 性格外向者

✪**eye** [aɪ] **I** *n* **1** [C] [解剖] 眼睛 **2** [C] (喻) 眼光 ◊ *He scrutinised the pages with a critical eye.* 他以挑剔的眼光细看了几页。**3** [C] [*of needle*] 孔 **4** [S] [*of tornado, hurricane*] 风眼 **II** *vt* (*look at*) 审视 ◊ *We eyed each other thoughtfully.* 我们仔细地审视了对方。♦**to keep an eye on sb/sth** 密切注意某人/某事 ♦**before** *or* **in front of** *or* **under one's eyes** 在某人的眼皮底下 ♦**to catch sb's eye** [*action, movement* +] 被某人看到；[*person* +] (*deliberately*) 引起某人的注意 ♦**to clap** *or* **lay** *or* **set eyes on sb/sth** [非正式] 看见某人/某事 ♦**to have one's eye on sth** [非正式] (*want*) 想要某物 ♦**to keep one's eyes open for** *or* **to keep an eye out for sb/sth** 留意某人/某事 ♦**to look sb in the eye** *or* **to meet**

sb's eyes 正视某人 ♦ **to see sth through sb's eyes** 从某人的角度看 ♦ **as far as the eye can see** 就视力所及的范围 ♦ **in the public eye** 广为人知 ♦ **to see eye to eye (with sb)** (与某人)看法完全一致 ♦ **to have an eye for sth** 具有对某物的鉴赏力 ♦ **there's more to this than meets the eye** 并不像看到的那么简单

eyeball ['aɪbɔːl] *n* [c] 眼球

eyebrow ['aɪbrau] *n* [c] 眉毛 ♦ **his behaviour raised a few eyebrows** 他的行为颇令某些人瞠目

eyedrops ['aɪdrɔps] *n* [*pl*] 眼药水

eyelash ['aɪlæʃ] *n* [c] 眼睫毛

eyelid ['aɪlɪd] *n* [c] 眼皮

eyeliner ['aɪlaɪnə(r)] *n* [c/u] 眼线笔

eyeshadow ['aɪʃædəu] *n* [c/u] 眼影

eyesight ['aɪsaɪt] *n* [u] 视力

eye witness *n* [c] (*to crime, accident*) 目击者

Ff

F¹, **f** [ɛf] **I** *n* [c/u] (*letter*) 英语的第六个字母 **II** *abbr* (= ***female***) 女性

F² [ɛf] **I** *n* [c/u] [音] C大调音阶中的第四个音符 **II** *abbr* (= ***Fahrenheit***) 华氏

fable ['feɪbl] *n* **1** [c] (*story*) 寓言 **2** [c/u] (*myth*) 传说

fabric ['fæbrɪk] *n* **1** [c/u] (*cloth*) 织物 **2** [s] [*of society*] 结构 **3** [s] [正式] [*of building*] 结构

fabricate ['fæbrɪkeɪt] *vt* **1** [+ *evidence, story*] 编造 **2** [+ *parts, equipment*] 制造

fabulous ['fæbjuləs] *adj* **1** [非正式] (*fantastic*) [+ *person, looks, mood*] 极好的 **2** (*extraordinary*) [+ *beauty, wealth, success*] 格外的 **3** (*mythical*) 传说中的

✪ **face** [feɪs] **I** *n* **1** [c] [解剖] 脸 ◊ *She had a beautiful face.* 她的脸很漂亮。**2** [c] (*expression*) 表情 ◊ *He looked at her with a puzzled face.* 他用疑惑的表情看着她。**3** [c] [*of clock*] 正面 **4** [c] [*of mountain, cliff*] 陡面 ◊ *the north face of Mount Tai* 泰山朝北的陡面；[*of building*] 面 **5** [c] (*side*) [*of cube, dice etc*] 面 **6** [s] (*aspect*) [*of belief, system*] 一面 ◊ *the ugly face of capitalism* 资本主义的丑恶的一面；[*of city, institution*] 面貌 ◊ *The face of a city can change completely in a year.* 城市的面貌一年一个样。**II** *vt* **1** [+ *direction*] [*person* +] 面向；[*building, seat, car* +] 朝 **2** (*confront*) 面临 ◊ *We are faced with a serious problem.* 我们正面临一个严重的问题。**3** [+ *unpleasant situation*] 面对；[+ *truth, facts*] 正视 ◊ *Williams faces life in prison if convicted.* 如果被定罪的话，威廉姆斯将面对终生监禁。◊ *We simply must face facts.* 我们显然必须得正视现实。**III** *vi* [*person* +] 面向；[*building, seat, car* +] 朝 ◊ *He was facing forwards.* 他面向前方。◊ *The garden faces south.* 这座花园朝南。♦ **I can't** *or* **couldn't face it** 我应付不了 ♦ **to be** *or* **lie face down/up** [*person* +] 俯卧／仰卧；[*card* +] 正面 ♦ **to lose/save face** 丢／挽回面子 ♦ **to make** *or* [英] **pull a face (at sb)** (对某人) 做鬼脸 ♦ **in the face of** [+ *difficulties, opposition*] 面对 ♦ **on the face of it** (*superficially*) 表面看来 ♦ **to come face to face with** [+ *person*] 与…面对面；[+ *problem*] 正视

❑ **face up to** *vt* [不可拆分] **1** [+ *truth, facts*] 接受 **2** [+ *responsibilities, duties*] 承担

face cloth [英] *n* [c] 洗脸毛巾 [美= **washcloth**]

facelift ['feɪslɪft] *n* [c] **1** [*of person*] 面部拉皮整容手术 **2** [*of place, building*] 翻新 ♦ **to have a facelift** 做面部拉皮整容手术 ♦ **to give a room a facelift** 翻修房间

face pack [英] *n* [c] 面膜

facet ['fæsɪt] *n* [c] **1** [*of question, personality*] 方面 **2** [*of gem*] 琢面

face value *n* **1** [c] [*of coin, banknote, ticket*] 票面价值 **2** ♦ **to take sth at face value** (*accept unquestioningly*) 认为真如其显示的那样

facial ['feɪʃl] **I** *adj* [+ *hair, expression*] 面部的 **II** *n* [c] 面部按摩 ♦ **to have a facial** 做面部按摩

facilitate [fə'sɪlɪteɪt] *vt* [+ *action, process*] 使容易

facility [fə'sɪlɪtɪ] *n* [c] **1** (*feature*) 设施 **2** (*service*) 设施 ♦ **to have a facility for sth** (*skill, aptitude*) 有做某事的天分

✪ **fact** [fækt] *n* **1** [c] (*piece of information*) 真相 ◊ *It may help you to know the full facts of the case.* 了解本案的全部真相会对你有所帮助。**2** [u] (*truth*) 事实 ◊ *I don't know whether the rumour was based on fact or not.* 我不知道这个传闻是否基于事实。♦ **in (actual) fact** *or* **as a matter of fact** (*for emphasis*) 实际上；(*when disagreeing*) 其实 ◊ *In fact, I'm not at all sure that Freud was correct.* 其实，我一点儿也不肯定弗洛伊德是正确的。；(*when* *qualifying statement*) 事实上 ◊ *It was terribly cold weather, a blizzard in fact.* 天气异常冷，事实上，是暴风雪。 ♦ **to know for a fact (that) ...** 肯定… ♦ **the fact (of the matter) is (that) ...** 事实是… ♦ **the facts of life** 性知识 ♦ **a fact of life** 无法改变的事实 ♦ **facts and figures** 精确的资料

faction [ˈfækʃən] [宗, 政治] *n* [c] (*group*) 派系

factor [ˈfæktə(r)] *n* [c] **1** [*of problem, decision etc*] 因素 **2** [数] 因数
❑ **factor in** *vt* [+ *cost*] 把…作为因素考虑

factory [ˈfæktərɪ] *n* [c] 工厂

factual [ˈfæktjuəl] *adj* [+ *account, error*] 事实的

faculty [ˈfækəltɪ] *n* **1** [c] (*sense, ability*) 官能 **2** [c/u] [英] [*of university*] 学院 **3** [c/u] [美] (*teaching staff*) 全体教师

fad [fæd] *n* [c] (*craze*) 时尚

fade [feɪd] **I 1** *vi* [*colour, wallpaper, photograph* +] 褪色; [*sound, light* +] 渐弱 **2** [*memory, interest* +] 逐渐消失; [*hope* +] 破灭 ◊ *Hopes are fading for the success of the cease-fire.* 停火协议能够成功的希望即将破灭。; [*prospects* +] 暗淡; [*possibilities* +] 减少 **II** *vt* [+ *colour*] 使褪色
❑ **fade away** *vi* **1** [*music, sound* +] 慢慢减弱 **2** [*image* +] 变模糊 **3** (喻) 逐渐消失
❑ **fade in** *vt* [+ *picture, sound*] 使淡入
❑ **fade out** *vi* **1** [+ *light, image, sound*] 逐渐减弱 **2** (喻) 逐渐消失

faeces [ˈfiːsiːz] (美 **feces**) [正式] *n* [*pl*] 粪便

fag [fæg] [非正式] *n* [c] **1** [英] (*cigarette*) 香烟 **2** [美; 非正式, 疑讳] (*homosexual*) 男同性恋

Fahrenheit [ˈfærənhaɪt] **I** *adj* 华氏的 **II** *n* 华氏温度计

✪ **fail** [feɪl] **I** *vt* **1** [+ *exam, test*] 没有通过 ◊ *I failed my driving test twice.* 我两次驾驶考试都没合格。 **2** [+ *candidate*] 评定…不及格 ◊ *One of the examiners wanted to fail him.* 其中一位考官想要评定他不及格。 **3** [*leader, system* +] 使失望 ◊ *Our leaders have failed us.* 我们的领导使我们失望。 **4** [*courage, memory* +] 失去 ◊ *At the last minute his courage failed him.* 在关键时刻，他失去了勇气。 **II** *vi* **1** [*candidate* +] 没通过 ◊ *"Did you pass?" – "No, I failed."* "你过了吗？" "没过。" **2** [*attempt, plan, remedy* +] 失败 ◊ *The attempt to bribe the clerk had failed.* 贿赂职员的尝试失败了。 **3** [*brakes* +] 失灵 ◊ *The brakes failed and his car crashed into a tree.* 由于刹车失灵，他的车撞树上了。 **4** [*eyesight, health* +] 衰退 ◊ *They go and read to people whose sight is failing.* 他们给那些视力衰退的人读书听。 **5** [*light* +] 变暗 ◊ *In a few hours the light will fail.* 几个小时以后，天色就会变暗。 ♦ **to fail to do sth** (*not succeed*) 未能做某事 ◊ *The England team failed to win a place in the finals.* 英格兰队未能进入决赛。; (*neglect*) 没有做某事 ◊ *The bomb failed to explode.* 炸弹没有爆炸。 ♦ **without fail** (*definitely*) 一定 ◊ *Don't worry, I'll be there without fail.* 别担心，我一定会去。; (*without exception*) 毫无例外 ◊ *He attended every meeting without fail.* 他每次会议都参加，没有例外的。

failing [ˈfeɪlɪŋ] **I** *n* [c] (*weakness*) 缺陷 **II** *prep* ♦ **failing that** 不然的话

failure [ˈfeɪljə(r)] *n* **1** [c/u] (*lack of success*) 失败 **2** [c] (*person*) 废物 **3** [c/u] (*mechanical, electrical*) 故障 **4** [c/u] [*of crops*] 歉收 ♦ **failure to do sth** 没有做某事 ♦ **heart/kidney failure** 心力/肾衰竭 ♦ **it was a (complete) failure** 那是个(彻底的)失败

faint [feɪnt] **I** *adj* **1** [+ *sound, light, smell, hope*] 微弱的 **2** [+ *recollection, smile*] 淡淡的 **3** [+ *mark, trace*] 隐约的 **4** [+ *breeze*] 轻柔的 **II** *n* [c] [医] 昏倒 **III** *vi* [医] 晕倒 ♦ **to feel faint** 感到眩晕

faintest [ˈfeɪntɪst] *adj, n* ♦ **I haven't the faintest (idea)** 我一点儿也不知道

faintly [ˈfeɪntlɪ] *adv* **1** (*slightly*) 有些 **2** (*weakly*) 微弱地

fair [fɛə(r)] **I** *adj* **1** (*just, right*) [+ *person, decision, trial*] 公平的

2 *(quite large)* [+ *size, number, distance, amount*] 相当的 **3** *(quite good)* [+ *chance, guess, idea*] 大体的 **4** [+ *skin, complexion*] 白皙的; [+ *hair*] 金色的 **5** [正式][+ *weather*] 晴朗的 **II** *adv* ♦**to play fair** 公平行事 **III** *n* [c] **1** *(trade fair)* 交易会 **2** [英](*also:* **funfair**) 游乐场 [美= **carnival**] ♦**it's not fair!** 太不公平了！♦**a fair amount of** 不少

fairground ['fɛəgraund] *n* [c] 游乐场

fair-haired [fɛə'hɛəd] *adj* [+ *person*] 金色毛发的

fairly ['fɛəlɪ] *adv* **1** *(justly)* [*share, distribute* +] 公平地 **2** *(quite)* [+ *heavy, fast, good*] 相当

fairness ['fɛənɪs] *n* [U] *(justice, impartiality)* 公正 ♦**in all fairness** 公正地说

fairway ['fɛəweɪ] [高尔夫] *n* [c] 球座与终点间经过修整的草地

fairy ['fɛərɪ] *n* [c] 仙女

fairy tale *n* [c] 童话

faith [feɪθ] *n* **1** [U] *(trust)* 信任 **2** [c] *(specific religion)* 宗教 **3** [U] *(religious belief)* 信仰 ♦**to have faith in sb/sth** 相信某人/某事 ♦**in good faith** 真心实意的

faithful ['feɪθful] *adj* **1** *(loyal)* [+ *service, supporter, friend*] 忠实的 **2** *(sexually)* [+ *husband, wife, lover*] 忠诚的 **3** *(accurate)* [+ *account, version, copy*] 真实的 ♦**to be faithful to** [+ *book, film*] 忠实于; *(sexually)* [+ *husband, wife*] 忠诚于

faithfully ['feɪθfəlɪ] *adv* **1** *(loyally)* [*serve, promise, follow* +] 忠实地 **2** *(accurately)* [*restore, record, copy* +] 精确地 ♦**Yours faithfully** [英] 您忠实的 [美= **Sincerely yours**]

fake [feɪk] **I** *n* [c] **1** *(painting, antique, document)* 赝品 **2** *(person)* 骗子 **II** *adj* [+ *painting, document*] 假的 **III** *vt* **1** [+ *painting, antique, document*] 伪造 **2** [+ *emotion, reaction*] 假装; [+ *death, injury*] 佯装

falcon ['fɔːlkən] *n* [c] 猎鹰

✪**fall** [fɔːl] *(pt* **fell**, *pp* **fallen)** **I** *vi* **1** [*person, object* +] 掉 ◊ *Bombs fell in the town.* 炸弹掉进城里。◊ *Her father fell into the sea.* 她父亲掉到海里了。**2** *(fall over)* [*person, building* +] 倒下 ◊ *She gripped his shoulders to stop herself from falling.* 她抓住他的肩膀以防自己倒下。**3** [*snow, rain* +] 下 ◊ *An inch of rain fell within 15 minutes.* 15 分钟内下了1英寸的雨。**4** [*price, temperature, currency* +] 下降 ◊ *Oil prices fell by 0.2 per cent.* 油价下降了0.2%。**5** [*government, leader, country* +] 下台 ◊ *The prime minister fell from power.* 首相下台了。**6** [*night, darkness* +] 降临 ◊ *as darkness fell* 当黑暗降临时 **7** [*light, shadow* +] 投射 ◊ *A shadow fell over her book.* 一道阴影投射到她的书上。**8** [*silence, sadness, tiredness* +] 降临 ◊ *Silence fell on the passengers as the police checked identity cards.* 警察检查身份证的时候，沉默降临到每个乘客身上。**II** *n* **1** [c] [*of person*] 摔倒 ◊ *He had a nasty fall.* 他摔得不轻。**2** [c] *(in price, temperature)* 下降 ◊ *There has been a sharp fall in the value of the pound.* 英镑值急剧下降。**3** [s] [*of government, leader*] 垮台 ◊ *a debate which led to the Government's fall* 一场导致政府垮台的辩论 **4** [c] [*of rain, snow*] 场 ◊ *a heavy fall of snow* 一场大雪 **5** [c/U] [美] *(autumn)* 秋天 ◊ *in the fall of 1991* 1991年秋天 [英 = **autumn**] **III falls** *n* [*pl*] *(waterfall)* 瀑布 ◊ *Niagara Falls* 尼亚加拉大瀑布 ♦**Christmas falls on a Sunday** 圣诞节适逢星期天 ♦**to fall in love (with sb/sth)** 爱上（某人/某事）♦**to fall flat** [*joke* +] 毫无效果 ♦**to fall short of the required amount** 达不到要求的数量 ♦**to fall ill/pregnant** 生病/怀孕 ♦**which group do you fall into?** 你属于哪一组？

❑**fall apart** *vi* **1** [*building, structure* +] 破碎 **2** [*system, organization* +] 瓦解 **3** [非正式] *(emotionally)* 崩溃

❑**fall back** *vi* *(retreat)* 撤退

❑**fall back on** *vt* [不可拆分] *(resort to)* 依靠

❑**fall behind** *vi* 落后 ♦**to fall behind with one's payments** 逾期不付款

❑**fall down** *vi* **1** [*person* +] 摔倒

2 [*building* +] 倒塌
❑**fall for** *vt* [不可拆分] **1** [+ *trick, story, lie*] 上…的当 **2** [+ *person*] 爱上
❑**fall in** *vi* **1** [*roof, ceiling* +] 塌陷 **2** [军] 集合
❑**fall in with** *vt* [不可拆分][+ *sb's plans*] 赞成
❑**fall off** *vi* **1** [*person, object* +] 掉下 **2** (*diminish*) [*takings, attendance* +] 减少
❑**fall out** *vi* **1** [*hair, teeth* +] 掉 **2** [*friends* +] 争吵 ♦**to fall out with sb** 与某人争吵
❑**fall over I** *vi* [*person, object* +] 跌倒 **II** *vt* [不可拆分] ♦**to fall over o.s. to do sth** [非正式] 想方设法做某事
❑**fall through** *vi* [*plan* +] 落空
❑**fall to** *vt* [不可拆分] ♦**to fall to sb to do sth** [*responsibility* +] 做某事的责任落在某人身上

fallacy ['fæləsɪ] *n* [C/U] (*misconception*) 谬论

fallen ['fɔːlən] *pp of* **fall**

fallout ['fɔːlaut] *n* [U] (*radiation*) 放射尘

false [fɔːls] *adj* **1** (*artificial*) 假的 **2** (*untrue*) [+ *statement, accusation, name*] 假的 **3** (*mistaken*) [+ *impression*] 错误的 **4** (*insincere*) [+ *person, smile, promise*] 假装的 ♦**under false pretences** [法] 以欺诈手段 ♦**false negative/positive** [医] 误诊阴性/阳性

false alarm *n* [C] 虚惊

false teeth [英] *n* [*pl*] 假牙

falter ['fɔːltə(r)] *vi* **1** (*be unsteady*) [*voice* +] 颤抖; [*person* +] 犹豫; [*steps* +] 蹒跚 **2** (*weaken*) [*person* +] 迟疑; [*demand* +] 下降; [*interest* +] 减少

fame [feɪm] *n* [U] 声誉

familiar [fə'mɪlɪə(r)] *adj* **1** (*well-known*) [+ *face, voice, name*] 熟悉的 **2** (*intimate*) [+ *behaviour, tone*] 亲密的 ♦**to be familiar with** [+ *subject*] 对…熟悉 ♦**to be on familiar terms (with sb)** (与某人)交情好

familiarize [fə'mɪlɪəraɪz] *vt* ♦**to familiarize o.s. with sth** 熟悉某事

✪**family** ['fæmɪlɪ] **I** *n* [C] **1** (*relations*) 家庭 ◊ *the Adams Family* 亚当斯一家 **2** (*children*) 孩子 ◊ *couples with large families* 有很多孩子的夫妇们 **3** (*ancestors*) 祖先 ◊ *Her family came to Los Angeles at the turn of the century.* 她的祖先在世纪初时来到洛杉矶。**II** *cpd* [复合词] [+ *members, home, life, business*] 家庭

family doctor [英] *n* [C] 家庭医生

family planning *n* [U] 计划生育 ♦**family planning clinic** 计划生育诊所

famine ['fæmɪn] *n* [C/U] 饥荒 ♦**famine relief** 赈济饥荒

famous ['feɪməs] *adj* 著名的 ♦**to be famous for sth** 因某事而闻名

> 📖 **famous** 的人或事物比 **well-known** 的人或事物更出名。**notorious** 的人或事物是因不好的名声而出名，即臭名昭著。**infamous** 不是 **famous** 的反义词，词义和 **notorious** 相近，但语气更强。**notable** 的人或事物是重要的或让人感兴趣的人或事物。

fan [fæn] **I** *n* [C] **1** (*admirer*) [*of pop star*] 迷; [体育] 球迷 **2** [电子] 风扇 **3** (*handheld*) 扇子 **II** *vt* **1** [+ *face, person*] 扇 **2** [+ *fire*] 煽 **3** (喻) [+ *fears, hatred*] 煽动
❑**fan out** *vi* (*spread out*) 散开

fanatic [fə'nætɪk] *n* [C] **1** (*extremist*) 狂热者 **2** (*enthusiast*) 迷恋…的人

fan belt [汽车] *n* [C] 风扇皮带

fanciful ['fænsɪful] *adj* **1** (*unrealistic*) [+ *notion, idea*] 不切实际的 **2** (*elaborate*) [+ *design, name*] 新颖奇特的

fan club *n* [C] …迷俱乐部

fancy ['fænsɪ] **I** *adj* **1** (*elaborate*) [+ *jewellery, clothes, hat*] 别致的 **2** (*high-quality, expensive*) [+ *school, hotel, food*] 高档的 **II** *vt* **1** [尤英: 非正式] (*feel like, want*) 想要 **2** (*think, imagine*) 认为 **3** [非正式] [+ *person*] 喜欢 **III** *n* **1** [C/U] (*imagination*) 想象力 **2** [C] (*whim*) 幻想 **3** [C/U] (*fantasy*) 幻想 ◊ *Fancy seeing you here!* 真想不到在这见到你！♦**to fancy o.s.** [贬] 高估自己 ♦**to take a fancy to sb/sth** 喜欢上某人/某事 ♦**when the fancy takes him** 当他突发奇想时 ♦**a passing fancy** 心血来潮

♦**to take** *or* **tickle sb's fancy** 吸引某人

fancy dress *n* [U] 奇装异服

fancy-dress party ['fænsɪdrɛs-] *n* [C] 化装舞会

fang [fæŋ] *n* [C] [*of snake, wolf etc*] 獠牙

fanlight ['fænlaɪt] *n* [C] 气窗

fantasize ['fæntəsaɪz] *vi* ♦**to fantasize about (doing) sth** 幻想（做）某事 ♦**to fantasize that ...** 幻想…

fantastic [fæn'tæstɪk] *adj* **1** (*wonderful*) [+ *person, film, meal*] 极好的 **2** (*enormous*) [+ *sum, amount, profit*] 巨大的 **3** (*also:* ***fantastical***) (*strange, incredible*) 荒诞的

fantasy ['fæntəsɪ] *n* **1** [C] (*dream*) 幻想 **2** [C/U] (*film, story*) 虚构 **3** [U] (*imagination*) 想像

fanzine ['fænzi:n] *n* [C] 迷友杂志

FAO *abbr* (= ***for the attention of***) 请…亲自处理

FAQ *n abbr* (= ***frequently asked question***) 常见问题

✪**far** [fɑ:(r)] **I** *adj* **1** (*distant*) 远的 ◊ *Yes, it's quite far.* 是的，是挺远。 **2** (*extreme*) ♦**the far end/side** 尽头的 **II** *adv* **1** (*a long way*) (*in space*) 远 ◊ *He didn't hit the ball very far.* 他没把球打得很远。；(*in time*) 久远地 ◊ *if we look far into the future* 如果我们展望久远的未来 **2** (*much, greatly*) …得多 ◊ *His new house is far bigger.* 他的新房子要大得多。 ♦**as far as ...** 一直到… ◊ *Go as far as the church.* 一直走到教堂。 ♦**as far as possible** 尽可能 ♦**as far as I know** 据我所知 ♦**by far** …得多 ◊ *She was by far the best swimmer.* 她显然是最好的游泳者。 ♦**so far** 迄今为止 ♦**far from** 一点也不 ◊ *His hands were far from clean.* 他的手一点也不干净。 ◊ *Far from speeding up, the tank came to a halt.* 坦克不但没有加速，反而停了下来。 ♦**is it far to London?** 离伦敦远吗？ ♦**it's not far from here** 离这里不远 ♦**how far?** (*in distance*) 多远？ ◊ *How far is the Great Wall from here?* 长城离这里有多远？；(*in degree*) 到什么程度 ◊ *How far can he be trusted?* 他的可信度有多少？；(*in progress*) 进展如何 ◊ *How far have you got with the work?* 你工作进展如何？ ♦**far away** 遥远 ◊ *He sat as far away from the others as possible.* 他坐在尽可能远离他人的地方。 ♦**far off** (*in time*) 遥远 ♦**far better** 好得多 ♦**at the far end (of)** [*of table*] 在（…的）另一边；[*of room, theatre*] 在（…的）那一边；[*of field*] 在（…的）对面 ♦**at the far side (of)** 在（…的）那一边 ♦**as far back as the 13th century** 早在13世纪 ♦**to go too far** （喻）做得过分 ♦**he went so far as to resign** 他甚至辞职了 ♦**far and away** 无疑 ◊ *This is far and away the most important point.* 这无疑是最重要的一点。 ♦**from far and wide** 从四面八方 ♦**far from it** 远非如此 ♦**far be it from me to criticize** 我并不想指责谁 ♦**the far left/right** [政治] 极左/右

faraway ['fɑ:rəweɪ] *adj* **1** [+ *place*] 遥远的 **2** [+ *look, smile, voice*] 恍惚的

farce [fɑ:s] *n* [C] **1** [戏剧] 滑稽剧 **2** （喻）闹剧

fare [fɛə(r)] **I** *n* **1** [C] (*price*) (*on train, bus*) 票价；(*in taxi*) 乘客 **2** [U] [正式] (*food*) 食物 **II** *vi* 进展 ♦**how did you fare?** 你过得怎么样？ ♦**half/full fare** 半/全价

Far East *n* ♦**the Far East** 远东

farewell [fɛə'wɛl] [过时：文] **I** *int* 再见 ♦**to bid sb farewell** 向某人告别 **II** *n* [C] 告别 **III** *cpd* [复合词] [+ *party, gift*] 送别

farm [fɑ:m] **I** *n* [C] 农场 **II** *vt* [+ *land*] 耕种 **III** *vi* 务农
❑**farm out** *vt* [+ *work etc*] 招人承包

farmer ['fɑ:mə(r)] *n* [C] 农民

farmhouse ['fɑ:mhaus] *n* [C] 农舍

farming ['fɑ:mɪŋ] *n* [U] (*agriculture*) 农业 ♦**sheep farming** 养羊

farmland ['fɑ:mlænd] *n* [U] (*being farmed*) 耕地；(*suitable for farming*) 适于耕种的土地

farmyard ['fɑ:mjɑ:d] *n* [C] 农家的庭院

far-reaching ['fɑ:'ri:tʃɪŋ] *adj* [+ *reforms, effects, implications*] 意义深远的

far-sighted ['fɑ:'saɪtɪd] [美] *adj* 远视的 [英 = **long-sighted**]

fart [fɑːt] [非正式，疑讳] **I** *vi* 放屁 **II** *n* [c] **1** 屁 **2**（喻）*(person)* ♦**old fart** 讨厌的老家伙

farther [ˈfɑːðə(r)] **I** *adv* **1** *(in distance, time)* 更远地 **2** *(in degree)* 更多 **II** *adj* [文][+ *shore, side*] 更远的

> **farther** 和 **further** 都是 **'far'** 的比较级形式，并且两者都可以用作形容词和副词。**farther** 和 **further** 都可用来表示距离和时间。*Birds were able to find food by flying farther and farther…He must have found a window open further along the balcony…The use of animals by man stretches farther back in time than we had previously imagined.*
> 只有 **further** 可以用来表示事物的程度或者范围。如果进行 **further discussions**，就是进行 **more discussions**。若某情况 **further worsened**，表示某个本已糟糕的情况 **becomes worse**。*It was agreed to call a further meeting on the 10th…The government announced further changes to the scheme…aspects of advanced technology which complicate the world further…*

farthest [ˈfɑːðɪst] *adv* **I 1** *(in distance)* 最远地 **2** *(in time)* 最久远地 **3** *(in degree)* 最多 **II** *adj* [+ *point, extent*] 最远的

fascinate [ˈfæsɪneɪt] *vt (intrigue, interest)* 使着迷

fascinated [ˈfæsɪneɪtɪd] *adj* 入迷的

fascinating [ˈfæsɪneɪtɪŋ] *adj* [+ *story, person, place*] 迷人的

fascination [fæsɪˈneɪʃən] *n* [U/S] 着迷

fascist [ˈfæʃɪst] **I** *n* [c] **1** [政治] 法西斯主义者 **2**（喻）极端分子 **II** *adj* [政治] 法西斯主义的

fashion [ˈfæʃən] **I** *n* **1** [U/S] *(trend) (in clothes, thought, behaviour)* 流行的式样 **2** [c] *(clothes)* 时装 **3** [s] *(manner)* 方式 **II** *vt* [正式]*(make)* 制作 ♦**in fashion** 流行 ♦**to be/go out of fashion** 过时 ♦**after a fashion** [*finish, manage* +] 勉强算是

fashionable [ˈfæʃnəbl] *adj* [+ *clothes, restaurant, resort*] 流行的; [+ *writer, director*] 受欢迎的

fast [fɑːst] **I** *adj* **1** [+ *runner, car, progress*] 快的 ◊ *He was a very fast driver.* 他开车很快。**2** [+ *dye, colour*] 不褪色的 **II** *adv* **1** [*run, act, think* +] 快 **2** [*stick, hold* +] 紧紧地 **III** *n* [c] [宗] 禁食 **IV** *vi* [宗] 禁食 ♦**to be fast** [*clock, watch* +] 快 ♦**my watch is 5 minutes fast** 我的表快 5 分钟。♦**fast asleep** 酣睡 ♦**to hold fast to sth**（喻）坚持某事 ♦**to stand fast**（喻）不让步 ♦**as fast as I can** 我尽快 ♦**to make a boat fast** [英] 把船拴牢

fasten [ˈfɑːsn] **I** *vt* **1** *(tie, join)* 固定 **2** [+ *coat, jacket, belt*] 系 **II** *vi* [*coat, jacket* +] 扣上
❑ **fasten (up)on** *vt* [不可拆分] [+ *idea, scheme*] 集中在…

fastener [ˈfɑːsnə(r)] *n* [c] *(button, clasp, zip etc)* 紧固物

fast food I *n* [U] *(burger etc)* 快餐 **II** *cpd* [复合词] [+ *restaurant, industry etc*] 快餐

fastidious [fæsˈtɪdɪəs] *adj (fussy)* 挑剔的

fat [fæt] **I** *adj* **1** [+ *person*] 肥胖的; [+ *animal*] 肥的 **2** [+ *book*] 厚的; [+ *wallet*] 装得满满的 **3** [非正式] [+ *profit, fee*] 大量的 **II** *n* **1** [U] *(on person, animal, meat)* 脂肪 **2** [C/U] *(for cooking)* 食用油 **3** [化] 脂肪 ♦**to live off the fat of the land** 锦衣玉食 ♦**that's a fat lot of good** *or* **help** [非正式] 这有什么屁用

> 用 **fat** 形容某人胖，显得过于直接，甚至有些粗鲁。比较礼貌而又含蓄的说法是 **plump** 或 **chubby**，后者更为正式。**overweight** 和 **obese** 暗示某人因为肥胖而有健康问题。**obese** 是医学术语，表示某人极度肥胖或超重。一般而言，应尽量避免当面使用任何表示肥胖的词语。

fatal [ˈfeɪtl] *adj* **1** [+ *accident, injury, illness*] 致命的 **2**（喻）[+ *mistake*] 严重的

fatality [fəˈtælɪtɪ] *n* [c] *(death, victim)* 死亡

fatally ['feɪtəlɪ] *adv* **1** [+ *wounded, injured*] 致命地 **2** (喻) 严重地

fate [feɪt] *n* **1** [U] (*destiny*) 天意 **2** [C] [*of person, company, plan*] 命运

fateful ['feɪtful] *adj* [+ *moment, decision*] 决定命运的

✪ **father** ['fɑːðə(r)] *n* [C] **1** (*parent*) 父亲 **2** (喻) (*originator*) 鼻祖 ◊ *the father of modern photography* 现代摄影艺术的鼻祖 **3** [宗] 神父 ◊ *Father William* 神父威廉

Father Christmas [英] *n* 圣诞老人 [美 = **Santa Claus**]

father-in-law ['fɑːðərənlɔː] (*pl* **fathers-in-law**) *n* [C] [*of woman*] 公公; [*of man*] 岳父

Father's Day *n* [C/U] 父亲节

fathom ['fæðəm] **I** *n* [C] [航海] 英寻 **II** *vt* (*also:* ***fathom out***) [+ *meaning, mystery, reason*] 领悟

fatigue [fə'tiːg] **I** *n* [U] (*tiredness*) 疲劳 **II fatigues** *n* [*pl*] [军] 制服 ♦ **metal fatigue** 金属疲劳

fattening ['fætnɪŋ] *adj* 容易让人长胖的

fatty ['fætɪ] **I** *adj* **1** [+ *food*] 含脂肪多的 **2** [+ *acids, tissue*] 脂肪的 **II** *n* [C] [非正式] (*man, woman*) 胖子

faucet ['fɔːsɪt] [美] *n* [C] 水龙头 [英 = **tap**]

fault [fɔːlt] **I** *n* **1** [S] (*mistake*) 错误 **2** [C] (*defect*) (*in person*) 缺点; (*in machine*) 故障 **3** [C] [地理] (*crack*) 断层 **4** [C] [网球] 失误 **II** *vt* (*criticize*) 挑剔 ♦ **it's my fault** 是我的错 ♦ **at fault** 有责任 ♦ **to find fault with sb/sth** 找某人/某事的错 ♦ **through no fault of one's own** 不是自身的过失 ♦ **generous/modest to a fault** 过分慷慨/谦虚

faultless ['fɔːltlɪs] *adj* (*perfect*) 无懈可击的

faulty ['fɔːltɪ] *adj* [+ *machine*] 有故障的

fauna ['fɔːnə] *n* [U]/PL 动物群

fava bean ['fɑːvə(r)-] [美] *n* [C] 蚕豆 [英 = **broad bean**]

favour ['feɪvə(r)] (美 **favor**) **I** *n* **1** [U] (*approval*) 赞成 **2** [C] (*act of kindness*) 恩惠 **II** *vt* **1** (*prefer*) [+ *solution*] 赞成; [+ *person*] 偏爱 **2** (*be advantageous to*) 对…有利 ♦ **to ask a favour of sb** 请求某人帮忙 ♦ **to do sb a favour** 帮某人的忙 ♦ **to be in favour of sth/doing sth** 赞成某事/做某事 ♦ **to be in/out of favour** 得到/失去赞同 ♦ **to reject sth in favour of sth else** 拒绝某事转而选择另外某事 ♦ **to rule in sb's favour** [法] 裁决对某人有利 ♦ **biased in favour of** 偏袒 ♦ **to find favour with sb** [*suggestion, plan* +] 受到某人的青睐 ♦ **to win sb's favour** 赢得某人的好感

favourable ['feɪvrəbl] (美 **favorable**) *adj* **1** [+ *comment, reaction, impression*] 赞成的 **2** [+ *comparison*] 好的 **3** [+ *terms, conditions*] 有利的 ♦ **to be favourable to sth** 赞同某事 ♦ **to be favourable to sb** 对某人有利

favourite ['feɪvrɪt] (美 **favorite**) **I** *adj* [+ *author, film, food, colour*] 最喜欢的 **II** *n* [C] **1** (*thing, person*) 偏爱 **2** (*in race*) 最有希望的获胜者

fawn [fɔːn] **I** *n* [C] (*young deer*) 幼鹿 **II** *adj* (*also:* ***fawn-coloured***) 浅黄褐色的 **III** *vi* ♦ **to fawn over** *or* **(up)on sb** 巴结某人

fax [fæks] **I** *n* [C] **1** (*document*) 传真 **2** (*also:* ***fax machine***) 传真机 **II** *vt* [+ *document*] 用传真发送

FBI [美] *n abbr* (= ***Federal Bureau of Investigation***) 联邦调查局

FDA [美] *n abbr* (= ***Food and Drug Administration***) ♦ **the FDA** 食品及药物管理局

✪ **fear** [fɪə(r)] **I** *n* **1** [C/U] (*terror*) 害怕 ◊ *I stood there crying and shaking with fear.* 我站在那里，因为害怕而哭泣着，颤抖着。◊ *She was brought up with no fear of animals.* 她从小到大都不怕动物。**2** [C/U] (*anxiety*) 焦虑 ◊ *My worst fears were quickly realized.* 最令我焦虑的事情很快就发生了。**II** *vt* **1** (*be scared of*) 害怕 ◊ *a woman whom he disliked and feared* 一个他不喜欢而且害怕的女人 **2** (*be worried about*) 担心 ◊ *An epidemic of plague was feared.* 人们担心将会流行瘟疫。**III** *vi* ♦ **to fear for sb/sth** 为某人/某事担忧 ♦ **fear of heights/the dark** 怕高/黑 ♦ **for fear of doing sth** 以免做某事 ◊ *They did not mention it for fear of offending him.* 他们没有提那件

事以免触犯了他。♦**to fear that ...** 恐怕…

fearful ['fɪəful] *adj* **1** (*frightened*) 害怕的 **2** [正式] (*dreadful*) [+ *risk, accident*] 可怕的 **3** [非正式: 过时] (*terrible*) [+ *sight, noise*] 极坏的 ♦**to be fearful of sth** 害怕某事

fearless ['fɪəlɪs] *adj* [+ *person*] 无所畏惧的

feasible ['fiːzəbl] *adj* [+ *proposal, idea*] 可行的

feast [fiːst] **I** *n* [c] **1** (*banquet*) 宴会 **2** [宗] (*festival*) 节日 **II** *vi* [文] 宴饮 ♦**a feast of** (喻) 许许多多的 ♦**to feast on sth** 尽情地享用某物 ♦**to feast one's eyes (up)on sb/sth** 尽情观赏某人/某物

feat [fiːt] *n* [c] (*achievement*) 技艺 ♦**a brilliant feat of engineering** 工程上的高超技艺

feather ['fɛðə(r)] **I** *n* [c] [*of bird*] 羽毛 **II** *cpd* [复合词] [+ *mattress, bed, pillow*] 羽绒 **III** *vt* ♦**to feather one's nest** 中饱私囊 ♦**a feather in one's cap** 引以为豪的成就

feature ['fiːtʃə(r)] **I** *n* [c] **1** (*characteristic*) 特点 ◊ *safety features* 安全装置 ◊ *This is a common feature of modern life.* 这是现代生活的共同特点。**2** [出版, 电视] 专题 **3** [影院] (*also: **feature film***) 故事片 **II** *vt* [*film, exhibition* +] 由…主演 **III** *vi* ♦**to feature in** [+ *situation, exhibition, magazine*] 被包括在…内 **IV features** *n* [*pl*] [*of face*] 五官

feature film *n* [c] 故事片

Feb. *abbr* (= ***February***) 二月

February ['fɛbruərɪ] *n* [c/u] 二月 *see also* **July**

feces ['fiːsiːz] [美] *n* [*pl*] = **faeces**

fed [fɛd] *pt, pp of* **feed**

federal ['fɛdərəl] *adj* [+ *country, system*] 联邦制的; [+ *government, judge*] 联邦的

federation [fɛdə'reɪʃən] *n* [c] (*association*) 联合会

fed up [非正式] *adj* ♦**to be fed up** 厌倦

fee [fiː] *n* [c] (*payment*) 费; [+ *of doctor, lawyer*] 费用; (*for examination, registration*) 费 ♦**school fees** 学费 ♦**entrance fee** 门票费 ♦**membership fee** 会员费 ♦**for a small fee** 收少许费用

feeble ['fiːbl] *adj* **1** (*weak*) [+ *person, animal, voice*] 虚弱的 **2** (*ineffectual*) [+ *attempt, excuse, argument*] 无力的; [+ *joke*] 不好笑的

feed [fiːd] (*pt, pp* **fed**) **I** *vt* **1** [+ *baby, invalid, dog*] 喂 **2** [+ *family, guests*] 供给…食物 **II** *vi* **1** [*baby* +] 喝奶 **2** [*animal* +] 吃 **III** *n* **1** [u] [*of animal*] 饲料 **2** [c] [*of baby*] 喂奶 ♦**to feed sth into** [+ *document, tape*] 把某事放进…里; [+ *data, information*] 把某物输入…; [+ *coins, money*] 把某物放入…

❑ **feed on** *vt* [不可拆分] **1** (*live on*) 以…为食 ◊ *Not all bats feed on insects.* 不是所有的蝙蝠都以昆虫为食物。**2** (喻) 助长

feedback ['fiːdbæk] *n* [u] **1** (*information*) 反馈 **2** (*noise*) 噪声

✪ **feel** [fiːl] (*pt, pp* **felt**) **I** *vt* **1** (*touch*) [+ *object, face*] 摸 ◊ *Eric felt his face. "Am I bleeding?"* 埃里克摸着自己的脸。"我在流血吗？" **2** (*experience*) [+ *desire, anger, grief*] 觉得 ◊ *Mrs Oliver felt a sudden desire to burst out crying.* 奥利弗夫人突然觉得很想哭出来。; [+ *pain*] 感到 ◊ *He felt a sudden pain in his leg.* 他突然感到一阵腿疼。**3** (*be aware of*) 发觉 ◊ *He felt her leg against his.* 他发觉她的腿正抵着他的腿。**4** (*sense*) 感觉到 **5** (*think, believe*) 认为 ◊ *She knew how I felt about the subject.* 她知道我对这事的看法。◊ *We felt she would win.* 我们认为她会赢。**III** *n* [s] **1** [*of substance, cloth*] 摸上去的感觉 ◊ *He remembered the feel of her skin.* 他记得她皮肤摸上去的感觉。**2** (*impression*) 感觉 ◊ *The room has a warm, cosy feel.* 这个房间有种温暖舒适的感觉。♦**to feel that ...** 感到… ◊ *I feel I'm neglecting my duty.* 我感到我失职了。♦**to feel hungry** 觉得饿 ♦**to feel cold** 觉得冷 ♦**to feel the cold/the heat** 怕冷/热 ♦**to feel lonely/better** 感到孤独/感觉好多了 ♦**I don't feel well** 我觉得身体不适 ♦**to feel sorry for sb** 同情某人 ♦**it feels soft** 这摸上去软软的 ♦**it feels**

colder here 这儿感觉更冷些 ♦ **it feels like velvet** 它摸上去像天鹅绒 ♦ **to feel like** (*want*) 想要 ◊ *I feel like a stroll.* 我想散散步。; (*consider o.s.*) 觉得自己像 ◊ *I felt like a murderer.* 我觉得自己像是杀人犯。♦ **it feels like** *or* **it feels as if ...** 仿佛觉得… ♦ **to have a feel of sth** 摸一摸某物 ♦ **to get the feel of sth** 开始熟悉某事 ♦ **to have the feel of sth** (*impression*) 有种好似某事的感觉 ♦ **I'm still feeling my way** 我仍然在摸索前进 ♦ **I don't feel myself** 我觉得身体不舒服

❑ **feel about, feel around** *vi* (*in pocket, bag, the dark*) 摸索

❑ **feel for** *vt* [不可拆分] **1** (*grope for*) 摸索着找 ◊ *I felt for my wallet.* 我摸索着找我的钱包。**2** (*sympathize with*) 同情 ◊ *I really feel for you.* 我真的同情你。

feeling ['fiːlɪŋ] **I** *n* **1** [c] (*emotion*) 感受 **2** [c] (*physical sensation*) 感觉 **3** [u] (*sense of touch*) 触觉 **4** [s] (*impression*) 感觉 **5** [u] (*sympathy*) 同情 **II feelings** *n* [*pl*] **1** (*attitude*) 看法 **2** (*emotions*) 情感 ♦ **feelings were running high** 群情激愤 ♦ **what are your feelings about the matter?** 你对这事的看法是什么？ ♦ **I have a feeling that ...** 我有种感觉… ♦ **my feeling is that ...** 我的感觉是… ♦ **bad** *or* **ill feeling** 反感 ♦ **to hurt sb's feelings** 伤害某人的感情

feet [fiːt] *n* [*pl*] *of* **foot**

feign [feɪn] *vt* [正式] [+ *illness, interest*] 假装

fell [fɛl] **I** *pt of* **fall II** *vt* **1** [+ *tree*] 砍倒 **2** [+ *opponent*] 打倒 **III the fells** *n* [*pl*] [英] (*moorland*) 沼泽地 **IV** *adj* ♦ **in one fell swoop** 一下子

fellow ['fɛləu] **I** *n* [c] **1** [过时, 非正式] (*man*) 小伙子 **2** [正式] (*comrade*) 同事 **3** [*of learned society*] 会员 **4** [*of university*] 研究员 **II** *cpd* [复合词] ♦ **their fellow prisoners/students** 他们的狱友/同学 ♦ **her fellow workers** 她的同事们

fellowship ['fɛləuʃɪp] *n* **1** [c] (*society*) 团体 **2** [c] [大学] 研究员职位 **3** [u] (*comradeship*) 友谊

felony ['fɛlənɪ] [法] *n* [c] 重罪

felt [fɛlt] **I** *pt, pp of* **feel II** *n* [u] (*fabric*) 毛毡

felt-tip pen ['fɛlttɪp-], **felt-tip** *n* [c] 毡头墨水笔

female ['fiːmeɪl] **I** *n* [c] **1** [动] 雌兽 **2** (*woman*) 女性 **II** *adj* **1** [动] 雌性的 **2** [+ *sex, character, child*] 女性的 **3** (*relating to women*) 妇女的 ♦ **male and female students** 男女学生

feminine ['fɛmɪnɪn] *adj* **1** [+ *clothes, behaviour*] 女性的 **2** [语言] 阴性的

feminist ['fɛmɪnɪst] **I** *n* [c] 女权主义者 **II** *adj* 女权主义的

fence [fɛns] **I** *n* [c] (*barrier*) 篱笆 **II** *vt* **1** (*also:* ***fence in***) [+ *land*] 把…用篱笆围起 **2** (*also:* ***fence off***) 把…用篱笆圈起 **III** *vi* [体育] 击剑 ♦ **to sit on the fence** (喻) 持观望态度

fencing ['fɛnsɪŋ] *n* [u] **1** [体育] 击剑 **2** (*material for fences*) 筑栅栏的材料

fend [fɛnd] *vi* ♦ **to fend for o.s.** 自谋生计

❑ **fend off** *vt* **1** (*physically*) [+ *attack, attacker, blow*] 挡开 **2** (*verbally*) [+ *questions, requests, person*] 回避

fender ['fɛndə(r)] *n* [c] **1** [*of fireplace*] 围栏 **2** [美] [*of car*] 挡泥板 [英= **wing**] **3** [美] [*of car*] 保险杠 [英= **bumper**] **4** (*on boat*) 护舷物

fennel ['fɛnl] *n* [u] 茴香

ferment [*vb* fə'mɛnt, *n* 'fəːmɛnt] **I** *vi* [*beer, dough, fruit* +] 发酵 **II** *vt* [+ *beer, dough, fruit*] 使发酵 **III** *n* [u] (*unrest*) 骚动 ♦ **to be in ferment** 处于动荡不安中

fern [fəːn] *n* [c] 蕨

ferocious [fə'rəuʃəs] *adj* **1** [+ *animal, assault*] 凶猛的 **2** [+ *battle, competition, argument*] 激烈的

ferret ['fɛrɪt] *n* [c] 雪貂

❑ **ferret about, ferret around** *vi* [英: 非正式] [*person, animal* +] 到处搜寻

❑ **ferret out** [非正式] *vt* [+ *information*] 查出

ferry ['fɛrɪ] **I** *n* [c] (*small*) 摆渡; (*large*) (*also:* ***ferryboat***) 渡船 **II** *vt* (*transport*) (*by sea, air, road*) 运送 ♦ **to ferry sth/sb across** *or* **over** 载某物/某人渡过

fertile ['fəːtaɪl] *adj* **1** [+ *land, soil*] 肥沃的; [+ *woman*] 能生育的

2 [+ *imagination, mind*] 丰富的 ♦**fertile ground**（喻）沃土

fertilize ['fəːtɪlaɪz] *vt* **1** [生物] 使受精 **2** [农] [+ *land*] 施肥于

fertilizer ['fəːtɪlaɪzə(r)] *n* [c/u] (*for plants, land*) 肥料

fervent ['fəːvənt] *adj* [+ *admirer, supporter*] 强烈的; [+ *belief, hope*] 热切的

fervour ['fəːvə(r)] (美 **fervor**) *n* [u] 热情

fester ['fɛstə(r)] *vi* [文] **1** [*sore, wound* +] 化脓 **2**（喻）[*resentment* +] 加剧

festival ['fɛstɪvəl] *n* [c] **1** [宗] 节日 **2** [戏剧, 音] 艺术节

festive ['fɛstɪv] *adj* **1** [+ *mood, atmosphere*] 喜庆的 **2** (*relating to Christmas*) 节日的 ♦**the festive season** 节日期

festoon [fɛs'tuːn] *vt* ♦**to be festooned with** 给…饰以花饰

fetch [fɛtʃ] *vt* **1** (*bring*) 去拿来 **2** (*sell for*) 卖得 ♦**to fetch sth for sb, fetch sb sth** 去给某人拿来某物 ♦**how much did it fetch?** 这个卖多少钱？

❑**fetch up** [非正式] *vi* 到达

fête [feɪt] **I** *n* [c] (*at church, school*) 游园会 **II** *vt* 特别款待

feud [fjuːd] **I** *n* [c] (*quarrel*) 长期不和 **II** *vi* 长期不和 ♦**to feud with sb** 与某人结怨 ♦**a family feud** 家族世仇

feudal ['fjuːdl] *adj* [+ *system, society, lord*] 封建的

fever ['fiːvə(r)] *n* **1** [c/u] [医] 发烧 **2**（喻）(*frenzy*) ♦**a fever of excitement/anxiety** 激动若狂／极度不安 ♦**he has a fever** 他发烧了

fever blister [美: 医] *n* [c] 疱疹 [英 = **cold sore**]

feverish ['fiːvərɪʃ] *adj* **1** [医] 发烧的 **2**（喻）[+ *emotion, activity*] 狂热的

✪**few** [fjuː] **I** *adj* **1** (*not many*) 少数的 ◊ *She has few friends.* 她的朋友不多。**2** ♦**a few** (*some*) 几个 ◊ *She has a few friends.* 她有几个朋友。 **II** *pron* **1** ♦**a few** (*some*) 几个 ◊ *Many of us tried and a few succeeded.* 我们中的许多人都试了，只有几个成功了。; (*not many*) 很少几个 ◊ *Many of us tried but few succeeded.* 我们中的许多人都试了，但很少几个成功了。**2** ♦**in the next few days** 在接下来的几天里 ♦**in the past few days** 在过去的几天里 ♦**every few days/months** 每几天／几个月 ♦**a few of us/them** 我们／他们中的几个 ♦**a few more** 再多几个 ♦**very few survive** 极少幸存 ♦**a good few** *or* **quite a few** 相当多 ♦**as few as** 竟少到 ♦**they are few and far between** 他们简直是凤毛麟角

> 📖 **few** 和 **a few** 都用在可数名词的复数形式之前，但意义不同。例如，*I have a few friends* 表示肯定含义，表示你有一些朋友。然而，*I have few friends* 表示否定含义，即你几乎没有朋友。

fewer ['fjuːə(r)] *adj* 较少的 ♦**no fewer than** 不少于 ♦**there are fewer buses on Sundays** 星期天公共汽车比较少
📖 用法参见 **less**

fewest ['fjuːɪst] *adj* 最少的

fiancé [fɪ'ɔnseɪ] *n* [c] 未婚夫

fiancée [fɪ'ɔnseɪ] *n* [c] 未婚妻

fiasco [fɪ'æskəu] (*pl* **fiascos**) *n* [c] (*disaster*) 惨败

fib [fɪb] [非正式] **I** *n* [c] (*lie*) 小谎 **II** *vi* 撒小谎

fibre ['faɪbə(r)] (美 **fiber**) *n* **1** [c] (*thread*) 纤维 **2** [c/u] (*cloth*) 纤维制品 **3** [u] (*roughage*) 纤维质 **4** [c] [解剖] (*tissue*) 纤维

fibreglass ['faɪbəglɑːs] (美 **fiberglass**) *n* [u] 玻璃纤维

fickle ['fɪkl] *adj* [+ *person*] 易变的; [+ *weather*] 无常的

fiction ['fɪkʃən] *n* **1** [u] (*novels, stories*) 小说 **2** [u] (*invention*) 虚构的事 **3** [c] (*lie*) 杜撰

fictional ['fɪkʃənl] *adj* [+ *character, event*] 虚构的

fictitious [fɪk'tɪʃəs] *adj* **1** (*non-existent*) 杜撰的 **2** (*imaginary*) [+ *character, event*] 虚构的

fiddle ['fɪdl] **I** *n* [c] **1** [音] 小提琴 **2** [英: 非正式] (*fraud, swindle*) 诓骗 **II** *vt* [英: 非正式] [+ *books, accounts,*

taxes] 篡改 ♦ **tax fiddle** 骗税
❑ **fiddle with** *vt* [不可拆分] 不停拨弄

fiddler ['fɪdlə(r)] *n* [c] [音] 小提琴手

fidelity [fɪ'dɛlɪtɪ] *n* [u] [正式] **1** [*of spouse, dog*] 忠诚 **2** (*accuracy*) [*of report, translation*] 精确

field [fiːld] **I** *n* [c] **1** (*grassland*) 草地 **2** (*cultivated*) 田地 **3** [体育] (*pitch*) 场地 **4** (*subject, area of interest*) 领域 **5** (*range*) [*of gravitation, magnetism*] 场 **6** [矿] 矿区 **7** [计算机] 字段 **II** *vi* [板球] 接球 **III** *cpd* [复合词] [+ *study, trip*] 实地 ♦ **the field** (*competitors, entrants*) 全体出场参赛者 ♦ **to lead the field** [体育] 领头; (喻) 一马当先 ♦ **field of vision** 视野 ♦ **to have a field day** 忙得不亦乐乎

fielder ['fiːldə(r)] [板球, 棒球] *n* [c] 外野手

field marshal *n* [c] 陆军元帅

fieldwork ['fiːldwəːk] *n* [u] (*research*) 实地考察

fierce [fɪəs] *adj* **1** [+ *animal*] 凶猛的; [+ *warrior, enemy*] 凶恶的; [+ *battle*] 猛烈的 **2** [+ *loyalty, resistance, competition*] 强烈的; [+ *wind, heat, storm*] 强劲的

fiery ['faɪərɪ] *adj* **1** (字) 着火的; [+ *red, orange*] 如火的 **2** (喻) [+ *person, temper, speech*] 火爆的

✪ **fifteen** [fɪf'tiːn] *num* 十五 ♦ **that will be fifteen pounds, please** 请付15英镑 ♦ **she's fifteen (years old)** 她15岁了 ♦ **there are fifteen of us** 我们有15个人 ♦ **all fifteen of them** 他们15个人都

fifteenth [fɪf'tiːnθ] *num* 第十五 *see also* **fifth**

fifth [fɪfθ] **I** *num* **1** (*in series*) 第五 **2** (*fraction*) 五分之一 **II** *n* [汽车] (*also: **fifth gear***) 第五挡 **III** *adv* ♦ **to come fifth** (*in race, competition*) 名列第五名 ♦ **on July fifth, on the fifth of July** 在7月5日 ♦ **Charles the fifth** 查尔斯五世

✪ **fifty** ['fɪftɪ] *num* 五十 ♦ **he's in his fifties** 他50多岁 ♦ **during the fifties** 在50年代

fifty-fifty ['fɪftɪ'fɪftɪ] [非正式] **I** *adj* 各半的 **II** *adv* [*divide, share, split* +] 各半地 ♦ **to have a fifty-fifty chance (of success)** 有百分之五十(成功)的机会

fig [fɪg] *n* [c] **1** (*fruit*) 无花果 **2** (*also: **fig tree***) 无花果树 ♦ **I don't care** *or* **give a fig** [过时:非正式] 我毫不在意

✪ **fight** [faɪt] (*pt, pp* **fought**) **I** *n* [c] **1** (字) 斗殴 ◊ *There were sometimes fights between the workers.* 有时工人之间会发生斗殴。 **2** [拳击] 拳击赛 **3** (喻) (*against disease, alcoholism, prejudice*) 斗争 ◊ *the fight against drug abuse* 与滥用毒品所作的斗争 **4** (*quarrel*) 争吵 ◊ *He had a big fight with his dad.* 他和他的父亲大吵了一架。 **II** *vt* **1** [+ *person, enemy, army*] 与…对打 ◊ *I fought him, and I won.* 我跟他对打，我赢了。 **2** [+ *battle*] 与…战斗 ◊ *Police fought a gun battle with the gang.* 警察与歹徒展开一场枪击战。 **3** [+ *disease, prejudice etc*] 与…斗争 ◊ *She devoted her life to fighting poverty.* 她一生都在与贫穷作斗争。 **4** [+ *fire*] 与…搏斗 ◊ *They fought the fire for three days.* 他们与大火搏斗了3天。 **5** [+ *urge, impulse*] 抑制 ◊ *He fought the urge to cry.* 他抑制住了想哭的冲动。 **6** [法] [+ *case*] 为…极力争辩 ◊ *He fought his case in various courts.* 他在各个法庭为他的案子据理力争。 **7** [+ *election*] 力争 ◊ *the parties fighting the election* 力争获选的各个政党 **8** [拳击] 与…进行拳击赛 ◊ *I'd like to fight him for the title.* 我想与他进行拳击赛争夺冠军头衔。 **III** *vi* **1** [*people, enemies, armies* +] 战斗 ◊ *He fought in the war.* 他在战争中作战。 **2** (*quarrel*) 争吵 ◊ *They fight about who pays the bills.* 他们为谁付账而争吵。 **3** (*struggle*) 奋斗 ◊ *We had fought to hold on to the company.* 我们曾经为保住公司而奋斗。 ♦ **to put up a fight** 开展斗争 ♦ **to fight with sb** 跟某人打架 ♦ **to fight for/against sth** 为支持/反对某事而斗争 ♦ **to fight one's way through a crowd/the undergrowth** 费力地穿过人群/丛林
❑ **fight back** **I** *vi* 回击 **II** *vt* [+ *tears, fear*] 抑制住
❑ **fight down** *vt* [+ *urge*] 努力抑制

❑**fight off** *vt* **1** [+ *attacker*] 击退 **2** [+ *disease*] 消除 **3** [+ *sleep, urge*] 克制

❑**fight out** *vt* ♦**to fight it out** 一决雌雄

fighter ['faɪtə(r)] *n* [c] **1** (*boxer etc*) 拳击手 **2** (*also:* ***fighter plane***) 战斗机 **3** (*courageous person*) 勇士

fighting ['faɪtɪŋ] *n* [U] (*battle, violence*) 搏斗

figurative ['fɪgjurətɪv] *adj* [+ *painting, style*] 华美的 ♦**in a figurative sense** 用比喻意

✪**figure** ['fɪgə(r)] **I** *n* [c] **1** [绘画, 几何] 图形 ◊ *A hexagon is a six-sided figure.* 六边形是有6个边的图形。**2** (*number, statistic*) 统计数字 ◊ *unemployment figures* 失业统计数字 **3** (*digit*) 数字 ◊ *The second figure looks like a five.* 第二个数字看起来像5。**4** (*body, shape*) 身材 ◊ *She's got a fabulous figure.* 她的身材棒极了。**5** (*person*) 轮廓 ◊ *the figure of a man silhouetted against the skyline* 被天际衬托着的男人轮廓 **6** [艺术] 画像 ◊ *a life-size figure of a woman* 与真人同样大小的女人画像 **7** (*personality*) 人物 ◊ *He's a controversial figure.* 他是一个颇有争议的人物。**II** *vt* [尤美:非正式] (*reckon*) 估计 ◊ *They figured it was better to stay where they were.* 他们估计最好还是待在原处。**III** *vi* (*feature*) 出现 ◊ *Loneliness figures a lot in his conversation.* 孤独在他的谈话中出现了好几次。♦**in single/double figures** 以单位数/双位数 ♦**I couldn't put a figure on it** 我说不出它的确切数字 ♦**public figure** 公众人物 ♦**a hero/mother** *etc* **figure** 英雄/母亲{等}式的人物 ♦**that figures** [非正式] 那不足为怪

❑**figure out** [非正式] *vt* (*work out*) 弄清楚 ◊ *She had not yet figured out what she was going to do.* 她还没有弄清楚她要做什么。

figurehead ['fɪgəhɛd] *n* [c] **1** [*of organization*] 傀儡 **2** [航海] 船头雕饰

file [faɪl] **I** *n* [c] **1** (*dossier*) 档案 **2** (*folder*) 文件夹 **3** (*for loose leaf*) 卷宗 **4** [计算机] 文件 **5** (*tool*) 锉刀 **II** *vt* **1** (*also:* ***file away***) [+ *papers, document*] 把…归档 **2** [法] [+ *accusation, complaint, request*] 把…备案 **3** [+ *wood, metal, fingernails*] 把…锉平 **III** *vi* ♦**to file in/out/past** 鱼贯而入/出/过 ♦**to file for divorce** 申请离婚

filing cabinet *n* [c] 档案柜

Filipino [fɪlɪ'piːnəu] (*pl* **Filipinos**) **I** *adj* 菲律宾的 **II** *n* [c] (*person*) 菲律宾人

fill [fɪl] **I** *vt* **1** [+ *container*] 装满 **2** [+ *space, area*] 占满 **3** [+ *crack, hole*] 塞满 **4** [+ *tooth*] 补 **5** [+ *role, position*] 担任 **6** [+ *job vacancy*] [*company* +] 选人补上; [*candidate* +] 补上 **7** [+ *gap, need*] 弥补 **II** *vi* [*room, hall* +] 挤满 **III** *n* ♦**to have had one's fill of sth** 已经受够了某事 ♦**to eat/drink one's fill** 吃个饱/喝个够 ♦**to fill sth with sth** 用某物填满某物 ♦**to be filled with anger/resentment** 满腔怒火/憎恨

❑**fill in I** *vt* **1** [+ *hole, crack*] 填满 **2** [尤英] [+ *form, name*] 填写 [美 = **fill out**] ♦**to fill sb in on sth** [非正式] 给某人提供关于某事的详情 **II** *vi* ♦**to fill in for sb** 临时补某人的缺

❑**fill out** *vt* [+ *form*] 填写

❑**fill up I** *vt* **1** [*food* +] [+ *person*] 使…有饱胀的感觉 **2** (*occupy*) [+ *container, space*] 占满 **3** [+ *cup, saucepan*] 倒满 **II** *vi* [*room, stadium* +] 挤满 ♦**fill it** *or* **her up, please** [汽车] 请加满油

filler ['fɪlə(r)] *n* [C/U] (*for wood, plaster*) 填充物

fillet ['fɪlɪt] **I** *n* [C/U] [*of meat, fish*] 片 **II** *vt* [+ *fish, meat*] 把…切成片

fillet steak *n* [C/U] 牛肉片

filling ['fɪlɪŋ] **I** *n* **1** [c] (*in tooth*) 填补物 **2** [C/U] [*of cake, pie, sandwich*] 馅 **II** *adj* [+ *food*] 易使人饱的

filling station [尤英] *n* [c] 加油站 [美 = **gas station**]

✪**film** [fɪlm] **I** *n* **1** [c] [尤英:影院, 电视] 影片 [美 = **movie**] **2** [C/U] [摄影] 胶卷 ◊ *a roll of film* 一卷胶卷 **3** [c] [*of dust, tears, grease*] 薄层 ◊ *A film of dust covered every surface.* 薄薄的一层灰尘覆盖了每一处表面。**4** [U] [英] (*also:* ***clingfilm***) 薄膜 **II** *vt*

[+ scene, person, book] 把…拍成影片 **III** *vi* 拍摄 ◊ *The TV crews couldn't film at night.* 电视剧组人员晚上无法拍摄。

film star *n* [c] [尤英] 影星

filter ['fɪltə(r)] **I** *n* [c] **1** (*for water, oil*) 过滤器 **2** [摄影] 滤器 **II** *vt* [+ *water, soil etc*] 过滤

❑ **filter into** *vt* [不可拆分] [*sound, light* +] 微微透入

❑ **filter through** *vi* [*news, information* +] 慢慢传开

filter lane [英:汽车] *n* [c] 转弯车道

filth [fɪlθ] *n* [U] **1** (*dirt*) 污物 **2** (*smut*) 污秽内容

filthy ['fɪlθɪ] *adj* **1** (*dirty*) [+ *object, person*] 污秽的 **2** (*disgusting*) [+ *language, book, habit*] 污秽的

fin [fɪn] *n* [c] **1** [*of fish*] 鳍 **2** [*of aircraft*] 翼

✪ **final** ['faɪnl] **I** *adj* **1** (*last*) 最后的 ◊ *Astronauts will make a final attempt to rescue the satellite.* 宇航员将做出最后的努力抢救卫星。 **2** (*definitive*) [+ *decision, offer*] 不可变更的 ◊ *The judges' decision is final.* 法官的决定是不可变更的。 **3** (*ultimate*) [+ *irony, humiliation*] 莫大的 ◊ *Being sacked was the final humiliation.* 被解雇是莫大的羞辱。 **II** *n* [c] [体育] 决赛 **III finals** *n* [*pl*] **1** [大学] 期末考试 **2** [体育] 决赛 ♦ **to sit one's finals** 参加大学毕业考试

finale [fɪ'nɑːlɪ] *n* [c] **1** [戏剧] 最后一幕; [音] 终曲 **2** (喻) 收场

finalist ['faɪnəlɪst] *n* [c] 决赛选手

finalize ['faɪnəlaɪz] *vt* [+ *plans, deal, arrangements*] 最终确定

finally ['faɪnəlɪ] *adv* **1** (*eventually*) 终于 **2** (*lastly*) 最后 **3** (*in conclusion*) 总之 **4** (*irrevocably*) 确定地

🕮 用法参见 **eventually**

finance [faɪ'næns] **I** *n* [U] **1** (*money, backing*) 资金 **2** (*money management*) 财政 **II** *vt* (*back, fund*) 为…提供资金 **III finances** *n* [*pl*] 财力

✪ **financial** [faɪ'nænʃəl] *adj* [+ *difficulties, adviser*] 财政的 ◊ *The company is in financial difficulties.* 公司正处于财政困难时期。

financial year *n* [c] 财政年度

financier [faɪ'nænsɪə(r)] *n* [c] 出资人

✪ **find** [faɪnd] (*pt, pp* **found**) **I** *vt* **1** (*locate*) [+ *person, object, exit*] 找到 ◊ *The police found a pistol at his home.* 警察在他家里找到一支手枪。; [+ *lost object*] 找回 ◊ *He eventually found the book under his bed.* 他终于在床下找回了那本书。 **2** (*discover*) [+ *answer, solution*] 找出 ◊ *There is a genuine effort to find a solution.* 人们真心实意地努力寻找一条解决的途径。; [+ *object, person*] 发现 ◊ *When she got home she found a six-page letter from Tom.* 她到家时发现了一封汤姆写给她的6页的信。 **3** (*consider*) 认为 ◊ *I don't find that funny at all.* 我认为那一点都没什么好玩的。 **4** (*get*) [+ *work, job*] 得到 ◊ *He cannot find work.* 他没能得到工作。; [+ *money*] 筹集 ◊ *Some families cannot even find enough money for basic needs.* 有些家庭甚至筹不到满足基本需要的钱。; [+ *time*] 有 ◊ *How do you find time to write these books?* 你怎么有时间写这些书? **II** *n* [c] (*discovery*) 难得之才 ◊ *They've got a new singer, and she's a real find.* 他们已经找到了一位新歌手，她是一个真正的难得之才。 ♦ **to find sb guilty/not guilty** 判决某人有罪/无罪 ♦ **to find one's way** 认得路 ♦ **many exotic species are found there** 那儿有许多奇异的物种 ♦ **I found myself starting to laugh** 我不由自主地笑了起来 ♦ **to find that ...** 发觉… ◊ *When I woke up, I found I couldn't move my legs.* 醒来时，我发觉腿动不了了。 ♦ **to find sth easy/difficult** 觉得某事容易/难

🕮 用法参见 **discover**

❑ **find out I** *vt* **1** [+ *fact, truth*] 查明 ◊ *You'll have to watch next week to find out what happens.* 让你们等到下周看看会怎样。 **2** [+ *person*] (*in wrongdoing*) 发现 ◊ *I wondered for a moment if she'd found me out.* 我一度想知道她是否已经发现我了。 **II** *vi* ♦ **to find out about sth** (*deliberately*) 获知某事; (*by chance*) 偶然发现某物

findings ['faɪndɪŋz] *n* [*pl*] [*of report*] 调查结果; [*of court, committee*] 裁决

fine [faɪn] **I** *adj* **1** (*satisfactory*) 还不错的 **2** (*excellent*) [+ *object, person*] 好的 **3** (*in texture*) [+ *hair, thread, powder, sand*] 细的 **4** (*pleasant*) [+ *weather, day*] 晴朗的 **5** (*subtle*) [+ *adjustment, detail, distinction*] 细微的 **II** *adv* **1** (*well*) 不错地 **2** (*thinly*) 细地 **III** *n* [c] [法] 罚款 **IV** *vt* [法] 处…以罚金 ♦ **(I'm) fine** (我) 很好 ♦ **(that's) fine** (那) 好吧 ♦ **to cut it fine** (*in time*) 扣得紧 ♦ **you're doing fine** 你做得很好

fine art *n* [u] (*also:* **fine arts**) 美术 ♦ **he's got it down to a fine art** 他对此游刃有余

finger ['fɪŋgə(r)] **I** *n* [c] [解剖] 手指 **II** *vt* (*touch*) 触摸 ♦ **to keep one's fingers crossed** (喻) 祈愿好运 ♦ **to cross one's fingers** 食指与中指交叉重叠 ♦ **to point the finger at sb** (喻) 指责某人 ♦ **to put one's finger on sth** (喻) 对某事有充分把握

fingernail ['fɪŋgəneɪl] *n* [c] 指甲

fingerprint ['fɪŋgəprɪnt] **I** *n* [c] 指纹 **II** *vt* [+ *person*] 取…的指纹 ♦ **to take sb's fingerprints** 取下某人的指纹

fingertip ['fɪŋgətɪp] *n* [c] 指尖 ♦ **to have sth at one's fingertips** (*at one's disposal*) 轻而易举地得到某物; (*know well*) 对某事了如指掌

finish ['fɪnɪʃ] **I** *n* **1** [s] (*end*) 结束 **2** [c] [体育] 终点 **3** [c] (*appearance, texture*) 末道漆 **II** *vt* [+ *work*] 结束; [+ *task, report, book*] 完成; [+ *drink*] 喝完; [+ *sandwich*] 吃完; [+ *cigarette*] 吸完 **III** *vi* **1** [*course, event* +] 结束 **2** [*person* +] 说完 ♦ **a close finish** [体育] 扣人心弦的终场 ♦ **to finish doing sth** 做完某事 ♦ **to finish third** (*in race, competition*) 最后得了第三名 ♦ **to put the finishing touches to sth** 最后完结某事 ♦ **she's finished with him** [非正式] 她已经跟他分手了

❑ **finish off** *vt* **1** [+ *job, report*] 完成; [+ *dinner, wine*] 吃/喝光 **2** [非正式] (*kill*) 干掉

❑ **finish up I** *vi* (*end up*) 告终 **II** *vt* **1** [+ *meal*] 吃完; [+ *drink*] 喝完 **2** [美] (*finish off*) 完成

finite ['faɪnaɪt] *adj* **1** [+ *number, amount*] 有限的 **2** [+ *verb*] 限定的

Finland ['fɪnlənd] *n* 芬兰

Finn [fɪn] *n* [c] 芬兰人

Finnish ['fɪnɪʃ] **I** *adj* 芬兰的 **II** *n* [u] (*language*) 芬兰语

fir [fəː(r)] *n* [c] (*also:* **fir tree**) 冷杉

fire ['faɪə(r)] **I** *n* **1** [u] (*flames*) 火 **2** [c] (*in fireplace, hearth etc*) 炉火 **3** [c/u] (*accidental*) 火灾 **4** [u] (*shots*) 射击 **II** *vt* **1** (*shoot*) [+ *gun, bullet, shot, arrow*] 射出 **2** (*stimulate*) [+ *imagination, enthusiasm*] 激起 **3** [非正式] (*dismiss*) [+ *employee*] 解雇 **III** *vi* (*shoot*) 开火 ♦ **on fire** 起火 ♦ **to set fire to sth, set sth on fire** 放火烧某物 ♦ **electric/gas fire** [尤英] 电/煤气炉 [美 = **heater**] ♦ **to come/be under fire (from)** 遭到 (来自…的) 射击 ♦ **to catch fire** 着火 ♦ **to open fire (on sb)** (向某人) 开火 ♦ **to fire questions at sb** 向某人急速地连续发问

fire alarm *n* [c] 火警警报

firearm ['faɪərɑːm] *n* [c] 枪支

fire brigade *n* [c] 消防队

fire department [美] *n* = **fire service**

fire engine [英] *n* [c] 救火车 [美 = **fire truck**]

fire escape *n* [c] 太平梯

fire exit *n* [c] 安全出口

fire extinguisher *n* [c] 灭火器

fireman ['faɪəmən] (*pl* **firemen**) *n* [c] 消防队员

fireplace ['faɪəpleɪs] *n* [c] 壁炉

fire service [英] *n* [c] 消防部门

fire station *n* [c] 消防站

fire truck [美] *n* [c] 救火车 [英 = **fire engine**]

firewall ['faɪəwɔːl] [计算机] *n* [c] 防火墙

firewood ['faɪəwud] *n* [u] 木柴

firework ['faɪəwəːk] **I** *n* [c] (*explosive*) 烟火 **II fireworks** *n* [*pl*] (*display*) 烟火表演

firing line ['faɪərɪŋ-] *n* ♦ **to be in the firing line** (喻) 在第一线

✪ **firm** [fəːm] **I** *adj* **1** [+ *mattress, ground*] 硬实的 **2** [+ *person*] 坚定的 **3** [+ *grasp, hold, grip*] (字) 稳定而有力的 ◊ *I took a firm hold on the rope.* 我牢牢地抓着绳子。; (喻) 毫不动摇的 ◊ *He has a firm grasp of the* *principles.* 他毫不动摇地坚持原则。**4** [+ *views, leadership*] 强有力的 **5** [+ *offer*] 确定的 **6** [+ *decision, opinion*] 坚决的 ◊ *He made a firm decision to leave.* 他作出坚决的决定要离开。**7** [+ *evidence, news, information*] 确凿的 ◊ *We have no firm evidence.* 我们没有确凿的证据。**II** *n* [c] (*company*) 公司 ♦**to be firm with sb** 严格对待某人 ♦**to stand firm** 立场坚定 ♦**to be a firm believer in sth** 是某事坚定的信仰者

firmly [ˈfəːmlɪ] *adv* **1** [*rest, stand* +] 牢牢地; [*push, pull, hold* +] 紧紧地 **2** [*believe* +] 坚定地 **3** [*say, tell* +] 坚决地

✪**first** [fəːst] **I** *adj* **1** (*in series*) 第一的 ◊ *For the first time in our lives ...* 我们生命中的第一次… **2** (*initial*) [+ *reaction, impression*] 最初的 ◊ *My first reaction was one of horror.* 我最初的反应是害怕。**3** (*top*) [+ *prize, division*] 头等的 ◊ *She won first prize.* 她得了头等奖。 **4** (*front*) [+ *row*] 第一的 ◊ *We had seats in the first row.* 我们的座位在第一排。**5** (*main*) [+ *duty, responsibility*] 首要的 ◊ *My first duty is to my patients.* 我首先要对病人负责。**II** *adv* **1** (*before anyone else*) [*speak, arrive* +] 首先 ◊ *Jenny spoke first.* 詹妮首先发言。**2** (*before other things*) 首先 ◊ *But first I had to get a visa.* 但是首先我得先拿到签证。**3** (*when listing reasons*) 第一 ◊ *There were several reasons for this. First, four submarines had been sighted.* 这有几个原因。第一，发现了4艘潜水艇。**4** (*for the first time*) 第一次 ◊ *Sophie and Dave first met in the summer of 1910.* 索菲和戴夫第一次是在1910年夏天相遇。**5** (*in race, competition*) [*come, finish* +] 第一名 ◊ *Johnson came first in the one hundred metres.* 约翰逊在一百米跑比赛中获得第一名。**III** *n* **1** [U] [汽车] (*also:* ***first gear***) 一挡 ◊ *I changed down into first.* 我换到了一挡。**2** [c] [英:大学] 甲等 ◊ *He got a first in French.* 他的法语得了甲等。**3** [c] (*event*) 首次 ◊ *The meeting between financial analysts was a first for the company.* 金融分析家之间的会议在公司里是首次。♦**at first** 起先 ♦**first of all** 首先 ♦**the first of January** 1月1号 ♦**in the first instance** 起初 ♦**I'll do it first thing tomorrow** 明天我首先做这件事 ♦**from the (very) first** 从（最）一开始 ♦**to put sb/sth first** 把某人/某事放在第一位 ♦**at first hand** 直接地 ♦**the first I heard/knew of it** 最初我所听到的/所知道的

first aid *n* [U] 急救

first-aid kit [fəːstˈeɪd-] *n* [c] 急救包

first-class [fəːstˈklɑːs] **I** *adj* **1** (*excellent*) [+ *worker, piece of work*] 第一流的 **2** [+ *carriage, ticket, stamp*] 一类的 **II** *adv* [*travel, send* +] 作为一类

first-hand [fəːstˈhænd] *adj* [+ *knowledge, experience*] 第一手的

first lady *n* [c] 第一夫人 ♦**the first lady of jazz** 爵士乐之后

firstly [ˈfəːstlɪ] *adv* 首先

first name *n* [c] 名 ♦**to be on first-name terms (with sb)** （与某人）关系亲密

first-rate [fəːstˈreɪt] *adj* [+ *actor, swimmer, performance*] 第一流的

fiscal [ˈfɪskl] *adj* [+ *year, policy*] 财政的

fish [fɪʃ] **I** *n* **1** [c] [动] 鱼 **2** [U] (*food*) 鱼肉 **II** *vt* [+ *river, area*] 捕 **III** *vi* (*commercially*) 捕鱼; (*as sport, hobby*) 钓鱼 ♦**to go fishing** 去钓鱼

> **FISH AND CHIPS**
> **fish and chips** 是一种英国传统的外卖食品，由卷着面糊的大块炸鱼排和炸薯条组成，用醋或辣酱调味。**fish and chips** 可以在 **chip shop**［参见 **chip shop**］里买到。你可以买回家吃，也可以在街上吃。鱼一般用鳕鱼、黑斑鳕鱼或鲽鱼。

❑**fish out** [非正式] *vt* (*from water*) 打捞; (*from box, bag etc*) 掏出

fish and chips [英] *n* [U] 炸鱼排加炸薯条

fisherman [ˈfɪʃəmən] (*pl* **fishermen**) *n* [c] 渔民

fishery [ˈfɪʃərɪ] *n* [c] **1** (*fishing grounds*) 渔场 **2** (*fish farm*) 养鱼场

fish fingers [英] *n* [*pl*] 炸鱼条

fishing [ˈfɪʃɪŋ] *n* [U] 钓鱼
fishing boat [ˈfɪʃɪŋ-] *n* [C] 渔船
fishing line *n* [C] (*line*) 钓丝
fishing rod *n* [C] 钓竿
fishmonger [ˈfɪʃmʌŋɡə(r)], **fishmonger's** [尤英] *n* [C] 鱼贩
fish sticks [美] *n* [*pl*] = **fish fingers**
fishy [ˈfɪʃɪ] *adj* **1** [+ *taste, smell*] 鱼味的 **2** [非正式] (*suspicious*) 可疑的
fist [fɪst] *n* [C] 拳
fit [fɪt] **I** *adj* **1** (*suitable*) 合适的 **2** (*healthy*) 健康的 **II** *vt* **1** [*clothes, shoes* +] 合…的身 **2** (*attach*) [+ *lock, wheels*] 安装 **3** (*be suitable for*) [+ *needs, aims*] 与…相协调 **4** (*match*) [+ *facts, theory, description*] 与…相符 **III** *vi* **1** [*clothes, shoes* +] 合身 **2** (*in space, gap*) 适合 **IV** *n* [C] [医] 发作 ♦ **to be fit to** [非正式] (*about to*) 马上就 ♦ **to be fit for** (*suitable for*) 适于 ♦ **to keep fit** 保持健康 ♦ **to see fit to do sth** 认为做某事合适 ♦ **a fit of rage** 一阵怒火 ♦ **a fit of giggles** 一阵咯咯的笑 ♦ **a fit of hysterics** 一阵歇斯底里的发作 ♦ **to have a fit** [医] 癫痫病发作; [非正式](喻) 震惊 ♦ **to be a good fit** 很合身 ♦ **in** *or* **by fits and starts** 一阵一阵的 ♦ **to fit sth with sth** 给某物安装某物
❑ **fit in I** *vi* **1** (字) [*person, object* +] 容纳 **2** (喻) [*person* +] 接纳 **II** *vt* (喻) [+ *appointment, visitor*] 定时间于 ♦ **to fit in with sb's plans** 正合某人的计划
❑ **fit into** *vt* **1** [+ *hole, gap*] 刚好放下 **2** [+ *suitcase, room*] 放得下 **3** [*person* +] [+ *group*] 合群
❑ **fit out, fit up** *vt* (*equip*) 提供装备
fitment [ˈfɪtmənt] *n* [C] (*furnishing*) 家具; (*equipment*) 设备
fitness [ˈfɪtnɪs] *n* [U] **1** [医] 健康 **2** (*suitability*) 适合
fitted [ˈfɪtɪd] *adj* [+ *jacket*] 合身的; [+ *carpet, wardrobe*] 定做的 ♦ **fitted with** 配备…的
fitted carpet *n* [C] 按照房间尺寸铺好的地毯
fitted kitchen [英] *n* [C] 有固定设备的厨房
fitted sheet *n* [C] 四角缝紧兜住床垫的床单
fitter [ˈfɪtə(r)] *n* [C] (*person*) 装备工
fitting [ˈfɪtɪŋ] **I** *adj* (*appropriate*) [+ *tribute, conclusion*] 恰当的 **II** *n* [C] **1** (*for clothes*) 试穿 **2** (*handle, tap*) 配件 **III fittings** *n* [*pl*] (*in building*) 装置
fitting room *n* [C] (*in shop*) 试衣间
✪ **five** [faɪv] *num* 五 ♦ **that will be five pounds, please** 请付5镑 ♦ **she's five (years old)** 她5岁了 ♦ **it's five o'clock** 5点了 ♦ **no later than five (o'clock)** 不迟于5点 ♦ **there are five of us** 我们有5个人 ♦ **all five of them** 他们5个人都 ♦ **five hundred/thousand children** 五百/千名儿童
fiver [ˈfaɪvə(r)] [英] [非正式] *n* [C] 五镑钞票
fix [fɪks] **I** *vt* **1** (*set*) [+ *date, price, meeting*] 确定 **2** (*mend*) [+ *machine, leak, fault*] 修理 **3** (*resolve*) [+ *problem*] 解决 **4** (*prepare*) [+ *meal, drink*] 准备 **5** [非正式] [+ *game, election, result*] 操纵 **II** *n* [非正式] **1** ♦ **to be in a fix** 陷入进退维谷的境地 **2** [C] [非正式] (*injection*) 毒品注射 ♦ **a fix of coffee/chocolate** [非正式] 我每天需要定量的咖啡/巧克力 ♦ **the fight was a fix** 这场拳击赛受到了操纵 ♦ **to fix sth to/on sth** (*attach*) 把某物安装在某物上 ♦ **to fix one's eyes on sb/sth** 盯着某人/某事 ♦ **to fix one's attention on sb/sth** 将注意力集中于某人/某物
❑ **fix up** *vt* (*arrange*) [+ *meeting, appointment*] 安排 ♦ **to fix sb up with sth** 给某人提供某物
fixed [fɪkst] *adj* **1** [+ *price, amount, intervals*] 固定的 **2** [+ *ideas*] 固执的 **3** [+ *smile*] 呆板的 ♦ **there's a fixed charge** 收费固定 ♦ **how are you fixed for money/time?** 经济情况如何/有时间吗? ♦ **of no fixed address** *or* [英] **abode** [正式] 没有固定的住所
fixture [ˈfɪkstʃə(r)] *n* [C] **1** (*bath, sink, cupboard*) 固定装置 **2** [英: 体育] 预定日期的比赛项目 ♦ **she is a fixture in New York's nightclubs** 她是纽约夜总会的常客 ♦ **sold with fixtures and fittings** 连同家具和设备一同出售的
fizzy [ˈfɪzɪ] [英] *adj* [+ *drink*] 带气的

[美= **carbonated**]

flag [flæg] **I** *n* [c] **1** 旗 **2** (*also: **flagstone***) 石板 **II** *vi* [*person* +] 疲倦; [*spirits, enthusiasm* +] 衰退 ♦**to fly the flag** (喻) 表示拥护和支持 ♦**flag of convenience** 方便旗，为减少运费或逃避本国其他规章制度而在他国注册后悬挂的他国的旗帜

❑**flag down** *vt* [+ *taxi, car*] 挥手示意…停下

flagpole ['flægpəul] *n* [c] 旗杆

flair [flɛə(r)] *n* **1** ♦**to have a flair for sth** 对某事有天分 **2** [U] (*panache*) 气派

flak [flæk] *n* [U] **1** [军] 高射炮 **2** (喻) (*criticism*) 批评

flake [fleɪk] **I** *n* [c] **1** [*of rust, paint*] 薄片 **2** [*of snow*] 片 **II** *vi* (*also: **flake off***) [*paint, enamel* +] 剥落

❑**flake out** [非正式] *vi* [*person* +] 累得瘫倒

flamboyant [flæm'bɔɪənt] *adj* [+ *clothes, style*] 艳丽的; [+ *person*] 派头十足的

flame [fleɪm] *n* [C/U] [*of fire*] 火焰 ♦**to burst into flames** 烧起来 ♦**in flames** 燃烧着 ♦**an old flame** [非正式] 老情人

flamingo [flə'mɪŋgəu] (*pl* **flamingos** *or* **flamingoes**) *n* [c] 火烈鸟

flammable ['flæməbl] *adj* [+ *gas, fabric*] 易燃的

flan [flæn] *n* [c] 果酱饼

flank [flæŋk] **I** *n* [c] **1** [*of animal*] 胁腹 **2** [*of army*] 侧翼 **II** *vt* ♦**to be flanked by sb/sth** 某人/某物在…的旁边

flannel ['flænl] **I** *n* **1** [U] (*fabric*) 法兰绒 **2** [c] [英] (*also: **face flannel***) 面巾 [美=**washcloth**] **3** [U] [英:非正式] (*waffle*) 兜圈子 **II flannels** *n* [*pl*] [过时] 法兰绒裤子

flap [flæp] **I** *n* [c] [*of pocket, envelope, skin*] 盖 **II** *vt* [+ *arms, wings*] 摆动 **III** *vi* [*sail, flag* +] 摆动 ♦**to be in a flap (about** *or* **over sth)** [非正式] (对某事) 慌作一团

flare [flɛə(r)] **I** *n* [c] (*signal*) 信号弹 **II** *vi* (*also: **flare up***) **1** [*fire, match* +] 火焰突然变旺 **2** (*also: **flare up***) [*fighting, violence, trouble* +] 突然爆发 **3** [*tempers* +] 突然发怒 **4** [*nostrils* +] 鼓起

❑**flare up** *vi* [*disease, injury* +] 突然发作 **III flares** *n* [*pl*] (*trousers*) 喇叭裤

flash [flæʃ] **I** *vt* **1** [+ *light*] 使闪光 **2** (*send*) [+ *news, message*] 传送 **3** [+ *look, smile*] 闪过 **II** *vi* **1** [*lightning, light* +] 闪光 **2** [文] [*eyes* +] 闪烁 **III** *n* [c] **1** [*of light, lightning*] 闪光 **2** [摄影] 闪光灯 **3** [美:非正式] (*also: **flashlight***) 闪光信号灯 [英=**torch**] **IV** *adj* [非正式] [+ *restaurant, car*] 浮华的 ♦**in a flash** 一刹那间 ♦**quick as a flash** 极快 ♦**a flash of inspiration/anger** 突如其来的灵感/怒气 ♦**to flash one's headlights** 亮起车头灯 ♦**the thought flashed through his mind** 一个想法在他脑子里突然闪现 ♦**to flash by** *or* **past** 一闪而过

flashback ['flæʃbæk] *n* [c] **1** [影院] 闪回 **2** [心理] 回想

flashbulb ['flæʃbʌlb] *n* [c] 闪光灯泡

flashlight ['flæʃlaɪt] [尤美] *n* [c] 手电筒 [英=**torch**]

flashy ['flæʃɪ] [非正式:贬] *adj* 华丽而俗气的

flask [flɑːsk] *n* [c] **1** (*also: **vacuum flask***) 保温瓶 **2** (*bottle*) 携带式酒瓶 **3** [化] 烧瓶

flat [flæt] **I** *adj* **1** (*level*) [+ *ground, surface*] 平的 **2** (*shallow*) 浅的 **3** [+ *tyre, ball*] 气不足的 **4** [英] [+ *battery*] 没电的 [美=**dead**] **5** [+ *beer, champagne*] 跑了气的 **6** [+ *refusal, rejection, denial*] 断然的 **7** [音] [+ *singing, instrument*] 降音的 **8** [+ *rate, fee*] 统一的 **9** (*without emotion*) [+ *voice*] 无精打采的 **II** *n* [c] **1** [英] (*in building*) 公寓 [美=**apartment**] **2** [汽车] 漏气车胎 **3** [音] 降号 **III** *adv* **1** [*lie* +] 平地 **2** [音] [*sing, play* +] 降音地 ♦**to work flat out** [英] 尽全力工作 ♦**in 10 minutes flat** 就10分钟 ♦**to fall flat** [*joke, attempt* +] 毫无效果 ♦**the flat of one's hand** 手掌 ♦**B/A flat** [音] 降B/A音

flatten ['flætn] **I** *vt* **1** (*also: **flatten out***) 使变平 **2** (*destroy*) [+ *building, crop, city*] 夷平 **II** *vi* (*also: **flatten out***)

平展 ♦ **to flatten o.s. against a wall** 自己平倚着墙

flatter ['flætə(r)] *vt* **1** (*praise*) 奉承 **2** [*dress, photograph* +] 使更漂亮 ♦ **to be flattered (that …)** (对于…)感到荣幸 ♦ **to flatter o.s. (that …)** (对…)自我感觉良好

flattering ['flætərɪŋ] *adj* **1** [+ *comment*] 奉承的 **2** [+ *dress, photograph*] 使美过其实的

flaunt [flɔːnt] *vt* [+ *wealth, possessions*] 炫耀

flavour ['fleɪvə(r)] (美 **flavor**) **I** *n* [C/U] [*of food, drink*] 味 **II** *vt* [+ *food, drink*] 给…调味 ♦ **strawberry-flavoured** 草莓味的 ♦ **music with an African flavour** 具有非洲风情的音乐

flavoured ['fleɪvəd] *adj* 经调味的 ♦ **flavoured with** 加了…调味的

flavouring ['fleɪvərɪŋ] (美 **flavoring**) *n* [C/U] 调味品

flaw [flɔː] *n* [C] (*in argument, theory*) 缺陷; (*in character*) 缺点; (*in cloth, pattern*) 瑕疵

flawless ['flɔːlɪs] *adj* [+ *performance, complexion*] 完美无瑕的

flea [fliː] *n* [C] 跳蚤

fleck [flɛk] **I** *n* [C] **1** [*of mud, paint, colour*] 斑点 **2** (*pattern*) 点 **II** *vt* ♦ **to be flecked with mud/blood** *etc* 溅有泥点/血斑{等} ♦ **brown flecked with white** 夹杂白色斑点的褐色 ♦ **flecks of dust/blood** 尘粒/血斑

flee [fliː] (*pt, pp* **fled**) **I** *vt* [+ *danger, famine, country*] 逃离 **II** *vi* [*refugees, escapees* +] 逃走

fleece [fliːs] **I** *n* [C] **1** (*sheep's wool*) 羊毛; (*sheep's coat*) 羊的皮毛 **2** (*garment*) 毛呢衣物 **II** *vt* [非正式] (*cheat*) 诈取

fleet [fliːt] *n* [C] [*of ships, lorries, buses*] 队

fleeting ['fliːtɪŋ] *adj* [+ *glimpse, visit, happiness*] 短暂的

Flemish ['flɛmɪʃ] **I** *adj* 佛兰芒的 **II** *n* [U] (*language*) 佛兰芒语

flesh [flɛʃ] *n* [U] **1** [解剖] 肉 **2** (*skin*) 肉体 **3** [*of fruit, vegetable*] 果肉 ♦ **in the flesh** 亲自 ♦ **she's my own flesh and blood** 她是我的亲骨肉

❑ **flesh out** *vt* [+ *proposal, account*] 充实

flew [fluː] *pt of* **fly**

flex [flɛks] **I** *n* [C/U] [英] [*of appliance*] 电线 [美 = **cord**] **II** *vt* [+ *muscles, fingers*] 屈曲

flexibility [flɛksɪ'bɪlɪtɪ] *n* [U] **1** [*of object, material*] 柔韧性 **2** [*of ideas, approach*] 灵活性

flexible ['flɛksəbl] *adj* **1** [+ *material*] 柔韧的 **2** [+ *response, policy*] 灵活的 **3** [+ *person, schedule*] 机动的

flexitime ['flɛksɪtaɪm] [英] *n* [U] 弹性工作制 ♦ **to work flexitime, be on flexitime** 按弹性工作制工作 [美 = **flextime**]

flick [flɪk] **I** *vt* (*with fingers*) 轻弹; [+ *whip, towel*] 轻拂; [+ *cigarette ash*] 弹去; [+ *switch*] 拨 **II** *vi* 快而轻地移动 **III** *n* [C] [*of finger, hand*] 轻拂; [*of whip*] 轻打; (*through book, pages*) 快速翻阅 **4 the flicks** *n* [*pl*] [英:非正式] 电影院

❑ **flick through** *vt* [不可拆分] [+ *book, pages*] 快速翻阅

flicker ['flɪkə(r)] **I** *vi* **1** [*light, candle* +] 闪烁 **2** [*smile, look* +] 闪过 **II** *n* [C] **1** [*of light, flames*] 闪烁 **2** [*of pain, fear*] 一丝 **3** [*of smile*] 闪现

flight [flaɪt] *n* **1** [U] (*action*) [*of plane*] 飞行; [*of birds*] 飞翔 **2** [C] [航空] (*journey*) 航班; (*plane*) 班机 **3** [U] (*escape*) 逃逸 **4** [C] (*also:* ***flight of stairs, flight of steps***) 一段楼梯 ♦ **to take flight** 逃跑 ♦ **a flight of fancy** 异想天开

flight attendant *n* [C] (*male*) 男空服人员; (*female*) 空姐

flight deck *n* [C] **1** [航空] 驾驶舱 **2** [航海] 飞行甲板

flimsy ['flɪmzɪ] *adj* **1** [+ *structure, door, lock*] 不结实的; [+ *clothes, shoes*] 轻薄的 **2** [+ *excuse, evidence*] 不足信的

flinch [flɪntʃ] *vi* (*in pain*) 退缩 ♦ **to flinch from** [+ *unpleasant duty, decision*] 逃避

fling [flɪŋ] (*pt, pp* **flung**) **I** *vt* [+ *ball, stone, hat*] 掷; [+ *one's arms, oneself*] 猛然移动 **II** *n* [非正式] **1** [C] (*love affair*) 一时的行乐 **2** [S] (*spree*) 放纵

flint [flɪnt] *n* **1** [U] (*stone*) 燧石 **2** [U] (*in cigarette lighter*) 打火石

flip [flɪp] **I** *vt* **1** [+ *lights, switch*] 捻

2 (*also: **flip over***) 快速地翻转 **II** *vi* 一下翻转 ♦**to flip a coin** 抛硬币 ♦**to flip a pancake** 翻烙饼
❑**flip through** *vt* [不可拆分] [+ *book, pages*] 快速翻阅

flip-flops ['flɪpflɔps] [尤英] *n* [*pl*] 夹趾拖鞋 [美=**thongs**]

flipper ['flɪpə(r)] *n* [c] **1** [*of seal, penguin*] 鳍状肢 **2** (*for swimming*) 脚蹼

flirt [flə:t] **I** *vi* (*with person*) 调情 **II** *n* [c] 调情者 ♦**to flirt with an idea** 对某个想法只是想想而已

flit [flɪt] *vi* **1** [*person* +] 换来换去; [*bird, butterfly* +] 飞来飞去 **2** [*expression, smile* +] 掠过

float [fləut] **I** *vi* **1** (*on water*) [*object* +] 漂浮 **2** (*through air*) [*paper, feather* +] 飘浮 **3** [文] [*sound, smell* +] 飘散 **4** (*stay afloat*) [*swimmer, object* +] 浮着 **5** [商] [*currency* +] 浮动 **II** *vt* **1** [商] [+ *currency*] 使浮动 **2** [商] [+ *company*] 以公开发行股票的办法开办新公司 **3** [+ *idea, plan*] 提出 **III** *n* [c] **1** (*for fishing*) 鱼漂 **2** (*for swimming*) 浮板 **3** (*in carnival*) 彩车 **4** [英] (*money*) 周转零款
❑**float around** *vi* [*idea, rumour* +] 广为流传

flock [flɔk] **I** *n* [c] **1** [*of sheep, birds*] 群 **2** [过时:宗] 同一牧师管辖下的全体教徒 **II** *vi* [*people* +] 成群结队 ♦**flocks of journalists** 众多的新闻记者

flog [flɔg] *vt* **1** (*whip*) 抽打 **2** [英:非正式] (*sell*) 卖

flood [flʌd] **I** *n* **1** [c/u] [*of water*] 洪水 **2** [c] [*of letters, requests, imports*] 大量 **II** *vt* **1** (*through forces of nature*) 淹没 **2** (*intentionally*) 浇灌 **3** [汽车] [+ *engine*] 使…溢流 **III** *vi* **1** [*place* +] 为水所淹 **2** [*people, goods* +] ♦**to flood into** 洪水般涌入 ♦**to flood the market** [商] 充斥市场 ♦**in flood** 泛滥

flooding ['flʌdɪŋ] *n* [u] 泛滥

floodlight ['flʌdlaɪt] **I** *n* [c] 泛光灯 **II** *vt* 用泛光灯照亮

floor [flɔ:(r)] *n* **I** **1** [c] [*of room*] 地板 **2** [c] (*storey*) 楼层 **3** [s] [*of sea, valley*] 底 **II** *vt* **1** (*knock down*) 把…打翻在地 **2** (*surprise*) [*question, remark* +] 使惊得无以应付 ♦**on the floor** 在地板上 ♦**ground floor** [英] 一楼 ♦**first floor** [英] 二楼; [美] 一楼 ♦**top floor** 顶层 ♦**to take the floor** [*speaker* +] 开始发言

> 在英式英语中，建筑的 **ground floor** 是指紧贴地面的那个楼层。它上面的一层叫 **first floor**。在美式英语中，**first floor** 是指紧贴地面的楼层，它上面的一层是 **second floor**。

floorboard ['flɔ:bɔ:d] *n* [c] 地板块

flooring ['flɔ:rɪŋ] *n* [u] 地板材料

floor show *n* [c] 夜总会的文娱表演

flop [flɔp] **I** *vi* **1** (*into chair, onto floor etc*) 猛落 **2** [非正式] (*fail*) 失败 **II** *n* [c] [非正式] (*failure*) 失败

floppy ['flɔpɪ] **I** *adj* [+ *hat, bow*] 松垂的 **II** *n* [c] (*also: **floppy disk***) 软盘

flora ['flɔ:rə] *n* [c] 植物群

floral ['flɔ:rl] *adj* [+ *dress, pattern*] 花卉的 ♦**a floral arrangement** 花饰

florist ['flɔrɪst] *n* [c] **1** (*shopkeeper*) 花商 **2** ***florist's*** 花店

flotation [fləu'teɪʃən] *n* [c/u] [*of company*] 股票发行

flounder (*pl* **flounder** *or* **flounders**) ['flaundə(r)] **I** *vi* **1** [*swimmer* +] 挣扎 **2** [*career, economy* +] 垂死挣扎; [*person, speaker* +] 漫无目的 **II** *n* [c/u] [动] 鲆鲽

flour ['flauə(r)] *n* [u] 面粉

flourish ['flʌrɪʃ] **I** *vi* **1** [*business, economy, arts* +] 繁荣 **2** [*plant, animal* +] 兴旺 **II** *vt* [+ *document, handkerchief*] 挥舞 **III** *n* ♦**with a flourish** 用花哨的动作

flout [flaut] *vt* [+ *law, convention*] 蔑视

flow [fləu] **I** *vi* **1** [*liquid, gas, electricity* +] 流动 **2** [*traffic, people* +] 川流不息 **3** [*money, information* +] 流通 **4** [文] [*clothes, hair* +] 飘垂 **II** *n* [c/u] **1** [*of liquid, gas, electricity*] 流动 **2** [*of traffic*] 川流不息 **3** [*of money, information*] 流通 **4** [*of tide*] 涨潮 **5** [*of thought, speech*] 流畅

flower ['flauə(r)] **I** *n* [c] 花 **II** *vi* **1** [*plant, tree* +] 开花 **2** (喻) (*blossom*) 成熟 ♦**in flower** 正开着花

flower bed *n* [c] 花坛
flowerpot ['flauəpɔt] *n* [c] 花盆
flown [fləun] *pp of* **fly**
flu [flu:] *n* [U] 流感
fluctuate ['flʌktjueɪt] *vi* [*price, rate, temperature* +] 波动; [*opinions, attitudes* +] 动摇
fluent ['flu:ənt] *adj* [+ *speech, reading, writing*] 流畅的 ♦ **he's a fluent speaker/reader** 他是个说话/阅读流利的人 ♦ **to speak fluent French, be fluent in French** 讲流利的法语
fluff [flʌf] **I** *n* [U] **1** (*on clothes, carpet*) 绒毛 **2** (*fur*) [*of kitten, chick*] 绒毛 **II** *vt* **1** [非正式] [+ *speech, interview*] 将…搞糟 **2** (*also:* ***fluff up***) [+ *hair, pillow, feathers*] 抖松
fluffy ['flʌfɪ] *adj* **1** [+ *towel, sweater*] 蓬松的 **2** [+ *cake*] 松软的 ♦ **fluffy toy** 绒毛玩具
fluid ['flu:ɪd] **I** *n* [C/U] (*liquid*) 流体 **II** *adj* **1** [+ *movement*] 流畅的 **2** (喻) [+ *situation, arrangement*] 易变的
fluke [flu:k] [非正式] *n* [c] 侥幸
flung [flʌŋ] *pt, pp of* **fling**
fluorescent [fluə'rɛsnt] *adj* [+ *material, colour*] 发荧光的; [+ *light*] 荧光的
fluoride ['fluəraɪd] *n* [U] 氟化物
flurry ['flʌrɪ] *n* [c] [*of snow, wind*] 一阵 ♦ **a flurry of activity** 一阵活动 ♦ **a flurry of excitement** 一阵激动
flush [flʌʃ] **I** *n* [c] **1** (*on face*) 红晕 **2** [*of toilet*] 冲水 **3** [纸牌] 同花 **II** *vt* ♦ **to flush the toilet** 冲厕所 **III** *vi* **1** (*become red*) 脸红 **2** [*toilet* +] 冲水 **IV** *adj* ♦ **flush with** 与…齐平的 ♦ **in the first flush of freedom** 获得自由的最初兴奋期 ♦ **in the first flush of youth** 在风华正茂的青春时期
❑ **flush out** *vt* [+ *animals, birds*] 赶出; [+ *criminal*] 逐出
flute [flu:t] *n* [c] 长笛
flutter ['flʌtə(r)] **I** *vi* **1** [*bird* +] 拍翅; [*flag, clothes* +] 飘动 **2** [*heart, stomach* +] 悸动 **II** *vt* [*wings* +] 拍 **III** *n* [s] **1** [*of wings*] 拍动; [*of cloth*] 飘动 **2** [*of panic, excitement*] 一阵心绪不宁
flux [flʌks] *n* ♦ **in a state of flux** 处于不断变化之中

✪ **fly** [flaɪ] (*pt* **flew**, *pp* **flown**) **I** *vt* **1** [+ *plane*] 驾驶 ◊ *He flew a small plane to Cuba.* 他驾驶一架小飞机去古巴了。**2** [+ *passengers, cargo*] 空运 ◊ *The supplies are being flown from Pisa.* 补给品正从比萨空运过来。**3** [+ *distance*] 飞行 ◊ *He flew thousands of miles just to be with her.* 他飞行数千英里，只是为了和她在一起。**4** [+ *kite*] 放 **II** *vi* **1** [*bird, insect, plane* +] 飞 ◊ *No other creature can fly as far as birds.* 没有比鸟飞得更远的动物。◊ *The planes flew through the clouds.* 飞机飞过云层。**3** [*passengers* +] 乘飞机 ◊ *He flew back to London.* 他乘飞机回伦敦了。**4** [*pilot* +] 驾驶飞机 ◊ *She is learning to fly.* 她在学习驾驶飞机。**5** (*rush*) 飞奔 ◊ *I flew downstairs.* 我飞奔到楼下。**6** (*dash away*) 快走 ◊ *I'm sorry, I must fly.* 对不起，我得赶快走。**7** [文] (*flee*) 逃跑 ◊ *By the time they returned, their prisoner had flown.* 等他们回来时，他们的囚犯已经逃跑了。**8** [*flag, hair* +] 飘动 ◊ *A red flag was flying from the balcony.* 一面红旗在阳台上飘动着。**III** *n* [c] **1** (*insect*) 苍蝇 **2** (*also:* ***flies***) (*on trousers*) 有拉锁/纽扣的开口 ◊ *His flies were undone.* 他裤子的拉锁没拉上。♦ **to fly open** 猛地突然打开 ♦ **to fly off the handle** 发火 ♦ **to go flying** 横飞出去 ♦ **to send sb flying** 将某人抛了出去 ♦ **she came flying into the room** 她飞快地跑进房间 ♦ **her glasses flew off** 她的眼镜突然跌落 ♦ **to fly into a rage** 勃然大怒
❑ **fly away** *vi* [*bird, insect* +] 飞走
❑ **fly in** *vi* **1** [*plane* +] 降落 **2** [*person* +] 飞抵
❑ **fly off** *vi* = **fly away**
❑ **fly out** *vi* **1** [*plane* +] 飞离 **2** [*person* +] 乘机离开
fly-drive ['flaɪdraɪv] *adj* ♦ **fly-drive holiday** 空陆联程的旅游方式，即乘飞机到达目的地机场后，驾驶租用的汽车前往其他地方
flyer ['flaɪə(r)] *n* [c] **1** (*notice*) 传单 **2** [航空] (*passenger*) 乘客
flying ['flaɪɪŋ] **I** *n* [U] (*activity*) 飞行; (*going by plane*) 乘飞机 **II** *adj* [+ *insect, animal*] 会飞的 ♦ **a flying**

visit 短暂的访问 ♦ **to get off to a flying start** 开端良好 ♦ **he doesn't like flying** 他不喜欢坐飞机 ♦ **with flying colours** 大获全胜地

flying saucer [过时] *n* [c] 飞碟

flyover ['flaɪəuvə(r)] [英] *n* [c] 立交桥 [美=**overpass**]

FM *abbr* [广播] (= ***frequency modulation***) 调频

foal [fəul] *n* [c] 驹子

foam [fəum] **I** *n* [u] **1** (*on liquid, soap, beer, coffee*) 泡沫 **2** (*also:* ***foam rubber***) 泡沫橡胶 **II** *vi* [*soapy water, champagne* +] 起泡沫 ♦ **to be foaming at the mouth** (喻) 大怒

fob [fɔb] **I** *vt* ♦ **to fob sb off** 搪塞某人 **II** *n* [c] (*also:* ***watch fob***) 怀表链

focal point ['fəukl-] *n* [c] [*of room, activity, lens*] 焦点

focus ['fəukəs] (*pl* **focuses**) **I** *n* **1** [u] [摄影] 聚焦 **2** [c] (喻) (*subject*) 重点 **3** [c] (喻) (*attention*) 关注点 **II** *vt* **1** [+ *camera, telescope*] 调节…的焦距 **2** [+ *light rays*] 使聚焦 **3** [+ *eyes*] 使注视 **III** *vi* ♦ **to focus (on)** (*with camera*) 聚焦（于）; [*eyes* +] 注视（于）; (喻) (*concentrate on*) 集中（于） ♦ **in focus/out of focus** 焦点对准/没对准 ♦ **to be the focus of attention** 为关注的焦点 ♦ **to focus (one's) attention on sb/sth** 把精力集中于某人/某事

fodder ['fɔdə(r)] *n* [u] (*food*) 饲料

foe [fəu] [文] *n* [c] 敌人

foetus ['fiːtəs] (美 **fetus**) *n* [c] 胎儿

fog [fɔg] *n* [c/u] 雾

foggy ['fɔgɪ] *adj* [+ *day, climate*] 有雾的 ♦ **it's foggy** 今天有雾 ♦ **I haven't the foggiest (idea)** [非正式] 我一点也不知道

fog lamp (美 **fog light**) *n* [c] 雾灯

foil [fɔɪl] **I** *vt* [+ *attempt, plan*] 阻止 **II** *n* **1** [u] (*also:* ***kitchen foil***) 箔纸 **2** [c] (喻) (*complement*) 陪衬 **3** [c] [击剑] 花剑 ♦ **to act as a foil to** (喻) 作…的陪衬

fold [fəuld] **I** *n* **1** [c] (*in paper, cloth*) 折叠 **2** [c] (*in dress*) 褶 **3** [c] (*for sheep*) 羊栏 **4** [宗] ♦ **the fold** 信徒 **II** *vt* **1** (*also:* ***fold up***) [+ *cloth, clothes, paper, map*] 折叠 **2** (*also:* ***fold up***) [+ *chair, table*] 折 **3** [+ *one's arms, hands*] 交叠 **III** *vi* **1** [尤英] [*business, organization* +] 关停 **2** (*also:* ***fold up***) [*map, chair, table* +] 折叠起来

folder ['fəuldə(r)] *n* [c] (*for papers*) 文件夹

folding ['fəuldɪŋ] *adj* [+ *chair, bed*] 折叠的

foliage ['fəulɪɪdʒ] *n* [u] 叶子

folk [fəuk] **I** *n* [*pl*] (*also:* ***folks***) (*people*) 人们 **II** *cpd* [复合词] [+ *art, tales, medicine*] 民间 **III** ♦ **my folks** *n* [*pl*] [非正式] 我的家人

folklore ['fəuklɔː(r)] *n* [u] 民俗

folk music *n* [u] 民间音乐

folk song *n* [c] 民歌

✪ **follow** ['fɔləu] **I** *vt* **1** [+ *person, car*] (*go behind*) 跟随 ◊ *We followed him up the steps.* 我们跟随他上了台阶。**2** [+ *person*] (*join later*) 跟着到来 ◊ *He followed Julie to New York.* 他跟着朱莉到了纽约。**3** (*come after*) [+ *event, activity, time*] 继之而来 ◊ *the rioting that followed the verdict* 裁定后继之而来的暴乱 **4** (*take heed of*) [+ *example, advice, instructions*] 遵循 ◊ *She promised to follow his advice.* 她承诺要遵循他的忠告。**5** [+ *route, path*] 沿着…行进 ◊ *We followed a path along the creek.* 我们沿着小溪边的一条小路行进。**6** (*understand*) [+ *event, story*] 领会 ◊ *They were having some difficulty in following the plot.* 他们在理解情节上有困难。**7** (*take an interest in*) [+*sport, TV serial*] 对…感兴趣 ◊ *Millions of people follow football.* 成百上万的人对足球感兴趣。**8** (*with eyes*) 追随 ◊ *Suzy's eyes followed a police car as it drove slowly past.* 苏西的眼睛追随着一辆慢慢驶过的警车。**II** *vi* **1** [*person* +] 跟随 ◊ *They took him into a small room and I followed.* 他们把他带进一间小屋里，我跟了进去。**2** [*event, activity, time* +] 接下来 ◊ *He was arrested in the confusion which followed.* 他在接下来的一片混乱中被捕了。**3** (*result*) [*conclusion, benefit* +] 必然发生 ◊ *If the explanation is right, two things follow ...* 如果这一解释正确的话，两件事情必然发生… ♦ **to follow in sb's footsteps** 步某人后尘 ♦ **I don't quite follow you** 我不

太理解你的意思 ♦**it follows that ...** 一定是… ♦**as follows** (*when listing*) 如下◊ *The winners are as follows: ...* 获奖者如下: … ; (*in this way*) 按如下方式◊ *The sum will be calculated as follows ...* 总额将按如下方式计算… ♦**to follow suit**(喻)照样去做 ♦**to follow one thing (up) with another thing** 紧接着一件事做另一件事 ♦**followed by** 接着是
❑**follow on** *vi* (*continue*) 继续下去
❑**follow through** *vt* [+ *plan, idea*] 将…进行到底
❑**follow up** *vt* **1** [+ *letter, offer*] 对…采取进一步行动◊ *I followed up an advertisement for a second-hand Volkswagen.* 看了广告后，我对二手的大众车作了进一步了解。**2** [+ *idea, suggestion*] 把…探究到底◊ *The police are following up several leads.* 警方正顺着几个线索追查到底。

follower ['fɔləuə(r)] *n* [c] [*of person, belief*] 拥护者

following ['fɔləuɪŋ] **I** *prep* (*after*) 在…之后 **II** *adj* **1** (*next*) [+ *day, week*] 接着的 **2** (*next-mentioned*) [+ *way, list etc*] 下述的 **III** *n* [c] [*of party, religion, group*] 一批拥护者

follow-on call ['fɔləuɔn-] [通信] *n* [c] 继续拨叫电话

follow-up ['fɔləuʌp] **I** *n* [c] 后续 **II** *adj* [+ *treatment, survey, programme*] 后续的

folly ['fɔlɪ] *n* **1** [c/u] (*foolishness*) 愚蠢 **2** [c] (*building*) 装饰性建筑

fond [fɔnd] *adj* **1** ♦**to be fond of** [+ *person*] 喜爱; [+ *food, walking etc*] 喜欢 **2** [+ *memory*] 美好的; [+ *smile, look*] 深情的; [+ *hope, wish*] 不切实际的

✪**food** [fu:d] *n* [c/u] 食物 ♦**food for thought** 引人深思的事

food mixer *n* [c] 食物搅拌器

food poisoning *n* [u] 食物中毒

food processor [-prəusɛsə(r)] *n* [c] 食品加工机

food stamp *n* [c] [美] 政府发给低收入者的食品券，可用于换取食物

fool [fu:l] **I** *n* **1** [c] (*idiot*) 白痴 **2** [c/u] [英:烹饪] 奶油拌果子泥甜点 **II** *vt* (*deceive*) 欺骗 **III** *vi* ♦**to fool with sb/sth** 戏弄某人/摆弄某物 ♦**to make a fool of sb** (*ridicule*) 嘲弄某人 ♦**to make a fool of o.s.** 使自己出丑 ♦**you can't fool me** 你骗不了我
❑**fool about, fool around** [贬] *vi* (*behave foolishly*) 做蠢事

foolish ['fu:lɪʃ] *adj* **1** (*ridiculous*) 愚蠢的 **2** (*unwise*) 不明智的

foolproof ['fu:lpru:f] *adj* [+ *plan etc*] 万无一失的

✪**foot** [fut] (*pl* **feet**) **I** *n* **1** [c] (*measure*) 英尺◊ *a man over 6 feet tall* 一个6英尺多高的男子 **2** [c] [*of person*] 脚 **3** [c] [*of animal*] 蹄 **4** [c] [*of bed*] 放脚的一头 **5** [s] [*of cliff, hill, stairs*] 最底部 **II** *vt* ♦**to foot the bill** 付账 ♦**on foot** 步行 ♦**to be on one's feet** (*standing*) 站起来 ♦**to get** *or* **rise to one's feet** 站起来 ♦**to get back on one's feet** (*after illness, bad experience*) 恢复元气 ♦**to find one's feet**(喻)适应 ♦**to put one's foot down** (*in car*) (*accelerate*) 踩油门; (*say no*) 坚决反对 ♦**to put one's feet up** (*relax*) 双脚平搁起来休息 ♦**to set foot somewhere** 去某处 ♦**to stand on one's own two feet** 自力更生 ♦**at the foot of the page** 在页脚

footage ['futɪdʒ] [影院] *n* [u] 镜头

football ['futbɔ:l] *n* **1** [c] (*ball*) 足球 **2** [u] (*sport*) [英] 足球 [美=**soccer**] [美] 美式足球 [英=**American football**]

football boots [英] *n* [*pl*] 足球鞋

footballer ['futbɔ:lə(r)] [英] *n* [c] 足球运动员

football match [英] *n* [c] 足球赛

footbrake ['futbreɪk] *n* [c] 脚刹车

footbridge ['futbrɪdʒ] *n* [c] 步行桥

foothills ['futhɪlz] *n* [*pl*] 山麓小丘

foothold ['futhəuld] *n* [c] **1** [登山] 立足处 **2** (喻) 立足点

footing ['futɪŋ] *n* [c] (*basis*) ♦**on a more formal/scientific footing** 在更正式/科学的基础上 ♦**to lose one's footing** 失去平衡 ♦**on an equal footing** 在平等的基础上

footnote ['futnəut] *n* [c] (*in book*) 脚注

footpath ['futpɑ:θ] *n* [c] 人行小径

footprint ['futprɪnt] *n* [c] [*of person, animal*] 足迹

footstep ['futstɛp] *n* [c] (*sound*) 脚步声

footwear ['futwɛə(r)] *n* [u] 鞋类

for

KEYWORD

[fɔː(r)]

I *prep*

1 (*recipient*) 为 ♦**is this for me?** 这是为我准备的吗？ ♦**a table for two** 供两人用的桌子 ♦**it's meant for children rather than adults** 专门用于儿童而非成人 ♦**skiing is not for me** 滑雪不适合我

2 (*purpose*) 为了 ♦**what's it for?** 它有什么用途？ ♦**it's time for lunch** 该吃午饭了 ♦**what for?** 为什么呢？ ♦**a knife for chopping vegetables** 用于切菜的刀 ♦**have you got time for a coffee?** 你有时间喝杯咖啡吗？ ♦**a tricycle designed for use on the road** 公路专用三轮车

3 (*time*) ♦**he was away for two years** 他离开两年了 ♦**she will be away for a month** 她将离开一个月 ♦**can you do it for tomorrow?** 你能明天前做完吗？ ♦**it hasn't rained for three weeks** 已经有3周没下雨了 ♦**the trip is scheduled for June 5** 旅行安排在6月5日

4 (*in exchange for*) ♦**I sold it for £50** 我以五十镑卖掉了它 ♦**to pay 50 pence for a ticket** 花50便士买张票 ♦**pound for pound/dollar for dollar** 物有所值

5 (*reason*) 因为 ♦**for this reason** 由于这个原因 ♦**for lack of sth** 由于缺乏某物 ♦**our reasons for doing this** 我们这么做的原因

6 (*on behalf of, representing*) 为 ♦**he works for a local firm** 他为一家当地公司工作 ♦**the MP for ...** 代表…的国会议员 ♦**I'll do it for you** 我会替你做的 ♦**G for George** George 中的G

7 (*destination*) 前往 ♦**the train for London** 开往伦敦的火车 ♦**he left for Rome** 他前往罗马

8 (*with infinitive clause*) ♦**it is not for me to decide** 这不是由我来决定的 ♦**it would be best for you to leave** 你最好离开 ♦**there is still time for you to do it** 你还有时间去做

9 (*to get*) 欲知 ♦**for further information, see ...** 欲知进一步的信息，见… ♦**he went for the paper** 他去找报纸了

10 (*in spite of*) 尽管 ♦**for all his complaints, he is very fond of her** 尽管他牢骚满腹，他还是很喜欢她

11 (*with regard to*) 就…而言 ♦**it's cold for July** 对7月而言这算冷天了 ♦**he's mature for his age** 对他的年龄而言他算是成熟的 ♦**for scientists, this is less important** 对于科学家来说，这不太重要 ♦**another word for this is ...** 对于这个的另一种说法是… ♦**what's the French for "flower"?** "flower"用法语怎么说？

12 (*in favour of*) 赞成 ♦**are you for or against us?** 你是赞成还是反对我们？ ♦**I'm all for it** 我完全赞成 ♦**vote for X** 投票赞成X

13 (*referring to distance*) 达 ♦**there are roadworks for 50 km** 长跑练习长达50公里 ♦**we walked for miles** 我们走了几英里

14 (*with "if"*) ♦**I wouldn't be alive today, if it weren't for him** 若不是由于他，我不会活到今天的 ♦**had it not been for Bill, we'd have been late** 若不是比尔，我们一定迟到了

II *conj* [文] (*since, as*) 因为 ♦**she was very angry, for he was late again** 她非常生气，因为他又迟到了

📖 用法参见 **since**

📖 **for** 和 **to** 都可用于表示某人的目的，但后接不同的语言结构。**for** 用于表示目的时，后面必须跟名词。*Occasionally I go to the pub for a drink.* **for** 通常不用在动词前面。不能说 *I go to the pub for to have a drink*。**for** 用在 -ing 形式前表示某物的用途。*...a small* *machine for weighing the letters...* 与动词连用时，不定式前不加 **for** 。*She went off to fetch help.*

forage [ˈfɔrɪdʒ] **I** *vi* (*search*) (*for food*) 觅食 **II** *n* [U] 饲料 ♦**to forage for sth** [*person, animal* +] 搜寻某物

foray [ˈfɔreɪ] *n* [C] **1** [军] (*raid*) 偷袭 **2** (*venture*) 冒险 ♦**to make a foray into** [军] 对…进行袭击; (喻) 对…进行初步尝试

forbid [fəˈbɪd] (*pt* **forbad(e)**, *pp* **forbidden**) *vt* (*prohibit*) [+ *sale, marriage, event*] 禁止; (*make impossible*) 阻止 ♦**to forbid sb to do sth** (*prohibit*) 禁止某人做某事; (*make impossible*) 阻止某人做某事

forbidden [fəˈbɪdn] **I** *pp of* **forbid** **II** *adj* [+ *subject*] 被禁止的 ♦**forbidden fruit** (喻) 禁果

✪**force** [fɔːs] **I** *n* **1** [U] (*violence*) 武力 ◊ *We have renounced the use of force to settle our disputes.* 我们摈弃使用武力解决我们的争端。**2** [U] (*strength*) 力量 ◊ *The force of the explosion shattered the windows.* 爆炸的力量击碎了窗玻璃。**3** [C] (*power, influence*) 势力 ◊ *the forces of evil* 邪恶势力 **4** [C/U] [物] 力 ◊ *the earth's gravitational force* 地球的重力 **II** *vt* **1** (*drive, compel*) 强迫 ◊ *Ought he to be forced out of the Presidency?* 应该强迫他离任总统一职吗？ **2** (*push*) 用力推 ◊ *I forced his head back.* 我用力把他的头往后推开了。**3** (*break open*) [+ *lock, door*] 强行打开 ◊ *They had to force the lock on the trunk.* 他们不得不强行打开箱子上的锁。**III forces** *n* [*pl*] [军] **1** 部队 ◊ *the deployment of American forces in the region* 美国部队在该地区的部署 **2** ♦**the Forces** [英] 军队 ♦**in force** (*in large numbers*) 大批地 ◊ *Animal rights campaigners turned up in force.* 动物权利运动参与者们大批涌现。♦**to be in force** [*law, system* +] 正在施行中 ♦**to come into force** [*law, system* +] 生效 ♦**to join forces (with sb)** （与某人）联合 ♦**a force 5 gale** 5 级风 ♦**the sales force** [商] 推销人员 ♦**through** *or* **from force of habit** 出于习惯 ♦**to force o.s. to do sth** 强迫自己做某事 ♦**to force sb to do sth** 强迫某人做某事 ♦**to force sth (up)on sb** 将某事强加于某人 ♦**to force o.s. (up)on sb** 试图强暴某人 ♦**to force a smile/laugh** 强作笑脸/强颜欢笑

❑**force back** *vt* [+ *tears, urge*] 强忍住

forced [fɔːst] *adj* **1** [+ *labour*] 强迫的; [+ *landing*] 被迫的 **2** [+ *smile, gesture*] 勉强的

forceful [ˈfɔːsful] *adj* [+ *person*] 坚定有力的; [+ *impression, reminder*] 有力的

ford [fɔːd] **I** *n* [C] (*in river*) 浅滩 **II** *vt* [+ *river, stream*] 涉过

fore [fɔː(r)] **I** *n* [C] ♦**to come to the fore** 涌现出来 **II** *adj* [航海，航空] 在前部的 **III** *adv* [航海，航空] 在前部

forearm [ˈfɔːrɑːm] *n* [C] 前臂

forecast [ˈfɔːkɑːst] (*pt, pp* **forecast** *or* **forecasted**) **I** *n* [C] **1** [*of weather*] 预报 **2** [*of profits, prices*] 预测 **II** *vt* (*predict*) 预测 ♦**to forecast that...** 预测到…

forecourt [ˈfɔːkɔːt] [尤英] *n* [C] [*of garage*] 前院

forefinger [ˈfɔːfɪŋgə(r)] *n* [C] 食指

forefront [ˈfɔːfrʌnt] *n* [C] ♦**at the forefront of** [+ *industry, campaign*] 在…的最前锋

foregone [ˈfɔːgɔn] *adj* ♦**it's a foregone conclusion** 这是个预料之中的必然结局

foreground [ˈfɔːgraund] *n* [C/U] [*of painting*] 前景 ♦**to be in/come to the foreground** (喻) 处于/取得突出地位

forehead [ˈfɔrɪd, ˈfɔːhɛd] *n* [C] 额

✪**foreign** [ˈfɔrɪn] *adj* **1** [+ *country, holiday, language*] 外国的 **2** [+ *trade, policy*] 对外的 ♦**foreign to** 对…陌生

foreign currency *n* [C/U] 外币

foreigner [ˈfɔrɪnə(r)] *n* [C] 外国人

foreign exchange *n* **1** [C] (*system*) 国际汇兑 **2** [U] (*money*) 外汇

Foreign Office [英] *n* [C] ♦**the Foreign Office** 外交部

Foreign Secretary [英] *n* [C] 外交部长

foreman ['fɔːmən] (*pl* **foremen**) *n* [c] 1 [*of factory, building site*] 领班 2 [*of jury*] 陪审长

foremost ['fɔːməust] I *adj* (*most important*) 首屈一指的 II *adv* ♦ **first and foremost** 首要地

forename ['fɔːneɪm] *n* [c] 名

forensic [fə'rɛnsɪk] *adj* [+ *expert, test, evidence*] 法庭的

forerunner ['fɔːrʌnə(r)] *n* [c] ♦ **the forerunner of** …的前身

foresee [fɔː'siː] (*pt* **foresaw**, *pp* **foreseen**) *vt* [+ *problem, development*] 预见

foreseeable [fɔː'siːəbl] *adj* ♦ **in the foreseeable future** 在可预见的未来

foresight ['fɔːsaɪt] *n* [u] 先见之明

forest ['fɔrɪst] *n* [c/u] 森林

forestall [fɔː'stɔːl] *vt* [+ *person*] 抢在…之前行动; [+ *event*] 阻止

forestry ['fɔrɪstrɪ] *n* [u] (*science*) 林学; (*skill*) 造林术

forever [fə'rɛvə(r)] *adv* 1 (*permanently*) 永远 2 (*always*) 一直 ♦ **it has gone forever** 它已经一去不复返了 ♦ **it will last forever** 它会一直持续下去的 ♦ **you're forever finding difficulties** 你总是自寻烦恼

foreword ['fɔːrwəːd] *n* [c] 前言

forfeit ['fɔːfɪt] I *n* [c] (*price, fine*) 罚金 II *vt* (*lose*) [+ *right, chance, privilege*] 丧失; (*give up*) [+ *one's happiness, health, income*] 放弃

forgave [fə'geɪv] *pt of* **forgive**

forge [fɔːdʒ] I *vt* 1 (*fraudulently*) [+ *signature, banknote*] 伪造 2 (*create*) [+ *alliance, relationship, links*] 创建 3 [+ *wrought iron*] 锻造 II *n* [c] (*smithy*) 铁匠铺
❑ **forge ahead** *vi* ♦ **forge ahead with sth** 在某方面稳步前进

forger ['fɔːdʒə(r)] *n* [c] 伪造者

forgery ['fɔːdʒərɪ] *n* 1 [u] (*crime*) 伪造罪 2 [c] (*document, painting etc*) 伪造品

forget [fə'gɛt] (*pt* **forgot**, *pp* **forgotten**) I *vt* 1 [+ *fact, face, skill, appointment*] 忘记 2 (*leave behind*) [+ *object*] 忘带 3 (*put out of mind*) [+ *quarrel, person*] 忘掉 II *vi* (*fail to remember*) 忘记 ♦ **to forget to do sth** 忘记做某事 ♦ **to forget how to do sth** 忘记如何做某事 ♦ **to forget that ...** 忘记… ♦ **to forget o.s.** 忘乎所以

forgetful [fə'gɛtful] *adj* [+ *person*] 健忘的

forgive [fə'gɪv] (*pt* **forgave**, *pp* **forgiven**) *vt* (*pardon*) 原谅 ♦ **to forgive sb for sth** 原谅某人某事 ♦ **forgive my ignorance, but ...** 请原谅我的无知，但是… ♦ **they could be forgiven for thinking that ...** 他们认为…也不为过 ♦ **to forgive and forget** 不记前嫌

forgiveness [fə'gɪvnɪs] *n* [u] 宽恕 ♦ **to ask** *or* **beg for forgiveness** 请求{或}乞求原谅

forgot [fə'gɔt] *pt of* **forget**

forgotten [fə'gɔtn] *pp of* **forget**

fork [fɔːk] I *n* [c] 1 (*for eating*) 餐叉 2 (*for gardening*) 耙子 3 (*in road, river, railway*) 岔路 II *vi* [*road, river* +] 岔开
❑ **fork out** [非正式] I *vi* (*pay*) 支付 II *vt* 花费

forlorn [fə'lɔːn] *adj* [文] 1 [+ *person*] 孤苦伶仃的 2 [+ *attempt, hope*] 几乎无望的 3 [+ *place*] 荒凉的

✪ **form** [fɔːm] I *n* 1 [c] (*type*) 类型 ◊ *The symptoms take various forms.* 症状有多种类型。◊ *a rare form of cancer* 一种罕见的癌症类型 2 [c] (*manner*) 形式 ◊ *She didn't like the form in which the questions were written.* 她不喜欢这些问题的书写形式。3 [c] (*body*) 体态 ◊ *She gazed at his slumbering form.* 她注视着他沉睡时的体态。4 [c] [英：教育] (*class*) 年级 ◊ *the sixth form* 六年级 5 [c] (*document*) 表格 ◊ *You will be asked to fill in a form.* 你需要填一份表格。6 [u] [体育] 竞技状态 ◊ *His form this season has been brilliant.* 他本季的竞技状态极佳。II *vt* 1 (*make*) [+ *shape, queue, object*] 组成 ◊ *Form a circle please, children.* 孩子们，请组成一个圈。2 (*cause to exist*) 形成 ◊ *The islands were formed comparatively recently.* 这些岛屿是在比较近的年代形成的。3 (*comprise*) 构成 ◊ *Cereals form their staple diet.* 谷物构成了他们的主食。4 (*create*) [+ *group, organization, company*] 成立 ◊ *The League was* *formed in 1959.* 该俱乐部是于1959 年成立的。**5** [+ *idea, impression*] 形成 ◊ *the impression I'd formed of Jack* 我对杰克形成的印象 **6** [+ *habit*] 养成 ◊ *He formed the habit of taking long solitary walks.* 他养成了独自长途徒步走的习惯。**7** [+ *relationship*] 建立 ◊ *He is wary of forming another close relationship.* 他对再与人建立密切关系非常谨慎。**III** *vi* **1** [*shape, queue* +] 产生 ◊ *A scab had formed on his knee.* 他的膝盖上结了个痂。◊ *That's why this natural phenomenon forms.* 那就是这个自然现象产生的原因。**2** (*begin to exist*) [*stars, mountains* +] 形成 ◊ *The stars must have formed around 10 billion years ago.* 星星一定是在大约一百亿年前形成的。♦ **in the form of** 通过…方式 ◊ *She is taking lots of exercise in the form of walks or swimming.* 她正通过走路或者游泳的方式作大量的锻炼。♦ **to take the form of** 以…形式 ◊ *The broadcast took the form of an interview.* 这个节目是以采访的形式进行的。♦ **to form part of sth** 构成某事的一部分 ♦ **to be in good** *or* **top form** [体育] 处于良好的竞技状态 {或} 巅峰状态；[英] (喻) 处于良好的精神状态 ♦ **to be on/off form** [体育] 竞技状态良好/不好；[英] (喻) 能/不能发挥正常水平

formal ['fɔːməl] *adj* **1** [+ *offer, approval, occasion, dinner*] 正式的 **2** [+ *speech, behaviour*] 合礼仪的 **3** [+ *education, qualifications*] 正规的 **4** [+ *approach, style*] 有条理的 ♦ **formal dress** (*evening dress*) 礼服 ♦ **formal gardens** 官方公园

formality [fɔː'mælɪtɪ] **I** *n* **1** [c] 形式 **2** [U] (*politeness*) 礼节 **II formalities** *n* [*pl*] (*procedures*) 手续

formally ['fɔːməlɪ] *adv* **1** [*announce, approve, dress, behave* +] 正式地 ♦ **to be formally invited** 受到正式邀请

format ['fɔːmæt] **I** *n* [c] **1** (*form, style*) 形式 **2** [*of software, recording*] 格式 **II** *vt* [计算机] [+ *disk*] 将…格式化

formation [fɔː'meɪʃən] *n* **1** [U] [*of organization, business*] 组成；[*of idea, relationship, rocks, clouds*] 形成 **2** [c] (*pattern*) 结构 ♦ **to fly in formation** [航空] 编队飞行

formative ['fɔːmətɪv] *adj* [+ *influence, experience*] 形成的 ♦ **one's formative years** 性格形成时期

✪ **former** ['fɔːmə(r)] **I** *adj* **1** [+ *husband, president etc*] 前任的 ◊ *He's a former army officer.* 他是位前任军官。**2** (*earlier*) [+ *power, authority*] 以前的 ◊ *They have lost much of their former authority.* 他们失去了许多以前的权利。**II** *pron* ♦ **the former** 前者 ◊ *The former believe in a strong centralized government.* 前者信仰强有力的中央集权制的政府。♦ **in former times/years** 以前

> 请勿将 **former** 和 **previous** 混淆。**former** 是指某人曾经拥有的某个特定的工作、职位或角色，或者指某个曾经存在，但现已消失的状况。… *former President Bill Clinton…He murdered his former wife.* **previous** 用来指先前，即说话前所发生的事情或存在的事物。*She has a teenage daughter from a previous marriage... Crime increased in 2001 compared with the previous year.*

formerly ['fɔːməlɪ] *adv* (*previously*) 从前

formidable ['fɔːmɪdəbl] *adj* [+ *task*] 艰巨的；[+ *opponent*] 难以对付的

formula ['fɔːmjulə] (*pl* **formulae** ['fɔːmjuliː] *or* **formulas**) *n* **1** [c] [数] 公式 **2** [c] [化] 分子式 **3** [c] (*plan*) 方案 **4** [U] (*also:* ***formula milk***) 配方奶粉 ♦ **Formula One** [汽车] 一级方程式赛车

formulate ['fɔːmjuleɪt] *vt* **1** [+ *plan, proposal*] 构想出 **2** (*express*) [+ *thought, opinion*] 表达

formulation [fɔːmju'leɪʃən] *n* **1** [c/U] [*of medicine, cosmetic*] 配制 **2** [U] [*of policy, plan*] 制订 **3** [c] /[U] [正式] (*form of words*) 表达方式

fort [fɔːt] *n* [c] 堡垒 ♦ **to hold the fort** *or* [美] **hold down the fort** (喻) 暂时代人维持现状

forth [fɔːθ] *adv* [文] ♦**to go forth** 向前 ♦**back and forth** 来回 ♦**to go back and forth** 来来回回 ♦**to bring forth** [文] 提出 ♦**and so forth** 等等

forthcoming [fɔːθ'kʌmɪŋ] *adj* **1** [+ *event*] 临近的 **2** [正式] [+ *help, money, information*] 随要随到的 **3** [+ *person*] 乐于助人的

forthright ['fɔːθraɪt] *adj* [+ *person, language*] 直率的; [+ *condemnation, opposition*] 直言不讳的

fortieth ['fɔːtɪɪθ] *num* 第四十

fortify ['fɔːtɪfaɪ] *vt* **1** [+ *place*] 设防于 **2** [+ *food, drink*] 使…加强 **3** [+ *person*] [*food, drink* +] 使精力旺盛

fortnight ['fɔːtnaɪt] [英] *n* [c] 两星期 ♦**it's a fortnight since ...** 自从…已经过了两个星期了

fortnightly ['fɔːtnaɪtlɪ] [英] **I** *adj* [+ *meeting, magazine*] 每两星期一次的 **II** *adv* [*meet, publish* +] 每两星期一次地

fortress ['fɔːtrɪs] *n* [c] 堡垒

fortunate ['fɔːtʃənɪt] *adj* [+ *person, coincidence, escape*] 幸运的 ♦**he was fortunate to survive** 他幸运地活了下来 ♦**it is fortunate that ...** 幸亏…

fortunately ['fɔːtʃənɪtlɪ] *adv* 幸运的是

fortune ['fɔːtʃən] **I** *n* **1** [U] (*also:* ***good fortune***) (*luck*) 好运 **2** [c] (*wealth*) 大笔钱 **II fortunes** *n* [*pl*] 时运 ♦**to make a fortune** 发大财 ♦**to tell sb's fortune** 给某人算命

fortune-teller ['fɔːtʃəntɛlə(r)] *n* [c] 算命者

✪ **forty** ['fɔːtɪ] *num* 四十

forum ['fɔːrəm] *n* [c] **1** (*for discussion*) 论坛 **2** (*Roman square*) 公共集会场所

forward ['fɔːwəd] **I** *adj* **1** (*in position*) 前部的 **2** (*in movement*) 向前的 **3** (*not shy*) 冒失的 **II** *n* [c] [体育] 前锋 **III** *vt* **1** [+ *letter, goods*] 转递 **2** (*further*) [+ *career, plans*] 促进 ♦**"please forward"** "请转交" **IV** *adv* = **forwards** ♦**forward planning** 预先计划

forwards ['fɔːwədz] *adv* (*in space, time*) 向前

fossil ['fɔsl] *n* [c] 化石

foster ['fɔstə(r)] **I** *vt* **1** [+ *child*] 领养 **2** [+ *idea, activity, feeling*] 培养 **II** *cpd* [复合词] [+ *parent, mother, child*] 寄养

fought [fɔːt] *pt, pp of* **fight**

foul [faul] **I** *adj* **1** (*filthy*) [+ *state, taste, smell*] 令人作呕的; [+ *place*] 污秽的 **2** (*dreadful*) [+ *temper, mood*] 坏透的; [+ *day, time, luck*] 糟透的; [+ *weather*] 恶劣的 **3** (*obscene*) [+ *language*] 下流的 **II** *n* [c] [体育] 犯规 **III** *vt* **1** (*dirty*) 弄脏 **2** [*dog* +] 弄脏 **3** [体育] 对…犯规 **4** (*entangle*) [+ *anchor, propeller*] 缠住 ♦**to fall foul of sb** [尤英] 与某人发生冲突

foul play *n* [U] **1** [法] 暴力行径 **2** [体育] 犯规行为

found [faund] **I** *pt, pp of* **find** **II** *vt* [+ *organization, company*] 创办

foundation [faun'deɪʃən] **I** *n* **1** [U] [*of organization, company, city*] 成立 **2** [c] (*basis*) [*of belief, way of life*] 基础 **3** [U] (*substance*) (喻) 根据 **4** [c] (*organization*) 基金会 **5** [U/C] (*also:* ***foundation cream***) 粉底霜 **II foundations** *n* [*pl*] [*of building*] 地基 ♦**without foundation** 没有根据 ♦**to lay the foundations of sth** 为某事奠定基础

founder ['faundə(r)] **I** *n* [c] [*of institution, organization*] 创始人 **II** *vi* **1** [*ship* +] 沉没 **2** [*plan, project* +] 失败

founding ['faundɪŋ] *adj* ♦**founding father** [历史] (*in US*) 开国者; (喻) [*of institution, organization*] 创始人

fountain ['fauntɪn] *n* [c] **1** (字) 喷泉 **2** [文] (喻) [*of liquid*] 大量

fountain pen *n* [c] 自来水笔

✪ **four** [fɔː(r)] *num* 四 ♦**on all fours** 爬着地 *see also* **five**

four-letter word ['fɔːlɛtə-] *n* [c] (*swear word*) 脏话

four-poster ['fɔː'pəustə(r)] *n* [c] (*also:* ***four-poster bed***) 有四根帷柱的床

✪ **fourteen** ['fɔː'tiːn] *num* 十四 *see also* **fifteen**

fourteenth ['fɔː'tiːnθ] *num* 第十四 *see also* **fifth**

fourth ['fɔːθ] **I** *num* **1** 第四 **2** [美] (*quarter*) 四分之一 [英 = **quarter**] **II** *n* [c] [汽车] (*also:* ***fourth gear***) 第

四挡 *see also* **fifth**
four-wheel drive ['fɔːwiːl-] *n* [c] ［汽车］四轮驱动
fowl [faul] *n* [c] 禽
fox [fɔks] **I** *n* [c] 狐狸 **II** *vt* ［英］ (*baffle*) 使迷惑
foyer ['fɔɪeɪ] *n* [c] [*of hotel, theatre, cinema*] 门厅
Fr. ［宗］*abbr* (= ***father***) 神父
fraction ['frækʃən] *n* [c] **1** (*portion*) 小部分 **2** ［数］分数
fracture ['fræktʃə(r)] **I** *n* [c] [*of bone*] 断裂 **II** *vt* [+ *bone*] 折断 **III** *vi* [*bone* +] 断裂
fragile ['frædʒaɪl] *adj* **1** [+ *object, structure*] 易损的 **2** [+ *economy, peace*] 薄弱的 **3** (*delicate*) 纤巧的 **4** (*unwell*) [+ *person*] 虚弱的
fragment [*n* 'frægmənt, *vb* fræg'mɛnt] **I** *n* [c] **1** [*of bone, glass etc*] 碎片 **2** [*of conversation, poem etc*] 片断 **II** *vi* **1** (字) 裂成碎片 **2** (喻) 分裂 **III** *vt* 分裂
fragrance ['freɪgrəns] *n* [c/u] (*smell*) 香气
fragrant ['freɪgrənt] *adj* 芳香的
frail [freɪl] *adj* **1** [+ *person, invalid*] 虚弱的 **2** [+ *structure*] 易破碎的
frame [freɪm] **I** *n* [c] **1** [*of building, structure*] 框架 **2** [*of body*] 骨架 **3** [*of picture, mirror, door, window*] 框 **5** (*also:* ***frames***) [*of spectacles*] 眼镜架 **6** (影院) 画面 **II** *vt* **1** [+ *picture, photograph*] 给…镶框 **2** [+ *reply, law, theory*] 表达 **3** ［非正式］(*incriminate*) 诬陷
frame of mind (*pl* **frames of mind**) *n* [c] 心境
framework ['freɪmwəːk] *n* [c] **1** (*structure*) 结构 **2** (喻) 框架
France [frɑːns] *n* 法国
franchise ['fræntʃaɪz] **I** *n* [c] **1** ［商］特许经营 **2** ［政治］选举权 **II** *vt* ［商］授予…特许权
frank [fræŋk] *adj* **I 1** [+ *person*] 坦率的 **2** [+ *discussion, admission*] 坦诚的 **II** *vt* [+ *letter*] 盖邮资已付戳于
frankly ['fræŋklɪ] *adv* **1** (*honestly*) [*say, admit* +] 坦白地 **2** (*introducing statement*) 说实话
frantic ['fræntɪk] *adj* **1** [+ *person*] 发疯的 **2** [+ *rush, pace, search*] 狂乱的
fraternity [frə'təːnɪtɪ] *n* **1** [u] (*feeling*) 友爱 **2** [c] (*group of people*) 同人 **3** [c] ［美：大学］联谊会
fraud [frɔːd] *n* **1** [c/u] (*crime*) 诈骗 **2** [c] (*person*) 骗子
fraudulent ['frɔːdjulənt] *adj* [+ *scheme, claim*] 欺骗的
fraught [frɔːt] *adj* **1** ♦ **fraught with danger/problems** 充满危险/问题 **2** (*tense, anxious*) [+ *situation, evening, meeting*] 令人焦虑的
fray [freɪ] **I** *vi* [*cloth, rope* +] 磨损 **II** *n* [c] ♦ **to join** *or* **enter the fray** 参加角逐 ♦ **tempers were frayed** 发火了 ♦ **her nerves were frayed** 她神经非常紧张
freak [friːk] **I** *n* [c] **1** (*person*) (*in attitude, behaviour*) 怪人; (*in appearance*) 怪物 **2** ［非正式］(*fanatic*) ♦ **health/fitness freak** 健康/健身狂 **II** *cpd* ［复合词］[+ *accident, storm*] 反常 **III** *vi* ［非正式］(*also:* ***freak out***) 躁动不安 **IV** *vt* ［非正式］(*also:* ***freak out***) 使躁动不安
freckle ['frɛkl] *n* [c] 雀斑
✪ **free** [friː] **I** *adj* **1** (*costing nothing*) [+ *meal, ticket etc*] 免费的 ◊ *The coffee was free.* 咖啡是免费的。 **2** [+ *person*] 自由的 ◊ *The slave escaped and became a free man.* 奴隶逃跑了，成了自由人。 **3** [+ *time*] 空闲的 ◊ *They don't have much free time.* 他们没有多少空闲时间。 **4** [+ *seat, table*] 空余的 ◊ *Is that seat free?* 那个座位是空的吗？ **5** (*unrestricted*) [+ *choice, press, speech, elections*] 自由的 ◊ *It's their free choice.* 那是他们的自由选择。 ◊ *We can't do that if we haven't got a free press.* 如果没有自由的新闻界，我们根本做不到。; [+ *passage, movement*] 畅通的 **6** [+ *hand, arm*] 闲着的 ◊ *He buttoned his overcoat with his free hand.* 他用闲着的那只手扣上了外衣的扣子。 **II** *vt* **1** (*release*) [+ *prisoner, slave*] 释放 ◊ *They were freed by their kidnappers unharmed.* 他们被绑匪释放了，并没有受到伤害。; [+ *injured person*] 解救 ◊ *Firemen tried to free the injured.* 消防队员尽力解救受伤人员。; [+ *jammed object*] 使脱开 ◊ *He used a screwdriver to free the lock.* 他用螺丝刀打开了锁。

2 [+ *person*] (*from responsibility, duty*) 摆脱 ◊ *His contract will run out shortly, freeing him to pursue his own projects.* 他的合同很快就要到期了，这样他得以摆脱来发展自己的项目。♦ **free (of charge), for free** 免费 ♦ **to give sb a free hand** 给某人自主权 ♦ **free and easy** 自由自在的 ♦ **admission free** 免费进入 ♦ **to be free of** *or* **from sth** 没有某物 ◊ *The area will be free of pollution by the year 2006.* 到2006年，这个地区将没有污染。♦ **to be free to do sth** 随意做某事 ◊ *Women should be free to dress as they please.* 女性应该任其喜好随意穿戴。♦ **to free sb of sth** 使某人摆脱某物 ♦ **feel free** 随便

freedom ['fri:dəm] *n* [U] **1** (*liberty*) 自由 **2** [*of prisoner, slave, movement*] 自由 **3** (*political*) 自由 **4** (*from poverty, disease, hunger*) 免受

Freefone® ['fri:fəun] [英] *n* [C] ♦ **call Freefone 0800** 拨打免费电话 0800 [美=**toll-free**]

free gift *n* [C] 赠品

free kick [足球] *n* [C] 任意球

freelance ['fri:lɑ:ns] **I** *adj* [+ *journalist, photographer, work*] 自由职业的 **II** *adv* ♦ **to work freelance** 做自由职业工作

freely ['fri:lɪ] *adv* **1** (*without restriction*) [*move* +] 自由地; [*talk* +] 无拘束地 **2** (*liberally*) [*spend, give* +] 大手大脚地; [*perspire* +]大量地 **3** (*willingly*) [*share, admit* +] 自愿地 ♦ **to be freely available** 随意获得

Freepost® ['fri:pəust] [英] *n* [U] 免费邮寄

free-range ['fri:'reɪndʒ] *adj* [+ *eggs, chickens*] 放养的

freeway ['fri:weɪ] [美] *n* [C] 高速公路 [英=**motorway**]

free will *n* [C] ♦ **of one's own free will** 自觉自愿地

freeze [fri:z] (*pt* **froze**, *pp* **frozen**) **I** *vi* **1** [*liquid, weather* +] 结冰 **2** [*pipe* +] 冻住 **3** [*person* +] (*with cold*) 冻僵 **4** (喻) (*from fear, shock*) 呆住 **II** *vt* **1** [+ *water, lake*] 使结冰 **2** [+ *food*] 冷冻 **3** [*wages, prices, bank account, assets*] 冻结 **III** *n* [C] **1** (*cold weather*) 霜冻 **2** (*on wages, prices*) 冻结 ♦ **it may freeze tonight** 今晚可能会结冰
❏ **freeze out** *vt* ♦ **to freeze sb out of sth** 把某人从某处挤走
❏ **freeze over** *vi* **1** [*river, lake* +] 结冰 **2** [*windscreen, windows* +] 结霜

freezer ['fri:zə(r)] *n* [C] 冰柜

freezing ['fri:zɪŋ] *adj* (*also:* ***freezing cold***) [+ *day, weather*] 极冷的; [+ *water, place, room*] 冰冷的; [+ *person, hands*] 冰凉的 ♦ **3 degrees below freezing** 零下3度 ♦ **I'm freezing** 冻死我了 ♦ **it's freezing outside** 外面特别冷
📖 用法参见 **cold**

freezing point *n* [C/U] 冰点

freight [freɪt] *n* [U] (*goods*) 货物 ♦ **by air/sea freight** 通过空/海运

freight train *n* [C] 货运列车

French [frentʃ] **I** *adj*] 法国的 **II** *n* [U] (*language*) 法语 **III the French** *n* [*pl*] (*people*) 法国人

French bean [英] *n* [C] 菜豆 [美= **string bean**]

French bread *n* [U] 法式棍子面包

French dressing] *n* [U] 法式色拉调料

French fries [-fraɪz] [尤美] *n* [*pl*] 炸薯条 [英=**chips**]

Frenchman ['frentʃmən] (*pl* **Frenchmen**) *n* [C] 法国男人

French stick *n* [C] 法式棍子面包

French window *n* [C] 落地窗

Frenchwoman ['frentʃwumən] (*pl* **Frenchwomen**) *n* [C] 法国女人

frenzy ['frenzɪ] *n* [C/U] 狂热 ♦ **a frenzy of activity/excitement** 活动的/兴奋得狂乱 ♦ **to drive sb into a frenzy** 把某人逼得发狂 ♦ **to be in a frenzy** 发狂地

frequency ['fri:kwənsɪ] *n* **1** [U] [*of event*] 频繁性 **2** [C/U] [广播] 频率 ♦ **to increase in frequency** 频率增加

frequent [*adj* 'fri:kwənt, *vb* frɪ'kwent] **I** *adj* [+ *occurrence, visitor*] 频繁的 **II** *vt* [正式] [+ *pub, restaurant*] 常去

frequently ['fri:kwəntlɪ] *adv* 时常地

fresh [freʃ] *adj* **1** [+ *food, bread, vegetables*] 新鲜的 **2** [+ *paint, footprints*] 新的 **3** [+ *water*] 淡的 **4** (*new*) [+ *approach, way*] 新颖的 **5** (*recent*) [+ *instructions, inquiries*] 附

加的; [+ *memories*] 鲜明的 **6** (*cheeky*) [+ *person*] 冒失的 ♦ **fresh air** 新鲜空气 ♦ **to make a fresh start** 重新开始 ♦ **he's fresh from** *or* **out of university** 他刚刚大学毕业 ♦ **to be fresh out of sth** [非正式] 刚刚用完某物

freshen ['frɛʃən] *vi* [*wind* +] 变强
❑ **freshen up** *vi* [*person* +] 梳洗一番

fresher ['frɛʃə(r)] [英:大学,非正式] *n* [c] 大学一年级新生

freshly ['frɛʃlɪ] *adv* [+ *made, cooked, painted*] 刚刚

freshman ['frɛʃmən] [美] (*pl* **freshmen**) *n* [c] 大学一年级学生

freshwater ['frɛʃwɔːtə(r)] *adj* [+ *lake, fish*] 淡水的

fret [frɛt] *vi* (*worry*) 担心

Fri. *abbr* (= ***Friday***) 星期五

friar ['fraɪə(r)] *n* [c] 修道士

friction ['frɪkʃən] *n* [u] **1** [物] (*resistance*) 摩擦力 **2** (*rubbing*) 摩擦 **3** (喻) (*conflict*) (*also:* ***frictions***) 冲突

Friday ['fraɪdɪ] *n* [c/u] 星期五 *see also* **Tuesday**

fridge [frɪdʒ] [英] *n* [c] 冰箱 [美= **refrigerator**]

fried [fraɪd] **I** *pt, pp of* **fry II** *adj* [+ *food*] 炒的

✪ **friend** [frɛnd] *n* [c] 朋友 ♦ **to be friends** 是朋友 ♦ **to be friends with sb** 是某人的朋友 ♦ **to make friends** 交朋友 ♦ **to make friends with sb** 与某人交朋友 ♦ **the friends of Birmingham Royal Ballet** 伯明翰皇家芭蕾舞团的赞助者

friendly ['frɛndlɪ] **I** *adj* **1** [+ *person*] 友善的; [+ *tone, hug, atmosphere, government*] 友好的 **2** [英:体育] [+ *game, match*] 友谊的 **II** *n* [c] [英:体育] 友谊比赛 ♦ **to be friendly with** 跟…友好 ♦ **to be friendly to** 对…友好

friendship ['frɛndʃɪp] *n* **1** [c] (*relationship*) 友情 **2** [u] (*state*) 友爱

frieze [friːz] *n* [c] 中楣

frigate ['frɪgɪt] *n* [c] 护卫舰

fright [fraɪt] *n* **1** [u] (*terror*) 恐惧 **2** [c] (*shock*) 惊吓 ♦ **to take fright** 受惊 ♦ **to give sb a fright** 吓唬某人一下 ♦ **to look a fright** [非正式] 看起来怪得吓人

frighten ['fraɪtn] *vt* 使惊恐
❑ **frighten away** *vt* **1** [+ *birds, children etc*] 吓跑 **2** (喻) (*deter*) 使踌躇
❑ **frighten into** *vt* ♦ **to frighten sb into doing sth** 吓得某人去做某事
❑ **frighten off** *vt* = **frighten away**

frightened ['fraɪtnd] *adj* **1** [+ *person, animal*] ♦ **to be frightened** 被吓倒 **2** [+ *eyes, expression*] 恐惧的 ♦ **to be frightened of sth/of doing sth** *or* **to do sth** 害怕某事/做某事

> 📖 请勿将 **frightened** 和 **frightening** 混淆。如果你感到 **frightened**，表示你感到恐惧或紧张。*I think he was truly frightened of me at times…I was more frightened than I had ever been in my life.* 如果某事物 **frightening**，表示它让人感到恐惧。*Do you ever have frightening dreams?…It was a strange, rather frightening place.*

frightening ['fraɪtnɪŋ] *adj* [+ *experience, prospect*] 令人恐惧的 📖 用法参见 **frightened**

frightful ['fraɪtful] [过时] *adj* **1** (*dreadful*) [+ *smell, mistake*] 可怕的 **2** [非正式] (*emphatic use*) 极大的

frill [frɪl] *n* [c] (*on dress, shirt*) 褶边 ♦ **with no** *or* **without frills** 毫无虚饰的

fringe [frɪndʒ] *n* [c] **1** [英] (*hair*) 刘海 [美= **bangs**] **2** (*on shawl, lampshade*) 流苏 **3** (*edge*) [*of town, forest*] 外围 **4** (喻) [*of activity, organization*] 次要部分

Frisbee® ['frɪzbɪ] *n* [c] 飞盘

fritter ['frɪtə(r)] *n* [c] 油煎饼
❑ **fritter away** *vt* [+ *time, money*] 浪费掉

frivolous ['frɪvələs] *adj* [+ *conduct, person*] 轻浮的; [+ *activity*] 无所谓的

fro [frəu] *adv see* **to**

frock [frɔk] [过时] *n* [c] (*dress*) 女服

frog [frɔg] [动] *n* [c] 青蛙 ♦ **to have a frog in one's throat** 声音嘶哑

frogman ['frɔgmən] (*pl* **frogmen**) *n* [c] 蛙人

frolic ['frɔlɪk] *vi* [*animals, children* +] 嬉戏

✪ **from**

KEYWORD

[frɔm] *prep*

1 (*indicating starting place*) 来自 ♦ **where are you from?** 你来自哪里？ ♦ **to run away from home** 离家出走 ♦ **from London to Glasgow** 从伦敦到格拉斯哥 ♦ **to be back from Spain/Paris** *etc* 从西班牙/巴黎{等}回来 ♦ **viewed from above** 从上鸟瞰 ♦ **a light bulb hung from the ceiling** 从天花板上垂下的灯泡

2 (*indicating origin*) 来自 ♦ **a present/telephone call/letter from sb** 来自某人的礼物/电话/信 ♦ **to take sth from sb/sth** 从某人/某物处拿某物

3 (*with time, distance, price, numbers*) 从 ♦ **from January (on)** 从1月(开始) ♦ **from one o'clock to** *or* **until two** 从1点直到2点 ♦ **it's 1 km from the beach** 从海滩到这儿有1公里 ♦ **a long way from home** 离家很远 ♦ **prices starting from £10** 从10镑起价 ♦ **unemployment has fallen from 7.5% to 7.2%** 失业率已经从7.5%降至7.2% ♦ **six from ten leaves four** 10减去6还剩4

4 (*because of, on the basis of*) 根据 ♦ **from what he says** 根据他所说的 ♦ **from what I understand** 据我所了解

5 (*out of*) ♦ **made from** 用…做成

✪ **front** [frʌnt] **I** *n* **1** [c] [*of house, dress*] 前面 ◊ *jackets with buttons down the front* 前面有纽扣的上衣；[*of coach, train, car*] 前部 ◊ *The cop searched the front of the car.* 警方搜查了汽车的前部。**2** [c] [军] 前线 ◊ *Her husband is fighting at the front.* 她的丈夫在前线打仗。**3** [c] [气象] 锋 ◊ *a cold/warm front* 冷/暖锋 **4** [s] (*also:* ***sea front***) 海滨人行道 ◊ *a stroll along the front* 沿海滨人行道的散步 **5** [c] (*pretence*) 装模作样 ◊ *Richard kept up a brave front.* 理查德一直装作一副勇敢的样子。**6** [c] (*disguise*) 幌子 ◊ *The organization was used as a front for drug trafficking.* 该组织被用作毒品贩运的幌子。**II** *adj* **1** [+ *seat, garden, entrance etc*] 前面的 **2** [+ *tooth*] 前部的 **III** *vi* ♦ **to front onto sth** [*house* +] 面向某物 ◊ *houses that front directly onto little courtyards* 直接面向小庭院的房子 **IV** *vt* **1** [英] [+ *organization*] 当…的头儿 [美 = **head**] **2** [+ *pop group*] 做…的主唱 ♦ **in front** (*in moving line*) 在前面 ◊ *He was driving too close to the car in front.* 他车开得离前面的车太近。；(*in race, contest*) 领先 ◊ *David is in front in the jockeys' title race.* 大卫在马术冠军赛中居领先位置。♦ **in front of** (*facing*) 在…前面 ◊ *A car drew up in front of the house.* 一辆汽车在房子前面停了下来。；(*in the presence of*) 在…面前 ◊ *They never argued in front of their children.* 他们从来不在孩子面前吵架。♦ **on the political/economic front** 在政治/经济方面 ♦ **to put on a front** 装腔作势

front door *n* [c] 前门

frontier ['frʌntɪə(r)] *n* [c] **1** [英] (*between countries*) 国界 [美 = **border**] **2** (喻) 界限

front page [出版] *n* [c] 头版 ♦ **to make the front page** 成为头条新闻

frost [frɔst] *n* [c] **1** [c] (*weather*) 霜 **2** [U] (*ice*) 冰霜

frostbite ['frɔstbaɪt] *n* [U] 冻伤

frosting ['frɔstɪŋ] *n* [U] (*on cake*) 糖霜 [英 = **icing**]

frosty ['frɔstɪ] *adj* **1** [+ *day, night, weather*] 有霜冻的; [+ *grass, window*] 结霜的 **2** [+ *reception, look*] 冷淡的

froth [frɔθ] **I** *n* [U] (*on liquid*) 泡沫 **II** *vi* [*liquid* +] 起泡沫

frown [fraun] **I** *n* [c] 皱眉 **II** *vi* 皱眉

❏ **frown (up)on** *vt* [不可拆分] (喻) 不赞成

froze [frəuz] *pt of* **freeze**

frozen ['frəuzn] **I** *pp of* **freeze** **II** *adj* **1** [+ *food*] 冷冻的; [+ *ground, lake*] 结冰的 **2** [+ *person, fingers*] 冰冷的 **3** [商] [+ *assets*] 冻结的

frugal ['fruːgl] *adj* [+ *person*] 节俭的;

[+ *meal*] 廉价的

fruit [fruːt] (*pl* **fruit** *or* **fruits**) *n* [C/U] **1** 水果 **2** (喻)(*results*) 成果 ♦**to bear fruit** (喻) 取得成果

fruitful ['fruːtful] *adj* [+ *meeting, discussion*] 富有成效的

fruition [fruː'ɪʃən] *n* [C] ♦**to come to fruition** [正式] 得以实现

fruit juice *n* [C/U] 果汁 ♦**I'd like a fruit juice** 我想要杯果汁

fruit machine [英] *n* [C] 吃角子老虎机 [美=**slot machine**]

fruit salad *n* [C/U] 水果色拉

frustrate [frʌs'treɪt] *vt* **1** [+ *person*] 使沮丧 **2** [+ *plan, attempt*] 阻碍

frustrated [frʌs'treɪtɪd] *adj* 泄气的

fry [fraɪ] (*pt, pp* **fried**) **I** *vt* [烹饪] 油煎 **II fries** *n* [*pl*] [烹饪] = **French fries** 📖用法参见 **cook**

frying pan ['fraɪɪŋ-] *n* [C] 平底煎锅

ft. *abbr* (= ***foot, feet***) 英尺

fudge [fʌdʒ] **I** *n* [U] [烹饪] 软糖 **II** *vt* [+ *issue, problem*] 规避

fuel ['fjuəl] **I** *n* [C/U] (*for heating etc*) 燃料 **II** *vt* **1** [+ *furnace, aircraft*] 由…作燃料 **2** (喻) [+ *rumours, dispute*] 加剧

fugitive ['fjuːdʒɪtɪv] *n* [C] 逃亡者

fulfil [ful'fɪl] (美 **fulfill**) *vt* **1** [+ *function, role, task*] 完成; [+ *condition, requirement*] 满足; [+ *ambition, dream, promise*] 实现 **2** (*satisfy*) [+ *person*] 令…满足

fulfilment [ful'fɪlmənt] (美 **fulfillment**) *n* [U] **1** (*satisfaction*) 满足 **2** [*of promise, threat, request*] 实行; [*of hope, dream, ambition*] 实现

✪ **full** [ful] **I** *adj* **1** [+ *container, cup*] 满的 ◊ *The bucket is almost full.* 桶要满了。; [+ *cinema, car, restaurant*] 满的 ◊ *All the car parks are full.* 所有的停车场都满了。**2** (*maximum*) [+ *use, volume, price*] 最大限度的 ◊ *The radio was playing at full volume.* 收音机以最大音量播放着。**3** (*complete*) [+ *details*] 全部的 ◊ *Full details will be sent to you.* 全部的具体情况会发给你。; [+ *information, name*] 完全的 ◊ *I haven't got his full name.* 我没有他的全名。**4** [+ *flavour*] 醇厚的 **5** [+ *skirt, sleeves*] 肥大的 **6** [+ *life*] 充实的 ◊ *a very full and interesting life* 非常充实而有趣的生活 **7** [+ *impact, implication*] 所有的 ◊ *I paused to allow the full impact of this to register.* 我停下来，以便仔细感受这一切带来的所有影响。 **II** *adv* ♦**to know full well that …** 完全清楚地了解… ♦**full up** [+ *hotel etc*] 爆满 ♦**I'm full (up)** 我吃饱了 ♦**a full week/month** 整整一个星期/月 ◊ *For a full week we did not eat.* 整整一个星期，我们没吃东西。♦**in full view of sb** 完全看得见某人 ♦**full marks** [英: 教育] 满分 ♦**at full speed** 以全速 ♦**full of** [+ *objects, people*] 充满 ◊ *His office was full of policemen.* 他的办公室里满是警察。; [+ *confidence, hope*] 充满 ◊ *I was full of confidence.* 我充满了信心。♦**in full** [*reproduce, quote, pay* +] 全部地 ◊ *The bill has been paid in full.* 账单全部付清了。♦**to write one's name in full** 写出自己的全名 ♦**to strike sb full in the face** 正打在某人的脸上 ♦**to do sth to the full** 充分地做某事

full employment *n* [U] 充分就业

full-length ['ful'lɛŋθ] **I** *adj* **1** [+ *book, film*] 未删节的 **2** [+ *coat, skirt*] 长及脚踝的 **3** [+ *portrait, mirror*] 全身的 **II** *adv* [*lie* +] 直直地

full moon *n* [S] 满月

full-scale ['fulskeɪl] *adj* **1** [+ *war, search, inquiry*] 全面的 **2** [+ *model, drawing*] 与原物同样大的

full stop [英] *n* [C] 句号 [美=**period**] ♦**to come to a full stop** (喻) 完全停止

full-time ['ful'taɪm] **I** *adj* [+ *work, study*] 全职的; [+ *student, staff*] 全日制的 **II** *adv* [*work, study* +] 全日地

fully ['fulɪ] *adv* **1** (*completely*) [*understand, recover* +] 完全地; [+ *automatic*] 完全地; [+ *trained, qualified*] 全面地 **2** (*in full*) [*answer, describe* +] 充分地 **3** (*as many as*) 整整

fully-fledged ['fulɪ'flɛdʒd] *adj* [+ *member, atheist etc*] 完全的

fully-licensed ['fulɪ'laɪsnst] [英] *adj* [+ *hotel, restaurant*] 可以售酒的

fumble ['fʌmbl] *vi* ♦**to fumble for** 笨手笨脚地摸索

❑**fumble with** *vt* [不可拆分][+ *key, pen*] 笨手笨脚地抓住

fume [fjuːm] *vi* (*rage*) 大怒

fumes [fjuːmz] *n* [*pl*] [*of fire, fuel, car*] 浓烈的烟气

fumigate ['fjuːmɪgeɪt] *vt* [+ *house, clothes*] 烟熏

fun [fʌn] *n* [U] 乐趣 ♦**to have fun** 玩得开心 ♦**to get a lot of fun out of sth** 从某事中得到许多乐趣 ♦**he's good fun (to be with)** 跟他(在一起)很有趣 ♦**it was a lot of fun** 非常开心 ♦**it's not much fun** 没什么劲儿 ♦**to do sth for fun** 为找乐而做某事 ♦**to do sth in fun** 开玩笑地做某事 ♦**to make fun of sb/sth** 取笑某人/某物

function ['fʌŋkʃən] **I** *n* [C] **1** (*role*) 作用 **2** [正式](*product*) ♦**to be a function of sth** 取决于某物 **3** (*social occasion*) 社交聚会 **II** *vi* [*system, process* +] 运行; [*device* +] 运转 ♦**to function as** 起…的作用

functional ['fʌŋkʃənl] *adj* **1** (*practical*) [+ *furniture, design etc*] 实用的 **2** [+ *working*] [+ *equipment, device*] 在运转的

✪**fund** [fʌnd] **I** *n* [C] **1** [*of money*] 基金 ◊ *the disaster fund* 救灾基金 **2** (*source, store*) [*of knowledge, experience*] 储备 ◊ *a large fund of scientific knowledge* 大量科学知识的储备 **II** *vt* 资助 ◊ *The work is funded by private industry.* 这项工作是由私人企业资助的。**III funds** *n* [*pl*] (*money*) 资金

fundamental [fʌndə'mɛntl] *adj* **1** (*essential*) [+ *principle, concept*] 根本的 **2** (*basic*) [+ *change, difference, error*] 基本的 ♦**fundamental to** 对…是必要的

funeral ['fjuːnərəl] *n* [C] 葬礼

funeral home *n* = **funeral parlour**

funeral parlour [英] *n* [C] 殡仪馆

funfair ['fʌnfɛə(r)] [英] *n* [C] 露天游乐场 [美= **carnival**]

fungus ['fʌŋgəs] (*pl* **fungi**) *n* **1** [C] (*plant*) 真菌 **2** [U] (*mould*) 霉

funnel ['fʌnl] **I** *n* [C] **1** (*for pouring*) 漏斗 **2** [*of ship*] 烟囱 **II** *vi* [*water, wind* +] 汇集 **III** *vt* **1** [+ *water, wind*] 使汇集 **2** (喻) [+ *money, resources*] 汇集

funny ['fʌnɪ] *adj* **1** (*amusing*) 可笑的 **2** (*strange*) 奇怪的 ♦**to feel funny** [非正式](*unwell*) 稍感不适

fur [fəː(r)] **I** *n* **1** [C/U] [*of animal*] 毛 **2** [C] (*garment*) 毛皮大衣 **3** [U] [英] (*in kettle*) 水锈 **II** *cpd* [复合词] [+ *hat, collar etc*] 毛皮

fur coat *n* [C] 毛皮大衣

furious ['fjuərɪəs] *adj* **1** [+ *person*] 大发雷霆的 **2** [+ *row, argument*] 激烈的 **3** [+ *effort, speed*] 强劲的 ♦**to be furious with sb** 对某人大发雷霆 📖 用法参见 **angry**

furlong ['fəːlɔŋ] *n* [C] 长度单位弗隆，相当于201.167米

furnace ['fəːnɪs] *n* [C] 熔炉

furnish ['fəːnɪʃ] *vt* **1** [+ *room, building*] 布置 **2** [正式](*supply*) 提供 ♦**to furnish sb with sth** [正式]给某人提供某物 ♦**furnished flat** *or* [美] **apartment** 带家具的公寓

furnishings ['fəːnɪʃɪŋz] *n* [*pl*] 陈设

furniture ['fəːnɪtʃə(r)] *n* [U] 家具 ♦**a piece of furniture** 一件家具

furrow ['fʌrəu] **I** *n* [C] **1** (*in field*) 垄沟 **2** (*in skin*) 皱纹 **II** *vt* [+ *brow*] 使起皱纹 **III** *vi* [*brow* +] 起皱纹

furry ['fəːrɪ] *adj* [+ *animal, tail, toy*] 毛茸茸的; [+ *coat, hat*] 毛皮的

✪**further** ['fəːðə(r)] **I** *adj* [+ *additional*] 进一步的 ◊ *Doctors are carrying out further tests.* 医生们在做进一步的检查。**II** *adv* **1** (*farther*) (*in distance, time*) 更远地 ◊ *further along the beach* 沿着海滨更远处 ◊ *It has its origins much further back in time.* 它的起源在时间上要追溯得更远。; (*in degree*) 更深地 ◊ *He sank further into debt.* 他更加深陷债务中。; (*in development*) 进一步地 ◊ *He did not develop that idea any further.* 他没有再进一步发展那个设想。**2** [正式](*furthermore*) 此外 **III** *vt* [+ *career, project, cause*] 促进 ◊ *a plot by Morris to further his career* 莫里斯促进其事业的一个计划 ♦**to further one's/sb's interests** 增进自己/某人的利益 ♦**until further notice** 直到另行通知 ♦**how much further is it?** 还有多远？ ♦**further to your letter of ...** [英:正式:商]鉴于你…的来信 📖 用法参见 **farther**

further education *n* [U] 继续教育
furthermore [fəːðəˈmɔː(r)] *adv* 此外
furthest [ˈfəːðɪst] **I** *superl of* **far** **II** *adv* (*farthest*) (*in distance*) 最远地; (*in time*) 最久远地; (*in degree*) 最大程度地 **III** *adj* 最远的
furtive [ˈfəːtɪv] *adj* [+ *glance, manner*] 鬼鬼祟祟的
fury [ˈfjuərɪ] *n* [U/S] 狂怒 ♦ **in a fury** 勃然大怒地
fuse [fjuːz] (美 **fuze**) **I** *n* [C] **1** [电子] (*in plug, circuit*) 保险丝 **2** (*for bomb, firework*) 导火线 **II** *vt* **1** [英: 电子] 使短路 **2** (*join together*) [+ *substances, metals*] 熔合 **3** [+ *ideas, systems*] 结合 **III** *vi* **1** [英: 电子] 短路 **2** (*join together*) [*substances, metals* +] 熔合 **3** [*ideas, systems* +] 结合 ♦ **a fuse has blown** 保险丝烧断了
fuse box *n* [C] 保险丝盒
fuselage [ˈfjuːzəlɑːʒ] *n* [C] 机身
fusion [ˈfjuːʒən] *n* **1** [C/U] [*of ideas, qualities*] 融合 **2** [U] [物] (*also:* ***nuclear fusion***) 核聚变
fuss [fʌs] **I** *n* **1** [S/U] (*bother*) 大惊小怪 **2** [C] (*disturbance*) 慌乱 **II** *vi* (*fret*) 大惊小怪 ♦ **to make** *or* **kick up a fuss (about sth)** [非正式] (对某事) 小题大做 ♦ **to make a fuss of sb** [英] 对某人过分关心
❑ **fuss over** *vt* [不可拆分] **1** [+ *person*] 娇宠 **2** [+ *health, appearance, details*] 过分注意
fussy [ˈfʌsɪ] *adj* **1** [+ *person*] 挑剔的 **2** [+ *clothes, decorations*] 过分装饰的 ♦ **I'm not fussy** (*I don't mind*) 我无所谓
futile [ˈfjuːtaɪl] *adj* [+ *attempt, gesture, search*] 无效的
✪ **future** [ˈfjuːtʃə(r)] **I** *adj* 将来的 ◊ *at some future date* 在将来的某一天; [+ *president, spouse*] 未来的 ◊ *She met her future husband at the party.* 她是在那个晚会上认识她未来的丈夫的。 **II** *n* **1** (*time to come*) ♦ **the future** 未来 ◊ *We will have to see what the future holds.* 我们还得看未来的发展如何。 **2** [C] (*prospects*) 前途 ◊ *I decided that my future lay in medicine.* 我决心把我的前途放在医学方面。 **3** [语言] (*also:* ***future tense***) ♦ **the future** 将来时 **III futures** *n* [*pl*] [经济] 期货交易 ♦ **in (the) future** (*from now on*) 从今以后 ♦ **in the future** (*not now*) 将来 ♦ **in the near/foreseeable future** 在不久/可预见的未来 ♦ **there's no future in this idea** 这个设想没有前途
fuze [fjuːz] [美] *n* [C], *vt, vi* = **fuse**
fuzzy [ˈfʌzɪ] *adj* **1** (*blurred*) [+ *photo, image*] 模糊的 **2** [+ *hair*] 毛茸茸的 **3** (*confused*) [+ *thoughts, ideas*] 含糊不清的
fuzzy logic [计算机] *n* [U] 模糊逻辑
FYI *abbr* (= ***for your information/ interest***) 供参考

Gg

G[1], **g**[1] [dʒiː] *n* [C/U] (*letter*) 英语的第七个字母

G[2] [dʒiː] **I** *n* [C/U] [音] C 大调音阶中的第五音 **II** *n abbr* **1** [英：教育] (= ***good***) 优 **2** [美：电影] (= ***general audience***) 各种年龄段都可观看

g[2] *abbr* **1** (= ***gram***) 克 **2** [物] (= ***gravity***) 重力

gable ['geɪbl] *n* [C] [*of building*] 三角墙

gadget ['gædʒɪt] *n* [C] 小装置

Gaelic ['geɪlɪk] **I** *adj* 盖尔人的 **II** *n* [U] (*language*) 盖尔语

> **GAELIC**
> 爱尔兰和苏格兰西北部的一部分人说**Gaelic**（盖尔语）。爱尔兰盖尔语和苏格兰盖尔语稍有差别，但是两者都和威尔士语有关。100 多万人说爱尔兰盖尔语，爱尔兰宪法将其定为第一官方语言。在苏格兰，说盖尔语的人数在急速下降，近来降到了5 万人以下。

gag [gæg] **I** *n* [C] **1** (*on mouth*) 塞口物 **2** (*joke*) 笑话 **II** *vt* **1** [+ *prisoner*] 塞住…的嘴 **2** (喻) 使缄默 **III** *vi* (*choke*) 作呕 ♦ **to gag on sth** 被某物卡住喉咙

gain [geɪn] **I** *vt* **1** [+ *speed, weight, confidence*] 增加 **2** (*obtain*) 获得 **II** *vi* [*clock, watch* +] 走快 **III** *n* [C/U] (*increase, improvement*) 获益 ♦ **to gain in value/popularity** 增值/提高声望 ♦ **to gain ground** [*idea* +] 开始被人接受 ♦ **to gain on sb** 赶上某人 ♦ **weight gain** 体重增加 ♦ **to gain 3lbs (in weight)** (体重) 增加 3 磅 ♦ **to do sth for gain** (*for profit*) 为获利而做某事 ♦ **to gain from sth** [+ *money*] 从某事中获利; [+ *knowledge*] 从某事中获益 ♦ **a gain in efficiency/productivity** 效率/生产力的提高 ♦ **a gain of 10%** 10% 的增长

gal. *abbr* (= ***gallon***) 加仑

gala ['gɑːlə] *n* [C] (*festival*) 盛会 ♦ **a swimming/sports gala** 游泳/体育大赛

galaxy ['gæləksɪ] *n* **1** [C] 星系 **2** ♦ **the Galaxy** 银河系

gale [geɪl] *n* [C] (*wind*) 大风 ♦ **to be blowing a gale** 刮大风 ♦ **gale force 10** *or* **force 10 gale** 10 级大风 ♦ **gales of laughter** 阵阵笑声

gale-force wind ['geɪlfɔːs] *n* [C] 7 至10 级大风

gall. *abbr* (= ***gallon***) 加仑

gallant ['gælənt] *adj* **1** (*brave*) [+ *person, fight, effort*] 英勇的 **2** (*polite*) [过时] 献殷勤的

gall bladder *n* [C] 胆囊

gallery ['gælərɪ] *n* [C] **1** (*also:* ***art gallery***) (*public*) 美术馆; (*private*) 画廊 **2** (*in hall, church, theatre*) 廊台

galley ['gælɪ] *n* [C] **1** (*kitchen*) [*of ship, aircraft*] 厨房 **2** (*ship*) 大型划船

gallon ['gælən] *n* [C] (= *8 pints; BRIT = 4.5l; US = 3.8l*) 加仑

gallop ['gæləp] **I** *vi* [*horse* +] 飞跑; [*rider* +] 骑马奔驰 **II** *n* [C] **1** (*ride*) 骑马奔驰 **2** [*of horse*] 飞跑 ♦ **at a gallop** 飞奔

gallstone ['gɔːlstəun] *n* [C] 胆石

galore [gə'lɔː(r)] *adj* ♦ **bargains/prizes galore** 大量的便宜货/奖品

Gambia ['gæmbɪə] *n* 冈比亚

gamble ['gæmbl] **I** *vi* **1** (*bet*) 赌博 **2** (*take a risk*) 投机 **II** *vt* [+ *money*] 赌 **III** *n* [C] (*risk*) 冒险 ♦ **to gamble on sth** 对某事打赌; [+ *horses, race*] 对某物下赌注; [+ *success, outcome*] 对某事冒险 ♦ **to take a gamble** 冒险行事

❑ **gamble away** *vt* [+ *money*] 输光

gambler ['gæmblə(r)] *n* [C] **1** (*person who bets*) 赌博者 **2** (*risk-taker*) 投机者

gambling ['gæmblɪŋ] *n* [U] 赌博

✪ **game** [geɪm] **I** *n* **1** [C] (*sport*) 运动 ◊ *the wonderful game of football* 精彩的足球运动 **2** [C] (*activity*) (*children's*) 游戏 ◊ *This is a great game for children's parties.* 这是孩子们聚

会上的一个绝妙的游戏。**3** [c] (*also:* ***board game***) 棋盘游戏◊ *a box of toys, games, and books* 一箱玩具、游戏器具和书；(*also:* ***computer game***) 电脑游戏 **4** [c] (*match*) 比赛◊ *a game of cricket against Birkenhead School* 一场对伯肯黑德学校的板球比赛 **5** [c] 一局◊ *Sampras leads by four games to one.* 桑普拉斯在局数上以4比1领先 **6** [c] (*strategy, scheme*) 花招 ◊ *The government is playing a very shrewd political game.* 政府在玩弄一出非常狡猾的政治花招。**7** [u] (*animals, birds*) 猎物 **II** *adj* (*willing*) ♦**game for** 敢作敢为的◊ *I'm game for anything!* 我什么都敢干！**III games** *n* [*pl*] [英:教育] 体育活动◊ *I was hopeless at games.* 我对学校的体育活动都不在行。♦**a game of football/tennis** 一场足球/网球赛 ♦**big game** (*animals*) 大猎物 ♦**to give the game away** 露出马脚 ♦**to beat sb at his own game** 将计就计地战胜某人 ♦**the name of the game** 头等大事 ♦**to be on the game** [英:非正式] 从事卖淫嫖娼活动 ♦**to play games (with sb)** (喻) (对某人) 耍花招

games console ['geɪmz-] [计算机] *n* [c] 游戏机

game show I *n* [c] 电视竞赛游戏 **II** *cpd* [复合词] [+ *host, contestant*] 电视竞赛游戏

gammon ['gæmən] [英] *n* [u] 熏猪腿

gang [gæŋ] *n* [c] **1** [*of criminals, hooligans*] 一帮 **2** [*of friends, colleagues*] 一伙 **3** [*of workmen*] 一组 ❑**gang up** *vi* ♦**to gang up on sb** 联合起来对付某人

gangster ['gæŋstə(r)] *n* [c] 歹徒

gaol [dʒeɪl] [英] *n, vt* = **jail**

gap [gæp] *n* [c] **1** (*in space*) 缝隙 **2** (*in time*) 间隔 **3** (*in knowledge, coverage, records*) 空白 **4** (*difference*) 差距 ♦**a gap in the market** 市场空白

> **GAP YEAR**
> 在高中毕业以后、进入大学继续接受高等教育之前，学生可以休息一年，这一年被称为**gap year**。在**gap year**其间，很多人选择去旅游或去国外生活，也有人更愿意工作。无论如何选择，他们都能从学校学习生活之外获得宝贵的生活经验。

gape [geɪp] *vi* **1** (*stare*) 目瞪口呆地凝视 **2** [*shirt, hole* +] 裂开

gaping ['geɪpɪŋ] *adj* [+ *hole, wound*] 裂开的

gap year [英] *n* [c] 高中和大学之间的空隙年

garage ['gærɑːʒ] *n* [c] **1** (*of private house*) 车库 **2** (*for car repairs*) 汽车修理厂 **3** [英] (*petrol station*) 加油站

garbage ['gɑːbɪdʒ] *n* [u] **1** [尤美] (*rubbish*) 垃圾 **2** (*nonsense*) 废话 **3** (*bad film, book etc*) 拙劣作品

garbage bag [美] *n* [c] 垃圾袋

garbage can [美] *n* [c] 垃圾箱 [英=**dustbin**]

garbage man (*pl* **garbage men**) [美] *n* [c] 清洁工 [英=**dustman**]

garden ['gɑːdn] **I** *n* [c] 花园 **II** *vi* 收拾花园 **III gardens** *n* [*pl*] **1** (*public park*) 公园 **2** (*private, in street names*) 花园

garden centre (美 **garden center**) *n* [c] 园艺中心

gardener ['gɑːdnə(r)] *n* [c] (*professional*) 园丁；(*amateur*) 园艺爱好者

gardening ['gɑːdnɪŋ] *n* [u] (*non-professional*) 园艺；(*professional*) 园艺学 ♦**to do the gardening** 侍弄花草

garish ['gɛərɪʃ] *adj* [+ *colour, clothing, decor*] 俗艳的

garland ['gɑːlənd] *n* [c] [*of flowers*] 花环

garlic ['gɑːlɪk] **I** *n* [u] 大蒜 **II** *cpd* [复合词] [+ *puree, salt*] 大蒜；[+ *mayonnaise*] 有大蒜味的

garment ['gɑːmənt] *n* [c] 衣服

garnish ['gɑːnɪʃ] **I** *vt* [+ *food*] 加饰菜于 **II** *n* [c/u] 装饰菜

garrison ['gærɪsn] *n* [c] (*soldiers*) 卫戍部队；(*building*) 卫戍区

garters ['gɑːtəz] *n* [*pl*] 吊袜带 [英=**suspenders**]

gas [gæs] **I** *n* **1** [c/u] [化] 气体 **2** [u] (*for cooking, heating*) 煤气 **3** [u] [美:非正式] (*also:* ***gasoline***) 汽油 [英=**petrol**] **4** [u] (*anaesthetic*) 麻醉气 **II** *vt* (*kill*) 用毒气处死

gas cooker [英] *n* [c] 煤气炉
gas cylinder *n* [c] 煤气罐
gas fire [英] *n* [c] 煤气取暖器
gash [gæʃ] **I** *n* [c] (*wound, tear*) 深长的伤口 **II** *vt* (*wound*) 在…上划深长切口
gasket ['gæskɪt] *n* [c] 垫圈
gasoline ['gæsəliːn] [美] *n* [u] 汽油 [英=**petrol**]
gasp [gɑːsp] **I** *n* [c] **1** (*breath*) 喘息 **2** [*of pain, astonishment, in surprise*] 上气不接下气 **II** *vi* **1** (*pant*) 喘息 **2** (*in surprise*) 猛地吸口气 ♦**to gasp for breath/air** 气喘 ♦**to be gasping for a drink/cigarette** [英：非正式] 口渴/烟瘾难熬
gas pedal [尤美] *n* [c] 油门
gas station [美] *n* [c] 加油站 [英=**filling** *or* **petrol station**]
gas tank [美] *n* [c] 汽油罐 [英=**petrol tank**]
gate [geɪt] *n* [c] **1** (*of garden, field*) 门; (*of building*) 大门 **2** (*at airport*) 登机口 **3** (*at level-crossing*) 栅门 **4** (*at sporting event*) 观众数
gateau ['gætəu] (*pl* **gateaux**) [尤英] *n* [c] 奶油蛋糕
gatecrash ['geɪtkræʃ] **I** *vt* [+ *party*] 擅自进入 **II** *vi* 不请自来
gateway ['geɪtweɪ] *n* [c] (*entrance*) 门口 ♦**the gateway to the continent** 通向大陆的门户 ♦**a gateway to success/stardom** 成功/成名之道
gather ['gæðə(r)] **I** *vt* **1** (*pick, collect*) [+ *flowers, fruit, wood*] 采集 **2** (*also: **gather up***) (*put together*) [+ *papers, clothes*] 收拢 **3** (*assemble*) [+ *information, evidence*] 搜集 **4** (*understand*) ♦**to gather (that) ...** 获悉… **II** *vi* **1** (*assemble*) 聚集 **2** [*dust* +] 积聚 **3** [*clouds* +] 密集 ♦**to gather speed** 逐渐加速 ♦**to gather momentum/force** 势头渐猛/逐渐加强力量 ♦**to gather one's thoughts** 集中思想 ♦**as far as I can gather** 据我推测 ♦**to gather dust** (喻) 束之高阁
gathering ['gæðərɪŋ] *n* [c] 集会 ♦**family gathering** 家庭聚会
gauge [geɪdʒ] **I** *n* [c] **1** (*measuring device*) 量表 **2** [铁路] 轨距 **II** *vt* [+ *distance, speed*] 测量; [+ *feelings, reaction*] 揣测 ♦**pressure/temperature gauge** 压力/温度仪 ♦**fuel** *or* **petrol** *or* [美] **gas gauge** 燃料表
gaunt [gɔːnt] *adj* **1** (*haggard*) [+ *person, face, appearance*] 憔悴的 **2** (*grim, desolate*) [+ *place, outline*] 荒凉的
gave [geɪv] *pt of* **give**
gay [geɪ] **I** *adj* **1** (*homosexual*) 同性恋的 **2** (*cheerful*) [+ *person*] 欢快的; [+ *colour, music, dress*] 明快的 **II** *n* [c] (*homosexual*) 同性恋
gaze [geɪz] **I** *vi* ♦**to gaze at sth/sb** 凝视着某物/某人 **II** *n* (*stare*) 凝视
GB *abbr* (= ***Great Britain***) 大不列颠
GCSE [英] *n abbr* (= ***General Certificate of Secondary Education***) 普通中等教育证书
Gdns. *abbr* (= **Gardens**) 花园
GDP *n abbr* (= ***gross domestic product***) 国内生产总值
gear [gɪə(r)] **I** *n* **1** [c] [术语] [*of machine*] 齿轮; [*of car, bicycle*] 排挡 **2** [u] (*equipment*) 装备 **3** [u] (*clothing*) 服装 **II** *vt* ♦**to be geared to** *or* **towards** 使适应 ♦**to be in first/second** *etc* **gear** 第一/二{等}挡 ♦**to leave the car in gear** 摘挡停车 ♦**to change** *or* [美] **shift gear** 换挡
❑ **gear up** *vi* ♦**to gear (o.s.) up to do sth** (自己)作好做某事的心理准备 ♦**to gear o.s. up for sth** (自己)为某事做好心理准备
gearbox ['gɪəbɔks] *n* [c] 变速箱
gear lever, gear stick [英] *n* [c] 换挡杆 [美=**gearshift**]
gearshift ['gɪəʃɪft] [美] *n* [c] 换挡杆 [英=**gear lever, gear stick**]
geese [giːs] *n* [*pl*] *of* **goose**
gel [dʒɛl] **I** *n* [c/u] (*for hair, washing, shaving*) 啫喱 **II** *vi* **1** [*people* +] 凝聚 **2** [*thought, idea* +] 变得明朗 ♦**to gel with sb** 与某人配合融洽 ♦**bath/shower gel** 浴液
gem [dʒɛm] *n* [c] **1** (*stone*) 宝石 **2** (喻) 难能可贵的人
Gemini ['dʒɛmɪnaɪ] *n* **1** [u] (*sign*) 双子座 **2** [c] (*person*) 属双子座的人 ♦**I'm (a) Gemini** 我是双子座的
gen. *abbr* = **general, generally**

gender ['dʒɛndə(r)] *n* [c/u] **1** (*sex*) 性 **2** [语言] 性

gene [dʒiːn] *n* [c] 基因

✪ **general** ['dʒɛnərl] **I** *adj* **1** (*overall*) [+ *situation*] 总的; [+ *decline, standard*] 一般的 ◊ *the general standard of education in England* 英格兰教育的一般标准; [+ *performance*] 总体的 **2** (*widespread*) [+ *interest, awareness, feeling*] 普遍的 ◊ *a topic of general interest* 普遍感兴趣的话题 ◊ *a general feeling of optimism* 普遍的乐观情绪 **3** (*non-specific*) [+ *terms, outline, idea*] 笼统的 ◊ *principles that are stated in very general terms* 非常笼统地注明的原则 **4** (*miscellaneous*) [+ *expenses, details*] 常规的 ◊ *general expenses such as meals and phone calls* 常规消费例如饭费和电话费 **II** *n* [军] 将军 ◊ *General Montgomery* 蒙哥马利将军 ♦ **in general** (*as a whole*) 总的来说 ◊ *Teachers in general are pleased with the new scheme.* 总的来说教师们对新方案比较满意。; (*on the whole*) 一般来说 ◊ *In general, it was the young who voted in the election.* 一般来说是年轻人在选举中投票。♦ **as a general rule** 一般而言 ♦ **in general terms** 大致上说 ♦ **the general public** 广大公众

general anaesthetic (美 **general anesthetic**) *n* [c/u] 全身麻醉 ♦ **to have a general anaesthetic** 被全身麻醉

general election *n* [c] (*in Britain, United States*) 大选

generalize ['dʒɛnrəlaɪz] *vi* 笼统概括

generally ['dʒɛnrəlɪ] *adv* **1** (*on the whole*) 大体上 **2** (*widely*) 普遍地 **3** (*usually*) 通常 ♦ **generally speaking** 一般说来 ◊ *He generally gets up very early.* 他通常很早起床。

generate ['dʒɛnəreɪt] *vt* **1** [+ *power, electricity*] 产生 **2** [+ *income, profits, jobs*] 创造; [+ *interest*] 引起

generation [dʒɛnə'reɪʃən] *n* **1** [c] (*of people, family*) 一代人 **2** [c] (*period of time*) 代 **3** [c] (*series*) [*of computers, mobile phones*] 代 **4** [u] (*production*) (*of electricity, power*) 产生

generator ['dʒɛnəreɪtə(r)] [电子] *n* [c] 发电机

generosity [dʒɛnə'rɔsɪtɪ] *n* [u] 慷慨

generous ['dʒɛnərəs] *adj* **1** [+ *person*] 大方的 **2** (*sizeable*) [+ *measure, gift*] 大量的

genetic [dʒɪ'nɛtɪk] *adj* 遗传的

genetically modified [dʒɪ'nɛtɪklɪ 'mɔdɪfaɪd] *adj* 转基因的

genetics [dʒɪ'nɛtɪks] *n* [u] (*science*) 遗传学

genial ['dʒiːnɪəl] *adj* [+ *person*] 和蔼可亲的; [+ *face, personality*] 亲切的

genitals ['dʒɛnɪtlz] *n* [*pl*] 生殖器

genius ['dʒiːnɪəs] *n* [c] **1** (*person*) 天才 **2** [u] (*ability, skill*) 天赋 ♦ **a stroke of genius** 天才之举

gent [dʒɛnt] [英:非正式] *n* 绅士 *see also* **gents**

gentle ['dʒɛntl] *adj* **1** [+ *person, nature*] 温和的 **2** (*light*) [+ *movement, breeze, shake*] 轻柔的 **3** [+ *slope, curve*] 平缓的 **4** [烹饪] [+ *heat*] 文 **5** [+ *soap*] 柔和的 ♦ **to give sb a gentle hint/reminder** 给某人一个善意的暗示/提醒

gentleman ['dʒɛntlmən] (*pl* **gentlemen**) *n* [c] **1** (*man*) 先生 **2** (*well-mannered man*) 绅士 **3** (*referring to social position*) 有身份的人 ♦ **a real gentleman** 一位真正的绅士 ♦ **gentleman's agreement** 君子协定

gently ['dʒɛntlɪ] *adv* **1** [*touch, move* +] 温柔地; [*say, smile* +] 温和地 **2** [*slope, curve* +] 平缓地 **3** [烹饪] [*cook, heat* +] 用文火地

gentry ['dʒɛntrɪ] *n* [*pl*] ♦ **the gentry** (*aristocracy*) 贵族

gents [dʒɛnts] *n* ♦ **the gents** [英:非正式] (*men's toilet*) 男厕

genuine ['dʒɛnjuɪn] *adj* **1** (*real*) [+ *antique, leather*] 真正的 **2** (*sincere*) [+ *person*] 真诚的; [+ *emotion, interest*] 实实在在的

genuinely ['dʒɛnjuɪnlɪ] *adv* [+ *interested, concerned*] 真地

geographical [dʒɪə'græfɪkl] *adj* 地理的

geography [dʒɪ'ɔgrəfɪ] *n* [u] **1** [*of country, region*] 地理 **2** (*school/university subject*) 地理学

geological [dʒɪə'lɔdʒɪkl] *adj* 地质的

geology [dʒɪ'ɔlədʒɪ] *n* [U] 1 [*of area, rock*] 地质 2 (*university subject*) 地质学

geometric [dʒɪə'mɛtrɪk] *adj* 1 (*mathematical*) [+ *law, problem*] 几何的 2 (*regular*) [+ *shape, design, pattern*] 几何图形的

geometry [dʒɪ'ɔmətrɪ] *n* [U] 1 (*science*) 几何学 2 (*shape, proportions*) 几何图形

geranium [dʒɪ'reɪnɪəm] *n* [C] 天竺葵

geriatric [dʒɛrɪ'ætrɪk] *adj* [+ *patient, hospital, medicine*] 老年病学的

germ [dʒəːm] [生物] *n* [C] 细菌 ♦ **the germ of an idea** 一个想法的萌芽

German ['dʒəːmən] **I** *adj* 德国的 **II** *n* 1 [C] (*person*) 德国人 2 [U] (*language*) 德语

German measles [英] *n* [U] (*rubella*) 风疹

Germany ['dʒəːmənɪ] *n* 德国

gesture ['dʒɛstjə(r)] **I** *n* [C] 1 (*movement*) 表情动作 2 (*symbolic*) 姿态 **II** *vi* (*wave, point*) 用动作表示 ♦ **to make a gesture** (字) 做手势 ♦ **a gesture of goodwill/support** 善意/支持的姿态

✪ **get**

KEYWORD

[gɛt] (*pt, pp* **got**, 美 *pp* **gotten**)

I *vt*

1 ♦ **to have got** *see* **have, got**

2 (*obtain, find*) [+ *money, permission, results, information*] 获得; [+ *job, flat, room*] 得到 ♦ **he got a job in London** 他在伦敦得到一份工作 ♦ **we can get something to eat on the train** 我们可以在火车上弄点儿吃的 ♦ **to get a look at sth/sb** 看看某物/某人

3 (*fetch*) [+ *person, doctor, object*] 去拿 ♦ **to get sth for sb** 为某人去拿某物 ♦ **could you get me my coat please?** 请你把我的外套拿来好吗? ♦ **can I get you a coffee?** 要我给你拿杯咖啡吗? ♦ **I'll come and get you** 我会来接你的

4 (*receive*) [+ *present, letter, prize, TV channel*] 收到; [+ *price*] 得到 ◊ *He got a good price for the car.* 他把车卖了个好价钱。♦ **what did you get for your birthday?** 你生日时得到了什么礼物? ♦ **how much did you get for the painting?** 你这幅画卖了多少钱? ♦ **he gets a lot of pleasure from music** 他从音乐中得到了很大乐趣

5 (*board*) [+ *plane, bus etc*] 乘坐 ♦ **I'll get the bus** 我会乘坐公共汽车

6 (*prepare*) [+ *meal*] 准备 ♦ **I'll get lunch** 我来准备午餐

7 (*cause to be/become*) ♦ **to get sth/sb ready** 使某事/某人准备就绪 ♦ **to get sb drunk/into trouble** 使某人喝醉/陷入麻烦 ♦ **did you get the answer right?** 你的答案正确吗?

8 (*seize, catch*) 抓住 ♦ **get him!** 抓住他! ♦ **the police will get him eventually** 警察最终会抓住他的

9 (*hit*) [+ *target etc*] 击中

10 (*take, move*) 把…送到 ♦ **we must get him to hospital** 我们必须把他送到医院 ♦ **I'll get you there somehow** 我会设法让你到那儿 ♦ **do you think we'll get it through the door?** 你觉得我们能把它弄进门吗? ♦ **to get sth to sb** 为某人取得某物

11 (*buy*) 买; (*regularly*) 买到 ♦ **I'll get some milk from the supermarket** 我要去超市买牛奶 ♦ **we don't get a newspaper** 我们没买到报纸 ♦ **let me get you a drink** 让我给你来杯喝的吧

12 (*be infected by*) [+ *cold, measles etc*] 染上 ♦ **you'll get a cold** 你会得感冒的

13 (*understand*) [+ *joke, point*] 领会

14 (*hear*) 听见 ♦ **I didn't get your name** 我没听见你的名字

15 (*have*) [+ *time, opportunity*] 有 ♦ **I get the impression that ...** 我有…的印象 ♦ **I got a shock when I saw him** 当我看见他时我惊呆了

16 ♦ **to get sth done** (*do oneself*) 做某事; (*have done*) 完成某事 ♦ **to get the washing/dishes done** 洗好衣物/餐具 ♦ **to get one's hair cut** 理发 ♦ **to get the car going** *or* **to go** 使汽车发动起来 ♦ **to get sb to do sth** 让某人做某事

17 [非正式] (*annoy*) 使…恼火

♦ **what gets me is his attitude** 是他的态度让我恼火
II *vi*
1 (*become, be*) (+ *adj*) 变得 ♦ **to get old/tired/cold/dirty** 变老/变得疲倦/变冷/变脏 ♦ **to get drunk** 喝醉了 ♦ **to get bored** 变得无聊 ♦ **it's getting late** 不早了
2 (*go*) ♦ **to get to work/the airport/Beijing** *etc* 到办公室/到达机场/到达北京{等} ♦ **how did you get here?** 你是怎么到这儿的? ♦ **he didn't get home till 10pm** 他直到晚上10点才到家 ♦ **how long does it take to get from London to Paris?** 从伦敦到巴黎需要多久? ♦ **the talks are getting nowhere** 会谈毫无进展
3 (*begin*) ♦ **to get to know sb** 开始了解某人 ♦ **let's get going** *or* **started!** 开始吧!
4 (*manage*) ♦ **how often do you get to see him?** 你多久见他一次?
5 (*in expressions*) ♦ **don't let it get to you** 别受它的影响 ♦ **get lost!** 走开! ♦ **how crazy/stupid can you get?** 你怎么变得这样疯狂/愚蠢呢?
III *aux vb*
1 ♦ **to have got to** *see* **have, got**
2 (*passive use*) 作为构成被动语态的助动词 ♦ **to get killed** 被杀 ♦ **to get paid** 拿薪水
❑ **get about** *vi* 1 [*person* +] (*travel*) 旅行; (*move about*) 各处走动 ♦ **I can't get about as much as I used to** 我不能再像我过去那样到处走动了 2 [尤英] [*news, rumour* +] 流传
❑ **get across** *vt* [+ *message, meaning, idea*] 使…被理解
❑ **get along** *vi* 1 (*be friends*) 相处 ♦ **to get along well with sb** 与某人相处融洽 2 (*manage*) 过活 3 (*depart*) 离开 ♦ **I'd better be getting along soon** 我最好尽快离开
❑ **get around I** *vt* [不可拆分] [+ *problem*] 克服; [+ *law, rule*] 规避; [+ *person*] 说服 **II** *vi* 传开来
❑ **get around to** *vt* [不可拆分] ♦ **to get around to sth/to doing sth** 终于有时间做某事
❑ **get at** [英:非正式] *vt* [不可拆分]
1 (*attack, criticize*) 不断指责 ♦ **you're always getting at me** 你总是数落我 2 (*reach*) 够着 ◊ *We want to get at the truth.* 我们想了解真相。3 (*insinuate*) ♦ **what are you getting at?** 你讲这话什么意思?
❑ **get away** *vi* (*leave*) 脱身; (*on holiday*) 去度假; (*escape*) 逃跑
❑ **get away with** *vt* [不可拆分] 不因…而受惩罚 ♦ **to get away with doing sth** 不因做某事而受惩罚 ♦ **he'll never get away with it!** 他决不会逃脱干系的!
❑ **get back I** *vi* 1 (*return*) 回来 2 (*move away*) ♦ **get back!** 快回来! **II** *vt* (*reclaim*) 重新得到 ◊ *All he wanted was to get his girlfriend back.* 他所想的一切都是让女朋友再回到身边。
❑ **get back at** *vt* [不可拆分] ♦ **to get back at sb (for sth)** (因某事)对某人进行报复
❑ **get back to** *vt* [不可拆分]
1 (*return to*) [+ *activity, work*] 回到; [+ *normality*] 恢复; [+ *subject*] 重新回到 ♦ **to get back to sleep** 重又睡着 2 (*contact again*) 再与…联络
❑ **get by** *vi* 1 (*manage*) 过得去 ♦ **I can get by in Dutch** 我的荷兰语还凑合 ♦ **to get by on a small salary** 靠微薄的薪水勉强度日
2 (*pass*) 过去
❑ **get down I** *vi* 趴下 **II** *vt*
1 (*depress*) [+ *person*] 使…沮丧
2 (*write*) 记下来 3 (*swallow*) [+ *food, pill*] 吞下
❑ **get down to** *vt* [不可拆分] [+ *work*] 开始认真处理 ♦ **to get down to business** (喻)安心处理事务
❑ **get in I** *vi* 1 (*be elected*) [*candidate, party* +] 当选 2 (*arrive*) [*train, bus, plane* +] 抵达 3 (*arrive home*) 到家
II *vt* 1 (*bring in*) [+ *shopping, supplies*] 购买; [+ *harvest*] 收获 2 ♦ **I couldn't get a word in** 我一句话也插不进
❑ **get into** *vt* [不可拆分] 1 (*become part of*) [+ *conversation, argument, fight*] 进行; [+ *sphere of activity*] 开始从事; [+ *university, school*] 进入
2 [+ *vehicle*] 乘坐 3 [+ *clothes*] 穿上
4 (*in expressions*) ♦ **to get into bed**

上床 ♦ **I don't know what has got into him** 我不知道他是怎么回事
❑ **get off** I *vi* 1 (*from train, bus*) 下车 2 (*leave*) 离开 3 (*escape*) 从轻处罚 ♦ **he got off with a £50 fine** 他只被罚了50英镑而已 4 ♦ **to get off to a good start** 开头顺利 II *vt* 1 (*remove*) [+ *clothes*] 脱下; [+ *stain*] 消除 2 (*as holiday*) [+ *day, week*] 放假 ♦ **we get three days off at Christmas** 圣诞节时我们放了3天假 III *vt* [不可拆分] (*leave*) [+ *train, bus*] 从…下来; [+ *bed, table*] 从…起身
❑ **get off with** [英:非正式] *vt* [不可拆分] 与…有染
❑ **get on** I *vi* 1 (*be friends*) 和睦相处 ♦ **to get on well with sb** 与某人相处融洽 2 (*progress*) 进展 ♦ **how are you getting on?** 你过得怎么样? ♦ **to get on well with sth** 在某方面进展顺利 ♦ **time is getting on** 不早了 II *vt* [不可拆分] [+ *bus, train*] 上
❑ **get on to** *vt* [不可拆分] 1 [+ *subject, topic*] 开始涉及 2 [尤英] (*contact*) [+ *person*] 与…联系
❑ **get on with** *vt* [不可拆分] 1 (*be friends with*) [+ *person*] 与…和睦相处 2 (*continue, start*) [+ *meeting, work etc*] 开始继续做
❑ **get out** I *vi* [*person* +] (*of place*) 离开; (*of vehicle*) 下车; (*to enjoy o.s.*) 尽情享乐; [*news etc* +] 泄露 II *vt* 1 (*take out*) [+ *book, object etc*] 拿出 2 (*remove*) [+ *stain*] 消除
❑ **get out of** I *vt* [不可拆分] 1 [+ *vehicle*] 从…下来 2 (*avoid*) [+ *duty etc*] 摆脱 ♦ **to get out of doing sth** 逃避做某事 II *vt* 1 (*from bank*) [+ *money*] 提取 ♦ **I need to get some money out of the bank** 我需要去银行取些钱 2 (*extract*) [+ *confession, details etc*] 打探出 ♦ **we finally got the name out of him** 我们终于从他那里打探出了名字 3 (*derive*) [+ *pleasure, benefit*] 获得
❑ **get over** I *vt* [不可拆分] 1 [+ *illness, shock*] 从…中恢复过来 II *vt* 2 (*communicate*) [+ *idea etc*] 使…明白 3 ♦ **to get it over with** 尽快从…中解脱
❑ **get round** = **get around**
❑ **get through** I *vi* [通信] 接通 II *vt* [不可拆分] 1 (*finish*) [+ *work, book*] 完成 2 [尤英] (*use up*) 用完 3 (*survive*) 捱过
❑ **get through to** *vt* [不可拆分] 1 [通信] 接通 2 (*make understand*) 使…理解
❑ **get together** I *vi* [*people* +] 聚在一起 II *vt* 1 (*amass*) [+ *money*] 积累 2 (*gather up*) 把…收拾起来 3 (*organize*) [+ *project, plan etc*] 组织筹备
❑ **get up** I *vi* (*rise*) (*from chair, sofa*) 站起来; (*out of bed*) 起床 II *vt* ♦ **to get up enthusiasm for sth** 对某事产生热情
❑ **get up to** [尤英] *vt* [不可拆分] [+ *prank etc*] 搞 ◊ *What has he been getting up to?* 他在搞什么花样?

getaway ['gɛtəweɪ] *n* ♦ **to make a** *or* **one's getaway** 逃跑
Ghana ['gɑːnə] *n* 加纳
Ghanaian [gɑː'neɪən] I *adj* 加纳的 II *n* [c] (*person*) 加纳人
ghastly ['gɑːstlɪ] *adj* [+ *person, behaviour*] 糟透的; [+ *event, crime*] 可怕的
ghetto ['gɛtəu] (*pl* **ghettos** *or* **ghettoes**) *n* [c] 贫民窟
ghost [gəust] I *n* [c] (*spirit*) 鬼神 II *vt* 为…捉刀 ♦ **to give up the ghost** [*person* +] 绝望; [*machine* +] 停止运转 ♦ **the ghost of a chance (of doing sth)** 只有很少机会(做某事)
giant ['dʒaɪənt] I *n* [c] 1 (*in stories*) 巨人 2 (*large company*) 巨头 II *adj* (*huge*) 巨大的 ♦ **an opera/a football giant** 歌剧/足球巨星
giddy ['gɪdɪ] *adj* ♦ **to be** *or* **feel giddy** (*faint, dizzy*) 感到头晕 ♦ **to feel giddy with excitement/delight** 激动/高兴得晕头转向
gift [gɪft] *n* [c] 1 (*present*) 礼物 2 (*talent*) 天赋 ♦ **to have a gift for sth** (*talent*) 对某事有天赋
gifted ['gɪftɪd] *adj* [+ *person*] 有天赋的 ♦ **gifted children** 天资聪颖的孩子
gift shop (美 **gift store**) *n* [c] 礼品店

gift token, gift voucher *n* [c] 礼品券
gig [gɪg] *n* [c] (*show*) 现场演出
gigabyte ['dʒɪgəbaɪt] [计算机] *n* [c] 千兆字节 ♦**a ten-gigabyte hard drive** 10 千兆字节硬盘
gigantic [dʒaɪ'gæntɪk] *adj* 庞大的
giggle ['gɪgl] **I** *vi* 咯咯地笑 **II** *n* [c] 咯咯笑
gills [gɪlz] *n* [*pl*] 鳃
gilt [gɪlt] **I** *adj* [+ *frame, jewellery*] 镀金的 **II** *n* [u] 镀金
gimmick ['gɪmɪk] *n* [c] 花招
gin [dʒɪn] *n* [u] (*alcohol*) 杜松子酒 ♦**a gin and tonic** 杜松子酒加奎宁水
ginger ['dʒɪndʒə(r)] **I** *n* [u] (*spice*) 姜 **II** *adj* (*colour*) [+ *hair, moustache*] 姜色的
❑**ginger up** *vt* (*liven up*) 使有活力
gingerly ['dʒɪndʒəlɪ] *adv* (*cautiously*) 小心翼翼地
gipsy ['dʒɪpsɪ] *n* = **gypsy**
giraffe [dʒɪ'rɑːf] *n* [c] 长颈鹿
✪**girl** [gəːl] *n* [c] **1** (*child*) 女孩；(*young woman, woman*) 姑娘 ◊ *She's a good-looking girl.* 她是个漂亮的姑娘。 **2** (*daughter*) 女儿 ◊ *She has two girls and a boy.* 她有两个女儿和一个儿子。
girlfriend ['gəːlfrɛnd] *n* **1** [c] (*of girl*) 女性朋友 **2** (*of boy*) 女朋友
Girl Scout [美] *n* **1 the Girl Scouts** (*organization*) 女童子军 **2** (*person*) 女童子军成员
gist [dʒɪst] *n* ♦**the gist of his speech/article** 他讲话/文章的主旨

✪**give**
KEYWORD
[gɪv] (*pt* **gave**, *pp* **given**)
I *vt*
1 (*hand over*) ♦**to give sb sth, give sth to sb** 给某人某物；(*as gift*) 送给某人某物 ♦**I gave David the book, I gave the book to David** 我把这本书送给了戴维 ♦**give it to him** 把它送给他
2 (*provide*) [+ *advice, details*] 提供 ♦**to give sb sth** [+ *opportunity, surprise, shock, job*] 给某人某物 ♦**I gave him the chance to deny it** 我给他机会拒绝 ♦**you'll need to give me more time** 你需要给我更多的时间 ♦**to give sb the impression that ...** 给某人…的印象
3 (*deliver*) ♦**to give a speech/a lecture** 做演讲/讲座
4 (*organize*) ♦**to give a party/dinner party** *etc* 做东办一个聚会/宴会{等}
5 (*used with noun to replace a verb*) ♦**to give a sigh/cry/shout** *etc* 叹了口气/哭了出来/大叫了一声{等} ♦**to give a shrug/push** 耸了耸肩/推了一把
II *vi*
1 (*also:* ***give way***) (*break, collapse*) 支撑不住 ♦**his legs gave beneath him** 他腿软了 ♦**the roof/floor gave as I stepped on it** 我刚一踩上去屋顶/地板就塌了
2 (*stretch*) [*fabric, shoes* +] 变松
❑**give away** *vt* **1** [+ *money, object, prize*] 赠送 **2** (*betray*) [+ *secret, information, person*] 泄露 **3** [+ *bride*] 在婚礼上把新娘交给新郎
❑**give back** *vt* [+ *money, book etc*] 交还 ♦**to give sth back to sb** 把某物交还给某人
❑**give in I** *vi* (*yield*) 屈服 ♦**to give in to sth** 屈服于某事 **II** *vt* [+ *essay etc*] 上交
❑**give off** *vt* [+ *heat, smoke, smell*] 散发
❑**give out I** *vt* (*distribute*) [+ *prizes, books, drinks etc*] 分发 **II** *vi* **1** (*run out*) [*supplies* +] 用完 **2** (*fail*) 出故障
❑**give up I** *vi* (*stop trying*) 放弃 **II** *vt* **1** [+ *job*] 辞掉；[+ *hobby*] 抛弃；[+ *idea, hope, right, territory*] 放弃 ♦**to give up smoking** 戒烟 **2** (*surrender*) ♦**to give o.s. up** 投案自首

given ['gɪvn] **I** *pp of* **give II** *adj* (*fixed*) [+ *time, amount*] 一定的 **III** *prep* (*taking into account*) ♦**given the circumstances ...** 考虑到当时的情况… ♦**given that ...** 考虑到…
glacier ['glæsɪə(r)] *n* [c] 冰川
glad [glæd] *adj* (*happy, pleased*) 高兴的 ♦**to be glad about sth** 对某事高兴 ♦**to be glad that ...** 很高兴… ♦**to be glad of sth** 因某事而高

兴 ♦ **I'm glad to see you** 我非常高兴见到你 ♦ **I'd be glad to help you** 我很愿意帮助你

gladly ['glædlɪ] *adv* **1** (*happily*) 高兴地 **2** (*willingly*) 乐意地

glamor ['glæmə(r)] [美] *n* = **glamour**

glamorous ['glæmərəs] *adj* 富有魅力的

glamour (美 **glamor**) ['glæmə(r)] *n* [U] 魅力

glance [glɑːns] **I** *n* [C] (*look*) 扫视 **II** *vi* 瞥 ♦ **to glance at sb/sth** 看某人/某物一眼 ♦ **at a glance** 一瞥之下 ♦ **at first glance** 乍一看
❑ **glance off** *vt* [不可拆分] 擦过

gland [glænd] *n* [C] 腺

glare [glɛə(r)] **I** *n* **1** [U] [*of light*] 强光 **2** [C] (*angry look*) 怒视 **II** *vi* **1** [*light* +] 眩目地照射 **2** [*person* +] 怒目而视 ♦ **the glare of publicity** 众目睽睽 ♦ **to glare at sb** 怒视某人

glaring ['glɛərɪŋ] *adj* [+ *error, example, omission*] 明显的

glass [glɑːs] *n* **I 1** [U] (*substance*) 玻璃 **2** [C] (*container*) 玻璃杯 **3** [C] (*glassful*) 一杯 **II glasses** *n* [*pl*] (*spectacles*) 眼镜 ♦ **a pair of glasses** 一副眼镜

glaze [gleɪz] **I** *vt* **1** [+ *pottery*] 上釉于 **2** [+ *bread, pastry*] 浇在…上 **II** *n* [C/U] (*on pottery*) 釉
❑ **glaze over** 显得呆滞

gleam [gliːm] **I** *vi* **1** [*light, eyes* +] 闪烁 **2** [*polished surface* +] 发光 **II** *n* [C] (*from polished surface*) 亮光 ♦ **a gleam in sb's eye** 某人眼里闪烁的光芒

gleaming ['gliːmɪŋ] *adj* (*shiny*) 闪闪发亮的

glean [gliːn] *vt* [+ *information, ideas*] 搜集

glee [gliː] *n* [U] (*joy*) 欣喜

glen [glɛn] *n* [C] 峡谷

glide [glaɪd] *vi* **1** [*person, snake* +] 滑行 **2** [*bird, aeroplane* +] 滑翔

glider ['glaɪdə(r)] *n* [C] (*aircraft*) 滑翔机

gliding ['glaɪdɪŋ] *n* (*in aircraft*) 滑翔运动 ♦ **to go gliding** 去滑翔

glimmer ['glɪmə(r)] **I** *n* [C] [*of light*] 微光 **II** *vi* [*light* +] 发微光 ♦ **a glimmer of hope/interest** 一线希望/一丝兴趣

glimpse [glɪmps] **I** *n* ♦ **a glimpse of** [*person, place, object*] 一瞥 **II** *vt* [+ *person, place, object*] 瞥见 ♦ **to catch a glimpse of sb/sth** 瞥见某人/某事

glint [glɪnt] **I** *vi* **1** [*light, shiny surface* +] 闪闪发光 **2** [*eyes* +] 闪烁 **II** *n* [C] **1** [*of metal, light*] 反光 **2** (*in eyes*) 光芒

glisten ['glɪsn] *vi* (*with sweat, rain, oil etc*) 闪闪发光 ♦ **to glisten with sth** 某物晶莹发亮

glitter ['glɪtə(r)] **I** *vi* [*light, shiny surface* +] 闪闪发光; [*eyes* +] 闪烁 **II** *n* [U] (*decoration*) 小发光物

gloat [gləut] *vi* 幸灾乐祸 ♦ **to gloat over** *or* **about sth** 对某事幸灾乐祸

global ['gləubl] *adj* **1** (*worldwide*) 全球的 **2** (*overall*) 综合的

global warming [-'wɔːmɪŋ] *n* [U] 全球变暖

globe [gləub] *n* **1** ♦ **the globe** (*the world*) 世界 **2** [C] (*model*) 地球仪 ♦ **around the globe** 全世界

gloom [gluːm] *n* **1** (*dark*) ♦ **the gloom** 黑暗 **2** [U] (*sadness*) 忧郁 ♦ **economic gloom** 经济萧条

gloomy ['gluːmɪ] *adj* **1** (*dark*) [+ *place, weather*] 黑暗的 **2** (*sad*) [+ *person, situation, news*] 忧郁的

glorify ['glɔːrɪfaɪ] *vt* (*glamorize*) 颂扬

glorious ['glɔːrɪəs] *adj* **1** [+ *sunshine, day, weather*] 灿烂的 **2** [+ *victory, occasion, career*] 光荣的

glory ['glɔːrɪ] *n* **I 1** [U] (*prestige*) 荣誉 **2** [C/U] (*splendour*) 壮观 **II** *vi* ♦ **to glory in** 自豪于 ♦ **moment of glory** 光荣时刻

gloss [glɔs] *n* **1** [S/U] (*shine*) 光泽 **2** [C/U] (*also: **gloss paint***) 光泽涂料
❑ **gloss over** *vt* [不可拆分] [+ *problem, error*] 掩饰

glossary ['glɔsərɪ] *n* [C] 词汇表

glossy ['glɔsɪ] *adj* **1** [+ *hair, surface*] 有光泽的 **2** [+ *magazine, brochure*] 光纸印刷的

glove [glʌv] *n* [C] 手套 ♦ **a pair of gloves** 一副手套 ♦ **to fit like a glove** 正合适

glove compartment *n* [C] 汽车仪表板上的小贮藏箱

glow [gləu] **I** *vi* **1** [*embers, stars* +] 发

光 **2** [*face, skin, cheeks* +] 发红 **II** *n* [s] **1** [*of embers, stars*] 光亮 **2** [*of face, cheeks, skin*] 红润 ♦**a glow of pride/satisfaction** 自豪/满意的心情 ♦**to glow with pleasure/pride** 洋溢着喜悦/自豪之情

glowing ['gləuɪŋ] *adj* **1** [+ *fire*] 红彤彤的 **2** [+ *complexion*] 容光焕发的 **3** (*excellent*) [+ *tribute, report, description*] 热烈的

glucose ['glu:kəus] *n* [U] 葡萄糖

glue [glu:] **I** *n* [C/U] 胶 **II** *vt* 粘贴 ♦**to glue sth together** 把某物粘在一起 ♦**to glue sth to sth** 把某物粘在某物上 ♦**to be glued to the television** 紧盯着电视

glum [glʌm] *adj* (*miserable*) [+ *person, face, expression*] 忧郁的

glut [glʌt] **I** *n* [C] 供应过剩 **II** *vt* ♦**to be glutted (with...)** [*market, economy* +] 充斥着(…) ♦**a glut of oil/fruit** 油/水果供应过剩

GM *adj abbr* (= ***genetically modified***) 转基因的

gm (*pl* **gm** *or* **gms**) *abbr* (= ***gram***) 克

GMT *abbr* (= ***Greenwich Mean Time***) 格林尼治标准时间

gnaw [nɔ:] **I** *vt* [+ *bone*] 啃 **II** *vi* ♦**to gnaw at** [*guilt, doubt* +] 折磨

GNP *n abbr* (= ***Gross National Product***) 国民生产总值

GNVQ [英:教育] *n abbr* (= ***general national vocational qualification***) 国家职业技能综合考试

✪ **go**

KEYWORD

[gəu] (*pt* **went**, *pp* **gone**, *pl* **goes**)

I *vi*

1 (*travel, move*) 去 ♦**he's going to New York** 他要去纽约 ♦**where's he gone?** 他去哪儿了? ♦**shall we go by car or train?** 我们开车去还是坐火车去? ♦**to go to do sth, go and do sth** [英] 去做某事

2 (*depart*) 离开 ♦**let's go** 我们走吧 ♦**I must be going** 我必须得走了 ♦**they came at eight and went at nine** 他们8点来9点走的 ♦**our plane goes at 11pm** 我们的飞机晚上11点起飞

3 (*disappear*) 消失 ♦**all her jewellery had gone** 她所有的珠宝首饰都不见了 ♦**where's the tea gone?** 茶怎么不见了?

4 (*attend*) ♦**to go to school/university** 上学/上大学 ♦**to go to evening classes** 去上夜校

5 (*with activity*) ♦**to go for a walk** 去散步 ♦**to go on a trip** 去旅行 ♦**to go swimming** 去游泳

6 (*work*) [*clock, video etc* +] 运转 ◊ *I can't believe your watch is still going after all these years.* 我真不能相信你的表这么多年后还在走。; [*bell* +] 敲响

7 (*become*) ♦**to go pale/mouldy/bald** 变得苍白/发霉/秃顶 ♦**she went red** 她脸红了

8 (*be sold*) ♦**to go for £10** 卖10镑

9 (*be about to, intend to*) ♦**are you going to come?** 你要来吗? ♦**I think it's going to rain** 我想天要下雨了 ♦**I'm going to be a doctor when I grow up** 我长大后想成为一名医生

10 (*progress*) [*time, event, activity* +] 进行 ♦**time went very slowly/quickly** 时间过得很慢/很快 ♦**how did it go?** 这事进展如何?

11 (*be placed*) ♦**where does this cup go?** 把这个茶杯放在哪儿? ♦**the milk goes in the fridge** 牛奶放在冰箱里 ♦**it won't go in** 放不进去

12 (*lead*) [*road, path* +] 通向

13 (*pass*) 归 ♦**the job is to go to someone else** 这份工作将归别人所得 ♦**and the prize goes to ...** 奖品归…

14 (*fail*) [*sight, hearing* +] 减退; [*clutch, battery* +] 衰竭 ♦**the battery's going** 电池没电了

15 (*be removed*) [*object* +] 被丢弃; [*jobs* +] 被取消; [*employee* +] 被辞退 ♦**more jobs are to go at the factory** 这家工厂会有更多的工作被取消

16 (*combine well*) [*colours, clothes, foods* +] 相配

17 (*say*) [*story, poem, saying* +] 正如…所说 ♦**as the story goes** 如故事中所讲的

18 (*be available*) ♦**there's a flat going downstairs** 楼下有间空的公寓 ♦**I'll take whatever's going**

无论什么样的我都要
19 (*to take away*) ♦ **a hamburger and fries to go** [美] 汉堡包和炸薯条外卖
20 (*in other expressions*) ♦ **there's still a week to go before the exams** 考试前还有一个星期的时间 ♦ **he has a lot going for him** 他有很多有利条件 ♦ **to get going** 走 ◊ *Give me the keys. I've got to get going.* 给我钥匙。我得走了。♦ **to keep going** 继续下去
II *vt* (*travel*) [+ *distance*] 走
III *n*
1 (*try*) 尝试 ♦ **to have a go (at sth/at doing sth)** 试一下(某事/做某事)
2 (*turn*) 轮流 ♦ **whose go is it?** 轮到谁了? ♦ **it's your go** 轮到你了
3 ♦ **to have sth on the go** 手头上正忙着某事
4 [尤英:非正式] (*move*) ♦ **to be on the go** 忙忙碌碌的
❑ **go about I** *vt* [不可拆分] (*tackle*) 处理 ♦ **how do I go about doing this?** 我该怎样着手做这事呢?
II *vi* 1 [*rumour* +] 传开 ♦ **there's a rumour going about that ...** 一条关于…的谣言正流传开来
2 (*manner*) ♦ **he goes about in a white suit** 他总是穿着白西装
❑ **go after** *vt* [不可拆分] 1 (*pursue*) [+ *person*] 追赶 2 (*try to get*) [+ *job*] 设法得到; [+ *record*] 设法打破
❑ **go against** *vt* [不可拆分] 1 (*be unfavourable to*) 不利于 2 (*disregard*) [+ *advice, wishes etc*] 违背
❑ **go ahead** *vi* 1 (*take place*) [*event* +] 发生 2 (*press on*) ♦ **to go ahead with sth** 着手做某事 ♦ **go ahead!** (*encouraging*) 干吧!
❑ **go along** *vi* 去
❑ **go along with** *vt* [不可拆分] (*agree with*) [+ *plan, idea, decision*] 赞同; [+ *person*] 同意
❑ **go around** *vi* 1 (*circulate*) [*news, rumour* +] 传播 2 (*revolve*) 转动 3 [尤英] (*visit*) ♦ **to go around (to sb's)** 拜访(某人的家) 4 (*suffice*) 够每人一份 5 (*as a habit*) 习惯于 ♦ **he goes around in an orange baseball cap** 他总是戴着一顶橘黄色的棒球帽
❑ **go away** *vi* 1 (*leave*) 离开 2 (*on holiday*) 外出
❑ **go back** *vi* (*return*) 返回
❑ **go back on** *vt* [不可拆分] [+ *promise, agreement*] 背弃
❑ **go back to** *vt* [不可拆分] [+ *activity, work, school*] 回到
❑ **go by I** *vi* [*vehicle, years, time* +] 过去 **II** *vt* [不可拆分] [+ *rule etc*] 遵照
❑ **go down I** *vi* 1 (*fall*) [*price, level, amount* +] 下降 2 (*set*) [*sun* +] 落下 3 (*sink*) [*ship* +] 沉没 4 (*crash*) [*computer* +] 死机; [*plane* +] 坠毁 5 [体育] (*lose*) 输掉; (*be relegated*) 降级 ♦ **we went down to Newcastle** 我们输给了纽卡斯尔队 6 ♦ **to go down well/badly** [*speech, remark, idea* +] 受到/不受欢迎 7 ♦ **to go down with flu** 得流感 **II** *vt* [不可拆分] [+ *stairs, ladder*] 从…下来
❑ **go for** *vt* [不可拆分] 1 (*fetch*) 去取 2 (*opt for*) 选择 3 (*be attracted by*) 喜欢 4 (*attack*) 攻击 5 (*apply to*) 适用于 ♦ **that goes for me too** 那也适用于我
❑ **go in** *vi* (*enter*) 进去
❑ **go in for** *vt* [不可拆分]
1 [+ *competition*] 参加 2 (*like*) 爱好 ♦ **he doesn't go in for compliments** 他不喜欢恭维
❑ **go into** *vt* [不可拆分] 1 (*enter*) [+ *building, room*] 进入 2 (*examine*) [+ *subject, details*] 探究 3 (*embark on*) [+ *career*] 从事
❑ **go off I** *vt* [不可拆分] [尤英] (*begin to dislike*) [+ *person, place, idea etc*] 不再喜欢 **II** *vi* 1 (*leave*) 离去 ♦ **he's gone off to work** 他已经去上班了 2 (*explode*) [*bomb, gun* +] 爆炸 3 (*sound*) [*alarm* +] 响起 4 (*pass off*) [*event* +] 进行 ♦ **the wedding went off without a hitch** 婚礼进行得非常顺利 5 (*switch off*) [*lights etc* +] 熄灭 6 [尤英] [*food, milk, meat* +] 变质
❑ **go off with** *vt* [不可拆分] 1 (*run away with*) [+ *lover*] 同…私奔 2 (*take*) [+ *object*] 抢走
❑ **go on I** *vi* 1 (*continue*) 继续 ♦ **to go on with one's work** 继续自己的工作 ♦ **we have enough to be going on with** [尤英] 目前我们够了 ♦ **to go on doing sth** 继续做某事 2 (*happen*) 发生 ♦ **what's going on here?** 这里发生什么事了?

3 (*come on*) [*lights etc* +] 打开 4 ♦**to go on to do sth** 接着做某事 **II** *vt* [不可拆分] **1** (*be guided by*) [+ *evidence etc*] 把…作为依据 ♦**there isn't much to go on** 没有太多可以依据的东西 **2** (*approach*) ♦**he's going on 50** 他马上就要50岁了

❑**go on about** *vt* [不可拆分] 对…唠唠叨叨

❑**go on at** [英:非正式] *vt* [不可拆分] (*nag*) 向…唠唠叨叨 ♦**she's always going on at me to tidy my room** 她总是唠唠叨叨地要我清理房间

❑**go out** *vi* **1** [*person* +] 离开; (*to party, club etc*) 出去消遣 ♦**to go out of** 离开 ♦**are you going out tonight?** 你今晚出去吗？ **2** [*couple* +] 和…交往 ♦**they've been going out for 3 years and have just got engaged** 他们已经交往3年了，并且刚刚订婚 ♦**to go out with sb** 和某人交往 **3** (*be extinguished*) [*light, fire* +] 熄灭

❑**go over I** *vi* 过去 **II** *vt* (*check*) 仔细检查 ♦**to go over sth in one's mind** 在脑子里过一遍

❑**go round** *vi* = **go around**

❑**go through** *vt* [不可拆分] **1** [+ *place, town*] 路过 **2** (*undergo*) 经历 ♦**he's going through a difficult time** 他正经历着困难时期 **3** (*search through*) 翻遍 **4** (*run through*) [+ *list, book, story*] 仔细查看 **5** (*perform*) [+ *routine, procedure, exercise*] 履行

❑**go through with** *vt* [不可拆分] [+ *plan, crime*] 做到 ♦**I couldn't go through with it** 我无法把它做完

❑**go together** *vi* [*colours, clothes, foods* +] 相配

❑**go towards** *vt* [不可拆分] [*money* +] 作为…的部分付款

❑**go under** *vi* **1** (*sink*) [*ship, person* +] 沉没 **2** [*business, project* +] 失败

❑**go up** *vi* **1** (*rise*) [*price, level, value* +] 上涨 **2** (*go upstairs*) 上楼

❑**go up to** *vt* [不可拆分] 向…走过去

❑**go with** *vt* [不可拆分] **1** (*combine well with*) [*colours, clothes, foods* +] 与…协调 **2** (*accompany*) 与…相伴共存

❑**go without** *vt* [不可拆分] [+ *food, treats*] 没有

go-ahead [ˈgəuəhɛd] **I** *n* ♦**the go-ahead** (*for project*) 许可 ♦**to give sb/sth the go-ahead** 准许某人做某事/某事得以进行 **II** *adj* [+ *person, firm*] 有进取心的

goal [gəul] **I** *n* [c] **1** [体育] (*point scored*) 进球得分; (*on pitch*) 球门 **2** (*aim*) 目标 ♦**to score a goal** 进一球

goalkeeper [ˈgəulkiːpə(r)] *n* [c] 守门员

goalpost [ˈgəulpəust] *n* [c] 门柱 ♦**to move** *or* **shift the goalposts** 改变规则

goat [gəut] *n* [c] 山羊

gobble [ˈgɔbl] *vt* 狼吞虎咽

❑**gobble down** *vt* 大口吞下

God [gɔd] **I** *n* 上帝 **II** *int* 天啊 ♦**to play God** [贬] 以上帝自居

god [gɔd] *n* [c] 天神 ♦**the god of thunder** 雷神

godchild [ˈgɔdtʃaɪld] (*pl* **godchildren**) *n* [c] (*male*) 教子; (*female*) 教女

goddaughter [ˈgɔddɔːtə(r)] *n* [c] 教女

goddess [ˈgɔdɪs] *n* [c] (字) 女神 ♦**the moon goddess** 月神 ♦**sex/screen goddess** 性感/银屏女神

godfather [ˈgɔdfɑːðə(r)] *n* [c] **1** (*male godparent*) 教父 **2** (*gangster*) 帮头

godmother [ˈgɔdmʌðə(r)] *n* [c] 教母

godparent [ˈgɔdpɛərənt] *n* [c] 教父教母

godson [ˈgɔdsʌn] *n* [c] 教子

goggles [ˈgɔglz] *n* [*pl*] 护目镜

✪**going** [ˈgəuɪŋ] **I** *present participle of* **go II** *adj* ♦**the going rate/price** 现行率/时价 **III** *n* ♦**the going** (*progress*) 进展 ◊ *The going was becoming easier as the talks progressed.* 随着对话的进行进展变得更加顺利。; (*conditions*) 路况 ◊ *The going became more difficult as the rain became heavier.* 雨越下越大，路况变得更差了。 ♦**when the going gets tough** 当情况艰难时 ♦**while the going is good** 趁

情况顺利时 ♦**it was hard** *or* **tough** *or* **heavy going** 困难重重 ♦**that's good** *or* **not bad going** 还不错 ♦**a going concern** 运作正常的公司

gold [gəuld] **I** *n* **1** [U] (*metal*) 黄金 **2** [U] (*jewellery*) 金饰品 **3** [U] (*colour*) 金色 **4** [C] [体育：非正式] (*also:* ***gold medal***) 金牌 **II** *adj* **1** (*made of gold*) [+ *ring, watch, tooth*] 金的 **2** (*gold-coloured*) 金色的 ♦**as good as gold** 很乖

golden ['gəuldən] *adj* **1** (*made of gold*) 金制的 **2** (*colour*) 金色的 **3** (*wonderful*) [+ *opportunity, future*] 绝妙的

goldfish ['gəuldfɪʃ] (*pl* **goldfish**) *n* [C] 金鱼

goldmine ['gəuldmaɪn] *n* [S] (喻) 金矿

gold-plated ['gəuld'pleɪtɪd] *adj* 包金的

golf [gɔlf] *n* [U] 高尔夫球 ♦**to play golf** 打高尔夫球

golf ball *n* [C] 高尔夫球

golf club *n* [C] **1** (*stick*) 高尔夫球棍 **2** (*organization*) 高尔夫球俱乐部

golf course *n* [C] 高尔夫球场

golfer ['gɔlfə(r)] *n* [C] 高尔夫球运动员

gone [gɔn] **I** *pp of* **go** **II** *adj* 离去的 **III** *prep* [英：非正式] (*after*) 过 ♦**the food's all gone** 食物都没了

gong [gɔŋ] *n* [C] 锣

✪ **good** [gud] **I** *adj* **1** (*pleasant*) 令人愉快的 ◊ *They had a really good time.* 他们玩得很开心。**2** (*high quality*) [+ *food, school, job*] 好的 ◊ *She speaks very good English.* 她英语说得很好。**3** (*well-behaved*) [+ *boy, girl, dog*] 乖的 ◊ *Were the kids good?* 孩子们乖吗？ **4** (*sensible*) [+ *idea, reason, advice*] 好的 ◊ *It was a good idea to bring a torch.* 带手电筒是个好主意。**5** (*skilful*) 好的 ◊ *He's a good footballer.* 他是个很好的足球运动员。**6** (*positive*) [+ *news, luck, example*] 好的 ◊ *a piece of good news* 一条好消息 **7** (*cheerful*) [+ *mood, temper*] 愉快的 ◊ *She's in a good mood!* 她心情很好！ ◊ *She had a good time in Italy.* 她在意大利度过了一段愉快的时光。**8** (*morally correct*) 公正的 ◊ *The president is a good man.* 总统是个公正的人。 **II** *n* [U] (*right*) 善 ◊ *the battle between good and evil* 善恶之争 ♦**good!** 好！ ♦**to be good at (doing) sth** 精于(做)某事 ♦**to be no good at (doing) sth** 不擅长(做)某事 ♦**to be good for doing sth** (*useful*) 对做某事有帮助 ♦**it's no good doing...** 做…没有用 ♦**it didn't do any good** 没什么用处 ♦**to be up to no good** 不怀好意 ♦**it's good for you** (*healthy, beneficial*) 对你有益 ♦**to be good to sb** (*kind*) 对某人很好 ◊ *He's always been very good to me.* 他总是对我很好。 ♦**to be good with people/with figures** 擅长与人/数字打交道 ♦**to be good with one's hands** 手很灵巧 ♦**is it any good?** (*will it do?*) 这行吗？ ◊ *There's no honey – is sugar any good?* 没有蜂蜜 – 糖行吗？；(*what's it like?*) 怎么样？ ◊ *Is her new novel any good?* 她的新小说怎么样？ ♦**it's good to see you** 很高兴见到你 ♦**it's a good thing you were there, it's a good job you were there** [英] 幸亏你在那儿 ♦**that's very good of you** 你实在太好了 ♦**would you be good enough to ...?** 可不可以请您…？ ♦**good morning/afternoon!** 早上/下午好！ ♦**good evening!** 晚上好！ ♦**good night!** (*before going home*) 再见！；(*before going to bed*) 晚安！ ♦**to feel good** (*happy*) 感到高兴 ♦**to make good** [+ *damage, loss*] 弥补 ◊ *Three years was a short time in which to make good the deficiencies.* 弥补这些不足，3 年的时间是很短的。；(*succeed*) 成功 ♦**to take a good look** 好好看一看 ♦**a good while ago** 很久以前 ♦**as good as** (*almost*) 几乎相当于 ♦**for good** (*forever*) 永久地 ♦**for the good of sb** 为了某人的利益 ♦**it's for your own good** 是为了你自己好 ♦**to do sb good** 对某人有益 ♦**not until I'm good and ready** 直到我彻底准备好时才 *see also* **goods**

> 请勿将**be good for**和**be good to**混淆。若某事**be good for**某个个人或组织，即它有益于该人或组织。*The policy is good for company morale.* 如果某人**be good to**你，表示他对你很友好，很体贴。*Phil cannot replace my dad but he has been very good to me.*

goodbye [gud'baɪ] *int* 再见 ♦**to say goodbye** 告别

Good Friday *n* [U] 耶稣受难日，即复活节前的星期五

good-looking ['gud'lukɪŋ] *adj* 好看的

good-natured ['gud'neɪtʃəd] *adj* [+ *person*] 性情温和的; [+ *discussion*] 和善的

goodness ['gudnɪs] **I** *n* [U] (*of person*) 善良 **II** *int* ♦**(my) goodness!** (我的)天哪！ ♦**for goodness sake!** 看在老天爷的份上！ ♦**goodness gracious!** 天哪！ ♦**thank goodness!** 谢天谢地！ ♦**out of the goodness of his heart** 出于他的好心

goods [guds] *n* [*pl*] **1** [商] 商品 **2** (*possessions*) 动产 ♦**to come up with** *or* **deliver the goods** 达到要求

goods train [英] *n* [C] 货物列车 [美=**freight train**]

goodwill [gud'wɪl] *n* [U] 善意 ♦**a gesture of goodwill** 善意的表示

goose [guːs] (*pl* **geese**) *n* [C] 鹅

gooseberry ['guzbərɪ] *n* [C] (*fruit*) 醋栗 ♦**to play gooseberry** [英] 当电灯泡

goose bumps *n* [*pl*] 鸡皮疙瘩 ♦**to get goose bumps** 起鸡皮疙瘩

gooseflesh ['guːsflɛʃ] *n* [U] = **goose bumps**

goose pimples *n* [*pl*] = **goose bumps**

gorge [gɔːdʒ] **I** *n* [C] (*valley*) 峡谷 **II** *vt* ♦**to gorge o.s. (on sth)** 狼吞虎咽(吃某物)

gorgeous ['gɔːdʒəs] *adj* **1** [+ *necklace, dress*] 华丽的; [+ *weather, day*] 宜人的 **2** [+ *person*] 光彩夺目的

gorilla [gə'rɪlə] *n* [C] (*animal*) 大猩猩

gory ['gɔːrɪ] *adj* 血淋淋的 ♦**the gory details** 令人毛骨悚然的细节

gosh [gɔʃ] *int* 啊呀！

gospel ['gɔspl] *n* **1** [C] [宗] 福音书 **2** [C] (*doctrine*) 信条 **3** [U] (*also:* ***gospel music***) 福音音乐 **4** [U] (*also:* ***gospel truth***) 绝对真理 ♦**the gospel** (*Christ's teachings*) 福音书

gossip ['gɔsɪp] **I** *n* **1** [U] (*rumours*) 流言蜚语 **2** [C] (*chat*) 闲谈 **3** [C] (*busybody*) 爱飞短流长的人 **II** *vi* (*chat*) 闲谈 ♦**to gossip with sb** 和某人闲谈

✪ **got** [gɔt] *pt, pp of* **get** ♦**have you got your umbrella?** 你有伞吗？ ♦**he has got to accept the situation** 他只得接受现状 ♦**he's got to be guilty** 他肯定有罪

gotten ['gɔtn] [美] *pp of* **get**

gourmet ['guəmeɪ] **I** *n* [C] (*person*) 美食家 **II** *adj* [+ *food, cooking*] 精美的

govern ['gʌvən] **I** *vt* **1** [+ *country*] 统治 **2** [+ *event, conduct*] 控制 **II** *vi* 统治

✪ **government** ['gʌvnmənt] **I** *n* **1** [C] (*institution*) 政府 ◊ *The Government is in the wrong.* 是政府的错误。 **2** [U] (*act of governing*) 执政 ◊ *He had no previous experience of government.* 他以前没有执政的经验。 **II** *cpd* [复合词] [+ *grant, report, official, policy*] 政府

governor ['gʌvənə(r)] *n* [C] **1** [*of state*] 州长; [*of colony*] 总督 **2** [*of bank, school, hospital*] 董事 ◊ *the Board of Governors* 理事会 **3** [英] [*of prison*] 狱长

Govt *abbr* (= ***government***) 政府

gown [gaun] *n* [C] **1** (*dress*) 礼服 **2** [英] [*of teacher, judge*] 礼袍

GP *n abbr* [C] (= ***general practitioner***) 家庭医生

GR8 *abbr* = (**great**) 太好了

grab [græb] **I** *vt* **1** (*seize*) 抓住 **2** [+ *food, drink, sleep*] 抓紧做 **3** [+ *chance, opportunity*] 抓住 **4** [+ *attention*] 吸引 **II** *vi* ♦**to grab at sth** 抢某物 **III** *n* ♦**to make a grab for sth** 向某物抓去 ♦**to grab hold of sth/sb** 抓住某物/某人

grace [greɪs] **I** *n* [U] **1** (*gracefulness*) 优雅 **2** (*dignified behaviour*) 体面

II *vt* (*adorn*) 使增光 ♦**his fall from grace** 他的不得势 ♦**to fall from grace** 不得势 ♦**5 days' grace** 5 天的宽限 ♦**with (a) good/bad grace** 欣然地/勉强地 ♦**to say grace** 谢恩祈祷

graceful ['greɪsful] *adj* **1** [+ *animal, athlete, movement, style*] 优美的 **2** (*polite*) 得体的

gracious ['greɪʃəs] **I** *adj* **1** (*courteous*) [+ *person*] 有礼的; [+ *speech, smile*] 亲切的 **2** (*elegant*) [+ *era, lifestyle*] 高雅的 **II** *int* ♦**(good** *or* **goodness) gracious!** 天哪！

grade [greɪd] **I** *n* [c] **1** (*quality*) [*of goods, product*] 等级 **2** (*rank*) (*in company, organization*) 级别 **3** (*school mark*) 分数 **4** [美] (*school class*) 年级 **5** [美] (*gradient*) 坡 **II** *vt* (*rank, class*) 分等次 ♦**to make the grade** 达到标准

grade crossing [美] *n* [c] 铁路线与公路交叉处 [英=**level crossing**]

grade school [美] *n* [c/u] 小学 [英=**primary school**]

gradient ['greɪdɪənt] [英] *n* [c] [*of road, slope*] 坡度 [美=**grade**]

gradual ['grædjuəl] *adj* [+ *change, process, improvement*] 逐渐的

gradually ['grædjuəlɪ] *adv* 逐渐地

graduate [*n* 'grædjuɪt, *vb* 'grædjueɪt] **I** *n* [c] **1** (*person with degree*) 毕业生 **2** [美] ♦**high school/elementary school graduate** 中学/小学毕业生 **II** *vi* **1** (*from university*) 毕业 **2** [美] (*from high school/elementary school etc*) 毕业 **3** (*progress*) 发展 ♦**a philosophy graduate, a graduate in philosophy** [英] 哲学专业毕业生

graduation [grædju'eɪʃən] *n* **1** [u] (*from university*) 毕业 **2** [u] [美] (*from high school, elementary school etc*) 毕业 **3** [c/u] (*also:* ***graduation ceremony***) (*after degree*) 毕业典礼; [美] (*after high school, elementary school etc*) 毕业典礼

graffiti [grə'fiːtɪ] *n* [u] 涂鸦

graft [grɑːft] **I** *n* **1** [c] [*of skin, bone*] 移植物 **2** [u] [英: 非正式] (*hard work*) 苦差 **3** [u] [美] (*bribery*) 贿赂 **II** *vt* ♦**to graft (onto)** [+ *skin, bone*] 移植(到); [+ *plant*] 嫁接(到) ♦**skin/bone graft** 皮肤/骨移植

grain [greɪn] *n* **1** [c] [*of wheat, rice*] 谷粒 **2** [c/u] (*cereals*) 谷物 **3** [u] [美] (*corn*) 玉米 **4** [c] [*of sand, salt, sugar*] 颗粒 **5** ♦**the grain** [*of wood*] 纹理 ♦**it goes against the grain** 格格不入 ♦**a grain of truth** 一点真实性

gram [græm] *n* [c] 克

grammar ['græmə(r)] *n* [u] **1** (*rules of language*) 语法 **2** (*use of rules*) 语法运用

grammar school [英] *n* [c] 文法学校，11 到18 岁孩子就学的公立学校，学生成绩一般都比较优秀

gramme [græm] [英] *n* = **gram**

gran [græn] *n* [c] (*on mother's side*) 外婆; (*on father's side*) 奶奶

grand [grænd] **I** *adj* **1** (*impressive*) [+ *building, landscape*] 壮丽的; [+ *scheme, design*] 宏伟的 **2** (*wonderful*) 美好的 **II** *n* (*a thousand pounds/dollars*) 1000 英镑/美元 ♦**grand total** 总数

grandad, granddad ['grændæd] *n* [c] (*on mother's side*) 外公; (*on father's side*) 爷爷

grandchild ['græntʃaɪld] (*pl* **grandchildren**) *n* [c] (*male on father's side*) 孙子; (*female on father's side*) 孙女; (*male on mother's side*) 外孙; (*female on mother's side*) 外孙女

granddaughter ['grændɔːtə(r)] *n* [c] (*on father's side*) 孙女; (*on mother's side*) 外孙女

grandfather ['grændfɑːðə(r)] *n* [c] (*on mother's side*) 外公; (*on father's side*) 爷爷

grandiose ['grændɪəus] *adj* 浮夸的

grandma ['grænmɑː] *n* [c] (*on mother's side*) 外婆; (*on father's side*) 奶奶

grandmother ['grænmʌðə(r)] *n* [c] (*on father's side*) 外婆; (*on father's side*) 奶奶

grandpa ['grænpɑː] *n* [c] (*on mother's side*) 外公; (*on father's side*) 爷爷

grandparents ['grændpɛərənts] *n* [*pl*] (*on mother's side*) 外公外婆; (*on father's side*) 爷爷奶奶

grand piano *n* [c] 大钢琴

Grand Prix ['grɑːn'priː] (*pl* **Grands Prix** *or* **Grand Prix**) *n* (*motor racing*) 国际汽车大奖赛

grandson ['grænsʌn] *n* [c] (*on father's side*) 孙子; (*on mother's side*) 外孙
granite ['grænɪt] *n* [u] 花岗石
granny, grannie ['grænɪ] *n* [c] (*on mother's side*) 外婆; (*on father's side*) 奶奶
grant [grɑːnt] **I** *vt* [+ *request, visa, permission*] 授予 **II** *n* [c] (*award*) 拨款 ♦ **to take sb for granted** 认为某人做的事情是理所当然 ♦ **to take sth for granted** 想当然地认为某事 ♦ **to take it for granted that ...** 认为…是理所当然 ♦ **to grant that ...** 承认… ♦ **I grant (you) that ...** 我(向你)承认…
grape [greɪp] *n* [c] 葡萄 ♦ **a bunch of grapes** 一串葡萄 ♦ **sour grapes** 酸葡萄
grapefruit ['greɪpfruːt] (**grapefruit** *or* **grapefruits**) *n* [c/u] 葡萄柚
graph [grɑːf] *n* [c] 图表
graphic ['græfɪk] *adj* **1** [+ *account, description, scene*] 生动的 **2** [+ *art, design*] 绘画艺术的 *see also* **graphics**
graphic designer *n* [c] 平面造型设计师
graphics ['græfɪks] **I** *n* [u] (*design*) 制图学 **II** *n* [*pl*] (*images*) 图形
grapple ['græpl] *vi* **1** ♦ **to grapple with sb** 与某人搏斗 **2** ♦ **to grapple with** [+ *problem*] 设法解决
grasp [grɑːsp] **I** *vt* **1** (*hold, seize*) 抓住 **2** (*understand*) 理解 **II** *n* [s] **1** (*grip*) 紧握 **2** (*understanding*) 理解力 ♦ **to slip from sb's grasp** 从某人手中溜掉 ♦ **within/beyond sb's grasp** 为某人力所能及/力所不及 ♦ **to grasp at…** [+ *rope, handle*] 向…抓去
grass [grɑːs] **I** *n* **1** [c/u] [植] 草 **2** [c] [英:非正式] (*informer*) 告密者 **3** [u] (*marijuana*) 大麻 **II** *vi* ♦ **to grass on sb** [英:非正式] 告某人的密 ♦ **the grass** (*the lawn*) 草坪
grasshopper ['grɑːshɔpə(r)] *n* [c] 蚱蜢
grass roots ['grɑːsruːts] **I** *n* [*pl*] ♦ **the grass roots** 基层 **II** *cpd* [复合词] [+ *level, opinion, support*] 基层群众
grate [greɪt] **I** *vi* **1** ♦ **to grate (on sth)** (*scrape*) (磨到某物)发出刮擦声 **2** ♦ **to grate on sb** (*annoy*) 使某人烦躁 **II** *vt* [+ *food*] 磨碎 **III** *n* [c] (*for fire*) 炉栅
grateful ['greɪtful] *adj* [+ *person*] 感激的 ♦ **to be grateful to sb** 感激某人 ♦ **to be grateful for** [+ *help, opportunity*] 感激… ♦ **to be grateful to sb for sth** 为某事感激某人
grater ['greɪtə(r)] *n* [c] 磨碎器 ♦ **cheese/nutmeg grater** 奶酪/肉豆蔻磨碎器
gratifying ['grætɪfaɪɪŋ] *adj* (*pleasing, satisfying*) 令人满意的 ♦ **it is gratifying to ...** …是令人满足的 ♦ **it is gratifying that ...** 令人满足的是…
gratitude ['grætɪtjuːd] *n* [u] 感激
grave [greɪv] **I** *n* [c] (*tomb*) 坟墓 **II** *adj* **1** [+ *situation, crisis*] 严重的; [+ *concern, danger*] 重大的 **2** [+ *expression, person*] 严肃的
gravel ['grævl] *n* [u] 砾石
gravestone ['greɪvstəun] *n* [c] 墓碑
graveyard ['greɪvjɑːd] *n* [c] 墓地
gravity ['grævɪtɪ] *n* [u] **1** [物] 重力 **2** (*seriousness*) 严重性
gravy ['greɪvɪ] *n* [u] (*sauce*) 肉卤
gray [greɪ] [美] *adj* = **grey**
graze [greɪz] **I** *vi* [*animal* +] 吃草 **II** *vt* **1** (*scrape*) [+ *arm, leg, knee*] 擦伤 **2** (*touch lightly*) 擦过 **III** *n* (*wound*) 擦伤
grease [griːs] **I** *n* [u] **1** (*lubricant*) 润滑油 **2** (*fat*) 油脂 **3** (*dirt*) 油污 **II** *vt* **1** (*lubricate*) 上润滑油于 **2** [+ *cooking dish*] 给…涂油脂
greasy ['griːsɪ] *adj* **1** [+ *tools, hands*] 油污的 **2** [+ *food*] 油腻的 **3** [+ *skin, hair*] 多油脂的
✪ **great** [greɪt] **I** *adj* **1** (*large*) [+ *area, amount, number*] 巨大的 ◊ *a great black cloud of smoke* 一团巨大的黑烟 ◊ *a great number of people* 很多人 **2** (*considerable*) [+ *success, achievement*] 重大的; [+ *pleasure, difficulty, value*] 极大的; [+ *risk*] 超乎寻常的 **3** (*intense*) [+ *heat, pain*] 强烈的 ◊ *The heat was so great I took off my shirt.* 实在太热了，于是我脱下了我的衬衫。◊ *David had a great desire to live in the countryside.* 大卫有住在乡下的强烈愿望。;

[+ *love*] 深的 **4** (*important, famous*) [+ *city, person, work of art*] 伟大的 ◊ *the great novels of the 19th century* 19 世纪的伟大小说 ◊ *Shakespeare was a great man.* 莎士比亚是个伟人。**5** (*terrific*) [+ *person, place*] 好极了的；[+ *idea*] 棒极了的 ◊ *It's a great idea.* 这是个棒极了的主意。**6** (*ardent*) [+ *believer, supporter*] 十足的 **II** *int* ♦ **great!** (*enthusiastically*) 太好了！；(*sarcastically*) 天啊！ **III** *n* (*success*) (*person*) 伟人 ◊ *She is one of the greats of modern cinema.* 她是当今电影界的巨星之一。；(*work of art, film, literature*) 巨作 ◊ *the greats of feminist literature* 女权文学的巨作 ♦ **I feel great** 我感觉好极了 ♦ **they're great friends** 他们是挚友 ♦ **we had a great time** 我们玩得很快活

Great Britain *n* 大不列颠

great-grandfather [greɪt'grænfɑːðə(r)] *n* [c] 曾祖父

great-grandmother [greɪt'grænmʌðə(r)] *n* [c] 曾祖母

greatly ['greɪtlɪ] *adv* [+ *surprised, amused, honoured*] 非常；[*benefit, improve, increase, reduce* +] 大大地

Greece [griːs] *n* 希腊

greed [griːd] *n* [u] 贪婪 ♦ **greed for sth** 对某物贪得无厌

greedy ['griːdɪ] *adj* 贪心的 ♦ **to be greedy for** [+ *money, power*] 贪图；[+ *affection*] 渴望

Greek [griːk] **I** *adj* 希腊的 **II** *n* **1** [c] (*person*) 希腊人 **2** [u] (*modern language*) 希腊语 **3** [u] (*also:* ***ancient Greek***) 古希腊语

✪ **green** [griːn] **I** *adj* **1** (*colour*) 绿色的 **2** (*inexperienced*) 缺乏经验的 ◊ *He was very green, straight out of college.* 他刚毕业，没什么经验。**3** (*environmental*) 环保的 ◊ *green activists* 环保分子 **II** *n* **1** [c/u] (*colour*) 绿色 ◊ *The walls were a bright green.* 墙是鲜绿色的。**2** [c] [高尔夫] 球穴区 **3** [c] (*also:* ***village green***) 村庄公共绿地 **III greens** *n* [*pl*] **1** (*vegetables*) 绿叶菜 **2** [政治] ♦ **the Greens** 绿党成员 ♦ **to have green fingers** *or* [美] **a green thumb** 擅长侍弄花草 ♦ **to give sb/sth the green light** 准许某人做某事/某事的发生 ♦ **to be green with envy** 十分妒忌

green card [美] *n* [c] (*work permit*) 绿卡

greenery ['griːnərɪ] *n* [u] 绿色植物

greengage ['griːngeɪdʒ] *n* [c] (*fruit*) 西洋李子

greengrocer ['griːngrəusə(r)] [尤英] *n* [c] **1** (*person*) 蔬菜水果商 **2** (*shop*) (*also:* ***greengrocer's***) 果蔬店

greenhouse ['griːnhaus] **I** *n* [c] 暖房 **II** *cpd* [复合词] [+ *gas, emissions*] 温室

greenhouse effect *n* ♦ **the greenhouse effect** 温室效应

Greenland ['griːnlənd] *n* 格陵兰岛

Greenlander ['griːnləndə(r)] *n* [c] 格陵兰岛人

green salad *n* [c/u] 蔬菜色拉

greet [griːt] *vt* **1** (*welcome*) [+ *person*] 欢迎 **2** (*receive*) [+ *announcement, news*] 回应

greeting ['griːtɪŋ] *n* [c] (*welcome*) 问候 ♦ **Christmas/birthday greetings** 圣诞节/生日祝福 ♦ **Season's greetings** 节日问候

greetings card, greeting card *n* [c] 贺卡

grew [gruː] *pt of* **grow**

grey (美 **gray**) [greɪ] **I** *adj* **1** (*colour*) 灰色的；[+ *hair*] 灰白的 **2** (*dull*) [+ *weather, day*] 阴沉的 **3** (喻) (*faceless*) 了无生趣的 **II** *n* [c/u] (*colour*) 灰色 ♦ **to go grey** [*person, hair* +] 变灰白

grey-haired [greɪ'hɛəd] *adj* 灰白头发的

grid [grɪd] *n* **1** [c] (*pattern*) 网格状 **2** ♦ **the (National) Grid** (国家) 输电网 **3** [c] (*cover for drain*) 阴沟铁栅 **4** [c] (*diagram*) 坐标方格

gridlock ['grɪdlɔk] **I** *n* [u] **1** (*traffic jam*) 大堵塞 **2** (*stalemate*) 僵局 **II** *vt* ♦ **to be gridlocked** [*roads* +] 陷入交通大堵塞；[*talks, process* +] 陷入僵局

grief [griːf] *n* [u] (*distress, sorrow*) 悲痛 ♦ **to come to grief** [*plan* +] 归于失败；[*person* +] 遭到不幸 ♦ **good grief!** 哎呀！

grievance ['griːvəns] *n* [c/u] (*complaint*) 抱怨

grieve [griːv] I *vi* (*feel sad*) 伤心 II *vt* (*sadden*) 使伤心 ♦**to grieve for sb** 因某人亡故而伤心 ♦**to grieve over sth** 因某事伤心
grievous ['griːvəs] *adj* [+ *loss, mistake, blow*] 沉痛的 ♦**grievous bodily harm** [法] 严重的人身伤害
grill [grɪl] I *n* [c] [英] (*on cooker*) 烤架 [美 = **broiler**] II *vt* 1 [英] [+ *food*] 烤 [美 = **broil**] 2 (*question*) 严厉盘问
grille [grɪl] *n* [c] (*screen*) (*on window, counter*) 格栅 ♦**radiator grille** (*on car*) 散热器护栅
grim [grɪm] *adj* 1 (*unpleasant*) [+ *situation, news*] 严酷的 2 (*unattractive*) [+ *place*] 阴森的 3 (*serious, stern*) [+ *person, expression*] 令人生畏的 ♦**grim reality** 严酷的现实
grime [graɪm] *n* [u] (*dirt*) 污垢
grin [grɪn] I *n* [c] (*smile*) 露齿的笑 II *vi* 露齿而笑 ♦**to grin and bear it** 逆来顺受
grind [graɪnd] (*pt, pp* **ground**) I *vt* 1 (*crush*) [+ *coffee, pepper*] 磨碎 2 (*squash*) 碾 3 [美] [+ *meat*] 绞碎 4 (*sharpen*) [+ *knife, blade*] 磨快 II *vi* [*vehicle, gears* +] 轰鸣着缓慢行进 III *n* ♦**the grind** (*work*) 苦差 ♦**to grind one's teeth** 咬牙切齿 ♦**to grind to a halt** [*vehicle* +] 嘎嘎作响地慢慢停下; [*talks, production* +] 逐渐停滞
❑**grind down** (喻) *vt* [+ *person*] 消磨…的意志
❑**grind out** *vt* (*churn out*) 费心劳力地做出
grip [grɪp] I *n* 1 [c] (*hold*) 紧握 2 [s] (*control*) 支配 3 [u/s] [*of tyre, shoe*] 抓力 II *vt* 1 [+ *object*] 紧握 2 [+ *audience, attention*] 吸引住 ♦**to come** *or* **get to grips with** [+ *problem, difficulty*] 认真对付 ♦**to lose one's grip (on)** (喻) 失去控制 ♦**to get a grip on** 把握住 ♦**in the grip of** 笼罩在…中
gripping ['grɪpɪŋ] *adj* [+ *story, film*] 扣人心弦的
grisly ['grɪzlɪ] *adj* [+ *death, murder*] 恐怖的
grit [grɪt] I *n* [u] 1 (*sand, gravel*) 沙粒 2 (*determination*) 勇气 II *vt* [+ *road*] 用沙子覆盖 III **grits** *n* [*pl*] [美: 烹饪] 粗玉米粉 ♦**to grit one's teeth** (字) 咬紧牙; (喻) 咬紧牙关
groan [grəun] I *n* [c] (*of pain*) 呻吟; (*of unhappiness*) 哼声; (*of disappointment, disapproval*) 嘘声 II *vi* 1 (*in pain*) 呻吟; (*with disapproval*) 嘟囔 2 [*tree, floorboard* +] 发出嘎吱声 III *vt* ♦**"not again!" he groaned** "够了!" 他抱怨道
grocer ['grəusə(r)] *n* [c] 1 (*person*) 食品杂货商 2 (*shop*) (*also: **grocer's***) 食品杂货店
grocery ['grəusərɪ] I *n* [c] (*also: **grocery shop***) [英] (*also: **grocery store***) [尤美] 食品杂货店 II **groceries** *n* [*pl*] (*provisions*) 食品杂货
groin [grɔɪn] *n* [c] 腹股沟
groom [gruːm] I *n* [c] 1 (*for horse*) 马夫 2 (*also: **bridegroom***) 新郎 II *vt* [+ *horse*] 给…刷毛 ♦**to be groomed for sth** 接受做某事的培养 ♦**well-groomed** [+ *person*] 服饰整洁的
groove [gruːv] *n* [c] 1 (*in record, surface*) 槽 2 (*rhythm*) 节奏
grope [grəup] *vi* 1 ♦**to grope for** (字) (*feel for*) 摸索; (喻) (*try to think of*) [+ *word, phrase*] 搜寻 2 (*molest*) 性骚扰 ♦**to grope one's way through/towards sth** 摸索着通过/走向某物
gross [grəus] I *adj* 1 (*extreme*) [+ *misconduct, indecency, negligence*] 严重的 2 (*horrible*) 粗俗的 3 [商] [+ *weight*] 毛的; [+ *income, profit, interest*] 总的 II *n* [*pl*] (*twelve dozen*) 罗 III *vt* [商] ♦**to gross £500,000** 获得50万英镑的总收入 IV *adv* [商] 税前地
grossly ['grəuslɪ] *adv* (*greatly*) [+ *unfair, exaggerated, inadequate*] 十分地
grotesque [grə'tɛsk] *adj* 1 (*shocking*) 荒唐的 2 (*ugly*) 丑陋的
✪**ground** [graund] I *pt, pp of* **grind** II *n* 1 (*floor*) ♦**the ground** 地面 ◊ *He picked his coat up from the ground.* 他从地上拾起大衣。 2 (*earth, soil, land*) ♦**the ground** 土地 ◊ *The ground was very wet and soft.* 土地非常潮湿松软。◊ *a*

rocky piece of ground 一块多岩石的土地 **3** [c] [体育] 场 ◊ *Manchester United's football ground* 曼联队的足球场 **4** [c] [美: 电子] 接地装置 [英 = **earth**] **III grounds** *n* [*pl*] **1** (*gardens etc*) 庭园 ◊ *the palace grounds* 宫殿庭园 **2** (*reasons, basis*) 理由 **3** (*also: **coffee grounds***) 咖啡渣 **IV** *vt* **1** [+ *plane*] 使停飞 **2** [+ *child*] 限制出门 ◊ *His father grounded him for a month.* 他爸爸整个月都限制他出门。 **3** [美: 电子] 使接地 [英 = **earth**] **V** *adj* **1** [+ *coffee, almonds, spice, pepper*] 磨碎的 **2** [美] [+ *meat*] 绞碎的 **VI** *vi* [*ship* +] 搁浅 ◊ *the rocks where the ship had grounded* 船搁浅处的礁石 ♦ **on the ground** 在地面上 ♦ **the facilities on the ground** 地面设备 ♦ **below/above ground** 地下/上 ♦ **common ground** 共同点 ♦ **to gain/lose ground** (喻) 越来越看好/渐失优势 ♦ **to get off the ground** (喻) 开始进行 ♦ **to stand** *or* **hold one's ground** 坚持立场 ♦ **to be thin on the ground** [英] 为数不多 ♦ **to break new ground** 开辟新天地 ♦ **to burn/raze sth to the ground** 把某物烧成平地/夷为平地 ♦ **to go to ground** 躲了起来 ♦ **to find the middle ground** 找到中间立场 ♦ **to prepare the ground for sth** 为某事铺平道路 ♦ **to shift** *or* **change one's ground** 改变立场 ♦ **it suits him down to the ground** [英: 非正式] 这完全适合他 ♦ **grounds for** [+ *optimism, hope, concern*] …的原因; [+ *divorce, appeal, complaint*] …的理由 ♦ **grounds for doing sth** 做某事的根据 ♦ **on (the) grounds of** 以…为理由 ♦ **on the grounds that ...** 以…为理由 ♦ **on medical/humanitarian grounds** 基于人道主义/健康状况 ♦ **burial/hunting ground(s)** 坟地/猎场

groundcloth ['graundklɔθ] [美] *n* [c] 铺地防潮布 [英 = **groundsheet**]

ground floor *n* [c] 一楼 [美 = **first floor**]

grounding ['graundɪŋ] *n* (*foundation*) ♦ **a grounding in** …的基础

groundsheet ['graundʃiːt] [英] *n* [c] 铺地防潮布 [美 = **groundcloth**]

groundwork ['graundwəːk] *n* [U] (*preparation*) 基础 ♦ **to lay the groundwork for sth** 为某事打下基础

✪ **group** [gruːp] **I** *n* [c] **1** (*of people, buildings etc*) 组 ◊ *dinner with a small group of friends* 和几个朋友吃的晚饭 ◊ *A group of experts are on the case.* 一组专家正在解决问题。 **2** (*organization*) 团体 ◊ *members of an environmental group* 一个环保团体的成员 **3** (*also: **pop group, rock group***) 组合 **4** [商] (*of businesses*) 集团 **II** *vt* (*organize, arrange*) 把…分组 ♦ **in groups** 成组地 ♦ **age/income group** 年龄/收入组 ♦ **newspaper/property group** 报纸/房地产集团

❑ **group together** *vi* (*band together*) 团结起来 ◊ *They encouraged the workers to group together.* 他们鼓励工人们团结起来。

grouse [graus] **I** *n* **1** (*game bird*) 松鸡 **2** (*complaint*) 牢骚 **II** *vi* (*complain*) 发牢骚

grovel ['grɔvl] *vi* **1** (*be humble*) 奴颜婢膝 **2** (*crawl about*) 爬行 ♦ **to grovel to sb** 向某人卑躬屈膝

✪ **grow** [grəu] (*pt* **grew**, *pp* **grown**) **I** *vi* **1** [*plant, tree* +] 生长 ◊ *the oak tree growing at the end of the lane* 长在小巷尽头的橡树; [*person, animal* +] 长大 ◊ *He's grown a lot since I last saw him.* 自从我上次见他，他长大了许多。; [*hair, nails* +] 留 **2** (*increase*) [*amount, feeling, problem* +] 扩大 ◊ *Their influence is steadily growing.* 他们的影响在稳步扩大。; [*economy, business* +] 发展 **II** *vt* [+ *flowers, vegetables*] 栽种 ◊ *I'm growing leeks in my garden.* 我在花园里种韭葱。; [+ *beard, hair*] 留 ◊ *I've decided to grow my hair.* 我决定留头发。 ♦ **to grow (by) 20cm** 长了20厘米 ♦ **to grow by 10%** 增长10%。 ♦ **to grow rich/old/impatient** 变富/变老/变得不耐烦

❑ **grow apart** *vi* 变得有隔阂

❑ **grow into** *vt* [不可拆分] (*become*) 变成

❑ **grow on** *vt* [不可拆分] ♦ **to grow**

on sb 越来越为某人喜欢◊ *That painting is growing on me.* 我越来越喜欢那幅画。

❑**grow out of** *vt* [不可拆分] [+ *clothes*] 长得穿不下; [+ *habit*] 逐渐放弃◊ *Many children suck their thumbs. Most of them grow out of it.* 很多孩子嘬大拇指，但大多数大了就不会了。◊ *He grew out of his late night coffee habit.* 他逐渐放弃了晚上喝咖啡的习惯。

❑**grow up** *vi* (*be brought up*) 长大◊ *She grew up in Japan.* 她在日本长大。; (*be mature*) 成熟◊ *It's time you grew up.* 你到了应该成熟的时候了。

grower ['grəuə(r)] *n* [c] ♦**fruit/vegetable growers** 果/菜农

growing ['grəuɪŋ] *adj* **1** [+ *number*] 日趋增多的; [+ *concern, pressure, demand*] 越来越多的; [+ *interest, awareness*] 日益增强的; [+ *problem, evidence*] 日趋严重的 **2** [+ *child, plant*] 生长中的 ♦**fast-growing** [+ *business, market*] 高速发展的

growl [graul] **I** *vi* **1** [*dog, bear, lion* +] 嗥叫 **2** [*person* +] 咆哮 **II** *vt* [*person* +] 低吼 **III** *n* [c] **1** [*of dog, bear, lion*] 嗥叫 **2** [*of person*] 低吼

grown [grəun] **I** *pp of* **grow** **II** *adj* [+ *man, woman*] 成年的

grown-up [grəun'ʌp] **I** *n* [c] (*adult*) 成年人 **II** *adj* **1** (*fully grown*) 成人的 **2** (*mature*) 成熟的

growth [grəuθ] **I** *n* **1** [u/s] [*of economy, industry*] 发展 **2** [u] [*of child, animal, plant*] 生长 **3** [c] (*tumour*) 肿块 ♦**a growth in sth** 某方面的发展 ♦**population/earnings/sales growth** 人口/收入/销售量的增长 **II** *cpd* [复合词] [+ *industry, area*] 成长型

grub [grʌb] *n* **1** [c] (*larva*) 蛴螬 **2** [u] (*food*) 食物

grubby ['grʌbɪ] *adj* **1** (*dirty*) [+ *person, clothes*] 肮脏的 **2** (*sordid*) [+ *business, tactics*] 卑鄙的

grudge [grʌdʒ] *n* [c] (*grievance*) 积怨 ♦**to have** *or* **bear a grudge (against sb)** 对(某人)怀恨在心

grudging ['grʌdʒɪŋ] *adj* [+ *respect, admiration, acceptance*] 勉强的

gruelling (美 **grueling**) ['gruəlɪŋ] *adj* [+ *experience, activity, schedule*] 折磨人的

gruesome ['gru:səm] *adj* [+ *murder, discovery, details*] 令人毛骨悚然的

grumble ['grʌmbl] **I** *vi* (*complain*) 抱怨 **II** *vt* (*complain*) 表示不满 ♦**to grumble that ...** 抱怨… **III** *n* [c] (*complaint*) 抱怨

grumpy ['grʌmpɪ] *adj* 脾气坏的

grunt [grʌnt] **I** *vi* [*person* +] 发哼哼声; [*pig, bear* +] 发出呼噜声 **II** *vt* 咕哝着表示 **III** *n* [c] [*of person*] 咕哝声; [*of pig, bear*] 呼噜声

GSOH *abbr* (= ***good sense of humour***) 有幽默感

guarantee [gærən'ti:] **I** *n* [c] **1** (*assurance*) 保证 **2** [商] (*warranty*) 质保承诺 **II** *vt* **1** (*promise*) [+ *success, safety, happiness*] 确保 **2** (*ensure*) 保证 **3** [商] [+ *product, work*] 担保 ♦**a/no guarantee that ...** 有/没有…的保证 ♦**to guarantee (that) ...** 保证… ♦**to guarantee to do sth** 保证做某事

guaranteed [gærən'ti:d] *adj* [+ *income, price, rate*] 有保证的; [+ *success, satisfaction*] 确保的

guard [gɑ:d] **I** *n* **1** [c] (*sentry*) 警卫 **2** [u] (*squad*) 保卫队 **3** [c] [英: 铁路] 列车员 **4** [c] (*protective cover*) 防护装置 **II** *vt* [+ *building, entrance, door*] 守卫; [+ *person*] 保护; [+ *prisoner*] 看守 ♦**to be on one's guard (against)** 提防 ♦**to lower** *or* **drop one's guard** 放松警惕 ♦**to catch sb off (their) guard** 乘某人不备 ♦**to be on guard** 值班 ♦**to stand guard** 站岗 ♦**I will guard it with my life** 我将尽最大努力保护它

❑**guard against** *vt* [不可拆分] [+ *disease, damage*] 防止; [+ *complacency*] 警惕

guarded ['gɑ:dɪd] *adj* [+ *person, statement*] 谨慎的; [+ *optimism*] 有保留的 ♦**a closely guarded secret** 一个严格保守的秘密 ♦**the entrance was heavily guarded** 入口处戒备森严

guardian ['gɑ:dɪən] *n* [c] **1** [法] [*of minor*] 监护人 **2** (*defender*) 保护者

Guatemala [gwɑːtɪˈmɑːlə] *n* 危地马拉

Guatemalan [gwɑːtɪˈmɑːlən] **I** *adj* 危地马拉的 **II** *n* [c] 危地马拉人

guerrilla [gəˈrɪlə] **I** *n* [c] 游击队员 **II** *cpd* [复合词] [+ *group, war*] 游击队

guess [gɛs] **I** *vt, vi* **1** (*conjecture*) 猜测 **2** (*work out*) 推测 **II** *n* [c] 猜测 ♦ **I guess so** 我想是吧 ♦ **to guess (that) ...** (*conjecture*) 猜测…; (*work out*) 推测…; (*suppose*) 想… ♦ **to keep sb guessing** 让某人捉摸不定 ♦ **guess what** 没想到吧 ♦ **guess what I did last night** 猜猜我昨晚干什么了 ♦ **you're right, I guess** 我想你是对的 ♦ **my guess is (that) ...** 我的猜测是… ♦ **to take** *or* **have** *or* **make a guess** 猜猜看 ♦ **I'll give you three guesses** 我让你猜3次 ♦ **why it happened is anyone's** *or* **anybody's guess** 没人拿得准究竟是怎么回事 ♦ **best guess** 最佳猜测

❑ **guess at** *vt* [不可拆分] (*estimate*) 估计

guesswork [ˈgɛswəːk] *n* [u] (*speculation*) 猜测 ♦ **to take the guesswork out of sth** 排除某事中的不定因素

guest [gɛst] **I** *n* [c] (*at home*) 客人; (*on TV, radio show*) 特邀嘉宾; (*at special event*) 宾客; (*in hotel*) 房客 **II** *vi* 作特邀嘉宾 ♦ **be my guest** 请便 **III** *cpd* [复合词] [+ *speaker, appearance*] 特邀

guest house [ˈgɛsthaus] [英] *n* [c] 招待所

guest room *n* 客房

guidance [ˈgaɪdəns] *n* [u] (*advice*) 指导 ♦ **guidance on (doing) sth** (做) 某事的指导

guide [gaɪd] **I** *n* [c] **1** (*tour guide*) 导游 **2** (*local guide*) 向导 **3** (*also:* ***guide book***) 指南 **4** ♦ **Guide** [英] (*group member*) 女童子军成员 **II Guides** *n* [*pl*] [英] (*youth group*) 女童子军 [美=**Girl Scouts**] **III** *vt* **1** (*round city, museum etc*) 给…导游 **2** (*lead*) 给…领路 **3** (*with advice*) ♦ **to guide sb through sth** 指引某人做某事 **4** (*influence*) [*conscience, principles* +] 指引 **5** (*direct*) 引导

> **GUIDES**
> **Guides**（女童子军）是英国的 **Girl Guides** 或美国的 **Girl Scouts** 的成员，年龄一般在10到15岁之间（美国为10到14岁之间）。她们分成小组活动，培养实践能力和提高独立性。她们帮助社区其他成员，保护环境并了解不同的文化。活动主要围绕运动、户外技能、急救和看护动物等展开。

guidebook [ˈgaɪdbuk] *n* [c] 旅游指南

guided tour [ˈgaɪdɪd-] *n* [c] 有导游的游览

guide dog [英] *n* [c] 导盲犬 [美=**seeing-eye dog**]

guidelines [ˈgaɪdlaɪnz] *n* [*pl*] 指导方针

guild [gɪld] *n* [c] (*association*) 协会

guilt [gɪlt] *n* [u] **1** (*remorse*) 内疚 **2** (*responsibility*) 有罪

guilty [ˈgɪltɪ] *adj* **1** (*remorseful*) [+ *person, feelings*] 内疚的 **2** [+ *expression, smile*] 心虚的; [+ *secret, conscience*] 自知有过错的 **3** (*responsible*) 有过失的 **4** [法] 有罪的 ♦ **guilty of murder/manslaughter** 谋杀/误杀罪

Guinea [ˈgɪnɪ] *n* ♦ **Republic of Guinea** 几内亚

guinea pig [ˈgɪnɪ-] *n* **1** (*animal*) 豚鼠 **2** (*person*) 实验品

guise [gaɪz] *n* ♦ **in** *or* **under the guise of** 在…的幌子下 ♦ **in a different guise** 在不同的伪装下

guitar [gɪˈtɑː(r)] *n* [c] 吉他

gulf [gʌlf] **I** *n* **1** [c] (*bay*) 海湾 **2** [c] (*difference*) 鸿沟 **3** ♦ **the Gulf** 海湾地区 **II** *cpd* [复合词] ♦ **Gulf** [+ *war, crisis*] 海湾

gull [gʌl] *n* [c] (*seagull*) 海鸥

gullible [ˈgʌlɪbl] *adj* 易上当的

gully [ˈgʌlɪ] *n* [c] (*ravine*) 隘谷

gulp [gʌlp] **I** *vt* (*also:* ***gulp down***) [+ *food*] 狼吞虎咽地吞下; [+ *drink*] 大口地饮 **II** *vi* (*from nerves, excitement*) 哽住 **III** *n* [c] (*of air*) 一大口; (*of drink, food*) 吞咽 ♦ **to swallow sth in one gulp** [+ *food*] 将某物一口吞下; [+ *drink*] 将某物一饮而尽

gum [gʌm] *n* **1** [c] [解剖] 牙床 **2** [U] (*glue*) 胶 **3** [U] (*also:* ***chewing gum/ bubblegum***) 口香糖 **4** [c] (*also:* ***gumdrop***) (*sweet*) 胶姆糖
❑ **gum up** *vt* 使出毛病
gun [gʌn] *n* [c] (*small, medium-sized*) 枪; (*large*) 炮 ♦ **to stick to one's guns** 固执己见
❑ **gun down** *vt* 枪杀
❑ **gun for** *vt* [不可拆分] 伺机攻击
gunfire ['gʌnfaɪə(r)] *n* [U] 炮火
gunman ['gʌnmən] (*pl* **gunmen**) *n* [c] 持枪歹徒
gunpoint ['gʌnpɔɪnt] *n* ♦ **at gunpoint** 在枪口威胁下
gunpowder ['gʌnpaudə(r)] *n* [U] 火药
gunshot ['gʌnʃɔt] **I** *n* [c] (*act, sound*) 射击 **II** *cpd* [复合词] [+ *wound*] 枪击
gurney ['gəːnɪ] *n* [c] 有轮子的病床 [英 = **trolley**]
gush [gʌʃ] **I** *vi* **1** [*blood, water, oil* +] 喷出 **2** [*person* +] 表现过火 **II** *n* [s] [*of water*] 涌流
gust [gʌst] **I** *n* [c] [*of wind*] 一阵 **II** *vi* [*wind* +] 狂风大作
gut [gʌt] **I** *n* **1** [c] (*intestine*) 肠子 **2** [U] [音, 体育] (*also:* ***catgut***) 羊肠线 **3** [c] (*pot belly*) 肚子 **II** *vt* **1** [+ *animal, fish*] 取出…的内脏 **2** [+ *building*] 损毁…的内部 **III guts** *n* [*pl*] **1** [解剖] [*of person, animal*] 内脏 **2** (*courage*) 勇气 ♦ **to hate sb's guts** 对某人恨之入骨 **IV** *cpd* [复合词] [+ *feeling, reaction, instinct*] 直觉
gutter ['gʌtə(r)] *n* [c] **1** (*in street*) 阴沟 **2** (*of roof*) 檐槽 ♦ **to end up in the gutter** 最终落得一无所有
guy [gaɪ] *n* [c] **1** (*man*) 家伙 **2** [英] (*effigy*) 盖伊•福克斯像 **3** (*also:* ***guy rope***) 支索 ♦ **(you) guys** 伙计们
Guy Fawkes Night [gaɪ'fɔːks-] (英) *n* U 篝火之夜

> **Guy Fawkes Night**
> 每年的11月5日，是英国人纪念揭穿盖•福克斯（Guy Fawkes）Gunpowder Plot（火药阴谋）的日子—1605年11月5日，盖•福克斯企图引爆英国国会两院。孩子们用旧衣服做成盖•福克斯的头像（称为guys），并向过路人要钱，用以在Guy Fawkes Night购买烟花。这个节日也被叫做Bonfire Night，人们在公园和花园里点燃篝火，并在篝火上焚烧盖•福克斯的头像。

Guyana [gaɪ'ænə] *n* 圭亚那
guzzle ['gʌzl] *vt* [+ *drink*] 狂饮; [+ *food*] 大吃
gym [dʒɪm] *n* **1** [c] (*also:* ***gymnasium***) 健身房 **2** [U] (*also:* ***gymnastics***) 体操
gymnast ['dʒɪmnæst] *n* [c] 体操运动员
gymnastics [dʒɪm'næstɪks] *n* [U] 体操
gym shoes *n* [*pl*] 体操鞋
gynaecologist (美 **gynecologist**) [gaɪnɪ'kɔlədʒɪst] *n* [c] 妇科医生
gypsy ['dʒɪpsɪ] *n* [c] 吉卜赛人

Hh

H, h [eɪtʃ] *n* [c/u] (*letter*) 英语的第八个字母

habit ['hæbɪt] *n* **1** [c/u] (*custom, practice*) 习惯 **2** [c] (*also:* ***drug habit***) 瘾 **3** [c] [宗] (*costume*) 宗袍 ♦**to be in the habit of doing sth** 有做某事的习惯 ♦**to have a habit of doing sth** 习惯做某事 ♦**to get out of/into the habit of doing sth** 改掉/养成做某事的习惯 ♦**to do sth out of habit** 出于习惯做某事 ♦**don't make a habit of it** 别经常这么做 ♦**a bad habit** 坏习惯

habitat ['hæbɪtæt] *n* [c/u] 栖息地

habitual [hə'bɪtjuəl] *adj* **1** [+ *action*] 通常的 **2** [+ *drinker, criminal, liar*] 积习已深的

habitually [hə'bɪtjuəlɪ] *adv* [+ *late, untidy etc*] 习惯性地

hack [hæk] **I** *vt, vi* 砍 **II** *n* [c] [贬] (*writer*) 雇佣文人 ♦**to hack (away) at sth with a knife** 用刀乱砍某物 ♦**to hack (one's way/a path) through the jungle** 从丛林中开出条路来 ♦**to hack sb to death** 乱刀砍死某人 ♦**to hack sb/sth to pieces** 把某人/某物砍碎 ♦**he can't hack it as a singer** [非正式] 他没本事做歌手

❑**hack into** *vt* [不可拆分] [+ *computer system*] 窃入

❑**hack off** *vt* 砍下

hacker ['hækə(r)] [计算机] *n* [c] 黑客

had [hæd] *pt, pp of* **have**

haddock ['hædək] (*pl* **haddock**) *n* [c/u] 黑线鳕 ♦**smoked haddock** 熏鳕鱼

hadn't ['hædnt] = **had not**

haemorrhage (美 **hemorrhage**) ['hɛmərɪdʒ] **I** *n* [c/u] 出血 **II** *vi* 出血 ♦**to have a brain haemorrhage** 大脑内出血

haemorrhoids (美 **hemorrhoids**) ['hɛmərɔɪdz] *n* [*pl*] 痔疮

haggle ['hægl] *vi* **1** (*bargain*) 讨价还价 **2** (*argue*) 争论 ♦**to haggle over the price of sth** 就某物讨价还价

hail [heɪl] **I** *n* [u] 冰雹 **II** *vt* [+ *taxi*] 招手叫停; [文] [+ *person*] 招呼 **III** *vi* 下雹 ♦**he died in a hail of bullets** 他死于一阵弹雨 ♦**the meeting was hailed as a triumph** 会议被认为是一大成功 ♦**he hails from Scotland** 他来自苏格兰

hailstone ['heɪlstəun] *n* [c] 冰雹

hair [hɛə(r)] *n* **1** (*human*) [u] (*on head*) 头发; [u] (*on body*) 汗毛; [c] (*single strand*) 毛发 **2** [c/u] (*animal*) (*on body, single strand*) 毛毛 **3** [c] (*on plants and insects*) 绒毛 ♦**to do one's hair** 梳头 ♦**to have** *or* **get one's hair done** (*styled*) 打理头发 ♦**to have** *or* **get one's hair cut** 剪头发 ♦**by a hair's breadth** (喻) 极端的距离 ♦**to let one's hair down** (喻) 放松一点 ♦**to make sb's hair stand on end** (喻) 使某人毛骨悚然 ♦**not a hair out of place** 衣着一丝不乱 ♦**he didn't turn a hair** 泰然处之 ♦**to get in sb's hair** 惹恼某人

hairbrush ['hɛəbrʌʃ] *n* [c] 发刷

haircut ['hɛəkʌt] *n* [c] **1** (*at hairdresser's etc*) 理发 **2** (*hairstyle*) 发型 ♦**to have** *or* **get a haircut** 剪头发

hairdo ['hɛədu:] [非正式] *n* [c] 发型

hairdresser ['hɛədrɛsə(r)] *n* [c] **1** (*person*) 美发师 **2** (*also:* ***hairdresser's***) 发廊

hairdryer ['hɛədraɪə(r)] *n* [c] 吹风机

hair gel *n* [u] 发胶

hairspray ['hɛəspreɪ] *n* [u] 喷发定型剂

hairstyle ['hɛəstaɪl] *n* [c] 发型

hairy ['hɛərɪ] *adj* **1** [+ *person, arms, animal*] 多毛的 **2** [+ *leaf, stem*] 毛茸茸的 **3** [非正式] [+ *situation*] 惊险的

Haiti ['heɪtɪ] *n* 海地

hake [heɪk] (*pl* **hake**) *n* [c/u] 狗鳕

✪**half** [hɑ:f] (*pl* **halves**) **I** *n* [c], *pron* **1** [*of amount, object*] 一半 ◊ *Just give me half (of) that, please.* 请给我一半。◊ *We ate half (of) the cake.* 我们吃了蛋糕的一半。◊ *The bridge was re-built in two halves.* 桥是分开两半重建的。**2** [c] [英] [*of beer etc*]

半品脱 ◊ *a half of lager* 半品脱贮藏啤酒 **3** [C] [英] (*child's ticket*) 半票 ◊ *A half to Oxford Street, please.* 请给一张到牛津街的半价票。**II** *adj* [+ *bottle*] 一半的 ◊ *a half bottle of wine* 半瓶葡萄酒 **III** *adv* [非正式] [+ *empty, closed, open, asleep*] 半 ◊ *By the end of his speech the room was half empty.* 他讲完话时，人已走了一半了。♦ **the two halves of the brain** 左右脑 ♦ **the first/second half** [体育] 上/下半场 ♦ **to cut sth in half** 把某物切成两半 ♦ **two/three** *etc* **and a half** 二/三{等}点五 ♦ **half a pound/kilo/mile** *etc* 半磅/公斤/英里{等} ♦ **half a pint** 半品脱 ♦ **a day/week/pound** *etc* **and a half** 一天/星期/磅{等}半 ♦ **half a dozen** 半打 ♦ **half an hour** 半小时 ♦ **half past three/four** *etc* 三/四{等}点半 ♦ **half three/four** *etc* [英:非正式] 三/四{等}点半 ♦ **he was drunk half the time** [非正式] 他大部分时候都是喝醉的 ♦ **to be half German/Irish** *etc* 有一半德国/爱尔兰{等}血统的 ♦ **half as much (as)** …的一半 ♦ **to go halves (with sb on sth)** (与某人)平摊(某物的费用) ♦ **she never does things by halves** 她做事总是很彻底的 ♦ **she's half his age** 她的年龄是他的一半 ♦ **he's too clever by half!** 他聪明过头了！

half board [尤英] *n* [U] 半膳宿

half-brother ['hɑːfbrʌðə(r)] *n* [C] (*same mother, different father*) 同母异父的兄弟; (*same father, different mother*) 同父异母的兄弟

half day *n* [C] 半日

half fare *n* [C] (*on bus, train etc*) 半票

half-hearted ['hɑːf'hɑːtɪd] *adj* [+ *attempt, apology*] 心不在焉的

half-hour [hɑːf'auə(r)] **I** *n* [C] 半小时 **II** *cpd* [复合词] [+ *programme, film, drive*] 半小时

half price ['hɑːf'praɪs] **I** *adj* 半价的 **II** *adv* 半价地 **III** *n* [U] ♦ **we sold them at half price** 我们把它们半价卖了 ♦ **we got it for half price** 我们半价买的

half-sister ['hɑːfsɪstə(r)] *n* [C] (*same mother, different father*) 同母异父的姐妹; (*same father, different mother*) 同父异母的姐妹

half-term [hɑːf'təːm] [英:教育] *n* [C/U] 期中假 ♦ **at half-term** 期中假时

half-time [hɑːf'taɪm] [体育] *n* [U] 半场 ♦ **at half-time** 半场时

halfway ['hɑːf'weɪ] *adv* (*between two points*) 到一半 ♦ **to meet sb halfway** (喻)和某人折中妥协 ♦ **halfway through sth** 在某事过了一半时 ♦ **the halfway point** *or* **stage of a race** 比赛中点时

halibut ['hælɪbət] (*pl* **halibut**) *n* [C/U] 大比目鱼

hall [hɔːl] *n* **1** [C] [尤英] (*entrance*) 门厅 [美=**entrance hall**] **2** [C] (*room*) 礼堂 **3** [大学] ♦ **to live in hall** [英], **to live in a hall** [美] 住宿舍

hallmark ['hɔːlmɑːk] *n* [C] **1** (*on metal*) 纯度印记 **2** [*of writer, artist, style*] 特征

hallo [hə'ləu] *int* = **hello**

hall of residence [英] (*pl* **halls of residence**) *n* [C] 宿舍

Halloween ['hæləu'iːn] *n* [U] 万圣节

> **HALLOWEEN**
> 很早以前，人们相信在 **Halloween**（10月31日万圣节）的夜晚，死人的灵魂会重返人间。如今，万圣节为孩子们装扮成巫婆和鬼魂提供了一个好机会。孩子们去敲邻居的门，问邻居是要给 **treat** 还是要 **trick**。如果没有糖果或钱（即 **treat**），孩子们就会威胁要玩把戏（即 **trick**）来捉弄你。

hallucination [həluːsɪ'neɪʃən] *n* [C/U] 幻觉

hallway ['hɔːlweɪ] [英] *n* [C] (*vestibule*) 门厅

halo ['heɪləu] *n* [C] [*of saint, angel*] 光轮; (*around object, planet*) 晕

halt [hɔːlt] **I** *vt* [+ *person, vehicle, movement*] 使停止; [+ *progress, activity, growth*] 阻止 **II** *vi* [*person, vehicle* +] 停止; [*progress, activity, growth* +] 阻止 ♦ **to call a halt to sth** 命令停止 ♦ **to come to a halt** 停了下来 ♦ **to bring sth to a halt** 制止某事

halve [hɑːv] **I** *vt* **1** (*reduce*) 将…减半 **2** (*divide in two*) 将…分成两半 **II** *vi* (*decrease by half*) 减半

halves [hɑːvz] *pl of* **half**

ham [hæm] **I** *n* **1** (*meat, joint*) 火腿 **2** [非正式] (*actor*) 蹩脚演员 **II** *cpd* [复合词] [+ *sandwich, roll, salad*] 火腿

hamburger [ˈhæmbəːgə(r)] *n* [c] 汉堡包

hamlet [ˈhæmlɪt] *n* [c] 小村庄

hammer [ˈhæmə(r)] **I** *n* [c] (*tool*) 锤子 **II** *vt* **1** [+ *nail*] 锤击 **2** [尤英：非正式] (*attack*) 严厉批评 **3** [英：非正式] (*beat*) 击败 **III** *vi* (*on door, table, surface*) 接连捶打 ♦**to hammer an idea into sb** *or* **across to sb** 反复地向某人灌输一个观点 ♦**to hammer away at sth** [+ *subject, theme*] 不断地致力于某事
❑**hammer in** *vt* [+ *nail*] 锤击
❑**hammer out** *vt* (喻) [+ *solution, agreement*] 推敲出

hammock [ˈhæmək] *n* [c] 吊床

hamper [ˈhæmpə(r)] **I** *vt* [+ *person, movement, effort*] 阻碍 **II** *n* [c] 食品篮

hamster [ˈhæmstə(r)] *n* [c] 仓鼠

hamstring [ˈhæmstrɪŋ] **I** *n* [c] 腘腱 **II** *vt* [+ *person, development*] 使受挫

✪**hand** [hænd] **I** *n* **1** [c] [解剖] 手 **2** [c] [*of clock*] 指针 **3** [c] (*worker*) 工人 **4** [U] [文] (*handwriting*) 手迹 ◊ *The manuscripts were written in Bach's own hand.* 这些手稿是巴赫本人的手迹。**5** [c] [*of cards*] 一手牌 **6** [c] (*measurement*) 一手之宽 **II** *vt* (*pass, give*) 递 ◊ *He handed me a piece of paper.* 他递给我一张纸。♦**to do sth by hand** 手工制作 ♦**"hands off!"** 别碰！♦**in sb's hands** 在某人照管下 ♦**to be in safe hands/the wrong hands** 在可靠/不可靠的人手中 **to get** *or* **lay one's hands on sth** [非正式] 找到某物 ♦**to join hands** 手拉手 ♦**hand in hand** (*holding hands*) 手拉手 ♦**to go hand in hand (with sth)** (和某事) 密切关联地 ♦**to have one's hands full (with sth)** 手头忙于 (某事) ♦**to give** *or* **lend sb a hand (with sth)** 帮某人 (做某事) ♦**to have a hand in sth** 参与某事 ♦**to be (near** *or* **close) at hand** 在附近 ♦**Hughes finished with 15 seconds in hand** [英] 休斯完成时还剩下15秒 ♦**the job in hand** 手头的工作 ♦**we have the matter in hand** 我们控制了局势 ♦**to be on hand** [*person, services etc* +] 在近处 ♦**to reject/dismiss sth out of hand** 不假思索地拒绝/抛弃某事 ♦**to have sth to hand** [+ *information etc*] 手头有某物 ♦**on the one hand ..., on the other hand ...** 一方面…，另一方面…
❑**hand around** *vt* (*distribute*) 传递
❑**hand down** *vt* [+ *knowledge, possessions*] 传下去
❑**hand in** *vt* 上交
❑**hand out** *vt* 分配
❑**hand over** *vt* [+ *object, present, letter*] 交给; [+ *prisoner, hostage*] 移交
❑**hand over to** *vt* 移交
❑**hand round** [英] *vt* = **hand around**

handbag [ˈhændbæg] [英] *n* [c] 手包 [美 = **purse**]

hand baggage *n* [U] 手提行李

handbook [ˈhændbuk] *n* [c] 手册

handbrake [ˈhændbreɪk] [尤英] *n* [c] 手闸 [美 = **emergency brake**]

handcuffs [ˈhændkʌfs] *n* [*pl*] 手铐 ♦**in handcuffs** 带手铐

handful [ˈhændful] *n* [c] [*of soil, stones, sand*] 一把 ♦**a handful of** [+ *people, places etc*] 少数 ♦**she's quite a handful** [非正式] 她真难管

handicap [ˈhændɪkæp] **I** *n* [c] **1** (*disability*) 残疾 **2** (*disadvantage*) 不利条件 **3** [高尔夫] 差点 **II** *vt* (*hamper*) 妨碍

handicapped [ˈhændɪkæpt] *adj* 有残疾的 ♦**mentally/physically handicapped** 心理/身体残疾的

handkerchief [ˈhæŋkətʃɪf] *n* [c] 手帕

handle [ˈhændl] **I** *n* [c] [*of bag*] 把手; [*of cup, knife, paintbrush, broom, spade*] 柄; [*of door, window*] 拉手 **II** *vt* **1** (*hold*) [+ *object, ornament*] 拿; [+ *baby*] 抱 **2** (*operate*) [+ *gun, car*] 操纵 **3** (*deal with*) [+ *problem, job, responsibility*] 处理; [+ *people*] 对付 **III** *vi* (*perform*) 操作 ♦**to fly off the handle** [非正式] 勃然大怒 ♦**to get a handle on a problem** [非正式] 控

制某个问题 ♦ **"handle with care"** 小心轻放

handlebars ['hændlbɑː(z)] *n* [*pl*] 把手

hand luggage *n* [U] 手提行李

handmade ['hænd'meɪd] *adj* 手工制作的

handout ['hændaut] *n* [C] (*money, clothing, food etc*) 接济物; (*notes*) (*at lecture, meeting etc*) 讲义; (*publicity leaflet*) 传单

hands-free kit ['hændz'friː-] *n* [C] 手机车载免提套件

handsome ['hænsəm] *adj* 1 (*attractive*) [+ *man*] 英俊的; [+ *woman*] 健美的; [+ *building*] 堂皇的 2 (*good*) [+ *profit, return*] 大方的 ◊ *They made a handsome profit on the sale of the flat.* 他们从卖房中获得相当大的利润。; [+ *victory*] 出色的

handwriting ['hændraɪtɪŋ] *n* [U] 笔迹

handy ['hændɪ] *adj* 1 (*useful*) 方便的 2 (*close at hand*) 手边的 3 ♦ **to be handy with sth** 巧于某事 ♦ **to come in handy** 迟早有用 ♦ **to be handy for doing sth** 对做某事有用

hang [hæŋ] (*pt, pp* **hung**) **I** *vt* 1 [+ *clothes, light, picture*] 挂 2 (*execute*) [+ *criminal*] (*pt, pp* **hanged**) 吊死 **II** *vi* 1 (*be suspended*) [*clothes, light, picture* +] 悬挂; [*breath, smoke, smell* +] 飘浮 2 (*fall*) [*clothing, fabric, hair* +] 垂 ♦ **to hang one's head (in shame)** (羞愧得)低下头 ♦ **the walls are hung with old pictures** 墙上挂着旧画 ♦ **to hang loose** [*hair* +] 披散; [*arms* +] 轻松下垂 ♦ **to hang open** [*door, mouth* +] 开着 **III** *n* ♦ **to get the hang of sth** [非正式] 掌握某事的方法

❑ **hang about** *vi* = **hang around**

❑ **hang around** [非正式] **I** *vi* 闲荡 **II** *vt* [不可拆分] 闲荡

❑ **hang back** *vi* (*hesitate*) 踌躇不前

❑ **hang down** *vi* 吊下来

❑ **hang on I** *vi* (*wait*) 稍等 **II** *vt* [不可拆分] (*depend on*) 有赖于

❑ **hang onto, hang on to** *vt* [不可拆分] 1 (*grasp*) 紧紧抓住 2 [非正式: 喻] (*keep*) 保留

❑ **hang out I** *vt* [+ *washing*] 晾 **II** *vi* 1 [*washing* +] 晾 2 [非正式] (*go*) 闲荡

❑ **hang round** [英] *vi* = **hang around**

❑ **hang together** *vi* [*argument, story* +] 一致

❑ **hang up I** *vi* [通信] 挂断电话 **II** *vt* [+ *coat, hat, clothes*] 挂起

❑ **hang up on** *vt* [不可拆分] [通信] 挂断…电话

hanger ['hæŋə(r)] *n* [C] (*also:* ***coat hanger***) 衣架

hang-gliding ['hæŋglaɪdɪŋ] *n* [U] 悬挂式滑翔运动 ♦ **to go hang-gliding** 做悬挂式滑翔运动

hangover ['hæŋəuvə(r)] *n* [C] (*after drinking*) 宿醉 ♦ **a hangover from the past** 遗留物

hankie ['hæŋkɪ] [非正式] *n* = **hanky**

hanky ['hæŋkɪ] [非正式] *n* 手帕

haphazard [hæp'hæzəd] *adj* [+ *system, arrangement*] 杂乱的

✪ **happen** ['hæpən] *vi* (*occur, result*) [*incident, accident* +] 发生 ◊ *What's happening?* 发生什么事? ♦ **what will happen if ...?** 如果…会怎么样? ♦ **tell me what happened** 告诉我发生了什么事 ♦ **to happen to do sth** 刚巧做某事 ♦ **as it happens** 碰巧 ♦ **it's the best thing that ever happened to me** 我从未遇上这么好的事情

❑ **happen (up)on** *vt* [不可拆分] 偶然发现

happily ['hæpɪlɪ] *adv* 1 (*fortunately*) 幸运地 2 (*cheerfully*) 愉快地 ♦ **happily married** 婚姻幸福 ♦ **I will happily do it for you** 我很高兴帮你做这件事 ♦ **and they all lived happily ever after** 他们永远幸福地生活下去

happiness ['hæpɪnɪs] *n* [U] 幸福

happy ['hæpɪ] *adj* 1 (*contented*) [+ *person, mood*] 高兴的; [+ *face*] 愉快的 ◊ *I was happy to hear that you passed your exams.* 非常高兴听到你考试通过了。 2 (*cheerful*) [+ *life, childhood, marriage, place*] 美满的 3 (*fortunate*) [+ *coincidence*] 幸运的 ♦ **to be happy with sth** (*satisfied*) 对某事满意 ♦ **to be happy to do sth** (*willing*) 乐意做某事 ♦ **to be happy for sb to do sth** 乐意让某人做某

事 ♦ **to be happy for sb** (*delighted*) 为某人高兴 ♦ **to have a happy ending** [*story* +] 有个美满的结局; [*incident* +] 有个圆满的结局 ♦ **happy birthday!** 生日快乐! ♦ **happy Christmas!** 圣诞快乐! ♦ **happy Easter!** 复活节快乐! ♦ **happy anniversary!** 周年纪念日快乐!

harass [ˈhærəs] *vt* (*annoy, pester*) 骚扰

harassment [ˈhærəsmənt] *n* [U] 骚扰 ♦ **sexual harassment** 性骚扰

harbour (美 **harbor**) [ˈhɑːbə(r)] **I** *n* [C] [航海] 港口 **II** *vt* **1** [+ *hope, fear*] 心怀 **2** [+ *criminal, fugitive*] 藏匿 ♦ **to harbour a grudge against sb** 对某人心怀怨恨

✪ **hard** [hɑːd] **I** *adj* **1** (*not soft*) [+ *surface, object*] 硬的 ◊ *the hard wooden floor* 硬木地板 **2** (*not easy*) [+ *question, problem*] 困难的 ◊ *That is a very hard question to answer.* 那个问题很难回答。; [+ *work*] 费力的 ◊ *Their work is hard and dangerous.* 他们的工作既费力又危险。; [+ *life, time*] 艰辛的 ◊ *He's had a very hard life.* 他的生活很艰难。 **3** (*violent*) [+ *push, punch, kick*] 用力的 **4** (*severe*) [+ *person, expression*] 苛刻的 **5** [化] [+ *water*] 硬的 **6** (*cold*) [+ *winter, frost*] 寒冷的 **II** *adv* **1** [*work, try, think* +] 努力地 ◊ *I've been working hard all day.* 我已努力地工作了一整天。 **2** [*laugh, rain, snow* +] 猛烈地 ◊ *I've never seen Terry laugh so hard.* 我从没见过特里笑得那么厉害。 ♦ **the wind is blowing hard** 风猛烈地刮着 **3** (*violently*) [*hit, punch, kick* +] 用力地 ♦ **it is hard to understand what is happening** 很难理解现在发生了什么事情 ♦ **it's hard to tell/say/know** 很难讲/说/知道 ♦ **such events are hard to understand** 这种事很难理解 ♦ **to be hard to please** 难以取悦 ♦ **to find it hard to do sth** 觉得做某事困难 ♦ **it's hard work serving in a shop** 商店工作很难做 ♦ **hard luck!** 真倒霉! ♦ **to be hard on sb** [*person* +] 对某人过分严厉; [*situation* +] 对某人来说有害 ♦ **no hard feelings!** 别记仇! ♦ **to be hard of hearing** 听力不佳 ♦ **to feel hard done by** [英] 觉得受到不公平待遇 ♦ **hard evidence/facts** 铁证/客观的事实 ♦ **be hard put** *or* **pushed to do sth** 难以做某事 ♦ **to look hard at** (*stare at*) [+ *person*] 盯着; (*consider*) [+ *idea, problem, situation*] 认真考虑

hardback [ˈhɑːdbæk] *n* [C] (*book*) 精装本 ♦ **it's only available in hardback** 只有精装本

hard-boiled egg [ˈhɑːdˈbɔɪld-] *n* [C] 煮老了的鸡蛋

hard disk [计算机] *n* [C] 硬盘

hard drugs *n* [*pl*] 烈性毒品

harden [ˈhɑːdn] **I** *vt* **1** [+ *wax, glue etc*] 使变硬 **2** [+ *person, attitude, resolve*] 使变得冷酷无情 **II** *vi* **1** [*wax, glue etc* +] 变硬 **2** [*person, attitude, resolve* +] 变得冷酷无情 ♦ **to harden one's heart** 使心肠变硬

hardly [ˈhɑːdlɪ] *adv* **1** (*scarcely*) 几乎不 **2** (*no sooner*) ♦ **he had hardly sat down when the door burst open** 他一坐下门就被猛地打开了 ♦ **hardly ever/any/anyone** 几乎从不/没有/没有任何人 ♦ **I can hardly believe it** 我简直不能相信 ♦ **it's hardly surprising** 并不出奇

hardship [ˈhɑːdʃɪp] *n* [C/U] 困难

hard shoulder [尤英] *n* [C] 高速公路紧急停车带 [美=**shoulder**]

hard up [非正式] *adj* 拮据的

hardware [ˈhɑːdwɛə(r)] *n* [U] **1** (*ironmongery*) 五金制品 **2** [计算机] 硬件 **3** [军] 重武器

hardware store *n* [C] 五金商店

hardworking [hɑːdˈwəːkɪŋ] *adj* [+ *employee, student*] 勤奋的

hardy [ˈhɑːdɪ] *adj* [+ *animal, person*] 能吃苦的; [+ *plant*] 耐寒的

hare [hɛə(r)] *n* **1** [C] (*animal*) 野兔 **2** [U] (*meat*) 野兔肉
❑ **hare off** [英: 非正式] *vi* 飞跑

harm [hɑːm] **I** *vt* **1** (*damage*) 损坏 **2** (*injure*) 伤害 **II** *n* [U] **1** (*damage*) 损害 **2** (*injury*) 伤害 ♦ **to mean no harm** 没有恶意 ♦ **out of harm's way** 在安全的地方 ♦ **there's no harm (in) trying** 试一试也无妨 ♦ **to come to no harm** 平安无事 ♦ **to do more harm than good** 得

不偿失 ♦**it wouldn't do any harm (for you) to get an answerphone** 买个录音电话(对你)没什么害处

harmful ['hɑːmful] *adj* [+ *effect, chemical, influence*] 有害的 ♦**to be harmful to sb/sth** 对某人/某物有害

harmless ['hɑːmlɪs] *adj* 1 (*safe*) 无害的 2 (*inoffensive*) [+ *person, joke, pleasure, activity*] 无恶意的

harmonica [hɑː'mɔnɪkə] *n* [C] 口琴

harmonious [hɑː'məunɪəs] *adj* 1 [+ *discussion, relationship*] 和睦的 2 [+ *balance, layout, pattern*] 协调的 3 [+ *sound, tune*] 悦耳的

harmony ['hɑːmənɪ] *n* [U] 1 (*accord*) 和睦 2 [音] 和声 ♦**in harmony (with)** [*work, live* +] 与…协调一致

harness ['hɑːnɪs] **I** *n* [C] 1 (*for horse, dog etc*) 挽具 2 (*safety harness*) 安全带 **II** *vt* 1 [+ *resources, energy*] 利用 2 [+ *horse, dog*] 套上

harp [hɑːp] **I** *n* [C] [音] 竖琴 **II** *vi* ♦**to harp on (about sth)** [贬] (对某事)唠唠叨叨

harrowing ['hærəuɪŋ] *adj* [+ *film, experience*] 令人伤心的

harsh [hɑːʃ] *adj* 1 [+ *criticism, sentence, treatment*] 严酷的 2 [+ *conditions, climate, winter*] 恶劣的 3 [+ *sound, light*] 刺耳的; [+ *chemical*] 刺激性的

harvest ['hɑːvɪst] **I** *n* 1 [C/U] (*harvest time*) 收获 2 [C] (*crop*) 收成 **II** *vt* [+ *wheat, fruit, potatoes*] 收割

has [hæz] *vb see* **have**

hasn't ['hæznt] = **has not**

hassle ['hæsl] [非正式] **I** *n* [C/U] (*bother*) 麻烦 **II** *vt* [+ *person*] 打扰

haste [heɪst] *n* [U] 仓促 ♦**in haste** 匆忙地 ♦**to make haste (to)** [过时] 赶快

hasten ['heɪsn] **I** *vt* [+ *decision, downfall, process etc*] 加速 **II** *vi* [文] 赶快 ♦**to hasten to do sth** 赶快做某事 ♦**I hasten to add ...** 我急忙补充说… ♦**to hasten to say ...** 忙不迭地说…

hastily ['heɪstɪlɪ] *adv* 1 (*hurriedly*) 赶快地 2 (*rashly*) 仓促地

hasty ['heɪstɪ] *adj* 1 (*hurried*) [+ *departure, return*] 仓促的 2 (*rash*) [+ *decision, reply*] 草率的 ♦**don't be hasty** 别性急

hat [hæt] *n* [C] 帽子 ♦**to keep sth under one's hat** 对某事保守秘密 ♦**at the drop of a hat** 毫不迟疑地 ♦**that's old hat now** 那已经过时了 ♦**to take one's hat off to sb** 向某人表示赞赏 ♦**to talk through one's hat** 胡说

hatch [hætʃ] **I** *n* [C] 1 [航海] 舱口 2 [尤英] (*also:* ***serving hatch***) 小窗口 **II** *vi* 1 [*bird* +] 出壳 2 [*egg* +] 孵化 **III** *vt* 1 [+ *egg*] 孵 2 [+ *plot, scheme*] 策划 ♦**to be hatched** 孵出

hatchback ['hætʃbæk] *n* [C] 有仓门式后背的汽车

hate [heɪt] **I** *vt* [+ *person*] 恨; [+ *food, activity, sensation*] 讨厌 **II** *n* [U] 仇恨 ♦**to hate doing/to do sth** 不喜欢做某事 ♦**I hate to trouble you, but ...** 我本不愿意麻烦你，但是… ♦**I hate to tell you this, but ...** 我抱歉地告诉你…

hatred ['heɪtrɪd] *n* [U] 仇恨

haul [hɔːl] **I** *vt* ♦**to haul sth/sb up/out** *etc* 用力拉某物/某人起来/出来{等} **II** *n* [C] [*of stolen goods*] 被窃物 ♦**to haul o.s. out of sth** 把自己硬拉出某物 ♦**to be hauled (up) before the court** 被送上法庭 ♦**a long haul** 长久战

haunt [hɔːnt] **I** *vt* 1 [*ghost, spirit* +] 常出没于 2 [*problem, memory, fear* +] 萦绕在心头 **II** *n* [C] 常去的地方

haunted ['hɔːntɪd] *adj* 1 [+ *house, building*] 闹鬼的 2 [+ *expression*] 愁容满面的

✪ **have**

KEYWORD

[hæv] (*pt, pp* **had**)

I *vt*

1 (*possess*) 有 ♦**he has** *or* **he has got blue eyes/dark hair** 他长着蓝眼睛/黑头发 ♦**do you have** *or* **have you got a car/phone?** 你有车/电话吗? ♦**I have** *or* **I have got an idea** 我有个主意 ♦**to have** *or* **have got sth to do** 有必须得做的事 ♦**she had her eyes closed** 她闭上了眼睛

2 (*with meals, drinks*) ♦**to have breakfast** 吃早饭 ♦**to have a**

drink/a cigarette 喝一杯/抽支烟
3 (*with activity*) ♦**to have a swim/bath** 游泳/洗澡 ♦**to have a meeting/party** 开会/开派对
4 (*receive, obtain*) 得到 ♦**can I have a packet of sugar, please?** 请给我一包糖，好吗？♦**can I have your address?** 能告诉我你的地址吗？♦**you can have it for £5** 付5英磅它就是你的了 ♦**I must have it by tomorrow** 明天以前我必须得到它
5 (*give birth to*) ♦**to have a baby** 生孩子
6 (*allow*) 容忍 ♦**I won't have it!** 我绝不允许！♦**we can't have that** 我们绝不允许那样
7 ♦**to have sth done** 指使/安排做某事 ♦**to have one's hair cut** 理发
8 (*experience, suffer*) ♦**to have a headache** 头痛 ♦**to have a cold/flu/diabetes** 得感冒/流感/糖尿病 ♦**to have a heart attack** 心脏病发作 ♦**to have an operation** 动手术 ♦**she had her bag stolen/her arm broken** 她的包被偷了/她的胳膊断了
9 [非正式] (*dupe*) ♦**to be had** 被骗 ♦**you've been had!** 你被骗了！
10 [非正式] ♦**to have had it** (*be in trouble*) 没希望了
II *aux vb*
1 ♦**to have arrived/gone** 已到了/走了 ♦**has he told you?** 他已经告诉你了吗？♦**when she had dressed, she went downstairs** 穿好衣服后，她下了楼 ♦**having lived abroad for years, I wasn't familiar with ...** 已在国外呆了多年，我都对…不熟悉了 ♦**I haven't seen him for ages/since July** 我已经很久/自7月以来就没见过他了
2 (*in tag questions*) ♦**you've done it, haven't you?** 你已经做了，是不是？♦**he hasn't done it, has he?** 他还没做，是吗？
3 (*in short answers and questions*) ♦**yes, I have** 是的，我有/已做了 ♦**no I haven't!** 不，我还没有/没做呢！ ♦**so have I!** 我也一样！ ♦**neither have I** 我也没有过 ♦**"I've seen this movie before" – "oh have you?"** "我以前看过这部电影"–"噢，是吗？" ♦**"we haven't been there before" – "oh haven't you?"** "我们以前没去过那儿"–"噢，是吗？" ♦**I've finished, have you?** 我已经完成了，你呢？
4 (*be obliged*) ♦**to have (got) to do sth** 不得不做某事 ♦**she has (got) to do it** 她必须得这么做 ♦**this has (got) to be a mistake** 这一定是个错误 ♦**he had to go away** 他必须得走
❑**have in** [非正式] *vt* ♦**to have it in for sb** 对某人怀恨在心
❑**have on** *vt* 1 [+ *clothes*] 穿着 ♦**he didn't have anything on** 他什么都没穿 ♦**I don't have any money on me** 我一点钱都没带 2 [英:非正式] (*tease*) 逗 ♦**you're having me on!** 你在逗我！ 3 ♦**to have sth on** 已安排了某事 ♦**do you have anything on tomorrow?** 你明天有事吗？
❑**have out** *vt* ♦**to have it out with sb** 同某人辩个明白

haven ['heɪvn] *n* [c] 避难处
haven't ['hævnt] = **have not**
havoc ['hævək] *n* [u] 大破坏 ♦**to cause havoc** 使混乱 ♦**to play havoc with** *or* **wreak havoc on sth** 扰乱某事
Hawaii [hə'waɪiː] *n* 夏威夷
Hawaiian [hə'waɪjən] **I** *adj* 夏威夷的 **II** *n* 1 [c] (*person*) 夏威夷人 2 [u] (*language*) 夏威夷语
hawk [hɔːk] **I** *n* [c] 1 (*bird*) 鹰 2 (*person*) 主战分子 **II** *vt* [贬] (*sell*) 硬卖 ♦**to watch sb like a hawk** 看某人看得很紧
hawthorn ['hɔːθɔːn] *n* [c/u] 山楂
hay [heɪ] *n* [u] 干草
hay fever *n* [u] 花粉病
haystack ['heɪstæk] *n* [c] 大干草垛
hazard ['hæzəd] **I** *n* [c] 危险 **II** *vt* ♦**to hazard a guess that ...** 试着猜猜… ♦**to be a hazard to sb** 对某人构成危险 ♦**to be a health/fire hazard** 健康/火灾上的危害
hazardous ['hæzədəs] *adj* (*dangerous*) 危险的

hazard (warning) lights [汽车] *n* [*pl*] 警报灯

haze [heɪz] *n* [s/u] 薄雾 ♦**a haze of cigarette smoke** 香烟的烟雾

hazel ['heɪzl] **I** *n* [c] (*tree*) 榛树 **II** *adj* [+ *eyes*] 淡褐色的

hazelnut ['heɪzlnʌt] *n* [c] 榛子

hazy ['heɪzɪ] *adj* **1** (*indistinct*) [+ *sky, day, sunshine*] 雾蒙蒙的; [+ *outline, view*] 朦胧的 **2** (*vague*) [+ *idea, memory*] 模糊的 ♦**he's rather hazy about the details** 他对细节有点遮遮掩掩

✪**he** [hiː] *pron* **1** (*man, boy*) 他 ◊ *He didn't do it. I did.* 他没做，我做了。**2** (*male animal*) 它 ◊ *He's a good dog.* 它是只好狗。

✪**head** [hɛd] **I** *n* [c] **1** [解剖] 头 **2** (*mind*) 头脑 **3** [*of company, organization, department*] 领导 **4** [英] (*head teacher*) 校长 **5** [*of table*] 首 **6** [*of queue, list*] 最前面 **7** (*on tape recorder, video*) 磁头 **8** (*on beer*) 泡沫 **II** *vt* **1** [+ *list, group*] 打头 ◊ *The list of most polluted cities is headed by London.* 污染最严重的城市列表以伦敦打头。**2** [+ *group, company*] 领导 ◊ *The firm is headed by John Murray.* 公司是由约翰•麦瑞领导的。**3** [足球] [+ *ball*] 用头顶 ♦**he fell head first into the river** 他头向下地栽到水里 ♦**to go** *or* **fall head over heels** (字) 头朝下跌倒 ♦**to fall head over heels (in love)** (喻) 神魂颠倒地坠入(情网) ♦**10 pounds a** *or* **per head** 每人10英镑 ♦**she's got a head for figures/heights** 她有算术才能/能登高 ♦**I have no head for heights/figures** 我登高/算数不灵 ♦**to come to a head/to be brought to a head** [*situation* +] 到了紧要关头 ♦**let's put our heads together** 咱们共同商量 ♦**off the top of my head** 我估计 ♦**on your own head be it!** 由你自负后果 ♦**to bite** *or* **snap sb's head off** 对某人大发脾气 ♦**it went to his head** [*alcohol* +] 喝得他晕头转向; [*success, power* +] 冲昏了他的头脑 ♦**to keep one's head** 保持镇定 ♦**to lose one's head** 仓皇失措 ♦**I can't make head or** *or* **nor tail of this** [非正式] 我对这件事一点也摸不着头脑 ♦**to go/be off one's head** [尤英:非正式] 发疯了 ♦**to be off** *or* **out of one's head** (*on drink, drugs*) 神志不清 ♦**to have got it into one's head that ...** (*be under impression that*) 固执地认为…; (*have understood that*) 明白了… ♦**from head to foot** *or* **toe** 从头到脚 ♦**to laugh/scream one's head off** 狂笑/狂呼不已 ♦**to go over sb's head** 令某人不能理解 ♦**heads or tails?** 正面还是反面? ♦**it's heads** 硬币正面

❑**head for** *vt* [不可拆分] [+ *place*] 前往 ◊ *What's the name of the place we're heading for?* 我们要去的地方叫什么? ◊ *They are heading for the airport.* 他们正前往机场。♦**to be heading** *or* **headed for Glasgow** 正前往格拉斯哥 ♦**to be heading** *or* **headed for disaster** 快要碰到灾祸

❑**head off I** *vt* **1** [+ *person, vehicle*] 上前拦住 **2** [+ *threat, danger*] 防止 ◊ *They did this in order to head off a strike.* 他们这样做是为了防止罢工的发生。**II** *vi* (*leave*) 出发 ◊ *I think we'd better be heading off.* 我们该出发了。

❑**head up** *vt* [+ *organization, investigation*] 领导 ◊ *Judge Samuel Evans headed up the investigation.* 塞缪尔•爱文斯法官领导这项调查。

headache ['hɛdeɪk] *n* [c] **1** (*pain*) 头痛 **2** (*problem*) 令人头疼的问题 ♦**to have a headache** 头痛 ♦**to be a headache (for sb)** (*problem*) 是件(令某人)头痛的事

heading ['hɛdɪŋ] *n* [c] [*of chapter, article*] 标题

headlamp ['hɛdlæmp] [英] *n* = **headlight**

headlight ['hɛdlaɪt] *n* [c] 前灯

headline ['hɛdlaɪn] *n* [c] 标题 ♦**the headlines** [出版] 头条新闻; [电视, 广播] 内容提要 ♦**to hit the headlines** 成为头条新闻 ♦**it was headline news** 是头条新闻

headmaster [hɛd'mɑːstə(r)] [英] *n* [c] 校长

headmistress [hɛd'mɪstrɪs] [英] *n* [c] 女校长

head office *n* [C/U] [*of company*] 总部

head of state (*pl* **heads of state**) *n* [C] 元首

headphones ['hɛdfəunz] *n* [*pl*] 耳机

headquarters ['hɛdkwɔːtəz] *n* [*pl*] 1 [*of company, organization*] 总部 2 [军] 指挥部

headroom ['hɛdrum] *n* [U] (*in car, under bridge*) 净空高度 ♦ **"Max. Headroom: 3.4 metres"** "高度限制：3.4 米"

headscarf ['hɛdskɑːf] (*pl* **headscarves**) *n* [C] [英] 头巾; (*worn by Muslim women*) 包头巾

headset ['hɛdsɛt] *n* [C] 耳机

head teacher [英] *n* [C] 校长

headway ['hɛdweɪ] *n* ♦ **to make headway** 取得进展

heal [hiːl] **I** *vt* 1 [+ *injury*] 愈合; [+ *sick person*] 治愈 2 (*emotionally*) 治愈 3 [+ *rift, disagreement*] 调解 **II** *vi* 1 (*physically*) 痊愈 2 (*emotionally*) 愈合

✪ **health** [hɛlθ] *n* [U] 1 健康 ◊ *Her health has never been very good.* 她的健康从来都不好。2 (*prosperity*) 发达 ♦ **to be good/bad for one's health** 对某人的健康有益/不利 ♦ **to be in good/poor health** 身体健康/不好 ♦ **to drink (to) sb's health** 举杯祝某人健康

health care I *n* [U] 保健 **II** *cpd* [复合词] [+ *system, worker, services*] 保健

health centre (美 **health center**) *n* [C] 医疗中心

health food *n* [C/U] 保健食品

Health Service [英] *n* ♦ **the (National) Health Service** 国民保健制度

healthy ['hɛlθɪ] *adj* 1 [+ *person, teeth, organ, skin*] 健康的 2 (*hearty*) [+ *appetite*] 好的 3 (*health-promoting*) [+ *diet, lifestyle*] 对健康有益的 4 (*good*) [+ *profit, turnover*] 相当大的 5 (*successful*) [+ *economy, company, account*] 兴旺发达的

heap [hiːp] **I** *n* [C] (*pile*) [*of clothes, papers*] 堆 **II** *vt* ♦ **to heap sth on sth** [+ *sand, earth, clothes*] 将某物堆在某物上; [+ *food*] 将某物装满某物 ♦ **heaps** *or* **a heap of** [非正式] [+ *time, work, money etc*] 大量 ♦ **to heap praise/criticism on sb** 对某人大加赞赏/批评

❑ **heap up** *vt* [+ *stones, sand*] 堆起

✪ **hear** [hɪə(r)] (*pt, pp* **heard**) *vt* 1 [+ *sound, voice, music*] 听见 ◊ *He heard voices in the garden.* 他听见从花园里传来的声音。2 (*listen to*) [+ *news, lecture, concert*] 听 ◊ *I heard the news on the radio this morning.* 我今天早上听了新闻广播。◊ *We went to hear the Berlin Philharmonic.* 我们去听了柏林交响乐团。3 [法] [+ *case, evidence*] 审理 ♦ **to hear sb doing sth** 听见某人做某事 ♦ **to hear that ...** 听说… ♦ **I've heard it all before** 我早就听了多少遍了 ♦ **to hear about sth/sb** 听说某事/某人 ♦ **to hear from sb** 得到某人的消息 ♦ **have you heard of Damien Hirst?** 你有没有听说过戴米安•赫斯特? ♦ **I've never heard of him** 我从来没听说过他 ♦ **I wouldn't** *or* **won't hear of it!** 我坚决不同意! ♦ **hear, hear** [英:正式] 说的好，说的好

❑ **hear out** *vt* ♦ **to hear sb out** 听某人讲完

heard [həːd] *pt, pp of* **hear**

hearing ['hɪərɪŋ] *n* 1 [U] (*sense*) 听力 2 [C] [法] 开审 ♦ **in** *or* **within sb's hearing** 在某人听得到的范围内 ♦ **to give sb a (fair) hearing** [英] (公正地)听取某人的申诉

hearing aid *n* [C] 助听器

hearse [həːs] *n* [C] 灵车

heart [hɑːt] **I** *n* 1 [C] [解剖] 心脏 2 [C] (*emotions*) 感情 3 [C/U] (*character, attitude*) 心灵 4 [C] (*shape*) 心形物 5 [C] [*of lettuce*] 菜心 **II hearts** *n* [*pl*] [纸牌] 红桃 ♦ **to learn/know sth (off) by heart** 背诵某事 ♦ **I knew in my heart (of hearts) it was true** 在我内心深处我知道这是对的 ♦ **(at) the heart of the problem/debate** （在）问题/争论的实质 ♦ **the heart of London** 伦敦中心 ♦ **at heart** (*basically*) 本质上 ♦ **to have a soft/hard heart** 心肠软/硬 ♦ **to lose heart** 失去信心 ♦ **to take heart (from sth)** (从某事)受到鼓舞 ♦ **she set her heart on being a lawyer** 她一心想当律师

♦**the heart of the matter** 问题的关键 ♦**my heart went out to them** 我非常同情他们 ♦**matters** *or* **affairs of the heart** 感情问题 ♦**with all one's heart** [*believe* +] 全心全意地; [*love* +] 真心实意地 ♦**to break sb's heart** 使某人伤心 ♦**to have a broken heart** 心碎了 ♦**to have a change of heart** 改变主意 ♦**be close** *or* **dear to one's heart** 是某人所关心的 ♦**I thanked him from the bottom of my heart** 我从心底里感激他 ♦**my heart sank** 我心头一沉 ♦**to take sth to heart** 对某事耿耿于怀 ♦**to one's heart's content** 尽情地

heart attack *n* [c] 心脏病发作 ♦**to have a heart attack** 心脏病发作

heartbeat ['hɑːtbiːt] *n* **1** [s] (*beating*) 心跳 **2** [c] (*single beat*) 心跳

heartbreaking ['hɑːtbreɪkɪŋ] *adj* [+ *news, story*] 令人伤心的 ♦**it was heartbreaking to watch** 看着真让人心碎

heartbroken ['hɑːtbrəukən] *adj* 心碎的

heartburn ['hɑːtbəːn] *n* [u] 胃灼热 ♦**I've got heartburn** 我有胃灼热

heart disease *n* [u] 心脏病

hearth [hɑːθ] *n* [c] (*fireplace*) 壁炉炉床

heartily ['hɑːtɪlɪ] *adv* **1** [*laugh* +] 起劲地 **2** [*eat, drink* +] 尽情地 **3** [*agree, dislike* +] 非常; [+ *glad, sick, sorry*] 非常

heartless ['hɑːtlɪs] *adj* [+ *person, attitude*] 无情的

hearty ['hɑːtɪ] *adj* **1** (*cheerful*) [+ *person, laugh*] 开心快活的 **2** (*satisfying*) [+ *meal*] 丰盛的 **3** [+ *appetite*] 大的 **4** (*strong*) [+ *agreement, dislike*] 强烈的

heat [hiːt] **I** *n* **1** [u] (*warmth*) 热 **2** [u] (*temperature*) 热度 **3** [u] (*hob, flame etc*) 热源 **4** [c] [体育] (*also:* ***qualifying heat***) 预赛 **II** *vt* [+ *water, food*] 加热; [+ *room, house*] 取暖 ♦**in the heat of the election campaign** 在选举竞争的白热阶段 ♦**in the heat of the moment** 一时激动之下 ♦**to be on** *or* (美) **in heat** [动] 正在发情 ♦**I find the heat unbearable** 热得我实在受不了

❑**heat up I** *vi* [*water, room* +] 热起来 **II** *vt* [+ *food*] 加热

heated ['hiːtɪd] *adj* **1** [+ *pool, room*] 加热的 **2** [+ *argument, debate*] 激烈的

heater ['hiːtə(r)] *n* [c] (*electric heater, gas heater*) 供暖装置; (*in car*) 暖气设备

heather ['hɛðə(r)] *n* [u] 石南属植物

heating ['hiːtɪŋ] *n* [u] **1** (*process*) 供暖 **2** (*system*) 暖气

heatwave ['hiːtweɪv] *n* [c] 酷暑时期

heave [hiːv] **I** *vt* ♦**to heave sth/sb onto sth** 将某物/某人用力移动到某物上 **II** *vi* **1** [*chest, sea* +] 起伏 **2** (*retch*) [*person, stomach* +] 恶心 **III** *n* [c] (*pull*) 拉 (*push*) 推; (*lift*) 举 ♦**to heave o.s. up** 拉自己起来 ♦**to heave a sigh** 叹了一口气 ♦**to heave a sigh of relief** 松了一口气

❑**heave to** (*pt, pp* **hove**) [航海] *vi* 停航

heaven ['hɛvn] **I** *n* [u] [宗, 非正式] 天堂 **II heavens** *n* [*pl*] ♦**the heavens** [文] 天空 ♦**the heavens opened** 下了一场倾盆大雨 ♦**to move heaven and earth to do sth** 竭尽全力做某事 ♦**heaven forbid!** 千万不要!

heavenly ['hɛvnlɪ] *adj* **1** [宗] (*celestial*) 天堂的 **2** [非正式] (*wonderful*) [+ *day, place, occasion*] 无比快乐的

heavily ['hɛvɪlɪ] *adv* **1** [*land, fall, sigh* +] 沉重地 **2** (*a lot*) [*drink, smoke* +] 大量地; [*rain, snow* +] 大 **3** [+ *armed, guarded*] 大量; [+ *sedated*] 厉害地 **4** [*criticize* +] 严厉地 ♦**to be heavily made up** 浓妆艳抹的 ♦**heavily pregnant** 怀孕后期 ♦**to rely heavily on** *or* **be heavily reliant on sb/sth** 过分依赖某人/某物 ♦**he was very heavily built** 他身材庞大

heavy ['hɛvɪ] *adj* **1** (*in weight*) [+ *load, suitcase*] 重的 **2** (*well-built*) [+ *person*] 壮实的 **3** (*thick*) [+ *material, door etc*] 厚的 **4** (*in amount, number etc*) [+ *responsibility, commitment*] 重大的; [+ *casualties*] 大量的; [+ *fighting*] 激烈的; [+ *traffic*] 拥挤的; [+ *fine,* *penalty, sentence*] 重的; [+ *drinking, smoking, gambling*] 过度的; [+ *rain, snow*] 大的; [+ *blow, fall*] 沉重有力的; [+ *breathing*] 沉重的; [+ *schedule, week*] 繁忙的 **5** (*physically demanding*) [+ *work*] 繁重的 **6** (*rich*) [+ *food, meal*] 难消化的 **7** [非正式] (*difficult*) [+ *situation*] 难办的; [+ *discussion*] 沉重的 ♦**how heavy are you/is it?** 你/它有多重? ♦**it's ten times heavier than** *or* **ten times as heavy as we estimated** 比我们预计的要重10倍 ♦**a heavy drinker/smoker** 酒/烟鬼 ♦**to make heavy weather of sth** 对某事小题大做 ♦**with a heavy heart** [文] 沉重的心情 ♦**tanks are very heavy on fuel** 坦克很耗油 ♦**the air was heavy with moisture** [文] 空气湿度很大

Hebrew ['hiːbruː] **I** *adj* 希伯来的 **II** *n* [U] (*language*) 希伯来语

hectare ['hɛktɑː(r)] *n* [C] 公顷

hectic ['hɛktɪk] *adj* [+ *schedule, pace, life etc*] 繁忙的

he'd [hiːd] = **he would, he had**

hedge [hɛdʒ] **I** *n* [C] 树篱 **II** *vi* (*stall*) 闪烁其词 ♦**a hedge against inflation** 防止通货膨胀的手段 ♦**to hedge one's bets** 两面下注

hedgehog ['hɛdʒhɔg] *n* [C] 刺猬

heed [hiːd] *vt* [正式] [+ *advice, warning*] 听从 ♦**to pay (no) heed to** *or* **take (no) heed of** (不)听取

heel [hiːl] **I** *n* [C] **1** [*of foot*] 脚后跟 **2** [*of shoe*] 鞋跟 **II heels** *n* [*pl*] (*also: **high heels***) 高跟鞋 ♦**to bring sb to heel** 使某人屈服 ♦**to take to one's heels** [文] 逃跑 ♦**to turn on one's heel** 急转身

hefty ['hɛftɪ] [非正式] *adj* **1** [+ *person*] 强壮的 **2** [+ *push*] 有力的 **3** [+ *profit, fine*] 可观的

height [haɪt] **I** *n* **1** [C/U] [*of person, tree, building*] 高度 **2** [C] (*altitude*) 高处 **II heights** *n* [*pl*] (*altitude*) 高; (*high ground*) 高地 ♦**of average/medium height** 平均/中等高度 ♦**what height are you?** 你有多高? ♦**the cliff is 100m in height** 悬崖有100米高 ♦**to gain/lose height** 升高/降低高度 ♦**flying at a height of 5000 m** 在5000米的高空飞行 ♦**at knee/waist/shoulder height** 齐膝盖/腰/肩膀 ♦**from a (great) height** 从(很)高处 ♦**at the height of the summer** 在盛夏之际 ♦**a writer at the height of his powers** 一名处于巅峰状态的作家 ♦**it is the height of fashion/good taste** 那是最时髦/最有品位的 ♦**at its height, ...** 在鼎盛时期, …

heighten ['haɪtn] *vt* [+ *awareness, tension, fears, interest*] 增加

heir [ɛə(r)] *n* [C] 继承人 ♦**to be (the) heir to sth** 是某物的继承人 ♦**the heir to the throne** 王位的继承人

heiress ['ɛərɛs] *n* [C] 女继承人

held [hɛld] *pt, pp of* **hold**

helicopter ['hɛlɪkɔptə(r)] *n* [C] 直升飞机

hell [hɛl] **I** *n* **1** [U] [宗] 地狱 **2** [C/U] (喻) (*life, situation*) 活受罪 **II** *int* [非正式, 疑讳] 天啊 ♦**(just) for the hell of it** [非正式] 仅为取乐 ♦**to give sb hell** [非正式] (*tell off*) 狠狠地数落某人; (*cause pain*) 使某人吃苦头; (*cause trouble for*) 给某人找麻烦 ♦**all hell broke loose** [非正式] 突然之间闹翻天 ♦**a** *or* **one hell of a job/time etc** [非正式] 一份很难的工作/一段难熬的时光 ♦**a** *or* **one hell of a lot of** [非正式] 好多 ♦**to go to hell** [宗] 下地狱; (喻: 非正式, 疑讳) 见鬼去吧 ♦**it was hell** [非正式] 糟糕极了 ♦**the babysitter/neighbour from hell** [非正式] 糟透了的保姆/邻居 ♦**what/where/who the hell** [非正式] 究竟什么/哪里/谁 ♦**to run like hell** [非正式] 拼命地跑 ♦**oh, to hell with it!** [非正式] 见鬼吧!

he'll [hiːl] = **he will, he shall**

hello [hə'ləu] *int* (*as greeting*) 你好; [通信] 喂; (*to attract attention*) 劳驾; (*expressing surprise*) 嘿

helmet ['hɛlmɪt] *n* [C] [*of motorcyclist, cyclist, astronaut*] 头盔; [*of soldier, policeman, fireman*] 钢盔

✪**help** [hɛlp] **I** *n* [U] 帮助 ◊ *Thanks for your help.* 多谢你的帮助。; (*when in danger*) 救命 ◊ *He was screaming for help.* 他大叫救命。**II** *vt* **1** [+ *person*] 帮助 ◊ *His car wouldn't start, so I helped him.* 他的车起动不

了，所以我帮助了他。**2** (*improve*) 改善 ◊ *The new law does little to help the environment.* 新法律在改善环境方面没起什么作用。**III** *vi* **1** (*assist*) 帮忙 ◊ *Can I help?* 我能帮忙吗？**2** (*be useful*) 有用 ◊ *The right style of swimsuit can help by hiding bulges.* 款式适当的游泳衣有助于掩饰肥胖部位。◊ *Does that help?* 那有用吗？ ♦**she needs help to get up the stairs** 她需要帮助才能上楼梯 ♦**the book wasn't much help** 这本书没什么用 ♦**thanks, you've been a great help** 谢谢，你帮了很大忙 ♦**with the help of sb/sth** 在某人/某物的帮助下 ♦**to be of help (to sb)** (对某人)有所帮助 ♦**I helped him (to) fix his car** 我帮助他修了他的车 ♦**I helped her to her feet** 我帮她站起来 ♦**help!** 救命！ ♦**can I help you?** (*in shop*) 我能为您效劳吗？ ♦**people who can help themselves** (*be independent*) 能自立的人 ♦**to help o.s. to sth** (*serve oneself*) 随意用某物；[非正式] (*steal*) 顺手牵羊拿某物 ♦**he can't help it** 他毫无办法 ♦**I can't help feeling sorry for him** 我情不自禁地同情他 ♦**it can't be helped** 没办法

❑**help out** **I** *vi* 帮忙 ♦**to help out with sth** 帮忙做某事 ◊ *I help out with the secretarial work.* 我帮忙做秘书工作。**II** *vt* 帮忙 ◊ *I had no money, but my mum helped me out.* 我没钱，但我妈妈帮了我的忙。

helper ['hɛlpə(r)] *n* [c] 帮手

helpful ['hɛlpful] *adj* [+ *person*] 有用的；[+ *advice, suggestion*] 有建设性的

helping ['hɛlpɪŋ] *n* [c] [*of food*] 一份

helpless ['hɛlplɪs] *adj* (*defenceless*) 无依无靠的 ♦**he was helpless to resist** 他无法抵制

helpline ['hɛlplaɪn] *n* [c] (*for emergencies, information*) 热线

hem [hɛm] **I** *n* [c] [*of skirt, dress*] 褶边 **II** *vt* [+ *skirt, dress etc*] 给…缝边

❑**hem in** *vt* 包围

hemisphere ['hɛmɪsfɪə(r)] *n* [c] **1** [地理] 半球 **2** [*of brain*] 大脑半球 ♦**the northern/southern hemisphere** 北/南半球

hemorrhage ['hɛmərɪdʒ] [美] *n* = **haemorrhage**

hemorrhoids ['hɛmərɔɪdz] [美] *n* [*pl*] = **haemorrhoids**

hen [hɛn] *n* [c] **1** (*chicken*) 母鸡 **2** (*of other species*) 雌禽 ♦**a hen pheasant/chaffinch etc** 一只雌雉/花鸡{等}

hence [hɛns] *adv* (*therefore*) 因此 ♦**2 years hence** 今后两年

henceforth [hɛns'fɔːθ] *adv* 今后

hen night [英] *n* [c] 婚礼前新娘与女伴们的聚会

hepatitis [hɛpə'taɪtɪs] *n* [u] 肝炎

✪**her** [hɜː(r)] **I** *pron* **1** (*of woman, girl*) 她 ◊ *I haven't seen her.* 我还没见到她。◊ *They gave her the job.* 他们给了她那份工作。◊ *Tell her that I'll be late.* 告诉她我会晚到。◊ *You could write her a letter.* 你可以给她写封信。◊ *"Not her again," said Peter.* 彼得说："又是她。" ◊ *I was at school with her.* 我和她是同学。**2** (*of female animal*) 它 ◊ *You'll have to take her to the vet.* 你得带它去看兽医。**II** *adj* **1** (*of woman, girl*) 她的 ◊ *Her face was very red.* 她的脸很红。**2** (*referring to female animal*) 它的 ◊ *a cow and her calf* 母牛和它的小牛

herb [həːb, (美) əːrb] *n* [c] 草本植物

herbal ['həːbl, (美) 'əːrbl] *adj* [+ *medicine, remedy*] 药草的

herbal tea *n* [c/u] **1** 药茶

herd [həːd] **I** *n* [c] [*of cattle, goats*] 牧群 **II** *vt* (*drive*) [+ *animals*] 牧放；[+ *people*] 驱赶

✪**here** [hɪə(r)] *adv* **1** (*in/to this place*) 在这里 **2** (*near me*) 到这里 **3** (*at this point*) 这时 ♦**"here!"** (*present*) "在这儿！" ♦**here's my phone number** 这是我的电话号码 ♦**here's your taxi** 你的出租车来了 ♦**here he is** (*he's just arrived*) 他到了 ♦**here you are** (*take this*) 给你 ♦**here we are!** (*found it!*) 找到了！ ♦**here and there** 各处 ♦**"here's to ..."** (*toast*) "为…干杯" ♦**I'm here to help you** 我是来帮你的 ♦**ok here goes, I'll try it** 好，来吧，我来试试 ♦**here we go (again)** [非正

式] 噢，(又) 来了 ♦**(in the) here and now** 现在

hereditary [hɪ'rɛdɪtrɪ] *adj* 1 [+ *disease*] 遗传的 2 [+ *title*] 世袭的

heritage ['hɛrɪtɪdʒ] **I** *n* [U/S] 遗产 **II** *cpd* [复合词] [英] [+ *centre, industry, site*] 文化遗产

hernia ['həːnɪə] *n* [C] 疝

hero ['hɪərəu] (*pl* **heroes**) *n* [C] 1 [*in book, film*] 男主人公 2 [*of battle, struggle etc*] 英雄 ♦**Clint Eastwood is my hero** 克林特•伊斯特伍德是我崇拜的偶像

heroic [hɪ'rəuɪk] *adj* 英勇的

heroin ['hɛrəuɪn] *n* [U] 海洛因

heroine ['hɛrəuɪn] *n* [C] 1 (*in book, film*) 女主人公 2 [*of battle, struggle etc*] 女英雄 ♦**Elizabeth Taylor was my heroine** 伊丽莎白• 泰勒是我崇拜的偶像

heroism ['hɛrəuɪzəm] *n* [U] 英勇 ♦**an act of heroism** 英雄行为

heron ['hɛrən] *n* [C] 鹭

herring ['hɛrɪŋ] (*pl* **herring** *or* **herrings**) *n* [C/U] 鲱鱼

hers [həːz] *pron* 1 (*of woman, girl*) 她的 ◊ *This is hers.* 这是她的。 2 (*of female animal*) 它的 ◊ *Which bowl is hers?* 哪个食盆是它的？ ♦**a friend of hers** 她的一个朋友

✪ **herself** [həː'sɛlf] *pron* 1 她自己 ◊ *She hurt herself.* 她伤了自己。 ◊ *She made the dress herself.* 她自己做的这件连衣裙。 ◊ *She'll have to try it out for herself.* 她必须得自己试试。 2 (*emphatic*) 她本人 ◊ *She herself lives in London.* 她本人住在伦敦。 ♦**by herself** (*unaided*) 她独立地 ◊ *She painted the house by herself.* 她自己一个人粉刷了房子。; (*alone*) 她独自地 ◊ *She lives by herself.* 她独自一人住。

he's [hiːz] = **he is, he has**

hesitant ['hɛzɪtənt] *adj* [+ *smile, reaction*] 迟疑不决的 ♦**to be hesitant about doing** *or* **to do sth** 对于做某事犹豫不决

hesitate ['hɛzɪteɪt] *vi* 犹豫 ♦**I would hesitate to say yes at this stage** 我目前还不太想给肯定的答复 ♦**he did not hesitate to take action** 他毫不迟疑地采取了行动 ♦**don't hesitate to contact me** 请务必和我联系

hesitation [hɛzɪ'teɪʃən] *n* [C/U] 1 (*delay*) 犹豫 2 (*in speech*) 迟疑 3 (*unwillingness*) 不愿意 ♦**I have no hesitation in agreeing with him** 我毫不犹豫地同意了他的意见 ♦**he accepted without hesitation** 他毫不犹豫地接受了

heterosexual ['hɛtərəu'sɛksjuəl] **I** *adj* [+ *person, relationship*] 异性的 **II** *n* [C] 异性恋者

hexagon ['hɛksəgən] *n* [C] 六角形

hey [heɪ] *int* 1 (*to attract attention*) 喂 2 (*showing surprise, interest, anger*) 嘿

heyday ['heɪdeɪ] *n* ♦**the heyday of the railways** 铁路的黄金时代 ♦**in its heyday, ...** 在最兴旺发达的时候，…

HGV [英] *n abbr* (= ***heavy goods vehicle***) 载重车辆

hi [haɪ] *int* (*as greeting*) 嘿; (*in e-mail*) 你好

hibernate ['haɪbəneɪt] *vi* 冬眠

hiccough ['hɪkʌp] *vi* = **hiccup**

hiccup ['hɪkʌp] **I** *vi* 打嗝 **II** *n* [C] (*problem*) 小问题 **III hiccups** *n* [*pl*] ♦**to have/get (the) hiccups** 打嗝

hid [hɪd] *pt of* **hide**

hidden ['hɪdn] **I** *pp of* **hide** **II** *adj* [+ *feelings, dangers, facts*] 暗藏的; [+ *place, camera, microphone*] 隐秘的 ♦**there are no hidden charges** 没有变相的额外费用 ♦**hidden agenda** 隐藏的动机

hide [haɪd] (*pt* **hid**, *pp* **hidden**) **I** *n* [C/U] (*skin*) 兽皮 **II** *vt* 1 (*conceal*) [+ *object, person*] 隐藏; [+ *feeling, information*] 隐瞒 2 (*obscure*) [+ *sun, view*] 遮挡 **III** *vi* 藏起来 ♦**to hide from sb** 躲着某人 ♦**to hide o.s.** 躲起来 ♦**to hide sth from sb** (字) 让某人找不到某物; (喻) 对某人隐瞒某事 ♦**he hid his face in his hands** 他用手遮住自己的脸 ♦**I have nothing to hide** 我没什么可隐瞒的

hideous ['hɪdɪəs] *adj* [+ *painting, face*] 极丑的; [+ *conditions, mistake*] 令人惊骇的

hiding ['haɪdɪŋ] *n* 1 ♦**to give sb/get a (good) hiding** [非正式] (痛) 打某人/被 (痛) 打一顿 2 ♦**go into/be in hiding** 躲藏起来 ♦**to**

come out of hiding 从躲藏处出来

hi-fi ['haɪfaɪ] *n* [c] 高保真音响设备

✪**high** [haɪ] **I** *adj* **1** (*tall*) [+ *mountain, building, wall, heel etc*] 高的 ◊ *the high walls of the prison* 监狱的高墙 **2** (*not low down*) [+ *ceiling, shelf, sun, collar*] 高的 **3** (*in degree, quantity*) [+ *level, price, speed, temperature etc*] 高的; [+ *risk*] 极大的 ◊ *a high risk of failure* 极高的失败的风险; [+ *wind*] 强烈的 ◊ *High winds have damaged the power lines.* 强风已毁坏了电缆。**4** (*high-pitched*) [+ *voice, note*] 尖锐的 **5** (*high-ranking*) [+ *official*] 高级的 ◊ *someone very high in the government* 在政府里地位极高的某人 **6** (*good*) [+ *principles, standards, morals*] 高的 ◊ *He was a man of the highest principles.* 他是个非常有原则的人。◊ *The standard was very high.* 标准很高。; [+ *quality, standard*] 高的 ◊ *The standard of university education is very high.* 大学教育的标准是非常高的。**7** [非正式] (*on drugs*) 醉的 **8** [烹饪] [+ *meat, game*] 略微腐坏的 **II** *adv* [*reach, throw* +] 高高地 ◊ *He threw the ball high in the air.* 他把球高高地扔到空中。; [*fly, climb* +] 高 **III** *n* [c] 最高记录 ◊ *Exports have reached a new high.* 出口已创一个新记录。♦ **it is 20 m high** 有20米高 ♦ **how high is the door?** 门有多高? ♦ **foods that are high in fat** 脂肪含量高的食品 ♦ **the temperature was in the high eighties** 气温高达85至90度 ♦ **safety has always been our highest priority** 安全一直是我们最重视的问题 ♦ **I have a very high opinion of him** 我对他的评价很高 ♦ **to have high expectations (of sb/sth)** (对某人/某事)有很高的期望 ♦ **to be in high spirits** 情绪很高 ♦ **to be high on** [+ *drug*] 因…而神情恍惚 ♦ **sales of vodka have reached an all-time high** 伏特加酒的销售量创历史最高记录 ♦ **to pay a high price for sth** (喻)为某事付出很高的代价 ♦ **it's high time you learned how to do it** 这是你该学怎么做的时候了 ♦ **to aim high** (喻)力争上游 ♦ **plates piled high with food** 碟子里高高地堆着食物 ♦ **economic reform is high on our agenda** *or* **list** 经济改革是我们的日程表上非常重要的问题 ♦ **high up** (*above the ground*) 离地面高的; (*in rank*) 居高位的 ♦ **to search** *or* **look high and low for sth** 到处寻找某物

> **high** 不能用于描写人，动物和植物，而应用 **tall**。
> *She was rather tall for a woman.* **tall** 还可以用来描写建筑物，如摩天大楼等，以及其他高度大于宽度的东西。*…tall pine trees… a tall glass vase*

high chair *n* [c] 高脚椅

high-class ['haɪ'klɑːs] *adj* [+ *performer, service*] 第一流的; [+ *shop, neighbourhood, hotel*] 高级的

higher education *n* [U] 高等教育

high heels *n* [*pl*] (*shoes*) 高跟鞋

high jump *n* [体育] ♦ **the high jump** 跳高 ♦ **you'll be for the high jump** (喻)你将受到严厉惩罚

highlands ['haɪləndz] *n* [*pl*] 高原地区 ♦ **the Highlands (of Scotland)** (苏格兰)高地

highlight ['haɪlaɪt] **I** *n* [c] (*best part*) 最精彩的部分 **II** *vt* [+ *problem, need*] 强调 **III highlights** *n* [*pl*] **1** [电视] 最精彩的场面 **2** (*in hair*) 挑染

highlighter ['haɪlaɪtə(r)] *n* [c] (*pen*) 荧光记号笔

highly ['haɪlɪ] *adv* (*extremely*) [+ *unlikely, critical, confidential, successful*] 非常 ♦ **highly paid** 高薪 ♦ **highly skilled** [+ *person*] 技巧非常熟练的; [+ *job*] 熟练 ♦ **to speak/think highly of sb** 赞扬/尊重某人 ♦ **to be highly regarded** *or* **thought of** 倍受尊重的

highness ['haɪnɪs] *n* ♦ **His/Your Highness** 殿下

high-rise ['haɪraɪz] **I** *adj* [+ *flats, offices*] 高层的 **II** *n* [c] 高层建筑

high school *n* [c/U] **1** [英] (*for students aged 11-18*) 中学 **2** [美] (*for students aged 14-18*) 中学

high season [英] *n* ♦ **the high**

season 旺季

high street [尤英] **I** *n* [c] 大街 [美= **main street**] **II** *adj* [尤英] 大街的

high-tech, hi-tech ['haɪ'tɛk] *adj* [+ *industry, company, equipment*] 高科技的

highway ['haɪweɪ] [尤美] *n* [c] 公路

Highway Code [英] *n* ♦ **the Highway Code** 公路法规

hijack ['haɪdʒæk] **I** *vt* [+ *plane, idea, event*] 劫持 **II** *n* 劫持

hijacker ['haɪdʒækə(r)] *n* [c] 劫持者

hike [haɪk] **I** *vi* (*go walking*) 步行 **II** *vt* [非正式] (*raise*) 突然提高 **III** *n* [c] **1** (*walk*) 徒步旅行 **2** [非正式] (*in prices etc*) 突然上涨 ♦ **to go for a hike** 做徒步旅行 ♦ **to go hiking** 做徒步旅行

❑ **hike up** *vt* [非正式] **1** (*pull up*) [+ *trousers, skirt*] 提起 **2** (*raise*) 急剧提高

hiker ['haɪkə(r)] *n* [c] 徒步旅行者

hiking ['haɪkɪŋ] *n* [U] 步行

hilarious [hɪ'lɛərɪəs] *adj* [+ *account, adventure*] 滑稽的

hill [hɪl] *n* [c] (*hillock*) 小山; (*slope*) 坡 ♦ **to be over the hill** [非正式] 过了巅峰时期

hillside ['hɪlsaɪd] *n* [c] 山坡

hill-walking ['hɪlwɔːkɪŋ] *n* [U] 登山 ♦ **to go hill-walking** 登山

hilly ['hɪlɪ] *adj* [+ *country, area*] 多小山的

✪ **him** [hɪm] *pron* **1** (*of man, boy*) 他 ◊ *I haven't seen him.* 我还没看见他。◊ *They gave him the job.* 他们给了他那份工作。◊ *Not him again!* 又是他! ◊ *I was at school with him.* 我和他是同学。◊ *I gave the bag to him.* 我把包给了他。**2** (*male animal*) 它 ◊ *You'll have to take him to the vet.* 你得带它去看兽医。

✪ **himself** [hɪm'sɛlf] *pron* **1** 他自己 ◊ *He hurt himself.* 他伤了自己。◊ *He prepared the supper himself.* 他自己准备了晚餐。◊ *He'll have to try it out for himself.* 他必须得自己试试。**2** (*emphatic*) 他本人 ◊ *He himself lives in London.* 他本人住在伦敦。♦ **by himself** (*unaided*) 他独立地 ◊ *He painted the house by himself.* 他自己一个人粉刷了房子。; (*alone*) 他独自地 ◊ *He lives by himself.* 他独自一人住。

hind [haɪnd] **I** *adj* (*rear*) [+ *legs, quarters*] 后面的 **II** *n* (*female deer*) 雌鹿

hinder ['hɪndə(r)] *vt* [+ *progress, movement, person*] 阻碍 ♦ **to hinder sb from doing sth** 妨碍某人做某事

hindsight ['haɪndsaɪt] *n* ♦ **with hindsight, we'd have done it differently** 事后想来，我们本该换个方法 ♦ **in hindsight, this was a mistake** 事后想来，这是个错误

Hindu ['hɪnduː] **I** *n* [c] 印度教信徒 **II** *adj* 与印度教有关的

Hinduism ['hɪnduːɪzm] *n* [U] 印度教

hinge [hɪndʒ] *n* [c] 铰链

❑ **hinge on** *vt* [不可拆分] (*depend on*) 取决于

hint [hɪnt] **I** *n* **1** [c] (*suggestion*) 暗示 **2** [c] (*advice*) 建议 **3** [s] (*sign, trace*) 迹象 **II** *vt* ♦ **to hint that ...** (*suggest*) 暗示… ♦ **to give a hint that ...** 暗示… ♦ **to take a hint** 理会了暗示

❑ **hint at** *vt* [不可拆分] 暗示

hip [hɪp] **I** *n* [c] [解剖] 髋部 **II** *adj* [非正式] (*trendy*) 赶时髦的

hippie ['hɪpɪ] *n* [c] 嬉皮士

hippo ['hɪpəu] [非正式] *n* [c] 河马

hippopotamus [hɪpə'pɔtəməs] (*pl* **hippopotamuses** *or* **hippopotami** [hɪpə'pɔtəmɪ]) *n* [c] 河马

hippy ['hɪpɪ] *n* = **hippie**

hire ['haɪə(r)] **I** *vt* [尤英] [+ *car, equipment, hall*] 租用 [美= **rent**]; [+ *worker*] 雇用 **II** *n* [U] [英] [*of car, hall etc*] 租用 [美= **rental**] ♦ **for hire** [尤英] [*car, boat, building* +] 供出租; [*taxi* +] 空车 ♦ **the car is on hire** 这辆车已被租用

❑ **hire out** *vt* [+ *cars, equipment, hall*] 出租; [+ *cleaners, security guards*] 出雇

hire car [英] *n* [c] 租的车 [美= **rental car**]

✪ **his** [hɪz] **I** *adj* **1** (*of man, boy*) 他的 ◊ *His face was very red.* 他的脸很红。**2** (*of animal*) 它的 ◊ *The dog is having his dinner.* 狗正在吃晚餐。**II** *pron* **1** (*of man, boy*) 他的 ◊ *These are his.* 这些是他的。**2** (*of male animal*) 它的 ◊ *Which bowl is his?* 哪个食盆是它的? ♦ **a friend of his**

他的一个朋友

Hispanic [hɪs'pænɪk] I *adj* 拉丁裔美国人的 II *n* [c] 拉丁裔美国人

hiss [hɪs] I *vi* [*snake, cat, steam, fat in pan etc* +] 发出嘶嘶声; [*person, audience* +] 发尖利的嘘声 II *vt* 压低嗓门地说 ◊ *"Be quiet!" she hissed.* "别说话！"她压低了嗓门斥责道。III *n* [c] [*of snake, steam, fat etc*] 嘶嘶声; [*of person, audience*] 嘘声 ♦ **to hiss at sb/sth** (*in disapproval*) 对某人/某物发嘘声

historian [hɪ'stɔːrɪən] *n* [c] 历史学家

historic [hɪ'stɔrɪk] *adj* (*important*) [+ *change, achievement, moment*] 历史性的

historical [hɪ'stɔrɪkl] *adj* [+ *figure, event, novel, film*] 历史的

✪ **history** ['hɪstərɪ] *n* **1** [u] [*of town, country, person*] 历史 ◊ *one of the most dramatic moments in Polish history* 波兰历史上最激动人心的时刻之一 **2** [u] [教育] 历史 **3** [c] (*record*) 历史 ◊ *a college with a tremendous sporting history* 一家有了不起的体育史的学院 ♦ **to have a history of sth/doing sth** 有某事/做某事的前科 ♦ **that's history** 那已成为历史了 ♦ **the rest is history** 后来的事就众所周知了 ♦ **to make history** 创造历史

✪ **hit** [hɪt] (*pt, pp* **hit**) I *vt* **1** (*strike*) [+ *person, thing*] 打 ◊ *He hit me on the head.* 他打了我的头。**2** (*collide with*) [+ *car, tree, wall*] 碰撞 ◊ *The truck had hit a wall.* 卡车撞了墙。**3** [+ *target*] [*bomb, bullet* +] 击中 ◊ *a missile that could hit its target with deadly accuracy* 一个命中率极高的导弹; [*bomber, gunner* +] 命中 ◊ *He hit the bull's eye and won the prize.* 他命中了靶心，赢了奖。**4** (*appear in*) [+ *news, newspapers*] 登出 **5** (*affect*) [+ *person, services, event etc*] 打击 ◊ *Consumers will be hit hard by the rise in prices.* 物价上涨对消费者打击重大。**6** (*occur to*) 想出 ◊ *Then the answer hit me.* 我一下子想出了答案。II *n* [c] **1** (*knock*) 击 **2** (*on website*) 点击 **3** (*hit song*) 成功而风行一时的事物 ♦ **to be/become a hit** [*song, film, play* +] 是/成为成功而风行一时的

❑ **hit back** I *vi* **1** (字) (*strike*) 回击 **2** (喻) (*counterattack*) ♦ **to hit back (at sb)** 回击(某人) II *vt* 回击

❑ **hit off** *vt* ♦ **to hit it off (with sb)** [非正式] (与某人)相处很好

❑ **hit out at** [尤英] *vt* [不可拆分] **1** (字) 猛打 ◊ *Ralph hit out at his assailant.* 拉尔夫猛打攻击他的人。**2** (喻) ♦ **to hit out at sb** 猛烈抨击某人 ◊ *The Prime Minister hit out at his colleagues.* 首相猛烈抨击他的同事。

❑ **hit (up)on** *vt* [不可拆分] [+ *solution*] 灵机一动地想出

hitch [hɪtʃ] I *vi* [非正式] (*hitchhike*) 搭便车旅行 II *n* [c] (*difficulty*) 障碍 ♦ **to hitch a ride** *or* **lift** [非正式] 搭便车 ♦ **to hitch sth (on) to sth** (*fasten*) 将某物拴在某物上 ♦ **to get hitched (to sb)** [非正式] (与某人)结婚 ♦ **technical hitch** 技术故障

❑ **hitch up** *vt* **1** [+ *trousers, skirt*] 急速拉起 **2** [+ *horse and cart*] 套车

hitchhike ['hɪtʃhaɪk] *vi* 搭便车旅行 ♦ **to hitchhike to New York** 搭便车到纽约去

hitchhiker ['hɪtʃhaɪkə(r)] *n* [c] 搭便车旅行者

hitchhiking ['hɪtʃhaɪkɪŋ] *n* [u] 搭便车旅行

hi-tech ['haɪ'tɛk] *adj* = **high-tech**

hitman ['hɪtmæn] (*pl* **hitmen**) [非正式] *n* 职业杀手

HIV *n abbr* (= ***human immunodeficiency virus***) 艾滋病病毒 ♦ **to be HIV positive/negative** 携带艾滋病病毒/未受艾滋病病毒感染

hive [haɪv] *n* [c] (*beehive*) 蜂箱 ♦ **a hive of activity/industry** 紧张繁忙的场所/喧闹的工业区

❑ **hive off** [尤英:非正式] *vt* [+ *company*] 使分立出来

HMS [英] *abbr* (= ***His/Her Majesty's Ship***) 英国皇家海军舰艇

HNC [英] *n abbr* (= ***Higher National Certificate***) 国家高等合格证书

HND [英] *n abbr* (= ***Higher National Diploma***) 国家高等技术学校毕业证书

hoard [hɔːd] I *n* [c] [*of food, money,*

treasure] 秘藏物 **II** *vt* [+ *food, money, treasure*] 储藏 **III** *vi* 积聚

hoarse [hɔːs] *adj* [+ *person, voice, whisper*] 嘶哑的

hoax [həuks] *n* [c] 戏弄

hob [hɔb] [英] *n* [c] (*on cooker, stove*) 炉盘

hobble ['hɔbl] *vi* 跛行

hobby ['hɔbɪ] *n* [c] 爱好

hobo ['həubəu] [美] *n* [c] 流浪汉

hockey ['hɔkɪ] *n* [u] **1** [英] (*on grass*) 曲棍球 [美 = **field hockey**] **2** [美] (*on ice*) 冰球 [英 = **ice hockey**]

hockey stick ['hɔkɪstɪk] *n* [c] 曲棍球球棍

hog [hɔg] **I** *n* [c] **1** [英] (*boar*) 阉公猪 **2** [美] (*pig*) 猪 **II** *vt* [+ *road, telephone etc*] 占用 ♦**to go the whole hog** [非正式] 彻底地干

> **HOGMANAY**
> **New Year's Eve**（新年前夜）是即将过去的一年的最后一天，在苏格兰被称为 **Hogmanay**。在苏格兰，除夕的庆典尤为重要。全家和朋友们汇聚一堂，一起聆听午夜的钟声，然后争当 **first-foot**（第一个拜年的人）。在拜访友人和邻居时，人们会随身带上酒（一般是威士忌），还有一块煤，据说这样能为来年带来好运气。

hoist [hɔɪst] **I** *n* [c] (*apparatus*) 起重机 **II** *vt* [+ *heavy object*] 举起; [+ *flag, sail*] 升起 ♦**to hoist o.s. onto a table** 自己爬到桌子上了
❑ **hoist up** *vt* [+ *person, thing*] 举起 ♦**to hoist o.s. up** 往上爬

✪ **hold** [həuld] (*pt, pp* **held**) **I** *vt* **1** (*grip*) [+ *bag, umbrella, box etc*] 拿 ◊ *Hold the baby while I load the car.* 我装车时帮我抱着婴儿。◊ *I held the box tightly.* 我紧紧地拿着盒子。 **2** (*keep*) [+ *hand, arm, head etc*] 保持 ◊ *Hold your hands in front of your face.* 把你的双手举在面前。 ◊ *Hold your arms still.* 胳膊保持不动。 **3** (*contain*) [*room, box, bottle etc* +] 容纳 ◊ *Each bottle will hold a litre.* 每个瓶子有一升的容量。 **4** (*have*) [+ *office, power*] 担任 ◊ *She has never held ministerial office.* 她从来没有担任过部长级职位。; [+ *ticket, licence, opinion*] 持有 ◊ *He did not hold a firearms licence.* 他没有持枪执照。◊ *I myself hold the view that ...* 我本人持有的观点是…; [+ *meeting, interview, election*] 举行 ◊ *The government said it would hold an investigation.* 政府表示将会进行一项调查。 **5** (*detain*) 拘留 ◊ *I was held overnight in a cell.* 我整个晚上被拘留在牢房。 **II** *vi* **1** (*withstand pressure*) 支持得住 ◊ *How long will the roof hold?* 屋顶能支持多久？ **2** (*be valid*) [*argument, theory* +] 有根据 ◊ *Your argument doesn't hold.* 你的论点立不住。 **3** (*stay same*) [*offer, invitation* +] 有效 ◊ *Will you tell her the offer still holds.* 你能告诉她邀请仍然有效吗？; [*luck, weather, ceasefire* +] 持续 ◊ *If my luck continues to hold, I think I've got a fair chance.* 如果我继续走运，我想我的机会不小。 **4** [通信] 等着 ◊ *The line's engaged: will you hold?* 电话占线，你能等一下吗？ **III** *n* [c] **1** (*grasp*) 握 ◊ *He released his hold on the camera.* 他撒手放开照相机。 **2** [*of ship, plane*] 货舱 ♦**to hold one's head up** 抬起头; (喻) 保持信心 ♦**to hold sb responsible/liable/accountable** 要求某人负责 ♦**hold the line!** [通信] 别挂线！ ♦**to hold one's breath** 屏息 ♦**don't hold your breath!** [非正式] 别指望！ ♦**to hold one's own (against sb)** (喻) (和某人) 不相上下 ♦**to hold sth shut/open** 使某物保持关着的/开着的状态 ♦**to hold sb prisoner/hostage** 扣留某人作为囚犯/人质 ♦**I don't hold with all this modern art** 我不赞同现代艺术 ♦**hold it!** 别动！ ♦**to hold sb's interest** *or* **attention** 保持某人的兴趣 {或} 注意力 ♦**hold still** *or* **hold steady** 静止不动 ♦**to have a hold over sb** 影响某人 ♦**to get/grab/take hold of sb/sth** 紧紧拿着/抓着/握着某人/某物 ♦**I need to get hold of Bob** 我需要找到鲍勃 ♦**to take hold of sb** (*overwhelm*) 征服某人 ♦**to put sth on hold** 暂时不做某事
❑ **hold against** *vt* ♦**to hold sth**

against sb 因某事对某人记仇 ◊ *He lost the case, but never held it against me.* 他输了这场官司，但从未因此而记恨过我。

❑ **hold back** *vt* **1** [+ *person, progress*] 阻拦 ◊ *She's very ambitious, so don't try to hold her back.* 她很有野心，别阻拦她。**2** [+ *secret, information*] 隐瞒 ◊ *I want the truth, now, with nothing held back.* 我现在要的是真相，没有一点隐瞒。

❑ **hold down** *vt* **1** (*restrain*) [+ *person*] 把…按倒在地上 ◊ *It took three men to hold him down.* 要3个男人才把他按在地上。**2** (*manage*) [+ *job*] 保持住 ◊ *He could never hold down a regular job.* 他从来都保不住一份稳定的工作。

❑ **hold forth** *vi* 滔滔不绝地讲 ◊ *Jenkins was there, holding forth on his favourite subject.* 詹金斯在那儿，滔滔不绝地讲述他最喜欢的话题。

❑ **hold off I** *vt* [+ *challenge*] 使不能接近 ◊ *Alesi drove magnificently, holding off the challenge from Berger.* 阿勒西开得棒极了，使勃克不能接近。**II** *vi* 拖延 ◊ *They threatened military action but have held off until now.* 他们以军事行动相威胁，但一直拖到现在。; [*rain* +] 不下 ♦ **to hold off doing sth** 推迟做某事

❑ **hold on** *vi* **1** (*keep hold*) 抓牢 ◊ *The rope was wet, but Nancy held on.* 绳子湿了，但南希仍然牢牢地抓着。**2** [非正式] (*wait*) 等一会儿 ◊ *Hold on a moment, please.* 请等一会儿。

❑ **hold on to** *vt* [不可拆分] **1** (*grasp*) 抓住 ◊ *He had to hold on to the chair to steady himself.* 他不得不抓住椅子使自己站稳。**2** (*keep*) 保留 ◊ *Will you hold on to this for me for a couple of days?* 这个你能帮我保留几天吗？

❑ **hold out I** *vt* **1** [+ *hand*] 伸出 ◊ *Sam held out his hand for the briefcase.* 山姆伸手拿公文包。**2** [+ *hope, prospect*] 带来 ◊ *Science may hold out some prospect of feeding the hungry.* 科学为解决饥饿问题带来了希望。**II** *vi* ♦ **to hold out (for sth)** 坚决要求（某物）◊ *I should have held out for a better deal.* 我本该要求更好的待遇。

❑ **hold over** *vt* (*postpone*) 推迟

❑ **hold up** *vt* **1** (*lift up*) 举起 ◊ *The Englishman held up the rifle.* 英国人举起了手枪。**2** (*support*) 支撑 ◊ *These books hold the bed up.* 这些书支撑着床。**3** (*delay*) 阻碍 ◊ *Why were you holding everyone up?* 你为什么要阻碍其他人？**4** (*rob*) [+ *person, bank*] 抢劫 ◊ *He held me up at gunpoint.* 他持枪抢劫了我。

holder ['həuldə(r)] *n* [c] **1** (*container*) 容器 **2** (*owner*) [*of ticket, licence*] 持有者; [*of title, record*] 保持者

hold-up ['həuldʌp] *n* [c] **1** (*robbery*) 持械抢劫 **2** (*delay*) 延搁; (*in traffic*) 交通阻塞

hole [həul] **I** *n* [c] **1** (*space, gap*) 洞 **2** (*tear*) (*in clothing, pocket, bag*) 破洞 **3** (*for rabbit, mouse etc*) 洞穴 **4** [非正式] (*unpleasant place*) 陋室 **5** [高尔夫] 球洞 **II** *vt* [+ *ship, building etc*] 打洞 ♦ **hole in the heart** [医] 心脏穿孔 ♦ **to pick holes (in sth)** [非正式: 喻] 找某物（中）的漏洞 ♦ **a hole in one** 一击入洞

❑ **hole up** *vi* 躲藏

holiday ['hɔlɪdeɪ] [英] *n* [c/u] 假期 [美 = **vacation**] ♦ **public holiday** 公共假期 ♦ **the school/summer/Christmas holidays** [英: 教育] 学校/暑/圣诞假期 [美 = **vacation**] ♦ **to be on holiday** 在度假

holidaymaker ['hɔlɪdɪmeɪkə(r)] [英] *n* [c] 度假者

holiday resort *n* [c] 旅游胜地

Holland ['hɔlənd] *n* 荷兰

hollow ['hɔləu] **I** *adj* **1** (*not solid*) [+ *container, log, tree*] 空的 **2** (*sunken*) [+ *cheeks, eyes*] 凹陷的 **3** (*empty*) [+ *claim, threat*] 空洞的 **4** (*dull*) [+ *sound, laugh*] 沉闷的 **II** *n* [c] (*in ground*) 凹地

❑ **hollow out** *vt* 挖空

holly ['hɔlɪ] *n* [u] 冬青

Hollywood ['hɔlɪwud] **I** *n* 好莱坞 **II** *cpd* [复合词] [+ *studio, star, film*] 好莱坞

holocaust ['hɔləkɔːst] *n* [c] 大屠杀

♦**the Holocaust** [历史] 第二次世界大战期间纳粹对犹太人的大屠杀

holy ['həulı] *adj* [+ *picture, place, water*] 神圣的; [+ *person*] 圣洁的

homage ['hɔmıdʒ] *n* [U] 敬意 ♦**to pay homage to sb/sth** 向某人/某物表示敬意

✪**home** [həum] **I** *n* **1** [C/U] (*house*) 家 ◊ *His home is in Hampstead.* 他家在汉姆斯塔德。**2** [C/U] (*country, area*) 家乡 ◊ *Jack often dreamed of home from his prison cell.* 杰克在监狱牢房里常常梦见家乡。**3** [C] (*institution*) 收容院 ◊ *a home for handicapped children* 残疾儿童收容院 **II** *adj* **1** (*made at home*) 家庭的 ◊ *home cooking* 家庭式烹调 **2** [经济, 政治] (*domestic*) 国内的 ◊ *the expansion of the home market* 国内市场的扩大 **3** [体育] [+ *team, game*] 主场的 ◊ *They are Celtic fans, and attend all home games.* 他们是凯特人队的球迷，观看所有的主场比赛。**III** *adv* [*be, go, get etc* +] 在家 ◊ *I want to go home.* 我想回家。◊ *I'll phone you as soon as I get home.* 我一回家就打电话给你。♦**at home** (*in house*) 在家 ◊ *She went out to work, while he stayed at home to care for the children.* 她出去工作，而他则在家照顾孩子。; [体育] 在主场 ◊ *Our team are at home this weekend.* 这个周末我们的球队是主场。; (*comfortable*) 自在 ◊ *I felt at home at once, because I recognized familiar faces.* 我立即感到自在，因为我见到熟悉的面孔。♦**make yourself at home** 请不要拘束 ♦**the home of free enterprise/the blues** 自由企业/蓝调音乐的起源地 ♦**home and dry** [英], **home free** [美] 大功告成 ♦**a home from** *or* (美) **away from home** 像家一样舒适的地方 ♦**to bring sth home to sb** 使某人认识到某事 ♦**to drive/hammer sth home** (喻) 强调某事; (字) 全部砸进去

❑**home in on** *vt* [不可拆分] **1** (*locate*) [*missile, equipment* +] 自动追击 ◊ *The Sidewinder missile can home in on its target with pinpoint accuracy.* 响尾蛇导弹能非常准确地追击目标。**2** (*concentrate on*) 把注意力集中于 ◊ *Critics immediately homed in on the group's greatest weakness.* 评论家立即针对该团体的最薄弱环节进攻。◊ *He homed in on the details.* 他把注意力集中于细节方面。

home address *n* [C] 家庭地址

home economics *n* [U] 家政学

homeland ['həumlænd] *n* [C] 祖国

homeless ['həumlıs] **I** *adj* [+ *family, refugee*] 无家可归的 **II** *n* [*pl*] ♦**the homeless** 无家可归的人 ♦**to be made homeless** 被弄成无家可归

homely ['həumlı] *adj* **1** [英] (*comfortable*) 令人感到舒适的 [美 = **homey**] **2** [美] (*in looks*) 相貌平平的

home-made [həum'meıd] *adj* [+ *bread, bomb*] 自制的

Home Office [英] *n* ♦**the Home Office** 内政部

homeopathic [həumıəu'pæθık] *adj* 顺势疗法的

homeowner *n* [C] 房产主

homepage ['həumpeıdʒ] [计算机] *n* [C] 主页

Home Secretary [英] *n* ♦**the Home Secretary** 内政部长

homesick ['həumsık] *adj* 想家的

home town *n* [C] 家乡

homework ['həumwəːk] *n* [U] 家庭作业 ♦**to do one's homework** (字) 做家庭作业; (喻) 做必要的准备工作

homey ['həumı] [美] *adj* 舒适的 [英 = **homely**]

homicide ['hɔmısaıd] [美] *n* [C/U] 杀人 [英 = **murder**]

homoeopathic [həumıəu'pæθık] [英] *adj* = **homeopathic**

homosexual [hɔməu'sɛksjuəl] **I** *adj* [+ *person, relationship*] 同性恋的 **II** *n* [C] (*man, woman*) 同性恋者

Honduras [hɔn'djuərəs] *n* 洪都拉斯

honest ['ɔnıst] **I** *adj* **1** (*truthful*) 诚实的 **2** (*trustworthy*) 可信的 **II** *adv* [非正式] (*honestly*) 老实说 ♦**to be honest, ...** 说实话，…

honestly ['ɔnıstlı] *adv* **1** (*with integrity*) 正直地 **2** (*bluntly*) 坦白地 **3** (*emphasizing sth*) 真的 ♦**I honestly**

don't know 我真的不知道 ♦ **oh, honestly!** 真是的！
honesty ['ɔnɪstɪ] *n* [U] 1 (*integrity*) 诚实 2 (*bluntness*) 坦白 ♦ **in all honesty** 说实话
honey ['hʌnɪ] *n* [U] 1 (*food*) 蜂蜜 2 [尤美:非正式] (*darling*) 宝贝
honeymoon ['hʌnɪmuːn] *n* [C] 1 蜜月 2 (喻) 早期的和谐时期 ♦ **to be on (one's) honeymoon** [*couple* +] 在度蜜月 ♦ **the honeymoon period is over** 初期的和谐时期已经过去了
honeysuckle ['hʌnɪsʌkl] *n* [U] 金银花
Hong Kong ['hɔŋ'kɔŋ] *n* 香港
honor ['ɔnə(r)] [美] *vt, n* = **honour**
honorable ['ɔnərəbl] [美] *adj* = **honourable**
honorary ['ɔnərərɪ] *adj* 1 [+ *job, secretary*] 名誉的 2 [+ *title, degree*] 荣誉的
honour (美 **honor**) ['ɔnə(r)] **I** *vt* 1 [+ *hero, leader*] 向… 表示敬意 2 [+ *commitment, promise*] 遵守 **II** *n* 1 [U] (*pride, self-respect*) 自尊 2 [C] (*tribute*) 荣誉 ♦ **I would be honoured to accept** 我将非常荣幸地接受 ♦ **a festival in honour of David Hockney** 为了对大卫·霍可尼表示敬意而举行的庆祝活动 ♦ **it is an honour to work with her** 和她一起工作是很光荣的 ♦ **the honour of hosting the Olympic Games** 主办奥林匹克运动会的光荣 ♦ **to do the honours** [非正式] 尽主人之谊 ♦ **on my honour** 用我的名誉担保 ♦ **your/his honour** [法] 阁下
honourable ['ɔnərəbl] (美 **honorable**) *adj* 1 [+ *person, action, defeat*] 高尚的 2 (*in parliament*) 尊敬的
honours degree *n* [C] 优等成绩学位
hood [hud] *n* [C] 1 [*of coat etc*] 兜帽 2 (*mask, blindfold*) 面罩 3 [美:汽车] 发动机罩 [英 = **bonnet**] 4 (*cover*) 罩 5 [*of cooker*] 排油烟机
hoof [huːf] (*pl* **hooves**) *n* 蹄
hook [huk] **I** *n* [C] (*for coats, fishing, curtains etc, on dress*) 钩 **II** *vt* 1 (*fasten*) 钩住 2 ♦ **to hook one's arm around sth** 用胳膊钩住某物 **III** *vi* (*fasten*) ♦ **to hook onto sth** 挂在某物上 ♦ **left/right hook** 左/右钩拳 ♦ **to get sb off the hook** 使某人脱离困境 ♦ **to be off the hook** 脱身 ♦ **to take the phone off the hook** 不把电话听筒挂上
❑ **hook up** *vt* [广播, 电视等] 联机
hooligan ['huːlɪgən] *n* [C] 流氓
hoop [huːp] *n* [C] 1 (*ring*) 圈 2 (*in basketball*) 篮圈 3 (*for croquet*) 拱门 ♦ **to jump through a hoop** *or* **hoops** 受磨炼
hooray [huː'reɪ] *int* 好哇
hoot [huːt] **I** *vi* 1 [*driver, car, siren* +] 鸣响; [*owl* +] 鸣叫 2 (*laugh, jeer*) 哈哈大笑 **II** *vt* [+ *horn*] 按 **III** *n* [C] [*of horn*] 汽车喇叭声; [*of owl*] 猫头鹰的叫声 ♦ **to hoot with laughter** 呵呵大笑 ♦ **a hoot of laughter** 呵呵大笑 ♦ **it's/he's a hoot** [非正式] 这是滑稽的/他是个滑稽的人
Hoover® ['huːvə(r)] [英] **I** *n* [C] 吸尘器 **II** *vt* [+ *carpet*] 用吸尘器吸
hooves [huːvz] *n* [*pl*] *of* **hoof**
hop [hɔp] **I** *vi* 1 (*jump*) [*person* +] 单脚跳; [*bird* +] 双脚跳 2 [非正式] (*move quickly*) 飞奔 ◊ *I hopped out of bed.* 我跳下床。 **II** *n* [C] (*by person*) 单脚跳; (*by bird*) 双爪跳 ♦ **to be hopping mad** [非正式] 气得暴跳如雷 ♦ **to catch sb on the hop** [英:非正式] 使某人措手不及 *see also* **hops**
✪ **hope** [həup] **I** *vt* 希望 ◊ *I sat down, hoping to remain unnoticed.* 我坐下，希望没有被人注意到。 ◊ *They hope that a vaccine will be available soon.* 他们希望很快能有疫苗。 **II** *vi* 盼望 ◊ *Nothing can be done except to wait, hope, and pray.* 除了等待、期望和祈祷外，什么都没用。 **III** *n* 1 [U] 希望 ◊ *She never completely gave up hope.* 她从来没有完全放弃希望。 2 [C] (*aspiration*) 期望 ◊ *the hopes and dreams of reformers* 改革者的期望和梦想 ♦ **I hope so/not** 希望是这样/希望不会 ♦ **to hope that ...** 希望… ♦ **I hope you don't mind** 希望你不介意 ♦ **to hope to do sth** 希望能做某事 ♦ **to hope for the best** 保持乐观 ♦ **to have no hope**

of sth/doing sth 对某事/做某事不抱希望 ♦**in the hope of/that** 希望… ♦**to hope against hope that ...** 抱有一线希望…

hopeful ['həupful] **I** *adj* **1** (*optimistic*) [+ *person*] 乐观的 **2** (*promising*) [+ *situation, sign*] 鼓舞人心的 **II** *n* [c] 有前途的人 ♦**to be hopeful that ...** 对…抱有希望 ♦**surgeons are hopeful of saving her** 外科医生对挽救她抱有希望

hopefully ['həupfulɪ] *adv* (*expectantly*) 怀着希望地 ♦**hopefully, ...** 如果运气好…

hopeless ['həuplɪs] *adj* **1** (*in despair*) 绝望的 **2** (*dismal*) [+ *situation, position*] 糟糕的 **3** [非正式] (*useless*) [+ *teacher, driver, service*] 无能的 ♦**to be hopeless at doing sth** 实在不会做某事 ♦**I'm hopeless at cooking** 我做饭实在不行

hops [hɔps] *n* [*pl*] 啤酒花

horizon [hə'raɪzn] **I** *n* (*skyline*) ♦**the horizon** 地平线 **II horizons** *n* [*pl*] 眼界 ♦**on the horizon** (喻) 即将发生的

horizontal [hɔrɪ'zɔntl] *adj* 水平的

hormone ['hɔːməun] *n* [c] 激素

horn [hɔːn] *n* **1** [c] [*of animal*] 角 **2** [u] (*substance*) 角质物 **3** [c] [音] 号 **4** [c] [汽车] 喇叭

horoscope ['hɔrəskəup] *n* [c] 占星术

horrendous [hə'rɛndəs] *adj* [+ *crime, error*] 恐怖的

horrible ['hɔrɪbl] *adj* [+ *colour, food, mess*] 糟透的; [+ *accident, crime*] 可怕的; [+ *experience, moment, situation, dream*] 令人恐惧的

horrid ['hɔrɪd] *adj* [+ *person, place, thing*] 极糟的 ♦**to be horrid to sb** 对某人极不友好

horrific [hɔ'rɪfɪk] *adj* [+ *injury, accident, crime*] 极其可怕的

horrified ['hɔrɪfaɪd] *adj* 受惊吓的 ♦**to be horrified at sth** 对某事感到震惊

horrifying ['hɔrɪfaɪɪŋ] *adj* [+ *experience, crime*] 极其恐怖的

horror ['hɔrə(r)] *n* [u] (*alarm*) 恐怖 ♦**to have a horror of sth** 痛恨某事 ♦**the horrors of war** 战争的恐怖

horror film *n* [c] 恐怖片

hors d'oeuvre [ɔː'dəːvrə] *n* [c/u] 餐前的开胃小吃

horse [hɔːs] *n* [c] 马

horseback ['hɔːsbæk] *n* ♦**on horseback** 骑着马

horse chestnut *n* [c] **1** (*tree*) 七叶树 **2** (*conker*) 七叶树坚果

horsepower ['hɔːspauə(r)] *n* [u] [*of engine, car etc*] 马力

horse racing *n* [u] 赛马

horseradish ['hɔːsrædɪʃ] *n* [c/u] 辣根

horse riding *n* [u] 骑马

hose [həuz] *n* [c] (*also:* ***hosepipe***) 输水软管
❑**hose down** *vt* 用软管输水冲洗

hospitable ['hɔspɪtəbl] *adj* **1** [+ *person, behaviour*] 好客的 **2** [+ *climate*] 宜人的

✪**hospital** ['hɔspɪtl] *n* [c/u] 医院 ♦**to be in hospital** *or* (美) **in the hospital** 住院

hospitality [hɔspɪ'tælɪtɪ] *n* [u] **1** [*of host, welcome*] 好客 **2** [商] (*food, drink*) 招待

✪**host** [həust] **I** *n* [c] **1** (*at party, dinner*) 主人 **2** [电视, 广播] [*of television programme*] 主持人 **3** (*for festival, conference etc*) 东道主 **II** *adj* [+ *country, organization*] 东道主的 **III** *vt* **1** [+ *party, dinner*] 举行 **2** [电视, 广播] [+ *show*] 主持 **3** [+ *festival, conference*] 主办 ♦**a whole host of problems** 许多问题 ♦**the host** [宗] 圣饼

hostage ['hɔstɪdʒ] *n* [c] (*prisoner*) 人质 ♦**to be taken/held hostage** 被绑架/扣押做人质

hostel ['hɔstl] [尤英] *n* [c] (*for homeless etc*) 招待所

hostess ['həustɪs] *n* [c] **1** (*at party, dinner etc*) 女主人 **2** (*in night club*) 女招待

hostile ['hɔstaɪl] *adj* **1** (*aggressive*) [+ *person, attitude*] 不友好的 **2** [+ *conditions, environment*] 恶劣的 **3** (*enemy*) 敌方的 ♦**to be hostile to** *or* **towards sb** 对某人不友善

hostility [hɔ'stɪlɪtɪ] **I** *n* [u] (*aggression*) 敌意 **II hostilities** *n* [*pl*] (*fighting*) 交战

hot [hɔt] *adj* **1** [+ *object*] 烫的;

[+ *weather, person*] 热的 **2** (*spicy*) [+ *food*] 辣的 **3** [非正式] (*up-to-the-moment*) 热门的 **4** (*fierce*) [+ *temper*] 暴躁的 ♦ **he's not so hot on physics** [非正式] 他物理不怎么好 ♦ **hot and bothered** 焦躁不安的 ❑ **hot up** [英:非正式] **I** *vi* [*situation, party* +] 热闹起来 **II** *vt* [+ *pace*] 使增加

> 📖 在非正式英语中，**boiling** 或 **scorching** 可用于强调天气非常炎热。在冬天，如果气温比平均气温要高，可以用 **mild**。一般而言，**hot** 所表达的气温要高于 **warm**。**warm** 的东西是热得令人感到舒服的东西。...*a warm evening*...

hot chocolate *n* [U] 热巧克力

hot dog *n* [C] 热狗

hotel [həu'tɛl] *n* [C] 旅馆 ♦ **to stay at a hotel** 住旅馆

hotline ['hɔtlaɪn] *n* [C] 热线

hotly ['hɔtlɪ] *adv* **1** [*speak* +] 生气地 **2** [*contest, pursue* +] 激烈地 ♦ **a claim which he has hotly denied** 他极力否认的说法

hot-water bottle [hɔt'wɔːtə(r)-] *n* [C] 热水袋

hound [haund] **I** *n* [C] (*dog*) 猎狗 **II** *vt* (*harass, persecute*) 不断烦扰

✪ **hour** ['auə(r)] **I** *n* **1** [C] 小时 **2** [S] [正式] (*time*) 时间 ◊ *The hour of his execution was approaching.* 处决他的时间快到了。**II hours** *n* [*pl*] **1** (*ages*) 很长时间 ◊ *Getting there would take hours.* 去那儿要花很长时间。**2** (*in job*) 工作时间 ◊ *I worked quite irregular hours.* 我的工作时间很不固定。♦ **office/visiting hours** 办公/参观时间 ♦ **the buses leave on the hour** 每小时正点有一班公共汽车 ♦ **in the early** *or* **small hours** 凌晨 ♦ **after hours** 工作结束后 ♦ **at all hours of the day and night** 白天和晚上任何时候 ♦ **for three/four hours** 三/四个小时 ◊ *They slept for two hours.* 他们睡了两个小时。♦ **(at) 60 kilometres/miles an** *or* **per hour** 每小时60 公里/英里 ♦ **to pay sb by the hour** 按小时付费给某人 ♦ **lunch hour** 午餐时间

hourly ['auəlɪ] **I** *adv* (*once each hour*) 每小时 **II** *adj* **1** (*once each hour*) 每小时一次的 **2** (*per hour*) [+ *rate, income*] 每小时的

✪ **house** [*n* haus, *vt* hauz] **I** *n* **1** [C] (*home*) 家 **2** [S] (*household*) 全家 ◊ *The noise woke the whole house.* 那个声音吵醒了全家。**3** [C] (*company*) ♦ **publishing house/steak house** 出版社/牛肉馆 **4** [C] [政治] 议院 **5** [C] [戏剧] 观众 **6** [C] (*dynasty*) 王室 ◊ *the House of Windsor* 英国王室 **II** *vt* **1** [+ *person*] 提供住房 ◊ *Too many married couples are waiting to be housed.* 太多已婚夫妻正等着提供住房。**2** [+ *collection*] 储藏 ◊ *This is the building which houses the library.* 这就是藏书的那个建筑。♦ **at/to my house** 在/到我家 ♦ **to get** *or* **put** *or* **set one's house in order** 把自己的事情处理妥当 ♦ **to bring the house down** [非正式] 博得全场喝彩 ♦ **to get on like a house on fire** [非正式] 意气相投 ♦ **drinks are on the house** 饮料免费 ♦ **to keep house** 料理家务

household ['haushəuld] *n* [C] **1** (*family*) 家庭 **2** (*home*) 家 ♦ **to be a household name** 是家喻户晓的名字

housekeeper ['hauskiːpə(r)] *n* [C] 管家

housekeeping ['hauskiːpɪŋ] *n* [U] **1** (*work*) 管理家务 **2** [英] (*money*) 持家费

House of Commons *n* ♦ **the House of Commons** 下议院

House of Lords *n* ♦ **the House of Lords** 上议院

House of Representatives *n* ♦ **the House of Representatives** 众议院

Houses of Parliament *n* [*pl*] ♦ **the Houses of Parliament** 议院

housewife ['hauswaɪf] (*pl* **housewives**) *n* [C] 家庭主妇

house wine *n* [C/U] 饭馆、酒吧提供的最便宜的葡萄酒

housework ['hauswəːk] *n* [U] 家务劳动

housing ['hauzɪŋ] **I** *n* [U] **1** (*houses*) 房屋 **2** (*provision*) 住房 **II** *cpd* [复合

词] [+ *problem, shortage*] 住房

housing estate [英] *n* [c] 住宅区

housing project [美] *n* [c] 安居工程

hove [həuv] *pt, pp of* **heave to**

hover ['hɔvə(r)] *vi* **1** [*bird, insect* +] 翱翔; [*helicopter* +] 盘旋 **2** [*person* +] 徘徊

hovercraft ['hɔvəkrɑːft] (*pl* **hovercraft**) *n* [c] 气垫船

✪ **how**

KEYWORD

[hau]

I *adv*

1 (*in questions*) 怎样 ♦ **how did you do it?** 你是怎么做的？♦ **how was the film?** 电影怎么样？♦ **how are you?** 你好吗？♦ **how can you be so unkind?** 你怎么能如此刻薄呢？♦ **"how do you do?" – "how do you do?"** "你好！" "你好！" ♦ **how long have you lived here?** 你在这儿住了多久了？♦ **how much milk/many people?** 有多少奶/人？♦ **how old are you?** 你多大了？♦ **how tall is he?** 他有多高？♦ **how well do you know her?** 你对她了解有多少？

2 (*in exclamations*) ♦ **how lovely/awful!** 太可爱/糟了！

3 (*in suggestions*) ♦ **how about a cup of tea/a walk** *etc*? 来杯茶/去散步{等}好吗？♦ **how about going to the cinema?** 去看电影好吗？♦ **how would you like to eat out tonight?** 今天晚上出去吃好吗？

4 (*avoiding repetition*) ♦ **how about you?** 你呢？

II *conj* 怎么 ♦ **I know how you did it** 我知道你怎么做的 ♦ **to know how to do sth** 知道如何做某事 ♦ **it's amazing how he always seems to understand** 他总是如此善解人意真是太了不起了

✪ **however** [hau'ɛvə(r)] **I** *adv* **1** (*but*) 但是 ◊ *I hoped he might offer me a job. However, he didn't.* 我希望他能给我一份工作。但是他并没有这么做。**2** (*with adj, adv*) 不管怎样 ◊ *However hard she tried, nothing seemed to work.* 不管她怎样努力，都不行。**3** (*in questions*) 究竟怎样 ◊ *However did you find me?* 你究竟怎样找到我的？**II** *conj* (*no matter how*) 无论 ◊ *Wear your hair however you want.* 你想梳什么发型都行。◊ *I will wait for you however late you are.* 无论多晚我都会等你 。

howl [haul] **I** *vi* [*animal* +] 嗥叫; [*baby, person* +] 嚎哭; (*laugh*) 狂笑; [*wind* +] 呼啸 **II** *n* [c] (*of animal*) 嗥叫; (*of baby, person*) 嚎哭; (*of laughter*) 狂笑

hp [汽车] *abbr* (= ***horsepower***) 马力

HQ *abbr* (= ***headquarters***) 总部

HRH [英] *abbr* (= ***His/Her Royal Highness***) 殿下

hr(s) *abbr* (= ***hour(s)***) 小时

HST [美] *abbr* (= ***Hawaiian Standard Time***) 夏威夷标准时间

hubcap ['hʌbkæp] *n* [c] 毂盖

huddle ['hʌdl] **I** *vi* 蜷缩 **II** *n* [c] 挤作一团 ♦ **to huddle together** 挤作一团 ♦ **to huddle around sth** 围着某物

huff [hʌf] *n* ♦ **to be in a huff** 发怒

hug [hʌg] **I** *vt* **1** [+ *person*] 拥抱 **2** [+ *object*] 紧抱 **II** *n* [c] 拥抱 ♦ **to give sb a hug** 拥抱某人

huge [hjuːdʒ] *adj* [+ *crowd, skyscraper, wardrobe*] 巨大的; [+ *amount, profit, debt*] 巨额的; [+ *task*] 庞大的

hull [hʌl] **I** *n* [c] **1** [航海] 船体; [*of nut*] 壳 **2** [*of strawberry etc*] 花萼 **II** *vt* [+ *fruit*] 除去…花萼

hum [hʌm] **I** *vt* [+ *tune, song*] 哼 **II** *vi* [*person* +] 哼; [*machine, insect* +] 发出嗡嗡声 **III** *n* [s] [*of traffic, machines, voices*] 嗡嗡声

✪ **human** ['hjuːmən] **I** *adj* [+ *body, behaviour*] 人的 ◊ *the human body* 人体; [+ *weakness, emotion*] 有人性的 **II** *n* [c] (*also:* ***human being***) 人 ◊ *Could a computer ever beat a human at chess?* 下象棋电脑能打败人吗？♦ **the human race** 人类 ♦ **human nature** 人性 ♦ **human error** 人为错误 ♦ **we're only human** 我们只是普通人

humane [hjuː'meɪn] *adj* [+ *treatment, slaughter*] 人道的

humanitarian [hjuːmænɪ'tɛərɪən] *adj* [+ *aid, principles*] 人道主义的

♦**on humanitarian grounds** 以人道主义的原则

humanity [hjuːˈmænɪtɪ] **I** *n* [U] **1** (*mankind*) 人类 **2** (*kindness*) 博爱 **3** (*humanness*) 人性 **II the humanities** *n* [*pl*] 人文学科

human rights *n* [*pl*] 人权

humble [ˈhʌmbl] **I** *adj* **1** (*modest*) [+ *person*] 谦虚的 **2** (*lowly*) [+ *background*] 卑贱的 **II** *vt* (*humiliate, crush*) 使谦卑 ♦**to humble sb's pride** 打掉某人的傲气

humid [ˈhjuːmɪd] *adj* [+ *atmosphere, climate*] 潮湿的

humidity [hjuːˈmɪdɪtɪ] *n* [U] [*of atmosphere, climate*] 湿度

humiliate [hjuːˈmɪlɪeɪt] *vt* [+ *rival, person*] 羞辱

humiliating [hjuːˈmɪlɪeɪtɪŋ] *adj* [+ *experience, defeat*] 丢脸的

humiliation [hjuːmɪlɪˈeɪʃən] *n* **1** [U] (*feeling*) 羞辱 **2** [C] (*situation, experience*) 丢脸

humility [hjuːˈmɪlɪtɪ] *n* [U] (*modesty*) 谦恭

humor [ˈhjuːmə(r)] [美] *n* = **humour**

humorous [ˈhjuːmərəs] *adj* [+ *remark, book, person*] 幽默的

humour (美**humor**) [ˈhjuːmə(r)] **I** *n* [U] 幽默 **II** *vt* [+ *person*] 迎合 ♦**sense of humour** 幽默感 ♦**to be in good/bad humour** 情绪好/不好

hump [hʌmp] **I** *n* [C] (*in ground*) 丘陵; (*to restrict speed*) 凸面; [*of camel*] 峰; (*deformity*) 驼背 **II** *vt* 扛 ♦**to get the hump** [英:非正式] 闷闷不乐

hunch [hʌntʃ] **I** *n* [C] (*intuition*) 直觉 ♦**I have a hunch that ...** 我的直觉是… **II** *vt* ♦**to hunch one's shoulders** 耸起双肩

✪**hundred** [ˈhʌndrəd] **I** *num* 百 **II hundreds** *n* [*pl*] 几百 ◊ *He handed me hundreds of forms.* 他递给我几百张表格。♦**a** *or* **one hundred books/people/dollars** 一百本书/个人/美元 ♦**a** *or* **one hundred per cent** 百分之百

hundredth [ˈhʌndrədθ] **I** *adj* 第一百的 **II** *n* ♦**a hundreth (of a)** 百分之一

hung [hʌŋ] **I** *pt, pp of* **hang** **II** *adj* ♦**a hung parliament** 各党势均力敌的议院

Hungarian [hʌŋˈgɛərɪən] **I** *adj* 匈牙利的 **II** *n* **1** [C] (*person*) 匈牙利人 **2** [U] (*language*) 匈牙利语

Hungary [ˈhʌŋgərɪ] *n* 匈牙利

hunger [ˈhʌŋgə(r)] **I** *n* [U] **1** (*lack of food*) 饿 **2** (*starvation*) 饥饿 **II** *vi* ♦**they hunger for adventure** 他们渴望冒险 ♦**his hunger for adventure** 他想冒险的强烈愿望

hungry [ˈhʌŋgrɪ] *adj* 饥饿的 ♦**to be hungry** 饿了 ♦**to be hungry for success** 渴望成功 ♦**to go hungry** 挨饿

hunt [hʌnt] **I** *vt* **1** (*for food, sport*) 打猎 **2** [+ *criminal, fugitive*] 追捕 **II** *vi* **1** (*for food, sport*) 打猎 **2** [英] (*for foxes*) 猎狐 **III** *n* [C] **1** (*for food, sport*) 狩猎 **2** [英] (*group of fox hunters*) 猎狐队 **3** (*for missing person*) 搜寻 **4** (*for criminal*) 追捕 ♦**detectives are hunting for clues** 刑警们在寻找线索

❑**hunt down** *vt* 追捕到

hunter [ˈhʌntə(r)] *n* [C] (*for food, sport*) 猎手 ♦**bargain/house hunter** 寻便宜货/屋者

hunting [ˈhʌntɪŋ] *n* [U] (*for food, sport*) 打猎 ♦**job/house/bargain hunting** 到处找工作/住房/便宜货

hurdle [ˈhəːdl] **I** *n* [C] (*difficulty*) 障碍 **II hurdles** *n* [*pl*] [体育] 跳栏

hurl [həːl] *vt* **1** [+ *object*] 用力投掷 **2** [+ *insult, abuse*] 叫嚷

hurrah [huˈrɑː] *int* = **hooray**

hurray [huˈreɪ] *int* = **hooray**

hurricane [ˈhʌrɪkən] *n* [C] 飓风 ♦**hurricane Charley/Tessa** 查理/特萨号台风

hurriedly [ˈhʌrɪdlɪ] *adv* 匆忙地

hurry [ˈhʌrɪ] **I** *vi* 赶紧 **II** *vt* [+ *person*] 催 **III** *n* ♦**to be in a hurry (to do sth)** 急于(做某事) ♦**to hurry in/off/home** 赶着进来/走/回家 ♦**they hurried to help him** 他们赶紧去帮他 ♦**to do sth in a hurry** 匆忙地做某事 ♦**there's** *or* **I'm in no hurry** 不着急{或}我不着急 ♦**what's the hurry?** 着什么急?

❑**hurry along** *vt* 加速

❑**hurry up** I *vi* 赶快 II *vt* 使赶紧

hurt [hɜːt] (*pt, pp* **hurt**) I *vt* 1 (*cause pain to*) 弄痛 2 (*injure*) [+ *arm, leg, finger etc*] 使受伤 3 (*emotionally*) 使伤心 II *vi* (*be painful*) 痛 III *adj* 1 (*injured*) 受伤的 2 (*emotionally*) 受委屈的 ♦**to hurt o.s.** 伤了自己 ♦**I didn't want to hurt your feelings** 我并不想伤害你的感情 ♦**where does it hurt?** 哪儿疼？

hurtful ['hɜːtful] *adj* [+ *remark*] 刻薄的

✪**husband** ['hʌzbənd] I *n* [c] 丈夫 II *vt* [文] [*resources*] 节省

hush [hʌʃ] I *int* 嘘 II *vi* (*be quiet*) 安静下来 III *vt* (*quieten*) 使安静 IV *n* ♦**a hush fell over the crowd** 人群顿时一片寂静

❑**hush up** *vt* [+ *scandal etc*] 不让张扬

husky ['hʌskɪ] I *adj* [+ *voice*] 嘶哑的 II *n* [c] (*dog*) 爱斯基摩狗

hut [hʌt] *n* [c] 1 (*house*) 简陋的小屋 2 (*shed*) 木棚

hyacinth ['haɪəsɪnθ] *n* [c] 风信子

hydrofoil ['haɪdrəfɔɪl] *n* [c] (*boat*) 水翼船

hydrogen ['haɪdrədʒən] [化] *n* [U] 氢

hygiene ['haɪdʒiːn] *n* [U] 卫生

hygienic [haɪ'dʒiːnɪk] *adj* 卫生的

hymn [hɪm] *n* [c] 赞美诗

hype [haɪp] [非正式] I *n* [U] 炒作 II *vt* 炒作

hyphen ['haɪfn] *n* [c] 连字符

hypnosis [hɪp'nəusɪs] *n* [U] 1 (*state*) 催眠状态 2 (*hypnotism*) 催眠术 ♦**under hypnosis** 处于被催眠状态

hypnotize ['hɪpnətaɪz] *vt* 1 (字) 使进入催眠状态 2 (喻) (*fascinate*) 使着迷

hypocrite ['hɪpəkrɪt] *n* [c] 伪君子

hypocritical [hɪpə'krɪtɪkl] *adj* [+ *person, behaviour*] 虚伪的

hypothesis [haɪ'pɔθɪsɪs] (*pl* **hypotheses** [haɪ'pɔθɪsiiz]) [正式] *n* [c] (*theory*) 假设

hysterical [hɪ'stɛrɪkl] *adj* 1 [+ *person, laughter*] 歇斯底里的 2 [非正式] (*hilarious*) 歇斯底里的

hysterics [hɪ'stɛrɪks] [非正式] *n* [*pl*] ♦**to be in/have hysterics** (*panic, be angry*) 歇斯底里发作; (*laugh loudly*) 不可控制的狂笑

Ii

I[1], i [aɪ] *n* [c/u] (*letter*) 英语的第九个字母

I[2] [aɪ] *pron* 我

I[3] *abbr* (= **island, isle**) 岛

IC [手机短信] *abbr* (= ***I see***) 知道了

ice [aɪs] **I** *n* **1** [u] (*on lake, river, road*) 冰; (*for drink*) 冰块 **2** [c] [英: 过时] (*ice cream*) 冰淇淋 **II** *vt* [+ *cake*] 在…撒上糖霜 **III** *vi* (*also:* ***ice over, ice up***) [*road, window* +] 结冰 ♦**to put sth on ice** (喻) 搁置某事 ♦**to break the ice** (喻) 使气氛活跃起来 ♦**to cut no ice (with sb)** (喻) (对某人) 不起作用 ♦**to be (skating) on thin ice** (喻) 如履薄冰

iceberg ['aɪsbəːg] *n* [c] 冰山 ♦**the tip of the iceberg** (喻) 冰山一角

ice cream *n* [c/u] 冰淇淋

ice cube *n* [c] 冰块

iced [aɪst] *adj* **1** [+ *drink*] 冰的 **2** [+ *cake*] 有糖霜的

ice hockey [尤英] *n* [u] 冰球 [美= **hockey**]

Iceland ['aɪslənd] *n* 冰岛

Icelander ['aɪsləndə(r)] *n* [c] 冰岛人

Icelandic [aɪs'lændɪk] **I** *adj* 冰岛的 **II** *n* [u] (*language*) 冰岛语

ice lolly [英] *n* [c] 冰棍 [美= **Popsicle**]

ice rink *n* [c] 溜冰场

ice-skating ['aɪsskeɪtɪŋ] *n* [u] 溜冰; (*figure skating*) 花样滑冰 ♦**to go ice-skating** 去溜冰

icing ['aɪsɪŋ] [烹饪] *n* [u] 糖霜 ♦**the icing on the cake** (喻) 锦上添花

icing sugar [英] *n* [u] 糖粉 [美= **confectioners' sugar**]

icon ['aɪkɔn] *n* [c] **1** (*religious*) 圣像 **2** [计算机] 图符 **3** (喻) (*symbol*) 偶像

ICT [英] *n abbr* (= ***Information and Communication Technology***) 通信技术

icy ['aɪsɪ] *adj* [+ *air, water, temperature*] 冰冷的; [+ *road*] 结冰的

ID *n abbr* (= ***identification***) 身份证明 ♦**do you have any ID?** 你有证件吗?

I'd [aɪd] = **I would, I had**

ID card *n* = **identity card**

✪idea [aɪ'dɪə] *n* **1** [c] (*scheme*) 主意 ◊ *I had a brilliant idea.* 我有个绝妙主意。**2** [c] (*opinion, theory*) 看法 ◊ *People had some odd ideas about us.* 人们对我们有些古怪的看法。**3** [c/u] (*notion*) 概念 ◊ *Have you any idea how much it would cost?* 你知道大概是多少钱吗? ◊ *Do you have any idea how big the project is going to be?* 你对项目规模有概念吗? **4** [s] (*objective*) 目的 ◊ *The idea is to try and avoid further expense.* 目的是尽量避免更多的开销。♦**once you get the idea** 一旦你明白了 ♦**(what a) good idea!** (真是个) 好主意! ♦**to have a good/clear idea of sth** 非常了解某事 ♦**I haven't the slightest** *or* **faintest idea** 我根本就不知道 ♦**that's not my idea of fun** 那不是我的兴趣所在

ideal [aɪ'dɪəl] **I** *adj* [+ *person, world*] 理想的 **II** *n* **1** [c] (*principle*) 理想 **2** [s] (*epitome*) 完美典范

ideally [aɪ'dɪəlɪ] *adv* **1** [+ *suited, located, qualified*] 理想地 **2** (*preferably*) 按理想说

identical [aɪ'dɛntɪkl] *adj* 完全相同的 ♦**identical to** 和…完全相同

identification [aɪdɛntɪfɪ'keɪʃən] *n* [u] **1** (*pinpointing*) 识别 **2** (*of person, dead body, disease*) 确认 **3** (*proof of identity*) 身份证明 **4** (*association*) 关联 **5** (*empathy*) 息息相通感

identify [aɪ'dɛntɪfaɪ] *vt* (*recognize*) 识别 ♦**to identify with sb/sth** (*empathize*) 与某人/某物认同 ♦**to identify sb/sth with** (*associate*) 与某人/某物相关联

identity [aɪ'dɛntɪtɪ] *n* [c/u] **1** [*of person, culprit*] 身份 **2** [*of group, culture, nation, place*] 特性

identity card *n* [c] 身份证

ideological [aɪdɪə'lɔdʒɪkl] *adj* 思想上的

ideology [aɪdɪ'ɔlədʒɪ] *n* [c/u] (*beliefs*) 意识形态

idiom [ˈɪdɪəm] *n* **1** [c] (*saying*) 习语 **2** [c/u] [正式] (*style*) 风格

idiot [ˈɪdɪət] *n* [c] 傻子

idle [ˈaɪdl] **I** *adj* **1** (*inactive*) 闲散的 **2** (*lazy*) 懒惰的 **3** [+ *conversation, curiosity*] 无用的 **4** [+ *threat, boast*] 虚张声势的 ◊ *This is no idle threat.* 这不是随便说说吓唬人的。 **5** [+ *machinery, factory*] 闲置的 **6** [+ *worker*] 无所事事的 **II** *vi* [*machine, engine* +] 闲置 ♦ **to lie** *or* **stand idle** [*factory, machinery* +] 被搁置不用

❑ **idle away** *vt* ♦ **to idle away the time** 虚度光阴

idol [ˈaɪdl] *n* [c] **1** (*hero*) 偶像 **2** (*religious*) 圣像

idyllic [ɪˈdɪlɪk] *adj* [+ *place, situation, childhood*] 质朴宜人的

i.e. *abbr* (= ***id est***) 也就是

✪ **if**

KEYWORD

[ɪf] *conj*

1 (*conditional use*) 如果 ♦ **I'll go if you come with me** 如果你和我一起的话我就去 ♦ **if anyone comes in ...** 如果有人来… ♦ **if I were you** 如果我是你的话 ♦ **if necessary** 如有必要 ♦ **if so** 如果是这样的话 ♦ **if not** 如果不行的话

2 (*stating facts*) 即使 ♦ **she understood his meaning if not his words** 虽然不懂他的话，她明白他的意思

3 (*whenever*) 无论何时 ♦ **if we are in Hong Kong, we always go to see her** 我们无论何时去香港，都会去看她

4 (***also: even if***) 即使 ♦ **I'll get this sorted if it's the last thing I do!** 无论怎样我都会把这事解决好！

5 (*whether*) 是否 ♦ **I don't know if he's in** 我不知道他是否会在 ♦ **ask him if he can come** 问他是否能来

6 (*in requests*) 请 ♦ **if you could sign here, please** 请在这儿签名，好吗

7 (*in expressions*) ♦ **if ever** 要是有 ◊ *If ever a man needed help, it was I.* 要是有人需要帮助的话，那就是我。 ♦ **if only** (*giving reason*) 即使只是; (*expressing wish*) 要是…就好了 ♦ **let's invite her here, if only to find out what she's doing** 我们邀请她来这儿吧，即使只是问问她在忙些什么 ♦ **if only we had more time!** 要是我们再多点时间就好了！

ignite [ɪɡˈnaɪt] **I** *vt* **1** (*cause to burn*) [+ *explosive, petrol*] 点燃; [+ *fire*] 点 **2** (喻) [+ *interest, passion*] 使激动; [+ *war, debate*] 激起 **II** *vi* 着火

ignition [ɪɡˈnɪʃən] [汽车] *n* **1** [u] (*process*) 发火 **2** [c] (*mechanism*) 发火装置 ♦ **turn the ignition on/off** 开/关点火装置

ignorance [ˈɪɡnərəns] *n* [u] (*lack of knowledge*) 无知 ♦ **to keep sb in ignorance of sth** 不让某人知道某事

ignorant [ˈɪɡnərənt] *adj* **1** (*uninformed, unaware*) 无知的 **2** (*rude*) 粗鲁无礼的 ♦ **to be ignorant of** [+ *subject, events*] 不知道的

ignore [ɪɡˈnɔː(r)] *vt* **1** (*pay no attention to*) [+ *person*] 不理; [+ *advice, event*] 不顾 **2** (*overlook*) [+ *fact*] 忽视

I'll [aɪl] = **I will, I shall**

ill [ɪl] **I** *adj* **1** (*sick*) 有病的 **2** (*harmful*) [+ *effects, luck, fortune*] 坏的 **II** *n* [文] (*evil*) 恶意 **III the ill** *n* [*pl*] ♦ **the mentally/terminally ill** 精神/晚期病人 **IV ills** *n* [*pl*] [正式, 文] (*troubles*) 弊病 **V** *adv* [正式] ♦ **to speak/think ill of sb** 讲某人坏话/认为某人坏 ♦ **to fall** *or* **be taken ill** 生病

> 📖 单词 **ill** 和 **sick** 在语意上很相近，但使用方法略有不同。**ill** 通常不用在名词前，但可用在动词词组中，比如 **fall ill** 和 **be taken ill** 。*He fell ill shortly before Christmas...One of the jury members was taken ill.* **sick** 经常用在名词前。*...sick children...* 在英式英语中，**ill** 比 **sick** 更为文雅和委婉。**sick** 常常指实际的身体病痛，例如晕船或呕吐。*I spent the next 24 hours in bed,*

groaning and being sick. 美式英语中，**sick**经常用在英国人说**ill**的地方。*Some people get hurt in accidents or get sick.*

illegal [ɪ'liːgl] *adj* 非法的 ♦**it is illegal to ...** 做…是非法的
illegible [ɪ'lɛdʒɪbl] *adj* [+ *writing*] 难以辨认的
illegitimate [ɪlɪ'dʒɪtɪmət] *adj* **1** [+ *child*] 私生的 **2** [+ *activity*] 违法的
ill health *n* [U] 健康状况不佳
illiterate [ɪ'lɪtərət] *adj* **1** [+ *person*] 文盲的 **2** [+ *letter, writing*] 语言错误的
illness ['ɪlnɪs] *n* [C/U] 病
illuminate [ɪ'luːmɪneɪt] *vt* **1** [+ *room, street, building*] 照明 **2** (*explain*) 解释
illuminated [ɪ'luːmɪneɪtɪd] *adj* **1** [+ *sign, building*] 被照明的 **2** [+ *manuscript*] 加了彩饰的
illusion [ɪ'luːʒən] *n* [C] **1** (*false idea*) 幻想 **2** (*false appearance*) 错觉 ♦**to have no illusions about sth** 对某事不抱有幻想 ♦**to be under the illusion that ...** 对…存有幻想
illustrate ['ɪləstreɪt] *vt* **1** (*demonstrate*) 显示 **2** [+ *point, argument*] 说明 **3** [+ *book*] 用插图装饰
illustration [ɪlə'streɪʃən] *n* **1** [C] (*picture*) 插图 **2** [C/U] (*example*) 实例
I'm [aɪm] = **I am**
image ['ɪmɪdʒ] *n* [C] **1** (*mental picture*) 印象 **2** (*picture*) 图像 **3** (*reflection*) 映像 **4** (*public face*) 形象 **5** (*in poem, novel*) 意象 ♦**to project an** *or* **the image of ...** 给人的印象是…
imaginary [ɪ'mædʒɪnərɪ] *adj* **1** [+ *danger*] 虚构的 **2** [+ *being, place*] 想象中的
imagination [ɪmædʒɪ'neɪʃən] *n* **1** [C/U] 想象力 **2** [C] (*mind's eye*) 想象 ♦**a lack of imagination** 缺乏想象力 ♦**it's just your imagination** 只是你的想象而已
imaginative [ɪ'mædʒɪnətɪv] *adj* **1** [+ *person*] 富于想象的 **2** [+ *idea, approach, solution*] 新颖的
imagine [ɪ'mædʒɪn] *vt* **1** (*envisage*) 想象 **2** (*dream*) 幻想 **3** (*suppose*) 设想
imbalance [ɪm'bæləns] *n* [C/U] 不平衡
IMF *n abbr* (= ***International Monetary Fund***) ♦**the IMF** 国际货币基金组织
imitate ['ɪmɪteɪt] *vt* **1** (*copy*) 效仿 **2** (*mimic*) [+ *person, sound, gesture*] 模仿
imitation [ɪmɪ'teɪʃən] **I** *n* **1** [U] (*act*) 模仿 **2** [C] (*copy*) 仿制品 **II** *adj* 仿制的 ♦**to do an imitation of sb** 模仿某人
immaculate [ɪ'mækjulət] *adj* **1** [+ *room, appearance*] 无瑕疵的 **2** [+ *performance*] 完美的 ♦**the Immaculate Conception** 圣灵怀胎说
immature [ɪmə'tjuə(r)] *adj* **1** [+ *organ, organism*] 发育未全的 **2** (*childish*) [+ *person, behaviour*] 不成熟的
immediate [ɪ'miːdɪət] *adj* **1** [+ *reaction, effect, result*] 立即的 **2** (*urgent*) [+ *need, problem*] 当前的 **3** (*nearest*) [+ *family, superior, vicinity*] 最近的
immediately [ɪ'miːdɪətlɪ] **I** *adv* **1** (*at once*) 立即地 **2** [+ *apparent, obvious*] 直接地 **3** (*directly*) 紧接地 **II** *conj* ♦**immediately he had said it, he regretted it** 他刚一说完马上就后悔了 ♦**immediately next to** 紧靠着 ♦**immediately before/after** 紧接着…之前/后
immense [ɪ'mɛns] *adj* 巨大的
immensely [ɪ'mɛnslɪ] *adv* [*like, help* +] 非常; [+ *popular, grateful*] 非常
immerse [ɪ'məːs] *vt* (*submerge*) 浸没 ♦**to immerse sth in water** *etc* 把某物浸没在水{等}里 ♦**to immerse o.s. in sth** [+ *work, thought, subject*] 沉浸于某事之中
immigrant ['ɪmɪgrənt] *n* [C] 移民
immigration [ɪmɪ'greɪʃən] **I** *n* [U] **1** (*process*) 移民 **2** (*also:* ***immigration control***) (*at airport, port, border*) 移民局检查 **II** *cpd* [复合词] [+ *authorities, policy, controls, officer*] 移民
imminent ['ɪmɪnənt] *adj* [+ *danger, death, arrival, departure*] 逼近的
immoral [ɪ'mɔrəl] *adj* [+ *person, behaviour, idea*] 不道德的 ♦**it is immoral to ...** …是不道德的

immortal [ɪ'mɔːtl] **I** *adj* **1** [+ *god, being*] 不朽的 **2** [+ *poetry, words*] 流芳百世的 **II** *n* **1** 不朽者 **2** (*famous person*) 流芳百世的人

immune [ɪ'mjuːn] *adj* ♦ **immune to 1** [+ *disease*] 对…有免疫力 **2** [+ *flattery, criticism, attack*] 不受…影响的 ♦ **immune from** [+ *prosecution, scandal*] 免除…

immune system *n* [C] 免疫系统

immunize ['ɪmjunaɪz] *vt* 使免疫 ♦ **to immunize sb against sth** 使某人免患某病

impact [*n* 'ɪmpækt, *vb* ɪm'pækt] **I** *n* **1** [C/U] [*of collision, blow*] 冲击 **2** [C] [*of law, change, situation*] 影响 **II** *vi* ♦ **to impact (up)on sb/sth** 冲击某人/某物 ♦ **to have an impact (up)on sb/sth** 对某人/某物产生影响 ♦ **to make an impact** 产生影响 ♦ **(up)on impact** 在碰撞时

impair [ɪm'pɛə(r)] *vt* [+ *faculties, vision, judgement*] 削弱

impartial [ɪm'pɑːʃl] *adj* **1** [+ *judge, observer*] 公正的; [+ *advice*] 不偏不倚的

impasse ['ɪm'pɑːs] *n* [S] (*in war, negotiations*) 僵局 ♦ **to reach an impasse** 陷入僵局

impatience [ɪm'peɪʃəns] *n* [U] **1** (*annoyance at waiting*) 急躁 **2** (*irritation*) 不耐烦 **3** (*eagerness*) 急切

impatient [ɪm'peɪʃənt] *adj* **1** (*at waiting*) 急躁的 **2** (*irritable*) 不耐烦的 ♦ **to get impatient (at** *or* **with sth)** (对某事) 不耐烦 ♦ **to be impatient for sth/to do sth** 渴望某事/做某事

impeccable [ɪm'pɛkəbl] *adj* [+ *dress, manners, taste*] 无瑕疵的; [+ *credentials, reputation*] 勿容置疑的

impede [ɪm'piːd] *vt* [+ *progress, development, movement*] 妨碍

impending [ɪm'pɛndɪŋ] *adj* [+ *war, marriage*] 即将来临的; [+ *doom, disaster*] 逼近的

imperative [ɪm'pɛrətɪv] **I** *adj* 绝对必要的 **II** *n* [C] **1** [正式] (*necessity*) 要务 **2** [语言] 祈使语气 ♦ **it is imperative to stick to your budget** 绝对不能超过预算 ♦ **it is imperative for us to act quickly** 我们必须要立即行动 ♦ **it is imperative that ...** …是非常重要的 ♦ **in the imperative** [语言] 用祈使语气

imperfect [ɪm'pəːfɪkt] **I** *adj* [+ *goods*] 有瑕疵的; [+ *system, understanding, world*] 不完美的 **II** *n* (*also:* ***imperfect tense***) ♦ **the imperfect** 未完成时态 ♦ **in the imperfect** 用未完成时态

imperial [ɪm'pɪərɪəl] *adj* **1** [+ *palace, family*] 皇帝的; [+ *power*] 帝国的 **2** [英] [+ *measure*] 英制的

impersonal [ɪm'pəːsənl] *adj* **1** [+ *place, organization*] 没人情味的 **2** (*objective*) [+ *basis*] 客观的

impersonate [ɪm'pəːsəneɪt] *vt* **1** (*fraudulently*) 冒充 **2** (*for entertainment*) 模仿

impetus ['ɪmpətəs] *n* [U/S] 动力

implant [*vb* ɪm'plɑːnt, *n* 'ɪmplɑːnt] **I** *vt* **1** [+ *embryo, tissue, cells*] 植入 **2** [+ *idea, principle*] 灌输 **II** *n* [C] 植入物

implement [*vb* ɪmplɪ'mɛnt, *n* 'ɪmplɪmənt] **I** *vt* [+ *plan, regulation*] 实施 **II** *n* [C] (*tool*) 器具

implicate ['ɪmplɪkeɪt] *vt* 牵连 ♦ **to be implicated in sth** 牵连在某事中

implication [ɪmplɪ'keɪʃən] *n* **1** [C] (*possible consequence*) 牵扯的后果 **2** [C/U] (*inference*) 含意 **3** [U] (*involvement*) 牵连 ♦ **by implication** 含蓄地

implicit [ɪm'plɪsɪt] *adj* **1** (*implied*) [+ *threat, meaning, criticism*] 含蓄的 **2** (*absolute*) [+ *belief, trust*] 绝对的 **3** (*inherent*) 内含的

imply [ɪm'plaɪ] *vt* **1** [*person* +] (*suggest*) 暗示 ♦ **to imply that ...** 暗示… **2** [*fact* +] (*mean*) 意味

impolite [ɪmpə'laɪt] *adj* 没礼貌的 ♦ **it would be impolite to refuse the invitation** 拒绝邀请将会是没礼貌的

import [*vb* ɪm'pɔːt, *n*, *cpd* 'ɪmpɔːt] **I** *vt* [+ *goods*] 进口 **II** *n* **1** [C] (*sth imported*) 进口商品 **2** [U] (*importation*) 进口 **3** [S] (*significance*) 重要性 **III** *cpd* [复合词] [+ *duty, licence, restrictions*] 进口 ♦ **of little/**

no import 无关紧要

importance [ɪm'pɔːtns] *n* [U] 1 (*significance*) 重要性 2 (*influence*) 影响 ♦ **of importance** 有影响的 ♦ **of great/little importance** 至关重要/无关紧要

✪ **important** [ɪm'pɔːtənt] *adj* 1 (*significant*) [+ *thing, factor, decision*] 重要的 ◊ *That is a very important point that you've raised.*你提的问题是很重要的。2 (*influential*) 有影响的 ◊ *the list of important people who are coming* 到场的要人名单 ◊ *a very important criminal lawyer* 一个非常有影响的刑事辩护律师 ♦ **it is important to eat sensibly** 合理进食是很重要的 ♦ **it is important for them to understand that ...** 他们一定要懂得… ♦ **it is important that ...** …是非常重要的 ♦ **it's not important** 不重要的

importer [ɪm'pɔːtə(r)] *n* [C] 进口商

impose [ɪm'pəuz] **I** *vt* [+ *sanctions, restrictions, fine*] 施加 **II** *vi* ♦ **to impose on sb** 强加于某人

imposing [ɪm'pəuzɪŋ] *adj* [+ *building*] 壮观的; [+ *person, manner*] 威严的

impossible [ɪm'pɔsɪbl] *adj* 1 [+ *task, demand*] 不可能的 2 (*difficult*) [+ *situation, position*] 无法忍受的; [+ *person*] 难以对付的 ♦ **it is impossible to understand what's going on** 不可能了解事情的进展情况 ♦ **these feelings are impossible to ignore** 不能忽视这些情感 ♦ **it's impossible for me to leave now** 我现在走不了 ♦ **the impossible** 不可能的事

impotent ['ɪmpətənt] *adj* 1 [正式] (*powerless*) [+ *person, group*] 无力的; [+ *rage*] 不起作用的 2 (*sexually*) 阳萎的

impoverished [ɪm'pɔvərɪʃt] *adj* [+ *country, area, person*] 贫困的

impractical [ɪm'præktɪkl] *adj* 1 [+ *idea, plan*] 不切实际的 2 [+ *person*] 实践能力差的

impress [ɪm'prɛs] *vt* [+ *person*] 给…极深的印象 ♦ **to be impressed by** *or* **with sb/sth** 对某人/某物印象深刻 ♦ **to impress sth (up)on sb** 使某人铭记某事

impression [ɪm'prɛʃən] *n* [C] 1 [*of place, situation, person*] 印象 2 (*mark*) [*of stamp, seal, foot*] 印记 3 (*imitation*) 滑稽模仿 ♦ **to be under the impression that ...** 以为… ♦ **first impressions** 第一印象 ♦ **to make** *or* **create a good/bad impression** 留下好/不良印象 ♦ **to give the impression of/that ...** 给人的印象是…

impressive [ɪm'prɛsɪv] *adj* [+ *reputation, achievement, performance*] 给人深刻印象的

imprison [ɪm'prɪzn] *vt* 监禁

imprisonment [ɪm'prɪznmənt] *n* [U] 监禁

improbable [ɪm'prɔbəbl] *adj* 1 (*unlikely*) [+ *outcome, explanation, story*] 不大可能的 2 (*strange*) [+ *event, story*] 未必可信的 ♦ **it is improbable that ...** …是不大可能的

improper [ɪm'prɔpə(r)] *adj* 1 (*unsuitable*) [+ *procedure*] 不适当的 2 (*dishonest*) [+ *activities*] 不正当的 3 [过时] (*rude*) 不合适的 ♦ **It would be improper to ...** …是不适当的

improve [ɪm'pruːv] **I** *vt* [+ *quality, conditions, situation*] 改进 **II** *vi* [*weather, situation* +] 改善; [*pupil, performance* +] 进步; [*patient, health* +] 改善

❑ **improve on** *vt* [不可拆分] 改进

improvement [ɪm'pruːvmənt] *n* [C/U] 改进 ♦ **improvement in** [+ *person, thing*] 进步 ♦ **to be an improvement (on sb/sth)** 比(某人/某物)有进步 ♦ **to make improvements to sth** 改进某物

improvise ['ɪmprəvaɪz] **I** *vi* 1 (*make do*) 临时凑合 2 [戏剧, 音] 即兴创作 **II** *vt* 1 [+ *bed, meal, shelter*] 临时凑成 2 [戏剧, 音] 即兴创作

impulse ['ɪmpʌls] *n* 1 [C/U] (*urge*) 冲动 2 [C] [电子] 脉冲 ♦ **to have an impulse to do sth** 有做某事的冲动 ♦ **to do sth on impulse** 一时冲动做某事 ♦ **to act on impulse** 凭一时冲动行事

impulsive [ɪm'pʌlsɪv] *adj* [+ *person*] 冲动的; [+ *purchase, decision*] 凭冲动的

in

KEYWORD

[ɪn]

I *prep*

1 (*indicating place, position*) 在…里 ♦ **it's in the house/garden/box** 它在房子/花园/盒子里 ♦ **put it in the house/garden/box** 把它放在房子/花园/盒子里 ♦ **in here/there** 在这儿/那儿 ♦ **there's a crack in the wall** 墙上有个裂缝

2 (*with place names*) 在 ♦ **in London/England** 在伦敦/英格兰

3 (*time*) (*during*) 在; (*within*) (*referring to future*) 在…之后; (*referring to past*) 在…之内 ♦ **in 1988/May** 在1988 年/5 月 ♦ **in spring/summer** 在春天/夏天 ♦ **in the morning/afternoon** 在上午/下午 ♦ **in term time/the holidays** 在学期/假期中 ♦ **in the nineties** 在90 年代 ♦ **I'll see you in two weeks' time** *or* **in two weeks** 我两周后见你 ♦ **I did it in 3 hours/days** 我花了3 小时/天完成 ♦ **most people can do this in half an hour** 大多数人能够在半小时内完成 **4** (*indicating manner, style etc*) 以 ♦ **in a loud/soft voice** 大声地/用柔和的声音 ♦ **in pencil/ink** 用铅笔/墨水笔 ♦ **the boy in the blue shirt** 穿蓝衬衫的男孩儿 ♦ **a tall woman, dressed in blue** 一位身穿蓝衣的高个女子 ♦ **in the sun/rain** 在阳光下/雨中

5 (*with languages*) 用 ♦ **in English/French** 用英语/法语

6 (*mood, state*) 处于 ♦ **he looked up in surprise** 他吃惊地往上看 ♦ **to be in a mood/a bad temper** 心情/脾气不好 ♦ **in good condition** 状况良好地

7 (*with ratios, numbers*) 每 ♦ **one in ten people** 十分之一的人 ♦ **20 pence in the pound** 每1 英镑中的20 便士 ♦ **they lined up in twos** 他们排成两排 ♦ **people came in their thousands** 数以千计的人们涌了进来

8 (*in book, film, activity*) 在 ♦ **I read it in a newspaper** 我在报纸上看到的 ♦ **in (the works of) Dickens** 在狄更斯(的作品)中 ♦ **to be in teaching/publishing** 从事教育/出版业

9 (*amongst*) [+ *group, collection*] 在…中 ♦ **the best athlete in the team** 该队中最好的运动员 ♦ **the disease is common in children** 这种病在儿童中是常见的

10 (*with present participle*) 通过 ♦ **in saying this** 通过这么一说

II *adv*

1 ♦ **to be in** (*at home, work etc*) 在 ◊ *My flatmate was in at the time.* 我寓友那时候在家。; (*in fashion*) 流行地; (*in station, port*) 到达 ♦ **miniskirts are in again this year** 迷你裙今年又流行了 ♦ **the train isn't in yet** 火车还没到站 ♦ **to ask sb in** 把某人请到家中

2 ♦ **to be in for sth** [+ *shock, surprise*] 即将体验到某事

III *n* ♦ **the ins and outs** [*of proposal, situation etc*] 来龙去脉

in. (*pl* **in.** or **ins**) *abbr* (= ***inch***) 英寸

inability [ɪnə'bɪlɪtɪ] *n* ♦ **my/his inability (to do sth)** 我/他没能力(做某事)

inaccurate [ɪn'ækjurət] *adj* 不准确的

inadequacy [ɪn'ædɪkwəsɪ] *n* [C/U]
1 [*of system, preparations*] 不充分
2 [*of person*] 不胜任

inadequate [ɪn'ædɪkwət] *adj*
1 [+ *income, amount, supply*] 不充分的 **2** [+ *person*] 不能胜任的

inadvertently [ɪnəd'vəːtntlɪ] *adv* 漫不经心地

inappropriate [ɪnə'prəuprɪət] *adj*
1 (*unsuitable*) 不适当的 **2** (*improper*) [+ *remark, behaviour*] 不相宜的 ♦ **it would be inappropriate to comment** 进行评论将是不恰当的 ♦ **it would be inappropriate for me to interfere** 我干涉将是不恰当的 ♦ **to be inappropriate to sth** 对某事不相宜

inaugurate [ɪ'nɔːgjureɪt] *vt*
1 [+ *president, official*] 为…举行就职典礼 **2** [+ *system, measure*] 开创

Inc. [尤美] *abbr* (= ***incorporated***) 有限公司

inc. *abbr* (= ***including***) 包括

incapable [ɪn'keɪpəbl] *adj* ♦ **to be incapable of sth/doing sth** 不会

某事/做某事

incense [*n* 'ɪnsɛns, *vb* ɪn'sɛns] **I** *n* [U] (*perfume*) 香 **II** *vt* (*enrage*) 激怒

incentive [ɪn'sɛntɪv] **I** *n* [C/U] 刺激 ♦**tax incentives** 税收鼓励 **II** *cpd* [复合词] [商] [+ *payment, plan*] 激励

inch [ɪntʃ] **I** *n* [C] 英寸 **II** *vi* ♦**to inch forward/up** 一点一点地向前/上 **III** *vt* ♦**to inch sth forward/up** 一点一点地使某物向前/上 ♦**we searched every inch of the house** 我们彻底地搜查了那间房子 ♦**he didn't give an inch** (*back down, yield*) 他寸步不让

incidence ['ɪnsɪdns] *n* [C/U] [*of crime, disease*] 发生率

incident ['ɪnsɪdnt] *n* [C] (*event*) 事件

incidentally [ɪnsɪ'dɛntəlɪ] *adv* (*by the way*) 顺便提一句

incl. *abbr* = **inc.**

inclination [ɪnklɪ'neɪʃən] *n* [C/U] (*desire*) 倾向

incline [*n* 'ɪnklaɪn, *vb* ɪn'klaɪn] **I** *n* [C] (*slope*) 斜坡 **II** *vt* (*bend*) [+ *head*] 低 **III** *vi* [*surface* +] 倾斜 ♦**I incline to the view that ...** [正式] 我倾向于…的观点

inclined [ɪn'klaɪnd] *adj* ♦**to be inclined to do sth** (*tend to*) 倾向于做某事; (*want to*) 想做某事 ♦**to be mathematically/artistically inclined** 在数学/艺术方面有天赋

✪**include** [ɪn'klu:d] *vt* 包括 ◊ *The four-man crew included one Briton.* 四人小组包括一个英国人。◊ *Carpets and curtains are included in the purchase price.* 地毯和窗帘包括在购物价格里。

included [ɪn'klu:dɪd] *adj* 包括在内的 ♦**myself included** 包括我在内 ♦**service is not included** 不含小费 ♦**included in the price** 包括在价格内

✪**including** [ɪn'klu:dɪŋ] *prep* 包括 ♦**it costs £15.50, including postage and packing** 价格15英镑50便士，邮资和包装费包括在内 ♦**nine people were injured, including two Britons** 九个人受了伤，包括两个英国人 ♦**up to and including** 直到并包括 ♦**including service charge** 内含小费

inclusion [ɪn'klu:ʒən] *n* [U] 包括

inclusive [ɪn'klu:sɪv] **I** *adj* **1** [+ *price*] 一切费用包括在内的 **2** [+ *organization, society*] 包罗广泛的 **II** *adv* 包括一切费用在内地 ♦**inclusive of tax** 含税 ♦**Monday to Friday inclusive** 从周一到周五，包括首尾两天

income ['ɪnkʌm] *n* [C/U] 收入 ♦**gross/net income** 总/净收入 ♦**income bracket** 收入类别

income tax *n* [U] 所得税

incoming ['ɪnkʌmɪŋ] *adj* **1** [+ *flight, call, tide*] 进来的; [+ *missile*] 正袭来的 **2** [+ *government, president*] 即将就任的

incompatible [ɪnkəm'pætɪbl] *adj* **1** [+ *lifestyles, systems, aims*] 不相容的; [+ *people*] 合不来的 **2** [+ *computers, software*] 不兼容的 ♦**incompatible with** 与…不相容

incompetence [ɪn'kɔmpɪtns] *n* [U] 不胜任

incompetent [ɪn'kɔmpɪtnt] *adj* 不胜任的

incomplete [ɪnkəm'pli:t] *adj* **1** (*unfinished*) [+ *book, painting, process*] 未完成的 **2** (*partial*) [+ *success, achievement*] 不彻底的

inconsistent [ɪnkən'sɪstnt] *adj* **1** [+ *behaviour, action, person*] 反复无常的 **2** [+ *statements*] 前后矛盾的 ♦**inconsistent with** 与…不一致

inconvenience [ɪnkən'vi:njəns] **I** *n* [C/U] 不便 **II** *vt* 打扰

inconvenient [ɪnkən'vi:njənt] *adj* [+ *time, moment*] 不合时宜的; [+ *journey, place*] 不方便的 ♦**that's very inconvenient for me** 那对我来说是很不方便的

incorporate [ɪn'kɔ:pəreɪt] *vt* (*include*) 包含

Incorporated [ɪn'kɔ:pəreɪtɪd] *adj* [美:商] 组成公司的

incorrect [ɪnkə'rɛkt] *adj* **1** [+ *information, answer*] 错误的 **2** [+ *posture, diet*] 不适当的

✪**increase** [*n* 'ɪnkri:s, *vb* ɪn'kri:s] **I** *n* [C] 增长 ◊ *a sharp increase in productivity* 生产率的急剧增长 ◊ *an increase of 2 per cent in the volume of sales* 销售量增长了百分

之二 **II** *vi* [*price, level, productivity* +] 增长 ◊ *The population continues to increase.* 人口不断增长。**III** *vt* [+ *price, number, level*] 提高 ◊ *The company has increased the price of its cars.* 公司提高了汽车价格。♦ **a 5% increase, an increase of 5%** 百分之五的增长 ♦ **a tax/price increase** 加税/价 ♦ **to be on the increase** 在增加中 ♦ **to increase by 3%** 增长了百分之三

increasingly [ɪn'kriːsɪŋlɪ] *adv* (*with adj*) 越来越; (*with verb*) 日益

incredible [ɪn'krɛdɪbl] *adj*
1 (*amazing, wonderful*) 不可思议的
2 (*unbelievable*) 难以置信的
3 (*enormous*) 惊人的

incredibly [ɪn'krɛdɪblɪ] *adv*
1 (*surprisingly*) 难以置信地
2 (*extremely*) 非常地

incur [ɪn'kəː(r)] [正式] *vt* [+ *expenses, loss, debt*] 遭受; [+ *disapproval, anger*] 招致

indecent [ɪn'diːsnt] *adj*
1 [+ *behaviour, suggestion, photo*] 下流的 2 [+ *haste*] 不合适的

indeed [ɪn'diːd] *adv* 1 (*certainly*) 确实 2 (*as a reply*) 是的 3 (*as intensifier*) 实在 4 (*in fact*) 实际上 ♦ **yes indeed!** 的确如此！

indefinitely [ɪn'dɛfɪnɪtlɪ] *adv* [*postpone, continue, wait* +] 无限期地

independence [ɪndɪ'pɛndns] *n* [U] 独立 ♦ **to declare independence** 宣布独立 ♦ **independence of mind/spirit** 思想/精神独立

Independence Day *n* [C/U] 独立纪念日

✪ **independent** [ɪndɪ'pɛndnt] *adj*
1 [+ *country, person, inquiry, organization*] 独立的 ◊ *Two independent studies came to the same conclusions.* 两个独立的研究得出了相同的结论。2 [英] [+ *school*] 私立的 ♦ **financially independent** 经济自立的 ♦ **independent of each other** 相互独立

index ['ɪndɛks] (*pl* **indexes**) **I** *n* [C]
1 (*in book, library etc*) 索引 2 (*sign*) 指数 **II** *vt* [+ *book, information*] 编索引

India ['ɪndɪə] *n* 印度

Indian ['ɪndɪən] **I** *adj* 印度的 **II** *n* [C]
1 (*person from India*) 印度人 2 [过时] (*Native American*) 印第安人

indicate ['ɪndɪkeɪt] **I** *vt* 1 (*show*) 表明 2 (*point to*) 指向 3 (*mention*) 暗示 **II** *vi* [英] (*in car*) ♦ **to indicate left/right** 打左/右转向灯 [美 = **signal**]

indication [ɪndɪ'keɪʃən] *n* [C/U] (*sign*) 迹象 ♦ **to give an/no indication that ...** 显示/不显示出… ♦ **all the indications are that ...** 所有的迹象显示…

indicator ['ɪndɪkeɪtə(r)] *n* [C] 1 [英] [*on car*] 指示器 [美 = **turn signal**]
2 (*measurement*) 指标 ♦ **an indicator of health/economic activity** 健康/经济活动指标

indict [ɪn'daɪt] [尤美：法] *vt* 控告 ♦ **to be indicted for murder** 被告谋杀罪

indictment [ɪn'daɪtmənt] *n* 1 [C] (*condemnation*) 谴责 2 [C/U] [尤美：法] 起诉

indifference [ɪn'dɪfrəns] *n* [U] (*lack of interest*) 冷淡

indifferent [ɪn'dɪfrənt] *adj*
1 (*uninterested*) 没兴趣的
2 (*mediocre*) 平庸的 ♦ **to be indifferent to sth** 不关心某事

indigestion [ɪndɪ'dʒɛstʃən] *n* [U] 消化不良

indignant [ɪn'dɪgnənt] *adj*
♦ **indignant (at sth/that ...)** (对某事/…) 感到气愤

indirect [ɪndɪ'rɛkt] *adj* 1 [+ *result, effect*] 间接的 2 [+ *route, journey*] 迂回的 3 [+ *answer, reference*] 非直截了当的

indirectly [ɪndɪ'rɛktlɪ] *adv*
1 [+ *responsible*] 间接地 2 [*refer to, cause* +] 间接地

indispensable [ɪndɪs'pɛnsəbl] *adj* 必不可少的 ♦ **indispensable to/for** 对…必需的

individual [ɪndɪ'vɪdjuəl] **I** *n* (*single person*) 个人 **II** *adj* 1 (*personal*) 个人的 2 (*particular*) 单个的 3 (*unique*) 独特的 ♦ **he is an unpleasant/interesting individual** 他是个讨厌的/有趣的人

individuality [ɪndɪvɪdju'ælɪtɪ] *n* [U] 个性

individually [ɪndɪ'vɪdjuəlɪ] *adv*
1 (*by oneself*) 单独地 2 (*separately*) 个别地

Indonesia [ɪndəˈniːzɪə] *n* 印度尼西亚
Indonesian [ɪndəˈniːzɪən] **I** *adj* 印度尼西亚的 **II** *n* **1** [c] (*person*) 印度尼西亚人 **2** [u] (*language*) 印度尼西亚语
indoor [ˈɪndɔː(r)] *adj* 室内的

> 📖 请勿将**indoor**和**indoors**混淆。**indoor**是形容词，用在名词之前。它可以描述存在于建筑物内部的东西或者发生在建筑物内的事情。*...an indoor swimming pool...Table tennis, chess and cards are all indoor games.* **indoors**是副词。如果去**indoors**，就是去建筑物的内部。如果某事发生在**indoors**，表示它发生在建筑物内部。*He ran indoors and up the stairs to pack his bag...On a rainy day, the children were forced to play indoors.*

indoors [ɪnˈdɔːz] *adv* 在室内
📖 用法参见**indoor**
induce [ɪnˈdjuːs] *vt* **1** (*cause*) 导致 **2** [+ *birth, labour*] 人工引导 ♦ **to induce sb to do sth** 引诱某人做某事
indulge [ɪnˈdʌldʒ] **I** *vt* **1** [+ *desire, passion*] 纵情享受 **2** [+ *person, child*] 纵容 **II** *vi* ♦ **to indulge (in)** [+ *luxury, hobby, vice*] 沉溺（于）♦ **to indulge o.s.** 纵情享受
indulgence [ɪnˈdʌldʒəns] *n* **1** [u] (*leniency*) 纵容 **2** [c] (*pleasure*) 嗜好
indulgent [ɪnˈdʌldʒənt] *adj* [+ *parent*] 溺爱的; [+ *smile*] 宽容的
industrial [ɪnˈdʌstrɪəl] *adj* [+ *equipment, production, waste, society*] 工业的; [+ *accident*] 因工的
industrial estate [英] *n* [c] 工业区 [美=**industrial park**]
industrialist [ɪnˈdʌstrɪəlɪst] *n* [c] 工业家
industrialized [ɪnˈdʌstrɪəlaɪzd] *adj* 工业化的
industrial park [美] *n* [c] 工业区 [英=**industrial estate**]
✪ **industry** [ˈɪndəstrɪ] *n* **1** [u] (*manufacturing*) 工业 ◊ *Industry is making increasing use of robots.* 工业生产越来越多地利用机器人。 **2** [c] (*business*) 行业 ◊ *the film industry* 电影业 **3** [u] (*diligence*) 勤劳 ◊ *No one doubted his industry.* 没人怀疑他的勤劳。
ineffective [ɪnɪˈfɛktɪv] *adj* [+ *policy, system*] 无效的
inefficiency [ɪnɪˈfɪʃənsɪ] *n* [u] [*of person, machine, system*] 无效率
inefficient [ɪnɪˈfɪʃənt] *adj* [+ *person, machine, system*] 效率低的
inept [ɪˈnɛpt] *adj* [+ *politician, management*] 无能的 ♦ **to be inept at sth** 不擅长某事
inequality [ɪnɪˈkwɔlɪtɪ] *n* [c/u] 不平等
inevitable [ɪnˈɛvɪtəbl] **I** *adj* [+ *outcome, result, consequence*] 不可避免的 **II** *n* ♦ **the inevitable** 不可避免的事情
inevitably [ɪnˈɛvɪtəblɪ] *adv* 必然地
inexpensive [ɪnɪkˈspɛnsɪv] *adj* 便宜的
inexperienced [ɪnɪkˈspɪərɪənst] *adj* 无经验的
inexplicable [ɪnɪkˈsplɪkəbl] *adj* [+ *decision, mistake*] 莫名其妙的
infamous [ˈɪnfəməs] *adj* [+ *crime, murderer*] 臭名昭著的
📖 用法参见**famous**
infancy [ˈɪnfənsɪ] *n* [u] [*of person*] 婴儿期 ♦ **to die in infancy** 夭折 ♦ **to be in its infancy** [*research, organization* +] 处于初创阶段
infant [ˈɪnfənt] **I** *n* [c] **1** (*baby*) 婴儿 **2** (*young child*) 幼儿 **II** *cpd* [复合词] **1** [+ *food, seat*] 婴儿 **2** [+ *son, daughter*] 年幼
infantry [ˈɪnfəntrɪ] [军] *n* ♦ **the infantry** 步兵
infect [ɪnˈfɛkt] *vt* **1** [+ *person, animal, plant*] 感染 **2** [*vice, enthusiasm* +] 感染 ♦ **to become infected** [*wound* +] 感染了; [*person* +] 染上了
infection [ɪnˈfɛkʃən] *n* **1** [c] (*disease*) 感染 **2** [u] (*contagion*) 传染 ♦ **to have an ear/throat infection** 耳朵/咽喉感染
infectious [ɪnˈfɛkʃəs] *adj* **1** [+ *disease*] 传染的 **2** [+ *enthusiasm, laughter*] 有感染力的
infer [ɪnˈfəː(r)] *vt* **1** (*deduce*) 推断 **2** (*imply*) 暗示
inferior [ɪnˈfɪərɪə(r)] **I** *adj* **1** (*lower in*

hierarchy) 低等的 **2** (*in worth*) [+ *work, person*] 差的; [+ *goods*] 次的 **II** *n* [C] **1** (*in hierarchy*) 下级 **2** (*in worth*) 低下的人 ♦ **to be inferior to** 比…低一等 ♦ **to feel inferior (to)** 感到（比…）低一等

infertile [ɪn'fəːtaɪl] *adj* **1** [+ *man, woman, animal*] 不能生育的 **2** [+ *soil, land*] 贫瘠的

infertility [ɪnfəː'tɪlɪtɪ] **I** *n* [U] **1** [*of man, woman, animal*] 不育症 **2** [*of soil*] 贫瘠 **II** *cpd* [复合词] [+ *clinic, specialist*] 不育症

infested [ɪn'fɛstɪd] *adj* [+ *plant, animal*] 被侵扰的 ♦ **to be infested with** 被…侵扰

infinite ['ɪnfɪnɪt] *adj* **1** (*very great*) [+ *variety, patience*] 极大的 **2** (*limitless*) [+ *universe, number*] 无限的

infinitely ['ɪnfɪnɪtlɪ] *adv* (*with adj*) 非常地; (*with comparative*) …得多

infirmary [ɪn'fəːmərɪ] *n* [C] 医院

inflame [ɪn'fleɪm] *vt* [+ *situation, passions*] 使火上浇油

inflamed [ɪn'fleɪmd] *adj* [+ *throat, appendix, joint*] 发炎的 ♦ **to become inflamed** 发炎了

inflammation [ɪnflə'meɪʃən] *n* [U] 发炎

inflatable [ɪn'fleɪtəbl] *adj* [+ *life jacket, dinghy, ball*] 充气的

inflate [ɪn'fleɪt] **I** *vt* **1** [+ *tyre, balloon*] 使充气 **2** [+ *price*] 抬高 **3** (*exaggerate*) [+ *amount, effect*] 夸大 **II** *vi* [*tyre, balloon* +] 膨胀

inflated [ɪn'fleɪtɪd] *adj* [+ *price*] 飞涨的; [+ *opinion, idea*] 夸大的

inflation [ɪn'fleɪʃən] *n* [U] 通货膨胀

inflexible [ɪn'flɛksɪbl] *adj* **1** [+ *rule, system*] 固定的 **2** [+ *person*] 不灵活的 **3** [+ *object, material*] 不可弯曲的

inflict [ɪn'flɪkt] *vt* ♦ **to inflict sth on sb** [+ *damage, suffering*] 使某人遭受某事

influence ['ɪnfluəns] **I** *n* **1** [C/U] (*power*) 权势 **2** [C] (*effect*) 影响 **II** *vt* [+ *person, situation, choice*] 影响 ♦ **to be/have an influence on sb** 对某人有影响 ♦ **to be a good/bad influence on sb** 对某人有好/坏的影响 ♦ **to have a good/bad influence on sb** 对某人有好/坏的影响 ♦ **under the influence of alcohol/drugs** 在酒精/毒品的作用下

influential [ɪnflu'ɛnʃl] *adj* [+ *politician, critic*] 有权势的 ♦ **to be influential in doing sth** 对做某事有影响

influx ['ɪnflʌks] *n* [C] [*of people*] 涌入; [*of funds, goods*] 流入

info ['ɪnfəu] [非正式] *n* [U] 信息

inform [ɪn'fɔːm] **I** *vt* **1** (*tell*) 告诉 **2** [正式] (*give form to*) 贯穿 **II** *vi* ♦ **to inform on sb** (*to police, authorities*) 告发某人 ♦ **to inform sb of sth** 把某事通知某人 ♦ **to inform sb that ...** 告诉某人…

informal [ɪn'fɔːml] *adj* **1** (*relaxed*) [+ *person, speech, behaviour*] 不拘礼节的 **2** (*casual*) [+ *clothes, party*] 日常的 **3** (*unofficial*) [+ *meeting, discussions, agreement*] 非正式的

✪ **information** [ɪnfə'meɪʃən] *n* [U] 信息 ◊ *For further information, contact the number below.* 如需详情，请打以下电话。◊ *If you have any new information, please let us know.* 如果有任何新信息，请告诉我们。 ♦ **a piece of information** 一条信息 ♦ **for your information** 供参考

information technology *n* [U] 信息技术

informative [ɪn'fɔːmətɪv] *adj* [+ *report, article*] 增长见闻的

informed [ɪn'fɔːmd] *adj* [+ *person*] 有见识的 ♦ **to be well/poorly informed** 见多识广的/孤陋寡闻的 ♦ **an informed guess/choice** 有根据的猜测/选择

infra-red [ɪnfrə'rɛd] *adj* [+ *rays, light, equipment*] 红外线的

infrastructure ['ɪnfrəstrʌktʃə(r)] *n* [C/U] [*of country, organization*] 基础结构

infrequent [ɪn'friːkwənt] *adj* [+ *buses*] 稀少的; [+ *visits*] 不经常的

infuriate [ɪn'fjuərɪeɪt] *vt* [+ *person*] 激怒

infuriating [ɪn'fjuərɪeɪtɪŋ] *adj* 令人讨厌的

ingenious [ɪn'dʒiːnjəs] *adj* [+ *idea, solution*] 有独创性的; [+ *invention, device*] 精巧的

ingredient [ɪn'griːdɪənt] *n* [C] **1** (*in

food) 配料 **2** (*in situation*) 要素

inhabit [ɪn'hæbɪt] *vt* 居住

inhabitant [ɪn'hæbɪtənt] *n* [c] 居民

inhale [ɪn'heɪl] **I** *vt* [+ *smoke, gas*] 吸入 **II** *vi* **1** 吸气 **2** (*when smoking*) 吸入肺部

inhaler [ɪn'heɪlə(r)] *n* [c] 吸入器

inherent [ɪn'hɪərənt] *adj* [+ *danger, problem, qualities*] 内在的 ♦ **to be inherent in** *or* **to sth** 某物内在固有的

inherit [ɪn'hɛrɪt] **1** *vt* [+ *property, money*] 继承 **2** [+ *characteristic, disease*] 由遗传而得 **3** [+ *situation*] 接手

inheritance [ɪn'hɛrɪtəns] *n* **1** [c/u] (*property, money*) 继承 **2** [u/s] (*genetic*) 遗传 **3** [u/s]（喻）(*legacy*) 遗产

inhibit [ɪn'hɪbɪt] *vt* **1** (*slow down, stop*) 阻止 **2** ♦ **to inhibit sb from doing sth** (*discourage*) 阻止某人做某事

inhibited [ɪn'hɪbɪtɪd] *adj* 拘束的

inhibition [ɪnhɪ'bɪʃən] *n* **1** [c] (*hang-up*) 抑制 **2** [u] (*restraint*) 约束

initial [ɪ'nɪʃl] **I** *adj* [+ *stage, reaction, meeting*] 初步的 **II** *n* [c] (*letter*) 首字母 **III** *vt* [+ *document*] 草签 **IV initials** *n* [*pl*] [*of name*] 首字母

initially [ɪ'nɪʃəlɪ] *adv* 最初

initiate [*vb* ɪ'nɪʃɪeɪt, *n* ɪ'nɪʃɪɪt] **I** *vt* (*begin*) [+ *talks, process*] 发动 **II** *n* (*member*) 新入会的人 ♦ **to initiate sb into** [+ *religion, mysteries, secrets*] 把…传授给某人; [+ *society, organization*] 接纳某人加入 ♦ **to initiate proceedings against sb** 开始提起对某人的诉讼

initiation [ɪnɪʃɪ'eɪʃən] *n* [c/u] **1** (*start*) 开创 **2** (*into group, organization*) 加入仪式

initiative [ɪ'nɪʃətɪv] *n* **1** [c] (*idea, measure*) 倡议 **2** [u] (*resourcefulness*) 主动性 ♦ **to take the initiative** 采取主动 ♦ **to act on one's own initiative** 主动采取行动 ♦ **to have the initiative** 掌握主动权 ♦ **to have the initiative to do sth** 有做某事的主动性

inject [ɪn'dʒɛkt] **I** *vt* **1** [+ *drugs, poison*] 注射 **2** ♦ **to inject fun/interest into sth** 给某物注入乐趣/兴趣 ♦ **to inject money into sth** 把资金投入某事 **II** *vi* [*drug user* +] 注射 ♦ **to inject sb with sth** 给某人注射某物

injection [ɪn'dʒɛkʃən] *n* [c] **1** [医] 注射 **2** [*of money*] 投入 ♦ **to give sb an injection** 给某人注射 ♦ **to have an injection** 打针

injure ['ɪndʒə(r)] *vt* [+ *person*] 伤害; [+ *leg, arm, hand*] 伤 ♦ **to injure o.s.** 伤害自己 ♦ **he was badly injured in the attack** 他在进攻中受了重伤

injured ['ɪndʒəd] **I** *adj* **1** [+ *person, part of body*] 受伤的 **2** [+ *pride, feelings*] 受伤的 **II** *n* [*pl*] ♦ **the injured** 受伤者 ♦ **the injured party** [法] 受害方

injury ['ɪndʒərɪ] *n* [c/u] (*wound*) 伤害 ♦ **to do o.s. an injury** 伤害自己 ♦ **to escape without injury** 安然脱险

injustice [ɪn'dʒʌstɪs] *n* [c/u] 不公正 ♦ **you do me an injustice** 你让我受委屈了

ink [ɪŋk] **I** *n* [c/u] (*in pen*) 墨水; (*in printing*) 油墨 **II** *vt* 涂墨于

inland [*adj* 'ɪnlənd, *adv* ɪn'lænd] **I** *adj* [+ *lake, sea, waterway*] 内陆的 **II** *adv* [*travel, live* +] 在内陆

Inland Revenue [英] *n* ♦ **the Inland Revenue** 国内税收部 [美 = **Internal Revenue Service, IRS**]

in-laws ['ɪnlɔːz] *n* [*pl*] 姻亲

inmate ['ɪnmeɪt] *n* [c] [*of prison, psychiatric hospital*] 同住者

inn [ɪn] *n* [c] 小旅馆

innate [ɪ'neɪt] *adj* [+ *skill, quality, characteristic*] 天生的

inner ['ɪnə(r)] *adj* **1** [+ *office, courtyard*] 内部的 **2** [+ *calm, feelings*] 内心的

inner city *n* [c] 旧城区，尤其指社会和经济问题较严重的市中心

inner-city ['ɪnəsɪtɪ] *adj* 旧城区的

inning ['ɪnɪŋ] [棒球] *n* [c] 局

innings (*pl* **innings**) ['ɪnɪŋz] [板球] *n* [c] 局 ♦ **he's had a good innings**（喻）他一生幸福而长寿

innocence ['ɪnəsns] *n* [u] **1** [法] 清白 **2** (*naivety*) 单纯

innocent ['ɪnəsnt] **I** *adj* **1** (*not guilty*) 清白的 **2** (*naive*) [+ *child, person*] 单

纯的 **3** (*not involved*) 无辜的 **4** [+ *remark, question*] 无恶意的 **II** *n* [C] (*naive person*) 幼稚的人 ♦ **to be innocent of a crime** 无罪 ♦ **to play the innocent** 假装无知

innocently ['ɪnəsntlɪ] **1** *adv* (*trustingly*) 天真地 **2** (*feigning innocence*) [*say, act* +] 假装无心地

innovation [ɪnəu'veɪʃən] *n* [C/U] 创新

innovative ['ɪnəvətɪv] *adj* **1** [+ *product, design*] 新颖的 **2** [+ *person*] 富有创新精神的

innuendo [ɪnju'ɛndəu] (*pl* **innuendoes** *or* **innuendos**) *n* [C/U] 影射 ♦ **sexual innuendo** 性暗示

in-patient ['ɪnpeɪʃənt] *n* [C] 住院病人

input ['ɪnput] **I** *n* **1** [C/U] [*of resources*] 投入 **2** [U] [计算机] 输入 **II** *vt* [计算机] 输入

inquest ['ɪnkwɛst] *n* [C] **1** (*on sb's death*) 审讯 **2** (喻) (*into defeat, failure*) 调查

inquire [ɪn'kwaɪə(r)] *vt, vi* 询问 ♦ **to inquire about** [+ *person, fact*] 打听 ♦ **to inquire where/what/whether** 询问哪里/什么/是否
❑ **inquire after** *vt* [不可拆分] ♦ **to inquire after sb/sb's health** 问起某人/某人的健康情况
❑ **inquire into** *vt* [不可拆分] [+ *death, circumstances*] 调查

inquiry [ɪn'kwaɪərɪ] *n* **1** [C] (*question*) 询问; (*about advertisement*) 咨询 **2** [C] (*investigation*) 调查 **3** [U] [警察] 质询 ♦ **to make inquiries** 进行调查 ♦ **public inquiry** 公开调查 ♦ **to hold an inquiry into sth** 对某事进行调查 ♦ **a court of inquiry** 调查庭

ins *abbr* (= **inches**) 英寸

insane [ɪn'seɪn] **I** *adj* **1** (*clinically*) [+ *person*] 精神错乱的 **2** (*foolish*) [+ *idea, scheme*] 愚蠢的 **II** *n* [*pl*] ♦ **the insane** 精神病患者 ♦ **to go insane** 疯了

insanity [ɪn'sænɪtɪ] *n* [U] **1** (*clinical*) 精神病 **2** [*of idea, decision, action*] 荒谬

insect ['ɪnsɛkt] *n* [C] 昆虫

insect repellent *n* [C/U] 杀虫剂

insecure [ɪnsɪ'kjuə(r)] *adj* **1** [+ *person*] 缺乏自信的 **2** [+ *job, system*] 无保障的

insecurity [ɪnsɪ'kjuərɪtɪ] *n* **1** [C/U] [*of person*] 不安全感 **2** [U] [*of job, finances*] 无保障

insensitive [ɪn'sɛnsɪtɪv] *adj* (*uncaring*) [+ *person*] 不敏感的; [+ *remark*] 麻木不仁的

insert [*vb* ɪn'səːt, *n* 'ɪnsəːt] **I** *vt* **1** [+ *object*] (*into sth*) 插入; (*between two things*) 夹 **2** [+ *word*] (*into text*) 插入 **II** *n* [C] (*in magazine, book*) 插页

inside ['ɪn'saɪd] **I** *n* 内部 **II** *adj* **1** [+ *wall, surface*] 内部的; [+ *lavatory*] 室内的; [+ *pocket*] 里面的 **2** [+ *knowledge, information, story*] 内幕的 **III** *adv* **1** [*go* +] 里面; [*be* +] 在里面 **2** (*indoors*) 在屋内 **IV** *prep* **1** [+ *place, container*] 在…的里面 **2** [+ *time*] 在…之内 **3** [+ *organization*] 在内部 **V** **insides** *n* [*pl*] [非正式] (*stomach*) [+ *of person, animal*] 内脏

inside lane *n* [C] 里道

inside out *adv* 里面朝外地 ♦ **to know sth/sb inside out** 透彻了解某事/某人 ♦ **to turn sth inside out** (字) 把某物的里面翻到外面; (喻) 彻底查看某物

insider [ɪn'saɪdə(r)] *n* [C] 内部人士

insight ['ɪnsaɪt] *n* **1** [C/U] (*into situation, problem*) 见识 **2** [U] (*understanding*) 洞察力 ♦ **to gain/give an insight into sth** 对某事了解/使了解某事

insignificant [ɪnsɪg'nɪfɪknt] *adj* 无足轻重的

insincere [ɪnsɪn'sɪə(r)] *adj* [+ *person*] 不诚恳的; [+ *words, flattery*] 虚假的; [+ *smile*] 虚伪的

insist [ɪn'sɪst] *vi, vt* 坚持 ♦ **to insist that ...** (*claim*) 坚持…; (*demand*) 坚决要求… ♦ **to insist on sth/doing sth** 坚持要求某事/做某事

insistence [ɪn'sɪstəns] *n* [U] 坚决主张 ♦ **at his insistence** 经他坚决要求 ♦ **his insistence on sth/doing sth** 他坚决主张某事/做某事

insistent [ɪn'sɪstənt] *adj* **1** (*determined*) [+ *person*] 坚持的 **2** (*continual*) [+ *noise, rhythm*] 不断的 ♦ **to be insistent that ...** 一再坚持…

insomnia [ɪn'sɔmnɪə] *n* [U] 失眠
inspect [ɪn'spɛkt] *vt* **1** (*examine*) 检查 **2** (*officially*) [+ *premises, equipment, troops*] 视察
inspection [ɪn'spɛkʃən] *n* [C/U] **1** (*examination*) 检查 **2** (*official*) [*of premises, equipment, troops*] 视察 ♦ **to carry out an inspection (of sth)** 检查(某物)
inspector [ɪn'spɛktə(r)] *n* [C] **1** (*official*) 检查员 **2** [英：警察] 巡官 **3** [英] (*also:* ***ticket inspector***) 查票员
inspiration [ɪnspə'reɪʃən] *n* **1** [U] (*encouragement*) 鼓舞 **2** [S] (*stimulus*) 灵感 **3** [S] (*inspiring person, action*) 鼓舞人心的人/物 **4** [C] (*idea*) 妙想 ♦ **to be the inspiration for sth** 是某事的灵感起源 ♦ **to be an inspiration to sb** 是对某人的鼓舞
inspirational [ɪnspə'reɪʃənl] *adj* 激发灵感的
inspire [ɪn'spaɪə(r)] *vt* **1** [+ *person*] 激励 **2** [+ *work of art*] 给予灵感 **3** [+ *confidence, hope, respect*] 唤起 ♦ **to inspire sb to do sth** 鼓舞某人做某事
inspiring [ɪn'spaɪərɪŋ] *adj* 鼓舞人心的
instability [ɪnstə'bɪlɪtɪ] *n* [U] [*of place, situation, person*] 不稳定性
install, instal [ɪn'stɔːl] *vt* **1** [+ *equipment, software*] 安装 **2** [+ *official*] 使…就职
installation [ɪnstə'leɪʃən] *n* **1** [U] [*of machine, equipment*] 安装 **2** [C] (*place*) 设施
instalment (美 **installment**) [ɪn'stɔːlmənt] *n* [C] **1** (*payment*) 分期付款 **2** [*of story, TV serial*] 连载的一部分 ♦ **in instalments** [*pay, receive* +] 分期付款
instance ['ɪnstəns] *n* [C] (*example*) 例子 ♦ **for instance** 例如 ♦ **in many instances** 很多情况下 ♦ **in the first instance** 首先
instant ['ɪnstənt] **I** *n* [C] (*moment*) 瞬息 **II** *adj* **1** [+ *reaction, success*] 立即的 **2** [+ *coffee, soup, noodles*] 速食的 ♦ **she called the police the instant he left** 他一走，她就叫警察了 ♦ **at that instant** 在那一瞬间 ♦ **for an instant** 一瞬间 ♦ **in an instant** 立即
instantly ['ɪnstəntlɪ] *adv* (*with verb*) 立即; (*with adjective*) 即刻
instead [ɪn'stɛd] *adv* 代替 ♦ **instead of** 而不是
instinct ['ɪnstɪŋkt] *n* [C/U] **1** (*biological*) 本能 **2** (*inclination*) 直觉 ♦ **survival/killer instinct** 求生本能/嗜杀本性
instinctive [ɪn'stɪŋktɪv] *adj* [+ *reaction, feeling*] 本能的
institute ['ɪnstɪtjuːt] **I** *n* [C] **1** (*research or teaching organization*) 学院 **2** (*professional body*) [*of architects, planners etc*] 协会 **II** *vt* [+ *system, rule, measure*] 设立; [+ *inquiry*] 着手 ♦ **to institute proceedings against sb** 对某人提出诉讼
institution [ɪnstɪ'tjuːʃən] *n* **1** [C] (*custom, tradition*) 风俗 **2** [C] (*organization*) 公共机构 **3** [C] (*mental hospital, children's home*) 收容所 **4** [U] (*putting in place*) [*of system, rule*] 设立
institutional [ɪnstɪ'tjuːʃənl] *adj* 机构性的 ♦ **to be in institutional care** 在慈善机构的收容照顾下
instruct [ɪn'strʌkt] *vt* **1** (*tell*) ♦ **to instruct sb to do sth** 命令某人做某事 **2** (*teach*) ♦ **to instruct sb in sth** 教某人某事
instruction [ɪn'strʌkʃən] **I** *n* [U] (*teaching*) 教育 **II** *cpd* [复合词] [+ *manual, leaflet*] 说明 **III instructions** *n* [*pl*] **1** (*orders*) 指示 **2** (*directions*) (*on label, in manual*) 说明
instructor [ɪn'strʌktə(r)] *n* [C] (*for skiing, swimming, driving*) 教员
instrument ['ɪnstrumənt] *n* [C] **1** (*tool, device*) 器械 **2** [音] 乐器 ♦ **an instrument of diplomacy/repression** 外交/镇压手段
instrumental [ɪnstru'mɛntl] **I** *adj* [+ *music, piece*] 乐器的 **II** *n* [C] (*piece of music*) 器乐 ♦ **to be instrumental in (doing) sth** 在(做)某事中起到关键作用
insufficient [ɪnsə'fɪʃənt] *adj* [+ *funds, evidence*] 不足的
insulate ['ɪnsjuleɪt] *vt* **1** [+ *house, body*] (*against cold*) 使…隔热 **2** [+ *room, studio*] (*against sound*) 使…隔音 **3** [+ *equipment*] (*against

electricity) 使绝缘 **4** （喻） ♦ **to insulate sb/o.s. from** *or* **against sth** 使某人/自己与某物隔离 ♦ **to insulate sth from** *or* **against** [+ *cold*] 使某物不受…; [+ *sound*] 使某物与…隔离

insulation [ɪnsju'leɪʃən] *n* [U] **1** (*against cold*) (*action*) 防寒; (*material*) 防寒材料 **2** （喻） [*of person, group*] 隔绝

insulin ['ɪnsjulɪn] *n* [U] 胰岛素 ♦ **to be on insulin** 用胰岛素

insult [*n* 'ɪnsʌlt, *vb* ɪn'sʌlt] **I** *n* [C] 侮辱 **II** *vt* 侮辱 ♦ **to be an insult to sth** 对某物的亵渎 ♦ **to add insult to injury** 雪上加霜

insulting [ɪn'sʌltɪŋ] *adj* [+ *attitude, remark*] 侮辱的; [+ *person*] 无礼的

insurance [ɪn'ʃuərəns] *n* [U] 保险 ♦ **fire/life/health insurance** 火/人寿/健康险 ♦ **to take out insurance (against)** 买（防备…的）保险 ♦ **as (an) insurance against** （喻）作为预防…的措施

insurance policy *n* [C] **1** （字）保险单 **2** （喻）保险措施 ♦ **life/health/travel insurance policy** 人寿/健康/旅行保险单 ♦ **to take out an insurance policy** 买保险

insure [ɪn'ʃuə(r)] *vt* [+ *house, car*] 给…保险 ♦ **to be insured for 5000 pounds** 上了5000英磅保险 ♦ **to be insured against fire** 保火险

insurer [ɪn'ʃuərə(r)] *n* [C] 承保人

intact [ɪn'tækt] *adj* **1** (*whole*) 完整的 **2** (*unchanged*) 完好无损的

intake ['ɪnteɪk] *n* **1** [S] [*of food, water, air*] 摄取 **2** [C] [*of students, recruits*] 招收

integral ['ɪntɪgrəl] *adj* 构成整体所必需的 ♦ **an integral part of** …的组成部分 ♦ **integral to** 对…是不可缺的

integrate ['ɪntɪgreɪt] **I** *vt* **1** [+ *newcomer*] ♦ **to integrate sb into sth** 使某人与某物融为一体 **2** [+ *ideas, systems*] 使结合 **II** *vi* [*groups, individuals* +] 融成一体

integrity [ɪn'tɛgrɪtɪ] *n* [U] **1** (*honesty*) 刚正不阿 **2** (*purity*) [*of culture, group*] 完整

intellect ['ɪntəlɛkt] *n* [C/U] **1** (*thinking*) 智力 **2** (*intelligence*) 才智

intellectual [ɪntə'lɛktjuəl] **I** *adj* **1** [+ *activity, interest, pursuit*] 智力的 **2** (*clever*) 高智商的 **II** *n* [C] (*person*) 知识分子

intelligence [ɪn'tɛlɪdʒəns] *n* [U] **1** (*intellect*) 才智 **2** (*understanding*) 理解力 **3** [军] (*service*) 情报机构 **4** [军] (*information*) 情报

intelligent [ɪn'tɛlɪdʒənt] *adj* **1** [+ *person*] 聪明的 **2** [+ *decision, conversation*] 明智的 **3** [+ *machine, life*] 智能的

intend [ɪn'tɛnd] *vt* ♦ **to intend to do sth** 打算做某事 ♦ **to intend doing sth** 打算做某事 ♦ **to intend that ...** 打算… ♦ **to be intended to do sth** 用来做某事 ♦ **to be intended for sb/sth** [*gift, money* +] 专门用于某人/某事 ♦ **to be intended as sth** [*announcement, declaration* +] 被有意作为某物

intense [ɪn'tɛns] *adj* **1** (*great*) [+ *heat, pain*] 剧烈的; [+ *anger, joy, desire*] 强烈的; [+ *competition*] 激烈的 **2** [+ *person*] 认真的

intensely [ɪn'tɛnslɪ] *adv* (*extremely*) 非常地

intensify [ɪn'tɛnsɪfaɪ] **I** *vt* [+ *efforts, pressure*] 加强 **II** *vi* [*efforts, pressure* +] 加剧

intensity [ɪn'tɛnsɪtɪ] *n* [U] [*of heat, anger, desire*] 强度; [*of debate, attack*] 激烈

intensive [ɪn'tɛnsɪv] *adj* [+ *training, study, talks*] 深入细致的; [+ *efforts*] 集中的; [+ *treatment, therapy*] 强化的

intensive care *n* ♦ **to be in intensive care** 接受重病特别护理

intent [ɪn'tɛnt] **I** *n* [U] [正式] 意图 **II** *adj* **1** ♦ **to be intent on sth** (*absorbed in*) 专心致志于某事 **2** ♦ **to be intent on doing sth** (*determined*) 一心想做某事 ♦ **to all intents (and purposes)** 实际上

intention [ɪn'tɛnʃən] *n* [C/U] 打算 ♦ **with the best (of) intentions** 好心好意地 ♦ **to have no/every intention of doing sth** 根本没有做某事的意图/打定主意做某事

intentional [ɪn'tɛnʃənl] *adj* 故意的

intentionally [ɪn'tɛnʃnəlɪ] *adv* 故意地

interact [ɪntər'ækt] *vi* 互相影响 ♦**to interact with** 与…接合

interaction [ɪntər'ækʃən] *n* [c/u] **1** [*of people*] 互相联系 **2** [*of ideas, objects*] 相互影响

interactive [ɪntər'æktɪv] *adj* **1** [+ *television, computer, game*] 交互的 **2** [+ *group, teaching*] 互动的

intercept [ɪntə'sɛpt] *vt* [+ *person, car*] 截住; [+ *message, supplies*] 截取; [+ *plane, missile*] 截获

interchange [*n* 'ɪntətʃeɪndʒ, *vb* ɪntə'tʃeɪndʒ] **I** *n* **1** [c/u] (*exchange*) [*of ideas, information*] 交换 **2** [c] (*on motorway, freeway*) 立体交叉道 **II** *vt* 交换

intercourse ['ɪntəkɔːs] *n* [u] **1** [正式] (*also:* ***sexual intercourse***) 性交 **2** ♦**social intercourse** [过时] 社交 ♦**to have (sexual) intercourse** 性交

✪**interest** ['ɪntrɪst] **I** *n* **1** [u/s] (*in subject, idea, person*) 兴趣 ◊ *There has been a lively interest in the elections.* 大家对选举兴致颇高。**2** [c] (*pastime, hobby*) 爱好 ◊ *His interests include cooking and photography.* 他的爱好包括烹调和摄影。**3** [c] (*advantage, profit*) 利益 ◊ *They would protect the interests of their members.* 他们将保护成员的利益。**4** [u] (*on loan, savings*) 利息 ◊ *Does your current account pay interest?* 你的活期存款账户付利息吗？◊ *the interest you pay on your mortgage* 你付贷款的利息 **II interests** *n* [*pl*] [商] (*in a company*) 股权 ◊ *Her business interests include a theme park.* 她的公司股权包括一个主题公园。**III** *vt* [*work, subject, idea* +] 使感兴趣 ◊ *These are the stories that interest me.* 这些是使我感兴趣的故事。♦**to take an interest in sth/sb** 对某事/某人感兴趣 ♦**to show an interest in sth/sb** 显露对某事/某人的兴趣 ♦**to lose interest (in sth/sb)** 对（某事/某人）失去兴趣 ♦**controlling interest** [商] 控股权益 ♦**to be in sb's interests** 对某人有益 ♦**in the interests of stability/security** 为稳定/安全起见 ♦**to interest sb in sth** 使某人对某事发生兴趣

interested ['ɪntrɪstɪd] *adj* **1** ♦**to be interested (in sth/doing sth)** 对（某事/做某事）有兴趣 **2** [+ *party, body*] 有关的

> 📖 请勿将 **interested** 和 **interesting** 混淆。如果你 **interested in** 某事，说明你对它很感兴趣，很想了解或知道更多关于它的事情，或者想花更多的时间来做这件事。*Not all of the children were interested in animals...She asked him how he became interested in politics.* 如果你发现某事 **interesting**，表示它令人感兴趣，引人注意，使你乐于更多地了解这件事或者去做这件事。*It must be an awfully interesting job...The interesting thing is that this is exactly the answer we got before.*

interesting ['ɪntrɪstɪŋ] *adj* [+ *idea, place, person*] 有趣的 ♦**it is interesting that ...** 令人关注的是… ♦**it will be interesting to see how he reacts** 看他怎么反应会是很有趣的
📖 用法参见 **interested**

interestingly ['ɪntrɪstɪŋlɪ] *adv* 有趣的是

interest rate *n* [c] 利率

interface ['ɪntəfeɪs] **I** *n* [c] **1** [计算机] 界面 **2** (*area of contact*) 接合处 **II** *vi* [正式] (*interact*) ♦**to interface (with sth)** （与某物）互相影响

interfere [ɪntə'fɪə(r)] *vi* **1** (*meddle*) (*in situation, sb's affairs*) 干涉 **2** (*disrupt*) 妨碍 ♦**to interfere in sth** 干预某事 ♦**to interfere with sth** [+ *plans, career, duty*] 妨碍某事

interference [ɪntə'fɪərəns] *n* [u] **1** (*meddling*) 干涉 **2** [广播, 电视] 干扰

interim ['ɪntərɪm] **I** *adj* [+ *agreement, report*] 临时的; [+ *results, profits*] 中期的; [+ *government*] 过渡的 **II** *n* ♦**in the interim** 在此期间

interior [ɪn'tɪərɪə(r)] **I** *n* **1** [c] [*of building, car, box*] 内部 **2** [s] [*of country*] 内地 **II** *adj* **1** [+ *door, window, room*] 内部的 **2** [+ *minister,* *department*] 内政的 ♦ **Minister/Ministry of the Interior** 内政部长/部

interior design *n* [U] 室内设计

intermediate [ɪntəˈmiːdɪət] *adj* **1** [+ *stage, position*] 中间的 **2** [+ *student, course, level*] 中级的

intermission [ɪntəˈmɪʃən] *n* [C] [电影] 休息时间; [美:戏剧, 音] 幕间休息 [英=**interval**]

intern [*vb* ɪnˈtəːn, *n* ˈɪntəːn] **I** *vt* (*imprison*) 拘留 **II** *n* [C] [美:医, 政治] 实习生

internal [ɪnˈtəːnl] *adj* **1** [+ *wall, dispute, reform, mail*] 内部的 **2** [+ *bleeding, injury, examination*] 内的 **3** [+ *security, politics*] 国内的

internally [ɪnˈtəːnəlɪ] *adv* **1** (*within*) 在内部 **2** [医] 在体内 **3** (*within a company*) 从内部 ♦ **"not to be taken internally"** "切勿内服"

Internal Revenue Service [美] *n* ♦ **the Internal Revenue Service** 国税局 [英=**Inland Revenue**]

✪ **international** [ɪntəˈnæʃənl] **I** *adj* 国际的 **II** *n* [C] [英:体育] **1** (*match*) 国际比赛 **2** (*player*) 国际比赛选手

international relations *n* [*pl*] 国际关系

Internet [ˈɪntənɛt] *n* ♦ **the Internet** 因特网

Internet café *n* [C] 网吧

Internet service provider *n* [C] 因特网服务提供者

interpret [ɪnˈtəːprɪt] **I** *vt* **1** (*explain*) [+ *message, poem*] 把…理解为; [+ *behaviour, statement*] 阐释 **2** (*translate*) 口译 **II** *vi* (*translate*) 口译 ♦ **to interpret sth as sth** 把某事理解为某事

interpretation [ɪntəːprɪˈteɪʃən] *n* **1** [C/U] (*explanation, understanding*) 解释 **2** [C] [戏剧, 音] 艺术表现

interpreter [ɪnˈtəːprɪtə(r)] *n* [C] 口译者

interrogate [ɪnˈtɛrəgeɪt] *vt* [+ *witness, prisoner, suspect*] 审问

interrogation [ɪntɛrəˈgeɪʃən] *n* **1** [U] (*activity*) 审问 **2** [C] (*period of questioning*) 审讯期

interrupt [ɪntəˈrʌpt] **I** *vt* **1** [+ *speaker, conversation*] 打断 **2** [+ *activity*] 中断 **II** *vi* (*in conversation*) 打岔 📖 用法参见**disturb**

interruption [ɪntəˈrʌpʃən] *n* [C/U] 打扰

intersection [ɪntəˈsɛkʃən] *n* [C] [*of roads*] 交叉口

interstate [ˈɪntəsteɪt] **I** *adj* 州与州之间的 **II** *n* [C] [美] 州际公路

interval [ˈɪntəvl] *n* [C] **1** (*break, pause*) 间隔 **2** [英:戏剧, 音, 体育] 幕间休息 [美=**intermission**] ♦ **at intervals** (*in time*) 不时; (*in space*) 每隔一定距离 ♦ **sunny intervals** 偶尔出太阳

intervene [ɪntəˈviːn] *vi* **1** [*person* +] 干预 **2** [*event* +] 介入 **3** [*time* +] 介于 **4** (*in speech*) 打断

intervention [ɪntəˈvɛnʃən] *n* [C/U] [*by person*] 干预; (*military*) 干涉

interview [ˈɪntəvjuː] **I** *n* [C/U] **1** (*for job*) 面试 **2** [出版, 广播, 电视] 采访 **II** *vt* **1** (*for job*) 面试 **2** [出版, 广播, 电视] 采访 **3** [警察] 盘问 ♦ **to go for/have an interview** 参加面试 ♦ **to give an interview** 接受采访

interviewer [ˈɪntəvjuə(r)] *n* [C] **1** [广播, 电视] 采访者 **2** [*of job applicant*] 面试者

intimacy [ˈɪntɪməsɪ] *n* [U] **1** (*mental*) 亲密 **2** (*physical*) 亲昵

intimate [*adj* ˈɪntɪmət, *vb* ˈɪntɪmeɪt] **I** *adj* **1** (*very close*) [+ *friend, relationship*] 亲密的 **2** (*sexual*) [+ *relationship*] 暧昧的 **3** (*private*) [+ *conversation, details*] 私人的 **4** (*cosy*) [+ *restaurant, atmosphere*] 惬意的 **5** (*thorough*) [+ *knowledge*] 精通的 **II** *vt* [正式] (*hint at*) 暗示 ♦ **to be intimate (with sb)** (*sexually*) 和(某人)关系暧昧 ♦ **to have an intimate knowledge of sth** 对某事造诣很深 ♦ **to intimate that ...** [正式] 暗示…

intimidate [ɪnˈtɪmɪdeɪt] *vt* 恐吓 ♦ **to intimidate sb into doing sth** 胁迫某人做某事

intimidated [ɪnˈtɪmɪdeɪtɪd] *adj* 被胁迫的

intimidating [ɪnˈtɪmɪdeɪtɪŋ] *adj* [+ *atmosphere, place, experience*] 恐怖的; [+ *person*] 可怕的

into
KEYWORD
['ɪntu]
prep (*indicating motion, direction*) 到…里面 ♦ **come into the house/garden** 走进房子/花园里 ♦ **get into the car** 进入车子 ♦ **he threw some socks into his case** 他把几只袜子扔进了箱子里 ♦ **let's go into town** 我们进城吧 ♦ **she poured some tea into the cup** 她把一些茶倒进了杯子里 ♦ **to translate Chinese into French** 把汉语翻译成法语 ♦ **it broke into pieces** 它碎成一片片的了 ♦ **research into cancer** 对癌症的深入研究 ♦ **he worked late into the night** 他工作到深夜 ♦ **they got into trouble** 他们陷入麻烦之中 ♦ **I'd like to change some dollars into euros** 我想把一些美元换成欧元

intolerable [ɪn'tɔlərəbl] *adj* [+ *behaviour, situation, burden*] 无法忍受的

intolerant [ɪn'tɔlərənt] *adj* [+ *person, society*] 偏狭的; [+ *attitude*] 不容忍的 ♦ **to be intolerant of sth/sb** 不能容忍某事/某人

intranet ['ɪntrənɛt] *n* [C] 内联网

intricate ['ɪntrɪkət] *adj* [+ *pattern, design*] 复杂的

intrigue [*n* 'ɪntri:g, *vb* ɪn'tri:g] **I** *n* [C/U] 阴谋 **II** *vt* (*fascinate*) 使…感兴趣

intrigued [ɪn'tri:gd] *adj* 被迷住的 ♦ **I would be intrigued to hear more** 我有兴趣接着听

intriguing [ɪn'tri:gɪŋ] *adj* 引人入胜的

introduce [ɪntrə'dju:s] *vt* **1** [+ *new idea, measure, technology*] 引进 **2** [+ *speaker, TV show, radio programme*] 介绍 **3** ♦ **to introduce sb (to sb)** 给某人介绍(某人) **4** ♦ **to introduce sb to sth** [+ *pastime, technique*] 引导某人做某事 ♦ **may I introduce you (to ...)?** 让我介绍你(认识…)好吗?

introduction [ɪntrə'dʌkʃən] *n* **1** [U] [*of new idea, measure, technology*] 引进 **2** [C] [*of person*] 介绍 **3** [C] (*beginning*) [*of book, talk*] 引言 **4** (*first experience of sth*) ♦ **China's introduction to British ballet** 中国首次接触英国芭蕾 **5** (*presentation of basic facts*) ♦ **an introduction to linguistics** 语言学入门 ♦ **letter of introduction** 介绍信

introductory [ɪntrə'dʌktərɪ] *adj* **1** [+ *remarks, course*] 介绍性的 **2** [+ *offer, price*] 试销的

intrude [ɪn'tru:d] *vi* **1** [*person* +] 侵入 **2** ♦ **to intrude on** [*person, thing* +] [+ *conversation, grief, party*] 打扰 ♦ **am I intruding?** 我没有打扰吧?

intruder [ɪn'tru:də(r)] *n* [C] 闯入者

intuition [ɪntju:'ɪʃən] *n* [C/U] 直觉

inundate ['ɪnʌndeɪt] *vt* ♦ **to be inundated with** [+ *calls, letters, requests*] …多得应接不暇

invade [ɪn'veɪd] *vt* **1** [军] 侵略 **2** (喻) [*people, animals* +] 涌入

invalid [*n* 'ɪnvəlɪd, *adj* ɪn'vælɪd] **I** *n* [C] 病弱者 **II** *adj* [+ *procedure, document, argument*] 无效的

invaluable [ɪn'væljuəbl] *adj* [+ *experience, advice*] 无价的

> 特别注意，请勿将单词 **invaluable**，**priceless** 和 **worthless** 混淆。某事物 **invaluable**，表示该事物非常有价值。*Their advice to me was invaluable at that stage of my work.* **priceless** 表示事物非常珍贵，是无价之宝。*...priceless masterpieces by Van Gogh...* 与之相反，**worthless** 表示某事物没有什么价值。*I'm afraid your shares are now worthless.*

invariably [ɪn'vɛərɪəblɪ] *adv* 不变地

invasion [ɪn'veɪʒən] *n* [C/U] **1** [军] 入侵 **2** (喻) 侵袭 **3** ♦ **an invasion of privacy** 对隐私的侵犯

invent [ɪn'vɛnt] *vt* **1** [+ *machine, system, game, word*] 发明 **2** [+ *lie, excuse*] 捏造

invention [ɪn'vɛnʃən] *n* **1** [C] (*machine, system*) 发明 **2** [C] (*untrue story*) 捏造 **3** [U] (*act of inventing*) [*of* *machine, system*] 发明

inventive [ɪn'ventɪv] *adj* [+ *person, mind, idea*] 有发明才能的

inventor [ɪn'ventə(r)] *n* [c] [*of machine, system*] 发明家

inventory ['ɪnvəntrɪ] *n* **1** [c] [*of house, ship*] 清单 **2** [c/u] [美] (*supply, stock*) 库存

inverted commas [ɪn'vəːtɪd-] [英] *n* [*pl*] 引号 ♦**in inverted commas** (字) 用引号标志; (喻) 所谓的 [美 = **quotation marks**]

invest [ɪn'vest] **I** *vt* **1** [+ *money*] 投资 **2** [+ *time, energy*] 投入 **II** *vi* ♦**invest in** [商] 投资于; (喻) [+ *product, system*] 购买 ♦**to invest sb with rights/responsibilities** [正式] 授予某人权利/责任 ♦**by the powers invested in me** [正式] 根据授予我的权力

investigate [ɪn'vestɪgeɪt] *vt* 调查

investigation [ɪnvestɪ'geɪʃən] *n* [c/u] 调查 ♦**to be under investigation (for sth)** (由于某事) 接受调查

investigator [ɪn'vestɪgeɪtə(r)] *n* [c] 调查员

investment [ɪn'vestmənt] *n* **1** [u] (*activity*) 投资 **2** [c] (*amount of money*) 投资额 **3** [c] (*property, painting etc*) 投资 ◊ *I bought a flat as an investment.* 我买了一套公寓作为投资。 **4** [u/s] (喻) 投资

investor [ɪn'vestə(r)] [经济] *n* [c] 投资者

invisible [ɪn'vɪzɪbl] *adj* **1** 看不见的 **2** [+ *problem, situation*] 被忽略的 **3** [+ *exports, earnings, assets*] 无形的

invitation [ɪnvɪ'teɪʃən] *n* **1** [c] 邀请 **2** [c] (*card*) 请柬 **3** ♦**an invitation to disaster/crime** 招致灾难/犯罪的诱因 ♦**by invitation only** 凭柬入场 ♦**at sb's invitation** 应某人的邀请

invite [*vb* ɪn'vaɪt, *n* 'ɪnvaɪt] **I** *vt* **1** 邀请 **2** (*encourage*) [+ *trouble, criticism*] 招致 **II** *n* [c] [非正式] (*invitation*) 邀请 ♦**to invite sb to do sth** 邀请某人做某事 ♦**to invite sb to dinner** 请某人赴宴

❑**invite out** *vt* 将…请去

inviting [ɪn'vaɪtɪŋ] *adj* 吸引人的

invoice ['ɪnvɔɪs] **I** *n* [c] 发票 **II** *vt* [+ *person*] 开发票 ♦**to invoice sb for goods** 给某人开物品发票

invoke [ɪn'vəuk] *vt* **1** [+ *law, saying, famous person*] 援引 **2** (*evoke*) [+ *feelings, memories*] 唤起

involve [ɪn'vɔlv] *vt* **1** (*entail*) 包含 **2** (*concern, affect*) 使卷入 ♦**to involve sb (in sth)** 使某人参与(某事)

involved [ɪn'vɔlvd] *adj* **1** (*complicated*) 复杂的 **2** ♦**to be involved in** (*take part in*) 参与; (*be engrossed in*) 专心于 **3** (*be entailed by*) …所需的 ♦**to feel involved in sth** 感到成为某事的一部分 ♦**to be involved with sb** 和某人关系亲密

involvement [ɪn'vɔlvmənt] *n* **1** [u] (*participation*) 参与 **2** [u] (*concern, enthusiasm*) 眷顾 **3** [c/u] (*relationship*) 牵连

inward ['ɪnwəd] **I** *adj* **1** [+ *movement*] 向内的 **2** [+ *thoughts, feelings*] 内心的 **II** *adv* = **inwards**

inwards ['ɪnwədz] *adv* [*move, face* +] 向内

iodine ['aɪəudiːn] *n* [u] 碘

IOU *n abbr* (= ***I owe you***) 借条

IQ *n abbr* (= ***intelligence quotient***) 智商

IRA *n abbr* **1** (= ***Irish Republican Army***) 爱尔兰共和军 **2** [美] (= ***individual retirement account***) 个人退休账户

Iran [ɪ'rɑːn] *n* 伊朗

Iranian [ɪ'reɪnɪən] **I** *adj* 伊朗的 **II** *n* **1** [c] (*person*) 伊朗人 **2** [u] (*language*) 伊朗语

Iraq [ɪ'rɑːk] *n* 伊拉克

Iraqi [ɪ'rɑːkɪ] **I** *adj* 伊拉克的 **II** *n* [c] (*person*) 伊拉克人

Ireland ['aɪələnd] *n* 爱尔兰 ♦**the Republic of Ireland** 爱尔兰共和国

iris ['aɪrɪs] *n* [c] **1** (*of eye*) 虹膜 **2** (*flower*) 蝴蝶花

Irish ['aɪrɪʃ] **I** *adj* 爱尔兰的 **II** *n* [u] (*language*) 爱尔兰语 **III the Irish** *n* [*pl*] 爱尔兰人

Irishman ['aɪrɪʃmən] (*pl* **Irishmen**) *n* [c] 爱尔兰男人

Irishwoman ['aɪrɪʃwumən] (*pl* **Irishwomen**) *n* [c] 爱尔兰女人

iron ['aɪən] **I** *n* **1** [U] (*metal*) 铁 **2** [C] (*for clothes*) 熨斗 **II** *adj* **1** [+ *bar, railings*] 铁的 **2** (喻) [+ *will, discipline*] 刚强的 **III** *vt* [+ *clothes*] 熨 **IV irons** *n* [*pl*] (*chains*) 镣铐 ♦**to clap sb in irons** 给某人戴上镣铐
❑**iron out** *vt* [+ *problems*] 消除

ironic [aɪ'rɔnɪk] *adj* **1** [+ *remark, smile*] 挖苦的 **2** [+ *situation*] 令人啼笑皆非的 ♦**it is ironic that ...** 具有讽刺性的是…

ironically [aɪ'rɔnɪklɪ] *adv* **1** [*say* +] 挖苦地 **2** ♦**ironically (enough) ...** (极)具有讽刺性的是…

ironing ['aɪənɪŋ] *n* [U] **1** (*activity*) 熨烫 **2** (*clothes*) 要熨烫的衣服 ♦**to do the ironing** 熨衣服

ironing board *n* [C] 熨衣板

irony ['aɪrənɪ] *n* **1** [U] (*in speech*) 讽刺 **2** [C/U] [*of situation*] 讥讽

irrational [ɪ'ræʃənl] *adj* [+ *feelings, behaviour*] 无理性的

irregular [ɪ'rɛgjulə(r)] *adj* **1** [+ *surface, pattern*] 不整齐的 **2** (*not set*) [+ *hours, times*] 不定期的; [+ *meals, periods*] 不规律的; [+ *heartbeat, pulse*] 不规则的 **3** (*not acceptable*) [+ *behaviour*] 不正当的 **4** [语言] [+ *verb, noun, adjective*] 不规则的 ♦**at irregular intervals** 不定时的间隔

irrelevant [ɪ'rɛləvənt] *adj* 不相干的 ♦**irrelevant to sb/sth** 与某人/某事无关

irresistible [ɪrɪ'zɪstɪbl] *adj* **1** [+ *urge, desire*] 压不住的 **2** [+ *person, charm, food*] 无法抗拒的 **3** [+ *force, pressure*] 不可抗拒的

irrespective [ɪrɪ'spɛktɪv] ♦**irrespective of** *prep* 不论

irresponsible [ɪrɪ'spɔnsɪbl] *adj* [+ *person, driver*] 无责任感的; [+ *attitude, behaviour*] 不负责任的 ♦**it is irresponsible to drive when tired** 疲劳驾车是很不负责任的

irreversible [ɪrɪ'vəːsəbl] *adj* [+ *damage, change*] 不可扭转的

irrigation [ɪrɪ'geɪʃən] *n* [U] 灌溉

irritable ['ɪrɪtəbl] *adj* [+ *person*] 易激怒的
📖 用法参见**angry**

irritate ['ɪrɪteɪt] *vt* **1** [+ *person*] 使烦躁 **2** [+ *skin, eyes*] 使不舒服

irritating ['ɪrɪteɪtɪŋ] *adj* [+ *person, habit, noise*] 烦人的

irritation [ɪrɪ'teɪʃən] *n* **1** [U] (*feeling of annoyance*) 恼怒 **2** [C] (*annoying thing*) 恼人的事 **3** [C/U] [*of skin, eyes*] 刺激

IRS [美] *n abbr* (= ***Internal Revenue Service***) ♦**the IRS** 国税局

is [ɪz] *vb see* **be**

Islam ['ɪzlɑːm] *n* [U] 伊斯兰教

Islamic [ɪz'læmɪk] *adj* [+ *law, faith*] 伊斯兰教的; [+ *country*] 伊斯兰的

island ['aɪlənd] *n* [C] **1** [地理] 岛 **2** (*also:* ***traffic island***) 交通岛

islander ['aɪləndə(r)] *n* [C] 岛上居民

isle [aɪl] *n* [C] 岛

isn't ['ɪznt] = **is not**

isolate ['aɪsəleɪt] *vt* **1** [+ *person, country*] 孤立 **2** [+ *substance, sick person, animal*] 隔离

isolated ['aɪsəleɪtɪd] *adj* **1** [+ *place*] 孤零零的 **2** [+ *person*] 孤立的 **3** (*single*) [+ *incident, case, example*] 个别的

isolation [aɪsə'leɪʃən] *n* [U] **1** [*of person*] 孤立 **2** ♦**to consider sth in isolation** 孤立地看待某事

ISP *n abbr* (= ***Internet service provider***) 因特网服务提供者

Israel ['ɪzreɪl] *n* 以色列

Israeli [ɪz'reɪlɪ] **I** *adj* 以色列的 **II** *n* [C] (*person*) 以色列人

✪**issue** ['ɪʃjuː] **I** *n* **1** [C] (*problem, subject*) 问题 ◊ *the issue of human rights* 人权问题 **2** ♦**the issue** (*most important part*) 要点 ◊ *That's not the issue.* 那不是问题所在。**3** [C] [*of magazine, newspaper*] 期 ◊ *the latest issue of the magazine* 最新一期杂志 **4** [C] (*pl* **issue**) [过时] (*offspring*) 子女 ◊ *He died without issue.* 他死后无子女。**II** *vt* **1** [+ *rations, equipment, documents*] 发给 ◊ *Who issued the travel documents?* 谁签发旅行证件? **2** [+ *statement*] 发表 ◊ *We need to issue some sort of statement.* 我们要发表某种声明。**III** *vi* [正式] ♦**to issue (from)** [*liquid, sound, smell* +] (从…)出来 ♦**to avoid the issue** 回避问题 ♦**to confuse** *or* **cloud the issue** 混淆问题 ♦**to take issue with sb** 与某人争论 ♦**to make an issue of sth** 把某事

看得极为重要 ♦**to be at issue** 在争议中的 ♦**to issue sth to sb** 给某人发放某物 ♦**to issue sb with sth** 给某人发放某物

IT *n abbr* (= ***Information Technology***) 信息技术

✪**it** [ɪt] *pron* **1** (*object or animal*) 它 ◊ *"Where's my pen?" – "It's on the table."* "我的钢笔在哪儿呢?" – "在桌子上。" ◊ *I can't find it.* 我找不到。◊ *Give it to me.* 把它给我。◊ *I spoke to him about it.* 我跟他说了这事儿。; (*referring to baby*) 他/她 ◊ *Is it a boy or a girl?* 是男孩儿还是女孩儿? **2** (*weather, date, time*) ◊ *It's raining.* 正在下雨。◊ *It's very cold in winter here.* 这里的冬天很冷。◊ *It's Friday.* 今天星期五。◊ *It's 6 o'clock.* 现在6点。◊ *It's August 10th.* 今天是8月10日。 **3** (*impersonal*) ◊ *It doesn't matter.* 没关系。◊ *It's easy to see why you left.* 你离开的原因显而易见。◊ *It was John who spoke to them.* 是约翰告诉他们的。 ♦**what is it?** (*thing*) 是什么东西?; (*what's the matter?*) 怎么了? ♦**"who is it?" – "it's me"** "是谁?" "是我。"

Italian [ɪ'tæljən] **I** *adj* 意大利的 **II** *n* **1** [c] (*person*) 意大利人 **2** [u] (*language*) 意大利语

italics [ɪ'tælɪks] *n* [*pl*] 斜体字 ♦**in italics** 用斜体

Italy ['ɪtəlɪ] *n* 意大利

itch [ɪtʃ] **I** *n* [c] (*on skin*) 痒 **II** *vi* [*person, part of body* +] 发痒 ♦**to be itching to do sth** [非正式] 渴望做某事

itchy ['ɪtʃɪ] *adj* [+ *skin, nose, eyes, scalp etc*] 发痒的; [+ *piece of clothing*] 使人发痒的 ♦**to have itchy feet** 渴望漫游

it'd ['ɪtd] = **it would, it had**

item ['aɪtəm] *n* [c] **1** (*on list, agenda*) 项目; (*on bill*) 项; (*in collection, object*) 物品 **2** (*in newspaper, on TV*) 新闻 ♦**items of clothing** 几件衣服

itinerary [aɪ'tɪnərərɪ] *n* [c] 旅行计划

it'll ['ɪtl] = **it will**

✪**its** [ɪts] *adj* **1** (*of animal*) 它的 ◊ *The horse lifted its head.* 马抬起头来。 **2** (*of baby*) 他/她的 ◊ *The baby was sucking its thumb.* 宝宝吮着大拇指。

> 📖 请勿将**its**和**it's**混淆。**its** 意为"它的"。**it's**是*it is*或者*it has*的缩略形式。*The dog wagged its tail...It's hot in here... It's stopped raining.*

it's [ɪts] = **it is, it has**
📖 用法参见**its**

✪**itself** [ɪt'sɛlf] *pron* **1** (*reflexive*) 它自己 ◊ *It switches itself on automatically.* 它自动接通。**2** (*emphatic*) 本身 ◊ *I think life itself is a learning process.* 我认为生活本身是个学习的过程。 ♦**the baby can hold the toy itself** 宝宝自己能拿住玩具 ♦**she is kindness/politeness itself** 她是仁慈/礼貌的化身 ♦**in itself** 本身 ◊ *Stress in itself is not necessarily harmful.* 压力本身并不一定是有害的。 ♦**by itself** (*unaided*) 自己独立地 ◊ *The cat managed to climb down the tree itself.* 猫自己设法爬下了树。◊ *The wound will heal by itself.* 伤口会自己愈合的。; (*alone*) 单独地 ◊ *The dog shouldn't have been left at home by itself.* 狗不该被单独留在家里。

ITV [英:电视] *n abbr* (= ***Independent Television***) 独立电视台

IUD *n abbr* (= ***intra-uterine device***) 避孕环

I've [aɪv] = **I have**

ivory ['aɪvərɪ] *n* [u] **1** (*substance*) 象牙 **2** (*colour*) 乳白色

ivy ['aɪvɪ] *n* [u] 常春藤

> **Ivy League**
> 美国东北部的8所一流大学被称作**Ivy League**(常青藤盟校)。哈佛大学、耶鲁大学、宾夕法尼亚大学、普林斯顿大学、哥伦比亚大学、布朗大学、达特莫斯大学和康奈尔大学最初常聚到一起举行体育比赛。这个名字据称是取之于爬满了老楼墙壁的常青藤。另一种说法是,最初只有4所大学,罗马数字的4是IV,发音近似于**ivy**。

Jj

J, j [dʒeɪ] *n* [C/U] (*letter*) 英语的第十个字母

jab [dʒæb] **I** *vt* ♦ **to jab sb (in the arm/back/eye) with sth** 用某物戳某人(的胳膊/背部/眼睛) **II** *vi* ♦ **to jab at sb with sth** 用某物戳某人 **III** *n* [C] [英:非正式] (*injection*) 注射 ♦ **to jab one's finger/stick at sb** 用手指/棍子戳某人 ♦ **to jab sth into sth/sb** 把某物刺入某物/某人 ♦ **to have a flu/tetanus jab** [英:非正式] 打感冒/破伤风预防针 ♦ **to give sb a jab** [英:非正式] 给某人打针

jack [dʒæk] *n* [C] **1** [汽车] 千斤顶 **2** [纸牌] 杰克 **3** [滚木球] 靶子球
❑ **jack in** [非正式] *vt* 放弃
❑ **jack up** *vt* **1** [汽车] 用千斤顶顶起 **2** [非正式] [+ *price, amount*] 提高

jacket ['dʒækɪt] *n* [C] **1** (*garment*) 夹克 **2** [尤美] (*also:* ***dust jacket***) 护封 ♦ **potatoes in their jackets, jacket potatoes** [英] 带皮的马铃薯 [美= **baked potatoes**]

jackpot ['dʒækpɔt] *n* [C] 头彩 ♦ **to hit the jackpot** [非正式] (喻) 获得最大成功

Jacuzzi® [dʒə'ku:zɪ] *n* [C] 一种用于涡流式沐浴或用于在浴池中产生旋涡的装置的商标

jade [dʒeɪd] **I** *n* [U] (*stone*) 玉 **II** *adj* (*also:* ***jade green***) 碧绿的 **III** *cpd* [复合词] [+ *necklace, ornament*] 玉的

jagged ['dʒægɪd] *adj* [+ *outline, edge, rocks*] 参差不齐的

jail [dʒeɪl] **I** *n* [C/U] 监狱 **II** *vt* 监禁 ♦ **in jail** 在监狱 ◊ *He was sentenced to two years in jail.* 他被判两年监禁。♦ **to go to jail** 入狱

jail sentence *n* [C] 监狱刑期

jam [dʒæm] **I** *n* **1** [C/U] [英] (*preserve*) 果酱 [美= **jelly**] **2** [C] (*also:* ***traffic jam***) 交通堵塞 **II** *vt* **1** ♦ **to jam sth into/on sth** 将某物塞进/扣住某物 **2** (*fill*) [+ *road, square etc*] 拥塞 **3** (*immobilize*) [+ *mechanism, drawer etc*] 使卡住 **4** (*inundate*) [+ *switchboard, phone lines*] 使塞满 **5** [广播] (*prevent from broadcasting*) 干扰 **III** *vi* **1** (*get stuck*) [*drawer, mechanism, gun* +] 卡住 **2** ♦ **to jam into a stadium/hall** *etc* 涌进体育馆/大厅{等} **3** [非正式] [音] 即兴演奏 ♦ **to be in a jam** [非正式] (*in difficulty*) 陷入困境 ♦ **to get sb out of a jam** [非正式] 使某人摆脱困境

Jamaica [dʒə'meɪkə] *n* 牙买加

Jamaican [dʒə'meɪkən] **I** *adj* 牙买加的 **II** *n* [C] (*person*) 牙买加人

jammed [dʒæmd] *adj* **1** [+ *roads*] 堵塞的 **2** [+ *mechanism, machine*] 卡住的 **3** [+ *switchboard, phone lines*] 应接不暇的 ♦ **to be jammed with people/cars** 挤满了人/汽车

Jan. *abbr* (= ***January***) 一月

janitor ['dʒænɪtə(r)] *n* [C] 看门人

January ['dʒænjuərɪ] *n* [C/U] 一月 *see also* **July**

Japan [dʒə'pæn] *n* 日本

Japanese [dʒæpə'ni:z] (*pl* **Japanese**) **I** *adj* 日本的 **II** *n* **1** [C] (*person*) 日本人 **2** [U] (*language*) 日语

jar [dʒɑ:(r)] **I** *n* [C] **1** (*container*) 广口瓶 **2** (*contents*) 罐装物 **II** *vi* **1** ♦ **to jar (on sb)** [*sound, remark* +] 给(某人)不愉快的感觉 **2** (*move*) 颠簸 **III** *vt* **1** (*shake, knock*) 使震伤 **2** (*grate on*) [*sound, remark* +] 刺激

jargon ['dʒɑ:gən] *n* [U] 行话

javelin ['dʒævlɪn] *n* **1** [C] (*spear*) 标枪 **2** (*competition*) ♦ **the javelin** 标枪赛

jaw [dʒɔ:] [解剖] **I** *n* [C] [*of person*] 颌 **II jaws** *n* [*pl*] [*of person, animal*] 嘴巴 ♦ **his jaw dropped** 他大吃一惊

jazz [dʒæz] *n* [U] [音] 爵士乐 ♦ **and all that jazz** [非正式] 诸如此类的事情
❑ **jazz up** *vt* [非正式] [+ *food, party, one's image*] 使有趣

jealous ['dʒɛləs] *adj* **1** (*possessive*) [+ *husband, wife etc*] 爱妒忌的 **2** (*envious*) 妒忌的 ♦ **to be jealous of sb/sth** 忌妒某人/某事

jealousy ['dʒɛləsɪ] *n* [U] **1** (*possessiveness*) [*of husband, wife etc*] 嫉妒 **2** (*envy*) 妒忌

jeans [dʒiːnz] *n* [*pl*] 牛仔裤 ♦**a pair of jeans** 一条牛仔裤
jeep® [dʒiːp] *n* [c] 吉普车
jelly ['dʒɛlɪ] *n* [c/u] **1** [英] (*dessert*) 果冻 [美=**Jell-O**®] **2** [美] (*preserve*) 果酱 [英=**jam**]
Jell-O® ['dʒɛləu] [美] *n* [u] 果冻 [英=**jelly**]
jellyfish ['dʒɛlɪfɪʃ] (*pl* **jellyfish**) *n* [c] 海蜇
jeopardize ['dʒɛpədaɪz] *vt* [+ *job, relationship, outcome*] 危害
jerk [dʒəːk] **I** *vt* (*pull*) ♦**to jerk sth up/away/back** 将某物猛地拉上/开/回 **II** *vi* ♦**to jerk up/back** 猛然向上/后一动 **III** *n* [c] **1** (*jolt*) 急动 **2** [非正式, 疑讳] (*idiot*) 呆子 ♦**the bus jerked to a halt** 汽车猛地停住了 ♦**the train started with a jerk** 火车颠簸着起动了 ♦**with a jerk of his head** 扭动一下他的头 ♦**to give a jerk** 抖了一下
jersey ['dʒəːzɪ] **I** *n* **1** [c] [过时] (*pullover*) 针织毛衫 **2** [u] (*fabric*) 细毛纱 **II** *cpd* [复合词] [+ *dress, top*] 针织紧身衣
Jesus ['dʒiːzəs] *n* [宗] 耶稣 ♦**Jesus Christ** 耶稣基督 ♦**Jesus!** [非正式, 疑讳] 天哪!
jet [dʒɛt] **I** *n* **1** [c] [*of gas, liquid*] 喷射流 **2** [c] (*aeroplane*) 喷气式飞机 **3** [u] (*stone*) 黑玉 **II** *vi* ♦**to jet off to Paris/on holiday** 飞往巴黎/度假 **III** *cpd* [复合词] [+ *earring, necklace*] 黑玉
jet engine *n* [c] 喷气发动机
jet lag *n* [u] 时差反应
jetty ['dʒɛtɪ] *n* [c] 码头
Jew [dʒuː] *n* [c] 犹太人
jewel ['dʒuːəl] *n* [c] **1** (*gem*) 宝石 **2** (喻) 珍宝 ♦**it's the jewel in the/sb's crown** 是/某人的宝中之宝
jeweller (美 **jeweler**) ['dʒuːələ(r)] *n* [c] **1** (*person*) 珠宝商 **2** (*also: **jeweller's***) 珠宝店
jewellery (美 **jewelry**) ['dʒuːəlrɪ] *n* [u] 首饰
Jewish ['dʒuːɪʃ] *adj* 犹太的
jigsaw ['dʒɪgsɔː] *n* **1** [c] (*also: **jigsaw puzzle***) 拼图玩具 **2** (喻) 错综复杂的局势 **3** (*tool*) 竖锯
✪**job** [dʒɔb] *n* [c] **1** (*position*) 工作 ◊ *Gladys got a job as a secretary.* 格拉迪斯找到了一份秘书工作。 **2** (*task*) 任务 ◊ *We managed to finish the entire job in three months.* 我们花了3个月的时间完成了全部任务。 **3** (*function*) 职责 ◊ *It's not my job to look after your children.* 给你看孩子不是我的职责。 ♦**it's a good job that ...** 幸好… ♦**to do** *or* [英] **make a good job of sth** 把事情做好 ♦**I had a job finding it** 我好不容易才找到 ♦**on the job** [*learn, teach* +] 工作着 ♦**a part-time/full-time job** 半职/全职工作 ♦**he's only doing his job** 他只是在履行职责 ♦**it's just the job** [英:非正式] 正是想要的
📖 用法参见 **position**
job centre [英] *n* [c] 职业介绍所
jobless ['dʒɔblɪs] **I** *adj* 失业的 **II** *n* [*pl*] ♦**the jobless** 失业者
jockey ['dʒɔkɪ] **I** *n* [c] [体育] 赛马骑师 **II** *vi* ♦**to jockey for position** [*rivals, competitors* +] 运用手段谋取利益
jog [dʒɔg] **I** *vt* 轻碰 **II** *vi* 慢跑 **III** *n* ♦**to go for a jog** 去慢跑 ♦**to jog sb's memory** 唤起某人的记忆 ♦**to go jogging** 去慢跑
jogging ['dʒɔgɪŋ] *n* [u] 慢跑
✪**join** [dʒɔɪn] **I** *vt* **1** (*become member of*) [+ *club, party, army, navy, queue*] 加入 ◊ *We both joined the Labour Party.* 我们俩都加入了工党。 **2** (*connect*) [+ *things, places*] 连接 ◊ *Draw a straight line joining these two points.* 画一直线, 将这两点连接起来。 **3** (*meet*) [+ *person*] 会面 ◊ *She flew out to join him in Africa.* 她飞往非洲与他会面。 **4** [+ *road, river*] 汇合 ◊ *This road joins the motorway at junction 16.* 这条路在16号岔路口与高速公路汇合。 **II** *vi* [*roads, rivers* +] 汇合 ◊ *The two streams join and form a river.* 两条小溪汇合, 形成河流。 **III** *n* [c] 接缝 ♦**to join forces (with sb)** (与某人) 通力合作 ♦**will you join us for dinner?** 你想不想和我们一起吃晚饭? ♦**I'll join you later** 我一会儿过来
❏**join in** **I** *vi* 参与 **II** *vt* [不可拆分] [+ *work, discussion etc*] 参加
❏**join up** *vi* **1** [军] 参军 **2** (*meet*) ♦**to**

join up (with sb) （与某人）联合起来

joiner ['dʒɔɪnə(r)] [英] *n* [C] 细木工人

joint [dʒɔɪnt] **I** *n* [C] **1** [解剖] 关节 **2** [术语] (*in woodwork, pipe etc*) 连接处 **3** [英：烹饪] [*of beef, lamb*] 大块肉 [美=**roast**] **4** [非正式] (*bar, club*) 低级场所 **5** [非正式：药品] 含大麻的香烟 **II** *adj* **1** (*shared*) [+ *effort, decision*] 共同的; [+ *owners*] 联合的 ♦**to be out of joint** 不协调的

joint account *n* [C] 共有帐户

jointly ['dʒɔɪntlɪ] *adv* [*own, run, fund, produce* +] 共同地; [+ *responsible*] 共同地

joke [dʒəuk] **I** *n* [C] **1** (*funny story*) 笑话 **2** (*prank*) 玩笑 **II** *vi* 开玩笑 ♦**the decision was a joke** [非正式] 这个决定真是荒唐 ♦**it's no joke** [非正式] 不是闹着玩儿的 ♦**to play a joke on sb** 开某人的玩笑 ♦**to joke about sth** 以某事为笑柄 ♦**you're joking** *or* **you must be joking!** [非正式] 你在开玩笑｛或｝你一定在开玩笑吧！

joker ['dʒəukə(r)] *n* [C] **1** [纸牌] 百搭 **2** (*person*) 爱开玩笑的人

jolly ['dʒɔlɪ] **I** *adj* **1** (*merry*) [+ *person, laugh*] 愉快的 **2** (*enjoyable*) [+ *time, party*] 欢乐的 **II** *adv* [英：过时，非正式] 非常 **III** *vt* [英] ♦**to jolly sb along** 哄某人开心 ♦**jolly good** [英] 太好了

jolt [dʒəult] **I** *n* [C] **1** (*jerk*) 颠簸 **2** (*shock*) 震惊 **II** *vt* **1** (*physically*) 摇晃 **2** (*emotionally*) 使震惊 **III** *vi* 颠簸 ♦**to give sb a jolt** (*emotionally*) 使某人震惊 ♦**I realized with a jolt that ...** 我猛然意识到…

Jordan ['dʒɔːdən] *n* **1** (*country*) 约旦 **2** ♦**the (River) Jordan** 约旦河

Jordanian [dʒɔː'deɪnɪən] **I** *adj* 约旦的 **II** *n* [C] 约旦人

journal ['dʒəːnl] *n* [C] **1** (*publication*) 报刊 **2** (*diary*) 日记 ♦**to keep a journal (of sth)** 记（关于某事的）日记

journalism ['dʒəːnəlɪzəm] *n* [U] (*profession*) 新闻业 ♦**piece of journalism** 报导

journalist ['dʒəːnəlɪst] *n* [C] 新闻工作者

journey ['dʒəːnɪ] **I** *n* [C] 旅程 **II** *vi* [正式] 旅行 ♦**a 5-hour journey** 5个小时的路程 ♦**to go on a journey** 去旅行

> 请勿将**journey, voyage**和**trip**混淆。**journey**是指从一地搭乘车船或飞机到另一地的过程。*...a journey of over 2000 miles...* 如果你**journey to**某地，你就是去那里。这是书面的用法。*The nights became colder as they journeyed north.* **voyage**是指从一地到另一地的长途行程，通常指乘船旅行或者太空旅行。*...the voyage to the moon in 1972...* **trip**是指从一地到另一地的旅行过程，在目的地做短暂的停留后返回。*...a business trip to Milan...*

joy [dʒɔɪ] *n* **1** [U] (*happiness*) 快乐 **2** [C] (*delight*) 愉悦

joyrider ['dʒɔɪraɪdə(r)] *n* [C] 开偷来的车去兜风的人

joystick ['dʒɔɪstɪk] *n* [C] **1** [航空] 操纵杆 **2** [计算机] 控制杆

JP [英] *n abbr* (= ***Justice of the Peace***) 地方执法官

Jr (美 **Jr.**) *abbr* (*in names*) (= ***junior***) 小

judge [dʒʌdʒ] **I** *n* [C] **1** [法] 法官 **2** (*in competition*) 裁判 **II** *vt* **1** [+ *exhibits, competition etc*] 评定 **2** (*evaluate*) [+ *effect, impact*] 评估; [+ *person*] 评判 **3** (*estimate*) [+ *age, weight, size*] 判断 **4** [正式] (*consider*) 断定 **III** *vi* (*form opinion*) 判断 ♦**I'll be the judge of that** 这由我说了算 ♦**judging by** *or* **from his expression** 从他的表情上判断 ♦**as** *or* **so far as I can judge** 依我看 ♦**to be a good judge of sth** 很会判断某事

judg(e)ment ['dʒʌdʒmənt] *n* **1** [C/U] (*view, opinion*) 看法 **2** [U] (*discernment*) 判断力 **3** [C/U] [法] 审判 ♦**in my judgment** 依我来看 ♦**to pass judgment (on sb/sth)** [法]（对某人/某事）作出判决;（喻）评论（某人/某事）♦**an error of judgment** 判断失误

judo ['dʒuːdəu] *n* [U] 柔道

jug [dʒʌg] *n* [C] **1** (*container*) 壶

2 *(contents)* 壶

juggle ['dʒʌgl] **I** *vi* 玩杂耍 **II** *vt* **1** (字) 连续抛接 **2** (喻) [+ *demands, priorities*] 同时兼顾 ♦ **to juggle with sth** [+ *balls, plates etc*] 连续抛接某物; [+ *figures, numbers*] 窜改某物

juggler ['dʒʌglə(r)] *n* [c] 杂耍演员

juice [dʒuːs] **I** *n* **1** [c/u] *(from fruit)* 汁 **2** [u] [非正式] *(petrol)* 汽油 **II juices** *n* [*pl*] [*of meat*] 汁; *(digestive)* 液

juicy ['dʒuːsɪ] *adj* **1** [+ *fruit, steak*] 多汁液的 **2** [非正式] *(scandalous)* [+ *details, rumours, gossip*] 绘声绘色的

Jul. *abbr* (= ***July***) 七月

July [dʒuː'laɪ] *n* [c/u] 七月 ♦ **the first of July** 七月一日 ♦ **(on) the eleventh of July** (在) 七月十一日 ♦ **in the month of July** 在七月份 ♦ **at the beginning/end of July** 在七月初/末 ♦ **in the middle of July** 在七月中旬 ♦ **during July** 在七月份期间 ♦ **in July of next year** 在明年七月 ♦ **each** *or* **every July** 每年七月 ♦ **July was wet this year** 今年七月份多雨

jumble ['dʒʌmbl] **I** *n* **1** [s] *(muddle)* 杂乱 **2** [u] [英] *(items for sale)* 义卖的旧杂物 [美 = **rummage**] **II** *vt* *(also: **jumble up**)* 使混乱

jumble sale [英] *n* [c] 杂物义卖 [美 = **rummage sale**]

> **JUMBLE SALE**
> 在学校或教堂里举行 **jumble sale** (杂物拍卖) 可以为慈善机构、学校 (例如，为了购买电脑) 或教会 (或许为了修葺屋顶) 筹措资金。人们捐出不需要的衣物、玩具、图书和其他家庭用品，有意者前来观看，以期"掏到"便宜的二手货。

jumbo ['dʒʌmbəu] **I** *n* [c] *(also: **jumbo jet**)* 大型喷气式客机 **II** *adj* *(also: **jumbo-size(d)**)* 特大的

jump [dʒʌmp] **I** *vi* **1** *(into air)* 跳 **2** *(from seat etc)* 跳起来 **3** *(with fear, surprise)* 突然跃起 **4** *(increase)* 暴涨 **II** *vt* [+ *fence, stream*] 跳过 **III** *n* [c] **1** *(leap)* 跳 **2** *(increase)* 猛增 ♦ **to jump over sth** 跳过某物 ♦ **to jump out of a window** 从窗户跳下 ♦ **to jump on/off sth** 跳上/下某物 ♦ **to jump to one's feet** 噌地站起来 ♦ **to jump the queue** [英] 加塞儿 ♦ **to get a** *or* **the jump on sb/sth** [美] 抢在某人/某事之前行动

❏ **jump at** *vt* [不可拆分] [+ *chance, offer*] 欣然接受

❏ **jump up** *vi* 突然站立

jumper ['dʒʌmpə(r)] *n* [c] **1** [英] *(sweater)* 毛衣 [美 = **sweater**] **2** [美] *(dress)* 无袖连衣裙 [英 = **pinafore**] **3** [体育] ♦ **a long/high jumper** 跳远/跳高运动员

Jun. *abbr* (= ***June***) 六月

junction ['dʒʌŋkʃən] [英] *n* [c] **1** [*of roads*] 交叉点 [美 = **intersection**] **2** [铁路] 联轨点

June [dʒuːn] *n* [c/u] 六月 *see also* **July**

jungle ['dʒʌŋgl] *n* **1** [c/u] 丛林 **2** [s] (喻) 混乱 ♦ **the law of the jungle** 弱肉强食的原则

junior ['dʒuːnɪə(r)] **I** *adj* 级别低的 **II** *n* [c] **1** *(subordinate)* 下级 **2** [英: 教育] 小学生 ♦ **he's my junior by 2 years, he's 2 years my junior** 他比我小两岁 ♦ **to be junior to sb** 是某人的下属 ♦ **George Bush Junior** [美] 小乔治·布什

junior high (美 **junior high school**) *n* [c/u] 初中

junior school [英] *n* [c/u] 小学

junk [dʒʌŋk] **I** *n* **1** [u] [非正式] *(rubbish)* 废旧杂物 **2** [u] *(antiques)* 古董 **3** [c] *(ship)* 平底帆船 **II** *vt* [非正式] 扔掉

junk food *n* [u] 垃圾食品

junkie ['dʒʌŋkɪ] [非正式] *n* [c] 吸毒者

junk mail *n* [u] 垃圾邮件

Jupiter ['dʒuːpɪtə(r)] *n* [u] *(planet)* 木星

jurisdiction [dʒuərɪs'dɪkʃən] *n* [u] 司法权 ♦ **to have jurisdiction over** 对…有管辖权 ♦ **it falls** *or* **comes within/outside my jurisdiction** 这件事在我的权限之内/之外

jury ['dʒuərɪ] *n* [c] **1** [法] 陪审团 **2** *(in competition)* 评审团 ♦ **the jury is (still) out** 陪审团 (仍) 在合议

✪**just** [dʒʌst] **I** *adj* **1** [正式] (*fair*) [+ *decision, punishment, reward*] 公平的 ◊ *Was Pollard's life sentence just or was it too severe?* 判波拉德无期徒刑公平呢，还是太重了？; [+ *society, cause*] 公正的 ◊ *a just and civilized society* 一个公正文明的社会 **II** *adv* **1** (*exactly*) 正好 ◊ *That's just what I wanted to hear.* 那正好是我想要听的。**2** (*merely*) 仅仅 ◊ *It's not true, it's just a story.* 这不是真的，仅仅是个故事。**3** (*barely*) 刚刚 ◊ *Her hand was just visible.* 刚刚能看见她的手。**4** (*for emphasis*) 简直 ◊ *She just won't relax.* 她就是无法放松。**5** (*in instructions, requests*) (*only*) 只是 ◊ *I just want some information on ferries, please.* 劳驾，我只是想要一些有关渡船的信息。♦ **it's just right** 正合适 ♦ **I'm just finishing this** 我马上就做完了 ♦ **we were just going** 我们正要走 ♦ **I was just about to phone** *or* **I was just going to phone** 我正要打电话 ♦ **to have just done sth** 刚刚做完某事 ◊ *He has just left.* 他刚走。♦ **just now** (*a moment ago*) 刚才; (*at the present time*) 现在 ♦ **just about everything/everyone** 差不多所有东西/所有人 ♦ **it's just about big enough** 差不多够大了 ♦ **we can just about get there in time** 我们可能刚刚能准时赶到那里 ♦ **it's just that ...** 不过… ♦ **she's just as clever as you** 她跟你一样聪明 ♦ **just as I expected** 正如我所预料的那样 ♦ **just as he was leaving** 就在他要离开时 ♦ **just before/after ...** 就在…以前/以后 ♦ **just enough time/money** 时间/钱正好够 ♦ **he just missed** (*failed to hit target*) 他差点就打中目标 ♦ **he just missed the wall** (*avoided crashing into*) 他差点撞到墙上 ♦ **not just now** 不是现在 ♦ **just a minute, just one moment** (*asking someone to wait*) 等一下; (*interrupting*) 慢着

justice ['dʒʌstɪs] *n* **1** [U] [法] (*system*) 司法 **2** [U] (*fairness*) 正义 **3** [U] (*legitimacy*) [*of cause, complaint*] 正当 **4** [C] [美] (*judge*) 法官 ♦ **Lord Chief Justice** [英:法] 首席大法官 ♦ **to do justice to sb/sth** 使某人/某物达到最佳效果 ◊ *The photograph I had seen didn't do her justice.* 照片没有她本人好看。♦ **she didn't do herself justice** 她没有充分发挥自己的才能 ♦ **to bring sb to justice** 把某人缉拿归案

justifiable [dʒʌstɪ'faɪəbl] *adj* 有理的

justification [dʒʌstɪfɪ'keɪʃən] *n* [C/U] 正当理由

justify ['dʒʌstɪfaɪ] *vt* **1** [+ *action, decision*] 证明…是有理由的 ♦ **he is justified in doing it** 他这么做是有理由的 ♦ **to justify o.s.** 为自己辩护

jut [dʒʌt] *vi* (*also: **jut out***) 突出

juvenile ['dʒuːvənaɪl] **I** *adj* **1** [+ *crime, offender, court*] 青少年的 **2** [贬] [+ *humour, mentality, person*] 幼稚的 **II** *n* [C] [正式] 青少年

Kk

K¹, k [keɪ] *n* [c/u] (*letter*) 英语的第十一个字母

K² *abbr* **1** [非正式] (= ***thousand*(*s*)**) 千 **2** [计算机] (= ***kilobyte*(*s*)**) 千字节

kabob [kə'bɔb] [美] *n* [c] **1** (*on stick*) 烤肉串 **2** (*in bread*) 夹烤肉饼 [英= **kebab**]

Kampuchea [kæmpu'tʃɪə] [旧] *n* 柬埔寨

Kampuchean [kæmpu'tʃɪən] [旧] *adj* 柬埔寨的

kangaroo [kæŋgə'ruː] *n* [c] 袋鼠

karaoke [kɑːrə'əukɪ] *n* [u] 卡拉OK

karate [kə'rɑːtɪ] *n* [u] 空手道

Kazakhstan [kæzæk'stɑːn] *n* 哈萨克斯坦

kebab [kə'bæb] *n* [c] **1** (*on stick*) 烤肉串 **2** (*in bread*) 夹烤肉饼 [美= **kabob**]

keel [kiːl] **I** *n* [c] [航海] 龙骨 ♦ **to keep sb/sth on an even keel** 使某人/某物保持稳定 ♦ **to get** *or* **put sth back on an even keel** 使某物恢复稳定

❑ **keel over** [非正式] *vi* [*person* +] 倒下

keen [kiːn] *adj* **1** (*enthusiastic*) 热衷的 **2** [+ *interest, desire*] 强烈的 **3** [+ *sense, mind, intelligence*] 敏锐的 **4** [+ *competition*] 激烈的 ♦ **to have a keen eye for detail** 对细节有敏锐的观察力 ♦ **to be keen to do sth** 渴望做某事 ♦ **to be keen for sb to do sth** 极力要求某人做某事 ♦ **to be keen that ...** 积极主张… ♦ **to be keen on sth** 热衷于某事 ♦ **to be keen on doing sth** (*enjoy doing*) 喜欢做某事; (*eager to do*) 很想做某事 ♦ **to be keen on sb** 喜爱某人

✪ **keep** [kiːp] (*pt, pp* **kept**) **I** *vt* **1** (*retain*) [+ *receipt, money, job*] 保留 ◊ *Make sure you always keep your receipts.* 记住留着收据。**2** (*store*) 保存 ◊ *Keep your card in a safe place.* 把你的卡保存好。◊ *The rubbish is kept in the basement.* 垃圾是放在地下室的。**3** (*detain*) 留 ◊ *They kept her in hospital overnight.* 他们留她在医院过夜。**4** (*hold*) 保持 ◊ *Keep your back straight.* 别驼背。◊ *Keep costs to a minimum.* 尽量减低费用。**5** (*manage*) [+ *shop, guest house*] 经营 ◊ *My aunt kept a sweetshop.* 我姨妈经营糖果店。**6** (*look after*) [+ *chickens, bees etc*] 饲养 **7** [+ *accounts, diary*] 记 ◊ *As a young girl I used to keep a diary.* 当我是小女孩时我常记日记。**8** (*support*) [+ *family*] 养 **II** *vi* **1** (*stay*) 保持 ◊ *It's not always easy to keep warm.* 保暖并不总是那么容易的。**2** (*last*) [*food* +] 保鲜 ◊ *Homemade muesli keeps for ages.* 自己作的穆兹利可以保鲜很长时间。◊ *Fish doesn't keep well, even in the fridge.* 就算把鱼放在冰箱里也不容易保鲜。**III** *n* **1** [s] (*expenses*) 生活费 ◊ *I need to give my parents money for my keep.* 我需要给父母我的生活费。**2** [c] [*of castle*] 要塞 ♦ **to keep doing sth** (*repeatedly*) 总是做某事; (*continuously*) 不停做某事 ♦ **to keep sb happy** 让某人高兴 ♦ **to keep sb waiting** 让某人等着 ♦ **to keep the room tidy** 保持房间整洁 ♦ **to keep sth to o.s.** 保守秘密 ♦ **to keep an appointment** 守约 ♦ **to keep a promise** 履行诺言 ♦ **to keep one's word** 履行诺言 ♦ **can you keep a secret?** 你能保守秘密吗？♦ **to keep a record (of sth)** 记录（某事）♦ **to keep o.s.** 供养自己 ♦ **to keep (good) time** [*clock* +] 准时 ♦ **what kept you?** 怎么会晚了？♦ **how are you keeping?** [非正式] 你还好吗？♦ **to keep at it** (*persevere*) 坚持干

❑ **keep away I** *vt* ♦ **to keep sth/sb away (from sth)** 使某物/某人不要来（某处）◊ *Keep animals away from the kitchen.* 别让动物到厨房里。**II** *vi* ♦ **to keep away (from sth)** 不接近（某处）◊ *They kept away from the forest.* 他们不接近森林。

❑ **keep back I** *vt* **1** (*reserve*) [+ *paint,*

ingredients] 保留◊ *Keep back enough juice to make the sauce.* 留足够的汁做调味汁。**2** (*conceal*) [+ *information*] 隐瞒◊ *I can't help feeling he's keeping something back.* 我总觉得他在隐瞒着什么。**II** *vi* 不靠近◊ *Keep back or I'll shoot.* 别向前，不然我就开枪了。

❑ **keep down** *vt* **1** (*control*) [+ *prices, spending*] 控制◊ *We want to try and keep costs down.* 我们想尽量压缩费用。**2** (*not vomit*) [+ *food*] 咽下◊ *I can't keep anything down, not even water.* 我什么都咽不下，连水都不行。

❑ **keep from I** *vt* [不可拆分] ♦ **to keep from doing sth** 克制◊ *She bit her lip to keep from crying.* 她咬着嘴唇克制着自己不要哭。**II** *vt* ♦ **to keep sb/sth from doing sth** 不让某人/某物做某事◊ *Can't you keep your children from stealing my apples?* 你不能不让你孩子偷我的苹果吗？

❑ **keep in** *vt* [+ *invalid, child*] 不让外出；(*as punishment*) 关禁闭

❑ **keep in with** [尤英] *vt* [不可拆分] 搞好关系◊ *Now he is getting old he wishes he had kept in with his family.* 他年纪大了，后悔当初没有多亲近家人。

❑ **keep off I** *vt* 使不接近◊ *a bamboo shelter to keep the rain off* 挡雨的竹棚◊ *Keep your dog off my lawn!* 别让你的狗接近我的草坪！ ♦ **Keep your hands off me!** 别碰我！ **II** *vt* [不可拆分] ♦ **keep off the grass!** 请勿进入草坪！ **III** *vi* [*rain* +] 不下（雨）◊ *Luckily the rain kept off.* 幸好没有下雨。

❑ **keep on** *vi* ♦ **to keep on doing sth** 继续做某事◊ *They kept on walking for a while in silence.* 他们继续走了一会儿，谁都没说话。

❑ **keep out** *vt* [+ *intruder, unwelcome visitor*] 阻拦◊ *a guard dog to keep out intruders* 阻止闯入者的看家狗

❑ **keep to** *vt* [不可拆分] (*observe*) [+ *agreement*] 遵守；[+ *limit*] 局限于◊ *You've got to keep to the speed limit.* 你绝对不能超速。

❑ **keep up I** *vt* **1** (*maintain*) [+ *standards*] 维持◊ *It's important to keep up our standards.* 维持水准是很重要的。**2** (*continue*) [+ *payments, diet*] 继续◊ *He was unable to keep up the payments.* 他没能力继续付款。**3** (*prevent from sleeping*)（使）熬夜◊ *We were kept up by the noise from next door.* 隔壁的噪音使我们睡不着觉。♦ **to keep up appearances** 撑场面 **II** *vi* ♦ **to keep up** (*with walker, vehicle*) 跟上；(*with demand, inflation*) 跟上；(*in work*) 跟上 ♦ **to keep up with sb** (*walking, moving*) 跟上某人；(*in work*) 跟上某人 ♦ **to keep up with demand/inflation** 跟上需求/通货膨胀

keeper [ˈkiːpə(r)] *n* [c] **1** (*at zoo*) 饲养员 **2** [c] [英：非正式] (*goalkeeper*) 守门员

keep fit [尤英] *n* [u] 健身运动

keep-fit *cpd* [复合词] [+ *class, session, course*] 健身

keeping [ˈkiːpɪŋ] *n* [u] ♦ **in keeping with** [+ *image, surroundings*] 与…协调；[+ *regulation, law*] 与…一致 ♦ **out of keeping with** 与…不协调

kennel [ˈkɛnl] **I** *n* [c] [英] (*dog house*) 狗窝 **II** (***also kennels***) *n* [*pl*] (*establishment*) 养狗场

Kenya [ˈkɛnjə] *n* 肯尼亚

Kenyan [ˈkɛnjən] **I** *adj* 肯尼亚的 **II** *n* (*person*) 肯尼亚人

kept [kɛpt] *pt, pp of* **keep**

kerb (美 **curb**) [kəːb] *n* [c] 路缘

kerosene [ˈkɛrəsiːn] *n* [u] **1** (*aviation fuel*) 航空燃料 **2** [美] (*for heater, lamp*) 煤油 [英= **paraffin**]

ketchup [ˈkɛtʃəp] *n* [u] 番茄酱

kettle [ˈkɛtl] *n* [c] 水壶 ♦ **to put the kettle on** 烧水 ♦ **the kettle's boiling** 水开了

key [kiː] **I** *n* [c] **1** (*for lock, mechanism*) 钥匙 **2** [*of computer, typewriter, piano*] 键 **3** [音] 调 **4** ♦ **the key (to sth)** (*to success, victory, peace, mystery*)（某事的）关键 **II** *adj* [+ *issue, factor etc*] 关键的 **III** *vt* (***also key in***) 输入 ♦ **to hold the key to sth** 掌握某事的关键 ♦ **the key to doing sth** 做某事的关键

keyboard [ˈkiːbɔːd] **I** *n* [c] [*of computer, typewriter, piano*] 键盘 **II keyboards** *n* [*pl*] 键盘乐器

keyhole [ˈkiːhəul] *n* [c] 钥匙孔

key ring *n* [c] 钥匙环
kg *abbr* (= ***kilogram(s)***) 公斤
khaki ['kɑːkɪ] **I** *n* [U] **1** (*colour*) 土黄色 **2** (*material*) 卡其布 **II** *adj* **1** (*colour*) 土黄色的 **2** (*material*) 卡其布的
kHz *abbr* (= ***kilohertz***) 千赫兹
kick [kɪk] **I** *vt* [+ *person, ball*] 踢 **II** *vi* [*person, horse* +] 踢 **III** *n* [c] **1** (*blow from person, animal*) 踢 **2** [体育] 踢 **3** [*of rifle*] 反冲 ♦**to give sb a kick** 踢某人 ♦**to get a kick out of sth** 从某事中获得乐趣 ♦**to do sth for kicks** [非正式] 为刺激而做某事 ♦**to kick the habit** [非正式] 戒除恶习 ♦**to kick the bucket** [非正式] 翘辫子 ♦**I could have kicked myself!** [非正式] 我真后悔！
❑**kick about** *vt, vi* = **kick around**
❑**kick around** [非正式] **I** *vi* 在 **II** *vt* [+ *ideas*] 随便谈一谈
❑**kick in** *vi* (*take effect*) [*electrical device* +] 开启; [*medicine* +] 起作用
❑**kick off I** *vi* **1** [体育] 开赛 **2** [非正式] (*begin*) 开始 **II** *vt* 开始
❑**kick up** *vt* [不可拆分] ♦**to kick up a fuss (about sth)** (为某事) 大发牢骚
kick-off ['kɪkɔf] [体育] *n* [s] 开场时间
kid [kɪd] **I** *n* [c] **1** [非正式] (*child*) 小孩; (*teenager*) 年轻人 **2** (*goat*) 小山羊 **II** *vi* [非正式] (*joke*) 开玩笑 ♦**you're kidding!** 你一定是在开玩笑吧！ ♦**kid brother** [非正式] 弟 ♦**kid sister** [非正式] 妹
kidnap ['kɪdnæp] **I** *vt* 绑架 **II** *n* [c/U] 绑架
kidnapping ['kɪdnæpɪŋ] *n* [c/U] 绑架
kidney ['kɪdnɪ] *n* **1** [c] [解剖] 肾脏 **2** [c/U] [烹饪] 腰子
kidney bean *n* [c] 云豆
✪ **kill** [kɪl] **I** *vt* **1** [+ *person, animal, plant*] 致死 ◊ *Her mother was killed in a car crash.* 她母亲死于车祸。 **2** (*murder*) 谋杀 ◊ *She killed him with a hammer.* 她用锤子杀死了他。 **3** (喻) [+ *rumor, hope, idea*] 扼杀 **4** [非正式] [+ *lights, motor*] 关掉 **5** [+ *pain*] 止痛 ◊ *I'll give you something to kill the pain.* 我给你点止痛的药。 **II** *n* [s] (*after hunt*) 捕杀 ♦**my back's killing me** [非正式] 我的背疼死了 ♦**to kill time** 消磨时间 ♦**he certainly hasn't been killing himself** [非正式:喻] 他肯定没有竭尽全力 ♦**to kill o.s. (laughing** *or* **with laughter)** [非正式:喻] 笑得前仰后合 ♦**to go** *or* **move in for the kill** (喻) 出致命的一击
❑**kill off** *vt* **1** [+ *bacteria, species*] 灭绝 **2** [+ *hope, idea*] 扼杀

> 📖 有几个词和 **kill** 语意相近。**murder** 是蓄意谋杀。**assassinate** 是指出于政治目而暗杀某重要人物。**slaughter** 和 **massacre** 表示大屠杀，**slaughter** 还可以指宰杀动物用以食用。

killer ['kɪlə(r)] *n* [c] **1** (*murderer*) 凶手 **2** (*disease, activity*) 杀灭物 ♦**learning English vocabulary is a killer** 学习英文单词真是难死人了
killing ['kɪlɪŋ] *n* [c] 谋杀 ♦**to make a killing** [非正式] 发大财
kiln [kɪln] *n* [c] 窑
kilo ['kiːləu] *n* [c] 公斤
kilobyte ['kɪləubaɪt] [计算机] *n* [c] 千字节
kilogram(me) ['kɪləugræm] *n* [c] 公斤
kilometre (美 **kilometer**) ['kɪləmiːtə(r)] *n* [c] 公里
kilowatt ['kɪləuwɔt] *n* [c] 千瓦
kilt [kɪlt] *n* [c] 苏格兰短裙
kin [kɪn] [过时] *n* [*pl*] 亲戚
✪ **kind** [kaɪnd] **I** *adj* [+ *person, action, smile, voice*] 友好的 ◊ *They are all extremely kind and helpful.* 他们都很友好，乐于助人。◊ *Thank you. You've been very kind.* 谢谢，你太好心了。 **II** *n* [c] (*type, sort*) 种类 ◊ *an opportunity to meet all kinds of people* 与各种各样的人见面的机会 ♦**it was kind of them to help** 他们来帮忙真是太好了 ♦**would you be kind enough to** *or* **so kind as to close the window?** 麻烦你把窗户关上好吗？ ♦**he's a kind of explorer** 他可以说是个探险者 ♦**she's kind of cute** [非正式] 她还算可爱 ♦**in kind** (*similarly*) 以牙还牙; (*not in money*) 以物偿付

♦ **payment in kind** 以货代款 ♦ **to be two/three/four of a kind** 两/三/四个都属同一类

kindergarten ['kɪndəgɑːtn] *n* [c] 幼儿园

kindly ['kaɪndlɪ] **I** *adj* [+ *person, tone, interest*] 友善的 **II** *adv* [*say, smile, treat* +] 亲切地; [+ *agree, offer*] 友善地 ♦ **will you kindly stop shouting at me!** 请别冲着我大喊大叫! ♦ **he doesn't take kindly to criticism/people criticizing him** 他不乐意接受批评

kindness ['kaɪndnɪs] *n* **1** [U] (*quality*) 仁慈 **2** [c] (*act*) 友好的行为

king [kɪŋ] *n* [c] **1** 国王 **2** [纸牌] 老K **3** [国际象棋] 王 ♦ **the king of the jungle/rock 'n' roll** 森林/摇滚乐之王

kingdom ['kɪŋdəm] *n* [c] 王国 ♦ **the animal/plant kingdom** 动/植物王国

kingfisher ['kɪŋfɪʃə(r)] *n* [c] 翠鸟

king-size(d) ['kɪŋsaɪz(d)] *adj* 特大的

kiosk ['kiːɔsk] *n* [c] **1** (*shop*) 售货亭 **2** [英] (*phone box*) 电话亭

kipper ['kɪpə(r)] *n* [c] 熏制鲱鱼

kiss [kɪs] **I** *n* [c] 吻 **II** *vt* 吻 **III** *vi* 接吻 ♦ **to give sb a kiss** 吻某人一下 ♦ **to kiss sb goodbye/goodnight** 与某人吻别/吻某人一下，道晚安

kiss of life [英] *n* [s] 口对口人工呼吸

kit [kɪt] **I** *n* **1** [U] [尤英] (*equipment*) 成套用品; (*clothing*) 服装; [军] 装备 **2** [c] (*set*) 用品包 **3** [c] (*for assembly*) 配套元件

❑ **kit out** [英:非正式] *vt* ♦ **to kit sb out (with/in sth)** (用某物) 装备某人 ♦ **to be kitted out with/in sth** 全副武装地穿着某物 ♦ **to kit o.s. out with/in sth** 全副武装地穿着某物

kitchen ['kɪtʃɪn] *n* [c] 厨房

kitchen sink *n* [c] 厨房洗涤池

kite [kaɪt] *n* [c] **1** (*toy*) 风筝 **2** [动] 鸢 ♦ **as high as a kite** 晕乎乎的

kitten ['kɪtn] *n* [c] 小猫

kiwi fruit ['kiːwiː-] *n* [c] 猕猴桃

Kleenex® ['kliːnɛks] *n* [c] (*pl* **Kleenex**) 纸巾

km *abbr* (= ***kilometre(s)***) 公里

km/h *abbr* (= ***kilometres per hour***) 每小时…公里

knack [næk] *n* [c] ♦ **to have the knack of doing sth** 掌握做某事的诀窍 ♦ **there's a knack to doing this** 干这个是有诀窍的

knee [niː] **I** *n* [c] 膝盖 **II** *vt* 用膝盖撞击 ♦ **to bring sb to his/her knees** 迫使某人屈服 ♦ **(to sit/be) on sb's knee** (坐)在某人的膝上 ♦ **to be on one's knees** 跪着 ♦ **to fall to one's knees** 跪倒

kneecap ['niːkæp] **I** *n* [c] 膝盖骨 **II** *vt* 用枪击穿膝盖骨

kneel [niːl] (*pt, pp* **knelt**) *vi* (*also* ***kneel down***) 跪下 ♦ **to be kneeling** 跪着

knelt [nɛlt] *pt, pp of* **kneel**

knew [njuː] *pt of* **know**

knickers ['nɪkəz] [英] *n* [*pl*] 女式内裤 [美 = **panties**] ♦ **a pair of knickers** 一条女式内裤 ♦ **to get one's knickers in a twist** [英:非正式] 恼火

knife [naɪf] (*pl* **knives**) **I** *n* [c] 刀 **II** *vt* 用刀刺 ♦ **knife and fork** 刀叉 ♦ **to go under the knife** 动手术 ♦ **the knives are out for him** [英] 他成为众矢之的

knight [naɪt] **I** *n* [c] **1** [历史] 骑士 **2** [国际象棋] 马 **II** *vt* 封…为爵士

knit [nɪt] **I** *vt* [+ *garment*] 织 **II** *vi* **1** (*with wool*) 织 **2** [*bones* +] 愈合

knitted ['nɪtɪd] *adj* [+ *garment*] 针织的

knitting ['nɪtɪŋ] *n* [U] **1** (*activity*) 织 **2** (*garments*) 编织物 ♦ **to do one's knitting** 织东西

knitting needle *n* [c] 编织针

knitwear ['nɪtwɛə(r)] *n* [U] 针织品

knives [naɪvz] *n* [*pl*] *of* **knife**

knob [nɔb] *n* [c] **1** [*on door*] 球形把手 **2** (*on radio, TV etc*) 旋钮 **3** [*on gatepost, stick, umbrella*] 圆把儿 ♦ **a knob of butter** [英] 一小块黄油

knock [nɔk] **I** *vt* **1** (*strike*) 碰撞 **2** [非正式] (*criticize*) 批评 **II** *vi* **1** (*on door, window*) 敲 **2** [*engine* +] 发出爆震声; [*pipes* +] 嘭嘭作响 **III** *n* [c] **1** (*blow, bump*) 碰撞 **2** (*on door*) 敲门声 ♦ **to knock a nail into sth** 在某处钉钉子 ♦ **to knock a hole in sth** 在某处

打个洞 ♦**he knocked the drink out of my hand** 他碰掉了我手里的饮料 ♦**to knock sb to the ground/floor** [*blow, blast, person* +] 把某人击倒在地 ♦**to knock sb unconscious** [*blow, blast* +] 把某人打昏; [*person* +] 打昏某人 ♦**to knock some sense into sb** 让某人明事理 ♦**knock it off!** [非正式] 别胡闹了！ ♦**he knocked on** *or* **at the door** 他敲了门

❑**knock about** [非正式] **I** *vt* [+ *person*] 不断打 **II** *vi* ♦**knock about with sb** 和某人厮混

❑**knock around** *vt, vi* = **knock about**

❑**knock back** [非正式] *vt* [+ *drink*] 一饮而尽

❑**knock down** *vt* **1** (*run over*) 撞倒 **2** (*demolish*) 拆除 **3** [尤美] [+ *price*] 减

❑**knock off I** *vi* [非正式] (*finish work*) 下班 **II** *vt* **1** [+ *percentage, amount*] 减价 **2** [英:非正式] (*steal*) 偷

❑**knock out** *vt* **1** (*make unconscious*) [*blow, person* +] 打昏; [*drug* +] 使丧失知觉; (*cause to sleep*) [*sedative* +] 使入睡 **2** [拳击] 击昏 **3** (*eliminate*) (*in game, competition*) 淘汰

❑**knock over** *vt* 撞倒

knockout ['nɔkaut] **I** *n* [c] **1** [拳击] 击倒对手获胜 **2** [非正式] (*sensation*) (*person*) 令人倾倒的人; (*thing*) 引人注目的东西 **II** *adj* [英] [+ *competition*] 淘汰赛

knot [nɔt] **I** *n* [c] **1** (*in rope, string*) 结; (*in hair*) 髻 **2** (*in wood*) 节瘤 **3** [航海] 节 **II** *vt* 将…打个结 ♦**to tie a knot** 打个结 ♦**to tie the knot** (*get married*) 结婚 ♦**to have a knot in one's stomach** 感到心里一阵紧揪

✪ **know** [nəu] (*pt* **knew**, *pp* **known**) *vt* **1** [+ *facts, dates etc*] 知道 ◊ *I don't know her address.* 我不知道她的地址。**2** [+ *language*] 懂 ◊ *I don't know Chinese very well.* 我不怎么懂汉语。**3** (*be acquainted with*) [+ *person, place, subject*] 认识 ◊ *I've known David for years.* 我认识戴维很多年了。*He didn't know London very well.* 他不怎么熟悉伦敦。**4** (*recognize*) 识别 ◊ *He knew a good bargain when he saw one.* 他很会识别便宜货。♦**to know that ...** 知道… ◊ *I knew that he lived in Glasgow.* 我知道他住在格拉斯哥。◊ *I knew at once that something was wrong.* 我马上就知道有点不对头。♦**to know where/when** 知道何处/何时… ♦**do you know how to swim?** 你会游泳吗？♦**everyone knew him as Robert** 每个人都叫他罗伯特 ♦**to get to know sb** 逐渐开始了解某人 ♦**to let it be known that ...** 使人们间接了解到… ♦**to know sth about sb/sth** 知道某人/某事的情况 ◊ *She didn't know anything about music.* 她对音乐一窍不通。♦**to know about sth** 听说过某事 ♦**I don't know about that** 我不这么认为 ♦**yes, I know** 对，的确如此 ♦**you never know** 很难讲 ♦**to know of sth/sb** 听说过某事/某人 ♦**you know** (*used for emphasis*) 你得知道 ◊ *The conditions in there are awful, you know.* 你得知道，那里的条件很差。; (*in explanations*) 你知道的 ◊ *the white dress, you know, the one with the short sleeves* 白色连衣裙，你知道的，就是短袖的那件 ♦**to know better (than to do sth)** 明白而不至于(做某事) ♦**you should know better than to do that** 你应该知道不该那样做 ♦**to be in the know** 知情

know-all ['nəuɔːl] [英:非正式, 贬] *n* [c] 自以为无所不知的人 [美 = **know-it-all**]

know-how ['nəuhau] [非正式] *n* [u] 技能

knowing ['nəuɪŋ] *adj* [+ *smile, look*] 心照不宣的

knowingly ['nəuɪŋlɪ] *adv* **1** (*intentionally*) 蓄意地 **2** [*smile, look* +] 会意地

know-it-all ['nəuɪtɔːl] [美:非正式, 贬] *n* [c] 自以为无所不知的人 [英 = **know-all**]

knowledge ['nɔlɪdʒ] *n* [u] 知识 ♦**to (the best of) my knowledge** 据我所知 ♦**it is common knowledge that ...** 众所周知… ♦**safe in the knowledge that ...** 对…心中有数

knowledgeable ['nɔlɪdʒəbl] *adj* 知识渊博的 ♦**to be knowledgeable about sth** 对某事在行

known [nəun] **I** *pp of* **know II** *adj*

[+ *criminal, cure*] 已知的 ♦**to be known for sth** 因某事而出名

knuckle ['nʌkl] *n* [c] 指节

❑**knuckle down** [非正式] *vi* 开始认真工作 ♦**to knuckle down to sth** 埋头做某事

❑**knuckle under** [非正式] *vi* 屈服

koala [kəu'ɑːlə] *n* [c] 树袋熊

Koran [kɔ'rɑːn] *n* ♦**the Koran** 《古兰经》

Korea [kə'rɪə] *n see* **North Korea, South Korea**

Korean [kə'rɪən] **I** *adj* [地理] 朝鲜的 **II** *n* **1** (*person*) 朝鲜人 **2** (*language*) 朝鲜语

kosher ['kəuʃə(r)] *adj* **1** (字) [+ *meat, restaurant*] 按犹太教规的 **2** [非正式:喻] 正确的

Kremlin ['krɛmlɪn] *n* ♦**the Kremlin** (*building*) 克里姆林宫; (*government*) 俄罗斯政府

Kurd [kəːd] *n* 库尔德人

Kuwait [ku'weɪt] *n* 科威特

Kuwaiti [ku'weɪtɪ] **I** *adj* 科威特的 **II** *n* (*person*) 科威特人

kW, KW *abbr* (= ***kilowatt***) 千瓦

Kyrgyzstan [kəːgɪ'stɑːn] *n* 吉尔吉斯斯坦

Ll

L[1], **l** [ɛl] *n* (*letter*) 英语的第十二个字母

L[2] *abbr* **1** [英:汽车] (= ***learner***) 驾驶学员 **2** (= ***large***) 大的

L., l. *abbr* **1** (= ***lake***) 湖 **2** (= ***left***) 左的

l *abbr* (= ***litre(s)***) 升

L8R [手机短信] *abbr* = **later**

lab [læb] [非正式] *n* (*laboratory*) 试验室

label ['leɪbl] **I** *n* [c] **1** (字) (*on suitcase, clothing, bottle, tin etc*) 标签 **2** (喻) 绰号 **3** [音] [*of record*] 原指贴在唱片上的标签，现专指唱片公司 **II** *vt* **1** (字) [+ *object*] 用标签标明 **2** (喻) [+ *person*] 把…称为

labor *etc* ['leɪbə(r)] [美] *n* = **labour** *etc*

laboratory [lə'bɔrətərɪ] *n* [c] **1** (*for analysis, research*) 研究室 **2** (*in school*) 实验室

Labor Day [美] *n* [U] 劳动节

laborious [lə'bɔːrɪəs] *adj* 艰苦的

labor union [美] *n* [c] 工会 [英 = **trade union**]

✪ **labour** (美 **labor**) ['leɪbə(r)] **I** *n* **1** [U] (*hard work*) 劳动 ◊ *the culmination of fifteen months' labour* 15个月劳动的终结 **2** [U] (*manpower*) 劳动力 ◊ *a shortage of skilled labour* 熟练劳动力的缺乏 **3** [U] [工业] (*work done by work force*) 工作 ◊ *They are threatening a withdrawal of labour.* 他们威胁要撤回完成的工作。**4** [U] [医] 分娩 **5** [U] ♦ **Labour** (*Labour Party*) 工党 **II** *adj* ♦ **Labour** [+ *politician, voter*] 工党 **III** *vi* ♦ **to labour to do sth** 不辞辛劳地做某事 **IV** *vt* ♦ **to labour a point** 一再重复 ♦ **to labour under a delusion/an illusion** 抱着错觉不放 ♦ **to be in labour** [医] 处于阵痛期 ♦ **to vote Labour** 投工党的票

labo(u)rer ['leɪbərə(r)] *n* [c] 劳动者

Labour Party [英] *n* 工党

lace [leɪs] **I** *n* [U] **1** (*fabric*) 花边 **2** [c] [*of shoe etc*] 系带 **II** *adj* [+ *curtains, handkerchief, garment*] 有花边的 **III** *vt* **1** (*also: **lace up***) [+ *shoe etc*] 系紧 **2** ♦ **to lace sth with** [+ *alcohol, poison*] 搀某物于

lack [læk] **I** *n* [S/U] (*absence*) 缺乏 **II** *vt* [+ *means, skills, experience, confidence*] 缺乏 ♦ **through** *or* **for lack of sth** 因缺乏某物 ♦ **to be lacking** 不足 ♦ **to be lacking in sth** [+ *confidence, imagination, talent*] 缺乏某物

lacquer ['lækə(r)] *n* [C/U] **1** (*finish*) 漆 **2** [英] (*also: **hair lacquer***) 发胶 [美 = **hairspray**]

lacy ['leɪsɪ] *adj* [+ *dress, nightdress, tights etc*] 花边的; [+ *flowers, pattern*] 花边似的

lad [læd] [非正式] *n* [c] (*boy*) 小伙子; (*young man*) 青年男子

ladder ['lædə(r)] **I** *n* [c] **1** (*for climbing*) 梯子 **2** [英] (*in tights*) 抽丝 [美 = **run**] **II** *vt, vi* [英] [+ *tights*] 抽丝 ♦ **the social/career ladder** (喻) 社会/事业阶梯

ladle ['leɪdl] **I** *n* [c] 长柄勺子 **II** *vt* ♦ **to ladle sth into/onto sth** 把某物舀到某物里/上

❑ **ladle out** *vt* (喻) [+ *advice, money etc*] 慷慨地提供

lady ['leɪdɪ] *n* [c] **1** (*woman*) 女士 **2** (*educated woman*) 淑女 **3** [英] (*title*) 夫人 ♦ **Our Lady** [宗] 圣母 ♦ **ladies and gentlemen ...** 女士们，先生们… ♦ **young lady** 小姐 ♦ **the ladies'** [英], **the ladies' room** [美] 女厕所

ladybird ['leɪdɪbəːd] [英] *n* [c] 瓢虫 [美 = **ladybug**]

ladybug ['leɪdɪbʌg] [美] *n* = **ladybird**

lag [læg] [尤英] *vt* [+ *pipes etc*] 给…加上外套

❑ **lag behind I** *vi* 落后 **II** *vt* [不可拆分] ♦ **to lag behind sb** (*in league tables, studies, technology*) 落后于某人

lager ['lɑːgə(r)] [英] *n* [C/U] 淡啤酒

lagoon [lə'guːn] *n* [c] 潟湖

laid [leɪd] *pt, pp of* **lay**

laid-back [leɪd'bæk] [非正式] *adj* 松弛的

lain [leɪn] *pp of* **lie**

lake [leɪk] *n* [c] 湖 ♦**the wine/milk lake** 欧盟储备的多余葡萄酒/牛奶

lamb [læm] *n* **1** [c] (*animal*) 羔羊 **2** [u] (*meat*) 羔羊肉

lame [leɪm] *adj* **1** [+ *person, animal*] 跛的 **2** (*weak*) [+ *excuse, argument*] 站不住脚的 ♦**to go lame** [*horse* +] 变成瘸子

lament [lə'mɛnt] [正式] **I** *n* [c] (*complaint*) 悲伤 **II** *vt* (*regret*) 为…而痛惜; [+ *sb's death*] 哀悼 ♦**to lament (the fact) that ...** 哀叹…(的事实) ♦**"prices have dropped," he lamented** "价格下跌了," 他哀叹道

lamp [læmp] *n* [c] 灯

lamp-post ['læmppəust] [英] *n* [c] 路灯柱 [美=**street lamp, street light**]

lampshade ['læmpʃeɪd] *n* [c] 灯罩

✪**land** [lænd] **I** *n* **1** [u] (*area of open ground*) 土地 ◊ *agricultural land* 田地 **2** [u] (*property, estate*) 田产 ◊ *Their home is on his father's land.* 他们的屋宅也列在父亲的田产中。**3** [u] (*not sea*) 陆地 ◊ *We turned away from land and headed out to sea.* 我们离开陆地，向海洋进发。**4** [c] [文] (*country, nation*) 国家 ◊ *a foreign land* 外国 **II lands** *n* [*pl*] [文] 地产 **III** *vi* **1** (*fall*) 落下 ◊ *Three shells had landed close to a crowd of people.* 3颗炮弹在人群附近落下。**2** [航空，宇航] 降落 ◊ *His plane lands at six-thirty.* 他的飞机于6点30分降落。**3** (*from ship*) 登陆 ◊ *Three divisions of troops landed in Malaysia.* 3个师的部队在马来西亚登陆。**4** (喻) (*arrive unexpectedly*) [*object, item* +] 不期而至 ◊ *The report landed on his desk.* 那份报告不期然地落到他的办公桌上。**IV** *vt* **1** [+ *plane, spacecraft*] 使降落; [+ *ship*] 使登陆 **2** [尤英] [+ *goods, fish*] 卸 ◊ *The catch was landed at Liverpool.* 捕获物在利物浦卸上岸。**3** [+ *job, place*] 捞到 ◊ *He landed a place on the graduate training scheme.* 他在毕业生培训项目中捞到一个位置。**4** [+ *blow, punch*] 打 ◊ *He landed a blow on the Italian's chin.* 他在那个意大利人的下颌上打了一拳。♦**to own land** 拥有田产 ♦**to go/travel by land** 从陆路去/陆路旅行 ♦**on dry land** 陆地上 ♦**to land sb with sth/sb** [英:非正式] 把某事/某人硬推给某人 ♦**to land sb in trouble** [英:非正式] 使某人陷入麻烦

❑**land up** [尤英:非正式] *vi* 落得 ◊ *You'll land up in jail if you aren't careful.* 如果你不小心的话，你就得落得个入狱的下场。

landing ['lændɪŋ] *n* **1** [c] (*on stairs*) 楼梯平台 **2** [c/u] [航空] 降落

landing card [航空，航海] *n* [c] 入境登记卡

landlady ['lændleɪdɪ] *n* [c] **1** [*of rented house, flat, room*] 女房东 **2** [英] [*of pub*] 女店主

landlord ['lændlɔːd] *n* [c] **1** [*of rented house, flat, room*] 男房东 **2** [英] [*of pub*] 男店主

landmark ['lændmɑːk] *n* [c] **1** (*building, hill etc*) 界标 **2** (喻) 里程碑

landowner ['lændəunə(r)] *n* [c] 土地所有者

landscape ['lændskeɪp] **I** *n* **1** [c/u] 风景 **2** [c] [艺术] 风景画 **II** *vt* 使自然美化

landslide ['lændslaɪd] *n* [c] **1** (字) 塌方 **2** (喻) (*electoral*) 竞选选票的一面倒 ♦**to win by a landslide** 大获全胜

lane [leɪn] *n* [c] **1** (*in country*) 小路 **2** (*in town*) 巷 **3** [汽车] [*of road*] 车道 **4** [*of athletics track, swimming pool*] 道

language ['læŋgwɪdʒ] *n* **1** [c] (*English, Russian etc*) 语言 **2** [u] (*speech*) 语言表达能力 **3** [u] (*specialized terminology*) 术语 **4** [u] (*style*) [*of writing, speech*] 措辞

language laboratory *n* [c] 语言实验室

lantern ['læntən] *n* [c] 灯笼

Laos [laus] [地理] *n* 老挝

Laotian ['lauʃn] [地理] **I** *adj* 老挝的 **II** *n* **1** [c] (*person*) 老挝人 **2** [u] (*language*) 老挝语

lap [læp] **I** *n* [c] **1** [*of person*] 大腿的上方 **2** (*in race*) 圈 **II** *vt* **1** (*also:* ***lap up***) [+ *milk etc*] 舔 **2** (*also:* ***lap against***) [+ *shore, cliff, pier*] 拍打; [+ *competitor*] (*in race*) 领先…一圈 **III** *vi* ♦**to lap against sth** [*waves, water* +] 拍打某物

❑**lap up** *vt* (字) [+ *milk etc*] 舔; (喻) [+ *flattery, news story*] 欣然接受

lapel [lə'pɛl] *n* [c] 翻领

Lapland ['læplænd] [地理] *n* 拉普兰

Lapp [læp] **I** *adj* [地理] 拉普的 **II** *n* **1** [c] (*person*) 拉普人 **2** [u] (*language*) 拉普语

lapse [læps] **I** *n* [c] **1** (*bad behaviour*) 差错 **2** [*of memory, concentration*] 丧失 **3** [*of time*] 流逝 **II** *vi* **1** [*time* +] 流逝 **2** (*expire*) [*contract* +] 失效; [*membership* +] 丧失 **3** [宗] [*person* +] 背离 ♦**to lapse into silence** 陷入沉默

laptop ['læptɔp] *n* [c] (*also:* ***laptop computer***) 笔记本电脑

lard [lɑːd] *n* [u] 猪油

larder ['lɑːdə(r)] [尤英] *n* [c] 食品室

✪**large** [lɑːdʒ] *adj* **1** (*big*) [+ *house, person etc*] 大的; [+ *number, amount*] 大量的 ◊ *a large number of people* 许多人 ◊ *We are facing a large number of problems.* 我们面临大量的问题。**2** (*serious*) [+ *problem, question*] 重大的 ♦**at large** (*as a whole*) 整个 ◊ *their attitude to the world at large* 他们对整个世界的态度 ♦**to be at large** 逍遥自在 ◊ *There were three convicts still at large.* 3 名囚犯仍逍遥法外。♦**by and large** 总的来说

largely ['lɑːdʒlɪ] *adv* (*mostly*) 大体上 ♦**largely because of** 主要是因为

large-scale ['lɑːdʒ'skeɪl] *adj* **1** [+ *action, event*] 大规模的 **2** [+ *map, diagram*] 大比例的

lark [lɑːk] *n* [c] **1** (*bird*) 云雀 **2** [英: 非正式] (*fun*) 戏谑 ♦**to do sth for a lark** [英] 为闹着玩而做某事

❑**lark around, lark about** *vi* 胡闹

larva ['lɑːvə] (*pl* **larvae**) *n* [c] 幼虫

laryngitis [lærɪn'dʒaɪtɪs] [医] *n* [u] 喉炎

laser ['leɪzə(r)] *n* **1** [c/u] (*beam*) 激光 **2** [c] (*machine*) 激光器

lash [læʃ] **I** *vt* **1** (*tie*) ♦**to lash sth to sth** 把某物紧紧系在某物上 **2** [文] [*rain, wind* +] 抽打 **3** (*whip*) 鞭打 **II** *n* [c] (*blow of whip*) 鞭打 **III lashes** *n* [*pl*] (*eyelashes*) 睫毛

❑**lash down I** *vt* (*tie*) 捆紧 **II** *vi* [*rain* +] 猛烈冲击

❑**lash out** *vi* ♦**to lash out (at sb)** (*strike out*) 痛打(某人) ♦**to lash out at sb** (*verbally*) 严厉斥责某人

lass [læs] [英: 非正式] *n* [c] 少女

✪**last** [lɑːst] **I** *adj* **1** (*most recent*) [+ *visit, trip, letter*] 最近的 ◊ *Much had changed since my last visit.* 自我最近一次拜访以后，那里发生了很大的变化。; [+ *Monday, July, weekend etc*] 上 ◊ *last Monday* 上个星期一 **2** (*final*) [+ *bus, hope etc*] 最后的 ◊ *He missed the last bus home.* 他错过了回家的最后一班车。; (*of series, row*) 最后的 ◊ *the last classroom along the passage* 走廊里的最后一个教室 ◊ *the last three pages of the chapter* 这一章的最后 3 页 **3** (*remaining*) [+ *traces, piece etc*] 剩下的 ◊ *the last piece of pizza* 剩下的一块比萨饼 **4** (*for emphasis*) 最不的 ◊ *The last thing I wanted to do was teach.* 我最不想做的事就是教书了。◊ *You are the last person I'd confide in!* 你是我最不信任的人！**II** *pron* **1** (*previous one*) 上一个 ◊ *The next tide would be even higher than the last.* 下一次的潮水要比上一次的还高。**2** (*final one(s)*) 最后一个 ◊ *Which address is the last on your list?* 你单子上的最后一个地址是哪一个？◊ *The trickiest bits are the last on the list.* 最棘手的是单子上的最后一个。**3** (*for emphasis*) 最后一个 ◊ *I would be the last to say that science has explained everything.* 我绝对不觉得科学已经解释了所有事情。◊ *He is the last person I would think of.* 他是我最不会考虑的一个人。**4** (*remainder*) 剩下的 ◊ *He finished off the last of the wine.* 他把剩下的葡萄酒喝完了。◊ *We've eaten the last of the pineapples.* 我们把剩下的菠萝都吃了。**III** *adv* **1** (*most recently*) 最近 ◊ *They last saw their homeland nine years ago.* 他们最近一次看到故乡是9 年以前了。**2** (*at the end*) 最后 ◊ *He added the milk last.* 他最后把牛奶加进去。**3** (*in final position*) 最后 **IV** *vi* **1** (*continue*) 持续 ◊ *Their marriage only lasted six months.* 他们

的婚姻只持续了6个月。◊ *The war in Croatia lasted until January 1992.* 克罗地亚的战争一直持续到1992年1月。**2** (*stay fresh*) 保鲜 ◊ *A fresh pepper lasts about three weeks.* 新鲜的辣椒能保鲜约3个星期。**3** (*be sufficient*) [*money, commodity* +] 够用 ◊ *The curry lasted for two nights.* 这些咖喱饭够两个晚上用了。♦ **last week** 上个星期 ◊ *I had lunch with him last week.* 我上个星期跟他一起吃的午饭。♦ **last night** (*yesterday evening*) 昨晚; (*during the night*) 昨天夜里 ♦ **the last time** (*the final time*) 最后一次; (*the previous time*) 上一次 ♦ **at (long) last** (*finally*) 终于 ♦ **the last I heard** 最近一次我听到的是 ♦ **I'm always the last to find out** 我总是最后一个知道 ♦ **the night/Christmas before last** 前天晚上/前年圣诞节 ♦ **our house is the last but one** 我们的房子是倒数第二个 ♦ **the last president but one** 倒数第二个总统 ♦ **last but not least** 最后一个，但不是不重要的 ♦ **it lasts (for) 2 hours** 持续了两个小时 ♦ **it can't/won't last** 它不会持久

last-ditch ['lɑːst'dɪtʃ] *adj* ♦ **a last-ditch attempt** 孤注一掷

lasting ['lɑːstɪŋ] *adj* [+ *impression, solution*] 持久的

lastly ['lɑːstlɪ] *adv* 最后

last-minute ['lɑːstmɪnɪt] *adj* [+ *decision, appeal etc*] 最后一刻的

last name *n* [C] 姓

latch [lætʃ] *n* [C] (*on door, gate*) 闩 ♦ **on/off the latch** 上/没上闩
❑ **latch on to** *vt* [不可拆分] **1** [非正式] (*take interest in*) [+ *person*] 缠住不放; [+ *idea*] 关注 **2** (*attach to*) [+ *object*] 附着

✪ **late** [leɪt] **I** *adj* **1** (*at an advanced point of*) 晚的 ◊ *in the late afternoon* 傍晚 **2** (*not on time*) 迟的 ◊ *I apologize for my late arrival.* 真抱歉，我迟到了。**3** (*after the usual time*) 稍晚的 ◊ *They had a late lunch.* 他们午餐吃得比较晚。**4** (*deceased*) ♦ **the late Mr Parkin** 已故的帕金先生 **II** *adv* **1** (*at an advanced point of*) 晚 ◊ *The case is expected to end late next week.* 该案可望于下周晚些时候结束。**2** (*not on time*) 迟 ◊ *Steve arrived late.* 斯蒂夫迟到了。**3** (*after the usual time*) 晚 ◊ *We went to bed very late.* 我们很晚才睡觉。♦ **we're late** 我们迟到了 ♦ **sorry I'm late** 对不起，我迟到了 ♦ **to be 10 minutes late** 迟到10分钟 ♦ **it's late** 太迟了 ♦ **to be in one's late thirties/forties** 接近40/50岁 ♦ **late of** [正式] (*until recently of*) 直到最近 ◊ *Jane Smith, late of Bristol* 简·史密斯，直到最近一直住在布里斯托尔 ♦ **to work late** 工作到很晚 ♦ **late in life** 晚年 ♦ **of late** [正式] (*recently*) 近来 ♦ **in late May** 5月下旬 ♦ **late in the day** (喻) 为时已晚

latecomer ['leɪtkʌmə(r)] *n* [C] 迟到者

lately ['leɪtlɪ] *adv* (*recently*) 最近

latent ['leɪtnt] *adj* [+ *energy, skill, ability*] 潜在的

✪ **later** ['leɪtə(r)] **I** *adj* [+ *time, date, meeting etc*] 较晚的 ◊ *An inquest will be held at a later date.* 审讯将于再晚些时候进行。; [+ *version, edition*] 以后的 ◊ *He changed his approach in later editions.* 在以后的版本中，他改变了方法。**II** *adv* 以后 ◊ *I'll join you later.* 我一会儿就来。♦ **in later life** 在晚年 ♦ **some time/weeks/years later** 一些时候/几个星期/几年以后 ♦ **later on** 以后 📖 用法参见 **after**

latest ['leɪtɪst] *adj* **1** (*most recent*) [+ *book, film, news etc*] 最新的 **2** (*most up-to-date*) [+ *fashion*] 最新式的 ♦ **at the latest** 最迟

lather ['lɑːðə(r)] **I** *n* [S/U] (*soapy*) 泡沫 **II** *vt* [+ *hair, fabric*] 涂泡沫于 **III** *vi* [*soap etc* +] 起泡沫 ♦ **to get in a lather** *or* **to work o.s. up into a lather (over** *or* **about sth)** (对某事) 过分焦躁不安

Latin ['lætɪn] **I** *n* **1** [U] (*language*) 拉丁语 **2** [C] (*person*) 拉丁人 **II** *adj* 拉丁的

Latin America *n* 拉丁美洲

Latin American I *adj* 拉丁美洲的 **II** *n* [C] (*person*) 拉丁美洲人

latitude ['lætɪtjuːd] *n* **1** [C/U] [地理] 纬度 **2** [U] (*freedom*) 自由

latter ['lætə(r)] **I** *adj* **1** (*not former*) 后者的 **2** (*later*) [+ *part, half*] 后半的 **II** *n* ♦**the latter** 后者
Latvia ['lætvɪə] [地理] *n* 拉脱维亚
Latvian ['lætvɪən] **I** *adj* 拉脱维亚的 **II** *n* **1** [c] (*person*) 拉脱维亚人 **2** [u] (*language*) 拉脱维亚语
✪ **laugh** [lɑːf] **I** *n* [c] 笑 **II** *vi* 笑 ♦**to give a laugh** 发笑 ♦**to do sth for a laugh** *or* **for laughs** 做某事取乐 ♦**to have the last laugh** 取得最后胜利
❑ **laugh at** *vt* [不可拆分] **1** (字) 对…发笑 **2** (喻) (*mock*) 嘲笑
❑ **laugh off** *vt* [+ *criticism, problem*] 对…一笑置之
laughable ['lɑːfəbl] *adj* [+ *attempt, idea, proposition*] 可笑的
laughter ['lɑːftə(r)] *n* [u] 笑声
launch [lɔːntʃ] **I** *vt* **1** [航海] (*on maiden voyage*) [+ *ship, liner*] 使下水; (*for rescue*) [+ *lifeboat*] 放下 **2** [宇航] [+ *rocket, missile, satellite*] 发射 **3** (喻) [+ *product, publication*] 推出; [+ *campaign*] 发起 **II** *n* [c] **1** [航海] [*of ship*] 下水; [*of lifeboat*] 放下 **2** [航天] [*of rocket, missile, satellite*] 发射 **3** (喻) [+ *of product, publication*] 首次推出; [*of campaign*] 发起 **4** (*motorboat*) 汽艇
❑ **launch into** *vt* [不可拆分] [+ *speech, activity*] 开始
launder ['lɔːndə(r)] *vt* **1** [过时] [+ *clothes, sheets*] 洗熨 **2** (喻) [+ *money*] 洗 ◊ *banks that launder drug money* 洗毒品赃款的银行
Launderette® [lɔːn'drɛt] (英 **laundrette**, 美 **Laundromat®** ['lɔːndrəmæt]) *n* [c] 自助洗衣店
laundry ['lɔːndrɪ] *n* **1** [u] (*dirty washing*) 待洗的衣物; (*clean washing*) 洗好的衣物 **2** [c] (*business*) 洗衣店 **3** [c] (*also: **laundry room***) 洗衣房 ♦**to do the laundry** 洗烫衣物
laundry detergent [美] *n* [u/c] 洗衣粉 [英 = **soap powder, laundry detergent**]
lava ['lɑːvə] *n* [u] 熔岩
lavatory ['lævətərɪ] [英: 过时] *n* [c] 卫生间 [美 = **bathroom**]
lavender ['lævəndə(r)] **I** *n* [u] **1** (*plant*) 熏衣草 **2** (*colour*) 淡紫色 **II** *adj* (*lavender-coloured*) 淡紫色的 **III** *cpd* [复合词] [+ *oil*] 熏衣草
lavish ['lævɪʃ] **I** *adj* **1** (*grand*) [+ *meal*] 丰盛的; [+ *party*] 盛大的; [+ *production*] 大量的 **2** (*generous*) [+ *lifestyle, spending, gift*] 奢华的; [+ *praise*] 慷慨的 **II** *vt* ♦**to lavish sth on sb** [+ *gifts, praise*] 将某物慷慨赠予某人 ◊ *The prince lavished gifts on his guests.* 王子将礼物赠予到访客人。; [+ *time, attention*] 将某物花在某人身上 ♦**to be lavish with sth** 在某物上非常大方 ♦**to be lavish in one's praise of sth** 对某物赞不绝口
✪ **law** [lɔː] **I** *n* **1** [s/u] (*legal system*) 法律 ◊ *Changes in the law are needed.* 有必要修改法律。**2** [u] (*profession*) 司法界 ◊ *a career in law* 在司法界的事业 **3** [u] [大学] 法学 ◊ *a degree in law* 法学学位 **4** [c] (*regulation*) 法规 ◊ *Britain's blasphemy laws* 英国的有关亵渎神祇的法规 **5** [c] (*code*) 规范 ◊ *inflexible moral laws* 固定的道德规范 **6** [c] [*of nature, science*] 定律 ◊ *the law of gravity* 引力定律 **II laws** *n* [*pl*] (*rules*) [*of organization, activity*] 规则 ♦**against the law** 违法 ♦**to break the law** 违法 ♦**by law** 依照法律 ♦**to be above the law** 凌驾于法律之上 ♦**criminal/company law** 刑/公司法 ♦**to take the law into one's own hands** 越过法律权限擅自处理 ♦**to study law** 学习法律 ♦**to go to law** [尤英] 诉诸法律 ♦**law and order** 治安
lawful ['lɔːful] *adj* [+ *activity, organization*] 合法的
lawless ['lɔːlɪs] *adj* [+ *action*] 不法的
lawn [lɔːn] *n* [c] 草坪
lawn bowling [英] *n* [u] 地滚球戏 [英 = **bowls**]
lawnmower ['lɔːnməuə(r)] *n* [c] 割草机
law school [美] *n* [c/u] 法律学校 ♦**to go to law school** 进法律学校
lawsuit ['lɔːsuːt] *n* [c] [正式] 诉讼
lawyer ['lɔːjə(r)] *n* [c] 律师
lax [læks] *adj* [+ *behaviour, standards*] 不严格的
laxative ['læksətɪv] **I** *n* [c] 泻药 **II** *adj* 缓泻的
lay [leɪ] (*pt, pp* **laid**) **I** *pt of* **lie II** *vt*

1 (*put*) 放 2 (*put down*) [+ *carpet, cable etc*] 铺 3 (*set*) [+ *trap*] 设置 4 [+ *egg*] 产 III *adj* (*secular*) [+ *preacher*] 非神职的 ♦**to lay the table** 摆放餐具 ♦**to lay the blame for sth on sb** 因某事责怪某人 ♦**to lay charges** 提出指控 ♦**to lay the foundations/basis for sth** 为某事奠定基础 ♦**to lay a trap for sb** 为某人设置圈套 ♦**to get laid** [非正式，疑讳] 性交 ♦**the lay person** 外行

❑**lay aside** *vt* 1 [+ *object*] 把…放在一边 2 [+ *feeling, belief*] 放弃

❑**lay down** *vt* 1 (*put down*) 放下 2 [+ *rules, laws etc*] 制定 ♦**to lay down the law** 定下规矩 ♦**to lay down one's life for sb** [文] (*in war etc*) 为某人而牺牲自己的生命

❑**lay in** *vt* [+ *supply*] 储存

❑**lay into** *vt* [不可拆分] 1 (*attack physically*) 痛打 2 (*criticize*) 斥责

❑**lay off** I *vt* [+ *workers*] 解雇 II *vi* [非正式] 住手

❑**lay on** *vt* [+ *meal, entertainment etc*] 提供 ◊ *Mrs Kaul had laid on dinner.* 考尔太太设了宴席。

❑**lay out** *vt* 1 (*spread out*) [+ *objects*] 摊开 2 (*present*) [+ *ideas, plans*] 陈述 3 (*design*) [+ *land, building*] 设计 4 [非正式] (*spend*) 耗费 5 [+ *corpse*] 为…做殡葬准备

❑**lay up** *vt* ♦**to be laid up (with sth)** [非正式] (*with illness*) (因…而) 卧床

lay-by ['leɪbaɪ] [英] *n* [c] 路侧停车处 [美=**pull-off**]

layer ['leɪə(r)] I *n* [c] 1 [*of substance, material*] 层 2 (喻) [*of system, idea*] 层 II *vt* 把…分层

layman ['leɪmən] (*pl* **laymen**) *n* [c] 外行 ♦**in layman's terms** 用非专业的语言

lay-off ['leɪɔf] [工业] *n* [c] 下岗

layout ['leɪaut] *n* [c] 1 [*of building, garden*] 布局 2 [*of report, article*] 设计

lazy ['leɪzɪ] *adj* 1 [+ *person*] 懒惰的 2 (*relaxed*) [+ *day, lunch*] 懒散的; [+ *movement, drawl*] 缓慢的

lb *abbr* (= ***pound***) 磅

LCD *n abbr* (= ***liquid crystal display***) 液晶显示屏

✪**lead**[1] [liːd] (*pt, pp* **led**) I *n* 1 [s] (*in race, competition*) (*front position*) 领先 2 [c] (喻) (*example*) 榜样 3 [c] (*clue*) 线索 ◊ *The police were following up several leads.* 警方顺着几条线索进一步调查。4 [c] [电影，戏剧] (*part*) 主角 ◊ *Richard is to play the lead in their new film.* 理查德将在他们的新片中扮演主角。; (*actor, actress*) 主演 5 [c] [尤英] [*for dog*] 皮带 [美=**leash**] 6 [c] [电子] 导线; (*to battery*) 导线 II *vt* 1 (*guide*) 带领 ◊ *The nurse led me to a large room.* 护士把我带到一个大房间。2 (*be at the head of*) [+ *group, party, organization*] 领导 ◊ *He led the country between 1949 and 1984.* 他于1949至1984年领导这个国家。; [+ *march, demonstration, parade*] 带领 ◊ *He led a demonstration through the city.* 游行队伍在他的带领下穿过市区。3 (*spearhead*) [+ *campaign, activity*] 指挥; (*start*) [+ *move*] 发起 ◊ *The educated middle class led the move towards independence.* 受过教育的中产阶级发起了走向独立的运动。4 (*direct*) [+ *discussion, conversation*] 引向 ◊ *After a while I led the conversation around to her job.* 过了一会，我把谈话内容引向了她的工作。III *vi* 1 [*walker, rider, driver* +] 领路 ◊ *Tom was leading; I followed behind.* 汤姆领路；我跟在后面。2 (*in race, competition*) 领先 ◊ *Spurs lead by four goals to two.* 斯帕思队以4比2领先。3 [*road, pipe, wire etc* +] 通往 ◊ *A path leads straight to Stonehenge.* 一直通往巨石阵的小径。♦**to be in the lead** (*in race, competition, poll*) 领先 ♦**to go into the lead** 进入领先位置 ♦**to take the lead** [体育] 领先; (喻) 起带头作用 ◊ *They took the lead in the development of naval aviation.* 他们在海军航空学的发展中起了带头作用。♦**to have a lead of 5 points** [体育] 领先5分 ♦**to follow sb's lead** 仿效某人的做法 ◊ *Many others followed his lead.* 许多人效仿了他的做法。♦**to lead a busy/active life** 过着繁忙/活跃的生活 ♦**to lead the way** (字) 引路; (喻) 率先 ♦**to lead sb to believe that ...** 使某人相信… ♦**to lead sb to do sth** 促使某人做

某事◊ *What led you to do this work?* 什么促使你做这项工作？

❑**lead away** *vt* [+ *prisoner etc*] 带走

❑**lead back** *vi* 带回

❑**lead off** **I** *vi* (*in game, conversation, meeting etc*) 开始◊ *She led off with a few of her old hit songs.* 她以她的几首流行的旧歌开始了演出。**II** *vt* [不可拆分] (*also:* ***lead off from***) [*road, room, door* +] 由…通向

❑**lead on** *vt* (*deceive*) [+ *person*] 劝诱◊ *I bet she led him on.* 我想她一定引诱他了。

❑**lead on to** [尤英] *vt* [不可拆分] (*result in*) 引起

❑**lead to** *vt* [不可拆分] (*result in*) 导致

❑**lead up to** *vt* [不可拆分] **1** (*culminate in*) [+ *situation*] 导致 ◊ *the events that led up to her death* 导致她死亡的事件 **2** (*precede*) [+ *time, event*] 临近◊ *the weeks leading up to Christmas* 临近圣诞节前的几个星期 **3** (*in conversation*) 渐渐引到◊ *Since you came in you've been leading up to this question.* 自你进来后，一直在渐渐引向这个问题。

✪**lead**[2] [lɛd] **I** *n* **1** [U] (*metal*) 铅 **2** [C/U] (*in pencil*) 铅笔心 **II** *cpd* [复合词] [+ *pipe, roof*] 铅

leaded ['lɛdɪd] *adj* **1** [+ *petrol*] 含铅的 **2** [+ *window, glass*] 铅框的

✪**leader** ['liːdə(r)] *n* [C] **1** [*of group, organization*] 领导人 **2** [体育] 领先者 **3** [英] (*in newspaper*) 社论 [美 = **editorial**] **4** ♦**Leader of the House of Commons/Lords** [英: 议会] 下/上议院议长

leadership ['liːdəʃɪp] *n* [U] **1** (*leading people*) 领导人 **2** (*position*) 领导 **3** (*quality*) 领导能力

lead-free ['lɛdfriː] *adj* [+ *petrol, paint*] 无铅的

leading ['liːdɪŋ] *adj* **1** (*most important*) [+ *person, thing*] 主导的 **2** [戏剧, 电影] [+ *role, part*] 主要的 **3** (*front*) 引领的

lead singer [liːd-] *n* [C] (*in pop group*) 主唱

leaf [liːf] (*pl* **leaves**) *n* [C] **1** [*of tree, plant*] 叶 **2** [*of table*] 活动桌板 ♦**to turn over a new leaf** 翻开新的篇章 ♦**to take a leaf out of sb's book** 模仿某人

❑**leaf through** *vt* [不可拆分] [+ *book, magazine*] 翻阅

leaflet ['liːflɪt] **I** *n* [C] (*booklet*) 小册子; (*single sheet*) 传单 **II** *vt* [+ *place*] 向…散发传单

league [liːg] *n* [C] **1** (*like-minded group*) 联盟 **2** [体育] 联赛 ♦**to be in league with sb** 与某人勾结 ♦**to be in the same league as sb** (*comparing*) 与某人同类 ♦**out of sb's league** (喻) 与某人不是一类人

leak [liːk] **I** *n* [C] **1** [*of liquid, gas*] 裂隙 **2** (*hole*) (*in roof, pipe etc*) 漏洞 **3** [*of document, information*] 泄露 **II** *vi* [*shoes, pipe, liquid, gas* +] 漏 **III** *vt* **1** [+ *liquid, gas*] 漏 **2** [+ *document, information*] 泄露

❑**leak out** *vi* [*news, information* +] 泄露

lean [liːn] (*pt, pp* **leaned** *or* **leant**) **I** *vt* ♦**to lean sth on/against sth** 把某物靠在某物上 **II** *vi* (*slope*) 倾斜 **III** *adj* **1** [+ *person*] 精瘦的 **2** [+ *meat*] 瘦的 **3** [+ *period of time*] 不景气的 ♦**to lean against sth** [*person* +] 靠在某物上 ♦**to lean forward/back** 向前/后倾

❑**lean on** *vt* [不可拆分] **1** (*rest against*) [+ *person, object*] 倚 **2** (喻) [+ *person*] 依赖 **3** [非正式] (*threaten*) 威胁

❑**lean towards** *vt* [不可拆分] [+ *idea, belief, right, left*] 倾向于

leaning ['liːnɪŋ] *n* [C] 倾向

leant [lɛnt] *pt, pp of* **lean**

leap [liːp] (*pt, pp* **leaped** *or* **leapt**) **I** *n* [C] **1** (*jump*) 跳 **2** (*increase*) (*in price, number etc*) 激增 **II** *vi* **1** (*jump*) 跳 **2** ♦**to leap into/onto sth** 迅速跳进/上某物 **3** (*increase*) [*price, number etc* +] 激增 ♦**to take a leap of faith** 碰运气 ♦**by** *or* **in leaps and bounds** 突飞猛进地 ♦**my heart leapt** (*with happiness*) 我的心狂跳不已; (*with fear*) 我的心突突直跳

❑**leap at** *vt* [不可拆分] [+ *offer, chance*] 迫不及待地接受

❑**leap up** *vi* **1** [*person* +] 一跃而起 **2** (*increase*) [*price, amount* +] 激增

leapt [lɛpt] *pt, pp of* **leap**

leap year *n* [c] 闰年

✪ **learn** [ləːn] (*pt, pp* **learned** *or* **learnt**) **I** *vt* **1** (*study*) [+ *skill*] 学 ◊ *Children learn foreign languages very easily.* 孩子学外语非常容易。; [+ *poem, song*] 背 ◊ *We have to learn the whole poem by heart.* 我们得把整首诗背下来。**2** (*find out*) [+ *news, fact*] 得知 ◊ *I remember when I learned the terrible news.* 我还记得什么时候得知这条坏消息的。**II** *vi* 学 ◊ *Experienced teachers help you learn quickly.* 经验丰富的老师帮你学得快。♦**to learn about sth** (*study*) 学到某物 ♦**to learn to do sth/how to do sth** (*by studying*) 学做某事/怎样做某事 ◊ *He is learning to play the piano.* 他在学弹钢琴。; (*through experience*) 学做某事/学习如何做某事 ◊ *He learned to conceal his views.* 他学会了隐瞒观点。♦**to learn of sth** (*find out*) 获悉某事 ♦**to learn that ...** (*find out*) 获悉… ♦**to learn from one's mistakes** 从错误中吸取教训

learned ['ləːnɪd] *adj* **1** [+ *person*] 博学的 **2** [+ *book, paper*] 学术性的

learner ['ləːnə(r)] *n* [c] **1** (*student*) 学习者 **2** [英] (*also:* ***learner driver***) 驾驶学员

learning ['ləːnɪŋ] *n* [u] (*study*) 学习

learnt [ləːnt] *pt, pp of* **learn**

lease [liːs] **I** *n* [c] (*legal agreement, contract*) (*on flat, car*) 租约 **II** *vt* [+ *flat, car*] 租 ♦**on lease (to)** 被租给 ♦**to give sb a new lease of life** 给某人注入新的活力 ♦**to lease sth to sb** [+ *flat, car, land*] 把某物租给某人

leash [liːʃ] *n* [c] 皮带 ♦**on a leash** 拴在链条上

✪ **least** [liːst] **I** *adj* (+ *noun*) 最少的 ◊ *the area where there is least unemployment* 失业率最低的地区 **II** *adv* **1** (+ *adjective*) ♦**the least expensive/attractive/interesting** 最便宜/没有魅力/没趣的 ◊ *the least interesting of all his theories* 他所有理论中最没趣的 **2** (+ *verb*) 最不 ◊ *He came out when I least expected it.* 在我最意想不到的时候，他出现了。◊ *those who need help the least* 最不需要帮助的那些人 **III** *pron* ♦**the least** 最少 ◊ *the gap between those earning the most and those earning the least* 收入最多的人与收入最少的人之间的差距 ♦**at least** (*in expressions of quantity, comparisons*) 至少 ◊ *I must have slept twelve hours at least.* 我一定至少睡了12个小时。; (*still*) 无论如何 ◊ *It looks difficult but at least it is not dangerous.* 看起来很困难，但无论如何没有什么危险。; (*or rather*) 起码 ◊ *I spotted my ex-wife; at least I thought I did.* 我看见我前妻了；起码我认为是的。; (*at the very minimum*) 至少 ◊ *You could at least have written.* 你至少应该写信吧。♦**not in the least** 一点也不 ♦**it was the least I could do** 是我力所能及的 ♦**not least because** 尤其是因为 ♦**to say the least** 至少可以说 ♦**least of all** 尤其

leather ['lɛðə(r)] **I** *n* [u] 皮革 **II** *cpd* [复合词] [+ *jacket, shoes, chair*] 皮

✪ **leave** [liːv] (*pt, pp* **left**) **I** *vt* **1** (*depart from*) [+ *place*] 离开 ◊ *They left the house after tea.* 吃过茶点后，他们离开了家。**2** (*give up*) [+ *school, job, group*] 放弃 ◊ *He left school with no qualifications.* 他弃学了，没有拿到任何文凭。**3** (*take leave of*) [+ *person*] 与…分开 ◊ *I simply couldn't bear to leave my little girl.* 我就是忍受不了与我的小女儿分开。**4** (*abandon*) [+ *wife, family*] 抛弃 ◊ *My husband left me for another woman.* 我丈夫为了另一个女人抛弃了我。**5** (*cause*) [+ *mark, stain, impression*] 留下 ◊ *Coffee leaves a stain.* 咖啡会留下污迹。**6** (*leave behind*) (*deliberately*) 留下 ◊ *Leave your key with a neighbour.* 把钥匙留给邻居。; (*accidentally*) 落 ◊ *I had left my raincoat in the restaurant.* 我把雨衣落在饭店里了。**7** [+ *message*] 留 ◊ *Can I leave a message for Jim?* 我能不能给吉姆留个口信？**8** (*keep back*) [+ *food, space, time*] 留 ◊ *Leave some of the stew for the boys.* 把炖菜给那几个男孩留一些。**9** (*waste*) [+ *food, drink*] 剩 **II** *vi* **1** (*depart*) [*person* +] 离开; [*bus, train* +] 出发 ◊ *My train leaves at 11.30.* 我坐的火车11点

30 分出发。2 (*give up school*) 辍学; (*give up job*) 辞职◊ *He hated his job, so he left.* 他憎恶他的工作，所以辞职了。III *n* [U] (*time off*) (*maternity/sick etc leave*) 休假◊ *Why don't you take a few days' leave?* 你为什么不休几天假？; [军] 假期 ◊ *How much leave do you get?* 你有多少探亲假？♦ **to leave sth to sb** [+ *money, property etc*] 把某物留给某人 ♦ **to leave sth until later** 把某事往后拖延 ♦ **to leave sb/sth alone** 不理会某人/某物 ♦ **to leave sb to do sth** 让某人做某事 ♦ **the accident left four people dead** 该事故造成4人死亡 ♦ **he leaves a wife and two children** 他死后留下了妻子和两个孩子 ♦ **to be left with sth** 被赠予某物 ◊ *When their mother died they were left with nothing.* 母亲死后没有留给他们任何遗产。♦ **to leave for** [+ *destination*] 前往◊ *My plan was to leave for the seaside.* 我的计划是前往海边。♦ **to take one's leave (of sb)** [正式] (向某人) 告别 ♦ **to be on leave** 在休假

❑ **leave behind** *vt* 1 (*forget*) 忘带 2 (*decide not to take*) 留下 3 (*say goodbye to*) [+ *person, place*] 永别 4 (*leave in one's wake*) [+ *situation*] 留下 5 (*advance beyond*) [+ *country, organization*] 超过

❑ **leave off** I *vt* 1 [+ *cover, lid*] 敞开 2 [+ *heating, light*] 关掉 3 (*omit*) (*from list*) 遗漏 II *vi* [非正式] (*stop*) 别… ◊ *Just leave off, will you!* 别烦了，行不行！

❑ **leave on** *vt* [+ *light, heating*] 开着

❑ **leave out** *vt* 删掉◊ *One or two scenes in the play were left out.* 剧中的一两个场景被删掉了。♦ **to leave sb/sth out of sth** 不把某人/某物包括在某物内

leaves [liːvz] *n* [*pl*] *of* **leaf**

Lebanese [lɛbəˈniːz]] (*pl* **Lebanese**) I *adj* 黎巴嫩的 II *n* (*person*) 黎巴嫩人

Lebanon, the Lebanon [ˈlɛbənən] *n* 黎巴嫩

lecture [ˈlɛktʃə(r)] I *n* [C] (*talk*) 讲座 II *vi* 做讲座 III *vt* (*scold*) ♦ **to lecture sb on *or* about sth** 告诫某人有关某事 ♦ **to give a lecture (on sth)** 作(某方面的) 讲座 ♦ **to give sb a lecture (on *or* about sth)** (*telling off*) (就某事) 斥责某人

lecture hall [美] = **lecture theatre** *n* 讲演厅

lecturer [ˈlɛktʃərə(r)] *n* [C] 讲师

lecture theatre [英] *n* [C] 讲演厅 [美 = **lecture hall**]

LED *n abbr* (= ***light-emitting diode***) 发光二级管

led [lɛd] *pt, pp of* **lead**[1]

ledge [lɛdʒ] *n* [C] 1 [*of mountain*] 岩石突出部 2 [*of window*] 台

leek [liːk] *n* [C] 韭葱

leer [lɪə(r)] I *vi* ♦ **to leer at sb** 色迷迷地看某人 II *n* [C] 斜眼一瞥

✪ **left**[1] [lɛft] I *adj* (*not right*) 左的◊ *his left eye* 他的左眼 II *n* ♦ **the left** 左侧◊ *There was a strong light coming from the left.* 有一道强光从左侧射来。III *adv* [*turn, go, look* +] 向左 ◊ *Turn left at the traffic lights.* 在红绿灯处向左拐。♦ **on the left** 在左边 ♦ **to the left** 靠左边 ♦ **the Left** [政治] 左翼

✪ **left**[2] [lɛft] I *pt, pp of* **leave** II *adj* ♦ **to be left** (*remain*) 剩下◊ *Is there any gin left?* 剩没剩杜松子酒？♦ **to have sth left** 还剩某物 ♦ **to be left over** [*food, money etc* +] 剩下

left-hand [ˈlɛfthænd] *adj* [+ *side, corner*] 左侧的

left-handed [lɛftˈhændɪd] *adj* 左撇子的

left-luggage [lɛftˈlʌgɪdʒ] [英] *n* [U] ♦ **left-luggage locker** 行李寄存柜 ♦ **left-luggage office** 行李寄存处

leftovers [ˈlɛftəuvəz] *n* [*pl*] [*of meal*] 剩饭

left-wing [ˈlɛftˈwɪŋ] [政治] I *adj* [+ *person, ideas*] 左翼的 II *n* ♦ **the left wing** 左翼

leg [lɛg] *n* 1 [C] [*of person, bird, table, chair*] 腿 2 [C] [*of trousers, shorts*] 腿部 ♦ **trouser legs** 裤腿 3 [C/U] [烹饪] [*of lamb, chicken*] 腿 ♦ **he doesn't have a leg to stand on** [非正式] 他完全站不住脚 ♦ **the first/second/last leg** [*of journey*] 第一/第二/最后一段行程; [尤英：体育] 一段赛程

legacy [ˈlɛgəsɪ] *n* [C] (*in will*) 遗产 ♦ **the legacy of** [+ *event, historical* *period*] …的后果

legal ['li:gl] *adj* **1** (*relating to law*) [+ *system, requirement*] 法律的 **2** (*allowed by law*) [+ *action, situation*] 合法的 ♦**to take legal action/proceedings against sb** 对某人采取法律行动/提出诉讼

legal holiday [美] *n* [C] 法定假期 [英=**bank holiday, public holiday**]

legalize ['li:gəlaɪz] *vt* 使合法化

legally ['li:gəlɪ] *adv* **1** (*as regards the law*) 在法律上 **2** (*according to the law*) 依照法律地 ♦**legally binding** 受法律约束

legend ['lɛdʒənd] *n* **1** [C/U] (*story*) 传奇 **2** [C] (喻)(*person*) 传奇人物

legendary ['lɛdʒəndərɪ] *adj* **1** (*from legend*) 传奇的 **2** (喻)(*very famous*) 传奇般的

leggings ['lɛgɪŋz] *n* [*pl*] **1** (*woman's*) 裤袜 **2** (*protective*) 绑腿

legible ['lɛdʒəbl] *adj* 易读的

legislate ['lɛdʒɪsleɪt] *vi* 立法 ♦**to legislate on sth** 就某事立法 ♦**to legislate against sth** 立法禁止某事

legislation [lɛdʒɪs'leɪʃən] *n* [U] 立法

legislative ['lɛdʒɪslətɪv] *adj* [+ *assembly, power, reform*] 立法的

legitimate [lɪ'dʒɪtɪmət] *adj* **1** (*reasonable*) [+ *fear, claim, excuse*] 合理的 **2** (*legal*) 合法的 **3** [+ *child*] 婚生的

leisure ['lɛʒə(r), (美) 'li:ʒə(r)] *n* [U] (*free time*) 闲暇 ♦**at (one's) leisure** 在闲暇的时候

leisure centre [英] *n* [C] 娱乐中心

leisurely ['lɛʒəlɪ] *adj* [+ *pace, walk*] 悠闲的

lemon ['lɛmən] **I** *n* [C] 柠檬 **II** *adj* (*also:* ***lemon yellow***) 柠檬黄色的

lemonade [lɛmə'neɪd] *n* [U] 柠檬汽水

lend [lɛnd] (*pt, pp* **lent**) *vt* **1** ♦**to lend sth to sb** 把某物借给某人 **2** (*loan*) [*bank etc* +] 贷 **3** [正式] ♦**to lend dignity to sth** 显示对某事的尊重 ♦**it lends itself to ...** 适宜于…

length [lɛŋθ] *n* **1** [C/U] (*size*) [*of object, animal*] 长度; [*of sentence, article*] 篇幅 **2** [C] (*piece*) [*of wood, string, cloth etc*] 一段 **3** [C] (*in swimming pool*) 长度 **4** [C/U] (*duration*) 期间 ♦**at length** (*for a long time*) 详尽地; [文] (*at last*) 最后 ♦**it is 10 metres in length** 10米长 ♦**to go to great lengths to do sth** 竭尽全力做某事 ♦**they travelled the length of the island** 他们走遍了整个岛屿

lengthen ['lɛŋθn] **I** *vt* 使延长 **II** *vi* 变长

lengthways ['lɛŋθweɪz], **lengthwise** ['lɛŋθwaɪz] *adv* [*slice, fold, lay* +] 纵向地

lengthy ['lɛŋθɪ] *adj* **1** [+ *process, procedure, meeting*] 漫长的 **2** [+ *report, book, document*] 冗长的

lenient ['li:nɪənt] *adj* [+ *person, attitude, punishment*] 宽大的

lens [lɛnz] *n* [C] [*of spectacles*] 镜片; [*of telescope, camera*] 镜头

Lent [lɛnt] *n* [U] 大斋节

lent [lɛnt] *pt, pp of* **lend**

lentil ['lɛntɪl] *n* [C] 小扁豆

Leo ['li:əu] *n* **1** [U] (*sign*) 狮子座 **2** [C] (*person*) 狮子座的人 ♦**I'm (a) Leo** 我是狮子座的

leopard ['lɛpəd] *n* [C] 豹

leotard ['li:ətɑ:d] *n* [C] 紧身衣

leprosy ['lɛprəsɪ] *n* [U] 麻风病

lesbian ['lɛzbɪən] **I** *adj* 女性同性恋的 **II** *n* [C] 女同性恋者

Lesotho [lɪ'su:tu:] *n* 莱索托

✪ **less** [lɛs] **I** *adj* (+ *noun*) 更少的 ◊ *A shower uses less water than a bath.* 淋浴比盆浴用的水更少。**II** *adv* **1** (+ *adjective/adverb*) 较少地 ◊ *He still eats cheese, but far less often.* 他还是吃奶酪，但不像以前那么频繁了。◊ *Malaria is less common in Britain.* 疟疾在英国较少见。 **2** (+ *verb*) 较少 ◊ *I visit him less than I should.* 我应该多去看他。◊ *He goes out less than he used to.* 他比以前出去得少了。**III** *pron* 较少的东西 ◊ *I've got less than you.* 我的比你的少。**IV** *prep* ♦**less tax/10% discount** 去掉税/10%的折扣 ♦**less of the money/time** 较少的钱/时间 ♦**I see less of them now they've moved** 他们搬家了，我与他们见面的机会少了 ♦**less than half** 不到一半 ♦**no less than 45% of the electorate** 不少于45%的全体选民 ♦**less than ever** 不比从前 ♦**less than perfect/helpful** 决不完美/决没有帮助 ♦**less and**

less (*as adj*) 越来越少的; (*as adv*) 越来越少地 ♦**the less he works, the more he complains** 他做的越少，抱怨的越多 ♦**the Prime Minister, no less** 居然是首相

> 📖 **less** 可以修饰不可数名词。*...less meat...* 修饰可数名词应该使用**fewer**。*...fewer potatoes...*

lessen ['lɛsn] **I** *vi* 减少 **II** *vt* 使减少

lesser ['lɛsə(r)] *adj* (*smaller*) (*in degree, importance, amount*) 次要的 ♦**to a lesser extent** *or* **degree** 在较小程度上

lesson ['lɛsn] *n* [c] **1** (*class*) (*in history, dancing etc*) 课 **2** (喻) 教训 ♦**to teach sb a lesson** (喻) 给某人一个教训

lest [lɛst] [正式] *conj* 以免

✪ **let** [lɛt] (*pt, pp* **let**) *vt* **1** ♦**to let sb do sth** (*give permission*) 允许某人做某事◊ *My parents wouldn't let me go out with boys.* 我父母不许我与男孩子们一起交往。**2** ♦**to let sth happen** 让某事发生◊ *People here let everyone else do the work.* 这里的人让别人做工作。**3** [英] (*also:* ***let out***) (*lease*) 出租◊ *She is thinking of letting her house to an American serviceman.* 她在想把房子租给一个美国军人。[美=**rent**] ♦**to let sb know that ...** 告诉某人… **4** ♦**to let sb in/out** 让某人进去/出去 ♦**let's go/eat** 我们走/吃吧◊ *I'm bored. Let's go home.* 我觉得无聊，我们回家吧。♦**let me explain/help** 让我来解释/帮忙 ♦**he can't afford his rent, let alone a holiday** 他付不起房租，更别提度假了 ♦**"to let"** “现房待租” ♦**to let go** (*release one's grip*) 松开 ♦**to let go of** (*stop holding*) 松开… ♦**to let sb/sth go** (*release*) 放走某人/某物◊ *Eventually I let the frog go.* 最后，我放走了青蛙。♦**to let o.s. go** (*relax*) 放得开; (*neglect o.s.*) 不修边幅

❑**let down** *vt* **1** (*fail*) [+ *person*] 令…失望◊ *Charlie's never let me down yet.* 查理从来没有令我失望过。**2** [尤英] [+ *tyre etc*] 给…放气 **3** [+ *dress, hem etc*] 放长

❑**let in** *vt* **1** [+ *water, air*] 允许进来 **2** (*open door for*) [+ *person*] 给…开门 ♦**to let sb in on a secret** 让某人知道一个秘密

❑**let off** *vt* **1** [+ *culprit*] 放过◊ *He let me off with a warning.* 他给我一个警告就放过我了。**2** (*excuse*) ♦**to let sb off sth** 允许某人不用做某事 **3** [+ *firework, gun, bomb*] 放

❑**let on** *vi* ♦**not to let on that ...** 不泄漏出去…

❑**let out 1** *vt* [+ *water, air, breath*] 放掉 **2** [+ *scream, cry*] 发出◊ *She let out a terrible shriek.* 她发出一声可怕的尖叫。**3** [英] (*lease*) 出租◊ *She is thinking of letting out her house to an American serviceman.* 她在想把她的房子租给一个美国军人。[美=**rent**]

❑**let up** *vi* **1** (*cease*) 停止◊ *We thought the rain would let up soon.* 我们觉得雨不久会停。**2** (*diminish*) 减缓◊ *Still the heat didn't let up.* 炎热依旧没有减缓。

lethal ['li:θl] *adj* [+ *weapon, chemical etc*] 致命的

✪ **letter** ['lɛtə(r)] *n* [c] **1** (*note*) 信 **2** [*of alphabet*] 字母◊ *the letter E* 字母E ♦**to the letter** 不折不扣地

letterbox ['lɛtəbɔks] [英] *n* [c] (*in door*) 信箱 [美=**mailbox**]

lettuce ['lɛtɪs] *n* [c/u] 生菜

leukaemia (美 **leukemia**) [lu:'ki:mɪə] *n* [u] 白血病

✪ **level** ['lɛvl] **I** *adj* **1** (*flat*) 平的◊ *The floor is quite level.* 地板很平。**2** [烹饪] [+ *spoonful*] 平的 **3** (*at same height*) 一样高的 *Amy knelt down so that their eyes were level.* 艾米蹲下身子，这样他们可以平视对方。◊ *The tree tops are level with the roof.* 树冠与屋顶一样高。**4** (*in points, goals etc*) 平的◊ *The teams were level at the end of extra time.* 加时赛结束时，两队比分平了。**II** *adv* ♦**to draw level with** [尤英] [+ *person, vehicle*] 与…平齐; [+ *team, opponent*] 与…比分拉平 **III** *n* [c] **1** (*amount, degree*) (*on scale*) 程度 ◊ *the lowest level of inflation for years* 多年来最低程度的通货膨胀率 **2** (*standard*) 水平◊ *The general level* *of training was not high.* 培训的总体水平不高。**3** (*height*) [*of lake, river*] 水位◊ *The level of the lake continues to rise.* 湖水的水位继续上升。**IV** *vt* (*flatten*) [+ *building, forest etc*] 把…弄平◊ *Tractors levelled more than 1000 acres of forest.* 拖拉机将1000多英亩的森林夷为平地。**V** *vi* ♦**to level with sb** [非正式] 对某人开诚布公 ♦**to be level with** [尤英] [+ *person, vehicle*] 与…平齐; [+ *team, opponent*] 与…并驾齐驱 ♦**at eye/waist** *etc* **level** 在与眼/腰{等}平齐的位置◊ *He held the gun at waist level.* 他把枪端在与腰平齐的位置上。♦**to be on the level** [非正式] [*plan etc* +] 真实可信; [*person* +] 诚恳 ♦**to level the score** [体育] 扳平比分 ♦**to level an accusation/a criticism at** *or* **against sb** 指控/批评某人 ♦**to level a gun at sb** 把枪对准某人 ♦**to do one's level best** 全力以赴

❑**level off** *vi* **1** [*prices etc* +] 稳定 **2** [*plane* +] 平飞

❑**level out** *vi* = **level off**

level crossing [英] *n* [c] 平交道口 [美=**railroad crossing**]

lever ['liːvə(r), (美) 'lɛvə(r)] **I** *n* [c] **1** (*to operate machine*) 杆 **2** (*to provide leverage*) 杠杆 **3** (喻) 手段 **II** *vt* ♦**to lever sth open** 撬开某物 ♦**to lever o.s. up** 把自己支撑起来

leverage ['liːvərɪdʒ, (美) 'lɛvərɪdʒ] *n* [u] **1** (*using bar, lever*) 杠杆作用 **2** (喻) (*influence*) 影响

levy ['lɛvɪ] **I** *n* (*tax, charge*) 税款 **II** *vt* [+ *tax, charge*] 征收

liability [laɪə'bɪlətɪ] **I** *n* **1** [c] (*burden, risk*) 负担 **2** [u] (*responsibility*) 责任 **II liabilities** *n* [*pl*] [商] 债务

liable ['laɪəbl] *adj* ♦**to be liable to sth/to do sth** [*person* +] 有…/做某事的倾向; [*thing* +] 可能会…/做某事 ♦**to be liable (for sth)** (*for damages, debt*) 负(某事的)责任

liaise [liː'eɪz] *vi* ♦**to liaise (with sb)** (*initiate contact*) (与某人)联络; (*maintain contact*) (与某人)保持联系

liar ['laɪə(r)] *n* [c] 说谎者

liberal ['lɪbərl] **I** *adj* **1** (*tolerant*) [+ *person, attitude*] 开明的 **2** (*generous*) [+ *use, amount*] 大方的 **3** [政治] ♦**Liberal** 自由党 **II** *n* [c] **1** (*tolerant person*) 开明的人 **2** [政治] ♦**Liberal** 自由党党员 ♦**to be liberal with sth** (*generous*) 慷慨提供某物

Liberal Democrat [英] *n* [c] 自由民主党党员 ♦**the Liberal Democrat Party** 自由民主党

liberate ['lɪbəreɪt] *vt* [+ *city, country*] 解放; [+ *oppressed people etc*] 使获自由; [+ *hostage, prisoner*] 释放

liberation [lɪbə'reɪʃən] *n* [u] [*of country, oppressed group*] 解放

Liberia [laɪ'bɪərɪə] *n* 利比里亚

Liberian [laɪ'bɪərɪən] **I** *adj* 利比里亚的 **II** *n* [c] (*person*) 利比里亚人

liberty ['lɪbətɪ] *n* [c/u] 自由 ♦**to be at liberty** [*criminal* +] 自由的 ♦**to be at liberty to do sth** 有权做某事 ♦**to take the liberty of doing sth** 冒昧地做某事

Libra ['liːbrə] *n* **1** [u] (*sign*) 天秤座 **2** [c] (*person*) 天秤座的人 ♦**I'm (a) Libra** 我是天秤座的

librarian [laɪ'brɛərɪən] *n* [c] 图书管理员

library ['laɪbrərɪ] *n* [c] **1** (*public*) 图书馆 **2** (*in private house*) 书斋 **3** (*private collection*) 收藏

Libya ['lɪbɪə] *n* 利比亚

Libyan ['lɪbɪən] **I** *adj* 利比亚的 **II** *n* [c] (*person*) 利比亚人

lice [laɪs] *n* [*pl*] *of* **louse**

licence (美 **license**) ['laɪsns] *n* **1** [c] (*permit*) 许可证 **2** [c] (*also:* ***driving licence***) 驾驶执照 **3** [c] [商] 特许 **4** [u] [贬] ♦**licence to do sth** 放肆地做某事 ♦**under licence** [商] 经特许

📖 用法参见**license**

license ['laɪsns] **I** *n* [美] = **licence** **II** *vt* ♦**to license sb/sth (to do sth)** 许可某人/某组织(做某事)

> 📖 请勿将**licence**和**license**混淆。在英式英语中，以**–ce**结尾的**licence**是名词。 *... a driver's licence ...* 以**–se**结尾的**license**是动词。*The restaurant*

was licensed to serve alcohol. 在美式英语中，后一种拼写也可用作名词。

licensed ['laɪsnst] *adj* **1** [+ *car, gun*] 领有许可证的 **2** [英][+ *restaurant, hotel*] (*to sell alcohol*) 领有卖酒许可证的

license number [美] *n* [c] 车牌号 [英=**registration number**]

license plate [美] *n* [c] 车牌照 [英=**number plate**]

lick [lɪk] **I** *vt* **1** [+ *stamp, fingers, lolly etc*] 舔 **2** [非正式] (*defeat*) 击败 **II** *n* [c] 舔 ♦**to lick one's lips** (字) 舔嘴唇; (喻) 垂涎欲滴 ♦**a lick of paint** [非正式] 少许涂料

lid [lɪd] *n* [c] **1** [*of box, case, pan*] 盖 **2** (*eyelid*) 眼睑 ♦**to keep a/the lid on sth** (喻) 隐瞒某事

lie[1] [laɪ] (*pt* **lay**, *pp* **lain**) *vi* **1** (*be horizontal*) [*person* +] 躺 **2** (*be situated*) [*place* +] 位于; [*object* +] 平放 **3** (喻) [*problem, cause etc* +] 在于 **4** [英] (*be placed*) (*in race, league etc*) 处于 **5** ♦**to lie hidden/forgotten** 被遗忘 ♦**to lie ahead** 摆在面前 ♦**to lie low** (喻) 隐藏

❏**lie about** [英] *vi* = **lie around**

❏**lie around** *vi* **1** [*things* +] 乱放 **2** [*people* +] 懒懒散散

❏**lie back** *vi* [*person* +] 向后靠

❏**lie behind** *vt* [不可拆分] (*cause*) 是…的缘由

❏**lie down** *vi* [*person* +] 躺下 ♦**to take sth lying down** 对某事俯首屈服

lie[2] [laɪ] **I** *vi* (*tell lies*) 说谎 **II** *n* [c] 谎言 ♦**to tell lies** 说谎 ♦**to live a lie** 过着虚伪的生活

Liechtenstein ['lɪktənstaɪn] [地理] *n* 列支敦士登

lie-in ['laɪɪn] [英: 非正式] *n* ♦**to have a lie-in** 睡懒觉

lieutenant [lɛf'tɛnənt, (美) luː'tɛnənt] *n* [c] 中尉

✪ **life** [laɪf] (*pl* **lives**) *n* **1** [c/u] (*living, existence*) 生命 ◊ *her last hours of life* 她生命的最后时刻 **2** [u] (*living things*) 生物 ◊ *Is there life on Mars?* 火星上有生物吗？◊ *Your life is in danger.* 你的生命处于危险之中。**3** [c] (*lifespan*) [*of person*] 一生 ◊ *People spend their lives worrying about money.* 人的一生都在为钱而担忧。; [*of machine, organization*] 寿命 ◊ *The repairs did not increase the life of the equipment.* 维修并没有增加设备的使用寿命。**4** [u] (*events, experience*) 生活 ◊ *Life had not been kind to her.* 生活没有善待她。**5** [u] (*vitality*) [*of person, place*] 活力 ◊ *The town was full of life.* 这座城市充满了活力。**6** [u] [非正式] (*also:* ***life imprisonment***) 无期徒刑 ◊ *He could get life, if convicted.* 如果定罪，他会被判无期徒刑。♦**to paint from life** 写生 ♦**to fight for one's life** 与生命抗争 ♦**to be jailed/scarred for life** 遭受终生监禁/创伤 ♦**his personal/working life** 他的个人/工作生活 ♦**to come to life** [*person, party etc* +] 苏醒过来 ♦**to take sb's life/one's own life** [正式] 杀害某人/自杀

lifebelt ['laɪfbɛlt] *n* [c] 救生带

lifeboat ['laɪfbəut] *n* [c] 救生船

lifeguard ['laɪfgɑːd] *n* [c] (*at beach, swimming pool*) 救生员

life insurance *n* [u] 人寿保险

life jacket *n* [c] 救生衣

lifelike ['laɪflaɪk] *adj* **1** [+ *model, dummy etc*] 逼真的 **2** (*realistic*) [+ *painting, character*] 栩栩如生的

life preserver [-prɪ'zəːvə(r)] [美] *n* [c] (*lifebelt*) 救生用具; (*life jacket*) 救生衣

life sentence *n* [c] 无期徒刑

lifestyle ['laɪfstaɪl] *n* [c/u] 生活方式

lifetime ['laɪftaɪm] *n* **1** [c] [*of person*] 一生 **2** [s] [*of product, organization*] 寿命 ♦**the chance of a lifetime** 千载难逢的机会

lift [lɪft] **I** *vt* **1** (*raise*) [+ *thing, part of body*] 举起 **2** (*end*) [+ *ban, sanctions, embargo*] 解除 **3** (*increase*) [+ *rate, price*] 提高 **4** [非正式] (*copy*) 抄袭 **II** *vi* [*fog* +] 消散 **III** *n* [c] [英] 电梯 [美=**elevator**] ♦**to give sb a lift** [尤英: 汽车] 让某人搭便车

❏**lift off** *vi* [*rocket, aircraft* +] 起飞

❏**lift up** *vt* [+ *person, thing*] 举起

lift-off ['lɪftɔf] *n* [c/u] [*of rocket*] 起飞

light [laɪt] (*pt, pp* **lit**) **I** *n* **1** [u] (*from sun, moon, lamp, fire*) 光 **2** [c] [电子, 汽车] 灯 **3** [s] (*for cigarette etc*) 打火机

II *vt* **1** (*set alight*) [+ *candle, fire, cigarette*] 点燃 **2** [+ *room*] 照亮 **III** *adj* **1** (*pale*) [+ *colour*] 淡的 **2** (*bright*) [+ *building, room*] 明亮的 **3** (*not dark*) [+ *evening, morning*] 亮的 **4** (*not heavy*) [+ *object*] 轻的 **5** (*not intensive*) [+ *rain, traffic, sleep*] 小量的 **6** (*not strenuous*) [+ *work*] 容易做的 **7** (*graceful, gentle*) [+ *movement, action*] 轻快的 **8** (*lenient*) [+ *sentence*] 从轻的 **9** (*not serious*) [+ *book, music*] 轻松的; [+ *discussion etc*] 轻松的 **IV** *adv* [*travel* +] 轻装地 **V lights** *n* [*pl*] **1** [汽车] (*also:* ***traffic lights***) 交通指示灯 ♦**to turn** *or* **switch the light on/off** 开/关灯 ♦**to cast** *or* **shed** *or* **throw light on sth** (喻) 使某事清楚明白地显示出来 ♦**to present sth in a favourable/an unfavourable light** 表现某物宜人/不宜人之处 ♦**to set light to sth** [尤英] 点燃某物 [美 = **set fire to**] ♦**to come** *or* **be brought to light** [*fact, information* +] 暴露 ♦**in the light of** [+ *discussions, new evidence etc*] 鉴于 ♦**to make light of sth** 对某事不以为意

❑**light up I** *vi* **1** (*illuminate*) 变亮 **2** [*face, eyes* +] 放光彩 **II** *vt* (*illuminate*) 照亮

light bulb *n* [c] 灯泡

lighten ['laɪtn] **I** *vt* **1** (*make less heavy*) 使变轻 **2** (*make less difficult*) [+ *load, burden*] 减轻 **3** (*make less serious*) [+ *situation, atmosphere, mood*] 使轻松 **4** (*make less dark*) 使变浅 **II** *vi* **1** (*become more cheerful*) [*mood* +] 变得愉快 **2** (*become less dark*) 变浅

lighter ['laɪtə(r)] *n* [c] (*also:* ***cigarette lighter***) 打火机

light-hearted [laɪt'hɑːtɪd] *adj* [+ *person*] 轻松愉快的; [+ *question, remark etc*] 轻松的

lighthouse ['laɪthaus] *n* [c] 灯塔

lighting ['laɪtɪŋ] *n* [u] (*on roads, in theatre*) 照明设备

lightly ['laɪtlɪ] *adv* **1** (*gently*) [*kiss, touch* +] 轻轻地 **2** (*not heavily*) [*sleep, eat* +] 轻微地 **3** [烹饪] [*cook, brown, steam* +] 稍微地 **4** (*not seriously*) 轻率地 ♦**to get off lightly** 从轻发落

lightning ['laɪtnɪŋ] **I** *n* [u] (*in sky*) 闪电 **II** *adj* ♦**with lightning speed** 闪电般的

lightweight ['laɪtweɪt] **I** *adj* **1** [+ *fabric, product*] 重量轻的 **2** (喻) [+ *person*] 无足轻重的 **II** *n* [c] **1** [拳击] 轻量级运动员 **2** (喻) (*person*) 无足轻重的人

✪**like¹** [laɪk] *prep* **1** (*similar to*) 像 ◊ *a house like ours* 像我们这样的房子 **2** (*in similes*) 像…一样 ◊ *I was trembling like a leaf.* 我抖得像片叶子一样。**3** (*such as*) 如 ◊ *big countries like Australia and India* 如澳大利亚和印度这样的大国 ♦**something like that** 差不多 ♦**to be like sth/sb** 像某物/某人 ♦**what's he/the weather like?** 他/天气怎么样? ♦**to look like** [+ *person*] 长得像; [+ *thing*] 类似 ♦**to sound/taste like** 听/尝起来像 ♦**what does it look/sound/taste like?** 看/听/尝起来怎么样? ♦**he was acting like an idiot** 他做事像白痴一样 ♦**there's nothing like ...** 什么也比不上… ♦**that's just like him** 他就是这样 ♦**like this** 像这样 ♦**and the like** 诸如此类

✪**like²** [laɪk] **I** *vt* **1** (*find attractive, enjoyable*) [+ *person, thing*] 喜欢 ◊ *I can't think why Grace doesn't like me.* 我不明白格雷丝为什么不喜欢我。**2** (*approve of*) [+ *action, behaviour*] 赞同 **II** *n* ♦**his likes and dislikes** 他的好恶 ♦**to like doing sth** 喜欢做某事 ♦**to like to do sth** 喜欢做某事 ◊ *I like to go to bed early during the week.* 不是周末的时候，我喜欢早点上床休息。◊ *She doesn't like him working so hard.* 她不愿意他工作得那么辛苦。◊ *His wife didn't like him drinking so much.* 他妻子不愿意他喝这么多酒。♦**I would** *or* **I'd like an ice-cream/to go for a walk** 我想吃个冰淇淋/去散步 ♦**would you like a coffee?** 你想不想来杯咖啡? ♦**if you like** (*in offers, suggestions*) 如果你愿意的话 ◊ *You can stay here if you like.* 如果你愿意的话，你可以呆在这里。; (*in other words*) 换句话说

likeable ['laɪkəbl] *adj* [+ *person*] 可

爱的

likelihood ['laɪklɪhud] *n* [U/S] 可能性 ♦**there is every likelihood that ...** 非常有可能… ♦**in all likelihood** 十有八九

✪**likely** ['laɪklɪ] *adj* **1** (*probable*) 很可能的◊ *A "yes" vote is still the likely outcome.* 结果仍很有可能是赞成票。**2** [*+ person, place, thing*] 合适的 ◊ *He seemed a likely candidate to become Prime Minister.* 他似乎是成为首相的合适人选。♦**it is likely that ...** 有可能… ♦**to be likely to do sth** 很有可能做某事 ♦**not likely!** [非正式] 太不可能！

likeness ['laɪknɪs] *n* [S] (*similarity*) 相似 ♦**that's a good likeness** (*photo, portrait*) 那活像本人

likewise ['laɪkwaɪz] *adv* (*similarly*) 同样地 ♦**to do likewise** 照样做

liking ['laɪkɪŋ] *n* ♦**to have a liking for sb/sth** 喜爱某人/某物 ♦**to be to sb's liking** 合某人意 ♦**it's too big for my liking** 对我来说太大了 ♦**to take a liking to sb** 对某人产生好感

lilac ['laɪlək] **I** *n* **1** [C] [植] 丁香树; **2** [C/U] (*flower*) 丁香花 **3** [U] (*colour*) 淡紫色 **II** *adj* 淡紫色的

lily ['lɪlɪ] *n* [C] (*plant*) 百合属; (*flower*) 百合花

limb [lɪm] *n* [C] **1** [解剖] 四肢 **2** [文] [*of tree*] 大枝 ♦**to go out on a limb** (喻) 惹是生非

limbo ['lɪmbəu] *n* ♦**to be in limbo** 处于不定状态

lime [laɪm] *n* **1** [C] (*fruit*) 酸橙 **2** [C] (*also:* ***lime tree***) (*linden*) 椴树; (*bearing limes*) 酸橙树 **3** [C/U] (*also:* ***lime juice***) 酸橙汁 **4** (*for soil*) 石灰

limelight ['laɪmlaɪt] *n* ♦**to be in the limelight** 为公众所瞩目

limestone ['laɪmstəun] *n* [U] 石灰岩

limit ['lɪmɪt] **I** *vt* [*+ production, expense etc*] 限制 **II** *n* [C] **1** (*maximum point*) 限度 **2** [*of area, city*] 界线 **3** (*restriction*) (*on time, money etc*) 限定 ♦**to limit o.s. to sth** 自我限定某物 ♦**to be off limits (to sb)** 禁止(某人)入内 ♦**to be over the limit** [英] 饮酒过量 ♦**within limits** 适度地

limitation [lɪmɪ'teɪʃən] **I** *n* [U] (*control*) 限制 **II limitations** *n* [*pl*] (*shortcomings*) 局限 ♦**a limitation on sth** 对某事的限额

limited ['lɪmɪtɪd] *adj* [*+ choice, resources etc*] 有限的 ♦**to be limited to sth/sb** 只限于某物/某人

limousine ['lɪməziːn] *n* [C] 豪华轿车

limp [lɪmp] **I** *n* [C] 跛行 **II** *vi* [*person, animal +*] 跛行 **III** *adj* [*+ body, material etc*] 柔软的 ♦**to have a limp** 腿瘸 ♦**to walk with a limp** 一瘸一拐地走

✪**line** [laɪn] **I** *n* [C] **1** (*long thin mark*) 线 **2** (*wrinkle*) 皱纹 **3** (*row*) *of people, things*) 排◊ *a line of women queueing for bread* 一排妇女在排队等面包 ◊ *long lines of trees* 长排的树木 **4** [*+ of words*] (*written, printed*) 行◊ *I only read the first few lines.* 我只读了前几行。; (*in poem, song*) 句◊ *the most famous line in English poetry* 英语诗歌中最有名的一句 **5** [戏剧, 电影] 台词◊ *He's learning his lines for the school play.* 他在为学校里的一出剧背台词。**6** (*rope, cord*) 线; (*also:* ***washing line***) 晾衣绳◊ *She hung her washing on the line.* 她把衣服挂到晾衣绳上。; (*also:* ***fishing line***) 钓鱼线; [电子] (*wire*) 电线◊ *High winds had brought the lines down.* 猛烈的风把电线刮断了。; [通信] 线路 ◊ *The line was dead.* 线路不通。**7** (*railway track*) 铁路线路◊ *repairs to the line* 对铁路线路的维修 **8** (*bus, coach, train route*) 路线◊ *They had taken the wrong line on the London Tube.* 他们在伦敦地铁坐错了线。**9** (*boundary*) 界线◊ *just across the state line in Nevada* 刚刚越过内华达州的州界 **10** [文] (*edge, contour*) 曲线◊ *an evening dress that follows the lines of the body* 显现身体曲线的晚礼服 **11** (*attitude, policy*) 方针◊ *the official line of the Labour Party* 工党的方针 **12** (*also:* ***line of business, line of work***) 生产线◊ *What line are you in?* 你在哪一条生产线上？**13** [商] (*of product*) 种◊ *a new line of computer printers* 一种新的电脑打印机 **II** *vt* **1** (*form rows along*) [*people, trees +*] 沿…排成行◊ *Crowds lined the route.*

一群人沿路排成一行。**2** (*form layer inside*) 覆盖…的里层 ◊ *Moisture lined the walls of the cave.* 湿气覆盖洞穴内壁。◊ *the muscles that line the intestines* 肠内壁的肌肉 **3** (*put lining in*) [+ *clothing*] 加里衬于; [+ *container*] 放在…的内壁 ♦ **to line sth with sth** 把某物放在某物的内壁 ♦ **hold the line please!** [通信] 请稍等! ♦ **to stand** *or* **wait in line** [尤美] 排队等候 [英=**queue**] ♦ **in line with** (*according to*) 与…一致 ♦ **to be in line for sth** 即将获得某事物 **4** ♦ **somewhere along** *or* **down the line** 在某个时期 ♦ **to bring sth into line with sth** 使某物与某物一致 ♦ **to be on the line** [*job, reputation* +] 面临威胁 ♦ **on the right lines** 大体正确 ♦ **to be/step out of line** (喻) 越轨 ♦ **to draw the line at doing sth** 拒绝做某事 ♦ **to take a hard line on sth** 对某事态度强硬

❑ **line up I** *vi* (*form queue*) 排队 **II** *vt* **1** [+ *people, objects*] 使排队 ◊ *The men were lined up against a wall.* 这些男子们被靠墙排成排。**2** (*organize*) [+ *event, celebration*] 安排 ◊ *A formal party was lined up.* 人们正在安排一场正式的晚会。**3** ♦ **to line sb up (for sth)** (为某事) 安排组织好某人 ◊ *I had lined up a wonderful cast.* 我已经安排好一组优秀的演员到场。♦ **to have sb/sth lined up** 安排某人/某事

linear [ˈlɪnɪə(r)] *adj* **1** [+ *process, sequence*] 线性的 **2** [+ *shape, form*] 直线的

lined [laɪnd] *adj* **1** [+ *face, skin*] 褶皱的 **2** [+ *paper*] 带横格的 **3** [+ *skirt, jacket etc*] 带衬里的

linen [ˈlɪnɪn] **I** *n* [U] **1** (*cloth*) 亚麻布 **2** (*tablecloths, sheets etc*) 亚麻制品 **II** *cpd* [复合词] [+ *jacket, sheets, etc*] 亚麻料

liner [ˈlaɪnə(r)] *n* [C] (*ship*) 班轮

line-up [ˈlaɪnʌp] *n* [C] **1** (*chosen group*) [体育] 阵容; (*at concert, festival*) 演出名单 **2** (*identity parade*) 等待检查的一排人

linger [ˈlɪŋgə(r)] *vi* [*smell, tradition, feelings* +] 继续存留; [*person* +] 逗留

lingerie [ˈlænʒəriː] *n* [U] 女内衣

lingering [ˈlɪŋgərɪŋ] *adj* [+ *sense, feeling, doubt*] 继续存在的; [+ *death*] 拖久的

linguist [ˈlɪŋgwɪst] *n* [C] **1** (*knowing languages*) 通晓数国语言的人 **2** (*knowing linguistics*) 语言学家

linguistic [lɪŋˈgwɪstɪk] *adj* [+ *ability, awareness, studies etc*] 语言学的

linguistics [lɪŋˈgwɪstɪks] *n* [U] 语言学

lining [ˈlaɪnɪŋ] *n* **1** [C/U] [*of garment*] 衬里 **2** [C] [解剖] [*of stomach etc*] 膜

link [lɪŋk] **I** *n* [C] **1** (*relationship*) 关系 **2** (*connection*) (*between people, organizations*) 联系 **3** [计算机] (*also: **hyperlink***) 超链接 **4** (*means of transport/communication*) 线路 **5** [*of chain*] 环节 **II** *vt* **1** (*join*) [+ *places, objects*] 连接 **2** (*relate*) [+ *people, situations*] 联系 **3** [+ *arms, hands*] 挽住 **III links** *n* [*pl*] [高尔夫] 球场

❑ **link up I** *vt* [+ *machines, systems*] 联接 **II** *vi* [*people, groups* +] 联合

lion [ˈlaɪən] *n* [C] 狮子 ♦ **the lion's share of sth** 某物的最大一部分

lioness [ˈlaɪənɪs] *n* [C] 母狮

lip [lɪp] *n* **1** [C] [解剖] 唇 **2** [C] [*of cup, jug etc*] 边缘 **3** [U] [非正式] (*insolence*) 唐突无礼的话

lip-read [ˈlɪpriːd] *vi* 唇读

lipstick [ˈlɪpstɪk] *n* [C/U] 口红

liqueur [lɪˈkjuə(r), (美) lɪˈkɜː(r)] *n* [C/U] 饭后饮用的甜的烈性酒

liquid [ˈlɪkwɪd] **I** *n* [C/U] 液体 **II** *adj* 液体的

liquidize [ˈlɪkwɪdaɪz] [烹饪] *vt* 使液化

liquidizer [ˈlɪkwɪdaɪzə(r)] [尤英: 烹饪] *n* 榨汁机

liquor [ˈlɪkə(r)] [美] *n* [U] 酒 ♦ **hard liquor** 烈性酒 [英=**spirits**]

liquor store [美] *n* [C] 酒店 [英=**off-licence**]

lisp [lɪsp] **I** *n* [C] 咬舌 **II** *vi* 咬着舌说 ♦ **to speak with a lisp** 口齿不清地说

✪ **list** [lɪst] **I** *n* [C] 单子 ◊ *There were six names on the list.* 单子上有6个名字。**II** *vt* **1** (*record*) [*person* +] 列出 ◊ *The pupils listed their favourite sports.* 小学生们把他们最喜好的运动列了出来。**2** (*show*)

[*document, label* +] 标明◊ *There was a label on each case listing its contents.* 每个箱子都有一个标签标明箱内东西。**3** [计算机] 列出 ◊ *Have you tried listing your other directories?* 你有没有试着把其他的目录列出来？**4** (*include on list*) 列在…之内◊ *He is not listed in the phone book.* 他的名字没列在电话簿内。**III** *vi* [*ship* +] 倾斜

listen ['lɪsn] **I** *vi* **1** (*try to hear*) (*to sound, music*) 听; (*to speaker*) 听…说 **2** (*follow advice*) 听从 ♦**to listen to sb** (*pay attention to*) 留神听某人说话; (*follow advice of*) 听从某人 ♦**to listen to sth** 听某事 ♦**listen!** (*to a sound*) 你听！; (*pay attention to me*) 听着！♦**to listen for** (*also: **listen out for***) [英] 注意听
❑**listen in** *vi* ♦**listen in on** *or* **to** (*eavesdrop*) 偷听

listener ['lɪsnə(r)] [广播] *n* [c] 听众 ♦**to be a good listener** 会倾听的人

lit [lɪt] *pt, pp* **of light**

liter ['liːtə(r)] [美] *n* = **litre**

literacy ['lɪtərəsɪ] *n* [U] 读写能力

literal ['lɪtərəl] *adj* [+ *sense, meaning*] 字面的; [+ *translation*] 直译的

literally ['lɪtrəlɪ] *adv* **1** (*used for emphasis*) 确实地 **2** [*translate* +] 逐字地

literary ['lɪtərərɪ] *adj* [+ *work, criticism, theory*] 文学的; [+ *word, expression, language*] 书面的

literate ['lɪtərət] *adj* (*able to read and write*) 有读写能力的; (*well-educated*) 有文化修养的

literature ['lɪtrɪtʃə(r)] *n* [U] **1** (*novels, plays, poetry*) 文学 **2** (*printed information*) 印刷品 **3** (*publications*) 文献

Lithuania [lɪθju'eɪnɪə] [地理] *n* 立陶宛

Lithuanian [lɪθju'eɪnɪən] **I** *adj* 立陶宛的 **II** *n* **1** [c] (*person*) 立陶宛人 **2** [U] (*language*) 立陶宛语

litre (美 **liter**) ['liːtə(r)] *n* [c] 升

litter ['lɪtə(r)] **I** *n* **1** [U] (*rubbish*) 垃圾 **2** [c] [+ *of dogs, cats, pigs etc*] 一窝 **II** *vt* 使…布满杂乱东西

litter bin [英] *n* [c] 垃圾箱 [美 = **trash can**]

littered ['lɪtəd] *adj* ♦**littered with** [+ *papers, debris*] 胡乱堆满; [+ *mistakes, references*] 布满

✪**little** ['lɪtl] **I** *adj* **1** (*small*) [+ *thing, person*] 小的◊ *a little house* 小房子 **2** (*young*) [+ *child*] 小的◊ *a little boy of 8* 一个8岁的小男孩 **3** (*younger*) ♦**little brother/sister** 弟弟/妹妹 **4** (*short*) [+ *distance, time, event*] 短的 ◊ *a little while longer* 过一段时间 ◊ *There is very little time left.* 只剩下很短的时间了。**5** (*trivial*) 琐碎的 ◊ *Harry would often get angry over little things.* 哈利总是为琐事动怒。**6** (*quantifier*) ♦**to have little time/money** 没有多少时间/金钱 **II** *adv* 少◊ *I have seen him very little recently.* 最近我很少见到他。◊ *We tried to interfere as little as possible.* 我们尽可能不干预。♦**a little** (*small amount*) 一点; (+ *noun*) 一点; [*sleep, eat* +] 一点◊ *Try to persuade her to eat a little.* 试着劝她吃点东西。♦**a little bit** (+ *adj*) 有点 ♦**little by little** 逐渐地

> **little** 和 **a little** 都用在不可数名词前，但是意义不同。例如，如果说 **I have a little money**，这是一个肯定的表达，说明你有钱。然而，如果说 **I have little money**，它就是一个否定的表达，意思是基本上没钱。

little finger *n* [c] 小指

✪**live**[1] [lɪv] **I** *vi* **1** (*reside*) (*in house, town, country*) 住◊ *I used to live in Grange Road.* 我曾经住在格兰治路。**2** (*lead one's life*) 生活◊ *people who live in poverty* 生活在贫困中的人们 **3** (*survive*) 活着◊ *We need water to live.* 我们需要水来维持生命。◊ *Do you work to live or live to work?* 你是为活着而工作还是为工作而活着？**II** *vt* [+ *life*] 过◊ *We can start living a normal life again.* 我们可以重新开始过正常的生活。♦**to live by hunting/fishing** 以狩猎/捕鱼为生
❑**live down** *vt* [+ *defeat, error, failure*] 使人淡忘
❑**live for** *vt* [不可拆分] [+ *work,*

pleasure] 为…而生活
❑**live in I** *vi* [*student* +] 住学校公寓; [*maid, nurse etc* +] 住在雇主家里
❑**live off** *vt* [不可拆分] **1** [+ *money*] 靠…生活 **2** [+ *food*] 以…为主食 ◊ *We lived off fruit for a week.* 我们一个星期都以水果为主食。
3 [+ *parents etc*] 依靠…生活 ◊ *I was living off my parents.* 我依靠父母生活。
❑**live on I** *vt* [不可拆分]
1 [+ *money*] 靠…维持生活 ◊ *I don't have enough money to live on.* 我的钱不够维持生活。**2** [+ *food*] 以…为主食 ◊ *The children live on chips.* 孩子们把薯条当主食。**II** *vi* (*survive*) (*in memory, history*) 留下印记
❑**live out** *vt* **1** ♦**to live out one's days** *or* **life** 度过一生 **2** [+ *dream, fantasy*] 付诸实践
❑**live through** *vt* [不可拆分] [+ *war, crisis etc*] 历经
❑**live together** *vi* 同居
❑**live up** *vt* ♦**to live it up** [非正式] 狂欢
❑**live up to** *vt* [不可拆分] [+ *expectations*] 符合
❑**live with** *vt* [不可拆分] [+ *partner*] 与…同居

✪**live**² [laɪv] **I** *adj* **1** [+ *animal, plant*] 活的 **2** [+ *pictures, broadcast*] 实况的; [+ *performance*] 现场的 **3** [电子] [+ *wire*] 带电的 **4** [+ *bullet*] 未爆炸的 **II** *adv* **1** [*broadcast* +] 实况地 **2** [*perform, play* +] 现场地

livelihood ['laɪvlɪhud] *n* [C/U] (*source of income*) 生计

lively ['laɪvlɪ] *adj* [+ *person*] 活泼的; [+ *place, event, discussion*] 活跃的 ♦**to take a lively interest in sth** (*enthusiastic*) 对某物有浓厚的兴趣

liven up ['laɪvn-] **I** *vt* [+ *place, discussion, evening etc*] 使有生气; [+ *person*] 使活跃 **II** *vi* [*place, discussion, evening, person etc* +] 活跃起来

liver ['lɪvə(r)] *n* **1** [C] [解剖] 肝脏 **2** [C/U] [烹饪] 肝

lives [laɪvz] *n* [*pl*] *of* **life**

livestock ['laɪvstɔk] *n* [U] 家畜

living ['lɪvɪŋ] **I** *adj* [+ *author, relative*] 在世的 **II** *n* **1** [U] (*life*) 生活 **III the living** *n* [*pl*] 活着的人们 ♦**for a living** 作为谋生之道 ♦**to earn** *or* **make a/one's living** 谋生 ♦**within living memory** 就当今人们所能记住的

living room *n* [C] 起居室

lizard ['lɪzəd] *n* [C] 蜥蜴

LMT [美] *abbr* (= ***Local Mean Time***) 地方平均时

load [ləud] **I** *n* [C] **1** (*thing carried*) [*of person, animal*] 负荷; [*of vehicle*] 装载量 **2** (*weight*) 负重 **3** [电子, 科技] 负荷 **4** (*workload*) 工作量 **II** *vt* **1** (*also: **load up***) [+ *vehicle, ship etc*] 装 **2** [计算机] [+ *program, data*] 下载 **3** [+ *gun*] 给…上子弹; [+ *camera*] 把胶卷装入 ♦**loads of** *or* **a load of money/people** [非正式] 很多钱/人 ♦**a load of nonsense** [非正式] 一派胡言

loaded ['ləudɪd] *adj* **1** [+ *gun*] 装有子弹的 **2** [+ *question, word*] 别有用意的 **3** [非正式] (*rich*) 很有钱的 ♦**to be loaded in favour of/against sb** (*biased*) 一味地偏爱/反对某人 ♦**to be loaded with sth** [+ *goods*] 满载某物 **4** [+ *humour, irony*] 充满某事

loaf [ləuf] (*pl* **loaves**) **I** *n* [C] ♦**a loaf (of bread)** 一条(面包) **II** *vi* **1** (*also: **loaf about, loaf around***) 闲逛 ♦**use your loaf!** [英:非正式] 动动脑筋!

loan [ləun] **I** *n* **1** [C] (*sum of money*) 贷款 **2** [S] [*of book, car, house etc*] 借出 **II** *vt* ♦**to loan sth (out) to sb** [+ *money, thing*] 把某物借给某人 ♦**to be on loan (to/from sb/sth)** (从某人/某处)借来 ♦**to give/offer sb the loan of sth** 主动提出借给某人某物

loathe [ləuð] *vt* 憎恨 ♦**to loathe doing sth** 极讨厌做某事

loaves [ləuvz] *n* [*pl*] *of* **loaf**

lobby ['lɔbɪ] **I** *n* [C] **1** [*of building*] 大厅 **2** [政治] (*pressure group*) 游说团 **II** *vt* [+ *MP, councillor*] 游说 **III** *vi* ♦**to lobby for sth** 为某事而游说

lobster ['lɔbstə(r)] *n* **1** [C] [动] 龙虾 **2** [C/U] [烹饪] 龙虾肉

✪**local** ['ləukl] **I** *adj* **1** [+ *council, newspaper, library*] 当地的; [+ *residents*] 本地的 **2** [通信] [+ *call*] 本地的 **II** *n* [C] [英:非正式] (*pub*) 当

地酒店 **III the locals** *n* [*pl*] (*people*) 当地人

local anaesthetic *n* [c/u] 局部麻醉

local authority [英] *n* [c] 地方当局 [美=**local government**]

local government *n* **1** [u] (*system*) 地方政府 **2** [c] [美] (*organization*) 地方当局 [英=**local authority**]

locally ['ləukəlɪ] *adv* **1** (*not nationally*) 在地方 **2** (*in the neighbourhood*) 在附近

local time *n* [u] 当地时间

locate [ləu'keɪt] *vt* [正式] (*find*) [+ *person, thing*] 找到 ♦**to be located** [正式] (*situated*) 位于

location [ləu'keɪʃən] *n* **1** [c] (*place*) 地点 **2** [c/u] [电影] 外景 **3** [c/u] (*setting*) 位置 **4** [c] (*whereabouts*) 位置 ♦**on location** [电影] 外景拍摄

loch [lɔx] *n* [c] 湖

lock [lɔk] **I** *n* [c] **1** [*of door, drawer, suitcase*] 锁 **2** (*on canal*) 水闸 **3** (*also: **lock of hair***) 一绺头发 **II** *vt* **1** [+ *door, drawer, suitcase*] 锁 **2** [计算机] [+ *screen*] 锁 **III** *vi* **1** [*door etc* +] 锁得上 **2** (*jam*) [*wheels, knee, mechanism* +] 卡住 **3** ♦**to lock (into place)** 挤住 **IV locks** *n* [*pl*] [文] (*hair*) 头发 ♦**lock, stock and barrel** 全部地

❑**lock away** *vt* **1** [+ *valuables*] 将…锁藏起来 **2** [+ *criminal*] 把…关起来

❑**lock in** *vt* [+ *person, object*] (*in room, safe*) 把…锁起来 ♦**to lock sb in** 关某人禁闭

❑**lock out** *vt* **1** [+ *person*] (*deliberately*) 把…锁在外面 ♦**to lock o.s. out** 把自己锁在外面 **2** [工业] 不准工人进厂以威胁工人接受条件

❑**lock up I** *vt* **1** [+ *house, car*] 锁好 **2** [+ *criminal*] 把…监禁起来 [+ *mental patient*] 把…关进精神病院 **II** *vi* 锁好门窗

locked [lɔkt] *adj* 上了锁的

locker ['lɔkə(r)] *n* [c] 小柜

locksmith ['lɔksmɪθ] *n* [c] 锁匠

locomotive [ləukə'məutɪv] *n* [c] [正式] 机车

lodge [lɔdʒ] **I** *vi* **1** [*person* +] ♦**to lodge (with)** 寄宿 **2** (*get stuck*) [*bullet* +] 射入 **II** *vt* [+ *complaint, protest, appeal*] 提出 **III** *n* [c] **1** (*at entrance*) 小屋 **2** (*hunting lodge*) 小屋

lodger ['lɔdʒə(r)] *n* [c] 房客

lodging ['lɔdʒɪŋ] **I** *n* **1** [u] (*accommodation*) 宿处 **II lodgings** *n* [*pl*] 租住的房子

loft [lɔft] *n* [c] **1** (*attic*) 阁楼 **2** (*apartment*) 顶楼公寓

log [lɔg] **I** *n* [c] **1** (*from tree*) (*trunk*) 原木; (*for fuel etc*) 木柴 **2** (*diary*) 日志 **II** *n abbr* (= ***logarithm***) [数] 对数 **III** *vt* [+ *event, fact*] 记录 ♦**to keep a log (of sth)** 登记某事

❑**log in, log on** [计算机] *vi* 登录

❑**log into** [计算机] *vt* [不可拆分] 登入

❑**log out, log off** [计算机] *vi* 退出系统

logic ['lɔdʒɪk] *n* [u] **1** [哲] 逻辑 **2** (*judgment*) 逻辑性

logical ['lɔdʒɪkl] *adj* [+ *argument, analysis*] 逻辑的; [+ *conclusion, result*] 合逻辑的; [+ *course of action*] 合乎情理的 ♦**it is logical to assume that ...** 假定…是合乎情理的

logistics [lɔ'dʒɪstɪks] *n* [*pl*] 后勤

logo ['ləugəu] *n* [c] [*of firm, organization*] 标识

lollipop ['lɔlɪpɔp] *n* [c] 棒棒糖

lollipop lady [英] *n* [c] 为保证儿童安全过马路手持暂停指挥牌的女交通管理员

lollipop man [英] (*pl* **lollipop men**) *n* [c] 为保证儿童安全过马路手持暂停指挥牌的男交通管理员

lolly ['lɔlɪ] [英:非正式] *n* [c] (*lollipop*) 棒棒糖 *see also* **ice lolly**

London ['lʌndən] *n* 伦敦

Londoner ['lʌndənə(r)] *n* [c] 伦敦人

lone [ləun] *adj* [+ *person, thing*] 孤独的 ♦**a lone voice** 自持一个观点

loneliness ['ləunlɪnɪs] *n* [u] 孤独

lonely ['ləunlɪ] *adj* **1** (*sad*) [+ *person*] 孤独的; [+ *situation, period*] 孤寂的 **2** (*unfrequented*) [+ *place*] 人迹罕至的

loner ['ləunə(r)] *n* [c] 喜独处的人

✪**long** [lɔŋ] **I** *adj* **1** (*in distance*) [+ *rope, hair, table, tunnel etc*] 长的 **2** (*in time*) [+ *meeting, discussion, film, time*] 长的 ◊ *It was a long meeting.* 这个会议很长。**3** (*in words*) [+ *book, poem*] 长的 **II** *adv* (*time*) 长久 ◊ *Have you been* *here long?* 你在这里时间长吗？ **III** *vi* ♦**to long for sth/to do sth** 渴望某物/做某事 ♦**how long is the tunnel?** 这个隧道有多长？ ♦**how long is the lesson?** 这节课多长时间？ ♦**6 metres long** 6米长 ♦**the film is three hours long** 这部电影长达3个小时 ♦**all day/night long** 整天/夜 ♦**so** *or* **as long as** (*provided*) 只要; (*while*) 在…同时◊ *You can't turn the heat off as long as the system is on.* 在系统开着的同时，不能中断供暖。♦**he no longer comes** *or* **he doesn't come any longer** 他不再来了 ♦**long ago** 很久以前 ♦**long before/after** 很久以前/以后 ♦**before long** (+ *future*) 不久 ◊ *They're bound to catch him before long.* 不久，他们一定会抓到他。; (+ *past*) 很快◊ *Before long we were all safely back home.* 很快，我们就都安全到家了。♦**for long** 很久 ♦**it won't take long** 这不需花很多时间 ♦**it won't be long before/until ...** 很快就… ♦**I won't be long** 我很快就来 ♦**at long last** 终于 ♦**a long way** 很远 ♦**so long!** [非正式] 再见！ ♦**the long and the short of it is that ...** 总而言之…

long-distance [lɔŋ'dɪstəns] **I** *adj* [+ *journey, phone call*] 长途的; [+ *race, runner*] 长跑的 **II** *adv* [*phone* +] 通过长途电话

long-haul ['lɔŋhɔːl] *adj* [*flight, route* +] 长途的

longing ['lɔŋɪŋ] *n* [c/u] ♦**longing (for)** (对…的)渴望

longitude ['lɔŋgɪtjuːd] *n* [c/u] 经度 ♦**250 degrees longitude** 经度250度

long jump [体育] *n* ♦**the long jump** 跳远

long-life ['lɔŋlaɪf] *adj* [+ *milk*] 可长久保存的; [+ *batteries, bulb*] 耐用的

long-sighted ['lɔŋ'saɪtɪd] [英] *adj* 远视的[美=**far-sighted**]

long-standing ['lɔŋ'stændɪŋ] *adj* [+ *tradition, problem, dispute*] 长期存在的; [+ *relationship*] 长久的

long-term ['lɔŋtəːm] *adj* [+ *effects, prospects, future*] 长远的; [+ *plan, project, solution*] 长久的; [+ *memory*] 长期的 ♦**the long-term unemployed** 长期失业

long wave *n* [u] 长波

loo [luː] [英:非正式] *n* [c] 厕所[美=**bathroom**]

✪**look** [luk] **I** *vi* **1** (*glance, gaze*) 看 **2** (*search*) 找◊ *Have you looked behind the sofa?* 你找没找沙发后面？**3** (*seem, appear*) 看起来◊ *He looked scared.* 他看起来害怕了。◊ *It looks all right to me.* 我看可以。**II** *n* **1** (*expression*) 表情◊ *There was a worried look on his face.* 他脸上有一种担忧的表情。**2** (*appearance*) 装扮◊ *the punk look* 朋克式装扮 **III looks** *n* [*pl*] (*appearance*) 外表; (*good looks*) 美貌 ♦**to look out of the window** 望向窗外 ♦**to look south/onto the sea** [*building, window, garden* +] 面向南方/大海 ♦**look (here)!** (*expressing annoyance etc*) 喂！ ♦**look!** (*expressing surprise*) 看！ ♦**look out!** 当心！ ♦**to look like sb** (*in appearance*) 长得像某人 ♦**it looks like Jim** (*it may be him*) 看起来像吉姆 ♦**to look like sth** (*in appearance*) 看起来像某物 ♦**it looks like rain** 看来要下雨了 ♦**it looks as if ...** 看来…◊ *It looks about 4 metres long.* 看起来约有4米长。♦**to have** *or* **take a look at** (*examine*) 看一看; (*consider*) 细看 ♦**to give sb a quizzical/puzzled look** 揶揄地/疑惑地看某人一眼 ♦**to have a look for sth/sb** 找某物/某人 ♦**by the look** *or* **looks of it** 根据外表来判断 ♦**I don't like the look of it/him** 看它/他的样子就不舒服

❏**look after** *vt* [不可拆分] **1** (*care for*) 照顾 **2** (*deal with*) 照管

❏**look ahead** *vi* (*in time*) 向前看

❏**look around** = **look round**

❏**look at** *vt* [不可拆分] **1** (*gaze at*) 看一看 **2** (*consider*) [+ *problem, subject etc*] 考虑

❏**look back** *vi* **1** (*think back*) 回顾 ◊ *The past always seems better when you look back on it.* 当你回顾往事的时候，过去总是那么美好。**2** (*glance back*) 回头看 ♦**to look back at sth/sb** 回头看某物/某人

♦ **looking back, ...** 回想起来,…
❑ **look down on, look down upon** *vt* [不可拆分] 轻视
❑ **look for** *vt* [不可拆分] (*seek*) [+ *person, thing*] 寻找
❑ **look forward to** *vt* [不可拆分] 盼望 ♦ **to look forward to doing sth** 盼望做某事 ♦ **we look forward to hearing from you** 我们盼望收到你的回音
❑ **look in** *vi* ♦ **to look in on sb** 顺便看望某人
❑ **look into** *vt* [不可拆分] (*investigate*) 调查 ♦ **to look into doing sth** 为做某事作调查准备
❑ **look on I** *vi* (*watch*) 旁观 **II** *vt* [不可拆分] (*also:* ***look upon***) (*consider*) 看待 ◊ *Employers look favourably on applicants who have work experience.* 雇主对有工作经验的申请者另眼看待。♦ **to look on sb as sth** 把某人当作某物看待
❑ **look out for** *vt* [不可拆分] (*pay attention to*) 留心
❑ **look over** *vt* (*examine*) [+ *document, essay*] 检查; [+ *building*] 查看
❑ **look round, look around I** *vi* **1** (*turn head*) 环顾 **2** (*in building etc*) 看看 **II** *vt* [不可拆分] [+ *place, building*] 游览
❑ **look through** *vt* [不可拆分] [+ *book, magazine, papers*] 翻阅
❑ **look to** *vt* [不可拆分] ♦ **to look to sb for sth/to do sth** 指望某人提供某事/做某事
❑ **look up I** *vi* **1** (*raise eyes*) 抬眼看 **2** [非正式] ♦ **things are looking up** 事情有好转了 **II** *vt* **1** [+ *information, meaning etc*] 查 **2** [+ *person*] 看望
❑ **look upon** = **look on**
❑ **look up to** *vt* [不可拆分] [+ *hero, idol*] 敬佩

lookout ['lukaut] **I** *n* [c] **1** (*person*) 看守 **2** (*place*) 瞭望台 ♦ **to be on the lookout for sth** 留心某事 ♦ **to keep a lookout (for sb/sth)** 密切注视(某人/某事) **II** *cpd* [复合词] [+ *post, tower, point*] 瞭望

loom [lu:m] **I** *vi* **1** (*also:* ***loom up***) [*object, shape* +] 隐隐出现 **2** [*event* +] 逼近 **II** *n* (*for weaving*) 织布机 ♦ **to loom large** 赫然显现

loony ['lu:nɪ] [非正式] **I** *adj* 发疯的 **II** *n* [c] 疯子

loop [lu:p] **I** *n* [c] **1** (*in string, ribbon etc*) 圈 **2** [计算机] 重复指令 **II** *vt* ♦ **to loop sth around/over sth** 把某物缠绕在某物上 **III** *vi* 环绕

loophole ['lu:phəul] *n* [c] (*in law*) 漏洞

loose [lu:s] **I** *adj* **1** (*not firm*) [+ *screw, connection, tooth*] 松动的 **2** (*not tied back*) [+ *hair*] 散开的 **3** (*not tight*) [+ *clothes, trousers etc*] 宽松的; [+ *coalition, arrangement*] 松散的 **4** (*vague*) [+ *definition, translation*] 不精确的 **5** [过时] (*promiscuous*) [+ *woman, morals*] 放荡的 **II** *n* ♦ **to be on the loose** [*prisoner, animal* +] 行动不受限制 **III** *vt* **1** [正式] (*free*) [+ *animal, prisoner*] 把…放开 ♦ **to set sb/sth loose** 释放某人/某物 ♦ **to let sb loose on sth** 放任某人做某事 ♦ **to break loose** 挣脱出来

loosely ['lu:slɪ] *adv* **1** [*hold, hang, tie* +] 松散地 **2** [*organized, arranged*] 不周密地 **3** [*define, translate* +] 粗略地 ♦ **loosely speaking** 笼统地说

loosen ['lu:sn] *vt* **1** (*undo*) [+ *screw, nuts*] 拧松; [+ *clothing, belt, tie etc*] 松开 **2** (*relax*) [+ *restrictions, laws*] 放松 ♦ **to loosen one's grip on sth** [+ *object*] 对紧抓的某物稍稍松手; [+ *power, people*] 放松对某物的掌控
❑ **loosen up** *vi* **1** (*exercise*) 放松 **2** (*relax*) 松弛下来

loot [lu:t] **I** *vt* [+ *shops, homes*] 洗劫 **II** *n* [U] [非正式] 掠夺品

lopsided ['lɔp'saɪdɪd] *adj* (*crooked*) 歪斜的

lord [lɔ:d] [英] *n* [c] (*peer*) 贵族 ♦ **Lord Smith** 史密斯阁下 ♦ **the Lord** [宗] 上帝 ♦ **my lord** [英] (*to bishop, noble*) 大人; (*to judge*) 阁下 ♦ **good Lord!** 我的天! ♦ **the Lords** [英] 上议院

lorry ['lɔrɪ] [英] *n* [c] 卡车 [美 = **truck**]

lorry driver [英] *n* [c] 卡车司机 [美 = **truck driver**]

✪ **lose** [lu:z] (*pt, pp* **lost**) **I** *vt* **1** (*mislay*) [+ *keys, pen etc*] 丢失 ◊ *I lost my keys.* 我把钥匙丢了。**2** (*not win*) [+ *contest, fight, argument*] 输 **3** (*be*

dismissed from) [+ *job, place*] 丢掉 ◊ *He lost his place in the team.* 他丢掉了在队里的位置。**4** (*through death*) [+ *relative, wife etc*] 失去 ◊ *He had just lost his wife.* 他刚刚失去了妻子。**5** (*waste*) [+ *time, opportunity*] 浪费 **6** [商] [+ *money*] 亏损 ◊ *The company was losing a million pounds a week.* 该公司一个星期亏损100万英镑。**7** (*through injury, disease*) [+ *blood, tooth, leg*] 失掉; [+ *voice, sight etc*] 丧失 **8** (*run out of*) [+ *confidence, control etc*] 丧失 **9** (*shake off*) [+ *pursuers*] 摆脱 ◊ *He managed to lose his pursuers in the maze of streets.* 在繁杂的街道上，他竭力摆脱了跟踪者。**II** *vi* (*in competition, argument*) 输 ♦ **to lose o.s. in sth** 沉湎于某事 ♦ **to lose weight** 减重 ♦ **to lose no time in doing sth** 马上着手做某事 ◊ *Bill lost no time in telling me about his idea.* 比尔赶紧和我讲他的想法。♦ **to lose (time)** [*clock* +] 慢(时间) ♦ **to lose sight of sth** (*no longer see*) 看不见某物; (*forget*) 忽略某事
❑ **lose out** *vi* 受损失

loser [ˈluːzə(r)] *n* [c] **1** (*in game, contest*) 失败者 **2** [非正式] (*failure*) 不成器的人 ♦ **to be a good/bad loser** 输得起/不起的人

loss [lɔs] **I** *n* **1** [c/u] 丧失 **2** [c/u] (*death*) 失去 **II losses** *n* [*pl*] [军] 伤亡 ♦ **loss of life** 丧生 ♦ **to make a loss** [*company* +] 亏损 ♦ **to sell sth at a loss** 亏本卖某物 ♦ **to cut one's losses** 赶紧罢手以免更大损失 ♦ **to be at a loss (as to how/why** *etc* **...)** (对如何/为何{等}…)不知所措

lost [lɔst] **I** *pt, pp of* **lose II** *adj* [+ *object*] 丢失的; [+ *person, animal*] 走失的 ♦ **to be lost** (*having lost one's way*) 迷路 ♦ **to get lost** (*lose one's way*) 迷路 ♦ **to feel lost** 不知所措 ♦ **get lost!** [非正式] (*go away*) 走开! ♦ **to be lost in thought** 陷入沉思 ♦ **to be lost on sb** [*advice, words* +] 对某人不起作用

lost and found [美] *n* = **lost property**

lost property *n* [u] **1** (*things*) 招领的失物 **2** [英] (*office*) 失物招领处 [美 = **lost and found**]

✪ **lot** [lɔt] *n* [c] **1** (*set, group*) (*of papers, books, people etc*) 批 ◊ *We've just sacked one lot of builders.* 我们刚解雇了一批建筑工人。**2** [美] (*land*) 地皮 (*see also* **parking lot**) **3** (*at auction*) 批件 ◊ *lot no. 359* 批件号为359 **4** (*destiny*) 命运 ◊ *attempts by the workers to improve their lot* 工人为改变自身命运所做的努力 ♦ **a lot** (*many*) [*of books etc*] 许多 ◊ *Have one of mine, I've got a lot.* 给你一个吧，我有很多。; (*much*) [*of money etc*] 很多 ◊ *We still owe quite a lot.* 我们还是欠很多钱。♦ **a lot of** (*many, much*) 许多 ◊ *a lot of people* 许多人 ◊ *I drink a lot of coffee.* 我喝许多咖啡。♦ **lots of** [+ *things, people*] 许多 ♦ **he reads/smokes a lot** 他书读得/烟抽得很多 ♦ **I like you a lot** 我非常喜欢你 ♦ **the lot** [非正式] (*everything*) 全部 ◊ *She's taken the lot!* 她全部都拿走了! ♦ **they're a boring/friendly lot** [非正式] 他们这些人很无聊/友好 ♦ **to draw lots** 抽签

lotion [ˈləuʃən] *n* [c/u] 洗液

lottery [ˈlɔtərɪ] *n* [c] **1** (*game*) 彩票 **2** (喻) 难料的事

loud [laud] **I** *adj* **1** [+ *noise, voice, laugh*] 响亮的 **2** (*gaudy*) [+ *clothes*] 俗艳的 **II** *adv* [*speak etc* +] 大声地 ♦ **out loud** [*read, laugh etc* +] 出声地 ♦ **to be loud in one's support/condemnation of sth** 大力支持/强烈谴责某事

loudly [ˈlaudlɪ] *adv* 大声地

loudspeaker [laudˈspiːkə(r)] *n* [c] 扬声器

lounge [laundʒ] **I** *n* [c] **1** (*in hotel*) 休息室 **2** (*at airport, station*) 等候室 **3** [尤英] (*in house*) 起居室 **4** [英] (*also:* **lounge bar**) 豪华酒吧 **II** *vi* 懒洋洋地倚靠着
❑ **lounge about** (英 **lounge around**) *vi* 闲逛 ♦ **to lounge around the house/pool** 在家/游泳池消磨时间

louse [laus] (*pl* **lice**) *n* [c] 虱子
❑ **louse up** [非正式] *vt* 搞糟

lousy [ˈlauzɪ] [非正式] *adj* [+ *show, meal, weather etc*] 糟糕的; [+ *cook, singer, teacher etc*] 乏善可陈的 ♦ **to**

feel lousy (*ill*) 感觉不舒服

lout [laut] *n* [c] 粗人

lovable ['lʌvəbl] *adj* 可爱的

✪ **love** [lʌv] **I** *n* [U] **1** (*for partner, sweetheart*) 爱情; (*for child, pet*) 爱 ◊ *my love for my children* 我对孩子的爱 **2** [英:非正式](*term of address*) 对不相识者的客气称呼 ◊ *Are you OK, love?* 你没事吧? **II** *vt* [+ *partner, child, pet*] 爱 ◊ *I love you.* 我爱你。; [+ *thing, food, activity*] 热爱 ♦ **sb's love for sb** 某人对某人的爱 ♦ **to be in love (with sb)** (与某人)恋爱 ♦ **to fall in love (with sb)** 爱上(某人) ♦ **to make love** 做爱 ♦ **love at first sight** 一见钟情 ♦ **love (from) Anne** (*on letter*) 爱你的,安妮 ♦ **to send one's love to sb** 向某人问候 ♦ **a love of music/football/animals** 对音乐/足球/动物的热爱 ♦ **"15 love"** [网球] 15比0 ♦ **to love doing/to do sth** 喜爱做某事 ♦ **I'd love to come** 我非常想来 ♦ **I'd love you to come** *or* **I'd love it if you came** 你要是来真是太好了 📖 用法参见**nought**

love affair *n* [c] 风流韵事

love life *n* [c/U] 爱情生活

lovely ['lʌvlɪ] [尤英] *adj* **1** (*beautiful*) [+ *place, person, music etc*] 漂亮的 **2** (*delightful*) [+ *holiday, meal, present*] 令人愉快的; [+ *person*] 可爱的 ♦ **how lovely to see you!** 见到你真是高兴!

lover ['lʌvə(r)] *n* [c] **1** (*sexual partner*) 情人 **2** [文](*person in love*) 情侣 ♦ **a lover of art** *or* **an art lover** 钟爱艺术的人

loving ['lʌvɪŋ] *adj* [+ *person*] 表示爱的; [+ *relationship*] 充满爱的; [+ *care, support*] 细心周到的 ♦ **in loving memory of ...** 充满爱意地追念…

✪ **low** [ləu] **I** *adj* **1** (*not tall*) [+ *wall, hill, heel etc*] 矮的 **2** (*not high up*) [+ *ceiling, shelf, sun, neckline*] 低的 **3** (*deep*) [+ *bow, curtsey*] 深的 **4** (*in degree*) [+ *temperature, price, level, speed etc*] 低的 **5** (*in intensity*) [+ *heat, light, volume*] 低的 **6** (*poor*) [+ *standard, quality*] 低劣的 ◊ *work of very low quality* 质量低劣的工作 ◊ *The standard of child care is very low in many homes.* 在许多家庭里,对孩子的照顾是不足的。**7** (*low-pitched*) [+ *voice, note*] 低音的 ◊ *a long low note* 长长的低音音调 **8** (*quiet*) [+ *voice, whisper, murmur*] 低声的 **9** (*depressed*) [+ *person, morale*] 情绪低落的 ◊ *I was really low after my father died.* 我父亲去世以后,我的情绪非常低落。**II** *adv* [*fly* +] 低 ◊ *I asked him to fly low over the beach.* 我让他在海滩上方低飞。**III** *n* [c] **1** [气象] 低气压区 **2** (*low point*) 低点 ♦ **to be/run low on sth** 快用完某物 ♦ **low in calories/salt/fat** 低卡路里/盐/脂肪

low-alcohol ['ləu'ælkəhɔl] *adj* [+ *wine, beer*] 低度酒的

low-calorie ['ləu'kælərɪ] *adj* [+ *food*] 低卡路里的

lower ['ləuə(r)] **I** *vt* **1** ♦ **to lower sth into/to/onto sth** 把某物向下移到某物里/上 **2** (*reduce*) [+ *rate, level, price etc*] 降低 **3** (*make less loud*) [+ *voice*] 放低; [+ *volume*] 减低 **4** (*bow*) [+ *head, eyes*] 低垂 **II** *adj* **1** (*bottom*) [+ *deck, lip*] 下层的 **2** (*less important*) [+ *court, rank*] 下级的 ♦ **the lower sixth** [英:教育] 中学六年级 ♦ **to lower o.s. into a chair/onto a bed** 屈身坐在椅子/躺在床上

low-fat ['ləu'fæt] *adj* [+ *food, yogurt, diet*] 低脂肪的

loyal ['lɔɪəl] *adj* [+ *friend, supporter, customer etc*] 忠实的 ♦ **to be/remain loyal to sb** 对某人保持忠诚

loyalty ['lɔɪəltɪ] *n* [U] 忠诚 ♦ **sb's loyalty to sb** 某人对某人的忠诚 ♦ **out of loyalty to sb** 出于对某人的忠诚 ♦ **to have strong/divided loyalties** 非常忠诚/部分的忠诚

LP *n abbr* (= ***long-playing record***) 慢转密纹唱片

L-plates ['ɛlpleɪts] [英:汽车] *n* [*pl*] L车牌(以提示其他司机该车由学员驾驶员驾驶)

> **L-PLATES**
> 按照英国法律,学员驾驶员在未通过考试以前,要在他驾驶的任何车辆前后贴上**L-plate**标志。**L-plate** 是塑料或金属的方

形牌子，白底，带有一个大大的红色L（意为learner）。学员驾驶员驾驶车辆时，必须有合格的司机陪同。在通过考试前，驾车上高速公路是违法的。

LSAT [美] *n abbr* (= ***Law School Admissions Test***) 法学院入学考试
Ltd [商] *abbr* (= ***limited company***) 股份有限公司
lubricate ['luːbrɪkeɪt] *vt* [+ *part of machine, chain etc*] 给…上油
luck [lʌk] *n* [U] **1** (*chance*) 运气 **2** (*good fortune*) 幸运 ♦**good luck** 好运 ♦**good luck!** *or* **best of luck!** 祝你好运！♦**bad luck** 不走运 ♦**bad** *or* **hard** *or* **tough luck!** (*showing sympathy*) 真不走运！♦**hard** *or* **tough luck!** (*not showing sympathy*) 活该倒霉！♦**to be in luck** 走运 ♦**to be out of luck** 不走运 ♦**to have no luck (doing sth)** 没有(做某事的)运气 ♦**to try one's luck (at sth/at doing sth)** 碰碰(某事/做某事的)运气 ♦**with (any) luck** 如果幸运的话
luckily ['lʌkɪlɪ] *adv* 幸运的是 ♦**luckily for me/us** 我/我们挺运气的
lucky ['lʌkɪ] *adj* **1** [+ *person*] 幸运的 **2** [+ *charm, number*] 吉祥的 ♦**to be lucky** [*person* +] 走运 ♦**I'm lucky to be alive** 我很庆幸我活着 ♦**to be lucky enough to do sth** 有幸做某事 ♦**it is lucky that ...** 侥幸的是… ♦**today's your lucky day** 今天是你的吉日 ♦**to have a lucky escape** 侥幸逃脱 ♦**lucky break** 命运的转机 ♦**you'll be lucky!** [非正式] 你会有好运的！♦**you'll be lucky if ...** [非正式] 如果…就算你走运了
lucrative ['luːkrətɪv] *adj* [+ *contract, business, market*] 有利的
ludicrous ['luːdɪkrəs] *adj* (*ridiculous*) [+ *situation, idea, price etc*] 荒唐的 ♦**it is ludicrous to suggest that ...** 建议…真是荒唐 ♦**it's ludicrous that ...** …真是荒唐
luggage ['lʌɡɪdʒ] *n* [U] 行李 ♦**piece of luggage** 一件行李
luggage rack *n* [C] **1** (*in train, coach*) 行李架 **2** [美] (*on car*) 车顶架 [英 = **roof rack**]
lukewarm ['luːkwɔːm] *adj* **1** (*tepid*) 微温的 **2** (*unenthusiastic*) [+ *reaction, welcome*] 冷淡的 ♦**to be lukewarm about sth/doing sth** 对某事/做某事热情不高 ♦**to be lukewarm towards sb** 对某人不冷不热
lull [lʌl] **I** *n* (*break*) (*in conversation, fighting etc*) 间歇 **II** *vt* ♦**to lull sb to sleep** [*sound, motion* +] 哄某人睡觉 ♦**to be lulled into sth/doing sth** 被哄得产生某事/被哄得做某事
lullaby ['lʌləbaɪ] *n* [C] 催眠曲
lumber ['lʌmbə(r)] **I** *n* [U] **1** [尤美] (*wood*) 木材 [英 = **timber**] **2** [英:过时] (*junk*) 废旧杂物 **II** *vi* ♦**to lumber into view/across the square** [*person, animal* +] 笨重缓慢地走进视野/通过广场; [*truck, tank* +] 缓缓地移动进入视野/穿过广场
❑**lumber with** *vt* [英:非正式] ♦**to be/get lumbered with sb/sth** 为某人/某事所累 ♦**to be/get lumbered with doing sth** 苦于无奈做某事
luminous ['luːmɪnəs] *adj* **1** [+ *hands, dial, paint, etc*] 发光的 ◊ *the luminous dial on the clock* 钟表上的夜光指针 **2** (*bright*) 明亮的
lump [lʌmp] **I** *n* [C] **1** (*piece*) [*of clay, butter, wood, sugar etc*] 块 **2** (*protrusion*) (*on body*) 肿块 **II** *vt* ♦**to lump together** [非正式] [+ *things, places*] 杂凑在一起; [+ *people*] 混在一起
lump sum *n* [C] 一次性付的钱
lumpy ['lʌmpɪ] *adj* [+ *rice, sauce*] 多块的; [+ *bed, mattress*] 凹凸不平的
lunar ['luːnə(r)] *adj* [+ *landscape, module, landing etc*] 月的
lunatic ['luːnətɪk] **I** *n* [C] **1** [非正式] (*fool*) 疯子 **2** [过时] (*mentally ill*) 精神失常者 **II** *adj* [+ *behaviour*] 疯的
lunch [lʌntʃ] **I** *n* **1** [C/U] (*meal*) 午餐 **2** [U] (*lunchtime*) 午餐时间 **II** *vi* [正式] 吃午饭 ♦**to have lunch (with sb)** (与某人)共进午餐 ♦**to have sth for lunch** 午餐吃某物 ♦**to invite sb to lunch** 邀请某人共进午餐
📖 用法参见 **meal**
lunch break *n* [C] 午休时间 ♦**to be**

on one's lunch break 在午休
lunch hour *n* [C] = **lunch break**
lunchtime ['lʌntʃtaɪm] *n* [C/U] 午餐时间 ♦**at lunchtime** 午休时候
lung [lʌŋ] *n* [C] 肺
lure [luə(r)] **I** *vt* (*entice, tempt*) ♦**to lure sb into/to sth** 引诱某人进入某处/做某事 **II** *n* [C] **1** (*attraction*) 魅力 **2** [钓鱼, 狩猎] 饵
❑**lure away** *vt* 诱惑
lurk [lɜːk] *vi* **1** [*animal, person* +] 暗藏 **2** (喻) [*danger, suspicion, doubt* +] 潜伏
lush [lʌʃ] *adj* [+ *fields, gardens*] 茂盛的; [+ *grass, vegetation*] 繁茂的
lust [lʌst] **I** *n* **1** [U] (*sexual*) 性欲 **2** [U/S] ♦**lust for money/power/revenge** 金钱/权力/复仇欲 **II** *vi* **1** ♦**to lust after sb** 贪恋某人 **2** ♦**to lust for** *or* **after sth** [+ *power, money*] 对某物有强烈的欲望
Luxembourg ['lʌksəmbɜːg] [地理] *n* 卢森堡
luxurious [lʌg'zjuərɪəs] *adj* [+ *hotel, surroundings, lifestyle*] 豪华的
luxury ['lʌkʃərɪ] **I** *n* **1** [U] (*comfort*) 奢华 **2** [C] (*extra*) 奢侈品 **3** [S] (*pleasure*) 奢侈享受 **II** *cpd* [复合词] [+ *hotel, car, goods etc*] 豪华 ♦**to live in luxury** 过奢华的生活 ♦**it's a luxury (for me/us) to be able to lie in** (对我/我们来说)睡懒觉简直是一种奢侈
LW [广播] *abbr* (= ***long wave***) 长波
Lycra ® ['laɪkrə] **I** *n* [U] 莱卡 **II** *cpd* [复合词] [+ *clothes, shorts*] 莱卡
lying ['laɪɪŋ] **I** *vb see* **lie**[1] **lie**[2] **II** *n* [U] 说谎 **III** *adj* 好说谎的
lyric ['lɪrɪk] **I** *adj* [+ *poetry*] 抒情的 **II lyrics** *n* [*pl*] [*of song*] 词句

Mm

M¹, m¹ [ɛm] **I** *n* (*letter*) 英语的第十三个字母 **II** *abbr* (= ***male***) 男性
M² **I** *abbr* (= ***medium***) 中等的 **II** *n abbr* [英] (= ***motorway***) ♦ **the M1** 1号高速公路
m² *abbr* **1** (= ***metre(s)***) 米 **2** (= ***million***) 百万
MA *n abbr* (= ***Master of Arts***) (*qualification*) 文学硕士学位; (*person*) 文学硕士
ma [mɑː] [非正式] *n* [c] 妈
mac [mæk] [英:非正式] *n* [c] 雨衣
macaroni [mækə'rəunɪ] *n* [U] 通心粉 ♦ **macaroni cheese** *or* [美] **macaroni and cheese** 干酪通心粉布丁
Macedonia [mæsɪ'dəunɪə] *n* 马其顿
Macedonian [mæsɪ'dəunɪən] **I** *adj* 马其顿的 **II** *n* **1** [c] (*person*) 马其顿人 **2** [U] (*language*) 马其顿语
machine [mə'ʃiːn] **I** *n* [c] **1** 机器 **2** (*system*) [*party, war, propaganda*] 机构 **3** (*automaton*) 自动装置 **II** *vt* **1** [术语] 机械加工 **2** [+ *dress etc*] 用缝纫机制作 ♦ **by machine** 用机器制造
machine gun *n* [c] 机关枪
machinery [mə'ʃiːnərɪ] *n* [U] **1** 机器 **2** (*of government*) 体系
machine washable [mə'ʃɪːn'wɔʃəbl] *adj* 可机洗的
macho ['mætʃəu] *adj* [+ *man, attitude, approach*] 大男子气概的
mackerel ['mækrl] *n* [c/U] (*pl* **mackerel**) 鲭鱼
mackintosh ['mækɪntɔʃ] [英] *n* [c] 雨衣
mad [mæd] *adj* **1** (*insane*) 精神失常的 **2** (*foolish*) 愚蠢的 **3** (*wild*) 疯狂的 **4** [非正式] (*angry*) 恼怒的 ♦ **to go mad** [非正式] (*go insane*) 发疯; (= *get angry*) 发火 ♦ **you are/must be mad (to do that)** 你(那么做)准是犯傻了 ♦ **to drive sb mad** [非正式] 逼得某人发疯 ♦ **to be mad at sb** [非正式] 对某人很恼火 ♦ **to be mad about** *or* **on sth** [非正式] 狂热地爱好某物 ♦ **to be mad about** *or* **on sb** [非正式] 迷恋某人 ♦ **like mad** [非正式] 拼命
Madagascar [mædə'gæskə(r)] *n* 马达加斯加
madam ['mædəm] *n* **1** (*form of address*) 女士 **2** [c] [尤英] (*child*) 任性的大小姐 ♦ **Madam Chairman/Speaker** 主席/议长女士 ♦ **Dear Madam** 尊敬的女士
mad cow disease [尤英] *n* [U] (*BSE*) 疯牛病
made [meɪd] **I** *pt, pp of* **make** **II** *adj* ♦ **a British-made car** 一辆英国制造的汽车
made-to-measure ['meɪdtə'mɛʒə(r)] [英] *adj* 量身定做的
made-up ['meɪd'ʌp] *adj* **1** (*wearing make-up*) 化了妆的 **2** (*invented*) [+ *word, name, story*] 编造的
madly ['mædlɪ] *adv* **1** (*frantically*) [*grin, scream, rush* +] 疯狂地 **2** (*extremely*) [+ *jealous, angry*] 极其地 ♦ **madly in love** 深深地爱恋
madman ['mædmən] (*pl* **madmen**) *n* [c] 疯子 ♦ **like a madman** 像个疯子一样
madness ['mædnɪs] *n* [U] **1** (*insanity*) 疯狂 **2** (*foolishness*) 愚蠢 ♦ **it would be madness to do that** 那么做真是愚蠢之极
Mafia ['mæfɪə] *n* ♦ **the Mafia** 黑手党
mag [mæg] [英:非正式] *n* (*magazine*) 杂志
magazine [mægə'ziːn] *n* [c] **1** [出版, 广播, 电视] 杂志 **2** [*of firearm*] 弹匣 **3** [军] (*store*) 弹药库
maggot ['mægət] *n* [c] 蛆
magic ['mædʒɪk] **I** *n* [U] **1** (*supernatural power*) 魔法 **2** (*wonder*) 魔力 **3** (*conjuring*) 魔术 **II** *adj* **1** [+ *formula, solution, cure*] 神奇的 **2** (*special*) [+ *place, moment, experience*] 迷人的 **3** (*supernatural*) 魔法的 ♦ **as if by/like magic** 不可思议 ♦ **the magic number/word** 神

奇数字/咒语

magical ['mædʒɪkl] *adj* 1 (*supernatural*) 魔力的 2 (*wonderful*) 迷人的

magician [mə'dʒɪʃən] *n* [c] (*wizard, conjurer*)魔术师

magistrate ['mædʒɪstreɪt] *n* [c] 地方法官

magnet ['mægnɪt] *n* [c] 1 磁铁 2 ♦**a magnet for** (*attraction*) 吸引物

magnetic [mæg'nɛtɪk] *adj* 1 [物]有磁性的 2 [+ *tape, strip, disk*] 磁的 2 [+ *personality*] 有魅力的

magnificent [mæg'nɪfɪsnt] *adj* (*excellent*) [+ *book, painting*] 极棒的; (*impressive*) [+ *work, performance*] 出色的; (*beautiful*) [+ *building, view, costume*] 华丽的

magnify ['mægnɪfaɪ] *vt* 1 (*enlarge*) [+ *object*] 放大 2 (*amplify*) [+ *sound*] 扩大 3 (*increase*) 加强

magnifying glass ['mægnɪfaɪɪŋ-] *n* [c] 放大镜

magpie ['mægpaɪ] *n* [c] 喜鹊

mahogany [mə'hɔgənɪ] I *n* [U] 红木 II *cpd* [复合词] [+ *table, desk*] 红木

maid [meɪd] *n* [c] (*servant*) 女仆

maiden name *n* [c] 娘家姓

mail [meɪl] I *n* [U] 1 ♦**the mail** (*the post*) 邮政 2 (*letters*) 邮件 3 (*e-mail*) 电子邮件 II *vt* 1 [尤美](*post*) 寄出 [英=**post**] 2 (*e-mail*) 发电邮给 ♦**your cheque is in the mail** 你的支票已寄出 ♦**by mail** 以邮寄方式

mailbox ['meɪlbɔks] *n* [c] 1 [美](*for letters etc*) 信箱 [英=**letterbox**] 2 [美] 邮筒 [英=**post box**] 3 [计算机] 电子信箱

mailing list ['meɪlɪŋ-] *n* [c] 邮寄名单

mailman ['meɪlmæn] (*pl* **mailmen**) [美] *n* [c] 邮差 [英=**postman**]

mail order I *n* [U] (*system*) 邮购 II *cpd* [复合词] ♦**mail-order** [+ *firm, catalogue*] 邮购

mailwoman ['meɪlwumən] (*pl* **mailwomen**) [美] *n* [c] 女邮递员 [英=**postwoman**]

✪ **main** [meɪn] I *adj* [+ *reason, place, entrance, meal*] 主要的 ◊ *My main concern is to protect the children.* 保护孩子们是我主要关心的事。◊ *Mrs Foster hurried through the main entrance.* 福斯特太太匆匆忙忙地从主入口进来了。II *n* (*pipe*) [+ *water, gas*] 总管道 ◊ *A bulldozer had severed a gas main.* 推土机切断了一条煤气总管道。♦**in the main** (*in general*) 大体上

main course *n* [c] 主菜

mainland ['meɪnlənd] I *n* ♦**the mainland** 大陆 II *adj* 大陆的

mainly ['meɪnlɪ] *adv* 主要地

main road *n* [c] 主干道

mains [meɪnz] I *n* [*pl*] [电子] 总输送网 II *cpd* [复合词] [+ *electricity, water, drainage*] 干线

mainstream ['meɪnstriːm] I *n* ♦**the mainstream** 主流 II *adj* [+ *cinema, politics etc*] 主流的

main street [美] *n* [c] 大街 [英 =**high street**]

maintain [meɪn'teɪn] *vt* 1 (*preserve*) [+ *friendship, peace*] 保持 2 (*keep up*) [+ *momentum, output*] 维持 3 (*look after*) [+ *building, equipment*] 保养 4 (*affirm*) [+ *belief, opinion, innocence*] 坚持 5 (*provide for*) [+ *dependant*] 赡养 ♦**to maintain that ...** 坚称… ♦**to maintain o.s.** 养活自己

maintenance ['meɪntənəns] *n* [U] 1 (*running*) [*of building, equipment*] 保养 2 (*preservation*) [*of peace, system*] 维持 3 [法](*alimony*) 赡养费

maize [meɪz] [尤英] *n* [U] 玉米 [美 =**corn**]

majestic [mə'dʒɛstɪk] *adj* 壮观的

majesty ['mædʒɪstɪ] *n* 1 [c] (*title*) ♦**Your/His/Her Majesty** 陛下 2 [U] (*splendour*) 雄伟

✪ **major** ['meɪdʒə(r)] I *adj* 1 (*important, significant*) [+ *event, factor*] 重要的 ◊ *Exercise has a major part to play in preventing disease.* 锻炼对于预防疾病有重要作用。2 [音] [+ *key, scale*] 大调 II *n* [c] 1 [军] 少校 2 [美:教育](*main subject*) 专业 3 ♦**a history major** [美:教育](*student*) 历史专业学生 III *vi* ♦**to major in sth** [美:教育] 主修某专业 ◊ *I decided to major in French.* 我决定主修法语。♦**(symphony/concerto) in C major** C大调(交响乐/协奏曲)

majority [mə'dʒɔrɪtɪ] I *n* 1 [S + PL VB] [*of people, things*] 大多数 2 [c]

(*margin*) [*of votes*] 多数票 **3** [U] (*adulthood*) 成年 **II** *cpd* [复合词] [+ *verdict, holding*] 多数 ♦ **to be in a** *or* **the majority** 占多数 ♦ **the (vast) majority of ...** (绝)大多数…

✪ **make** [meɪk] (*pt, pp* **made**) **I** *vt* **1** (*produce, form*) [+ *object, clothes, cake*] 做 ◊ *Sheila makes her own bread.* 希拉自己做面包。; [+ *noise*] 制造 ◊ *We made a terrible racket as we came out of the club.* 我们大声喧哗着出了夜总会。; [+ *speech*] 发表 ◊ *He made a speech about the need for unity.* 他发表了有关统一之必要的演讲。; [+ *remark, suggestion*] 提出 ◊ *May I make a suggestion?* 我能提个建议吗？; [+ *mistake*] 犯 ◊ *You have made a terrible mistake.* 你犯了个严重的错误。**2** (*manufacture*) [+ *goods*] 生产 ◊ *The firm makes a wide range of electrical goods.* 这家公司生产各种电器产品。**3** (*cause to be*) ♦ **to make sb sad** 使某人难过 ◊ *The whole business makes me really angry.* 整件事使我实在恼火。**4** ♦ **to make sb famous** 使某人成名 ◊ *James Bond, the role that made Sean Connery a star* 詹姆士·邦德，这个使肖恩·康纳利成名的角色 **5** ♦ **to make sth into sth** 将某物改成某物 ◊ *a disused factory that was made into an art gallery* 一座废弃的工厂被改成了美术馆 **6** (*force*) ♦ **to make sb do sth** 促使某人做某事 **7** (*earn*) [+ *money*] 挣 ◊ *He was making nine hundred dollars a week.* 他一周挣900美元。**8** (*equal*) ♦ **2 and 2 make 4** 2加2等于4 **9** [+ *friend, enemy*] 结交 ◊ *I made some good friends at the conference.* 我在会上结交了一些好朋友。◊ *On his first day at school he made friends with a girl called Janet.* 他在上学的头一天结交了一位叫珍妮特的女孩。**10** (*cause to be successful*) 使成功 ◊ *What really makes the book are the illustrations.* 真正使这本书成功的是它的插图。◊ *Meeting you has really made my day!* 能认识你实在是我今天最高兴的事！**11** (*be, constitute*) 成为 ◊ *She'll make a good teacher.* 她将会成为一名好老师。**II** *n* [C] (*brand*) 牌子 ◊ *She couldn't tell what make of car he was driving.* 她看不出他开的是辆什么牌子的车。♦ **to make a profit/loss** 赢利/赔钱 ♦ **to make one's bed** 铺床 ♦ **to make a fool of sb** 愚弄某人 ♦ **to make it** (*arrive*) 及时抵达; (*succeed*) 达成目标; (*in life*) 成功 ♦ **what time do you make it?** 你表几点了？♦ **to make good** (*succeed*) 有成就 ◊ *He was born poor but made good and went to the States.* 他出身贫苦，但后来颇有成就并去了美国。; (*carry out*) [+ *threat, promise*] 履行 ◊ *Arkoff made good his promise.* 阿考夫履行了他的诺言。; (*put right*) [+ *damage, loss*] 弥补 ◊ *Three years was a short time in which to make good the deficiencies.* 用3年时间弥补亏空是很短的。♦ **to make do with sth** 将就某事 ♦ **it's made (out) of glass** 是玻璃做的 ♦ **to have (got) it made** [非正式] 有成功的把握

❑ **make for** *vt* [不可拆分] [+ *place*] 走向 ◊ *He rose from his seat and made for the door.* 他从座位上起身，向门走去。

❑ **make of** *vt* [不可拆分] 看待 ◊ *What did you make of the Prime Minister's speech last night?* 你怎么看待昨晚首相的讲话？

❑ **make off** *vi* 逃走

❑ **make off with** *vt* [不可拆分] 偷走

❑ **make out** *vt* **1** (*understand*) 明白 ◊ *It's difficult to make out what he says.* 他说的话很难让人明白。**2** (*see*) 看出 ◊ *I could just make out the outline of the house.* 我只能看出房子的轮廓。**3** (*write*) [+ *cheque*] 开出 ◊ *I made a cheque out for 300 pounds.* 我开出一张300英镑的支票。**4** (*pretend*) ♦ **to make out that ...** 假装… **5** (*claim, imply*) ♦ **to make sb out to be rich/talented** 把某人说成很富有/有才华 ◊ *He's not as hard as people make out.* 他并不像人们说的那么强硬。♦ **to make out a case for sth** 提出理由证实某事

❑ **make over** *vt* (*assign*) ♦ **to make sth over (to sb)** 把某物的所有权

转让（给某人）◊ *The land was made over to the Council for building purposes.* 这块地的所有权已转让给市议会作为建筑用地。

❑ **make up** I *vt* **1** (*constitute*) 构成 ◊ *Women make up two-fifths of the British labour force.* 妇女构成英国劳动力人数的五分之二。♦ **to be made up of** 由…组成 **2** (*invent*) [+ *story, excuse*] 捏造 ◊ *He was very good at making up excuses.* 他对捏造借口很在行。**3** (*prepare*) [+ *bed*] 准备 **4** (*with cosmetics*) 化妆 ◊ *She spent too much time making herself up.* 她花太多的时间来化妆。
II *vi* (*after quarrel*) 和好 ◊ *She came back and they made up.* 她回来了，他们和好如初。♦ **to make up one's mind** 下定决心 ♦ **to make it up to sb** 对某人作出补偿 ◊ *I'll make it up to you, I promise.* 我保证对你作出补偿。♦ **to make o.s. up** 化妆

❑ **make up for** *vt* ［不可拆分］ [+ *deficiency*] 弥补 ◊ *What the country lacks in natural resources it makes up for in bright ideas.* 国家在自然资源方面的缺乏由明智的决策加以弥补。; [+ *loss, disappointment*] 补偿 ◊ *I'm sorry I broke your vase – I'll make up for it.* 很抱歉打碎了你的花瓶，我会做出补偿的。

makeover ['meɪkəuvə(r)] *n* [c] **1** (*facelift*) [*of person*] 整容; [*of room*] 翻新 **2** (*improvement*) 革新

maker ['meɪkə(r)] *n* [c] **1** (*person*) [*of programme, film etc*] 制作者 **2** (*manufacturer*) 制造商

makeshift ['meɪkʃɪft] *adj* (*temporary*) 临时凑合的

make-up ['meɪkʌp] *n* **1** [u] (*cosmetics*) 化妆品 **2** [s] (*personality*) 性格 **3** [s] (*composition*) 组成

making ['meɪkɪŋ] *n* [u] 制作 ♦ **a star in the making** 一个成长中的明星 ♦ **to have (all) the makings of** 具备…的（所有）素质 ♦ **of one's own making** 自作自受 ♦ **to be the making of sb/sth** 某人/某事成功的因素

malaria [mə'lɛərɪə] *n* [u] 疟疾

Malawi [mə'lɑːwɪ] *n* 马拉维

Malaysia [mə'leɪzɪə] *n* 马来西亚

Malaysian [mə'leɪzɪən] I *adj* 马来西亚的 II *n* [c] (*person*) 马来西亚人

Maldives ['mɔːldaɪvz] *n* [*pl*] ♦ **the Maldives** 马尔代夫群岛

male [meɪl] I *n* [c] **1** (*man*) 男子 **2** ［生物］雄性动物 II *adj* **1** (*in gender*) [+ *employee, child, model, friend, population*] 男的; [+ *animal, insect, plant, tree etc*] 雄性的; **2** (*relating to men*) [+ *role, characteristic, behaviour*] 男性的

male nurse *n* [c] 男护士

malfunction [mæl'fʌŋkʃən] I *n* [c] [*of computer, machine*] 故障 II *vi* [*computer, machine* +] 发生故障

Mali ['mɑːlɪ] *n* 马里

malicious [mə'lɪʃəs] *adj* [+ *person, gossip*] 恶意的

malignant [mə'lɪgnənt] *adj* **1** ［医］ [+ *tumour, growth*] 恶性的 **2** (*harmful, cruel*) [+ *behaviour, intention*] 恶毒的

mall [mɔːl] *n* [c] (*also* : ***shopping mall***) 大型购物中心

mallet ['mælɪt] *n* [c] 木槌

malnutrition [mælnjuː'trɪʃən] *n* [u] 营养不良

malpractice [mæl'præktɪs] *n* [c/u] 渎职

malt [mɔːlt] *n* **1** [u] (*grain*) 麦芽 **2** [c/u] (*also* : ***malt whisky***) 麦芽威士忌酒

Malta ['mɔːltə] *n* 马耳他

Maltese [mɔːl'tiːz] (*pl* **Maltese**) I *adj* 马耳他的 II *n* **1** [c] (*person*) 马耳他人 **2** [u] (*language*) 马耳他语

mammal ['mæml] *n* [c] 哺乳动物

mammoth ['mæməθ] I *adj* (*enormous*) [+ *task*] 巨大的 II *n* [c] ［动］猛犸

✪ **man** [mæn] (*pl* **men**) I *n* **1** [c] (*person*) 男人 ◊ *Larry was a handsome man in his early fifties.* 50刚出头的拉里是个帅气的男人。**2** [u] (*mankind*) 人类 ◊ *the most dangerous substance known to man* 人类所知的最危险的物质 **3** (*form of address*) 老兄 ◊ *Hey man, where d'you get those boots?* 嗨，老兄，你从哪儿搞来的这些靴子？**4** [c] (*in board game*) (*piece*) 棋子 ◊ *Both players begin with the same number of men.* 双方选手以同样数目的棋子开始比赛。II *vt* (*staff*) 在…值班 ◊ *The station is*

seldom manned in the evening. 这个车站晚上很少有人值班。
III men *n* [*pl*] (*troops, workers*) 雇员 ◊ *The men voted to accept the pay offer.* 雇员们投票决定接受工资条件。 ♦**a betting/outdoors man** 好赌博/户外活动的人 ♦**man and wife** 夫妻

manage ['mænɪdʒ] **I** *vt* (*run, control*) [+ *business, shop, time, money*] 管理 **II** *vi* (*cope*) 应付 ♦**to manage to do sth** 设法做到某事 ♦**to manage without sb/sth** 在没有某人/某物的情况下设法对付过去 ♦**he managed a smile** 他勉强一笑

manageable ['mænɪdʒəbl] *adj* [+ *task, number, problem*] 易处理的

management ['mænɪdʒmənt] *n* **1** [U] (*managing*) 管理 **2** [U/S] (*managers*) 管理人员 ♦**under new management** 在新的领导下

manager ['mænɪdʒə(r)] *n* [C] **1** [*of business, department etc*] 经理 **2** [*of entertainer*] 经纪人 **3** [体育] 球队经理 ♦**sales manager** 销售经理

manageress [mænɪdʒə'rɛs] *n* [C] 女经理

managerial [mænɪ'dʒɪərɪəl] *adj* [+ *position, role, skills*] 管理的 ♦**managerial staff** 管理人员

managing director ['mænɪdʒɪŋ-] *n* [C] 总裁

mandarin ['mændərɪn] *n* **1** [U] ♦**Mandarin (Chinese)** 普通话 **2** [C] (*Chinese official*) 官人 **3** [C] [英] (*civil servant*) 内务官员 **4** [C] (*also* : ***mandarin orange***) 柑橘

mandate ['mændeɪt] **I** *n* [C] **1** [政治] 委任 **2** (*authority*) 授权 **II** *vt* ♦**to be mandated to do sth** 被授权做某事

mandatory ['mændətərɪ] *adj* (*obligatory*) 强制的

mane [meɪn] *n* [C] **1** [*of horse*] 马鬃 **2** [*of lion*] 狮鬣 **3** [*of person*] 厚密的头发

maneuver [mə'nuːvə(r)] [美] *vt, vi, n* = **manoeuvre**

mangetout ['mɔnʒ'tuː] [英] *n* [C] 可连荚吃的豆

mangle ['mæŋgl] *vt* (*twist, crush*) 压损

mango ['mæŋgəu] (*pl* **mangoes**) **I** *n* [C] (*fruit*) 芒果 **II** *cpd* [复合词] [+ *juice, yoghurt*] 芒果

manhole ['mænhəul] *n* [C] 检修孔 ♦**manhole cover** 窖井盖

manhood ['mænhud] *n* [U] **1** (*adulthood*) 成年 **2** (*masculinity*) 男子气概

mania ['meɪnɪə] *n* **1** [C] (*craze*) 狂热 **2** [U] (*illness*) 躁狂症

maniac ['meɪnɪæk] *n* [C] **1** (*lunatic*) 疯子 **2** (*idiot*) 傻子 **3** (*freak*) ♦**a baseball/religious maniac** 棒球迷/宗教狂

manic ['mænɪk] *adj* [+ *behaviour, activity*] 疯狂的

manicure ['mænɪkjuə(r)] **I** *n* [C] 修指甲 **II** *vt* 修 ♦**to have a manicure** 修指甲

manifest ['mænɪfɛst] [正式] **I** *vt* (*show, display*) 表明 **II** *adj* (*evident, obvious*) [+ *failure, injustice*] 明显的 **III** *n* [C] [航空, 航海] 舱单 ♦**it manifests itself** 显现出来 ♦**to be/become** *or* **be made manifest** 明了/变得明了

manifesto [mænɪ'fɛstəu] *n* [C] 宣言

manipulate [mə'nɪpjuleɪt] *vt* **1** (*influence*) [+ *person, situation, events*] 操纵; [+ *nature*] 控制 **2** (*handle*) [+ *object, substance*] 熟练使用 **3** [医] [+ *joint*] 推拿 **4** (*operate*) [+ *machine, controls*] 操作

manipulation [mənɪpju'leɪʃən] *n* [C/U] **1** (*influencing*) [*of person, situation, events*] 操纵; [*of nature*] 调控 **2** (*handling*) [*of object, substance*] 使用 **3** [医] 推拿 **4** (*operation*) [*of machine, controls*] 操作

mankind [mæn'kaɪnd] *n* [U] (*human beings*) 人类

manly ['mænlɪ] *adj* [+ *quality, feeling*] 男子气的; [+ *activity*] 适合男子的; [+ *person, appearance*] 男子汉的

man-made ['mæn'meɪd] *adj* 人造的

manner ['mænə(r)] **I** *n* [S] **1** (*way*) 方式 **2** (*behaviour*) 举止 **II manners** *n* [*pl*] (*polite behaviour*) 礼貌 ♦**in a manner of speaking** 在某种意义上 ♦**all manner of objects/things** 各种各样的东西 ♦**to have good/bad manners** 有礼貌/无礼 ♦**it's good/bad manners to arrive on time** 准时是有礼貌/无礼的表现

manoeuvre (美 **maneuver**) [mə'nuːvə(r)] **I** *vt* **1** (*move*) [+ *vehicle, bulky object*] 设法移动 **2** (*manipulate*) [+ *person, things*] 操纵 **II** *vi* (*move*) [*driver, vehicle* +] 驶 **III** *n* [C] **1** (*movement*) 动作 **2** (*move*) 策略 **IV manoeuvres** *n* [*pl*] [军] 演习 ♦**room for manoeuvre** 回旋的余地

manpower ['mænpauə(r)] *n* [U] 人力

mansion ['mænʃən] *n* [C] 宅第

manslaughter ['mænslɔːtə(r)] *n* [U] 过失杀人

mantelpiece ['mæntlpiːs] *n* [C] 壁炉台

manual ['mænjuəl] **I** *adj* **1** [+ *work, worker*] 手工的 **2** (*hand-operated*) [+ *controls, car, gearbox*] 手动的 **3** (*relating to hands*) [+ *dexterity*] 手的 **II** *n* [C] (*handbook*) 手册

manually ['mænjuəlɪ] *adv* [*operate* +] 人工地

manufacture [mænju'fæktʃə(r)] **I** *vt* **1** (*make, produce*) [+ *goods*] 生产 **2** (*fabricate*) [+ *information*] 捏造 **II** *n* [U] (*making*) 生产

manufacturer [mænju'fæktʃərə(r)] *n* [C] 制造商

manure [mə'njuə(r)] *n* [U] 粪肥

manuscript ['mænjuskrɪpt] *n* [C] **1** [*of book, report*] 底稿 **2** (*old document*) 手稿

✪ **many** ['mɛnɪ] **I** *adj* (*a lot of*) [+ *people, things, ideas*] 许多的 ◊ *Many people have been killed.* 许多人被杀害。 ◊ *Not many films are made in Finland.* 芬兰出品的电影不是很多。 **II** *pron* 许多的 ◊ *Some find jobs, but many are forced to beg.* 一些人找到了工作，但许多人被迫去乞讨。 ♦**how many** (*direct question*) 多少 ◊ *How many cigarettes do you smoke a day?* 你一天抽多少支香烟？; (*indirect question*) 多少 ◊ *No-one knows how many people were killed.* 没有人知道有多少人被杀害。 ♦**as many as you can** (*maximum amount*) 尽可能多 ♦**twice as many (as)** (*comparison*) (是…的) 两倍 ◊ *We produce ten times as many tractors as the United States.*我们生产的拖拉机是美国的10 倍。 ♦**as many as ten thousand people** (*emphatic*) 一万人之多 ♦**a good** *or* **great many** 相当多 ♦**many a time** 许多次

map [mæp] **I** *n* [C] 地图 **II** *vt* (*make a map of*) 绘制…的地图

❑ **map out** *vt* **1** [+ *plan, task*] 筹划 **2** [+ *career*] 安排

maple ['meɪpl] **I** *n* **1** [C/U] (*tree*) 枫树 **2** [U] (*wood*) 枫木 **II** *cpd* [复合词] [+ *wood, tree, leaf*] 枫

Mar. *abbr* (= ***March***) 三月

mar [mɑː(r)] *vt* (*spoil*) 毁坏

marathon ['mærəθən] **I** *n* [C] (*race*) 马拉松长跑 **II** *adj* 马拉松式的

marble ['mɑːbl] **I** *n* **1** [U] (*stone*) 大理石 **2** [C] (*glass ball*) 弹子 **II** *cpd* [复合词] [+ *tiles, statue, fireplace*] 大理石 **III marbles** *n* [*pl*] (*game*) 弹子游戏 ♦**to lose one's marbles** [非正式] 丧失理智

✪ **March** [mɑːtʃ] *n* [C/U] 三月 *see also* **July**

march [mɑːtʃ] **I** *vi* **1** [军] [*soldiers* +] 行军 **2** [*protesters* +] 行进 **3** (*walk briskly*) 快步走 **II** *vt* **1** 使行军 **2** 迫使前进 **III** *n* [C] **1** [军] 行军 **2** (*demonstration*) 游行示威 **3** ♦**the march of progress** 事情的进展

> **MARDI GRAS**
> **Mardi Gras** 即为基督教的 **Shrove Tuesday**（忏悔星期二），是 **Lent**（大斋节）开始的前一天。复活节之前的40 天为 **Lent**，基督徒有在这个期间斋戒的传统 。**Mardi Gras** 的名称来自法语，原意为 **fat Tuesday**，因为在这一天，人们在斋戒前要吃掉所有油腻的食物。在某些地方，比如，美国新奥尔良的南部城市，这天是人们纵情狂欢的时刻，人们穿上五颜六色的盛装，在街头载歌载舞。

mare [mɛə(r)] *n* [C] 母马

margarine [mɑːdʒə'riːn] *n* [U] 人造黄油

margin ['mɑːdʒɪn] *n* [C] **1** (*difference*) (*of votes, points*) 差数 **2** (*extra amount*) (*for safety, error etc*) 余地 **3** (*space*) [*of page*] 页边空白 **4** (*edge*) 边缘 ♦**(on) the margins (of sth)** （在）（某事

物的）边缘

marginal ['mɑːdʒɪnl] **I** *adj* **1** (*minor*) [+ *increase, improvement*] 微小的 **2** [+ *person, group*] (*socially excluded*) 边缘的 **II** [英] *n* (*also* : ***marginal seat***) 边座

marginally ['mɑːdʒɪnəlɪ] *adv* [+ *different, better etc*] 稍许; [*improve, increase, etc* +] 稍微

marigold ['mærɪgəuld] *n* [c] 金盏花

marijuana [mærɪ'wɑːnə] *n* [u] 大麻

marina [mə'riːnə] *n* [c] 小艇船坞

marinade ['mærɪneɪd] **I** *n* [c] 腌泡汁 **II** *vt, vi* = **marinate**

marinate ['mærɪneɪt] **I** *vt* 使浸泡 **II** *vi* 腌泡

marine [mə'riːn] **I** *adj* **1** [+ *life, plant, biology*] 海洋的 **2** (*maritime*) [+ *engineering, law, insurance*] 海事的 **II** *n* [c] (*soldier*) 海军陆战队士兵

marital ['mærɪtl] *adj* 婚姻的

marital status *n* [u] 婚姻状况

maritime ['mærɪtaɪm] *adj* [+ *nation, museum*] 海洋的 ♦**maritime law** 海事法

marjoram ['mɑːdʒərəm] *n* [u] 墨角兰

mark [mɑːk] **I** *n* **1** [c] (*cross, tick etc*) 记号 **2** [c] (*stain*) 污点 **3** [c] (*trace*) [*of shoes, fingers, tyres*] 印迹 **4** [s] (*token*) 特征 **5** [c] [英] (*grade, score*) 分数 **6** (*level, stage*) ♦**the halfway mark** 中点标志 **7** (*version, model*) ♦**Mark 3 Ford Escort** 福特护卫者3型 **II** *vt* **1** (*with word, symbol*) 标明 **2** (*stain, damage*) [+ *clothes, furniture*] 留痕迹于 **3** (*indicate*) [+ *place*] 标示 **4** (*signal*) [+ *event*] 标志 **5** (*characterize*) 以…为特征 **6** [英:教育] 评分 **7** [尤英:体育] [+ *player*] 盯住 **III** *vi* (*stain*) 留下痕迹 ♦**to leave your** *or* **a mark** 留下你的/深远影响 ♦**to make one's mark** 成名 ♦**"on your marks** *or* [美] **mark"** [体育] "各就各位" ◊ *On your marks, get set, go!* 各就各位，预备，跑！ ♦**to be up to the mark** 达到要求的标准 ♦**to be quick/slow off the mark (in doing sth)** 不失时机地/慢吞吞地开始（做某事） ♦**to be wide of the mark** [*claim, estimate* +] 毫不相干 ♦**to mark time** 原地踏步

❑**mark down** *vt* **1** (*reduce*) [+ *prices, goods*] 削价 **2** (*write down*) 记下

❑**mark off** *vt* (*tick off*) 标记出

❑**mark out** *vt* **1** [+ *area, road*] 划出 **2** [+ *person, place*] 区别

❑**mark up** *vt* (*increase*) [+ *price, goods*] 标高

marked [mɑːkt] *adj* (*obvious*) 显著的 ♦**in marked contrast to...** 与…形成鲜明对照 ♦**he is a marked man** 他被盯上了

marker ['mɑːkə(r)] *n* [c] **1** (*sign*) 标识 **2** (*also* : ***marker pen***) 记号笔

✪**market** ['mɑːkɪt] **I** *n* [c] **1** (*in town, village etc*) (*place*) 市场; (*event*) 集市 **2** (*demand*) 市场 ◊ *The foreign market was increasingly important.* 国外市场日益重要起来。 **II** *vt* 销售 ♦**to be on/come onto the market** 在市场上出售 ♦**on the open market** 在开放的市场上 ♦**to play the market** [经济] 投机倒把

marketing ['mɑːkɪtɪŋ] **I** *n* [u] 市场营销 **II** *cpd* [复合词] [+ *campaign, director*] 销售

marketplace ['mɑːkɪtpleɪs] *n* [c] **1** [商] ♦**the marketplace** 市场 **2** (*area, site*) 集市场

market research *n* [u] 市场调查

marmalade ['mɑːməleɪd] *n* [c/u] 橘子酱

> **MARMALADE**
>
> **marmalade**（橘子酱）是由略带苦味的橘子，有时也用柠檬或柚子，腌制而成。**marmalade** 澄亮透明，往往还带着碎碎的橘子皮。在早餐时，将**marmalade** 涂抹在面包或烤面包片上食用。

maroon [mə'ruːn] **I** *adj* (*colour*) 褐红色的 **II** *vt* ♦**to be marooned** (*stranded*) 被困

marquee [mɑː'kiː] *n* [c]大帐篷

marriage ['mærɪdʒ] *n* **1** [c/u] (*relationship, institution*) 婚姻 **2** [c] (*wedding*) 婚礼 ♦**marriage of convenience** 权宜婚姻

marriage certificate *n* [c] 结婚证书

married ['mærɪd] *adj* **1** [+ *man, woman*] 已婚的 **2** [+ *life*] 婚姻的 ♦**a**

married man/woman 有妇之夫/有夫之妇 ♦ **to be married to sb** 和某人结婚 ♦ **to get married** 结婚
marrow [ˈmærəu] *n* 1 [c/u] (*vegetable*) 西葫芦 2 [u] (*bone marrow*) 骨髓
marry [ˈmærɪ] **I** *vt* 1 [*man, woman* +] 和…结婚 2 [*priest, registrar* +] 为…主持婚礼 **II** *vi* 结婚
Mars [mɑːz] *n* (*planet*) 火星
marsh [mɑːʃ] *n* [c/u] (*bog*) 沼泽
marshal [ˈmɑːʃl] **I** *n* [c] 1 (*official*) (*at sports meeting etc*) 典礼官 2 [美:警察] 执法官 3 [军] (*also* : ***field marshal, air marshal***) 元帅 **II** *vt* 1 (*organize*) [+ *resources, support*] 聚集 2 [+ *soldiers*] 集结
martial art [ˈmɑːʃl-] *n* [c] 武术 ♦ **the martial arts** 武术
martyr [ˈmɑːtə(r)] **I** *n* [c] 殉道者 **II** *vt* (*kill*) 使成为殉道者
marvel [ˈmɑːvl] **I** *n* [c] (*wonder*) 奇迹 **II** *vi* ♦ **to marvel at sth** 对某事感到大为惊讶
marvellous (美 **marvelous**) [ˈmɑːvləs] *adj* 极好的
Marxism [ˈmɑːksɪzəm] *n* [u] 马克思主义
Marxist [ˈmɑːksɪst] **I** *adj* 马克思主义的 **II** *n* [c] 马克思主义者
marzipan [ˈmɑːzɪpæn] *n* [u] 杏仁蛋白糊
mascara [mæsˈkɑːrə] *n* [u] 睫毛膏
mascot [ˈmæskət] *n* [c] 吉祥物
masculine [ˈmæskjulɪn] *adj* 1 (*of men*) [+ *characteristic, value etc*] 男性的 2 (*manly*) [+ *man, woman, image*] 男子气的; [+ *room, clothes*] 男性化的 3 [语言] [+ *pronoun etc*] 阳性的
mash [mæʃ] [烹饪] **I** *vt* (*also* : ***mash up***) 把…捣成糊状 **II** *n* [u] [英:非正式] (*mashed potato*) 土豆泥
mashed potato [mæʃt-] *n* [c/u] 土豆泥
mask [mɑːsk] **I** *n* [c] 1 (*disguise*) 面罩 2 (*protection*) 口罩 3 (*concealing emotions*) 伪装 **II** *vt* (*hide*) [+ *feelings*] 掩饰; [+ *object*] 遮住 ♦ **a masked man** (*robber etc*) 戴面具的人
mason [ˈmeɪsn] *n* [c] 1 (*also* : ***stone mason***) 石匠 2 (*also* : ***freemason***) 共济会会员
masonry [ˈmeɪsnrɪ] *n* [u] (*stonework*) 砖石结构
mass [mæs] **I** *n* 1 [c] (*large amount, number*) [*of objects, people, substance*] 大量 2 [c] (*area, volume*) [*of air, water, land*] 团 3 [c/u] [物] [*of object*] 体积 4 [c/u] [宗] ♦ **Mass** 弥撒 **II** *cpd* [复合词] [+ *communication, unemployment etc*] 大规模 **III** *vi* [*troops, protesters* +] 聚集 **IV** *vt* [+ *troops*] 集结 **V the masses** *n* [*pl*] 群众 ♦ **masses of** [非正式] 大量 ♦ **to go to Mass** 去做弥撒
massacre [ˈmæsəkə(r)] **I** *n* [c/u] 大屠杀 **II** *vt* 大规模屠杀
📖 用法参见 **kill**
massage [ˈmæsɑːʒ] **I** *n* [c/u] 按摩 **II** *vt* 1 按摩 2 (*manipulate*) [+ *statistics*] 篡改 ♦ **to give sb a massage** 为某人按摩
massive [ˈmæsɪv] *adj* 1 (*huge*) [+ *amount, increase etc*] 巨大的; [+ *explosion*] 大规模的 2 [+ *heart attack, haemorrhage*] 严重的 3 [非正式] (*emphatic*) 极大的
mass media *n* ♦ **the mass media** 大众传媒
mass-produce [ˈmæsprəˈdjuːs] *vt* [+ *goods, cars etc*] 批量生产
mass-produced [ˈmæsprəˈdjuːst] *adj* 批量生产的
mast [mɑːst] *n* [c] 1 [航海] 船桅 2 (*for radio, television etc*) 天线杆
master [ˈmɑːstə(r)] **I** *n* [c] 1 [*of servant, dog*] 主人 2 [*of situation*] 主宰者 3 [过时] (*teacher*) (*in secondary school*) 男教师 4 [过时] ♦ **Master Simon** 西蒙少爷 5 [过时] (*on envelope*) ♦ **Master Simon Fisher** 西蒙・费舍先生 6 [艺术,音等] 大师 7 (*also* : ***master copy***) 母版 8 ♦ **master's (degree)** 硕士(学位) **II** *cpd* [复合词] [+ *baker, craftsman, builder etc*] 师傅 **III** *vt* 1 (*overcome*) [+ *situation, difficulty, feeling*] 控制 2 (*learn*) [+ *skill, language*] 掌握
mastermind [ˈmɑːstəmaɪnd] **I** *vt* 策划 **II** *n* [c] 策划者
Master of Arts *n* [s] 1 (*degree*) 文学硕士学位 2 (*person*) 文学硕士
Master of Science *n* [s] 1 (*degree*) 理学硕士学位 2 (*person*) 理学硕士
masterpiece [ˈmɑːstəpiːs] *n* [c] 1 (*great work*) 杰作 2 (*greatest work*)

♦ **sb's masterpiece** 某人最杰出的作品 **3** (*superb example*) ♦ **a masterpiece of sth** 某事的典范

mat [mæt] **I** *n* [c] **1** (*on floor*) 席 **2** (*also : **doormat***) 门口地垫 **3** (*also : **table mat***) 桌垫 **II** *adj* = **matt**

✪ **match** [mætʃ] **I** *n* **1** [c] (*game*) [*of football, tennis etc*] 比赛 **2** [c] (*for lighting fire etc*) 火柴 **3** (*combination*) ♦ **to be a good/perfect match** [*colours, clothes* +] 很/非常相称 ◊ *Helen's choice of lipstick was a good match for her skin-tone.* 海伦选的唇膏和她的肤色非常相称。**II** *vt* **1** (*go well with*) [*colours, clothes* +] 和…相配 ◊ *The lampshades matched the curtains.* 灯罩和窗帘很相配。**2** ♦ **to match sth to** *or* **with sth** (*coordinate*) 使某物和某物相配 ◊ *She likes to match her lipstick with her outfit.* 她喜欢用和她的服饰相配的口红。; (*put together*) 使某物和某物相匹配 ◊ *an organization which matches job seekers with vacancies* 把求职者安排在相应空缺岗位上的机构 **3** (*also : **match up***) [+ *socks, gloves etc*] 配成对 ◊ *She was trying to match all the odd socks that were lying about.* 她正试着把散落四处的单只袜子配成对。**4** (*equal*) 比得上 ◊ *efforts to match ever-increasing demand by building new schools* 建立新学校以努力满足不断增长的需求 **5** (*correspond to*) 和…一致 ◊ *check that the buyer's name matches the name on the credit card* 检查一下买主姓名是否和信用卡上的姓名一致 **III** *vi* **1** (*go together*) [*colours, materials* +] 相配 ◊ *All the chairs matched.* 所有的椅子都很搭配。**2** (*correspond*) 相符合 ◊ *The sale will only go ahead if the serial numbers match.* 只有当序号都相符合时，销售才能继续进行。♦ **to be no match for sb/sth** 同某人/某物没法相比 ♦ **to be** *or* **make a good match** [*couple* +] 很般配的一对 ◊ *Don't they make a good match?* 他们真是很般配的一对！♦ **to meet one's match** 遇到对手 ♦ **with shoes to match** 配以合适的鞋子

❑ **match up to** *vt* [不可拆分] 配得上

matchbox [ˈmætʃbɔks] *n* [c] 火柴盒

matching [ˈmætʃɪŋ] *adj* [+ *clothes, curtains etc*] 相称的

mate [meɪt] **I** *n* [c] **1** [英:非正式] (*friend*) 伙伴 **2** (*animal*) 配偶 **3** [航海] (*also : **first mate***) 大副; [军] (*junior officer*) 军士 **4** (*assistant*) 助手 **II** *vi* [*animals* +] 交配

material [məˈtɪərɪəl] **I** *n* **1** [c/u] (*substance*) 材料 **2** [c/u] (*cloth*) 衣料 **3** [u] (*information, data*) 资料 **II** *adj* **1** (*physical*) 物质的 **2** [正式] (*relevant*) [+ *evidence*] 决定性的 **III materials** *n* [*pl*] (*equipment*) 用具

materialize [məˈtɪərɪəlaɪz] *vi* **1** (*happen*) [*problem, event* +] 出现 **2** (*suddenly appear*) 突然出现

maternal [məˈtəːnl] *adj* **1** [+ *feelings, role*] 母亲的 **2** [+ *grandfather, aunt etc*] 母系的

maternity [məˈtəːnɪtɪ] **I** *n* [u] (*motherhood*) 母亲身份 **II** *cpd* [复合词] [+ *clothes, ward, care*] 孕产妇

maternity hospital *n* [c] 产科医院

maternity leave *n* [u] 产假 ♦ **to be on maternity leave** 休产假

math [mæθ] [美] *n* = **maths**

mathematical [mæθəˈmætɪkl] *adj* **1** [+ *formula, calculation*] 数学的 **2** [+ *mind, abilities*] 数学方面的

mathematician [mæθəməˈtɪʃən] *n* [c] **1** (*by career*) 数学家 **2** (*mathematically gifted person*) 数学好的人

mathematics [mæθəˈmætɪks] [正式] *n* [u] 数学

maths [mæθs] [英] *n* [u] 数学 [美 = **math**]

matinée [ˈmætɪneɪ] **I** *n* [c] 午后的演出 **II** *cpd* [复合词] [+ *performance*] 下午场

matron [ˈmeɪtrən] [英] *n* [c] **1** (*in nursing home, hospital*) 护士长 **2** (*in school*) 女舍监

matt, matte, mat [mæt] *adj* [+ *colour, finish, paint*] 无光泽的

matted [ˈmætɪd] *adj* [+ *hair*] 缠结的

✪ **matter** [ˈmætə(r)] **I** *n* **1** [c] (*affair, situation, problem*) 事件 ◊ *Will you report the matter to the authorities?* 你会将该事件报告给当局吗？**2** [u] [物] 物质 ◊ *An atom is the*

smallest indivisible particle of matter. 原子是最小的不可分的物质微粒。**3** [U] ♦**waste/vegetable matter** 废物/植物 **II** *vi* (*be important*) 要紧 ◊ *Your happiness is the only thing that matters.* 你的幸福是惟一要紧的事。**III matters** *n* [*pl*] 事态 ◊ *It is hard to see how this would improve matters.* 很难看出这会对事态有怎样的改善。
♦**what's the matter (with ...)?** (…)怎么了? ♦**in a matter of days/weeks** 仅几天/几周 ♦**as a matter of urgency** *or* **priority** 作为紧急{或}优先考虑的事情 ♦**no matter what** (*whatever happens*) 不管发生什么 ♦**another** *or* **a different matter** 另一回事 ♦**it is only a matter of time** 这仅仅是时间问题 ♦**as a matter of course** 理所当然的事 ♦**as a matter of fact** 事实上 ♦**for that matter** (*used for emphasis*) 而且 ♦**no matter how/what/who**不管怎样/无论什么/无论谁 ♦**it doesn't matter** 没关系

matter-of-fact ['mætərəv'fækt] *adj* [+ *person, voice, attitude etc*] 不带感情的

mattress ['mætrɪs] *n* [C] 床垫

mature [mə'tjuə(r)] **I** *adj* **1** (*not childlike*) 成熟的 **2** (*fully grown*) 成年的 **3** (*ripe*) [+ *cheese, wine*] 酿熟的 **II** *vi* **1** (*grow up*) [*person* +] 长成 **2** (*develop*) [*artist, style* +] 成熟 **3** (*ripen, age*) [*cheese, wine etc* +] 酿熟 **4** [经济] 到期 **III** *vt* [+ *wine, cheese*] 使酿熟 ♦**mature cheddar (cheese)** 浓味切达干酪

mature student [英] *n* [C] 成年学生

maturity [mə'tjuərɪtɪ] *n* [U] (*adulthood, wisdom*) 成熟

maul [mɔːl] *vt* **1** [*lion, bear, dog etc* +] 伤害 **2** (*criticize*) 抨击

Mauritania [mɔːrɪ'teɪnɪə] *n* 毛里塔尼亚

Mauritius [mə'rɪʃəs] *n* 毛里求斯

mauve [məuv] *adj* 淡紫色的

maverick ['mævrɪk] **I** *n* [C] 自行其是的人 **II** *adj* 自行其是的

max. *abbr* = **maximum**

maximize ['mæksɪmaɪz] *vt* **1** [+ *profit, output, efficiency etc*] 使增至最大限度 **2** [计算机] 使…最大化 ◊ *Click on the square icon to maximize the window.* 点击方形图标使窗口最大化。

maximum ['mæksɪməm] **I** *adj* **1** (*highest, greatest*) [+ *speed, height*] 最高的; [+ *weight*] 最重的; [+ *sentence*] 最严厉的 **2** (*great*) 最大的 **II** *n* [C] 最大量 ♦**a maximum of two years** 至多两年 ♦**six weeks maximum** 6 星期的最高极限

✪ **May** [meɪ] *n* [C/U] 五月 *see also* **July**

✪ **may**

KEYWORD

[meɪ] *aux vb*

1 (*possibility*) ♦**it may rain later** 等会儿可能要下雨 ♦**we may not be able to come** 我们可能来不了 ♦**he may be out** 他可能出去了 ♦**he may have hurt himself** 他可能伤了自己 ♦**the coat may be worn with or without the hood** 外套可以连帽穿也可以不连帽穿

2 (*permission*) ♦**may I come in?** 我可以进来吗? ♦**may I offer you a glass of wine?** 给你来一杯酒好吗? ♦**you may go now** 你现在可以走了

3 (*conceding*) ♦**I may be old, but I'm not stupid** 我也许是老了,但绝不愚蠢; (*expressing wishes*) 祝愿 ♦**may you be very happy together!** 祝愿你们百年好合!

4 (*in expressions*) ♦**you may as well go** 你不妨也去 ♦**come what may** 无论发生什么事

maybe ['meɪbiː] *adv* **1** (*indicating uncertainty, concession*) 可能 **2** (*making suggestions*) 也许 **3** (*estimating*) 大概 ♦**maybe so/not** 也许如此/不是

May Day *n* [U] 五一节

mayhem ['meɪhɛm] *n* [U] 混乱

mayonnaise [meɪə'neɪz] *n* [U] 蛋黄酱 ♦**egg/tuna mayonnaise** 蛋黄酱鸡蛋/金枪鱼

mayor [mɛə(r)] *n* [C] 市长

mayoress ['mɛərɛs] [英] *n* [C] **1** (*female mayor*) 女市长 **2** (*wife of mayor*) 市长夫人

maze [meɪz] *n* [c] **1** (*puzzle*) 迷宫 **2** ♦**maze of streets/corridors** 迷宫似的街道/走廊 **3** ♦**maze of rules/jargon** 错综复杂的规则/术语

MBA *n abbr* (= ***Master of Business Administration***) (*qualification*) 工商管理硕士学位; (*person*) 工商管理硕士

MD *n abbr* **1** (= ***Doctor of Medicine***) (*with doctorate*) 医学博士; [美] (*with degree*) 医学博士 **2** [尤英: 商] (= ***Managing Director***) 总经理 **3** = **MiniDisc®**

MDT [美] *abbr* (= ***Mountain Daylight Time***) 山区时间

✪ **me** [miː] *pron* 我 ◊ *He loves me.* 他爱我。◊ *Give me the key.* 把钥匙给我。♦**it's me** 是我

meadow [ˈmɛdəu] *n* [c] 草地

meagre (美 **meager**) [ˈmiːgə(r)] *adj* 微薄的

meal [miːl] *n* **1** [c] (*occasion*) 一餐 **2** [c] (*food*) 膳食 **3** [u] (*flour*) 粗磨粉 ♦**to go out for a meal** 出去吃饭 ♦**to make a meal of sth** [英: 非正式] 对某事做得太过分

> 📖 每天的第一顿饭叫做 **breakfast**。午餐最常用的表达法是 **lunch**，但是在英国的某些地方，或在某些场合下，也可以用 **dinner**。*He seldom has lunch at all ... school dinners ... Christmas dinner.* **dinner** 通常用来指晚餐。在英式英语里，它还可以指正式的或特殊的一餐。*In the evening they had a dinner to celebrate.* **supper** 和 **tea** 有时也被用来表示晚餐，但也有人用 **supper** 表示夜宵，用 **tea** 表示下午小餐。

mealtime [ˈmiːltaɪm] *n* [c/u] 吃饭时间

✪ **mean** [miːn] (*pt, pp* **meant**) **I** *vt* **1** (*signify*) 表示…意思 ◊ *What does "imperialism" mean?* "imperialism"是什么意思？◊ *In modern Welsh, "glas" means "blue".* 在现代威尔士语中，"glas"表示的意思是蓝色。**2** (*refer to*) 意指 ◊ *I thought you meant her, not me.* 我想你指的是她，不是我。**3** (*involve*) 意味着 ◊ *Becoming a millionaire didn't mean an end to his money worries.* 成为百万富翁并不意味着他不再被钱困扰。**4** (*intend*) ♦**to mean to do sth** 意欲做某事 **5** ♦**a film meant for adults** 针对成人的电影 **II** *adj* **1** (*not generous*) 吝啬的 **2** (*unkind*) [+ *person*] 刻薄的 **3** [美: 非正式] (*cruel*) [+ *person, animal*] 残忍的 **4** (*shabby*) [+ *street, lodgings*] 破旧的 ♦**I mean it, I mean what I say** 我是当真的 ♦**what do you mean?** 你什么意思？♦**do you mean it?** 你当真吗？♦**to mean a lot to sb** 对某人很重要 ♦**I mean** 我是说 ♦**he's meant to be an expert** (*reputed*) 他被公认为专家 ♦**to be mean with sth** (*ungenerous*) 在某事上很吝啬 ♦**to be mean to sb** (*unkind*) 对某人刻薄 ♦**he plays a mean guitar** [非正式] 他弹吉他很出色 ♦**he's no mean pianist/footballer** 他是位很好的钢琴家/足球运动员 *see also* **means**

meaning [ˈmiːnɪŋ] *n* **1** [c/u] (*sense, signification*) [*of word, expression*] 意思; [*of symbol, dream, gesture*] 含义 **2** [u] (*purpose, value*) 意义

meaningful [ˈmiːnɪŋful] *adj* **1** [+ *result, explanation*] 有意义的 **2** [+ *glance, remark*] 意味深长的 **3** [+ *relationship, occasion*] 有意义的

meaningless [ˈmiːnɪŋlɪs] *adj* **1** (*nonsensical*) 无意义的 **2** (*pointless*) 无目的的

means [miːnz] (*pl* **means**) **I** *n* [c] (*method*) 方法 **II** *n* [*pl*] [正式] (*money*) 财富 ♦**by means of** 通过 ♦**by all means!** 当然！♦**by no means** 决不

meant [mɛnt] *pt, pp of* **mean**

meantime [ˈmiːntaɪm] **I** *n* ♦**in the meantime** 同时 **II** *adv* [美] 在此期间

meanwhile [ˈmiːnwaɪl] *adv* 同时

measles [ˈmiːzlz] *n* [u] 麻疹

measure [ˈmɛʒə(r)] **I** *vt* **1** [+ *size, distance, temperature etc*] 测量 **2** (*evaluate*) [+ *impact, success, performance*] 衡量 **II** *vi* [*room, person, object* +] 有 **III** *n* **1** [c] (*step*) 措施 **2** [正式] (*degree, amount*) ♦**a** *or* **some**

measure of 相当程度的 **3** ♦ **a/the measure of** [+ *achievement, situation*] 一定程度的 **4** [c] (*serving*) [*of whisky, brandy etc*] 固定量 **5** [c] [美:音] 小节 [英=**bar**] ♦ **to take measures to do sth** [正式] 采取措施以应对某事 ♦ **for good measure** 另外 ♦ **beyond measure** (*used for emphasis*) 非常地
❑ **measure up** *vi* ♦ **to measure up (to sth)** 符合(某标准)

measurement ['mɛʒəmənt] **I** *n* **1** [c] (*length, width etc*) 尺寸 **2** [u] (*process of measuring*) 测量
II measurements *n* [*pl*] [*of person*] 三围 ♦ **chest/hip measurement** 胸围/臀围 ♦ **to take measurements** 量尺寸

meat [miːt] **I** *n* [u] 肉 **II** *cpd* [复合词] [+ *product, dish, pie*] 肉类 ♦ **crab meat** 蟹肉

meatball ['miːtbɔːl] *n* [c] 肉丸

Mecca ['mɛkə] *n* **1** [地理] 麦加 **2** [c] (喻) ♦ **mecca** 向往的地方

mechanic [mɪ'kænɪk] *n* [c] 机械工

mechanical [mɪ'kænɪkl] *adj* **1** [+ *device, problem, work*] 机械的 **2** (*automatic*) [+ *gestures*] 呆板的

mechanical engineering *n* [u] (*science*) 机械工程

mechanics [mɪ'kænɪks] **I** *n* [u] [物] 力学 **II** *n* [*pl*] [*of process, system, government*] 构成

mechanism ['mɛkənɪzəm] *n* [c] **1** (*device*) 机械装置 **2** (*procedure*) 途径 **3** (*reflex*) 本能反应

medal ['mɛdl] *n* [c] (*award*) 奖章

medallist (美 **medalist**) ['mɛdlɪst] *n* [c] 奖牌获得者 ♦ **gold/silver medallist** 金牌/银牌获得者

meddle ['mɛdl] *vi* ♦ **to meddle** 干预 ♦ **to meddle with** *or* **in sth** 干预某事

media ['miːdɪə] **I** *pl of* **medium II** *n* [*pl*] ♦ **the media** 媒体 **III** *cpd* [复合词] [+ *coverage, attention, bias*] 媒体

mediaeval [mɛdɪ'iːvl] *adj* = **medieval**

median strip ['miːdɪən-] [美:汽车] *n* [c] 中央分车带 [英=**central reservation**]

mediate ['miːdɪeɪt] *vi* 调停

medical ['mɛdɪkl] **I** *adj* [+ *treatment, care*] 医疗的 **II** *n* [c] (*examination*) 体格检查

medical certificate *n* [c] 诊断书

medical student *n* [c] 医科学生

medicated ['mɛdɪkeɪtɪd] *adj* [+ *soap, shampoo*] 含药物的

medication [mɛdɪ'keɪʃən] *n* [c/u] 药物 ♦ **to be on medication** 进行药物治疗

medicinal [mɛ'dɪsɪnl] *adj* [+ *substance*] 药用的; [+ *qualities, effects*] 药疗的

medicine ['mɛdsɪn] *n* **1** [u] (*science*) 医学 **2** [c/u] (*medication*) 药

medieval, mediaeval [mɛdɪ'iːvl] *adj* 中世纪的

mediocre [miːdɪ'əukə(r)] *adj* 平庸的

meditate ['mɛdɪteɪt] *vi* **1** 冥想 **2** (*reflect*) 沉思 ♦ **to meditate on sth** 对某事进行深思

meditation [mɛdɪ'teɪʃən] *n* **1** [u] (*ritual*) 冥想 **2** [c] (*thought*) 沉思

Mediterranean [mɛdɪtə'reɪnɪən] **I** *n* ♦ **the Mediterranean** (*sea*) 地中海; (*region*) 地中海沿岸地区 **II** *adj* [+ *climate, diet*] 地中海地区的

medium ['miːdɪəm] (*pl* **media** *or* **mediums**) **I** *adj* **1** (*average*) [+ *size, height*] 中等的 **2** (*clothing size*) 中码的 **II** *n* [c] **1** (*means*) [*of communication*] 媒介 **2** (*substance, material*) 传导体 **3** (*pl* **mediums**) (*person*) 灵媒 ♦ **to strike** *or* **find a happy medium** 找到一种折中办法

medium-sized ['miːdɪəm'saɪzd] *adj* 中等大小的

medium wave [尤英] *n* [u] 中波

meek [miːk] *adj* 温顺的

✪ **meet** [miːt] (*pt, pp* **met**) **I** *vt* **1** [+ *friend*] (*accidentally*) 遇见 ◊ *I met Dave this morning while I was out shopping.* 我今天早晨出去购物的时候遇见了戴夫。; (*by arrangement*) 和…见面 ◊ *I could meet you for a drink after work.* 我可以下班后和你见面去喝一杯。 **2** [+ *stranger*] (*for the first time*) 结识 ◊ *I met a Swedish girl on the train from Copenhagen.* 我在从哥本哈根开出的火车上结识了一位瑞典女孩。; (*be introduced to*) 认识 ◊ *Hey, Terry, come and meet my Dad.* 嗨，特里，来介绍你认识我爸爸。

3 (*go and fetch*) (*at station, airport*) 接 ◊ *Dan came to the airport to meet me.* 丹来机场接我。4 [+ *opponent*] 对抗 ◊ *Arsenal meet Liverpool in the next round of the Cup.* 在足总杯下一轮的比赛中，阿森纳队将和利物浦队对抗。5 (*satisfy*) [+ *need, condition*] 达到 ◊ *Certain standards must be met by all applicants.* 所有的申请者都必须达到这些标准。6 (*deal with*) [+ *problem, challenge, deadline*] 应付 ◊ *It is going to be difficult to meet the deadline.* 很难在截止日期前完成。7 (*pay*) [+ *expenses, bill, cost*] 支付 ◊ *The government will meet the cost of any damage.* 政府将支付任何损失费用。8 (*join*) [*line, road, area* +] 汇合 ◊ *where the Atlantic meets the Indian Ocean* 大西洋和印度洋汇合的地方 9 (*touch*) 接触 ◊ *The plane jolted as the wheels met the ground.* 轮子触地后飞机颠簸前行。10 [+ *eyes, gaze*] 正视 ◊ *Nina's eyes met her sister's across the table.* 尼娜和坐在桌子另一边的姐姐互相对视着。**II** *vi* 1 [*friends* +] (*accidentally*) 相遇 ◊ *They met again while walking their dogs in Hyde Park.* 他们在海德公园遛狗的时候又相遇了。; (*by arrangement*) 见面 ◊ *After that they met every day.* 此后他们天天见面。2 [*strangers* +] (*for the first time*) 认识 ◊ *I don't think we've met, have we?* 我想我们不认识，对吧？ 3 [*club, committee etc* +] (*for talks, discussion*) 开会 ◊ *The committee meets four times a year.* 委员会一年开4次会。4 (*join*) [*lines, roads, areas* +] 相交 ◊ *Parallel lines never meet.* 平行线永远不会相交。5 [*opponents* +] 交手 ◊ *The two women will meet tomorrow in the final.* 这两位女选手将在明天的决赛中交手。6 (*touch*) 相碰 ◊ *Their mouths met.* 他们相吻了。7 [*eyes* +] 相遇 ◊ *Our eyes met.* 我们的目光相遇了。**III** *n* [c] 1 [英] (*in hunting*) 集合 2 [美:体育] 比赛 ◊ *a track meet* 一场田径比赛 ♦ **pleased to meet you** 见到你很高兴 ♦ **nice to have met you** 很高兴认识你

❑ **meet up** *vi* (*by arrangement*) 会面 ◊ *We meet up for lunch once a week.* 我们每周会面一次共进午餐。; (*accidentally*) 偶遇

❑ **meet up with** *vt* [不可拆分] (*by arrangement*) 和…会面; (*accidentally*) 和…偶遇

❑ **meet with** *vt* [不可拆分] 1 [+ *difficulty, success*] 经历 ◊ *The strikes met with little success.* 罢工不太成功。2 (*have meeting with*) [+ *person*] 与…会面

✪ **meeting** ['miːtɪŋ] *n* 1 [c] (*assembly*) [*of club, committee etc*] 会议 ◊ *There is a different chairman at each meeting.* 每次会议都有不同的主席。2 [s] (*people*) 与会者 ◊ *The meeting decided that further efforts were needed.* 与会者决定要进一步努力。3 [c] (*encounter*) 会面 ◊ *Christopher remembers his first meeting with Alice.* 克里斯托弗记得他和艾丽斯的第一次会面。◊ *a chance meeting on the way to the office* 去办公室途中的一次偶遇 ♦ **to call a meeting** 召集一次会议 ♦ **she's in** *or* **at a meeting** 她在开会

meeting place ['miːtɪŋpleɪs] *n* [c] 会场

megabyte ['mɛgəbaɪt] *n* [c] 兆字节

megaphone ['mɛgəfəun] *n* [c] 扩音器

melancholy ['mɛlənkəlɪ] **I** *adj* (*sad*) 忧郁的 **II** *n* [u] (*sadness*) 忧郁

melody ['mɛlədɪ] *n* 1 [c] (*tune*) 旋律 2 [u] (*tunefulness*) 抑扬顿挫

melon ['mɛlən] *n* [c/u] 瓜

melt [mɛlt] **I** *vi* 1 [*metal, ice, snow, butter, chocolate* +] 融化 2 ♦ **melt into** [+ *darkness, crowd*] 消失 **II** *vt* [+ *metal, ice, snow, butter, chocolate*] 使融化 **III** *n* [c] [美:烹饪] 烤的奶酪加肉面包 ♦ **my heart melted** 我的心软了

❑ **melt away** *vi* 1 [*people* +] 逐渐散去 2 [*doubts* +] 消除

❑ **melt down** *vt* 熔毁

✪ **member** ['mɛmbə(r)] *n* [c] 1 [*of family, staff, public*] 一员 ◊ *He refused to name the members of staff involved.* 他拒绝说出职工中参加者的姓名。2 [*of club, party*] 成员 ◊ *Britain is a member of NATO.* 英国是北大西洋公约组织的成员。

3 [*of parliament, assembly*] 议员 ◊ *He was elected to Parliament as the Member for Leeds.* 他被选为代表利兹市的议会议员。 ♦ **member country/state** 成员国/州

Member of Congress [美] *n* [C] 国会议员

Member of Parliament [英] *n* [C] 下院议员

Member of the European Parliament *n* [C] 欧洲议会议员

membership ['mɛmbəʃɪp] *n* [U] **1** (*member status*) 会员身份 **2** [S + PL VB] (*members*) 全体会员 **3** [C] (*number of members*) 会员人数

membership card *n* [C] 会员证

memento [mə'mɛntəu] (*pl* **mementos** *or* **mementoes**) *n* [C] 纪念品

memo ['mɛməu] *n* [C] 备忘录

memorabilia [mɛmərə'bɪlɪə] *n* [*pl*] 纪念品

memorable ['mɛmərəbl] *adj* 难忘的

memorandum [mɛmə'rændəm] [正式] *n* [C] 备忘录

memorial [mɪ'mɔːrɪəl] **I** *n* [C] 纪念碑 **II** *adj* [+ *service, prize*] 纪念仪式的

memorize ['mɛməraɪz] *vt* 记住

memory ['mɛmərɪ] *n* **1** [C/U] (*ability to remember*) 记忆力 **2** [C] (*thing remembered*) 记忆 **3** [C] [+ *of dead person*] 追忆 **4** [C/U] [计算机] 存储器 ♦ **to have a good/bad memory (for sth)** (对某事)记忆力好/差 ♦ **to lose one's memory** 丧失记忆 ♦ **loss of memory** *or* **memory loss** 失忆 ♦ **to do sth from memory** 凭记忆做某事 ♦ **in memory of** 以纪念

men [mɛn] *n* [*pl*] *of* **man**

menace ['mɛnɪs] **I** *n* **1** [C] (*source of danger*) 威胁 **2** [U] (*feeling of danger*) 危险 **3** [非正式] (*nuisance*) ♦ **to be a menace** 讨厌的东西 **II** *vt* (*threaten*) 威胁

menacing ['mɛnɪsɪŋ] *adj* [+ *person, gesture, expression*] 凶恶的

mend [mɛnd] *vt* **1** (*repair*) [+ *object*] 修理 **2** (*heal*) [+ *division, quarrel*] 弥合 ♦ **to mend one's ways** 改善自己的行为方式 ♦ **to be on the mend** [非正式] 在好转中

menial ['miːnɪəl] *adj* (*lowly*) [+ *work, tasks*] 卑下的

meningitis [mɛnɪn'dʒaɪtɪs] *n* [U] 脑膜炎

menopause ['mɛnəupɔːz] *n* ♦ **the menopause** 绝经期

men's room [美] *n* [C] (*men's toilet*) 男厕所

menstruation [mɛnstru'eɪʃən] *n* [U] 月经

menswear ['mɛnzwɛə(r)] *n* [U] 男装

mental ['mɛntl] *adj* **1** [+ *ability, effort, development*] 智力的 **2** [+ *illness, health*] 精神的 **3** [英:非正式] (*crazy, mad*) 发疯的 ♦ **mental arithmetic** 心算

mental hospital *n* [C] 精神病院

mentality [mɛn'tælɪtɪ] *n* [C] 心态

mentally ['mɛntlɪ] *adv* [+ *disturbed, unstable, exhausted*] 精神上 ♦ **to be mentally handicapped** 智力发育不全 ♦ **to be mentally ill** 精神失常

menthol ['mɛnθɔl] *n* [U] 薄荷醇

mention ['mɛnʃən] **I** *vt* 提到 **II** *n* [C/U] (*reference*) 提及 ♦ **to mention that ...** 谈到… ♦ **don't mention it!** 不客气! ♦ **not to mention ...** 更不必说… ♦ **to make no mention of sth** 未提及某事

📖 用法参见 **comment**

menu ['mɛnjuː] *n* [C] **1** (*list of dishes*) 菜单 **2** (*also* : **set menu**) (*meal*) 套餐 **3** [计算机] 选择菜单

MEP *n abbr* (= ***Member of the European Parliament***) 欧洲议会议员

mercenary ['məːsɪnərɪ] **I** *n* [C] (*soldier*) 雇佣兵 **II** *adj* [贬] [+ *person*] 惟利是图的

merchandise ['məːtʃəndaɪz] *n* [U] 商品

merchant ['məːtʃənt] **I** *n* [C] 商人 **II** *adj* [+ *seaman, ship, fleet*] 商业的

merchant marine [美] *n* = **merchant navy**

merchant navy *n* ♦ **the merchant navy** 商船队

merciless ['məːsɪlɪs] *adj* 冷酷无情的

mercury ['məːkjurɪ] *n* **1** [U] 水银 **2** ♦ **Mercury** [天文] 水星

mercy ['məːsɪ] *n* [U] 宽恕 ♦ **to beg** *or* **plead for mercy** 乞求宽恕 ♦ **to**

have mercy on sb 怜悯某人 ♦**to be at the mercy of sb** 任凭某人的摆布

mere [mɪə(r)] *adj* **1** (*simple*) 仅仅的 **2** (*slightest*) 微不足道的 ♦**a mere 2%** 仅仅2%

merely ['mɪəlɪ] *adv* 只不过 ♦**not merely... but...** 不仅…而且…

merge [məːdʒ] **I** *vt* 合并 **II** *vi* **1** (*combine*) [*objects, organizations* +] 联合 **2** (*blend*) [*colours, sounds, shapes* +] 融合 ♦**to merge sth with sth** 将某物和某物结合 ♦**to merge with sth** (*combine*) [*object, organization* +] 和某物结合; (*blend*) [*colour, sound, shape etc* +] 和某物融合

merger ['məːdʒə(r)] *n* [c] 合并

meringue [mə'ræŋ] *n* [c/u]蛋白酥皮饼

merit ['mɛrɪt] **I** *n* [u] (*worth, value*) 价值 **II** *vt* [正式](*deserve*) 值得 **III merits** *n* [*pl*] (*advantages*) 优点 ♦**on merit** *or* **on its/their merits** 根据实际功过{或}根据是非曲直

mermaid ['məːmeɪd] *n* [c] 美人鱼

merry ['mɛrɪ] *adj* **1** (*happy*) [+ *person, mood*] 快乐的 **2** (*cheerful*) [+ *tune*] 欢快的 **3** [英:非正式](*tipsy*) 微醉的 ♦**Merry Christmas!** 圣诞快乐!

merry-go-round ['mɛrɪgəuraund] *n* [c] **1** (*roundabout*) 旋转木马 **2** (*whirl*) 走马灯似的更迭

mesh [mɛʃ] **I** *n* [c/u] (*net*) 网 **II** *vi* 紧密配合 ♦**to mesh with sth** 与某物协调一致

mess [mɛs] *n* **1** [s/u] (*untidiness*) 凌乱 **2** [s/u] (*chaotic situation*) 混乱的局面 **3** [s/u] (*filth*) 脏东西 **4** [c] [军] 食堂 ♦**what a mess!** (*house, room*) 真是又脏又乱!; (*situation*) 真是乱七八糟! ♦**to be a mess** [*room, house* +] 又脏又乱; [*life, situation* +] 一团糟 ♦**to be in a mess** [*hair, room* +] 乱七八糟地; [*organization, country* +] 陷入困境 ♦**to get o.s. in a mess** 使自己陷入困境

❏**mess about, mess around** [非正式] **I** *vi* **1** (*waste time*) 混日子 **2** (*joke*) ♦**to be messing about** 开玩笑 **II** *vt* [尤英](*treat unfairly*) 玩弄

❏**mess about with, mess around with** [非正式] *vt* [不可拆分] (*interfere with*) 干预

❏**mess up** [非正式] **I** *vt* **1** (*spoil*) [+ *plan, system*] 毁掉 **2** (*make untidy*) [+ *house, room, things*] 弄乱 **3** (*make dirty*) [+ *room, floor*] 搞脏 **II** *vi* (*make a mistake*) 搞砸

❏**mess with** [非正式] *vt* [不可拆分] 插手

message ['mɛsɪdʒ] *n* [c] **1** (*to sb*) 消息 **2** (*meaning*) [*of play, book etc*] 主旨 ♦**to leave (sb) a message** (给某人)留个信 ♦**to get the message** [非正式] 领会 ♦**to get the/one's message across** 使人理解这个/自己的意思

messenger ['mɛsɪndʒə(r)] *n* [c] 通信员

messy ['mɛsɪ] *adj* **1** (*untidy*) [+ *person, activity*] 邋遢的; [+ *thing, place*] 凌乱的 **2** (*awkward*) [+ *situation*] 棘手的

met [mɛt] *pt, pp of* **meet**

metabolism [mɛ'tæbəlɪzəm] *n* [c/u] 新陈代谢

metal ['mɛtl] **I** *n* [c/u] 金属 **II** *cpd* [复合词] [+ *plate, bar, rod*] 金属

metallic [mɪ'tælɪk] *adj* **1** [+ *sound*] 金属的 **2** (*made of metal*) 金属制的 **3** [+ *paint, colour*] 像金属的 **4** [+ *taste*] 有金属腥味的

metaphor ['mɛtəfə(r)] *n* [c/u] 隐喻

meteor ['miːtɪə(r)] *n* [c] 流星

meteorite ['miːtɪəraɪt] *n* [c] 陨星

meteorology [miːtɪə'rɔlədʒɪ] *n* [u] 气象学

meter ['miːtə(r)] **I** *n* [c] **1** (*instrument*) (*for gas, water, electricity*) 仪表; (*also*: ***parking meter***) 停车计时器 **2** [美] (*unit*) = **metre** **II** *vt* [+ *gas, water, electricity*] 用表计量

> 📖 请勿将 **meter** 和 **metre** 混淆。在英式英语里,以 **-er** 结尾的 **meter**,是用来测量或记录某事的工具,而以 **-re** 结尾的 **metre**,是测量单位 。在美式英语中,**meter** 对于这两个含义都适用。

method ['mɛθəd] *n* [c/u] (*way*) 方法 ♦**method of payment** *or* **payment method** 付款方式

methodical [mɪ'θɔdɪkl] *adj* 有条不

紊的

meths [mɛθs] [英:非正式] *n* [U] 甲基化酒精

methylated spirits [mɛθəleɪtɪd-] [英:正式] *n* [U]甲基化酒精

meticulous [mɪ'tɪkjuləs] *adj* [+ *person, detail*] 严谨的; [+ *care*] 过度重视细节的 ♦**to be meticulous about sth/about doing sth** 对某事/做某事非常谨慎

metre (美 **meter**) ['miːtə(r)] *n* [C] (*unit*) 米

📖 用法参见 **meter**

metric ['mɛtrɪk] **I** *adj* 公制的 **II** *n* ♦**to think/work in metric** [非正式] 用公制考虑/工作 ♦**to go metric** 采用公制

metro ['mɛtrəu] *n* ♦**the metro** 地铁

metropolitan [mɛtrə'pɔlɪtn] *adj* 大都市的

Mexican ['mɛksɪkən] **I** *adj* 墨西哥的 **II** *n* [C] (*person*) 墨西哥人

Mexico ['mɛksɪkəu] *n* 墨西哥

mg *abbr* (= ***milligram***) 毫克

MHz *abbr* (= ***megahertz***) 兆赫

mice [maɪs] *n* [*pl*] *of* **mouse**

microchip ['maɪkrəutʃɪp] *n* [C] 集成电路块

microphone ['maɪkrəfəun] *n* [C] 话筒

microscope ['maɪkrəskəup] *n* [C] 显微镜 ♦**under the microscope** (喻) 仔细审查

microwave ['maɪkrəuweɪv] **I** *n* [C] (*also* : ***microwave oven***) 微波炉 **II** *vt* 用微波炉烹调

mid- [mɪd] *adj* 中的 ♦**he's in his mid-thirties/forties** 他大约三十五六/四十五六岁

mid-air ['mɪdɛə(r)] **I** *n* ♦**in mid-air** 在空中 **II** *adj* 空中的

midday [mɪd'deɪ] **I** *n* [U] **1** (*noon*) 正午 **2** (*middle of the day*) 中午 **II** *adj* 中午的 ♦**at midday** (*at noon*) 在正午; (*in the middle of the day*) 在中午

✪**middle** ['mɪdl] **I** *n* **1** [C] (*centre*) 中央 ◊ *Howard stood in the middle of the room.* 霍华德站在房间中央。 **2** [S] (*half-way point*) [*of month, event*] 中 ◊ *in the middle of the morning* 上午10点左右 ◊ *in the middle of the party* 舞会中 **3** [C] [非正式] (*waist*) 腰部 **II** *adj* **1** [+ *position, event, period*] 中间的 ◊ *She was the middle child of three.* 她在3个孩子中排行老二。◊ *the middle month of each quarter* 每一季的中间那个月份 **2** (*moderate*) [+ *course, way, path*] 中间派的 ◊ *a middle course between free enterprise and state intervention* 介于自由企业与政府干预之间的中间道路 ♦**in the middle of the night** 在半夜 ♦**to be in the middle of sth/of doing sth** 正忙于某事/做某事

middle-aged [mɪdl'eɪdʒd] *adj* **1** (*neither young nor old*) 中年的 **2** (*stuffy, boring*) 老气的

Middle Ages *n* [*pl*] ♦**the Middle Ages** 中世纪 ♦**in the Middle Ages** 在中世纪时期

middle class [mɪdl'klɑːs] **I** *n* ♦**the middle class(es)** 中产阶级 **II** *adj* (*also* : ***middle-class***) **1** (*sociologically*) 中层社会的 **2** [贬] (*bourgeois*) 中产阶级的

Middle East *n* ♦**the Middle East** 中东

Middle Eastern *adj* 中东的

middle name *n* [C] 中间名字 ♦**trouble is her middle name** 麻烦是她的突出特征

> **MIDDLE NAME**
>
> **first name** 是由父母取的名字。**last name** 或 **surname** 是家族的姓氏。在说英语的国家中，名在姓之前。在 **first name** 和 **last name** 之间，还可能有 **middle name**（中名），这是你父母给你取的第二个"名"。**middle name** 通常只用于正式场合，例如，选课或签署文件时。

midge [mɪdʒ] *n* [C] 蠓

midget ['mɪdʒɪt] **I** *n* [C] 矮人 **II** *adj* (*miniature*) 袖珍的

midnight ['mɪdnaɪt] **I** *n* [U] 半夜 **II** *cpd* [复合词] 午夜的 ♦**at midnight** 在午夜

midst [mɪdst] *n* ♦**in the midst of** [+ *situation, event*] 在…之际; [+ *crowd, group*] 在…中 ♦**to be in the midst of doing sth** 正在做某事

midsummer [mɪd'sʌmə(r)] *n* [U] 仲夏

midway [mɪd'weɪ] I *adj* ♦**the midway point** (*in space*) 中间位置; (*in time*) 到一半的时候 II *adv* **1** (*in space*) ♦**midway between sth and sth** 某地与某地的中间 **2** (*in time*) ♦**midway through sth** 某事中途

midweek [mɪd'wiːk] I *adj* 一周中间的 II *adv* 一周中间

midwife ['mɪdwaɪf] (*pl* **midwives**) *n* [c] 助产士

midwinter [mɪd'wɪntə(r)] *n* [u] 仲冬

✪**might** [maɪt] I *aux vb* **1** (*possibility*) ♦**I might get home late** 我可能会晚回家 ♦**you might be right** 你也许是对的 ♦**it might have been an accident** 可能是个事故 ♦**you might have been killed!** 你差点儿没命了! **2** (*suggestions*) ♦**you might try the bookshop** 你可以试一下书店 **3** (*permission*) ♦**might I make a suggestion?** 我可以提个建议吗? **4** (*in expressions*) ♦**I might have known** *or* **guessed** 我早就该知道{或}猜到 ♦**you might as well go** 你不妨也去 II *n* (*power*) 力量 ♦**with all one's might** 竭尽全力地

mighty ['maɪtɪ] I *adj* (*powerful*) 强大的 II *adv* [美: 非正式](*very*) 很

migraine ['miːgreɪn] *n* [c/u] 偏头痛

migrant ['maɪgrənt] I *n* [c] **1** (*person*) 移民 **2** (*animal*) 迁徙动物 II *cpd* [复合词] [+ *worker*] 流动; [+ *animal*] 迁徙

migrate [maɪ'greɪt] *vi* **1** [*person* +] 迁移 **2** [*bird* +] 迁徙

migration [maɪ'greɪʃən] *n* [c/u] **1** [+ *of people*] 移居 **2** [+ *of birds*] 迁徙

mike [maɪk] [非正式] *n* (*microphone*) 麦克风

mild [maɪld] I *adj* **1** (*slight*) [+ *feeling, tone*] 温和的 **2** (*not severe*) [+ *infection, illness*] 轻微的 **3** (*gentle*) [+ *person, nature*] 和善的 **4** (*moderate*) [+ *climate, weather*] 温暖的 **5** (*not harsh*) [+ *soap, cosmetic*] 温和的 **6** (*not strong*) [+ *curry, cheese*] 淡味的 II *n* [英](*beer*) 淡啤酒

📖 用法参见 **hot**

mildew ['mɪldjuː] *n* [u] 霉

mildly ['maɪldlɪ] *adv* **1** (*slightly*) 稍微 **2** (*gently*) [*say, remark* +] 温和地 **3** (*not strongly*) [+ *spiced, flavoured*] 适度地 ♦**to put it mildly** 说得婉转些

mile [maɪl] I *n* [c] 英里 II **miles** *n* [*pl*] [非正式](*a long way*) 很远的距离 ♦**to do 30 miles to the gallon** 1加仑油可跑30英里 ♦**70 miles per** *or* **an hour** 每小时70英里 ♦**to win by a mile** *or* **miles** [非正式] 远远胜出 ♦**to be miles away** [非正式] (*distracted*) 心不在焉 ♦**miles better/too slow** [非正式] 好得多/过分慢

mileage ['maɪlɪdʒ] *n* [c/u] **1** (*number of miles*) 英里里程 **2** (*fuel efficiency*) 燃油效率 **3** ♦**to get a lot of mileage out of sth** 从某事中获取大量好处

mileometer, milometer [maɪ'lɔmɪtə(r)] *n* [c] 计程器

milestone ['maɪlstəun] *n* [c] (*important event*) 里程碑

militant ['mɪlɪtnt] I *adj* (*politically active*) 激进的 II *n* [c] (*political activist*) 激进分子

✪**military** ['mɪlɪtərɪ] I *adj* [+ *leader, action*] 军事的 II *n* ♦**the military** 军队

militia [mɪ'lɪʃə] *n* [c] 民兵

milk [mɪlk] I *n* [u] 奶 II *vt* **1** [+ *cow, goat*] 挤…的奶 **2** (*exploit*) [+ *situation, person*] 榨取

milk chocolate *n* [u] 牛奶巧克力

milkman ['mɪlkmən] (*pl* **milkmen**) *n* [c] 送牛奶的人

milkshake ['mɪlkʃeɪk] *n* [c/u] 奶昔

milky ['mɪlkɪ] *adj* **1** (*in colour*) 乳白色的 **2** [+ *drink*] 掺奶的

mill [mɪl] I *n* [c] **1** (*for grain*) 磨坊 **2** (*for coffee, pepper*) 碾磨器 **3** (*factory*) 厂 II *vt* (*grind*) [+ *grain, flour*] 磨

❑**mill about, mill around** *vi* [*people, crowd* +] 乱转

millennium [mɪ'lenɪəm] (*pl* **millenniums** *or* **millennia**) *n* [c] **1** (*1000 years*) 一千年 **2** ♦**the Millennium** (*year 2000*) 千禧年

milligram (英 **milligramme**) ['mɪlɪgræm] *n* [c] 毫克

millilitre (美 **milliliter**) ['mɪlɪliːtə(r)] *n* [c] 毫升

millimetre (美 **millimeter**) ['mɪlɪmiːtə(r)] *n* [c] 毫米

✪**million** ['mɪljən] I *num* 百万 ◊ *three*

million pounds 300 万英镑 **II millions** *n* [*pl*]（字）数百万；[非正式]（喻）无数 ♦**a** *or* **one million books/people/dollars** 100 万本书/个人/元 ♦**millions are starving** 数以百万的人正在忍受饥饿 ♦**millions of people/things** *(loads of)* 无数的人/物

millionaire [mɪljə'nɛə(r)] *n* [c] 百万富翁

millionth ['mɪljənθ] **I** *adj* 第一百万的 **II** *n* [c] *(millionth part)* 百万分之一

milometer [maɪ'lɔmɪtə(r)] *n* **= mileometer**

mime [maɪm] **I** *vt* **1** 假唱 **2** *(act out)* 模仿 **II** *vi* **1** 假装 **2** *(act)* 用手比划表示 **III** *n* **1** [U] *(art form)* 哑剧 **2** [C] *(performance)* 哑剧表演 **IV** *cpd* [复合词] [+ *artist*] 哑剧

mimic ['mɪmɪk] **I** *vt* 模仿 **II** *n* [c] 善于模仿的人

min. (*pl* **min.** *or* **mins**) *n abbr* **1** (= ***minute***) 分钟 **2 = minimum**

mince [mɪns] **I** *n* [U] [英:烹饪] 肉末 [美 = **ground beef**] **II** *vt* [英] [+ *meat*] 绞碎 [美 = **grind**] **III** *vi* *(in walking)* 扭扭捏捏地走 ♦**he doesn't mince (his) words** 他直言不讳

mincemeat ['mɪnsmiːt] *n* [U] **1** *(fruit)* 百果馅 **2** [英] *(meat)* 肉末 [美 = **ground beef, hamburger meat**] ♦**to make mincemeat of sb** 彻底击败某人

mince pie *n* [C/U] 百果馅饼

✪**mind** [maɪnd] **I** *n* [c] **1** *(thoughts)* 脑海 ◊ *He couldn't get her out of his mind.* 他无法将她从脑海中摆脱。**2** *(intellect)* 智力 ◊ *Studying stretched my mind and got me thinking.* 学习开发了我的智力并让我勤于思考。**3** *(mentality)* 头脑 ◊ *Andrew, you have a very suspicious mind.* 安德鲁，你有个善猜疑的头脑。**4** *(thinker)* 有才智的人 ◊ *a team of the brightest minds available* 才智出众的人组成的团队 **II** *vt* **1** [英] *(look after)* [+ *child, shop*] 照看 ◊ *My mother is minding the office.* 我母亲正照看着办公室。**2** *(be careful of)* 当心 ◊ *Mind your head!* 当心头！ **3** *(object to)* 介意 ◊ *I don't mind walking.* 我不介意走路。**4** *(have a preference)* ♦**I don't mind (what/who ...)** 我不在乎（什么/谁…）◊ *I don't mind what we have for dinner.* 我不在乎我们晚饭吃什么。**5** ♦**do/would you mind (if ...)?**（如果…）你介意吗？◊ *Would you mind waiting outside for a moment?* 你介意在外面等一会儿吗？♦**to be out of one's mind** 发疯 ♦**to have a lot on one's mind** 有许多事牵肠挂肚 ♦**to my mind** *(in my opinion)* 据我看来 ♦**to make up one's mind** *or* **make one's mind up** 下定决心 ♦**to change one's/sb's mind** 改变主意 ♦**to be in** *or* [美] **of two minds about sth** 对某事犹豫不决 ♦**what do you have in mind?** 你有什么主意？♦**to bear** *or* **keep sth in mind** 记住某事 ♦**it slipped my mind** 我忘了 ♦**it never crossed my mind** 我从未想过 ♦**in my mind's eye** 在我的想像中 ♦**to come** *or* **spring to mind** 在脑海中闪现 ♦**my mind was on other things** 我的心思在其他事情上 ♦**to have** *or* **keep an open mind** 暂不作决定 ♦**state of mind** 精神状况 ♦**to take one's mind off sth** 暂时丢开不想 ♦**mind you, ...** *(admittedly)* 说真的，…♦**never mind** 不要紧 ♦**I wouldn't mind a coffee** 我挺想喝杯咖啡 ♦**mind your own business** [非正式, 疑讳] 别多管闲事 ♦**mind the step** 小心脚下

minder ['maɪndə(r)] *n* [c] **1** *(bodyguard)* 保镖 **2** [英] *(also: **childminder**)* 保育员

mindful ['maɪndful] [正式] *adj* ♦**mindful of** 留神的

mindless ['maɪndlɪs] *adj* **1** *(senseless)* [+ *violence*] 盲目的 **2** *(stupid)* [+ *person*] 没头脑的 **3** *(boring)* [+ *work*] 无需动脑的

✪**mine**[1] [maɪn] *pron* 我的 ♦**a friend of mine** 我的一个朋友 ♦**this is mine** 这是我的 ♦**these are mine** 这些是我的

✪**mine**[2] [maɪn] **I** *n* [c] **1** *(for coal, gold etc)* 矿 **2** *(bomb)* 地雷 **II** *vt* **1** *(dig out)* [+ *coal, gold etc*] 开采 **2** *(lay mines in)* [+ *area*] 布雷于 ♦**he's a real mine**

of information 他真是一本活字典

minefield ['maɪnfiːld] *n* [c] **1** (*area*) 雷区 **2** (*situation*) 危险地带

miner ['maɪnə(r)] *n* [c] 矿工

mineral ['mɪnərəl] **I** *n* [c] 矿物 **II** *cpd* [复合词] [+ *deposit, resources*] 矿物

mineral water *n* [U/C] 矿泉水

mingle ['mɪŋgl] *vi* **1** ♦ **to mingle (with sth)** (*mix*) [*sounds, smells etc* +] (和某物) 混杂 **2** [*person* +] (*at party*) 交往

miniature ['mɪnətʃə(r)] **I** *adj* 微型的 **II** *n* [c] **1** (*painting*) 微型画 **2** (*bottle*) 小瓶装的酒 ♦ **in miniature** 缩影的

minibar ['mɪnɪbɑː(r)] *n* [c] 客房内酒吧

minibus ['mɪnɪbʌs] *n* [c] 小公共汽车

minicab ['mɪnɪkæb] [英] *n* [c] 必须得事先预定的出租车

MiniDisc®, minidisc ['mɪnɪdɪsk] *n* **1** [U] (*system*) MD 格式 **2** [c] (*disc*) 迷你光碟 **3** [c] (*also* : ***MiniDisc® player***) 微型唱片机

minimal ['mɪnɪml] *adj* 最低限度的

minimize ['mɪnɪmaɪz] *vt* **1** (*reduce*) [+ *risks, disease*] 使…减少到最低 **2** (*play down*) [+ *role, weakness*] 贬低 **3** [计算机] 把…最小化

minimum ['mɪnɪməm] **I** *adj* **1** (*lowest, smallest*) 最低的 **2** (*little*) 最少的 **II** *n* [c] 最少量 ♦ **to reduce/keep sth to a minimum** 将某物降到/保持在最低限度 ♦ **a minimum of ...** 最少的… ♦ **three months minimum** 最少3个月

mining ['maɪnɪŋ] **I** *n* [U] 矿业 **II** *cpd* [复合词] [+ *village, expert*] 采矿

miniskirt ['mɪnɪskəːt] *n* [c] 超短裙

✪ **minister** ['mɪnɪstə(r)] **I** *n* [c] **1** [英 : 政治] 部长 ◊ *the new Defence Minister* 新国防部部长 **2** [宗] 牧师 **II** *vi* ♦ **to minister to** [+ *people, needs*] 照料

ministry ['mɪnɪstrɪ] *n* **1** [c] [英 : 政治] 部 **2** [宗] ♦ **the ministry** 牧师 ♦ **the Ministry of Defence/Agriculture** [英] 国防部/农业部

minor ['maɪnə(r)] **I** *adj* **1** (*unimportant*) [+ *repairs, changes*] 不重要的; [+ *injuries*] 不严重的 **2** [音] [+ *key, scale*] 小调的 **II** *n* [c] **1** (*under-age child*) 未成年人 **2** [美 : 教育] (*subject*) 辅修科目 **3** [美 : 教育] (*student*) ♦ **a history minor** 历史辅修生 **III** *vi* [美 : 教育] ♦ **to minor in sth** 辅修某科 ♦ **Chopin's Scherzo in B flat minor** 用降B小调演奏肖邦的谐谑曲

minority [maɪ'nɔrɪtɪ] **I** *n* **1** [S + PL VB] [*of group, society*] 少数 **2** [c] (*ethnic, cultural, religious*) 少数民族 **II** *cpd* [复合词] [+ *shareholder, verdict*] 少数 ♦ **to be in a** *or* **the minority** 占少数 ♦ **a (small) minority of** (极)少数的

mint [mɪnt] **I** *n* **1** [U] (*plant*) 薄荷 **2** [U] (*sweet*) 薄荷糖 **3** ♦ **the (Royal) Mint,** [美] **the Mint** (英国皇家)铸币局, (美国)铸币局 **II** *vt* [+ *coins*] 铸造 ♦ **in mint condition** 状况完好

minus ['maɪnəs] **I** *n* [c] **1** (*also* : ***minus sign***) 负号 **2** (*disadvantage*) 不足 **II** *prep* [非正式] (*without*) 没有 ♦ **12 minus 3 (is** *or* **equals 9)** 12减3(等于9) ♦ **minus 24 (degrees C/F)** (*temperature*) 零下24 (摄氏/华氏度) ♦ **minus 24** [数] 负24 ♦ **B minus** [教育] B减

✪ **minute**[1] [maɪ'njuːt] *adj* [+ *amount*] 极小的 ♦ **in minute detail** 细枝末节

✪ **minute**[2] ['mɪnɪt] **I** *n* [c] **1** (*unit*) 分钟 **2** (喻) (*short time*) 一会儿 ◊ *Will you excuse me if I sit down for a minute?* 我可以坐一会儿吗? **II minutes** *n* [*pl*] [*of meeting*] 会议记录 ♦ **5 minutes past 3** 3点过5分 ♦ **wait** *or* **just a minute!** 等一会儿! ♦ **(at) any minute** *or* **any minute (now)** 随时 ♦ **the minute (that) ...** 一…就… ♦ **this minute** [非正式] 立刻 ♦ **(at/until) the last minute** (在/到)最后一刻

miracle ['mɪrəkl] **I** *n* [c] **1** [宗] 圣迹 **2** (*marvel*) 奇迹 **II** *cpd* [复合词] [+ *cure, drug*] 特效 ♦ **it's a miracle (that) ...** …真是个奇迹

miraculous [mɪ'rækjuləs] *adj* **1** 奇迹般的 **2** [宗] 圣迹般的

mirage ['mɪrɑːʒ] *n* [c] **1** (*optical illusion*) 海市蜃楼 **2** (*delusion*) 幻影

mirror ['mɪrə(r)] **I** *n* [c] 镜子; [*in car*] 后视镜 **II** *vt* 反映

misbehave [mɪsbɪ'heɪv] *vi* 行为无礼

misc. *abbr* = **miscellaneous**

miscalculate [mɪs'kælkjuleɪt] **I** *vt* 错误估计 **II** *vi* 算错

miscarriage ['mɪskærɪdʒ] *n* [c] [医] 流产 ♦**to have a miscarriage** 流产 ♦**miscarriage of justice** 误判

miscellaneous [mɪsə'leɪnɪəs] *adj* [+ *people, objects*] 形形色色的 ♦**miscellaneous expenses** 各种花销

mischief ['mɪstʃɪf] *n* [U] **1** (*playfulness, fun*) 顽皮 **2** (*trouble, harm*) 损害 ♦**to get into** *or* **up to mischief** 胡闹 ♦**to do o.s. a mischief** [非正式] 使自己受伤

mischievous ['mɪstʃɪvəs] *adj* **1** (*playful, fun-loving*) 淘气的 **2** (*malicious*) 恶意的

misconception ['mɪskən'sɛpʃən] *n* [c] 误解

misconduct [mɪs'kɔndʌkt] *n* [U] (*misbehaviour*) 行为不端

miser ['maɪzə(r)] [贬] *n* [c] 守财奴

miserable ['mɪzərəbl] *adj* **1** (*unhappy*) [+ *person*] 痛苦的 **2** (*wretched*) [+ *conditions, place*] 破败的 **3** (*unpleasant*) [+ *weather, day*] 恶劣的 **4** (*bad-tempered, unfriendly*) [+ *person, nature*] 坏脾气的 **5** (*meagre*) [+ *amount*] 少得可怜的 **6** (*hopeless*) [+ *failure*] 悲惨的 ♦**to feel miserable** 感到痛苦

misery ['mɪzərɪ] *n* **1** [U] (*unhappiness*) 痛苦 **2** [U] (*wretchedness*) 穷困 **3** [c] [尤英: 非正式] (*person*) 爱发牢骚的人 ♦**to put sb out of their misery** [非正式] 解开某人心中的疑团 ♦**to put sth out of its misery** 杀死某动物以结束其痛苦 ♦**to make sb's life a misery** 使某人日子不好过

misfortune [mɪs'fɔːtʃən] *n* [C/U] 不幸

misgiving [mɪs'gɪvɪŋ] *n* [C/U] ♦**to have misgivings about sth** 对某事感到担心 ♦**to be filled with misgiving about sth** 对某事疑虑重重

misguided [mɪs'gaɪdɪd] *adj* [+ *opinion, attempt*] 误导的; [+ *person*] 误入歧途的

mishandle [mɪs'hændl] *vt* [+ *situation, project*] 错误处理

mishap ['mɪshæp] *n* [c] 小小的不幸 ♦**without mishap** 毫无波折

mishear [mɪs'hɪə(r)] (*pt, pp* **misheard**) **I** *vt* [+ *person, remark*] 听错 **II** *vi* 听错

misheard [mɪs'həːd] *pt, pp of* **mishear**

misinterpret [mɪsɪn'təːprɪt] *vt* 曲解

misjudge [mɪs'dʒʌdʒ] *vt* [+ *person, situation*] 错误判断

mislay [mɪs'leɪ] (*pt, pp* **mislaid**) *vt* 忘记把…放在何处

mislead [mɪs'liːd] (*pt, pp* **misled**) *vt* 误导 ♦**to mislead sb about sth** 在某事上误导某人

misleading [mɪs'liːdɪŋ] *adj* 使人误解的

misled [mɪs'lɛd] *pt, pp of* **mislead**

misplace [mɪs'pleɪs] [正式] *vt* (*mislay*) 误置

misprint ['mɪsprɪnt] *n* [c] 印刷错误

misrepresent [mɪsrɛprɪ'zɛnt] *vt* [+ *person, views*] 歪曲

Miss [mɪs] *n* **1** (*before surname*) 小姐 **2** [尤英] (*as form of address*) 小姐 ♦**Dear Miss Smith** 亲爱的史密斯小姐 ♦**Miss World** (*in beauty contests*) 世界小姐

> **MISS, MRS, MS**
> 在说英语的国家中，**Mrs**（夫人）用于已婚女士的姓名前。**Miss**（小姐）用于未婚女士的姓名前。有些女士认为，让人们知道她是否结婚并不重要，所以往往用**Ms**（女士）称呼自己。与**Mr**（先生）类似，**Ms**不表明任何婚姻状况。

✪**miss** [mɪs] **I** *vt* **1** (*fail to hit*) 未击中 ◊ *She threw an ashtray across the room, narrowly missing my head.* 她从房间那端扔过来一只烟灰缸，差点击中我的头。**2** [体育] [+ *shot, penalty*] 打偏 ◊ *He scored four goals but missed a penalty.* 他进了4个球，却踢偏了1个点球。**3** (*fail to catch*) [+ *train, bus, plane*] 错过

◊ *Daniel nearly missed his flight.* 丹尼尔差点错过他的航班。**4** (*notice loss of*) [+ *money etc*] 发觉丢失 ◊ *He didn't miss his wallet until he was on the plane.* 直到上了飞机他才发觉丢失了钱包。**5** (*fail to notice*) 忽视 ◊ *Captain Cobbins was an experienced officer and didn't miss much.* 科宾斯上尉是个有经验的军官，不会忽视太多东西。**6** (*feel the absence of*) [+ *person, thing*] 想念 ◊ *Did you miss me?* 你想念我吗？◊ *If I moved into a flat I'd really miss my garden.* 如果我搬到公寓去住，我肯定会很想念我的花园。**7** (*fail to take*) [+ *chance, opportunity*] 错过 ◊ *It was too good an opportunity to miss.* 这个机会好得不容错过。**8** (*fail to attend*) [+ *class, meeting*] 缺席 ◊ *I couldn't miss a departmental meeting.* 系里开会我不可以缺席。**II** *vi* (*fail to hit*) [*person* +] 没打中 ◊ *She threw her plate at his head and missed.* 她把盘子朝他的头扔去，但没打中。**III** *n* [c] **1** (*failure to hit*) 击不中 ◊ *After more misses, they shot the lion in the chest.* 又有几次没击中后，他们射中了狮子的胸部。**2** [体育] 失误 ◊ *Striker Marcus Smith's miss cost them the match.* 前锋马库斯•史密斯的失误使他们输掉了这场比赛。♦**to just miss sth** 刚好错过某事 ♦**you can't miss it** 你不会找不到 ♦**to miss the point** 没领会要点 ♦**his shirt was missing a button** [非正式] 他的衬衫少了一粒纽扣 ♦**to give sth a miss** [英: 非正式] 避开某事

❑**miss out** [英] **I** *vt* (*accidentally*) 遗漏 ◊ *It's easy to miss out a comma when you're writing quickly.* 在你飞快地书写的时候很容易会遗漏一个逗号。[美=**leave out**] **II** *vi* (*lose out*) 错过机会

❑**miss out on** *vt* [不可拆分] [+ *opportunity, fun*] 错过

missile ['mɪsaɪl] *n* [c] **1** [军] 导弹 **2** (*object thrown*) 投掷物

missing ['mɪsɪŋ] *adj* (*absent, lost*) [+ *person*] 失踪的; [+ *object*] 丢失的 ♦**to go missing** 不知去向 ♦**missing person** 失踪人员 ♦**missing in action** 作战中失踪

mission ['mɪʃən] *n* [c] **1** (*task*) 任务 **2** (*aim*) 使命 **3** (*official representatives*) 代表团 **4** [军, 航空] (*flight*) 飞行任务 **5** [宗] (*campaign*) 传教活动; (*building*) 教区

missionary ['mɪʃənrɪ] *n* [c] 传教士

misspell ['mɪs'spɛl] (*pt, pp* **misspelt** (英) *or* **misspelled**) *vt* 拼错

mist [mɪst] *n* [c/u] 薄雾

❑**mist over, mist up I** *vi* [*window, glasses* +] 被蒙上水汽 ♦**his eyes misted over** 他泪眼模糊 **II** *vt* [+ *window, glasses*] 使蒙上水汽

mistake [mɪs'teɪk] (*pt* **mistook**, *pp* **mistaken**) **I** *n* [c] **1** (*error*) (*in calculations, text etc*) 错误 **2** (*blunder*) 过失 **II** *vt* (*be wrong about*) 弄错 ♦**to make a mistake** 犯错 ♦**you're making a big mistake** 你正在犯一个严重的错误 ♦**to make the mistake of doing sth** 误做某事 ♦**it's a (big) mistake to do that** 那么做是个(严重的)错误 ♦**there must be some mistake** 一定是搞错了 ♦**to do sth by mistake** 误做某事 ♦**to mistake A for B** 把A误认为B ♦**there is no mistaking ...** …不可能被弄错

mistaken [mɪs'teɪkən] **I** *pp of* **mistake II** *adj* [+ *idea, belief etc*] 错误的 ♦**to be mistaken (about sth)** [*person* +] (把某事)搞错 ♦**if I'm not** *or* **unless I'm mistaken** 如果我没弄错的话

mister ['mɪstə(r)] *n* [非正式] 先生 *see* **Mr**

mistletoe ['mɪsltəu] *n* [u] 槲寄生

mistletoe 是一种灌木，绿色茎叶和蜡白色浆果。在英国和美国，被用作圣诞节装饰物。根据传统，人们在槲寄生下面亲吻。

mistook [mɪs'tuk] *pt of* **mistake**

mistress ['mɪstrɪs] *n* [c] **1** (*lover*) 情妇 **2** [英: 过时, 教育] (*teacher*) 女教师 **3** (*owner*) 女主人 **4** [*of house, servant*] 女主人

mistrust [mɪs'trʌst] **I** *n* [u] ♦**mistrust (of sth/sb)** (对某事/某人)不信任 **II** *vt* 不相信

misty ['mɪstɪ] *adj* [+ *day, weather*] 有雾的 ♦**it's misty** 有雾

misunderstand [mɪsʌndə'stænd]

(*pt, pp* **misunderstood**) *vt, vi* 误解
misunderstanding ['mɪsʌndə'stændɪŋ] *n* **1** [c/u] 误会 **2** [c] (*disagreement*) 争执
misunderstood [mɪsʌndə'stud] **I** *pt, pp of* **misunderstand** **II** *adj* 被误解的
misuse [*n* mɪs'juːs, *vb* mɪs'juːz] **I** *n* [c/u] 滥用 **II** *vt* 误用
mitt [mɪts] *n* [c] **1** [非正式](*mitten*) 连指手套 **2** [棒球](*glove*) 棒球手套 **3** [非正式](*hand*) 手
mitten ['mɪtn] *n* [c] 连指手套
mix [mɪks] **I** *vt* **1** (*combine*) [+ *liquids, ingredients, colours*] 混合 **2** (*prepare*) [+ *cake, sauce*] 拌和; [+ *cement*] 搅拌 **3** [+ *sounds, tracks*] 混 **II** *vi* **1** 混合 **2** (*socially*) ♦**to mix (with sb)** (和某人)相处 **III** *n* **1** [c] (*combination*) 混合 **2** [c/u] (*powder*) 混合料 ♦**to mix sth with sth** [+ *activities*] 将某物同某物混淆 ♦**to mix business with pleasure** 把生意和娱乐相结合 ♦**to mix sb a drink** 给某人调制一杯饮料 ♦**politics and sport don't mix** 政治和运动互不相容
❑**mix in** *vt* [+ *eggs etc*] 搅拌加入
❑**mix up** *vt* (*confuse*) [+ *people*] 分辨不出; [+ *things*] 混淆
mixed [mɪkst] *adj* **1** (*varying*) [+ *reactions, signals*] 复杂的 **2** (*combined*) [+ *salad, herbs*] 什锦的 **3** (*diverse*) [+ *group, community*] 形形色色的 **4** [+ *race*] 混血的 **5** [+ *marriage*] 异族的 **6** (*coeducational*) [+ *school, education*] 男女混合的 ♦**to have mixed feelings (about sth)** (对于某事)百感交集
mixed grill [英:烹饪] *n* [c] 烤杂排
mixed up [mɪkst'ʌp] *adj* (*confused*) 糊涂的 ♦**to get mixed up (about sth)** (把某事)混淆起来 ♦**to get sth mixed up** [+ *facts, dates*] 把某事弄混 ♦**to be** *or* **get mixed up in sth** 被卷入某事
mixer ['mɪksə(r)] *n* [c] **1** (*also :* ***food mixer***) 搅拌器 **2** (*drink*) 调酒用的饮料 **3** (*person*) ♦**to be a good mixer** 是交际能手
mixture ['mɪkstʃə(r)] *n* [c/u] 混合物
mix-up ['mɪksʌp] [非正式] *n* [c] 混乱
mm *abbr* (= ***millimetre(s)***) 毫米
moan [məun] **I** *vi* **1** (*groan*) 呻吟 **2** [非正式](*complain*) ♦**to moan (about sth)** 抱怨(某事) **3** (*say*) 呻吟着说 **II** *n* [c] **1** (*groan*) 呻吟 **2** (*complaint*) 抱怨
moat [məut] *n* [c] 护城河
mob [mɔb] **I** *n* **1** [c] (*disorderly crowd*) 暴民 **2** [c] [非正式](*gang, crew*) 团伙 **3** [非正式](*mafia*) ♦**the Mob** 黑手党 **II** *vt* [+ *person*] 成群围住 **III** *cpd* [复合词] [+ *violence, rule*] 暴民
mobile ['məubaɪl] **I** *adj* **1** [+ *library, studio, office*] 流动的 **2** [+ *person*] (*having transport*) 有私人的代步工具的; (*able to walk*) 能活动的 **3** [+ *workforce, population*] 流动的 **II** *n* [c] **1** [英:非正式](*mobile phone*) 手机 **2** (*decoration*) 风动饰物
mobile home *n* [c] 活动住房
mobile phone [英] *n* [c] 手机 [美 = **cellphone, cellular phone**]
mobility [məu'bɪlɪtɪ] *n* [u] **1** [*of person*] (*through transport*) 机动性; (*ability to walk*) 行走能力 **2** [*of workforce, population*] 流动性
mobilize ['məubɪlaɪz] **I** *vt* **1** (*organize*) [+ *people, support*] 动员 **2** [军][+ *army*] 调动 **II** *vi* [军] [*country, army* +] 动员起来
mock [mɔk] **I** *vt* (*ridicule*) 嘲笑 **II** *adj* **1** (*artificial, false*) [+ *style, material*] 仿制的 **2** (*pretend*) [+ *emotion*] 假装的 **3** (*staged*) [+ *battle, execution*] 模拟的 **III mocks** *n* [*pl*] [英](*also :* ***mock exams, mock examinations***) 模拟考试
mockery ['mɔkərɪ] *n* [u] 嘲弄 ♦**to make a mockery of sth** 使某事成为笑柄
mocking ['mɔkɪŋ] *adj* 讥讽的
mod cons ['mɔd'kɔnz] [英:非正式] *n* [*pl*] *abbr* (= ***modern conveniences***) 现代化生活设备
mode [məud] [正式] *n* [c] **1** (*form*) 形式 **2** (*setting*) 模式
model ['mɔdl] **I** *n* [c] **1** [*of boat, building etc*] 模型 **2** (*fashion model*) 时装模特 **3** (*artist's model*) 模特 **4** (*example*) ♦**a model of ...** …的典范 **II** *adj* **1** (*exemplary*) [+ *teacher, mother, farm etc*] 模范的 **2** (*miniature*) ♦**model aircraft/train** 模型飞机/火车 **III** *vt* **1** [+ *clothes*] 展示

2 (*sculpt*) 塑造 **IV** *vi* (*for designer, photographer etc*) 当模特 ♦ **to model o.s. on sb** 以某人为榜样
modem ['məudɛm] *n* [c] 调制解调器
moderate [*adj*, *n* 'mɔdərət, *vb* 'mɔdəreɪt] **I** *adj* **1** (*not extreme*) [+ *views, people*] 中庸的 **2** (*not big, not small*) [+ *amount, improvement*] 适度的 **II** *n* [c] [政治] 温和派 **III** *vt* **1** [+ *tone of voice, language*] 使缓和 **2** [+ *demands*] 减轻; [+ *views*] 使温和 **IV** *vi* (*abate*) [*storm, crisis etc* +] 变温和
moderation [mɔdə'reɪʃən] *n* [u] 中庸 ♦ **in moderation** 适度
modern ['mɔdən] *adj* **1** (*present-day*) [+ *world, times, society etc*] 现代的 **2** (*up-to-date*) [+ *technology, design etc*] 新式的
modern languages *n* [*pl*] 现代语言
modernize ['mɔdənaɪz] *vt* 使现代化
modest ['mɔdɪst] *adj* **1** (*small*) [+ *amount, improvement*] 少量的; [+ *house, flat*] 朴素的 **2** (*not boastful*) [+ *person*] 谦虚的 **3** (*decent*) [+ *woman, clothes, behaviour*] 端庄的
modesty ['mɔdɪstɪ] *n* [u] **1** (*humility*) 谦逊 **2** (*smallness*) 小 **3** (*simplicity*) 朴实 **4** (*decency*) 端庄
modification [mɔdɪfɪ'keɪʃən] *n* [c/u] (*to machine*) 改装; (*to policy, plan*) 修改 ♦ **to make modifications to sth** 对某物进行修改
modify ['mɔdɪfaɪ] *vt* [+ *machine*] 改装; [+ *policy, plan*] 修改
module ['mɔdju:l] *n* [c] **1** [教育] 单元 **2** [航天] 舱 **3** [*of building*] 部件 **4** [*of machine*] 组件
mohair ['məuhɛə(r)] **I** *n* [u] 马海毛 **II** *cpd* [复合词] [+ *jumper, scarf, dress*] 马海毛
Mohammed [mə'hæmɛd] *n* 穆罕默德
moist [mɔɪst] *adj* 潮湿的
moisten ['mɔɪsn] *vt* 弄湿
moisture ['mɔɪstʃə(r)] *n* [u] 水分
moisturizer ['mɔɪstʃəraɪzə(r)] *n* [c/u] 保湿霜
molasses [mə'læsɪz] *n* [u] 糖浆
mold *etc* [məuld] [美] *n, vt* = **mould** *etc*
Moldova [mɔl'dəuvə] *n* 摩尔多瓦
Moldovan [mɔl'dəuvən] **I** *adj* 摩尔多瓦的 **II** *n* **1** [c] (*person*) 摩尔多瓦人 **2** [u] (*language*) 摩尔多瓦语
mole [məul] *n* [c] **1** (*on skin*) 痣 **2** (*animal*) 鼹鼠 **3** (*spy*) 间谍
molecule ['mɔlɪkju:l] *n* [c] 分子
molest [mə'lɛst] *vt* (*sexually*) 猥亵
molten ['məultən] *adj* [+ *metal, glass, rock*] 熔化的
mom [mɔm] [美: 非正式] *n* [c] 妈妈 [英 = **mum**]
✪ **moment** ['məumənt] *n* **1** [c] (*period of time*) 片刻 ◊ *It lasted only a moment.* 只持续了片刻。**2** [c] (*point in time*) 瞬间 ◊ *That was the moment I understood.* 在那一瞬间我明白了。**3** [u] [正式] (*importance*) 重要 ◊ *a matter of the greatest moment* 最重要的一件事 ♦ **for a** *or* **one moment** (*showing disbelief*) 一刻 ◊ *I don't for a moment think there'll be a divorce.* 我一刻都没想过会离婚。; (*showing relief*) 有那么一刻 ◊ *For a moment I thought he wasn't going to make it.* 有那么一刻我还以为他不会来了。; (*briefly*) 一会儿 ◊ *She stared at him for a moment, then turned away.* 她盯着他看了一会儿，然后转过身。♦ **for the moment** 暂时 ♦ **in a moment** (*explaining when*) 马上; (*explaining duration*) 一瞬间 ♦ **one moment, please** (*on the telephone*) 请稍等 ♦ **the moment (that) ...** 一…，就… ♦ **at that moment** 当时 ♦ **at the/this (present) moment** 此刻/当前 ♦ **(at) any moment (now)** 随时 ♦ **at the last moment** 在最后一刻
momentarily ['məuməntrɪlɪ] *adv* **1** [英] (*for a moment*) 短暂地 **2** [美] (*very soon*) 立即
momentary ['məuməntərɪ] *adj* 短暂的
momentous [məu'mɛntəs] *adj* 重大的
momentum [məu'mɛntəm] *n* [u] **1** [*of events, change, political movement*] 势头 **2** [物] 动量 ♦ **to gather** *or* **gain momentum** [*process* +] 势头增长; [*object, vehicle* +] 积聚动力
mommy ['mɔmɪ] [美: 非正式] *n* [c]

妈妈

Mon. *abbr* (= ***Monday***) 星期一

monarch ['mɔnək] *n* [c] 君主

monarchy ['mɔnəkɪ] *n* 1 [u] (*system*) 君主制 2 [c] (*country*) 君主制国家 3 ♦**the monarchy** (*royal family*) 皇室

monastery ['mɔnəstərɪ] *n* [c] 寺院

Monday ['mʌndɪ] *n* [c/u] 星期一 *see also* **Tuesday**

monetary ['mʌnɪtərɪ] *adj* [+ *system, policy, control*] 货币的

✪**money** ['mʌnɪ] **I** *n* [u] 1 (*cash*) 钱 ◊ *Do you have any money on you?* 你身边带钱了吗? 2 (*in the bank*) 存款 ◊ *I spent all my money on the house.* 我把存款都用来买房子了。3 (*currency*) 货币 ◊ *They might not accept British money.* 他们可能不接受英国货币。**II monies** *n* [*pl*] [正式] 款项 ◊ *the investment and management of monies by pension funds* 退休基金各款项的投资及管理 ♦**to make money** [*person, business* +] 赚钱 ♦**to be in the money** [非正式] 有钱 ♦**to get your money's worth** 物有所值

money belt *n* [c] 腰包

money order [美] *n* [c] 汇票 [英 = **postal order**]

Mongol ['mɔŋgəl] **I** *n* [c] 蒙古人 **II** *adj* 蒙古的

Mongolia [mɔŋ'gəulɪə] *n* 蒙古

Mongolian [mɔŋ'gəulɪən] **I** *adj* 蒙古的 **II** *n* 1 [c] (*person*) 蒙古人 2 [u] (*language*) 蒙古语

mongrel ['mʌŋgrəl] *n* [c] (*dog*) 杂种狗

monitor ['mɔnɪtə(r)] **I** *n* [c] 1 (*screen*) [计算机] 显示屏; [*of video, television*] 监视器 2 [医] (*machine*) 监控器 3 (*observer*) 监察员 4 [教育] 导生 **II** *vt* 1 [+ *progress, situation*] 监控 2 [+ *broadcasts*] 监听

monk [mʌŋk] *n* [c] 僧侣

monkey ['mʌŋkɪ] *n* [c] 1 [动] 猴 2 [非正式] (*scamp*) 淘气鬼

monologue ['mɔnəlɔg] *n* 1 [c/u] (*speech*) 独白 2 [c] (*rant*) 长篇大论

monopoly [mə'nɔpəlɪ] *n* [c] 1 (*control*) ♦**monopoly (over/on sth)** (对某事的) 垄断 2 (*company*) 垄断企业 ♦**to have a monopoly on/over sth** 对某事实行垄断 ♦**doctors don't have a monopoly on morality** 并非只有医生才有道德规范

monosodium glutamate [mɔnə'səudɪəm'gluːtəmeɪt] *n* [u] 味精

monotonous [mə'nɔtənəs] *adj* [+ *life, job etc, voice, tune*] 单调的

monotony [mə'nɔtənɪ] *n* [u] [*of life, job etc*] 一成不变; [*of voice, tune*] 单调

monsoon [mɔn'suːn] *n* [c] 1 (*also*: ***monsoon season***) ♦**the monsoon** 季风季节 2 (*rainstorm*) 季风雨

monster ['mɔnstə(r)] **I** *n* [c] 1 (*imaginary creature*) 怪物 2 (*large thing*) 庞然大物 3 (*evil person*) (*cruel, frightening*) 恶人 **II** *adj* [非正式] (*massive*) 巨大的

✪**month** [mʌnθ] *n* [c] 1 (*calendar month*) 月 2 (*four-week period*) 一个月的时间 ♦**every month** 每个月 ♦**300 dollars a month** 一个月300美元

monthly ['mʌnθlɪ] **I** *adj* 每月的 **II** *adv* (*every month*) 按月 **III** *n* [c] 月刊

monument ['mɔnjumənt] *n* [c] 1 (*memorial*) 纪念碑 2 (*historical building*) 历史遗迹 ♦**a monument to sb/sth** (*structure*) 某人/某事的纪念碑; (喻) 某人/某事的典范

mood [muːd] *n* 1 [c] [*of person*] 心情; [*of crowd, group*] 氛围 2 [s] [*of place*] 气氛 ♦**to be in a mood** 心情不好 ♦**to be in a good/bad/awkward mood** 心情好/坏/不痛快 ♦**I'm (not) in the mood to do this** 我想做这个 (没有心思做这个)

moody ['muːdɪ] *adj* 1 (*unpredictable*) [+ *person*] 喜怒无常的 2 (*atmospheric*) [+ *film, music*] 忧郁的

moon [muːn] **I** *n* 1 ♦**the moon** 月球 2 [c] [*of other planets*] 卫星 **II** *vi* [英: 非正式] 亮出光屁股 ♦**to be over the moon** [非正式] 非常喜悦 ♦**once in a blue moon** 千载难逢 ◊ *Once in a blue moon you get some problems.* 偶尔你也碰到一些麻烦。

❑**moon about** *vi* = **moon around**

❑**moon around** **I** *vi* [非正式] 闲混 **II** *vt* [不可拆分] 闲逛

moonlight ['muːnlaɪt] **I** *n* [U] 月光 **II** *vi* [非正式](*work*) 兼职 ♦**in the moonlight** 在月光下

moor [muə(r)] **I** *n* [C] [尤英](*heath*) 荒泽 **II** *vt* [+ *boat, ship*] 系泊 **III** *vi* 停泊

moose [muːs] (*pl* **moose**) *n* 麋

mop [mɔp] **I** *n* [C] **1** (*for floors*) 拖把 **2** ♦**mop (of hair)** 蓬乱的(头发) **II** *vt* **1** [+ *floor*] 用拖把擦洗 **2** [+ *brow, forehead*] 擦

❑**mop up** *vt* **1** [+ *liquid*] 擦干净 **2** [非正式](*deal with*) 处理

mope [məup] *vi* 郁闷

❑**mope about** *vi, vt* = **mope around**

❑**mope around I** *vi* 闷闷不乐 **II** *vt* [不可拆分][+ *house, office*] 没精打采地闲逛

moped ['məupɛd] *n* [C] 机动自行车

moral ['mɔrəl] **I** *adj* [+ *issues, values*] 道德的; [+ *courage, duty*] 道义的; [+ *behaviour, person*] 品行端正的 **II** *n* [C] [*of story*] 寓意 **III morals** *n* [*pl*] (*principles, values*) 道德规范 ♦**(to give sb) moral support** (*encouragement*) (给某人以)道义上的支持

morale [mɔ'rɑːl] *n* [U] [*of army, staff*] 士气

morality [mə'rælɪtɪ] *n* **1** [U] (*ethics*) 道德伦理 **2** [C] (*system of morals*) 道德观 **3** [U] [*of something*] 道德性

morally ['mɔrəlɪ] *adv* **1** (*from a moral perspective*) [+ *right, wrong, justifiable*] 从道德观点看; [+ *superior*] 道德上 **2** (*in a moral way*) [*live, behave* +] 品行端正地

morbid ['mɔːbɪd] *adj* [+ *person, interest, subject*] 病态的

✪ **more**

KEYWORD

[mɔː(r)]

I *adj*

1 (*in comparisons*) (*with uncount noun, plural noun*) 更多的 ♦**I get more money/holidays than you do** 我比你有更多的钱/假期 ♦**there are more problems than solutions** 问题多于解决方案

2 (*additional*) (*with uncount noun, plural noun*) 再一些的 ♦**would you like some more tea/peanuts?** 你要再来点茶/花生吗？♦**is there any more wine?** 还有酒吗？♦**are there any more cakes?** 还有蛋糕吗？♦**I have no more** *or* **I don't have any more milk/pencils** 我没有牛奶/铅笔了 ♦**a few more weeks** 再几个星期

II *pron*

1 (*in comparisons*) (*more in quantity, number*) 更多的量 ♦**there's/there are more than I thought** 比我想得更多 ♦**it cost more than we expected** 比我们预料得更贵 ♦**more than 20** 大于20 ♦**she's got more than me** 她比我得到的多

2 (*further, additional*) (*in quantity*) 额外的量 ♦**is there/are there any more?** 还有多的吗？♦**there isn't/there aren't any more left** 没有多余的了 ♦**have you got any more of it/them?** 你还有吗？♦**a little/a few more** 多一点点 ♦**much/many more** 多得多

III *adv*

1 (*to form comparative*) 更 ♦**more dangerous/difficult (than)** (比…)更危险/难 ♦**more easily/quickly (than)** (比…)更容易/快 ♦**I go out more than I used to** 我比过去出去得多了

2 (*in expressions*) ♦**more and more** 越来越 ♦**more or less** (+ *adj, adv*) 差不多; (*at end of sentence*) 或多或少 ♦**more than ever** 空前的多 ♦**once more** 再一次 ♦**what's more** 更有甚者

moreover [mɔː'rəuvə(r)] *adv* 而且

morgue [mɔːg] *n* [C] 停尸房

✪ **morning** ['mɔːnɪŋ] **I** *n* [C/U] *(early in the moring)* 早晨 *(later in the morning)* 上午 ◊ *We spent all morning cleaning the kitchen.* 我们花了一上午时间来打扫厨房。**II** *cpd* [复合词] [+ *paper, sun, walk*] *(early in the moring)* 早晨 *(later in the morning)* 上午 ♦**good morning!** 早上好！♦**he'll phone back in the morning** 他会在明天上午回电话 ♦**at 3 o'clock/7 o'clock in the morning** 凌晨3点/早上7点

♦**this morning** 今天上午 ♦**the next morning** 第二天早上 ♦**on Monday morning** 星期一上午

morning sickness *n* [U] 孕妇晨吐

Moroccan [mə'rɔkən] **I** *adj* 摩洛哥的 **II** *n* [C] (*person*) 摩洛哥人

Morocco [mə'rɔkəu] *n* 摩洛哥

moron ['mɔːrɔn] [非正式, 疑讳] *n* [C] 蠢货

morphine ['mɔːfiːn] *n* [U] 吗啡

Morse [mɔːs] *n* [U] (*also* : **Morse code**) 莫尔斯电码

mortal ['mɔːtl] **I** *adj* **1** (*not immortal*) 终有一死的 **2** [+ *danger, enemy, combat*] 致命的 **II** *n* ♦**a mere/an ordinary mortal** 凡人/普通人

mortar ['mɔːtə(r)] *n* **1** [U] [建筑] 砂浆 **2** [C] [军] 迫击炮 **3** [C] [烹饪] (*bowl*) 研钵 ♦**pestle and mortar** 杵和臼

mortgage ['mɔːgɪdʒ] **I** *n* [C] 抵押贷款 **II** *vt* [+ *house, property*] 抵押 ♦**to take out a mortgage (on sth)** 用抵押贷款(购置某物)

mortician [mɔː'tɪʃən] [美] *n* [C] 殡葬业者

mortified ['mɔːtɪfaɪd] [非正式] *adj* (*embarrassed*) ♦**to be mortified** 感到羞辱

mortuary ['mɔːtjuərɪ] *n* [C] 太平间

mosaic [məu'zeɪɪk] *n* [C] 镶嵌图案

Moslem ['mɔzləm] *adj, n* = **Muslim**

mosque [mɔsk] *n* [C] 清真寺

mosquito [mɔs'kiːtəu] (*pl* **mosquitoes**) *n* [C] 蚊

mosquito net *n* [C] 蚊帐

moss [mɔs] *n* [C/U] 苔藓

✪ **most**

KEYWORD

[məust]

I *adj*

1 (*almost all*) (*with uncount noun, plural noun*) 大部分的 ♦**most people** 大多数人

2 (*in comparisons*) ♦**(the) most** (*with uncount noun, plural noun*) 最 ♦**who won the most money/prizes?** 谁赢了最多的钱/奖品? ♦**we see each other most days** 我们大多数时间都见面

II *pron* (*uncount*) 大部分; (*plural*) 大多数 ♦**most of it/them** 它/他们的大部分 ♦**I paid the most** 我付了大部分 ♦**to make the most of sth** 充分利用某物 ♦**at the (very) most** 顶多

III *adv* (*superlative*)

1 (*with verb*) ♦**(the) most** 最 ♦**what I miss (the) most is ...** 我最想念的是…

2 (*with adj*) ♦**the most comfortable/expensive sofa in the shop** 店里最舒服/贵的沙发

3 (*with adv*) ♦**most efficiently/effectively** 最有效率/有效地 ♦**most of all** 最起码的

4 (*very*) [*polite, interesting etc*] 很 ♦**a most interesting book** 一本很有趣的书

注意，可以说 *Most children love sweets*，但不能说 *Most of children love sweets*。然而，如果后接代词，就可以说 *Most of them love sweets*。

mostly ['məustlɪ] *adv* **1** (*chiefly*) 主要 **2** (*usually*) 通常

MOT [ɛməu'tiː] [英] *n* 旧车性能测试

motel [məu'tɛl] *n* [C] 汽车旅馆

moth [mɔθ] *n* [C] 蛾

✪ **mother** ['mʌðə(r)] **I** *n* **1** [C] (*parent*) 母亲 **2** (*as address*) ♦**Mother** 妈妈 **II** *vt* **1** (*be mother to*) 抚养 **2** (*pamper, protect*) 慈母般照顾 ◊ *She mothers all her lodgers.* 她慈母般照顾所有的房客。

motherhood ['mʌðəhud] *n* [U] 母亲身份

mother-in-law (*pl* **mothers-in-law**) ['mʌðərɪnlɔː] *n* [C] [*of woman*] 婆婆; [*of man*] 岳母

motherly ['mʌðəlɪ] *adj* [+ *feeling, behaviour*] 母亲的; [+ *person, figure*] 母亲般的

mother-of-pearl ['mʌðərəv'pəːl] *n* [U] 珠母层

Mother's Day [英] *n* [C/U] 母亲节

mother-to-be ['mʌðətə'biː] (*pl* **mothers-to-be**) *n* [C] 孕妇

mother tongue *n* [C] 母语

motif [məu'tiːf] *n* [C] **1** (*design*) 基调 **2** (*theme*) 主题

motion ['məuʃən] **I** *n* **1** [U] 运动 **2** [C]

(*gesture*) 动作 **3** [c] (*in meeting*) 动议 **4** [c] [英] (*also*: **bowel motion**) 大便 [美=**movement**] **II** *vi* ♦**to motion to sb (to do sth)** (*gesture, signal*) 示意某人(做某事) ♦**to be in motion** [*process, event* +] 在进行中; [*vehicle, device* +] 在行驶中 ♦**to set sth in motion** [+ *process, event*] 使某事开始进行; [+ *device*]使某物开始运转 ♦**to go through the motions** 敷衍了事

motionless ['məuʃənlɪs] *adj* 不动的

motion picture [尤美] *n* [c] 电影

motivate ['məutɪveɪt] *vt* **1** (*prompt, drive*) ♦**to be motivated by sth** [*act, decision* +] 受某事的驱使; [*person* +] 受到某事的激发 **2** [+ *worker, student etc*] 激励 ♦**to motivate sb to do sth** 激励某人做某事 ◊ *What motivates athletes to take drugs?* 什么驱使运动员服用禁药? ♦**a racially motivated attack** 带有种族动机的攻击行动

motivated ['məutɪveɪtɪd] *adj* 士气高涨的

motivation [məutɪ'veɪʃən] *n* [U] **1** (*motive*) 动机 **2** (*commitment*) 动力

motive ['məutɪv] **I** *n* [c] (*reason*) 动机 **II** *adj* [+ *power, force*] 产生运动的

motor ['məutə(r)] **I** *n* [c] **1** [*of machine, vehicle*] 发动机 **2** [英:非正式] (*car*) 汽车 **II** *adj* [+ *industry, trade*] 机动车辆的 **III** *vi* [过时] (*drive*) 开汽车

motorbike ['məutəbaɪk] *n* [c] 摩托车

motorboat ['məutəbəut] *n* [c] 摩托艇

motor car [英] [正式] *n* [c] 汽车

motorcycle ['məutəsaɪkl] [正式] *n* [c] 摩托车

motorcyclist ['məutəsaɪklɪst] *n* [c] 摩托车手

motoring ['məutərɪŋ] [尤英] **I** *n* [U] (*activity*) 驾驶汽车 **II** *adj* [+ *offence, organization*] 汽车驾驶的 [美=**automobile, driving**]

motorist ['məutərɪst] [尤英] *n* [c] 开汽车的人 [美=**driver**]

motor racing [英] *n* [U] 赛车

motorway ['məutəweɪ] [英] **I** *n* [c] 高速公路 [美=**freeway**] **II** *cpd* [复合词] [+ *traffic, network*] 高速公路

motto ['mɔtəu] (*pl* **mottoes**) *n* [c] **1** (*slogan*) [*of school, regiment*] 格言 **2** (*principle*) [*of person*] 座右铭

mould (美 **mold**) [məuld] **I** *n* **1** [c] (*cast*) (*for jelly, metal*) 模子 **2** [U] (*fungus*) 霉菌 **II** *vt* **1** (*shape*) [+ *plastic, clay etc*] 使成形 **2** (*influence*) [+ *public opinion, character*] 影响

mouldy (美 **moldy**) ['məuldɪ] *adj* [+ *bread, cheese*] 发霉的

mound [maund] *n* [c] **1** [*of earth*] 土堆 **2** (*heap*) [*of objects*] 堆 **3** [棒球] 投球区土墩

mount [maunt] **I** *vt* **1** (*organize*) [+ *attack, campaign*] 发起; [+ *exhibition, display*] 举办 **2** (*fix*) [+ *jewel, picture*] 安放 **3** (*get onto*) [+ *horse, cycle*] 骑上 **4** [正式] (*climb*) [+ *staircase, platform*] 登上 **II** *vi* **1** (*increase*) [*tension, problems* +] 加剧 **2** (*pile up*) 增加 **3** (*get onto horse or cycle*) 骑 **III** *n* **1** (*mountain*) (*in names*) ♦**Mount Rushmore** 拉什莫尔山 **2** [c] [正式] (*horse*) 坐骑 **3** [c] (*for picture, photograph etc*) 框 ♦**the car mounted the pavement** 汽车轧上人行道 ♦**mounting debts/bills** 成堆的债务/账单

❑**mount up** *vi* 不断增加

mountain ['mauntɪn] **I** *n* [c] 山 **II** *cpd* [复合词] [+ *road, stream*] 山 ♦**a mountain of sth** [+ *papers, work*] 一大堆某物 ♦**to make a mountain out of a molehill** 小题大做

mountain bike *n* [c] 山地自行车

mountaineer [mauntɪ'nɪə(r)] *n* [c] 登山能手

mountaineering [mauntɪ'nɪərɪŋ] *n* [U] 登山运动 ♦**to go mountaineering** 爬山

mountainous ['mauntɪnəs] *adj* [+ *country, area*] 多山的

mountain range *n* [c] 山脉

mountainside ['mauntɪnsaɪd] *n* [c] 山坡

mourn [mɔːn] **I** *vt* **1** [+ *death*] 哀悼; [+ *person*] 悼念 **2** [+ *loss of something*] 为…感到痛心 **II** *vi* ♦**to mourn for** [+ *person*] 悼念; [+ *thing, time*] 为…感到惋惜

mourner ['mɔːnə(r)] *n* [c] 送葬者

mourning ['mɔːnɪŋ] *n* [U] 哀悼 ♦**to be in mourning** 服丧

mouse [maus] (*pl* **mice**) *n* [c] **1** [动] 鼠 **2** [计算机] 鼠标

mouse mat *n* [c] 鼠标垫
moussaka [mu'sɑːkə] *n* [u] 碎肉茄子蛋
mousse [muːs] *n* [c/u] **1** [烹饪] 奶油冻 **2** (*foam*) 摩丝
moustache (美 **mustache**) [məs'tɑːʃ] *n* [c] 髭
mouth [*n* mauθ, *vb* mauð] **I** *n* [c] **1** [+ *of person, animal*] 嘴 **2** (*way of talking*) 说话方式 **3** [*of river*] 河口 **4** [*of cave, tunnel*] 口 **II** *vt* **1** (*mime*) 唇语 **2** (*trot out*) 言不由衷地说
mouthful ['mauθful] *n* **1** [c] [*of food*] 一口 **2** [s] [非正式] (*word*) 拗口的词
mouth organ [尤英] *n* [c] 口琴
mouthpiece ['mauθpiːs] *n* [c] **1** [*of telephone*] 送话口; [*of trumpet etc*] 吹口 **2** (*spokesman*) 代言人
mouthwash ['mauθwɔʃ] *n* [c/u] 漱口剂
✪ **move** [muːv] **I** *vi* **1** (*change position*) [*vehicle* +] 行进 ◊ *The train began to move.* 火车开始开动了。; [*person, object* +] 动 **2** (*relocate*) 搬家 ◊ *She had often considered moving to London.* 她常考虑搬到伦敦去住。**3** (*also* : ***move on***) (*from job*) 换 ◊ *Christina moved to another job to get more experience.* 克里斯蒂娜换了另一份工作以获得更多的经验。; (*from activity*) 改换 **4** (*shift*) ♦ **to move to(wards)** 倾向于 ◊ *The Labour Party has moved to the right.* 工党已倾向于右派立场。**5** (*develop*) [*situation, events* +] 进展 ◊ *Events are moving fast.* 事情进展迅速。**II** *vt* **1** (*change position of*) [+ *furniture, car etc*] 挪动 ◊ *Workmen were moving a heavy wardrobe down the stairs.* 工人们正把一个很重的衣橱挪到楼下去。**2** (*transfer*) [+ *worker*] 调动 ◊ *His superiors moved him to another department.* 他的上司把他调到另一个部门。**3** (*change*) ♦ **to move sth (to)** [+ *event, date*] 改(到) ◊ *The club has moved its meeting to January 22nd.* 俱乐部已把聚会的日期改到1月22日。**4** (*affect emotionally*) [+ *person*] 感动 ◊ *The whole incident had moved her profoundly.* 整个事件深深地感动了她。**5** ♦ **to move sb to do sth** (*motivate*) 促使某人做某事 ◊ *What has moved the President to take this step?* 是什么促使总统采取这一举措？**6** ♦ **to move that ...** [政治] 提议… ◊ *She moved that the meeting be adjourned.* 她提议休会。**III** *n* [c] **1** (*movement*) 动作 ◊ *Daniel's eyes followed her every move.* 丹尼尔的眼光紧随她的每一个动作。**2** (*act*) 行动 ◊ *A government move to drop the plan could affect share prices.* 政府终止这项计划的行动将会影响到股票价格。**3** (*change*) [*of house*] 搬家 ◊ *The move to Prague was a daunting prospect.* 搬家至布拉格，其前景颇令人沮丧。**4** (*change*) [*of job, belief*] 变动 ◊ *His move to the personnel department was no surprise.* 他被调到人事部门的变动并不令人吃惊。**5** (*in game*) (*go, turn*) 一步; (*change of position*) 一步棋 ♦ **to move house/jobs/offices** 搬家/换工作/更换办公地点 ♦ **a good/bad move** 好/糟糕的一步 ♦ **one false move** 不明智的行为 ♦ **to get a move on** [非正式] 快点 ♦ **to be on the move** 迁移中 ♦ **to make a move** (*take action*) 采取行动; (*leave*) 离去
❑ **move about, move around** *vi* **1** (*change position*) 走来走去 **2** (*change residence, job*) 不断迁移 ◊ *I was born in Fort Worth but we moved about a lot.* 我出生在沃思堡，但我们不断在各地迁移。
❑ **move along I** *vi* **1** (*develop*) 发展 ◊ *Research tends to move along at a slow but orderly pace.* 研究趋于缓慢而有序地发展。**2** (*keep walking*) 走开 ◊ *Move along there, please.* 请走开。**II** *vt* **1** (*cause to develop*) 使进展 ◊ *I hope we can move things along without too much delay.* 我希望我们能使事情有所进展而不致有太多延误。**2** (*order to move*) [*police* +] 命令走开 ◊ *Our officers are moving them along and not allowing them to gather in large groups.* 我们的官员命令他们走开，不允许他们聚众。
❑ **move around** *vi* = **move about**
❑ **move away** *vi* (*from town, area*) 离开 ◊ *He moved away and lost contact*

with the family. 他离开家，和家人失去了联系。; (*from window, door*) 走开 ◊ *She moved away from the window.* 她从窗户处走开。

❑ **move back** I *vi* **1** (*return*) (*to town, area*) 回来 **2** (*backwards*) [*person, troops, vehicle* +] 后退 II *vt* [+ *crowd*] 使后退; [+ *object*] (*less far forward*) 往后移; (*to original position*) 使回原位; (*in board game*) 后退 ◊ *Move back three squares.* 后退3格。

❑ **move down** *vi* 下降

❑ **move forward** I *vi* [*person, troops, vehicle* +] 向前移动; (*in board game*) 前进 II *vt* [+ *object*] 使向前移

❑ **move in** *vi* **1** (*into house*) 搬入 ◊ *The house wasn't ready when she moved in.* 她搬进去的时候房子还没装修好。**2** [*police, soldiers* +] 开进来 ◊ *The troops moved in to stop the riot.* 军队开进来镇压暴乱。

❑ **move in on** *vt* [不可拆分] 开始参与

❑ **move into** *vt* [不可拆分] [+ *house, area*] 搬进

❑ **move in with** *vt* [不可拆分] 和…同居 ◊ *Her husband had moved in with a younger woman.* 她的丈夫和一个比她年轻的女人同居了。

❑ **move off** *vi* [*car* +] 开走 ◊ *Gil waved his hand and the car moved off.* 吉尔挥了挥手，车开走了。

❑ **move on** I *vi* **1** (*leave*) 启程前往 ◊ *After three weeks in Hong Kong, we moved on to Japan.* 在香港逗留了3个星期后，我们启程前往日本。**2** (*progress*) 进行 ◊ *Now, can we move on and discuss productivity.* 好，让我们进行下一项，讨论生产率问题。II *vt* **1** (*order to move*) 命令走开 ◊ *I used to busk, but I was always being moved on by the police.* 我以前常在街头卖艺，但警察总是命令我走开。**2** (*cause to develop*) 使有所进展 ◊ *I think we need to move things on a bit.* 我认为我们应该使情况略有所进展。

❑ **move out** *vi* (*of house*) 搬出去 ◊ *The guy that lived there moved out a month ago.* 以前住在那儿的家伙一个月前搬出去了。

❑ **move over** *vi* (*to make room*) 让开些 ◊ *Move over and let me drive.* 让开些，让我来开车。

❑ **move up** *vi* **1** (*on sofa etc*) 靠拢 ◊ *Move up, John, and make room for the lady.* 靠拢点，约翰，给那位女士挪个地方。**2** [+ *employee, pupil*] 升级

movement ['muːvmənt] I *n* **1** [C] [宗, 政治] (*group of people*) 团体 **2** [C/U] (*moving*) 动静 **3** [C] (*gesture*) 动作 **4** [C/U] (*transport, travel*) [*of goods, people*] 运输 **5** [C/U] (*shift*) (*in attitude, policy*) 动向 **6** [C] [音] 乐章 **7** [C] (*also* : ***bowel movement***) 排便 II **movements** *n* [*pl*] [*of person*] 活动

movie ['muːvɪ] [美] *n* [C] 电影 [英 = **film**] ♦ **the movies** 电影 [英 = **the cinema**]

movie theater [美] *n* [C] 电影院 [英 = **cinema**]

moving ['muːvɪŋ] *adj* **1** (*emotionally*) 动人的 **2** (*not static*) 活动的

mow [məu] (*pt* **mowed**, *pp* **mowed** *or* **mown**) *vt* [+ *grass, lawn*] 刈

❑ **mow down** *vt* (*kill*) [+ *person*] [*driver* +] 撞死; [*gunman* +] 枪杀

mower ['məuə(r)] *n* [C] (*also* : ***lawnmower***) 割草机

Mozambique [məuzəm'biːk] *n* 莫桑比克

MP *n abbr* **1** [英] (= ***Member of Parliament***) 下院议员 **2** (= ***Military Police***) 军警

MP3 [ɛmpiː'θriː] *n* **1** (*format*) 一种音频压缩格式 **2** (*file*) 以这种音频压缩格式储存的声音文件

mph *abbr* (= ***miles per hour***) 每小时…英里

Mr (美 **Mr.**) ['mɪstə(r)] *n* ♦ **Mr Smith** 史密斯先生

Mrs (美 **Mrs.**) ['mɪsɪz] *n* ♦ **Mrs Smith** 史密斯太太

MS *n abbr* **1** [美] (= ***Master of Science***) = **MSc** **2** (= ***multiple sclerosis***) 多发性硬化

Ms (美 **Ms.**) [mɪz] *n* (*Miss or Mrs*) ♦ **Ms Smith** 史密斯女士

MSc *n abbr* (= ***Master of Science***) (*qualification*) 理学硕士学位; (*person*) 理学硕士

MSG I [手机短信] *abbr* = **message** II *n abbr* (= ***monosodium glutamate***) 味精

MSP *n abbr* (= ***Member of the Scottish***

Parliament) 苏格兰下院议员
MST [美] *abbr* (= ***Mountain Standard Time***) 山区标准时间
Mt, Mt. [尤美] (*pl* **Mts**) *abbr* (= ***mount***) 山

much
KEYWORD
[mʌtʃ]
I *adj* 大量的 ♦ **we haven't got much time/money** 我们没有多少时间/钱
II *pron* 大量 ♦ **there isn't much left** 剩下的不多了 ♦ **he doesn't do much at the weekends** 周末他不做太多事 ♦ **much of the time/his life** 大多数时间/他人生的大部分
III *adv*
1 (*a great deal*) 许多 ♦ **he hasn't changed much** 他没变很多 ♦ **"did you like her?" – "not much"** "你喜欢她吗？" "不太喜欢" ♦ **much as I like him ...** 尽管我喜欢他，但是… ♦ **however much you may try to forget ...** 无论你怎么竭力想忘掉都…
2 (*far*) …得多 ♦ **I'm much better now** 我感觉好多了 ♦ **it's much the biggest publishing company in Europe** 它是欧洲最大的出版公司 ♦ **those trousers are much too big for you** 那些裤子对你而言实在太肥了
3 (*often*) 经常 ♦ **do you go out much?** 你经常出去吗？
4 (*almost*) 几乎 ♦ **the two books are much the same** 这两本书几乎是一样的 ♦ **"how are you feeling?" – "much the same"** "你感觉怎么样？" "几乎没变"

muck [mʌk] *n* [U] [非正式] (*dirt*) 污垢
❑ **muck about** [英:非正式] **I** *vi* **1** (*fool about*) 鬼混 **2** ♦ **to muck about with sth** 瞎摆弄某物 **II** *vt* [+ *person*] 耍弄
❑ **muck around** *vi* = **muck about**
❑ **muck in** [英:非正式] *vi* 一起出力
❑ **muck out I** *vt* 清除 **II** *vi* 打扫畜舍
❑ **muck up** [英:非正式] *vt* [+ *exam, interview etc*] 搞糟 [美 = **screw up**]
mucky ['mʌkɪ] [非正式] *adj* [+ *boots, field*] 肮脏的
mucus ['mjuːkəs] *n* [U] 黏液
mud [mʌd] *n* [U] 泥
muddle ['mʌdl] **I** *n* [C/U] **1** [*of papers, figures, things*] 混乱状态 **2** (*situation*) 糟糕局面 **II** *vt* (*also*: **muddle up**) [+ *things*] 把…弄乱; [+ *words, names*] 混淆; [+ *person*] 使糊涂 ♦ **to be in a muddle** 一片混乱 ♦ **to get in a muddle** [*person* +] 弄糊涂了; [*objects* +] 搞得一团糟 ♦ **to muddle sb/sth (up) with sb/sth** 将某人和某人/某物和某物搞混
❑ **muddle along** *vi* [非正式] (*drift*) 混日子
❑ **muddle through** [非正式] *vi* (*get by*) 对付过去
muddled *adj* (*confused*) [+ *person, thinking, ideas*] 糊涂的
muddy ['mʌdɪ] **I** *adj* **1** [+ *floor, field*] 沾满烂泥的 **2** [+ *colour, green*] 灰暗的 **II** *vt* (*dirty*) 使沾上烂泥
mudguard ['mʌdgɑːd] [尤英] *n* [C] 挡泥板
muesli ['mjuːzlɪ] *n* [U] 穆兹利，和干水果混在一起的燕麦早餐
muffin ['mʌfɪn] *n* [C] **1** 松饼 **2** [英] 英式松饼
muffle ['mʌfl] *vt* [+ *sound*] 使低沉
muffled ['mʌfld] *adj* **1** [+ *sound*] 低沉的 **2** (*against cold*) 裹住的
muffler ['mʌflə(r)] *n* [C] **1** [美:汽车] 消音器 **2** [过时] (*scarf*) 围巾
mug [mʌg] **I** *n* [C] **1** (*large cup*) (*for drinks*) 大杯子; (*for beer*) 啤酒杯 **2** (*contents*) 一大杯的量 **3** [非正式] (*face*) 脸 **4** [英:非正式] (*fool*) 傻瓜 **II** *vt* (*rob*) 行凶抢劫 ♦ **it's a mug's game** [英:非正式] 这是桩无利可图的事
❑ **mug up** [英:非正式] *vt* (*also*: **mug up on**) 突击学习
mugger ['mʌgə(r)] *n* [C] 抢劫犯
mugging ['mʌgɪŋ] *n* [C/U] (*assault*) 行凶抢劫
muggy ['mʌgɪ] *adj* [+ *weather, day*] 闷热而潮湿的 ♦ **it's muggy today** 今天天气很闷热
mule [mjuːl] *n* [C] **1** [动] 骡 **2** (*shoe*) 拖鞋
multicoloured (美 **multicolored**) ['mʌltɪkʌləd] *adj* 多色的
multi-level [mʌltɪ'lɛvl] [美] *adj*

[+ *building, car park*] 多层的［英 =**multi-storey**］
multimedia [mʌltɪ'miːdɪə] **I** *n* [U] **1**［计算机］多媒体 **2**［教育］多媒体教学 **II** *adj* 多媒体的
multinational [mʌltɪ'næʃənl] **I** *adj* **1** [+ *company, corporation*] 跨国的 **2** [+ *force*] 多国的 **II** *n* [C] 跨国公司
multiple ['mʌltɪpl] **I** *adj* [+ *injuries*] 多次的; [+ *collision*] 多重的; [+ *birth*] 多胎的 **II** *n* [C]［数］倍数
multiple-choice ['mʌltɪpltʃɔɪs] *adj* [+ *exam, question*] 多项选择的
multiple sclerosis [-sklɪ'rəusɪs] *n* [U] 多发性硬化
multiplex ['mʌltɪplɛks] *n* [C] (*also*: ***multiplex cinema***) 多剧场影剧院
multiplication [mʌltɪplɪ'keɪʃən] *n* **1** [U]［数］乘法 **2** [S] (*increase*) 倍增
multiply ['mʌltɪplaɪ] **I** *vt*［数］♦**to multiply sth (by sth)**（某数）乘以某数 **II** *vi* **1** (*increase*) 增加 **2** (*reproduce*) 繁殖 **3**［数］做乘法
multiracial [mʌltɪ'reɪʃl] *adj* [+ *school, society*] 多种族的
multi-storey [mʌltɪ'stɔːrɪ] **I** *adj* [+ *building, car park*] 多层的 **II** *n* [C] (*car park*) 多层停车场
multitude ['mʌltɪtjuːd] *n* **1** ♦**a multitude of** [+ *reasons, ideas*] 许多 **2** [C]［文］(*crowd*) 人群 ♦**to cover** *or* **hide a multitude of sins** 掩盖种种罪恶
mum [mʌm] **I** *n*［英：非正式］(*mother*) 妈妈［美 =**mom**］**II** *adj* ♦**to keep mum** 保密 ♦**mum's the word** 别声张
mumble ['mʌmbl] **I** *vt* 含糊地说 **II** *vi* 咕哝 **III** *n* [C] 咕哝
mummy ['mʌmɪ] *n* [C] **1**［英：非正式］(*mother*) 妈妈［美 =**mommy**］**2** (*embalmed body*) 木乃伊
mumps [mʌmps] *n* [U] 腮腺炎
munch [mʌntʃ] **I** *vt* 大嚼 **II** *vi* 出声咀嚼
municipal [mjuː'nɪsɪpl] *adj* 市政的
mural ['mjuərəl] *n* [C] 壁画
murder ['məːdə(r)] **I** *n* [C/U] (*killing*) 谋杀 **II** *vt* **1** (*kill*) 谋杀 **2** (*spoil*) [+ *piece of music, language*] 糟蹋 ♦**to get away with murder**［非正式］为所欲为 ♦**the traffic was murder!**［非正式］交通真要命！♦**I could murder him!** 我真该杀了他！
📖 用法参见 **kill**
murderer ['məːdərə(r)] *n* [C] 凶手
murky ['məːkɪ] *adj* **1** [+ *street, night*] 昏暗的 **2** [+ *water*] 混浊的 **3**［英］(*shady, shadowy*) 不可告人的 **4** (*hazy, unclear*) 晦涩难懂的
murmur ['məːmə(r)] **I** *vt* (*say quietly*) 小声说 **II** *vi* (*speak quietly*) 小声说话 **III** *n* **1** [C] (*voice*) 低语 **2** [S] (*low sound*) [*of voices*] 窃窃低语声; [*of wind, waves*] 细声 **3** [C]［医］(*also*: ***heart murmur***) 杂音 ♦**without a murmur** 毫无怨言
muscle ['mʌsl] *n* **1** [C/U]［解剖］肌肉 **2** [U] (*power*) 实力 ♦**he didn't move a muscle** 他一动不动 ♦**to flex one's muscles** 显示力量
❑**muscle in** *vi* 强行挤入
❑**muscle in on** *vt*［不可拆分］强行插足
muscular ['mʌskjulə(r)] *adj* [+ *person, body*] 肌肉发达的; [+ *pain, weakness*] 肌肉的
museum [mjuː'zɪəm] *n* [C] 博物馆
mushroom ['mʌʃrum] **I** *n* [C] (*edible*) 蘑菇; (*poisonous*) 毒蘑菇 **II** *vi* [*town, organization* +] 迅速发展 **III** *cpd*［复合词］[+ *soup, omelette, pizza*] 蘑菇
✪**music** ['mjuːzɪk] *n* [U] **1** (*sound*) 音乐 ◊ *classical music* 古典音乐 **2** (*activity*) 音乐艺术 ◊ *He plans to make his career in music.* 他打算在音乐艺术方面发展。**3**［教育，大学］音乐课 **4** (*score*) 乐谱 ◊ *He's never been able to read music.* 他一向不识乐谱。♦**to face the music** 承担自己行为的后果 ♦**to be music to sb's ears** 佳音
musical ['mjuːzɪkl] **I** *adj* **1** (*related to music*) [+ *career, skills*] 音乐的 **2** (*musically gifted*) [+ *person*] 有音乐天赋的 **3** (*resembling music*) [+ *tone, voice, accent*] 悦耳的 **II** *n* [C] (*show, film*) 音乐剧
musical instrument *n* [C] 乐器
musician [mjuː'zɪʃən] *n* [C] 音乐家
Muslim, Moslem ['muzlɪm] **I** *n* [C] 穆斯林 **II** *adj* 穆斯林的
muslin ['mʌzlɪn] *n* [U] 平纹细布
mussel ['mʌsl] *n* [C] 贻贝
✪**must** [mʌst] **I** *aux vb* **1** (*expressing*

importance or necessity) 必须◊ *The doctor must allow the patient to decide.* 医生必须让病人来决定。**2** (*expressing intention*) 得◊ *I really must be getting back.* 我真得回去了。**3** (*expressing forceful suggestion*) 一定要◊ *You must see my new guitar.* 你一定要看看我的新吉他。**4** (*expressing anger in question*) 偏要◊ *Must you be so careless?* 你偏要这么粗心吗？**5** (*expressing presumption*) 一定◊ *Russell must be one of the youngest ever Wembley referees.* 拉塞尔一定是温布利体育场上历来最年轻的裁判之一。◊ *He must have forgotten to pick up the tickets.* 他一定忘记去取票了。**6** (*expressing sympathy*) 一定◊ *Sit down, you must be exhausted.* 坐吧，你一定累坏了。**7** (*expressing surprise or shock*) ♦**you must be joking** 你准是在开玩笑◊ *I must be mad!* 我准是疯了！ **II** *n* [非正式] (*necessity*) ♦**to be a must** 是必备之物◊ *Rubber gloves are a must if your skin is sensitive.* 橡胶手套对于敏感皮肤是必备之物。♦**if you must** (*expressing reluctant agreement*) 如果你坚持要 ♦**if you must know** (*expressing reluctance to tell sb sth*) 如果你一定要知道的话

mustache ['mʌstæʃ] [美] *n* **= moustache**

mustard ['mʌstəd] *n* [U] 芥末

mustn't ['mʌsnt] **= must not**

mute [mjuːt] **I** *adj* (*silent*) 缄默的 **II** *vt* (*reduce*) 抑制

mutilate ['mjuːtɪleɪt] *vt* [+ *person, corpse*] 毁伤

mutiny ['mjuːtɪnɪ] **I** *n* [C/U] [*of soldiers, sailors*] 哗变 **II** *vi* [*soldiers, sailors* +] 反叛

mutter ['mʌtə(r)] **I** *vi* 嘟哝 **II** *vt* 低声说 **III** *n* [C] 低语

mutton ['mʌtn] *n* [U] (*meat*) 羊肉 ♦**mutton dressed (up) as lamb** [英:非正式] 老来俏

mutual ['mjuːtʃuəl] *adj* (*shared*) [+ *feeling, attraction*] 共有的; [+ *benefit, interest*] 共同的 ♦**a mutual friend** 共同的朋友 ♦**the feeling is mutual** 有同感

mutually ['mjuːtʃuəlɪ] *adv* [+ *convenient, acceptable*] 彼此 ♦**mutually exclusive** 互不相容

muzzle ['mʌzl] **I** *n* [C] **1** (*restraint*) (*for dog*) 口套 **2** (*nose and mouth*) [*of dog*] 鼻口部分 **3** [*of gun*] 枪口 **II** *vt* **1** [+ *dog*] 给…套口套 **2** (*gag*) [+ *press, person*] 使缄默

MW [广播] *abbr* (**= *medium wave***) 中波

✪ **my** [maɪ] *adj* 我的◊ *my parents* 我的父母◊ *I've washed my hair.* 我洗了头。

Myanmar ['maɪænmɑː], **Myanma** [mjænmɑː] *n* 缅甸

myself [maɪ'sɛlf] *pron* **1** 我自己◊ *I hurt myself.* 我伤了自己。◊ *I prepared the dinner myself.* 我自己做的晚餐。◊ *I bought myself a new CD.* 我给自己买了张新唱片。◊ *I want to try it out for myself.* 我想自己试一下。**2** (*emphatic*) 我本人◊ *I myself live in London.* 我本人住在伦敦。**3** (*me*) 我◊ *a complete beginner like myself* 像我这样的一个初学者 ♦**by myself** (*unaided*) 我独力地◊ *I did it all by myself.* 这都是我自己一个人独力做的。; (*alone*) 我独自◊ *I live by myself.* 我独自一个人住。

mysterious [mɪs'tɪərɪəs] *adj* **1** (*strange*) 神秘的 **2** (*enigmatic*) ♦**to be mysterious about sth** 对某事卖弄玄虚

mystery ['mɪstərɪ] **I** *n* **1** [C] (*puzzle*) 谜 **2** [U] (*strangeness*) [*of place, person*] 离奇 **3** [C] (*story*) 推理作品 **II** *adj* (*unknown, mysterious*) 神秘的

mystical ['mɪstɪkl] *adj* [+ *experience, cult, rite*] 玄妙的

mystify ['mɪstɪfaɪ] *vt* 使困惑

myth [mɪθ] *n* [C] **1** (*legend, story*) 神话 **2** (*fallacy*) 谬论

mythical ['mɪθɪkl] *adj* **1** [+ *beast, monster*] 神话中的 **2** [+ *jobs, opportunities etc*] 虚构的

mythology [mɪ'θɔlədʒɪ] *n* [C/U] 神话

Nn

N¹, n [ɛn] *n* [c/u] (*letter*) 英语的第十四个字母

N² *abbr* (= **north**) 北方

n/a *abbr* (= **not applicable**) 不适用

nag [næg] **I** *vt* (*go on at*) 唠叨 **II** *vi* 唠叨 **III** *n* [c] **1** [非正式] (*horse*) 马 **2** [贬] (*person*) 喋喋不休的人 ♦**to nag at sb** [*worry, doubt, feeling* +] 令某人烦恼 ♦**to nag (at) sb to do sth** 唠叨某人做某事 ♦**to nag sb into doing sth** 非叫某人做某事不可

nagging ['nægɪŋ] **I** *adj* [+ *doubt, suspicion*] 挥之不去的; [+ *pain*] 令人心烦的 **II** *n* [u] 纠缠不休

nail [neɪl] **I** *n* [c] **1** [*of finger, toe*] 指甲 **2** (*for hammering*) 钉子 **II** *vt* **1** (*attach*) ♦**to nail sth to/on sth** 把某物钉在某物上 **2** [非正式] [+ *thief*] 抓住 ♦**to be nailed shut** 用钉子钉死

❑**nail down** *vt* **1** (*identify*) 确定 **2** (*agree on*) 达成 **3** (*attach*) 钉牢 ♦**to nail sb down to a date/price** 要某人确定日期/价格

nailfile ['neɪlfaɪl] *n* [c] 指甲锉

nail polish *n* [u] 指甲油

nail polish remover *n* [u] 洗甲水

nail varnish [英] *n* = **nail polish**

naive, naïve [naɪ'iːv] *adj* [+ *person, ideas*] 天真的 ♦**it was naive of him to believe her** 他真是天真，竟然相信了她

naked ['neɪkɪd] *adj* **1** [+ *person, body*] 裸体的 **2** [+ *flame, light*] 无遮蔽的 **3** [+ *fear, hatred*] 分明的 ♦**visible to the naked eye** 肉眼可见的 ♦**to see sth with the naked eye** 肉眼可见某物

✪**name** [neɪm] **I** *n* [c] **1** [*of person, thing*] 名字 **2** (*reputation*) 名声 **II** *vt* **1** (*give name to*) [+ *child, ship*] 取名 ◊ *Have they named the baby yet?* 他们给孩子取名了吗？ **2** (*identify*) [+ *accomplice, victim, criminal*] 确定 ◊ *The victims have not been named.* 遇难者的身份还没有确定。 **3** (*specify*) [+ *date, place, price*] 说定 ◊ *Name the place, we'll be there.* 说定个地方，我们会在那儿。 ♦**what's your name?** 你叫什么名字？ ♦**my name is Peter** 我叫彼得 ♦**to mention sb by name** 指名道姓 ♦**in sb's name** 以某人的名义 ♦**crimes committed in the name of freedom** 以自由为名违法犯罪 ♦**to call sb names** 嘲弄某人 ♦**to give one's name and address** 留下姓名和地址 ♦**to make a name for o.s.** 成名 ♦**to give sb/sth a bad name** 损害某人/某事的声誉 ♦**the name of the game** [非正式] 最要紧的方面 ♦**to be named after** *or* [美] **for sb/sth** 以某人/某事物的名字命名 ♦**to name sb as sb** 确认某人是某人 ◊ *The victim was named as John Smith.* 遇难者被确认是约翰•史密斯。 ♦**to name sb as sth** 任命某人某种职务 ◊ *McGovern was named as the new chairman.* 麦戈文被任命为新的主席。

namely ['neɪmlɪ] *adv* 即 ♦**namely that ...** 就是说…

nanny ['nænɪ] *n* [c] 保姆

nap [næp] **I** *n* **1** [c] (*sleep*) 小睡 **2** [s] [*of fabric*] 绒毛 **II** *vi* [非正式] ♦**to be caught napping** 被察觉有失误之处 ♦**to have a nap** 小睡一会儿

napkin ['næpkɪn] *n* [c] (*serviette*) 餐巾

nappy ['næpɪ] [英] *n* [c] 尿布 [美 = **diaper**]

narcotic [nɑː'kɔtɪk] **I** *adj* [+ *drug, effects*] 麻醉的 **II** *n* [c] (*type of drug*) 麻醉药 **III narcotics** *n* [*pl*] [尤美] (*illegal drugs*) 毒品

narrative ['nærətɪv] *n* [c/u] 叙述

narrator [nə'reɪtə(r)] *n* [c] **1** (*in novel, play*) 叙述者 **2** [电影, 电视, 广播] 解说员

narrow ['nærəu] **I** *adj* **1** [+ *road, ledge, feet*] 窄的 **2** [+ *majority, victory, defeat*] 勉强的 **3** [+ *ideas, view*] 狭隘的 **II** *vi* **1** [*road, river* +] 变窄 **2** [*gap, difference* +] 缩小 **3** [*eyes* +] 眯 **III** *vt* **1** [+ *gap, difference*] 缩小 **2** [+ *eyes*] 眯

起 ♦**to have a narrow escape** 勉强逃脱 ♦**in the narrow sense of the word** 就该词的狭义来说

❑**narrow down** *vt* [+ *choice, possibility*] 减少 ♦**to narrow the list down (to three)** 把名单减少(到3个)

narrowly ['nærəulɪ] *adv* [+ *avoid, escape, miss*] 勉强地

narrow-minded [nærəu'maɪndɪd] *adj* [+ *person*] 心胸狭窄的; [+ *attitude*] 狭隘偏执的

NASA ['næsə] [美] *n abbr* (= ***National Aeronautics and Space Administration***) 国家航空和宇宙航行局

nasal ['neɪzl] *adj* **1** [解剖, 医] [+ *passage, cavity, congestion*] 鼻的 **2** [+ *voice*] 带鼻音的

nasty ['nɑːstɪ] *adj* **1** (*obnoxious*) [+ *person*] 令人憎恶的; [+ *remark*] 恶意的 **2** (*bad*) [+ *taste, smell*] 恶心的; [+ *weather, temper, shock*] 讨厌的 **3** (*serious*) [+ *injury, accident, disease*] 严重的; [+ *problem*] 难的 ♦**to be nasty to sb** 待某人不好 ♦**to turn nasty** [*person* +] 露出凶相 ♦**a nasty business** 令人难受的事

✪**nation** ['neɪʃən] *n* **1** [c] (*country*) 国家 **2** ♦**the nation** (*people*) 国民

✪**national** ['næʃənl] **I** *adj* [+ *election, newspaper, interest*] 国家的; [+ *characteristic, hobby*] 民族的 **II** *n* [c] (*citizen*) 公民

national anthem *n* [c] 国歌

national dress *n* [u] 民族服装

National Health Service [英] *n* ♦**the National Health Service** 英国国民医疗服务制度 ♦**on the National Health Service** 由国民保健署提供

national holiday [美] *n* [c] 法定假期 [英 = **bank holiday**]

National Insurance [英] **I** *n* [u] 英国国民保险制度 **II** *cpd* [复合词] [+ *contributions, card*] 国民保险

nationalism ['næʃnəlɪzəm] *n* [u] 民族主义

nationalist ['næʃnəlɪst] **I** *adj* 民族主义的 **II** *n* [c] 民族主义者

nationality [næʃə'nælɪtɪ] *n* [c/u] 国籍 ♦**What nationality is he?** 他是哪国人?

nationalize ['næʃnəlaɪz] *vt* 使国有化

nationally ['næʃnəlɪ] *adv* [*broadcast, agree* +] 全国性地; [*available* +] 在全国范围内

national park *n* [c] 国家公园

National Trust [英] *n* ♦**the National Trust** 全国名胜古迹托管协会

nationwide ['neɪʃənwaɪd] **I** *adj* [+ *problem, tour, campaign, search etc*] 全国性的 **II** *adv* [*distribute, broadcast, campaign etc* +] 全国性地; [*available* +] 在全国范围内

native ['neɪtɪv] **I** *adj* [+ *country*] 本国的; [+ *language, tongue*] 母语的; [+ *plant, species*] 土生的 **II** *n* [c] 当地人 ♦**to be a native of Canada/France** [*person* +] 加拿大/法国本地人 ♦**to be native to Canada/France** [*plant, animal* +] 加拿大/法国本土的

Native American **I** *n* [c] 印第安人 **II** *adj* 印第安人的

> **NATIVE AMERICAN**
>
> **Native American** (美洲印第安人)由许多部族组成,例如,科曼奇族、阿帕契族和苏人族,他们在欧洲人到来之前就一直居住在北美洲。继欧洲人之后,后来非洲人和亚洲人也陆续来到北美大陆。**Native American** 最初被西方人称为 **Indian**,因为人们错误地认为发现者克里斯托弗·哥伦布到达了东印度而不是北美大陆。切不可使用带有种族歧视色彩的字眼 **Red Indian** 或 **redskin** 等。

native speaker *n* [c] 讲母语的人 ♦**a native speaker of English, an English native speaker** 以英语为母语的人

NATO ['neɪtəu] *n abbr* (= ***North Atlantic Treaty Organization***) 北约

natural ['nætʃrəl] *adj* **1** (*normal*) 正常的 **2** (*instinctive*) [+ *inclination, instinct*] 出于本性的 **3** (*innate*) [+ *flair, aptitude, talent*] 天生的 **4** (*unaffected*) [+ *person, manner*] 自然的 **5** (*not man-made*) [+ *material,* *product, food*] 天然的; [+ *disaster*] 大自然的 **6** [音] 本位音的 **7** (*biological*) [+ *father, parent, sister*] 亲生的 ♦ **it's natural to worry about one's children** 担心自己的孩子是很自然的 ♦ **it is natural for us to want excitement** 对我们来说，寻求刺激是很自然的 ♦ **to die of natural causes** 自然死亡 ♦ **Martin is a natural musician** 马丁是个天生的音乐家

natural gas *n* [U] 天然气

natural history *n* [U] 博物学

naturally ['nætʃrəlɪ] *adv* **1** (*unsurprisingly*) 自然地 **2** [*behave, lead, arise, result* +] 自然地 **3** [*occur, happen* +] 自然而然地 **4** (*by nature*) 天生地 ♦ **"naturally!"** "当然啦！" ♦ **to come naturally (to sb)** (对某人来说)很容易

natural resources *n* [*pl*] 自然资源

nature ['neɪtʃə(r)] *n* **1** [U] (*also:* ***Nature***) 自然界 **2** (*character*) [*of thing*] [S/U] 特性; [*of person*] [C/U] 天性 ♦ **the protests were political in nature** 那些抗议都是政治性的 ♦ **it was not in her nature to tell lies** 她生性不会说谎 ♦ **I am an optimist by nature** 我天生是个乐天派 ♦ **by its (very) nature** 理所当然 ♦ **documents of a confidential nature** 机密文件 ♦ **or something of that nature** 或者类似性质的事物

naught [nɔːt] *n* = **nought**

naughty ['nɔːtɪ] *adj* **1** (*disobedient*) [+ *child*] 淘气的 **2** (*rude*) [+ *magazine, film*] 低级的; [+ *word*] 下流的

nausea ['nɔːsɪə] *n* [U] 恶心

naval ['neɪvl] *adj* [+ *uniform, battle, forces*] 海军的

navel ['neɪvl] *n* [C] 肚脐

navigate ['nævɪgeɪt] **I** *vt* **1** [+ *ship, aircraft*] 导航 **2** [+ *river, ocean*] 在…航行 **II** *vi* (*in a car*) 指路; [*birds, fish* +] 找到正确的方向 ♦ **to navigate (one's way) around sth** [字] 绕过某物 ♦ **to navigate (a path) through sth** [喻] 找到解决的方法

navigation [nævɪ'geɪʃən] *n* [U] **1** (*action*) 航行 **2** (*science*) 航行学

navy ['neɪvɪ] **I** *n* **1** ♦ **the navy** (*service*) 海军 **2** [C] (*ships*) 海军舰队 **3** [U] (*also:* ***navy-blue***) 藏青色 **II** *adj* (*also:* ***navy-blue***) 藏青色的 ♦ **to be in the navy** 在海军服役 ♦ **to join the navy** 参加海军 ♦ **the Department of the Navy** [美] 海军部

Nazi ['nɑːtsɪ] **I** *n* [C] 纳粹分子 **II** *cpd* [复合词] [+ *party, propaganda, sympathizer*] 纳粹

NB *abbr* (= **nota bene**) 注意

NBA [美] *n abbr* (= ***National Basketball Association***) 全国篮球协会

NBC [美] *n abbr* (= ***National Broadcasting Company***) 国家广播公司

NE *abbr* (= ***north-east***) 东北

✪ **near** [nɪə(r)] **I** *adj* **1** (*physically, in time*) 近的 ◊ *The nearest shops are 5 km away.* 最近的商店离这里有5公里远。◊ *My office is quite near.* 我的办公室离这儿不远。◊ *Christmas is quite near now.* 圣诞节很近了。**2** (*not complete*) [+ *darkness, tragedy*] 几乎 ◊ *We were sitting in near darkness.* 我们几乎是在黑暗中坐着。**II** *adv* **1** (*close*) 近 ◊ *He must live quite near.* 他一定住得很近。**2** (*almost*) [+ *disastrous, perfect, impossible, fatal*] 几乎 ◊ *a near fatal accident* 一场几乎致命的事故 **III** *prep* (*also:* ***near to***) **1** (*physically*) 近 ◊ *I stood very near them.* 我站得离他们很近。**2** (*just before/after*) 临近 ◊ *It happened near the beginning of the game.* 这件事发生在临近比赛的时候。**3** (*bordering on*) [+ *completion, truth, collapse*] 接近 ◊ *Her views were fairly near the truth.* 她的观点相当接近真相。**IV** *vt* **1** [+ *place, end, age, time*] 接近 ◊ *He was nearing the door when the light went on.* 他接近门的时候，灯亮了。◊ *They were nearing the end of their training.* 他们的训练接近尾声了。**2** (*border on*) 近于 ◊ *The crisis neared a critical point last week.* 上星期，危机近于顶点。♦ **25,000 pounds or nearest offer** [英] 25,000 英镑或者是与之相似的报价 ♦ **in the near future** 在不远的将来 ♦ **to draw near** [*event,* *time* +] 临近◊ *The wedding day drew near.* 婚礼快到了。♦**near enough** 将近 ♦**she's nowhere near ready** 她根本没准备好 ♦**don't go/come any nearer!** 不许再走/靠近了！♦**don't come near me!** 别走近我！♦**he won't (even) go near a hospital** 他(怎么也)不愿意去医院 ♦**the building is nearing completion** 这座楼房要竣工了

nearby [nɪə'baɪ] **I** *adj* 附近的 **II** *adv* 在附近

nearly ['nɪəlɪ] *adv* 差不多 ♦**you're nearly as tall as I am** 你跟我差不多高了 ♦**the film isn't nearly as good as the book** 电影拍得没有书好看 ♦**it's not nearly big enough** 根本不够大 ♦**I (very) nearly fell over** 我差点摔倒了 ♦**nearly always** 几乎总是 ♦**she was nearly in tears** 她差点要哭了

near-sighted [nɪə'saɪtɪd] [美] *adj* (*short-sighted*) 近视的

neat [niːt] *adj* **1** (*tidy*) [+ *house, desk, pile, clothes*] 整洁的; [+ *handwriting*] 工整的 **2** [+ *person*] (*organized*) 爱整洁的; (*in appearance*) 干净得体的 **3** (*simple, effective*) [+ *plan, solution, description*] 简明的 **4** [尤英] (*undiluted*) [+ *whisky, gin etc*] 纯的◊ *I drink my whisky neat.* 我爱喝纯威士忌酒。**5** [美:非正式] (*great*) 绝妙的

neatly ['niːtlɪ] *adv* (*tidily, conveniently*) 整齐地

necessarily ['nɛsɪsrɪlɪ] *adv* (*inevitably*) 必然 ♦**not necessarily** 未必

necessary ['nɛsɪsrɪ] *adj* **1** (*required*) [+ *skill, quality, item*] 必要的 **2** (*inevitable*) [+ *consequence, connection*] 必然的 ♦**if/when/where necessary** 如有必要/必要时/在必要处 ♦**I don't want to stay longer than necessary** 我不想呆得太久 ♦**it may be necessary (for us) to buy a new cooker** (我们)可能应该买一个新的炊具

necessity [nɪ'sɛsɪtɪ] *n* **1** [U] (*need*) 需要 **2** [C] (*essential item*) 必需品 **3** [C] (*essential measure*) 不可避免的事情 ♦**there is no necessity for us to do anything** 我们没有必要做什么 ♦**of necessity** [正式] 必定 ♦**out of necessity** 迫不得已 ♦**the necessity of doing sth** 做某事的必要性

neck [nɛk] **I** *n* [C] **1** [解剖] [*of person, animal*] 颈 **2** [*of shirt, dress, jumper*] 领子 **3** (*narrow part*) [*of bottle*] 颈部; [*of guitar, violin*] 颈状部位 **II** *vi* [非正式] 盘颈亲昵 ♦**to be breathing down sb's neck** 紧紧盯着某人 ♦**to be neck and neck** 并驾齐驱 ♦**to stick one's neck out** [非正式] 担风险

necklace ['nɛklɪs] *n* [C] 项链

necktie ['nɛktaɪ] [美] *n* [C] 领带 [英 = **tie**]

nectarine ['nɛktərɪn] *n* [C] (*fruit*) 油桃

✪**need** [niːd] **I** *vt* **1** (*require*) 需要◊ *You need glasses.* 你得戴眼镜。◊ *The animals need food supplements throughout the winter.* 动物整个冬天都需要食物补给。**2** (*want*) [+ *drink, holiday, cigarette*] 想要◊ *I need a holiday.* 我想要去度假。**3** (*could do with*) [+ *a haircut, a bath, a wash*] 得◊ *The car needs a wash.* 这车得洗洗了。**II** *n* [S] **1** (*demand*) 需求◊ *These groups are obviously answering a need.* 这些团体显然是在满足一种需求。**2** (*necessity*) 必要◊ *There's a need for more information.* 有必要再寻求一些信息。**3 needs** *n* [*pl*] (*requirements*) 需求◊ *He had not been able to satisfy her emotional needs.* 他没能满足她感情上的需求。◊ *the needs of industry* 工业的需求 ♦**to need to do sth** 必须做某事◊ *You need to see a doctor.* 你必须去看医生。♦**the car needs servicing** 这辆车需要维修了 ♦**you don't need (to have) a degree to see what's going on** 你很容易就能知道发生了什么 ♦**he doesn't need to know** *or* **he needn't know** 他不必知道 ♦**"need I stay?" – "no, you needn't"** "需要我留下吗？" "不必了" ♦**to be in need** 有困难 ♦**to be (badly) in need of sth**

(急)需某物 ♦ **(there's) no need** *(it's not necessary)* (那)不用了 ♦ **there's no need to shout** *(please don't)* 别嚷嚷 ♦ **there's no need for us to finish this** 我们没有必要做完 ♦ **he has no need to work** 他没有必要工作 ♦ **to feel the need to do sth** 觉得应该做某事

needle ['niːdl] I *n* [c] **1** *(for sewing)* 针 **2** *(for knitting)* 编织针 **3** *(for injections)* 注射针 **4** *(on record player)* 唱针 **5** *(on dial)* 指针 **6** *(on pine tree)* 针叶 II *vt* [非正式] *(nag)* 刺激

needless ['niːdlɪs] *adj* [+ *death, suffering, worry, risk etc*] 不必要的 ♦ **needless to say** 不用说

needlework ['niːdlwəːk] *n* [u] 针线活

needn't ['niːdnt] = **need not**

needy ['niːdɪ] I *adj* 贫困的 II *n* [*pl*] ♦ **the needy** 贫困的人

negative ['nɛgətɪv] I *adj* **1** [+ *effect, news*] 负面的 **2** [+ *test, result*] 阴性的 **3** *(gloomy)* [+ *person, attitude, view*] 消极的 **4** *(not affirmative)* [+ *answer, response*] 否定的 **5** [电子][+ *charge, current*] 负极的 **6** [数] 负的 II *n* [c] **1** [摄影] 底片 **2** [语言] 否定词 ♦ **why do you have to be so negative about everything?** 你怎么对什么都这么消极呢? ♦ **to answer in the negative** 作否定的回答

neglect [nɪ'glɛkt] I *vt* **1** *(not care for)* [+ *child, area, house, garden*] 忽略 **2** *(not pay attention to)* [+ *person*] 怠慢; [+ *work, duty*] 疏忽 **3** *(overlook)* [+ *writer, artist*] 忽视 II *n* [u] **1** [*of child*] 疏忽 **2** [*of area, house, garden*] 疏于照顾 ♦ **to neglect to do sth** 漏做某事

neglected [nɪ'glɛktɪd] *adj* **1** *(uncared for)* [+ *animal, child, garden*] 未被妥善照管的 **2** *(ignored)* [+ *family, wife*] 被冷落的 ◊ *She's feeling rather neglected.* 她感到倍受冷落。 **3** *(overlooked)* [+ *writer, artist*] 被忽视的; [+ *aspect*] 被忽略的

negligence ['nɛglɪdʒəns] [正式] *n* [u] *(carelessness)* 玩忽职守

negligible ['nɛglɪdʒɪbl] *adj* [+ *risk, amount, level*] 无足轻重的

negotiate [nɪ'gəuʃɪeɪt] I *vi* 商讨 II *vt* **1** [+ *treaty, contract*] 谈判 **2** [+ *obstacle, hill, bend*] 顺利通过 ♦ **to negotiate with sb (for sth)** (就某事)与某人协商

negotiation [nɪgəuʃɪ'eɪʃən] I *n* [u] *(bargaining)* 谈判 II **negotiations** *n* [*pl*] *(discussions)* 洽谈

negotiator [nɪ'gəuʃɪeɪtə(r)] *n* [c] 谈判人

neighbour (美 **neighbor**) ['neɪbə(r)] *n* [c] **1** *(person living nearby)* 邻居 **2** *(person next to you)* 旁边的人

neighbourhood (美 **neighborhood**) ['neɪbəhud] *n* [c] **1** *(place)* 地区 **2** *(people)* 邻里 ♦ **in the neighbourhood of sth** [+ *place*] 邻近某处; [+ *amount*] 大约某数量

neighbouring (美 **neighboring**) ['neɪbərɪŋ] *adj* [+ *town, state, house, building*] 邻近的

neither ['naɪðə(r)] I *pron* *(person)* 两人都不; *(thing)* 两者都不 II *conj* ♦ **I didn't move and neither did John** 我和约翰都没动 ♦ **neither do/have I** 我也不/没 ♦ **neither ... nor ...** 既不…也不… ♦ **that is neither here nor there** 不相干

> **neither** 和 **none** 作代词的时候用法不同。用 **neither** 指两个人或事物，表示否定含义。*Neither had close friends at university.* **neither of** 的用法与之相同，后接代词或名词词组。*Neither of them spoke...Neither of these options is desirable.* 注意，也可以把 **neither** 用在单数可数名词之前。*Neither side can win.* **none** 可以指代三个或者三个以上的人或事物，表示否定含义。*None could afford the food.* **none of** 的用法与之相同，后接代词或名词词组。*None of them had learned anything...None of his companions answered.*

neon ['niːɔn] I *n* [u] 氖 II *cpd* [复合词] [+ *light, sign*] 霓虹

Nepal [nɪ'pɔːl] *n* 尼泊尔

Nepalese [nɛpəl'iːz] (*pl* **Nepalese**) I *adj* 尼泊尔的 II *n* **1** [u] *(language)* 尼泊尔语 **2** [c] *(person)* 尼泊尔人 ♦ **the Nepalese** *(people)*

尼泊尔人

Nepali [nɪ'pɔːlɪ] **I** *adj* 尼泊尔的 **II** *n* **1** [u] (*language*) 尼泊尔语 **2** [c] (*person*) 尼泊尔人

nephew ['nɛvjuː] *n* [c] (*brother's son*) 侄子; (*sister's son*) 外甥 ♦ **my nieces and nephews** 我的甥侄辈

nerve [nəːv] *n* **1** [c] [解剖] 神经 **2** [u] (*courage*) 勇气 **3 nerves** *n* [*pl*] (*anxiety*) 神经紧张; (*strength of character*) 精神力量 ♦ **to lose one's nerve** 失去勇气 ♦ **to have the nerve to do sth** (*courage*) 有胆量做某事; (*cheek*) 厚颜无耻地做某事 ♦ **you've got a nerve!** [非正式] 你真有脸！ ♦ **what a nerve!** 真有胆量！ ♦ **to get on sb's nerves** 使某人心烦

nervous ['nəːvəs] *adj* **1** (*worried*) 紧张的 **2** (*by nature*) [+ *person, animal, disposition*] 神经质的 **3** (*mental*) [+ *strain, tension, disorder*] 神经的 ♦ **to be nervous about sth/about doing sth** 对某事/做某事感到紧张不安 ♦ **to be nervous of sb/sth** 对某事/某人心中不安

nervous breakdown *n* [c] 精神崩溃 ♦ **to have a nervous breakdown** 精神崩溃

nervousness ['nəːvəsnɪs] *n* [u] (*anxiety*) 焦虑

nervous system *n* [c] 神经系统

nest [nɛst] **I** *n* [c] [*of bird*] 巢; [*of insect, animal*] 穴 **II** *vi* 筑巢

net [nɛt] **I** *n* **1** [c] (*for fishing, trapping, in games*) 网 **2** [c] (*for protecting plants, pram*) 网罩 **3** [u] (*fabric*) 网眼织物 **4** [计算机] ♦ **the Net** 网络 **II** *vt* **1** [+ *fish, butterfly*] 用网捕 **2** [+ *sum of money*] 净得 **III** *adj* **1** (*also: **nett***) [+ *assets, income, profit*] 净的 **2** (*final*) [+ *result, effect*] 最终的 ♦ **to slip through the net** (*escape arrest*) 漏网; (*miss out*) 漏掉 ♦ **to cast/spread one's net wider** 抛开/撒开大网 ♦ **an income/profit of 10,000 pounds net** 纯收入/利润10,000英镑 ♦ **net weight 250g** 净重250克 ♦ **250g net** 净重250克

netball ['nɛtbɔːl] *n* [u] 无挡板篮球

Netherlands ['nɛðələndz] *n* [*pl*] ♦ **the Netherlands** 荷兰

nett [nɛt] [英] *adj* = **net**

nettle ['nɛtl] *n* [c] 荨麻 ♦ **to grasp the nettle** [尤英] 果断处理棘手问题

network ['nɛtwəːk] **I** *n* [c] **1** [*of roads, veins etc*] 网状系统 **2** [*of people, offices, shops*] 联络网 **3** (*system*) 网络 **4** [电视, 广播] (*company*) 网 **II** *vi* **1** (*socialize*) 建立关系 **2** ♦ **to be networked** [广播, 电视] 联播

neurotic [njuə'rɔtɪk] **I** *adj* [+ *person, behaviour*] 神经质的 **II** *n* 神经质者 ♦ **to be/become neurotic about sth** 对某事极为焦虑

neuter ['njuːtə(r)] **I** *vt* [+ *male*] 阉割; [+ *female*] 骟 **II** *adj* [语言] 中性的

neutral ['njuːtrəl] **I** *adj* **1** [+ *person, country, position*] 中立的 **2** (*impassive*) [+ *voice, language, expression*] 不带感情色彩的 **3** [+ *colour*] 暗淡的 **4** [电子] [+ *wire*] 不带电的 **II** *n* (*in vehicle*) ♦ **in/into neutral** 处于空挡位置 ♦ **to remain neutral** 保持中立

✪ **never** ['nɛvə(r)] *adv* **1** (*not at any time*) 从未 ◊ *I never met him.* 我从未见过他。 **2** (*emphatic*) 决不 ◊ *I would never do anything to hurt him.* 我决不会做任何伤害他的事情。 ♦ **never again!** 下次绝对不许了！ ♦ **we never saw him again** 我们再没有见过他 ♦ **never ever** [非正式] 永不 ♦ **never in my life** 我从未 ◊ *Never in my life have I seen anyone drink as much as you.* 我从未见过任何人有你这么能喝酒。 ♦ **well I never!** [非正式, 过时] 真没想到！

never-ending [nɛvər'ɛndɪŋ] *adj* [+ *supply, quest, struggle*] 永无休止的

nevertheless [nɛvəðə'lɛs] *adv* [正式] 不过

✪ **new** [njuː] *adj* **1** (*brand new*) 崭新的 ◊ *smart new houses* 漂亮的新居 ◊ *We have just bought a new television.* 我们刚买了一台崭新的电视。 **2** (*recent*) [+ *product, system, method etc*] 新式的 ◊ *a new type of bandage* 一种新式绷带 **3** (*different*) [+ *job, address, boss, president*] 新的 ◊ *He's got a new job.* 他找到了一个新工作。 **4** (*recently found*) [+ *star, country, friend, evidence*] 新发现的 ◊ *New evidence has come to light.* 有

新的证据出现了。**5** (*inexperienced*) [*+ mother, member*] 无经验的 ◊ *The society welcomes new members.* 协会欢迎新成员。 ♦ **this concept is new to me** 我对这个概念不熟悉 ♦ **I'm new to this way of doing things** 我不熟悉这种做事方式 ♦ **I'm new here** 我是新来的

New Age *adj* 新世纪的

newborn ['njuːbɔːn] *adj* [*+ baby, lamb*] 新生的

newcomer ['njuːkʌmə(r)] *n* [c] (*to area, organization, activity*) 新来的人 ♦ **to be a newcomer to sth** 某领域的新手

newly ['njuːlɪ] *adv* [*+ formed, discovered, acquired*] 新近地

✪ **news** [njuːz] *n* [u] 消息 ◊ *News travels pretty fast around here.* 在这里，消息传得很快。 ♦ **a piece of news** 一条消息 ♦ **good/bad news** 好/坏消息 ♦ **to be good/bad news (to/for sb)** 对某人有利/不利 ♦ **the news** [电视，广播] 新闻 ♦ **to be on the news** 在新闻中播出 ♦ **to be in the news** 被作为新闻报道

> 注意，尽管 **news** 看起来像是复数，事实上它是一个不可数名词。*Good news is always worth waiting for.* 不能说 **a news**，但是可以说 **a piece of news**，指某个具体的事实或消息。*One of my colleagues told me a very exciting piece of news.* 当谈到电视、广播或者报纸新闻的时候，可以把一个独立的故事或报道叫做 **a news item**。

news agency *n* [c] 通讯社

newsagent ['njuːzeɪdʒənt] [英] *n* [c] **1** (*person*) 报刊经销人 **2** (*also: **newsagent's***) 报刊店

newscaster ['njuːzkɑːstə(r)] [美] *n* [c] 播音员 [英=**newsreader**]

newsletter ['njuːzlɛtə(r)] *n* [c] 通讯

newspaper ['njuːzpeɪpə(r)] *n* **1** [c] (*publication*) 报纸 **2** [c] (*organization*) 报社 **3** [u] (*sheets of paper*) 报纸 ♦ **in the newspaper** 在报上 ♦ **to be in the newspapers** 在报上报道

newsreader ['njuːzriːdə(r)] [英] *n* [c] 播音员 [美=**newscaster**]

newt [njuːt] *n* [c] 水螈

New Year *n* [u] ♦ **(the) New Year** 新年 ♦ **in the New Year** 在新的一年中 ♦ **Happy New Year!** 新年快乐！ ♦ **to wish sb a happy new year** 祝愿某人新年快乐

New Year's Day (美 **New Year's**) *n* [u] 元旦 ♦ **on New Year's Day** 在元旦那天

New Year's Eve (美 **New Year's**) *n* [u] 元旦前夜

New Zealand [-'ziːlənd] **I** *n* 新西兰 **II** *adj* 新西兰的

New Zealander [-'ziːləndə(r)] *n* [c] 新西兰人

✪ **next** [nɛkst] **I** *adj* **1** (*in time*) 下一个的 ◊ *I've got a meeting next Friday.* 下星期五我有个会。◊ *I'm getting married next year.* 明年我结婚。 **2** (*adjacent*) [*+ house, street, room*] 旁边的 ◊ *The telephone was ringing in the next room.* 隔壁房间的电话在响。◊ *He is talking with the next person.* 他正在和旁边的人说话。**3** (*in queue, series, list*) 下一个的 ◊ *the next person in the queue* 队伍中的下一个人 **II** *adv* 接下来地 ◊ *Allow the sauce to cool. Next, add the parsley.* 先冷却调味汁。接下来，放入欧芹。◊ *The news is next.* 接下来是新闻。**III** *pron* 下一个 ◊ *I don't want to be the next to go.* 我不想是下一个要走的人。 ♦ **the next day/morning** 第2天/天早晨 ♦ **the next five years/weeks will be very important** 接下来的5年/周将是至关重要的 ♦ **the next five days/weeks were a nightmare** 接下来的5天/周简直是恶梦一场 ♦ **the next flight/prime minister** 下一次航班/下一任首相 ♦ **next time, be a bit more careful** 下一次，要更谨慎些 ♦ **who's next?** 下一位是谁？ ♦ **when next I saw him ...** 当我再一次看到他的时候… ♦ **next to nothing** [*cost, do, know +*] 几乎不 ♦ **the next best thing** 仅次于最好的 ♦ **the next largest category** 第二大范畴 ♦ **the next thing I knew** [非正式] 突然发现 ♦ **the week after next** 下下个星期 ♦ **next to** *(beside)* 旁边 ♦**next on the right/left** 右/左面第一个 ♦**next (please)!** *(at doctor's etc)* 下一位！

next door I *adv* *(in neighbouring building, room etc)* 隔壁 **II** *adj* [+ *building, house, flat, room*] 隔壁的 ♦**my next door neighbour** 我的隔壁邻居 ♦**the people/family next door** 隔壁的人/人家

next of kin ['nɛkstəv'kɪn] [正式] **I** *n* [U] *(individual)* 直系亲属 **II** *n* [*pl*] *(family)* 家人

NFL [美] *n abbr* (= ***National Football League***) 全国橄榄球联盟

NHS [英] *n abbr* (= ***National Health Service***) ♦**the NHS** 英国国民医疗服务制度

nibble ['nɪbl] *vt* **1** *(bite)* 轻咬 **2** *(eat)* 啃 ♦**to nibble (away) on** *or* **at sth** 一点一点地咬某物

Nicaragua [nɪkə'rægjuə] *n* 尼加拉瓜

Nicaraguan [nɪkə'rægjuən] **I** *adj* 尼加拉瓜的 **II** *n* [C] 尼加拉瓜人

nice [naɪs] *adj* **1** *(good)* [+ *time, holiday, meal, weather etc*] 好的 **2** [+ *person*] *(likeable)* 和蔼的; *(friendly)* 友好的 **3** *(kind)* [+ *remark, act*] 善意的 **4** (+ *adj*) *(lovely)* 宜人的 ♦**to look nice** [*person, place* +] 看上去不错 ♦**it's nice to see you** 很高兴见到你 ♦**it's nice that ...** 太好了… ♦**to be nice to sb** 对某人好 ♦**it's nice of you to ask ...** 谢谢你问起… ♦**it's nice and warm/bright in here** 这里真好，挺温暖/明亮的

nicely ['naɪslɪ] *adv* **1** *(satisfactorily)* [*work, run* +] 令人满意地 **2** *(attractively)* [*dress, arrange* +] 好看地 ♦**you can have a biscuit if you ask nicely** 如果你好好问的话，你可以吃一块饼干 ♦**that will do nicely** 对我来说就够了 ♦**she's doing (very) nicely** 她过得(很)好

niche [niːʃ] *n* [C] **1** *(for statue)* 壁龛 **2** *(in market, organization, field)* 空白 ♦**to find one's niche** 找到自己的位置 ♦**to carve a niche for o.s.** 为自己寻求发展的空间

nick [nɪk] **I** *vt* **1** [英:非正式] *(steal)* 偷 **2** [英:非正式] *(arrest)* 抓获 **3** *(cut)* 刮破 **II** *n* [C] *(scratch)* 小伤口 ♦**to be nicked for doing sth** [英:非正式] 因做某事而被捕 ♦**in good nick** [英:非正式] 状况良好 ♦**the nick** [英:非正式] 监狱 ♦**in the nick of time** 正当紧要关头

nickel ['nɪkl] *n* [C] **1** *(metal)* 镍 **2** [美] *(coin)* 5美分硬币

nickname ['nɪkneɪm] **I** *n* [C] 绰号 **II** *vt* ♦**to nickname sb sth** 给某人起某个绰号

nicotine ['nɪkətiːn] *n* [U] 尼古丁

niece [niːs] *n* [C] *(brother's daughter)* 侄女; *(sister's daughter)* 甥女 ♦**my nieces and nephews** 我的甥侄辈

Niger *n* **1** [niː'ʒeə(r)] *(country)* 尼日尔 **2** ['naɪdʒə(r)] *(river)* 尼日尔河

Nigeria [naɪ'dʒɪərɪə] *n* 尼日利亚

Nigerian [naɪ'dʒɪərɪən] **I** *adj* 尼日利亚的 **II** *n* [C] 尼日利亚人

✪**night** [naɪt] *n* **1** [C/U] *(period of darkness)* 黑夜 **2** [C] *(evening)* 晚上 ♦**at night** 夜间 ♦**from nine o'clock at night until nine in the morning** 从晚上9点到早上9点 ♦**by night** 夜间 ◊ *They travelled by night to avoid detection.* 他们夜间赶路以免被人察觉。♦**in/during the night** 夜里 ♦**the night before last** 前天晚上 ♦**the night before (sth)** 前一天晚上 ♦**night and day** *or* **day and night** 日日夜夜 ♦**night was falling** 夜幕降临了

nightclub ['naɪtklʌb] *n* [C] 夜总会

nightdress ['naɪtdrɛs] [英] *n* [C] 睡衣 [美=**nightgown**]

nightfall ['naɪtfɔːl] *n* [U] 黄昏 ♦**at nightfall** 在傍晚

nightgown ['naɪtgaun] [尤美] *n* [C] 睡衣 [英=**nightdress**]

nightie ['naɪtɪ] *n* = **nightdress**

nightingale ['naɪtɪŋgeɪl] *n* [C] 夜莺

nightlife ['naɪtlaɪf] *n* [U] 夜生活

nightly ['naɪtlɪ] **I** *adj* 晚间的 **II** *adv* 每晚

nightmare ['naɪtmɛə(r)] *n* [C] 恶梦 ♦**to have a nightmare** 做恶梦 ♦**the bus journey was a nightmare** 乘公共汽车旅行真是一场恶梦

night school *n* [C/U] 夜校 ♦**to go to night school** 上夜校

night shift *n* [C] **1** *(hours)* 夜班 **2** *(people)* 夜班工作人员 ♦**to do**

the night shift 值夜班 ♦ to be on night shift 值夜班

night-time ['naɪttaɪm] **I** *n* [U] 夜间 ♦ **at night-time** 在晚上 **II** *cpd* [复合词] [+ *curfew, raid, activity*] 夜间

nil [nɪl] *n* **1** [U] [英: 体育] 零 ♦ **they lost two nil to Italy** 他们以0比2输给意大利队 **2** ♦ **their chances of survival are nil** 他们没有幸存的可能

📖 用法参见 **nought**

nimble ['nɪmbl] *adj* [+ *person, fingers, movements*] 灵巧的; [+ *mind*] 敏锐的

✪ **nine** [naɪn] *num* 九 *see also* **five**

✪ **nineteen** ['naɪn'tiːn] *num* 十九 *see also* **fifteen**

nineteenth [naɪn'tiːnθ] *num* 第十九 *see also* **fifth**

ninetieth ['naɪntɪəθ] *num* 第九十

✪ **ninety** ['naɪntɪ] *num* 九十 *see also* **fifty**

ninth [naɪnθ] *num* **1** (*in series*) 第九 **2** (*fraction*) 九分之一 *see also* **fifth**

nip [nɪp] **I** *vt* (*bite*) 咬 **II** *n* **1** (*bite*) ♦ **to give sb a nip** 轻咬某人 **2** [C] (*drink*) 少量 ♦ **to nip to a place** [英: 非正式] 快去某处 ♦ **to nip out/down/up (to do sth)** [英: 非正式] 快点去/下去/上去 (做某事)

nipple ['nɪpl] *n* [C] **1** (*on body*) 乳头 **2** [美] (*on bottle*) 橡皮奶头 [英= **teat**]

nitrogen ['naɪtrədʒən] *n* [U] 氮

✪ **no**

KEYWORD

[nəu] (*pl* **noes**)

I *adv* (*opposite of "yes"*) 不 ♦ **"did you see it?" – "no (I didn't)"** "你看见了吗?" — "不 (我没见到)" ♦ **no thank you, no thanks** 不用，谢谢你 ♦ **oh no!** 噢不! ♦ **no fewer/more than** 不少/多于

II *adj* (*not any*) 没有 ♦ **I have no milk/books** 我没有牛奶/书 ♦ **I've no time** 我没时间 ♦ **there's no other solution** 没有其他办法 ♦ **"no entry"** "严禁入内" ♦ **"no smoking"** "严禁吸烟" ♦ **no way!** 没门儿!

III *n* 否决 ♦ **there were 20 noes and one "don't know"** 有二十个说 "不"，一个说 "不确定" ♦ **I won't take no for an answer** 我不会接受否定的答复

no. (*pl* **nos.**) *abbr* (= **number**) 编号

nobility [nəu'bɪlɪtɪ] *n* **1** [U] (*quality*) 高尚 **2** ♦ **the nobility** 贵族

noble ['nəubl] **I** *adj* **1** (*admirable*) [+ *person, character*] 高尚的 **2** (*aristocratic*) [+ *family, birth*] 贵族的 **II** *n* [C] 贵族

nobody ['nəubədɪ] *pron* 没有人 ♦ **he's a nobody** 他是个无名小卒

nod [nɔd] **I** *vi* (*to show agreement*) 点头; (*as greeting*) 点头打招呼; (*indicating sth/sb*) 点头示意 **II** *vt* ♦ **to nod one's head** (*to show agreement*) 点头表示同意; (*as greeting*) 点头招呼; (*indicating sth/sb*) 点头示意 **III** *n* [C] (*to show agreement*) 点头同意; (*as greeting*) 点头打招呼; (*indicating sth/sb*) 点头示意 ♦ **to nod to sb** (*as greeting*) 对某人点头打招呼 ♦ **to nod the ball into the net/over the line** [英: 非正式] 把球顶入网/顶过线 ♦ **to give a nod** (*to show agreement*) 点头同意; (*as greeting*) 点头打招呼

❑ **nod off** [非正式] *vi* (*also*: **nod off to sleep**) 打瞌睡

noise [nɔɪz] *n* **1** [C] (*sound*) 响声 **2** [U] (*din*) 噪音 ♦ **to make a noise** 发出响声 ♦ **Try not to make so much noise.** 尽量不要弄出这么多响声。

noisy ['nɔɪzɪ] *adj* [+ *people, machine*] 嘈杂的; [+ *place*] 喧闹的

nominal ['nɔmɪnl] *adj* **1** [+ *leader, head, Christian*] 名义上的 **2** [+ *fee, sum, amount*] 微不足道的

nominate ['nɔmɪneɪt] *vt* **1** (*propose*) (*for job, award*) 提名 **2** (*appoint*) 任命 ♦ **to nominate sb for sth** [+ *post, position*] 任命某人担任某职位 ♦ **to nominate sb/sth for sth** [+ *award, prize*] 提名某人/某事获得某物 ♦ **to nominate sb to sth** [+ *body, organization*] 为某团体选任某人

nomination [nɔmɪ'neɪʃən] *n* **1** [C] (*proposal*) (*for post, award*) 提名 **2** [C/U] (*appointment*) 任命

nominee [nɔmɪ'niː] *n* [C] 被提名者

non-alcoholic [nɔnælkə'hɔlɪk] *adj* 不含酒精的

none [nʌn] *pron* **1** (*not one*) 没有一个 **2** (*not any*) 没有一点儿 ♦ **none**

of us/them 我们/他们谁也没 ♦ **I've/there are none left** (*not one*) 我一个也没有了/一个也没剩 ♦ **I've/there's none left** (*not any*)我一点也没有了/一点也没剩 ♦ **none at all** (*not any*) 一点儿都没有了; (*not one*) 根本没有 ♦ **I was none the wiser** 我还是不明白 ♦ **she would have none of it** [非正式] 她决不接受 ♦ **it was none other than Jim Murdoch** 不是别人，正是吉姆·默多克 ♦ **to be none too pleased about sth** 对某事很不高兴 ♦ **none but** [正式] 只有
📖 用法参见 **neither**

nonetheless ['nʌnðə'lɛs] *adv* 不过

non-existent [nɒnɪg'zɪstənt] *adj* 不存在的

non-fiction [nɒn'fɪkʃən] **I** *n* [U] 非小说类文学 **II** *cpd* [复合词] [+ *book, prize*] 写实的

nonsense ['nɒnsəns] *n* [U] **1** (*rubbish*) 胡说八道 **2** (*gibberish*) 无意义的词语 ♦ **nonsense!** 胡说！♦ **to make a nonsense of sth** 使某事变得荒谬

non-smoker ['nɒn'sməukə(r)] *n* [C] 不吸烟的人

non-smoking ['nɒn'sməukɪŋ] *adj* [+ *area, carriage*] 禁烟的

non-stick ['nɒn'stɪk] *adj* [+ *pan, surface*] 不粘的

non-stop ['nɒn'stɒp] **I** *adj* [+ *activity, music*] 不停的; [+ *flight*] 直达的 **II** *adv* **1** (*ceaselessly*) 不断地 **2** (*without interruption*) [*fly, drive* +] 不停地

noodles ['nu:dlz] *n* [*pl*] 面条

noon [nu:n] **I** *n* [U] 中午 **II** *cpd* [复合词] 正午的 ♦ **at noon** 中午

no-one ['nəuwʌn] *pron* = **nobody**

nor [nɔ:(r)] *conj* 也不 ♦ **nor me!** 我也不是！*see also* **neither**

norm [nɔ:m] *n* [C] **1** (*convention*) 规范 **2** (*rule, requirement*) 标准 ♦ **to be the norm** 是正常现象

normal ['nɔ:məl] *adj* [+ *life, behaviour, circumstances, person*] 正常的 ♦ **in normal circumstances ...** 在正常情况下… ♦ **to get back** *or* **return to normal** 恢复正常 ♦ **to continue as normal** 照常继续 ♦ **more/higher/worse than normal** 比正常的多/高/糟糕

normally ['nɔ:məlɪ] *adv* **1** (*usually*) 通常地 **2** (*conventionally*) [*act, behave* +] 正常地 ♦ **to be working normally** 正常运作

✪ **north** [nɔ:θ] **I** *n* [U/S] 北方 **II** *adj* 北部的 **III** *adv* 向北方 ♦ **the north of France** 法国北部 ♦ **to the north** 以北 ♦ **the north wind** 北风 ♦ **north of ...** 以北 ◊ *It's 15 miles or so north of Oxford.* 在牛津以北15英里左右。

North America *n* 北美

North American **I** *adj* 北美的 **II** *n* [C] 北美人

north-east [nɔ:θ'i:st] **I** *n* 东北 **II** *adj* 东北的 **III** *adv* 向东北

north-eastern ['nɔ:θ'i:stən] *adj* 东北的

northern ['nɔ:ðən] *adj* 北方的 ♦ **the northern hemisphere**北半球

Northern Ireland *n* 北爱尔兰

North Korea *n* 朝鲜

North Korean **I** *adj* 朝鲜的 **II** *n* [C] 朝鲜人

North Pole *n* ♦ **the North Pole** 北极

North Sea *n* ♦ **the North Sea** 北海

northward(s) ['nɔ:θwəd(z)] *adv* 向北

north-west [nɔ:θ'wɛst] **I** *n* 西北 **II** *adj* 西北的 **III** *adv* 向西北

north-western ['nɔ:θ'westən] *adj* 西北的

Norway ['nɔ:weɪ] *n* 挪威

Norwegian [nɔ:'wi:dʒən] **I** *adj* 挪威的 **II** *n* **1** [C] (*person*) 挪威人 **2** [U] (*language*) 挪威语

nos. *abbr* (= ***numbers***) 编号

nose [nəuz] **I** *n* [C] **1** (*on face*) 鼻子; (*sense of smell*) 嗅觉 **2** [*of aircraft*] 机头 **II** *vi* ♦ **to nose forward/out** 缓慢前行/驶出 ♦ **just follow your nose** 凭本能行事 ♦ **to get (right) up sb's nose** [英:非正式] (真是)使某人恼怒 ♦ **to have a (good) nose for sth** 善于觉察某事 ♦ **to keep one's nose clean** [非正式] 洁身自好 ♦ **to look down one's nose at sb/sth** [非正式] 小看某人/某事 ♦ **to pay through the nose (for sth)** [非正式]付出过高价格(买某物) ♦ **to rub sb's nose in sth** [非正

式]哪壶不开提哪壶 ♦**to turn one's nose up at sth** [非正式]对某事不屑一顾 ♦**to be happening/going on under sb's nose** 在某人眼皮底下发生/进行 ♦**to poke** *or* **stick one's nose into sth** [非正式]干预某事

❑**nose around, nose about** [非正式] **I** *vi* 察看 **II** *vt* [不可拆分]考察

nosebleed ['nəuzbli:d] *n* [C] 鼻出血 ♦**to have a nosebleed** 流鼻血

nosey ['nəuzɪ] [非正式] *adj* = **nosy**

nostalgia [nɔs'tældʒɪə] *n* [U] 怀旧 ♦**nostalgia for sth** 对某事物的怀恋

nostalgic [nɔs'tældʒɪk] *adj* [+ *person*] 怀旧的; [+ *trip, memory, song, book*] 令人怀旧的 ♦**to be nostalgic about/for sth** 怀恋某事物

nostril ['nɔstrɪl] *n* [C] 鼻孔

nosy ['nəuzɪ] [非正式] *adj* 爱多管闲事的

✪**not** [nɔt] *adv* 不 ♦**he is not** *or* **isn't here** 他不在这儿 ♦**I do not** *or* **don't want to go out tonight** 我今晚不想出去 ♦**it's too late, isn't it?** 现在太晚了，不是吗？♦**he asked me not to do it** 他叫我不要这么做 ♦**are you coming or not?** 你来不来？♦**not at all** (*in answer to question*) 一点也不; (*in answer to thanks*) 不客气 ♦**I'm not at all tired** 我一点也不累 ♦**not yet/now** 还没/现在不 ♦**not really** 并不是的 ♦**not everyone has the time to cook** 不是所有人都有时间下厨的

notable ['nəutəbl] **I** *adj* [+ *success, achievement, example*] 显著的 **II** *n* [正式]要人 ♦**to be notable for sth** 因某事而著称 ♦**it is notable that ...** 值得注意的是… ♦**with a few notable exceptions** 除了个别明显的例外

🕮用法参见 **famous**

notably ['nəutəblɪ] *adv* **1** (*particularly*)尤其 **2** (*noticeably*) 显著地 ♦**most notably** 最为显著地

notch [nɔtʃ] *n* [C] **1** (*in wood, blade*) 凹口 **2** (*level*) 等级

❑**notch up** *vt* [+ *victory, sales, profit*] 取得

note [nəut] **I** *n* [C] **1** (*message*) 便条 **2** (*to remind o.s.*) 笔记 **3** (*in book, article*) 注释 **4** [英](*banknote*) 纸币 [美=**bill**] **5** [音](*sound*) 音; (*printed, written*) 音符 **II** *vt* **1** (*observe*) 留意 **2** (*point out*) 指出 **3** (*also: **note down***) 记下 **III notes** *n* [*pl*] (*from or for lecture etc*) 笔记 ♦**to make a note of sth** 记下某事 ♦**to take notes** 记笔记 ♦**to compare notes** 交换意见 ♦**the film ends on a positive note** 影片以大团圆的结局告终 ♦**to sound/strike a note of caution** 听起来有/带着一种警告的语气 ♦**there was a note of triumph in her voice** 她说话时带着一种胜利的口吻 ♦**to take note (of sth)** 留意到（某事）♦**of note** 有名望 ♦**to note that ...** 指出… ♦**(please) note that . . .**（请）注意…

notebook ['nəutbuk] *n* [C] 笔记本

noted ['nəutɪd] *adj* (*famous*) 知名的 ♦**to be noted for sth** 以某事物而著名

notepad ['nəutpæd] *n* [C] **1** (*pad of paper*) 记事本 **2** [计算机]记事簿

notepaper ['nəutpeɪpə(r)] *n* [U] 信纸

noteworthy ['nəutwə:ðɪ] [正式] *adj* [+ *fact, event*] 值得注意的 ♦**it is noteworthy that ...** 值得注意的是…

✪**nothing** ['nʌθɪŋ] *pron* **1** (*not anything*) 什么也没有 ◊ *I pressed the button but nothing happened.* 我按了按钮，但什么都没有发生。◊ *The man nodded but said nothing.* 男子点了点头，但什么也没有说。**2** (*something trivial*) 无关紧要 ◊ *a fight that started over nothing* 因无关紧要的事而打架 ♦**nothing new/serious/to worry about** 没有什么新的/要紧的/值得担忧的 ♦**there's nothing better/worse (than ...)** 没有（比…）更好/更糟糕的 ♦**nothing much** 没有什么 ♦**nothing else** 没有别的 ♦**for nothing** (*free*) 免费; (*cheap*) 便宜; (*in vain*) 白白地 ♦**to be worth nothing** 一文不值 ♦**nothing at all** 什么也没有 ◊ *"What did you say?" – "Nothing. Nothing at all."* "你说什么？" – "没有。什么也没

说。” ♦**nothing but** 只 ♦**he's nothing if not well-organized** [正式] 他条理分明之极 ♦**it's nothing less than outrageous!** 简直是蛮横无理！ ♦**he's nothing less than a thief!** 他简直是个贼！ ♦**it was nothing of the sort** *or* **kind** 根本没有那回事

notice ['nəutɪs] **I** *vt* (*observe*) 注意到 **II** *n* **1** [C] (*sign*) 公告 **2** [U] (*warning*) 通知 **3** [C] [英] (*review*) [*of play, film*] 评论 ♦**to notice that ...** 注意到… ♦**to bring sth to sb's notice** 引起某人对某事的注意 ♦**to take no notice of sb/sth** 不理某人/某事 ♦**to escape sb's notice** 躲过某人的注意 ♦**it has come to my notice that ...** 我察觉到… ♦**to give sb notice of sth** 事先通知某人有关某事 ♦**without notice** 不事先通知 ♦**advance notice** 提前通知 ♦**at short/a moment's/24 hours' notice** 一经通知就/马上就/24小时内就 ♦**until further notice** 直到另行通知 ♦**to hand in** *or* **give in one's notice** 递交辞呈 ♦**to be given one's notice** 接到解雇通知

noticeable ['nəutɪsəbl] *adj* [+ *effect, difference, improvement*] 明显的 ♦**it is noticeable that ...** 可以明显注意到…

noticeably ['nəutɪsəblɪ] *adv* 明显地 ♦**most noticeably** 最明显地

noticeboard ['nəutɪsbɔːd] [英] *n* [C] 布告栏 ♦**on the noticeboard** 在布告栏上 [美=**bulletin board**]

notification [nəutɪfɪ'keɪʃən] *n* [U] 通知 ♦**to be given** *or* **receive notification of sth** 收到有关某事的通知

notify ['nəutɪfaɪ] *vt* ♦**to notify sb (of sth)** 将（某事）通知某人 ♦**to notify sb that ...** 告诫某人…

notion ['nəuʃən] **I** *n* [C] (*idea*) 概念 **II notions** *n* [*pl*] [美] 小件针线用品

notorious [nəu'tɔːrɪəs] *adj* [+ *case, criminal, murderer, womanizer*] 声名狼籍的 ♦**to be notorious for sth/for doing sth** 因某事/做某事而臭名远扬

📖 用法参见 **famous**

notoriously [nəu'tɔːrɪəslɪ] *adv* [+ *unreliable, inefficient*] 人所共知地

notwithstanding [nɔtwɪθ'stændɪŋ] *prep, adv* 尽管

nought [nɔːt] [尤英] *num* 零 [美=**zero**]

> 📖 在英式英语的口语中，**nought** 比 **zero** 常用得多。*...from nought to 60 miles per hour...* 在科技性内容中，**zero** 通常作为数字使用。当你想显得精确时，通常也使用 **zero**。在美式英语中，一般使用 **zero**，而不用 **nought**。在报电话号码时，用 **o**（[əu]）。在体育评论中，尤其是表示足球比分时，多用 **nil**。*England beat Poland two-nil at Wembley.* 网球运动中，通常用 **love** 表示零的含义。*...a two-games-to-love lead...*

noun [naun] *n* [C] 名词

nourish ['nʌrɪʃ] *vt* [+ *person*] 养育; [+ *plant*] 滋养

nourishment ['nʌrɪʃmənt] *n* [U] (*food*) 营养

Nov. *abbr* (= **November**) 十一月

novel ['nɔvl] **I** *n* [C] 小说 **II** *adj* [+ *idea, approach*] 新颖的

novelist ['nɔvəlɪst] *n* [C] 小说家

novelty ['nɔvəltɪ] **I** *n* **1** [U] (*newness*) 新奇 **2** [C] (*new concept, experience*) 新奇的事物 **II novelties** *n* [*pl*] (*knick-knacks*) 小玩意

November [nəu'vɛmbə(r)] *n* [C/U] 十一月 *see also* **July**

novice ['nɔvɪs] *n* [C] **1** (*beginner*) 新手 **2** [宗] (*female*) 见习修女; (*male*) 见习修士 ♦**to be a novice at sth** 对某物不熟悉

✪ **now** [nau] **I** *adv* **1** (*at the present time*) 现在 ◊ *It is now just after one o'clock.* 现在刚过1点钟。◊ *I'm going home now.* 我要回家了。**2** (*these days*) 如今 ◊ *Most schoolchildren now own calculators.* 如今大多数学童都有计算器。**3** (*under the circumstances*) 看来 ◊ *I was hoping to go tomorrow. That won't be possible now.* 我本来想明天走。看来这不可能了。**4** (*specifying length of time*) 到现在为止 ◊ *They've been married now for 30 years.* 到现在为止，他们已经结

婚30年了。5 (*introducing new information*) 喂◊ *Now, I hadn't told him this, so he must have found out for himself.* 喂，这件事我没告诉他，他一定是自己发现的。
II *conj* ♦**now (that)** 既然◊ *Now that he's feeling better, he can go back to work.* 既然他感觉好些了，就可以去上班了。♦**right now** 这时 ◊ *What if a shark came along right now?* 这时，如果来了鲨鱼该怎么办呢？♦**by now** 到现在◊ *He should be here by now.* 他现在应该到了。◊ *By now he'll be home and in bed.* 现在，他一定到了家，上床休息了。♦**just now** (*at the moment*) 眼下◊ *I'm pretty busy just now.* 眼下我很忙。♦**(every) now and then** *or* **again** 时而 ♦**from now on** 从现在起 ♦**in 3 days from now** 从现在起3天后 ♦**between now and Monday** 从现在到星期一 ♦**that's all for now** 就到这里 ♦**any day/moment/time now** 不日/随时/任何时候 ♦**now then** 喂(以引起注意)

nowadays ['nauədeɪz] *adv* 现今

nowhere ['nəuwɛə(r)] *adv* (*no place*) 无处; (*emphatic*) 没有地方 ♦**nowhere else** (*no place else*) 没有其他地方; (*emphatic*) 不在任何其他地方 ♦**to come/appear from** *or* **out of nowhere** 不知从什么地方突然冒出来/出现 ♦**this is getting us nowhere, we're getting nowhere with this** 这么做我们只能一无所获 ♦**in the middle of nowhere** 前不着村，后不着店

nozzle ['nɔzl] *n* [c] 喷嘴

nuclear ['njuːklɪə(r)] *adj* [+ *fission, physics, weapon, power*] 核能的

nucleus ['njuːklɪəs] (*pl* **nuclei** ['njuːklɪiː]) *n* [c] **1** [*of atom, cell*] 核 **2** [*of group*] 核心人物

nude [njuːd] **I** *adj* 裸体的 **II** *n* [c] (*picture*) 裸体画; (*sculpture*) 裸体雕像 ♦**in the nude** (*naked*) 裸体

nudge [nʌdʒ] **I** *vt* 用肘轻推 **II** *n* [c] 轻推 ♦**to give sb a nudge** 用肘轻推某人

nudist ['njuːdɪst] **I** *n* [c] 裸体主义者 **II** *cpd* [复合词] [+ *beach*] 裸体

nudity ['njuːdɪtɪ] *n* [u] 裸体

nugget ['nʌgɪt] *n* [c] **1** [*of gold*] 小块 **2** [烹饪] 碎块 **3** [*of information*] 有价值的东西

nuisance ['njuːsns] *n* ♦**to be a nuisance** [*thing* +] 讨厌的东西; [*person* +] 讨厌的人 ♦**it's a nuisance that ...** 真是讨厌… ♦**what a nuisance!** 真讨厌！

numb [nʌm] **I** *adj* **1** [+ *fingers, toes, arm etc*] 麻木的 **2** (*through fear, shock*) 僵住的 **II** *vt* **1** (字) [+ *fingers, part of body*] 麻痹 **2** [+ *person, senses*] 使失去知觉 ♦**to go numb** [*fingers, toes, arm* +] 变麻 ♦**to be numb with shock/fear/grief** 因震惊/恐惧/悲痛而失去知觉 ♦**to numb the pain** 麻痹疼痛

✪**number** ['nʌmbə(r)] **I** *n* **1** [c] [数] 数 ◊ *Think of a number between one and ten.* 在1至10之间想一个数。**2** [c] (*telephone number*) 电话号码 **3** [c] [*of house, bank account, bus etc*] 号◊ *He lives at number 3, Argyll Street.* 他住在阿盖尔街3号。**4** [c/u] (*quantity*) [*of things, people*] 数量◊ *The number of traffic accidents has fallen.* 交通事故的数量已经减少。◊ *A surprising number of men never marry.* 男性不结婚的人数惊人的多。**II** *vt* **1** [+ *pages*] 给…标号码 ◊ *Number the pages before you start.* 在开始之前，先把页码标上。**2** (*amount to*) 总计◊ *The force numbered almost a quarter of a million men.* 该部队总计约有25万男子。♦**their album reached number twenty three** 他们的唱片在排行榜上名列23 ♦**a number of** (*several*) 几个 ♦**a large/small number of** 大量/少数 ♦**any number of** [+ *things, reasons*] 许多 ♦**to be numbered among** [正式] 属于

number one *adj* [+ *priority, position, choice, issue*] 首要的

number plate [英] *n* [c] 车号牌 [美 = **license plate**]

Number Ten [英] *n* (*10 Downing Street*) 唐宁街10号是指英国伦敦唐宁街10号，即英国首相的办公住所。

numerical [njuː'mɛrɪkl] *adj* [+ *value*]

数字的; [+ *advantage, superiority*] 人数的 ♦ **in numerical order** 按数字顺序

numerous ['nju:mərəs] *adj* [+ *examples, attempts etc*] 许多的 ♦ **on numerous occasions** 许多次

nun [nʌn] *n* [C] 修女

nurse [nə:s] **I** *n* [C] **1** (*in hospital*) 护士 **2** [过时] (*nanny*) 保姆 **II** *vt* **1** [+ *patient*] 照料 **2** [+ *cold, injury*] 护理 ♦ **to nurse a grudge against sb** 对某人怀恨在心

nursery ['nə:sərɪ] *n* [C] **1** (*kindergarten*) 幼儿园 **2** (*room*) 保育室 **3** (*garden*) 苗圃; (*garden centre*) 花卉商店

nursery rhyme *n* [C] 儿歌

nursery school *n* [C/U] 幼儿园

nursing ['nə:sɪŋ] **I** *n* [U] (*profession, care*) 护理 **II** *cpd* [复合词] **1** [+ *staff, profession, care*] 护理 **2** [+ *mother*] 喂奶

nursing home *n* [C] 私人疗养院

nurture ['nə:tʃə(r)] *vt* [+ *child, talent, relationship, new player*] 培养; [+ *plant*] 培育; [+ *hopes, ambition, dream*] 抱有

nut [nʌt] *n* [C] **1** [植, 烹饪] 坚果 **2** [科技] 螺母 **3** [非正式] (*lunatic*) 疯子 ♦ **the nuts and bolts of sth** 某事的基本要点 *see also* **nuts**

nutmeg ['nʌtmɛg] *n* [U] 肉豆蔻

nutrient ['nju:trɪənt] **I** *n* [C] 营养 **II** *adj* 有营养的

nutrition [nju:'trɪʃən] *n* [U] (*nourishment*) 营养

nutritious [nju:'trɪʃəs] *adj* [+ *food, meal*] 有营养的

nuts [nʌts] [非正式] *adj* ♦ **to be nuts** 发疯的 ♦ **to be nuts about sth/sb** 迷恋某物/某人 ♦ **to go nuts** (*get angry*) 暴跳如雷; (*become crazed*) 发疯 *see also* **nut**

NVQ [英: 教育] *n abbr* (= ***national vocational qualification***) 国家职业考试

NW *abbr* (= ***north-west***) 西北

nylon ['naɪlɔn] **I** *n* [U] 尼龙 **II** *cpd* [复合词] [+ *shirt, sheets*] 尼龙

NZ *abbr* (= ***New Zealand***) 新西兰

Oo

O, o [əu] *n* [c/u] **1** (*letter*) 英语的第十五个字母 **2** [美:教育] (*outstanding*) 优秀 **3** [通信等] (*number*) 零
📖 用法参见 **nought**

oak [əuk] **I** *n* **1** [c] (*also:* ***oak tree***) 橡树 **2** [u] (*wood*) 橡木 **II** *cpd* [复合词] [+ *furniture, door*] 橡木

OAP [英] *n abbr* (= ***old-age pensioner***) 拿退休金的人

oar [ɔː(r)] *n* [c] 桨 ♦**to put** *or* **shove one's oar in** [非正式] (*interfere*) 干预

oasis [əu'eɪsɪs] (*pl* **oases** [əu'eɪsiːz]) *n* [c] **1** (*in desert*) 绿洲 **2** (*sanctuary*) 慰藉

oath [əuθ] *n* [c] **1** (*promise*) 誓言 **2** [过时] (*swearword*) 咒骂 ♦**on** [英] *or* **under oath** 在发誓的情况下 ♦**to take the oath** [法] 宣誓

oatmeal ['əutmiːl] *n* [u] **1** (*for cooking*) 燕麦粉 **2** [尤美] (*porridge*) 燕麦粥 [英 = **porridge**]

oats [əuts] *n* [*pl*] 燕麦

obedience [ə'biːdɪəns] *n* [u] 服从 ♦**in obedience to** 遵从

obedient [ə'biːdɪənt] *adj* [+ *child, dog*] 顺从的

obese [ə'biːs] *adj* 肥胖的
📖 用法参见 **fat**

obesity [ə'biːsɪtɪ] *n* [u] 肥胖症

obey [ə'beɪ] **I** *vt* [+ *person, orders*] 听从; [+ *law, regulations*] 服从 **II** *vi* 服从

obituary [ə'bɪtjuərɪ] *n* [c] 讣告

object [*n* 'ɔbdʒɛkt, *vb* əb'dʒɛkt] **I** *n* [c] **1** (*thing*) 物体 **2** (*aim, purpose*) 目的 **3** ♦**an object of ridicule/the object of his affection** 嘲笑的对象/他爱慕的对象 **4** [语言] 宾语 **II** *vi* 反对 ♦**money/distance is no object** 金钱/距离不成问题 ♦**to object to sth** 反对某事 ♦**to object that ...** 反对说… ♦**I object!** 我反对!

objection [əb'dʒɛkʃən] *n* [c] 异议 ♦**to make** *or* **raise an objection** 提出异议 ♦**to have no objection to sth** 不反对某事

objective [əb'dʒɛktɪv] **I** *adj* 客观的 **II** *n* [c] (*goal*) 目标

obligation [ɔblɪ'geɪʃən] *n* [c/u] 责任 ♦**to have an obligation to do sth** 有责任做某事 ♦**to have an obligation to sb (to do sth)** 对某人有(做某事)的责任 ♦**to be under an obligation to do sth** 有义务做某事 ♦**to be under an obligation to sb** 对某人有义务

obligatory [ə'blɪgətərɪ] *adj* 强制性的

oblige [ə'blaɪdʒ] **I** *vt* **1** (*compel*) ♦**to oblige sb to do sth** 迫使某人做某事 **2** (*do a favour for*) 施惠于 **II** *vi* (*cooperate*) 帮忙 ♦**to feel obliged to do sth** 感到必须得做某事 ♦**to be (much) obliged to sb (for sth)** [正式, 过时] (*grateful*) (由于某事)(非常)感激某人 ♦**I would be obliged if ...** [正式] 烦请您…

oblique [ə'bliːk] **I** *adj* **1** (*indirect*) [+ *reference, warning*] 间接的 **2** [+ *angle*] 斜的 **II** *n* [c] [英:排版] 斜线 ♦**at an oblique angle (to sth)** (与某物)呈斜角

oblivion [ə'blɪvɪən] *n* [u] 遗忘 ♦**to be consigned to oblivion** 被忘却

oblivious [ə'blɪvɪəs] *adj* ♦**oblivious of** *or* **to sth** 忘却某事

oblong ['ɔblɔŋ] **I** *n* [c] 长方形 **II** *adj* 长方形的

obnoxious [əb'nɔkʃəs] *adj* [+ *behaviour, person, smell*] 讨厌的

oboe ['əubəu] *n* [c] 双簧管

obscene [əb'siːn] *adj* **1** (*offensive*) [+ *gesture, remark, image*] 猥亵的 **2** (*immoral*) [+ *wealth, income etc*] 可憎的

obscenity [əb'sɛnɪtɪ] *n* **1** [u] (*behaviour*) 淫行 **2** [c] (*swearword*) 脏话

obscure [əb'skjuə(r)] **I** *adj* **1** (*little-known*) [+ *place, author etc*] 不知名的 **2** (*difficult to understand*) 晦涩的 **II** *vt* **1** (*conceal*) [+ *view, object*] 遮蔽; [+ *truth, meaning etc*] 混淆

observant [əb'zəːvənt] *adj* 观察力

敏锐的

observation [ɔbzə'veɪʃən] *n* 1 [c] (*remark*) 评论 2 [u] (*act of observing*) 观察 3 [u] [医] 观察 ♦**powers of observation** 观察力 ♦**she's under observation** 她受到严密监视

observatory [əb'zəːvətrɪ] *n* [c] 天文台

observe [əb'zəːv] *vt* 1 (*watch*) 观察 2 [正式] (*notice*) 注意到 3 (*comment*) 评论 4 (*abide by*) [+ *rule, convention*] 遵守 ♦**to observe that …** 评述说…

observer [əb'zəːvə(r)] *n* [c] 1 (*onlooker*) 旁观者 2 (*commentator*) 评论员

obsess [əb'sɛs] *vt* 使着迷 ♦**to be obsessed by** *or* **with sb/sth** 被某人/某事迷住心窍

obsession [əb'sɛʃən] *n* [c] 着迷

obsessive [əb'sɛsɪv] *adj* [+ *person*] 着迷的; [+ *behaviour, interest*] 着魔的 ♦**to be obsessive about sth** 对某物着迷

obsolete ['ɔbsəliːt] *adj* 不再用的

obstacle ['ɔbstəkl] *n* [c] 1 (*physical barrier*) 障碍 2 (*difficulty*) 阻碍 ♦**an obstacle to sth/to doing sth** 某事/做某事的障碍

obstinate ['ɔbstɪnɪt] *adj* 1 (*stubborn*) [+ *person*] 固执的; [+ *resistance, refusal*] 顽固的 2 (*troublesome*) [+ *problem, stain etc*] 难对付的

obstruct [əb'strʌkt] *vt* 1 (*block*) [+ *road, path*] 堵塞 2 (*hinder*) [+ *justice, progress*] 阻碍

obstruction [əb'strʌkʃən] *n* 1 [c] (*blockage*) 障碍物 2 [u] [*of plan, law*] 阻碍

obtain [əb'teɪn] [正式] **I** *vt* (*get*) [+ *book, information, degree etc*] 获得 **II** *vi* (*exist, be the case*) 通行

obvious ['ɔbvɪəs] *adj* 明显的 ♦**it's obvious that …** 很明显… ♦**for obvious reasons** 由于显然的理由

obviously ['ɔbvɪəslɪ] *adv* 1 (*of course*) 显然地 2 (*noticeably*) 明显地 ♦**obviously!** 当然! ♦**obviously not** 显然不是 ♦**he was obviously not drunk** 很显然，他没醉 ♦**he was not obviously drunk** 他醉得不明显

occasion [ə'keɪʒən] **I** *n* [c] 1 (*moment*) 时刻 2 (*event, celebration*) 场合 3 (*opportunity*) ♦**an occasion for sth/for doing sth** 某事/做某事的机会 **II** *vt* [正式] (*cause*) 引起 ♦**on occasion(s)** 有时 ♦**to rise to the occasion** 应付自如 ♦**a sense of occasion** 隆重感

occasional [ə'keɪʒənl] *adj* 偶尔的 ♦**I like the occasional drink** 我喜欢偶尔喝点酒

occasionally [ə'keɪʒənəlɪ] *adv* 偶尔地 ♦**very occasionally** 非常偶然地

occult [ɔ'kʌlt] **I** *n* ♦**the occult** 神鬼之事 **II** *adj* [+ *subject, powers*] 玄妙的

occupant ['ɔkjupənt] *n* [c] 1 (*long-term*) [*of house*] 占用者 2 (*short-term*) [*of car, room etc*] 使用者

occupation [ɔkju'peɪʃən] *n* 1 [c] (*job*) 职业 2 [c] (*pastime*) 消遣 3 [u] (*annexation*) [*of building, country etc*] 占领

occupier ['ɔkjupaɪə(r)] [正式] *n* [c] 占用者

occupy ['ɔkjupaɪ] *vt* 1 (*inhabit*) [+ *house, office*] 占用 2 ♦**to be occupied** [*seat, place etc* +] 被占用 3 (*take possession of*) [+ *building, country etc*] 占领 4 (*take up*) [+ *attention, mind*] 填满; [+ *space*] 占 5 (*fill*) [+ *time*] 占用; [+ *position, post*] 担任 ♦**to occupy o.s. (with sth/doing sth)** (*to be busy*) 使自己忙于(某事/做某事) ♦**to be occupied with sth/doing sth** 忙于某事/做某事

occur [ə'kəː(r)] *vi* 1 (*happen*) 发生 2 (*be found*) 出现 ♦**to occur to sb** 某人想到

occurrence [ə'kʌrəns] [正式] *n* [c] 1 (*event*) 事件 2 (*incidence*) 事故 ♦**an everyday/daily occurrence** 每天/日常发生的事情

ocean ['əuʃən] *n* [c] 海洋 ♦**oceans of** [非正式] 许多 ♦**it's a drop in the ocean** 沧海一粟

o'clock [ə'klɔk] *adv* ♦**six o'clock** 6点钟

Oct. *abbr* (= **October**) 十月

October [ɔk'təubə(r)] *n* [c/u] 十月 *see also* **July**

octopus ['ɔktəpəs] *n* [c] 章鱼

odd [ɔd] *adj* 1 (*strange*) 奇怪的 2 (*not

paired) [+ *sock, glove, shoe etc*] 单只的
3 (*assorted, unspecified*) 任意的
4 [+ *number*] 奇数的 ♦**to be the odd man/woman/one out** 落单的男人/女人/一人 ♦**the odd drink/walk/holiday** 偶尔的饮酒/散步/度假 ♦**sixty odd** 六十几个 *see also* **odds**

oddly ['ɔdlɪ] *adv* **1** (*strangely*) [*behave, dress* +] 古怪地 **2** *see also* **enough**

odds [ɔdz] *n* [*pl*] **1** 可能性 **2** (*in betting*) 赌注赔率 ♦**the odds are in favour of/against him** 形势对他有利/不利 ♦**against all (the) odds** 克服各种不利条件 ♦**odds and ends** [非正式] 零碎的东西 ♦**it makes no odds** [非正式] 没有区别 ♦**to be at odds (with)** (*in disagreement*) (与) 不和; (*at variance*) (与) 不相称

odometer [ɔ'dɔmɪtə(r)] [美] *n* [c] 里程表

odour (美 **odor**) ['əudə(r)] *n* [c/u] 气味

of
KEYWORD
[ɔv, əv]
I *prep*
1 (*gen*) 的 ♦**the history of China** 中国历史 ♦**at the end of the street** 在街的尽头 ♦**the president of France** 法国总统 ♦**a friend of ours/mine** 我们/我的一个朋友 ♦**the city of New York** 纽约城 ♦**south of Madrid** 马德里的南部 ♦**how silly of him not to say anything!** 他只字未提真是太傻了！
2 (*expressing quantity, amount*) ♦**a kilo of flour** 一公斤面粉 ♦**a cup of tea/vase of flowers** 一杯茶/一瓶花 ♦**a slice of bread** 一片面包 ♦**there were three of them** 他们有3个 ♦**three of us went** 我们3人去了 ♦**can some of you help?** 你们中有人能帮忙吗？♦**I'll eat half of it** 我要吃一半 ♦**the number of road accidents** 交通事故的数量 ♦**an annual income of $30,000** 每年3万美元的收入
3 (*made of*) 由…制成 ♦**made of wood** 木制的
4 (*in dates*) ♦**the 5th of July** 7月5日 ♦**the winter of 2001** 2001年的冬天
5 [美] (*in times*) ♦**at five of three** 3点差5分

off
KEYWORD
[ɔf]
I *adj*
1 (*not turned on*) [+ *machine, light, engine, tap*] 关着的
2 (*cancelled*) [+ *meeting, match, agreement*] 取消的
3 [英] [+ *milk, cheese, meat etc*] 不新鲜的 ♦**the milk's off** 牛奶变质了
4 (*in expressions*) ♦**on the off chance** (*just in case*) 怀着渺茫的希望 ♦**to have an off day** [非正式] 状态欠佳
II *adv*
1 (*away*) ♦**I must be off** 我必须得走了 ♦**where are you off to?** 你上哪儿去？♦**to go off to Paris/Italy** 去巴黎/意大利 ♦**it's a long way off** (*in distance*) 它在很远的地方; (*in time*) 它还远未结束 ♦**the game is three days off** 3天后开赛
2 (*not at work*) ♦**to be off** (*on holiday*) 在休假; (*due to illness*) 休病假 ♦**I'm off on Fridays** 我周五不上班 ♦**to have a day off** (*as holiday*) 休假一天; (*because ill*) 休病假一天
3 [商] ♦**10% off** 10%的折扣
4 (*removed, detached*) 脱落/掉 ♦**there's a button off** 一颗扣子掉了
III *prep*
1 (*indicating motion, removal etc*) ♦**to take a picture off the wall** 把画像从墙上取下来 ♦**to fall/jump off a cliff** 摔/跳下悬崖 ♦**to get off a bus/train** 下公共汽车/火车
2 (*distant from*) ♦**it's just off the motorway** 它就在高速公路边上 ♦**it's 15 km off the main road** 它离主干道15公里远 ♦**an island off the coast** 海岸边的一个小岛
3 (*not enjoying*) ♦**to be off meat/beer** *etc* 不想吃肉/喝啤酒{等}

off-colour ['ɔf'kʌlə(r)] [英] *adj* (*ill*) 身体不舒服的 ♦**to feel off-colour**

感觉不适

off-duty ['ɔf'dju:tɪ] *adj* 不当班的

offence (美 **offense**) [ə'fɛns] *n* **1** [c] (*crime*) 罪行 **2** [u] (*hurt feelings*) 冒犯 **3** [美:体育] ♦**the offense** 进攻方 ♦**to commit an offence** 犯罪 ♦**to give** *or* **cause offence (to sb)** 冒犯(某人) ♦**to take offence (at sth)** (因某事而)生气 ♦**no offence, but ...** 不要见怪，但…

offend [ə'fɛnd] **I** *vt* (*upset*) 得罪 **II** *vi* (*commit an offence*) 犯罪 ♦**to offend against** [+ *law, rule*] 违反

offender [ə'fɛndə(r)] *n* [c] **1** (*criminal*) 罪犯 **2** (*culprit*) 作祟的人/物

offense [ə'fɛns] [美] *n* [c] = **offence**

offensive [ə'fɛnsɪv] **I** *adj* **1** [+ *remark, behaviour*] 无礼的 **2** [美:体育] 攻方的 **II** *n* [c] [军] 进攻 ♦**to be offensive to sb** 得罪某人 ♦**offensive weapon** 进攻性武器 ♦**to go on the offensive** 采取攻势

✪**offer** ['ɔfə(r)] **I** *vt* **1** (*making invitation*) 给 ◊ *I was offered a place at Harvard University.* 哈佛大学给了我一次入学机会。◊ *Meadows stood up and offered her his chair.* 梅多斯站起来把座位让给了她。 **2** (*bid*) [+ *money*] 出价 ◊ *They offered Ramon 2,000 pesos an acre for his farm.* 他们向拉蒙出价一英亩2000比索来购买他的农场。 **3** (*provide*) [+ *service, product*] 提供 ◊ *We are successful because we offer a quality service.* 我们的成功在于我们提供优质的服务。 **4** (*give*) [+ *advice, help, congratulations*] 提出 ◊ *Do you have any advice to offer parents?* 你有什么建议要向家长提吗？ **II** *n* [c] **1** (*proposal*) 提议 ◊ *Anne would not accept Steele's offer.* 安妮将不会接受斯蒂尔的提议。 **2** (*special deal*) 特价 ◊ *today's special offer* 今天的特价商品 **3** (*bid*) 报价 ♦**to make (sb) an offer (for sth)** (就某物)向(某人)报价 ◊ *I'll make you one final offer.* 我将给你一个最终报价。 ♦**to be on offer** [商] (*available*) 供出售的

off-hand [ɔf'hænd] **I** *adj* 随便的 **II** *adv* 当下 ♦**I can't tell you** *or* **say off-hand** 我不能即刻告诉你

✪**office** ['ɔfɪs] *n* **1** [c] (*room*) 办公室 ◊ *He called me into his office.* 他把我叫进他的办公室。 **2** [c] (*department*) 部门 **3** [c] [美] [*of doctor, dentist*] 诊所 [英 = **surgery**] **4** [u] (*job, position*) 职务 ♦**Office of Fair Trading** [英] 公平贸易部 ♦**to be in** *or* **hold office** 担任要职 ♦**to run for office** 竞选公职 ♦**to take office** 就职 ♦**through his good offices** [正式] 通过他的斡旋

office block *n* [c] 办公大楼

office building *n* [c] 办公大楼

office hours *n* [*pl*] **1** [商] 办公时间 **2** [美:医] 门诊时间 ♦**during/outside office hours** 上班/下班时间

✪**officer** ['ɔfɪsə(r)] *n* [c] **1** [军] 军官 **2** (*also:* ***police officer***) 警官 **3** (*official*) 官员

office worker *n* [c] 职员

✪**official** [ə'fɪʃl] **I** *adj* **1** (*approved*) 官方的 ◊ *the official unemployment figures* 官方的失业统计数据 **2** (*job-related*) [+ *residence, visit*] 公务的 ◊ *the Irish President's official residence* 爱尔兰总统的官邸 ◊ *Tony Blair is currently on an official visit to Hungary.* 托尼•布莱尔正在对匈牙利进行正式访问。 **II** *n* [c] (*in government, organization etc*) 官员

off-licence ['ɔflaɪsns] [英] *n* [c] (*shop*) 有卖酒许可的店 [美 = **liquor store**]

offline [ɔf'laɪn], **off-line** [计算机] **I** *adj* **1** 脱机的 **2** (*switched off*) 关机的 **II** *adv* 脱机地

off-peak ['ɔf'pi:k] **I** *adj* [+ *heating, telephone calls, train, ticket*] 非高峰时间的 **II** *adv* [*call, travel* +] 非高峰时间地

off-putting ['ɔfputɪŋ] [英] *adj* 令人讨厌的

off-season ['ɔf'si:zn] **I** *n* ♦**the off season** 淡季 **II** *adj* [+ *holiday, booking, ticket*] 淡季的 **III** *adv* [*travel, book etc* +] 淡季地

offset ['ɔfsɛt] (*pt, pp* **offset**) *vt* (*counteract*) 抵销

offshore [ɔf'ʃɔ:(r)] **I** *adj* [+ *rig, wind, fishing*] 离岸的; [+ *company, bank, investment*] 海外的 **II** *adv* 近海地

offside ['ɔf'saɪd] **I** *adj* **1** [汽车] (*right*)

右侧的; (*left*) 左侧的 **2** [体育] 越位的 **II** *adv* [体育] 越位地 **III** *n* ♦ **the offside** [汽车] (*right*) 右侧; (*left*) 左侧

offspring ['ɔfsprɪŋ] (*pl* **offspring**) [正式] *n* 后代

✪ **often** ['ɔfn] *adv* **1** (*frequently*) 经常 ◊ *She didn't write very often.* 她不经常写信。♦ **how often do you wash the car?** 你多久洗一次车? ♦ **I wash up twice as often as them** *or* **as they do** 我洗碗的次数是他们的两倍 **2** ♦ **more often than not** *or* **as often as not** 往往 ♦ **every so often** 时常 ♦ **it's not often that ...** 并不经常…

> 不能用 **often** 来表示在短期内发生了几次的事情。例如，不能说 *I often phoned her yesterday*，而是说 *I phoned her several times yesterday* 或 *I kept phoning her yesterday*。

oh [əu] *int* **1** (*beginning reply*) 哦 **2** (*expressing feelings*) 啊

OHP *n abbr* (= ***overhead projector***) 高架投影仪

✪ **oil** [ɔɪl] **I** *n* [C/U] **1** 油 **2 II** *vt* [+ *engine, machine*] 给…加油; [+ *wood, skin*] 给…涂油

oil filter [汽车] *n* [C] 滤油器

oil painting *n* [C] (*picture*) 油画

oil refinery *n* [C] 炼油厂

oil rig *n* [C] **1** (*on land*) 石油钻塔; (*at sea*) 钻井平台

oil slick *n* [C] 浮油

oil tanker *n* [C] (*ship*) 油轮

oil well *n* [C] 油井

oily ['ɔɪlɪ] *adj* **1** [+ *rag, substance*] 多油的 **2** [+ *food*] 油腻的

ointment ['ɔɪntmənt] *n* [C] 油膏

OK [əu'keɪ] = **okay**

okay [əu'keɪ] [非正式] **I** *adj* **1** (*acceptable*) 可以的 **2** (*safe and well*) 好的 **II** *adv* (*acceptably*) 不错 **III** *int* **1** (*expressing agreement*) 行 **2** (*in questions*) 好吗 **3** (*granted*) 好吧 **IV** *vt* (*approve*) 批准 **V** *n* ♦ **to give sb/sth the okay** 同意某人/某事 ♦ **are you okay?** 你还好吗? ♦ **are you okay for money?** 你钱够用吗? ♦ **it's okay with** *or* **by me** 这对我没问题

✪ **old** [əuld] *adj* **1** (*aged*) [+ *person*] 年老的 ◊ *an old lady* 一位年老的女士 **2** (*talking about age*) 岁数的 ◊ *He wasn't old enough to understand.* 他还没到能明白的岁数。**3** (*not new, not recent*) 古老的 ◊ *an old proverb* 古老的谚语 **4** (*worn out*) 破旧的 ◊ *an old toothbrush lying on the window sill* 窗台上有一把破牙刷 **5** (*former*) 以前的 ◊ *his old job at the town hall* 他以前在市政厅的工作 **6** (*long-standing*) [+ *friend, enemy, rival*] 老的 ◊ *Pete's an old friend of mine.* 彼得是我的一个老朋友。♦ **how old are you?** 你多大了? ♦ **he's 10 years old** 他10岁了 ♦ **older brother/sister** 哥哥/姐姐 ♦ **any old thing** [非正式] 随便什么东西

old age *n* [U] **1** (*state*) 老年 **2** (*time of life*) 晚年

old age pension [英] *n* [C] (*state pension*) 退休金 [美 = **social security benefit, social security payment**]

old age pensioner [英] *n* [C] (*senior citizen*) 拿退休金的人 [美 = **senior citizen, retiree**]

old-fashioned ['əuld'fæʃnd] *adj* [+ *object, custom, idea*] 老式的; [+ *person*] 守旧的

old people's home [尤英] *n* [C] 养老院

olive ['ɔlɪv] **I** *n* [C] **1** (*fruit*) 橄榄 **2** (*also:* ***olive tree***) 橄榄树 **II** *adj* (*also:* ***olive-green***) 橄榄绿的 ♦ **to offer an olive branch to sb** 向某人提出和解的建议

olive oil *n* [U] 橄榄油

Olympic [əu'lɪmpɪk] **I** *adj* 奥林匹克的 **II the Olympics** *n* [*pl*] 奥林匹克运动会

Olympic Games *n* [*pl*] 奥林匹克运动会

Oman [əu'mɑːn] *n* [C] 阿曼

omelette (美 **omelet**) ['ɔmlɪt] *n* [C] 煎蛋饼 ♦ **ham/cheese omelet(te)** 火腿/奶酪煎蛋饼

omen ['əumən] *n* [C] (*sign*) 预兆 ♦ **a good/bad omen** 一个好的/坏的预兆

ominous ['ɔmɪnəs] *adj* [+ *sign, event, silence, warning*] 不祥的; [+ *clouds, smoke*] 预示的

omit [əu'mɪt] [正式] *vt* 删去 ♦**to omit to do sth** 忽略做某事

✪ **on**
KEYWORD
[ɔn]
I *prep*
1 (*indicating position*) 在…上 ♦**it's on the table/wall** 它在桌上/墙上 ♦**he put the book on the shelf** 他把书放到架子上 ♦**the house is on the main road** 房子在主路旁 ♦**to live on a farm/an island** 住在一个农场里/岛上 ♦**on the left/right** 在左边/右边 ♦**on the top floor** 在顶楼 ♦**she was lying on her back/stomach** 她仰面躺着/俯卧着
2 (*indicating means, method, condition etc*) ♦**on foot** 步行 ♦**on the train/bus** [*be, sit* +] 在火车/公共汽车上; [*travel, go* +] 乘坐 ♦**on the television/radio** 在电视上/广播中 ♦**she's on the telephone** (*engaged*) 她正在打电话 ♦**on the Internet** 在因特网上 ♦**to be on antibiotics** 定期服用抗生素 ♦**to be away on business** 出差
3 (*referring to time*) 在 ♦**on Friday** 在星期五 ♦**on Fridays** 在每个星期五 ♦**on June 20th** 在6月20日 ♦**on Friday, June 20th** 在6月20日，星期五 ♦**on Christmas Day** 在圣诞日 ♦**a week on Friday** 下个星期五 ♦**on arrival** 到了后 ♦**on seeing this** 看到这个以后
4 (*about, concerning*) 关于 ♦**information on train services** 火车服务信息
II *adv*
1 (*clothes*) ♦**to have one's coat on** 穿着外套 ♦**what's she got on?** 她穿着什么？
2 (*covering, lid etc*) ♦**screw the lid on tightly** 把盖子旋紧
3 (*onwards, further*) ♦**to walk/read on** 继续走/读 ♦**from now/that day on** 从此/那一天以后 ♦**on and on** 不停地
III *adj*
1 (*turned on*) [+ *machine, light, engine, tap*] 打开的
2 (*happening*) ♦**is the meeting still on?** 会议还在进行吗？♦**there's a good film on at the cinema** 电影院正在上映一部好电影 ♦**the weather forecast will be on in a minute** 马上就有天气预报
3 [非正式] ♦**that's not on!** 那可不行！

✪ **once** [wʌns] **I** *adv* 1 (*one time only*) 一次 2 (*at one time*) 曾经 ◊ *Texas was once ruled by Mexico.* 德克萨斯州曾经受墨西哥管辖。3 (*on one occasion*) 有一次 ◊ *I went to Portugal once.* 我去过一次葡萄牙。
II *conj* 1 (*as soon as*) 一旦 ♦**at once** (*immediately*) 立刻; (*simultaneously*) 同时 ♦**once a** *or* **every month** 每月一次 ♦**once more** *or* **again** 再一次 ♦**once and for all** 一劳永逸地 ♦**once upon a time** (*in stories*) 很久以前; (*in the past*) 从前 ♦**once in a while** 偶尔 ♦**all at once** (*suddenly*) 突然 ♦**for once** 就这一次 ♦**just this once** [非正式] 就这一次 ♦**once or twice** (*a few times*) 一两次

oncoming ['ɔnkʌmɪŋ] *adj* (*approaching*) [+ *traffic, car*] 迎面而来的

one
KEYWORD
[wʌn]
I *adj*
1 (*number*) 一 ♦**he's one year old** 他1岁 ♦**it's one o'clock** 现在1点 ♦**one hundred/thousand children** 100/1000个孩子 ♦**one hundred and fifty** 150 ♦**we'll go there one day** 总有一天我们会去那儿的 ♦**there will be one or two changes** 会有一两个改动 ♦**one thing I don't understand is why ...** 我不明白的一件事是为什么…
2 (*sole*) 唯一的 ♦**my one hope is that ...** 我唯一的希望是…
3 (*instead of "a"*) 一个
4 (*same*) 同一的 ♦**shall I put it all on the one plate?** 要我把它都放在同一个盘子里吗？
II *pron*
1 (*number*) 一 ♦**I've already got one** 我已经有一个了 ♦**one of them/of the boys** 他们中的一个/男孩中的一个 ♦**it's one of**

the biggest airports in the world 这是世界上最大的飞机场之一 ♦**two coffees, not one** 两杯咖啡，而不是一杯 ♦**one by one** 一个一个地 ♦**all in one** 合为一体的
2 (*with adj*) 一个 ♦**I've already got a red one.** 我已经有一个红的了。♦**you are the only one who can do it** 你是唯一可以做这事的人
3 (*in generalizations*) 人人 ♦**what can one do?** 一个人能做什么呢？♦**one's** (*possessive*) 本人的 ♦**to cut one's finger/hair** 割破手指/剪头发 ♦**this one** 这个 ♦**that one** 那个 ♦**one another** (*us*) 相互; (*you, them*) 彼此 ♦**one never knows** 没有人会知道 ♦**to be at one (with sb)** (与某人) 一致 ♦**to be/get one up on sb** 胜某人一筹
III *n*
(*numeral*) 一

one-off [wʌn'ɔf] [尤英] **I** *adj* 一次性的 **II** *n* [c] [非正式] 一次性事件

oneself [wʌn'sɛlf] *pron* 自己 ◊ *It's important to give oneself time to think.* 给自己一些时间思考是很重要的。♦**to hurt oneself** 伤了自己 ♦**to keep sth for oneself** 把某物留给自己 ♦**to talk to oneself** 自言自语 ♦**by oneself** (*unaided*) 独力地 ◊ *One should learn to deal with one's problems by oneself.* 每个人应该学会自己独立解决问题。; (*alone*) 独自 ◊ *Living by oneself is very lonely.* 独自一个人生活很孤单。

one-sided [wʌn'saɪdɪd] *adj* 1 (*unequal*) [+ *contest, relationship*] 一边倒的 2 (*biased*) 片面的

one-to-one ['wʌntəwʌn] **I** *adj* [+ *relationship, tuition*] 一对一的 **II** *adv* [+ *talk, deal with*] 一对一地

one-way ['wʌnweɪ] *adj* 1 [+ *street, traffic*] 单行的 2 [+ *ticket, trip*] 单程的

ongoing ['ɔngəuɪŋ] *adj* [+ *project, situation etc*] 持续的

onion ['ʌnjən] **I** *n* [c] 洋葱 **II** *cpd* [复合词] [+ *soup*] 洋葱 ♦**to know one's onions** [非正式] 精明干练

online ['ɔnlaɪn], **on-line** [计算机] **I** *adj* 1 (*connected to the Internet*) [+ *person, computer*] 在线的 2 (*available on the Internet*) [+ *service*] 在线的 **II** *adv* (*on the Internet*) 网上 ♦**to go online** (*connect to the Internet*) [*person* +] 上网; (*become available on the Internet*) [*person, organization* +] 在线

onlooker ['ɔnlukə(r)] *n* [c] 旁观者

✪ **only** ['əunlɪ] **I** *adv* 1 (*emphasizing one thing*) 仅仅 ◊ *I'm only interested in finding out the facts.* 我仅仅对找出事实真相有兴趣。◊ *The video is to be used for teaching purposes only.* 该录像仅供教学使用。
2 (*emphasizing sth must happen*) 只有 ◊ *The lawyer is paid only if he wins.* 律师只有赢了官司才能拿钱。
3 (*emphasizing insignificance*) 只 ◊ *I was only joking.* 我只是在开玩笑。**II** *adj* (*sole*) 唯一的 ◊ *He was the only survivor.* 他是唯一的幸存者。**III** *conj* (*but*) 可是 ♦**I saw her only last week** 我上周才见了她 ♦**I'd be only too pleased** *or* **happy to help** 我非常乐意来帮忙 ♦**I know only too well ...** 我太了解… ♦**it's only fair/natural** 这很公平/自然 ♦**we asked for her autograph only to be ignored** 我们要她的签名却被置之不理 ♦**only just** (*recently*) 刚刚 ◊ *I've only just arrived* 我刚刚才到; (*barely*) 勉强 ◊ *Farmers have only just managed to survive* 农民们只是勉强维持生计 ♦**not only ... but (also) ...** 不但…而且… ◊ *Chimps not only use tools but make them.* 黑猩猩不但使用而且制造工具。♦**the only one** (*person*) 唯一; (*thing*) 唯一 ♦**an only child** 独生子女

o.n.o. [英] *abbr* (= ***or nearest offer***) 或依买方接近售价的出价

on-screen, onscreen ['ɔnskriːn] **I** *adj* 1 [计算机] 在屏幕上的 2 [电视, 电影] 银屏上的 3 [电视, 电影] 银幕的 **II** *adv* 1 [计算机] 在屏幕上 2 [电视, 电影] 银幕上

onset ['ɔnsɛt] *n* [s] [*of war, winter, illness*] 开始

onstage [ɔn'steɪdʒ] *adv* [*appear, walk* +] 舞台上

onto ['ɔntu], **on to** *prep* 到…上

♦ **to get onto sth** [+ *bus, train, plane*] 上某交通工具; [+ *subject, matter*] 开始谈论某事 ♦ **to hold/hang/cling onto sth** 紧紧抓/握/揪住某物 ♦ **to be onto something** [非正式] 将要揭示某事 ♦ **to be onto sb** [非正式] 追究某人

onward ['ɔnwəd] **I** *adj* **1** [+ *journey, flight*] 延续的 **2** [+ *progress*] 前进的 **II** *adv* = **onwards**

onwards ['ɔnwədz] *adv* **1** *(on journey, walk etc)* [*continue, go* +] 向前地 **2** *(in development)* [*move, progress* +] 前进地 ♦ **from that time onwards** 从那一时刻起

oops [ups] [非正式] *int* 哎呀

ooze [u:z] **I** *vi* [*mud, water, slime* +] 渗出 **II** *vt* **1** [+ *pus, blood etc*] 渗出 **2** [*person* +] [+ *confidence, sex appeal*] 散发出

op [ɔp] [非正式] *n* [c] **1** [尤英:医] 手术 **2** [军] 行动 **3** *(opportunity)* 机会 ♦ **photo op** 拍照机会

opaque [əu'peɪk] *adj* **1** [+ *substance, glass, window*] 不透明的 **2** [+ *comment, language*] 晦涩的

OPEC ['əupɛk] *n abbr* (= ***Organization of Petroleum-Exporting Countries***) 石油输出国组织

✪ **open** ['əupn] **I** *adj* **1** *(unfastened, unsealed)* [+ *door, window*] 开着的 ◊ *He climbed through the open window.* 他从开着的窗户中爬了进来。; [+ *container*] 打开的 ◊ *an open packet of cigarettes* 一包打开的香烟; [+ *mouth, eyes*] 张着的 ◊ *Angelica looked at me with her mouth open.* 安吉莉卡张着嘴看着我。**2** *(accessible to the public)* [+ *shop*] 营业的 ◊ *The bank won't be open for another half-hour.* 这家银行再过半个小时就不营业了。**3** [+ *countryside, road*] 开阔的 ◊ *The road stretched across open country.* 道路穿过开阔地带向前延伸。**4** *(frank)* [+ *nature, character*] 坦率的 ◊ *Judy had an open and trusting nature.* 朱迪天性坦率、易信赖他人。**5** *(not reserved)* [+ *ticket, return*] 日期待定的 ◊ *I can stay as long as I want, I've got an open ticket.* 我想呆多久就呆，我买了张日期待定的票。**6** *(available)* [+ *offer, vacancy*] 可得到的 ◊ *I'm afraid the vacancy is no longer open.* 我恐怕这个职位空缺没了。◊ *We should use all the opportunities open to us.* 我们应该利用一切可得到的机会。**II** *vt* **1** *(unfasten, unseal)* [+ *container*] 打开 ◊ *I opened a can of beans.* 我打开了一罐豆子。; [+ *door, lid*] 开 ◊ *She opened the door with her key.* 她用钥匙开了门。; [+ *letter*] 拆开 ◊ *I'll open the mail after breakfast.* 我会在早饭后拆开信件。; [+ *book, hand, mouth, eyes*] 开 ◊ *He opened the heavy Bible.* 他翻开厚重的圣经。◊ *He opened his mouth and yawned.* 他张开嘴打了个哈欠。◊ *She opened her eyes and looked around.* 她睁开眼睛向四周望了望。**2** *(launch, declare operational)* 宣布营业 ◊ *The leisure centre was opened by the Queen in 1976.* 这个休闲中心是在1976年由女王宣布开业的。**III** *vi* **1** *(come unfastened or unsealed)* [*door, lid* +] 开 ◊ *The door opened and a tall man entered the room.* 门开了，一个高个子男人走进了房间。; [*container* +] 开 ◊ *The box opened and the books fell out.* 盒子开了，里面的书掉了出来。**2** [*book, hand, mouth, eye, flower* +] 张开 ◊ *The officer's mouth opened in astonishment.* 这个官员吃惊地张大了嘴。◊ *Her eyes opened and she woke up.* 她的眼睛睁开了，她醒过来了。**3** [*public building* +] *(each day)* 开门 ◊ *He was waiting for the bar to open.* 他等着酒吧开门。; *(for first time)* 开始营运 ◊ *The original railway station opened in 1854.* 最早的火车站于1854年开始营运。**4** *(have first night)* [*film, play* +] 首演 ◊ *The new Spielberg film has opened in New York.* 斯皮尔伯格的新电影已在纽约首映。**IV** *n* ♦ **(out) in the open** *(not secret)* 公开 ♦ **an open question** 容许争论的问题 ♦ **an open secret** 公开的秘密 ♦ **an open fire** 未封上的炉火 ♦ **in the open (air)** 在户外 ♦ **the open sea/ocean** 远海/洋 ♦ **to open one's mouth** *(speak)* 张口说话 ♦ **to be open to** [+ *suggestions, ideas*] 乐意接受; [+ *criticism, abuse*] 容易受到

♦**open to the public seven days a week** 一周向公众开放7天 ♦**to open an account** 开立账户

❑**open onto** *vt* [不可拆分] [*room, door* +] 通向

❑**open up I** *vt* **1** [+ *country, market, opportunities*] 开放◊ *If the agreement is to succeed, the EU must open up its markets.* 如能达成协议，欧盟必须开放其市场。**2** (*unlock*) 打开 **II** *vi* **1** (*unlock*) 开门◊ *Open up! It's freezing out here.* 开门！外面很冷。**2** (*confide*) 倾诉◊ *She was disappointed that he hadn't opened up more.* 他未能倾诉更多的情况，为此她很失望。**3** [*country, market, opportunities* +] 展现◊ *New opportunities are opening up for investors who want ...* 新的机会正展现给那些想…的投资者们。

open-air [əupn'ɛə(r)] *adj* [+ *concert, swimming pool*] 户外的

opener ['əupnə(r)] *n* [c] **1** (*also:* ***tin opener, can opener***) 开启工具 **2** (*also:* ***bottle opener***) 开瓶器

opening ['əupnɪŋ] **I** *adj* (*initial*) [+ *remarks, stages, scene*] 开始的 **II** *n* [c] **1** (*gap, hole*) 开口 **2** (*beginning*) [*of play, book etc*] 开头 **3** (*ceremony*) [*of building, bridge etc*] 开放 **4** (*opportunity*) 机会 **5** (*job*) 空缺

opening hours *n* [*pl*] 营业时间

openly ['əupnlɪ] *adv* [*speak, cry* +] 公开地 ♦**to be openly gay** 公开同性恋

open-minded [əupn'maɪndɪd] *adj* 开明的

open-necked ['əupnnɛkt] *adj* [+ *shirt*] 开领的

openness ['əupnnɪs] *n* [U] **1** (*frankness*) 坦率 **2** (*receptiveness*) 开放

open-plan ['əupn'plæn] *adj* [+ *office*] 开敞式布置

Open University [英] *n* ♦**the Open University** 开放大学

> **OPEN UNIVERSITY**
> 英国 **Open University** 的学生在家里完成大部分的学业，通过广播和电视节目接受函授辅导，通过邮件收到作业。他们可以不时地在普通大学中和辅导老师见面，也可以参加夏季学校。**Open University** 又称为 **OU**，可以使不具备正式资格或无法参加传统课程的人们获得学位。许多成年人报名入学。

opera ['ɔpərə] *n* **1** [c] (*individual work*) 歌剧 **2** [U] (*art form*) 歌剧

opera house *n* [c] 歌剧院

opera singer *n* [c] 歌剧演唱者

✪**operate** ['ɔpəreɪt] **I** *vt* (*work*) [+ *machine, vehicle, system*] 操作; [+ *company, organization*] 经营 **II** *vi* **1** (*work*) [*machine, vehicle, system* +] 工作◊ *Calculators and computers operate on the same principle.* 计算器和计算机是按同样的原理工作的。; [*company, organization* +] 运作◊ *the multinational companies which operate in their country* 在他们国家做生意的跨国公司; [*laws, forces* +] 生效◊ *Laws of the same kind operate in nature.* 同样的法则也在自然界起作用。**2** [医] 动手术◊ *They operated but it was too late.* 他们动了手术，但已经太迟了。♦**to operate on sb** [医] 给某人动手术

operating room ['ɔpəreɪtɪŋ-] [美：医] *n* [c] 手术室

operating system [计算机] *n* [c] 操作系统

operating table [医] *n* [c] 手术台 ♦**to be on the operating table** 在手术台上

operating theatre [英] [医] *n* [c] 手术室 [美= **operating room**]

✪**operation** [ɔpə'reɪʃən] *n* **1** [c] (*procedure*) 实施步骤◊ *the risks at each stage of the operation* 各个实施步骤的风险 **2** [c] [军，警察等] 行动◊ *the most successful customs operation of the year* 本年度最成功的海关行动 **3** [c] [医] 手术◊ *a major heart operation* 一次大的心脏手术 **4** [U] (*use*) [*of machine, vehicle etc*] 操作◊ *a guide to the operation of the machine* 机器操作指南 **5** [c] [商] (*business*) 企业◊ *The two groups now run their business as a single combined operation.* 两个集团现作为一个单一的联合企业经营业

务。♦**to be in operation** [*law, scheme* +] 在实施中; [*machine, device* +] 运转着 ♦**to come into operation** 生效 ♦**to bring** *or* **put sth into operation** 使某事开始实施 ♦**to have an operation** [医]接受手术 ♦**to perform** *or* **carry out an operation** [医]施行手术◊ *Dr Jones will perform the operation.* 琼斯医生将施行这次手术。

operational [ɔpə'reɪʃənl] *adj* [+ *machine, vehicle, system*] 可使用的

operative ['ɔpərətɪv] **I** *adj* [+ *machine, measure, system*] 有效的 **II** *n* [c] **1** (*worker*) 工人 **2** [美] (*government agent*) 特工 ♦**the operative word** 关键词

operator ['ɔpəreɪtə(r)] *n* [c] **1** [通信]接线员 **2** [*of machine*] 操作员 **3** (*business*) 经营者

opinion [ə'pɪnjən] *n* **1** [c] (*individual view*) 观点 **2** [U] (*collective view*) 见解 ♦**in my/her opinion** 按我的/她的意见 ♦**to have a good** *or* **high opinion of sb** 对某人评价好{或}高 ♦**to have a good** *or* **high opinion of o.s.** 自视很好{或}很高 ♦**to be of the opinion that ...** [正式]认为…

opinionated [ə'pɪnjəneɪtɪd] *adj* 固执己见的

opinion poll *n* [c] 民意测验

opium ['əupɪəm] *n* [U] 鸦片

opponent [ə'pəunənt] *n* [c] **1** (*adversary*) (*in competition, fight, election*) 对手 **2** (*enemy*) [*of government*] 政敌 **3** [*of course of action*] 反对者

opportunity [ɔpə'tjuːnɪtɪ] *n* [c/U] 机会 ♦**to take the opportunity of doing sth** *or* **to do sth** 趁机会做某事 ♦**at the first opportunity** 一有机会

oppose [ə'pəuz] *vt* [+ *person, idea*] 反对 ♦**to be opposed to sth** 反对某事 ♦**as opposed to** 而不是

opposing [ə'pəuzɪŋ] *adj* **1** [+ *side, team*] 对立的 **2** [+ *ideas, tendencies*] 相反的

opposite ['ɔpəzɪt] **I** *adj* **1** (*facing*) [+ *side, house*] 对面的 **2** (*farthest*) [+ *end, corner*] 最远的 **3** (*contrary*) [+ *meaning, direction*] 相反的 **II** *adv* [*live, work, sit* +] 在对面 **III** *prep* **1** (*across from*) 在…的对面 **2** (*corresponding to*) (*on list, form etc*) 对应 **IV** *n* ♦**the opposite** 对立面 ♦**the opposite sex** 异性

opposition [ɔpə'zɪʃən] *n* **1** [U] (*resistance*) 反对 **2** ♦**the opposition** [体育] (*opponents*) 对手 ♦**the Opposition** [英:政治]反对派

oppress [ə'prɛs] *vt* 压迫

opt [ɔpt] *vi* ♦**to opt for sth** 选择某事 ♦**to opt to do sth** 选择做某事

❑**opt out** *vi* ♦**to opt out (of sth)** 决定退出(某事)

optician [ɔp'tɪʃən] *n* [c] **1** (*person*) 眼镜商 **2** (*also:* ***optician's***) 眼镜店

optimism ['ɔptɪmɪzəm] *n* [U] 乐观

optimist ['ɔptɪmɪst] *n* [c] 乐观主义者

optimistic [ɔptɪ'mɪstɪk] *adj* 乐观的

optimum ['ɔptɪməm] *adj* [+ *conditions, number, size etc*] 最佳的

option ['ɔpʃən] *n* [c] **1** (*choice*) 选择 **2** [教育,大学]选修课 **3** [商]买卖权 ♦**to keep one's options open** 暂不做决定 ♦**to have no other option (but to ...)** (除…之外)别无选择 ♦**I'm afraid that's not an option** 我恐怕那样行不通

optional ['ɔpʃənl] *adj* 可选的 ♦**optional extras** 选装配件

✪**or** [ɔː(r)] *conj* **1** (*linking alternatives*) 还是◊ *Would you like tea or coffee?* 你要茶还是咖啡? **2** (*also:* ***or else***) 否则◊ *Don't put plastic dishes in the oven or they'll melt.* 别把塑料盘子放进烤箱,否则它们会熔化的。**3** (*qualifying previous statement*) 或者说◊ *The man was a fool, or at least incompetent.* 那人是个傻瓜,或者说,至少很无能。 **4** (*giving approximate amount*) 大约◊ *five or ten minutes* 大约5到10分钟

oral ['ɔːrəl] **I** *adj* **1** (*spoken*) [+ *test, report*] 口头的 **2** [+ *vaccine, medicine, contraceptive*] 口服的 **II** *n* [c] (*spoken examination*) 口试 ♦**oral sex** 口交

orange ['ɔrɪndʒ] **I** *n* **1** [c] (*fruit*) 柑橘 **2** [U] (*drink*) 橙汁 **II** *adj* (*in colour*) 橙色的

orange juice *n* [U] 橘子汁

orange squash *n* [U] 浓缩橙汁

orange tree *n* [c] 橘树

orbit ['ɔːbɪt] **I** *n* [c] [*of planet, satellite etc*] 轨道 **II** *vt* [*+ earth, moon etc*] 环绕…运行 ♦**to put a satellite into orbit** 将卫星送入轨道

orchard ['ɔːtʃəd] *n* [c] 果园

orchestra ['ɔːkɪstrə] *n* **1** [c] (*players*) 管弦乐队 **2** [美] (*stalls*) ♦**the orchestra** 剧场正厅前座 [英= **stalls**]

orchid ['ɔːkɪd] *n* [c] 兰花

ordeal [ɔː'diːl] *n* [c] 煎熬

✪**order** ['ɔːdə(r)] **I** *n* **1** [c] (*command*) 命令 **2** [c] [商] (*from shop, company*) 定货; (*in restaurant*) 点菜◊ *A waiter came to take their order.* 一位服务员过来请他们点菜。**3** [u] (*sequence*) 次序 **4** [u] (*stability*) 常规 **5** [u] (*peace*) 秩序◊ *Troops were sent to the islands to restore order.* 军队被派往岛上以恢复秩序。**6** [s] (*system*) 制度◊ *questioning the existing social order* 质疑现行社会制度 **7** [c] [宗] 修道会 **II** *vt* **1** (*command*) 命令◊ *Sherman ordered an investigation into the deaths.* 舍曼下令对死亡事件进行调查。**2** [商] (*from shop, company*) 定购◊ *She phoned the shop and ordered a couple of CDs.* 她给商店打电话定购了两张CD。◊ *Davis ordered a pizza.* 戴维斯定了一份比萨饼。; (*in restaurant*) 点菜 **3** (*arrange*) 整理◊ *He spent five minutes ordering the notes for his speech.* 他花了5分钟整理演讲稿。**III** *vi* (*in restaurant*) 点菜◊ *Are you ready to order?* 可以点菜了吗? ♦**to be under orders to do sth** 奉命做某事 ♦**to take orders** 接受命令◊ *I'm not taking orders from you or anyone else!* 我不会接受你或其他任何人的命令! ♦**to place an order for sth with sb** 向某人定购某物◊ *She placed an order for a carton of fresh cream with the milkman.* 她向卖牛奶的人定购了一盒新鲜奶油。♦**made/done to order** [商] 定制 ♦**on order** [商] 已定而尚未交货的 ♦**in order** (*in sequence*) 按顺序; (*correct*) 妥当的◊ *Thank you, sir, your papers seem to be in order.* 谢谢您,先生,您的资料看起来都很妥当。♦**in order of size** 按尺寸大小 ♦**in alphabetical/numerical order** 按字母/数字顺序 ♦**in short order** 迅速地 ♦**in (good) working order** 运转(良好) ♦**out of order** (*not working*) 已坏停用; (*in the wrong sequence*) 顺序颠倒◊ *It's hopeless, the pages are all out of order.* 全完了,所有页码顺序都颠倒了。♦**in order to do sth** 为了做某事◊ *He had to hurry in order to catch his train.* 为了赶上火车他得快点了。♦**in order for sth to happen** 为了成就某事 ♦**in order that ...** 以便… ♦**to the order of** [经济] 面值◊ *a cheque to the order of five thousand pounds* 一张面值5000英镑的支票 ♦**of** *or* **in the order of** (*approximately*) 大约 ♦**to order sb to do sth** 命令某人做某事◊ *He ordered me to leave the building.* 他命令我离开大楼。

❑**order around** *vt* (*also:* ***order about***) 支使

order form *n* [c] 定货单

orderly ['ɔːdəlɪ] **I** *adj* (*well-organized*) [*+ manner, sequence, system*] 有秩序的 **II** *n* [c] **1** [医] 勤杂工 **2** [军] 勤务兵

ordinary ['ɔːdnrɪ] *adj* **1** (*everyday*) 普通的 **2** [贬] (*mediocre*) 平常的 ♦**out of the ordinary** (*exceptional*) 非凡的

ore [ɔː(r)] *n* [c/u] 矿石

oregano [ɔrɪ'gɑːnəu, (美) ə'rɛgənəu] *n* [u] 牛至

organ ['ɔːgən] *n* [c] **1** [解剖] 器官 **2** [音] 管风琴

organic [ɔː'gænɪk] *adj* **1** [*+ food, farming*] 有机的 **2** [*+ substance*] 有机物的

organism ['ɔːgənɪzəm] *n* [c] 生物体

organization [ɔːgənaɪ'zeɪʃən] *n* **1** [c] (*business, club, society, arranging*) 组织 **2** [u] (*order*) 条理

organize ['ɔːgənaɪz] *vt* **1** (*arrange*) [*+ activity, event*] 组织 **2** (*order*) 整理

organized ['ɔːgənaɪzd] *adj* **1** (*structured*) 有组织的 **2** (*efficient*) 井然有序的

organizer ['ɔːgənaɪzə(r)] *n* [c] [*of conference, party etc*] 组织者

orgasm ['ɔːgæzəm] *n* [c/u] 性高潮

♦**to have an orgasm** 达到性高潮
orgy [ˈɔːdʒɪ] *n* [c] 纵酒狂欢 ♦**an orgy of violence/destruction** 极度暴力/破坏
oriental [ɔːrɪˈɛntl] *adj* 东方的
orientation [ɔːrɪənˈteɪʃən] *n* [c/u] (*beliefs, preferences*) 定位 ♦**orientation course** 迎新情况介绍
origin [ˈɔrɪdʒɪn] *n* [c/u] **1** (*source*) 起源 **2** (*ancestry*) 出身 ♦**country of origin** 祖国 ♦**people of Indian origin**印度人
original [əˈrɪdʒɪnl] **I** *adj* **1** (*first, earliest*) 最初的 **2** (*authentic*) [+ *art, writing, music*] 原作的 **3** (*imaginative*) [+ *artist, idea*] 独创的 **II** *n* [c] (*not a copy*) [*of painting, document etc*] 原作
originally [əˈrɪdʒɪnəlɪ] *adv* (*at first*) 起初
originate [əˈrɪdʒɪneɪt] *vi* ♦**to originate in** [*idea, custom etc* +] 发源于 ♦**to originate with** *or* **from** 由…首创
ornament [ˈɔːnəmənt] *n* **1** [c] (*object*) 装饰物 **2** [u] (*decorations*) 装饰
ornamental [ɔːnəˈmɛntl] *adj* (*decorative*) [+ *pond, tree*] 装饰的
ornate [ɔːˈneɪt] *adj* (*highly decorative*) [+ *necklace, design*] 装饰华丽的
orphan [ˈɔːfn] **I** *n* [c] 孤儿 **II** *vt* ♦**to be orphaned** 成为孤儿
orthodox [ˈɔːθədɔks] *adj* **1** (*conventional, accepted*) [+ *beliefs, methods*] 正统的 **2** (*conservative, traditional*) [+ *person*] 保守的 **3** ♦**Orthodox** [宗] 东正教的
orthopaedic (美 **orthopedic**) [ɔːθəˈpiːdɪk] *adj* [+ *surgeon, ward, shoes*] 矫形的
ostentatious [ɔstɛnˈteɪʃəs] *adj* [+ *building, car etc*] 装饰花哨的; [+ *person*] 卖弄的
osteopath [ˈɔstɪəpæθ] *n* [c] 整骨医生
ostrich [ˈɔstrɪtʃ] *n* [c] 鸵鸟
✪**other** [ˈʌðə(r)] **I** *adj* **1** (*additional*) 另外的 ◊ *May I make one other point?* 我能再另外讲一点吗？**2** (*not this one*) 其他的 ◊ *Calls are cheaper in the evening than at other times.* 晚上打电话比其他时间打便宜。◊ *toys, paints, books and other equipment* 玩具、颜料、书和其他装备 **3** ♦**the other ...** (*of two things or people*) 另一… ◊ *the other side of the street* 街道的另一边 **4** (*apart from oneself*) 其他的 ◊ *She likes to be with other people.* 她喜欢和其他人在一起。**II** *pron* **1** (*additional one, different one*) 其他 ◊ *in our family, as in many others* 在我们的家庭，就像在许多其他家庭一样 ◊ *Some projects are shorter than others.* 某些项目比其他的工期短。◊ *He and two others were sentenced to death.* 他和其他两个人被判死刑。**2** (*of two things or people*) ♦**the other** 另一个 ◊ *his papers in one hand, his hat in the other* 他一只手拿着报纸，另一只拿着帽子 **3** ♦**others** (*other people*) 他人 ◊ *a brave man who died helping others* 一个为拯救他人而死的勇士 ♦**the others** (*people*) 其他人; (*things*) 其余 ♦**other than** (*apart from*) 除了 ♦**the other day/week** [非正式] (*recently*) 几天/星期前 ♦**somebody/something or other** [非正式] 某个人/某件事 ♦**none other than** 不是别人而正是
otherwise [ˈʌðəwaɪz] *adv* **1** (*if not*) 否则 **2** (*apart from that*) 除此以外 **3** (*differently*) 别样 ♦**otherwise known as ...** 又以…为人们所熟知
otter [ˈɔtə(r)] *n* [c] 水獭
OU [英] *n abbr* (= ***Open University***) ♦**the OU** 开放大学
ouch [autʃ] *int* 哎哟
ought [ɔːt] (*pt* **ought**) *aux vb* **1** (*indicating advisability*) ♦**you ought to see a doctor** 你应该去看医生 **2** (*indicating likelihood*) ♦**he ought to be there now** 他现在应该到那儿了 ♦**this ought to be easy** (*but it isn't*) 这本该挺容易的 ♦**you ought to have been more careful** 你早该更当心点的 ♦**he ought to have arrived by now** 他这会儿该到了
ounce [auns] *n* [c] (*unit of weight*) 盎司 ♦**an** *or* **every ounce of** 一点{或}每一分

✪ **our** ['auə(r)] *adj* 我们的 ◊ *our apartment* 我们的公寓
ours ['auəz] *pron* 我们的 ♦ **this is ours** 这是我们的 ♦ **a friend of ours** 我们的一个朋友
ourselves [auə'sɛlvz] *pron* [*pl*] 我们自己 ◊ *We didn't hurt ourselves.* 我们没伤到自己。◊ *We built the house ourselves.* 我们自己盖了房子。◊ *We ourselves live in London.* 我们本人住在伦敦。◊ *We bought ourselves a new car.* 我们给自己买了辆新车。♦ **by ourselves** (*unaided*) 我们独力地 ◊ *We're learning to play the guitar by ourselves.* 我们在自学吉他。; (*alone*) 我们单独地 ◊ *We were left by ourselves.* 我们单独留了下来。
oust [aust] *vt* (*forcibly remove*) [+ *government, MP etc*] 驱逐

✪ **out**
KEYWORD
[aut]
I *adv*
1 (*outside*) 在外面 ♦ **it's sunny/cold out** 外面阳光明媚/冷 ♦ **out here/there** 这儿/那儿 ♦ **to pull sth out** 把某物拿开 ♦ **to be/get out and about** 四处走动
2 (*absent, not in*) 不在 ♦ **Mr Green is out at the moment** 格林先生这会儿不在 ♦ **to have a day/night out** 外出玩一天/一晚
3 (*indicating distance*) 出发地 ♦ **the boat was 25 km out** 船开出了25公里 ♦ **three days out from Plymouth** 从普利茅斯出发3天的路程
4 [体育] 出界地 ♦ **the ball was out** 球出界了 ♦ **out!** 出界！
II *adj*
1 ♦ **to be out** (*unconscious*) 不省人事的; (*out of game*) 出局的; (*out of fashion*) 过时的; (*in flower*) 盛开的; (*known*) [*news, secret* +] 被泄露的; (*available*) [*book, CD* +] 有售的; (*extinguished*) [*fire, light, gas* +] 熄灭的; (*impossible*) 不可行的; [非正式] (*on strike*) 在罢工中的; [*tide* +] 退潮的 ♦ **before the week was out** 在这周结束前
2 [非正式] ♦ **to be out to do sth** (*intend*) 力求做某事
3 (*wrong*) ♦ **to be out in one's calculations** 计算有错误
III *vt* [+ *homosexual*] 揭露…的性倾向
IV ♦ **out of** *prep*
1 (*outside*) (*with movement*) 出; (*beyond*) 朝…外 ♦ **to go/come out of the house** 从房子里走出去/来 ♦ **to take sth out of a box/bag** *etc* 把某物从盒子/包{等}里拿出来 ♦ **to look out of the window** 向窗外望去 ♦ **to drink sth out of a cup** 用杯子喝某物 ♦ **to copy sth out of a book** 从书中直接摘录某物 ♦ **to be out of danger** 脱离危险 ♦ **to stay out of the sun/rain** 避免日晒/躲雨
2 (*with cause, motive*) 出于 ♦ **out of curiosity/fear/greed** 出于好奇/害怕/贪心
3 (*from among*) …中的 ♦ **one out of every three smokers** 每3个烟民中的1个 ♦ **out of 100 cars sold, only one had any faults** 100辆售出的车中，只有1辆有问题
4 (*without*) ♦ **to be out of milk/petrol** 牛奶喝完了/汽油用完了

outback ['autbæk] *n* ♦ **the outback** 内地
outbound ['autbaund] *adj* [+ *flight, journey*] 开往外地的
outbreak ['autbreɪk] *n* [c] [*of war, disease, violence*] 爆发
outburst ['autbəːst] *n* [c] **1** (*fit*) [*of rage, temper, joy etc*] 爆发 **2** (*period*) [*of violence*] 突发
outcast ['autkɑːst] *n* [c] 被遗弃的人
outcome ['autkʌm] *n* [c] 结果
outcry ['autkraɪ] *n* [c] 强烈抗议
outdated [aut'deɪtɪd] *adj* [+ *custom, idea, method*] 过时的
outdo [aut'duː] (*pt* **outdid**, *pp* **outdone**) *vt* 胜过 ♦ **not to be outdone** 为了不相形见绌
outdoor [aut'dɔː(r)] *adj* **1** (*taking place outdoors*) [+ *activity*] 户外的 **2** (*for use outdoors*) [+ *swimming pool, toilet*] 露天的; [+ *clothes*] 室外的 **3** [+ *person*] 爱好户外活动的

> 📖 请勿将**outdoor**和**outdoors**混淆。**outdoor**是用在名词前面的形容词。它是用来描述发生或存在于户外而非室内的事情。*David enjoyed outdoor activities, such as sailing, climbing and cycling…In summer when it's really hot, we go swimming at the outdoor pool.*
> **outdoors**是副词。如果某事发生或存在于**outdoors**，它发生在户外而非室内。*It was such a beautiful day that I decided it would do him good to be outdoors… Outdoors, the children played happily, while the adults talked inside the house.*

outdoors [aut'dɔːz] **I** *adv* (*in the open air*) [*play, stay, sleep* +] 在户外 **II** *n* ♦ **the (great) outdoors** 野外活动
📖 用法参见 **outdoor**

outer ['autə(r)] *adj* 外部的

outer space *n* [U] 太空

outfit ['autfɪt] **I** *n* [C] **1** (*clothes and accessories*) 全套衣装 **2** (*suit of clothes*) 套装 **3** [非正式] (*firm*) 组织 **II** *vt* [美] 装备

outgoing ['autgəuɪŋ] *adj* **1** (*extrovert*) 开朗的 **2** (*leaving office*) [+ *president, mayor etc*] 将离任的 **3** [+ *mail, call, flight*] 外发的

outgoings ['autgəuɪŋz] [英] *n* [*pl*] 开销

outgrow [aut'grəu] (*pt* **outgrew**, *pp* **outgrown**) *vt* **1** [+ *clothes*] 因长大而穿不下 **2** [+ *behaviour, idea, taste*] 因成长而不再有

outhouse ['authaus] *n* [C] **1** (*building*) 外屋 **2** [美] (*toilet*) 户外厕所

outing ['autɪŋ] *n* [C] (*excursion*) 出游

outlaw ['autlɔː] **I** *vt* [+ *activity, organization*] 宣布…为非法… **II** *n* [C] 逃犯

outlay ['autleɪ] [正式] *n* [C] 支出

outlet ['autlɛt] *n* [C] **1** (*hole, pipe*) 排放口 **2** [美：电子] 电源插座 [英 = **socket**] **3** [商] (*also*: ***retail outlet***) 经销店 **4** (*for feelings, anger, talents, energy*) 发泄途径

outline ['autlaɪn] **I** *n* [C] **1** (*shape*) [*of object, person, house etc*] 轮廓 **2** (*brief explanation*) [*of plan, subject*] 概要 **II** *vt* **1** (*explain briefly*) 概括 **2** (*silhouette*) 衬出轮廓

outlook ['autluk] *n* **1** [C] (*attitude*) 看法 **2** [S] (*prospects, weather forecast*) 前景

outlying ['autlaɪɪŋ] *adj* 远离中心的

outnumber [aut'nʌmbə(r)] *vt* 在数量上超过 ♦ **they outnumbered us (by) five to one** 他们的人数是我们的5倍

out-of-date [autəv'deɪt] *adj* **1** (*expired*) [+ *passport, ticket etc*] 过期的 **2** (*old-fashioned*) [+ *book, object, idea*] 过时的

out of doors [autəv'dɔːz] *adv* [*play, eat, sit* +] 在户外

out-of-the-way ['autəvðə'weɪ] *adj* **1** (*remote*) [+ *place*] 偏僻的 **2** (*little-known*) 不知名的

out-of-town ['autəvtaun] *adj* [+ *shop, supermarket*] 郊区的

out-of-work ['autəvwəːk] *adj* 失业的

outpatient ['autpeɪʃənt] *n* [C] 门诊病人

outpost ['autpəust] *n* [C] **1** [军] 前哨 **2** [商] 边远分部

output ['autput] **I** *n* [C/U] **1** (*production*) [*of factory, mine, writer etc*] 产量 **2** [计算机] 输出 **II** *vt* [计算机] [*program, computer* +] 输出

outrage ['autreɪdʒ] **I** *n* **1** [C] (*scandal*) 引起义愤的事 **2** [C] (*atrocity*) 暴行 **3** [U] (*anger*) 愤慨 **II** *vt* (*shock, anger*) 使义愤

outrageous [aut'reɪdʒəs] *adj* **1** (*appalling*) [+ *remark, behaviour*] 惊人的 **2** (*daring, flamboyant*) [+ *clothes*] 大胆的

outright [*adv* aut'raɪt, *adj* 'autraɪt] **I** *adv* **1** (*absolutely*) [*reject, condemn* +] 彻底地 **2** (*openly*) [*ask, deny, refuse* +] 直率地 **II** *adj* **1** (*absolute*) [+ *winner, victory*] 完全的 **2** (*open*) [+ *refusal, denial, hostility*] 无保留的 ♦ **to be killed outright** 当场毙命

outset ['autsɛt] *n* (*start*) ♦ **at the outset** 在开始时 ♦ **from the outset** 从一开始

✪ **outside** [aut'saɪd] **I** *n* [C] (*exterior*) [*of container*] 外面；[*of building*] 外表

II *adj* **1** (*exterior*) [+ *wall, surface*] 外部的 ◊ *a long wooden shed that stood against the outside wall* 紧靠外墙的一个长长的木棚 **2** (*outdoor*) [+ *toilet*] 户外的 ◊ *We only had an outside toilet.* 我们只有一个户外厕所。**3** (*independent*) 外界的 ◊ *a report prepared by a group of outside consultants* 由一组外界顾问准备的报告 **III** *adv* **1** [*be, wait* +] 在外面 ◊ *It was dark outside.* 外面很黑。**2** [*go* +] 向外面 ◊ *Let's go outside.* 我们到外面去吧。**IV** *prep* **1** (*on the outside of*) [+ *place*] 在…外 ◊ *There was a demonstration outside the embassy.* 在大使馆外有示威游行。; [+ *organization*] 在…以外 ◊ *He is hoping to recruit a chairman from outside the company.* 他希望在公司以外招聘一位主席。**2** (*not included in*) [+ *period*] 在…以外 ◊ *You'll have to do it outside office hours.* 你得在办公时间以外做这件事。; [+ *price range*] 超出 ◊ *a beautiful guitar, but way outside my price range* 是把漂亮的吉他，但超出了我能承受的价格范围 **3** (*near to*) [+ *larger place*] 在…附近 ◊ *a small village just outside Birmingham* 在伯明翰附近的小村庄 **4** ♦ **an outside chance** 微乎其微的机会 ◊ *He's got an outside chance of winning.* 他赢的机会微乎其微。♦ **at the outside** (*at the most*) 最多; (*at the latest*) 最迟 ♦ **the outside world** 外界 ♦ **outside of** (*apart from*) 除了

outside lane *n* [c] (*right-hand side of road*) 右边车道; (*left-hand side of the road*) 左边车道

outside line [通信] *n* [c] 外线

outsider [aut'saɪdə(r)] *n* [c] **1** (*stranger*) 外人 **2** (*odd man out*) 局外人 **3** (*in race etc*) 不被看好的选手

outsize ['autsaɪz] [英] *adj* **1** (*extra-large*) [+ *clothes*] 特大的 **2** (*huge*) 巨大的

outskirts ['autskəːts] *n* [*pl*] ♦ **the outskirts** 郊区 ♦ **on the outskirts of ...** 在…的郊区

outspoken [aut'spəukən] *adj* [+ *person, critic*] 直言不讳的; [+ *statement, criticism*] 坦率的

outstanding [aut'stændɪŋ] *adj* **1** (*excellent*) 杰出的 **2** (*remaining*) [+ *debt*] 未付款的; [+ *work, problem*] 未解决的 **3** (*obvious*) [+ *example*] 显著的

outward ['autwəd] *adj* **1** (*external*) [+ *sign, appearances*] 外表的 **2** (*outbound*) [+ *journey*] 外出的

outwardly ['autwədlɪ] *adv* 外表上

outward(s) ['autwəd(z)] *adv* 向外

outweigh [aut'weɪ] [正式] *vt* ♦ **the advantages (far) outweigh the disadvantages** 利(远远)大于弊

oval ['əuvl] **I** *adj* [+ *table, mirror, face*] 椭圆形的 **II** *n* [c] 椭圆 ♦ **the Oval Office** [美] 白宫椭圆形办公室

ovary ['əuvərɪ] *n* [c] 卵巢

oven ['ʌvn] *n* [c] 烤箱

ovenproof ['ʌvnpruːf] *adj* 耐热的

oven-ready ['ʌvnrɛdɪ] *adj* 即可入炉烤制的

over
KEYWORD
['əuvə(r)]
I *adj* (*finished*) [+ *game, life, relationship etc*] 结束的 **II** *prep* **1** (*more than*) 超过 ♦ **over 200 people came** 超过二百人来了 **2** (*indicating position*) (*above, on top of*) 在…上; (*spanning*) 横跨; (*across*) 穿过; (*on the other side of*) 在…对面 ♦ **there's a picture over the fireplace** 壁炉上挂着一幅画 ♦ **a bridge over the river** 横跨河流的一座桥 ♦ **a helicopter flew over the building** 一架直升机在大楼上方飞过 ♦ **to climb over a wall** 爬过一堵墙 ♦ **pour the sauce over the mushrooms** 把汁浇在蘑菇上 ♦ **the pub over the road** 街对面的酒吧 **3** (*during*) 在…期间 ♦ **we talked about it over dinner** 我们边吃晚饭边讨论 ♦ **let's discuss it over a drink** (*invitation*) 我们边喝东西边商议吧 ♦ **over the weekend** 在周末 **4** (*recovered from*) [+ *illness, shock, trauma*] 康复 ♦ **he's over the flu** 他流感好了 **5** (*about*) 关于 ♦ **concern over**

recent events 对最近事态的关心
6 ♦**all over the town/house/floor** 全镇/满屋子/满地
III *adv*
1 (*across*) [*walk, jump, fly etc* +] 过 ♦**to cross over to the other side of the road** 穿过马路到另一边 ♦**over here/there** 在这里/那里 ♦**to ask** *or* **invite sb over** (*to one's house*) 邀请某人来作客 ♦**I'll drive over to her place later** 我过会儿会开车去她那儿
2 ♦**to fall/turn over** 跌倒/打翻
3 (*remaining*) (*money, food etc*) 剩下 ♦**there are three over** 还剩3个 ♦**is there any cake (left) over?** 还有蛋糕剩下吗?
4 (*more, above*) 超过 ♦**people aged 65 and over** 65岁及以上年龄的人
5 (*very*) [+ *clever, rich, generous etc*] 过于 ♦**not over intelligent** 不太聪明
6 [美](*again*) 再 ♦**if she'd had the chance to do it over** 如果她有机会再做一次的话 ♦**twice over** 再次
7 (*in expressions*) ♦**all over** (*everywhere*) 到处 ♦**all over again** 重新 ♦**over and over (again)** 三番五次

overall [*adj, n* 'əuvərɔːl, *adv* əuvər'ɔːl] **I** *adj* **1** (*total*) [+ *length, cost etc*] 全部的 **2** (*general*) [+ *impression, view*] 总体的 **II** *adv* 总的说来 **III** *n* [c] [英](*woman's, child's, painter's*) 罩衫 **IV overalls** *n* [*pl*] (*protective clothing*) 工装裤

overboard ['əuvəbɔːd] [航海] *adv* 向船外 ♦**to go overboard (on sth)** [非正式] (对某事) 走极端

overbooked [əuvə'bukt] *adj* 超员预订的

overcame [əuvə'keɪm] *pt of* **overcome**

overcast ['əuvəkɑːst] *adj* 多云的

overcharge [əuvə'tʃɑːdʒ] *vt, vi* 要价太高

overcoat ['əuvəkəut] *n* [c] 大衣

overcome [əuvə'kʌm] (*pt* **overcame**, *pp* **overcome**) *vt* **1** [+ *difficulty, problem, fear*] 战胜 **2** ♦**to be overcome by sth** (*emotionally*) 因某事而不能自持; (*physically*) 受不了某物 ♦**to be overcome with grief** 悲痛不已

overcrowded [əuvə'kraudɪd] *adj* 过度拥挤的

overcrowding [əuvə'kraudɪŋ] *n* [u] 过度拥挤

overdo [əuvə'duː] (*pt* **overdid**, *pp* **overdone**) *vt* **1** (*take to extremes*) [+ *exercise*] 做得过多; [+ *whisky, beer, eating*] 过度饮食; [+ *praise*] 过度使用 **2** (*overcook*) 煮得过久 ♦**to overdo it** [非正式] (*overtax oneself*) 工作过度; (*exaggerate*) 夸张

overdone [əuvə'dʌn] *adj* [+ *food*] 煮得过久的

overdose ['əuvədəus] **I** *n* [c] 过量用药 **II** *vi* ♦**to overdose (on sth)** 过量用(某药物) ♦**to take an overdose** 服药过量

overdraft ['əuvədrɑːft] *n* [c] 透支额

overdrawn [əuvə'drɔːn] *adj* [+ *account, person*] 透支的

overdue [əuvə'djuː] *adj* **1** (*late*) [+ *person, bus, train*] 迟到的 **2** (*much needed*) [+ *change, reform*] 期待已久的 **3** (*late*) [+ *library book, rented video*] 过期的 **4** (*outstanding*) [+ *bill, rent*] 过期未付的 ♦**to be long overdue** [*reform* +] 早该实行的 ♦**to be two weeks overdue** [*library book, rented video* +] 过期两周的

overestimate [*vb* əuvər'ɛstɪmeɪt, *n* əuvər'ɛstɪmət] **I** *vt* 过高估计 **II** *n* [c] 过高的估计

overexcited [əuvərɪk'saɪtɪd] *adj* 过度兴奋的

overflow [*vb* əuvə'fləu, *n* 'əuvəfləu] **I** *vi* **1** [*sink, bath, jug* +] 满得溢出; [*river* +] 泛滥 **2** [*liquid* +] 溢出 **3** (喻) ♦**to be overflowing (with sth/sb)** 挤满(某物/某人) **4** (*become apparent*) [*emotion* +] 爆发 **5** ♦**to overflow with sth** [+ *emotion*] 满怀某事 **II** *n* [c] **1** (*hole, pipe*) 溢流口 **2** (*excess*) 过剩之物或人 ♦**to be full to overflowing** 满得要溢出来

overgrown [əuvə'grəun] *adj* [+ *garden*] 蔓生的 ♦**an overgrown child** 思想言行幼稚的成年人

overhaul [*vb* əuvə'hɔːl, *n* 'əuvəhɔːl] **I** *vt* **1** [+ *engine*] 大修 **2** [+ *system,* *method*] 彻底革新 **II** *n* [c] **1** [*of engine etc*] 大修 **2** [+ *of system*] 检查修正

overhead [*adv* əuvə'hɛd, *adj* 'əuvəhɛd] **I** *adv* **1** (*above*) 在头顶上 **2** (*in the sky*) 在空中 **II** *adj* **1** [+ *light, lighting*] 头顶上的 **2** [+ *cables, railway*] 高架的

overheads ['əuvəhɛdz] *n* [*pl*] (*expenses*) 经费

overhead projector *n* [c] 高架投影仪

overhear [əuvə'hɪə(r)] (*pt, pp* **overheard**) *vt* [+ *person*] 偶然听到; [+ *conversation*] 无意听到

overheat [əuvə'hiːt] *vi* **1** [*engine* +] 变得过热 **2** [*economy* +] 发展过热

overjoyed [əuvə'dʒɔɪd] *adj* 极度高兴的 ♦ **to be overjoyed at sth** 因某事而欣喜若狂

overland ['əuvəlænd] **I** *adj* [+ *journey*] 经由陆路的 **II** *adv* [*travel* +] 经陆路

overlap [*vb* əuvə'læp, *n* 'əuvəlæp] **I** *vi* **1** (*physically*) [*objects, areas* +] 重叠 **2** (*coincide*) [*ideas, activities, events* +] 巧合 **II** *vt* **1** (*go over*) 部分重叠 **2** (*put over*) 交搭 **III** *n* [c] 重叠部分

❑ **overlap with** *vt* [不可拆分] 与…重叠

overleaf [əuvə'liːf] *adv* 在背面

overload [əuvə'ləud] **I** *vt* **1** [+ *vehicle*] 使超载 **2** ♦ **to overload sb with sth** 使某人负载过多某物 **3** [电子] [+ *circuit*] 使超负荷 **II** *n* [U] [*of information, work*] 过重的负担 ♦ **to be overloaded (with sth)** [*vehicle* +] (因某物而) 超载; [*person, system* +] (因某物而) 负荷过重

overlook [əuvə'luk] *vt* **1** (*have view over*) 俯瞰 **2** (*fail to notice*) 忽略 **3** (*forgive*) 宽容

overnight [*adv* əuvə'naɪt, *adj* 'əuvənaɪt] **I** *adv* **1** (*during the whole night*) [*sleep, stay* +] 一整夜 **2** (喻) (*suddenly*) 一下子 **II** *adj* (*for a night*) [+ *accommodation*] 过夜的 ♦ **an overnight success** 突如其来的成功 ♦ **overnight stop** *or* **stay** 过一夜

overnight bag *n* [c] 短途旅行包

overpass ['əuvəpɑːs] [尤美] *n* [c] 立交桥 [英 = **flyover**]

overpay [əuvə'peɪ] *vt* 多付

overpower [əuvə'pauə(r)] *vt* (*physically*) [+ *thief, assailant*] 制服; [+ *team, opponent*] 打败

overpowering [əuvə'pauərɪŋ] *adj* **1** [+ *smell, sound, taste*] 极其强烈的 **2** [+ *desire, urge*] 难以抑制的 **3** (*imposing*) 强悍的

overreact [əuvəri'ækt] *vi* 反应过火

overrule [əuvə'ruːl] *vt* [+ *person, decision*] 否决

overrun [əuvə'rʌn] (*pt* **overran**, *pp* **overrun**) **I** *vt* [*army, rebels* +] [+ *area*] 横行于 **II** *vi* ♦ **to overrun (by 10 minutes)** 超出 (10 分钟) ♦ **to be overrun by** *or* **with sth** 某物泛滥成灾的

oversaw [əuvə'sɔː] *pt of* **oversee**

overseas [əuvə'siːz] **I** *adv* 向海外 **II** *adj* (*foreign*) [+ *market, trade*] 海外的; [+ *student, visitor*] 在国外的

oversee [əuvə'siː] (*pt* **oversaw**, *pp* **overseen**) *vt* (*supervise*) 监督

overshadow [əuvə'ʃædəu] *vt* **1** (*cloud*) 给…蒙上阴影 **2** (*eclipse*) ♦ **to be overshadowed by sb/sth** 与某人/某物相比黯然失色 **3** (*tower over*) 高出

oversight ['əuvəsaɪt] *n* [c] 疏忽 ♦ **due to an oversight** 由于疏忽

oversleep [əuvə'sliːp] (*pt, pp* **overslept**) *vi* 睡过头

overspend [əuvə'spɛnd] (*pt, pp* **overspent**) *vi* 超支 ♦ **we have overspent by 5,000 dollars** 我们超支了5000美元

overt [əu'vəːt] *adj* 公开的

overtake [əuvə'teɪk] (*pt* **overtook**, *pp* **overtaken**) **I** *vt* **1** [尤英: 汽车] 超过 [美 = **pass**] **2** [*event, change* +] [+ *person, place*] 突然降临 **3** [*emotion, weakness* +] [+ *person*] 压倒 **II** *vi* [尤英: 汽车] 超车 [美 = **pass**]

overthrow [*vt* əuvə'θrəu, *n* 'əuvəθrəu] (*pt* **overthrew**, *pp* **overthrown**) **I** *vt* [+ *government, leader*] 推翻 **II** *n* [s] 推翻

overtime ['əuvətaɪm] *n* [U] **1** 加班时间 **2** [美: 体育] 加时赛 ♦ **to do** *or* **work overtime** 加班 ♦ **to work overtime to do sth** [非正式] 加班加点地做某事

overtook [əuvəˈtuk] *pt of* **overtake**
overturn [əuvəˈtəːn] **I** *vt* **1** [+ *glass, chair*] 打翻 **2** (*reverse*) [+ *decision, ruling*] 推翻 **3** [+ *government, system*] 颠覆 **II** *vi* [*vehicle* +] 翻倒; [*boat* +] 翻了
overweight [əuvəˈweɪt] *adj* [+ *person*] 超重的
📖 用法参见 **fat**
overwhelm [əuvəˈwɛlm] *vt* **1** (*affect deeply*) [*feelings, emotions* +] 使不知所措 **2** (*defeat*) [+ *opponent, enemy etc*] 制服
overwhelming [əuvəˈwɛlmɪŋ] *adj* **1** [+ *desire, sense*] 极其强烈的 **2** [+ *majority, victory*] 压倒性的
overwork [əuvəˈwəːk] **I** *n* [U] 过分劳累 **II** *vt* [+ *person*] 使工作过度 **III** *vi* 工作过度
overworked [əuvəˈwəːkt] *adj* **1** [+ *person*] 过度劳累的 **2** [+ *word, expression*] 使用过滥的
ow [au] *int* 哎哟
owe [əu] *vt* [+ *money*] 欠 ♦**to owe sb sth** [+ *money*] 欠某人某物; [+ *apology, explanation*] 应给予某人某物 ♦**to owe sth to sb** [+ *success, life*] 应把某事归功于某人 ♦**to owe it to sb/o.s. (to do sth)** 该为某人/自己(做某事)
owing to [ˈəuɪŋ-] *prep* (*because of*) 因为
owl [aul] *n* [C] 猫头鹰
✪**own** [əun] **I** *adj* (*emphasizing possession, individual action*) 自己的 ◊ *I decided I wanted to have my own shop.* 我决定要拥有自己的商店。◊ *They will be expected to make their own beds.* 他们被要求自己铺床。**II** *pron* (*emphasizing possession, individual action*) 自己的 ◊ *Did she hire skis or take her own?* 她是租的滑雪板还是拿的自己的？◊ *There's no career structure, you have to create your own.* 并没有什么职业模式，你得创造出你自己的。**III** *vt* (*possess*) [+ *house, land, car etc*] 拥有 ◊ *Julie's father owned a pub.* 朱莉的父亲拥有一家酒吧。♦**a room of my own** 我自己的房间 ♦**to get one's own back (on sb)** [尤英：非正式] (*take revenge*)（向某人）报复 [美 = **get even (with sb)**] ♦**on one's own** (*alone*) 独自地 ◊ *She lived on her own.* 她独自一人住。; (*without help*) 独立地 ◊ *We can't solve this problem on our own.* 我们无法独立解决这个问题。♦**a place to call one's own** 一个属于自己的地方 ♦**to come into one's own** 进入鼎盛时期 ♦**as if** *or* **like he owns the place** [非正式] 好像他是这儿的主人似的
❑**own up** *vi* (*confess*) 坦白 ◊ *Come on, own up! Who did it?* 得了，坦白吧！是谁干的？
❑**own up to** *vt* [不可拆分] 承认 ♦**to own up to having done sth** 承认干了某事
owner [ˈəunə(r)] *n* [C] 物主
ownership [ˈəunəʃɪp] *n* [U] 所有权
ox [ɔks] (*pl* **oxen**) *n* [C] 公牛
Oxbridge [ˈɔksbrɪdʒ] [英] *n* [U] (*Oxford and Cambridge universities*) 牛津和剑桥大学

> **OXBRIDGE**
> **Oxbridge** 是英国两所久副盛名的大学牛津大学和剑桥大学的合称。这两所大学的历史都可以追溯到12 世纪。其间任何一所学院中的教育都被认为具备世界一流水平。许多 **Oxbridge** 的毕业生进入政治、商务以及外交领域，开始他们辉煌的职业生涯。

oxen [ˈɔksn] *n* [*pl*] *of* **ox**
oxtail soup [ˈɔksteɪl-] *n* [U] 牛尾汤
oxygen [ˈɔksɪdʒən] *n* [U] 氧气
oyster [ˈɔɪstə(r)] *n* [C] 牡蛎 ♦**the world is your oyster** 这个世界是你的
oz *abbr* (= ***ounce***) 盎司
ozone [ˈəuzəun] *n* [U] 臭氧
ozone-friendly [əuzəunˈfrɛndlɪ] *adj* 无害臭氧层的
ozone layer *n* [C] 臭氧层

Pp

P, p[1] [piː] *n* [C/U] (*letter*) 英语的第十六个字母
p[2] [英] *abbr* (= **penny/pence**) 便士
p. (*pl* **pp.**) *abbr* (= **page**) 页
PA *n abbr* **1** (= ***personal assistant***) 私人助理 **2** ♦**PA (system)** (= ***public address system***) 有线广播系统
p.a. *abbr* (= ***per annum***) 每年
pace [peɪs] **I** *n* **1** [S] (*speed*) [*of change, life etc*] 速度; [*of walker, runner*] 步速 **2** [C] (*as measurement*) 步 **II** *vt* (*also:* ***pace around***) [+ *room*] 踱步于 ♦**to set the pace** (*in race*) 定步速 ♦**to keep pace with** [+ *person*] 与…并驾齐驱; [+ *events*] 与…同步 ♦**to do sth at one's own pace** 按自己的步调做某事 ♦**to take a pace forwards/backwards** 进一步/退一步 ♦**to put sb through his/her paces** 考察某人的能力 ♦**to pace up and down** 踱来踱去
pacemaker [ˈpeɪsmeɪkə(r)] *n* [C] **1** [医] 起搏器 **2** [体育] 定步速者
Pacific [pəˈsɪfɪk] *n* ♦**the Pacific (Ocean)** 太平洋
pacifier [ˈpæsɪfaɪə(r)] [美] *n* [C] (*for sucking*) 橡皮奶头 [英 = **dummy**]
pacifist [ˈpæsɪfɪst] *n* [C] 和平主义者
pack [pæk] **I** *vt* **1** [+ *clothes*] 把…打包 **2** [+ *suitcase, bag*] 把…装箱 **3** [+ *hole*] (*with earth, cement*) 填塞 **II** *vi* 打点行装 **III** *n* [C] **1** (*bundle*) [*of goods*] 捆; [*of documents*] 包 **2** [美] [*of cigarettes*] 包 **3** (*group*) [*of hounds*] 群; [*of people*] 伙 **4** (*back pack*) 背包 **5** [*of cards*] 副 ♦**to pack one's bags** (喻) 卷铺盖走人 ♦**to pack sb/sth into sth** (*cram*) 把某人/某物塞满某物 ♦**to pack sth into/around sth** (*compress*) 把某物塞进某物/在某物周围压紧 ♦**to send sb packing** [非正式] 把某人赶走
❑**pack in** [英: 非正式] *vt* [+ *job*] 放弃 ♦**pack it in!** (*stop it!*) 停止!
❑**pack off** [非正式] *vt* ♦**to pack sb off to school/bed** *etc* 打发某人上学/上床睡觉{等}
❑**pack up I** *vi* **1** [英: 非正式] (*stop working*) 停止工作 **2** [英] (*put things away*) 打点行装 **II** *vt* [+ *belongings, clothes*] 打包
package [ˈpækɪdʒ] **I** *n* [C] **1** (*parcel*) 包裹 **2** [*of measures, proposals*] 一揽子 **3** [计算机] 程序包 **II** *vt* [+ *goods*] 包装
package deal *n* [C] **1** (*set of proposals*) 一揽子交易 **2** (*holiday*) 包价旅游
package holiday [英] *n* [C] 包价旅游 [美 = **package tour**]
package tour *n* = **package holiday**
packaging [ˈpækɪdʒɪŋ] *n* [U] 包装
packed [pækt] *adj* **1** (*crowded*) 拥挤的 **2** (*compacted*) [+ *snow, earth*] 压坚实的 ♦**packed solid** (*with people*) 挤得水泄不通
packed lunch [英] *n* [C] 盒装午餐
packet [ˈpækɪt] *n* [C] [*of cigarettes, biscuits*] 盒; [*of crisps, sweets, seeds*] 袋; [*of cereals*] 包 ♦**to make a packet** [英: 非正式] 赚大钱
packing [ˈpækɪŋ] *n* [U] **1** (*act*) 打包 **2** (*wrapping*) 包装材料 ♦**to do one's/the packing** 打包
pact [pækt] *n* [C] 合同
pad [pæd] **I** *n* [C] **1** [*of paper*] 便笺簿 **2** (*to prevent friction, damage*) 垫 **3** (*for cleaning*) 抹布 **4** [非正式] (*home*) 住所 **II** *vt* [+ *cushion, shoulders, upholstery*] 填塞 **III** *vi* ♦**to pad about/out** *etc* 踱来踱去/踱出{等} ♦**elbow/knee pad** 护肘/护膝
padded [ˈpædɪd] *adj* [+ *jacket, shoulder, collar*] 加有衬垫的
padding [ˈpædɪŋ] *n* [U] **1** (*material*) 填塞物 **2** (喻) 冗词赘句
paddle [ˈpædl] **I** *n* [C] **1** (*for canoe*) 短桨 **2** [美] (*for table tennis*) 球拍 [英 = **bat**] **II** *vt* [+ *boat, canoe*] 用桨划 **III** *vi* (*at seaside*) 戏水 ♦**to go for a paddle** 去戏水
paddling pool [ˈpædlɪŋ-] [英] *n* [C] 浅水池 [美 = **wading pool**]
paddock [ˈpædək] *n* [C] (*field*) 围场; (*at race course*) 马的集中场

padlock [ˈpædlɔk] **I** *n* [c] 挂锁 **II** *vt* 锁上

paedophile (美 **pedophile**) [ˈpiːdəufaɪl] **I** *n* [c] 恋童癖者 **II** *adj* [+ *ring, network, activity*] 恋童癖的

✪ **page** [peɪdʒ] **I** *n* [c] **1** [*of book, magazine, newspaper*] 页 **2** (*also:* **page boy**) (*in hotel*) 男听差; (*at wedding*) 小男傧相 **II** *vt* (*in hotel, place of work*) [+ *person*] 广播找

pager [ˈpeɪdʒə(r)] *n* [c] 寻呼机

paid [peɪd] **I** *pt, pp of* **pay II** *adj* [+ *work*] 有薪金的; [+ *holiday*] 带薪的; [+ *staff, official*] 受雇用的 ♦**well paid** [+ *person*] 拿高薪的; [+ *job*] 薪金丰厚的 ♦**badly** *or* **poorly paid** [+ *person*] 拿低薪的; [+ *job*] 低收入的 ♦**to put paid to sth** [英] 结束某事

pain [peɪn] *n* **1** [c/u] (*physical*) 疼痛 **2** [u] (喻) (*unhappiness*) 痛苦 **3** [非正式] (*nuisance*) ♦**to be a pain (in the neck)** 讨厌的家伙 ♦**to have a pain in one's chest/arm** 胸痛/胳膊疼 ♦**to be in pain** 在苦恼中 ♦**to take (great) pains to do sth** 尽力做某事 ♦**to take (great) pains with/over sth** 对某事煞费苦心 ♦**what a pain!** [非正式] 真讨厌! ♦**on pain of death/imprisonment** 违者以死/监禁论处

painful [ˈpeɪnful] *adj* **1** (*physically*) [+ *back, joint, swelling etc*] 疼痛的; [+ *treatment, blow, spasm etc*] 痛苦的 **2** (*upsetting, unpleasant*) [+ *memory, decision, situation, sight*] 讨厌的 **3** [非正式] (*embarrassing*) [+ *performance, interview*] 令人难堪的

painfully [ˈpeɪnfəlɪ] *adv* [+ *aware, obvious, shy*] 痛苦地; [+ *slow*] 使人心烦地

painkiller [ˈpeɪnkɪlə(r)] *n* [c] 止痛药

painless [ˈpeɪnlɪs] *adj* **1** [+ *treatment, operation, childbirth*] 无痛的 **2** (喻) [+ *solution, method, process*] 不费力的

painstaking [ˈpeɪnzteɪkɪŋ] *adj* [+ *work, research, investigation*] 艰苦的; [+ *person*] 勤奋努力的

paint [peɪnt] **I** *n* [c/u] **1** (*decorator's*) 油漆 **2** (*artist's*) 颜料 **II** *vt* **1** (*decorate*) [+ *wall, door, house*] 油漆 **2** (*portray*) [+ *person, object*] 描绘 **3** (*create*) [+ *picture, portrait*] 用颜料画 **III** *vi* (*creatively*) 绘画 ♦**a tin of paint** 一罐颜料 ♦**to paint sth blue/white etc** 把某物涂成蓝色/白色{等} ♦**to paint a grim/gloomy/vivid picture of sth** 将某物描绘成一副凄凉/灰暗/生动的景象 ♦**to paint in oils** 画油画

paintbrush [ˈpeɪntbrʌʃ] *n* [c] **1** (*decorator's*) 漆刷 **2** (*artist's*) 画笔

painter [ˈpeɪntə(r)] *n* [c] **1** (*artist*) 画家 **2** (*decorator*) 油漆工

painting [ˈpeɪntɪŋ] *n* **1** [u] (*activity*) (*artistic*) 绘画; (*decorating walls, doors etc*) 上油漆 **2** [c] (*picture*) 画

paintwork [ˈpeɪntwəːk] *n* [u] 漆面

pair [pɛə(r)] *n* [c] **1** [*of shoes, gloves, socks*] 双 **2** (*two people*) 对 ♦**a pair of scissors** 一把剪刀 ♦**a pair of trousers** 一条裤子 ♦**in pairs** 成对地

❑**pair off** *vi* ♦**to pair off with sb** 与某人成双成对

> 📖 名词**pair**后既可跟动词单数形式也可跟动词复数形式，具体用法取决于它所指的两个事物或人是被看作一个整体还是两者的集合。*A good pair of trainers is essential...The pair are still friends and meet regularly.*

pajamas [pəˈdʒɑːməz] [美] *n* [*pl*] = **pyjamas**

Pakistan [pɑːkɪˈstɑːn] *n* 巴基斯坦

Pakistani [pɑːkɪˈstɑːnɪ] **I** *adj* 巴基斯坦的 **II** *n* [c] 巴基斯坦人

pal [pæl] [非正式] *n* [c] 好友

palace [ˈpæləs] *n* [c] 宫殿 ♦**Buckingham Palace** 白金汉宫

pale [peɪl] **I** *adj* **1** (*light*) [+ *wall, wood*] 灰暗的; [+ *colour*] 淡的 **2** (*milky*) [+ *light, sky*] 昏暗的 **3** (*fair*) [+ *skin, complexion*] 白皙的 **4** (*from sickness, fear*) [+ *face, person*] 苍白的 **II** *n* [c] ♦**beyond the pale** 越轨的 **III** *vi* [*cheeks* +] 变苍白 ♦**pale blue/pink/green** 淡蓝色/粉红色/绿色 ♦**to grow** *or* **turn** *or* **go pale** 变得苍白 ♦**to pale into insignificance (beside sth)** (与某事比) 微不足道

Palestine ['pælɪstaɪn] *n* 巴勒斯坦
Palestinian [pælɪs'tɪnɪən] **I** *adj* 巴勒斯坦的 **II** *n* [c] 巴勒斯坦人
palette ['pælɪt] *n* [c] **1** (*for mixing paints*) 调色盘 **2** (*range of colours*) 一套颜料
palm [pɑːm] *n* [c] **1** (*also: **palm tree***) 棕榈树 **2** [*of hand*] 手掌
❑ **palm off** [非正式] *vt* ♦ **to palm sth off on sb** 把某物硬塞给某人
palmtop ['pɑːmtɔp] *n* [c] 掌上电脑
pamper ['pæmpə(r)] *vt* [+ *child, pet*] 纵容 ♦ **to pamper o.s.** 放纵自己
pamphlet ['pæmflət] *n* [c] 小册子
pan [pæn] **I** *n* [c] **1** (*also: **saucepan***) 炖锅 **2** [美] (*for baking*) 平底锅 **II** *vi* [电影, 电视] 摇镜头 **III** *vt* [非正式] [+ *book, film*] 严厉批评 ♦ **to pan for gold** 淘金
Panama ['pænəmɑː] *n* 巴拿马
pancake ['pænkeɪk] *n* [c] 薄煎饼

> **PANCAKE**
> 如果你要求英国厨师和美国厨师为你做一张 **pancake**，饼的样子决不会是一模一样。在这两个国家，**pancake** 都呈扁平圆形，用牛奶、面粉和鸡蛋打成面糊，油炸后，趁热吃。英国的饼很薄，经常卷起来，或者夹有甜味或其他口味的馅儿。很多人在 **Shrove Tuesday**（忏悔星期二）即 **Lent**（大斋节）开始前的一天吃饼，这一天就是人们熟知的 **Pancake Day**（煎饼节）。（**Lent** 是指复活节前的40天，从前基督教徒有在这段时间里斋戒的传统。）在美国，**pancake** 相对较小、较厚，通常在早餐时，就着黄油和枫糖吃。

panda ['pændə] *n* [c] 熊猫
pander ['pændə(r)] *vi* ♦ **to pander to** [+ *person, whim, desire, opinion*] 迎合
p & h [美] *abbr* (= ***postage and handling***) = **p & p**
p & p [英] *abbr* (= ***postage and packing***) 邮费及包装费 [美 = **p & h**]
pane [peɪn] *n* [c] [*of glass*] 窗格玻璃
panel ['pænl] *n* [c] **1** [*of wood, metal etc*] 板 **2** (*group of judges, experts*) 专门小组 ♦ **control** *or* **instrument panel** 控制板 {或} 仪表板
panelled (美 **paneled**) ['pænld] *adj* [+ *room, wall, door*] 有镶板的
panelling (美 **paneling**) ['pænəlɪŋ] *n* [U] 镶板
pang [pæŋ] *n* [c] [*of regret, sadness, guilt, conscience*] 悲痛 ♦ **hunger pangs** 一阵饥饿感
panhandler ['pænhændlə(r)] [美:非正式] *n* [c] 乞丐 [英 = **beggar**]
panic ['pænɪk] **I** *n* **1** [U] (*anxiety*) 惊恐 **2** [c] (*scare*) 恐慌 **II** *vi* [*person, crowd* +] 惊慌 **III** *vt* [+ *person*] 使惊慌 ♦ **to be in a panic** 处于焦虑不安中 ♦ **to do sth in a panic** 惊慌失措地做某事 ♦ **to get into a panic** 陷入恐慌
panorama [pænə'rɑːmə] *n* [c] 全景
pansy ['pænzɪ] *n* [c] (*flower*) 三色紫罗兰
pant [pænt] *vi* [*person* +] 喘气; [*animal* +] 气喘吁吁
panther ['pænθə(r)] *n* [c] 豹
panties ['pæntɪz] [尤美] *n* [*pl*] 短衬裤 [英 = **pants, knickers**]
pantomime ['pæntəmaɪm] [英] *n* [c/U] 童话剧

> **PANTOMIME**
> 作为圣诞节期间的特殊节目，英国家长会带孩子去看一场 **pantomime**，又称为 **panto**，一种取材于童话传说或传统故事的戏剧。演员穿着奇特的戏装，还有很多歌曲和舞蹈表演。观众的参与受到鼓励。孩子们给反派角色喝倒彩，使劲给男女主人公鼓劲。男主人公可能会由年轻的女演员反串，而男演员则反串岁数较大的女性角色（常常是男主人公的母亲）。

pants [pænts] *n* [*pl*] **1** [英] (*underwear*) 内裤 [美 = **underpants**] **2** [美] (*trousers*) 裤子 [英 = **trousers**] ♦ **a pair of pants** [英] (*underwear*) (*woman's, man's*) 一条内裤; [美] (*trousers*) 一条裤子
pantyhose ['pæntɪhəuz] [美] *n* [*pl*] 连裤袜 ♦ **a pair of pantyhose** 一条

连裤袜［英= **tights**］

✪**paper** ['peɪpə(r)] **I** *n* **1** [U] 纸 **2** [C] (*also:* ***newspaper***) 报纸 **3** [C] (*exam*) 试卷 **4** [C] (*academic essay*) (*spoken*) 论文; (*written*) 文章 **5** [C] (*official report*) 文件 **6** [U] (*wallpaper*) 壁纸 **II** *adj* [+ *hat, aeroplane, cup, plate, towel*] 纸制的 **III** *vt* [+ *room*] 贴壁纸于 **IV papers** *n* [*pl*] **1** (*also:* ***identity papers***) 身份证件 **2** (*documents*) 文件 ♦**a piece of paper** (*odd bit*) 一张纸; (*sheet*) 一张纸 ♦**to put sth down on paper** 把某事写下来

paperback ['peɪpəbæk] **I** *n* [C] 平装书 **II** *adj* ♦**paperback edition** 平装版

paper bag *n* [C] 纸制购物袋

paper clip *n* [C] 回形针

paper handkerchief *n* [C] 面巾纸

paper hanky ［非正式］*n* [C] 面巾纸

paperweight ['peɪpəweɪt] *n* [C] 压纸器

paperwork ['peɪpəwə:k] *n* [U] 文书工作

paprika ['pæprɪkə] *n* [U] 辣椒粉

pap smear, pap test [pæp-] *n* [C] 子宫颈涂片检查［英= **smear (test)**］

par [pɑ:(r)] *n* [U] **1** (*standard*) ♦**to be below par** 一般水平以下 **2**［高尔夫］标准杆数 ♦**to be on a par with** 与…同等水平 ♦**to feel below** *or* **under par** 感觉身体不适 ♦**under/over par**［高尔夫］低于/高于标准杆数 ♦**to be par for the course**（喻）不出所料的

paracetamol [pærə'si:təmɔl] *n* [C/U] 扑热息痛

parachute ['pærəʃu:t] **I** *n* [C] 降落伞 **II** *vi* 跳伞 **III** *vt* 伞投 ♦**to parachute sb/sth into** [+ *country, region*] 用降落伞将某人/某物空投到

parade [pə'reɪd] **I** *n* [C] 游行 **II** *vt* **1** [+ *prisoners*] 使…游街 **2** (*show off*) [+ *object, person, wealth, knowledge*] 炫耀 **III** *vi* 游行

paradise ['pærədaɪs] *n* **1** [U]［宗］(*heaven*) 天堂 **2** [C/U]（喻）乐园

paradox ['pærədɔks] *n* [C] **1** (*situation*) 自相矛盾 **2** (*statement*) 反论

paradoxically [pærə'dɔksɪklɪ] *adv* 自相矛盾地

paraffin ['pærəfɪn]［英］*n* [U] (*also:* ***paraffin oil***) 石蜡［美= **kerosene**］

paragraph ['pærəgrɑ:f] *n* [C] 段落 ♦**to begin a new paragraph** 开始一个新的段落

Paraguay ['pærəgwaɪ] *n* **1** (*country*) 巴拉圭 **2** (*river*) ♦**the Paraguay** 巴拉圭河

Paraguayan [pærə'gwaɪən] **I** *adj* 巴拉圭的 **II** *n* [C] 巴拉圭人

parallel ['pærəlɛl] **I** *adj* **1** [+ *lines, walls, streets*] 平行的 **2**（喻）(*similar*) 相似的; (*simultaneous*) 同时的 **3**［计算机］并行的 **II** *n* [C] **1** (*similarity*) 相似 **2**［地理］纬度圈 **III** *vt* 与…相似 ♦**to be parallel to sth** 与某物平行 ♦**to run parallel (with** *or* **to)**（字）（与…）平行;（喻）（与…）同时发生 ♦**in parallel (with sth)**（与某事）同时 ♦**to draw parallels between/with** 从…中/与…找到相似之处

paralyse（美 **paralyze**）['pærəlaɪz] *vt* **1**［医］使瘫痪 **2**（喻）[+ *airport, organization, production*] 使瘫痪 ♦**to be paralysed with** *or* **by fear/indecision** 害怕/优柔寡断得不知所措

paralysed（美 **paralyzed**）['pærəlaɪzd]［医］*adj* [+ *person, limb*] 瘫痪的

paralysis [pə'rælɪsɪs]［医］*n* [U] 瘫痪

paralyze ['pærəlaɪz]［美］*vt* = **paralyse**

paramedic [pærə'mɛdɪk] *n* [C] 护理人员

paramount ['pærəmaunt] *adj* 最高的 ♦**of paramount importance** 至关重要

paranoid ['pærənɔɪd]［非正式］*adj* (*suspicious*) 多疑的

parasite ['pærəsaɪt] *n* [C] **1**（字）(*insect*) 寄生虫; (*plant*) 寄生植物 **2**（喻）(*person*) 寄生虫

parcel ['pɑ:sl] **I** *n* [C] (*package*) 包裹［美= **package**］**II** *vt* (*also:* ***parcel up***) 打包

❑**parcel out** *vt* [+ *land*] 瓜分

pardon ['pɑ:dn] **I** *vt* **1**［法］[+ *prisoner*] 赦免 **2** (*forgive*) [+ *sin, error, person*] 原谅 **II** *n* [C]［法］赦免 ♦**to pardon sb for sth/for doing**

sth 原谅某人某事/做某事 ♦ **I beg your pardon!, pardon me!** (*I'm sorry!*) 对不起！♦ **(I beg your) pardon?,** (美) **pardon me?** (*what did you say?*) 请问您刚才说什么？ ♦ **pardon me!** [尤英] (*to get attention*) 劳驾

✪ **parent** ['pɛərənt] **I** *n* [c] **1** (*father*) 父亲 **2** (*mother*) 母亲 **II parents** *n* [*pl*] 父母

parental [pə'rɛntl] *adj* [+ *guidance, responsibility*] 父母的

parish ['pærɪʃ] *n* [c] **1** [*of church*] 教区 **2** (*civil*) 行政堂区

park [pɑːk] **I** *n* [c] **1** (*public garden*) 公园 **2** [英] (*private*) 私家庄园 **II** *vt* 停放 **III** *vi* 停车

parked ['pɑːkt] *adj* [+ *driver, car*] 停着的

parking ['pɑːkɪŋ] *n* [U] 停车 ♦ **"no parking"** "严禁停车"

parking lights [美] *n* [*pl*] 边灯 [英= **sidelights**]

parking lot [美] *n* [c] 停车场 [英= **car park**]

parking meter *n* [c] 停车计时器

parking ticket *n* [c] 违章停车罚款单

parliament ['pɑːləmənt] [英] *n* [c/U] 议会

parliamentary [pɑːlə'mɛntərɪ] *adj* 议会的

parlour (美 **parlor**) ['pɑːlə(r)] *n* [c] **1** (*in house*) 起居室 **2** (*shop*) ♦ **pizza/ice-cream parlour** 比萨饼/冰淇淋店

Parmesan [pɑːmɪ'zæn] *n* [U] (*also:* ***Parmesan cheese***) 巴尔马干酪

parole [pə'rəul] **I** *n* [U] 假释 **II** *vt* 假释 ♦ **to be on parole** 宣誓后获释

parrot ['pærət] *n* [c] 鹦鹉

parsley ['pɑːslɪ] *n* [U] 欧芹

parsnip ['pɑːsnɪp] *n* [c] 欧洲防风根

parson ['pɑːsn] [过时] *n* [c] (*Church of England*) 教区牧师; (*in other church*) 牧师

✪ **part** [pɑːt] **I** *n* **1** [c/U] (*section, division*) 部分 ◊ *This is still a major problem in some parts of the world.* 这仍然是世界上某些地方的一个主要问题。◊ *She spent the first part of her honeymoon in hospital.* 她蜜月的头一部分是在医院里度过的。◊ *The exam is divided into two parts.* 考试分为两部分。**2** [c] (*piece*) [*of machine, vehicle*] 部件 ◊ *a group of workers who make parts for generators* 一组生产发电机部件的工人 **3** [c] [戏剧, 电影, 电视, 广播] (*role*) 角色 ◊ *King Lear is certainly the most difficult part in the play.* 李尔王无疑是这部戏中最难的角色。**4** [s] (*involvement*) 份儿 ◊ *If only he could conceal his part in the accident.* 但愿他会隐瞒他在事故中也有份儿。**5** [c] (*of serialized story, play*) 分部 **6** [c] [美] (*in hair*) 分缝 [英= **parting**] **7** [c] [音] 声部 **II** *adv* = **partly III** *vt* **1** (*separate*) [+ *objects*] 分开; [+ *couple, family members*] 使分开; [+ *fighters*] 拉开 **2** (*divide*) [+ *hair*] 分 **IV** *vi* **1** (*leave each other*) [*couple* +] 分手 **2** (*take one's leave*) [*people* +] 分别 **3** (*divide*) [*crowd* +] 分开 ♦ **to take part in** (*participate in*) 参加 ♦ **to play a part in** (*be part of*) 在…中起作用 ♦ **to look the part** 仪表得体 ♦ **to take sth in good part** 不因某事而见怪 ♦ **to take sb's part** 支持某人 ♦ **on sb's part** 在某人方面 ♦ **for my/his part** 就我/他来说 ♦ **for the most part** (*usually, generally*) 大抵 ♦ **in part** 在某种程度上 ♦ **for the better** *or* **best part of the day** 一天中大部分时间 ♦ **to be part and parcel of sth** 某事物的主要组成部分

❑ **part with** *vt* [不可拆分] [+ *possessions*] 放弃; [+ *money, cash*] 花

partial ['pɑːʃl] *adj* **1** (*incomplete*) [+ *victory, support, solution*] 部分的 **2** (*unjust*) 偏袒的 **3** ♦ **to be partial to sb/sth** 偏爱某人/某事

partially ['pɑːʃəlɪ] *adv* (*partly*) 部分地 ♦ **partially sighted/deaf** 半盲/聋

participant [pɑː'tɪsɪpənt] *n* [c] (*in activity, debate, on course etc*) 参加者

participate [pɑː'tɪsɪpeɪt] *vi* 参与 ♦ **to participate in sth** [+ *activity, discussion*] 参加某事

participation [pɑːtɪsɪ'peɪʃən] *n* [U] (*in competition, discussion*) 参与

particle ['pɑːtɪkl] *n* [c] [*of dust, metal*] 微粒; [*of food*] 小粒

particular [pə'tɪkjulə(r)] **I** *adj* **1** (*specific*) [+ *person, thing, time, place*] 特定的 **2** (*special*) 特有的 **3** (*great*) 特别的 **II particulars** *n* [*pl*] (*details*) 细节; (*name, address etc*) 详情 ♦ **in particular** 尤其 ♦ **to be very particular about sth** (*fussy, demanding*) 对某事很挑剔

particularly [pə'tɪkjuləlɪ] *adv* **1** (*especially*) 尤其 **2** (*really*) [+ *difficult, good, beautiful, badly*] 特别地; [*like, dislike, want* +] 格外地

parting ['pɑːtɪŋ] **I** *n* **1** [C/U] (*leave-taking*) 分离 **2** [C/U] (*separation*) 分界 **3** [C] [英] (*in hair*) 分缝 [美 = **part**] **II** *adj* [+ *words, gift, kiss*] 临别的 ♦ **parting shot** 临别恶语

partition [pɑː'tɪʃən] **I** *n* **1** [C] (*wall, screen*) 分隔物 **2** [U] [*of country*] 分裂 **II** *vt* **1** [+ *room, office*] 分隔 **2** [+ *country*] 分裂

partly ['pɑːtlɪ] *adv* (*to some extent*) 部分地

partner ['pɑːtnə(r)] **I** *n* [C] **1** (*wife, husband, girlfriend, boyfriend*) 伴侣 **2** (*in firm*) 合伙人 **3** (*in treaty, agreement etc*) 合作者 **4** [体育] 搭档 **5** (*for cards, games*) 对家 **6** (*at dance*) 舞伴 **II** *vt* [+ *person*] (*at dance*) 做…的舞伴; (*in card game*) 做…的对家 ♦ **business partner** 生意伙伴

partnership ['pɑːtnəʃɪp] *n* [C/U] **1** (*between people, organizations*) 合伙关系 **2** (*in firm, business*) 合伙人身份 ♦ **to go into partnership** *or* **form a partnership (with sb)** (与某人)合伙做生意

part of speech *n* [C] 词性

partridge ['pɑːtrɪdʒ] *n* [C] 山鹑

part-time ['pɑːt'taɪm] **I** *adj* [+ *work, staff, course, student*] 兼职的 **II** *adv* [*work, study* +] 部分时间地

✪ **party** ['pɑːtɪ] *n* [C] **1** [政治] 党 **2** (*social event*) 聚会 **3** (*group*) 群 **4** [法] 一方 ♦ **birthday party** 生日聚会 ♦ **dinner party** 家宴 ♦ **to give** *or* **throw** *or* **have a party** 举行晚会 ♦ **to be (a) party to sth** [+ *crime, undertaking*] 参与某事

✪ **pass** [pɑːs] **I** *vt* **1** (*spend*) [+ *time*] 度过 ◊ *The children passed the time playing in the street.* 孩子们在街上玩以消磨时间。 **2** (*hand*) ♦ **to pass sb sth** [+ *salt, glass, newspaper, tool*] 把某物递给某人 ◊ *She passed me her glass.* 她把她的玻璃杯递给我。 **3** (*go past*) [+ *place, person*] 经过 ◊ *We passed the new hotel.* 我们经过了那家新旅馆。 **4** (*move*) ♦ **to pass sth through/around/over sth** 将某物穿过/围住/跨过某物 **5** (*overtake, exceed*) [+ *vehicle*] 超过 ◊ *We got behind a tractor and couldn't pass it.* 我们跟在一辆拖拉机后面，没法超过。 ◊ *Contributions for 1986 have already passed the £3 million mark.* 1986 年的捐款额已超过了300 万英镑的数目。 **6** [+ *exam, test*] 通过 ◊ *Kevin has just passed his driving test.* 凯文刚刚通过驾驶测试。 **7** (*approve*) [+ *law, proposal*] 批准 ◊ *Many of the laws passed by Parliament are never enforced.* 国会批准的许多法案从未强制执行。 **8** [体育] ♦ **to pass sb the ball** 把球传给某人 **II** *vi* **1** (*go by*) [*time* +] 过去 ◊ *Several minutes passed.* 几分钟过去了。 **2** (*go past*) [*vehicles, people* +] 经过 ◊ *The ships sounded their hooters as they passed.* 船只经过时鸣汽笛。 **3** (*go*) ♦ **to pass through/over/near sth** 穿过/跨过/移近某物 **4** (*in exam*) 及格 ◊ *She told me that I had passed.* 她告诉我我及格了。 **5** ♦ **to pass to sb** [*inheritance, estate* +] 传给某人 **III** *n* [C] **1** (*permit*) 许可证 **2** (*in mountains*) 隘口 **3** [体育] 传球 ♦ **to pass without comment** 默许 ♦ **to pass unnoticed** 被忽略过去 ♦ **to pass for 25** 被认为有25 岁 ♦ **to pass as sth/sb** 当作某事/某人 ♦ **I'll pass, thanks** [非正式] 不用了，谢谢 ♦ **to get a pass (in sth)** [教育, 大学] (某考试) 达到及格标准 ♦ **to make a pass at sb** [非正式] 向某人调情 ♦ **things have come to a pretty pass** [英: 非正式] 事情到了如此糟糕的境地

❑ **pass around, pass round** *vt* 传递

❑ **pass away** *vi* (*die*) 去世

❑ **pass by I** *vi* 走过 **II** *vt* [*life, love* +] 漠视

❑ **pass down** *vt* [+ *customs, inheritance*] 把…往下传

❑**pass off** *vi* [*event, demonstration* +] 完成
❑**pass off as** *vt* [+ *person, object*] 冒充作 ◊ *She passed him off as her young brother.* 她把他冒充作自己的弟弟。◊ *horse meat passed off as beef* 将马肉假冒作牛肉 ♦**to pass o.s. off as sth** 自己冒充作某物
❑**pass on I** *vt* ♦**to pass sth on (to sb)** [+ *news, information, message*] 把某物传给(某人); [+ *illness*] 把某病传染给(某人); [+ *benefits, costs, price rises*] 将某事波及(某人) **II** *vi* (*die*) 去世
❑**pass out** *vi* **1** (*faint*) 昏厥 **2** [英:军] 毕业
❑**pass over I** *vt* (*ignore*) 不予考虑 **II** *vi* (*die*) 去世
❑**pass round** *vt* = **pass around**
❑**pass up** *vt* [+ *opportunity, chance*] 放弃

passable ['pɑːsəbl] *adj* **1** [+ *road*] 可通行的 **2** (*acceptable*) [+ *restaurant, attempt, quality*] 尚可的

passage ['pæsɪdʒ] *n* **1** [c] (*corridor*) 走廊 **2** [c] (*in book, speech, piece of music*) 段 **3** [c] [解剖] 通道 **4** [U] (*movement, progress*) 通过 **5** [c] (*on boat*) (*journey*) 航行 ♦**to clear a passage (through sth)** (从某事物中)开出一条路 ♦**the passage of time** 时间的推移

passageway ['pæsɪdʒweɪ] *n* [c] 走廊

passenger ['pæsɪndʒə(r)] *n* [c] (*in car, boat, plane etc*) 乘客

passer-by [pɑːsə'baɪ] (*pl* **passers-by**) *n* [c] 过路人

passing ['pɑːsɪŋ] **I** *adj* [+ *comment, glimpse, thought*] 短暂的; [+ *moment*] 飞逝的 **II** *n* [U] [*of person*] 去世; [*of era, years, custom*] 消逝 ♦**a passing interest in sb/sth** 对某人/某事短暂的兴趣 ♦**to bear a passing resemblance to sth/sb** 与某事/某人非常相似 ♦**in passing** [*mention, note* +] 顺便地

passing place [英] *n* [c]窄路会车时车辆的停靠处

passion ['pæʃən] *n* **1** [U] (*for person*) 情爱 **2** [c] (*for cars, sport, politics*) 酷爱 **3** [U] (*fervour*) 激情 ♦**to have a passion for sth** 酷爱某事

passionate ['pæʃənɪt] *adj* **1** [+ *person*] (*fervent*) 充满激情的; (*loving*) 热恋的 **2** [+ *affair, embrace*] 感情强烈的

passion fruit (*pl* **passion fruit**) *n* [c] 西番莲果

passive ['pæsɪv] **I** *adj* [+ *person, attitude*] 消极的 **II** *n* ♦**the passive** [语言] 被动语态 ♦**passive resistance** 消极抵抗

passport ['pɑːspɔːt] *n* **1** [c] 护照 **2** (喻) ♦**a/the passport to** …的保障

passport control *n* [U] 验照处

passport office *n* [c] 护照管理局

password ['pɑːswəːd] *n* [c] 密码

✪**past** [pɑːst] **I** *prep* (*in front of, beyond, later than*) 过 ◊ *He walked past the hat shop.* 他走过了这家帽子店。◊ *The farm was just past the village.* 过了村庄就是农场。◊ *I think we must have gone past the turn.* 我想我们已经过了转弯处。◊ *It's long past bedtime.* 早过了就寝的时间了。**II** *adv* (*by*) ♦**to go/walk/drive past** 经/走/开过 **III** *adj* (*previous*) [+ *life, experience, government*] 过去的; [+ *week, month, year etc*] 刚过去的 **IV** *n* [c] **1** ♦**the past** 过去; (*tense*) 过去时 **2** [*of person, country*] 过去 ♦**he ran past me** 他从我身边跑过 ♦**he's past forty** 他40多岁了 ♦**it's past midnight** 过了午夜 ♦**ten/(a) quarter past eight** 8点10/15分 ♦**I'm past caring** 我已不在乎了 ♦**to be past it** [英:非正式] [*person, thing* +] 老而无用了 ♦**for the past few/3 days** 过去几/3天以来 ♦**the past tense** 过去时 ♦**in the past** (*before now*) 在过去; (*in the past tense*) 用过去时态

pasta ['pæstə] *n* [U] 意大利面食

paste [peɪst] **I** *n* **1** [c/U] (*wet mixture*) 浆糊 **2** [U] (*jewellery*) 人造宝石 **3** [U] [烹饪] ♦**fish/meat/tomato** *etc* **paste** 鱼/肉/番茄{等} 酱 **II** *vt* **1** (*stick*) ♦**to paste sth on/to sth** [+ *paper, label, poster*] 把某物贴在某物上 **2** [计算机] ♦**to paste sth into a file** 把某物粘贴在文件里 ♦**wallpaper paste** 壁纸胶

pastel ['pæstl] **I** *adj* [+ *colour*] 浅色的 **II** *n* **1** [c/U] (*chalk*) 彩色粉笔 **2** [c]

(*picture*) 彩色粉笔画
pasteurized ['pæstʃəraɪzd] *adj* [+ *milk, cream*] 巴氏杀菌法的
pastime ['pɑːstaɪm] *n* [c] 消遣
pastor ['pɑːstə(r)] *n* [c] 牧师
past participle *n* [c] 过去分词
pastry ['peɪstrɪ] *n* **1** [u] (*dough*) 油酥面团 **2** [c] (*cake*) 酥皮糕点
pasture ['pɑːstʃə(r)] *n* **1** [u] (*grazing land*) 牧草 **2** [c] (*field*) 牧场
pasty [*n* 'pæstɪ, *adj* 'peɪstɪ] **I** *n* [c] [英] 馅饼 **II** *adj* [+ *complexion, face*] 苍白的
pat [pæt] **I** *vt* [+ *hand, shoulder, dog*] 轻拍 **II** *n* [c] ♦**to give sb a pat (on the shoulder/arm)** (在某人肩/臂上)轻拍一下 **III** *adj* [+ *answer, remark*] 敷衍了事的 ♦**to pat sb on the head/arm** 拍拍某人的头/胳膊 ♦**to give sb/o.s. a pat on the back** (喻)对某人/自己表示赞同 ♦**he knows it off pat,** (美) **he has it down pat** 他对这事了如指掌
patch [pætʃ] **I** *n* [c] **1** (*piece of material*) 补钉 **2** (*over eye*) 罩 **3** (*area*) 斑片 **II** *vt* [+ *clothes, roof, tyre*] 补 ♦**vegetable/cabbage** *etc* **patch** 蔬菜/卷心菜{等}地 ♦**(to go through) a bad/rough patch** 经受不幸/困难时期
❑**patch up** *vt* **1** [+ *clothes, roof, tyre*] 修补 **2** (喻) [+ *marriage, relationship*] 弥合; [+ *quarrel*] 平息
patchy ['pætʃɪ] *adj* **1** (*uneven*) [+ *colour, lawn, fog, rain*] 不均匀的; [+ *performance, progress, education*] 杂凑的 **2** (*incomplete*) [+ *information, knowledge, results*] 不调和的
pâté ['pæteɪ] *n* [c/u] 肉酱
patent ['peɪtnt] **I** *n* [c] 专利权 **II** *vt* 取得…的专利权 **III** *adj* [+ *nonsense, lie*] 显而易见的
paternal [pə'təːnl] *adj* [+ *responsibility, love*] 父亲般的 ♦**paternal grandmother/grandfather** 祖母/父
path [pɑːθ] *n* [c] **1** (*track*) 小路; (*in garden*) 小径 **2** [*of bullet, planet, car, person*] 路线 **3** (喻) (*way*) 道路 ♦**garden path** 公园小径
pathetic [pə'θɛtɪk] *adj* **1** (*pitiful*) [+ *person, animal*] 可怜的; [+ *sight, cries*] 哀怜的 **2** (*very poor*) [+ *excuse, effort, attempt*] 不足道的
pathway ['pɑːθweɪ] *n* [c] **1** (*path*) 小路 **2** (喻) (*to success, good career etc*) 途径
patience ['peɪʃns] *n* [u] **1** (*tolerance*) 耐心 **2** [英:纸牌] 单人纸牌戏 ♦**to lose (one's) patience** 失去耐心
patient ['peɪʃnt] **I** *n* [c] [医] 病人 **II** *adj* [+ *person*] 耐心的 ♦**to be patient with sb** 对某人有耐心
patio ['pætɪəu] *n* [c] 露台
patriotic [pætrɪ'ɔtɪk] *adj* [+ *person, song, speech*] 爱国的
patrol [pə'trəul] **I** *n* **1** [c] (*group*) 巡逻队 **2** [c/u] (*activity*) 巡逻 **II** *vt* [+ *city, streets, area*] 在…巡逻 ♦**to be on patrol** 在巡逻中 ♦**to do a patrol (of sth)** (对某处)进行巡逻
patron ['peɪtrən] *n* [c] **1** (*customer*) [*of pub, hotel*] 主顾 **2** (*benefactor*) [*of charity, campaign, group*] 赞助人 ♦**patron of the arts** 提倡艺术的人
patronize ['pætrənaɪz] *vt* **1** (*treat condescendingly*) 居高临下地对待 **2** (*support*) [+ *artist, writer, musician*] 资助 **3** [正式] [+ *shop, firm, restaurant*] 惠顾
patronizing ['pætrənaɪzɪŋ] *adj* [+ *person*] 居高临下的; [+ *tone, comment*] 屈尊俯就的
patter ['pætə(r)] **I** *n* **1** [s] (*sound*) [*of feet, rain*] 嗒嗒声 **2** [u/s] (*talk*) 珠玑妙语 **II** *vi* [*footsteps, person* +] 嗒嗒地行走; [*rain* +] 发出嗒嗒声
pattern ['pætən] *n* [c] **1** (*design*) (*on material, carpet*) 花样 **2** [*of behaviour, activity*] 方式 **3** [*for sewing, knitting*] 样式 **4** (*model*) 模范 ♦**patterns of behaviour** 行为模式
patterned ['pætənd] *adj* [+ *fabric, carpet*] 有图案的
pause [pɔːz] **I** *n* [c] **1** (*temporary halt*) 停顿 **2** [音] 延长号 **II** *vi* (*when speaking*) 停顿; (*when doing sth*) 暂停 ♦**to pause for breath** 停下来喘口气
pave [peɪv] *vt* [+ *street, yard, path*] 铺砌 ♦**to pave the way for sth** 为某事铺平道路
pavement ['peɪvmənt] *n* [c] **1** [英] (*for pedestrians*) 人行道 [美= **sidewalk**] **2** [美] (*road surface*) 铺筑

过的路面

pavilion [pəˈvɪlɪən] [英] *n* [c] 1 (*building*) 休息处 2 (*temporary structure*) 搭建物

paving [ˈpeɪvɪŋ] *n* [u] (*material*) 铺筑材料

paw [pɔː] I *n* [c] [*of cat, dog, lion, bear*] 爪子 II *vt* (*also:* ***paw at***) (*with paw*) 抓挠; (*with hoof*) 扒; [贬] (*touch*) 粗鲁地摸弄

pawn [pɔːn] I *n* [c] 1 [国际象棋] 卒 2 (喻) 工具 II *vt* 典当

pawnbroker [ˈpɔːnbrəukə(r)] *n* [c] 当铺老板

✪ **pay** [peɪ] (*pt, pp* **paid**) I *n* [u] (*wage, salary*) 工资 ◊ *The pay is dreadful.* 工资低微。II *vt* 1 [+ *debt, bill, tax*] 付 2 [+ *person*] (*as wage, salary*) ♦ **to get paid** 发工资; (*for goods, services*) 付给 3 ♦ **to pay sb sth** (*as wage, salary, for goods, services*) 付给某人某物 III *vi* [*be profitable, beneficial*] 有利 ♦ **how much did you pay for it?** 你买那个花了多少钱? ♦ **I paid 10 pounds for that record** 我买那张唱片花了10英镑 ♦ **to pay the price** *or* **penalty for sth** (喻) 为某事付出代价 ♦ **to pay one's way** 自谋生路 ♦ **it pays to be cautious** 小心谨慎不吃亏

❑ **pay back** *vt* 1 [+ *money, loan*] 偿还 2 [+ *person*] (*with money*) 还给

❑ **pay for** *vt* [不可拆分] 1 [+ *purchases*] 买 2 (喻) [+ *mistake*] 为…付出代价

❑ **pay in** *vt* [+ *money, cheque*] 存入账户

❑ **pay off** I *vt* 1 [+ *debt, mortgage*] 还清 2 [+ *creditor etc*] 付清 II *vi* [*scheme, decision, patience* +] 得益

❑ **pay out** *vt* 1 [+ *rope*] 松出 2 [+ *money*] 付出

❑ **pay up** *vi* [*person, company* +] 付清

payable [ˈpeɪəbl] *adj* [+ *tax, interest*] 应付的 ♦ **to make a cheque payable to sb** 开一张可由某人兑现的支票

pay day *n* [u] 发薪日

pay envelope [美] *n* [c] 工资袋 [英 = **pay packet**]

payment [ˈpeɪmənt] *n* 1 [c] (*sum of money*) 付款额 2 [u] (*act of paying*) 支付 ♦ **advance payment** 预付款 ♦ **monthly payment** 月付 ♦ **on payment of** 在支付…的情况下

payout [ˈpeɪaut] *n* [c] 支出

pay packet [英] *n* [c] 工资袋 [美 = **pay envelope**]

payphone [ˈpeɪfəun] *n* [c] 公用电话

payroll [ˈpeɪrəul] *n* [c] 工资名单 ♦ **to be on the/sb's payroll** 受雇/于某公司

pay slip [英] *n* [c] 薪水单

PC I *n abbr* 1 (= ***personal computer***) 个人电脑 2 [英] (= ***police constable***) 普通警员 II *adj abbr* (= ***politically correct***) 不会造成冒犯的

pc I *abbr* (= ***per cent***) 百分之 II *n abbr* (= ***postcard***) 明信片

PDA *n abbr* (= ***personal digital assistant***) 掌上电脑

PDT [美] *abbr* (= ***Pacific Daylight Time***) 太平洋夏令时间

PE [教育] *n abbr* (= ***physical education***) 体育

pea [piː] *n* [c] 豌豆

✪ **peace** [piːs] *n* [u] 1 (*not war*) 和平 ◊ 2 (*calm*) [*of place, surroundings*] 宁静 ◊ *He chose to return to the relative peace of his childhood village.* 他选择回到相对宁静的童年时的村子。; (*personal*) 平静 ◊ *the search for this elusive inner peace* 寻找难得的内心平静 ♦ **to be at peace with sb/sth** 对某人/某事平和处之 ♦ **to keep the peace** [*police* +] 维持治安; [*ordinary person* +] 守规矩

peaceful [ˈpiːsful] *adj* 1 [+ *place, time*] 安静的 2 [+ *person*] 平和的

peach [piːtʃ] I *n* [c] 桃 II *adj* (*in colour*) 桃色的

peacock [ˈpiːkɔk] *n* [c] 孔雀

peak [piːk] I *n* [c] 1 [*of mountain*] 山顶 2 [*of cap*] 舌 3 (喻) [*of powers, career, fame etc*] 顶峰 II *adj* [+ *level, times*] 高峰的 III *vi* [*person, temperature, crisis, career* +] 达到顶峰

peanut [ˈpiːnʌt] *n* [c] 花生

peanut butter *n* [u] 花生酱

pear [pɛə(r)] *n* [c] 梨

pearl [pəːl] *n* [c] 珍珠

peasant [ˈpɛznt] *n* [c] 农民

peat [piːt] *n* [u] 泥煤

pebble [ˈpɛbl] *n* [c] 卵石

peck [pɛk] I *vt* [*bird* +] 啄 II *vi* ♦ **to**

peck at sth [*bird* +] 啄某物 **III** *n* [c] 1 [*of bird*] 啄 2 (*kiss*) 匆匆地吻 ♦ **to peck a hole in sth** 在某物上啄一个洞 ♦ **to peck sb on the cheek, give sb a peck on the cheek** 轻吻某人面颊

peckish [ˈpɛkɪʃ] [英:非正式] *adj* ♦ **to be** *or* **feel peckish** 觉得有点饿

peculiar [pɪˈkjuːlɪə(r)] *adj* (*strange*) [+ *person, taste, shape, idea*] 奇怪的 ♦ **peculiar to sth/sb** 为某事/某人所特有

peculiarity [pɪkjuːlɪˈærɪtɪ] *n* [c] 1 (*habit*) [*of person*] 怪癖 2 (*characteristic*) [*of person, place, style*] 特质

pedal [ˈpɛdl] **I** *n* [c] 1 (*on bicycle*) 脚蹬子 2 [*in car, on piano*] 踏板 **II** *vi* 踩踏板

pedestal [ˈpɛdəstl] *n* [c] 基座 ♦ **to put sb on a pedestal** 把某人当偶像崇拜

pedestrian [pɪˈdɛstrɪən] **I** *n* [c] 行人 **II** *adj* 1 [+ *street, traffic*] 步行的 2 (*prosaic*) 乏味的

pedestrian crossing [英] *n* [c] 人行横道

pedestrianized [pɪˈdɛstrɪənaɪzd] *adj* 步行的

pedestrian precinct [英] *n* [c] 步行区

pedigree [ˈpɛdɪgriː] *n* [c] 1 [*of animal*] 系谱 2 [*of person*] 门第 3 (*track record*) [*of person, sports team*] 记录 ♦ **pedigree dog/cattle** 纯种狗/牛

pedophile [ˈpiːdəufaɪl] [美] *n, adj* = **paedophile**

pee [piː] [非正式] **I** *vi* 撒尿 **II** *n* ♦ **to have a pee** 撒尿 ♦ **to need a pee** 要撒尿

peek [piːk] **I** *vi* ♦ **to peek at/over/into** *etc* 向/从上/向里{等}窥视 **II** *n* ♦ **to have** *or* **take a peek (at sth/sb)** 瞥(某物/某人)一眼

peel [piːl] **I** *n* [U] [*of orange, potato*] 皮 **II** *vt* [+ *vegetables, fruit*] 削 **III** *vi* [*paint, wallpaper* +] 剥落; (*after sunburn etc*) [*skin, back, person* +] 脱皮

❑ **peel back** *vt* 剥开

❑ **peel off** *vt* [+ *label, wrapping etc*] 剥掉

peep [piːp] **I** *n* ♦ **to have** *or* **take a peep (at sth/sb)** 瞥(某物/某人)一眼 **II** *vi* (*look*) 窥视 ♦ **I didn't hear a peep from him** [非正式] 我没有听到他一点声响

❑ **peep out** *vi* (*be visible*) 慢慢露出

peer [pɪə(r)] **I** *n* [c] 1 [英] (*noble*) 贵族 2 (*equal*) 同等的人 3 (*contemporary*) 同龄人 **II** *vi* ♦ **to peer at sb/sth** 盯着看某人/某事

peg [pɛg] **I** *n* [c] 1 (*for coat, hat, bag*) 挂钉 2 [英] (*also: **clothes peg***) 衣夹 3 (*also: **tent peg***) 系帐篷的桩 **II** *vt* ♦ **to peg sth at/to sth** [+ *price, rate, level*] 将某物固定于某物 ♦ **to peg the washing on the line** 把洗好的衣服夹在晾衣绳上

pelican [ˈpɛlɪkən] *n* [c] 鹈鹕

pelican crossing [英] *n* [c] 自控人行横道

pellet [ˈpɛlɪt] *n* [c] 1 [*of paper, mud, dung*] 小团 2 (*for shotgun*) 小弹丸 3 [*of animal feed*] 丸

pelt [pɛlt] **I** *vt* ♦ **to pelt sb with sth** 向某人扔某物 **II** *vi* [非正式] (*run*) 飞奔 **III** *n* [c] (*animal skin*) 毛皮 ♦ **it is** *or* **the rain is pelting down** [非正式] 大雨倾盆

pelvis [ˈpɛlvɪs] *n* [c] 骨盆

pen [pɛn] **I** *n* 1 [c] (*for writing*) 笔; (*also: **fountain pen***) 自来水笔; (*also: **ballpoint pen***) 圆珠笔 2 [c] (*enclosure*) (*for sheep, pigs*) 栏 3 [美:非正式] (*prison*) ♦ **the pen** 监狱 **II** *vt* [正式] [+ *letter, note, article*] 写 ♦ **to put pen to paper** 下笔 ♦ **to be penned in** *or* **up** [*person, animal* +] 被关起来

penalize [ˈpiːnəlaɪz] *vt* 1 ♦ **to penalize sb (for sth/for doing sth)** [体育] (因某事/做某事)判罚某人; (*in exam*) (因某事/做某事)扣某人分; (*disadvantage*) (因某事/做某事)使某人处不利地位 2 [+ *activity, attitude*] 处罚

penalty [ˈpɛnltɪ] *n* [c] 1 (*punishment, fine*) 处罚 2 [足球, 橄榄球] 罚球

pence [pɛns] [英] *n* [*pl*] *of* **penny**

pencil [ˈpɛnsl] *n* [c] 铅笔

❑ **pencil in** *vt* [+ *appointment, person*] 暂定为

pencil case *n* [c] 铅笔盒

pencil sharpener *n* [c] 铅笔刀

pendant [ˈpɛndnt] *n* [c] 垂饰

pending ['pɛndɪŋ] **I** *prep* 直至 **II** *adj* [正式] [+ *business, lawsuit, divorce*] 未决的

penetrate ['pɛnɪtreɪt] *vt* [*light, water, sound* +] 透过; [*person* +] [+*territory, forest*] 进入; [+ *profession, organisation*] 进入; [+ *enemy group etc*] 打入

penfriend ['pɛnfrɛnd] [英] *n* [c] 笔友 [美= **pen pal**]

penguin ['pɛŋgwɪn] *n* [c] 企鹅

penicillin [pɛnɪ'sɪlɪn] *n* [u] 青霉素

peninsula [pə'nɪnsjulə] *n* [c] 半岛

penis ['pi:nɪs] *n* [c] 阴茎

penitentiary [pɛnɪ'tɛnʃərɪ] [美] *n* [c] 监狱

penknife ['pɛnnaɪf] *n* [c] 小刀

penniless ['pɛnɪlɪs] *adj* [+ *person*] 身无分文的

penny ['pɛnɪ] (*pl* **pennies** *or* (英) **pence**) *n* [c] **1** [英] (*after 1971*) 便士 **2** [美: 非正式] 分 ♦**it was worth every penny** 那非常值得 ♦**it won't cost you a penny** 这不会花你一分一厘

pen pal [美] *n* [c] 笔友 [英= **penfriend**]

pension ['pɛnʃən] *n* [c] (*from state*) 养老金; (*from employer*) 退休金; ❑**pension off** *vt* 发给…养老金使其退休

pensioner ['pɛnʃənə(r)] [英] *n* [c] 领养老金的人 [美= **retiree**]

Pentagon ['pɛntəgən] [美] *n* ♦**the Pentagon** 五角大楼

penthouse ['pɛnthaus] *n* [c] 屋顶公寓

penultimate [pɛ'nʌltɪmət] *adj* [+ *paragraph, day*] 倒数第二的

✪**people** ['pi:pl] **I** *n* [*pl*] **1** (*individuals*) 人◊ *There were 120 people at the lecture.* 120 人去听了讲座。 **2** (*generalizing*) 人们◊ *There has been a complete change in people's ideas on the subject.* 人们完全改变了对这个问题的看法 。**3** ♦**the people** (*ordinary people*) 人民◊ *a rift between the people and their leadership* 人民和领导层的不和; [政治] 国民 **II** *n* [c] (*nation, race*) 民族◊ *the native peoples of Central America* 中美洲的土著民族 **III** *vt* (*populate*) 居住于 ♦**old people** 老人 ♦**young people** 年轻人 ♦**many people** 许多人 ♦**people say that ...** 有人说… ♦**a man of the people** 同人民打成一片的人

📖 用法参见 **person**

pepper ['pɛpə(r)] **I** *n* **1** [u] (*spice*) 胡椒粉 **2** [c] (*vegetable*) 胡椒 **II** *vt* ♦**to pepper sth with sth** 将某物接二连三地点缀于某物

peppermint ['pɛpəmɪnt] *n* **1** [c] (*sweet, candy*) 薄荷糖 **2** [u] (*plant*) 胡椒薄荷

per [pə:(r)] *prep* 每 ♦**per day** 每天 ♦**per person** 每人 ♦**per hour** 每小时 ♦**per kilo** 每公斤 ♦**per annum** 每年 ♦**per capita** 每人 ♦**as per your instructions** [正式] 按照你的指示

perceive [pə'si:v] *vt* **1** [+ *sound, light, difference*] 察觉 **2** (*understand*) 理解 ♦**to perceive sb/sth as being/doing sth** 认为某人/某物为/做某事

✪**per cent, percent** (*pl* **per cent**) *n* [c] 百分之… ♦**a 20 per cent discount** 优惠20% ♦**by 15 per cent** 以15%的比例

percentage [pə'sɛntɪdʒ] *n* [c] (*amount*) 百分数 ♦**to be paid on a percentage basis** 按百分比支付

perception [pə'sɛpʃən] *n* **1** [u] (*perspicacity*) 悟性 **2** [c] (*idea*) 看法 **3** [c] (*way of thinking*) 感知

perceptive [pə'sɛptɪv] *adj* **1** [+ *person*] 观察敏锐的 **2** [+ *comment, analysis*] 富有见地的

perch [pə:tʃ] **I** *n* **1** [c] (*for bird*) 栖息地 **2** [c] (*pl* **perch**) (*fish*) 鲈鱼 **II** *vi* **1** [*bird* +] 栖息 **2** [*person* +] 坐

percussion [pə'kʌʃən] *n* [u] 打击乐器

perfect [*adj*, *n* 'pə:fɪkt, *vb* pə'fɛkt] **I** *adj* **1** (*faultless*) [+ *weather, behaviour*] 完美的; [+ *sauce, skin, teeth*] 无瑕的 **2** (*ideal*) [+ *crime, solution, example*] 理想的 **3** (*complete*) [+ *sense, nonsense, madness*] 完全的; [+ *idiot, fool, stranger*] 绝对的 **II** *vt* [+ *technique, skill*] 使完善 **III** *n* ♦**the perfect (tense)** 完成(时) ♦**perfect for sb/sth** 对某人/某事完全合适 ♦**he's a perfect stranger to me** 对我来

说他完全是个陌生人

perfection [pə'fɛkʃən] *n* [U] (*faultlessness*) 完美 ♦**to perfection** [*done, cooked* +] 恰到好处

perfectly ['pəːfɪktlɪ] *adv* **1** [*perform, work, do, speak* +] 非常好地 **2** [*suit, capture* +] 完美地 **3** (*emphatic*) [+ *honest, reasonable, clear*] 绝对地 ♦**I'm perfectly happy with the situation** 我对这个情况完全满意 ♦**you know perfectly well that ...** 你知道得很清楚…

perform [pə'fɔːm] **I** *vt* **1** [+ *task*] 执行; [+ *operation*] 施行; [+ *ceremony*] 举行 **2** [+ *piece of music, dance, play*] 表演 **II** *vi* **1** (*function*) [*person, organization, business* +] 表现; [*instrument, vehicle* +] 运转 **2** [*actor, musician, singer, dancer* +] 演出

performance [pə'fɔːməns] *n* **1** [C] [戏剧, 电影等] (*by actor, musician, singer, dancer*) 表演; [*of play, show*] 演出 **2** [U] [*of employee, surgeon, athlete, team*] 表现; [*of company, economy*] 运作; [*of car, engine*] 性能 ♦**the team put up a good performance** 该队表现良好

performer [pə'fɔːmə(r)] *n* [C] (*actor, musician, singer, dancer*) 表演者 ♦**to be a good/poor performer** 有造诣/水平差的表演者

perfume ['pəːfjuːm] **I** *n* **1** [C/U] 香水 **2** [C] [文] (*smell*) [*of flowers, spices*] 芳香 **II** *vt* [文] [+ *air, room*] 使…散发香味; (*intentionally*) 洒香水

✪**perhaps** [pə'hæps] *adv* 可能 ♦**perhaps he'll come** 他可能会来 ♦**perhaps not** 未必

perimeter [pə'rɪmɪtə(r)] *n* [C] 周边

period ['pɪərɪəd] **I** *n* [C] **1** (*interval, stretch*) 周期 **2** (*time*) 时期 **3** (*era*) 时代 **4** [教育] 课时 **5** [尤美] (*punctuation mark*) 句号 [英 = **full stop**] **6** (*also: **menstrual period***) 月经期 **II** *adj* [+ *costume, furniture etc*] 古式的 ♦**for a period of three weeks** 3 周的时间 ♦**the holiday period** [英] 假期 ♦**I won't do it. Period.** 我不愿意做。就这样。 ♦**to have one's period** 来例假

periodic [pɪərɪ'ɔdɪk] *adj* [+ *event, occurrence*] 周期性的

periodical [pɪərɪ'ɔdɪkl] **I** *n* [C] 期刊 **II** *adj* 定期的

periodically [pɪərɪ'ɔdɪklɪ] *adv* 定期地

peripheral [pə'rɪfərəl] **I** *adj* **1** [+ *issue, activity*] 边缘的 **2** [+ *area, vision*] 外围的 **II** *n* [C] [计算机] 外围设备 ♦**to be peripheral to sth** 对某事不重要

perish ['pɛrɪʃ] *vi* **1** (*die*) 死亡 **2** [尤英] [*rubber, elastic, leather* +] 老化

perjury ['pəːdʒərɪ] *n* [U] 伪证 ♦**to commit perjury** 作伪证

perk [pəːk] [非正式] *n* [C] 好处

❑**perk up** **I** *vi* (*cheer up*) 活跃起来 **II** *vt* 使快活

perm [pəːm] **I** *n* [C] [英] 烫发 [美 = **permanent**] **II** *vt* ♦**to have one's hair permed** 烫头发

permanent ['pəːmənənt] **I** *adj* [+ *relationship, feature, solution*] 持久的; [+ *damage*] 永久的 [+ *state, job, position*] 长期的 ♦**permanent address** 固定地址 ♦**I'm not permanent here** 我不会一直呆在这里 **II** *n* [美] = **perm**

permanently ['pəːmənəntlɪ] *adv* **1** (*for ever*) [*affect, damage* +] 永远地 **2** [*stay, live* +] 一直地; [+ *locked, open, frozen*] 长期地

permissible [pə'mɪsɪbl] *adj* 容许的

permission [pə'mɪʃən] *n* [U] **1** (*consent*) 准许 **2** (*official authorization*) 批准 ♦**to give sb permission to do sth** (*consent*) 许可某人做某事; (*official authorization*) 批准某人做某事

permit [*n* 'pəːmɪt, *vb* pə'mɪt] **I** *n* [C] (*authorization*) 许可证 **II** *vt* [正式] **1** (*allow*) 允许 **2** (*make possible*) 容许 ♦**fishing permit** 捕鱼许可证 ♦**to permit sb to do sth** (*allow*) 允许某人做某事; (*make possible*) 使某人可能做某事 ♦**weather permitting** 天气许可的话

perpendicular [pəːpən'dɪkjulə(r)] **I** *adj* [+ *line, surface*] 垂直的 **II** *n* [C] ♦**the perpendicular** [几何] 垂直线 ♦**perpendicular to** 垂直于

perplex [pə'plɛks] *vt* 使…迷惑

persecute ['pəːsɪkjuːt] *vt* 迫害

persecution [pəːsɪ'kjuːʃən] *n* [U] 迫害

persevere [pəːsɪ'vɪə(r)] *vi* ♦**to**

persevere (with sth) 百折不挠地（做某事）

Persian ['pəːʃən] I *adj* 波斯的 II *n* 1 [U] (*language*) 波斯语 2 [C] (*person*) 波斯人

Persian Gulf *n* ♦ **the Persian Gulf** 波斯湾

persist [pə'sɪst] *vi* [*rain, problem, symptom etc* +] 持续 ♦ **to persist with sth** 执意坚持某事 ♦ **to persist in doing sth** 坚持不懈地做某事

persistence [pə'sɪstəns] *n* [U] 1 (*determination*) 坚持不懈 2 (*continuing existence*) 持续

persistent [pə'sɪstənt] *adj* 1 [+ *smell, noise*] 不断的 [+ *problem, rain, wind*] 持续的; [+ *symptom, cough*] 顽固性的; [+ *rumour, report*] 连续不断的 2 [+ *person*] 坚持不懈的

✪ **person** ['pəːsn] (*pl gen* **people**) *n* [C] 人 ♦ **in person** [*appear, collect, sing* +] 亲自 ♦ **on** *or* **about one's person** 带在身上 ♦ **first/second/third person** 第一/二/三人称

> 📖 **person** 的复数形式通常为 **people**。 *They were both lovely, friendly people... There were a lot of people at the party.* **persons** 只用于正式场合和法律用语中。*Persons who wish to adopt a child may contact their local social services department.*

personal ['pəːsnl] *adj* 1 (*individual*) [+ *telephone number, bodyguard*] 私人的; [+ *opinion, habits*] 个人的; [+ *care, contact, appearance, appeal*] 亲自的 2 (*private*) [+ *life, matter, relationship*] 私人的 3 (*against sb*) [+ *remark, attack*] 人身的 ♦ **personal belongings** *or* **property** 私人物品 ♦ **nothing personal!** 不针对个人！

personal assistant *n* [C] 私人秘书

personal computer *n* [C] 个人电脑

personal details *n* [*pl*] 个人信息

personality [pəːsə'nælɪtɪ] *n* 1 [C/U] (*character*) 个性 2 [C] (*famous person*) 名人

personally ['pəːsnəlɪ] *adv* 1 (*for my part*) 就我个人来说 2 (*in person*) 亲自 3 [*meet, know* +] 个人地 ♦ **to take sth personally** 认为某事是针对个人的

personal organizer *n* [C] 个人备忘录

personal stereo *n* [C] 随身听

personify [pəː'sɔnɪfaɪ] *vt* 1 (*embody*) 是…的化身 2 (*represent*) [+ *quality*] 象征

personnel [pəːsə'nɛl] I *n* [*pl*] (*staff*) 人员 II *n* [U] (*department*) 人事部门

perspective [pə'spɛktɪv] 1 [C] (*way of thinking*) 视角 2 [U] [艺术] 透视法 ♦ **to put sth into perspective** （喻）正确地看待某物

perspiration [pəːspɪ'reɪʃən] *n* [U] 汗

persuade [pə'sweɪd] *vt* ♦ **to persuade sb to do sth** 劝说某人做某事 ♦ **to persuade sb that ...** 说服某人… ♦ **to be persuaded of sth** (*certain*) 确信某事

persuasion [pə'sweɪʒən] *n* 1 [U] 说服 2 [C] [正式] (*belief*) 信仰 ♦ **people of all political persuasions** 持各种政见的人们

persuasive [pə'sweɪsɪv] *adj* [+ *person*] 有说服力的; [+ *argument, evidence*] 令人信服的

Peru [pə'ruː] *n* 秘鲁

Peruvian [pə'ruːvjən] I *adj* 秘鲁的 II *n* [C] 秘鲁人

perverse [pə'vəːs] *adj* [+ *person*] 刚愎的; [+ *behaviour, remark*] 背理的; [+ *delight, pleasure*] 违反常情的

pervert [*n* 'pəːvəːt, *vt* pə'vəːt] I *n* [C] 堕落者 II *vt* [正式] 1 (*corrupt*) [+ *person, mind*] 腐蚀 2 (*distort*) [+ *truth, custom*] 曲解 ♦ **to pervert the course of justice** 滥用司法程序

pessimist ['pɛsɪmɪst] *n* [C] 悲观主义者

pessimistic [pɛsɪ'mɪstɪk] *adj* [+ *person, attitude*] 悲观的 ♦ **to be pessimistic about sth** 对某事感到悲观

pest [pɛst] *n* [C] 1 (*insect*) 害虫 2 [非正式:喻] (*nuisance*) (*person*) 讨厌的人

pester ['pɛstə(r)] *vt* 烦扰 ♦ **to pester sb for sth** 缠着某人要某物 ♦ **to pester sb to do sth** 缠住某

人做某事

pesticide ['pɛstɪsaɪd] *n* [c] 杀虫剂

pet [pɛt] **I** *n* [c] 宠物 **II** *adj* [+ *theory, subject, project*] 特别的 **III** *vt* (*stroke*) [+ *person, animal*] 抚摸 **IV** *vi* (*sexually*) 爱抚 ♦ **teacher's pet** (*favourite*) 老师的宠儿 ♦ **pet dog/rabbit** *etc* 宠物狗/兔{等} ♦ **pet hate** 特别讨厌的事物

petal ['pɛtl] *n* [c] 花瓣

peter out ['piːtə-] *vi* [*road, stream* +] 逐渐消失; [*conversation, meeting* +] 逐渐停息

petite [pə'tiːt] *adj* [+ *woman*] 娇小的

petition [pə'tɪʃən] **I** *n* [c] **1** (*signed document*) 请愿书 **2** [法] 诉状 **II** *vt* [法] 请愿 **III** *vi* [法] ♦ **to petition for divorce** 起诉离婚 ♦ **to petition to do sth** 申请做某事

petrified ['pɛtrɪfaɪd] (喻) *adj* (*terrified*) 吓呆的 ♦ **to be petrified of sth** 很害怕某事

petrify ['pɛtrɪfaɪ] *vt* (*terrify*) 使吓呆

petrol ['pɛtrəl] [英] *n* [U] 汽油 [美 = **gas, gasoline**]

petroleum [pə'trəulɪəm] *n* [U] 石油

petrol pump [英] *n* [c] **1** (*at petrol station*) 加油泵 [美 = **gas pump**] **2** (*in engine*) 油泵

petrol station [英] *n* [c] 加油站 [美 = **gas station**]

petrol tank [英] *n* [c] 汽油罐 [美 = **gas tank**]

petticoat ['pɛtɪkəut] [过时] *n* [c] (*full length*) 裙子; (*underskirt*) 衬裙

petty ['pɛtɪ] *adj* **1** (*trivial*) 琐碎的 **2** (*small-minded*) 狭隘的 **3** (*minor*) [+ *crime, criminal, theft*] 不严重的

pew [pjuː] *n* [c] (*in church*) 靠背长凳

pewter ['pjuːtə(r)] *n* [U] 白蜡

PG [英: 电影] *n abbr* (= ***parental guidance***) 宜在家长指导下观看

PG13 [美: 电影] *n abbr* (= ***parental guidance***) 13 岁以下儿童宜在家长指导下观看

phantom ['fæntəm] **I** *n* [c] (*ghost*) 幽灵 **II** *adj* (喻) 幻想的

pharmacist ['fɑːməsɪst] *n* [c] **1** (*person*) 药剂师 **2** (*shop*) (*also: **pharmacist's***) 药店

pharmacy ['fɑːməsɪ] *n* **1** [c] (*shop*) 药店 **2** [U] (*science*) 药学
📖 用法参见 **chemist**

phase [feɪz] **I** *n* [c] 阶段 **II** *vt* [+ *action, change*] 分阶段进行
❑ **phase in** *vt* 分阶段引进
❑ **phase out** *vt* 分阶段结束

PhD *n abbr* (= ***Doctor of Philosophy***) (*qualification*) 博士学位; (*person*) 博士

pheasant ['fɛznt] *n* **1** [c] (*bird*) 雉 **2** [U] (*meat*) 雉肉

phenomena [fə'nɔmɪnə] *n* [*pl*] *of* **phenomenon**

phenomenal [fə'nɔmɪnl] *adj* [+ *increase, talent, success*] 非凡的

phenomenon [fə'nɔmɪnən] (*pl* **phenomena**) *n* [c] 现象 ♦ **a natural phenomenon** 自然现象

Philippines ['fɪlɪpiːnz] *n* ♦ **the Philippines** (*also: **Republic of the Philippines***) 菲律宾

philosopher [fɪ'lɔsəfə(r)] *n* [c] 哲学家

philosophical [fɪlə'sɔfɪkl] *adj* **1** [+ *ideas, discussion, debate*] 哲学的 **2** (*calm, resigned*) 达观的 ♦ **to be philosophical about sth** 对某事泰然处之

philosophy [fɪ'lɔsəfɪ] *n* **1** [U] (*subject*) 哲学 **2** [c] (*set of ideas*) [*of philosopher*] 哲学体系 **3** [c] (*personal beliefs*) 人生观

phlegm [flɛm] *n* [U] 痰

phobia ['fəubjə] *n* [c] 恐惧 ♦ **a phobia about sth/about doing sth** 对某事/做某事的恐惧症

phone [fəun] **I** *n* **1** [U] (*system*) ***the phone*** 电话 **2** [c] (*object*) 电话 **II** *vt* [+ *person, organization*] 打电话给 **III** *vi* 打电话 ♦ **to be on the phone** (*possess a phone*) 装有电话; (*be calling*) 在通话 ♦ **by phone** 通过电话 ♦ **over the phone** 通过电话
❑ **phone back I** *vt* **1** (*return call of*) 给…回电话 **2** (*call again*) 再给…打电话 **II** *vi* **1** (*return call*) 回电 **2** (*call again*) 再打电话
❑ **phone up I** *vt* 给…打电话 **II** *vi* 打电话

phone bill *n* [c] 话费单

phone book *n* [c] 电话簿

phone booth [美] *n* = **phone box**

phone box [英] *n* [c] 电话亭 [美 = **phone booth**]

phone call *n* [c] 电话 ♦ **to make a**

phone call 打电话
phonecard ['fəunkɑːd] *n* [c] 电话卡
phone number *n* [c] 电话号码
phonetics [fə'nɛtɪks] *n* [u] 语音学
phoney ['fəunɪ] [非正式] **I** *adj* [+ *address, accent*] 伪造的; [+ *person*] 冒充的 **II** *n* [c] 冒充者
✪**photo** ['fəutəu] [非正式] *n* [c] 照片 ♦**to take a photo (of sb/sth)** 给(某人/某物)拍照片
photocopier ['fəutəukɔpɪə(r)] *n* [c] 影印机
photocopy ['fəutəukɔpɪ] **I** *n* [c] 影印本 **II** *vt* [+ *document, picture*] 影印
photograph ['fəutəgræf] **I** *n* [c] 照片 **II** *vt* [+ *person, object, place*] 给…拍照 ♦**to take a photograph of sb/sth** 给某人/某物拍照
photographer [fə'tɔgrəfə(r)] *n* [c] 摄影师
photographic [fəutə'græfɪk] *adj* [+ *equipment, paper, evidence*] 摄影的
photography [fə'tɔgrəfɪ] *n* [u] 摄影
phrase [freɪz] **I** *n* [c] **1** (*expression*) 习语 **2** (*in phrase book, dictionary*) 短语 **3** (*not clause*) 词组 **4** (*quotation*) 警句 **5** [音] 短句 **II** *vt* (*word*) (*in speech*) 表达; (*in writing*) 措辞 ♦**set phrase** 固定词组 ♦**turn of phrase** 措辞
phrase book *n* [c] 常用词手册
physical ['fɪzɪkl] **I** *adj* **1** (*not mental*) [+ *needs, harm, exercise, strength*] 生理的 **2** [+ *geography, properties*] 自然的 **3** (*material*) [+ *object, world*] 物质的 **4** (*scientific*) [+ *law, explanation*] 物理的 **5** (*sexual*) [+ *love, relationship, attraction*] 肉体上的 **II** *n* [c] 体格检查
physical education *n* [u] 体育
physically ['fɪzɪklɪ] *adv* [+ *fit, attractive*] 身体上地
physician [fɪ'zɪʃən] [美] *n* [c] 医生
physicist ['fɪzɪsɪst] *n* [c] 物理学家
physics ['fɪzɪks] *n* [u] 物理学
physiotherapist [fɪzɪəu'θɛrəpɪst] *n* [c] 理疗师
physiotherapy [fɪzɪəu'θɛrəpɪ] *n* [u] 物理疗法
physique [fɪ'ziːk] *n* [c] 体格
pianist ['piːənɪst] *n* [c] (*professional*) 钢琴家; (*amateur*) 钢琴演奏者
piano [pɪ'ænəu] *n* [c] 钢琴
pick [pɪk] **I** *n* **1** [c] (*also:* ***pickaxe***) 镐 **2** ♦**the pick of** …的精华 **II** *vt* **1** (*choose*) 选择 **2** (*gather*) [+ *fruit, flowers*] 采摘 **3** (*remove, take*) ♦**to pick sth off/out of/from sth** 把某物从某物中摘下/挑出/拣出 **4** [+ *lock*] 拨开 **5** [+ *scab, spot*] 除掉 ♦**take your pick** 随意挑选 ♦**to pick one's nose** 挖鼻孔 ♦**to pick one's teeth** 剔牙 ♦**to pick sb's brains** [非正式] 向某人请教 ♦**to pick sb's pocket** 扒窃某人的口袋 ♦**to pick a fight/argument (with sb)** (向某人)挑起争斗/争论 ♦**to pick one's way across/through sth** 谨慎地通过某物
❑**pick at** *vt* [不可拆分] [+ *food*] 一点点地吃
❑**pick off** *vt* (*shoot*) [+ *people, aircraft*] 瞄准射击
❑**pick on** [非正式] *vt* [不可拆分] 找…的碴
❑**pick out** *vt* **1** (*make out*) [+ *person, thing*] 分辨出 **2** (*select*) [+ *person, thing*] 挑中
❑**pick up I** *vi* (*improve*) [*health* +] 恢复; [*economy, business etc* +] 好转 **II** *vt* **1** [+ *object*] (*take hold of*) 拿起; (*from floor, ground*) 捡起 **2** (*collect*) [+ *person, parcel*] 接 **3** (*catch*) [+ *illness*] 获得 **4** [+ *hitchhiker*] 搭载 **5** [非正式] [+ *person*] (*for sexual encounter*) 随便结识 **6** [非正式] (*learn*) [+ *language, skill, idea*] 学会 **7** (*arrest*) 逮捕 **8** (*receive*) [+ *signal, radio station*] 收到 ♦**to pick up where one left off** 从停下来的地方继续 ♦**to pick o.s. up** (*after falling*) 自己站起来 ♦**to pick up speed** 加速
pickle ['pɪkl] **I** *n* [c/u] (*preserve*) 腌菜 **II** *vt* (*in vinegar*) 腌渍; (*in brine*) 腌制 **III pickles** *n* [*pl*] 腌菜 ♦**to be/get in a pickle** [非正式] 处于/进入进退两难的境地
pickpocket ['pɪkpɔkɪt] *n* [c] 扒手
pick-up ['pɪkʌp] *n* [c] (*also:* ***pick-up truck***) 轻型小货车
picnic ['pɪknɪk] **I** *n* [c] (*meal*) 野餐 **II** *vi* 去野餐 ♦**to have a picnic** 野餐 ♦**to go on** *or* **for a picnic** 去野餐
picnic area *n* [c] 野餐区
picture ['pɪktʃə(r)] **I** *n* [c] **1** (*painting, drawing, print*) 画 **2** (*photograph*) 照片 **3** [电视] 图像 **4** (*film, movie*) 电影

5（喻）(*description*) 描绘; (*situation*) 局面 **II** *vt* (*imagine*) 想像 **III the pictures** *n* [*pl*] [英: 非正式] (*the cinema*) 电影院 [美 = **the movies**] ♦**to take a picture of sb/sth** 给某人/某物拍照 ♦**to paint a vivid/gloomy/bleak** *etc* **picture (of sth)** 描绘了(某事的)一副生动/灰暗/凄凉{等}的景象 ♦**to put sb in the picture** 使某人非常了解情况 ♦**to get the picture** [非正式] 了解情况 ♦**to have a picture of sth** (*mentally*) 非常明白某事 ♦**to be pictured** 登了照片

picture messaging [-ˈmɛsɪdʒɪŋ] *n* [U] 彩信

picturesque [pɪktʃəˈrɛsk] *adj* [+ *village, building*] 美丽如画的

pie [paɪ] *n* [C/U] 派

piece [piːs] *n* [C] **1** (*fragment*) 块 **2** (*length*) [*of string, ribbon, sticky tape*] 段 **3** (*portion*) [*of cake, bread, chocolate*] 块 **4** (*article, work of art, composition*) 篇 **5** (*for game, chess, draughts*) 棋子 ♦**in pieces** 破碎 ♦**to take sth to pieces** (*dismantle*) 把某物全部拆开来 ♦**to be in one piece** [*object* +] 完整无损; [*person* +] 安然无恙 ♦**piece by piece** 一点一点地 ♦**to pick up the pieces** 重新振作起来 ♦**to go to pieces** [非正式] 崩溃 ♦**a piece of paper** 一张纸 ♦**a piece of clothing** 一块布 ♦**a piece of furniture** 一件家具 ♦**a piece of machinery** 一部机器 ♦**a piece of advice** 一条建议 ♦**a piece of research** 一项调查 ♦**a twenty-piece dinner service** 20 人的套餐服务 ♦**to say one's piece** 吐出心里话 ♦**a 10p piece** [英] 一枚10 便士硬币

❑**piece together** *vt* **1** [+ *information, truth*] 搜集 **2** [+ *object*] 拼合

pie chart *n* [C] 饼形图

pier [pɪə(r)] *n* [C] 码头

pierce [pɪəs] *vt* [+ *surface, material, skin*] 刺 ♦**to have one's ears pierced** 扎耳洞

pierced [pɪəst] *adj* [+ *ears, nose, lip*] 穿孔的

piercing [ˈpɪəsɪŋ] *adj* **1** [+ *cry, scream*] 尖锐的 **2** [+ *eyes, stare*] 敏锐的 **3** [+ *wind*] 刺骨的 **II** *n* [C] 人体穿孔

pig [pɪg] *n* [C] **1** 猪 **2** [非正式] (*person*) (*unkind*) 粗俗的人; (*greedy*) 贪吃的人

pigeon [ˈpɪdʒən] *n* [C] 鸽子

piggy bank [ˈpɪgɪ-] *n* [C] 储蓄罐

pigpen [美] *n* = **pigsty**

pigsty [ˈpɪgstaɪ] [尤英] *n* [C] **1** (*on farm*) 猪圈 [美 = **pigpen**] **2** [非正式] (*room, house*) 邋遢的房子

pigtail [ˈpɪgteɪl] *n* [C] 辫子

pike [paɪk] (*pl* **pike** *or* **pikes**) *n* [C] (*fish*) 狗鱼

pilchard [ˈpɪltʃəd] *n* [C] 沙丁鱼

pile [paɪl] **I** *n* [C] **1** [*of earth, leaves, boxes, clothes etc*] 堆 **2** [*of carpet*] 绒面 **3** (*pillar*) 桩 **II** *vt* [+ *objects*] 堆起 **III piles** *n* [*pl*] (*haemorrhoids*) 痔疮 ♦**piles of** *or* **a pile of sth** [非正式] 一大堆某物 ♦**in a pile** 堆成堆 ♦**to pile into/out of sth** [非正式] [+ *vehicle, building*] 一窝蜂地进入/离开某处

❑**pile on** *vt* ♦**to pile it on** [非正式] 夸张

❑**pile up** *vi* **1** [*papers* +] 堆积 **2** [*problems, work* +] 积累

pile-up [ˈpaɪlʌp] *n* [C] 数辆车同时碰撞事件

pilgrimage [ˈpɪlgrɪmɪdʒ] *n* [C] 朝圣 ♦**to go on** *or* **make a pilgrimage to** 前去朝圣

pill [pɪl] *n* [C] 药丸 ♦**the pill** (*contraceptive pill*) 避孕药 ♦**to be on the pill** 服避孕药

pillar [ˈpɪlə(r)] *n* [C] 柱子 ♦**a pillar of society/of the community** 社会/社区的支柱

pillow [ˈpɪləu] *n* [C] 枕头

pillowcase [ˈpɪləukeɪs] *n* [C] 枕套

pilot [ˈpaɪlət] **I** *n* [C] **1** [航空] 飞行员 **2** [航海] 领航员 **3** [电视] (*also:* ***pilot episode***) 试播片断 **II** *adj* [+ *scheme, study*] 试验性的 **III** *vt* [+ *aircraft*] 驾驶 ♦**to pilot a scheme/programme** 试行计划/项目

pimple [ˈpɪmpl] *n* [C] 粉刺

PIN [pɪn] *n abbr* (= ***personal identification number***) (***also PIN number***) 密码

pin [pɪn] **I** *n* [C] **1** (*used in sewing*) 大头针 **2** (*badge*) 饰针 **3** (*in wheel,* *machine*) 轴钉 **4** (*in bone*) 骨钉 **5** (*in grenade*) 保险针 **6** [英：电子] ♦**a 3-pin plug** 三相插头 **II** *vt* **1** (*on wall, door, board*) 钉住; (*to clothes*) 别住 **2** [+ *person, part of body*] (*in position*) 使不能动 ♦**pins and needles** 发麻 ♦**to pin sth on sb** 把某事归罪于某人 ♦**to pin the blame on sb** 推说是某人的责任 ♦**to pin one's hopes on sth/sb** 寄希望于某事/某人

❑**pin down** *vt* **1** ♦**to pin sb down (to sth)** 迫使某人履行(某事) **2** (*identify*) [+ *date, location, source of problem*] 确定

pinafore ['pɪnəfɔː(r)] [尤英] *n* [c] **1** (*also: **pinafore dress***) 无袖女裙 **2** (*apron*) 围涎

pinch [pɪntʃ] **I** *n* **1** [c] [*of spice, salt, sugar*] 一撮 **2** ♦**to give sb a pinch** 捏某人 **II** *vt* **1** [+ *person*] (*with finger and thumb*) 捏 **2** [非正式] (*steal*) 偷窃 **III** *vi* [*shoe* +] 夹脚 ♦**at a pinch** 必要时 ♦**to feel the pinch** 感到缺钱

pine [paɪn] **I** *n* **1** [c] (*also: **pine tree***) 松树 **2** [u] (*wood*) 松木 **II** *vi* ♦**to pine (for sb/sth)** [+ *person, place*] 朝思暮想(某人/某物)

❑**pine away** *vi* 憔悴

pineapple ['paɪnæpl] *n* [c] 菠萝

ping [pɪŋ] *n* [c] (*noise*) 砰

ping-pong® ['pɪŋpɔŋ] [非正式] *n* [u] 乒乓球

pink [pɪŋk] **I** *adj* 粉红色的 **II** *n* [c/u] 粉红色

pinpoint ['pɪnpɔɪnt] *vt* [+ *cause, problem*] 查明; [+ *position, place*] 指出

pint [paɪnt] *n* [c] **1** (*measure*) [英] (*568 cc*) 品脱; [美] (*473 cc*) 品脱 **2** [英：非正式] (*beer*) 一品脱啤酒 ♦**to go for a pint** [英：非正式] 去酒吧喝酒

pioneer [paɪə'nɪə(r)] **I** *n* [c] **1** [*of scheme, science, method*] 先驱 **2** (*early settler*) 拓荒者 **II** *vt* [+ *technique, invention*] 倡导

pious ['paɪəs] *adj* **1** (*religious*) 虔诚的 **2** (*sanctimonious*) 虚伪的 **3** (*empty*) [+ *hopes, words*] 空洞的

pip [pɪp] **I** *n* [c] [*of apple, orange*] 种子 **II** *vt* [英] (喻) ♦**to be pipped at the post** 最后一刻败北 **III the pips** *n* [*pl*] [英] (*time signal on radio*) 报时信号; (*during phone call*) 嘟嘟声

pipe [paɪp] **I** *n* [c] **1** (*for water, gas*) 管子 **2** (*for smoking*) 烟斗 **3** [音] (*instrument*) 管乐器; [*of organ*] 管 **II** *vt* [+ *water, gas, oil*] 管道输送 **III pipes** *n* [c]*pl* (*also: **bagpipes***) 风笛

❑**pipe down** [非正式] *vi* (*be quiet*) 安静下来

pipeline ['paɪplaɪn] *n* [c] (*for oil, gas*) 管道 ♦**to be in the pipeline** 在酝酿中

piper ['paɪpə(r)] *n* [c] 风笛手

piping ['paɪpɪŋ] **I** *n* [u] **1** (*pipes*) 管道 **2** (*on clothes*) 滚边 **II** *adv* ♦**piping hot** [+ *water, food, coffee*] 滚烫

pirate ['paɪərət] **I** *n* [c] 海盗 **II** *vt* [+ *video, CD, software etc*] 盗版

pirated ['paɪərətɪd] [商] *adj* [+ *video, CD, software etc*] 盗版的

Pisces ['paɪsiːz] *n* **1** [u] (*sign*) 双鱼座 **2** [c] (*person*) 属双鱼座的人 ♦**I'm (a) Pisces** 我是双鱼座的

piss [pɪs] [非正式，疑讳] **I** *vi* (*urinate*) 撒尿 **II** *n* [u] (*urine*) 尿 ♦**it's pissing down** [英] (*raining*) 下大雨 ♦**piss off!** 滚开！♦**to piss o.s. (laughing)** [英] 大笑不止 ♦**to be pissed off (with sb/sth)** (*annoyed*) 厌烦(某人/某事) ♦**to take the piss (out of sb)** [英] 取笑(某人)

pissed [pɪst] [非正式，疑讳] *adj* (*drunk*) 醉的

pistol ['pɪstl] *n* [c] 手枪

piston ['pɪstən] *n* [c] 活塞

pit [pɪt] **I** *n* [c] **1** (*coal mine*) 矿井 **2** (*hole*) (*in ground, road*) 坑 **3** (*also: **gravel pit***) 采石场 **4** [美] (*fruit stone*) 核 **5** (*also: **orchestra pit***) 乐队池 **II** *vt* ♦**to pit one's wits/skills against sb** 与某人较量才智/技能 **III the pits** *n* [*pl*] [汽车] 维修加油站 ♦**in the pit of one's stomach** 在内心深处 ♦**to be pitted against sb/sth** 与某人/某事较量

pitch [pɪtʃ] **I** *n* **1** [c] [英：体育] (*field*) 球场 [美 = **field**] **2** [s/u] [*of note, sound, voice*] 音高 **3** [s] (喻) (*level, degree*) [*of feeling, situation*] 程度 **4** [u] (*tar*) 沥青 **5** [c] (*also: **sales pitch***) 推销商品的行话 **6** [u] [航海] [*of boat*] 颠簸 **II** *vt* **1** [+ *tent*] 搭 **2** (*throw*)

[+ *ball, object*] 投 **3** (*knock*) [+ *person*] 摔出 **4** (*set*) [+ *price, message*] 定位 **III** *vi* **1** (*fall forwards*) 重重倒下 **2** [航海] [*boat* +] 颠簸
❑ **pitch in** [非正式] *vi* [*person* +] 起劲地干

pitch-black ['pɪtʃ'blæk] *adj* [+ *night, place*] 漆黑的

pitcher ['pɪtʃə(r)] *n* [c] **1** [尤美] (*jug*) 大罐 **2** [美: 棒球] 投手

pitfall ['pɪtfɔːl] *n* [c] 隐患

pith [pɪθ] *n* [u] **1** [*of orange, lemon*] 髓 **2** (喻) [*of matter, question*] 精髓

pitiful ['pɪtɪful] *adj* **1** (*touching*) [+ *person, appearance, sight etc*] 可怜的 **2** (*lamentable*) [+ *excuse, attempt, effort etc*] 可鄙的

pity ['pɪtɪ] **I** *n* **1** [u] (*compassion*) 同情 **2** (*misfortune*) ♦ **it is a pity that ...** 真遗憾… **II** *vt* [+ *person*] 同情 ♦ **to take pity on sb** 怜悯某人 ♦ **what a pity!** 真可惜!

pizza ['piːtsə] *n* [c] 比萨饼

placard ['plækɑːd] *n* [c] (*outside shop*) 招贴; (*in demonstration*) 标语牌

placate [plə'keɪt] [正式] *vt* [+ *person*] 安慰; [+ *opposition, anger*] 平息

✪ **place** [pleɪs] **I** *n* **1** [c] (*location*) 地方 ◊ *We were looking for a good place to camp.* 我们寻找露营的地方。◊ *The cellar was a very dark place.* 地窖是个很黑的地方。◊ *They seem to have scheduled the president to be in two places at once.* 他们似乎想让总统同时出现在两个不同的地方。◊ *The pain was always in the same place.* 总是在一个地方疼。◊ *I keep these cards in a very safe place.* 我把卡片放在一个非常安全的地方。**2** [c] (*empty*) (*space*) 空位 ◊ *I found a place to park.* 我找到了一个空位停车。; (*seat*) 座位 ◊ *There was only one place left for him to sit.* 只有一个座位留给他。; (*at university, on course, on committee, in team*) 名额 ◊ *I got a place at a teachers' training college nearby.* 我得到了附近师范学院的一个名额。**3** [s] [非正式] (*home*) 家 ◊ *Do you want to meet at your place or mine?* 你想在你家还是我家见面? **4** (*in street names*) 路 ◊ *Laurel Place* 劳瑞尔路 **5** [s] (*role*) (*in society, system, world*) 地位 ◊ *Britain's place in the world* 英国在世界上的地位 **6** [c] (*in competition*) 名次 ◊ *Britain won third place at the games in Barcelona.* 英国在巴塞罗那奥运会上得了第3名。**7** [美: 非正式] ♦ **some/every/no/any place** 某些/每个/没有/任何地方 ◊ *The poor guy obviously didn't have any place to go.* 那个可怜的家伙显然没有任何地方可去。**II** *vt* **1** (*put*) [+ *object*] 放 ◊ *She placed the music on the piano and sat down.* 她把乐谱放在钢琴上,坐了下来。**2** (*classify*) [+ *person, work, drug*] 归类 ◊ *Some place him on a par with Einstein.* 有人将他归为与爱因斯坦比肩的人。**3** (*identify*) [+ *person*] 记起 ◊ *She was looking at me as if she could not quite place me.* 她看着我好像记不起我是谁了。 ♦ **from place to place** 从一个地方到另一个地方 ♦ **all over the place** (*everywhere*) 到处 ♦ **in places** 有几处 ♦ **in the first place** (*first of all*) 首先; (*originally*) 原先 ♦ **to change places with sb** (喻) 与某人交换位置 ♦ **at sb's place** (*home*) 在某人的家里 ♦ **to sb's place** 到某人的家里 ♦ **he's going places** 他正飞黄腾达 ♦ **in sb's/sth's place** 代替某人/某物 ♦ **to take sb's/sth's place** 代替某人/某物 ♦ **it's not my place to do it** 我无权这么做 ♦ **to put sb in his/her place** (喻) 煞住他/她的傲气 ♦ **to fall into place** (*become clear*) 开始有头绪; (*go well*) 开始明朗化 ♦ **in place** (*in correct place*) 到位; (*ready*) 就绪 ♦ **out of place** (*in wrong place*) 不在应在的地方; (*inappropriate*) 不适当的 ♦ **to feel out of place** 感到不自在的 ♦ **to take place** (*happen*) 发生 ♦ **to place an order** 订购 ♦ **to place an advertisement** 打广告 ♦ **to be placed third** *etc* (*in race, exam*) 得第3名{等} ♦ **to place one's faith in/hopes on sth** 对某事寄于信任/希望 ♦ **how are you placed?** 你有什么安排吗?

placement ['pleɪsmənt] *n* **1** [c] (*job*) 职位 **2** [u] (*placing*) [*of object*] 放置; (*in home, school*) [*of person*] 安置

place of birth *n* [c] 出生地
placid ['plæsɪd] *adj* **1** [+ *person*] 平静的 **2** [+ *place, river, life*] 宁静的
plague [pleɪg] **I** *n* **1** [c] (*disease*) 瘟疫 **2**（喻）[*of locusts, rats*] 灾难; [*of robberies, attacks*] 祸患 **II** *vt*（喻）[*problems, difficulties* +] 烦扰 ♦ **to plague sb with questions** 不断向某人发问
plaice [pleɪs] (*pl* **plaice**) *n* [c/u] 鲽鱼
plain [pleɪn] **I** *adj* **1** (*not patterned*) 无图案花纹的 **2** (*simple*) [+ *dress, food, design*] 简单的 **3** (*clear, easily understood*) 清楚的 **4** (*not beautiful*) [+ *girl, woman*] 不漂亮的 **II** *adv* [+ *wrong, stupid, terrible etc*] 简直 **III** *n* [c] **1** (*area of land*) 平原 **2** (*in knitting*) ♦ **one plain, one purl** 一针平织，一针反织 ♦ **in plain clothes** [警察]身穿便服 ♦ **it is plain that ...** 显然… ♦ **to make it plain to sb that ...** 对某人明确表示…
plain chocolate *n* [u] 纯巧克力 [美= **dark chocolate**]
plainly ['pleɪnlɪ] *adv* **1** (*obviously*) 显然地 **2** (*distinctly*) [*hear, see, recognize* +] 清楚地; [*state* +] 明确地
plaintiff ['pleɪntɪf] [法] *n* [c] 原告
plait [plæt] **I** *n* [c] [*of hair*] 辫子; [*of rope, leather*] 辫状物 [美= **braid**] **II** *vt* [+ *hair, rope, leather*] 编 [美= **braid**]
✪ **plan** [plæn] **I** *n* [c] **1** (*scheme, project*) 计划 **2** (*drawing*) 详图 **II** *vt* **1** [+ *crime, holiday, future etc*] 计划 **2** (*design*) [+ *building, garden etc*] 设计 **III** *vi* (*think ahead*) 打算 ◊ *We must plan for the future.* 我们必须为将来做打算。**IV plans** *n* [c]*pl* (*intentions*) 计划 ◊ *Do you have any plans for the weekend?* 你周末有什么计划吗？ ♦ **to go according to plan** 按计划进行 ♦ **to plan to do sth** 计划做某事 ♦ **how long do you plan to stay?** 你准备住多久？ ♦ **to plan for** *or* **on sth** (*expect*) 预先想到某事 ♦ **to plan on doing sth** 意欲做某事
plane [pleɪn] **I** *n* [c] **1** 飞机 **2** [数] 平面 **3**（喻）(*level*) [*of existence, consciousness*] 水平 **4** (*tool*) 刨子 **5** (*also: **plane tree***) 悬铃木 **II** *vt* [+ *wood*] 刨
planet ['plænɪt] *n* [c] 行星
plank [plæŋk] *n* [c] **1** [*of wood*] 板 **2** ♦ **the main/central plank** [*of policy, argument*] 主要/中心政纲准则
planning ['plænɪŋ] *n* [u] **1** (*organization*) 计划 **2** (*town planning*) 规划
✪ **plant** [plɑːnt] **I** *n* **1** [c] 植物 **2** [u] (*machinery*) 机器 ◊ *new plant and equipment* 新的机器设备 **3** [c] (*factory, power station*) 工厂 **II** *vt* **1** [+ *flower, tree, crop etc*] 栽种; [+ *field, garden*] 种植 ◊ *Alongside the road was a field planted with maize.* 路的两边是种了玉米的田地。**2** (*put secretly*) [+ *microphone, bomb*] 安放 ◊ *They had planted the bomb beneath the house.* 他们在房子下安放了炸弹。; [+ *incriminating evidence*] 栽赃 ◊ *I'm convinced the evidence was planted in John's flat.* 我相信在约翰房里发现的证据是栽赃的。**3** (*place*) [+ *object, kiss*] 放置
plantation [plæn'teɪʃən] *n* [c] **1** (*for tea, rubber, sugar*) 种植园 **2** [*of trees*] 人工林
plaque [plæk] *n* **1** [c] (*on building, wall*) 饰板 **2** [u] (*on teeth*) 斑
plaster ['plɑːstə(r)] **I** *n* **1** [u] (*for walls, ceilings*) 灰泥 **2** [u] (*also: **plaster of Paris***) 熟石灰 **3** [c/u] [英] (*also: **sticking plaster***) 橡皮膏 [美= **Band-Aid**] **II** *vt* **1** [+ *wall*] 用灰泥涂抹 **2** (*cover*) ♦ **to plaster sth with sth** 用某物贴满某物 ♦ **in plaster** [英] 打了石膏的
plaster cast [医] *n* [c] 石膏绷带
plastic ['plæstɪk] **I** *n* [c/u] 塑料 **II** *adj* **1** [+ *bucket, chair, cup*] 塑料的 **2** (*flexible*) 可塑的
plastic bag *n* [c] 塑料袋
plastic surgery *n* [u] 整形手术
plastic wrap [美] *n* [u] 保鲜膜 [英= **clingfilm**]
plate [pleɪt] *n* **1** [c] (*dish*) 碟; (*for serving*) 托盘 **2** [c] (*on door*) 牌 **3** [c] (*on machine*) 金属牌 **4** [u] (*metal objects*) (*also: **gold plate***) 镀金餐具; (*also: **silver plate***) 银餐具 **5** [c] [排版] (*for printing*) 印版 **6** [c] (*picture, photograph*) 整页插图 **7** [c] (*number plate*) 牌照 **8** [c] (*dental plate*) 托牙板 ♦ **a plate of cakes/biscuits** 一盘蛋

糕/饼干

plateau ['plætəu] (*pl* **plateaus** *or* **plateaux**) *n* [c] **1** 高原 **2** (喻) [*of activity, process*] 稳定状态

platform ['plætfɔːm] *n* [c] **1** (*stage*) 平台 **2** (*for landing on*) 平台 **3** [铁路] 站台 **4** [政治] 政纲 **5** [英] [*of bus*] 出入口平台 ♦ **the train leaves from platform 7** 火车从7号站台出发

platinum ['plætɪnəm] *n* [u] 白金

platoon [plə'tuːn] *n* [c] 排

platter ['plætə(r)] *n* [c] 大浅盘

plausible ['plɔːzɪbl] *adj* [+ *theory, explanation*] 似乎有理的; [+ *person, rogue, liar*] 花言巧语的

✪ **play** [pleɪ] **I** *n* **1** [c] [戏剧, 电视, 广播] 戏剧 **2** [u] (*activity*) (*with toys, games etc*) 游戏; (*sport*) 活动 ◊ *Rain again interrupted play at Wimbledon today.* 温布尔登赛事又受到下雨的干扰。**II** *vt* **1** [+ *game, chess*] 玩 ◊ *Let's play a game.* 咱们玩游戏吧。; [*football*] 踢; [*cricket, tennis*] 打 **2** (*compete against*) [+ *team, opponent*] 同…比赛 **3** (*in play, film*) [+ *part, role, character*] 扮演 **4** [音] [+ *instrument, piece of music*] 演奏 **5** (*listen to*) [+ *CD, record, tape*] 播放 **III** *vi* **1** [*children* +] 玩耍 ◊ *Polly was playing with her teddy bear.* 波丽在玩她的玩具熊。**2** [*orchestra, band* +] 演奏 **3** [*CD, record, tape, radio* +] 播放 ◊ *There was classical music playing in the background.* 古典音乐正作为背景音乐播放。 ♦ **a play on words** 双关语 ♦ **to bring into play** 调动 ♦ **to play cards** 玩纸牌 ♦ **to play a trick on sb** 对某人耍花招 ♦ **to play a part** *or* **role in sth** (喻) 在某事中起作用 ♦ **to play (it) safe** 谨慎行事 ♦ **to play for time** 为争取时间而拖延 ♦ **to play into sb's hands** 让某人占便宜

❑ **play about with** *vt* [不可拆分] = **play around with**

❑ **play along with** *vt* [不可拆分] [+ *person*] 同…合作; [+ *idea, charade*] 依照…行事

❑ **play around** [非正式] *vi* (*be silly*) 胡闹

❑ **play around with, play about with** [非正式] *vt* [不可拆分] [+ *idea, problem*] 摆弄

❑ **play at** *vt* [不可拆分] ♦ **to play at (doing/being) sth** (*do half-heartedly*) 敷衍地做某事; (*as game*) 装扮某事 ◊ *They played at (being) soldiers.* 他们装扮士兵。 ♦ **what's he playing at?** 他在胡闹些什么?

❑ **play back** *vt* [+ *recording, message, video*] 回放

❑ **play down** *vt* 减低

❑ **play off against** *vt* 挑拨离间

❑ **play on** *vt* [不可拆分] [+ *sb's feelings, fears*] 利用 ♦ **to play on sb's mind** 萦绕某人的心头

❑ **play up** [非正式] *vi* **1** [*machine, part of body* +] 出毛病 **2** [*child* +] 调皮捣乱

✪ **player** ['pleɪə(r)] *n* [c] **1** [体育] 选手 ◊ *He was a good tennis player.* 他是名优秀的网球选手。**2** [音] ♦ **a trumpet/flute/piano player** 小号/长笛/钢琴演奏者 **3** [戏剧] 演员 **4** [商, 政治] (*party involved*) 参与者 ◊ *America is a key player in the negotiations.* 美国是这次谈判的主要参与者。

playful ['pleɪful] *adj* [+ *person, gesture*] 开玩笑的; [+ *animal*] 顽皮的

playground ['pleɪgraund] *n* [c] (*at school*) 运动场; (*in park*) 游戏场

playgroup ['pleɪgruːp] *n* [c] 幼儿园

playing card ['pleɪɪŋ-] *n* [c] 纸牌

playing field *n* [c] 运动场 ♦ **a level playing field** (喻) 公平竞争

playschool ['pleɪskuːl] *n* = **playgroup**

playtime ['pleɪtaɪm] *n* [u] 游戏时间

playwright ['pleɪraɪt] *n* [c] 剧作家

plc [英] *abbr* (= ***public limited company***) 股票上市公司

plea [pliː] *n* [c] **1** (*request*) ♦ **plea (for sth)** 恳求(某事) **2** [法] (*in court*) 抗辩 **3** (*excuse*) 托词 ♦ **a plea for help** 请求帮助 ♦ **a plea for sb to do sth** 请求某人做某事

plead [pliːd] **I** *vt* **1** [法] [+ *case, cause*] 为…辩护 **2** (*give as excuse*) [+ *ignorance, ill health, poverty*] 以…为借口 **II** *vi* [法] (*in court*) 辩护 ♦ **to plead with sb (to do sth)** 恳求某人(做某事) ♦ **to plead for sth** 恳求某物 ♦ **to plead guilty** 服罪 ♦ **to**

plead not guilty 不服罪

pleasant ['plɛznt] *adj* **1** (*agreeable*) 令人愉快的 **2** (*friendly*) 友善的

pleasantly ['plɛzntlɪ] *adv* [+ *warm, tired, relaxed*] 愉快地; [*say, behave, spend time* +] 亲切地 ♦ **to be pleasantly surprised** 感到惊喜的

please [pliːz] **I** *int* **1** (*in polite requests, written instructions*) 请 **2** (*accepting sth*) 好的 **3** (*to attract attention*) 劳驾 **II** *vt* (*satisfy*) 使高兴 **III** *vi* (*give pleasure, satisfaction*) 满意 ♦ **yes, please** 好的 ♦ **my bill, please** 请给我账单 ♦ **please don't cry!** 拜托，别哭了！♦ **it pleased them to ...** …让他们开心 ♦ **please yourself!** [非正式] 请便！♦ **do as you please** 按你喜欢的做

pleased [pliːzd] *adj* (*happy, satisfied*) 开心的 ♦ **to be pleased that ...** 对…感到高兴 ♦ **to be pleased to help** 乐意相助 ♦ **pleased to meet you** 见到你很高兴 ♦ **pleased with sth** 对某事满意 ♦ **we are pleased to inform you that ...** 我们荣幸地告诉你…

pleasing ['pliːzɪŋ] *adj* [+ *situation, picture, person*] 令人愉快的 ♦ **it's pleasing to see/know that ...** 高兴地看到/知道…

pleasurable ['plɛʒərəbl] *adj* [+ *experience, sensation*] 令人愉快的

pleasure ['plɛʒə(r)] *n* **1** [U] (*happiness, satisfaction*) 高兴 **2** [U] (*fun*) 享乐 **3** [C] (*enjoyable experience*) 乐事 ♦ **to take pleasure in sth/in doing sth** 乐于某事/做某事 ♦ **to give sb great pleasure** 使某人很高兴 ♦ **"it's a pleasure", "my pleasure"** "乐意效劳" ♦ **with pleasure** 非常愿意 ♦ **is this trip for business or pleasure?** 这趟旅行是出公差还是度假?

pleat [pliːt] *n* [C] 褶

pleated ['pliːtɪd] *adj* 有褶的 ◊ *a pleated skirt* 百褶裙

pledge [plɛdʒ] **I** *n* [C] (*promise*) 誓言 **II** *vt* (*promise*) [+ *money, support, help*] 发誓 ♦ **to pledge that ...** 保证… ♦ **to pledge to do sth** 保证做某事 ♦ **to pledge sb to secrecy** 叫某人发誓保密 ♦ **to pledge o.s. to sth** 保证某事

plentiful ['plɛntɪful] *adj* [+ *food, supply, resources*] 大量的

plenty ['plɛntɪ] *pron* **1** (*lots*) 大量 **2** (*sufficient*) 充足 ♦ **plenty of** [+ *food, money, time*] 很多; [+ *jobs, people, houses*] 许多 ♦ **we've got plenty of time to get there** 我们有充足的时间去那里

pliers ['plaɪəz] *n* [*pl*] 钳子 ♦ **a pair of pliers** 一把钳子

plight [plaɪt] *n* [S] [*of person, country*] 困境

plod [plɔd] *vi* 沉重而缓慢地走 ♦ **to plod up/down the stairs** 拖着脚步走上/下楼梯

❑ **plod along, plod on** *vi* [*work, production* +] 缓慢进行

❑ **plod along with, plod on with** *vt* [不可拆分] 努力从事

plonk [plɔŋk] **I** *n* [U] [英:非正式] (*wine*) 劣质酒 **II** *vt* ♦ **to plonk sth down on sth** 把某物重重地放在某物上 ♦ **to plonk o.s. down (on sth)** 猛地坐下(坐在某处)

plot [plɔt] **I** *n* **1** [C] (*secret plan*) ♦ **a plot (to do sth)** (做某事的) 阴谋 **2** [C/U] [*of story, play, film*] 情节 **3** [C] (*also: **plot of land***) 小块地皮 **4** [C] (*for gardening*) 小块土地 **II** *vt* **1** [+ *sb's downfall, overthrow*] 密谋 **2** [+ *strategy*] 谋划 **3** [航空, 航海] [+ *position, course*] 标绘 **4** [数] [+ *point on graph*] 绘制 **III** *vi* (*conspire*) 密谋 ♦ **to plot to do sth** 密谋做某事

plough (美 **plow**) [plau] **I** *n* [C] 犁 **II** *vt* [+ *field, land*] 耕

❑ **plough back** *vt* ♦ **to plough sth back (into sth)** [+ *profits*] 把某事再投资(于某事)

❑ **plough into I** *vt* [不可拆分] [+ *crowd*] 猛力撞入 **II** *vt* (*invest*) ♦ **to plough money into sth** 把钱投资于某事

❑ **plough through** *vt* [不可拆分] [+ *meal, work, meeting*] 费力而缓慢地进行

ploughman's lunch ['plaumənz-] [英] *n* [C] 酒吧供应的农夫午餐，包括面包、奶酪、色拉和泡菜

plow [plau] [美] *n, vt* = **plough**

ploy [plɔɪ] *n* [C] ♦ **ploy (to do sth)** (做某事的) 花招

pls *abbr* (= ***please***) 请
pluck [plʌk] **I** *vt* **1** [+ *fruit, flower, leaf*] 采摘 **2** (*seize*) 扯 **3** [+ *guitar, strings*] 拨 **4** [+ *chicken, turkey, goose*] 拔…的毛 **5** [+ *eyebrows*] 拔 **II** *n* [U] (*courage*) 勇气 ♦ **to be plucked from danger** 脱离危险 ♦ **to be plucked to safety** 转危为安 ♦ **to pluck up (the) courage (to do sth)** 鼓起勇气(做某事)
❑ **pluck at** *vt* [不可拆分] 抓住
plug [plʌg] **I** *n* [C] **1** [电子] (*on appliance*) 插头; [非正式] (*socket*) 插座 **2** (*in sink, bath*) 塞子 **3** (*also: **spark(ing) plug***) 火花塞 **4** [+ *of flush toilet*] ♦ **to pull the plug** 冲厕所 **5** (*advertisement*) ♦ **to give sb/sth a plug** 大肆宣传某人/某物 **II** *vt* **1** [+ *hole, leak*] 塞住 **2** [非正式] (*advertise*) 推销 ♦ **to pull the plug (on sth)** [非正式] [+ *project, deal*] 停止(某事)
❑ **plug in** [电子] **I** *vt* 插上…的插头 **II** *vi* 插上插头
plughole ['plʌghəul] [英] *n* [C] 排水孔 ♦ **to go down the plughole** [非正式] 付诸东流
plum [plʌm] **I** *n* [C] (*fruit*) 梅子 **II** *adj* [非正式] ♦ **a plum job** 美差
plumber ['plʌmə(r)] *n* [C] 管子工
plumbing ['plʌmɪŋ] *n* [U] **1** (*piping*) 管道装置 **2** (*trade, work*) 管道装修
plummet ['plʌmɪt] *vi* **1** [*price, amount, rate* +] 暴跌 **2** [*aircraft, bird etc* +] 俯冲
plump [plʌmp] *adj* [+ *person, arm, chicken, fruit*] 丰满的
📖 用法参见 **fat**
❑ **plump for** [非正式] *vt* [不可拆分] 选定
❑ **plump up** *vt* [+ *cushion, pillow*] 使鼓起
plunder ['plʌndə(r)] **I** *vt* [正式] **1** (*steal from*) [+ *city, tomb*] 抢劫 **2** (*take*) 取得 **II** *n* [U] **1** (*activity*) 抢劫 **2** (*stolen things*) 赃物
plunge [plʌndʒ] **I** *n* [C] **1** (*fall*) [*of person*] 跳入 **2** [*in prices, rates*] 猛跌 **II** *vt* **1** ♦ **to plunge sth into sth** [+ *knife, hand etc*] 把某物猛插入另一物 **2** ♦ **to be plunged into darkness/chaos** 陷入黑暗/混乱 **III** *vi* **1** ♦ **to plunge into sth** (*fall*) 撞入某处; (*leap*) 跳入某处 **2** [*economy, interest rates* +] ♦ **to plunge (to sth)** 猛然跌入(某状态) **3** [*bird* +] 俯冲 ♦ **to take the plunge** (喻) 采取断然行动 ♦ **to plunge (o.s.)/be plunged into sth** (*become involved*) 全身心投入某事
plural ['pluərl] **I** *adj* 复数的 **II** *n* [C] 复数
plus [plʌs] **I** *conj* **1** (*added to*) 加 **2** (*as well as*) 和 **II** *adj* (*positive*) [+ *number*] 正的 **III** *adv* (*additionally*) 此外 **IV** *n* [C] [非正式] ♦ **it's a plus** 这是个附加的好处 ♦ **ten/twenty plus** 十几/二十多 ♦ **B plus** [教育] B加
ply [plaɪ] **I** *vt* **1** (*offer*) ♦ **to ply sb with food/drink** 反复给某人食物/饮料 **2** (*bombard*) ♦ **to ply sb with questions** 向某人问个不休 **3** [+ *tool*] 使用 **4** [*ship, aircraft, vehicle* +] [+ *route*] 定期来回 **II** *vi* ♦ **to ply between ... and ...** [*ship, aircraft, vehicle* +] 在…和…之间定期来回 **III** *n* [C] [*of wool, rope*] 股 ♦ **to ply one's trade** 从事自己的工作
plywood ['plaɪwud] *n* [U] 胶合板
PM [英: 非正式] *n abbr* (= ***Prime Minister***) ♦ **the PM** 总理
p.m. *adv abbr* (= ***post meridiem***) 下午
pneumatic drill [nju:'mætɪk-] *n* [C] 风钻
pneumonia [nju:'məunɪə] *n* [U] 肺炎
poach [pəutʃ] **I** *vt* **1** (*steal*) [+ *fish, animals, birds*] 偷猎 **2** [+ *person*] 挖人 **3** [+ *idea*] 窃取 **4** (*cook*) [+ *egg*] 水煮; [+ *fish, chicken, fruit*] 炖 **II** *vi* (*steal*) 偷猎
poached [pəutʃt] *adj* [+ *egg, salmon*] 煮的
PO Box *n abbr* (= ***Post Office Box***) 邮箱
pocket ['pɔkɪt] **I** *n* [C] **1** (*in jacket, trousers, shirt, skirt*) 口袋 **2** (*in suitcase, car door, handbag*) 袋子 **3** (喻) (*small area*) [*of air, resistance*] 小范围 **II** *cpd* [复合词] [+ *calculator, dictionary*] 袖珍的 **III** *vt* **1** (*take*) 把…据为己有 **2** (*steal*) [+ *money, document*] 据为己有 ♦ **to put money in sb's pocket** 把钱放入某人腰包 ♦ **to be out of pocket** [英] 赔钱

pocketbook [ˈpɔkɪtbuk] *n* [c] **1** [美] (*wallet*) 皮夹 **2** [美] (*handbag*) 手提包 **3** (*notebook*) 袖珍记事本

pocket money [尤英] *n* [u] 零花钱 [美 = **allowance**]

pod [pɔd] *n* [c] (*on plant*) 豆荚

podgy [ˈpɔdʒɪ] [非正式] *adj* [+ *person, cheeks, arms etc*] 矮胖的

podiatrist [pɔˈdiːətrɪst] [尤美] *n* [c] 足病医生

podium [ˈpəudɪəm] *n* [c] 指挥台

poem [ˈpəuɪm] *n* [c] 诗

poet [ˈpəuɪt] *n* [c] 诗人

poetic [pəuˈɛtɪk] *adj* **1** [+ *drama, language, description*] 有诗意的 **2** [+ *tradition*] 诗的

poetry [ˈpəuɪtrɪ] *n* [u] **1** (*poems*) 诗 **2** (*form of literature*) 诗歌

poignant [ˈpɔɪnjənt] *adj* 心酸的

✪ **point** [pɔɪnt] **I** *n* **1** [c] (*in report, lecture, interview*) 论点 ◊ *The research made some valid points.* 研究得出了一些有效的论点。**2** [s] (*significant part*) [*of argument, discussion*] 要害 ◊ *He came straight to the point.* 他切中要害。**3** [s] (*purpose*) [*of action*] 目的 ◊ *What was the point in getting married?* 结婚目的何在？ **4** [c] (*aspect*) [*of report, project, situation*] 点 ◊ *The most interesting point about the village was its religion.* 关于这个村庄最有趣的一点是它的宗教。**5** [c] (*place*) 位置 ◊ *We were nearing the point where the lane curved round to the right.* 我们在道路向右转弯这个位置附近。**6** [s] (*moment*) 时刻 ◊ *At this point the girl slowly sat up on the sofa.* 就在这时女孩在沙发上慢慢坐起。**7** [c] (*sharp end*) [*of needle, knife, instrument*] 尖端 **8** [c] (*in score, competition, game, sport*) 分 ◊ *New Zealand have beaten Scotland by 21 points to 18.* 新西兰以21 分比18 分赢了苏格兰。**9** [c] (*also:* ***power point***) 插座 **10** [c] (*also:* ***decimal point***) 小数点 ◊ *seven point eight per cent* 百分之七点八 **II** *vi* (*with finger, stick*) 指出 **III** *vt* ♦ **to point sth at sb** [+ *gun, finger, stick*] 把某物瞄准某人 **IV points** *n* [*pl*] **1** [汽车] 接触点 **2** [英: 铁路] 道岔 ♦ **there's no point (in doing that)** (那样做) 毫无意义 ♦ **good/bad points** [*of person*] 优/缺点 ♦ **a strong point** 长处 ♦ **the train stops at Carlisle and all points south** 火车停靠卡莱尔及其以南的所有站点 ♦ **at that point** 那时 ♦ **up to a point** 在某种程度上 ♦ **two point five** (*2.5*) 二点五 ♦ **to be on the point of doing sth** 正要做某事时 ♦ **to make a point of doing sth** 特意做某事 ♦ **to get/miss the point** 理解/不理解要点 ♦ **to come/get to the point** 切中要点 ♦ **to make one's point** 使他人领会自己的意思 ♦ **to prove one's point** 证明某人的观点 ♦ **that's the whole point!** 正是这个意思！ ♦ **to be beside the point** 不切题的 ♦ **you've got a point there!** 你言之有理！ ♦ **I take/see your point** 我接受/理解你的看法 ♦ **in point of fact** 事实上 ♦ **the points of the compass** 罗盘上的罗经点 ♦ **to point at sth/sb** (*with finger, stick*) 指着某物/某人 ♦ **to point to sth/sb** (*with finger/stick*) 指向某物/某人 ◊ *Mr Jones pointed to a chair and asked her to sit down.* 琼斯先生指指椅子请她坐下。 ♦ **to point to** *or* **towards sth** [*sign, needle, arrow* +] 指向某物 ♦ **to point to sth** [*fact* +] 暗示某事; [*speaker* +] 指出 ◊ *They pointed proudly to the administration's success in recent years.* 他们自豪地指出近年来在管理上的成功。 ♦ **to point forwards/north** 指向前/北 ♦ **to point the way forward** 标引前方道路

❑ **point out** *vt* [+ *person, place, mistake, fact*] 指出 ♦ **to point out that ...** 指出…

❑ **point to** *vt* [不可拆分] 暗示

point-blank [ˈpɔɪntˈblæŋk] **I** *adv* **1** [*refuse, say, ask* +] 直截了当地 **2** (*also:* ***at point-blank range***) 短射程 **II** *adj* [+ *refusal*] 直截了当的

pointed [ˈpɔɪntɪd] *adj* **1** [+ *stick, nose, roof, shoes*] 尖的 **2** (喻) [+ *remark, question*] 一针见血的

pointedly [ˈpɔɪntɪdlɪ] *adv* [*ask, reply* +] 直截了当地

pointer [ˈpɔɪntə(r)] *n* [c] **1** (*tip*) 点子 **2** (*indication*) 暗示 **3** (*needle*) (*on* *machine*) 指针 **4** (*stick*) 教鞭 **5** (*dog*) 指示犬

pointless [ˈpɔɪntlɪs] *adj* 无意义的 ♦ **it is pointless to complain** 抱怨无用

point of view *n* [c] 观点 ♦ **from the point of view of ...** 从…的观点来看 ♦ **from a practical point of view** 从现实的角度看

poison [ˈpɔɪzn] **I** *n* [c/u] 毒药 **II** *vt* **1** [+ *person, animal*] 下毒 **2** [+ *relationship, atmosphere*] 毒害

poisoning [ˈpɔɪznɪŋ] *n* [u] 下毒 ♦ **lead/alcohol poisoning** 铅/酒精中毒

poisonous [ˈpɔɪznəs] *adj* **1** (字) [+ *animal, plant, fumes, chemicals*] 有毒的 **2** (喻) [+ *rumours, comments*] 恶毒的

poke [pəuk] **I** *vt* **1** (*jab*) (*with finger, stick*) 戳 **2** (*put*) ♦ **to poke sth in (to) sth** 把某物戳到另一物中 **II** *n* ♦ **to give sb/sth a poke** 捅捅某人/某物 ♦ **to poke the fire** 拨火 ♦ **to poke one's head out of the window/around the door** *etc* 把头探出窗户/门{等} ♦ **to poke fun at sb/sth** 嘲笑某人/某物

❑ **poke about, poke around** [非正式] *vi* (*search*) ♦ **to poke about (for sth)** 摸索着找(某物)

❑ **poke at** *vt* [不可拆分] (*prod*) 拨弄

❑ **poke out** *vi* (*stick out*) 露出

poker [ˈpəukə(r)] *n* **1** [u] [纸牌] 扑克牌戏 **2** [c] (*for fire*) 拨火棒

Poland [ˈpəulənd] *n* 波兰

polar [ˈpəulə(r)] *adj* [+ *ice-cap, region*] 地极的

polar bear *n* [c] 北极熊

Pole [pəul] *n* [c] 波兰人

pole [pəul] *n* [c] **1** (*stick*) 杆 **2** [地理] 地极 **3** [电子] 电极 ♦ **to be poles apart** 截然相反 ♦ **to be in pole position** (*in motor racing*) 在跑道内圈

pole bean [美] *n* [c] (*runner bean*) 蔓生菜豆

pole vault *n* [s] ♦ **the pole vault** 撑杆跳高

✪ **police** [pəˈliːs] **I** *n* [*pl*] **1** (*organization*) 警方 **2** (*members*) 警察 **II** *vt* [+ *street, area, event*] 维持治安

police car *n* [c] 警车

police force *n* [c] 警力

policeman [pəˈliːsmən] (*pl* **policemen**) *n* [c] 男警察

police officer *n* [c] 警察

police station *n* [c] 警察局

policewoman [pəˈliːswumən] (*pl* **policewomen**) *n* [c] 女警察

✪ **policy** [ˈpɔlɪsɪ] *n* **1** [c/u] [*of government, council*] 政策 ◊ *What is their policy on nuclear testing?* 他们对核试验的政策是什么?; [*of company, newspaper*] 方针 **2** [c] (*also: **insurance policy***) 保单 ♦ **to take out a policy** [保险] 买保险

polio [ˈpəulɪəu] *n* [u] 小儿麻痹症

Polish [ˈpəulɪʃ] **I** *adj* 波兰的 **II** *n* [u] (*language*) 波兰语

polish [ˈpɔlɪʃ] **I** *n* **1** [c/u] (*for shoes, furniture, floor*) 上光剂 **2** [u] (*shine*) (*on shoes, furniture, floor*) 光泽 **3** [u] (喻) (*refinement*) 优雅 **II** *vt* [+ *shoes*] 擦亮; [+ *furniture, floor*] 上光

❑ **polish off** [非正式] *vt* [+ *food, drink*] 吃/喝掉

polished [ˈpɔlɪʃt] *adj* **1** [+ *furniture, floor*] 擦亮的 **2** (喻) [+ *person*] 优雅的; [+ *performance, style*] 优美的

polite [pəˈlaɪt] *adj* **1** (*well-mannered*) [+ *person, behaviour*] 有礼貌的 **2** (*refined*) [+ *company, society*] 上流的 ♦ **to make polite conversation** 谈吐斯文 ♦ **it isn't polite to do that** 那样做是不礼貌的

politeness [pəˈlaɪtnɪs] *n* [u] 礼貌 ♦ **to do sth out of politeness** 出于礼貌做某事

✪ **political** [pəˈlɪtɪkl] *adj* **1** [+ *system, party, issue, agenda, crisis etc*] 政治的 **2** [+ *person*] 从事政治的

politically [pəˈlɪtɪklɪ] *adv* [+ *motivated, sensitive*] 政治上 ♦ **politically correct** [+ *person, word*] 得体的 ♦ **politically incorrect** 不得体的

politician [pɔlɪˈtɪʃən] *n* [c] 政治家

politics [ˈpɔlɪtɪks] **I** *n* [u] **1** (*activity*) 政治 **2** (*subject*) 政治学 **II** *n* [*pl*] (*beliefs, opinions*) 政见 ♦ **office politics** 人际关系

poll [pəul] **I** *n* [c] (*also: **opinion poll***) 民意调查 **II** *vt* **1** [+ *people*] (*in opinion poll*) 向…提问 **2** (*number of* *votes*) 获得选票 **III polls** *n* [C] *pl* (*election*) 选举投票 ♦**to go to the polls** [*voters* +] 去投票; [*government* +] 进行选举 ♦**the polls have closed** 投票结束了

pollen [ˈpɔlən] *n* [U] 花粉

polling station [ˈpəulɪŋ-] [英] *n* [C] 投票站

pollute [pəˈluːt] *vt* [+ *air, water, land*] 污染

polluted [pəˈluːtɪd] *adj* [+ *river, beach, water*] 被污染的

pollution [pəˈluːʃən] *n* [U] **1** (*process*) 污染 **2** (*substances*) 污染物

polo [ˈpəuləu] *n* [U] [体育] 马球

polo neck [英] *n* [C] 圆高领

polo shirt *n* [C] 短袖有领的运动T恤衫

polyester [pɔlɪˈɛstə(r)] *n* [U] 聚酯

polystyrene [pɔlɪˈstaɪriːn] **I** *n* [U] 聚苯乙烯 **II** *cpd* [复合词] [+ *cup, tile*] 聚苯乙烯

polytechnic [pɔlɪˈtɛknɪk] [英:历史] *n* [C] 专科学校

polythene [ˈpɔlɪθiːn] *n* [U] 聚乙烯

polythene bag *n* [C] 聚乙烯塑料袋

pomegranate [ˈpɔmɪgrænɪt] *n* [C] 石榴

pompous [ˈpɔmpəs] [贬] *adj* [+ *person*] 自大的; [+ *speech, comment, article, gesture*] 浮夸的

pond [pɔnd] *n* [C] 池塘

ponder [ˈpɔndə(r)] **I** *vt* (*think about*) 深思 **II** *vi* 沉思

pony [ˈpəunɪ] *n* [C] 小马

ponytail [ˈpəunɪteɪl] *n* [C] 马尾辫 ♦**to have one's hair in a ponytail** 梳成马尾辫

pony trekking [-trɛkɪŋ] [英] *n* [U] 骑小型马出游 ♦**to go pony trekking** 骑小型马出游

poodle [ˈpuːdl] *n* [C] 卷毛狮子狗

pool [puːl] **I** *n* **1** [C] (*pond*) 水塘 **2** [C] (*also: **swimming pool***) 游泳池 **3** (喻) ♦**pool of light/blood** 一滩亮光/血 **4** [C] (*amount, number*) [*of cash*] 公库; [*of secretaries, workers, vehicles*] 储备 **5** [C] [纸牌] (*kitty*) 全部赌注 **6** [U] (*game*) 普儿弹子戏 **II** *vt* [+ *money, knowledge, resources, ideas*] 集中 **III pools** *n* [*pl*] [英] (*also: **football pools***) 足球彩票 ♦**car pool** 合伙用车 ♦**typing pool,** (美) **secretary pool** 秘书组 ♦**to do the (football) pools** 赌足球彩票

poor [puə(r)] **I** *adj* **1** (*not rich*) [+ *person*] 贫穷的; [+ *country, area*] 贫困的 **2** (*bad*) [+ *quality, performance*] 低水平的; [+ *eyesight, memory, health*] 不好的; [+ *swimmer, reader*] 糟糕的; [+ *wages, conditions, results, attendance*] 差的 **II** *n* [*pl*] ♦**the poor** 穷人 ♦**to be poor in sth** [+ *resources, vitamins*] 缺乏某物 ♦**to be poor at doing sth** 不善于做某事 ♦**poor (old) Bill** 可怜的(老)比尔

poorly [ˈpuəlɪ] **I** *adj* [非正式] (*ill*) 身体不适的 **II** *adv* [+ *designed, paid, furnished, educated etc*] 不足地; [*play, sell, perform* +] 糟糕地

pop [pɔp] **I** *n* **1** [U] [音] 流行音乐 **2** [U] [英:非正式] (*fizzy drinks*) 汽水 [美= **soda pop**] **3** [C] [美:非正式] (*father*) 爸爸 **4** [C] (*sound*) 爆破声 **II** *vi* **1** [*balloon, cork* +] 爆开 **2** [非正式] [*eyes* +] 张大 **III** *vt* [非正式] ♦**to pop sth into/onto sth** 快速地将某物放进某物里/放在某处 ♦**to go pop** [非正式] 发出爆裂声 ♦**she popped her head out of the window** 她猛地从窗户里探出头
❑**pop in** [非正式] *vi* 来/去一会儿
❑**pop out** [非正式] *vi* 出去一会儿
❑**pop up** [非正式] *vi* 突然出现

popcorn [ˈpɔpkɔːn] *n* [U] 爆玉米花

pope [pəup] *n* [C] 教皇

poplar [ˈpɔplə(r)] *n* [C] 杨树

popper [ˈpɔpə(r)] *n* [C] **1** [英:非正式] (*for fastening*) 摁扣儿 **2** [尤美] (*for popcorn*) 爆玉米花的器皿

poppy [ˈpɔpɪ] *n* [C] 罂粟

Popsicle® [ˈpɔpsɪkl] [美] *n* [C] 冰棒 [英= **ice lolly**]

pop star *n* [C] 明星

popular [ˈpɔpjulə(r)] *adj* **1** (*well-liked*) [+ *person, place, thing*] 流行的 **2** (*general*) [+ *idea, belief, appeal*] 普遍的 **3** (*fashionable*) [+ *name, activity*] 时髦的 **4** (*not elitist*) [+ *books, newspapers, TV programmes*] 通俗的 **5** [政治] [+ *movement, activity*] 民众的 ♦**to be popular with sb** [*food, activity etc* +] 某人所喜欢的; [*person* +] 受某人欢迎的

popularity [pɔpju'lærɪtɪ] *n* [U] [*of person*] 名望 [*of thing, activity*] 普及
popularly ['pɔpjuləlɪ] *adv* [+ *called, known as*] 一般地; [+ *believed, supposed*] 普遍地
population [pɔpju'leɪʃən] *n* [C] 1 (*inhabitants*) 人口 2 ♦**the male/civilian/elephant population** 男性/平民/大象的数量 ♦**a prison population of 44,000** 44, 000 名囚犯
porcelain ['pɔːslɪn] *n* [U] 瓷
porch [pɔːtʃ] *n* [C] 1 (*entrance*) [*of house*] 门廊; [*of church*] 柱廊 2 [美] (*veranda*) 走廊
pore [pɔː(r)] I *n* [C] 1 [解剖] 毛孔 2 [植] 气孔 II *vi* ♦**to pore over** *or* **through sth** [+ *book, article*] 钻研某物
pork [pɔːk] *n* [U] 猪肉
pork chop *n* [C] 猪排
porn [pɔːn] [非正式] *n* [U] 色情作品
pornographic [pɔːnə'græfɪk] *adj* [+ *film, book, magazine*] 色情的
pornography [pɔː'nɔgrəfɪ] *n* [U] 色情作品
porridge ['pɔrɪdʒ] *n* [U] 麦片粥
port [pɔːt] I *n* 1 [C] (*harbour*) 港口 2 [C] (*town*) 港市 3 [U] [航海] (*left side*) 左舷 4 [U] (*wine*) 波尔图葡萄酒 5 [C] [计算机] 端口 II *adj* [航海] [+ *side*] 左舷的 ♦**port of call** [航海] 停靠港 ♦**to port** [航海] 向左舷
portable ['pɔːtəbl] *adj* [+ *television, computer etc*] 便携式的
porter ['pɔːtə(r)] *n* [C] 1 (*for luggage*) 搬运工 2 [英] (*doorkeeper*) 门房 [美 = **doorman**] 3 [英] (*in hospital*) 勤杂工 [美 = **orderly**] 4 [美] (*on train*) 列车员 [美 = **attendant**]
portfolio [pɔːt'fəulɪəu] *n* [C] 1 (*case*) 公事包 2 (*work*) [*of artist, student*] 文件夹 3 [政治] 部长职责 4 [经济] 投资组合
portion ['pɔːʃən] *n* [C] 1 (*part*) 部分 2 (*helping of food*) 份
portrait ['pɔːtreɪt] *n* [C] (*picture*) 画像
portray [pɔː'treɪ] *vt* 1 (*depict*) 描绘 2 (*play*) [*actor* +] 扮演
portrayal [pɔː'treɪəl] *n* [C] 1 (*depiction*) 描述 2 (*actor's*) 表演
Portugal ['pɔːtjugl] *n* 葡萄牙
Portuguese [pɔːtju'giːz] (*pl* **Portuguese**) I *adj* 葡萄牙的 II *n* 1 [C] (*person*) 葡萄牙人 2 [U] (*language*) 葡萄牙语
pose [pəuz] I *n* [C] 姿势 II *vt* 1 [+ *question*] (*ask*) 问; (*raise*) 提出 2 [+ *problem, danger*] 引发 III *vi* ♦**to pose as sb** 摆出某人的样子 ♦**to pose for sth** [+ *painting, photograph*] 为某事摆姿势 ♦**to strike a pose** 装样子
posh [pɔʃ] [非正式] *adj* 1 (*smart*) [+ *hotel, restaurant, car*] 豪华的 2 (*upper-class*) [+ *person, voice*] 上流的 ♦**to talk posh** 装腔作势地说话
✪**position** [pə'zɪʃən] I *n* [C] 1 (*place*) [*of house, person, thing*] 位置 ◊ *The house is in a very exposed position.* 房子处在一个显眼的位置。; [*of sun, stars*] 方位 2 (*posture*) [*of person's body*] 姿势 ◊ *She remained in that position.* 她保持那种姿势。3 [正式] (*job*) 职位 4 (*role*) [*in society*] 地位 5 (*in race, competition*) 名 6 (*attitude*) 观点 7 (*situation*) 处境 II *vt* [+ *person, thing*] 放置 ♦**to be in position** 在适当的位置 ♦**to be in a position to do sth** 能做某事

> 请勿将 **position**， **post** 和 **title** 混淆。某人拥有的固定工作，在正式的英语被称为 **position** 或 **post**。在招聘广告中，工作职位通常被称为 **position** 或 **post**，人们申请工作时，通常可以使用这两者中的任何一个。*He left a career in teaching to take up a position with a charity... She is well qualified for the post.* 在会话中，用 **job** 一词。*He's afraid of losing his job.* 某人的 **title** 是指他在某组织机构中的地位或职位。*"Can you tell me your official job title?" – "It's Sales Manager."*

positive ['pɔzɪtɪv] *adj* 1 (*hopeful, confident*) [+ *person, attitude*] 积极的 2 (*good*) [+ *situation, experience*] 有益的 3 (*decisive*) [+ *decision, action, step*] 明确的 4 [+ *response*] 正面的 5 (*affirmative*) [+ *test, result*] 阳性的 6 (*clear*) [+ *proof, evidence*] 确定的 7 (*sure*) ♦**to be positive (about**

sth) 确信(某事) **8** [数] 正的 **9** [电子] 正极的 ♦**positive thinking** 乐观的想法 ♦**to be positive that ...** (*sure*) 确信…

positively ['pɔzɪtɪvlɪ] *adv* **1** (*really*) 确实地 **2** (*encouragingly*) 积极地

possess [pə'zɛs] *vt* **1** (*own*) [+ *car, watch, radio*] 拥有 **2** (*have*) [+ *quality, ability*] 具有 **3** [文] (*take hold of*) 支配 ♦**like a man possessed** 像着了魔似的男人 ♦**whatever possessed you (to do it)?** 什么想法促使你(去干这事)?

possession [pə'zɛʃən] **I** *n* [U] (*act, state*) 拥有 **II possessions** *n* [*pl*] 财产 ♦**to be in possession of sth** [正式] [+ *facts, information, documents*] 掌握某事 ♦**to take possession of sth** [军] 占领某处; [*new owner* +] 获得某物 ♦**to be in the possession of sb** 被某人所拥有

possessive [pə'zɛsɪv] **I** *adj* 占有欲强的 **II** *n* [C] [语言] 所有格 ♦**to be possessive about sb** 对某人有强烈的占有欲 ♦**to be possessive about sth** 独占某物

possibility [pɔsɪ'bɪlɪtɪ] *n* [C] **1** (*chance*) (*that sth is true*) 可能性; (*of sth happening*) 可能的事 **2** (*option*) 可选性

✪**possible** ['pɔsɪbl] *adj* (*conceivable*) [+ *event, reaction, effect, consequence*] 可能的; [+ *risk, danger*] 潜在的; [+ *answer, cause, solution*] 可接受的 ♦**it's possible (that ...)** 可能(…) ♦**if it's possible to do that** 如有可能做的话 ♦**if possible** 如有可能 ♦**as far as possible** 尽可能地 ♦**to do everything possible** 竭尽所能 ♦**as soon as possible** 尽快 ♦**as much as possible** 尽可能多地 ♦**the best possible/the worst possible time/option** *etc* 再好/再糟不过的时候/选择{等}

possibly ['pɔsɪblɪ] *adv* **1** (*perhaps*) 大概 **2** (*conceivably*) (*expressing surprise*) 到底 ♦**to do everything one possibly can** 尽最大的能力 ♦**if you possibly can** 你尽可能 ♦**I can't possibly do that** 我无论如何也不会做那事的

post [pəust] **I** *n* **1** [英] ♦**the post** (*service, system*) 邮政; [*letters, delivery*] 邮件 [美 = **mail**] **2** [C] (*pole*) 柱子 **3** [C] (*job*) 职位 **4** [C] [军] 岗哨 **5** [C] (*also: **trading post***) 贸易站 **6** [C] (*also: **goalpost***) 球门柱 **II** *vt* **1** [英] [+ *letter*] 邮寄 [美 = **mail**] **2** [军] 让…站岗 ♦**in the post** 邮递中 ♦**by post** [英] 以邮件的方式 ♦**by return of post** [英] 由下一班回程邮递立即回信 ♦**to post sb to Paris/Spain** *etc* (*assign*) 派某人到巴黎/西班牙{等} ♦**to keep sb posted (on sth)** 使某人知情(某事)

❑**post up** *vt* 张贴

📖 用法参见 **position**

postage ['pəustɪdʒ] *n* [U] (*charge*) 邮资 ♦**postage and packing** 邮费及包装费

postal ['pəustl] *adj* [+ *charges, service, strike, worker*] 邮政的

postal order [英] *n* [C] 邮政汇票

postbox ['pəustbɔks] [英] *n* [C] (*in street*) 邮筒

postcard ['pəustkɑːd] *n* [C] 明信片

postcode ['pəustkəud] [英] *n* [C] 邮政编码 [美 = **zip code**]

poster ['pəustə(r)] *n* [C] 海报

postgraduate ['pəust'grædjuət] [英] *n* [C] 研究生

postman ['pəustmən] (*pl* **postmen**) [英] *n* [C] 邮递员 [美 = **mailman**]

postmark ['pəustmɑːk] *n* [C] 邮戳

post-mortem [pəust'mɔːtəm] *n* [C] **1** (*autopsy*) 验尸 **2** (喻) 事后剖析

post office *n* **1** [C] (*building*) 邮局 **2** ♦**the Post Office** (*organization*) 邮局

postpone [pəus'pəun] *vt* 推迟

posture ['pɔstʃə(r)] **I** *n* **1** [C/U] (*physical*) 姿势 **2** [C] [正式] (喻) (*attitude*) 态度 **II** *vi* 摆姿势

postwoman ['pəustwumən] (*pl* **postwomen**) [英] *n* [C] 女邮递员 [美 = **mailwoman**]

pot [pɔt] **I** *n* **1** [C] (*for cooking*) 锅 **2** [C] (*also: **teapot***) 茶壶 **3** [C] (*also: **pot of tea***) 一壶茶 **4** [C] (*also: **coffeepot***) 咖啡壶 **5** [C] (*also: **pot of coffee***) 一壶咖啡 **6** [C] (*for paint, jam, marmalade, honey*) 罐 **7** [C] (*also: **chamber pot***) 尿壶 **8** [C] (*also: **flowerpot***) 花盆 **9** [U] [非正式] (*marijuana*) 大麻 **II** *vt* [+ *plant*] 把…栽在盆里 ♦**pots of money** [英: 非正式] 大笔钱 ♦**to go**

to pot [非正式] [*work, performance* +] 垮掉

potato [pəˈteɪtəu] (*pl* **potatoes**) *n* [c/u] 马铃薯

potato chips [美] *n* [*pl*] 马铃薯片 [英= **crisps**]

potato peeler [-ˈpiːlə(r)] *n* [c] 马铃薯削皮器

potent [ˈpəutnt] *adj* **1** (*powerful*) [+ *argument, symbol, mix*] 有说服力的; [+ *drug*] 有效力的; [+ *drink*] 烈性的 **2** [+ *man*] 有性交能力的 ♦ **a potent weapon** 强有力的武器

potential [pəˈtɛnʃl] **I** *adj* [+ *sales, advantage, problem*] 潜在的 **II** *n* [u] **1** (*aptitude*) ♦ **potential (for sth)** (对某事的)可能性 **2** (*capability*) [*of person*] 潜质 **3** (*possibilities*) [*of thing*] 潜力 ♦ **to have potential** 有潜力 ♦ **to achieve one's potential** 发挥潜力

potentially [pəˈtɛnʃəlɪ] *adv* 可能地

pothole [ˈpɔthəul] *n* [c] **1** (*in road*) 坑洼 **2** (*cave*) 壶穴

pot plant [英] *n* [c] 盆栽植物

potter [ˈpɔtə(r)] **I** *n* [c] 陶工 **II** *vi* ♦ **to potter around, potter about** [英] 磨磨蹭蹭地做琐事 ♦ **to potter around the house** [英] 在房里闲逛

pottery [ˈpɔtərɪ] *n* **1** [u] (*pots, dishes*) 陶器 **2** [u] (*work, hobby*) 陶艺 **3** [c] (*factory, workshop*) 制陶厂 ♦ **a piece of pottery** 一件陶器

potty [ˈpɔtɪ] [非正式] **I** *adj* (*mad*) 傻的 **II** *n* [c] (*for child*) 尿壶 ♦ **to go potty** [非正式] 发疯

pouch [pautʃ] *n* [c] **1** (*for tobacco, coins*) 小袋 **2** [动] 育儿袋

poultry [ˈpəultrɪ] *n* [u] **1** (*birds*) 家禽 **2** (*meat*) 家禽肉

pounce [pauns] *vi* **1** 猛扑 **2** ♦ **to pounce on sb/sth** [*animal, person* +] 猛扑向某人/某物 **3** ♦ **to pounce on** (*criticize*) [+ *mistake, suggestion, comment*] 抨击

✪ **pound** [paund] **I** *n* [c] **1** (*unit of money*) 镑 **2** (*unit of weight*) 磅 **3** (*for dogs, cats*) 认领所; (*for cars*) 认领场 **II** *vt* **1** (*beat*) [+ *table, wall, door etc*] 猛击 **2** (*crush*) [+ *spice, grain etc*] 捣 **III** *vi* **1** [*heart* +] 剧烈跳动 **2** [*head* +] 剧痛 ♦ **a pound coin** 1 镑硬币 ♦ **a five-pound note** 5 镑纸币 ♦ **half a pound (of sth)** 半磅(某物)

pound sterling *n* [c] 英镑

pour [pɔː(r)] **I** *vt* ♦ **to pour sth (into/onto sth)** [+ *liquid*] 灌某物(到某物里/上); [+ *powder*] 倒某物(到某物里/上) **II** *vi* **1** ♦ **to pour (from sth)** [*water, blood, smoke* +] (从某物)涌出 **2** ♦ **to pour into/out of sth** [*people* +] 涌进/出某地 ♦ **to pour sb/o.s. a drink** 给某人/自己倒了一杯喝的 ♦ **tears/sweat poured down his face** 眼泪/汗水顺着他的面颊流了下来 ♦ **it is pouring (with rain), it is pouring down** 大雨如注
❑ **pour away** *vt* [+ *liquid*] 倒掉
❑ **pour in** **I** *vi* [*news, letters* +] 滚滚而来 **II** *vt* [+ *water, milk, eggs*] 倒入
❑ **pour out** *vt* **1** [+ *tea, wine etc*] 倒出 **2** (喻) [+ *thoughts, feelings, worries*] 倾诉

pouring [ˈpɔːrɪŋ] *adj* ♦ **pouring rain** 倾盆大雨

pout [paut] *vi* 撅嘴

poverty [ˈpɔvətɪ] *n* [u] 贫穷 ♦ **to live in poverty** 生活贫困

POW *n abbr* (= ***prisoner of war***) 战俘

powder [ˈpaudə(r)] **I** *n* **1** [c/u] 粉 **2** [u] (*also:* ***face powder***) 扑面粉 **II** *vt* ♦ **to powder one's face** 在脸上擦粉 ♦ **to powder one's nose** 上厕所

powdered milk [ˈpaudəd-] *n* [u] 奶粉

✪ **power** [ˈpauə(r)] **I** *n* [u] **1** (*control*) (*over people, activities*) 权力 **2** (*ability*) 能力 **3** (*legal right*) 权限 **4** [*of ideas, words*] 影响力 **5** (*force, energy*) [*of explosion, engine*] 效力; [*of person, muscle*] 力量 **6** (*electricity*) 电力 **II** *vt* [+ *machine*] 为…提供动力 ♦ **to do everything in one's power to help** 竭尽全力帮助 ♦ **a world power** 世界大国 ♦ **the powers that be** 当权者 ♦ **to be in power** [政治] 掌权 ♦ **to take power** 夺取政权 ♦ **to come to power** 开始执政 ♦ **2 to the power of 3** [数] 2 的 3 次幂 ♦ **a power breakfast/lunch** 早/午餐高层汇报会

power cut [英] *n* [c] 停电 [美= **outage**]

powered ['pauəd] *adj* ♦**powered by sth** 由某物提供动力的 ♦**nuclear-powered submarine** 核动力潜艇

power failure *n* [c] 断电

powerful ['pauəful] *adj* **1** (*influential*) [+ *person, organization*] 有影响力的 **2** (*physically strong*) [+ *person, body, animal*] 强健的 **3** (*forceful*) [+ *blow, kick*] 有力的 **4** [+ *engine, machine*] 大功率的; [+ *substance, cleaner, drug*] 强效的 **5** [+ *smell*] 浓的 **6** [+ *voice*] 巨大的 **7** [+ *argument, evidence*] 令人信服的; [+ *writing, speech, work of art, performance*] 有感染力的 **8** [+ *emotion*] 强烈的

powerless ['pauəlɪs] *adj* 无力的 ♦**to be powerless to do sth** 对做某事无能为力

power point [英] *n* [c] 电源插座 [美= **outlet**]

power station *n* [c] 发电厂

pp *abbr* (= ***per procurationem***) 以…的名义

pp. *abbr* (= ***pages***) 页

PR *n abbr* **1** (= ***public relations***) 公共关系 **2** (= ***proportional representation***) 比例代表制

practical ['præktɪkl] **I** *adj* **1** (*not theoretical*) [+ *difficulties, experience*] 实践的 **2** [+ *ideas, methods, advice, suggestions*] 切合实际的 **3** (*sensible*) (*person, mind*) 有实际经验的 **4** (*good with hands*) 动手能力强的 **5** (*functional*) [+ *clothes, things*] 实用的 **II** *n* [c] **1** (*examination*) 实践考试 **2** (*lesson*) 实习课

practical joke *n* [c] 恶作剧

practically ['præktɪklɪ] *adv* **1** (*almost*) 几乎 **2** (*not theoretically*) 实际上

practice ['præktɪs] **I** *n* **1** [c] (*custom*) 习俗 **2** [c/u] (*way of operating*) 惯例 **3** [u] (*not theory*) 实践 **4** [u] (*exercise, training*) 练习 **5** [c] (*training session*) 实习 **6** [u] [*of religion*] 信奉活动 **7** [医, 法] (*business*) [c] 从业; (*work*) [u] 工作 **II** *vt, vi* [美] **(= practise)** ♦**it's normal** *or* **standard practice** 这是通常{或}标准做法 ♦**in practice** (*in reality*) 实际上 ♦**to put sth into practice** 应用某事 ♦**to be out of practice** 荒疏 ♦**2 hours' piano practice** 2小时的练琴时间

practise (美 **practice**) ['præktɪs] **I** *vt* **1** (*work on*) [+ *sport, technique, musical instrument, piece of music*] 练习 **2** (*carry out*) [+ *custom, activity, craft, religion*] 实行 ◊ *Acupuncture was first practised in China in the third millennium BC.* 公元前3000年中国人首次使用针灸。**3** [+ *medicine, law*] 从业 **II** *vi* **1** (*train*) (*in music, theatre, sport*) 练习 **2** [*lawyer, doctor, dentist* +] 从业 ♦**to practise as a lawyer** 开业做律师

practising ['præktɪsɪŋ] *adj* [+ *Christian, Jew, Muslim*] 笃信的; [+ *doctor, dentist, lawyer*] 从业的; [+ *homosexual*] 有实际性行为的

practitioner [præk'tɪʃənə(r)] [正式] *n* [c] (*also:* ***general practitioner***) 开业者 ♦**alternative practitioner** 使用非传统治疗方式的从业者 ♦**legal practitioner** 从业律师

pragmatic [præg'mætɪk] *adj* [+ *person, approach etc*] 务实的

prairie ['prɛərɪ] *n* [c] 大草原 ♦**the prairies** 北美洲大草原

praise [preɪz] **I** *n* [u] **1** 赞扬 **2** (*to God*) 赞美 **II** *vt* **1** 称赞 **2** [宗] [+ *God*] 颂扬 ♦**to sing sb's praises** 称颂某人 ♦**to praise sb for sth/for doing sth** 因某事赞扬某人/赞扬某人做某事

pram [præm] [英] *n* [c] 婴儿车 [美= **baby carriage**]

prank [præŋk] [过时] *n* [c] 恶作剧

prawn [prɔːn] [英] *n* [c] 虾 [美= **shrimp**]

prawn cocktail [英] *n* [c/u] 冷盘虾 [美= **shrimp cocktail**]

pray [preɪ] *vi* 祷告 ♦**to pray for/that** [宗] 为…祈祷/祈祷… ♦**I pray that she'll never find out** [非正式] (喻) 我祈祷她永远不会发现

prayer [prɛə(r)] [宗] **I** *n* **1** [u] (*activity*) 祷告 **2** [c] (*words*) 祈祷文 **II prayers** *n* [*pl*] (*service*) 祈祷式 ♦**to say one's prayers** 祈祷

preach [priːtʃ] **I** *vi* **1** [*priest, vicar* +] 布道 **2** (*moralize*) 说教 **II** *vt* **1** [+ *sermon*] 讲道 **2** (*advocate*) 宣扬 ♦**to preach at sb** (喻) 对某人说教 ♦**to be preaching to the converted** (喻) 对人们宣传他们

早已持有的观点 ♦ **to preach the Gospel** 传播福音

preacher ['priːtʃə(r)] *n* [c] 传教士

precarious [prɪ'kɛərɪəs] *adj* 1 (*dangerous*) 危险的 2 (喻) [+ *position, situation, job*] 不确定的

precaution [prɪ'kɔːʃən] *n* [c] 预防措施 ♦ **as a precaution** 以防万一 ♦ **to take precautions** 采取防范措施

precede [prɪ'siːd] *vt* 1 (*in time*) [+ *event*] 早于 2 (*in space*) [+ *person*] 先于 3 [*words, sentences, section* +] 在…之前

precedent ['prɛsɪdənt] [正式] *n* [c/u] 1 先例 2 [法] 判例 ♦ **to establish** *or* **set a precedent** 开创先例; [法] 援为判例

preceding [prɪ'siːdɪŋ] *adj* [+ *chapter, programme, day etc*] 在前的

precinct ['priːsɪŋkt] **I** *n* [c] 1 [英] (*also:* ***shopping precinct***) 购物区 2 [美] (*part of city*) 管辖区 **II precincts** *n* [*pl*] [正式] [*of cathedral, college*] 周围地区 ♦ **pedestrian precinct** [英] 行人专用区

precious ['prɛʃəs] *adj* 1 (*valuable*) [+ *time, resource, memories*] 宝贵的; (*financially*) 贵重的 2 (*important*) ♦ **precious (to sb)** (对某人) 珍贵 3 [贬] [+ *person, writing, style*] 矫揉造作的 4 [非正式] (*damned*) 该死的 5 [非正式] ♦ **precious little/few** 极少

precise [prɪ'saɪs] *adj* 1 [+ *time, nature, position, circumstances*] 精确的; [+ *figure, definition*] 准确的; [+ *explanation*] 清晰的 2 (*detailed*) [+ *instructions, plans*] 详尽的 ♦ **to be precise** (*in fact*) 确切地说

precisely [prɪ'saɪslɪ] *adv* (*exactly*) 确切地; (*referring to time*) 正好 ♦ **precisely!** 的确如此!

precision [prɪ'sɪʒən] *n* [u] 精确

precocious [prɪ'kəuʃəs] *adj* 1 [+ *child*] 早熟的; (*talented*) 过早发展的 2 [+ *talent*] 早慧的

predator ['prɛdətə(r)] *n* [c] 1 [动] 肉食动物 2 (喻) (*person, organization*) 掠夺者

predecessor ['priːdɪsɛsə(r)] *n* [c] 1 (*person*) (*in job*) 前任 2 (*machine, object*) 被替代的事物

predicament [prɪ'dɪkəmənt] *n* [c] 困境 ♦ **to be in a predicament** 处于困境之中

predict [prɪ'dɪkt] *vt* [+ *event, death etc*] 预言 ♦ **to predict that ...** 预言…

predictable [prɪ'dɪktəbl] *adj* [+ *outcome, behaviour, remark etc*] 可预料的; [+ *person*] 平庸的

prediction [prɪ'dɪkʃən] *n* [c] 预言

predominantly [prɪ'dɔmɪnəntlɪ] *adv* 主要地

preface ['prɛfəs] **I** *n* [c] 序言 **II** *vt* ♦ **to preface sth with sth** [+ *speech, action*] 以某物开启某物 ♦ **he prefaced his remark by saying that ...** 以说…作为他的开场白 ♦ **to be prefaced by sth** 以某事作为开场

prefect ['priːfɛkt] [英] *n* [c] (*in school*) 级长

prefer [prɪ'fəː(r)] *vt* 偏爱 ♦ **to prefer coffee to tea** 喜欢咖啡胜于茶 ♦ **to prefer doing sth** 更喜欢做某事 ♦ **I'd prefer to go by train** 我宁愿坐火车去 ♦ **I'd prefer him to go to university** 我宁可他上大学 ♦ **to prefer charges** 提出控告

preferable ['prɛfrəbl] *adj* ♦ **preferable (to sth/to doing sth)** (比某事/做某事) 更可取 ♦ **it is preferable to discuss matters openly** 公开地讨论事情会更好

preferably ['prɛfrəblɪ] *adv* 最好

preference ['prɛfrəns] *n* [c/u] 偏爱 ♦ **to have a preference for sth/for doing sth** 偏爱某物/做某事 ♦ **in preference to sth** 更倾向于某事 ♦ **to give preference to sb** 给某人以优待

preferential [prɛfə'rɛnʃəl] *adj* [+ *treatment, arrangement*] 优待的

prefix ['priːfɪks] [语言] *n* [c] 前缀

pregnancy ['prɛgnənsɪ] *n* 1 [u] (*condition*) 孕期 2 [c] (*instance*) 怀孕

pregnant ['prɛgnənt] *adj* 1 [+ *woman, animal*] 怀孕的 2 (喻) [+ *pause, silence*] 耐人寻味的 ♦ **3 months pregnant** 怀孕3个月 ♦ **when I was pregnant with Stephen** 当我怀着史蒂芬的时候 ♦ **to get pregnant** 怀孕了

prehistoric ['priːhɪs'tɔrɪk] *adj* 史前的

prejudice ['prɛdʒudɪs] **I** *n* [C/U] (*bias*) 偏见 **II** *vt* **1** (*influence*) [+ *person, result, case*] 使有偏见 **2** (*compromise*) [+ *situation, health etc*] 侵害 ♦ **prejudice against/in favour of sb** 对某人有偏见/偏爱某人 ♦ **without prejudice to** [正式] 无损于 ♦ **to prejudice sb against/in favour of sth** 使某人对某事抱有偏见/怀有好感

prejudiced ['prɛdʒudɪst] *adj* (*biased*) [+ *person*] 有偏见的; [+ *view, opinion, information*] 偏颇的 ♦ **to be prejudiced in favour of sb/sth** 偏向于某人/某事 ♦ **to be prejudiced against sb/sth** 对某人/某事存有偏见

preliminary [prɪ'lɪmɪnərɪ] **I** *adj* [+ *talks, results etc*] 预备性的 **II** *n* [C] [体育] 预赛 ♦ **preliminary round** [体育] 分组预选赛 ♦ **as a preliminary to sth/to doing sth** 作为某事/做某事的预备

prelude ['prɛljuːd] *n* [C] **1** [音] 前奏曲 **2** ♦ **a prelude to sth/to doing sth** 某事/做某事的前奏

premature ['prɛmətʃuə(r)] *adj* [+ *baby*] 早产的; [+ *death, arrival, congratulations*] 过早的 ♦ **you're being a little premature** 你有点草率

premier ['prɛmɪə(r)] **I** *adj* (*best*) 首位的 **II** *n* [C] [政治] 首相

première ['prɛmɪɛə(r)] *n* [C] [*of film, play, musical*] 首次公演

Premier League [英:足球] *n* ♦ **the Premier League** 超级联赛

premise ['prɛmɪs] [正式] **I** *n* [C] [*of argument*] 前提 **II** **premises** *n* [*pl*] [*of business, institution, school*] 地产 ♦ **on the premises** (*in the buildings*) 在屋内; (*outside*) 在房屋周围

premium ['priːmɪəm] **I** *n* [C] **1** [商] (*additional sum*) 额外费用 **2** [保险] 保险费 **II** *adj* (*also:* ***premium-quality***) [+ *product, service*] 质量一流的 ♦ **to be at a premium** (*expensive*) 稀有而昂贵的; (*hard to get*) 稀缺的

premonition [prɛmə'nɪʃən] *n* [C] 预感 ♦ **to have a premonition that ...** 预感到…

preoccupied [priː'ɔkjupaɪd] *adj* [+ *person*] 全神贯注的 ♦ **to be preoccupied with sth** 对某事心事重重

prep [prɛp] **I** *vt* [尤美] **1** (*prepare*) 预备 **2** [医] [+ *patient*] 为…作术前准备 **II** *n* [U] [英] (*homework*) 课外作业 ♦ **to do one's prep** 做课外作业

prepaid [priː'peɪd] *adj* [+ *fee, activity, funeral*] 预付的; [+ *envelope, phone card*] 预先付讫的

preparation [prɛpə'reɪʃən] **I** *n* **1** [U] (*activity*) 准备 **2** [C] (*food, medicine, cosmetic*) 配制品 **II** **preparations** *n* [*pl*] (*arrangements*) ♦ **preparations (for sth)** (为某事的)准备工作 ♦ **in preparation for sth** 为某事而准备的 ♦ **to make preparations for sth** 为某事做好准备

preparatory school [prɪ'pærətərɪ-] *n* = **prep school**

prepare [prɪ'pɛə(r)] **I** *vt* [+ *speech, room, report, object etc*] 准备; [+ *food, meal*] 预备 **II** *vi* ♦ **to prepare (for sth)** [+ *event, exam, interview*] (为某事)做准备 ♦ **to prepare o.s. for sth** [+ *shock, meeting, event*] 使自己对某事有所准备 ♦ **to prepare to do sth** (*get ready*) 准备好做某事 ♦ **to prepare for action** 准备战斗

prepared [prɪ'pɛəd] *adj* ♦ **to be prepared to do sth** (*willing*) 有意做某事 ♦ **prepared (for sth)** (*ready*) (对某事)有所准备的

preposition [prɛpə'zɪʃən] *n* [C] 介词

prep school *n* [C/U] **1** [英] 只收男生或女生的私立小学 **2** [美] 预科学校

prerequisite [priː'rɛkwɪzɪt] *n* [C] 先决条件

preschool ['priː'skuːl] *adj* [+ *age, child, education*] 学龄前的

prescribe [prɪ'skraɪb] *vt* **1** [医] 开 **2** (*state*) 规定 ♦ **to prescribe sth for sb/sth** 给某人/因为某事开某物

prescription [prɪ'skrɪpʃən] *n* [C] [医] (*slip of paper*) 处方; (*medicine*) 药方 ♦ **to make up a prescription** 配方 ♦ **to give sb a prescription for sth** 给某人开用于某事的处方 ♦ **"only available on prescription"** "凭处方购买"

presence ['prɛzns] *n* **1** [U] (*existence,*

attendance) 到场 **2** [u]（喻）(*personality*) 风度 **3** [c] (*spirit, invisible influence*) 存在 ♦**in sb's presence** 当着某人的面 ♦**to make one's presence felt** 让人感到自身的存在

present [*adj*, *n* 'prɛznt, *vb* prɪ'zɛnt] **I** *adj* **1** (*current*) 现有的 **2** (*in attendance*) 在场的 **II** *n* **1** (*not past*) ♦**the present** 目前 **2** [c] (*gift*) 礼物 **3** ♦**the present** (*also:* ***present tense***) 现在时态 **III** *vt* **1** (*give*) ♦**to present sth (to sb)** [+ *prize, award*] 授予（某人）某事 **2** (*cause, provide*) [+ *problem, threat*] 产生; [+ *challenge, opportunity*] 呈现 **3** (*introduce*) [+ *information, view*] 表述; [+ *person*] 介绍 **4** (*portray*) [+ *person, thing*] 描述 **5** [广播, 电视] [+ *programme*] 主持 ♦**the present day** 当今 ♦**to be present at sth** 出席某事 ♦**to be present in sth** 存在于某事中 ♦**all those present** 全体在场人员 ♦**at present** 现在 ♦**to give sb a present** 给某人礼物 ♦**to present sb with sth** [+ *prize, award*] 授予某人某物; [+ *choice, option*] 给予某人某物; [+ *difficulty, problem, threat*] 给某人带来某物 ♦**to present o.s. as being ...** 将自己表述为… ♦**to present itself** [*opportunity* +] 出现

presentable [prɪ'zɛntəbl] *adj* [+ *person*] 中看的

presentation [prɛzn'teɪʃən] *n* **1** [c] [*of award, prize*] 授予 **2** [u] (*appearance*) [*of product, food*] 外观; [*of essay, report*] 观感 **3** [c] (*lecture, talk*) 陈述 **4** [c] [戏剧] (*production*) 演出 ♦**to give a presentation** 做陈述 ♦**on presentation of...** [+ *voucher, invitation*] 一经出示…

present-day ['prɛzntdeɪ] *adj* 当前的

presenter [prɪ'zɛntə(r)] *n* [c] (*on radio, TV*) 节目主持人

presently ['prɛzntlɪ] *adv* **1** (*after a while*) 一会儿 **2** (*shortly*) 马上 **3** (*currently*) 目前

present participle *n* [c] 现在分词

preservation [prɛzə'veɪʃən] *n* [u] **1** (*continuation*) [*of peace, standards, life etc*] 保持 **2** (*maintenance*) [*of building, monument, furniture etc*] 保存

preservative [prɪ'zəːvətɪv] *n* [c/u] (*for food, wood*) 防腐剂

preserve [prɪ'zəːv] **I** *vt* **1** [+ *customs, independence, peace*] 维护; [+ *building, artefact*] 保存; [+ *character, area, forest*] 保护 **2** (*in salt, syrup, vinegar etc*) [+ *food*] 防腐 **II** *n* **1** [c/u] (*jam, marmalade, chutney*) 果酱 **2** [c] (*for game, fish*) 私人渔猎区 **3** [c] ♦**a male/working class preserve** 男性/工人阶级所独有 ♦**strawberry preserve** 草莓酱

preside [prɪ'zaɪd] *vi* ♦**to preside over sth** [+ *meeting, event*] 主持某事

✪**president** ['prɛzɪdənt] *n* [c] **1** [政治] 总统 **2** [+ *of society, club, institution*] 主席 **3** [美] [*of company*] 总裁

presidential [prɛzɪ'dɛnʃl] *adj* [政治] [+ *election, candidate*] 总统职位的; [+ *adviser, representative*] 总统的

✪**press** [prɛs] **I** *n* **1** (*newspapers, journalists*) ♦**the press** 新闻界 **2** [c] (*for wine*) 榨汁机 **3** [c] (*also:* ***printing press***) 印刷机 **II** *vt* **1** [+ *button, switch, bell*] 按; [+ *accelerator*] 踏 **2** (*squeeze*) 挤 **3** (*iron*) [+ *clothes, sheets etc*] 熨平 **4** (*put pressure on*) ♦**to press sb for sth/to do sth** 催逼某人某事/做某事 **5** (*express*) [+ *claim, views, point*] 坚持 **III** *vi* (*squeeze*) 挤 ♦**to go to press** [*newspaper* +] 付印 ♦**to give sth a press** [+ *switch, button, bell*] 按某物 ♦**at the press of a switch** 按了开关后 ♦**to press sb about sth** 从某人处打探某事 ♦**to press sb for an answer** 催某人回答 ♦**to press sb into doing sth** (*urge*) 迫切要求某人做某事 ♦**to press sth (up)on sb** (*force*) 迫使某人接受某事 ♦**to press charges (against sb)** [法] 起诉（某人）♦**to be pressed for time/money** 时间紧迫/手头紧 ♦**to press (down) on sth**（向下）压某物 ♦**to press for sth** [+ *changes etc*] 迫切要求某事

❑**press ahead, press on** *vi* 勇往直前 ♦**to press on with sth** 加紧某事

press conference *n* [c] 新闻发布会

pressing ['prɛsɪŋ] *adj* [+ *problem, issue*] 紧迫的

press stud [英] *n* [c] 揿扣儿

press-up [ˈprɛsʌp] [英] *n* [c] 俯卧撑

✪**pressure** [ˈprɛʃə(r)] **I** *n* **1** [u] (*physical force*) 压力 **2** [u] [*of air, gas, water*] 压强 **3** [u] (喻) (*coercion*) ♦**pressure (to do sth)** (做某事的)压力 **4** [c/u] (*stress*) 压力 **II** *vt* ♦**to pressure sb (to do sth)** 强使某人(做某事) ♦**high/low pressure** 高/低压 ♦**to put pressure on sb (to do sth)** 对某人施加压力(去做某事) ♦**under pressure** (*with stress*) 在压力下 ♦**to be under pressure to do sth** 被迫做某事 ♦**to pressure sb into doing sth** 迫使某人做某事

pressure cooker *n* [c] 高压锅

pressure group *n* [c] 压力集团

prestige [prɛsˈtiːʒ] *n* [u] [*of person, organization, job*] 威望

prestigious [prɛsˈtɪdʒəs] *adj* [+ *institution, job*] 有威望的

presumably [prɪˈzjuːməblɪ] *adv* 据推测

presume [prɪˈzjuːm] *vt* **1** (*assume*) ♦**to presume (that ...)** 认定(…) **2** (*dare*) ♦**to presume to do sth** 擅自做某事 ♦**I presume so** 我认为是的 ♦**to be presumed dead** 被认定死亡

pretence (美 **pretense**) [prɪˈtɛns] *n* [c/u] 假装 ♦**under false pretences** 虚情假意地 ♦**to make a pretence of doing sth** 假装做某事

pretend [prɪˈtɛnd] **I** *vt* ♦**to pretend to do sth/pretend that ...** (*make believe*) 假装做某事/假装… ◊ *The children were pretending to be pirates.* 孩子们扮成海盗。◊ *She can sunbathe and pretend she's in Spain.* 她能照日光浴，想像着她是在西班牙。**II** *vi* 假装 ♦**I don't pretend to understand it** (*claim*) 我不会不懂装懂的

pretense [prɪˈtɛns] [美] *n* = **pretence**

pretentious [prɪˈtɛnʃəs] *adj* [+ *person, play, restaurant etc*] 矫饰的

pretext [ˈpriːtɛkst] *n* [c] 借口 ♦**on** *or* **under the pretext of sth/of doing sth** 以某事/做某事为借口

pretty [ˈprɪtɪ] **I** *adj* [+ *person, face, house, dress*] 漂亮的 **II** *adv* [非正式] (*quite*) [+ *good, happy, soon etc*] 相当 ♦**to look pretty** 看上去漂亮 ♦**pretty much/pretty well** [非正式] (*more or less*) 差不多

prevail [prɪˈveɪl] *vi* **1** (*be current*) [*custom, belief, conditions, fashion* +] 盛行 **2** (*triumph*) ♦**to prevail (over sth)** 胜过(某事) ♦**to prevail upon sb to do sth** 说服某人做某事

prevailing [prɪˈveɪlɪŋ] *adj* **1** [+ *wind*] 盛行的 **2** (*dominant*) [+ *view, opinion*] 主导的

prevalent [ˈprɛvələnt] *adj* [+ *belief, custom, attitude*] 普遍的

prevent [prɪˈvɛnt] *vt* [+ *war, disease, situation*] 阻止; [+ *accident, fire*] 防止 ♦**to prevent sb (from) doing sth** 阻止某人做某事 ♦**to prevent sth (from) happening** 防止某事发生

preventable [prɪˈvɛntəbl] *adj* [+ *disease, death, accident*] 可预防的

prevention [prɪˈvɛnʃən] *n* [u] 预防

preventive [prɪˈvɛntɪv] *adj* [+ *measures, medicine*] 预防的

preview [ˈpriːvjuː] *n* [c] [*of film, exhibition*] 预演

previous [ˈpriːvɪəs] *adj* **1** (*prior*) [+ *marriage, relationship, experience, owner*] 前的 **2** (*preceding*) [+ *chapter, week, day*] 以前的 ♦**previous to** (*before*) 在…之前

📖 用法参见 **former**

previously [ˈpriːvɪəslɪ] *adv* **1** 以前 **2** ♦**10 days previously** 10 天前

pre-war [priːˈwɔː(r)] *adj* 二战前的

prey [preɪ] *n* [u] 猎物 ♦**to fall prey to sth** (喻) 受某事折磨 ♦**to be prey to sth** 为某事而受苦

❑**prey on** *vt* [不可拆分] [*animal* +] 捕食 ♦**to prey on sb's mind** 烦扰某人

✪**price** [praɪs] **I** *n* [c/u] 价格 **II** *vt* [+ *goods*] 定价 ♦**what is the price of ...?** …多少钱？ ♦**to go up** *or* **rise in price** 涨价 ♦**you can't put a price on friendship/your health** 友谊/健康无价 ♦**to pay a high price for sth** (喻) 为某事付出很高代价 ♦**it's a small price to pay for freedom** 这是为自由付出的小小代价 ♦**at a price** 以很高代价 ♦**what price he'll change his mind?** 他改变主意的可能性有

多少？ ♦**to be priced at** 定价为 ♦**to price o.s. out of the market** 漫天要价以至无人问津

priceless ['praɪslɪs] *adj* **1** [+ *diamond, painting*] 无价的 **2** (*very useful*) [+ *experience, skill, assistance*] 宝贵的 **3** [非正式] (*amusing*) [+ *person, comment*] 很有趣的
📖 用法参见 **invaluable**

price list *n* [c] 价目表

prick [prɪk] **I** *n* [c] **1** (*sting*) 刺 **2** [非正式，疑讳] (*penis*) 阴茎; (*idiot*) 蠢人 **II** *vt* **1** (*scratch*) (*on thorn, with needle*) 刺 **2** (*also:* ***prick holes in***) 刺孔于 ♦**to prick o.s. (on/with sth)** 被（某物）刺到 ♦**to prick up one's ears** (*listen*) 侧耳倾听

prickly ['prɪklɪ] *adj* **1** [+ *plant, fabric, animal*] 多刺的 **2** (*irritable*) [+ *person*] 易怒的

pride [praɪd] **I** *n* [U] **1** (*satisfaction, dignity, self-respect*) 自豪 **2** (*arrogance*) 傲慢 **II** *vt* ♦**to pride o.s. on sth/on doing sth** 因某事/做某事而自豪 ♦**to take (a) pride in sb/sth** 因某人/某事而自豪 ♦**to take a pride in doing sth** 以做某事为豪 ♦**to have** *or* **take pride of place** [英] 占据头等重要的位置

priest [priːst] *n* [c] 神职人员

primarily ['praɪmərɪlɪ] *adv* 主要地

primary ['praɪmərɪ] **I** *adj* **1** (*principal*) [+ *reason, aim, cause*] 主要的 **2** [英] [+ *education, teacher*] 小学的 **II** *n* [c] (*in US*) (*also:* ***primary election***) 初选

primary school [英] *n* [c/U] 小学 [美= **elementary school, grade school**]

prime [praɪm] **I** *adj* **1** (*major*) [+ *cause, concern, target*] 首要的 **2** (*best*) [+ *condition, position*] 第一流的 **II** *n* [c] ♦**in one's prime** 处于黄金时期 **III** *vt* **1** (*prepare*) ♦**to prime sb (to do sth)** 事先使某人准备好（做某事）**2** [+ *gun*] 装 **3** [+ *wood*] 给…上底漆 ♦**of prime importance** 最重要 ♦**prime beef** 上等牛肉 ♦**a prime example of ...** …最典型的例子 ♦**in the prime of life** 处于壮年时期

Prime Minister *n* [c] 总理

primitive ['prɪmɪtɪv] *adj* **1** (*simple*) [+ *tribe, society, tool*] 原始的 **2** (*early*) [+ *man, life form, instinct*] 早期的 **3** (*crude*) [+ *conditions, technique*] 简陋的

primrose ['prɪmrəuz] *n* [c] 报春花

prince [prɪns] *n* [c] 王子

princess [prɪn'sɛs] *n* [c] 公主

principal ['prɪnsɪpl] **I** *adj* **1** (*main*) [+ *reason, aim*] 主要的 **2** [戏剧] [+ *role, part, character*] 主要的 **II** *n* **1** [c] (*head teacher*) [*of school, college*] 校长 **2** [c] [戏剧] 主角 **3** [s] [经济] (*sum*) 资本

principally ['prɪnsɪplɪ] *adv* 主要地

principle ['prɪnsɪpl] *n* **1** [c/U] (*moral belief*) 正直 **2** [c/U] [*of philosophy, theory*] 原理 **3** [c] (*basic law*) 原则 ♦**in principle** (*in theory*) 原则上 ♦**to agree to/approve of sth in principle** 原则上同意/批准某事 ♦**on principle** 根据原则

print [prɪnt] **I** *n* **1** [U] (*type*) 印刷字体 **2** [c] (*picture*) 图片 **3** [c] (*photograph*) 照片 **4** [c] (*fabric*) 印花布 **II** *vt* **1** (*produce*) [+ *book, newspaper, leaflet*] 印刷 **2** (*publish*) [+ *story, article*] 出版 **3** (*stamp*) [+ *word, number, pattern*] 印 **4** (*write*) 用印刷体写 **5** [计算机] 打印 **III** *vi* (*write*) 用印刷体写 **IV prints** *n* [*pl*] (*fingerprints*) 指纹 ♦**the fine** *or* **small print** 小号印刷体 ♦**to appear in print/get into print** 刊登出 ♦**to be in print** [*book* +] 在销售的 ♦**to be out of print** [*book* +] 绝版的
❑**print out** *vt* [计算机] [+ *document, file*] 打印出

printer ['prɪntə(r)] *n* [c] **1** (*machine*) 打印机 **2** (*person*) 印刷工 **3** (*firm*) (*also:* ***printer's***) 印刷所

printout ['prɪntaut] *n* [c] 打印输出

prior ['praɪə(r)] **I** *adj* **1** (*previous*) [+ *knowledge, engagement, consent*] 在先的 **2** (*more important*) [+ *duty, commitment*] 更重要的 **II** *n* [c] [宗] (*head monk*) 小修道院院长; (*deputy head monk*)大修道院副院长 ♦**I have a prior engagement** 我有另一个约会在先 ♦**without prior warning** 没有事先警告 ♦**prior to sth/to doing sth** 在某事/做某事之前 ♦**to have a prior claim on**

sth 对某事有优先要求权

priority [praɪˈɔrɪtɪ] **I** *n* [c] (*concern*) 重点 **II priorities** *n* [*pl*] 优先考虑的事 ♦**to take** *or* **have priority (over sth/sb)** (比某事/某人) 具有优先权 ♦**to give priority to sth/sb** 给某事/某人以优先权

prison [ˈprɪzn] *n* **1** [c/u] (*institution*) 监狱 **2** [u] (*imprisonment*) 坐牢 **3** [c] (喻) 束缚 ♦**in prison** 坐牢

prisoner [ˈprɪznə(r)] *n* [c] 囚犯; (*during war*) 战俘 ♦**the prisoner at the bar** [法] 被告 ♦**to take sb prisoner** 俘虏某人 ♦**to hold sb prisoner** 关押某人

prison officer *n* [c] 狱官

prisoner of war *n* [c] 战俘

pristine [ˈprɪstiːn] *adj* [+ *house, clothes*] 纯净的 ♦**in pristine condition** 一尘不染的

privacy [ˈprɪvəsɪ] *n* [u] 隐私 ♦**in the privacy of one's own home** 在自家私下里 ♦**an invasion of privacy** 对隐私的侵犯

private [ˈpraɪvɪt] **I** *adj* **1** (*not public*) [+ *property, land, plane*] 私人的; [+ *performance, ceremony*] 非公开的 **2** (*not state-owned*) [+ *education, housing, health care, industries*] 私有的 **3** (*confidential*) [+ *papers, discussion, conversation, meeting*] 秘密的 **4** (*not professional*) [+ *correspondence, life*] 个人的 **5** (*personal*) [+ *life, thoughts, plans, affairs, belongings*] 私人的 **6** (*secluded*) [+ *place*] 幽僻的 **7** (*secretive*) [+ *person*] 内敛的 **II** *n* [c] [军] 士兵 ♦**to be in private practice** [医] 私人开业行医 ♦**in (his) private life** 在他的私生活中 ♦**in private** 私下

privately [ˈpraɪvɪtlɪ] *adv* **1** (*in private*) 私下地 **2** (*secretly*) 秘密地 ♦**privately owned** 私人所有

private property *n* [u] 私人财产

private school *n* [c/u] (*fee-paying*) 私立学校

privatize [ˈpraɪvɪtaɪz] *vt* [+ *company, industry*] 私有化

privilege [ˈprɪvɪlɪdʒ] *n* **1** [c] (*benefit*) 优惠 **2** [s] (*honour*) 荣幸 **3** [u] (*due to background*) 特权

privileged [ˈprɪvɪlɪdʒd] *adj* **1** [+ *person, position*] 享有特权的 **2** [+ *information*] 特许的 ♦**to be/feel privileged to do sth** 有幸做某事

privy [ˈprɪvɪ] [正式] *adj* ♦**to be privy to sth** [+ *information, facts*] 私下知悉某事

prize [praɪz] **I** *n* [c] **1** (*in competition, sport*) 奖 **2** [教育, 大学] (*for achievement*) 奖励 **II** *adj* 一流的 **III** *vt* 珍藏

prize-giving [ˈpraɪzgɪvɪŋ] *n* [c] **1** (*after competition*) 颁奖仪式 **2** [教育] (*for achievement*) 颁奖

prizewinner [ˈpraɪzwɪnə(r)] *n* [c] **1** (*in competition*) 获奖者 **2** [教育, 大学] (*for achievement*) 获奖者

pro [prəu] **I** *n* **1** [c] (*professional*) 职业选手 **2** ♦**the pros and cons (of sth/of doing sth)** (某事/做某事的) 利弊 **II** *prep* (*in favour of*) 赞成

probability [prɔbəˈbɪlɪtɪ] *n* [c/u] ♦**probability (of sth/that ...)** (某事/…的) 可能性 ♦**the probability of sth happening** 某事发生的可能性 ♦**the probability is that ...** 可能性是… ♦**in all probability** 极有可能

probable [ˈprɔbəbl] *adj* 可能的 ♦**it is/seems probable that ...** 可能…/似乎可能…

✪**probably** [ˈprɔbəblɪ] *adv* 可能 ◊ *You probably won't understand this word.* 你可能不理解这个词。 ♦**probably!/probably not!** 很可能! /很可能不是!

probation [prəˈbeɪʃən] *n* [u] **1** (*for criminal*) 缓刑 **2** (*for employee*) 试用期 ♦**to be on probation** [*criminal* +] 在缓刑中; [*employee* +] 在试用期中 ♦**to put sb on probation** [+ *criminal*] 判某人缓刑

probe [prəub] **I** *n* [c] **1** [医] 探针 **2** (*also: **space probe***) 航天探测器 **3** (*enquiry*) (*into corruption, illegal practices*) 探究 **II** *vt* **1** (*investigate*) [+ *financial situation, practices, mystery, death*] 调查 **2** (*search*) 探查 **3** [医] (*with instrument*) [+ *wound*] 检查 **III** *vi* **1** (*investigate*) ♦**to probe (into sth)** 探究(某事) **2** [医] (*with instrument*) 探查

✪**problem** [ˈprɔbləm] *n* [c] **1** (*difficulty*) 难题 **2** (*puzzle*) 疑惑 ♦**to have**

problems with sth 对某事有疑惑 ♦**what's the problem?** 有什么问题吗？ ♦**I had no problem finding her** 我要找她不难 ♦**no problem!** [非正式]没问题！

problematic(al) [prɔblə'mætɪk(l)] *adj* [+ *activity, situation, relationship*] 成问题的

procedure [prə'siːdʒə(r)] *n* **1** [C] (*process*) 步骤 **2** [C/U] (*customary method*) 程序

proceed [prə'siːd] *vi* **1** (*continue*) 继续 **2** [正式] (*go*) (*on foot*) 走; (*in car*) 前进; [*car, vehicle* +] 行进 ♦**to proceed with sth** 继续某事 ♦**to proceed to do sth** 开始做某事

proceedings [prə'siːdɪŋz] *n* [*pl*] **1** (*events*) 活动 **2** [法] 诉讼 **3** (*minutes*) [*of conference, meeting*] 记录

proceeds ['prəusiːdz] *n* [*pl*] 收入

✪**process** ['prəusɛs] **I** *n* [C] **1** (*procedure*) 过程 **2** [生物, 化] 过程 **II** *vt* **1** [+ *raw materials, food*] 加工 **2** [+ *application*] (*for job, visa, benefit*) 办理 **3** [计算机] [+ *data*] 处理 ♦**by a process of elimination** 通过一系列的筛选 ♦**in the process** 在过程中 ♦**to be in the process of doing sth** 在从事某事的过程中

procession [prə'sɛʃən] *n* [C] 队伍 ♦**wedding/funeral procession** 迎亲/送葬队伍

proclaim [prə'kleɪm] *vt* 宣告 ♦**to proclaim that ...** 声明… ♦**to proclaim o.s. sth** 公开宣称自己的某立场

prod [prɔd] **I** *vt* **1** (*push*) (*with finger, stick, knife*) 戳 **2** (*encourage*) ♦**to prod sb into sth/into doing sth** 促使某人做某事 **II** *n* [C] **1** (*with finger, stick, knife*) ♦**to give sb/sth a prod** 戳某人/某物一下 **2** (*reminder*) ♦**to give sb a prod** 提醒某人一下 ♦**to prod sb to do sth** 促使某人做某事

prodigy ['prɔdɪdʒɪ] *n* [C] 天才 ♦**child prodigy** 神童

✪**produce** [*n* 'prɔdjuːs, *vb* prə'djuːs] **I** *n* [U] 产品 ◊ *organic produce* 绿色产品 **II** *vt* **1** (*bring about*) [+ *effect, result etc*] 促成 ◊ *All our efforts have failed to produce an agreement.* 我们所有的努力都没能促成一致意见。 **2** (*make*) [+ *goods, commodity*] 生产 ◊ *The company produces components for the aerospace industry.* 这家公司为航空业生产零部件。 **3** [生物, 化] [+ *gas, toxins etc*] 产生 **4** (*provide*) [+ *evidence, argument*] 提出 ◊ *Scientists have produced powerful arguments against his ideas.* 科学家们提出了辩驳他的想法的有力论据。 **5** (*show*) [+ *passport, knife etc*] 出示 **6** [+ *play, film, programme*] 上演

producer [prə'djuːsə(r)] *n* [C] **1** [戏剧, 电影, 音] [*of film, play, programme*] 制片人; [*of record*] 制作人 **2** [*of food, material*] (*country*) 产地; (*company*) 制造商

✪**product** ['prɔdʌkt] *n* [C] **1** 产品 **2** (*result*) 产物

production [prə'dʌkʃən] *n* **1** [U] [工业, 农] (*process*) 生产; (*amount produced, amount grown*) 产量 **2** [U] [生物] [*of cells, hormones etc*] 繁殖 **3** [C] (*play, show*) 作品 **4** [U] [*of film, programme, play*] 制作 ♦**to go into production** [*goods* +] 投产 ♦**on production of** 一经出示

productive [prə'dʌktɪv] *adj* **1** [+ *workforce, factory, writer*] 多产的 **2** [+ *discussion, meeting, relationship*] 富有成效的

productivity [prɔdʌk'tɪvɪtɪ] *n* [U] 生产力

profession [prə'fɛʃən] *n* [C] **1** (*job*) 职业 **2** (*people*) (*medical, legal etc*) 从业人员

professional [prə'fɛʃənl] **I** *adj* **1** (*work-related*) [+ *activity, context, capacity*] 业务的 **2** (*not amateur*) [+ *photographer, musician, footballer*] 职业的; [+ *advice, help*] 专业的 **3** (*correct*) [+ *person, attitude*] 内行的 **4** (*skilful*) [+ *performance, piece of work*] 专业水平的 **II** *n* [C] **1** (*doctor, lawyer, teacher*) 专业人士 **2** [体育] 职业运动员 **3** (*competent person*) 内行 ♦**professional misconduct** 渎职 ♦**to seek/take professional advice** 寻求/采纳专家建议

professionally [prə'fɛʃnəlɪ] *adv* **1** (*as a professional*) [*qualified* +] 专业上; [*play* +] 职业地 **2** (*correctly*) [*behave* +] 内行地 **3** (*skilfully*) [*produce, make etc* +] 专业地 ♦ **speaking professionally** 从专业上讲 ♦ **personally and professionally** 从个人生活和工作来说

professor [prəˈfɛsə(r)] *n* [c] **1** [英] 教授 **2** [美] 教员

profile [ˈprəufaɪl] *n* [c] **1** [*of person's face*] 侧面 **2** (喻) (*biography*) 简介 ♦ **to keep a low profile** [*person* +] 保持低调 ♦ **a high profile** [*of person, organization*] 引人注目的形象

profit [ˈprɔfɪt] **I** *n* [c/u] 利润 **II** *vi* ♦ **to profit from sth** 从某事中获益 ♦ **to make a profit** 赚钱 ♦ **to sell (sth) at a profit** 出售(某物)而获利

profitable [ˈprɔfɪtəbl] *adj* **1** [+ *business, deal, activity*] 有利润的 **2** [+ *discussion, meeting*] 有益的

profound [prəˈfaund] *adj* **1** (*great*) [+ *effect, change, implications*] 深远的; [+ *differences*] 极大的; [+ *shock, sense, feeling, respect*] 深深的 **2** (*intellectual*) [+ *idea, book, mind*] 深刻的

program [ˈprəugræm] **I** *n* [c] **1** (*also: **computer program***) 程序 **2** [美] = **programme** **II** *vt* **1** [计算机] ♦ **to program sth (to do sth)** 为某物编程(做某事) **2** [美] = **programme**

✪ **programme** (美 **program**) [ˈprəugræm] **I** *n* [c] **1** [广播, 电视] 节目 **2** (*for theatre, concert*) 节目宣传册 **3** (*list*) [*of talks, events, performances*] 节目单 **4** (*scheme*) 计划 **II** *vt* ♦ **to programme sth (to do sth)** [+ *machine, system*] 设定某事(做某事) *see also* **program**

programmer [ˈprəugræmə(r)] [计算机] *n* [c] 程序员

progress [*n* ˈprəugrɛs, *vb* prəˈgrɛs] **I** *n* [u] **1** (*headway*) 进展 **2** (*advances*) 进步 **3** (*development*) [*of event, match, talks, disease*] 发展 **II** *vi* **1** (*make headway*) 进展 **2** ♦ **to progress (to sth/to doing sth)** 提高(到某事/到做某事) **3** (*move on*) [*career, day, disease* +] 推进 ♦ **to make progress (with sth)** (对某事)取得进步 ♦ **in progress** [*meeting, battle, match* +] 正在进展中

progression [prəˈgrɛʃən] *n* **1** [u/s] (*advancement*) (*in career, course*) 进展 **2** [c] (*development*) (*of events, disease, career*) 进程 **3** [c] (*series*) 系列

progressive [prəˈgrɛsɪv] **I** *adj* **1** (*enlightened*) [+ *person, school, policy*] 先进的 **2** (*gradual*) [+ *loss, decline, change*] 逐渐的 **II** *n* [c] (*person*) 改革派人士

prohibit [prəˈhɪbɪt] [正式] *vt* 禁止 ♦ **to prohibit sb from doing sth** 严禁某人做某事 ♦ **"smoking prohibited"** "严禁吸烟"

project [*n* ˈprɔdʒɛkt, *vb* prəˈdʒɛkt] **I** *n* [c] **1** (*plan, scheme*) 工程 **2** [教育, 大学] 课题 **II** *vt* **1** (*plan*) 计划 **2** (*estimate*) [+ *figure, amount*] 估计 **3** [+ *light, film, picture*] 投射 **4** [+ *feeling, quality, image*] 表露 **5** ♦ **to project sb/o.s. as sth** 突出某人/自己作为某物的形象 **III** *vi* (*stick out*) 突出

projection [prəˈdʒɛkʃən] *n* **1** [c] (*estimate*) 预测 **2** [c] (*overhang*) 凸出物 **3** [u] [*of film, movie*] 投影

projector [prəˈdʒɛktə(r)] *n* [c] 放映机

prolific [prəˈlɪfɪk] *adj* [+ *artist, composer, writer*] 多产的

prologue (美 **prolog**) [ˈprəulɔg] *n* [c] [*of play, book*] 序

prolong [prəˈlɔŋ] *vt* 延长

prom [prɔm] *n* [c] **1** [英] (*by sea*) 海滨大道 **2** [美] (*dance*) 学生的正式舞会

PROM

在英国，**prom**（即 **promenade concert** 的略称）是由一系列古典音乐会组成。每年夏天，由 **Royal Albert Hall** 在伦敦举办的 **prom** 最为著名。每季的最后一场音乐会，**Last Night of the Proms**，通常会有电视转播，并总要演奏一些爱国歌曲。在场的听众一边站着挥舞手中的英国国旗，一边纵情歌唱。美国人对 **prom** 的理解却不大相同，其含义为高中或大学学年末举行的一场正式舞会。**senior prom** 标志着 **high school** 的结束。对于美国年轻人而言，这也是成长历程中一个重要的典礼。

promenade [prɔmə'nɑːd] **I** *n* [c] 海滨大道 **II** *vi* [*person* +] 散步

prominence ['prɔmɪnəns] *n* [u] (*importance*) 卓越 ♦**to give prominence to sth** 重视某事 ♦**to rise to prominence** 崭露头角

prominent ['prɔmɪnənt] *adj* **1** (*important*) 重要的 **2** (*noticeable*) 显著的

promiscuous [prə'mɪskjuəs] *adj* [+ *person, behaviour*] 滥交的

promise ['prɔmɪs] **I** *n* **1** [c] 许诺 **2** [u] (*potential*) [*of person*] 有前途; [*of thing*] 前景 **II** *vi* 保证 **III** *vt* ♦**to promise sb sth, promise sth to sb** 保证给某人某物 ♦**to make a promise (to do sth)** 保证(做某事) ♦**to break/keep a promise (to do sth)** 违背/遵守(做某事的)诺言 ♦**a young man of promise** 有希望的小伙子 ♦**to promise (sb) that ...** (向某人)保证… ♦**to promise to do sth** 保证做某事 ♦**it promises to be lively** 这看来很来劲

promising ['prɔmɪsɪŋ] *adj* [+ *person, career*] 有希望的

promote [prə'məut] *vt* **1** [+ *employee*] 晋升 **2** (*publicize*) [+ *record, film, book, product*] 促销 **3** (*encourage*) [+ *understanding, peace*] 促进 **4** (*sponsor, organize*) [+ *event*] 赞助 ♦**the team was promoted to the first division** [英:体育]该队升到第一级别

promoter [prə'məutə(r)] *n* [c] **1** [*of concert, sporting event*] 赞助人 **2** [*of cause, idea*] 推广人

promotion [prə'məuʃən] *n* **1** [c/u] (*at work*) 晋级 **2** [u] (*pushing*) [*of product*] 促销 **3** [c] (*publicity campaign*) 推广 **4** [u] [英:体育]升级

prompt [prɔmpt] **I** *adj* **1** (*on time*) 干脆的 **2** (*rapid*) [+ *action, response*] 迅速的 **II** *n* [c] **1** [戏剧] ♦**to give sb a prompt** 给某人提词 **2** [计算机]提示符 **III** *vt* **1** (*cause*) [+ *action, plan*] 引发 **2** (*when talking*) 提示 **3** [戏剧]提词 ♦**to be prompt to do sth** 立刻做某事 ♦**at 8 o'clock prompt** 8点整 ♦**to prompt sb to do sth** 促使某人做某事

promptly ['prɔmptlɪ] *adv* **1** (*immediately*) 立刻 **2** (*punctually*) 准时地

prone [prəun] *adj* **1** ♦**to be prone to sth** 易于某事的 **2** (*face down*) ♦**to lie prone** 俯卧 ♦**she is prone to burst into tears if ...** 如果…她动辄就哭 ♦**accident-/injury-prone** 易出事/受伤的

prong [prɔŋ] *n* [c] [*of fork*] 尖齿

pronoun ['prəunaun] *n* [c] 代词

pronounce [prə'nauns] **I** *vt* **1** [+ *word, name*] 发音 **2** [正式] [+ *verdict, sentence*] 宣布 **3** [正式] (*opine*) 断言 **II** *vi* [正式] ♦**to pronounce (up)on sth** 就某事发表意见 ♦**to pronounce sb fit/dead** 宣布某人康复/死亡 ♦**to pronounce o.s. satisfied** 表示满意

pronunciation [prənʌnsɪ'eɪʃən] *n* [c/u] 发音

proof [pruːf] **I** *n* [u] 证据 **II** [正式] *adj* ♦**to be proof against sth** 不受某事影响的 **III proofs** *n* [*pl*] [排版]校样 ♦**to be 70% proof** [*alcohol* +] 70% 的标准酒精度

prop [prɔp] **I** *n* [c] **1** (*stick, post*) 支柱 **2** (喻) (*person, thing*) 靠山 **II** *vt* (*also: **prop up***) (*lean*) ♦**to prop sth (up) against/on sth** 把某物靠在某物上 **III props** *n* [*pl*] [戏剧]道具
❑**prop up** *vt* **1** (字) (*lean*) 支撑 **2** (喻) [+ *government, industry, currency*] 支持

propaganda [prɔpə'gændə] *n* [u] 宣传

propel [prə'pɛl] *vt* **1** [+ *vehicle, boat, machine, person*] 推动 **2** (喻) ♦**to propel sb into sth** 促使某人做某事

propeller [prə'pɛlə(r)] *n* [c] 推进器

proper ['prɔpə(r)] *adj* **1** (*genuine*) [+ *job, meal, teacher etc*] 适当的 **2** (*correct*) [+ *procedure, place, word*] 恰当的 **3** (*socially acceptable*) [+ *behaviour, job*] 适宜的 **4** [非正式] (*real*) [+ *idiot, thug etc*] 十足的 ♦**to go through the proper channels** 通过正当渠道 ♦**the town/city proper** 城/市区

properly ['prɔpəlɪ] *adv* **1** (*adequately*) [*eat, work, concentrate* +] 充分地 **2** (*decently*) [*behave* +] 体面地

proper noun *n* [C] 专有名词
property ['prɔpətɪ] *n* **1** [U] (*possessions*) 财产 **2** [C/U] (*buildings and land*) 地产 **3** [C] (*characteristic*) [*of substance, material*] 特性
prophecy ['prɔfɪsɪ] *n* [C] 预言
prophet ['prɔfɪt] *n* [C] [宗] 先知 ♦**prophet of doom** 悲观预言家
proportion [prə'pɔːʃən] **I** *n* **1** [C] [正式] (*part*) [*of group, amount*] 部分 **2** [C] (*number*) [*of people, things*] 比例 **3** [C/U] (*ratio*) ♦**proportion (of sth to sth)** (某物与某物的)比例 **II proportions** *n* [*pl*] (*dimensions*) [*of building, design*] 比例; (喻)程度 ♦**in (direct) proportion to sth** (*at the same rate as*) 与某事成(正)比; (*in relation to*) 与某事相称 ♦**to keep sth in proportion** 如实对待某事 ♦**to get sth out of proportion** 无根据地夸大某事 ♦**to be out of all proportion to sth** 完完全全与某事不相称 ♦**to have a sense of proportion** 具有辨别轻重缓急的能力
proportional [prə'pɔːʃənl] *adj* ♦**proportional to sth** 与某物成比例的
proportionate [prə'pɔːʃənɪt] *adj* = **proportional**
proposal [prə'pəuzl] *n* [C] **1** (*plan*) 提案 **2** (*also: **proposal of marriage***) 求婚
propose [prə'pəuz] **I** *vt* **1** [+ *plan, idea*] 提出 **2** [+ *motion*] 提议 **II** *vi* (*offer marriage*) 求婚 ♦**to propose to do** *or* **doing sth** (*intend*) 意欲做某事 ♦**to propose that ...** (*suggest*) 建议…; (*in debate*) 提出… ♦**to propose a toast** 提议干杯
proposition [prɔpə'zɪʃən] **I** *n* [C] **1** (*idea*) ♦**a difficult/attractive proposition** 一个棘手/有趣的问题 **2** (*offer, suggestion*) 提议 **3** [正式] (*statement*) 主张 **II** *vt* ♦**to proposition sb** 向某人提出猥亵的要求 ♦**to make sb a proposition** 向某人提议
proprietor [prə'praɪətə(r)] *n* [C] [*of hotel, shop, newspaper*] 业主
prose [prəuz] *n* [U] 散文
prosecute ['prɔsɪkjuːt] **I** *vt* **1** ♦**to prosecute sb (for sth/for doing sth)** (因某事/做某事而)起诉某人 **2** [+ *case*] 起诉 **II** *vi* 起诉
prosecution [prɔsɪ'kjuːʃən] *n* **1** [C/U] [*of person*] 起诉 **2** (*accusing side*) ♦**the prosecution** 原告
prosecutor ['prɔsɪkjuːtə(r)] *n* [C] 起诉人
prospect [*n* 'prɔspɛkt, *vb* prə'spɛkt] **I** *n* **1** [C/U] (*likelihood*) 可能 **2** [S] (*thought*) 期望 **II** *vi* ♦**to prospect (for sth)** [+ *gold, oil, minerals*] 勘探(某物) **III prospects** *n* [*pl*] (*for work, marriage*) 前景
prospective [prə'spɛktɪv] *adj* [+ *husband, employer, buyer etc*] 可能的
prospectus [prə'spɛktəs] *n* [C] **1** [*of university, school*] 简介 **2** [*of company*] 计划书
prosper ['prɔspə(r)] [正式] *vi* [*person, business, city* +] 兴隆
prosperity [prɔ'spɛrɪtɪ] *n* [U] 繁荣
prosperous ['prɔspərəs] *adj* [+ *person, business, city*] 繁荣的
prostitute ['prɔstɪtjuːt] **I** *n* [C] (*female*) 妓女 **II** *vt* ♦**to prostitute o.s./one's talents** (喻)作践自己/自己的才华 ♦**a male prostitute** 男妓
protect [prə'tɛkt] *vt* [+ *person, floor, rights, freedom*] 保护 ♦**to protect sb/sth from** *or* **against sth** 保护某人/某物不受某物的伤害 ♦**to protect o.s. from** *or* **against sth** 保护自己不受某物的伤害
protection [prə'tɛkʃən] *n* **1** [C/U] ♦**protection (from** *or* **against sth)** [*of person, floor, plant*] (免受某物侵害的)保护 **2** [U] [*of rights, freedom, interests*] 保护 **3** [U] [保险] ♦**protection (against sth)** (防止某事的)保险 ♦**to be offered police protection** 被提供了警方保护的
protective [prə'tɛktɪv] *adj* **1** [+ *clothing, layer*] 保护性的 **2** [+ *person*] 给予保护的 ♦**protective custody** [法] 保护性拘留
protein ['prəutiːn] *n* [C/U] 蛋白质
protest [*n* 'prəutɛst, *vb* prə'tɛst] **I** *n* [C/U] 抗议 **II** *vi* ♦**to protest about/against/at sth** [英] 抗议某事 **III** *vt*

1 (*claim*) 申辩 2 [美] (*voice opposition to*) 示威 ♦ **to protest that ...** 坚决声明…

Protestant ['prɔtɪstənt] **I** *n* [c] 新教徒 **II** *adj* 新教的

protester [prə'tɛstə(r)] *n* [c] 抗议者

protractor [prə'træktə(r)] *n* [c] 量角器

proud [praud] *adj* 1 [+ *parents, owner*] 自豪的 2 (*arrogant*) 骄傲的 3 (*dignified*) [+ *person, people*] 自尊心强的 ♦ **to be proud of sb/sth** 为某人/某事感到自豪 ♦ **to be proud to do sth** 以做某事为荣 ♦ **to be proud that ...** 为…感到自豪 ♦ **to do sb proud** [非正式] 盛情款待某人

prove [pruːv] **I** *vt* [+ *idea, theory*] 证明 **II** *vi* ♦ **to prove (to be) correct** *etc* 证明是对的{等} ♦ **to prove that ...** [*person* +] 证明…; [*situation, experiment, calculations* +] 显示… ♦ **to prove sb right/wrong** 证明某人是对的/错的 ♦ **to prove o.s. (to be) useful** *etc* 证明自己是有用的{等}

proverb ['prɔvəːb] *n* [c] 谚语

✪ **provide** [prə'vaɪd] *vt* 1 [+ *food, money, shelter*] 供应; [+ *answer, opportunity, details*] 提供 2 ♦ **to provide that ...** [*law, agreement* +] 规定… ♦ **to provide sb with sth** [+ *food, job, resources*] 提供某人某物 ♦ **to be provided with** [+ *person*] 具有; [+ *thing*] 有

❑ **provide for** *vt* [不可拆分] 1 [+ *person*] 供养 2 [+ *future event*] 提前准备 ♦ **to be well provided for** 保障生活无忧的 ♦ **to provide for sth (to happen)** [*law, agreement* +] 规定某事(发生)

provided (that) [prə'vaɪdɪd-] *conj* 假如

providing [prə'vaɪdɪŋ] *conj* ♦ **providing (that)** 假如

province ['prɔvɪns] **I** *n* 1 [c] [*of country*] 省 2 [s] (*area of responsibility etc*) [*of person*] 本分 **II the provinces** *n* [*pl*] 首都以外的地方

provincial [prə'vɪnʃəl] *adj* 1 [+ *town, newspaper etc*] 省的 2 (*unsophisticated*) 偏狭的

provision [prə'vɪʒən] **I** *n* 1 [u] [*of service*] 供应 2 [c/u] (*arrangement*) (*for potential need*) 准备 3 [c] (*stipulation*) (*in contract, agreement*) 规定 **II provisions** *n* [*pl*] (*food*) 食物 ♦ **to make provision for** [+ *sb's future, family*] 为…做准备; [+ *security, defences*] 为…做好安排

provisional [prə'vɪʒənl] *adj* [+ *government, agreement, arrangement etc*] 临时的

provocative [prə'vɔkətɪv] *adj* 1 [+ *remark, article, behaviour, action*] 挑衅的 2 (*sexually*) [+ *clothing, behaviour, gesture*] 挑逗的

provoke [prə'vəuk] *vt* 1 (*annoy*) [+ *person*] 激怒 2 (*cause*) [+ *fight, reaction, anger*] 挑起 ♦ **to provoke sb into doing sth** 刺激某人做某事

prowl [praul] **I** *vi* [*animal, person* +] 潜行 **II** *n* 1 (字) ♦ **to be on the prowl** [*animal* +] 潜行觅食 2 (喻) ♦ **to be on the prowl (for sth)** [*person* +] 来回寻觅(某物)

proximity [prɔk'sɪmɪtɪ] *n* [u] ♦ **proximity (to sth/sb)** 邻近(某物/某人)

proxy ['prɔksɪ] *n* ♦ **by proxy** 由代理人

prudent ['pruːdnt] *adj* 慎重的

prudently ['pruːdntlɪ] *adv* [*act, behave* +] 谨慎地

prune [pruːn] **I** *n* [c] 梅干 **II** *vt* [+ *bush, plant, tree*] 修剪

pry [praɪ] *vi* ♦ **to pry (into sth)** 刺探(某事) ♦ **safe from prying eyes** 躲开窥视的眼睛

PS *abbr* (= ***postscript***) 附言

pseudonym ['sjuːdənɪm] *n* [c] 笔名 ♦ **under a pseudonym** 以笔名

PST [美] *abbr* (= ***Pacific Standard Time***) 太平洋标准时间

psychiatric [saɪkɪ'ætrɪk] *adj* 精神病学的

psychiatrist [saɪ'kaɪətrɪst] *n* [c] 精神病医生

psychic ['saɪkɪk] *adj* [+ *person, powers*] 特异功能的 ♦ **I'm not psychic!** 我没有特异功能!

psychoanalysis [saɪkəuə'nælɪsɪs] *n* [u] 精神分析学

psychoanalyst [saɪkəu'ænəlɪst] *n* [c] 精神分析学家

psychological [saɪkə'lɔdʒɪkl] *adj* **1** (*mental*) [+ *effect, problem, disorder*] 心理的 **2** (*relating to psychology*) [+ *test, treatment*] 心理学的
psychologist [saɪ'kɔlədʒɪst] *n* [c] 心理学家
psychology [saɪ'kɔlədʒɪ] *n* **1** [u] (*science*) 心理学 **2** [c/u] (*character*) 心理
psychotherapist [saɪkəu'θɛrəpɪst] *n* [c] 精神治疗师
psychotherapy [saɪkəu'θɛrəpɪ] *n* [u] 心理疗法
PTO *abbr* (= ***please turn over***) 请翻过来
pub [pʌb] [英] *n* [c] 酒吧
puberty ['pjuːbətɪ] *n* [u] 青春期
✪ **public** ['pʌblɪk] **I** *adj* **1** (*from people*) [+ *support, opinion, interest*] 公众的 **2** (*for people*) [+ *building, service, library*] 公共的 **3** (*not private*) [+ *announcement, meeting*] 公开的; [+ *figure, life*] 社会的 **4** (*state*) [+ *funding, spending, service*] 国家的 **II** *n* [s + PL VB] **1** ♦ **the (general) public** 民众 **2** (*audience, fans*) ♦ **sb's public** 某人的支持公众 ♦ **it's public knowledge** 众所周知 ♦ **in/out of the public eye** 常/不常在公开场合露面的 ♦ **to make sth public** 将某事公布于世 ♦ **to become public** 变得公开的 ♦ **to go public** [商] 上市 ♦ **in public** [*speak, smoke, drink* +] 公开地
publication [pʌblɪ'keɪʃən] *n* **1** [u] [*of book, magazine, article*] 出版 **2** [c] (*book, magazine*) 刊物
public company *n* [c] 上市公司
public convenience [英: 正式] *n* [c] 公共厕所
public holiday *n* [c] 法定假期
public house [英] *n* = **pub**
publicity [pʌb'lɪsɪtɪ] *n* [u] **1** (*information, advertising*) 宣传 **2** (*attention*) 关注
publicize ['pʌblɪsaɪz] *vt* [+ *fact, event, book*] 宣传
public limited company *n* [c] 上市有限公司
publicly ['pʌblɪklɪ] *adv* **1** [*say, announce, deny* +] 公开地 **2** (*state*) [+ *owned, run, funded*] 由公众
public opinion *n* [u] 舆论
public relations *n* [*pl*] [u] 公共关系 ♦ **a public relations exercise** 公关演习
public school *n* [c/u] **1** [英] (*private school*) 私立中学 **2** [美] (*state school*) 公立学校
public transport *n* [u] 公共交通
publish ['pʌblɪʃ] *vt* **1** [*company* +] [+ *book, magazine*] 出版 **2** [*newspaper, magazine* +] [+ *letter, article*] 刊登 **3** [*writer* +] [+ *article, story*] 发表
publisher ['pʌblɪʃə(r)] *n* [c] **1** (*person*) 出版商 **2** (*company*) 出版社
publishing ['pʌblɪʃɪŋ] *n* [u] 出版
pub lunch [英] *n* [c] 由酒吧提供的午餐
pudding ['pudɪŋ] *n* **1** [c/u] (*type of dessert*) 布丁 **2** [c/u] [英] (*dessert in general*) 甜点 ♦ **rice pudding** 米饭布丁 ♦ **black pudding,** (美) **blood pudding** 黑血肠
puddle ['pʌdl] *n* [c] **1** [*of rain*] 水坑 **2** [*of blood, oil*] 滩
Puerto Rico ['pwəːtəu'riːkəu] *n* 波多黎各
puff [pʌf] **I** *n* [c] **1** (*on cigarette, pipe*) ♦ **to take a puff** 吸一口 **2** (*gasp*) 喘息 **II** *vi* **1** (*pant*) 喘气 **2** ♦ **to puff on** *or* **at sth** [+ *cigarette, pipe*] 吸某物 ♦ **a puff of wind/air/smoke** 一阵风/空气/烟
❑ **puff out** *vt* [+ *one's chest, cheeks*] 鼓起
puff pastry *n* [u] 松饼
pull [pul] **I** *vt* **1** [+ *rope, hair*] 拖; [+ *handle, door, cart, carriage*] 拉 **2** (*draw*) [+ *curtain, blind*] 拉 **3** (*squeeze*) [+ *trigger*] 扣 **4** [非正式] (*attract*) [+ *people*] 吸引; [+ *sexual partner*] 勾引 **5** [+ *pint of beer*] 灌 **II** *vi* 猛拉 **III** *n* **1** [c] (*tug*) ♦ **to give sth a pull** 拉一下某物 **2** [s] [*of moon, magnet, current*] 牵引力 **3** [s] (喻) [+ *of homeland, past*] 吸引力 ♦ **to pull sth free/out of sth** [+ *arm, hand, foot*] 将某物从某物中抽出来 ◊ *She pulled her feet out of the wet boots.* 她把脚从湿靴子中抽了出来。 ♦ **to pull a muscle** 扭伤肌肉 ♦ **to pull a face** 夸张地做表情 ♦ **to pull sth to pieces** (*criticize*) 将某事批得体无完肤 ♦ **to pull o.s.**

together 振作起来 ♦ **to pull sb's leg**（喻）开某人的玩笑 ♦ **to pull strings (for sb)**（为某人）暗中操作

❏**pull apart** *vt* **1** (*separate*) [+ *fighters*] 拉开 **2** (*destroy*) 扯坏

❏**pull away** *vi* **1** [*vehicle, driver* +] 驰离 **2** [*person* +] (*from sb*) 疏远

❏**pull back** *vi* **1** (*retreat*) [*troops* +] 撤退 **2** (*change mind*) ♦ **to pull back (from sth/from doing sth)** 中止（某事/做某事）

❏**pull down** *vt* [+ *building*] 拆毁

❏**pull in** **I** *vi* **1** (*at the kerb*) 停了下来 **2** [*train* +] 到站 **II** *vt* **1** [非正式] [+ *money*] 赚 **2** [+ *crowds, people*] 吸引 **3** [*police* +] ♦ **to pull sb in (for sth/for doing sth)**（为某事/做某事）拘捕某人

❏**pull into** *vt* [不可拆分] [*driver, vehicle* +] [+ *road, drive*] 拐入

❏**pull off** *vt* **1** (*take off*) [+ *clothes*] 脱下 **2**（喻）[+ *plan, deal, trick, victory*] 实现 ♦ **to pull it off** 成功

❏**pull out** **I** *vi* **1** [汽车] (*from kerb*) 开出; (*when overtaking*) 超车 **2** [*train* +] 离站 **3** (*withdraw*) (*from agreement, contest*) 退出; [*troops* +] 撤离 **II** *vt* (*extract*) [+ *file, information*] 调出

❏**pull over** **I** *vi* 靠边停下 **II** *vt* ♦ **the police pulled him over** 警察叫他停车

❏**pull through** *vi* (*from illness*) 恢复健康; (*from difficulties*) 渡过难关

❏**pull together** *vi* 同心协力

❏**pull up** **I** *vi* (*stop*) [*driver, vehicle* +] 停下 **II** *vt* **1** (*raise*) [+ *socks, trousers*] 拉起 **2** (*uproot*) [+ *plant, weed*] 拔除 ♦ **to pull up a chair** 拖把椅子过来

pulley [ˈpulɪ] *n* [c] 滑轮

pull-off [ˈpulɔf] [美] *n* [c] 路侧停车处 [英 = **lay-by**]

pullover [ˈpuləuvə(r)] *n* [c] 套头衫

pulp [pʌlp] **I** *n* [u] **1** [*of fruit*] (*inside*) 果肉; (*crushed*) 浆 **2** (*for paper*) 浆 **II** *adj* [贬] [+ *magazine, novel*] 低劣的 **III** *vt* [+ *paper, documents*] 销毁 ♦ **to beat sb to a pulp** 把某人打得遍体鳞伤

pulp fiction *n* [c] 低俗小说

pulpit [ˈpulpɪt] *n* [c] 讲坛

pulse [pʌls] **I** *n* [c] **1** [解剖] 脉搏 **2** (*rhythm*) 节奏 **3** [术语] 脉冲 **II** *vi* 有节奏地跳动 **III** **pulses** *n* [*pl*] [烹饪] 豆子 ♦ **to take** *or* **feel sb's pulse** 给某人诊脉 ♦ **to have one's finger on the pulse (of sth)** 了解（某物）最新动态

puma [ˈpjuːmə] *n* [c] (*mountain lion*) 美洲狮

pump [pʌmp] **I** *n* [c] **1** (*for liquid, gas*) 泵 **2** (*for getting water*) 抽水机 **3** (*for inflating sth*) 打气筒 **4** [尤英] (*shoe*) 浅口无带皮鞋 **II** *vt* **1** (*move*) ♦ **to pump sth into/out of/up from sth** [+ *liquid, gas*] 把某物从某物抽入/抽出/抽上去 **2** (*obtain*) [+ *oil, water, gas*] 用泵抽 ♦ **water/petrol pump** 水/油泵 ♦ **to pump money into sth** [非正式] 不断把钱投入某事 ♦ **to have one's stomach pumped** 洗胃 ♦ **to pump sb for information** [非正式] 从某人处探出消息

❏**pump out** *vt* (*supply*) 源源不断供应

❏**pump up** *vt* (*inflate*) 打气

pumpkin [ˈpʌmpkɪn] *n* [c] 南瓜

pun [pʌn] *n* [c] 双关

punch [pʌntʃ] **I** *n* **1** [c] (*blow*) 拳打 **2** [u]（喻）(*force*) 力量 **3** [c] (*tool*) (*for making holes*) 打孔器 **4** [c/u] (*drink*) 混合饮料 **II** *vt* **1** (*hit*) 用拳打击 **2** [+ *button, keyboard*] 敲击 **3** (*make a hole in*) [+ *ticket, paper*] 在…上打孔 ♦ **he didn't pull his** *or* **any punches** 他直言不讳 ♦ **to punch sb on the nose/in the eye** 拳打某人的鼻子/眼睛 ♦ **to punch a hole in sth** 在某物上打孔

❏**punch in** *vt* 敲入

❏**punch out** [美] *vt* (*hit*) 拳打

punchline [ˈpʌntʃlaɪn] *n* [c] 妙语

punch-up [ˈpʌntʃʌp] [英：非正式] *n* [c] 打架

punctual [ˈpʌŋktjuəl] *adj* 准时的

punctuation [pʌŋktjuˈeɪʃən] *n* [u] 标点

puncture [ˈpʌŋktʃə(r)] **I** *n* [c] 刺孔 **II** *vt* [+ *tyre, lung*] 戳破 ♦ **to have a puncture** 轮胎被扎破了

pundit [ˈpʌndɪt] *n* [c] 专家

punish [ˈpʌnɪʃ] *vt* **1** [+ *person*] 惩罚 **2** [+ *crime*] 处罚 ♦ **to punish sb for sth/for doing sth** 因某事/做某事而惩罚某人

punishment ['pʌnɪʃmənt] *n* **1** [U] 惩罚 **2** [C/U] (*penalty*) 处罚 ♦**to take a lot of punishment** (喻) [*car, machine, person, body* +] 受到很大损伤

punk [pʌŋk] *n* **1** [C] (*also:* ***punk rocker***) 朋克音乐的表演者/追随者 **2** [U] (*also:* ***punk rock***) 朋克摇滚乐 **3** [C] [美:非正式] (*hoodlum*) 小阿飞

punter ['pʌntə(r)] [英:非正式] *n* [C] **1** (*gambler*) 下赌注的人 **2** (*customer*) 顾客

pup [pʌp] *n* [C] **1** (*young dog*) 小狗 **2** [*of seal, otter*] 幼兽

pupil ['pjuːpl] *n* [C] **1** (*student*) 学生 **2** [*of eye*] 瞳孔

puppet ['pʌpɪt] *n* [C] **1** (*on strings*) 木偶 **2** (*also:* ***glove puppet***) 布袋式木偶 **3** (喻) (*person, government*) 傀儡

puppy ['pʌpɪ] *n* [C] 小狗

purchase ['pəːtʃɪs] [正式] **I** *vt* 购买 **II** *n* **1** [U] (*act of buying*) 购买 **2** [C] (*item bought*) 购买物 **3** (*grip*) ♦**to get** *or* **gain (a) purchase on sth** 牢牢抓住某物

pure [pjuə(r)] *adj* **1** [+ *silk, gold, wool*] 纯的 **2** (*clean*) [+ *water, air*] 纯净的 **3** (*chaste*) [+ *woman, girl*] 纯洁的 **4** (*theoretical*) [+ *maths, science, research*] 纯理论的 **5** (*complete*) [+ *coincidence, luck, joy, speculation*] 完全的 ♦**a pure wool jumper** 纯毛套衫 ♦**this is fraud, pure and simple** 这完完全全是欺诈

puree ['pjuəreɪ] *n* [C/U] 酱

purely ['pjuəlɪ] *adv* (*wholly*) 完全地

purify ['pjuərɪfaɪ] *vt* [+ *air, water, gold*] 净化

purity ['pjuərɪtɪ] *n* [U] **1** [*of air, water*] 纯净 **2** [*of woman, girl*] 纯洁

purple ['pəːpl] **I** *adj* 紫色的 **II** *n* [C/U] 紫色

purpose ['pəːpəs] *n* [C] **1** [*of person*] 目的 **2** [*of act, meeting, visit*] 意义 ♦**a sense of purpose** (*in life*) 意义感; (*in activity*) 目标感 ♦**for that purpose** 出于那种目的 ♦**for medicinal/propaganda** *etc* **purposes** 出于医疗/宣传{等}的目的 ♦**for all practical purposes, to all intents and purposes** 实际上 ♦**to little/no purpose** 徒劳无益的 ♦**on purpose** 故意地

purposeful ['pəːpəsful] *adj* [+ *person, look, gesture*] 坚定的

purr [pəː(r)] **I** *vi* **1** [*cat* +] 呜呜叫 **2** [*engine, car* +] 发出隆隆声 **3** [*person* +] 呢喃 **II** *n* [C] [*of cat*] 呜呜声; [*of engine, car*] 隆隆声

purse [pəːs] **I** *n* [C] **1** [英] (*for money*) 钱包 **2** [美] (*handbag*) 手袋 [英= **handbag**] **II** *vt* ♦**to purse one's lips** 撅起嘴

pursue [pə'sjuː] [正式] *vt* **1** (*follow*) [+ *person, car*] 追赶 **2** (*involve o.s. in*) [+ *activity, interest, policy, career*] 继续 **3** (*try to obtain*) [+ *aim, objective*] 追求 **4** (*follow up*) [+ *matter, claim*] 穷追不舍; [+ *topic, possibility, idea*] 探究

pursuit [pə'sjuːt] *n* **1** ♦**the pursuit of** [+ *happiness, pleasure, excellence*] 对…的追求 **2** [C] (*pastime*) 消遣 ♦**in pursuit of** [+ *happiness, pleasure*] 追求; [+ *person, car, animal*] 穷追 ♦**in hot pursuit** 紧紧追赶

pus [pʌs] *n* [U] 脓

push [puʃ] **I** *n* [C] **1** 推 **2** (*encouragement*) 鼓励 **II** *vt* **1** (*press*) [+ *button*] 按 **2** (*shove*) [+ *car, door, person*] 推 **3** (*put pressure on*) [+ *person*] 逼迫 **4** (*promote*) [+ *product, project*] 推销; [+ *case, argument*] 努力争取 **5** [非正式] (*sell*) [+ *drugs*] 贩卖 **III** *vi* **1** (*press*) 按 **2** (*shove*) 推 ♦**to give sth/sb a push** (*with hand*) 推了某物/某人一下 ♦**at the push of a button** 只要按一下按钮 ♦**at a push** [英:非正式] 紧急情况下 ♦**to push one's way through the crowd** 挤过人群 ♦**to push sth/sb out of the way** 把某物/某人推开 ♦**to push a door open/shut** 把门推开/上 ♦**"push"** (*on door*) "推" ♦**to push sb to do sth** 促使某人做某事 ♦**to push sb into doing sth** 迫使某人做某事 ♦**to push o.s. to the limit** 将自己推到极限 ♦**to be pushed for time/money** [非正式] 赶时间/缺钱 ♦**she's pushing fifty** [非正式] 她将近50岁了 ♦**to push forward/push through the crowd** 挤向/过人群
❑**push ahead** *vi* (*make progress*) ♦**to push ahead (with sth)** 推进

(某事)
❑**push around** [非正式] *vt* (*bully*) 摆布
❑**push aside** *vt* [+ *idea, thought*] 忽略
❑**push back** *vt* [+ *chair, hair*] 往后推
❑**push down** *vt* [+ *total, prices*] 降低
❑**push for** *vt* [不可拆分] 迫切要求
❑**push forward** = **push ahead**
❑**push in** *vi* (*in queue*) 插队
❑**push off** [非正式] *vi* (*leave*) 走开 ♦**push off!** 滚开！
❑**push on** *vi* (*continue*) ♦**to push on (with sth)** 加紧(做某事)
❑**push over** *vt* [+ *person, wall, furniture*] 推倒
❑**push through** *vt* [+ *measure, scheme*] 促成
❑**push up** *vt* [+ *total, prices*] 提高

pushchair ['puʃtʃɛə(r)] [英] *n* [c] 幼儿车 [美 = **stroller**]

pusher ['puʃə(r)] [非正式] *n* [c] (*drug dealer*) 毒品贩子

push-up ['puʃʌp] [美] *n* [c] 俯卧撑 ♦**to do push-ups** 做俯卧撑

pushy ['puʃɪ] [贬] *adj* (*assertive*) 好胜且好卖弄的

pussy ['pusɪ] *n* [c] [非正式] (*also: **pussycat***) 小猫咪

✪**put** [put] (*pt, pp* **put**) *vt* **1** (*place*) [+ *thing*] 放 ◊ *I put her suitcase on the table.* 我把她的手提箱放在桌上。; [+ *person*] (*in institution*) 安置 ◊ *They had to put him in an asylum.* 他们只得把他安置在收容所里。◊ *He'd been put in jail.* 他被投入了监牢。; [+ *confidence, trust, faith*] (*in person, thing*) 投入 ◊ *Are we right to put our confidence in computers?* 我们是否应该对计算机有信心？ **2** (*cause to be*) [+ *person, thing*] (*in state, situation*) 使处于 ◊ *It puts me in a rather difficult position.* 这使我处于一个非常为难的处境。 **3** (*express*) [+ *idea, remark*] 表述 ◊ *He didn't put it quite as crudely as that.* 他表述得并没那么拙劣。 **4** (*present*) ♦**to put sth (to sb)** [+ *case, view, suggestion*] (向某人)陈述某事 ◊ *He should have known how to put his case.* 他早该知道如何陈述他的情况。**5** (*classify*) 看作 ◊ *I wouldn't put him in the same class as Verdi.* 我没把他看作是与维迪一个级别的。**6** (*write, type*) [+ *word, information*] 写 ♦**to put a lot of time/energy/effort into sth/into doing sth** 投入大量的时间/精力/努力于某事/做某事 ♦**to put money on a horse** 赌马 ♦**to stay put** 留在原处 ♦**how shall I put it?** 我该怎么说呢？ ♦**let me put it this way** 让我这么说吧 ♦**to put a question (to sb)** (向某人)提问 ♦**I put it to you that ...** [英:正式] 我认为… ♦**the cost is now put at 20 million pounds** 现在成本估计为20亿英镑
❑**put about I** *vt* [英] [+ *rumour*] 散布 **II** *vi* [航海] 改变方向
❑**put across, put over** *vt* [+ *ideas, argument*] 讲清
❑**put aside** *vt* **1** [+ *work, object*] 放在一边 ◊ *My aunt put aside her sewing and picked up her book.* 我舅妈把针线活放在一边开始看书。**2** (*disregard*) [+ *idea, problem, remark*] 置之不理 ◊ *It's a problem which they usually put aside.* 这是他们通常置之不理的问题。**3** (*save*) [+ *sum of money*] 存 ◊ *She put aside a small sum every week to pay for her annual holiday.* 她每星期存一点钱用于每年的度假。
❑**put away** *vt* **1** (*store, unpack*) 把…收起 ◊ *I put away the shopping.* 我把买的东西收起来了。**2** [非正式] (*imprison*) 把…关起 ◊ *They put him away for ten years.* 他们把他关了10年。**3** (*save*) [+ *money*] 存 ◊ *I've got a thousand pounds put away for a rainy day.* 我存了1000镑以备不时之需。**4** [非正式] (*consume*) [+ *food, drink*] 吃喝掉
❑**put back** *vt* **1** (*replace*) 放回 ◊ *I put the book back on the shelf.* 我把书放回书架。**2** (*postpone*) 推迟 **3** (*delay*) 使延误 **4** [+ *watch, clock*] 倒拨
❑**put by** *vt* [+ *money, supplies*] 存储…备用
❑**put down** *vt* **1** (*on floor, table*) 放下 **2** (*in writing*) 写下 **3** [+ *money, deposit*] 支付 **4** (*quell*) [+ *riot, rebellion*] 镇压 **5** [非正式] (*humiliate*) [+ *person*] 羞辱 **6** (*put to sleep*) [+ *animal*] 宰杀

❑**put down to** *vt* (*attribute*) ♦**to put sth down to sth** 把某事归因于某事◊ *I put it down to arthritis.* 我把它归因于关节炎。

❑**put forward** *vt* **1** [+ *ideas, proposal, name*] 提出◊ *These were the arguments which Jenny put forward.* 这些是詹妮提出的论点。
2 [+ *watch, clock*] 向前拨

❑**put in I** *vt* **1** (*make*) [+ *request, complaint, application*] 提出
2 (*dedicate*) [+ *time, effort, work*] 投入
3 (*install*) [+ *gas, electricity, sink*] 安装
II *vi* [航海] ♦**to put in (at)** 进港

❑**put in for** *vt* [不可拆分] [+ *promotion, leave*] 申请

❑**put off** *vt* **1** [+ *event*] (*delay*) 推迟
2 [+ *person*] (*ask to wait*) 使等待◊ *They wanted to come this evening but I put them off until tomorrow.* 他们今晚想来，但我让他们等到明天。; [英] (*distract*) 使分心◊ *Every time Peter served, a man in the crowd coughed and put him off.* 每次轮到彼得时，人群中就有人咳嗽让他分心。; (*discourage*) 使失去兴趣◊ *His personal habits put her off.* 他的个人习惯使她失去了兴趣。 ♦**to put off doing sth** (*postpone*) 推迟做某事 ♦**to put sb off sth/sb** (*alienate from*) 使某人摆脱某事/某人 ♦**to put sb off doing sth** 使不再喜欢做某事

❑**put on** *vt* **1** [+ *clothes, make-up, glasses*] 穿戴 **2** (*switch on*) [+ *light, TV, radio, oven*] 开; [+ *CD, video*] 放; [+ *dinner*] 做; [+ *kettle*] 用…烧水
3 (*organize*) [+ *play, exhibition*] 举行; [+ *extra bus, train*] 安排 **4** (*adopt*) [+ *look, accent, act*] 假装 ♦**to put on weight/three kilos** *etc* 增重/增加了3公斤{等} ♦**you're putting it on** (*pretending*) 你是假装的

❑**put onto** *vt* ♦**to put sb onto sb/sth** 向某人引荐某人/某物

❑**put out I** *vt* **1** (*extinguish*) [+ *candle, cigarette*] 熄灭; [+ *fire, blaze*] 扑灭 **2** (*switch off*) [+ *electric light*] 关 **3** (*lay out*) 摆放 **4** (*take outside*) [+ *rubbish, cat*] 放出 **5** [+ *one's hand*] (*to greet, touch, for help, protection*) 伸出 **6** (*make public*) [+ *story, statement*] 公布 **7** [英] (*dislocate*) [+ *back, shoulder*] 使…脱臼 **8** [非正式] (*inconvenience*) [+ *person*] 麻烦 **II** *vi* [航海] ♦**to put out to sea** 出海 ♦**to put out from Plymouth** 从普利茅斯启航 ♦**to put out one's tongue** 伸出舌头 ♦**to put o.s. out** 难为自己

❑**put over** *vt* = **put across**

❑**put through** *vt* **1** [通信] [+ *person, phone call*] 接通◊ *"Data Room, please." – "I'll put you through."* "请接资料室。" "我给你接通。"
2 (*cause to experience*) ♦**to put sb through sth** 使某人经受某事
3 (*carry out*) [+ *plan, agreement*] 完成 ♦**put me through to Miss Blair** 请帮我接布莱尔小姐

❑**put together** *vt* [+ *furniture, machine*] 装配; [+ *team, collection*] 组成; [+ *plan, campaign*] 组织 ♦**more than the rest of them put together** 比其他所有人的总和都多

❑**put up** *vt* **1** [+ *fence, building, tent*] 建造; [+ *poster, sign*] 张贴
2 [+ *umbrella, hood*] 撑起 **3** (*provide*) [+ *money*] 提供 **4** (*increase*) [+ *price, cost*] 增加 **5** (*accommodate*) 为…提供住宿 ♦**to put up one's hand** 举手 ♦**to put up resistance/a fight** 进行抵抗/战斗 ♦**to put sb up to sth/to doing sth** (*incite*) 唆使某人做某事 ♦**to put sth up for sale** 出售某物

❑**put upon** *vt* [不可拆分] ♦**to be put upon** 被利用

❑**put up with** *vt* [不可拆分] 容忍

putt [pʌt] **I** *vt* 轻击 **II** *n* [c] 轻击

putting green ['pʌtɪŋ-] *n* [c] 高尔夫球场中球洞草坪区

puzzle ['pʌzl] **I** *n* **1** [c] (*for entertainment*) (*riddle, conundrum*) 谜; (*game*) 测智游戏; (*toy*) 测智玩具
2 [s] (*mystery*) 谜团 **II** *vt* (*baffle*) 使困惑 **III** *vi* ♦**to puzzle over sth** 对某事冥思苦想

puzzled ['pʌzld] *adj* [+ *person, expression, frown*] 茫然的 ♦**to be puzzled by** *or* **about sth** 对某事感到困惑 ♦**to be puzzled as to why ...** 对于为什么…感到困惑

puzzling ['pʌzlɪŋ] *adj* [+ *statement, action, behaviour*] 令人困惑的

PVC *n abbr* (= ***polyvinyl chloride***) 聚氯乙烯

PW [美] *n abbr* = **POW**

pyjamas (美 **pajamas**) [pə'dʒɑːməz] *n* [*pl*] 睡衣裤 ♦ **a pair of pyjamas** 一套睡衣裤

pylon ['paɪlən] *n* [c] 电缆塔

pyramid ['pɪrəmɪd] *n* [c]
1 (*monument*) 金字塔 **2** [几何] 锥体
3 (*pile*) [*of objects*] 一堆

Qq

Q, q [kjuː] *n* [C/U] (*letter*) 英语的第十七个字母
QC [英:法] *n abbr* (= ***Queen's Counsel***) 皇室法律顾问
quack [kwæk] **I** *n* [C] **1** [*of duck*] 嘎嘎声 **2** [非正式, 贬] (*doctor*) 庸医 **II** *vi* 嘎嘎叫 **III** *adj* [非正式, 贬] [+ *remedy*] 冒牌的
quad [kwɔd] *n* **1** (*quadrangle*) 四边形 **2** (*quadruplet*) ♦**quads** 四胞胎
quadruple [kwɔ'druːpl] **I** *vt* 使成四倍 **II** *vi* 成四倍
quail [kweɪl] **I** *n* [C] (*bird*) 鹌鹑 **II** *vi* [文] ♦**to quail (at sth)** (对某事)感到不寒而栗
quaint [kweɪnt] *adj* **1** [+ *house, village*] 古雅的 **2** [+ *ideas, customs, times*] 离奇的
quake [kweɪk] **I** *vi* (*tremble*) 战栗 **II** *n* [C] [非正式] (*also:* ***earthquake***) 地震
qualification [kwɔlɪfɪ'keɪʃən] *n* **1** [C] (*degree, diploma etc*) 资格证明; (*skill*) 素质 **2** [C/U] (*reservation*) 条件 **3** [U] (*graduation*) 取得资格
qualified ['kwɔlɪfaɪd] *adj* **1** (*trained*) [+ *doctor, teacher, nurse etc*] 合格的 **2** (*limited*) [+ *support, praise*] 有保留的 ♦**fully qualified** 完全合格的 ♦**he's not qualified for the job** 他不胜任这项工作 ♦**to be/feel qualified to do sth** (*fit, competent*) 有/感到有资格做某事 ♦**it was a qualified success** 这是一次有限的胜利
qualify ['kwɔlɪfaɪ] **I** *vi* **1** (*pass examination(s)*) 取得资格 **2** (*in competition*) 具备资格 **3** ♦**to qualify for sth** (*be eligible for*) 符合某事的条件 **II** *vt* **1** ♦**to qualify sb for sth/to do sth** 使某人对某事/做某事有资格 **2** (*modify*) [+ *statement*] 缓和 ♦**to qualify as an engineer/a nurse** *etc* 取得工程师/护士{等}的资格
quality ['kwɔlɪtɪ] **I** *n* **1** [U] (*standard*) [*of work, product*] 质量 **2** [C] (*characteristic*) [*of person*] 素质; [*of wood, stone etc*] 特质 **II** *adj* [+ *goods, product, service*] 优质的 ♦**of good/poor quality** 质量好/坏的 ♦**quality of life** 生活质量 ♦**quality time** 休闲时光
qualm [kwɑːm] *n* [C] 疑虑 ♦**to have no qualms about doing sth** 对于做某事毫无疑虑
quantify ['kwɔntɪfaɪ] *vt* 量化
quantity ['kwɔntɪtɪ] *n* **1** [C/U] (*amount*) 数量 **2** [U] (*volume*) 容量 ♦**in large/small quantities** 大/少量 ♦**in quantity** (*in bulk*) 大批量
quarantine ['kwɔrəntiːn] *n* [U] 检疫 ♦**in quarantine** 被隔离
quarrel ['kwɔrəl] **I** *n* [C] 吵架 **II** *vi* 争吵 ♦**to have a quarrel with sb** 跟某人争吵 ♦**I can't quarrel with that** 我对此无可争辩
quarry ['kwɔrɪ] **I** *n* **1** [C] (*for stone, minerals*) 采石场 **2** [S] (*prey*) 猎物 **II** *vt* [+ *stone, minerals*] 开采
quart [kwɔːt] [美] *n* [C] 夸脱
quarter ['kwɔːtə(r)] **I** *n* [C] **1** (*fourth part*) 四分之一 **2** (*three months*) 季度 **3** (*district*) 地区 **4** [美] (*coin*) 25 美分硬币 **II** *vt* **1** (*cut into four*) 把…切成4片 **2** (*divide by four*) 把…4等分 **3** ♦**to be quartered** (*accommodated*) 被安置 **III** *adj* 四分之一的 **IV quarters** *n* [C] *pl* 宿舍 ♦**to cut/divide sth into quarters** 把某物切/分为4份 ♦**a quarter of an hour** 一刻钟 ♦**it's a quarter to three** *or* [美] **of three** 现在是三点差一刻 ♦**it's a quarter past three** *or* [美] **after three** 现在是三点一刻 ♦**at close quarters** 近距离地
quarter-final ['kwɔːtə'faɪnl] *n* [C] 四分之一决赛
quarterly ['kwɔːtəlɪ] **I** *adj* [+ *meeting, payment, report*] 季度的 **II** *adv* [*meet, pay* +] 季度地 **III** *n* [C] (*magazine*) 季刊
quarter-pounder ['kwɔːtə'paʊndə(r)] *n* [C] 四分之一磅重的大汉堡

quartet [kwɔː'tɛt] *n* [c] **1** (*group*) 四人表演组合 **2** (*piece of music*) 四声部曲

quartz [kwɔːts] **I** *n* [u] 石英 **II** *cpd* [复合词] [+ *watch, clock*] 石英

quay [kiː] *n* [c] 码头

queasy ['kwiːzɪ] [非正式] *adj* (*nauseous*) ♦ **to feel queasy** 感到恶心

queen [kwiːn] *n* [c] **1** (*monarch*) 女王 **2** (*king's wife*) 王后 **3** ♦ **the queen of crime fiction** 犯罪小说之冠 **4** [动] 雌后 **5** [非正式, 讳] (*homosexual*) 男同性恋者 **6** [纸牌] 皇后 **7** [国际象棋] 王后 ♦ **Queen Victoria** 维多利亚女王 ♦ **the queen of hearts/spades** 红桃/黑桃皇后

Queen Mother *n* ♦ **the Queen Mother** 太后

queer [kwɪə(r)] **I** *adj* **1** [过时] (*odd*) [+ *feeling, story, place*] 奇怪的 **2** [非正式, 讳] (*homosexual*) 同性恋的 **II** *n* [c] [非正式, 讳] (*homosexual*) 同性恋者

quell [kwɛl] *vt* [+ *riot*] 镇压; [+ *unease, fears*] 消除

quench [kwɛntʃ] *vt* ♦ **to quench one's thirst** 解渴

query ['kwɪərɪ] **I** *n* [c] (*question*) 疑问 **II** *vt* **1** (*check*) [+ *figures, bill, expenses etc*] 询问 **2** (*ask*) ♦ **to query whether/why/what** *etc* 询问是否/为何/什么{等}

quest [kwɛst] *n* [c] ♦ **quest (for sth)** (对某物的)探寻

✪ **question** ['kwɛstʃən] **I** *n* **1** [c] (*query*) 问题 ◊ *A panel of experts attempted to answer our questions.* 专家组试图回答我们的问题。 **2** [u] (*doubt*) 疑问 ◊ *There was no question about the diagnosis: she had lung cancer.* 诊断结果已经没有疑问：她患了肺癌。 **3** [c] (*issue*) 议题 ◊ *the nuclear power question* 核能源议题 **4** [c] (*in written exam*) 试题 ◊ *You have to answer four questions in two hours.* 你得在两小时内回答四道题。 **II** *vt* **1** (*interrogate*) 盘问 ◊ *A man is being questioned by police in connection with the attack.* 一名与该袭击有关的男子正受到警方盘问。 **2** (*doubt*) 怀疑 ◊ *It never occurs to them to question the doctor's decisions.* 他们从未想过要怀疑医生的决定。 ♦ **to ask sb a question, to put a question to sb** 问某人一个问题，向某人提出问题 ♦ **to be in question** 出问题的 ♦ **to bring** *or* **call sth into question** 对某事提出质疑 ♦ **to be open to question** 令人怀疑的 ♦ **to be beyond question** 不成问题的 ♦ **without question** (*unquestioningly*) 毫无异议; (*without doubt*) 毫无疑问 ♦ **the question is ...** 问题是… ♦ **there's no question of a compromise/them agreeing** 妥协/他们同意是不可能的 ♦ **to be out of the question** 不可能的 ♦ **the person/night in question** 谈及的人/夜晚 ♦ **to question whether ...** 询问是否…

questionable ['kwɛstʃənəbl] *adj* [+ *value, quality*] 可疑的; [+ *taste*] 成问题的; [+ *motive, behaviour, practice*] 靠不住的; [+ *decision*] 不确定的 ♦ **it is questionable whether ...** 是否…还不确定

question mark *n* [c] 问号

questionnaire [kwɛstʃə'nɛə(r)] *n* [c] 问卷

queue [kjuː] [尤英] **I** *n* [c] 队 [美 = line] **II** *vi* (*also:* ***queue up***) 排队 [美 = line up] ♦ **to jump the queue** 加塞儿 ♦ **to queue for sth** 为某事排队 ♦ **to be queueing up for sth/to do sth** (喻) 为某事/做某事排队等候

quiche [kiːʃ] *n* [c/u] 什锦烘饼

✪ **quick** [kwɪk] **I** *adj* **1** (*fast*) [+ *person, movement etc*] 快的 ◊ *You'll have to be quick. The flight leaves in about three hours.* 你得快点。航班大约3小时后起飞。 ◊ *He was a very quick learner.* 他学东西很快。 **2** (*sharp*) [+ *mind, wit*] 敏捷的 **3** (*brief*) [+ *look*] 快速的; [+ *visit*] 短时间的 **4** (*swift*) [+ *reply, response, decision*] 迅速的 ◊ *a quick end to the war* 战争的迅速收场 **II** *adv* [非正式] (*quickly*) 快地 ◊ *Come quick!* 快点来！ ♦ **be quick!** 快点！ ♦ **to be quick to do sth** 立马做某事 ♦ **to have a quick temper** 脾气急躁

quicken ['kwɪkən] **I** *vt* [+ *pace, step*] 加快 **II** *vi* [*pace, step, pulse* +] 加速

quickly ['kwɪklɪ] *adv* **1** (*at speed*) [*walk, grow, speak, work* +] 快地 **2** (*swiftly*) [*realize, change, react, finish* +] 迅速地; [*die* +] 快速地

quick-witted [kwɪk'wɪtɪd] *adj* 机敏的

quid [kwɪd] (*pl* **quid**) [英:非正式] *n* [c] 1 英镑

quiet ['kwaɪət] **I** *adj* **1** (*not noisy*) [+ *voice, music*] 悄声的; [+ *engine, aircraft*] 无噪音的; [+ *place*] 安静的 **2** (*tranquil*) [+ *place, situation, time*] 宁静的 **3** (*reserved*) [+ *person*] 平静的 **4** (*silent*) ♦ **to be quiet** [*person* +] 沉默的 **5** (*not busy*) [+ *business, day*] 冷清的 **6** (*discreet*) [+ *wedding, celebration*] 私下的 **II** *n* [u] **1** (*peacefulness*) 宁静 **2** (*silence*) 安静 **III** *vt* **1** [美] (*silence*) 使安静 [英 = **quieten**] **2** [美] (*calm*) [+ *fears*] 安抚 **IV** *vi* [美] 沉静下来 [英 = **quieten**] ♦ **be quiet!** 请安静！♦ **to go quiet** 哑口无言 ♦ **to keep quiet about sth/keep sth quiet** 保守某事的秘密/将某事保密 ♦ **I'll have a quiet word with him** 我要私下跟他谈谈 ♦ **on the quiet** 私下里

quieten ['kwaɪətn] [英] (*also:* ***quieten down***) **I** *vi* **1** (*grow calm*) 平静下来 **2** (*grow silent*) 安静下来 [美 = **quiet**] **II** *vt* [+ *person, animal*] 使…安静 [美 = **quiet**]

quietly ['kwaɪətlɪ] *adv* **1** [*speak, play* +] 安静地 **2** (*silently*) 默默地 **3** (*calmly*) 平静地 ♦ **quietly confident** 沉稳自信

quilt [kwɪlt] *n* [c] **1** (*covering*) 被子 **2** [英] (*duvet*) 羽绒被

quirk [kwəːk] *n* [c] **1** (*idiosyncrasy*) 怪癖 **2** (*chance event*) 异常的事 ♦ **a quirk of fate** 命运难料

quirky ['kwəːkɪ] *adj* [+ *person, humour, film*] 怪诞的

quit [kwɪt] (*pt, pp* **quit** *or* **quitted**) **I** *vt* **1** [尤美] (*give up*) [+ *habit, activity*] 摆脱 **2** [非正式] (*leave*) [+ *job*] 辞去; [+ *place, premises*] 离开 **II** *vi* **1** (*give up*) 放弃 **2** (*resign*) 辞职 ♦ **to quit doing sth** 戒除做某事 ♦ **quit doing that!** [美:非正式] 别再干那个了！♦ **notice to quit** [英] 请辞报告

✪ **quite** [kwaɪt] *adv* **1** (*rather*) 相当 ◊ *He was quite young.* 他相当年轻。◊ *He calls quite often.* 他常常打电话。◊ *I quite like it.* 我相当喜欢它。**2** (*completely*) 十分 ◊ *I stood quite still.* 我十分安静地站着。◊ *I'm not quite sure.* 我不十分肯定。◊ *It's quite clear that this won't work.* 十分清楚的是，这方法不奏效。♦ **I see them quite a lot** 我常常见到他们 ♦ **it costs quite a lot to go to the States** 去美国相当贵 ♦ **quite a lot of money** 很多钱 ♦ **quite a few** 相当多 ♦ **it's not quite finished** 像是还没结束 ♦ **it's not quite the same** 不十分相同 ♦ **there aren't quite enough glasses** 杯子不太够 ♦ **I can't quite remember** 我不太记得了 ♦ **I didn't buy quite as many as last time** 我没买上次那么多 ♦ **I quite understand** 我相当明白 ♦ **quite (so)!** 的确（是这样）！♦ **it was quite a sight** 景色十分了得

> 📖 **quite** 可用在 **a** 或 **an** 之前，后接形容词加名词结构。例如，可以说 *It's quite an old car* 或者 *The car is quite old*，以及 *It was quite a warm day* 或者 *The day was quite warm*。如前例所示，**quite** 应放在不定冠词之前。例如，不能说 *It's a quite old car*。**quite** 可以用来修饰形容词和副词，而且程度比 **fairly** 更强烈，但是比 **very** 弱。**quite** 暗示某事物的某种特性超出预料。*Nobody here's ever heard of it but it is actually quite common.* 注意，不要混淆 **quite** 和 **quiet** 。

quits [kwɪts] *adj* ♦ **we're quits** 我们互不相欠了 ♦ **let's call it quits** 让我们就此罢手

quiver ['kwɪvə(r)] *vi* (*tremble*) [*lip, voice* +] 颤抖 ♦ **to quiver with fear/rage** 因恐惧/愤怒而颤抖

quiz [kwɪz] **I** *n* [c] (*game*) 测验 **II** *vt* [非正式] (*question*) 盘问

quota ['kwəʊtə] *n* [c] **1** (*allowance*) 定额 **2** (*share*) 配额

quotation [kwəʊ'teɪʃən] *n* [c] **1** (*from book, play, interview*) 引语 **2** (*estimate*) 报价

quotation marks *n* [*pl*] 引号 ♦ **in**

quotation marks 带引号

quote [kwəʊt] **I** *vt* **1** [+ *politician, author etc*] 引用;[+ *line*] 引述;[+ *reference number*] 援引;[+ *law, statistics*] 引证 **2** ♦ **to quote a price/figure for sth** 为某事物报出价格/数字 **II** *n* [c] **1** (*from book, play, interview, person*) 引语 **2** (*estimate*) 报价 **III quotes** *n* [*pl*] [非正式] (*quotation marks*) 引号 ♦ **to quote sb as saying that ...** 引用某人的话说… ♦ **in quotes** 在引号里

Rr

R[1], **r** [ɑː(r)] *n* [C/U] (*letter*) 英语的第十八个字母
R[2] [美:电影] *abbr* **1** (= ***restricted***) 17岁限制级 **2** [手机短信] = **are**
R. [美:政治] *abbr* = **republican**
R., r. *abbr* **1** (= ***river***) 河 **2** (= ***right***) 右边的
rabbi ['ræbaɪ] *n* [C] 拉比(犹太教教师或法学导师)
rabbit ['ræbɪt] **I** *n* **1** [C] (*animal*) 兔子 **2** [U] (*meat*) 兔肉 **II** *vi* [英:非正式] (*also:* ***to rabbit on***) 唠叨
rabies ['reɪbiːz] *n* [U] 狂犬病
raccoon [rə'kuːn] *n* [C] 浣熊
✪**race** [reɪs] **I** *n* **1** [C] (*speed contest*) 速度竞赛 **2** [C] (*for power, control*) 竞赛 **3** [C/U] (*ethnic group*) 种族 **II** *vi* **1** (*compete in races*) 参赛 **2** (*hurry*) 快速行进 **3** [*pulse, heart* +] 剧烈跳动; [*mind* +] 飞快地转 **4** [*engine* +] 快速运转 **III** *vt* **1** [+ *person*] 与…进行速度竞赛 **2** (*enter for races*) [+ *horse, dog*] 使参赛; [+ *car, boat*] 赛 ♦**a race against time** 抢时间 ♦**he raced across the road** 他快速穿过马路 ♦**to race in/out** 快速进/出
race car [美] *n* = **racing car**
racecourse ['reɪskɔːs] [英] *n* [C] 赛马场 [美 = **racetrack**]
racehorse ['reɪshɔːs] *n* [C] 赛马
racetrack ['reɪstræk] *n* [C] (*for cars*) 赛道; [美] (*for horses*) 赛马场 [英 = **racecourse**]
racial ['reɪʃl] *adj* [+ *discrimination, prejudice, equality*] 种族的
racing ['reɪsɪŋ] *n* [U] 比赛
racing car [英] *n* [C] 赛车
racing driver [英] *n* [C] 赛车手
racism ['reɪsɪzəm] *n* [U] 种族歧视
racist ['reɪsɪst]] **I** *adj* [+ *policy, attack, behaviour, idea*] 种族主义的; [+ *person, organization*] 有种族偏见的 **II** *n* 种族主义者
rack [ræk] **I** *n* [C] **1** (*also:* ***luggage rack***) 行李架 **2** [*for hanging clothes, dishes*] 架 **II** *vt* ♦**racked by** *or* **with** [+ *pain, anxiety, doubts*] 被/受折磨 ♦**magazine rack** 报刊架 ♦**to go to rack and ruin** [*building* +] 荒废; [*business, country* +] 衰败 ♦**to rack one's brains** 绞尽脑汁
racket ['rækɪt] *n* **1** [C] (*for tennis, squash etc*) 球拍 **2** [S] (*noise*) [非正式] 吵闹 **3** [C] (*swindle*) [非正式] 非法勾当
racquet ['rækɪt] *n* [C] 球拍
radar ['reɪdɑː(r)] **I** *n* [C/U] 雷达 **II** *cpd* [复合词] [+ *screen, antenna, system*] 雷达
radiant ['reɪdɪənt] *adj* **1** [+ *smile, person*] 容光焕发的 **2** [+ *object*] 光辉灿烂的 **3** [物] 辐射的
radiation [reɪdɪ'eɪʃən] *n* [U] **1** (*radioactivity*) 辐射 **2** (*radio waves*) 射线
radiator ['reɪdɪeɪtə(r)] *n* [C] **1** (*on wall*) 暖气片 **2** (*in car*) 散热器
radical ['rædɪkl] **I** *adj* **1** (*fundamental*) [+ *change, reform, disagreement*] 根本的 **2** [政治] [+ *person, organization, views*] 激进的 **II** *n* [C] [政治] (*person*) 激进分子
✪**radio** ['reɪdɪəu] **I** *n* **1** [C] (*receiver*) 收音机 **2** [C] (*two-way*) 无线电收发报机 **3** [U] (*broadcasting*) 广播 **4** [U] (*communication system*) 无线通讯 **II** *vi* 用无线电发送 **III** *vt* **1** (*contact by radio*) [+ *person*] 用无线电联系 **2** (*send by radio*) [+ *information, message*] 广播 ♦**on the radio** 广播中
radioactive ['reɪdɪəu'æktɪv] *adj* 放射性的
radioactive waste *n* [U] 放射性废物
radio-controlled ['reɪdɪəu-kən'trəuld] *adj* 无线电遥控的
radio station *n* [C] 广播电台
radish ['rædɪʃ] *n* [C] 萝卜
RAF [英] *n abbr* (= ***Royal Air Force***) ♦**the RAF** 皇家空军
raffle ['ræfl] **I** *n* [C] 对奖 **II** *vt* [+ *prize*] 抽中
raft [rɑːft] *n* [C] **1** (*also:* ***life raft***) 皮艇 **2** (*improvised*) 筏 ♦**a raft of** 大量
rag [ræg] **I** *n* **1** [C/U] (*piece of cloth*) 破

布 **2** [c] [非正式:贬] (*newspaper*) 小报 **II** *vt* [英] (*tease*) 戏弄 **III rags** *n* [*pl*] (*torn clothes*) 破旧衣服 ♦**in rags** 衣衫褴褛 ♦**a rags-to-riches story** 从赤贫到暴富的故事

rage [reɪdʒ] **I** *n* [c/u] (*fury*) 盛怒 **II** *vi* **1** [*person* +] 发怒 **2** [*storm* +] 肆虐; [*debate* +] 持续 ♦**it's all the rage** (*very fashionable*) 风靡一时 ♦**to fly into a rage** 勃然大怒

ragged ['rægɪd] *adj* **1** (*untidy*) [+ *clothes, person*] 破烂不堪的 **2** (*uneven*) [+ *edge, line*] 凸凹不平的

raid [reɪd] **I** *n* [c] [*by soldiers, police*] 突袭; (*by criminal*) 袭击 **II** *vt* [*soldiers, police* +] 突袭; [*criminal* +] 袭击

rail [reɪl] **I** *n* [c] **1** (*for safety*) (*on stairs*) 扶手; (*on bridge, balcony*) 横栏; (*on ship*) 栏杆 **2** (*for hanging clothes*) 横杆 **3** (*also:* ***curtain rail***) 窗帘横杆 **4** (*for trains*) 铁轨 **II** *cpd* [复合词] [+ *travel, transport, strike*] 铁路 ♦**by rail** (*by train*) 乘火车

railcard ['reɪlkɑːd] [英] *n* [c] 火车票优惠卡

railing(s) ['reɪlɪŋ(z)] *n* [*pl*] 围栏

railroad ['reɪlrəud] [美] *n* [c] = **railway**

railway ['reɪlweɪ] [英] *n* [c] **1** (*system*) 铁路 **2** (*line*) 铁道 **3** (*company*) 铁路公司

railway line [英] *n* [c] 铁路线

railway station [英] *n* [c] 火车站

rain [reɪn] **I** *n* [u] 雨 **II** *vi* **1** 下雨 ♦**in the rain** 在雨中 ♦**as right as rain** [非正式] 完全康复了 ♦**it's raining** 正在下雨 ♦**it's raining cats and dogs** 下着倾盆大雨 ♦**to be rained off** 因雨暂停

rainbow ['reɪnbəu] *n* [c] 彩虹

raincoat ['reɪnkəut] *n* [c] 雨衣

raindrop ['reɪndrɔp] *n* [c] 雨滴

rainfall ['reɪnfɔːl] *n* [c/u] 降雨量

rainforest ['reɪnfɔrɪst] *n* [c/u] 雨林

rainy ['reɪnɪ] *adj* [+ *day, night, area*] 多雨的 ♦**rainy season** 雨季 ♦**to save sth for a rainy day** 存储某物以备不时之需

✪**raise** [reɪz] **I** *vt* **1** (*lift*) [+ *hand, glass*] 举起; [+ *window*] 打开 **2** (*increase*) [+ *salary, rate, speed limit*] 增加; [+ *morale, standards*] 提高 **3** (*bring up*) [+ *subject, question, objection*] 提出; [+ *doubts, hopes*] 引起 **4** [+ *money, loan*] 筹集 **5** (*rear*) [+ *child, family*] 抚养; [+ *cattle, chickens*] 饲养; [+ *crop*] 种植 **6** (*end*) [+ *siege, embargo*] 解除 **II** *n* [c] [美] (*payrise*) 加薪 [英 = **rise**] ♦**to raise a glass to sb/sth** 为某人/某事举杯庆贺 ♦**to raise sb's hopes** 使某人满怀希望 ♦**to raise a smile/laugh** 引来微笑/大笑 ♦**to raise one's voice** 提高某人的声音

raisin ['reɪzn] *n* [c] 葡萄干

rake [reɪk] **I** *n* [c] **1** (*tool*) 耙 **2** [过时] (*person*) 花花公子 **II** *vt* **1** [+ *soil*] 耙 **2** [+ *leaves, lawn*] 耙拢 **3** [*light, gun* +] [+ *area*] 扫射 ♦**he's raking it in** [非正式] 他发大财了

rally ['rælɪ] **I** *n* [c] **1** (*public meeting*) 集会 **2** [汽车] 拉力赛 **3** [网球] 连续对打 **II** *vt* [+ *support*] 集合 **III** *vi* **1** (*unite*) 联合 **2** [*sick person* +] 康复 **3** [*Stock Exchange* +] 回升

❑**rally round I** *vi* 团结一致 **II** *vt* [不可拆分] 团结在…周围

RAM [ræm] [计算机] *n abbr* (= ***random access memory***) 随机存储器

ram [ræm] **I** *n* [c] (*sheep*) 公羊 **II** *vt* **1** (*crash into*) 撞击 **2** (*push*) [+ *bolt, fist etc*] 捅

ramble ['ræmbl] **I** *n* [c] (*walk*) 散步 **II** *vi* **1** (*hike*) 漫步 **2** (*also:* ***ramble on***) (*talk*) 闲扯

rambler ['ræmblə(r)] *n* [c] **1** [英] (*walker*) 漫步者 **2** [植] 攀缘植物

rambling ['ræmblɪŋ] **I** *n* [u] 散步 **II** *adj* **1** [+ *speech, letter*] 漫无边际的 **2** [+ *house*] 杂乱无章的 **3** [植] 攀缘的

ramp [ræmp] *n* [c] **1** [*for cars, wheelchairs etc, in garage*] 坡道 ♦**on/off ramp** [美:汽车] 上/下坡道

rampage [ræm'peɪdʒ] **I** *n* ♦**to go on the rampage** 横冲直撞 **II** *vi* 横冲直撞

ran [ræn] *pt of* **run**

ranch [rɑːntʃ] *n* [c] 牧场

rancid ['rænsɪd] *adj* 有腐臭的

R & D *n abbr* (= ***research and development***) 研究与开发

random ['rændəm] **I** *adj* **1** [+ *arrangement, selection*] 随机的 **2** (*haphazard*) 任意的 **II** *n* ♦**at**

random 随意

rang [ræŋ] *pt of* **ring**

range [reɪndʒ] **I** *n* [c] **1** [c] (*variety*) [*of ages, prices*] 范围; [*of subjects, possibilities*] 系列 **2** [商] (*selection*) 范围 **3** (*reach*) [*of missile, vision*] 射程 **4** (*also:* ***mountain range***) 山脉 **5** (*also:* ***kitchen range***) [英] 炉灶 **II** *vt* (*place in a line*) 排列 **III** *vi* ♦**to range over ...** [*writing, speech* +] 涉及… ♦**at close range** 近距离 ♦**price range** 价格范围 ♦**within (firing) range** 在(射击)距离内 ♦**out of range** 超出范围 ♦**to range from ... to ...** 在…到…之间 ♦**ranged right/left** [*text* +] 靠右/左对齐

ranger ['reɪndʒə(r)] *n* [c] 护林员

rank [ræŋk] **I** *n* **1** [c] (*row*) 行 **2** [c/u] (*status*) 等级 **3** [c/u] (*social class*) [正式] 阶层 **4** [c] [英] (*also:* ***taxi rank***) 出租车候客站 **II** *vi* ♦**to rank as ...** 被列为… **III** *vt* ♦**he is ranked third in the world** 他在世界上排名第三 **IV** *adj* **1** (*stinking*) 发臭的 **2** (*utter*) [+ *hypocrisy, stupidity etc*] 极度的 **V the ranks** *n* [*pl*] **1** [军] 士兵 **2** (*group*) 行列 ♦**the rank and file** (*ordinary members*) 普通成员 ♦**to rank among ...** 列入…当中 ♦**to close ranks** 紧密团结 ♦**to break ranks** 打破阶层

ransom ['rænsəm] *n* [c/u] (*money*) 赎金 ♦**to hold to ransom** [+ *hostage etc*] 勒取赎金; (喻) [+ *nation, company*] 要挟

rant [rænt] **I** *vi* 咆哮 **II** *n* [c] 咆哮 ♦**to rant and rave** 大嚷大叫

rap [ræp] **I** *vt* (*tap*) 敲打 **II** *vi* **1** (*tap*) 敲击 **2** (*perform rap song*) 说唱表演 **III** *n* **1** [c] (*tap*) 敲打声 **2** [u] (*also:* ***rap music***) 说唱音乐 ♦**to rap sb's knuckles** *or* **to rap sb on the knuckles** 斥责某人

rape [reɪp] **I** *n* **1** [c/u] (*crime*) 强奸 **2** [u] [植] = **oilseed rape** **II** *vt* 强奸

rapid ['ræpɪd] *adj* [+ *growth, development, change*] 迅速的; [+ *heartbeat, steps*] 快的

rapidly ['ræpɪdlɪ] *adv* [*grow, change, walk, move* +] 迅速地

rapids *n* [*pl*] 湍流

rapist ['reɪpɪst] *n* [c] 强奸犯

rapport [ræ'pɔː(r)] *n* [s] 和睦关系

rare [rɛə(r)] *adj* **1** (*uncommon*) 稀有的 **2** (*lightly cooked*) [+ *steak*] 半熟的 ♦**it is rare to find ...** 难得找到…

rarely ['rɛəlɪ] *adv* 很少

rash [ræʃ] **I** *n* **1** [c] (*on skin*) 皮疹 **2** [s] (*spate*) [*of events, robberies*] 一连串 **II** *adj* **1** [+ *person*] 轻率的 **2** [+ *promise, act*] 草率的 ♦**to come out in a rash** 出皮疹

rasher ['ræʃə(r)] [英] *n* [c] 熏肉片 [美 = **slice**]

raspberry ['rɑːzbərɪ] *n* [c] **1** (*fruit*) 山莓 ♦**to blow a raspberry** [非正式] 咂舌头嘲笑某人

rat [ræt] *n* [c] **1** [动] 田鼠 **2** [非正式] (*person*) 卑鄙小人

✪**rate** [reɪt] **I** *n* [c] **1** (*speed*) 速率 **2** (*level*) [*of interest, taxation, inflation*] 率 **3** (*ratio*) 比率 **II** *vt* **1** (*value*) 评价 **2** (*estimate*) 评估 **3** (*price*) 对…估价 **III rates** *n* [*pl*] **1** [英:旧] (*property tax*) 房地产税 ♦**at a rate of 60 kph** 以每小时60公里的速度 ♦**rate of growth** [经济] 增长率 ♦**rate of return** [经济] 回报率 ♦**at this/that rate** 照这种/那种情况继续 ♦**at any rate** (*at least*) 无论如何 ♦**to rate sb/sth as** 把某人/某事物评价成 ♦**to rate sb/sth as sth** 把某人/某事物评为某事物 ♦**to rate sb/sth among** 把某人/某事物归类于 ♦**to rate sb/sth highly** 给某人/某事物高度评价

✪**rather** ['rɑːðə(r)] *adv* **1** (*somewhat*) 相当 **2** (*instead*) 而 ♦**rather a lot** 相当多 ♦**I would rather go than stay** 我宁愿走而不愿留下来 ♦**I'd rather not say** 我宁可不说 ♦**rather than** (*instead of*) 而不是 ♦**or rather** (*more accurately*) 或者更确切地 ♦**I rather think he won't come** 我的确认为他不会来

rating ['reɪtɪŋ] **I** *n* [c] **1** (*score*) 等级 **2** (*assessment*) 评定 **3** [英:航海] (*sailor*) 水兵 **II ratings** *n* [*pl*] [广播] 收听率; [电视] 收视率

ratio ['reɪʃɪəu] *n* [c] 比例 ♦**a ratio of 5 to 1** 5比1的比例 ♦**the ratio of ... to ...** …对…的比例

ration ['ræʃən] **I** *n* [c] (*allowance*) [*of food, petrol etc*] 配给限额 **II** *vt* [+ *food, petrol etc*] 定量供应 **III rations** *n* [*pl*] [军] 口粮

rational ['ræʃənl] *adj* [+ *decision, explanation*] 合理的; [+ *person*] 理性的

rationalize ['ræʃnəlaɪz] *vt* **1** (*justify*) 使有合理依据 **2** (*streamline*) [+ *company, system*] 使合理化

rattle ['rætl] **I** *n* [c] **1** (*baby's toy*) 拨浪鼓 **2** (*noise*) [*of door, window*] 格格响; [*of train, car, engine etc*] 轰鸣声; [*of bottles*] 格格响; [*of chain*] 哗啦声 **II** *vi* **1** [*door, window* +] 哐啷哐啷作响; [*bottles* +] 格格作响; [*chains* +] 哗啦作响; [*train, car, engine* +] 轰隆作响 **III** *vt* **1** (*shake*) 使颤动出声 **2** [非正式] (*unsettle*) 使不安 ♦**to rattle along** [*car, bus* +] 轰鸣而过

❑**rattle off** *vt* 急促而不假思索地说

raucous ['rɔːkəs] *adj* 沙哑的

rave [reɪv] **I** *vi* (*talk wildly*) 胡言乱语 **II** *adj* [非正式] [+ *review*] 热烈的 **III** *n* [c] [英: 非正式] (*dance*) 狂欢舞会

❑**rave about** *vt* [不可拆分] [非正式] 极力赞美

raven ['reɪvən] *n* [c] 渡鸦

ravine [rə'viːn] *n* [c] 深谷

raw [rɔː] *adj* **1** (*uncooked*) [+ *meat, vegetables*] 生的 **2** (*unprocessed*) [+ *cotton, sugar etc*] 未加工的 **3** (*sore*) 摩擦得疼的 **4** (*inexperienced*) 生手的 **5** [+ *weather, day*] 湿冷的 ♦**to get a raw deal** 受到不公待遇

raw materials *n* [*pl*] 原材料

ray [reɪ] *n* [c] **1** [*of light*] 光线 **2** [*of heat*] 辐射 ♦**a ray of hope** 一线希望

razor ['reɪzə(r)] *n* [c] **1** (*also:* ***safety razor***) 剃须刀 **2** (*also:* ***electric razor***) 电动剃须刀

razor blade *n* [c] 剃须刀刀片

RC *adj abbr* (= ***Roman Catholic***) 天主教的

Rd, (尤美 **Rd.**) *abbr* (= ***road***) 路

RDA *n abbr* (= ***recommended daily amount***) 推荐日摄取量

RE [英: 教育] *n abbr* (= ***religious education***) 宗教教育

re [riː] *prep* (*with regard to*) 关于

✪**reach** [riːtʃ] **I** *vt* **1** (*arrive at*) [+ *place, destination*] 到达; [+ *conclusion, agreement, decision*] 达成; [+ *stage, level, age*] 达到 **2** (*be able to touch*) 够着 **3** (*get hold of*) 联络 **II** *vi* (*stretch out one's arm*) 伸手 **III** *n* [U] (*range*) [*of arm*] 伸手可及的范围 **IV reaches** *n* [*pl*] [*of river*] 游 ♦**within reach** 伸手可及 ♦**out of reach** 远离 ♦**within reach of ...** 离…近 ♦**within easy reach of...**离…很近 ♦**beyond the reach of sb/sth** (喻) 超出某人/某事能力之外 ♦**"keep out of the reach of children"** "远离儿童"

❑**reach out** **I** *vi* 伸手 **II** *vt* [+ *hand*] 伸出 ♦**to reach out for sth** 伸手拿某物

> **reach** 和 **arrive** 都可以指到达某个地方。**reach** 后可以直接加表示地点的名词或代词，而且强调需要很大努力才能到达。*To reach the capital might not be easy.* **arrive at** 和 **reach** 还可以表示某人最终做了决定或找到了答案。*It took hours to arrive at a decision...They were unable to reach a decision.*

react [riː'ækt] *vi* **1** (*respond*) 反应 **2** (*rebel*) ♦**to react against sth** 反抗某事 **3** [化] ♦**to react (with)** (和…) 起反应 **4** [医] (对…) 有反应

reaction [riː'ækʃən] **I** *n* **1** [C/U] (*response*) 反应 **2** [C] [医, 化] 反应 **3** [U] (*conservatism*) 极端保守 **II reactions** *n* [*pl*] (*reflexes*) 反应能力 ♦**a reaction against sth** 反对某事

reactor [riː'æktə(r)] *n* [c] 反应器

✪**read** [riːd] (*pt, pp* **read**) **I** *vi* **1** [*person* +] 阅读 **2** [*piece of writing* +] 读起来 **II** *vt* **1** [+ *book, newspaper etc*] 读 **2** [+ *music*] 看懂 **3** (*understand*) [+ *mood, thoughts*] 了解 **4** [+ *meter, thermometer etc*] 识读 **5** (*carry stated message*) [*notice, sign* +] 写着; [*meter, thermometer etc* +] 显示 **6** (*study at university*) [英] 攻读 **III** *n* ♦**to have a read** 阅读 ♦**to read sb's mind** 了解某人的想法 ♦**to take sth as read** 把某事当作是不容置疑的 ♦**to read sth into sb's remarks** 从某人的话中读出某种含义 ♦**it's a good read** 这是本好的读物

❑**read out** *vt* 朗读
❑**read over** *vt* 细读
❑**read through** *vt* **1** (*quickly*) 浏览 **2** (*thoroughly*) 仔细阅读
❑**read up on** *vt* [不可拆分] 研读
reader ['riːdə(r)] *n* [C] **1** [*of book, newspaper etc*] 读者 **2** (*beginner's book*) 初级读本 **3** [英:大学] 高级讲师
readily ['rɛdɪlɪ] *adv* **1** (*without hesitation*) 欣然 **2** (*without difficulty*) 容易地
reading ['riːdɪŋ] *n* **1** [U] [*of books, newspapers etc*] (*activity*) 阅读 **2** [U] (*material read*) 阅读材料 **3** [C] (*literary event*) 朗读会 **4** [C] (*on meter, thermometer etc*) 读数 **5** [C] (*interpretation*) ♦**my reading of the situation is that ...** 我对于这种情况的理解是… **6** [C] (*in church*) 朗诵会 **7** [C] (*text from Bible etc*) 朗读
ready ['rɛdɪ] **I** *adj* **1** (*prepared, available*) 做好准备的 **2** (*willing*) 乐意的 **3** (*easy, quick*) 就绪的 **II** *n* ♦**at the ready** 准备好 **III** *vt* 准备 ♦**to get ready** (*prepare o.s.*) 准备好 ♦**to get sb/sth ready** 使某人/某物准备就绪 ♦**to be ready to do sth** (*prepared*) 准备做某事; (*willing*) 愿意做某事 **to be ready for sth** (*prepared for*) 已为某事准备好; (*wanting*) 想要某物 ♦**ready for use** 待用
ready-made ['rɛdɪ'meɪd] *adj* **1** [+ *clothes*] 现成的 **2** (*useful*) 可用的
✪**real** [rɪəl] **I** *adj* **1** (*not artificial*) [+ *leather, gold etc*] 真正的 **2** (*not feigned*) [+ *reason, interest, name*] 真实的 **3** (*not imaginary*) [+ *life, feeling*] 真实的 **4** (*for emphasis*) 真的 ◊ *It's a real shame.* 真是遗憾。**II** *adv* [美:非正式] (*very*) 很 ♦**for real** 当真 ♦**the real thing** 真家伙 ♦**in real life** 现实生活中 ♦**in real terms** 实际上
real estate I *n* [U] 不动产 **II** *cpd* [复合词] [美] [+ *agent, business etc*] 房地产
realistic [rɪə'lɪstɪk] *adj* **1** (*sensible*) 现实的 **2** (*convincing*) [+ *book, film, portrayal etc*] 逼真的
reality [riː'ælɪtɪ] *n* **1** [U] (*real things*) 现实 **2** [C/U] (*realness*) 真相 ♦**in reality** 事实上
reality TV *n* [U] 真人电视秀
realization [rɪəlaɪ'zeɪʃən] *n* **1** [S/U] (*understanding*) 认识 **2** [U] (*fulfilment*) [*of dreams, hopes, fears*] 实现 **3** [C/U] [经济] [*of asset*] 变卖
realize ['rɪəlaɪz] *vt* **1** (*understand*) 意识到 **2** (*fulfil*) [+ *dream, ambition, fears*] 实现; [+ *design, idea*] 体现 **3** [经济] [+ *amount, profit*] 变卖 ♦**to realize that ...** 意识到…
✪**really** ['rɪəlɪ] *adv* **1** (*very*) ♦**really good/delighted** 真好/真高兴 **2** (*genuinely*) 确实 **3** (*after negative*) 真正地 ♦**really?** (*indicating surprise, interest*) 真的吗? ♦**really!** (*indicating annoyance*) [英] 哎呀! 📖 用法参见 **actually**
realm [rɛlm] *n* [C] (*domain*) 领域
realtor ['rɪəltɔː(r)] [美] *n* [C] 房地产商 [英=**estate agent**]
reappear [riːə'pɪə(r)] *vi* 重现
rear [rɪə(r)] **I** *adj* **1** (*back*) [+ *end, entrance*] 后面的 **II** *n* **1** [S] (*back*) 后面 **2** [C] (*buttocks*) [非正式] 臀部 **III** *vt* (*raise*) [+ *cattle, chickens*] [尤英] 饲养 [美=**raise**]; [+ *family, children*] 抚养 **IV** *vi* (*also:* ***rear up***) [*horse* +] 用后腿站立
rearrange [riːə'reɪndʒ] *vt* **1** [+ *objects*] 重新安置 **2** [+ *meeting*] 重新安排
rear-view mirror ['rɪəvjuː-] *n* [C] 后视镜
✪**reason** ['riːzn] **I** *n* **1** [C] (*cause*) 原因 **2** [U] (*rationality*) 理性 **II** *vi* ♦**to reason with sb** 与某人理论 **III** *vt* 推理 ♦**the reason for sth** 某事的动机 ♦**the reason why** …的原因 ♦**to have reason to do sth** [正式] 有理由做某事 ♦**by reason of** [正式] 因为 ♦**with good reason** 合乎情理 ♦**within reason** 在合理的范围内
reasonable ['riːznəbl] *adj* **1** (*moderate, sensible*) [+ *person, decision*] 合情合理的; [+ *number, amount*] 相当的; [+ *price*] 合理的 **2** (*not bad*) 凑合的 **3** (*rational*) [+ *explanation, request*] 合理的 ♦**be reasonable!** 理智些!
reasonably ['riːznəblɪ] *adv* **1** (*moderately*) 相当地 **2** (*sensibly*) 明

智地

reasoning ['riːznɪŋ] *n* [U] 推理

reassurance [riːə'ʃuərəns] *n* **1** [U] (*comfort*) 放心 **2** [C] (*guarantee*) 保证

reassure [riːə'ʃuə(r)] *vt* 使安心

rebate ['riːbeɪt] *n* [C] 部分退款

rebel [*n* 'rɛbl, *vb* rɪ'bɛl] **I** *n* [C] **1** (*against society, parents*) 反叛者 **2** (*in uprising*) 起义者 **3** (*in politics*) 持不同政见者 **II** *vi* **1** (*against society, parents*) 反叛 **2** (*in uprising*) 起义 **3** (*in politics*) 反对

rebellion [rɪ'bɛljən] *n* [C/U] (*uprising*) 叛乱; (*against society, parents*) 反叛; (*in politics*) 反抗

rebellious [rɪ'bɛljəs] *adj* [+ *person*] 叛逆的; [+ *behaviour*] 反叛的; [+ *politician*] 反对的

rebuild [riː'bɪld] (*pt, pp* **rebuilt**) *vt* **1** [+ *town, building*] 重建 **2** [+ *economy, confidence*] 恢复

recall [*vb* rɪ'kɔːl, *n* 'riːkɔl] **I** *vt* **1** (*remember*) 记起 **2** (*recount*) 回忆起 **3** (*call back*) [+ *parliament, ambassador etc*] 召回; [+ *product*] 收回 **II** *n* **1** [U] [*of memories*] 回忆 **2** [S] [*of ambassador etc*] 召回 ♦ **beyond recall** 无法恢复

receding [rɪ'siːdɪŋ] *adj* [+ *hair*] 后移的

receipt [rɪ'siːt] **I** *n* **1** [C] (*for purchases*) 收据 **2** [C] (*for deposit*) 收条 **3** [U] (*act of receiving*) 收到 **II receipts** *n* [*pl*] (*monies received*) 收入 ♦ **on receipt of** [正式] 收到…时 ♦ **to be in receipt of sth** [正式] 已收到某物

✪ **receive** [rɪ'siːv] *vt* **1** (*get*) [+ *money, letter etc*] 收到; [+ *injury, treatment*] 受到; [+ *criticism, acclaim*] 遭受 **2** [广播, 电视] 接收 **3** [正式] (*welcome*) [+ *visitor, guest*] 接待 **4** (*react to*) 接受到 ♦ **"received with thanks"** [商] "钱款已收到, 谢谢" ♦ **to be on the receiving end of sth** 遭受某事

receiver [rɪ'siːvə(r)] *n* [C] **1** (*of telephone*) 听筒 **2** [广播, 电视] 接收器 **3** [法法, 商] 破产管理人

✪ **recent** ['riːsnt] *adj* [+ *event*] 最近的 ♦ **in recent years** *or* **times** 近年来 {或} 近一段时期

recently ['riːsntlɪ] *adv* **1** (*lately, not long ago*) 最近 ♦ **until recently** 直到最近

reception [rɪ'sɛpʃən] *n* **1** [S] (*in public building*) 接待处 **2** [C] (*party*) 欢迎会 **3** [U] [广播, 电视] 接收 **4** [C] (*welcome*) 反响

reception desk *n* [S] **1** 接待处

receptionist [rɪ'sɛpʃənɪst] [尤英] *n* [C] 接待员 [美=**desk clerk**]

recession [rɪ'sɛʃən] *n* [C/U] 衰退

recharge [riː'tʃɑːdʒ] *vt* 充电

recipe ['rɛsɪpɪ] [烹饪] *n* [C] 食谱 ♦ **a recipe for disaster/success** 造成灾难的因素/成功的秘诀

recipient [rɪ'sɪpɪənt] *n* [C] 接受者

recital [rɪ'saɪtl] *n* [C] 独自表演

recite [rɪ'saɪt] *vt* **1** [+ *poem*] 背诵 **2** (*enumerate*) [+ *complaints etc*] 列举

reckless ['rɛkləs] *adj* [+ *person, behaviour*] 鲁莽的

reckon ['rɛkən] **I** *vt* **1** (*consider*) 认为 **2** (*calculate*) 计算 **II** *vi* ♦ **he is somebody to be reckoned with** 他是一个得认真对付的人 ♦ **to reckon without sb/sth** 未考虑到某人/某事物 ♦ **I reckon that ...** (*think*) [非正式] 我估计…

❑ **reckon on** *vt* [不可拆分] (*expect*) 期望

reclaim [rɪ'kleɪm] *vt* **1** [+ *luggage, tax etc*] 取回 **2** [+ *land*] (*from sea*) 开垦

recline [rɪ'klaɪn] **I** *vi* **1** [*person* +] 斜倚 **2** [*seat* +] 向后倾斜 **II** *vt* [+ *seat*] 使倾斜

recognition [rɛkəg'nɪʃən] *n* [U] **1** (*identification*) [*of person, place*] 认出 **2** (*understanding*) [*of problem, fact*] 承认 **3** (*approval*) [*of achievement*] 认可 ♦ **to change beyond recognition** 变化得使人认不出来 ♦ **in recognition of** 为酬答…而 ♦ **to gain recognition** 得到承认

recognizable ['rɛkəgnaɪzəbl] *adj* 可辨认的

recognize ['rɛkəgnaɪz] *vt* **1** [+ *person, place, voice*] 认出; [+ *sign, symptom*] 识别; [+ *problem, need*] 承认 **2** (*accept validity of*) [+ *qualifications*] 认可; [+ *government*] 承认 **3** (*show appreciation of*) [+ *achievement*] 认可 ♦ **to recognize sb by/as** 通过…认出某人/把某人认作…

recollect [rɛkə'lɛkt] *vt* 想起

recollection [rɛkə'lɛkʃən] *n* **1** [c] (*memory*) 记忆 **2** [u] (*remembering*) 回忆 ♦ **to the best of my recollection** 如果我没有记错

recommend [rɛkə'mɛnd] *vt* **1** [+ *book, shop, person*] 推荐 **2** [+ *course of action*] 建议 ♦ **she has a lot to recommend her** 她有许多值得称道的地方 ♦ **to recommend sb for promotion** 推荐某人升职

recommendation [rɛkəmɛn'deɪʃən] *n* [c/u] 推荐 ♦ **on the recommendation of** 在…建议下

reconcile ['rɛkənsaɪl] *vt* **1** [+ *two people*] 和解 **2** [+ *two facts, beliefs*] 调和 ♦ **to reconcile o.s. to sth** [+ *unpleasant situation etc*] 使自己接受某事

reconsider [riːkən'sɪdə(r)] *vt, vi* 重新考虑

reconstruct [riːkən'strʌkt] *vt* **1** (*rebuild*) 重建 **2** (*form picture of*) [+ *event, crime*] 重现

✪ **record** [*n* 'rɛkɔːd, *vb* rɪ'kɔːd] **I** *n* [c] **1** (*written account*) 记载 **2** (*also:* ***track record***) 记录 **3** (*sound-recording*) 唱片 **4** (*unbeaten statistic*) 记录 **II records** *n* [*pl*] 记录 **III** *vt* **1** (*make record of, document*) 记录 **2** (*show, register*) [*thermometer, clock etc* +] 显示 **3** (*make recording of*) 录制 **IV** *adj* [+ *sales, profits, levels*] 创记录的 ♦ **in record time** 破记录地 ♦ **to keep sth on record** 把某事物记录保存下来 ♦ **to have a good/poor record** 有良好/不好的记录 ♦ **to keep a record of sth** 记录某事 ♦ **to set** *or* **put the record straight** 澄清事实 ♦ **to be on record** 正式记录的 ♦ **off the record** [*speak* +] 私下里

recorded delivery [rɪ'kɔːdɪd-] [英] *n* [u] 挂号邮递

recorder [rɪ'kɔːdə(r)] *n* [c] **1** [音] (*instrument*) 八孔竖笛 **2** [法法] 法官

recording [rɪ'kɔːdɪŋ] *n* **1** [c] (*recorded music, voice etc*) 录音 **2** [u] (*process of recording*) 录制

record player *n* [c] 唱机

recount [rɪ'kaunt] *vt* [+ *story, event*] 描述

recover [rɪ'kʌvə(r)] **I** *vi* **1** (*from illness, shock, experience*) 恢复 **2** [*country, economy* +] 复原 **II** *vt* **1** [+ *stolen goods, lost items*] 找回 **2** [+ *body*] 找到 **3** [+ *financial loss*] 挽回 **4** [+ *consciousness*] 恢复

recovery [rɪ'kʌvərɪ] *n* **1** [c/u] (*from illness, operation*) 康复 **2** [u] [*of stolen, lost items*] 挽回 **3** [c/u] (*in economy, finances*) 恢复 **4** [u] [*of physical/mental state*] 恢复 ♦ **to be in recovery** (*from addiction etc*) 在恢复中

recreate [riːkrɪ'eɪt] *vt* 重现

recreation [rɛkrɪ'eɪʃən] *n* [u] 消遣

recreational [rɛkrɪ'eɪʃənl] *adj* 娱乐的

recruit [rɪ'kruːt] **I** *n* [c] **1** [军] 新兵 **2** (*in company, organization*) 新成员 **II** *vt* **1** [军] 招募 **2** [+ *staff, new members*] 招收

recruitment [rɪ'kruːtmənt] *n* [u] 招收

rectangle ['rɛktæŋgl] *n* [c] 长方形

rectangular [rɛk'tæŋgjulə(r)] *adj* 长方形的

rectify ['rɛktɪfaɪ] *vt* 改正

rector ['rɛktə(r)] *n* [c] 教区长

recur [rɪ'kəː(r)] *vi* **1** [*error, event* +] 再发生 **2** [*illness, pain* +] 复发

recurring [rɪ'kəːrɪŋ] **I** *adj* (*recurrent*) [+ *problem, dream*] 重复的 **II** *adv* (*in decimals*) 循环

recycle [riː'saɪkl] *vt* 再生利用

recycling [riː'saɪklɪŋ] *n* [u] 循环利用

✪ **red** [rɛd] **I** *adj* **1** 红色的 **2** [+ *face, person*] 涨红的 **3** [+ *hair*] 红褐色的 **4** [+ *wine*] 红的 **II** *n* [c/u] 红色 ♦ **to be in the red** [非正式] [*bank account, business* +] 负债 ♦ **to see red** [非正式] 暴怒

Red Cross *n* ♦ **the Red Cross** 红十字会

redcurrant ['rɛdkʌrənt] [英:植,烹饪] *n* [c] 小红浆果; (*also:* ***redcurrant bush***) 红浆果树

redeem [rɪ'diːm] *vt* **1** [+ *situation*] 挽回 **2** [+ *sth in pawn, loan*] 赎回 **3** [宗] [+ *person*] 拯救 ♦ **to redeem o.s.** 弥补自己的过失

red-haired [rɛd'hɛəd] *adj* 红棕色头发的

redhead ['rɛdhɛd] *n* [c] 有红棕色头发的人

red-hot [rɛd'hɔt] *adj* **1** (*very hot*) 炽热的 **2** [非正式](*very popular*) 热门的 **3** [非正式](*passionate*) 狂热的 ♦ **the red-hot favourite** [非正式] 大热门

red light *n* ♦ **to go through a red light** 闯红灯

red-light district ['rɛdlaɪt-] *n* [c] 红灯区

red meat *n* [c/u] 牛羊肉

redo [riː'duː] *vt pt* **redid** *pp* **redone** 重做

reduce [rɪ'djuːs] *vt* [+ *spending, numbers, risk etc*] 减少 ♦ **to reduce sb to sth** 使某人沦落到某种状态 ♦ **to reduce sth to sth** 使某事陷入某种状态 ♦ **to reduce sth by/to** 将某物减少…/将某物减少到… ♦ **to reduce sb to tears** 使某人伤心流泪 ♦ **to reduce sb to silence** 使某人沉默 ♦ **"reduce speed now"** [汽车] "现在减速"

reduced [rɪ'djuːst] *adj* [+ *goods, ticket etc*] 减少的 ♦ **"greatly reduced prices"** "大减价"

reduction [rɪ'dʌkʃən] *n* **1** [c/u] (*decrease*) 减少 **2** [c] (*discount*) 减价

redundancy [rɪ'dʌndənsɪ] [英] *n* **1** [c] (*dismissal*) 冗员 [美= **layoff**] **2** [u] (*being dismissed*) 裁员 ♦ **compulsory redundancy** 强行裁员 ♦ **voluntary redundancy** 自愿减员

redundant [rɪ'dʌndnt] *adj* [英] **1** (*unemployed*) [+ *worker*] 被裁员的 **2** (*superfluous*) [+ *skills, buildings*] 冗余的 ♦ **to be made redundant** [*worker* +] 被裁员

reed [riːd] [植] *n* [c] 芦苇

reef [riːf] *n* [c] 暗礁

reel [riːl] **I** *n* [c] **1** [*of thread, cable, film, tape*] 卷轴 **2** [电影] 盘 **3** (*on fishing-rod*) 钓丝螺旋轮 **4** (*dance*) 里尔舞 (一种轻快的苏格兰或爱尔兰舞) **II** *vi* **1** (*sway*) 摇晃地移动 **2** (*from shock*) 眩晕 ♦ **my head is reeling** 我头昏脑胀

❑ **reel in** *vt* [*fish*] 收线钓到; [*line*] 绕

❑ **reel off** *vt* (*say*) 一口气说出

ref [rɛf] [体育] [非正式] *n* [c] (*referee*) 裁判员

ref. *abbr* (= ***reference***) 参考号

refectory [rɪ'fɛktərɪ] *n* [c] **1** (*in school, university*) 食堂 **2** (*in monastery*) 斋房

refer [rɪ'fəː(r)] *vt* ♦ **to refer sb to** [+ *book*] 叫某人参看; [+ *manager*] 叫某人去…寻求帮助; [+ *doctor, hospital*] 将某人交由…治疗 ♦ **to refer sth to** (*pass on*) [+ *task, problem*] 把某事提交给

❑ **refer to** *vt* [不可拆分] **1** (*mention*) 提到 **2** (*by a name*) 说起 **3** (*relate to*) 指 **4** (*mean*) 意为 **5** (*consult*) 参考

referee [rɛfə'riː] **I** *n* [c] **1** [体育] 裁判员 **2** [英] (*for job application*) 证明人 [美= **reference**] **II** *vt* [+ *football match etc*] 当裁判

reference ['rɛfrəns] *n* [c] **1** (*mention*) 提到 **2** (*in book, article*) 参考 **3** (*number, name*) 参考号 ◊ *a map reference* 地图图例 **4** (*for job application*) (*letter*) 证明人 ♦ **with reference to** *or* **in reference to** (*in letter*) 关于… ♦ **"please quote this reference"** [商] "请注明此编号"

reference number *n* [c] 参考号

refill [*vb* riː'fɪl, *n* 'riːfɪl] **I** *vt* 再装满 **II** *n* [c] **1** [*of ink*] 替芯; [*of detergent*] 替换装 **2** [*of drink*] 续杯

refine [rɪ'faɪn] *vt* **1** (*purify*) [+ *substance*] 精炼 **2** (*improve*) [+ *theory, method*] 改良

refined [rɪ'faɪnd] *adj* **1** (*cultured*) [+ *person, taste*] 有教养的 **2** (*purified*) [+ *substance*] 精炼的

refinery [rɪ'faɪnərɪ] *n* [c] 精炼厂

reflect [rɪ'flɛkt] **I** *vt* **1** (*bounce back*) [+ *image*] 映出; [+ *light, heat*] 反射 **2** (*mirror*) [+ *situation, attitude*] 反映 **II** *vi* (*think*) 沉思

❑ **reflect on** *vt* [不可拆分] 带来

reflection [rɪ'flɛkʃən] **I** *n* **1** [c] (*image*) 影像 **2** [u] [*of light, heat*] 反射 **3** [c] (*indication*) [*of situation, attitude*] 反映 **4** [u] (*thought*) 沉思 **II reflections** *n* [*pl*] 考虑 ♦ **on reflection** 再经考虑 ♦ **to be a reflection on sb/sth** (*criticism*) 有损于某人/某事

reflex ['riːflɛks] **I** *n* [c] **1** [生理] (*action, movement*) 反射动作 **2** (*habit*) 反射作用 **II** *adj* [+ *action, movement*] (*also:* ***reflex action***) 反射动作的 **III reflexes** *n* [*pl*] (*speed of reaction*) 反应

reform [rɪˈfɔːm] **I** *n* **1** [U] [*of law, system*] 改革 **2** [C] (*process, result*) 改革 **II** *vt* [+ *law, system*] 改革 **III** *vi* [*criminal, alcoholic* +] 改过

refrain [rɪˈfreɪn] **I** *vi* 克制 **II** *n* [C] [*of song*] 叠句 ♦**to refrain from doing sth** 克制而不做某事

refresh [rɪˈfrɛʃ] *vt* [*sleep, drink, rest* +] 使恢复 ♦**to refresh sb's memory** 唤起某人的记忆

refreshing [rɪˈfrɛʃɪŋ] *adj* **1** [+ *drink, sleep*] 提神的 **2** [+ *fact, idea etc*] 令人耳目一新的

refreshments [rɪˈfrɛʃmənts] *n* [*pl*] 饮料及小吃

refrigerator [rɪˈfrɪdʒəreɪtə(r)] *n* [C] 冰箱

refuel [riːˈfjuəl] **I** *vi* [*aircraft, car* +] 加燃料 **II** *vt* [+ *aircraft, car*] 给…加燃料

refuelling [riːˈfjuəlɪŋ] *n* [U] 加燃料

refuge [ˈrɛfjuːdʒ] *n* **1** [U] (*source of protection*) 庇护 **2** [C] (*hut*) 庇护所 **3** [C] (*safe house*) 避难所 ♦**to seek** *or* **take refuge in silence/drink** 从缄默/饮酒中寻求慰藉

refugee [rɛfjuˈdʒiː] *n* [C] 难民 ♦**a political refugee** 政治难民

refund [*n* ˈriːfʌnd, *vb* rɪˈfʌnd] **I** *n* [C] 退款 **II** *vt* [+ *money*] 偿还

refurbish [riːˈfəːbɪʃ] *vt* 重新装饰

refusal [rɪˈfjuːzəl] *n* [C/U] 拒绝 ♦**to give/offer sb first refusal** (*option*) 给某人优先取舍权

refuse[1] [rɪˈfjuːz] *vt, vi* 拒绝 ♦**to refuse to do sth** 拒绝做某事 ♦**to refuse sb sth** 拒绝给某人某物 ♦**to refuse sb permission** 不批准某人

refuse[2] [ˈrɛfjuːs] *n* [U] 垃圾

refuse collection *n* [C/U] 垃圾收集

regain [rɪˈgeɪn] *vt* [+ *power, control*] 重新取得; [+ *health, confidence*] 恢复

regard [rɪˈgɑːd] **I** *vt* **1** (*consider, view*) 认为 **II** *n* [U] (*esteem*) 尊敬 ♦**to give one's regards to** 向…表示问候 ♦**"with kindest regards"** "谨此致候" ♦**as regards, with regard to, in regard to** [正式] 关于 ♦**in this/that regard** 在这/那方面

regarding [rɪˈgɑːdɪŋ] *prep* [正式] 关于

regardless [rɪˈgɑːdlɪs] *adv* [*carry on, continue* +] 无论如何 ♦**regardless of** 不管

regenerate [rɪˈdʒɛnəreɪt] **I** *vt* 复兴 **II** *vi* [生物] 再生

reggae [ˈrɛgeɪ] *n* [U] 西印度群岛的节奏很强的流行音乐和舞蹈

regime [reɪˈʒiːm] *n* [C] **1** (*system of government*) 政体 **2** (*diet, exercise*) 养生法

regiment [*n* ˈrɛdʒɪmənt, *vt* ˈrɛdʒɪmɛnt] **I** *n* [C] [军] 团 **II** *vt* [+ *people*] 严格控制

region [ˈriːdʒən] *n* [C] **1** (*area*) 区域 **2** (*administrative division*) 地区 ♦**in the region of** [正式] (*approximately*) 大约

regional [ˈriːdʒənl] *adj* 地区的

register [ˈrɛdʒɪstə(r)] **I** *n* [C] **1** (*at hotel*) 登记 **2** (*in school*) 注册 **3** (*official record*) 记录 **II** *vt* **1** [+ *birth, death, marriage*] 登记 **2** [+ *letter*] 挂号邮寄 **3** (*indicate*) [+ *amount, measurement*] 显示为; [+ *feeling, opinion*] 流露出 **III** *vi* **1** (*sign up*) (*at hotel*) 登记; (*at doctor's, dentist's, for work, class*) 注册 **2** (*show*) [*amount, measurement* +] 显示 **3** (*make impression*) 留有印象 ♦**to register a protest** 以示抗议

registered [ˈrɛdʒɪstəd] *adj* **1** [邮政] [+ *letter, mail*] 挂号的 **2** [+ *drug addict*] 有记录的 **3** [+ *childminder etc*] 注册的

registrar [ˈrɛdʒɪstrɑː(r)] *n* [C] **1** (*in registry office*) 登记员 **2** [英] (*in hospital*) 专科住院医师 **3** (*in college, university*) 大学中主管招生、考试等事务的负责人

registration [rɛdʒɪsˈtreɪʃən] *n* [C/U] [*of birth, death, students etc*] 登记

registration number [英] *n* [C] 牌照号码 [美 = **license number**]

registry office [ˈrɛdʒɪstrɪ-] [英] *n* [C] 户籍登记处 ♦**to get married in a registry office** 在户籍登记处公证结婚

regret [rɪˈgrɛt] **I** *n* [C/U] 遗憾 **II** *vt* **1** [+ *one's action*] 后悔 **2** [+ *event*] 对…表示遗憾 ♦**with regret** 遗憾地 ♦**to have no regrets** 没有遗憾 ♦**to regret that ...** 对…感到后悔 ♦**we regret to inform you that ...** 我们遗憾地通知您…

regrettable [rɪ'grɛtəbl] *adj* [正式] 令人遗憾的

regrettably [rɪ'grɛtəblɪ] *adv* [正式] 可惜地

regular ['rɛgjulə(r)] **I** *adj* **1** (*even*) [+ *breathing, intervals*] 有规律的; [+ *features, shape etc*] 匀称的 **2** (*frequent*) [+ *event*] 有规律的; [+ *visitor*] 经常的 **3** (*usual*) 固定的 **4** (*normal*) 正常的 **5** [+ *soldier*] 正规的 **6** [语言] [+ *verb etc*] 规则的 **II** *n* [C] (*client etc*) (*in bar, restaurant, shop*) 常客

regularly ['rɛgjuləlɪ] *adv* **1** (*frequently*) 经常 **2** (*at set intervals*) 定期地 **3** (*smoothly, evenly*) [+ *spaced, distributed*] 均匀地 **4** (*symmetrically*) [+ *shaped etc*] 匀称地

regulate ['rɛgjuleɪt] *vt* **1** (*control*) 管制 **2** (*adjust*) [+ *machine, oven*] 调整

regulation [rɛgju'leɪʃən] *n* **1** [C] (*rule*) 规章 **2** [U] (*control*) [*of process, expenditure, speed*] 法规

rehabilitation ['riːəbɪlɪ'teɪʃən] *n* [U] [*of criminal, drug addict, invalid*] 康复

rehearsal [rɪ'həːsəl] *n* [C/U] 排练

rehearse [rɪ'həːs] *vt, vi* 排练

reign [reɪn] **I** *n* [C] [*of monarch*] 统治 **II** *vi* **1** [*monarch* +] 统治 **2** [*peace, calm, silence etc* +] 笼罩 ♦ **a reign of terror** 恐怖时期 ♦ **to reign supreme** 占绝对优势

reimburse [riːɪm'bəːs] *vt* 偿还

rein [reɪn] *n* [C] (*for horse*) 缰绳 ♦ **to give sb free rein** 给予某人充分自由 ♦ **to keep a tight rein on sth** 严密地控制某事

❑ **rein in** *vt* 控制

reincarnation [riːɪnkɑː'neɪʃən] *n* **1** [U] (*belief*) 转世 **2** [C] (*reincarnated being*) 转世化身

reindeer ['reɪndɪə(r)] (*pl* **reindeer**) *n* 驯鹿

reinforce [riːɪn'fɔːs] *vt* **1** (*strengthen*) 加固 **2** (*back up*) [+ *idea, statement, prejudice*] 加强

reinforcement [riːɪn'fɔːsmənt] **I** *n* [C/U] **1** (*strengthening*) 加固 **2** (*backing up*) [*of attitude, prejudice*] 加强 **II reinforcements** *n* [*pl*] [军] 增援

reinstate [riːɪn'steɪt] *vt* **1** [+ *tax, law, practice*] 恢复 **2** [+ *employee*] 恢复职位

reject [*n* 'riːdʒɛkt, *vb* rɪ'dʒɛkt] **I** *vt* **1** [+ *plan, belief, idea, goods*] 拒绝接受 **2** [+ *applicant, admirer*] 拒绝 **3** [*machine* +] [+ *coin*] 不接受 **4** [医] [+ *heart, kidney*] 排斥 **II** *n* [C] 退货产品

rejection [rɪ'dʒɛkʃən] *n* [C/U] **1** [*of plan, belief etc*] 拒绝接受 **2** [*of applicant*] 拒绝 **3** (*feeling*) 拒绝 **4** [医] [*of heart, kidney*] 排斥

rejoice [rɪ'dʒɔɪs] *vi* ♦ **to rejoice at** *or* **over sth** 因某事感到高兴

relate [rɪ'leɪt] **I** *vi* ♦ **to relate to** (*empathize with*) [+ *person*] 与…交往; (*concern*) [+ *subject*] 与…有关 **II** *vt* **1** (*tell*) [+ *story etc*] [正式] 讲述 **2** (*connect*) 将…联系起来

related [rɪ'leɪtɪd] *adj* **1** [+ *questions, issues*] 有联系的 **2** [+ *people*] 有亲缘关系的 **3** [+ *species, languages*] 属同一种类的 ♦ **to be related to sb** 和某人有关连 ♦ **to be related to sth** [*species, language* +] 和某事有关连

relating to [rɪ'leɪtɪŋ-] *prep* 关于

relation [rɪ'leɪʃən] **I** *n* [C] **1** (*relative*) 亲戚 **2** (*connection*) 关系 **II relations** *n* [*pl*] (*rapport*) 关系 ♦ **diplomatic/international relations** 外交/国际关系 ♦ **to bear no relation to** 和…无关 ♦ **in relation to** 与…相比

relationship [rɪ'leɪʃənʃɪp] *n* [C] **1** (*connection*) 关系 **2** (*rapport*) (*between two people, countries*) 关系 **3** (*affair*) 亲密的关系 ♦ **to have a good relationship** 关系亲密

relative ['rɛlətɪv] **I** *n* [C] (*member of family*) 亲戚 **II** *adj* (*comparative*) 相对的 ♦ **relative to** 相对于 ♦ **it's all relative** 都是相对而言

relatively ['rɛlətɪvlɪ] *adv* 相对

relax [rɪ'læks] **I** *vi* **1** [*person* +] (*unwind*) 放松 **2** [*body, muscle* +] 松弛 **II** *vt* **1** [+ *person, mind*] 使放松 **2** [+ *one's grip, muscles*] 使松弛 **3** [+ *rule, control*] 放宽

relaxation [riːlæk'seɪʃən] *n* [U] **1** (*rest*) 消遣 **2** [*of rule, control etc*] 放宽

relaxed [rɪ'lækst] *adj* [+ *person*] 放松的; [+ *discussion, atmosphere*] 轻松的

relaxing [rɪ'læksɪŋ] *adj* 令人放松的

relay [*n* ˈriːleɪ, *vb* rɪˈleɪ] **I** *n* [C] (*also:* ***relay race***) 接力赛 **II** *vt* **1** [*+ message, news*] 转述 **2** [*+ programme, broadcast*] 转播

✪ **release** [rɪˈliːs] **I** *n* **1** [C] [*of prisoner*] 释放 **2** [C] [*of documents, funds etc*] 公开 **3** [C] [*of gas, water etc*] 排放 **4** [U] (*from obligation, situation*) 免除 **5** [U] [*of film, record*] 发行 **6** [C] (*record, film*) 发行 **7** [C] [术语] (*device*) 释放器 **II** *vt* **1** [*+ person*] (*from captivity*) 释放; (*from wreckage etc*) 解救; (*from obligation, responsibility*) 免除 **2** [*+ gas etc*] 排放 **3** (*let go of*) 放开 **4** [术语] [*+ catch, spring etc*] 放开; [汽车] [*+ clutch, brake*] 松开 **5** [*+ record, film*] 发行 **6** [*+ report, news, figures*] 发表 ♦ **"on general release"** [*film +*] "公开上映"

relegate [ˈrɛləgeɪt] *vt* **1** [英: 体育] ♦ **to be relegated** 被降级 **2** (*downgrade*) ♦ **to relegate sth to ...** 把某物降级到…

relent [rɪˈlɛnt] *vi* 让步

relentless [rɪˈlɛntlɪs] *adj* **1** [*+ heat, noise, pressure*] 不断的 **2** [*+ tyrant, enemy*] 残忍的

relevant [ˈrɛləvənt] *adj* **1** [*+ fact, information, question*] 切题的 **2** [*+ chapter, area*] 相关的 ♦ **relevant to** 和…有关的

reliable [rɪˈlaɪəbl] *adj* [*+ person, firm, news, information*] 可靠的; [*+ method, machine*] 可信赖的

relic [ˈrɛlɪk] *n* [C] **1** [*of the past*] 遗物 **2** (*historical object*) 纪念物 **3** [宗] 圣者遗物

relief [rɪˈliːf] **I** *n* **1** [U] (*alleviation*) 缓解 **2** [U] (*gladness*) 如释重负 **3** [U] (*aid*) (*to country etc*) 救援 **4** [C] [艺术] 浮雕 **5** [U] [地理] 地势起伏 **II** *cpd* [复合词] [*+ bus, driver*] 后备 ♦ **in relief** [艺术] 浮雕

relieve [rɪˈliːv] *vt* **1** (*alleviate*) [*+ pain, worry*] 减轻 **2** (*take over from*) [*+ colleague*] 换班 ♦ **to relieve sb of sth** [*+ load*] 替某人拿某物; [*+ duties, post*] 免除 ♦ **to relieve o.s.** (*euphemism*) 解大小便

relieved [rɪˈliːvd] *adj* 宽慰的 ♦ **to be relieved that ...** 对…感到放心 ♦ **I'm relieved to hear it** 听到这么说我感到宽慰

religion [rɪˈlɪdʒən] *n* **1** [U] (*belief*) 宗教信仰 **2** [C] (*set of beliefs*) 宗教

religious [rɪˈlɪdʒəs] *adj* **1** [*+ activities, faith*] 宗教的 **2** [*+ person*] 笃信宗教的 **3** [*+ book*] 有关宗教的

religious education *n* [U] 宗教教育

relinquish [rɪˈlɪŋkwɪʃ] *vt* [*+ authority, control, claim*] 放弃

relish [ˈrɛlɪʃ] **I** *n* **1** [C/U] [烹饪] 调味品 **2** [U] (*enjoyment*) 乐趣 **II** *vt* (*enjoy*) [*+ challenge, competition*] 享受; [*+ idea, thought, prospect*] 喜欢 ♦ **to relish doing sth** 乐于做某事

relocate [riːləuˈkeɪt] **I** *vt* [*+ business, staff*] 调动 **II** *vi* 迁往别处

reluctance [rɪˈlʌktəns] *n* [U] 不情愿

reluctant [rɪˈlʌktənt] *adj* (*unwilling*) 不情愿的 ♦ **to be reluctant to do sth** 不愿做某事

reluctantly [rɪˈlʌktəntlɪ] *adv* 不情愿地

rely on [rɪˈlaɪ-] *vt* [不可拆分] **1** (*be dependent on*) 依赖 **2** (*trust*) 信赖

✪ **remain** [rɪˈmeɪn] *vi* **1** (*continue to be*) 仍然是 **2** (*stay*) 逗留 **3** (*survive*) 遗留 ♦ **to remain silent/in control** 保持沉默/仍然控制局面 ♦ **much remains to be done** 还有许多事情要做 ♦ **the fact remains that ...** 事实上情况是… ♦ **it remains to be seen whether ...** 是否…，以后可见分晓

remainder [rɪˈmeɪndə(r)] **I** *n* [S] (*rest*) 剩余部分 **II** *vt* [商] 清仓抛售

remaining [rɪˈmeɪnɪŋ] *adj* 剩下的

remains [rɪˈmeɪnz] *n* [*pl*] **1** (*remnants*) [*of object, building, meal*] 剩余物 **2** (*relics*) 遗迹 **3** [*of dead person*] 遗体

remand [rɪˈmɑːnd] **I** *n* ♦ **to be on remand** 被还押 **II** *vt* **1** ♦ **to be remanded in custody** 被还押 **2** ♦ **to be remanded on bail** 被保释候审

remark [rɪˈmɑːk] **I** *n* [C] (*comment*) 评论 **II** *vt* (*comment*) 评论 ♦ **to remark that...** 说… ♦ **to remark on sth** 谈论某事

📖 用法参见 **comment**

remarkable [rɪˈmɑːkəbl] *adj* 不寻常的

remarkably [rɪˈmɑːkəblɪ] *adv* 极其地

remarry [riːˈmærɪ] *vi* 再婚
remedy [ˈrɛmədɪ] **I** *n* [c] **1** (*for illness*) 治疗法 **2** (*for situation*) 补救的方法 **II** *vt* **1** [+ *mistake, injustice*] 改正 **2** [+ *situation*] 补救
✪ **remember** [rɪˈmɛmbə(r)] *vt* **1** (*still have in mind*) [+ *person, name, event etc*] 记住 **2** (*bring back to mind*) 回想起 **3** (*bear in mind*) 牢记 ♦ **remember me to him** (*send greetings*) 代我向他问候 ♦ **to remember doing sth** *or* **having done sth** 记得做过某事 ♦ **she remembered to do it** 她记得要做某事
remembrance [rɪˈmɛmbrəns] *n* **1** (*memory*) ♦ **in remembrance of** 纪念 **2** [c/u] (*souvenir*) [*of place, event*] 纪念物
Remembrance Day, Remembrance Sunday [英] *n* 阵亡将士纪念日

> **REMEMBRANCE SUNDAY**
> Remembrance Sunday 是最接近11月11日的那个星期天，在这一天人们纪念在两次世界大战中阵亡的将士。

remind [rɪˈmaɪnd] *vt* 提醒 ♦ **to remind sb to do sth** 提醒某人做某事 ♦ **to remind sb that ...** 提醒某人… ♦ **to remind sb of sth** (*issue reminder*) 提醒某人某事 ♦ **to remind sb of sb/sth** (*be reminiscent of*) 使某人想起某人/某事 ♦ **that reminds me!** 我记起来了！
reminder [rɪˈmaɪndə(r)] *n* [c] **1** [*of person, place, event*] 唤起记忆的事物 **2** (*aide-memoire*) 提醒物 **3** (*official letter*) 催缴单
reminiscent [rɛmɪˈnɪsnt] *adj* ♦ **to be reminiscent of sth** 使人想起某事
remnant [ˈrɛmnənt] *n* [c] **1** (*relic*) 残余 **2** [商] [*of cloth*] 碎布头
remorse [rɪˈmɔːs] *n* [u] 悔恨
remote [rɪˈməut] *adj* **1** (*isolated*) [+ *place*] 遥远的 **2** (*distant*) [+ *person*] 冷淡的 **3** (*slight*) [+ *possibility, chance*] 微小的 ♦ **in the remote past** 在遥远的过去 ♦ **there is a remote possibility that ...** …的可能性极小 ♦ **to be remote from** 与…无关
remote control *n* **1** [c] (*device*) (*for TV etc*) 遥控器 **2** [u] (*system*) 遥控
remotely [rɪˈməutlɪ] *adv* (*slightly*) 丝毫
removal [rɪˈmuːvəl] *n* **1** [u] (*of object, stain*) 去除 **2** [u] [*of threat, suspicion*] 排除 **3** [c/u] [英] (*from building*) 搬迁 **4** [u] (*dismissal*) (*from office*) 免职
removal man (*pl* **removal men**) [英] *n* [c] 搬运工
removal van [英] *n* [c] 搬迁专用车
remove [rɪˈmuːv] *vt* **1** [+ *object, organ*] 移走 **2** [+ *clothing, bandage etc*] 脱下 **3** [+ *stain*] 清除 **4** [+ *obstacle, problem, suspicion, threat*] 消除 **5** [+ *official*] 免职 **6** [+ *name*] (*from list*) 删除 ♦ **my first cousin once removed** 我堂亲/表亲的子女
rename [riːˈneɪm] *vt* 重新命名
render [ˈrɛndə(r)] [正式] *vt* **1** (*give*) [+ *service, aid*] 提供 **2** ♦ **to render sth harmless/worthless** 使某物无害/一文不值 **3** (*submit*) [+ *account*] 翻译
rendezvous [ˈrɔndɪvuː] (*pl* **rendezvous** [ˈrɔndɪvuːz]) **I** *n* [c] **1** (*meeting*) 约会 **2** (*place*) 约会地点 **II** *vi* **1** [*people, spacecraft* +] 会合 ♦ **to rendezvous with sb** 与某人在约定地点相会
renew [rɪˈnjuː] *vt* **1** [+ *efforts, attack, talks*] 重新开始 **2** [+ *loan, contract*] 延长 **3** [+ *acquaintance, relationship*] 重建
renewal [rɪˈnjuːəl] *n* **1** [c/u] [*of licence, contract etc*] 更新 **2** [s] [*of hostilities, conflict*] 重新开始
renewed [rɪˈnjuːd] *adj* 复兴的
renovate [ˈrɛnəveɪt] *vt* 修复
renowned [rɪˈnaund] *adj* 著名的 ♦ **to be renowned for sth** 由于某事而知名
rent [rɛnt] **I** *n* [c/u] (*for building, room, land*) 租金 **II** *vt* **1** (*hire*) [+ *building, room, land, car*] 租用 **2** (*also:* ***rent out***) [+ *house, room*] 出租
rental [ˈrɛntl] **I** *n* **1** [c] (*charge*) 租金 **2** [u] (*act of renting*) 租赁 **II** *adj* 出租的
rental car [美] *n* [c] 租的车 [英= **hire car**]
reorganize [riːˈɔːgənaɪz] *vt* 重组

rep [rɛp] *n* 1 (*representative*) (*for group*) 代表; (*also:* ***sales rep***) 商品经销代理 2 [戏剧] (*repertory*) 仓库

Rep. [美:政治] *abbr* 1 (= ***representative***) 众议院议员 2 (= ***republican***) 共和党的

repair [rɪ'pɛə(r)] I *n* [c/u] 修理 II *vt* 1 [+ *object, building*] 修补 2 [+ *damage*] 维修 ♦ **in good/bad repair** 维修良好/不善 ♦ **to be beyond repair** 无法修复 ♦ **under repair** (*road etc*) 在修理中

repair kit *n* [c] 成套维修工具

repay [riː'peɪ] *pt, pp* **repaid** *vt* 1 [*loan, debt, person*] 偿还 2 [+ *favour*] 报答 3 [+ *sb's efforts, attention*] 值得

repayment [riː'peɪmənt] *n* 1 [c] (*sum of money*) 还款 2 [u] (*action of repaying*) 偿还

repeat [rɪ'piːt] I *vt* 1 [+ *statement, question*] 重复 2 [+ *action, mistake*] 重做 3 [广播, 电视] 重播 4 [教育] [+ *class, course*] 重修 5 [+ *pattern*] 重复 II *vi* ♦ **I repeat** 我重申 III *n* [c] 1 [广播, 电视] 重播 2 [*of event*] 重演 ♦ **to repeat o.s.** 一再重述 ♦ **to repeat itself** 再次发生

repeatedly [rɪ'piːtɪdlɪ] *adv* 反复地

repeat prescription *n* [c] 同样药方

repellent [rɪ'pɛlənt] *adj* 令人厌恶的

repetition [rɛpɪ'tɪʃən] *n* [c/u] (*repeat occurrence*) 重复

repetitive [rɪ'pɛtɪtɪv] *adj* [+ *movements, work, music*] 反复的

replace [rɪ'pleɪs] *vt* 1 (*put back*) 将…放回 2 (*supply replacement for*) [+ *sth damaged, lost, worn out*] 替换 3 (*take the place of*) 代替 ♦ **to replace sth with sth else** 用某物代替某物

replacement [rɪ'pleɪsmənt] *n* 1 [c] (*substitute person*) 代替人 2 [c] (*substitute object*) 代替物 3 [u] (*act of replacing*) 代替

replay [*n* 'riːpleɪ, *vb* riː'pleɪ] I *n* [c] 1 [电视] (*repeat showing*) 重放 2 [*of match*] 重新比赛 II *vt* [+ *track, song*] (*on tape*) 重新播放 ♦ **to replay a match** 重新比赛

replica ['rɛplɪkə] I *n* [c] 复制品 II *adj* 复制的

reply [rɪ'plaɪ] I *n* [c] 1 (*answer*) 回答 2 (*retaliation*) 反应 II *vi* 1 (*to question, letter*) 答复 2 (*retaliation*) (*to attack etc*) 回应 ♦ **in reply to your question ...** 就你的问题而言… ♦ **"in reply to your letter ..."** "对您来信的回复…" ♦ **there's no reply** [通信] 无人接听

✪ **report** [rɪ'pɔːt] I *n* [c] 1 (*account*) 报告 2 [出版, 电视] (*bulletin*) 报道 3 [英] (*also:* ***school report***) 成绩单 4 [*of gun*] 爆炸声 II *vt* 1 (*state*) 汇报 2 [出版, 电视] 报道 3 (*bring to notice*) [+ *theft, accident, death*] 报案; [+ *person*] 告发 III *vi* (*make a report*) 汇报 ♦ **to report to sb** (*present o.s. to*) 向某人报到; (*be responsible to*) 对某人负责 ♦ **to report on sth** 报告某事 ♦ **to report sick** 报病 ♦ **it is reported that ...** 据报道…

report card [美] *n* [c] 学生成绩报告单 [英 = **report**]

reportedly [rɪ'pɔːtɪdlɪ] *adv* 据说

reporter [rɪ'pɔːtə(r)] *n* [c] 记者

represent [rɛprɪ'zɛnt] *vt* 1 (*act on behalf of*) [+ *person, nation*] 代表 2 (*reflect*) [+ *view, belief*] 体现 3 (*stand for*) [+ *word, object*] 表示 4 (*constitute*) 体现 ♦ **to represent sb/sth as** (*describe*) 把某人/某事描绘成

representation [rɛprɪzɛn'teɪʃən] I *n* 1 [u] (*representatives*) 代表 2 [c] (*depiction*) 描绘 II **representations** *n* [*pl*] (*protest*) 抗议

representative [rɛprɪ'zɛntətɪv] I *n* [c] 1 [*of person, nation*] 代表 2 [商] 代理 3 [美:政治] 众议院议员 II *adj* [+ *group, survey, cross-section*] 有代表性的 ♦ **representative of** 典型的

repress [rɪ'prɛs] *vt* [+ *people, revolt*] 压制; [+ *feeling, impulse*] 压抑

repression [rɪ'prɛʃən] *n* 1 [c/u] [*of people, country*] 镇压 2 [c] [*of feelings*] 压抑

reprimand ['rɛprɪmɑːnd] I *n* [c] 训斥 II *vt* 训斥

reproduce [riːprə'djuːs] I *vt* 复制 II *vi* (*breed*) 繁殖

reproduction [riːprə'dʌkʃən] *n* 1 [c] (*copy*) [*of document*] 拷贝件; [*of painting, furniture*] 复制品 2 [u] (*copying*) 复印 3 [u] (*breeding*) 繁殖 4 [u] [*of sound*] 录制

reptile ['rɛptaɪl] *n* [c] 爬行动物

republic [rɪ'pʌblɪk] *n* [c] 共和国
republican [rɪ'pʌblɪkən] **I** *adj* 1 [+ *system, government etc*] 共和政体的 2 [美：政治] ♦**Republican** 共和党的 **II** *n* [c] 1 (*anti-monarchist*) 共和主义者 2 [美：政治] ♦**Republican** 共和党党员
reputable ['rɛpjutəbl] *adj* 声誉好的
reputation [rɛpju'teɪʃən] *n* [c] 名声 ♦**to have a reputation for** 因…而闻名
reputed [rɪ'pjuːtɪd] *adj* 据说的
request [rɪ'kwɛst] **I** *n* [c] 1 (*polite demand*) 要求 2 [广播] 点播 **II** *vt* 要求 ♦**on request** 应要求 ♦**at the request of** 应…的要求 ♦**Mr and Mrs X request the pleasure of your company...** [正式] X 先生和夫人敬请您的大驾光临…
require [rɪ'kwaɪə(r)] *vt* 1 (*need*) 需要 2 (*demand*) 要求 ♦**to be required** [*approval, permission* +] 必须有 ♦**to require sb to do sth** 要求某人做某事 ♦**if required** 如有需要 ♦**required by law** 法律规定
requirement [rɪ'kwaɪəmənt] *n* [c] 1 (*need*) 需要的事物 2 (*condition*) 必备条件 ♦**to meet sb's requirements** 符合某人的要求
rescue ['rɛskjuː] **I** *n* [c/u] 1 营救 **II** *vt* 1 解救 ♦**to go/come to sb's rescue** 前往/来营救某人 ♦**to rescue sb from sth** 从某事中解救某人
✪**research** [rɪ'səːtʃ] **I** *n* [u] 1 研究 **II** *vt* [+ *story, subject*] 研究 **III** *vi* ♦**to research into sth** 研究某事 ♦**to do research** 从事研究 ♦**a piece of research** 一个研究课题 ♦**research and development** 研究与开发
resemblance [rɪ'zɛmbləns] *n* [c/u] (*likeness*) 相似 ♦**to bear a strong resemblance to** 与…极其相似 ♦**it bears no resemblance to ...** 与…毫无相似之处
resemble [rɪ'zɛmbl] *vt* 与…相似
resent [rɪ'zɛnt] *vt* [+ *attitude, treatment*] 憎恶; [+ *person*] 怨恨
resentful [rɪ'zɛntful] *adj* 憎恨的
resentment [rɪ'zɛntmənt] *n* [c/u] 憎恨
reservation [rɛzə'veɪʃən] *n* 1 [c] (*booking*) 预定 2 [c/u] (*doubt*) 保留 3 [c] (*land*) 保留地 ♦**with reservation(s)** (*doubts*) 持保留意见 ♦**to make a reservation** (*in hotel, restaurant, on train*) 预定
reservation desk [美] *n* [c] (*in hotel*) 预定台
reserve [rɪ'zəːv] **I** *vt* 1 [+ *seat, table, ticket etc*] 预定 2 (*keep*) 保留 **II** *n* [c] 1 (*store*) [*of food, fuel, energy, talent etc*] 储备 2 [c] [英：体育] 候补队员 3 [c] (*also: **nature reserve***) 自然保护区 4 [u] (*restraint*) 矜持 **II** **reserves** *n* [*pl*] [军] 后备军 ♦**in reserve** 备用
reserved [rɪ'zəːvd] *adj* 1 (*unavailable*) [+ *seat*] 已预定的 2 (*restrained*) 矜持的
reservoir ['rɛzəvwɑː(r)] *n* [c] 1 [*of water*] 水库 2 [*of talent etc*] 储备
residence ['rɛzɪdəns] *n* 1 [c] [正式] (*home*) 居所 2 [u] (*length of stay*) 居住 ♦**to take up residence** 开始居住 ♦**to be in residence** (*queen etc*) 居住 ♦**writer/artist in residence** 常驻作家/艺术家 ♦**place of residence** [正式] 居住地
residence permit [英] *n* [c] 居留许可
resident ['rɛzɪdənt] **I** *n* [c] 1 [*of country, town, house*] 居民 2 [*of hotel*] 房客 **II** *adj* 1 [正式] (*residing*) 居住的 2 [+ *population*] 居住的
residential [rɛzɪ'dɛnʃəl] *adj* 1 [+ *area*] 住宅的 2 [+ *course*] 寄宿制的 3 [+ *staff*] 住宿的 4 [+ *home*] 居住的
residue ['rɛzɪdjuː] [化] *n* [c] 残余
resign [rɪ'zaɪn] **I** *vt* [+ *one's job*] 辞去 **II** *vi* 辞职 ♦**to resign o.s. to sth** [+ *situation, fact*] 听任某事
resignation [rɛzɪg'neɪʃən] *n* 1 [c/u] (*from job*) 辞呈 2 [u] (*state of mind*) 达观 ♦**to tender one's resignation** 宣布辞职
resilient [rɪ'zɪlɪənt] *adj* 1 [+ *material*] 有弹性的 2 [+ *person*] 适应力强的
resin ['rɛzɪn] *n* [c/u] 1 (*natural*) 树脂 2 (*synthetic*) 合成树脂
resist [rɪ'zɪst] *vt* 1 (*withstand*) [+ *change, demand*] 抗拒; [+ *enemy, attack, damage, cold*] 抵抗; [+ *temptation, urge*] 克制 2 (*withstand temptation of*) 抗拒

resistance [rɪ'zɪstəns] *n* **1** [s/u] (*opposition*) (*to change, demand*) 抵制 **2** [s/u] [医] (*to illness, infection*) 抵抗力 **3** [s/u] [军] 抵抗 **4** [u] [电子] 电阻

resistant [rɪ'zɪstənt] *adj* **1** (*to change etc*) 抵制的 **2** (*to chemical, disease, antibiotics*) 有抵抗力的

resit [*n* 'riːsɪt, *vb* riː'sɪt] [英] **I** *vt* [+ *exam*] 补考 **II** *n* 补考

resolute ['rɛzəluːt] *adj* [+ *person*] 坚定的; [+ *refusal, action*] 果断的

resolution [rɛzə'luːʃən] *n* **1** [c/u] (*vow, determination*) 决心 **2** [c] (*formal decision*) 决议 **3** [s] (*solution*) [*of problem, difficulty*] 解决 ♦ **to make a resolution** 下决心 ♦ **New Year's resolution** 新年决心

resolve [rɪ'zɔlv] **I** *vt* [+ *problem, difficulty*] 解决 **II** *vi* ♦ **to resolve to do sth** 下决心去做某事 **III** *n* [u] (*determination*) 决心

resort [rɪ'zɔːt] **I** *n* **1** [c] (*also:* ***holiday resort***) 度假胜地 **2** (*recourse*) ♦ **without resort to** 不诉诸于 **II** *vi* ♦ **to resort to sth** 最终诉诸于某事 ♦ **a seaside/winter sports resort** 海边/冬季运动胜地 ♦ **as a last resort** 作为最后手段 ♦ **in the last resort** 最终还得

resource [rɪ'zɔːs] **I** *n* [c] (*raw material*) 资源 **II resources** *n* [*pl*] **1** (*coal, iron, oil etc*) 资源 **2** (*money*) 财力 **III** *vt* [英] ♦ **to be adequately/poorly resourced** 设备充足/不足 ♦ **natural resources** 自然资源

resourceful [rɪ'zɔːsful] *adj* 机敏的

respect [rɪs'pɛkt] **I** *n* [u] (*consideration, esteem*) 尊敬 **II** *vt* [+ *person*] 尊敬; [+ *sb's wishes, beliefs*] 考虑到; [+ *custom, tradition*] 尊重 **III respects** *n* [*pl*] (*regards*) 问候 ♦ **to have respect for sb/sth** 对某人/某事怀有敬意 ♦ **to show sb/sth respect** 对某人/某事表示尊敬 ♦ **with respect to** *or* **in respect of** [正式] 关于 ♦ **in this respect** 就此而言 ♦ **in some/many respects** 在某些/许多方面 ♦ **with (all due) respect** 尊重您的意见，但是 ♦ **to pay one's respects** [正式] 表示某人的敬意

respectable [rɪs'pɛktəbl] *adj* **1** [+ *area, background*] 体面的 **2** [+ *person*] 受人尊敬的 **3** (*adequate*) [+ *amount, income*] 过得去的; [+ *standard, mark etc*] 相当好的

respectful [rɪs'pɛktful] *adj* 恭敬的

respective [rɪs'pɛktɪv] *adj* 分别的

respectively [rɪs'pɛktɪvlɪ] *adv* 分别 ♦ **France and Britain were 3rd and 4th respectively** 法国和英国分别名列第3和第4

respite ['rɛspaɪt] *n* [s/u] (*rest*) 暂缓

respond [rɪs'pɔnd] *vi* **1** (*answer*) 回应 **2** (*react*) (*to pressure, criticism*) 回应; (*to treatment*) 反应

response [rɪs'pɔns] *n* [c] **1** (*answer*) (*to question, remark*) 回答 **2** (*reaction*) (*to situation, event*) 反应 ♦ **in response to** 作为回应

responsibility [rɪspɔnsɪ'bɪlɪtɪ] **I** *n* **1** [u] (*liability*) 责任 **2** [s] (*duty*) 职责 **3** [u] (*obligation*) 义务 **II responsibilities** *n* [*pl*] 责任 ♦ **to take responsibility for sth/sb** 对某事/某人负责

responsible [rɪs'pɔnsɪbl] *adj* **1** (*at fault*) 负有责任的 **2** (*in charge*) 负责的 **3** (*sensible, trustworthy*) [+ *person*] 可靠的; [+ *job*] 责任重大的 ♦ **to be responsible for sth/doing sth** 为某事/做某事负责 ♦ **to be responsible to sb** 对某人负责

> 请勿将**responsible for**和**responsible to**混淆。如果你**responsible for**某事物，表示你有责任处理此事，并做出与之有关的决定。*We cannot be responsible for delays between sending and receipt of e-mails.* **responsible for**也可表示某人是导致某事发生的原因，或应对此承担责任。*He still felt responsible for her death.* 如果你**responsible to**某个人或某个组织，表明他们是你的上级，你需要向他们进行汇报。*I'm responsible to my board of directors.*

responsibly [rɪs'pɔnsɪblɪ] *adv* 明事理地

responsive [rɪs'pɔnsɪv] *adj* **1** (*receptive*) 积极响应的 **2** (*to sb's needs, interests etc*) 反应灵敏的

rest [rɛst] **I** *n* **1** [U] (*relaxation*) 休息 **2** [C] (*break*) 休息 **3** [S] (*remainder*) 剩余 **4** [C] (*support*) 支架 **II** *vi* **1** (*relax*) 休息 **2** (*be supported*) 依靠 **III** *vt* (*relax*) [+ *eyes, legs, muscles*] 休息 ♦ **to rest sth on/against sth** (*lean*) 把某物靠在某物上 ♦ **to rest on sth** (*lean on*) 靠在某物上; (*be based on*) 依据某物 ♦ **the rest (of them)** (*people, objects*) (他们当中) 其余的 ♦ **and the rest/all the rest of it** 以及其余/其余所有的 ♦ **to put** *or* **set sb's mind at rest** 使某人免于忧虑 ♦ **to rest one's eyes** *or* **gaze on sth** 将目光停留在某物上 ♦ **to come to rest** [*object* +] 停下来 ♦ **to lay sb to rest** 安葬某人 ♦ **to let the matter rest** 使事情到此为止 ♦ **I won't rest until ...** 直到…我才会停止 ♦ **I rest my case** (*hum*) 我无需多说了

rest area [美] *n* [C] 路边服务站 [英 = **service station**]

restaurant [ˈrɛstərɔŋ] *n* [C] 餐馆

restaurant car [英] *n* [C] 餐车 [美 = **dining car**]

restful [ˈrɛstful] *adj* [+ *music, lighting, atmosphere*] 令人放松的

restless [ˈrɛstlɪs] *adj* **1** (*dissatisfied*) 焦躁不安的 **2** (*fidgety*) 坐立不安的

restoration [rɛstəˈreɪʃən] *n* **1** [C/U] [*of painting, church etc*] 修复 **2** [U] [*of rights, of law and order*] 恢复 **3** [U] [*of land*] 复原 **4** [U] [*of health, sight, etc*] 恢复 **5** [历史] ♦ **the Restoration** 1660 年英国查理二世王权复辟

restore [rɪˈstɔː(r)] *vt* **1** [+ *painting, building etc*] 修复 **2** [+ *law and order*] 恢复 **3** [+ *faith, confidence*] 重建 **4** (*to power, former state*) 使…复位 **5** [+ *land*] 恢复 **6** (*return*) [正式] 归还 **7** [+ *health, sight*] 恢复

restrain [rɪsˈtreɪn] *vt* **1** [+ *person*] 阻止 **2** [+ *curiosity, anger*] 抑制 **3** [+ *growth, inflation*] 遏制 ♦ **to restrain sb from doing sth** 阻止某人做某事 ♦ **to restrain o.s. from doing sth** 克制自己做某事

restraint [rɪsˈtreɪnt] *n* **1** [C/U] (*restriction*) 约束 **2** [U] (*moderation*) 克制 ♦ **wage restraint** 工资限额政策

restrict [rɪsˈtrɪkt] *vt* **1** [+ *growth, membership, privilege*] 限制 **2** [+ *vision, movements*] 阻碍 **3** [+ *activities*] 约束

restriction [rɪsˈtrɪkʃən] *n* [C] 限制

rest room [美] *n* [C] 洗手间 [英 = **toilet, lavatory**]

restructure [riːˈstrʌktʃə(r)] *vt* **1** [+ *organization, system*] 改组 **2** [+ *debt*] 重组

✪ **result** [rɪˈzʌlt] **I** *n* [C] [*of event, action*] 后果; [*of match, election, exam, competition*] 结果; [*of calculation*] 答案 **II** *vi* 产生 ♦ **to result in** 导致 ♦ **as a result of** 由于 ♦ **to result from** 因…而产生 ♦ **as a result it is...** 因此是…

resume [rɪˈzjuːm] **I** *vt* **1** [+ *work, journey*] 继续 **II** *vi* (*start again*) 继续 ♦ **to resume one's seat** [正式] 回到原座

résumé [ˈreɪzjuːmeɪ] *n* [C] **1** (*summary*) 摘要 **2** [美] (*CV*) 简历 [英 = **CV**]

resuscitate [rɪˈsʌsɪteɪt] *vt* **1** [医] 使…苏醒 **2** [+ *plan, idea*] 重新启动

retail [ˈriːteɪl] **I** *adj* [+ *trade, sales*] 零售的 **II** *adv* 零卖地 **III** *vt* (*sell*) 零售 **IV** *vi* ♦ **to retail at** *or* **for...** 以…价格零售

retailer [ˈriːteɪlə(r)] *n* [C] 零售商

retail price *n* [C] 零售价

retain [rɪˈteɪn] *vt* [+ *independence, humour, heat*] 保持; [+ *ticket, souvenir*] 保留

retaliate [rɪˈtælɪeɪt] *vi* 报复

retaliation [rɪtælɪˈeɪʃən] *n* [U] 报复 ♦ **in retaliation for** 为…复仇

retarded [rɪˈtɑːdɪd] *adj* **1** [+ *child*] 智力迟缓的 **2** [+ *development, growth*] 发育迟缓的 ♦ **mentally retarded** 智力迟缓的

retire [rɪˈtaɪə(r)] *vi* **1** (*give up work*) 退休 **2** [正式] (*withdraw*) 离开 **3** [正式] (*go to bed*) 就寝

retired [rɪˈtaɪəd] *adj* 退休的

retiree [rɪtaɪəˈriː] [美] *n* [C] 领养老金的人 [英 = **pensioner**]

retirement [rɪˈtaɪəmənt] *n* [C/U] 退休

retort [rɪˈtɔːt] **I** *vi* 反驳 **II** *n* [C] (*reply*) 反驳

retreat [rɪˈtriːt] **I** *n* **1** [C] (*place*) 隐居处 **2** [C/U] (*act*) 退避 **3** [C/U] [军] 撤退 **II** *vi* **1** (*from danger, enemy*) 退避 **2** (*from promise etc*) 放弃 **3** [军] 撤退

♦**to beat a hasty retreat** 迅速逃离
retrieve [rɪ'triːv] **I** *vt* **1** [+ *object*] 取回 **2** (*put right*) [+ *situation, error*] 挽回 **3** [计算机] 检索
retrospect ['rɛtrəspɛkt] *n* ♦**in retrospect** 回顾
✪**return** [rɪ'tə:n] **I** *vi* [*person* +] 返回 ◊ *I returned to my hotel.* 我返回到我住的酒店。; [*situation, symptom* +] 再出现 ◊ *If the pain returns, repeat the treatment.* 如果疼痛再出现，则重复疗程。**II** *vt* **1** [+ *something borrowed or stolen*] 归还 ◊ *He returned her passport.* 他归还了她的护照。**2** [+ *favour, feeling, greeting*] 回 **3** [法法][+ *verdict*] 裁决 **4** [政治] [+ *candidate*] 当选 **5** [+ *ball*] 回传 **III** *n* **1** [s] [*of person*] 返回 **2** [s] [*of something borrowed or stolen*] 归还 **3** [s] (*to activity, to a state*) 回到 **4** [c/u] [经济] (*from land, shares, investment*) 盈利 **5** [s] [*of merchandise*] 退货 **6** [u] [计算机] (*key*) 回车键 **IV returns** *n* [*pl*] [商] 利润 ♦**in return (for)** 作为（对…）的回报 ♦**by return of post** 请即赐复 ♦**many happy returns (of the day)!** 生日快乐！**V** *cpd* [复合词] **1** [英][+ *journey, ticket*] 往返 **2** [+ *match*] [英] 回访
❏**return to** *vt* [不可拆分] **1** [+ *consciousness, power*] 恢复 **2** [+ *subject, activity*] 回到
reunion [riː'juːnɪən] *n* **1** [c] [*of family, school, class etc*] 团聚 **2** [c/u] [*of two people*] 重聚
reunite [riːjuː'naɪt] *vt* **1** [+ *people*] 重聚 **2** [+ *organization, country etc*] 使…重新团结
rev [rɛv] [汽车] *n abbr* (= ***revolution***) 旋转
revamp [riː'væmp] *vt* 更新
rev counter [英:汽车] *n* [c] 转速计数器
Rev(d). [宗] *abbr* (= ***reverend***) 牧师
reveal [rɪ'viːl] *vt* **1** (*make known*) 透露 **2** (*make visible*) 展现
revealing [rɪ'viːlɪŋ] *adj* **1** [+ *comment, action*] 揭露事实的 **2** [+ *clothes*] 暴露的
revel ['rɛvl] *vi* ♦**to revel in sth** 尽情享受某事物
revelation [rɛvə'leɪʃən] **I** *n* **1** [c] (*fact*) 透露出来的事 **2** [s] (*surprise*) 揭露 **3** [c/u] (*disclosure*) [*of fact*] 揭露 **II Revelations** *n* [*pl*] (*in Bible*) 启示录
revenge [rɪ'vɛndʒ] **I** *n* [u] 复仇 **II** *vt* [+ *defeat, injustice*] 报复 ♦**to get one's revenge (for sth)** （为某事）进行报复 ♦**to take (one's) revenge (on sb)** （对某人）进行报复 ♦**to revenge o.s. (on sb)** （向某人）进行报复
revenue ['rɛvənjuː] *n* [c/u] 岁入
Reverend ['rɛvərənd] *adj* 牧师的 ♦**the Reverend John Smith** 约翰•史密斯牧师; (*Catholic*) 修道院院长; (*Lutheran*) 牧师
reversal [rɪ'və:sl] *n* [c] **1** (*turnaround*) 翻转 **2** (*setback*) 挫败
reverse [rɪ'və:s] **I** *n* **1** [s] (*opposite*) 相反 **2** [u] [汽车] (*also:* ***reverse gear***) 倒退挡 **3** [s] (*back*) [*of cloth, coin, medal*] 反面; [*of paper*] 背面 **4** [c] (*setback, defeat*) 挫败 **II** *adj* **1** [+ *process, effect*] 相反的 **2** [+ *side*] 反面的 **III** *vt* **1** [+ *order, position, direction*] 使反转 **2** [+ *process, decision, trend*] 彻底转变 **3** [法法][+ *judgement, verdict*] 撤销 **4** [+ *roles*] 互换 **5** [+ *car*] [尤英] 倒退行驶 [美 = **back up**] **IV** *vi* [英:汽车] 倒退行驶 [美 = **back up**] ♦**in reverse** (*action, process*) 顺序相反; [汽车] 挂倒挡 ♦**in reverse order** 逆序 ♦**to go into reverse** [*trend* +] 逆转; (*in car*) 挂倒挡
reverse-charge call [rɪ'və:stʃɑːdʒ-] [英] *n* [c] 受话人付费电话 [美 = **collect call**]
reversing lights [rɪ'və:sɪŋ-] [英] *n* [*pl*] 倒车灯
revert [rɪ'və:t] *vi* **1** ♦**to revert to** [+ *former state*] 回到 **2** [法法] [*money, property* +] 物归原主
review [rɪ'vjuː] **I** *n* [c] **1** (*evaluation*) [*of book, film etc*] 评论 **2** (*examination*) [*of situation, policy etc*] 审查 **3** (*magazine*) 评论刊物 **4** [军] 检阅 **II** *vt* **1** [+ *book, film etc*] 评论 **2** [+ *situation, policy etc*] 审查 **3** [军] [+ *troops*] 检阅 ♦**to be/come under review** 受到审查
reviewer [rɪ'vjuːə(r)] *n* [c] 评论家
revise [rɪ'vaɪz] **I** *vt* (*alter, adapt*) [+ *manuscript, article*] 修改;

[+ *opinion, attitude*] 修正; [+ *procedure*] 改进; (*study*) 复习 **II** *vi* (*study*) [英] 复习 ♦**revised edition** 修订本

revision [rɪˈvɪʒən] *n* **1** [C/U] (*alteration, adaptation*) 修改 **2** [U] [英] (*studying*) 复习

revival [rɪˈvaɪvəl] *n* [C] **1** (*renewed popularity*) 复兴 **2** (*economic*) 复苏 **3** [戏剧] 重新上演

revive [rɪˈvaɪv] **I** *vt* **1** [+ *person*] 使苏醒 **2** [+ *economy, industry*] 复苏 **3** [+ *custom*] 复兴 **4** [+ *hope, courage, interest etc*] 唤起 **5** [+ *play*] 重演 **II** *vi* **1** [*person* +] 苏醒 **2** [*activity, economy, faith, interest etc* +] 复苏

revolt [rɪˈvəult] **I** *n* [C/U] **1** (*rebellion*) 造反 **2** (*rejection*) 反叛 **II** *vi* 起义 **III** *vt* 使憎恶 ♦**to revolt against sb/sth** 反抗某人/某物

revolting [rɪˈvəultɪŋ] *adj* 令人厌恶的

revolution [rɛvəˈluːʃən] *n* **1** [C/U] [政治] 革命 **2** [C] (*change*) (*in industry, education etc*) 变革 **3** [C/U] (*rotation*) 旋转一周

revolutionary [rɛvəˈluːʃənrɪ] **I** *adj* **1** [+ *method, idea, concept*] 创新的 **2** [政治] [+ *leader, army, movement*] 革命的 **II** *n* [C] [政治] 革命者

revolutionize [rɛvəˈluːʃənaɪz] *vt* 彻底改变

revolve [rɪˈvɔlv] *vi* [*wheel, propeller etc* +] 旋转 ♦**to revolve (a)round sth** **1** [*earth, moon* +] 围绕某物旋转 **2** [*life, discussion* +] 以某物为中心

revolver [rɪˈvɔlvə(r)] *n* [C] 左轮手枪

reward [rɪˈwɔːd] **I** *n* [C] **1** (*for service, merit, work*) 奖励 **2** [警察] (*for capture of criminal, information*) 赏金 **3** (*satisfaction*) 回报 **II** *vt* **1** [+ *person*] 奖赏 **2** [+ *patience, determination etc*] 报偿

rewarding [rɪˈwɔːdɪŋ] *adj* (*worthwhile*) [+ *experience, job etc*] 值得做的 ♦**financially rewarding** 报酬丰厚

rewind [riːˈwaɪnd] (*pt, pp* **rewound**) *vt* 倒带

rewrite [riːˈraɪt] (*pt* **rewrote** *pp* **rewritten**) *vt* 改写

rheumatism [ˈruːmətɪzəm] *n* [U] 风湿病

rhinoceros [raɪˈnɔsərəs] *n* [C] 犀牛

rhubarb [ˈruːbɑːb] *n* [U] 大黄

rhyme [raɪm] **I** *n* **1** [C] (*sound, word*) 同韵词 **2** [C] (*verse*) 押韵诗 **3** [U] (*technique*) 押韵 **II** *vi* 押韵 ♦**without rhyme or reason** 毫无道理 ♦**to rhyme with sth** 与某词押韵

rhythm [ˈrɪðm] *n* **1** [C/U] [*of drums, music*] 节奏 **2** [C] [*of body, tides, seasons*] 周期

RI *n abbr* (= ***religious instruction***) [英:教育] 宗教教育

rib [rɪb] **I** *n* [C] [解剖] 肋骨 **II** *vt* (*mock*) [非正式] 逗弄

ribbon [ˈrɪbən] *n* **1** [C/U] (*for hair*) 饰带; (*for decoration*) 捆扎带 **2** [C] [*of typewriter*] 色带 ♦**in ribbons** (*torn*) 破烂不堪

rice [raɪs] *n* [C/U] **1** (*grain*) 大米 **2** (*when cooked*) 米饭

rice pudding *n* [C/U] 米饭布丁

rich [rɪtʃ] **I** *adj* **1** [+ *person, country*] 富有的 **2** [+ *food, diet*] 油腻的 **3** [+ *soil*] 肥沃的 **4** [+ *colour*] 深的 **5** [+ *voice*] 深沉的 **6** [+ *experience, life, history*] 丰富的 **7** [+ *tapestries, silks*] 贵重的 **II** *n* [*pl*] ♦**the rich** 富人 ♦**rich in** [+ *minerals, resources etc*] 富含

riches [ˈrɪtʃɪz] *n* [*pl*] 财富

richly [ˈrɪtʃlɪ] *adv* **1** [+ *decorated, carved*] 华丽地 **2** [+ *coloured, flavoured*] 浓厚地 **3** [*reward, benefit* +] 丰厚地 **4** [+ *deserved, earned*] 完全地

rid [rɪd] (*pt, pp* **rid**) *vt* ♦**to rid sb/sth of sth** 使某人/某物摆脱某事物 ♦**to get rid of sth/sb** [+ *smell, dirt, car etc*] 摆脱某事物/某人 ♦**to be rid of sth/sb** 摆脱某事物/某人

riddle [ˈrɪdl] *n* [C] **1** (*conundrum*) 谜语 **2** (*mystery*) 谜

riddled [ˈrɪdld] *adj* ♦**to be riddled with** **1** [+ *guilt, doubts, errors*] 充斥着 **2** [+ *holes, bullets*] 被弄得千疮百孔

ride [raɪd] (*pt* **rode**, *pp* **ridden**) **I** *n* [C] **1** (*in car, on bicycle*) 兜风 **2** (*on horse, bus, train*) 出行 **3** (*track, path*) 供骑马用的小径 **II** *vi* **1** (*travel*) (*on horse*) 骑马; (*on bicycle*) 骑车; (*in car*) 乘坐 **III** *vt* **1** [+ *horse, bicycle, motorcycle*] 骑 **2** [+ *distance*] 行进 ♦**a**

horse/car ride 骑马/乘车出游 ♦**to go for a ride** 出游 ♦**to give sb a ride** [美] 让某人搭车 ♦**to take sb for a ride** (喻) 欺骗某人 ♦**to be riding high** 声明显赫 ♦**a rough ride** [非正式] 艰难的处境

❑**ride out** *vt* ♦**to ride out the storm** 安然度过

rider ['raɪdə(r)] *n* [C] **1** (*on horse*) 骑师; (*on bicycle*) 骑自行车的人; (*on motorcycle*) 骑手 **2** (*addendum*) 附加意见

ridge [rɪdʒ] *n* [C] **1** 隆起 **2** [*of hill*] 脊

ridicule ['rɪdɪkjuːl] **I** *vt* **1** (*mock*) [+*person, proposal*] 嘲讽 **II** *n* [U] 嘲笑 ♦**to be the object of ridicule** 成为嘲笑的对象

ridiculous [rɪ'dɪkjuləs] *adj* 荒谬的

riding ['raɪdɪŋ] *n* [U] 骑马 ♦**to go riding** 去骑马

rife [raɪf] *adj* [*corruption, superstition, disease etc* +] 普遍的 ♦**to be rife with** [+ *rumours, fears etc*] 充斥着

rifle ['raɪfl] **I** *n* [C] (*gun*) 步枪 **II** *vt* (*also:* ***rifle through***) [+ *papers, clothing, bag etc*] 搜劫

rift [rɪft] *n* [C] **1** (*split*) (*in ground*) 裂缝 **2** (*disagreement*) 裂痕

rig [rɪg] **I** *n* [C] **1** (*also:* ***oil rig***) 钻井台 **II** *vt* [+ *election, game etc*] 暗箱操纵

❑**rig out** [英:非正式] *vt* ♦**to rig sb out as/in** 将某人打扮成/使某人穿戴着

❑**rig up** *vt* [+ *device, net*] 拼凑做成

✪**right** [raɪt] **I** *adj* **1** (*not left*) 右边的 ◊ *her right hand* 她的右手 **2** (*correct*) [+ *answer, size, person*] 正确的 ◊ *the right answer* 正确答案; (*appropriate*) [+ *person, place, clothes*] 合适的; [+ *decision, direction, time*] 最适宜的 **3** (*proper, fair*) 恰当的 **4** [+ *side*] (*of material*) 正面的 **5** (*socially acceptable*) 适当的 **6** (*emphasizing*) [英:非正式] 不折不扣的 **II** *n* **1** [S] (*not left*) 右边 **2** [U] (*what is morally right*) 正确 **3** [C] (*entitlement*) 权利 **III** *adv* **1** (*correctly*) 正确地 **2** (*properly, fairly*) 恰当 **3** (*not to/on the left*) 右边地 **4** (*directly, exactly*) 就 **IV** *vt* **1** (*put right way up*) [+ *ship, car etc*] 使…回到正确的位置 **2** (*correct*) [+ *fault, situation, wrong*] 纠正 **V** *int* 好 **VI rights** *n* [*pl*] [出版] 版权 ♦**this is not the right time for...** 这时间不合适做… ♦**do you have the right time?** 你的表几点了? ♦**the Right** [政治] 右派 ♦**to be right** [*person* +] 正确; [*answer, fact* +] 对; [*clock* +] 准确 ♦**to get sth right** 做对某事 ♦**let's get it right this time!** 这次别再出错了! ♦**you did the right thing** 你做得对 ♦**to put sth right** [+ *mistake, injustice etc*] 纠正某事 ♦**right now** [非正式] 当即 ♦**right before/after** 刚好在之前/之后 ♦**right against the wall** 正好靠墙 ♦**right in the middle** 正中间 ♦**right ahead** 正前方 ♦**by rights** 按道理 ♦**to** *or* **on the right** (*position*) 靠{或}在右侧 ♦**to the right** (*movement*) 向右 ♦**to be in the right** 有道理 ♦**right away** *or* **right off** (*immediately*) 立刻 ♦**to be within one's rights** 不超越权限 ♦**in his/her own right** 依靠他/她自身的能力 ♦**to go right to the end of sth** 一直走到某物的尽头 ♦**film rights** 电影拍摄权

right angle *n* [C] 直角 ♦**at right angles** 垂直

rightful ['raɪtful] *adj* [+ *heir, owner, place, share*] 合法的

right-hand drive ['raɪthænd-] **I** *n* [U] 右侧驾驶 **II** *adj* [+ *vehicle*] 右侧驾驶的

right-handed [raɪt'hændɪd] *adj* 惯用右手的

right-hand side *n* [S] 右侧

rightly ['raɪtlɪ] *adv* (*with reason*) 恰当地 ♦**if I remember rightly** [英] 如果我没记错

right of way *n* [C] **1** (*public path*) 通行权 **2** [汽车] (*priority*) 先行权

right-wing [raɪt'wɪŋ] **I** *adj* 右翼的 **II** *n* [S] (*of political party*) 右翼势力

rigid ['rɪdʒɪd] *adj* **1** [+ *structure, back etc*] 坚硬的 **2** [+ *attitude, principle, views etc*] 僵化的 **3** [+ *control*] 严格的

rigorous ['rɪgərəs] *adj* [+ *control, test, training*] 严格的

rim [rɪm] *n* [C] **1** [*of glass, dish*] 边缘 **2** [*of wheel*] 辋圈

rind [raɪnd] *n* [C/U] [*of bacon, fruit, cheese*] 皮

ring [rɪŋ] (*pt* **rang**, *pp* **rung**) **I** *n* [C]

1 (*on finger*) 戒指 2 [*of people, objects, light, smoke etc*] 圈 3 [*of spies, drug-dealers etc*] 团伙 4 (*for boxing*) 拳击台 5 [*of circus*] 马戏场 6 (*bullring*) 斗牛场 7 (*sound of telephone, bell*) 铃声 8 (*on cooker*) [尤英] 灶眼 **II** *vi* 1 [*bell* +] 鸣响 2 [*telephone* +] 响 3 [英:通信] (*call*) 打电话 [美=**call**] 4 (*also: **ring out***) [*voice, words, shot* +] 鸣响 **III** *vt* 1 [+ *bell, doorbell*] 使…响 2 [英:通信] 给…打电话 3 (*circle*) 圈出 4 (*surround*) 环绕 ♦**there was a ring at the door, the doorbell rang** 有人按门铃 ♦**to give sb a ring** [英:通信] 给某人打电话 ♦**that has a ring of truth about it** 那听上去是真的 ♦**to run rings (a)round sb** [非正式] 远远胜过某人 ♦**my ears are ringing** 我耳中嗡嗡作响 ♦**to ring true/false** 听起来正确/错误

❑**ring back** [英:通信] **I** *vt* 回电话 [美=**call back**] **II** *vi* 再打电话 [美=**call back**]

❑**ring off** [英:通信] *vi* 挂断电话 [美=**hang up**]

❑**ring up** [英:通信] *vt* 给…打电话

ringing ['rɪŋɪŋ] **I** *adj* [+ *crash*] 清脆的 **II** *n* [U] 1 [*of telephone, bell*] 鸣响 2 (*in ears*) 嗡嗡作响

ringing tone [英] *n* [C] 铃声

ring road [英:汽车] *n* [C] 环路

rink [rɪŋk] *n* [C] 1 (*also: **ice rink***) 溜冰场 2 (*also: **roller skating rink***) 旱冰场

rinse [rɪns] **I** *n* [C] [*of dishes, clothes*] 漂洗; [*of hair, hands*] 冲洗; (*hair dye*) 染发剂 **II** *vt* [+ *dishes, clothes*] 漂洗; [+ *hair, hands etc*] 冲洗; (*also: **rinse out***) [+ *mouth*] 漱

riot ['raɪət] **I** *n* [C] (*disturbance*) 暴乱 **II** *vi* 闹事 ◊ *They rioted in protest against the Government.* 他们在反对政府的抗议中闹事。♦**to run riot** [*children, football fans etc* +] 撒野 ♦**a riot of colour(s)** 五彩缤纷

RIP *abbr* (= ***rest in peace***) 愿灵安眠

rip [rɪp] **I** *n* [C] 裂口 **II** *vt* 撕裂 **III** *vi* 裂开

❑**rip off** *vt* 1 [+ *clothes*] 迅速脱掉 2 [非正式] (*swindle*) 欺骗

❑**rip up** *vt* 把…撕成碎片

ripe [raɪp] *adj* 1 [+ *fruit, corn*] 成熟的 ; [+ *cheese*] 发酵好的 ♦**to be ripe for sth** 某事的时机已成熟 ♦**the time is ripe** 时机已成熟 ♦**he lived to a ripe old age** 他活到高龄

ripen ['raɪpn] **I** *vi* [*sun* +] [+ *fruit, crop*] 成熟 **II** *vt* [*fruit, crop* +] 使…成熟

rip-off ['rɪpɔf] [非正式] *n* [C] 1 敲竹杠 2 (*copy*) [*of song, film*] 抄袭

ripple ['rɪpl] **I** *n* [C] 1 (*on water*) 涟漪 2 [*of laughter, applause*] 微弱的一阵 **II** *vi* 1 [*water* +] 起涟漪 2 [*muscles* +] 凸起 **III** *vt* [+ *surface*] 使…泛起涟漪

✪**rise** [raɪz] (*pt* **rose**, *pp* **risen**) **I** *n* 1 [C] (*incline*) 斜坡 2 [C] [英] (*salary increase*) 加薪 3 [C] (*in prices, temperature, crime rate etc*) 上升 4 [S] (*to power, fame etc*) 兴起 **II** *vi* 1 (*move upwards*) 上升 2 [*prices, numbers* +] 上升 3 [*water* +] 上涨 4 [*sun, moon* +] 升起 5 [*wind* +] 刮起来 6 [正式] [*person* +] (*get up*) 起床 7 (*from chair*) 起身 8 [*sound, voice* +] (*in pitch*) 提高 9 [*land* +] 隆起 10 (*also: **rise up***) [*tower, building* +] 矗立 11 (*revolt*) 反抗 12 (*in rank*) 升职 ♦**to rise to power** 掌权 ♦**to rise above sth** 不受某事的影响 ♦**to give rise to sth** 引起某事

rising ['raɪzɪŋ] *adj* 1 (*increasing*) 增加的 2 [+ *tide*] 上涨的 3 (*up-and-coming*) [+ *film star, politician etc*] 崭露头角的

risk [rɪsk] **I** *n* 1 [C/U] (*danger*) 危险 2 [C] (*possibility, chance*) 风险 3 [C] (*dangerous person or thing*) 危险事物 **II** *vt* 1 (*endanger*) 冒…危险 2 (*take the chance of*) 冒险做 ♦**to take a risk** 担风险 ♦**to run the risk of sth/doing sth** 冒着某事/做某事的危险 ♦**at risk** 处于危险 ♦**at one's own risk** 风险自负 ♦**to risk it** [非正式] 冒险一试

risky ['rɪskɪ] *adj* 有风险的

rite [raɪt] *n* [C] 仪式 ♦**rite of passage** 人生大事

ritual ['rɪtjuəl] **I** *adj* [+ *dance, murder*] 仪式上的 **II** *n* [C/U] 1 [宗] 仪式程序 2 (*procedure*) 程序

rival ['raɪvl] **I** *n* [C] 1 (*in competition, election, business*) 竞争对手 2 (*in love*) 情敌 **II** *adj* 1 [+ *firm, newspaper etc*] 竞争的 2 [+ *teams, groups,* *supporters etc*] 对立的 **III** *vt* (*match*) 与…匹敌

rivalry [ˈraɪvlrɪ] *n* [c/u] 竞争

river [ˈrɪvə(r)] **I** *n* [c] **1** 河 **2** [*of blood etc*] 涌出 **II** *cpd* [复合词] [+ *port, traffic*] 河 ♦**up/down river** 河流上游/下游

river bank *n* [c] 河岸

river bed *n* [c] 河床

rivet [ˈrɪvɪt] **I** *n* [c] (*bolt*) 铆钉 **II** *vt* [+ *person, attention*] 吸引

✪**road** [rəud] **I** *n* [c] **1** (*in country*) 公路 **2** (*in town*) 路 **3** (喻) 道路 **II** *cpd* [复合词] [+ *accident, sense*] 交通 ♦**it takes four hours by road** 要花4小时的车程 ♦**let's hit the road** [非正式] 我们启程吧 ♦**to be on the road** [*person* +] 在旅途中; [*pop group* +] 在巡回演出中 ♦**on the road to success/recovery** 在获得成功/康复的过程中 ♦**major/minor road** 主干道/非主干道

roadblock [ˈrəudblɔk] *n* [c] 路障

road map *n* [c] 道路图

road rage *n* [u] 行车纠纷

road safety *n* [u] 道路安全

roadside [ˈrəudsaɪd] **I** *n* [c] 路边 **II** *cpd* [复合词] [+ *building, sign etc*] 路边 ♦**at** *or* **by the roadside** 在路边

road sign *n* [c] 交通标志

roadway [ˈrəudweɪ] *n* [c] 车行道

roadworks *n* [*pl*] 道路施工

roam [rəum] **I** *vi* 漫无目的地走动 **II** *vt* [+ *streets, countryside*] 漫步

roar [rɔː(r)] **I** *n* [c] **1** [*of animal*] 吼叫声 **2** [*of crowd*] 喧哗 **3** [*of traffic, storm*] 喧闹声 **II** *vi* **1** [*animal* +] 吼叫 **2** [*person, crowd* +] 大喊大叫 **3** [*engine, wind etc* +] 咆哮 ♦**to roar with laughter** 哈哈大笑 ♦**roar of laughter** 大笑声

roast [rəust] **I** *n* [c] (*meat dish*) 烤肉 **II** *vt* **1** [+ *food*] 烤 **2** [+ *coffee*] 烘焙

🕮 用法参见 **cook**

roast beef *n* [u] 烤牛肉

rob [rɔb] *vt* [+ *person, house, bank*] 抢劫 ♦**to rob sb of sth** 剥夺某人的某物

🕮 用法参见 **steal**

robber [ˈrɔbə(r)] *n* [c] 强盗

🕮 用法参见 **thief**

robbery [ˈrɔbərɪ] *n* [c/u] 抢劫

robe [rəub] *n* [c] **1** (*for ceremony etc*) 礼袍 **2** (*also:* ***bath robe***) 浴袍 **3** [美] (*dressing-gown*) 睡袍

robin [ˈrɔbɪn] *n* [c] 知更鸟

robot [ˈrəubɔt] *n* [c] 机器人

robust [rəuˈbʌst] *adj* **1** [+ *person*] 强健的 **2** [+ *object, machine*] 结实的 **3** [+ *appetite, health, economy*] 旺盛的

rock [rɔk] **I** *n* **1** [u] (*substance*) 岩 **2** [c] (*boulder*) 巨石 **3** [c] [尤美] (*small stone*) 小石子 **4** [u] [音] (*also:* ***rock music***) 摇滚乐 **5** [u] [英] (*candy*) 硬棒糖 **II** *vt* **1** (*swing gently*) [+ *cradle*] 摇晃; [+ *child*] 轻摇 **2** (*shake*) [*explosion* +] 使剧烈震动; (*shock*) [*news, crime* +] 使震惊 **III** *vi* **1** [*object* +] 摇晃 **2** [*person* +] 轻轻摇摆 ♦**on the rocks** [非正式] [*drink* +] (*with ice*) 加冰块的; [*marriage* +] (*in difficulties*) 濒于破裂; [*business* +] (*in difficulties*) 濒临破产

rock and roll *n* [u] 摇滚乐

rock-bottom [ˈrɔkˈbɔtəm] **I** *n* ♦**to reach** *or* **touch** *or* **hit rock-bottom** [*person* +] 处于最糟的境地; [*prices* +] 降至最低点 **II** *adj* [+ *prices*] 最低的

rock climbing *n* [u] 攀岩运动

rocket [ˈrɔkɪt] **I** *n* [c] **1** [航天] 火箭 **2** [军] 火箭式导弹 **3** (*firework*) 火箭式礼花 **II** *vi* (*also:* ***sky-rocket***) 剧增

rocking chair [ˈrɔkɪŋ-] *n* [c] 摇椅

rocking horse *n* [c] 木马

rocky [ˈrɔkɪ] *adj* **1** [+ *path, shore, ground*] 岩石的 **2** [非正式] [+ *business, marriage*] 不稳定

rod [rɔd] *n* [c] **1** (*pole*) 杆 **2** (*also:* ***fishing rod***) 钓鱼竿

rode [rəud] *pt of* **ride**

rodent [ˈrəudnt] *n* [c] 啮齿目动物

rogue [rəug] *n* [c] 无赖

✪**role** [rəul] *n* [c] **1** (*function*) [*of person, country, organization*] 作用 **2** [戏剧] (*part*) 角色

role model *n* [c] 榜样

roll [rəul] **I** *n* [c] **1** [*of paper, cloth, film etc*] 一卷 **2** [*of banknotes*] 一叠 **3** (*also:* ***bread roll***) 小圆面包 **4** (*register, list*) 花名册 **5** (*sound*) [*of drums, thunder*] 持续而平稳的振动声 **II** *vt* **1** [+ *ball, stone, dice etc*] 使滚动 **2** (*also:* ***roll up***) [+ *carpet, string*] 绕; [+ *sleeves, cigarette*] 卷 **3** [+ *eyes*] 转

动 **4** (*also:* ***roll out***) [+ *pastry*] 擀 **5** (*flatten*) [+ *lawn, road, surface*] 碾平 **III** *vi* **1** [*ball, stone etc* +] 滚动 **2** [*drums, thunder* +] 发出隆隆声 **3** [*vehicle* +] 缓行 **4** [*ship* +] 左右摇晃 **5** [*tears, sweat* +] 滚落 **6** [*camera, printing press* +] 运转 ♦**cheese/ham roll** 奶酪/火腿面包卷 ♦**to be rolling in it** [非正式] 赚大笔的钱 ♦**on a roll** [非正式] 好运连连 ♦**rolled into one** [非正式] 合为一体的

❑**roll about, roll around** *vi* 打滚

❑**roll in** *vi* [非正式] [*money, invitations* +] 滚滚而来

❑**roll over** *vi* 翻滚

❑**roll up I** *vt* [+ *carpet, newspaper, string*] 卷起 **II** *vi* [非正式] (*arrive*) 到达

roll call *n* [c/u] 点名

roller ['rəulə(r)] *n* [c] **1** (*in machine*) 滚筒 **2** (*for moving heavy object*) 滚轮 **3** (*for lawn*) 辊草坪机 **4** (*for road*) 轧路机 **5** (*for hair*) 卷发筒

rollerblades ['rəuləbleɪdz] *n* [*pl*] 直排轮溜冰鞋

roller coaster *n* [c] (*at funfair*) 过山车 ♦**on a roller coaster** 急转突变

roller skates *n* [*pl*] 旱冰鞋

roller skating *n* [u] 穿旱冰鞋滑行

rolling pin *n* [c] 擀面杖

ROM [rɔm] *n abbr* (= ***read-only memory***) 只读存储器

Roman ['rəumən] **I** *adj* **1** (*of ancient Rome*) 古罗马的 **2** (*of modern Rome*) 罗马的 **II** *n* [c] (*in ancient Rome*) 古罗马人

Roman Catholic I *adj* 天主教的 **II** *n* [c] 天主教教徒

romance [rə'mæns] *n* **1** [c] (*affair*) 恋情 **2** [u] (*romantic actions, feelings*) 浪漫 **3** [u] (*charm, excitement*) 迷人之处 **4** [c] (*novel*) 爱情小说

Romania [rə'meɪnɪə] *n* 罗马尼亚

Romanian [rə'meɪnɪən] **I** *adj* 罗马尼亚的 **II** *n* **1** [c] (*person*) 罗马尼亚人 **2** [u] (*language*) 罗马尼亚语

Roman numeral *n* [c] 罗马数字

romantic [rə'mæntɪk] *adj* **1** [+ *person*] 浪漫的 **2** (*connected with love*) [+ *play, story etc*] 爱情的 **3** (*charming, exciting*) [+ *setting, holiday, dinner etc*] 浪漫的 **4** (*naive, idealized*) [+ *view, idea*] 理想主义的

rompers ['rɔmpəz] *n* [*pl*] 幼儿连衫裤

romper suit ['rɔmpəsuːt] *n* [c] 幼儿连衫裤

roof [ruːf] **I** *n* [c] **1** [*of building*] 屋顶 **2** [*of cave, mine, vehicle*] 顶 ♦**to go through the roof** [非正式] [*level, price* +] 突飞猛涨 ♦**to hit the roof** *or* **to go through the roof** [非正式] (*lose one's temper*) 怒气冲天

roof rack [英:汽车] *n* [c] 车顶架 [美 = **luggage rack**]

rook [ruk] *n* [c] **1** (*bird*) 秃鼻乌鸦 **2** [国际象棋] 车

✪**room** [ruːm] **I** *n* **1** [c] (*in house*) 室 **2** [c] (*also:* ***bedroom***) 卧室 **3** [u] (*space*) 空间 **II** *vi* ♦**to room with sb** [尤美] 和某人一起租住 ♦**single/double room** 单人/双人间 ♦**to make room for sb** 给某人让出地方

roommate ['ruːmmeɪt] *n* [c] 室友

room service *n* [u] 客房送餐服务

roomy ['ruːmɪ] *adj* 宽敞的

rooster ['ruːstə(r)] [尤美] *n* [c] 公鸡 [英 = **cock**]

root [ruːt] **I** *n* [c] **1** [植] 根 **2** [数] 方根 **3** [*of hair, tooth*] 根 **4** [*of problem, belief*] 根源 **II** *vi* [*plant* +] 生根 **III** *vt* ♦**to be rooted in** [*ideas, attitudes* +] 根源于 **IV roots** *n* [*pl*] (*family origins*) 祖先 ♦**to take root** [*plant* +] 生根; [*idea* +] 扎根

❑**root about** *vi* (喻) (*search*) 翻寻

❑**root for** *vt* [不可拆分] (*support*) 给…加油

❑**root out** *vt* 不遗余力地寻找

rope [rəup] **I** *n* [c/u] **1** 绳子 **II** *vt* **1** (*tie*) 将…拴在 **2** (*also:* ***rope together***) [+ *climbers etc*] 用绳捆绑 ♦**to know the ropes** 掌握诀窍

❑**rope in** *vt* [非正式] [+ *person*] 说服…参加

❑**rope off** *vt* [+ *area*] 用绳围起

rop(e)y ['rəupɪ] [英:非正式] *adj* 劣质的

rosary ['rəuzərɪ] *n* [c] (*beads*) 念珠

rose [rəuz] **I** *pt of* **rise II** *n* [c] (*flower*) 玫瑰 **III** *adj* (*pink*) 玫瑰色的

rosé ['rəuzeɪ] *n* [c/u] 玫瑰红葡萄酒

rosemary ['rəuzmərɪ] *n* [u] 迷迭香

rosy ['rəuzɪ] *adj* **1** (*pink*) 红扑扑的

2 [+ *situation*] 令人鼓舞的 ♦**a rosy future** 美好的未来

rot [rɔt] **I** *n* [U] 1 (*decay*) 腐烂 2 [英:非正式,过时](*rubbish*) 蠢话 **II** *vt* (*cause to decay*) 使腐坏 **III** *vi* (*decay*) [*teeth, wood, fruit etc* +] 腐烂 ♦**to stop the rot** [英] 力挽狂澜

❑**rot away** *vi* 朽烂

rota ['rəutə] *n* [C] 勤务轮值表 ♦**on a rota basis** 轮流当值

rotate [rəu'teɪt] **I** *vt* 1 (*spin*) 转动 2 (*change round*) [+ *crops*] 轮种 **II** *vi* 1 (*revolve*) 旋转 2 (*take turns*) 轮换

rotating [rəu'teɪtɪŋ] *adj* 1 [+ *movement*] 旋转的 2 [+ *drum, mirror*] 可旋转的

rotation [rəu'teɪʃən] *n* 1 [C/U] [*of planet, drum etc*] 旋转 2 [U] [*of crops*] 轮种 3 [U] [*of jobs*] 轮流 ♦**in rotation** 轮流地

rotten ['rɔtn] *adj* 1 (*decayed*) [+ *food*] 腐烂的; [+ *wood*] 朽烂的; [+ *teeth*] 蛀烂的 2 [非正式](*awful*) 糟透的 ♦**to feel rotten** (*ill*) [非正式] 感觉不适

rouble, ruble ['ruːbl] *n* [C] 卢布

rough [rʌf] **I** *adj* 1 [+ *skin, surface, cloth*] 粗糙的 2 [+ *terrain*] 崎岖的 3 [+ *sea, crossing*] 波涛汹涌的 4 (*violent*) [+ *person*] 粗鲁的; [+ *town, area*] 治安混乱的; [+ *treatment, handling*] 粗暴的 5 (*hard*) [+ *life, conditions, journey*] 艰难的 6 (*approximate*) [+ *outline, plan, idea*] 粗略的; [+ *sketch, drawing*] 初步的 **II** *vt* ♦**to rough it** [非正式] 将就着过 ♦**to have a rough time** 处境艰难 ♦**to sleep rough** [英] [*homeless person* +] 露宿街头 ♦**to feel rough** [英:非正式] 感觉不适

❑**rough out** *vt* [+ *drawing*] 勾勒; [+ *idea, article*] 拟出…的草案

roughly ['rʌflɪ] *adv* 1 (*violently*) [*handle, grab, push etc* +] 粗暴地 2 (*aggressively*) [*speak* +] 粗鲁地 3 [*make, construct* +] 粗糙地 4 (*approximately*) 大约 ♦**roughly speaking** 粗略地说

roulette [ruː'lɛt] *n* [U] 轮盘赌

round [raund] **I** *adj* 1 (*circular*) 圆的 2 (*spherical*) 球形的 3 (*approximate*) [+ *figure, sum*] 不计尾数的 **II** *n* [C] 1 (*journey*) [*of milkman, paper boy*] [尤英] 投递路线; [*of doctor*] 巡回出诊或查房 2 (*stage*) (*in competition*) 一轮 3 [*of drinks*] 一轮 4 [高尔夫] 一场 5 [拳击] 回合 6 [*of ammunition*] 一发 7 [*of talks*] 一轮 **III** *vt* [+ *corner, bend*] 绕过 **IV** *prep* 1 (*surrounding*) 围绕 2 (*near*) 在…附近 3 (*on or from the other side of*) 绕过 4 (*indicating circular movement*) ♦**to move round the room/sail round the world** 绕房间一周/环球航行 ♦**all round** 在…周围 ♦**to go round** (*rotate*) 转动 ♦**to go round (sth)** 绕过(某物) ♦**to get round sth** [+ *problem, difficulty*] 绕过某事 ♦**to go round to sb's (house)** 造访某人(的家) ♦**enough to go round** 够每个人分的 ♦**to go round the back** 绕到背面 ♦**to come/go the long way round** 绕远路来/去 ♦**all (the) year round** 一年到头 ♦**the wrong way round** 反了 ♦**in round figures** 用约整数表示 ♦**to ask sb round** 邀请某人来家 ♦**I'll be round at 6 o'clock** 我会在6点钟到你家 ♦**round about** [尤英] (*approximately*) 大约 ♦**round the clock** [非正式] 连续24小时 ♦**the daily round** (喻) 每天例行的公事 ♦**a round of applause** 掌声雷动 ♦**a round of toast/sandwiches** [英] 一份土司/三明治

❑**round down** *vt* 把…调低为整数

❑**round off** *vt* 1 [+ *meal, evening etc*] 圆满结束 2 [+ *price, figure*] 把…四舍五入

❑**round on** [英] *vt* [不可拆分] 责骂 [美=**turn on**]

❑**round up** *vt* 1 [+ *cattle, sheep*] 驱拢 2 [+ *people*] 围捕 3 [+ *price, figure*] 把…调高为整数

roundabout ['raundəbaut] **I** *n* [C] [英] 1 [汽车] 环形交叉路 [美=**traffic circle**] 2 (*at funfair*) 旋转木马 3 (*in playground*) 旋转盘 **II** *adj* 1 [+ *route*] 绕道的 2 [+ *way, means*] 拐弯抹角的

round trip **I** *n* [C] 往返旅行 **II** *adj* [美] 往返的 [英=**return**]

roundup ['raundʌp] *n* [C] 1 [*of news, information*] 综述 2 [*of criminals*] 搜捕

rouse [rauz] *vt* 1 (*wake up*) [正式] 叫

醒 2 (*stir up*) 使激动 ♦**to rouse o.s.** 醒来 ♦**to rouse sb to anger** 激怒某人

route [ruːt] **I** *n* [c] **1** (*path, journey*) 路 **2** [*of bus, train*] 路线; [*of ship*] 航线 **3** (*means*) 途径 **II** *vt* 按路线发送 ♦**"all routes"** [汽车] "所有车辆按路线行驶"

routine [ruːˈtiːn] **I** *adj* [+ *work, job*] 常规的; [+ *check, inquiries*] 例行的 **II** *n* **1** [c/u] (*procedure*) 例行公事 **2** [c/u] (*drudgery*) 日常琐事 **3** [c] [戏剧] 保留节目

row¹ [rəu] **I** *n* [c] **1** (*line*) [*of people, houses, etc*] 一排 **2** [*of seats in theatre, cinema*] 一排 **II** *vi* (*in boat*) 划船 **III** *vt* [+ *boat*] 划 ♦**in a row** 连续

row² [rau] **I** *n* **1** [s] (*noise*) [英: 非正式] 吵闹声 **2** [c] (*noisy quarrel*) 吵架 **3** [c] (*dispute*) 争执 **II** *vi* (*argue*) 争吵 ♦**to have a row** 吵架

rowboat [ˈrəubəut] [美] *n* [c] 划艇 [英=**rowing boat**]

rowing [ˈrəuɪŋ] [体育] *n* [u] 赛艇运动

rowing boat [英] *n* [c] 划艇 [美=**rowboat**]

royal [ˈrɔɪəl] *adj* 皇家的 ♦**the royal family** 王室

> **ROYAL FAMILY**
> **royal family** (英国王室)以伊丽莎白女王二世为首。女王于 1953 年登基。她的丈夫是菲利普亲王,即爱丁堡公爵。他们育有四名成年子女:查尔斯王子、安妮公主、安德鲁王子和爱德华王子。查尔斯王子,即威尔士亲王是王位的继承人。他有两个孩子,威廉王子和哈利王子。他们的母亲是已故的威尔士王妃戴安娜。

Royal Air Force [英] *n* ♦**the Royal Air Force** 皇家空军

royalty [ˈrɔɪəltɪ] **I** *n* [u] (*royal persons*) 王室成员 **II royalties** *n* [*pl*] (*to author*) 版税; (*to inventor*) 专利权使用费

RRP [英] *n abbr* (= ***recommended retail price***) 建议零售价

RSI [医] *n abbr* (= ***repetitive strain injury***) 肢体重复性劳损

RSVP *abbr* (= ***répondez s'il vous plaît***) 请赐复

RU [手机短信] *abbr* = **are you**

rub [rʌb] **I** *vt* (*with hand, fingers*) 揉; (*with cloth, substance*) 擦 ♦**to rub sth with sth** 将某物涂抹在某物上 ♦**to rub sth onto** *or* **into sth** 用某物揉擦某物 ♦**to rub one's hands (together)** 搓手 ♦**to rub sb up** *or* [美] **rub sb the wrong way** [非正式] 惹恼某人

❑**rub down** *vt* [+ *body*] 擦干; [+ *horse*] 擦刷干净

❑**rub in** *vt* [+ *ointment*] 将…揉搓进… ♦**don't rub it in!** [非正式] 别老提了!

❑**rub off I** *vi* [*paint* +] 被擦掉 **II** *vt* [+ *paint, mark etc*] 擦掉

❑**rub off on** [非正式] *vt* [不可拆分] 影响

❑**rub out** *vt* (*erase*) 擦掉

rubber [ˈrʌbə(r)] *n* **1** [u] (*substance*) 橡胶 **2** [c] [英] 橡皮擦 [美=**eraser**] **3** [c] [美: 非正式] 安全套 [英=**condom**]

rubber band *n* [c] 橡皮筋

rubber boot [美] *n* [c] 橡胶长统靴 [英=**wellington**]

rubbish [ˈrʌbɪʃ] [英] **I** *n* [u] **1** (*refuse*) 垃圾 [美=**garbage, trash**] **2** (*inferior material*) 垃圾 **3** (*nonsense*) 废话 **II** *adj* [英: 非正式] ♦**I'm rubbish at golf** 我高尔夫球打得很糟糕 **III** *vt* 贬低 ♦**rubbish!** 胡说!

rubbish bin [英] *n* [c] 垃圾箱

rubbish dump [英] *n* [c] 垃圾堆存处

rubble [ˈrʌbl] *n* [u] **1** 碎石

ruby [ˈruːbɪ] **I** *n* [c] (*gem*) 红宝石 **II** *adj* (*red*) 深红色的

rucksack [ˈrʌksæk] *n* [c] 背包

rudder [ˈrʌdə(r)] *n* [c] **1** [*of ship*] 舵 **2** [*of plane*] 方向舵

rude [ruːd] *adj* **1** [+ *person, behaviour, remark*] 无礼的 **2** (*vulgar*) [+ *word, joke, noise*] 粗鄙的 **3** (*brutal*) [+ *shock, surprise*] 突然的 **4** (*crude*) [+ *table, shelter etc*] 简陋 ♦**to be rude to sb** 对某人无礼

rudely [ˈruːdlɪ] *adv* [*interrupt, say, push* +] 无礼地

ruffle [ˈrʌfl] **I** *vt* **1** [+ *hair*] 抚弄 **2** [+ *water*] 吹皱 **3** [*bird* +] [+ *feathers*]

竖起 **4** [+ *person*] 使心烦意乱
II ruffles *n* [*pl*] 皱边
rug [rʌg] *n* [c] **1** (*carpet*) 小地毯 **2** [英] (*blanket*) 小毛毯
rugby ['rʌgbɪ] *n* [u] (*also:* ***rugby football***) 英式橄榄球
rugged ['rʌgɪd] *adj* **1** [+ *man, features, face*] 粗野的 **2** [+ *piece of equipment*] 结实的 **3** [+ *landscape*] 崎岖多岩的 **4** [+ *determination, independence*] 坚强的 **5** [+ *character*] 坚忍的
ruin ['ruːɪn] **I** *n* **1** [u] (*destruction*) [*of building*] 毁坏; [*of hopes, plans etc*] 破灭 **2** [u] (*downfall*) [*of person*] 落泊 **3** [u] (*bankruptcy*) 破产 **4** [c] (*old building*) 废墟 **II** *vt* **1** (*spoil*) [+ *clothes, carpet etc*] 毁坏; [+ *plans, prospects etc*] 葬送; [+ *eyesight, health*] 损害 **2** (*bankrupt*) [+ *person*] 使破产 **III ruins** *n* [*pl*] [*of building, castle etc*] 废墟 ♦**to be in ruins** [*building, town* +] 破败不堪; [*life, plans etc* +] 严重受损
✪**rule** [ruːl] **I** *n* **1** [c] (*regulation*) 规则 **2** [s] (*norm*) 惯例 **3** [c] [*of language, science*] 规则 **4** [u] (*government*) 统治 **5** [c] (*for measuring*) 尺 **II** *vt* [+ *country, people*] 统治 **III** *vi* **1** [*leader, monarch etc* +] 统治 **2** (*on subject*) 作出裁决 ♦**to rule in favour of/against/on** [法法] 判定…/否决…/对…作出裁决 ♦**to rule that...** [*umpire, judge etc* +] 裁决… ♦**it's against the rules** 这是不合规定的 ♦**as a rule of thumb** 凭经验行事 ♦**under British rule** 在英国的统治下 ♦**to bend the rules** 通融一下 ♦**to rule over sb/sth** [+ *country, people*] 统治某人/某地 ♦**as a rule** 通常
❑**rule out** *vt* [+ *idea, possibility etc*] 排除; [+ *situation, competition*] 使成为不可能 ♦**murder cannot be ruled out** 不排除他杀的可能性
ruler ['ruːlə(r)] *n* [c] **1** (*for measuring*) 直尺 **2** (*sovereign*) 统治者
ruling ['ruːlɪŋ] **I** *adj* [+ *party, body*] 执政的 **II** *n* [c] [法法] 裁决 ♦**the ruling class** 统治阶级
rum [rʌm] *n* [u] 朗姆酒
Rumania *etc* [ruː'meɪnɪə] *n* = **Romania** *etc*
rumble ['rʌmbl] **I** *n* [c] [*of thunder, traffic, guns*] 隆隆声 **II** *vi* **1** [*stomach* +] 咕噜作响 **2** [*thunder, guns, traffic* +] 发隆隆声 **3** (*also:* ***rumble along***) 隆隆地行进
rummage ['rʌmɪdʒ] **I** *n* [u] 翻找 **II** *vi* (*search*) 翻找
rumour (美 **rumor**) ['ruːmə(r)] **I** *n* [c/u] 谣言 **II** *vt* ♦**it is rumoured that ...** 据谣传…
rump steak *n* [c/u] 后腿部牛排
✪**run** [rʌn] (*pt* **ran**, *pp* **run**) **I** *n* [c] **1** (*as exercise, sport*) 跑步 **2** (*in car*) 旅行 **3** (*regular journey*) [*of train, bus etc*] 路线 **4** (*series*) [*of victories, defeats etc*] 连续 **5** [板球, 棒球] 跑动得分 **6** [戏剧] 持续的演出 **7** (*in tights, stockings*) 抽丝 **II** *vt* **1** [+ *race, distance*] 跑 **2** (*operate*) [+ *business, shop, country*] 经营; [+ *competition, course*] 开办; [+ *country*] 治理 **3** [+ *water, bath*] 流 **4** (*pass*) [+ *hand, fingers*] 移动 **5** (*operate*) [+ *machine*] 使运转 **6** (*perform*) [+ *program, test*] 进行; (*own, maintain*) [+ *car, machine*] 使用 **7** [出版] [+ *feature, article*] 刊登 **III** *vi* **1** [*person, animal* +] 跑 **2** (*flee*) 逃跑 **3** (*work*) [*machine* +] 运转 **4** (*operate*) [*system, organization, etc* +] 运作 **5** [*bus, train* +] (*operate*) 行驶 **6** (*continue*) [*play, show etc* +] 连续上演; [*contract* +] 有效 **7** (*flow*) [*river, tears, nose* +] 流 **8** [美] (*in election*) 竞选 [英=**stand**] **9** [*road, railway etc* +] 伸展 **10** [*colours, washing* +] 掉色 **11** (*in combination*) 变得 ♦**to go for a run** (*as exercise*) 跑步锻炼 ♦**to break into a run** 突然奔跑起来 ♦**a run of good/bad luck** 接二连三的好运/厄运 ♦**to have the run of sb's house** 被允许随意进出某人的住宅 ♦**there was a run on ...** [+ *meat, tickets*] 有…的需求 ♦**in the long run** 终究 ♦**in the short run** 从短期看 ♦**on the run** [*fugitive* +] 逃跑 ♦**I'll run you to the station** 我开车送你去车站 ♦**to make a run for it** [非正式] 试图迅速逃跑 ♦**to run on** *or* **off petrol/batteries** 以汽油/电池为能源 ♦**to run for president** 竞选总统 ♦**to run dry** [*well etc* +] 干涸 ♦**tempers were running high** 情绪变得激动起来

♦unemployment is running at 20 per cent 失业率为20% **♦it runs in the family** 这是家族遗传 **♦to be run off one's feet** [英] 忙碌不堪

❑**run across** *vt* [不可拆分] (*find*) 不期而遇

❑**run after** *vt* [不可拆分] (*chase*) 追赶

❑**run away** *vi* (*from home, situation*) 出走

❑**run away with** *vt* [不可拆分] 不受…控制

❑**run by** *vt* **♦to run sth by sb** [非正式] 看某人对某事的反应

❑**run down I** *vt* **1** [尤英] [+ *production, factory*] 逐渐停止 **2** [汽车] [+ *person*] 撞伤 **3** (*criticize*) 诋毁 **II** *vi* [*battery* +] 耗尽 **♦to be run down** [*person* +] (*tired*) 筋疲力尽

❑**run in** [英] *vt* [+ *car*] 小心试用

❑**run into** *vt* [不可拆分] **1** (*meet*) [+ *person*] 偶然碰见; [+ *trouble, problems*] 遭遇 **2** (*collide with*) 撞上 **♦to run into debt** 陷入债务 **♦their losses ran into millions** 他们的损失达到数百万

❑**run off I** *vi* **1** [*person, animal* +] 跑掉 **2** (*with sb*) 私奔 **II** *vt* **1** [+ *liquid*] 使流掉 **2** [+ *copies*] 复印一下

❑**run out** *vi* **1** [*time, money, luck* +] 用完 ◊ *Time is running out.* 快没时间了。**2** [*lease, passport* +] 到期

❑**run out of** *vt* [不可拆分] 耗尽

❑**run over I** *vt* [汽车] [+ *person*] 撞倒 **II** *vt* [不可拆分] (*repeat*) 再来一遍 **III** *vi* [*bath, sink, water* +] 溢出

❑**run through** *vt* [不可拆分] **1** [+ *instructions*] 扫视 **2** (*rehearse*) [+ *scene, lines*] 排练

❑**run up** *vt* [+ *debt*] 积欠

❑**run up against** *vt* [不可拆分] [+ *difficulties*] 遇到

runaway ['rʌnəweɪ] **I** *adj* [+ *truck, train*] 失控的; [+ *horse*] 脱缰的; [+ *inflation, success*] 势不可挡的 **II** *n* [c] (*child*) 离家出走者

rung [rʌŋ] **I** *pp of* **ring II** *n* [c] **1** [*of ladder*] 横档 **2** (*in organization*) 级别

runner ['rʌnə(r)] *n* [c] **1** (*in race*) (*person*) 赛跑者; (*horse*) 赛马 **2** (*on sledge, etc*) 滑板 **3** (*on drawer*) 滑槽 **♦drugs/gun runner** 毒品/枪支走私者

runner bean [英] *n* [c] 红花菜豆

runner-up [rʌnər'ʌp] *n* [c] 亚军

running ['rʌnɪŋ] **I** *n* **1** [u] (*sport*) 赛跑 **2** [s] [*of business, organization*] 管理 **3** [s] [*of machine etc*] 维修保养 **II** *adj* [+ *water, stream*] 流动的 **♦to be in the running for sth** 有希望得到某物 **♦to be out of the running for sth** 没有希望得到某物 **♦6 days running** 连续6天 **♦to give a running commentary on sth** 对某事做连续报导 **♦to have a running battle with sb** 和某人不断争吵 **♦a running total** 累积总计 **♦to be up and running** [*system etc* +] 运作正常

runny ['rʌnɪ] *adj* **1** [+ *egg, butter*] 流质的 **2** [+ *nose*] 流鼻涕的; [+ *eyes*] 流泪的

run-up ['rʌnʌp] *n* **1** **♦the run-up to...** [+ *election etc*] …的前期 **2** [c] (*before a jump*) 助跑

runway ['rʌnweɪ] *n* [c] 跑道

rupture ['rʌptʃə(r)] **I** *n* [c] **1** [医] 破裂 **2** (*conflict*) 决裂 **II** *vt* **1** [+ *part of body*] 使破裂 **2** [+ *relations*] 破坏 **3** **♦to rupture o.s.** [医] 发疝气

rural ['ruərl] *adj* **1** [+ *area, accent*] 乡村的 **2** [+ *economy, problems*] 农村的

rush [rʌʃ] **I** *n* [s] (*hurry*) 匆忙; [*of water, air*] 冲; [*of feeling, emotion*] 突发; (*sudden demand*) **♦a rush (on)** 抢购 **II** *vt* (*hurry*) [+ *lunch, job etc*] 赶紧做; [+ *person*] (*to hospital etc*) 急速赶往; [+ *supplies, order*] (*to person, place*) 急速发送 **III** *vi* **1** [*person* +] 急速前往 ◊ *Russian banks rushed to buy as many dollars as they could.* 俄国银行赶紧买入尽可能多的美元。**2** [*air, water* +] 急泻 **♦don't rush me!** 别催我！**♦to rush sth off** (*send*) 紧急发送某物 **♦what's the rush?** 什么事那么急？**♦to be in a rush (to do sth)** 仓促(地做某事) **♦to rush sb into doing sth** 催促某人做某事

❑**rush through** *vt* [+ *order, application*] 赶紧处理

rush hour *n* [c] 高峰时间

Russia ['rʌʃə] *n* 俄罗斯

Russian ['rʌʃən] **I** *adj* 俄罗斯的 **II** *n* **1** [c] (*person*) 俄罗斯人 **2** [u] (*language*) 俄语

Russian Federation *n* ♦**the Russian Federation** 俄罗斯联邦
rust [rʌst] **I** *n* [U] 铁锈 **II** *vi* [*iron, car etc* +] 生锈 **III** *vt* [+ *iron, car etc*] 使生锈
rusty ['rʌstɪ] *adj* **1** [+ *surface, object*] 生锈的 **2** [+ *skill*] 荒疏的
rutabaga [ruːtə'beɪgə] 〔美〕*n* [C/U] 芜菁甘蓝〔英=**swede**〕
ruthless ['ruːθlɪs] *adj* [+ *person*] 冷酷的; [+ *determination, efficiency*] 坚决的
RV 〔美〕*n abbr* (= ***recreational vehicle***) 娱乐车
Rwanda [ru'ændə] *n* 卢旺达
Rwandan [ru'ændən] **I** *adj* 卢旺达的 **II** *n* [C] (*person*) 卢旺达人
rye [raɪ] *n* [U] (*cereal*) 黑麦

Ss

S[1], **s** [ɛs] *n* [C/U] **1** (*letter*) 英语的第十九个字母 **2** [美:教育] (*satisfactory*) 成绩"满意"

S[2] *abbr* **1** (= ***south***) 南方 **2** (= ***small***) 小的 **3** (*pl* **SS**) (= ***saint***) 圣徒

Sabbath ['sæbəθ] *n* [C] 安息日

sabotage ['sæbətɑːʒ] **I** *n* [U] 蓄意破坏 **II** *vt* [+ *machine, bridge etc*] 破坏; [+ *plan, meeting, relationship etc*] 毁 ♦**an act of sabotage** 破坏行为

saccharin ['sækərɪn] *n* [U] 糖精

sachet ['sæʃeɪ] *n* [C] [*of shampoo, sugar etc*] 小袋

sack [sæk] **I** *n* [C] (*bag*) 麻袋 **II** *vt* **1** (*dismiss*) 解雇 **2** (*plunder*) 洗劫 ♦**to get the sack** 被解雇 ♦**to give sb the sack** 解雇某人 ♦**to sack sb for sth/for doing sth** 因某事/做某事解雇某人

sacred ['seɪkrɪd] *adj* **1** (*religious*) [+ *music, art*] 宗教的 ◊ *sacred songs or music* 圣歌或圣乐 **2** (*holy*) [+ *animal, place, writings*] 神圣的 **3** (喻) (*sacrosanct*) 神圣不可侵犯的

sacrifice ['sækrɪfaɪs] **I** *n* **1** [C] [宗] [*of animal, person*] 献祭 **2** [C/U] (喻) 牺牲 **II** *vt* **1** [宗] [+ *animal*] 用…祭祀 **2** (*forfeit*) [+ *health, career, human lives*] 牺牲 ♦**to make sacrifices (for sb/sth)** (为某人/某事)做出牺牲 ♦**to sacrifice sth for sb/sth** 为某人/某事牺牲某物

sad [sæd] *adj* **1** (*unhappy*) 伤心的 **2** (*distressing*) 令人悲伤的 **3** (*regrettable*) 令人遗憾的 **4** [非正式] (*pathetic*) 可悲的 ♦**to be sad about sth** 因某事难过 ♦**I'm sad that ...** …使我伤心 ♦**he was sad to see her go** 看着她走, 他很伤心 ♦**it is sad that ...** 很遗憾…

sadden ['sædn] *vt* [+ *person*] 使伤心 ♦**I was saddened to learn of his death** 得知他去世令我很悲痛

saddle ['sædl] **I** *n* [C] (*for horse*) 马鞍; (*on bike, motorbike*) 车座 **II** *vt* **1** (*also: **saddle up***) 给…装鞍 **2** ♦**to saddle sb with sth** 使某人承担某项责任 ♦**in the saddle** (*on horse*) 骑着马; (*in control*) 掌权

❑**saddle up** *vt* 给…装鞍

sadistic [sə'dɪstɪk] *adj* 施虐狂的

sadly ['sædlɪ] *adv* **1** (*unhappily*) 难过地 **2** (*unfortunately*) 可惜地 **3** (*seriously*) [*mistaken, neglected*] 完全地 ◊ *If you think I'm going to leave, you are sadly mistaken.* 如果你以为我会离开, 你就完全错了。♦**to be sadly lacking (in sth)** 丝毫没有(某物) ♦**he will be sadly missed** 大家会很想他的

sadness ['sædnɪs] *n* [U] 悲痛

s.a.e. [英] *abbr* (= ***stamped addressed envelope***) 贴有邮票并写好地址的信封 [美 = **SASE**]

safari [sə'fɑːrɪ] *n* [C] 游猎 ♦**to go on safari** 去游猎

safe [seɪf] **I** *adj* **1** (*not dangerous*) 安全的 **2** (*out of danger*) 脱险的 **3** (*secure*) [+ *place*] 保险的 **4** (*trouble-free*) [+ *journey, delivery*] 无损的 **5** (*without risk*) [+ *option, action*] 无风险的 **6** [贬] (*tame*) 沉闷的 **II** *n* [C] 保险箱 ♦**safe from sth** 不受到某事的攻击 ♦**safe and sound** 安然无恙 ♦**safe journey!** 一路平安! ♦**(just) to be on the safe side** 为谨慎起见 ♦**it is safe to say that ...** 可以有把握地说… ♦**in safe hands** 在可靠的人手中

safeguard ['seɪfgɑːd] **I** *n* [C] 保护措施 **II** *vt* 保护

safely ['seɪflɪ] *adv* **1** (*without harm*) [*drive, arrive etc* +] 安全地 **2** (*securely*) [*lock up, hide* +] 万无一失地 **3** (*reliably*) ♦**I can safely say/assume that ...** 我可以有把握地说/认为…

safe sex *n* [U] 安全性交

safety ['seɪftɪ] **I** *n* [U] **1** [*of plane, roads, factory*] 安全 **2** (*wellbeing*) [*of person, crew*] 平安 **3** (*harmful potential*) [*of object, substance*] 安全性 **4** (*safe place*) 安全场所 **II** *cpd* [复合词] [+ *features, measures*] 安全

safety pin *n* [C] 安全别针

saffron ['sæfrən] **I** *n* [U] (*spice*) 藏红花 **II** *adj* (*in colour*) 橘黄的
sag [sæg] *vi* **1** [*bed, roof* +] 下陷; [*breasts, bottom* +] 松弛而下垂 **2** (喻) [*spirits* +] 萎靡不振; [*demand* +] 下跌
sage [seɪdʒ] **I** *n* **1** [U] (*herb*) 鼠尾草 **2** [C] [文] (*wise man*) 圣贤 **II** *adj* [文] 贤明的
Sagittarius [sædʒɪ'tɛərɪəs] *n* **1** [U] (*sign*) 人马座 **2** [C] (*person*) 人马座的人 ♦ **I'm (a) Sagittarius** 我是人马座的
Sahara [sə'hɑːrə] *n* ♦ **the Sahara (Desert)** 撒哈拉(大沙漠)
said [sɛd] *pt, pp of* **say**
sail [seɪl] **I** *n* [C] [*of boat, yacht*] 帆 **II** *vt* [+ *boat, yacht*] 驾驶 **III** *vi* **1** (*travel*) [*ship* +] 航行; [*sailor* +] 扬帆行驶; [*passenger* +] 乘船航行 **2** (*begin voyage*) 启航 **3** (*fly*) ♦ **to sail over/across/up to sth** 飞过/飞越/上升到某处 ♦ **to set sail** 起航 ♦ **to sail for** *or* **to set sail for** 起航前往 ♦ **to go sailing** 去航行
❑ **sail through** *vt* [不可拆分] [+ *exams, interview etc*] 顺利地通过
sailboat ['seɪlbəut] [美] *n* [C] 帆船 [英 = **sailing boat**]
sailing ['seɪlɪŋ] *n* **1** [U] [体育] 帆船运动 **2** [C] (*departure*) 轮船航班 ♦ **it wasn't all plain sailing** 并不都是一帆风顺
sailing boat [英] *n* [C] 帆船 [美 = **sailboat**]
sailor ['seɪlə(r)] *n* [C] 水手
saint [seɪnt] *n* [C] **1** [宗] 圣徒 **2** (*good person*) 圣人 ♦ **he's no saint** 他并不是十全十美
sake [seɪk] *n* ♦ **for the sake of** [+ *health, career, person etc*] 为了 ♦ **do it for my sake!** 看在我的情份上做吧! ♦ **for its own sake** 纯粹为此而已 ♦ **he enjoys talking for talking's sake** 他喜欢为了说话而说话 ♦ **for argument's sake, for the sake of argument** 为了便于讨论 ♦ **for goodness** *or* **heaven's sake!** [非正式] 看在上帝份上!
salad ['sæləd] *n* [C/U] 色拉 ♦ **green/tomato salad** 蔬菜/西红柿色拉 ♦ **ham/chicken/cheese salad** 火腿/鸡肉/干酪色拉 ♦ **potato/pasta/rice salad** 土豆/意大利粉/米饭色拉
salad cream [英] *n* [U] 色拉酱
salad dressing *n* [C/U] 色拉调味料
salami [sə'lɑːmɪ] *n* [C/U] 萨拉米香肠
salary ['sælərɪ] *n* [C/U] 薪水 ♦ **to be on a good/modest salary** 拿高薪/适中的薪水
✪ **sale** [seɪl] **I** *n* **1** [S] (*selling*) 出售 ◊ *new laws to control the sale of guns* 控制枪支出售的新法律 **2** [C] (*with reductions*) 贱卖 **3** [C] (*auction*) 拍卖 ◊ *a cattle sale* 牛拍卖 **II sales** *n* [*pl*] **1** (*quantity sold*) 销售量 ◊ *Car sales are down.* 小汽车销售量有所下降。**2** (*department*) 销售部 **3** ♦ **the sales** 降价期 **4** (*in compounds*) [+ *campaign, drive, figures, target*] 销售; [+ *conference, meeting*] 与销售有关的 ♦ **to be (up) for sale** 待售 ♦ **to be on sale** [英] (*available*) 上市; [美] (*reduced*) 廉价出售 ♦ **(on) sale or return** 卖不出去可以退货 ♦ **closing-down** *or* [美] **liquidation sale** 清仓大甩卖
sales assistant [英] *n* [C] 售货员 [美 = **sales clerk**]
sales clerk [美] *n* [C] 售货员 [英 = **sales assistant**]
salesman ['seɪlzmən] (*pl* **salesmen**) *n* [C] **1** (*representative*) 推销员 **2** (*in shop, showroom*) 售货员
salesperson ['seɪlzpəːsn] (*pl* **salespeople**) *n* [C] **1** (*representative*) 推销员 **2** (*in shop, showroom*) 售货员
sales rep [-rɛp] *n* [C] 推销员
saleswoman ['seɪlzwumən] (*pl* **saleswomen**) *n* [C] **1** (*representative*) 女推销员 **2** (*in shop, showroom*) 女售货员
saline ['seɪlaɪn] **I** *adj* [+ *water, solution*] 含盐的 **II** *n* [U] 生理盐水
saliva [sə'laɪvə] *n* [U] 唾液
salmon ['sæmən] (*pl* **salmon**) *n* [C/U] 大马哈鱼 ♦ **smoked salmon** 熏制的大马哈鱼
salon ['sælɔn] *n* [C] **1** (*also: **hairdressing salon***) 美发廊 **2** (*also: **beauty salon***) 美容院
saloon [sə'luːn] *n* [C] **1** [美] (*bar*) 酒吧; [英:过时] (*lounge bar*) (*also: **saloon bar***) 雅座酒吧 **2** [英:汽车] 可

容纳4至7位乘客的轿车[美=**sedan**]

salt [sɔːlt] **I** *n* [U] 盐 **II** *vt* **1** (*flavour*) 加盐于 **2** (*preserve*) 用盐腌 **III** *cpd* [复合词][+ *lake, deposits*] 盐 ♦**to take sth with a pinch** *or* **grain of salt** 对某事半信半疑 ♦**the salt of the earth** 社会中坚分子 ♦**worth one's salt** 称职

salt cellar [英] *n* [C] 盐瓶[美=**salt shaker**]

salt shaker [美] *n* [C] 盐瓶[英=**salt cellar**]

saltwater ['sɔːltwɔːtə(r)] *adj* [+ *fish, lake*] 咸水的

salty ['sɔːltɪ] *adj* [+ *food*] 咸的; [+ *air*] 有海洋气息的

salute [sə'luːt] **I** *n* [C] **1** (*with hand*) 敬礼 **2** (*with guns*) 礼炮 **3** (*in greeting*) 致意 **4** (*expressing admiration*) ♦**a salute to** 向…的致敬 **II** *vt* **1** [+ *officer, flag*] 向…行军礼 **2** (*praise*) 祝贺 **III** *vi* (*with hand*) 行礼 ♦**to salute sb for sth** (喻)因某事对某人表示赞赏

salvage ['sælvɪdʒ] **I** *n* [U] **1** (*saving*) 抢救 **2** (*things saved*) 抢救出的财物 **II** *vt* (*from ship, building*) 抢救; [+ *pride, reputation*] 挽救 ♦**to salvage sth (from sth)** (从某事中)挽回某物

salvation [sæl'veɪʃən] *n* [U] **1** [宗] 拯救 **2** (喻) [*of person, institution*] 救星 ♦**to be beyond salvation** 无可救药

Salvation Army *n* ♦**the Salvation Army** 救世军

✪**same** [seɪm] **I** *adj* **1** (*similar*) [+ *size, colour, age etc*] 相同的 ◊ *He and Tom were the same age.* 他和汤姆年龄相同。**2** (*very same*) [+ *place, person, time etc*] 同一个的 ◊ *We stay in the same hotel every year.* 我们每年总是住在同一个旅馆。**3** (*aforementioned*) 上述的 ◊ *I had the same experience myself.* 我自己也有上述的经历。**II** *pron* ♦**the same 1** (*similar*) 一样 ◊ *The houses were all the same.* 房子都一样。**2** (*unchanged*) 一成不变的状况 ◊ *Nothing ever stays the same.* 事情不可能是一成不变的。**3** (*also:* ***the same thing***) 同样 ◊ *We like him very much and he says the same about us.* 我们很喜欢他，他说他也同样喜欢我们。♦**the same as** 与…一样 ♦**the same book/place as** 与…一样的书/地方 ♦**on the same day** 在同一天 ♦**at the same time** (*simultaneously*) 同时 ◊ *They started moving at the same time.* 他们同时开始移动。; (*paradoxically*) 同时 ◊ *They want to stay but at the same time they want to go.* 他们想留下，但同时又想走。; (*notwithstanding*) 尽管如此 ◊ *At the same time, I'd like to be sure it's true.* 尽管如此，我还是想证实它的真实性。♦**all** *or* **just the same** 仍然 ♦**to do the same (as sb)** 也（像某人）那么做 ♦**(the) same to you!** (*after greeting*) 祝你也一样！; (*after insult*) 你也是！♦**same here!** [非正式]我也一样！♦**they're one and the same** 他们完全一样 ♦**(the) same again** 同样的再来一份 ♦**"Do you want some tea?" – "No, but thanks all the same"** "你要茶吗？" "不，但还是要谢谢。"

sample ['sɑːmpl] **I** *n* [C] [*of work, merchandise*] 样品; [医] [*of blood, urine*] 采样; [*of people, things*] 抽样 **II** *vt* [+ *food, wine*] 品尝; [+ *place, situation, way of life*] 体验 ♦**free sample** 免费赠样

sanction ['sæŋkʃən] **I** *n* **1** [C] (*punishment*) 制裁 **2** [U] (*approval*) 批准 **II** *vt* (*give approval to*) 批准 **III sanctions** *n* [*pl*] [政治] 国际制裁 ♦**sanctions against** 对…的制裁 ♦**to impose sanctions (on** *or* **against)** (对…)实施制裁

sanctuary ['sæŋktjuərɪ] *n* **1** [C] (*for birds, animals*) 禁猎区 **2** [C] (*place of safety*) 避难所 **3** [U] (*safety*) 避难

sand [sænd] **I** *n* [U] 沙子 **II** *vt* (*also:* ***sand down***) 打磨 **III sands** *n* [*pl*] (*beach*) 沙滩

❑**sand down** *vt* 打磨

sandal ['sændl] *n* [C] 凉鞋

sandbox ['sændbɔks] [美] *n* [C] (*for children*) 沙坑[英=**sandpit**]

sand castle ['sændkɑːsl] *n* [C] 沙堡

sand dune *n* [C] 沙丘

sandpaper ['sændpeɪpə(r)] *n* [U] 砂

纸

sandpit ['sændpɪt] [英] *n* [C] (*for children*) 沙坑 [美 = **sandbox**]

sandstone ['sændstəun] **I** *n* [U] 砂岩 **II** *cpd* [复合词] [+ *building, wall, cliff*] 砂岩质

sandwich ['sændwɪtʃ] **I** *n* [C] 三明治 **II** *vt* ♦ **to be sandwiched between** 被夹在…之间 ♦ **a cheese/ham/jam sandwich** 奶酪/火腿/果酱三明治

sandy ['sændɪ] *adj* **1** [+ *beach*] 覆盖着沙的 **2** (*in colour*) [+ *hair*] 沙色的

sane [seɪn] *adj* **1** (*not crazy*) 神志正常的 **2** (*reasonable*) [+ *action, policy, idea*] 明智的

sang [sæŋ] *pt of* **sing**

sanitary napkin ['sænɪtərɪ-] [美] *n* [C] 卫生巾 [英 = **sanitary towel**]

sanitary towel ['sænɪtərɪ-] [英] *n* [C] 卫生巾 [美 = **sanitary napkin**]

sanity ['sænɪtɪ] *n* [U] **1** (*mental health*) 精神健全 **2** (*sense*) 明智

sank [sæŋk] *pt of* **sink**

Santa (Claus) ['sæntə('klɔːz)] *n* 圣诞老人

sap [sæp] **I** *n* [U] [*of plants*] 汁 **II** *vt* ♦ **to sap sb's strength/confidence** 使某人筋疲力尽/挫伤某人的自信心

sapphire ['sæfaɪə(r)] *n* [C/U] 蓝宝石

sarcasm ['sɑːkæzm] *n* [U] 讽刺

sarcastic [sɑː'kæstɪk] *adj* [+ *person*] 尖刻的; [+ *remark*] 讽刺的

sardine [sɑː'diːn] *n* [C] 沙丁鱼

SARS *n abbr* (= ***severe acute respiratory syndrome***) 非典型性肺炎

SASE [美] *n abbr* (= ***self-addressed stamped envelope***) 贴足邮资写明发信人自己的姓名地址的回信信封 [英 = **s.a.e.**]

sash [sæʃ] *n* [C] **1** (*around waist*) 腰带; (*over shoulder*) 肩带 **2** [*of window*] 窗框

SAT *n abbr* **1** [美] (= ***Scholastic Aptitude Test***) 学业能力倾向测试 **2** [英] (= ***Standard Assessment Task***) 小学标准评估

sat [sæt] *pt, pp of* **sit**

Sat. *abbr* (= ***Saturday***) 星期六

satchel ['sætʃl] *n* [C] 书包

satellite ['sætəlaɪt] *n* **1** [C] (*for communications*) 人造卫星 **2** [U] (*also:* ***satellite television***) 卫星电视 **3** [C] [天文] (*moon*) 卫星 **4** [C] [政治] (*also:* ***satellite state***) 卫星国 ♦ **on satellite** 在卫星电视上

satellite dish *n* [C] 圆盘式卫星电视接收器

satellite television *n* [U] 卫星电视

satin ['sætɪn] **I** *n* [U] 缎子 **II** *cpd* [复合词] [+ *ribbon, dress*] 缎子 ♦ **with a satin finish** 有缎子光泽

satire ['sætaɪə(r)] *n* **1** [U] (*humour*) 讽刺 **2** [C] (*novel, play*) 讽刺作品

satisfaction [sætɪs'fækʃən] *n* [U] **1** (*contentment*) 满足感 **2** (*for wrong, injustice*) ♦ **to get satisfaction (from sb)** (从某人那里)得到赔偿 ♦ **satisfaction with** 对…的满意 ♦ **has it been done to your satisfaction?** 您对此满意吗?

satisfactory [sætɪs'fæktərɪ] *adj* 令人满意的 ♦ **in a satisfactory condition** [医] 病情稳定

satisfied ['sætɪsfaɪd] *adj* **1** (*pleased*) 满足的 **2** (*convinced*) 确信的 ♦ **to be satisfied with sth** (*pleased*) 对某事满意 ♦ **to be satisfied that ...** 确信…

satisfy ['sætɪsfaɪ] *vt* **1** (*please*) [+ *person*] 使满足 **2** [+ *curiosity*] 满足 **3** [+ *demand*] 满足; [+ *requirements, conditions*] 符合 **4** (*convince*) ♦ **to satisfy sb that ...** 使人相信… ♦ **to satisfy o.s. that ...** 使自己确信…

satisfying ['sætɪsfaɪɪŋ] *adj* [+ *task*] 令人满意的; [+ *meal*] 令人心满意足的

Saturday ['sætədɪ] *n* [C/U] 星期六 *see also* **Tuesday**

sauce [sɔːs] *n* [C/U] (*savoury*) 酱; (*sweet*) 汁

saucepan ['sɔːspən] *n* [C] 深平底锅

saucer ['sɔːsə(r)] *n* [C] 茶杯碟

Saudi ['saudɪ] **I** *adj* (*also:* ***Saudi Arabian***) 沙特阿拉伯的 **II** *n* [C] (*person*) (*also:* ***Saudi Arabian***) 沙特阿拉伯人

Saudi Arabia [saudɪə'reɪbɪə] *n* 沙特阿拉伯

sauna ['sɔːnə] *n* [C] **1** (*act*) 桑拿浴 **2** (*room*) 桑拿浴室 ♦ **to have a sauna** 洗桑拿

sausage ['sɔsɪdʒ] *n* [C/U] 香肠

sausage roll [英] *n* [c] 香肠卷

sauté ['səuteɪ] **I** *vt* 快炸 **II** *adj* (*also:* ***sautéed***) [+ *potatoes, mushrooms*] 炸的

savage ['sævɪdʒ] **I** *adj* [+ *animal*] 凶猛的; [+ *attack*] 恶毒的 **II** *n* [c] [过时, 贬] 野蛮人 **III** *vt* **1** (*maul*) 凶猛地攻击 **2** (*criticize*) 猛烈抨击 ♦ **he was savaged to death** 他被残害致死

save [seɪv] **I** *vt* **1** (*rescue*) [+ *person*] 救 **2** (*preserve*) [+ *job, marriage, environment*] 保全 **3** (*put by*) [+ *money*] 积攒 **4** (*economize on*) [+ *money, time*] 节省 **5** (*keep*) [+ *receipts etc*] 保存; [+ *food, drink etc*] 留着; [+ *seat*] 保留 **6** [计算机] 存储 **7** [体育] 救球 **II** *vi* (*also:* ***save up***) 积攒 **III** *n* [c] 救球 **IV** *prep* [正式] (*also:* ***save for***) 除…外 ♦ **to save sb from sth** 挽救某人免于某事 ♦ **to save sb's life** 挽救某人的生命 ♦ **to save (up) for sth** 为某物储蓄 ♦ **to save sb/o.s. some work/time/expense** 对某人/自己来说省事/节省时间/节省开支 ♦ **to save sth for sth** 为某事留某物 ♦ **to save sb from doing sth** 使某人免于做某事 ♦ **God save the Queen!** 上帝保佑女王! ♦ **to make a save** [体育] 救球
❑ **save up** *vi* 积攒

saving ['seɪvɪŋ] **I** *n* [c] [*of time, money*] 节约 **II savings** *n* [*pl*] (*money*) 存款 ♦ **to make a saving (on sth)** (在某物上) 节省

savings account *n* [c] 储蓄账户

savings and loan association [美] *n* [c] 房屋储蓄借贷联合会 [英 = **building society**]

saviour (美 **savior**) ['seɪvjə(r)] *n* [c] **1** 救星 **2** ♦ **the Saviour** 救世主

savoury (美 **savory**) ['seɪvərɪ] **I** *adj* [+ *food, dish*] 咸辣的 **II savouries** *n* [*pl*] [英] 小吃

saw [sɔː] (*pt* **sawed**, *pp* **sawed** *or* **sawn**) **I** *pt of* **see** **II** *vt* 锯 **III** *vi* ♦ **to saw through sth** 锯断某物 **IV** *n* [c] 锯子 ♦ **to saw sth in half** 将某物锯成两半
❑ **saw up** *vt* 把…锯成小块

sawdust ['sɔːdʌst] *n* [u] 锯末

sawn [sɔːn] *pp of* **saw**

sax [sæks] [非正式] *n* [c] 萨克斯管

saxophone ['sæksəfəun] *n* [c] 萨克斯管

✪ **say** [seɪ] (*pt, pp* **said**) **I** *vt* **1** (*utter*) 说 ◊ *I couldn't understand what they were saying.* 我不明白他们在说什么。 **2** (*indicate*) [*clock, watch, barometer* +] 表明 ◊ *My watch says 3 o'clock.* 我的手表3点了。; [*sign* +] 写着 **II** *n* ♦ **to have one's say** 表达个人的意见 ♦ **to say that ...** (*in speech*) 说… ◊ *She said that I was to give you this.* 她叫我把这个给你。◊ *He said that he'd broken his arm.* 他说他的手臂断了。; (*in writing*) [*person* +] 说…; [*book, article* +] 写明… ♦ **to say sth to sb** 告诉某人某事 ♦ **to say sth to o.s.** 暗自思量某事 ♦ **to say yes/no** 同意/不同意 ♦ **to say goodbye/sorry (to sb)** (向某人) 告别/道歉 ♦ **when all is said and done** 归根结底 ♦ **there is something/a lot to be said for it** 有一些/很多优点 ♦ **it says something/a lot about her state of mind** 这在某种/很大程度上显露了她的想法 ♦ **you can say that again!** [非正式] 我太同意你说的了! ♦ **that is to say** 就是说 ♦ **that goes without saying** 那自不消说 ♦ **I can't say I'm sorry** 我并不感到内疚 ♦ **I must say that ...** 依我看… ♦ **to say nothing of** 更不用说 ♦ **that says it all** 不言自明 ♦ **say that ...** (*suppose*) 假设… ◊ *Say you won a million pounds.* 假设你赢了100万英镑。 ♦ **come for dinner at, say, 8 o'clock** 来吃晚饭吧，先定8点吧 ♦ **shall we say Tuesday?** 星期二好吗? ♦ **to have a** *or* **some say in sth** 对某事有发言权

saying ['seɪɪŋ] *n* [c] 格言

scab [skæb] *n* [c] **1** (*on wound*) 痂 **2** [非正式, 贬] (*strike-breaker*) 工贼

scaffolding ['skæfəldɪŋ] *n* [u] 脚手架

scald [skɔːld] **I** *vt* 烫伤 **II** *n* [c] 烫伤 ♦ **to scald o.s.** 烫伤自己

scale [skeɪl] **I** *n* **1** [s] (*size, extent*) 规模 **2** [c] (*measuring system*) (*for temperature etc*) 标度 **3** [c] [英] [*of salaries, fees etc*] 级别 **4** [c] [*of map,*

model] 比例 **5** [c] [音] 音阶 **6** [c] [*of fish, reptile*] 鳞 **II** *cpd* [复合词] [+ *model, drawing*] 按比例制作的 **III** *vt* (*climb*) 攀登 **IV scales** *n* [*pl*] (*for weighing*) (*also:* ***bathroom scales, kitchen scales***) 秤; (*for heavier things*) 磅秤 ♦**a pair** *or* **set of scales** 一架天平 ♦**on a scale of 1 to 10** 从1到10各等级地 ♦**to scale** 按比例 ♦**on a large/small scale** 以大/小规模
❏**scale down** *vt* 相应缩减

scallion ['skæljən] [美: 烹饪, 植] *n* [c] 葱 [英 = **spring onion**]

scallop ['skɔləp] *n* [c] (*shellfish*) 扇贝

scalp [skælp] **I** *n* [c] 头皮 **II** *vt* 削下…的头皮

scalpel ['skælpl] *n* [c] (*for surgery*) 手术刀; (*for artwork*) 雕刻刀

scam [skæm] [非正式] *n* [c] 骗局

scampi ['skæmpɪ] [英] *n* [*pl*] 大虾

scan [skæn] **I** *vt* **1** (*examine closely*) [+ *area, room, horizon, group*] 仔细察看 **2** (*glance quickly over*) [+ *newspaper, article, page*] 浏览 **3** [*radar* +] 扫描 **4** [计算机] [+ *document, picture*] 扫描 **5** (*with x-ray, ultrasound etc*) [+ *luggage*] 查验; [医] 扫描检查 **II** *vi* [*poem* +] 符合格律 **III** *n* [c] [医] 扫描; [*of pregnant woman*] 超声波检查 ♦**to scan sth into a computer** 将某物扫描入电脑

scandal ['skændl] *n* **1** [c] (*shocking event*) 丑闻 **2** [u] (*gossip*) 流言飞语 **3** [c] (*disgrace*) 耻辱 ♦**it is a scandal that …** …真是个耻辱

Scandinavia [skændɪ'neɪvɪə] *n* 斯堪的纳维亚

Scandinavian [skændɪ'neɪvɪən] **I** *adj* 斯堪的纳维亚的 **II** *n* [c] (*person*) 斯堪的纳维亚人

scanner ['skænə(r)] *n* [c] **1** (*in hospital*) 扫描器 **2** (*for security*) 扫描检测装置 **3** [计算机] 扫描仪

scapegoat ['skeɪpgəut] **I** *n* [c] 替罪羊 **II** *vt* ♦**to scapegoat sb (for sth)** 使某人(成为某事的)替罪羊 ♦**to make sb a scapegoat (for sth)** 使某人成为(某事的)替罪羊

scar [skɑː(r)] **I** *n* [c] **1** (*on skin*) 伤疤 **2** (*mental, emotional*) 创伤 **II** *vt* **1** (*skin*) 给…留下伤痕 **2** [+ *mind*] 给…留下创伤 **3** [+ *place*] 在…留下痕迹 ♦**to scar sb for life** (*physically*) 给某人留下终生的伤疤; (*emotionally*) 给某人留下终生的创伤

scarce [skɛəs] *adj* 短缺的 ♦**to make o.s. scarce** [非正式] 溜走

scarcely ['skɛəslɪ] *adv* **1** (*barely*) 几乎不 **2** (*certainly not*) 决不 ♦**scarcely anybody** 几乎没人 ♦**I can scarcely believe it** 我简直不能相信 ♦**scarcely had I arrived when the phone rang** 我刚到电话就响了

scare [skɛə(r)] **I** *vt* 使害怕 **II** *n* [c] **1** (*fright*) ♦**to give sb/have a scare** 把某人吓了一跳/吓了一跳 **2** (*public panic*) 恐慌 ♦**a bomb/security scare** 炸弹/安全恐慌
❏**scare away, scare off** *vt* **1** [+ *intruder, visitor, animal etc*] 把…吓跑 **2** (*put off*) [+ *boyfriend, voter etc*] 吓跑

scarecrow ['skɛəkrəu] *n* [c] 稻草人

scared ['skɛəd] *adj* **1** (*frightened*) ♦**to be scared (of sb/sth)** 害怕(某人/某物) **2** (*worried*) ♦**to be scared of sth/that …** 担心某事/… ♦**to be scared of doing sth** (*frightened of*) 害怕做某事; (*worried about*) 担心做某事 ♦**to be scared to do sth** 害怕做某事 ♦**to be scared stiff** *or* **scared to death** 吓得要命

scarf [skɑːf] (*pl* **scarfs** *or* **scarves**) *n* [c] (*long*) 围巾; (*square*) 头巾

scarlet ['skɑːlɪt] *adj* 鲜红的

scarves [skɑːvz] *n* [*pl*] *of* **scarf**

scary ['skɛərɪ] [非正式] *adj* 令人害怕的

scatter ['skætə(r)] **I** *vt* **1** (*drop*) ♦**to scatter sth over/on sth** 将某物撒在某处 **2** (*untidily*) 乱放 **3** (*disperse*) 驱散 **II** *vi* 分散

scenario [sɪ'nɑːrɪəu] *n* [c] **1** (*development*) 局面 **2** [电影, 戏剧] 剧本提纲

scene [siːn] *n* [c] **1** (*in play, film, book*) 一场 **2** [*of crime, accident*] 现场 **3** (*picture*) 景象 **4** (*event*) 场面 **5** [非正式] (*fuss*) 当众吵闹 ♦**behind the scenes** 秘密地 ♦**to appear on the scene** 到场 ♦**the political scene** 政治舞台 ♦**to set the scene for sth** 为某事的发生做准备 ♦**to make a**

scene [非正式](*fuss*) 大吵大闹
scenery ['siːnərɪ] *n* [U] **1** (*landscape*) 风景 **2** [戏剧] 舞台布景
scenic ['siːnɪk] *adj* [+ *location etc*] 风景优美的 ♦ **to take the scenic route** 走风景优美的那条路
scent [sɛnt] **I** *n* **1** [C] [*of flowers, herbs etc*] 香味 **2** [C/U] (*used for tracking*) [*of person, animal*] 气味 **3** [C/U] [英] (*perfume*) 香水 [美 = **perfume**] **II** *vt* (*catch smell of*) 嗅到 ♦ **to put** *or* **throw sb off the scent** 使某人失去线索
scented ['sɛntɪd] *adj* [+ *flower, candle, soap etc*] 芳香的
sceptical (美 **skeptical**) ['skɛptɪkl] *adj* 怀疑的 ♦ **to be sceptical about sth** 对某事持怀疑态度
schedule ['ʃɛdjuːl, (美) 'skɛdjuːl] **I** *n* [C] **1** (*agenda*) 日程安排 **2** [美] [*of trains, buses*] 时间表 [英 = **timetable**] **3** (*list of prices, details etc*) 清单 **II** *vt* ♦ **to be scheduled to do sth** 安排做某事 ♦ **on schedule** 准时 ♦ **to be ahead of/behind schedule** 提前/落后于计划 ♦ **we are working to a very tight schedule** 我们的工作日程很紧 ♦ **everything went according to schedule** 所有事情都按预定计划进行了 ♦ **to be scheduled for next week/2 o'clock** 被排在下星期/两点钟进行
scheduled flight ['ʃɛdjuːld-, (美) 'skɛdjuːld-] *n* [C] 定期航班
scheme [skiːm] **I** *n* [C] **1** [尤英] 计划 [美 = **program**] **2** (*plan*) 方案 **II** *vi* 图谋
schizophrenic [skɪtsə'frɛnɪk] **I** *adj* 精神分裂的 **II** *n* [C] 精神分裂症患者
scholar ['skɔlə(r)] *n* [C] (*learned person*) 学者
scholarship ['skɔləʃɪp] *n* **1** [C] (*grant*) 奖学金 **2** [U] (*knowledge*) 学术成就
✪ **school** [skuːl] **I** *n* **1** [C/U] (*place*) 学校; (*pupils and staff*) 全体师生 ◊ *The whole school's going to hate you.* 全体师生都会恨你的。**2** [U] (*school time, experience*) 上学 **3** [C/U] (*university department*) 学院 ◊ *the art school* 艺术学院 **4** [C/U] [美: 非正式] (*university*) 大学 **5** [C] (*specialist academy*) ♦ **riding/driving school** 骑术/驾驶学校 **6** [C] [*of fish, dolphins*] 群 **II** *cpd* [复合词] [+ *uniform, shoes, year*] 学校的 ♦ **to go to school** [*child* +] 上学; [美] (*university*) 上大学 ♦ **to leave school** [*child* +] 结束义务教育 ♦ **to be at law/medical school** 攻读法律/医学 ♦ **to go to law/medical school** 上法/医学院
school book ['skuːlbuk] *n* [C] 教科书
schoolboy ['skuːlbɔɪ] *n* [C] 男生
schoolchildren ['skuːltʃɪldrən] *n* [*pl*] 学童
schoolgirl ['skuːlgəːl] *n* [C] 女生
schooling ['skuːlɪŋ] *n* [U] 学校教育
schoolteacher ['skuːltiːtʃə(r)] *n* [C] 教师
science ['saɪəns] *n* **1** [U] (*scientific study*) 科学 **2** [C/U] (*branch of science, school subject*) 学科 ♦ **the sciences** 理科
science fiction *n* [U] 科幻小说
scientific [saɪən'tɪfɪk] *adj* **1** (*relating to science*) 科学的 **2** (*methodical*) 符合科学定律的
scientist ['saɪəntɪst] *n* [C] 科学家
sci-fi ['saɪfaɪ] *n abbr* (= ***science fiction***) 科幻小说
scissors ['sɪzəz] *n* [*pl*] 剪刀 ♦ **a pair of scissors** 一把剪刀
scold [skəuld] *vt* 责骂
scone [skɔn] [尤英] *n* [C] 烤饼
scoop [skuːp] **I** *n* [C] **1** (*implement*) 球形勺 **2** (*portion*) ♦ **a scoop (of sth)** 一勺(的某物) **3** [出版] 独家新闻 **II** *vt* **1** (*lift*) ♦ **to scoop sb/sth into one's arms** 把某人/某物揽在怀里 **2** (*with spoon, hands*) ♦ **to scoop sth into sth** 把某物舀入某物中 **3** [+ *prize, award*] 赢得
❑ **scoop out** *vt* 舀出
❑ **scoop up** *vt* 捞起
scooter ['skuːtə(r)] *n* [C] **1** (*also: **motor scooter***) 小型摩托车 **2** (*child's*) 踏板车
scope [skəup] *n* **1** [U] (*opportunity, potential*) ♦ **scope (for sth/to do sth)** (某事/做某事的)余地 **2** [S] (*range*) 范围 ♦ **there is plenty of scope for improvement** [英] 还有很大的改进余地

scorching ['skɔːtʃɪŋ] [非正式] *adj* (*also:* ***scorching hot***) [+ *day, weather*] 炎热的 ♦**it's scorching today** 今天是个大热天
📖 用法参见**hot**

score [skɔː(r)] **I** *n* [c] **1** (*points*) 比分 **2** [音] 配乐 **3** [文] (*twenty*) 二十 **II** *vt* **1** [+ *goal, point*] 得 **2** (*achieve*) [+ *success, victory*] 取得 **3** (*cut*) [+ *card, leather*] 划; [+ *line, mark*] 刻 **4** [非正式] [+ *drug*] 非法取得 **III** *vi* (*in game, sport*) 得分 ♦**scores (of)** 许多 ♦**a score of** 几个 ♦**on that/this score** 在那/这一点上 ♦**to score 6 out of 10** 10 分中得6 分 ♦**to score a point over sb/score points off sb** (喻) 驳倒某人 ♦**to score a hit** 命中 ♦**to score low/high** 获低/高分

scoreboard ['skɔːbɔːd] *n* [c] 记分牌

scorer ['skɔːrə(r)] *n* [c] **1** [*of goal, point, run etc*] 得分者 **2** (*person keeping score*) 记分员

scorn [skɔːn] **I** *n* [u] 鄙视 **II** *vt* **1** (*despise*) 瞧不起 **2** (*reject*) 拒绝

Scorpio ['skɔːpɪəu] *n* **1** [u] (*sign*) 天蝎座 **2** [c] (*person*) 天蝎座的人 ♦**I'm (a) Scorpio** 我是天蝎座的

scorpion ['skɔːpɪən] *n* [c] 蝎子

Scot [skɔt] *n* [c] 苏格兰人

Scotch [skɔtʃ] *n* **1** [u] (*also:* ***Scotch whisky***) 苏格兰威士忌 **2** [c] (*measure of whisky*) 一杯威士忌

Scotch tape® [美] *n* [u] 透明胶带

Scotland ['skɔtlənd] *n* 苏格兰

Scots [skɔts] **I** *adj* 苏格兰的 **II** *n* [u] (*dialect*) 苏格兰英语

Scotsman ['skɔtsmən] (*pl* **Scotsmen**) *n* [c] 苏格兰男人

Scotswoman ['skɔtswumən] (*pl* **Scotswomen**) *n* [c] 苏格兰女人

Scottish ['skɔtɪʃ] *adj* 苏格兰的

scout [skaut] **I** *n* [c] **1** (*also:* ***boy scout***) 男童子军成员 **2** [军] 侦察员 **II** *vt* ♦**to scout an area (for sth)** 搜索某个地区 (寻找某物) **III** *vi* ♦**to scout for sth** 物色某物
IV the Scouts *n* [*pl*] 童子军
❑**scout around** (英 **scout round**) *vi* 到处找

scowl [skaul] **I** *vi* 横眉怒目 **II** *n* [c] 怒容 ♦**to scowl at sb** 怒视某人

scramble ['skræmbl] **I** *vi* (*clamber*) ♦**to scramble up/down/over sth** 爬上/下/过某物 ♦**to scramble into/out of sth** 仓促进入/出某处 ♦**to scramble for sth/to do sth** (*compete*) 争抢某物/做某事 **II** *vt* [+ *eggs*] 炒 **III** *n* [c] **1** ♦**scramble (for sth)** (*struggle, rush*) 争夺 (某物) **2** (*climb*) 攀登 ♦**he scrambled to his feet** 他腾地站起来 ♦**to go scrambling** [英: 体育] 参加摩托车越野赛

scrambled egg ['skræmbld-] *n* [c/u] 炒鸡蛋

scrap [skræp] **I** *n* **1** [c] [*of paper, cloth*] 碎屑; [*of truth, evidence*] 一丁点 **2** [u] (*also:* ***scrap metal***) 废铜烂铁 **3** [c] [非正式] (*quarrel*) 争吵; (*fight*) 打架 **II** *vt* **1** [+ *car, ship*] 报废 **2** [+ *project, idea, system, tax*] 废弃 **III** *vi* [非正式] (*quarrel*) 争吵; (*fight*) 打架
IV scraps *n* [*pl*] [*of food*] 残羹剩饭 ♦**to sell sth for scrap** 把某物作为废品出售

scrapbook ['skræpbuk] *n* [c] 剪贴簿

scrape [skreɪp] **I** *vt* **1** (*clean*) 擦净 **2** (*hurt*) 擦伤 **3** (*damage*) 刮坏 **II** *vi* 刮 **III** *n* **1** [s] (*sound*) 刮擦声 **2** [c] [非正式, 过时] (*difficulty*) 窘境 ♦**to scrape sth off/from sth** 从某物刮掉/刮去某物
❑**scrape through** *vt* [不可拆分] *vi* 勉强通过
❑**scrape together** *vt* 凑集

scrap paper *n* [u] 废纸 ♦**a piece of scrap paper** 一张废纸

scratch [skrætʃ] **I** *n* [c] **1** (*on car, furniture etc*) 刮痕 **2** (*on body*) 擦伤 **II** *vt* **1** (*damage*) [+ *car, furniture, etc*] 划破 **2** (*because of itch*) 搔 **3** (*claw*) 抓 **III** *vi* 搔痒 ♦**to do sth from scratch** 白手起家做某事 ♦**to be up to scratch** 合格 ♦**to scratch the surface (of sth)** (对某事) 浅尝辄止 ♦**to scratch o.s.** 挠自己

scratch card ['skrætʃkɑːd] [英] *n* [c] 刮卡

scrawl [skrɔːl] **I** *vt* 潦草地写 **II** *n* [c/u] 潦草的笔迹

scream [skriːm] **I** *n* [c] 尖叫声 **II** *vi* 尖声喊叫 **III** *vt* ♦**to scream sth (at sb)** (冲着某人) 大喊某事 ♦**to let out a scream** 发出尖叫 ♦**he's/it's**

a scream [非正式] 他/这滑稽透顶了 ♦**to scream at sb** 大骂某人 ♦**to scream at sb to do sth** 大声喝叫某人去做某事

screech [skriːtʃ] **I** *vi* **1** [*car, tyres, brakes* +] 发出刺耳的声音 **2** [*bird* +] 尖叫 **3** [*person* +] ♦**to screech (at sb)** (冲某人)尖叫 **II** *vt* 尖声喊出 **III** *n* [C] **1** [*of car, tyres, brakes*] 刺耳的声音 **2** [*of bird, person*] 尖叫 ♦**to screech to a halt** 嘎然刹住

screen [skriːn] **I** *n* [C] **1** (*at cinema*) 银幕 **2** [*of television, computer*] 屏幕 **3** (*partition*) 屏风 **4** (*for illegal activity*) 掩护 **II** *vt* **1** (*conceal*) 遮蔽 **2** [+ *film*] (*in the cinema*) 上映; (*on television*) 播放 **3** (*check*) [+ *candidates*] 筛选 ♦**to screen sb for sth** (*for disease*) 对某人进行某病的检查; (*for security reasons*) 对某人进行某安全事项检查 ♦**to screen sth from sth** 把某物与某物挡开

screening [ˈskriːnɪŋ] *n* **1** [C] [*of film*] (*in the cinema*) 上映; (*on television*) 播放 **2** [C/U] [医] 检查 **3** [U] (*for security*) 审查

screenplay [ˈskriːnpleɪ] *n* [C] 电影剧本

screensaver [ˈskriːnseɪvə(r)] *n* [C] 屏幕保护

screw [skruː] **I** *n* [C] 螺丝 **II** *vt* **1** (*fasten*) ♦**to screw sth on/to sth** [+ *shelf etc*] 用螺丝把某物固定在某物上 **2** (*twist into position*) ♦**to screw sth on/into sth** 将某物拧在/入某物 **3** [非正式, 疑讳] (*have sex with*) 与…性交 ♦**to put the screw(s) on** [非正式] 威逼 ♦**to turn** *or* **tighten the screw(s) on sb** [非正式] 对某人增加压力 ♦**to screw one's eyes/face into a grimace** 眯起双眼/皱起面孔做怪相 ♦**to screw sth out of sb** [尤英: 非正式] 逼迫某人拿出某物 ♦**to have one's head screwed on** [非正式] 保持头脑清醒
❑**screw down** *vt* 用螺丝固定
❑**screw in** *vt* 拧入
❑**screw up I** *vt* **1** [英] [+ *paper*] 把…揉成一团 [美 = **crush**] **2** [非正式] (*ruin*) 把…弄得一团糟 **II** *vi* [非正式] (*fail*) 弄糟 ♦**to screw up one's eyes/face** 眯起眼睛/皱起眉头

screwdriver [ˈskruːdraɪvə(r)] *n* [C] 螺丝起子

scribble [ˈskrɪbl] **I** *vt* [+ *note*] 潦草书写 **II** *vi* **1** (*write quickly*) 潦草书写 **2** (*make marks*) 乱涂 **III** *n* [C/U] **1** (*note*) 草草写成的便条 **2** (*drawing*) 涂鸦之作
❑**scribble down** *vt* 草草写下

script [skrɪpt] *n* **1** [C] [*of play, film*] 剧本 **2** [C/U] (*writing*) 文字体系

scroll [skrəul] **I** *n* [C] **1** [*of paper, parchment*] 卷轴 **2** (*decoration*) 涡卷形装饰 **II** *vi* ♦**to scroll up/down** 逐渐上移/下移

scrounge [skraundʒ] [非正式] **I** *vt* ♦**to scrounge sth (off sb)** (从某人处)乞讨某物 **II** *vi* ♦**to scrounge (off sb)** (向某人)乞讨 **III** *n* ♦**to be on the scrounge** 在行骗

scrub [skrʌb] **I** *vt* [+ *floor, pan, clothes*] 擦洗; [+ *vegetables, one's hands*] 刷洗 **II** *vi* 用力擦洗 **III** *n* **1** [U] (*land*) 低矮丛林地 **2** [S] (*wash*) 擦洗 ♦**to scrub sth clean** 将某物擦净 ♦**to give sth a scrub** 刷净某物
❑**scrub off** *vt* 擦掉

scruffy [ˈskrʌfɪ] *adj* [+ *person, appearance*] 邋遢的; [+ *clothes, house*] 不整洁的

scrum [skrʌm] *n* [C] 橄榄球赛中两队前锋并排用肩膀相抵，用腿争夺扔进中间空隙中的球

scrutiny [ˈskruːtɪnɪ] *n* [U] 仔细检查 ♦**to come under scrutiny** 受到密切注意

scuba diving [ˈskuːbə-] *n* [U] 带水下呼吸器潜水 ♦**to go scuba diving** 去潜水

scuffle [ˈskʌfl] **I** *n* [C] 混战 **II** *vi* 扭打 ♦**to scuffle with sb** 与某人混战

sculptor [ˈskʌlptə(r)] *n* [C] 雕塑家

sculpture [ˈskʌlptʃə(r)] *n* **1** [U] (*art*) 雕塑 **2** [C] (*object*) 塑像

scum [skʌm] *n* **1** [U] (*on liquid*) 浮渣 **2** [PL] [非正式] (*people*) 渣滓

scurry [ˈskʌrɪ] *vi* 急赶
❑**scurry around** *vi* 奔忙
❑**scurry off** *vi* 匆忙离开

scythe [saɪð] *n* [C] 长柄大镰刀

SE *abbr* (= ***south-east***) 东南部

sea [siː] **I** *n* **1** ♦**the sea** 海洋 **2** (*in names*) ♦**the North/Irish/Dead Sea**

北/爱尔兰/死海 **II** *cpd* [复合词] [+ *breeze, air*] 海 ♦**beside** *or* **by the sea** 在海边 ♦**by sea** 由海路 ♦**at sea** (字) 在海上 ♦**to be all at sea (with sth)** (对某事) 不知所措 ♦**to be swept out to sea** 被大海卷走 ♦**to look out to sea** 瞭望大海 ♦**heavy** *or* **rough sea(s)** 波涛汹涌 ♦**a sea of faces/glasses** 数不清的面孔/玻璃杯

seafood ['siːfuːd] *n* [U] 海味

seafront ['siːfrʌnt] *n* ♦**the seafront** 滨海区

seagull ['siːgʌl] *n* [C] 海鸥

seal [siːl] **I** *n* [C] **1** (*animal*) 海豹 **2** (*official stamp*) 印章 **3** (*in fridge, machine*) 密封装置 **4** (*sealed condition*) 密封 **II** *vt* **1** (*close*) [+ *envelope*] 封讫; [+ *container, opening*] 密封 **2** (*finalize*) [+ *agreement*] 使定局 ♦**to give sth one's seal of approval** 正式认可某物 ♦**to seal sb's fate** 注定某人的命运

❑**seal off** *vt* 封锁

sea level *n* [U] 海平面 ♦**100 metres above/below sea level** 海拔/低于海平面 100 米

seam [siːm] *n* [C] **1** (*stitches*) 缝 **2** [*of coal etc*] 层 ♦**to be bursting at the seams** 拥挤不堪

search [sɜːtʃ] **I** *n* [C] **1** (*for missing person*) 搜寻 **2** [*of place*] 搜查 **3** [计算机] 检索 **II** *vt* [+ *place, suitcase, person*] 搜查 **III** *vi* ♦**to search (for sb/sth)** 寻找 (某人/某物) ♦**a search for** [+ *object, person*] 寻找; [+ *solution, settlement*] 寻求 ♦**in search of** 寻求 ♦**to search sb/sth for sth** 为找某物搜查某人/某物 ♦**to search one's mind for sth** 绞尽脑汁想某事

❑**search through** *vt* [不可拆分] 彻底搜寻

search engine [计算机] *n* [C] 搜索引擎

search party *n* [C] 搜索队 ♦**to send out a search party (for sb)** 派搜索队 (寻找某人)

seashore ['siːʃɔː(r)] *n* [C] 海岸 ♦**on the seashore** 在海边

seasick ['siːsɪk] *adj* 晕船的 ♦**to be** *or* **feel seasick** 感到晕船恶心 ♦**to be seasick** (*vomit*) 晕船呕吐

seaside ['siːsaɪd] [英] *n* ♦**the seaside** 海边 ♦**at the seaside** 在海边 ♦**to go to the seaside** 去海边

✪**season** ['siːzn] **I** *n* [C] **1** [*of year*] 季节 **2** (*for activity*) 时节 ◊ *the planting season* 种植时节 ◊ *the football season* 足球赛季 ◊ *the rainy season* 雨季 **3** (*series*) [*of films etc*] 上映期 ◊ *a new season of horror films* 恐怖片新的上映期 **II** *vt* ♦**to season sth (with sth)** (用某物) 给某物调味 ♦**raspberries are in season/out of season** 红莓正当令/下市

seasonal ['siːznl] *adj* [+ *factors, variations*] 季节性的; [+ *staff*] 节令性的

seasoning ['siːznɪŋ] *n* [C/U] 调味品

season ticket *n* [C] 季票

seat [siːt] **I** *n* [C] **1** (*chair*) 椅子; (*in car, theatre, cinema*) 座; **2** (*place*) (*in theatre, bus, train*) 座位 **3** [*of MP*] 议席 **4** (*on committee*) 席位 **5** (*part*) [*of chair*] 座部; [*of trousers*] 臀; (*buttocks*) 臀部 **6** (*centre*) [*of government, learning etc*] 中心 **II** *vt* **1** (*put*) 使就座 **2** (*have room for*) 容纳 ♦**are there any seats left?** 还有位子吗? ♦**to take a/one's seat** 就座 ♦**to be in the driver's** *or* **driving seat** 处于控制地位 ♦**to seat o.s.** 坐下 ♦**to be seated** (*be sitting*) 坐下 ♦**please be seated** [正式] 请坐

seat belt *n* [C] 安全带

seating ['siːtɪŋ] *n* [U] 座位

sea turtle [美] *n* [C] 海龟 [英= **turtle**]

sea water *n* [U] 海水

seaweed ['siːwiːd] *n* [C/U] 海草

sec [非正式] *n* [C] 一会儿 ♦**I'll just be a sec** 我只要一会儿

sec., sec *n abbr* (= ***second***(**s**)) 秒

secluded [sɪ'kluːdɪd] *adj* [+ *place, life*] 僻静的

✪**second** ['sɛkənd] **I** *adj* 第二的 ◊ *his second marriage* 他的第二次婚姻 **II** *adv* **1** (*after someone else*) [*perform* +] 第二地; (*in race, contest*) [*come, finish* +] 第二名地 **2** (*secondly*) 再者 **III** *n* **1** [C] (*unit of time*) 秒 **2** (*short time*) ♦**seconds/a second** 片刻 ◊ *It'll only take a second.* 一会儿就行。◊ *Wait a* *second!* 稍等片刻！**3** [U] (*also:* ***second gear***) 第二挡 **4** [C] (*imperfect product*) 次品 ◊ *Some of the articles are seconds.* 有些东西是次品。**IV** *vt* **1** (*in formal meeting*) [+ *motion, nomination*] 附议 **2** (*back*) [+ *call*] 赞同 **3** [英] [教育] ♦ **upper/lower second** 中上/中下 ♦ **second floor** [英] 三层; [美] 二层 ♦ **to be second nature to sb** 某人的第二天性 ♦ **to be second to none** 首屈一指的 ♦ **to be second only to sth/sb** 仅次于某物/某人 ♦ **Charles the Second** 查理二世 ♦ **just a second!** 就一会儿！

secondary ['sɛkəndərɪ] **I** *adj* **1** (*less important*) [+ *issue, role*] 次要的; [+ *road*] 支路的 **2** (*subsequent*) [+ *effect*] 随后的; [+ *infection, tumour*] 继发性的 **II** *cpd* [复合词] [+ *pupil, curriculum*] 中学 ♦ **of secondary importance** 次要的

secondary school *n* [C/U] 中学

second-class ['sɛkənd'klɑːs] **I** *adj* **1** [+ *citizen, education etc*] 二等的 **2** [+ *stamp, letter*] 第二级的 **3** [+ *ticket, carriage*] 二等的 **II** *adv* **1** [*travel* +] 乘坐二等 **2** [*send, post* +] 作为第二级邮件 **III** *n* [U] 二等

second-hand ['sɛkənd'hænd] **I** *adj* **1** [+ *car, books, clothes*] 二手的 **2** [+ *information, opinions*] 间接的 **II** *adv* [*buy* +] 作为二手货 ♦ **to hear sth (at) second-hand** 间接地得知某事 **III** *cpd* [复合词] [+ *shop, bookshop*] 经营旧货

secondly ['sɛkəndlɪ] *adv* 其次

second-rate ['sɛkənd'reɪt] *adj* 平庸的

second thought *n* ♦ **to have second thoughts about sth/about doing sth** 重新考虑某事/做某事 ♦ **without a second thought** 不加思索地 ♦ **on second thoughts** *or* [美] **thought** 经重新考虑后

Second World War *n* ♦ **the Second World War** 第二次世界大战

secrecy ['siːkrəsɪ] *n* [U] 保密 ♦ **in secrecy** 秘密地

secret ['siːkrɪt] **I** *adj* [+ *plan, activity, place etc*] 秘密的 **II** *n* [C] 秘密 ♦ **to keep sth secret (from sb)** (对某人)保密某事 ♦ **a secret admirer** (*romantic*) 暗恋者 ♦ **can you keep a secret?** 你能保守秘密吗？ ♦ **to make no secret of sth** 不隐瞒某事 ♦ **in secret** 暗地里 ♦ **the secret of (sb's) success** (某人)成功的秘诀

secretarial [sɛkrɪ'tɛərɪəl] *adj* [+ *work, assistance*] 秘书的; [+ *course*] 有关秘书事务的; [+ *staff*] 秘书处的

✪ **secretary** ['sɛkrətərɪ] *n* [C] **1** (*in office*) 秘书 **2** [*of organization*] (*committee member*) 书记; (*manager*) 干事 **3** (*company secretary*) 文书 ♦ **Secretary of State (for sth)** [英] (某部)部长 ♦ **Secretary of State** [美] 国务卿 ♦ **the Transport/Health Secretary** [英] 交通/卫生大臣

secretive ['siːkrətɪv] *adj* 爱保密的 ♦ **to be secretive about sth** 对某事守口如瓶

secretly ['siːkrɪtlɪ] *adv* [*act* +] 秘密地; [*hope* +] 暗自地

secret service *n* [C] 情报机关

sect [sɛkt] *n* [C] 派别

section ['sɛkʃən] *n* [C] **1** (*part*) 部分 **2** (*department*) 部门 **3** [*of document*] 节 **4** (*cross-section*) 剖面图 ♦ **the business section** 商业版

sector ['sɛktə(r)] *n* [C] **1** 部分 **2** [军] 防御地段 ♦ **the public/private sector** 政府机构/私营部门

secular ['sɛkjulə(r)] *adj* 非宗教的

secure [sɪ'kjuə(r)] **I** *adj* **1** (*impregnable*) [+ *house, windows*] 紧闭的; [+ *prison, hospital*] 拘留性的; [+ *border*] 固若金汤的; [+ *data, communication, transaction*] 安全的 **2** (*dependable*) [+ *job, future*] 稳定的 **3** (*firmly fixed*) 牢固的 **4** (*emotionally*) 无忧虑的 **II** *vt* **1** (*fasten*) [+ *rope, shelf*] 缚牢 **2** (*get*) [+ *contract, votes*] 获得 **3** (*make safe*) [+ *place*] 使安全 **4** ♦ **to secure a loan against sth** 用某物担保贷款 ♦ **to be financially secure** 经济上无忧无虑 ♦ **to secure sth to sth** 将某物缚在某物上 ♦ **to secure sth for sb** 为某人弄到某物

✪ **security** [sɪ'kjuərɪtɪ] **I** *n* [U] **1** (*precautions*) 保安措施 ◊ *The*

Queen's visit was marked by tight security. 女王的到访以保安严密著称。**2** [*of country, border, building, person*] 安全; [*of data, transaction*] 妥善保管 **3** [*of job etc*] 稳定性 ◊ *fears about job security* 对工作稳定性的担忧 **4** (*emotional*) 安全感 ◊ *a sense of security* 安全感 **5** (*for loan*) 抵押品 **II securities** *n* [*pl*] [经济] 证券 ♦**to increase/tighten security** 增加/加强保安

security guard *n* [c] (*at building*) 保安人员; (*transporting money*) 押钞人员

sedan [sə'dæn] [美:汽车] *n* [c] 箱式小客车 [英= **saloon**]

sedate [sɪ'deɪt] **I** *adj* [+ *person*] 安祥的; [+ *life*] 平静的; [+ *pace*] 稳健的 **II** *vt* 给…服镇静剂

sedative ['sɛdɪtɪv] *n* [c] 镇静剂

seduce [sɪ'djuːs] *vt* (*sexually*) 勾引; (*tempt*) 引诱; (*delight*) 吸引 ♦**to seduce sb into doing sth** 引诱某人做某事

seductive [sɪ'dʌktɪv] *adj* [+ *person*] 性感的; [+ *offer, argument*] 诱惑的

✪ **see** [siː] (*pt* **saw**, *pp* **seen**) **I** *vt* **1** 看见 ◊ *Did you see what happened?* 你看见发生的事了吗？**2** (*meet*) [+ *person*] 见 ◊ *I'll see you at the cinema.* 我在电影院见你。◊ *You need to see a doctor.* 你需要去看医生。**3** (*watch*) [+ *film, play etc*] 看 ◊ *the best film I've ever seen* 我看过的最好的电影 **4** (*look at*) [+ *letter, document, picture etc*] 看 ◊ *Did you see the article by Professor Gray?* 你看了格雷教授的文章了吗？**5** (*understand*) 明白 ◊ *I see what you mean.* 我明白你的意思了。**6** (*notice*) 意识到 **7** (*find out*) 查明 **8** (*imagine*) 想像 **9** (*regard*) 把…当作 ◊ *He saw her as a rival.* 他把她当成一个对手。**10** (*witness*) [+ *change, event*] 目睹 ◊ *Yesterday saw the resignation of the disgraced Minister.* 昨天威望扫地的部长辞职了。**II** *vi* 看见 ◊ *It's dark and I can't see.* 太黑了，我看不见。♦**I can see something** 我能看见某物 ♦**to see sb doing/do sth** 看见某人做某事 ♦**there was nobody to be seen** 看不见任何人 ♦**have you seen my glasses?** 你看见我的眼镜了吗？♦**I don't know what she sees in him** 我不知道她看中他哪一点 ♦**to go and see sb** 去见某人 ♦**see Chapter 6** 参见第6章 ♦**to see that ...** (*realize, notice*) 意识到…◊ *I could see she was lonely.* 我察觉到她很孤独。; (*ensure*) 确保 ♦**to see if** (*find out if*) 查看…是否 ◊ *I'll see if she's available.* 我去看看她是否有空。♦**I can see him doing really well** (*envisage*) 我可以想像他将干得不错 ♦**see you (soon)!** [非正式] 再见！♦**see you later!** 一会儿见！♦**to see sb to the door** 送某人出门 ♦**I'll see what I can do** 我会看看能做些什么 ♦**let me see, let's see** (*show me*) 让我看看吧; (*let me think*) 让我想一想 ♦**I see** 我明白 ♦**you see** (*in explanations*) 你知道 ♦**we'll see** 看看再说 ♦**see for yourself** 你自己看看 ♦**as far as I can see** 就我看来

❑ **see about** *vt* [不可拆分] (*deal with*) 处理

❑ **see off** *vt* **1** (*say goodbye to*) 向…告别 **2** [英] (*defeat*) [+ *opponent, challenge*] 击败

❑ **see out** *vt* (*see to the door*) 送 ♦**I'll see myself out** 不用送了

❑ **see through I** *vt* (*help*) [+ *person*] 帮助…渡过难关 ◊ *$50 should see you through.* 50美金应该能够帮你渡过难关。◊ *He saw me through the hard times.* 他曾帮我度过艰难岁月。**II** *vt* [不可拆分] (*understand*) [+ *person*] 看穿; [+ *plan*] 识破 ◊ *The jailers saw through my scheme.* 看守们识破了我的计划。

❑ **see to** *vt* [不可拆分] (*deal with*) 处理 ◊ *Franklin saw to the luggage.* 福兰克林负责照管行李。♦**to see to it that ...** 确保…

seed [siːd] **I** *n* **1** [c/u] [*of plant, fruit*] 籽 **2** [c] (*beginning*) 萌芽 **3** [c] [网球] 种子选手 **II** *vt* ♦**to be seeded nine/fifteenth** *etc* 第9/15{等}号种子选手 ♦**to plant** *or* **sow a seed** (*in ground*) 播种; (*in sb's mind*) 播下…的种子 ♦**to go** *or* **run to seed** [*plant* +] 花谢结籽; [*person, institution* +] 走下坡路

seeing ['siːɪŋ] *conj* ♦**seeing as** *or*

that 鉴于

seeing-eye dog [美] *n* [c] 导盲犬 [英 = **guide dog**]

seek [siːk] (*pt, pp* **sought**) *vt* **1** [+ *truth, revenge, shelter, compensation*] 寻求 **2** [+ *work, job*] 寻找 ♦**to seek advice/help (from sb)** (向某人)求教/求助 ♦**to seek to do sth** 试图做某事

❑**seek out** *vt* 搜寻出

✪**seem** [siːm] *vi* 似乎 ◊ *Everyone seems busy.* 每个人似乎都挺忙。♦**it seems like ...** 看起来像是… ♦**it seems as if ...** 好像… ♦**to seem (to be) happy/interested** 好像(是)高兴/感兴趣 ♦**to seem to do sth** 好像做某事 ♦**how did she seem to you?** 你觉得她看起来怎么样? ♦**there seems to be ...** 好像有… ♦**it seems that ...** 看来… ♦**it seems to me that ...** 我觉得… ♦**she couldn't seem to stop crying** 她看来是哭不停了 ♦**I seem to have mislaid it** 我好像忘记把它放在哪里了

seemingly ['siːmɪŋlɪ] *adv* 表面上

seen [siːn] *pp of* **see**

seesaw ['siːsɔː] **I** *n* [c] 跷跷板 **II** *vi* 反复多变

seethe [siːð] *vi* **1** [*person* +] 怒火中烧 **2** ♦**to be seething (with)** (*crowded*) 拥挤不堪 ♦**to seethe at sth** 为某事发怒 ♦**to seethe with anger** 火冒三丈

see-through ['siːθruː] *adj* [+ *blouse, dress*] 薄如蝉翼的

segment ['sɛgmənt] *n* [c] [*of population, society*] 阶层; [*of market, economy etc*] 部分; [*of orange*] 瓣

segregate ['sɛgrɪgeɪt] *vt* (*divide*) 使隔离; (*isolate*) 使孤立 ♦**to segregate sb from sb** 将某人与某人分开

seize [siːz] *vt* **1** [+ *person, object, opportunity*] 抓住 **2** [+ *power, control*] 夺取; [+ *building, territory*] 占据 **3** [+ *hostage*] 俘获 **4** [+ *property*] 没收

❑**seize up** *vi* [*engine* +] 卡住; [*part of body* +] 僵住

❑**seize (up)on** *vt* [不可拆分] 大肆利用

seizure ['siːʒə(r)] *n* [c] **1** [医] 发作 **2** (*taking*) [*of power, land*] 夺取 **3** (*confiscation*) [*of drugs etc*] 没收

seldom ['sɛldəm] *adv* 不常

select [sɪ'lɛkt] **I** *vt* 挑选 **II** *adj* 第一流的 ♦**a select group** 精选的一群 ♦**a select few** 精选的几个

selection [sɪ'lɛkʃən] *n* **1** [U] (*being chosen*) 挑选 **2** [c] [商] (*range*) 供选择的范围 **3** [c] (*collection*) 选集

selective [sɪ'lɛktɪv] *adj* **1** (*discerning*) 精挑细选的 **2** (*based on selection*) [+ *education, school, breeding etc*] 选择性的

self [sɛlf] (*pl* **selves**) *n* ♦**the self** (*ego*) 自身 ♦**I feel my old** *or* **normal self again** 我感到和以前一模一样

self-assured [sɛlfə'ʃuəd] *adj* 自信的

self-catering [sɛlf'keɪtərɪŋ] [英] *adj* [+ *holiday, accommodation*] 自供伙食的

self-centred (美 **self-centered**) [sɛlf'sɛntəd] *adj* 以自我为中心的

self-confidence [sɛlf'kɔnfɪdns] *n* [U] 自信心

self-conscious [sɛlf'kɔnʃəs] *adj* 容易难为情的 ♦**to be self-conscious about sth** 极为在意某事

self-contained [sɛlfkən'teɪnd] *adj* [+ *flat*] 有独立设施的; [+ *person*] 不与他人往来的

self-control [sɛlfkən'trəul] *n* [U] 自制力

self-defence (美 **self-defense**) [sɛlfdɪ'fɛns] *n* [U] 自卫 ♦**in self-defence** 出于自卫

self-discipline [sɛlf'dɪsɪplɪn] *n* [U] 自我约束

self-drive [sɛlf'draɪv] [英] *adj* ♦**a self-drive car** 由承租人驾驶的车 ♦**a self-drive holiday** 自己租车驾驶的旅行

self-employed [sɛlfɪm'plɔɪd] **I** *adj* 个体的 **II** *n* [*pl*] ♦**the self-employed** 个体户

self-esteem [sɛlfɪs'tiːm] *n* [U] 自尊心 ♦**to have low/high self-esteem** 自尊心差/强

self-indulgent [sɛlfɪn'dʌldʒənt] *adj* 放纵自己的

self-interest [sɛlf'ɪntrɪst] *n* [U] 自身利益

selfish ['sɛlfɪʃ] *adj* [+ *person, reason, behaviour*] 自私的 ♦**it was a selfish**

decision 这是一个自私的决定

selfless ['sɛlflɪs] *adj* [+ *person, act, behaviour*] 无私的

self-pity [sɛlf'pɪtɪ] *n* [U] 自怜

self-raising [sɛlf'reɪzɪŋ] [英] *adj* ♦**self-raising flour** 自发面粉 [美=**self-rising**]

self-respect [sɛlfrɪs'pɛkt] *n* [U] 自尊心

self-rising [sɛlf'raɪzɪŋ] [美] *adj* ♦**self-rising flour** 自发面粉 [英=**self-raising**]

self-service [sɛlf'səːvɪs] *adj* [+ *shop, restaurant, garage*] 自助的

✪**sell** [sɛl] (*pt, pp* **sold**) **I** *vt* **1** 卖◊ *I sold the house for 80,000 pounds.* 我的房子卖了8万英镑。◊ *Do you sell flowers?* 你们这儿卖花吗？◊ *We sell rubber products.* 我们经销橡胶制品。**2** (喻) [+ *idea*] 使接受◊ *She is hoping she can sell the idea to clients.* 她希望能够让客户接受这个主意。**II** *vi* [*goods, product* +] 有销路◊ *I'm not sure if it will sell.* 我不能肯定是否有销路。♦**to sell at** *or* **for 10 pounds** 售价10英镑 ♦**to sell sb sth, sell sth to sb** 将某物卖给某人 ♦**to sell o.s.** 自我推销

❑**sell off** *vt* 卖掉

❑**sell out** *vi* **1** (字) [*shop* +] 卖光存货; [*book, tickets etc* +] 卖光◊ *The tickets have sold out.* 票卖光了。**2** (喻) (*betray principles*) 放弃原则 **3** [美] (*sell everything*) 出售所有财物 ♦**to sell out of sth** 卖光某物 ◊ *The shop had sold out of ice creams.* 那家商店的冰淇淋卖光了。

❑**sell up** [英] *vi* 出售所有财物

sell-by date ['sɛlbaɪ-] [英] *n* [C] 商品必须售出的截止日期

seller ['sɛlə(r)] *n* [C] (*person, company*) 销售者 ♦**to be a big seller** 畅销品 ♦**it's a seller's market** 这是卖方市场

Sellotape® ['sɛləuteɪp] [英] **I** *n* [U] 透明胶带 [美=**Scotch tape**] **II** *vt* ♦**to sellotape sth to sth** 用透明胶带将某物粘贴在某物上 ♦**to sellotape things together** 用透明胶带将东西粘在一起 [美=**tape**]

selves [sɛlvz] *pl of* **self**

semester [sɪ'mɛstə(r)] [尤美] *n* [C] 学期

semicircle ['sɛmɪsəːkl] *n* [C] 半圆

semi-colon [sɛmɪ'kəulən] *n* [C] 分号

semi-detached [sɛmɪdɪ'tætʃt] [英] *adj* 半独立式的

semi-final [sɛmɪ'faɪnl] *n* [C] 半决赛

seminar ['sɛmɪnɑː(r)] *n* [C] 专题讨论会

semi-skimmed (milk) [sɛmɪ'skɪmd] [英] *n* [U] 半脱脂奶 [美=**two-percent milk**]

Sen. [美] *abbr* **1** (= ***senator***) 参议院议员 **2** (*in names*) (= ***senior***) 老

senate ['sɛnɪt] *n* **1** [政治] ♦**the Senate** 参议院 **2** [大学] (*also:* ***the Senate***) 理事会

senator ['sɛnɪtə(r)] [美] *n* [C] 参议院议员

✪**send** [sɛnd] (*pt, pp* **sent**) *vt* **1** ♦**to send sth (to sb)** [+ *letter, money etc*] 将某物发送(给某人)◊ *I promised I would send her the money.* 我答应会将钱给她送去的。**2** [+ *person*] 派遣◊ *The government sent troops to the region.* 政府派遣军队去那个地区。**3** (*transmit*) [+ *signal, picture*] 传送◊ *the pictures that the satellite sent back* 卫星传送回来的照片 ♦**to send sth by post** *or* [美] **mail** 邮寄某物 ♦**to send sb for** [+ *check-up, scan etc*] 叫某人去; [+ *bread, water etc*] 差某人去送 ♦**he was sent there to fight terrorists** 他被派到那儿去对付恐怖分子 ♦**to send word that ...** 捎信说… ♦**she sends (you) her love** 她(向你)问候 ♦**to send sb to sleep** 使某人入睡 ♦**to send sth flying** 把某物撞飞

❑**send away** *vt* [+ *unwelcome visitor*] 把…打发走

❑**send away for** *vt* [不可拆分] 函购

❑**send back** *vt* [+ *goods*] 退还

❑**send for** *vt* [不可拆分] **1** (*also:* ***send away for, send off for***) (*by post*) 函购 **2** [+ *doctor, police*] 差人去叫

❑**send in** *vt* [+ *report, application etc*] 寄送

❑**send off** *vt* **1** ♦**to send sth off (to sb)** [+ *goods, parcel*] 将某物邮寄(给某人) **2** [体育] [+ *player*] 将…罚出场

❑**send off for** *vt* [不可拆分] 函购

❑ **send on** *vt* [+ *letter*] 转送; [+ *luggage etc*] (*in advance*) 先行发走; (*afterwards*) 转送

❑ **send out** I *vt* 1 [+ *invitation, leaflet*] 发出 2 (*emit*) [+ *light, heat, signal*] 发送出 II *vi* ♦ **to send out for sth** [+ *pizza, curry*] 电话订购某物

❑ **send round** *vt* ♦ **to send sth round (to sb)** [+ *letter, document etc*] 分发某物(给某人)

❑ **send up** *vt* 1 (*raise*) [+ *price, blood pressure*] 使上升 2 [英:非正式] (*parody*) 通过模仿取笑

sender ['sɛndə(r)] *n* [c] [*of letter, package, radio message*] 发送人

send-off ['sɛndɔf] [非正式] *n* ♦ **to give sb a good send-off** 为某人饯行

Senegal [sɛnɪ'gɔːl] *n* 塞内加尔

Senegalese [sɛnɪgə'liːz] (*pl* **Senegalese**) I *adj* 塞内加尔的 II *n* [c] (*person*) 塞内加尔人

senile ['siːnaɪl] *adj* 老态龙钟的

senior ['siːnɪə(r)] *adj* [+ *staff, manager, officer*] 高级的; [+ *job, position*] 上级的 ♦ **to be senior to sb, be sb's senior** (*in company*) 是某人的上级 ♦ **she is 15 years his senior** 她比他年长15岁 ♦ **Jones Senior** [尤美] 老琼斯

senior citizen *n* [c] 已届退休年龄的公民

senior high (美 **senior high school**) *n* [c] 高中

sensation [sɛn'seɪʃən] *n* 1 [c] (*physical, mental*) 感觉 2 [u] (*sense of touch*) 触觉 3 (*great success*) ♦ **to be a sensation** 轰动一时的人物/事件 ♦ **to cause a sensation** 引起轰动

sensational [sɛn'seɪʃənl] *adj* 1 (*wonderful*) 极好的 2 (*surprising*) [+ *event*] 轰动性的 3 (*exaggerated*) [+ *story, report*] 耸人听闻的

✪ **sense** [sɛns] I *n* 1 [c] [*of sight, smell, taste etc*] 感觉官能 ◊ *a keen sense of smell* 嗅觉灵敏 ◊ *the five senses* 5种感觉官能 2 [s] (*feeling*) [*of guilt, shame etc*] 感觉 ◊ *I was overcome by a sense of failure.* 我被失败感所压倒。3 [u] (*good sense*) 明智 4 [c] (*meaning*) [*of word*] 释义 ◊ *a noun which has two senses* 一个有两种释义的名词 II *vt* (*become aware of*) 觉察到 ♦ **to have the sense to do sth** 明智地做某事 ◊ *They sometimes have the sense to seek help.* 他们有时很明智，知道求助。♦ **it makes sense** (*can be understood*) 讲得通; (*is sensible*) 合情合理 ♦ **there is no sense in doing that** 那么做是不明智的 ♦ **to come to one's senses** (*become reasonable*) 恢复理智 ♦ **to take leave of one's senses** 发疯 ♦ **to talk sense** 说话有道理 ♦ **to make sense of sth** 理解某事 ♦ **in a sense** 从某种意义上说 ♦ **to sense that ...** 察觉到… ◊ *He sensed that she did not like him.* 他察觉到她不喜欢他。

senseless ['sɛnslɪs] *adj* 1 (*pointless*) 毫无意义的 2 (*unconscious*) 不省人事的 ♦ **to be beaten senseless** 被打得失去知觉

sense of humour *n* [s] 幽默感

sensible ['sɛnsɪbl] *adj* [+ *person*] 通情达理的; [+ *decision, suggestion*] 明智的; [+ *shoes, clothes*] 实用耐穿的 ♦ **it would be sensible to go to bed early** 早上床睡觉是明智的

sensitive ['sɛnsɪtɪv] *adj* 1 [+ *person*] (*understanding*) 善解人意的; (*over-sensitive*) 过于敏感的 2 [+ *subject*] 棘手的 3 [+ *skin*] 敏感的 4 [+ *instrument*] 灵敏的 ♦ **to be sensitive to sth** [+ *sb's needs, feelings, heat, light etc*] 对某物敏感 ♦ **to be sensitive about sth** 对某事敏感

sensitivity [sɛnsɪ'tɪvɪtɪ] I *n* 1 [c/u] [*of person*] (*to sb's feelings, needs*) 敏感性; (*over-sensitive nature*) 神经过敏 2 [u] [*of device, organism etc*] (*to heat, light etc*) 灵敏性 3 [u] [*of issue*] 棘手 II **sensitivities** *n* [*pl*] 感情

sensual ['sɛnsjuəl] *adj* 1 [+ *pleasure, experience*] 感官的 2 [+ *person*] 性感的

sensuous ['sɛnsjuəs] *adj* 1 [+ *experience, pleasure, fabric*] 给感官以快感的 2 [+ *person, voice, lips*] 性感的

sent [sɛnt] *pt, pp of* **send**

sentence ['sɛntns] I *n* 1 [c] [语言] 句子 2 [c/u] [法] 刑罚 II *vt* ♦ **to**

sentence sb to death/to 5 years in prison 判某人死刑/5 年囚禁 ♦**to pass sentence on sb** 宣布对某人的判决

sentiment ['sɛntɪmənt] *n* **1** [c] (*opinion*) 观点 **2** [u] (*emotion*) 多愁善感

sentimental [sɛntɪ'mɛntl] *adj* [+ *person*] 多愁善感的; [+ *song, story*] 充满柔情的; [+ *value, reasons*] 情感的

separate [*adj* 'sɛprɪt, *vb* 'sɛpəreɪt] **I** *adj* [+ *section, piece, pile*] 分开的; [+ *occasion, incident*] 不同的; [+ *existence, organization, species, entity*] 独立的; [+ *rooms*] 单独的; [+ *issue, question*] 不相关的 **II** *vt* **1** (*split up*) [+ *people, things*] 分开 **2** (*make a distinction between*) [+ *ideas, facts*] 区分 **3** (*exist between*) 分隔 **III** *vi* **1** (*move apart*) 分开 **2** (*split up*) [*parents, couple* +] 分居 **3** (*also: **separate out***) [*mixture, sauce, colours* +] 分离 **IV separates** *n* [*pl*] (*clothes*) 单件衣物 ♦**they went their separate ways** (*to different places*) 他们分道扬镳了; (*ended their relationship*) 他们分手了 ♦**to keep sth separate from** 将某物与…分开 ♦**to remain separate from** 保持与…分离 ♦**to separate from** [+ *object, surface*] 与…分开; [+ *husband, wife*] 分居 ♦**to separate sth from sth** (*move apart*) 把某物与某物分开; (*make a distinction between*) 把某物从某物中识别出来; (*make different*) 将某物与某物区分; (*form a barrier between*) 把某物与某物分隔 ♦**to be separated** [*couple* +] 分居 ♦**to separate (people/things) into groups** 将(人/物)分成组

separated ['sɛpəreɪtɪd] *adj* (*not divorced*) 分居的

separately ['sɛprɪtlɪ] *adv* 分开地

separation [sɛpə'reɪʃən] *n* [c/u] **1** [*of things, groups*] 分开; (*process of separating*) 分离 **2** (*division*) (*into smaller parts*) 分隔 **3** (*time apart*) (*from loved ones*) 分离 **4** (*split-up*) [*of couple*] 分居

Sept. *abbr* (= ***September***) 九月

September [sɛp'tɛmbə(r)] *n* [c/u] 九月 *see also* **July**

septic ['sɛptɪk] *adj* [+ *wound, finger etc*] 脓毒性的 ♦**to go septic** 化脓

sequel ['siːkwl] *n* [c] **1** (*to film, story*) 续集 **2** (*aftermath*) 后果

sequence ['siːkwəns] *n* [c] **1** (*series*) 一连串 **2** (*order*) 顺序 **3** [电影] 连续镜头 ♦**sequence of events** 一连串事件 ♦**in sequence** 按顺序

sequin ['siːkwɪn] *n* [c] 装饰性亮片

Serb [səːb] *adj, n* = **Serbian**

Serbia ['səːbɪə] *n* 塞尔维亚

Serbian ['səːbɪən] **I** *adj* 塞尔维亚的 **II** *n* **1** [c] (*person*) 塞尔维亚人 **2** [u] (*language*) 塞尔维亚语

serene [sɪ'riːn] *adj* [+ *person, smile*] 安祥的; [+ *place*] 宁静的

sergeant ['sɑːdʒənt] *n* [c] **1** [军] 中士 **2** [英:警察] 小队长; [美] 巡佐

serial ['sɪərɪəl] **I** *n* [c] (*on TV, radio*) 连续剧; (*in magazine*) 连载 **II** *adj* [+ *rapist, adulterer, murder etc*] 连续的

serial killer *n* [c] 连环杀手

serial number *n* [c] 编号

series ['sɪərɪz] (*pl* **series**) *n* [c] **1** [*of events, things*] 一系列 **2** (*on TV, radio*) 系列节目

✪**serious** ['sɪərɪəs] *adj* **1** [+ *problem, accident, illness*] 严重的 **2** (*not frivolous*) [+ *matter*] 严肃的 ◊ *I think this is a serious point.* 我认为这是个严肃的问题。; [+ *thought, consideration*] 认真的 **3** [+ *person*] (*sincere*) 当真的 ◊ *You really are serious about this, aren't you?* 你是当真的，是不是？◊ *I hope you're not serious.* 我希望你不是当真的。; (*solemn*) 严肃的 ♦**are you serious?** 你是认真的吗？

seriously ['sɪərɪəslɪ] *adv* **1** [*injure, ill, damage* +] 严重地 **2** [*talk, think* +] 认真地; [*deal with* +] 严肃地 **3** (*sincerely*) [*hope, believe* +] 真诚地 **4** (*truth to tell*) 说真的 ♦**to take sb/sth seriously** 认真对待某人/某事 ♦**seriously rich** [非正式] 极其富有的

seriousness ['sɪərɪəsnɪs] *n* [u] **1** [*of problem, situation*] 严重性 **2** [*of person*] 严肃 ♦**in all seriousness** 说实在的

sermon ['səːmən] *n* [c] **1** [宗] 布道 **2** (喻) 说教

servant ['səːvənt] *n* [c] **1** (*worker*) 佣人 **2** (喻) 工具

serve [səːv] **I** *vt* **1** [+ *country, community, organization*] 供职于 **2** [+ *people, area*] [*hospital, business, library etc* +] 为…服务 **3** (*in shop, bar etc*) 招待 **4** [+ *food, drink, meal*] 端上 **5** (*satisfy*) [+ *purpose*] 达到 **6** [+ *apprenticeship*] 当; [+ *prison term*] 服 **II** *vi* **1** (*at table*) 侍奉用餐 **2** [网球] 发球 **3** (*do duty*) [*official* +] 供职; [*soldier* +] 服役 **4** (*function*) ♦**to serve as sth** 当作某物用 **III** *n* [c] [网球] 发球 ♦**are you being served?** 有人接待您吗？ ♦**it serves you right** 你活该 ♦**to serve on a committee/jury** 是委员会/陪审团的成员 ♦**to serve to do sth** 有助于做某事
❑**serve out** *vt* [+ *contract*] 做到期满; [+ *term*] 供职到任期结束; [+ *prison sentence*] 服满
❑**serve up** *vt* [+ *food*] 端上

server ['səːvə(r)] *n* [c] **1** [计算机] 服务器 **2** [网球] 发球员

✪**service** ['səːvɪs] **I** *n* **1** [c] (*facility*) 服务◊ *a one hour dry-cleaning service* 一小时干洗服务 **2** [u] (*in hotel, restaurant*) 服务◊ *The service isn't very good.* 服务不怎么好。 **3** [c] (*train/bus service*) 火车/公共汽车营运◊ *The service is better than it used to be.* 营运服务比以前好。 **4** [u] (*employment*) 任职◊ *Pat is leaving the company after 12 years service.* 在任职12年后，帕特将离开公司。 **5** [c] (*organization, system*) 公共服务业务◊ *the postal service* 邮政服务 **6** [c] [宗] (*ceremony*) 仪式◊ *A religious service is currently underway.* 一场宗教仪式正在进行中。◊ *the Sunday evening service* 星期日的晚祷仪式 **7** [c] [汽车] 维修◊ *The car is due for a service.* 这车该维修了。 **8** [c] [网球] (*serve*) 轮到的发球权 **9** ♦**a dinner/tea service** 整套餐/茶具 **II** *vt* [+ *vehicle, machine*] 检修 **III services** *n* [*pl*] (*help*) 帮助◊ *Their services are no longer required.* 不再需要他们的帮助了。 **IV the Services** *n* [*pl*] [军] 三军 ♦**military** *or* [尤英] **national service** 义务兵役 ♦**service included/not included** (*on menu*) 含/不含小费 ♦**to be of service to sb** 为某人效劳 ♦**to do sb a service** 帮某人的忙 ♦**to be in/out of service** [*machine, vehicle* +] 在使用中/停止使用 ♦**to have one's car serviced** 把某人的车送去维修 *see also* **services**

service area [英] *n* [c] (*on motorway*) 路边服务区

service charge *n* [c] 服务费

serviceman ['səːvɪsmən] (*pl* **servicemen**) *n* [c] 军人

services ['səːvɪsɪz] (*pl* **services**) [英] *n* [c] (*on motorway*) 路边服务站

service station *n* [c] **1** (*petrol station*) 加油站 **2** [英] (*on motorway*) 路边服务站 [美 = **rest area**]

serviette [səːvɪ'ɛt] [英] *n* [c] 餐巾 [美 = **napkin**]

serving ['səːvɪŋ] *n* [c] 一份

sesame ['sɛsəmɪ] **I** *n* [c] 芝麻 **II** *cpd* [复合词] [+ *seeds, oil*] 芝麻

session ['sɛʃən] *n* [c] **1** (*period of activity*) 一段时间◊ *a recording session* 录制时间 **2** (*sitting*) [*of court*] 开庭; [*of parliament*] 会议 **3** [美] (*academic year*) 学年; (*term*) 学期 ♦**to be in session** (*at court*) 开庭; (*in council, parliament*) 开会; (*over period of months, weeks etc*) 开会期

✪**set** [sɛt] (*pt, pp* **set**) **I** *n* **1** [c] [*of problems, questions*] 系列◊ *a new set of problems* 一系列新问题; [*of cutlery, saucepans, books, keys*] 套; [*of golf clubs, spanners*] 成套 **2** [c] [电视, 广播] (*also:* ***television set***) 电视机 **3** [c] [网球] 局 **4** [s] (*group of people*) 群◊ *the yachting set* 一群快艇爱好者 **5** [c] (*also:* ***film set***) 摄影场 **6** [c] [戏剧, 电影] (*stage*) 舞台; (*scenery*) 布景 **7** [c] (*at hairdresser's*) 做头发◊ *a shampoo and set* 洗头和做头发 **8** [c] [数] 集 **II** *adj* (*fixed*) [+ *routine, time, price*] 规定的◊ *Meals are at set times.* 在规定时间进餐。 **III** *vt* **1** (*put*) 放◊ *He set the glass on the counter.* 他把玻璃杯放在柜台上。 **2** (*lay*) [+ *table*] 摆放◊ *Shall I set the table for supper?* 要我为晚餐摆放餐具吗？ **3** (*fix*) [+ *time, price, rules etc*] 确定◊ *They haven't yet set a date* *for the wedding.* 他们还没确定婚礼的日期。**4** (*establish*) [*+ record*] 创造 ◊ *She set a new world record in the 400 metres.* 她创造了新的400米世界记录。; [*+ precedent*] 开创; [*+ example*] 树立 **5** (*adjust*) [*+ alarm*] 设定 ◊ *He set his alarm clock for four a.m.* 他把闹钟设定在早晨4点。; [*+ heating, volume etc*] 调整 **6** [英] (*make up*) [*+ exam*] 出试题 **7** (*impose*) [*+ task, challenge, target, deadline*] 规定 ◊ *We have set ourselves an ambitious target.* 我们为自己制定了一个雄心勃勃的目标。**8** (*typeset*) 排版 ◊ *the deadline for setting the text* 文字排版的最后期限 **IV** *vi* **1** [*sun +*] 落山 **2** [*jam, jelly, concrete, glue +*] 凝固 ◊ *He held the board in place while the glue set.* 他举着板子等着胶水干。**3** [*bone +*] 接合长好 ◊ *It'll take six weeks for the bone to set.* 骨头接合长好要用6个星期。♦ **a set of false teeth** 一副假牙 ♦ **a set of dining-room furniture** 一套饭厅家具 ♦ **these chairs are only available as a set** 这些椅子只成套出售 ♦ **a chess set** 一副国际象棋 ♦ **to be set in one's ways** 积习难改 ♦ **a set phrase** 一个固定词组 ♦ **to be set on doing sth** 决心做某事 ♦ **to be set to do sth** (*likely to*) 很有可能做某事; (*about to*) 将做某事 ♦ **all set for sth/to do sth** (*ready*) 为某事做好准备 ♦ **a house set in parkland** 座落在开阔草坪上的房屋 ♦ **a novel set in Rome** 以罗马为背景的小说 ♦ **a gate set into the wall** 嵌在墙里的大门 ♦ **to set sth to music** 为…谱曲 ♦ **to set the scene** *or* **stage for sth** 为某事创造条件 ♦ **to set sb free** 给某人自由

❑ **set about** *vt* [不可拆分] (*embark on*) ♦ **to set about sth/doing sth** 着手某事/做某事

❑ **set against** *vt* **1** ♦ **to set sth against sth** [*+ argument, fact*] 把某事和某事作比较 **2** ♦ **to set sb against sb** 使某人反对某人

❑ **set apart** *vt* 使显得与众不同

❑ **set aside** *vt* **1** [*+ money, time*] 留出 **2** [*+ belief, emotion*] 不理会

❑ **set back** *vt* **1** (*cost*) ♦ **to set sb back 5 pounds** [非正式] 花了某人5英镑 **2** (*delay*) ♦ **to set sb/sth back** 耽搁某人/某事 ◊ *Bad weather set us back by about three weeks.* 恶劣的天气耽搁了我们3个星期。**3** (*situate*) ♦ **a house set back from the road** 远离公路的一幢房子

❑ **set down** *vt* [*+ rules, guidelines*] 制定

❑ **set forth** [正式] *vt* [*+ argument, case*] 陈述

❑ **set in** *vi* [*winter, bad weather +*] 到来; [*panic, infection +*] 开始并持续 ♦ **the rain has set in for the day** 今天雨会下一整天

❑ **set off I** *vi* (*depart*) ♦ **to set off (for)** 启程 (前往) **II** *vt* **1** (*start*) [*+ bomb*] 使爆炸; [*+ alarm*] 触发; [*+ chain of events*] 导致 **2** (*show up well*) [*colour, flavour +*] 衬托得更有吸引力 ◊ *a red dress that set off her marvellous complexion* 一件衬托出她绝好气色的红色连衣裙

❑ **set out I** *vi* (*depart*) 出发 **II** *vt* **1** (*arrange*) [*+ chairs, plates, goods etc*] 摆放 **2** (*state*) [*+ argument, theory etc*] 阐述 ♦ **to set out to do sth** 开始做某事 ♦ **to set out from home** 从家里出发

❑ **set up I** *vt* **1** (*start*) [*+ organization, service*] 设立 **2** (*erect*) [*+ tent*] 搭; [*+ roadblock*] 设置 **II** *vi* (*in business*) 成立 ♦ **to set o.s. up** (*in business*) 开业 ♦ **to set up shop/home** 开店/定居

setback ['sɛtbæk] *n* [c] (*hitch*) 挫折; (*in health*) 复发

set menu *n* [c] 套餐

settee [sɛ'tiː] *n* [c] 长沙发椅

setting ['sɛtɪŋ] *n* [c] **1** [*of controls*] 挡 **2** (*location*) 环境 **3** [*of jewel*] 底座

settle ['sɛtl] **I** *vt* **1** [*+ argument, question*] 解决; [*+ affairs*] 料理 **2** (*pay*) [*+ bill, account, debt*] 支付 **II** *vi* **1** [*sand, dust +*] 沉积 **2** [*sediment +*] 沉淀 **3** ♦ **to settle on sth** [*insect, bird +*] 停落在某物上 **4** (*go to live*) 定居 **5 = settle down** ♦ **they have settled their differences** 他们已经解决了他们之间的分歧 ♦ **to settle a score** *or* **an old score (with**

sb) (与某人)算旧账 ♦**that's settled then!** 那么事情就这样定了! ♦**to settle o.s. (into ...)** (在…)坐下来 ♦**it'll settle your stomach** 这会使你的胃舒服一点 ♦**to wait for the dust to settle** (喻)等到尘埃落定
❑**settle down** I *vi* 1 (*live stable life*) 开始过安稳的日子 2 (*make o.s. comfortable*) 舒舒服服地歇下来 3 (*become calm*) [*person* +] 适应; [*situation* +] 平静下来 ♦**to settle down to do sth** 定下心来做某事
❑**settle for** *vt* [不可拆分] 勉强认可
❑**settle in** *vi* 适应
❑**settle into** *vt* [不可拆分] 1 [+ *school, job etc*] 习惯于 2 [+ *chair*] 舒舒服服地坐下
❑**settle on** *vt* [不可拆分] (*decide on*) [+ *object*] 决定; [+ *action, name*] 选定
❑**settle up** *vi* ♦**to settle up (with sb)** 付清欠(某人的)账

settlement ['sɛtlmənt] *n* 1 [c] (*agreement*) 协议 2 [u] (*payment*) 清偿 3 [c] (*village, town*) 定居点 4 [u] (*colonization*) 殖民地的开拓 ♦**in settlement of our account** 结清我们的账目

setup ['sɛtʌp] [非正式] *n* [c] (*organization*) 机构; (*system, situation*) 组织情况

✪**seven** ['sɛvn] *num* 七 *see also* **five**

✪**seventeen** [sɛvn'tiːn] *num* 十七 *see also* **fifteen**

seventeenth [sɛvn'tiːnθ] *num* 第十七 *see also* **fifth**

seventh ['sɛvnθ] *num* 第七 *see also* **fifth**

seventieth ['sɛvntɪɪθ] *num* 第七十

✪**seventy** ['sɛvntɪ] *num* 七十 *see also* **fifty**

sever ['sɛvə(r)] *vt* 1 [+ *limb, pipe*] 切断 2 [+ *links, relations*] 断绝

✪**several** ['sɛvərl] *adj, pron* 几个 ◊ *several hours later* 几个小时后 ♦**several times** 几次 ♦**several of us** 我们中的几个

severe [sɪ'vɪə(r)] *adj* 1 [+ *pain, damage, shortage*] 严重的 2 [+ *punishment, criticism*] 严厉的; [+ *winter, climate*] 严酷的 4 (*stern*) [+ *person, expression*] 严肃的 5 (*austere*) [+ *architecture, dress*] 简朴的

severity [sɪ'vɛrɪtɪ] *n* [u] 1 [*of pain, damage, shortage, injury, illness*] 严重 2 [*of punishment*] 严厉; [*of winter, weather*] 严酷 3 (*sternness*) [*of manner, voice*] 严肃 4 (*austerity*) [*of architecture, dress*] 简朴

sew [səu] (*pt* **sewed**, *pp* **sewn**) *vi, vt* 缝 ♦**to sew sth together** 缝合某物
❑**sew up** *vt* 1 [+ *garment*] 把…缝起来 2 [非正式] [+ *deal, contest*] 顺利完成

sewage ['suːɪdʒ] *n* [u] 污物

sewer ['suːə(r)] *n* [c] 排污管

sewing ['səuɪŋ] *n* [u] 1 (*activity*) 缝纫 2 (*items being sewn*) 缝制品

sewing machine *n* [c] 缝纫机

sewn [səun] *pp of* **sew**

sex [sɛks] *n* 1 [c] (*gender*) 性别 2 [u] (*lovemaking*) 性交 ♦**to have sex (with sb)** (和某人)性交

sex education *n* [u] 性教育

sexism ['sɛksɪzəm] *n* [u] 性别歧视

sexist ['sɛksɪst] I *adj* [+ *person, attitude, behaviour*] 性别歧视的 II *n* [c] (*person*) 性别歧视者

sexual ['sɛksjuəl] *adj* [+ *attraction, relationship, health*] 性的; [+ *differences, discrimination*] 性别的; [+ *reproduction, maturity*] 生殖的

sexuality [sɛksju'ælɪtɪ] *n* [u] 1 (*sexual feelings*) 性欲 2 (*sexual orientation*) 性倾向

sexy ['sɛksɪ] *adj* 性感的

Seychelles [seɪ'ʃɛl(z)] *n* [*pl*] ♦**the Seychelles** 塞舌尔群岛

Sgt (尤美 **Sgt.**) *abbr* (= ***sergeant***) (*in army*) 中士; [英] (*in police*) 巡佐

shabby ['ʃæbɪ] *adj* 1 [+ *clothes, place*] 破旧的; [+ *person*] 衣衫褴褛的 2 [+ *treatment, behaviour*] 不公正的

shack [ʃæk] *n* [c] 棚屋
❑**shack up** [非正式] *vi* ♦**to shack up (with sb)** (与某人)同居

shade [ʃeɪd] I *n* 1 [u] (*shelter*) 阴凉处 2 [u] (*in painting, photo*) 阴影 3 [c] (*hue*) [*of colour*] 色度 4 [c] (*also:* ***lampshade***) 灯罩 5 [c] [美] (*on window*) 遮阳窗帘 [英 = **blind**] II *vt* [+ *place*] 遮蔽; [+ *eyes*] 为…挡光 III **shades** *n* [*pl*] [非正式] 太阳镜 ♦**in the shade** 在阴凉处 ♦**a**

shade ... 有点… ♦**shades of meaning/opinion** 有细微差别的意思/意见 ♦**to shade sth from the light/sun** 遮住某物以使不受光线/阳光照射
❑**shade into** *vt* [不可拆分] 逐渐变成

shadow ['ʃædəu] **I** *n* **1** [c] 影子 **2** [u] (*shade*) 阴影 **II** *vt* 跟踪 **III** [英] *cpd* [复合词] [政治] [+ *minister, chancellor*] 影子 ♦**in shadow** 在阴影中 ♦**in the shadow of sth** 在某物的影子下 ♦**in sb's shadow** 在某人的阴影下 ♦**without** *or* **beyond a shadow of (a) doubt** 毫无疑问

shadow cabinet [英] *n* ♦**the Shadow Cabinet** 影子内阁

shady ['ʃeɪdɪ] *adj* **1** [+ *place*] 背阴的; [+ *tree*] 成荫的 **2** (*dishonest*) [+ *person*] 不正当的; [+ *activity, deal*] 见不得人的

shaft [ʃɑːft] *n* [c] **1** [*of mine, lift*] 井状通道 **2** [*of axe, club, spear etc*] 柄 **3** (*in machine*) 轴 **4** [*of light*] 束

shaggy ['ʃægɪ] *adj* [+ *hair, sweater, dog etc*] 蓬乱的

shake [ʃeɪk] (*pt* **shook**, *pp* **shaken**) **I** *vt* **1** [+ *dice, rug, person*] 猛摇; [+ *bottle, cocktail, medicine*] 摇晃; [+ *buildings, ground*] 使震动 **2** (*affect*) [+ *person*] 使震惊 **3** (*undermine*) [+ *belief, confidence*] 使动摇 **II** *vi* [*person, part of the body* +] 发抖; [*voice* +] 颤抖; [*building, table* +] 震动; [*ground* +] 震颤 **III** *n* **1** ♦**to give sth/sb a shake** 猛摇一下某物/某人 **2** [c] (*also:* ***milkshake***) 奶昔 ♦**to shake one's head** (*in refusal*) 摇头拒绝; (*in dismay*) 摇摇头 ♦**to shake one's fist (at sb)** (朝某人)挥拳头 ♦**to shake hands (with sb)** (和某人)握手 ♦**to shake with fear/rage/laughter** [*person* +] 怕/气/笑得发抖; [*voice* +] 怕/气/笑得颤抖 ♦**he declined with a shake of his head** 他摇摇头拒绝了
❑**shake down** [美] *vt* [+ *person*] 勒索
❑**shake off** *vt* **1** [+ *person, sb's hand*] 摆脱 **2** [+ *pursuer*] 甩掉 **3** [+ *illness, habit*] 克服
❑**shake up** *vt* **1** (*reorganize*) 重组 **2** (*upset*) 使受惊吓

shaky ['ʃeɪkɪ] *adj* **1** [+ *hand*] 发抖的; [+ *voice*] 颤抖的 **2** (*weak*) [+ *situation, start, economy*] 不稳定的 **3** (*unreliable*) [+ *memory*] 不可靠的; [+ *knowledge, understanding*] 成问题的

shall [ʃæl] *aux vb* **1** (*indicating future in 1st person*) ♦**I shall go** 我要走了 **2** (*in 1st person questions*) ♦**shall I/we open the door?** 我/我们把门打开好吗? **3** (*in 1st person tag questions*) ♦**I'll get some, shall I?** 我去拿一些，好吗? **4** (*indicating inevitability*) 一定 ♦**the president shall hold office for five years** [正式] 总统要任职5年

shallow ['ʃæləu] **I** *adj* **1** [+ *water, ditch, grave*] 浅的; [+ *container*] 浅口的; [+ *breathing*] 浅的 **2** (*superficial*) [+ *person, argument, idea*] 肤浅的 **II shallows** *n* [*pl*] ♦**the shallows** 浅水处

sham [ʃæm] **I** *n* [c] 假象 **II** *cpd* [复合词] [+ *marriage, fight*] 假

shambles ['ʃæmblz] *n* ♦**to be a shambles** [*place* +] 乱七八糟; [*event, situation* +] 一塌糊涂 ♦**what a shambles!** 真是一团糟!

shame [ʃeɪm] **I** *n* [u] **1** (*embarrassment*) 羞耻 **2** (*disgrace*) 耻辱 **II** *vt* 使感到羞耻 ♦**it is a shame that ...** …真遗憾 ♦**it would be a shame to waste this** 把这浪费掉太可惜了 ♦**what a shame!** 太遗憾了! ♦**to put sb/sth to shame** 使某人/某事相形见绌 ♦**it shamed him to admit ...** 他羞愧地承认… ♦**to shame sb into sth/into doing sth** 使某人羞愧地做某事

shameful ['ʃeɪmful] *adj* [+ *action, episode*] 可耻的 ♦**it is shameful that ...** …是可耻的

shameless ['ʃeɪmlɪs] *adj* [+ *person, behaviour*] 无耻的

shampoo [ʃæm'puː] **I** *n* [c/u] (*substance*) 洗发液 **II** *vt* 用洗发液洗

shandy ['ʃændɪ] [英] *n* **1** [u] (*type of drink*) 搀柠檬汁的啤酒 **2** [c] (*glass*) 一杯搀柠檬汁的啤酒

shan't [ʃɑːnt] = **shall not**

shape [ʃeɪp] **I** *n* **1** [c] (*form, circle, triangle etc*) 形状 **2** [s] (喻) [*of plan, organization*] 模式 **II** *vt* **1** (字) (*fashion, form*) 塑造 **2** (*determine*) [+ *ideas, life*] 决定 ♦ **to take shape** [*idea, plan etc* +] 成形 ♦ **in the shape of a heart** 呈心形 ♦ **I can't bear gardening in any shape or form** 我受不了任何形式的园艺 ♦ **to be in (good) shape** [*person* +] 体形好 ♦ **to be out of shape** [*person* +] 体质差 ♦ **to get (o.s.) into shape** 锻炼身体
❑ **shape up** *vi* (*progress*) [*events* +] 进展; [*person* +] 表现

shapeless [ˈʃeɪplɪs] *adj* 不成形的

✪ **share** [ʃɛə(r)] **I** *n* [c] **1** (*part*) 一份 **2** [商, 经济] (*in company*) 股票 ◊ *The firm's shares jumped to 114p.* 公司的股票涨到114便士。 **II** *vt* **1** (*have in common*) [+ *room, bed, taxi*] 合用; [+ *feature, quality*] 共有 ◊ *two tribes who share a common language* 说同一种语言的两个部落 **2** (*be jointly responsible for*) [+ *job, cooking, task*] 分担 **3** (*divide*) ♦ **to share sth among/between** 把某物分给… ◊ *Share the sweets between the children.* 把糖分给孩子们吃。 ♦ **to do one's share** 尽自己的责任 ◊ *It helps when a father does his share at home.* 父亲在家中尽自己的责任会有很大帮助。 ♦ **to get one's share** 得到自己应得的一份 ♦ **to share sth with sb** [+ *room, bed, taxi*] 和某人合用某物 ◊ *the huge house that he shared with his sisters* 他和姊妹们合住的大房子; [+ *feature, quality*] 和某人共有某特性; [+ *cost*] 和某人分摊某开销; [+ *job, cooking, task*] 和某人分担某事; (*allow to use*) 和某人分享某物 ♦ **to share in** [+ *success, profits, benefits*] 分享; [+ *responsibility, work*] 分担
❑ **share out** *vt* 平均分配

shareholder [ˈʃɛəhəuldə(r)] *n* [c] 股东 [美 = **stockholder**]

shark [ʃɑːk] *n* **1** [c/U] (*fish*) 鲨鱼 **2** [c] [非正式] (*person*) 骗子

sharp [ʃɑːp] **I** *adj* **1** [+ *knife, teeth*] 锋利的; [+ *point, edge*] 尖锐的 **2** (*pointed*) [+ *nose, chin*] 尖的 **3** (*abrupt*) [+ *increase, change*] 急剧的; [+ *curve, bend*] 急转的 **4** (*clear*) [+ *image, distinction*] 清晰的 **5** (*acute*) [+ *pain, cold*] 剧烈的 **6** (*severe*) [+ *reply, criticism*] 严厉的 **7** (*strong*) [+ *taste, smell*] 浓烈的 **8** (*quick-witted*) [+ *person*] 机敏的 **9** [音] 升半音的 **II** *n* [c] [音] 半升音 **III** *adv* (*precisely*) ♦ **at 2 o'clock sharp** 两点整 ♦ **turn sharp left** 向左急转弯 ♦ **to be sharp with sb** 对某人刻薄 ♦ **C sharp/F sharp** 升C调/升F调 ♦ **sharp practice** 不正当的手段

sharpen [ˈʃɑːpn] *vt* **1** (字) [+ *stick, pencil*] 削尖; [+ *knife*] 磨快 **2** (喻) [+ *skill, understanding*] 磨练

sharpener [ˈʃɑːpnə(r)] *n* [c] (*also:* ***pencil sharpener***) 卷笔刀; (*also:* ***knife sharpener***) 磨具

sharply [ˈʃɑːplɪ] *adv* **1** (*abruptly*) [*turn* +] 突然地 **2** (*steeply*) [*rise, fall* +] 急剧地 **3** (*greatly*) [*contrast* +] 鲜明地 **4** (*severely*) [*speak* +] 严厉地

shatter [ˈʃætə(r)] *vt, vi* **1** (*break*) 粉碎 **2** (喻) (*ruin*) [+ *hopes, confidence*] 粉碎

shattered [ˈʃætəd] *adj* **1** (*overwhelmed, grief-stricken*) 感到震骇的 **2** [非正式] (*exhausted*) 筋疲力尽的

shave [ʃeɪv] **I** *vt* [+ *head, legs*] 剃毛发; [+ *person*] 剃须 **II** *vi* 刮脸 **III** *n* ♦ **to have a shave** 刮脸
❑ **shave off** *vt* [+ *beard*] 剃去

shaver [ˈʃeɪvə(r)] *n* [c] (*also:* ***electric shaver***) 电动剃刀

shaving [ˈʃeɪvɪŋ] **I** *n* [U] (*action*) 剃须 **II** *cpd* [复合词] [+ *gel, things*] 剃须 **III shavings** *n* [*pl*] 刨花

shaving cream *n* [U] 剃须膏

shaving foam *n* [U] 泡沫剃须膏

shawl [ʃɔːl] *n* [c] 披肩

✪ **she** [ʃiː] *pron* **1** (*woman, girl*) 她 ◊ *She didn't do it. I did.* 她没做。是我做的。 **2** (*animal*) 它 ◊ *She's a good dog.* 它是只好狗。

sheath [ʃiːθ] *n* [c] **1** (*for knife*) 鞘 **2** [英] (*condom*) 避孕套

shed [ʃɛd] (*pt, pp* **shed**) **I** *n* [c] **1** (*in garden*) 棚 **2** (*by railway, factory*) 棚式外廊 **II** *vt* **1** (*naturally*) [+ *skin, leaves, hair*] 脱落 **2** (*get rid of*) 摆脱 ♦ **to shed tears** 流泪 ♦ **to shed blood**

杀人 ♦**to shed jobs** 裁员 ♦**a lorry has shed its load** [英] 一辆大卡车掉落了货物

she'd [ʃiːd] = **she had, she would**

sheep [ʃiːp] (*pl* **sheep**) *n* [C] 绵羊

sheepdog ['ʃiːpdɔg] *n* [C] **1** (*for controlling sheep*) 牧羊犬 **2** (*type of dog*) 牧羊犬

sheepskin ['ʃiːpskɪn] **I** *n* [C/U] 绵羊皮 **II** *cpd* [复合词] [+ *coat, gloves*] 绵羊皮

sheer [ʃɪə(r)] *adj* **1** [+ *joy, delight, beauty*] 纯粹的; [+ *determination, brilliance*] 绝对的; [+ *terror, desperation*] 彻底的; [+ *size, scale, volume*] 巨大的 **2** (*steep*) [+ *cliff, drop*] 陡峭的 **3** (*thin*) 纤薄的 ♦**by sheer chance** 纯属偶然 ♦**it was sheer luck** 这纯粹是运气

sheet [ʃiːt] *n* [C] **1** (*on bed*) 床单 **2** [*of paper*] 一张; [*of glass, metal, wood, ice*] 一片

sheik(h) [ʃeɪk, (美) ʃiːk] *n* [C] 酋长

shelf [ʃɛlf] (*pl* **shelves**) *n* [C] (*bookshelf*) 架子; (*in cupboard*) 搁板; (*in oven*) 层 ♦**a set of shelves** 一整套架子 ♦**to be left on the shelf** [非正式] [*person* +] 嫁不出去的

shell [ʃɛl] **I** *n* [C] **1** (*on beach*) 贝壳 **2** [*of tortoise, snail, crab, egg, nut*] 壳 **3** (*explosive*) 炮弹 **4** (*frame*) [*of building, boat, car*] 框架 **II** *vt* **1** (*prepare*) [+ *nuts, peas, prawns*] 去壳 **2** (*fire shells at*) 炮击

❑**shell out** [非正式] **I** *vt* [不可拆分] ♦**to shell out money (for sth/on sth/to do sth)** (为某物/就某物/为做某事)破费 **II** *vi* ♦**to shell out (for sth/on sth/to do sth)** (为某物/就某物/为做某事)花钱

she'll [ʃiːl] = **she will**

shellfish ['ʃɛlfɪʃ] (*pl* **shellfish**) **I** *n* [C/U] 贝类海产 **II** *n* [*pl*] (*as food*) 贝类海鲜

shelter ['ʃɛltə(r)] **I** *n* **1** [C] (*building*) (*against bad weather*) 遮蔽处; (*against bombs*) 防空洞; (*for homeless*) 收容所 **2** [U] (*protection*) [*from rain*] 躲避; (*from danger*) 避难 **II** *vt* **1** (*protect*) (*from wind and rain*) 遮蔽 **2** (*give lodging to*) [+ *fugitive*] 收容 **III** *vi* 躲避 ♦**to take shelter (from sth)** 躲避(某事)

sheltered ['ʃɛltəd] *adj* **1** [+ *bay, harbour*] 遮风避雨的 **2** [+ *life, upbringing*] 受庇护的 ♦**sheltered housing** *or* **accommodation** 福利院

shelves [ʃɛlvz] *n* [*pl*] *of* **shelf**

shepherd ['ʃɛpəd] **I** *n* [C] 牧羊人 **II** *vt* ♦**to shepherd sb towards/onto** *etc* **sth** 护送某人去/上{等}某处

shepherd's pie [英] *n* [C/U] 肉馅土豆泥饼

sheriff ['ʃɛrɪf] [美] *n* [C] **1** (*modern*) 县治安官 **2** (*in Wild West*) 镇上警长

sherry ['ʃɛrɪ] *n* **1** [C/U] (*substance*) 雪利酒 **2** [C] (*also:* ***glass of sherry***) 一杯雪利酒

she's [ʃiːz] = **she is, she has**

shield [ʃiːld] **I** *n* [C] **1** (*soldier's*) 盾牌 **2** (*trophy*) 盾形锦标 **3** [术语] (*protective device*) 防护板 **4** ♦**a shield against sth** 免受某物侵害的屏障 **II** *vt* ♦**to shield sb/sth (from sth)** (*physically*) 把某人/某物(与某物)遮挡开; (喻)保护某人/某物(免于某事)

shift [ʃɪft] **I** *n* [C] **1** (*change*) 转变 **2** (*period of work*) 轮班 **3** (*group of workers*) 轮班职工 **II** *vt* **1** (*move*) 移动 **2** (*change*) [+ *opinion, policy, emphasis*] 改变 **3** (*remove*) [+ *stain*] 去除 **III** *vi* **1** (*move*) [*cargo, load* +] 移动; [*wind* +] 转向; [*person, eyes* +] 转移 **2** (*change*) [*opinion, policy* +] 改变 ♦**to shift gears** [美:汽车] 换挡 [英 = **change gears**] ♦**to shift up/down** [美:汽车] 升一挡/降一挡 [英 = **change**]

shift work *n* [U] 轮班工作 ♦**to do shift work** 做轮班工作

shin [ʃɪn] **I** *n* [C] 胫部 **II** *vi* ♦**to shin up a tree** 爬上树

shine [ʃaɪn] (*pt, pp* **shone**) **I** *vi* **1** [*sun, light* +] 照耀 **2** [*eyes, hair* +] 发光 **3** (*excel*) ♦**to shine (at sth)** (在某方面)很出色 **II** *vt* **1** [+ *torch, light*] 用…照 **2** (*pt, pp* **shined**) (*polish*) [+ *shoes, furniture etc*] 擦亮 **III** *n* [S/U] (*of surface*) 光泽

shingles ['ʃɪŋglz] *n* [U] 带状疱疹

shiny ['ʃaɪnɪ] *adj* 闪闪发光的

ship [ʃɪp] **I** *n* [C] 船 **II** *vt* ♦**to ship sb/sth to** 运送某人/某物到 ♦**to**

be on board ship 在船上

shipment ['ʃɪpmənt] *n* [c] [*of goods*] (*by ship*) 船运货物; (*by train, plane etc*) 运输的货物

shipping ['ʃɪpɪŋ] *n* [u] **1** (*business*) 航运业 **2** (*cost of transport*) 船运费 **3** (*ships*) 船舶

shipwreck ['ʃɪprɛk] **I** *n* **1** [c/u] (*event*) 海难 **2** [c] (*ship*) 失事的船只 **II** *vt* ♦**to be shipwrecked** 遭海难

shipyard ['ʃɪpjɑːd] *n* [c] 船坞

shirt [ʃəːt] *n* [c] 衬衫

shit [ʃɪt] [非正式, 疑讳] **I** *int* 该死 **II** *n* [u] **1** (*faeces*) 粪便 **2** (*rubbish, nonsense*) 狗屎

shiver ['ʃɪvə(r)] **I** *n* [c] 颤抖 **II** *vi* 发抖 ♦**to shiver with fear/cold** 怕得/冷得发抖

shoal [ʃəul] *n* [c] [*of fish*] 群

shock [ʃɔk] **I** *n* **1** [c] (*unpleasant surprise*) 震骇 **2** [c] (*surprise*) 震惊 **3** [u] (*condition*) (*emotional*) 令人震惊的状况; [医] 休克 **4** [c/u] (*impact*) 震动 **5** [c] (*also: **electric shock***) 触电 **II** *vt* **1** (*upset*) 使震惊 **2** (*offend, scandalize*) 使厌恶 ♦**it came as a shock (to hear that ...)** (听到…) 令人震惊 ♦**to be in shock** [医] 处于休克状态

shocked [ʃɔkt] *adj* **1** (*upset*) 受到打击的 **2** (*offended, scandalized*) 感到不快的 ♦**I was shocked to learn that ...** 听说…我很震惊

shocking ['ʃɔkɪŋ] *adj* **1** (*outrageous*) 骇人听闻的 **2** [非正式] (*very bad*) 糟透的 ♦**it is shocking that ...** 令人吃惊的是…

shoe [ʃuː] (*pt, pp* **shod**) **I** *n* [c] **1** (*for person*) 鞋 **2** (*for horse*) 马蹄铁 **II** *vt* 钉马蹄铁 ♦**a pair of shoes** 一双鞋 ♦**I wouldn't want to be in his shoes** 我不想处于他的境地

shoelace ['ʃuːleɪs] *n* [c] 鞋带 ♦**to do up** *or* **tie** *or* **fasten one's shoelaces** 系鞋带

shoe polish *n* [u] 鞋油

shoe shop *n* [c] 鞋店

shone [ʃɔn] *pt, pp of* **shine**

shook [ʃuk] *pt of* **shake**

shoot [ʃuːt] (*pt, pp* **shot**) **I** *n* [c] **1** (*on branch, seedling*) 嫩芽 **2** [电影, 摄影] 拍摄 **II** *vt* **1** (*kill*) [+ *person, animal*] 向…开枪 **2** [英] (*hunt*) 射猎 [美= **hunt**] **3** (*execute*) 枪决 **4** [+ *film*] 拍摄 **III** *vi* **1** (*with gun, bow*) ♦**to shoot (at sb/sth)** (朝某人/某物) 射击 **2** [足球等] 射门 ♦**to shoot sb in the back/leg** *etc* 射中某人的背部/腿 {等} ♦**to shoot o.s.** 射中自己 ♦**to shoot o.s. in the head/leg** *etc* 射中自己的头/腿 {等} ♦**to shoot past/into/through sth** *etc* (*move*) 飞快经过/进入/穿过某物 {等}

❑**shoot down** *vt* **1** [+ *plane*] 击落 **2** (喻) [+ *person*] 批驳; [+ *idea, rumour etc*] 驳倒

❑**shoot up** *vi* **1** (*increase*) 暴涨 **2** (*inject drugs*) 注射毒品

shooting ['ʃuːtɪŋ] *n* [c] **1** (*attack, murder, shots*) 枪击 **2** [*of film*] 拍摄 **3** [英] (*hunting*) 射猎 [美= **hunting**]

shop [ʃɔp] **I** *n* [c] **1** [尤英] 商店 [美= **store**] **2** (*workshop*) 车间 **II** *vi* 购物 **III** *vt* [英: 非正式] [+ *person*] 告发 ♦**to talk shop** 三句话不离本行 ♦**to go shopping** 去买东西

❑**shop around** *vi* 仔细选购 ♦**to shop around for sth** 到处物色某物

shop assistant [英] *n* [c] 店员 [美= **sales clerk**]

shopkeeper ['ʃɔpkiːpə(r)] [英] *n* [c] 店主 [美= **storekeeper**]

shoplifting ['ʃɔplɪftɪŋ] *n* [u] 商店货物扒窃

shopper ['ʃɔpə(r)] *n* [c] 购物者

shopping ['ʃɔpɪŋ] *n* [u] **1** (*activity*) 购物 **2** (*goods*) 所购之物 ♦**to do the shopping** 买东西 *see also* **shop**

shopping bag *n* [c] 购物袋

shopping cart [美] *n* [c] 购物手推车 [英= **shopping trolley**]

shopping centre (美 **shopping center**) *n* [c] 购物中心

shopping list *n* [c] **1** (*for purchases*) 购物单 **2** (*wish list*) 心愿表

shopping mall *n* [c] 购物大厦

shopping trolley [英] *n* [c] 购物手推车 [美= **shopping cart**]

shop window *n* [c] 商店橱窗

shore [ʃɔː(r)] *n* [c] 岸 ♦**the shore(s) of ...** …的岸边 ♦**on shore** 在陆上

❑**shore up** *vt* [+ *wall*] 支撑; [+ *system*] 加强

✪**short** [ʃɔːt] **I** *adj* **1** (*in time*) 短暂的 ◊ *We had a short meeting.* 我们的会

面很短暂。2 (*in length*) 短的◊ *His black hair was very short.* 他的黑头发很短。3 (*not tall*) 矮的◊ *I'm tall and thin and he's short and fat.* 我又高又瘦，他又矮又胖。4 (*scarce*) 短缺的◊ *Money is short.* 钱不够。5 (*curt*) ♦**to be short (with sb)**（对某人）粗暴无礼◊ *I'm sorry I was so short with you.* 对不起，我对你太粗暴无礼了。**II** *n* [c] 1［英］(*drink*) 少量烈酒 2 (*film*) 短片 **III shorts** *n* [*pl*] 1 (*short trousers*) 短裤 2［尤美］(*underpants*) 男用短衬裤 ♦**a short time ago** 不久以前 ♦**at short notice** 临时通知 ♦**in short** 简而言之 ♦**to have a short temper** 脾气暴躁 ♦**to be short of sth** 缺乏某物 ♦**I'm 3 short** 我还缺3个 ♦**Fred is short for Frederick** 弗雷德是弗雷德里克的简称 ♦**a pair of shorts** 一条短裤 ♦**to cut short** 缩短 ♦**to run short of** 所剩不多了 ♦**to fall short of** 未达到 ♦**short of doing ...** 除了做…外 ♦**nothing/little short of ...** 不亚于/简直就是… ♦**to stop short** 突然停住 ♦**to stop short of doing sth** 差点儿就要做某事

shortage [ˈʃɔːtɪdʒ] *n* [c/u] 短缺

shortbread [ˈʃɔːtbrɛd] *n* [c/u] 白脱甜酥饼

short-circuit [ʃɔːtˈsəːkɪt] **I** *vi* 发生短路 **II** *vt* 1［电子］使短路 2 (喻) [+ *process, system*] 避开 **III** *n* [c] 短路

shortcoming [ˈʃɔːtkʌmɪŋ] *n* [c] 缺点

shortcrust pastry [ˈʃɔːtkrʌst-]［英］*n* [u] 松脆馅饼底盘

short cut *n* [c] 1 (*route*) 近路 2 (*method*) 捷径

shorten [ˈʃɔːtn] **I** *vt* 1 [+ *holiday, life, book, letter*] 缩短 2 [+ *clothes, plank etc*] 截短 **II** *vi* 变短

shortfall [ˈʃɔːtfɔːl] *n* [c] 赤字

shorthand [ˈʃɔːthænd] *n* [u] 1 (*system*) 速记 2 (*quick name*) 简略表达 ♦**in shorthand** 用速记记录

shortlist **I** *n* [c] 最后一轮候选名单 **II** *vt*［尤英］进入最后一轮候选名单

short-lived [ˈʃɔːtˈlɪvd] *adj* 短暂的

shortly [ˈʃɔːtlɪ] *adv* 马上 ♦**shortly after/before sth** 某事后/前不久 ♦**shortly after/before doing sth** 做某事后/前不久

short-sighted [ʃɔːtˈsaɪtɪd] *adj* 1［英］近视的［美 = **near-sighted**］2 (*misguided*) 目光短浅的

short-sleeved [ˈʃɔːtsliːvd] *adj* 短袖的

short story *n* [c] 短篇小说

short-tempered [ʃɔːtˈtɛmpəd] *adj* 易怒的

short-term [ˈʃɔːttəːm] *adj* [+ *solution, gain*] 短期的; [+ *memory*] 短暂的

short wave *n* [u] 短波

shot [ʃɔt] **I** *pt, pp of* **shoot** **II** *n* 1 [c] (*from gun*) 射击 2 [u] (*shotgun pellets*) 铅沙弹 3 [c]［足球］射门 4 [c] (*injection*) 皮下注射 5 [c]［电影，摄影］镜头 ♦**to fire a shot (at sb/sth)**（朝某人/某物）开枪 ♦**a good/poor shot** (*person*) 一位神枪手/不高明的射手 ♦**a shot in the arm** (喻)起鼓舞作用的事物 ♦**to have a shot at sth/at doing sth**［非正式］尝试某事/做某事 ♦**to give sth one's best shot**［非正式］对某事尽自己最大的努力 ♦**to do sth like a shot**［非正式］立刻做某事 ♦**to call the shots** 发号施令 ♦**it's a long shot** 这是大胆的尝试 ♦**to get shot of sb/sth**［非正式］摆脱某人/某物

shotgun [ˈʃɔtgʌn] *n* [c] 霰弹枪

✪**should** [ʃud] *aux vb* 1 (*indicating advisability*) ♦**I should go now** 我现在应该走了 2 (*indicating obligation*) 应当 3 (*indicating likelihood*) ♦**he should be there by now/he should get there soon** 他现在该到那儿了/他该很快就到那儿了 4［正式］(*would*) ♦**I should go if he asked me** 如果他要求，我会走的 5 (*after 'that'*) ♦**it's not right that we should be fined** 我们竟会被罚款，这是不对的 ♦**you should have been more careful** 你本该更加小心 ♦**he should have arrived by now** 他现在应该到了 ♦**I should go if I were you** 我要是你就走了 ♦**I should like to** 我很乐意 ♦**I should like to invite them**

to dinner 我想要请他们吃晚餐 ♦**I should like a strawberry ice cream** 我想要一份草莓冰淇淋 ♦**should he phone** *or* **if he should phone ...** 如果他打电话来…

shoulder ['ʃəuldə(r)] **I** *n* [c] 肩膀 **II** *vt* [+ *responsibility, blame*] 承担 ♦**to look over one's shoulder** (*feel anxious*) 焦虑不安 ♦**to rub shoulders with sb** (*mix with*) 和某人有交往 ♦**to work shoulder to shoulder** (*co-operate*) 齐心协力地工作 ♦**we will stand shoulder to shoulder with our allies** 我们将与我们的同盟并肩协力

shoulder blade *n* [c] 肩胛骨

shouldn't ['ʃudnt] = **should not**

shout [ʃaut] **I** *n* [c] 喊叫声 **II** *vt* (*also:* ***shout out***) 呼喊 **III** *vi* (*also:* ***shout out***) 喊叫 ♦**to give sb a shout** [非正式] 让某人知道 ❑**shout down** *vt* [+ *speaker*] 用叫喊声压倒

shouting ['ʃautɪŋ] *n* [U] (*quarrelling*) 叫喊

shove [ʃʌv] **I** *vt* 撞 **II** *n* [c] ♦**to give sb/sth a shove** 猛推某人/某物 ♦**to shove sth into/under sth** [非正式] (*put*) 把某物塞进某物/塞到某物下 ♦**he shoved me out of the way** 他把我推到一边 ❑**shove off** [非正式] *vi* 走开

shovel ['ʃʌvl] **I** *n* [c] 铲 **II** *vt* **1** [+ *snow, coal, earth*] 铲 **2** (*push*) 把…胡乱塞入

✪**show** [ʃəu] (*pt* **showed**, *pp* **shown**) **I** *n* [c] **1** (*display*) [*of emotion, support, strength*] 表示◊ *Miners gathered in a show of support for the government.* 矿工们聚集在一起以表示对政府的支持。**2** (*exhibition*) 展览 **3** [戏剧] 演出 **4** [电视, 广播] 节目 **II** *vt* **1** (*indicate*) 表明 ♦**to show sb sth** *or* **to show sth to sb** 给某人看某物{或}把某物给某人看◊ *Cut out this article and show it to your bank manager.* 剪下这篇文章，把它给你的银行经理看一下。**2** (*demonstrate*) 展示 **3** (*display*) [+ *signs*] 显示; [+ *respect, interest etc*] 表示◊ *The peace talks showed signs of progress.* 和平谈判显示出进展的迹象。**4** (*put on*) [+ *programme, film*] 播映◊ *The ceremony was shown on BBC1.* 典礼在BBC1 台播映。**5** (*illustrate, depict*) [*picture, graph, film etc* +] 描述◊ *Figure 4.1 shows the respiratory system.* 图示4. 1 显示的是呼吸系统。**6** ♦**to show sb in/out** 带某人进来/出去 **7** (*exhibit*) [+ *painting etc*] 展出 **III** *vi* **1** (*be evident*) 显而易见◊ *Ferguson was unhappy and it showed.* 弗格森不太高兴，这是显而易见的。**2** (*be visible*) 看得见 **3** [尤美] (*arrive, appear*) 露面 ♦**a show of hands** 举手表决 ♦**who's running the show here?** 谁在这儿掌管一切？ ♦**for show** 为装门面 ♦**on show** [*exhibits etc* +] 在展览中 ♦**to show that ...** 表明…◊ *The post-mortem shows that death was due to natural causes.* 验尸情况证实死亡是由于自然原因造成的。♦**to show sb how to do sth** 示范某人如何做某事 ♦**to show a profit/loss** [商] 赢利/亏损 ♦**to show sb to his seat/to the door** 领某人到他的座位/门口 ♦**to have something/nothing to show for sth** 在某方面有所建树/毫无成果 ♦**it just goes to show that ...** 这证明… ❑**show around** *vt* [+ *person*] 带…参观 ❑**show off I** *vi* 卖弄 **II** *vt* 炫耀 ❑**show up I** *vi* **1** (*be visible, noticeable*) 显露 **2** (*arrive, appear*) 露面 **II** *vt* **1** (*make visible, noticeable*) [+ *imperfections etc*] 使显现 **2** (*embarrass*) 使难堪

show business *n* [U] 娱乐界

shower ['ʃauə(r)] **I** *n* [c] **1** (*rain*) 阵雨 **2** [*of stones, sparks etc*] 一阵 **3** (*for washing*) 淋浴器 **4** [美] (*party*) 送礼会 **II** *vi* 洗淋浴 **III** *vt* ♦**to shower sb with sth** [+ *confetti, rice*] 把某物撒向某人; [+ *gifts, kisses*] 送某人大量的某物 ♦**to have** *or* **take a shower** 洗淋浴

shower cap *n* [c] 浴帽

shower gel *n* [U] 沐浴露

showing ['ʃəuɪŋ] *n* [c] [*of film*] 放映

show jumping [-dʒʌmpɪŋ] *n* [U] 赛马中的障碍赛

shown [ʃəun] *pp of* **show**

show-off ['ʃəuɔf] *n* [c] 爱卖弄的人

showroom [ˈʃəuruːm] *n* [c] 陈列室

shrank [ʃræŋk] *pt of* **shrink**

shred [ʃrɛd] **I** *n* [c] **1** (*piece*) 细条 **2** ♦ **not a shred of evidence/truth** 无丝毫证据/事实 **II** *vt* [+ *food*] 切碎; [+ *paper, documents*] 撕碎

shrewd [ʃruːd] *adj* [+ *person*] 精明的; [+ *investment*] 高明的

shriek [ʃriːk] **I** *vi* 尖叫 **II** *n* [c] 尖叫声 ♦ **to shriek with laughter** 尖声大笑

shrimp [ʃrɪmp] *n* [c] (*small*) 小虾; [美] (*bigger*) 虾 [英 = **prawn**]

shrimp cocktail [美] *n* [c] 冷盘虾 [英 = **prawn cocktail**]

shrine [ʃraɪn] *n* [c] **1** (*religious*) 圣坛 **2** (*to sb's memory*) 圣地

shrink [ʃrɪŋk] (*pt* **shrank**, *pp* **shrunk**) **I** *vi* **1** [*cloth* +] 缩水 **2** [*forests, profits, audiences etc* +] 减少 **3** ♦ **to shrink away/back** 退缩/畏缩 **II** *vt* [+ *cloth*] 使皱缩 **III** *n* [c] [非正式, 贬] 精神病医生 ♦ **not to shrink from sth** 不回避某事

shrivel [ˈʃrɪvl] (*also:* ***shrivel up***) **I** *vi* 枯萎 **II** *vt* 使干枯

shroud [ʃraud] **I** *n* [c] 裹尸布 **II** *vt* **1** ♦ **to be shrouded in mist/smoke** *etc* 被雾/烟{等}笼罩 **2** ♦ **to be shrouded in mystery** 笼罩着神秘色彩

shrub [ʃrʌb] *n* [c] 灌木

shrug [ʃrʌg] **I** *vi* 耸肩 **II** *vt* ♦ **to shrug one's shoulders** 耸耸肩 **III** *n* [c] 耸肩

❏ **shrug off** *vt* [+ *criticism, problem, illness*] 对…不予理会

shrunk [ʃrʌŋk] *pp of* **shrink**

shudder [ˈʃʌdə(r)] **I** *vi* [*person* +] 颤抖; [*vehicle, machine* +] 剧烈摇晃 **II** *n* [c] 颤抖 ♦ **to shudder with fear/cold** *etc* 吓得/冷得{等}发抖 ♦ **to shudder to a halt** 随着一阵颤动停了下来 ♦ **I shudder to think what would have happened if ...** 我不敢设想如果…将会发生什么 ♦ **to give a shudder** 浑身颤抖

shuffle [ˈʃʌfl] **I** *vi* **1** ♦ **to shuffle along/in/out** *etc* 拖着脚走来走去/走进来/走出去{等} **2** (*fidget*) ♦ **to shuffle around** 坐立不安 **II** *vt* **1** [+ *cards*] 洗 **2** [+ *papers*] 乱翻 **3** ♦ **to shuffle one's feet** 来回地挪动双脚 **III** *n* [s] 曳足而行

shun [ʃʌn] *vt* [+ *publicity, neighbours etc*] 回避

shut [ʃʌt] (*pt, pp* **shut**) **I** *vt* [+ *door, drawer*] 关上; [+ *shop*] 关门; [+ *mouth, eyes*] 闭上 **II** *vi* [*door, drawer* +] 关上; [*shop* +] 打烊; [*mouth, eyes* +] 闭上 **III** *adj* [+ *door, drawer*] 关闭的; [+ *shop*] 打烊的; [+ *mouth, eyes*] 闭着的

❏ **shut away** *vt* ♦ **to shut o.s. away** 把自己关起来

❏ **shut down I** *vt* **1** [+ *factory etc*] 使停业 **2** [+ *machine*] 关闭 **II** *vi* [*factory etc* +] 停业

❏ **shut in** *vt* 把…关起来

❏ **shut off** *vt* [+ *supply, water, engine*] 切断

❏ **shut out** *vt* **1** [+ *person*] 把…关在外面; [+ *cold, noise etc*] 把…隔绝在外 **2** (*block*) [+ *view*] 挡住; [+ *thought, memory*] 排除

❏ **shut up I** *vi* [非正式]住口 **II** *vt* [+ *person*] 使住口 ♦ **shut up!** [非正式]闭嘴!

shutter [ˈʃʌtə(r)] *n* [c] **1** (*on window*) 百叶窗 **2** (*on camera*) 快门

shuttle [ˈʃʌtl] **I** *n* [c] **1** (*plane, bus etc*) 穿梭班机/班车 **2** (*also:* ***space shuttle***) 航天飞机 **3** (*for weaving*) 梭 **II** *vi* [*vehicle, person* +] ♦ **to shuttle back and forth between** 在…间穿梭往返 **III** *vt* 穿梭

shuttlecock [ˈʃʌtlkɔk] [体育] *n* [c] 羽毛球

shy [ʃaɪ] **I** *adj* [+ *person*] 害羞的; [+ *animal*] 易受惊的 **II** *vi* [*horse* +] 惊退 ♦ **to be shy of doing sth** 对做某事有顾忌

❏ **shy away from** *vt* [不可拆分] ♦ **to shy away from sth/from doing sth** 因顾忌而回避某事/做某事

Siberia [saɪˈbɪərɪə] *n* 西伯利亚

sibling [ˈsɪblɪŋ] [正式] *n* [c] 兄弟姐妹 ♦ **sibling rivalry** 手足相争

Sicilian [sɪˈsɪlɪən] **I** *adj* 西西里的 **II** *n* [c] (*person*) 西西里人

Sicily [ˈsɪsɪlɪ] *n* 西西里岛

sick [sɪk] **I** *adj* **1** (*physically*) 患病的; (*mentally*) 令人讨厌的 **2** ♦ **to be sick** (*vomit*) 呕吐 **3** [+ *humour, joke*] 病态的 **II** *n* [u] [英] (*vomit*) 呕吐物

III *n* [*pl*] ♦**the sick** 病人 ♦**to feel sick** 感觉恶心 ♦**to fall sick** 患病 ♦**to be off sick** 因病缺席 ♦**to make sb sick** [非正式] 使某人感到厌恶 ♦**to be sick of sth/of doing sth** [非正式] 讨厌某事/做某事 📖用法参见**ill**

sicken ['sɪkn] *vt* (*disgust*) 使作呕

sickening ['sɪknɪŋ] *adj* 令人作呕的

sick leave *n* [U] 病假 ♦**to be on sick leave** 休病假

sickly ['sɪklɪ] *adj* **1** [+ *child, plant*] 多病的 **2** [+ *smell, taste*] 令人作呕的

sickness ['sɪknɪs] *n* [U] **1** (*illness*) 患病 **2** (*vomiting*) 呕吐 ♦**radiation/altitude/motion sickness** 放射病/高空病/晕动病

✪**side** [saɪd] **I** *n* [C] **1** 边◊ *on both sides of the border* 边境两边 **2** (*surface*) [*of cube*] 面 **3** (*not back or front*) [*of building, vehicle*] 侧面◊ *a van with his name on the side* 侧面写有他名字的货车; [*of body*] 体侧 **4** (*half*) [*of paper, face, brain etc*] 一面◊ *on the other side of the page* 这页纸的另一面上; [*of tape, record*] 面◊ *We want to hear side A.* 我们想听A面。 **5** (*edge*) [*of road, bed etc*] 边缘◊ *Park on the side of the road.* 把车停在路边。 **6** [*of hill, valley*] 坡◊ *narrow valleys with steep sides* 两面陡坡的狭窄山谷 **7** (*aspect*) 方面◊ *Anxiety has a mental and a physical side.* 焦虑有精神方面的因素也有身体方面的因素。 **8** [英] (*team*) 队◊ *the Scottish First Division side* 苏格兰甲级队 [美 = **team**] **9** (*in conflict, contest*) 一方◊ *They sold arms to both sides.* 他们向双方出售军火。 **10** [*of argument, debate*] 派◊ *people on both sides of the issue* 针对该议题的两派人 **II** *adj* [+ *door, entrance*] 旁边的 **III** *vi* ♦**to side with sb** 支持某人 ♦**on either side of sth** 在某物的任一边 ♦**on the other side of sth** 在某物的另一边 ♦**the right/wrong side of sth** 某物正确的/错误的一边 ♦**from side to side** 从一边到另一边 ♦**to lie on one's side** [*person* +] 侧卧; [*thing* +] 侧放 ♦**by the side of** 在…旁边 ♦**side by side** 肩并肩 ♦**she never left my side** 她从没离开过我身边 ♦**to be at** *or* **by sb's side** 在某人身旁 ♦**to get on the right/wrong side of sb** (喻) 讨某人喜欢/不讨某人喜欢 ♦**they are on our side** 他们站在我们这边 ♦**to take sides** 偏袒 ♦**to put sth to one side** 把某事暂搁一边 ♦**to earn some money on the side** 赚额外的收入 ♦**a side of beef** 牛的肋肉

sideboard ['saɪdbɔːd] **I** *n* [C] 餐具柜 **II sideboards** *n* [*pl*] [英] = **sideburns**

sideburns ['saɪdbəːnz] *n* [*pl*] 连鬓胡子

side-effect ['saɪdɪfɛkt] *n* [C] **1** [*of drug*] 副作用 **2** [*of situation*] 意外后果

sidelight ['saɪdlaɪt] *n* [C] **1** [英] (*on front of vehicle*) 示宽灯 [美 = **parking light**] **2** [美] (*on side of vehicle*) 边灯

sideline ['saɪdlaɪn] **I** *n* [C] **1** (*extra job*) 副业 **2** [体育] 边线 **II** *vt* **1** (*keep back*) [+ *person, policy*] 使靠边 **2** [+ *player*] 使…退出比赛 ♦**on the sidelines** (*not involved*) 当局外人

side order *n* [C] 与主菜同时上的附加菜

side street *n* [C] 小街

sidetrack ['saɪdtræk] *vt* 使…转移目标

sideview mirror ['saɪdvjuː-] [美] *n* [C] 后视镜 [英 = **wing mirror**]

sidewalk ['saɪdwɔːk] [美] *n* [C] 人行道 [英 = **pavement**]

sideways ['saɪdweɪz] **I** *adv* [*move* +] 向一边; [*look, face* +] 斜侧 **II** *adj* [+ *glance, movement*] 向一侧的

siege [siːdʒ] *n* [C] 围困 ♦**to lift a siege** 解围 ♦**to be under siege** 被围困 ♦**to lay siege to** [*police, soldiers* +] 围攻; [*journalists* +] 包围

Sierra Leone [sɪ'ɛrəlɪ'əun] *n* 塞拉利昂

sieve [sɪv] **I** *n* [C] (*for flour etc*) 筛子; (*for liquid*) 滤器; (*garden sieve*) 筛网 **II** *vt* [+ *flour, soil etc*] 筛; [+ *liquid*] 滤 ♦**to have a memory** *or* **mind like a sieve** 记性极差

sift [sɪft] *vt* 筛

❏**sift through** *vt* [不可拆分] [+ *evidence, wreckage*] 详查

sigh [saɪ] **I** *n* [C] 叹息 **II** *vi* 叹气 ♦**to breathe** *or* **heave a sigh of relief**

松一口气

sight [saɪt] **I** *n* **1** [U] (*faculty*) 视力 **2** [C] (*spectacle*) 景象 **3** [C] (*on gun*) 瞄准器 **II sights** *n* [*pl*] (*places of interest*) ♦**the sights** 景点 **III** *vt* 看见 ♦**to catch sight of sb/sth** 瞧见某人/某物 ♦**to lose sight of sth** (喻) 忽略某事 ♦**the sight of sth** 一看见某物 ♦**to set one's sights on sth** 立志拥有某物 ♦**in sight** (字) 看得见 ♦**out of sight** 看不见 ♦**to be in** *or* **within sight** (喻) 在望 ♦**at first sight** 乍一看 ♦**I know her by sight** 我看到她就知道她是谁 ♦**on sight** [*shoot, arrest* +] 一看见就… ♦**a sight better/worse** [非正式] 好/坏得多

sightseeing ['saɪtsiːɪŋ] *n* [U] 观光 ♦**to go sightseeing** 观光游览

✪**sign** [saɪn] **I** *n* **1** [C] (*notice*) 指示牌 ◊ *a sign saying "No Exit"* 一块写着"禁止入内"的指示牌 **2** [C] (*also: **road sign***) 路标 **3** [C] (*gesture*) (*with hand etc*) 手势 ◊ *the V-for-victory sign* 代表胜利的V字手势 **4** [C] [数, 音] (*symbol*) 符号 ◊ *an equals sign* 一个等于号 **5** [C/U] (*indication, evidence*) 迹象 ◊ *The sky is clear and there's no sign of rain.* 天空晴朗，丝毫没有要下雨的迹象。**6** [C] [占星术] 星座 **II** *vt* **1** [+ *document*] 签署 **2** [+ *TV programme*] (*for deaf people*) 用手语演播 **3** [足球] [+ *player*] 与…签约 **III** *vi* **1** (*use sign language*) 使用手语 **2** [足球] [*player* +] 签约 ♦**to make a sign** 做手势 ♦**a plus/minus sign** 正/负号 ♦**there's no sign of her changing her mind** 她没有任何要改变主意的表示 ♦**he was showing signs of improvement** 他的身体有好转的迹象 ♦**a sign of the times** 时代的特征 ♦**it's a good/bad sign** 这是个好/坏兆头 ♦**to sign one's name** 签名

❑**sign away** *vt* [+ *rights etc*] 签字放弃

❑**sign for** *vt* [不可拆分] [+ *goods*] 签收

❑**sign in** *vi* (*at hotel etc*) 签到

❑**sign off** *vi* **1** [广播, 电视] 结束播放 **2** (*in letter*) 就此搁笔 **3** [英] (*as unemployed*) 退出失业救济

❑**sign on** [英] *vi* (*as unemployed*) 申请失业救济 ♦**to sign on for sth** [+ *course*] 签约做某事

❑**sign out** *vi* (*from hotel etc*) 签名离开

❑**sign over** *vt* ♦**to sign sth over to sb** 将某物签约转让给某人

❑**sign up I** *vi* (*for job, course, trip etc*) 签约受雇 **II** *vt* [+ *player, recruit*] 签约雇用 ♦**to sign up for** [+ *job, course, trip etc*] 签约从事

signal ['sɪgnl] **I** *n* [C] **1** (*to do sth*) 信号 **2** (*indication*) 暗示 **3** [铁路] 信号机 **4** [电子] 信号 **II** *vi* **1** (*with gesture, sound*) ♦**to signal (to sb)** (向某人) 示意 **2** [汽车] (*with indicator*) 开信号灯示意 **III** *vt* **1** [+ *message*] 用信号示意; [+ *person*] 向…打手势示意 **2** (*indicate*) 标志着 **IV** *adj* [正式] [+ *triumph, failure*] 显著的

signature ['sɪgnətʃə(r)] *n* [C] 签名

significance [sɪg'nɪfɪkəns] *n* [U] 重要性 ♦**of no/some significance** 毫无/有一定重要意义

significant [sɪg'nɪfɪkənt] *adj* **1** (*important*) 重要的 **2** (*considerable*) [+ *amount, number, effect*] 相当大的 **3** (*meaningful*) [+ *look, glance etc*] 意味深长的 ♦**it is significant that ...** 值得注意的是…

signify ['sɪgnɪfaɪ] *vt* **1** (*represent*) [*symbol, number* +] 表示 **2** (*indicate*) [*event* +] 意味 **3** (*make known*) [*person* +] 示意 ♦**to signify that ...** 意味着…

sign language *n* [C/U] 手势语; (*for deaf people*) 手语

signpost ['saɪnpəust] *n* [C] **1** (*road sign*) 路标 **2** (*indicator*) 指标

Sikh [siːk] **I** *n* [C] 锡克教信徒 **II** *adj* 锡克教的

silence ['saɪləns] **I** *n* [C/U] 寂静 **II** *vt* [+ *person*] 使安静; [+ *opposition*] 压制 ♦**in silence** 鸦雀无声 ♦**to break one's silence** 开口讲话

silent ['saɪlənt] *adj* [+ *person*] (*on particular occasion*) 沉默的; (*as character trait*) 沉默寡言的; [+ *place, object*] 安静的; [+ *prayer, emotion*] 默默的; [+ *film*] 无声的 ♦**to fall silent** (*stop talking*) 不作声; (*stop making noise*) 安静下来 ♦**to be/remain silent about sth** 对某事守口如瓶

silhouette [sɪluː'ɛt] **I** *n* [C] 黑色轮

廓 **II** *vt* ♦**to be silhouetted against sth** 某物衬出…的轮廓

silicon ['sɪlɪkən] *n* [U] 硅

silicon chip *n* [C] 硅片

silicone ['sɪlɪkəun] **I** *n* [U] 硅酮 **II** *cpd* [复合词] [+ *implant, coating*] 硅酮

silk [sɪlk] **I** *n* [C/U] 丝绸 **II** *cpd* [复合词] [+ *scarf, shirt etc*] 丝绸

silky ['sɪlkɪ] *adj* [+ *material*] 丝质的; [+ *skin*] 柔软光洁的

silly ['sɪlɪ] *adj* [+ *person*] 愚蠢的; [+ *idea, object*] 可笑的 ♦**he's silly to be upset** 他这么难过真是太傻了 ♦**it would be silly to waste it** 把它浪费了就太愚蠢了

silver ['sɪlvə(r)] **I** *n* [U] **1** 银 **2** (*silverware*) 银器 **3** (*coins*) 银币 **II** *adj* **1** (*in colour*) [+ *hair*] 银白色的 **2** (*made of silver*) [+ *spoon, necklace etc*] 银的 ♦**silver-grey** 银灰色

silver-plated [sɪlvə'pleɪtɪd] *adj* 镀银的

SIM card ['sɪm-] *n* [C] 手机智能卡

similar ['sɪmɪlə(r)] *adj* 相似的 ♦**to be similar to sth** 和某事物类似

similarity [sɪmɪ'lærɪtɪ] *n* **1** [U] (*resemblance*) 相似 **2** [C] (*similar feature*) 相似之处

similarly ['sɪmɪləlɪ] *adv* **1** (*in a similar way*) 类似地 **2** (*likewise*) 同样地

simmer ['sɪmə(r)] **I** *vi* 炖 **II** *vt* 煨
❑**simmer down** *vi* (*calm down*) 安静下来; [*situation* +] 平静下来

simple ['sɪmpl] *adj* **1** (*easy*) 简单的 **2** (*basic*) [+ *meal, life, cottage etc*] 简朴的 **3** (*mere*) 纯粹的 **4** [语言] [+ *tense*] 简单的 **5** [过时] (*not intelligent*) 智能低的 ♦**it would be simpler to move house** 搬家会更容易些

simplicity [sɪm'plɪsɪtɪ] *n* [U] **1** (*lack of complexity*) 简易 **2** [*of design, style etc*] 朴素

simplify ['sɪmplɪfaɪ] *vt* 简化

simply ['sɪmplɪ] *adv* **1** (*merely*) 仅仅 **2** [*live, say, dress etc* +] 简单地 **3** (*absolutely*) 完全

simulate ['sɪmjuleɪt] *vt* [+ *action, feeling*] 假装; [+ *substance, noise*] 模仿

simultaneous [sɪməl'teɪnɪəs] *adj* 同时的; [+ *translation*] 同声的; [+ *broadcast*] 同步的

sin [sɪn] **I** *n* [C/U] 罪孽 **II** *vi* 有罪

✪**since** [sɪns] **I** *adv* **1** (*from then onwards*) 此后 ◊ *They went to college together and have done business together since.* 他们一起上的大学并从此后一起做生意。**2** (*latterly*) 后来 ◊ *6,000 people were arrested, several hundred of whom have since been released.* 6000 人被逮捕，其中几百人后来被释放。**II** *prep* **1** (*from*) 自…以来 ◊ *I've been here since the end of June.* 我自6月底以来一直在这儿。**2** (*after*) 从…以后 ◊ *I haven't seen powdered eggs since the war.* 自战后我从未见过鸡蛋粉。**III** *conj* **1** (*from when*) 自从 ◊ *I've been wearing glasses since I was three.* 我从3岁起就戴眼镜。**2** (*after*) 从…以后 ◊ *So much has changed in the sport since I was a teenager.* 自我十几岁起，这项运动已经改变了很多。**3** (*as*) 因为 ◊ *Since it was Saturday, he stayed in bed an extra hour.* 因为是星期六，他在床上多呆了一小时。♦**since then** *or* **ever since** 从那时起 ♦**long since** 很久以前

> **for** 用来表示过去、现在或将来某事持续的时间的长短，或未发生某事的时间的长短。*She slept for eight hours...He will be away for three weeks...I hadn't seen him for four years.* 表示某个时间段开始时，用 **since**。*She has been with the group since it began...the first civilian president since the coup 17 years ago...* **since** 还可以表示某事发生的最后时间，或者未发生某事的时间的长短。*She hadn't eaten since breakfast...It was a long time since she had been to church.*

sincere [sɪn'sɪə(r)] *adj* [+ *person*] 真诚的; [+ *belief, apology*] 诚挚的

sincerely [sɪn'sɪəlɪ] *adv* 由衷地 ♦**Yours sincerely** *or* [美] **Sincerely yours** 谨上

sing [sɪŋ] (*pt* **sang**, *pp* **sung**) **I** *vi* [*person* +] 唱歌; [*bird* +] 鸣 **II** *vt* [+ *song*] [*person* +]唱; [*bird* +] 鸣唱 ♦**to sing sb sth, sing sth to sb** 为

某人唱某歌
❑**sing along** *vi* ♦**to sing along (with/to)** (和着···)一起唱
Singapore [sɪŋgə'pɔː(r)] *n* 新加坡
singer ['sɪŋə(r)] *n* [c] 歌手
singing ['sɪŋɪŋ] *n* [u] (*activity*) 唱歌; (*sounds*) 歌声
✪**single** ['sɪŋgl] **I** *adj* **1** (*solitary*) 单个的◊ *We heard a single shot.* 我们听到一声枪响。**2** (*individual*) 惟一的 ◊ *the world's single most important source of oil* 世界上惟一最重要的石油来源 **3** (*unmarried*) 单身的◊ *a single woman* 一位单身女子 **4** (*for one person, car etc*) [*+ sheet, garage*] 单人的 **II** *n* [c] [英] **1** (*also: **single ticket***) 单程票 [美= **one-way ticket**] **2** (*record*) 单曲唱片 ♦**not a single one was left** 一个都没剩 ♦**every single day** 每一天 ♦**single spacing** [排版] 单倍行距
❑**single out** *vt* (*choose*) 选出 ♦**to single sb out for sth** 为某事选出某人
single bed *n* [c] 单人床
single file *n* ♦**in single file** 一列纵队
single-handed [sɪŋgl'hændɪd] *adv* 独自一人地
single-minded [sɪŋgl'maɪndɪd] *adj* 一心一意的
single parent *n* [c] 单亲
single room *n* [c] 单人房
singles ['sɪŋglz] [网球] *n* [u] 单打比赛
singular ['sɪŋgjulə(r)] **I** *adj* **1** [语言] 单数的 **2** (*remarkable*) 非凡的 **2** [过时] (*strange*) 奇怪的 **II** *n* ♦**the singular** 单数形式 ♦**in the singular** 用单数
sinister ['sɪnɪstə(r)] *adj* [*+ event, figure, reason*] 邪恶的
sink [sɪŋk] (*pt* **sank**, *pp* **sunk**) **I** *n* [c] 洗涤槽 **II** *vt* **1** [*+ ship*] 使下沉 **2** [*+ well, mine*] 挖掘 **III** *vi* **1** (*in water*) [*ship +*] 沉没; [*object +*] 下沉 **2** (*subside*) [*ground, building, foundation +*] 下陷 **3** (*drop*) [*level, price +*] 下跌 ♦**to sink sth into sth** [*+ teeth, claws, knife, needle*] 将某物插入某物 ♦**to sink to ...** [*prices, pay increases etc +*] 下降至··· ♦**the sun was sinking** 太阳落山了 ♦**she sank to her knees** 她跪下了 ♦**to sink into a chair** 瘫在椅子上 ♦**to sink into depression/a coma** 陷入消沉/昏迷 ♦**my heart sank** 我心头一沉 ♦**her voice sank to a whisper** 她的声音减小成耳语
❑**sink in** *vi* [*words +*] 被理解
sinus ['saɪnəs] *n* [c] 鼻窦
sip [sɪp] **I** *n* [c] 一小口 **II** *vt* 抿 **III** *vi* 小口地喝 ♦**to take** *or* **have a sip (of sth)** 抿一口(某饮料)
sir [səː(r)] *n* (*as address*) 先生 ♦**yes, sir** 是,先生 ♦**Dear Sir** 亲爱的先生 ♦**Dear Sirs** 诸位先生 ♦**Dear Sir or Madam** 亲爱的先生或女士 ♦**Sir John Smith** 约翰·史密斯爵士
siren ['saɪərn] *n* [c] 警报器
sirloin ['səːlɔɪn] *n* [c/u] (*also: **sirloin steak***) 牛腰上部的肉
✪**sister** ['sɪstə(r)] **I** *n* [c] **1** 姐妹; (*elder*) 姐姐; (*younger*) 妹妹 **2** (*nun*) 修女 **3** [英] (*nurse*) 护士长 **II** *cpd* [复合词] ♦**sister organization/ship** 姐妹组织/船 ♦**my brothers and sisters** 我的兄弟姐妹们
sister-in-law ['sɪstərɪnlɔː] (*pl* **sisters-in-law**) *n* [c] (*husband or wife's older sister*) 姑子; (*husband or wife's younger sister*) 姨子; (*older brother's wife*) 嫂子; (*younger brother's wife*) 弟媳
✪**sit** [sɪt] (*pt, pp* **sat**) **I** *vi* **1** (*also: **sit down***) 坐下◊ *A woman came and sat next to her.* 一位女子进来,紧挨她坐下。**2** (*be sitting*) 坐◊ *She was sitting on the edge of the bed.* 她正坐在床沿上。**3** [*parliament, court +*] 开会◊ *Parliament sits for only 28 weeks out of 52.* 议会一年52周里只开28周的会。**4** (*for painter*) 当模特 ◊ *She had sat for famous painters like Rossetti.* 她为罗塞蒂等著名画家当过模特。**II** *vt* **1** (*position*) 使坐 ◊ *He used to sit me on his lap.* 他以前常让我坐在他腿上。**2** (*invite to sit*) 使就座 **3** [英] [*+ exam*] 参加 [美= **take**] ♦**to sit on a committee** 成为委员会成员◊ *Sit tight! I'll be right back.* 等一下!我马上就回来。
❑**sit about** [英:非正式] *vi* = **sit around**
❑**sit around** [非正式] *vi* 闲坐着

❑ **sit back** [非正式] *vi* (喻) 在一旁闲着
❑ **sit down** *vi* (*from standing*) 坐下 ♦ **to be sitting down** 就座
❑ **sit in on** *vt* [不可拆分] [+ *meeting, lesson*] 旁听
❑ **sit on** [非正式] *vt* [不可拆分] (*keep to oneself*) [+ *report etc*] 搁置
❑ **sit out** *vt* [+ *event*] 挨到…结束
❑ **sit through** *vt* [+ *film, lecture etc*] 耐着性子到…结束
❑ **sit up** *vi* **1** (*from lying*) 坐起来 **2** (*straighten*) 坐直 **3** (*stay up late*) 熬夜

sitcom ['sɪtkɔm] *n* [c] 情景喜剧

site [saɪt] **I** *n* [c] **1** [*of event*] 地点 **2** (*building site*) 工地 **3** (*archaeological*) 遗址 **4** (*also:* ***website***) 网址 **II** *vt* [+ *factory, missiles*] 设置

sitting ['sɪtɪŋ] *n* [c] **1** [*of assembly etc*] 开会 **2** (*in canteen*) 分批就餐 ♦ **to do sth at a single sitting** 一口气做完某事

sitting room [英] *n* [c] 起居室 [美 = **living room**]

situated ['sɪtjueɪtɪd] *adj* ♦ **to be situated in/on/near sth** 位于某物中/上/旁

✪ **situation** [sɪtju'eɪʃən] *n* [c] **1** (*circumstances*) 情况 ◊ *It's an impossible situation.* 这情况真是难以应付。**2** (*location*) 环境 ◊ *The city is in a beautiful situation.* 这座城市环境优美。**3** [过时] (*job*) 工作 ◊ *It's not so easy to find another situation.* 另找份工作并不那么容易。 ♦ **"situations vacant"** [英] "招聘" [美 = **Employment**]

✪ **six** [sɪks] *num* 六 *see also* **five**

✪ **sixteen** [sɪks'tiːn] *num* 十六 *see also* **fifteen**

sixteenth [sɪks'tiːnθ] *num* 第十六 *see also* **fifth**

sixth [sɪksθ] *num* **1** (*in series*) 第六 **2** (*fraction*) 六分之一 ♦ **the upper/lower sixth** [英:教育] 高级/初级六年级，英国中学教育的最后两年，在此期间学生准备A level考试，以取得大学入学资格 *see also* **fifth**

sixth form [英] *n* ♦ **the sixth form** 六年级，英国中学教育的最后两年，在此期间学生准备A level考试，以取得大学入学资格

sixth form college [英] *n* [c] 第六级学校，为16岁以上的学生提供A level考试及相关的课程

sixtieth ['sɪkstɪɪθ] *num* 第六十

✪ **sixty** ['sɪkstɪ] *num* 六十 *see also* **fifty**

size [saɪz] *n* **1** [c/u] [*of object*] 大小; [*of clothing, shoes*] 尺码 **2** [c/u] [*of loan, business*] 多少 **3** [u] [*of area, building, task, loss etc*] 大 ♦ **I take size 12** (*dress, shirt etc*) 我穿12号 ♦ **what size shoes do you take?** 你穿几号的鞋？ ♦ **it's the size of ...** 相当于…的大小 ♦ **to cut sth to size** 将某物改至一定大小
❑ **size up** [非正式] *vt* [+ *person, situation*] 评估

sizeable ['saɪzəbl] *adj* [+ *amount, number*] 相当大的; [+ *problem, operation*] 大的; [+ *object, company, estate*] 颇大的; [+ *majority, minority*] 相当数量的

sizzle ['sɪzl] *vi* 咝咝作响

skate [skeɪt] **I** *n* **1** [c] (*ice skate*) 溜冰鞋 **2** [c] (*roller skate*) 旱冰鞋 **3** [c/u] (*pl* **skate**) (*fish*) 鳐鱼 **II** *vi* **1** (*ice skate*) 溜冰 **2** (*roller skate*) 溜旱冰 ♦ **to go skating** (*on ice skates*) 去溜冰; (*on roller skates*) 去溜旱冰
❑ **skate around, skate over, skate round** *vt* [不可拆分] [+ *problem, issue*] 一带而过

skateboard ['skeɪtbɔːd] *n* [c] 滑板

skateboarding ['skeɪtbɔːdɪŋ] *n* [u] 滑板运动

skater ['skeɪtə(r)] *n* [c] 滑冰者

skating ['skeɪtɪŋ] *n* [u] (*ice-skating*) 冰上运动 *see also* **skate**

skating rink *n* [c] (*ice rink*) 溜冰场

skeleton ['skɛlɪtn] *n* [c] **1** (*bones*) 骨骼 **2** (*frame*) [*of building*] 框架 **3** (*framework*) [*of plan*] 提纲

skeptical ['skɛptɪkl] [美] *adj* = **sceptical**

sketch [skɛtʃ] **I** *n* [c] **1** (*drawing*) 素描 **2** (*outline*) 概述 **3** [戏剧, 电视, 广播] 诙谐短剧 **II** *vt* **1** [+ *drawing, landscape, figure, map*] 给…画速写 **2** (*also:* ***sketch out***) [+ *ideas, plan*] 概述

sketchy ['skɛtʃɪ] *adj* 粗略的

skewer ['skjuːə(r)] **I** *n* [c] 串肉扦 **II** *vt* 刺穿

ski [skiː] **I** *n* [c] 滑雪板 **II** *vi* 滑雪 ♦**to go skiing** 去滑雪
ski boot *n* [c] 滑雪鞋
skid [skɪd] **I** *vi* ♦**to skid (into/across** *etc* **sth)** [*person* +] 滑着(冲向/穿过{等}某物); [*car, driver* +] 打滑 **II** *n* [c] ♦**to go into a skid** 打滑
skier ['skiːə(r)] *n* [c] 滑雪者
skiing ['skiːɪŋ] *n* [U] **1** (*activity*) 滑雪 **2** (*competition*) 滑雪比赛 *see also* **ski**
skilful (美 **skillful**) ['skɪlful] *adj* [+ *person, player*] 老练的; [+ *use, choice, management*] 技巧娴熟的 ♦**to be skilful at doing sth** 能熟练地做某事
ski lift *n* [c] 载送滑雪者上坡的装置
skill [skɪl] *n* **1** [U] (*ability*) 技巧 **2** [c] (*acquired*) 技能
skilled [skɪld] *adj* [+ *person*] 熟练的; [+ *work*] 技术性的
skillful ['skɪlful] [美] *adj* = **skilful**
skim [skɪm] *vt* **1** ♦**to skim sth from** *or* **off sth** [+ *fat, cream*] 从某物上撇去某物 **2** (*also:* ***skim over***) [+ *ground, water, wave*] 掠过 **3** (*also:* ***skim through***) [+ *book, article*] 浏览
skim milk [美] *n* [U] 脱脂牛奶 [英 = **skimmed milk**]
skimmed milk [skɪmd-] [英] *n* [U] 脱脂牛奶 [美 = **skim milk**]
skimpy ['skɪmpɪ] *adj* **1** [+ *meal*] 不足的 **2** [+ *clothes*] 用料少的
skin [skɪn] **I** *n* **1** [C/U] [*of person*] 皮肤; [*of animal*] 皮; (*complexion*) 肤色 **2** [C/U] [*of fruit, vegetable*] 外皮 **3** [s] (*on liquid*) 薄层 **II** *vt* 剥去…的皮 ♦**to be soaked** *or* **drenched to the skin** 全身都湿透了
skin cancer *n* [C/U] 皮肤癌
skinhead ['skɪnhɛd] [英] *n* [c] 留平头的人(一般被认为有暴力倾向)
skinny ['skɪnɪ] [非正式] *adj* [+ *person*] 极瘦的; [+ *arms, legs*] 皮包骨的
skip [skɪp] **I** *vi* **1** (*hop*) 蹦跳 **2** [尤英] (*with rope*) 跳绳 [美 = **skip rope**] **II** *vt* **1** (*miss*) [+ *lunch, lecture*] 故意不做; [+ *school*] 逃学 **2** (*also:* ***skip over***) [+ *boring parts*] 略过 **III** *n* [c] **1** (*movement*) 蹦跳 **2** [英] (*container*) 无盖用以装运工地废料的废料桶 [美 = **Dumpster®**]
ski pass *n* [c] 滑雪证
skipper ['skɪpə(r)] **I** *n* [c] [*of ship*] 船长; [*of team*] 队长 **II** *vt* [+ *boat*] 当…的船长; [+ *team*] 当…的队长
skipping rope ['skɪpɪŋ-] [英] *n* [c] 跳绳 [美 = **skip rope**]
skip rope [美] *n* [c] 跳绳 [英 = **skipping rope**]
skirt [skəːt] **I** *n* [c] 裙子 **II** *vt* **1** [+ *area*] [*path, road etc* +] 环绕; [*person* +] 绕…的边缘走 **2** [+ *problem, question*] 避而不谈
❑**skirt around, skirt round** *vt* [不可拆分] = **skirt**
skirting board ['skəːtɪŋ-] [英] *n* [C/U] 踢脚板 [美 = **baseboard**]
ski slope *n* [c] 滑雪坡
skive [skaɪv] [英:非正式] *vi* 逃避劳动
❑**skive off** [英:非正式] **I** *vt* [不可拆分] [+ *school, work*] 逃避 **II** *vi* 逃避劳动
skull [skʌl] *n* [c] 颅骨
skunk [skʌŋk] *n* [c] 臭鼬
sky [skaɪ] *n* [C/U] 天空 ♦**to praise sb to the skies** 把某人捧上了天
skyscraper ['skaɪskreɪpə(r)] *n* [c] 摩天大厦
slab [slæb] *n* [c] [*of stone, concrete*] 厚板; [*of meat*] 厚片
slack [slæk] **I** *adj* **1** [+ *rope, skin*] 松弛的 **2** [+ *market, demand, business*] 不景气的; [+ *period*] 萧条的 **3** [+ *worker*] 懈怠的 **4** [+ *security, discipline*] 马虎的 **II** *n* [U] (*in rope etc*) 松弛部分 **III slacks** *n* [*pl*] [过时] (*trousers*) 宽松的裤子
slacken ['slækn] **I** *vi* **1** [*rope* +] 变松 **2** (*also:* ***slacken off***) [*speed* +] 放慢; [*demand, situation* +] 减缓; [*rain* +] 变小 **II** *vt* [+ *grip*] 放松; [+ *speed*] 放慢
slain [sleɪn] *pp of* **slay**
slam [slæm] **I** *vt* **1** [+ *door*] 使劲关 **2** (*throw*) ♦**to slam sth down** 砰地放下某物 **3** (*criticize*) 猛烈抨击 **II** *vi* [*door* +] 砰地关上 ♦**to slam sth against/into sth** 用某物猛击某物/将某物使劲扔进某物 ♦**to slam on the brakes** 猛踩刹车 ♦**to slam into sth** 猛然撞上某物

slander ['slɑːndə(r)] I *n* [c/u] [法] 诽谤 II *vt* 诋毁

slang [slæŋ] *n* [u] 俚语 ♦**military/prison slang** 军队/监狱俚语

slant [slɑːnt] I *vi* [*floor, ceiling, handwriting* +] 倾斜; [*sunlight* +] 斜照 II *vt* [+ *information, programme*] 有倾向性地报导 III *n* [s] 1 [*of eyes, shoulders, handwriting, hill*] 倾斜 2 (喻) (*approach*) 有偏向性的观点

slap [slæp] I *n* [c] 掌击 II *vt* [+ *child, face, bottom*] 掴 III *adv* [非正式] (*directly*) 直接地 ♦**to give sb a slap** 打某人一巴掌 ♦**a slap in the face** (喻) 污辱 ♦**to slap sb on the back** 拍拍某人的后背 ♦**to slap sth (down) on sth** 啪的一声把某物扔到某物上 ♦**to slap some paint on a wall** 往墙上涂些油漆 ♦**slap-bang** *or* **slap in the middle of sth** [英: 非正式] 在某物的正中央

slash [slæʃ] I *vt* 1 [+ *tyres, face*] 划破 2 [+ *prices, costs*] 大幅削减 II *n* [c] 1 (*slit*) 划口 2 (*also:* ***forward slash***) 斜线号 ♦**to slash one's wrists** 割腕 ♦**to slash at sb/sth** 朝某人/某物猛砍

slate [sleɪt] I *n* 1 [u] 板岩 2 [c] (*on roof*) 石板瓦 II *vt* [英] (*criticize*) 严厉批评

slaughter ['slɔːtə(r)] I *n* [u] [*of people*] 屠杀; [*of wildlife*] 杀戮; [*of cows, sheep, pigs etc*] 屠宰 II *vt* [+ *people*] 屠杀; [+ *wildlife*] 杀戮; [+ *cows, sheep, pigs etc*] 屠宰
📖 用法参见 **kill**

slaughterhouse ['slɔːtəhaus] *n* [c] 屠宰场

Slav [slɑːv] *n* [c] 斯拉夫人

slave [sleɪv] I *n* [c] 奴隶 ♦**to work like a slave** 像奴隶般工作 ♦**a slave to sth** 受某物掌控
❑**slave away** *vi* 苦干
❑**slave over** *vt* [不可拆分] 拼命地干 ♦**to slave over a hot stove** 在灼热的炉子前忙碌

slavery ['sleɪvərɪ] *n* [u] 奴隶制

slay [sleɪ] (*pt* **slew**, *pp* **slain**) *vt* 1 [文] [+ *dragon*] 杀死; [+ *person*] 杀害 2 [尤美] (*murder*) 谋杀

sleazy ['sliːzɪ] [非正式] *adj* [+ *place*] 肮脏的; [+ *magazine, person*] 淫秽的

sled [slɛd] [美] I *n* [c] 雪橇 [英 = **sledge**] II *vi* ♦**to go sledding** 乘雪橇 [英 = **go sledging**]

sledge [slɛdʒ] [英] I *n* [c] 雪橇 [美 = **sled**] II *vi* ♦**to go sledging** 乘雪橇 [美 = **go sledding**]

sleek [sliːk] *adj* 1 [+ *hair, fur*] 油亮的 2 [+ *car, boat etc*] 锃亮的 3 [+ *person*] 考究的

sleep [sliːp] (*pt, pp* **slept**) I *n* 1 [u] 睡眠 2 [c] (*nap*) 睡觉 II *vi* (*be asleep*) 睡; (*fall asleep*) 入睡; (*spend the night*) 过夜 III *vt* ♦**the house sleeps 4** 这个房子可供4个人睡 ♦**to go to sleep** 去睡觉 ♦**to have a good night's sleep** 睡个好觉 ♦**to put a cat/dog** *etc* **to sleep** 把猫/狗{等}人道地杀死 ♦**I didn't lose any sleep over it** (喻) 我并没有为这事忧虑过
❑**sleep around** [非正式] *vi* 乱搞男女关系
❑**sleep in** [英] *vi* 睡懒觉
❑**sleep off** *vt* 以睡眠消除
❑**sleep through** *vt* [不可拆分] [+ *noise*] 不被…吵醒
❑**sleep together** *vi* 有性关系
❑**sleep with** *vt* [不可拆分] 和…有性关系

sleeper ['sliːpə(r)] *n* [c] 1 [英] (*train*) 卧车; (*carriage*) 卧铺车厢; (*berth*) 卧铺 2 [英] (*on track*) 枕木 3 ♦**I'm a light/heavy sleeper** 我是个睡觉警醒/沉的人

sleeping bag ['sliːpɪŋ-] *n* [c] 睡袋

sleeping car *n* [c] 火车卧铺车厢

sleeping pill *n* [c] 安眠药

sleepless ['sliːplɪs] *adj* [+ *person*] 失眠的 ♦**to have a sleepless night** 过了个不眠之夜

sleepwalk ['sliːpwɔːk] *vi* 梦游

sleepy ['sliːpɪ] *adj* 1 [+ *person*] 瞌睡的 2 [+ *village, town*] 冷清的

sleet [sliːt] *n* [u] 雨夹雪

sleeve [sliːv] *n* [c] 1 [*of jacket, sweater etc*] 袖子 2 [尤英] [*of record*] 唱片套 [美 = **jacket**] ♦**with long/short sleeves** 长袖/短袖 ♦**to have sth up one's sleeve** (喻) 暗藏某物以备不时之需

sleeveless ['sliːvlɪs] *adj* 无袖的

sleigh [sleɪ] *n* [c] 雪橇

slender ['slɛndə(r)] *adj* 1 [+ *person, legs*] 修长的 2 [+ *chance, means,*

majority] 微弱的
slept [slɛpt] *pt, pp of* **sleep**
slew [sluː] **I** *pt of* **slay** **II** *vi* [*vehicle* +] 旋转 **III** *vt* [+ *vehicle*] 使旋转 **IV** *n* [尤美] ♦**a slew of** 大量
slice [slaɪs] **I** *n* [c] **1** [*of meat, bread, lemon*] 片 **2** (*share*) 份额 **II** *vt* 把…切成片 **III** *vi* ♦**to slice through sth** 划开某物 ♦**sliced bread** 切片面包 ♦**it's the best thing since sliced bread** 这是极好的东西
slick [slɪk] **I** *adj* **1** [+ *performance, advertisement*] 巧妙的; [+ *movement, gear change*] 娴熟的 **2** [贬] (*clever*) 圆滑的 **II** *n* [c] 浮油
slide [slaɪd] (*pt, pp* **slid**) **I** *n* [c] **1** (*in playground*) 滑梯 **2** [摄影] 幻灯片 **3** [英] (*also:* ***hair slide***) 发夹 **4** (*microscope slide*) 载物片 **5** (*in prices, earnings*) 下滑 **II** *vt* 使…滑动 **III** *vi* **1** (*slip*) ♦**to slide down/off/into sth** 滑下/离/进某物 **2** (*quietly*) ♦**to slide into/out of sth** 悄悄溜进/出某处 ♦**to slide into chaos/a depression** 渐渐陷入混乱/消沉 ♦**to let standards/things slide** 听任标准下降/事情变糟
❑**slide away** *vi* 溜走
sliding ['slaɪdɪŋ] *adj* [+ *door*] 滑动的
slight [slaɪt] **I** *adj* **1** [+ *increase, problem*] 微小的 **2** (*slim*) [+ *person*] 娇小的 **3** (*insubstantial*) 无足轻重的 **II** *vt* (*insult*) 怠慢 **III** *n* [c] (*insult*) 污辱 ♦**the slightest noise/problem** *etc* 极轻微的声响/极小的问题{等} ♦**not the slightest bit** 一点也不 ♦**not in the slightest** 一点也不
slightly ['slaɪtlɪ] *adv* (*a bit*) 略微地 ♦**slightly built** 体格纤弱
slim [slɪm] **I** *adj* **1** [+ *figure*] 苗条的; [+ *book, wallet*] 薄的 **2** [+ *chance*] 小的 **II** *vi* (*lose weight*) 节食减肥
❑**slim down I** *vi* [*company* +] 精简机构 **II** *vt* [+ *company*] 精简
slimming ['slɪmɪŋ] *n* [u] 减肥
slimy ['slaɪmɪ] *adj* **1** [+ *substance*] 泥浆的; (*object*) 有泥浆的 **2** [英] [+ *person*] 谄媚的
sling [slɪŋ] (*pt, pp* **slung**) **I** *n* [c] **1** (*for arm*) 悬带 **2** (*for baby*) 背带 **II** *vt* **1** (*throw*) 扔 **2** (*suspend*) 悬挂 ♦**to have one's arm in a sling** 胳膊用悬带吊着 ♦**to sling sth over sth** 将某物挂在某物上
slip [slɪp] **I** *vt* (*put*) ♦**to slip sth into/under sth** 将某物悄悄塞入某物/到某物下面 **II** *vi* **1** (*slide*) [*person* +] 滑跤; [*object* +] 滑落 **2** (*decline*) 下降 **III** *n* [c] **1** (*fall*) 滑倒 **2** (*mistake*) 差错 **3** [*of paper*] 细条 **4** (*underskirt*) 衬裙; (*with top part*) 连身衬裙 ♦**to slip sth on/off** [+ *clothes, shoes*] 迅速穿上/脱下某物 ♦**to slip sth to sb, slip sb sth** 偷偷将某物塞给某人 ♦**it slipped my mind** 我忘了 ♦**to slip into/out of sth** [+ *room, house*] 悄悄溜进/出某处; [+ *clothes, shoes*] 迅速穿上/脱下某物 ♦**to slip into a habit/routine** 逐渐养成习惯/规律 ♦**to let slip that ...** 无意中透露… ♦**a slip of the tongue** 口误 ♦**to give sb the slip** [非正式] 甩掉某人
❑**slip away** *vi* (*go*) 悄悄溜走
❑**slip out** *vi* (*go out*) 出去一下
❑**slip up** *vi* (*make mistake*) 出差错
slipper ['slɪpə(r)] *n* [c] 拖鞋
slippery ['slɪpərɪ] *adj* **1** [+ *surface*] 滑的 **2** [+ *person*] 狡猾的 ♦**to be on a slippery slope to ruin/anarchy** 将导致毁灭/混乱
slip road [英] *n* [c] (*to motorway*) 连接高速公路的岔道 [美 = **entrance ramp, exit ramp**]
slit [slɪt] (*pt, pp* **slit**) **I** *n* [c] **1** (*cut*) 划口 **2** (*opening*) 缝 **II** *vt* (*make a cut in*) 切开 ♦**to slit sb's throat** 割开某人的喉咙
slog [slɔg] [英: 非正式] **I** *vi* (*also:* ***slog away***) 勤恳地工作 **II** *n* [s] **1** (*effort*) (*also:* ***hard slog***) 艰辛的事 **2** (*journey*) 长途跋涉
slogan ['sləugən] *n* [c] 口号
slope [sləup] **I** *n* [c] **1** (*gentle hill*) 斜坡 **2** (*side of mountain*) 坡 **3** (*slant*) 坡度 **4** (*ski slope*) 滑雪坡 **II** *vi* ♦**to slope down** 向下倾斜 ♦**on a slope** 在斜坡上 ♦**to slope to the right/left** 向右/左倾斜
sloping ['sləupɪŋ] *adj* [+ *ground, roof*] 斜的
sloppy ['slɔpɪ] *adj* **1** (*careless*) 马虎的 **2** (*sentimental*) 感伤的
slot [slɔt] **I** *n* [c] **1** (*in machine*) 狭槽 **2** (喻) (*in timetable*) 时段; [广播, 电

视]档期**II** *vt* ♦**to slot sth into sth** [+ *money, card, cassette*] 把某物放入某处**III** *vi* ♦**to slot into sth** 放入某物

❑**slot in I** *vt* [+ *money, card, cassette*] 把…放入 ♦**to slot sb in** 把某人安排进去**II** *vi* 安放

slot machine *n* [c] 投币机; (*for gambling*) 吃角子老虎机

slouch [slautʃ] **I** *vi* **1** (*have poor posture*) ♦**to slouch (over sth)** 无精打采地靠着(某物) **2** (*walk*) ♦**to slouch in/out** 没精打采地走进/走出**II** *n* [s] 低头垂肩的姿态 ♦**she was slouched in a chair** 她没精打采地坐在椅子上

❑**slouch around** *vi* 懒散地闲逛

Slovak ['sləuvæk] **I** *adj* 斯洛伐克的**II** *n* **1** [c] (*person*) 斯洛伐克人 **2** [u] (*language*) 斯洛伐克语 ♦**the Slovak Republic** 斯洛伐克共和国

Slovakia [sləu'vækɪə] *n* 斯洛伐克

Slovakian [sləu'vækɪən] *adj, n* = **Slovak**

Slovene ['sləuviːn] **I** *adj* 斯洛文尼亚的**II** *n* **1** [c] (*person*) 斯洛文尼亚人 **2** [u] (*language*) 斯洛文尼亚语

Slovenia [sləu'viːnɪə] *n* 斯洛文尼亚

Slovenian [sləu'viːnɪən] *adj, n* = **Slovene**

slow [sləu] **I** *adj* **1** [+ *music, journey, process, speed etc*] 慢的; [+ *driver, swimmer, learner*] 迟钝的 **2** (*not clever*) [+ *person*] 愚钝的 **3** (*not exciting*) [+ *place, activity*] 乏味的 **II** *adv* [非正式] 缓慢地**III** *vt* (*also: **slow down, slow up***) [+ *vehicle, driver, business*] 放慢**IV** *vi* (*also: **slow down, slow up***) [*vehicle, driver, business* +] 减速 ♦**to be slow to act/decide** 行动/决定迟了 ♦**to be slow** [*watch* +] 慢了 ♦**my watch is 20 minutes slow** 我的表慢了20分钟 ♦**business is slow** 生意清淡 ♦**I began to walk slower and slower** 我开始越走越慢 ♦**"slow"** (*road sign*) "缓行"

❑**slow down I** *vi* (*become less active*) [*person* +] 放松**II** *vt* (*make less active*) [+ *person*] 使放松

slowly ['sləulɪ] *adv* **1** [*walk, move* +] 慢慢地 **2** (*gradually*) 逐渐地

slow motion *n* ♦**in slow motion** 以慢动作

slug [slʌg] *n* [c] **1** 鼻涕虫 **2** [美:非正式] (*bullet*) 子弹

sluggish ['slʌgɪʃ] *adj* [+ *circulation, stream*] 迟缓的; [+ *economy, growth*] 萧条的

slum [slʌm] **I** *n* [c] (*house*) 陋室; (*area*) 贫民窟**II** *vt, vi* ♦**to be slumming (it)** 过贫穷的生活

slump [slʌmp] **I** *n* [c] **1** (*drop*) (*in sales, demand etc*) 暴跌 **2** [经济] (*recession*) 经济萧条**II** *vi* **1** [*person* +] ♦**to slump (into/onto sth)** 猛地倒(在某物里/上) **2** [*sales, demand etc* +] 暴跌 ♦**he was slumped over the wheel** 他猛地倒在方向盘上

slung [slʌŋ] *pt, pp of* **sling**

slur [sləː(r)] **I** *n* (*insult*) ♦**a slur (on sb/sth)** (对某人/某物的)诽谤 **II** *vt* ♦**to slur one's speech** 说话含糊

sly [slaɪ] *adj* [+ *smile, expression, remark*] 会意的; [+ *person*] 狡诈的 ♦**on the sly** [非正式] 秘密地

smack [smæk] **I** *n* [c] 巴掌**II** *vt* [+ *face, person*] 掴; (*as punishment*) 打 **III** *vi* ♦**to smack of sth** 带有某事的意味**IV** *adv* [非正式] ♦**smack in the middle** 在正中间 ♦**to smack one's lips** 咂嘴

✪**small** [smɔːl] **I** *adj* **1** [+ *person, object, quantity, number*] 小的 ◊ *the smallest church in England* 英格兰最小的教堂 ◊ *a small amount of money* 一小笔钱 **2** (*young*) [+ *child*] 年幼的 ◊ *She had two small children.* 她有两个年幼的孩子。**3** (*minor*) [+ *mistake, problem, change*] 微不足道的 ◊ *He made a lot of small mistakes.* 他犯过很多小错。**II** *n* [c] ♦**the small of the** *or* **one's back** 后腰 ♦**to get** *or* **grow smaller** [*thing* +] 变小; [*population, number* +] 变少 ♦**to make sth smaller** [+ *object, garment*] 使某物变小些 ♦**a small business/businessman** 小本生意/商人 ♦**to make sb look/feel small** 使某人显得/觉得渺小

smart [smɑːt] **I** *adj* **1** [尤英] (*neat, tidy*) [+ *person, clothes*] 漂亮的; [+ *place*] 整洁的 **2** (*fashionable*) [+ *house, area, party*] 时髦的 **3** (*clever*) [+ *person, idea*] 聪明的 **4** [军]

[+ *bomb, weapon*] 精确制导的 **II** *vi* **1** (*sting*) [*eyes, wound* +] 感到刺痛 **2** (*feel upset*) ♦**to smart from sth** *or* **over sth** 对某事感到痛苦 ♦**the smart set** 时髦的阔人 ♦**don't get smart with me!** 别对我耍小聪明！

smart card *n* [c] 智能卡

smarten up ['smɑːtn-] **I** *vt* [+ *place*] 整理 **II** *vi* [*person* +] 打扮起来 ♦**to smarten o.s. up** 打扮自己

smash [smæʃ] **I** *n* [c] **1** [非正式] (*car crash*) 撞车 **2** (*also:* ***smash hit***) (*song, play, film*) 轰动的演出 **3** [网球] 高压球 **II** *vt* **1** [+ *bottle, window etc*] 打碎 **2** (*beat*) [+ *record*] 打破 **3** (*destroy*) [+ *life, hope*] 破灭；[+ *organization, system*] 消灭 **III** *vi* (*break*) [*bottle, window etc* +] 打碎 ♦**to smash sth into/against sth** 用某物猛击某物 ♦**to smash sth (in)to pieces** *or* **bits** 将某物击成碎片 ♦**to smash through sth** 撞穿某物

❑**smash up** *vt* [+ *room, furniture, car etc*] 撞毁

smashing ['smæʃɪŋ] [英：非正式] *adj* (*wonderful*) 极好的

smear [smɪə(r)] **I** *n* [c] **1** (*mark*) 污迹 **2** (*insult*) 诽谤 **3** [英] (*also:* ***smear test***) 子宫颈涂片检查 [美 = **pap smear**] **II** *vt* **1** (*spread*) [+ *cream, ointment, paint etc*] 涂抹 **2** (*make dirty with*) 弄脏 **3** (*insult*) 诽谤 ♦**his hands were smeared with oil/ink** 他的手上沾满了油/墨水

smell [smɛl] (*pt, pp* **smelled** *or* **smelt**) **I** *n* **1** [c] (*aroma, odour*) 气味 **2** [u] (*sense*) 嗅觉 **II** *vt* **1** (*notice the smell of*) 闻到 **2** (*sniff*) 嗅 **3** (*have instinct for*) 察觉 **III** *vi* **1** (*have unpleasant odour*) 发臭 **2** ♦**to smell nice/delicious/spicy** *etc* 闻起来香/好吃/辣{等} ♦**sense of smell** 嗅觉 ♦**to smell of** 有…气味

smelly ['smɛlɪ] [贬] *adj* (*not fragrant*) 难闻的；[+ *cheese*] 气味强烈的

smelt [smɛlt] **I** *pt, pp of* **smell II** *vt* [+ *ore*] 熔炼

smile [smaɪl] **I** *n* [c] 微笑 **II** *vi* ♦**to smile (at sb)** （对某人）微笑 **III** *vt* 用微笑表示

smiling ['smaɪlɪŋ] *adj* [+ *face, person*] 微笑的

smirk [sməːk] [贬] **I** *n* [c] 傻笑 **II** *vi* 傻笑

smog [smɔg] *n* [u] 烟雾

smoke [sməuk] **I** *n* [u] 烟 **II** *vi* **1** [*person* +] 吸烟 **2** [*chimney* +] 冒烟 **III** *vt* **1** [+ *cigarette, cigar, pipe*] 抽 **2** [+ *fish, meat*] 熏制 ♦**to have a smoke/go for a smoke** 抽根烟/去抽根烟 ♦**to go up in smoke** [*house etc* +] 被烧光；（喻）突然破灭 ♦**do you smoke?** 你抽烟吗？

smoke alarm *n* [c] 烟雾报警器

smoked [sməukt] *adj* [+ *bacon, salmon*] 熏制的；[+ *glass*] 烟熏过的

smoker ['sməukə(r)] *n* [c] (*person*) 吸烟者

smoking ['sməukɪŋ] **I** *n* [u] 吸烟 **II** *adj* [+ *area, compartment*] 吸烟的 ♦**"no smoking"** "禁止吸烟"

smoky ['sməukɪ] *adj* [+ *atmosphere, room*] 烟雾弥漫的；[+ *taste*] 烟熏的

smooth [smuːð] **I** *adj* **1** (*not rough*) [+ *surface, skin*] 光滑的 **2** (*not lumpy*) [+ *sauce, mixture*] 无颗粒的 **3** (*not harsh*) [+ *flavour, whisky*] 醇和的 **4** (*not jerky*) [+ *movement*] 流畅的 **5** (*not bumpy*) [+ *landing, take-off, flight*] 平稳的 **6** (*successful*) [+ *transition, running, process*] 顺利的 **7** [贬] [+ *man*] 圆滑的 **II** *vt* (*also:* ***smooth out, smooth down***) [+ *skirt, piece of paper etc*] 使平滑 ♦**to smooth the path** *or* **way (for sth)** （为某事）铺平道路

❑**smooth out** *vt* [+ *difficulties*] 消除 *see also* **smooth**

❑**smooth over** *vt* = **smooth out**

smother ['smʌðə(r)] *vt* **1** [+ *fire, flames*] 把…闷熄 **2** (*suffocate*) [+ *person*] 使窒息 **3** (*over-protect*) [+ *person*] 溺爱 **4** (*repress*) [+ *emotions*] 抑制 ♦**to smother sth/sb with sth** (*cover*) 用某物将某物/某人覆盖 ♦**smothered with** *or* **in sth** 以{或}被某物覆盖

SMS *n abbr* (= ***short message service***) 短信息服务

smudge [smʌdʒ] **I** *n* [c] 污迹 **II** *vt* 弄脏

smug [smʌg] [贬] *adj* [+ *person, expression*] 沾沾自喜的

smuggle ['smʌgl] *vt* [+ *goods, drugs, refugees*] 走私 ♦**to smuggle sth in/out** 走私进口/出口某物

smuggler ['smʌglə(r)] *n* [c] 走私者
smuggling ['smʌglɪŋ] *n* [u] 走私
snack [snæk] **I** *n* [c] 小吃 **II** *vi* 吃零食 ♦**to have a snack** 吃点零食
snack bar *n* [c] 小吃部
snag [snæg] **I** *n* [c] (*problem*) 麻烦 **II** *vt* [+ *clothes*] 钩破
snail [sneɪl] *n* [c] 蜗牛 ♦**at a snail's pace** 极慢地
snake [sneɪk] **I** *n* [c] 蛇 **II** *vi* [文] ♦**to snake (through sth)** 蜿蜒(穿过某物)
snap [snæp] **I** *n* **1** [s] (*sound*) 劈啪声 **2** [c] [非正式] (*photograph*) 照片 **II** *adj* [+ *decision, judgement*] 仓促的 **III** *vt* **1** [+ *rope, stick etc*] 把…啪地拉断 **2** [非正式] (*photograph*) 给…拍照 **IV** *vi* **1** [*rope, stick etc* +] 啪地绷断 **2** (喻) (*lose control*) 崩溃 ♦**a cold snap** 寒潮 ♦**to snap one's fingers** (字) 打响指; (喻) 轻而易举 ◊ *I can get anything I want just by snapping my fingers.* 我可以轻而易举地得到任何想要的东西。♦**to snap open/shut** [*trap, jaws, bag etc* +] 啪地一声打开/合上
❑ **snap at** *vt* [不可拆分] **1** [*dog* +] 一下咬住 **2** [*person* +] 厉声对…说
❑ **snap off I** *vt* 折断 **II** *vi* 断掉
❑ **snap out of** *vt* [不可拆分] ♦**to snap out of sth** 很快摆脱某心境 ♦**to snap out of it** 摆脱沮丧的情绪
❑ **snap up** *vt* [+ *bargain*] 抢购
snapshot ['snæpʃɔt] *n* [c] **1** (*photo*) 快照 **2** (*impression*) 简单印象
snarl [snɑːl] **I** *vi* [*animal* +] 嗥叫 **II** *vt* [*person* +] 咆哮道 **III** *n* [c] [*of animal*] 嗥叫
❑ **snarl up** *vt* [+ *plan etc*] 搅乱
snatch [snætʃ] **I** *n* [c] [*of conversation, song etc*] 片段 **II** *vt* **1** (*grab*) 抢夺 **2** (*seize*) [+ *child, hostage*] 劫 **3** (*steal*) [+ *handbag etc*] 抢走 **4** (*take*) [+ *opportunity, look, time etc*] 抓住 **III** *vi* ♦**don't snatch!** 别抢! ♦**to snatch a sandwich** 抓紧时间吃个三明治 ♦**to snatch some sleep** 抓紧时间睡会儿觉
❑ **snatch up** *vt* 一把抓住
sneak [sniːk] (*pt* (美) *also* **snuck**) **I** *vi* ♦**to sneak in/out** 偷偷溜进/出 **II** *vt* ♦**to sneak a look at sth** 偷看一眼某物 ♦**to sneak sb/sth into a place** 将某人/某物偷带进一个地方 **III** *n* [c] [非正式] (*telltale*) 告密者
❑ **sneak up** *vi* ♦**to sneak up on sb** 悄悄地接近某人
sneakers ['sniːkəz] [美] *n* [*pl*] 胶底运动鞋 [英 = **trainers**]
sneaky ['sniːkɪ] [非正式] *adj* [+ *person, action*] 鬼鬼祟祟的
sneer [snɪə(r)] **I** *vi* 讥笑 **II** *n* [c] 嘲讽 ♦**to sneer at sb/sth** (*mock*) 嘲笑某人/某事
sneeze [sniːz] **I** *vi* 打喷嚏 **II** *n* [c] 喷嚏 ♦**it's not to be sneezed at** [非正式] 这可不应被轻视
sniff [snɪf] **I** *n* [c] **1** (*from cold, crying*) 抽鼻子; (*disapproving*) 嗤之以鼻 **II** *vi* 抽鼻子 **III** *vt* [+ *perfume, air*] 嗅; [+ *glue*] 吸入 ♦**to take a sniff of sth** (*smell*) 闻一下某物
❑ **sniff out I** *vt* **1** [+ *drugs etc*] 嗅出 **2** [非正式] [+ *scandal, bargain*] 找出
snigger ['snɪgə(r)] *vi* 窃笑
snip [snɪp] **I** *vt* 剪断 **II** *vi* ♦**to snip at sth** 剪某物 **II** *n* **1** [c] 剪 **2** [s] [英: 非正式] (*bargain*) 便宜货
sniper ['snaɪpə(r)] *n* [c] 狙击手
snob [snɔb] [贬] *n* [c] 势利小人
snooker ['snuːkə(r)] **I** *n* [u] [体育] 英式台球 **II** *vt* [英: 非正式] ♦**to be snookered** 处于困境
snoop [snuːp] *vi* ♦**to snoop around** 到处窥探 ♦**to snoop on sb** 窥探某人
snooze [snuːz] [非正式] **I** *n* [c] 小睡 **II** *vi* 打盹 ♦**to have a snooze** 打个盹
snore [snɔː(r)] **I** *vi* 打鼾 **II** *n* [c] 鼾声
snorkel ['snɔːkl] **I** *n* [c] 潜水通气管 **II** *vi* 戴潜水通气管潜泳 ♦**to go snorkelling** 去潜泳
snort [snɔːt] **I** *n* [c] [*of person*] 哼的一声; [*of animal*] 喷鼻息的声音 **II** *vi* [*person* +] 哼一声; [*animal* +] 喷鼻息 **III** *vt* [非正式] [+ *cocaine*] 从鼻孔吸入
snow [snəu] **I** *n* [u] 雪 **II** *vi* 下雪 **III** *vt* ♦**to be snowed under with work** [非正式] 忙得不可开交 ♦**it's snowing** 下雪了
snowball ['snəubɔːl] **I** *n* [c] 雪球 **II** *vi* [*problem, campaign* +] 滚雪球般地扩大
snowboard ['snəubɔːd] **I** *n* [c] 滑雪

板 **II** *vi* 用滑雪板滑雪 ♦**to go snowboarding** 去滑滑雪板

snowboarding ['snəubɔːdɪŋ] *n* [U] 滑雪板运动 *see also* **snowboard**

snub [snʌb] **I** *vt* [+ *person*] 怠慢 **II** *n* [C] 怠慢

snug [snʌg] *adj* **1** [+ *place*] 温暖舒适的; [+ *person*] 安适的 **2** (*well-fitting*) [+ *garment*] 紧身的 ♦**a snug fit** 合体

so

KEYWORD

[səu]

I *adv*

1 (*thus, likewise*) 这样 ♦**they do so because ...** 他们这样做是因为… ♦**if you don't want to go, say so** 如果你不想去，就说你不想去 ♦**if so** 如果这样 ♦**"it's five o'clock" - "so it is!"** "5点了。" "的确是！" ♦**I hope/think so** 我希望/认为如此 ♦**so far** (*up to now*) 迄今为止; (*up to then*) 到那时为止 ♦**and so on** 等等

2 (*also*) ♦**so do I/so am I** 我也一样

3 (*in comparisons*) (*to such a degree*) 如此 ♦**so quickly/big (that)** 如此快/大（以至于）♦**not so clever (as)** 不（如…）那么聪明

4 (*very*) 非常 ♦**we were so worried** 我们非常担心 ♦**so much** 那么多 ♦**there's so much work to do** 有那么多工作要做 ♦**I love you so much** 我非常爱你 ♦**so many** 那么多 ♦**I've got so many things to do** 我有那么多事情要做

5 (*linking events*) 于是 ♦**so I was right after all** 那终究我是对的 ♦**so how was your day?** 那你今天过得怎么样？

6 [非正式] ♦**so (what)?** 那又怎么样？

7 (*in approximations*) ♦**ten or so** 10个左右

8 [非正式] ♦**so long!** 再见！

II *conj*

1 (*expressing purpose*) ♦**so (that)** 为的是 ♦**I brought it so (that) you could see it** 我带过来给你看 ♦**so as to** 以便

2 (*expressing result*) 因此 ♦**he didn't come so I left** 他没来，因此我走了

soak [səuk] **I** *vt* **1** (*drench*) 使湿透 **2** (*leave in water*) 浸泡 **II** *vi* **1** [*dirty washing, dishes* +] 浸泡 **2** [*person* +] (*in bath*) 泡一泡 ♦**to soak through sth** 浸透某物 ♦**to have a soak** (*in bath*) 泡一泡

❑**soak in** *vi* [*liquid* +] 吸收

❑**soak up** *vt* [+ *liquid*] 吸收

soaked [səukt] *adj* (*also:* ***soaked through***) [+ *person, clothes*] 湿透的

soaking ['səukɪŋ] *adj* (*also:* ***soaking wet***) [+ *person*] 湿透的; [+ *clothes*] 湿淋淋的

so-and-so ['səuənsəu] [非正式] *n* [C] (*somebody*) 某某人; (*something*) 某某事 ♦**Mr/Mrs So-and-so** 某某先生/太太 ♦**the little so-and-so!** [贬] 讨厌的家伙！

soap [səup] *n* [C/U] **1** 肥皂 **2** = **soap opera**

soap opera *n* [C] 肥皂剧

soap powder *n* [C/U] 皂粉

soar [sɔː(r)] *vi* **1** [*bird* +] 翱翔; [*aircraft* +] 升入 **2** [*temperature, price* +] 骤升 **3** [*building, tree etc* +] 高耸

sob [sɔb] **I** *n* [C] 啜泣 **II** *vi* 啜泣

sober ['səubə(r)] *adj* **1** 未醉的 **2** (*serious*) [+ *person*] 郑重的; [+ *attitude*] 清醒的 **3** [+ *colours, clothes*] 素净的 ♦**to stay sober** 保持清醒

❑**sober up** **I** *vi* 清醒起来 **II** *vt* 使醒酒

so-called ['səu'kɔːld] *adj* **1** (*before name, title*) 号称的 **2** (*falsely named*) 所谓的

soccer ['sɔkə(r)] *n* [U] 足球 [英 = **football**]

sociable ['səuʃəbl] *adj* 好交际的

social ['səuʃl] **I** *adj* **1** [+ *problems, injustice, change, structure*] 社会的 **2** [+ *event, function*] 社交的 ◊ *We ought to organize more social events.* 我们应该组织更多的社交活动。**3** [+ *animals, insects*] 群居的 **II** *n* [C] [过时] 社交聚会

socialism ['səuʃəlɪzəm] *n* [U] 社会主义

socialist ['səuʃəlɪst] **I** *adj* [+ *party, state*] 社会主义的 **II** *n* [C] 社会主义者

socialize ['səuʃəlaɪz] *vi* 参加社交

♦**to socialize with** 与…交往
social life *n* [c] 社交生活
socially ['səuʃəlɪ] *adv* [*meet, know* +] 社会上 ♦**socially acceptable** 社会上可以接受的 ♦**socially deprived/disadvantaged** 在全社会中贫困的/处于社会不利地位的
social security [英] *n* [U] (*payment*) 社会保障 [美 = **welfare**] ♦**Department of Social Security** 社会保障部 ♦**to be on social security** 靠社会救济金为生的 [美 = **to be on welfare**]
social services [-'sə:vɪsɪz] *n* [*pl*] 社会福利事业
social work *n* [U] 社会福利工作
social worker *n* [c] 社会福利工作者
✪**society** [sə'saɪətɪ] **I** *n* **1** [U] (*people in general*) 社会 ◊ *Women must have equal status in society.* 妇女在社会上必须有平等的地位。**2** [c/U] (*community*) 社会 ◊ *a multi-racial society* 多种族社会 **3** [c] (*club*) 社团 ◊ *the local film society* 当地影视协会 **II** *cpd* [复合词] [+ *wedding*] 社交界
sociology [səusɪ'ɔlədʒɪ] *n* [U] 社会学
sock [sɔk] **I** *n* [c] 袜子 **II** *vt* [非正式] ♦**to sock sb in the mouth/on the jaw** 猛击某人的嘴巴/下巴 ♦**to pull one's socks up** (喻) 加紧努力
socket ['sɔkɪt] *n* [c] **1** [英: 电子] 插座 [美 = **outlet**] **2** (*also:* ***eye socket***) 眼窝; (*also:* ***hip socket*** *etc*) 髋关节 {等}
soda ['səudə] *n* [U] **1** (*also:* ***soda water***) 苏打水 **2** [美] (*also:* ***soda pop***) 汽水
sodium ['səudɪəm] *n* [U] 钠
sofa ['səufə] *n* [c] 沙发
sofa bed *n* [c] 沙发床
soft [sɔft] *adj* **1** [+ *towel*] 松软的; [+ *skin*] 柔滑的 **2** [+ *bed, paste*] 柔软的 **3** [+ *voice, music*] 轻柔的 **4** [+ *light, colour*] 柔和的 **5** (*lenient*) 温和的 ♦**to have a soft spot for sb** 对某人有好感 ♦**to be soft on sb** 对某人宽厚
soft drink *n* [c] 软性饮料
soft drugs *n* [*pl*] 软毒品
soften ['sɔfn] **I** *vt* **1** [+ *food*] 使变软 **2** [+ *impact, blow*] 使缓和 **3** [+ *position, attitude*] 使软化 **4** [+ *voice, expression*] 使柔和 **II** *vi* **1** (*also:* ***soften up***) [*food, material* +] 变软 **2** [*position, attitude* +] 变缓和 **3** [*voice, expression* +] 变温和
❑**soften up** **I** *vt* (喻) [+ *person*] 使软化 **II** *vi* [*food, material* +] 变软
softly ['sɔftlɪ] *adv* **1** (*gently*) 轻轻地 **2** (*quietly*) 温柔地
softness ['sɔftnɪs] *n* [U] [*of hair, skin*] 柔性
software ['sɔftwɛə(r)] *n* [U] 软件
soggy ['sɔgɪ] *adj* [+ *food*] 水份太多的; [+ *clothes*] 湿透的 ♦**to go soggy** 受潮
soil [sɔɪl] **I** *n* **1** [c/U] (*earth*) 土壤 **2** [U] (*territory*) 领土 **II** *vt* (*make dirty*) 弄脏
solar ['səulə(r)] *adj* 太阳的
solar power *n* [U] 太阳能
solar system *n* [c] 太阳系
sold [səuld] *pt, pp of* **sell**
soldier ['səuldʒə(r)] *n* [c] 士兵
❑**soldier on** *vi* 顽强地坚持下去
sold out *adj* [+ *tickets*] 卖光的; [+ *concert, show*] 客满的 ♦**to be sold out of sth** 某物全部卖光了
sole [səul] **I** *n* **1** [c] [*of foot, shoe*] 底 **2** [c/U] (*pl* **sole**) (*fish*) 鳎鱼 **II** *adj* **1** (*only*) [+ *aim, purpose, reason*] 惟一的 **2** (*exclusive*) [+ *ownership, responsibility*] 专有的
solely ['səullɪ] *adv* 惟一地 ♦**I will hold you solely responsible** 我要你个人负责
solemn ['sɔləm] *adj* **1** [+ *person, expression*] 一本正经的 **2** [+ *music*] 庄严的 **3** [+ *promise, agreement*] 郑重的
solicitor [sə'lɪsɪtə(r)] [英] *n* [c] 律师
solid ['sɔlɪd] **I** *adj* **1** (*not soft*) 坚实的 **2** (*without gaps*) 紧密的 **3** (*not liquid*) 固体的 **4** (*reliable*) [+ *person*] 可信赖的; [+ *advice, experience*] 确实的; [+ *evidence, information*] 有根据的 **5** (*strong*) [+ *structure*] 牢固的 **6** (*unbroken*) [+ *months, years*] 整整的 **7** (*pure*) [+ *gold, oak etc*] 纯质的 **II** *adv* ♦**I read for 2 hours solid** 我阅读了整整两个小时 **III** *n* [c] 固体 **IV** **solids** *n* [*pl*] (*food*) 非流食
solidarity [sɔlɪ'dærɪtɪ] *n* [U] 团结一致 ♦**to show solidarity (with sb)** 显示(同某人)站在一起
solitary ['sɔlɪtərɪ] *adj* **1** [+ *person, animal, life*] 孤僻的 **2** [+ *activity*] 单独的 **3** (*single*) 无伴的
solitude ['sɔlɪtju:d] *n* [U] 独处 ♦**to**

live in solitude 离群索居

solo ['səuləu] **I** *n* [c] (*piece of music*) 独奏; (*song*) 独唱; (*dance*) 独舞 **II** *adj* [+ *flight, album, career*] 单独的 **III** *adv* [*fly, play, perform* +] 单独地

soloist ['səuləuɪst] *n* [c] (*instrumentalist*) 独奏演员; (*singer*) 独唱演员

soluble ['sɔljubl] *adj* 可溶的

solution [sə'luːʃən] *n* [c] **1** (*to problem*) 解决方案 **2** (*to crossword, riddle*) 答案 **3** (*liquid*) 溶液

solve [sɔlv] *vt* **1** [+ *mystery, case*] 破解 **2** [+ *problem*] 解决 **3** [+ *puzzle, riddle*] 解答

solvent ['sɔlvənt] **I** *adj* [商] 有偿付能力的 **II** *n* [c/u] [化] 溶剂

Somali [sə'mɑːlɪ] **I** *adj* 索马里的 **II** *n* [c] (*person*) 索马里人

Somalia [sə'mɑːlɪə] *n* 索马里

sombre (美 **somber**) ['sɔmbə(r)] *adj* **1** [+ *colour, place*] 暗淡的 **2** [+ *person, mood, expression*] 忧郁的

✪ **some**

KEYWORD

[sʌm] *adj*

1 (*a little, a few*) 一些 ♦**some milk/books** 一些牛奶/书 ♦**would you like some wine?** 你来点葡萄酒吗？ ♦**we've got some time but not much** 我们还有些时间，但不太多了 ♦**there must be some steps we can take** 我们一定能采取些什么措施

2 (*certain, in contrasts*) 某些 ♦**some people say that ...** 有些人说… ♦**some people hate fish, while others love it** 有些人讨厌鱼，而有些人喜欢

3 (*unspecified*) ♦**some (or other)** 某一 ♦**he was asking for some book (or other)** 他要某本书 ♦**some woman was asking for you** 有位女士找你 ♦**some day** 某天 ♦**we'll meet again some day** 有一天我们会再见面的 ♦**shall we meet some day next week?** 我们在下个星期的某天见面好吗？

4 (*considerable*) 相当的

5 [非正式] (*emphatic*) 了不得的 ♦**that was some party!** 那个聚会好棒！

III *pron* (*a certain amount, certain number*) 一些 ♦**I've got some** 我有一些 ♦**there was/were some left** 还剩下一些 ♦**some of it/them** 它的一部分/他们中的一些 ♦**some of the play was good** 戏剧中的某些部分是好的 ♦**could I have some of that cheese?** 给我点儿那种奶酪好吗？ ♦**I've read some of the book** 那本书我读了一些

IV *adv*

1 (*approximately*) ♦**some 10 people** 大约10人

2 [美] (*to a degree*) 一点儿 ♦**we can walk some** 我们可以走一走

somebody ['sʌmbədɪ] *pron* = **someone**

somehow ['sʌmhau] *adv* (*in some way*) 不知怎样地

someone ['sʌmwʌn] *pron* 某人 ♦**there's someone coming** 有人来了 ♦**I saw someone in the garden** 我看见花园里有人 ♦**someone else** 别人

someplace ['sʌmpleɪs] [美] *adv* = **somewhere**

✪ **something** ['sʌmθɪŋ] *pron* 某事物 ♦**let's do something nice for your birthday** 咱们得好好过过你的生日 ♦**there was obviously something wrong** 显然有些事情不对劲 ♦**something to do** 有事要做 ♦**something else** 其他事情 ♦**would you like a sandwich or something?** 你要来点三明治或其他什么东西吗？ ♦**it's something of a mystery** 这是件神秘的事 ♦**they make up something like two-thirds of the population** 他们占了差不多三分之二的人口

sometime ['sʌmtaɪm] *adv* 某个时候

> 请勿将**sometimes** 和 **sometime** 混淆。**sometimes** 表示某事物只发生在某些时候，而不是总是发生。*Do you visit your sister? – Sometimes.... Sometimes I wish I still lived in Australia.* **sometimes** 还可以表示某事物发生在特定情况下，而不是在任何情况下都

会发生。*Sometimes they stay for a week, sometimes just for the weekend.*
sometime 表示未来或过去某个不确定或未指明的时间。*(Can I come and see you sometime?…He started his new job sometime last month.)*

sometimes ['sʌmtaɪmz] *adv* 有时 📖 用法参见 **sometime**

somewhat ['sʌmwɔt] *adv* 有点 ♦ **somewhat to my surprise** 让我有点奇怪的是

somewhere ['sʌmwɛə(r)] *adv* (*place*) 在某处 ♦ **I need somewhere to live** 我需要找个地方住 ♦ **I must have lost it somewhere** 我一定把它丢在哪儿了 ♦ **it's somewhere in Italy** 这是意大利的某个地方 ♦ **let's go somewhere quiet** 我们去个安静的地方吧 ♦ **somewhere else** 别的地方 ♦ **to be getting somewhere** (*making progress*) 有些进展 ♦ **he's somewhere between 65 and 70** 他的年纪大约在65至70之间

✪ **son** [sʌn] *n* [c] 儿子

song [sɔŋ] *n* **1** [c] 歌曲 **2** [c] [*of bird*] 鸣叫 **3** [u] (*singing*) 唱歌 ♦ **to be on song** [英] [*sportsperson* +] 处于良好竞技状态

son-in-law ['sʌnɪnlɔː] (*pl* **sons-in-law**) *n* [c] 女婿

✪ **soon** [suːn] *adv* **1** (*in a short time*) 不久 ◊ *It will soon be Christmas.* 不久圣诞节就要到了。**2** (*a short time later*) 很快 ◊ *I soon forgot about our conversation.* 我很快就忘了我们的谈话内容。**3** (*early*) 早 ◊ *It's too soon to talk about leaving.* 谈离开的事还太早。♦ **soon afterwards** 不久后 ♦ **as soon as** 一…就… ♦ **quite soon** 很快 ♦ **how soon?** 多快？♦ **see you soon!** 再见！

sooner ['suːnə(r)] *adv* ♦ **I would sooner ...** 我宁愿… ♦ **sooner or later** 迟早 ♦ **the sooner the better** 越快越好 ♦ **no sooner said than done** 说到做到 ♦ **no sooner had we left than ...** 我们一离开就…

soothe [suːð] *vt* **1** [+ *person, animal*] 使…平静 **2** [+ *pain*] 使…缓和

soothing ['suːðɪŋ] *adj* **1** [+ *ointment*] 镇痛的 **2** [+ *words, manner*] 令人安慰的 **3** [+ *music, bath*] 令人心旷神怡的

sophisticated [sə'fɪstɪkeɪtɪd] *adj* **1** [+ *person*] 老于世故的; [+ *lifestyle, taste*] 高雅时髦的 **2** [+ *machinery, system*] 精密的

sophomore ['sɔfəmɔː(r)] [美] *n* [c] 二年级学生

soprano [sə'prɑːnəu] *n* [c] (*woman, girl*) 女高音歌手; (*boy*) 男童声最高音歌手

sorbet ['sɔːbeɪ] [英] *n* [c/u] 果汁冰糕

sordid ['sɔːdɪd] *adj* **1** [+ *place*] 污秽的 **2** [+ *behaviour*] 卑鄙的

sore [sɔː(r)] **I** *adj* **1** (*painful*) 痛的 **2** [美:非正式] (*angry*) 恼火的 **II** *n* [c] 痛处 ♦ **it's a sore point (with him)** 这是(他的一个)痛处 ♦ **to be sore about sth** [美:非正式] 因某事生气 ♦ **to be sore at sb** [美:非正式] 生某人的气

sorely ['sɔːlɪ] *adv* **1** ♦ **to be sorely tempted (to do sth)** 极想(做某事) **2** ♦ **he'll be sorely missed** 人们会非常想念他

sorrow ['sɔrəu] **I** *n* [c] 悲伤 **II sorrows** *n* [*pl*] 烦恼

sorry ['sɔrɪ] *adj* **1** (*regretful*) 懊悔的 **2** (*wretched*) [+ *condition, excuse*] 拙劣的 ♦ **(I'm) sorry!** (*apology*) 对不起！♦ **sorry?** (*pardon?*) 请再讲一遍 ♦ **to feel sorry for sb** 对某人表示同情 ♦ **to be sorry about sth** 对某事表示歉意 ♦ **I'm sorry if I offended you** 如果我冒犯了你，我很抱歉 ♦ **I'm sorry to hear that ...** 听到…我很伤心 ♦ **a sorry sight** 悲惨景象

✪ **sort** [sɔːt] **I** *n* **1** [c] ♦ **sort (of)** 种类 ◊ *What sort of school did you go to?* 你去了哪种学校？◊ *What sort do you want?* 你要哪一种？**2** [c] (*make, brand*) [*of coffee, car etc*] 品牌 **3** [s] (*person*) 人 ◊ *He seemed to be just the right sort for the job.* 他看起来是做这份工作的合适人选。**II** *vt* **1** (*arrange*) [+ *papers, mail, belongings*] 把…分类 ◊ *Minnie was alone in the post office, sorting mail.* 明妮独自在邮局，将邮件分类。

2 (*separate*) 分开 ◊ *The students are sorted into three ability groups.* 将学生按能力分成3个组。3 [非正式] (*solve*) [+ *problem*] 解决 ◊ *These problems have now been sorted.* 这些问题已经被解决了。4 [计算机] 整理 ♦ **sort of** [非正式] 有点儿 ◊ *It's a sort of yellowish colour.* 有点儿发黄的颜色。♦ **all sorts of** 各种不同的 ♦ **a career/an education of sorts** 不怎么样的职业/教育
❑ **sort out** *vt* 1 (*separate*) 区别 ◊ *the difficulty of trying to sort out fact from fiction* 区别事实与虚构的困难
2 (*solve*) [+ *problem*] 解决

SOS [ɛsəu'ɛs] *n* 紧急求救

so-so ['səusəu] [非正式] **I** *adj* (*in quality*) 马马虎虎的 **II** *adv* ♦ **'How are you?' – 'So-so.'** "你好吗？" "还凑合。"

sought [sɔːt] *pt, pp of* **seek**

soul [səul] *n* 1 [c] [宗] 灵魂 2 [s] (喻) 精力 3 [c] (*person*) 人 4 [u] [音] 爵士灵歌 ♦ **I didn't see a soul** 我一个人都没看见 ♦ **poor soul** 可怜的人

✪ **sound** [saund] **I** *adj* 1 (*healthy*) 健康的 ◊ *My heart is basically sound.* 我的心脏基本上是健康的。2 (*not damaged*) [+ *building*] 完好无损的 ◊ *The house was surprisingly sound after the explosion.* 爆炸发生后，这所房子令人吃惊地完好无损。3 (*sensible*) [+ *advice*] 明智的
4 (*safe*) [+ *investment*] 可靠的
5 (*reliable, thorough*) 牢固的 ◊ *a sound theoretical foundation* 牢固的理论基础 6 (*valid*) [+ *argument, policy, claim*] 合理的 ◊ *His argument is basically sound.* 他的论点基本上是合理的。**II** *adv* ♦ **sound asleep** 酣睡 **III** *n* 1 [c] (*noise*) 声音 ◊ *the sound of footsteps* 脚步声 2 [s] (*volume*) (*on TV, radio etc*) 音量 ◊ *Morris turned down the sound.* 莫里斯把音量调小了。3 [u] [物] 声 ◊ *twice the speed of sound* 声速的两倍 **IV** *vt* [+ *alarm, bell*] 敲响 ◊ *Sound the alarm!* 敲警钟！ **V** *vi* 1 [*alarm, bell* +] 响 ◊ *The buzzer sounded in Daniel's office.* 丹尼尔办公室的门铃响了。2 (*seem*) 听起来 ◊ *She sounded a bit worried.* 她听起来有点担心。♦ **to be of sound mind** 心理健康的 ♦ **to make a sound** 出声 ♦ **I don't like the sound of that** 我不喜欢那种语气 ♦ **that sounds like an explosion** 听起来像是爆炸声的 ♦ **she sounds like the Queen** (*in voice, manner*) 她的语气听上去像是女皇 ♦ **that sounds like a great idea** 这主意听起来妙极了 ♦ **it sounds as if ...** 听起来似乎…
❑ **sound off** [非正式] *vi* ♦ **to sound off (about sth)** (就某事) 夸夸其谈
❑ **sound out** *vt* [+ *person*] 试探

soundly ['saundlɪ] *adv* 1 [*sleep* +] 酣畅地 2 [*be based* +] 稳固地
3 [*defeat* +] 彻底地

soundtrack ['saundtræk] *n* [c] 声道

soup [suːp] *n* [c/u] 汤

sour ['sauə(r)] **I** *adj* 1 (*bitter-tasting*) 酸的 2 [+ *milk*] 酸的 3 (*bad-tempered*) 愠怒的 **II** *vt* [+ *relationship, attitude*] 使恶化 **II** *vi* [*relationship, attitude* +] 变坏 ♦ **to go** *or* **turn sour** [*milk, wine* +] 变馊; [*relationship* +] 变糟 ♦ **it's sour grapes** 这是酸葡萄

source [sɔːs] *n* [c] 1 [*of money, resources, energy*] 来源 2 (*person*) 消息提供者 3 (*book*) 原始资料 4 [*of river*] 源头 5 [*of problem, anxiety*] 根源

✪ **south** [sauθ] **I** *n* [s/u] 南方 **II** *adj* 南部的 **III** *adv* 向南方 ♦ **the south of France** 法国南部 ♦ **to the south** 以南 ♦ **the south wind** 南风
♦ **south of ...** 在…以南 ◊ *It's 15 miles or so south of Glasgow.* 它位于格拉斯哥以南15英里左右。

South Africa *n* 南非

South African I *adj* 南非的 **II** *n* [c] (*person*) 南非人

South America *n* 南美洲

South American I *adj* 南美洲的 **II** *n* [c] (*person*) 南美洲人

south-east [sauθ'iːst] **I** *n* 东南 **II** *adj* 东南的 **III** *adv* 向东南

South-East Asia *n* 东南亚

south-eastern [sauθ'iːstən] *adj* 东南的

southern ['sʌðən] *adj* 南方的 ♦ **the southern hemisphere** 南半球

South Korea *n* 韩国

South Pole *n* ♦**the South Pole** 南极
southward(s) ['sauθwəd(z)] *adv* 向南
south-west [sauθ'wɛst] **I** *n* [s/u] 西南 **II** *adj* 西南的 **III** *adv* 向西南
south-western [sauθ'wɛstən] *adj* 西南的
souvenir [suːvə'nɪə(r)] *n* [c] 纪念品
sovereign ['sɔvrɪn] **I** *n* [c] [正式] (*king, queen*) 君主 **II** *adj* **1** [+ *state, country*] 独立自主的 **2** [+ *power, right*] 拥有最高权力的
sow [səu] (*pt* **sowed**, *pp* **sown**) *vt* **1** [+ *seeds*] 播种 **2** [+ *suspicion, doubts etc*] 传播
soy [sɔɪ] [美] *n* [u] 黄豆 [英 = **soya**]
soya ['sɔɪə] [英] *n* [u] 黄豆 [美 = **soy**]
soya bean [英] *n* [c] 黄豆 [美 = **soybean**]
soybean ['sɔɪbiːn] [美] *n* [c] 黄豆 [英 = **soya bean**]
soy sauce *n* [u] 酱油
spa [spɑː] *n* [c] **1** (*town*) 矿泉胜地 **2** [美] (*also:* ***health spa***) 美容健身院
space [speɪs] **I** *n* **1** [c/u] (*gap, place*) 空隙 **2** [c/u] (*room*) 空间 **3** [u] (*beyond Earth*) 太空 **II** *cpd* [复合词] 太空 **III** *vt* (*also:* ***space out***) [+ *text, visits*] 把…分隔开; [+ *payments*] 把…均匀分配 ♦**to clear a space for sth** 为某物腾地方 ♦**in a short space of time** (*from now*) 片刻后; (*in past*) 很快 ♦**(with)in the space of an hour** 在一小时内
spacecraft ['speɪskrɑːft] (*pl* **spacecraft**) *n* [c] 宇宙飞船
spaceship ['speɪsʃɪp] *n* = **spacecraft**
spacious ['speɪʃəs] *adj* 宽敞的
spade [speɪd] **I** *n* [c] **1** (*tool*) 锹 **2** (*child's*) 小铲 **II spades** *n* [*pl*] [纸牌] 黑桃
spaghetti [spə'gɛtɪ] *n* [u] 意大利面
Spain [speɪn] *n* 西班牙
spam [spæm] [计算机] *n* [u] 垃圾邮件
span [spæn] **I** *vt* **1** [+ *river, lake*] 横跨 **2** [+ *time*] 跨越 **II** *n* [c] **1** [*of wings*] 翼展 **2** [*of arch*] 跨度 **3** (*in time*) 一段时间
Spaniard ['spænjəd] *n* [c] 西班牙人
Spanish ['spænɪʃ] **I** *adj* 西班牙的 **II** *n* [u] (*language*) 西班牙语 **III the Spanish** *n* [*pl*] 西班牙人
spank [spæŋk] *vt* [+ *person, bottom*] 打
spanner ['spænə(r)] [英] *n* [c] 扳钳 [美 = **wrench**]
spare [spɛə(r)] **I** *adj* **1** (*free*) 多余的 **2** (*extra*) 备用的 **II** *n* [c] = **spare part III** *vt* **1** ♦**to spare sb the trouble/pain/details** 避免某人的麻烦/让某人知道详情 **2** (*make available*) 抽出 **3** (*afford to give*) 出让 **4** (*not harm*) 幸免 ♦**these two are going spare** 这两个是闲着的 ♦**to have time/money to spare** 有剩余的时间/金钱 ♦**to spare no expense** 不惜工本 ♦**I can spare (you) 5 minutes** 我能(为你)抽出5分钟
spare part *n* [c] 备件
spare time *n* [u] 业余时间
spark [spɑːk] **I** *n* [c] **1** (*from fire, electricity*) 火花 **2** [*of wit, interest, imagination*] 一点儿 **II** *vt* (*also:* ***spark off***) 触发
spark plug *n* [c] 火花塞
sparkle ['spɑːkl] **I** *n* [u] 光亮 **II** *vi* **1** [*diamonds* +] 闪耀 **2** [*water* +] 闪闪发光 **3** [*eyes* +] 发亮
sparkling water *n* [u] 苏打水
sparkling wine *n* [u] 汽酒
sparrow ['spærəu] *n* [c] 麻雀
sparse [spɑːs] *adj* **1** [+ *vegetation, traffic*] 稀少的 **2** [+ *hair*] 稀疏的
spasm ['spæzəm] *n* **1** [c/u] [医] 抽搐 **2** [c] [*of anger etc*] 一阵
spat [spæt] **I** *pt, pp of* **spit II** *n* [c] [美] (*quarrel*) 争端
spate [speɪt] *n* ♦**a spate of** 大量 ♦**to be in spate** [*river* +] 猛涨
spatula ['spætjulə] *n* [c] **1** [烹饪] 刮刀 **2** [医] 压舌板
✪**speak** [spiːk] (*pt* **spoke**, *pp* **spoken**) **I** *vt* **1** [+ *language*] 讲 ◊ *They both spoke English.* 他们两个都讲英语。**2** ♦**to speak the truth** 说实话 **II** *vi* **1** 讲话 ◊ *Simon opened his mouth to speak.* 西蒙开口讲话了。**2** (*make a speech*) 演说 ◊ *The Prime Minister spoke to the nation on television.* 总理在电视上向全国人民作演说。♦**they're not speaking** 他们不再讲话了 ♦**she's not speaking to me** 她不再和我讲话了 ♦**to speak of** *or* **about sb/**

sth 提到某人/某事 ♦**to speak to sb about sth** 和某人谈某事 ♦**to speak well** *or* **highly of sb** 赞扬某人 ♦**to speak ill of sb** 说某人的坏话 ♦**no food/money to speak of** 不值一提的食物/金钱 ♦**so to speak** 也就是说 ♦**generally/technically** *etc* **speaking** 总的/从技术上{等}来说 ♦**speaking of ...** 提到… ♦**speaking as a parent/teacher, ...** 作为家长/老师来说…

❑**speak for** *vt* [不可拆分][+ *other people*] 代表…讲话◊ *I think I can speak for everyone here when I express my sincere apologies.* 我想我能够代表这里的所有人表示由衷的歉意。♦**it speaks for itself** 这不言而喻 ♦**speak for yourself!** [非正式]谈你自己的意见! ♦**that picture is already spoken for** (*reserved*) 那幅画已经有人要了
❑**speak out** *vi* 畅所欲言
❑**speak up** *vi* ♦**speak up!** 大声点儿!

speaker ['spiːkə(r)] *n* [C] **1** (*in debate etc*) 演讲者 **2** (*also:* ***loudspeaker***) 扬声器 **3** ♦**the Speaker** (*in UK House of Parliament*) 下议院议长; (*in US House of Representatives*) 众议院议长 ♦**a French/Russian speaker** 讲法语/俄语的人

speaking ['spiːkɪŋ] **I** *n* [U] (*in debate, meeting*) 演讲 **II** *adj* ♦**Italian-speaking people** 讲意大利语的人士 ♦**to be on speaking terms (with sb)** (和某人)关系好

spear [spɪə(r)] **I** *n* [C] (*weapon*) 矛 **II** *vt* [+ *person*] 用矛刺; [+ *object*] 叉

✪**special** ['spɛʃl] **I** *adj* **1** (*important*) 特别的◊ *We only use these plates on special occasions.* 我们只在特别场合才用这些碟子。**2** (*different*) 异常的◊ *Did you notice anything special about him?* 你有没有注意到他有什么异常的地方? **3** (*particular*) 专门的◊ *To marry a foreigner, special permission has to be obtained.* 与外国人结婚,须经专门许可。**4** (*extra*) [+ *effort, favour*] 额外的◊ *a law which provides special assistance to those with large families* 为大家庭提供额外帮助的一项法律 **II** *n* [C] **1** (*in restaurant*) 特色菜 **2** [电视, 广播]特别节目 **3** (*train*) 专列 ♦**to take special care** 格外小心 ♦**it's nothing special** 没什么特别的

special delivery *n* ♦**by special delivery** 用特快专递

special effects [电影] *n* [*pl*] 特技效果

specialist ['spɛʃəlɪst] *n* [C] **1** (*expert*) ♦**a specialist in** *or* **on** 一位…方面的专家 **2** [医]专科医生

speciality [spɛʃɪ'ælɪtɪ] (美 **specialty** ['spɛʃəltɪ]) *n* [C] **1** (*food*) 特制品; (*product*) 特产 **2** (*subject area*) 专业

specialize ['spɛʃəlaɪz] *vi* ♦**to specialize in** [+ *subject*] 专攻; [+ *food*] 擅长于

specially ['spɛʃlɪ] *adv* **1** (*specifically*) 专门地 **2** [非正式](*particularly*) 尤其

special needs *n* [*pl*] ♦**children with special needs** [英]有特殊需要的儿童

special offer [商] *n* [C] 特价品

specialty ['spɛʃəltɪ] [美] *n* = **speciality**

species ['spiːʃiːz] *n* [C] 种

specific [spə'sɪfɪk] *adj* **1** (*fixed*) 特定的 **2** (*exact*) 具体的 **3** ♦**to be specific to** 对…特有的

specifically [spə'sɪfɪklɪ] *adv* **1** (*specially*) 特别地; (*exclusively*) 特定的 **2** (*exactly*) 明确的 ♦**(more) specifically** (更)具体地说

specify ['spɛsɪfaɪ] *vt* 指定 ♦**unless otherwise specified** 除非额外注明

specimen ['spɛsɪmən] *n* [C] **1** [*of plant, animal*] 标本 **2** [*of handwriting, signature*] 实例 **3** [*of blood, urine*] 抽样

speck [spɛk] *n* [C] [*of dirt, dust*] 斑点 ◊ *a tiny speck of dust* 一小粒灰尘

spectacle ['spɛktəkl] **I** *n* **1** [C] (*scene*) 奇观 **2** [C/U] (*event, performance*) 场面 **II spectacles** *n* [*pl*] (*glasses*) 眼镜

spectacular [spɛk'tækjulə(r)] **I** *adj* [+ *view, scenery*] 壮丽的; [+ *rise, growth*] 惊人的◊ *a spectacular rise in house prices* 房价的暴涨; [+ *success, result*] 引人注目的 **II** *n* [C] (*performance*) 场面浩大的表演

spectator [spɛk'teɪtə(r)] *n* [C] 观众

spectrum ['spɛktrəm] (*pl* **spectra** ['spɛktrə]) *n* [c] **1** (*of colours, radio waves*) 谱 **2** [*of opinion, emotion etc*] 范围

speculate ['spɛkjuleɪt] *vi* **1** [经济] 投机 **2** ♦**to speculate (about)** 猜测(关于…) ♦**to speculate that ...** 推测…

speech [spiːtʃ] *n* **1** [c] (*formal talk*) 演说 **2** [u] (*faculty*) 说话能力 **3** [s] (*manner of speaking*) 说话方式 **4** [u] (*spoken language*) 口语 **5** [c] [戏剧] 台词

speechless ['spiːtʃlɪs] *adj* 讲不出话的 ♦**to be speechless with rage/astonishment** 气/惊讶得讲不出话来

speed [spiːd] (*pt, pp* **sped**) **I** *n* **1** [c/u] (*rate, promptness*) 速度 **2** [u] (*fast movement*) 快速 **3** [c] (*rapidity*) 迅速 **4** [c] [*of typing, shorthand*] 速度 **II** *vi* **1** ♦**to speed along/by** *etc* 沿着{等}…迅速行进 **2** (*drive too fast*) 超速行驶 ♦**at full** *or* **top speed** 以最高速度 ♦**at a speed of 70km/h** 以时速70公里 ♦**a five-speed gearbox** 5速变速箱

❑**speed up** (*pt, pp* **speeded up**) **I** *vi* **1** [*car, runner etc* +] 加快速度 **2** [*process* +] 加速 **II** *vt* 加快…的速度

speedboat ['spiːdbəut] *n* [c] 快艇

speeding ['spiːdɪŋ] [法] *n* [u] 超速行驶

speed limit [法] *n* [c] 速度极限

speedy ['spiːdɪ] *adj* [+ *recovery, return, conclusion*] 迅速的; [+ *sale, trial*] 快的

spell [spɛl] (*pt, pp* **spelled** *or* **spelt**) **I** *n* [c] **1** (*period*) 一段时间 **2** (*also:* ***magic spell***) 咒语 **II** *vt* **1** [+ *word*] 用字母拼 **2** [+ *disaster, trouble*] 招致 ♦**to cast a spell on sb** [*witch* +] 用咒语迷惑某人; (喻) 迷住某人 ♦**to be/fall under sb's spell** 被某人迷住 ♦**he can't spell** 他不会拼写

❑**spell out** *vt* **1** [+ *feelings, intentions etc*] 详细说明 **2** [+ *word*] 把…的字母拼写出

spelling ['spɛlɪŋ] *n* **1** [c] [*of word*] 拼法 **2** [u] (*ability to spell*) 拼写 ♦**spelling mistake** 拼写错误

spelt [spɛlt] *pt, pp of* **spell**

✪**spend** [spɛnd] (*pt, pp* **spent**) *vt* **1** [+ *money*] 花费 ◊ *I spent a hundred pounds on clothes.* 我花了100英镑买衣服。**2** [+ *time, life*] 度过 ◊ *I have spent all my life in this town.* 我在这个镇上度过了一生。♦**to spend time/energy on sth** 在某事上花时间/精力 ♦**to spend time/energy doing sth** 花时间/精力做某事 ♦**to spend the night in a hotel** 在旅馆度过一晚

spending ['spɛndɪŋ] *n* [u] 开支

spent [spɛnt] **I** *pt, pp of* **spend** **II** *adj* **1** [+ *cartridge, bullets*] 失去效能的 **2** [+ *matches*] 已用过的

sperm [spəːm] *n* **1** [c] (*cell*) 精子 **2** [u] (*fluid*) 精液

sphere [sfɪə(r)] *n* [c] **1** 球体 **2** (*area*) 领域

spice [spaɪs] **I** *n* [c/u] 香料 **II** *vt* ♦**to spice sth (up) with** (喻) 用…为某物增添趣味

spicy ['spaɪsɪ] *adj* [+ *food*] 辛辣的

spider ['spaɪdə(r)] *n* [c] 蜘蛛 ♦**spider's web** 蜘蛛网

spike [spaɪk] **I** *n* [c] **1** (*of metal*) 尖钉 **2** (喻) 尖状物 **II spikes** *n* [*pl*] [体育] (*shoes*) 钉鞋 **III** *vt* [非正式] [+ *drink*] 搀加

spike heels [美] *n* [*pl*] 细高跟鞋 [英 = **stilettos**]

spill [spɪl] (*pt, pp* **spilt** *or* **spilled**) **I** *vt* [+ *liquid*] 使溢出 **II** *vi* [*liquid* +] 溢出 ♦**to spill sth on/over sth** 将某物洒在某物上

❑**spill out** *vi* **1** [*people* +] 蜂拥 **2** [*things* +] 流出 **3** (*from container*) 散落

❑**spill over** *vi* **1** [*liquid* +] 溢出 **2** ♦**spill over into** [*conflict, tension* +] 发展成

spin [spɪn] (*pt* **spun, span**, *pp* **spun**) **I** *n* **1** [c/u] [*of wheel etc*] 旋转 **2** [s] (*in car*) 兜风 **3** [s] [航空] 急剧下降 **4** [s] (*interpretation*) 添油加醋 **5** [u] [贬: 政治] 添油加醋 **6** [c/u] [*of ball*] 旋转 **II** *vt* **1** [+ *wheel, ball, coin*] 使…旋转 **2** [+ *wool, cotton*] 纺; **3** [英] (*also:* ***spin-dry***) 甩干 **III** *vi* **1** [*person* +] 转身 **2** [*wheel, ball etc* +] 打转 **3** (*make thread*) 纺纱 ♦**my head's spinning** 我头昏脑胀 ♦**to spin a yarn** 编造奇闻轶事

❑**spin out** *vt* [+ *speech etc*] 拖长时间

spinach ['spɪnɪtʃ] *n* [U] 菠菜

spinal ['spaɪnl] *adj* 脊柱的

spine [spaɪn] *n* [C] **1** (*backbone*) 脊柱 **2** (*on plant, animal*) 刺 **3** [*of book*] 书脊

spiral ['spaɪrəl] **I** *n* [C] 螺旋 **II** *vi* **1** ♦**to spiral (upwards)** [*smoke* +] 盘旋(上升) **2** [*prices etc* +] 不断急剧上升 **3** ♦**to spiral downwards** [*prices, rates* +] 不断急剧下降; [*person* +] 每况愈下 ♦**a spiral of debt** 一连串债务 ♦**a downward spiral** 一连串的倒霉事

spire ['spaɪə(r)] *n* [C] 塔尖

spirit ['spɪrɪt] **I** *n* **1** [C] (*soul*) 精神 **2** [C] (*ghost*) 幽灵 **3** [U] (*energy, courage*) 勇气 **4** [S] [*of law, agreement*] 精神实质 **5** [S] (*frame of mind*) 心态 **II** *vt* ♦**to be spirited away** 被迅速而神秘地带走 **III spirits** *n* [*pl*] **1** [英] (*whisky etc*) 烈酒 [美 = **liquor**] **2** (*frame of mind*) 情绪 ♦**community spirit** 社区精神 ♦**in good spirits** 心境好的

spiritual ['spɪrɪtjuəl] **I** *adj* **1** (*of the spirit*) 精神上的 **2** (*religious*) 宗教的 **II** *n* [C] (*song*) 灵歌

spit [spɪt] (*pt, pp* **spat**) **I** *n* **1** [C] (*for roasting*) 烤肉叉 **2** [U] (*saliva*) 唾液 **II** *vi* **1** [*person, animal* +] 吐唾液 **2** [*fire, cooking food* +] 乱崩 **3** ♦**it's spitting** [英] 天正下着毛毛雨 [美 = **sprinkle**] **III** *vt* [+ *water, food*] 吐出

❑**spit out** *vt* 吐出

spite [spaɪt] **I** *n* [U] 恶意 **II** *vt* 激怒 ♦**in spite of** 尽管 ♦**to do sth in spite of o.s.** 不由自主地做某事

spiteful ['spaɪtful] *adj* [+ *person, behaviour*] 怀有恶意的

splash [splæʃ] **I** *n* [C] **1** (*sound*) 溅泼声 **2** [*of liquid*] 少许 **3** [*of colour*] 斑点 **II** *int* 扑通 **III** *vt* 溅 **IV** *vi* **1** (*also:* ***splash about***) (*in sea*) 嬉水 **2** [*water, rain* +] 噼噼啪啪落下 ♦**to splash paint on the floor** 把油漆泼在地板上 ♦**to make a splash** [非正式: 喻] 引起轰动

❑**splash out** [英: 非正式] *vi* ♦**to splash out (on)** 大手大脚地花钱(在)

splendid ['splɛndɪd] *adj* **1** (*excellent*) [+ *idea, work*] 极好的 **2** (*impressive*) [+ *architecture, work of art*] 辉煌的

splendour (美 **splendor**) ['splɛndə(r)] **I** *n* [U] 壮观 **II splendours** *n* [*pl*] 辉煌

splinter ['splɪntə(r)] **I** *n* [C] **1** [*of wood*] 刺 **2** [*of glass*] 碎片 **II** *vi* 裂成碎片

split [splɪt] (*pt, pp* **split**) **I** *n* **1** [C] (*crack, tear*) 裂缝 **2** [S] (*division*) 划分 **3** [C] (*disagreement*) 分裂 **II** *vt* **1** (*divide*) 把…划分 **2** (*cause to divide*) [+ *party, group*] 使分裂 **3** (*share equally*) [+ *work, profits*] 平分 **III** *vi* **1** ♦**to split (into)** (*divide*) 划分(成) **2** [*party, group* +] 分裂 **3** (*crack, tear*) [*wood, garment* +] 裂开 ♦**to do the splits** 劈叉 ♦**let's split the difference** 让我们分担差额吧 ♦**to split hairs** 在鸡毛蒜皮上争辩

❑**split up I** *vi* **1** [*couple, group* +] 分手 **II** *vt* 把…分割

splutter ['splʌtə(r)] *vi* **1** [*engine, flame* +] 发噼啪声 **2** [*person* +] 结结巴巴地说 **3** (*sound angry*) 急促而含糊地说

spoil [spɔɪl] (*pt, pp* **spoiled** *or* **spoilt**) **I** *vt* **1** (*damage*) 损害 **2** [+ *child*] 溺爱 **3** (*indulge*) [+ *person*] 宠爱 **4** [英] [+ *ballot paper*] 作废 **II** *vi* ♦**to be spoiling for a fight** 一心想打架 ♦**to spoil o.s.** 犒劳自己

spoilt [spɔɪlt] **I** *pt, pp of* **spoil II** *adj* **1** [+ *child*] 宠坏的 **2** [英] [+ *ballot paper*] 作废的

spoke [spəuk] **I** *pt of* **speak II** *n* [C] [*of wheel*] 辐条

spoken ['spəukn] *pp of* **speak**

spokesman ['spəuksmən] (*pl* **spokesmen**) *n* [C] 男发言人

spokesperson ['spəukspəːsn] (*pl* **spokespeople**) *n* [C] 发言人

spokeswoman ['spəukswumən] (*pl* **spokeswomen**) *n* [C] 女发言人

sponge [spʌndʒ] **I** *n* **1** [U] (*substance*) (*man-made, natural*) 海绵 **2** [C] (*for washing*) 海绵擦 **3** [C/U] (*also:* ***sponge cake***) 松糕 **II** *vt* (*wipe*) 用海绵擦 **III** *vi* ♦**to sponge off** *or* **on sb** [非正式] 白吃白喝某人

sponsor ['spɔnsə(r)] **I** *n* [C] **1** [*of player, event, TV programme*] 赞助者

2 [英] (*for charity*) 出资者 3 (*for application, bill in parliament etc*) 倡议者 II *vt* 1 [+ *player, event, TV programme*] 赞助 2 [英] (*for charity*) 赞助 3 [+ *proposal, bill etc*] 倡议

sponsorship ['spɔnsəʃɪp] *n* [U] 资助

spontaneous [spɔn'teɪnɪəs] *adj* 1 (*unplanned*) 自然而然的 2 [+ *explosion, miscarriage*] 自然的

spooky ['spuːkɪ] [非正式] *adj* 阴森森的

spoon [spuːn] I *n* [C] 匙 II *vt* ♦ **to spoon sth into/onto/over** 用匙将某物放入/放在…上/浇在…上

spoonful ['spuːnful] *n* [C] ♦ **a spoonful of** 一匙

sport [spɔːt] I *n* 1 [C] (*particular game*) 运动 2 [U] (*generally*) 体育 II *vt* [+ *clothes*] 穿着; [+ *jewellery*] 戴着 ♦ **she's a (good) sport** [过时] 她是一个大度的人

sporting ['spɔːtɪŋ] *adj* 1 [+ *event etc*] 体育运动的 2 [过时] (*generous*) [+ *act, gesture*] 大度的 ♦ **to have a sporting chance of doing sth** 有可能做某事

sport jacket [美] *n* [C] 粗呢夹克 [英 = **sports jacket**]

sports car *n* [C] 跑车

sports jacket [英] *n* [C] 粗呢夹克 [美 = **sport jacket**]

sportsman ['spɔːtsmən] (*pl* **sportsmen**) *n* [C] 男运动员

sportswear ['spɔːtswɛə(r)] *n* [U] 运动服

sportswoman ['spɔːtswumən] (*pl* **sportswomen**) *n* [C] 女运动员

sporty ['spɔːtɪ] *adj* 1 [+ *person*] 爱运动的 2 [+ *car*] 像赛车的

spot [spɔt] I *n* [C] 1 (*mark*) 斑点 2 (*dot*) 点 3 (*pimple*) 疵点 4 [*of rain*] 一滴 5 (*place*) 地点 6 [广播, 电视] 短小节目 7 ♦ **a spot of** [尤英] (*small amount*) [+ *lunch, activity*] 少量; [+ *trouble, bother*] 处境 II *vt* (*notice*) 发现 ♦ **on the spot** (*in that place*) 在现场; (*immediately*) 当场 ♦ **to be in a tight spot** [非正式] 处于困境中 ♦ **to put sb on the spot** 使某人处于难堪地位

spotless ['spɔtlɪs] *adj* 一尘不染的

spotlight ['spɔtlaɪt] I *n* [C] 1 (*on stage*) 聚光灯 2 (*in room*) 照明灯 II *vt* 使突出醒目

spouse [spaus] *n* [C] 配偶

sprain [spreɪn] I *vt* ♦ **to sprain one's ankle/wrist** 扭伤脚踝/手腕 II *n* [C] 扭伤

sprang [spræŋ] *pt of* **spring**

sprawl [sprɔːl] I *vi* 1 [*person* +] 伸开四肢躺/坐 2 [*place* +] 扩展 II *n* [U] ♦ **urban sprawl** 城镇漫无计划地扩展 ♦ **to send sb sprawling** 把某人摔趴在地上

spray [spreɪ] I *n* 1 [C/U] [*of water*] 水花 2 [C/U] (*in can*) 喷剂 3 [C] (*in garden*) 喷雾器 4 [C] [*of flowers*] 小枝 II *vt* 1 (*sprinkle*) [+ *liquid*] 喷; [+ *glass etc*] 向…溅射 2 (*with pesticide*) [+ *crops*] 向…喷杀虫剂 3 (*with paint*) 喷涂 4 [+ *bullets*] 向…扫射 III *vi* 1 [*liquid* +] 溅散 2 (*with pesticide*) 喷杀虫剂

spread [sprɛd] (*pt, pp* **spread**) I *n* 1 [S] (*increase*) 扩展 2 [S] (*range, distribution*) 各种 3 [C/U] (*on bread*) 涂抹酱 4 [C] [非正式] (*meal*) 盛宴 5 [C] [出版, 排版] 横贯两版的篇幅 II *vt* 1 ♦ **to spread sth on/over** 把某物摊在…上 2 [+ *butter, jam etc*] 涂 3 [+ *wings, arms, sails*] 张开 4 (*scatter*) 撒 5 (*distribute*) [+ *workload, wealth*] 分摊 6 (*distribute*) [+ *repayments, job losses*] 把…分期 7 [+ *disease*] 传播 III *vi* 1 [*news* +] 不胫而走; [*disease* +] 传播 2 [*liquid, gas, fire* +] 蔓延 ♦ **to spread bread/toast with butter** 把黄油抹在面包/烤面包上

❑ **spread out** I *vi* 1 (*move apart*) [*people, animals, vehicles* +] 散开 2 (*stretch out*) [*person* +] 伸开四肢 II *vt* (*arrange*) 摊开

spreadsheet ['sprɛdʃiːt] *n* [C] 电子表格

spree [spriː] *n* [C] ♦ **to go on a spending/drinking spree** 无节制地花钱/酗酒

spring [sprɪŋ] (*pt* **sprang**, *pp* **sprung**) I *n* 1 [C/U] (*season*) 春季 2 [C] (*wire coil*) 弹簧 3 [C] [*of water*] 泉 II *vi* 1 (*leap*) 跳 2 (*move suddenly*) 弹 III *vt* ♦ **to spring a leak** [*pipe etc* +] 出现裂缝 ♦ **in (the) spring** 在春季 ♦ **to walk with a spring in one's step** 轻快有力地走路 ♦ **to spring into**

action 迅速行动起来 ♦**to spring from** 起源于 ♦**he sprang the news on me** 他突然向我宣布了这条消息

❑**spring up** *vi* (*suddenly appear*) 突然出现

spring onion [英] *n* [c] 小葱 [美= **scallion**]

sprinkle ['sprɪŋkl] **I** *vt* **1** (*with liquid*) 洒 **2** (*with powder*) 撒 ♦**to sprinkle water on sth, sprinkle sth with water** 把水洒在某物上 **II** *vi* ♦**it's sprinkling** [美] 天正下着毛毛雨 [英= **spit**]

sprint [sprɪnt] **I** *n* [c] (*race*) 短跑 **II** *vi* 全速奔跑 ♦**to break into a sprint** 突然开始奔跑

sprinter ['sprɪntə(r)] *n* [c] 短跑运动员

sprout [spraut] **I** *vi* **1** (*produce shoots*) 发芽 **2** (*grow*) 长出 **II** *vt* [+ *hair, wings*] 长出 **III sprouts** *n* [*pl*] 球芽甘蓝

sprung [sprʌŋ] *pp of* **spring**

spun [spʌn] *pt, pp of* **spin**

spur [spəː(r)] **I** *n* **1** ♦**a spur to sth** 某物的刺激物 **2** [c] (*on rider's boot*) 靴刺 **II** *vt* ♦**to spur sb into (doing) sth** 激励某人去(做)某事 ♦**on the spur of the moment** 一时冲动之下

❑**spur on** *vt* 激励

spurt [spəːt] **I** *n* [c] **1** [*of blood etc*] 喷射 **2** [*of energy*] 迸发 **II** *vi* **1** ♦**to spurt from sth** [*blood, flame* +] 从某物中喷出 **2** ♦**to spurt up/along** [*person, thing* +] 突然加速 ♦**to put on a spurt** (*in race*) 全力冲刺; (*in work*) 全力以赴

spy [spaɪ] **I** *n* [c] 间谍 **II** *vi* **1** ♦**to spy on** (*watch*) 暗中监视 **2** (*get information about*) 刺探 **III** *vt* [文] (*notice*) 发现 **IV** *cpd* [复合词] **1** [+ *film, story*] 间谍 **2** [+ *satellite, plane*] 侦探 ♦**to spy for** 为…充当间谍

spying ['spaɪɪŋ] *n* [u] 当间谍

Sq (尤美 **Sq.**) *abbr* (= ***square***) (*in addresses*) 广场

sq. *abbr* = **square** 平方

squabble ['skwɔbl] **I** *vi* 发生口角 **II** *n* [c] 口角 ♦**to squabble with sb** 与某人发生口角

squad [skwɔd] *n* [c] **1** [军, 警察] 班 **2** [体育] 队

squadron ['skwɔdrn] *n* [c] **1** (*in air force, navy*) 中队 **2** (*in army*) 连

squander ['skwɔndə(r)] *vt* [+ *money, resources*] 浪费

square [skwɛə(r)] **I** *n* [c] **1** 正方形 **2** (*in town*) 广场 **3** [数] 平方 **4** [美] (*block of houses*) 街区 **5** [非正式, 过时] (*person*) 老古板 **II** *adj* (*in shape*) 正方形的 **III** *vt* **1** [数] 使自乘 **2** (*arrange*) 调正 **3** ♦**to square sth with sth** 使某事与某事一致 **4** ♦**to square sth with sb** [非正式] 就某事获得某人的许可 **IV** *vi* **1** ♦**to square with** 符合 ♦**we're back to square one** 我们又得从头来过 ♦**to be all square** [非正式] [*people* +] 扯平; [*match* +] 打平 ♦**a square meal** 一顿丰盛的饭菜 ♦**2 metres square** 2米见方 ♦**2 square metres** 2平方米

❑**square up** [英] *vi* (*settle bill, debt*) 结清 ♦**to square up with sb** 和某人结清账

squarely ['skwɛəlɪ] *adv* **1** (*directly*) [*fall, land etc* +] 正对着地 **2** (*fully*) [*face, confront* +] 直面地

square root *n* [c] 平方根

squash [skwɔʃ] **I** *n* **1** [u] [英] ♦**orange squash** 浓缩橙汁, 需加水再喝 **2** [c/u] [美] (*vegetable*) 南瓜 **3** [u] [体育] 壁球 **II** *vt* **1** (*crush*) 把…压碎 **2** ♦**to squash sb/sth into** 将某人/某物硬塞入 ♦**to squash sb/sth against** 将某人/某物挤到 ♦**to squash sth flat** 将某物压扁

squat [skwɔt] **I** *vi* **1** (*also:* ***squat down***) 蹲下 **2** (*be sitting*) 蹲坐 **3** (*on property*) 擅自占用 **II** *n* [c] (*illegally occupied building*) 擅自占用的建筑 **III** *adj* [+ *person*] 矮胖的; [+ *shape*] 低矮的

squatter ['skwɔtə(r)] *n* [c] 擅自占地者

squeak [skwiːk] **I** *vi* **1** [*door* +] 嘎吱作响 **2** [*mouse* +] 吱吱叫 **II** *n* [c] **1** [*of hinge*] 嘎吱声 **2** [*of mouse*] 吱吱声

❑**squeak by, squeak through** [非正式] *vi* 勉强通过

squeal [skwiːl] **I** *vi* **1** [*person* +] 发出长而尖的叫声 **2** [*brakes, tyres* +] 发

出尖锐刺耳声 **II** *n* [c] **1** [*of person*] 尖叫声 **2** [*of brakes, tyres*] 刺耳声

squeeze [skwi:z] **I** *n* [c] **1** [*of hand etc*] 紧握 **2** [经济] 银根紧缩 **II** *vt* **1** 用力捏 **2** ♦**to squeeze sth under/through sth** 将某物硬挤到某物下面/过某物 **III** *vi* ♦**to squeeze under/through sth** 硬挤到某物下面/过某物 ♦**to give sth a squeeze** 用力捏了捏某物 ♦**a squeeze of lemon** 一点榨出的柠檬汁

❑**squeeze out** *vt* **1** [+ *juice, paste etc*] 榨出 **2** (喻) (*exclude*) [+ *person*] 排挤出

squid [skwɪd] *n* [c/u] 鱿鱼

squint [skwɪnt] **I** *vi* 眯着眼看 **II** *n* [c] [医] 斜视

squirm [skwə:m] *vi* **1** (*wriggle*) 扭动 **2** (喻) (*with embarrassment*) 局促不安

squirrel ['skwɪrəl] *n* [c] 松鼠

squirt [skwə:t] **I** *vi* ♦**to squirt out** 喷射出 **II** *vt* ♦**to squirt sth into/onto sth** 将某物喷入某物/到某物上 **III** *n* [c] [*of liquid*] 喷流

Sr (尤美 **Sr.**) *abbr* (= ***senior***) 老

Sri Lanka [srɪ'læŋkə] *n* 斯里兰卡

St (尤美 **St.**) *abbr* **1** (= ***street***) 街 **2** (*pl* **SS**) (= ***saint***) 圣人

stab [stæb] **I** *vt* [+ *person*] 刺 **II** *vi* 戳 **III** *n* **1** [c] (*with knife etc*) 刺 **2** ♦**a stab of pain/pity/jealousy** 一阵疼痛/怜悯/嫉妒 **3** ♦**to have a stab at (doing) sth** [非正式] 试图 (做) 某事 ♦**to stab sb to death** 刺死某人 ♦**to stab sb in the back** (喻) 暗箭伤人 ♦**to stab sth with sth** 用某物戳某物

stability [stə'bɪlɪtɪ] *n* [u] **1** [*of government, economy etc*] 稳定 **2** [*of object*] 稳定性

stabilize ['steɪbəlaɪz] **I** *vt* [+ *prices, rates*] 保持…的稳定 **II** *vi* [*prices, rates, patient's condition* +] 稳定

stable ['steɪbl] **I** *adj* **1** [+ *prices, relationship, personality, condition*] 稳定的 **2** [+ *object*] 稳固的 **II** *n* [c] (*also:* ***stables***) **1** (*for horse*) 马厩 **2** (*in horse-racing*) 赛马训练场 **III** *vt* [+ *horse*] 把…拴进马厩

stack [stæk] **I** *n* [c] (*pile*) 堆 **II** *vt* (*also:* ***stack up***) [+ *chairs, books etc*] 把…堆起来 ♦**to be stacked with …** 堆满了… ♦**stacks of time/money** [英: 非正式] 大量时间/钱 ♦**the odds are stacked against them** 他们的胜算不大

stadium ['steɪdɪəm] (*pl* **stadia** ['steɪdɪə] *or* **stadiums**) *n* [c] 体育场

✪**staff** [stɑ:f] **I** *n* [c] **1** (*workforce*) 职员 ◊ *an error by one of his staff* 他的一名职员犯的过失 **2** [文] (*stick*) 棍棒 **II** *vt* 为…配备职员 ◊ *It was staffed by engineers.* 为其配备了工程师。

stag [stæg] *n* [c] 牡鹿

✪**stage** [steɪdʒ] **I** *n* [c] **1** (*in theatre*) 舞台 **2** (*platform*) 平台 **3** (*period*) 阶段 ◊ *the final stage of a world tour* 环球旅行的最后阶段 **II** *vt* **1** [+ *play*] 上演 **2** [+ *demonstration, strike*] 举行 ♦**to do sth in stages** 分期做某事 ♦**the stage** [戏剧] 剧坛 ♦**in the early/final stages** 在早/晚期 ♦**he staged a remarkable recovery** 他奇迹般地康复了

stagger ['stægə(r)] **I** *vi* 跌跌撞撞 **II** *vt* **1** (*amaze*) 使震惊 **2** [+ *hours, holidays*] 使错开

staggering ['stægərɪŋ] *adj* 令人吃惊的

stagnant ['stægnənt] *adj* **1** [+ *economy, business*] 萧条的 **2** [+ *water*] 停滞的

stag night *n* [c] 婚礼前新郎与男伴们的聚会

stain [steɪn] **I** *n* [c] (*mark*) 污迹 **II** *vt* **1** (*mark*) 沾污 **2** [+ *wood*] 给…染色

stained glass [steɪnd-] *n* [u] 彩色玻璃

stainless steel ['steɪnlɪs-] *n* [u] 不锈钢

stair [stɛə(r)] **I** *n* [c] (*step*) 梯级 **II stairs** *n* [*pl*] (*flight of steps*) 楼梯

staircase ['stɛəkeɪs] *n* [c] 楼梯

stairway ['stɛəweɪ] *n* [c] 楼梯

stake [steɪk] **I** *n* [c] **1** (*post*) 桩 **2** (*interest*) 股份 **3** (*in gambling*) 赌注 **4** (*in risky situation*) 利害关系 **II** *vt* ♦**to stake money on sth** 对某事押赌注 ♦**to stake one's reputation on sth** 把某人的声誉押在某事上 ♦**to stake a claim to sth** 声明对某物拥有所有权 ♦**to have a stake in sth** 与某事有利害关系 ♦**to raise the stakes** (喻) 冒更大

的风险 ♦ **there's a lot at stake** 很多事情可能受到很大影响 ♦ **I wouldn't stake my life on it** 我并不肯定

❑ **stake out** *vt* [+ *position, claim*] 申明

stale [steɪl] *adj* **1** [+ *bread, food*] 陈的 **2** [+ *smell, air*] 污浊的 **3** (喻) [+ *relationship, person, ideas*] 乏味的

stalk [stɔːk] **I** *n* [c] [*of flower, leaf*] 梗; [*of fruit*] 柄 **II** *vt* **1** [+ *animal*] 潜步追踪 **2** [+ *person*] 骚扰 **III** *vi* ♦ **to stalk out/off** 昂首阔步地走出/离开

stall [stɔːl] **I** *n* [c] **1** (*in street, market etc*) 货摊 **2** (*in stable*) 牲畜棚 **II** *vt* **1** [+ *car*] 使熄火 **2** (*delay*) [+ *person*] 拖住; [+ *process*] 拖延 **III** *vi* **1** [*engine, car* +] 熄火 **2** [*person* +] 拖延 **IV the stalls** *n* [*pl*] [英] (*in cinema, theatre*) 正厅前座

stamina ['stæmɪnə] *n* [U] 耐力

stammer ['stæmə(r)] **I** *n* [c] 结巴 **II** *vi* 结巴地说话

stamp [stæmp] **I** *n* [c] **1** 邮票 **2** (*rubber stamp*) 图章 **3** (*in passport etc*) 章 **II** *vi* (*with foot*) 跺脚 **III** *vt* [+ *passport, visa etc*] 盖章于 ♦ **to bear the stamp of sth** (喻) 有某物的特征 ♦ **to stamp one's foot** 跺脚 ♦ **to stamp a mark/word on sth** 在某物上盖印/字

❑ **stamp out** *vt* [+ *bullying, discrimination etc*] 消灭

stampede [stæm'piːd] **I** *n* [c] **1** [*of animals*] 惊跑 **2** [*of people*] 蜂拥 **II** *vi* **1** [*animals* +] 惊跑 **2** [*people* +] 蜂拥

stance [stæns] *n* [c] **1** (*posture*) 站立姿势 **2** (*attitude*) 态度

✪ **stand** [stænd] (*pt, pp* **stood**) **I** *n* [c] **1** (*stall*) 摊子 ◊ *a newspaper stand* 报摊 **2** (*at exhibition*) 展台 **3** [英] (*in stadium, arena*) 看台 **4** (*for holding things*) 架子 ◊ *A number of hats hung from a stand.* 架子上挂了几顶帽子。 **II** *vi* **1** (*be upright*) 站立 ◊ *She was standing at the bus stop.* 她站在公共汽车站。 **2** (*rise*) 站起来 ◊ *The judge asked us all to stand.* 法官让我们都站起来。 **3** (*be situated*) [*object, building* +] 耸立 ◊ *The house stands alone on top of a hill.* 那幢房子傲然耸立在山顶上。 **4** (*remain*) [*decision, offer* +] 保持有效 ◊ *Our original offer stands.* 我们当初的提议仍然有效。 **5** [英] (*in election*) 当候选人 ◊ *She was invited to stand as the Liberal candidate.* 她被邀请做自由党候选人。 [美 = **run**] **6** ♦ **to stand aside/back** 让开/退后 **7** ♦ **where** *or* **how does he stand on ...?** 他对…持什么态度？ **III** *vt* **1** ♦ **to stand sth on/in sth** 将某物竖放在某物上/中 **2** (*withstand, tolerate*) 经受住 ◊ *The economy will not stand another rise in interest rates.* 经济将经受不起利息的再次上升。 **3** ♦ **I can't stand him/it** 我无法容忍他/它 ♦ **to take the stand** [美:法] 出庭作证 ♦ **to make a stand against sth** 反抗某物 ♦ **to take a stand on sth** 对某事表明立场 ♦ **sb's last stand** 某人的最后一搏 ♦ **to stand at** [*value, level, score etc* +] 处于 ◊ *Unemployment now stands at 20%.* 目前失业率处于20%的水平。 ♦ **as things stand** 照这种样子 ♦ **it stands to reason** 那是显而易见的 ♦ **to stand to gain/lose sth** 很可能会获得/失去某物 ♦ **to stand for parliament** [英] 竞选议员 ♦ **to stand sb a drink/meal** [非正式] 请某人喝一杯/吃一顿 ♦ **to stand trial** 受审判

❑ **stand by I** *vi* **1** (*be ready*) 作好准备 **2** (*fail to help*) 袖手旁观 ◊ *We cannot stand by and watch while our allies are attacked.* 我们不能袖手旁观，眼睁睁看着盟军遭到进攻。 **II** *vt* [不可拆分] **1** [+ *promise, decision*] 遵守 **2** [+ *person*] 支持

❑ **stand down** *vi* 辞职

❑ **stand for** *vt* [不可拆分] **1** (*signify*) 主张 ◊ *He hates us and everything we stand for.* 他恨我们以及我们主张的一切。 **2** [*abbreviation* +] 代表 ◊ *What does CSE stand for?* CSE 代表什么？ **3** ♦ **I will not stand for it** 我不会容忍这个

❑ **stand in for** *vt* [不可拆分] [+ *teacher etc*] 代替

❑ **stand out** *vi* (*be prominent*) 醒目 ◊ *The name on the van stood out clearly.* 货车上的名字非常醒目。

❑ **stand up** *vi* **1** [*person* +] (*rise*) 起立 ◊ *I put down my glass and stood up.*

我把玻璃杯放下，站起来。
2 [*person* +] (*be on one's feet*) 站立◊ *a shop assistant who has to stand up all day* 整天都得站着的售货员
3 [*claim, evidence* +] 站得住脚◊ *He made wild accusations that did not stand up.* 他做了无根无据、根本站不住脚的指控。
❑**stand up for** *vt* [不可拆分] [+ *person*] 坚持; [+ *one's rights*] 维护
❑**stand up to** *vt* [不可拆分]
1 (*withstand*) 经得起◊ *Will this building stand up to the gales?* 这座建筑会经得起狂风吗?
2 [+ *person*] 勇敢地面对◊ *He's too weak to stand up to her.* 他太软弱了，根本无法面对她。

standard ['stændəd] **I** *n* [c] **1** (*level*) 水平 **2** (*norm, criterion*) 标准 **3** (*flag*) 旗子 **II** *adj* **1** [+ *size etc*] 普通的 **2** [+ *procedure, practice*] 标准的 **3** [+ *model, feature*] 规范的 **4** [+ *textbook, work*] 权威性的 **III standards** *n* [*pl*] 规范 ♦**to be up to standard** 达到标准

standardize ['stændədaɪz] *vt* 标准化

standard of living *n* [c] 生活水平

stand-by, standby ['stændbaɪ] **I** *n* [c] 后备 **II** *cpd* [复合词] [+ *ticket, seat*] 剩余 ♦**to be on stand-by** [*doctor, crew, firemen etc* +] 待命

standing ['stændɪŋ] **I** *n* **1** [u] (*status*) 身份 **2** [c] (*reputation*) 声誉 **II** *adj* **1** ♦**a standing invitation** 长期有效的邀请◊ *Remember that you have a standing invitation to stay with us.* 记住你随时可以来我们这里住。**2** [+ *army*] 常备的 ♦**of many years' standing** 持续多年的 ♦**a standing ovation** 起立长时间鼓掌

standing order [英:经济] *n* [c] 长期有效委托书

standpoint ['stændpɔɪnt] *n* ♦**from a military/economic standpoint** 从军事/经济的立场出发

standstill ['stændstɪl] *n* ♦**to be at a standstill** [*traffic, negotiations* +] 停滞不前的 ♦**to come** *or* **be brought to a standstill** [*traffic* +] 停滞下来; [*production, progress* +] 被迫停顿

stank [stæŋk] *pt of* **stink**

staple ['steɪpl] **I** *n* [c] **1** (*for fastening paper*) 订书钉 **2** (*food*) 主食 **II** *adj* [+ *diet, goods*] 基本的 **III** *vt* (*fasten*) 用订书钉钉 ♦**to be a staple of sth** [*product, activity* +] 为某物的一个主要成分

✪**star** [stɑː(r)] **I** *n* [c] **1** (*in sky*) 星 **2** (*shape*) 星形物 **3** (*celebrity*) 明星 **II** *vt* [*play, film* +] [+ *actor, actress*] 使主演◊ *The movie starred Lana Turner.* 莱娜·特纳担任那部电影的主角。**III** *vi* ♦**to star (in)** [+ *play, film*] (在…中)主演 **IV the stars** *n* [*pl*] [非正式] (*horoscope*) 星象 ♦**a 4-star hotel** 4星级旅馆

starboard ['stɑːbɔːd] *adj* [+ *side*] 右舷的 ♦**to starboard** 距离右舷

starch [stɑːtʃ] *n* **1** [c/u] (*in food*) 淀粉 **2** [u] (*for stiffening clothes*) 淀粉浆

stardom ['stɑːdəm] *n* [u] 明星地位

stare [stɛə(r)] **I** *vi* ♦**to stare (at sb/sth)** 盯着(某人/某物) **II** *n* [c] 凝视 ♦**to give sb a stare** 盯某人一眼

stark [stɑːk] **I** *adj* **1** [+ *room, object, landscape*] 光秃秃的 **2** [+ *warning, choice*] 严峻的 **3** ♦**to be in stark contrast to sth** 和某物形成鲜明对比 **II** *adv* ♦**stark naked** 一丝不挂地

✪**start** [stɑːt] **I** *n* [c] **1** 开始◊ *the start of the year* 年初◊ *the start of the project* 项目的开始 **2** (*departure*) 开端◊ *We need a fresh start.* 我们要有个新的开端。**3** (*sudden movement*) 惊跳◊ *He awoke with a start.* 他猛然惊醒。**4** (*lead*) 先行◊ *You must give me fifty metres start.* 你一定要让我先行50米。**II** *vt* **1** (*begin*) 开始◊ *My father started work when he was ten.* 我父亲10岁时开始工作。**2** (*cause*) [+ *fire, panic*] 使产生◊ *I started a fire.* 我生了火。**3** (*found*) [+ *business etc*] 创建◊ *He raised the money to start a restaurant.* 他筹资创建了一家餐馆。**4** [+ *engine, car*] 启动 **III** *vi* **1** (*begin*) 开始◊ *The meeting starts at 7.* 会议7点开始。**2** (*with fright*) 惊起◊ *It caused her to start back in terror.* 她被惊吓得往后跳了一下。**3** [*engine, car* +] 启动◊ *The car wouldn't start.* 那辆车启动不了。**4** ♦**to start as sth** 从做某事发迹◊ *Mr. Dunbar started as an assistant.* 邓伯先生从当助理起家。♦**at the start** (*at first*) 一开

始 ♦**for a start** (*firstly*) 首先 ♦**from the start** 从一开始 ♦**to get off to a good/bad start** 开头顺利/开头不顺利 ♦**to make an early start** 一早出发 ♦**from start to finish** 从头至尾 ♦**to start doing** *or* **to do sth** 开始做某事 ♦**to start (off) with** (*initially*) 开始时

❑**start off** *vi* **1** (*begin*) 开始从事 ◊ *He started off as an assistant.* 他从助理做起。**2** (*begin moving*) 动身 ♦**to start off by doing sth** 首先做某事

❑**start on** *vt* [不可拆分] 开始

❑**start out** *vi* (*begin*) 开始 ◊ *It started out as fun, but it became hard work.* 开始很好玩，但后来变得很费劲。♦**to start out by doing sth** 最先做某事

❑**start over** [美] *vi, vt* 重新开始

❑**start up I** *vt* **1** [+ *business etc*] 创办 **2** [+ *engine, car*] 发动 **II** *vi* [*engine, car* +] 发动

starter ['stɑːtə(r)] *n* [c] **1** (*in car*) 起动装置 **2** (*race official*) 发令员 **3** (*horse, athlete*) 参赛者 **4** [英] (*in meal*) 开胃菜 ♦**for starters** [非正式] 首先

starting point ['stɑːtɪŋ-] *n* [c] **1** (*for journey*) 起始点 **2** (*for discussion, idea*) 开端

startle ['stɑːtl] *vt* 使吓一跳

startling ['stɑːtlɪŋ] *adj* 惊人的

starvation [stɑː'veɪʃən] *n* [u] 饥饿 ♦**to die of** *or* **from starvation** 饿死

starve [stɑːv] **I** *vi* **1** (*be very hungry*) 挨饿 **2** (*die from hunger*) 饿死 **II** *vt* [+ *person, animal*] 使挨饿 ♦**I'm starving** [非正式] 我饿极了 ♦**to starve to death** 饿死 ♦**to be starved of ...** [+ *investment, love*] 匮乏…的

✪**state** [steɪt] **I** *n* **1** [c] (*condition*) 状态 ◊ *They are concerned about the state of the house.* 他们对房子的状态有所担心。**2** [c] (*country*) 国家 ◊ *Europe's only remaining communist state* 欧洲惟一尚存的共产主义国家 **3** [c] (*part of country*) 州 ◊ *the Southern states* 美国南部各州 **4** [s] (*government*) 政府 ◊ *The state does not collect enough revenue to cover its expenditure.* 政府征收的税收不能满足支出。**II** *cpd* [复合词] **1** (*government-controlled*) 政府 ◊ *the state social-security system* 政府社会保障系统 **2** (*involving head of state*) 国事 ◊ *a state visit to India* 对印度的国事访问 **III** *vt* (*say, declare*) 申明 ◊ *Please state your name.* 请申明您的姓名。**IV the States** *n* [*pl*] [非正式] 美国 ♦**to be in a state** 处于焦虑状态 ♦**to get into a state** 陷入紧张不安的状态 ♦**to lie in state** 受公众瞻仰 ♦**a state of emergency** [政治] 紧急状态 ♦**state of affairs** 事态 ♦**state of mind** 心情 ♦**to state that ...** 声明…

stately ['steɪtlɪ] *adj* **1** [+ *building*] 宏伟的 **2** [+ *pace*] 庄重的

statement ['steɪtmənt] *n* [c] **1** (*declaration*) 声明 **2** (*also:* ***bank statement***) 银行结单

state school [英] *n* [c] 公立学校 [美 = **public school**]

statesman ['steɪtsmən] (*pl* **statesmen**) *n* [c] 政治家

static ['stætɪk] **I** *n* [u] **1** (*on radio, TV*) 静电干扰 **2** (*also:* ***static electricity***) 静电 **II** *adj* 静止的 ♦**to remain static** [*numbers, prices etc* +] 保持稳定

station ['steɪʃən] **I** *n* [c] **1** (*railway station*) 车站 **2** (*police station*) 警察局 **3** (*on radio*) 电台 **II** *vt* **1** (*position*) 安置 **2** [军] (*base*) 驻扎 ♦**to marry/be educated above one's station** [过时] 与高于本人地位的人结婚/受到高于本人地位的教育 ♦**to station o.s. somewhere** 呆在某处

stationary ['steɪʃnərɪ] *adj* 停滞的

stationery ['steɪʃnərɪ] *n* [u] 文具

station wagon [美] *n* [c] 旅行车 [英 = **estate car**]

statistic [stə'tɪstɪk] *n* [c] 统计资料

statistical [stə'tɪstɪkl] *adj* [+ *analysis, evidence, information*] 统计的

statistics *n* [u] (*subject*) 统计学

statue ['stætjuː] *n* [c] 塑像

stature ['stætʃə(r)] *n* [u] **1** (*height*) 身高 **2** (*reputation*) 名望

status ['steɪtəs] *n* [u] **1** (*position*) 地位 **2** (*official classification*) 身份 **3** (*importance*) 重要地位

status quo [-'kwəu] [正式] *n* ♦**the status quo** 现状

statutory ['stætjutrɪ] [正式] *adj* 法定的

staunch [stɔːntʃ] **I** *adj* [+ *supporter, ally*] 坚定的 **II** [正式] *vt* **1** [+ *flow*] 阻止 **2** [+ *blood, wound*] 使止住

✪ **stay** [steɪ] **I** *n* [C] **1** 逗留 ◊ *We want to make your stay as enjoyable as possible.* 我们想尽量令你的逗留愉快。**2** (*in institution*) 暂住 ◊ *an overnight stay in hospital* 在医院里暂住的一夜 **II** *vi* **1** (*in place, position*) 呆 ◊ *"Stay here," Kate said. "I'll bring the car."* "呆在这里，" 凯特说，"我把车开过来。" **2** (*in town, hotel, someone's house*) 逗留 ◊ *How long can you stay in Brussels?* 你能在布鲁塞尔逗留多长时间？**3** (*in state, situation*) 保持 ◊ *information on how to stay healthy* 有关如何保持健康的资料 **III** *vt* ♦ **to stay the night** 过夜 ♦ **to stay with sb** 在某人家暂住 ♦ **computers are here to stay** 电脑将深深扎下根来 ♦ **to stay put** 固定不动 ♦ **to stay ahead of sth/sb** 领先于某物/某人

❑ **stay away** *vi* **1** (*from place*) 不接近 **2** (*from person, activity*) 远离

❑ **stay behind** *vi* 留在后面

❑ **stay in** *vi* 呆在家里

❑ **stay on** *vi* (*in place, job*) 继续留下

❑ **stay out** *vi* 夜不归宿 ◊ *She stayed out all night.* 她彻夜未归。♦ **stay out of it!** 别介入这件事！

❑ **stay up** *vi* 不去睡

steadily ['stɛdɪlɪ] *adv* **1** (*continuously*) 不断地 **2** (*calmly*) [*look, stare* +] 镇定地

steady ['stɛdɪ] **I** *adj* **1** (*continuous*) [+ *progress, increase, fall*] 稳定的 **2** (*regular*) [+ *job, income*] 固定的 **3** (*uniform*) [+ *speed*] 规律的 **4** (*stable*) [+ *relationship*] 稳定的 **5** (*reliable*) [+ *person*] 踏踏实实的 **6** (*firm*) [+ *object, hand etc*] 稳的 **7** (*calm*) [+ *look, voice*] 镇定的 **II** *vt* (*stabilize*) 使平稳 **III** *vi* (*stabilize*) 稳定下来 ♦ **to steady o.s.** (*mentally*) 使自己镇定下来; (*physically*) 使自己不摇晃 ♦ **to steady one's nerves** 稳定自己的情绪

steak [steɪk] *n* **1** [C/U] (*beef*) 牛排 **2** [C] (*fish, pork etc*) 厚片

steal [stiːl] (*pt* **stole**, *pp* **stolen**) **I** *vt* 偷窃 **II** *vi* **1** 行窃 **2** ♦ **to steal away/out** 悄悄溜走 ♦ **he stole it from me** 他从我这里把它偷走了

> 📖 请勿将**rob**和**steal**混淆。如果你**steal**某物，例如钱或车，你未经允许就将他人的物品据为己有，并且不打算归还。*My car was stolen on Friday evening.* 注意，不能说某人steal某人，只能说steal from某人。某人**rob**某人或某个地方，即使用暴力将他人或某个地方的东西据为己有，并且不打算归还。*They planned to rob an old woman...They joined forces to rob a factory.* **rob**后可以跟**of**加被强占的物品。*The two men were robbed of more than £700.* 注意，**rob**后可以直接跟被抢劫的对象，即可以说rob某人。

steam [stiːm] **I** *n* [U] **1** 蒸汽 **2** (*on window*) 水汽 **II** *cpd* [复合词] 蒸汽 **III** *vt* 蒸 **IV** *vi* 冒蒸汽 ♦ **to run out of steam** 失去劲头 ♦ **under one's own steam** 靠自己的力量 ♦ **to let off steam** 发泄

❑ **steam up** *vi* [*window, mirror, spectacles* +] 蒙上水汽 ♦ **to get steamed up about sth** [非正式] 因某事而恼火

📖 用法参见 **cook**

steamy ['stiːmɪ] *adj* **1** [+ *room*] 蒸汽弥漫的 **2** [非正式] [+ *film, book, scene*] 色情的

steel [stiːl] **I** *n* [U] 钢铁 **II** *cpd* [复合词] **1** (*made from steel*) 钢制 **2** (*producing steel*) 钢铁生产 **III** *vt* ♦ **to steel o.s. (to do sth)** 狠下心（做某事）

steep [stiːp] **I** *adj* **1** [+ *hill, staircase*] 陡的 **2** [+ *increase, rise*] 急剧的 **3** [非正式] (*expensive*) 过高的 **II** *vt* ♦ **to steep sth in liquid** 将某物浸泡在液体中 ♦ **to be steeped in history** 充满历史气息

steeple ['stiːpl] *n* [C] 尖塔

steer [stɪə(r)] **I** *vt* **1** [+ *car, boat, plane*] 驾驶 **2** ♦ **to steer sb to/towards** 带领某人去/向…方向发展 **II** *vi* [*car, boat, plane* +] 行驶 ♦ **to steer**

clear of sb/sth 避开某人/某事

steering ['stɪərɪŋ] *n* [U] (*in car etc*) 转向装置

steering wheel *n* [C] 方向盘

stem [stɛm] **I** *n* [C] **1** [*of plant*] 茎 **2** [*of leaf, fruit*] 梗 **3** [*of glass*] 柄脚 **4** [*of pipe*] 柄 **II** *vt* **1** (*stop*) [+ *flow, tide*] 堵住; [+ *illegal drugs, violence*] 遏制 **2** [+ *bleeding*] 止住

❑ **stem from** *vt* [不可拆分] 起源于

stench [stɛntʃ] *n* [C] 恶臭

✪ **step** [stɛp] **I** *n* **1** [C] (*footstep*) 脚步 ◊ *He heard steps in the corridor.* 他听见走廊里的脚步声。**2** [C] (*in dance*) 舞步 **3** [C] (*action*) 步骤 ◊ *the first step towards peace* 通向和平的第一步 **4** [C] (*stage*) [*of process*] 阶段 ◊ *The next step is to put the theory into practice.* 下一阶段是将理论付诸于实践。**5** [C] [*of stairs*] 梯级 ◊ *She was sitting on the top step.* 她坐在最高的一级楼梯上。**6** [C] (*outside door*) 台阶 **7** [U] (*also:* ***step aerobics***) 阶梯健身运动 **II** *vi* **1** ♦ **to step forward/backward** *etc* 向前/后{等}迈步 **2** ♦ **to step on/over sth** (*tread*) 踩在某物上/跨过某物 **III steps** *n* [*pl*] [英] = **stepladder** ♦ **step by step** 逐步地 ♦ **to stay** *or* **keep one step ahead of sb/sth** 保持比某人/某物领先一步 ♦ **to take a step** (字) 迈一步 ♦ **to take steps to do sth** (喻) 采取措施做某事 ♦ **to be in step/out of step with sb** (喻) 与某人一致/不一致 ♦ **to walk in step/out of step (with sb)** (与某人) 步伐一致/不一致

❑ **step aside** = **step down**

❑ **step back** *vi* ♦ **to step back (from sth)** (喻) 跳出 (某事) 来看

❑ **step down, step aside** *vi* 辞职

❑ **step in** *vi* (*intervene*) 介入

❑ **step off** *vt* [不可拆分] [+ *plane, platform*] 走下来

❑ **step up** *vt* (*increase*) [+ *efforts, pace etc*] 增加

stepbrother ['stɛpbrʌðə(r)] *n* [C] (*with shared father*) 异母兄弟; (*with shared mother*) 异父兄弟

stepchild ['stɛptʃaɪld] (*pl* **stepchildren**) *n* [C] (*of woman*) 丈夫与前妻所生的子女; (*of man*) 妻子与前夫所生的子女

stepdaughter ['stɛpdɔːtə(r)] *n* [C] 继女

stepfather ['stɛpfɑːðə(r)] *n* [C] 继父

stepladder ['stɛplædə(r)] *n* [C] 活梯

stepmother ['stɛpmʌðə(r)] *n* [C] 继母

stepsister ['stɛpsɪstə(r)] *n* [C] (*with shared father*) 异母姐妹; (*with shared mother*) 异父姐妹

stepson ['stɛpsʌn] *n* [C] 继子

stereo ['stɛrɪəu] **I** *n* [C] 立体声装置 **II** *adj* 立体声的 ♦ **in stereo** 用立体声

stereotype ['stɪərɪətaɪp] **I** *n* [C] 老套 **II** *vt* 使模式化

sterile ['stɛraɪl] *adj* **1** [+ *bandage, needle*] 消过毒的 **2** [+ *person, animal*] 不育的 **3** [+ *debate, ideas*] 枯燥乏味的

sterilize ['stɛrɪlaɪz] *vt* **1** [+ *object*] 消毒 **2** [+ *person, animal*] 使绝育

sterling ['stəːlɪŋ] **I** *n* [U] (*currency*) 英国货币 **II** *adj* **1** [+ *silver*] 纯的 **2** [+ *efforts, character*] 优秀的 ♦ **one pound sterling** 一英镑

stern [stəːn] **I** *adj* **1** [+ *warning, measures*] 严厉的 **2** [+ *person*] 严格的 **II** *n* [C] [*of boat*] 船尾

steroid ['stɪərɔɪd] *n* [C] 类固醇

stew [stjuː] **I** *n* [C/U] 炖的食物 **II** *vt, vi* **1** [+ *meat, vegetables*] 炖 **2** [+ *fruit*] 煨 ♦ **stewed tea** 泡过久的茶

steward ['stjuːəd] *n* [C] **1** (*on ship, plane, train*) 乘务员 **2** (*at race, march, in club*) 干事

stewardess ['stjuədɛs] *n* [C] 女乘务员

stick [stɪk] (*pt, pp* **stuck**) **I** *n* [C] **1** [*of wood*] 枯枝 **2** (*as weapon*) 棍棒 **3** (*walking stick*) 拐杖 **4** [*of chalk, dynamite, celery*] 条 **II** *vt* **1** ♦ **to stick sth on** *or* **to sth** (*with glue etc*) 将某物粘贴在某物上 **2** ♦ **to stick sth in/through sth** [非正式] (*put*) 随手将某物戳进/放进某物中 **3** ♦ **to stick sth in** *or* **into sth** (*push*) 将某物刺入某物中 **4** [英: 非正式] (*tolerate*) 忍受 **III** *vi* **1** ♦ **to stick (to sth)** [*stamp, sticker* +] 粘贴 (在某物上) **2** [*substance, paste* +] 粘在 **3** (*remain*) [*name* +] 长久保留 ◊ *I nicknamed him "Rex", a name which stuck.* 我给他起了个外号叫

Rex，一直叫到现在。4 (*get jammed*) [*door, lift* +] 卡住 ♦**to get (hold of) the wrong end of the stick** [非正式] 误解 ♦**to stick in one's mind** [*thought etc* +] 铭记在某人的心中
❑**stick around** [非正式] *vi* 呆在附近
❑**stick by** *vt* [不可拆分] [+ *person*] 忠于
❑**stick out I** *vi* (*protrude*) 伸出 **II** *vt* 1 (*extend*) [+ *tongue, hand*] 伸出 2 ♦**to stick it out** [非正式] 坚持到底
❑**stick to** *vt* [不可拆分] 1 [+ *one's word, agreement*] 信守 2 [+ *the truth, facts*] 紧扣 3 (*continue on*) [+ *road*] 沿着 4 [+ *job*] 坚持
❑**stick together** *vi* [*people* +] 团结一致
❑**stick up I** *vi* (*extend upwards*) 竖起 **II** *vt* [+ *picture, notice*] 张贴
❑**stick up for** *vt* [不可拆分] [+ *person, idea*] 为…辩护
❑**stick with** *vt* [不可拆分] [+ *person, job*] 忠于

sticker ['stɪkə(r)] *n* [c] 不干胶标签

sticky ['stɪkɪ] *adj* 1 [+ *substance*] 黏的 2 [+ *bottle, tube etc*] 胶黏的 3 (*adhesive*) [+ *tape, paper*] 黏性的 4 [+ *weather, day*] 湿热的 5 [非正式] (*difficult*) 棘手的

stiff [stɪf] **I** *adj* 1 [+ *brush, trousers*] 硬挺的 2 [+ *paste*] 稠的 3 (*with aching muscles*) [+ *person*] 酸痛的；[+ *neck, arm etc*] 僵硬的 4 [+ *door, drawer, zip etc*] 紧的 5 [+ *manner, smile*] 生硬的 6 [+ *competition*] 激烈的；[+ *sentence, law*] 严厉的 7 [+ *whisky, brandy*] 烈性的；[+ *breeze*] 强劲的 **II** *adv* ♦**to be bored/scared stiff** 讨厌/害怕极了 ♦**to keep a stiff upper lip** [英] 感情不外露

stiffen ['stɪfn] **I** *vi* 1 [*person, body* +] 变僵直 2 (*also:* ***stiffen up***) [*muscles, joints* +] 变僵硬 3 [*attitudes, behaviour* +] 变得坚定 **II** *vt* 1 [+ *cloth*] 使变挺 2 [+ *attitude, behaviour*] 加强

stifle ['staɪfl] *vt* 1 [+ *yawn, laugh*] 忍住 2 [+ *debate, creativity*] 抑制

stifling ['staɪflɪŋ] *adj* 1 [+ *heat*] 令人窒息的 2 (喻) [+ *situation*] 沉闷的

stigma ['stɪgmə] *n* 1 [c/u] (*disgrace*) 耻辱 2 [c] [植] [*of flower*] 柱头

stilettos [stɪ'lɛtəuz] [英] *n* [*pl*] 细高跟鞋 [美 = **spike heels**]

✪**still** [stɪl] **I** *adj* 1 [+ *person, hands, etc*] 不动的 ◊ *He sat very still for several minutes.* 他一动也不动地坐了几分钟。◊ *His hands were never still.* 他双手从不停歇。2 (*tranquil*) [+ *place, water, air*] 平静的 ◊ *The night air was very still.* 夜空非常寂静。◊ *a still lake* 平静的湖 3 [英] (*not fizzy*) 无气泡的 ◊ *a bottle of still water* 一瓶无气泡的水 **II** *adv* 1 (*up to the present*) 仍然 ◊ *She still lives in London.* 她仍住在伦敦。2 (*possibly*) 还是 ◊ *We could still make it if we rush.* 如果我们快点，还能赶上。3 (*even*) 更 ◊ *They could delay the flight still further.* 他们能将航班拖延得更久。4 (*yet*) 还 ◊ *There are ten weeks still to go.* 还有10个星期呢。5 (*nonetheless*) 尽管如此 ◊ *I didn't win. Still, it was fun.* 我没赢。尽管如此，却玩得很开心。6 (*for emphasis*) 还是 ◊ *Despite the ruling, he was still found guilty.* 尽管有那个裁决，他还是被定了罪。**III** *n* [c] [电影] 剧照 ♦**to stand/keep still** 站着别动/别动 ♦**he still hasn't arrived** 他还没到 ♦**better still** 更好

stimulate ['stɪmjuleɪt] *vt* 1 [+ *economy, interest, demand*] 激励 2 [+ *person*] 激发 3 [+ *part of body*] 促进

stimulus ['stɪmjuləs] (*pl* **stimuli** ['stɪmjulɪ]) *n* 1 [c/u] (*incentive*) 刺激 2 [c] [生物, 心理] 刺激因素

sting [stɪŋ] (*pt, pp* **stung**) **I** *n* [c] 1 (*pain, bite*) 刺 2 (*part*) [*of insect*] 螯刺 3 [非正式] (*by police*) 精心设置的圈套 **II** *vt* 1 [*insect, nettle* +] 刺 2 [*substance* +] 灼痛 3 [*wind, remarks* +] 刺痛 **III** *vi* 1 [*insect, nettle* +] 叮 2 [*ointment* +] 引起刺痛 3 [*skin* +] 感到灼痛

stink [stɪŋk] (*pt* **stank**, *pp* **stunk**) **I** *n* [c] 恶臭 **II** *vi* 发臭 ♦**to stink of sth** 有某物的气味 ♦**that idea stinks!** [非正式] 那个主意糟透了！

stint [stɪnt] **I** *n* [c] 时间 **II** *vi* ♦**don't stint on ...** 别舍不得…

stir [stəː(r)] **I** *n* [s] (*fuss*) 轰动 **II** *vt*

1 [+ tea, sauce etc] 搅动 2 (move) [+ person] 打动；[+ emotion] 激起 **III** *vi* (move slightly) [leaves etc +] 微动；[person +] 挪动 ♦ **to give sth a stir** 搅动某物

❑ **stir up** *vt* 1 [+ trouble] 挑起 2 [+ dust, mud] 扬起

stir-fry ['stəː'fraɪ] **I** *vt* 煸 **II** *n* [c] 炒菜

stitch [stɪtʃ] **I** *n* 1 [c] (in sewing) 针脚 2 [c] (in knitting) 针 3 [c] [医] 缝针 4 [s] (pain) 突然剧痛 **II** *vt* 1 ♦ **to stitch sth together/to stitch sth to sth** 将某物缝起来/将某物缝在某物上 2 [医] (also: **stitch up**) [+ wound] 缝合

❑ **stitch up** *vt* 1 [医] [+ wound] 缝合 2 [英：非正式] (trick, frame) 诬陷

stock [stɔk] **I** *n* 1 [c] (supply) 供应物 2 [U] (in shop) 库存 3 [c/U] [经济] 股票 4 [U] (gravy) 汤汁 5 [U] [正式] (origin) 血统 **II** *n* [pl] (livestock) 牲畜 **III** *adj* [+ answer, response] 老一套的 **IV** *vt* [shop +] [+ goods] 储备 ♦ **in/out of stock** 有/无存货 ♦ **stocks and shares** 股票 ♦ **to take stock (of sth)** 斟酌（某事） ♦ **well-stocked** 储备丰富

❑ **stock up** *vi* ♦ **to stock up (on** *or* **with sth)** 储备（某物）

stockbroker ['stɔkbrəukə(r)] *n* [c] 股票经纪人

stock exchange *n* [c] 股票交易所

stockholder ['stɔkhəuldə(r)] [美] *n* [c] 股东 [英 = **shareholder**]

stocking ['stɔkɪŋ] *n* [c] 长统袜

stock market *n* [c] 股票市场

stoke [stəuk] *vt* 1 (also: **stoke up**) [+ fire, furnace] 添燃料 2 (also: **stoke up**) [+ feeling] 煽动

stole [stəul] **I** *pt of* **steal II** *n* [c] (shawl) 披肩

stolen ['stəuln] *pp of* **steal**

stomach ['stʌmək] **I** *n* [c] 1 (organ) 胃 2 (abdomen) 腹部 **II** *vt* 容忍

stomach ache *n* [c/U] 胃痛

stone [stəun] **I** *n* 1 [U] 石头 2 [c] (pebble) 石子 3 [c] (gem) 宝石 4 [c] [英] (in fruit) 核 [美 = **pit**] 5 [c] [英] (weight) 英石，等于14磅或6.35公斤 **II** *cpd* [复合词] (made of stone) 石制 **III** *vt* 1 (throw stones at) 向…扔石头 2 [英] [+ fruit] 去核 [美 = **pit**]

♦ **within a stone's throw of** 与…只有一箭之遥

stood [stud] *pt, pp of* **stand**

stool [stuːl] *n* [c] 1 (chair) 凳子 2 [医] (faeces) 大便

stoop [stuːp] **I** *vi* 1 (also: **stoop down, stoop over**) (bend) 弯腰 2 (walk with a stoop) 驼背 **II** *n* 驼背 ♦ **to stoop to (doing) sth** 堕落到（做出）某事

✪ **stop** [stɔp] **I** *vt* 1 停止 ◊ *Stop the car and let me out.* 停车让我下车。 2 (prevent) 阻止 ◊ *Does putting people in prison stop crime?* 把人关在监狱里能阻止犯罪吗？ 3 [+ cheque] 停止兑现 **II** *vi* 1 [person, vehicle +] 停下来 ◊ *She stopped and stared at the poster.* 她停下来盯着海报看。 2 (stop working) [watch, engine, heart +] 停 ◊ *My watch has stopped.* 我的手表停了。 3 [rain, noise, activity +] 停 ◊ *The rain had stopped.* 雨停了。 4 (also: **stop off**) (on journey) 逗留 **III** *n* [c] 1 (on journey) (place) 站；(time) 停留 ◊ *Their first stop was a hotel outside Paris.* 他们旅程中的第一站是巴黎郊外的一家旅馆。 2 (for bus, train) 车站 ◊ *We'll get off at the next stop.* 我们将在下一站下车。 ♦ **to stop doing sth** 停止做某事 ♦ **to stop sb (from) doing sth** 阻止某人做某事 ♦ **stop it!** 住手！ ♦ **to come to a stop** [car, train etc +] 停下来 ♦ **to put a stop to sth** 使某事停止

❑ **stop by I** *vi* 顺便过访 **II** *vt* [不可拆分] [+ place] 顺道去

❑ **stop up** *vt* [+ hole, leak] 堵塞

stoplight ['stɔplaɪt] [美] *n* [c] 1 (in road) 交通信号灯 [英 = **traffic light**] 2 (on vehicle) 刹车灯

stopover ['stɔpəuvə(r)] *n* [c] 1 (on journey) 中途停留 2 (on plane journey) 转机停留

stoppage ['stɔpɪdʒ] *n* [c] 1 (strike) 停工 2 [英：体育] 暂停 [美 = **time out**] 3 (from salary) 扣除

storage ['stɔːrɪdʒ] *n* [U] 1 贮藏 2 [计算机] 存储

store [stɔː(r)] **I** *n* [c] 1 [of food etc] 储备 2 [of knowledge, jokes etc] 丰富 3 (depot) 仓库 4 [英] (large shop) 大商店 5 [美] (shop) 店铺 [英 = **shop**]

II *vt* **1** (*also:* ***store away***) [+ *provisions, information etc*] 存放 **2** [*computer, brain* +] [+ *information*] 存储
III stores *n* [*pl*] (*provisions*) 补给品
♦ **to be** *or* **lie in store (for sb)** 等待着(某人) ♦ **to set great/little store by sth** [正式] 重视/轻视某物
❑ **store up** *vt* [+ *food, money*] 储备; [+ *memories*] 积聚

storekeeper ['stɔːkiːpə(r)] [美] *n* [C] 店主 [英= **shopkeeper**]

storey (美 **story**) ['stɔːrɪ] *n* [C] 层

storm [stɔːm] **I** *n* [C] **1** 暴风雨 **2** [*of criticism, protest*] 爆发 **II** *vi* ♦ **to storm in/out** 猛冲而入/出 **III** *vt* (*attack*) [+ *place*] 猛攻 ♦ **to take sth by storm** 轰动

stormy ['stɔːmɪ] *adj* **1** [+ *weather*] 有暴风雨的 **2** [+ *relationship*] 多风波的; [+ *debate*] 激烈的

✪ **story** ['stɔːrɪ] *n* [C] **1** (*account*) 描述 ◊ *I told her the story of my life.* 我向她描述了我的生活。◊ *the story of the women's movement in Ireland* 对于爱尔兰妇女运动的描述 **2** (*tale*) 故事 ◊ *a ghost story* 一个鬼故事 **3** (*in newspaper, on news broadcast*) 报道 ◊ *Those are some of the top stories in the news.* 那些是新闻中最重要的报道。**4** (*lie*) 谎话 ◊ *He invented some story about a friend.* 他编造了个有关一个朋友的谎话。**5** [美] [*of building*] = **storey** ♦ **it's a different story** 那是另一回事 ♦ **the (same) old story** 老一套 ♦ **that's only part of** *or* **not the whole story** 那不是事实的全部 ♦ **my side of the story** 我的叙述

stout [staut] **I** *adj* **1** [+ *shoes*] 耐穿的; [+ *branch*] 粗大的 **2** [+ *person*] 肥胖的 **3** [+ *resistance, defence*] 顽强的 **II** *n* [C/U] [英] (*beer*) 黑啤酒

stove [stəuv] *n* [C] **1** (*for cooking*) 炉子 **2** (*for heating*) 加热器 **3** [美] (*top of cooker*) 炉

straddle ['strædl] *vt* **1** [+ *chair, fence etc*] (*sitting*) 跨坐; (*standing*) 跨立 **2** [*bridge, town* +] [+ *border, road*] 横跨 **3** [+ *period, activity*] 跨越

straight [streɪt] **I** *adj* **1** (*not curving*) 笔直的 **2** [+ *hair*] 直的 **3** (*honest*) [+ *answer*] 直截了当的 **4** (*simple*) [+ *fight, choice*] 非此即彼的 **5** (*uninterrupted*) [+ *hours, victories*] 连续的 **6** [戏剧] (*serious*) [+ *role, play*] 朴实无华的 **7** [非正式] (*heterosexual*) 异性恋的 **8** [+ *whisky etc*] 纯的 **II** *adv* **1** [*walk, stand, look* +] 直 **2** (*immediately*) 直接地 **3** (*without an interval*) 连续不断地 **III** *n* [C] **1** (*on racetrack*) 直道 ♦ **to be straight with sb** (*honest*) 坦诚地对待某人 ♦ **to put sth straight** (*make it clear*) 澄清某事 ♦ **to get sth straight** 彻底了解某事 ♦ **let's get this straight** 让我们把事情搞清楚 ♦ **straight away, straight off** 马上 ♦ **to tell sb sth straight (out)** 坦率地告诉某人某事

straighten ['streɪtn] **I** *vt* (*also:* ***straighten out***) [+ *picture, hair*] 弄直 **II** *vi* (*also:* ***straighten out***) [*road etc* +] 变直
❑ **straighten out I** *vi* = **straighten II** *vt* **1** = **straighten 2** [+ *problem, situation*] 弄清楚
❑ **straighten up** *vi* (*stand straight*) 直起身子

straightforward [streɪt'fɔːwəd] *adj* **1** (*simple*) 简单的 **2** (*honest*) [+ *person, behaviour*] 直截了当的

strain [streɪn] **I** *n* **1** [C/U] (*pressure*) 负担 **2** [C/U] (*tension*) 紧张 **3** [U] [术语] 作用力 **4** [C] [*of virus, plant*] 系 **5** [C/U] ♦ **back/muscle strain** 背部/肌肉扭伤 **II** *vt* **1** [+ *back, muscle*] 扭伤 **2** (*overload*) [+ *resources, system*] 使超过负荷 **3** [+ *food*] 过滤 **III** *vi* ♦ **to strain to do sth** 尽力去做某事 **IV strains** *n* [*pl*] [文] [*of music*] 乐曲 ♦ **to be under great strain** [*person* +] 处于极度紧张之中; [*organization* +] 负担过重 ♦ **to put a strain on sth/sb** 给某事/某人增加负担

strained [streɪnd] *adj* **1** [+ *back, muscle*] 劳损的 **2** [+ *voice, laugh etc*] 勉强的 **3** [+ *relations*] 紧张的

strainer ['streɪnə(r)] *n* [C] 滤网

strait [streɪt] **I** *n* [C] [地理] (*also:* ***straits***) 海峡 **II straits** *n* [*pl*] ♦ **to be in dire** *or* **desperate straits** 处于艰难的境地

strand [strænd] *n* [C] **1** [*of wire, wool*] 股 **2** [*of hair*] 缕 **3** [*of plan, theory, story*] 一个组成部分

stranded ['strændɪd] *adj* 1 [+ *traveller*] 受困无援的 2 [+ *ship, animal*] 搁浅的

strange [streɪndʒ] *adj* 1 (*odd*) 奇怪的 2 (*unfamiliar*) [+ *person, place*] 陌生的

strangely ['streɪndʒlɪ] *adv* 奇怪地 ♦ **strangely (enough)** 奇怪的是

stranger ['streɪndʒə(r)] *n* [c] 1 (*unknown person*) 陌生人 2 (*from another area*) 异乡人 ♦ **they are strangers** 他们互相不认识 ♦ **to be a stranger to sth** 很不习惯某事

strangle ['stræŋgl] *vt* 1 (*kill*) 扼死 2 (喻) (*stifle*) 压制

strap [stræp] **I** *n* [c] 1 [*of watch, bag*] 带 2 [*of slip, dress*] 肩带 **II** *vt* ♦ **to strap sb/sth in/on** 用带子将某人/某物捆在…里/上

strategic [strə'tiːdʒɪk] *adj* 1 [+ *position*] 关键的 2 [+ *plan, site*] 有战略意义的 3 [+ *weapons, arms*] 战略的

strategy ['strætɪdʒɪ] *n* 1 [c/u] (*plan*) 行动计划 2 [u] [军] 战略

straw [strɔː] *n* 1 [u] 稻草 2 [c] (*drinking straw*) 吸管 ♦ **that's the last straw!** 那是最后的极限！

strawberry ['strɔːbərɪ] **I** *n* [c] 草莓 **II** *cpd* [复合词] 草莓

stray [streɪ] **I** *adj* 1 [+ *cat, dog*] 迷失的 2 [+ *bullet, hair*] 零星的 3 (*scattered*) 偶尔发生的 **II** *vi* 1 ♦ **to stray into/onto** 误入 2 (喻) [*thoughts, mind* +] 走神; [*eyes* +] 不由自主地移动 **III** *n* [c] (*dog, cat*) 走失的动物

streak [striːk] **I** *n* [c] 1 (*stripe*) 条纹 2 (*in hair*) 缕 3 [*of madness, jealousy etc*] 个性特征 **II** *vt* 在…上留下条纹 **III** *vi* ♦ **to streak past** 划过 ♦ **to have streaks in one's hair** 头发有不同颜色的条缕 ♦ **a winning/losing streak** 接连赢/失败 ♦ **to be streaked with sth** 夹杂着某物

stream [striːm] **I** *n* [c] 1 (*small river*) 溪流 2 (*current*) 水流 3 (*series*) [*of people, vehicles*] 川流不息; [*of questions, insults etc*] 一连串 4 [英:教育] 能力小组 **II** *vt* [英:教育] 把学生分成能力小组 **III** *vi* [*water, oil, blood* +] 涌流 ♦ **to come on stream** [*factory etc* +] 投入生产 ♦ **to stream in/out** [*people* +] 涌入/出

✪ **street** [striːt] *n* [c] 街道 ♦ **on the street(s)** (*homeless*) 无家可归的; (*outdoors*) 户外 ♦ **the man in the street** 普通人

streetcar ['striːtkɑː(r)] [美] *n* [c] 有轨电车 [英 = **tram**]

strength [strɛŋθ] *n* 1 [u] (*physical*) 力气 2 [u] [*of object, material*] 强度 3 [u] (*power, influence*) [*of person, organization, country*] 实力 4 [u] (*courage, determination*) 勇气 5 [c/u] (*quality, ability*) 长处 6 [u] (*intensity*) [*of feeling, opinion, belief*] 力量 7 [u] (*number of people*) 人数 8 [c/u] [*of drink, chemical*] 浓度 ♦ **on the strength of** 依凭 ♦ **to go from strength to strength** 不断取得成功 ♦ **at full strength** (*fully staffed*) 全体 ♦ **below strength** [*staff, army, team* +] 人手不足 ♦ **strength of mind/character** 充足的信心/坚强的性格

strengthen ['strɛŋθn] *vt* 1 [+ *building, machine*] 加固 2 [+ *muscle*] 使…有力 3 [+ *economy, currency, relationship*] 加强 4 [+ *argument*] 增强

strenuous ['strɛnjuəs] *adj* 1 [+ *exercise, walk*] 激烈的 2 [+ *efforts*] 努力的

stress [strɛs] **I** *n* [c/u] 1 (*mental strain*) 压力 2 (*force, pressure*) 重压 3 (*on word, syllable*) 重音 4 (*emphasis*) 强调 **II** *vt* 1 [+ *point, importance*] 强调 2 [+ *word, syllable*] 重读 ♦ **to be under stress** 有压力 ♦ **to lay great stress on sth** 极其强调某物 ♦ **to stress that ...** 强调…

stressed *adj* (*tense*) 紧张的

stressful ['strɛsful] *adj* [+ *job, situation*] 紧张的

stretch [strɛtʃ] **I** *n* [c] 1 [*of road, sand, water*] 连绵的一片; 2 (*period*) 一段时间 **II** *vi* 1 [*person, animal* +] 伸懒腰 2 (*extend*) [*land, area* +] 延伸 3 (*be flexible*) [*elastic, garment etc* +] 伸缩 **III** *vt* 1 [+ *arm, leg*] 伸直 2 (*pull*) [+ *elastic, garment*] 拉 3 (*over-extend*) [+ *resources*] 使紧张 4 [*job, task* +] [+ *person*] 使倾注全力 ♦ **for several days/weeks at a stretch** 连续几

天/星期 ♦**by no/any stretch of the imagination** 无论怎样/任凭如何异想天开 ♦**to stretch one's legs** 散散步
❑**stretch out I** *vi* 舒展着身子躺 **II** *vt* [+ *arm, leg*] 伸出 ♦**to stretch o.s. out** 舒展着身子躺
❑**stretch to** *vt* [不可拆分] [*money, food* +] 支付得起

stretcher ['strɛtʃə(r)] **I** *n* [c] 担架 **II** *vt* 用担架抬

strict [strɪkt] *adj* **1** [+ *rule, instruction*] 严格的 **2** [+ *person*] 严厉的 ♦**in the strict(est) sense of the word** 就某字精确的意义而言 ♦**a strict vegetarian** 绝对的素食主义者 ♦**to tell sb sth in the strictest confidence** 极秘密地将某事告诉某人

strictly ['strɪktlɪ] *adv* **1** (*severely*) 严格地 **2** (*exactly*) 完全地 **3** (*exclusively*) 绝对地 ♦**strictly confidential** 绝密 ♦**strictly speaking** 严格地说 ♦**strictly between ourselves** 只有我们两个人知道

stride [straɪd] (*pt, pp* **strode**) **I** *n* [c] 大步 **II** *vi* ♦**to stride across/off** 大步流星地穿过/走开 ♦**to take sth in one's stride** *or* [美] **in stride** 从容处理某事 ♦**to make strides** 取得进步

strike [straɪk] (*pt, pp* **struck**) **I** *n* [c] **1** [*of workers*] 罢工 **2** [军] 袭击 **II** *vt* **1** [正式] (*hit*) [+ *person, thing*] 打 **2** [正式] (*collide with*) 碰撞 **3** (*affect*) 侵袭 **4** [*idea, thought* +] 突然想到 **5** [+ *oil, gold*] 发现 **6** [+ *bargain, deal*] 达成 **7** [+ *match*] 擦 **8** ♦**to strike fear/terror into people** [文] 引起人们的恐惧/惊恐 **III** *vi* **1** (*go on strike*) 罢工 **2** [*illness, disaster* +] 降临 **3** [*clock* +] 报时 **4** [*killer* +] 袭击; [*snake* +] 咬 ♦**to be on strike** 在罢工 ♦**to go on strike** 参加罢工 ♦**to call a strike** 号召罢工 ♦**to be struck by lightning** 遭到雷击 ♦**to be struck by sth** 某事给…印象深刻 ♦**it struck me that ...** 我突然想到… ♦**he struck me as very serious/clever** 我感到他很严肃/聪明 ♦**the clock struck nine** 钟敲了9点 ♦**to strike a balance (between two things)** (把两者) 折中
❑**strike back** *vi* **1** [军] 反击 **2** [*person* +] (*retaliate*) 回击
❑**strike down** *vt* (*kill*) 打倒; (*injure*) 使病得厉害
❑**strike off** *vt* **1** (*from list*) 除名 **2** [+ *doctor, lawyer*] 取消从业资格
❑**strike out I** *vi* **1** (*speak out*) 抨击 **2** (*hit out*) 猛力打击 **3** (*become independent*) 独闯新路 **4** [文] (*in particular direction*) 行进 **5** [棒球] 使三击不中出局 **6** [美:非正式] (*fail*) 失败 **II** *vt* [+ *word, sentence*] 删去
❑**strike up** *vt* **1** [+ *conversation*] 开始 **2** [+ *friendship*] 开始建立 **3** [*band, orchestra* +] [+ *music*] 开始演奏

striker ['straɪkə(r)] *n* [c] **1** (*person on strike*) 罢工者 **2** [足球] 前锋

striking ['straɪkɪŋ] *adj* **1** (*noticeable*) 突出的 **2** (*attractive*) 出众的

string [strɪŋ] (*pt, pp* **strung**) **I** *n* **1** [c/u] 细绳 **2** [c] [*of beads, onions*] 串 **3** [c] [*of islands*] 一系列 **4** [c] [*of disasters, excuses*] 一连串 **5** [c] [计算机] 字符串 **6** [c] (*on guitar, violin*) 弦 **II** *vt* ♦**to string sth across sth** 把某物挂在某物上 **III the strings** *n* [*pl*] (*in orchestra*) 弦乐器 ♦**to pull strings** 运用影响以达目的 ♦**with no strings (attached)** 不加附带条件
❑**string along** *vt* [+ *person*] 愚弄
❑**string together** *vt* [+ *words etc*] 把…连接在一起

string bean [美] *n* [c] 菜豆 [英=**French bean**]

strip [strɪp] **I** *n* [c] **1** [*of paper, cloth*] 狭条 **2** [*of metal, wood*] 条 **3** [*of land, water*] 带状 **4** [体育] (*team colours*) 彩条球衣 **5** [美] (*comic strip*) 连环画 **II** *vt* **1** (*undress*) 脱光…的衣服 **2** [+ *bed*] 取下 **3** [+ *paint*] 刮去 **4** [+ *engine, machine*] 拆开 **5** ♦**to strip sb of** [+ *property, rights, title*] 剥夺某人的 **III** *vi* (*undress*) 脱光衣服; (*as entertainer*) 表演脱衣舞
❑**strip away** *vt* (喻) 揭除
❑**strip off I** *vi* (*undress*) 脱光衣服 **II** *vt* [+ *clothes*] 脱下

stripe [straɪp] **I** *n* [c] 条纹 **II stripes** *n* [*pl*] (*on uniform*) 制服上表示军衔或服役时间的条纹

striped [straɪpt] *adj* 有条纹的
stripper ['strɪpə(r)] *n* [c] (*strip-tease artist*) 脱衣舞表演者
strip-search ['strɪpsəːtʃ] **I** *n* [c] 光身搜查 **II** *vt* 对…进行光身搜查
strive [straɪv] (*pt* **strove**, *pp* **striven** ['strɪvn]) *vi* ♦**to strive for sth/to do sth** 力争某事/做某事
strode [strəud] *pt of* **stride**
stroke [strəuk] **I** *n* [c] **1** (*blow*) 击 **2** (*in swimming*) (*single movement*) 两臂划水一周; (*style*) 泳姿 **4** [医] 中风 **5** [网球, 板球, 高尔夫] 击球 **6** [*of clock*] 鸣响 **7** [*of paintbrush, pen*] 笔划 **II** *vt* [+ *person, animal etc*] 抚摸 ♦**at a stroke, in one stroke** 一下子 ♦**a stroke of luck** 好运 ♦**on the stroke of midnight** 子时 ♦**a 2-stroke engine** 双冲程发动机
stroll [strəul] **I** *n* [c] 散步 **II** *vi* 散步 ♦**to go for a stroll** 去散步 ♦**to have** *or* **take a stroll** 去散步
stroller ['strəulə(r)] [美] *n* [c] 婴儿小推车 [英 = **pushchair**]
✪**strong** [strɔŋ] **I** *adj* **1** [+ *person, arms, grip*] 有力的 **2** (*healthy*) 强健的 ◊ *Next week you may travel, when you are a little stronger.* 下星期你身体稍稍好一些就可以出去旅行了。◊ *He was very strong when he was young.* 他年轻时身体很强壮。**3** [+ *object, material*] 牢固的 **4** [+ *wind, current*] 强劲的 **5** [+ *drug*] 强劲的; [+ *alcoholic drink*] 烈性的; [+ *chemical, non-alcoholic drink*] 浓的 **6** [+ *impression, influence*] 感染力强的 **7** [+ *opinion, view, supporter*] 坚定的 **8** [+ *smell, taste, flavour*] 浓郁的 **9** [+ *protest, measures*] 激烈的 **10** [+ *personality*] 强的 **11** [+ *desire, reaction*] 强烈的 **12** (*likely to succeed*) 强有力的 ◊ *She is a strong contender for the team.* 她是入选队伍强有力的竞争者。**II** *adv* ♦**to be going strong** [*place, activity* +] 状态良好; [*person* +] 身体硬朗 ♦**strong language** 激烈的措辞 ♦**his/her strong point(s)** 他/她的长处 ♦**they were 50 strong** 他们多达50人
stronghold ['strɔŋhəuld] *n* [c] [*of attitude, belief*] 坚固据点
strongly ['strɔŋlɪ] *adv* **1** [+ *made, built*] 牢固 **2** [*defend, advise, argue* +] 坚决 **3** [*feel, believe* +] 坚定 **4** [*impress, influence* +] 强大 **5** [*taste, smell* +] 浓重 ♦**I feel strongly about it** 我对此有强烈的看法
strove [strəuv] *pt of* **strive**
struck [strʌk] *pt, pp of* **strike**
structural ['strʌktʃrəl] *adj* [+ *changes, damage*] 结构的
structural engineer *n* [c] 房产检视员
structure ['strʌktʃə(r)] **I** *n* **1** [c/u] [*of organization, society, book etc*] 体系 **2** [c] (*building*) 建筑物 **II** *vt* 安排
struggle ['strʌgl] **I** *n* **1** [c] (*fight*) 搏斗 **2** [c/u] (*attempt to do sth*) 斗争 **3** [c] (*difficulty*) 难事 **II** *vi* **1** (*try hard*) 尽力 **2** (*fight*) 搏斗 **3** (*try to free o.s.*) 挣扎 **4** (*have difficulty*) 艰难地应付 ♦**to have a struggle to do sth** 艰难地做某事
strung [strʌŋ] *pt, pp of* **string**
stub [stʌb] **I** *n* [c] [*of cheque, ticket etc*] 存根 ♦**pencil stub** 铅笔头 ♦**cigarette stub** 烟蒂 **II** *vt* ♦**to stub one's toe** 踢到了脚趾
❑**stub out** *vt* [+ *cigarette*] 捻熄
stubble ['stʌbl] *n* [u] **1** (*on chin*) 胡子茬 **2** (*in field*) 残株
stubborn ['stʌbən] *adj* **1** [+ *person*] 倔强的; [+ *resistance*] 顽强的 **2** [+ *stain, illness*] 难对付的
stuck [stʌk] **I** *pt, pp of* **stick** **II** *adj* ♦**to be stuck** (*unable to move*) [*object* +] 卡住; [*person* +] 陷于; (*unable to continue*) 卡住了 ♦**to get stuck** (*physically*) 被卡住; (*with work*) 被难住
stud [stʌd] **I** *n* [c] **1** (*on clothing etc*) 饰钉 **2** (*earring*) 耳钉 **3** [英] (*on soles of boots*) 鞋钉 **4** (*stud farm*) 种马场 **5** [非正式] (*man*) 性欲旺盛的男子 **II** *vt* ♦**studded with** 镶有
✪**student** ['stjuːdənt] **I** *n* [c] **1** (*at university*) 大学生 **2** (*at school*) 中学生 **II** *cpd* [复合词] [+ *life, pub*] 学生; [+ *friends*] 同学 ♦**a law/medical student** 一名法律/医学学生 ♦**a student nurse/teacher** 一名实习护士/教师
student driver [美] *n* [c] 见习司机
studio ['stjuːdɪəu] *n* [c] **1** [电视, 广播, 音] 摄影室 **2** [*of artist*] 画室; [*of*

photographer] 摄影室
studio apartment [美] *n* [c] 带有厨房和卫生间的小型套房 [英= **studio flat**]
studio flat [英] *n* [c] 带有厨房和卫生间的小型套房 [美= **studio apartment**]
✪ **study** ['stʌdɪ] **I** *n* **1** [u] (*activity*) 学习 ◊ *rooms set aside for study* 专供学习的房间 **2** [c] (*piece of research*) 研究 ◊ *the first study of the drug's effects* 第一项探讨药物作用的研究 **3** [c] (*room*) 书房 **II** *vt* **1** [+ *subject*] 攻读 **2** [+ *sb's face, evidence*] 仔细察看 **III** *vi* 学习 **IV studies** *n* [*pl*] 学业 ♦ **to make a study of sth** 研究某事 ♦ **business/European studies** 商务/欧洲研究
stuff [stʌf] **I** *n* [u] **1** (*things*) 物品 **2** (*substance*) 东西 **II** *vt* **1** ♦ **to stuff sth in/under sth** 把某物塞入某物内/塞到某物下面 **2** ♦ **to stuff sth with sth** 用某物装满某物 **3** [烹饪] [+ *peppers, mushrooms*] 给…装馅; [+ *chicken, turkey*] 把填料塞入 **4** [+ *toy, pillow*] 填塞 **5** [+ *dead animal*] 制成标本 **6** ♦ **my nose is stuffed up** 我鼻子堵了 ♦ **get stuffed!** [英: 非正式, 疑讳] 去你的!
stuffing ['stʌfɪŋ] *n* [u] (*in sofa, chicken etc*) 填料
stuffy ['stʌfɪ] *adj* **1** [+ *room*] 闷热的 **2** [+ *person, ideas*] 古板的
stumble ['stʌmbl] *vi* **1** (*while moving*) 绊脚 **2** (*while speaking*) 结巴
❑ **stumble across, stumble on** *vt* [不可拆分] 偶然遇到
stump [stʌmp] **I** *n* [c] **1** [*of tree*] 树桩 **2** [*of limb*] 残肢 **II** *vt* ♦ **to be stumped** 被难倒
❑ **stump up** *vt* [英: 非正式] [+ *money*] 付清
stun [stʌn] *vt* **1** (*shock*) 使震惊 **2** (*daze*) 使昏迷
stung [stʌŋ] *pt, pp of* **sting**
stunk [stʌŋk] *pp of* **stink**
stunned [stʌnd] *adj* (*shocked*) 目瞪口呆的 ♦ **a stunned silence** 哑口无言
stunning ['stʌnɪŋ] *adj* **1** (*impressive*) 惊人的 **2** (*beautiful*) [+ *person, dress etc*] 极漂亮的
stunt [stʌnt] **I** *n* [c] **1** (*in film*) 惊险动作 **2** (*publicity stunt*) 噱头 **II** *vt* [+ *growth, development*] 阻碍…的正常发育
stupid ['stjuːpɪd] *adj* **1** [+ *person*] 笨的 **2** [+ *question, idea, mistake*] 愚蠢的 **3** [非正式] 乏味的
stupidity [stjuː'pɪdɪtɪ] *n* [u] 愚蠢
sturdy ['stəːdɪ] *adj* **1** [+ *object*] 结实的 **2** [+ *person*] 健壮的
stutter ['stʌtə(r)] **I** *n* [c] 口吃 **II** *vi* 结结巴巴地说 ♦ **to have a stutter, speak with a stutter** 结结巴巴地说
style [staɪl] **I** *n* **1** [c] (*type*) 方式 **2** [u] (*elegance*) 风度 **3** [c/u] (*design*) 样式 **II** *vt* **1** [+ *hair*] 打理 **2** [+ *clothes*] 使符合特定款式 ♦ **in the latest style** 最新式样
stylish ['staɪlɪʃ] *adj* 时髦的
stylist ['staɪlɪst] *n* [c] **1** (*hair stylist*) 发型师 **2** (*literary*) 文体家
sub... [sʌb] *prefix* **1** 下 **2** 分支 **3** 次于
subconscious [sʌb'kɔnʃəs] **I** *n* [s] 潜意识 **II** *adj* 潜意识的
subdued [səb'djuːd] *adj* **1** [+ *person*] 闷闷不乐的 **2** [+ *light*] 柔和的
subject [*n* 'sʌbdʒɪkt, *vb* səb'dʒɛkt] **I** *n* [c] **1** (*matter*) 主题 **2** [教育] 科目 **3** [*of country*] 国民 **4** [语法] 主语 **II** *vt* ♦ **to subject sb to sth** 使某人经受某事 **III** *adj* ♦ **to be subject to** 遭到 ♦ **to change the subject** 改变话题 ♦ **subject to availability** 以可取得为准 ♦ **prices may be subject to alteration** 价格可能会有变动
subjective [səb'dʒɛktɪv] *adj* 主观的
subject matter *n* [u] 题材
submarine [sʌbmə'riːn] *n* [c] 潜水艇
submerge [səb'məːdʒ] **I** *vt* 使淹没 **II** *vi* [*submarine* +] 潜入水中 ♦ **to submerge o.s. in sth** (喻) 献身于某事
submission [səb'mɪʃən] *n* **1** [u] (*subjection*) 屈服 **2** [u] [正式] [*of document*] 提交 **3** [c] (*proposal*) 呈递材料
submit [səb'mɪt] **I** *vt* [+ *proposal, application, claim etc*] 提交 **II** *vi* ♦ **to submit to sth** 屈服于某物
subordinate [*n, adj* sə'bɔːdɪnət, *vt* sə'bɔːdɪneɪt] **I** *n* [c] 下属 **II** *adj* **1** [+ *officer, position, role*] 下级的

2 ♦**to be subordinate to sb** 是某人的下属 3 ♦**to be subordinate to sth** 从属于某事物 **III** *vt* ♦**to subordinate sth to sth** 使某物服从某物

subordinate clause *n* 从句

subscribe [səb'skraɪb] *vi* ♦**to subscribe (to sth)** [+ *magazine etc*] 订阅; [+ *fund, charity*] 定期捐款 ♦**I don't subscribe to that view** 我不赞成那个看法

subscriber [səb'skraɪbə(r)] *n* [c] 1 (*to magazine, newspaper*) 订阅者 2 (*to service*) 用户

subscription [səb'skrɪpʃən] *n* [c] 1 (*to magazine, service*) 订阅 2 (*money paid*) 订阅费 3 (*membership dues*) 注册费 4 (*to charity*) 捐赠 ♦**to take out a subscription to** [+ *organization*] 注册; [+ *magazine etc*] 订阅

subsequent ['sʌbsɪkwənt] [正式] *adj* 1 (*later*) [+ *events, generations*] 随后的 2 (*further*) [+ *research, investigations*] 进一步的 ♦**subsequent to** 在…之后

subsequently ['sʌbsɪkwəntlɪ] [正式] *adv* 后来

subside [səb'saɪd] *vi* 1 [*feeling* +] 平息 2 [*flood, river* +] 减退 3 [*earth, building* +] 下陷

subsidiary [səb'sɪdɪərɪ] **I** *adj* 1 [+ *question, role*] 次要的 2 [英: 大学] [+ *subject*] 辅助的 **II** *n* [c] 1 (*subsidiary company*) 子公司 2 [英: 大学] (*subsidiary subject*) 辅助科目

subsidize ['sʌbsɪdaɪz] *vt* 给…补助金

subsidy ['sʌbsɪdɪ] *n* [c] 补助金

substance ['sʌbstəns] *n* 1 [c] (*matter*) 物质 2 [s] [正式] [*of speech, article etc*] 要旨 3 [u] [正式] (*truth*) 根据 4 [u] (*importance, significance*) 实质 ♦**a man of substance** [正式] 要人 ♦**to lack substance** [*speech, article etc* +] 缺乏实质性内容

substantial [səb'stænʃl] *adj* 1 [+ *building*] 牢固的 2 [+ *meal*] 丰盛的; [+ *improvement*] 重大的; [+ *reward, amount*] 相当数额的

substantially [səb'stænʃəlɪ] [正式] *adv* 1 (*by a large amount*) 在很大程度上 2 (*in essence*) 基本上

substitute ['sʌbstɪtjuːt] **I** *n* [c] 1 (*person*) 代替者 2 (*thing*) 代用品 3 [足球] 替补队员 **II** *vt* ♦**to substitute sth (for sth)** 用某物代替(某物) **III** *vi* ♦**to substitute for** [*person* +] 接替 [*thing* +] 代替

substitution [sʌbstɪ'tjuːʃən] *n* [c/u] 代替; [足球] 替换

subtitles ['sʌbtaɪtlz] *n* [*pl*] 字幕

subtle ['sʌtl] *adj* 1 [+ *change, difference*] 细微的 2 [+ *smell, sound, etc*] 隐约的; [+ *scent*] 淡雅的 3 (*indirect*) [+ *person*] 敏锐的

subtlety ['sʌtltɪ] *n* 1 [c] (*nuance*) 细微差别 2 [u] (*indirect methods*) 含蓄的方式 3 [u] (*art of being subtle*) 微妙之处

subtract [səb'trækt] *vt* ♦**to subtract sth (from sth)** (从某数中)减去某数

suburb ['sʌbəːb] **I** *n* [c] 郊区 **II the suburbs** *n* [*pl*] 郊区

suburban [sə'bəːbən] *adj* 1 [+ *shopping centre, train etc*] 郊区的 2 [贬] [+ *clothes, lifestyle*] 古板的

subway ['sʌbweɪ] *n* [c] 1 [美] (*underground railway*) 地铁 [英 = **underground**] 2 [英] (*underpass*) 地下通道 [美 = **underpass**]

succeed [sək'siːd] **I** *vi* [*plan, person* +] 成功; [*marriage* +] 美满 **II** *vt* 1 [+ *person*] (*in job*) 接替 2 (*follow*) 继…之后 ♦**to succeed in doing sth** 成功地做某事 ♦**to succeed to the throne** 继承王位

success [sək'sɛs] *n* [u/c] 成功 ♦**without success** 一无所成

successful [sək'sɛsful] *adj* 1 [+ *attempt, film, product*] 成功的 2 [+ *writer, lawyer*] 有成就的 ♦**the successful candidate** 获胜的候选人 ♦**to be successful in doing sth** 在做某事方面成功

successfully [sək'sɛsfəlɪ] *adv* 成功地

succession [sək'sɛʃən] *n* 1 [s] (*series*) 一连串 2 [u] (*to throne etc*) 继承 ♦**for the third year in succession** 连续3年 ♦**in quick succession** 紧接着

successive [sək'sɛsɪv] *adj* [+ *governments, years, attempts*] 接连的 ♦**on 3 successive days** 接连3天

successor [sək'sɛsə(r)] *n* [c] 继任者 ♦**to be the successor to sb** 做某人的接班人

succumb [sə'kʌm] [正式] *vi* ♦**to succumb (to)** (*to temptation*) 抵挡不住 ♦**to succumb to illness** 被疾病压垮

✪**such** [sʌtʃ] *adj* **1** (*of this kind*) 此类的 ◊ *Such a book should be praised, not banned.* 此类书应该得到赞扬，而不应被禁止。**2** (*emphasizing similarity*) 诸如此类◊ *It was in Brighton or Bournemouth or some such place.* 是在布赖顿或伯恩茅斯，或诸如此类的地方。**3** (*so much*) 这等◊ *He showed such courage in the face of adversity.* 他在厄运面前显示出这等勇气。♦**such a(n)** 那么◊ *It was such a lovely day.* 那一天天气那么好。♦**such a lot of** 那么多 ♦**in such a way that ...** 以致于… ♦**such as** (*like*) 像◊ *countries such as France, Germany, and Italy* 像法国、德国、意大利等国家 ♦**you're welcome to borrow such books as I have** 我只有这些书，但是你尽管借 ♦**I said no such thing** 我没有这样讲 ♦**such as it is** 尽管价值不过尔尔 ♦**as such** (*exactly*) 如所指的◊ *I am not a learner as such: I used to ride a bike years ago.* 我并不完全是个初学者，许多年前也常常骑自行车。◊ *He's not lazy as such: he just lacks energy.* 他并不像所说的那样懒：他只是缺少活力。; (*on its own*) 就其本身而言◊ *He is not very interested in politics as such.* 他对政治本身并不大感兴趣。

> 📖 **such** 修饰单数可数名词时，后面跟**a** 或**an** 。*...such a pleasant surprise... such an old car...* 修饰名词复数或不可数名词时，后面不加**a** 或**an** 。*...such beautiful girls...such power...* 不能用**such** 指代在现场的某事物或说话人所在地，而要用**like that** 或**like this** 。例如，你称赞某人的手表时，不能说*I'd like such a watch*，而应说*I'd like a watch like that*。同样，谈到目前你所居住的城镇时，不能说*There's not much to do in such a town*，而应说*There's not much to do in a town like this.*

such-and-such ['sʌtʃənsʌtʃ] *adj* 某某

suck [sʌk] **I** *vt* **1** [+ *ice-lolly, sweet*] 含在嘴里舔吃; [+ *dummy, thumb*] 吮 **3** [*pump, machine* +] 抽吸 **II** *vi* ♦**to suck (on/at sth)** 吮（某物）

Sudan [su'dɑːn] *n* 苏丹

Sudanese [suːdə'niːz] **I** *adj* 苏丹的 **II** *n* [c] (*person*) 苏丹人

sudden ['sʌdn] *adj* 意外的 ♦**all of a sudden** 出乎意料

suddenly ['sʌdnlɪ] *adv* 突然

sue [suː] **I** *vt* 起诉 **II** *vi* 提起诉讼 ♦**to sue sb for damages** 控告某人要求赔偿

suede [sweɪd] **I** *n* [u] 仿麂皮 **II** *cpd* [复合词][+ *shoes, handbag*] 仿麂皮

suffer ['sʌfə(r)] **I** *vt* **1** [+ *blow, setback*] 遭受 **2** [+ *pain, illness*] 承受 **II** *vi* **1** (*due to pain, illness poverty etc*) [*activity* +] 受损失 **2** (*be badly affected*) [*person* +] 受苦难 ♦**to suffer from shock/diarrhoea** 受惊吓/患腹泻

sufferer ['sʌfərə(r)] *n* [c] 患者

suffering ['sʌfərɪŋ] *n* [c/u] 痛苦

suffice [sə'faɪs] [正式] *vi* 足够 ♦**suffice it to say that ...** 只要说…就够了

sufficient [sə'fɪʃənt] *adj* **1** 足够的 **2** [正式][+ *condition, cause*] 充足的 ♦**to be sufficient for sth** 对某事来说足够了 ♦**to be sufficient to do sth** 足够做某事 ♦**sufficient money to do sth/for sth** 足够的资金来做某事/付某笔费用

sufficiently [sə'fɪʃəntlɪ] *adv* **1** [*recover, provide* +] 充分地 **2** [+ *large, powerful*] 足够地

suffocate ['sʌfəkeɪt] **I** *vi* **1** (*die*) 闷死 **2** (*have difficulty breathing*) 呼吸困难 **II** *vt* 使窒息

sugar ['ʃugə(r)] **I** *n* [u/c] 糖 **II** *vt* [+ *tea etc*] 加糖

✪**suggest** [sə'dʒɛst] *vt* **1** (*propose*) 建议◊ *We have to suggest possible topics for next term's class.* 我们需要就下学期的课题提些建议。**2** (*indicate*) 显示出◊ *His expression* *suggested some pleasure at the fact that I had come.* 他的表情显示出他对我的到来有些好感。♦**to suggest that ...** (*propose*) 建议…◊ *I suggested that we walk to the park.* 我建议走路去公园。; (*indicate*) 显示出…◊ *Early reports suggested that he would lose heavily.* 早期报告显示出他会惨败。; (*imply*) 暗示 ◊ *I'm not suggesting (that) that is what is happening.* 我并未暗示说现在就是这样。

suggestion [sə'dʒɛstʃən] *n* [c] **1** (*proposal*) 建议 **2** (*indication*) 暗示 **3** (*association*) 联想 ♦**a suggestion of sth** 细微的迹象 ♦**to make a suggestion** 提建议

suggestive [sə'dʒɛstɪv] *adj* [+ *remark*] 挑逗的 ♦**to be suggestive of sth** 使人联想起某物

suicide ['suɪsaɪd] **I** *n* **1** [c/u] 自杀 **2** [u] (*harmful action*) 自取灭亡 **3** [c] (*person*) 自杀者 **II** *cpd* [复合词] [+ *attack, mission*] 自杀性 ◊ *a suicide bomber* 人肉炸弹 ♦**to commit suicide** 自杀

suit [su:t] **I** *n* [c] **1** (*man's, woman's*) 西装 **2** (*for particular activity*) 套装 **3** [法] 讼案 **4** [纸牌] 一组同样花色的纸牌 **II** *vt* **1** (*be convenient, appropriate*) 对…合适 **2** [*colour, clothes* +] [+ *person*] 适合 ♦**to file** *or* **bring a suit against sb** [美:法] 起诉某人 ♦**to follow suit** (*do the same*) 跟着做 ♦**to suit sth to sb/sth** (*adapt*) 使某物适合于某人/某物 ♦**to be suited to doing sth** 适宜于做某事 ♦**to suit o.s.** 随自己的意愿行事 ♦**suit yourself!** 自便！ ♦**to be well suited (to each other)** (互相) 很搭配

suitable ['su:təbl] *adj* **1** (*convenient*) [+ *time, place*] 合适的 **2** (*appropriate*) [+ *person, clothes etc*] 适合的

suitably ['su:təblɪ] *adv* **1** [+ *dressed, qualified*] 适当地 **2** [+ *impressed, amazed*] 适宜地

suitcase ['su:tkeɪs] *n* [c] 手提箱

suite [swi:t] *n* [c] **1** (*in hotel, large building*) 套间 *see also* **en suite** **2** (*furniture*) 一套家具 ♦**a bedroom/dining room suite** 一套卧室/饭厅家具 ♦**a bathroom suite** 一套浴具

sulfur ['sʌlfə(r)] [美] *n* = **sulphur**

sulk [sʌlk] **I** *n* [c] 生闷气 **II** *vi* 生闷气 ♦**to be in a sulk** 生闷气

sulphur (美 **sulfur**) ['sʌlfə(r)] *n* [u] 硫磺

sultana [sʌl'tɑ:nə] [英] *n* [c] 无核小葡萄干

sum [sʌm] **I** *n* [c] **1** (*amount*) 数额 **2** (*calculation*) 算术题 **3** [数] (*total*) 总数 ♦**to do a sum** 算算术 ♦**in sum** [正式] 简而言之

❑**sum up I** *vt* **1** (*describe briefly*) 概括 **2** (*epitomize*) 代表 **II** *vi* 总结

summarize ['sʌməraɪz] **I** *vt* 概括 **II** *vi* 总结

summary ['sʌmərɪ] **I** *n* [c] 摘要 **II** *adj* [正式] [+ *justice, execution*] 草率的 ♦**in summary** 概括地说

summer ['sʌmə(r)] **I** *n* [c/u] 夏季 **II** *cpd* [复合词] [+ *dress, weather, sunshine*] 夏季 ♦**in (the) summer** 在夏季

summertime ['sʌmətaɪm] *n* [u] 夏季

summit ['sʌmɪt] *n* [c] **1** [*of mountain*] 峰顶 **2** [政治] (*meeting*) 高峰会议

summon ['sʌmən] *vt* **1** [+ *person, police, help*] 召唤 **2** [法] 传讯 **3** (*also:* ***summon up***) [+ *strength, courage*] 鼓起

Sun. *abbr* (= ***Sunday***) 星期天

sun [sʌn] *n* **1** [s/c] (*in the sky*) 太阳 **2** [u] (*heat*) 太阳的光和热; (*light*) 阳光 ♦**to sit/lie in the sun** 坐/躺在阳光下 ♦**to catch the sun** 被晒黑 ♦**everything under the sun** 世上万物

sunbathe ['sʌnbeɪð] *vi* 晒日光浴

sunblock ['sʌnblɔk] *n* [c/u] 防晒霜

sunburn ['sʌnbə:n] *n* [u] 晒斑

sunburnt ['sʌnbə:nt] *adj* = **sunburned**

sunburned, sunburnt ['sʌnbə:nd] *adj* 晒伤的

Sunday ['sʌndɪ] *n* [c/u] 星期天 *see also* **Tuesday**

SUNDAY LUNCH

英国传统的Sunday lunch以大块烤肉为主菜，如牛肉、猪肉、羊肉或鸡肉。除肉类之外，还

配有烤土豆、蔬菜，可能还有 **Yorkshire pudding** 一一种用加牛奶、鸡蛋的面糊做成的脆皮可口的饼，要在炉里烤到表层胀起才算好。**gravy**（调味肉汁）也会在餐桌上见到。自己不想做也没关系，许多酒吧和餐馆提供**Sunday lunch** 。

sunflower ['sʌnflauə(r)] *n* [c] 向日葵
sung [sʌŋ] *pp of* **sing**
sunglasses ['sʌŋglɑːsɪz] *n* [*pl*] 墨镜
sunk [sʌŋk] *pp of* **sink**
sunlight ['sʌnlaɪt] *n* [u] 阳光
sunny ['sʌnɪ] *adj* **1** [+ *weather, day*] 晴朗的 **2** [+ *place*] 阳光充足的 **3** [+ *disposition, person*] 乐观的 ♦**it is sunny** 天气晴朗
sunrise ['sʌnraɪz] *n* **1** [u] (*time*) 拂晓 **2** [c] (*sky*) 日出 ♦**at sunrise** 拂晓时分
sun roof *n* [c] (*on car*) 遮阳篷顶
sun screen *n* [c/u] 遮光屏
sunset ['sʌnsɛt] *n* **1** [u] (*time*) 傍晚 **2** [c] (*sky*) 日落 ♦**at sunset** 傍晚时
sunshine ['sʌnʃaɪn] *n* [u] 阳光
suntan ['sʌntæn] **I** *n* [c] 晒黑 **II** *cpd* [复合词][+ *lotion, cream*] 防晒 ♦**to get a suntan** 皮肤晒黑
super ['suːpə(r)] [英:非正式] *adj* 极好的
superb [suː'pəːb] *adj* 极好的
superficial [suːpə'fɪʃəl] *adj* **1** [+ *wound, injury, damage*] 表皮的 **2** [+ *knowledge, analysis*] 表面性的 **3** [贬][+ *person*] 肤浅的
superintendent [suːpərɪn'tɛndənt] *n* [c] **1** [警察][英] 警督; [美] 警长 **2** [*of place, activity*] 主管人 **3** [美][*of building, school*] 看门人 [英= **caretaker**]
superior [su'pɪərɪə(r)] **I** *adj* **1** (*better*) 优秀的 **2** (*more senior*) 上级的 **3** [贬] (*smug*) 高傲的 **II** *n* [c] (*in rank*) 上级 ♦**superior to** 优于
superiority [supɪərɪ'ɔrɪtɪ] *n* [u] 优势
supermarket ['suːpəmɑːkɪt] *n* [u] 超级市场
supernatural [suːpə'nætʃərəl] **I** *adj* [+ *creature, powers*] 神奇的 **II** *n* ♦**the supernatural** 超自然事物
superpower ['suːpəpauə(r)] [政治] *n* [c] 超级大国
superstition [suːpə'stɪʃən] *n* [c/u] 迷信
superstitious [suːpə'stɪʃəs] *adj* [+ *person, fear, belief*] 迷信的
supervise ['suːpəvaɪz] *vt* [+ *person, activity*] 监督
supervision [suːpə'vɪʒən] *n* [u] [*of person*] 管理; [*of activity*] 监督 ♦**under medical supervision** 遵循医嘱
supervisor ['suːpəvaɪzə(r)] *n* [c] **1** [*of workers*] 监工 **2** [*of student*] 导师
supper ['sʌpə(r)] *n* [c/u] **1** (*early evening*) 晚餐 **2** (*late evening*) 夜宵 ♦**to have supper** 吃晚餐
📖 用法参见 **meal**
supple ['sʌpl] *adj* **1** [+ *object, material*] 柔韧的 **2** [+ *person, body*] 轻盈的
supplement [*n* 'sʌplɪmənt, *vb* 'sʌplɪmɛnt] **I** *n* [c] **1** (*additional amount*) [*of vitamins, money etc*] 补充 **2** [*of book*] 补编 **3** [*of newspaper, magazine*] 增刊 **II** *vt* 补充
supplier [sə'plaɪə(r)] *n* [c] 供应商
supply [sə'plaɪ] **I** *vt* **1** (*provide*) 提供 **2** [商](*deliver*) 送货 **II** *n* **1** [c/u] (*stock*) 供应量 **2** [u] (*supplying*) 供应 **III supplies** *n* [*pl*] **1** (*food*) 供给 **2** [军] 军需品 ♦**to supply sth to sb** 为某人提供某物 ♦**to supply sb/sth with sth** 为某人/某物提供某物 ♦**it comes supplied with an adaptor** 内含变压器 ♦**food is in short supply** 食品供应不足 ♦**the electricity/gas supply** 电力/煤气供应 ♦**supply and demand** [经济] 供求
✪**support** [sə'pɔːt] **I** *n* **1** [u] (*moral*) 支持 ◊ *The prime minister gave his full support to the reforms.* 首相对改革给予大力支持。**2** [u] (*financial*) 资助 ◊ *the proposal to cut agricultural support by 15%* 削减15%的农业资助的提议 **3** [u] (*kindness, help*) 帮助 ◊ *mentally ill people in need of support* 患心理疾病的人士需要帮助 **4** [c] (*for object, structure*) 支承 **5** [u] (*balance*) 支撑物 ◊ *Alice was leaning against him for support.* 艾丽斯把他当支撑物靠着。**6** [u] (*evidence*) (*for theory, statement*) 依据

◊ *History offers some support for this view.* 历史为此观点提供了某些依据。**II** *vt* **1** (*morally*) [+ *policy, strike etc*] 支持 ◊ *He thanked everyone who had supported the strike.* 他对支持罢工的所有人士表示感谢。**2** (*financially*) 供养 ◊ *He has a wife and three children to support.* 他需要供养妻子和3个孩子。**3** (*hold up*) [+ *object, structure*] 支承 ◊ *the girders that supported the walkway* 支承着人行道的大梁 **4** (*hold up*) [+ *person*] 撑着 ◊ *Let your baby sit on the floor with cushions to support him.* 让你的婴儿坐在地上，用坐垫撑着他。**5** (*substantiate*) [+ *theory, statement*] 证实 ◊ *There was no evidence to support such a theory.* 没有证据来证实这一理论。**6** [+ *football team*] 支持 ◊ *Tim supports Manchester United.* 蒂姆支持曼联队。♦ **in support of** 支持 ♦ **to support o.s.** (*financially*) 养活自己

supporter [sə'pɔːtə(r)] *n* [C] **1** [*of politician, policy*] 支持者 **2** [*of team*] 追随者

suppose [sə'pəuz] *vt* 认为 ♦ **I suppose** 我想 ♦ **it was worse than she'd supposed** 事情比她想像的要糟 ♦ **I don't suppose she'll come** 我想她不会来 ♦ **he's about sixty, I suppose** 我想他大概60岁 ♦ **I suppose so/not** 我看是/不是这样 ♦ **suppose he was right** 假定他是对的 ♦ **he is supposed to do it** (*duty*) 他应该做的 ♦ **he's supposed to be an expert** 人们以为他是个专家

supposedly [sə'pəuzɪdlɪ] *adv* 据称

supposing [sə'pəuzɪŋ] *conj* 假使

suppress [sə'prɛs] *vt* **1** [+ *religion*] 禁止; [+ *revolt*] 镇压 **2** [+ *information, publication*] 封锁 **3** [+ *feelings*] 抑制 **4** [+ *yawn, laugh, sneeze*] 忍住

supreme [su'priːm] *adj* **1** (*in titles*) 最高的 **2** (*great*) 极度的

Supt (尤美 **Supt.**) [警察] *abbr* (= ***superintendent***) 警长

surcharge ['səːtʃɑːdʒ] *n* [C] 附加费

✪ **sure** [ʃuə(r)] **I** *adj* **1** (*definite, convinced*) 有把握的 ◊ *How can you be so sure?* 你怎么这么有把握？**2** (*reliable*) [+ *remedy*] 有效的; [+ *sign*] 准确无误的 ◊ *She has a sure grasp of social issues.* 她对社会问题掌握得准确无误。**3** ♦ **to be sure to do sth** (*certain*) 肯定做某事 ◊ *Kids are sure to love crawling through the tunnel.* 孩子们肯定喜欢爬隧道。**II** *adv* ♦ **she sure is pretty** [尤美:非正式] 她确实很漂亮 ♦ **to make sure that ...** (*take action*) 保证… ◊ *Make sure that you follow the instructions carefully.* 你一定要仔细按照说明书做。◊ *You must make sure that you finish your work on time.* 你必须保证按时完成工作。; (*check*) 查明… ◊ *He looked in the bathroom to make sure that he was alone.* 他看了看洗澡间，确定是否只有他一个人。♦ **sure!** [非正式] (*of course*) 当然了！♦ **sure enough** 果然 ♦ **to be sure of (doing) sth** 有把握(做)某事 ♦ **that's for sure** 毫无疑问 ♦ **I'm sure of it** 我确信 ♦ **I'm not sure how/why/when** 我不能肯定如何/为什么/什么时候 ♦ **to be sure of o.s.** 有自信心

surely ['ʃuəlɪ] *adv* (*for emphasis*) 想必; [正式] (*certainly*) 肯定 ♦ **surely you don't mean that!** 你肯定不是这个意思！♦ **slowly but surely** 缓慢而稳步地

surf [səːf] **I** *n* [U] 拍岸的浪花 **II** *vi* 冲浪 **III** *vt* ♦ **to surf the Internet** 网上冲浪 ♦ **to go surfing** 去冲浪

surface ['səːfɪs] **I** *n* **1** [C] [*of object*] 表面 **2** [C] (*top layer*) 表层 **3** [C] [*of lake, pond*] 水面 **4** [S] [*of mind, emotions*] 外表 **II** *vi* **1** [*fish, diver* +] 浮出水面 **2** [*news* +] 被揭露; [*feeling* +] 显露 **3** [非正式] (*rise from bed*) 起床 **III** *vt* [+ *road*] 铺路 ♦ **on the surface** 在表面上

surfboard ['səːfbɔːd] *n* [C] 冲浪板

surfing ['səːfɪŋ] *n* [U] 冲浪 *see also* **surf**

surge [səːdʒ] **I** *n* [C] **1** (*in demand, interest*) 急剧上升 **2** (*in flow*) 汹涌 **3** [*of emotion*] 一阵 ♦ **a surge of electricity** 电涌 **II** *vi* **1** [*water* +] 奔腾 **2** [*people, vehicles* +] 涌 **3** [*level, rate* +] 急剧上升 **4** [文] [*emotion* +] 翻腾 **5** [电子] 突然增加 ♦ **to surge**

forward 蜂拥向前
surgeon ['sɜːdʒən] *n* [c] 外科医师
surgery ['sɜːdʒərɪ] *n* **1** [u] (*treatment*) 外科手术 **2** [c] [英] (*room*) [*of doctor, dentist*] 诊所 **3** [c] [英] (*also:* ***surgery hours***) [*of doctor, dentist*] 门诊时间 **4** [c] [英] [*of MP etc*] 接待时间
surgical ['sɜːdʒɪkl] *adj* **1** [+ *instrument, mask etc*] 外科手术用的 **2** [+ *treatment, operation*] 外科的
surname ['sɜːneɪm] *n* [c] 姓
surpass [sɜː'pɑːs] [正式] *vt* 超过
surplus ['sɜːpləs] **I** *n* [c] ♦**a surplus (of sth)** 过剩的(某物) **II** *adj* [+ *stock, grain etc*] 过剩的 ♦**a trade surplus** 贸易顺差 ♦**it is surplus to our requirements** [正式] 超过我们的需要
surprise [sə'praɪz] **I** *n* **1** [c] (*unexpected event*) 意想不到的事物 **2** [u] (*astonishment*) 诧异 **II** *adj* [+ *visit, announcement etc*] 出人意料的 **III** *vt* **1** (*astonish*) 使感到意外 **2** (*catch unawares*) 使震惊 ♦**it came as a surprise (to me)** 这出乎(我的)意料 ♦**to take sb by surprise** 使某人吃惊 ♦**to my (great) surprise** 使我(很)惊奇的是 ♦**it surprised me that ...** 令我吃惊的是… ♦**it wouldn't surprise me if ...** 如果…我不会感到吃惊
surprised [sə'praɪzd] *adj* 惊讶的 ♦**to be surprised to find/see sth** 真没想到会发现/看到某物 ♦**to be surprised at sth** 对某事感到吃惊 ♦**to be surprised that ...** 对…感到惊讶

> 📖 请勿将**surprised** 和 **surprising** 混淆。在发生意外或异常情况时，可以说你感到**surprised**。*I'm surprised at your behaviour...I was surprised that it was so cold in August...* **surprising** 的事物让人感到**surprised**。*A surprising number of customers complained...It's not surprising that she was disappointed when he didn't arrive.*

surprising [sə'praɪzɪŋ] *adj* [+ *situation, announcement*] 出人意外的 ♦**it is surprising how/that ...** 真没想到如此/是… 📖 用法参见**surprised**
surprisingly [sə'praɪzɪŋlɪ] *adv* 出人意外地 ♦**(somewhat) surprisingly, he agreed** 他(有点)出人意外地同意了
surrender [sə'rɛndə(r)] **I** *n* **1** [c/u] (*act*) 投降 **2** [u] [*of weapons*] 交出 **II** *vi* 投降 **III** *vt* **1** [+ *weapons, territory*] 交出 **2** [+ *claim, right*] 放弃
surrogate ['sʌrəgɪt] **I** *n* [c] 替代品 **II** *adj* (*substitute*) 替代的
surround [sə'raund] *vt* **1** [*walls, circumstances* +] 围绕 **2** [*police, soldiers* +] 包围 ♦**to surround o.s. with people/things** 周围都是人/物
surrounding [sə'raundɪŋ] *adj* 周围的
surroundings [sə'raundɪŋz] *n* [*pl*] 环境
surveillance [sɜː'veɪləns] *n* [u] 监视 ♦**under surveillance** 在监视下
survey [*n* 'sɜːveɪ, *vb* sɜː'veɪ] **I** *n* [c] **1** [尤英] [*of house*] 查勘 [美 = **inspection**] **2** [*of land*] 测量 **3** (*poll*) 民意测验 **II** *vt* **1** [尤英] [+ *house*] 查勘 [美 = **inspect**] **2** (*examine, measure*) [+ *land*] 测量 **3** (*carry out survey on*) [+ *people, organizations*] 调查 **4** (*look at*) [+ *scene, work etc*] 审视
surveyor [sə'veɪə(r)] *n* [c] **1** [*of land*] 勘测员 **2** [英] [*of buildings*] 房产检视员 [美 = **structural engineer**]
survival [sə'vaɪvl] **I** *n* [u] [*of person, company*] 生存 **II** *cpd* [复合词] [+ *course, kit, guide*] 救生
survive [sə'vaɪv] **I** *vi* **1** [*person, animal* +] 幸存 **2** [*custom* +] 继续存在 **II** *vt* **1** (*outlive*) [+ *person*] 比…活得长 **2** [+ *accident, illness etc*] 从…中逃生 ♦**to survive on £80 a week** 每周靠80英镑过活
survivor [sə'vaɪvə(r)] *n* [c] **1** [*of illness, accident*] 幸存者 **2** [*of incest, abuse*] 生还者 ♦**the only survivor from the 1990 team** 1990年队伍的惟一幸存者
susceptible [sə'sɛptəbl] *adj* **1** ♦**susceptible (to)** [+ *heat, injury*] 易受的; [+ *flattery, pressure*] 易受…影响的 **2** [+ *person*] 易受感动的

suspect [*adj*, *n* 'sʌspɛkt, *vb* səs'pɛkt] **I** *adj* 可疑的 **II** *n* [c] (*in crime*) 嫌疑犯 **III** *vt* **1** [+ *person*] 怀疑 **2** [+ *sb's motives etc*] 质疑 **3** (*think*) 猜想 ♦**to suspect sb of doing sth** 怀疑某人做某事 ♦**to suspect that ...** 怀疑…
suspend [səs'pɛnd] *vt* **1** (*hang*) 悬挂 **2** (*delay, stop*) 暂停 **3** (*from employment*) 暂令停职
suspended sentence [səs'pɛndɪd-] *n* [c] 缓刑
suspenders [səs'pɛndəz] *n* [*pl*] **1** [英] 吊袜带 [美 = **garters**] **2** [美] 背带 [英 = **braces**]
suspense [səs'pɛns] *n* [U] **1** (*uncertainty*) 焦虑 **2** (*in novel, film etc*) 悬念 ♦**to keep sb in suspense** 使某人处于紧张状态
suspension [səs'pɛnʃən] *n* **1** [C/U] (*from job, team*) 暂令停职 **2** [U] (*in car etc*) 减震装置 **3** [U] [*of payment, flight etc*] 暂停
suspension bridge *n* [c] 吊桥
suspicion [səs'pɪʃən] *n* **1** [C/U] (*about crime, wrongdoing*) 怀疑 **2** [C/U] (*distrust*) 怀疑 **3** [C] (*idea*) 模糊的想法 **4** [S] (*trace, hint*) 一点儿 ♦**to be arrested on suspicion of murder** 因谋杀嫌疑被逮捕 ♦**to be under suspicion** 受到怀疑
suspicious [səs'pɪʃəs] *adj* **1** [+ *look*] 表示怀疑的; [+ *nature*] 多疑的 **2** [+ *circumstances, death, package*] 可疑的 ♦**to be suspicious of** *or* **about sb/sth** 对某人/某事起疑心
sustain [səs'teɪn] *vt* **1** [+ *interest, growth, life etc*] 维持 **2** [+ *person*] 支撑 **3** [正式] [+ *injury, loss, defeat*] 遭受
SUV *n abbr* (= ***sport*(*s*) *utility vehicle***) 越野车
SW *abbr* **1** (= ***south-west***) 西南部 **2** [广播] (= ***short wave***) 短波
swagger ['swægə(r)] **I** *n* [s] 昂首阔步 **II** *vi* 大摇大摆
swallow ['swɔləu] **I** *n* [c] **1** (*bird*) 燕子 **2** [*of food, drink*] 吞咽 **II** *vt* **1** [+ *food, drink, pills*] 吞下 **2** [+ *story, statement*] 轻信 **III** *vi* 吞咽 ♦**to swallow one's pride** 放下架子
❑**swallow up** *vt* **1** [+ *money, resources*] 耗尽 **2** [+ *company*] 吞并
swam [swæm] *pt of* **swim**
swamp [swɔmp] **I** *n* [C/U] 沼泽 **II** *vt* (*flood*) 浸没 ♦**to be swamped with sth** 某物多得难以招架
swan [swɔn] *n* [c] 天鹅
swap [swɔp] **I** *n* [c] 交换 **II** *vt* **1** ♦**to swap sth (for)** (*exchange (for)*) (以某物) 作交换; (*replace (with)*) 以…替代某物 **2** [+ *stories, opinions*] 交换 ♦**to do a swap (with sb)** (与某人) 交换 ♦**to swap places (with sb)** (与某人) 换位子
swarm [swɔːm] **I** *n* [c] [*of bees, ants, people*] 群 **II** *vi* **1** [*bees, ants* +] 成群地行进 **2** [*people* +] 蜂拥 ♦**to be swarming with** 挤满
sway [sweɪ] **I** *vi* [*person, tree* +] 摇摆 **II** *vt* (*influence*) 动摇 **III** *n* ♦**to hold sway (over sb/sth)** 有支配 (某人/某物) 的力量
Swaziland ['swɑːzɪlænd] *n* 斯威士兰
swear [swɛə(r)] (*pt* **swore**, *pp* **sworn**) **I** *vi* (*curse*) 咒骂 **II** *vt* (*promise*) 宣誓 ♦**to swear that ...** (*promise*) 发誓…; (*confirm*) 起誓保证… ♦**to swear to do sth** 宣誓做某事 ♦**to swear an oath** 起誓 ♦**to be sworn to secrecy/silence** 发誓保守秘密/保持沉默
❑**swear by** *vt* [不可拆分] ♦**I swear by it/them** 我极其信赖某事/他们
❑**swear in** *vt* [+ *person*] 使宣誓就职
swear word *n* [c] 骂人的话
sweat [swɛt] **I** *n* [U] 汗水 **II** *vi* 出汗 ♦**to be in a (cold) sweat** (字) 出了一身 (冷) 汗; (喻) 吓得出了一身 (冷) 汗
sweater ['swɛtə(r)] *n* [c] 毛衣
sweatshirt ['swɛtʃəːt] *n* [c] 棉毛衫
sweatsuit ['swɛtsuːt] *n* [c] 运动服
sweaty ['swɛtɪ] *adj* 满是汗的
Swede [swiːd] *n* [c] 瑞典人
swede [swiːd] [英] *n* [C/U] 洋大头菜 [美 = **rutabaga**]
Sweden ['swiːdn] *n* 瑞典
Swedish ['swiːdɪʃ] **I** *adj* 瑞典的 **II** *n* [U] (*language*) 瑞典语
sweep [swiːp] (*pt, pp* **swept**) **I** *n* [c] **1** ♦**the floor could do with a sweep** 地板该扫了 **2** (*curve*) 蜿蜒 **3** (*range*) 广度 **II** *vt* **1** (*with brush*) 扫

2 (*with hand*) 拂去; [+ *one's hair*] 掠 3 [*wind* +] 吹; [*water, crowd* +] 冲 4 [*eyes, lights* +] [+ *place*] 扫视 **III** *vi* 1 ♦ **to sweep in/out/past** [*person* +] 昂首阔步地进来/出去/走过 2 [*hand, arm* +] 挥舞 3 [*wind* +] 吹 ♦ **to sweep sth under the carpet** *or* **rug** (喻) 隐瞒某事

❑ **sweep aside, sweep away** *vt* 一扫而空

❑ **sweep up I** *vi* 清扫 **II** *vt* [+ *dirt, rubbish etc*] 扫去

sweet [swiːt] **I** *n* [英] 1 [C] (*chocolate, mint etc*) 糖果 [美 = **candy**] 2 [C/U] (*pudding*) 甜点 [美 = **dessert**] **II** *adj* 1 (*sugary*) 甜的 2 (*fragrant*) 芳香的 3 [+ *sound*] 悦耳的 4 [+ *air, water*] 清新的 5 (*kind*) 和蔼的 6 [非正式] (*cute*) 可爱的 7 [+ *revenge*] 令人满意的 ♦ **to smell/taste sweet** 闻/尝起来甜美 ♦ **sweet and sour** 糖醋

sweetcorn ['swiːtkɔːn] *n* [U] 1 [植] 甜玉米 2 [烹饪] 玉米粒

sweeten ['swiːtn] *vt* 使变甜

sweetener ['swiːtnə(r)] *n* [C] 1 (*sugar substitute*) 代糖 2 (喻) 甜头

sweetheart ['swiːthɑːt] *n* [C] 1 (*boyfriend/girlfriend*) 心上人 2 (*form of address*) 亲爱的

sweetness ['swiːtnɪs] *n* [U] [*of food, drink*] 甜

swell [swɛl] (*pt* **swelled**, *pp* **swollen** *or* **swelled**) **I** *vi* 1 (*also:* ***swell up***) [*face, ankle etc* +] 肿胀 2 (*increase*) [*amount, size* +] 增加 3 [文] (*get louder*) 变响亮 **II** *vt* 使增加 **III** *n* [S] [*of sea*] 海面波浪 **IV** *adj* [美: 非正式] (*excellent*) 出色的 ♦ **to swell with pride** [文] 充满自豪

swelling ['swɛlɪŋ] *n* [C/U] 肿块肿胀

swept [swɛpt] *pt, pp of* **sweep**

swerve [swəːv] **I** *n* [C] (*in car etc*) 改变方向 **II** *vi* [*car etc* +] 突然转向 **III** *vt* [+ *car etc*] 使突然转向

swift [swɪft] **I** *adj* 1 [+ *recovery*] 快速的; [+ *response, decision*] 敏捷的 2 [+ *stream, movement*] 速度快的 **II** *n* [C] (*bird*) 褐雨燕 ♦ **to be swift to do sth** 迅速地做某事

swim [swɪm] (*pt* **swam**, *pp* **swum**) **I** *vi* 1 [*person, animal* +] 游水 2 (*as sport*) 游泳 3 (喻) [*room* +] 旋转 **II** *vt* 1 [+ *river etc*] 游过 2 [+ *distance*] 游 **III** *n* [C] ♦ **to go for a swim** 去游泳 ♦ **to go swimming** 去游泳 ♦ **my head is swimming** 我头晕

swimmer ['swɪmə(r)] *n* [C] 1 游泳者 2 (*sportsperson*) 游泳运动员 ♦ **he's a good swimmer** 他是个游泳好手

swimming ['swɪmɪŋ] *n* [U] 游泳

swimming pool *n* [C] 游泳池

swimming trunks [英] *n* [*pl*] 游泳裤 [美 = **trunks**]

swimsuit ['swɪmsuːt] *n* [C] 游泳衣

swing [swɪŋ] (*pt, pp* **swung**) **I** *n* 1 [C] (*in playground*) 秋千 2 [C] (*movement*) 摇摆 3 [C] (*in opinions etc*) 剧变 4 [U] [音] 强节奏爵士音乐 **II** *vt* 1 [+ *arms, legs*] 摆动 2 [+ *vehicle etc*] 使转向 **III** *vi* 1 [*pendulum etc* +] 晃动 2 [*door etc* +] 转动 3 [*vehicle* +] 转向 4 [*person* +] 摇摆 5 [*opinions, attitudes* +] 剧变 ♦ **a swing to the left** [政治] 改向左派 ♦ **to get into the swing of things** 积极投入某事 ♦ **to be in full swing** [*party etc* +] 正处于全盛时期 ♦ **to take a swing at sb/sth** (*try to hit*) 挥拳打某人/某物

❑ **swing at** *vt* [不可拆分] (*try to hit*) 挥拳打

swipe [swaɪp] **I** *vt* 1 [非正式] (*steal*) 偷 2 (*through machine*) [+ *card*] 刷卡 **II** *vi* ♦ **to swipe at** 猛打 **II** *n* ♦ **to take a swipe at sb/sth** (字) 挥臂猛击某人/某物; (喻) (*criticize*) 含沙射影地攻击某人/某物

swirl [swəːl] **I** *vi* [*water, leaves* +] 打旋 **II** *vt* 使旋动 **III** *n* [C] 打旋

Swiss [swɪs] (*pl* **Swiss**) **I** *adj* 瑞士的 **II** *n* [C] (*person*) 瑞士人

switch [swɪtʃ] **I** *n* [C] 1 (*for light, radio etc*) 开关 2 (*change*) 转变 **II** *vt* 1 (*change*) 改变 2 (*exchange*) 调换 **III** *vi* (*change*) 转变 ♦ **to switch two things round** *or* **over** 交换两样东西的位置

❑ **switch off I** *vt* [+ *light, engine, radio etc*] 关掉 **II** *vi* [非正式] (*stop paying attention*) 失去兴趣

❑ **switch on** *vt* [+ *light, engine, radio etc*] 开启

switchboard ['swɪtʃbɔːd] *n* [C] 交换台

Switzerland ['swɪtsələnd] *n* 瑞士

swivel ['swɪvl] **I** *vi* ♦**to swivel round** 转动 **II** *vt* ♦**to swivel sth round** 使某物转动
swollen ['swəulən] **I** *pp of* **swell II** *adj* **1** [+ *ankle, eyes etc*] 肿胀的 **2** [+ *lake, river etc*] 涨水的
swoop [swu:p] **I** *n* [c] **1** (*by police, soldiers*) 突袭 **2** [*of bird, aircraft*] 飞扑 **II** *vi* **1** [*bird, aircraft* +] 突然下落 **2** [*police, soldiers* +] 突袭 ♦**in** *or* **at one fell swoop** 一下子
swop [swɔp] *n, vt* = **swap**
sword [sɔ:d] *n* [c] 剑
swordfish ['sɔ:dfɪʃ] (*pl* **swordfish**) *n* [c/u] 箭鱼
swore [swɔ:(r)] *pt of* **swear**
sworn [swɔ:n] **I** *pp of* **swear II** *adj* ♦**a sworn statement** 宣誓证词 ♦**to be sworn enemies** 是不共戴天的仇敌
swum [swʌm] *pp of* **swim**
swung [swʌŋ] *pt, pp of* **swing**
syllable ['sɪləbl] *n* [c] 音节
syllabus ['sɪləbəs] [尤英] *n* [c] 教学大纲 ♦**on the syllabus** 含在教学大纲内
symbol ['sɪmbl] *n* [c] **1** (*sign*) 象征 **2** [数, 化] 符号 **3** (*representation*) 标志
symbolic [sɪm'bɔlɪk], **symbolical** [sɪm'bɔlɪkl] *adj* **1** [+ *importance, value, gesture*] 象征性的 **2** [+ *language, representation*] 象征主义的 ♦**to be symbolic of sth** 是某物的象征
symmetrical [sɪ'mɛtrɪkl] *adj* 对称的
symmetry ['sɪmɪtrɪ] *n* [c/u] 对称性
sympathetic [sɪmpə'θɛtɪk] *adj* **1** (*understanding*) 有同情心的 **2** (*likeable*) [+ *person, character*] 意气相投的 **3** (*supportive*) 赞同的 ♦**to be sympathetic to sth** (*supportive*) 赞同某事; (*understanding*) 同情某事
sympathize ['sɪmpəθaɪz] *vi* ♦**to sympathize (with)** (*express sorrow for*) [+ *person*] (对…) 表示同情; (*understand*) [+ *sb's feelings*] 体谅; (*support*) [+ *organization, cause, idea*] 支持
sympathy ['sɪmpəθɪ] **I** *n* [u] 同情心 **II sympathies** *n* [*pl*] (*support*) 支持; (*condolences*) 慰问 ♦**to have** *or* **feel sympathy for sb** 同情某人 ♦**to have sympathy with** [+ *idea, attitude*] 赞同 ♦**with deepest sympathy** 深表慰问 ♦**to come out in sympathy (with sb)** [*workers* +] 声援 (某人)
symphony ['sɪmfənɪ] *n* [c] 交响乐
symptom ['sɪmptəm] *n* [c] **1** [医] 症状 **2** (*indication*) 征兆
synagogue ['sɪnəgɔg] *n* [c] 犹太教堂
synchronize ['sɪŋkrənaɪz] **I** *vt* [+ *watches, movements*] 使…在时间上一致 **II** *vi* ♦**to synchronize with** 与…一致 ♦**to synchronize sth with sth** 使某物与某物一致
syndicate [*n* 'sɪndɪkɪt, *vt* 'sɪndɪkeɪt] **I** *n* [c] [*of people, businesses, newspapers*] 辛迪加 **II** *vt* ♦**to be syndicated (to)** [*article* +] 联网发表; [*programme* +] 联网播放
syndrome ['sɪndrəum] *n* [c] **1** [医] 综合征 **2** (喻) 种种表现
synonym ['sɪnənɪm] *n* [c] 同义词
synthetic [sɪn'θɛtɪk] **I** *adj* [+ *material, chemical*] 合成的 **II** *n* [*pl*] ♦**synthetics** (*fabrics etc*) 合成纤维
Syria ['sɪrɪə] *n* 叙利亚
Syrian ['sɪrɪən] **I** *adj* 叙利亚的 **II** *n* [c] (*person*) 叙利亚人
syringe [sɪ'rɪndʒ] *n* [c] 注射器
syrup ['sɪrəp] *n* [u] **1** (*in cooking*) 糖浆 **2** [医] 糖浆剂 **3** (*also: golden syrup*) 糖浆
✪ **system** ['sɪstəm] *n* [c] **1** (*organization, set*) 系统 ◊ *a new administrative system* 新的行政系统 ◊ *a computer system* 电脑系统 **2** (*method*) 方法 ◊ *a simple filing system* 简单的文件归档方法 **3** [解剖, 法, 数] 系统 ◊ *the digestive system* 消化系统 ◊ *the legal system* 法律系统 ◊ *the decimal system* 十进制 **4** (*body*) 身体 ◊ *The strenuous exercise made great demands on her system.* 艰苦的锻炼使她的身体付出很大的代价。♦**the system** (*government*) 制度 ♦**it was a shock to his system** 对他震动很大 ♦**to get sth out of one's system** 把某事发泄出来
systematic [sɪstə'mætɪk] *adj* 有系统的

Tt

T, t [tiː] *n* [C/U] (*letter*) 英语的第二十个字母

ta [tɑː] [英:非正式] *int* 谢谢

tab [tæb] *n* [C] **1** (*on drinks can*) 拉环 **2** (*on garment*) 标签 **3** [美] (*bill*) 账单 ♦**to pick up the tab** [非正式] 付账 ♦**to keep tabs on** [非正式] [+ *person, sb's movements*] 监视

table ['teɪbl] **I** *n* [C] **1** (*piece of furniture*) 桌子 **2** (*chart*) 表格 **II** *vt* [英] [+ *motion, proposal etc*] 提议 ♦**to lay** *or* **set the table** 摆餐桌 ♦**to clear the table** 清理餐桌 ♦**to turn the tables on sb** 转而占了某人的上风

tablecloth ['teɪblklɔθ] *n* [C] 桌布

table d'hôte [tɑːbl'dəut] *n* [C] 套餐

table lamp *n* [C] 台灯

table mat *n* [C] **1** (*for plate*) 桌垫 **2** (*for hot dish*) 盘垫

tablespoon ['teɪblspuːn] *n* [C] **1** (*spoon*) 餐匙 **2** (*amount*) 一餐匙的量

tablespoonful ['teɪblspuːnful] *n* [C] 一餐匙的量

tablet ['tæblɪt] *n* [C] **1** [医] 药片 **2** [历史] (*for writing*) 写字版 ♦**a tablet of soap** [英:正式] 一块肥皂

table tennis [体育] *n* [U] 乒乓球

tabloid ['tæblɔɪd] *n* [C] 小报 ♦**the tabloids** 各种小报

taboo [tə'buː] **I** *n* [C] (*religious, social*) 禁忌 **II** *adj* [+ *subject, place, name etc*] 忌讳的

tack [tæk] **I** *n* [C] (*nail*) 图钉 **II** *vt* **1** (*nail*) 用图钉钉 **2** (*stitch*) 粗缝 **III** *vi* [航海] 抢风航行 ♦**to change tack, try a different tack** 改变方针 ♦**to tack sth on to (the end of) sth** [+ *note, clause*] 把某事物附加到某事物(的末尾)
❑**tack up** *vt* 粗缝

tackle ['tækl] **I** *n* **1** [U] (*for fishing*) 用具 **2** [U] (*for lifting*) 滑轮 **3** [C] [足球] 抢球; [橄榄球] 擒抱 **II** *vt* **1** (*deal with*) [+ *problem*] 解决 **2** (*challenge*) [+ *person*] 坦诚面对 **3** [足球, 橄榄球] 截球

tacky ['tækɪ] *adj* **1** (*sticky*) 黏的 **2** [贬] (*cheap-looking*) 俗气的

tact [tækt] *n* [U] 机智

tactful ['tæktful] *adj* 老练的

tactical ['tæktɪkl] *adj* **1** [+ *move, withdrawal, error*] 策略的 **2** [军] [+ *weapons*] 战术的; [+ *policy, bombing etc*] 战略的 ♦**tactical voting** [英] 策略性投票

tactics ['tæktɪks] *n* [*pl*] 策略

tactless ['tæktlɪs] *adj* 不得体的

tadpole ['tædpəul] *n* [C] 蝌蚪

taffy ['tæfɪ] [美] *n* [U] 太妃糖 [英 = **toffee**]

tag [tæg] **I** *n* [C] **1** (*label*) 标签 **2** (*electronic*) 标签 **II** *vt* **1** (*label*) [+ *object*] 加标签于 **2** (*describe*) [+ *person*] 把… 称为 ♦**a price/name tag** 价格/姓名标签
❑**tag along** *vi* 尾随

Tahiti [tɑː'hiːtɪ] *n* 塔希提

tail [teɪl] **I** *n* [C] **1** [*of animal*] 尾巴 **2** [*of plane*] 尾部 **3** [*of shirt, coat*] 下摆 **II** *vt* (*follow*) [+ *person, vehicle*] 尾随 **III tails** *n* [C] *pl* (*formal suit*) 燕尾服 ♦**to turn tail (and run)** 掉头(逃跑) ♦**"heads or tails?" – "tails"** "正面还是背面?" "背面"
❑**tail off** *vi* **1** (*in size, quality etc*) 逐渐减少 **2** (*also: **tail away***) [*voice* +] 逐渐消失

tailor ['teɪlə(r)] **I** *n* [C] **1** (*person*) 裁缝 **2** (*also: **tailor's***) 裁缝店 **II** *vt* ♦**to tailor sth (to)** 修改某物(以适应)

tainted ['teɪntɪd] *adj* **1** [+ *food, water, air*] 被污染的 **2** (喻) [+ *reputation etc*] 被玷污的

Tajikistan [tɑːdʒɪkɪ'stɑːn] *n* 塔吉克斯坦

✪**take** [teɪk] (*pt* **took**, *pp* **taken**) **I** *vt* **1** [+ *holiday, vacation*] 度; [+ *shower, bath*] 洗; [+ *decision*] 做 **2** (*take hold of*) [+ *sb's arm etc*] 拿 ◊ *Let me take your coat.* 让我来拿你的外套吧。 **3** (*steal*) 偷走 ◊ *Someone's taken my pen.* 有人偷走了我的钢笔。

4 (*require*) [+ *effort, courage etc*] 需要 ◊ *It took a lot of courage to admit his mistake.* 他需要很大勇气去承认错误。**5** (*tolerate*) [+ *pain, criticism etc*] 忍受 ◊ *I can't take any more.* 我不能再忍受了。**6** (*hold*) [+ *passengers, spectators etc*] 容纳 ◊ *The new stadium can take about 8000 people.* 新的体育场大约可以容纳8000人。**7** (*accompany*) [+ *person*] 送 ◊ *He offered to take her home in a taxi.* 他提出乘出租车送她回家。**8** [+ *prisoner*] 俘获 ◊ *Marines went in, taking 15 prisoners.* 海军陆战队员进去了，俘获了15名犯人。**9** (*accept*) [+ *job, position*] 接受 ◊ *I eagerly took the job.* 我兴冲冲地接受了这份工作。**10** (*carry, bring*) [+ *object*] 携带 ◊ *Don't forget to take your umbrella.* 别忘了带雨伞。**11** (*travel along*) [+ *road*] 走 ◊ *Take the Chester Road out of town.* 走切斯特路出城。**12** [+ *car, train etc*] 乘坐 ◊ *She took the train to New York.* 她乘火车去纽约。**13** [+ *size*] 穿 ◊ *What size do you take?* 你穿多大号？**14** [+ *time*] 花费 ◊ *The sauce takes 25 minutes to prepare.* 做调味汁要花25分钟。**15** (*react to*) 看待 ◊ *How did he take the news?* 他怎样看待这个消息？◊ *No one took my message seriously.* 没有人认真看待我的讯息。**16** [+ *exam, test*] 参加 ◊ *She's not yet taken her driving test.* 她还没考驾照。**17** [+ *drug, pill etc*] 服用 ◊ *I took a couple of aspirins.* 我服下几片阿斯匹林。**18** [尤英] (*teach*) [+ *subject, class*] 教 ◊ *She took them for geography.* 她教他们地理。**19** (*study*) [+ *subject, course*] 修 ◊ *I'm taking history at university.* 我在大学修历史。**II** *vi* (*have effect*) [*dye, injection, drug* +] 见效 ◊ *You need a few minutes for cortisone to take.* 你得等几分钟让可的松见效。**III** *n* [c] **1** [电影] 镜头 ◊ *She had to do several takes to get it right.* 她拍了好几个镜头才得到满意的效果。**2** [非正式] (*viewpoint*) 看法 ◊ *What's your take on this?* 你对这件事的看法是什么？♦**to take sth from** [+ *drawer, box etc*] 把某物从…拿出来 ♦**I take it that ...** 我的理解是… ♦**take it or leave it** 接不接受随便 ♦**to take sb for ...** (*mistake*) 把某人误认为… ◊ *I took him for a doctor.* 我把他误认为医生了。♦**to take sb's hand, take sb by the hand/arm** 拉某人的手，牵某人的手/挽某人的胳膊 ♦**to take sb for a walk** 带某人去散步 ♦**to take it on** *or* **upon o.s. to do sth** 将做某事的责任揽到自己身上 ♦**to take to doing sth** 开始有规律地做某事

❑**take after** *vt* [不可拆分] (*resemble*) 像 ◊ *He takes after his dad.* 他像他的爸爸。

❑**take apart** *vt* (*dismantle*) [+ *bicycle, radio, machine*] 拆开

❑**take away I** *vt* **1** (*remove*) 拿走 **2** (*carry off*) 带走 **3** [数] 减去 ◊ *What's 35 take away 10?* 35减去10等于多少？**II** *vi* ♦**to take away from** (*detract from*) 减损

❑**take back** *vt* **1** (*return*) [+ *goods*] 退回 **2** (*retract*) [+ *one's words*] 收回

❑**take down** *vt* **1** (*write down*) 记录 **2** (*dismantle*) [+ *wall, fence etc*] 拆除

❑**take in I** *vt* **1** (*deceive*) [+ *person*] 蒙骗 ◊ *I wasn't going to be taken in by his charm.* 我不会被他的魅力所蒙骗。**2** (*understand*) 明白 ◊ *Robert took it all in without needing explanations.* 罗伯特没用任何解释就全明白了。**3** (*include*) 容纳 ◊ *The university has expanded to take in the school of art.* 为了容纳艺术学院，大学进行了扩张。**4** [+ *lodger*] 留宿 **5** [+ *orphan, refugee, stray dog*] 收容 **6** [+ *dress, waistband*] 改窄

❑**take off I** *vi* **1** [*aircraft* +] 起飞 **2** (*also: **take o.s off***) (*go away*) 动身外出 ◊ *They took off for a weekend in the country.* 他们动身去乡下度周末。**II** *vt* **1** [+ *time from work*] 休假 ◊ *She took two days off work.* 她休了两天假。**2** [+ *clothes, glasses, make-up*] 脱下 **3** [尤英] (*imitate*) [+ *person*] 模仿

❑**take on** *vt* **1** (*undertake*) [+ *work, responsibility*] 承担 ◊ *Don't take on any more responsibilities.* 不要再承担更多的责任了。**2** [+ *employee*] 雇用 ◊ *The company has taken on more staff.* 公司雇用了更多员

工。**3** (*compete against*) 与…较量 ◊ *I knew I couldn't take him on.* 我知道自己没法跟他较量。**4** (*develop*) 越来越显示出 ◊ *His writing took on a greater intensity.* 他的写作越来越显示出深度。

❑**take out** *vt* **1** (*invite*) [+ *person*] 邀请 ◊ *He took her out for a meal.* 他邀请她出去吃饭。**2** (*remove*) [+ *tooth*] 拔除 **3** [+ *loan, mortgage, licence etc*] 取得

❑**take out on** *vt* ♦**to take one's anger/feelings out on sb** 向某人发泄怒气/情感

❑**take over I** *vt* **1** [+ *business, country*] 接管 **2** [+ *job*] 接手 ◊ *His widow has taken over the running of the company.* 他的遗孀接手经营这家公司。**II** *vi* ♦**to take over from sb** 从某人手中接管

❑**take to** *vt* [不可拆分] **1** (*like*) 喜欢上 ◊ *I immediately took to Alan.* 我立刻喜欢上了艾伦。**2** (*begin*) 开始常做 ◊ *He's recently taken to fishing.* 他最近开始常去钓鱼。

❑**take up I** *vt* **1** (*start*) [+ *hobby, sport*] 开始 **2** [+ *job*] 从事 **3** (*occupy*) [+ *time, space*] 占用 ◊ *I won't take up any more of your time.* 我不会再占用你更多的时间。**4** (*deal with*) 着手处理 ◊ *He intends to take up the proposal with the prime minister.* 他打算与首相着手处理该提议。**5** (*continue*) [+ *task, story*] 继续 ◊ *David was taking up where he had left off.* 戴维接着上次中断的地方继续。**6** (*shorten*) [+ *hem, garment*] 改短 **II** *vi* (*befriend*) ♦**to take up with sb** 开始和某人鬼混 ♦**to take sb up on an offer** 接受某人提出的建议

takeaway ['teɪkəweɪ] [英] *n* [c] **1** (*shop, restaurant*) 外卖店 [美 = **takeout**] **2** (*food*) 外卖餐 [美 = **takeout**]

taken ['teɪkən] **I** *pp of* **take II** *adj* ♦**to be taken with sb/sth** (*attracted to*) 被某人/某事迷住

takeoff ['teɪkɔf] *n* [c] [*of plane*] 起飞

takeout ['teɪkaut] [美] *n* [c] **1** (*shop, restaurant*) 外卖店 [英 = **takeaway**] **2** (*food*) 外卖餐 [英 = **takeaway**]

takeover ['teɪkəuvə(r)] *n* [c] **1** (*of company*) 接管 **2** (*of country*) 占领

takings ['teɪkɪŋz] [英：商] *n* [*pl*] (*from sales*) 营业收入

talc [tælk] *n* [u] (*also:* ***talcum powder***) 爽身粉

tale [teɪl] *n* [c] **1** (*story*) 故事 **2** (*account*) 传闻 ♦**to tell tales** [*child* +] 打小报告

talent ['tælnt] *n* [c/u] 才能 ♦**to have a talent for sth** 在某事上有天分

talented ['tæləntɪd] *adj* [+ *person, actor etc*] 有才能的

✪**talk** [tɔːk] **I** *n* **1** [c] (*prepared speech*) 讲话 ◊ *a talk on careers abroad* 关于海外事业发展的讲话 **2** [u] (*conversation*) 谈话 ◊ *I will not have that kind of talk at the table!* 我不会在餐桌上进行这类谈话的！**3** [u] (*gossip*) 谣言 ◊ *There is talk that the president may be deposed.* 有谣言说总统可能被罢免。**4** [c] (*discussion*) 交谈 ◊ *I want to have a long talk with her.* 我想跟她长谈一次。**II** *vi* **1** (*speak*) 说话 **2** (*chat*) 聊 ◊ *We talked for hours.* 我们聊了几个小时。**3** (*give information*) 招供 ◊ *They'll talk, they'll name me.* 他们会招供的，他们会供出我的。**4** (*gossip*) 说闲话 ◊ *We don't want the neighbours to talk.* 我们不想让邻居说闲话。**III** *vt* [+ *politics, sport etc*] 谈论 ◊ *Let's talk business.* 咱们谈论正事吧。**IV talks** *n* [*pl*] [政治等] 会谈 ♦**to give a talk** 作讲座; [*politician* +] 发表讲话 ♦**to talk to** *or* **with sb** 跟某人谈话 ♦**to talk about sth** 谈论某事 ♦**talking of ...** 谈到…

❑**talk down** *vt* (*denigrate*) 贬低

❑**talk into** *vt* ♦**to talk sb into (doing) sth** 说服某人做某事

❑**talk out of** *vt* ♦**to talk sb out of (doing) sth** 说服某人不做某事

❑**talk over, talk through** *vt* [+ *problem etc*] 仔细商讨

❑**talk up** *vt* (*exaggerate*) 夸耀

talkative ['tɔːkətɪv] *adj* 健谈的

talk show [电视，广播] *n* [c] **1** [美] 脱口秀 [英 = **chat show**] **2** (*discussion programme*) 访谈节目

tall [tɔːl] *adj* 高的 ♦**how tall are you?** 你有多高？♦**he's 6 feet tall** 他6英尺高 ♦**a tall order** 苛求

📖 用法参见 **high**

tambourine [tæmbəˈriːn] *n* [c] 铃鼓

tame [teɪm] **I** *adj* **1** [+ *animal, bird*] 驯服的 **2**（喻）[+ *story, party*] 乏味的 **II** *vt* [+ *animal, bird*] 驯养

tamper [ˈtæmpə(r)] *vi* ♦**to tamper with sth** 乱动某物

tampon [ˈtæmpɔn] *n* [c] 月经棉栓

tan [tæn] **I** *n* [c] (*also:* ***suntan***) 晒黑的肤色 **II** *vi* **1** [*person* +] 晒黑 **III** *vt* [+ *hide, animal skin*] 鞣 **IV** *adj* (*colour*) 黄褐色的 ♦**to get a tan** 晒黑

tandem [ˈtændəm] *n* [c] 双人脚踏车 ♦**in tandem (with)**（与…）紧密配合

tangerine [tændʒəˈriːn] **I** *n* [c] (*fruit*) 红橘 **II** *adj* (*colour*) 橘红的

tangle [ˈtæŋgl] **I** *n* [c] [*of branches, knots, wire*] 缠结 **II** *vt* ♦**to be/get tangled (up)** 乱成一团 ♦**in a tangle** [*wires, string etc* +] 乱成一团；（喻）错综复杂

tank [tæŋk] *n* [c] **1**［军］坦克 **2** (*for petrol, water*) 箱 **3** (*also:* ***fish tank***) 缸

tanker [ˈtæŋkə(r)] *n* [c] **1** (*ship*) 油轮 **2** (*truck*) 油罐车 **3**［铁路］运油火车

tanned [tænd] *adj* [+ *skin, person*] 晒黑的

tantrum [ˈtæntrəm] *n* [c] 发脾气 ♦**to have a tantrum** [*child* +] 耍脾气 ♦**to throw a tantrum** [*adult* +] 发脾气

Tanzania [tænzəˈnɪə] *n* 坦桑尼亚

Tanzanian [tænzəˈnɪən] **I** *adj* 坦桑尼亚的 **II** *n* [c] (*person*) 坦桑尼亚人

tap [tæp] **I** *n* [c] **1**［尤英］(*on sink, pipe etc*) 龙头［美 = **faucet**］**2** (*gentle blow*) 轻敲 **II** *vt* **1** (*hit gently*) 轻拍 **2** [+ *resources, energy*] 利用 **3** [+ *telephone*] 窃听 ♦**on tap**［非正式］[*resources, information* +] 现成的；[*beer* +] 扎啤

tap-dancing [ˈtæpdɑːnsɪŋ] *n* [u] 踢踏舞

tape [teɪp] **I** *n* **1** [u] (*in cassette etc*) 带 **2** [c] (*cassette*) 磁带 **3** [u] (*adhesive*) 胶带 **4** [c/u] (*for tying*) 绑带 **5** [c] (*tag*) (*on clothes*) 标签 **II** *vt* **1** (*record*) 录制 **2** (*attach*) 贴
❑**tape up** *vt* (*fasten with tape*) 捆扎

tape measure *n* [c] 卷尺

tape recorder *n* [c] 录音机

tapestry [ˈtæpɪstrɪ] *n* **1** [c/u] (*on wall*) 挂毯 **2** [c]［文］多彩景象

tar [tɑː] *n* [u] **1** (*on road etc*) 沥青 **2** (*in cigarettes*) 焦油

target [ˈtɑːgɪt] **I** *n* [c] **1** (*of missile etc*) 目标 **2**（喻）(*of criticism, abuse*) 对象 **3** (*aim*) 目标 **II** *vt* **1** (*attack*) [+ *troops etc*] 瞄准 **2** (*try to solve*) [+ *problem*] 尽力解决 **3** (*criticize*) [+ *person*] 抨击 **4** [+ *audience, market*] 把…作为目标 ♦**to be on target** [*project, work, sales* +] 按计划进行

tariff [ˈtærɪf] *n* [c] **1** (*tax*) 关税 **2**［英：正式］(*in hotel, restaurant*) 价目

tarmac® [ˈtɑːmæk] **I** *n* [u] **1**［英］(*on road*) 沥青碎石路面［美 = **blacktop**］**2**［航空］♦**the tarmac** 柏油路面 **II** *vt*［英］[+ *road*] 用柏油铺

tarpaulin [tɑːˈpɔːlɪn] *n* [c/u] 油布

tarragon [ˈtærəgən] *n* [u] 龙蒿

tart [tɑːt] **I** *n* [c] **1** (*cake*) 果馅饼 **2**［英：非正式，讳］(*prostitute*) 妓女 **II** *adj* (*bitter*) 酸的
❑**tart up**［英：非正式］*vt* [+ *room, building*] 艳俗地装饰 ♦**to tart o.s. up**［非正式］打扮

tartan [ˈtɑːtn] **I** *n* [c/u] 苏格兰方格呢 **II** *adj* [+ *rug, scarf etc*] 苏格兰方格的

> **TARTAN**
>
> **tartan** 是一种有图案的厚羊毛布料，其图案是由不同宽度和颜色的直线条垂直交叉组成。**tartan** 用来做 **kilt** ——一种苏格兰成年男子和男孩子在正式场合穿的特别的短裙。这种布料起源于 **Highlands**（苏格兰高地）—即苏格兰群山连绵的西北部。在那里，**tartan** 被作为反抗英国王室的标志，并因此在1747 年至1782 年期间被禁用。不同的颜色和图案代表着苏格兰的不同地区。

tartar(e) sauce [ˈtɑːtə-] *n* [u] 塔塔沙司

task [tɑːsk] *n* [c] 任务 ♦**to take sb to task** (*rebuke, scold*) 责备某人

taste [teɪst] **I** *n* **1** [u] (*sense*) 味觉 **2** [c] (*flavour*) 味道 **3** [c] (*sample*) 尝试 **4** [s]（喻）[*of suffering, freedom etc*] 体验 **5** [u] (*choice, liking*) 品位 **II** *vt* **1** (*get flavour of*) 尝 **2** (*test, detect*) 品尝

III *vi* ♦**to taste of/like sth** 有/像某物的味道 ♦**to develop** *or* **acquire a taste for sth** 养成对某物的爱好 ♦**to have good/bad taste** 品位好/差 ♦**to be in good/bad taste** [*remark, joke* +] 格调高雅/低俗 ♦**to taste delicious/bitter** 尝起来好吃/苦

tasteful ['teɪstful] *adj* [+ *clothes, furnishings*] 高雅的

tasteless ['teɪstlɪs] *adj* **1** [+ *food*] 无味的 **2** [+ *remark, joke*] 不雅的 **3** [+ *furniture, decor etc*] 低俗的

tasty ['teɪstɪ] *adj* [+ *food*] 味美的

tattered ['tætəd] *adj* **1** [+ *clothes*] 褴褛的 **2** (喻) [+ *hopes*] 潦倒的

tatters ['tætəz] *n* ♦**to be in tatters** [*clothes* +] 破烂的; [*plan, relationship* +] 千疮百孔的

tattoo [tə'tuː] **I** *n* [c] **1** (*on skin*) 纹身 **2** [英] (*military display*) 军乐队表演 **II** *vt* ♦**to tattoo sth on sth** 将某物纹刺在某处

taught [tɔːt] *pt, pp of* **teach**

taunt [tɔːnt] **I** *vt* [+ *person*] 讥笑 **II** *n* [c] (*insult*) 侮辱 ♦**to taunt sb with/about sth** 用/就某事嘲弄某人

Taurus ['tɔːrəs] *n* **1** [U] (*sign*) 金牛座 **2** [c] (*person*) 金牛座的人 ♦**I'm (a) Taurus** 我是金牛座的

taut [tɔːt] *adj* [+ *skin, thread etc*] 紧绷的

✪ **tax** [tæks] **I** *n* [C/U] (*on goods, income etc*) 税 **II** *vt* **1** [+ *earnings, goods etc*] 对…征税 **2** (*test*) [+ *person, memory, patience*] 考验 ◊ *That question really taxed him.* 那个问题对他真是个考验。♦**before/after tax** 税前/后 ♦**free of tax** 免税的

taxation [tæk'seɪʃən] *n* [U] **1** (*system*) 税制 **2** (*money paid*) 税额

tax-free ['tæksfriː] *adj* 免税的

taxi ['tæksɪ] **I** *n* [c] 出租车 **II** *vi* [*plane* +] 滑行

taxi driver *n* [c] 出租司机

taxi rank [英] *n* [c] 出租车候客站 [美= **taxi stand**]

taxi stand [美] *n* [c] 出租车候客站 [英= **taxi rank**]

taxpayer ['tækspeɪə(r)] *n* [c] 纳税人

TB *n abbr* (= ***tuberculosis***) 肺结核

tbc *abbr* (= ***to be confirmed***) 有待确认

tea [tiː] *n* [C/U] **1** (*drink*) 茶 **2** (*dried leaves*) 茶叶 **3** [英] (*evening meal*) 晚饭 ♦**(afternoon) tea** [英] (下午) 茶

📖 用法参见 **meal**

> **TEA**
>
> 英国人和美国人喝的茶大多是红茶。通常茶里要加牛奶，可能还加糖，当然也可以在茶里只放一小片柠檬。花草茶（**herbal tea**），如薄荷或甘菊茶，正风行起来。**tea** 还可以指下午小餐，通常有三明治、蛋糕，还有茶。在英国的一些地方，**tea** 还可以指晚上的正餐。

tea bag *n* [c] 袋茶

tea break [英] *n* [c] 茶点时间 [美= **coffee break**]

teach [tiːtʃ] (*pt, pp* **taught**) **I** *vt* **1** ♦**to teach sb sth, teach sth to sb** 教某人某事，将某事教给某人 **2** (*in school*) [+ *pupils, subject*] 教 **3** (*educate*) 教育 **II** *vi* (*be a teacher*) 教书 ♦**to teach sb to do sth/how to do sth** 教某人做某事/怎样做某事

teacher ['tiːtʃə(r)] *n* [c] 教师

teaching ['tiːtʃɪŋ] **I** *n* [U] (*job*) 教学 **II teachings** *n* [*pl*] 教导

tea cloth [英] *n* [c] 擦拭布 [美= **dishcloth**]

teacup ['tiːkʌp] *n* [c] 茶杯

tea leaves *n* [*pl*] 茶叶

✪ **team** [tiːm] *n* [c] **1** [*of people, experts, horses*] 组 ◊ *a team of scientists* 一组科学家 **2** [体育] 队
❑**team up** *vi* 合作 ♦**to team up with sb** 与某人协作

teamwork ['tiːmwəːk] *n* [U] 协力合作

teapot ['tiːpɔt] *n* [c] 茶壶

tear[1] [tɛə(r)] (*pt* **tore**, *pp* **torn**) **I** *n* [c] (*rip, hole*) 裂口 **II** *vt* **1** (*rip*) 撕裂 **2** (*remove violently*) 扯 **III** *vi* **1** (*become torn*) 撕破 **2** (*rush*) 飞奔 ♦**to tear sth to pieces** *or* **to bits** *or* **to shreds** [+ *paper, letter, clothes*] 把某物撕成片{或}小块{或}条 ♦**to tear sb to pieces** (喻) 与某人激烈争吵
❑**tear along** *vi* [*driver, vehicle* +] 疾驰
❑**tear apart** *vt* **1** (*upset*) [+ *person*] 使

心神不安 **2** (*divide*) [+ *group of people*] 使分裂

❑ **tear away** *vt* ♦ **to tear o.s. away (from sth)** 强迫自己离开(某事物)

❑ **tear down** *vt* [+ *building, statue*] 拆除

❑ **tear off** *vt* [+ *clothes*] 脱掉

❑ **tear up** *vt* [+ *sheet of paper, cheque*] 撕毁

tear[2] [tɪə(r)] *n* [c] (*when crying*) 眼泪 ♦ **to be in tears** 哭泣 ♦ **to burst into tears** 哭起来

tearful ['tɪəful] *adj* [+ *person, face*] 含泪的

tear gas *n* [u] 催泪弹

tease [tiːz] **I** *vt* 逗弄 **II** *n* [c] (*person*) 爱开玩笑的人

teaspoon ['tiːspuːn] *n* [c] (*spoon, amount*) 茶匙

teaspoonful ['tiːspuːnful] *n* [c] 一茶匙的量

teatime ['tiːtaɪm] [英] *n* [u] 茶点时间

tea towel [英] *n* [c] 擦拭布 [美 = **dish towel**]

technical ['tɛknɪkl] *adj* **1** [+ *problems, advances*] 技术的 **2** [+ *terms, language*] 专业的 **3** [+ *skills, ability etc*] 专业技能的

technically ['tɛknɪklɪ] *adv* **1** [+ *advanced, demanding*] 科技地 **2** (*strictly speaking*) 严格说来

technician [tɛk'nɪʃən] *n* [c] 技师

technique [tɛk'niːk] *n* **1** [c] (*method*) 手法 **2** [u] (*skill*) 技术

technological [tɛknə'lɔdʒɪkl] *adj* 工艺的

technology [tɛk'nɔlədʒɪ] *n* [c/u] 工艺学

teddy (bear) ['tɛdɪ(-)] *n* [c] 玩具熊

tedious ['tiːdɪəs] *adj* 乏味的

tee [tiː] *n* [c] [高尔夫] 球座

❑ **tee off** *vi* [高尔夫] 开球

teem [tiːm] *vi* ♦ **to be teeming with** [+ *visitors, tourists etc*] 充满

teen [tiːn] *adj* (*teenage*) 青少年的 *see also* **teens**

teenage ['tiːneɪdʒ] *adj* [+ *children, fashions etc*] 十几岁的

teenager ['tiːneɪdʒə(r)] *n* [c] 青少年

teens [tiːnz] *n* [*pl*] ♦ **to be in one's teens** 在少年时代

tee-shirt ['tiːʃəːt] *n* = **T-shirt**

teeth [tiːθ] *n* [*pl*] *of* **tooth**

teetotal ['tiː'təutl] *adj* [+ *person*] 滴酒不沾的

tel. *abbr* (= ***telephone number***) 电话号码

telecommunications ['tɛlɪkəmjuːnɪ'keɪʃənz] *n* [u] 电信

telegram ['tɛlɪgræm] *n* [c] 电报

telegraph pole ['tɛlɪgrɑːf-] *n* [c] 电话线杆

telephone ['tɛlɪfəun] **I** *n* **1** [u] (*system*) 电话 **2** [c] (*piece of equipment*) 电话 **II** *vt, vi* 打电话 ♦ **to be on the telephone** (*talking*) 正在打电话; [英] (*connected to phone system*) 装电话

telephone box [英] *n* [c] 电话亭 [美 = **phone booth**]

telephone call *n* [c] 电话 ♦ **to make a telephone call** 打电话

telephone book, telephone directory *n* [c] 电话簿

telephone number *n* [c] 电话号码

telesales ['tɛlɪseɪlz] *n* [u] 电话销售

telescope ['tɛlɪskəup] *n* [c] 望远镜

televise ['tɛlɪvaɪz] *vt* 电视播放

television ['tɛlɪvɪʒən] *n* **1** [c] (*also: **television set***) 电视机 [u] (*system*) 电视 **3** [u] (*business*) 电视业 ♦ **to be on television** [*programme* +] 由电视播放; [*person* +] 上电视

television programme *n* [c] 电视节目

✪ **tell** [tɛl] (*pt, pp* **told**) **I** *vt* **1** (*inform*) ♦ **to tell sb sth** 告诉某人某事 ◊ *They told us the news.* 他们告诉了我们这个消息。**2** (*relate*) [+ *story, joke*] 讲 ◊ *Will you tell me a story?* 你能给我讲个故事吗? **3** (*distinguish*) ♦ **to tell sth from sth** 把某物和某物区分开 **4** (*know*) 确定 ◊ *I couldn't tell what they were thinking.* 我不能确定他们在想什么。**5** (*reveal*) 表明 ◊ *The facts tell us that this is not true.* 事实向我们表明这不是真的。**II** *vi* (*have an effect*) 影响 ◊ *The late nights were beginning to tell on my health.* 熬夜开始影响我的健康了。♦ **to tell sb to do sth** 指示某人做某事 ♦ **to tell sb that ...** 告诉某人说… ♦ **to tell sb about** *or* **of sth** 给某人讲述某事 ♦ **to tell**

the time 看时间 ♦ **(I) tell you what ...** [非正式]（我）提议… ♦ **to do as one is told** 按吩咐做事

❑ **tell apart** *vt* (*distinguish*) 分辨出

❑ **tell off** *vt* ♦ **to tell sb off** 斥责某人

❑ **tell on** *vt* [不可拆分] [非正式] (*inform against*) 揭发

teller ['tɛlə(r)] [美] *n* [c] (*in bank*) 出纳员

telly ['tɛlɪ] [英:非正式] *n* [c/u] 电视 ♦ **on telly** 在电视上播放 ♦ **to watch telly** 看电视 [美=**TV**]

temp [tɛmp] **I** *n* [c] 临时雇员 **II** *vi* 做临时工

temper ['tɛmpə(r)] **I** *n* [c/u] 脾气 **II** *vt* [正式] (*moderate*) 使缓和 ♦ **to be in a good/bad temper** 情绪好/坏 ♦ **to lose one's temper** 发怒 ♦ **to have a bad temper** 脾气坏

temperament ['tɛmprəmənt] *n* [c/u] 性情

temperamental [tɛmprə'mɛntl] *adj* **1** [+ *person*] 喜怒无常的 **2** [+ *car, machine*] 时好时坏的

temperature ['tɛmprətʃə(r)] *n* **1** [c/u] [*of place*] 气温 **2** [u] [*of person*] 体温 ♦ **to have** *or* **be running a temperature** 发烧 ♦ **to take sb's temperature** 测某人的体温

temple ['tɛmpl] *n* [c] **1** (*building*) 庙宇 **2** (*at side of head*) 太阳穴

temporarily ['tɛmpərərɪlɪ] *adv* 临时地

temporary ['tɛmpərərɪ] *adj* 临时的 ♦ **temporary secretary/teacher** 临时秘书/代课教师

tempt [tɛmpt] *vt* 诱使 ♦ **to tempt sb into doing sth** *or* **to do sth** 诱使某人做某事 ♦ **to be tempted to do sth** 受到引诱去做某事

temptation [tɛmp'teɪʃən] *n* [c/u] 诱惑

tempting ['tɛmptɪŋ] *adj* 诱人的

✪ **ten** [tɛn] *num* 十 ♦ **tens of thousands** 好几万

tenant ['tɛnənt] *n* [c] 房客

tend [tɛnd] **I** *vt* **1** [正式] [+ *plants, crops*] 看护 **2** [正式] [+ *sick person*] 照料 **II** *vi* **1** ♦ **to tend to do sth** 倾向于做某事 **2** ♦ **to tend towards sth** 趋于某事 **3** ♦ **to tend to sb/sth** 照料某人/某事物

tendency ['tɛndənsɪ] *n* [c] 倾向 ♦ **a tendency to do sth** 做某事的倾向

tender ['tɛndə(r)] **I** *adj* **1** (*loving*) [+ *person, care*] 温柔的 **2** (*sore*) [+ *arm, leg etc*] 有触痛的 **3** [+ *meat, vegetables*] 嫩的 **4** [+ *age*] 年幼的 **II** *n* [c] [商] (*offer*) 投标 **III** *vt* [正式] [+ *offer, resignation, apology*] 提出 **IV** *vi* ♦ **to tender for sth** [商] 为某事投标 ♦ **to put in a tender (for)** （参加某项）投标 ♦ **to put work out to tender** [英] 对工程进行招标

tendon ['tɛndən] *n* [c] 腱

tenner ['tɛnə(r)] [英:非正式] *n* [c] (*ten pounds*) 10 英镑; (*ten-pound note*) 面值10 英镑的钞票

tennis ['tɛnɪs] *n* [u] 网球运动

tennis ball *n* [c] 网球

tennis court *n* [c] 网球场

tennis match *n* [c] 网球赛

tennis player *n* [c] 网球手

tennis racket *n* [c] 网球拍

tenor ['tɛnə(r)] *n* **1** [c] [音] 男高音歌手 **2** [s] [*of speech, reply etc*] 大意

tenpin bowling ['tɛnpɪn-] [尤英] *n* [u] 十柱保龄球

tense [tɛns] **I** *adj* **1** [+ *person, smile, period, situation*] 紧张的 **2** [+ *muscle*] 紧绷的 **II** *n* [c] [语言] 时态 **III** *vt, vi* (*also:* ***tense up***) (*tighten*) 绷紧

tension ['tɛnʃən] *n* **1** [c/u] (*of situation*) 紧张的局势 **2** [u] (*of person*) 焦虑 **3** [u] (*between ropes, wires*) 张力

tent [tɛnt] *n* [c] 帐篷

tentative ['tɛntətɪv] *adj* **1** [+ *person*] 犹豫不决的 **2** [+ *step, smile*] 试探性的 **3** [+ *conclusion, agreement, plan*] 暂定的

tenth [tɛnθ] *num* **1** (*in series*) 第十 **2** (*fraction*) 十分之一 *see also* **fifth**

tent peg *n* [c] 帐篷桩

tent pole *n* [c] 帐篷支柱

tepid ['tɛpɪd] *adj* **1** [+ *liquid*] 微温的 **2**（喻）[+ *reaction, applause*] 不热烈的

✪ **term** [tə:m] **I** *n* [c] **1** (*word, expression*) 词语 ◊ *a term of abuse* 骂人的词语 **2** (*period*) 期间 ◊ *Blair's second term of office as Premier* 布莱尔作为首相的第二个任期 **3** (*at school, university*) 学期 **II** *vt* (*call*) 将…称作

◊ *The press termed the visit a triumph.* 媒体称这次访问非常成功。
III terms *n* [c] *pl* (*conditions*) [*of agreement, treaty etc*] 条款 ♦**in simple/economic terms** 简单/就经济而言 ♦**in terms of the climate/economy** 就气候/经济而言 ♦**on easy terms** [商] 以分期付款方式 ♦**in the short/long term** 短/长期 ♦**to think/talk in terms of doing sth** 就做某事的角度来考虑/说 ♦**to be on good terms** 关系好 ♦**to be on good terms with sb** 与某人关系好 ♦**on equal** *or* **the same terms** 按同样条件 ♦**to come to terms with sth** 接受某事为事实

terminal ['tɜːmɪnl] **I** *adj* [+ *disease, patient*] 晚期的 **II** *n* [c] **1** [计算机] 终端 **2** [电子] 接头处 **3** [商] (*for oil, ore etc*) 储备区 **4** (*at airport*) 终点站

terminally ['tɜːmɪnlɪ] *adv* ♦**terminally ill** 病入膏肓的

terminate ['tɜːmɪneɪt] **I** *vt* **1** [正式] [+ *discussion etc*] 终结 **2** [+ *contract, pregnancy*] 终止 **II** *vi* [*contract* +] 终止 ♦**this train terminates in ...** [正式] 本次列车的终点站是…

termini ['tɜːmɪnaɪ] *n* [*pl*] *of* **terminus**

terminology [tɜːmɪ'nɔlədʒɪ] *n* [c/u] 术语

terminus ['tɜːmɪnəs] (*pl* **termini**) *n* [c] (*for buses, trains*) 终点站

Ter(r). *abbr* (= ***terrace***) 地

terrace ['tɛrəs] **I** *n* [c] **1** [英] (*row of houses*) 成排的房屋 **2** (*patio*) 平台 **3** [农] 梯田 **II terraces** *n* [*pl*] [英:体育] ♦**the terraces** 球场看台

terraced ['tɛrəst] *adj* **1** [+ *house*] 成排的 **2** [+ *garden*] 梯状的

terrain [tɛ'reɪn] *n* [c/u] 地势

terrible ['tɛrɪbl] *adj* **1** [+ *accident, winter*] 可怕的 **2** (*very poor*) 糟糕的 **3** [非正式] (*awful*) 糟透的

terribly ['tɛrɪblɪ] *adv* **1** (*very*) 非常 **2** (*very badly*) 差劲地

terrier ['tɛrɪə(r)] *n* [c] (*dog*) 活泼的小狗

terrific [tə'rɪfɪk] *adj* **1** (*very great*) [+ *amount, thunderstorm, speed*] 惊人的 **2** (*wonderful*) [+ *time, party, idea etc*] 极好的

terrified ['tɛrɪfaɪd] *adj* 吓坏的 ♦**to be terrified of sth** 被某事吓破胆

terrify ['tɛrɪfaɪ] *vt* 使惧怕

terrifying ['tɛrɪfaɪɪŋ] *adj* 令人害怕的

territorial [tɛrɪ'tɔːrɪəl] **I** *adj* [+ *waters, boundaries, dispute*] 领土的 **II** *n* [c] [英:军] 英国义务兵

territory ['tɛrɪtərɪ] *n* [c/u] **1** (*land*) 领土 **2** (喻) 范围

terror ['tɛrə(r)] *n* [u] (*great fear*) 恐惧 ♦**in terror of sth** 对某事胆战心惊 ♦**to have a terror of (doing) sth** 害怕(做)某事

terrorism ['tɛrərɪzəm] *n* [u] 恐怖主义

terrorist ['tɛrərɪst] **I** *n* [c] 恐怖分子 **II** *adj* 恐怖分子的

✪**test** [tɛst] **I** *n* [c] **1** (*trial, check*) 试验 ◊ *a nuclear test* 核试验 **2** [*of person, courage etc*] 判断标准 ◊ *The test of any civilised society is how it treats its minorities.* 对于任何文明社会的判断标准是它怎样对待少数民族。**3** [医] 检验 ◊ *a blood test* 验血 **4** [化] 化验 ◊ *They carried out tests on the water.* 他们对水域进行化验。**5** [教育] 测验 **6** [*of intelligence*] 测验 ◊ *an intelligence test* 智力测验 **7** (*also:* ***driving test***) 驾驶考试 **II** *vt* **1** (*try out*) 试验 ◊ *The drug was tested on gorillas.* 药品在大猩猩身上进行了试验。**2** [医] 检测 ◊ *They tested her blood type.* 他们检测了她的血型。**3** [教育] 测试 ◊ *I will test you on your knowledge of French.* 我要测试一下你的法语。♦**to put sth to the test** 将某物加以考验 ♦**to test water for impurities** 测试水的纯度

testicle ['tɛstɪkl] *n* [c] 睾丸

testify ['tɛstɪfaɪ] **I** *vi* **1** [法] 作证 **II** *vt* [法] ♦**to testify that ...** 证实… ♦**to testify to sth** [*person* +] 证实某事; [*fact* +] 证明某事

testimony ['tɛstɪmənɪ] *n* [c/u] **1** [法] 证词 **2** ♦**to be (a) testimony to sth** 是对某事物的(一个)证明

test match [英:板球, 橄榄球] *n* [c] 国际锦标赛

test tube *n* [c] 试管

tetanus ['tɛtənəs] [医] *n* [u] 破伤风

text [tɛkst] **I** *n* **1** [u] (*written material*) 正文 **2** [c] (*book*) 课本 **3** [c] (*also:* ***text***

message) 手机短信 II *vt* (*on mobile phone*) 发短消息
textbook ['tɛkstbuk] *n* [c] 课本
textile ['tɛkstaɪl] I *n* [c] 纺织品 II **textiles** *n* [*pl*] (*industries*) 纺织厂
text message *n* [c] 短信
text messaging [-'mɛsɪdʒɪŋ] *n* [U] 发短信
texture ['tɛkstʃə(r)] *n* [C/U] [*of cloth, skin, soil*] 质地
Thai [taɪ] I *adj* 泰国的 II *n* 1 [c] (*person*) 泰国人 2 [U] (*language*) 泰语
Thailand ['taɪlænd] *n* 泰国
✪**than** [ðæn, ðən] I *prep* 1 (*in comparisons*) 比 ◊ *She's taller than her husband.* 她比丈夫高。◊ *We've got less than three weeks.* 我们只有不到3周的时间了。◊ *This year my salary is more than twice what it was last year.* 我今年的薪水是去年的两倍多。II *conj* 比 ◊ *He loves her more than she loves him.* 他对她的爱比她对他的爱要多。♦ **it's smaller than a matchbox** 它比一个火柴盒还小 ♦ **more/less than Paul** 比保罗多/少 ♦ **more than 20** 多于20 ♦ **more than once** 不止一次 ♦ **she's older than you think** 她比你想像的年纪要大 ♦ **I'd rather stay in than go out** 我宁可呆在家里而不愿出去
✪**thank** [θæŋk] *vt* [+ *person*] 感谢 ♦ **thank you (very much)** (非常)感谢你 ♦ **no, thank you** 不，谢谢 ♦ **thank God, thank Goodness, thank heavens** 感谢上帝 ♦ **to thank sb for (doing) sth** 感谢某人(做)某事 ♦ **I don't need any help, thank you** 我自己来，谢谢你
thankful ['θæŋkful] *adj* ♦ **to be thankful (for sth)** 感激(某事) ♦ **to be thankful that/to be ...** 庆幸…
thankfully ['θæŋkfəlɪ] *adv* 幸亏 ♦ **thankfully, there were few victims** 幸亏受害者不多
thanks [θæŋks] I *n* [*pl*] 感谢 II *int* [非正式] 谢谢 ♦ **to give sb one's thanks** [正式] 向某人表示感谢 ♦ **many thanks, thanks a lot** 多谢 ♦ **no, thanks** 不了，谢谢 ♦ **thanks to sb/sth** 多亏某人/某事
Thanksgiving (Day) ['θæŋksgɪvɪŋ(-)] [美] *n* [C/U] 感恩节

> **THANKSGIVING**
> 每年11月的第4个星期四是 **Thanksgiving**(感恩节)，是美国一个重要的全国性节日，对于每个家庭也是个值得庆祝的日子。感恩节是为了纪念第一批到达北美大陆的英国定居者 — **pilgrims**(英国清教徒)。感恩节名字的由来可以追溯到1621年，清教徒们因为第一次丰收而向上帝表示感谢。传统的感恩节大餐以烤火鸡为主菜，以**pumpkin pie** 为甜点。

✪ **that**
KEYWORD
[ðæt] (*demonstrative adj, pron: pl* **those**)
I *adj* 那 ♦ **that man/woman/book** 那个男人/女人/那本书 ♦ **that place** 那个地方 ♦ **that one** 那一个 ♦ **that one over there** 那边的那个
II *pron*
1 (*demonstrative*) 那 ♦ **who's/what's that?** 那是谁/那是什么? ♦ **is that you?** 是你吗? ♦ **I prefer this to that** 两相比较，我更喜欢这个 ♦ **will you eat all that?** 你会把那个都吃完吗? ♦ **that's my house** 那是我的房子 ♦ **that's what he said** 那是他所说的 ♦ **that is (to say)** 也就是(说) ♦ **that's it** (*finished*) 就这样; (*exactly*) 没错 ♦ **that's that** 就这样了
2 (*relative*) …的 ♦ **the girl that came in** 进来的那个女孩 ♦ **the man that I saw** 我见过的那个男的 ♦ **the woman that you spoke to** 你说过话的那个女的 ♦ **all that I have** 我所有的一切 ♦ **the day that he came** 他来的那天
III *conj* 引导宾语从句的关系代词 ♦ **he thought that I was ill** 他以为我病了 ♦ **it's interesting that you should agree** 有趣的是你竟然同意了 ♦ **I'm so happy that I could sing for joy** 我高兴得唱起了歌
IV *adv* (*so*) 如此 ♦ **that much/bad/high** 如此多/糟糕/高

thatched [θætʃt] *adj* [+ *roof, cottage*] 茅草屋顶的

thaw [θɔː] **I** *n* **1** [c] [*of ice, snow*] 解冻 **2** [s] (喻) (*in relations*) 缓和 **II** *vi* **1** [*ice, snow* +] 融化 **2** (喻) [*relations* +] 缓和 **III** *vt* **1** (*also:* ***thaw out***) [+ *frozen food*] 解冻 **2** (喻) [+ *atmosphere, relations*] 缓和 ♦ **it's thawing** (*weather*) 雪化了

✪ **the**

KEYWORD

[ðiː, ðə] *def art*

1 定冠词，用于指代已知的人或物 ♦ **the man/girl/house/book** 男人/女孩/房子/书 ♦ **the men/women/houses/books** 男人/女孩/房子/书 ♦ **the yellow dress, not the green one** 那件黄色的衣服，不是绿色的 ♦ **the Germans and the French** 德国人和法国人 ♦ **the history of France** 法国史 ♦ **I haven't the time/money** 我没钱/时间 ♦ **the best solution** 最好的解决方案 ♦ **to play the piano/violin** 弹钢琴/拉小提琴 ♦ **the age of the computer** 计算机时代 ♦ **I got it from the teacher** 我从老师那儿得来的 ♦ **I'm going to the butcher's/the cinema** 我要去肉店/电影院 ♦ **can you give it to the nurse?** 你能把它交给那位护士吗？

2 (+ *adjective*) (*forming uncount noun*) 用于形容词前表示不可数的一类物; (*forming plural noun*) 用于形容词前构成复数，表示一类人或物 ♦ **to attempt the impossible** 尝试不可能的事 ♦ **the rich and the poor** 穷人和富人

3 (*in dates, decades*) 表示具体时间 ♦ **the fifth of March** 3月5日 ♦ **the nineties** 90年代

4 (*in titles*) 用于称谓中 ♦ **Elizabeth the First** 伊丽莎白一世 ♦ **Peter the Great** 彼得大帝

5 (*in comparisons*) ♦ **the faster he works, the more mistakes he makes** 他工作得越快，犯的错误就越多 ♦ **the more I look at it the less I like it** 我越看越不喜欢 ♦ **two dollars to the pound** 两美元兑换一英镑

theatre (美 **theater**) [ˈθɪətə(r)] *n* **1** [c] (*building*) 剧院 **2** [u] (*entertainment*) 戏剧 **3** [c] [医] (*also:* ***operating theatre***) 手术室 **4** [c] [美] (*also:* ***movie theater***) 电影院 [英 = **cinema**] ♦ **to go to the theatre** 去看戏

theatrical [θɪˈætrɪkl] *adj* **1** [+ *event, production, performance*] 戏剧的 **2** (喻) [+ *gesture, behaviour*] 矫揉造作的

theft [θɛft] *n* [c/u] 盗窃

✪ **their** [ðɛə(r)] *adj* **1** (*of men, boys, mixed group*) 他们的 ◊ *Their children grew up in the countryside.* 他们的孩子在乡间长大。; (*of women, girls*) 她们的 ◊ *The girls went out with their boyfriends.* 女孩们和她们的男朋友们一起出去了。; (*of things, animals*) 它们的 ◊ *The trees shed their leaves every autumn.* 这些树每年秋天都落叶。 **2** (*his or her*) 他/她的 ◊ *Does anyone need any help with their homework?* 谁做家庭作业需要帮助？

📖 用法参见 **there**

theirs [ðɛəz] *pron* **1** (*of men, boys, mixed group*) 他们的; (*of women, girls*) 她们的; (*of animals*) 它们的 **2** (*his or hers*) 他/她的 ◊ *I don't know whose handkerchief it is. Somebody must have left theirs.* 我不知道那是谁的手帕。一定是谁把它落在这儿了。 ♦ **it's theirs** 是他们/她们的 ♦ **a friend of theirs** 他们/她们的一个朋友

✪ **them** [ðɛm, ðəm] *pron* **1** (*plural*) (*referring to men, boys, mixed group*) 他们; (*referring to women, girls*) 她们 ◊ *I'll phone them later.* 我过一会儿给他们/她们打电话。 ◊ *If you see your parents, do give them my best wishes.* 如果你见到你的父母，一定代我向他们问好。 ◊ *Not them again.* 又是他们/她们。 ◊ *I was at school with them.* 我和他们/她们是校友。; (*referring to things and animals*) 它们 ◊ *He took off his glasses and put them in his pocket.* 他摘下眼镜，把它放进口袋。 **2** (*singular*) (*him or her*) 他/她 ◊ *If anyone phones, please tell them I'm out.* 如果有人打电话，告诉他/

她我出去了。

theme [θiːm] *n* [c] **1** [*of speech, article, book etc*] 主题 **2** [音] 主旋律

theme park *n* [c] 主题公园

✪ **themselves** [ðəm'sɛlvz] **I** *pl pron* **1** (*referring to men, boys, mixed group*) 他们自己; (*referring to girls, women*) 她们自己 ◊ *Have they hurt themselves?* 他们/她们伤了自己吗? ◊ *They all enjoyed themselves.* 他们/她们都玩得很开心。◊ *They cooked the meal themselves.* 他们/她们自己做的饭。◊ *They only care about themselves.* 他们只关心自己。; (*referring to animals*) 它们自己 ◊ *Cats wash themselves.* 猫自己清洗自己。**2** (*emphatic*) (*referring to men, boys, mixed group*) 他们本人; (*referring to women, girls*) 她们本人 ◊ *They themselves live in London.* 他们/她们本人住在伦敦。**3** (*singular*) (*himself or herself*) 他/她自己 ◊ *Anyone who has a problem should deal with it themselves.* 任何人有问题都应该自己解决。♦ **by themselves** (*unaided*) 他/她们独立地 ◊ *They built the house by themselves.* 他/她们自己盖了房子。; (*alone*) 他/她们独自地 ◊ *They live by themselves.* 他们自己住。

✪ **then** [ðɛn] **I** *adv* **1** (*at that time*) (*past*) 当时 ◊ *Life was simpler then.* 当时的生活较为简单。; (*future*) 那时 ◊ *I'm coming up on Friday so I'll see you then.* 我星期五会来的，那就那时见吧。**2** (*after that*) 之后 ◊ *He thought a bit and then answered.* 他想了一会儿之后答应了。◊ *I'll give him a call and then we'll know what's happening.* 我给他打个电话，之后我们就会知道是什么事了。**3** (*therefore*) 就是 ◊ *This, then, is what you must do.* 这就是你要做的。**II** *adj* 当时的 ◊ *the then president* 当时的总统 ♦ **by then** 到那时 ♦ **from then on** 从那时起 ♦ **before then** 在那之前 ♦ **until then** 直到那时 ♦ **since then** 自从那时 ♦ **but then** (*however*) 不过 ♦ **well/OK then** 好吧 ♦ **if ... then ...** 如果…就…

theology [θɪ'ɔlədʒɪ] *n* [U] 神学

theoretical [θɪə'rɛtɪkl] *adj* **1** [+ *explanation, subject*] 理论的 **2** [+ *possibility, risk*] 假设的

theory ['θɪərɪ] *n* [C/U] 理论 ♦ **in theory** 就理论而言

therapist ['θɛrəpɪst] *n* [C] 治疗专家

therapy ['θɛrəpɪ] *n* [U] 治疗 ♦ **to be in therapy** 接受治疗

✪ **there** [ðɛə(r)] **I** *adv* (*referring to place, pointing, indicating*) 那儿 ♦ **they've lived there for 30 years** 他们在那儿住了30年 ♦ **he went there on Friday** 他是星期五去那儿的 ♦ **is Shirley there please?** (*on telephone*) 请问雪莉在吗? ♦ **it's over there** 在那边 ♦ **it's in/down there** 就在那边 ♦ **put it in/down there** 就把它放在那边 ♦ **that book there** 在那边的那本书 ♦ **there he is!** 他在那儿呐! ♦ **there you are** (*offering something*) 给你 ♦ **that's what it's there for** 那就是它存在的原因 ♦ **there is/there are** 有 ♦ **there has been an accident** 发生了一个事故 ♦ **there are 3 of them** 他们中有3个 ♦ **hello there, hi there** 你好啊 ♦ **there!** 嘿! ♦ **there, there** (*comforting*) 好了，好了

> 📖 请勿将**there**，**their** 和 **they're** 混淆。**there** 表示某事物的存在，引起对某事物的注意，或表示某事物在某地或将要到达某地。*There is nothing to be afraid of...There she is...I'll meet them there later.* **their** 表示某物属于上文提到的某人或某物，或与上文提到的某人或某物有关。*They walked their dog together every day...It wasn't their fault that they were late.* **they're** 是**they are** 的缩略形式。*They're nice people.*

thereabouts ['ðɛərə'bauts] *adv* ♦ **or thereabouts 1** (*place*) 或其附近 **2** (*amount*) 大约如此

thereafter [ðɛər'ɑːftə(r)] [正式] *adv* 此后

thereby ['ðɛəbaɪ] [正式] *adv* 因此

therefore ['ðɛəfɔː(r)] *adv* 因此

there's ['ðɛəz] = **there is, there has**

thermal ['θəːml] *adj* **1** [+ *springs,*

baths] 温的 **2** [+ *power, insulation*] 热量的 **3** [+ *underwear*] 保暖的 **4** [+ *paper, printer*] 热敏的

thermometer [θəˈmɔmɪtə(r)] *n* [C] 温度计

Thermos® [ˈθəːməs] *n* [C] (*also:* ***Thermos flask***) 保温瓶

thermostat [ˈθəːməustæt] *n* [C] 恒温器

✪**these** [ðiːz] **I** *pl adj* (*demonstrative*) 这些 **II** *pl pron* 这些 ♦**these ones are cheaper than those ones** 这些比那些便宜 ♦**these days** 目前 ♦**which are better? these or those?** 哪些更好？这些还是那些？

thesis [ˈθiːsɪs] (*pl* **theses** [ˈθiːsiːz]) *n* [C] **1** (*for degree*) 论文 **2** (*argument*) 论点

✪**they** [ðeɪ] *pl pron* **1** (*referring to men, boys, mixed group*) 他们 ◊ *They haven't arrived yet.* 他们还没到。; (*referring to women, girls*) 她们 ◊ *They're pretty girls.* 她们是漂亮的女孩。; (*referring to animals, things*) 它们 ◊ *They are healthy animals.* 它们是健康的动物。 **2** (*in generalizations*) 人们 ◊ *They say that there are plenty of opportunities.* 人们都说有很多机会。 **3** (*he or she*) 他/她 ◊ *If anyone has any problems they can come to Mary for help.* 如果谁有任何问题，可以向玛丽寻求帮助。

they'd [ðeɪd] = **they had, they would**

they'll [ðeɪl] = **they shall, they will**

they're [ðɛə(r)] = **they are**

they've [ðeɪv] = **they have**

thick [θɪk] *adj* **1** [+ *slice, line, book, clothes etc*] 厚的 **2** [+ *sauce, mud, fog*] 浓的 **3** [+ *forest, hair etc*] 浓密的 **4** [英:非正式] (*stupid*) 笨的 ♦**it's 20 cm thick** 有20厘米粗 ♦**thick and fast** 席卷而来 ♦**in the thick of it** 深陷某事 ♦**through thick and thin** 在任何情况下

thicken [ˈθɪkn] **I** *vi* **1** [*sauce etc* +] 变稠 **2** [*crowd etc* +] 聚集 **II** *vt* [+ *sauce etc*] 使变稠 ♦**the plot thickens** 事情变得复杂了

thickness [ˈθɪknɪs] *n* [C/U] **1** [*of rope, wire*] 厚度 **2** (*layer*) 层

thief [θiːf] (*pl* **thieves**) *n* [C] 贼

> 📖 任何将他人物品未经许可就据为己有的人，都可被叫做 **thief**。**robber** 是指用暴力的手段，或以暴力相威胁，将他人的物品据为己有，例如抢劫银行或商店等。**burglar** 是指入室抢劫者。

thigh [θaɪ] *n* [C] 大腿

thin [θɪn] **I** *adj* **1** [+ *slice, line, book, material etc*] 薄的 **2** [+ *soup, sauce*] 稀的 **3** [+ *person, animal*] 瘦的 **4** [+ *hair*] 稀疏的 **5** [+ *crowd*] 少的 **II** *vt* (*also:* ***thin down***) [+ *sauce, paint*] 使变稀 **III** *vi* (*also:* ***thin out***) [*crowd, vegetation* +] 减少 ♦**thin on the ground** 寥寥无几的 ♦**his hair is thinning** 他的头发变得稀疏了

✪**thing** [θɪŋ] **I** *n* [C] **1** 事 ◊ *A strange thing happened.* 发生一件很奇怪的事。 **2** (*physical object*) 物品 ◊ *A baby's not a thing. It's a human being!* 婴儿不是物品，是人！ **3** (*matter, subject, anything*) 事情 ◊ *Don't bother me with little things like that.* 别用那些小事烦我。◊ *Don't you worry about a thing.* 别担心任何事。 **II things** *n* [*pl*] **1** (*belongings*) 东西 ◊ *I like my own things around me.* 我喜欢我的东西都在我旁边。 **2** (*in general*) 情形 ◊ *How are things going?* 情形如何？ ♦**the thing is ...** 是这样… ♦**for one thing** 一则 ♦**the best thing would be to ...** 最好的方式是… ♦**first thing (in the morning)** (早晨)头件事 ♦**last thing (at night)** (晚上)最后做的事 ♦**to have a thing about** [非正式] (*like*) 喜爱; (*dislike*) 厌恶 ♦**to do one's own thing** [非正式] 自由行事 ♦**you lucky/silly thing** [非正式] 你这个幸运的/傻人

✪**think** [θɪŋk] (*pt, pp* **thought**) **I** *vi* **1** (*reflect*) 思考 ◊ *He thought for a moment, but said nothing.* 他思考了一会，没说什么。 **2** (*reason*) 想 ◊ *People didn't think this way 20 years ago.* 人们20年前不这么想。 **II** *vt* **1** (*be of the opinion, believe*) 认为 **2** (*believe*) 以为 ◊ *How old do you*

think I am? 你以为我多大？
3 (*reflect*) 想 ◊ *"What are you thinking?" – "I am thinking how lovely you look".* "你在想什么？""我在想你是多么好看。" 4 (*conceive, imagine*) 想出 III *n* ♦ **to have a think about sth** 考虑某事 ♦ **to think of** (*reflect upon*) 想着；(*recall*) 记起；(*show consideration for*) 考虑；(*conceive of*) 想到 ♦ **what do you think of ...?** 你认为…怎么样？♦ **to think about sth/sb** 想着某事物/某人 ♦ **I'll think about it** 我要考虑一下 ♦ **to think of doing sth** 考虑做某事 ♦ **to think highly of sb** 看重某人 ♦ **to think nothing of doing sth** 认为做某事没什么了不起 ♦ **to think aloud** 自言自语 ♦ **think again!** 别想！♦ **he is thought to have survived** 人们认为他活了下来 ♦ **I think so/not** 我想是/不是的
❑ **think back** *vi* ♦ **to think back (to sth)** 回想起（某事）
❑ **think over** *vt* [+ *offer, suggestion*] 仔细考虑
❑ **think through** *vt* 全面考虑
❑ **think up** *vt* [+ *plan, scheme, excuse*] 想出

thinking ['θɪŋkɪŋ] *n* [U] 1 (*ideas*) 想法 2 (*thought*) 思考 ♦ **to my (way of) thinking** 依我看来

third [θəːd] I *num* 1 (*in series*) 第三 2 (*fraction*) 三份 II *n* 1 [U] [汽车] (*also: **third gear***) 第三挡 2 [C] [英：大学] (*degree*) 学位考试最低及格成绩 ♦ **a third of** 三分之一 *see also* **fifth**

thirdly ['θəːdlɪ] *adv* 第三

third party insurance [英] *n* [U] 第三方保险

Third World I *n* ♦ **the Third World** 第三世界 II *adj* [+ *country, debt*] 第三世界的

thirst [θəːst] *n* 1 [C/U] (*feeling*) 口渴 2 [U] (*condition*) 干渴 ♦ **a thirst for...** [+ *success, learning etc*] 渴望…

thirsty ['θəːstɪ] *adj* 渴的 ♦ **gardening is thirsty work** 园艺是辛苦的工作

✪ **thirteen** [θəː'tiːn] *num* 十三 *see also* **fifteen**

thirteenth [θəː'tiːnθ] *num* 第十三 *see also* **fifth**

thirtieth ['θəːtɪɪθ] *num* 第三十

✪ **thirty** ['θəːtɪ] *num* 三十 *see also* **fifty**

✪ **this**

KEYWORD

[ðɪs] (*pl* **these**)
I *adj*
1 (*demonstrative*) 这 ♦ **this man** 这个男人 ♦ **this house** 这座房子 ♦ **this one is better than that one** 这个比那个好
2 (*with days, months, years*) 这个 ♦ **this Sunday/month/year** 这个星期天/月/今年
II *pron* 这个 ♦ **who's/what's this?** 这是谁/什么？♦ **this is where I live** 这是我住的地方 ♦ **this is how you do it** 你应该这么做 ♦ **this is what he said** 这是他所说的 ♦ **this is Janet** (*in introduction*) 这是珍妮特；(*on telephone*) 我是珍妮特 ♦ **like this** 像这个一样的
III *adv* (*demonstrative*) ♦ **this much/high/long** 这么多/高/长 ♦ **it was about this big** 它大约有这么大 ♦ **we can't stop now we've gone this far** 我们已经走了这么远了，停不下来了

thistle ['θɪsl] *n* [C] 蓟

thongs [θɔŋz] [美] *n* [*pl*] (*open shoes*) 夹趾拖鞋 [英 = **flip-flops**]

thorn [θɔːn] *n* [C] 刺

thorough ['θʌrə] *adj* 1 [+ *search, investigation etc*] 彻底的 2 [+ *knowledge, research*] 详尽的 3 (*methodical*) [+ *person*] 细致的 4 (*complete*) 完全的

thoroughly ['θʌrəlɪ] *adv* 1 [*examine, study* +] 全面地 2 [*wash, search* +] 彻底地 3 (*very, very much*) 十分地 ♦ **I thoroughly agree** 我完全同意

✪ **those** [ðəuz] I *pl adj* 1 那些 II *pl pron* 那些 ♦ **those people/books** 那些人/书 ♦ **I prefer those ones to these** 与这些相比我更喜欢那些 ♦ **are those yours?** 那些是你的吗？

✪ **though** [ðəu] I *conj* (*although*) 虽然 ◊ *Though he hadn't stopped working all day, he wasn't tired.* 虽然

一整天都在工作，他却不累。**II** *adv* 但是◊ *It's not easy, though.* 但是不容易啊。♦**even though** 尽管

> **though** 和 **although** 都用在从句中，引出某个意外的情况或跟另一事实形成对照的情况。**though** 不用于非常正式的英语中。*Though he was noisy and sometimes arrogant, I quite liked him…It was certainly not paper, though it looked very much like it…Although she said she was hungry, she refused food and drink…The street is much the same, although there are some rather smart new shops.*
> **even though** 可用于强调令人吃惊的事实。*She wore a fur coat, even though it was a very hot day.*
> **as though** 通过对比或解释的方式来描述某个情形。*He looked at me as though I was a total stranger…The furniture looked as though it had come out of somebody's attic.* **though** 也可以表示 'however' 的含义。但这种用法非常不正式。*At weekends, though, the atmosphere changes…He was dressed neatly, though.*

✪**thought** [θɔːt] **I** *pt, pp of* **think** **II** *n* **1** [c] (*idea*) 想法◊ *The thought never crossed my mind.* 我从来没有这种想法。**2** [u] (*reflection*) 沉思◊ *She frowned as though deep in thought.* 她皱着眉头好像陷入深深的沉思。**3** [u] (*way of thinking*) 观点◊ *This school of thought argues that depression is best treated by drugs.* 这个学术派的观点认为抑郁最好用药物治疗。**4** [c] (*intention*) 念头◊ *Her one thought was to get back to Derek.* 她惟一的念头是回到德里克身边。**III** **thoughts** *n* [*pl*] (*opinions*) 看法◊ *Tom disclosed his thoughts on Britain.* 汤姆透露了他对英国的看法。♦**after much thought** 经慎重考虑后 ♦**to give sth some thought** 琢磨某事

thoughtful ['θɔːtful] *adj* **1** (*deep in thought*) 深思的 **2** (*considerate*) 体贴的

thoughtless ['θɔːtlɪs] *adj* (*inconsiderate*) [+ *behaviour, words, person*] 不体贴的

✪**thousand** ['θauzənd] *num* ♦**a** *or* **one thousand** 一千 ♦**thousands of** 许许多多◊ *thousands of dollars* 许多美元

thousandth ['θauzəntθ] *num* (*in series*) 第一千

thrash [θræʃ] *vt* **1** (*hit*) 鞭打 **2** [非正式] (*defeat*) 击溃
❑**thrash about, thrash around** *vi* 乱冲乱撞
❑**thrash out** *vt* [非正式] [+ *problem, differences*] 推敲

thread [θrɛd] **I** *n* **1** [c/u] (*yarn*) 线 **2** [c] [*of screw*] 螺纹 **3** [c] (*of story, account*) 思路 **II** *vt* **1** [+ *needle*] 穿 **2** (*join with string*) 串 ♦**to thread one's way between/through** 小心翼翼地穿过

threat [θrɛt] *n* [c/u] 威胁 ♦**to make a threat (against sb)** 威胁（某人）♦**to be under threat (of/from sth)** 受到（某物的）威胁 ♦**a threat to sth** 对某物的威胁

threaten ['θrɛtn] **I** *vi* [*storm, danger* +] 似将发生 **II** *vt* **1** (*make a threat against*) [+ *person*] 威胁 **2** (*endanger*) [+ *life, livelihood etc*] 使受到威胁 ♦**to threaten sb with a knife/gun** 用刀/枪威胁某人 ♦**to be threatened with imprisonment/extinction** 受到监禁/覆灭的威胁 ♦**to threaten to do sth** (*promise*) 扬言做某事; (*seem likely*) 可能发生某事

threatening ['θrɛtnɪŋ] *adj* [+ *behaviour, person, letter*] 威胁的

✪**three** [θriː] *num* 三 *see also* **five**

three-dimensional [θriːdɪ'mɛnʃənl] *adj* **1** [+ *object*] 三维的 **2** [+ *film, picture, image*] 立体的

three-piece suite [尤英] *n* [c] 三件一套的沙发

three-quarters [θriː'kwɔːtəz] **I** *n* [*pl*] 四分之三 **II** *adv* ♦**three-quarters full/empty** 四分之三满/空 **III** *pron* 四分之三 ♦**three-quarters of an hour** 45 分钟

threshold ['θrɛʃhəuld] *n* [c] **1** [*of building, room*] 门槛 **2** (喻) (*on scale*) 限度 ♦**to be on the threshold of**

(喻)正处在…的开端
threw [θru:] *pt of* **throw**
thrift shop [美] *n* [c] 慈善商店 [英= **charity shop**]
thrifty ['θrɪftɪ] *adj* [+ *person*] 节俭的
thrill [θrɪl] **I** *n* [c] (*excitement*) 兴奋 **II** *vi* ♦**to thrill at/to sth** 因某事而兴奋 **III** *vt* [+ *person, audience*] 使兴奋 ♦**to give sb a thrill** 使某人兴奋 ♦**a thrill of anticipation/surprise** 一阵期望/惊奇 ♦**to be thrilled with sth/to do sth/that ...** 对于某事/做某事/…感到兴奋
thriller ['θrɪlə(r)] *n* [c] (*novel, play, film*) 惊险
thrilling ['θrɪlɪŋ] *adj* [+ *performance, news etc*] 令人兴奋的
thriving ['θraɪvɪŋ] *adj* [+ *business, community*] 繁荣的
throat [θrəut] *n* [c] **1** (*gullet*) 咽喉 **2** (*neck*) 脖子 ♦**to clear one's throat** 清清嗓子 ♦**to have a sore throat** 嗓子疼
throb [θrɔb] **I** *n* [s] **1** [*of heart*] 悸动 **2** [*of pain*] 一跳跳的疼 **3** [*of engine, music*] 振动 **II** *vi* **1** [*head, foot etc* +] 一跳一跳地疼 **2** [*heart* +] 悸动 **3** [*engine, music* +] 振动
throne [θrəun] *n* [c] **1** (*chair*) 宝座 **2** (喻) 皇位
throng ['θrɔŋ] **I** *n* [c] (*crowd*) 大群 **II** *vt* [*people* +] [+ *streets, beaches etc*] 蜂拥而至 **III** *vi* ♦**to throng to/into/around** 拥向/入/在周围
✪**through** [θru:] **I** *prep* **1** [+ *place*] 穿过 ◊ *The rain poured through a hole in the roof.* 雨在屋顶上穿了一个洞。**2** (*throughout*) [+ *time*] 整个 ◊ *trips for older people all through the year* 整年都为老年人安排的旅行 **3** (*coming from the other side of*) 穿过 ◊ *They could hear music through the walls of the house.* 他们能听到音乐穿墙而来。**4** (*by means of*) 通过 ◊ *They were opposed to change through violence.* 他们反对通过暴力变革。**5** (*because of*) 由于 ◊ *The discovery of adrenalin came about through a mistake.* 由于一个错误导致了肾上腺素的发现。**II** *adv* **1** (*in space*) 穿过 ◊ *We decided to drive straight through to Birmingham.* 我们决定开车直接去伯明翰。**2** (*in time*) 整个 ◊ *hard work right through the summer* 持续了整个夏天的辛苦工作 **III** *adj* [+ *ticket, train*] 直达的 ♦**(from) Monday through Friday** [美](从)周一到周五 [英= **to**] ♦**to be through** (*on telephone*) 被接通 ◊ *You're through.* 已为您接通 ◊ *You're through to the accounts department.* 已为你接到会计部。♦**to be through with sb/sth** 与某人断绝往来/再也不做某事 ♦**"no through road"** [英] "此路不通" ♦**"no through traffic"** [美] "此路不通"
throughout [θru:'aut] **I** *prep* **1** [+ *place*] 遍及 **2** [+ *time*] 贯穿 **II** *adv* **1** (*everywhere*) 全部 **2** (*the whole time*) 始终
throw [θrəu] (*pt* **threw**, *pp* **thrown**) **I** *n* [c] 投掷 **II** *vt* **1** (*toss*) [+ *stone, ball etc*] 丢 **2** (*place carelessly*) 扔 **3** [+ *person*] 抛 **4** [+ *one's head, arms etc*] 甩 **5** [*horse* +] [+ *rider*] 摔出 **6** [+ *fit, tantrum*] 发作 **7** (喻) (*confuse*) 惊扰 ♦**to throw one's energy/money into sth** 把大量的精力/金钱投入某事 ♦**to throw o.s. into sth** 积极投入某事 ♦**to throw o.s. somewhere** 重重地倒在某处 ♦**to be thrown in(to) jail** *or* **prison** 被投入监狱 ♦**to be thrown into turmoil/confusion** 陷入混乱/迷惑 ♦**to throw open** [+ *doors, windows*] 使大开着; [+ *debate*] 使公开 ♦**to throw a party** [非正式] 开个派对
❑**throw about, throw around** [非正式] *vt* (喻) [+ *money*] 挥霍
❑**throw away** *vt* **1** [+ *rubbish*] 扔掉 **2** [+ *opportunity*] 错过
❑**throw in** *vt* [非正式] (*include*) 免费供应
❑**throw off** *vt* (*get rid of*) 摆脱
❑**throw out** *vt* **1** [+ *rubbish*] 扔掉 **2** (*from team, organization*) 赶走 **3** [+ *case, request*] 否决
❑**throw up** [非正式] *vi* (*vomit*) 呕吐
thrown [θrəun] *pp of* **throw**
thru [θru:] [美] = **through**
thrush [θrʌʃ] *n* **1** [c] (*bird*) 画眉鸟 **2** [u] [医] 鹅口疮
thrust [θrʌst] (*pt, pp* **thrust**) **I** *n* **1** [u] [术语] 推力 **2** [c] (*push*) 猛推 **3** [s]

(*impetus*) 要点 **II** *vt* **1** [+ *person, object*] 猛推 **2** [+ *hand, sword*] 戳
thud [θʌd] **I** *n* [c] 砰的一声 **II** *vi* 砰然作响
thug [θʌg] *n* [c] 暴徒
thumb [θʌm] **I** *n* [c] (*on hand*) 大拇指 **II** *vt* ♦**to thumb a lift/ride** 搭便车 ♦**to give sb/sth the thumbs down** [非正式]不同意某人/某事 ♦**to give sb/sth the thumbs up** [非正式]同意某人/某事
❑**thumb through** *vt* [不可拆分] [+ *book, magazine*] 翻阅
thumbtack ['θʌmtæk] [美] *n* [c] 图钉 [英 = **drawing pin**]
thump [θʌmp] **I** *n* [c] **1** (*blow*) 重击 **2** (*sound*) 砰的一声 **II** *vt* **1** [尤英: 非正式] (*hit*) [+ *person*] 揍 **2** [+ *object, table*] 撞击 **III** *vi* **1** ♦**to thump on sth** 撞击某物 **2** [*heart etc* +] 砰砰作响
thunder ['θʌndə(r)] **I** *n* [U] **1** (*in sky*) 雷 **2** (喻) [*of guns, waterfall etc*] 隆隆声 **II** *vi* **1** ♦**it was thundering** 打雷了 **2** [*guns, train etc* +] 轰隆作响 **III** *vt* (*shout*) 大嚷大叫 ♦**to thunder past** [*train etc* +] 像雷电一样通过
thunderstorm ['θʌndəstɔːm] *n* [c] 雷雨
Thu. *abbr* (= ***Thursday***) 星期四
Thur(s). *abbr* (= ***Thursday***) 星期四
Thursday ['θəːzdɪ] *n* [c/U] 星期四 *see also* **Tuesday**
thus [ðʌs] [正式] *adv* **1** (*therefore*) 因此 **2** (*in this way*) 就这样
thwart [θwɔːt] *vt* **1** [+ *person, plans*] 阻挠
thx *abbr* (= ***thanks***) 谢谢
thyme [taɪm] *n* [U] (*herb*) 百里香
tick [tɪk] **I** *n* **1** [c] [尤英] (*mark*) 勾号 [美 = **check**] **2** [c] [*of clock*] 嘀嗒声 **3** [c] [动] 扁虱 **4** [c] [英: 非正式] (*moment*) 一刹那 **5** [英: 非正式] (*credit*) ♦**to buy sth on tick** 赊账购买某物 **II** *vi* [*clock, watch* +] 嘀嗒作响 **III** *vt* [尤英] [+ *item on list*] 打勾 [美 = **check off**] ♦**what makes him tick?** [非正式]什么使他成为这个样子的?
❑**tick away, tick by** *vi* [*clock, time, seconds* +] 时间嘀嗒流逝
❑**tick off** *vt* **1** [尤英] [+ *item on list*] 打勾 [美 = **check off**] **2** [英: 非正式] (*scold*) 责骂 **3** [美: 非正式] (*annoy*) 使厌烦
❑**tick over** *vi* [*business etc* +] 照常进行
ticket ['tɪkɪt] *n* **1** [c] (*for public transport, theatre, raffle etc*) 票 **2** [c] [汽车] (*also:* ***parking ticket***) 违章停车罚单 **3** [c] (*price label*) 标价牌 **4** [s] [美: 政治] 候选人名单
ticket barrier *n* [c] (*automatic*) 检票口
ticket collector *n* [c] (*on train, bus*) 检票员
ticket inspector *n* [c] (*on train, bus*) 查票员
ticket machine *n* [c] 售票机
ticket office *n* [c] 售票处
tickle ['tɪkl] **I** *vt* **1** [+ *person*] 挠 **2** (喻) (*amuse*) 逗乐 **II** *vi* [*feather, hair etc* +] 发痒
ticklish ['tɪklɪʃ] *adj* **1** [+ *person*] 怕痒的 **2** [+ *problem, decision, issue etc*] 棘手的
tide [taɪd] **I** *n* **1** [c] (*in sea*) 潮汐 **2** [s] (喻) [*of events, fashion, opinion*] 趋向 ♦**high/low tide** 涨/落潮
❑**tide over** *vt* (*with loan etc*) 渡过
tidy ['taɪdɪ] **I** *adj* **1** [+ *room, desk, person*] 整洁的 **2** [非正式] [+ *sum, profit*] 可观的 **II** *vt* (*also:* ***tidy up***) [+ *room, house etc*] 整理
❑**tidy away** *vt* 整理
❑**tidy up** *vt, vi* 整理
tie [taɪ] **I** *n* [c] **1** (*clothing*) 领带 **2** (*string etc*) 带子 **3** (*link*) 联系 **4** [尤英: 体育] (*match*) 淘汰赛 **5** (*draw*) (*in competition*) 平局 **II** *vt* **1** (*also:* ***tie up***) [+ *shoelaces etc*] 扎 **2** (*also:* ***tie together***) [+ *ropes etc*] 拴 **3** (*link*) 紧密相关 **III** *vi* ♦**to tie (with sb)** [体育等] (与某人) 打成平局 ♦**to tie sth in a bow/knot** 将某物打成蝴蝶结/打结 ♦**to tie string/ribbon around sth** 把绳/丝带绕着某物打结
❑**tie down** *vt* (喻) (*restrict*) [+ *person*] 束缚 ♦**to tie sb down to a date/price** 为某人定死日期/价钱
❑**tie in** *vi* ♦**to tie in with** 与…相符
❑**tie up** *vt* **1** [+ *parcel etc*] 捆绑 **2** [+ *dog*] 拴 **3** [+ *person*] 捆绑 **4** (*settle*) [+ *arrangements, deal etc*] 了结 ♦**to**

be tied up [非正式] (*busy*) 忙得不可开交

tier [tɪə(r)] *n* [c] **1** [*of stadium etc*] 排 **2** [*of cake*] 层

tiger ['taɪgə(r)] *n* [c] 老虎

tight [taɪt] **I** *adj* **1** (*not loose*) [+ *string, skin, cloth*] 紧绷的 **2** (*compact*) 紧密的 **3** (*firm*) [+ *hold, grip*] 紧的 **4** (*close-fitting*) [+ *shoes, clothes*] 紧身的 **5** (*sharp*) [+ *bend*] 急转的 **6** (*strict*) [+ *budget, schedule*] 紧张的; [+ *security, controls*] 严格的 **7** (*scarce*) [+ *money*] 短缺的 **8** [非正式] (*stingy*) 小气的 **9** [非正式] (*drunk*) 醉了的 **II** *adv* [*hold, squeeze, shut* +] 紧紧地 ♦**to be packed tight** [*suitcase* +] 塞满; [*people* +] 靠紧

tighten ['taɪtn] **I** *vt* **1** [+ *rope, strap*] 拉紧 **2** [+ *screw, bolt*] 弄紧 **3** [+ *grip, security, rules etc*] 加紧 **II** *vi* **1** [*grip* +] 握紧 **2** [*rope, strap etc* +] 拉紧 ❑**tighten up** *vt* [+ *screw, bolt*] 弄紧

tightly ['taɪtlɪ] *adv* **1** (*firmly, tautly*) [*grasp, cling, close, seal* +] 紧紧地 **2** (*closely*) 紧密地 **3** (*rigorously*) [*control, regulate* +] 严格地 ♦**a tightly knit community** 内部联系密切的社区

tights [taɪts] [英] *n* [*pl*] 连裤袜 [美 = **pantyhose**]

tile [taɪl] **I** *n* [c] **1** (*on roof*) 瓦 **2** (*on floor, wall*) 砖 **II** *vt* [+ *floor, bathroom etc*] 给…铺砖

till [tɪl] **I** *n* [c] [英] (*in shop etc*) 收银台 [美 = **cash register**] **II** *vt* (*cultivate*) [+ *land, soil*] 耕种 **III** *prep, conj* = **until**

tilt [tɪlt] **I** *vt* **1** [+ *object*] 翘起 **2** [+ *part of body*] 仰起 **II** *vi* **1** [*object* +] 倾斜 **2** [*part of body* +] 抬起 **III** *n* [c] (*slope*) 倾斜 ♦**(at) full tilt** 全速地

timber ['tɪmbə(r)] [英] *n* [u] (*material*) 木料 [美 = **lumber**]

✪**time** [taɪm] **I** *n* **1** [u] 时间 ◊ *a period of time* 一段时间 ◊ *I haven't got much time.* 我没太多时间。**2** [u] (*period*) 时候 ◊ *during my time in Toronto* 我在多伦多的时候 **3** [c] (*day*) 时期 ◊ *in these difficult times* 在这段困难时期 **4** [s] (*by clock*) 时间 ◊ *I will see you at the same time next week.* 下星期和你在同一时间见面。**5** [c] (*occasion*) 次 ◊ *the last time I saw her* 我最后一次见到她 **6** [u] [音] 节拍 **II** *vt* **1** (*measure time of*) 计时 ◊ *They timed his rate of breathing.* 他们计算他呼吸的频率。◊ *He timed his speech.* 他对自己的演讲进行了计时。**2** (*fix moment for*) [+ *visit etc*] 定于 ◊ *They timed the attack for six o'clock.* 他们定于6点发动攻击。♦**it is time for sth/to do sth** 是做某事的时候 ♦**to have a good/bad time** 度过一段愉快/不愉快的时光 ♦**to spend time** 花时间 ♦**to spend one's time doing sth** 花时间做某事 ♦**three times a day** 一日三次 ♦**three times the size of sth** 某物大小的3倍 ♦**four at a time** 一次4个 ♦**for a time** 好一段时间 ♦**all the time** 总是 ♦**for the time being** 暂时 ♦**from time to time** 偶尔 ♦**time after time, time and again** 一次次 ♦**at one time** (*in the past*) 曾经 ♦**at the same time** (*nevertheless*) 然而; (*simultaneously*) 同时 ♦**at times** (*sometimes*) 有时 ♦**in time** (*eventually*) 到时 ♦**to be in time** [音] [*singers, dancers etc* +] 合拍 ♦**in time (for)** 正好赶上(…) ♦**in a week's/month's time** 一周/月以后 ♦**in no time, in next to no time** 立刻 ♦**it's about time ...** *or* **it's high time ...** 早就该… ♦**the best/worst film of all time** 有史以来最好/最差的电影 ♦**any time** 任何时候 ♦**on time** 准时 ♦**once upon a time** 很久以前 ♦**to be 30 minutes behind time/ahead of time** 晚了/提前30分钟 ♦**by the time he arrived** 到他到达时 ♦**5 times 5 is 25** 5乘5等于25 ♦**what time is it?, what's the time?** 几点了? ♦**to ask sb the time** 问某人时间 ♦**time off** (*from work*) 休假 ♦**to have a hard time** 受苦受难 ♦**time's up!** 时间到了! ♦**to have no time for sth** (喻) 没有时间关注某事 ♦**in one's own (good) time** (*without being hurried*) 从容地 ♦**in** *or* (美) **on one's own time** (*out of working hours*) 业余时间 ♦**to take one's time** 慢慢来 ♦**to take time** 需要时间 ♦**to be behind the times** 落伍 ♦**to be ahead of** *or*

before one's time 领先于某人的时代 ♦**to time sth well/badly** 把某段时间计划得好/糟糕 ♦**to be timed to happen** 定于发生

timeless ['taɪmlɪs] *adj* 永恒的

time limit *n* [c] 期限

timely ['taɪmlɪ] *adj* [+ *arrival, reminder*] 及时的

time out [美:体育] *n* [c] 休场 [英= **stoppage**]

timer ['taɪmə(r)] *n* [c] 定时器

timetable ['taɪmteɪbl] *n* [c] **1** [英:铁路等] 时刻表 [美= **schedule**] **2** [英:教育] 课程表 [美= **class schedule**] **3** (*programme of events*) 计划表

time zone *n* [c] 时区

timid ['tɪmɪd] *adj* [+ *person, animal*] 胆小的

timing ['taɪmɪŋ] *n* [u] **1** (*skill*) 时间把握 **2** [*of announcement*] 时间安排

tin [tɪn] *n* **1** [u] (*metal*) 锡 **2** [c] [英] (*can*) 罐 [美= **can**] **3** [c] (*container*) (*for biscuits, tobacco etc*) 听 **4** [c] [英] (*for baking*) 锡盒 [美= **pan**]

tinfoil ['tɪnfɔɪl] *n* [u] (*foil*) 锡纸

tingle ['tɪŋgl] **I** *vi* (*when circulation returns, with cold*) 刺痛; (*with excitement*) 激动起来 **II** *n* ♦**a tingle of excitement** 一阵兴奋

tinker ['tɪŋkə(r)] **I** *vi* ♦**to tinker with sth** 随意乱修某物 **II** *n* [c] **1** (*pot mender*) 补锅匠 **2** [英:非正式,疑讳] (*gipsy*) 浪人

tinned [tɪnd] [英] *adj* [+ *food*] 罐装的 [美= **canned**]

tin opener [-əupnə(r)] [英] *n* [c] 开罐器 [美= **can opener**]

tint [tɪnt] **I** *n* [c] **1** (*colour*) 淡色 **2** (*for hair*) 染色 **II** *vt* [+ *hair*] 染

tinted ['tɪntɪd] *adj* [+ *hair, spectacles, glass*] 泛…色的

tiny ['taɪnɪ] *adj* 极小的 ♦**a tiny bit** 微乎其微

tip [tɪp] **I** *n* [c] **1** [*of branch, paintbrush etc*] 顶端 **2** (*protective*) (*on umbrella, walking stick*) 尖端 **3** (*to waiter etc*) 小费 **4** [英] (*for rubbish*) 弃置场 **5** [英] (*for coal*) 堆 **6** (*advice*) 提示 **II** *vt* **1** [+ *waiter*] 给…小费 **2** (*pour*) 倒出 **3** (*also: **tip over***) (*overturn*) 翻转 **4** (*predict*) [+ *winner etc*] 猜测 **5** (*tilt*) [+ *object, part of body*] 倾斜 **III** *vi* (*also: **tip over***) [*object, part of body* +] 倾斜 ♦**the tip of the iceberg** (喻) 冰山一角

❑**tip off** *vt* [+ *person*] 提醒

tiptoe ['tɪptəu] *vi* 踮着脚走 ♦**on tiptoe** 踮着脚走

tire ['taɪə(r)] **I** *n* [美] = **tyre II** *vt* (*also: **tire out***) (*make tired*) 使疲劳 **III** *vi* (*become tired*) 疲劳 ♦**to tire of sth** 对某事感到厌倦了

tired ['taɪəd] *adj* 累的 ♦**to be tired of (doing) sth** 厌倦于(做)某事

> 📖 请勿将**tired**与**tiring**混淆。如果你**tired**，说明你感到疲劳，需要休息。*Do you mind if I sit down? I'm feeling very tired.* **tiring**的任务或旅途让人感到**tired**。*Looking after young children is very tiring...I went to bed early after the long and tiring journey.*

tiresome ['taɪəsəm] *adj* 讨厌的

tiring ['taɪərɪŋ] *adj* [+ *work, day etc*] 令人疲劳的

📖 用法参见 **tired**

tissue ['tɪʃuː] *n* **1** [u] [解剖,生物] 组织 **2** [c] (*paper handkerchief*) 纸巾

tissue paper *n* [u] 绵纸

tit [tɪt] *n* [c] **1** [非正式,疑讳] (*breast*) 乳房 **2** (*bird*) 山雀 ♦**tit for tat** 以牙还牙

title ['taɪtl] *n* **1** [c] [*of book, play etc*] 标题 **2** [c] (*rank*) 称号 **3** [c] [体育] 冠军 **4** [u] [法] (*right*) ♦**title to** 所有权

📖 用法参见 **position**

T-junction ['tiː'dʒʌŋkʃən] *n* [c] 丁字路口

✪ **to**

KEYWORD

[tuː, tə]

I *prep*

1 (*direction*) 到 ♦**to France/London/school/the station** 去法国/伦敦/学校/车站 ♦**we went to a party last night** 我们昨晚去参加了一个聚会 ♦**the road to Manchester** 通往曼彻斯特的路

2 (*as far as*) ♦**from here to London** 从这儿到伦敦 ♦**to count to ten** 数到10

3 (*position*) 向 ♦**to the north/south** 朝北/南 ♦**to the left/right** 向左/

右 ♦**nailed/stuck to the wall** 钉/粘在墙上
4 (*in time expressions*) ♦**it's five/ten/a quarter to five** 差5分/10 分/一刻5 点
5 (*for, of*) 的 ♦**the key to the front door** 前门的钥匙 ♦**a letter to his wife** 给他妻子的一封信 ♦**she is secretary to the director** 她是主管的秘书
6 (*indirect object*) ♦**to give sth to sb** 给某人某物 ♦**to talk to sb** 对某人说 ♦**I sold it to a friend** 我把它卖给了一个朋友 ♦**you've done something to your hair** 你打理了你的头发 ♦**it was clear to me that ...** 对我来说这显而易见…; (*after noun*) (*involving*) ♦**damage to sth** 对某物的损害 ♦**a danger to sb** 对某人的危险 ♦**repairs to sth** 对某物的修理
7 (*towards*) ♦**to be friendly/kind/loyal to sb** 对某人友好/仁慈/忠实
8 (*in relation to*) ♦**30 miles to the gallon** 每加仑可行30 英里 ♦**A is to B as C is to D** A 与B的关系就像C与D的关系 ♦**three goals to two** 3 比2
9 (*purpose, result*) ♦**to come to sb's aid** 来帮某人的忙 ♦**to sentence sb to death** 判某人死刑
10 (*indicating range, extent*) ♦**from ... to** 从…到… ♦**everything from seeds to vegetables** 从种子到蔬菜的每样东西 ♦**from May to September** 从5月到9月
11 (*with*) ♦**to enter to the sound of drums** 随着鼓声进入
II *with verb*
1 (*simple infinitive*) 与原形动词一起构成动词不定式 ♦**to go/eat** 走/吃 ♦**to want/to try to do sth** 想/试着做某事
2 (*with vb omitted*) 用来代替动词不定式或不定式短语，避免重复 ♦**I don't want to** 我不想 ♦**you ought to** 你应该
3 (*in order to*) 为了 ♦**I did it to help you** 我这么做是为了帮你 ♦**measures to help developing nations** 用以帮助发展中国家的措施
4 (*equivalent to relative clause*) 用作定语 ♦**I have things to do** 我有事要做 ♦**he has a lot to lose** 他要失去很多
5 (*after adjective etc*) 用于某些动词、名词、形容词后构成不定式 ♦**to be ready to go** 准备走 ♦**it's great to see you** 见到你太好了 ♦**too old/young to do sth** 年纪太大/太小以至于不能做某事 ♦**it's too heavy to lift** 它太重了根本提不动 ♦**to be old/young enough to do sth** 到了做某事的年龄/足够年轻做某事
6 (*and*) ♦**he awoke/arrived to find that everyone had gone** 他醒来/到了发现大家都走了
III *adv* ♦**to push/pull the door to** 把门掩上 ♦**to and fro** 来来回回地

toad [təud] *n* [c] 蟾蜍
toadstool ['təudstu:l] *n* [c] 毒菌
toast [təust] **I** *n* **1** [U] [烹饪] 烤面包 **2** [c] (*drink*) 祝酒 **II** *vt* **1** [烹饪] [+ *bread etc*] 烤 **2** (*drink to*) 为…祝酒 ♦**a piece** *or* **slice of toast** 一片烤面包 ♦**to drink a toast to sb** 为某人干杯
📖 用法参见 **cook**
toaster ['təustə(r)] *n* [c] 烤面包机
tobacco [tə'bækəu] *n* [U] 烟草
tobacconist's (shop) [tə'bækənɪsts-] *n* [c] 烟草店
toboggan [tə'bɔgən] *n* [c] 平底雪橇
✪ **today** [tə'deɪ] **I** *adv* **1** 今天 ◊ *I hope you're feeling better today.* 我希望你今天感觉好些。**2** (*at the present time*) 现在 ◊ *This is the best translation available today.* 这是现存的最好的翻译。**II** *n* [U] **1** 今天 ◊ *Today is Thursday.* 今天星期四。**2** (*the present time*) 现今 ◊ *the Africa of today* 现今的非洲 ♦**what day is it today?** 今天星期几？♦**a week ago today** 上星期的今天 ♦**today is the 4th of March** 今天是3月4日 ♦**today's paper** 今天的报纸
toddler ['tɔdlə(r)] *n* [c] 学步的小孩
toe [təu] *n* [c] **1** [*of foot*] 脚趾 **2** [*of shoe, sock*] 脚趾处 ♦**big/little toe** 大/小脚趾 ♦**to toe the line** 听从命令

TOEFL *n abbr* ['tɔfəl] (= ***Test of English as a Foreign Language***) 托福
toenail ['təuneɪl] *n* [c] 脚指甲
toffee ['tɔfɪ] *n* **1** [u] [英] (*substance*) 太妃糖 [美 = **taffy**] **2** [c] (*sweet*) 乳脂糖
✪ **together** [tə'gɛðə(r)] *adv* **1** (*with each other*) 一起 ◊ *We went on long bicycle rides together.* 我们一起骑了很长一段时间的自行车。**2** (*in the same place*) 在一起 ◊ *The trees grew close together.* 这些树长拢在一起。**3** (*at the same time*) 同时 ◊ *Three horses crossed the finish line together.* 3匹马同时越过终点线。**4** (*in a group*) 合在一起 ◊ *Mix the ingredients together thoroughly.* 把这些原料充分地合在一起。**5** (*combined*) 加起来 ◊ *The two opposition parties together won 29 per cent of the vote.* 两个反对党加起来赢得29%的选票。♦**together with** 连同
Togo ['təugəu] *n* 多哥
toilet ['tɔɪlət] **I** *n* [c] **1** (*apparatus*) 抽水马桶 **2** [英] (*room*) 卫生间 [美 = **bathroom**] **II** *cpd* [复合词] [+ *kit, accessories etc*] 厕所 ♦**to go to the toilet** [尤英] 上厕所
toilet bag [英] *n* [c] 洗漱包
toilet paper *n* [u] 卫生纸
toiletries ['tɔɪlətrɪz] *n* [*pl*] 卫生用品
toilet roll *n* [c/u] 卫生卷纸
token ['təukən] **I** *n* [c] **1** (*sign*) 象征 **2** (*instead of money*) 代金券 **II** *adj* [+ *strike, payment, gesture*] 象征性的 ♦**by the same token** 同样
told [təuld] *pt, pp of* **tell**
tolerable ['tɔlərəbl] *adj* **1** (*bearable*) 可忍受的 **2** [正式] (*fairly good*) 相当好的
tolerant ['tɔlərnt] *adj* 宽容的 ♦**to be tolerant of** 对…宽容
tolerate ['tɔləreɪt] *vt* **1** [+ *pain, noise etc*] 忍受 **2** (*accept*) 容忍
toll [təul] **I** *n* [c] **1** [*of casualties, accidents*] 伤亡人数 **2** (*on road, bridge*) 通行费 **II** *vi* [*bell* +] 鸣响 ♦**the work took its toll on us** 这工作让我们受尽折磨
toll-free ['təulfriː] [美: 通信] **I** *adj* [+ *number*] 免费的 [英 = **freephone**] **II** *adv* ♦**to call toll-free** 拨打免费电话
tomato [tə'mɑːtəu] (*pl* **tomatoes**) *n* [c/u] 西红柿
tomato sauce [烹饪] *n* [u] (*ketchup*) 西红柿酱
tomb [tuːm] *n* [c] 坟墓
tombstone ['tuːmstəun] *n* [c] 墓碑
tomorrow [tə'mɔrəu] **I** *adv* **1** 明天 **2** (*in the future*) 未来 **II** *n* **1** [u] 明天 **2** [c/u] (*future*) 将来 ♦**a week tomorrow, tomorrow week** 下星期的明天 ♦**the day after tomorrow** 后天 ♦**tomorrow morning** 明天早晨
ton [tʌn] *n* [c] **1** [英] 英吨 **2** [美] (*also:* ***short ton***) 美吨 **3** (*metric ton*) 公吨 ♦**tons of** [非正式] 大量的
tone [təun] **I** *n* **1** [c] [*of sound*] 音质 **2** [c] [*of voice*] 腔调 **3** [s] [*of speech, article etc*] 基调 **4** [c/u] [*of colour*] 色调 **5** [s] [通信] 声音 **II** *vt* (*also:* ***tone up***) [+ *muscles*] 增强
❑ **tone down** *vt* **1** [+ *criticism etc*] 缓和 **2** [+ *colour, flavour*] 调和
❑ **tone in with, tone with** [尤英] *vt* [不可拆分] 搭配
Tonga ['tɔŋə] *n* 汤加
tongs [tɔŋz] *n* [*pl*] 夹子
tongue [tʌŋ] *n* **1** [c] [解剖] 舌头 **2** [u] [烹饪] 口条 **3** [c] [正式] (*language*) 语言 ♦**tongue in cheek** 毫无诚意的
tonic ['tɔnɪk] *n* **1** [u] (*also:* ***tonic water***) 奎宁水 **2** [c/u] [医] 滋补品 **3** [c] (喻) (*boost*) 有兴奋作用的东西
tonight [tə'naɪt] *adv, n* [u] 今晚
tonsil ['tɔnsl] *n* [c] 扁桃体 ♦**to have one's tonsils out** 切除扁桃体
tonsillitis [tɔnsɪ'laɪtɪs] *n* [u] 扁桃腺炎
✪ **too** [tuː] **I** *adv* **1** (*excessively*) 太 ◊ *It was too far to walk.* 要是走路就太远了。**2** (*also*) 也 ◊ *You're from Brooklyn? Me too!* 你从布鲁克林来？我也是！ **3** (*for emphasis*) 并且 ◊ *We did learn to read, and quickly too.* 我们确实学会了阅读，并且学得很快。♦**too bad!** 很遗憾！ ♦**I'm not too happy with it** 我对此并不是很高兴 ♦**all too well/recently, only too well/recently** 好/近得不能再好/近

用法参见 **also**

took [tuk] *pt of* **take**

tool [tuːl] *n* [c] **1** (*implement*) 用具 **2** (喻) 工具 **3** [贬] (*person*) 爪牙

tool box *n* [c] 工具箱

tool kit *n* [c] 工具包

tooth [tuːθ] (*pl* **teeth**) *n* [c] **1** [解剖] 牙齿 **2** [*of comb, saw, zip*] 齿 ♦**to have a tooth out** *or* (美) **pulled** 拔牙 ♦**to brush one's teeth** 刷牙

toothache [ˈtuːθeɪk] *n* [c/u] 牙痛 ♦**to have toothache** 牙痛

toothbrush [ˈtuːθbrʌʃ] *n* [c] 牙刷

toothpaste [ˈtuːθpeɪst] *n* [c/u] 牙膏

toothpick [ˈtuːθpɪk] *n* [c] 牙签

✪**top** [tɔp] **I** *n* **1** [c] [*of mountain, building, tree, stairs*] 顶部 **2** [c] [*of page*] 顶端 ◊ *Go back to the top of the page.* 回到本页的顶端。**3** [c] [*of cupboard*] 顶层 **4** [c] [*of surface, table*] 表面 **5** [s] [尤英] [*of street*] 尽头 **6** [c] (*lid*) [*of box, jar, bottle*] 盖子 **7** [s] [*of table, league*] 榜首 **8** [u] [汽车] (*also: **top gear***) 最高挡 **9** [c] (*blouse etc*) 上衣 **II** *adj* **1** [+ *shelf, step, storey, marks*] 最高的 **2** [+ *executive, golfer etc*] 顶级的 ♦**top speed** 全速 **III** *vt* **1** (*be first in*) [+ *poll, vote, list*] 获第一名 **2** (*exceed*) [+ *estimate, speed etc*] 超过 ◊ *US investments here topped fifty million dollars.* 美国的投资超过5000万美元。♦**at the top of the stairs/page/street** 在楼梯/页面的顶端/街道的尽头 ♦**at the top of the list** 居于榜首 ♦**to get to the top** (*in profession etc*) 取得高层地位 ♦**on top of** (*above*) 在…上面 ◊ *She laid her hand on top of his.* 她把手放在他的手上。; (*in addition to*) 除…之外 ◊ *700 jobs are being cut on top of the 2000 that were lost last year.* 除了去年2000人失去工作之外，又有700个工作职位被削减。♦**to get on top of sth** (喻) 圆满地处理某事 ♦**from top to bottom** 彻底 ♦**from top to toe** [英] 从头到脚 ♦**at the top of one's voice** 扯着嗓子叫喊 ♦**to be/go over the top** [英:非正式] 过分 ♦**top priority** 最优先 ♦**to be** *or* **come top** 独占鳌头

❑**top up** *vt* **1** [+ *drink*] 加满 **2** [+ *salary, loan*] 增加

top hat *n* [c] 大礼帽

topic [ˈtɔpɪk] *n* [c] 话题

topical [ˈtɔpɪkl] *adj* [+ *issue, question*] 热门的

topless [ˈtɔplɪs] *adj* [+ *bather, waitress, dancer*] 袒胸的

topping [ˈtɔpɪŋ] [烹饪] *n* [c/u] 配料

topple [ˈtɔpl] **I** *vt* [+ *government, leader*] 推翻 **II** *vi* (*also: **topple over***) [*person, object* +] 翻倒

torch [tɔːtʃ] *n* [c] **1** [英] (*electric*) 手电筒 [美=**flashlight**] **2** (*with flame*) 火把

tore [tɔː(r)] *pt of* **tear**[1]

torment [*n* ˈtɔːmɛnt, *vb* tɔːˈmɛnt] **I** *n* [c/u] 折磨 **II** *vt* **1** [*feelings, guilt* +] 折磨 **2** (*annoy*) 折磨 ♦**in torment** 在折磨中

torn [tɔːn] **I** *pp of* **tear**[1] **II** *adj* ♦**to be torn between** 在两者中游移不定

tornado [tɔːˈneɪdəu] (*pl* **tornadoes**) *n* [c] 飓风

torpedo [tɔːˈpiːdəu] (*pl* **torpedoes**) *n* [c] 鱼雷

torrent [ˈtɔrnt] *n* [c] **1** (*flood*) 急流 **2** (喻) ♦**a torrent of abuse/questions** 一片谩骂/成堆的问题

torrential [tɔˈrɛnʃl] *adj* [+ *rain*] 滂沱的

tortoise [ˈtɔːtəs] *n* [c] 乌龟

torture [ˈtɔːtʃə(r)] **I** *n* [u] **1** 酷刑 **2** (*torment*) 折磨 **II** *vt* **1** 对…施以酷刑 **2** (*torment*) 使痛苦

Tory [ˈtɔːrɪ] [英:政治] **I** *adj* 保守党的 **II** *n* [c] 保守党党员

toss [tɔs] **I** *vt* **1** 扔 **2** [*wind, sea* +] [+ *boat etc*] 使颠簸 **3** [+ *salad*] 拌 **4** [+ *pancake*] 抛起使翻转 **II** *n* **1** ♦**with a toss of her head** 她把头往后一仰 **2** ♦**to decide sth by the toss of a coin** 抛硬币决定某事 ♦**to toss a coin** 掷硬币 ♦**to toss one's head** 一摆头 ♦**to win/lose the toss** [体育] 掷硬币占上风/落下风 ♦**I don't give a toss** [英:非正式] 我不在乎 ♦**to toss and turn** (*in bed*) 辗转反侧

❑**toss up** *vi* 掷硬币决定

✪**total** [ˈtəutl] **I** *adj* **1** [+ *number, workforce, cost etc*] 总的 **2** (*complete*) [+ *failure, wreck, stranger*] 完全的 **II** *n* [c] (*sum of money, number*) 总数 ◊ *The*

companies have a total of 1776 employees. 公司总共有1776名员工。**II** *vt* **1** (*add up*) 加起来◊ *Votes cast for each candidate will be totalled.* 每个候选人的选票要被加起来。**2** (*add up to*) 总计◊ *1980 revenues totalled 18 billion dollars.* 1980年税收总计180亿美元。
♦in total 总共

totalitarian [təutælɪ'tɛərɪən] *adj* [+ *regime, state*] 极权主义的

totally ['təutəlɪ] *adv* **1** [*agree, destroy* +] 完全地 **2** [+ *different, new*] 绝对地

touch [tʌtʃ] **I** *n* **1** [U] (*sense of touch*) 触觉 **2** [C] (*contact*) 触摸 **3** [C] (*detail*) 修饰 **II** *vt* **1** (*with hand, foot*) 触摸 **2** (*tamper with*) 瞎搞 **3** (*make contact with*) 碰到 **4** (*move*) (*emotionally*) 感动 **5** (*use, consume*) 碰过 **III** *vi* (*be in contact*) 接触 **♦a personal touch** 独特的方法 **♦to put the finishing touches to sth** 对某物做最后的润色 **♦a touch of frost/flu** *etc* 些微的霜/有点儿感冒{等} **♦to be out of touch** 落伍的 **♦to be/keep in touch with sth** 与某事物保持联系 **♦to be/keep in touch (with sb)** (与某人)保持联系 **♦to get in touch with sb** 与某人联系 **♦to lose touch (with sb)** (与某人)失去联系
❑**touch down** *vi* [*aircraft* +] 着陆
❑**touch on** *vt* [不可拆分] (*mention*) 提及
❑**touch up** *vt* (*paint*) 修饰

touchdown ['tʌtʃdaun] *n* **1** [C/U] [*of aircraft, spacecraft*] 着陆 **2** [C] [体育] 触地得分

touched [tʌtʃt] *adj* (*emotionally*) 感动的

touching ['tʌtʃɪŋ] *adj* (*moving*) [+ *scene, story etc*] 使人感动的

touchline ['tʌtʃlaɪn] [体育] *n* [S] 边线

touch-sensitive ['tʌtʃ'sɛnsɪtɪv] *adj* [+ *screen*] 触摸感应的

touchy ['tʌtʃɪ] *adj* **1** [+ *person*] 敏感的 **2** [+ *subject*] 棘手的

tough [tʌf] *adj* **1** (*strong, hard-wearing*) [+ *material*] 坚韧的 **2** [+ *meat*] 老的 **3** [+ *person, animal*] (*physically*) 强壮的 **4** (*mentally*) 顽强的 **5** (*difficult*) [+ *task, problem, way of life*] 艰辛的 **6** [+ *time*] 倒霉的 **7** (*firm*) [+ *stance, negotiations, policies*] 严格的 **8** (*rough*) 无法无天的 **♦tough (luck)!** 倒霉!

tour ['tuə(r)] **I** *n* [C] **1** (*journey*) 旅行 **2** [*of town, factory, museum*] 观光 **3** (*by pop group, sports team etc*) 巡回表演 **II** *vt* [+ *country, city etc*] 观光◊ *The Prime Minister toured the poorest area of Liverpool.* 首相巡视了利物浦最贫穷的地区。**♦to go on a tour of** [+ *museum etc*] 去游览…; [+ *region*] 去… 旅行 **♦to go/be on tour** [*pop group, theatre company etc* +] 进行巡回演出

tour director [美] *n* [C] 导游

tour guide *n* [C] 导游 [美 = **tour director**]

tourism ['tuərɪzm] *n* [U] 旅游业

tourist ['tuərɪst] **I** *n* [C] 游客 **II** *cpd* [复合词] [+ *season, attraction*] 旅游
♦the tourist trade 旅游业

tourist office *n* [C] 旅游咨询处

tournament ['tuənəmənt] *n* [C] 锦标赛

tow [təu] **I** *vt* [+ *vehicle, trailer*] 拖 **II** *n* [汽车] **♦to give sb a tow** 帮某人拖车 **♦to have sb in tow** [非正式] 带着某人 **♦"on** *or* (美) **in tow"** [汽车] "被拖着"
❑**tow away** *vt* [+ *vehicle*] 拖走

✪**toward(s)** [tə'wɔːd(z)] *prep* **1** (*in direction of*) (字) 朝着◊ *He saw his mother running toward(s) him.* 他看见妈妈朝着他跑来。; (喻) 向着◊ *the trend toward(s) couples living together rather than marrying* 向着同居而不结婚方向发展的趋势 **2** (*with regard to*) 对于◊ *There has been a change of attitude toward(s) science.* 对于科学有态度上的转变。**3** (*near*) 接近◊ *Their home was toward(s) the top of the hill.* 他们的家接近山顶。**4** (*as contribution to*) 为◊ *He gave them £20,000 toward(s) a house.* 他为他们的房子捐助两万英镑。**5** (*in time*) 接近◊ *towards the end of the year* 接近年底时

towel ['tauəl] **I** *n* [C] 毛巾 **II** *vt* [+ *hair*] 用毛巾擦 **♦to throw in the towel** (喻) 认输 **♦to towel o.s. dry** 用毛巾擦干自己

towelling ['tauəlɪŋ] *n* [U] (*fabric*) 毛巾布
tower ['tauə(r)] **I** *n* [C] 塔 **II** *vi* [*building, mountain* +] 耸立 ♦**to tower above** *or* **over sb/sth** 比某人/某物高得多
tower block [英] *n* [C] 高楼大厦
✪**town** [taun] *n* **1** [C] 城镇 **2** [U] (*one's home town*) 家乡 ◊ *She left town.* 她离开了家乡。♦**to go to town** (喻) 以极大的精力去做 ♦**in town** 在市中心 ♦**to be out of town** 出城
town centre [英] *n* [C] 市中心
town hall [英] *n* [C] 市政厅
tow rope ['təurəup] *n* [C] 拖绳
tow truck [美] *n* [C] (*breakdown lorry*) 拖车
toxic ['tɔksɪk] *adj* [+ *fumes, waste etc*] 有毒的
toy [tɔɪ] **I** *n* [C] 玩具 **II** *cpd* [复合词] [+ *train, car etc*] 玩具
❑**toy with** *vt* [不可拆分] **1** [+ *object, food*] 心不在焉地摆弄 **2** [+ *idea*] 漫不经心地考虑
toyshop ['tɔɪʃɔp] *n* [C] 玩具店
trace [treɪs] **I** *n* [C] **1** (*sign*) [*of substance*] 痕迹; [*of person*] 踪迹 **2** (*small amount*) ♦**a trace of** 微量的 **II** *vt* **1** (*draw*) [+ *picture*] 描摹 **2** (*with finger*) 勾画 **3** (*also:* ***trace back***) [+ *development, progress etc*] 追溯 **4** (*locate*) [+ *person, letter*] 追踪; [+ *cause*] 探究 ♦**to vanish** *or* **disappear without trace** 消失得无影无踪
track [træk] **I** *n* [C] **1** (*path*) 小径 **2** [*of bullet etc*] 轨迹 **3** [*of suspect, animal*] 足迹 **4** [铁路] 轨道 **5** (*on tape, record*) 曲目 **6** [体育] 跑道 **II** *vt* (*follow*) [+ *animal, person*] 追踪 ♦**to keep/lose track of sb/sth** 掌握/跟不上某人/某物的动态 ♦**to be on the right track** (喻) 方向正确
❑**track down** *vt* [+ *prey, criminal*] 追踪到
tracksuit ['træksu:t] [英] *n* [C] 运动服 [美= **sweatsuit**]
tractor ['træktə(r)] *n* [C] 拖拉机
✪**trade** [treɪd] **I** *n* **1** [U] (*buying and selling*) 贸易 **2** [C] (*skill, job*) 谋生之道 **3** [C] (*specific kind of work*) 行业 ◊ *the book trade* 图书业 **II** *vi* (*do business*) 做生意 **III** *vt* **1** (*exchange*) ♦**to trade sth (for sth)** [尤美] 用某物交换(某物) ♦**to trade with** [+ *country, company*] 与…进行贸易 ♦**to trade in** [+ *merchandise*] 从业于
❑**trade in** *vt* [+ *old car etc*] 以旧换新
trademark ['treɪdmɑ:k] *n* [C] 商标
trader ['treɪdə(r)] *n* [C] 商人
tradesman ['treɪdzmən] (*pl* **tradesmen**) *n* [C] **1** (*workman*) 工匠 **2** (*shopkeeper*) 小业主
trade union [尤英] *n* [C] 工会 [美= **labor union**]
trading ['treɪdɪŋ] *n* [U] 交易
tradition [trə'dɪʃən] *n* [C/U] 传统
traditional [trə'dɪʃənl] *adj* [+ *costume, music, method etc*] 传统的
traffic ['træfɪk] **I** *n* [U] **1** (*vehicles*) 交通 **2** [*in drugs etc*] 非法交易 **3** (*air traffic, sea traffic etc*) 航行 **II** *vi* ♦**to traffic in** [+ *liquor, drugs*] 贩卖
traffic circle [美] *n* [C] 转盘 [英= **roundabout**]
traffic jam *n* [C] 交通阻塞
traffic lights *n* [*pl*] 红绿灯
traffic warden [尤英] *n* [C] 交通管理员
tragedy ['trædʒədɪ] *n* [C/U] **1** (*disaster*) 极大的不幸 **2** [戏剧] 悲剧
tragic ['trædʒɪk] *adj* **1** [+ *death, consequences, accident*] 悲惨的 **2** [戏剧] [+ *play, hero etc*] 悲剧的
trail [treɪl] **I** *n* [C] **1** (*path*) 小路 **2** [*of footprints etc*] 串 **II** *vt* **1** (*drag*) [+ *scarf, coat, fingers*] 拖 **2** (*follow*) [+ *person, animal*] 跟踪 **III** *vi* **1** (*drag*) [*scarf, coat, fingers* +] 拖曳 **2** (*move slowly*) 拖着步子走 **3** (*in game, contest*) 落后 ♦**to be on the trail of sb/sth, be on sb's trail** 追踪某人/某物
❑**trail away, trail off** *vi* [*sound, voice* +] 渐弱至无声
trailer ['treɪlə(r)] *n* [C] **1** [汽车] 拖车 **2** [美] (*caravan*) 房式拖车 [英= **caravan**] **3** [电影, 电视] 预告片
trailer park [美] *n* [C] 活动住房停放处 [英= **caravan site**]
train [treɪn] **I** *n* [C] **1** [铁路] 火车 **2** [*of dress*] 裙裾 **II** *vt* **1** (*teach skills to*) 培训 **2** [+ *dog*] 训练 **3** [+ *athlete*] 培养 **4** (*educate*) [+ *mind*] 开发 **5** [+ *plant*] 给…整枝 ♦**to train sth on sb/sth**

[+ *camera, hose, gun etc*] 把某物对准某人/某物 **III** *vi* **1** (*learn a skill*) 受训练 **2** [体育] 锻炼 ♦ **train of thought** 思路 ♦ **a train of events** 一系列的事件

trained [treɪnd] *adj* **1** [+ *worker, teacher*] 经专门训练的 **2** [+ *animal*] 驯化的 ♦ **to the trained eye** 经专业眼光鉴定

trainee [treɪ'niː] *n* [c] **1** (*apprentice*) 受训者 **2** (*in office, management job*) 实习生

trainer ['treɪnə(r)] *n* [c] **1** [体育] 教练 **2** [英] (*shoe*) 运动鞋 [美 = **sneaker**] **3** [*of animals*] 驯兽师

training ['treɪnɪŋ] *n* [U] **1** (*for occupation*) 培训 **2** [体育] 训练 ♦ **to be in training for sth** [体育] 为某事进行训练

training course *n* [c] 培训班

trait [treɪt] *n* [c] 特性

traitor ['treɪtə(r)] *n* [c] 叛徒

tram [træm] [英] *n* [c] (*also: **tramcar***) 有轨电车 [美 = **streetcar**] ♦ **to go by tram** 乘有轨电车去

tramp [træmp] **I** *n* [c] **1** (*vagrant*) 流浪者 **2** [尤美：非正式，贬] (*woman*) 荡妇 **II** *vi* (*walk slowly*) 踏 **III** *vt* [+ *town, streets*] 踏遍

trample ['træmpl] **I** *vt* **1** [+ *grass, plants*] 践踏 **2** [+ *person*] 踩 **II** *vi* ♦ **to trample on** 践踏在 ♦ **to trample on sb's feelings** 伤害某人的感情

trampoline ['træmpəliːn] *n* [c] 蹦床

trance [trɑːns] *n* [c] 恍惚 ♦ **to be in/go into a trance** 在/陷入迷睡状态

tranquil ['træŋkwɪl] *adj* 宁静的

tranquillity (美 **tranquility**) [træŋ'kwɪlɪtɪ] *n* [U] 安谧

tranquillizer (美 **tranquilizer**) ['træŋkwɪlaɪzə(r)] *n* [c] 镇静剂

transaction [træn'zækʃən] *n* [c] (*piece of business*) 交易

transatlantic ['trænzət'læntɪk] *adj* **1** [+ *trade, phone-call, flight etc*] 跨越大西洋的 **2** [英] (*American*) 大西洋彼岸的

transcript ['trænskrɪpt] *n* [c] [*of tape, notes*] 讲稿

transfer [*n* 'trænsfə(r), *vb* træns'fəː(r)] **I** *n* **1** [C/U] [*of money, documents etc*] 转移 **2** [C/U] [*of employee*] 调任 **3** [C/U] [政治] [*of power*] 移交 **4** [c] [体育] 转会 **5** [c] [英] (*picture, design*) 转印 [美 = **decal**] **II** *vt* **1** [+ *employee*] 调任 **2** [+ *money, documents etc*] 转移 **3** [政治] [+ *power, ownership*] 移交 ♦ **by bank transfer** 通过银行转账 ♦ **to transfer the charges** [英：通信] 收费转移

transform [træns'fɔːm] *vt* [+ *person, situation etc*] 完全改变 ♦ **to transform sb/sth into** 使某人/某事变成

transformation [trænsfə'meɪʃən] *n* [C/U] 改变 ♦ **transformation into sth** 改变成某事物

transfusion [træns'fjuːʒən] *n* [C/U] (*also: **blood transfusion***) 输血

transit ['trænzɪt] **I** *n* **1** ♦ **in transit** [*people* +] 在途中; [*things* +] 运送中 **2** [U] [美] 运输 **II** *adj* [+ *area, building*] 中转的

transition [træn'zɪʃən] *n* [C/U] 过渡 ♦ **transition from/to sth** 从/向某事物过渡

translate [trænz'leɪt] *vt* **1** [+ *word, book etc*] 翻译 **2** (*convert*) 转化 ♦ **to translate a book from English into French** 把一本书从英语翻译成法语

translation [trænz'leɪʃən] *n* **1** [c] (*text*) 译文 **2** [U] (*act of translating*) 翻译 ♦ **to read sth in translation** 读某物的译文

translator [trænz'leɪtə(r)] *n* [c] 译者

transmission [trænz'mɪʃən] *n* **1** [U] [*of information, disease*] 传播 **2** [c] [电视，广播] (*broadcast*) 播送 **3** [U] (*act of transmitting*) 播出 **4** [C/U] [汽车] 传动装置

transmit [trænz'mɪt] *vt* **1** [+ *message, signal*] 发送 **2** [正式] [+ *disease*] 传播 **3** [电视，广播] [+ *programme*] 播出

transmitter [trænz'mɪtə(r)] [电视，广播] *n* [c] 发射机

transparent [træns'pærnt] *adj* **1** [+ *blouse, plastic*] 透明的 **2** (喻) [+ *lie, pretence*] 显而易见的; [+ *costs, activity*] 清楚的

transplant [*vb* træns'plɑːnt, *n* 'trænsplɑːnt] **I** *vt* **1** [医] [+ *organ*] 移植 **2** (*move*) 使迁移 **3** [+ *plant*] 移栽 **II** *n* **1** [C/U] [医] (*operation*) 移植 **2** [c]

[医] (*organ*) 移植器官 ♦**to have a heart/liver transplant** 进行心脏/肝脏移植

transport [*n* 'trænspɔːt, *vb* træns'pɔːt] **I** *n* [U] **1** [*of people, goods*] 运输 **2** (*transportation*) 交通工具 **II** *vt* (*move*) 运送 ♦**to have one's own transport** 有自己的交通工具 ♦**public transport** [尤英] 公共交通 ♦**Department of Transport** [英] 交通部

transportation ['trænspɔː'teɪʃən] *n* [U] **1** [美] (*transport*) 运输 **2** (*means of transport*) 交通工具 ♦**Department of Transportation** [美] 交通部

transvestite [trænz'vɛstaɪt] *n* [C] 爱穿着异性衣物的人

trap [træp] **I** *n* [C] **1** (*for animals*) 陷阱 **2** (*trick*) 圈套 **3** (*carriage*) 双轮马车 **II** *vt* **1** [+ *animal*] 诱捕 **2** (*trick*) [+ *person*] 诱导 **3** (*confine*) (*in bad marriage etc*) 使陷入 **4** (*in building etc*) 困住 **5** (*capture*) [+ *gas, water, energy*] 使不泄漏 ♦**to set** *or* **lay a trap for sb** 为某人设陷阱 ♦**to trap one's finger in the door** 某人的手指被门缝夹了一下

trash [træʃ] *n* [U] **1** [美] 废物 [英 = **rubbish**] **2** [贬] (*nonsense*) 胡说八道

trash can [美] *n* [C] 垃圾桶 [英 = **(dust) bin**]

trauma ['trɔːmə] *n* [C/U] 创伤

traumatic [trɔː'mætɪk] *adj* 创伤的

travel ['trævl] **I** *n* [U] (*travelling*) 旅行 **II** *vi* **1** [*person* +] 前往 **2** [*light, sound, news* +] 传播 **III** *vt* [+ *distance*] 走过 **IV travels** *n* [C] *pl* 游历 ♦**news travels fast** 消息传得快 ♦**this wine doesn't travel well** 这酒不宜长途运输

travel agency *n* [C] 旅行社

travel agent *n* [C] **1** (*shop, office*) 旅行中介 **2** (*person*) 旅行代理人

traveller (美 **traveler**) ['trævlə(r)] *n* [C] **1** 旅行者 **2** [英] (*gypsy*) 漂泊者

traveller's cheque (美 **traveler's check**) *n* [C] 旅行支票

travelling (美 **traveling**) ['trævlɪŋ] **I** *n* [U] 行程 **II** *cpd* [复合词] [+ *circus, exhibition*] 巡回 ♦**travelling expenses** 旅费

travel insurance *n* [U] 旅行保险

travel rep *n* [C] 全陪导游

travel sick *adj* 晕车/船/机的

travel sickness *n* [U] 晕车/船/机症

tray [treɪ] *n* [C] **1** (*for food, drink*) 托盘 **2** (*on desk*) 文件盘

treacherous ['trɛtʃərəs] *adj* **1** [+ *person*] 不忠的 **2** [+ *ground, conditions, current*] 危险的

treacle ['triːkl] [英] *n* [U] (*also:* ***black treacle***) 糖浆 [美 = **molasses**]

tread [trɛd] (*pt* **trod**, *pp* **trodden**) **I** *n* **1** [S] (*footstep*) 脚步声 **2** [C/U] [*of tyre*] 轮胎面 **II** *vi* 走 ♦**to tread carefully** (喻) 小心行事

❑**tread on** *vt* [不可拆分] 踩上

treasure ['trɛʒə(r)] **I** *n* **1** [U] (*gold, jewels etc*) 宝藏 **2** [C] [非正式] (*person*) 宝贝 **II** *vt* (*value*) [+ *object, memory, friendship*] 珍惜 **III treasures** *n* [*pl*] 珍品

treasurer ['trɛʒərə(r)] *n* [C] 财务总管

treasury ['trɛʒərɪ] *n* ♦**the Treasury,** (美) **the Treasury Department** 财政部

treat [triːt] **I** *n* [C] **1** (*gift, outing etc*) 待遇 **2** (*luxury*) 礼遇 **II** *vt* **1** (*behave towards*) [+ *person, object*] 对待 **2** [医] [+ *patient, illness*] 医治 **3** [术语] [+ *substance, material*] 处理 ♦**to treat sth as a joke** 把某事当作笑话 ♦**to treat sb for a wound/injury** 给某人治疗伤口/伤处 ♦**to treat a substance/material with sth** 用某物处理某种物质/材料 ♦**to treat sb to sth** 用某物款待某人 ♦**to treat o.s. to sth** 使自己享受某物

treatment ['triːtmənt] *n* **1** [U] (*attention*) 对待 **2** [C/U] [医] 治疗 ♦**to have** *or* **receive treatment for sth** [医] 因某病接受治疗

treaty ['triːtɪ] *n* [C] 条约

treble ['trɛbl] **I** *adj* **1** (*triple*) 三倍的 **2** [音] [+ *instrument*] 高音; [+ *voice, part*] 高音部 **II** *n* [C] **1** (*singer*) 高音歌手 **2** (*on hi-fi, radio etc*) 高音部 **III** *vt* 使成三倍 **IV** *vi* 增至三倍 ♦**to be treble the amount/size of sth** 是某物数量/大小的三倍

tree [triː] *n* [C] 树

trek [trɛk] **I** *n* [C] 跋涉 **II** *vi* 徒步穿越

tremble ['trɛmbl] *vi* **1** [*voice* +] (*with fear etc*) 颤抖 **2** [*body* +] (*with fear, cold etc*) 战栗 **3** [*ground, trees* +] 抖动

tremendous [trɪ'mɛndəs] *adj* **1** (*enormous*) [+ *amount, success etc*] 极大的 **2** (*excellent*) 极棒的

trench [trɛntʃ] *n* [c] **1** 沟 **2** (*in battlefield*) 战壕

trend [trɛnd] *n* [c] **1** (*tendency*) 趋势 **2** (*fashion*) 潮流 ♦**a trend towards/away from (doing) sth** （做）某事/背离某事的倾向 ♦**to set a trend** 领导潮流

trendy ['trɛndɪ] [非正式] *adj* [+ *idea, person, clothes, place*] 时髦的

trespass ['trɛspəs] *vi* ♦**to trespass on** 擅入 ♦**"no trespassing"** "禁止擅入"

trial ['traɪəl] **I** *n* [c/u] **1** [法] 审理 **2** [*of machine, drug etc*] 试验 **II trials** *n* [*pl*] (*ordeal*) 麻烦 ♦**horse trials** 马术比赛 ♦**trial by jury** 陪审团审理 ♦**to be sent for trial** 送审 ♦**on trial** [法] 受审; (*on approval*) 试验 ♦**by trial and error** 反复试验

trial period *n* [c] (*for employee, product*) 试用期

triangle ['traɪæŋgl] *n* [c] **1** [数] 三角 **2** [音] 三角铁

triangular [traɪ'æŋgjulə(r)] *adj* 三角形的

tribe [traɪb] *n* [c] 部落

tribunal [traɪ'bjuːnl] *n* [c] 特别法庭

tribute ['trɪbjuːt] *n* [c/u] 赞赏 ♦**to be a tribute to sth** 归功于某事 ♦**to pay tribute to sb/sth** 对某人/某事表示敬意

trick [trɪk] **I** *n* [c] **1** (*by conjuror*) 戏法 **2** (*deception*) 伎俩 **3** (*skill, knack*) 诀窍 **4** [纸牌] 一圈牌 **II** *vt* (*deceive*) 耍花招 ♦**to play a trick on sb** 对某人耍花招 ♦**a trick of the light** 光引起的幻觉 ♦**that should do the trick** [非正式] 这应该奏效 ♦**to trick sb into doing sth** 用计诱使某人做某事

trickle ['trɪkl] **I** *vi* **1** [*water, tears, blood* +] 一滴滴地流 **2** [*people, things* +] 相继走 **II** *n* [c] [*of water, blood*] 细流

tricky ['trɪkɪ] *adj* [+ *job, problem*] 棘手的

tricycle ['traɪsɪkl] *n* [c] 三轮车

trifle ['traɪfl] **I** *n* **1** [c] (*small detail*) 琐事 **2** [c/u] [烹饪] 水果蛋糕 **II** *adv* ♦**a trifle long/short** 有点长/短 **III** *vi* ♦**to trifle with sb/sth** 耍某人/不重视某事

trigger ['trɪgə(r)] **I** *n* [c] **1** [*of gun*] 扳机 **2** [*of bomb*] 导火索 **3** (*cause*) 诱因 **II** *vt* **1** [+ *alarm, bomb*] 启动 **2** (*also:* ***trigger off***) [+ *reaction, riot*] 引发

trim [trɪm] **I** *adj* **1** [+ *garden etc*] 整齐的 **2** [+ *figure, person*] 苗条的 **II** *n* **1** [c] (*haircut*) 修剪 **2** [c/u] (*decoration*) (*on clothes*) 镶边; (*on car*) 饰边 **III** *vt* **1** (*cut*) [+ *hair, beard*] 剪短 **2** (*decorate*) ♦**to trim (with)** （以…）装饰 **3** [航海] [+ *sail*] 整帆 ♦**to keep in (good) trim** 保持身体健康
❑**trim off** *vt* 除去

trimmings ['trɪmɪŋz] *n* [*pl*] **1** [烹饪] 花色配菜 **2** [*of pastry etc*] 边角料

Trinidad and Tobago ['trɪnɪdædntə'beɪgəu] *n* 特立尼达和多巴哥

trio ['triːəu] *n* [c] **1** [音] [*of musicians*] 三重奏 **2** [音] (*composition*) 三重奏曲 **3** (*group of three*) 三人组

trip [trɪp] **I** *n* [c] **1** (*journey*) 出行 **2** (*outing*) 外出 **II** *vi* **1** (*also:* ***trip up***) (*stumble*) 绊倒 **2** [文] (*walk lightly*) 轻快地走 **III** *vt* (*also:* ***trip up***) (*cause to fall*) 把…绊倒 ♦**to go on a trip** 外出旅行
❑**trip over** *vt* [不可拆分] [+ *stone, root etc*] 绊倒
❑**trip up I** *vi* **1** = **trip 2** （喻）(*make a mistake*) 出差错 **II** *vt* **1** = **trip 2** （喻）(*cause to make a mistake*) 使犯错
📖 用法参见 **journey**

triple ['trɪpl] **I** *adj* 三部分的 **II** *adv* ♦**triple the distance/size** 三倍的距离/尺寸 **III** *vt* 使增至三倍 **IV** *vi* 三倍于

triplets ['trɪplɪts] *n* [*pl*] 三胞胎

tripod ['traɪpɔd] *n* [c] (*for camera, telescope*) 三脚架

triumph ['traɪʌmf] **I** *n* **1** [c] (*great achievement*) 巨大的成功 **2** [u] (*satisfaction*) 得意 **II** *vi* ♦**to triumph (over)** **1** [+ *problem, disability etc*] 胜（过） **2** [+ *opponent*] 战胜

triumphant [traɪ'ʌmfənt] *adj* [+ *person, team*] 得胜的; [+ *wave, return*] 凯旋的

trivia ['trɪvɪə] *n* [*pl*] 琐事
trivial ['trɪvɪəl] *adj* 琐碎的
trod [trɔd] *pt of* **tread**
trodden [trɔdn] *pp of* **tread**
trolley ['trɔlɪ] *n* [c] **1** [英] (*for luggage, in supermarket*) 手推车 [美 = **cart**] **2** [英] (*table on wheels*) 茶具车 [美 = **cart**] **3** [英] (*in hospital*) 有轮子的病床 [美 = **gurney**] **4** [美] (*vehicle*) 电车 [英 = **tram**]
trombone [trɔm'bəun] *n* [c] 长号
troop [tru:p] **I** *n* [c] **1** [*of people, animals*] 群 **2** [*of soldiers*] 队 **II** *vi* ♦ **to troop in/out** 结队进/出 **III troops** *n* [c] *pl* [军] 部队
trophy ['trəufɪ] *n* [c] (*cup, shield etc*) 奖品
tropical ['trɔpɪkl] *adj* [+ *rainforest, disease, climate*] 热带的
trot [trɔt] **I** *n* [s] **1** [*of person*] 小步快跑 **2** [*of horse*] 小跑 **II** *vi* [*horse, person* +] 小步快跑 ♦ **on the trot** [英: 非正式] (*in succession*) 一个接一个地
❑ **trot out** [非正式] *vt* [+ *excuse, information*] 重复
trouble ['trʌbl] **I** *n* **1** [c/u] (*difficulties, bother, effort*) 麻烦 **2** [s] (*problem*) 问题 **3** [u] (*unrest*) 骚乱 **II** *vt* **1** (*worry*) 使担忧 **2** (*disturb*) 打扰 **III** *vi* ♦ **to trouble to do sth** 费心做某事 **IV troubles** *n* [*pl*] 忧虑 ♦ **to be in trouble** (*with police, authorities*) 惹麻烦; [*ship, climber etc* +] 陷入困境 ♦ **to have trouble doing sth** 做某事有困难 ♦ **what's the trouble?** 怎么了? ♦ **the trouble is ...** 问题是… ♦ **stomach/back trouble** 胃部/背部毛病 ♦ **it's no trouble!** 没问题! ♦ **to go to the trouble of doing sth, take the trouble to do sth** 不辞劳苦地做某事 ♦ **please don't trouble yourself** 不麻烦您了
troubled ['trʌbld] *adj* **1** [+ *person*] 焦虑的 **2** [+ *place, times*] 多事的
troublemaker ['trʌblmeɪkə(r)] *n* [c] 闹事者
troublesome ['trʌblsəm] *adj* [+ *child etc*] 烦人的; [+ *injury, cough etc*] 麻烦的
trough [trɔf] *n* [c] **1** (*for feeding animals*) 槽 **2** (喻) (*low point*) 低谷 ♦ **a trough of low pressure** [气象] 低压槽
trousers ['trauzəz] [英] *n* [*pl*] 裤子 [美 = **pants**] ♦ **a pair of trousers** 一条裤子
trout [traut] *n* **1** [c/u] 鳟鱼 **2** [u] (*food*) 鳟鱼肉
trowel ['trauəl] *n* [c] **1** (*garden tool*) 小铲子 **2** (*builder's tool*) 瓦刀
truant ['truənt] **I** *n* **1** ♦ **to play truant** 逃学 **2** [c] (*pupil*) 逃学生 **II** *vi* 逃学
truce [tru:s] *n* [c] 休战 ♦ **to call a truce** 宣布休战
truck [trʌk] *n* **1** [c] [尤美] 卡车 [英 = **lorry**] **2** [c] [英: 铁路] 货车 **3** ♦ **to have no truck with sb/sth** 拒不与某人打交道/参与某事
truck driver [尤美] *n* [c] 卡车司机 [英 = **lorry driver**]
true [tru:] *adj* **1** [+ *story, motive, feelings*] 真实的 **2** (*genuine, typical*) 真正的 **3** (*accurate*) [+ *likeness*] 准确的 ♦ **it is true that ...** …是真的 ♦ **to come true** [*dream, prediction* +] 实现 ♦ **to hold true** 适用 ♦ **to be true to sb** 对某人忠诚 ♦ **to be true to sth** (*to idea, cause*) 忠于某事 ♦ **true to form** 一如既往 ♦ **true to life** 逼真的
truly ['tru:lɪ] *adv* **1** (*genuinely*) 确实地 **2** (*for emphasis*) 相当地 **3** (*truthfully*) 的确地 ♦ **yours truly** (*in letter*) 您忠诚的
trumpet ['trʌmpɪt] *n* [c] 小号
trunk [trʌŋk] **I** *n* [c] **1** [*of tree*] 树干 **2** [*of elephant*] 象鼻 **3** (*case*) 箱子 **4** [美] (*of car*) 后备箱 [英 = **boot**] **5** [正式] [*of person*] 躯干 **II trunks** *n* [*pl*] (*also:* ***swimming trunks***) 游泳裤
trust [trʌst] **I** *n* **1** [u] 信任 **2** [c] [经济] 信托 **3** [c] [英] (*also:* ***trust hospital***) 由政府出资独立经营的医院 **II** *vt* **1** (*have confidence in*) [+ *person*] 信任 **2** (*consider reliable*) [+ *legs, voice etc*] 信赖 **3** [+ *sb's judgement, advice*] 相信 ♦ **sb's trust in sb** 某人对某人的信任 ♦ **a position of trust** 重任 ♦ **to take sth on trust** [+ *advice, information*] 未经查证就相信某事 ♦ **to hold sth in trust** [法] 受托保管某物 ♦ **to trust sb to do sth** 信任某人做某事 ♦ **to trust sb with sth** 把某物托付给某人 ♦ **to trust**

(that) ... [正式] (*hope*) 相信…
trusted ['trʌstɪd] *adj* [+ *friend, advisor*] 可靠的
trusting ['trʌstɪŋ] *adj* [+ *person, nature*] 相信别人的
trustworthy ['trʌstwəːðɪ] *adj* [+ *person*] 可靠的
truth [truːθ] (*pl* **truths** [truːðz]) *n* **1** [U] (*facts*) 事实 **2** [U] (*truthfulness*) 真实性 **3** [C] (*principle*) 真理
truthful ['truːθful] *adj* **1** [+ *person*] 诚实的 **2** [+ *answer, account*] 如实的
✪**try** [traɪ] **I** *n* [C] **1** 尝试 ◊ *It's worth a try.* 这值得一试。**2** [橄榄球] 触球 **II** *vt* **1** (*attempt*) 试 ◊ *I tried a different approach to the problem.* 我试着用不同的方法来解决这个问题。**2** (*test*) 尝试 ◊ *I've tried herbal cigarettes but I don't like them.* 我尝试过草烟但不喜欢。**3** [法] [+ *case, person*] 审理 **4** [+ *person, place*] 试 ◊ *Have you tried the local music shops?* 你试过当地的音乐商店吗? **III** *vi* (*make effort*) 努力 ◊ *You can do it if you try.* 如果你努力就能够做到。♦ **to have a try at sth, give sth a try** 尝试做某事 ♦ **to try to do sth, try doing sth** 尽力做某事 ♦ **to try one's best** *or* **hardest to do sth** 尽某人最大的能力做某事
❑**try on** *vt* [+ *dress, hat, shoes*] 试穿 ♦ **to try it on (with sb)** [英: 非正式] 试探(某人)
❑**try out** *vt* (*test*) 试验
trying ['traɪɪŋ] *adj* **1** [+ *person*] 难对付的 **2** [+ *experience, situation*] 令人厌烦的
T-shirt ['tiːʃəːt] *n* [C] 短袖衫
tub [tʌb] *n* [C] **1** (*container*) 缸 **2** [美] 浴缸 [英 = **bath**]
tube [tjuːb] *n* **1** [C] (*pipe*) 管子 **2** [C] (*container*) 筒 **3** [英] ♦ **the tube** (*underground*) 地铁 [美 = **subway**] **4** [美: 非正式] ♦ **the tube** (*television*) 电视 [英 = **the box**] ♦ **to travel by tube** 乘地铁
tuberculosis [tjubəːkju'ləusɪs] *n* [U] 肺结核
tube station [英] *n* [C] 地铁站
tuck [tʌk] **I** *vt* **1** (*put*) 夹 **II** *n* [C] [缝纫] 褶
❑**tuck away** *vt* (*store*) 妥善保存 ♦ **to be tucked away** [*building etc* +] 隐蔽起来
❑**tuck in I** *vt* **1** [+ *clothing*] 塞进 **2** [+ *child*] 给…盖好被子 **II** *vi* [英: 非正式] (*eat*) 尽情吃
❑**tuck into** [英: 非正式] *vt* [不可拆分] [+ *meal*] 大吃
❑**tuck up** [英] *vt* [+ *invalid, child*] 给…盖好被子
tuck shop [英] *n* [C] 糖果铺
Tue(s). *abbr* (= ***Tuesday***) 星期二
Tuesday ['tjuːzdɪ] *n* [C/U] 星期二 ♦ **it is Tuesday 23rd March** 今天是3月23号, 星期二 ♦ **on Tuesday** 在星期二 ♦ **on Tuesdays** 每个星期二 ♦ **every Tuesday** 每逢星期二 ♦ **every other Tuesday** 隔周星期二 ♦ **last/next Tuesday** 上个/下个星期二 ♦ **the following Tuesday** 下个星期二 ♦ **Tuesday's newspaper** 星期二的报纸 ♦ **a week/fortnight on Tuesday** 一周/两周后的星期二 ♦ **the Tuesday before last** 上上个星期二 ♦ **the Tuesday after next** 下下个星期二 ♦ **Tuesday morning/afternoon/evening** 星期二早晨/下午/晚上
tug [tʌg] **I** *vt* 拉 **II** *vi* ♦ **to tug at** 拉 **III** *n* **1** ♦ **to give sth a tug** 猛拽某物 **2** [C] (*ship*) 拖船
tuition [tjuː'ɪʃən] *n* [U] **1** 教学 **2** (*fees*) 学费
tulip ['tjuːlɪp] *n* [C] 郁金香
tumble ['tʌmbl] **I** *n* [C] 跌倒 **II** *vi* [*person, object* +] 滚落; [*water* +] 翻滚; [*prices, levels* +] 跌 ♦ **to have** *or* **take a tumble** 跌跤
❑**tumble to** [非正式] *vt* [不可拆分] ♦ **he tumbled to the fact that ...** 他突然明白事实是…
tumble dryer [英] *n* [C] 滚筒干衣机 [美 = **dryer**]
tumbler ['tʌmblə(r)] *n* [C] (*glass*) 平底玻璃杯
tummy ['tʌmɪ] [非正式] *n* [C] 肚子
tumour (美 **tumor**) ['tjuːmə(r)] [医] *n* [C] 肿瘤
tuna ['tjuːnə] *n* [C/U] (*also:* ***tuna fish***) 金枪鱼
tune [tjuːn] **I** *n* [C] (*melody*) 曲调 **II** *vt* **1** [音] [+ *instrument*] 调 **2** [+ *engine, machine*] 调试 **3** [+ *radio, TV*] 调台 ♦ **to be in/out of tune** [*instrument* +] 调子正确/不正确; [*singer* +] 合/

跑调 ♦ **to be in/out of tune with** (喻) 与…协调/不协调 ♦ **to change one's tune** 转变态度 ♦ **to the tune of 10,000 pounds** 最大限额到1万镑
❑ **tune in** *vi* [广播, 电视] 收听/看
❑ **tune up** *vi* [*musician, orchestra* +] 调音

tunic ['tjuːnɪk] *n* [c] 无袖上衣

Tunisia [tjuː'nɪzɪə] *n* 突尼斯

Tunisian [tjuː'nɪzɪən] **I** *adj* 突尼斯的 **II** *n* [c] (*person*) 突尼斯人

tunnel ['tʌnl] **I** *n* [c] **1** 隧道 **2** (*in mine*) 坑道 **II** *vi* 挖地道

turbulence ['təːbjuləns] *n* [U] 猛烈而不稳定的水流/气流

turf [təːf] **I** *n* **1** [U] (*grass*) 草坪 **2** [c] (*square of grass*) 草皮 **II** *vt* [+ *area*] 铺
❑ **turf out** [英: 非正式] *vt* [+ *person*] 赶走

Turk [təːk] *n* [c] 土耳其人

Turkey ['təːkɪ] *n* 土耳其

turkey ['təːkɪ] *n* **1** [c] (*bird*) 火鸡 **2** [U] (*meat*) 火鸡肉

Turkish ['təːkɪʃ] **I** *adj* 土耳其的 **II** *n* [U] (*language*) 土耳其语

Turkmenistan ['təːkmɛnɪstɑːn] *n* 土库曼斯坦

turmeric ['təːmərɪk] [烹饪] *n* [U] 姜黄

turmoil ['təːmɔɪl] *n* [S/U] 混乱 ♦ **in turmoil** 处于混乱状态

✪ **turn** [təːn] **I** *n* [c] **1** (*change*) 转变 ◊ *every twist and turn in government policy* 政府政策的每一次扭转 **2** (*in road*) 转弯 **3** (*performance*) 表演 ◊ *a comedy turn* 喜剧表演 **4** (*in game, queue, series*) 机会 ◊ *He stood in the queue waiting his turn.* 他排队等着轮到他。 **5** [英: 非正式: 医] 发病 ◊ *Mrs Reilly is having one of her turns.* 瑞利夫人的病发作了。 **II** *vt* **1** [+ *part of body*] 转动 ◊ *He turned his head left and right.* 他把头左右转动。 **2** [+ *object*] 调转 ◊ *She turned the bedside chair to face the door.* 她把床边的椅子转向门口。 **3** [+ *handle, key*] 转动 **4** [+ *page*] 翻 **5** (*shape*) [+ *wood, metal*] 打制 **III** *vi* **1** (*rotate*) [*object, wheel* +] 旋转 ◊ *The cog wheels started to turn.* 齿轮开始旋转。 **2** (*change direction*) [*person* +] 转身 ◊ *He turned abruptly and walked away.* 他突然转身走开了。 **3** [*vehicle* +] 转向 ◊ *You come over a bridge and turn sharply to the right.* 你走到桥边然后照直向右转。 **4** (*become sour*) [*milk* +] 变质 ♦ **to take a turn for the worse** [*situations, events* +] 恶化 ♦ **"no left turn"** "禁止左转" ♦ **it's my turn to ...** 轮到我做… ♦ **to take turns** *or* **to take it in turns (to do sth)** 轮流做(某事) ♦ **in turn** (*one after the other*) 轮流; (*then, afterwards*) 依次 ♦ **turn of events** 事态变迁 ♦ **it gave me quite a turn** [非正式] 吓了我一跳 ♦ **at the turn of the century/year** 在世纪/新年之交 ♦ **to do sb a good turn** 帮某人大忙 ♦ **to turn forty** 满40岁 ♦ **to turn grey** [*person, hair* +] 变灰白 ♦ **to turn green/blue** *etc* 变绿/蓝{等} ♦ **to turn nasty** 变糟
❑ **turn against** *vt* [不可拆分] 转而反对
❑ **turn around** *vi* = **turn round**
❑ **turn away** **I** *vi* 放弃 **II** *vt* **1** [+ *applicants*] 拒绝 **2** [+ *business*] 放弃
❑ **turn back** **I** *vi* 往回走 **II** *vt* [+ *person, vehicle*] 掉头
❑ **turn down** *vt* **1** [+ *request, offer*] 拒绝 **2** [+ *heat, sound*] 调低 **3** [+ *bedclothes*] 垂放
❑ **turn in** **I** *vi* [非正式] (*go to bed*) 睡觉 **II** *vt* [+ *oneself*] (*to police*) 自首; [+ *sb else*] (*to police*) 告发
❑ **turn into** **I** *vt* [不可拆分] 变成 ◊ *The water turns into steam.* 水变成了蒸汽。 **II** *vt* 使变成 ◊ *Don't turn a drama into a crisis.* 别把戏剧变成闹剧。
❑ **turn off** **I** *vi* (*from road*) 拐弯 **II** *vt* **1** [+ *light, radio, tap etc*] 关 **2** [+ *engine*] 关掉
❑ **turn on** **I** *vt* **1** [+ *light, radio, tap etc*] 打开 **2** [+ *engine*] 发动 **II** *vt* [不可拆分] [+ *person*] 攻击
❑ **turn out** **I** *vt* [+ *light, gas*] 关掉 **II** *vi* [*voters etc* +] 到场 ♦ **to turn out to be** (*prove to be*) 原来是 ♦ **to turn out well/badly** 结果很好/很糟
❑ **turn over** **I** *vi* [*person* +] 翻身 **II** *vt* **1** [+ *object, page*] 翻转 **2** (*give*) 移交 ◊ *He had refused to turn over funds that had belonged to Potter.* 他拒绝

移交属于伯特的款项。♦**to turn sth over to** (*change function of*) 把某物改变成

❑**turn round, turn around** I *vi* 1 [*person, vehicle* +] 调转 2 (*rotate*) 转动 II *vt* [*person, vehicle* +] 调头

❑**turn to** I *vt* [不可拆分] 1 [+ *page*] 翻到 2 [+ *person*] 求助于 II *vt* [+ *attention, thoughts*] 转到 ◊ *We turn now to the British news.* 我们现在转到英国新闻。

❑**turn up** I *vi* 1 (*arrive*) [*person* +] 露面 2 (*be found*) [*lost object* +] 出现 II *vt* 1 [+ *collar, sleeves*] 竖起 2 [+ *radio, heater etc*] 开大 3 [+ *hem*] 改短

turning ['tə:nɪŋ] *n* [c] (*in road*) 拐弯

turning point *n* [c] 转弯处

turnip ['tə:nɪp] *n* [c/u] 萝卜

turnout ['tə:naut] *n* [c] [*of people, voters etc*] 全部参与人（数）

turnover ['tə:nəuvə(r)] *n* [c/u] 1 [商] (*amount of money*) 营业额 2 [商] [*of staff*] 人事变动率 3 [烹饪] 糖三角 ♦**there is a rapid turnover in staff** 人员变动很快

turn signal [美] *n* [u] 指示器 [英= **indicator**]

turnstile ['tə:nstaɪl] *n* [c] 旋转栅门

turn-up ['tə:nʌp] *n* [c] 1 [英] (*on trousers*) 卷边 [美= **cuff**] 2 ♦**that's a turn-up for the books!** [非正式] 真是意想不到的事！

turquoise ['tə:kwɔɪz] I *n* [c] (*stone*) 绿松石 II *adj* [+ *colour*] 青绿色的

turtle ['tə:tl] [英] *n* [c] 龟 [美= **sea turtle**]

tusk [tʌsk] *n* [c] [*of elephant, boar etc*] 长牙

tutor ['tju:tə(r)] I *n* [c] 1 [英:教育] 助教 2 (*private tutor*) 家庭教师 II *vt* (*teach*) 教

tutorial [tju:'tɔ:rɪəl] *n* [c] 辅导课

tuxedo [tʌk'si:dəu] [美] *n* [c] 男式晚礼服 [英= **dinner jacket, DJ**]

TV *n abbr* (= ***television***) 电视 ♦**on TV** 在电视上播放 ♦**to watch TV** 看电视

tweed [twi:d] I *n* [c/u] 粗花呢 II *adj* [+ *jacket, skirt*] 粗花呢的

tweezers ['twi:zəz] *n* [*pl*] 镊子 ♦**a pair of tweezers** 一把镊子

twelfth [twɛlfθ] *num* 1 (*in series*) 第十二 2 (*fraction*) 十二分之一

✪**twelve** [twɛlv] *num* 十二 ♦**at twelve (o'clock)** (*midday*) 中午12点; (*midnight*) 凌晨零点 *see also* **five**

twentieth ['twɛntɪɪθ] *num* 第二十

✪**twenty** ['twɛntɪ] *num* 二十 ♦**twenty-one** 二十一 *see also* **fifty**

twenty-four-seven, 24/7 ['twɛntɪfɔ:sɛvn] [非正式] *adv* 夜以继日地 ♦**to do sth twenty-four-seven** 夜以继日地做某事

✪**twice** [twaɪs] *adv* 两次 ♦**twice as much/long as** 多/长至两倍 ♦**twice a week** 一周两次 ♦**she is twice your age** 她年纪比你大一倍

twig [twɪg] I *n* [c] 嫩枝 II *vi* [英:非正式] (*realize*) 明白 III *vt* [英:非正式] (*realize*) 恍然大悟

twilight ['twaɪlaɪt] *n* [u] 1 (*evening*) 黄昏 2 (*light*) 暮色

twin [twɪn] I *adj* 1 [+ *sister, brother*] 孪生的 2 [+ *spires, towers etc*] 成双的 II *n* [c] 1 (*person*) 双胞胎 2 (*also: twin room*) 双人房 III *vt* [英] [+ *towns etc*] ♦**to be twinned with** 与…结对子

twin beds *n* [*pl*] 成对的单人床

twinkle ['twɪŋkl] I *vi* [*star, light, eyes* +] 闪烁 II *n* [s] 光芒

twin room *n* [c] 有两张单人床的房间

twirl [twə:l] I *vt* 使旋转 II *vi* 1 (*twist*) 缠绕 2 (*move round and round*) 转圈 III *n* ♦**to do a twirl** 转一圈

twist [twɪst] I *n* [c] 1 (*action*) 拧 2 (*in road, track etc*) 弯曲处 3 (*in coil, flex etc*) 螺旋状 4 (*in story*) 转变 II *vt* 1 (*turn*) 扭 2 (*turn the ends of*) 使成螺旋状 3 (*injure*) [+ *ankle etc*] 扭伤 4 [+ *sb's arm, hand etc*] 扭 5 (*turn*) [+ *object*] 扭转 6 （喻）[+ *meaning, words*] 曲解 III *vi* 1 [*road, river* +] 盘旋 2 [*arm, leg etc* +] 扭曲

twit [twɪt] [非正式] *n* [c] 笨蛋

twitch [twɪtʃ] I *n* [c] 抽动 II *vi* [*muscle, body* +] 颤动

✪**two** [tu:] *num* 二 ♦**two by two, in twos** 两两成群 ♦**to put two and two together** （喻）根据事实推断 *see also* **five**

two-percent milk [美] *n* [u] 半脱脂奶 [英= **semi-skimmed (milk)**]

TXT [手机短信] *abbr* = **text**
type [taɪp] **I** *n* **1** [c] (*category, example*) 种类 **2** [c] (*sort, kind*) 类型 **3** [c] [*person* +] 型 **4** [u] [排版] 字体 **II** *vt, vi* 打字
❑ **type into** *vt* 录入
❑ **type up** *vt* 打印
typewriter ['taɪpraɪtə(r)] *n* [c] 打字机
typhoid ['taɪfɔɪd] *n* [u] 伤寒
typhoon [taɪ'fuːn] *n* [c] 台风
typical ['tɪpɪkl] *adj* [+ *behaviour, weather etc*] 典型的 ♦ **typical of** 典型的 ♦ **that's typical!** 一向如此！
typically *adv* **1** (*generally*) 通常地 **2** (*very*) [+ *English, Chinese etc*] 典型地 **3** (*as usual*) 向来
typing ['taɪpɪŋ] *n* [u] 打字
typist ['taɪpɪst] *n* [c] 打字员
tyre (美 **tire**) ['taɪə(r)] *n* [c] 轮胎
tyre pressure (美 **tire pressure**) *n* [c] 轮胎气压

Uu

U, u [juː] *n* [C/U] (*letter*) 英语的第二十一个字母
UFO *n abbr* (= ***unidentified flying object***) 不明飞行物
Uganda [juːˈgændə] *n* 乌干达
Ugandan [juːˈgændən] **I** *adj* 乌干达的 **II** *n* [C] (*person*) 乌干达人
ugly [ˈʌglɪ] *adj* **1** [+ *person, dress, building*] 丑陋的 **2** (*unpleasant*) [+ *situation, incident*] 令人不快的
UHT *adj abbr* (= ***ultra-heat treated***) 超高温处理
UK *n abbr* (= ***United Kingdom***) ♦**the UK** 大不列颠及北爱尔兰联合王国
Ukraine [juːˈkreɪn] *n* ♦**(the) Ukraine** 乌克兰
Ukrainian [juːˈkreɪnɪən] **I** *adj* 乌克兰的 **II** *n* **1** [C] (*person*) 乌克兰人 **2** [U] (*language*) 乌克兰语
ulcer [ˈʌlsə(r)] *n* [C] 溃疡
ultimate [ˈʌltɪmət] **I** *adj* **1** (*final*) [+ *aim, success, result*] 最终的 **2** (*greatest*) [+ *responsibility, authority*] 最大的 **II** *n* ♦**the ultimate in luxury** *etc* 最奢华{等}之物
ultimately [ˈʌltɪmətlɪ] *adv* **1** (*finally*) 最终地 **2** (*basically*) 根本地
ultimatum [ʌltɪˈmeɪtəm] (*pl* **ultimatums** *or* **ultimata** [ʌltɪˈmeɪtə]) *n* [C] 最后通牒 ♦**to give sb an ultimatum** 给某人下最后通牒
ultrasound [ˈʌltrəsaund] *n* **1** [C] (*also:* ***ultrasound scan***) 超声 **2** [U] (*sound waves*) 超声波
ultraviolet [ˈʌltrəˈvaɪəlɪt] *adj* [+ *rays, light, radiation*] 紫外的
umbrella [ʌmˈbrɛlə] **I** *n* [C] **1** 伞 **2** (喻) ♦**under the umbrella of** 在…的庇护下 **II** *adj* **1** [+ *group, organization*] 包罗万象的 **2** [+ *term, word*] 集合的
umpire [ˈʌmpaɪə(r)] **I** *n* [C] [网球, 板球] 裁判员 **II** *vt* [+ *game*] 当…的裁判
UN *n abbr* (= ***United Nations***) ♦**the UN** 联合国
unable [ʌnˈeɪbl] *adj* ♦**to be unable to do sth** 不能做某事
unacceptable [ʌnəkˈsɛptəbl] *adj* 不能接受的 ♦**it is unacceptable for ministers to tell lies** 部长撒谎是不能接受的
unaccompanied [ʌnəˈkʌmpənɪd] *adj* **1** [+ *child*] 无人陪同的 **2** [+ *voice, instrument*] 无伴奏的
unaccustomed [ʌnəˈkʌstəmd] *adj* **1** ♦**to be unaccustomed to sth** 对某事不习惯 **2** (*unusual*) 不寻常的 ♦**to be unaccustomed to doing sth** 不习惯做某事
unanimous [juːˈnænɪməs] *adj* [+ *decision*] 一致同意的 ♦**to be unanimous in sth/in doing sth** 一致同意某事/做某事
unarmed [ʌnˈɑːmd] *adj* 无武装的 ♦**unarmed combat** 徒手搏击
unattended [ʌnəˈtɛndɪd] *adj* [+ *luggage etc*] 无人看管的 ♦**to leave sth/sb unattended** 单独撇下某物/某人
unattractive [ʌnəˈtræktɪv] *adj* **1** [+ *person, character*] 没有魅力的 **2** [+ *building, place*] 乏味的 **3** [+ *prospect, idea*] 讨厌的 ♦**to be unattractive to sb** [*plan, idea* +] 对某人没有吸引力
unauthorized [ʌnˈɔːθəraɪzd] *adj* **1** [+ *visit, use*] 未经批准的 **2** [+ *version, biography*] 未经授权的
unavailable [ʌnəˈveɪləbl] *adj* **1** [+ *product, book*] 不可获得的 **2** [+ *person*] 联系不上的 ♦**to be unavailable for comment** 无法发表评论
unavoidable [ʌnəˈvɔɪdəbl] *adj* [+ *delay, job losses etc*] 不可避免的
unaware [ʌnəˈwɛə(r)] *adj* ♦**to be unaware of sth** 不知道某事 ♦**to be unaware that ...** 没有意识到…
unawares [ʌnəˈwɛəz] *adv* ♦**to catch** *or* **take sb unawares** 使某人吃惊
unbearable [ʌnˈbɛərəbl] *adj* **1** [+ *heat, pain*] 难以忍受的 **2** [+ *person*] 不能容忍的 ♦**to**

become unbearable [*heat, pain, life* +] 变得难以忍受

unbeatable [ʌnˈbiːtəbl] *adj* 1 [+ *person, team*] 难以战胜的 2 [+ *price, value, quality*] 无与伦比的

unbelievable [ʌnbɪˈliːvəbl] *adj* 1 不可信的 2 (*amazing*) 难以置信的 ♦ **it is unbelievable that ...** … 真是难以置信

unbias(s)ed [ʌnˈbaɪəst] *adj* [+ *person, opinion*] 公正的

unborn [ʌnˈbɔːn] *adj* [+ *child*] 未出生的

unbreakable [ʌnˈbreɪkəbl] *adj* 不易打碎的

unbutton [ʌnˈbʌtn] *vt* [+ *coat, shirt etc*] 解开… 的纽扣

uncalled-for [ʌnˈkɔːldfɔː(r)] *adj* [+ *remark, criticism etc*] 无理由的

uncanny [ʌnˈkænɪ] *adj* [+ *resemblance, ability, feeling*] 异乎寻常的 ♦ **it's uncanny** 这真怪异

uncertain [ʌnˈsəːtn] *adj* [+ *future, outcome*] 不确定的 ♦ **to be uncertain about sth** 对某事心无定数 ♦ **to be uncertain how/whether to do sth** 拿不准该如何做某事/是否要做某事 ♦ **it's uncertain whether ...** 是否…仍无法确定 ♦ **in no uncertain terms** 毫不含糊地

uncertainty [ʌnˈsəːtntɪ] *n* [U] (*confusion*) 不确定

unchanged [ʌnˈtʃeɪndʒd] *adj* 未改变的

uncivilized [ʌnˈsɪvɪlaɪzd] *adj* 1 (字) [+ *country, people*] 未开化的 2 (喻) [+ *person, behaviour, hour*] 无教养的

uncle [ˈʌŋkl] *n* [C] (*father's older brother*) 伯父; (*father's younger brother*) 叔父; (*father's sister's husband*) 姑父; (*mother's brother*) 舅父; (*mother's sister's husband*) 姨父

unclear [ʌnˈklɪə(r)] *adj* 1 [+ *reason, implications*] 不清楚的 2 [+ *instructions, answer*] 含糊的 ♦ **it is** *or* **remains unclear whether ...** 是否…仍不确定 ♦ **to be unclear about sth** 对某事不甚明了

uncomfortable [ʌnˈkʌmfətəbl] *adj* 1 (*physically*) [+ *person*] 不舒服的; [+ *chair, room, journey*] 不舒适的 2 (*uneasy*) [+ *person*] 不安的 3 (*unpleasant*) [+ *situation, fact*] 不利的

uncommon [ʌnˈkɔmən] *adj* 罕见的

unconditional [ʌnkənˈdɪʃənl] *adj* [+ *love, acceptance, surrender*] 无条件的

unconscious [ʌnˈkɔnʃəs] **I** *adj* 1 (*not awake*) 失去知觉的 2 (*not deliberate*) 无意识的 3 (*unaware*) ♦ **unconscious of** 未察觉的 **II** *n* ♦ **the unconscious** 潜意识 ♦ **to knock/beat sb unconscious** 把某人打昏过去

uncontrollable [ʌnkənˈtrəuləbl] *adj* 1 [+ *person*] 不受管束的 2 [+ *temper, laughter*] 控制不住的

unconventional [ʌnkənˈvɛnʃənl] *adj* [+ *person, behaviour*] 反传统的

uncover [ʌnˈkʌvə(r)] *vt* 1 (*remove covering from*) 露出 2 (*discover*) [+ *plot, evidence*] 发现

undecided [ʌndɪˈsaɪdɪd] *adj* 1 [+ *person*] 犹豫不决的 2 [+ *question*] 未决定的 ♦ **to be undecided about sth** 对某事拿不定主意

undeniable [ʌndɪˈnaɪəbl] *adj* [+ *fact, evidence*] 不可否认的

✪ **under** [ˈʌndə(r)] **I** *prep* 1 (*beneath*) 在…下面 ◊ *the cupboard under the sink* 在水槽下面的橱柜 2 (*less than*) [+ *age, price*] 不到 ◊ *He's still under 18.* 他还不到18岁。 3 (*according to*) [+ *law, agreement*] 根据 ◊ *Equal pay for men and women is guaranteed under English law.* 根据英格兰法律，应保证男女同工同酬。 4 [+ *sb's leadership*] 在…的领导下 ◊ *China under Chairman Mao* 毛主席领导下的中国 5 [+ *chapter, heading etc*] 在…中 ◊ *It's filed under letter C.* 它被归在字母C中。 **II** *adv* 1 [*go, fly etc* +] 从下面 2 (*in age, price etc*) 以下 ◊ *children aged 12 and under* 12岁及以下的儿童 ♦ **she writes under the name Jan Hunt** 她以简•亨特这个名字写东西

under-age [ʌndərˈeɪdʒ] *adj* [+ *person*] 未成年的 ♦ **under-age drinking/sex** 未成年人的饮酒/性行为

underbush [ˈʌndəbuʃ] [美] *n* [U] 下

层灌木丛［英 = **undergrowth**］

undercover [ʌndəˈkʌvə(r)] **I** *adj* [+ *operation, work, agent*] 秘密的 **II** *adv* [*work* +] 暗中的

underdone [ʌndəˈdʌn] *adj* 半生不熟的

underestimate [*vb* ˈʌndərˈɛstɪmeɪt, *n* ˈʌndərˈɛstɪmət] **I** *vt* [+ *importance, amount, person*] 低估 **II** *n* [c] 低估

undergo [ʌndəˈgəu] (*pt* **underwent**, *pp* **undergone**) *vt* [+ *surgery, test, treatment, training*] 经受

undergraduate [ʌndəˈgrædjuɪt] **I** *n* [c] 本科生 **II** *cpd*［复合词］[+ *course, degree etc*] 本科

underground [ˈʌndəgraund] **I** *n* ♦**the underground 1**［英］(*railway*) 地铁［美 = **subway**］**2**［政治］地下组织 **II** *adj* [+ *car park, cables, newspaper, activities*] 地下的 **III** *adv* **1** (*below ground*) 在地下 **2** (*secretly*) 秘密地

undergrowth [ˈʌndəgrəuθ]［英］*n* [u] 下层灌木丛［美 = **underbush**］

underline [ʌndəˈlaɪn]［英］*vt* **1** [+ *word, sentence*] 在…下面划线［美 = **underscore**］**2** (*emphasize*) 强调［美 = **underscore**］

undermine [ʌndəˈmaɪn] *vt* [+ *sb's confidence, authority*] 逐渐削弱

underneath [ʌndəˈniːθ] **I** *adv* **1** (*below*) 在下面 **2**（喻）(*at heart*) 心底里 **II** *prep* **1** (*below*) 在…下面 **2**（喻）在…背后 **III** *n* ♦**the underneath** 底部

underpants [ˈʌndəpænts] *n* [*pl*] 内裤

underpass [ˈʌndəpɑːs] *n* [c] **1** (*for pedestrians*) 地下通道 **2** (*road under motorway*) 高架桥下通道

underscore [ʌndəˈskɔː(r)] *vt* **1** (*highlight*) 强调 **2** (*with line*) [+ *word, phrase etc*] 在…下面划线

undershirt [ˈʌndəʃəːt]［美］*n* [c] 贴身内衣［英 = **vest**］

underside [ˈʌndəsaɪd] *n* [c] 底面

underskirt [ˈʌndəskəːt]［英］*n* [c] 衬裙

✪ **understand** [ʌndəˈstænd] (*pt, pp* **understood**) *vt* [+ *speaker, sb's words, meaning*] 明白；[+ *foreign language*] 懂；[+ *book, subject, behaviour*] 理解 ◊ *They are too young to understand what is going on.* 他们太年轻，无法理解所发生的一切。◊ *His wife doesn't understand him.* 他的妻子不理解他。♦**to understand that ...** (*believe*) 获悉… ♦**he is understood to be in Italy** 人们认为他在意大利 ♦**to make o.s. understood** 将自己的意思表达清楚

understandable [ʌndəˈstændəbl] *adj* 可以理解的 ♦**it is understandable that ...** …是可以理解的

understanding [ʌndəˈstændɪŋ] **I** *adj* 通情达理的 **II** *n* [c/u] **1** (*knowledge*) 了解 **2** [u] (*sympathy*) 同情 **3** [c] (*agreement*) 协定 **4** [u] (*trust*) 相互理解 ♦**to come to an understanding with sb (about sth)**（就某事）和某人达成协议 ♦**to have an understanding of sth** 对某事有一定的了解 ♦**on the understanding that ...** 在…条件下

understate [ʌndəˈsteɪt] *vt* 轻描淡写

understatement [ˈʌndəsteɪtmənt] *n* [c/u] 轻描淡写的陈述

understood [ʌndəˈstud] **I** *pt, pp of* **understand II** *adj* **1** (*agreed*) 取得同意的 **2** (*implied*) 不言而喻的 ♦**it is understood that ...** 不言而喻的是…

undertake [ʌndəˈteɪk] (*pt* **undertook**, *pp* **undertaken**) *vt* [+ *task, job*] 承担 ♦**to undertake to do sth**［正式］保证做某事

undertaker [ˈʌndəteɪkə(r)]［英］*n* [c] 丧事承办人［美 = **mortician**］

undertaking [ˈʌndəteɪkɪŋ] *n* [c] (*task*) 任务 ♦**to give an undertaking to do sth** 承诺做某事 ♦**to give an undertaking that ...** 承诺…

underwater [ˈʌndəˈwɔːtə(r)] **I** *adv* [*swim etc* +] 在水下 **II** *adj* [+ *exploration, camera etc*] 水下的

underway [ʌndəˈweɪ] *adj* 在进行中的 ♦**to get underway** 开始

underwear [ˈʌndəwɛə(r)] *n* [u] 内衣

underworld [ˈʌndəwəːld] *n* ♦**the underworld 1** (*criminal*) 黑社会 **2**［神］阴间

undesirable [ʌndɪˈzaɪərəbl] *adj*

[+ *person, effects, behaviour*] 不良的 ♦**it is undesirable that ...** …令人不快

undisputed ['ʌndɪs'pjuːtɪd] *adj* **1** [+ *fact*] 无可置疑的 **2** [+ *champion*] 无可争辩的

undo [ʌn'duː] (*pt* **undid**, *pp* **undone**) *vt* **1** [+ *shoelaces, knot, buttons, trousers*] 解开 **2** (*spoil*) [+ *work*] 使无效 **3** [+ *damage*] 消除

undone [ʌn'dʌn] **I** *pp of* **undo II** *adj* **1** [+ *work, tasks etc*] 未做的 **2** [+ *shoelaces, zip, button*] 松开的; [+ *blouse, dress*] 解开的 ♦**to leave sth undone** 未完成某事 ♦**to come undone** [*shoelaces, zip, button* +] 开了; [*blouse, dress* +] 解开了 ◊ *His shoelaces came undone.* 他的鞋带开了。

undoubtedly [ʌn'dautɪdlɪ] *adv* 毋庸置疑地

undress [ʌn'drɛs] **I** *vi* 脱衣服 **II** *vt* 脱去…的衣服

unearth [ʌn'əːθ] *vt* **1** [+ *remains, treasure etc*] 发掘 **2** [+ *secrets, evidence*] 发现

uneasy [ʌn'iːzɪ] *adj* **1** (*worried*) [+ *person, feeling*] 不安的 **2** (*fragile*) [+ *peace, truce, relationship*] 令人不安的 ♦**to be uneasy about sth** 为某事忧虑

unemployed [ʌnɪm'plɔɪd] **I** *adj* [+ *person*] 失业的 **II** *n* [*pl*] ♦**the unemployed** 失业者

unemployment [ʌnɪm'plɔɪmənt] *n* [U] 失业

unequal [ʌn'iːkwəl] *adj* **1** [+ *lengths, amounts*] 不同的 **2** [+ *system, situation*] 不平等的 ♦**to be/feel unequal to sth** [正式]不胜任某事/感觉难以胜任某事

UNESCO [juː'nɛskəu] *n abbr* (= ***United Nations Educational, Scientific and Cultural Organization***) 联合国教科文组织

uneven [ʌn'iːvn] *adj* **1** [+ *teeth, road, surface*] 高低不平的 **2** [+ *breathing*] 紊乱的; [+ *rate*] 有差异的 **3** (*inconsistent*) [+ *performance*] 不稳定的

unexpected [ʌnɪks'pɛktɪd] *adj* 意外的

unexpectedly [ʌnɪks'pɛktɪdlɪ] *adv* 意外地

unfair [ʌn'fɛə(r)] *adj* [+ *system, situation, act, person*] 不公平的 ♦**to be unfair to sb** 对某人不公平 ♦**it's unfair that ...** …是不公平的 ♦**it is unfair to generalize** 笼统地概括是不公平的 ♦**to gain an unfair advantage** 获取不正当的利益

unfaithful [ʌn'feɪθful] *adj* [+ *husband, wife*] 不忠的 ♦**to be unfaithful to sb** 对某人不忠

unfamiliar [ʌnfə'mɪlɪə(r)] *adj* [+ *place, person, subject*] 陌生的 ♦**to be unfamiliar to sb** 对某人来说不熟悉 ♦**to be unfamiliar with sth** 不熟悉某事

unfashionable [ʌn'fæʃnəbl] *adj* [+ *clothes, ideas*] 过时的; [+ *place*] 不流行的

unfasten [ʌn'fɑːsn] *vt* **1** [+ *strap, belt, button, clothes*] 解开 **2** [+ *lock, latch*] 打开

unfavourable (美 **unfavorable**) [ʌn'feɪvrəbl] *adj* **1** [+ *conditions, impression*] 不利的 **2** [+ *review, reaction*] 不赞同的 ♦**to be unfavourable to sb** [*terms, conditions* +] 不利于某人

unfinished [ʌn'fɪnɪʃt] *adj* 未完成的 ♦**unfinished business** 未做完的事情

unfit [ʌn'fɪt] *adj* (*physically*) 不太健康的 ♦**to be unfit for sth/to do sth** 不胜任某事/不适合做某事 ♦**unfit for work** 身体不佳无法工作 ♦**unfit for human consumption** 不宜给人食用

unfold [ʌn'fəuld] **I** *vt* [+ *sheet, map*] 展开 **II** *vi* [*situation, story, facts* +] 展现

unforgettable [ʌnfə'gɛtəbl] *adj* 难忘的

unfortunate [ʌn'fɔːtʃənət] *adj* **1** (*unlucky*) [+ *person, accident*] 不幸的 **2** (*regrettable*) [+ *event, remark*] 令人遗憾的 ♦**it is unfortunate that ...** 不幸的是…

unfortunately [ʌn'fɔːtʃənətlɪ] *adv* 可惜

unfounded [ʌn'faundɪd] *adj* [+ *allegations, fears*] 没有根据的

unfriendly [ʌn'frɛndlɪ] *adj*

1 [+ *person*] 不友善的 **2** [+ *behaviour, remark*] 不友好的 ♦**to be unfriendly to sb** 对某人不友好

unfurnished [ʌn'fəːnɪʃt] *adj* [+ *house, flat*] 无家具设备的

ungrateful [ʌn'greɪtful] *adj* 不领情的

unhappiness [ʌn'hæpɪnɪs] *n* [U] 不幸

unhappy [ʌn'hæpɪ] *adj* **1** [+ *person*] 愁苦的 **2** (*unfortunate*) [+ *accident, event*] 不幸的 **3** [+ *childhood*] 悲惨的 ♦**to be unhappy about** *or* **with sth** (*dissatisfied*) 对某事不满

unhealthy [ʌn'hɛlθɪ] *adj* **1** [+ *person*] 身体不佳的 **2** [+ *place, diet, lifestyle*] 不利于健康的 **3** [+ *interest*] 不健康的

unheard-of [ʌn'həːdɔv] *adj* **1** (*unknown*) 无先例的 **2** (*exceptional*) 前所未闻的

unhelpful [ʌn'hɛlpful] *adj* **1** [+ *person*] 不予帮助的 **2** [+ *advice*] 无用的 ♦**to be unhelpful to sb** [*person* +] 对某人毫无帮助; [*situation, system* +] 对某人是无益的

unhurt [ʌn'həːt] *adj* 没有受伤的 ♦**to escape unhurt** 安然逃脱

unhygienic ['ʌnhaɪ'dʒiːnɪk] *adj* 不卫生的

unidentified [ʌnaɪ'dɛntɪfaɪd] *adj* 无法识别的

uniform ['juːnɪfɔːm] **I** *n* [C/U] 制服 **II** *adj* **1** (*regular*) [+ *length, width etc*] 统一的 **2** (*similar*) [+ *objects*] 相同的 **3** [+ *result, rise, growth*] 一致的 ♦**in uniform** 穿着制服

unify ['juːnɪfaɪ] *vt* 使统一

unimportant [ʌnɪm'pɔːtənt] *adj* 微不足道的

uninhabited [ʌnɪn'hæbɪtɪd] *adj* [+ *area,island, house etc*] 无人居住的

unintentional [ʌnɪn'tɛnʃənəl] *adj* 无心的

✪ **union** ['juːnjən] **I** *n* **1** [U] (*unification*) 合并 ◊ *We are working for the union of the two countries.* 我们正为这两个国家的合并而努力。**2** [C] (*also: **trade union***) 工会 **II** *cpd* [复合词] [+ *activities, representative etc*] 协会

Union Jack *n* [C] 英国国旗

unique [juː'niːk] *adj* **1** (*individual*) [+ *number, pattern etc*] 独一无二的 **2** (*distinctive*) [+ *ability, skill, performance*] 罕有的 ♦**to be unique to sb/sth** 某人/某物独有的

unisex ['juːnɪsɛks] *adj* [+ *hair salon, clothing*] 不分男女的

unit ['juːnɪt] *n* [C] **1** (*single whole*) 单位 **2** (*group, centre*) 小组 **3** (*measurement*) 单位 **4** (*machine*) 部件 **5** (*section*) [*of furniture etc*] 组合件 **6** [军] 分队 **7** (*in course book*) 单元

unite [juː'naɪt] **I** *vt* [+ *people, party*] 使联合 **II** *vi* [*people, party* +] 联合行动

united [juː'naɪtɪd] *adj* **1** [+ *group*] 和睦的 **2** [+ *effort*] 共同的 **3** [政治] [+ *country*] 统一的 ♦**to be united in sth** [+ *desire, belief, dislike*] 在某事上保持一致 ♦**to be united on sth** [+ *issue, need*] 就某事达成一致 ♦**to be united against sb/sth** 团结起来对抗某人/某事

United Arab Emirates *n* [*pl*] ♦**the United Arab Emirates** 阿拉伯联合酋长国

United Kingdom *n* ♦**the United Kingdom** 大不列颠及北爱尔兰联合王国

United Nations *n* ♦**the United Nations** 联合国

United States (of America) *n* ♦**the United States (of America)** 美利坚合众国

unity ['juːnɪtɪ] *n* [U] **1** (*solidarity*) 团结 **2** (*unification*) 统一

Univ. *abbr* (= ***university***) 大学

universal [juːnɪ'vəːsl] *adj* 普遍的

universe ['juːnɪvəːs] *n* [C] 宇宙

✪ **university** [juːnɪ'vəːsɪtɪ] **I** *n* [C/U] 大学 ♦**to go to university** 上大学 **II** *cpd* [复合词] [+ *student, professor, education, year*] 大学

unjust [ʌn'dʒʌst] *adj* [+ *action, treatment, society, law*] 不公正的

unkind [ʌn'kaɪnd] *adj* 刻薄的 ♦**to be unkind to sb** 对某人刻薄 ♦**it is unkind to make fun of people** 取笑他人是不友好的 ♦**it was unkind of him to say that** 他那么说是不友好的

unknown [ʌn'nəun] **I** *adj* **1** [+ *fact, number*] 未知的 **2** [+ *writer, artist*] 名不见经传的 **3** (*unidentified*) [+ *person*] 陌生的 **II** *n* **1** [C] (*person*)

无名小卒 **2** [s] (*thing*) 未知事物 ♦ **he was unknown to me** 我不认识他 ♦ **unknown to me, he ...** 不为我所知，他… ♦ **it is not unknown for travellers to forget their passports** 旅客忘带护照的事并不少见 ♦ **an unknown quantity** 一个未知数 ♦ **fear of the unknown** 对未知事物的恐惧

unlawful [ʌn'lɔːful] *adj* 非法的

unleaded [ʌn'lɛdɪd] **I** *adj* 无铅的 **II** *n* [U] 无铅燃料

unleash [ʌn'liːʃ] *vt* [+ *feeling, force etc*] 激起；[+ *missile*] 发射

unless [ʌn'lɛs] *conj* 除非 ♦ **unless otherwise stated** 除非另有说明

unlike [ʌn'laɪk] **I** *adj* (*not alike*) 不相似的 **II** *prep* **1** (*in contrast to*) 与…相反 **2** (*different from*) 不同于 **3** (*not typical of*) 无…的特征

unlikely [ʌn'laɪklɪ] *adj* **1** 未必会发生的 **2** [+ *combination, circumstances*] 不大可能的 ♦ **in the unlikely event that ...** 万一有…情况 ♦ **in the unlikely event of anything going wrong** 万一有事不顺 ♦ **it is unlikely that ...** …是不大可能的 ♦ **he is unlikely to win** 他获胜的希望不大

unlimited [ʌn'lɪmɪtɪd] *adj* [+ *supply, resources*] 无限制的；[+ *money, travel*] 无限量的

unlisted ['ʌn'lɪstɪd] *adj* **1** [美：通信] [+ *person, number*] 未列入电话簿的 [英 = **ex-directory**] **2** [经济] 不上市的

unload [ʌn'ləud] *vt* **1** [+ *objects*] 卸 **2** [+ *car, lorry etc*] 从…上卸货

unlock [ʌn'lɔk] *vt* [+ *door, car, suitcase*] 开

unlucky [ʌn'lʌkɪ] *adj* **1** [+ *person*] 不幸的 **2** [+ *object, number*] 不吉利的 ♦ **he was unlucky enough to lose his wallet** 他丢了钱包，真是太倒霉了 ♦ **we were unlucky not to win** 真不走运，我们没赢

unmarried [ʌn'mærɪd] *adj* 未婚的

unmistak(e)able [ʌnmɪs'teɪkəbl] *adj* 明显的

unnatural [ʌn'nætʃrəl] *adj* **1** (*not normal*) 反常的 **2** (*not sincere*) 做作的 ♦ **it is not unnatural that ...** …是很正常的 ♦ **it is unnatural to keep the sexes apart** 将两性分开是不合人情的 ♦ **it would be unnatural for two people to agree all the time** 要两个人总是意见一致是不正常的

unnecessary [ʌn'nɛsəsərɪ] *adj* 不必要的 ♦ **it was unnecessary to do anything** 什么都不必做

unnoticed [ʌn'nəutɪst] *adj* ♦ **it went** *or* **passed unnoticed** 没有人察觉

unofficial [ʌnə'fɪʃl] *adj* **1** [+ *estimate, report*] 非官方的 **2** [+ *strike*] 未经工会同意的

unpack [ʌn'pæk] **I** *vi* 开包 **II** *vt* [+ *suitcase, bag*] 打开…取出东西

unpaid [ʌn'peɪd] *adj* **1** [+ *bill, tax*] 未支付的 **2** [+ *holiday, leave*] 无薪的 **3** [+ *work*] 无报酬的 **4** [+ *worker*] 无酬服务的

unpleasant [ʌn'plɛznt] *adj* [+ *experience, task, situation, sensation*] 使人不愉快的；[+ *person, manner*] 令人讨厌的 ♦ **to be unpleasant to sb** 跟某人过不去 ♦ **she's unpleasant to work with** 她很难一起共事 ♦ **it is very unpleasant to be criticized** 受到批评让人很不高兴

unplug [ʌn'plʌg] *vt* 拔去…的插头

unpopular [ʌn'pɔpjulə(r)] *adj* [+ *person, decision*] 不受欢迎的 ♦ **to be unpopular with sb** 不受某人的欢迎 ♦ **to make sb/o.s. unpopular (with sb)** 使某人/自己不受(某人的)欢迎

unprecedented [ʌn'prɛsɪdɛntɪd] *adj* **1** [+ *decision, event, increase*] 前所未有的 **2** [+ *success*] 空前的

unpredictable [ʌnprɪ'dɪktəbl] *adj* [+ *person, weather, result*] 易变的

unprofessional [ʌnprə'fɛʃənl] *adj* [+ *attitude, conduct, act*] 不专业的

unprotected ['ʌnprə'tɛktɪd] *adj* **1** (*not defended*) 不设防的 **2** (*not covered*) 无保护的 ♦ **unprotected sex** 无防范措施的性行为 ♦ **to be unprotected from sth** 未经保护地暴露于某物

unqualified [ʌn'kwɔlɪfaɪd] *adj* **1** [+ *teacher, nurse etc*] 不合格的 **2** (*complete*) [+ *disaster, success, support*] 完全的 ♦ **to be unqualified for** 不能胜任 ♦ **to be unqualified**

to do sth 没资格做某事
unravel [ʌn'rævl] **I** *vt* **1** [+ *string, wool*] 解开 **2** [+ *mystery, truth*] 弄清 **II** *vi* [*mystery, puzzle* +] 明朗
unreal [ʌn'rɪəl] *adj* **1** (*artificial*) 假的 **2** (*bizarre*) 离谱的
unrealistic ['ʌnrɪə'lɪstɪk] *adj* [+ *person, expectation, idea, view*] 不切实际的 ♦ **it is unrealistic to expect that ...** 指望…是不切实际的
unreasonable [ʌn'riːznəbl] *adj* **1** [+ *person, attitude*] 无理的 **2** [+ *decision, price, amount*] 不合理的 ♦ **it is unreasonable to expect that ...** 指望…是荒谬的 ♦ **it is not unreasonable that ...** …并不过分
unrelated [ʌnrɪ'leɪtɪd] *adj* **1** [+ *incident, cause*] 不相关的 **2** [+ *people*] 无亲缘关系的 ♦ **unrelated to sth** 和某物无关 ♦ **unrelated to sb** 和某人无亲缘关系的
unreliable [ʌnrɪ'laɪəbl] *adj* **1** [+ *person, firm*] 不可信赖的 **2** [+ *machine, method*] 不可靠的
unrest [ʌn'rɛst] *n* [U] 动荡
unroll [ʌn'rəul] *vt* 展开
unruly [ʌn'ruːlɪ] *adj* **1** [+ *child, behaviour*] 任性的 **2** [+ *hair*] 不服帖的
unsafe [ʌn'seɪf] *adj* **1** (*in danger*) [+ *person*] 不安全的 **2** (*dangerous*) [+ *machine, bridge, conditions*] 危险的 **3** [英:法] [+ *conviction*] 不成立的 ♦ **it is unsafe to play here** 在这儿玩不安全 ♦ **the car was unsafe to drive** 开这辆车不安全 ♦ **unsafe to eat/drink** 食用/饮用不安全 ♦ **unsafe sex** 无防范措施的性行为
unsatisfactory ['ʌnsætɪs'fæktərɪ] *adj* 令人不满意的
unscrew [ʌn'skruː] *vt* [+ *lid, cap*] 旋开
unsettled [ʌn'sɛtld] *adj* **1** [+ *person*] 不安的 **2** [+ *situation, future*] 不稳定的 **3** [+ *question, argument, issue etc*] 未解决的 **4** [+ *weather*] 易变的
unsettling [ʌn'sɛtlɪŋ] *adj* 使人不安的
unshaven [ʌn'ʃeɪvn] *adj* [+ *man, face*] 胡子未刮的
unskilled [ʌn'skɪld] *adj* **1** [+ *worker*] 不熟练的 **2** [+ *work, job*] 无需特殊技能的
unstable [ʌn'steɪbl] *adj* **1** [+ *ladder*] 不牢固的 **2** [+ *government, situation*] 不稳固的 **3** [+ *person*] 反复无常的 **4** [化, 物] [+ *substance*] 不稳定的
unsteady [ʌn'stɛdɪ] *adj* **1** [+ *step, voice*] 不平稳的 **2** [+ *person*] 摇晃的 **3** [+ *ladder etc*] 不稳固的 ♦ **to be unsteady on one's feet** 走路摇摇晃晃
unsuccessful [ʌnsək'sɛsful] *adj* **1** [+ *attempt, application*] 失败的 **2** [+ *person, applicant*] 不成功的 ♦ **to be unsuccessful in** *or* **at doing sth** 做某事没有成功
unsuitable [ʌn'suːtəbl] *adj* **1** [+ *place, time, clothes*] 不适宜的 **2** [+ *candidate, applicant*] 不合适的 **3** [+ *friend, husband, partner*] 不相称的 ♦ **to be unsuitable for sth/for doing sth** 不适于某事/做某事 ♦ **to be unsuitable for sb** 对某人不合适
unsure [ʌn'ʃuə(r)] *adj* 没有把握的 ♦ **to be unsure about sth** 对某事没有把握 ♦ **to be unsure of o.s.** 对自己缺乏信心
unsympathetic ['ʌnsɪmpə'θɛtɪk] *adj* **1** (*uncaring*) 无动于衷的 **2** (*unlikeable*) 冷淡的 ♦ **to be unsympathetic to(wards) sth** 对某事不表同情
untidy [ʌn'taɪdɪ] *adj* **1** [+ *room*] 不整洁的 **2** [+ *person, appearance*] 邋遢的
untie [ʌn'taɪ] *vt* **1** [+ *rope, knot*] 解开 **2** [+ *prisoner, dog*] 松开 **3** [+ *sb's hands, feet*] 给…松绑
✪ **until** [ən'tɪl] **I** *prep* 直到…时 ◊ *They didn't find her until the next day.* 他们直到第二天才找到她。**II** *conj* 到…为止 ◊ *She waited until he had gone.* 她一直等到他走为止。 ♦ **until now** 直到现在 ♦ **not until now** 直到现在才 ♦ **until then** 届时 ♦ **not until then** 直到那时…才
untrue [ʌn'truː] *adj* 不正确的 ♦ **it is untrue that ...** …与事实不符 ♦ **it would be untrue to say that ...** 说…就不对了
unused[1] [ʌn'juːzd] *adj* 闲置的
unused[2] [ʌn'juːst] *adj* ♦ **to be unused to sth/to doing sth** 不习惯某事/做某事

unusual [ʌn'juːʒuəl] *adj* **1** 不寻常的 **2** (*distinctive*) 与众不同的 ♦**it's unusual to see someone so tall** 难得见到这么高的人

unusually [ʌn'juːʒuəlɪ] *adv* 异乎寻常地

unveil [ʌn'veɪl] *vt* **1** [+ *statue, plaque*] 为…揭幕 **2** [+ *plan*] 透露

unwanted [ʌn'wɔntɪd] *adj* **1** [+ *clothing, animal*] 没人要的 **2** [+ *child, pregnancy*] 不想要的

unwelcome [ʌn'wɛlkəm] *adj* **1** [+ *guest*] 不受欢迎的 **2** [+ *news*] 讨厌的 ♦**to feel unwelcome** 感到不受欢迎

unwell [ʌn'wɛl] *adj* ♦**to feel/be unwell** 觉得/身体不适

unwilling [ʌn'wɪlɪŋ] *adj* ♦**to be unwilling to do sth** 不愿做某事

unwind [ʌn'waɪnd] (*pt, pp* **unwound**) **I** *vt* [*bandage, scarf etc*] 解开 **II** *vi* (*relax*) 放松

unwise [ʌn'waɪz] *adj* **1** [+ *decision, choice*] 愚蠢的 **2** [+ *person*] 不明智的 ♦**it would be unwise to expect too much** 期望过多是不明智的 ♦**to be unwise enough to do sth** 做某事真是傻

unwittingly [ʌn'wɪtɪŋlɪ] *adv* 无意地

unwrap [ʌn'ræp] *vt* 打开…的包装

unzip [ʌn'zɪp] *vt* 拉开

up
KEYWORD
[ʌp]

I *prep*

1 (*to higher point on*) [+ *hill, slope, ladder, stairs*] 沿…向上 ♦**he went up the stairs/the hill/the ladder** 他上了楼/山/梯子

2 (*along*) [+ *road, river*] 沿着 ♦**a bus came/went up the road** 一辆公共汽车沿着路开过来/去

3 (*at higher point on*) [+ *hill, ladder, tree*] 在…高处; [+ *road*] 在…高远处; [+ *river*] 在…上游 ♦**the cat was up a tree** 猫在树上 ♦**they live further up the street** 他们住在这条街那边儿

II *adv* **1** (*towards higher point*) 往上 ♦**the lift only goes up to the 12th floor** 电梯只到12层楼以上 ♦**to pace up and down** 走来走去

2 (*at higher point*) 高高地 ♦**up in the sky** 在天上 ♦**up here/there** 这/那上面 ♦**up above** 再往上

3 ♦**to be up** (*be out of bed*) 起床; (*be at an end*) [*time* +] 结束; (*be on the increase*) [*price, level, amount* +] 上升 ♦**what's up?** [非正式] 怎么了? ♦**what's up with him?** 他怎么了?

4 (*to/in the north*) 在/向北方 ♦**he often comes up to Scotland** 他常北上去苏格兰 ♦**how long are you staying up here?** 你在那儿住了多久了?

5 (*approaching*) ♦**to go/come/run up (to sb)** (朝某人)走去/过来/跑去

6 ♦**up to** (*as far as*) 直到; (*in approximations*) 多达 ♦**the water came up to his knees** 水到他的膝盖了 ♦**I can spend up to £100** 我可以花到100英镑 ♦**up to 100 people** 多达100人

7 ♦**up to or until** 直到 ♦**I'll be here up to or until 5.30 pm** 我会一直呆到下午5点30分 ♦**up to now** 直到现在

8 ♦**it is up to you (to decide)** 随便你(决定)

9 ♦**to be up to sth** [非正式] (*be doing*) 忙于做某件坏事 ♦**what is he up to?** 他在搞什么鬼?

10 ♦**to be up to sth** (*adequate for*) [+ *task*] 足够某事; [+ *standard*] 达到某事 ♦**his work is not up to the required standard** 他的工作未能达到要求的标准 ♦**to be up to doing sth** 胜任做某事

11 ♦**to feel up to sth/to doing sth** 感到能胜任某事/感到有力气做某事

12 (*in other expressions*) ♦**to be up against sb/sth** 面临某人/某事 ♦**to be up for discussion** 即将讨论

III *vt* (*increase*) 增加

IV *vi* [非正式] ♦**she upped and left** 她突然起身离开了

V *n* [*pl*] ♦**ups and downs** (*in life, career*) 起起伏伏 ♦**we all have our ups and downs** 我们都有盛衰浮沉

up-and-coming [ʌpənd'kʌmɪŋ] *adj* [+ *actor, musician, company*] 有前途的

upbringing ['ʌpbrɪŋɪŋ] *n* [c] 教养
update [*vb* ʌp'deɪt, *n* 'ʌpdeɪt] **I** *vt* [+ *records, information*] 更新 **II** *n* [c] 最新信息 ♦**to update sb on sth** 告知某人某事最新动态
upfront [ʌp'frʌnt] **I** *adj* **1** [+ *person*] 坦率的 **2** (*advance*) [+ *charge, cost*] 提前支付的 **II** *adv* [*pay, charge* +] 提前地 ♦**to be upfront about sth** 对某事很坦率 ♦**to be upfront about being gay/divorced** *etc* 公开表示自己是同性恋/已离婚{等}
upgrade [*vb* ʌp'greɪd, *n* 'ʌpgreɪd] **I** *vt* **1** [+ *computer etc*] 使升级 **2** [+ *employee*] 提升 **II** *n* [c] 升级 ♦**to upgrade sth/sb to sth** 将某物升级为某物/将某人升为某职 ♦**an upgrade to sth** 提升到某个等级
upheaval [ʌp'hiːvl] *n* [c] 剧变
uphill ['ʌp'hɪl] **I** *adj* **1** [+ *climb, journey*] 上坡的 **2** (喻) [+ *task*] 艰难的 **II** *adv* [*walk, push* +] 往坡上 ♦**an uphill struggle** *or* **battle (to do sth)** (做某事的) 艰苦奋斗
uphold [ʌp'həuld] (*pt, pp* **upheld**) *vt* [+ *law, principle, decision*] 维护
upholstery [ʌp'həulstərɪ] *n* [u] 软垫
upkeep ['ʌpkiːp] *n* [u] **1** [*of building, place*] 维护 **2** [*of person, service*] 供养
upload [ʌp'ləud] *vt* 上载
upmarket [ʌp'mɑːkɪt] [英] *adj* [+ *product, hotel*] 高档的 [美= **upscale**]
upon [ə'pɔn] [正式] *prep* 在…上面 ♦**upon doing sth** 在做某事之时 ♦**Christmas/the football season is upon us** 圣诞节/足球赛季就要来了 ♦**row upon row/layer upon layer of** 一排排的/一层层的…
upper ['ʌpə(r)] **I** *adj* **1** [+ *floor, deck, shelf*] 上层的 **2** [+ *lip*] 上面的 **3** [+ *part*] 较高的 **4** [+ *arm, back, body*] 上部的 **II** *n* [c] [*of shoe*] 鞋帮 ♦**the upper sixth** [英:教育] 中学七年级 (英国中学教育的最后一年,在此其间,学生参加大学升学资格的考试)
upper class I *n* ♦**the upper class(es)** 上流社会 **II** *adj* (*also: upper-class*) 上流社会的
upright ['ʌpraɪt] **I** *adj* **1** (*vertical*) [+ *freezer, vacuum cleaner*] 立式的 **2** (*honest*) [+ *person*] 正直的 **II** *adv* [*sit, stand* +] 挺直地 **III** *n* [c] [建筑] 垂直的构件 ♦**to remain upright** 保持直立
uprising ['ʌpraɪzɪŋ] *n* [c] 起义
uproar ['ʌprɔː(r)] *n* [u] **1** (*shouting*) 喧嚣 **2** (*protest*) 骚乱 ♦**an uproar over** *or* **about sth** 因某事引起的骚乱
upscale ['ʌpskeɪl] [美] *adj* [+ *product, hotel*] 高档的 [英= **upmarket**]
upset [*vb, adj* ʌp'sɛt, *n* 'ʌpsɛt] (*pt, pp* **upset**) **I** *vt* **1** (*make unhappy*) [+ *person*] 使苦恼 **2** (*knock over*) [+ *glass etc*] 打翻 **3** (*disturb*) [+ *routine, plan*] 打乱 **II** *adj* **1** (*unhappy*) 心烦意乱的 **2** [+ *stomach*] 不舒服的 **III** *n* ♦**to have/get a stomach upset** [英] 感到肠胃不适 ♦**to be upset about sth** 为某事感到烦恼 ♦**to get upset** (*sad*) 感到难过; (*offended*) 感到生气
upside down [ʌpsaɪd-] **I** *adv* [*hang, hold, turn* +] 上下颠倒地 **II** *adj* 上下颠倒的 ♦**to turn a place upside down** 把某地方翻得乱七八糟 ♦**to turn sb's life** *or* **world upside down** 把某人的生活搞得天翻地覆
upstairs [ʌp'stɛəz] **I** *adv* **1** [*be* +] 在楼上 **2** [*go* +] 往楼上 **II** *adj* [+ *window, room*] 楼上的 **III** *n* [s] [*of building*] 楼上
up-to-date ['ʌptə'deɪt] *adj* **1** (*modern*) 最新的 **2** (*well-informed*) 掌握最新信息的 ♦**to keep up-to-date (with sth)** 跟上(某事的)最新发展 ♦**to keep sb up-to-date (with** *or* **on sth)** 为某人提供(关于某事的)最新信息 ♦**to keep sth up-to-date** 不断更新某物
uptown ['ʌptaun] [美] **I** *adv* **1** [*be* +] 在市镇外围的住宅区 **2** [*go* +] 去市镇外围的住宅区 **II** *adj* 住宅区的
upward ['ʌpwəd] **I** *adj* 向上的 **II** *adv* = **upwards** ♦**upward of** (*more than*) 多于…
upwards ['ʌpwədz] *adv* 向上
uranium [juə'reɪnɪəm] *n* [u] 铀
Uranus [juə'reɪnəs] *n* 天王星
urban ['əːbən] *adj* [+ *area, development*] 城市的
urge [əːdʒ] **I** *n* [c] 冲动 **II** *vt* **1** ♦**to urge sb to do sth** 怂恿某人做某

事2 ♦**to urge caution** 强调要谨慎 ♦**to have an urge to do sth** 强烈地想要做某事 ♦**an urge for revenge** 复仇的强烈欲望
❑**urge on** *vt* 激励

urgency ['əːdʒənsɪ] *n* [U] [*of task*] 紧迫 ♦**a note of urgency** (*in voice*) 急迫的语气 ♦**sense of urgency** 紧迫感 ♦**as a matter of urgency** 作为紧急事件

urgent ['əːdʒənt] *adj* **1** [+ *letter, message etc*] 紧急的 **2** [+ *need, voice*] 急迫的

urinal ['juərɪnl] *n* [C] 小便池

urinate ['juərɪneɪt] *vi* 排尿

urine ['juərɪn] *n* [U] 尿

URL [计算机] *n abbr* (= ***Uniform Resource Locator***) 在互联网上的WWW 服务程序上用于指定信息位置的表示方法

urn [əːn] *n* [C] **1** (*pot*) 瓮 **2** (*for ashes*) 骨灰瓮 **3** (*also:* ***tea urn***) 茶水壶

Uruguay ['juərəgwaɪ] *n* 乌拉圭

Uruguayan [juərə'gwaɪən] **I** *adj* 乌拉圭的 **II** *n* [C] (*person*) 乌拉圭人

US *n abbr* (= ***United States***) ♦**the US** 美国

✪**us** [ʌs] *pron* 我们 ◊ *They need us.* 他们需要我们。◊ *He brought us a present.* 他带给我们一份礼物。◊ *He lives with us.* 他和我们住在一起。

USA *n abbr* (= ***United States of America***) ♦**the USA** 美国

✪**use** [*n* juːs, *vb* juːz] **I** *n* **1** [U/S] (*using*) 使用 ◊ *the use of artificial drugs* 人造药品的使用 **2** [C/U] (*purpose*) 用途 ◊ *Metal detectors have many uses.* 金属探测器有很多用途。**3** [C] [*of word*] 用法 ◊ *Old uses of some words are dying out.* 一些词的旧用法正逐渐消失。**II** *vt* **1** [+ *object, tool*] 使用 **2** [+ *word, phrase*] 应用 **3** [贬] [+ *person*] 利用 **4** (*also:* ***use up***) [+ *supply*] 用完 ◊ *You've used all the ice cubes.* 你用掉了所有的冰块。♦**to be in use** 正被使用 ♦**to go out of use** 不再被使用 ♦**to be of use (to sb)** (对某人) 有用 ♦**to make use of sth** 利用某物 ♦**it's no use** 没用的 ♦**it's no use arguing/crying** *etc* 吵/哭{等}是没用的 ♦**what's the use!** 有什么用呢! ♦**to be no use (to sb)** (对某人) 毫无用处 ♦**to have a use for sth** 用得着某物 ♦**to have the use of sth** 使用某物 ♦**she used to do it** 她过去是这么做的 ♦**I didn't use to** *or* **I used not to worry so much** 我过去不这么焦虑 ♦**to be used to sth/to doing sth** 习惯于某事/做某事 ♦**to get used to sth/to doing sth** 开始习惯于某事/做某事
❑**use up** *vt see* **use**

used [juːzd] *adj* **1** [+ *tissue, glass, envelope*] 用过的 **2** [+ *car*] 旧的

useful ['juːsful] *adj* 有用的 ♦**to be useful to** *or* **for sb** 对某人有用的 ♦**to be useful for sth/doing sth** 对某事/做某事有帮助的 ♦**it's useful to keep a diary** 写日记很有助益 ♦**it would be useful for us to have more information** 得到更多的信息会对我们很有用 ♦**to come in useful** 有帮助

useless ['juːslɪs] *adj* **1** (*unusable*) 无用的 **2** (*pointless*) 徒劳的 **3** [非正式] (*hopeless*) 无能的 ♦**it's useless to complain** 抱怨是无用的 ♦**to be useless at sth/at doing sth** [非正式] 对某事/做某事非常差劲

user ['juːzə(r)] *n* [C] **1** [*of product, service*] 使用者 **2** (*consumer*) [*of petrol, gas etc*] 用户

user-friendly ['juːzə'frɛndlɪ] *adj* 易于使用的

USS *abbr* (= ***United States Ship***) 美国军舰

usual ['juːʒuəl] *adj* [+ *time, place etc*] 惯常的 ♦**as usual** (*as normally happens*) 像往常一样; (*just the same*) 像平常一样 ♦**warmer/colder than usual** 比平常暖和/冷 ♦**it is usual to tip waiters** 给侍者小费是很平常的

usually ['juːʒuəlɪ] *adv* 通常地

utensil [juː'tɛnsl] *n* [C] 用具 ♦**cooking/kitchen utensils** 烹饪/厨房用具

utility [juː'tɪlɪtɪ] *n* **1** [C] (*also:* ***public utility***) 公共设施 **2** [U] [正式] (*usefulness*) 效用

utilize ['juːtɪlaɪz] [正式] *vt* 利用

utmost ['ʌtməust] **I** *adj* 极度的 **II** *n* ♦**to do one's utmost (to do sth)** 竭尽全力(做某事) ♦**of the utmost**

importance 最重要的
utter ['ʌtə(r)] **I** *adj* (*total*) [+ *amazement, nonsense, fool*] 绝对的 **II** *vt* [文] [+ *sounds, words*] 说
utterly ['ʌtəlɪ] *adv* (*totally*) 全然
U-turn ['juː'təːn] *n* [c] **1** (*when driving*) U 形转弯 **2** (喻) 彻底转变
♦**to do a U-turn** (*in vehicle*) 180 度掉头; (喻) 彻底转变
Uzbek ['ʌzbɛk] **I** *adj* 乌兹别克的 **II** *n* **1** [c] (*person*) 乌兹别克人 **2** [u] (*language*) 乌兹别克语
Uzbekistan [ʌzbɛkɪ'stɑːn] *n* 乌兹别克

Vv

V[1], **v** [viː] *n* [c/u] (*letter*) 英语的第二十二个字母
V[2] [手机短信] *abbr* (= ***very***) 很
v. *abbr* **1** (= ***versus***) 对 **2** (= ***volt***) 伏特 **3** (= ***verse***) 诗
vacancy ['veɪkənsɪ] *n* [c] (*job*) 空缺; (*hotel room*) 空房 ♦ **"no vacancies"** "客满" ♦ **have you any vacancies?** (*hotel*) 你们有空房吗?
vacant ['veɪkənt] *adj* **1** [+ *seat, bathroom*] 空着的 **2** [+ *look, expression*] 茫然的 **3** [+ *job*] 空缺的
vacate [və'keɪt] [正式] *vt* [+ *house, seat*] 空出; [+ *job*] 辞去
vacation [və'keɪʃən] *n* [c] **1** [尤美] 休假 [英 = **holiday**] **2** (*at university etc*) 假期 ♦ **to take a vacation** 休假 ♦ **to be/go on vacation** 在/去度假
vaccinate ['væksɪneɪt] *vt* ♦ **to vaccinate sb (against sth)** 给某人接种疫苗(预防某疾病)
vaccination [væksɪ'neɪʃən] *n* **1** [u] (*immunization*) 疫苗接种 **2** [c] (*injection*) 预防针 ♦ **a vaccination against smallpox/tetanus** 天花疫苗接种/破伤风预防针
vaccine ['væksiːn] *n* [c/u] 疫苗
vacuum ['vækjum] **I** *n* [c] **1** 真空 **2** (喻) 空白 **II** *vt* [+ *room, carpet etc*] 用吸尘器打扫
vacuum cleaner *n* [c] (*also:* ***vacuum***) 真空吸尘器
vagina [və'dʒaɪnə] *n* [c] 阴道
vague [veɪg] *adj* **1** [+ *memory, idea*] 不清楚的; [+ *shape, outline*] 模糊的; [+ *talk, instructions*] 含糊的 **2** (*evasive*) [+ *person, promise*] 含糊其辞的 **3** (*distracted*) [+ *person, look*] 茫然的 ♦ **I haven't the vaguest idea** 我一无所知
vaguely ['veɪglɪ] *adv* **1** (*unclearly*) 含糊地 **2** (*evasively*) 闪烁其辞地 **3** (*slightly*) 略微地
vain [veɪn] *adj* **1** (*conceited*) [+ *person*] 自负的 **2** (*useless*) [+ *attempt, action, hope*] 徒劳的 ♦ **in vain** 徒然 ♦ **to die in vain** 白白死去
Valentine's Day ['væləntaɪnz-] *n* [c/u] 情人节
valiant ['vælɪənt] *adj* 勇敢的
valid ['vælɪd] *adj* **1** [+ *ticket, document*] 有效的 **2** [+ *argument, reason*] 令人信服的
valley ['vælɪ] *n* [c] 山谷
valuable ['væljuəbl] **I** *adj* **1** [+ *jewels, painting etc*] 贵重的 **2** (*useful*) [+ *lesson, contribution*] 有价值的 **II valuables** *n* [*pl*] 贵重物品
valuation [vælju'eɪʃən] *n* [c] [*of house etc*] 估价
✪**value** ['væljuː] **I** *n* **1** [c/u] (*financial worth*) 价值 **2** [u] (*importance*) 重要性 ◊ *The value of this experience should not be underestimated.* 这次经历的重要性不应被低估。**3** [u] (*worth in relation to price*) 价格 ◊ *Both offer excellent value at around £50 for a double room.* 对一间双人房双方都报出50英镑左右的优惠价格。 **II** *vt* **1** (*assess the worth of*) 给…估价 ◊ *jewellery valued at around $10,000* 估价在1万美元左右的珠宝 **2** (*appreciate*) 重视 ◊ *She genuinely values his opinion.* 她确实很重视他的看法。**III values** *n* [*pl*] (*principles, beliefs*) 价值观念 ♦ **value for money** 物有所值 ♦ **to lose (in) value** [*currency, property* +] 贬值 ♦ **to gain (in) value** [*currency, property* +] 升值 ♦ **to be of value to sb** 对某人有益
valued ['væljuːd] *adj* 受重视的
valve [vælv] *n* [c] (*in pipe, tube*) 阀; (*in heart, vein*) 瓣膜
vampire ['væmpaɪə(r)] *n* [c] 吸血鬼
van [væn] *n* [c] **1** [汽车] 厢式运货车 **2** [英: 铁路] 铁路货车厢
vandal ['vændl] *n* [c] 蓄意破坏公物者
vandalism ['vændəlɪzəm] *n* [u] 蓄意破坏公物的行为
vandalize ['vændəlaɪz] *vt* 肆意毁坏
vanilla [və'nɪlə] *n* [u] 香草
vanish ['vænɪʃ] *vi* **1** [*person, aircraft* +] 消失 **2** (*cease to exist*) [*tradition, system, species* +] 灭绝

vanity ['vænɪtɪ] *n* [U] 虚荣
vapour (美 **vapor**) ['veɪpə(r)] *n* [C/U] 蒸汽
variable ['vɛərɪəbl] **I** *adj* **1** (*likely to change*) [+ *mood, quality, climate*] 易变的 **2** (*able to be changed*) [+ *temperature, height, speed*] 可变的 **II** *n* [C] **1** [数] 变量 **2** (*factor*) 可变因素
variant ['vɛərɪənt] *n* [C] 变体
variation [vɛərɪ'eɪʃən] *n* **1** [C/U] (*in price, level, amount*) 变动 **2** [C] [*of plot, musical theme etc*] 变化
varied ['vɛərɪd] *adj* **1** (*diverse*) [+ *opinions, reasons*] 各种各样的 **2** (*full of variety*) [+ *career, work, diet*] 丰富多彩的
variety [və'raɪətɪ] *n* **1** [U] (*diversity*) 多样性 **2** [S] (*range*) [*of objects*] 若干 **3** [C] (*type*) 种类 ♦ **a wide variety of ...** 种类繁多的… ♦ **for a variety of reasons** 由于种种原因
various ['vɛərɪəs] *adj* **1** (*several*) 不同的 **2** (*different*) 各种各样的
varnish ['vɑːnɪʃ] **I** *n* [C/U] 清漆 **II** *vt* 给…涂清漆 ♦ **to varnish one's nails** 给指甲涂指甲油
vary ['vɛərɪ] **I** *vt* (*make changes to*) [+ *routine, diet*] 更改 **II** *vi* (*be different*) [*amount, sizes, colours* +] 有差异 ♦ **to vary with** [+ *weather, season, age etc*] 随…而变化
vase [vɑːz, (美) veɪs] *n* [C] 花瓶
Vaseline® ['væsɪliːn] *n* [U] 凡士林
vast [vɑːst] *adj* **1** [+ *area*] 广阔的 **2** [+ *knowledge*] 渊博的 **3** [+ *expense*] 巨额的
VAT [viːeɪ'tiː, væt] [英] *n abbr* (= ***value added tax***) 增值税
vault [vɔːlt] **I** *n* [C] **1** (*tomb*) 地下墓室 **2** (*in bank*) 保险库 **3** [*of roof*] 拱顶 **II** *vt* (*also:* ***vault over***) 跃过
VCR *n abbr* (= ***video cassette recorder***) 录像机
VD *n abbr* (= ***venereal disease***) 性病
VDT [美] *n abbr* (= ***visual display terminal***) = **VDU**
VDU [英] *n abbr* (= ***visual display unit***) 视频显示装置 [美 = **VDT**]
veal [viːl] *n* [U] 小牛肉
veer [vɪə(r)] *vi* **1** [*vehicle* +] 突然转向 **2** [*wind* +] 转向
vegan ['viːgən] **I** *n* [C] 纯素食主义者 **II** *adj* 纯素食主义者的
vegetable ['vɛdʒtəbl] **I** *n* [C] 蔬菜 **II** *cpd* [复合词] [+ *oil, dish*] 蔬菜
vegetarian [vɛdʒɪ'tɛərɪən] **I** *n* [C] 素食者 **II** *adj* [+ *diet, restaurant etc*] 素的
vegetation [vɛdʒɪ'teɪʃən] [正式] *n* [U] 植物
veggieburger ['vɛdʒɪbəːgə(r)] *n* [C] 素食汉堡包
vehement ['viːɪmənt] *adj* 激烈的
vehicle ['viːɪkl] *n* [C] **1** (*car, bus etc*) 机动车 **2** [正式] (*means*) 工具
veil [veɪl] *n* [C] **1** (*covering*) 面纱 **2** (喻) [*of secrecy, silence*] 掩盖
vein [veɪn] *n* [C] **1** (*in body*) 静脉 **2** [*of leaf*] 叶脉 **3** [*of metal, mineral*] 矿脉 **4** (*mood, style*) 风格
Velcro® ['vɛlkrəu] *n* [U] 尼龙搭扣
velocity [vɪ'lɔsɪtɪ] *n* [C/U] 速度
velvet ['vɛlvɪt] **I** *n* [C/U] 天鹅绒 **II** *adj* 天鹅绒的
vending machine ['vɛndɪŋ-] *n* [C] 自动售货机
vendor ['vɛndə(r)] *n* [C] **1** (*in street*) 小贩 **2** [法] [*of house, land*] 卖主
Venezuela [vɛnɛ'zweɪlə] *n* 委内瑞拉
Venezuelan [vɛnɛ'zweɪlən] **I** *adj* 委内瑞拉的 **II** *n* [C] (*person*) 委内瑞拉人
vengeance ['vɛndʒəns] *n* [U] 报复 ♦ **to do sth with a vengeance** 加倍努力地做某事
venison ['vɛnɪsn] *n* [U] 鹿肉
venom ['vɛnəm] *n* [U] **1** [*of snake, insect*] 毒液 **2** (喻) (*bitterness*) 怨恨
vent [vɛnt] **I** *n* [C] (*for air, smoke etc*) 孔 **II** *vt* [+ *feelings, anger*] 发泄 ♦ **to give vent to** [+ *feelings, anger*] 发泄
ventilate ['vɛntɪleɪt] *vt* 使通风
venture ['vɛntʃə(r)] **I** *n* [C] 探险 **II** *vt* [+ *opinion, sentence*] [正式] 冒昧地表示 **III** *vi* 冒险前往 ♦ **business venture** 企业 ♦ **to venture to do sth** 冒险做某事 ♦ **to venture into sth** 大胆尝试某事
venue ['vɛnjuː] *n* [C] 举行场所
Venus ['viːnəs] *n* (*planet*) 金星
verb [vəːb] *n* [C] 动词
verbal ['vəːbl] *adj* **1** [+ *skills, translation etc*] 语言的 **2** [+ *attack*] 口头的 **3** [语言] 动词的

verdict ['vəːdɪkt] *n* [c] **1** [法] 裁定 **2** (*opinion*) 定论 ♦**a verdict of guilty/not guilty** 有罪/无罪的裁定

verge [vəːdʒ] *n* [c] **1** [英] [*of road*] 路边草带 **2** ♦**to be on the verge of sth/of doing sth** 即将发生某事/即将做某事

❑**verge on** *vt* [不可拆分] 濒临

verify ['vɛrɪfaɪ] *vt* 证实 ♦**to verify that ...** 证实…

versatile ['vəːsətaɪl] *adj* **1** [+ *person*] 多才多艺的 **2** [+ *substance, machine*] 多功能的

verse [vəːs] *n* **1** [U] (*poetry*) 诗 **2** [c] [*of poem, song*] 诗节 **3** [c] (*in bible*) 节 ♦**to write in verse** 用韵文写

version ['vəːʃən] *n* [c] **1** [*of book, design*] 版本 **2** [*of event, incident*] 说法

versus ['vəːsəs] *prep* 与…相对; (*in competition*) 对

vertical ['vəːtɪkl] **I** *adj* 垂直的 **II** *n* ♦**the vertical** 垂直方向

✪**very** ['vɛrɪ] **I** *adv* **1** 很 ◊ *a very good idea* 一个很好的主意 **2** ♦**the very end/beginning** 最终/一开始 **II** *adj* ♦**those were his very words** 那就是他的原话 ♦**the very thought (of it) alarms me** 一想起(它)就让我惊恐不安 ♦**at the very least** 至少 ♦**very well** (*agreeing*) 那好吧 ♦**very much so** 确实如此 ♦**very little** 极少的 ♦**there isn't very much (of ...)** (…)不太多了 ♦**I like him very much** 我非常喜欢他

vessel ['vɛsl] [正式] *n* [c] **1** (*boat*) 轮船 **2** (*container*) 容器

vest [vɛst] **I** *n* [c] **1** [英] (*underwear*) 汗衫 [美 = **undershirt**] **2** [美] (*waistcoat*) 马甲 [英 = **waistcoat**] **II** *vt* [正式] ♦**to be vested with sth** 被赋予某物 ♦**to be vested in sb** 被给予某人

vet [vɛt] **I** *n* [c] **1** [尤英] (*veterinary surgeon*) 兽医 [美 = **veterinarian**] **2** [美: 非正式] (*veteran*) 老兵 **II** *vt* [英] (*check*) 审查

veteran ['vɛtərn] **I** *n* [c] [*of war*] 老兵 **II** *adj* [+ *MP, campaigner*] 经验丰富的

veterinarian [vɛtrɪ'nɛərɪən] [美] *n* [c] 兽医 [英 = **vet, veterinary surgeon**]

veterinary ['vɛtrɪnərɪ] *adj* 兽医的

veterinary surgeon [正式: 英] *n* [c] 兽医 [美 = **veterinarian**]

veto ['viːtəu] (*pl* **vetoes**) **I** *n* [c] 否决 **II** *vt* 否决 ♦**power of veto** 否决权 ♦**to put a veto on** 禁止

VHF [广播] *n abbr* (= ***very high frequency***) 特高频

via ['vaɪə] *prep* **1** [+ *place*] 经由 **2** (*by means of*) 通过

viable ['vaɪəbl] *adj* 可行的

vibrate [vaɪ'breɪt] **I** *vi* 震颤 **II** *vt* 使震动

vibration [vaɪ'breɪʃən] *n* **1** [U] (*movement*) 震动 **2** [c] (*instance*) 颤动

vicar ['vɪkə(r)] *n* [c] 教区牧师

vice [vaɪs] *n* **1** [c] (*moral fault*) 恶习 **2** [U] (*criminal activities*) 毒品色情犯罪 **3** [c] [英] (*tool*) 老虎钳 [美 = **vise**]

vice-chairman [vaɪs'tʃɛəmən] *n* [c] 副主席

vice president *n* [c] **1** [政治] 副总统 **2** [*of club*] 副会长

vice versa ['vaɪsɪ'vəːsə] *adv* 反之亦然

vicinity [vɪ'sɪnɪtɪ] *n* ♦**in the vicinity (of)** 在(…)附近

vicious ['vɪʃəs] *adj* **1** [+ *attack, blow*] 剧烈的 **2** [+ *person, dog*] 凶残的 **3** [+ *words, look, letter*] 恶毒的

victim ['vɪktɪm] *n* [c] [*of accident etc*] 受害者 ♦**to be the victim of** [+ *attack etc*] 成为…的受害者

victimize ['vɪktɪmaɪz] *vt* 欺负

victor ['vɪktə(r)] [文] *n* [c] 胜利者

Victorian [vɪk'tɔːrɪən] **I** *adj* **1** [+ *house, furniture etc*] 维多利亚时代的 **2** (*old-fashioned*) [+ *values etc*] 古板守旧的 **II** *n* [c] (*person*) 维多利亚时代的人

victorious [vɪk'tɔːrɪəs] *adj* 胜利的

victory ['vɪktərɪ] *n* [c/U] 胜利 ♦**to win a victory over sb** 击败某人获胜

video ['vɪdɪəu] **I** *n* **1** [c] (*film*) 录像 **2** [U] (*system*) 录像 **3** [c] (*cassette*) 录像带 **4** [c] [尤英] (*machine*) 录像机 [美 = **VCR**] **II** *cpd* [复合词] [+ *equipment etc*] 录像 **III** *vt* [尤英] 录下 [美 = **tape, videotape**]

video camera *n* [c] 摄像机

video game *n* [c] 电子游戏

video recorder *n* [c] 录像机
video shop [英] *n* [c] 录像带租赁店
videotape ['vɪdɪəuteɪp] **I** *n* [c/u] 录像带 **II** *vt* (*record*) 录
vie [vaɪ] [正式] *vi* ♦**to vie (with sb) (for sth/to do sth)** (与某人)争夺(某物)/争(做某事)
Vietnam [vjɛt'næm] *n* 越南
Vietnamese [vjɛtnə'mi:z] (*pl* **Vietnamese**) **I** *adj* 越南的 **II** *n* **1** [c] (*person*) 越南人 **2** [u] (*language*) 越南语
✪**view** [vju:] **I** *n* [c] **1** (*from window, hilltop etc*) 景色 **2** (*outlook*) 见解 **3** (*ability to see sth*) 看 ◊ *They pushed forward for a better view.* 他们用力朝前挤，想看得清楚些。 **4** (*opinion*) 看法 ◊ *his views on women* 他对女人的看法 **II** *vt* **1** [正式] (*look at*) 看 **2** (*consider*) 看待 ◊ *How do you view the matter?* 你如何看待这件事？ ♦**to block sb's view** 挡住某人的视线 ♦**on view** (*in museum etc*) 在展出 ♦**in full view (of)** (…)全都看得见的 ♦**to take the view that ...** 认为… ♦**in view of the weather/the fact that ...** 考虑到天气/…这个事实 ♦**in my view** 在我看来 ♦**with a view to ...** 是为了…
viewer ['vju:ə(r)] *n* [c] [*of TV*] 观众
viewpoint ['vju:pɔɪnt] *n* [c] **1** (*attitude*) 角度 **2** (*place*) 观察位置
vigilant ['vɪdʒɪlənt] *adj* 警惕的
vigorous ['vɪgərəs] *adj* **1** [+ *exercise*] 充满活力的 **2** [+ *campaign, action*] 积极的
vile [vaɪl] *adj* **1** (*offensive*) [+ *behaviour, language*] 可恶的 **2** (*unpleasant*) [+ *weather, food, temper*] 极坏的
villa ['vɪlə] *n* [c] **1** (*in countryside*) 乡间别墅 **2** (*in town*) 市郊独立的别墅
village ['vɪlɪdʒ] *n* [c] 村庄
villager ['vɪlɪdʒə(r)] *n* [c] 村民
villain ['vɪlən] *n* [c] **1** (*scoundrel*) 恶棍 **2** (*in novel, play etc*) 反面人物 **3** [英] (*criminal*) 职业罪犯
vindictive [vɪn'dɪktɪv] *adj* [+ *person, action*] 报复性的
vine [vaɪn] *n* [c] **1** (*producing grapes*) 葡萄藤 **2** (*in jungle*) 藤本植物
vinegar ['vɪnɪgə(r)] *n* [c/u] 醋
vineyard ['vɪnjɑ:d] *n* [c] 葡萄园
vintage ['vɪntɪdʒ] **I** *n* [c] (*of wine*) 酿造年份及产地 **II** *adj* **1** [+ *wine*] 上等的 **2** [+ *car, aeroplane*] 古老而享有声誉的 **3** [+ *comedy, performance etc*] 经典的 ♦**the 1970 vintage** (*of wine*) 1970 年产的葡萄酒
vinyl ['vaɪnl] *n* [u] **1** (*material*) 乙烯基 **2** (*records*) 唱片
viola [vɪ'əulə] *n* [c] 中提琴
violate ['vaɪəleɪt] [正式] *vt* **1** [+ *law, agreement*] 违背 **2** [+ *peace, privacy*] 侵犯 **3** [+ *tomb*] 亵渎
violation [vaɪə'leɪʃən] *n* [c/u] **1** [*of agreement, law*] 违反 **2** [*of tomb*] 亵渎 ♦**in violation of** [+ *rule, law*] 违背
violence ['vaɪələns] *n* [u] **1** 暴力 **2** [文] (*strength*) 猛力
violent ['vaɪələnt] *adj* **1** [+ *person, crime*] 暴力的 **2** [+ *death, explosion*] 猛烈的 **3** [+ *opposition, pain, emotion*] 强烈的
violet ['vaɪələt] **I** *adj* [+ *light, glow, sky*] 紫罗兰色的 **II** *n* [c] (*flower*) 紫罗兰
violin [vaɪə'lɪn] *n* [c] 小提琴
violinist [vaɪə'lɪnɪst] *n* [c] 小提琴手
VIP [vi:aɪ'pi:] *n abbr* (= ***very important person***) 要人
virgin ['və:dʒɪn] **I** *n* [c] 处女 **II** *adj* [+ *snow, forest*] 原始的
Virgo ['və:gəu] *n* **1** [u] (*sign*) 处女座 **2** [c] (*person*) 处女座的人 ♦**I'm (a) Virgo** 我是处女座的
virtual ['və:tjuəl] *adj* **1** 实际上的 **2** [计算机] 虚拟的 ♦**it's a virtual certainty/impossibility** 这实际上是件已确定的事/不可能的事
virtually ['və:tjuəlɪ] *adv* 事实上 ♦**it is virtually impossible** 事实上这是不可能的
virtual reality *n* [u] 虚拟现实
virtue ['və:tju:] *n* **1** [u] (*moral correctness*) 美德 **2** [c] (*good quality*) 优点 **3** [c] (*advantage*) 优势 ♦**by virtue of** [正式] 由于
virus ['vaɪərəs] [医, 计算机] *n* [c] 病毒
visa ['vi:zə] *n* [c] 签证
vise [vaɪs] [美] *n* = **vice**
visibility [vɪzɪ'bɪlɪtɪ] *n* [u] **1** 能见度 **2** (喻) (*prominence*) 瞩目
visible ['vɪzəbl] *adj* **1** (*able to be seen*) 可见的 **2** (喻) (*noticeable*) 明显的

vision ['vɪʒən] *n* **1** [U] (*sight*) 视力 **2** [C] (*hope for the future*) 想像 **3** [C] (*in dream etc*) 幻象

✪**visit** ['vɪzɪt] **I** *n* [C] **1** (*to person*) 拜访 **2** (*to place*) 访问 **II** *vt* **1** [+ *person*] 拜访 **2** [+ *place*] 游览 ♦**to pay sb a visit** 拜访某人 ♦**on a private/official visit** 进行私人性/官方的访问

❑**visit with** [美] *vt* [不可拆分] 拜访

visiting hours ['vɪzɪtɪŋ-] *n* [*pl*] (*in hospital*) 探视时间

visitor ['vɪzɪtə(r)] *n* [C] **1** (*to city, country*) 游客 **2** (*to person, house*) 来客

visitor centre (美 **visitor center**) *n* [C] 游客中心

visual ['vɪzjuəl] *adj* 视觉的

visualize ['vɪzjuəlaɪz] *vt* **1** (*imagine*) 设想 **2** (*envisage*) 想像

vital ['vaɪtl] *adj* **1** (*essential*) 至关重要的 **2** (*full of life*) [+ *person*] 有活力的 ♦**it is vital to .../that ...** 对…/…是至关重要的 ♦**to be of vital importance (to sb/sth)** (对某人/某事) 极其重要 ♦**vital organs** 重要器官

vitality [vaɪ'tælɪtɪ] *n* [U] (*liveliness*) 生命力

vitamin ['vɪtəmɪn, (美) 'vaɪtəmɪn] **I** *n* [C] 维生素 **II** *cpd* [复合词] [+ *pill, supplement*] 维生素

vivid ['vɪvɪd] *adj* **1** [+ *description, memory*] 生动的 **2** [+ *colour, light*] 鲜艳的 ♦**a vivid imagination** 生动的想象力

V-neck ['viːnɛk] *n* [C] **1** (*also:* ***V-neck sweater***) V 领衫 **2** (*collar*) V 字领

vocabulary [vəu'kæbjulərɪ] *n* **1** [C/U] [*of person*] 词汇量 **2** [C] [*of language*] 词汇

vocal ['vəukl] *adj* **1** (字) 嗓音的 **2** (喻) (*outspoken*) 直言不讳的

vocation [vəu'keɪʃən] *n* [C] 职业

vocational [vəu'keɪʃənl] *adj* [+ *training, course, skills*] 职业的

vodka ['vɔdkə] *n* [C/U] 伏特加酒

vogue [vəug] *n* ♦**the vogue for** … 的新潮流 ♦**to be in vogue** 正在流行 ♦**to come into vogue** 开始流行

voice [vɔɪs] **I** *n* [C] **1** 嗓音 **2** (*opinion*) 意见 **II** *vt* [+ *opinion, anger, concern*] 表达 ♦**in a loud/soft voice** 大声地/柔声地 ♦**to have a voice in sth** 对某事有发言权 ♦**to give voice to** [+ *doubt, wish etc*] 表露 ♦**the active/passive voice** 主动/被动语态

voice mail *n* [U] 语音留言

void [vɔɪd] **I** *n* [C] **1** (*space*) 空间 **2** (喻) (*emptiness*) 空虚 **II** *adj* (*invalid*) [+ *vote, contract*] 无效的 ♦**to be void of sth** [正式] 缺乏某物

vol. *abbr* (= **volume**) 册

volatile ['vɔlətaɪl] *adj* **1** [+ *situation*] 不稳定的 **2** [+ *person, temper*] 多变的 **3** [术语] [+ *liquid, substance*] 易挥发的

volcano [vɔl'keɪnəu] (*pl* **volcanoes**) *n* [C] 火山

volleyball ['vɔlɪbɔːl] *n* [U] 排球

volt [vəult] *n* [C] 伏特

voltage ['vəultɪdʒ] *n* [C/U] 电压 ♦**high/low voltage** 高压/低压

volume ['vɔljuːm] *n* **1** [C] [*of object, gas etc*] 体积 **2** [C] [*of sales, traffic*] 量 **3** [C] [正式] (*book*) 卷; (*in series*) 册 **4** [U] (*sound level*) [*of TV, radio, stereo*] 音量 ♦**volume one/two** [*of book*] 第一/二册 ♦**the way she looked at him spoke volumes** 她看他的眼神意味深长

voluntarily ['vɔləntrɪlɪ] *adv* 主动地

voluntary ['vɔləntərɪ] *adj* **1** (*not compulsory*) 自愿的 **2** [+ *work, worker*] 志愿的 **3** [+ *organization*] 自愿的

volunteer [vɔlən'tɪə(r)] **I** *n* [C] **1** (*unpaid worker*) 志愿者 **2** (*helper*) 自愿参加者 **3** (*to army etc*) 志愿兵 **II** *vt* [正式] [+ *information, explanation*] 主动提供 **II** *vi* (*for army etc*) 自愿 ♦**to volunteer to do sth** 自愿做某事

vomit ['vɔmɪt] **I** *n* [U] 呕吐物 **II** *vt* [+ *blood etc*] 吐 **III** *vi* 呕吐

✪**vote** [vəut] **I** *n* [C] **1** 选票 **2** ♦**the vote** (*votes cast*) 选票总数; (*right to vote*) 选举权 ◊ *They captured 13 per cent of the vote.* 他们获得了百分之十三的选票。◊ *Women have had the vote for over fifty years.* 妇女获得选举权已有五十多年了。**II** *vt* ♦**to vote Labour/Green** *etc* 投票给工党/绿党{等} **III** *vi* 投票 ♦**to cast one's vote** 投票 ♦**to put sth to the vote** 将某事交付表决 ♦**to take a vote on sth** 就某事进行表

决 ♦**to vote to do sth** 投票决定做某事 ♦**to vote yes/no to sth** 投票赞成/反对某事 ♦**to be voted chairman** *etc* 被投票选为主席{等} ♦**to vote for sb** 投某人票 ♦**to vote for/against sth** 投票支持/反对某事 ♦**to vote on sth** 投票表决某事

voter ['vəutə(r)] *n* [c] 选举人

voting ['vəutɪŋ] *n* [u] 选举

voucher ['vautʃə(r)] *n* [c] 代金券

vow [vau] **I** *n* [c] 誓言 **II** *vt* ♦**to vow to do sth** 发誓做某事 ♦**to take** *or* **make a vow to do sth** 立誓要做某事 ♦**to vow that ...** 立誓…

vowel ['vauəl] *n* [c] 元音

voyage ['vɔɪɪdʒ] **I** *n* [c] 航行 **II** *vi* [正式] 航行
📖 用法参见 **journey**

vulgar ['vʌlgə(r)] *adj* **1** (*rude*) [+ *person, joke, gesture*] 粗俗的 **2** (*tasteless*) [+ *decor, design*] 庸俗的

vulnerable ['vʌlnərəbl] *adj* **1** [+ *person*] 易受伤的 **2** [+ *position, target*] 脆弱的 ♦**to be vulnerable to sth** 易受某物伤害

vulture ['vʌltʃə(r)] *n* [c] **1** 秃鹫 **2** [贬] (*person*) 乘人之危者

Ww

W¹, w ['dʌbljuː] *n* [c/u] (*letter*) 英语的第二十三个字母
W² *abbr* **1** (= **west**) 西方 **2** [电子] (= **watt**) 瓦
waddle ['wɔdl] *vi* [*duck, fat person* +] 摇摇摆摆地行走
wade [weɪd] *vi* **1** (*in water, mud*) ♦ **to wade across/through sth** 跋涉而过某地 **2** (喻) ♦ **to wade through** [+ *book, report*] 吃力地看完
❑ **wade in** *vi* 插手
wading pool [美] *n* [c] 浅水池 [英 = **paddling pool**]
wafer ['weɪfə(r)] *n* [c] (*biscuit*) 威化饼
waffle ['wɔfl] **I** *n* **1** [c] [烹饪] 蛋奶烘饼 **2** [u] (*empty talk*) 空话 **II** *vi* (*also:* ***waffle on***) 胡扯
wag [wæg] **I** *vt* **1** [+ *finger*] 摇动 **2** [+ *tail*] 摇 **II** *vi* [*tail* +] 摇
wage [weɪdʒ] **I** *n* [c] (*also:* ***wages***) 工资 **II** *vt* [+ *war, campaign*] 发动 ♦ **a day's wages** 一天的工资 ♦ **to wage war (against** *or* **on sth)** (对某事) 开战
wage packet [尤英] *n* [c] 工资袋
wager ['weɪdʒə(r)] **I** *n* [c] 赌注 **II** *vt* 以…为赌注 ♦ **I'll wager that ...** [非正式] 我打赌…
wagon (尤英 **waggon**) ['wægən] *n* [c] **1** (*horse-drawn*) 四轮运货马车 **2** [英: 铁路] 货车 ♦ **to be on the wagon** [非正式] 戒酒
wail [weɪl] **I** *n* [c] **1** [*of person*] 嚎啕声 **2** [*of siren*] 呼啸声 **II** *vi* **1** [*person* +] 嚎啕 **2** [*siren* +] 呼啸 **III** *vt* 哀诉
waist [weɪst] *n* [c] **1** 腰 **2** [*of clothing*] 腰身
waistcoat ['weɪskəut] [英] *n* [c] 马甲 [美 = **vest**]
✪ **wait** [weɪt] **I** *vi* 等待 **II** *n* [c] (*interval*) 等待时间 ◊ *There was a long wait.* 等待时间很长。♦ **to wait for sb/sth** 等候某人/某物 ♦ **there was a letter waiting for me** 有封信等我去取 ♦ **I can't wait** *or* **I can hardly wait to tell her** 我等不及要告诉她 ♦ **it can wait** 这可以过会儿再说 ♦ **wait a minute!** 等一下! ♦ **"repairs while you wait"** "修补, 立等可取" ♦ **to keep sb waiting** 让某人等着 ♦ **to lie in wait for sb** 埋伏着等待某人
❑ **wait around, wait about** *vi* ♦ **to wait around** *or* **about for sth** 无所事事地等待某事
❑ **wait behind** *vi* 留下来等候
❑ **wait on** *vt* [不可拆分] (*in restaurant, hotel etc*) 侍候
❑ **wait up** *vi* 熬夜等待 ♦ **don't wait up for me** 不要熬夜等我
waiter ['weɪtə(r)] *n* [c] 男服务员
waiting list ['weɪtɪŋ-] *n* [c] 等候者名单 ♦ **to be on the waiting list (for sth)** 被列于 (某事的) 等候者名单
waiting room *n* [c] 等候室
waitress ['weɪtrɪs] *n* [c] 女服务员
waive [weɪv] *vt* **1** [+ *rule, fee*] 取消 **2** [+ *right*] 放弃
wake [weɪk] (*pt* **woke, waked**, *pp* **woken, waked**) **I** *vt* (*also:* ***wake up***) 唤醒 **II** *vi* (*also:* ***wake up***) 醒来 **III** *n* [c] **1** (*for dead person*) 守灵 **2** [*of boat*] 尾波 ♦ **in the wake of sth** 紧随某事而来 ♦ **to follow in sb's wake** 紧随某人 ♦ **to leave sth in one's wake** 走后留下某物
❑ **wake up I** *vt* 唤醒 **II** *vi* 醒来 ♦ **to wake up to sth** 意识到某事
waken ['weɪkn] *vt, vi* = **wake**
Wales [weɪlz] *n* 威尔士 ♦ **the Prince of Wales** 威尔士王子
✪ **walk** [wɔːk] **I** *n* **1** [c] 散步 **2** [s] (*gait*) 步态 **3** [c] (*route*) 散步场所 **II** *vi* 走 **III** *vt* **1** [+ *distance*] 走 **2** [+ *dog*] 遛 ♦ **it's 10 minutes' walk from here** 从这儿走有10分钟的路程 ♦ **to go for a walk** 去散步 ♦ **to slow to a walk** 放慢速度改为步行 ♦ **people from all walks of life** 各界人士 ♦ **to walk in one's sleep** 梦游 ♦ **I'll walk you home** 我陪你走回家
❑ **walk off with** [非正式] *vt* [不可拆分] **1** (*steal*) 顺手拿走 **2** (*win*) [+ *prize*]

轻易赢得
❑walk out *vi* 1 ♦**to walk out (of sth)** 退出（某事）2 ♦**to walk out (on sb)** 离开（某人）3 (*strike*) 罢工
walker ['wɔːkə(r)] *n* [c] 散步者
walkie-talkie ['wɔːkɪ'tɔːkɪ] *n* [c] 步话机
walking ['wɔːkɪŋ] *n* [U] 步行 ♦**it's within walking distance** 只有几步路
walking stick *n* [c] 手杖
Walkman® ['wɔːkmən] *n* [c] 随身听
walkway ['wɔːkweɪ] *n* [c] 人行道
✪**wall** [wɔːl] *n* [c] 1 [*of building, room*] 墙 2 (*around city*) 城墙；(*around garden, field*) 围墙 3 (*side*) [*of tunnel, cave*] 内壁；[*of stomach, artery*] 壁 ♦**to go to the wall** [非正式] 破产
❑**wall in** *vt* 用墙围住
Wall Street *n* 华尔街
wallet ['wɔlɪt] *n* [c] 钱包
wallpaper ['wɔːlpeɪpə(r)] **I** *n* [c/U] 1 墙纸 2 [计算机] 桌面 **II** *vt* 糊墙纸于
walnut ['wɔːlnʌt] **I** *n* 1 [c] (*nut*) 核桃 2 [c] (*also:* ***walnut tree***) 胡桃树 3 [U] (*wood*) 胡桃木 **II** *cpd* [复合词] [+ *desk, table etc*] 胡桃
walrus ['wɔːlrəs] (*pl* **walrus** *or* **walruses**) *n* [c] 海象
waltz [wɔːlts] **I** *n* [c] (*music*) 圆舞曲；(*dance*) 华尔兹舞 **II** *vi* 1 (*dance*) 跳华尔兹舞 2 [非正式] ♦**to waltz in/off** *etc* 大摇大摆地走进/离开{等}
wand [wɔnd] *n* [c] (*also:* ***magic wand***) 魔杖
wander ['wɔndə(r)] **I** *vi* 1 (*roam*) 漫游；(*because lost*) 迷失 2 [*mind, thoughts* +] 恍惚 **II** *vt* [+ *streets, countryside*] 在…闲逛 **III** *n* [s] 漫步 ♦**to wander off/away** 走失/走散 ♦**to have** *or* **go for** *or* **take a wander** 出去逛逛
wane [weɪn] **I** *vi* 1 [*moon* +] 亏缺 2 [*interest, influence etc* +] 减弱 **II** *n* ♦**to be on the wane** 日益衰落
✪**want** [wɔnt] **I** *vt* 1 (*wish for*) 想要 2 [非正式] (*need*) 需要 **II** *n* [s] [正式] (*lack*) ♦**want of** 缺乏 **III wants** *n* [*pl*] (*needs*) 需求 ♦**to want to do sth** 想要做某事 ♦**to want sb to do sth** 希望某人做某事 ♦**to want sth done** 要别人把某事做好 ♦**your hair wants cutting/washing** 你的头发要剪剪/洗洗了 ♦**you want to be more careful** [非正式] 你要多加小心 ♦**you're wanted on the phone** 有你的电话 ♦**he is wanted by the police** 他被警察通缉 ♦**"cook wanted"** "招聘厨师" ♦**if you want** 如果你乐意的话 ♦**to want out** [非正式] (*of deal etc*) 想退出 ♦**to want in** [非正式] (*on deal etc*) 想要加入 ♦**for want of** 因为缺乏
wanted ['wɔntɪd] *adj* [+ *criminal, man*] 受通缉的
✪**war** [wɔː(r)] *n* [c/U] 1 (*fighting*) 战争 2 (喻) (*competition*) 战争 ◊ *a trade/price war* 一场贸易/价格战 ♦**to be at war (with sb)** (与某人) 进行战争 ♦**to go to war** 开战 ♦**to make war on sb/sth** 向某人/某事开战 ♦**a war on drugs/crime** 同毒品/犯罪的斗争 ♦**war of words** 口诛笔伐
ward [wɔːd] *n* [c] 1 (*in hospital*) 病房 2 [政治] (*district*) 行政区 3 [法] (*child*) 被监护人
❑**ward off** *vt* [+ *threat, danger*] 防止；[+ *attacker*] 避开
warden ['wɔːdn] *n* [c] 1 (*in park, game reserve*) 管理员 2 (*at jail*) [英] 看守；[美] 监狱长 [英 = **governor**] 3 [英] (*at youth hostel*) 舍监
wardrobe ['wɔːdrəub] *n* 1 [c] (*cupboard*) 衣橱 2 [c] (*clothes*) 衣服 3 [U] [电影, 戏剧] 戏装
warehouse ['wɛəhaus] *n* [c] 仓库
warfare ['wɔːfɛə(r)] *n* [U] 战争
warhead ['wɔːhɛd] *n* [c] 弹头
warm [wɔːm] **I** *adj* 1 [+ *meal, soup, water*] 温热的；[+ *day, weather*] 暖和的 2 [+ *clothes, blankets*] 保暖的 3 [+ *applause, welcome*] 热情的 4 (*friendly*) [+ *person*] 友爱的 **II** *vt* 使暖和 ♦**it's warm** 天很暖和 ♦**are you warm enough?** 你觉得够暖和吗？♦**to keep warm** 保暖 ♦**to keep sth warm** [+ *food*] 使某物保温；[+ *building, house etc*] 使某物保持温暖 ♦**with my warmest thanks** 顺致我最诚挚的谢意 ♦**to warm one's hands/feet** 暖暖手/脚 ♦**to warm to sb/sth** 对某人/某

事产生好感
📖用法参见**hot**
❑**warm up** I *vi* 1 [*room, weather* +] 暖起来; [*water, substance etc* +] 变热 2 [*athlete, pianist etc* +] 热身 3 [*engine, photocopier etc* +] 预热 II *vt* 1 [+ *food*] 加热 2 [+ *person*] 使暖起来
warmly ['wɔːmlɪ] *adv* 1 [*welcome, greet, applaud* +] 热情地 2 [*dress, wrap up* +] 暖和地
warmth [wɔːmθ] *n* [U] 1 [*of fire*] 温暖 2 [*of clothing, blanket*] 暖和 3 (*friendliness*) 热情 ♦**we huddled together for warmth** 我们挤在一起取暖
warm-up ['wɔːmʌp] *n* [C] 1 [体育] 热身活动 2 (喻) (*rehearsal*) 预演 ♦**a warm-up match** *or* **game** 一场热身赛
warn [wɔːn] I *vt* ♦**to warn sb that** 警告某人… II *vi* ♦**to warn of sth** 警告提防某事 ♦**"War may break out," he warned** "战争可能会爆发，"他警告道 ♦**to warn sb not to do sth** 告诫某人不要做某事 ♦**to warn sb of sth** 警告某人某事 ♦**to warn sb against sth** 告诫某人提防某事 ♦**to warn against doing sth** 告诫不准做某事
warning ['wɔːnɪŋ] *n* 1 [C] (*action, words, sign*) 警告 2 [C/U] (*notice*) 预兆 ♦**to give sb a warning** 给某人一个警告 ♦**let this be a warning to you** 让这事成为你的鉴诫 ♦**without (any) warning** (*suddenly*) 出人意料地; (*without notice*) 毫无征兆地
warrant ['wɔrnt] I *n* [C] 1 (*for arrest*) 逮捕令 2 (*also:* ***search warrant***) 搜查令 II *vt* (*merit*) 应受到
warranty ['wɔrəntɪ] *n* [C] 担保 ♦**under warranty** 在质保期内
warrior ['wɔrɪə(r)] *n* [C] 战士
warship ['wɔːʃɪp] *n* [C] 军舰
wart [wɔːt] *n* [C] 疣
wartime ['wɔːtaɪm] I *n* ♦**in wartime** 在战时 II *adj* 战时的
wary ['wɛərɪ] *adj* ♦**to be wary (of sb/sth)** 提防(某人/某事) ♦**to be wary about** *or* **of doing sth** 对做某事很谨慎
was [wɔz] *pt of* **be**
wash [wɔʃ] I *vt* 1 [+ *clothes, dishes, paintbrush*] 洗 2 (*carry*) ♦**to be washed ashore/out to sea** *etc* 被冲到岸边/冲向大海{等} II *vi* 1 [*person* +] 洗净 2 [*sea, waves etc* +] ♦**to wash over/against sth** 冲过/拍打某物 III *n* 1 [C] (*clean*) 洗 2 [S] [*of ship*] 涡流 ♦**to wash one's face/hands/hair** 洗脸/手/头发 ♦**to wash one's hands of sth/sb** 洗手不干某事/断绝与某人的关系 ♦**to wash sth out of sth** 将某物从某物上冲掉 ♦**to have a wash** 洗一下 ♦**to give sth a wash** 洗一洗某物 ♦**to be in the wash** 正在洗
❑**wash away** *vt* [+ *bridge, building, village etc*] 冲走
❑**wash down** *vt* 1 (*with wine, lager etc*) [+ *food*] 吞下 2 (*clean*) [+ *wall, path*] 冲洗
❑**wash off** *vi, vt* 洗掉
❑**wash out** I *vi* [*dye, colour* +] 洗褪色; [*dirt, stain* +] 洗掉 II *vt* [+ *tank, bucket etc*] 刷洗
❑**wash up** I *vi* 1 [英] (*wash dishes*) 洗餐具 2 [美] (*have a wash*) 洗一洗 II *vt* 1 [英] [+ *plates*] 洗 2 (*onto land*) 把…冲上岸
washbasin ['wɔʃbeɪsn] *n* [C] 脸盆
washcloth ['wɔʃklɔθ] [美] *n* [C] 毛巾 [英 = **face cloth, flannel**]
washer ['wɔʃə(r)] *n* [C] (*on tap etc*) 垫圈
washing ['wɔʃɪŋ] *n* [U] 1 (*dirty*) 待洗衣物 2 (*clean*) 洗好的衣物 ♦**to do the washing** 洗衣服
washing line [英] *n* [C] 晾衣绳
washing machine *n* [C] 洗衣机
washing powder [英] *n* [C/U] 洗衣粉 [美 = **soap powder, laundry detergent**]
washing-up [wɔʃɪŋ'ʌp] [英] *n* [U] 待洗餐具 [美 = **dirty dishes**] ♦**to do the washing-up** 洗餐具 [美 = **wash the dishes**]
washing-up liquid [英] *n* [U] 洗洁剂 [美 = **dishwashing liquid**]
washroom ['wɔʃrum] *n* [C] 盥洗室
wasn't ['wɔznt] = **was not**
wasp [wɔsp] *n* [C] 黄蜂
waste [weɪst] I *n* 1 [S/U] [*of resources, food, money*] 浪费 2 [U] (*rubbish*) 废料 II *adj* [+ *material*] 废的 III *vt* [+ *money, energy, time*] 浪费;

[+ *opportunity*] 失去 **IV wastes** *n* [*pl*] (*land*) 荒地 ♦ **what a waste!** 真可惜！♦ **it's a waste of money** 这是白费钱 ♦ **it's a waste of time** 这是浪费时间 ♦ **you're wasting your time** 你是在浪费时间 ♦ **to go to waste** 浪费掉 ♦ **to lay waste (to) sth** 毁坏某物

❑ **waste away** *vi* 消瘦下去

waste ground [英] *n* [U] 荒地

wastepaper basket ['weɪstpeɪpə-] [英] *n* [C] 废纸篓

✪ **watch** [wɔtʃ] **I** *n* [C] **1** (*wristwatch*) 手表 **2** (*guards*) 警卫 **3** (*spell of duty*) 值班 **II** *vt* **1** (*look at*) [+ *people, objects*] 注视；[+ *match, programme, TV*] 看 **2** (*spy on, guard*) 监视 **3** (*pay attention to*) 关注 **4** (*be careful of*) 留意 **III** *vi* 注视 ♦ **to keep watch** 放哨 ♦ **to keep a close watch on sb/sth** 密切注意某人/某事 ♦ **on watch** 放哨 ♦ **to be under watch** 被监视 ♦ **to watch sb do/doing sth** 看着某人做某事 ♦ **watch what you're doing/how you drive** 小心你现在做的事/小心驾驶 ♦ **watch it!** [非正式] 当心！

❑ **watch for, watch out for** *vt* [不可拆分] 留心

❑ **watch out** *vi* 提防 ♦ **watch out!** [非正式] 小心！

❑ **watch out for** *vt* [不可拆分] = **watch for**

watchdog ['wɔtʃdɔg] *n* [C] (*authority*) 监察人员

watchstrap ['wɔtʃstræp] *n* [C] 表带

✪ **water** ['wɔːtə(r)] **I** *n* [U] 水 **II** *vt* [+ *plant*] 给…浇水 **III** *vi* **1** [*eyes* +] 流泪 **2** [*mouth* +] 流口水 **IV waters** *n* [*pl*] (*area of water*) 水域 ♦ **a drink of water** 一杯水 ♦ **to pass water** 小便 ♦ **the water's edge** 水边 ♦ **in British waters** 在英国海域

❑ **water down** *vt* **1** [+ *drink, paint*] 搀水冲淡 **2** [+ *article, proposal*] 使缓和

watercolour (美 **watercolor**) ['wɔːtəkʌlə(r)] **I** *n* [C] (*painting*) 水彩画 **II watercolours** *n* [*pl*] (*paints*) 水彩颜料

watercress ['wɔːtəkrɛs] *n* [U] 水田芥

waterfall ['wɔːtəfɔːl] *n* [C] 瀑布

watering can ['wɔːtərɪŋ-] *n* [C] 喷壶

watermelon ['wɔːtəmɛlən] *n* [C] 西瓜

waterproof ['wɔːtəpruːf] *adj* 防水的

water-skiing ['wɔːtəskiːɪŋ] *n* [U] ♦ **to go water-skiing** 去滑水

water sports *n* [*pl*] 水上运动

watery ['wɔːtərɪ] *adj* **1** (*thin*) [+ *coffee, soup etc*] 稀的 **2** (*resembling water*) [+ *liquid, substance, discharge etc*] 水状的 **3** [+ *eyes*] 眼泪汪汪的 **4** (*pale*) [+ *light*] 淡淡的

watt [wɔt] *n* [C] 瓦 ♦ **a 100-watt light-bulb** 一只100瓦的灯泡

wave [weɪv] **I** *n* [C] **1** [*of hand*] 挥动 **2** (*on water*) 波浪 **3** [广播] 波 **4** (*in hair*) 拳曲 **5** [*of emotion, panic, anger*] 高涨；[*of violence, attacks, strikes*] 风潮 **II** *vi* **1** (*gesture*) 挥手示意 **2** [*branches, grass* +] 摆动；[*flag* +] 飘动 **III** *vt* **1** (*motion with*) [+ *hand*] 挥；[+ *flag, handkerchief*] 挥动 **2** (*brandish*) [+ *weapon, gun, spear*] 挥舞；[+ *letter, newspaper, photo*] 晃动 ♦ **to give sb a wave** 向某人挥挥手 ♦ **the pain came in waves** 痛感阵阵袭来 ♦ **to wave to/at sb** 对/向某人挥手 ♦ **to wave goodbye to sb, wave sb goodbye** 向某人挥手告别 ♦ **he waved me away/over** 他挥手让我离开/过来

❑ **wave aside** *vt* [+ *suggestion, objection*] 对…置之不理

wavelength ['weɪvlɛŋθ] *n* [C] [广播, 物] [*of light, sound*] 波长 ♦ **to be on the same wavelength** 和谐融洽

waver ['weɪvə(r)] *vi* **1** [*voice* +] 颤抖；[*flame, shadow* +] 摇曳 **2** [*feeling* +] 动摇 **3** (*hesitate*) [*person* +] 犹豫不决

wavy ['weɪvɪ] *adj* [+ *line*] 波浪式的；[+ *hair*] 拳曲的

wax [wæks] **I** *n* [U] **1** (*in candles, polish*) 蜡 **2** (*earwax*) 耳垢 **II** *vt* [+ *floor, car*] 给…打蜡 **III** *vi* [*moon* +] 渐圆

✪ **way** [weɪ] **I** *n* **1** [C] (*route*) 路 ◊ *A man asked me the way to St Paul's.* 有一个人问我去圣保罗教堂的路怎么走。**2** [C] (*path, access*) 路线 ◊ *This is the way in.* 这是进来的路线。**3** [S] (*distance*) 距离 ◊ *We've a fair way to go yet.* 我们还颇有一段距离要

走。4 [c] (*direction*) 方向◊ *Which way did she go?* 她朝哪个方向去了？5 [c] (*manner*) 方式◊ *She smiled in a friendly way.* 她友好地笑了笑。◊ *Do you like the way he dealt with the problem?* 你喜欢他处理这个问题的方式吗？6 [c] (*method*) 方法◊ *different ways of cooking fish* 不同的烹调鱼的方法 **II** *adv* (*far, a lot*) 远远地◊ *We'll have to decide way in advance.* 我们得早早地提前作决定。◊ *He was way behind.* 他远远落在了后面。**III ways** *n* [*pl*] (*habits*) 习俗 ♦**which way?/this way** 往哪边？/这边 ♦**on the way** 在路上 ♦**to be on one's way** 在途中 ♦**to fight one's way through a crowd** 费劲地挤过人群 ♦**to keep out of sb's way** 别去惹某人 ♦**it's a long way away** 离这儿很远 ♦**all the way/most of the way/half the way** 完全地/大部分地/一半地 ♦**to go out of one's way to do sth** 不辞辛苦地做某事 ♦**to be in the way** 挡道的 ♦**out of the way** (*finished*) 解决掉的；(*secluded*) 偏远的 ♦**to lose one's way** 迷路 ♦**under way** [*activity, project etc* +] 在进行中 ♦**the way back** 回去的路 ♦**to make way (for sb/sth)** 让位（给某人/某物） ♦**to get one's (own) way, have one's (own) way** 自主行事 ♦**to give way** (*break, collapse*) 倒塌；(*stop resisting*) 屈服 ♦**the right/wrong way up** [英]正面/反面朝上 ♦**the wrong way round** [英]刚好相反 ♦**he's in a bad way** [非正式]他健康状况不佳 ♦**you can't have it both ways** 你不能两者兼得 ♦**to have a way of doing sth** 善于做某事 ♦**in a way** 在某种程度上 ♦**in some ways** 在某些方面 ♦**no way!** [非正式]没门！♦**by the way ...** 顺便提一下… ♦**"way in"** [英]"入口" ♦**"way out"** [英]"出口" ♦**"give way"** [英]"减速让车" ♦**way of life** 生活方式 ♦**do it this way** 这么做 ♦**I had no idea you felt that way (about it)** 我不知道你（对这事）是那样想的

WC [英] *n abbr* (= ***water closet***) 厕所

✪**we** [wiː] *pl pron* 我们◊ *We live in London.* 我们住在伦敦。

weak [wiːk] *adj* **1** [+ *person, muscle, back etc*] 虚弱的；[+ *heart, voice, eyesight*] 衰弱的；[+ *object, material*] 易坏的 **2** (*morally*) [+ *person*] 懦弱的 **3** [经济] [+ *currency, pound, dollar etc*] 疲软的 **4** (*poor*) [+ *performance*] 差的；[+ *position*] 软弱的 **5** (*not convincing*) [+ *argument, evidence*] 不充分的 **6** (*low-strength*) [+ *tea, coffee, substance etc*] 淡的 **7** [+ *smile*] 淡淡的

weaken [ˈwiːkn] **I** *vi* [*resolve, person* +] 变得优柔寡断；[*influence, power* +] 变弱 **II** *vt* [+ *person*] 使虚弱；[+ *institution*] 削弱

weakness [ˈwiːknɪs] *n* **1** [c] (*frailty*) 虚弱 **2** [u] [*of system, method*] 薄弱；[*of economy, currency, market*] 疲软；[*of sound, signal*] 微弱 **3** [c] (*problem*) 缺点 ♦**to have a weakness for sth** 特别偏爱某物

wealth [wɛlθ] *n* [c] **1** (*riches*) 财富 **2** (*prosperity*) 富裕 **3** ♦**a wealth of ...** 大量的…

wealthy [ˈwɛlθɪ] **I** *adj* 富有的 **II** *n* [*pl*] ♦**the wealthy** 富人

weapon [ˈwɛpən] *n* [c] **1**（字）武器 **2**（喻）手段

wear [wɛə(r)] (*pt* **wore**, *pp* **worn**) **I** *n* [u] **1** (*use*) 使用 **2** (*damage*) 磨损 **3** (*clothing*) ♦**evening/beach wear** 晚装/沙滩装 **II** *vt* [+ *clothes, shoes*] 穿着；[+ *spectacles, jewellery*] 戴着 **III** *vi* (*become shabby*) 磨损 ♦**to wear one's hair up/long/loose** *etc* 把头发梳上去/留着长发/松散着头发{等} ♦**to wear a hole in sth** 在某物上磨出一个洞 ♦**I can't decide what to wear** 我拿不定主意该穿什么 ♦**to wear well** 经久耐用 ♦**to wear thin** [*material* +] 磨薄；[*excuse, joke* +] 渐失效力；[*patience* +] 快磨没了

❑**wear away I** *vt* 使磨损 **II** *vi* 磨损

❑**wear down** *vt* **1** [+ *heel*] 使磨薄 **2** [+ *person*] 使精疲力竭

❑**wear off** *vi* 逐渐消失

❑**wear on** *vi* 消逝

❑**wear out I** *vt* **1** [+ *shoes, clothing*] 穿破 **2** (*tire*) [非正式]使疲乏 **II** *vi* 耗尽

weary [ˈwɪərɪ] **I** *adj* (*tired*) 疲劳的

II *vi* ♦ **to weary of sb/sth** 厌烦某人/某事 ♦ **to be weary of sb/sth** 厌倦某人/某事

weasel ['wiːzl] *n* [c] 鼬

weather ['wɛðə(r)] **I** *n* [u] 天气 **II** *vt* **1** [+ *crisis*] 经受住 **2** [+ *wood, rock*] 使经风历雨 **III** *vi* 褪色 ♦ **what's the weather like?** 天气怎么样？ ♦ **under the weather** 不舒服 ♦ **to weather the storm** 经受住风暴的袭击

weather forecast *n* [c] 天气预报

weatherman ['wɛðəmæn] (*pl* **weathermen**) *n* [c] 天气预报员

weave [wiːv] (*pt* **wove**, *pp* **woven**) **I** *vt* [+ *cloth*] 织; [+ *basket*] 编 **II** *vi* (*pt, pp* ***weaved***) ♦ **to weave in and out of/among** 在…中穿进穿出/在…中迂回行进 **III** *n* [c] 织法

web [wɛb] *n* [c] **1** [*of spider*] 网 **2** [*of paths*] 网; [*of reasons, lies*] 一套 **3** ♦ **the Web** 互联网 ♦ **on the Web** 在互联网上

web page *n* [c] 网页

website ['wɛbsaɪt] *n* [c] 网址

wed [wɛd] (*pt* **wed**, *pp* **wedded** *or* **wed**) **I** *vt* 与…结婚 **II** *vi* 结婚

we'd [wiːd] = **we had, we would**

Wed(s). *abbr* (= ***Wednesday***) 星期三

wedding ['wɛdɪŋ] *n* [c] 婚礼

wedding anniversary *n* [c] 结婚纪念日

wedding day *n* [c] 婚礼日

wedding dress *n* [c] 婚纱

wedding ring *n* [c] 结婚戒指

wedge [wɛdʒ] **I** *n* [c] **1** (*under door etc*) 三角木 **2** [*of cheese, cake etc*] 楔形 **3** (*tool*) 楔子 **II** *vt* **1** ♦ **to wedge sth open/shut** 顶住某物使之开着/关着 **2** (*push*) ♦ **to wedge sth in sth** 将某物楔入某物 ♦ **to be wedged (in) between** 被紧紧地夹在…中间 ♦ **to drive a wedge between** 在…之间挑拨离间

Wednesday ['wɛnzdɪ] *n* [c/u] 星期三 *see also* **Tuesday**

wee [wiː] **I** *adj* [苏格兰] 很小的 **II** *vi* [英:非正式] 撒尿 **III** *n* [c] [英:非正式] **1** (*urine*) 尿 **2** (*act*) 撒尿 ♦ **to have a wee** [英:非正式] 去小便

weed [wiːd] **I** *n* [c] **1** (*plant*) 杂草 **2** [非正式, 贬] (*person*) 孱弱的人 **II** *vt* [+ *garden*] 给…除杂草

❑ **weed out** *vt* 淘汰

weedkiller ['wiːdkɪlə(r)] *n* [c/u] 除草剂

✪ **week** [wiːk] *n* [c] **1** 星期 ◊ *I had a letter from my mother last week.* 上星期我收到一封我母亲的信。 **2** (*working week*) 工作周 ◊ *workers on a three-day week* 实行3天制工作周的工人 **3** (*Monday to Friday*) ♦ **the week** 工作日 ♦ **this/next/last week** 本/下/上周 ♦ **once/twice a week** 一周一次/两次 ♦ **in two weeks' time** 在两周后 ♦ **a week today/on Friday** 下星期的今天/下星期五 ♦ **during the week** 在工作日期间

weekday ['wiːkdeɪ] *n* [c] 工作日 ♦ **on weekdays** 在工作日

weekend [wiːk'ɛnd] *n* [c] 周末 ♦ **at the weekend** 在周末 ♦ **this/next/last weekend** 这个周末/下周末/上周末

weekly ['wiːklɪ] **I** *adv* 每周 **II** *adj* [+ *newspaper, magazine*] 每周一期的; [+ *payment, meeting, visit etc*] 按周的 **III** *n* [c] **1** (*newspaper*) 周报 **2** (*magazine*) 周刊

weep [wiːp] (*pt, pp* **wept**) **I** *vi* **1** [*person* +] 哭泣 **2** [*wound* +] 渗出液体 **II** *n* [c] ♦ **to have a weep** 大哭一场

weigh [weɪ] **I** *vt* **1** [+ *parcel, baby, flour*] 称…的重量 **2** (*consider*) [+ *evidence, facts, risks etc*] 权衡 **II** *vi* ♦ **she weighs 50kg** 她的体重为50公斤 ♦ **how much do you weigh?** 你有多重？ ♦ **to weigh on sb** 使某人心情沉重 ♦ **to weigh anchor** 起锚

❑ **weigh down** *vt* **1** (*physically*) 压垮 **2** (*with worry, problems*) ♦ **to be weighed down with** *or* **by sth** 深受某事重压之苦

❑ **weigh out** *vt* 称出

❑ **weigh up** [尤英] *vt* [+ *evidence, alternatives*] 掂量; [+ *person*] 评价

weight [weɪt] **I** *n* **1** [u] 重量 **2** [c] (*heavy object*) 重物 **3** [c] (*for scales*) 砝码 **4** [c] (*problem, responsibility*) 重压 **II** *vt* ♦ **to be weighted in favour of sb/sth** 设置得有利于某人/某事 **III** **weights** *n* [*pl*] (*in gym*) 举重器械 ♦ **sold by weight** 按分量出售

♦**to lose weight** 体重减轻 ♦**to put on weight** 体重增加 ♦**to throw one's weight behind sth/sb** 全力支持某事/某人 ♦**to pull one's weight** 做好本分工作 ♦**weights and measures** 度量衡
❑**weight down** *vt* 压住

weightlifting ['weɪtlɪftɪŋ] *n* [U] 举重

weir [wɪə(r)] *n* [C] 堰

weird [wɪəd] *adj* [+ *object, situation, effect*] 奇特的; [+ *person*] 古怪的

welcome ['wɛlkəm] **I** *adj* [+ *visitor, news, change etc*] 受欢迎的 **II** *n* [C] 欢迎 **III** *vt* **1** [+ *visitor, speaker etc*] 欢迎 **2** [+ *news, change etc*] 欢迎 ♦**welcome to Beijing!** 欢迎到北京来! ♦**to make sb (feel) welcome** 使某人(感到)受欢迎 ♦**to be welcome to do sth** 欢迎做某事 ♦**"thank you" – "you're welcome!"** "谢谢你。" "别客气!" ♦**to give sb a warm welcome** 热烈欢迎某人

weld [wɛld] **I** *vt* 焊接 **II** *n* [C] 焊接点 ♦**to weld sth to sth** 将某物同某物结合起来

welder ['wɛldə(r)] *n* [C] 焊工

welfare ['wɛlfɛə(r)] **I** *n* [U] **1** (*well-being*) 幸福 **2** [美] (*social aid*) 福利救济 [英 = **social security**] **II** *cpd* [复合词] [+ *system, services*] 福利的

welfare state *n* ♦**the welfare state** 福利国家

✪**well** [wɛl] **I** *n* [C] **1** (*for water*) 井 **2** (*oil well*) 油井 **II** *adv* **1** (*to a high standard*) 好 ◊ *She speaks French well.* 她法语说得好。**2** (*completely*) 充分地 ◊ *Mix all the ingredients well.* 将所有的配料充分混合。◊ *I don't know him well.* 我不是很了解他。**3** (*emphatic*) (*with adv, adj, phrase*) 很 ◊ *The film is well worth seeing.* 这部电影很值得一看。**III** *adj* (*healthy*) 身体好的 ◊ *He's not very well.* 他身体不太好。**IV** *vi* [*tears* +] 涌上 **V** *int* 唔 ◊ *Well! I don't know what to say to that.* 唔,我不知道对此该说些什么。♦**to do well** [*person* +] 做得好; [*business* +] 进展顺利 ♦**well done!** 棒极了! ♦**well done** [+ *meat*] 煮得老的 ♦**he did as well as he could** 他尽可能做得好 ♦**how well do you know him?** 你对他有多了解? ♦**as well** (*in addition*) 也 ♦**X as well as Y** (*in addition to*) 除了Y还有X ♦**you might** *or* **may as well tell me** 你还是告诉我吧 ♦**you may** *or* **could well be right** 你很可能是对的 ♦**it's just as well** 幸好 ♦**well and truly** 确实地 ♦**I don't feel well** 我觉得不舒服 ♦**get well soon!** 早日康复! ♦**well, as I was saying ...** 那么,像我刚才所说的… ♦**oh well** 噢,那好吧
❑**well up** *vi* [*tears, emotions etc* +] 涌上

we'll [wi:l] = **we will, we shall**

well-behaved ['wɛlbɪ'heɪvd] *adj* 行为端正的

well-being ['wɛl'bi:ɪŋ] *n* [U] 康乐

well-built ['wɛl'bɪlt] *adj* [+ *person*] 体格健美的

well-dressed ['wɛl'drɛst] *adj* 穿着考究的

wellington ['wɛlɪŋtənz] [尤英] *n* [C] (*also:* ***wellington boot***) 橡胶长统靴 [美 = **rubber boot**]

well-known ['wɛl'nəun] *adj* [+ *person*] 有名的; [+ *fact, brand*] 众所周知的 ♦**to be well-known for sth** 因某事而著名 ♦**it is well-known that ...** …是众所周知的
📖 用法参见 **famous**

well-off ['wɛl'ɔf] *adj* 富裕的

well-paid ['wɛl'peɪd] *adj* [+ *person*] 报酬优厚的; [+ *job*] 高薪的

welly ['wɛlɪ] [英:非正式] *n* [C] 橡胶长统靴 [美 = **rubber boot**]

Welsh [wɛlʃ] **I** *adj* 威尔士的 **II** *n* [U] (*language*) 威尔士语 **III** *n* [*pl*] ♦**the Welsh** 威尔士人

Welshman ['wɛlʃmən] (*pl* **Welshmen**) *n* [C] 威尔士男子

Welshwoman ['wɛlʃwumən] (*pl* **Welshwomen**) *n* [C] 威尔士女子

went [wɛnt] *pt of* **go**

wept [wɛpt] *pt, pp of* **weep**

were [wə:(r)] *pt of* **be**

we're [wɪə(r)] = **we are**

weren't [wə:nt] = **were not**

✪**west** [wɛst] **I** *n* **1** [U/S] (*direction*) 西方 **2** ♦**the West** [政治] 西方国家 **II** *adj* 西部的 **III** *adv* 向西 ♦**the west of Ireland** 爱尔兰西部 ♦**to**

the west 以西 ♦**the west wind** 西风 ♦**west of** … 以西◊ *It's 15 miles or so west of Oxford.* 它位于牛津以西15英里左右。

western ['wɛstən] **I** *adj* **1** [地理] 西部的 **2** [政治] 西方国家的 **II** *n* [c] 西部影片

West Indian I *adj* 西印度群岛的 **II** *n* [c] 西印度群岛人

West Indies [-'ɪndɪz] *n* [*pl*] ♦**the West Indies** 西印度群岛

westward(s) ['wɛstwəd(z)] *adv* 向西

wet [wɛt] **I** *adj* **1** [+ *person, clothes*] 湿的; [+ *paint, cement, glue*] 未干的 **2** (*rainy*) [+ *weather, day*] 多雨的 **II** *n* [c] [英:政治] 采取自由主义的保守党成员 **III** *vt* (*dampen*) 把…弄湿 ♦**soaking wet** 湿透了 ♦**to get wet** 弄湿 ♦**to get sth wet** 把某物弄湿 ♦**his face was wet with tears** 他泪流满面 ♦**"wet paint"** "油漆未干" ♦**wet blanket** 扫兴的人 ♦**to wet one's pants** *or* **o.s.** 尿裤子 ♦**to wet the bed** 尿床

wet suit *n* [c] 紧身潜水衣

we've [wiːv] = **we have**

whack [wæk] *vt* 猛击

whale [weɪl] *n* [c] 鲸

wharf [wɔːf] (*pl* **wharves**) *n* [c] 码头

✪ **what**

KEYWORD

[wɔt]

I *pron*

1 (*interrogative*) (*subject, object, object of prep*) 什么 ♦**what is happening?** 发生了什么事? ♦**what is it?** 那是什么? ♦**what are you doing?** 你在干什么? ♦**what are you talking about?** 你在说什么? ♦**what?, what did you say?** 什么? ♦**what about me?** 那我呢? ♦**what about going to a movie?** 去看电影怎么样?

2 (*in indirect questions/speech*) (*subject, object*) 什么 ♦**do you know what's happening?** 你知道发生了什么事吗? ♦**tell me what he said** 告诉我他说了什么

3 (*relative*) 所…的 ♦**I saw what was on the table** 我看见了桌上的东西 ♦**what you say is wrong** 你所说的是错的

II *adj*

1 (*interrogative, in indirect questions/speech*) 什么 ♦**what time is it?** 几点了? ♦**what size is this shirt?** 这件衬衫是几码的? ♦**what number do I dial?** 我要拨什么号码? ♦**what books do you need?** 你需要什么书?

2 (*in exclamations*) 多么 ♦**what a mess!** 真是一团糟! ♦**what a lovely day!** 多么好的天气啊! ♦**what a fool I am!** 我真是个傻子!

III *int* (*disbelieving*) 什么 ♦**what, no coffee!** 什么,没咖啡了!

> 📖 对某人或某事物的外表或外形特征进行提问时,应该用**what**或**like**引导的问句,而不能用**how**引导的问句。例如,*How is Susan?*,可以用来询问**Susan**的健康状况。如果想知道她的外貌,则应问*What does Susan look like?*如果想了解她的个性,可以问*What is Susan like?*

whatever [wɔt'ɛvə(r)] **I** *adj* (*any*) 任何的 **II** *conj* (*no matter what*) 无论什么 **III** *adv* (*whatsoever*) 任何 **IV** *pron* **1** (*indicating vagueness*) 不论什么 **2** (*what*) 究竟什么 **3** ♦**do whatever is necessary/you want** 做任何必要的/你想做的事情 ♦**whatever happens** 无论发生什么 ♦**no reason whatever** 没有任何原因 ♦**nothing whatever** 根本没有什么

whatsoever [wɔtsəu'ɛvə(r)] *adv* = **whatever**

wheat [wiːt] *n* [U] 小麦

wheel [wiːl] **I** *n* [c] **1** 轮 **2** (*also:* ***steering wheel***) 方向盘 **3** (*on ship*) 舵轮 **II** *vt* 推 **III** *vi* ♦**to wheel around** 猛地转过身 ♦**at the wheel** 正在开车

wheelbarrow ['wiːlbærəu] *n* [c] 独轮车

wheelchair ['wiːltʃɛə(r)] *n* [c] 轮椅

wheel clamp [英] *n* [c] 车轮固定夹 [美= **Denver boot**]

wheeze [wiːz] **I** *vi* 气喘 **II** *n* [C] [英:过时,非正式] (*scheme*) 巧妙主意

✪ **when**
KEYWORD
[wɛn]
I *adv* (*interrogative*) 什么时候 ♦ **when did it happen?** 什么时候发生的?
II *pron* (*relative*) ♦ **the day when** 当…的那一天
III *conj*
1 (*in time clauses*) 当…时 ♦ **when you've read it, tell me what you think** 当你读过之后,告诉我你是怎么想的 ♦ **be careful when you cross the road** 过马路时要当心 ♦ **that was when we needed you** 那是我们需要你的时候 ♦ **she was reading when I came in** 当我进来时她正在阅读 ♦ **I know when it happened** 我知道什么时候发生的
2 (*whereas*) 而 ♦ **you said I was wrong when in fact I was right** 你说我是错的而事实上我是对的
3 (*considering*) 既然 ♦ **why did you buy that when you can't afford it?** 既然你买不起为什么还要买?

whenever [wɛn'ɛvə(r)] **I** *conj* **1** (*any time that*) 无论何时 **2** (*every time that*) 每当 **3** (*showing uncertainty*) 任何什么时候 **II** *adv* 随便什么时候

✪ **where** [wɛə(r)] **I** *adv* (*in or to what place*) 在哪里 ◊ *Where's Jane?* 简在哪里? **II** *conj* **1** (*the place in which*) 哪里 ◊ *Do you know where he is?* 你知道他在哪里吗? ◊ *People looked to see where the noise was coming from.* 人们想弄清噪音是从哪里传来的。**2** (*relating to phase*) 在…阶段 ◊ *The government is at a stage where it is willing to talk.* 政府正处于乐于进行会谈的阶段。*That's where you're wrong!* 那就是你的错误所在! **3** (*whereas*) 然而 ◊ *Sometimes a teacher will be listened to, where a parent might not.* 有时老师的话听得进去,而父母的可能就不行了。♦ **where are you from?** 你是哪里人? ♦ **where will it all end?** 到哪儿才是个头? ♦ **this is where ...** (字) 这是…的地方; (喻) 这是…之处 ♦ **where possible** 如有可能的话

whereabouts [*adv* wɛərə'bauts, *n* 'wɛərəbauts] **I** *adv* 在哪里 **II** *n* ♦ **the whereabouts of sb/sth** 某人的下落/某物的所在

whereas [wɛər'æz] *conj* 而

whereby [wɛə'baɪ] *adv* ♦ **a system whereby we ...** 我们借以…的一种制度

wherever [wɛər'ɛvə(r)] **I** *conj* **1** (*no matter where*) 无论在哪里 **2** (*not knowing where*) 不管在哪里 **II** *adv* (*showing surprise*) 究竟在哪里 ♦ **sit wherever you like** 你喜欢坐哪儿就坐哪儿

✪ **whether** ['wɛðə(r)] *conj* 是否 ◊ *I can't tell whether she loves me or she hates me.* 我搞不清她是爱我还是恨我。♦ **I don't know whether to accept or not** 我不知道是接受还是不接受 ♦ **whether we like it or not** 无论我们喜欢与否 ♦ **it's doubtful whether ...** 是否…还不肯定

✪ **which**
KEYWORD
[wɪtʃ]
I *adj*
1 (*interrogative*) (*singular*) 哪个; (*plural*) 哪些 ♦ **which picture do you want?** 你要哪幅画? ♦ **which books are yours?** 哪些书是你的? ♦ **which one/ones?** 哪个/些? ♦ **which one of you did it?** 你们中的哪个人做的?
2 (*in indirect questions/speech*) (*singular*) 哪个; (*plural*) 哪些 ♦ **he asked which book I wanted** 他问我要哪本书
3 (*relative*) ♦ **in which case** 在这种情况下 ♦ **by which time** 到那时为止
II *pron*
1 (*interrogative*) (*subject, object*) 哪个 ♦ **which of these is yours?** 这些中的哪个是你的? ♦ **which of you are coming?** 你们中的哪些人会来? ♦ **which do you want?** (*singular*) 你要哪个?; (*plural*) 你要哪些?
2 (*in indirect questions/speech*) (*subject, object*) 哪个 ♦ **ask him which of the**

models is the best 问他哪种型号是最好的 ♦**tell me which you want** *(singular)* 告诉我你要哪个; *(plural)* 告诉我你要哪些 ♦**I don't mind which** 哪个都行
3 *(relative) (subject, object)* …的那个… ♦**the shot which you heard/which killed him** 你听到的那一枪/杀死他的那一枪 ♦**the chair on which you are sitting** 你正坐着的那把椅子 ♦**he said he knew, which is true** 他说他知道，事实的确如此 ♦**after which** 在那以后

whichever [wɪtʃ'ɛvə(r)] **I** *adj (any... that)* 无论哪个 **II** *pron* 1 *(no matter which)* 无论哪个 2 *(specifying)* …的那一个 ♦**whichever way you look at it** 无论你以何种方式看待它

✪**while** [waɪl] **I** *n* [s] 一会儿 ◊ *a book that I read a little while ago* 我不久前刚看的一本书 **II** *conj* 1 *(at the same time as)* 当…的时候 ◊ *While I was in London she was in Paris.* 当我在伦敦的时候，她在巴黎。
2 *(during the time that)* 在…时 ◊ *Someone opened the door while he was making his speech.* 在他演讲时有人打开了门。3 *(although)* 虽然 ◊ *While I'm very fond of him, I don't actually want to marry him.* 虽然我很喜欢他，但我真的不想嫁给他。4 *(but)* 而 ◊ *The first two services are free, while the third costs £35.* 头两次服务是免费的，而第3次要花费35镑。♦**for a while** 有一会儿 ♦**in a while** 过一会儿 ♦**all the while** 一直
❑**while away** *vt* 消磨 ◊ *They whiled away the hours telling stories.* 他们讲故事以消磨时间。

whilst [waɪlst] *conj* = **while**

whim [wɪm] *n* [c] 一时的兴致 ♦**on a whim** 一时心血来潮 ♦**at the whim of** 由…随心所欲地

whimper ['wɪmpə(r)] **I** *n* [c] 呜咽声 **II** *vi* 呜咽 ♦**without a whimper** *(without complaining)* 一声不吭地

whine [waɪn] **I** *n* [c] 1 *[from person, animal]* 哀鸣 2 *[of engine, siren]* 呜呜声 **II** *vi* 1 *[person, animal +]* 哀叫
2 *[engine, siren +]* 发呜呜声
3 *(complain)* 发牢骚 ♦**to whine about sth** 没完没了地抱怨某事

whip [wɪp] **I** *n* [c] 1 *(for hitting)* 鞭子; *(riding crop)* 马鞭 2 [政治] *(person)* 组织秘书 **II** *vt* 1 *(hit)* [+ *person, animal*] 鞭打 2 *(beat)* [+ *cream, eggs*] 搅打
3 *(snatch)* ♦**to whip sth out/off/away** 猛地掏出/脱下/拿走
4 ♦**to whip sb into hysteria/a frenzy** 煽动得某人歇斯底里/如痴如狂
❑**whip up** *vt* 1 [+ *cream*] 搅打 2 [非正式] [+ *meal, dress*] 迅速做好
3 [+ *support, hatred, hysteria etc*] 煽动

whipped cream [wɪpt-] *n* [U] 泡沫奶油

whirl [wəːl] **I** *vt* 使旋转 **II** *vi* [*snow, leaves etc* +] 回旋; [*dancer, object* +] 旋转 **III** *n* [s] [*of activity, pleasure*] 一连串 ♦**her mind** *or* **head is in a whirl** 她的思绪一片纷乱 ♦**to give sth a whirl** [非正式] *(try)* 试一试某事
❑**whirl around I** *vi* 1 *(turn)* 猛地转身 2 *(move)* [*dancer* +] 旋转起舞; [*snow, leaves etc* +] 飞旋 **II** *vt* 使旋转

whisk [wɪsk] **I** *n* [c] 打蛋器 **II** *vt* [+ *cream, eggs*] 搅打 ♦**to whisk sb away** *or* **off** 飞快地把某人送走

whiskers ['wɪskəz] *n* [*pl*] [*of animal*] 须; [*of man*] 髯

whisky (美 **whiskey**) ['wɪskɪ] *n* [c/U] 威士忌酒

whisper ['wɪspə(r)] **I** *n* [c] 1 低语
2 [文] [*of wind, leaves*] 沙沙声 **II** *vi* 低语 **III** *vt* 悄声说出 ♦**to say sth/speak in a whisper** 小声说某事/小声说话 ♦**to whisper sth to sb** 低声对某人说某事

whistle ['wɪsl] **I** *vi* 1 [*person* +] *(melodiously)* 吹口哨; *(in surprise)* 吹了声口哨; [*bird* +] 啭鸣 2 [*kettle, train* +] 鸣笛 3 [*bullet* +] 呼啸而行 **II** *vt* [+ *tune*] 用口哨吹出 **III** *n* [c]
1 *(device)* 哨子 2 *(sound)* 口哨声

✪**white** [waɪt] **I** *adj* 1 雪白的; [+ *wine*] 白的 2 *(with milk)* [+ *coffee*] 加奶的
3 [+ *person*] *(racially)* 白种人的; *(with fear, anger, illness etc)* 苍白的 **II** *n*
1 [U] *(colour)* 白色 ◊ *A woman dressed in white came up to me.* 一位身穿白色衣服的女子朝我走来。2 [c] *(person)* 白人 3 [c/U] [*of egg*] 蛋白
4 [c] [*of eye*] 眼白 **III whites** *n* [*pl*] *(washing)* 白色衣物 ♦**to go white**

(*with fear, anger, illness etc*) 脸色变得煞白; (*lose hair colour*) [*person, hair* +] 头发变白

white coffee [英] *n* [C/U] 加奶咖啡

White House *n* ♦ **the White House** 白宫

whitewash ['waɪtwɔʃ] **I** *n* **1** [U] (*paint*) 白涂料 **2** [C/U] (*cover-up*) 粉饰 **3** [C] [非正式: 体育] 得零分的惨败 **II** *vt* **1** (*paint*) 粉刷 **2** (*cover up*) 粉饰

whiting ['waɪtɪŋ] (*pl* **whitings** *or* **whiting**) *n* [C/U] 牙鳕

whittle ['wɪtl] *vt* ♦ **to whittle sth down/away** 削减/消耗某物

whizz [wɪz] *vi* ♦ **to whizz past (sth)** 飕飕地飞过(某物)

WHO *n abbr* (= ***World Health Organization***) ♦ **the WHO** 国际卫生组织

✪ **who**

KEYWORD

[huː] *pron*

1 (*interrogative*) (*subject, object, object of prep*) 谁 ♦ **who is it?** 是谁? ♦ **who's there?** 是谁? ♦ **who are you?** 你是谁? ♦ **who did you call?** 你给谁打电话了? ♦ **who did you discuss it with?** 你和谁讨论了?

2 (*in indirect questions/speech*) (*subject, object, after preposition*) 谁 ♦ **I told her who I was** 我告诉了她我是谁 ♦ **can you tell me who lives here?** 你能告诉我谁住在这儿吗? ♦ **tell me who you invited** 告诉我你邀请了谁 ♦ **I don't know who he gave it to** 我不知道他把它给了谁

3 (*relative*) (*subject, object*) …的那个… ♦ **the girl who came in** 进来的那个女孩 ♦ **the man who we met in Sydney** 我们在悉尼遇到的那个男子 ♦ **my cousin who lives in New York** 我住在纽约的表亲 ♦ **Nicole, who you've met, is getting married** 你所见过的那个尼科尔, 就要结婚了

whoever [huː'ɛvə(r)] *pron* **1** (*the person who*) 谁 **2** (*anyone*) 无论谁 **3** (*no matter who*) 不管什么人 **4** (*in questions*) (*who*) ♦ **whoever told you that?** 那事究竟是谁告诉你的?

✪ **whole** [həul] **I** *adj* **1** (*entire*) (字) 整个的 ◊ *We spent the whole summer in Italy.* 我们整个夏天都是在意大利过的。; (喻) (*emphatic*) 完全的 ◊ *a whole new way of doing business* 一个全新的商业运作方式 **2** (*unbroken*) 完整的 ◊ *He swallowed it whole.* 他把它完整地吞了下去。 **II** *n* **1** [C] (*entirety*) 整体 **2** ♦ **the whole of sth** 某物的全部 ♦ **the whole (of the) time** 所有的时间 ♦ **the whole lot (of it)** 全部 ♦ **the whole lot (of them)** 全部 ♦ **as a whole** 整个看来 ♦ **on the whole** 大体上

wholefood(s) ['həulfuːd(z)] *n* [*pl*] [尤英] 天然食品

wholeheartedly [həul'hɑːtɪdlɪ] *adv* [*agree, support etc* +] 全心全意地

wholemeal ['həulmiːl] [英] *adj* [+ *bread, flour, pasta*] 全麦的

wholesale ['həulseɪl] **I** *n* [C] 批发 **II** *adj* **1** [+ *price, market*] 批发的 **2** (*widespread*) 大规模的 **III** *adv* [*buy, sell* +] 以批发价

wholesome ['həulsəm] *adj* **1** [+ *food*] 健康的 **2** (*innocent*) 健康向上的

wholewheat ['həulwiːt] *adj* = **wholemeal**

wholly ['həulɪ] *adv* 完全地

whom [huːm] [正式] *pron* **1** (*interrogative*) 谁 **2** (*relative*) 所…的那个… ♦ **whom did you see?** 你见到谁了? ♦ **to whom did you give it?** 你把它给谁了? ♦ **tell me from whom you received it** 告诉我你从谁那儿得来的 ♦ **the man whom I saw/to whom I spoke** 我见到的/我跟他说过话的那个男的 ♦ **her brother, whom you've met, is a gifted pianist** 你所见过的她哥哥, 是位有天赋的钢琴家

whore [hɔː(r)] [非正式, 贬] *n* [C] 娼妓

✪ **whose** [huːz] **I** *adj* **1** (*interrogative*) 谁的 **2** (*relative*) …的 **II** *pron* 谁的 ♦ **whose is this?** 这是谁的? ♦ **whose are these?** 这些是谁的? ♦ **whose book is this/coats are these?** 这本书是谁的/这些外套是谁的? ♦ **whose tent did you borrow?** 你借了谁的帐篷?

♦**the woman whose car was stolen** 汽车给偷走的那个女的 ♦**Jane Smith, whose voice you liked so much, is performing live** 她的嗓音为你所喜欢的简·史密斯，正在做现场表演 ♦**I know whose it is** 我知道这是谁的

✪ **why**

KEYWORD

[waɪ]

I *adv* 为什么 ♦**why is he always late?** 为什么他总是迟到？♦**why not?** 为什么不呢？♦**why not do it now?** 为什么不现在做呢？♦**I don't know why** 我不知道为什么 ♦**can you tell me the reason why?** 你能告诉我为什么吗？

II *conj* 为什么 ♦**I wonder why he said that** 我想知道他为什么那么说 ♦**the reason why he did it** 他那么做的原因 ♦**that's not the reason why I'm here** 那不是我在这儿的原因

III *int* (*expressing surprise, shock, annoyance*) 嗯; (*explaining*) 那么 ♦**why, it's you!** 呦，是你呀！♦**why, that's impossible!** 嗯，那是不可能的！♦**"I don't understand" – "why, it's obvious!"** "我不明白" "嗨，这是显而易见的！"

wicked ['wɪkɪd] *adj* **1** (*evil*) [+ *person*] 邪恶的; [+ *act, crime*] 罪恶的 **2** (*mischievous*) [+ *smile, sense of humour*] 顽皮的 **3** [非正式] (*terrible*) 可怕的

wicket ['wɪkɪt] *n* [c] **1** (*stumps*) 三柱门 **2** (*area*) 三柱门之间的场地 ♦**to take a wicket** 使一个击球员出局

✪ **wide** [waɪd] **I** *adj* **1** [+ *road, river, area etc*] 宽的 **2** [+ *range, variety, publicity, choice etc*] 广泛的 **II** *adv* ♦**to open sth wide** [+ *window, mouth*] 张大某物 ♦**to go wide** [*shot etc* +] 打偏 ♦**how wide is it?** 它有多宽？♦**it's 3 metres wide** 它有3米宽

widely ['waɪdlɪ] *adv* **1** [*differ, vary* +] 大大地; [*travel* +] 范围广地 **2** [+ *spaced, separated*] 相距远地 **3** [+ *believed, known*] 广泛地 ♦**to be widely read** 博览群书

widen ['waɪdn] **I** *vt* **1** [+ *road, river etc*] 拓宽 **2** [+ *experience, horizons etc*] 扩展 **3** [+ *gap, difference etc*] 扩大 **II** *vi* **1** [*road, river etc* +] 变宽 **2** [*gap, difference etc* +] 扩大

wide open *adj* [+ *eyes, mouth*] 大张的; [+ *window*] 大开的

widespread ['waɪdsprɛd] *adj* [+ *use, practice, belief, feeling*] 分布广的; [+ *support, opposition*] 普遍的

widow ['wɪdəu] *n* [c] 寡妇

widowed ['wɪdəud] *adj* 丧偶的

widower ['wɪdəuə(r)] *n* [c] 鳏夫

width [wɪdθ] *n* **1** [c/u] 宽度 **2** [c] (*in swimming pool*) 池宽 ♦**it's 7 metres in width** 它的宽度为7米

wield [wiːld] *vt* **1** [+ *sword, knife*] 持 **2** [+ *power, influence*] 行使

✪ **wife** [waɪf] (*pl* **wives**) *n* [c] 妻子

wig [wɪg] *n* [c] 假发; (*worn in court*) 假发套

wiggle ['wɪgl] **I** *vt, vi* 扭动 **II** *n* [c] 扭动

wild [waɪld] **I** *adj* **1** [+ *animal, plant*] 野生的 **2** (*uncultivated*) [+ *area*] 荒芜的 **3** [+ *weather, sea*] 暴风雨的 **4** [+ *person, behaviour*] 狂野的 **5** [非正式] (*angry*) 愤怒的 **6** [+ *idea, guess*] 轻率的 **7** [+ *applause, cheers*] 狂热的 **II** *n* ♦**in the wild** 在野生状态下 **III the wilds** *n* [*pl*] 偏僻地区 ♦**to run wild** 毫无管束 ♦**I'm not wild about it** [非正式] 我对此无多大兴趣 ♦**the audience went wild** 观众变得非常狂热

wilderness ['wɪldənɪs] *n* [c] 荒野

wildlife ['waɪldlaɪf] *n* [u] 野生动物

wildly ['waɪldlɪ] *adv* **1** [*applaud, cheer* +] 狂热地 **2** [*wave, shake* +] 剧烈地 **3** (*very*) [+ *different, successful, optimistic etc*] 极度地 **4** (*very much*) [*vary, fluctuate* +] 极大地

✪ **will**

KEYWORD

[wɪl]

I *aux vb*

1 (*forming future tense*) ♦**I will call you tonight** 我今晚会给你打电话的 ♦**what will you do next?** 下面你要做什么？♦**will you do it? – yes I will/no I won't** 你会做吗？–是的，我会的/不，我不会 ♦**I**

will have finished it by tomorrow 我明天前可以做完
2 (*in conjectures, predictions*) 该是 ♦ **he'll be there by now** 他现在该到了 ♦ **that will be the postman** 那准是邮差 ♦ **he will have left by now** 他现在一定已经离开了
3 (*in commands, requests, offers*) ♦ **will you be quiet!** 你安静点！♦ **will you help me?** 你帮帮我好吗？♦ **will you have a cup of tea?** 你要来杯茶吗？
4 (*be prepared to*) 会 ♦ **I won't put up with it!** 我不会容忍它的！
5 (*characteristic behaviour*) 会 ♦ **it will dissolve in water** 它会溶解在水中
6 (*emphatic annoyance*) 总是 ♦ **he *will* leave the gate open** 他总是开着门
II *vt* ♦ **to will sb to do sth** 用意志力促成某人做某事 ♦ **he willed himself to go on** 他尽力使自己继续
III *n*
1 (*volition*) 意志 ♦ **she lost her will to live** 她失去了活下去的意志 ♦ **against his will** 违背他的意愿
2 (*testament*) 遗嘱 ♦ **to make a will** 立遗嘱

willing ['wɪlɪŋ] *adj* 1 ♦ **to be willing to do sth** 愿意做某事 2 (*enthusiastic*) 热切的 3 [+ *helper, participant etc*] 积极肯干的 ♦ **to show willing** 表现得乐意
willingly ['wɪlɪŋlɪ] *adv* 乐意地
willingness ['wɪlɪŋnɪs] *n* [c] 1 (*readiness*) 愿意 2 (*enthusiasm*) 热切
willow ['wɪləu] *n* 1 [c] (*tree*) 柳树 2 [u] (*wood*) 柳木
willpower ['wɪl'pauə(r)] *n* [u] 意志力
wilt [wɪlt] *vi* 枯萎
✪ **win** [wɪn] (*pt, pp* **won**) I *n* [c] 胜利 II *vt* 1 [+ *game, fight, argument, election*] 在…中获胜 2 [+ *prize, medal*] 赢得；[+ *support, popularity, order*] 获得 III *vi* 获胜
❑ **win over** *vt* [+ *person*] 争取过来
❑ **win round** [英] *vt* = **win over**
wince [wɪns] I *vi* 咧嘴 II *n* [c] 咧嘴
wind[1] [wɪnd] I *n* 1 [c/u] 风 2 [u] (*flatulence*) 肠胃气胀 3 [u] (*breath*) 呼吸 II *vt* 使呼吸困难 ♦ **into or against the wind** 逆风 ♦ **to get wind of sth** [非正式] 听到某事的风声 ♦ **the wind (section)** [音] 管乐器(部) ♦ **to break wind** 放屁
wind[2] [waɪnd] (*pt, pp* **wound**) I *vt* 1 ♦ **to wind sth around sth** [+ *rope, bandage*] 把某物绕在某物上 2 [+ *watch, clock, toy*] 给…上发条 II *vi* ♦ **to wind through/uphill** *etc* 蜿蜒穿过/上坡{等}
❑ **wind down** *vt* 1 [+ *window*] 摇下 2 (*cut back*) [+ *activity*] 逐步减少
❑ **wind up** I *vt* 1 [+ *watch, clock, toy*] 给…上发条 2 [+ *window*] 摇上 3 [+ *firm*] 停业 4 [+ *meeting, discussion*] 结束 5 [英] [非正式] (*tease*) 哄骗；(*annoy*) 烦扰 II *vi* 告终
windfall ['wɪndfɔːl] *n* [c] 1 (*money*) 意外收获 2 (*apple*) 落果
winding ['waɪndɪŋ] *adj* [+ *road, river*] 蜿蜒的 ♦ **a winding staircase** 盘旋式楼梯
wind instrument ['wɪnd-] *n* [c] 管乐器
windmill ['wɪndmɪl] *n* [c] 风车
window ['wɪndəu] *n* [c] 1 (*in house, building*) 窗户；(*in shop*) 橱窗；(*in car, train*) 窗 2 (*pane*) 窗玻璃 3 [计算机] 视窗
window box *n* [c] 窗台花箱
window cleaner *n* [c] 擦窗工人
window pane *n* [c] 窗玻璃
windowsill ['wɪndəusɪl] *n* [c] 窗台
wind power ['wɪnd-] *n* [u] 风力
windscreen ['wɪndskriːn] [英] *n* [c] 挡风玻璃 [美 = **windshield**]
windscreen wiper [-waɪpə(r)] [英] *n* [c] 挡风玻璃雨刮器 [美 = **windshield wiper**]
windshield ['wɪndʃiːld] [美] *n* [c] 挡风玻璃 [英 = **windscreen**]
windshield wiper [-waɪpə(r)] [美] *n* [c] 挡风玻璃雨刮器 [英 = **windscreen wiper**]
windsurfing ['wɪndsəːfɪŋ] *n* [u] 帆板运动
windy ['wɪndɪ] *adj* [+ *weather, day*] 有风的 ♦ **it's windy** 今天风很大
wine [waɪn] I *n* [c/u] 1 (*from grapes*) 葡萄酒 2 (*from other fruits etc*) 果酒 II *vt* ♦ **to wine and dine sb** 以酒宴款待某人

wine bar *n* [c] 酒吧
wine glass *n* [c] 酒杯
wine list *n* [c] 酒水单
wing [wɪŋ] **I** *n* [c] **1** [*of bird, insect*] 翅膀; [*of aeroplane*] 机翼 **2** [*of building*] 侧楼 **3** [*of organization*] 派系 **4** [英] [*of car*] 挡泥板 [美 = **fender**] **II the wings** *n* [*pl*] [戏剧] 舞台的侧面
winger ['wɪŋə(r)] *n* [c] 边锋
wing mirror [英] *n* [c] 侧视镜 [美 = **sideview mirror**]
wink [wɪŋk] **I** *n* [c] [*of eye*] 眨眼 **II** *vi* **1** [*person* +] 眨眼 **2** [*light* +] 闪烁 ♦ **to give sb a wink, wink at sb** 向某人眨了眨眼
winner ['wɪnə(r)] *n* [c] 获胜者
winning ['wɪnɪŋ] *adj* **1** [+ *team, entry*] 获胜的; [+ *shot, goal*] 致胜的 **2** (*attractive*) [+ *smile, personality*] 迷人的 *see also* **winnings**
winnings ['wɪnɪŋz] *n* [*pl*] 赢得的钱
winter ['wɪntə(r)] **I** *n* [c/u] 冬季 **II** *vi* 过冬 ♦ **in (the) winter** 在冬季
wipe [waɪp] **I** *vt* **1** (*dry, clean*) 擦 **2** (*remove*) 擦去 **3** (*erase*) [+ *tape*] 抹掉 **II** *n* [c] ♦ **to give sth a wipe** 把某物擦一擦 ♦ **to wipe one's nose** 揩揩鼻子
❑ **wipe away** *vt* [+ *tears*] 擦去; [+ *mark*] 除去
❑ **wipe off** *vt* 擦掉
❑ **wipe out** *vt* (*destroy*) [+ *city, population, wildlife*] 消灭
❑ **wipe up** *vt* 把…揩干净
wire ['waɪə(r)] **I** *n* **1** [c/u] (*metal*) 金属丝 **2** [c] [电子] (*uninsulated*) 电线; (*insulated*) 电缆 **3** [c] [尤美] (*telegram*) 电报 **II** *vt* **1** [美] (*with telegram*) 发电报给 **2** (*also:* **wire up**) [电子] [+ *building*] 给…布线; [+ *appliance, plug*] (*put cables in*) 给…接线; (*connect*) 给…连线
wiring ['waɪərɪŋ] *n* [u] 线路
wisdom ['wɪzdəm] *n* [u] [*of person*] 智慧; [*of action, remark*] 明智
wisdom tooth (*pl* **wisdom teeth**) *n* [c] 智齿
wise [waɪz] *adj* [+ *person*] 睿智的; [+ *action, remark*] 明智的 ♦ **I'm none the wiser** 我仍然糊里糊涂 ♦ **it would be wise to do it now** 现在去做这件事应是明智之举
❑ **wise up** [非正式] *vi* ♦ **to wise up to sth** 了解某事
wish [wɪʃ] **I** *n* [c] 愿望 **II** *vt* 但愿 ♦ **to make a wish** (*silently*) 默默地许愿; (*out loud*) 大声地许愿 ♦ **we have no wish to cause problems** 我们并不想引起麻烦 ♦ **best wishes** (*on birthday, promotion etc*) 良好的祝愿 ♦ **with best wishes** (*in letter*) 祝好 ♦ **give her my best wishes** 代我向她致意 ♦ **to wish to do sth** 想要做某事 ♦ **to wish sb goodbye/good night** 向某人告别/道晚安 ♦ **to wish sb well** 祝某人一切顺利 ♦ **to wish sth on sb** 想让某事发生在某人身上 ♦ **to wish for sth** 想望某物
wishful ['wɪʃful] *adj* ♦ **wishful thinking** 痴心妄想
wistful ['wɪstful] *adj* 憧憬的
wit [wɪt] **I** *n* **1** [u] (*wittiness*) 风趣 **2** [c] (*person*) 风趣的人 **3** [u] (*sense*) 颖悟力 **II wits** *n* [*pl*] (*intelligence*) 才智 ♦ **to be at one's wits' end** 智穷计尽 ♦ **to have one's wits about one** 保持头脑清醒
witch [wɪtʃ] *n* [c] 女巫

✪ **with**
KEYWORD
[wɪð, wɪθ] *prep*
1 (*together with, at the house of*) 和…在一起 ♦ **I was with him** 我和他在一起 ♦ **I'll be with you in a minute** 请稍等 ♦ **we'll take the children with us** 我们会带着孩子们的 ♦ **mix the sugar with the eggs** 把糖和鸡蛋混在一起 ♦ **we stayed with friends** 我们和朋友们呆在一起 ♦ **a waiter came round with some wine** 服务员拿着酒过来了 ♦ **I'm with you** [非正式] (*I understand*) 我明白你的意思 ♦ **to argue/fight/compete with sb** 与某人争论/斗争/竞争
2 (*indicating feature, possession*) 有 ♦ **a room with a view** 能观景的房间 ♦ **the man with the grey hat/blue eyes** 戴着灰帽子/有蓝眼睛的男人
3 (*indicating manner*) 带着 ♦ **with tears in her eyes** 眼睛里含着泪水地 ♦ **with a sigh/laugh** 叹了口气/笑着地 ♦ **she stood with her**

hands on her hips 她叉着腰站着
4 (*indicating means, substance*) 用 ♦**to walk with a stick** 拄着拐杖走 ♦**you can open the door with this key** 你可以用这把钥匙开门 ♦**he was covered with bruises/mud** 他满身淤伤/泥巴 ♦**to fill sth with water** 在某物里装满水
5 (*indicating cause*) ♦**red with anger** 气得涨红了脸 ♦**to shake with fear** 怕得发抖 ♦**he spent a week in bed with flu** 他因为流感卧病在床一星期
6 (*in relation to*) 后接 **with** 的动词，例如**to deal with**，**to cope with**，参阅动词。♦**to be bored/pleased with sth/sb** 因某事/某人而觉得闷/高兴 ♦**to deal/cope with sth** 对付/应付某事 ♦**to have a problem with money** 在经济上有麻烦
7 (*according to*) 随着 ♦**it will improve with time** 它会随着时间而改进

withdraw [wɪθ'drɔː] (*pt* **withdrew**, *pp* **withdrawn**) **I** *vt* **1** (*take away*) [+ *object*] 抽回 **2** [正式] (*take back*) [+ *offer, remark*] 收回 **3** ♦**to withdraw money** (*from bank*) 提款 **II** *vi* **1** [*troops* +] 撤回 **2** (*from activity, organization*) 退出 **3** (*from room*) 离开 ♦**to withdraw into o.s.** 变得孤僻

withdrawal [wɪθ'drɔːəl] *n* **1** [C/U] (*removal*) [*of troops*] 撤退; [*of offer, remark*] 收回; [*of services*] 撤销 **2** [U] (*from activity, organization*) 退出 **3** [C/U] [经济] [*of money*] 提款 **4** [U] [医] (*following addiction*) 戒毒期 **5** [U] [心理] (*uncommunicative behaviour*) 社交冷漠

withdrawn [wɪθ'drɔːn] **I** *pp of* **withdraw II** *adj* 性格内向的

wither ['wɪðə(r)] *vi* **1** [*flower, plant* +] 枯萎 **2** (*become weak*) 衰败
❑**wither away** *vi* 消亡

withhold [wɪθ'həuld] (*pt, pp* **withheld**) *vt* [+ *money, aid*] 拒给; [+ *permission*] 不给; [+ *information, facts*] 拒绝提供

✪**within** [wɪð'ɪn] **I** *prep* **1** [+ *place*] 在…里面; [+ *society, organization*] 在…内部; [+ *person*] 在…内心 **2** [+ *time, distance*] 在…之内 **3** [+ *limit, budget*] 在…限度以内 **II** *adv* (*in place, area, object*) 在里面; (*in society, organization*) 在内部 ♦**within reach (of sb)** 在(某人)伸手可及的地方 ♦**within sight (of sth)** 在看得到(某物)的地方 ♦**within the week** 在本周内 ♦**within a mile of sth** 在离某地不出一英里的地方 ♦**within an hour of his arrival** 在他到达后一小时内 ♦**within the law** 合法的

✪**without** [wɪð'aut] *prep* 没有 ♦**without a coat** 未穿外套 ♦**without speaking** 不曾说话 ♦**it goes without saying** 这不消说 ♦**without anyone knowing** 不为人知地

withstand [wɪθ'stænd] (*pt, pp* **withstood**) *vt* 经受住

witness ['wɪtnɪs] **I** *n* [C] (*gen, also in court*) 目击者; (*to document*) 联署人 **II** *vt* **1** (*see*) [+ *event*] 目击; (喻) (*experience*) 经历 **2** (*confirm*) [+ *signature*] 联署 ♦**witness for the prosecution** 控方证人 ♦**witness for the defence** 辩方证人 ♦**to be (a) witness to sth** 为某事的目击者 ♦**to bear witness to sth** 表明某事 ♦**to witness to sth** 为某事作证

witty ['wɪtɪ] *adj* 诙谐的

wives [waɪvz] *n* [*pl*] *of* **wife**

wizard ['wɪzəd] *n* [C] **1** (*with magical powers*) 男巫 **2** [非正式] (*expert*) 奇才

wk *abbr* (= ***week***) 星期

WKND [手机短信] *abbr* (= ***weekend***) 周末

WLTM *abbr* (= ***would like to meet***) 想结识

wobble ['wɔbl] *vi* [*object, table, jelly* +] 摇晃; [*person, knees* +] 颤抖

woe [wəu] **I** *n* [U] (*sorrow*) 悲哀 **II woes** *n* [*pl*] (*misfortunes*) 不幸

woke [wəuk] *pt of* **wake**

woken ['wəukn] *pp of* **wake**

wolf [wulf] (*pl* **wolves** [wulvz]) **I** *n* [C] 狼 **II** *vt* [非正式] (*also:* ***wolf down***) 狼吞虎咽地吃下

✪**woman** ['wumən] (*pl* **women**) *n* [C] 妇女 ♦**young woman** 年轻女子 ♦**woman doctor/friend** 女医生/女性朋友

womb [wuːm] *n* [c] 子宫
women ['wɪmɪn] *n* [*pl*] *of* **woman**
won [wʌn] *pt, pp of* **win**
wonder ['wʌndə(r)] **I** *n* **1** [c] (*miracle*) 奇迹 **2** [u] (*awe*) 惊奇 **II** *vt* ♦ **to wonder whether/why** *etc* 想知道是否/为什么{等} **III** *vi* 感到奇怪 ♦ **it's a wonder that ...** 奇怪的是… ♦ **(it's) no/little/small wonder that ...** (这)难怪… ♦ **to work** *or* **do wonders** 创造奇迹 ♦ **to wonder about sth** 对某事感到疑惑 ♦ **to wonder at sth** 对某事感到诧异 ♦ **I wonder if you could help me** 不知你是否可以帮我
wonderful ['wʌndəful] *adj* 绝妙的 ♦ **it's wonderful to see you** 见到你真是太好了
won't [wəunt] = **will not**
wood [wud] *n* **1** [u] 木材 **2** [c] (*forest*) 树林
wooden ['wudn] *adj* **1** [+ *object*] 木制的 **2** (喻) [+ *performance, actor*] 呆板的
woodwind ['wudwɪnd] *adj* [+ *instrument*] 木管乐器的 ♦ **the woodwind (section)** [音] 木管乐器(部)
woodwork ['wudwəːk] *n* [u] **1** (*craft*) 木工手艺 **2** (*wooden parts*) 木制品
wool [wul] *n* [u] 羊毛 ♦ **to pull the wool over sb's eyes** 蒙骗某人
woollen (美 **woolen**) ['wulən] *adj* 羊毛的
woolly (美 **wooly**) ['wulɪ] *adj* **1** [+ *socks, hat etc*] 羊毛的 **2** (*confused*) [+ *ideas, person*] 糊涂的
✪ **word** [wəːd] **I** *n* **1** [c] 词 **2** [s] (*promise*) 诺言 **3** [u/s] (*news*) 消息 **II** *vt* 措辞 ♦ **what's the word for "pen" in French?** "钢笔"这个词在法语里怎么说? ♦ **word for word** (*verbatim*) 一字不变地; (*in translation*) 逐字地 ♦ **to put sth into words** 用语言表达某事 ♦ **not a word** 一句也不 ♦ **in a word** 简而言之 ♦ **in other words** 换句话说 ♦ **to have a word (with sb)** (和某人)谈谈 ♦ **to have words (with sb)** (和某人)争论 ♦ **I'll take your word for it** 我相信你说的话 ♦ **by word of mouth** 口头地 ♦ **a word of warning/thanks** *etc* 警告/感谢{等}的话 ♦ **the last word** 定论 ♦ **in so many words** 直截了当地 ♦ **to break one's word** 食言 ♦ **to give sb one's word** 对某人许下诺言 ♦ **to keep one's word** 遵守诺言 ♦ **to send word of sb/sth** 转告某人/某事的消息 ♦ **to leave word (with sb/for sb) that ...** (通过某人/给某人)留个口信儿…
wording ['wəːdɪŋ] *n* [u] 措辞
word processing [-'prəusɛsɪŋ] *n* [u] 文字处理
word processor [-'prəusɛsə(r)] *n* [c] **1** (*machine*) 文字处理器 **2** (*software*) 文字处理软件
wore [wɔː(r)] *pt of* **wear**
✪ **work** [wəːk] **I** *n* **1** [u] (*tasks, duties*) 事情 ◊ *I must go, I've got loads of work to do.* 我得走了,我有一大堆事情要做。**2** [u] (*job*) 工作 ◊ *The work of a doctor is very interesting and varied.* 医生的工作非常有趣而且丰富多彩。**3** [u] (*place*) 工作场所 **4** [c] [艺术, 文学] 作品 ◊ *Chopin's works* 萧邦的作品 **II** *vi* **1** (*have job, do tasks*) 工作 ◊ *She works for a drug company.* 她在一家药品公司工作。◊ *We were working 24 hours a day.* 我们曾一天工作24 小时。**2** (*function*) [*mechanism, machine* +] 运行 ◊ *The traffic lights weren't working.* 红绿灯坏了。◊ *The new machine is working well.* 新机器运行良好。**3** (*take effect*) [*medicine etc* +] 见效 ◊ *How long does a sleeping pill take to work?* 一颗安眠药要多长时间开始见效? **4** (*be successful*) [*idea, method* +] 起作用 ◊ *95% of these diets do not work.* 95% 的这些减肥食谱都不起作用。**III** *vt* **1** (*shape*) [+ *clay, wood, leather etc*] 加工 **2** (*exploit*) [+ *mine*] 开采; [+ *land*] 耕种 **3** (*operate*) [+ *machine*] 操作 **4** (*cause*) [+ *miracle*] 创造 ◊ *I can't work miracles, you know.* 你要知道,我不能创造奇迹。**IV works** *n* [*pl*] (*activities*) 作业 *see also* **works** ♦ **to set to work** *or* **start work (on sth)** 着手做(某项工作) ♦ **to be at work (on sth)** 在做(某项)工作 ♦ **to go to work** 去上班 ♦ **to be out of work** 失业 ♦ **to be in work** 有工作 ♦ **to have your work cut**

out 面临艰巨的任务 ♦**to work hard** 努力工作 ♦**to work on the principle that ...** 按照…原则行事 ♦**to work one's way to the top** 费力地一点点爬到高职 ♦**to work loose** [*part, knot* +] 渐渐变松 ♦**to work sth into sth/work sth in** [+ *substance*] 将某物和进某物/将某物和进去

❑**work off** *vt* [+ *energy, anger*] 发泄

❑**work on** *vt* [不可拆分] **1** (*busy o.s. with*) 从事于 **2** (*try to influence*) [+ *person*] 设法说服

❑**work out I** *vi* **1** [体育] 锻炼 **2** (*progress*) [*job, plans etc* +] 发展 **II** *vt* [+ *answer, solution*] 努力找出; [+ *plan, details*] 制订出 ♦**it works out at 100 pounds** 算下来达100磅 ♦**I can't work out why ...** 我弄不懂为什么…

❑**work up** *vt* [+ *courage, enthusiasm*] 激发 ♦**to get worked up (about sth)** (对某事)很激动

✪**worker** ['wəːkə(r)] *n* [c] (*employed person*) 工人 ◊ *The dispute affected relations between management and workers.* 这场争端影响到管理层和工人的关系。♦**a hard/good worker** 工作努力/良好的人 ♦**factory/postal/health** *etc* **worker** 工厂工人/邮政/医疗工作者{等}

work experience *n* [u] 工作经历

workforce ['wəːkfɔːs] *n* [c] [*of region, country*] 劳动力; [*of company*] 职工总数

✪**working** ['wəːkɪŋ] **I** *adj* **1** [+ *person, population, mother*] 在职的 **2** [+ *life, clothes*] 工作的; [+ *hours, conditions, practice*] 工作上的 **3** (*moving*) [+ *part*] 运行的 **4** (*functioning*) [+ *model*] 发挥机能的 **5** (*temporary*) [+ *title, definition*] 暂行的 **II workings** *n* [*pl*] [*of device, brain*] 运转; [*of institution*] 运作 ♦**to have a working knowledge of sth** 具有足够运用的某方面的知识 ♦**to have a good working relationship with sb** 和某人有良好的工作关系

working class I *n* ♦**the working class(es)** 工人阶级 **II** *adj* (*also: **working-class***) 工人阶级的

working day [尤英] *n* [c] (*not holiday*) 工作日; (*working hours*) 工作时间

working week [尤英] *n* [c] 工作周

workman ['wəːkmən] (*pl* **workmen**) *n* [c] 劳动者

workout ['wəːkaut] *n* [c] 锻炼 ♦**to go for a workout** 去健身

work permit *n* [c] 工作许可证

workplace ['wəːkpleɪs] *n* [c] 工作场所

works [wəːks] (*pl* **works**) [英] *n* [c] **1** (*factory*) 工厂 **2** [非正式] ♦**the works** 相关的所有事物

worksheet ['wəːkʃiːt] *n* [c] 工作表

workshop ['wəːkʃɔp] *n* [c] **1** (*building*) 车间 **2** (*session*) 专题研讨会

workstation ['wəːksteɪʃən] *n* [c] **1** (*desk*) 工作台 **2** (*computer*) 工作站

work surface *n* [c] 厨房橱柜上的操作面

worktop ['wəːktɔp] [英] *n* [c] 厨房橱柜上的操作面 [美= **countertop**]

✪**world** [wəːld] **I** *n* **1** (*earth*) ♦**the world** 世界 ◊ *in many parts of the world* 在世界的许多地方 **2** [c] (*planet*) 星球 **3** [c] (*everyday existence*) 生活 ◊ *It was as if my world had collapsed.* 这就好像我的生活已经崩溃了。**4** [c] (*sphere*) 界 ◊ *The world of football is very competitive.* 足球界竞争很激烈。**II** *cpd* [复合词] [+ *champion, record, power, authority*] 世界; [+ *tour*] 环球 ♦**all over the world** 全世界 ♦**to think the world of sb** 非常看重某人 ♦**what in the world is he doing?** 他究竟在做什么? ♦**it'll do you a** *or* **the world of good** [非正式] 这会对你大有好处 ♦**out of this world** [非正式] 无与伦比的 ♦**World War One/Two** 第一次/第二次世界大战

World Cup [足球] *n* ♦**the World Cup** 世界杯足球赛

worldwide ['wəːld'waɪd] **I** *adj* 世界范围的 **II** *adv* 在全世界

World-Wide Web [wəːld'waɪd-] *n* ♦**the World-Wide Web** 万维网

worm [wəːm] **I** *n* [c] **1** (*also: **earthworm***) 蚯蚓 **2** [计算机] 蠕虫病毒 **II** *vt* 给…驱肠虫 ♦**to have worms** 患有寄生虫病 ♦**to worm**

one's way into sth [+ *position*] 费尽心机地钻入某处; [+ *sb's affections*] 千方百计地获取某事 ♦ **to worm sth out of sb** 从某人口中慢慢探出某事

worn [wɔːn] **I** *pp of* **wear** **II** *adj* [+ *carpet, shoe, patch, brakes etc*] 用旧的

worn-out ['wɔːnaut] *adj*
1 (*damaged*) [+ *object*] 破旧的
2 (*exhausted*) [+ *person*] 疲惫不堪的

worried ['wʌrɪd] *adj* 闷闷不乐的 ♦ **to be worried about sth/sb** 担心某事/某人 ♦ **to be worried that ...** 担心…

worry ['wʌrɪ] **I** *n* **1** [U] (*feeling of anxiety*) 忧虑 **2** [C] (*cause of anxiety*) 担心 **II** *vt* 使担心 **III** *vi* 担心 ♦ **to worry about** *or* **over sth/sb** 担心某事/某人

worrying ['wʌrɪɪŋ] *adj* 令人担心的

worse [wəːs] **I** *adj* (*comparative of bad*) 更坏的 **II** *adv* (*comparative of badly*) 更糟地 **III** *n* [U] 更坏的事 ♦ **to get worse** 逐渐恶化 ♦ **to go from bad to worse** 每况愈下 ♦ **you could do worse (than to ...)** (做…) 还是不错的 ♦ **a change for the worse** 向更坏方向的转变 ♦ **he is none the worse for it** 他并未因此怎么样 ♦ **so much the worse for you!** 那你就更加不妙!

worsen ['wəːsn] **I** *vt* 使变得更坏 **II** *vi* 变得更坏

worse off *adj* **1** (*financially*) 收入变少的 **2** (*not as good*) 变得更糟糕的 ♦ **he is now worse off than before** (*in situation*) 他现在的情况比以前更糟糕

worship ['wəːʃɪp] **I** *n* [U] 礼拜 **II** *vt* **1** [+ *god*] 敬奉 **2** (*adore*) [+ *person, thing*] 崇拜 ♦ **Your Worship** [英] (*to mayor*) 阁下; (*to judge*) 法官大人

worst [wəːst] **I** *adj* (*superlative of bad*) 最坏的 **II** *adv* (*superlative of badly*) 最糟地 **III** *n* [S/U] 最坏的事 ♦ **at worst** 在最坏的情况下 ♦ **if the worst comes to the worst** 如果最坏的事情发生 ♦ **at one's worst** 在最糟糕的状态下

worth [wəːθ] **I** *n* [U] 价值 **II** *adj* ♦ **to be worth £50** 值50英镑 ♦ **it's worth it** 这是值得的 ♦ **how much is it worth?** 它值多少钱? ♦ **400 dollars' worth of damage** 价值400美元的损失 ♦ **50 pence worth of apples** 50便士的苹果 ♦ **it would be worth your while to do something about the problem** 花工夫处理这个问题是值得的 ♦ **it would be (well) worth doing ...** (很) 值得做…

worthless ['wəːθlɪs] *adj* 毫无价值的
📖 用法参见 **invaluable**

worthwhile ['wəːθ'waɪl] *adj* [+ *activity*] 值得做的; [+ *cause, job*] 有价值的 ♦ **it might be worthwhile to write to them** 给他们写信是值得的

worthy ['wəːðɪ] *adj* **1** (*respectable*) [+ *person*] 可敬的; [+ *motive, goal*] 高尚的 **2** (*deserving*) [+ *winner, successor*] 相称的 ♦ **to be worthy of sth/sb** (*deserving of*) 值得某物/配得上某人; (*reminiscent of*) 和某物/某人相称的

✪ **would**
KEYWORD

[wud] *aux vb*
1 (*conditional tense*) ♦ **I would love to go to Italy** 我很愿意去意大利 ♦ **you would never guess that ...** 你永远猜不到… ♦ **I'm sure he wouldn't do that** 我确定他不会那么做的 ♦ **if you asked him he would do it** 如果你要求的话他会做的 ♦ **if you had asked him he would have done it** 如果你问过他的话，他早就会做了
2 (*in offers, invitations, requests*) ♦ **would you like a biscuit?** 你要来块饼干吗? ♦ **would you ask him to come in?** 你要叫他进来吗? ♦ **would it be all right if I sat down?** 我可以坐下吗? ♦ **he asked me if I would go with him** 他问我是否愿意和他一起去
3 (*be willing to*) ♦ **she wouldn't help me** 她不愿意帮助我 ♦ **she wouldn't behave** 她不会老老实实的 ♦ **the door wouldn't open** 门是打不开的 ♦ **I wish you would tidy your room** 但愿你会收拾你

的房间
4 (*in indirect speech*) ♦ **he said he would be at home later** 他说他晚点儿会在家的 ♦ **she asked me if I would be angry if ...** 她问我如果…我是否会生气
5 (*used to*) ♦ **he would spend every day on the beach** 他以前天天都呆在沙滩上
6 (*conjecture*) ♦ **you wouldn't know him** 你一定认不出他的 ♦ **it would have been midnight** 可能已经是半夜了
7 (*emphatic annoyance*) 老是 ♦ **it *would* have to snow today!** 今天又得下雪！♦ **you *would* say that, wouldn't you!** 你会那么说，是不是！
8 (*insistence*) ♦ **I didn't want her to, but she would do it** 我不想她这么做，但她会的

wouldn't ['wudnt] = **would not**
wound[1] [waund] *pt, pp of* **wind**[2]
wound[2] [wu:nd] **I** *n* [c] 伤口 **II** *vt* **1** (*physically*) 使受伤 **2** (*emotionally*) 伤害 ♦ **to be wounded in the leg/arm** *etc* 腿部/手臂{等}受伤
wove [wəuv] *pt of* **weave**
woven ['wəuvn] *pp of* **weave**
WPC [英] *n abbr* (= ***woman police constable***) 女警官
wrap [ræp] **I** *n* [c] (*shawl*) 披肩; (*cape*) 斗篷 **II** *vt* **1** (*cover*) 包 **2** ♦ **to wrap sth around sth/sb** [+ *paper, scarf, cloth etc*] 用某物把某物/某人裹起来; [+ *arms, legs etc*] 用某物紧紧环绕着某物/某人 ♦ **under wraps** [*plan, scheme* +] 保密
❑ **wrap up I** *vi* (*warmly*) 穿得暖和 **II** *vt* **1** (*pack*) 包起来 **2** (*complete*) [+ *deal, agreement*] 完成
wrapper ['ræpə(r)] *n* [c] **1** (*on food, goods*) 包装纸 **2** [英] [*of book*] 书皮
wrapping paper ['ræpɪŋ-] *n* [U] (*brown*) 牛皮纸; (*gift wrap*) 包装纸
wreath [ri:θ] (*pl* **wreaths** [ri:ðz]) *n* [c] **1** (*funeral wreath*) 花圈 **2** (*garland*) 花环
wreck [rɛk] **I** *n* [c] **1** (*wreckage*) [*of vehicle, ship*] 残骸 **2** [美] (*accident*) 事故 [英 = **crash**] **3** [非正式] (*person*) 憔悴的人 **II** *vt* **1** (*ruin*) [+ *equipment, room etc*] 毁坏; [+ *process, life, chances, marriage*] 破坏 **2** (*sink*) [+ *ship*] 使失事 **3** (*destroy*) [+ *car, building*] 摧毁
wreckage ['rɛkɪdʒ] *n* [S/U] [*of car, plane, ship etc*] 残骸; [*of building*] 废墟
wren [rɛn] *n* [c] 鹪鹩
wrench [rɛntʃ] **I** *n* **1** [c] (*tool*) 扳手 **2** [S] (*tug*) 猛扭 **3** [S] (*sadness*) 痛苦 **II** *vt* **1** (*pull*) ♦ **to wrench sth away/out** *etc* 猛力将某物挣开/拔出{等} **2** (*injure*) [+ *arm, back, ankle etc*] 扭伤 ♦ **to wrench sth from sb** 从某人手里抢走某物 ♦ **to wrench sth open** 用力扭开某物 ♦ **to wrench o.s. free** 用力挣脱
wrestle ['rɛsl] *vi* **1** ♦ **to wrestle (with sb)** [体育] (和某人) 摔跤; (*fight*) (和某人) 打架 **2** ♦ **to wrestle with sth** [+ *problem, issue, question*] 努力解决某事; [+ *conscience*] 与某事做苦苦挣扎
wrestler ['rɛslə(r)] *n* [c] 摔跤选手
wrestling ['rɛslɪŋ] *n* [U] 摔跤
wretched ['rɛtʃɪd] *adj* **1** (*miserable*) 悲惨的 **2** (*bad*) 糟糕的 **3** (*expressing irritation*) (*damned*) 讨厌的 **4** (*unhappy*) ♦ **to be wretched** 感到苦恼
wriggle ['rɪgl] **I** *vi* (*also:* ***wriggle about***) 扭动 **II** *vt* [+ *one's toes, fingers*] 扭动 **III** *n* [c] 扭动
❑ **wriggle out of** *vt* [不可拆分] [非正式] ♦ **to wriggle out of sth/of doing sth** 摆脱某事/做某事
wring [rɪŋ] (*pt, pp* **wrung**) *vt* **1** [+ *neck*] 扭 **2** ♦ **to wring one's hands** (字) 扭绞双手; (喻) 无能为力 **3** ♦ **to wring sth out of sb** 千方百计从某人处索取某物
❑ **wring out** *vt* [+ *cloth etc*] 绞干
wrinkle ['rɪŋkl] **I** *n* [c] (*on skin*) 皱纹; (*in paper, cloth etc*) 褶皱 **II** *vt* [+ *forehead*] 皱起 **III** *vi* [*skin* +] 起皱纹; [*paint, paper etc* +] 有皱痕 ♦ **to wrinkle one's nose (at sth)** (对某事) 皱鼻子
wrinkled ['rɪŋkld] *adj* [+ *skin, face*] 布满皱纹的; [+ *person*] 满脸皱纹的; [+ *clothing, fabric, paper*] 起皱的
wrist [rɪst] *n* [c] 手腕
✪ **write** [raɪt] (*pt* **wrote**, *pp* **written**) **I** *vt*

1 (*note down*) [+ *address, number etc*] 写下 **2** (*compose*) [+ *letter, note*] 写 **3** (*create*) [+ *novel, music etc*] 创作 **4** (*also: **write out***) [+ *cheque, receipt, prescription*] 开 **II** *vi* 写字 ♦ **to write sb a letter, write a letter to sb** 给某人写信 ♦ **to write to sb** 写信给某人

❑ **write away** *vi* ♦ **to write away for sth** [+ *information*] 发信索要某物; [+ *goods*] 函购某物

❑ **write down** *vt* 记下

❑ **write in** *vi* 发函

❑ **write into** *vt* ♦ **to write sth into sth** [+ *contract, agreement*] 把某事写入某物

❑ **write off I** *vt* **1** [+ *debt, money*] 注销 **2** [+ *person*] 把…看作不存在 **3** [+ *plan, project*] 取消 **4** [英] (*wreck*) [+ *vehicle*] 报废 **II** *vi* ♦ **to write off for sth** [+ *information*] 写信索要某物; [+ *goods*] 函购某物

❑ **write out** *vt* **1** [+ *list, name and address, report*] 写下 **2** (*copy out*) 誊写 **3** [+ *cheque, receipt etc*] 开

❑ **write up** *vt* [+ *minutes, report, findings*] 把…整理成文; [+ *event, visit etc*] 详细记述

write-off ['raɪtɔf] *n* [c] 报废物

writer ['raɪtə(r)] *n* [c] **1** (*author*) 作家 **2** [*of report, document etc*] 作者

writing ['raɪtɪŋ] *n* [U] **1** (*sth written*) 文字 **2** (*handwriting*) 笔迹 **3** (*style*) 文风 **4** (*activity*) 写作 ♦ **in writing** 以书面形式

writing paper *n* [U] 信纸

written ['rɪtn] *pp of* **write**

wrong [rɔŋ] **I** *adj* **1** (*inappropriate*) [+ *choice, action, decision*] 不恰当的; [+ *person, equipment, kind, job*] 不合适的 **2** (*incorrect*) [+ *answer, information, report*] 错误的 **3** (*unsatisfactory*) 不好的 **4** (*morally bad*) 不道德的 **II** *adv* (*incorrectly*) [*do, spell etc* +] 错误地 **III** *n* **1** [c] (*injustice*) 不公 **2** [U] (*evil*) 邪恶 **IV** *vt* (*treat unfairly*) 冤枉 ♦ **you've got it wrong** 你搞错了 ♦ **to be wrong** [*answer* +] 是错的; [*person* +] (*about sth*) 弄错的; (*in doing, saying sth*) 搞错了 ♦ **to be wrong to do sth** [*person* +] 做某事是不对的 ♦ **it is wrong to steal, stealing is wrong** 偷窃是不道德的 ♦ **what's wrong?** 出了什么事? ♦ **what's wrong with you?** 你怎么了? ♦ **there's nothing wrong** 没问题 ♦ **to go wrong** [*plan* +] 失败; [*machine* +] 发生故障 ♦ **where did I go wrong?** 我错在哪里了? ♦ **to be in the wrong** 做错

wrongful ['rɔŋful] *adj* 不正当的

wrongly ['rɔŋlɪ] *adv* **1** (*incorrectly*) [*answer, translate, spell, believe* +] 错误地 **2** (*by mistake*) [*diagnose, identify* +] 错误地 **3** (*unjustly*) [*accuse, imprison* +] 不公正地 **4** (*inappropriately*) [+ *dressed, arranged*] 不恰当地 ♦ **she supposed, wrongly, that ...** 她错误地假定…

wrong number *n* [c] ♦ **you've got the wrong number** 你打错了 ♦ **it was a wrong number** 这个电话号码是错的

wrote [rəut] *pt of* **write**

wrung [rʌŋ] *pt, pp of* **wring**

WWW [计算机] *n abbr* (= ***World-Wide Web***) 万维网

Xx

X, x [ɛks] *n* [C/U] (*letter*) 英语的第二十四个字母
XL *abbr* (= ***extra large***) 特大号
Xmas ['ɛksməs] *n abbr* (= ***Christmas***) 圣诞节
X-ray ['ɛksreɪ] **I** *n* [C] **1** (*ray*) X 射线 **2** (*photo*) X 光照片 **II** *vt* 用X 光检查 ♦**to have an X-ray** 作一次X 光检查 ♦**to take an X-ray of sth** 对某物做X 光检查
xylophone ['zaɪləfəun] *n* [C] 木琴

Yy

Y, y [waɪ] *n* [C/U] (*letter*) 英语的第二十五个字母
Y [手机短信] *abbr* (= **why**) 为什么
yacht [jɔt] *n* [C] **1** (*sailing boat*) 帆船 **2** (*luxury craft*) 游艇
yachting ['jɔtɪŋ] *n* [U] 帆船驾驶运动
yard [jɑːd] *n* **1** [C/U] (*paved area*) 院子 **2** [C] [美] (*garden*) 庭院 [英 = **garden**] **3** (*measure*) 码,长度单位。一码等于3 英尺或0.9144 米 ♦**builder's yard** 建筑工地
yarn [jɑːn] *n* **1** [C/U] (*thread*) 纱线 **2** [C] [非正式] (*tale*) 奇谈
yawn [jɔːn] **I** *vi* 打呵欠 **II** *n* [C] 呵欠
yd *abbr* (= **yard**) 码,长度单位。一码等于3 英尺或0.9144 米
✪**yeah** [jɛə] [非正式] *adv* 是的
✪**year** [jɪə(r)] *n* [C] **1** 年 **2** [教育, 大学] 学年 **3** [商] 年度 **4** [*of wine*] 年份 ♦**in the year 2000** 在2000 年 ♦**every year** 每年 ♦**this year** 今年 ♦**last year** 去年 ♦**next year** 明年 ♦**a** *or* **per year** 每年 ♦**all year round** 一年到头 ♦**year in, year out** 年复一年 ♦**he's 8 years old** 他8 岁 ♦**an eight-year-old child** 一个8 岁的小孩 ♦**I hadn't seen him for** *or* **in years** 我有好多年没见他了 ♦**we lived there for years** 我们住在那儿有好多年了
yearly ['jɪəlɪ] **I** *adj* **1** [+ *event, meeting etc*] 一年一度的 **2** [+ *rate, income etc*] 一年的 **II** *adv* **1** (*once a year*) 一年一次地 **2** (*every year*) 每年地 ♦**twice yearly** (*as adv*) 一年两次地; (*as adj*) 一年两次的
yearn [jəːn] *vi* ♦**to yearn for sth** 渴望某事 ♦**to yearn to do sth** 渴望做某事
yeast [jiːst] *n* [U] 酵母
yell [jɛl] **I** *n* [C] 叫喊 **II** *vi* 叫喊 **III** *vt* 叫喊着说 ♦**to let out a yell** 大喊一声 ♦**to yell at sb** (*scold*) 对某人大喊大叫
✪**yellow** ['jɛləu] **I** *adj* 黄色的 **II** *n* [C/U] 黄色 **III** *vi* 变黄
Yellow Pages® *n* [*pl*] ♦**the Yellow Pages®** 黄页电话号码簿
Yemen ['jɛmən] *n* 也门
Yemeni ['jɛmənɪ] **I** *adj* 也门的 **II** *n* [C] (*person*) 也门人
✪**yes** [jɛs] **I** *adv* **1** (*replying to question*) 是的 **2** (*contradicting*) 不 *"That isn't possible." – "Oh yes it is!"* "那是不可能的。" – "不, 是可能的!" **II** *n* [C] **1** (*vote*) 赞成 **2** (*answer*) 是 **3** (*person*) 投赞成票者 ♦**to say yes** 同意
✪**yesterday** ['jɛstədɪ] **I** *adv* 昨天 ◊ *She left yesterday.* 她昨天走的。**II** *n* [U] 昨天 ♦**all day yesterday** 昨天一整天 ♦**the day before yesterday** 前天 ♦**yesterday morning/afternoon** 昨天上午/下午
✪**yet** [jɛt] **I** *adv* **1** (*up to now*) (*with negative*) 还; (*in questions*) 已经 ◊ *They haven't finished yet.* 他们还没完工。◊ *Have you written to him yet?* 你已经写信给他了吗? **2** (*now*) (*in negatives*) 还 ◊ *He hasn't arrived yet.* 他还没来呢。◊ *Don't get up yet.* 先别起床。**3** (*still*) 仍然 ◊ *There may yet be time.* 仍有时间。**II** *conj* 然而 ♦**not just yet** 现在不 ♦**the best yet** 迄今最好的 ♦**as yet** 迄今为止 ♦**a few days yet** 还有几天 ♦**to have yet to do sth** 还没做某事 ♦**yet another** 又一个 ♦**yet again** 又一次
yew [juː] *n* **1** [C] (*tree*) 紫杉 **2** [U] (*wood*) 紫杉木
yield [jiːld] **I** *n* [C] **1** [农] 产量 **2** [商] 利润 **II** *vt* **1** (*give up*) [+ *control, responsibility*] 让出 **2** (*produce*) [+ *harvest*] 出产; [+ *results, profit*] 产生 **III** *vi* **1** (*surrender*) ♦**to yield (to sth)** 屈服(于某事) **2** [*door, lock* +] 弯曲 **3** [美] (*in car etc*) 让路 [英 = **give way**] ♦**a yield of 5%** 5% 的利润
YMCA *n abbr* (= ***Young Men's Christian Association***) (*hostel*) 由基督教青年会运营的供男子住宿的旅馆
yob [jɔb] [英: 非正式, 贬] *n* [C] 粗俗

的男人

yoga ['jəugə] *n* [U] 瑜珈

yog(h)urt ['jəugət] *n* **1** [C/U] (*substance*) 酸奶 **2** [C] (*also: **pot of yog(h)urt***) 一盒酸奶

yolk [jəuk] *n* [C/U] 蛋黄

✪**you** [juː] *pron* **1** (*singular*) 你; (*plural*) 你们 ◊ *Do you know her?* 你/你们认识她吗? ◊ *I like you.* 我喜欢你/你们。◊ *I'll send you the photos when I've got them.* 我拿到照片后会寄给你/你们的。◊ *I gave it to you.* 我把它给你/你们。◊ *It's for you.* 是给你/你们的。**2** (*in generalizations*) (*one*) 任何人 ◊ *You can't put metal dishes in a microwave.* 金属制的碟子不能用于微波炉。♦**you never know** 谁知道

you'd [juːd] = **you had, you would**

you'll [juːl] = **you will, you shall**

✪**young** [jʌŋ] **I** *adj* 幼小的 **II the young** *n* [*pl*] (*people*) 年轻人; [*of animal*] 幼仔 ♦**a young man** 一个小伙子 ♦**a young lady** 一位少女 ♦**my younger brother/sister** 我的弟弟/妹妹 ♦**the younger generation** 年轻一代 ♦**in my younger days** 在我年轻的时候

youngster ['jʌŋstə(r)] *n* [C] 小孩

✪**your** [jɔː(r)] *adj* (*of one person*) 你的; (*of more than one person*) 你们的 ◊ *your house* 你/你们的房子 ◊ *Have you cleaned your teeth?* 你/你们刷牙了吗?

> 📖 请勿将 **your** 和 **you're** 混淆。**your** 是指与正在和你谈话的人相关，或从属于他们的某事物。*Is that your brother?...Your spelling is terrible.* **your** 也可用来泛指与人有关的事物。*I've heard that diets can be bad for your health.*
> **you're** 是 **you are** 的缩略形式。*If you're not well, you should go to bed.*

you're [juə(r)] = **you are**
📖 用法参见 **your**

yours [jɔːz] *pron* (*of one person*) 你的; (*of more than one person*) 你们的 ♦**is this yours?** 这是你/你们的吗? ♦**a friend of yours** 你/你们的一个朋友 ♦**yours sincerely/faithfully** 你真挚的/忠实的 ♦**yours** (*in letter*) 谨上

yourself [jɔː'sɛlf] *pron* **1** 你自己 ◊ *Have you hurt yourself?* 你伤到自己了吗? ◊ *Did you paint the room yourself?* 你自己粉刷了房间? ◊ *Buy yourself something nice.* 给你自己买点好东西。◊ *Be honest with yourself.* 你得正视自己。**2** (*emphatic*) 你本人 ◊ *So you yourself live in London, do you?* 那你本人住在伦敦，是吗? **3** (*you*) 你 ◊ *an intelligent person like yourself* 像你一样有智慧的人 ♦**by yourself** (*unaided*) 独立地 ◊ *Did you make the cake by yourself?* 你自己一个人做了蛋糕?; (*alone*) 独自地 ◊ *Do you live by yourself?* 你独自一个人住吗?

yourselves [jɔː'sɛlvz] *pl pron* **1** 你们自己 ◊ *Have you hurt yourselves?* 你们伤到自己了吗? ◊ *Did you paint the house yourselves?* 你们自己粉刷了房子? ◊ *Buy yourselves something nice.* 给你们自己买点好东西。**2** (*emphatic*) 你们本人 ◊ *So you yourselves live in London, do you?* 那你们本人住在伦敦，是吗? **3** (*you*) 你们 ◊ *intelligent people like yourselves* 像你们一样有智慧的人 ♦**by yourselves** (*unaided*) 独力地 ◊ *Did you make the cake by yourselves?* 你们自己做了蛋糕?; (*alone*) 独自地 ◊ *Do you live by yourselves?* 你们自己单独住吗?

youth [juːθ] **I** *n* **1** [U] (*young days*) 青少年时期 **2** [U] (*being young*) 年轻 **3** [C] (*young man*) 男青年 **II the youth** *n* [*pl*] 青年人 ♦**in my youth** 在我的青年时代

youth club *n* [C] 青年俱乐部

youthful ['juːθful] *adj* [+ *appearance, enthusiasm etc*] 年轻的; [+ *indiscretion*] 不成熟的

youth hostel *n* [C] 青年招待所

you've [juːv] = **you have**

YR [手机短信] *abbr* (= ***your***) 你的

yr *abbr* (= ***year***) 年

YWCA *n abbr* (= ***Young Women's Christian Association***) (*hostel*) 由基督教青年会运营的供女子住宿的旅馆

Zz

Z, z [zɛd,（美）ziː] *n* [C/U] (*letter*) 英语的第二十六个字母
Zambia [ˈzæmbɪə] *n* 赞比亚
Zambian [ˈzæmbɪən] **I** *adj* 赞比亚的 **II** *n* [C] (*person*) 赞比亚人
zeal [ziːl] *n* [U] 热情
zebra [ˈziːbrə] *n* [C] 斑马
zebra crossing [英] *n* [C] 斑马线
zero [ˈzɪərəu] (*pl* **zero** *or* **zeroes**) **I** *n* **1** [U/C] (*number*) 零 **2** [U] (*nothing*) 没有 ◊ *Visibility at the city's airport came down to zero.* 这个城市机场的能见度降为零。**II** *adj* 为零的 ♦**5 degrees below zero** 零下5度 🕮 用法参见 **nought**
❑ **zero in on** *vt* [不可拆分] 瞄准
zest [zɛst] *n* **1** [U] (*enthusiasm*) 热忱 **2** [U/S] (*excitement*) 兴趣 **3** [U] [*of orange, lemon*] 外皮 ♦**zest for life** 对生命的热情
zigzag [ˈzɪgzæg] **I** *n* [C] 弯弯曲曲的线条 **II** *vi* 曲折前进
Zimbabwe [zɪmˈbɑːbwɪ] *n* 津巴布韦
Zimbabwean [zɪmˈbɑːbwɪən] **I** *adj* 津巴布韦的 **II** *n* [C] (*person*) 津巴布韦人
zinc [zɪŋk] *n* [U] 锌
zip [zɪp] **I** *n* [C] [英] (*fastener*) 拉链 [美 = **zipper**] **II** *vt* (*also:* ***zip up***) 拉…的拉链
zip code [美] *n* [C] 邮政编码 [英 = **post code**]
zipper [ˈzɪpə(r)] [美] *n* [C] 拉链 [英 = **zip**]
zit [zɪt] [非正式] *n* [C] (*pimple*) 青春痘
zodiac [ˈzəudɪæk] *n* ♦**the zodiac** 黄道十二宫图
zone [zəun] *n* [C] (*area*) 地带
zoo [zuː] (*pl* **zoos**) *n* [C] 动物园
zoology [zuːˈɔlədʒɪ] *n* [U] 动物学
zoom [zuːm] *vi* **1** ♦**to zoom past/along** 疾驰而过/沿…疾驰 **2** ♦**to zoom in (on sth/sb)** [摄影, 电影]（对准某物/某人）拉近镜头
zucchini [zuːˈkiːnɪ] (*pl* **zucchini** *or* **zucchinis**) [美] *n* [C/U] 绿皮密生西葫芦 [英 = **courgette**]

部 首 检 字 表
RADICAL INDEX

检字方法说明：

（1）根据字的部首在部首目录中查到该部首所在检字表中的号码；

（2）按此号码在检字表中找到该部首，并根据字的笔画（字的笔画数不含其部首）查到该字的汉语拼音。

How to use this index:

(1) Use pages 1 and 2 to identify the radical. Note the number preceding it.

(2) In the index on pages 3-36, use this number to find all the characters appearing in this dictionary which contain the radical. Characters are ordered according to the number of strokes. The pinyin given will lead you to the correct entry.

部 首 目 录

一 画

(1) 一
(2) 丨
(3) 丿
(4) 丶
(5) 乙（乚 乛㇆）

二 画

(6) 二
(7) 十
(8) 厂
(9) 匚
(10) 刂
(11) 卜
(12) 冂
(13) 亻
(14) 八
(15) 人（入）
(16) 勹
(17) 几
(18) 儿
(19) 亠
(20) 冫
(21) 冖
(22) 讠（言）
(23) 卩
(24) 阝（在左）
(25) 阝（在右）
(26) 凵
(27) 刀
(28) 力
(29) 厶
(30) 又
(31) 廴

三 画

(32) 工
(33) 土
(34) 士
(35) 扌
(36) 艹
(37) 寸
(38) 弋
(39) 廾（在下）
(40) 大
(41) 尢
(42) 小
(43) 口
(44) 囗
(45) 巾
(46) 山
(47) 彳
(48) 彡
(49) 犭
(50) 夕
(51) 夂
(52) 饣
(53) 丬
(54) 广
(55) 忄
(56) 门
(57) 氵
(58) 宀
(59) 辶
(60) 彐（彑）
(61) 尸
(62) 己（巳）

(63) 弓
(64) 子
(65) 女
(66) 纟
(67) 马
(68) 幺
(69) 巛

四 画

(70) 王
(71) 韦
(72) 木
(73) 犬
(74) 歹
(75) 车
(76) 戈
(77) 比
(78) 瓦
(79) 止
(80) 支
(81) 日
(82) 曰
(83) 水
(84) 贝
(85) 见
(86) 牛(牜)
(87) 手
(88) 毛
(89) 气
(90) 攵
(91) 片
(92) 斤
(93) 爪(爫)
(94) 父
(95) 月
(96) 欠
(97) 风
(98) 殳
(99) 文
(100) 方
(101) 火
(102) 斗
(103) 灬
(104) 户
(105) 礻
(106) 心
(107) 肀(聿)
(108) 毌(毋母)

五 画

(109) 示
(110) 石
(111) 龙
(112) 业
(113) 目
(114) 田
(115) 罒
(116) 皿
(117) 钅
(118) 矢
(119) 禾
(120) 白
(121) 瓜
(122) 用
(123) 鸟
(124) 疒
(125) 立
(126) 穴
(127) 衤
(128) 疋
(129) 皮
(130) 矛

六 画

(131) 耒
(132) 老(耂)
(133) 耳
(134) 西(覀)
(135) 页
(136) 虍
(137) 虫
(138) 缶
(139) 舌
(140) ⺮(竹)
(141) 臼
(142) 自
(143) 血
(144) 舟
(145) 衣
(146) 羊
(147) 米
(148) 艮
(149) 羽
(150) 糸

七 画

(151) 走
(152) 赤
(153) 豆
(154) 酉
(155) 辰
(156) 卤
(157) 里
(158) 足
(159) 身
(160) 采
(161) 谷
(162) 豸
(163) 角
(164) 言(訁见讠)
(165) 辛

八 画

(166) 青
(167) 雨
(168) 齿
(169) 隹
(170) 金
(171) 鱼

九 画

(172) 革
(173) 骨
(174) 鬼
(175) 食
(176) 音

十 画

(177) 髟

十一画

(178) 麻
(179) 鹿

十二画

(180) 黑

十三画

(181) 鼠

十四画

(182) 鼻

检字表

(1) 一部

一 yī

一画

丁 dīng
七 qī

二画

三 sān
干 gān;gàn
于 yú
下 xià
丈 zhàng
与 yǔ
才 cái
万 wàn
上 shàng

三画

丰 fēng
井 jǐng
开 kāi
夫 fū
天 tiān
无 wú
专 zhuān
丐 gài
五 wǔ
不 bù
屯 tún
互 hù
牙 yá
丑 chǒu

四画

末 mò
未 wèi
击 jī
正 zhēng
zhèng
甘 gān
世 shì
可 kě
丙 bǐng
平 píng
东 dōng
且 qiě
册 cè
丝 sī

五画

亚 yà
亘 gèn
吏 lì
再 zài
百 bǎi
而 ér
夹 gā;jiā;jiá

六画

严 yán
巫 wū
更 gēng;gèng
束 shù
两 liǎng
丽 lì
来 lái
求 qiú

七画

表 biǎo
事 shì
枣 zǎo

八画

奏 zòu
甚 shèn
巷 hàng;xiàng
柬 jiǎn
歪 wāi
面 miàn
韭 jiǔ
昼 zhòu

九画

艳 yàn
哥 gē
孬 nāo

十一画

棘 jí

十五画

噩 è
整 zhěng
臻 zhēn

二十一画

囊 náng

(2) 丨部

三画

中 zhōng
zhòng
内 nèi

四画

北 běi
凸 tū
旧 jiù
甲 jiǎ
申 shēn
电 diàn
由 yóu
史 shǐ
央 yāng
冉 rǎn
凹 āo
出 chū

五画

师 shī
曳 yè
曲 qū;qǔ
肉 ròu

六画

串 chuàn

七画

非 fēi
畅 chàng

八画

临 lín

(3) 丿部

一画

九 jiǔ
匕 bǐ
乃 nǎi

二画

千 qiān
川 chuān
及 jí
久 jiǔ

三画

午 wǔ
升 shēng
夭 yāo
长 cháng
zhǎng
币 bì
反 fǎn
乏 fá
氏 shì
丹 dān
乌 wū

四画

生 shēng
失 shī
乍 zhà
丘 qiū
甩 shuǎi

(4)

丶部

(5)

乙(乚乛𠃍)部

(6)

二部

(7)

十部

(8)

厂部

八画

原 yuán

九画

厢 xiāng
厩 jiù

十画

厨 chú
厦 shà
雁 yàn
厥 jué

十四画

赝 yàn

(9) 匚部

二画

区 qū
匹 pǐ
巨 jù

四画

臣 chén
匠 jiàng

五画

匣 xiá
医 yī

八画

匿 nì
匪 fěi

九画

匮 kuì

(10) 刂部

三画

刊 kān

四画

刑 xíng
列 liè
划 huá;huà
刚 gāng
则 zé
创 chuāng
chuàng
刎 wěn
刘 liú

五画

别 bié;biè
利 lì
删 shān
刨 bào;páo
判 pàn

六画

刺 cī;cì
到 dào
制 zhì
刮 guā
刽 guì
刹 chà;shā
剁 duò
剂 jì
刻 kè
刷 shuā;shuà

七画

荆 jīng
削 xiāo;xuē
剐 guǎ
剑 jiàn
前 qián
剃 tì

八画

剔 tī
剖 pōu
剜 wān
剥 bāo;bō
剧 jù

九画

副 fù

十画

剩 shèng
割 gē

十一画

剽 piāo

十三画

劐 huō

(11) 卜部

卜 bo;bǔ

三画

卡 kǎ;qiǎ
占 zhān;zhàn
外 wài

四画

贞 zhēn

六画

卦 guà
卧 wò

八画

桌 zhuō

(12) 冂部

二画

冈 gāng

四画

同 tóng
网 wǎng

(13) 亻部

一画

亿 yì

二画

仁 rén
什 shén;shí
仆 pú
仇 chóu
化 huà
仍 réng
仅 jǐn

三画

仨 sā
仕 shì
仗 zhàng
代 dài
付 fù
仙 xiān
仟 qiān
仪 yí
他 tā
仔 zǐ

四画

伟 wěi
传 chuán
zhuàn
休 xiū
伍 wǔ
伎 jì
伏 fú
优 yōu
伐 fá
仲 zhòng
件 jiàn
任 rèn
伤 shāng
价 jià
伦 lún
份 fèn
仰 yǎng
伉 kàng
仿 fǎng
伙 huǒ
伪 wěi
伫 zhù
伊 yī
似 shì;sì

五画

估 gū
体 tǐ
何 hé
佐 zuǒ
但 dàn
伸 shēn
作 zuō;zuò
伯 bó
伶 líng

佣 yōng;yòng
低 dī
你 nǐ
住 zhù
位 wèi
伴 bàn
伺 cì;sì
佛 fó

六画

佳 jiā
侍 shì
佬 lǎo
供 gōng;gòng
使 shǐ
佰 bǎi
例 lì
侠 xiá
侥 jiǎo
侄 zhí
侦 zhēn
侣 lǚ
侃 kǎn
侧 cè
侏 zhū
侨 qiáo
佩 pèi
侈 chǐ
佼 jiǎo
依 yī
佯 yáng

七画

俨 yǎn
便 biàn;pián
俩 liǎ
俪 lì
修 xiū
俏 qiào
俚 lǐ
保 bǎo
促 cù
俄 é
侮 wǔ
俭 jiǎn
俗 sú
俘 fú
信 xìn
侵 qīn
侯 hóu
俑 yǒng
俊 jùn

八画

俸 fèng
债 zhài
借 jiè
偌 ruò
值 zhí
倚 yǐ
倾 qīng
倒 dǎo;dào
倘 tǎng
俱 jù
倡 chàng
候 hòu
俯 fǔ
倍 bèi
倦 juàn
健 jiàn
倔 jué;juè

九画

做 zuò
偃 yǎn
偕 xié
偿 cháng
偶 ǒu
偎 wēi
傀 kuǐ
偷 tōu
停 tíng
偏 piān
假 jiǎ;jià

十画

傲 ào
傅 fù
傍 bàng
傧 bīn
储 chǔ

十一画

催 cuī
傻 shǎ
像 xiàng

十二画

僚 liáo
僧 sēng

十三画

僵 jiāng
僻 pì

十四画

儒 rú

(14)
八 部

八 bā

二画

分 fēn;fèn
公 gōng

三画

只 zhī;zhǐ
兰 lán

四画

共 gòng
并 bìng
关 guān

五画

兵 bīng
谷 gǔ
兑 duì
弟 dì

六画

其 qí
具 jù
典 diǎn
卷 juǎn;juàn
单 dān

七画

养 yǎng
酋 qiú
首 shǒu

八画

翁 wēng
益 yì
兼 jiān

九画

黄 huáng
兽 shòu

十画

普 pǔ
奠 diàn
曾 céng;zēng

十二画

舆 yú

十四画

冀 jì

(15)
人(入)部

人 rén
入 rù

一画

个 gè

二画

介 jiè
从 cóng
今 jīn
仓 cāng
以 yǐ

三画

丛 cóng
令 lìng

四画

全 quán
会 huì;kuài
合 hé
企 qǐ
众 zhòng
伞 sǎn
氽 tǔn

五画

余 yú

含 hán
六画
舍 shě;shè
命 mìng
八画
拿 ná
九画
盒 hé
十画
舒 shū
禽 qín

(16)
勹部

一画
勺 sháo
二画
勿 wù
匀 yún
勾 gōu;gòu
三画
句 jù
匆 cōng
包 bāo
四画
旬 xún
七画
匍 pú
九画
够 gòu

(17)
几部

几 jī;jǐ
一画
凡 fán
二画
凤 fèng
四画
朵 duǒ
夙 sù
凫 fú
五画
壳 ké;qiào
秃 tū
六画
咒 zhòu
凯 kǎi
凭 píng
十二画
凳 dèng

(18)
儿部

儿 ér
二画
允 yǔn
三画
兄 xiōng
四画
光 guāng
先 xiān
八画
党 dǎng
九画
兜 dōu

(19)
亠部

一画
亡 wáng
二画
六 liù
亢 kàng
三画
市 shì
玄 xuán
四画
交 jiāo
产 chǎn
充 chōng
妄 wàng
五画
亨 hēng
弃 qì
六画
变 biàn
京 jīng
享 xiǎng
夜 yè
七画
哀 āi
亭 tíng
亮 liàng
帝 dì
八画
衰 shuāi
衷 zhōng
高 gāo
离 lí
旁 páng
九画
毫 háo
烹 pēng
商 shāng
率 shuài
十画
亵 xiè
就 jiù
十一画
禀 bǐng
雍 yōng
十二画
裹 guǒ
豪 háo
膏 gāo
十三画
褒 bāo
十五画
襄 xiāng
嬴 yíng

(20)
冫部

二画
斗 dǒu;dòu
四画
冲 chōng
chòng
次 cì
决 jué
冰 bīng
五画
冻 dòng
况 kuàng
冷 lěng
冶 yě
六画
净 jìng
八画
凌 líng
凄 qī
准 zhǔn
凋 diāo
凉 liáng;liàng
九画
凑 còu
减 jiǎn
十画
寒 hán
十三画
凛 lǐn
十四画
凝 níng

(21)
冖部

二画
冗 rǒng
三画
写 xiě
四画
军 jūn
五画
罕 hǎn
七画
冠 guān;guàn

八画
冥 míng
冤 yuān
十画
幂 mì

(22) 讠(言)部

二画
计 jì
订 dìng
讣 fù
认 rèn
讥 jī
三画
讨 tǎo
让 ràng
讪 shàn
训 xùn
议 yì
讯 xùn
记 jì
四画
讲 jiǎng
讳 huì
讴 ōu
许 xǔ
讹 é
论 lùn
讼 sòng
讽 fěng
设 shè
访 fǎng
诀 jué
五画
证 zhèng
评 píng
诅 zǔ
识 shí
诈 zhà
诉 sù
诊 zhěn
诋 dǐ
词 cí
译 yì
六画
诓 kuāng
试 shì
诗 shī
诘 jí;jié
诙 huī
诚 chéng
话 huà
诞 dàn
诠 quán
诡 guǐ
询 xún
该 gāi
详 xiáng
诧 chà
诩 xǔ
七画
诫 jiè
诬 wū
语 yǔ;yù
误 wù
诱 yòu
诲 huì
说 shuì;shuō
诵 sòng
八画
请 qǐng
诸 zhū
诺 nuò
读 dú
诽 fěi
课 kè
调 diào;tiáo
谄 chǎn
谅 liàng
谆 zhūn
谈 tán
谊 yì
九画
谋 móu
谍 dié
谎 huǎng
谐 xié
谓 wèi
谗 chán
谙 ān
谚 yàn
谜 mí
十画
谢 xiè
谣 yáo
谤 bàng
谦 qiān
十一画
谨 jǐn
谩 màn
谬 miù
十二画
谱 pǔ
十三画
谴 qiǎn

(23) 卩部

一画
卫 wèi
三画
叩 kòu
印 yìn
四画
危 wēi
五画
却 què
即 jí
七画
卸 xiè

(24) 阝(在左)部

二画
队 duì
四画
阱 jǐng
阵 zhèn
阳 yáng
阶 jiē
阴 yīn
防 fáng
五画
陆 liù;lù
际 jì
阿 ā;ē
陈 chén
阻 zǔ
附 fù
六画
陋 lòu
陌 mò
降 jiàng;xiáng
限 xiàn
七画
陡 dǒu
陛 bì
陨 yǔn
除 chú
险 xiǎn
院 yuàn
八画
陵 líng
陶 táo
陷 xiàn
陪 péi
九画
随 suí
隅 yú
隆 lóng
隐 yǐn
十画
隔 gé
隙 xì
隘 ài

撤 chè
撰 zhuàn

十三画

擀 gǎn
撼 hàn
擂 lèi
操 cāo
擅 shàn

十四画

擦 cā

十六画

攒 cuán;zǎn

二十画

攫 jué

(36)

艹 部

一画

艺 yì

二画

艾 ài
节 jiē;jié

三画

芋 yù
芝 zhī

四画

芙 fú
芜 wú
苇 wěi
芸 yún
芽 yá
花 huā
芹 qín
芥 jiè
芬 fēn
苍 cāng
芳 fāng
芦 lú
芭 bā
苏 sū

五画

茉 mò
苦 kǔ
苛 kē
若 ruò
茂 mào
苹 píng
苗 miáo
英 yīng
苟 gǒu
苑 yuàn
苞 bāo
范 fàn
茁 zhuó
茄 jiā;qié
茎 jīng
苔 tái
茅 máo

六画

茸 róng
茬 chá
荐 jiàn
草 cǎo
茧 jiǎn
茵 yīn
茴 huí
荞 qiáo
荏 rěn
荟 huì
茶 chá
荒 huāng
茫 máng
荡 dàng
荣 róng
荤 hūn
荧 yíng
荫 yìn
荔 lì
药 yào

七画

莽 mǎng
莲 lián
莫 mò
莴 wō
荷 hé;hè
莅 lì
获 huò

八画

菁 jīng
著 zhù
菱 líng
萋 qī
菲 fěi
萌 méng
萝 luó
菌 jūn
萎 wěi
菜 cài
菊 jú
萃 cuì
菩 pú
萍 píng
菠 bō
萤 yíng
营 yíng
萦 yíng
萧 xiāo
菇 gū

九画

葫 hú
葬 zàng
募 mù
董 dǒng
葆 bǎo
葡 pú
葱 cōng
蒂 dì
落 là;lào;luò
葵 kuí

十画

蒜 suàn
蓝 lán
幕 mù
蓦 mò
蓓 bèi
蓬 péng
蓄 xù
蒙 mēng
méng
Měng
蒸 zhēng

十一画

蔫 niān
蔷 qiáng
蔽 bì
暮 mù
摹 mó
蔓 màn
蔑 miè
蔗 zhè
蔼 ǎi
蔚 wèi

十二画

蕉 jiāo
蕊 ruǐ
蔬 shū
蕴 yùn

十三画

蕾 lěi
薯 shǔ
薪 xīn
薄 báo;bó;bò

十四画

藏 cáng;zàng
藐 miǎo

十五画

藕 ǒu
藤 téng

十六画

孽 niè
蘑 mó

十九画

蘸 zhàn

(37)

寸 部

寸 cùn

呱 guā
呼 hū
鸣 míng
咆 páo
呢 ne;ní
咄 duō
咖 gā;kā
呦 yōu
知 zhī
和 hé;huó;huò
咎 jiù

六画

咸 xián
哇 wā
哄 hōng
hǒng
hòng
哑 yǎ
咧 liē;liě;lie
咣 guāng
虽 suī
品 pǐn
咽 yān;yàn
哗 huā;huá
咱 zán
咿 yī
响 xiǎng
哈 hā;hǎ
咯 gē
哆 duō
咬 yǎo
咳 hāi;ké
咪 mī
哪 nǎ
哟 yō
咨 zī

七画

唇 chún
哲 zhé
哮 xiào
唠 lào
哺 bǔ
哽 gěng
哨 shào
哭 kū
哦 ó;ò
唤 huàn
唁 yàn
哼 hēng
唧 jī
啊 ā;á;à
唉 āi;ài
唆 suō

八画

啧 zé
喵 miāo
啄 zhuó
啪 pā
啦 lā;la
啃 kěn
唬 hǔ
唱 chàng
唾 tuò
唯 wěi
啤 pí
啐 cuì
啸 xiào
啜 chuò
售 shòu

九画

喷 pēn;pèn
喋 dié
喳 chā;zhā
喇 lǎ
喊 hǎn
喝 hē;hè
喂 wèi
喘 chuǎn
嗖 sōu
喉 hóu
喻 yù
啼 tí
嗟 jiē
喧 xuān
喙 huì
善 shàn

十画

嗷 áo
嘟 dū
嗜 shì
嗔 chēn
嗝 gé
嗅 xiù
嗳 ǎi
嗡 wēng
嗤 chī
嗓 sǎng

十一画

嘈 cáo
嗽 sòu
嘎 gā
嘘 shī;xū
嘣 bēng
嘛 ma
嘀 dī;dí

十二画

嘻 xī
噎 yē
嘶 sī
嘲 cháo
嘹 liáo
嘿 hēi
噙 qín
嘱 zhǔ
噔 dēng

十三画

噢 ǒ
噤 jìn
嘴 zuǐ
器 qì
噪 zào

十四画

嚎 háo

十五画

嚣 xiāo

十七画

嚼 jiáo;jué
嚷 rāng;rǎng

(44)
囗部

二画

囚 qiú
四 sì

三画

因 yīn
团 tuán
回 huí

四画

园 yuán
围 wéi
困 kùn
囤 tún
囫 hú

五画

国 guó
固 gù
囹 líng
图 tú

六画

囿 yòu

七画

圃 pǔ
圆 yuán

八画

圈 juān
juàn
quān

(45)
巾部

巾 jīn

二画

布 bù
帅 shuài

三画

帆 fān

四画

帐 zhàng

希 xī

五画

帖 tiē;tiě;tiè
帜 zhì
帕 pà
帛 bó
帘 lián
帚 zhǒu

六画

帮 bāng
带 dài

八画

帷 wéi

九画

幅 fú
帽 mào

十画

幌 huǎng

十二画

幢 zhuàng

(46) 山部

山 shān

三画

屿 yǔ
屹 yì
岁 suì
岂 qǐ

四画

岗 gǎng
岔 chà
岛 dǎo

五画

岸 àn
岬 jiǎ
岭 lǐng
岳 yuè

六画

炭 tàn
峡 xiá
峥 zhēng

七画

峭 qiào
峰 fēng
峻 jùn

八画

崖 yá
崎 qí
崭 zhǎn
崩 bēng
崇 chóng
崛 jué

九画

嵌 qiàn
崴 wǎi

十二画

嶙 lín

十六画

巅 diān

十七画

巍 wēi

(47) 彳部

三画

行 háng;xíng

四画

彻 chè
役 yì
彷 páng

五画

征 zhēng
往 wǎng
彼 bǐ
径 jìng

六画

待 dāi;dài
徇 xùn
衍 yǎn
律 lǜ
很 hěn

七画

徒 tú
徐 xú

八画

徜 cháng
得 dé;de;děi
衔 xián

九画

街 jiē
御 yù
循 xún

十画

微 wēi

十二画

德 dé

十三画

衡 héng

十四画

徽 huī

(48) 彡部

四画

形 xíng
杉 shān

五画

衫 shān

六画

须 xū

八画

彬 bīn
彪 biāo
彩 cǎi

十一画

彰 zhāng

十二画

影 yǐng

(49) 犭部

二画

犯 fàn

三画

犷 guǎng

四画

狂 kuáng
犹 yóu

五画

狙 jū
狐 hú
狗 gǒu
狞 níng
狒 fèi

六画

狭 xiá
狮 shī
独 dú
狰 zhēng
狡 jiǎo
狩 shòu
狱 yù
狠 hěn

七画

狼 láng

八画

猜 cāi
猪 zhū
猎 liè
猫 māo
猖 chāng
猝 cù
猕 mí
猛 měng

九画

猩 xīng
猥 wěi
猾 huá
猴 hóu

十画

猿 yuán

十三画

獭 tǎ

(50) 夕部

夕 xī

三画

多 duō

五画

罗 luó

八画

梦 mèng

(51)
夂部

二画

处 chǔ;chù
冬 dōng

四画

麦 mài
条 tiáo

五画

备 bèi

七画

夏 xià

九画

惫 bèi

(52)
饣部

二画

饥 jī

四画

饬 chì
饭 fàn
饮 yǐn

五画

饯 jiàn
饰 shì
饱 bǎo
饲 sì

六画

饵 ěr
饶 ráo
蚀 shí
饺 jiǎo
饼 bǐng

七画

饿 è
馁 něi

八画

馄 hún
馅 xiàn

九画

馈 kuì
馊 sōu
馋 chán

十画

馏 liù

十一画

馒 mán

(53)
丬部

三画

壮 zhuàng
妆 zhuāng

四画

状 zhuàng

六画

将 jiāng;jiàng

(54)
广部

广 guǎng

三画

庄 zhuāng
庆 qìng

四画

床 chuáng
库 kù
庇 bì
应 yīng;yìng
庐 lú
序 xù

五画

庞 páng
店 diàn
庙 miào
府 fǔ
底 de;dǐ
废 fèi

六画

度 dù;duó
庭 tíng

七画

席 xí
座 zuò
唐 táng

八画

庵 ān
廊 láng
庸 yōng
康 kāng
鹿 lù

十画

廉 lián

十一画

腐 fǔ

十五画

鹰 yīng

(55)
忄部

一画

忆 yì

三画

忏 chàn
忙 máng

四画

怀 huái
怄 òu
忧 yōu
忡 chōng
怅 chàng
忱 chén
快 kuài

五画

怔 zhēng
怯 qiè
怦 pēng
性 xìng
怕 pà
怜 lián
怪 guài
怡 yí

六画

恒 héng
恢 huī
恍 huǎng
恬 tián
恤 xù
恰 qià
恪 kè
恼 nǎo
恨 hèn

七画

恭 gōng
悖 bèi
悚 sǒng
悟 wù
悄 qiāo;qiǎo
悍 hàn
悔 huǐ
悦 yuè

八画

情 qíng
惬 qiè
惜 xī
惭 cán
悼 dào
惧 jù
悸 jì
惟 wéi
惆 chóu
惊 jīng
惦 diàn
惋 wǎn
惨 cǎn
惯 guàn

九画

愤 fèn

慌 huāng
惰 duò
惺 xīng
愕 è
惴 zhuì
愣 lèng
惶 huáng
愧 kuì
愉 yú
慨 kǎi

十画

慑 shè
慎 shèn

十一画

慕 mù
慢 màn
慷 kāng

十二画

懂 dǒng
憔 qiáo
懊 ào
憧 chōng
憎 zēng

十三画

懒 lǎn
憾 hàn
懈 xiè

十四画

懦 nuò

十五画

懵 měng

(56) 门部

门 mén

一画

闩 shuān

二画

闪 shǎn

三画

闭 bì
问 wèn
闯 chuǎng

四画

闰 rùn
闲 xián
间 jiān;jiàn
闷 mēn;mèn

五画

闸 zhá
闹 nào

六画

闺 guī
闻 wén
阀 fá
阁 gé

七画

阄 jiū
阅 yuè

八画

阉 yān
阐 chǎn

九画

阑 lán
阔 kuò

(57) 氵部

二画

汁 zhī
汇 huì
汉 hàn

三画

汗 hán;hàn
污 wū
江 jiāng
汲 jí
汐 xī
汛 xùn
池 chí
汤 tāng

四画

汪 wāng
沐 mù
沥 lì
沏 qī
沙 shā
汩 gǔ
汽 qì
沦 lún
汹 xiōng
泛 fàn
沧 cāng
沟 gōu
没 méi;mò
沆 hàng
沉 chén
沁 qìn

五画

沫 mò
浅 qiǎn
法 fǎ
泄 xiè
沽 gū
河 hé
沾 zhān
沮 jǔ
泪 lèi
油 yóu
泊 bó
沿 yán
泡 pào
注 zhù
泣 qì
泻 xiè
泌 mì
泳 yǒng
泥 ní
泯 mǐn
沸 fèi
沼 zhǎo
波 bō
泼 pō
泽 zé
泾 jīng
治 zhì

六画

洼 wā
洁 jié
洪 hóng
洒 sǎ
浇 jiāo
浊 zhuó
洞 dòng
洇 yīn
测 cè
洗 xǐ
活 huó
涎 xián
派 pài
洽 qià
浏 liú
济 jǐ;jì
洋 yáng
洲 zhōu
浑 hún
浓 nóng
津 jīn

七画

涛 tāo
涝 lào
酒 jiǔ
涟 lián
涉 shè
消 xiāo
涓 juān
涡 wō
浩 hào
海 hǎi
涂 tú
浴 yù
浮 fú
涣 huàn
涤 dí
流 liú
润 rùn
涧 jiàn
涕 tì

(58)

宀部

(67)
马 部

(68)
幺 部

(69)
巛 部

(70)
王 部

(71)
韦 部

(72)
木 部

三画
杆 gān;gǎn
杜 dù
杠 gàng
杖 zhàng
材 cái
村 cūn
杏 xìng
极 jí
杨 yáng
杈 chà
李 lǐ
四画
枉 wǎng
林 lín
枝 zhī
杯 bēi
枢 shū
柜 guì
杳 yǎo
枚 méi
析 xī
板 bǎn
松 sōng
枪 qiāng
枫 fēng
构 gòu
枕 zhěn
果 guǒ
采 cǎi
五画
某 mǒu
标 biāo
柑 gān
枯 kū
柄 bǐng
栋 dòng
查 chá
相 xiāng;xiàng
柏 bǎi
栅 zhà
柳 liǔ
栎 lì
柿 shì
栏 lán
柠 níng
枷 jiā
树 shù
亲 qīn
柒 qī
染 rǎn
架 jià
柔 róu
六画
栽 zāi
框 kuàng
桂 guì
栖 qī;xī
桎 zhì
档 dàng
株 zhū
桥 qiáo
桦 huà
栓 shuān
桃 táo
桅 wéi
格 gé
桩 zhuāng
校 jiào;xiào
核 hé
样 yàng
根 gēn
栩 xǔ
栗 lì
柴 chái
桀 jié
桨 jiǎng
案 àn
七画
械 xiè
梗 gěng
梧 wú
梢 shāo
梏 gù
梅 méi
检 jiǎn
梳 shū
梯 tī
桶 tǒng
梭 suō
梨 lí
梁 liáng
八画
棒 bàng
棱 léng
棋 qí
椰 yē
植 zhí
森 sēn
椅 yǐ
椒 jiāo
棵 kē
棍 gùn
棉 mián
棚 péng
棕 zōng
棺 guān
榔 láng
椭 tuǒ
集 jí
九画
楔 xiē
楚 chǔ
楷 kǎi
槐 huái
楼 lóu
概 gài
十画
模 mó;mú
榜 bǎng
榨 zhà
十一画
横 héng;hèng
槽 cáo
樱 yīng
橡 xiàng
樟 zhāng
橄 gǎn
十二画
橱 chú
橛 jué
橇 qiāo
橙 chéng
橘 jú
十三画
檐 yán
檀 tán

(73)
犬部

犬 quǎn
六画
臭 chòu;xiù
九画
献 xiàn

(74)
歹部

歹 dǎi
二画
死 sǐ
三画
歼 jiān
五画
残 cán
六画
殊 shū
殉 xùn
毙 bì
七画
殓 liàn
八画
殖 zhí
十画
殡 bìn

(75)
车部

车 chē;jū
一画
轧 yà;zhá
二画
轨 guǐ
三画
轩 xuān
四画
轰 hōng
转 zhuǎn
zhuàn
轭 è
斩 zhǎn
轮 lún
软 ruǎn
五画
轱 gū
轴 zhóu
轶 yì
轻 qīng
六画
轿 jiào
较 jiào
七画
辅 fǔ
辆 liàng
八画
辍 chuò
辈 bèi
九画
辐 fú
辑 jí
输 shū
十画
辖 xiá
辗 zhǎn
十一画
辘 lù
十二画
辙 zhé

(76)
戈部

二画
戎 róng
戍 shù
成 chéng
三画
戒 jiè
四画
或 huò
五画
战 zhàn
六画
载 zǎi;zài
七画
戚 qī
戛 jiá
八画
裁 cái
十画
截 jié
十一画
戮 lù
十三画
戴 dài
十四画
戳 chuō

(77)
比部

比 bǐ
五画
皆 jiē
毗 pí

(78)
瓦部

瓦 wǎ
四画
瓮 wèng
六画
瓶 píng
瓷 cí

(79)
止部

止 zhǐ
二画
此 cǐ
三画
步 bù
四画
武 wǔ
歧 qí
肯 kěn
六画
耻 chǐ

(80)
支部

十画
敲 qiāo

(81)
日部

日 rì
一画
旦 dàn
二画
早 zǎo
旭 xù
三画
旱 hàn
时 shí
旷 kuàng
四画
昔 xī
旺 wàng
昆 kūn
昌 chāng
明 míng
易 yì
昂 áng
昏 hūn
五画
春 chūn
昧 mèi
是 shì
显 xiǎn
映 yìng
星 xīng
昨 zuó
昵 nì
昭 zhāo
香 xiāng
六画
晋 jìn
晒 shài
晓 xiǎo
晃 huǎng
huàng
晌 shǎng
晕 yūn;yùn
七画
匙 chí
晤 wù
晨 chén
晦 huì
晚 wǎn
八画
暂 zàn
晴 qíng
暑 shǔ
晰 xī
量 liáng;liàng
晶 jīng
景 jǐng
晾 liàng
智 zhì
九画
暖 nuǎn

八画
氮 dàn
氯 lǜ

(90)
攵部

二画
收 shōu
三画
改 gǎi
五画
政 zhèng
故 gù
六画
致 zhì
敌 dí
效 xiào
七画
赦 shè
教 jiāo;jiào
敕 chì
救 jiù
敝 bì
敏 mǐn
敛 liǎn
敢 gǎn
八画
散 sǎn;sàn
敬 jìng
敞 chǎng
敦 dūn
九画
数 shǔ;shù
十一画
敷 fū

(91)
片部

片 piān;piàn
四画
版 bǎn
八画
牍 dú
牌 pái
九画
牒 dié

(92)
斤部

斤 jīn
一画
斥 chì
四画
欣 xīn
七画
断 duàn
八画
斯 sī
九画
新 xīn

(93)
爪(爫)部

爪 zhǎo;zhuǎ
四画
爬 pá
六画
舀 yǎo
爱 ài

(94)
父部

父 fù
二画
爷 yé
四画
斧 fǔ
爸 bà
六画
釜 fǔ
爹 diē

(95)
月部

月 yuè
二画
有 yǒu
肌 jī
肋 lèi
三画
肝 gān
肚 dù
肛 gāng
肘 zhǒu
肠 cháng
四画
肾 shèn
肴 yáo
肤 fū
肺 fèi
肢 zhī
肿 zhǒng
服 fú;fù
胀 zhàng
朋 péng
股 gǔ
肮 āng
肥 féi
胁 xié
育 yù
五画
胡 hú
背 bēi;bèi
胃 wèi
胚 pēi
胆 dǎn
胜 shèng
胞 bāo
胖 pàng
脉 mài;mò
胫 jìng
胎 tāi
六画
胯 kuà
胭 yān
脍 kuài
脆 cuì
脂 zhī
胸 xiōng
胳 gē
脏 zāng;zàng
脐 qí
胶 jiāo
脑 nǎo
脓 nóng
脊 jǐ
朗 lǎng
七画
脚 jiǎo
脖 bó
脯 pú
脸 liǎn
脱 tuō
八画
期 jī;qī
朝 cháo;zhāo
腊 là
腌 yān
脾 pí
腋 yè
腔 qiāng
腕 wàn
腱 jiàn
九画
腻 nì
腰 yāo
腼 miǎn
腥 xīng
腮 sāi
腭 è
腹 fù
腺 xiàn
鹏 péng
腾 téng

(110) 石部

石 shí

三画

矿 kuàng
码 mǎ

四画

研 yán
砖 zhuān
砒 pī
砌 qì
砂 shā
砚 yàn
砍 kǎn

五画

砝 fǎ
砸 zá
砰 pēng
砾 lì
础 chǔ
破 pò

六画

硕 shuò

七画

硬 yìng
确 què
硫 liú

八画

碍 ài
碘 diǎn
碑 bēi
碎 suì
碰 pèng
碗 wǎn
碌 liù;lù

九画

碧 bì
碟 dié
碱 jiǎn
碳 tàn
磋 cuō
磁 cí

十画

磕 kē
磊 lěi
磅 bàng;páng
碾 niǎn
磐 pán

十一画

磺 huáng
磨 mó;mò

十二画

礁 jiāo
磷 lín

(111) 龙部

六画

聋 lóng
袭 xí

(112) 业部

业 yè

(113) 目部

目 mù

二画

盯 dīng

三画

盲 máng

四画

盹 dǔn
盼 pàn
眨 zhǎ
看 kān;kàn
盾 dùn
眉 méi

五画

眩 xuàn
眠 mián

六画

眶 kuàng
眺 tiào
睁 zhēng
眯 mī;mí
眼 yǎn
眸 móu
眷 juàn

七画

睐 lài
鼎 dǐng

八画

督 dū
睛 jīng
睹 dǔ
睦 mù
瞄 miáo
睫 jié
睡 shuì
睬 cǎi

九画

睿 ruì
瞅 chǒu

十画

瞌 kē
瞒 mán
瞎 xiā
瞑 míng

十一画

瞥 piē
瞟 piǎo
瞠 chēng

十二画

瞧 qiáo
瞬 shùn
瞳 tóng
瞩 zhǔ
瞪 dèng

十三画

瞻 zhān

(114) 田部

田 tián

四画

畏 wèi
界 jiè

五画

畔 pàn
留 liú
畜 chù;xù

六画

略 lüè
累 léi;lěi;lèi

七画

畴 chóu
番 fān

八画

畸 jī

(115) 罒部

四画

罚 fá

五画

罢 bà

八画

署 shǔ
置 zhì
罪 zuì
罩 zhào

十一画

罹 lí

十二画

羁 jī

(116) 皿部

三画

盂 yú

十三画

馥 fù

(120) 白部

白 bái

二画

皂 zào

三画

的 de;dí;dì

六画

皑 ái

皎 jiǎo

九画

魄 pò

(121) 瓜部

瓜 guā

十一画

瓢 piáo

十四画

瓣 bàn

十七画

瓤 ráng

(122) 用部

用 yòng

四画

甭 béng

(123) 鸟部

鸟 niǎo

四画

鸥 ōu

鸦 yā

五画

鸭 yā

鸵 tuó

鸳 yuān

六画

鸽 gē

七画

鹅 é

八画

鹊 què

鹌 ān

十画

鹤 hè

十一画

鹦 yīng

十二画

鹬 yù

(124) 疒部

二画

疖 jiē

疗 liáo

三画

疟 nüè

疙 gē

疚 jiù

四画

疥 jiè

疮 chuāng

疯 fēng

疫 yì

疤 bā

五画

症 zhēng
zhèng

病 bìng

疾 jí

疹 zhěn

疼 téng

疱 pào

痂 jiā

疲 pí

痉 jìng

六画

痔 zhì

疵 cī

痊 quán

痒 yǎng

痕 hén

七画

痣 zhì

痨 láo

痘 dòu

痞 pǐ

痢 lì

痤 cuó

痛 tòng

八画

痱 fèi

痼 gù

痴 chī

瘁 cuì

痰 tán

九画

瘟 wēn

瘦 shòu

瘊 hóu

瘙 sào

十画

瘪 biē;biě

瘤 liú

瘠 jí

瘫 tān

十一画

瘾 yǐn

瘸 qué

十二画

癌 ái

十三画

癖 pǐ

十六画

癫 diān

(125) 立部

立 lì

四画

竖 shù

五画

站 zhàn

竞 jìng

六画

章 zhāng

竟 jìng

翌 yì

七画

童 tóng

竣 jùn

九画

竭 jié

端 duān

(126) 穴部

穴 xué

二画

究 jiū

穷 qióng

三画

空 kōng;kòng

四画

突 tū

穿 chuān

窃 qiè

五画

窍 qiào

窄 zhǎi

容 róng

窈 yǎo

六画

窒 zhì

窑 yáo

七画

窜 cuàn

窝 wō

窖 jiào

窗 chuāng

窘 jiǒng

八画

窥 kuī
窦 dòu
窠 kē
窟 kū

(127)

衤部

二画

补 bǔ

三画

衬 chèn

四画

袄 ǎo

五画

袜 wà
袒 tǎn
袖 xiù
袍 páo
被 bèi

七画

裕 yù
裤 kù
裙 qún

八画

裱 biǎo
褂 guà
裸 luǒ
裨 bì

九画

褐 hè
褪 tuì;tùn

十画

褥 rù
褴 lán

十一画

褶 zhě

十二画

襁 qiǎng

十三画

襟 jīn

(128)

疋部

六画

蛋 dàn

七画

疏 shū

(129)

皮部

皮 pí

五画

皱 zhòu

六画

皲 jūn
颇 pō

七画

皴 cūn

(130)

矛部

矛 máo

四画

矜 jīn

(131)

耒部

四画

耕 gēng
耘 yún
耗 hào
耙 bà;pá

(132)

老(耂)部

老 lǎo

(133)

耳部

耳 ěr

四画

耽 dān
耸 sǒng

五画

职 zhí
聆 líng
聊 liáo

六画

联 lián

七画

聘 pìn

八画

聚 jù

九画

聪 cōng

(134)

西(覀)部

西 xī

十二画

覆 fù

(135)

页部

页 yè

二画

顶 dǐng
顷 qǐng

三画

顺 shùn

四画

顽 wán
顾 gù
顿 dùn
颁 bān
颂 sòng
预 yù

五画

颅 lú
领 lǐng
颈 jǐng

六画

颊 jiá
颌 hé

七画

颐 yí
频 pín

八画

颗 kē

九画

题 tí
颜 yán
额 é

十画

颠 diān

十三画

颤 chàn;zhàn

十七画

颧 quán

(136)

虍部

二画

虎 hǔ
虏 lǔ

三画

虐 nüè

五画

虚 xū

(137)

虫部

虫 chóng

二画

虱 shī

三画

虹 hóng

五画

酣 hān
酥 sū

六画

酬 chóu
酱 jiàng

七画

酵 jiào
酷 kù
酶 méi
酿 niàng
酸 suān

八画

醋 cù
醇 chún
醉 zuì

九画

醒 xǐng

(155) 辰部

辰 chén

(156) 卤部

卤 lǔ

(157) 里部

里 lǐ;li

四画

野 yě

(158) 足部

足 zú

二画

趴 pā

三画

趸 dǔn
趿 tā

四画

距 jù
趾 zhǐ
跃 yuè

五画

践 jiàn
跋 bá
跌 diē
跑 pǎo
跛 bǒ

六画

跨 kuà
跷 qiāo
跳 tiào
跺 duò
跪 guì
路 lù
跻 jī
跤 jiāo
跟 gēn

七画

踌 chóu
踉 liàng
踊 yǒng

八画

踝 huái
踢 tī
踟 chí
踩 cǎi
踮 diǎn
踪 zōng
踞 jù
踏 tà

九画

踹 chuài
踱 duó
蹄 tí
蹉 cuō
蹂 róu

十画

蹑 niè
蹒 pán
蹈 dǎo
蹊 qī;xī

十一画

蹙 cù
蹩 bié
蹦 bèng

十二画

蹶 jué
蹴 cù
蹲 dūn
蹭 cèng
蹿 cuān
蹬 dēng

十三画

躁 zào

(159) 身部

身 shēn

三画

躬 gōng

四画

躯 qū

六画

躲 duǒ

八画

躺 tǎng

(160) 采部

五画

释 shì

(161) 谷部

十画

豁 huō;huò

(162) 豸部

三画

豺 chái
豹 bào

七画

貌 mào

(163) 角部

角 jiǎo;jué

六画

触 chù
解 jiě;jiè

(164) 言(訁见讠)部

言 yán

六画

誊 téng
誉 yù

七画

誓 shì

十二画

警 jǐng

十三画

譬 pì

(165) 辛部

辛 xīn

五画

辜 gū

六画

辟 bì;pì

七画

辣 là

九画

辨 biàn
辩 biàn

十画

辫 biàn

(166) 青部

青 qīng

六画

静 jìng

八画

靛 diàn

(167) 雨部

雨 yǔ

三画

雪 xuě

五画

雷 léi

零 líng

雾 wù

雹 báo

六画

需 xū

七画

震 zhèn

霄 xiāo

霉 méi

八画

霖 lín

霓 ní

霍 huò

霎 shà

九画

霜 shuāng

霞 xiá

十一画

霭 ǎi

十三画

霸 bà

露 lòu;lù

霹 pī

(168) 齿部

齿 chǐ

五画

龃 jǔ

龄 líng

龅 bāo

六画

龇 zī

龈 yín

九画

龋 qǔ

龌 wò

(169) 隹部

二画

隽 jùn

四画

雄 xióng

雅 yǎ

五画

雏 chú

六画

雌 cí

八画

雕 diāo

(170) 金部

五画

鉴 jiàn

八画

錾 zàn

十一画

鏖 áo

(171) 鱼部

鱼 yú

四画

鱿 yóu

鲁 lǔ

六画

鲜 xiān

七画

鲢 lián

鲤 lǐ

鲨 shā

八画

鲱 fēi

鲸 jīng

九画

鳄 è

十画

鳍 qí

鳏 guān

十一画

鳖 biē

十二画

鳝 shàn

鳞 lín

(172) 革部

革 gé

二画

勒 lè;lēi

四画

靴 xuē

靶 bǎ

六画

鞋 xié

鞍 ān

七画

鞘 qiào

八画

鞠 jū

九画

鞭 biān

(173) 骨部

骨 gū;gǔ

五画

骷 kū

六画

骸 hái

十二画

髓 suǐ

(174) 鬼部

鬼 guǐ

四画

魂 hún

魁 kuí

五画

魅 mèi

十一画

魔 mó

(175) 食部

食 shí

七画

餐 cān

(176) 音部

音 yīn

四画

韵 yùn

(177) 髟部

五画

髯 rán

Aa

阿 ā [前缀] (方) ♦阿爸 dad ♦阿妹 little sister
▷另见 ē

阿斗 Ā Dǒu [名] (喻) incompetent ◇他这个经理真是个阿斗。He's really an incompetent manager.

阿拉伯数字 Ālābó shùzì [名] Arabic numerals

阿姨 āyí [名] **1** (指年长妇女) auntie ◇李阿姨是妈妈的好朋友。Auntie Li is a good friend of Mum's. **2** (女保育员) carer

啊 ā [叹] oh ◇啊！着火了！ Oh! It's caught fire! ◇啊！我考过了！ Wow! I passed the exam!

啊 ǎ [叹] huh ◇啊？你在这儿干吗？ Huh? What are you doing here?

啊 à [叹] **1** (表示应诺) all right ◇啊，这样可以。All right, that's fine. **2** (表示醒悟) aha ◇啊，现在我知道了。Aha! Now I understand. **3** (表示惊异或赞叹) ah ◇啊，大海！ Ah, the sea!

哎 āi [叹] **1** (表示惊讶或不满) oh ◇哎！这么贵！ Oh! It's so expensive! **2** (表示提醒) hey ◇哎！别踩了那朵花。Hey! Careful not to tread on that flower.

哎呀 āiyā [叹] oh ◇哎呀，这条路真难走！ Oh, this road is hard going! ◇哎呀，电脑又有病毒了。Oh no, the computer has been infected by a virus again.

哎哟 āiyō [叹] **1** (表示惊讶) oh ◇哎哟！都这么晚了！ Oh, it's so late! **2** (表示痛苦) ow **3** (表示惋惜) oh no

哀 āi **I** [形] (悲痛) sad **II** [动] **1** (悼念) mourn **2** (怜悯) pity

哀愁 āichóu [名] sorrow

哀悼 āidào [动] mourn

哀怜 āilián [名] compassion

哀求 āiqiú [动] plead ◇哀求饶命 plead for one's life

哀伤 āishāng [名] grief

哀叹 āitàn [动] sigh

哀痛 āitòng [动] grieve ◇他哀痛失去了最好的朋友。He is grieving for the loss of his best friend.

哀怨 āiyuàn [名] grief and resentment

哀乐 āiyuè [名] funeral music

埃 āi [名] dust

挨 āi [动] **1** (靠近) be next to ◇网吧挨着一家礼品店。The Internet café is next to a gift shop. ◇两个孩子挨着门坐。The two children sat by the door. **2** (逐个) ◇警察挨门搜查。The police conducted a house-to-house search.
▷另见 ái

挨个儿 āigèr [副] one by one ◇请大家排好队，挨个儿上车。Please will everyone line up and get on the bus one by one.

挨近 āijìn [动] be close to ◇我们学校挨近一家电影院。Our school is close to a cinema.

挨门挨户 āimén-āihù house-to-house ◇你对挨门挨户推销的做法有什么看法？ What do you think of the door-to-door sales method?

唉 āi [叹] **1** (表示答应) mm **2** (表示叹息) oh
▷另见 ài

唉声叹气 āi shēng tàn qì sigh deeply

挨 ái [动] **1** (遭受) suffer ♦挨饿 suffer from hunger ♦挨骂 get told off **2** (艰难度过) endure ◇那么困难的年代我们都挨过来了，这不算什么。We have all endured such difficult times that this seems insignificant. **3** (拖延) put … off (*pt, pp* put)
▷另见 āi

挨打 áidǎ [动] be beaten up

挨整 áizhěng [动] be the target of attack

皑 ái [形] 见下文

皑皑 ái'ái [形] snow-white

癌 ái [名] cancer

癌变 áibiàn [动] become cancerous (*pt* became, *pp* become)

癌症 áizhèng [名] cancer

嗳 ǎi [叹] oh

矮 ǎi [形] **1** (指人) short ◇我矮他一头。I'm a head shorter than him. **2** (指物) low

矮小 ǎixiǎo [形] **1** (身材) short **2** (树木、草棚等) low

矮子 ǎizi [名] dwarf

蔼 ǎi [形] friendly

霭 ǎi [名] mist

艾 ài **I** [名] (植) mugwort **II** [动] (书) end

艾滋病 àizībìng [名] AIDS

唉 ài [叹] **1** (表伤感或惋惜) oh **2** (表示回应命令) OK
▷另见 āi

爱 ài [动] **1** (恋) love ◇我爱你。I love you. ◇爱祖国 love one's country ◇他爱上了一个女孩。He fell in love with a girl. **2** (喜欢) enjoy ◇爱上网 enjoy surfing the net ◇爱逛街 enjoy strolling around the streets **3** (爱惜) care about ◇爱公物 respect public property **4** (容易) ◇她爱晕车。She tends to get car sick. ◇爱发脾气 be hot-tempered

爱不释手 ài bù shì shǒu be attached ◇他对那台笔记本电脑爱不释手。He's very attached to that laptop.

爱称 àichēng [名] pet name

爱戴 àidài [动] love and esteem

爱抚 àifǔ [动] fondle

爱好 àihào [动] be keen on ◇爱好集邮 be keen on stamp collecting ◇她有广泛的爱好。She has many hobbies.

爱护 àihù [动] take care of (*pt* took, *pp* taken)

爱怜 àilián [动] coo over ◇这只小狗真惹人爱怜。The puppy made everyone coo.

爱莫能助 ài mò néng zhù have one's hands tied ◇他有很多困难，但我爱莫能助。He's having a lot of problems, but my hands are tied.

爱慕 àimù [动] adore ◇她爱慕她丈夫。She adores her husband. ◇那女人爱慕虚荣。That woman is very vain.

爱情 àiqíng [名] love ◇爱情是无价的。Love is priceless.

爱屋及乌 ài wū jí wū love me, love my dog ◇他真是爱屋及乌，竟然喜欢上了女友听的音乐。This really is a case of love me, love my dog. Now he's suddenly started to like his girlfriend's music.

爱惜 àixī [动] value ◇爱惜时间 value one's time

爱心 àixīn [名] affection

隘 ài **I** [形] narrow ♦隘巷 narrow alley **II** [名] pass ♦要隘 pass

碍 ài [动] be in the way ◇你干你的，我干我的，碍你啥了？ You get on with your business and I'll get on with mine. I'm not in your way, am I?

碍口 àikǒu [动] be too embarrassing for words ◇跟老师借钱真碍口！Borrowing money from a teacher is too embarrassing for words!

碍面子 ài miànzi ◇碍着上级的面子，他没提啥意见。To avoid his superiors losing face, he didn't make any suggestions.

碍事 àishì **I** [动] matter ◇他出席不了会议不碍事。It didn't matter that he couldn't attend the meeting. **II** [形] serious ◇他的病不碍事。His illness isn't serious.

碍手碍脚 ài shǒu ài jiǎo get in the way ◇我正忙着呢，别在这里碍手碍脚的。I'm really busy – stop getting in the way.

碍眼 àiyǎn [形] **1** (不顺眼) ugly ◇这些花花绿绿的标牌立在校园里，怪碍眼的。These gaudy signs all over campus are a real eyesore. **2** (不便) in the way ◇人家正忙着呢，我们在这里碍眼，快走吧！Everyone's very busy. We're in the way here – let's go!

嗳 ài [叹] oh

暧 ài [形] (书) dim

暧昧 àimèi [形] **1** (含糊) vague **2** (关系) ambiguous

安 ān **I** [形] **1** (安定) quiet ◇坐立不安 be unable to sit still ◇心神不安 feel uneasy **2** (平安) safe ◆治安 public order ◇安抵目的地 arrive safely at one's destination **II** [动] **1** (使安静) calm ◆安心 calm the nerves **2** (满足) be content with ◇安于现状 be content with the way things are **3** (放置) place ◇把他安在哪里合适呢？ Where would be a good place to put him? **4** (安装) fit ◇安窗户 fit a window ◇门上安把锁 fit a lock on the door **5** (设立) set … up (*pt*, *pp* set) ◇这里安了个收费站。A toll booth has been set up here. **6** (加上) bring (*pt*, *pp* brought) ◇安罪名 bring a charge **7** (怀着) harbour (英), harbor (美) ◇安坏心 harbour (英) 或 harbor (美) evil intentions ◇你安的什么心？ What are you plotting?

安插 ānchā [动] **1** (人) install ◇安插亲信 install in place a trusted friend **2** (东西) insert ◇安插增刊 insert supplements

安定 āndìng **I** [形] stable **II** [动] stabilize ◇安定局面 stabilize the situation ◇安定民心 reassure the public

安顿 āndùn **I** [动] (表示安排妥当) (人) make arrangements for ◇安顿家小 make arrangements for the family **II** [形] (安稳) peaceful ◇这儿太嘈杂，我睡不安顿。It's too noisy here – I can't sleep properly.

安放 ānfàng [动] put … in a safe place (*pt*, *pp* put) ◇把贵重物品安放好。Put your valuables in a safe place.

安分 ānfèn [形] contented

安好 ānhǎo [形] safe and sound

安家 ānjiā [动] **1** (安置家庭) settle ◇他们在北京安了家。They settled in Beijing. **2** (结婚) get married

安检 ānjiǎn [名] security check ◇经过安检 go through security ◇乘客登机前必须安检。Passengers must go through security before boarding.

安静 ānjìng [形] **1** (无声) quiet **2** (平静) peaceful ◇婴儿在小床上睡得很安静。The baby was sleeping peacefully in its cot.

安乐 ānlè [形] comfortable

安乐死 ānlèsǐ [名] euthanasia

安宁 ānníng [形] **1** (秩序正常) undisturbed **2** (宁静) calm ◇我心里天天不得安宁。I never feel at ease.

安排 ānpái [动] arrange

安全 ānquán [形] safe ◇居民区有保安巡逻，比较安全。There are security patrols in this district, so it is fairly safe. ◇安全驾驶 drive safely ◇一人出门在外，注意安全。When you are away from home, be sure to take care. ◇人身安全 personal safety

安全套 ānquántào [名] condom

安然 ānrán [形] **1** (平安) safe ◇安然无恙 safe and sound **2** (平静) peaceful ◇知道门已关好，她安然入睡了。Once she knew that the door had been locked, she fell asleep peacefully.

安身 ānshēn [动] settle down

安生 ānshēng [形] **1** (安定) peaceful **2** (安静) quiet

安慰 ānwèi **I** [动] comfort ◇我安慰了他几句。I said a few comforting words to him. **II** [形] reassured ◇听了你讲的话，我心里很安慰。After hearing what you had to say, I felt reassured.

安稳 ānwěn [形] **1** (稳当) steady **2** (方) (沉静) calm

安息 ānxī [动] **1** (休息) rest **2** (悼念用语) rest in peace

安详 ānxiáng [形] composed

安心 ānxīn [动] **1** (形容心情) stop worrying ◇得知家中一切都好，我也就安心了。Once I knew that everything was fine at home, I stopped worrying. **2** (居心不善) plot ◇你安的什么心？ What are you plotting? **3** (不分心) keep one's mind on (*pt*, *pp* kept)

安逸 ānyì [形] comfortable

安葬 ānzàng [动] bury

安置 ānzhì [动] make arrangements for

安装 ānzhuāng [动] install

庵 ān [名] 1 (书) (小草屋) hut 2 (佛寺) nunnery

谙 ān [动] (书) be familiar with

谙熟 ānshú [动] have a good knowledge of

鹌 ān 见下文

鹌鹑 ānchún [名] quail

鞍 ān [名] saddle

岸 àn I [名] edge ♦河岸 river bank ♦海岸 seashore II [形] (书) 1 (崇高) lofty ♦伟岸 strapping 2 (骄傲) proud ♦傲岸 proud

按 àn I [动] 1 (用手压) press ◊按电钮 press a button ◊按门铃 push a doorbell ◊按手印 make a fingerprint 2 (人) push … down ◊他把小偷按倒在地。He pushed the thief to the ground. 3 (搁下) shelve ◊按下此事不说 put the matter aside 4 (抑制) restrain ◊按不住心头怒火 be unable to restrain one's fury II [介] (依照) according to ◊按制度办事 do things by the book ◊按质定价 price on the basis of quality

按部就班 àn bù jiù bān stick to the rules ◊时间不够了，不能这样按部就班。There's not enough time, so we will have to break the rules.

按揭 ànjiē [名] mortgage

按摩 ànmó [动] massage

按捺 ànnà [动] restrain

按图索骥 àn tú suǒ jì be rigid in one's approach ◊他做什么事情都是按图索骥，效率太低。He's ineffective because his approach is too rigid.

按照 ànzhào [介] according to ◊按照课本 according to the text book ◊方案按照大家的建议修改了。The plan was changed in line with everyone's recommendations.

案 àn [名] 1 (桌子) table 2 (案件) case 3 (案卷) file 4 (提案) proposal

案件 ànjiàn [名] case

案卷 ànjuàn [名] file

案子 ànzi [名] 1 (家具) counter ◊熨衣案子 ironing board 2 (案件) case

暗 àn I [形] 1 (昏暗) dim ◊今晚月光很暗。Tonight the moon is dim. 2 (秘密) underhand ◊明人不做暗事。An honest person does nothing underhand. II [副] secretly

暗暗 àn'àn [副] secretly

暗藏 àncáng [动] conceal

暗淡 àndàn [形] 1 (昏暗) dim 2 (不明朗) dismal

暗害 ànhài [动] 1 (暗杀) murder 2 (陷害) stab … in the back

暗号 ànhào [名] secret signal

暗杀 ànshā [动] assassinate

暗示 ànshì [动] hint ◊他暗示我赶快离开。He hinted that I should leave soon. ◊他没明白我的暗示。He didn't pick up on my hint.

暗算 ànsuàn [动] plot against ◊他总是暗算别人。He's always plotting against people. ◊他常常遭人暗算。He frequently falls prey to other people's machinations.

暗无天日 àn wú tiān rì anarchy ◊当时的社会暗无天日。There was complete anarchy in society at that time.

暗语 ànyǔ [名] code word

暗中 ànzhōng I [名] the dark ◊我在暗中什么也看不见。I couldn't see anything in the dark. II [副] surreptitiously ◊他暗中操纵选举。He surreptitiously fixed the election.

暗自 ànzì [副] secretly

黯 àn 见下文

黯然 ànrán [形] 1 (昏暗) dim 2 (低落) dejected

肮 āng 见下文

肮脏 āngzāng [形] 1 (不干净) filthy ◊地板很肮脏。The floor is filthy. 2 (喻) (不道德) vile ◊他思想肮脏。His way of thinking is vile. ◊这是一笔肮脏的交易。It's a dirty deal.

昂 áng [动] 1 (抬) lift ◊昂起头 hold one's head high 2 (高涨) be high ◊她情绪高昂。She's high in spirits.

昂然 ángrán [形] resolute

昂首阔步 áng shǒu kuò bù stride with one's head held high ◇他昂首阔步地前进。He strode forward with his head held high.

昂扬 ángyáng [形] upbeat

盎 àng [形] (书) abundant

盎然 àngrán [形] abundant

盎司 àngsī [量] ounce

凹 āo [形] sunken

凹陷 āoxiàn [动] sink (*pt* sank, *pp* sunk)

遨 áo 见下文

遨游 áoyóu [动] travel

嗷 áo 见下文

嗷嗷 áo'áo [拟] ◇他疼得嗷嗷叫。He howled with pain. ◇成群的雁在头顶嗷嗷叫着。Flocks of geese honked overhead.

熬 áo [动] **1** (煮) stew ♦熬粥 make porridge **2** (提取) decoct **3** (忍受) endure

熬煎 áojiān [名] suffering

熬夜 áoyè [动] stay up late

翱 áo 见下文

翱翔 áoxiáng [动] soar

鏖 áo 见下文

鏖战 áozhàn [动] fight hard (*pt, pp* fought)

袄 ǎo [名] coat ♦棉袄 padded jacket

拗 ào [动] awkward
▷另见 niù

拗口 àokǒu [形] hard to pronounce

傲 ào [形] proud

傲骨 àogǔ [名] pride

傲慢 àomàn [形] arrogant

傲气 àoqì [名] arrogance ◇他有股傲气。He is a bit arrogant.

傲然 àorán **I** [形] lofty **II** [副] proudly

奥 ào [形] profound

奥林匹克运动会 Àolínpǐkè yùndònghuì [名] Olympic Games (*pl*)

奥秘 àomì [名] mystery ◇揭示大自然的奥秘 reveal Nature's mysteries

奥妙 àomiào [形] mysterious ◇这问题很好理解，其中并无奥妙。This can be easily explained – there's nothing mysterious about it at all.

澳 ào [名] bay

懊 ào [形] **1** (后悔) regretful **2** (恼怒) annoyed

懊悔 àohuǐ [动] regret ◇他错过了这个好机会，懊悔不已。He really regretted having missed such a good opportunity.

懊恼 àonǎo [形] upset ◇他因没考好而懊恼。He was upset that he didn't get a better mark in the exam.

懊丧 àosàng [形] despondent ◇他因失业而懊丧。Losing his job left him rather despondent.

Bb

八 bā [数] eight

八方 bāfāng [名] all directions

八股 bāgǔ [名] lifeless writing

八九不离十 bā jiǔ bù lí shí (口) pretty close ◇你的答案八九不离十。Your answer is pretty close.

八面玲珑 bāmiàn línglóng be a smooth operator

八仙过海，各显神通 bāxiān guòhǎi, gè xiǎn shéntōng compete to demonstrate one's talents ◇他们大搞技术创新，真是八仙过海，各显神通。They have been very innovative technically – each competing with the other to demonstrate their talents.

巴 bā **I** [动] **1** (盼望) hope ♦巴望 look forward to **2** (粘住) cling to (*pt, pp* clung) ◇葡萄藤巴在架子上。The vine clung to the trellis. **3** (方) (张开) open ◇巴着眼 with eyes open **II** [名] **1** (粘结物) crust ♦锅巴 rice crust ♦泥巴 mud **2** (器官) ♦下巴 chin ♦尾巴 tail ♦嘴巴 mouth

巴结 bājie [动] suck up to ◇巴结上司 suck up to the boss

巴士 bāshì [名] bus

巴望 bāwàng [动] look forward to ◇他巴望着能来信。He was looking forward to getting a letter.

巴掌 bāzhang [名] (手掌) palm ◇拍巴掌 clap

扒 bā [动] **1** (挖) dig ... up (*pt, pp* dug) ◇她把埋的陶器扒了出来。She dug up buried pottery. **2** (拆) pull ... down ◇扒房子 pull down a house **3** (攀缘) lean on ◇两个邻居扒在墙头上聊天。The two neighbours (英) 或 neighbors (美) leaned on the wall chatting. **4** (拨动) push ... aside **5** (剥下) take ... off (*pt* took, *pp* taken) ◇扒下袜子 take off one's socks
▷另见 pá

扒拉 bāla [动] brush ◇把土扒拉一边去 brush the earth to one side

芭 bā [名] banana

芭蕉 bājiāo [名] banana

芭蕾舞 bālěiwǔ [名] ballet

吧 bā **I** [拟] crack ◇吧！枪响了。The gun went off with a crack. **II** [名] bar **III** [动] take a drag (*pt* took, *pp* taken) ◇他吧了一口烟。He took a drag on his cigarette.

吧嗒 bāda [拟] click ◇门吧嗒一声关上了。The door closed with a click.

吧女 bānǚ [名] barmaid

疤 bā [名] **1** (疤痕) scar ◇他脸上有疤。He had a scar on his face. **2** (痕迹) mark

疤痕 bāhén [名] scar ◇这件事给他心里留下一个疤痕。This event left him psychologically scarred.

捌 bā [数] eight

笆 bā [名] basketry

笆斗 bādǒu [名] basket

拔 bá [动] **1** (抽出) pull ... up ♦拔草 weed **2** (取下) pull ... out ◇拔牙 pull out a tooth **3** (吸出) draw ... out (*pt* drew, *pp* drawn) **4** (挑选) choose (*pt* chose, *pp* chosen) ◇选拔人才 select talented people **5** (提高) raise **6** (超出) exceed ♦海拔 height above sea level ◇出类拔萃 outstanding **7** (夺取) capture ◇连拔三城 capture three towns in succession **8** (冷却) cool ◇用冰水拔啤酒 cool beer in iced water

拔高 bágāo [动] raise ◇拔高嗓门 raise one's voice

拔河 báhé [名] tug-of-war

拔尖儿 bájiānr [形] excellent

拔苗助长 bá miáo zhù zhǎng damage by applying too much pressure ◇用这种方法教育孩子，简直是拔苗助长。Teaching children in this way simply means applying too much pressure and damaging them.

跋 bá **I** [动] cross ♦跋山 cross

mountains II [名] postscript

跋扈 báhù [形] domineering

跋山涉水 bá shān shè shuǐ cross mountains and rivers

跋涉 báshè [动] trek ◇长途跋涉 make a long trek

把 bǎ I [动] 1 (握住) hold (*pt, pp* held) ◇把住栏杆 hold onto the rails 2 (看守) guard ◇把大门 guard the gate 3 (控制) control ◇把舵 be at the helm 4 (拿) take (*pt* took, *pp* taken) ◇别把这当回事。Don't take this too seriously. 5 (紧靠) be near to ◇把着十字路口有家超市。There is a supermarket near the crossroads. 6 (束缚) secure ◇把住裂口 secure a breach II [名] 1 (把手) handle 2 (捆) bundle ♦草把 a bundle of straw III [量] ◇一把刀 a knife ◇一把米 a handful of rice IV [介] ◇把门关好 shut the door ◇把作业做完 finish doing one's homework ◇她把书放在桌子上了。She put the book on the table. V [副] about ◇个把月 about one month
▷另见 bà

把柄 bǎbǐng [名] hold ◇他抓住了我的把柄。He's got a hold over me.

把持 bǎchí [动] 1 (独占) monopolize ◇把持高位 monopolize power 2 (控制) control ◇她被伤害得这么厉害, 我怕她把持不住。She has been hurt so badly, I'm worried she may not be able to keep her feelings under control.

把关 bǎguān [动] 1 (把守关口) hold a pass (*pt, pp* held) 2 (严守标准) ensure standards (*pl*) ◇把好质量关 ensure quality standards

把势 bǎshi [名] 1 (武术) martial arts (*pl*) 2 (能手) skilled worker ◇干庄稼活儿，他是个好把势。He is a skilled farmer.

把守 bǎshǒu [动] guard ◇把守边境 guard the border

把手 bǎshǒu [名] handle

把握 bǎwò I [动] grasp ◇把握实质 have a grasp of the facts ◇把握时机 seize the opportunity II [名] certainty ◇没把握 there is no certainty ◇我对自己的未来毫无把握。My future is very uncertain.

把戏 bǎxì [名] 1 (杂耍) acrobatics (*pl*) 2 (花招) trick ◇他耍的把戏很难看穿。It's not easy to see through his tricks.

把兄弟 bǎxiōngdì [名] sworn brothers

靶 bǎ [名] target

靶子 bǎzi [名] target ◇你还未射中靶子。You haven't hit the target yet. ◇她因说错话而被当作攻击的靶子。Because she made a mistake she became the target of attack.

把 bà [名] 1 (手柄) handle ♦镐把 pickaxe handle 2 (茎秆) stem ♦花把 stem 3 (话柄) butt ◇话把儿 the butt of ridicule
▷另见 bǎ

把子 bàzi [名] handle ◇刀把子 knife handle

坝 bà [名] 1 (水闸) dam 2 (堤坝) dyke

爸 bà [名] father

爸爸 bàba [名] dad

耙 bà I [名] harrow II [动] harrow
▷另见 pá

罢 bà [动] 1 (停) stop ◇欲罢不能 compelled to carry on 2 (免去) dismiss ♦罢免 recall 3 (完毕) finish ◇听罢，他哈哈大笑。After listening, he laughed out loud. 4 (算了) give up (*pt* gave, *pp* given)

罢工 bàgōng [动] strike (*pt, pp* struck) ◇工人们罢工要求增加工资。The workers are striking for higher wages.

罢了 bàle [助] ◇我的水平并不高，只是尽自己的努力罢了。My average is not high, but I put in my best effort; that's all there is to it.

罢了 bàliǎo [动] let it pass (*pt, pp* let)

罢免 bàmiǎn [动] recall

罢手 bàshǒu [动] give up (*pt* gave, *pp* given)

罢休 bàxiū [动] give up (*pt* gave, *pp* given)

霸 bà I [名] 1 (指人) tyrant ♦恶霸 local tyrant 2 (指国家) hegemonist power ♦争霸 struggle for hegemony **II** [动] tyrannize ◊独霸一方 tyrannize a region **III** [形] tyrannical ♦霸气 domineering

霸道 bàdào [形] overbearing ◊横行霸道 tyrannize

霸道 bàdao [形] potent

霸权 bàquán [名] hegemony

霸王 bàwáng [名] despot

霸业 bàyè [名] position of supremacy

霸占 bàzhàn [动] seize

掰 bāi [动] break … off (*pt* broke, *pp* broken) ◊农民们在田地里正掰玉米呢。The farmers are picking maize in the fields.

掰腕子 bāi wànzi [动] arm wrestle

白 bái **I** [形] **1** (白色) white ♦苍白 pale **2** (清楚) clear ◊真相大白 the truth has come out **3** (明亮) bright ♦白天 daytime **4** (平淡) plain ◊白开水 boiled water **II** [动] state ♦辩白 argue **III** [副] **1** (无结果) in vain ◊我们这些试验是白做了。Our experiments were in vain. **2** (无偿地) free of charge ◊那些政客就喜欢白吃白喝。Those politicians just like eating and drinking, free of charge.

白白 báibái [副] in vain ◊不要白白浪费钱。Don't waste your money on nothing.

白璧微瑕 bái bì wēi xiá minor flaw

白菜 báicài [名] Chinese cabbage

白痴 báichī [名] **1** (病症) idiocy **2** (病人) idiot **3** (贬) (傻瓜) moron

白费 báifèi [动] waste ◊我们的努力没有白费。Our efforts have not been wasted. ◊你不要白费心思。Don't strain your brain for nothing.

白宫 Báigōng [名] the White House

白话 báihuà [名] unfounded statement

白金 báijīn [名] platinum

白净 báijing [形] fair and clear

白酒 báijiǔ [名] clear spirit

白卷 báijuàn [名] unanswered examination paper

白领 báilǐng [名] ◊白领职员 white-collar worker

白马王子 báimǎ wángzǐ knight in shining armour (英) 或 armor (美)

白米饭 báimǐfàn [名] boiled rice

白描 báimiáo [名] **1** (指美术) line drawing **2** (指写作) straightforward style of writing

白皮书 báipíshū [名] White Paper

白热 báirè [形] white-hot

白人 báirén [名] white people (*pl*) ◊他是白人。He's white.

白日做梦 báirì zuò mèng daydream

白色 báisè [名] **1** (字) white **2** (喻) counterrevolutionary ◊白色政权 counterrevolutionary regime

白手起家 báishǒu qǐ jiā build up from nothing (*pt, pp* built) ◊他们夫妻是白手起家。The couple started out their business from scratch.

白糖 báitáng [名] white sugar

白天 báitiān [名] daytime, day

白条 báitiáo [名] IOU

白头偕老 báitóu xié lǎo live together to a ripe old age ◊祝愿这对新人白头偕老，永远幸福。May the bride and groom live happily ever after to a ripe old age.

白血病 báixuèbìng [名] leukaemia (英), leukemia (美)

白眼 báiyǎn [名] disdainful look ◊他恨遭人白眼。He hates being treated with disdain.

白银 báiyín [名] silver

白昼 báizhòu [名] daytime

白字 báizì [名] wrong character

百 bǎi **I** [数] hundred **II** [形] numerous ◊千方百计 in every way possible

百般 bǎibān [副] in every possible way

百出 bǎichū [动] be full of

百废俱兴 bǎi fèi jù xīng all neglected tasks are being dealt with

百分比 bǎifēnbǐ [名] percentage

百分点 bǎifēndiǎn [名] percentage point

百分制 bǎifēnzhì [名] percentage system

百分之百 bǎi fēn zhī bǎi absolutely ◇他百分之百会来。He will definitely come.

百花齐放 bǎi huā qí fàng blossom freely ◇我们国家的文艺事业百花齐放。Our country's literature and fine arts scenes are blossoming freely.

百货 bǎihuò [名] general goods (*pl*) ◇百货商店 department store

百科全书 bǎikē quánshū [名] encyclopaedia (英), encyclopedia (美)

百里挑一 bǎi lǐ tiāo yī one in a hundred ◇这小伙儿真是百里挑一。This lad is really one in a hundred.

百炼成钢 bǎi liàn chéng gāng experience makes you stronger ◇这支军队百炼成钢。This army has been toughened up by its experience.

百年大计 bǎinián dàjì [名] landmark event

百年树人 bǎinián shùrén it takes a long time to cultivate people

百万 bǎiwàn [数] million ◇百万富翁 millionaire

百闻不如一见 bǎi wén bù rú yī jiàn seeing is believing

百无聊赖 bǎi wú liáolài bored stiff

百姓 bǎixìng [名] the common people

百依百顺 bǎiyī bǎishùn very obedient ◇他对妻子百依百顺。He obeys his wife in everything.

百折不挠 bǎi zhé bù náo indomitable

佰 bǎi [名] hundred

柏 bǎi [名] cypress

柏油 bǎiyóu [名] tar ◇柏油路 asphalt road

摆 bǎi I [动] **1** (放置) arrange ◇请把桌子摆好。Please lay the table. **2** (陈述) state **3** (显示) assume ◇他总是摆出一副官架子。He's always assuming official airs. **4** (摇动) wave ◇摆手 beckon II [名] **1** (部件) pendulum **2** (下幅) hem

摆布 bǎibù [动] **1** (操纵) order … around **2** (布置) arrange

摆动 bǎidòng [动] sway

摆放 bǎifàng [动] place

摆阔 bǎikuò [动] be ostentatious

摆弄 bǎinòng [动] **1** (玩弄) fiddle with **2** (运用) manipulate ◇他善于摆弄权力。He is adept at manipulation.

摆平 bǎipíng [动] treat … equally ◇我们对双方要摆平。We want to treat both parties equally.

摆谱儿 bǎipǔr [动] show off (*pt* showed, *pp* shown)

摆设 bǎishè [动] furnish and decorate ◇客厅里摆设得很有品位。The living room is tastefully furnished and decorated.

摆设儿 bǎisher [名] ornament

摆脱 bǎituō [动] break free from (*pt* broke, *pp* broken) ◇我们终于摆脱了贫困。We have finally broken free from poverty.

败 bài I [动] **1** (打败) defeat ◇大败敌人 defeat the enemy ◇我们败于主队。We lost to the home team. **2** (消除) counteract ◇败毒 counteract a poison **3** (毁坏) ruin II [形] withered

败北 bàiběi [动] be defeated

败笔 bàibǐ [名] artistic defect

败坏 bàihuài I [动] corrupt II [形] corrupt ◇这些人道德品质败坏。These people are morally corrupt.

败家子 bàijiāzǐ [名] spendthrift

败局 bàijú [名] defeat

败类 bàilèi [名] scum

败露 bàilù [动] be exposed

败落 bàiluò [动] decline ◇这个大家族逐渐败落了。The great family gradually went into decline.

败诉 bàisù [动] lose a lawsuit (*pt, pp* lost)

败仗 bàizhàng [名] defeat ◇这位将军从未打过败仗。This general has never suffered defeat.

拜 bài [动] **1** (会见) pay a visit (*pt, pp* paid) ♦拜会 pay an official call **2** (结拜) acknowledge ◊我拜他为师。I acknowledge him as my master. ◊结拜兄弟 sworn brothers

拜访 bàifǎng [动] call on

拜会 bàihuì [动] pay an official call (*pt, pp* paid)

拜年 bàinián [动] pay a New Year call (*pt, pp* paid)

拜托 bàituō [动] ◊拜托您给看会儿我女儿。Would you be kind enough to look after my daughter for a while.

拜谒 bàiyè [动] **1** (拜见) pay a formal visit (*pt, pp* paid) **2** (瞻仰) pay homage

扳 bān [动] **1** (拉动) pull ◊扳闸 pull a switch **2** (扭转) turn ◊双方扳成平局。The score is now equal.

扳子 bānzi [名] spanner

班 bān I [名] **1** (班级) class **2** (班组) team **3** (轮班) shift **4** (军) squad II [量] ◊下一班船 the next boat III [形] regular ◊班车 regular bus IV [动] deploy

班房 bānfáng [名] prison

班机 bānjī [名] **1** (指飞机) airliner **2** (指航班) scheduled flight

班级 bānjí [名] classes (*pl*)

班门弄斧 Bān mén nòng fǔ show oneself up in front of an expert

班子 bānzi [名] **1** (组织) group **2** (剧团) troupe

般 bān [名] sort

般配 bānpèi [动] be well matched

颁 bān 见下文

颁布 bānbù [动] promulgate

颁发 bānfā [动] **1** (发布) issue **2** (授予) award

斑 bān [名] spot

斑白 bānbái [形] greying (英), graying (美)

斑斓 bānlán [形] brightly-coloured (英), brightly-colored (美)

斑马线 bānmǎxiàn [名] zebra crossing

搬 bān [动] **1** (移动) take … away (*pt* took, *pp* taken) ◊把这些东西搬走。Take these things away. **2** (迁移) move ◊搬家 move house **3** (套用) copy mechanically

搬弄 bānnòng [动] **1** (搬动) fiddle with ◊不要搬弄枪。Don't fiddle with the gun. **2** (挑拨) stir … up ◊搬弄是非 make mischief **3** (炫耀) show … off (*pt* showed, *pp* shown) ◊搬弄知识 show off one's knowledge

搬迁 bānqiān [动] relocate

搬运 bānyùn [动] transport

板 bǎn I [名] **1** (片状硬物) board ♦天花板 ceiling **2** (音) beat ◊有板有眼 rhythmical II [形] **1** (指人) stiff ♦古板 inflexible **2** (指物) hard ◊地太板了。The ground is very hard. III [动] put on a stern expression (*pt, pp* put) ◊我们经理老板着脸。Our manager always looks stern.

板子 bǎnzi [名] board

版 bǎn [名] **1** (底版) printing plate ♦排版 typesetting **2** (版本) edition ♦初版 first edition **3** (版面) page ♦头版 front page

版本 bǎnběn [名] edition

版权 bǎnquán [名] copyright ◊版权所有 all rights reserved

版式 bǎnshì [名] format

版税 bǎnshuì [名] royalty

版图 bǎntú [名] territory

办 bàn I [动] **1** (处理) handle ♦办事 handle affairs **2** (创设) set … up (*pt, pp* set) ◊去年他们办了一个工厂。Last year they set up a factory. **3** (经营) run (*pt* ran, *pp* run) ◊校办产业 school-run industry **4** (展览) stage ◊办画展 stage an art exhibition **5** (采购) purchase **6** (惩治) punish II [名] office

办法 bànfǎ [名] way ◊想办法解决问题 find a way to solve the problem ◊这个办法可行。This is a feasible solution. ◊老师拿不努力的学生没办法。Teachers can do nothing about lazy students. ◊你办法多，帮帮我们。You always know how to sort things out – give us a hand. ◊联系办法 means of contact

办公 bàngōng [动] work

办理 bànlǐ [动] handle ◇办理丧事 handle funeral arrangements

办学 bànxué [动] run a school (*pt* ran, *pp* run)

办罪 bànzuì [动] punish

半 bàn **I** [数] **1** (二分之一) half ◇半价 half price **2** (很少) very few ◇他半个字都没写。He'd hardly written anything. **II** [名] middle ♦半夜 midnight **III** [副] partially ◇半新 almost new ◇他合上半开着的书。He closed the half-open book.

半半拉拉 bànbanlālā (口) leave things unfinished

半辈子 bànbèizi [名] half a lifetime ◇他当了半辈子的教师。He had spent half a lifetime as a teacher.

半壁江山 bànbì jiāngshān half the country ◇半壁江山沦落敌手。Half the country has fallen into the hands of the enemy. ◇他拥有这家公司的半壁江山。He owns half of the company.

半边天 bànbiāntiān [名] **1** (指天空) half the sky **2** (指妇女) women (*pl*)

半…不… bàn…bù… neither … nor ♦半新不旧 nearly new ♦半懂不懂 not quite clear

半成品 bànchéngpǐn [名] semi-finished product

半导体 bàndǎotǐ [名] **1** (指物质) semiconductor **2** (收音机) transistor radio

半岛 bàndǎo [名] peninsula

半吊子 bàndiàozi [名] **1** (指言行举止) blunderer **2** (指水平) incompetent ◇半吊子的老师怎么能教出好学生呢？How can that incompetent of a teacher produce good students? **3** (指处事态度) no-hoper

半斤八两 bàn jīn bā liǎng (口) six of one and half a dozen of the other ◇这两个人半斤八两，都不能胜任这份工作。They're six of one and half a dozen of the other – neither of them are competent enough to do the job.

半径 bànjìng [名] radius (*pl* radii)

半路出家 bànlù chūjiā (喻) have a complete career change

半瓶醋 bànpíngcù [名] (贬) ignoramus

半球 bànqiú [名] hemisphere ◇南半球 the Southern Hemisphere

半死不活 bàn sǐ bù huó lifeless

半途 bàntú [名] (书) halfway point

半途而废 bàntú ér fèi give up halfway ◇我们一定要坚持到底，不能半途而废。We must persevere – we can't give up halfway.

扮 bàn [动] **1** (饰演) play ◇他在影片中扮坏人。He played the villain in the film. **2** (指表情) pull ◇别冲我扮鬼脸。Don't pull faces at me.

扮相 bànxiàng [名] look ◇我喜欢戏中女主角的扮相。I liked the look of the female character in the play.

扮演 bànyǎn [动] act

伴 bàn **I** [名] company ◇我会和你做伴的。I will keep you company. ◇我和约翰搭伴去伦敦。John and I travelled to London together. **II** [动] accompany ◇在他的陪伴下，我回到了故乡。He accompanied me back to my hometown.

伴唱 bànchàng [动] accompany

伴侣 bànlǚ [名] **1** (爱人) partner **2** (伙伴) companion

伴娘 bànniáng [名] bridesmaid

伴随 bànsuí [动] follow

伴舞 bànwǔ [动] ◇她过去是伴舞的。She used to be a backing dancer.

伴奏 bànzòu [动] accompany ◇你唱支歌，我来给你用手风琴伴奏。Give us a song - I'll accompany you on the accordion.

拌 bàn [动] **1** (搅和) mix **2** (争吵) quarrel

拌嘴 bànzuǐ [动] quarrel

绊 bàn [动] **1** (使跌倒) trip ◇他下楼时绊了一跤。He tripped over on his way downstairs. **2** (妨碍) get in the way **3** (缠住) hold … up (*pt, pp* held) ◇他可能又被什么事情绊住了。Maybe something's held him up again.

绊脚石 bànjiǎoshí [名] stumbling block

瓣 bàn I [名] 1 (指花儿) petal 2 (指果实或球茎) segment 3 (碎片) fragment II [量] 1 (指花、叶、果实等) ◇几瓣蒜 a few cloves of garlic ◇一瓣橘子 a segment of orange 2 (部分) part

瓣膜 bànmó [名] (医) valve

邦 bāng [名] country

邦交 bāngjiāo [名] diplomatic relations (*pl*) ◇断绝邦交 break off diplomatic relations

帮 bāng I [动] 1 (帮助) help ◇我帮他修改文章。I helped him to improve his essay. 2 (被雇用) be hired ◆帮短工 be hired for short-term work II [名] 1 (物体周围的面) side ◆鞋帮 shoe upper 2 (菜帮子) outer leaf (*pl* leaves) 3 (团伙) gang III [量] group ◇一帮小伙子 a group of young men

帮厨 bāngchú [动] help out in the kitchen

帮倒忙 bāng dàománg [动] do … a disservice ◇他这么说其实是在给我帮倒忙。Actually what he said did me quite a disservice.

帮会 bānghuì [名] (旧) secret society

帮教 bāngjiào [动] help and teach (*pt, pp* taught)

帮忙 bāngmáng [动] help ◇请您帮我个忙。Please can you help me out?

帮派 bāngpài [名] faction

帮腔 bāngqiāng [动] stick up for (*pt, pp* stuck) ◇你为什么总给他帮腔? Why are you always sticking up for him?

帮手 bāngshǒu [名] assistant

帮凶 bāngxiōng [名] accessory

帮助 bāngzhù [动] help ◇护士长帮助他做手术。The head nurse helped him carry out the operation. ◇他帮助我们渡过难关。He helped us through a difficult time. ◇水果帮助消化。Fruit aids the digestion. ◇我们需要专家的帮助。We need the help of an expert. ◇谢谢您的帮助 Thank you for your help.

帮子 bāngzi [名] outer leaf (*pl* leaves)

绑 bǎng [动] tie up

绑架 bǎngjià [动] kidnap

绑票 bǎngpiào [动] kidnap

榜 bǎng [名] list of names ◇光荣榜 roll of honour (英) 或 honor (美)

榜样 bǎngyàng [名] model

膀 bǎng [名] 1 (肩膀) shoulder 2 (翅膀) wing
▷另见 páng

膀子 bǎngzi [名] 1 (手臂上部) upper arm ◇光着膀子 be stripped to the waist 2 (翅膀) wing

蚌 bàng [名] clam

棒 bàng I [名] 1 (棍子) cudgel 2 (棍状物) rod II [形] (口) great ◇他英语说得很棒。He speaks great English.

棒槌 bàngchui [名] 1 (木棒) club 2 (外行) amateur

棒子 bàngzi [名] 1 (棍子) club 2 (玉米) corn (英), maize (美)

傍 bàng I [动] be close to II [介] near

傍大款 bàng dàkuǎn (口) be a gold-digger

傍晚 bàngwǎn [副] at dusk

谤 bàng [动] (书) slander

磅 bàng I [量] pound II [名] scales (*pl*) III [动] weigh
▷另见 páng

镑 bàng [名] pound

包 bāo I [动] 1 (包裹) wrap 2 (包围) surround 3 (包含) include ◇这笔钱只是旅费，不包食宿。This money is just for travel expenses. It doesn't include food and lodgings. 4 (承诺完成) be contracted ◇我们包下了这个工程。We've been contracted to do this project. 5 (担保) guarantee 6 (约定专用) hire ◇包车 hire a car ◇包飞机 charter a plane II [名] 1 (包裹) parcel ◆背包 backpack 2 (口袋) bag ◆钱包 wallet 3 (疙瘩) lump 4 (隆起物) hump 5 (帐篷) tent III [量] ◇一包烟 a pack of cigarettes ◇一包茶 a packet of tea

包办 bāobàn [动] 1 (单独负责) take

sole charge of (*pt* took, *pp* taken) **2** (独断办理) monopolize ◇包办婚姻 arranged marriage

包庇 bāobì [动] cover up ◇包庇朋友 cover up for one's friends

包藏 bāocáng [动] harbour (英), harbor (美) ◇包藏杀机 harbour murderous intentions

包场 bāochǎng [动] make a block booking

包袱 bāofu [名] **1** (布) bundle **2** (喻) (负担) burden ◇孩子不应是成就事业的包袱。Children shouldn't get in the way of a successful career.

包干儿 bāogānr [动] see a task through (*pt* saw, *pp* seen)

包工 bāogōng **I** [动] contract ◇这座桥由一家北京建筑公司包工。A Beijing building company has been contracted to build the bridge. **II** [名] contractor

包裹 bāoguǒ **I** [动] wrap **II** [名] parcel

包含 bāohán [动] contain

包涵 bāohán [动] forgive (*pt* forgave, *pp* forgiven) ◇招待不周，请多包涵！ Please forgive me for giving you such a poor reception.

包括 bāokuò [动] include ◇月租450元，不包括取暖费。The rent is 450 yuan a month, but this doesn't include heating. ◇医疗队包括10个医生和一辆救护车。The medical team is comprised of ten doctors and one ambulance. ◇餐费包括百分之十的服务费。The bill includes a ten percent service charge.

包揽 bāolǎn [动] take sole charge of (*pt* took, *pp* taken)

包罗万象 bāoluó wànxiàng all-inclusive

包票 bāopiào [名] guarantee ◇我敢打包票，他肯定来。I can guarantee that he'll be coming.

包容 bāoróng [动] **1** (宽容) tolerate **2** (容纳) hold (*pt*, *pp* held)

包围 bāowéi [动] surround ◇这座城市四周被群山包围着。The city is surrounded by mountains on all sides.

包厢 bāoxiāng [名] box

包圆儿 bāoyuánr [动] **1** (全部买下) buy ... up (*pt*, *pp* bought) **2** (全部承担) finish ... off ◇这点活儿我们包圆儿了。We're going to finish this job off.

包扎 bāozā [动] bind (*pt*, *pp* bound)

包装 bāozhuāng **I** [动] package ... up **II** [名] package

苞 bāo [名] bud

苞米 bāomǐ [名] (方) corn (英), maize (美)

孢 bāo 见下文

孢子 bāozǐ [名] spore

炮 bāo [动] (烹调方法) sauté ▷另见 páo, pào

胞 bāo [名] **1** (指同父母) blood ◇胞兄 full brother **2** (指同国家、同民族) fellow countryman (*pl* countrymen)

剥 bāo [动] peel ◇剥香蕉 peel a banana ◇剥豌豆 shell peas ▷另见 bō

龅 bāo 见下文

龅牙 bāoyá [名] buck teeth (*pl*)

褒 bāo [动] praise

褒贬 bāobiǎn [动] pass judgement on ◇不要随便褒贬人。You can't pass judgment on people without proper consideration.

褒奖 bāojiǎng [动] laud ◇这种行为应当受到褒奖。This kind of behaviour should be lauded.

褒扬 bāoyáng [动] praise

雹 báo [名] hail

雹子 báozi [名] hailstone

薄 báo [形] **1** (不厚) thin **2** (不浓) weak **3** (冷淡) cold ◇我对她不薄。I treat her very well. **4** (贫瘠) infertile ◇薄地 poor land ▷另见 bó, bò

宝 bǎo **I** [名] treasure ♦国宝 national treasure **II** [形] precious

宝宝 bǎobǎo [名] darling

宝贝 bǎobèi [名] **1** (珍奇之物) treasure

2 (爱称) darling 3 (无能之人) idiot

宝贵 bǎoguì I [形] valuable ◇宝贵首饰 valuable jewellery ◇宝贵意见 valuable suggestion ◇宝贵文物 precious historical relics II [动] value ◇这玩意儿你不稀罕，他可宝贵得很。You don't care about it, but he values it dearly.

宝藏 bǎozàng [名] (矿产) precious minerals (*pl*)

宝座 bǎozuò [名] throne

饱 bǎo I [形] full ◇我吃饱了。I am full. II [副] fully ◇饱读美国文学 be well-read in American literature III [动] satisfy ◇精彩演出让观众大饱眼福。The audience feasted their eyes on the wonderful performance.

饱餐 bǎocān [动] eat one's fill (*pt* ate, *pp* eaten) ◇我们已饱餐了一顿。We've had a magnificent meal. ◇他们饱餐了一顿野味。They feasted on game.

饱尝 bǎocháng [动] 1 (吃饱) feast ◇饱尝美味佳肴 feast on fine food 2 (经历) experience

饱和 bǎohé [动] 1 (溶质) be saturated 2 (满) be full to capacity ◇政府机关的工作人员已经饱和了。The staff quota in the government organization is full. ◇冰箱的市场已经处于饱和状态。The market for refrigerators is already saturated.

饱经风霜 bǎo jīng fēngshuāng suffer hardship

饱满 bǎomǎn [形] 1 (丰满) plump 2 (充足) full ◇精神饱满 full of energy

饱学 bǎoxué [形] scholarly

保 bǎo I [动] 1 (保护) protect 2 (保持) keep (*pt, pp* kept) ◇这盒子可以用来保鲜。This box can be used to keep food fresh. 3 (保证) ensure ◇吃了这药，保你很快恢复健康。This medicine will ensure you a quick recovery. 4 (担保) stand guarantor (*pt, pp* stood) ♦保释 bail II [名] guarantor

保安 bǎo'ān I [动] 1 (保卫治安) ensure public security 2 (保护人身安全) ensure safety II [名] security guard

保镖 bǎobiāo [名] bodyguard

保藏 bǎocáng [动] conserve

保持 bǎochí [动] maintain ◇保持良好的秩序 maintain good order ◇保持警惕 stay vigilant ◇保持清醒的头脑 keep a clear head

保存 bǎocún [动] preserve

保单 bǎodān [名] insurance policy

保费 bǎofèi [名] (保险费) insurance premium

保管 bǎoguǎn I [动] (保藏管理) take care of (*pt* took, *pp* taken) II [名] storekeeper III [副] certainly ◇他做这件事保管能行。What he is doing is sure to work.

保护 bǎohù [动] protect ◇保护环境 protect the environment ◇保护眼睛 protect one's eyes ◇保护私人资料 data protection

保健 bǎojiàn [名] health care ◇保健食品 health food

保洁 bǎojié [动] keep the environment clean (*pt, pp* kept)

保龄球 bǎolíngqiú [名] 1 (体育运动) bowling 2 (球) bowl

保留 bǎoliú [动] 1 (保存不变) preserve ◇这座城市还保留着500多年前的寺庙。A temple more than 500 years old is preserved in the town. 2 (意见) hold back (*pt, pp* held) ◇各位可以保留自己的意见，下次开会再讨论。If everyone could hold back, we will discuss thoughts on this at the next meeting. 3 (不拿出来) retain

保密 bǎomì [动] keep … secret (*pt, pp* kept) ◇这个消息可要保密。This information must be kept secret.

保姆 bǎomǔ [名] 1 (做家务的女工) domestic help 2 (保育员) nanny

保全 bǎoquán [动] save

保释 bǎoshì [动] bail

保守 bǎoshǒu I [动] protect II [形] conservative

保送 bǎosòng [动] recommend … for a place ◇他儿子保送到清华大学。His son was recommended for admission to Qinghua University.

保外就医 bǎo wài jiù yī transfer a prisoner for medical attention

保卫 bǎowèi [动] defend

保险 bǎoxiǎn **I** [名] insurance **II** [形] safe **III** [副] certainly ◊你听我的，保险能行。If you do as I say it's sure to work.

保修 bǎoxiū [动] guarantee ◊这台电脑保修一年。This computer is guaranteed for one year.

保养 bǎoyǎng [动] **1** (身体) take care of one's health (*pt* took, *pp* taken) **2** (机器) maintain

保佑 bǎoyòu [动] bless

保育 bǎoyù [名] childcare ◊保育员 childcare worker ◊保育院 nursery school

保障 bǎozhàng [动] protect ◊保障公民的生命财产安全 protect people's lives and property ◊儿女多并不意味着晚年生活有保障。Having a lot of children certainly doesn't mean you will be protected in later life.

保证 bǎozhèng [动] guarantee ◊我保证能按时到达。I guarantee I will be there on time. ◊你的支持是我取得成功的保证。Your support is my guarantee of success.

保重 bǎozhòng [动] take care of oneself (*pt* took, *pp* taken)

葆 bǎo [动] preserve

堡 bǎo [名] fort

堡垒 bǎolěi [名] **1** (建筑物) fortress **2** (喻) (指难关) challenge **3** (指人) die-hard

报 bào **I** [动] **1** (告诉) report ◊报上级领导 report to one's superiors **2** (回答) respond ◊报以掌声 greet with applause **3** (报答) repay (*pt, pp* repaid) ♦报恩 repay a favour (英) 或 favor (美) **4** (报复) take revenge (*pt* took, *pp* taken) ♦报仇 take revenge **II** [名] **1** (报纸) newspaper ♦日报 daily **2** (刊物) periodical ♦画报 glossy magazine **3** (公告) report ◊公报 bulletin **4** (电报) telegram ♦发报 send a telegram

报案 bào'àn [动] report ◊接到居民报案后，警察以偷窃嫌疑将他逮捕。After a report from a local resident, the police arrested him on suspicion of theft.

报表 bàobiǎo [名] report form

报偿 bàocháng [动] repay (*pt, pp* repaid)

报仇 bàochóu [动] take revenge (*pt* took, *pp* taken)

报酬 bàochou [名] pay

报答 bàodá [动] repay (*pt, pp* repaid)

报到 bàodào [动] report

报道 bàodào **I** [动] report ◊电视台报道了这条新闻。The television station reported this item of news. **II** [名] report ◊一篇关于克隆人的报道 a report about human cloning ◊她负责体育新闻报道。She is in charge of sports coverage.

报废 bàofèi [动] discard ◊这辆汽车5年内报废。This car will have to be scrapped in five years.

报复 bàofù [动] retaliate

报告 bàogào **I** [动] report ◊有问题就向主管部门报告。If there is a problem just report it to the department responsible. **II** [名] report ◊在大会上作报告 give a talk at the conference

报关 bàoguān [动] declare

报价 bàojià [动] quote ◊这只手表报价500镑。This watch is quoted at £500. ◊你报价太高了。Your quotation is too high.

报捷 bàojié [动] report a success

报警 bàojǐng [动] report to the police

报刊 bàokān [名] newspapers and periodicals

报考 bàokǎo [动] take an entrance exam (*pt* took, *pp* taken)

报名 bàomíng [动] sign up ◊报名参加马拉松比赛 sign up for a marathon

报幕 bàomù [动] compere

报幕员 bàomùyuán [名] compere

报社 bàoshè [名] newspaper office

报失 bàoshī [动] report a loss ◊丢失信用卡要向警察报失。If you lose a credit card you should report it to the police.

报喜 bàoxǐ [动] give good news (*pt* gave, *pp* given) ◊报喜不报忧 give the good news but not the bad

报销 bàoxiāo [动] **1** (费用) claim for **2** (口) (除掉) demolish

报应 bàoyìng [名] just deserts ◇他迟早会遭报应。He'll get his just deserts sooner or later.

报账 bàozhàng [动] submit expenses

报纸 bàozhǐ [名] newspaper

刨 bào I [动] plane II [名] plane ▷另见 páo

抱 bào [动] **1** (手臂围住) carry in one's arms **2** (儿孙) ◇我们校长等着抱孙子呢！Our head teacher is going to be a grandmother! **3** (领养) adopt **4** (方) (结合) join together ◇抱成一团 stand together **5** (心里存有) cherish

抱病 bàobìng [动] be ill

抱残守缺 bào cán shǒu quē cling to the past ◇要强化创新意识，不能抱残守缺。We must emphasize creativity, and break the pattern of clinging to the past.

抱佛脚 bào fójiǎo leave … to the last minute ◇有些学生平时不努力，考前临时抱佛脚。Some students are lazy most of the time, and then try to cram just before the exams.

抱负 bàofù [名] ambition

抱恨 bàohèn [动] harbour (英) 或 harbor (美) regrets

抱歉 bàoqiàn [形] sorry ◇走时没来得及和你说一声，很抱歉。I'm sorry there was no time to speak with you before I left.

抱屈 bàoqū [动] feel wronged (*pt, pp* felt)

抱养 bàoyǎng [动] adopt

抱怨 bàoyuàn [动] complain ◇她报怨不平等的待遇。She complained about the unfair treatment. ◇小男孩报怨说爸爸脾气坏。The little boy complained that his dad had a bad temper. ◇多干点实事，少一点抱怨。Get on with it and stop grumbling.

豹 bào [名] leopard

暴 bào I [形] **1** (猛烈) violent **2** (凶狠) brutal **3** (急躁) vicious ◇她脾气很暴。She has a vicious temper. II [动] **1** (鼓起) bulge **2** (糟蹋) go to ruin (*pt* went, *pp* gone)

暴动 bàodòng [名] insurrection

暴发 bàofā [动] **1** (突然发作) break out (*pt* broke, *pp* broken) **2** (贬) (突然发财) strike it rich (*pt, pp* struck)

暴力 bàolì [名] violence

暴利 bàolì [名] enormous profit

暴烈 bàoliè [形] fierce

暴露 bàolù [动] reveal

暴乱 bàoluàn [名] riot

暴徒 bàotú [名] thug

暴行 bàoxíng [名] atrocity

暴躁 bàozào [形] irritable

暴卒 bàozú [动] die suddenly

爆 bào [动] **1** (猛然破裂) explode ◇炸弹爆炸了。The bomb exploded. ◇气球爆了。The balloon burst. **2** (突然发生) ◇一个无获胜希望的人爆了冷门。An outsider emerged as the winner. **3** (烹调方法) quick-fry

爆发 bàofā [动] **1** (迸发) erupt **2** (突发) break out (*pt* broke, *pp* broken)

爆满 bàomǎn [动] be completely packed

爆破 bàopò [动] blow … up (*pt* blew, *pp* blown)

爆炸 bàozhà [动] explode

杯 bēi I [名] **1** (杯子) cup ♦玻璃杯 glass ♦酒杯 wineglass **2** (酒) drink ◇再喝杯吧！ Have another drink! **3** (奖杯) cup ♦世界杯 World Cup II [量] cup ◇一杯咖啡 a cup of coffee ◇两杯水 two glasses of water

杯弓蛇影 bēi gōng shé yǐng suffer from imaginary fears

杯水车薪 bēi shuǐ chē xīn a drop in the ocean

卑 bēi [形] **1** (书) (谦恭) humble **2** (品质低劣) inferior

卑鄙 bēibǐ [形] contemptible

卑躬屈节 bēi gōng qū jié bow and scrape

卑贱 bēijiàn [形] **1** (地位低) lowly **2** (下贱) base

卑劣 bēiliè [形] despicable

背 bēi [动] **1** (驮) carry … on one's back ◇她背着书包走路。She walked along the road with her schoolbag on her back. **2** (担负) take … on (*pt* took, *pp* taken) ◇政治家背起了重大的责任。The politician has taken on great responsibility. ▷另见 bèi

背包袱 bēi bāofu have a load on one's mind

背负 bēifù [动] **1** (驮) carry on one's back **2** (担负) take … on (*pt* took, *pp* taken) ◇他背负着父母的期望。He has taken on his parents' aspirations.

背黑锅 bēi hēiguō carry the can

悲 bēi [形] **1** (悲伤) sad **2** (怜悯) compassionate ◇大慈大悲 infinitely merciful

悲哀 bēi'āi [形] sad

悲惨 bēicǎn [形] miserable

悲愤 bēifèn [名] grief and anger

悲观 bēiguān [形] pessimistic

悲伤 bēishāng [形] sad

悲天悯人 bēi tiān mǐn rén be concerned about corruption and social welfare

悲痛 bēitòng [形] sorrowful

悲壮 bēizhuàng [形] solemn and stirring

碑 bēi [名] tablet ◇纪念碑 monument ◇墓碑 tombstone

北 běi **I** [名] north ♦北方 the North **II** [动] (书) be defeated ♦败北 be defeated

北斗星 běidǒuxīng [名] the Plough (英), the Big Dipper (美)

北极 běijí [名] the North Pole

贝 bèi [名] shellfish

贝壳 bèiké [名] shell

备 bèi **I** [动] **1** (具备) have (*pt*, *pp* had) ◇柜台上备有样品。Samples are available on the counter. **2** (准备) prepare ◇佐料备齐了。The seasoning is prepared. **3** (防备) provide against **II** [名] equipment **III** [副] to the utmost ◇备受煎熬 endure the utmost suffering

备查 bèichá [动] be at hand for reference

备份 bèifèn [动](计算机) keep a backup copy (*pt*, *pp* kept)

备件 bèijiàn [名] spare part

备考 bèikǎo **I** [名] notes (*pl*) **II** [动] be at hand for reference ◇这个文件要录以备考。This document should be copied for future reference.

备课 bèikè [动] prepare a lesson ◇上完课后，老师又在备课了。When class was over the teacher prepared another lesson.

备料 bèiliào [动] **1** (准备材料) get materials ready ◇建这栋房子要备很多料。We have to get a lot of materials for building this house. **2** (准备饲料) prepare animal feed

备忘录 bèiwànglù [名] **1** (记事本) notepad **2** (外交文书) memorandum

备用 bèiyòng [动] backup ◇备用光盘 backup CD

备注 bèizhù [名] **1** (表格的栏) space for comments **2** (注解说明) notes (*pl*)

背 bèi **I** [名] back ♦背疼 backache ♦椅背 chairback **II** [动] **1** (指反向) have one's back to ◇他背着门站着。He is standing with his back to the door. **2** (离开) leave (*pt*, *pp* left) **3** (躲避) hide from (*pt* hid, *pp* hidden) ◇她有些背人的事。She has something to hide from people. ◇他总是背着父母说他们的坏话。He is always speaking badly of his parents behind their backs. **4** (背诵) recite ◇背首诗 recite a poem **5** (违背) go against (*pt* went, *pp* gone) **III** [形] **1** (偏僻) out-of-the-way **2** (口) (倒霉) unlucky **3** (听觉不灵) hard of hearing ▷另见 bēi

背道而驰 bèi dào ér chí go in the opposite direction

背井离乡 bèi jǐng lí xiāng be forced to leave one's home

背景 bèijǐng [名] **1** (布景) scenery **2** (指景物、情况) background ◇这张照片的背景是连绵的山脉。The photo shows a chain of mountains in the background. ◇我不知道他们的背景。I know nothing about their background.

背靠背 bèikàobèi back-to-back

背离 bèilí [动] **1** (离开) depart from **2** (违背) deviate from

背叛 bèipàn [动] betray ◇背叛祖国 betray one's country ◇回国之后他就变了心，背叛了女友。After coming back from abroad he ditched his girlfriend.

背弃 bèiqì [动] abandon ◇背弃信仰 abandon one's beliefs ◇背弃誓言 go back on one's word

背时 bèishí [形] (方) **1** (过时) outmoded **2** (倒霉) unlucky

背诵 bèisòng [动] recite

背信弃义 bèi xìn qì yì break faith with

背影 bèiyǐng [名] ◇我注视着他远去的背影。I gazed at his distant receding figure.

背运 bèiyùn **I** [名] bad luck **II** [动] be unlucky

悖 bèi **I** [动] (书) be contrary to **II** [形] perverse

悖谬 bèimiù [形] (书) irrational

被 bèi **I** [名] quilt ♦棉被 cotton-padded quilt **II** [动] meet with (*pt, pp* met) ♦被灾 meet with disaster **III** [介] ◇他被哥哥打了一顿。He was beaten up by his elder brother. **IV** [助] ◇被陷害 be framed ◇被跟踪 be followed

被动 bèidòng [形] passive

被告 bèigào [名] defendant

被迫 bèipò [动] be forced ◇她被迫卖掉首饰。She was forced to sell her jewellery.

倍 bèi **I** [名] times ◇这本书的厚度是那本书的3倍。This book is three times thicker than that one. ◇物价涨了两倍。Prices have doubled. **II** [形] double ◇事半功倍 get twice the result with half the effort

焙 bèi [动] dry ... over heat

焙烧 bèishāo [动] bake

辈 bèi [名] **1** (辈分) generation **2** (类) ◇无能之辈 people of no ability

辈出 bèichū [动] come forward in great numbers (*pt* came, *pp* come)

辈分 bèifen [名] seniority ◇我辈分比他小。I am junior to him in the family.

惫 bèi [形] exhausted

蓓 bèi 见下文

蓓蕾 bèilěi [名] bud

奔 bēn [动] **1** (急跑) speed (*pt, pp* sped) **2** (赶忙) hurry **3** (逃) flee (*pt, pp* fled)
▷另见 bèn

奔波 bēnbō [动] dash around

奔驰 bēnchí [动] speed (*pt, pp* sped) ◇汽车在高速公路上奔驰。The car is speeding along the motorway. ◇马在田野上奔驰。The horse is galloping across the fields.

奔放 bēnfàng [形] bold and unrestrained

奔赴 bēnfù [动] hurry towards

奔流 bēnliú **I** [动] rush **II** [名] swift current

奔忙 bēnmáng [动] rush around

奔命 bēnmìng [动] be always on the go

奔跑 bēnpǎo [动] dash

奔丧 bēnsāng [动] go home for a funeral (*pt* went, *pp* gone)

奔腾 bēnténg [动] **1** (奔跑) gallop **2** (奔流) surge

奔走 bēnzǒu [动] **1** (急走) run (*pt* ran, *pp* run) **2** (到处活动) rush about

本 běn **I** [名] **1** (根) root ♦木本 tree root **2** (根源) basis (*pl* bases) ◇本末倒置 put the cart before the horse **3** (本钱) capital ♦亏本 lose money in business **4** (本子) book ♦笔记本 notebook **5** (版本) edition ♦手抄本 hand-written copy **6** (底本) master copy ♦剧本 script **II** [形] **1** (主要) main ♦本部 headquarters (*pl*) **2** (原来) original ♦本意 original meaning **3** (自己的) one's own ♦本身 itself ♦本校 this school **4** (现今) this ♦本月 this month **III** [副] originally ◇我本

想亲自去一趟。I originally wanted to go myself. **IV** [量] ◇几本书 some books

本部 běnbù [名] headquarters

本地 běndì [名] locality ◇本地货 local goods ◇她是本地人。She is a native of this place.

本分 běnfèn **I** [名] duty **II** [形] dutiful

本行 běnháng [名] profession

本金 běnjīn [名] principal

本科 běnkē [名] undergraduate course ◇他本科毕业。He graduated with a bachelor's degree. ◇本科生 undergraduate

本来 běnlái **I** [形] original **II** [副] **1** (原先) at first **2** (理所当然) of course

本领 běnlǐng [名] skill

本末 běnmò [名] **1** (从头到尾) the whole story **2** (主要的和次要的) ◇本末倒置 put the cart before the horse

本能 běnnéng [名] instinct

本钱 běnqián [名] **1** (钱财) capital **2** (资历) prerequisite

本人 běnrén [名] **1** (我) | **2** (自己) oneself ◇我本人来处理这事。I will handle it myself. ◇你本人必须参加。You must take part yourself. ◇身份证要他本人来办。He has to apply for an ID card himself.

本色 běnsè [名] character

本色 běnshǎi [名] natural colour (英) 或 color (美)

本身 běnshēn [名] itself

本事 běnshi [名] ability

本土 běntǔ [名] (乡土) native land

本位 běnwèi [名] **1** (经济) (标准) standard **2** (自己的岗位) post

本性 běnxìng [名] nature

本义 běnyì [名] original meaning

本意 běnyì [名] intention

本职 běnzhí [名] job

本质 běnzhì [名] essence

畚 běn **I** [名] scoop **II** [动] (方) scoop up

畚箕 běnjī [名] (方) **1** (用于铲谷物) scoop **2** (用于扫垃圾) dustpan

奔 bèn **I** [动] **1** (走) head for ◇直奔教室 head straight for the classroom **2** (近) be getting on for ◇我是奔40的人了。I'm getting on for forty. **II** [介] towards ▷另见 bēn

奔命 bènmìng [动] rush

奔头儿 bèntour [名] prospect

笨 bèn [形] **1** (不聪明) stupid **2** (不灵巧) clumsy ◇他嘴很笨。He's quite inarticulate. **3** (笨重) cumbersome

笨蛋 bèndàn [名] (侮辱) idiot

笨口拙舌 bèn kǒu zhuō shé inarticulate

笨手笨脚 bèn shǒu bèn jiǎo clumsy ◇看你笨手笨脚的， 我来做吧。Look how clumsy you are, let me do it.

笨重 bènzhòng [形] heavy ◇笨重的家具 heavy furniture ◇笨重的体力劳动 heavy physical work

笨拙 bènzhuō [形] **1** (不灵巧) clumsy **2** (不聪明) stupid

崩 bēng [动] **1** (倒塌) collapse ◇雪崩 avalanche **2** (破裂) burst (*pt, pp* burst)

崩溃 bēngkuì [动] collapse ◇失恋后，她精神处于崩溃边缘。After the break-up she was close to nervous breakdown.

崩塌 bēngtā [动] collapse

绷 bēng [动] **1** (拉紧) pull ... tight ◇绳子绷紧了。The string is taut. **2** (弹) spring (*pt* sprang, *pp* sprung) ▷另见 běng, bèng

绷带 bēngdài [名] bandage

嘣 bēng [拟] bang ◇除夕晚上鞭炮嘣嘣响。On New Year's Eve there were lots of bangs from firecrackers. ◇他紧张得心里嘣嘣直跳。His heart was pounding with nervousness.

甭 béng [副] (方) ◇你甭去了。Don't bother going.

绷 běng [动] (方) scowl ▷另见 bēng, bèng

绷脸 běngliǎn [动] pull a lon

迸 bèng [动] spout

迸发 bèngfā [动] burst out (*pt, pp* burst) ◇老师的幽默使学生迸发出阵阵笑声。The teacher's jokes made the students burst out laughing.

泵 bèng [名] pump

绷 bèng [动] crack ◇木头门绷了几条缝。The wooden door has cracked in a few places.
▷另见 bēng, běng

蹦 bèng [动] leap

逼 bī [动] **1** (强迫) force **2** (强取) press for ◇逼债 press for repayment of a debt **3** (逼近) close in on

逼供 bīgòng [动] extract a confession

逼近 bījìn [动] close in on ◇敌军已逼近城门。The enemy have already closed in on the city gates.

逼迫 bīpò [动] force

逼债 bīzhài [动] press for repayment of a debt

逼真 bīzhēn [形] **1** (像真的) lifelike **2** (真切的) distinct

鼻 bí [名] **1** (鼻子) nose **2** (书) (首创) initiation ♦鼻祖 originator

鼻孔 bíkǒng [名] nostril

鼻梁 bíliáng [名] bridge of the nose

鼻涕 bítì [名] mucus

鼻子 bízi [名] nose

鼻祖 bízǔ [名] originator

匕 bǐ [名] 见下文

匕首 bǐshǒu [名] dagger

比 bǐ **I** [动] **1** (比较) compare ◇比比过去，我们现在的生活好多了。Life now is much better compared to the past. **2** (较量) compete ◇他们要比比谁游得快。They are competing to see who swims the fastest. **3** (比拟) compare ◇中国人喜欢把大地比作母亲。The Chinese like to compare the earth to a mother. **4** (仿照) copy ◇孩子们在比着图纸做飞机模型。The children are making model planes from diagrams. **5** (比画) gesture ◇她连说带比。She gesticulates as she talks. **II** [介] **1** (指得分) ◇两队最终以零比零战平。The two teams finally drew nil-nil. **2** (相对) ◇今年冬天比去年冷。It is colder this winter than last winter.

比比皆是 bǐbǐ jiēshì ubiquitous

比方 bǐfāng **I** [名] analogy ◇她打了个比方，把学英语比作建房子。She drew an analogy between learning English and building a house.
II [连] ◇你会有机会买房的，比方你中了彩。You would have the chance to buy a house – supposing you won the lottery.

比分 bǐfēn [名] score

比画 bǐhuà [动] gesture ◇英语老师讲课时爱比画。The English teacher likes making gestures when he is teaching. ◇裁缝拿布料在我胸前比画着。The dressmaker held the material in front of me to take a measurement.

比基尼 bǐjīní [名] bikini

比价 bǐjià [名] exchange rate

比较 bǐjiào **I** [动] compare ◇让我们比较一下两个民族的风俗习惯。Let us compare for a moment the customs of the two peoples. **II** [介] ◇国民生产总值比较去年有所增长。Compared to last year, gross national product has increased somewhat. **III** [副] relatively ◇这里的水果比较新鲜。The fruit here is relatively fresh. ◇广州的夏天比较热。Summers in Guangzhou are quite hot.

比例 bǐlì [名] **1** (指倍数) proportion **2** (指制图) scale ◇按比例制模型 make a scale model

比率 bǐlǜ [名] ratio

比拟 bǐnǐ [动] match

比如 bǐrú [连] for instance ◇小事情可以成为大新闻，比如人咬了狗。Small things can become big news, for instance if a person bites a dog. ◇有些人不适合做老师，比如小王。Some people are not suited to teaching, Xiao Wang for instance.

比赛 bǐsài [名] match ◇足球比赛 football match ◇演讲比赛 public speaking competition

比上不足，比下有余 bǐ shàng bùzú, bǐ xià yǒuyú reasonably well ◇咱们过的日子比上不足，比下有余。We have been living reasonably well.

比试 bǐshì [动] **1** (较量) have a competition **2** (做姿势) flourish ◇拿把剑比试一下 flourish a sword

比喻 bǐyù **I** [动] compare **II** [名] analogy

比照 bǐzhào [动] **1** (按照) base … on ◇教练比照对手的特点制订了一个方案。The coach based his strategy on the opponent's particular strengths and weaknesses. **2** (对照) contrast

比值 bǐzhí [名] ratio

比重 bǐzhòng [名] (比值) proportion

彼 bǐ [代] **1** (那个) that **2** (对方) the other side

彼岸 bǐ'àn [名] the opposite shore

彼此 bǐcǐ [代] **1** (双方) both sides ◇这对混双选手彼此并不太了解。This mixed-doubles pair don't know each other well. **2** (谦) ◇"你这次考得不错啊！" "彼此彼此！" You did really well in the exam! – You too! ◇"你看上去很棒啊！" "彼此彼此！" You look great! – Likewise!

笔 bǐ **I** [名] **1** (工具) pen ◇圆珠笔 ball-point pen **2** (笔法) calligraphic technique **3** (笔画) brush stroke **4** (话语) ◇文章结尾处应该再添几笔。The conclusion of the essay needs fleshing out a bit. **II** [动] write (*pt* wrote, *pp* written) ♦亲笔 one's own handwriting **III** [量] **1** (款项) ◇一笔钱 a sum of money **2** (书画) ◇一笔好字 a good hand

笔调 bǐdiào [名] tone

笔法 bǐfǎ [名] artistic technique

笔杆子 bǐgǎnzi [名] **1** (笔) shaft **2** (指写作) pen **3** (指作家) skilled writer

笔画 bǐhuà [名] brush stroke

笔迹 bǐjì [名] handwriting

笔记 bǐjì **I** [动] take down (*pt* took, *pp* taken) **II** [名] **1** (记录) note ◇记笔记 take notes **2** (指体裁) ◇笔记小说 literary sketches

笔记本电脑 bǐjìběn diànnǎo [名] laptop

笔名 bǐmíng [名] pen name

笔墨 bǐmò [名] words ◇写文章忌浪费笔墨。When writing an essay you should not waste words.

笔试 bǐshì [名] written examination

笔挺 bǐtǐng **I** [形] neatly pressed ◇笔挺的西装 a neatly pressed suit **II** [副] erect ◇卫兵们笔挺地站着。The guards stood erect.

笔头儿 bǐtóur [名] **1** (笔尖) nib **2** (写字) writing **3** (写作) writing ability

笔误 bǐwù [名] slip of the pen

笔译 bǐyì [名] written translation

笔者 bǐzhě [名] the author

笔直 bǐzhí [形] straight

鄙 bǐ **I** [形] **1** (粗俗) mean ♦卑鄙 mean **2** (自称) (谦) ◇鄙人 my humble self **II** [动] despise

鄙薄 bǐbó [动] despise

鄙陋 bǐlòu [形] shallow

鄙视 bǐshì [动] despise

币 bì [名] coin ♦货币 currency ♦外币 foreign currency

必 bì [副] **1** (必然) certainly **2** (必须) ◇必修科目 compulsory subjects

必定 bìdìng [副] surely ◇他必定知道真相。He surely knew the truth.

必恭必敬 bì gōng bì jìng very deferential

必然 bìrán **I** [形] inevitable **II** [名] necessity

必修课 bìxiūkè [名] compulsory course

必须 bìxū [副] ◇你们必须准时来上班。You must start work on time. ◇记者们必须撤离战区。The journalists have to evacuate the war zone.

必需 bìxū [动] need ◇考试时别忘带上必需的文具用品。Don't forget to bring the writing materials you need for the exam.

必要 bìyào [形] essential ◇开展反腐行动是必要的。It's essential

that we start a campaign against corruption.

闭 bì [动] **1** (关上) close **2** (堵塞) stop … up ◇闭气 airtight

闭路电视 bìlùdiànshì [名] closed-circuit television

闭门羹 bìméngēng [名] ◇吃闭门羹 be left out in the cold

闭门造车 bì mén zào chē divorce oneself from reality

闭幕 bìmù [动] **1** (指舞台) lower the curtain **2** (指会议) conclude

闭塞 bìsè [动] **1** (堵塞) obstruct **2** (不方便) be inaccessible

毕 bì **I** [动] finish **II** [副] fully

毕恭毕敬 bì gōng bì jìng 见 '必恭必敬'

毕竟 bìjìng [副] actually ◇和过去相比，我们的生活水平毕竟有了提高。If you compare with the past, actually our standard of living has improved.

毕生 bìshēng [名] lifetime

毕业 bìyè [动] graduate ◇她毕业于牛津大学法律系。She graduated in law from Oxford University.

毕业论文 bìyè lùnwén [名] thesis (*pl* theses)

庇 bì [动] shelter ♦包庇 shield

庇护 bìhù [动] shelter

陛 bì [名] (书) flight of steps

陛下 bìxià [名] Your Majesty

毙 bì [动] **1** (死) die **2** (枪杀) (口) shoot (*pt*, *pp* shot)

毙命 bìmìng [动] meet a violent death (*pt*, *pp* met)

敝 bì [形] **1** (破烂) ragged **2** (谦) (自己的) ◇敝人姓李。My surname is Li.

敝帚自珍 bì zhǒu zì zhēn attach sentimental value to

婢 bì [名] slave girl

婢女 bìnǚ [名] slave girl

裨 bì [名] (书) benefit

裨益 bìyì [名] (书) benefit ◇您的建议对我公司的发展大有裨益。Your recommendation will be of great benefit to the development of our company.

辟 bì [动] (书) ward … off
▷另见 pì

辟邪 bìxié [动] exorcize

碧 bì **I** [形] bluish green **II** [名] (书) green jade

碧绿 bìlǜ [形] dark green

碧玉 bìyù [名] jasper

蔽 bì [动] shelter ◇蔽雨 shelter from the rain

弊 bì [名] **1** (蒙骗) fraud ◇考试作弊 cheat in an exam **2** (害处) disadvantage

弊病 bìbìng [名] **1** (弊端) evil **2** (毛病) disadvantage

弊端 bìduān [名] abuse ◇市场经济和计划经济各有弊端。Abuses occur in both market and planned economies.

避 bì [动] **1** (躲开) avoid **2** (防止) prevent

避风 bìfēng [动] **1** (躲风) shelter from the wind **2** (躲麻烦) lie low (*pt* lay, *pp* lain)

避风港 bìfēnggǎng [名] haven

避免 bìmiǎn [动] avoid

避难 bìnàn [动] take refuge (*pt* took, *pp* taken)

避暑 bìshǔ [动] **1** (指去凉爽地方) go to a summer resort (*pt* went, *pp* gone) **2** (避免中暑) prevent sunstroke

避嫌 bìxián [动] avoid arousing suspicion

避孕 bìyùn [动] use contraceptives ◇避孕丸药 the pill

避重就轻 bì zhòng jiù qīng focus on small things, ignoring what's important ◇开会时我避重就轻，只谈小问题。At the meeting, I avoided the important issues, and spoke only about minor points. ◇首相答记者问时，老是避重就轻。When the prime minister answers journalists' questions he always evades the issue.

壁 bì [名] **1** (墙) wall **2** (山石) cliff

壁橱 bìchú [名] built-in cupboard (英) 或 closet (美)

壁灯 bìdēng [名] wall lamp

壁挂 bìguà [名] hanging

壁画 bìhuà [名] mural

壁垒 bìlěi [名] rampart ◇贸易壁垒 trade barrier

壁毯 bìtǎn [名] tapestry

壁纸 bìzhǐ [名] wallpaper

臂 bì [名] arm

臂膀 bìbǎng [名] arm

边 biān [名] **1** (边线) side ◇街两边 both sides of the street **2** (边缘) edge ◇碗边儿 edge of a bowl ◇路边 roadside ◇帽边儿 brim of a hat **3** (边界) border ◇边城 border town **4** (界限) limit ◇宇宙浩瀚无边。The universe is limitless.

边…边… biān…biān… ◇边吃边谈 talk while eating

边陲 biānchuí [名] (书) frontier

边防 biānfáng [名] border defence (英) 或 defense (美)

边关 biānguān [名] border pass

边际 biānjì [名] limit

边疆 biānjiāng [名] border area

边界 biānjiè [名] border

边境 biānjìng [名] border ◇边境冲突 border conflict

边卡 biānqiǎ [名] border checkpoint

边缘 biānyuán **I** [名] edge ◇这个国家正处于经济危机的边缘。This country is on the verge of economic crisis. **II** [形] marginal ◇边缘人群 fringe group

边缘科学 biānyuán kēxué [名] borderline science

边远 biānyuǎn [形] outlying

编 biān **I** [动] **1** (编织) weave (*pt* wove, *pp* woven) **2** (编排) organize ◇编组 put into groups **3** (编辑) edit ◇编词典 compile a dictionary **4** (创作) write (*pt* wrote, *pp* written) ◇编歌词 write lyrics **5** (捏造) fabricate **II** [名] book

编程 biānchéng [动] program

编辑 biānjí **I** [动] edit **II** [名] editor

编码 biānmǎ [动] encode ◇编码指令 coded instructions

编目 biānmù [动] catalogue

编排 biānpái [动] arrange

编审 biānshěn **I** [动] read and edit (*pt, pp* read) **II** [名] senior editor

编写 biānxiě [动] **1** (编著) compile **2** (创作) write (*pt* wrote, *pp* written)

编译 biānyì **I** [动] translate and edit **II** [名] translator–editor

编造 biānzào [动] **1** (报表、名册等) draw … up (*pt* drew, *pp* drawn) ◇编造预算 draw up a budget **2** (故事、谎言等) invent ◇编造谎言 invent a lie

编者 biānzhě [名] editor

编织 biānzhī [动] **1** (毛衣等) knit **2** (地毯等) weave (*pt* wove, *pp* woven)

编制 biānzhì **I** [动] **1** (编织) weave (*pt* wove, *pp* woven) **2** (制做) draw … up (*pt* drew, *pp* drawn) **II** [名] personnel quota ◇控制政府人员的编制 restrict the quota of government employees

编著 biānzhù [动] compile

编撰 biānzhuàn [动] compile

编组 biānzǔ [动] put into groups (*pt, pp* put)

编纂 biānzuǎn [动] compile

蝙 biān 见下文

蝙蝠 biānfú [名] bat

鞭 biān **I** [名] **1** (鞭子) whip **2** (教鞭) pointer **3** (爆竹) firecracker **II** [动] whip

鞭策 biāncè [动] spur on

鞭长莫及 biān cháng mò jí be beyond one's influence

鞭笞 biānchī [动] (书) flog

鞭打 biāndǎ [动] whip

鞭炮 biānpào [名] firecracker

鞭辟入里 biān pì rù lǐ incisive

鞭挞 biāntà [动] lash out at

贬 biǎn [动] **1** (降低) reduce ◇快要过期的食品会贬价出售。Foodstuffs getting close to their sell-by date need to be reduced in price. **2** (评价低) belittle ◇不要把别人贬得太低。You shouldn't belittle other people.

贬斥 biǎnchì [动] **1** (书) (降职) demote **2** (排斥) denigrate

贬义词 biǎnyì cí [名] derogatory expression

贬值 biǎnzhí [动] **1** (购买力下降) depreciate **2** (兑换率降低) devalue

扁 biǎn [形] flat
▷另见 piān

扁担 biǎndan [名] carrying pole

褊 biǎn [形] (书) narrow

褊狭 biǎnxiá [形] (书) cramped ◇住房褊狭 cramped living conditions ◇气量褊狭 small-minded

变 biàn **I** [动] **1** (改变) change ◇小城的面貌变了。The appearance of the town has changed. **2** (变成) become (*pt* became, *pp* become) ◇他变成熟了。He's become quite grown up. **3** (转换) transform ◇变乡村为城市 urbanize **II** [名] turn of events ◇情况可能有变。There may have been a change in circumstances.

变本加厉 biàn běn jiā lì become aggravated

变动 biàndòng [动] alter ◇会议安排变动了。The arrangements for the conference have altered.

变革 biàngé [动] transform ◇中国正在经历巨大的社会变革。China is currently undergoing a social transformation.

变更 biàngēng [动] modify

变故 biàngù [名] unforeseen event

变卦 biànguà [动] go back on one's word (*pt* went, *pp* gone)

变化 biànhuà [动] change

变幻 biànhuàn [动] fluctuate

变换 biànhuàn [动] vary

变脸 biànliǎn [动] turn hostile

变量 biànliàng [名] variable

变卖 biànmài [动] sell … off (*pt*, *pp* sold)

变迁 biànqiān [动] change

变色龙 biànsèlóng [名] chameleon

变数 biànshù [名] variable

变态 biàntài **I** [名](生物) metamorphosis **II** [形] abnormal

变天 biàntiān [动] **1** (指天气变化) ◇早上还有太阳，下午就变天了。It was sunny in the morning, but the weather changed in the afternoon. **2** (指政局变化) stage a comeback

变通 biàntōng [动] be flexible

变戏法 biàn xìfǎ [动] conjure

变相 biànxiàng [动] disguise

变心 biànxīn [动] cease to be loyal ◇他对女朋友变心了。He ceased to be loyal to his girlfriend.

变形 biànxíng [动] become deformed (*pt* became, *pp* become)

变性 biànxìng [动] **1** (化) denature **2** (改变性别) change sex

变异 biànyì [名] variation

变质 biànzhì [动] go bad (*pt* went, *pp* gone) ◇牛奶变质了。The milk has gone off.

便 biàn **I** [形] **1** (方便) convenient ♦轻便 portable **2** (简单) simple ♦便饭 simple meal **II** [名] **1** (方便之时) convenience ◇何时来讲学，悉听尊便。Please come and speak to us at your own convenience. **2** (粪便) excretion **III** [动] excrete ♦小便 urinate ♦大便 defecate **IV** [副] ◇稍等片刻演唱会便开始。The performance is about to start in a moment.
▷另见 pián

便当 biàndang [形] (口) handy

便道 biàndào [名] **1** (近路) shortcut **2** (人行道) pavement **3** (临时道路) temporary road

便饭 biànfàn [名] quick meal

便服 biànfú [名] **1** (平常服装) everyday clothes **2** (中式服装) Chinese dress

便捷 biànjié [形] **1** (直捷方便) quick and convenient **2** (轻快敏捷) nimble

便利 biànlì **I** [形] convenient **II** [动] facilitate

便士 biànshì [量] pence

便条 biàntiáo [名] note

便携式 biànxiéshì [形] portable

便衣 biànyī [名] 1 (指服装) plain clothes 2 (指人) plain-clothes policeman

便于 biànyú [动] be easy to ◇便于联系 be easy to contact

遍 biàn I [副] all over ◇我把柜子翻了个遍也没找着。I searched all through my wardrobe but couldn't find it. II [量] ◇我说了两遍。I said it twice.

遍布 biànbù [动] be found everywhere

遍地 biàndì [名] everywhere

遍及 biànjí [动] spread all over (*pt, pp* spread)

遍体鳞伤 biàn tǐ lín shāng beaten black and blue

辨 biàn [动] distinguish

辨别 biànbié [动] distinguish

辨认 biànrèn [动] identify

辨析 biànxī [动] discriminate ◇辨析同义词 discriminate between synonyms

辩 biàn [动] debate ◆争辩 contend

辩白 biànbái [动] plead innocence

辩驳 biànbó [动] refute

辩才 biàncái [名] eloquence

辩护 biànhù [动] 1 (辩解) defend 2 (申辩) plead ◇为被告人辩护 plead on the behalf of the accused

辩护人 biànhùrén [名] counsel

辩解 biànjiě [动] offer an explanation ◇不要为自己的错误行为辩解。Don't try to make excuses for your mistakes.

辩论 biànlùn [动] argue ◇我不想就这个问题与你辩论。I don't want to argue with you about this.

辫 biàn [名] plait

辫子 biànzi [名] 1 (发辫) plait 2 (把柄) handle

标 biāo I [名] 1 (记号) mark 2 (标准) standard 3 (奖品) prize 4 (出价) bid 5 (皮毛) symptom II [动] mark

标榜 biāobǎng [动] (贬) 1 (宣扬) flaunt 2 (吹捧) flatter

标本 biāoběn [名] 1 (样品) specimen 2 (代表) sample 3 (指问题、病) cause and effect ◇我们对这个问题得标本兼治。We need to tackle both the cause and effect of this problem.

标兵 biāobīng [名] (喻) (榜样) example

标底 biāodǐ [名] minimum bid

标的 biāodì [名] 1 (指合同) objective 2 (靶子) target

标点 biāodiǎn I [名] punctuation II [动] punctuate

标杆 biāogān [名] 1 (样板) model 2 (指测量工具) measuring pole

标记 biāojì [名] mark

标价 biāojià [名] marked price ◇这套西装标价为500镑。This suit is priced at £500.

标明 biāomíng [动] mark

标签 biāoqiān [名] label

标枪 biāoqiāng [名] (体育) javelin

标题 biāotí [名] 1 (指文章、书) title 2 (指新闻) headline

标新立异 biāo xīn lì yì break the mould

标语 biāoyǔ [名] slogan

标志 biāozhì I [名] sign II [动] mark

标致 biāozhì [形] beautiful

标准 biāozhǔn [名] I standard ◇道德标准 moral standard ◇不能把钱作为衡量幸福的惟一标准。You can't take money as the only standard for happiness. ◇当警察要达到一定的身高标准。In order to be a policeman you have to meet certain height requirements. ◇录取标准 entry requirements II [形] standard ◇标准时间 standard time ◇标准音 standard pronunciation

彪 biāo [名] (书) tiger cub

彪炳千古 biāobǐng qiāngǔ timeless

彪悍 biāohàn [形] valiant

彪形大汉 biāoxíng dàhàn [名] strapping man

膘 biāo [名] fat

镖 biāo [名] dart

飙 biāo [名] (书) whirlwind

飙升 biāoshēng [动] shoot up (*pt*, *pp* shot)

表 biǎo I [名] 1 (计时器) watch ◇手表 wristwatch 2 (计量器) meter ◇电表 electricity meter 3 (表格) form 4 (外表) appearance 5 (指亲戚) cousin ♦表哥 cousin 6 (榜样) model II [动] express

表白 biǎobái [动] express

表层 biǎocéng [名] surface

表达 biǎodá [动] express ◇他的表达能力很强。He's very good at expressing himself.

表格 biǎogé [名] form

表功 biǎogōng [动] (贬) talk oneself up ◇在经理面前，他使劲表功。When he was with his manager he did his best to talk himself up.

表决 biǎojué [动] vote

表里 biǎolǐ [名] (喻) (言行和思想) ◇这人表里不一。This man isn't what he appears. ◇她很可靠，表里如一。You can rely on her – what you see is what you get.

表露 biǎolù [动] reveal

表面 biǎomiàn [名] surface ◇我们不应只处理问题的表面。We shouldn't just be tackling the surface of the problem.

表面文章 biǎomiàn wénzhāng go through the motions ◇没有人真正遵守新规定，都在做表面文章。No one really respects the new regulations – they're all just going through the motions.

表明 biǎomíng [动] show (*pt* showed, *pp* shown)

表亲 biǎoqīn [名] cousin

表情 biǎoqíng [名] expression

表示 biǎoshì I [动] 1 (表达) express ◇表示衷心感谢 express heartfelt gratitude ◇表示歉意 express regret ◇举手表示赞成 raise one's hand to express approval 2 (显示) indicate ◇路上结冰了, 表示温度是零下。The road is iced up, which indicates that the temperature is below zero. II [名] 1 (言行或表情) gesture ◇他们不友好的表示激怒了我们。Their unfriendly gesture infuriated us. 2 (意见) attitude ◇对于这个决定, 他还未做明确的表示。He still hasn't given a clear indication of his attitude towards the decision.

表述 biǎoshù [动] express

表率 biǎoshuài [名] model

表态 biǎotài [动] make one's position known ◇在会上，每个人都要对这个问题表态。Everyone at the meeting had to make known their position on the problem.

表现 biǎoxiàn I [动] 1 (显出) show (*pt* showed, *pp* shown) 2 (贬) (炫耀) show off (*pt* showed, *pp* shown) II [名] (指行为、作风) performance

表演 biǎoyǎn [动] 1 (演出) perform ◇演员们的精彩表演赢得了观众的喝彩。The actors' wonderful performance won the audience's acclaim. 2 (演示) demonstrate

> **display** 是公共演出或其他意在娱乐大众的活动。它可能在室外进行。*a firework display... gymnastic displays...* **exhibition** 是指图片、雕塑、史料或者其他艺术品的展示, 例如在博物馆或者美术馆举办的展览。*an exhibition of modern art...* **performance** 或 **show** 是指演唱、舞蹈或者其他娱乐观众的表演形式。**performance** 通常指某个具体的活动, 而 **show** 可能是在一段时期内每晚都进行的演出。**show** 经常包含不同的项目, 譬如音乐、舞蹈或者喜剧表演。*They were giving a performance of Bizet's opera "Carmen"... How about going shopping and seeing a show in London?* **show** 也用来表示电视或者广播中的某个节目。*I had my own TV show.*

表扬 biǎoyáng [动] praise

表彰 biǎozhāng [动] commend

婊 biǎo 见下文

婊子 biǎozi [名] (贬) whore

裱 biǎo [动] mount

裱糊 biǎohú [动] paper

憋 biē [动] **1** (抑制) suppress **2** (憋闷) feel suffocated (*pt*, *pp* felt) ◊总呆在屋里憋得慌。Staying indoors all day will make you feel absolutely suffocated.

憋闷 biēmen [名] depression

憋气 biēqì [动] **1** (呼吸困难) feel suffocated (*pt*, *pp* felt) **2** (无法发泄) be frustrated

瘪 biē 见下文
▷另见 biě

瘪三 biēsān [名] (方) layabout

鳖 biē [名] soft-shelled turtle

别 bié **I** [动] **1** (离开) say goodbye (*pt*, *pp* said) ♦告别 part **2** (区分) differentiate ♦区别 distinguish **3** (固定) pin ◊胸针可以再别高一点。The brooch could be pinned a little bit higher. ◊他腰间别着一支枪。A gun was strapped round his waist. **II** [名] **1** (类别) category ◊请填写你的年龄、性别及政治派别。Please complete all parts of the form including age, gender and political party. **2** (差别) ◊天壤之别 worlds apart **III** [形] (其他) other ♦别人 other people **IV** [副] **1** (不要) ◊别听信谣言。Don't listen to gossip. ◊别忘了关灯。Don't forget to turn off the light. **2** (莫非) maybe ◊他肯定在家的，你别是敲错门了吧？ I'm sure he's at home. Maybe you knocked on the wrong door.
▷另见 biè

别称 biéchēng [名] alternative name

别出心裁 bié chū xīncái be original ◊朱莉别出心裁， 想要徒步走新疆。Julie had the original idea of touring Xinjiang on foot.

别号 biéhào [名] alternative name

别具匠心 bié jù jiàngxīn be completely original ◊他的画总是别具匠心。His paintings are always completely original.

别具一格 bié jù yī gé have a unique style ◊这座小城市有浓郁的地方特色，别具一格。This small town is rich in local specialities, which gives it its own unique style.

别开生面 bié kāi shēng miàn innovative

别离 biélí [动] leave (*pt*, *pp* left) ◊他别离了妻子，外出打工。He left his wife and went to look for work elsewhere.

别名 biémíng [名] alternative name

别人 biérén [名] other people ◊家里只有我，没有别人。There's only me at home, nobody else.

别树一帜 bié shù yī zhì found a new school of thought

别墅 biéshù [名] villa

别无长物 bié wú chángwù **1** (表示俭朴) own the mere bare necessities **2** (表示贫穷) not have a penny to one's name

别有风味 bié yǒu fēngwèi be unique

别有用心 bié yǒu yòngxīn have something up one's sleeve

别针 biézhēn [名] safety pin

别致 biézhì [形] unique ◊这辆车看上去很别致。This car has a unique look.

别字 biézì [名] misspelling

蹩 bié 见下文

蹩脚 biéjiǎo [形] shoddy ◊他写的文章很蹩脚。His essay was a pretty shoddy piece of work.

瘪 biě [形] **1** (表面下陷) dented ◊他把车头撞瘪了。He dented the front of the car. **2** (不饱满) shrivelled ◊大多数谷子已经瘪了。Most of the crop has shrivelled up.
▷另见 biē

别 biè [动] (方) talk … out of ◊这个人很倔强，我恐怕别不过他。This guy is too stubborn – I'm afraid I won't be able to talk him out of it.
▷另见 bié

别扭 bièniu **I** [形] **1** (指人、工具) difficult ◊在这种人手下工作真别扭。This kind of man is always difficult to work for. ◊这把钳子用起来很别扭。These pliers are very difficult to use. **2** (指文章、说话) awkward ◊这篇文章读起来有点别扭。This essay reads a little awkwardly. **II** [名] spat ◊他在和老

板闹别扭。He's having a spat with his boss.

宾 bīn [名] guest

宾馆 bīnguǎn [名] hotel

宾客 bīnkè [名] guest

宾至如归 bīn zhì rú guī feel at home ◇好的旅馆服务让游客有宾至如归的感觉。Good hotel service will make guests feel at home.

彬 bīn 见下文

彬彬有礼 bīnbīn yǒulǐ courteous

傧 bīn 见下文

傧相 bīnxiàng [名] **1** (伴娘) chief bridesmaid (英), maid of honour (美) **2** (伴郎) best man

滨 bīn **I** [名] ♦海滨 seashore **II** [动] border

缤 bīn 见下文

缤纷 bīnfēn [形] (书) ◇五彩缤纷 a dazzling array of colour

濒 bīn [动] **1** (紧挨) border on ◇濒临大海 border on the sea **2** (临近) be on the point of ♦濒死 on the point of death

濒临 bīnlín [动] border ◇中国濒临太平洋。China borders the Pacific.

濒危 bīnwēi [动] be endangered

摈 bìn [动] reject

摈除 bìnchú [动] discard

摈弃 bìnqì [动] abandon

殡 bìn [名] funeral ♦出殡 funeral procession

殡仪馆 bìnyíguǎn [名] funeral parlour (英) 或 parlor (美)

殡葬 bìnzàng [动] hold a funeral (*pt, pp* held)

膑 bìn [名] kneecap

鬓 bìn [名] sideburns (*pl*)

鬓发 bìnfà [名] sideburns (*pl*)

鬓角 bìnjiǎo [名] sideburns (*pl*)

冰 bīng **I** [名] ice **II** [动] **1** (使感觉寒冷) be freezing ◇这水冰手。This water is freezing. **2** (冰镇) cool ◇你去冰冷饮，我来煮咖啡。You cool the drinks and I'll make the coffee.

冰川 bīngchuān [名] glacier

冰点 bīngdiǎn [名] freezing point

冰冷 bīnglěng [形] freezing

冰凉 bīngliáng [形] ice-cold

冰淇淋 bīngqílín [名] ice cream

冰清玉洁 bīng qīng yù jié as pure as jade

冰霜 bīngshuāng [名] coldness

冰炭不相容 bīngtàn bù xiāng róng be completely incompatible

冰糖 bīngtáng [名] rock sugar

冰天雪地 bīng tiān xuě dì mind-numbingly cold

冰消瓦解 bīng xiāo wǎ jiě fall apart ◇头子被捕后，这个黑社会集团很快就冰消瓦解了。After their leader was caught, the underground gang soon fell apart.

冰镇 bīngzhèn [形] iced ◇冰镇啤酒 ice-cold beer

兵 bīng [名] **1** (军队) the army ♦骑兵 cavalry ◇当兵 join the army **2** (士兵) soldier **3** (兵器) arms (*pl*) ◇坚甲利兵 military strength **4** (兵法) military strategy ◇纸上谈兵 be an armchair strategist

兵变 bīngbiàn [名] mutiny

兵不血刃 bīng bù xuè rèn win without firing a shot

兵不厌诈 bīng bù yàn zhà all's fair in love and war

兵法 bīngfǎ [名] military tactics (*pl*)

兵荒马乱 bīng huāng mǎ luàn the turmoil of war

兵器 bīngqì [名] arms (*pl*)

兵强马壮 bīng qiáng mǎ zhuàng military might

兵团 bīngtuán [名] military corps (*pl* military corps)

兵役 bīngyì [名] military service ◇服兵役 do military service

兵营 bīngyíng [名] barracks (*pl*)

兵种 bīngzhǒng [名] military division

丙 bǐng [名] third ◇丙组的运动员先

上。The athletes in group three are to go first. ◇甲、乙、丙组 groups A, B and C

秉 bǐng [动] **1** (书) (拿) hold (*pt, pp* held) **2** (书) (掌握) preside over ♦秉权 be in power ◇康熙皇帝秉政61年。The Emperor Kangxi ruled for 61 years. **3** (书) (根据) be in accordance with

秉承 bǐngchéng [动] **1** (传统) carry ... on ◇我们要秉承公司的优秀传统。We must carry on the company's excellent traditions. **2** (意见) adopt

秉公 bǐnggōng [动] be impartial ◇秉公执法的法官 a judge who is impartial in enforcing the law ◇法制人员要秉公办事。Legal staff must be impartial about their work.

秉性 bǐngxìng [名] nature ◇她秉性坚强。She is strong by nature.

柄 bǐng [名] **1** (指器物) handle **2** (喻) (指言行) handle ♦笑柄 laughing stock ◇别让任何人抓住你的把柄。Don't let anyone get a handle on you. **3** (指植物) stem

饼 bǐng [名] **1** (指面食) cake ♦月饼 moon cake **2** (饼状物) ♦铁饼 discus ♦土豆饼 potato bread

饼干 bǐnggān [名] biscuit (英), cookie (美)

屏 bǐng [动] **1** (气、呼吸) hold (*pt, pp* held) **2** (除去) get rid of ◇屏弃坏习惯 get rid of bad habits ▷另见 píng

屏除 bǐngchú [动] discard

屏息 bǐngxī [动] hold one's breath (*pt, pp* held)

禀 bǐng [动] (书) consult

禀报 bǐngbào [动] (书) report

禀承 bǐngchéng [动] 见'秉承'

禀赋 bǐngfù [名] gift ◇他运动禀赋很高。He has a real gift for sports.

禀告 bǐnggào [动] (书) report

禀性 bǐngxìng [名] nature

并 bìng **I** [动] **1** (合并) merge ◇把两个部门并成一个 merge two departments into one **2** (并拢) bring ... together (*pt, pp* brought) ◇把脚并起来 bring your feet together **II** [副] **1** (平排) side by side ◇齐头并进 progress side by side **2** (同) simultaneously ◇人类能左右脑并用。Humans can use the left and right sides of their brains simultaneously. ♦相提并论 mention in the same breath **3** (表示强调) really ◇他今晚并不想出去。He really doesn't want to go out this evening. **III** [连] and ◇他会说法语，并在学习西班牙语。He can speak French, and he is studying Spanish at the moment.

并存 bìngcún [动] coexist

并蒂莲 bìngdìlián [名] (喻) (夫妻) devoted married couple

并发 bìngfā [动] develop into ◇他得了流感，现在并发了肺炎。He caught the flu, and now it has developed into pneumonia.

并发症 bìngfāzhèng [名] complication

并轨 bìngguǐ [动] merge ◇两种体制并轨。The two systems have merged.

并驾齐驱 bìng jià qí qū be on a level pegging ◇两国的经济发展并驾齐驱。The two countries are on a level pegging in terms of economic development.

并肩 bìngjiān [副] side by side ◇我们并肩在桥上走着。We were walking side by side on the bridge.

并举 bìngjǔ [动] develop simultaneously

并列 bìngliè [动] be equal ◇她俩期末考试并列第一。They came equal first in the end of term exams. ◇他俩并列冠军。They are joint champions.

并排 bìngpái [副] side by side ◇三个人并排骑着自行车。The three of them were cycling side by side.

并且 bìngqiě [连] **1** (和) and ◇她聪明并且用功。She is clever and diligent. **2** (此外) also ◇我们有信心，并且有实力赢得这场比赛。We have the confidence and also the ability to win the match.

并吞 bìngtūn [动] swallow ... up

并行 bìngxíng [动] **1** (指位置) run side by side (*pt* ran, *pp* run) **2** (指时间) run concurrently

并重 bìngzhòng [动] attach equal importance to

病 bìng **I** [名] **1** (疾病) disease ♦心脏病 heart disease **2** (错误) fault ◊这句话有语病。This sentence is not grammatical. ◊发音不好是这班同学的通病。Bad pronunciation is a common fault among students in this class. **II** [动] be ill ◊他病得不轻。He was seriously ill.

病变 bìngbiàn [名] pathological changes (*pl*)

病毒 bìngdú [名] virus

病房 bìngfáng [名] ward

病故 bìnggù [动] die of an illness

病号 bìnghào [名] patient

病句 bìngjù [名] ungrammatical sentence

病菌 bìngjūn [名] bacteria

病理 bìnglǐ [名] pathology

病历 bìnglì [名] medical record

病例 bìnglì [名] case ◊非典型病例 an atypical case

病魔 bìngmó [名] serious illness

病情 bìngqíng [名] condition ◊孩子的病情有好转。The child's condition has improved a lot.

病人 bìngrén [名] **1** (指医院里) patient **2** (指家里) invalid

病入膏肓 bìng rù gāo huāng beyond help

病态 bìngtài [名] illness ◊肥胖症是一种病态。Obesity is an illness.

病征 bìngzhēng [名] symptom

病症 bìngzhèng [名] illness

摒 bìng [动] exclude

摒弃 bìngqì [动] abandon

波 bō [名] **1** (指水、声音、电) wave **2** (喻) (意外变化) unexpected turn of events

波动 bōdòng [动] fluctuate

波段 bōduàn [名] wave ◊短波 short wave ◊中波 medium wave ◊长波 long wave

波及 bōjí [动] affect

波澜 bōlán [名] waves (*pl*) ◊情感的波澜 waves of emotion

波澜壮阔 bōlán zhuàngkuò magnificent

波浪 bōlàng [名] wave

波涛 bōtāo [名] billow

波折 bōzhé [名] setback

拨 bō **I** [动] **1** (号码) dial **2** (琴弦) pluck **3** (频道) change over to ◊请拨到中央一台好吗？ Can you change over to CCTV1 please? **4** (算盘) flick **5** (火) poke **6** (配给) allocate **II** [量] **1** (指人) group ◊我们公司为了新项目招了一拨人。Our company recruited a group of people for the new project. **2** (指物) batch ◊这两拨货昨天已经发出了。The two batches of goods were sent out yesterday.

拨款 bōkuǎn [动] allocate funds ◊政府拨款兴建了100所小学。The government allocated funds for the setting up of 100 primary schools. ◊教育拨款已经到位。The funding for education is already in place.

拨弄 bōnong [动] **1** (琴弦) pluck **2** (算盘) flick **3** (指用器具) poke around ◊我用筷子拨弄着鸡块。I poked at the chicken pieces with my chopsticks. **4** (挑拨) stir … up

玻 bō 见下文

玻璃 bōlí [名] glass

剥 bō 见下文
▷另见 bāo

剥夺 bōduó [动] strip … of ◊他被剥夺政治权利5年。He was stripped of his political rights for five years.

剥离 bōlí [动] come off (*pt* came, *pp* come)

剥削 bōxuē [动] exploit ◊残酷的剥削 ruthless exploitation ◊废除剥削制度 abolish exploitative systems

菠 bō 见下文

菠菜 bōcài [名] spinach

菠萝 bōluó [名] pineapple

播 bō [动] **1** (电视、收音机) broadcast

(*pt, pp* broadcast) **2** (播种) sow (*pt* sowed, *pp* sown)

播放 bōfàng [动] broadcast (*pt, pp* broadcast)

播弄 bōnong [动] 见 '拨弄'

播送 bōsòng [动] broadcast (*pt, pp* broadcast)

播音 bōyīn [动] broadcast (*pt, pp* broadcast)

播音员 bōyīnyuán [名] broadcaster

播种 bōzhǒng [动] sow (*pt* sowed, *pp* sown)

播种 bōzhòng [动] sow (*pt* sowed, *pp* sown) ◇农民在田里播种小麦。Farmers are sowing the field with wheat.

伯 bó [名] **1** (伯父) uncle **2** (大哥) eldest brother **3** (伯爵) earl

伯伯 bóbo [名] **1** (伯父) uncle **2** (用于称呼) uncle

> **uncle** 有时可作为对跟父亲同辈且年纪较大的男子的称呼，但不常用。伯伯后通常跟姓氏，例如：李伯伯；而**Uncle**后跟名字，例如：**Uncle Tom**。

伯乐 Bólè [名] talent scout

伯仲 bózhòng [名] (书) ◇他俩不分伯仲。There's little to choose between them. ◇他们的英语能力在伯仲之间。Their English is equally good.

驳 bó [动] refute

驳斥 bóchì [动] refute

驳杂 bózá [形] mixed

泊 bó [动] **1** (停靠) moor ♦泊船 moor a boat **2** (停留) stop over

泊位 bówèi [名] berth

帛 bó [名] (书) silks (*pl*)

勃 bó [形] (书) thriving

勃勃 bóbó [形] exuberant

勃然 bórán [副] suddenly

舶 bó [名] ocean liner

舶来品 bóláipǐn [名] import

脖 bó [名] neck

博 bó I [动] **1** (通晓) possess a wide knowledge of **2** (取得) gain II [形] abundant

博爱 bó'ài [名] universal love ◇自由、平等、博爱 liberty, equality and fraternity

博大精深 bó dà jīng shēn deep

博导 bódǎo [名] doctoral supervisor

博览 bólǎn [动] read widely (*pt, pp* read)

博览会 bólǎnhuì [名] fair

博士 bóshì [名] doctor

博士后 bóshìhòu [名] ◇我正在做博士后研究。I'm doing postdoctoral research at the moment.

博闻强记 bó wén qiáng jì be learned

博物 bówù [名] natural sciences (*pl*)

博物馆 bówùguǎn [名] museum

博学 bóxué [形] learned

搏 bó [动] **1** (搏斗) fight (*pt, pp* fought) **2** (跳动) beat (*pt* beat, *pp* beaten)

搏动 bódòng [动] beat (*pt* beat, *pp* beaten)

搏斗 bódòu I [动] **1** (对打) fight (*pt, pp* fought) **2** (斗争) struggle II [名] battle

箔 bó [名] foil ♦金箔 gold leaf

膊 bó [名] arm

薄 bó I [形] **1** (不强壮) weak **2** (少) meagre **3** (不厚道) mean **4** (不庄重) frivolous II [动] (轻视) look down on ▷另见 báo, bò

薄利 bólì [名] small profit

薄命 bómìng [形] ill-fated

薄情 bóqíng [形] heartless

薄弱 bóruò [形] weak

跛 bǒ [形] lame

跛子 bǒzi [名] ◇他是个跛子。He has a limp.

簸 bǒ [动] **1** (扬去) fan **2** (上下颠动) be bumpy
▷另见 bò

簸荡 bǒdàng [动] bump up and down

簸箩 bǒluo [名] wicker basket

薄 bò 见下文
▷另见 báo, bó

薄荷 bòhe [名] peppermint

簸 bò 见下文
▷另见 bǒ

簸箕 bòji [名] (指器具) dustpan

卜 bǔ [动] practice divination

补 bǔ [动] **1** (衣服、鞋、车胎、袜子) mend **2** (牙) fill **3** (增加) add ◇请把邮编补上。Please add the postcode. **4** (滋补) nourish

补办 bǔbàn [动] ◇我的身份证丢了，得去补办。I've lost my identity card and must replace it. ◇我错过了注册的时间，得以后补办。I missed the deadline for registration and had to deal with that at a later date.

补偿 bǔcháng [动] **1** (损失) compensate ◇补偿费 compensation **2** (欠缺、差额) make up for ◇公司给他5, 000美元以补偿他的损失。The company gave him US$5,000 in compensation for his injury.

补充 bǔchōng [动] add ◇补充说明 additional explanation

补丁 bǔding [名] patch

补给 bǔjǐ [名] supply

补救 bǔjiù [动] remedy ◇我们必须采取补救措施。We must adopt remedial measures.

补考 bǔkǎo [动] resit (*pt*, *pp* resat) ◇她下学期得补考数学。She has to resit her maths exam next term. ◇我下个月要参加补考。I will be taking resits next month.

补品 bǔpǐn [名] tonic

补贴 bǔtiē **I** [动] subsidize **II** [名] subsidy

补习 bǔxí [动] take extra lessons (*pt* took, *pp* taken)

补休 bǔxiū [名] time off in lieu

补养 bǔyǎng [动] nourish

补药 bǔyào [名] tonic

补助 bǔzhù [名] subsidy ◇学校每月补助他们200美元。The school gives them a subsidy of 200 dollars every month.

捕 bǔ [动] catch (*pt*, *pp* caught)

捕风捉影 bǔ fēng zhuō yǐng listen to hearsay

捕获 bǔhuò [动] capture

捕捞 bǔlāo [动] fish ◇捕捞牡蛎 fish for oysters

捕猎 búliè [动] hunt

捕捉 bǔzhuō [动] **1** (抓住) seize ◇捕捉良机 seize a golden opportunity **2** (捉拿) hunt down ◇捕捉逃犯 hunt down a convict

哺 bǔ [动] feed (*pt*, *pp* fed)

哺乳 bǔrǔ [动] breast-feed (*pt*, *pp* breast-fed)

哺乳动物 bǔrǔ dòngwù [名] mammal

哺育 bǔyù [动] **1** (喂养) feed (*pt*, *pp* fed) **2** (培养) nurture

不 bù [副] **1** (用于否定句) not ◇我不喜欢游泳。I don't like swimming. ♦不法 illegal ♦不轨 undisciplined ♦不诚实 dishonest ♦不人道 inhumane ◇他不抽烟。He doesn't smoke. **2** (用于否定回答) no ◇“你累了吧？” “不，不累。” Are you tired? – No, I'm not. ◇“你不忙吧？” “不，很忙”。You're not busy, are you? – Yes, I am. **3** (表示不能) ◇我吃不下。I can't eat it. ◇你找不到她吗？ Can't you find her? ◇他中文学不好。He's not good at Chinese. **4** (方) (用于问句) ◇你饿不？ Are you hungry? **5** (跟‘就是’搭配) ◇周末，她不是购物，就是看电视。If she doesn't go shopping at the weekend she'll watch TV. **6** (客套) (不用) ◇不客气。Please don't mention it. ◇不谢。You're welcome.

不安 bù'ān [形] **1** (指局势) unstable **2** (指情绪) uneasy **3** (客套) (表示歉意) ◇让您花这么多钱，真是不安。I'm sorry to make you spend so much money.

不白之冤 bù bái zhī yuān injustice

不卑不亢 bù bēi bù kàng neither overbearing nor self-effacing ◇他待人的态度一向不卑不亢。His manner with people is neither overbearing nor self-effacing.

不必 bùbì [副] ◇明天早上你们不必再来了。You don't have to come again tomorrow morning.

不…不… bù…bù… **1** (表示强式否定) ◇不知不觉 unwittingly ◇不慌不忙 unhurriedly ◇不折不扣 one hundred percent **2** (既不…也不…) neither … nor … ◇不亏不盈 neither too little nor too much ◇不大不小 just the right size ◇不死不活 half dead **3** (如果不…就不…) unless … then not ◇不破不立 without destruction there can be no construction ◇不见不散。See you there.

不测 bùcè **I** [形] (预料不到的) unexpected **II** [名] (意外) contingency

不曾 bùcéng [副] never ◇我不曾见过你。I've never met you.

不耻下问 bù chǐ xià wèn learn from those beneath one ◇老教授不耻下问，令人敬佩。It's admirable that the old professor is willing to learn from those beneath him.

不但 bùdàn [连] not only ◇这辆车的设计不但美观，而且实用。The design of this car is not only beautiful, it's also practical.

不当 bùdàng [形] inappropriate ◇用词不当 use inappropriate words ◇有不当之处，谨请包涵。Please excuse any improprieties.

不得了 bù déliǎo [形] **1** (表示惊讶) My God! ◇不得了，着火了！My God! It's on fire. ◇带孩子去酒吧，那可不得了。Taking children into bars is a shocking thing to do. **2** (表示程度) ◇这孩子淘气得不得了。This child is terribly naughty. ◇他难劝说得不得了。It is incredibly difficult to persuade him.

不得已 bùdéyǐ [动] have no alternative but to ◇这也是不得已而为之的事情。This is one of those things we have no alternative but to do.

不定 bùdìng **I** [副] ◇这货他们还不定要不要呢。It's still not certain whether they want these goods or not. **II** [形] ◇风向不定。The wind direction is changeable. ◇游移不定的目标 moving target

不断 bùduàn [副] continually ◇汽车不断减价。Cars are continually coming down in price. ◇沙漠不断扩大。The desert is expanding all the time. ◇人们的生活水平不断提高。The quality of people's lives goes on getting better.

不…而… bù…ér… ◇不劳而获 acquire without working ◇不言而喻 it goes without saying ◇不胫而走 spread like wildfire

不乏 bùfá [动] ◇这当中不乏知情者。There is no shortage of people in the know about this.

不凡 bùfán [形] extraordinary

不妨 bùfáng [副] ◇你不妨先说说你的想法。There's no harm in saying what you think.

不服 bùfú [动] not accept ◇你如果不服判决还可以上诉。If you don't accept the verdict, you can still appeal.

不敢 bùgǎn [动] not dare ◇她不敢说实话。She doesn't dare tell the truth.

不公 bùgōng [形] unfair

不苟 bùgǒu [形] careful ◇不苟言笑 serious in manner

不管 bùguǎn [连] ◇不管那女人怎么欺负我们，我们都不在乎。No matter how that woman bullies us, we just don't care. ◇不管你去什么地方，请一定和我保持联系。Wherever you go, please do keep in touch with me. ◇不管什么人求你帮忙，你不要拒绝他们。Whoever asks you for help, you shouldn't refuse them. ◇不管出什么事，我们都要保持镇定。Whatever happens, we must remain calm. ◇不管有多少人反对，他们都坚持原计划。It doesn't matter how many people disagree, they insist on implementing the original plan.

不轨 bùguǐ [形] irregular ◇这些人行为不轨引起了警察的注意。The irregular conduct of these people has attracted the attention of the police.

不过 bùguò I [副] 1 (仅仅) only ◊不过是点小伤，过几天就好了。It's only a slight injury. It'll be fine in a few days. ◊宝宝不过6个月大。The baby is only six months old. 2 (非常) ◊你要能帮忙，那就再好不过了！ If you were able to help, that couldn't be better. ◊这是最简单不过的方法。This is much the easiest method. II [连] but ◊他很喜欢新学校，不过离家太远了。He really likes his new school, but it's a very long way from home.

不及 bùjí [动] 1 (不如) be not as good as 2 (来不及) be too late

不计其数 bù jì qí shù countless

不假思索 bù jiǎ sīsuǒ without hesitation ◊他不假思索地给出了正确答案。He gave the correct answer without hesitation.

不禁 bùjīn [动] cannot help ◊我不禁失笑。I couldn't help laughing. ◊众人不禁欢呼起来。The crowd were unable to restrain a cheer.

不仅 bùjǐn [副] 1 (不止) not just ◊这不仅是学校的问题。This is not just the school's problem. 2 (不但) not only ◊这地毯不仅质量好，而且价格便宜。Not only is the carpet good quality, it's also cheap.

不胫而走 bù jìng ér zǒu spread like wildfire

不久 bùjiǔ [名] ◊在不久的将来 in the near future ◊这片田地不久前刚开垦。This land has only just been cultivated. ◊他们不久就要结婚了。They are getting married soon.

不拘 bùjū I [动] 1 (不拘泥) not confine oneself 2 (不计较) not worry about II [连] regardless of ◊不拘什么人，他都以礼相待。Regardless of who someone is, he is always polite.

不拘一格 bùjū yī gé not be limited to one type ◊选用人才要不拘一格。When selecting staff you mustn't be limited to just one type.

不堪 bùkān I [动] 1 (承受不了) cannot stand ◊不堪其苦 can't stand the hardship 2 (不能) not able ◊不堪设想 be inconceivable II [形] extreme

不可 bùkě [动] 1 (不可以) ◊不可一概而论。You can't generalize. ◊植物生长，水和阳光两者缺一不可。For plants to grow they must have both sun and water. ◊我们不可忽视年轻人的心理健康。We shouldn't overlook the mental health of young people. ◊我们对这些疾病不可不防。We mustn't fail to take steps against such diseases. 2 (与"非"连用) ◊今天非下雨不可。It will certainly rain today. ◊你非挨批不可。You are bound to be criticized. ◊我们非得解决这个问题不可。We absolutely have to sort this problem out.

不可救药 bù kě jiù yào be beyond help

不可思议 bù kě sīyì unbelievable

不可一世 bù kě yī shì be insufferably arrogant

不快 bùkuài [形] unhappy

不愧 bùkuì [动] be worthy of

不力 bùlì [形] 1 (不尽力) ◊领导常批评他办事不力。The boss frequently criticizes him for not doing his best. 2 (不得力) incompetent

不利 bùlì [形] 1 (不好) disadvantageous 2 (不顺) unsuccessful

不了了之 bù liǎo liǎo zhī leave unresolved ◊由于找不到嫌疑人，这个案件只能不了了之了。Since the suspect hasn't been found, the case simply had to be left unresolved.

不料 bùliào [动] not anticipate ◊不料下午下雨。I didn't anticipate it would rain in the afternoon. ◊我们本想和她开个玩笑，不料她却当真了。We had just wanted to have a laugh with her – we hadn't appreciated that she was serious.

不论 bùlùn I [连] no matter ◊不论是谁，都必须遵守法规。No matter who you are, you have to abide by the regulations. II [动] not consider

不满 bùmǎn [形] dissatisfied

不免 bùmiǎn [副] inevitably ◊竞争不免要有淘汰。In competitions there is inevitably elimination.

不明飞行物 bùmíng fēixíngwù [名] UFO

不谋而合 bù móu ér hé happen to coincide

不平 bùpíng I [形] unfair II [名] 1 (不公) injustice 2 (愤怒) resentment III [动] feel resentful (*pt, pp* felt)

不巧 bùqiǎo [形] unfortunate ◇你来得真不巧，王医生不在。Unfortunately, you haven't come at a good time – Dr Wang isn't here.

不求甚解 bù qiú shèn jiě be content with a superficial understanding ◇他学习一向不求甚解。He studies only to have a superficial understanding.

不屈 bùqū [动] not yield

不然 bùrán I [形] not so ◇这两件事看似一样，其实不然。These two seem the same, but in fact it is not so. II [连] otherwise ◇他家有老人，不然咱们倒可以去他家聚会。There is an elderly person in his family – otherwise we could get together at his house.

不忍 bùrěn [动] not bear

不如 bùrú [动] not be as good as ◇论跑步你不如她。You are not as good as her at running. ◇城里太吵，不如住在郊区。The city is too noisy – it's better living in the suburbs.

不三不四 bù sān bù sì 1 (不正经) shady 2 (不像样) neither one thing nor the other

不少 bùshǎo [形] a lot of ◇她有不少好朋友。She has a lot of good friends.

不胜 bùshèng I [动] cannot bear ◇不胜其苦 be unable to bear any more hardship ◇他不胜酒力，终于醉倒了。He had no tolerance for alcohol, and in the end fell down dead drunk. II [副] deeply ◇我对你的帮助不胜感激。I am deeply grateful for your help.

不是 bùshi [名] fault

不速之客 bù sù zhī kè uninvited guest ◇她是晚会上的不速之客。She was an uninvited guest at the party. ◇昨晚我家来了一位不速之客。Yesterday evening we had an unexpected guest.

不同 [形] different

不同凡响 bù tóng fánxiǎng outstanding

不外 bùwài [动] be limited to

不闻不问 bù wén bù wèn be indifferent ◇他对与己无关的事情一概不闻不问。He's indifferent to anything that doesn't have a bearing on him.

不相上下 bù xiāng shàng xià be about the same

不屑 bùxiè [动] disdain ◇不屑一顾 disdain to look at ◇他不屑金钱的诱惑。He's scornful of the temptations of money. ◇不屑的神情 a disdainful expression

不幸 bùxìng I [形] 1 (不幸运) unhappy 2 (出人意料) unfortunate ◇不幸被言中了。Unfortunately, it turned out to be true. II [名] disaster

不修边幅 bù xiū biānfú scruffy

不朽 bùxiǔ [形] immortal

不学无术 bù xué wú shù ignorant and incompetent ◇不学无术的人怎么能当校长？ How can someone ignorant and incompetent be head teacher?

不宜 bùyí [动] not be suitable for ◇这种菜不宜生食。This kind of vegetable is not suitable for serving raw.

不遗余力 bù yí yú lì do one's utmost ◇足球俱乐部不遗余力地引进外国球星。The football team did its utmost to attract foreign football stars.

不翼而飞 bù yì ér fēi disappear without trace

不约而同 bù yuē ér tóng happen to coincide ◇大家不约而同地投了赞成票。Everybody happened to vote in favour.

不择手段 bù zé shǒuduàn (贬) go to any lengths ◇为了发财，他不择手段。He'll go to any lengths to get rich.

不折不扣 bù zhé bù kòu through and through ◇他是不折不扣的球迷。He's a football fan through and through.

不知所措 bù zhī suǒ cuò be at a loss

不止 bùzhǐ [副] **1** (不停地) incessantly ◇大笑不止 laugh incessantly **2** (多于) more than ◇不止一次 on more than one occasion

不至于 bùzhìyú [副] ◇你不至于骗我吧？ You won't go so far as to cheat me, will you?

不自量力 bù zì liànglì overestimate one's abilities

布 bù **I** [名] cloth ◇布娃娃 rag doll **II** [动] **1** (宣告) publicize **2** (散布) spread (*pt, pp* spread) **3** (布置) arrange

布丁 bùdīng [名] pudding

布告 bùgào **I** [名] notice **II** [动] put up a notice (*pt, pp* put)

布景 bùjǐng [名] set

布局 bùjú [动] **1** (指结构) design ◇房间布局合理。The room is designed sensibly. ◇花园的布局很精巧。The layout of the garden is ingenious. **2** (指下棋) deploy

布匹 bùpǐ [名] cloth

布置 bùzhì [动] decorate

步 bù **I** [名] **1** (脚步) step **2** (阶段) stage **3** (地步) situation **II** [动] step **III** [量] move

步调 bùdiào [名] step ◇步调一致 stay in step

步伐 bùfá [名] pace ◇加快步伐 quicken one's pace

步人后尘 bù rén hòu chén follow in other people's footsteps

步行 bùxíng [动] go on foot (*pt* went, *pp* gone)

步骤 bùzhòu [名] step

部 bù **I** [名] **1** (部分) part ♦局部 part ♦头部 head **2** (部门) department ◇教育部 education department ♦总部 headquarters (*pl*) ♦分部 branch **3** (指军队) headquarters (*pl*) ♦司令部 army headquarters **II** [量] ◇一部字典 a dictionary ◇一部新型手机 a new style of mobile phone

部队 bùduì [名] armed forces (*pl*) ◇特种部队 special forces

部分 bùfen [名] part ◇我们只完成了项目的第一部分。We have only finished the first part of the project. ◇部分学生没有参加运动会。Some students didn't attend the sports meeting. ◇你要承担自己的那部分责任。You should shoulder your share of the responsibility. ◇我部分地同意他的观点。I partially agree with his view.

部件 bùjiàn [名] parts (*pl*)

部落 bùluò [名] tribe

部门 bùmén [名] department ◇政府部门 government department ◇邮政部门 post room ◇农业部门 department of agriculture

部署 bùshǔ [动] deploy

部位 bùwèi [名] place ◇手术部位 the place operated on

部下 bùxià [名] subordinate

埠 bù [名] port

簿 bù [名] book ♦练习簿 exercise book

簿子 bùzi [名] notebook

Cc

擦 cā [动] **1** (抹) wipe … clean ◇擦眼镜 wipe one's glasses clean ◇擦汗 wipe away one's sweat **2** (指用水) wash **3** (皮鞋) polish **4** (摩擦) rub ◇摩拳擦掌 be itching for a fight **5** (涂) apply ◇她粉底擦得太厚了。She has applied too much foundation. **6** (火柴) strike (*pt, pp* struck) **7** (破) scrape ♦擦伤 scrape **8** (挨着) brush ◇排球没发过去，擦网了。The volleyball didn't make it's way over – it just brushed the net. **9** (瓜果) shred

擦拭 cāshì [动] wipe … clean◇擦拭窗户 wipe a window clean◇擦拭银器 polish silverware

猜 cāi [动] **1** (猜测) guess **2** (猜疑) suspect

猜测 cāicè **I** [动] speculate ◇大家都在猜测谁能得奖。Everybody was speculating about who was going to win the prize. **II** [名] speculation

猜忌 cāijì [动] be suspicious

猜谜儿 cāimèir [动] guess

猜拳 cāiquán [动] *play a finger guessing game*

猜想 cāixiǎng [动] suppose

猜疑 cāiyí [动] have unfounded suspicions about

才 cái **I** [名] **1** (才能) ability ◇多才多艺 multi-talented **2** (人才) talent ♦奇才 extradordinary talent **II** [副] **1** (刚) just ◇我才到家，电话就响了。Just as I arrived home, the phone rang. **2** (表示晚) not…until ◇路上堵车，我10点才到单位上班。Because of the traffic jam, I did not arrive at work until ten. **3** (表示条件) only…if ◇学生只有用功，才能取得好成绩。Students will only be able to do well if they study hard. **4** (表示情况改变) only after◇他解释后，我才明白了他为什么那么难过。It was only after he explained that I understood why he was so sad. **5** (程度低) only ◇他才学会上网。He has only just learned how to use the Internet. **6** (表示强调) really ◇他才不愿意见你呢！ He really doesn't want to see you!

才干 cáigàn [名] ability

才华 cáihuá [名] talent

才貌 cáimào [名] ability and appearance

才能 cáinéng [名] ability ◇施展才能 put one's abilities to use ◇他有领导才能。He has leadership qualities.

才气 cáiqì [名] talent

才识 cáishí [名] ability and insight ◇他具有卓越的政治才识。He is a man of outstanding political ability and insight.

才学 cáixué [名] ability and learning

才子 cáizǐ [名] talented man (*pl* men)

材 cái [名] **1** (指物) material ♦建材 building material ♦教材 teaching material **2** (人才) talented person

材料 cáiliào [名] **1** (原料) material ◇建筑材料公司 building materials company ◇这件大衣是用什么材料做的？ What material is this coat made of? **2** (资料) material ◇我正为毕业论文搜集材料。I'm in the process of gathering material for my dissertation. **3** (人才) talent◇我不是经商的材料。I have no talent for business.

财 cái [名] wealth

财宝 cáibǎo [名] treasure

财阀 cáifá [名] tycoon

财富 cáifù [名] wealth

财经 cáijīng [名] finance and economics ◇财经学院 Institute of Finance and Economics

财路 cáilù [名] road to riches

财贸 cáimào [名] trade and finance

财神 cáishén [名] *the god of wealth*

财团 cáituán [名] consortium

财务 cáiwù [名] financial affairs (*pl*)

财物 cáiwù [名] assets (*pl*)

财政 cáizhèng [名] finance

财主 cáizhu [名] rich man (*pl* men)

裁 cái [动] **1** (衣服、纸) cut (*pt, pp* cut) **2** (减) cut (*pt, pp* cut) ♦裁员 cut staff **3** (判断) decide

裁定 cáidìng [动] adjudicate

裁缝 cáifeng [名] **1** (指男装) tailor **2** (指女装) dressmaker

裁决 cáijué [动] adjudicate

裁判 cáipàn **I** [名] judgment **II** [动] make a decision ◇我们要公平裁判这件事。We should make a fair decision on this matter.

裁员 cáiyuán [动] make redundancies ◇信息产业内刮起了一阵裁员风暴。There have been a wave of redundancies in the IT industry.

采 cǎi **I** [动] **1** (摘) pick **2** (选) choose (*pt* chose, *pp* chosen) **3** (开采) extract ♦采油 extract oil **4** (采集) gather **II** [名] spirit ♦风采 bearing

采伐 cǎifá [动] fell ◇过度的采伐会破坏森林。Excessive felling will destroy the forest.

采访 cǎifǎng [动] interview ◇记者采访了一位著名作家。The reporter interviewed a famous writer. ◇她已经做了十几年的新闻采访工作。She has already been working in investigative journalism for over ten years.

采购 cǎigòu **I** [动] purchase **II** [名] buyer

采光 cǎiguāng [名] lighting

采集 cǎijí [动] collect

采纳 cǎinà [动] adopt

采取 cǎiqǔ [动] adopt ◇政府采取紧急措施防止病毒传播。The government is adopting urgent measures to prevent the spread of disease. ◇我们采取主动，首先和新客户联络。We took the initiative and contacted the new client first.

采用 cǎiyòng [动] adopt ◇老师采用互动教学方式。The teacher has adopted an interactive method of teaching.

采摘 cǎizhāi [动] pick

彩 cǎi [名] **1** (颜色) colour (英), color (美) **2** (欢呼声) cheer **3** (花样) variety **4** (博彩) winnings (*pl*) ♦彩票 lottery ticket **5** (血) blood ♦挂彩 be wounded

彩电 cǎidiàn [名] colour (英) 或 color (美) TV

彩卷 cǎijuǎn [名] colour (英) 或 color (美) film

彩礼 cǎilǐ [名] wedding present

彩排 cǎipái [动] rehearse

彩票 cǎipiào [名] lottery ticket

彩色 cǎisè [名] colour (英), color (美)

睬 cǎi [动] take notice of (*pt* took, *pp* taken) ◇他太没人缘，晚会上没人睬他。He's not very good with people and no one takes any notice of him at parties.

踩 cǎi [动] **1** (脚) step on ◇跳舞时，我踩到他的脚了。During the dance I stepped on his foot. ◇我踩在椅子上擦窗户。I stood on a chair and cleaned the window. **2** (贬低) put … down (*pt, pp* put) ◇他不会夸人，只会踩人。He never praises people – he only puts them down.

菜 cài [名] **1** (植物) vegetable **2** (饭食) dish

菜单 càidān [名] menu

菜篮子 càilánzi [名] **1** (指买菜用的) shopping basket **2** (食品供应) food supply

菜谱 càipǔ [名] **1** (菜单) menu **2** (指书) cookbook

菜肴 càiyáo [名] dish

参 cān [动] **1** (加入) join ♦参军 enlist **2** (参考) refer to
▷另见 cēn, shēn

参拜 cānbài [动] bow before

参半 cānbàn [动] halve

参观 cānguān [动] tour ◇我们参观了故宫博物院。We toured the Forbidden City museum.

参加 cānjiā [动] take part in (*pt* took, *pp* taken) ◇参加演讲比赛 take part in a public speaking competition

◇参加新年晚会 attend a New Year's party ◇去年他参加了民主党。Last year he joined the Democratic Party.

参军 cānjūn [动] enlist ◇ 参军使他成熟了很多。Joining the army made him a lot more mature.

参考 cānkǎo I [动] consult ◇为了写毕业论文，我参考了几十本书。For my dissertation I had to consult dozens of different books. II [名] reference ◇参考书 reference book ◇以上观点仅供参考。The above advice is only for reference.

参谋 cānmóu I [名] 1 (顾问) advisor 2 (指军职) staff officer II [动] give advice (*pt* gave, *pp* given) ◇你帮我参谋一下，看他俩谁更优秀。I need you to give me some advice – who do you think is the best out of those two?

参数 cānshù [名] parameter

参议员 cānyìyuán [名] senator

参与 cānyù [动] participate in ◇参与竞选活动 participate in campaign activities ◇参与决策制定 participate in policy formulation ◇我参赛的态度是"重在参与，不重输赢"。My attitude towards competitions is: "It's not the winning, it's the taking part that counts."

参赞 cānzàn [名] attaché ◇美国大使馆文化参赞 the cultural attaché to the American embassy

参照 cānzhào [动] act in accordance with ◇我参照导师的意见修改了我的论文。I acted in accordance with the advice of my supervisor, and amended my thesis.

餐 cān I [名] meal II [量] meal

餐车 cānchē [名] 1 (指推车) food trolley 2 (指车厢) buffet (英) 或 dining (美) car

餐巾 cānjīn [名] napkin

餐具 cānjù [名] eating utensils (*pl*)

餐厅 cāntīng [名] canteen

残 cán I [形] 1 (指器物) defective 2 (指人或动物) disabled ◇这是匹好马，可惜残了。This is a good horse. It's a shame it's lame. 3 (剩余) remaining 4 (凶恶) cruel II [动] treat viciously

残暴 cánbào [形] cruel ◇侵略者的残暴 the cruelty of the invaders

残存 cáncún [动] survive ◇这是惟一残存的中国清代陶器样品。This is the only surviving example of Qing dynasty pottery in China. ◇公司里仍残存着性别歧视现象。Sexual discrimination still goes on in the company.

残废 cánfèi [动] be disabled ◇他中风后残废了。He was disabled by his stroke. ◇车祸使她成了残废。The car accident left her disabled.

残骸 cánhái [名] wreckage

残害 cánhài [动] devastate ◇战争残害了无数的人民。The war devastated the lives of countless people.

残疾 cánjí [名] disability ◇残疾人 people with disabilities ◇欢迎有残疾的人报名参加。People with disabilities are particularly encouraged to apply.

残局 cánjú [名] mess ◇公司倒闭后，只有经理在收拾残局。When the company closed only the manager was left to clear up the mess.

残酷 cánkù [形] brutal ◇残酷的市场竞争 brutal market competition ◇ 他被敌人残酷地杀害了。He was brutally murdered by the enemy.

残年 cánnián [名] final years (*pl*) ◇老人无儿无女，只能孤单单地度过残年。The old man had no children, and lived out his final years in loneliness.

残缺 cánquē [形] deficient

残忍 cánrěn [形] cruel

残杀 cánshā [动] brutally kill

残余 cányú [形] remaining ◇战败后，残余的部队逃回老家。After their defeat, the remaining troops fled home.

蚕 cán [名] silkworm

蚕豆 cándòu [名] broad (英) 或 fava (美) bean

蚕食 cánshí [动] encroach on ◇沙皇俄国对邻国采取了蚕食政策。

Tsarist Russia adopted a policy of encroaching on its neighbours.

惭 cán 见下文

惭愧 cánkuì [形] ashamed

惨 cǎn [形] **1** (悲惨) tragic **2** (厉害) severe **3** (凶恶) cruel

惨案 cǎn'àn [名] massacre

惨败 cǎnbài [动] suffer a disastrous defeat

惨不忍睹 cǎn bù rěn dǔ too horrible to look at

惨淡 cǎndàn [形] **1** (暗淡) dim **2** (萧条) dismal ◇几年的惨淡经营后，生意终于出现了转机。After several years' hard work, the business finally turned around.

惨绝人寰 cǎn jué rén huán horrific

惨痛 cǎntòng [形] bitter

惨无人道 cǎn wú rén dào barbaric

惨重 cǎnzhòng [形] disastrous

灿 càn 见下文

灿烂 cànlàn [形] glorious

仓 cāng [名] store ♦仓房 storehouse

仓储 cāngchǔ [动] store

仓促 cāngcù [形] hasty

仓皇 cānghuáng [形] panic-stricken

仓库 cāngkù [名] storehouse

苍 cāng [形] **1** (指天空) deep blue **2** (指植物) dark green **3** (指鬓发) grey (英), gray (美)

苍白 cāngbái [形] **1** (脸色) pale **2** (文章、表演等) bland

苍苍 cāngcāng [形] **1** (指天空) deep blue **2** (指植物) dark green **3** (指鬓发) grey (英), gray (美)

苍劲 cāngjìng [形] **1** (树) mighty **2** (书画) bold

苍老 cānglǎo [形] old

苍茫 cāngmáng [形] vast

苍生 cāngshēng [名] (书) the masses (*pl*)

苍天 cāngtiān [名] the heavens (*pl*)

苍蝇 cāngying [名] fly

沧 cāng [名] deep blue

沧海 cānghǎi [名] the sea

沧海桑田 cāng hǎi sāng tián radical changes ◇多年后重返故乡，真有种沧海桑田的感觉。Returning home after so many years, I had the impression that the place had undergone a complete transformation.

沧海一粟 cāng hǎi yī sù a drop in the ocean

沧桑 cāngsāng [名] all that life has to offer ◇在外漂泊了几十年，他已经饱经沧桑。He spent years drifting about, and has experienced all that life has to offer.

舱 cāng [名] **1** (用于载人) cabin ♦头等舱 first-class cabin **2** (用于装物) hold ♦货舱 cargo hold

藏 cáng [动] **1** (隐藏) hide (*pt* hid, *pp* hidden) **2** (储存) store **3** (收集) collect ♦藏书 collect books
▷另见 zàng

藏龙卧虎 cáng lóng wò hǔ hidden talent ◇人才招聘市场里藏龙卧虎。There is a lot of hidden talent on the job market.

藏匿 cángnì [动] conceal

藏书 cángshū **I** [动] collect books **II** [名] book collection

藏污纳垢 cáng wū nà gòu ◇这个地区真是个藏污纳垢之地。It's a really unsavoury area.

藏拙 cángzhuō [动] keep one's limitations to oneself (*pt, pp* kept) ◇他从不当众唱歌，只是为了藏拙。He never sings in public – he prefers to keep his limitations to himself. ◇她用化妆来藏拙。She uses make-up to cover her blemishes.

操 cāo **I** [动] **1** (拿) hold (*pt, pp* held) **2** (掌握) control **3** (从事) engage in **4** (语言、口音) speak (*pt* spoke, *pp* spoken) **II** [名] **1** (体育活动) exercise ◇早操有益于学生的身体健康。Morning exercises are beneficial to students' health. **2** (品行) conduct

操办 cāobàn [动] make arrangements ◇他父母给他操办

婚礼。His parents made all the arrangements for his wedding.

操场 cāochǎng [名] sports ground

操持 cāochí [动] **1** (处理) take charge of (*pt* took, *pp* taken) **2** (筹办) make arrangements for

操劳 cāoláo [动] work hard ◊校长为学生操劳过度，病倒了。The headteacher worked excessively hard for the pupils, and fell ill.

操练 cāoliàn [动] drill ◊教官正在操练新兵。The officer is putting the new soldiers through the drill.

操心 cāoxīn [动] concern ◊父母为他的身体操心。His parents were concerned about his health.

操行 cāoxíng [名] behaviour (英), behavior (美)

操之过急 cāo zhī guò jí be in too much of a rush ◊我们慢慢解决这个问题，不可操之过急。Let's take our time over this problem. We don't want to be in too much of a rush.

操纵 cāozòng [动] **1** (机器、仪器) operate **2** (贬) manipulate

操作 cāozuò [动] operate ◊工人熟练地操作着机器。The workers are operating the machine skilfully (英) 或 skillfully (美). ◊所有办公人员都能操作电脑。Everyone in the office knows how to use a computer. ◊操作说明 operating instructions (*pl*) ◊操作方法 how to use ◊安全操作手册 safety handbook

糙 cāo [形] poor ◊这条裤子做得太糙。These trousers are very poorly made. ◊这书印得太糙了。This book has been printed so shoddily.

嘈 cáo 见下文

嘈杂 cáozá [形] noisy

槽 cáo [名] **1** (下凹) groove **2** (用于盛液体) channel **3** (用于装饲料) trough

草 cǎo **I** [名] **1** (植物) grass **2** (用作材料) straw **II** [形] **1** (字) illegible **2** (初步) draft

草案 cǎo'àn [名] draft

草包 cǎobāo [名] **1** (人) waster **2** (物) straw sack

草本 cǎoběn [形] herbal

草草 cǎocǎo [副] hastily ◊我草草看了一遍笔记，就进了考场。I glanced hastily at my notes and went into the examination hall. ◊因为观众不多，所以演唱会草草收场了。Because there weren't enough people in the audience, the performance was brought to an abrupt end. ◊我们不能就这样草草了事，一定要找出问题的根源。This isn't something that we can just dash off – we're going to have to get to the root of the problem.

草创 cǎochuàng [动] set … up (*pt, pp* set) ◊我们市场部还处于草创阶段。Our marketing department is still just being set up.

草稿 cǎogǎo [名] rough draft

草菅人命 cǎo jiān rénmìng set little store by human life

草帽 cǎomào [名] straw hat

草莓 cǎoméi [名] strawberry

草木皆兵 cǎo mù jiē bīng be panic-stricken ◊战争即将打响，全国上下草木皆兵。Just before the war, the whole country was panic-stricken.

草拟 cǎonǐ [动] draft

草签 cǎoqiān [动] initial

草书 cǎoshū [名] cursive writing

草率 cǎoshuài [形] rash ◊他没有认真考虑，就草率地做了答复。He didn't think about it properly and came up with a careless reply. ◊写作文前要仔细构思，不要草率动笔。There's no point putting pen to paper before you have organised your thoughts. ◊结婚是人生大事，绝不能草率。Marriage is a big deal. You should never go into it rashly.

草图 cǎotú [名] sketch

草原 cǎoyuán [名] grasslands (*pl*)

草纸 cǎozhǐ [名] rough paper

册 cè **I** [名] book ♦手册 handbook ♦相册 photo album **II** [量] **1** (指同一本书) copy **2** (指不同本书) volume

册子 cèzi [名] brochure

厕 cè [名] toilet ♦公厕 public toilet

厕所 cèsuǒ [名] toilet

侧 cè I [名] side ◇步行街两侧是大大小小的商店。On either side of the pedestrian walkway there are shops of various sizes. II [动] turn ... away ◇我侧过脸去，不再理睬他。I turned my face away, and didn't take any more notice of him.

侧面 cèmiàn I [形] 1 (非官方) unofficial ◇侧面消息证明他已经提交了辞呈。Unofficial sources have confirmed that he has already handed in his notice. 2 (指方位) side ◇侧面的大楼是另外一个公司的。The building to the side here belongs to another company. II [名] side ◇船身的侧面遭到了猛烈的攻击。The side of the ship was heavily attacked. ◇我们从多个侧面分析市场的发展现状。We are looking at current market developments from many different angles.

侧目 cèmù [动] 1 (贬) shock ◇他无礼的行为令人侧目。Her rudeness shocked people. 2 (褒) surprise ◇泳坛小将的出色表现引起了老将的侧目。The outstanding performance by the new swimmers surprised the more experienced contenders.

侧身 cèshēn [动] turn sideways ◇她只能侧身过门。She had to turn sideways to get through the door.

侧重 cèzhòng [动] emphasize

测 cè [动] 1 (测量) measure 2 (推测) predict

测定 cèdìng [动] measure

测量 cèliáng I [动] measure II [名] survey

测评 cèpíng [动] evaluate ◇测评系统 evaluation system

测试 cèshì I [动] test II [名] test

测验 cèyàn I [动] test II [名] test

策 cè I [名] suggestion II [动] whip

策动 cèdòng [动] stir ... up

策划 cèhuà I [动] design II [名] planning

策略 cèlüè I [名] strategy II [形] strategic

策源地 cèyuándì [名] starting place ◇内战的策源地 the place where the civil war started

参 cēn 见下文
▷另见 cān, shēn

参差 cēncī [形] uneven ◇纪录片的质量参差不齐。The documentaries are uneven in quality.

层 céng I [量] 1 (指建筑物) floor ◇这幢摩天大楼有50层。This skyscraper is 50 floors high. 2 (指覆盖物) layer ◇电脑屏幕上有一层灰。There's a layer of dust on the computer screen. 3 (步) step ◇我们需要进一层研究。We need to investigate this further. 4 (指含义) layer ◇他的话还有一层深意。There is another layer of meaning in what he says. II [名] (指物、状态) layer ◇飞机穿过云层。The plane passed through layers of cloud.

> 在英式英语里，**ground floor** 是指紧贴地面的那个楼层。它上面的一层叫做 **first floor**。在美式英语中，**first floor** 是指紧贴地面的楼层，它上面的一层是 **second floor**.

层出不穷 céng chū bù qióng come thick and fast

层次 céngcì [名] 1 (指言语、文章) ◇他说话层次清楚。He speaks very clearly. ◇这篇报道层次混乱。This report has been put together very sloppily. 2 (指程度) level

层面 céngmiàn [名] 1 (范围) range ◇杂志的读者层面很广。Magazine readership is very broad. 2 (方面) aspect

曾 céng [副] once
▷另见 zēng

曾经 céngjīng [副] once ◇我曾经想出国留学。I once wanted to study abroad.

蹭 cèng [动] 1 (摩擦) rub ◇他在门垫上把鞋底的泥蹭掉了。He rubbed the mud off his shoe onto the doormat. 2 (沾上) smear ◇他离得太近，袖子上蹭到了油漆。He got too close to the wet paint and got his sleeve smeared. 3 (指速度) creep along (*pt, pp* crept) ◇路上很挤，

她一点一点地往前蹭。The roads were packed, so she crept along at a snail's pace. **4** (占便宜) scrounge ◊她已经工作了，可是还去父母家蹭饭吃。She has a job now, but still goes back to her parents' house to scrounge food.

叉 chā I [名] **1** (器具) fork **2** (餐具) fork **3** (符号) cross II [动] spear
▷另见 chǎ

叉腰 chāyāo [动] put one's hands on one's hips ◊她站着的时候习惯叉腰。When she was standing she liked to put her hands on her hips.

叉子 chāzi [名] **1** (符号) cross **2** (餐具) fork

差 chā [名] difference ◊这两个数的差是多少？ What's the difference between these two numbers?
▷另见 chà, chāi

差别 chābié [名] difference

差错 chācuò [名] **1** (错误) mistake **2** (意外) accident ◊万一他出了什么差错，他父母可承受不了。If he were ever to have any kind of accident, his parents wouldn't be able to bear it.

差额 chā'é [名] difference

差价 chājià [名] price difference

差距 chājù [名] difference

差强人意 chā qiáng rényì just passable ◊公司去年的效益差强人意。Last year the company's results were only just passable.

差异 chāyì [名] difference ◊中英文差异很大。The differences between Chinese and English are huge.

插 chā [动] insert ◊插插销 insert a plug ◊我能不能插一句？ Can I interrupt just a second? ◊他开始插手公司事务。He started meddling in the company's affairs.

插话 chāhuà I [动] interrupt II [名] interruption

插科打诨 chā kē dǎ hùn joke around

插曲 chāqǔ [名] **1** (音乐) incidental music **2** (事件) interlude

插入 chārù [动] insert

插手 chāshǒu [动] involve oneself in ◊雇主不应该插手职员的私事。Employers should not involve themselves in the private affairs of their staff.

插图 chātú [名] illustration

插销 chāxiāo [名] **1** (闩) bolt **2** (插头) electrical plug

插页 chāyè [名] insert

插足 chāzú [动] involve oneself in

插嘴 chāzuǐ [动] interrupt

插座 chāzuò [名] socket (英), outlet (美)

喳 chā 见下文
▷另见 zhā

喳喳 chāchā [拟] whisper

茬 chá [名] **1** (根茎) stubble **2** (次数) crop

茶 chá [名] tea ♦红茶 black tea ◊泡茶 make tea

茶点 chádiǎn [名] refreshments (*pl*)

茶话会 cháhuàhuì [名] tea party

茶具 chájù [名] tea set

茶叶 cháyè [名] tea leaves (*pl*)

茶余饭后 chá yú fàn hòu over a cup of tea ◊这个笑话成了茶余饭后的谈资。The joke became dinner-party material.

茶座 cházuò [名] tea house

查 chá [动] **1** (检查) inspect **2** (调查) investigate ◊这个案子还需要查一查。This case needs further investigation.

查抄 cháchāo [动] confiscate

查点 chádiǎn [动] check the quantity of ◊查点车上装载物品 check the quantity of goods in a vehicle

查对 cháduì [动] verify

查访 cháfǎng [动] make inquiries ◊查访民情 sound out public feeling

查封 cháfēng [动] seal … up

查号台 cháhàotái [名] directory inquiries (*sg*) (英) 或 assistance (美)

查看 chákàn [动] examine

查问 cháwèn [动] interrogate ◊警察正在查问嫌疑犯。The police are interrogating the suspect right now.

查询 cháxún [动] inquire about ◇网上查询 search the web

查阅 cháyuè [动] look … up ◇我去图书馆查阅资料。I'm going to the library to look up some information. ◇写论文前必须查阅大量书刊。Before writing a thesis it is necessary to consult a lot of material.

查账 cházhàng [动] check accounts

查找 cházhǎo [动] look for

查证 cházhèng [动] verify

搽 chá [动] apply ◇搽化妆品 apply cosmetics

察 chá [动] check ♦观察 observe

察访 cháfǎng [动] make inquiries

察觉 chájué [动] detect

察看 chákàn [动] examine ◇察看事故发生现场 examine the scene of the accident ◇察看工地 inspect a building site

察言观色 chá yán guān sè read people ◇他善于察言观色，讨好上司。He's very good at reading people and ingratiating himself with his superiors.

叉 chǎ [动] cross ◇叉着腿 with legs crossed
▷另见 chā

杈 chà [名] branch

岔 chà I [名] 1 (岔路) fork ◇三岔路口 a fork in the road 2 (毛病) accident ♦岔子 accident II [动] 1 (偏离方向) turn off ◇出租汽车岔上了小道。The taxi turned off onto a narrow track. 2 (分开) diverge ♦岔开 diverge

岔子 chàzi [名] 1 (岔路) side road 2 (事故) accident

刹 chà [名] Buddhist temple
▷另见 shā

刹那 chànà [名] instant ◇刹那间 in an instant

诧 chà [动] be surprised

诧异 chàyì [动] be surprised ◇他突然辞职，大家都很诧异。When he suddenly resigned everybody was very surprised.

差 chà I [动] 1 (不相同) ◇你和他比差得远了。You are not nearly as good as him. 2 (缺欠) ◇差3个人 be three people short ◇他还差我10镑钱。He still owes me ten pounds. II [形] 1 (错误) mistaken 2 (不好) poor ◇这些鞋的质量很差。These shoes are of poor quality.
▷另见 chā, chāi

差不多 chà bu duō I [形] very similar ◇这两块布颜色差不多。The colour (英) 或 color (美) of these two pieces of material is very similar. II [副] almost ◇晚饭差不多快做好了。Dinner is almost ready.

差劲 chàjìn [形] bad

姹 chà [形] beautiful

姹紫嫣红 chà zǐ yān hóng beautiful flowers (*pl*)

拆 chāi [动] 1 (打开) tear … open (*pt* tore, *pp* torn) ◇拆信 tear open a letter 2 (拆毁) dismantle ◇拆房子 demolish a house

拆穿 chāichuān [动] expose

拆毁 chāihuǐ [动] demolish

拆台 chāitái [动] undermine

差 chāi [动] send (*pt, pp* sent) ◇校长差他去参加研讨会。The principal is sending him to attend the seminar. ◇出差 go on a business trip
▷另见 chā, chà

差旅费 chāilǔfèi [名] travel expenses (*pl*)

差遣 chāiqiǎn [动] dispatch

差使 chāishǐ [动] assign

差使 chāishi [名] position

差事 chāishi [名] 1 (任务) assignment 2 (差使) position

柴 chái [名] firewood

柴火 cháihuo [名] firewood

柴油 cháiyóu [名] diesel

豺 chái [名] jackal

豺狼 cháiláng [名] 1 (豺和狼) jackals and wolves (*pl*) 2 (喻) (恶人) cruel and evil people (*pl*)

掺 chān [动] mix

搀 chān **1** (搀扶) support … by the arm ◇老两口相互搀着散步。The couple go walking arm in arm to support each other. **2** (混合) mix ◇咖啡里搀牛奶味道更佳。Coffee tastes nicer with milk.

搀扶 chānfú [动] support … by the arm

搀和 chānhuo [动] mix

搀杂 chānzá [动] mix

婵 chán 见下文

婵娟 chánjuān **I** [形] beautiful **II** [名] moon

谗 chán [动] slander

谗言 chányán [名] slander

馋 chán [形] greedy

馋涎欲滴 chánxián yù dī drool ◇牛肉的香味使我馋涎欲滴。The delicious smell of the beef made my mouth water.

禅 chán [名] (宗) **1** (静坐) meditation **2** (指佛事) ◇禅林 Buddhist temple ▷另见 shàn

禅宗 chánzōng [名] Zen

孱 chán [形] frail

孱弱 chánruò [形] (书) **1** (瘦弱) frail **2** (软弱) weak **3** (薄弱) faint

缠 chán [动] **1** (缠绕) twine **2** (纠缠) pester ◇别老缠着我，自己玩儿去。Stop pestering me, and go and play on your own. **3** (方) (应付) deal with (*pt*, *pp* dealt)

缠绵 chánmián [形] **1** (摆脱不开) lingering **2** (婉转动人) moving

蝉 chán [名] cicada

蝉联 chánlián [动] continue to hold a post ◇蝉联奥运会冠军 be the reigning Olympic champion

潺 chán 见下文

潺潺 chánchán [拟] babble ◇溪水潺潺 a babbling stream

蟾 chán [名] toad

蟾蜍 chánchú [名] toad

产 chǎn [动] **1** (生育) give birth to (*pt* gave, *pp* given) **2** (出产) produce ◇这里产石油。Oil is produced here. ◇荔枝产在南方。Lychees are grown in the South.

产地 chǎndì [名] producing area ◇菠萝产地 pineapple producing area

产妇 chǎnfù [名] *woman who is in labour or who has just given birth*

产量 chǎnliàng [名] yield

产品 chǎnpǐn [名] product ◇产品质量 product quality

产权 chǎnquán [名] property rights (*pl*) ◇知识产权 intellectual property

产生 chǎnshēng [动] produce ◇产生结果 produce a result ◇他的小说在读者中产生了很大反响。His novel created a big stir among readers. ◇他对电脑产生了浓厚的兴趣。He's become deeply interested in computers.

产物 chǎnwù [名] product

产业 chǎnyè [名] **1** (财产) property **2** (工业生产) industry ◇产业革命 the Industrial Revolution

产值 chǎnzhí [名] output value

谄 chǎn [动] flatter

谄媚 chǎnmèi [动] flatter

铲 chǎn **I** [名] shovel **II** [动] shovel

铲除 chǎnchú [动] eradicate

阐 chǎn [动] explain

阐明 chǎnmíng [动] expound

阐释 chǎnshì [动] explain ◇他对合同条款作了详细的阐释。He gave a detailed explanation of the clauses in the contract.

阐述 chǎnshù [动] expound

忏 chàn [动] repent

忏悔 chànhuǐ [动] repent

颤 chàn [动] tremble ▷另见 zhàn

颤抖 chàndǒu [动] shiver ◇他激动得浑身颤抖。He was trembling with excitement.

颤巍巍 chànwēiwēi [形] faltering ◇爷爷颤巍巍地端起碗。Grandpa

lifted his bowl unsteadily.

昌 chāng [形] flourishing

昌明 chāngmíng [形] thriving

昌盛 chāngshèng [形] prosperous

猖 chāng [形] aggressive

猖獗 chāngjué [形] rampant

猖狂 chāngkuáng [形] fierce

娼 chāng [名] prostitute

娼妓 chāngjì [名] prostitute

长 cháng I [形] long ◇长发 long hair II [名] 1 (长度) length ◇这张桌子有两米长。This table is two metres in length. 2 (长处) strong point ◇取长补短 learn from others' strong points
▷另见 zhǎng

长城 Chángchéng [名] the Great Wall

长处 chángchu [名] strong point

长此以往 cháng cǐ yǐ wǎng if things carry on this way ◇这些学生天天吸烟喝酒，长此以往肯定荒废学业。These students smoke and drink every day – if they carry on this way they'll certainly neglect their studies.

长度 chángdù [名] length

长短 chángduǎn [名] 1 (长度) length 2 (意外) accident

长方形 chángfāngxíng [名] rectangle

长话短说 cháng huà duǎn shuō cut a long story short ◇时间有限，我们就长话短说。There's not much time, so we'll keep it brief.

长假 chángjià [名] extended break

长江 Cháng Jiāng [名] the Yangtze

长久 chángjiǔ [形] long-term ◇长久之计 long-term plan

长空 chángkōng [名] vast sky

长眠 chángmián [动] (婉) die

长年累月 cháng nián lěi yuè year in year out

长跑 chángpǎo [动] go long-distance running (*pt* went, *pp* gone) ◇你参加过长跑比赛吗？ Have you ever taken part in any long-distance running competitions?

长篇大论 cháng piān dà lùn be long-winded

长篇小说 chángpiān xiǎoshuō [名] full-length novel

长生不老 chángshēng bù lǎo immortality

长逝 chángshì [动] pass away

长寿 chángshòu [形] long-lived ◇祝您长寿！ Here's to a long life!

长叹 chángtàn [动] sigh deeply

长途 chángtú [形] long-distance ◇长途电话 long-distance phone call ◇长途旅行 long journey

长项 chángxiàng [名] strong point

长于 chángyú [动] be good at

长远 chángyuǎn [形] long-term ◇长远利益 long-term benefits ◇长远眼光 long-term view

长治久安 cháng zhì jiǔ ān lasting stability and peace

长足 chángzú [形] rapid ◇职业教育取得了长足发展。There has been rapid development in vocational education.

场 cháng I [名] threshing ground II [量] ◇昨天下了一场大雨。Yesterday there was a downpour. ◇母亲生了一场病。Mother had an illness.
▷另见 chǎng

肠 cháng [名] intestines (*pl*)

肠子 chángzi [名] intestines (*pl*)

尝 cháng I [动] taste ♦品尝 taste II [副] (书) ever

尝试 chángshì [动] try

常 cháng I [形] 1 (平常) common ♦常态 normality 2 (经常) frequent ♦常客 regular guest II [副] often ◇我常去看戏。I often go to the theatre (英) 或 theater (美).

常常 chángcháng [副] often ◇我常常去北京出差。I often go to Beijing on business. ◇圣诞节人们常常互送礼物。At Christmas people usually give presents to each other.

常规 chángguī [名] 1 (规矩) convention ◇常规武器 conventional weapons (*pl*) 2 (医) routine

常轨 chángguǐ [名] normal practice

常客 chángkè [名] regular guest

常例 chánglì [名] common practice

常情 chángqíng [名] sense

常人 chángrén [名] ordinary person (*pl* people)

常任 chángrèn [形] permanent

常识 chángshí [名] **1** (非专业知识) general knowledge **2** (生活经验) common sense

常委 chángwěi [名] standing committee member

常务 chángwù [形] standing ◇常务委员会 standing committee

常言 chángyán [名] saying

偿 cháng [动] **1** (归还) repay (*pt*, *pp* repaid) ♦偿付 pay … back **2** (满足) fulfil ◇如愿以偿 fulfil one's dreams

偿还 chánghuán [动] repay (*pt*, *pp* repaid)

偿命 chángmìng [动] pay with one's life (*pt*, *pp* paid)

徜 cháng 见下文

徜徉 chángyáng [动] (书) wander about at one's leisure

厂 chǎng [名] **1** (工厂) factory ◇服装厂 clothing factory **2** (厂子) works (*sg*) ◇木材厂 timber yard (英), lumberyard (美)

厂家 chǎngjiā [名] factory

场 chǎng **I** [名] **1** (地方) ground ♦操场 sports ground ♦市场 market **2** (舞台) stage ◇上场 go on stage **3** (戏剧片段) scene ◇话剧的第一幕第二场 Act I, Scene II of the play **4** (物) field ◇电磁场 electromagnetic field **II** [量] ◇一场足球赛 a football match ◇一场戏 a play ▷另见 cháng

场地 chǎngdì [名] space ◇运动场地 sports area

场合 chǎnghé [名] occasion

场面 chǎngmiàn [名] **1** (戏剧景况) scene **2** (情景) occasion **3** (排场) front ◇撑场面 keep up appearances

场所 chǎngsuǒ [名] place ◇公共场所 public place

敞 chǎng **I** [形] spacious ♦宽敞 spacious **II** [动] be open ◇大门敞着。The main door is open.

敞亮 chǎngliàng [形] **1** (明亮) light and spacious **2** (喻) (开阔) clear ◇听了你的解释，我心里敞亮多了。Having heard your explanation, I'm much clearer now.

怅 chàng [形] disappointed

怅然 chàngrán [形] disappointed

怅惘 chàngwǎng [形] listless

畅 chàng **I** [形] **1** (无阻碍) smooth ♦畅通 unimpeded **2** (舒适) untroubled ◇他心情不畅。He's troubled by something. **II** [副] uninhibitedly ♦畅饮 drink one's fill

畅达 chàngdá [形] free-flowing

畅快 chàngkuài [形] carefree

畅所欲言 chàng suǒ yù yán speak freely

畅谈 chàngtán [动] talk happily

畅通 chàngtōng [动] be open ◇道路畅通 open road

畅销 chàngxiāo [动] have a ready market ◇这种新型洗衣机很畅销。There is a ready market for this new type of washing machine.

畅游 chàngyóu [动] **1** (游览) enjoy sightseeing **2** (游泳) enjoy a swim

倡 chàng [动] initiate

倡导 chàngdǎo [动] initiate

倡议 chàngyì [动] propose ◇这项倡议得到了大家的认同。This proposal met with everyone's agreement.

唱 chàng [动] **1** (发出乐音) sing (*pt* sang, *pp* sung) ♦独唱 solo ◇合唱 chorus **2** (大叫) cry

唱段 chàngduàn [名] aria

唱反调 chàng fǎndiào [动] express a contrary opinion

唱高调 chàng gāodiào [动] speak fine-sounding words (*pt* spoke, *pp* spoken)

唱歌 chànggē [动] sing (*pt* sang, *pp* sung)

唱腔 chàngqiāng [名] aria

唱戏 chàngxì [动] perform opera

唱主角 chàng zhǔjué [动] play the lead

抄 chāo [动] 1 (誊写) copy ◇抄诗 copy out a poem 2 (抄袭) plagiarize 3 (查收) raid ◇抄家 raid a home 4 (走近路) take a short cut (*pt* took, *pp* taken) ◇抄道 take a short cut 5 (插在袖子里) fold one's arms (*into one's sleeves*) ◇他抄着手站在那儿。He stood there with his arms folded.

抄家 chāojiā [动] search a home and confiscate possessions

抄录 chāolù [动] make a copy

抄袭 chāoxí [动] 1 (剽窃) plagiarize 2 (照搬) copy indiscriminately 3 (绕道袭击) launch a surprise attack

钞 chāo [名] banknote

钞票 chāopiào [名] banknote

超 chāo I [动] 1 (超过) exceed ◇超额 be above quota 2 (不受限制) transcend ◇超现实 transcend reality II [形] super ◇超低温 ultra-low temperature ◇超级明星 superstar

超编 chāobiān [动] overstaff

超标 chāobiāo [动] exceed limits

超常 chāocháng [形] extraordinary

超额 chāo'é [动] be above quota

超级 chāojí [形] super ◇超级大国 superpower ◇超级市场 supermarket

超群 chāoqún [动] be pre-eminent

超然 chāorán [形] aloof

超人 chāorén [名] superman (*pl* supermen)

超声波 chāoshēngbō [名] ultrasonic wave

超市 chāoshì [名] supermarket

超脱 chāotuō I [形] unconventional II [动] be detached from

超越 chāoyuè [动] overcome (*pt* overcame, *pp* overcome)

超载 chāozài [动] overload

超支 chāozhī [动] overspend (*pt*, *pp* overspent)

超重 chāozhòng [动] 1 (超过载重量) overload ◇货车超重了。The truck is overloaded. 2 (超过标准量) be overweight ◇他的行李超重了。His luggage is over the limit.

巢 cháo [名] nest

巢穴 cháoxué [名] 1 (指动物) nest 2 (指匪徒) lair

朝 cháo I [名] 1 (宫廷) imperial court 2 (朝代) dynasty 3 (王朝) reign ◇康熙王朝 Kangxi's reign II [动] face III [介] towards
▷另见 zhāo

朝拜 cháobài [动] 1 (皇帝) pay one's respects to (*pt*, *pp* paid) 2 (神) worship

朝代 cháodài [名] dynasty

朝圣 cháoshèng [动] make a pilgrimage

朝廷 cháotíng [名] 1 (听政的地方) court 2 (统治机构) imperial government

朝向 cháoxiàng [名] exposure

朝野 cháoyě [名] the government and the people

嘲 cháo [动] ridicule

嘲讽 cháofěng [动] sneer at ◇他总爱嘲讽他的同伴。He loved to sneer at his mates. ◇她用嘲讽的眼神瞥了他一眼。She glanced at him with a sneering expression.

嘲弄 cháonòng [动] mock ◇嘲弄历史定会被历史所嘲弄。Those who mock history will be mocked by history.

嘲笑 cháoxiào [动] laugh at ◇不要嘲笑别人的短处。You shouldn't laugh at other people's weaknesses.

潮 cháo I [名] 1 (潮汐) tide 2 (社会运动) movement ♦工潮 labour (英) 或 labor (美) movement ♦思潮 Zeitgeist II [形] damp

潮流 cháoliú [名] 1 (水流) tide 2 (发展趋势) trend

潮湿 cháoshī [形] humid

潮水 cháoshuǐ [名] tidal waters (*pl*)

潮汐 cháoxī [名] tide

吵 chǎo I [动] 1 (发出噪音) make a racket 2 (争吵) squabble II [形] noisy

吵架 chǎojià [动] quarrel

吵闹 chǎonào [动] 1 (争吵) bicker 2 (打扰) disturb

吵嘴 chǎozuǐ [动] bicker

炒 chǎo [动] 1 (烹调) stir-fry 2 (地皮、外汇等) speculate 3 (方) (解雇) sack ◇他被老板给炒了。He was sacked by the boss.

炒股 chǎogǔ [动] speculate in stocks and shares

炒汇 chǎohuì [动] speculate in foreign currency

炒货 chǎohuò [名] roasted snacks (*pl*)

炒冷饭 chǎo lěngfàn [动] rehash

炒买炒卖 chǎomǎi-chǎomài make a quick buck

炒鱿鱼 chǎo yóuyú [动] ◇她被炒了鱿鱼。She was given her marching orders.

炒作 chǎozuò [动] hype ◇她歌唱得很糟，但被炒作得很好。She's a hopeless singer but she's been really hyped.

车 chē [名] 1 (运输工具) vehicle ♦小汽车 car ♦公共汽车 bus 2 (带轮的装置) wheel♦风车 windmill 3 (机器) machine

车次 chēcì [名] 1 (火车的) train number 2 (长途汽车的) coach number

车费 chēfèi [名] fare

车祸 chēhuò [名] traffic accident

车间 chējiān [名] workshop

车库 chēkù [名] garage

车辆 chēliàng [名] vehicle

车轮 chēlún [名] wheel

车皮 chēpí [名] wagon

车水马龙 chē shuǐ mǎ lóng heavy traffic

车胎 chētāi [名] tyre

车厢 chēxiāng [名] coach

车载斗量 chē zài dǒu liáng ten a penny (英), a dime a dozen (美)

车站 chēzhàn [名] 1 (火车的) railway station 2 (汽车的) bus stop

车子 chēzi [名] 1 (小型运输车) vehicle 2 (自行车) bicycle

扯 chě [动] 1 (拉) pull ◇别扯我袖子。Stop pulling at my sleeve. 2 (撕) tear (*pt* tore, *pp* torn) 3 (闲谈) chat ♦闲扯 chat

扯谎 chěhuǎng [动] lie

扯皮 chěpí [动] wrangle

彻 chè [动] penetrate ♦透彻 penetrating ♦彻夜 all night

彻底 chèdǐ [形] thorough ◇房子打扫得很彻底。The room has been given a thorough cleaning. ◇他们的计划彻底落空了。Their plan was a complete failure.

彻头彻尾 chè tóu chè wěi outright

掣 chè [动] 1 (退) withdraw (*pt* withdrew, *pp* withdrawn) 2 (闪) flash by ◇风驰电掣 go like the wind

撤 chè [动] 1 (除去) take ... away (*pt* took, *pp* taken) ◇他的职务给撤了。He was dismissed from his job. 2 (退) move away ◇请向后撤一撤。Please move back a little.

撤除 chèchú [动] dismantle

撤换 chèhuàn [动] replace

撤离 chèlí [动] evacuate

撤诉 chèsù [动] drop charges

撤退 chètuì [动] withdraw (*pt* withdrew, *pp* withdrawn)

撤销 chèxiāo [动] 1 (职务) dismiss 2 (计划) cancel 3 (法令) rescind

撤职 chèzhí [动] dismiss (*from a post*)

澈 chè [形] clear

抻 chēn [动] stretch

嗔 chēn [动] 1 (生气) be angry 2 (埋怨) complain

嗔怪 chēnguài [动] rebuke

臣 chén 见下文

臣服 chénfú [动] acknowledge allegiance to

臣民 chénmín [名] subject

尘 chén [名] **1** (尘土) dirt ♦灰尘 dust **2** (尘世) the material world ♦红尘 worldly affairs (*pl*)

尘埃 chén'āi [名] dust

尘封 chénfēng [动] be dusty

尘世 chénshì [名] worldly affairs (*pl*)

尘土 chéntǔ [名] dust

辰 chén [名] **1** (星辰) heavenly body **2** (时间) birthday ♦寿辰 birthday

沉 chén **I** [动] **1** (向下落) sink (*pt* sank, *pp* sunk) ◊船沉到了海底。The ship sank to the bottom of the sea. **2** (指情绪) become grave (*pt* became, *pp* become) ◊遇到不如意的事，她马上就会沉下脸来。She pulls a long face as soon as anything happens to displease her. **II** [形] **1** (指程度深) deep ◊昨晚我睡得很沉。Last night I slept very deeply. **2** (重) heavy **3** (不舒服) heavy ◊我两条腿发沉。My legs feel heavy.

沉沉 chénchén [形] **1** (重) heavy **2** (程度深) deep ◊孩子们沉沉地睡了。Children sleep deeply.

沉甸甸 chéndiāndiān [形] **1** (重) heavy **2** (喻) worried ◊任务还没完成，我心里沉甸甸的。The job is not finished, and that worries me.

沉浮 chénfú **I** [动] drift **II** [名] vicissitude

沉积 chénjī [动] silt up

沉寂 chénjì [形] **1** (十分寂静) quiet **2** (没有消息) ◊他沉寂了很久后，突然给我们来了一封信。There was no news from him for ages, and then suddenly he sent us a letter. ◊那位小说家已沉寂了多年。We've heard nothing from the novelist for years.

沉浸 chénjìn [动] immerse

沉静 chénjìng [形] **1** (肃静) quiet **2** (指性格) placid

沉沦 chénlún [动] sink into (*pt* sank, *pp* sunk)

沉闷 chénmèn [形] **1** (天气、气氛) depressing **2** (心情) depressed ◊最近我心情很沉闷。I've been feeling really depressed lately. **3** (指性格) introverted

沉湎 chénmiǎn [动] indulge in

沉没 chénmò [动] sink (*pt* sank, *pp* sunk)

沉默 chénmò **I** [形] taciturn **II** [动] be silent

沉溺 chénnì [动] indulge in

沉睡 chénshuì [动] be fast asleep

沉思 chénsī [动] ponder ◊他为此事沉思了很久。He pondered this matter for a long time. ◊他陷入了沉思。He was lost in thought.

沉痛 chéntòng [形] **1** (心情) grieving **2** (教训) bitter

沉稳 chénwěn [形] **1** (稳重) steady **2** (安稳) peaceful ◊他一向睡得沉稳。He always sleeps peacefully.

沉重 chénzhòng [形] heavy

沉着 chénzhuó [形] calm ◊他处理问题沉着冷静。He deals with problems calmly and soberly.

沉醉 chénzuì [动] be intoxicated ◊他沉醉在成功的喜悦中。He was intoxicated with success.

忱 chén [名] sincerity ♦热忱 ardour (英), ardor (美)

陈 chén **I** [动] **1** (陈列) set … out (*pt*, *pp* set) **2** (陈述) state **II** [形] old

陈词滥调 chén cí làn diào clichés

陈腐 chénfǔ [形] dated

陈规 chénguī [名] outmoded conventions (*pl*)

陈旧 chénjiù [形] out-of-date

陈列 chénliè [动] display

陈年 chénnián [形] aged ◊陈年老酒 old wine

陈设 chénshè **I** [动] display ◊房间里陈设着几张古画。Some old pictures are on display in the room. **II** [名] furnishings (*pl*)

陈述 chénshù [动] state

晨 chén [名] morning ♦早晨 early morning ♦清晨 dawn

晨光 chénguāng [名] dawn

晨练 chénliàn [动] morning exercise

衬 chèn **I** [名] lining **II** [动] **1** (垫) line **2** (衬托) set … off (*pt*, *pp* set) **III** [形]

lining ♦衬布 lining material

衬托 chèntuō [动] set … off (*pt, pp* set)

称 chèn [动] match ♦相称 match ♦对称 be symmetrical ▷另见 chēng

称心 chènxīn [动] be satisfactory ◇这台电脑我买得称心。I am satisfied with the computer I bought.

称职 chènzhí [动] be competent ◇他担任这个职务很称职。He's very competent at his job.

趁 chèn [介] ◇趁这个机会我讲几句话。I would like to take this opportunity to say a few words. ◇趁年轻多学点知识。Learn something while you are young.

趁火打劫 chèn huǒ dǎ jié profit from other people's misfortunes

趁热打铁 chèn rè dǎ tiě strike while the iron is hot

趁势 chènshì [动] take the opportunity (*pt* took, *pp* taken)

称 chēng I [动] **1** (叫) call ◇我们都称他老王. We call him Old Wang. **2** (说) say (*pt, pp* said) ♦称谢 express one's gratitude **3** (测量) weigh II [名] name ♦简称 short form ▷另见 chèn

称病 chēngbìng [动] plead illness

称道 chēngdào [动] praise ◇他孝敬父母值得称道。The respect he shows towards his parents is worthy of praise.

称号 chēnghào [名] title

称呼 chēnghu I [动] call ◇我不知道怎么称呼他。I don't know what I should call him. II [名] form of address

称颂 chēngsòng [动] praise

称王称霸 chēngwáng chēngbà domineer

称谓 chēngwèi [名] title

称赞 chēngzàn [动] praise

撑 chēng [动] **1** (抵住) prop … up ◇他两手撑着下巴在深思。His chin was propped on his hands, and he was deep in thought. **2** (船) punt **3** (坚持住) keep … up (*pt, pp* kept) ◇他撑不住了，到底笑了。In the end, he couldn't help laughing. **4** (张开) open **5** (容不下) fill to bursting ◇少吃点吧，别撑着！ Don't eat so much, you'll burst!

撑腰 chēngyāo [动] support

瞠 chēng [动] stare

瞠目结舌 chēng mù jié shé be flabbergasted ◇他的回答令我瞠目结舌。I was flabbergasted at his reply.

成 chéng I [动] **1** (成功) accomplish ◇那件事成了。The job is done. **2** (成为) become (*pt* became, *pp* become) ◇两个人成了好朋友。The two of them became good friends. II [名] result III [形] **1** (成熟的) mature ♦成虫 adult **2** (现成的) established ♦成品 finished product **3** (表示数量) ◇成千上万 hundreds and thousands of ◇成批生产 bulk production **4** (可以) O.K. ◇成！就这么定了。O.K. – that's agreed.

成本 chéngběn [名] cost ◇生产成本 production costs (*pl*)

> 📖 请勿混淆 **cost** 和 **costs**。某事物的 **cost** 是指用于购买、完成或者制造它所需的费用。*…the cost of the telephone call… the total cost was over a million pounds…* 企业或者家庭的 **costs** 是指保证它们继续运转所需要的费用，包括电费、修理费用和税款。*…attempts to cut costs and boost profits…*

成材 chéngcái [动] become useful (*pt* became, *pp* become)

成分 chéngfèn [名] **1** (组成部分) composition ◇化学成分 chemical composition **2** (社会阶层) status

成功 chénggōng [动] succeed ◇他这次试验获得了成功。This time his experiment was successful. ◇本届运动会开得很成功。This year's sports event was a great success.

成果 chéngguǒ [名] achievement

成活 chénghuó [动] survive

成绩 chéngjì [名] success ◇我们在环境保护方面取得了很大成绩。We

have had considerable success in environmental protection. ◊他的学习成绩不理想。His school record is not satisfactory.

成家 chéngjiā [动] 1 (结婚) marry 2 (成为专家) become an authority (*pt* became, *pp* become)

成见 chéngjiàn [名] prejudice ◊他分明对我有成见。He is clearly prejudiced against me.

成交 chéngjiāo [动] strike a deal (*pt*, *pp* struck)

成就 chéngjiù I [名] achievement ◊他在事业上很有成就。He has achieved much in his career. II [动] achieve ◊他立志成就一番事业。He aspires to succeed in his career.

成立 chénglì [动] 1 (建立) found ◊联合国成立于1945年。The United Nations was founded in 1945. ◊一所新学校成立了。A new school has been established. 2 (有根据) be tenable ◊你的结论根本无法成立。Your conclusions are completely untenable.

成名成家 chéngmíng chéngjiā become an established authority

成年 chéngnián I [动] 1 (指动植物) mature 2 (指人) grow up (*pp* grew, *pt* grown) II [副] all year round

成品 chéngpǐn [名] end product

成气候 chéng qìhòu [动] get somewhere ◊这孩子将来能成气候。This child will really go places one day.

成器 chéngqì [动] grow up to be a useful person (*pp* grew, *pt* grown) ◊那孩子将来成不了器。That child is never going to get anywhere in life.

成亲 chéngqīn [动] marry

成全 chéngquán [动] help … get what he/she wants

成人 chéngrén I [名] adult II [动] grow up (*pp* grew, *pt* grown)

成人之美 chéng rén zhī měi help others achieve their goals

成熟 chéngshú [形] 1 (指果实) ripe 2 (指思想) mature 3 (指机会等) ripe

成为 chéngwéi [动] become (*pt* became, *pp* become)

成文 chéngwén I [名] existing writing ◊他抄袭成文。He is copying existing works. II [动] write (*pt* wrote, *pp* written) ◊这些规定必须成文。These provisions must be in writing.

成问题 chéng wèntí [动] be a problem

成效 chéngxiào [名] result

成心 chéngxīn [副] deliberately

成性 chéngxìng [动] become second nature (*pt* became, *pp* become)

成语 chéngyǔ [名] idiom

成员 chéngyuán [名] member ◊家庭成员 family member

成长 chéngzhǎng [动] grow up (*pp* grew, *pt* grown)

成竹在胸 chéng zhú zài xiōng have well-thought-out ideas

呈 chéng [动] 1 (呈现) assume ◊苹果呈圆型。Apples have a round form. 2 (呈送) present

呈报 chéngbào [动] submit a report

呈请 chéngqǐng [动] apply

呈现 chéngxiàn [动] appear

诚 chéng I [形] honest ♦忠诚 loyal ♦诚心 sincere II [副] really

诚惶诚恐 chéng huáng chéng kǒng in fear and trepidation

诚恳 chéngkěn [形] sincere ◊他诚恳地向她表示了感谢。He thanked her sincerely.

诚然 chéngrán [副] 1 (确实) truly ◊这孩子诚然懂礼貌。This child really does know how to be polite. 2 (固然) admittedly ◊困难诚然很多，但我们有信心克服。Admittedly there are many difficulties, but we are confident of overcoming them.

诚实 chéngshí [形] honest

诚心诚意 chéngxīn chéngyì in all sincerity

诚挚 chéngzhì [形] sincere

承 chéng [动] 1 (承受) bear (*pt* bore, *pp* borne) ◊这桥承不住这么重的货车。This bridge cannot bear the weight of such a heavy lorry. **2** (承担) undertake (*pt* undertook, *pp* undertaken) **3** (承蒙) be indebted to ◇承您夸奖。You're flattering me. **4** (继续) inherit ♦继承 be a successor to

承办 chéngbàn [动] undertake (*pt* undertook, *pp* undertaken)

承包 chéngbāo [动] contract

承保 chéngbǎo [动] underwrite (*pt* underwrote, *pp* underwritten)

承担 chéngdān [动] **1** (责任) bear (*pt* bore, *pp* borne) **2** (工作) undertake (*pt* undertook, *pp* undertaken) **3** (费用) bear (*pt* bore, *pp* borne)

承当 chéngdāng [动] bear (*pt* bore, *pp* borne) ◇一切责任都由我来承当。All responsibility will be borne by me.

承接 chéngjiē [动] **1** (接受) accept **2** (接续) continue

承揽 chénglǎn [动] contract◇我公司承揽房屋装修业务。My company's contracted to do the decorating work.

承蒙 chéngméng [动] (书) be indebted to

承诺 chéngnuò I [动] undertake (*pt* undertook, *pp* undertaken) II [名] commitment

承认 chéngrèn [动] **1** (认可) acknowledge **2** (政权) recognize

承上启下 chéng shàng qǐ xià link the preceding and the following ◇这段起了承上启下的作用。This paragraph is a link between the one before it and the one after it.

承受 chéngshòu [动] **1** (禁受) bear (*pt* bore, *pp* borne) ◇这木板承受不住100公斤的重量。This plank cannot bear a weight of 100 kilos. **2** (经受) experience

城 chéng [名] **1** (城墙) city wall ♦城外 outside the city **2** (城市) city ♦进城 go to town **3** (城镇) town

城堡 chéngbǎo [名] castle

城府 chéngfǔ [名] shrewdness ◇他城府很深。He's very shrewd.

城区 chéngqū [名] metropolitan area

城市 chéngshì [名] city

乘 chéng [动] **1** (搭坐) travel by ◇乘火车 travel by train **2** (利用) take advantage of (*pt* took, *pp* taken) ◇乘人之危 take advantage of sb's difficulties **3** (几倍于) multiply ◇8乘5等于40。Eight times five is forty.

乘法 chéngfǎ [名] multiplication

乘方 chéngfāng [名] (数) power

乘机 chéngjī [动] seize an opportunity

乘客 chéngkè [名] passenger

乘凉 chéngliáng [动] enjoy the cool

乘人之危 chéng rén zhī wēi take advantage of others' difficulties

乘务员 chéngwùyuán [名] conductor

乘虚而入 chéngxū'érrù exploit a weakness

盛 chéng [动] **1** (装) ladle … out ◇帮我盛碗饭。Give me a bowl of rice. **2** (容纳) contain ◇这袋子可盛50公斤。This bag can hold 50 kilos. ▷另见 shèng

程 chéng [名] **1** (规矩) rule ♦章程 constitution **2** (程序) procedure ♦议程 agenda ♦课程 curriculum **3** (距离) distance ♦路程 journey **4** (道路) journey ♦登程 set off

程度 chéngdù [名] **1** (水平) level **2** (限度) extent◇在一定程度上 to some extent

程控 chéngkòng [动] automate

程式 chéngshì [名] form

程序 chéngxù [名] **1** (次序) procedure **2** (计算机) program

惩 chéng [动] punish

惩办 chéngbàn [动] punish

惩处 chéngchǔ [动] punish

惩罚 chéngfá [动] punish ◇侵略者受到了应得的惩罚。The invaders got the punishment they deserved.

惩前毖后 chéng qián bì hòu learn from the past

澄 chéng I [形] clear ♦澄空 clear sky II [动] make … clear ♦澄清 purify ▷另见 dèng

澄清 chéngqīng I [形] clear II [动] clear … up ◇我们之间的误会澄

清了。We have cleared up our misunderstanding.

橙 chéng 见下文

橙子 chéngzi [名] orange

逞 chěng [动] **1** (夸耀) flaunt ◇逞威风 flaunt one's power **2** (达到目的) succeed ◆得逞 have one's way **3** (纵容) indulge ◆逞性 headstrong

逞能 chěngnéng [动] show off (*pt* showed, *pp* shown) ◇他为了逞能，喝酒醉得东倒西歪。He showed off by drinking until he was staggering about all over the place.

逞强 chěngqiáng [动] flaunt one's superiority

逞凶 chěngxiōng [动] behave violently

骋 chěng [动] **1** (跑) gallop ◆驰骋 gallop **2** (放任) give free rein to (*pt* gave, *pp* given)

骋目 chěngmù [动] (书) look into the distance

秤 chèng [名] balance

吃 chī [动] **1** (咀嚼吞咽) eat (*pt* ate, *pp* eaten) ◇吃面条 eat noodles ◇吃药 take medicine ◇吃奶 suckle **2** (就餐) eat in (*pt* ate, *pp* eaten) ◇我中午不做饭，吃食堂。I don't cook lunch – I eat in the canteen. **3** (依靠) live off ◇吃劳保 live off welfare ◇吃老本 rest on one's laurels **4** (消灭) wipe … out ◇吃掉一个棋子 take a chess piece **5** (耗费) withstand (*pt, pp* withstood) ◆吃力 strenuous ◇吃不消 unable to withstand **6** (吸收) absorb ◇棉布吃水。Cloth absorbs water. **7** (受) take (*pt* took, *pp* taken) ◇他胸口吃了一枪。He took a bullet in the chest. ◇吃亏 lose out

吃醋 chīcù [动] be jealous ◇我的女友好吃醋。My girlfriend gets jealous easily.

吃豆腐 chī dòufu [动] (喻) (方) be lecherous

吃官司 chī guānsi [动] be taken to court

吃喝玩乐 chī hē wán lè eat, drink and be merry

吃紧 chījǐn [形] **1** (紧张) tense ◇前线战事吃紧。The situation on the front line was tense. ◇节前火车票吃紧。In the run-up to the holiday, the ticket situation was tense. **2** (重要) important ◇做事最吃紧的是要专心。The most important thing is to concentrate on what you're doing.

吃惊 chījīng [动] surprise ◇她这么快就去了澳大利亚，让人吃了一惊。The speed with which she left for Australia surprised everyone.

吃苦 chīkǔ [动] put up with hardship (*pt, pp* put) ◇儿时的经历使我很能吃苦。My childhood experiences have helped me to put up with all kinds of hardship.

吃亏 chīkuī [动] **1** (受损失) lose out (*pt, pp* lost) ◇在谈判中我们吃亏了。We lost out in the negotiation. **2** (条件不利) be at a disadvantage

吃里爬外 chī lǐ pá wài double-cross

吃力 chīlì [形] **1** (费力) exhausting **2** (方) (疲劳) exhausted

吃请 chīqǐng [动] buy … off with a meal (*pt, pp* bought) ◇他为人廉洁，从不接受吃请。He's very straight-up, and would never be bought by a meal out.

吃素 chīsù [动] be vegetarian

吃香 chīxiāng [形] (口) popular

吃一堑，长一智 chī yī qiàn, zhǎng yī zhì experience is the mother of all wisdom

笞 chī [动] beat (*pt* beat, *pp* beaten) ◆鞭笞 whip

嗤 chī [动] (书) sneer

嗤笑 chīxiào [动] sneer at ◇他因为是文盲而遭人嗤笑。He was sneered at because he was illiterate.

嗤之以鼻 chī zhī yǐ bí turn one's nose up at

痴 chī **I** [形] idiotic ◇别理他，他在发痴。Don't listen to him – he's just being silly. **II** [名] obsession

痴呆 chīdāi [形] idiotic ◇老年痴呆症 senile dementia

痴迷 chīmí [形] infatuated

痴情 chīqíng **I** [名] passion **II** [形] deeply passionate

痴人说梦 chī rén shuō mèng unrealistic expectation

痴心妄想 chī xīn wàng xiǎng wishful thinking

池 chí [名] **1** (池塘) pond ◇养鱼池 fish pond **2** (指旁边高中间洼) pit ♦乐池 orchestra pit **3** (护城河) moat ♦城池 city moat

池塘 chítáng [名] pond

池鱼之殃 chí yú zhī yāng be involved in a disaster not of one's own making

弛 chí [动] (书) relax

弛缓 chíhuǎn **I** [动] calm down **II** [形] slackened

驰 chí [动] **1** (跑得快) speed (*pt, pp* sped) ♦奔驰 gallop **2** (传播) disseminate **3** (向往) long for ♦驰想 be lost in thought

驰骋 chíchěng [动] **1** (字) (快跑) gallop ◇驰骋辽阔草原 gallop across the wide plains **2** (喻) (活跃) be very active in ◇他驰骋于歌坛多年。He has been very active in the music world for years.

驰名 chímíng [动] become famous (*pt* became, *pp* become)

驰驱 chíqū [动] (骑马快跑) go at a gallop (*pt* went, *pp* gone)

迟 chí [形] **1** (慢) slow **2** (晚) late ◇对不起，迟了10分钟。Sorry, I'm ten minutes late. **3** (久) long ◇迟迟不做决定 dither

迟到 chídào [动] be late ◇上班迟到会扣奖金。If you're late for work your bonus can be docked.

迟钝 chídùn [形] (贬) slow ◇他对股市变化反应迟钝。He was slow to react to the changes on the stock exchange.

迟缓 chíhuǎn [形] slow

迟疑 chíyí [动] hesitate ◇她毫不迟疑地离开了家。She didn't hesitate to leave home.

迟早 chízǎo [副] sooner or later ◇他胡作非为，迟早要出事。His behaviour (英) 或 behavior (美) is outrageous. Sooner or later it'll end in disaster.

持 chí [动] **1** (拿着) hold (*pt, pp* held) ◇他手持护照。He held a passport in his hand. **2** (支持) support ♦坚持 maintain **3** (主管) manage ◇操持家务 manage the housework **4** (对抗) oppose ♦僵持 reach a stalemate

持久 chíjiǔ [形] protracted

持平 chípíng **I** [形] fair **II** [动] be equal ◇公司今年的利润与去年持平。This year's company profits are the same as last year's.

持续 chíxù [动] go on (*pt* went, *pp* gone) ◇高温天气持续了几天。The hot weather went on for some days. ◇该电视节目的收视率持续上升。The ratings for this TV programme (英) 或 program (美) continued to rise.

持之以恒 chí zhī yǐ héng persevere ◇英语学习要持之以恒。You must persevere with your English studies.

持之有故 chí zhī yǒu gù insist with good reason

匙 chí [名] spoon

踟 chí 见下文

踟蹰 chíchú [动] waver

尺 chǐ **I** [量] *unit of length, equal to a third of a metre* **II** [名] ruler

尺寸 chǐcun [名] **1** (长度) size **2** (口) (分寸) sense of propriety

尺牍 chǐdú [名] letter

尺度 chǐdù [名] yardstick

尺码 chǐmǎ [名] **1** (尺寸) size **2** (标准) standard

齿 chǐ **I** [名] **1** (器官) tooth (*pl* teeth) **2** (齿状物) protrusion ♦梳齿 teeth of a comb **II** [动] (书) mention

齿轮 chǐlún [名] gear wheel

侈 chǐ [形] (书) **1** (浪费) wasteful ♦奢侈 extravagant **2** (夸大) exaggerated

侈谈 chǐtán (书) **I** [动] brag **II** [名] extravagant flights of fancy

耻 chǐ [名] **1** (羞愧) shame **2** (耻辱) disgrace

耻辱 chǐrǔ [名] disgrace

耻笑 chǐxiào [动] mock

叱 chì [动] (书) rebuke

叱责 chìzé [动] scold

叱咤 chìzhà [动] (书) roar

叱咤风云 chì zhà fēng yún all-powerful

斥 chì [动] **1** (责备) denounce **2** (使离开) drive … away (*pt* drove, *pp* driven) ♦排斥 repel **3** (支付) fund **4** (扩展) expand

斥退 chìtuì [动] **1** (开除) dismiss ◇他被老板斥退了。He was dismissed by the boss. **2** (喝令退出) shout at … to go away ◇他斥退了手下。He shouted at his subordinate to go away.

斥责 chìzé [动] denounce

斥资 chìzī [动] fund

赤 chì **I** [形] **1** (红色) red **2** (表示革命) revolutionary **3** (忠诚) sincere **II** [动] bare

赤膊上阵 chì bó shàng zhèn **1** (字) do … bare-chested ◇参赛者身穿短裤，赤膊上阵。The competitors entered the field in shorts and with bare chests. **2** (喻) lay oneself bare (*pt, pp* laid)

赤诚 chìchéng [形] completely sincere

赤胆忠心 chì dǎn zhōng xīn utter devotion

赤道 chìdào [名] the equator

赤脚 chìjiǎo [动] be barefoot ◇赤脚走路 walk barefoot

赤裸裸 chìluǒluǒ [形] **1** (光身子) stark naked **2** (喻) (毫无掩饰) undisguised

赤贫 chìpín [形] utterly destitute ◇一个从赤贫走向成功的商业奇才 a commercial genius who rose from utter destitution to success

赤手空拳 chì shǒu kōng quán unarmed ◇赤手空拳地搏斗 engage in unarmed combat

赤条条 chìtiáotiáo [形] stark naked

赤子 chìzǐ [名] **1** (初生儿) newborn baby ◇赤子之心 pure and innocent **2** (爱国的人) patriot

赤字 chìzì [名] deficit ◇财政赤字 financial deficit

饬 chì **I** [动] **1** (命令) order **2** (整顿) reorganize **II** [形] prudent

饬令 chìlìng [动] order

炽 chì [形] **1** (书) (旺) ablaze **2** (热烈) fiery

炽烈 chìliè [形] **1** (字) (指火) raging **2** (喻) passionate ◇炽烈的情感 passionate emotions

炽热 chìrè [形] red-hot

翅 chì [名] **1** (翅膀) wing **2** (鳍) fin

翅膀 chìbǎng [名] wing

敕 chì [名] edict

冲 chōng **I** [名] important place ◇战略要冲 place of strategic importance **II** [动] **1** (向前闯) rush forward ◇横冲直撞 push one's way through **2** (猛撞) clash ♦冲撞 collide **3** (浇) pour boiling water on ◇这药需用开水冲服。This medicine should be taken mixed with boiled water. **4** (冲洗) rinse ◇冲一冲碗碟 rinse the dishes **5** (指胶片) develop ◇冲胶卷 develop a roll of film **6** (抵消) balance ♦冲账 balance the accounts
▷另见 chòng

冲刺 chōngcì [动] **1** (字) sprint ◇向终点冲刺 sprint to the finishing line **2** (喻) make a final spurt

冲动 chōngdòng [动] be impulsive ◇不要冲动，理智些吧。Don't be so impulsive – have some sense. ◇我当时有种购物的冲动。I had an impulse to go shopping.

冲锋 chōngfēng [动] charge

冲锋陷阵 chōng fēng xiàn zhèn **1** (作战英勇) charge the enemy lines **2** (喻) fight a brave battle

冲击 chōngjī [动] **1** (撞击) pound **2** (喻) (影响) have a big impact on ◇进入世界贸易组织将会冲击中国农业。Entering the World Trade Organisation will have a big impact on China's agriculture. **3** (冲锋) charge

冲剂 chōngjì [名] *medicine to be taken in water*

冲浪 chōnglàng [名] surf

冲天 chōngtiān [动] soar ◇怒火冲天 in a towering rage

冲突 chōngtū I [动] 1 (激烈争斗) conflict 2 (相抵触) clash ◇英语课和法语课冲突了。The English class clashes with the French class. II [名] (矛盾) conflict

冲洗 chōngxǐ [动] 1 (洗涤) wash ◇冲洗汽车 clean a car 2 (指胶片) develop ◇冲洗照片 develop a photograph

充 chōng [动] 1 (满) fill ♦充电 charge a battery ♦充其量 at most 2 (担任) act as ◇充当助理经理 act as assistant manager ◇充当配角 take a supporting role 3 (假装) pass ... off as ◇以次充好 pass things off as good quality

充斥 chōngchì [动] (贬) flood ◇市场上充斥着假货。The market is flooded with fake goods.

充当 chōngdāng [动] act as ◇朋友不懂英语，我充当翻译。My friend doesn't understand English, so I act as interpreter.

充电 chōngdiàn [动] 1 (字) charge 2 (喻) (指人) recharge one's batteries

充耳不闻 chōng ěr bù wén turn a deaf ear

充分 chōngfèn I [形] ample ◇做好充分的准备 make ample preparations II [副] fully ◇充分展示自己的才华 show one's talents to the full

充饥 chōngjī [动] alleviate one's hunger

充军 chōngjūn [动] banish ◇他被发配边疆充军。He was banished to the border area.

充满 chōngmǎn [动] 1 (填满) fill 2 (有) brim with ◇他的话充满自信。His speech brimmed with confidence.

充沛 chōngpèi [形] abundant

充其量 chōngqíliàng [副] at best

充实 chōngshí I [形] rich II [动] enrich

充数 chōngshù [动] make up the numbers

充裕 chōngyù [形] plentiful

充足 chōngzú [形] sufficient

忡 chōng 见下文

忡忡 chōngchōng [形] anxious ◇忧心忡忡 be worried sick

舂 chōng [动] pound ◇舂米 husk rice

憧 chōng 见下文

憧憬 chōngjǐng [动] look forward to

虫 chóng [名] insect

虫害 chónghài [名] pests (*pl*)

重 chóng I [动] 1 (重复) repeat ◇书买重了 buy two copies of the same book 2 (重叠) overlap II [副] again ◇他把作文重写了一遍。He wrote his essay all over again. ◇重返英国 return to Britain III [量] layer ◇万重山 range after range of mountains ◇一重重的困难 endless difficulties
▷另见 zhòng

重唱 chóngchàng [名] ensemble ♦二重唱 duo

重蹈覆辙 chóng dǎo fù zhé make the same old mistakes

重叠 chóngdié [形] overlapping

重逢 chóngféng [动] reunite ◇和好友重逢 be reunited with a good friend

重复 chóngfù [动] repeat

重婚 chónghūn [动] commit bigamy

重申 chóngshēn [动] reiterate

重新 chóngxīn [副] again ◇我把床重新铺了一遍。I made the bed again. ◇重新命名文件 rename a file ◇重新开始 start afresh

重洋 chóngyáng [名] the ocean

重奏 chóngzòu [名] ensemble

崇 chóng I [形] high II [动] think highly of (*pt, pp* thought) ♦推崇 hold ... in great esteem

崇拜 chóngbài [动] worship

崇高 chónggāo [形] lofty

崇敬 chóngjìng [动] respect ◇谁是你最崇敬的人？Who do you respect most?

崇山峻岭 chóng shān jùn lǐng towering mountains

崇尚 chóngshàng [动] advocate

宠 chǒng [动] spoil

宠爱 chǒng'ài [动] dote on

宠儿 chǒng'ér [名] favourite (英), favorite (美)

宠辱不惊 chǒng rǔ bù jīng be unflappable

宠物 chǒngwù [名] pet

冲 chòng **I** [形] **1** (指气味刺鼻) pungent ◊大蒜味很冲。Garlic is very pungent. **2** (劲儿足) vigorous ◊他说话挺冲的。He speaks quite bluntly. **II** [介] **1** (对着) at ◊他冲我做了个鬼脸。He made a face at me. ◊这些意见都是冲他提的。All the criticisms were aimed at him. **2** (凭) because of ◊顾客就是冲着这家超市的良好服务而来的。Customers go to that supermarket because of the excellent service. **III** [动] **1** (冲压) punch **2** (口) (正对) face ◊这道门冲南。This door faces south. ▷另见 chōng

冲劲儿 chòngjìnr [名] **1** (指人) vigour (英), vigor (美) **2** (刺激性) kick

抽 chōu [动] **1** (取出) take … out (*pt* took, *pp* taken) ◊他从钱夹中抽出一张钞票。He took a note (英) 或 bill (美) out of his wallet. **2** (取出部分) take (*pt* took, *pp* taken) ◊抽时间 find time **3** (长出) sprout ♦抽芽 sprout **4** (吸) inhale ♦抽烟 smoke ◊抽血 draw blood ◊抽水 pump water **5** (抽缩) shrink (*pt* shrank, *pp* shrunk) ◊棉布洗后会抽。Cotton shrinks after washing. **6** (打) whip ◊抽鞭子 whip

抽查 chōuchá [动] do a spot-check ◊产品质量抽查 do a spot-check on product quality

抽搐 chōuchù [动] twitch

抽风 chōufēng [动] **1** (指疾病) have convulsions **2** (喻) (不合常理) lose the plot (*pt, pp* lost)

抽奖 chōujiǎng [动] draw prizes (*pt* drew, *pp* drawn)

抽筋 chōujīn [动] (口) (肌肉痉挛) have cramp ◊脚抽筋 have cramp in one's foot

抽空 chōukòng [动] find the time (*pt, pp* found)

抽泣 chōuqì [动] sob

抽签 chōuqiān [动] draw lots (*pt* drew, *pp* drawn) ◊昨天我们是抽签决定谁洗碗的。Yesterday we drew lots to decide who was going to wash the dishes.

抽水 chōushuǐ [动] **1** (吸水) pump water **2** (缩水) shrink (*pt* shrank, *pp* shrunk) ◊这种布料不会抽水。This type of cloth doesn't shrink.

抽屉 chōuti [名] drawer

抽象 chōuxiàng [形] abstract

抽烟 chōuyān [动] smoke ◊他过去抽烟。He used to smoke.

抽样 chōuyàng [动] sample

仇 chóu [名] **1** (仇敌) enemy **2** (仇恨) hatred ♦报仇 avenge

仇敌 chóudí [名] enemy

仇恨 chóuhèn [动] hate

仇视 chóushì [动] be hostile to

惆 chóu [形] grief-stricken

惆怅 chóuchàng [形] melancholy

绸 chóu [名] silk ♦丝绸 silk

绸缎 chóuduàn [名] silk and satin

畴 chóu [名] (书) (种类) variety ♦范畴 category

酬 chóu **I** [动] **1** (书) (敬酒) toast **2** (报答) reward **3** (往来) socialize ♦应酬 socialize **4** (实现) realize **II** [名] payment

酬报 chóubào [动] reward ◊酬报好心人 reward good-hearted people ◊公司给每个员工500美金作为酬报。The company gave each of its employees a bonus of five hundred US dollars.

酬宾 chóubīn [动] have a sale ◊周末百货公司将有大酬宾活动。This weekend the department store is having a big sale.

酬金 chóujīn [名] remuneration

酬劳 chóuláo **I** [动] repay (*pt, pp* repaid) **II** [名] repayment

酬谢 chóuxiè [动] repay (*pt, pp* repaid)

稠 chóu [形] **1** (浓度大) thick **2** (稠密) dense

稠密 chóumì [形] dense

愁 chóu [动] be anxious ♦忧愁 be worried

愁眉苦脸 chóu méi kǔ liǎn pull a long face

愁闷 chóumèn [形] gloomy

筹 chóu **I** [名] **1** (小片) counter **2** (计策) plan ◇一筹莫展 be at one's wits end **II** [动] prepare

筹办 chóubàn [动] make preparations ◇筹办酒席 make preparations for a banquet

筹备 chóubèi [动] arrange

筹划 chóuhuà [动] plan

筹集 chóují [动] raise

筹码 chóumǎ [名] **1** (计数用具) counter **2** (喻) bargaining counter

踌 chóu 见下文

踌躇 chóuchú **I** [动] hesitate **II** [形] (书) complacent

踌躇满志 chóu chú mǎn zhì be full of pride

丑 chǒu [形] **1** (丑陋) ugly **2** (令人厌恶) disgraceful

丑八怪 chǒubāguài [名] (口) ◇他是个丑八怪。He's really ugly.

丑恶 chǒu'è [形] ugly

丑化 chǒuhuà [动] vilify

丑剧 chǒujù [名] farce

丑陋 chǒulòu [形] ugly

丑闻 chǒuwén [名] scandal

瞅 chǒu [动] (方) look at ◇我瞅了孩子一眼。I glanced at the child.

臭 chòu **I** [形] **1** (指气味) smelly **2** (惹人厌恶) disgusting **3** (拙劣) lousy **II** [副] severely
▷另见 xiù

臭虫 chòuchóng [名] bedbug

臭烘烘 chòuhōnghōng [形] foul-smelling

臭美 chòuměi [形] (贬) smug

臭名昭著 chòu míng zhāo zhù notorious

臭味相投 chòu wèi xiāng tóu be two of a kind

臭氧 chòuyǎng [名] ozone ◇臭氧层 ozone layer

出 chū **I** [动] **1** (与入相对) go out (*pt* went, *pp* gone) ♦出国 go abroad ♦出行 go on a journey ♦出游 go sightseeing **2** (来到) appear ♦出庭 appear in court ◇刚出台的法律 brand-new laws **3** (超出) exceed ♦出轨 derail ◇不出3天货就到了。The goods arrived within three days. **4** (给) give out (*pt* gave, *pp* given) ◇出考题 set an exam paper ◇他为此出了很多力。He put a lot of effort into this. **5** (产生) produce ◇这个学校出优秀教师。This college produces excellent teachers. **6** (发生) occur ♦出事 have an accident **7** (发出) come out (*pt* came, *pp* come) ♦出血 bleed ♦出汗 sweat **8** (显露) appear ♦出名 become famous **9** (支出) pay out (*pt*, *pp* paid) ◇量入为出 spend what one earns

出版 chūbǎn [动] publish

出殡 chūbìn [动] hold a funeral procession (*pt*, *pp* held)

出兵 chūbīng [动] dispatch troops

出差 chūchāi [动] go away on business (*pt* went, *pp* gone) ◇我经常去北京出差。I often go to Beijing on business.

出产 chūchǎn [动] produce

出丑 chūchǒu [动] make a fool of oneself ◇他表演失败，当众出丑了。His performance was a failure – he made a fool of himself in front of everyone.

出处 chūchù [名] source

出道 chūdào [动] launch one's career

出动 chūdòng [动] **1** (外出活动) set off (*pt*, *pp* set) **2** (派出) dispatch

出尔反尔 chū ěr fǎn ěr go back on one's word

出发 chūfā [动] **1** (离开) set out (*pt*, *pp* set) **2** (表示着眼点) take … as a starting point (*pt* took, *pp* taken) ◇从实际出发 take reality as one's starting point

出访 chūfǎng [动] travel on official business

出风头 chū fēngtou **1** (表示贬义) show off (*pt* showed, *pp* shown) **2** (抢眼)

steal the show (*pt* stole, *pp* stolen)

出格 chūgé [动] **1** (出众) be outstanding **2** (过分) step out of line ◇你的所作所为出格了。Your behaviour (英) 或 behavior (美) is out of line.

出活 chūhuó **I** [动] get work done ◇他花了很长时间，但就是不出活。He spent a lot of time on it, but didn't actually get any work done. **II** [形] efficient

出击 chūjī [动] attack

出家 chūjiā [动] **1** (当和尚) become a monk (*pt* became, *pp* become) **2** (当尼姑) become a nun (*pt* became, *pp* become)

出嫁 chūjià [动] marry

出境 chūjìng [动] **1** (指国境) leave the country (*pt*, *pp* left) **2** (指某一区域) leave a place

出局 chūjú [动] be knocked out

出口 chūkǒu **I** [动] **1** (说) utter **2** (指贸易) export **II** [名] exit

出口成章 chū kǒu chéng zhāng eloquent and articulate

出类拔萃 chū lèi bá cuì stand out from the crowd

出力 chūlì [动] put effort into (*pt*, *pp* put) ◇他为公司的创建出力不少。He put a lot of effort into establishing the company.

出笼 chūlóng [动] **1** (指蒸笼) come out of the steamer (*pt* came, *pp* come) **2** (喻) come out (*pt* came, *pp* come) ◇新政策出笼后，倍受抨击。When the new policies came out, they were heavily criticized.

出路 chūlù [名] **1** (指道路) way out **2** (前途) prospects (*pl*) **3** (销路) market

出落 chūluo [动] blossom

出马 chūmǎ [动] take the lead (*pt* took, *pp* taken) ◇厂长亲自出马谈这些生意。The factory director took the lead in these business discussions.

出卖 chūmài [动] **1** (卖) sell (*pt*, *pp* sold) **2** (贬) (背弃) betray

出面 chūmiàn [动] come out (*pt* came, *pp* come) ◇由董事会出面召集会议。The board of directors came out with a request for a meeting.

出名 chūmíng [动] become famous (*pt* became, *pp* become)

出没 chūmò [动] haunt

出纳 chūnà **I** [动] (指财务管理) keep the books (*pt*, *pp* kept) **II** [名] cashier

出品 chūpǐn **I** [动] produce **II** [名] product

出奇 chūqí [形] extraordinary

出奇制胜 chū qí zhì shèng seize victory through a surprise attack

出勤 chūqín [动] **1** (按时到) show up on time (*pt* showed, *pp* shown) ♦出勤率 ratio of attendance **2** (外出办公) go away for work (*pt* went, *pp* gone)

出让 chūràng [动] sell (*pt*, *pp* sold)

出人头地 chū rén tóu dì stand out

出任 chūrèn [动] (书) take up the post of (*pt* took, *pp* taken) ◇出任总理 take up the post of prime minister

出入 chūrù **I** [动] come and go **II** [名] discrepancy

出色 chūsè [形] outstanding

出山 chūshān [动] take up a post (*pt* took, *pp* taken)

出身 chūshēn **I** [动] come from (*pt* came, *pp* come) ◇他出身于一个富裕的家庭。He comes from a wealthy family. **II** [名] background ◇他是农民出身。He comes from a farming background.

出神入化 chū shén rù huà reach perfection

出生 chūshēng [动] be born ◇她出生在英国。She was born in Britain.

出生入死 chū shēng rù sǐ risk one's life

出师 chūshī [动] **1** (期满学成) finish one's apprenticeship **2** (书) (出兵) dispatch troops

出使 chūshǐ [动] be sent on a diplomatic mission

出世 chūshì [动] **1** (出生) be born ◇刚刚出世的婴儿 a new-born baby

2 (产生) arise (*pt* arose, *pp* arisen) 3 (超脱人世) be detached from the rest of the world

出手 chūshǒu I [动] 1 (卖出) sell (*pt, pp* sold) 2 (拿出) give … out (*pt* gave, *pp* given) 3 (行动) hit (*pt, pp* hit) II [名] (本领) skill

出售 chūshòu [动] sell (*pt, pp* sold)

出台 chūtái [动] 1 (上场) make an appearance 2 (公布实施) promulgate

出息 chūxi I [名] prospect II [动] come on (*pt* came, *pp* come) ◇他上大学后出息多了。He's really come on since going to university.

出席 chūxí [动] attend

出现 chūxiàn [动] appear ◇他没有出现在聚会上，朋友很失望。He didn't appear at the gathering and his friends were very disappointed. ◇她的出现令我感到意外。I was surprised by her unexpected appearance.

出血 chūxiě [动] 1 (字) bleed (*pt, pp* bled) 2 (喻) (花钱) blow a lot of money (*pt* blew, *pp* blown)

出洋相 chū yángxiàng [动] make a fool of oneself

出狱 chūyù [动] be released from prison

出院 chūyuàn [动] leave hospital (*pt, pp* left)

出众 chūzhòng [形] outstanding

出租 chūzū [动] let (*pt, pp* let) ◇有房出租 room to let

初 chū I [名] original ◇和好如初 become reconciled II [形] 1 (第一) first ♦初恋 first love ◇初次交往 first contact 2 (最低) primary ♦初级 primary 3 (开始) early ♦初冬 early winter

初步 chūbù [形] fundamental

初出茅庐 chū chū máolú be wet behind the ears

初级 chūjí [形] primary ◇初级阶段 initial stages

初期 chūqī [名] initial stage

初生之犊不怕虎 chū shēng zhī dú bù pà hǔ the young are fearless

初衷 chūzhōng [名] original intention

刍 chú I [名] hay II [动] (书) mow the lawn (*pt* mowed, *pp* mown) III [形] (书) (谦) meagre

刍议 chúyì [名] (谦) my humble opinion

除 chú I [动] 1 (去掉) get rid of ♦开除 dismiss ♦去除 remove 2 (指算术) divide ♦除法 division ◇16除以8等于2。Sixteen divided by eight is two. II [介] 1 (表示绝对排除关系) except ◇除彼得外大家都来了。Everyone came except Peter. 2 (表示并非惟一) apart from ◇除了珍妮，谁还去过上海？ Apart from Jenny, who else has been to Shanghai?

除非 chúfēi I [连] unless ◇除非天下雨，我通常晚饭后出去散步。Unless it's raining, I normally go for a walk after dinner. ◇除非他要我去，否则我不去。I won't go unless he wants me to. II [介] other than ◇这个秘方，除非他没人知道。Other than him, no one else knows the secret recipe.

除了 chúle [介] 1 (表示不包括) except ◇除了你其他人都参加了会议。Everyone else attended the meeting except you. 2 (除此以外) apart from ◇他除了学习英语， 还学习日语。Apart from studying English, he also studies Japanese. 3 (表示非此即彼) apart from … the only … ◇他的生活很简单，除了工作就是睡觉。His life is pretty simple – the only thing he does apart from work is sleep.

除名 chúmíng [动] strike ... off (*pt, pp* struck)

除外 chúwài [动] ◇班长除外，每个人都得写份报告。Everyone had to write a report except the class monitor. ◇雨天除外，他每天步行上班。He walks to work every day, except when it rains.

除夕 chúxī [名] New Year's Eve

厨 chú [名] 1 (厨房) kitchen 2 (厨师) cook

厨师 chúshī [名] cook

锄 chú I [名] hoe II [动] 1 (松土) hoe ♦锄地 hoe the fields 2 (铲除) wipe … out

锄头 chútou [名] hoe

雏 chú [形] (幼小) nestling

雏儿 chúr [名] (口) **1** (幼鸟) chick **2** (喻) (指人) innocent

雏形 chúxíng [名] **1** (最初形式) original state ◇公司的雏形不是这样的。The company didn't originally look like this. **2** (指模型) model

橱 chú [名] cabinet

橱窗 chúchuāng [名] **1** (指商店的展示窗) shop (英) 或 store (美) window **2** (用于展览图片等) display case

处 chǔ [动] **1** (交往) get on with **2** (在) be in ◇处于困境 be in a difficult position ◇他身处他乡，倍感孤独。When he's away from home he feels twice as lonely. **3** (办理) deal with (*pt, pp* dealt) **4** (处罚) penalize ♦惩处 penalize
▷另见 chù

处罚 chǔfá [动] punish

处方 chǔfāng [名] prescription

处分 chǔfèn **I** [动] punish **II** [名] punishment

处境 chǔjìng [名] situation

处决 chǔjué [动] **1** (执行死刑) execute **2** (决断) decide ◇提工资的事由董事会处决。Salary increases are decided on by the board of directors.

处理 chǔlǐ [动] **1** (解决) deal with (*pt, pp* dealt) ◇遇到问题应该及时处理。You should deal with problems as they arise. **2** (减价) sell … at a reduced price (*pt, pp* sold) ◇处理品 goods sold at a discount **3** (加工) treat ◇经高温处理过的牛奶 milk pasteurized at a high temperature

处女 chǔnǚ [名] virgin ♦处女地 virgin land ♦处女航 maiden voyage

处世 chǔshì [动] conduct oneself

处心积虑 chǔ xīn jī lǜ plot and scheme

处治 chǔzhì [动] punish

处置 chǔzhì [动] **1** (处理) deal with (*pt, pp* dealt) **2** (惩治) punish

础 chǔ [名] plinth

储 chǔ [动] store

储备 chǔbèi **I** [动] store … up **II** [名] reserve

储藏 chǔcáng [动] **1** (保藏) store **2** (蕴藏) contain ◇大量的石油储藏在这片沙漠中。Large reserves of oil are contained in this desert.

储存 chǔcún [动] stockpile

储蓄 chǔxù **I** [动] save **II** [名] savings (*pl*)

楚 chǔ **I** [名] (书) (痛苦) suffering **II** [形] (清晰) clear

楚楚 chǔchǔ [形] **1** (整洁) neat and tidy **2** (娇柔) dainty

处 chù [名] **1** (地方) place ♦暗处 secret place ♦益处 profit ◇四处都是人。There were people everywhere. **2** (部门) department ◇人事处 human resources department
▷另见 chǔ

处所 chùsuǒ [名] area

畜 chù [名] livestock
▷另见 xù

畜生 chùsheng [名] beast

触 chù [动] **1** (接触) touch **2** (触动) move

触动 chùdòng [动] **1** (碰撞) bump into **2** (损害) offend **3** (打动) stir … up

触犯 chùfàn [动] violate

触及 chùjí [动] touch

触角 chùjiǎo [名] tentacle

触类旁通 chù lèi páng tōng reason by analogy

触摸 chùmō [动] touch ◇触摸式屏幕 touch screen

触目惊心 chù mù jīng xīn shocking

黜 chù [动] (书) dismiss

黜免 chùmiǎn [动] (书) dismiss

矗 chù [动] (书) stand straight (*pt, pp* stood)

矗立 chùlì [动] stand majestically (*pt, pp* stood)

揣 chuāi [动] conceal … in one's clothes
▷另见 chuǎi

揣 chuǎi [动] (书) surmise
▷另见 chuāi

揣测 chuǎicè [动] guess

揣度 chuǎiduó [动] (书) speculate

揣摩 chuǎimó [动] speculate ◇我不停地揣摩他的心思。I kept speculating on what he might be thinking.

踹 chuài [动] **1** (踢) kick **2** (踩) tread (*pt* trod, *pp* trodden) ◇他踹到了狗屎。He trod in dog's mess.

川 chuān [名] **1** (河流) river **2** (平地) plain

川流不息 chuān liú bù xī endless streams ◇街上的人群川流不息。There were endless streams of people and cars on the road.

川资 chuānzī [名] travel expenses (*pl*)

穿 chuān [动] **1** (破) (纸) pierce **2** (谎言、事实) expose **3** (通过) pass through ◇周末的街头，行人穿行不息。Endless streams of people pass through the streets at the weekends . ◇穿针 thread a needle **4** (串) piece … together ◇把线索穿起来 piece together all the clues ◇穿珍珠 string pearls together **5** (衣服、鞋帽、首饰等) wear (*pt* wore, *pp* worn) ◇她喜欢穿金戴银。She likes to wear gold and silver. ◇他迅速穿上衣服。He put his clothes on very quickly. **6** (表示透彻) penetrate ◇看穿事情的真相 see through to the truth of a situation

穿插 chuānchā **I** [副] alternately ◇工作和休闲穿插进行 take turns to work and rest **II** [动] weave … in (*pt* wove, *pp* woven) ◇他在论文中穿插了些引文。He wove some quotations into his essay.

穿戴 chuāndài **I** [名] dress ◇他不讲究穿戴。He's not particular about what he wears. **II** [动] dress ◇全家穿戴整齐，准备去参加宴会。The whole family dressed up very smartly in preparation for the dinner party.

穿梭 chuānsuō [动] shuttle back and forth ◇机场大巴穿梭往来于机场和火车站。The airport bus shuttles back and forth between the airport and the train station.

穿小鞋 chuān xiǎoxié [动] (喻) make things hard for

穿越 chuānyuè [动] pass through

穿凿 chuānzáo [动] give a far-fetched account (*pt* gave, *pp* given)

穿着 chuānzhuó [名] outfit

传 chuán [动] **1** (交给) hand … down **2** (传授) pass … on **3** (传播) spread (*pt*, *pp* spread) **4** (传导) conduct **5** (表达) express ♦传情 express one's feelings ◇他们俩在会上眉目传情。They were eyeing each other up at the meeting. **6** (命令) summon **7** (传染) infect
▷另见 zhuàn

传播 chuánbō [动] disseminate

传达 chuándá **I** [动] pass … on ◇传达指示 pass on an instruction **II** [名] receptionist ◇传达室 reception room

传单 chuándān [名] leaflet

传递 chuándì [动] extend ◇传递祝福 extend good wishes ◇传递信息 transmit information

传媒 chuánméi [名] **1** (传播媒介) media ◇新闻传媒 the news media **2** (传染媒介) medium ◇苍蝇是许多疾病的传媒。Flies are the medium of many infections.

传票 chuánpiào [名] **1** (传唤凭证) summons (*sg*) **2** (账目凭单) voucher

传奇 chuánqí [形] legendary ◇传奇人物 legendary figure

传染 chuánrǎn [动] infect ◇蚊子传染疟疾。Mosquitoes carry the malaria infection.

传世 chuánshì [动] hand … down

传授 chuánshòu [动] pass … on ◇传授经验 pass on one's experience ◇传授知识 pass on knowledge

传说 chuánshuō **I** [动] ◇传说几百年前，这儿是一片海。People say that several hundred years ago this was all ocean. ◇传说他10年前就去了海外。It is said that he went abroad ten years ago. **II** [名] legend

传统 chuántǒng **I** [名] tradition **II** [形] **1** (世代相传) traditional ◇传统文化 traditional culture ◇传统医学 traditional medicine **2** (保守) conservative

传真 chuánzhēn [动] (指通讯方式) fax ◇我把文件传真给他了。I faxed the documents to him. ◇给我发个传真吧。Please send me a fax.

船 chuán [名] boat ◆渔船 fishing boat

船舶 chuánbó [名] shipping

船只 chuánzhī [名] vessels (*pl*)

喘 chuǎn **I** [动] gasp **II** [名] asthma

喘息 chuǎnxī [动] **1** (急促呼吸) pant **2** (短时休息) come up for air (*pt* came, *pp* come)

喘吁吁 chuǎnxūxū [形] puffing and panting

串 chuàn **I** [动] **1** (连贯) string ... together (*pt, pp* strung) ◇她把珍珠串了起来。She strung the pearls together. **2** (勾结) conspire **3** (指信号) get mixed up ◇电视串台了。The TV channels were all mixed up. ◇电话串线了。There was a crossed line. **4** (走动) drop by ◇他爱来我家串门。He likes to drop by my place. **5** (担任角色) act **II** [量] bunch ◇两串钥匙 two bunches of keys ◇一串珍珠 a string of pearls

串通 chuàntōng [动] (暗中勾结) collude ◇他俩串通作伪证。The two men colluded as false witnesses.

创 chuāng [名] wound ◆创痕 scar ◆创口 cut ◆创可贴 plaster (英), Band-Aid® (美)
▷另见 chuàng

创伤 chuāngshāng [名] **1** (指肉体上的) wound **2** (指精神上的) trauma

疮 chuāng [名] **1** (指疾病) ulcer ◆口疮 mouth ulcer ◆冻疮 chilblain **2** (指外伤) cut

疮疤 chuāngbā [名] **1** (疤痕) scar **2** (喻) weak point

疮痍 chuāngyí [名] (书) trauma

窗 chuāng [名] window ◆窗子 window

窗口 chuāngkǒu [名] **1** (字) window ◇售票窗口 ticket window **2** (喻) (渠道) vehicle **3** (喻) (反映处) window ◇眼睛是心灵的窗口。The eyes are a window on the soul.

窗口行业 chuāngkǒu hángyè [名] service industry

床 chuáng **I** [名] bed ◆单人床 single bed ◆河床 river bed ◆机床 lathe **II** [量] ◇一床棉被 a quilt

床位 chuángwèi [名] bed

闯 chuǎng [动] **1** (冲) rush **2** (磨炼) steel oneself **3** (惹) stir ... up ◆闯祸 cause trouble

闯荡 chuǎngdàng [动] steel oneself to face the outside world

闯祸 chuǎnghuò [动] cause trouble

闯江湖 chuǎng jiānghú lead a nomadic lifestyle (*pt, pp* led)

创 chuàng [动] create ◆独创 make an original creation ◇开创新纪元 create a new era ◇今年钢铁产量又创新高。This year steel production has reached new highs.
▷另见 chuāng

创见 chuàngjiàn [名] original idea

创建 chuàngjiàn [动] establish

创举 chuàngjǔ [名] pioneering work

创刊 chuàngkān [动] start publication

创立 chuànglì [动] establish ◇创立事业 establish a career ◇创立品牌 create a trademark

创始 chuàngshǐ [动] found

创业 chuàngyè [动] carve out a career

创意 chuàngyì [名] creativity

创造 chuàngzào [动] create ◇创造财富 create wealth

创作 chuàngzuò **I** [动] create **II** [名] work

吹 chuī [动] **1** (出气) blow (*pt* blew, *pp* blown) ◇吹灭蜡烛 blow out a candle **2** (演奏) play **3** (夸口) boast **4** (口) (破裂) fall through (*pt* fell, *pp* fallen) ◇他们去夏威夷的计划吹了。Their plan to go to Hawaii fell through. ◇我和女友吹了。I've broken up with my girlfriend.

吹风 chuīfēng [动] **1** (受风寒) catch a chill (*pt, pp* caught) **2** (吹干) blow-dry **3** (口) (透露) give advance warning (*pt* gave, *pp* given)

吹灰之力 chuī huī zhī lì [名] little effort ◇他不费吹灰之力就通过了考试。He got through the exam with very little effort.

吹毛求疵 chuī máo qiú cī find fault

吹牛 chuīniú [动] (书) brag

吹捧 chuīpěng [动] flatter

吹嘘 chuīxū [动] boast ◇吹嘘自己的长处 boast about one's strengths

炊 chuī [动] cook ◇炊具 cooking utensil ◇炊事 cooking

垂 chuí **I** [动] **1** (一头向下) hang down (*pt, pp* hung) **2** (敬) (长辈或上级) condescend **3** (书) (流传) hand ... down ◇永垂不朽 be everlasting **II** [副] (书) on the verge of ♦生命垂危 be on the verge of death

垂手 chuíshǒu [动] (表示恭敬) stand to attention (*pt, pp* stood)

垂手可得 chuí shǒu kě dé do... with one's eyes shut

垂头丧气 chuí tóu sàng qì be crestfallen

垂直 chuízhí [形] vertical

捶 chuí [动] pound

锤 chuí **I** [名] hammer **II** [动] hammer

锤炼 chuíliàn [动] **1** (冶金) hammer ... into shape **2** (磨炼) harden ◇锤炼意志 harden one's resolve ◇锤炼孩子的思考力 sharpen a child's powers of thought **3** (钻研琢磨) refine ◇锤炼写作技巧 refine one's writing skills

春 chūn [名] **1** (春季) spring **2** (情欲) sexual desire **3** (生机) vitality

春分 chūnfēn [名] spring equinox

春风得意 chūnfēng déyì take pride in one's successes

春风化雨 chūnfēng huàyǔ (喻) inspirational teaching

春光 chūnguāng [名] spring scenes (*pl*)

春节 Chūn Jié [名] Chinese New Year

春卷 chūnjuǎn [名] spring roll

春联 chūnlián [名] Spring Festival couplets (*pl*)

春秋 chūnqiū [名] year

春天 chūntiān [名] spring

春药 chūnyào [名] aphrodisiac

纯 chún [形] **1** (纯净) pure **2** (纯熟) skilful (英), skillful (美)

纯粹 chúncuì **I** [形] pure **II** [副] purely

纯洁 chúnjié **I** [形] pure **II** [动] purify

纯净 chúnjìng [形] pure

纯利 chúnlì [名] net profit

纯真 chúnzhēn [形] wholesome

纯正 chúnzhèng [形] **1** (纯粹) pure **2** (正当) unselfish ◇动机纯正 unselfish motivation

唇 chún [名] lip

唇舌 chúnshé [名] argument

唇亡齿寒 chún wáng chǐ hán share a common fate

淳 chún [形] (书) honest

淳朴 chúnpǔ [形] simple

醇 chún **I** [名] **1** (烈酒) spirit **2** (化) alcohol **II** [形] (书) pure

醇厚 chúnhòu [形] (纯正浓厚) rich

蠢 chǔn [形] **1** (愚蠢) stupid **2** (笨拙) clumsy

蠢蠢欲动 chǔnchǔn yù dòng on the point of stirring up trouble

戳 chuō **I** [动] **1** (穿过) poke ◇他不小心戳到了我的眼睛。He accidentally poked me in the eye. **2** (方) (损坏) pierce **II** [名] seal

戳穿 chuōchuān [动] **1** (刺穿) pierce **2** (揭穿) expose

戳子 chuōzi [名] seal

啜 chuò [动] (书) **1** (喝) sip **2** (抽噎) sob

啜泣 chuòqì [动] sob

绰 chuò [形] (书) **1** (宽绰) abundant **2** (柔美) graceful

绰绰有余 chuòchuò yǒu yú more than enough ◇用我的工资支付日常的生活绰绰有余。My wages are more than enough to pay for my daily outgoings.

绰号 chuòhào [名] nickname

辍 chuò [动] stop

辍笔 chuòbǐ [动] stop ◇辍笔5年后他又开始作画。Five years after he stopped painting he started up again. ◇他40岁时就辍笔了。He stopped writing at the age of forty.

辍学 chuòxué [动] give up one's studies (*pt* gave, *pp* given) ◇她被迫辍学。She was forced to give up her studies.

刺 cī [拟] whoosh
▷另见 cì

疵 cī [名] flaw

词 cí [名] **1** (语句) words (*pl*) ♦台词 lines **2** (指语言单位) word **3** (指韵文形式) *classical poetry using a set pattern*

词典 cídiǎn [名] dictionary ◇双语词典 bilingual dictionary

词典学 cídiǎnxué [名] lexicography

词法 cífǎ [名] morphology

词汇 cíhuì [名] vocabulary

词语 cíyǔ [名] term

词藻 cízǎo [名] rhetoric

词组 cízǔ [名] phrase

祠 cí [名] ancestral temple

祠堂 cítáng [名] ancestral temple

瓷 cí [名] porcelain

辞 cí **I** [名] **1** (语言) diction **2** (文学体裁) *early form of classical Chinese poetry* **II** [动] **1** (告别) bid ... farewell (*pt* bade, *pp* bidden) **2** (辞职) resign ◇他辞掉了市长的职务。He resigned from his position as mayor. **3** (辞退) dismiss ◇他被经理辞了。He was dismissed by the manager. **4** (躲避) decline

辞别 cíbié [动] bid ... farewell (*pt* bade, *pp* bidden) ◇他辞别了亲人去国外打工。He bade farewell to his relatives as he left to work overseas.

辞呈 cíchéng [名] letter of resignation ◇他向老板递交了辞呈。He gave his boss his letter of resignation.

辞典 cídiǎn [名] dictionary

辞令 cílìng [名] language ◇外交辞令 diplomatic language

辞世 císhì [动] pass away ◇因病辞世 pass away due to illness

辞书 císhū [名] reference books (*pl*)

辞退 cítuì [动] dismiss ◇他因工作不力，被老板辞退。He wasn't hardworking enough, and so was dismissed by the boss.

辞行 cíxíng [动] bid ... farewell (*pt* bade, *pp* bidden)

辞藻 cízǎo [名] rhetoric

辞章 cízhāng [名] **1** (韵文和散文) poetry and prose **2** (写作技巧) writing skills (*pl*)

辞职 cízhí [动] resign

> 请勿混淆 **resign** 和 **retire**。**resign** 表示某人在提出不愿再做某份工作后离职。*He resigned last week after a newspaper published claims that he had lied to get the job...She has threatened to resign from her well-paid job as a protest.* **retire** 表示离职并停止工作，通常此时是由于该人已达到领取养老金的年龄。*He retired in 1960... Her mum retired from her job as a teacher at the age of 60.* 当职业运动员不再从事职业体育运动，即使他们还非常年轻，也可以使用 **retire**。

慈 cí [形] kind

慈爱 cí'ài [形] affectionate

慈悲 cíbēi [名] compassion

慈善 císhàn [形] charitable

慈祥 cíxiáng [形] kind

磁 cí [名] (物) magnetism

磁场 cíchǎng [名] magnetic field

磁盘 cípán [名] disk

磁盘驱动器 cípán qūdòngqì [名] disk drive

雌 cí [形] female

雌雄 cíxióng [名] winners and losers (*pl*)

此 cǐ [代] (这) this (*pl* these) ◇此书 this book ◇此时此刻 right now ◇就此分手 part company now ◇由此向前 from now on ◇长此以往 if things continue like this

此起彼伏 cǐ qǐ bǐ fú continuously rising and falling

此外 cǐwài [连] apart from this ◇抽屉里就几件衣服，此外别无他物。There were just a few items of clothing in the drawer. Apart from that there was nothing.

此一时，彼一时 cǐ yī shí, bǐ yī shí things have changed ◇此一时，彼一时，现在家庭妇男越来越来越多了。Things have changed – there are more and more house-husbands around today.

次 cì **I** [名] ranking ♦档次 grade ♦层次 level ♦名次 position *(in a competition)* **II** [形] **1** (第二) second ♦次子 second son ♦次日 next day **2** (差) inferior ♦次品 inferior product ◇电影拍得太次了。The film was badly made. **III** [量] time ♦初次 first time ♦屡次 repeatedly

次序 cìxù [名] order ◇老师按字母次序点名。The teacher read the names out in alphabetical order.

次要 cìyào [形] secondary

伺 cì 见下文
▷另见 sì

伺候 cìhou [动] wait on ◇许多男人都希望老婆好好伺候他。A lot of men hope that their wives will wait on them.

刺 cì **I** [动] **1** (穿过) pierce **2** (刺激) irritate **3** (暗杀) assassinate **4** (侦探) spy **5** (讽刺) satirize **II** [名] sting
▷另见 cī

刺刺不休 cì cì bù xiū go on and on ◇他对此刺刺不休地说了一下午。He went on and on about it all afternoon.

刺耳 cì'ěr [形] **1** (指声音) ear-piercing **2** (喻) (指言语) jarring

刺骨 cìgǔ [动] be piercing ◇海水冰冷刺骨。The seawater was piercingly cold.

刺激 cìjī [动] **1** (指生物现象) stimulate **2** (推动) stimulate **3** (打击) provoke

刺客 cìkè [名] assassin

刺杀 cìshā [动] **1** (暗杀) assassinate **2** (拼杀) bayonet

刺探 cìtàn [动] spy ◇刺探商业情报 gather business intelligence

刺猬 cìwei [名] hedgehog

刺绣 cìxiù **I** [动] embroider **II** [名] embroidery

刺眼 cìyǎn [形] **1** (光线太强) dazzling **2** (扎眼) loud

赐 cì [动] **1** (赏赐) bestow ◇国王赐给他一箱黄金。The king bestowed a case of gold on him. **2** (敬) grant

赐教 cìjiào [动] (敬) give instructions (*pt* gave, *pp* given) ◇请高手赐教。Please give me instructions.

匆 cōng [副] hastily

匆匆 cōngcōng [形] hasty

匆促 cōngcù [形] hasty

匆忙 cōngmáng [形] hurried

葱 cōng **I** [名] spring onion **II** [形] green

葱翠 cōngcuì [形] lush green

聪 cōng **I** [名] hearing **II** [形] **1** (指听力) acute **2** (聪明) clever

聪明 cōngmíng [形] clever

从 cóng **I** [动] **1** (跟随) follow ♦从众 follow the crowd ♦从俗 follow convention **2** (顺从) comply with ♦服从 obey ◇言听计从 blindly follow **3** (从事) participate in ♦从戎 enlist **4** (采取) ◇从严治理 govern according to tougher principles ◇一切从简 do everything simply **II** [名] follower ♦仆从 attendant **III** [形] (从属) subordinate ♦从犯 accessory **IV** [介] **1** (起于) from ◇从前到后 from front to back ◇从

明天起 from tomorrow onwards ◇从山顶向远处眺望 look out into the distance from the top of the mountain ◇从东到西 from east to west **2** (经过) ◇轮船从桥下经过。The boat passed underneath the bridge. ◇飞机从我们头顶飞过。The plane passed over our heads. **V** [副] ♦从未 never ◇他从未见过大海。He's never seen the sea. ◇她从未到过苏格兰。She's never been to Scotland.

从此 cóngcǐ [副] after that ◇他们从此不再贫穷。After that they were no longer poor.

从而 cóng'ér [连] thus ◇公司决定裁员，从而削减成本。The company decided to lay people off, and thus reduce their costs.

从犯 cóngfàn [名] accessory

从军 cóngjūn [动] enlist

从来 cónglái [副] ◇我从来没去过美国。I've never been to the States. ◇她从来未说过。She never said it.

从命 cóngmìng [动] obey orders

从前 cóngqián [名] **1** (过去) ◇希望你比从前快乐。I hope you are happier than you were before. **2** (很久很久以前) once upon a time

从容 cóngróng [形] **1** (镇静) calm ◇神态从容 calm manner ◇从容应对 respond calmly **2** (宽裕) ample ◇时间从容。There's ample time.

从善如流 cóng shàn rú liú take good advice

从事 cóngshì [动] **1** (投身) undertake (*pt* undertook, *pp* undertaken) **2** (处理) deal with (*pt, pp* dealt)

从速 cóngsù [副] as soon as possible

从业 cóngyè [动] be employed ◇她从业于教育界。She is employed as a teacher.

丛 cóng **I** [动] crowd together **II** [名] **1** (指草木) thicket **2** (指人或物) crowd

丛书 cóngshū [名] series (*sg*)

淙 cóng 见下文

淙淙 cóngcóng [拟] gurgling

凑 còu [动] **1** (聚集) gather … together **2** (碰) encounter **3** (接近) approach

凑合 còuhe [动] **1** (聚集) gather … together **2** (拼凑) improvise **3** (将就) get by

凑巧 còuqiǎo [形] lucky ◇真不凑巧，没带多少现金。How unlucky – I didn't bring enough cash. ◇我凑巧也搭乘那趟火车。I happened to take the same train.

凑数 còushù [动] **1** (凑足数额) make enough ◇几个月的工资积攒下来凑数买了台电脑。My months of saving gave me enough to buy a computer. **2** (滥竽充数) make up the numbers ◇这张唱片中没有一首凑数之作。Not one song on this album is there just to make up the numbers.

粗 cū **I** [形] **1** (横剖面大) thick **2** (颗粒大) coarse **3** (指声音) gruff **4** (粗糙) crude **5** (疏忽) careless **6** (鲁莽) reckless **II** [副] sketchily ◇粗知一二 have a sketchy understanding

粗暴 cūbào [形] rough ◇他态度粗暴。He has a rough manner.

粗糙 cūcāo [形] **1** (不光滑) rough **2** (不细致) crude

粗茶淡饭 cū chá dàn fàn simple fare

粗放 cūfàng [形] extensive

粗犷 cūguǎng [形] **1** (粗野) crude **2** (粗豪) forthright

粗话 cūhuà [名] obscene language

粗粮 cūliáng [名] coarse grain

粗鲁 cūlǔ [形] crude

粗疏 cūshū [形] careless

粗俗 cūsú [形] obscene

粗心 cūxīn [形] careless

粗野 cūyě [形] rough

粗枝大叶 cū zhī dà yè slapdash

粗制滥造 cū zhì làn zào shoddy

促 cù **I** [形] urgent **II** [动] **1** (催) press ♦敦促 press **2** (靠近) be near

促成 cùchéng [动] bring about (*pt, pp* brought)

促进 cùjìn [动] promote

促使 cùshǐ [动] press for ◇促使

经济快速发展 press for speedy economic development

猝 cù [副] suddenly

猝然 cùrán [副] all of a sudden

醋 cù [名] 1 (指调味品) vinegar 2 (嫉妒) jealousy

簇 cù I [动] cluster II [量] bunch ◇一簇花 a bunch of flowers

簇新 cùxīn [形] brand new

簇拥 cùyōng [动] cluster round

蹙 cù I [形] urgent II [动] tighten ♦蹙额 knit one's brow

蹴 cù [动] 1 (踢) kick 2 (踏) tread (*pt* trod, *pp* trodden)

氽 cuān [动] blanch

镩 cuān I [名] ice pick II [动] hack

蹿 cuān [动] leap

攒 cuán [动] assemble ▷另见 zǎn

攒动 cuándòng [动] huddle together

窜 cuàn [动] 1 (乱跑) rush about 2 (改动) falsify

窜改 cuàngǎi [动] falsify

篡 cuàn [动] usurp

篡夺 cuànduó [动] usurp

篡改 cuàngǎi [动] falsify

催 cuī [动] 1 (敦促) hurry 2 (加快) speed ... up (*pt*, *pp* speeded)

催促 cuīcù [动] hurry ◇你不要老是催我。You've got to stop hurrying me all the time.

催化 cuīhuà [动] catalyze

催眠 cuīmián [动] hypnotize

摧 cuī [动] destroy

摧残 cuīcán [动] destroy

摧毁 cuīhuǐ [动] destroy

摧枯拉朽 cuī kū lā xiǔ with incredible ease

摧折 cuīzhé [动] 1 (折断) break (*pt* broke, *pp* broken) 2 (折磨) devastate ◇百姓饱受战火的摧折。The people were devastated by the war.

璀 cuǐ 见下文

璀璨 cuǐcàn [形] dazzling

脆 cuì [形] 1 (易碎) brittle 2 (指食物) crispy 3 (声音) crisp

脆弱 cuìruò [形] fragile

萃 cuì I [动] assemble II [名] gathering

萃集 cuìjí [动] cream ... off

啐 cuì [动] spit (*pt*, *pp* spat)

淬 cuì 见下文

淬火 cuìhuǒ [动] quench

瘁 cuì [形] (书) overwhelmed with work

粹 cuì I [形] pure II [名] essence

翠 cuì I [形] green II [名] jadeite

翠绿 cuìlǜ [形] emerald green

村 cūn I [名] village II [形] rustic

村落 cūnluò [名] village

村野 cūnyě I [名] countryside II [形] rustic

村庄 cūnzhuāng [名] village

皴 cūn [动] chapped

存 cún [动] 1 (存在) exist 2 (储存) store 3 (储蓄) save 4 (寄存) check ... in ◇存行李 check in one's bags 5 (保留) retain 6 (结存) be leftover ◇3年后公司净结存为零。After three years the company was left with nothing. 7 (心里怀着) harbour (英), harbor (美)

存储 cúnchǔ [动] store

存档 cúndàng [动] file

存放 cúnfàng [动] deposit ◇他将手提箱存放在朋友处。He deposited his suitcase at his friend's place.

存盘 cúnpán [动] save ◇打完文件后注意存盘。Make sure that you save your file after you've finished your keying in.

存心 cúnxīn I [动] ◇他对她存心不良。He has designs on her. II [副] deliberately ◇她存心叫我出丑。She deliberately made a fool of me.

存在 cúnzài [动] exist ◇这颗行星上可能存在生命。Life may exist on

this planet. ◇企业管理存在严重的缺陷。There are serious failings in the management of this enterprise. ◇各国政府在这个问题上存在分歧。Each country differs on this point. ◇他沉浸在往事的追忆中，忘记了我的存在。He was immersed in his recollection of the past and forgot about my existence.

存折 cúnzhé [名] passbook

寸 cùn **I** [量] *unit of length approximately 3 cm* **II** [形] tiny

寸步 cùnbù [名] tiny step

寸草不留 cùn cǎo bù liú raze to the ground

寸心 cùnxīn [名] **1** (内心) heart **2** (心意) feelings (*pl*)

搓 cuō [动] rub

磋 cuō [动] consult

磋商 cuōshāng [动] discuss

撮 cuō **I** [动] **1** (聚集) scoop ... up **2** (摘取) summarize **3** (方) (吃) grab a bite ◇上馆子撮一顿吧。Let's go to a restaurant to grab a bite to eat. **II** [量] **1** (指物) pinch ◇一撮面粉 a pinch of flour **2** (指人) clique

撮合 cuōhe [动] matchmake (*pt, pp* matchmade) ◇朋友撮合的婚姻 a marriage matchmade by friends

蹉 cuō 见下文

蹉跎 cuōtuó [动] waste time

痤 cuó 见下文

痤疮 cuóchuāng [名] acne

挫 cuò [动] **1** (挫折) defeat **2** (降低) wear ... down (*pt* wore, *pp* worn)

挫折 cuòzhé [名] setback

措 cuò [动] **1** (安排) handle **2** (筹划) make plans

措辞 cuòcí [动] diction

措施 cuòshī [名] measure ◇采取环保措施 take measures to protect the environment ◇预防措施 preventative measures

措手不及 cuò shǒu bù jí be caught off-guard

锉 cuò **I** [名] file **II** [动] file

错 cuò **I** [形] **1** (参差) interlocking **2** (不正确) incorrect **3** (糟糕) bad **II** [动] **1** (摩擦) grind (*pt, pp* ground) **2** (避开) miss ◇错过机会 miss an opportunity **3** (使不冲突) stagger ◇把上课和开会时间错开 stagger the time between classes and meetings **III** [名] fault

错爱 cuò'ài [动] (谦) ◇承蒙您错爱。You are too kind.

错怪 cuòguài [动] blame ... wrongly ◇对不起，是我错怪你了。Please accept my apologies for having wrongly blamed you.

错觉 cuòjué [名] illusion

错乱 cuòluàn [形] cluttered

错位 cuòwèi [动] displace

错误 cuòwù **I** [形] wrong **II** [名] mistake

错综复杂 cuòzōng fùzá complex ◇错综复杂的经济现象 complex economic phenomenon

Dd

耷 dā 见下文

耷拉 dāla [动] droop ◇她的眼皮耷拉着。Her eyelids were drooping.

搭 dā [动] **1** (建造) put … up (*pt*, *pp* put) ◇搭帐篷 put up a tent **2** (挂) hang (*pt*, *pp* hung) ◇我把大衣搭在胳膊上。I hung my overcoat over my arm. **3** (坐) take (*pt* took, *pp* taken) ◇他每个月搭飞机去上海。He takes the plane to Shanghai every month. ◇搭便车 get a lift **4** (连接) join ♦搭伙 join forces ◇两家公司终于搭上了关系。The two companies finally joined forces. **5** (加上) come up with (*pt* came, *pp* come) ◇再搭上点钱，我就能买辆新汽车。If I can come up with a bit more money, I'll be able to buy a new car. **6** (抬) carry ◇帮我把餐桌搭到厨房去。Help me carry the dining table into the kitchen.

搭档 dādàng **I** [名] partner **II** [动] team up ◇这个项目我和大卫搭档。I teamed up with David on the project. ◇咱们搭档开饭馆吧！ Let's open a restaurant together!

搭救 dājiù [动] rescue

搭配 dāpèi [动] **1** (安排) combine **2** (配合) pair up **3** (指语言) collocate

搭腔 dāqiāng [动] respond

答 dā [动] answer
▷另见 dá

答理 dāli [动] **1** (理睬) bother ◇她从不答理她不喜欢的人。She never bothers with people she doesn't like. ◇他性格古怪，别答理他。Don't take any notice of him – he's weird. **2** (打招呼) acknowledge ◇他跟我打招呼，我没答理他。He said hello to me, but I didn't acknowledge him.

答应 dāying [动] **1** (回答) answer **2** (同意) agree ◇我答应借他钱。I agreed to lend him money. **3** (承诺) promise

打 dá [量] dozen
▷另见 dǎ

达 dá [动] **1** (数量、目标) reach **2** (指时间) last ◇长达两个小时的报告 a report lasting two hours **3** (通) ◇这趟火车直达北京。This train is going direct to Beijing. ◇你要坐直达火车还是直达班机? Are you going by express train or direct flight? **4** (表示) express ♦转达 convey ◇请尽快把我的话转达给她。Please convey my message to her as soon as possible.

达标 dábiāo [动] reach a standard

达到 dádào [动] **1** (要求、水平、目的) achieve ◇达到目的 achieve an aim ◇达到要求 satisfy requirements **2** (指过程) reach ◇剧情达到高潮。The plot reached its climax.

达观 dáguān [形] philosophical

沓 dá [量] pile ◇一沓信 a pile of letters ◇两沓文件夹 two piles of files

答 dá [动] **1** (回答) answer ◇认真答题！ Answer the question properly! **2** (还报) repay (*pt*, *pp* repaid) ♦报答 repay ◇我怎么才能答谢你的帮助呀？ How can I repay you for all your help?
▷另见 dā

答案 dá'àn [名] answer

答辩 dábiàn [动] defend ◇法庭答辩 defend at court ◇我明天论文答辩。Tomorrow I have the viva for my thesis.

答复 dáfù [动] respond ◇等我仔细考虑后再答复你。I'll get back to you after I've thought it over. ◇这不是个令人满意的答复。This is not a satisfactory response.

答卷 dájuàn **I** [名] answer sheet **II** [动] answer exam questions

答谢 dáxiè [动] express appreciation

答疑 dáyí [动] take questions (*pt* took, *pp* taken)

打 dǎ **I** [动] **1** (指暴力) hit (*pt*, *pp* hit) ♦殴打 beat up **2** (敲) beat (*pt* beat, *pp* beaten) ◇打鼓 beat a drum

3 (破) break (*pt* broke, *pp* broken) ◇我把暖瓶给打了。I broke the Thermos flask®. **4** (发出) send (*pt*, *pp* sent) ◇打信号 send a signal ◇打电话 make a phone call ◇打手电 shine a torch **5** (做游戏) play ◇打篮球 play basketball **6** (表示动作) ♦打喷嚏 sneeze ◇小狗在雪堆里打滚。The little dog rolled about in the snow. **7** (建造) build (*pt*, *pp* built) **8** (涂抹) polish ◇鞋子得打油了。These shoes need a polish. ◇明天我要给汽车打蜡。Tomorrow I'm going to wax the car. **9** (交涉) deal with (*pt*, *pp* dealt) ◇我再也不和他打交道了。I don't want to have to deal with him any more. ◇打官司 file a lawsuit **10** (制造) make (*pt*, *pp* made) ◇打家具 make furniture **11** (搅拌) beat (*pt* beat, *pp* beaten) ◇打两个鸡蛋 beat two eggs **12** (编织) knit ◇打毛衣 knit a sweater **13** (捕捉) catch (*pt*, *pp* caught) ♦打猎 go hunting ◇他打了两只麻雀。He caught two sparrows. **14** (画) draw (*pt* drew, *pp* drawn) ◇打草稿 draw up a draft ◇他在纸上打横线。He drew horizontal lines on the paper. **15** (举) hold (*pt*, *pp* held) ◇打伞 hold an umbrella **16** (除去) get rid of **17** (买) buy (*pt*, *pp* bought) ◇请帮我去打瓶料酒。Please buy me a bottle of cooking wine. **18** (揭) open ◇打开礼物 open a present **19** (穿凿) dig (*pt*, *pp* dug) ◇打油井 dig an oil well ◇打耳洞 pierce one's ears **20** (证明、介绍信) issue **21** (舀) spoon out ◇你能帮我打碗汤吗？ Can you spoon me out a bowl of soup? **22** (收割) gather ◇打柴 gather firewood **23** (从事) do (*pt* did, *pp* done) ♦打杂儿 do odd jobs **24** (用) make (*pt*, *pp* made) ◇打比喻 make a comparison **25** (定罪名) convict ◇他被打成反动派。He was convicted of being a reactionary. **26** (捆) pack ◇打行李 pack one's bags **27** (计算) calculate ◇这笔费用应打入成本。This expenditure has to be factored into our costs. **28** (拨动) flick ◇他算盘打得很快。He's very quick with his abacus. **II** [介] from ◇打今儿起 from today ◇打这儿左转。Turn left just here.
▷另见 dá

打靶 dǎbǎ [动] practice shooting ◇打靶练习 target practice

打败 dǎbài [动] defeat

打扮 dǎban **I** [动] make oneself up **II** [名] look

打抱不平 dǎ bàobùpíng defend against an injustice

打草惊蛇 dǎ cǎo jīng shé give the game away

打岔 dǎchà [动] interrupt

打倒 dǎdǎo [动] **1** (击倒在地) knock down **2** (指口号) down with ◇打倒帝国主义！ Down with imperialism! **3** (推翻) overthrow

打的 dǎ dī [动] take a taxi (*pt* took, *pp* taken)

打点 dǎdian [动] **1** (收拾) organize ◇公司全靠他打点。The company left him to organize everything. ◇打点行装 pack one's bags **2** (贿赂) bribe

打动 dǎdòng [动] move

打赌 dǎdǔ [动] bet (*pt*, *pp* bet)

打发 dǎfa [动] **1** (时间) while away **2** (哄走) get rid of **3** (派) send (*pt*, *pp* sent)

打非 dǎfēi [动] crack down on illegal publications

打工 dǎgōng [动] temp ◇他在我们公司打了一个月的工。He temped in our company for a month. ◇打工妹 female migrant worker

打官司 dǎ guānsi [动] take legal action (*pt* took, *pp* taken)

打黑 dǎhēi [动] combat criminal organizations

打火 dǎhuǒ [动] **1** (发动) start ◇他的摩托车不打火。His motorbike wouldn't start. **2** (点燃) light (*pt*, *pp* lit)

打火机 dǎhuǒjī [名] lighter

打击 dǎjī **I** [动] crack down on **II** [名] **1** (指精神上) blow ◇高考落榜对他是一个沉重的打击。It was a major blow when he failed to pass the college entrance exams. **2** (指音乐) percussion ◇打击乐器 percussion instrument

打家劫舍 dǎ jiā jié shè loot

打假 dǎjiǎ [动] crack down on

counterfeiting ◊打假行动 a campaign to crack down on counterfeiting

打架 dǎjià [动] have a fight

打搅 dǎjiǎo [动] 1 (扰乱) disturb 2 (婉) disturb ◊对不起，打搅您一下！Sorry, may I disturb you for just a second?

打卡 dǎkǎ [动] 1 (指上班) clock in 2 (指下班) clock out 3 (付费) swipe

打开 dǎkāi [动] 1 (开启) open ◊请打开车门。Please open the car door. 2 (扩展) expand ◊打开局面 expand operations 3 (开) turn ... on ◊打开空调 turn on the air conditioning

打捞 dǎlāo [动] salvage

打量 dǎliang [动] size up

打猎 dǎliè [动] hunt

打乱 dǎluàn [动] disrupt ◊公司的计划被打乱了。The company's plans were disrupted.

打埋伏 dǎ máifu 1 (隐藏) lie in ambush 2 (隐瞒) cover-up

打破沙锅问到底 dǎpò shāguō wèn dào dǐ get to the bottom of things

打气 dǎqì [动] 1 (球、轮胎) inflate 2 (人) encourage

打趣 dǎqù [动] tease ◊别打趣我了。Don't tease me.

打拳 dǎquán [动] do shadow boxing

打扫 dǎsǎo [动] clean ◊妈妈花了整个下午在打扫厨房。Mum spent an entire afternoon cleaning the kitchen.

打手 dǎshou [名] hired thug

打算 dǎsuan I [动] plan ◊你明天打算干什么？ What are you planning to do tomorrow? II [名] plan

打听 dǎting [动] ask about

打消 dǎxiāo [动] give up (*pt* gave, *pp* given) ◊我打消了去参加晚会的念头。I gave up the idea of going to the party.

打小报告 dǎ xiǎobàogào (贬) tell tales

打雪仗 dǎ xuězhàng [动] have a snowball fight

打印 dǎyìn [动] print

打印机 dǎyìnjī [名] printer

打油诗 dǎyóushī [名] doggerel

打游击 dǎ yóujī [动] 1 (不固定) drift ◊他没有固定工作，四处打游击。He has no fixed work – he just drifts about. ◊他没钱租房子，到朋友家打游击。He doesn't have enough money to rent a flat so just drifts between friends' houses. 2 (战斗) fight a guerrilla war (*pt, pp* fought)

打杂儿 dǎ zár [动] do odd jobs

打仗 dǎzhàng [动] fight a war (*pt, pp* fought) ◊打败仗 be defeated ◊打胜仗 win a war

打招呼 dǎ zhāohu [动] 1 (问好) greet ◊他笑呵呵地和每个到场的人打招呼。He cheerily greeted everyone who came. 2 (通知) inform

打折扣 dǎ zhékòu [动] 1 (指做事情) fall short of a requirement (*pt* fell, *pp* fallen) 2 (降价) discount

大 dà [形] 1 (数量、体积、面积) big 2 (指力气) great ◊他劲儿真大！He's so strong! 3 (重要) important ◊法国是葡萄酒大国。France is an important wine-producing country. 4 (强) strong ◊大风 strong wind 5 (指声音) loud ◊音乐声太大，请关小一点。The music's too loud – could you turn it down a bit please? 6 (雨、雪) heavy ◊大雨 heavy rain 7 (指年龄) old ◊你多大了？ How old are you? ◊他比我大。He's older than me. 8 (指程度) ◊大笑 roar with laughter ◊大吃一惊 take a big shock ◊大哭 sob one's heart out 9 (老大) eldest ◊大姐 eldest sister 10 (敬) (名字、作品等) ◊请问尊姓大名？ Would you be kind enough to tell me your name? ▷另见 dài

big, large 和 **great** 都用来表示大小。一般而言, **large** 比 **big** 正式, 而 **great** 又比 **large**更为正式。**big** 和 **large** 通常用于描述物体。**big** 还表示某事物很重要或给人印象深刻。*...his influence over the big advertisers...* →

great 通常用于强调某人或某事物的重要性。*...the great artist, Van Gogh...* **great** 还可以暗示某事物因其大小而给人深刻的印象。*The great bird of prey soared into the sky.*
表示数量大可以用 **large** 或 **great**, 但不能用 **big**。*...a large amount of blood on the floor... the arrival of tourists in great numbers...* **big** 和 **great** 都可用于表示程度, **great** 比 **big** 更正式。*Most of them act like big fools... It gives me great pleasure to welcome you.* 注意, **great** 除了表示大小外还有其他的含义, 比如它可以表示某事物很独特, 非常好, 或很有趣。

大本营 dàběnyíng [名] base

大不了 dàbùliǎo I [副] at the worst II [形] serious ◇没考好没什么大不了，再努力点就是了。If you don't do well in your exams it's not serious – you'll just have to work a bit harder.

大步流星 dà bù liú xīng at a stride ◇老师大步流星地走进教室。The teacher came striding into the classroom.

大材小用 dà cái xiǎo yòng waste of talent

大吹大擂 dà chuī dà léi make a great noise

大打出手 dà dǎ chūshǒu come to blows

大胆 dàdǎn [形] bold

大刀阔斧 dà dāo kuò fǔ boldly

大抵 dàdǐ [副] generally

大地 dàdì [名] the land

大动干戈 dà dòng gāngē make a big fuss

大凡 dàfán [副] generally speaking

大方 dàfang [形] **1** (慷慨) generous **2** (不拘束) natural **3** (不俗气) tasteful ◇她穿着文雅大方。She dresses tastefully and elegantly.

大概 dàgài I [名] general idea II [形] approximate III [副] probably

大纲 dàgāng [名] outline

大公无私 dà gōng wú sī impartial

大功告成 dà gōng gào chéng complete successfully

大锅饭 dàguōfàn [名] extreme egalitarianism

大海捞针 dà hǎi lāo zhēn look for a needle in a haystack

大亨 dàhēng [名] magnate

大户 dàhù [名] important customer

大伙儿 dàhuǒr [代] everybody ◇我们大伙儿一起做饭。Everybody cooks together.

大惑不解 dà huò bù jiě be very puzzled

大家 dàjiā I [名] master ◇国画大家 a master of traditional Chinese painting II [代] everybody ◇大家都很喜欢这部电影。Everyone really likes this film. ◇大家都认为她是个好老师。Everybody thought she was a good teacher. ◇大家都会上网吗？Does everybody know how to get on to the Internet? ◇我们大家必须继续努力。We must all keep on trying.

大惊小怪 dà jīng xiǎo guài make a mountain out of a molehill

大局 dàjú [名] overall picture

大举 dàjǔ [形] large-scale

大快人心 dà kuài rén xīn to everybody's satisfaction

大款 dàkuǎn [名] (贬) moneybags (*sg*)

大理石 dàlǐshí [名] marble

大量 dàliàng [形] **1** (数量多) large amount of ◇这家公司吸引了大量的资金。This company attracted a large amount of investment. ◇公司准备大量裁员。The company is preparing to lay off a large number of people. **2** (气量大) generous ◇宽宏大量 broadminded

大陆 dàlù [名] **1** (指各大洲) continent ◇亚洲大陆 the Asian continent **2** (指中国) the mainland ◇中国大陆 mainland China

大路货 dàlùhuò [名] basic goods (*pl*)

大名 dàmíng [名] **1** (名字) full name **2** (名气) great reputation

大名鼎鼎 dàmíng dǐngdǐng

celebrated

大模大样 dà mú dà yàng haughtily

大逆不道 dà nì bù dào traitorous

大年 dànián [名] (丰年) bumper year

大排档 dàpáidàng [名] (方) market ◊夜间大排挡 night market

大牌 dàpái I [形] hotshot ◊大牌影星 hotshot movie star II [名] 1 (品牌) famous brand 2 (威风) airs and graces (*pl*)

大盘 dàpán [名] market index

大片 dàpiān [名] blockbuster

大起大落 dà qǐ dà luò wild fluctuations ◊股票价格大起大落。 Share prices are fluctuating wildly.

大气 dàqì I [名] 1 (气体) atmosphere 2 (呼吸) heavy breathing II [形] open-minded

大气候 dàqìhòu [名] climate

大器晚成 dà qì wǎn chéng great talent takes time to develop ◊她是位大器晚成的作家。She's a writer who will take time to develop.

大千世界 dàqiān-shìjiè the boundless universe

大人 dàren [名] adult

大赦 dàshè [动] amnesty

大失所望 dà shī suǒ wàng to one's great disappointment

大师 dàshī [名] master

大师傅 dàshifu [名] head chef

大使 dàshǐ [名] ambassador

大事 dàshì I [名] important event II [副] greatly

大势所趋 dàshì suǒ qū in tune with the general trend

大手笔 dàshǒubǐ [名] 1 (作品) masterpiece 2 (作家) well-known writer

大手大脚 dà shǒu dà jiǎo be extravagant ◊他花钱大手大脚的。He's very extravagant with money.

大提琴 dàtíqín [名] cello

大体 dàtǐ I [名] fundamental principle II [副] more or less ◊两国意见大体一致。The opinions of the two countries are more or less the same.

大庭广众 dà tíng guǎng zhòng in broad daylight

大同小异 dà tóng xiǎo yì much the same ◊他的新书和上本书大同小异。His new book is much the same as his last one.

大腕 dàwàn [名] big name ◊大腕级导演 a big-name director ◊他是歌坛的大腕。He's a big name in the singing world.

大喜过望 dà xǐ guò wàng pleased beyond expectation ◊她没有想到会得到这份工作，因此她大喜过望。She never thought she'd get the job, and so was pleased beyond all expectation.

大显身手 dà xiǎn shēnshǒu use one's talents to the full

大相径庭 dà xiāng jìngtíng as different as chalk and cheese

大小 dàxiǎo I [名] 1 (尺寸) size 2 (辈分) seniority ◊这女孩子说话真没大小！ The way this girl talks is so disrespectful! ◊全校不分大小，公平竞争。There are no distinctions of seniority at all on this campus – everyone competes on an equal footing. 3 (人口) people (*pl*) ◊全家大小共三口人。There are three people in my family altogether. 4 (大的和小的) total ◊我市大小超市有上百家。Our city has a total of over one hundred supermarkets. II [副] anyway ◊他大小是个经理，说话算数。Anyway, he's a manager so it's his word that counts.

大写 dàxiě I [名] 1 (指字母) capital letter 2 (指数字) *Chinese numeral written in full form* II [动] write in capitals (*pt* wrote, *pp* written)

大兴土木 dà xīng tǔmù carry out major building works

大型 dàxíng [形] large-scale ◊大型企业 large-scale enterprises ◊大型艺术展 large-scale art exhibition

大选 dàxuǎn [名] general election

大学 dàxué [名] university (英), college (美) ◊大学毕业 graduate from university (英) 或 college (美) ◊上大学 go to university (英) 或 college (美)

大学生 dàxuéshēng [名] university (英) 或 college (美) student

大雪 dàxuě [名] heavy snow ◊昨天下了场大雪。It snowed heavily yesterday.

大雅 dàyǎ [名] elegance

大言不惭 dà yán bù cán brag shamelessly

大意 dàyì [名] general idea

大意 dàyi [形] careless

大有作为 dà yǒu zuòwéi make the most of one's abilities

大雨 dàyǔ [名] downpour

大约 dàyuē [副] **1** (指数量) approximately ◊我大约有200块钱。I have approximately 200 yuan. **2** (可能) probably ◊他大约在上网。He's probably on the Internet.

大杂烩 dàzáhuì [名] **1** (指事物) mishmash **2** (指食物) hotchpotch

大张旗鼓 dà zhāng qí gǔ with great fanfare

大丈夫 dàzhàngfu [名] true man (*pl* men)

大致 dàzhì [副] **1** (大体上) approximately ◊两个人的水平大致相同。They are both at approximately the same level. **2** (大约) probably ◊他看上去大致20岁。By the look of him he's probably around 20 years old.

大众 dàzhòng [名] the people (*pl*) ◊大众文学 popular literature ◊大众品味 popular tastes

大众化 dàzhònghuà [名] popularization

大自然 dàzìrán [名] nature

大作 dàzuò [名] (敬) masterpiece

呆 dāi **I** [形] **1** (傻) slow-witted **2** (发愣) blank **3** (吓、惊) dumbstruck **II** [动] stay

呆板 dāibǎn [形] stiff

呆若木鸡 dāi ruò mù jī dumbstruck

呆账 dāizhàng [名] bad debt

呆子 dāizi [名] fool ◊书呆子 bookworm ◊他真是个呆子！He's such a fool!

待 dāi [动] stay ◊你再多待一会儿。Do stay a little longer. ◊她成天待在家里。She stays at home all day.

歹 dǎi [形] evil

歹毒 dǎidú [形] vicious

歹徒 dǎitú [名] gangster

逮 dǎi [动] catch (*pt, pp* caught) ▷另见 dài

大 dài 见下文

大夫 dàifu [名] doctor ▷另见 dà

代 dài **I** [动] **1** (替) do … on behalf of ◊经理病了，经理助理代他在会上发言。As the manager was ill, his assistant spoke on his behalf. ◊我代她在合同上签了字。I signed the contract on her behalf. **2** (指问候) ◊你见到他时，代我问好。When you see him, say hello from me. **3** (代理) act as ◊代校长 acting headmaster **II** [名] **1** (时代) times (*pl*) ♦古代 ancient times **2** (辈分) generation **3** (朝代) dynasty

代办 dàibàn [动] take … over (*pt* took, *pp* taken)

代笔 dàibǐ [动] write on behalf of (*pt* wrote, *pp* written) ◊我为他代笔写申请信。I wrote the application on his behalf.

代表 dàibiǎo **I** [名] representative ◊谈判代表 the delegate to the negotiations **II** [动] **1** (代替) stand in for (*pt, pp* stood) ◊副主任代表主任主持会议。The deputy director stood in for the director as chair of the meeting. **2** (委托) represent ◊他全权代表我们公司。He has full authority to represent our company. **3** (指意义、概念) be representative of ◊他的诗代表了时代精神。His poem is representative of the spirit of the age. **III** [形] archetypal ◊达芬奇是文艺复兴时期的代表人物。Da Vinci was an archetypal Renaissance figure.

代词 dàicí [名] pronoun

代沟 dàigōu [名] generation gap

代号 dàihào [名] code name

代价 dàijiàn [名] cost

代劳 dàiláo [动] help … out ◇打印的事就请您代劳了！ Could you help me out with the printing?

代理 dàilǐ [动] 1 (暂时替代) act on behalf of ◇代理经理 acting manager ◇代理校长 acting headmaster 2 (委托) represent

代理人 dàilǐrén [名] agent

代码 dàimǎ [名] code

代数 dàishù [名] algebra

代替 dàitì [动] substitute for

代谢 dàixiè [动] metabolize

代言人 dàiyánrén [名] spokesperson

玳 dài 见下文

玳瑁 dàimào [名] tortoiseshell

带 dài I [名] 1 (长条物) strap ♦皮带 leather belt ♦磁带 cassette ♦录像带 videotape 2 (轮胎) tyre (英), tire (美) ♦车带 car tyre (英) 或 tire (美) 3 (区域) zone ♦热带 the tropics ◇长江一带 the Yangtze region II [动] 1 (携带) take (*pt* took, *pp* taken) ◇别忘了带钱包！ Don't forget to take your wallet! 2 (捎带) ◇你出去时带点牛奶回来，好吗？ Can you buy some milk when you're out? ◇你去邮局时，能帮我带几张邮票吗？ If you're going to the post office, could you get me some stamps? 3 (呈现) wear (*pt* wore, *pp* worn) ◇面带笑容 wear a smile on one's face 4 (含有) have (*pt*, *pp* had) ◇这些豆子稍带苦味儿。These beans have a slightly bitter taste. ◇他这么说，是话里带刺儿。His remarks smacked of sarcasm. 5 (连带) come with (*pt* came, *pp* come) ◇买电脑，带免费打印机。When you buy a computer the printer comes free. ◇这本书带免费光盘吗？ Does the book come with a free CD? 6 (指导) direct ◇老教授带着两个博士生。The old professor was supervising two doctoral students. 7 (领) lead (*pt*, *pp* led) ◇她带着一组学生去野营。She led a group of students on a camping expedition. 8 (养) bring … up (*pt*, *pp* brought) ◇她是由奶奶带大的。She was brought up by her grandmother. 9 (带动) inspire ◇他带得我也爱运动了。He inspired my love of sport.

带动 dàidòng [动] 1 (指进步) drive (*pt* drove, *pp* driven) ◇高科技带动社会进步。Technology drives social progress. 2 (指机械动力) power

带劲 dàijìn [形] 1 (指兴致) interesting 2 (形容情绪高昂) energetic ◇他的演讲很带劲。He gave an impassioned speech.

带领 dàilǐng [动] 1 (领着) guide 2 (指挥) lead (*pt*, *pp* led)

带头 dàitóu [动] take the initiative (*pt* took, *pp* taken) ◇他带头捐书给图书馆。He took the initiative in donating books to the library.

待 dài [动] 1 (对待) treat ♦优待 treat 2 (招待) entertain 3 (等待) wait for ◇这个问题有待解决。This problem will have to wait for a solution.

待命 dàimìng [动] await orders

待人接物 dài rén jiē wù people skills

待业 dàiyè [动] be unemployed ◇待业青年 unemployed youth

待遇 dàiyù [名] pay

贷 dài I [动] 1 (指银行) lend (*pt*, *pp* lent) ◇银行贷给公司一笔款。The bank lent money to the company. 2 (指借钱方) take out a loan (*pt* took, *pp* taken) ◇公司向银行贷了一笔款。The company took out a loan from the bank. II [名] loan

贷款 dàikuǎn I [动] lend (*pt*, *pp* lent) ◇他向银行贷款买房。He took out a loan from the bank to buy a house. ◇这次银行拒绝贷款给他。The bank refused to lend him money this time. II [名] loan

怠 dài [形] 1 (懒惰) lazy 2 (不恭敬) disrespectful

怠工 dàigōng [动] go slow (*pt* went, *pp* gone)

怠慢 dàimàn I [动] slight ◇他怠慢了客人。He slighted the guests. II [形] (谦) remiss ◇如有怠慢之处，请多包涵。If I have been at all remiss, please accept my full apologies.

袋 dài I [名] bag II [量] bag

袋鼠 dàishǔ [名] kangaroo

逮 dài [动] capture
▷另见 dǎi

逮捕 dàibǔ [动] arrest

戴 dài [动] **1** (眼镜、帽子、小装饰品等) wear (*pt* wore, *pp* worn) **2** (拥护尊敬) support

戴罪立功 dài zuì lì gōng atone for one's crimes

丹 dān **I** [形] red **II** [名] pellet ◇灵丹妙药 panacea

丹青 dānqīng [名] (书) painting

丹心 dānxīn [名] loyalty

单 dān **I** [形] **1** (一个) single ◇单人床 single bed **2** (奇数) odd **3** (单独) solitary **4** (不复杂) simple **5** (薄弱) weak **6** (衣、裤) thin **II** [副] only ◇成功不能单凭运气。To be successful you can't rely only on luck. **III** [名] **1** (单子) sheet ◇床单 bed sheet **2** (列表) list ♦菜单 menu

单薄 dānbó [形] **1** (穿得少) flimsy **2** (瘦弱) frail **3** (薄弱) weak

单车 dānchē [名] (方) (自行车) bicycle

单程 dānchéng [名] single

单纯 dānchún **I** [形] simple **II** [副] merely ◇单纯地注入资金是无法挽救公司的. A mere cash injection isn't going to save the company.

单词 dāncí [名] word

单打 dāndǎ [名] singles (*pl*) ◇乒乓球女子单打 the women's table-tennis singles

单单 dāndān [副] only ◇别人都懂了，单单他不明白。The others all understood – only he didn't get it.

单调 dāndiào [形] monotonous

单独 dāndú [形] **1** (独自) alone **2** (独立) unaided ◇我能单独处理这事。I can handle this by myself.

单杠 dāngàng [名] horizontal bar

单价 dānjià [名] unit price

单间 dānjiān [名] separate room

单据 dānjù [名] receipt

单枪匹马 dān qiāng pǐ mǎ single-handedly

单亲 dānqīn [名] single parent ◇他来自单亲家庭。He comes from a single-parent family.

单身 dānshēn [名] single ♦单身汉 bachelor

单数 dānshù [名] **1** (指数字) odd number **2** (指词) singular ◇名词的单数形式 the singular form of the noun

单位 dānwèi [名] **1** (指标准量) unit ◇以平方米为测量单位 use square metres as the unit of measurement ◇单位人口密度 population density by area **2** (机构) unit ◇事业单位 work unit

单相思 dānxiāngsī [名] unrequited love

单一 dānyī [形] single

单音词 dānyīncí [名] monosyllabic word

单元 dānyuán [名] unit ◇单元房 self-contained flat (英) 或 apartment (美)

单子 dānzi [名] **1** (指床上用品) sheet **2** (列表) list

担 dān [动] **1** (挑) carry … on one's shoulder **2** (负) take … on (*pt* took, *pp* taken) ◇担起责任 take on a responsibility
▷另见 dàn

担保 dānbǎo [动] guarantee ◇他为我做担保。He acted as my guarantor. ◇我能担保产品质量。I can vouch for the quality of the product.

担待 dāndài [动] **1** (原谅) forgive (*pt* forgave, *pp* forgiven) **2** (负责) take responsibility (*pt* took, *pp* taken) ◇出了事儿， 她会担待的。If anything goes wrong, she will take responsibility for it.

担当 dāndāng [动] take … on (*pt* took, *pp* taken) ◇他勇于担当重任。He has the courage to take on important tasks.

担负 dānfù [动] shoulder

担架 dānjià [名] stretcher

担任 dānrèn [动] hold the post of (*pt*, *pp* held) ◇她担任经理助理。She holds the post of manager's assistant.

担心 dānxīn [动] worry ◇他担心母

亲的身体。He worried about his mother's health.

耽 dān 见下文

耽搁 dānge [动] **1** (拖延) delay ◇这事儿不能再耽搁了。This cannot be delayed any further. **2** (停留) stay ◇我不能在这儿再耽搁了。I can't stay here any longer.

耽误 dānwu [动] delay ◇因为机械故障， 耽误了飞机的起飞。The flight was delayed because of a mechanical fault. ◇别耽误时间！Don't waste time!

胆 dǎn [名] **1** (指器官) gall bladder **2** (胆量) courage **3** (指器皿) liner

胆敢 dǎngǎn [动] dare

胆固醇 dǎngùchún [名] cholesterol

胆量 dǎnliàng [名] guts (*pl*)

胆怯 dǎnqiè [形] timid

胆识 dǎnshí [名] courage and insight

胆战心惊 dǎn zhàn xīn jīng be scared out of one's wits

胆子 dǎnzi [名] guts (*pl*) ◇他胆子不小。He's got such guts.

掸 dǎn [动] brush

掸子 dǎnzi [名] duster

旦 dàn [名] **1** (书) (早晨) dawn **2** (天) day

旦夕 dànxī [名] short while ◇危在旦夕 in imminent danger

但 dàn **I** [连] but ◇她不很聪明，但很努力。She wasn't very clever, but she was very hardworking. ◇他有驾照，但没有车。He has a driver's licence, but no car. **II** [副] only ♦但愿 wish ◇晴空万里，但见骄阳。In the clear and boundless sky all you could see was the blazing sun.

但凡 dànfán [副] ◇但凡星期天，她都去游泳。She goes swimming every Sunday. ◇但凡中国人，都知道孔子。All Chinese people know about Confucius.

但是 dànshì [连] but ◇工作很忙，但是她还坚持锻炼。She was very busy at work, but she managed to stick to her exercise regime. ◇虽然下雨，但是不冷。Even though it's raining, it's not cold.

担 dàn **I** [名] load **II** [量] ◇一担水 two buckets of water
▷另见 dān

担子 dànzi [名] **1** (扁担) shoulder pole **2** (责任) responsibility

诞 dàn **I** [动] be born **II** [名] birthday **III** [形] absurd

诞辰 dànchén [名] birthday

诞生 dànshēng [动] be born ◇新一代手机诞生了。A new generation of mobile phones was born.

淡 dàn [形] **1** (指味道浓淡) weak **2** (指咸淡) bland **3** (颜色浅) light **4** (稀薄) light **5** (不热情) indifferent **6** (不红火) slack ◇最近生意很清淡。Business has been very slack lately.

淡泊 dànbó [动] (书) be unconcerned about

淡薄 dànbó [形] **1** (不浓厚) indifferent **2** (模糊) faint **3** (密度小) thin

淡化 dànhuà [动] **1** (指观念、感情、问题等) water down ◇淡化政治 watered-down politics **2** (水) desalinate ◇海水淡化工程 sea water desalination project

淡季 dànjì [名] low season ◇旅游淡季 the low tourist season ◇现在是西瓜的淡季。Watermelons are currently out of season.

淡漠 dànmò [形] **1** (冷淡) indifferent **2** (记忆、印象) faded

淡然 dànrán [形] (书) indifferent

淡然处之 dànrán chǔ zhī be unruffled ◇面对困难，他淡然处之。He was unruffled in the face of difficulty.

淡忘 dànwàng [动] fade from memory

蛋 dàn [名] **1** (卵) egg ♦鸡蛋 egg **2** (球状物) ball ♦鱼蛋 fish ball

蛋白质 dànbáizhì [名] protein

蛋糕 dàngāo [名] cake

弹 dàn [名] **1** (弹子) pellet **2** (子弹) bullet **3** (炸弹) bomb ♦原子弹 atomic bomb
▷另见 tán

弹丸 dànwán [名] **1** (丸) pellet **2** (书) (狭小之地) tiny place

弹药 dànyào [名] ammunition

氮 dàn [名] nitrogen

当 dāng **I** [助动] should ◊你有问题，当问就问。If you have questions that should be raised, then raise them. **II** [介] **1** (向) in front of ♦当众 in public ◊老师当着全班批评了班长 。The teacher criticized the class monitor in front of the whole class. **2** (正在) ◊当我们到时，电影已开始了。When we arrived the film had already started. ◊当他在美国时，他爷爷去世了。His grandfather passed away while he was in America. **III** [动] **1** (担任) act as ◊当经理 act as manager **2** (承当) deserve ◊不敢当！ I don't deserve it! **3** (掌管) be in charge ♦当家 rule the roost **4** (相当) match ◊门当户对 be well-matched **IV** [拟] **1** (指金属敲击声) chime ◊当当的钟声 the chiming of the bell **2** (指敲门声) knock
▷另见 dàng

当场 dāngchǎng [副] there and then ◊经理当场签了合同。The manager signed the contract there and then.

当初 dāngchū [名] those days ◊当初他俩就不和。Even in those days they didn't get on.

当代 dāngdài [名] the present ◊当代文学 contemporary literature

当道 dāngdào **I** [名] the middle of the road **II** [动] (贬) hold power (*pt, pp* held)

当地 dāngdì [名] locality ◊我在当地买了一所房子。I bought a house in the locality. ◊当地风俗 local customs

当机立断 dāng jī lì duàn make an on-the-spot decision

当即 dāngjí [副] immediately

当家 dāngjiā [动] rule the roost

当今 dāngjīn [名] the present

当局 dāngjú [名] authorities (*pl*)

当令 dānglìng [动] be in season ◊葡萄正当令。Grapes are currently in season.

当面 dāngmiàn [动] do … face to face ◊当面讨论 have a face-to-face discussion

当年 dāngnián **I** [名] **1** those days ◊想当年，我们都很幼稚。Thinking back to those days, we were all so naïve. **II** [动] be in the prime of one's life ◊三十多岁是男人正当年的时候。A man is in his prime when he's in his thirties.

当前 dāngqián **I** [动] be faced with **II** [名] present ◊当前的目标 the present aim

当权 dāngquán [动] hold power (*pt, pp* held)

当然 dāngrán **I** [副] of course ◊ "能帮个忙吗？" "当然可以！" Can you help me? – Of course!" ◊坐公共汽车当然要买票。Of course you have to buy a ticket if you want to take the bus. **II** [形] natural ◊你不努力，成绩差是当然的。If you don't work hard, it's only natural that you'll get low marks.

当仁不让 dāng rén bù ràng not shirk responsibility

当时 dāngshí [名] ◊他当时不知道犯了法。At the time he didn't know he'd broken the law. ◊我当时高兴极了。I was ecstatic at the time.

当头 dāngtóu [动] **1** (迎头) take … in the face (*pt* took, *pp* taken) ◊当头一拳 take a punch in the face **2** (在眼前) confront **3** (放在首位) prioritize ◊生意人是利字当头。Businesspeople prioritize profit above all else.

当务之急 dāng wù zhī jí top priority ◊我们的当务之急是解决资金问题。Our top priority is to resolve the issue of funding.

当心 dāngxīn [动] be careful

当选 dāngxuǎn [动] be elected ◊他当选为新一届主席。He was elected as the new chairman.

当政 dāngzhèng [动] be in power ◊他当政时，国泰民安。When he was in power the state was prosperous and the people were at peace.

当之无愧 dāng zhī wú kuì fully deserve ◊他是当之无愧的好领导。

He fully deserved the title of good leader.

当中 dāngzhōng [名] **1** (中间) ◇几个人当中，只有我信任她。Out of a number of people, I was the only one who believed her. ◇讨论当中，他言辞激烈。During the discussion he spoke forcefully. **2** (正中间) the centre (英) 或 center (美) ◇他站在舞台当中。He stood in the centre of the stage.

当众 dāngzhòng [副] publicly

挡 dǎng **I** [动] **1** (拦) keep off (*pt*, *pp* kept) ◇请别挡路! Keep off the road! **2** (遮蔽) shelter from **II** [名] (排挡) gear

挡箭牌 dǎngjiànpái [名] excuse

党 dǎng [名] **1** (政党) party **2** (集团) faction

党派 dǎngpài [名] clique

党羽 dǎngyǔ [名] (贬) adherents (*pl*)

当 dàng **I** [形] appropriate ♦妥当 appropriate ◇用词不当 an inappropriate choice of words **II** [动] **1** (作为) treat … as ◇我把妈妈当作最好的朋友。I treat my mother like my best friend. **2** (认为) assume ◇我当你明白了。I assumed you'd understood. **3** (抵押) pawn ◇他把手表给当了。He pawned his watch. **4** (指时间和地点) ♦当天 that day ♦当场 on the spot
▷另见 dāng

当年 dàngnián [名] that same year

当铺 dàngpù [名] pawnshop

当时 dàngshí [名] ◇他当时就在合同上签了字。He signed the contract there and then. ◇接到他的短信，我当时就给他回了电话。I called him back as soon as I received his text.

当天 dàngtiān [名] the same day ◇我明天去天津，当天就回来。I'm going to Tianjin tomorrow, and returning the same day.

当真 dàngzhēn **I** [动] take … seriously (*pt* took, *pp* taken) ◇别把他的话当真！ Don't take what he said seriously! **II** [形] serious **III** [副] really ◇他当真辞职了？ Did he really resign?

当作 dàngzuò [动] regard … as ◇人们经常把狗当作最忠实的朋友。People often regard dogs as their most loyal friends.

荡 dàng **I** [动] **1** (摇摆) sway **2** (闲逛) loaf about **3** (清除) clear … away **II** [形] **1** (广阔) vast **2** (放纵) loose in morals

荡妇 dàngfù [名] tart

荡气回肠 dàng qì huí cháng soul-stirring

荡然无存 dàngrán wú cún completely disappear

荡漾 dàngyàng [动] undulate

档 dàng [名] **1** (档案) file **2** (等级) grade

档案 dàng'àn [名] files (*pl*)

档次 dàngcì [名] grade

刀 dāo [名] **1** (指工具) knife (*pl* knives) **2** (刀状物) blade

刀枪 dāoqiāng [名] weapons (*pl*)

刀刃 dāorèn [名] **1** (字) knife edge **2** (喻) the most vital thing ◇他总能把钱花在刀刃上。He always spends his money on vital things.

刀山火海 dāo shān huǒ hǎi extremely dangerous place

叨 dāo 见下文

叨唠 dāolao [动] prattle on ◇别为了一点小事就叨唠。You really shouldn't prattle on about something so trivial.

导 dǎo [动] **1** (引导) guide ♦导游 guide **2** (传导) conduct **3** (开导) give guidance (*pt* gave, *pp* given) **4** (导演) direct

导播 dǎobō **I** [动] produce **II** [名] director

导弹 dǎodàn [名] missile

导电 dǎodiàn [动] conduct electricity

导购 dǎogòu [动] give shopping advice (*pt* gave, *pp* given) ◇导购小姐 salesgirl

导航 dǎoháng [动] navigate ◇雷达导航系统 radar navigation system

导火线 dǎohuǒxiàn [名] **1** (字) fuse **2** (喻) trigger

导论 dǎolùn [名] introduction

导师 dǎoshī [名] **1** (字) tutor **2** (喻) mentor

导体 dǎotǐ [名] conductor

导向 dǎoxiàng **I** [名] guidance **II** [动] lead to (*pt, pp* led)

导演 dǎoyǎn **I** [动] direct **II** [名] director

导游 dǎoyóu **I** [动] guide **II** [名] tour guide

导致 dǎozhì [动] lead to (*pt, pp* led) ◇首相的决定导致了暴动。The prime minister's decision led to rioting. ◇粗心导致她没考好。Because of her carelessness she failed the exam.

岛 dǎo [名] island ♦岛国 island nation ♦半岛 peninsula

岛屿 dǎoyǔ [名] islands (*pl*)

倒 dǎo **I** [动] **1** (横躺) fall (*pt* fell, *pp* fallen) ♦摔倒 fall down ♦卧倒 lie down ◇我倒在床上就睡。I collapsed into bed and fell asleep immediately. **2** (失败) fail ♦倒闭 go bankrupt ♦击倒竞争对手 beat a rival competitor **3** (食欲) spoil ◇倒胃口 lose one's appetite **4** (换) change ◇倒班 change shifts **5** (倒买倒卖) speculate **6** (嗓子) lose ◇歌唱家的嗓子倒了。The singer lost her voice. **II** [名] (贬) wheeler-dealer
▷另见 dào

倒闭 dǎobì [动] go bankrupt

倒戈 dǎogē [动] swap sides

倒买倒卖 dǎo mǎi dǎo mài speculate

倒霉 dǎoméi [形] unlucky

倒手 dǎoshǒu [动] **1** (换手) swap hands ◇他倒着手拎行李。He swapped the suitcase from one hand to the other. **2** (买卖货物) change hands

倒塌 dǎotā [动] collapse

倒台 dǎotái [动] fall from power (*pt* fell, *pp* fallen) ◇保守党政府倒台了。The Conservative government fell from power.

倒腾 dǎoteng [动] **1** (买进卖出) deal in (*pt, pp* dealt) ◇他在倒腾香烟。He deals in cigarettes. **2** (翻腾) rummage around

倒胃口 dǎowèikou [动] **1** (指食欲) lose one's appetite (*pt, pp* lost) **2** (使人生厌) put … off (*pt, pp* put) ◇他的所作所为让人倒胃口。People were really put off by what he had done.

捣 dǎo [动] **1** (捶打) crush **2** (搅乱) make trouble

捣鬼 dǎoguǐ [动] make mischief

捣毁 dǎohuǐ [动] destroy

捣乱 dǎoluàn [动] **1** (扰乱) disturb **2** (制造麻烦) make trouble

祷 dǎo [动] pray

祷告 dǎogào [动] pray

蹈 dǎo [动] **1** (跳动) skip ♦舞蹈 dancing **2** (书) (踩) tread (*pt* trod, *pp* trodden)

到 dào **I** [动] **1** (达到) arrive ◇火车到了。The train has arrived. ◇我是昨天到上海的。I arrived in Shanghai yesterday. ◇到点了，起床！ Time to get up! **2** (去) go (*pt* went, *pp* gone) ◇我到厦门旅游。I'm going to Xiamen on a tour. **3** (用作动词的补语) ◇听到这个消息我很吃惊。When I heard the news I was very surprised. ◇老师没想到我们会来医院看他。Our teacher hadn't imagined we would visit him in hospital. ◇真想不到他会离婚。I never would have thought he'd get divorced. ◇你的要求我办不到。I can't handle your demands. **II** [形] (周到) considerate

到处 dàochù [名] all places (*pl*) ◇这种植物到处都有。You can find this kind of plant everywhere.

到达 dàodá [动] arrive

到底 dàodǐ **I** [动] ◇坚持到底 keep going until the end ◇把改革进行到底 carry through reforms **II** [副] **1** (究竟) ◇你到底在干什么？ What on earth are you up to? ◇你到底还想不想上大学？ Do you actually want to go to university? **2** (毕竟) after all ◇他到底还只是个孩子。After all, he's still just a kid. **3** (终于) at last

到家 dàojiā [形] perfect

到位 dàowèi I [动] be in place ◇资金已经到位。The money is already in place. ◇货物一次到位。The goods will be sent in one go. II [形] precise ◇他回答得很到位。He answered very precisely.

到职 dàozhí [动] take office (*pt* took, *pp* taken)

倒 dào I [动] **1** (颠倒) ◇倒数第一 the very last ◇老师倒着点名。The teacher did the roll call in reverse order. ◇他把地图挂倒了。He hung the map up upside down. ◇姓和名写倒了。The first name and surname were written the wrong way round. **2** (后退) reverse ◇倒车 reverse a car **3** (倾倒) empty out ◇倒垃圾 empty the rubbish out ◇我来给您倒杯茶。Let me pour you a cup of tea. ◇在会上，他把所有的想法都倒了出来。He poured out all his ideas at the meeting. II [副] **1** (表示意料之外) unexpectedly **2** (反而) instead ◇她没哭，倒笑了。She didn't cry, but laughed instead. **3** (表示让步) though ◇这房子地段倒好，就是太小。Although the location of the house is good, it's still too small. ◇这部手提电脑新倒是新，就是太沉。Even though this laptop is new, it's just too heavy. **4** (表示转折) ◇他其貌不扬，倒是很聪明。He's not very attractive, but he's clever. ◇这包不漂亮，倒很实用。This bag isn't very smart, but it's practical. **5** (表示不耐烦) ◇你倒快点走啊！ Can you go a bit faster? ◇你倒是说呀！Can you get on with it please! **6** (表示责怪) ◇他说得倒漂亮，从没见他兑现过。He's all talk – he never lives up to his promises.
▷另见 dǎo

倒彩 dàocǎi [名] booing ◇喝倒彩 boo

倒插门 dàochāmén I [动] live off one's wife's family II [名] *son-in-law living off his wife's family*

倒打一耙 dào dǎ yī pá hit back unfairly ◇他倒打一耙，要求赔偿。He hit back with an unfair demand for compensation.

倒挂 dàoguà [动] **1** (颠倒地挂) hang ... upside down (*pt, pp* hung) **2** (价格等) be topsy-turvy ◇市场价与出厂价倒挂。The market prices are topsy-turvy in relation to factory prices.

倒立 dàolì [动] **1** (物) be upside down **2** (人) do a handstand

倒计时 dàojìshí [动] count down ◇奥运会进入了倒计时阶段。The countdown to the Olympics has begun.

倒贴 dàotiē [动] lose money unexpectedly (*pt, pp* lost)

倒退 dàotuì [动] go back (*pt* went, *pp* gone) ◇倒退5年，他只是个学徒。Going back five years, he was still a trainee. ◇她被吓得倒退了几步。She was so shocked that she had to take a few steps back.

倒影 dàoyǐng [名] reflection

倒置 dàozhì [动] reverse

悼 dào [动] mourn

悼词 dàocí [名] eulogy

悼念 dàoniàn [动] mourn

盗 dào I [动] rob ♦盗窃 steal II [名] robber ♦海盗 pirate

盗版 dàobǎn I [动] pirate ◇盗版软件 pirated software II [名] pirate copy

盗匪 dàofěi [名] robber

盗汗 dàohàn [名] night sweat

盗墓 dàomù [动] rob tombs

盗窃 dàoqiè [动] steal (*pt* stole, *pp* stolen)

盗用 dàoyòng [动] misappropriate

盗贼 dàozéi [名] thieves (*pl*)

道 dào I [名] **1** (路) road ♦近道 shortcut **2** (方法) way ◇生财之道 the road to riches **3** (德) morals **4** (技艺) art ♦茶道 tea ceremony **5** (道教) the Tao **6** (线) line ◇横道儿 horizontal line **7** (水流途径) channel ♦下水道 sewer II [量] **1** (用于长条形物体) ◇一道阳光 a beam of sunlight ◇两道泪痕 two tear streaks **2** (门、墙等) ◇第二道门 the second door ◇一道墙 a wall **3** (题目、命令) ◇三道题 three questions ◇两道命令 two orders

4 (次) ◊我还要办一道手续。I still need to complete one formality. ◊刷了两道漆 paint two coats

道别 dàobié [动] **1** (辞行) part ◊我们握手道别。We shook hands in parting. **2** (离别) say goodbye (*pt, pp* said) ◊临行前，他向全家道别。Before he left he said goodbye to everyone.

道德 dàodé [名] morals (*pl*) ◊偷东西真不道德。Stealing is so immoral.

道家 Dàojiā [名] Taoist school of thought

道教 dàojiào [名] Taoism

道具 dàojù [名] prop

道理 dàoli [名] **1** (规律) principle **2** (情理) sense

道路 dàolù [名] path

道貌岸然 dàomào ànrán (贬) be sanctimonious

道歉 dàoqiàn [动] apologize ◊我向你们道歉。I apologize to you all.

道士 dàoshi [名] Taoist priest

道听途说 dào tīng tú shuō hearsay

道谢 dàoxiè [动] thank

道学 dàoxué [名] **1** (理学) Neo-Confucianism **2** (古板迂腐) old school ◊她道学气太重。She's so old-school.

道义 dàoyì [名] morality and justice

稻 dào [名] paddy

稻子 dǎozi [名] rice

得 dé **I** [动] **1** (得到) get (*pt* got, *pp* got (英) 或 gotten (美)) ◊得奖 win a prize **2** (病) catch (*pt, pp* caught) ◊他得了流感。He caught flu. ◊她得了胃病。She's developed a stomach problem. **3** (计算) equal ◊四减二得二。Four minus two equals two. ◊三三得九。Three threes are nine. **4** (完成) be ready ◊晚饭得了。Dinner is ready. **5** (适合) be suitable ♦得体 appropriate **II** [叹] **1** (表示同意、禁止) OK ◊得，就这么决定了。OK, that's settled then. ◊得了，别再想了。That's enough. Stop thinking about it. **2** (表示无可奈何) Oh no! ◊得，我又没考及格！ Oh no, I failed again! **III** [助动] ◊版权所有，不得转载。All rights reserved, reprinting not allowed. ◊未经许可，不得擅自播放。Not to be transmitted without permission.
▷另见 de, děi

得便 débiàn [动] be convenient ◊我有个口信，请您得便转告他。I've a message – please pass it on to him when it's convenient.

得不偿失 dé bù cháng shī not be worth the effort

得逞 déchěng [动] (贬) succeed ◊他们的阴谋没能得逞。Their plot failed to succeed.

得寸进尺 dé cùn jìn chǐ be insatiably greedy

得当 dédàng [形] proper ◊这些问题处理得很得当。These issues have been dealt with properly.

得到 dédào [动] get (*pt* got, *pp* got (英) 或 gotten (美)) ◊得到表扬 win praise ◊得到奖学金 win a scholarship ◊得到帮助 get help ◊得到一张唱片 get hold of a record ◊得到提拔 get a promotion ◊他得到了一次出国的机会。He got an opportunity to go abroad.

得法 défǎ [动] have the right technique ◊老师教学得法，学生成绩大大提高。When a teacher has the right technique, the students get much better results.

得过且过 dé guò qiě guò drift along ◊他没有责任心，得过且过。He has no sense of responsibility – he just drifts along.

得力 délì **I** [动] benefit from **II** [形] competent

得失 déshī [名] ◊他太计较个人得失。He pays too much attention to personal gain.

得势 déshì [动] (贬) be in power

得手 déshǒu **I** [动] succeed **II** [副] smoothly

得体 détǐ [形] appropriate

得天独厚 dé tiān dú hòu enjoy great natural advantages ◊香港的地理位置得天独厚。Hong Kong enjoys great natural advantages.

得心应手 dé xīn yìng shǒu be very proficient ◊有了丰富的教学经验，

她教起书来得心应手。With her wealth of teaching experience, she is a very proficient teacher.

得意 déyì [形] pleased with oneself ◇他对自己的工作感到很得意。He has a high opinion of his own work.

得主 dézhǔ [名] winner

得罪 dézuì [动] offend

德 dé [名] **1** (品行) morality ♦品德 moral character ◇社会公德 public morals **2** (恩惠) kindness ♦恩德 kindness

德高望重 dé gāo wàng zhòng have integrity and a good reputation

德行 déxing [名] (贬) revolting behaviour (英) 或 behavior (美)

德育 déyù [名] ethics

地 de [助] ◇刻苦地学习 study hard ◇努力地工作 work hard ◇我们激烈地讨论了这个问题。We discussed the question heatedly. ◇委员会认真地考虑了雇员的意见。The committee took staff opinion into careful consideration. ◇学生大声地回答问题。The student answered questions loudly. ◇警察仔细地检查了小包。The police officer closely inspected the bag.
▷另见 dì

的 de [助] **1** (用于定语后面的) ◇昂贵的价格 high price ◇他的哥哥 his elder brother ◇经理的秘书 the manager's secretary ◇住在那座房子里的夫妇很少出去。The couple who live in that house rarely go out. ◇你买的书真有意思。The book you bought is really interesting. ◇进行的改革有一定的效力。The reforms that were brought in had some effect. ◇我最喜欢的裙子在这儿买不到。The skirt which I like the best is not on sale here. **2** (名词化) ◇画画的 painter ◇这是你的，那是我的。This is yours and that is mine. **3** (用于是…的强调结构) ◇我的嗓子是喊哑的。I shouted myself hoarse.
▷另见 dí, dì

的话 dehuà [助] ◇如果没有问题的话，会就开到这儿。If there are no questions, we can end the meeting here. ◇见到她的话，替我问好。Please give her my regards if you see her.

得 de [助] **1** (用于动词后面) ◇这种野菜吃得。This wild herb is edible. ◇这事太危险，我做不得。It's too dangerous – I shouldn't do it. **2** (动词或补语中间的) ◇她抬得动。She can carry it. ◇我写得完。I am able to finish writing it. **3** (动词和形容词后面) ◇他英语学得很快。He's learning English very quickly. ◇风大得很。The wind's very strong.
▷另见 dé, děi

得 děi **I** [动] (口) (需要) need ◇买房得多少钱？How much money do you need to buy a house? **II** [助动] (口) **1** (必要) must ◇要想成功，就得艰苦奋斗。If you want to succeed, you must work hard. ◇我们得6点出发。We have to leave at six. **2** (表示推测) will ◇再不听话，就得挨批评了。If you don't do as you are told, you will get a telling off. ◇快走，电影得开始了。Get a move on, the film's just about to start.
▷另见 dé, de

灯 dēng [名] light ♦台灯 desk lamp ♦红绿灯 traffic lights (*pl*)

灯红酒绿 dēng hóng jiǔ lù (喻) the high life ◇这座城市是个灯红酒绿的花花世界。The city is happening and has a great nightlife.

灯火 dēnghuǒ [名] lights (*pl*)

灯具 dēngjù [名] lighting

灯塔 dēngtǎ [名] lighthouse

登 dēng [动] **1** (由低到高) go up (*pt* went, *pp* gone) **2** (刊登) publish **3** (踩踏板) pedal **4** (踩) get up onto **5** (裤子、鞋) put … on (*pt, pp* put) ◇他登上鞋就出去了。He put his shoes on and went out.

登场 dēngchǎng [动] go on stage (*pt* went, *pp* gone)

登峰造极 dēng fēng zào jí attain the height of perfection

登记 dēngjì [动] register

登录 dēnglù [动] log in ◇登录网站 log in to a website

登门 dēngmén [动] call by ◇明天我

登门拜访你。I'll call by to see you tomorrow.

登时 dēngshí [副] immediately

登台 dēngtái [动] 1 (上场) go on stage (*pt* went, *pp* gone) ◇登台演出 perform on stage ◇登台演讲 go up to speak 2 (政治) enter politics

登载 dēngzǎi [动] publish

噔 dēng [拟] thud ◇他噔噔地跑上楼去。He thudded upstairs.

蹬 dēng [动] pedal

等 děng I [名] 1 (等级) grade ♦中等 medium ♦优等 outstanding ◇二等奖 second prize ◇一等品 first-rate goods 2 (类) kind ◇这等人 this kind of person II [动] 1 (相同) equal ♦等于 be equal to 2 (等待) wait ◇等车 wait for a bus III [连] (等到) when ◇等他来了，我们再讨论。We'll talk about it when he comes. IV [助] 1 (列举未尽的) etc. ◇他爱读诗歌、小说等等。He likes to read poems, novels, etc. 2 (煞尾的) namely ◇我喜欢足球、篮球、排球等三项运动。I enjoy three sports, namely football, basketball and volleyball.

等待 děngdài [动] wait ◇他耐心地等待时机。He patiently waited for an opportunity.

等到 děngdào [连] when

等等 děngděng [助] and so on ◇参赛国有英国、爱尔兰、法国等等。Countries taking part in the contest include Britain, Ireland, France, and so on.

等号 děnghào [名] (数) equals sign

等候 děnghòu [动] expect

等级 děngjí [名] grade

等量齐观 děng liàng qí guān equate

等式 děngshì [名] (数) equality

等同 děngtóng [动] equate

等闲 děngxián [形] (书) ordinary

等于 děngyú [动] 1 (相等于) equal 2 (等同) be equivalent to ◇保持沉默等于拒绝。To keep silent is equivalent to saying no.

凳 dèng [名] stool ♦板凳 wooden stool

澄 dèng [动] settle
▷另见 chéng

澄清 dèngqīng [动] become clear

瞪 dèng [动] 1 (表示生气) glare at 2 (睁大) open one's eyes wide

低 dī I [形] 1 (指高度、程度) low ◇房子的天花板很低。The house has a low ceiling. ◇蜻蜓飞得很低。Dragonflies fly very low. ◇水平低 low level ◇他们的工资低。Their wages are very low. ◇他喜欢低声说话。He likes to speak quietly. 2 (指等级) junior ◇她是低年级学生。She's a junior student. ◇我比她低两届。I am two years below her. II [动] (头) bend (*pt*, *pp* bent) ◇他低下了头。He bent his head.

低潮 dīcháo [名] low ebb ◇生意处于低潮。Business is at a low ebb.

低沉 dīchén [形] 1 (声音) deep ◇他声音低沉。He's got a deep voice. 2 (天空) overcast ◇低沉的夜空 an overcast night 3 (心情) ◇他情绪低沉。He's feeling a bit low.

低档 dīdàng [形] inferior

低调 dīdiào [形] low-key ◇问题处理得很低调。The problem was dealt with in a low-key way.

低谷 dīgǔ [名] doldrums ◇他的情绪陷入了低谷。He's in the doldrums.

低级 dījí [形] 1 (不高级) inferior 2 (庸俗) vulgar

低贱 dījiàn [形] humble

低廉 dīlián [形] cheap

低劣 dīliè [形] shoddy

低落 dīluò [形] depressed

低迷 dīmí [形] depressed

低能 dīnéng [名] low intelligence

低三下四 dī sān xià sì servile

低声下气 dī shēng xià qì meek

低下 dīxià [形] inferior

堤 dī [名] dyke

堤坝 dībà [名] water defences (英) 或 defenses (美) (*pl*)

提 dī [动] carry ◇提着行李 carry luggage
▷另见 tí

提防 dīfang [动] guard against

滴 dī **I** [动] drip ◇汗水从脑门上往下滴。Sweat kept dripping from his forehead. ◇我给他滴了几滴眼药水。I put some eye drops in his eyes. **II** [名] drop ♦水滴 drop of water **III** [量] drop ◇几滴墨水 a few drops of ink

滴答 dīdā [拟] **1** (指水滴) drip **2** (指钟表) tick

滴水不漏 dī shuǐ bù lòu be watertight ◇她的反驳滴水不漏。Her refutation is watertight.

嘀 dī 见下文
▷另见 dí

嘀嗒 dīdā [拟] 滴答

的 dí 见下文
▷另见 de, dì

的确 díquè [副] really ◇这的确是事实。This really is the truth.

的士 díshì [名] taxi

迪 dí [动] (书) enlighten

迪斯科 dísikē [名] disco

敌 dí **I** [名] enemy **II** [动] oppose **III** [形] equal

敌对 díduì [形] hostile

敌人 dírén [名] enemy

敌视 díshì [动] be hostile towards ◇敌视的态度 a hostile attitude

敌手 díshǒu [名] rival

敌意 díyì [名] hostility

涤 dí [动] wash

笛 dí [名] **1** (音) flute **2** (警笛) siren

笛子 dízi [名] bamboo flute

嘀 dí 见下文
▷另见 dī

嘀咕 dígu [动] **1** (小声说) whisper **2** (猜疑) have misgivings ◇我对是否考及格心里直嘀咕。I have misgivings about whether I'll pass the exam.

嫡 dí [形] **1** (指血统) blood ◇嫡亲 blood relation **2** (正宗) orthodox

嫡系 díxì [名] direct line of descent

诋 dǐ [动] (书) curse

诋毁 dǐhuǐ [动] defame

底 dǐ [名] **1** (最下部分) bottom ◇湖底 the bottom of a lake **2** (内情) ◇魔术师终于露了底。The magician finally showed how the trick worked. ◇会计向我们交了底，公司只赔不赚。The accountant let us see everything – the company simply can't pay. **3** (指文件) record ◇重要文件要留底儿。Records of important documents should be kept. **4** (末尾) end ◇年底 the end of the year **5** (衬托面) background ◇白底蓝花 blue flowers on a white background

底层 dǐcéng [名] **1** (指建筑) ground floor **2** (最下部) bottom ◇没受教育的人经常留在社会底层。Those without education are often left at the bottom of heap.

底稿 dǐgǎo [名] original

底价 dǐjià [名] reserve price

底牌 dǐpái [名] hand ◇谈判对手最后亮了底牌。The other side's negotiator came clean at last.

底气 dǐqì [名] lung power

底细 dǐxì [名] ◇我没摸清他的底细。I don't get where he's coming from. ◇事情的底细她没了解。She hasn't understood how the situation came about.

底子 dǐzi [名] **1** (最下部分) ◇我的鞋底子破了。I have a hole in the sole of my shoe. ◇她化妆底子颜色不好看。Her foundation is the wrong colour. **2** (内情) inside information **3** (基础) foundation ◇他的数学底子好。He has a good grounding in maths (英) 或 math (美). **4** (草稿) draft ◇画设计图前要打底子。Before you draw a design you must make a draft. **5** (衬托面) background

抵 dǐ [动] **1** (支撑) support **2** (抵抗) resist **3** (补偿) compensate for **4** (抵押) mortgage **5** (抵消) offset **6** (代替) be equal to

抵偿 dǐcháng [动] make good ◇我来抵偿损失。I'll make good the loss. ◇他们用实物抵偿欠款。They paid off their debt in kind.

抵触 dǐchù [动] clash ◇他们的意见

相抵触。They have a difference of opinion. ◇他与我在定期考核问题上抵触。We clashed on the question of regular assessment.

抵达 dǐdá [动] reach

抵挡 dǐdǎng [动] withstand (*pt, pp* withstood)

抵抗 dǐkàng [动] resist ◇我们应该坚持锻炼以增强对疾病的抵抗力。We should take exercise to build up resistance to disease.

抵赖 dǐlài [动] deny

抵消 dǐxiāo [动] ◇他的勤奋抵消了经验不足。His industriousness is enough to compensate for his inexperience. ◇正、负数抵消。Positive and negative numbers cancel each other out.

抵押 dǐyā [动] mortgage

抵御 dǐyù [动] resist

抵制 dǐzhì [动] resist

抵罪 dǐzuì [动] be punished for a crime

地 dì [名] **1** (地球) the Earth ◇地心 the Earth's core **2** (陆地) land ♦地下水 ground water **3** (土地) fields (*pl*) ◇农民们正在地里干活。The peasants are working in the fields. **4** (地点) location ♦目的地 destination **5** (路程) ◇车刚开了3英里就抛锚了。The car had only gone three miles when it broke down. ◇他家离城有5公里地。His home is five kilometres from the town. ◇从家到学校坐4站地。There are four stops between home and school. **6** (衬托面) background ◇白地儿红字 red characters on a white background
▷另见 de

地步 dìbù [名] **1** (处境) ◇你怎么到了这个地步了？ How did you get into such a state? ◇他竟落到沿街乞讨的地步。He was eventually reduced to begging in the street. **2** (程度) extent ◇她紧张到晕倒的地步。She was so nervous that she passed out.

地产 dìchǎn [名] property (英), real estate (美)

地大物博 dì dà wù bó a vast territory with rich resources

地带 dìdài [名] zone

地道 dìdào [名] tunnel

地道 dìdao [形] **1** (真正) genuine ◇一颗地道的珍珠 a genuine pearl **2** (纯正) pure ◇他的汉语说得真地道。His Chinese is very idiomatic. **3** (指质量) well done ◇这项工作干得真地道！ The work has been really well done.

地点 dìdiǎn [名] location

地段 dìduàn [名] area

地方 dìfāng [名] locality ◇地方政府 local government ◇地方方言 local accent

地方 dìfang [名] **1** (区域) place ◇这个地方真美。This place is beautiful. ◇你是哪个地方的人？ Where do you come from? **2** (空间) room ◇车里没地方了。There is no room in the car. **3** (身体部位) ◇我这个地方酸痛。I ache here. **4** (部分) part ◇有不明白的地方吗？ Are there any parts that are not clear?

地理 dìlǐ [名] geography ◇地理位置 geographical location

地利 dìlì [名] favourable geography

地面 dìmiàn [名] **1** (地表) the Earth's surface **2** (指房屋) floor

地盘 dìpán [名] territory

地皮 dìpí [名] building land

地平线 dìpíngxiàn [名] horizon ◇地平线上有一条船。There is a ship on the horizon.

地球 dìqiú [名] the Earth

地球村 dìqiúcūn [名] global village

地球仪 dìqiúyí [名] globe

地区 dìqū [名] area ◇北京地区普降大雨。The whole Beijing area gets a lot of rain. ◇贫困地区 poor area

地势 dìshì [名] topography

地摊 dìtān [名] stall

地毯 dìtǎn [名] carpet

地铁 dìtiě [名] **1** (地下铁道) underground (英), subway (美) **2** (列车) underground (英) 或 subway (美) train ◇他每天坐地铁上班。Every day he takes the underground (英) 或 subway (美) to work.

地图 dìtú [名] map

地位 dìwèi [名] position ◊学术地位 academic position ◊国际地位 international standing ◊平等的地位 equal status ◊历史地位 place in history

地下 dìxià [名] underground ◊地下管道 underground pipe ◊非法地下组织 an illegal underground organization

地下室 dìxiàshì [名] basement

地形 dìxíng [名] topography

地狱 dìyù [名] hell ◊孩子过着地狱般的生活。This child has had a hellish life.

地域 dìyù [名] **1** (领土) territory **2** (本土) locality

地震 dìzhèn [名] earthquake ◊新疆地震了。There has been an earthquake in Xinjiang.

地址 dìzhǐ [名] address ◊通信地址 postal address ◊家庭地址 home address ◊办公地址 business address ◊请留下您的地址。Please leave your address.

地址簿 dìzhǐbù [名] address book

地质 dìzhì [名] geology

地质学 dìzhìxué [名] geology

地主 dìzhǔ [名] landlord

弟 dì [名] younger brother ♦表弟 cousin

弟兄 dìxiong [名] brothers (*pl*)

弟子 dìzǐ [名] disciple

的 dì [名] target ♦目的 goal ▷另见 de, dí

帝 dì [名] **1** (神) God **2** (君主) emperor **3** (帝国主义) imperialism

帝国 dìguó [名] empire

帝国主义 dìguó zhǔyì [名] imperialism

帝王 dìwáng [名] emperor

递 dì **I** [动] (传送) pass ◊请把碗递给她。Please would you pass her the bowl. ◊能给她递个口信吗? Could you pass on a message to her? ◊他给我递了个眼色。He gave me a meaningful look. **II** [副] (顺次) in succession ♦递增 progressively increase

递补 dìbǔ [动] substitute ◊甲队员由乙队员递补。Player A was substituted by player B.

递交 dìjiāo [动] hand over

递进 dìjìn [动] progress ◊分层递进的教育方法 a teaching method that progresses in stages

递送 dìsòng [动] deliver ◊递送邮包 deliver parcels

第 dì [名] ◊第二次世界大战 the Second World War ◊得第一名 come first ♦第二职业 second job ♦第三产业 tertiary industry ♦第三世界 the Third World

第六感觉 dìliù gǎnjué [名] sixth sense

第三者 dìsānzhě [名] (破坏感情者) ◊因为第三者插足，他们分手了。They split up because of an affair.

第一夫人 dìyī fūrén [名] First Lady

第一手 dìyīshǒu [形] first-hand

蒂 dì [名] base

缔 dì [动] establish

缔交 dìjiāo [动] establish diplomatic relations

缔结 dìjié [动] conclude

缔约 dìyuē [动] conclude a treaty

缔造 dìzào [动] found

掂 diān [动] weigh in one's hand

掂量 diānliáng [动] **1** (字) weigh in one's hand ◊他掂量了一下邮件的重量。He weighed the mail in his hand. **2** (喻) (斟酌) consider ◊他仔细掂量了经理的话。He considered the manager's words carefully.

颠 diān [动] **1** (颠簸) jolt **2** (跌落) fall (*pt* fell, *pp* fallen)

颠簸 diānbǒ [动] toss

颠倒 diāndǎo [动] ◊这张照片上下颠倒了。The photo is upside down. ◊请把拖把颠倒过来放。Please could you put the mop the other way up.

颠覆 diānfù [动] overturn

颠扑不破 diān pū bù pò irrefutable

颠三倒四 diān sān dǎo sì incoherent ◇他说话颠三倒四的。He talks incoherently. ◇他做事颠三倒四的。When he tries to do something he always gets in a muddle.

巅 diān [名] summit

巅峰 diānfēng [名] summit

癫 diān [形] insane

癫痫 diānxián [名] epilepsy

典 diǎn I [名] **1** (标准) standard **2** (书籍) standard work ♦词典 dictionary **3** (典故) allusion **4** (典礼) ceremony II [动] pawn

典当 diǎndàng [动] ◇她典当房子以获得10万英镑贷款。She got a mortgage of £100,000 on her house.

典范 diǎnfàn [名] model

典故 diǎngù [名] allusion

典礼 diǎnlǐ [名] ceremony ◇毕业典礼 graduation ceremony ◇开幕典礼 opening ceremony ◇闭幕典礼 closing ceremony ◇结婚典礼 wedding ceremony

典型 diǎnxíng I [名] model II [形] (代表性) representative ◇典型案例 a representative case ◇典型文学作品 typical works of literature

典雅 diǎnyǎ [形] elegant

点 diǎn I [名] **1** (时间单位) o'clock ◇他早上8点上课。He starts class at eight o'clock in the morning. **2** (钟点) ◇到点了，该开会了。It's time for the meeting. **3** (小滴液体) drop ◇雨点 raindrops **4** (痕迹) stain ◇油点儿 oil stain **5** (指字、画) dot **6** (指几何) point ◇两点之间，直线最短。Between two points, a straight line is the shortest. **7** (小数点) decimal point ◇五点六 five point six (5.6) **8** (标志) point ♦终点 end point ♦沸点 boiling point **9** (方面) point ♦优点 strong point ♦重点 focal point ◇从这点看，他是对的。From this point of view he is right. ◇我对这点毫不怀疑。I have no doubts about that. II [动] **1** (画点) make a dot **2** (头) nod ♦点头 nod one's head **3** (药水等) ◇点眼药 apply eye drops **4** (查对) check ♦点名 call the register **5** (指定) select ◇点菜 order food **6** (灯、火、烟等) light (*pt, pp* lit) ◇点烟 light a cigarette **7** (点缀) decorate ◇客厅里点缀着彩灯。The sitting room is decorated with coloured lights. **8** (启发) hint ◇老师一点他就明白了。He quickly took the teacher's hint. III [量] **1** (少量) a little ◇有一点儿问题。There is a bit of a problem. ◇她会说一点日语。She can speak a little Japanese. ◇请给我一点糖。Could you give me some sugar? **2** (事项) item ◇议事日程上有6点。There are six items on the agenda. ◇领导的讲话主要有3点。There are three main points in the leader's speech. ◇我们有4点建议。We have four recommendations.

点拨 diǎnbo [动] instruct

点滴 diǎndī [名] bit ◇丰富的知识是点点滴滴积累成的。In-depth knowledge is accumulated bit by bit.

点击 diǎnjī [动] click

点题 diǎntí [动] set the theme (*pt, pp* set) ◇这段的第一句点了题。The first sentence of this section sets the theme.

点头 diǎntóu [动] nod

点头哈腰 diǎntóu-hāyāo bow and scrape

点心 diǎnxin [名] dim sum

点缀 diǎnzhuì [动] decorate

点子 diǎnzi [名] **1** (关键部分) key point **2** (主意) idea

碘 diǎn [名] iodine

踮 diǎn [动] stand on tiptoe (*pt, pp* stood)

电 diàn I [名] **1** (能源) electricity ♦电能 electric power ♦发电站 electric power station ◇停电了。There's been a power cut. **2** (电报) telegram ◇发急电 send an urgent telegram II [动] **1** (触电) get an electric shock **2** (发电报) send a telegram (*pt, pp* sent) ♦电贺 congratulate by telegram

电报 diànbào [名] telegram

电波 diànbō [名] electro-magnetic wave

电池 diànchí [名] battery

电动 diàndòng [形] electric ◇电动玩具 electric toy

电荷 diànhè [名] electric charge

电话 diànhuà [名] **1** (电话机) telephone ◇办公室的电话占线。The office phone is engaged (英) 或 busy (美). ◇别挂电话！ Don't hang up! **2** (打、接、回) call ◇我接到了妈妈的长途电话。I received a long-distance call from Mum. ◇上午有你的两个电话。This morning there were two calls for you.

电话号码 diànhuà hàomǎ [名] phone number

电力 diànlì [名] electricity ◇电力供应 electricity supply

电流 diànliú [名] electric current

电路 diànlù [名] electric circuit

电脑 diànnǎo [名] computer ◇台式电脑 desktop computer ◇手提电脑 laptop ◇电脑病毒 computer virus ◇他电脑专业毕业。He graduated in computing. ◇我在上电脑课。I'm taking a computer class.

电器 diànqì [名] electrical appliance ◇家用电器 home appliance

电视 diànshì [名] television, TV ◇彩色电视 colour (英) 或 color (美) television ◇卫星电视 satellite television ◇看电视 watch television ◇开电视 turn on the television ◇关电视 turn off the television

电台 diàntái [名] station

电信 diànxìn [名] telecommunications (*pl*)

电压 diànyā [名] voltage

电影 diànyǐng [名] film (英), movie (美)

电影院 diànyǐngyuàn [名] cinema

电源 diànyuán [名] power supply

电子 diànzǐ [名] electron ◇电子表 digital watch ◇电子游戏 electronic game ◇电子琴 electronic piano ◇电子音乐 electronic music

电子商务 diànzǐ shāngwù [名] e-commerce

电子图书 diànzǐ túshū [名] e-book

电子邮件 diànzǐ yóujiàn [名] e-mail ◇发电子邮件 send an e-mail

电阻 diànzǔ [名] resistance

店 diàn [名] **1** (商店) shop (英), store (美) **2** (旅店) hotel

店铺 diànpù [名] shop (英), store (美)

玷 diàn 见下文

玷污 diànwū [动] tarnish

垫 diàn **I** [名] cushion ♦椅垫 chair cushion ♦鞋垫 insole **II** [动] **1** (铺) insert ◇她在桌子腿下垫了点纸。She inserted a bit of paper under the table leg. **2** (付钱) pay (*pt, pp* paid) ◇书钱我先替你垫上。For now I'll pay for the book for you. **3** (填补) ◇吃点小菜，先垫垫肚子。Have a snack – it'll take the edge off.

淀 diàn 见下文

淀粉 diànfěn [名] starch

惦 diàn 见下文

惦记 diànjì [动] think about (*pt, pp* thought) ◇她老惦记着这些老人。She's always thinking about these old people.

惦念 diànniàn [动] worry about

奠 diàn [动] establish

奠定 diàndìng [动] establish

奠基 diànjī [动] lay a foundation (*pt, pp* laid) ◇奠基石 cornerstone

殿 diàn [名] palace ♦宫殿 palace

殿军 diànjūn [名] ◇他是殿军。He won the wooden spoon.

殿堂 diàntáng [名] hall

殿下 diànxià [名] (敬) Your Majesty

靛 diàn [名] indigo

靛蓝 diànlán [名] indigo

刁 diāo [形] **1** (狡猾) cunning **2** (方) (挑食的) fussy ◇孩子嘴真刁。The child is a really fussy eater.

刁难 diāonàn [动] make things difficult ◇他这是故意刁难我们。He is intentionally making things difficult for us.

刁钻 diāozuān [形] cunning

叼 diāo [动] have ... in one's mouth

凋 diāo [动] wither ♦凋零 wither ◇松柏常绿不凋。Pine trees are evergreen.

凋零 diāolíng [动] wither

凋谢 diāoxiè [动] wither

雕 diāo I [动] carve II [名] **1** (指艺术) sculpture ♦石雕 stone sculpture ♦浮雕 relief **2** (鸟) vulture

雕虫小技 diāo chóng xiǎo jì lesser talent

雕刻 diāokè I [动] carve II [名] carving

雕塑 diāosù [名] sculpture

雕琢 diāozhuó [动] **1** (雕刻) carve ◇用玉石雕琢成的荷花 a lotus flower carved in jade **2** (修饰) ◇这位作家爱过分雕琢文字。This writer writes in an overly ornate style.

吊 diào [动] **1** (悬挂) hang (*pt, pp* hung) ◇门前吊着一盏灯。A lamp is hanging at the doorway. **2** (提) hoist ... up **3** (收回) revoke ◇吊销执照 revoke a licence (英) 或 license (美) **4** (轻打) drop ◇他轻轻一吊，球过网了。He lightly dropped the ball over the net.

吊儿郎当 diào'erlángdāng fool around

吊胃口 diào wèikǒu [动] whet sb's appetite ◇这味道真吊胃口。The smell is really whetting my appetite.

吊销 diàoxiāo [动] revoke

吊唁 diàoyàn [动] express one's condolences

钓 diào [动] fish ♦钓鱼 go fishing ◇钓名利 fish for a compliment

钓饵 diào'ěr [名] bait

钓具 diàojù [名] fishing tackle

调 diào I [动] transfer ◇他被调到我们单位了。He was transferred to our unit. II [名] **1** (口音) accent ◇他说话有四川调。He has a Sichuan accent. **2** (曲调) melody ◇他唱走调了。He sings out of tune. ◇我不喜欢这个调。I don't like the melody. **3** (音) key ◇B调奏鸣曲 a sonata in the key of B **4** (声调) pitch ▷另见 tiáo

调兵遣将 diào bīng qiǎn jiàng deploy troops

调拨 diàobō [动] send (*pt, pp* sent)

调查 diàochá [动] investigate ◇这件事情一定要调查清楚。This matter must certainly be investigated and clarified.

调动 diàodòng [动] **1** (工作) transfer **2** (部队) deploy **3** (积极性) mobilize

调度 diàodù I [动] **1** (车辆) control **2** (生产、工作、人力) manage II [名] controller

调虎离山 diào hǔ lí shān entice ... out

调换 diàohuàn [动] swap

调门儿 diàoménr [名] **1** (声音) pitch ◇调门儿别太高了，我唱不上去。Don't pitch it too high. I won't be able to sing it. ◇她说话调门儿真高。She has a very high-pitched voice. **2** (论调) line ◇几篇评论文章的调门儿都一样。A number of reviews took the same line.

调配 diàopèi [动] deploy

调遣 diàoqiǎn [动] assign ◇我会听从组织的调遣。I'll accept the organization's assignment.

调子 diàozi [名] **1** (音) melody **2** (喻) tone ◇他的话语中带着悲观的调子。There is a pessimistic tone to what he is saying.

掉 diào [动] **1** (落下) fall (*pt* fell, *pp* fallen) ◇树叶纷纷从树上掉下来。The leaves are gradually falling from the trees. **2** (落后) fall behind (*pt* fell, *pp* fallen) **3** (遗失) lose (*pt, pp* lost) ◇我的上衣掉了一个扣子。I've lost a button off my shirt. **4** (减少) reduce **5** (转回) turn ... round ◇把车头掉过来 turn the car round **6** (互换) swap ◇我们掉一下座位好吗？ Let's swap seats, OK?

掉换 diàohuàn [动] swap

掉价 diàojià [动] **1** (指价格) come down in price (*pt* came, *pp* come) **2** (指身份) lose social status (*pt, pp* lost)

掉以轻心 diào yǐ qīng xīn treat … lightly ◇对安全问题千万不能掉以轻心。Safety issues should never be treated lightly.

爹 diē [名] (方) dad

跌 diē [动] fall down (*pt* fell, *pp* fallen)

跌宕 diēdàng [形] (书) twisting and turning

跌跌撞撞 diēdiezhuàngzhuàng staggering ◇他喝醉了，走路跌跌撞撞的。He's drunk and is staggering.

跌落 diēluò [动] (价格、产量) fall (*pt* fell, *pp* fallen) ◇最近物价有些跌落。Recently prices have fallen somewhat.

迭 dié **I** [动] alternate **II** [副] again and again ◇这种错误迭有发生。This sort of mistake is happening again and again.

迭起 diéqǐ [动] occur frequently

谍 dié [名] **1** (谍报) espionage **2** (间谍) spy

谍报 diébào [名] intelligence report

喋 dié 见下文

喋喋不休 diédié bù xiū witter on ◇他喋喋不休地谈着对未来的设想。He witters on and on about his plans for the future.

牒 dié [名] official document ◇最后通牒 ultimatum

叠 dié [动] **1** (一层加一层) pile … up **2** (信、纸、衣、被) fold

叠床架屋 dié chuáng jià wū duplication ◇写文章切忌叠床架屋。When you write an essay you should avoid repeating yourself.

碟 dié 见下文

碟子 diézi [名] small plate

蝶 dié [名] butterfly

丁 dīng [名] **1** (成年男子) man (*pl* men) **2** (人口) population **3** (小块) cube ♦肉丁 diced meat

丁当 dīngdāng [拟] **1** (瓷器、玉器) chink **2** (铃铛) tinkle **3** (指没钱) ◇他穷得丁当响。He's penniless.

丁零 dīnglíng [拟] tinkle

叮 dīng [动] **1** (蚊虫) bite (*pt* bit, *pp* bitten) **2** (叮嘱) warn

叮嘱 dīngzhǔ [动] warn ◇妈妈叮嘱我注意交通安全。Mother keeps warning me about watching the traffic.

盯 dīng [动] stare at

盯梢 dīngshāo [动] tail

钉 dīng **I** [名] nail **II** [动] **1** (紧跟) follow … closely **2** (督促) put pressure on (*pt*, *pp* put) ◇妈妈钉着他写作业。Mother is putting pressure on him to do his homework.
▷另见 dìng

顶 dǐng **I** [名] top ♦头顶 top of one's head ♦山顶 mountain top **II** [动] **1** (指用头) carry … on one's head ◇她头顶一个水罐。She is carrying a water pot on her head. **2** (拱起) lift … up ◇我们把汽车顶了起来。We lifted the car up. ◇小猫把土顶起来了。The kitten is pushing up the soil. **3** (支撑) prop … up **4** (撞) butt **5** (迎着) face ◇他们顶着烈日在训练。They do their training facing the sun. **6** (顶撞) be rude to **7** (承担) undertake (*pt* undertook, *pp* undertaken) **8** (相当) ◇他干活一个人能顶两个。He can do as much work as two people. **9** (顶替) take the place of (*pt* took, *pp* taken) **III** [量] ◇一顶帽子 a hat ◇一顶蚊帐 a mosquito net **IV** [副] extremely ◇顶好 extremely good

顶点 dǐngdiǎn [名] **1** (最高点) top ◇我们爬到了山的顶点。We reached the top of the mountain. **2** (数) node

顶峰 dǐngfēng [名] summit

顶呱呱 dǐngguāguā [形] first-rate

顶礼膜拜 dǐnglǐ móbài (贬) worship

顶牛儿 dǐngniúr [动] be at loggerheads with

顶替 dǐngtì [动] **1** (替代) take the place of (*pt* took, *pp* taken) ◇他走了，谁来顶替他的岗位？ After he's gone, who will take his place? **2** (冒名) pose as

顶天立地 dǐng tiān lì dì dauntless

顶头上司 dǐngtóu shàngsi direct superior

顶用 dǐngyòng [动] do the trick

顶嘴 dǐngzuǐ [动] answer back

鼎 dǐng I [名] tripod II [形] (书) (大) substantial

鼎鼎大名 dǐngdǐng dàmíng renowned

鼎沸 dǐngfèi [形] (书) tumultuous

鼎力 dǐnglì [动] (书) make a great effort

鼎盛 dǐngshèng [形] flourishing

订 dìng [动] **1** (确立) draw … up (*pt* drew, *pp* drawn) ◇我们必须订生产指标。We must draw up production targets. **2** (预订) order ◆订报 subscribe to a newspaper **3** (校正) revise **4** (装订) fasten … together

订单 dìngdān [名] order form

订购 dìnggòu [动] order

订婚 dìnghūn [动] get engaged

订货 dìnghuò [动] order goods

订交 dìngjiāo [动] establish relations

订金 dìngjīn [名] deposit

订立 dìnglì [动] establish

订正 dìngzhèng [动] correct

钉 dìng [动] **1** (固定) nail **2** (缝) sew … on (*pt* sewed, *pp* sewn) ▷另见 dīng

定 dìng I [形] **1** (平静) calm ◇她好像心神不定。She doesn't seem to be in a calm state of mind. **2** (不变的) settled ◆定论 final conclusion **3** (规定的) fixed ◆定义 definition II [动] **1** (决定) decide ◇我们必须尽快定计划。We must quickly decide on a plan. **2** (固定) settle ◇他们打算定居杭州。They plan to settle in Hangzhou. **3** (预定) order ◆定报 subscribe to a newspaper ◇他定了一批货。He ordered some goods. ◇我们定了音乐会的票。We booked tickets for the concert. III [副] definitely ◇我们的事业定会成功。Our project will definitely succeed.

定案 dìng'àn [动] reach a verdict

定夺 dìngduó [动] make a final decision

定额 dìng'é I [名] quota II [动] set a quota (*pt*, *pp* set)

定稿 dìnggǎo [动] finalize a manuscript

定购 dìnggòu [动] order

定婚 dìnghūn [动] get engaged

定货 dìnghuò [动] order goods

定价 dìngjià [动] set a price (*pt*, *pp* set)

定金 dìngjīn [名] deposit

定居 dìngjū [动] settle ◇他们准备定居国外。They are planning to settle abroad.

定局 dìngjú I [名] foregone conclusion II [动] make a final decision

定理 dìnglǐ [名] theorem

定量 dìngliàng I [动] **1** (规定数量) ration **2** (测定含量) quantify ◇我们对药物要进行定量分析。We need to do some quantitative analysis of the drugs. II [名] ration

定律 dìnglǜ [名] law

定论 dìnglùn [名] conclusion

定期 dìngqī I [动] set a date (*pt*, *pp* set) II [形] fixed

定情 dìngqíng [动] pledge one's love

定位 dìngwèi I [动] appraise II [名] position ◇我们必须找到这颗行星的定位。We must establish the exact position of the planet.

定型 dìngxíng [动] finalize a design

定性 dìngxìng [动] determine ◇我们对他的过失必须定性。We must determine what his error is.

定义 dìngyì [名] definition

定语 dìngyǔ [名] attribute

定罪 dìngzuì [动] convict

丢 diū [动] **1** (遗失) lose (*pt*, *pp* lost) **2** (扔掉) throw away (*pt* threw, *pp* thrown) **3** (投) toss ◇他丢给乞丐一便士。He tossed the beggar a penny. **4** (搁置) ◇这件事我丢不开。I can't let go of it. ◇我的日语丢了好

多年，都忘光了。I've not used my Japanese for years and have now forgotten it all. **5** (留下) leave … behind (*pt, pp* left)

丢丑 diūchǒu [动] lose face (*pt, pp* lost)

丢盔卸甲 diū kuī xiè jiǎ make a run for it

丢脸 diūliǎn [动] lose face (*pt, pp* lost)

丢人 diūrén [动] lose face (*pt, pp* lost)

丢三落四 diū sān là sì scatterbrained

丢卒保车 diu zú bǎo jū lose a pawn to save a castle

东 dōng [名] **1** (方向) east ♦东南亚 Southeast Asia ♦东风 east wind ◇中国东临太平洋。China borders on the Pacific Ocean to the east. **2** (主人) owner ♦房东 landlord ♦股东 shareholder **3** (东道主) host

东半球 dōngbànqiú [名] eastern hemisphere

东道 dōngdào [名] host

东道国 dōngdàoguó [名] host nation

东拉西扯 dōng lā xī chě rambling ◇你不要再东拉西扯了，快说正经事。Stop rambling and get to the point.

东跑西颠 dōng pǎo xī diān rush around

东拼西凑 dōng pīn xī còu scrimp and save ◇他就这样东拼西凑，硬把学费交上了。This is how he scrimped and saved, and managed to pay for the school fees.

东山再起 Dōng shān zài qǐ make a comeback

东西 dōngxī [名] east and west

东西 dōngxi [名] **1** (物品) thing ◇你把东西放在这儿吧。Why don't you leave your things here. ◇今天他买了不少东西。He did quite a bit of shopping today. **2** (家伙) ◇他这个小东西，真滑头！He's a slippery character! **3** (与'什么'一词连用) ◇我什么东西也看不见。I can't see anything. ◇他在大学里没学到什么东西。He didn't learn anything at university.

东…西… dōng … xī … ◇东倒西歪 walk unsteadily ◇他说话是东一句，西一句。He talks incoherently.

东张西望 dōng zhāng xī wàng look in all directions ◇他东张西望，也没找到出租车。He looked in all directions, but couldn't find a taxi. ◇考试时，不许东张西望。During exams it is not permitted to look around.

冬 dōng **I** [名] winter **II** [拟] knock

冬眠 dōngmián [动] hibernate

冬天 dōngtiān [名] winter

冬至 dōngzhì [名] winter solstice

董 dǒng [名] director

董事 dǒngshì [名] director

董事会 dǒngshìhuì [名] **1** (指企业) board of directors **2** (指学校) board of trustees

懂 dǒng [动] understand (*pt, pp* understood)

懂行 dǒngháng [动] (方) know the ropes (*pt* knew, *pp* known)

栋 dòng **I** [名] (书) ridgepole **II** [量] ◇一栋楼 a building

动 dòng [动] **1** (指改变位置) move ◇不要动我的书。Don't move my books. ◇不许动！Freeze! **2** (行动) act **3** (用作动补) ◇我提不动这个大箱子。I can't lift this case. ◇她太累了，走不动。She's too tired – she can't go on. ◇他能举得动100公斤的杠铃。He can lift barbells weighing 100 kilograms. **4** (使用) use ◇我们得动脑筋，想个办法。We must use our brains and think of a way. **5** (触动) affect **6** (感动) move ◇这首歌很动人。This song is very moving.

动产 dòngchǎn [名] movable property

动词 dòngcí [名] verb

动荡 dòngdàng [形] unstable

动工 dònggōng [动] begin construction (*pt* began, *pp* begun)

动机 dòngjī [名] motive

动静 dòngjìng [名] **1** (声音) sound **2** (情况) movement ◇敌军没有什么动静。There's no activity among the enemy troops.

动力 dònglì [名] **1** (指机械) power **2** (力量) strength

动乱 dòngluàn [名] unrest

动脉 dòngmài [名] artery

动情 dòngqíng [动] **1** (激动) be moving **2** (爱上) fall for (*pt* fell, *pp* fallen)

动人 dòngrén [形] moving ◊动人的故事 moving story

动身 dòngshēn [动] begin (*pt* began, *pp* begun)

动手 dòngshǒu [动] **1** (开始做) get to work **2** (用手摸) touch ◊只许看，不许动手。You can look, but don't touch. **3** (打人) strike a blow (*pt, pp* struck) ◊到底是谁先动手的？ So who struck the first blow?

动态 dòngtài [名] developments (*pl*)

动弹 dòngtan [动] move ◊我的腿麻了，动弹不了。My leg has gone to sleep. I can't move it.

动听 dōngtīng [形] ◊动听的音乐 beautiful music ◊动听的故事 interesting story

动武 dòngwǔ [动] use military force

动物 dòngwù [名] animal

动物园 dòngwùyuán [名] zoo

动向 dòngxiàng [名] trend

动心 dòngxīn [动] be affected

动摇 dòngyáo [动] shake (*pt* shook, *pp* shaken)

动议 dòngyì [名] motion

动用 dòngyòng [动] use

动员 dòngyuán [动] mobilize

动辄 dòngzhé [副] (书) readily ◊他动辄发火。He gets angry very readily.

动辄得咎 dòng zhé dé jiù be blamed no matter what one does

动作 dòngzuò **I** [名] movement **II** [动] make a move

冻 dòng **I** [动] freeze (*pt* froze, *pp* frozen) **II** [名] jelly

冻结 dòngjié [动] freeze ◊他的全部资产已被冻结。All his assets have been frozen.

洞 dòng **I** [名] **1** (孔) hole **2** (穴) cave **II** [副] thoroughly

洞察 dòngchá [动] see clearly (*pt* saw, *pp* seen)

洞房 dòngfáng [名] bridal suite

洞悉 dòngxī [动] understand ... clearly (*pt, pp* understood)

洞穴 dòngxué [名] cave

都 dōu [副] **1** (全部) all ◊全体成员都参加了会议。All the members attended the meeting. **2** (表示理由) all ◊都是他才酿成了车祸。The car crash was all his fault. **3** (甚至) even ◊老师待他比亲生父母都好。The teacher treated him even better than his parents. **4** (已经) already ◊都到寒冬了，他衣服还穿得很少。It's mid-winter already, but he's still lightly dressed.
▷另见 dū

兜 dōu **I** [名] **1** (衣袋) pocket ♦裤兜 trouser pocket **2** (拎兜) bag ♦网兜 string bag **II** [动] **1** (绕) ◊她说话爱兜圈子。She tends to skirt around the subject. **2** (招揽) canvass **3** (承担) take responsibility (*pt* took, *pp* taken) ◊这样做要是有差错，我兜着。If we do it this way and it's a mistake, I will take responsibility for it.

兜底 dōudǐ [动] expose ◊市长的风流韵事被兜了底。The mayor's illicit affair was exposed.

兜风 dōufēng [动] **1** (挡风) catch the wind (*pt, pp* caught) **2** (游逛) go for a spin (*pt* went, *pp* gone)

兜揽 dōulǎn [动] **1** (招揽) drum ... up ◊小贩在街头兜揽生意。The vendor drummed up business on the street corner. **2** (包揽) take ... on (*pt* took, *pp* taken) ◊我绝不随便兜揽这事。There's no way I'm taking this on lightly.

兜圈子 dōuquānzi [动] **1** (盘旋) circle **2** (喻) (拐弯抹角) beat about the bush (*pt* beat, *pp* beaten)

兜售 dōushòu [动] flog

斗 dǒu **I** [名] **1** (指容器) cup **2** (斗状物) ♦烟斗 pipe ♦漏斗 funnel **3** (北斗星) the Plough (英), the Big Dipper (美) **II** [量] *measurement of capacity, equal to 10 litres*
▷另见 dòu

斗胆 dǒudǎn [副] (用于自谦) boldly ◇容我斗胆评论一下你的工作。May I be so bold as to pass comment on your work?

抖 dǒu [动] **1** (颤抖) shiver **2** (甩动) shake (*pt* shook, *pp* shaken) ◇她把外套在门口抖了抖。She gave her coat a good shake in the doorway. **3** (倒出) bring ... to light (*pt, pp* brought) ◇首相受贿的丑闻被媒体给抖了出来。The media brought to light the scandal of the prime minister taking bribes. **4** (振作) gear...up ◇队员们抖起精神迎接下一场比赛。The players geared themselves up in preparation for the next match. **5** (贬) (得意) throw one's weight about (*pt* threw, *pp* thrown) ◇他发财后抖得不得了。After he'd made his fortune, he threw his weight about like you wouldn't believe.

抖动 dǒudòng [动] **1** (振动) shake (*pt* shook, *pp* shaken) **2** (颤动) tremble

抖擞 dǒusǒu [动] rouse ◇战士们精神抖擞地开往前线。The soldiers made their way to the front line with spirits roused.

陡 dǒu **I** [形] steep **II** [副] suddenly

陡峻 dǒujùn [形] precipitous

陡峭 dǒuqiào [形] steep ◇陡峭的悬崖 steep cliff

陡然 dǒurán [副] suddenly ◇总统竞选陡然升温。The presidential election is suddenly hotting up.

斗 dòu [动] **1** (打斗) fight (*pt, pp* fought) ♦斗鸡 cock fighting **2** (战胜) beat (*pt* beat, *pp* beaten)
▷另见 dǒu

斗殴 dòu'ōu [动] fight (*pt, pp* fought)

斗气 dòuqì [动] nurse a grudge ◇他正在和女朋友斗气。He's nursing a grudge against his girlfriend.

斗争 dòuzhēng [动] **1** (努力战胜) struggle ◇阶级斗争 class struggle **2** (打击) combat **3** (奋斗) fight for (*pt, pp* fought)

斗志 dòuzhì [名] will to fight

斗嘴 dòuzuǐ [动] **1** (吵架) quarrel **2** (耍嘴皮子) exchange banter

豆 dòu [名] bean

豆蔻年华 dòukòu niánhuá teenage

豆子 dòuzi [名] **1** (豆类作物) bean **2** (豆状物) bead

逗 dòu **I** [动] **1** (引逗) tease **2** (招引) attract **3** (逗留) stay **II** [形] amusing

逗号 dòuhào [名] comma

逗留 dòuliú [动] stay ◇她在巴黎逗留了3天。She stayed in Paris for three days.

逗趣儿 dòuqùr [动] amuse ◇她是个爱逗趣儿的人。She loves to make people laugh.

痘 dòu [名] **1** (痘苗) vaccine ♦种痘 vaccinate **2** (天花) smallpox

窦 dòu [名] **1** (洞) hole ♦疑窦 doubtful point **2** (医) (指器官) sinus ♦鼻窦 sinuses

都 dū [名] **1** (首都) capital **2** (大城市) major city ◇景德镇有瓷都之称。Jingdezhen is known as the porcelain city.
▷另见 dōu

都市 dūshì [名] metropolis ◇都市的夜生活丰富多彩。The city's nightlife is rich and varied.

嘟 dū **I** [拟] honk **II** [动] (方) pout ◇他嘟着嘴，在一旁生气。He pouted in annoyance.

嘟囔 dūnang [动] mumble ◇他一边嘟囔着一边走了出去。He mumbled to himself as he walked out.

督 dū [动] supervise

督察 dūchá **I** [动] supervise **II** [名] supervisor

督促 dūcù [动] watch over

毒 dú **I** [名] poison **II** [形] **1** (有毒) poisonous **2** (毒辣) malicious **III** [动] poison

毒害 dúhài [动] poison

毒辣 dúlà [形] malicious

毒品 dúpǐn [名] drug

毒手 dúshǒu [名] treachery

独 dú **I** [形] only ◇他是家里的独

子。He's the only son in the family. **II** [副] **1** (独自) alone ◇他现在独居。He lives alone. **2** (惟独) only ◇会议独缺山姆一人。Only Sam was missing from the meeting. **III** [名] old people without children

独霸 dúbà [动] dominate

独白 dúbái [名] soliloquy

独步 dúbù [动] **1** (无敌) be unrivalled (英) 或 unrivaled (美) ◇他在60年代独步文坛。In the sixties he was unrivalled in literary circles. **2** (独自行走) walk alone ◇他独步旅行，走遍了全国的城市。He travelled alone, visiting cities all over the country.

独裁 dúcái [动] dictate

独唱 dúchàng [名] solo

独出心裁 dú chū xīn cái be original

独创 dúchuàng [动] invent by oneself ◇他独创了新的风格。He invented this new style all by himself.

独当一面 dú dāng yī miàn take full responsibility

独到 dúdào [形] unique

独断独行 dú duàn dú xíng act autocratically

独家 dújiā [名] the only one ◇他独家生产这种设备。He's the only one who makes this equipment. ◇该报刊登了关于首相的独家新闻。The paper ran an exclusive on the prime minister.

独角戏 dújiǎoxì [名] one-man show

独具匠心 dú jù jiàngxīn have ingenuity

独揽 dúlǎn [动] have a monopoly on ◇在封建社会中，皇帝独揽大权。During feudal times, emperors had a monopoly on power.

独立 dúlì [动] **1** (指国家) declare independence ◇独立宣言 declaration of independence **2** (指个人) be independent **3** (单独站立) stand alone (*pt, pp* stood)

独木不成林 dú mù bù chéng lín many hands make light work

独木难支 dú mù nán zhī no one can save a difficult situation alone

独木桥 dúmùqiáo [名] **1** (字) single-plank bridge **2** (喻) rocky road

独辟蹊径 dú pì xī jìng be revolutionary

独身 dúshēn [动] be single ◇他独身多年后终于结婚了。After being single for many years, he finally got married.

独树一帜 dú shù yī zhì start a trend

独特 dútè [形] distinctive

独一无二 dú yī wú èr unparalleled

独占鳌头 dú zhàn áo tóu emerge as the winner

独自 dúzì [副] alone

读 dú [动] **1** (朗读) read (*pt, pp* read) ◇我每天给奶奶读报。I read the newspaper to my grandmother every day. **2** (阅读) read (*pt, pp* read) ◇大家需要仔细读这篇文章。Everyone should read this article carefully. **3** (上学) go to school (*pt* went, *pp* gone) ◇他因家庭生活困难只读完小学。His family were poor so he only managed to get through primary school.

读书 dúshū [动] **1** (阅读) read (*pt, pp* read) **2** (学习) study **3** (上学) go to school (*pt* went, *pp* gone)

读物 dúwù [名] reading material

读者 dúzhě [名] reader

渎 dú **I** [动] (书) show disrespect (*pt* showed, *pp* shown) ♦亵渎 blaspheme **II** [名] (书) drain

渎职 dúzhí [动] neglect one's duty

犊 dú [名] calf

牍 dú [名] **1** (木简) wooden writing tablet **2** (文件) documents

黩 dú [动] (书) **1** (轻举妄动) act wantonly ♦黩武 warlike **2** (玷污) blacken

笃 dǔ [形] **1** (忠诚) sincere **2** (危急) critical

笃实 dǔshí [形] **1** (忠诚老实) faithful **2** (实在) sound

笃学 dǔxué [动] be studious

堵 dǔ **I** [动] **1** (堵塞) block ◇水

管子堵了。The water pipe was blocked. ◇他们把漏水的地方给堵上了。They blocked up the leak. ◇因为车辆过多，公路上很堵。The road was blocked due to an excessive number of vehicles. **2** (发闷) suffocate ◇房间很闷，我胸口堵得很。The room was really stuffy and I felt quite suffocated. **II** [量] ◇一堵墙 a wall

堵截 dǔjié [动] intercept ◇他们堵截了敌人的运输车。They intercepted the enemy convoy.

堵塞 dǔsè [动] block up ◇用洗面奶清洁被堵塞的毛孔。You should use cleansing milk to clean blocked pores.

赌 dǔ [动] **1** (赌博) gamble **2** (打赌) bet (*pt*, *pp* bet)

赌博 dǔbó [动] gamble ◇他决心放弃赌博。He decided to give up gambling.

赌气 dǔqì [动] act rashly out of a sense of injustice

赌咒 dǔzhòu [动] swear (*pt* swore, *pp* sworn)

赌注 dǔzhù [名] bet

睹 dǔ [动] see (*pt* saw, *pp* seen)

睹物思人 dǔ wù sī rén ◇夫妻俩睹物思人，想起了远在他乡的儿子。The couple saw something that reminded them of their son who was far away from home.

杜 dù [动] shut … out (*pt*, *pp* shut)

杜绝 dùjué [动] put an end to (*pt*, *pp* put)

杜撰 dùzhuàn [动] make … up (*pt*, *pp* made) ◇这个故事纯属杜撰。This story is pure fabrication.

肚 dù [名] belly

肚子 dùzi [名] **1** (腹部) stomach **2** (圆而突起部分) ♦腿肚子 calf

妒 dù [动] envy

妒忌 dùjì [动] envy

度 dù **I** [名] **1** (限度) limit ◇他疲劳过度。He was totally exhausted. **2** (气量) tolerance ♦大度 magnanimous **3** (考虑) consideration ◇消防员们已把生死置之度外。The firemen didn't give a thought to their personal safety. **4** (程度) degree ♦厚度 thickness ♦亮度 brightness **II** [量] **1** (指经度或纬度) degree ◇北纬42度 latitude 42 degrees north **2** (指电量) kilowatt-hour ◇1度电 one kilowatt-hour **3** (指温度) degree ◇水的沸点为100度。The boiling point of water is 100 degrees. **4** (指弧度或角度) degree ◇直角为90 度。A right-angle is 90 degrees. **5** (次) time ◇一年一度的会议 annual meeting **III** [动] spend (*pt*, *pp* spent) ◇他们要去瑞士度周末。They are going to spend the weekend in Switzerland. ▷另见 duó

度量 dùliàng [名] tolerance

度日如年 dù rì rú nián drag on for years

渡 dù [动] **1** (越过) cross ◇横渡英吉利海峡 cross the English Channel **2** (指用船只) ferry **3** (喻) (通过) survive

渡口 dùkǒu [名] ferry crossing

镀 dù [动] plate

镀金 dùjīn [动] **1** (字) gold-plate **2** (喻) do … for show ◇他出国留学只不过是为镀金。His going abroad to study was really just for show.

端 duān **I** [名] **1** (头) end **2** (开头) beginning ♦开端 beginning **3** (方面) aspect **4** (理由) reason ◇他无端指责我。There was no reason for him to blame me. **II** [形] proper **III** [动] carry ◇他习惯端着碗喝汤。When he eats soup, he holds his bowl in both hands.

端倪 duānní [名] clue

端午节 Duānwǔjié [名] Dragon Boat Festival

端详 duānxiáng **I** [名] details (*pl*) **II** [形] dignified and serene

端详 duānxiang [动] look closely

端正 duānzhèng **I** [形] **1** (不歪斜) upright **2** (正派) proper **II** [动] correct

端庄 duānzhuāng [形] dignified

短 duǎn **I** [形] short ◇一封短信 a short letter **II** [动] owe ◇我不短你钱。I don't owe you money. **III** [名]

weakness ◇揭别人的短儿 expose other people's weaknesses

短兵相接 duǎn bīng xiāng jiē **1** (字) (指搏斗) engage in close combat **2** (喻) (针锋相对) tit for tat

短处 duǎnchu [名] weakness

短促 duǎncù [形] very brief

短见 duǎnjiàn [名] **1** (短浅的见识) short-sighted view **2** (自杀) suicide

短裤 duǎnkù [名] **1** (指女式内裤) pants (*pl*) **2** (指男式内裤) briefs (*pl*) **3** (指夏装) shorts (*pl*)

短路 duǎnlù [名] (电子) short circuit

短命 duǎnmìng [形] short-lived

短平快 duǎn píng kuài **I** [名] smash **II** [形] ◇此类项目以短平快著称。This type of project is famous for giving quick returns on your investment.

短评 duǎnpíng [名] brief comment

短浅 duǎnqiǎn [形] narrow and shallow ◇目光短浅 short-sighted

短缺 duǎnquē [动] lack ◇短缺商品 commodities in short supply

短视 duǎnshì [形] short-sighted

短途 duǎntú [名] short distance ◇短途旅行 short-haul trip

短小 duǎnxiǎo [形] short ◇他身材短小。He's short. ◇短小精悍的文章 a concise article

短信 duǎnxìn [名] text message

短暂 duǎnzàn [形] brief ◇短暂的分别 brief parting

段 duàn [量] **1** (用于长条物) ◇一段铁轨 a section of railway ◇一段木头 a chunk of wood **2** (指时间) period ◇一段时间 a period of time **3** (指路程) stretch ◇下一段路会很难走。The next stretch of road may be difficult to walk. **4** (部分) piece ◇一段对话 a piece of dialogue

段落 duànluò [名] **1** (指文章) paragraph **2** (阶段) stage

断 duàn **I** [动] **1** (分成段) break (*pt* broke, *pp* broken) **2** (断绝) break … off (*pt* broke, *pp* broken) **3** (判断) decide **II** [副] absolutely

断案 duàn'àn [动] settle a lawsuit

断层 duàncéng [名] **1** (指地质) fault **2** (不相衔接) gap

断代 duàndài [动] **1** (无后代) be childless **2** (喻) (后继无人) lack a successor

断代史 duàndàishǐ [名] dynastic history

断档 duàndàng [动] be sold out

断定 duàndìng [动] determine

断断续续 duànduànxùxù on and off ◇这本小说他断断续续地写了3年。He wrote the novel on and off for three years.

断交 duànjiāo [动] **1** (指国家) sever diplomatic relations ◇断交3年后，两国又重建外交关系。Three years after severing diplomatic relations, the two countries re-established their ties. **2** (指朋友) fall out (*pt* fell, *pp* fallen) ◇两人多年前就已断交了。The two friends fell out years ago.

断绝 duànjué [动] break … off (*pt* broke, *pp* broken) ◇断绝往来 break contact

断然 duànrán **I** [形] resolute **II** [副] categorically

断送 duànsòng [动] forfeit ◇断送前程 forfeit one's future

断言 duànyán [动] assert

断章取义 duàn zhāng qǔ yì quote out of context ◇他断章取义，曲解我的本意。He quoted me out of context and quite distorted my original meaning.

缎 duàn [名] satin

锻 duàn [动] forge

锻炼 duànliàn [动] **1** (指身体) work out **2** (磨炼) toughen ◇艰苦的环境锻炼人的意志。People are toughened by difficult experiences. **3** (冶炼) temper

堆 duī **I** [动] pile ◇别把垃圾堆在这里。Don't pile the rubbish up here. **II** [名] pile **III** [量] pile ◇一堆石头 a pile of stones

堆放 duīfàng [动] stack ◇房间里堆放着很多书。Scores of books were stacked in the room.

堆积 duījī [动] pile … up ◇粮食堆积如山。The grain was piled up like a mountain.

队 duì **I** [名] **1** (行列) line ◇列队欢迎 line up to welcome **2** (指集体) team ◇篮球队 basketball team **II** [量] troop ◇一队人马 an array of troops

队列 duìliè [名] formation

队伍 duìwu [名] **1** (军队) troops (*pl*) **2** (指集体) contingent **3** (行列) formation

对 duì **I** [动] **1** (回答) answer ♦对答 answer **2** (对待) treat ◇他对待他的父母很糟糕。He treated his parents horribly. **3** (朝着) face ◇对准目标 aim at the target **4** (接触) come into contact with (*pt* came, *pp* come) **5** (投合) suit ◇对脾气 suit one's temperament ◇今天的菜很对他的胃口。Today's meal was definitely to his liking. **6** (调整) adjust ◇对焦距 adjust the focus **7** (核对) check ◇对表 set one's watch **8** (加进) add ◇往酒里对点水 add some water to the alcohol **II** [形] **1** (对面) opposite ◇河对岸 the opposite side of the river **2** (正确) correct ◇这题我回答对了。I answered this question correctly. **3** (正常) normal **III** [介] **1** (朝) at ◇他对着她呵呵傻笑。He giggled at her. **2** (对于) ◇吸烟对健康有害。Smoking is harmful to your health. ◇他对自己的未来做了详尽的规划。He planned exhaustively for his future. ◇大家对选举的结果都很关心。Everyone was very concerned about the results of the election. **IV** [量] pair ◇一对绣花鞋 a pair of embroidered shoes ◇一对夫妻 a married couple

对白 duìbái [名] dialogue

对比 duìbǐ **I** [动] contrast ◇鲜明的对比 marked contrast **II** [名] ratio

对不起 duì bu qǐ [动] **1** (愧疚) be sorry ◇对不起， 我迟到了10分钟。Sorry, I'm ten minutes late. ◇对不起，请再说一遍。Sorry? Can you say that again please? ◇对不起，借过。Excuse me – may I just pass through?

对策 duìcè [名] countermeasure

对称 duìchèn [形] symmetrical

对答 duìdá [动] answer

对待 duìdài [动] treat

对等 duìděng [形] equal ◇两国在对等的基础上签定了条约。The two countries signed the agreement on an equal basis.

对调 duìdiào [动] swap ◇如果你不喜欢这个位置的话，我们可以对调。If you don't like your seat, we can swap.

对方 duìfāng [名] other side ◇恋爱中的男女很少介意对方的缺点。People who are in love rarely mind about their partner's weaknesses.

对付 duìfu [动] **1** (应对) deal with (*pt, pp* dealt)◇对付复杂局面 deal with a complicated situation ◇他不是一个好对付的人。He isn't easy to handle. **2** (将就) make do ◇没有别的，我们只好吃点方便面对付了。There's nothing else, so we'll just have to make do with some instant noodles.

对话 duìhuà **I** [名] dialogue ◇两国将就边境问题对话。The two countries will have a dialogue about the border issue. **II** [动] hold talks (*pt, pp* held) ◇劳资双方终于开始对话。Employers and employees began holding talks.

对讲机 duìjiǎngjī [名] intercom

对角线 duìjiǎoxiàn [名] diagonal

对接 duìjiē [动] link … up

对劲 duìjìn [形] **1** (合适) well-suited **2** (投缘) compatible **3** (正常) normal ◇这几天她好像不太对劲。She hasn't been altogether right these last few days.

对抗 duìkàng [动] **1** (对立) confront ◇两党之间的对抗并未消除。There are still some major disputes between the two parties. **2** (抵抗) oppose

对口 duìkǒu [动] be appropriate to ◇对口的工作 a job that is appropriate to one's training

对立 duìlì **I** [动] counter **II** [形] antagonistic

对路 duìlù [形] **1** (合适) suitable ◇该产品在法国市场不对路。This product is unsuitable for the French market. **2** (投缘) suited ◇两个人好像不对

路。These two don't seem very suited to each other.

对面 duìmiàn **I** [名] **1** (对过) the opposite ◇街对面有一家餐馆。There's a restaurant on the opposite side of the street. **2** (正前方) the front ◇对面跑过来一只小狗。A small dog ran up right in front of us. **II** [副] face to face ◇他们终于对面儿把事情说清楚了。They finally clarified the matter face to face.

对牛弹琴 duì niú tán qín preach to deaf ears

对手 duìshǒu [名] **1** (指比赛) opponent **2** (指能力) match ◇论工作能力，他根本不是你的对手。In terms of his professional abilities, he's just no match for you.

对头 duìtóu [形] **1** (正常) normal **2** (投合) compatible

对头 duìtou [名] **1** (仇人) enemy **2** (竞争对手) rival ◇她的对头也在竞争这个项目。Her rival is also competing for this project.

对象 duìxiàng [名] **1** (目标) object ◇爱丽斯是他爱慕的对象。Alice is the object of his affections. **2** (指男女朋友) partner

对应 duìyìng [动] correspond

对于 duìyú [介] ◇对于离婚，社会舆论反应不一。Society is divided in its opinion of divorce. ◇对于这篇文章，大家理解不一。Not everyone understands this article in the same way.

对照 duìzhào [动] compare

对症下药 duì zhèng xià yào use appropriate methods ◇治病要对症下药。When treating illnesses, appropriate methods must be used.

对峙 duìzhì [动] confront

兑 duì [动] **1** (互换) exchange **2** (汇兑) cash

兑付 duìfù [动] cash ◇兑付支票 cash a cheque (英) 或 check (美)

兑换 duìhuàn [动] convert ◇将欧元兑换成美元 convert euros into US dollars

兑现 duìxiàn [动] **1** (兑换现金) cash **2** (实现承诺) keep one's word (*pt, pp* kept)

吨 dūn [量] ton

吨位 dūnwèi [名] tonnage

敦 dūn [形] sincere

敦促 dūncù [动] urge

敦厚 dūnhòu [形] genuine

敦请 dūnqǐng [动] cordially invite

敦实 dūnshí [形] stocky ◇保镖长得通常都挺敦实。Bodyguards are usually very stocky.

墩 dūn [名] **1** (堆) mound **2** (墩子) block ♦桥墩 pier

蹲 dūn [动] **1** (弯腿) squat **2** (逗留) stay

盹 dǔn [名] nap ◇我得打个盹。I must take a nap.

趸 dǔn **I** [名] wholesale **II** [动] buy … wholesale (*pt, pp* bought)

趸批 dǔnpī [名] wholesale

炖 dùn [动] stew ◇土豆炖牛肉 stewed beef with potato

盾 dùn [名] (盾牌或盾形物) shield

盾牌 dùnpái [名] **1** (字) shield **2** (喻) pretext

钝 dùn [形] **1** (不锋利) blunt **2** (不灵活) dim

钝角 dùnjiǎo [名] obtuse angle

顿 dùn **I** [动] **1** (停顿) pause **2** (叩) kowtow ♦顿首 kowtow **3** (跺) stamp ♦顿足 stamp one's foot **4** (安置) arrange ♦安顿 settle down **II** [形] tired ♦劳顿 fatigued **III** [副] suddenly **IV** [量] ◇一顿饭 a meal ◇亨利昨晚挨了一顿打。Henry took quite a beating last night.

顿号 dùnhào [名] *Chinese serial comma*

顿时 dùnshí [副] immediately

遁 dùn [动] escape

遁词 dùncí [名] pretext

多 duō **I** [形] **1** (数量大) a lot of ◇很多书 a lot of books **2** (相差大) more

◇中国领土面积比日本大多了。China has a much bigger land mass than Japan. **3** (超出) too many ◇你多给了我2英镑。You gave me two pounds too much. ◇她喝多了。She drank too much. **4** (过分) excessive ♦多疑 over-suspicious **II** [数] ◇300多艘军舰 over three hundred warships ◇2年多前 over two years ago **III** [动] be more than ◇这个游戏多了2个人。We have two people too many for the game. ◇多个人就多份力量。The more people we have, the stronger we will be. **IV** [副] **1** (用在疑问句中) how ◇从北京到上海有多远？ How far is it from Beijing to Shanghai? ◇你儿子多大了？ How old is your son? **2** (表示感叹) how ◇多美的城市！ How beautiful this town is! ◇这女孩儿多聪明啊！ This girl is so clever! **3** (表示任何一种程度) however ◇无论多晚，她都会等他回家。However late it got, she would wait up for him to return home. ◇给我一把尺，多长都行。Give me a ruler – any length will do.

多半 duōbàn **I** [数] ◇这个班的学生多半英语好。Most of the students in this class have good English. ◇他的家庭成员多半赞同他的婚事。On the whole, most of his family were happy about his marriage. **II** [副] (大概) very likely ◇今天多半要下雨。It's very likely to rain today.

多边 duōbiān [名] ◇多边贸易谈判 multilateral trade talks ◇多边协议 multilateral agreement

多才多艺 duō cái duō yì versatile

多此一举 duō cǐ yī jǔ take unnecessary action

多愁善感 duō chóu shàn gǎn oversensitive

多多益善 duō duō yì shàn the more the better ◇你给我多少我都要，多多益善。Give me whatever you want, but the more the better.

多方 duōfāng [名] every way ◇多方协助 all manner of help

多亏 duōkuī [动] be lucky ◇多亏你把他送医院了。It's lucky that you took him to hospital. ◇多亏你告诉我们，不然我们就迷路了。It's lucky that you told us or we would have got lost.

多媒体 duōméitǐ [名] multimedia

多米诺骨牌 duōmǐnuò gǔpái [名] dominoes (*pl*)

多么 duōme [副] **1** (用于询问程度) how ◇他到底有多么聪明？ How clever is he really? **2** (用在感叹句) ◇多么蓝的天啊！ What a clear day! ◇海洋是多么广阔啊！The ocean is so vast! **3** (表示程度深) no matter how ◇不管天气多么寒冷，我们都要坚持锻炼。No matter how cold it gets, we must all stick to our exercise routine.

多面手 duōmiànshǒu [名] all-rounder

多谋善断 duō móu shàn duàn shrewd

多情 duōqíng [形] affectionate

多少 duōshǎo [副] **1** (或多或少) somewhat ◇经历了许多挫折后，他多少有些变化。After all the setbacks, he's somewhat changed. ◇这笔买卖多少能赚点钱。We're bound to earn some money from this deal. **2** (稍微) slightly

多少 duōshao **I** [代] (用于询问数量) ◇这台电视机多少钱? How much is this television? ◇今天有多少人到会? How many people attended the meeting today? **II** [数] ◇你们有多少我们要多少。We want everything you've got. ◇这样的电影， 没有多少人会喜欢的。There can't be many people who like this kind of film. ◇他的棋艺实在太高，多少人败在他的手下。He's just too good at chess – countless people have lost to him.

多事之秋 duō shì zhī qiū troubled times ◇今年真是多事之秋，家里接二连三地出事。This year we've had really troubled times – our family has had one problem after another.

多数 duōshù [名] the majority ◇多数民众参加了公投。The majority of people voted in the referendum.

多心 duōxīn [动] be oversensitive

多样 duōyàng [形] diverse

多余 duōyú [形] **1** (超出需要量的) surplus **2** (不必要的) redundant

多嘴 duōzuǐ [动] speak out of turn (*pt* spoke, *pp* spoken)

咄 duō [动] (书) scold

咄咄逼人 duōduō bī rén overbearing

咄咄怪事 duōduō guàishì strange goings-on

哆 duō 见下文

哆嗦 duōsuo [动] tremble ◇他气得直哆嗦。He trembled with rage. ◇她冷得直哆嗦。She was so cold she was shivering.

掇 duō [动] pick … up ♦拾掇 tidy … up

掇弄 duōnòng [动] (方) **1** (收拾) fix **2** (怂恿) provoke

夺 duó [动] **1** (抢) seize ◇夺门而出 force one's way out **2** (争取) compete for **3** (剥夺) deprive ◇父亲剥夺了我的继承权。My father deprived me of my inheritance. **4** (决定) resolve

夺标 duóbiāo [动] **1** (夺冠) win first prize (*pt*, *pp* won) **2** (中标) win a tender (*pt*, *pp* won)

夺冠 duóguàn [动] win the championship (*pt*, *pp* won)

夺目 duómù [形] dazzling

夺取 duóqǔ [动] **1** (武力强取) capture **2** (努力争取) strive for (*pt* strove, *pp* striven)

度 duó [动] (书) surmise
▷另见 dù

踱 duó [动] stroll

朵 duǒ [量] ◇朵朵白云 white clouds ◇几朵玫瑰 some roses

躲 duǒ [动] **1** (隐藏) hide (*pt* hid, *pp* hidden) **2** (避让) avoid ♦躲债 avoid a creditor

躲避 duǒbì [动] **1** (回避) run away from (*pt* ran, *pp* run) ◇躲避问题 run away from one's problems **2** (躲藏) hide (*pt* hid, *pp* hidden) ◇我不知道他躲避到哪里去了。I don't know where he had hidden himself.

躲藏 duǒcáng [动] hide (*pt* hid, *pp* hidden)

躲闪 duǒshǎn [动] dodge

驮 duò [名] load
▷另见 tuó

剁 duò [动] chop

垛 duò **I** [动] stack **II** [名] stack

舵 duò [名] helm

舵手 duòshǒu [名] helmsman

堕 duò [动] fall (*pt* fell, *pp* fallen)

堕落 duòluò [动] go to the bad (*pt* went, *pp* gone)

堕胎 duòtāi [动] have an abortion ◇堕胎在一些国家还是不合法的。Abortion is still illegal in some countries.

惰 duò [形] lazy ♦懒惰 indolent

惰性 duòxìng [名] **1** (消极态度) apathy **2** (指化学性质) inertia

跺 duò [动] stamp ◇他气得直跺脚。He was so angry that he stamped his feet repeatedly.

Ee

阿 ē [动] pander to ♦阿谀 flatter
▷另见 ā

阿谀奉承 ēyú fèngcheng creep and crawl ◊我讨厌那些阿谀奉承的人。I hate people who creep and crawl to others.

婀 ē 见下文

婀娜 ēnuó [形] graceful ◊婀娜多姿 lithe and graceful

讹 é **I** [名] error ◊以讹传讹 spread misinformation **II** [动] extort ◊他绑架的目的只是为了讹钱。He did the kidnapping as a way of extorting money.

讹传 échuán [名] hearsay

讹诈 ézhà [动] extort

俄 é **I** [名] (俄罗斯) Russia **II** [副] suddenly

俄顷 éqǐng [副] (书) presently

娥 é [名] pretty woman (*pl* women)

娥眉 éméi [名] **1** (字) beautiful eyebrows **2** (喻) (美女) beautiful woman (*pl* women)

鹅 é [名] goose (*pl* geese)

鹅毛 émáo [名] **1** (字) goose feather **2** (喻) trivial gift

蛾 é [名] moth

蛾子 ézi [名] moth

额 é [名] **1** (额头) forehead **2** (牌匾) board **3** (规定数目) quota

额度 édù [名] amount

额外 èwài [形] additional

恶 ě 见下文
▷另见 è, wù

恶心 ěxin **I** [动] feel nauseous (*pt, pp* felt) **II** [形] nauseating

厄 è **I** [名] **1** (书) (险要处) strategic place **2** (艰难困苦) disaster **II** [动] encounter difficulties

厄运 èyùn [名] misfortune

扼 è [动] **1** (用力掐) clutch **2** (把守) guard

扼杀 èshā [动] **1** (掐死) strangle **2** (喻) stifle

扼要 èyào [形] concise

扼制 èzhì [动] control

轭 è [名] yoke

垩 è [名] chalk

恶 è **I** [名] evil **II** [形] **1** (凶恶) ferocious **2** (恶劣) evil
▷另见 ě, wù

恶霸 èbà [名] local bully

恶毒 èdú [形] vicious

恶贯满盈 è guàn mǎn yíng evil and deserving of punishment

恶棍 ègùn [名] scoundrel

恶果 èguǒ [名] disastrous consequences (*pl*)

恶化 èhuà [动] deteriorate ◊两国关系恶化。Relations between the two countries deteriorated.

恶劣 èliè [形] bad

恶梦 èmèng [名] nightmare

恶魔 èmó [名] **1** (指宗教) demon **2** (喻) devil

恶习 èxí [名] vice

恶性 èxìng [形] **1** (疾病) malignant ◊恶性肿瘤 malignant tumour **2** (事故) horrific ◊恶性循环 vicious circle

恶浊 èzhuó [形] filthy

恶作剧 èzuòjù [名] practical joke ◊不要再搞恶作剧了。Don't play any more practical jokes.

饿 è **I** [形] hungry **II** [动] starve

饿虎扑食 è hǔ pū shí like a hungry tiger

遏 è [动] suppress

遏止 èzhǐ [动] check ◊民主化是不可遏止的趋势。The trend towards democracy cannot be checked. ◊遏止腐败现象 check corruption

遏制 èzhì [动] keep a check on (*pt, pp* kept)

愕 è [动] astound

愕然 èrán [形] (书) stunned

腭 è [名] palate

噩 è [形] terrifying

噩耗 èhào [名] devastating news (*sg*)

鳄 è [名] crocodile, alligator

恩 ēn [名] kindness ♦报恩 repay a favour (英) 或 favor (美)

恩爱 ēn'ài [形] loving ◇他们是一对恩爱夫妻。They are a devoted couple.

恩赐 ēn'cì [动] bestow ◇大丰收是上苍对我们的恩赐。A plentiful harvest is a gift from heaven.

恩德 ēndé [名] kindness

恩典 ēndiǎn **I** [名] favour (英), favor (美) **II** [动] bestow kindness on

恩惠 ēnhuì [名] favour (英), favor (美)

恩将仇报 ēn jiāng chóu bào bite the hand that feeds one

恩情 ēnqíng [名] great kindness

恩人 ēnrén [名] benefactor ◇他是我的大恩人。He is my saviour (英) 或 savior (美).

恩怨 ēnyuàn [名] a mixture of gratitude and resentment

摁 èn [动] press ◇请摁一下开关。Please press the switch.

儿 ér **I** [名] **1** (小孩子) child (*pl* children) **2** (年轻人) youngster ♦男儿 young man **3** (儿子) son **II** [形] male ♦儿马 stallion

儿歌 érgē [名] nursery rhyme

儿女 érnǚ [名] **1** (儿子和女儿) children **2** (青年男女) men and women (*pl*)

儿童 értóng [名] child (*pl* children)

儿戏 érxì [名] (喻) trivial thing ◇工作不是儿戏。Work is not a game.

而 ér [连] **1** (并且) and ◇美丽而聪明 beautiful and clever ◇抽烟有其害而无其利。Smoking does nothing but harm. **2** (但是) but ◇这种香水的香味儿浓而不劣。This perfume is strong but the smell is not overpowering. **3** (连接状语和动词) ◇夺门而逃 force the door and rush out **4** (如果) if ◇想成功而不努力，那是痴心妄想。It's just wishful thinking to imagine that you can be successful without putting in the work. **5** (到) to ◇由始而终 from start to finish

而后 érhòu [连] then ◇他去年来过一封信，而后再没联系过。Last year he sent a letter, but after that he didn't get in contact again.

而今 érjīn [名] today ◇原本荒凉的郊外，而今已是高楼林立。Today the old wasteland is a forest of skyscrapers.

而且 érqiě [连] and what's more ◇他会讲英语，而且讲得好。He can speak English, and what's more he speaks it very well. ◇他不但歌唱得好，而且还会作曲。He sings very well, and on top of that he can also write music.

而已 éryǐ [助] ◇我没别的意思，只是提醒你而已。All I'm doing is cautioning you. ◇她只是说说而已，不会真做的。She's all talk – she won't really do it.

尔 ěr [代] (书) **1** (你) you ◇非尔之过。It's not your fault. **2** (这样) so ♦果尔 if so **3** (那) that ◇尔日 on that day ◇尔时 at that time

尔虞我诈 ěr yú wǒ zhà each trying to cheat the other

耳 ěr [名] **1** (耳朵) ear **2** (耳状物) ear **3** (指位置) side

耳边风 ěrbiānfēng [名] deaf ear ◇她把妈妈的建议当作耳边风。She turned a deaf ear to her mother's advice.

耳聪目明 ěr cōng mù míng **1** (字) have good eyesight and hearing **2** (喻) have one's wits about one ◇他耳聪目明，极少上当。He has his wits about him and is rarely fooled.

耳光 ěrguāng [名] slap in the face

耳目 ěrmù [名] **1** (见闻) information ◇耳目闭塞 ill-informed **2** (密探) spy

耳目一新 ěr mù yī xīn refreshing

耳濡目染 ěr rú mù rǎn be subtly influenced

耳熟能详 ěr shú néng xiáng ◊这个曲子我耳熟能详。I've heard this tune so many times that I know it off by heart.

耳闻目睹 ěr wén mù dǔ witness … first-hand

耳语 ěryǔ [动] whisper

饵 ěr [名] **1** (糕饼) cake **2** (鱼饵) bait **II** [动] (书) entice

饵子 ěrzi [名] bait

二 èr **I** [数] two ◊第二次 the second time ◊一心二用 do two things at once **II** [动] ◊本店不二价。No bargaining in this shop.

二百五 èrbǎiwǔ [名] **1** (傻气的人) imbecile **2** (方) (半瓶醋) dabbler

二胡 èrhú [名] (中国乐器) erhu

二郎腿 èrlángtuǐ [名] cross-legged position ◊他坐着时老翘着二郎腿。He always sat cross-legged.

二流子 èrliúzi [名] layabout

二十 èrshí [数] twenty

二十四节气 èrshísì jiéqì [名] *the twenty-four Chinese solar terms*

二心 èrxīn [名] **1** (异心) disloyalty ◊他早就有了二心。He's been disloyal for a long time now. **2** (旁骛) half-heartedness

二一添作五 èr yī tiān zuò wǔ go fifty-fifty ◊我们二一添作五吧！Let's go fifty-fifty!

贰 èr [数] *an elaborate form of "two", used in writing cheques etc to prevent mistakes and forgery*

Ff

发 fā **I** [动] **1** (送出) send (*pt, pp* sent) ◇发电子邮件 send an e-mail ◇发货 deliver goods ◇发工资 pay wages **2** (发射) emit ♦发光 shine **3** (产生) produce ♦发电 generate electricity ♦发芽 sprout **4** (表达) express ♦发言 speak ◇发指示 give instructions **5** (扩大) develop ♦发扬 carry on **6** (兴旺) prosper ♦发家 make a family fortune **7** (使膨胀) ◇发面 leaven dough ◇蛋糕发起来了。The cake has risen. **8** (散开) spread (*pt, pp* spread) ♦发散 diverge ♦发挥 bring into play **9** (揭开) uncover ♦发现 discover ♦发掘 unearth ♦揭发 expose **10** (变得) become ♦发霉 go mouldy (英) 或 moldy (美) ♦发臭 smell bad **11** (流露) ♦发愁 worry ◇发脾气 lose one's temper **12** (感到) feel (*pt, pp* felt) ◇发冷 feel cold **13** (起程) leave (*pt, pp* left) ♦出发 set out **II** [量] ◇上千发子弹 thousands of bullets ▷另见fà

发榜 fābǎng [动] post up

发报 fābào [动] send a telegram (*pt, pp* sent)

发表 fābiǎo [动] **1** (宣布) announce ◇发表消息 announce the news ◇发表演说 make a speech **2** (刊登) publish

发布 fābù [动] issue

发财 fācái [动] make a fortune

发愁 fāchóu [动] worry

发出 fāchū [动] **1** (发送) send out (*pt, pp* sent) ◇发出求救信号 send out an SOS ◇发出传票 issue a summons **2** (散发) give out ◇发出光和热 give out light and heat

发达 fādá **I** [形] developed ◇他肌肉发达。He has well-developed muscles. **II** [动] promote

发呆 fādāi [动] be in a daze

发电 fādiàn [动] generate electricity

发电厂 fādiànchǎng [名] power station (英), power plant (美)

发动 fādòng [动] **1** (启动) start **2** (发起) launch **3** (鼓动) mobilize

发抖 fādǒu [动] **1** (因恐惧等) tremble **2** (因寒冷等) shiver

发放 fāfàng [动] grant ◇发放通行证 grant a pass

发愤 fāfèn [动] make a determined effort

发疯 fāfēng [动] go mad (*pt* went, *pp* gone)

发福 fāfú [动] put on weight (*pt, pp* put)

发稿 fāgǎo [动] file a report

发号施令 fā hào shī lìng go around issuing orders

发狠 fāhěn [动] **1** (下决心) make a determined effort **2** (恼火) be annoyed

发还 fāhuán [动] return ◇老师把作文发还给了学生。The teacher returned the essays to the students.

发慌 fāhuāng [动] be nervous

发挥 fāhuī [动] **1** (充分利用) bring ... into play (*pt, pp* brought) ◇这份工作使我充分发挥了专长。This job enabled me to make full use of my special skills. ◇发挥想象力 give one's imagination free rein ◇发挥电脑的作用 make the most of a computer **2** (详尽论述) elaborate ◇这一理论需要进一步发挥。This theory needs further elaboration.

发火 fāhuǒ [动] **1** (着火) catch fire (*pt, pp* caught) **2** (爆炸) detonate **3** (发脾气) lose one's temper (*pt, pp* lost)

发货 fāhuò [动] deliver goods

发迹 fājì [动] rise to power (*pt* rose, *pp* risen)

发家 fājiā [动] make a family fortune

发酵 fājiào [动] ferment ◇发酵饮料 fermented drink

发觉 fājué [动] discover ◇她发觉有错误。She discovered a mistake. ◇我发觉他有些不对劲。I realized there was something wrong with him.

发掘 fājué [动] unearth ◇发掘地下宝藏 unearth buried treasure ◇发掘潜力 discover hidden potential

发狂 fākuáng [动] go mad (*pt* went, *pp* gone)

发困 fākùn [动] feel sleepy (*pt*, *pp* felt)

发愣 fālèng [动] be in a daze

发霉 fāméi [动] go mouldy (英) 或 moldy (美) (*pt* went, *pp* gone)

发明 fāmíng [动] invent ◇计算机的发明是对人类的巨大贡献。The invention of the computer was of great benefit to humanity.

发难 fānàn [动] revolt ◇他们向政府发难。They revolted against the government.

发怒 fānù [动] get angry

发配 fāpèi [动] banish

发票 fāpiào [名] **1** (收据) receipt **2** (发货清单) invoice

发起 fāqǐ [动] **1** (倡议) sponsor **2** (发动) launch

发情 fāqíng [动] be in heat

发热 fārè [动] **1** (发烧) have a fever **2** (发出热量) give off heat (*pt* gave, *pp* given) **3** (不冷静) be hot-headed

发人深省 fā rén shēn xǐng give food for thought

发烧 fāshāo [动] have a temperature

发射 fāshè [动] launch

发生 fāshēng [动] happen ◇这是什么时候发生的? When did this happen? ◇近些年这座城市发生了很大变化。In recent years great changes have taken place in this city. ◇发生了一起车祸。There was a car accident.

发誓 fāshì [动] vow

发售 fāshòu [动] sell (*pt*, *pp* sold)

发条 fātiáo [名] spring ◇我的表上发条了。My watch is wound up.

发问 fāwèn [动] ask

发现 fāxiàn [动] discover ◇发现一个新油田 discover a new oilfield ◇发现线索 find clues ◇他在物理学上做出了很多重要发现。He made many important discoveries in physics.

发祥地 fāxiángdì [名] birthplace

发泄 fāxiè [动] vent

发行 fāxíng [动] publish ◇发行词典 publish a dictionary ◇发行影片 release a film ◇发行股票 issue stocks

发芽 fāyá [动] sprout

发言 fāyán [动] make a speech ◇工会主席的发言很精彩。The chairman of the trade union made a wonderful speech. ◇他要在明天的会上发言。He is going to speak at the meeting tomorrow.

发言人 fāyánrén [名] spokesperson (*pl* spokespersons)

发炎 fāyán [动] become inflamed

发扬 fāyáng [动] carry on

发音 fāyīn [动] pronounce ◇你这个单词发音不对。You pronounced this word wrong. ◇她的发音很标准。She has standard pronunciation.

发育 fāyù [动] develop ◇这些小鸡发育正常。These chicks are developing normally. ◇你要密切注意孩子智力的发育。You need to monitor children's intellectual development closely.

发源 fāyuán [动] rise (*pt* rose, *pp* risen)

发展 fāzhǎn [动] **1** (变化) develop ◇发展友好关系 develop friendly relations ◇中国的发展是对全球的重大贡献。The development of China has a lot to offer the world. **2** (扩大) expand

发作 fāzuò [动] **1** (突发) ◇激光唱机的老毛病发作了。The CD player is playing up again. ◇爷爷的心脏病又发作了。Grandpa had another heart attack. **2** (发脾气) flare up ◇他爱为小事发作。He is liable to flare up at trivial things.

乏 fá [动] **1** (缺乏) lack **2** (疲倦) be tired

乏味 fáwèi [形] dull

伐 fá [动] **1** (砍树) cut ... down (*pt*, *pp* cut) **2** (攻打) attack ♦讨伐 suppress

罚 fá [动] punish ♦罚款 fine ◊罚输者喝酒。The loser has to drink as a forfeit.

罚金 fájīn [名] fine ◊对他应处以罚金。A fine should be imposed on him.

罚款 fákuǎn I [动] fine II [名] fine

阀 fá [名] 1 (指人或家族) ♦军阀 warlord ♦财阀 tycoon 2 (指机器部件) valve

阀门 fámén [名] valve

筏 fá [名] raft

法 fǎ [名] 1 (法律) law ◊守法 abide by the law ◊犯法 break the law 2 (方法) method ♦用法 use 3 (标准) model ◊效法 follow an example 4 (佛理) Buddhism 5 (法术) magic ♦戏法 conjuring tricks

法办 fǎbàn [动] bring to justice (*pt, pp* brought)

法宝 fǎbǎo [名] magic weapon

法典 fǎdiǎn [名] statutes (*pl*)

法定 fǎdìng [形] statutory ◊法定假日 statutory holiday ◊法定继承权 legal right of inheritance

法官 fǎguān [名] judge

法规 fǎguī [名] laws and regulations (*pl*)

法理 fǎlǐ [名] legal principle

法令 fǎlìng [名] decree

法律 fǎlǜ [名] law

法门 fǎmén [名] Buddhism

法术 fǎshù [名] magic

法庭 fǎtíng [名] court ◊军事法庭 military court ◊民事法庭 civil court

法学 fǎxué [名] law

法医 fǎyī [名] forensic medical expert

法院 fǎyuàn [名] court

法则 fǎzé [名] law

法制 fǎzhì [名] legal system

法治 fǎzhì [名] rule of law

法子 fǎzi [名] way

砝 fǎ 见下文

砝码 fǎmǎ [名] weight

发 fà [名] hair ♦发辫 plait ▷另见 fā

> 📖 **hair** 既可以用作可数名词也可以用作不可数名词。在描述人时，**hair** 通常用作不可数名词。*She has long blonde hair and blue eyes… the girl with red hair and freckles…* 然而，当强调一根根或几簇头发或毛发时，可以将它用作可数名词。*There were some blonde hairs in the car.*

发廊 fàláng [名] hairdresser's

发型 fàxíng [名] hairstyle

珐 fà 见下文

珐琅 fàláng [名] enamel

帆 fān [名] sail

帆布 fānbù [名] canvas

帆船 fānchuán [名] sailing boat ◊帆船运动 sailing

番 fān [量] ◊我三番五次告诉他不要抽烟。I've told him time and time again he shouldn't smoke. ◊经过几番挫折他明白了许多道理。After a few false starts he picked up quite a lot. ◊他是出于一番好意才做的。He just did it out of a kind impulse. ◊这首曲子别有一番情调。This melody has an entirely different feel.

番茄 fānqié [名] tomato (*pl* tomatoes)

翻 fān [动] 1 (换位置) turn over ◊服务员把垫子翻过来。The staff turned the mattress over. ◊他在床上翻了个身。He turned over in bed. ◊车翻了。The car overturned. 2 (寻找) rummage ◊她正在屋里东找西翻。She is rummaging around in her room. 3 (推翻) reverse 4 (越过) get across 5 (增加) multiply 6 (翻译) translate 7 (翻脸) fall out (*pt* fell, *pp* fallen)

翻案 fān'àn [动] overturn a verdict

翻版 fānbǎn [名] reprint

翻番 fānfān [动] double

翻覆 fānfù [动] 1 (颠覆) overturn 2

(彻底变化) be transformed **3** (翻身) turn over

翻供 fāngòng [动] retract one's testimony

翻滚 fāngǔn [动] **1** (沸腾) seethe **2** (翻筋斗) roll

翻悔 fānhuǐ [动] back out ◇她说和我一起去,可又翻悔了。She said she'd go with me, but then backed out. ◇现在要翻悔你的承诺为时已晚。It's too late to go back on your promise.

翻江倒海 fān jiāng dǎo hǎi earth-shaking

翻来覆去 fān lái fù qù **1** (来回翻身) toss and turn **2** (反反复复) repeatedly

翻脸 fānliǎn [动] fall out (*pt* fell, *pp* fallen) ◇我和姐姐从没翻过脸。I've never fallen out with my sister.

翻身 fānshēn [动] **1** (转身) turn over **2** (解放) emancipate oneself

翻腾 fānténg [动] **1** (滚动) churn **2** (翻动) rummage **3** (思考) think over

翻天覆地 fān tiān fù dì earth-shattering

翻箱倒柜 fān xiāng dǎo guì search high and low

翻新 fānxīn [动] renovate ◇这所房子正在翻新。This house is being renovated. ◇皮沙发刚刚翻新过。The leather sofa has just been reconditioned. ◇花样翻新 in a new guise

翻译 fānyì **I** [动] translate **II** [名] translator

翻云覆雨 fān yún fù yǔ shifty

凡 fán **I** [名] **1** (人世间) mortal world **2** (大概) approximation **II** [形] ordinary **III** [副] **1** (凡是) ◇凡年满16周岁的，可申办身份证。All those who have reached the age of 16 can apply for an ID card. ◇凡坏人没有好下场。Bad people always come to a sticky end. **2** (总共) in all ◇全书凡6卷。The set contains six volumes in all.

凡人 fánrén [名] **1** (平常人) ordinary person **2** (俗人) mortal

凡是 fánshì [副] ◇凡是去过大连的人都说那儿好。Everyone who's been to Dalian says it's lovely. ◇凡是没洗干净的杯子都要放这儿。Any glasses that have not been washed properly should be put here.

烦 fán **I** [名] trouble ◇不厌其烦 not mind taking the trouble **II** [动] (谦) trouble ◇烦你给我弄杯水。May I trouble you to get me a glass of water? ◇烦请您给她捎个话儿? Could you please pass on a message to her? **III** [形] (厌烦) fed up ◇我烦那些人。I am fed up with those people. ◇这事真叫人烦！ It's so annoying!

烦劳 fánláo [动] trouble ◇烦劳您给孩子们读个故事。Would you mind reading a story to the children?

烦闷 fánmèn [形] depressed

烦恼 fánnǎo [形] worried ◇你不要为小事烦恼。You shouldn't worry about little things.

烦琐 fánsuǒ [形] over-elaborate

烦躁 fánzào [形] agitated

樊 fán [名] (书) fence

樊篱 fánlí [名] **1** (篱笆) fence **2** (喻) (形容限制) barrier

繁 fán **I** [形] numerous **II** [动] propagate

繁多 fánduō [形] numerous ◇名目繁多 numerous items ◇花样繁多 a great variety

繁复 fánfù [形] laborious and complicated

繁华 fánhuá [形] bustling

繁忙 fánmáng [形] busy

繁茂 fánmào [形] lush

繁荣 fánróng **I** [形] flourishing ◇经济在繁荣。The economy is booming. **II** [动] ◇繁荣市场 create a strong market

繁文缛节 fán wén rù jié bureaucracy

繁衍 fányǎn [动] multiply

繁杂 fánzá [形] diverse

繁殖 fánzhí [动] breed (*pt*, *pp* bred)

繁重 fánzhòng [形] strenuous ◇繁重的工作 strenuous work ◇繁重的任务 arduous tasks

反 fǎn I [名] 1 (相反) opposite ◊适得其反 lead to just the opposite 2 (造反) rebellion II [动] 1 (转换) turn ◊反败为胜 turn defeat into victory 2 (回) return 3 (反对) oppose 4 (背叛) rebel III [形] opposite IV [副] 1 (相反地) on the contrary ◊我觉得她不但不丑，反倒挺美。She is not ugly to me; on the contrary, I think she's beautiful. ◊他不安慰我，反伤我的感情。Instead of comforting me, he hurt my feelings. 2 (从反面) again ♦反顾 look back ♦反思 review

反驳 fǎnbó [动] refute

反差 fǎnchā [名] contrast

反常 fǎncháng [形] unusual

反衬 fǎnchèn [动] set … off (*pt, pp* set) ◊绿叶将花朵反衬得更加美丽。The green leaves set off the flowers beautifully.

反唇相讥 fǎn chún xiāng jī respond sharply

反倒 fǎndào [副] ◊让她等我，她反倒上车了。I asked her to wait for me, but instead she got on the bus. ◊雪停了，天反倒冷了。The snow has stopped, but the weather has turned colder.

反动 fǎndòng I [形] reactionary II [名] reaction

反对 fǎnduì [动] oppose

反而 fǎn'ér [副] instead ◊她不但没有平静下来，反而越来越激动。Instead of calming down, she became more and more agitated. ◊他不感到累，反而劲头更足。He didn't feel tired; on the contrary, he had even more energy.

反复 fǎnfù [副] 1 (重复) repeatedly 2 (多变) capriciously

反感 fǎngǎn [形] disgusted ◊我对他们的行为很反感。I'm disgusted by their behaviour.

反攻 fǎngōng [名] counterattack

反躬自问 fǎn gōng zì wèn ask oneself

反光 fǎnguāng I [动] reflect light II [名] reflected light

反话 fǎnhuà [名] irony

反悔 fǎnhuǐ [动] go back on one's word (*pt* went, *pp* gone) ◊答应别人的事可不能反悔。You can't go back on your promise.

反击 fǎnjī [动] fight back (*pt, pp* fought) ◊他们决定进行有力的反击。They decided to launch a major counterattack.

反抗 fǎnkàng [动] resist ◊反抗压迫 resist oppression ◊反抗精神 spirit of resistance

反恐怖主义 fǎn kǒngbù zhǔyì [名] anti-terrorism

反馈 fǎnkuì [动] give feedback (*pt* gave, *pp* given) ◊反馈意见 feedback

反面 fǎnmiàn I [名] other side II [形] negative

反目 fǎnmù [动] turn against

反派 fǎnpài [名] villain

反叛 fǎnpàn [动] revolt

反扑 fǎnpū [动] launch a counterattack

反其道而行之 fǎn qí dào ér xíng zhī do just the opposite

反射 fǎnshè I [动] reflect II [名] reflex ◊条件反射 conditioned reflex

反思 fǎnsī [动] review ◊对这次事故我们要进行深刻的反思。We need to have a full review of this accident.

反诉 fǎnsù [动] counterclaim

反问 fǎnwèn I [动] answer a question with a question ◊他没回答我的问题，却反问我一个。He didn't reply to my question, but answered with a question of his own. II [名] rhetorical question

反响 fǎnxiǎng [名] reverberation

反省 fǎnxǐng [动] question oneself ◊我们需要反省自己的行为。We need to question our own behaviour.

反义词 fǎnyìcí [名] opposite

反应 fǎnyìng [名] 1 (反响) response ◊上级对我们的意见很快有了反应。Management made a quick response to our suggestion. ◊观众对这部影片的反应不一。Audience reaction to the film varied. ◊这孩

子反应很快。The kid is quick-witted. **2** (指机体) reaction ◇过敏反应 allergic reaction **3** (指物理、化学) reaction ◇核反应 nuclear reaction

反映 fǎnyìng [动] **1** (反照) reflect **2** (汇报) report

反语 fǎnyǔ [名] irony

反正 fǎnzhèng [副] anyway ◇反正必须有人去，就让我去吧！ Since someone has to go anyway, why not let me go!

反之 fǎnzhī [连] otherwise ◇努力了我们就会成功，反之就难说了。If we work hard we will succeed – otherwise we may not.

返 fǎn [动] return

返潮 fǎncháo [动] get damp

返工 fǎngōng [动] redo

返航 fǎnháng [动] return

返回 fǎnhuí [动] come back (*pt* came, *pp* come)

返老还童 fǎn lǎo huán tóng regain one's youth

犯 fàn **I** [动] **1** (违犯) violate **2** (侵犯) attack **3** (发作) ◇他心脏病又犯了。He had another heart attack. **4** (错误、罪行等) commit **II** [名] criminal

犯病 fànbìng [动] have a relapse

犯愁 fànchóu [动] worry

犯法 fànfǎ [动] break the law (*pt* broke, *pp* broken)

犯规 fànguī [动] break the rules (*pt* broke, *pp* broken)

犯忌 fànjì [动] break a taboo (*pt* broke, *pp* broken)

犯禁 fànjìn [动] violate a prohibition

犯人 fànrén [名] prisoner

犯罪 fànzuì [动] commit a crime ◇犯罪心理 criminal mind

饭 fàn [名] **1** (餐) meal ♦早饭 breakfast ♦晚饭 supper **2** (米饭) rice

饭局 fànjú [名] dinner party

饭桶 fàntǒng [名] **1** (盛饭工具) rice container **2** (饭量大的人) big eater **3** (喻) (无用的人) imbecile

饭碗 fànwǎn [名] **1** (盛饭的碗) rice bowl **2**(口) (职业) job

泛 fàn **I** [动] **1** (书) (漂浮) float **2** (透出) suffuse ◇他脸上泛红。He blushed. **3** (泛滥) flood **II** [副] superficially

泛泛而谈 fànfàn ér tán talk generally

泛泛之交 fànfàn zhī jiāo acquaintance

泛滥 fànlàn [动] overflow

范 fàn [名] **1** (模范) model ♦典范 model **2** (范围) limit ♦规范 standard **3** (模子) pattern

范畴 fànchóu [名] category

范例 fànlì [名] example

范围 fànwéi [名] limit ◇管辖范围 limits of jurisdiction ◇势力范围 sphere of influence

范文 fànwén [名] model essay

贩 fàn **I** [动] deal in (*pt*, *pp* dealt) **II** [名] dealer

贩卖 fànmài [动] deal in (*pt*, *pp* dealt) ◇贩卖艺术品 deal in art ◇贩卖丝绸 be in the silk trade ◇贩卖人口 traffic in human beings

贩子 fànzi [名] dealer

方 fāng **I** [名] **1** (方向) direction ♦南方 the South **2** (方形) square ♦长方形 rectangle **3** (方面) side **4** (方法) method **5** (地方) place **6** (方子) prescription **7** (数) (乘方) power ◇3的4次方是81。Three to the power of four is 81. **II** [形] **1** (方形) square **2** (正直) honest **III** [副] **1**(书) (正当) ♦方今 nowadays ◇方兴未艾 be on the rise ◇来日方长 there is still time **2** (方才) just ◇如梦方醒 as if just awakened from a dream **IV** [量] **1** (指方形物) ◇一方豆腐 a piece of tofu ◇一方毛巾 a towel **2** (指平方或立方) ◇一方木材 a cubic metre of timber ◇办公室有30方。The office is 30 square metres.

方案 fāng'àn [名] plan ◇退休金方案 pension scheme ◇校长在制定本期工作方案。The head teacher is drawing up a work plan for the term.

方便 fāngbiàn [形] **1** (便利) convenient ◇上海的交通很方便。Transport in Shanghai is easy. ◇我

们应把方便留给他人。We should make things easy for people. **2** (适宜) appropriate ◊这里谈话不方便。It's not appropriate to talk here.

方才 fāngcái [副] just now ◊方才的事你不要放在心上。Don't take to heart what happened just now.

方程 fāngchéng [名] equation

方寸 fāngcùn [名] (心绪) mind ◊他乱了方寸。He felt very troubled.

方法 fāngfǎ [名] method

方法论 fāngfǎlùn [名] methodology

方略 fānglüè [名] strategy

方面 fāngmiàn [名] **1** (指人) side ◊优势在我们方面。 Our side has the advantage. **2** (指物) aspect ◊我们应该分析问题的所有方面。We should analyse all aspects of the problem.

方式 fāngshì [名] way ◊生活方式 way of life ◊生产方式 production method ◊她用简单的方式解决了问题。She solved the problem in a simple way.

方位 fāngwèi [名] position

方向 fāngxiàng [名] direction ◊你要朝那个方向走。You need to go in that direction. ◊他们在森林里迷失了方向。They got disoriented in the wood.

方兴未艾 fāng xīng wèi ài be on the rise

方言 fāngyán [名] dialect

方正 fāngzhèng [形] **1** (不歪斜) square **2** (正直) honest

方子 fāngzi [名] **1** (药方) prescription ◊开方子 write a prescription **2** (配方) formula

芳 fāng [名] **1** (香味) fragrance **2** (好名声) virtue

芳香 fāngxiāng [名] fragrance ◊芳香的花朵 fragrant flower

防 fáng **I** [动] **1** (防备) prevent ◊防冻 prevent frostbite ◊防盗 guard against theft **2** (防守) defend ◊海防 sea defences (英) 或 defenses (美) **II** [名] dyke

防暴 fángbào [动] ◊防暴警察 riot police

防备 fángbèi [动] guard against ◊防备敌人偷袭 guard against surprise attacks by the enemy ◊防备火灾 take precautions against fire

防不胜防 fáng bù shèng fáng be unable to defend

防范 fángfàn [动] keep a lookout (*pt, pp* kept)

防护 fánghù [动] protect

防患未然 fáng huàn wèi rán take preventative measures

防空 fángkōng [名] air defence (英) 或 defense (美) ◊防空导弹 air defence missile

防身 fángshēn [动] defend oneself

防微杜渐 fáng wēi dù jiàn nip in the bud

防卫 fánwèi [动] defend

防务 fángwù [名] defence (英), defense (美)

防线 fángxiàn [名] line of defence (英) 或 defense (美)

防御 fángyù [动] defend ◊修筑防御工事construct defences (英) 或 defenses (美)

防止 fángzhǐ [动] prevent ◊防止疾病扩散 prevent disease from spreading

防治 fángzhì [动] prevent and cure

坊 fáng [名] workshop

妨 fáng [动] obstruct ♦妨碍 obstruct

妨碍 fáng'ài [动] obstruct ◊车祸妨碍了交通。The car accident obstructed the traffic. ◊嘈杂声会妨碍他人学习。The noise will disturb those who are studying.

妨害 fánghài [动] jeopardize

房 fáng [名] **1** (房子) house ♦楼房 tower block **2** (房间) room ♦书房 study ♦卧房 bedroom **3** (像房子之物) ◊蜂房 beehive **4** (家族) ◊远房亲戚 a distant relative

房地产 fángdìchǎn [名] real estate

房东 fángdōng [名] landlord

房客 fángkè [名] tenant

房事 fángshì [名] sex

房屋 fángwū [名] building

仿 fǎng [动] **1** (仿效) copy **2** (类似) be like ◇他们两个人年龄相仿。They are both about the same age.

仿佛 fǎngfú **I** [连] as if **I** [形] similar

仿生学 fǎngshēngxué [名] bionics (*pl*)

仿效 fǎngxiào [动] imitate

仿造 fǎngzào [动] copy

仿照 fǎngzhào [动] copy ◇这个方法不错，我们可以仿照。That's a good method – let's copy it.

仿制 fǎngzhì [动] fake ◇这是仿制品。This is a fake.

访 fǎng [动] **1** (访问) call on ♦访友 call on a friend ♦访谈 call in for a chat **2** (调查) investigate ♦访查 investigate

访问 fǎngwèn [动] visit

纺 fǎng **I** [动] spin (*pt, pp* spun) **II** [名] silk

纺织 fǎngzhī [动] ◇纺织品 textiles (*pl*) ◇纺织工业 textile industry

放 fàng [动] **1** (使自由) release ♦释放 release ♦解放 free **2** (暂时停止) ◇下周我放两天假。I'll have two days off next week. ◇放学了。School is now over. **3** (放纵) let oneself go ◇放声歌唱 sing uninhibitedly ◇放言高论 speak without restraint **4** (赶牲畜吃草) graze ◇放牛 graze cattle **5** (驱逐) expel ♦流放 banish **6** (发出) send out (*pt, pp* sent) ♦放炮 fire a gun ♦放风筝 fly a kite **7** (点燃) set … off (*pt, pp* set) ◇放爆竹 set off firecrackers **8** (借出收息) lend (*pt, pp* lent) ◇放高利贷 practise (英) 或 practice (美) usury **9** (扩展) ◇把照片放大 enlarge a photo ◇把裙子放长 let down a skirt **10** (花开) bloom **11** (搁置) put … to one side (*pt, pp* put) **12** (弄倒) cut down (*pt, pp* cut) **13** (使处于) put (*pt, pp* put) ◇她把课本放在桌子上。She put the book on the table. **14** (加进) add ◇你往里放点糖就好喝。If you add some sugar it will taste better. **15** (控制自己) ◇放严肃点 become more serious **16** (放映) project ◇放电影 project a film **17** (保存) leave (*pt, pp* left) ◇把东西就放我这里吧。Leave your things with me.

放大 fàngdà [动] enlarge ◇把照片放大 enlarge a photo ◇把音量放大 turn up the volume

放荡 fàngdàng [形] dissipated

放风 fàngfēng [动] **1** (开窗通风) let in fresh air (*pt, pp* let) **2** (从牢房出来) let out for exercise **3** (散发消息) leak

放牧 fàngmù [动] graze

放屁 fàngpì [动] **1** (指生理现象) break wind (*pt* broke, *pp* broken) **2** (侮辱) (用来骂人) talk nonsense ◇放屁！(讳) That's complete crap!

放弃 fàngqì [动] give … up (*pt* gave, *pp* given)

放晴 fàngqíng [动] clear up

放任 fàngrèn [动] ignore ◇对错误的行为不能放任不管。Bad behaviour should not be ignored. ◇放任政策 laissez-faire policy

放射 fàngshè [动] radiate

放射性 fàngshèxìng [名] **1** (指原子能) radioactivity ◇放射性灰尘 radioactive dust **2** (指医学) radiation

放生 fàngshēng [动] release

放肆 fàngsì [形] wanton

放松 fàngsōng [动] relax

放心 fàngxīn [动] set one's mind at rest (*pt, pp* set) ◇孩子还没回来，我不放心。My mind won't rest because the child hasn't come back yet.

放眼 fangyǎn [动] survey

放逐 fàngzhú [动] banish

放纵 fàngzòng **I** [动] indulge ◇不要太放纵孩子。Don't be too indulgent with the children. **II** [形] undisciplined

飞 fēi **I** [动] (鸟、虫、飞机) fly (*pt* flew, *pp* flown) ◇这架飞机将由广州飞往北京。This plane is going from Guangzhou to Beijing. **2** (空中游动) flutter ◇叶子在空中飞着。The leaves are fluttering in the air. ◇飞雪花了。It's snowing. **3** (挥发) evaporate **II** [形] **1** (意外的) unexpected ♦飞祸 unexpected disaster **2** (凭空而来的) unfounded

◇流言飞语 unfounded rumours (英) 或 rumors (美) (*pl*) **III** [副] swiftly

飞驰 fēichí [动] speed (*pt, pp* sped)

飞碟 fēidié [名] UFO

飞短流长 fēi duǎn liú cháng tell stories

飞黄腾达 fēi huáng téng dá have a meteoric rise

飞机 fēijī [名] aeroplane (英), airplane (美)

飞快 fēikuài **I** [形] razor-sharp **II** [副] rapidly

飞毛腿 fēimáotuǐ [名] fast runner

飞速 fēisù [形] very fast

飞吻 fēiwěn [动] blow a kiss (*pt* blew, *pp* blown) ◇女孩儿给妈妈一个飞吻。The girl blew her mother a kiss.

飞翔 fēixiáng [动] hover

飞行 fēixíng [动] fly (*pt* flew, *pp* flown)

飞扬 fēiyáng [动] rise (*pt* rose, *pp* risen)

飞扬跋扈 fēi yáng bá hù pushy

飞跃 fēiyuè [动] leap ◇近几年，中国经济飞跃发展。China's economy has developed by leaps and bounds in recent years.

飞涨 fēizhǎng [动] soar

妃 fēi [名] concubine

非 fēi **I** [名] **1** (错误) wrong ♦是非 right and wrong **2** (非洲) Africa **II** [动] **1** (非议) blame ◇无可厚非 beyond reproach **2** (违反) run counter to (*pt* ran, *pp* run) ♦非法 illegal ♦非礼 impolite **3** (不是) not be ◇我非三言两语就能把这事说完的。I am not able to say it in a few words. **4** (强硬) insist on ◇他非要我参加。He insists on my taking part. ◇不行，我非得走。No, I must go. **III** [副] (必须) ◇我不让他去，他非去不可。I've tried to stop him, but he simply has to go. ◇要想通过考试，你非努力不行。You can't pass the exam without working hard.

非常 fēicháng **I** [形] exceptional **II** [副] very ◇你的同情让我非常感动。Your sympathy moved me very much. ◇这项工作非常难。This job is very hard. ◇你说的话非常重要。What you said is extremely important. ◇我非常抱歉。I'm terribly sorry.

非典 fēidiǎn [名] (非典型性肺炎) SARS

非法 fēifǎ [形] illegal

非凡 fēifán [形] outstanding

非…非… fēi...fēi... [连] neither... nor... ◇非亲非故 neither a relative nor a friend

非分 fēifèn [形] inappropriate

非金属 fēijīnshǔ [名] nonmetal

非礼 fēilǐ **I** [形] impolite **II** [动] sexually assault

非驴非马 fēi lǘ fēi mǎ be neither one thing nor the other

非难 fēinàn [动] censure

非人 fēirén [形] inhuman

非同小可 fēi tóng xiǎo kě no small matter

非议 fēiyì [动] reproach

绯 fēi [形] red

绯红 fēihóng [形] bright red ◇她脸蛋热得绯红。Her face was red with the heat.

扉 fēi [名] door

扉页 fēiyè [名] title page

蜚 见下文

蜚声 fēishēng [动] become famous

鲱 fēi [名] herring

肥 féi **I** [名] fertilizer **II** [动] **1** (使肥沃) fertilize **2** (暴富) get rich **III** [形] **1** (脂肪多) fat **2** (肥沃) fertile **3** (肥大) loose

肥大 féidà [形] **1** (宽大) loose **2** (肿大) swollen

肥料 féiliào [名] fertilizer

肥胖 féipàng [形] fat

肥沃 féiwò [形] fertile

肥皂 féizào [名] soap

肥壮 féizhuàng [形] stout

匪 fěi **I** [名] robber **II** [副] not ◇受益匪浅 gain quite significantly

匪徒 fěitú [名] gangster

匪夷所思 fěi yí suǒ sī fantastic

诽 fěi [动] slander

诽谤 fěibàng [动] slander

菲 fěi 见下文

菲薄 fěibó I [动] look down on II [形] humble

斐 fěi [形] brilliant

斐然 fěirán [形] brilliant

翡 fěi 见下文

翡翠 fěicuì [名] jadeite

吠 fèi [动] bark

肺 fèi [名] lung

肺腑 fèifǔ [名] heart ◊肺腑之言 heartfelt words ◊感人肺腑 deeply moving

狒 fèi 见下文

狒狒 fèifèi [名] baboon

废 fèi I [动] abandon II [形] **1** (不用的) waste **2** (没用的) useless **3** (残废的) disabled

废除 fèichú [动] abolish

废黜 fèichù [动] depose

废话 fèihuà [名] nonsense

废品 fèipǐn [名] **1** (不合格产品) reject **2** (废旧物品) waste

废弃 fèiqì [动] abandon

废寝忘食 fèi qǐn wàng shí forget to eat or sleep

废物 fèiwù [名] waste

废止 fèizhǐ [动] annul

废置 fèizhì [动] abandon

沸 fèi [形] boiling

沸点 fèidiǎn [名] boiling point

沸腾 fèiténg [动] **1** (汽化) boil **2** (喻) (指情绪) ◊大家沸腾起来。There was uproar.

费 fèi I [名] fee ◊车费 bus fare ◊医药费 medical expenses II [形] expensive III [动] **1** (花费) spend (*pt*, *pp* spent) ◊我费了好大的劲才明白他的意思。It was ages before I understood what he meant. ◊买这件皮大衣费了我很多钱。This leather coat cost me a lot of money. **2** (消耗过度) ◊这个牌子的冰箱很费电。This brand of refrigerator consumes too much electricity. ◊孩子们穿鞋太费。Children wear out their shoes too quickly.

费解 fèijiě [形] incomprehensible

费尽心机 fèi jìn xīnjī rack one's brains

费力 fèilì [动] take a lot of effort (*pt* took, *pp* taken) ◊我毫不费力地就把工作做完了。I got the job done without too much effort.

费神 fèishén [动] **1** (敬) ◊劳您费神把稿子看一下。Can I trouble you to take a look at this draft? **2** (耗费精神) put energy into (*pt*, *pp* put) ◊为写这篇文章我费了很大的神。I put a lot of energy into writing this article.

费事 fèishì [动] take trouble (*pt* took, *pp* taken) ◊他不怕费事，尽量做好会议的筹办工作。He is taking a lot of trouble in making arrangements for the meeting.

费心 fèixīn [动] **1** (敬) ◊您费心照看一会儿我的儿子好吗？Would you mind looking after my son for a while? ◊您费心帮我看看有没有错误。Can you check this for mistakes? **2** (耗费心思) devote a lot of care ◊我为他费了很多心。I devoted a lot of care to him.

费用 fèiyong [名] expense ◊生活费用 living expenses

痱 fèi [名] prickly heat

痱子 fèizi [名] prickly heat

分 fēn I [动] **1** (分开) divide ♦分离 separate ♦分散 scatter ♦分裂 split **2** (分配) assign ◊这些电脑已分给我们了。These computers have been assigned to us. **3** (辨别) distinguish ◊不分皂白 make no distinction between right and wrong II [名] **1** (分支) branch ◊分公司 branch of a company **2** (分数) fraction ♦分母 denominator III [量] **1** (分数) ◊四分之三 three quarters **2** (十分之一) one tenth ◊我们都怕老板三分。We are all a little afraid of the boss. **3** (长度单位) *unit of length, equivalent to 3mm* **4** (指货币) *unit of Chinese*

currency, equal to a hundredth of a yuan **5** (指时间) minute ◇5点过5分 5 minutes past 5 **6** (指弧度或角度) minute ◇36度20分角 36 degrees 20 minutes **7** (百分之一) per cent ◇月利1分 monthly interest of 1 per cent ◇他物理是93分。He got 93 per cent in physics.
▷另见fèn

分崩离析 fēn bēng lí xī fall to pieces

分辨 fēnbiàn [动] distinguish ◇分辨花样 distinguish one variety from another ◇我分辨不出这是什么颜色。I can't tell what colour it is.

分别 fēnbié **I** [动] **1** (离别) split up (*pt, pp* split) **2** (辨别) distinguish ◇分别善恶 distinguish the good from the bad **II** [名] difference

分布 fēnbù [动] distribute

分成 fēnchéng [动] divide

分词 fēncí [名] participle

分寸 fēncun [名] ◇经理说话很有分寸。The manager talks in a measured way.

分道扬镳 fēn dào yáng biāo each goes their own way

分割 fēngē [动] break apart (*pt* broke, *pp* broken)

分工 fēngōng [名] division of labour ◇社会分工 division of labour in society

分红 fēnhóng [动] get a bonus

分化 fēnhuà [动] **1** (分成) split up (*pt, pp* split) **2** (瓦解) break up (*pt* broke, *pp* broken) **3** (细胞、组织等) divide

分解 fēnjiě [动] **1** (数) break down (*pt* broke, *pp* broken) **2** (书) (解说) explain

分居 fēnjū [动] separate

分句 fēnjù [名] clause

分类 fēnlèi [动] classify ◇粗略的分类 rough classification

分离 fēnlí [动] **1** (分开) separate **2** (离别) part

分裂 fēnliè [动] **1** (分开) split (*pt, pp* split) **2**(生物)divide

分门别类 fēn mén bié lèi categorize

分泌 fēnmì [动] secrete

分娩 fēnmiǎn [动] give birth (*pt* gave, *pp* given)

分明 fēnmíng **I** [形] clear **II** [副] clearly

分派 fēnpài [动] assign

分配 fēnpèi [动] assign

分歧 fēnqí [名] difference

分散 fēnsàn [动] **1** (不集中) divert ◇不要分散你的注意力。Don't allow your attention to be diverted. **2** (散居) disperse

分身 fēnshēn [动] spare time

分神 fēnshén [动] ◇麻烦您分神帮我讲一讲这句话。Can I trouble you to help me with this speech?

分手 fēnshǒu [动] **1** (告别) say goodbye (*pt, pp* said) **2** (指男女关系) break up (*pt* broke, *pp* broken)

分数 fēnshù [名] fraction

分水岭 fēnshuǐlǐng [名] **1**(地理) watershed **2** (喻) (界限) dividing line

分摊 fēntān [动] share

分庭抗礼 fēn tíng kàng lǐ stand up to

分析 fēnxī [动] analyse (英), analyze (美) ◇对当前国际形势的透彻分析 a thorough analysis of recent international trends

分享 fēnxiǎng [动] share in ◇我们一起分享成功的欢乐。We will all share in the pleasure of success.

分晓 fēnxiǎo **I** [名] **1** (结果) solution **2** (道理) reason **II** [形] clear

分心 fēnxīn [动] **1** (分散注意力) be distracted **2** (费心) ◇这事让您分心了。Sorry to trouble you with this.

分忧 fēnyōu [动] ◇她始终帮我分忧。She always helps me through my problems.

分赃 fēnzāng [动] share the spoils

分支 fēnzhī [名] branch ◇学科的分支 branch of science ◇河流的分支 tributary

分子 fēnzǐ [名] **1** (数) numerator **2** (化) molecule

芬 fēn [名] fragrance ♦芬芳 fragrant

芬芳 fēnfāng [形] fragrant

吩 fēn 见下文

吩咐 fēnfù [动] instruct ◇母亲吩咐我看管好房子。Mother instructed me to look after the house.

纷 fēn [形] **1** (多) numerous ♦纷繁 numerous **2** (乱) confused ♦纷扰 confusion

纷繁 fēnfán [形] numerous

纷纷 fēnfēn I [形] diverse II [副] one after another

纷乱 fēnluàn [形] chaotic

纷纭 fēnyún [形] disorderly

纷争 fēnzhēng [名] dispute

纷至沓来 fēn zhì tà lái come thick and fast

氛 fēn [名] atmosphere

氛围 fēnwéi [名] atmosphere

坟 fén [名] grave

坟墓 fénmù [名] grave

焚 fén [动] burn

焚化 fénhuà [动] incinerate

焚烧 fénshāo [动] burn

粉 fěn I [名] **1** (粉末) powder **2** (粉丝) vermicelli II [动] **1** (成碎末) crumble ♦粉碎 crush **2** (变成粉状) pulverize III [形] **1** (白色) white **2** (粉红色) pink

粉红 fěnhóng [形] pink

粉末 fěnmò [名] powder

粉墨登场 fěn mò dēng chǎng **1** (贬) embark upon a political career **2** (产品、新人) be launched

粉饰 fěnshì [动] gloss over

粉刷 fěnshuā [动] whitewash

粉碎 fěnsuì I [形] crushed II [动] smash

分 fèn [名] **1** (成分) component ♦水分 water content **2** (限度) limit ♦过分 excessive ♦本分 duty **3** (情分) feelings (*pl*)
▷另见fēn

分量 fènliàng [名] weight ◇这两个西瓜是一样的分量。These two watermelons are the same weight. ◇他说的话很有分量。He speaks with authority.

分子 fènzǐ [名] ◇积极分子 activist ◇知识分子 intellectual ◇保守分子 conservative

份 fèn I [名] **1** (一部分) part ♦股份 share ◇他们把钱平分成4份。The money was divided equally between the four of them. **2** (指划分单位) ♦年份 year II [量] **1** (指食物) portion ◇一份快餐 a portion of fast food **2** (指报刊) copy

份额 fèn'é [名] share

份子 fènzi [名] share ◇出份子 club together

奋 fèn [动] **1** (振作) exert oneself ♦勤奋 diligent **2** (举起) raise

奋不顾身 fèn bù gù shēn act bravely and selflessly ◇抢险队员奋不顾身营救孩子们。The emergency worker showed great courage in rescuing the children.

奋斗 fèndòu [动] fight (*pt*, *pp* fought) ◇为前途而奋斗 fight for the future

奋发 fènfā [动] work hard

奋发图强 fèn fā tú qiáng work hard for success

奋勇 fènyǒng [动] act bravely ◇奋勇杀敌 fight the enemy bravely

粪 fèn [名] excrement

粪土 fèntǔ [名] rubbish

愤 fèn [形] indignant ♦气愤 indignant

愤慨 fènkǎi [形] indignant ◇这种无耻行为令人愤慨！This is outrageous behaviour (英) 或 behavior (美), quite infuriating!

愤怒 fènnù [形] angry ◇同事们愤怒谴责他卑鄙无耻的行径。His colleagues angrily condemned his despicable conduct.

愤世嫉俗 fèn shì jí sú detest the ways of the world

丰 fēng [形] **1** (丰富) abundant **2** (大) great **3** (貌美) good-looking

丰碑 fēngbēi [名] monument

丰富 fēngfù I [形] abundant ◇丰富多彩的生活 a full and interesting life II [动] enrich

丰功伟绩 fēng gōng wěi jì great achievements

丰厚 fēnghòu [形] abundant ◊丰厚的皮毛 thick fur ◊丰厚的薪水 a generous salary

丰满 fēngmǎn [形] **1** (指物品) plentiful **2** (指身材) well-developed ◊身体丰满匀称 a full and well-proportioned figure

丰年 fēngnián [名] good year ◊瑞雪兆丰年。Snow at the right time is a sign of a good harvest.

丰盛 fēngshèng [形] rich

丰收 fēngshōu [动] have a good harvest

丰硕 fēngshuò [形] substantial

丰衣足食 fēng yī zú shí be comfortably off

丰足 fēngzú [形] ample

风 fēng **I** [名] **1** (指空气流动) wind ♦狂风 gale ◊今天刮大风。It's very windy today. **2** (风气) trend **3** (景象) scene ♦风光 scenery **4** (态度) manner ♦风度 bearing **5** (消息) information ◊闻风而动 respond immediately **II** [形] rumoured (英), rumored (美) ◊风言风语 gossip **III** [动] air ♦风干 air-dry

风波 fēngbō [名] storm

风采 fēngcǎi [名] **1** (神采) elegance **2** (文采) writing talent

风餐露宿 fēng cān lù sù face the elements

风尘 fēngchén [名] (指旅行) travel weariness

风驰电掣 fēng chí diàn chè quick as lightning

风传 fēngchuán [动] be rumoured (英) 或 rumored (美)

风度 fēngdù [名] bearing

风格 fēnggé [名] **1** (气度) manner ◊高尚风格 refined manner **2** (特点) style ◊绘画风格 style of painting

风光 fēngguāng [名] scenery

风花雪月 fēng huā xuě yuè love affair

风华 fēnghuá [名] (书) elegance and talent ◊风华正茂 be in one's prime

风化 fēnghuà **I** [名] morals (*pl*) **II** [动] weather

风纪 fēngjì [名] discipline

风景 fēngjǐng [名] scenery

风浪 fēnglàng [名] **1** (风和波浪) rough waters (*pl*) **2** (遭遇) difficulties (*pl*) ◊久经风浪 have survived many troubles

风凉 fēngliáng [形] cool

风凉话 fēngliánghuà [名] sarcastic remark

风流 fēngliú [形] **1** (指功绩) outstanding **2** (指才学) free-spirited **3** (指男女关系) promiscuous ◊一夜风流 one night stand

风马牛不相及 fēng mǎ niú bù xiāng jí be completely at odds ◊这部电影的配乐与剧情风马牛不相及。The background music to this film is completely at odds with the storyline.

风貌 fēngmào [名] **1** (风格) style ◊民间艺术的风貌 folk-art style **2** (景象) scene

风靡一时 fēngmǐ yīshí be in fashion

风起云涌 fēng qǐ yún yǒng **1** (字) rising storm **2** (喻) upsurge ◊外资合作风起云涌。Joint ventures with foreign investment have really taken off.

风气 fēngqì [名] ◊社会风气越来越好。Social mores are improving. ◊全校出现了做早操的风气。Everyone at school has taken to doing morning exercises.

风情 fēngqíng [名] **1** (风向、风力) wind force and direction **2** (感情) expressions of love (*pl*) ◊卖弄风情 flirt **3** (风土人情) local customs (*pl*)

风趣 fēngqù [名] wit ◊他说话特别风趣。He is exceedingly witty.

风骚 fēngsāo **I** [名] literary brilliance **II** [形] flirtatious

风尚 fēngshàng [名] custom

风声 fēngshēng [名] **1** (指风) sound of the wind **2** (消息) rumour (英), rumor (美)

风水 fēngshuǐ [名] feng shui

风俗 fēngsú [名] custom

风调雨顺 fēng tiáo yǔ shùn favourable conditions

风头 fēngtou [名] 1 (情势) situation ◇看风头办事 act according to the situation 2 (出头露面) limelight ◇出风头 seek the limelight

风土 fēngtǔ [名] ◇风土人情 local landscape and customs

风味 fēngwèi [名] distinctive style ◇北京风味小吃 dishes in the Beijing style

风闻 fēngwén [动] hear a rumour (英) 或 rumor (美) (*pt, pp* heard)

风险 fēngxiǎn [名] risk

风向 fēngxiàng [名] wind direction

风行 fēngxíng [动] be in fashion

风雅 fēngyǎ [形] refined

风言风语 fēng yán fēng yǔ gossip

风雨 fēngyǔ [名] 1 (字) wind and rain 2 (喻) (困难) hardship

风雨同舟 fēngyǔ tóngzhōu stick together ◇风雨同舟共渡难关 stick together in difficulty

风云 fēngyún [名] turmoil ◇战争风云 the turmoil of war

风云人物 fēngyún rénwù influential person (*pl* people)

风韵 fēngyùn [名] charm

风姿 fēngzī [名] poise

枫 fēng [名] maple

封 fēng **I** [动] (封闭) seal ◇因车祸，路被封了。The road was sealed off because of the car accident. **II** [名] envelope **III** [量] ◇一封信 a letter

封闭 fēngbì [动] 1 (盖住) seal 2 (查封) seal off

封存 fēngcún [动] freeze (*pt* froze, *pp* frozen) ◇封存账号 freeze an account

封顶 fēngdǐng [动] cap ◇封顶价格 cap prices

封建 fēngjiàn **I** [名] feudalism **II** [形] feudal ◇封建社会 feudal society

封镜 fēngjìng [动] finish shooting

封杀 fēngshā [动] blacklist

封锁 fēngsuǒ [动] 1 (断绝联系) block ◇封锁经济 impose an economic blockade 2 (不能通行) seal off

疯 fēng **I** [形] mad **II** [副] madly ◇野草疯长。The weeds are out of control.

疯狂 fēngkuáng [形] crazy

疯子 fēngzi [名] lunatic ◇他是疯子。He's mad.

峰 fēng [名] 1 (山顶) peak 2 (喻) hump

峰会 fēnghuì [名] summit meeting

峰峦 fēngluán [名] a row of peaks

锋 fēng [名] 1 (尖端) point 2 (带头的) vanguard 3 (锋面) front ♦冷锋 cold front

锋利 fēnglì [形] 1 (工具) sharp 2 (言论) cutting ◇锋利的言辞 cutting remarks (*pl*)

锋芒 fēngmáng [名] 1 (尖利部分) the cutting edge ◇斗争锋芒直指官场腐败。The focus of attack is official corruption. 2 (才干) talent

蜂 fēng **I** [名] 1 (黄蜂) wasp 2 (蜜蜂) bee **II** [副] in swarms ◇蜂聚 gather in swarms

蜂蜜 fēngmì [名] honey

蜂拥 fēngyōng [动] swarm ◇球迷蜂拥而至。The football fans swarmed in.

逢 féng [动] come across (*pt* came, *pp* come)

逢场作戏 féng chǎng zuò xì enjoy the fun while it lasts ◇有的人把交朋友当作是逢场作戏。Some people regard friendship as a game.

逢凶化吉 féng xiōng huà jí land on one's feet

逢迎 féngyíng [动] (贬) ingratiate oneself with

缝 féng [动] sew (*pt* sewed, *pp* sewn)
▷另见fèng

缝纫 féngrèn [动] sew (*pt* sewed, *pp* sewn)

讽 fěng [动] mock ♦讥讽 satirize

讽刺 fěngcì [动] ridicule

凤 fèng [名] phoenix

凤毛麟角 fèng máo lín jiǎo as rare as hen's teeth

奉 fèng [动] **1** (献给) present **2** (接受) receive **3** (尊重) respect **4** (信仰) believe in **5** (伺候) attend to

奉承 fèngcheng [动] flatter

奉告 fènggào [动] (敬) inform

奉公守法 fèng gōng shǒu fǎ be public-spirited and respect the law

奉命 fèngmìng [动] be instructed ◇部委奉命紧急调查。Government departments were instructed to carry out an urgent investigation.

奉陪 fèngpéi [动] accompany ◇谁想下棋，我都愿奉陪。If anyone wants to play a game of chess, I'd be glad to join them.

奉若神明 fèng ruò shénmíng idolize

奉献 fèngxiàn [动] dedicate ◇为教育奉献生命 dedicate one's life to education

奉行 fèngxíng [动] pursue

俸 fèng [名] salary

俸禄 fènglù [名] official's salary

缝 fèng [名] **1** (接合处) seam ◇无缝长袜 seamless stockings **2** (缝隙) crack
▷另见 féng

缝隙 fèngxì [名] crack

佛 fó [名] **1** (佛教) Buddhism **2** (佛像) Buddha

佛教 fójiào [名] Buddhism

佛学 fóxué [名] Buddhism

否 fǒu **I** [动] deny **II** [副] **1**(书) (不) no **2** (是、能、可) or not ◇他明天是否参加聚会？ Is he coming to the party tomorrow or not?

否定 fǒudìng **I** [动] negate ◇事实否定了他说的话。The facts negate what he said. ◇我否定了他的建议。I refuted his suggestion. **II** [形] negative

否决 fǒujué [动] veto ◇否决提议 veto the motion

否认 fǒurèn [动] deny

否则 fǒuzé [连] otherwise ◇好好温习功课，否则考试通不过。Revise properly, otherwise you won't pass your exams.

夫 fū [名] **1** (丈夫) husband **2** (男子) man (*pl* men) **3** (劳动者) manual worker

夫妇 fūfù [名] husband and wife

夫人 fūrén [名] Mrs ◇胡夫人 Mrs Hu ◇第一夫人 First Lady

夫子 fūzǐ [名] **1** (学者) scholar **2**(贬) (陈腐的人) old fogey

肤 fū [名] skin

肤浅 fūqiǎn [形] superficial

孵 fū [动] hatch ◇孵小鸡 hatch chicks

敷 fū [动] **1** (涂) apply **2** (铺开) lay (*pt*, *pp* laid) **3** (足够) be sufficient for ◇入不敷出 income falls short of expenditure

敷设 fūshè [动] lay (*pt*, *pp* laid) ◇敷设电缆 lay an electric cable ◇敷设地雷 lay landmines

敷衍 fūyǎn [动] **1** (应付) go through the motions (*pt* went, *pp* gone) ◇敷衍了事 do a superficial job **2** (维持) get by ◇手里的钱还够敷衍几天。I have enough money to get by for a few days.

伏 fú **I** [动] **1** (趴) lean over **2** (低下去) fall (*pt* fell, *pp* fallen) **3** (隐藏) hide (*pt* hid, *pp* hidden) **4** (屈服) concede ◇伏输 concede defeat **5** (降伏) subdue **II** [名] the height of summer

伏案 fú'àn [动] hunch over one's desk

伏笔 fúbǐ [名] foreshadowing ◇故事的开端为悲剧性的结尾埋下了伏笔。The beginning of the story foreshadows the tragic ending.

伏兵 fúbīng [名] ambush

伏法 fúfǎ [动] be executed

伏击 fújī [动] ambush

伏侍 fúshi [动] look after

伏输 fúshū [动] concede defeat

伏特 fútè [量] volt

伏天 fútiān [名] the height of summer

伏帖 fútiē [形] **1** (舒服) content **2** (平整) neat ◇衣服熨烫得很伏帖。The clothes were ironed neatly.

伏罪 fúzuì [动] plead guilty

凫 fú **I** [名] wild duck **II** [动] swim (*pt* swam, *pp* swum)

芙 fú 见下文

芙蓉 fúróng [名] (荷花) lotus

扶 fú [动] **1** (稳住) steady ◇老太太扶着栏杆使自己站稳。The old woman steadied herself by holding on to the rail. ◇姑娘扶老大爷过马路。The girl helped the old man across the road. **2** (搀起) help up ◇护士把孩子扶起来。The nurse helped the child up. **3** (扶助) help

扶持 fúchí [动] support

扶贫 fúpín [动] help the poor

扶养 fúyǎng [动] **1** provide for ◇夫妻俩努力工作以扶养父母和孩子。The couple work hard to provide for their parents and children. **2** bring up (*pt, pp* brought) ◇他是由奶奶扶养大的。He was brought up by his grandmother.

扶摇直上 fúyáo zhí shàng rise sharply ◇公司产量扶摇直上。The company's output rose sharply.

扶植 fúzhí [动] foster

扶助 fúzhù [动] support

孚 fú [动] inspire confidence ◇深孚众望 inspire public confidence

拂 fú [动] **1** (轻擦) brush **2** (甩动) flick

拂拭 fúshì [动] wipe

拂晓 fúxiǎo [名] dawn

拂袖而去 fúxiù'érqù storm off

服 fú **I** [名] clothes (*pl*) ♦校服 school uniform **II** [动] **1** (吃) take (*pt* took, *pp* taken) ♦服药 take medicine **2** (担任) serve ♦服役 serve in the army **3** (服从) comply with ◇心服口服 be totally compliant **4** (使信服) convince **5** (适应) adapt ◇不服水土 not acclimatized
▷另见 fù

服从 fúcóng [动] obey

服毒 fúdú [动] take poison (*pt* took, *pp* taken)

服法 fúfǎ [名] directions (*pl*) ◇中药的服法 directions for using traditional Chinese medicine

服气 fúqì [动] accept ◇我对老师的批评感到不服气。I was unconvinced by the teacher's criticism.

服饰 fúshì [名] dress and accessories (*pl*)

服侍 fúshi [动] look after

服输 fúshū [动] concede

服帖 fútiē [形] **1** (驯服) docile **2** (妥当) proper ◇他把每件事安排得服服帖帖。He sorted everything into its proper place.

服务 fúwù [动] serve ◇很高兴为您服务。I am very happy to be of service to you.

服务员 fúwùyuán [名] **1** (指商店里) attendant **2** (指饭馆里) waiter, waitress **3** (指宾馆里) room attendant

服刑 fúxíng [动] serve a prison sentence ◇他在监狱中服了3年刑。He served a three-year prison sentence.

服药 fúyào [动] take medicine (*pt* took, *pp* taken)

服役 fúyì [动] serve (*in the forces*) ◇他的儿子在海军服役。His son is serving in the navy.

服用 fúyòng [动] (药) take (*pt* took, *pp* taken)

服装 fúzhuāng [名] clothing

俘 fú **I** [动] capture **II** [名] prisoner ♦战俘 prisoner of war

俘获 fúhuò [动] capture

俘虏 fúlǔ [名] prisoner

浮 fú **I** [动] float ◇她脸上浮现一丝笑容。She gave a faint smile. **II** [形] **1** (表面上) superficial ♦浮面 surface **2** (可移动) movable ♦浮财 movable assets (*pl*) **3** (暂时) temporary **4** (轻浮) slapdash **5** (空

虚) empty ♦浮夸 exaggerated **6** (多余) surplus

浮沉 fúchén [动] drift ◊与世浮沉 swim with the tide ◊商海浮沉 the ups and downs of business

浮动 fúdòng [动] **1** (流动) float **2** (不稳定) fluctuate

浮光掠影 fú guāng lüè yǐng fleeting ◊浮光掠影看厦门 make a fleeting visit to Xiamen

浮华 fúhuá [形] ostentatious

浮夸 fúkuā [动] exaggerate

浮力 fúlì [名] buoyancy

浮浅 fúqiǎn [形] shallow

浮现 fúxiàn [动] come back (*pt* came, *pp* come) ◊他的音容笑貌又浮现在眼前。His voice and smiling face came back to me.

浮想联翩 fúxiǎng liánpiān many thoughts run through one's mind

浮游 fúyóu [动] float

浮躁 fúzào [形] impulsive

浮肿 fúzhǒng [动] puff up ◊一夜没睡，他的眼睛有些浮肿。After a sleepless night, his eyes are a bit puffy.

符 fú **I** [名] **1** (标记) mark ♦音符 musical note **2** (图形) Daoist motif ◊护身符 talisman **II** [动] be in keeping with ◊他说的和做的不符。His words are out of keeping with his actions.

符号 fúhào [名] mark

符合 fúhé [动] match ◊符合招生条件 meet admission requirements

幅 fú **I** [名] **1** (指布) width **2** (泛指大小) size ♦幅度 range ◊大幅油画 a large oil painting **II** [量] ◊一幅窗帘 a curtain ◊一幅照片 a photograph

幅度 fúdù [名] range ◊两臂摆动的幅度不要太大。You must not swing your arms too much. ◊此次降价的幅度非常大。This time prices fell very sharply.

幅员 fúyuán [名] size ◊中国幅员辽阔。China is vast in size.

辐 fú [名] spoke

辐射 fúshè **I** [动] radiate **II** [名] radiation

蜉 fú 见下文

蜉蝣 fúyóu [名] mayfly

福 fú [名] good fortune

福分 fúfen [名] good fortune ◊有这么好的闺女，真是你的福分。You are really fortunate to have such a good daughter.

福利 fúlì [名] welfare ◊你们公司的福利好吗？Do you have good company benefits?

福气 fúqi [名] good fortune

福音 fúyīn [名] **1** (宗)(教义) Gospel **2** (好消息) good news

蝠 fú [名] bat ♦蝙蝠 bat

抚 fǔ [动] **1** (安慰) comfort ♦抚恤 give relief to (*pt* gave, *pp* given) **2** (保护) nurture **3** (按着) stroke

抚爱 fǔ'ài [动] cherish ◊缺乏抚爱的童年 a loveless childhood

抚今追昔 fǔ jīn zhuī xī evoke memories of the past

抚摩 fǔmó [动] stroke

抚弄 fǔnòng [动] fondle

抚慰 fǔwèi [动] comfort

抚恤 fǔxù [动] give relief to (*pt* gave, *pp* given)

抚养 fǔyǎng [动] bring … up (*pt*, *pp* brought)

抚育 fǔyù [动] **1** (人) raise **2** (动植物) tend

拊 fǔ [动] (书) clap

拊掌 fǔzhǎng [动] clap one's hands

斧 fǔ [名] axe (英), ax (美)

斧子 fǔzi [名] axe (英), ax (美)

府 fǔ [名] **1** (机关) government body ♦官府 the authorities ♦政府 government **2** (住宅) official residence

俯 fǔ [动] bend over (*pt*, *pp* bent) ♦俯伏 lie prone ♦俯冲 nose-dive

俯就 fǔjiù [动] **1** (敬) (担任) kindly accept ◊请您俯就经理一职。Please accept the position of director. **2** (迁就) go along with (*pt* went, *pp* gone)

俯瞰 fǔkàn [动] look down on ◇她从飞机上俯瞰长江。She looked down on the Yangtze from the plane.

俯拾即是 fǔ shí jí shì extremely common ◇民间故事俯拾即是。Folk tales are to be found everywhere.

俯视 fǔshì [动] look down on

俯首 fǔshǒu [动] bow one's head

俯首帖耳 fǔ shǒu tiē ěr be totally subservient ◇他对上司俯首帖耳。He's totally subservient to his boss.

釜 fǔ [名] pot

釜底抽薪 fǔ dǐ chōu xīn take drastic action

辅 fǔ [动] complement ◇相辅而行 complement each other

辅导 fǔdǎo [动] coach ◇辅导学生学习物理 coach students in physics

辅助 fǔzhù I [动] assist ◇他辅助我写这本书。He assisted me in writing this book. II [形] supplementary ◇辅助教材 supplementary teaching materials ◇辅助信息 additional information

辅佐 fǔzuǒ [动] assist ◇辅佐朝政 assist in the affairs of state

脯 fǔ [名] **1** (肉干) dried meat **2** (蜜饯) preserved fruit

腐 fǔ I [形] rotten II [名] beancurd ♦腐竹 roll of dried beancurd

腐败 fǔbài I [动] rot ◇腐败的食物 rotten food II [形] corrupt

腐化 fǔhuà [动] **1** (堕落) corrupt ◇贪污腐化 corruption **2** (腐烂) decompose

腐烂 fǔlàn I [动] rot II [形] decadent

腐蚀 fǔshí [动] **1** (消损) corrode ◇金属工具被腐蚀了。The metal tools have corroded. **2** (堕落) corrupt

腐朽 fǔxiǔ I [动] rot II [形] decadent

腐竹 fǔzhú [名] roll of dried beancurd

父 fù [名] **1** (父亲) father **2** (指男性长辈) *senior male relative* ♦祖父 grandfather

父老 fùlǎo [名] elder

父亲 fùqīn [名] father

父兄 fùxiōng [名] **1** (父亲和哥哥) father and elder brothers **2** (家长) head of the family

讣 fù I [动] announce a death II [名] obituary

讣告 fùgào I [动] announce a death II [名] obituary

付 fù [动] **1** (事物) hand over ♦托付 entrust ◇付诸实施 put into effect **2** (钱) pay (*pt*, *pp* paid) ♦偿付 pay back ◇付邮资 pay postage

付排 fùpái [动] have typeset

付托 fùtuō [动] entrust ◇付托重任 entrust with a heavy responsibility

付印 fùyìn [动] **1** (指交付出版社) submit for publication **2** (指交付印刷) go to press (*pt* went, *pp* gone)

付账 fùzhàng [动] pay the bill (*pt*, *pp* paid)

付之一炬 fù zhī yī jù be consumed by fire ◇失恋的女孩儿把男朋友的信付之一炬。The jilted girl burned all her boyfriend's letters.

付之一笑 fù zhī yī xiào brush off with a smile ◇他把感情得失，爱与不爱都付之一笑。He treats love and loss lightly.

付诸东流 fù zhū dōng liú waste ◇巨额投资付诸东流。A huge investment was wasted.

负 fù I [动] **1**(书) (背) carry on one's back ♦负重 carry a heavy load **2** (担负) bear (*pt* bore, *pp* borne) **3** (遭受) suffer ◇负伤 be wounded **4** (享有) enjoy **5** (拖欠) be in arrears ◇负债 be in debt **6** (背弃) turn one's back on **7** (失败) lose (*pt*, *pp* lost) ◇甲队0比2负于乙队。The A team lost to the B team two-nil. II [形] negative ♦负数 negative number

负担 fùdān I [动] bear (*pt* bore, *pp* borne) II [名] burden

负荷 fùhè I [动] (书) carry II [名] load

负荆请罪 fù jīng qǐng zuì humbly apologize

负疚 fùjiù [动] feel guilty (*pt*, *pp* felt)

负面效应 fùmiàn xiàoyìng [名] negative effect

负气 fùqì [动] ◇负气出走 leave in a fit of anger

负伤 fùshāng [动] be wounded

负心 fùxīn [动] be heartless

负隅顽抗 fù yú wán kàng put up a stiff resistance

负约 fùyuē [动] **1** (违背诺言) break a promise (*pt* broke, *pp* broken) **2** (失约) miss an appointment

负责 fùzé **I** [动] be responsible ◇谁应对这起事故负责？ Who should be held responsible for this accident? **II** [形] conscientious ◇他对工作很负责。 He is very conscientious about his work.

负债 fùzhài [动] be in debt

负重 fùzhòng [动] **1** (背着重物) carry a heavy load **2** (承担重任) take on an important task (*pt* took, *pp* taken)

妇 fù [名] **1** (妇女) woman (*pl* women) ♦妇科 gynaecology (英) gynecology (美) **2** (已婚妇女) married woman (*pl* women) **3** (妻) wife (*pl* wives)

妇科 fùkē [名] gynaecology (英) gynecology (美)

妇女 fùnǚ [名] woman (*pl* women)

附 fù [动] **1** (附带) attach **2** (靠近) get close to **3** (依从) depend on

附带 fùdài [动] add ◇附带说一句 mention in passing

附和 fùhè [动] echo ◇随声附和别人的说法 echo the views of others

附会 fùhuì [动] make a false analogy

附加 fùjiā [动] add ◇附加手续费 additional administrative charge

附件 fùjiàn [名] **1** (文件) attachment **2** (零件) spare parts (*pl*)

附近 fùjìn **I** [形] nearby **II** [名] vicinity ◇附近有电话亭吗？ Is there a telephone box in the vicinity?

附录 fùlù [名] appendix

附设 fùshè [动] add ◇办公楼里附设了个休息室。 A new lounge has been opened in the office building.

附属 fùshǔ **I** [动] attach to ◇该医院附属于一所大学。 This hospital is attached to a university. **II** [形] affiliated to

附议 fùyì [动] support a motion

附庸 fùyōng [名] dependency

附注 fùzhù [名] annotation

附着 fùzhuó [动] stick to (*pt*, *pp* stuck)

服 fù [量] dose
▷另见fú

赴 fù [动] go to (*pt* went, *pp* gone) ◇奔赴前线 rush to the front

赴任 fùrèn [动] take up a job (*pt* took, *pp* taken)

赴汤蹈火 fù tāng dǎo huǒ go through hell and high water

赴约 fùyuē [动] keep an appointment (*pt*, *pp* kept)

复 fù **I** [形] **1** (重复) duplicated ♦复制 reproduce **2** (繁复) complex
II [动] **1** (转) turn **2** (回答) reply **3** (恢复) recover **4** (报复) take revenge (*pt* took, *pp* taken)
III [副] again ♦复查 re-examine

复辟 fùbì [动] restore to power

复仇 fùchóu [动] take revenge (*pt* took, *pp* taken) ◇3年后他终于为死去的儿子复仇了。 After three years, he finally avenged his son's death.

复读 fùdú [动] retake

复发 fùfā [动] recur ◇病治愈后要防止复发。 After an illness is cured, you must prevent it from recurring.

复古 fùgǔ [动] go back to the old ways (*pt* went, *pp* gone)

复合 fùhé [形] compound

复活 fùhuó [动] revive

复活节 Fùhuó Jié [名] (宗) Easter

复句 fùjù [名] compound sentence

复述 fùshù [动] **1** (重复) repeat **2** (重新表达) retell

复数 fùshù [名] plural

复苏 fùsū [动] **1** (生物体) resuscitate **2** (经济) recover

复习 fùxí [动] revise ◇为考试而复习 revise for exams ◇复习功课 go over one's lessons

复兴 fùxīng [动] revive ◇文艺复兴 the Renaissance

复议 fùyì [动] reconsider

复印 fùyìn [动] photocopy

复员 fùyuán [动] **1** (转入和平) return to peacetime conditions **2** (退役) demobilize

复原 fùyuán [动] **1** (恢复健康) recover ◇老师病后身体已经复原。Our teacher has already recovered from his illness. **2** (恢复原样) restore

复杂 fùzá [形] complex

复制 fùzhì [动] reproduce

副 fù **I** [形] **1** (辅助) deputy ◇副局长 deputy director **2** (附带) subsidiary ♦副业 subsidiary business ◇副作用 side effect **II** [名] assistant ♦大副 first mate **III** [动] correspond to ◇名副其实 live up to its name **IV** [量] **1** (套) pair ◇一副耳机 a pair of headphones ◇一副手套 a pair of gloves **2** (指表情) ◇一副冷面孔 a cold expression

副本 fùběn [名] duplicate

副词 fùcí [名] adverb

副刊 fùkān [名] supplement

副食 fùshí [名] non-staple food

副手 fùshǒu [名] assistant

副业 fùyè [名] subsidiary business

副作用 fùzuòyòng [名] side effect

赋 fù **I** [动] **1** compose ◇赋诗一首 compose a poem **2** bestow **II** [名] (旧) tax ♦田赋 land tax

赋税 fùshuì [名] tax

赋闲 fùxián [动] be out of work

赋有 fùyǒu [动] possess ◇赋有朝气 possess vitality ◇赋有个性 have individuality

赋予 fùyǔ [动] give (*pt* gave, *pp* given) ◇赋予权利 grant rights

傅 fù [名] teacher

富 fù **I** [形] **1** (指财产) rich **2** (丰富的) abundant **II** [名] wealth **III** [动] enrich

富贵 fùguì [形] rich and influential

富豪 fùháo [名] rich and powerful person (*pl* people)

富丽堂皇 fù lì táng huáng splendid

富强 fùqiáng [形] prosperous and powerful

富饶 fùráo [形] abundant

富庶 fùshù [形] rich and populous

富翁 fùwēng [名] man of means (*pl* men) ◇百万富翁 millionaire

富有 fùyǒu **I** [形] wealthy **II** [动] be full of ◇富有创造力 be very creative

富裕 fùyù [形] prosperous ◇富裕地区 prosperous area ◇他家很富裕。His family is very well off.

富余 fùyu [形] surplus

富足 fùzú [形] comfortable

腹 fù [名] **1** (指躯干) stomach **2** (指物体) belly **3** (内心) mind ♦腹稿 mental outline

腹背受敌 fù bèi shòu dí be attacked from all sides

腹地 fùdì [名] hinterland

腹稿 fùgǎo [名] mental outline ◇演讲前先打个腹稿。Before making a speech, first have a mental outline.

缚 fù [动] bind (*pt, pp* bound) ◇作茧自缚 make a noose for one's own neck

覆 fù [动] **1** (盖住) cover **2** (翻过来) overturn

覆盖 fùgài [动] cover ◇地上覆盖着厚厚的白雪。The ground was covered in thick white snow.

覆灭 fùmiè [动] wipe out ◇全军覆灭。The whole army was wiped out.

覆没 fùmò [动] **1** (书) (指船) sink (*pt* sank, *pp* sunk) **2** (被消灭) annihilate

覆辙 fùzhé [名] ◇重蹈覆辙 take the same path to disaster

馥 fù [名] (书) fragrance

馥郁 fùyù [形] strongly scented

Gg

夹 gā 见下文
▷另见 jiā, jiá

夹肢窝 gāzhiwō [名] armpit

咖 gā 见下文
▷另见 kā

咖喱 gālí [名] curry

嘎 gā [拟] screech ◇火车嘎的一声停了下来。The train screeched to a halt.

嘎吱 gāzhī [拟] creak ◇小板凳被他压得嘎吱嘎吱地响。The stool creaked under his weight.

该 gāi **I** [动] **1** (应当) ought to **2** (轮到) be the turn of ◇这次该他主持会议了。It's his turn to chair the meeting this time. **3** (活该) serve … right ◇他睡懒觉误了火车，活该！He overslept and missed the train – serves him right! **II** [助动] **1** (应该) should ◇工作明天该完成了。The work should be finished by tomorrow. **2** (表示推测) ◇他还没回来，该不是又加班了吧？He's still not back – isn't he doing overtime? ◇再不吃的话，菜都该凉了。If we keep waiting the food is only going to get colder. **3** (用于加强语气) ◇房间里放些鲜花该多温馨啊！It would be so lovely to have some flowers in the room. ◇要是他能在这儿该多好啊！It would be great if he could be here. **III** [代] that, this

该当 gāidāng [动] deserve

该死 gāisǐ [形] damn

改 gǎi [动] **1** (改变) change **2** (修改) alter **3** (改正) correct

改编 gǎibiān [动] **1** (重写) adapt ◇将小说改编为电影 adapt a novel for the screen **2** (指编制) reorganise ◇改编军队 reorganize an army ◇改编预算体制 restructure a budgetary system

改变 gǎibiàn [动] change ◇安妮改变了主意，决定呆在家里。Annie changed her mind and decided to stay at home.

改朝换代 gǎi cháo huàn dài a change of regime

改动 gǎidòng [动] change

改恶从善 gǎi è cóng shàn turn over a new leaf

改革 gǎigé [动] reform ◇改革经济体制 reform the economic system

改观 gǎiguān [动] **1** (指面貌) take on a new look (*pt* took, *pp* taken) ◇城市的面貌改观了许多。The city has already taken on quite a new look. **2** (指观点) change one's attitude ◇家人对他完全改观了。His family completely changed their attitude towards him.

改过自新 gǎi guò zì xīn wipe the slate clean

改行 gǎiháng [动] change profession

改换 gǎihuàn [动] replace

改悔 gǎihuǐ [动] mend one's ways

改嫁 gǎijià [动] remarry ◇在中国封建社会里，改嫁是不被容许的。Remarriage wasn't acceptable in feudal Chinese society.

改进 gǎijìn [动] improve

改口 gǎikǒu [动] correct oneself

改良 gǎiliáng [动] **1** (改善) improve **2** (改进) reform

改善 gǎishàn [动] improve

改头换面 gǎi tóu huàn miàn make superficial changes

改弦更张 gǎi xián gēng zhāng make a fresh start

改邪归正 gǎi xié guī zhèng turn over a new leaf

改选 gǎixuǎn [动] re-elect

改造 gǎizào [动] **1** (指对自然) reclaim ◇改造农田 reclaim farmland **2** (彻底改变) transform ◇改造社会 transform society ◇改造罪犯 rehabilitate offenders

改正 gǎizhèng [动] correct ◇他改正了文中的错字。He corrected the

wrong characters in his essay. ◇改正缺点 mend one's ways

改组 gǎizǔ [动] reshuffle ◇政府改组 government reshuffle

丐 gài [名] beggar

钙 gài [名] (化) calcium

盖 gài I [名] 1 (指器皿) cover 2 (甲壳) shell II [动] 1 (蒙上) cover 2 (遮掩) cover up ◇他们想盖住丑闻。They wanted to cover the scandal up. 3 (打上) stamp 4 (压过) block out ◇汽车的噪音把我们的说话声盖下去了。The noise from the car blocked out the sound of our voices. 5 (建造) build (*pt, pp* built)

盖棺论定 gài guān lùn dìng only when a man is dead can he be judged

盖世 gàishì [动] be unparalleled ◇才华盖世 be of unparalleled talent

盖子 gàizi [名] (口) 1 (遮蔽物) lid 2 (甲壳) shell

概 gài I [名] 1 (大略) outline 2 (气度) bearing II [副] without exception

概况 gàikuàng [名] general situation

概括 gàikuò I [动] summarize II [形] brief

概率 gàilǜ [名] probability

概论 gàilùn [名] introduction

概貌 gàimào [名] general picture

概莫能外 gài mò néng wài without exception

概念 gàiniàn [名] concept

概念化 gàiniànhuà [动] conceptualize

概述 gàishù [动] summarize

概数 gàishù [名] approximate number

概要 gàiyào [名] outline

干 gān I [动] have to do with ♦干连 be responsible for ◇这不干我事。This has nothing to do with me. II [形] 1 (无水) dry 2 (不用水) dry ♦干洗 dry-clean 3 (干涸) dried-up 4 (空) empty ◇外强中干 outwardly strong but inwardly weak 5 (指拜认的关系) adoptive III [名] ♦笋干 dried bamboo shoots ♦豆腐干 dried tofu ♦葡萄干 raisin IV [副] 1 (只具形式) hollowly ♦干笑 laugh hollowly 2 (白白) in vain ◇他失约了，害得我干等了半天。He failed to make the appointment and I ended up wasting a long time waiting for him.
▷另见 gàn

干巴巴 gānbābā [形] 1 (干燥) dried-up 2 (不生动) bland

干杯 gānbēi [动] drink a toast (*pt* drank, *pp* drunk) ◇为我们成功的合作而干杯。Let's drink a toast to our successful cooperation. ◇"干杯！" "Cheers!"

干瘪 gānbiě [形] 1 (不丰满) shrivelled ◇干瘪的水果 shrivelled fruit ◇干瘪的老头子 a wizened old man 2 (枯燥) dull

干脆 gāncuì I [形] direct II [副] just ◇报酬这么低，干脆别干了。There's so little money in it – just give it up.

干戈 gāngē [名] arms ◇两国为了领土问题大动干戈。The two nations went to war over a territorial dispute.

干旱 gānhàn [形] arid

干涸 gānhé [形] dried-up

干货 gānhuò [名] dried food

干净 gānjìng [形] 1 (无尘) clean 2 (利落) clear ◇他干净利落地介绍完整个项目。He gave a clear and comprehensive introduction to the project. 3 (一点不剩) complete ◇请把汤喝干净。Please finish your soup.

干枯 gānkū [形] withered ◇干枯的叶子 withered leaves

干扰 gānrǎo [动] disturb ◇别干扰他学习。Don't disturb him when he's studying.

干涉 gānshè I [动] meddle ◇干涉别人私事 meddle in other people's affairs II [名] (关系) link

干洗 gānxǐ [动] dry-clean

干系 gānxì [名] responsibility ◇这件事故和他脱不了干系。He cannot escape responsibility for the accident.

干预 gānyù [动] interfere ◇干预总统选举 interfere in a presidential election

干燥 gānzào [形] dry

甘 gān I [形] 1 (指味觉) sweet 2 (幸福) fortunate II [副] willingly ◇他甘愿在家照看孩子。He willingly stayed at home to look after the children.

甘拜下风 gān bài xià fēng throw in the towel

甘苦 gānkǔ [名] 1 (美好和艰辛) ups and downs (*pl*) 2 (艰辛) hardship

甘甜 gāntián [形] sweet

甘心 gānxīn [动] 1 (愿意) be willing 2 (满意) be satisfied

甘休 gānxiū [动] take … lying down (*pt* took, *pp* taken) ◇他考试非得拿A才甘休。If he doesn't get an A in the exam he's not going to take it lying down.

甘于 gānyú [动] be willing to

甘愿 gānyuàn [动] be willing to

杆 gān [名] post
▷另见 gǎn

肝 gān [名] liver

肝胆 gāndǎn [名] 1 (真诚) sincerity 2 (勇气) courage

肝胆相照 gāndǎn xiāng zhào open one's heart

肝火 gānhuǒ [名] anger ◇不必为这点小事大动肝火。There is no need to get so angry over something so trivial.

肝脑涂地 gān nǎo tú dì lay down one's life

柑 gān [名] mandarin orange

竿 gān [名] pole

尴 gān 见下文

尴尬 gāngà [形] 1 (困难) awkward ◇尴尬的处境 an awkward situation 2 (方) (不自然) embarrassed ◇她看上去很尴尬。She looked very embarrassed.

杆 gǎn I [名] shaft II [量] ◇一杆笔 a pen ◇几杆枪 several guns
▷另见 gān

秆 gǎn [名] stalk

赶 gǎn I [动] 1 (追) catch (*pt*, *pp* caught) ◇赶公共汽车 catch a bus ◇赶潮流 catch up with the latest fashions 2 (加快) rush ◇赶功课 rush off an assignment ◇天黑了，学生们赶着回家。It was getting dark so the students rushed home. 3 (驱赶) drive (*pt* drove, *pp* driven) ◇赶着马车进城 drive a cart into town 4 (驱逐) drive out ◇赶走外来政权 drive out the foreign regime 5 (遇到) happen to ◇她的生日赶上是国庆节。Her birthday happened to be the same day as National Day. II [介] until ◇这株树赶明年春天再种吧。Let's not plant this tree until next spring.

赶场 gǎnchǎng [动] rush from one place to another

赶集 gǎnjí [动] go to market (*pt* went, *pp* gone)

赶紧 gǎnjǐn [副] quickly ◇下课后我赶紧回家。After class I quickly went home.

赶快 gǎnkuài [副] at once ◇我们得赶快走了！We must go at once!

赶浪头 gǎn làngtou follow the trend

赶路 gǎnlù [动] race ahead

赶忙 gǎnmáng [副] hurriedly

赶巧 gǎnqiǎo [副] by chance ◇我散步时赶巧遇见个老同学。I was out for a walk when I bumped into an old school friend. ◇他赶巧也在那儿。By chance he happened to be there as well.

赶时髦 gǎn shímáo be fashionable

赶鸭子上架 gǎn yāzi shàng jià set an impossible challenge

敢 gǎn I [形] courageous II [动] 1 (有胆量) dare 2 (有把握) be sure ◇我敢断定他在撒谎。I'm sure he is lying. 3 (谦) (请求) venture ◇敢问尊姓大名? May I ask your name?

敢于 gǎnyú [动] dare to ◇他敢于批评他的老板。He dared to criticize his boss.

敢作敢当 gǎn zuò gǎn dāng be ready to stand up and be counted

感 gǎn I [动] 1 (觉得) feel (*pt*, *pp* felt) 2 (感动) move ◇这个故事很感人。This story is very moving. ◇他被她的爱所感动。He was moved by her affection. ◇感人肺腑 extremely moving **3** (怀谢意) be grateful **4** (受) be affected by **5** (接触) be sensitive to **II** [名] sense ◇成就感 a sense of achievement ◇新鲜感 a breath of fresh air

感触 gǎnchù [名] emotion ◇对家乡的变化他深有感触。He was very emotional about the changes to his home town.

感动 gǎndòng [动] move ◇他很容易被感动。He's very easily moved.

感恩 gǎn'ēn [动] be grateful

感恩节 Gǎn'ēnjié [名] Thanksgiving

感官 gǎnguān [名] sense organs (*pl*)

感光 gǎnguāng [动] be light-sensitive

感化 gǎnhuà [动] reform

感激 gǎnjī [动] appreciate ◇我感激你所做的一切。I appreciate everything you have done.

感激涕零 gǎnjī tì líng shed tears of gratitude

感觉 gǎnjué **I** [名] feeling **II** [动] **1** (感到) feel (*pt, pp* felt) ◇感觉不舒服 feel below par ◇感觉轻松 feel relaxed **2** (认为) sense ◇他感觉到有点儿不对劲。He sensed that there was something wrong.

感慨 gǎnkǎi [动] sigh

感冒 gǎnmào [动] catch a cold (*pt, pp* caught)

感情 gǎnqíng [名] **1** (心理反应) emotion **2** (喜爱) feelings (*pl*) ◇他们感情一直没变。They never lost their feelings for each other.

感染 gǎnrǎn [动] **1** (传染) infect ◇伤口感染了。The cut was infected. **2** (引起共鸣) strike a chord (*pt, pp* struck) ◇他的演讲感染了在场的每个人。His speech struck a chord with everyone present.

感人肺腑 gǎn rén fèifǔ pull at one's heartstrings ◇这本书感人肺腑。This book really pulls at people's heartstrings.

感伤 gǎnshāng [动] be inconsolable

感受 gǎnshòu **I** [动] feel (*pt, pp* felt) **II** [名] impression ◇重返故乡后，他感受良多。His return home left a deep impression on him.

感叹 gǎntàn [动] sigh

感悟 gǎnwù [动] come to understand (*pt* came, *pp* come)

感想 gǎnxiǎng [名] thoughts (*pl*) ◇你对这些评论有何感想？ Did you have any particular thoughts on these comments?

感谢 gǎnxiè [动] thank ◇感谢您的指导。Thank you for your guidance.

感性 gǎnxìng [名] perception

感应 gǎnyìng [动] **1** (物理) induce **2** (感情变化) respond

感召 gǎnzhào [动] inspire

感知 gǎnzhī [动] perceive

橄 gǎn 见下文

橄榄 gǎnlǎn [名] olive

擀 gǎn [动] roll

擀面杖 gǎnmiànzhàng [名] rolling pin

干 gàn **I** [名] **1** (主体) trunk ◆躯干 trunk ◇公司骨干 the backbone of the company **2** (干部) cadre **II** [动] **1** (做) do (*pt* did, *pp* done) ◆干活 work **2** (担任) act as ◇他干过队长。He acted as team leader. **III** [形] capable
▷另见 gān

干部 gànbù [名] cadre

干才 gàncái [名] **1** (才能) ability **2** (指人) able person

> 请勿将 **ability**, **capability** 和 **capacity** 混淆。**ability** 通常表示某人有能力做好某事。*He had remarkable ability as a musician... the ability to bear hardship...*
> **capability** 表示某人做事的能力。*...a job that was beyond the capability of one man... the film director's ideas of the capability of the actor...*
> 如果某人有某种 **capacity**, 或 **capacity for something**, 或 **capacity to do something**, 表示他具备做此事的能力。**capacity** 比 **ability** 更为正式。*...their capacity for hard work... his capacity to see the other person's point of view...*

干将 gànjiàng [名] go-getter

干劲 gànjìn [名] vigour (英), vigor (美)

干警 gànjǐng [名] police

干练 gànliàn [形] capable and experienced

干流 gànliú [名] trunk stream

干线 gànxiàn [名] artery

冈 gāng [名] ridge

刚 gāng I [形] strong II [副] 1 (恰好) just ◇水温刚好。The temperature of the water was just right. 2 (仅仅) just ◇这儿刚够放一把椅子。There is just enough room for a chair. 3 (不久以前) only just ◇小宝宝刚会走路。The baby has only just started walking.

刚愎自用 gāng bì zì yòng obstinate

刚才 gāngcái [名] just now

刚刚 gānggāng [副] just ◇我刚刚吃完晚餐。I've just finished dinner.

刚好 gānghǎo I [形] just right II [副] luckily ◇我到车站的时候刚好有车。Luckily there was a bus when I got to the station.

刚健 gāngjiàn [形] bold

刚劲 gāngjìng [形] vigorous

刚烈 gāngliè [形] fiery

刚强 gāngqiáng [形] unyielding ◇刚强的性格 unyielding personality

刚毅 gāngyì [形] determined

刚正 gāngzhèng [形] principled

刚直 gāngzhí [形] upright

肛 gāng [名] anus

纲 gāng [名] 1 (总绳) headrope 2 (主体) key part 3 (生物群) class

纲举目张 gāng jǔ mù zhāng take care of the big things and the little things will take care of themselves

纲领 gānglǐng [名] guiding principle

纲目 gāngmù [名] detailed outline

纲要 gāngyào [名] outline

钢 gāng [名] steel

钢材 gāngcái [名] steel products (*pl*)

钢琴 gāngqín [名] piano

钢铁 gāngtiě [名] 1 (字) steel 2 (喻) iron ◇钢铁意志 an iron will

缸 gāng [名] 1 (器物) vat ♦鱼缸 fish bowl 2 (像缸之物) jar ♦汽缸 cylinder

岗 gǎng [名] 1 (土坡) ridge 2 (岗位) post ♦下岗 be laid-off

岗哨 gǎngshào [名] 1 (指处所) lookout post 2 (指人) sentry

岗位 gǎngwèi [名] post

港 gǎng [名] 1 (港湾) harbour (英), harbor (美) 2 (香港) Hong Kong

港币 gǎngbì [名] Hong Kong dollar

港口 gǎngkǒu [名] port

港湾 gǎngwān [名] harbour (英), harbor (美)

杠 gàng I [名] 1 (棍子) bar 2 (直线) thick line ◇在错误的地方划上红杠。Where there is a mistake, mark it with a thick red line. II [动] cross out

杠子 gàngzi [名] 1 (棍子) carrying pole 2 (直线) thick line

高 gāo [形] 1 (指高度) tall ♦高楼 tall building 2 (指标准或程度) high ♦高标准 high standard 3 (指等级) senior ♦高中 senior school 4 (指声音) high-pitched 5 (指年龄) old 6 (指价格) high 7 (敬) ◇您有何高见？ What is your opinion?

高矮 gāo'ǎi [名] height

高昂 gāo'áng [形] 1 (高起) elated 2 (昂贵) exorbitant

高傲 gāo'ào [形] arrogant

高不成，低不就 gāo bù chéng, dī bù jiù have ideas above one's station

高不可攀 gāo bù kě pān unattainable

高超 gāochāo [形] excellent

高潮 gāocháo [名] 1 (字) high tide 2 (喻) climax

高大 gāodà [形] 1 (字) huge 2 (喻) glorious

高档 gāodàng [形] top quality

高等 gāoděng [形] higher

高低 gāodī [名] **1** (高低程度) height **2** (高下) difference **3** (深浅) appropriateness

高地 gāodì [名] highlands

高调 gāodiào [名] big talk

高度 gāodù [名] altitude

高峰 gāofēng [名] summit ◇珠穆朗玛峰是世界第一高峰。Mount Qomolangma is the highest summit in the world. ◇上班高峰时间 morning rush hour

高峰会议 gāofēng huìyì [名] summit meeting

高峰时间 gāofēng shíjiān [名] rush hour

高高在上 gāo gāo zài shàng be superior

高官厚禄 gāo guān hòu lù plum job

高贵 gāoguì [形] **1** (指道德) dignified **2** (指地位) noble

高级 gāojí [形] **1** (指级别) senior ◇高级讲师 senior lecturer ◇高级法院 high court **2** (超过一般) high-quality ◇高级英语 advanced English ◇高级宾馆 luxury hotel

高架桥 gāojiàqiáo [名] flyover (英), overpass (美)

高见 gāojiàn [名] (敬) opinion

高洁 gāojié [形] noble

高就 gāojiù [动] (敬) be employed

高踞 gāojù [动] set oneself above (*pt, pp* set) ◇高踞榜首 take first place

高亢 gāokàng [形] resounding

高考 gāokǎo [名] college entrance examination

高科技 gāokējì [形] hi-tech

高科技 gāokējì yuánqū [形] hi-tech zone

高空 gāokōng [名] high altitude

高利贷 gāolìdài [名] usury

高龄 gāolíng **I** [名] (敬) old age **II** [形] older ◇高龄孕妇 women who are pregnant later in life

高论 gāolùn [名] (敬) brilliant remarks (*pl*)

高帽子 gāomàozi [名] flattery

高明 gāomíng **I** [形] wise **II** [名] expert

高攀 gāopān [动] be a social climber

高强 gāoqiáng [形] outstanding

高人 gāorén [名] master

高人一等 gāo rén yī děng regard oneself as a cut above the rest

高尚 gāoshàng [形] **1** (指道德) noble **2** (有意义的) respectable

高深 gāoshēn [形] profound

高深莫测 gāoshēn mò cè unfathomable

高手 gāoshǒu [名] expert

高寿 gāoshòu [名] **1** (敬) (年纪) age ◇您高寿了？May I ask how old you are? **2** (长寿) longevity

高速 gāosù [形] rapid ◇中国经济正高速发展。China's economy is developing rapidly.

高速公路 [名] gāosù gōnglù motorway (英), freeway (美)

高抬贵手 gāo tái guì shǒu be merciful

高谈阔论 gāo tán kuò lùn talk off the top of one's head

高屋建瓴 gāo wū jiàn líng be strategically situated

高下 gāoxià [名] superiority and inferiority

高兴 gāoxìng **I** [形] happy **II** [动] enjoy

高压 gāoyā **I** [名] **1** (指气压) high pressure **2** (指电压) high voltage **3** (指血压) high blood pressure **II** [形] high-handed ◇高压政策 high-handed policy

高雅 gāoyǎ [形] elegant

高原 gāoyuán [名] plateau (*pl* plateaux)

高瞻远瞩 gāo zhān yuǎn zhǔ far-sighted

高涨 gāozhǎng [动] rocket ◇物价高涨。Prices are rocketing.

高招 gāozhāo [名] bright ideas (*pl*)

高枕无忧 gāo zhěn wú yōu rest easy

高中 gāozhōng [名] (高级中学) senior school (英), high school (美)

高姿态 gāozītài [名] generous attitude

羔 gāo [名] young

羔羊 gāoyáng [名] lamb

膏 gāo [名] **1** (脂肪) grease **2** (糊状物) paste ♦药膏 ointment

膏药 gāoyao [名] plaster

糕 gāo [名] cake

糕点 gāodiǎn [名] pastries (*pl*)

搞 gǎo [动] **1** (干) do (*pt* did, *pp* done) **2** (弄) get (*pt* got, *pp* got (英) 或 gotten (美)) ◊搞到资金 secure funding ◊搞到消息 get information

搞定 gǎodìng [动] (口) sort out ◊这事一定要搞定！ This has really got to be sorted out!

搞鬼 gǎoguǐ [动] be up to mischief

稿 gǎo [名] draft

稿本 gǎoběn [名] manuscript

稿费 gǎofèi [名] fee

稿件 gǎojiàn [名] manuscript

稿子 gǎozi [名] **1** (草稿) draft **2** (诗文) manuscript **3** (计划) plan

告 gào [动] **1** (陈述) tell (*pt, pp* told) **2** (控诉) sue **3** (请求) request **4** (表明) announce ♦告辞 take one's leave **5** (宣布) declare

告白 gàobái [名] expression

告别 gàobié [动] say goodbye (*pt, pp* said)

告成 gàochéng [动] accomplish

告吹 gàochuī [动] come to nothing (*pt* came, *pp* come) ◊我们去大陆投资的计划告吹了。Our plans to invest on the mainland came to nothing.

告辞 gàocí [动] take leave (*pt* took, *pp* taken) ◊晚饭后他起身告辞。After the meal, he stood up and took his leave.

告发 gàofā [动] prosecute

告急 gàojí [动] report an emergency

告捷 gàojié [动] **1** (获胜) triumph **2** (报告胜利) report a victory

告诫 gàojiè [动] warn ◊我告诫孩子别太晚回家。I warned the children not to be too late home.

告警 gàojǐng [动] raise the alarm

告老还乡 gào lǎo huán xiāng retire to one's hometown

告密 gàomì [动] ◊她向当局告密说会有军事政变。She tipped off the authorities about the coup.

告罄 gàoqìng [动] run out (*pt* ran, *pp* run) ◊门票已告罄。There aren't any tickets left.

告饶 gàoráo [动] beg for mercy

告示 gàoshi [名] notification

告诉 gàosu [动] tell (*pt, pp* told)

> **tell** 表示告知某人某事。*The manufacturer told me that the product did not contain corn.* 动词 **tell** 通常可以带直接宾语，用来指受话方。*He told Alison he was suffering from leukaemia… What did she tell you?* 以下表达是错误的 *'What did she tell to you?'*。**tell** 后还可以加动词不定式，表示命令或指示。
>
> **say** 是表示某人说话最常用的词汇。请注意，在使用动词 **say** 时，表示受话方，应该使用介词 **to**。不能说 *'What did she say you?'*, 正确的说法是 *'What did she say to you?'*。

告退 gàotuì [动] request to leave

告知 gàozhī [动] let know (*pt, pp* let) ◊我写信告知父母我的近况。I wrote to my parents to let them know my latest news.

告终 gàozhōng [动] end up ◊以失败告终 end up in failure

告状 gàozhuàng [动] (口) **1** (起诉) file a lawsuit **2** (抱怨) complain ◊他向老板告状说我工作不卖力。He went to the boss to complain that I wasn't working hard enough.

疙 gē 见下文

疙瘩 gēda [名] **1** (指皮肤) pimple ◊起鸡皮疙瘩 come out in goosebumps

2 (小块) lump **3** (问题) unease ◇他们之间有点疙瘩。There was a certain amount of unease between them.

咯 gē 见下文

咯咯 gēgē [拟] chuckle

咯吱 gēzhī [拟] creak

哥 gē [名] **1** (哥哥) elder brother **2** (亲热称呼) brother

哥儿们 gērmen [名] **1** (弟兄) brothers (*pl*) **2** (朋友) mate (英), buddy (美)

胳 gē 见下文

胳膊 gēbo [名] arm

鸽 gē [名] dove

鸽子 gēzi [名] dove

搁 gē [动] **1** (放) put (*pt, pp* put) **2** (搁置) put aside

搁笔 gēbǐ [动] stop ◇那个画家已搁笔多年。That artist stopped painting a long time ago.

搁浅 gēqiǎn [动] **1** (字) be stranded **2** (喻) come to a standstill (*pt* came, *pp* come) ◇项目搁浅了。The project came to a standstill.

搁置 gēzhì [动] shelve ◇议案被搁置。The proposal was shelved.

割 gē [动] cut (*pt, pp* cut)

割爱 gē'ài [动] give up what one treasures (*pt* gave, *pp* given)

割裂 gēliè [动] separate

割让 gēràng [动] cede ◇割让领土 cede territory

割舍 gēshě [动] give up (*pt* gave, *pp* given)

歌 gē I [名] song II [动] sing (*pt* sang, *pp* sung)

歌唱 gēchàng [动] **1** (唱) sing (*pt* sang, *pp* sung) **2** (颂扬) sing the praises of

歌功颂德 gē gōng sòng dé sing the praises of

歌剧 gējù [名] opera

歌曲 gēqǔ [名] tune

歌手 gēshǒu [名] singer

歌颂 gēsòng [动] sing the praises of

歌坛 gētán [名] singing circles (*pl*) ◇他在歌坛很有名。He's very well-known in singing circles.

歌舞 gēwǔ [名] singing and dancing

歌星 gēxīng [名] pop star

歌谣 gēyáo [名] ballad

歌咏 gēyǒng [动] sing (*pt* sang, *pp* sung)

革 gé I [名] leather II [动] **1** (改变) change **2** (开除) expel

革除 géchú [动] **1** (铲除) eliminate **2** (开除) expel

革命 gémìng [动] revolutionize ◇工业革命 industrial revolution

革新 géxīn [动] innovate

革职 gézhí [动] dismiss

阁 gé [名] **1** (指建筑) pavilion **2** (内阁) cabinet ◇内阁成员 a member of the cabinet **3** (女子的居室) boudoir **4** (架子) shelf (*pl* shelves)

阁下 géxià [名] (敬) Your Excellency

格 gé [名] **1** (格子) check **2** (规格) standard **3** (品质) character

格调 gédiào [名] **1** (艺术特点) style **2** (书) (品格) character ◇他格调不高。He does not have nice character.

格斗 gédòu [动] wrestle

格格不入 gé gé bù rù be incompatible

格局 géjú [名] set-up

格式 géshi [名] format

格外 géwài [副] **1** (特别) especially **2** (额外) additionally ◇店里忙的时候就得格外找帮手。When the stall is busy we need additional staff .

格言 géyán [名] maxim

格子 gézi [名] shelf (*pl* shelves)

搁 gé [动] withstand (*pt, pp* withstood) ◇刚出土的文物搁不住阳光直射。Newly excavated cultural relics are unable to withstand direct sunshine.

蛤 gé [名] clam ▷另见 há

蛤蜊 gélí [名] clam

隔 gé [动] **1** (阻隔) separate **2** (间隔) be apart ◇两地相隔不远。The two places aren't far apart.

隔岸观火 gé àn guān huǒ stand by and watch

隔壁 gébì [名] next door ◇隔壁邻居 neighbour (英), neighbor (美)

隔阂 géhé [名] misunderstanding ◇文化隔阂 cultural misunderstanding ◇男女朋友间难免会有些隔阂。Misunderstandings are more or less inevitable in relationships.

隔绝 géjué [动] isolate ◇他在乡村过着与世隔绝的生活。He led a completely isolated life in the countryside. ◇两家隔绝往来已久。All contact between the two families stopped a long time ago.

隔离 gélí [动] quarantine ◇病人已被隔离观察。The patient has already been quarantined and observed. ◇种族隔离 racial segregation ◇南非种族隔离 apartheid

隔膜 gémó I [名] gulf ◇距离使两人产生隔膜。Distance created a gulf between them. II [形] (不了解) inept

隔墙有耳 gé qiáng yǒu ěr the walls have ears

隔靴搔痒 gé xuē sāo yǎng fail to get to the heart of a matter

隔音 géyīn [动] soundproof

嗝 gé [名] **1** (饱嗝) burp **2** (冷嗝) hiccup

个 gè I [名] (指身材或大小) size II [量] **1** (表示个数) ◇6个桃子 six peaches ◇两个月 two months **2** (表示约数) ◇俩人相差个两三岁。There's about two or three years between them. ◇她比她丈夫大个一两岁。She's about one or two years older than her husband. **3** (表示动量) ◇开个会 have a meeting ◇冲个澡 have a shower **4** (用在动补之间) ◇叫个不停 talk incessantly III [形] individual

个案 gè'àn [名] case ◇个案研究 case study

个别 gèbié [形] **1** (单个) individual **2** (少数) a couple ◇有个别人违反纪律。A couple of people broke the rules.

个人 gèrén I [名] individual II [代] oneself ◇就他个人而言 as far as he's concerned ◇在我个人看来，这是个好主意。As far as I'm concerned this is a good idea.

个体 gètǐ [名] **1** (指生物) individual ◇生物个体 each and every individual **2** (指经济形态) ◇个体所有制 private ownership ◇个体经营 private enterprise

个头儿 gètóur [名] **1** (指人) build ◇这男孩儿个头儿大。This boy is well-built. **2** (指物) size ◇大个头儿的西瓜 a big watermelon

个性 gèxìng [名] personality ◇他个性很强。He has a very strong personality.

个子 gèzi [名] stature ◇高个子女人 a tall woman

各 gè I [代] each ◇他们各取所好。Each of them will get what they want. II [副] individually

各奔前程 gè bèn qiánchéng go one's own way

各别 gèbié [形] **1** (不同) different **2** (方) (别致) unique **3** (特别) peculiar

各得其所 gè dé qí suǒ everyone in their proper place

各个 gègè I [代] each ◇各个成员 each member II [副] one by one ◇问题得各个解决。The problems need to be dealt with one by one.

各尽所能 gè jìn suǒ néng do what one can in one's role

各色 gèsè [形] all kinds of

各抒己见 gè shū jǐ jiàn everyone has their say

各行其是 gè xíng qí shì do as one pleases ◇这个部门的人各行其是。Everyone in this department does as they please.

各有千秋 gè yǒu qiān qiū each has its strong points

各自 gèzì [代] each

各自为政 gè zì wéi zhèng everyone does their own thing

给 gěi I [动] **1** (给予) give (*pt* gave, *pp*

given) ◊给我勇气 give me courage **2** (让) let (*pt, pp* let) ◊给他看看照片。Let him see the photos. **II** [介] **1** (为) for ◊我给妻子做早餐。I made breakfast for my wife. **2** (向) to ◊留给他 leave it to him ◊递给我 pass it to me **III** [助] ◊我把开会的事给忘了。I forgot about the meeting. ◊他把钥匙给掉了。He lost the key.
▷另见 jǐ

给以 gěiyǐ [动] give (*pt* gave, *pp* given) ◊给以资助 give financial support

根 gēn **I** [名] **1** (指植物) root **2** (子孙) offspring **3** (指物体) base **4** (本原) origin ♦祸根 the root of the problem **5** (依据) grounds (*pl*) ◊无根之谈 groundless claims **II** [副] thoroughly ♦根除 root out **III** [量] ◊一根绳子 a length of rope ◊几根稻草 some pieces of straw ◊一根头发 a hair

根本 gēnběn **I** [名] root **II** [形] fundamental **III** [副] **1** (完全) at all ◊根本没人告诉我。Nobody told me at all. **2** (彻底) thoroughly ◊根本转变态度 completely change one's attitude

根除 gēnchú [动] eliminate

根底 gēndǐ [名] **1** (基础) grounding ◊他数学根底不错。He has a good grounding in maths. **2** (底细) cause ◊灾祸的根底 the cause of the tragic accident

根基 gēnjī [名] **1** (字) foundations (*pl*) ◊建筑物的根基 the foundations of the building **2** (喻) foundation ◊事业的根基 the foundation of a career

根究 gēnjiū [动] get to the bottom of

根据 gēnjù **I** [介] according to **II** [名] basis (*pl* bases) ◊她的说法毫无根据。Her argument had absolutely no basis whatsoever. ◊文章的根据 the basis of the article

根绝 gēnjué [动] eradicate

根深蒂固 gēn shēn dì gù deep-rooted

根由 gēnyóu [名] cause

根源 gēnyuán [名] cause

根治 gēnzhì [动] bring to an end (*pt, pp* brought)

根子 gēnzi [名] (口) **1** (字) root **2** (喻) source

跟 gēn **I** [名] heel **II** [动] **1** (跟随) follow **2** (嫁) marry **III** [介] **1** (同) with ◊我跟朋友去公园了。I went to the park with friends. **2** (向) ◊跟我说说这件事。Tell me what happened. ◊婚姻大事得跟父母商量。When it comes to marriage you really should talk it through with your parents. **3** (表示比较) as ◊他的教育背景跟我相似。His educational background is similar to mine. **IV** [连] and ◊珍妮跟海伦都去上课了。Jenny and Helen both went to their lectures.

跟前 gēnqián [名] ◊他走到我跟前耳语了几句。He came close and whispered a few words. ◊有只猫蹲在窗户跟前。There's a cat sitting at the window.

跟随 gēnsuí [动] follow

跟头 gēntou [名] fall ◊跌了个跟头 have a fall ◊翻跟头 do a somersault

跟踪 gēnzōng [动] tail

亘 gèn [动] stretch

亘古未有 gèn gǔ wèi yǒu unprecedented

更 gēng **I** [动] **1** (改变) change **2** (书) (经历) experience **II** [名] watch
▷另见 gèng

更迭 gēngdié [动] alternate

更动 gēngdòng [动] change

更改 gēnggǎi [动] alter

更换 gēnghuàn [动] change

更生 gēngshēng [动] **1** (复兴) revive **2** (再生) regenerate ◊更生玻璃 recycled glass

更替 gēngtì [动] replace ◊这个国家政权更替频繁。This country's governments are constantly being replaced.

更新 gēngxīn [动] **1** (事物) replace ◊更新网站内容 update web content ◊更新设备 replace old equipment **2** (森林) renew

更衣 gēngyī [动] change one's clothes ◇更衣间 changing room

更正 gēngzhèng [动] correct ◇自我更正 correct oneself

耕 gēng [动] plough

耕耘 gēngyún [动] cultivate

耕作 gēngzuò [动] farm

羹 gēng [名] thick soup

羹匙 gēngchí [名] soup spoon

耿 gěng [形] upright

耿耿 gěnggěng [形] 1 (忠诚) devoted 2 (有心事) troubled

耿耿于怀 gěng gěng yú huái dwell on ◇她对同事的话一直耿耿于怀。She kept dwelling on what her colleague had said.

耿直 gěngzhí [形] upright

哽 gěng [动] choke

哽咽 gěngyè [动] choke down sobs

梗 gěng I [名] stalk II [动] 1 (挺直) straighten 2 (阻塞) obstruct

梗概 gěnggài [名] outline

梗塞 gěngsè [动] 1 (阻塞) block 2 (梗死) obstruct

梗阻 gěngzǔ [动] block

更 gèng [形] 1 (更加) even more ◇天更黑了。It's getting even darker. ◇她更漂亮了。She is becoming even more beautiful. 2 (书) (再) further ▷另见 gēng

更加 gèngjiā [副] even more ◇天气更加热了。The weather got even hotter.

工 gōng I [名] 1 (指人) worker ◆童工 child labour 2 (指阶级) the working class 3 (工作或劳动) work 4 (工程) project 5 (工业) industry 6 (指时间) man-day ◇这个工程得要7个工。This project will require seven man-days. 7 (技术) skill ◆做工 workmanship ◇他的唱工很好。He's a good singer. II [动] be skilled in III [形] exquisite

工本 gōngběn [名] production cost

工厂 gōngchǎng [名] factory

工场 gōngchǎng [名] workshop

工程 [名] gōngchéng engineering project ◇大兴土木工程 launch massive construction projects

工程师 gōngchéngshī [名] engineer

工夫 gōngfu [名] 1 (时间) time ◇这份作业很花工夫。The assignment took a long time to complete. 2 (空闲) spare time ◇有工夫到我这里来。If you have any spare time do come over to my place.

工会 gōnghuì [名] trade union

工匠 gōngjiàng [名] craftsman

工具 gōngjù [名] 1 (器具) tool ◇工具箱 toolbox ◇运输工具 means of transport 2 (喻) instrument ◇语言是交流的工具。Language is a means of communication.

工力 gōnglì [名] expertise

工期 gōngqī [名] time limit

工巧 gōngqiǎo [形] exquisite

工人 gōngrén [名] worker

工时 gōngshí [名] man-hour ◇他每天干8个工时的活。He works for eight hours a day.

工事 gōngshì [名] fortifications (*pl*)

工薪族 gōngxīnzú [名] wage earners (*pl*)

工序 gōngxù [名] process

工业 gōngyè [名] industry ◇石油工业 petroleum industry

工艺 gōngyì [名] 1 (技术) technology 2 (手工艺) craft

工友 gōngyǒu [名] 1 (同事) fellow worker 2 (勤杂工) caretaker

工于心计 gōng yú xīnjì calculating

工整 gōngzhěng [形] neat

工资 gōngzī [名] pay

> 📖 **pay** 是概括性的词汇，表示通过工作从雇主处得到的报酬。专业人员和办公室职员的工资是 **salary**，通常按月支付。然而，当谈论某人的 **salary** 时，通常是指年薪。*I'm paid a salary of £15,000 a year.* 体力劳动者的工资称为 **wages**，或 **a wage**。*Every week he handed all his wages in cash to his wife.* →

> **wages** 通常是以小时或星期计算。*...a wage of five dollars an hour...* **income** 指各种来源的收入的总和，其中也包括工资。*Only 25% of his income comes from his job, the rest is from investments.*

工作 gōngzuò [名] **1** (劳动) work ◇编译字典不是一件简单的工作。 Translating and editing a dictionary is not an easy job. ◇他做任何工作都很尽力。 He does his best on any work given to him. **2** (职业) job ◇我想找份好工作。 I am looking for a good job. **3** (业务) work ◇科研工作 scientific research work

弓 gōng **I** [名] bow **II** [动] bend (*pt, pp* bent)

弓箭 gōngjiàn [名] bow and arrow

公 gōng **I** [形] **1** (非私有) public ♦公共服务 public service **2** (共识) general **3** (共用) international **4** (公正) fair **5** (雄性) male **II** [动] make public **III** [名] **1** (公务) official business ◇因公出差 go on a business trip **2** (集体) authorities (*pl*) **3** (指爵位) duke **4** (敬) (老先生) ◇王公 Mr Wang **5** (丈夫的父亲) father-in-law

公安 gōng'ān [名] public security

公报 gōngbào [名] bulletin ◇新闻公报 news bulletin

公布 gōngbù [动] announce

公厕 gōngcè [名] public toilet

公道 gōngdào [形] fair

公德 gōngdé [名] social norms (*pl*)

公断 gōngduàn [动] arbitrate

公费 gōngfèi [名] public expense

公愤 gōngfèn [名] public outcry ◇他的暴行引起了公愤。 There was public outcry at his atrocious behaviour.

公干 gōnggàn [名] business

公告 gōnggào [名] proclamation ◇发布公告 issue a proclamation

公共 gōnggòng [形] public

公共汽车 gōnggòng qìchē [名] bus

公共汽车站 gōnggòng qìchēzhàn [名] **1** (指总站) bus station **2** (指路边站) bus stop

公共关系 gōnggòng guānxì [名] public relations (*pl*)

公关 gōngguān [名] (公共关系) public relations (*pl*)

公海 gōnghǎi [名] the high seas (*pl*)

公害 gōnghài [名] **1** (指对环境) environmental hazard **2** (指对社会) public hazard

公函 gōnghán [名] official correspondence

公家 gōngjia [名] the state

公开 gōngkāi **I** [形] public ◇公开演讲 public speech **II** [动] make public

公款 gōngkuǎn [名] public funds (*pl*)

公里 gōnglǐ [名] kilometre (英), kilometer (美)

公理 gōnglǐ [名] universal truth

公历 gōnglì [名] Gregorian calendar

公路 gōnglù [名] motorway

公论 gōnglùn [名] public opinion

公民 gōngmín [名] citizen

公墓 gōngmù [名] cemetery

公平 gōngpíng [形] fair

公婆 gōngpó [名] one's husband's parents

公仆 gōngpú [名] public servant ▷另见 gōng

公然 gōngrán [副] openly

公认 gōngrèn [动] acknowledge ◇他是大家公认的好学生。 He was generally acknowledged to be a good student.

公审 gōngshěn [动] put ... on trial (*pt, pp* put)

公式 gōngshì [名] formula (*pl* formulae)

公事 gōngshì [名] official business

公司 gōngsī [名] company ◇进出口公司 import-export company

公诉 gōngsù [动] (法) publicly prosecute

公文 gōngwén [名] official document

公务 gōngwù [名] official business

公物 gōngwù [名] public property

公休 gōngxiū [名] public holiday

公演 gōngyǎn [动] perform ◇这部歌剧一个月后将公演。The opera will be performed a month from now.

公益 gōngyì [名] public welfare

公有 gōngyǒu [形] public ◇公有土地 public land

公寓 gōngyù [名] **1** (旅馆) boarding house **2** (楼房) apartment

公元 gōngyuán [名] A.D. ◇公元2003年 2003 A.D.

公园 gōngyuán [名] park

公约 gōngyuē [名] treaty

公允 gōngyǔn [形] even-handed

公债 gōngzhài [名] government bonds (*pl*)

公章 gōngzhāng [名] official seal

公正 gōngzhèng [形] impartial

公证 gōngzhèng [名] authentication

公职 gōngzhí [名] public employment

公众 gōngzhòng [名] public

公主 gōngzhǔ [名] princess

功 gōng [名] **1** (功劳) contribution **2** (成效) achievement **3** (技术) skill

功败垂成 gōng bài chuí chéng fall at the last hurdle

功臣 gōngchén [名] hero (*pl* heroes)

功到自然成 gōng dào zìrán chéng success is born out of hard work

功德 gōngdé [名] merits (*pl*)

功底 gōngdǐ [名] grounding

功绩 gōngjì [名] contribution

功课 gōngkè [名] homework

功亏一篑 gōng kuī yī kuì fall at the last hurdle

功劳 gōngláo [名] contribution

功能 gōngnéng [名] function ◇电视有教育功能。Television has an educational function.

功效 gōngxiào [名] efficiency

功勋 gōngxūn [名] feats (*pl*)

功业 gōngyè [名] exploits (*pl*)

功用 gōngyòng [名] function

攻 gōng [动] **1** (攻打) attack **2** (驳斥) accuse **3** (学习) study hard

攻读 gōngdú [动] study hard ◇攻读学位 study for a degree

攻关 gōngguān [动] (突破难点) tackle a key problem

攻击 gōngjī [动] **1** (进攻) attack **2** (中伤) slander

攻克 gōngkè [动] capture

攻势 gōngshì [名] offensive

攻占 gōngzhàn [动] attack and occupy

供 gōng [动] **1** (供应) supply **2** (提供) provide
▷另见 gòng

供给 gōngjǐ [动] supply

供求 gōngqiú [名] supply and demand

供养 gōngyǎng [动] look after

供应 gōngyìng [动] supply

宫 gōng [名] **1** (皇宫) palace **2** (庙宇) temple **3** (文化娱乐场所) club

宫殿 gōngdiàn [名] palace

宫廷 gōngtíng [名] **1** (宫殿) palace **2** (统治集团) court

恭 gōng [形] respectful

恭贺 gōnghè [动] congratulate

恭敬 gōngjìng [形] respectful ◇他对老师非常恭敬。He was very respectful towards the teacher.

恭顺 gōngshùn [动] be respectful

恭维 gōngwei [动] flatter

恭喜 gōngxǐ [动] congratulate

躬 gōng **I** [动] (弯下身子) bow **II** [副] (自身) in person

巩 gǒng 见下文

巩固 gǒnggù **I** [形] solid **II** [动] strengthen

拱 gǒng [动] **1** (两手相合) join one's hands together **2** (环绕) encircle **3** (肢体弯曲) arch **4** (顶动) push ♦拱芽 sprout ◇拱开海外市场的大门 push open the doors to overseas markets

拱手 gǒngshǒu [动] cup one's hands

共 gòng **I** [形] common **II** [动] share **III** [副] **1** (一齐) together ◇共唱一首歌 sing a song together **2** (总共) altogether ◇该校共有学生8,000人。 This school has 8,000 students altogether. **IV** [名] (共产党) the communist party

共处 gòngchǔ [动] coexist ◇和平共处 peaceful coexistence

共存 gòngcún [动] coexist

共和 gònghé [名] republic

共聚一堂 gòng jù yī táng gather together ◇亲朋好友共聚一堂，祝贺他的成功。 His relatives and close friends gathered together to congratulate him on his success.

共鸣 gòngmíng [名] **1** (物) resonance **2** (指情绪) sympathy

共识 gòngshí [名] consensus

共事 gòngshì [动] work together ◇和她共事很愉快。 It's great working with her.

共通 gòngtōng [形] universal

共同 gòngtóng **I** [形] common ◇共同愿望 common aspiration **II** [副] together ◇共同生活 live together

共同体 gòngtóngtǐ [名] community

共性 gòngxìng [名] similarity

贡 gòng [名] tribute

贡品 gòngpǐn [名] tribute

贡献 gòngxiàn **I** [动] devote ◇他把一生贡献给了科学事业。 He devoted his whole life to science. **II** [名] contribution

供 gòng **I** [动] **1** (供奉) lay (*pt, pp* laid) ◇供奉祭品 lay offerings **2** (招供) confess ◇他供出了主犯的名字。 He confessed the name of the chief culprit. **II** [名] **1** (供品) offerings (*pl*) ◇上供 lay offerings **2** (口供) confession ◇翻供 withdraw a confession
▷另见 gōng

供词 gòngcí [名] confession

供奉 gòngfèng [动] make offerings to

供品 gòngpǐn [名] offerings (*pl*)

供认 gòngrèn [动] confess

供职 gòngzhí [动] hold a position (*pt, pp* held) ◇他供职于清华大学。 He held a position at Tsinghua University.

勾 gōu [动] **1** (删除) cross out ◇把这句话勾掉。 Cross out this sentence. **2** (描画) draw (*pt* drew, *pp* drawn) **3** (调和使黏) thicken ♦勾芡 thicken **4** (引起) evoke ◇勾起对往事的回忆 evoke memories of the past **5** (结合) gang up ◇他和坏人勾在一起。 He's got in with some bad people.
▷另见 gòu

勾搭 gōuda [动] **1** (串通) gang up **2** (引诱) seduce ◇他用花言巧语勾搭那个姑娘。 He used all kinds of sweet talk to seduce the girl.

勾画 gōuhuà [动] sketch

勾结 gōujié [动] collude ◇他与敌人相勾结。 He colluded with the enemy.

勾引 gōuyǐn [动] entice ◇勾引某人犯罪 entice sb to commit a crime

沟 gōu [名] **1** (指人工的) ditch **2** (指自然的) gully **3** (浅槽) groove

沟壑 gōuhè [名] gully

沟通 gōutōng [动] communicate ◇父母与子女应该经常沟通。 Parents should always communicate with their children.

钩 gōu **I** [名] **1** (钩子) hook **2** (汉字笔画) hooked stroke **3** (符号) tick **II** [动] **1** (用钩子挂) hook **2** (编织、缝) crochet

钩心斗角 gōu xīn dòu jiǎo scheme against one another

篝 gōu [名] (书) cage

篝火 gōuhuǒ [名] bonfire

苟 gǒu **I** [形] casual **II** [副] temporarily **III** [连] (书) provided

苟活 gǒuhuó [动] lead a dog's life (*pt, pp* led)

苟且 gǒuqiě [形] **1** (得过且过) drifting **2** (敷衍) perfunctory **3** (不正当) illicit

苟全 gǒuquán [动] barely manage to survive

苟同 gǒutóng [动] (书) agree without due consideration ◇你的观点我可

不能苟同。 I can't agree with you just like that.

狗 gǒu [名] dog

狗急跳墙 gǒu jí tiào qiáng clutch at straws ◊他狗急跳墙，口不择言。 He's really clutching at straws now – he'll say whatever it takes.

狗腿子 gǒutuǐzi [名] henchman

狗血喷头 gǒuxuè pēn tóu abusively

狗仔队 gǒuzǎiduì [名] paparazzi

勾 gòu 见下文
▷另见 gōu

勾当 gòudàng [名] dealings (*pl*) ◊罪恶勾当 criminal dealings

构 gòu I [动] **1** (组成) compose **2** (结成) form **3** (建造) construct II [名] **1** (结构) structure **2** (文艺作品) composition

构成 gòuchéng I [动] **1** (造成) constitute ◊他的行为已构成行贿。 His actions already constitute bribery. **2** (组成) compose ◊氢和氧构成水。 Water is composed of hydrogen and oxygen. II [名] line-up ◊这支队伍的成员构成很合理。 The team line-up made a lot of sense.

构件 gòujiàn [名] component part

构思 gòusī [动] compose

构想 gòuxiǎng I [动] compose II [名] concept

构造 gòuzào [名] structure

购 gòu [动] buy (*pt, pp* bought)

购买 gòumǎi [动] buy (*pt, pp* bought) ◊购买食品和药品 buy food and medicines

购物 gòuwù [动] go shopping (*pt* went, *pp* gone) ◊她爱购物。 She likes shopping. ◊我刚才去购物了。 I've just been shopping.

购销 gòuxiāo [名] buying and selling

购置 gòuzhì [动] purchase ◊学校又购置了一批计算机。 The school has purchased another batch of computers.

垢 gòu I [名] **1** (脏东西) filth **2** (书) (耻辱) insult II [形] (书) (污秽) filthy

够 gòu I [形] enough ◊5个就够了。 Five is enough. ◊只要你满意就够了。 As long as you are satisfied, that's enough. II [动] reach ◊我够不到顶层书架上的书。 I can't reach the books on the top shelf. ◊这些产品不够标准。 These products do not come up to standard. III [副] quite

够本 gòuběn [动] **1** (不输不赚) break even (*pt* broke, *pp* broken) **2** (喻) be worth the effort

够戗 gòuqiàng [形] (方) awful

够味儿 gòuwèir [形] (口) **1** (口味纯正) just right **2** (水平高) excellent

够意思 gòu yìsi [形] (口) wonderful

估 gū [动] guess

估计 gūjì [动] reckon ◊我估计明天能完工。 I reckon we should be able to finish tomorrow. ◊这是个保守的估计。 This is a conservative estimate.

估价 gūjià [动] **1** (对商品) estimate **2** (对人或事物) evaluate

估量 gūliáng [动] measure ◊这场火灾的损失难以估量。 It'll be hard to measure the damage caused by the fire.

估摸 gūmo [动] (口) reckon

估算 gūsuàn [动] guess

咕 gū [拟] coo

咕咚 gūdōng [拟] splash

咕嘟 gūdū [拟] **1** (指液体) bubble **2** (指喝水声) gulp ◊他咕嘟咕嘟地喝了一大杯水。 He gulped down a large glass of water.

咕唧 gūji [动] whisper

咕噜 gūlū [拟] rumble ◊我肚子咕噜咕噜直响。 My stomach rumbled.

呱 gū [拟] cry

沽 gū [动] (书) **1** (买) purchase **2** (卖) sell (*pt, pp* sold)

沽名钓誉 gū míng diào yù court publicity ◊他从不沽名钓誉。 He never courts publicity.

姑 gū I [名] **1** (姑母) aunt **2** (丈夫的姐妹) sister-in-law **3** (尼姑) nun II [副]

(姑且) for the time being

姑息 gūxī [动] appease

孤 gū [形] 1 (幼年丧父或父母双亡) orphaned 2 (孤单) alone

孤傲 gū'ào [形] aloof

孤单 gūdān [形] 1 (单薄) weak ◇工党在该选区势力孤单。 Support for the Labour Party is pretty weak in this constituency. 2 (寂寞) lonely ◇他时常感到孤单。 He often feels lonely.

孤独 gūdú [形] solitary

孤儿 gū'ér [名] orphan

孤芳自赏 gū fāng zì shǎng narcissistic

孤家寡人 gūjiā guǎrén loner

孤苦伶仃 gūkǔ língdīng lonely and wretched

孤立 gūlì I [形] 1 (无联系) isolated ◇这个案件绝对不是孤立的。 This is definitely not an isolated case. 2 (无助) unsupported II [动] isolate

孤零零 gūlínglíng [形] alone

孤陋寡闻 gū lòu guǎ wén out of touch

孤僻 gūpì [形] antisocial

孤掌难鸣 gū zhǎng nán míng hard to achieve by oneself

孤注一掷 gū zhù yī zhì put all one's eggs in one basket ◇他从不做孤注一掷的事。 He never puts all his eggs in one basket.

轱 gū 见下文

轱辘 gūlu [名] wheel

骨 gū 见下文
▷另见 gǔ

骨朵儿 gūduor [名] bud

菇 gū [名] mushroom

辜 gū [名] guilt

辜负 gūfù [动] fail to live up to ◇他辜负了家长和老师对他的期望。 He failed to live up to the expectations of his parents and teachers.

箍 gū I [名] hoop II [动] bind (*pt, pp* bound)

古 gǔ I [名] ancient times (*pl*) II [形] ancient ◇古文明 ancient civilization

古板 gǔbǎn [形] set in one's ways ◇他为人处事很古板。 He's so set in his ways.

古代 gǔdài [名] antiquity

古典 gǔdiǎn I [名] classics (*pl*) II [形] classical

古董 gǔdǒng [名] 1 (古代器物) antique 2 (喻) (指人) old fogey

古怪 gǔguài [形] bizarre

古籍 gǔjí [名] ancient books (*pl*)

古迹 gǔjì [名] historic site

古老 gǔlǎo [形] ancient

古朴 gǔpǔ [形] simple

古色古香 gǔ sè gǔ xiāng have an antique feel ◇故宫里的建筑物古色古香。 The architecture of the Forbidden City has a real antique feel to it.

古诗 gǔshī [名] ancient poetry

古玩 gǔwán [名] antiques (*pl*)

古往今来 gǔ wǎng jīn lái throughout the ages

古文 gǔwén [名] (文言文) classical prose

古稀 gǔxī [名] seventy years of age

古雅 gǔyǎ [形] quaint

古装 gǔzhuāng [名] ancient costume

谷 gǔ [名] 1 (山谷) valley 2 (谷类作物) grain 3 (谷子) millet 4 (方) (稻谷) unhusked rice

谷物 gǔwù [名] grain

谷子 gǔzi [名] millet

汩 gǔ [形] (书) gurgling

汩汩 gǔgǔ [拟] gurgle

股 gǔ I [名] 1 (大腿) thigh 2 (指组织单位) department 3 (指绳或线) strand 4 (股份) share II [量] 1 (指条状) ◇一股水流 a trickle of water ◇两股毛线 two strands of thread 2 (气体、气味) whiff

股东 gǔdōng [名] shareholder

股份 gǔfèn [名] share

股票 gǔpiào [名] share

股市 gǔshì [名] stock market

骨 gǔ [名] bone
▷另见 gū

骨干 gǔgàn [名] 1 (解剖) backbone 2 (起重要作用的力量) core

骨骼 gǔgé [名] (解剖) skeleton

骨架 gǔjià [名] 1 (骨头架子) skeleton 2 (支架) framework

骨气 gǔqì [名] integrity

骨肉 gǔròu [名] flesh and blood ◇这个孩子是他的亲骨肉。 The child is his flesh and blood.

骨头 gǔtou [名] 1 (字) bone 2 (喻) character

骨子里 gǔzilǐ [名] deep down ◇他表面答应，骨子里却另有打算。 He made a show of agreement but deep down he had other ideas.

牯 gǔ [名] bull

鼓 gǔ I [名] drum II [动] 1 (敲击) ◇鼓琴 play the zither ◇鼓掌 clap one's hands 2 (扇) blow (*pt* blew, *pp* blown) 3 (振奋) rouse 4 (拍打) beat (*pt* beat, *pp* beaten) 5 (凸起，胀大) bulge ◇他鼓着嘴。 He puffed his cheeks out. III [形] bulging ◇她的书包鼓鼓的。 Her schoolbag was full to bursting.

鼓吹 gǔchuī [动] 1 (宣传) advocate 2 (吹嘘) boast about ◇他鼓吹他所谓的发明。 He boasted about his so-called invention.

鼓动 gudòng [动] rouse

鼓励 gǔlì [动] encourage

鼓舞 gǔwǔ I [动] inspire II [形] inspiring

鼓掌 gǔzhǎng [动] applaud

固 gù I [形] strong ♦坚固 solid ♦稳固 stable ♦牢固 firm II [副] 1 (坚定) firmly 2 (本来) originally III [连] (固然) no doubt ◇中餐固好，西餐也不错。 There's no doubt that Chinese food is good, but Western cuisine isn't bad either. IV [动] 1 (使坚固) solidify 2 (防卫) strengthen

固步自封 gù bù zì fēng be a stick-in-the-mud

固定 gùdìng I [形] fixed II [动] fix ◇她把锻炼的时间固定在星期六下午。 She fixed the exercise time for Saturday afternoons.

固然 gùrán [连] 1 (虽然) admittedly ◇这样办固然可以，但就是需要时间。 Admittedly, you can do this but it will take time. 2 (的确) no doubt ◇事业固然重要，但家庭也不可忽视。 There's no doubt that work is important, but you can't neglect your family over it.

固守 gùshǒu [动] 1 (坚守) vigorously defend 2 (固执遵循) cling to (*pt, pp* clung) ◇固守陈规 cling to old-fashioned conventions

固体 gùtǐ [名] solid

固有 gùyǒu [形] inherent

固执 gùzhí [形] stubborn

固执己见 gùzhí jǐjiàn be stubborn

故 gù I [名] 1 (变故) incident 2 (原因) reason 3 (友情) friendship 4 (老友) old friend II [动] pass away III [形] 1 (表示老、旧) old 2 (亡故) deceased IV [副] on purpose V [连] therefore ◇他病了，故未参加会议。 He was ill, and therefore not at the meeting.

故步自封 gù bù zì fēng be complacent

故技 gùjì [名] old trick ◇故技重演 be up to one's old tricks

故居 gùjū [名] former home

故里 gùlǐ [名] home town

故弄玄虚 gù nòng xuánxū make a mystery of something ◇媒体总爱故弄玄虚。 The media always likes to make a mystery out of things.

故事 gùshi [名] story

故土 gùtǔ [名] native soil

故乡 gùxiāng [名] birthplace

故意 gùyì [副] deliberately ◇他故意气他的父亲。 He deliberately angered his father.

故障 gùzhàng [名] fault ◇这台机器出了故障。 This machine is faulty.

故作姿态 gù zuò zītài pose ◇别故作姿态了，赶快照吧！ Stop posing and let me take the picture!

顾 gù I [动] 1 (看) look ♦回顾 look back ♦环顾 look around 2 (注意, 照管) attend to ♦照顾 attend to ♦兼顾 give consideration to both sides 3 (拜访) visit 4 (光临) shop at ◇他爱光顾这家书店。 He likes to shop at this bookshop. II [副] (书) however

顾此失彼 gù cǐ shī bǐ let things slip

顾及 gùjí [动] consider

顾忌 gùjì [动] be guarded ◇他说话毫无顾忌。 He was never guarded about what he said.

顾客 gùkè [名] customer

顾虑 gùlǜ [名] misgivings (*pl*) ◇顾虑重重 have serious misgivings

顾名思义 gù míng sī yì as the name implies

顾盼 gùpàn [动] look around ◇他上课的时候老是左右顾盼。 He was always looking around in class.

顾全 gùquán [动] consider … fully

顾问 gùwèn [名] consultant

顾惜 gùxī [动] value

顾影自怜 gù yǐng zì lián 1 (孤独失意) self-pity 2 (自我欣赏) narcissism

梏 gù [名] wooden handcuffs (*pl*) ♦桎梏 fetters and handcuffs (*pl*)

雇 gù [动] 1 (雇佣) employ 2 (租赁) hire

雇佣 gùyōng [动] employ

雇员 gùyuán [名] employee

雇主 gùzhǔ [名] employer

痼 gù [形] 1 (难治愈) chronic 2 (难克服) inveterate

痼疾 gùjí [名] chronic illness

瓜 guā [名] (植) melon

瓜分 guāfēn [动] carve up ◇企图瓜分别国领土 plot to carve up other countries' territories

瓜葛 guāgé [名] association ◇我不想和这件事有任何瓜葛。 I don't want to be associated with this in any way.

瓜熟蒂落 guā shú dì luò everything works out when the time is right

呱 guā 见下文

呱呱 guāguā [拟] croak

呱呱叫 guāguājiào [形] (口) fantastic

刮 guā [动] 1 (指用刀) shave 2 (涂抹) smear 3 (搜刮) plunder 4 (风) blow

刮目相看 guāmù xiāng kàn look at someone with new eyes

剐 guǎ [动] cut (*pt, pp* cut)

寡 guǎ I [形] 1 (少) few 2 (淡而无味) bland II [名] 1 (寡妇) widow 2 (寡居) widowhood

寡妇 guǎfu [名] widow

寡廉鲜耻 guǎ lián xiǎn chǐ shameless

卦 guà [名] divinatory symbol

挂 guà [动] 1 (悬吊) hang 2 (中断电话) hang up ◇他愤怒地把电话挂了。 He hung up angrily. 3 (接通电话) connect ◇请挂传达室。 Can you please put me through to reception? 4 (钩) hitch … up

挂彩 guàcǎi [动] 1 (悬挂彩带) decorate 2 (受伤) be wounded

挂齿 guàchǐ [动] mention

挂钩 guàgōu I [名] hook II [动] link up with

挂号 guàhào [动] register

挂靠 guàkào [动] be affiliated to ◇挂靠在浙江大学 be affiliated to Zhejiang University

挂历 guàlì [名] calendar

挂名 guàmíng [动] be nominal ◇我只在该公司挂名而已。 I only have nominal responsibility for this company.

挂念 guàniàn [动] be concerned about ◇小张很挂念出国的妻子。 Xiao Zhang was very concerned about his wife, who had gone abroad.

挂拍 guàpāi [动] retire

挂失 guàshī [动] report the loss of

挂帅 guàshuài [动] take charge (*pt* took, *pp* taken)

挂图 guàtú [名] wall chart

挂靴 guàxuē [名] retire

挂一漏万 guà yī lòu wàn be far from exhaustive

褂 guà [名] gown

乖 guāi I [形] 1 (听话) well-behaved 2 (机灵) clever 3 (书) (不正常) abnormal II [动] (书) (违反) violate

乖戾 guāilì [形] (书) twisted ◇他的行为乖戾。 He's so twisted.

乖僻 guāipì [形] eccentric

乖巧 guāiqiǎo [形] 1 (机灵) clever 2 (惹人爱) lovable

拐 guǎi I [名] 1 (拐杖) walking stick 2 (拐角处) turning 3 (七) seven II [动] 1 (转变方向) turn ◇车从大路拐进一条小胡同。 The car left the main road and turned into a small alley. 2 (拐骗) swindle

拐卖 guǎimài [动] abduct and sell

拐骗 guǎipiàn [动] 1 (钱财) swindle 2 (妇女或儿童等) abduct

拐弯抹角 guǎi wān mò jiǎo 1 (道路不畅) twist and turn 2 (不直接) beat about the bush

怪 guài I [形] strange II [动] 1 (觉得奇怪) be surprised 2 (责怪) blame ◇这事也不能全怪他。 We can't blame this entirely on him. III [副] (口) really ◇这行李怪沉的。 This bag is really heavy. IV [名] monster

怪诞 guàidàn [形] uncanny

怪话 guàihuà [名] snide remark

怪模怪样 guài mú guài yàng grotesque

怪圈 guàiquān [名] strange phenomenon (*pl* phenomena)

怪异 guàiyì [形] weird

怪罪 guàizuì [动] blame

关 guān I [动] 1 (合拢) close ◇关窗户 close the window 2 (圈起来) imprison ◇战俘被关进集中营。 The prisoners of war were imprisoned in a concentration camp. ◇别让孩子整天关在家里。 Make sure the children aren't cooped up at home all day. 3 (停业) close down ◇这家公司早就关了。 The company closed down a long time ago. 5 (中断、终止) turn off ◇关灯 turn off the light 6 (牵连) concern ◇这不关他的事。 This matter does not concern him. II [名] 1 (守卫处所) pass 2 (出入境收税处) customs (*pl*) ♦海关 customs (*pl*) 3 (转折点) critical point ◇手术这一关他总算闯过去了。 His critical operation passed off safely. 4 (关联部分) ♦关节 joint ♦关键 key

关爱 guān'ài [动] cherish

关闭 guānbì [动] 1 (合拢) close 2 (歇业或停办) close down

关怀 guānhuái [动] be concerned about ◇关怀社会弱势群体 be concerned about disadvantaged social groups

关键 guānjiàn I [名] crux II [形] key

关节 guānjié [名] joint

关口 guānkǒu [名] 1 (必经之地) strategic pass 2 (关头) juncture

关联 guānlián [动] be interrelated ◇发展经济和保护环境是互相关联的。 Developing the economy and protecting the environment are interrelated.

关卡 guānqiǎ [名] checkpoint

关切 guānqiè I [形] deeply concerned II [动] be concerned

关税 guānshuì [名] customs duty

关头 guāntóu [名] juncture

关系 guānxì I [名] 1 (联系) relation ◇外交关系 diplomatic relations 2 (意义) bearing ◇此事关系重大。 This matter is of grave importance. 3 (原因) reason ◇由于健康关系，他提前退休了。 He retired early for reasons of ill health. 4 (证件) identification papers ◇出门把关系带上。 Take your papers with you when you go out. II [动] impact on ◇会议的决定关系到公司的未来。 The decisions made at this meeting will impact on the future of the company.

关心 guānxīn [动] be concerned ◇关心股市走向 be concerned about stock market trends

关押 guānyā [动] imprison

关于 guānyú [介] on ◇关于这个问题有很多争议。 There is a lot of controversy on this point.

关照 guānzhào [动] **1** (关心照顾) look after **2** (口头通知) tell

关注 guānzhù [动] pay close attention to (*pt, pp* paid) ◇社会都应该关注老年人问题。 Society should pay close attention to the problems of the elderly.

观 guān **I** [动] look ◆围观 gather round to watch ◆旁观 look on **II** [名] view ◆景观 sight ◆奇观 spectacle

观测 guāncè [动] observe

观察 guānchá [动] observe

观点 guāndiǎn [名] point of view

观感 guāngǎn [名] impressions (*pl*)

观光 guānguāng [动] go sightseeing (*pt* went, *pp* gone) ◇去巴黎观光 go sightseeing in Paris

观看 guānkàn [动] watch

观摩 guānmó [动] watch and learn

观念 guānniàn [名] concept

观赏 guānshǎng [动] stand back and enjoy

观望 guānwàng [动] wait and see ◇他们采取观望的态度。 They took a "wait-and-see" attitude.

观众 guānzhòng [名] spectator

官 guān [名] **1** (公职人员) official **2** (器官) organ

官场 guānchǎng [名] official circles ◇这在官场中很常见。 This is very common in official circles.

官邸 guāndǐ [名] official residence

官方 guānfāng [名] official

官官相护 guān guān xiāng hù ◇这种官官相护的情况必须制止。 The way that officials stick up for and protect one another has got to stop.

官吏 guānlì [名] (旧) official

官僚 guānliáo [名] bureaucrat ◇官僚作风 bureaucracy

官能 guānnéng [名] sense

官腔 guānqiāng [名] bureaucratic manner

官司 guānsi [名] lawsuit ◇和某人打官司 file a lawsuit against somebody

官员 guānyuán [名] official

官运亨通 guānyùn hēngtōng have a successful career as an official

官职 guānzhí [名] official position

冠 guān [名] **1** (帽子) hat **2** (帽状物) ◆鸡冠 crown ◆花冠 garland ▷另见 guàn

冠冕堂皇 guānmiǎn tánghuáng grandiose

棺 guān [名] coffin

鳏 guān [名] widower

鳏寡孤独 guān guǎ gū dú [名] people with no family to support them

管 guǎn **I** [名] **1** (管子) pipe ◆水管 water pipe **2** (乐器) wind instrument ◆双簧管 oboe **3** (管状物) tube ◆晶体管 transistor **4** (医) duct **II** [动] **1** (负责) be in charge of ◇管销售 be in charge of sales **2** (管辖) have jurisdiction over ◇这个市管3个区和5个县。 This city has jurisdiction over three districts and five counties. **3** (管教) discipline ◇把自己家的孩子管好 discipline one's children well **4** (过问) interfere ◇这事不用你管。 It's no use you interfering in this. **5** (担任) be in charge of ◇她管市场部。 She's in charge of the marketing department. **6** (保证) guarantee ◇管换管退。 The replacement or refund of defective goods is guaranteed. **7** (提供) provide ◇管吃管住 provide food and accommodation **III** [形] narrow ◆管见 in my humble opinion **IV** [介] ◇大家管他叫"小王"。 Everyone calls him "Xiao Wang".

管保 guǎnbǎo [动] guarantee

管道 guǎndào [名] pipeline ◇管道煤气 piped gas ◇石油运输管道 oil pipeline

管家 guǎnjiā [名] housekeeper

管教 guǎnjiào [动] discipline ◇管教子女是父母的责任。 It's the responsibility of parents to instil a sense of discipline in their children.

管理 guǎnlǐ **I** [动] **1** (负责) be in charge ◇管理财务 be in charge of finance **2** (保管) take care of (*pt* took, *pp* taken) ◇他管理计算机。 He takes care of the computers. **3** (看管) keep guard over (*pt, pp* kept) ◇管理犯人 keep guard over the prisoners ◇企业管理 business management

管事 guǎnshì [动] **1** (负责) be in charge **2** (有效) be effective

管束 guǎnshù [动] discipline

管辖 guǎnxiá [动] have jurisdiction over

管弦乐 guǎnxiányuè [名] orchestral music

管用 guǎnyòng [形] effective

管制 guǎnzhì **I** [名] control **II** [动] place under surveillance

贯 guàn **I** [动] **1** (贯穿) pass through **2** (连贯) keep following (*pt, pp* kept) **II** [名] ancestral home ♦籍贯 place of origin

贯彻 guànchè [动] implement

贯穿 guànchuān [动] run through ◇这项政策应该贯穿于整个工程。 This policy should run through the whole project. ◇这条铁路贯穿南北。 The railway runs from north to south.

贯串 guànchuàn [动] permeate

贯通 guàntōng [名] **1** (理解透彻) be well versed in **2** (连接) link up

贯注 guànzhù [动] concentrate ◇你应该全神贯注于工作。 You should concentrate fully on your work.

冠 guàn **I** [动] crown **II** [名] crown ▷另见 guān

冠词 guàncí [名] (语法) article

冠军 guànjūn [名] champion

惯 guàn [动] **1** (习惯) be used to ◇我吃西餐已经惯了。 I'm already used to Western food. **2** (纵容) spoil

惯犯 guànfàn [名] reoffender

惯技 guànjì [名] old trick

惯例 guànlì [名] convention

惯用 guànyòng **I** [动] often use ◇他惯用这种方法。 He often uses this sort of method. **II** [形] habitual

盥 guàn 见下文

盥洗 guànxǐ [动] wash (英), wash up (美)

灌 guàn [动] **1** (灌溉) irrigate **2** (注入) pour into ◇灌热水瓶 pour water into a flask **3** (强行劝酒) force … to drink ◇他把别人都灌醉了。 He got them all drunk. **4** (录音) record

灌溉 guàngài [动] irrigate

灌木 guànmù [名] (植) bush

灌输 guànshū [动] **1** (输水) divert water **2** (思想、知识) indoctrinate ◇有人向他灌输迷信思想。 Someone indoctrinated him with superstitious beliefs.

灌注 guànzhù [动] pour … into

罐 guàn 见下文

罐头 guàntou [名] tin

光 guāng **I** [名] **1** (指物质) light ◇月光 moonlight ◇阳光 sunlight **2** (景物) scenery ◇迷人的风光 enchanting scenery **3** (荣誉) glory ◇奥运冠军为国增光。 Olympic champions bring glory to their country. **4** (明亮) glint ◇他看到金子时两眼放光。 His eyes glinted when he saw the gold. **4** (好处) benefit **II** [动] **1** (光大) glorify ◇光耀门庭 bring glory to the family name **2** (露出) bare ◇大冬天他还光着上身。 He went bare-chested even in the depths of winter. **III** [形] **1** (光滑) smooth **2** (露着) bare ◇光脚 barefooted **3** (穷尽) used up ◇钱都用光了。 All the money's used up. **IV** [副] just ◇这件事光有热情是不够的。 This requires more than just enthusiasm. ◇他光说不做。 He's all talk.

光波 guāngbō [名] (物) light wave

光彩 guāngcǎi **I** [名] radiance **II** [形] glorious

光大 guāngdà [动] carry … forward

光复 guāngfù [动] recover

光顾 guānggù [动] shop at ◇欢迎光顾我店。 Welcome to our shop.

光怪陆离 guāng guài lù lí bizarre and fantastic

光棍 guānggùn [名] **1** (地痞) hooligan **2** (单身汉) bachelor

光滑 guānghuá [形] smooth

光辉 guānghuī I [名] radiance II [形] magnificent

光洁 guāngjié [形] bright and clean

光景 guāngjǐng I [名] 1 (情景) scene 2 (境况) situation II [副] 1 (大约) about ◊半夜光景下起了雪。 It started snowing about halfway through the night. 2 (很可能) probably ◊她很努力，将来光景有出息。 She's so hard-working – in the future she'll probably be very successful.

光亮 guāngliàng [形] shiny

光临 guānglín [动] be present

光溜溜 guāngliūliū [形] 1 (光滑) slippery 2 (无遮掩的) naked

光芒 guāngmáng [名] radiance

光芒万丈 guāngmáng wànzhàng resplendent

光明 guāngmíng I [名] light II [形] bright

光明正大 guāngmíng zhèngdà open and aboveboard

光盘 guāngpán [名] CD

光荣 guāngróng [形] glorious ◊光荣属于那些默默无闻的幕后工作者。 The glory should go to those who go unrecognised behind the scenes.

光天化日 guāng tiān huà rì in broad daylight

光秃秃 guāngtūtū [形] barren

光线 guāngxiàn [名] light

光阴 guāngyīn [名] time

光阴似箭 guāngyīn sì jiàn time flies

光泽 guāngzé [名] gloss

光照 guāngzhào [名] light

光宗耀祖 guāng zōng yào zǔ bring glory to one's ancestors

咣 guāng [拟] bang

广 guǎng [形] 1 (宽阔) broad 2 (多) numerous

广播 guǎngbō [动] broadcast (*pt, pp* broadcast) ◊他们正在广播找人。 They are currently broadcasting missing person announcements. ◊英语广播 English language broadcast

广博 guǎngbó [形] erudite

广场 guǎngchǎng [名] square

广大 guǎngdà [形] 1 (宽广) vast 2 (众多) numerous

广度 guǎngdù [名] range

广泛 guǎngfàn [形] wide-ranging ◊广泛的群众基础 broad popular base ◊广泛开展活动 initiate a wide range of activities

广告 guǎnggào [名] advertisement

广阔 guǎngkuò [形] broad

广义 guǎngyì [名] broad sense

犷 guǎng [形] uncouth ♦粗犷 rough and uncouth

犷悍 guǎnghàn [形] intrepid

逛 guàng [动] stroll

逛荡 guàngdang [动] loiter

归 guī [动] 1 (返回、还给) return 2 (合并) group together ◊我把书籍归类了。 I sorted out the books. 3 (属于) be under the charge of ◊这支部队归他指挥。 This team is under his charge. ◊这本书归他所有。 This book belongs to him.

归并 guībìng [动] 1 (并入) merge 2 (归拢) add up ◊费用归并后惊人得高。 When you add it all up it's prohibitively expensive.

归档 guīdàng [动] file ◊将这些资料归档备查。 Please file these materials away for future reference.

归根结底 guī gēn jié dǐ in the final analysis

归功 guīgōng [动] give credit to (*pt* gave, *pp* given) ◊成绩不能都归功于一个人。 You can't give one person the credit for all the success.

归还 guīhuán [动] return

归咎 guījiù [动] blame ◊不能把责任都归咎于他。 You can't lay the blame entirely on him.

归纳 guīnà [动] sum up

归属 guīshǔ [动] come under (*pt* came, *pp* come) ◊这个小组归属于人事部。 This team comes under the human resources department.

归顺 guīshùn [动] swear allegiance to (*pt* swore, *pp* sworn)

归降 guīxiáng [动] surrender

归心似箭 guīxīn sì jiàn long to return home

归于 guīyú [动] **1** (属于) attribute to ◇成功归于大家的努力。 The success is down to everyone's hard work. **2** (趋于) tend to

归置 guīzhi [动] (口) tidy up

龟 guī [名] tortoise
▷另见 jūn

龟甲 guījiǎ [名] tortoiseshell

龟缩 guīsuō [动] recoil ◇遇到困难我们不应该龟缩。 We shouldn't recoil in the face of difficulty.

规 guī I [名] **1** (工具) compasses (*pl*) **2** (规则) rule II [动] **1** (劝告) admonish ♦规劝 admonish **2** (谋划) plan ♦规划 plan

规程 guīchéng [名] rules (*pl*)

规定 guīdìng I [动] stipulate ◇请在规定的时间内完成。 Please complete this within the specified time. II [名] directive ◇这项规定过于苛刻。 This directive is excessively harsh.

规范 guīfàn [名] standard ◇良好的行为规范 standards of good conduct ◇他的汉语不规范。 His Chinese is not standard. ◇一定要规范市场秩序。 We must standardize the market economy.

规格 guīgé [名] specification

规划 guīhuà I [名] plan II [动] plan

规矩 guīju I [名] norm II [形] well-behaved ◇她的女儿很规矩。 Her daughter is so well-behaved. ◇他办事总是规矩。 He always plays by the rules.

规律 guīlǜ [名] law

规模 guīmó [名] scale

规劝 guīquàn [动] remonstrate

规则 guīzé I [名] regulation II [形] orderly

规章 guīzhāng [名] regulations (*pl*)

闺 guī [名] **1** (书) (门) gate **2** (闺房) boudoir

闺女 guīnü [名] **1** (未婚女子) girl **2** (女儿) daughter

瑰 guī [形] magnificent

瑰宝 guībǎo [名] treasure

瑰丽 guīlì [形] magnificent

轨 guǐ [名] **1** (轨道) rail **2** (秩序) course

轨道 guǐdào [名] **1** (指机车) track **2** (指天体) orbit **3** (秩序) course ◇这个项目已进入轨道。 The project is now on course.

轨迹 guǐjì [名] **1** (数) locus **2** (天文) orbit

诡 guǐ [形] **1** (奸猾) scheming **2** (奇异) eerie

诡辩 guǐbiàn [动] quibble ◇你实际上是在诡辩。 What you are really doing is quibbling. ◇诡辩改变不了事实。 Quibbling cannot change the facts.

诡计 guǐjì [名] intrigue

诡秘 guǐmì [形] surreptitious

诡异 guǐyì [形] strange

鬼 guǐ I [名] **1** (灵魂) ghost **2** (勾当) dirty trick **3** (不良行为者) ♦酒鬼 drunkard ♦色鬼 lech **4** (表示爱称) ♦机灵鬼 smart aleck II [形] **1** (不光明) secretive **2** (恶劣) damned **3** (机灵) clever

鬼把戏 guǐbǎxì [名] dirty trick

鬼点子 guǐdiǎnzi [名] wicked idea

鬼鬼祟祟 guǐguǐ suìsuì stealthy

鬼话 guǐhuà [名] lie

鬼混 guǐhùn [动] hang around ◇不要整天和不三不四的人鬼混。 You shouldn't be hanging around with such shady people.

鬼脸 guǐliǎn [名] grimace

鬼迷心窍 guǐ mí xīn qiào be obsessed

鬼使神差 guǐ shǐ shén chāi strange coincidence

柜 guì [名] **1** (柜子) cupboard ♦衣柜 wardrobe ♦保险柜 safe **2** (柜房) shop

柜台 guìtái [名] counter

刽 guì [动] cut off (*pt, pp* cut)

刽子手 guìzishǒu [名] **1** (死刑犯执行者) executioner **2** (屠杀者) butcher

贵 guì **I** [形] **1** (指价格) expensive **2** (值得珍视) valuable

贵宾 guìbīn [名] distinguished guest

贵干 guìgàn [名] business

贵人 guìrén [名] **1** (尊贵的人) eminent person **2** (好人) good person

贵重 guìzhòng [形] valuable

贵族 guìzú [名] aristocrat

桂 guì [名] laurel

桂冠 guìguān [名] laurel ◇桂冠诗人 Poet Laureate

跪 guì [动] kneel

跪拜 guìbài [动] worship on bended knee

滚 gǔn **I** [动] **1** (滚动) roll **2** (走开) get lost ◇你赶快滚！ Just get lost, will you! **3** (沸腾) boil **4** (指缝纫方法) hem **II** [形] **1** (滚动的) rolling **2** (沸腾的) boiling **III** [副] very

滚动 gǔndòng [动] roll

滚瓜烂熟 gǔnguā lànshú know off by heart ◇他把那首诗背得滚瓜烂熟。 He knew the whole poem off by heart.

滚滚 gǔngǔn [形] **1** (指河流) surging **2** (指财富) rolling ◇财源滚滚。 The money is rolling in.

滚热 gǔnrè [形] boiling hot

滚烫 gǔntàng [形] boiling

滚圆 gǔnyuán [形] perfectly round

棍 gùn [名] **1** (棍子) stick **2** (地痞) ruffian

锅 guō [名] **1** (指炊具) pot **2** (锅状物) bowl ♦火锅 hotpot

锅巴 guōbā [名] rice crust

锅台 guōtái [名] kitchen range

国 guó **I** [名] country **II** [形] **1** (国家) national ♦国徽 national emblem **2** (中国) Chinese ◇国剧 Chinese opera

国宝 guóbǎo [名] national treasure

国宾 guóbīn [名] guest of the state

国策 guócè [名] national policy

国产 guóchǎn [形] domestic

国粹 guócuì [名] the embodiment of a country

国都 guódū [名] capital

国度 guódù [名] country

国法 guófǎ [名] national law

国防 guófáng [名] national defence (英) 或 defense (美)

国歌 guógē [名] national anthem

国格 guógé [名] national dignity

国画 guóhuà [名] traditional Chinese painting

国徽 guóhuī [名] national emblem

国会 guóhuì [名] parliament

国货 guóhuò [名] domestic goods (*pl*)

国籍 guójí [名] nationality

国计民生 guó jì mín shēng the national economy and the people's livelihood

国际 guójì [形] international ◇国际和平与稳定 international peace and stability

国家 guójiā [名] state

国界 guójiè [名] national border

国境 guójìng [名] **1** (指范围) national territory **2** (边境) frontier

国库 guókù [名] treasury

国力 guólì [名] national strength

国门 guómén [名] border

国民 guómín [名] citizen

国民经济 guómín jīngjì [名] national economy

国难 guónàn [名] national crisis (*pl* crises)

国内 guónèi [形] domestic ◇国内生产总值 gross domestic product

国旗 guóqí [名] national flag

国企 guóqǐ [名] (国有企业) state-owned enterprise

国情 guóqíng [名] the state of the country

国庆 guóqìng [名] national day

国色天香 guósè tiānxiāng stunningly beautiful

国手 guóshǒu [名] national champion

国书 guóshū [名] credentials (*pl*)

国税 guóshuì [名] national taxation

国泰民安 guó tài mín ān a contented people living in a country at peace

国土 guótǔ [名] national territory

国王 guówáng [名] king

国威 guówēi [名] national prestige

国务 guówù [名] domestic affairs (*pl*)

国宴 guóyàn [名] state banquet

国营 guóyíng [形] state-run ◇国营企业 state-run enterprises

国有 guóyǒu [形] state-owned

国债 guózhài [名] national debt

果 guǒ **I** [名] **1** (果子) fruit **1** (结局) outcome ♦效果 result ♦成果 achievement **II** [动] be full **III** [形] resolute **IV** [副] naturally **V** [连] if

果不其然 guǒ bu qí rán as expected ◇果不其然, 他在图书馆看书。 As expected, he was in the library reading books.

果断 guǒduàn [形] resolute

果脯 guǒfǔ [名] preserved fruit

果敢 guǒgǎn [形] resolute and daring

果品 guǒpǐn [名] fruit

果然 guǒrán [副] really

果实 guǒshí [名] **1** (果子) fruit **2** (成果) fruits (*pl*) ◇成功的果实 the fruits of success

果真 guǒzhēn **I** [副] really ◇他果真是个勤奋的年轻人。 He really is a very hard-working young man. **II** [连] if

果子 guǒzi [名] fruit

裹 guǒ [动] **1** (缠绕) wrap ◇我把身子用毯子裹上。 I wrapped myself up in a blanket. **2** (夹带) smuggle away ◇他临走时裹走了一些首饰。 When he left he smuggled away some jewellery. **3** (方) (吸) suck

裹足不前 guǒ zú bù qián drag one's feet

过 guò **I** [动] **1** (经过) pass through **2** (度过) spend (*pt*, *pp* spent) ◇你假期怎么过的? How did you spend your holiday? **3** (过去) pass ◇几天过去了, 他还杳无音信。 Several days passed and still there was no news of him. **4** (处理) go over (*pt* went, *pp* gone) ◇这段文字还得过一遍。 This piece of text should be gone over again. **5** (转移到) transfer ◇过账 transfer from one account to another **6** (超过) be more than ◇工程已经过半。 The project is already more than half way through. ◇年过半百 over fifty years old **7** (生活) live ◇我们过得很好。 We live well. **8** (庆祝) celebrate ◇过生日 celebrate a birthday **II** [名] fault ◇将功补过 atone for one's crimes **III** [介] past ◇现在是9点过8分。 It is now eight minutes past nine.

过不去 guò bu qù [动] **1** (堵塞) be impassable **2** (为难) make things difficult for ◇他有意和我过不去。 He wanted to make things difficult for me. **3** (通不过) not get past ◇这在老板那儿一定过不去的。 This definitely isn't going to get past the boss. **4** (抱歉) feel sorry

过场 guòchǎng [名] interlude ◇走过场 (喻) do as a formality

过程 guòchéng [名] process ◇理解过程 process of understanding

过错 guòcuò [名] fault

过道 guòdào [名] corridor

过得去 guò de qù [动] **1** (可通过) be passable **2** (不错) be passable ◇饭菜还过得去。 The food is just passable. **3** (过意得去) feel at ease

过度 guòdù [形] excessive

过分 guòfèn [形] excessive

过关 guòguān [动] **1** (通过关口) cross a pass **2** (通过检验) pass a test

过河拆桥 guò hé chāi qiáo turn one's back on

过后 guòhòu [副] later ◇我们过后再谈。 Let's talk again later.

过户 guòhù [动] (法) transfer ownership

过火 guòhuǒ [形] excessive

过激 guòjī [形] extreme

过继 guòjì [动] adopt ◇他从小就过

继给了他的叔叔。 He was adopted by his uncle when he was little.

过奖 guòjiǎng [动] flatter

过街老鼠 guò jiē lǎoshǔ public enemy

过节儿 guòjiér [名] grudge

过客 guòkè [名] passer-by

过来 guòlái [动] come over (*pt* came, *pp* come) ◊你赶快过来，大家都等你呢！ Come straight over – everyone is waiting for you!

过来人 guòláirén [名] old hand

过量 guòliàng [形] excessive

过虑 guòlǜ [动] (过分担心) be overanxious ◊此事你不必过虑。 There's no need for you to get overanxious about this

过滤 guòlǜ [动] filter ◊过滤杂质filter out impurities

过门 guòmén [动] get married

过敏 guòmǐn [名] (医) allergy

过目 guòmù [动] look over

过目成诵 guò mù chéng sòng blessed with an extraordinary memory

过期 guòqī [动] expire

过谦 guòqiān [形] overly modest

过去 guòqù [名] the past ◊他比过去胖多了。 He weighs a lot more than he used to.

过去 guòqu [动] pass by ◊一辆车刚过去。 A car just went past.

过人 guòrén [动] excel

过日子 guò rìzi [动] live

过剩 guòshèng [形] excessive

过失 guòshī [名] mistake

过时 guòshí **I** [形] outdated **II** [动] pass time

过世 guòshì [动] pass away

过头 guòtóu [形] excessive

过往 guòwǎng [动] **1** (来去) come and go **2** (交往) associate with

过问 guòwèn [动] concern oneself with ◊这件事你就不必过问了。 There's no need for you to concern yourself with this.

过细 guòxì [形] meticulous

过眼云烟 guò yǎn yúnyān fleeting

过瘾 guòyǐn [动] do to one's heart's content ◊昨天我们玩得很过瘾。 Yesterday we played to our heart's content.

过硬 guòyìng [形] completely proficient

过于 guòyú [副] too

Hh

哈 hā I [叹] aha II [拟] ha ha ◇哈哈大笑 roar with laughter III [动] breathe out ◇他冲着手哈气，好暖和些。He breathed on his hands to warm them up.
▷另见 hǎ

哈欠 hāqian [名] yawn

哈腰 hāyāo [动] **1** (字) stoop ◇哈腰捡钱包 stoop to pick up one's wallet **2** (喻) suck up to

蛤 há 见下文
▷另见 gé

蛤蟆 háma [名] toad

哈 hǎ 见下文
▷另见 hā

哈巴狗 hǎbagǒu [名] **1** (字) Pekin(g)ese **2** (喻) sycophant

咳 hāi [叹] oh
▷另见 ké

还 hái [副] **1** (仍旧) still, yet ◇那家老饭店还很兴旺。The old restaurant is still thriving. ◇她还没回来。She hasn't come back yet. **2** (更加) even more ◇他比我还想家。He's even more homesick than I am. **3** (尚) still ◇她不聪明，但还算老实。She's no great brain, but still, she's honest. **4** (尚且) even ◇她还不着急，你急什么？ If even she isn't worried then why are you? **5** (居然) really ◇他这次考试还真的通过了。He really did pass the exam this time round. **6** (早在) as early as ◇当他还在襁褓中就被父母遗弃了。He was abandoned by his parents in infancy.
▷另见 huán

> 📖 **still** 用于强调对于某事的发生 或者对某事持续了如此长的时间而感到惊讶。*She was still looking at me… There are still plenty of horses round here.* **yet** 用于否定句和疑问句中，用于强调语气，暗示说话人对某事未发生，或者晚于预期时间发生而感到惊讶。*Have you seen it yet? … The troops could not yet see the shore … It isn't dark yet.*

还是 háishi I [副] **1** (仍然) still ◇尽管很危险，警察们还是冲了进去。In spite of the danger, the police still rushed on in. **2** (最好) had better ◇你还是先完成作业吧。You'd better finish your homework first. II [连] or ◇你是去巴黎还是去伦敦？ Are you going to Paris or London?

孩 hái [名] child (*pl* children)

孩提 háití [名] (书) early childhood

孩子 háizi [名] child (*pl* children)

骸 hái [名] **1** (骨) bones (*pl*) ♦骸骨 skeleton **2** (身体) body ♦形骸 human body ♦遗骸 remains (*pl*)

海 hǎi I [名] **1** (海洋) ocean ♦海岸线 coastline **2** (湖泊) lake **3** (喻) (指数量) sea ♦人海 sea of people ♦火海 inferno II [形] extra large ◇你先不要夸海口，事后再说。Don't go making wild boasts just yet – let's wait until after the event.

海岸 hǎi'àn [名] shore

海拔 hǎibá [名] elevation

海报 hǎibào [名] poster

海滨 hǎibīn [名] seaside

海底捞针 hǎidǐlāozhēn look for a needle in a haystack

海港 hǎigǎng [名] harbour (英), harbor (美)

海关 hǎiguān [名] customs (*pl*)

海货 hǎihuò [名] seafood

海疆 hǎijiāng [名] territorial waters (*pl*)

海军 hǎijūn [名] the navy

海枯石烂 hǎikūshílàn forever ◇他们发誓海枯石烂不变心。They vowed that they would always be faithful.

海阔天空 hǎikuòtiānkōng **1** (字) (指自然) boundless **2** (喻) (无拘束) anything and everything ◇他们海

阔天空地聊了起来。They started chatting about anything and everything.

海里 hǎilǐ [名] nautical mile

海量 hǎiliàng [名] **1** (敬) (大度) magnanimity ◇多谢您海量包涵。Thank you so much for your generosity. **2** (指酒量) tolerance ◇论喝酒，我可比不了您的海量。When it comes to alcohol, my tolerance just isn't as great as yours.

海洛因 hǎiluòyīn [名] heroin

海绵 hǎimián [名] sponge

海事 hǎishì [名] **1** (指事务) maritime affairs (*pl*) **2** (指事故) maritime accident

海誓山盟 hǎi shì shān méng pledge everlasting love

海外 hǎiwài [名] ◇海外学子 overseas student

海味 hǎiwèi [名] seafood

海峡 hǎixiá [名] strait ◇台湾海峡 the Taiwan Straits

海鲜 hǎixiān [名] seafood

海洋 hǎiyáng [名] ocean

海域 hǎiyù [名] waters (*pl*)

海员 hǎiyuán [名] sailor

骇 hài [动] shock

骇然 hàirán [形] dumbstruck

骇人听闻 hài rén tīng wén shocking

害 hài **I** [动] **1** (损害) harm ♦害人害己 harm others as well as oneself ◇他的失误害得公司破产。His mistake forced the company into bankruptcy. **2** (杀害) kill ♦遇害 be murdered **3** (指疾病) contract ♦害病 contract an illness **4** (感到) feel uneasy (*pt, pp* felt) ♦害羞 be shy **II** [名] harm ♦自然灾害 natural disaster **III** [形] harmful ♦害虫 pest

害处 hàichu [名] harm ◇多吃蔬菜没有害处。It won't do you any harm to eat more vegetables.

害怕 hàipà [动] be afraid

害群之马 hài qún zhī mǎ black sheep ◇她是这个班里的害群之马。She's the black sheep of the class.

害臊 hàisào [动] feel ashamed (*pt, pp* felt)

害羞 hàixiū [动] be shy

酣 hān 见下文

酣畅 hānchàng [形] unrestrained ◇笔墨酣畅 free-flowing writing

憨 hān [形] **1** (傻) silly ♦憨笑 simper **2** (朴实) naive ◇憨态可鞠 charmingly naive

憨厚 hānhòu [形] down-to-earth

憨笑 hānxiào [动] simper

鼾 hān [名] snore

鼾睡 hānshuì [动] be sound asleep

含 hán [动] **1** (用嘴) keep … in the mouth (*pt, pp* kept) ◇把温度计含在嘴巴里。Hold the thermometer in your mouth. **2** (包含) contain ◇含氟的牙膏 toothpaste with fluoride ◇这些烟不含尼古丁。These cigarettes do not contain nicotine. **3** (怀有) hold (*pt, pp* held) ♦含冤 suffer a gross injustice ♦含笑 with a smile

含苞 hánbāo [动] be in bud

含糊 hánhu [形] **1** (不清楚) vague **2** (马虎) careless ◇关键之处不可含糊。Make sure not to overlook the key points.

含混 hánhùn [形] ambiguous

含量 hánliàng [名] content

含情脉脉 hánqíng mòmò full of tender affection ◇他含情脉脉地望着新娘。He gazed at his bride with tender affection.

含沙射影 hán shā shè yǐng make insinuations

含辛茹苦 hán xīn rú kǔ endure hardship ◇她含辛茹苦地养大了5个孩子。She endured a lot of hardship bringing up her five children.

含蓄 hánxù **I** [动] be full of ◇文章中含蓄着深意。The essay had real depth. **II** [形] **1** (耐人寻味) measured **2** (内敛) reserved

含义 hányì [名] implication

函 hán [名] letter ♦公函 official letter

函电 hándiàn [名] correspondence

函授 hánshòu [动] teach by correspondence (*pt, pp* taught)

函数 hánshù [名] function

涵 hán [动] contain ♦涵盖 cover

涵养 hányǎng **I** [名] self-control **II** [动] conserve ◇树木有助于涵养水源。Trees are helpful in water conservation.

寒 hán **I** [形] **1** (冷) cold ♦春寒 spring chill ♦寒风 chilly wind **2** (贫穷) poor ♦贫寒 poverty-stricken ♦寒士 poor scholar **II** [动] tremble with fear ♦心寒 be bitterly disappointed

寒碜 hánchen **I** [形] **1** (丑) ugly **2** (丢脸) disgraceful ◇我考试没过，真寒碜！I failed the exam – what a disgrace! **II** [动] (讥笑) ridicule

寒窗 hánchuāng [名] difficult learning conditions (*pl*)

寒带 hándài [名] Frigid Zone

寒噤 hánjìn [名] shiver

寒冷 hánlěng [形] cold

寒流 hánliú [名] cold spell

寒酸 hánsuān [形] shabby ◇穿着寒酸 dress shabbily

寒心 hánxīn [动] be bitterly disappointed

寒暄 hánxuān [动] engage in small talk ◇我不善于与人寒暄。I'm no good at making small talk.

罕 hǎn 见下文

罕见 hǎnjiàn [形] rare

罕有 hǎnyǒu [形] rare

喊 hǎn [动] **1** (大声叫) shout ♦呼喊 yell **2** (叫) call ◇有人在喊你。Somebody's calling you.

喊叫 hǎnjiào [动] cry out

汉 hàn [名] **1** (汉族) the Han (*pl*) ♦汉人 the Han people (*pl*) **2** (男子) man (*pl* men) ♦庄稼汉 farmer ♦好汉 a real man

汉奸 hànjiān [名] traitor

汉学 hànxué [名] Sinology

汉语 Hànyǔ [名] Chinese

汉字 Hànzì [名] Chinese characters (*pl*)

汉子 hànzi [名] **1** (男子) man (*pl* men) **2** (方) (丈夫) husband

汉族 Hànzú [名] the Han (*pl*)

汗 hàn [名] sweat

汗流浃背 hàn liú jiā bèi sweat profusely

汗马功劳 hàn mǎ gōngláo distinguished service ◇他为公司的创建立下了汗马功劳。He distinguished himself in the work involved in setting up the company.

汗水 hànshuǐ [名] sweat

汗颜 hànyán [动] (书) feel ashamed (*pt, pp* felt)

旱 hàn [形] dry ♦旱季 dry season ♦旱田 non-irrigated land ♦旱冰 roller skating

旱涝保收 hàn lào bǎo shōu **1** (字) be sure of a stable yield **2** (喻) ensure a safe income ◇旱涝保收的工作 financially stable employment

旱灾 hànzāi [名] drought

悍 hàn [形] **1** (勇猛) brave **2** (凶狠) ferocious ♦凶悍 ferocious

悍然 hànrán [形] flagrant

捍 hàn [动] defend

捍卫 hànwèi [动] defend

焊 hàn [动] weld ◇他俩好得像是焊在了一起。The two of them go about as if they were joined at the hip.

焊接 hànjiē [动] weld

憾 hàn 见下文

憾事 hànshì [名] regret

撼 hàn [动] shake (*pt* shook, *pp* shaken)

撼动 hàndòng [动] vibrate

瀚 hàn [形] vast ♦浩瀚 vast

夯 hāng **I** [名] rammer ♦石夯 stone rammer **II** [动] **1** (砸) pound **2** (方) (击打) strike (*pt, pp* struck) ◇他被人用木棍夯倒了。Someone struck him down with a stick.

行 háng **I** [名] **1** (行列) row ♦第一行 first row ◇请把图标排成竖行。

Please arrange the icons in vertical rows. **2** (行业) profession ♦同行 people in the same profession ♦行规 industry rules **3** (机构) firm ♦银行 bank ♦车行 car dealer **II** [动] place ◊在家你行几？ Where do you come in your family? **III** [量] line ◊一行大雁 a line of wild geese ◊十四行诗 a sonnet
▷另见 xíng

行当 hángdang [名] **1** (口) (行业) line of work **2** (角色) role ◊他在戏班子里演好几个行当。He played several roles in the opera troupe.

行话 hánghuà [名] jargon

行家 hángjia [名] expert

行列 hángliè [名] ranks (*pl*)

行情 hángqíng [名] market conditions (*pl*)

行市 hángshi [名] prices (*pl*)

行伍 hángwǔ [名] the ranks (*pl*)

行业 hángyè [名] industry ◊服务行业 service industry ◊行业规则 industry rules

吭 háng throat ◊引吭高歌 belt out a song

航 háng **I** [名] (书) boat **II** [动] **1** (指船) sail ◊扬帆远航 set sail on a long voyage **2** (指飞机) fly (*pt* flew, *pp* flown) ♦航空公司 airline

航班 hángbān [名] **1** (指客轮) scheduled voyage **2** (指客机) scheduled flight

航程 hángchéng [名] voyage

航道 hángdào [名] channel

航海 hánghǎi [动] navigate

航空 hángkōng [动] fly (*pt* flew, *pp* flown) ♦航空信 airmail

航天 hángtiān [动] fly through the air (*pt* flew, *pp* flown)

航线 hángxiàn [名] route

航向 hángxiàng [名] course

航行 hángxíng [动] **1** (指船) sail **2** (指飞机) fly (*pt* flew, *pp* flown)

沆 hàng 见下文

沆瀣一气 hàng xiè yī qì (贬) be in cahoots with

巷 hàng 见下文
▷另见 xiàng

巷道 hàngdào [名] tunnel

号 háo [动] **1** (叫) yell **2** (哭) howl
▷另见 hào

号啕 háotáo [动] wail

蚝 háo [名] oyster

蚝油 háoyóu [名] oyster sauce

毫 háo **I** [名] **1** (细毛) fine hair **2** (笔) writing brush **3** (千分之一) ♦毫米 millimetre (英), millimeter (美) ♦毫升 millilitre (英), milliliter (美) **II** [形] (一点儿) tiny

毫毛 háomáo [名] body hair

豪 háo **I** [名] giant ♦文豪 literary giant **II** [形] **1** (指性格) unrestrained **2** (指语言) heroic **3** (指文笔) outstanding **4** (有权势) powerful ♦豪门 dynasty

豪放 háofàng [形] uninhibited

豪富 háofù [名] tycoon ◊非豪富买不起这里的别墅。Unless you're rolling in it, you won't be able to afford a villa around here.

豪华 háohuá [形] luxurious

豪杰 háojié [名] hero (*pl* heroes)

豪迈 háomài [形] heroic

豪门 háomén [名] dynasty

豪爽 háoshuǎng [形] straightforward

豪言壮语 háo yán zhuàng yǔ inspirational words ◊教练发豪言壮语，保证下场比赛能赢。The coach gave a really inspirational speech, guaranteeing that they could win the next match.

壕 háo [名] (指作战) moat

壕沟 háogōu [名] **1** (指作战) trench **2** (指大沟) ditch

嚎 háo [动] **1** (大声叫) howl **2** (大声哭) wail

嚎啕 háotáo [动] wail

好 hǎo **I** [形] **1** (令人满意) good ◊他脾气好。He's good-natured. ◊他为班里做了很多好事。He's done a lot of good things for the class. ◊汤很好闻。The soup smells good.

2 (容易) easy ◊这件事不好办。This won't be easy to manage. ◊英语好学吗？ Is English easy to learn? **3** (健康) well ◊你身体好吗？ Are you keeping well? **4** (亲密) good ◊我们是好朋友。We're good friends. **5** (表示问候) ◊你好！ Hello! ◊大家好。Hello everyone. **6** (表示完成) ◊工作找好了。I've found work. ◊衣服洗好了。The clothes have been washed. **7** (表示答应、结束等) ◊好，我们现在就去！ OK, let's go then! ◊好了，今天课就上到这里。Right, let's finish today's lesson here. **8** (表示反语) ◊好啊！你这下考砸了吧。Well done for going and flunking the exam. **II** [副] **1** (强调多或久) very ◊我等了好久她才来。I'd waited for a long time before she arrived. **2** (表示程度深) ◊好无礼的要求啊！ Such a rude request! ◊他话说得好快。He speaks so quickly. **III** [助动] (以便) ◊准备一下，我们好出发。Get yourself ready so that we can go out. **IV** [名] **1** (喝彩) cheer ◊他一唱完，全场叫好。As soon as he'd finished singing, everyone cheered. **2** (问候) regards (*pl*) ◊请代我向你太太问好。Please send my regards to your wife.
▷另见 hào

好比 hǎobǐ [动] be just like ◊情场好比战场。Affairs of the heart are just like battlefields.

好不 hǎobù [副] so ◊当时好不热闹。It was so lively then.

好处 hǎochu [名] **1** (益处) benefit **2** (利益) profit

好歹 hǎodǎi **I** [名] **1** (好坏) right and wrong ◊别理他，这人不知好歹。Don't listen to him – he doesn't know right from wrong. **2** (危险) the unthinkable **II** [副] **1** (将就) anyhow **2** (无论如何) at any rate ◊他好歹是你弟弟，这事就算了吧。At any rate, he's your brother, so just forget it.

好多 hǎoduō [形] many

好感 hǎogǎn [名] attraction ◊她对他有好感。She's attracted to him.

好汉 hǎohàn [名] brave man

好好先生 hǎohǎoxiānsheng yes man ◊他是个好好先生，谁都不想得罪。He's such a yes man – he doesn't like to offend anyone.

好久 hǎojiǔ [副] for a long time ◊我们好久没听到他的消息了。We haven't heard any news from him for a long time.

好看 hǎokàn [形] **1** (漂亮) nice-looking **2** (精彩) good ◊这本书很好看。This book is very good. **3** (光荣) proud ◊你成绩好，父母脸上也不知有多好看。If you get good results, your parents will be so proud. **4** (难堪) embarrassed ◊我要他好看！ I want to really embarrass him.

好了疮疤忘了疼 hǎole chuāngbā wàngle téng make the same mistakes all over again

好评 hǎopíng [名] high praise ◊他的小说大受好评。His novel was very highly praised.

好事 hǎoshì [名] (好事情) good deed ◊他为学校做了很多好事。He has done a lot of good deeds for the school.

好事多磨 hǎoshì duō mó it's never easy to get what you want

好手 hǎoshǒu [名] expert

好受 hǎoshòu [形] comfortable

好说 hǎoshuō [动] (没问题) be fine ◊你只要把钱交了，其他的事都好说。Just pay the fee – don't worry about the rest.

好似 hǎosì [副] ◊想起来那件事好似是昨天发生的。I think this is like what happened yesterday.

好听 hǎotīng [形] **1** (指声音、音乐) lovely **2** (指言语) nice

好像 hǎoxiàng [副] apparently ◊我们好像在哪儿见过。Apparently we've met somewhere before.

好笑 hǎoxiào [形] funny

好样儿的 hǎoyàngr de [名] ◊这些小伙子个个是好样儿的。These lads have got real guts.

好意 hǎoyì [名] kindness

好意思 hǎoyìsi [动] dare ◊这种话你也好意思说？ How dare you talk like this! ◊让您久等了，真不好意思。I'm very embarrassed for making you wait so long.

好在 hǎozài [副] luckily ◊他好在还有

个姐姐。Luckily he still has a sister.

好转 hǎozhuǎn [动] improve

号 hào I [名] 1 (名称) name ♦绰号 nickname 2 (商店) firm ♦商号 firm 3 (标记) sign ♦逗号 comma 4 (次序) number ◊我的座位在10号车厢。My seat is in coach ten. 5 (日期) date ◊今天几月几号? What's the date today? ◊6月1号是国际儿童节。The first of June is International Children's Day. 6 (大小) size ◊他得穿大号T恤衫。He needs a large-sized T-shirt. ◊我穿36号的鞋。I wear size thirty-six shoes. 7 (命令) order ◊他总向别人发号施令。He's always giving other people orders. 8 (乐器) brass instrument ♦小号 trumpet II [动] (脉) take (*pt* took, *pp* taken) ♦号脉 take a pulse
▷另见 háo

号称 hàochēng [动] 1 (著称) be known as 2 (声称) claim to be ◊军队实际八十万，号称百万。The army actually has 800,000 soldiers, but it claims to have a million.

号角 hàojiǎo [名] bugle

号令 hàolìng [名] order

号码 hàomǎ [名] number

号脉 hàomài [动] take a pulse (*pt* took, *pp* taken)

号召 hàozhào [动] appeal

好 hào [动] 1 (喜爱) like ◊他好集邮。He likes collecting stamps. ◊他好背后议论人。He likes discussing other people behind their backs. 2 (容易) be easy ◊天太热，人好中暑。It's too hot – you could easily get sunstroke.
▷另见 hǎo

好客 hàokè [形] hospitable

好奇 hàoqí [形] curious ◊好奇有时会引致灾祸。Curiosity can sometimes lead to disaster.

好强 hàoqiáng [形] ambitious

好胜 hàoshèng [形] competitive

好事 hàoshì [动] be nosy

好恶 hàowù [名] likes and dislikes (*pl*)

好学 hàoxué [形] studious

好逸恶劳 hào yì wù láo bone idle

耗 hào I [动] 1 (用) use 2 (方) (拖延) dawdle II [名] (坏消息) bad news (*sg*)

耗费 hàofèi [动] consume

耗损 hàosǔn [动] waste

耗子 hàozi [名] (方) mouse (*pl* mice)

浩 hào [形] 1 (大) great 2 (多) many

浩荡 hàodàng [形] mighty

浩浩荡荡 hàohào dàngdàng awesome

浩劫 hàojié [名] catastrophe

浩如烟海 hào rú yān hǎi myriad ◊中国古典诗歌浩如烟海。There are a myriad of Chinese ancient classical poems.

呵 hē [动] 1 (气) breathe out 2 (责备) scold

呵斥 hēchì [动] bawl ◊孩子还小，不要总呵斥他。The kid's still small – you shouldn't be bawling at him all the time.

呵护 hēhù [动] look after

喝 hē [动] drink (*pt* drank, *pp* drunk)
▷另见 hè

喝西北风 hē xīběifēng starve ◊他没了工作，全家只能喝西北风了。He lost his job, so the whole family is going to starve.

禾 hé 见下文

禾苗 hémiáo [名] grain seedling

合 hé I [动] 1 (闭) close ◊我把书合上了。I closed the book. 2 (合在一起) join ♦合资 joint venture 3 (折合) be equal to ◊一英镑合人民币多少钱? How much is a pound equal to in Renminbi? 4 (符合) tally with ◊他所说的不合事实。His story doesn't tally with the facts. ◊这段话不合逻辑。There's no logic in these words. II [形] whole ◊合家团聚 the whole family reunited

合并 hébìng [动] merge

合唱 héchàng [名] chorus

合成 héchéng [动] 1 (联合) merge 2 (化) synthesize

合法 héfǎ [形] legal

合格 hégé [形] qualified

合乎 héhū [动] conform to

合伙 héhuǒ [动] form a partnership

合计 héjì [动] add up to

合计 héji [动] **1** (琢磨) think (*pt, pp* thought) ◇他合计来合计去还是觉得不划算。He thought and thought about it and still reckoned it wasn't worth it. **2** (商量) discuss

合剂 héjì [名] mixture

合金 héjīn [名] alloy

合刊 hékān [名] combined issue

合理 hélǐ [形] rational

合流 héliú [动] (汇合) merge

合拍 hépāi **I** [形] in step with ◇他的生活方式与时代不太合拍。His lifestyle is not really in step with the times. **II** [动] co-produce

合情合理 hé qíng hé lǐ fair ◇他的做法合情合理。He has a fair way of doing things.

合群 héqún [形] gregarious

合身 héshēn [形] fitted ◇这些衣服很合身。These clothes are a good fit.

合适 héshì [形] appropriate

合算 hésuàn [动] be worthwhile

合同 hétong [名] contract

合意 héyì [形] suitable

合营 héyíng [动] co-own

合资 hézī [名] joint venture

合资公司 hézī gōngsī [名] joint venture company

合奏 hézòu [动] ensemble

合作 hézuò [动] cooperate ◇两家出版社合作出版了这套百科全书。Two publishing companies collaborated to publish this encyclopedia. ◇加强国际间的经济合作 increase international economic cooperation ◇我们是合作伙伴。We are partners in this collaboration.

何 hé [代] **1** (什么) ♦何时 when ♦何人 who **2** (哪里) ◇这消息从何而来？Where did this information come from?

何必 hébì [副] why

何不 hébù [副] why ... not ◇何不叫你女朋友一起来？Why don't you ask your girlfriend to come too? ◇既然有事，何不早说？You may have had things to do, but why didn't you say so earlier?

何尝 hécháng [副] ◇我何尝不想多学些英语，实在是没时间。It's not that I don't want to study English any more. I just don't have the time.

何等 héděng [副] how ◇他们何等幸福啊！How lucky are they!

何妨 héfáng **I** [动] (书) be no harm in ◇说说何妨? What's the harm in talking? **II** [副] why ◇你何妨不出国留学呢? Why don't you go abroad to study?

何苦 hékǔ [副] ◇你何苦这么做呢？Why are you bothering to do it? ◇你何苦去那么早呢？Why are you bothering to go so early?

何况 hékuàng [连] ◇那影片大人看了都害怕，何况儿童。Even adults find the film scary, never mind children. ◇山路很难走，何况还下着雨。The mountain pass is tricky, even when it's not raining.

何其 héqí [副] how ◇何其贪婪！How greedy!

何以 héyǐ [副] (书) **1** (怎么) how **2** (为什么) why

何止 hézhǐ [动] be far more than

和 hé **I** [连] and ◇他和我是同事。He and I are colleagues. ◇工作和学习 work and study **II** [介] with ◇这事和你没关系。This has nothing to do with you. **III** [形] **1** (平和) mild ♦温和 temperate **2** (暖) warm ♦暖和 warm **3** (和睦) on good terms ◇夫妻不和。The couple are not on good terms. **IV** [名] **1** (和解) reconciliation ♦讲和 talk of reconciliation **2** (和平) peace ◇维和部队 peace-keeping forces **3** (总数) total ◇5与5的和是10。5 and 5 is 10. **V** [动] draw (*pt* drew, *pp* drawn) ◇这场比赛和了。The match was a draw.
▷另见 huó, huò

和蔼 hé'ǎi [形] affable

和风 héfēng [名] light breeze

和服 héfú [名] kimono

和好 héhǎo [动] reconcile

和缓 héhuǎn I [形] gentle II [动] relax

和解 héjiě [动] settle … differences ◇尽管国际社会的调停两国终未和解。Despite the intervention of the international community, the two countries were ultimately unable to settle their differences.

和睦 hémù [形] harmonious

和盘托出 hé pán tuō chū tell the whole truth ◇她要将秘密和盘托出。She will tell the whole truth about her secrets.

和平 hépíng [名] (指战争) peace

和气 héqi I [形] polite II [名] peace

和善 héshàn [形] kind

和尚 héshang [名] Buddhist monk

和声 héshēng [名] (指音乐) chord

和事老 héshìlǎo [名] mediator

和数 héshù [名] sum

和谐 héxié [形] harmonious

和煦 héxù [形] warm

和颜悦色 hé yán yuè sè be all sweetness and light ◇老师对学生总是和颜悦色。The teacher is all sweetness and light with the students.

和约 héyuē [名] peace treaty

河 hé [名] **1** (河) river **2** (银河) galaxy

河川 héchuān [名] river

河道 hédào [名] river's course

河流 héliú [名] river

荷 hé [名] lotus
▷另见 hè

荷包蛋 hébāodàn [名] poached egg

核 hé I [名] **1** (指水果) stone **2** (指细胞、原子) nucleus II [动] examine ◆审核 examine and verify

核查 héchá [动] examine

核定 hédìng [动] verify

核对 héduì [动] check

核计 héjì [动] calculate

核实 héshí [动] verify

核算 hésuàn [动] calculate

核武器 héwǔqì [名] nuclear weapon

核心 héxīn [名] core

核准 hézhǔn [动] verify and approve

核子 hézǐ [名] nucleus

盒 hé [名] box

颌 hé [名] jaw

吓 hè I [动] scare II [叹] damn ◇吓，这是怎么搞的！ Damn! How has this happened?
▷另见 xià

贺 hè [动] congratulate

贺词 hècí [名] congratulatory speech

贺卡 hèkǎ [名] greetings card

贺年 hènián [动] extend New Year's greetings ◇贺年卡 New Year's card

贺喜 hèxǐ [动] congratulate

荷 hè I [动] (扛) shoulder II [名] load
▷另见 hé

荷枪实弹 hèqiāngshídàn armed ◇荷枪实弹的警察在巡逻。Armed police are on the beat.

喝 hè [动] shout
▷另见 hē

喝彩 hècǎi [动] cheer

喝倒彩 hè dàocǎi [动] boo

赫 hè I [形] conspicuous II [名] (赫兹) hertz

赫然 hèrán [副] (突然出现) impressively

赫兹 hèzī [名] hertz

褐 hè [名] (指颜色) brown

鹤 hè [名] crane

壑 hè [名] gully

黑 hēi [形] **1** (指颜色) black ◆黑板 blackboard **2** (暗) dark ◇天快黑了。It's nearly dark. **3** (秘密) secret ◆黑话 jargon **4** (狠毒) wicked ◇他的心真黑！ He's so wicked! **5** (反动) ◆黑社会 gangland ◆黑手党 the Mafia

黑暗 hēi'àn [形] **1** (指光线) dark **2** (腐败) corrupt

黑白 hēibái [名] **1** (颜色) black and white ◇黑白电视机 black and white television **2** (是非) right and wrong

黑帮 hēibāng [名] bunch of gangsters

黑道 hēidào [名] **1** (指路) dark street **2** (黑社会) gangland

黑话 hēihuà [名] jargon

黑客 hēikè [名] hacker

黑名单 hēimíngdān [名] blacklist

黑幕 hēimù [名] dark secret

黑钱 hēiqián [名] dirty money

黑人 Hēirén [名] black person (*pl* people)

黑色幽默 hēisè yōumò [名] black humour (英) 或 humor (美)

黑哨 hēishào [名] referee's biased call

黑社会 hēishèhuì [名] the underworld

黑市 hēishì [名] black market

黑手党 hēishǒudǎng [名] the Mafia

黑压压 hēiyāyā [形] masses of

黑油油 hēiyōuyōu [形] greasy

黑黝黝 hēiyōuyōu [形] shiny black

嘿 hēi **I** [叹] **1** (用于提起注意) hey ◇嘿，快来！ Hey, come quickly! **2** (表示得意) wow **3** (表示惊异) oh **II** [拟] ha ha

痕 hén [名] trace

痕迹 hénjì [名] **1** (印记) imprint **2** (迹象) trace

很 hěn [副] very ◇他个子很高。He is very tall. ◇她钢琴弹得很不错。She plays the piano very well. ◇我很了解他。I understand him very well. ◇伦敦的房价贵得很。House prices in London are very high.

狠 hěn **I** [形] **1** (凶恶) ruthless **2** (坚决) resolute **3** (厉害) relentless **II** [动] harden

狠毒 hěndú [形] cruel

狠心 hěnxīn [形] heartless

恨 hèn [动] **1** (憎恶) hate ◇他恨懒惰的人。He hates lazy people. **2** (后悔) regret ◇她恨当初和他结了婚。She regretted getting married to him in the first place.

恨铁不成钢 hèn tiě bù chéng gāng be cruel to be kind

恨之入骨 hènzhīrùgǔ detest ◇他对贪官恨之入骨。He detests corruption.

亨 hēng 见下文

亨通 hēngtōng [形] smooth

哼 hēng **I** [拟] moan **II** [动] **1** (唱) hum ◇他一边走一边哼着一只小曲。He hummed a tune as he walked. **2** (叫唤) groan

哼哧 hēngchī [拟] snort

恒 héng **I** [形] **1** (永久) permanent **2** (平常) common **II** [名] perseverance

恒量 héngliàng [名] constant

恒温 héngwēn [名] constant temperature

恒心 héngxīn [名] perseverance

恒星 héngxīng [名] star

横 héng **I** [名] horizontal **II** [形] **1** (梁、线、行) horizontal ◇横线 horizontal line **2** (左右向) sideways ◇他横躺在床上。He lay sideways on the bed. **3** (南北向) lengthways **4** (指横截) transverse ♦人行横道 zebra crossing **III** [副] **1** (纷杂) flowingly ◇妙趣横生 sparkle with wit **2** (蛮横) flagrantly ◇横行霸道 throw one's weight about **IV** [动] turn … lengthways ◇请把桌子横过来。Please turn the table lengthways. ▷另见 hèng

横冲直撞 héng chōng zhí zhuàng swerve about recklessly ◇巴士在车道里横冲直撞。The bus swerved about recklessly in the bus lane.

横七竖八 héng qī shù bā lying this way and that ◇门前横七竖八地停着很多自行车。Bicycles were lying this way and that in front of the door.

横扫 héngsǎo [动] sweep … away (*pt, pp* swept) ◇秋风横扫落叶。The autumn wind swept away the fallen leaves.

横竖 héngshù [副] in any case ◇我横竖会把那笔钱还给你的。I'll give you the money back in any case.

横向 héngxiàng [形] **1** (平行) horizontal **2** (指东西方向) lateral

横行 héngxíng [动] run wild (*pt* ran, *pp* run)

横行霸道 héngxíng bàdào terrorize ◊黑社会成员在社会上横行霸道。Members of the criminal underworld are terrorizing society.

衡 héng **I** [名] weight **II** [动] weigh

衡量 héngliáng [动] weigh

横 hèng [形] **1** (粗暴) harsh **2** (指意外) unexpected
▷另见 héng

横财 hèngcái [名] ill-gotten gains (*pl*) ◊发横财 get rich by foul means

哼 hng [叹] hmmph

轰 hōng **I** [拟] bang **II** [动] **1** (指炮) bang **2** (指火药) boom **3** (指雷) rumble **4** (动物) herd **5** (人) drive (*pt* drove, *pp* driven)

轰动 hōngdòng [动] take … by storm (*pt* took, *pp* taken) ◊轰动世界 take the world by storm

轰轰烈烈 hōnghōnglièliè vigorously ◊我们要轰轰烈烈地干一番事业。We are going to promote this cause vigorously.

轰隆 hōnglōng [拟] rumble

轰炸 hōngzhà [动] bomb
▷另见 hǒng, hòng

哄 hōng [拟] (形容大笑) roar

哄传 hōngchuán [动] spread (*pt, pp* spread) ◊人们在哄传地震的消息。People are spreading the news of the earthquake.

哄抢 hōngqiǎng [动] scramble for

哄堂大笑 hōngtáng dàxiào make everyone roar with laughter ◊他的笑话引得大家哄堂大笑。His joke made everyone roar with laughter.

烘 hōng [动] (烘烤) dry ◊她把衣服烘干了。She dried her clothes.

烘托 hōngtuō [动] (使突出) set … off (*pt, pp* set) ◊绿叶烘托着粉红色的花朵。The greenery set off the pink flowers.

弘 hóng **I** [形] great **II** [动] expand

弘扬 hóngyáng [动] promote

红 hóng **I** [形] **1** (指颜色) red **2** (形容受欢迎) popular ♦走红 be popular **3** (形容成功) successful ♦红运 lucky **4** (革命) red **II** [名] (红利) bonus ♦分红 get a bonus

红白喜事 hóng bái xǐshì [名] weddings and funerals (*pl*)

红包 hóngbāo [名] **1** (作为贺礼) lucky money **2** (贿赂) dirty money

红茶 hóngchá [名] black tea

红尘 hóngchén [名] the human world

红灯区 hóngdēngqū [名] red-light district

红火 hónghuo [形] flourishing

红利 hónglì [名] bonus

红领巾 hónglǐngjīn [名] red scarf *(worn by members of the Young Pioneers organization)*

红绿灯 hónglǜdēng [名] traffic lights (*pl*)

红马甲 hóngmǎjiǎ [名] stockbrocker

红娘 Hóngniáng [名] matchmaker

红旗 hóngqí [名] red flag

红人 hóngrén [名] rising star ◊他是剧团里的红人。He is the rising star of the theatrical troupe.

红润 hóngrùn [形] ruddy

红色 hóngsè [形] red ◊红色的头发 red hair ◊红色政权 revolutionary power

红十字会 Hóngshízìhuì [名] the Red Cross

红彤彤 hóngtōngtōng [形] scarlet

红外线 hóngwàixiàn [名] infrared rays

红眼 hóngyǎn [动] see red (*pt* saw, *pp* seen)

红眼病 hóngyǎnbìng [名] **1** (病) conjunctivitis **2** (嫉妒) jealousy

红艳艳 hóngyànyàn [形] scarlet

宏 hóng [形] great

宏大 hóngdà [形] grand

宏观 hóngguān [前缀] macro- ◊宏观经济 macroeconomics

宏论 hónglùn [名] bright idea

宏图 hóngtú [名] grand plan

宏伟 hóngwěi [形] magnificent

虹 hóng [名] rainbow

洪 hóng [名] (指洪水) flood

洪亮 hóngliàng [形] sonorous

洪水 hóngshuǐ [名] flood

鸿 hóng I [名] **1** (大雁) wild goose (*pl* geese) **2** (书信) letter II [形] vast

鸿沟 Hónggōu [名] gap

鸿雁 hóngyàn [名] (鸟) wild goose (*pl* geese)

鸿运 hóngyùn [名] fortune

哄 hǒng [动] **1** (哄骗) cheat **2** (安抚) calm ◊妈妈哄小孩睡觉。The mother calmed the child so that he could sleep.
▷另见 hōng, hòng

哄骗 hǒngpiàn [动] cheat

哄 hòng [动] cause an uproar
▷另见 hōng, hǒng

侯 hóu [名] **1** (贵族) nobleman (*pl* noblemen) **2** (侯爵) marquis

喉 hóu [名] throat

喉咙 hóulóng [名] throat

喉舌 hóushé [名] mouthpiece

猴 hóu [名] monkey

猴子 hóuzi [名] monkey

瘊 hóu 见下文

瘊子 hóuzi [名] wart

吼 hǒu [动] **1** (狮子、老虎) roar **2** (人、风) howl

吼叫 hǒujiào [动] howl

后 hòu [名] **1** (背面) the back ◊房后有个车库。At the back of the house is a garage. **2** (指时间) ♦后天 the day after tomorrow ◊后来的人没有位置坐。The people who arrive late won't get seats. **3** (指次序) the last ◊我坐在后排。I'm sitting in the last row. ◊他的考试成绩在全班后十名。His test mark puts him in the last ten of the class. **4** (子孙) children **5** (君主的妻子) empress ♦皇后 empress

后备 hòubèi [名] reserve

后辈 hòubèi [名] younger generation

后代 hòudài [名] **1** (指时代) later generations (*pl*) **2** (子孙) offspring

后盾 hòudùn [名] backup

后方 hòufāng [名] rear

后福 hòufú [名] future fortune

后顾之忧 hòu gù zhī yōu after-sales problems

后果 hòuguǒ [名] consequence

后患 hòuhuàn [名] bad consequences (*pl*)

后悔 hòuhuǐ [动] regret

后会有期 hòu huì yǒu qī we'll meet again someday

后继 hòujì [动] carry on

后进 hòujìn I [形] backward II [名] slowcoach

后劲 hòujìn [名] **1** (指酒) after-effects (*pl*) **2** (形容力量) stamina

后来 hòulái [副] afterwards ◊后来他们谁也不理谁。Afterwards they didn't talk to each other. ◊我后来再也没有见过他。I didn't see him again after that.

后路 hòulù [名] (指机会) way out

后面 hòumian I [名] back II [副] later

后怕 hòupà [动] have a lingering fear

后起之秀 hòu qǐ zhī xiù ◊他是文学界的后起之秀。He's up-and-coming in the literary world.

后勤 hòuqín [名] logistics (*pl*)

后人 hòurén [名] **1** (指非亲属) follower **2** (子孙) offspring

后任 hòurèn [名] successor

后事 hòushì [名] funeral

后手 hòushǒu [名] way out

后台 hòutái [名] **1** (指舞台) backstage **2** (喻) (指人或集团) backstage support

后天 hǒutiān [名] the day after tomorrow

后退 hòutuì [动] retreat

后卫 hòuwèi [名] rear

后裔 hòuyì [名] descendant

后援 hòuyuán [名] reinforcements (*pl*)

后缀 hòuzhuì [名] suffix

厚 hòu I [形] **1** (书、衣服、脸皮) thick ◇他脸皮真厚！ He's so thick-skinned! ◇厚被子 thick blanket **2** (雪、土) deep **3** (指感情) profound **4** (指性格) honourable **5** (指利润、礼品) extravagant **6** (指味道) rich **7** (指家产) loaded II [动] **1** (优待) favour (英), favor (美) **2** (重视) stress

厚爱 hòu'ài [名] adoration

厚道 hòudao [形] kind

厚望 hòuwàng [名] expectation

厚颜无耻 hòuyánwúchǐ shameless ◇厚颜无耻的叛徒 shameless turncoat

厚重 hòuzhòng [形] **1** (字典、大衣) thick **2** (奖赏、礼物) extravagant **3** (文化沉积) dignified

候 hòu I [动] **1** (等待) wait **1** (问好) inquire after II [名] **1** (时节) season **2** (情况) state

候补 hòubǔ [动] be a candidate for

候鸟 hòuniǎo [名] migratory bird

候选人 hòuxuǎnrén [名] candidate

呼 hū I [动] **1** (排气) exhale **2** (喊) shout **3** (叫) call II [拟] whistle

呼哧 hūchī [拟] pant

呼喊 hūhǎn [动] shout

呼号 hūháo [动] **1** (因悲伤) wail **2** (为求援) cry out

呼唤 hūhuàn [动] call

呼机 hūjī [名] pager

呼叫 hūjiào [动] **1** (指电台) call **2** (呼喊) shout

呼救 hūjiù [动] call for help

呼噜 hūlu [名] (口) snore

呼哨 hūshào [名] whistle

呼声 hūshēng [名] **1** (指声音) cry ◇震天动地的呼声 an earth-shattering cry **2** (意见) voice

呼吸 hūxī [动] breathe

呼啸 hūxiào [动] whistle ◇警车呼啸而过。The police car whistled past.

呼应 hūyìng [动] echo

呼吁 hūyù [动] call for ◇联合国呼吁双方停火。The United Nations is calling for a bilateral ceasefire.

忽 hū I [动] neglect II [副] suddenly

忽而 hū'ér [副] suddenly ◇远处的灯光忽而明，忽而暗。The lights in the distance flickered on and off.

忽略 hūlüè [动] overlook ◇易被忽略的细节 details that could be easily overlooked

忽然 hūrán [副] suddenly ◇天空忽然飘起了雪花。All at once the sky filled with snow.

忽视 hūshì [动] ignore

糊 hū [动] plaster ▷另见 hú, hù

囫 hú 见下文

囫囵吞枣 húlún tūn zǎo read without understanding

狐 hú [名] fox

狐假虎威 hú jiǎ hǔ wēi exploit another person's power

狐疑 húyí [动] suspect

弧 hú [名] arc

弧度 húdù [名] radian

弧形 húxíng [名] arc

胡 hú I [名] **1** (髭) moustache (英), mustache (美) **2** (长在下颚、两腮) beard II [副] recklessly

胡扯 húchě [动] talk nonsense ◇他尽胡扯。He is talking complete nonsense.

胡搅蛮缠 hú jiǎo mán chán pester incessantly

胡乱 húluàn [副] **1** (随便) casually ◇她胡乱地吃了两口就出门了。She grabbed a quick bite, then went out. **2** (任意) wilfully ◇他总是胡乱地发表意见。He 's always spouting off his opinions.

胡闹 húnào [动] play up ◇睡觉去吧，别胡闹了。Go to bed, and no playing up.

胡说 húshuō [动] talk nonsense

胡思乱想 hú sī luàn xiǎng let one's imagination run away with itself

胡同 hútòng [名] lane

胡言乱语 hú yán luàn yǔ talk nonsense ◇他一喝酒就会胡言乱语。Once he starts drinking he talks all sorts of nonsense.

胡子 húzi [名] 1 (髭) moustache (英), mustache (美) 2 (指长在下颚、两腮) beard 3 (方) (胡匪) bandit

胡作非为 hú zuò fēi wéi run amok

壶 hú [名] pot ◇一壶咖啡 a pot of coffee

葫 hú 见下文

葫芦 húlu [名] gourd

湖 hú [名] lake

湖泊 húpō [名] lake

煳 hú [动] burn ◇饭烧煳了。The rice is burnt.

蝴 hú 见下文

蝴蝶 húdié [名] butterfly

糊 hú [动] paste
▷另见 hū, hù

糊里糊涂 húlihútú confused

糊涂 hútu [形] 1 (不明白) confused 2 (混乱) chaotic ◇办公室里乱得一塌糊涂。The office was in complete chaos.

虎 hǔ I [名] tiger II [形] vigorous

虎口余生 hǔ kǒu yú shēng narrowly escape death

虎头蛇尾 hǔ tóu shé wěi peter out after a good start

唬 hǔ [动] intimidate

琥 hǔ 见下文

琥珀 hǔpò [名] amber

互 hù [副] mutually ◇两国领导定期互访。The leaders of the two countries met one another regularly in each place.

互补 hùbǔ [动] complement one another

互动 hùdòng [动] interact ◇教与学是互动的。There is interaction between teaching and learning.

互惠 hùhuì [动] reciprocate

互利 hùlì [动] be of mutual benefit

互联网 hùliánwǎng [名] the Internet

互通有无 hù tōng yǒuwú provide what another lacks

互相 hùxiāng [副] mutually

互助 hùzhù [动] help one another out

户 hù [名] 1 (门) door 2 (住户) family ◇几百户人家 several hundred families 3 (门第) social standing ◇门当户对 be well-matched 4 (户头) bank account ♦账户 account

户籍 hùjí [名] registered permanent residence

户口 hùkǒu [名] 1 (住户人口) number of households and total population 2 (户籍) registered permanent residence ◇迁户口 change one's permanent address

护 hù [动] 1 (保护) protect 2 (庇护) take sides (*pt* took, *pp* taken)

护城河 hùchénghé [名] moat

护短 hùduǎn [动] cover up ◇你不应该给他护短。You shouldn't have covered up for him.

护航 hùháng [动] escort

护理 hùlǐ [动] nurse ◇护理伤员 nurse the wounded

护身符 hùshēnfú [名] talisman

护士 hùshi [名] nurse

护送 hùsòng [动] escort

护卫 hùwèi [动] protect

护照 hùzhào [名] passport

糊 hù [名] paste
▷另见 hū, hú

糊弄 hùnong [动] (方) 1 (欺骗) fool ◇他爱编造谎言糊弄我。He loves to make up lies to fool me with. 2 (将就) make do with ◇粗茶淡饭，糊弄着吃吧。It's just simple fare, but I hope it will do.

花 huā I [名] 1 (指植物) flower 2 (花状物) ♦泪花 tear ♦雪花 snowflake ♦火花 spark 3 (烟火) fireworks (*pl*) 4 (花纹) pattern ◇印花布料 patterned material ◇白底红花 a red pattern on a white background 5 (精华)

pinnacle ◇艺术之花 the pinnacle of artistic achievement **6** (美女) beauty ♦校花 school beauties (*pl*) **7** (妓女) lady of the night ◇花街柳巷 red-light district **II** [形] **1** (多彩) multi-coloured (英), multi-colored (美) ◇花花绿绿 colourful (英), colorful (美) **2** (有花的) floral ♦花篮 basket of flowers ♦花车 float **3** (模糊) blurred ♦头昏眼花 muddle-headed and bleary-eyed **4** (虚假) superficial ♦花招 trick ◇花言巧语 smooth talk **III** [动] spend (*pt, pp* spent) ◇花钱 spend money ◇花工夫 put in effort

花白 huābái [形] grey (英), gray (美)

花边 huābiān [名] **1** (花纹) flowery border **2** (饰带) lace

花边新闻 huābiān xīnwén [名] tabloid gossip

花草 huācǎo [名] flowers and plants (*pl*)

花朵 huāduǒ [名] flower

花费 huāfei [动] spend (*pt, pp* spent) ◇花费心血 expend effort ◇留学的花费很大。It's very expensive to study abroad.

花好月圆 huā hǎo yuè yuán blissful harmony

花花公子 huāhuā-gōngzǐ playboy

花花绿绿 huāhuālǜlǜ [形] colourful (英), colorful (美)

花花世界 huāhuā-shìjiè world full of temptations

花卉 huāhuì [名] flowers and plants (*pl*)

花季 huājì [名] the flower of one's youth ◇花季少女 a young girl in the flower of her youth

花架子 huājiàzi [名] (喻) *something done merely for show*

花里胡哨 huālihúshào **1** (鲜艳) garish (美) **2** (浮华) showy

花柳病 huāliǔbìng [名] sexually transmitted disease

花名册 huāmíngcè [名] register

花容月貌 huā róng yuè mào stunningly beautiful

花色 huāsè [名] **1** (颜色) design and colour (英) 或 color (美) **2** (种类) variety

花哨 huāshao [形] **1** (颜色鲜艳) garish **2** (花样多) complex

花生 huāshēng [名] peanut

花束 huāshù [名] bouquet

花天酒地 huā tiān jiǔ dì lead a life of debauchery

花纹 huāwén [名] decorative design

花消 huāxiao [名] cost

花言巧语 huā yán qiǎo yǔ smooth talk

花样 huāyàng [名] **1** (式样) variety **2** (花招) trick

花椰菜 huāyēcài [名] broccoli

花园 huāyuán [名] garden

花招 huāzhāo [名] trick

花枝招展 huāzhī zhāozhǎn gaudily dressed

哗 huā [拟] ◇自来水哗哗地流。The water gushed out of the tap. ◇窗帘哗的一声拉上了。The curtains were pulled closed with a swoosh. ▷另见 huá

哗啦 huālā [拟] ◇他哗啦哗啦地翻着书。He sped through the book. ◇大桥哗啦一声就坍了。The bridge collapsed with a great crash.

划 huá [动] **1** (拨水) row ♦划桨 paddle **2** (合算) be worthwhile ◇划不来 not worth it **3** (擦) scratch ◇我把手指划破了。I've scratched my finger.
▷另见 huà

划算 huásuàn **I** [动] calculate **II** [形] good value

华 huá **I** [形] **1** (光彩) magnificent ♦华美 gorgeous **2** (繁盛) prosperous ♦繁华 flourishing **3** (奢侈) extravagant ♦浮华 flashy **4** (花白) grey (英), gray (美) ♦华发 grey (英) 或 gray (美) hair **II** [名] **1** (精华) the cream ♦才华 talent **2** (时光) time ◇青春年华 youth **3** (中国) China ♦华人 Chinese person

华灯 huádēng [名] decorated lantern

华而不实 huá ér bù shí showy

华发 huáfà [名] grey (英) 或 gray (美) hair

华贵 huáguì [形] **1** (华丽珍贵) sumptuous **2** (豪华富贵) luxurious

华丽 huálì [形] resplendent

华美 huáměi [形] resplendent

华侨 huáqiáo [名] overseas Chinese

华人 huárén [名] Chinese

华裔 huáyì [名] *person of Chinese origin*

哗 huá [动] make a noise
▷另见 huā

哗变 huábiàn [动] mutiny

哗然 huárán [形] in uproar

哗众取宠 huá zhòng qǔ chǒng play to the gallery

滑 huá **I** [形] **1** (光滑) slippery ◇路很滑。The road is very slippery. ◇她的皮肤很滑。Her skin is silky smooth. **2** (油滑) crafty **II** [动] slip

滑动 huádòng [动] slide (*pt, pp* slid)

滑稽 huájī [形] comical

滑溜 huáliu [形] smooth ◇滑溜的秀发 beautiful sleek hair

滑腻 huánì [形] silky-smooth

滑坡 huápō [动] **1** (字) slide (*pt, pp* slid) ◇昨天发生山体滑坡。Yesterday there was a landslide. **2** (喻) drop

滑润 huárùn [形] smooth

滑头 huátóu [名] sly old fox

滑翔 huáxiáng [动] glide

滑行 huáxíng [动] slide (*pt, pp* slid)

滑雪 huáxuě [动] ski

猾 huá [形] cunning

化 huà **I** [名] chemistry ♦化肥 chemical fertilizer **II** [动] **1** (变化) change ♦化装 make oneself up **2** (感化) convert ♦教化 educate **3** (融化) melt ◇积雪融化了。The piles of snow have melted. **4** (消化) digest ◇消化饼干 digestive biscuit **5** (烧化) burn ♦火化 cremate **6** (死) die

化工 huàgōng [名] chemical industry

化合 huàhé [动] chemically combine

化解 huàjiě [动] eliminate

化疗 huàliáo [动] treat … with chemotherapy

化名 huàmíng [名] pseudonym

化身 huàshēn [名] embodiment

化石 huàshí [名] fossil

化险为夷 huà xiǎn wéi yí head off a disaster

化学 huàxué [名] chemistry

化验 huàyàn [动] test

化妆 huàzhuāng [动] make oneself up

化装 huàzhuāng [动] **1** (修饰) get into costume **2** (假扮) disguise oneself

划 huà [动] **1** (划分) demarcate **2** (划拨) transfer **3** (计划) plan
▷另见 huá

划拨 huàbō [动] **1** (资金) transfer **2** (物品) allocate ◇政府把食品划拨给灾区。The government allocated food to the disaster zone.

划分 huàfēn [动] **1** (分成部分) divide **2** (区分) differentiate

划价 huàjià [动] get a prescription priced

划时代 huàshídài epoch-making

划一 huàyī [形] uniform

画 huà **I** [动] **1** (用铅笔) draw (*pt* drew, *pp* drawn) **2** (用刷状笔画) paint **II** [名] **1** (用铅笔) drawing **2** (用刷状笔画) painting ♦油画 oil painting **3** (笔画) stroke **III** [形] painted

画报 huàbào [名] pictorial

画饼充饥 huà bǐng chōng jī comfort oneself with illusions

画工 huàgōng [名] **1** (指人) painter **2** (指技法) drawing skill

画家 huàjiā [名] painter

画具 huàjù [名] painting utensil

画龙点睛 huà lóng diǎn jīng add the crowning touch

画面 huàmiàn [名] tableau (*pl* tableaux)

画蛇添足 huà shé tiān zú gild the lily

画坛 huàtán [名] artistic circles (*pl*)

画图 huàtú [名] picture

画外音 huàwàiyīn [名] voice-over

画像 huàxiàng [名] portrait

画押 huàyā [动] sign

画展 huàzhǎn [名] art exhibition

话 huà I [名] words (*pl*) ♦说话 talk ♦对话 conversation ♦谎话 lie II [动] talk about ♦话旧 reminisce ◇闲话家常 chat about everyday things

话别 huàbié [动] part ◇依依话别 be reluctant to part

话柄 huàbǐng [名] basis for attack

话旧 huàjiù [动] reminisce

话剧 huàjù [名] stage play

话题 huàtí [名] subject

话头 huàtóu [名] topic of conversation

话匣子 huàxiázi [名] chatterbox

话音 huàyīn [名] **1** (声音) voice **2** (言外之意) tone

话语 huàyǔ [名] words (*pl*)

桦 huà [名] birch

怀 huái I [名] **1** (胸前) bosom **2** (胸怀) mind ◇满怀壮志 have a head full of plans II [动] **1** (思念) think of (*pt, pp* thought) **2** (存有) keep ... in mind (*pt, pp* kept) **3** (有孕) become pregnant (*pt* became, *pp* become)

怀抱 huáibào I [动] **1** (抱在怀) hold ... in one's arms (*pt, pp* held) ◇女孩怀抱着猫咪。The girl held a cat in her arms. **2** (心里有) cherish II [名] bosom

怀才不遇 huái cái bù yù be unable to give full play to one's talent

怀春 huáichūn [动] have amorous thoughts

怀古 huáigǔ [动] ruminate on the past

怀恨 huáihèn [动] nurse a grudge

怀旧 huáijiù [动] ruminate on the past

怀念 huáiniàn [动] yearn for ◇怀念故乡 yearn for one's hometown

怀疑 huáiyí [动] **1** (认为是真) suspect ◇我怀疑她没说实话。I suspect that she's not telling the truth. **2** (认为不可能) doubt ◇我对他是否会来表示怀疑。I doubt he will come.

怀孕 huáiyùn [动] be pregnant

槐 huái [名] Chinese scholar tree

踝 huái [名] ankle

坏 huài I [形] **1** (不好) bad ♦坏蛋 bad egg ◇坏习惯 bad habit **2** (程度深) extreme ◇便宜的价格乐坏了顾客。The cheap prices made the customers extremely happy. II [动] go off (*pt* went, *pp* gone) ◇牛奶坏了。The milk has gone off. ◇空调坏了。The air-conditioning has broken down. III [名] dirty trick

坏处 huàichu [名] harm ◇多喝绿茶没坏处。There's no harm in drinking more green tea. ◇缺乏睡眠对身体有坏处。It's bad for you not to get enough sleep.

坏蛋 huàidàn [名] (讳) bastard

坏话 huàihuà [名] **1** (逆耳之言) honest truth ◇他好话坏话一并听。He's prepared to hear things he doesn't want to hear as well as that which is more welcome. **2** (不利的话) slur ◇他从不说老婆坏话。He never speaks ill of his wife.

坏事 huàishì I [名] bad things (*pl*) II [动] mess things up

坏水 huàishuǐ [名] evil idea

欢 huān [形] **1** (快乐) happy **2** (活跃) vigorous

欢畅 huānchàng [形] overjoyed

欢呼 huānhū [动] cheer

欢聚 huānjù [动] happily gather

欢快 huānkuài [形] cheerful ◇欢快的气氛 cheerful atmosphere

欢乐 huānlè [形] joyful

欢声笑语 huān shēng xiào yǔ happy chatter ◇校园里留下了我们的欢声笑语。Our happy chatter lingered in the schoolyard.

欢送 huānsòng [动] see ... off (*pt* saw, *pp* seen) ◇欢送代表团 see a delegation off

欢腾 huānténg [动] rejoice

欢天喜地 huān tiān xǐ dì with great joy ◇大家欢天喜地迎新年。Everyone welcomed in the new year with great joy.

欢喜 huānxǐ **I** [形] overjoyed ◊她满心欢喜地等他回来。Her heart was full of joy as she waited for him to return. **II** [动] be fond of

欢心 huānxīn [名] favour (英), favor (美) ◊她拼命想讨老师的欢心。She desperately wanted to gain favour with her teacher.

欢迎 huānyíng [动] welcome ◊欢迎光临！Welcome! ◊欢迎来中国。Welcome to China.

还 huán [动] **1** (回) return ♦还乡 return to one's hometown ♦生还 survive **2** (归还) return ♦还债 repay a debt ◊请把字典还给我。Please return the dictionary to me. **3** (回报) repay (*pt, pp* repaid) ♦还礼 return a gift with a gift ♦还价 make a counter-offer ♦还手 strike back ▷另见 hái

还本 huánběn [动] repay capital (*pt, pp* repaid)

还击 huánjī [动] fight back (*pt, pp* fought) ◊驻军奋起还击。The garrison readied itself for a counterattack.

还价 huánjià [动] make a counter-offer ◊讨价还价 haggle

还手 huánshǒu [动] retaliate ◊我还手打了他一巴掌。I slapped him in retaliation.

还原 huányuán [动] **1** (恢复) restore **2** (化) reduce

还愿 huányuàn [动] **1** (对神) thank the gods for answering one's prayers **2** (对人) fulfil a promise

环 huán **I** [名] **1** (圆圈) ring ♦耳环 earring **2** (环节) element ◊销售是重要的一个环节。Marketing is an important element. **II** [动] surround ◊四面环海 be surrounded by sea on all sides

环保 huánbǎo [名] (环境保护) environmental protection

环抱 huánbào [动] surround

环顾 huángù [动] look around

环节 huánjié [名] **1** (指事物) link **2** (指动物) segment

环境 huánjìng [名] environment ◊生活环境 living conditions (*pl*) ◊投资环境 investment environment

环境保护 huánjìng bǎohù [名] environmental protection

环球 huánqiú **I** [动] go round the world (*pt* went, *pp* gone) **II** [名] the whole world

环绕 huánrào [动] surround

环视 huánshì [动] look around

环行 huánxíng [动] circle

寰 huán [名] world

寰球 huánqiú [名] the whole world

缓 huǎn **I** [形] **1** (慢) slow **2** (缓和) relaxed **II** [动] **1** (推迟) delay **2** (恢复) revive

缓兵之计 huǎn bīng zhī jì delaying tactics

缓冲 huǎnchōng [动] buffer

缓和 huǎnhé [形] relaxed

缓急 huǎnjí [名] degree of urgency

缓解 huǎnjiě [动] alleviate

缓慢 huǎnmàn [形] slow

缓刑 huǎnxíng [动] suspend a sentence

幻 huàn **I** [形] unreal **II** [动] change majically

幻灯 huàndēng [名] **1** (幻灯片) slide **2** (幻灯机) slide projector

幻境 huànjìng [名] fairyland

幻觉 huànjué [名] illusion

幻灭 huànmiè [动] vanish into thin air

幻想 huànxiǎng **I** [动] dream ◊他幻想成为宇航员。He dreamed of becoming an astronaut. **II** [名] fantasy

幻影 huànyǐng [名] illusion

宦 huàn **I** [名] **1** (官吏) official **2** (太监) eunuch **II** [动] fill an office

宦官 huànguān [名] eunuch

宦海 huànhǎi [名] official circles (*pl*)

宦途 huàntú [名] official career

换 huàn [动] **1** (交换) exchange ◊我拿书换你的杂志。I've got this book to exchange for your magazine. ◊用美元换英镑 exchange US dollars for pounds **2** (更换) replace ◊家具换

成新的了。The furniture has been replaced.

换代 huàndài [动] (产品更新) upgrade

换季 huànjì [动] change clothes for the season

换届 huànjiè [动] reappoint ◇政府官员每隔5年换届。Government officials are reappointed to their jobs every five years.

换取 huànqǔ [动] exchange … for ◇该国用石油换取食品。The country provides oil in exchange for food.

换算 huànsuàn [动] convert ◇把外汇换算成人民币 convert foreign currency into Renminbi

换汤不换药 huàn tāng bù huàn yào make superficial changes

换血 huànxiě [动] (喻) introduce fresh blood

唤 huàn [名] summon

唤起 huànqǐ [动] **1** (号召) appeal ◇唤起民众的人权意识 appeal to people's awareness of human rights **2** (引起) call on

唤醒 huànxǐng [动] **1** (叫醒) wake up (*pt* woke, *pp* woken) ◇每天早晨闹钟把我唤醒。Every morning I am woken up by my alarm clock. **2** (使醒悟) awaken (*pt* awoke, *pp* awoken)

涣 huàn [动] vanish

涣然冰释 huànrán bīng shì melt away

涣散 huànsàn **I** [形] slack **II** [动] slacken

浣 huàn [动] wash

浣熊 huànxióng [名] racoon

患 huàn **I** [动] **1** (害) suffer from **2** (忧虑) worry **II** [名] trouble

患得患失 huàn dé huàn shī worry about personal gains and losses

患难 huànnàn [名] adversity

患者 huànzhě [名] sufferer

焕 huàn [形] shining

焕发 huànfā [动] **1** (有光彩) shine (*pt*, *pp* shone) **2** (振作) brace oneself

焕然一新 huànrán yī xīn take on an entirely new look

荒 huāng **I** [形] **1** (荒芜) waste **2** (荒凉) desolate **3** (短缺) short **4** (荒歉) famine **5** (非理性) ridiculous **II** [动] neglect **III** [名] wasteland

荒诞 huāngdàn [形] absurd

荒废 huāngfèi [动] **1** (没耕种) leave … uncultivated (*pt*, *pp* left) **2** (荒疏) neglect **3** (浪费) waste

荒郊 huāngjiāo [名] wilderness

荒凉 huāngliáng [形] desolate

荒谬 huāngmiù [形] ridiculous

荒漠 huāngmò **I** [形] deserted **II** [名] desert

荒年 huāngnián [名] famine year

荒疏 huāngshū [动] neglect

荒唐 huāngtáng [形] **1** (荒谬) absurd **2** (放荡) unconventional

荒无人烟 huāng wú rén yān desolate and uninhabited

荒芜 huāngwú [形] waste

荒淫 huāngyín [形] debauched

慌 huāng [形] nervous

慌乱 huāngluàn [形] flustered

慌忙 huāngmáng [形] hurried

慌张 huāngzhāng [形] nervous

皇 huáng [名] emperor

皇帝 huángdì [名] emperor

皇宫 huánggōng [名] palace

皇后 huánghòu [名] empress

皇家 huángjiā [名] royal family

皇历 huángli [名] (口) almanac

皇亲国戚 huáng qīn guó qì relatives of the emperor

黄 huáng **I** [形] **1** (指颜色) yellow **2** (色情) pornographic **II** [名] **1** (蛋黄) yolk **2** (黄金) gold

黄灿灿 huángcàncàn [形] golden

黄道吉日 huángdào jírì [名] auspicious day

黄澄澄 huángdēngdēng [形] golden

黄瓜 huángguā [名] cucumber

黄河 Huánghé [名] Yellow River

黄昏 huánghūn [名] dusk
黄金 huángjīn [名] gold
黄金时代 huángjīn shídài [名] **1** (繁荣时期) golden age **2** (指人生) the prime of one's life
黄粱美梦 huángliáng měimèng pipe dream
黄牛 huángniú [名] **1** (指动物) ox **2** (票贩子) ticket tout
黄牌 huángpái [名] yellow card
黄泉 huángquán [名] the underworld
黄色 huángsè [名] **1** (指颜色) yellow **2** (色情) pornographic
黄种 Huángzhǒng [名] Mongoloid race
惶 huáng [名] fear
惶惶 huánghuáng [形] on tenterhooks
惶惑 huánghuò [形] apprehensive
惶恐 huángkǒng [形] terrified
煌 huáng [形] bright
蝗 huáng 见下文
蝗虫 huángchóng [名] locust
磺 huáng [名] (化) sulphur (英), sulfur (美)
簧 huáng [名] **1** (指乐器) reed **2** (指器物) spring
恍 huǎng [副] **1** (恍然) suddenly **2** (仿佛) seemingly
恍惚 huǎnghū [形] **1** (神志不清) absent-minded **2** (不真切) faint
恍然大悟 huǎngrán dàwù suddenly see the light
恍如隔世 huǎng rú gé shì seem like a long time ago
晃 huǎng [动] **1** (闪耀) dazzle **2** (闪过) flash past
▷另见 huàng
晃眼 huǎngyǎn [动] **1** (耀眼) dazzle **2** (瞬间) happen in the blink of an eye
谎 huǎng [名] lie
谎言 huǎngyán [名] lie
幌 huǎng [名] (书) heavy curtain
幌子 huǎngzi [名] **1** (商品标志) shop (英) 或 store (美) sign **2** (名义) veneer
晃 huàng [动] shake (*pt* shook, *pp* shaken)
▷另见 huǎng
晃动 huàngdòng [动] rock
晃悠 huàngyou [动] **1** (摆动) sway **2** (闲逛) wander about
灰 huī **I** [名] **1** (灰烬) ash **2** (尘土) dust **3** (石灰) lime **II** [动] (消沉) be disheartened
灰暗 huī'àn [形] gloomy
灰尘 huīchén [名] dust
灰飞烟灭 huī fēi yān miè disappear
灰烬 huījìn [名] ashes (*pl*)
灰溜溜 huīliūliū [形] **1** (指颜色) dull grey (英) 或 gray (美) **2** (神情沮丧) dejected
灰蒙蒙 huīmēngmēng [形] overcast
灰色 huīsè [名] **1** (指颜色) grey (英), gray (美) **2** (喻) (颓废) melancholy
◇灰色的心情 melancholy emotions
◇灰色的电影 melancholy film
灰心 huīxīn [动] lose heart (*pt, pp* lost)
灰心丧气 huī xīn sàng qì down in the dumps
诙 huī 见下文
诙谐 huīxié [形] humorous
恢 huī [形] vast
恢复 huīfù [动] recover
恢弘 huīhóng [形] (书) extensive
恢恢 huīhuī [形] vast
挥 huī [动] **1** (挥舞) wave **2** (抹掉) wipe ... away **3** (指挥) command **4** (散出) scatter
挥发 huīfā [动] evaporate
挥汗如雨 huī hàn rú yǔ drip with sweat
挥霍 huīhuò [动] squander
挥金如土 huī jīn rú tǔ throw one's money about
挥舞 huīwǔ [动] wave
辉 huī **I** [名] splendour (英),

splendor (美) **II** [动] shine (*pt, pp* shone)

辉煌 huīhuáng [形] brilliant

辉映 huīyìng [动] reflect

徽 huī [名] badge

徽章 huīzhāng [名] badge

回 huí **I** [动] **1** (旋转) circle ♦巡回 make a circuit **2** (还) return ◊回国 return to one's country **3** (掉转) turn around ♦回头 turn one's head **4** (答复) reply ♦回信 reply to a letter **5** (回绝) decline ◊我回了他的邀请。I declined his invitation. **II** [量] **1** (次数) time ◊这是我第三回到杭州。This is my third time in Hangzhou. ◊我去过两回。I have been there twice. **2** (章) chapter ◊小说的第二回 the novel's second chapter

回报 huíbào [动] **1** (报告) report back **2** (报答) repay (*pt, pp* repaid) ◊回报父母 repay one's parents **3** (报复) retaliate

回避 huíbì [动] avoid

回肠荡气 huí cháng dàng qì soul-stirring

回潮 huícháo [动] **1** (字) get damp again **2** (喻) (重现) reappear

回车键 huíchējiàn [名] return key

回程 huíchéng [名] return (英) 或 round (美) trip

回答 huídá [动] answer

回荡 huídàng [动] reverberate

回复 huífù [动] **1** (答复) reply **2** (恢复) return ◊回复原状 return to a former state

回顾 huígù [动] look back

回光返照 huí guāng fǎn zhào brief revival before the end

回归 huíguī [动] return

回合 huíhé [名] round

回话 huíhuà [动] reply

回击 huíjī [动] counterattack

回敬 huíjìng [动] **1** (回报) do … in return ◊回敬你一杯 raise a glass in return **2** (回击) give tit-for-tat (*pt* gave, *pp* given)

回扣 huíkòu [名] commission

回老家 huílǎojiā **1** (字) return home **2** (喻) (诙谐) kick the bucket

回笼 huílóng [动] **1** (食物) reheat ◊把冷包子回笼 reheat cooled buns **2** (货币) withdraw … from circulation (*pt* withdrew, *pp* withdrawn) ◊货币回笼 withdraw currency from circulation

回落 huíluò [动] drop back

回马枪 huímǎqiāng [名] sudden retaliation

回迁 huíqiān [动] move back

回升 huíshēng [动] pick … up

回生 huíshēng [动] resurrect

回声 huíshēng [名] echo (*pl* echoes)

回收 huíshōu [动] **1** (再利用) recycle **2** (收回) retrieve ◊回收成本 retrieve one's costs

回首 huíshǒu [动] **1** (回头) look back **2** (书) (回忆) recollect

回天乏术 huí tiān fá shù be unable to turn around a hopeless situation

回条 huítiáo [名] receipt

回头 huítóu **I** [动] **1** (转头) turn around **2** (回来) return **3** (悔悟) repent **II** [副] in a moment ◊你先休息，回头我再找你吃晚饭。You have a rest just now, and in a moment I'll come back and get you for supper. ◊回头见。See you later.

回头客 huítóukè [名] returning customer

回头是岸 huí tóu shì àn never too late to mend one's ways

回味 huíwèi **I** [名] aftertaste **II** [动] reflect on

回响 huíxiǎng **I** [动] **1** (响应) respond **2** (回声) echo **II** [名] echo (*pl* echoes)

回想 huíxiǎng [动] recall

回心转意 huí xīn zhuǎn yì change one's mind

回旋 huíxuán [动] **1** (盘旋) circle **2** (进退) have room for manoeuvre

回忆 huíyì [动] recall

回音 huíyīn [名] **1** (回声) echo (*pl* echoes) **2** (答复) reply

回执 huízhí [名] receipt

茴 huí 见下文

茴香 huíxiāng [名] fennel

蛔 huí 见下文

蛔虫 huíchóng [名] roundworm

悔 huǐ [动] regret

悔不当初 huǐ bù dāng chū regret a decision

悔改 huǐgǎi [动] repent

悔过自新 huǐ guò zì xīn turn over a new leaf

悔恨 huǐhèn [动] deeply regret

悔悟 huǐwù [动] repent

毁 huǐ [动] **1** (破坏) destroy **2** (烧) burn **3** (诽谤) defame

毁谤 huǐbàng [动] slander

毁害 huǐhài [动] destroy

毁坏 huǐhuài [动] destroy ◇蓄意毁坏公物 vandalism

毁灭 huǐmiè [动] exterminate

毁容 huǐróng [动] disfigure

毁约 huǐyuē [动] go back on one's word (*pt* went, *pp* gone)

卉 huì [名] grass

汇 huì **I** [动] **1** (汇合) converge **2** (聚集) gather **3** (划拨) transfer **II** [名] **1** (外汇) foreign exchange **2** (聚集物) collection ♦词汇 vocabulary

汇报 huìbào [动] report

汇单 huìdān [名] remittance advice

汇兑 huìduì [动] remit

汇合 huìhé [动] **1** (水流) converge **2** (人群、意志、力量) come together (*pt* came, *pp* come)

汇集 huìjí [动] collect ◇人群汇集到广场上。A crowd gathered on the square.

汇率 huìlǜ [名] exchange rate

汇总 huìzǒng [动] collect

会 huì **I** [动] **1** (聚合) assemble ♦会诊 have a consultation **2** (见面) meet (*pt, pp* met) ♦会客 receive a guest **3** (理解) understand (*pt, pp* understood) ♦领会 understand **4** (通晓) be able to ◇会武术 be able to do martial arts **II** [助动] **1** (能做) can ◇我不会下象棋。I can't play chess. **2** (擅长) ◇会过日子 know how to economize ◇能说会道 be eloquent **3** (可能) might ◇明天会更热。Tomorrow might be hotter. **III** [名] **1** (集会) gathering ♦茶话会 tea party **2** (团体) association ♦学生会 student union **3** (城市) city ♦大都会 metropolis **4** (时机) opportunity ♦机会 opportunity **5** (庙会) fair ▷另见 kuài

会餐 huìcān [动] dine together

会合 huìhé [动] meet (*pt, pp* met)

会话 huìhuà [动] converse

会见 huìjiàn [动] meet (*pt, pp* met)

会聚 huìjù [动] assemble

会客 huìkè [动] receive a guest

会商 huìshāng [动] consult

会师 huìshī [动] join forces

会谈 huìtán [动] hold talks (*pt, pp* held)

会同 huìtóng [动] join together

会晤 huìwù [动] meet (*pt, pp* met)

会心 huìxīn [动] understand (*pt, pp* understood)

会议 huìyì [名] **1** (集会) meeting ◇首脑会议 summit meeting **2** (机构) council ◇政治协商会议 political consultation council

会员 huìyuán [名] member ◇会员注册 apply for membership

会战 huìzhàn [动] **1** (字) meet for a decisive battle (*pt, pp* met) **2** (喻) launch a campaign

会账 huìzhàng [动] pick up the bill

会诊 huìzhěn [动] consult

讳 huì **I** [动] regard … as taboo **II** [名] taboo

讳疾忌医 huì jí jì yī (喻) conceal one's shortcomings for fear of criticism

讳言 huìyán [动] be afraid to speak up

荟 huì [形] (书) lush

荟萃 huìcuì [动] assemble

诲 huì [动] teach (*pt, pp* taught)

诲人不倦 huì rén bù juàn teach tirelessly

绘 huì [动] 1 (用铅笔) draw (*pt* drew, *pp* drawn) 2 (用刷状笔画) paint

绘画 huìhuà [动] 1 (用铅笔) draw (*pt* drew, *pp* drawn) 2 (用刷状笔画) paint

绘声绘色 huì shēng huì sè vivid

绘制 huìzhì [动] draw (*pt* drew, *pp* drawn)

贿 huì [名] bribe

贿赂 huìlù [动] bribe ◊接受贿赂 accept a bribe

彗 huì [名] (书) broom

彗星 huìxīng [名] comet

晦 huì I [形] 1 (昏暗) dark 2 (不明显) unclear II [名] night

晦气 huìqì I [形] unlucky II [名] bad luck

晦涩 huìsè [形] obscure

秽 huì [形] 1 (肮脏) filthy 2 (丑恶) abominable 3 (淫乱) promiscuous

秽闻 huìwén [名] (书) notoriety

秽行 huìxíng [名] (书) debauched behaviour (英) 或 behavior (美)

秽语 huìyǔ [名] obscene language

惠 huì [动] (书) be beneficial ♦恩惠 kindness ◊互利互惠 mutually beneficial

惠顾 huìgù [动] patronize

惠临 huìlín [动] (敬) honour (英) 或 honor (美) … with one's presence

喙 huì [名] (书) 1 (鸟嘴) beak 2 (人嘴) mouth

慧 huì [形] intelligent

慧心 huìxīn [名] (智慧) wisdom

慧眼 huìyǎn [名] penetrating insight

昏 hūn I [名] dusk II [形] 1 (黑暗) dark 2 (迷糊) muddled III [动] faint

昏暗 hūn'àn [形] dim

昏沉 hūnchén [形] 1 (暗淡) murky 2 (昏乱) muddled

昏花 hūnhuā [形] poor ◊老眼昏花 poor eyesight in old age

昏黄 hūnhuáng [形] dim

昏厥 hūnjué [动] faint

昏聩 hūnkuì [形] (喻) (糊涂) muddle-headed

昏乱 hūnluàn [形] 1 (指头脑) confused 2 (书) (指社会) chaotic

昏迷 hūnmí [动] be unconscious

昏天黑地 hūn tiān hēi dì 1 (指天色) pitch-black 2 (神志不清) dizzy 3 (激烈) fiercely 5 (指社会混乱) chaotic

昏庸 hūnyōng [形] ineffectual

荤 hūn I [名] meat II [形] dirty ◊荤笑话 dirty jokes

荤腥 hūnxīng [名] meat

婚 hūn I [名] marriage II [动] marry

婚变 hūnbiàn [动] go through a marital breakdown

婚嫁 hūnjià [名] marriage

婚检 hūnjiǎn [动] have a pre-marital medical

婚礼 hūnlǐ [名] wedding ceremony

婚配 hūnpèi [动] get married

婚外恋 hūnwàiliàn [名] extra-marital relationship

婚姻 hūnyīn [名] marriage

浑 hún [形] 1 (浑浊) muddy 2 (糊涂) muddled 3 (天然) natural 4 (满) whole

浑蛋 húndàn [名] (讳) bastard

浑厚 húnhòu [形] 1 (指性格) straightforward 2 (指风格) powerful 3 (指声音) deep and resonant

浑浑噩噩 húnhún'è'è muddle-headed

浑朴 húnpǔ [形] straightforward

浑然一体 húnrán yītǐ completely blend in

浑水摸鱼 hún shuǐ mō yú fish in troubled waters

浑浊 húnzhuó [形] murky

馄 hún 见下文

馄饨 húntún [名] wonton

魂 hún [名] **1** (灵魂) soul **2** (精神) spirit

魂不附体 hún bù fù tǐ scared out of one's wits

魂魄 húnpò [名] soul

混 hùn **I** [动] **1** (搀杂) mix **2** (蒙混) pass off … as ◊鱼目混珠 pass off something fake as genuine **3** (苟且生活) drift ◊混日子 drift through the days **II** [副] aimlessly

混沌 hùndùn **I** [名] chaos **II** [形] ignorant

混合 hùnhé [动] mix

混混儿 hùnhùnr [名] rascal

混乱 hùnluàn [形] **1** (无秩序) chaotic **2** (无条理) disordered

混同 hùntóng [动] mix … up

混为一谈 hùn wéi yī tán confuse ◊你不能将这两个概念混为一谈。You mustn't lump these two concepts together.

混淆 hùnxiáo [动] confuse

混血儿 hùnxuè'ér [名] ◊马丁是个混血儿。Martin is mixed-race.

混杂 hùnzá [动] mix

混战 hùnzhàn [动] engage in long and complicated warfare

混浊 hùnzhuó [形] murky

劐 huō [动] slit (*pt*, *pp* slit)

豁 huō [动] **1** (裂开) break … open (*pt* broke, *pp* broken) **2** (舍弃) go all out (*pt* went, *pp* gone)
▷另见 huò

豁口 huōkǒu [名] breach

和 huó [动] mix … with liquid
▷另见 hé, huò

和面 huómiàn [动] knead dough

活 huó **I** [动] **1** (生存) live **2** (使生存) keep … alive (*pt*, *pp* kept) **II** [形] **1** (有生命) alive **2** (不固定) flexible ◊活期账号 current account **3** (不死板) lively **4** (逼真) lifelike **III** [副] completely ◊他活像个白痴。He acted like a complete idiot. **IV** [名] **1** (工作) work **2** (产品) product

活宝 huóbǎo [名] clown

活蹦乱跳 huó bèng luàn tiào lively and energetic

活动 huódòng **I** [动] **1** (运动) take exercise (*pt* took, *pp* taken) ◊我想到公园活动活动。I'd like to go to the park for a spot of exercise. **2** (行动) operate ◊黑帮常在该地区活动。The gang often operates in this area. **3** (动用关系) use connections ◊她为逃脱责任到处活动。She used all the connections she could to get herself out of trouble. **II** [名] activity ◊文娱活动 recreational activities **III** [形] movable

活该 huógāi [动] (口) serve … right ◊他和女朋友分手后很孤独—活该! He has been lonely after breaking up with his girlfriend – serves him right!

活活 huóhuó [副] when still alive

活计 huójì [名] **1** (体力劳动) manual labour (英) 或 labor (美) **2** (手工制品) handicrafts (*pl*)

活见鬼 huójiànguǐ preposterous

活口 huókǒu [名] **1** (指受害者) survivor **2** (指俘虏、罪犯) captive

活力 huólì [名] vitality

活灵活现 huó líng huó xiàn lifelike

活路 huólù [名] **1** (指道路) through pass **2** (生存之道) means of subsistence **3** (可行之道) feasible method

活络 huóluò [形] **1** (活动) wobbly **2** (不确定) uncertain **3** (灵活) quick ◊头脑活络 quick brain

活埋 huómái [动] bury … alive

活命 huómìng **I** [动] survive **II** [名] life (*pl* lives)

活泼 huópō [形] lively

活菩萨 huópúsa [名] (喻) angel

活期 huóqī [形] current ◊活期账号 current account

活塞 huósāi [名] piston

活生生 huóshēngshēng [形] **1** (真实) living **2** (活活) alive

活受罪 huóshòuzuì (口) suffer a living hell

活水 huóshuǐ [名] running water

活页 huóyè [名] ◊活页笔记本 loose-leaf notebook

活跃 huóyuè I [形] brisk II [动] 1 (使有生气) invigorate 2 (积极从事) be active

活捉 huózhuō [动] capture … alive

活字典 huózìdiǎn [名] walking dictionary

火 huǒ I [名] 1 (火焰) fire 2 (枪支弹药) ammunition 3 (医) (指内火) internal heat 4 (喻) (愤怒) rage II [动] be in a rage III [形] 1 (红色) flaming red 2 (兴旺) prosperous IV [副] urgently

火把 huǒbǎ [名] torch

火暴 huǒbào [形] (方) 1 (暴躁) fiery 2 (旺盛) bustling

火柴 huǒchái [名] match

火车 huǒchē [名] train

火红 huǒhóng [形] 1 (指颜色) flaming red 2 (旺盛) active ◊火红的生命 an active life

火候 huǒhou [名] 1 (火力) cooking power 2 (喻) (修养) level of attainment 3 (时机) crucial moment

火化 huǒhuà [动] cremate

火急 huǒjí [形] urgent

火警 huǒjǐng [名] fire alarm

火炬 huǒjù [名] torch

火坑 huǒkēng [名] (喻) living hell

火辣辣 huǒlālā [形] 1 (表示热) burning 2 (表示疼) burning 3 (表示激动) agitated 4 (泼辣尖锐) fiery ◊火辣辣的个性 a fiery character

火力 huǒlì [名] 1 (指燃料) thermal energy 2 (指弹药) firepower

火冒三丈 huǒ mào sān zhàng burn with rage

火气 huǒqì [名] 1 (医) (指病因) internal heat 2 (怒气) temper

火器 huǒqì [名] firearm

火热 huǒrè [形] 1 (极热) burning hot 2 (热烈) powerful ◊火热的表演 a powerful performance 3 (亲热) intimate ◊双方谈得火热。The two sides engaged in intense talks. 4 (激烈) energetic ◊两人辩论得火热。The two of them engaged in an energetic debate.

火山 huǒshān [名] volcano (*pl* volcanoes)

火上加油 huǒ shàng jiā yóu (喻) pour oil on the flames

火烧眉毛 huǒ shāo méimao (喻) be pressing

火速 huǒsù [副] at top speed

火腿 huǒtuǐ [名] ham

火险 huǒxiǎn [名] 1 (指保险) fire insurance 2 (火灾) fire risk

火眼金睛 huǒ yǎn jīn jīng eagle-eyed

火焰 huǒyàn [名] flame

火药 huǒyào [名] gunpowder

火药味 huǒyàowèi [名] (喻) belligerence

火葬 huǒzàng [动] cremate

伙 huǒ I [名] 1 (同伴) companion 2 (指集体) partnership 3 (伙食) meals (*pl*) II [量] group III [副] together with

伙伴 huǒbàn [名] companion

伙房 huǒfáng [名] kitchen

伙计 huǒji [名] 1 (伙伴) partner 2 (店员) shop assistant (英), sales clerk (美)

伙食 huǒshí [名] meals (*pl*)

伙同 huǒtóng [动] (贬) be in league with

或 huò I (书) [副] 1 (也许) probably ◊到下周或可完成任务。The task will probably be completed by next week. 2 (稍微) remotely ◊不可或缺 indispensable II [连] or ◊无论刮风或下雨，他都准时上班。Even when it's windy or rainy, he's always at work on time. ◊今天或明天，这份功课我一定得完成。I must finish this homework today or tomorrow.

或许 huòxǔ [副] perhaps

或者 huòzhě I [副] maybe ◊再给他发封信，或者会有回音的。If you send him another letter, maybe he'll reply. II [连] or ◊周末我或者在家做饭，或者出去吃。At the weekend I will either cook at home or go out to eat. ◊你先发言，或者他先发言都可以。Whether you speak first or he does doesn't really matter.

和 huò [动] mix
▷另见 hé, huó

货 huò [名] **1** (货币) currency **2** (货物) goods (*pl*) **3** (人) person (*pl* people)
♦蠢货 idiot

货币 huòbì [名] currency

货单 huòdān [名] invoice

货款 huòkuǎn [名] payment for goods

货色 huòsè [名] **1** (货物) goods (*pl*) **2** (贬) (指人或言行思想) rubbish (英), garbage (美)

货物 huòwù [名] goods (*pl*)

货真价实 huò zhēn jià shí **1** (字) high quality at a decent price ◇本店提供的服务货真价实。The service in this shop (英) 或 store (美) is of a high quality and it comes at a decent price. **2** (喻) through and through

获 huò [动] **1** (捉住) capture **2** (得到) obtain **3** (收割) reap ♦收获 harvest

获得 huòdé [动] gain ◇获得灵感 gain inspiration ◇获得冠军 win the championship

获取 huòqǔ [动] obtain

获释 huòshì [动] be set free

获悉 huòxī [动] (书) learn ◇我从朋友那里获悉他早已出国。I learned from friends that he had already gone abroad.

获准 huòzhǔn [动] get permission

祸 huò [名] **I** [名] misfortune **II** [动] harm

祸不单行 huò bù dān xíng it never rains but it pours

祸根 huògēn [名] root of the trouble

祸国殃民 huò guó yāng mín bring disaster upon the country and the people

祸害 huòhài **I** [名] **1** (祸患) disaster **2** (指人或事物) scourge **II** [动] destroy

祸患 huòhuàn [名] disaster

祸首 huòshǒu [名] chief culprit

祸水 huòshuǐ [名] (喻) culprit

惑 huò [动] **1** (疑惑) be puzzled **2** (蛊惑) delude

惑乱 huòluàn [动] befuddle

霍 huò [副] suddenly

霍地 huòdì [副] suddenly

霍霍 huòhuò **I** [拟] swish **II** [形] flash

霍乱 huòluàn [名] cholera

霍然 huòrán [副] suddenly

豁 huò **I** [形] **1** (指人) positive **2** (开阔) clear **II** [动] be exempt
▷另见 huō

豁达 huòdá [形] positive ◇妮科尔为人豁达。Nicole is such a positive person.

豁亮 huòliàng [形] **1** (敞亮) roomy and bright **2** (响亮) resonant

豁免 huòmiǎn [动] be exempt from ◇豁免关税 be exempt from import duty

豁然开朗 huòrán kāilǎng **1** (字) suddenly come across a panoramic scene **2** (喻) (突然领悟) suddenly see the light

Jj

几 jī **I** [名] small table ♦茶几 tea table ◊窗明几净 bright and clean **II** [副] (书) almost ◊当他到的时候几近3点。 It was almost three o'clock by the time he arrived. ▷另见 jǐ

几乎 jīhū [副] almost ◊从这儿到海边几乎有3公里。 It is almost three kilometres from here to the coast. ◊他几乎就要成功了。 He almost succeeded.

几率 jīlǜ [名] probability

讥 jī [动] mock ◊反唇相讥 retort sarcastically

讥讽 jīfěng [动] ridicule

讥笑 jīxiào [动] jeer

击 jī [动] **1** (打) strike (*pt, pp* struck) ◊用拳头猛击 pummel wildly ◊击鼓 beat a drum **2** (攻) attack ◊回击 launch a counterattack **3** (接触) meet (*pt, pp* met) ♦目击 witness ♦撞击 ram

击发 jīfā [动] fire

击掌 jīzhǎng [动] clap

击中要害 jīzhòng yàohài hit home ◊他的评论击中了要害。 His review hit home.

叽 jī [拟] chirp

叽咕 jīgu [动] whisper

叽叽喳喳 jījizhāzhā [拟] chirp

饥 jī **I** [形] hungry **II** [名] famine

饥饿 jī'è [形] starving

饥荒 jīhuang [名] **1** (粮灾) famine **2** (债务) debt

机 jī **I** [名] **1** (机器) machine ♦起重机 crane ♦发动机 engine **2** (飞机) aeroplane (英), airplane (美) ♦客机 airliner ♦直升机 helicopter **3** (枢纽) pivot ♦转机 turning point **4** (机会) opportunity ◊见机行事 play it by ear **5** (机能) ♦有机体 organism ◊无机化学 inorganic chemistry **II** [形] quick-witted ♦机智 ingenious

机场 jīchǎng [名] airport

机动 jīdòng [形] **1** (传动的) motorized ◊机动车 motor vehicle **2** (灵活) flexible **3** (备用的) reserve ◊机动兵力 reserve forces

机构 jīgòu [名] **1** (指机器) mechanism ◊传动机构 transmission **2** (指机关) body ◊管理机构 administrative body ◊科研机构 scientific research institute **3** (指内部) internal structure ◊机构调整 restructuring

机关 jīguān [名] **1** (部门) department ◊政府机关 government department **2** (机械) mechanism ◊启动机关 starting mechanism **3** (计谋) scheme

机关枪 jīguānqiāng [名] machine gun

机会 jīhuì [名] opportunity ◊抓住机会 grasp an opportunity ◊错过机会 miss an opportunity

机警 jījǐng [形] alert

机灵 jīling [形] clever

机能 jīnéng [名] function

机器 jīqì [名] **1** (指装置) machine **2** (指机构) apparatus

机巧 jīqiǎo [形] dexterous

机械 jīxiè **I** [名] machinery **II** [形] rigid ◊机械照搬他人的做法 copy someone else's method exactly

机械化 jīxièhuà [动] mechanize ◊农业机械化 agricultural mechanization

机要 jīyào [形] confidential

机遇 jīyù [名] opportunity

机智 jīzhì [形] resourceful

机组 jīzǔ [名] **1** (一组机器) set **2** (空勤人员) aircrew

肌 jī [名] muscle

肌肤 jīfū [名] skin

肌肉 jīròu [名] muscle

肌体 jītǐ [名] body

鸡 jī [名] chicken ♦公鸡 cock ♦母鸡 hen

鸡蛋 jīdàn [名] egg

鸡毛蒜皮 jīmáo suànpí trivial thing

鸡尾酒 jīwěijiǔ [名] cocktail

奇 jī [形] odd
▷另见 qí

奇数 jīshù [名] odd number

唧 jī [动] squirt

唧唧喳喳 jījī zhāzhā [拟] chirp

积 jī **I** [动] accumulate ◇积经验 accumulate experience **II** [形] long-standing ◇积习难改。Old habits die hard. **III** [名] (数) product

积存 jīcún [动] stockpile

积德 jīdé [动] do good deeds

积极 jījí [形] **1** (肯定的) positive **2** (热心的) active ◇她积极参加学校组织的活动。 She takes an active part in events organized by the college. ◇他上课发言很积极。 He participates actively in class.

积累 jīlěi [动] accumulate ◇资本积累 accumulation of capital

积习 jīxí [名] habit

积蓄 jīxù **I** [动] save **II** [名] savings

积压 jīyā [动] **1** (指物品) overstock ◇店里积压了大量商品。 The shop has overstocked on a lot of products. **2** (指情绪) ◇我积压了一肚子怒火。 I have a lot of pent-up anger.

积怨 jīyuàn [名] accumulated resentment

积攒 jīzǎn [动] save … bit by bit

积重难返 jī zhòng nán fǎn old habits die hard

基 jī **I** [名] base **II** [形] primary ♦基层 grass roots

基本 jīběn **I** [形] **1** (根本) basic ◇基本规律 basic norms **2** (主要) essential ◇基本特点 essential characteristics **3** (基础) elementary ◇基本知识 basic knowledge **II** [副] basically ◇饭菜基本准备好了。 The food is basically ready.

基本功 jīběngōng [名] basic skill

基础 jīchǔ **I** [名] foundation **II** [形] basic ◇基础知识 basic knowledge

基地 jīdì [名] base ◇军事基地 military base

基点 jīdiǎn [名] starting point

基调 jīdiào [名] **1** (基本精神) keynote **2** (音) main key

基督 Jīdū [名] Jesus

基督教 Jīdūjiào [名] Christianity

基建 jījiàn [名] infrastructure development

基金 jījīn [名] fund ◇助学基金 study fund

基石 jīshí [名] cornerstone

基数 jīshù [名] **1** (数) cardinal number **2** (统计) base

基因 jīyīn [名] gene ◇基因工程 genetic engineering

基于 jīyú [介] on the basis of ◇基于确凿的证据，他被判入狱。 On the basis of irrefutable evidence he was sent to jail.

犄 jī 见下文

犄角 jījiǎo [名] (角落) corner

犄角 jījiao [名] (指动物) horn

缉 jī [动] seize ♦侦缉 apprehend

缉捕 jībǔ [动] arrest

缉查 jīchá [动] raid

缉毒 jīdú [动] crack down on drug trafficking

缉拿 jīná [动] apprehend

缉私 jīsī [动] crack down on smuggling

畸 jī [形] **1** (不平衡) lopsided **2** (不正常) abnormal

畸轻畸重 jī qīng jī zhòng give more weight to one than the other

畸形 jīxíng [形] **1** (有缺陷的) deformed **2** (不正常的) unbalanced

跻 jī [动] mount

跻身 jīshēn [动] ascend

箕 jī [名] (指器具) dustpan

稽 jī [动] check ♦稽查 check

稽查 jīchá **I** [动] check **II** [名] customs officer

稽考 jīkǎo [动] ascertain

激 jī I [动] 1 (涌起) surge 2 (刺激) catch a chill (*pt, pp* caught) ◇他被大雨激了一下。 He caught a chill in the rain. 3 (唤起) excite ◇申奥成功激起了北京市民的热情。 The successful bid for the Olympic Games excited Beijingers' enthusiasm. 4 (冰) chill ◇把啤酒放凉水里激一下。 Put the beer in cold water to chill it a little. II [形] violent

激昂 jī'áng [形] aroused

激荡 jīdàng [动] inspire

激动 jīdòng [动] excite ◇激动的孩子 excited child ◇令人激动的电影 exciting film

激发 jīfā [动] arouse

激愤 jīfèn [形] indignant

激光 jīguāng [名] laser

激化 jīhuà [动] intensify

激活 jīhuó [动] activate

激进 jījìn [形] radical

激励 jīlì [动] inspire

激烈 jīliè [形] intense

激怒 jīnù [动] enrage

激情 jīqíng [名] passion

激素 jīsù [名] hormone

激增 jīzēng [动] shoot up (*pt, pp* shot) ◇电子产品在激增。 The quantity of electrical goods being produced has shot up.

羁 jī I [名] bridle II [动] 1 (拘束) restrain 2 (拦阻) delay

羁绊 jībàn [名] fetters (*pl*)

羁留 jīliú [动] 1 (逗留) stay 2 (拘留) detain

羁押 jīyā [动] detain

及 jí I [动] 1 (到达) reach ◇他过河时，水深及腰。 When he crossed the river, the water reached his waist. 2 (比得上) be as good as ◇我的法语水平不及她。 My French isn't as good as hers. 3 (赶上) be in time for ◇现在去看电影还来得及。 There is still time to get to the film. II [连] and ◇老师及学生 teachers and students

及格 jígé [动] pass

及时 jíshí I [形] timely ◇这场雨下得很及时。 This rain has come at the right time. II [副] without delay ◇有病要及时去就医。 If you are ill you should go to the doctor without delay.

及早 jízǎo [副] as soon as possible

吉 jí [形] lucky ♦吉祥 auspicious ◇逢凶化吉 land on one's feet

吉利 jílì [形] lucky

吉庆 jíqìng [形] auspicious

吉日 jírì [名] lucky day

吉他 jítā [名] guitar

吉祥 jíxiáng [形] auspicious

吉凶 jíxiōng [名] good and bad luck

汲 jí [动] draw (*pt* drew, *pp* drawn)

汲取 jíqǔ [动] derive

级 jí I [名] 1 (等级) level ◇各级政府部门 government departments of all levels 2 (年级) year (英), grade (美) ◇三年级 third year (英) 或 grade (美) 3 (台阶) step ◇石级 stone step 4 (语言) degree ◇比较级 the comparative degree II [量] step ◇100多级台阶 a staircase of more than 100 steps

级别 jíbié [名] level

极 jí I [名] 1 (顶点) extreme ◇真是荒谬之极。 This is absurd in the extreme. 2 (指地球或磁体) pole ◇南极 the South Pole ◇阴极 negative pole II [动] go to an extreme (*pt* went, *pp* gone) III [形] extreme ♦极限 limit IV [副] very ◇极少数 very few

极点 jídiǎn [名] 1 (极限) extreme 2 (指地球或磁体) pole

极度 jídù [副] extremely

极端 jíduān I [名] extreme ◇做什么事情都不要走极端。 You should exercise moderation in all that you do. II [形] absolute ◇极端仇视 absolute hostility

极力 jílì [副] to the utmost ◇极力劝说 do one's utmost to persuade

极其 jíqí [副] extremely

极限 jíxiàn [名] limit

极刑 jíxíng [名] death penalty

即 jí I [动] 1 (书) (就是) mean (*pt, pp* meant) ◇对她来说，结婚即生儿育女。 From her point of view, marriage means having children. 2 (靠近) approach ◇这个目标可望而不可即。 This goal is unattainable. 3 (到) ◇即位 ascend the throne 4 (就着) ◇即兴演唱 ad-lib II [形] present ♦即日 this very day III [副] immediately ◇我打个电话即到。 I will be there immediately – I just have to make a phone call.

即便 jíbiàn [连] even if ◇即便我忙，也要为你送行。 Even though I'm busy, I'll see you off.

即将 jíjiāng [副] soon

即刻 jíkè [副] immediately

即日 jírì [副] 1 (当天) this very day 2 (近几天) the next few days

即使 jíshǐ [连] even if ◇即使他不来，我们也照样干。 Even if he doesn't come, we'll go ahead as usual. ◇即使分手了，他们还是朋友。 Even though they've split up they're still friends.

即位 jíwèi [动] ascend the throne

即席 jíxí [形] impromptu ◇即席发言 make an impromptu speech

即兴 jíxìng [形] impromptu

亟 jí [副] urgently

急 jí I [形] 1 (着急) anxious ◇他急着赶火车。 He is anxious to catch the train. 2 (急躁) impatient 3 (猛烈) ◇雨下得真急。 It's raining really hard. ◇水流很急。 There's a strong current. 4 (紧急) urgent ◇这件事很急。 This matter is urgent. ◇急刹车 slam on the brakes II [名] priority ◇当务之急是解决难民的吃住问题。 Our top priority is to resolve the refugee accommodation and food supply problems. III [动] worry ◇他还没来，真急死人了。 He still hasn't arrived – we're worried to death.

急不可待 jí bù kě dài extremely anxious

急促 jícù [形] 1 (短促) rapid 2 (紧急) pressing ◇时间急促，我们赶快出发。 Time is pressing - we had better go.

急功近利 jí gōng jìn lì seek short-term benefits

急救 jíjiù [动] give first-aid (*pt* gave, *pp* given)

急剧 jíjù [副] rapidly ◇那座城市的环境急剧恶化。 The environment in the city is rapidly getting worse.

急忙 jímáng [副] hurriedly

急迫 jípò [形] urgent

急切 jíqiè [形] eager ◇我怀着急切的心情等他的来信。 I waited eagerly for his letter.

急速 jísù [副] rapidly ◇经济形势急速恶化。 The economy is deteriorating rapidly.

急性 jíxìng [形] acute

急性子 jíxìngzi [名] hothead

急于 jíyú [副] anxiously ◇他急于要走。 He is anxious to go. ◇不要急于下结论。 Don't be in such a hurry to pass judgment.

急躁 jízào [形] impatient

急诊 jízhěn [名] emergency treatment

急中生智 jí zhōng shēng zhì show resourcefulness in an emergency

疾 jí I [名] disease II [形] rapid

疾病 jíbìng [名] disease

棘 jí [名] thorn

棘手 jíshǒu [形] thorny

集 jí I [动] gather ◇集大家的智慧 draw on collective wisdom II [名] 1 (集市) market ◇赶集 go to market 2 (集子) anthology ◇诗集 an anthology of poems 3 (部分) part ◇该书分上下两集。 This book is divided into two parts.

集合 jíhé [动] assemble

集会 jíhuì [名] assembly

集结 jíjié [动] build … up (*pt, pp* built)

集权 jíquán [动] centralize

集散地 jísàndì [名] distribution centre (英) 或 center (美)

集市 jíshì [名] market

集思广益 jí sī guǎng yì pool knowledge

集体 jítǐ [名] collective

集团 jítuán [名] group

集腋成裘 jí yè chéng qiú every little helps

集镇 jízhèn [名] market town

集中 jízhōng [动] concentrate ◇大商场多集中在市中心。 Most of the department stores are concentrated in the city centre.

集装箱 jízhuāngxiāng [名] container

集资 jízī [动] raise funds

辑 jí I [动] edit II [名] volume

辑录 jílù [动] compile

嫉 jí [动] envy

嫉妒 jídù [动] envy ◇你不要嫉妒他人。 You shouldn't be jealous of other people.

嫉贤妒能 jí xián dù néng envy successful and talented people

瘠 jí [形] 1 (瘦弱) thin and weak 2 (瘠薄) barren

瘠田 jítián [名] infertile land

籍 jí [名] 1 (籍贯) native place 2 (书籍) book 3 (小册子) register 4 (身份) ◇国籍 nationality

籍贯 jíguàn [名] native place ◇他籍贯是福建厦门。 He was born in Xiamen in Fujian.

几 jǐ [数] 1 (用于疑问句) ◇昨天来了几位客人？ How many customers came yesterday? 2 (用于陈述句) ◇我在图书馆借了几本书。I borrowed several books from the library.
▷另见 jī

几何 jǐhé [名] geometry

几经 jǐjīng [副] ◇几经周折，他终于找到了失散多年的亲人。After much effort, he finally found the relatives he'd lost touch with for many years. ◇几经努力，她终于考上了重点大学。After much hard work, she finally got into a key university.

几时 jǐshí [代] 1 (什么时候) ◇你几时回来? When will you come back? ◇电脑几时修好？ When will the computer be fixed? 2 (任何时候) any time ◇我几时也没有说过这话。I never said anything of the sort.

己 jǐ [名] self ♦自己 oneself

挤 jǐ [动] 1 (紧紧靠拢) crowd ◇公共汽车很挤。The bus is very crowded. ◇过道里挤满了人。The passageway was packed with people. 2 (事情、会议、约会) be close ◇两个会议都挤在一起。The two meetings are very close to each other. ◇事情都挤在一块儿了。Everything's happening at the same time. 3 (推人) elbow one's way ◇他挤上拥挤的汽车。He elbowed his way onto the crowded bus. 4 (贬) (指社交) push one's way ◇她拼命想挤进上层社会。She worked hard to push her way into top society. 5 (牙膏、颜料) squeeze … out ♦挤奶 milk 6 (时间) make (*pt, pp* made) ◇他挤时间学英语。He made time to study English. 7 (排斥) rob … of ◇他的晋升机会被挤掉了。He was robbed of his opportunity for promotion.

济 jǐ 见下文
▷另见 jì

济济一堂 jǐjǐ yītáng assemble ◇研讨会上全国的语言学家济济一堂。Linguists from all over the country assembled at the symposium.

给 jǐ I [动] provide ♦补给 supply II [形] sufficient
▷另见 gěi

给养 jǐyǎng [名] supplies (*pl*)

给予 jǐyǔ [动] (书) give (*pt* gave, *pp* given) ◇他对我们给予了很大帮助。He has rendered us much help.

脊 jǐ [名] 1 (指人或动物) spine ♦脊柱 spinal column 2 (指物体) ridge ♦山脊 mountain ridge ♦书脊 spine

脊背 jǐbèi [名] back

脊梁 jǐliang [名] (脊背) back

脊髓 jǐsuǐ [名] spinal cord

脊椎 jǐzhuī [名] 1 (脊柱) spinal column ◇脊椎动物 vertebrates 2 (脊骨)

vertebra (*pl* vertebrae)

计 jì **I** [动] **1** (核算) calculate ♦共计 total **2** (打算) plan **3** (考虑) bother ◇他工作不计报酬。He's not bothered about what he's paid for his work. **II** [名] **1** (计谋) strategy **2** (测量仪器) gauge ♦温度计 thermometer

计策 jìcè [名] strategy

计划 jìhuà **I** [名] plan ◇你们应制定学习计划。You should devise a study plan. **II** [动] plan ◇你计划不周，怎么能成功呢？ If you don't plan properly, how can you succeed?

计较 jìjiào [动] **1** (在乎) bother ◇斤斤计较 quibble over every detail **2** (争论) argue ◇先不跟你计较，有空我再说。I won't argue with you now. Let's talk about it when I have time. **3** (计议) deliberate

计算 jìsuàn [动] **1** (数) calculate **2** (筹划) plan ◇做事没个计算可不行。It's no good taking action without a plan. **3** (暗算) scheme ◇小心别被人计算。Be careful others aren't scheming against you.

计算机 jìsuànjī [名] computer

计算器 jìsuànqì [名] calculator

记 jì **I** [动] **1** (指往事) remember **2** (写) record ◇记名字 record a name ◇记笔记 make notes ◇记账 keep accounts **II** [名] **1** (指书或文章) record ♦游记 travel journal ♦日记 diary **2** (标志) mark **3** (指皮肤) birthmark **III** [量] (方) ◇一记远射，球进了！ A long shot – and it's a goal! ◇他被打了一记耳光。He got a slap in the face.

> 📖 **remember** 后接带 **to** 的不定式或者动词的 **-ing** 形式。**remember to do something** 表示记得去做某事。*He remembered to buy his wife chocolates*。**remember doing something** 则表示记得已经做过某事。*I remember reading the newspaper aloud to my father at the age of five.*

记挂 jìguà [动] be concerned about

记过 jìguò [动] give … a black mark (*pt* gave, *pp* given) ◇他没完成任务，被记过一次。He didn't finish his work, and was given a black mark.

记号 jìhao [名] mark ◇在你不会的地方作个记号。Make a mark by the ones you are unable to do.

记录 jìlù **I** [动] (写下) write … down (*pt* wrote, *pp* written) ◇请把你的心得体会记录下来。Please write down what your own understanding is. **II** [名] **1** (材料) record ◇请整理一下会议记录。Please tidy up the minutes of the meeting. **2** (人) secretary ◇她是这次会议的记录。She is the secretary for this meeting. **3** (成绩) record ◇他打破了男子100米世界记录。He broke the world record for the men's 100 metres (英) 或 meters (美).

记名 jìmíng [动] register ◇总经理通过无记名投票选出。The general manager was elected by secret ballot.

记取 jìqǔ [动] remember

记事 jìshì **I** [动] keep a record (*pt, pp* kept) ◇记事本 notebook **II** [名] chronicles (*pl*)

记事儿 jìshìr [动] have memories ◇她打5岁起就记事儿了。Her memories start from when she was five.

记述 jìshù [动] tell (*pt, pp* told) ◇这部影片记述了一个真实的故事。This film tells a true story. ◇记者对此事进行了完整的记述。The journalist gave a full account of the event.

记性 jìxing [名] memory

记忆 jìyì **I** [动] remember **II** [名] memory ◇记忆犹新 the memory is fresh

记载 jìzǎi [动] record ◇这篇文章记载了当时的情况。This essay records the situation at that time. ◇请据实记载事情经过。Please write down exactly what happened.

记者 jìzhě [名] journalist ◇他是一名出色的摄影记者。He is a famous photo-journalist.

伎 jì 见下文

伎俩 jìliǎng [名] trick ◇逃票是他惯用的伎俩。Not buying tickets is his favourite trick. ◇我们识破了他的伎俩。We saw through his ploy.

纪 jì I [名] **1** age ♦中世纪 the Middle Ages (*pl*) **2** (指地质) period ♦侏罗纪 the Jurassic period **3** (纪律) discipline II [动] record

纪律 jìlǜ [名] discipline

纪念 jìniàn I [动] commemorate II [名] memento ◇送给你一支钢笔作纪念。Here is a pen as a memento. ◇给我签个名留作纪念吧。Please give me your autograph as a souvenir.

纪实 jìshí [名] record ◇纪实文学 literature based on actual events

纪要 jìyào [名] summary ◇请整理好会议纪要。Please put together a summary of the meeting.

纪元 jìyuán [名] era ◇新纪元 new era ◇公历从耶稣诞生的那年开始纪元。The Western calendar begins in the year of the birth of Christ.

技 jì [名] **1** (技艺) skill ♦技能 skill ♦技巧 technique **2** (本领) ability ♦绝技 unique ability

技能 jìnéng [名] skill

技巧 jìqiǎo [名] technique

技术 jìshù [名] technology ◇我们需要不断学习国际先进技术。We need to keep up with international advances in technology. ◇生产要与技术改造同时进行。Production must go hand in hand with technological improvement.

技艺 jìyì [名] skill

系 jì [动] **1** (打结) tie **2** (扣上) fasten ◇把领扣系好。Button up your collar.
▷另见 xì

忌 jì [动] **1** (嫉妒) envy ◇当领导决不能忌才。A leader should never be resentful of others' ability. **2** (害怕) fear ♦忌惮 dread **3** (避免) avoid **4** (戒除) give … up (*pt* gave, *pp* given) ♦忌酒 give up drinking ◇为了健康，你需要忌烟。You should give up smoking for the sake of your health.

忌妒 jìdu I [动] be jealous ◇他总是忌妒别人的成功。He is always jealous of other people's success. II [名] jealousy ◇她这么做是出于忌妒。She's done that out of jealousy.

忌讳 jìhuì [动] **1** (禁忌) be superstitious about **2** (避免) avoid ◇夜里我忌讳走墓地。At night I try to avoid walking by the graveyard.

际 jì [名] **1** (边缘) border ♦天际 horizon **2** (里边) interior ♦脑际 in one's mind **3** (彼此之间) ♦国际 international **4** (时候) occasion **5** (遭遇) lot

际遇 jìyù [名] (书) experience

妓 jì 见下文

妓女 jìnǚ [名] prostitute

季 jì [名] season ♦春季 spring ♦旺季 busy season ♦雨季 rainy season

季度 jìdù [名] quarter

季节 jìjié [名] season

季军 jìjūn [名] third place ◇她在这次写作大赛中获得季军。She came third in this major writing competition.

剂 jì I [名] **1** (指药、针、麻醉) preparation ♦针剂 injection **2** (指起化学物理作用) ♦杀虫剂 insecticide ♦除臭剂 deoderant II [量] (指配的汤药) dose ♦一剂药 a dose of medicine

剂量 jìliàng [名] dosage

迹 jì [名] **1** (印) trace ♦足迹 footprint ♦血迹 bloodstain ♦笔迹 writing **2** (遗留物) remains (*pl*) ♦古迹 historic sites (*pl*)

迹象 jìxiàng [名] indication ◇种种迹象表明他们不会来了。All the indications are that they won't come. ◇他还没有好转的迹象。He's still not showing any signs of improvement.

济 jì [动] **1** (渡过) cross ◇让我们同舟共济，共同努力吧。We're all in the same boat, so let's work together. **2** (救) help ♦接济 give aid **3** (有益) be of help ◇无济于事 be of no help
▷另见 jǐ

济事 jìshì [动] be of use ◊你这点儿钱根本不济事。This is simply not enough money to be of any use. ◊他去了也不济事。It won't be of any use even if he does go.

既 jì **I** [副] already ♦既定 fixed ◊既成事实 a fait accompli **II** [连] **1** (表示兼而有之) ◊他字写得既快又好。He writes both quickly and well. ◊他既高又壮。He's tall and strong. **2** (既然) since ◊既来之，则安之。Since we've come, let's make the best of it.

既然 jìrán [连] since ◊既然你知道错误了，为什么不及时纠正呢？Since you knew you'd made a mistake, why didn't you put it right immediately? ◊既然他执意要去，你就答应吧。Seeing as he's determined to go, why don't you just agree to it?

既往不咎 jì wǎng bù jiù let bygones be bygones

觊 jì 见下文

觊觎 jìyú [动] (书) covet

继 jì **I** [副] **1** (接续) continuously ♦继任 succeed to a post **2** (接连) successively ♦相继 one after another **II** [动] continue

继承 jìchéng [动] **1** (遗产、文化等) inherit **2** (遗志、未成事业) take … on (*pt* took, *pp* taken)

继而 jì'ér [副] then ◊他先是一愣，继而大笑。At first he was taken aback – then he burst out laughing.

继往开来 jì wǎng kāi lái forge ahead

继续 jìxù **I** [动] continue ◊你们要继续努力。You must continue to work hard. ◊我们继续昨天的话题接着谈。We'll continue with the topic we discussed yesterday. ◊身体痊愈后，他继续工作。After he recovered he went back to work. ◊我们继续往下读。Let's read on. **II** [名] continuation

祭 jì [动] **1** (祭祀) sacrifice ♦祭坛 sacrificial altar **2** (祭奠) hold a memorial service (*pt, pp* held)

祭奠 jìdiàn [动] hold a memorial service (*pt, pp* held)

祭祀 jìsì [动] sacrifice ◊一头小牛被用作祭祀。A young cow is used as a sacrifice.

祭文 jìwén [名] eulogy

悸 jì [动] (书) palpitate ◊想起那次历险，我到现在都心有余悸。When I think about the danger we were in, I still have palpitations.

悸动 jìdòng [动] pound

寄 jì [动] **1** (邮递) post (英), mail (美) ◊包裹已经寄走了。The package has already been posted (英) 或 mailed (美). **2** (付托) place ◊我寄希望于他。I pinned my hopes on him. **3** (依附) depend on ◊寄人篱下 be a dependant (英) 或 dependent (美)

寄存 jìcún [动] deposit ◊我把行李寄存在存包处了。I've checked my bag in.

寄放 jìfàng [动] leave (*pt, pp* left)

寄居 jìjū [动] live ◊她从小寄居在姑姑家。She has lived with her aunt ever since she was little.

寄生 jìshēng [动] be a parasite ◊真菌寄生在某些植物中。Fungus is a parasite on certain plants. ◊我们不能过寄生生活。We can't live as parasites.

寄宿 jìsù [动] **1** (借宿) stay ◊昨晚下大雨，我只好寄宿朋友家。With the heavy rain last night, I had no choice but to stay over at my friend's house. **2** (住校) board ◊我所在的学校是一所寄宿学校。The school I attended was a boarding school.

寄托 jìtuō [动] **1** (物品) leave (*pt, pp* left) **2** (理想、感情、希望) focus ◊葬礼是我们寄托感情的时刻。The funeral was an occasion for focusing our feelings. ◊她把希望寄托在女儿身上。Her hopes were pinned on her daughter.

寄养 jìyǎng [动] **1** (指人) foster **2** (指动植物) give … to look after (*pt* gave, *pp* given) ◊我把这盆花寄养在你这儿行吗？Would it be all right if I give you this plant to look after?

寄予 jìyǔ [动] **1** (寄托) place ◊父亲对他寄予了无限希望。His father places all his hopes in him. **2** (给

予) show (*pt* showed, *pp* shown) ◇全社区对他家的不幸寄予了无限的同情。The whole community showed boundless sympathy for the family's misfortunes. ◇他对年轻人寄予了无限关怀。He's deeply committed to young people.

寂 jì [形] **1** (静) quiet **2** (寂寞) lonely

寂静 jìjìng **I** [形] peaceful ◇尖叫声划破了寂静的夜晚。A scream broke the silence of the night. **II** [名] tranquillity

寂寞 jìmò [形] lonely

绩 jì [名] achievement ♦功绩 accomplishment ♦战绩 military success

髻 jì [名] chignon

冀 jì [动] (书) hope ♦冀望 long for

加 jiā [动] **1** (相加) ◇2加2等于4。Two plus two is four. ◇雪上加霜 one disaster after another **2** (增加) increase ◇老板要给我们加工资。The boss wants to increase our wages. **3** (添加) add ◇加点糖 add some sugar ◇请加一副碗筷。Can you give us another bowl and another set of chopsticks? **4** (加以) ◇我们对孩子要严加管教。We should be strict with children.

加班 jiābān [动] work overtime

加倍 jiābèi [动] double ◇下个月油价可能加倍。Next month the price of oil may double. ◇值夜班要加倍警惕。The night shift has to be doubly vigilant.

加法 jiāfǎ [名] addition

加封 jiāfēng [动] **1** (提升) grant **2** (查封) seal

加工 jiāgōng [动] **1** (制作) process **2** (完善) polish

加害 jiāhài [动] do … harm

加紧 jiājǐn [动] step up

加剧 jiājù [动] make … worse ◇谣言加剧了他们之间的矛盾。The allegation made the tension between them worse. ◇这项政策加剧了贫富差距。This policy exacerbates the gap between rich and poor.

加仑 jiālún [量] gallon

加码 jiāmǎ [动] **1** (加注) raise the stakes **2** (增加) increase a quota

加盟 jiāméng [动] join ◇本俱乐部欢迎青年人加盟。This club encourages young people to join.

加密 jiāmì [动] encrypt

加冕 jiāmiǎn [动] crown

加强 jiāqiáng [动] strengthen ◇加强防卫 strengthen defences (英) 或 defenses (美)

加入 jiārù [动] **1** (添加) add ◇汤里需要再加入点盐。You need to add a bit more salt to the soup. **2** (参加) join

加塞儿 jiāsāir [动] queue-jump (英), line-jump (美)

加速 jiāsù [动] accelerate

加以 jiāyǐ **I** [动] ◇旧的工作方法必须加以改进。The old working methods need to be improved. **II** [连] ◇这家商店离学校近，加以价格便宜，所以顾客很多。This shop is close to campus, and it's also cheap, so there are a lot of customers.

加油 jiāyóu [动] **1** (加燃料) refuel ◇飞机需要加油了。The plane needs to refuel. ◇我的汽车该加油了。I should get some petrol (英) 或 gas (美) for the car. **2** (加劲儿) make more effort ◇老板一再叮嘱大家加油干。The boss kept urging people to make more effort. ◇快，加油！Come on, come on!

夹 jiā **I** [动] **1** (钳) get hold of **2** (携带) carry … under one's arm ◇我们校长总是夹着公文包。Our head teacher always carries a briefcase under his arm. **3** (限制) ◇两边高楼夹着一条狭窄的街道。A narrow street hemmed in by tall buildings on either side. **4** (带) mix … with ◇笑声夹杂着哭声 laughter mixed with tears **II** [名] folder ◇文件夹 document folder
▷另见 gā, jiá

夹带 jiādài [动] smuggle

夹道 jiādào **I** [名] alleyway **II** [动] line the road

夹缝 jiāfèng [名] crevice

夹攻 jiāgōng [动] attack in a pincer movement

夹克 jiākè [名] jacket

夹生 jiāshēng [形] half-cooked

夹杂 jiāzá [动] be mixed with

茄 jiā 见下文
▷另见 qié

茄克 jiākè [名] jacket

佳 jiā [形] fine ◇佳音 good news ◇她最近身体欠佳。 She has recently been in poor health.

佳话 jiāhuà [名] talking point

佳节 jiājié [名] festival

佳境 jiājìng [名] beauty spot

佳丽 jiālì [名] beauty

佳偶 jiā'ǒu [名] happily married couple

佳期 jiāqī [名] wedding day

佳人 jiārén [名] beautiful woman (*pl* women)

佳肴 jiāyáo [名] delicacies (*pl*)

佳音 jiāyīn [名] good news (*sg*)

枷 jiā 见下文

枷锁 jiāsuǒ [名] fetters (*pl*)

痂 jiā [名] scab

家 jiā I [名] **1**(家庭) family **2**(住所) home ◇他一放假就回家。 As soon as the holiday started he went back home. **3**(学派) school of thought **4**(指人) ♦船家 boatman (*pl* boatmen) ♦农家 peasant ♦专家 expert ♦歌唱家 singer ♦画家 painter II [形] **1**(饲养的) domestic ♦家畜 domestic animal **2**(嫡亲的) ♦家兄 elder brother III [量] ◇一家公司 a company

家产 jiāchǎn [名] estate

家常 jiācháng [名] domestic affairs (*pl*)

家丑 jiāchǒu [名] family scandal

家畜 jiāchù [名] domestic animal

家传 jiāchuán [动] hand … down

家当 jiādàng [名] family possessions (*pl*)

家底 jiādǐ [名] property ◇他家底颇厚。 His family is quite wealthy.

家电 jiādiàn [名] domestic electrical appliance

家伙 jiāhuo [名] **1**(工具) tool **2**(武器) weapon **3**(人) guy

家计 jiājì [名] (书) family livelihood

家教 jiājiào I [动] bring … up (*pt, pp* brought) II [名] private tutor

家境 jiājìng [名] family circumstances (*pl*)

家具 jiājù [名] furniture

> 注意 **furniture** 只能用作不可数名词。不能说 'a furniture' 或 'furnitures'。如要具体指代桌子、椅子或床等家具，可以用 *a piece of furniture* 或 *an item of furniture*。

家眷 jiājuàn [名] wife and children

家禽 jiāqín [名] poultry (*pl*)

家室 jiāshì [名] **1**(妻子) wife (*pl* wives) ◇他已有家室。 He's married. **2**(家庭) family

家属 jiāshǔ [名] family members (*pl*)

家庭 jiātíng [名] family ◇他妻子很会处理家庭关系。 His wife is very good at sorting out relationships within the family. ◇我的家庭很和睦。 My household is harmonious.

家务 jiāwù [名] housework

家乡 jiāxiāng [名] hometown

家小 jiāxiǎo [名] wife and children

家业 jiāyè [名] family property

家用 jiāyòng I [名] living expenses (*pl*) II [形] domestic ◇家用电器 domestic electrical appliance ◇家用电脑 home computer

家喻户晓 jiā yù hù xiǎo be a household name

家园 jiāyuán [名] homeland

家长 jiāzhǎng [名] **1**(一家之长) head of the family **2**(父母) parent

家政 jiāzhèng [名] housekeeping

家族 jiāzú [名] family

嘉 jiā I [形] fine ♦嘉宾 honoured (英) 或 honored (美) guest II [动] praise

嘉宾 jiābīn [名] honoured (英) 或 honored (美) guest

嘉奖 jiājiǎng [动] commend

嘉许 jiāxǔ [动] praise

夹 jiá [形] lined ♦夹袄 padded jacket
▷另见 gā, jiā

戛 jiá 见下文

戛然而止 jiárán ér zhǐ stop suddenly

颊 jiá [名] cheek

甲 jiǎ [名] **1**(第一) ♦甲级品 A-grade **2**(动物硬壳) shell ♦龟甲 tortoiseshell **3**(角质硬壳) nail ♦指甲 fingernail **4**(装备) armour (英), armor (美) ♦装甲车 armoured (英) 或 armored (美) car

甲板 jiǎbǎn [名] deck

甲虫 jiǎchóng [名] beetle

岬 jiǎ [名] cape

岬角 jiǎjiǎo [名] headland

假 jiǎ **I** [形] **1**(虚伪) false ◇他表面上热情，其实特假。 He gives a false impression of being friendly. **2**(不真) artificial ♦假发 wig ♦假山 rockery ♦假话 lie **II** [连] if ♦假如 if **III**[动] borrow
▷另见 jià

假扮 jiǎbàn [动] dress up as

假充 jiǎchōng [动] pretend to be

假定 jiǎdìng [动] suppose ◇假定你中了大奖，你会做什么？ Supposing you won the jackpot, what would you do with it? ◇有外星人的说法只是一种假定。 The existence of extraterrestrials is just hypothesis.

假借 jiǎjiè [动] make use of

假冒 jiǎmào [动] pass oneself off as ◇他假冒总经理的名义诈骗银行。 He passed himself off as the managing director to defraud the bank. ◇假冒伪劣产品 fake, sub-standard goods

假面具 jiǎmiànjù [名] mask

假名 jiǎmíng [名] pseudonym

假如 jiǎrú [连] if

假设 jiǎshè **I** [动] suppose ◇假设这是真的，我们该怎么办? Supposing it's true, what should we do? **II** [名] hypothesis (*pl* hypotheses)

假使 jiǎshǐ [连] if

假释 jiǎshì [动] release … on parole

假象 jiǎxiàng [名] deceptive appearance ◇现在的经济繁荣只是一种假象。 The current apparent economic boom is deceptive.

假惺惺 jiǎxīngxīng [形] hypocritical

假意 jiǎyì **I** [名] insincerity ◇谁知道她是真情还是假意？ Who knows whether she is sincere or not? **II** [动] pretend ◇他假意吃惊。 He pretended to be surprised. ◇他假意笑着向我问好。 He greeted me with a false smile.

假装 jiǎzhuāng [动] pretend ◇我假装不懂他的意思。 I pretended not to understand what he meant.

价 jià [名] **1**(价格) price ♦物价 price **2**(价值) value

价格 jiàgé [名] price ◇价格标签 price tag

价目 jiàmù [名] marked price

价钱 jiàqian [名] price

价值 jiàzhí [名] value ◇价值观念 values ◇商业价值 market potential

价值连城 jiàzhí liánchéng priceless

驾 jià **I** [动] **1**(驾驭) harness **2**(驾驶) drive (*pt* drove, *pp* driven) ◇驾车 drive a car ◇驾飞机 fly a plane **II** [代] (敬) ♦劳驾 excuse me **III**[量] ◇3驾马车 three carts

驾轻就熟 jià qīng jiù shú be a piece of cake

驾驶 jiàshǐ [动] steer

驾驭 jiàyù [动] master

驾照 jiàzhào [名] driving licence (英) 或 driver's license (美)

架 jià **I** [名] **1**(架子) frame ♦书架 bookshelf ♦脚手架 scaffolding **2**(指行为) ♦吵架 quarrel ♦打架 fight **II** [动] **1**(撑起) support ◇架电线 carry electrical cables **2**(招架) ward … off **3**(绑架) kidnap ◇孩子被人架走了。 The child was kidnapped. **4**(搀扶) support … under the arm ◇我们把伤员架上了救护车。

Supporting the injured person under the arm, we helped him into the ambulance. III[量] ◇5架飞机 five planes ◇一架钢琴 a piano

架次 jiàcì [名] flight

架空 jiàkōng [动] build ... on stilts (*pt, pp* built)

架设 jiàshè [动] erect

架势 jiàshi [名] stance

架子 jiàzi [名] **1**(支撑物) rack ◇衣服架子 clothes rack **2**(指武术) position **3**(傲气) air ◇他一点都没有明星的架子。 He doesn't have the air of a star at all. **4**(结构) structure ◇这篇论文我已经搭好了架子。 I've already worked out the structure for this essay.

假 jià [名] holiday ♦暑假 summer holiday ♦病假 sick leave ▷另见 jiǎ

假期 jiàqī [名] holiday

假日 jiàrì [名] holiday

嫁 jià [动] **1**(结婚) marry **2**(转移) shift the blame

嫁祸于人 jià huò yú rén shift the blame onto another person ◇这是你自己的错，怎么能嫁祸于人？ It's your fault. How can you shift the blame onto someone else?

嫁接 jiàjiē [动] graft

嫁妆 jiàzhuang [名] dowry

尖 jiān I [形] **1**(锐利) pointed ◇这支铅笔削得太尖了。 This pencil is too sharp. **2**(指声音) shrill **3**(敏感) sensitive ◇他的眼睛很尖。 His eyesight is very acute. **4**(吝啬) stingy **5**(尖刻) biting II [动] ◇她尖着眼睛找别人的错。 She kept her eyes peeled in the search for peoples' mistakes. ◇这孩子尖着耳朵听父母说什么。 The child strained to hear what his parents were saying. III[名] **1**(尖端) tip ♦笔尖 pen tip **2**(精华) the best ◇他是我们中的尖子。 Of all of us he is the best.

尖端 jiānduān I [名] point ◇长矛的尖端 spearhead II [形] cutting-edge ◇尖端科技 the cutting edge of science and technology

尖刻 jiānkè [形] acrimonious

尖利 jiānlì [形] sharp

尖锐 jiānruì [形] **1**(锋利) sharp **2**(敏锐) penetrating ◇他的看法很尖锐。 He has insightful ideas. **3**(刺耳) shrill

尖酸刻薄 jiānsuān kèbó bitterly sarcastic

尖子 jiānzi [名] the best

奸 jiān I [形] **1**(奸诈) wicked ♦奸计 trickery **2**(不忠) treacherous ♦奸臣 treacherous official II [动] ♦通奸 adultery ♦强奸 rape III [名] traitor ♦内奸 traitor

奸猾 jiānhuá [名] treachery

奸计 jiānjì [名] trickery

奸商 jiānshāng [名] shark

奸污 jiānwū [动] rape

奸细 jiānxi [名] spy

奸险 jiānxiǎn [形] malicious

奸邪 jiānxié [形] crafty and evil

奸淫 jiānyín [动] rape

奸诈 jiānzhà [形] fraudulent

歼 jiān 见下文

歼灭 jiānmiè [动] annihilate

坚 jiān I [形] hard ♦坚冰 solid ice II [名] stronghold ◇坚不可摧 indestructible III[副] firmly ♦坚信 firmly believe

坚持 jiānchí [动] go on (*pt* went, *pp* gone) ◇你应该坚持锻炼身体。 You should go on taking exercise. ◇他坚持要我参加。 He insisted that I take part. ◇系主任一向坚持原则。 The head of department sticks to his principles.

坚定 jiāndìng [形] steadfast ◇我们要坚定地走正确的道路。 We must steadfastly keep to the correct path.

坚固 jiāngù [形] solid

坚果 jiānguǒ [名] nut

坚决 jiānjué [副] resolutely

坚强 jiānqiáng [形] strong ◇他意志坚强。 He is strong-willed.

坚韧 jiānrèn [形] tenacious

坚如磐石 jiān rú pánshí solid as a rock

坚实 jiānshí [形] solid

坚挺 jiāntǐng [形] strong

坚硬 jiānyìng [形] hard

坚贞 jiānzhēn [形] constant

间 jiān **I** [介] between ♦课间 between lessons **II** [名] **1**(范围) ♦晚间 in the evening ♦田间 field ◊人世间 in this world **2**(屋子) room ♦房间 room ◊洗手间 toilet ◊车间 workshop **III** [量] ◊两间客厅 two living rooms
▷另见 jiàn

间距 jiānjù [名] distance ◊高速行驶应注意行车间距。 When driving fast you must keep your distance from other cars.

肩 jiān 见下文

肩膀 jiānbǎng [名] shoulder

肩负 jiānfù [动] shoulder ◊父亲肩负着养家活口的责任。 Our father shoulders the responsibility of supporting the family. ◊他肩负了整项工程的组织工作。 He has taken on the administration of the whole project.

艰 jiān [形] difficult ♦艰辛 hardship

艰巨 jiānjù [形] formidable

艰苦 jiānkǔ [形] harsh

艰难 jiānnán [形] hard ◊他们生活艰难。 Their life is hard. ◊这位病人觉得走路很艰难。 The invalid finds it difficult to walk.

艰深 jiānshēn [形] abstruse

艰险 jiānxiǎn [形] hard and dangerous ◊路途极其艰险。 The journey is hard and dangerous.

监 jiān **I** [动] supervise ♦监视 keep watch **II** [名] **1**(监狱) prison ♦探监 visit a prison **2**(负责人) inspector ♦总监 chief-inspector

监测 jiāncè [动] monitor

监察 jiānchá [动] supervise

监督 jiāndū [动] supervise ◊舞台监督 stage manager

监工 jiāngōng **I** [动] oversee (*pt* oversaw, *pp* overseen) **II** [名] supervisor

监管 jiānguǎn [动] take charge of (*pt* took, *pp* taken)

监护 jiānhù [动] be a guardian ◊孩子由祖父母监护。 The child's grandparents are its guardians.

监禁 jiānjìn [动] take ... into custody (*pt* took, *pp* taken)

监考 jiānkǎo [动] invigilate

监控 jiānkòng [动] monitor and control

监牢 jiānláo [名] prison

监视 jiānshì [动] spy on

监听 jiāntīng [动] monitor ◊警方一直在监听罪犯。 The police are continuously monitoring criminals.

监狱 jiānyù [名] prison

兼 jiān [动] ◊这位董事长又兼着总经理的职位。 The Chairman of the Board is also the CEO.

兼并 jiānbìng [动] acquire

兼程 jiānchéng [动] advance at the double

兼而有之 jiān ér yǒu zhī be both ... and ... ◊一次学术性与娱乐性兼而有之的活动 an activity that is both educational and fun

兼顾 jiāngù [动] be concerned about both ... and ... ◊公司执行安全与效率兼顾的原则。 The company philosophy is to be concerned about both safety and efficiency.

兼任 jiānrèn [动] be concurrently

兼容 jiānróng [动] be compatible

兼容性 jiānróngxìng [名] compatibility

兼收并蓄 jiān shōu bìng xù incorporate diverse elements

兼职 jiānzhí [动] have more than one job ◊由于兼职太多，他终于累垮了。 Because he had too many jobs, he eventually collapsed with exhaustion. ◊兼职教师 part-time teacher

笺 jiān [名] writing paper ♦信笺 letter paper

缄 jiān 见下文

缄口 jiānkǒu [动] (书) hold one's tongue (*pt, pp* held)

缄默 jiānmò [动] (书) keep silent (*pt, pp* kept)

煎 jiān [动] **1**(油炸) fry ◇煎鸡蛋 fry an egg **2**(水煮) decoct

煎熬 jiān'áo [动] suffer ◇他承受了许多煎熬。He's experienced a lot of suffering.

拣 jiǎn [动] choose (*pt* chose, *pp* chosen)

拣选 jiǎnxuǎn [动] select

茧 jiǎn [名] **1**(指昆虫) cocoon ♦蚕茧 silkworm cocoon **2**(指手) callus

柬 jiǎn [名] card ♦请柬 invitation

柬帖 jiǎntiě [名] card

俭 jiǎn [形] frugal

俭朴 jiǎnpǔ [形] economical

俭省 jiǎnshěng [形] frugal

捡 jiǎn [动] pick ... up ◇谁捡到了我的手表? Who picked up my watch?

检 jiǎn [动] **1**(检查) examine ♦体检 medical examination **2**(检点) show restraint (*pt* showed, *pp* shown)

检测 jiǎncè [动] determine

检查 jiǎnchá **I** [动] examine ◇明天我要检查身体。I'm going to be medically examined tomorrow. **II** [名] self-criticism

检察 jiǎnchá [名] procuratorial work

检点 jiǎndiǎn **I** [动] check **II** [形] cautious

检举 jiǎnjǔ [动] accuse

检索 jiǎnsuǒ [动] look ... up ◇我喜欢在网上检索信息。I like to look up information on the Internet.

检讨 jiǎntǎo [动] examine

检修 jiǎnxiū [动] overhaul

检验 jiǎnyàn [动] inspect

检疫 jiǎnyì [动] quarantine

检阅 jiǎnyuè [动] inspect

减 jiǎn [动] **1**(减去) subtract ◇3减2等于1。Three minus two is one. **2**(减少) reduce ♦裁减 cut down **3**(降低) decrease ♦减退 fail

减产 jiǎnchǎn [动] ◇战争使石油大幅度减产。The war caused a large-scale drop in oil production.

减法 jiǎnfǎ [名] subtraction

减肥 jiǎnféi [动] slim ◇减肥食谱 diet

减缓 jiǎnhuǎn [动] slow down

减免 jiǎnmiǎn [动] reduce

减轻 jiǎnqīng [动] reduce

减色 jiǎnsè [动] spoil

减少 jiǎnshǎo [动] reduce

减员 jiǎnyuán [动] cut staff (*pt, pp* cut)

剪 jiǎn **I** [名] scissors (*pl*) **II** [动] **1**(铰) cut (*pt, pp* cut) ◇我该剪头了。I need to get my hair cut. ◇剪羊毛 shear a sheep **2**(除去) eliminate

剪裁 jiǎncái [动] cut (*pt, pp* cut) ◇文章太长，需要剪裁。The article is too long – it needs cutting. ◇这条裙子是我自己剪裁的。I made this skirt myself.

剪彩 jiǎncǎi [动] cut a ribbon (*pt, pp* cut) ◇市长将为开幕式剪彩。The mayor is cutting the ribbon at the opening ceremony.

剪辑 jiǎnjí [动] edit ◇电影剪辑 film editing

剪贴 jiǎntiē [动] cut and paste (*pt, pp* cut)

剪影 jiǎnyǐng [名] silhouette

简 jiǎn **I** [形] simple ♦简单 simple **II** [动] simplify ♦简化 simplify

简报 jiǎnbào [名] briefing ◇要闻简报 news bulletin

简编 jiǎnbiān [名] concise edition

简便 jiǎnbiàn [形] handy

简称 jiǎnchēng [名] abbreviation

简单 jiǎndān [形] **1**(不复杂) simple ◇他头脑简单。He's simple-minded. ◇医生简单地处理了他的伤口。The doctor treated his wound simply. **2**(草率) casual ◇不可用简单的方式对待学生的思想变化。Changes in student attitudes shouldn't be treated lightly. ◇简单从事 treat things casually **3**(平凡) ◇这孩子能说两门外语，真不简

单。 It is quite extraordinary that this child can speak two foreign languages.

简短 jiǎnduǎn [形] brief

简化 jiǎnhuà [动] simplify

简洁 jiǎnjié [形] concise

简捷 jiǎnjié [形] direct ◇这种简捷的方法真省时。 The direct method really saves time. ◇他说话简捷，从不拐弯抹角。 He always gets straight to the point and doesn't beat about the bush.

简介 jiǎnjiè [名] synopsis (*pl* synopses)

简历 jiǎnlì [名] CV (英), resumé (美)

简练 jiǎnliàn [形] concise

简陋 jiǎnlòu [形] crude

简略 jiǎnlüè [形] brief ◇他说话一贯很简略。 What he says is always very sketchy. ◇他简略介绍了公司的情况。 He gave a brief description of the situation at the company.

简明 jiǎnmíng [形] concise

简朴 jiǎnpǔ [形] simple ◇她穿着简朴。 She dresses simply.

简体字 jiǎntǐzì [名] simplified character

简写 jiǎnxiě [动] abridge

简要 jiǎnyào [形] brief

简易 jiǎnyì [形] simple

简直 jiǎnzhí [副] simply ◇这简直是浪费口舌。 This is simply a waste of breath.

简装 jiǎnzhuāng [名] standard edition

碱 jiǎn [名] alkali

见 jiàn **I** [动] **1**(看到) see (*pt* saw, *pp* seen) ♦常见 common ♦罕见 rare ◇我们俩好久没见了。 We have not seen each other in a long time. **2**(接触) come into contact with (*pt* came, *pp* come) ◇汽油见火就着。 Petrol ignites on contact with a flame. **3**(看得出) be visible ♦见效 take effect **4**(参照) see (*pt* saw, *pp* seen) ◇见上图 see the above diagram **5**(会见) meet (*pt, pp* met) ♦接见 receive ◇我下午见校长。 I'm meeting the principal this afternoon. **II** [名] opinion ♦偏见 prejudice **III**[助动] (书) ◇请见谅。 Please excuse me.

见不得 jiàn bu dé [动] **1**(不能接触) be unable to stand exposure to ◇这种细菌见不得光。 This type of bacteria can't stand exposure to light. **2**(不能公开) be unmentionable ◇这个政客做了很多见不得人的事。 This politician has done a lot of shameful things. **3**(不能忍受) be unable to endure ◇我见不得别人可怜的样子。 I can't bear seeing others suffer.

见长 jiàncháng [动] be good at

见地 jiàndì [名] insight ◇这篇文章颇有见地。 This essay is quite insightful.

见多识广 jiàn duō shí guǎng have wide experience

见方 jiànfāng [名] square

见缝插针 jiàn fèng chā zhēn take every opportunity

见怪 jiànguài [动] take offence (英) 或 offense (美) (*pt* took, *pp* taken) ◇他说话不得体，请别见怪。 He is talking inappropriately – please don't take offence.

见鬼 jiànguǐ [动] **1**(毁灭) go to hell ◇让陈旧的传统观念见鬼去吧！ To hell with those old-fashioned ideas! **2**(奇怪) odd

见好 jiànhǎo [动] get better ◇他的病见好了。 He is getting better.

见机行事 jiàn jī xíng shì play … by ear ◇情况复杂，你就见机行事吧。 It is a complex situation – you'd better play it by ear.

见解 jiànjiě [名] opinion

见面 jiànmiàn [动] meet (*pt, pp* met)

见仁见智 jiàn rén jiàn zhì have different opinions

见识 jiànshi **I** [动] experience **II** [名] experience ◇增长见识 widen one's experience

见外 jiànwài [形] treat … as a stranger ◇大家都是朋友，请别见外。 We are all friends – please don't stand on ceremony.

见微知著 jiàn wēi zhī zhù recognize telltale signs

见闻 jiànwén [名] information

见习 jiànxí [动] learn on the job ◇见习记者 trainee reporter

见笑 jiànxiào [动] laugh at

见义勇为 jiàn yì yǒng wéi stand up for what is right

见异思迁 jiàn yì sī qiān be fickle

见长 jiànzhǎng [动] shoot up (*pt, pp* shot)

见证 jiànzhèng **I** [动] witness **II** [名] clear proof

见证人 jiànzhèngrén [名] witness

件 jiàn **I** [量] item ◇一件衣裳 an item of clothing ◇两件事 two things **II** [名] correspondence ◇急件 urgent letter

间 jiàn **I** [名] space ♦间隙 interval ◇亲密无间 as thick as thieves **II** [动] **1**(使分隔) keep apart (*pt, pp* kept) ♦间隔 separate **2**(使不和) sow discord (*pt* sowed, *pp* sown) ♦离间 alienate **3**(使稀少) thin … out ▷另见 jiān

间谍 jiàndié [名] spy

间断 jiànduàn [动] interrupt ◇大雨一夜没有间断。The rain didn't let up all night.

间隔 jiàngé **I** [名] distance **II** [动] divide

间或 jiànhuò [副] (书) occasionally

间接 jiànjiē [形] indirect ◇这些经验我是间接得到的。I gained this experience indirectly.

间隙 jiànxì [名] gap ◇他们利用会议间隙到城里逛了逛。They took advantage of a gap between meetings to go into town.

间歇 jiànxiē [名] intermission

饯 见下文

饯行 jiànxíng [动] give a farewell dinner (*pt* gave, *pp* given)

建 jiàn [动] **1**(建造) build (*pt, pp* built) ♦扩建 extend **2**(建立) found ♦建国 found a new state **3**(提出) propose ♦建议 propose

建交 jiànjiāo [动] establish diplomatic relations

建立 jiànlì [动] establish ◇两个国家建立了友好关系。The two countries have established friendly relations.

建设 jiànshè [动] build (*pt, pp* built) ◇建设未来 build for the future

建树 jiànshù [名] contribution ◇他在物理研究方面颇有建树。He has made a significant contribution to physics.

建议 jiànyì [动] propose ◇他建议重新装修办公室。He proposed that we redecorate the office. ◇她提了很多合理的建议。She made a lot of sensible proposals.

建造 jiànzào [动] build (*pt, pp* built)

建制 jiànzhì [名] system ◇行政建制 administrative system

建筑 jiànzhù **I** [动] build (*pt, pp* built) ◇建筑房屋 build houses **II** [名] building ◇高层建筑 high-rise building ◇建筑工地 building site

建筑师 jiànzhùshī [名] architect

荐 jiàn [动] recommend ♦推荐 recommend ◇推荐信 letter of recommendation

荐举 jiànjǔ [动] recommend

贱 jiàn [形] **1**(便宜) cheap **2**(地位低) lowly ♦贫贱 poor and lowly **3**(卑鄙) contemptible ♦下贱 contemptible

贱民 jiànmín [名] rabble

剑 jiàn [名] sword

剑拔弩张 jiàn bá nǔ zhāng at each other's throats

涧 jiàn [名] gully ♦山涧 mountain stream

健 jiàn **I** [形] ♦强健 strong and healthy ♦健全 sound **II** [动] **1**(使强健) strengthen ♦健身 keep fit **2**(善于) be good at ♦健谈 be good at small-talk

健步如飞 jiàn bù rú fēi be a good walker

健儿 jiàn'ér [名] good athlete

健将 jiànjiàng [名] great sportsman

健康 jiànkāng [形] healthy ◇奶奶身体很健康。 Granny is very healthy. ◇他已经恢复了健康。 He's already recovered his health.

健美 jiànměi [形] strong and handsome ◇他体格健美。 His physique is very good.

健全 jiànquán [形] sound

健身 jiànshēn [动] keep fit (*pt, pp* kept) ◇健身运动 fitness activity

健谈 jiàntán [形] glib

健忘 jiànwàng [形] forgetful

健旺 jiànwàng [形] thriving

健在 jiànzài [动] be still alive

健壮 jiànzhuàng [形] robust

舰 jiàn [名] warship ◇巡洋舰 cruiser ♦舰队 fleet ◇航空母舰 aircraft-carrier

舰只 jiànzhī [名] naval vessel

渐 jiàn [副] gradually ◇天气渐暖。 The weather is getting warmer.

渐渐 jiànjiàn [副] gradually ◇物价渐渐上涨。 Prices are gradually going up.

渐进 jiànjìn [动] advance gradually ◇掌握一门语言是个渐进过程。 Mastering a language is a gradual process.

渐入佳境 jiàn rù jiājìng gradually improve

践 jiàn [动] 1 (踩) trample ♦践踏 trample 2 (履行) carry out ♦实践 carry out ♦践约 keep an appointment

践踏 jiàntà [动] trample ◇请勿践踏草地！ Keep off the grass!

践约 jiànyuē [动] keep an appointment (*pt, pp* kept)

毽 jiàn 见下文

毽子 jiànzi [名] shuttlecock

腱 jiàn [名] tendon

溅 jiàn [动] splash

溅落 jiànluò [动] splash down

鉴 jiàn I [动] 1 (照见) reflect ◇水清可鉴。 The water is so clear you can see reflections in it. 2 (细看) scrutinize ♦鉴别 distinguish II [名] warning ◇引以为鉴 take … as a warning

鉴别 jiànbié [动] distinguish ◇鉴别是非 distinguish between right and wrong

鉴定 jiàndìng [名] appraisal ◇经理对安娜的表现做了客观的鉴定。 The manager gave an objective appraisal of Anna's performance.

鉴赏 jiànshǎng [动] appreciate ◇鉴赏艺术作品 appreciate artworks

鉴于 jiànyú [连] ◇鉴于天气不好，我们决定取消比赛。 Seeing that the weather was bad, we decided to cancel the competition.

键 jiàn [名] key ♦键盘 keyboard ♦琴键 key

键盘 jiànpán [名] keyboard

箭 jiàn 见下文

箭步 jiànbù [名] big stride

江 jiāng [名] 1 (大河) river 2 (长江) Yangtze

江河日下 jiāng hé rì xià go from bad to worse

江湖 jiānghú [名] rivers and lakes (*pl*) ◇江湖艺人 itinerant entertainer

江郎才尽 Jiāngláng cái jìn lose one's touch

江山 jiāngshān [名] 1 (江河和山岭) rivers and mountains (*pl*) 2 (国家) the country

将 jiāng I [副] ◇他将成为一名医生。 He is going to become a doctor. II [助] ◇丑闻传将开来。 News of the scandal began to spread. ◇他把一本字典扔将过去。 He threw over a dictionary. III [动] 1 (下棋用语) check 2 (激) egg … on IV [介] with ◇将功折罪 atone for a crime with good deeds ◇请将车停在路边。 Please stop the car by the side of the road. ◇他将孩子送到了私立学校。 He sent the child to a private school.
▷另见 jiàng

将错就错 jiāng cuò jiù cuò make the

best of a bad situation

将功补过 jiāng gōng bǔ guò atone for a crime with good deeds

将计就计 jiāng jì jiù jì beat someone at their own game

将近 jiāngjìn [动] be approximately ◇这位足球明星的月收入将近3万镑。 This football star has a monthly income of approximately £30,000.

将就 jiāngjiu [动] make do with ◇饭菜不好，将就吃吧。 The food isn't great, but we'll just have to make do with it.

将军 jiāngjūn I [名] general II [动] challenge

将来 jiānglái [名] future ◇不远的将来，人类就能消灭艾滋病。 In the not-too-distant future, we are going to be able to wipe out AIDS.

将心比心 jiāng xīn bǐ xīn have empathy for

将信将疑 jiāng xìn jiāng yí only half believe

将要 jiāngyào [副] ◇她将要做妈妈了。 She is going to be a mother.

姜 jiāng [名] ginger

浆 jiāng I [名] paste ♦纸浆 pulp ♦糖浆 syrup II [动] starch ♦浆洗 starch

僵 jiāng [形] **1**(僵硬) stiff ◇我浑身冻僵了。 I'm frozen. **2**(相持不下) deadlocked ◇说话注意点，别把事情弄僵了。 Be careful what you say – you don't want to reach a deadlock.

僵持 jiāngchí [动] refuse to budge

僵化 jiānghuà [动] become rigid ◇他思想变得越来越僵化了。 He's becoming more and more rigid in the way he thinks.

僵局 jiāngjú [名] deadlock ◇谈判陷入僵局。 The talks reached a deadlock.

僵尸 jiāngshī [名] corpse

僵死 jiāngsǐ [动] be dead

僵硬 jiāngyìng [形] stiff ◇计算机前坐久了浑身会僵硬。 If you sit in front of a computer a long time you get stiff.

缰 jiāng [名] rein ♦缰绳 rein

疆 jiāng [名] border ♦边疆 frontier

疆场 jiāngchǎng [名] battlefield

疆界 jiāngjiè [名] border

疆土 jiāngtǔ [名] territory

疆域 jiāngyù [名] domain

讲 jiǎng [动] **1**(说) speak (*pt* spoke, *pp* spoken) ◇讲英语 speak English **2**(解释) explain ◇他在给我们讲计算机的用法。 He is explaining to us how to use the computer. **3**(谈) discuss ◇讲条件 discuss terms **4**(提及) ◇讲足球，他可是专家。 As for football, he's quite an expert. **5**(讲求) emphasize ◇讲卫生 pay attention to hygiene

讲和 jiǎnghé [动] make peace

讲话 jiǎnghuà [动] **1**(说话) speak (*pt* spoke, *pp* spoken) ◇上课不许讲话。 No talking in class. **2**(发言) address ◇校长要来给我们讲话。 The principal is coming to address us.

讲解 jiǎngjiě [动] explain

讲究 jiǎngjiu I [动] be particular about II [名] art ◇养花大有讲究。 Growing flowers is quite an art. III[形] exquisite ◇他穿着一向讲究。 He is always exquisitely dressed.

讲理 jiǎnglǐ [动] be reasonable ◇他这个人不讲理。 He is quite unreasonable.

讲排场 jiǎng páichang [动] be ostentatious

讲评 jiǎngpíng [动] critique

讲情 jiǎngqíng [动] intercede ◇她为逃学的儿子向老师讲情。 She interceded with the teacher for her son, who'd been playing truant.

讲师 jiǎngshī [名] lecturer

讲授 jiǎngshòu [动] teach (*pt, pp* taught)

讲述 jiǎngshù [动] relate

讲台 jiǎngtái [名] dais

讲坛 jiǎngtán [名] forum

讲学 jiǎngxué [动] give lectures (*pt* gave, *pt* given)

讲演 jiǎngyǎn [动] lecture ◊他的讲演很鼓舞人心。 His lectures are inspiring.

讲义 jiǎngyì [名] teaching materials (*pl*)

讲座 jiǎngzuò [名] course of lectures ◊系列讲座 lecture series

奖 jiǎng **I** [动] encourage ♦夸奖 praise **II** [名] award ♦奖品 prize

奖杯 jiǎngbēi [名] cup

奖惩 jiǎngchéng [名] reward and punish

奖金 jiǎngjīn [名] bonus

奖励 jiǎnglì [动] encourage and reward ◊物质奖励 material incentive

奖牌 jiǎngpái [名] medal

奖品 jiǎngpǐn [名] trophy

奖券 jiǎngquàn [名] lottery ticket

奖赏 jiǎngshǎng [动] reward ◊他因科研成果而获得奖赏。 He gained an award for his scientific achievements.

奖学金 jiǎngxuéjīn [名] scholarship

奖状 jiǎngzhuàng [名] certificate

桨 jiǎng [名] oar

匠 jiàng [名] **1**(工匠) craftsman (*pl* craftsmen) ♦木匠 carpenter **2**(书) (名家) master ♦文学巨匠 great literary master

匠人 jiàngrén [名] craftsman (*pl* craftsmen)

匠心 jiàngxīn [名] (书) craftsmanship

降 jiàng [动] **1**(落下) drop ♦降雪 snow **2**(降低) reduce ♦降价 reduce prices
▷另见 xiáng

降低 jiàngdī [动] reduce ◊降低生活开支 reduce living expenses

降格以求 jiàng gé yǐ qiú compromise one's standards

降落 jiàngluò [动] land

降生 jiàngshēng [动] be born

降温 jiàngwēn [动] **1**(变天) cool ◊明天开始降温。 It will start getting cooler tomorrow. **2**(缓和) wane ◊暑假结束后，旅游热开始降温。 Once the summer vacation is over, interest in travel starts to wane.

将 jiàng [名] **1**(军官) general ♦上将 general **2**(总指挥) commander-in-chief
▷另见 jiāng

将领 jiànglǐng [名] general

将士 jiàngshì [名] officers and men

绛 jiàng [形] crimson

强 jiàng [形] stubborn ♦倔强 stubborn
▷另见 qiáng, qiǎng

强嘴 jiàngzuǐ [动] answer … back

酱 jiàng **I** [名] **1**(调味品) soya bean (英) 或 soybean (美) paste ♦酱油 soy sauce **2**(糊状食品) paste ♦果酱 jam **II** [形] ♦酱肘子 knuckle of pork in soy sauce

酱菜 jiàngcài [名] vegetables in soy sauce

酱油 jiàngyóu [名] soy sauce

犟 jiàng [形] obstinate

犟劲 jiàngjìn [名] stubbornness

糨 jiàng [形] thick

糨糊 jiànghu [名] paste

交 jiāo **I** [动] **1**(交出) hand … in ◊请按时交作业。Please hand in your homework on time. **2**(付给) pay (*pt, pp* paid) ◊这个月的房租你交了吗？Have you paid this month's rent? **3**(托付) entrust ◊我要把这事交给他办。I am going to entrust it to him. **4**(交叉) cross ◊她站立不动，双臂交于胸前。She stood still, with her arms crossed in front of her. **5**(结交) associate with ♦交友 make friends **6**(书) (到) arrive at ◊时令已交立冬。It's already the beginning of winter. **II** [名] **1**(交情) friendship ♦深交 deep friendship **2**(交接处) boundary ◊小镇位于两省之交。The town is situated on the boundary between the two provinces. ◊此时正是秋冬之交。We are just on the cusp between autumn and winter.

III [副] ◇风雨交加的夜晚 a night of both wind and rain ◇她小时候过着饥寒交迫的生活。When she was young she experienced both hunger and cold.

交白卷 jiāo báijuàn [动] **1**(指考试) hand in a blank examination paper **2**(喻) ◇到现在还没开始，你想明天交白卷啊？ You still haven't even started. You won't have done it by tomorrow, will you?

交班 jiāobān [动] hand over to the next shift

交兵 jiāobīng [动] (书) engage militarily

交叉 jiāochā **I** [动] **1**(相交) intersect ◇一条公路与铁路在此交叉。A highway and a railway intersect here. **2**(穿插) alternate ◇各种体育活动交叉进行，学生会更感兴趣。If sports activities alternate with each other, students will find it more fun. **II** [形] overlapping ◇两篇论文有交叉的内容。The two theses overlap in content. ◇交叉学科 interdisciplinary subjects

交差 jiāochāi [动] report ◇工作完不成，我们没办法向上级交差。If we don't finish the work, we'll have nothing to report to management.

交错 jiāocuò [动] (书) crisscross

交代 jiāodài [动] **1**(移交) hand ... over ◇临走前，我已经向一位同事交代了工作。Before I left I handed my work over to a colleague. **2**(说明) explain ◇你要把有关政策交代清楚。You need to explain the relevant policy clearly. **3**(嘱咐) instruct

交底 jiāodǐ [动] lay one's cards on the table (*pt, pp* laid)

交点 jiāodiǎn [名] intersection ◇这里是两条铁路的交点。This is the intersection of two railway lines.

交锋 jiāofēng [动] **1**(交战) engage in combat **2**(比赛) compete ◇两支足球队将在上海交锋。The two football teams will compete in Shanghai.

交付 jiāofù [动] **1**(交纳) pay (*pt, pp* paid) ◇房客还没有交付租金。The tenant has not yet paid his rent. **2**(交给) hand ... over ◇交付任务 hand over a task ◇那座新的办公楼即将交付使用。That new office building is about to be made available for use.

交割 jiāogē [动] complete a transaction ◇双方已将每一笔货款交割清楚。The parties have completed payment transactions for the consignments.

交互 jiāohù [副] **1**(一起) together ◇做这项工作需要两种工具交互使用。For this job you need to use the two tools together. **2**(替换) in turn ◇队员们交互上场，免得过度劳累。The players took it in turns to go on, so as not to get too tired. **3**(互相) ◇老师让我们交互批改听写。The teacher asked us to correct each other's dictations.

交换 jiāohuàn [动] exchange ◇毕业前，同学们互相交换礼物。Before graduation, students exchange presents with each other. ◇我和她交换了座位。I swapped my seat with her. ◇农民们正在市场上交换农产品。The farmers trade agricultural produce in the market.

交火 jiāohuǒ [动] engage in battle

交集 jiāojí [动] mix ◇听到这个消息，她悲喜交集。On hearing the news, she had mixed feelings of joy and sorrow.

交际 jiāojì [动] socialize ◇他不善与人交际。He is not good at socializing. ◇语言是重要的交际工具。Language is an important tool for social interaction.

交加 jiāojiā [动] ◇在一个风雪交加的夜晚，他突然出现在村头。On a night of wind and snow, he suddenly appeared in the village.

交接 jiāojiē [动] **1**(连接) ◇现正是春夏交接之际。Now is the time when spring is turning into summer. **2**(移交) hand ... over **3**(结交) associate with ◇她交接的人都是上流社会的。The people she associates with are all upper class.

交界 jiāojiè [动] share a border

交警 jiāojǐng [名] traffic police

交口称誉 jiāo kǒu chēng yù be universally praised

交流 jiāoliú [动] exchange ◇交流学习经验 exchange learning techniques ◇老师们就传统教育问题交流了看法。The teachers exchanged views on traditional education.

交配 jiāopèi [动] (动物) mate

交情 jiāoqing [名] friendship

交涉 jiāoshè [动] negotiate ◇关于人质问题，双方已经过多次交涉。The two sides have negotiated several times over the hostage.

交手 jiāoshǒu [动] compete ◇我和他还从未交过手。I've never competed against him.

交谈 jiāotán [动] talk ◇两个好朋友交谈了一整夜。The two friends talked together the whole night.

交替 jiāotì [动] **1** (更换) ◇中国人常在新旧年交替时吃饺子。Chinese people often eat dumplings to see in the New Year. **2** (轮换) alternate ◇工作和休息应交替进行。One should alternate work and relaxation.

交通 jiāotōng [名] **1** (交流的工具) communications (*pl*) **2** (运输) traffic ◇这个地区的公路交通繁忙而有序。Road traffic in the area is heavy but well-regulated.

交头接耳 jiāo tóu jiē ěr (贬) whisper to each other ◇这俩学生在课堂上老是交头接耳。The two students are always whispering to each other in class.

交往 jiāowǎng [动] have contact ◇他与国际友人交往频繁。He is in frequent contact with international friends. ◇他交往了很多不三不四的朋友。He has relations with a lot of dubious characters. ◇这小伙子不爱交往。This young man is not very sociable. ◇我们与外界的交往日益广泛。Our contact with the outside world is becoming more and more extensive.

交响乐 jiāoxiǎngyuè [名] symphony

交椅 jiāoyǐ [名] **1** (折叠椅) folding chair **2** (喻) (地位) position ◇她在部门坐上了第一把交椅。She occupies the highest position in the department.

交易 jiāoyì **I** [动] trade ◇他们在交易股票。They are trading shares. ◇新产品开始上市交易。The new products have gone onto the market. ◇电子市场里交易很红火。Trade in the electronics market is flourishing. **II** [名] transaction ◇一笔划算的交易 a good deal

交谊 jiāoyì [名] (书) friendship

交战 jiāozhàn [动] engage in war

交织 jiāozhī [动] intertwine ◇两棵大树枝叶交织在一起。The branches of the two trees are intertwined. ◇喜悦和伤感交织在一起。Joy is mingled with sadness.

郊 jiāo [名] suburbs (*pl*) ♦市郊 suburbs (*pl*) ♦郊外 outskirts (*pl*) ◇他在北郊买了房子。He bought a house on the northern outskirts of the city.

郊区 jiāoqū [名] suburbs (*pl*) ◇他住在北京郊区。He lives in the Beijing suburbs.

浇 jiāo [动] **1** (灌溉) irrigate **2** (洒水) water ◇浇花 water the flowers **3** (浸透) soak ◇他被浇了一身雨。He was soaked in the rain. **4** (浇铸) cast (*pt, pp* cast)

浇灌 jiāoguàn [动] **1** (灌溉) irrigate ◇浇灌土地 irrigate the land ◇浇灌花园 water a garden **2** (灌注) pour ◇他们向墙体内浇灌了混凝土。They poured concrete into the wall frame.

娇 jiāo **I** [形] **1** (柔嫩) delicate ◇嫩红娇绿 delicate blossoms and leaves **2** (秀美) lovely ◇江山如此多娇。The scenery is so lovely. **3** (娇气) fragile **II** [动] spoil ◇这个女孩儿被父母娇坏了。The girl has been spoiled by her parents.

娇滴滴 jiāodīdī [形] coy

娇惯 jiāoguàn [动] pamper

娇贵 jiāogui [形] fragile ◇刚走一小段路就受不了，怎么这么娇贵？Walking just a short distance is too much for you – how come you are so fragile? ◇这个花瓶很娇贵，搬的时候要小心。This vase is fragile – be careful when you move it.

娇嫩 jiāonen [形] delicate

娇气 jiāoqì I [形] fragile II [名] fussiness ◇我们要想办法去掉这孩子的娇气。We've got to find a way of stopping the child from being so fussy.

娇生惯养 jiāo shēng guàn yǎng be pampered all one's life

娇小玲珑 jiāoxiǎo línglóng exquisite ◇她长得娇小玲珑。She looks exquisite.

娇纵 jiāozòng [动] indulge

姣 jiāo [形] (书) good-looking ♦姣美 beautiful

姣好 jiāohǎo [形] beautiful ◇她相貌姣好，身材苗条。She has a beautiful face and a slender figure.

骄 jiāo [形] 1(骄傲) arrogant ♦骄气 arrogance 2(书) (猛烈) fierce ◇7月的西安，骄阳似火。In Xi'an in July the sun is incredibly fierce.

骄傲 jiāo'ào I [形] 1(傲慢) arrogant 2(自豪) proud II [名] pride ◇5，000年悠久的历史是中国人民的骄傲。Their 5,000 years of history is the pride of the Chinese people.

骄横 jiāohèng [形] overbearing ◇他态度骄横，让人无法忍受。People can't stand his overbearing attitude.

骄气 jiāoqì [名] arrogance

骄奢淫逸 jiāoshēyínyì dissipated

骄子 jiāozǐ [名] favourite (英) 或 favorite (美) son

胶 jiāo I [名] 1(黏性物质) glue ♦万能胶 all-purpose glue ♦树胶 resin 2(橡胶) rubber ♦胶鞋 rubber boots (*pl*) II [动] glue ◇请把我的皮鞋胶上吧。Could you glue my shoes back together, please.

胶合 jiāohé [动] glue … together ◇把这两张纸胶合在一起吧。Let's glue these two pieces of paper together.

胶卷 jiāojuǎn [名] film ◇我买了一个彩色胶卷儿。I bought a roll of colour (英) 或 color (美) film.

胶囊 jiāonáng [名] capsule

胶着 jiāozhuó [动] (喻) stalemate

教 jiāo [动] teach (*pt, pp* taught) ◇他在中学教计算机。He teaches computing in a middle school. ◇我教孩子画画。I teach children drawing.
▷另见 jiào

教学 jiāoxué [动] teach (*pt, pp* taught) ◇他在一个小山村教学。He teaches in a mountain village.

椒 jiāo [名] 1(胡椒) pepper ♦胡椒 pepper 2(辣椒) chilli ♦辣椒 chilli

焦 jiāo I [形] 1(成黄黑色) burnt ◇米饭烧焦了。The rice is burnt. ◇孩子的衣服烤焦了。The child's clothes are scorched. ◇北京烤鸭外焦里嫩。Peking duck is charred on the outside and tender on the inside. 2(喻) (干) dry ◇她说得口焦舌燥。She spoke until her mouth was parched. 3(着急) agitated ♦心焦 feel agitated II [名] coke

焦点 jiāodiǎn [名] 1(物) focal point ◇主焦点 main focus 2(喻) (关键) focus ◇选课问题成了同学们议论的焦点。The problem of choosing courses has become a focus of discussion among the students. ◇她光彩夺目，成了晚会的焦点。She was stunningly beautiful and became the focus of attention at the party.

焦急 jiāojí [形] anxious ◇她为母亲的健康而感到焦急。She's anxious about her mother's health. ◇她焦急地等待着丈夫归来。She waited anxiously for her husband to return.

焦距 jiāojù [名] (物) focal length

焦虑 jiāolǜ [形] anxious

焦头烂额 jiāo tóu làn é be in a terrible way

焦躁 jiāozào [形] restless

焦灼 jiāozhuó [形] (书) anxious

跤 jiāo [名] fall ♦摔跤 fall down

蕉 jiāo [名] banana ♦香蕉 banana

礁 jiāo [名] reef

礁石 jiāoshí [名] reef

嚼 jiáo [动] chew
▷另见 jué

角 jiǎo [名] 1(指动物) horn ♦羊角 ram's horn 2(军号) bugle 3(数) angle ♦直角 right angle 4(角落) corner ♦墙角 corner of a wall
▷另见 jué

角度 jiǎodù [名] 1(数) angle 2(视角) point of view ◇从不同角度分析 analyze from different points of view ◇我们可以从多个角度来看待这个问题。We must look at this problem from different angles.

角落 jiǎoluò [名] corner ◇屋子的角落里挂了很多蜘蛛网。There were a lot of spider webs in the corner of the room.

侥 jiǎo 见下文

侥幸 jiǎoxìng [形] lucky ◇对考试不要心存侥幸。In exams you shouldn't put your faith in luck.

佼 jiǎo [形] (书) beautiful

佼佼 jiǎojiǎo [形] (书) outstanding ◇佼佼者 outstanding figure

狡 jiǎo [形] cunning ♦狡计 crafty trick

狡辩 jiǎobiàn [动] use specious arguments

狡猾 jiǎohuá [形] cunning

狡诈 jiǎozhà [形] deceitful

饺 jiǎo [名] Chinese dumpling ♦水饺儿 Chinese dumpling

绞 jiǎo [动] 1(扭) twist 2(勒死) hang (*pt, pp* hanged) ♦绞死 hang

绞杀 jiǎoshā [动] hang

绞刑 jiǎoxíng [名] hanging

铰 jiǎo [动] cut (*pt, pp* cut) ◇这张纸太大，用剪子铰一下。This piece of paper is too big, so let's cut it down with the scissors.

矫 jiǎo I [动] correct ♦矫正 correct ◇他现已痛矫前非。He's cleaned up his act now. II [形] strong

矫健 jiǎojiàn [形] vigorous

矫揉造作 jiǎo róu zào zuò forced ◇那个演员的表演矫揉造作。That actor's performance was very forced. ◇她矫揉造作的姿态令人反感。Her affected manners are off-putting.

矫枉过正 jiǎo wǎng guò zhèng overcompensate ◇因超重而节食固然不错，但如果矫枉过正，就会造成营养不良。It's good to go on a diet if you're overweight. But if you go too far you'll end up malnourished.

矫正 jiǎozhèng [动] correct ◇你应该好好矫正一下发音。You really should correct your pronunciation.

皎 jiǎo [形] bright ♦皎月 bright moon

皎洁 jiǎojié [形] bright

脚 jiǎo [名] 1(指人、动物) foot (*pl* feet) ♦脚印 footprint 2(指物体) base ♦墙脚 base of a wall ♦山脚 foot of a mountain

脚本 jiǎoběn [名] script ◇电视剧脚本 television script

脚步 jiǎobù [名] 1(步伐) step ◇重重的脚步声 the sound of heavy footsteps 2(速度) pace

脚镣 jiǎoliào [名] shackles (*pl*)

脚踏两只船 jiǎo tà liǎng zhī chuán (喻) (贬) sit on the fence

脚踏实地 jiǎo tà shídì keep one's feet on the ground ◇我们要脚踏实地地工作。It's important to have a down-to-earth attitude towards work.

脚注 jiǎozhù [名] footnote

搅 jiǎo [动] 1(搅拌) stir ◇把汤搅匀了再喝。Stir the soup before drinking it. 2(混杂) mix ◇不要把这两件事搅在一块儿。Don't mix these two things. 3(搅扰) disturb ◇噪音搅得我无法入睡。The noise disturbed me so much I couldn't sleep.

搅拌 jiǎobàn [动] stir ◇他往咖啡里加了点糖，搅拌了一下。He put some sugar in the coffee and stirred it. ◇把饺子馅儿搅拌均匀。Mix the dumpling filling until smooth.

搅和 jiǎohuo [动] 1(混合) mix ◇别把这两种东西搅和在一起。Don't mix these two things together 2(扰乱) mess ... up ◇这件事全让你给搅

和了！ You've completely messed it up!

缴 jiǎo [动] **1**(交纳) pay (*pt, pp* paid) ◊缴租金 pay the rent **2**(收缴) seize

缴获 jiǎohuò [动] seize

叫 jiào **I** [动] **1** (喊叫) shout ◊他们听到这个好消息都叫了起来。When they heard the good news they shouted for joy. **2** (招呼) call ◊他被人叫出去了。Somebody called him outside. **3** (菜、车) order ♦叫菜 order food ◊叫车 order a cab **4** (称为) be called ◊洛杉矶又叫天使之城。Los Angeles is also called the City of Angels. ◊你叫什么名字？What's your name? **5** (吩咐) order ◊大夫叫他卧床休息。The doctor ordered him to stay in bed and rest. **6** (叫牌) bid (*pt, pp* bid) ◊他叫3个黑桃。He bid three spades. **II** [形] male ◊叫驴 male donkey **III** [介] by ◊词典叫汤姆拿走了。The dictionary was taken away by Tom.

叫喊 jiàohǎn [动] yell

叫花子 jiàohuāzi [名] beggar

叫唤 jiàohuan [动] cry out

叫苦 jiàokǔ [动] moan

叫骂 jiàomà [动] hurl abuse

叫卖 jiàomài [动] peddle

叫牌 jiàopái [动] bid (*pt, pp* bid)

叫屈 jiàoqū [动] complain of unfair treatment

叫嚷 jiàorǎng [动] shout

叫嚣 jiàoxiāo [动] yell

叫座 jiàozuò [动] attract a crowd ◊这部电影很叫座。This show has pulled in quite an audience.

叫做 jiàozuò [动] be called

觉 jiào [名] sleep ◊希望你睡个好觉。I hope you'll have a good sleep.
▷另见 jué

校 jiào [动] check
▷另见 xiào

校订 jiàodìng [动] check

校对 jiàoduì **I** [动] proofread **II** [名] proofreader

校勘 jiàokān [动] cross-check

校样 jiàoyàng [名] proofs(*pl*)

轿 jiào [名] sedan chair

轿车 jiàochē [名] car

轿子 jiàozi [名] sedan chair

较 jiào [动] **1** (比较) compare ♦较量 test one's strength **2** (书) (计较) dispute

较劲儿 jiàojìnr [动] be competitive ◊不大的事，你较什么劲！ It's not that important. Why be so competitive?

较量 jiàoliàng [动] **1** (竞争) compete ◊我们无法和他们较量。There's no way we can compete with them. **2** (计较) dispute

较真儿 jiàozhēnr [形] serious ◊什么事情你不要太较真儿。You shouldn't take everything so seriously.

教 jiào **I** [动] teach (*pt, pp* taught) ♦教导 instruct **II** [名] religion ♦信教 be religious
▷另见 jiāo

教材 jiàocái [名] teaching materials (*pl*)

教程 jiàochéng [名] course

教导 jiàodǎo [动] instruct

教皇 jiàohuáng [名] the Pope

教会 jiàohuì [名] the Church

教诲 jiàohuì [名] teaching

教具 jiàojù [名] teaching aid

教科书 jiàokēshū [名] textbook

教练 jiàoliàn [名] coach

教师 jiàoshī [名] teacher ◊家庭教师 home tutor

教室 jiàoshì [名] classroom

教授 jiàoshòu **I** [名] professor **II** [动] lecture in ◊教授法学 lecture in Law

教唆 jiàosuō [动] incite

教堂 jiàotáng [名] church

教条 jiàotiáo [名] doctrine

教徒 jiàotú [名] disciple

教学 jiàoxué [名] **1** (知识传授) teaching **2** (教与学) teaching and study

教训 jiàoxun **I** [名] lesson ◊我从这

件事中吸取了教训。I drew lessons from this. **II** [动] teach … a lesson (*pt, pp* taught)

教养 jiàoyǎng [动] **1** (教育培养) bring … up(*pt, pp* brought) ◇这孩子很有教养。The child is well brought-up. **2** (感化) reform

教益 jiàoyì [名] benefit

教育 jiàoyù **I** [名] education **II** [动] educate ◇要教育青少年遵纪守法。We must educate young people to obey the law.

教育部 jiàoyùbù [名] the Ministry of Education

教员 jiàoyuán [名] teacher

窖 jiào **I** [名] cellar **II** [动] store … in a cellar

窖藏 jiàocáng [动] store … in a cellar

酵 jiào [动] ferment

酵母 jiàomǔ [名] yeast

节 jiē 见下文
▷另见 jié

节骨眼 jiēguyǎn [名] crucial moment

阶 jiē [名] **1** (台阶) step **2** (官阶) rank

阶层 jiēcéng [名] stratum(*pl* strata)

阶段 jiēduàn [名] stage ◇工程第一阶段已经完工。The first stage of the project has already been completed.

阶级 jiējí [名] class ◇有产阶级 the propertied class

阶梯 jiētī [名] **1** (梯子) ladder **2** (楼梯) flight of stairs

阶下囚 jiēxiàqiú [名] prisoner

疖 jiē [名] boil

皆 jiē [副] all ◇这个消息人人皆知。Everyone knows all about it.

皆大欢喜 jiē dà huān xǐ everyone's happy

结 jiē [动] bear (*pt* bore, *pp* borne)
♦结果 bear fruit
▷另见 jié

结巴 jiēba [动] stutter

结实 jiēshi [形] **1** (坚固耐用) sturdy **2** (健壮) strong ◇我儿子体格结实。My son has a strong build.

接 jiē [动] **1** (靠近) draw near (*pt* drew, *pp* drawn) ♦接近 be close to **2** (连接) connect ◇接电线 connect a cable **3** (托住) catch (*pt, pp* caught) ◇接球 catch a ball **4** (接收) receive ◇接到一封信 receive a letter ◇接电话 answer the phone **5** (迎接) meet (*pt, pp* met) ◇去火车站接人 meet someone at the station **6** (接替) take over (*pt* took, *pp* taken) ◇接工作 take over a job

接班 jiēbān [动] come on shift (*pt* came, *pp* come)

接触 jiēchù [动] **1** (交往) come into contact with (*pt* came, *pp* come) **2** (冲突) clash **3** (遇到) encounter

接待 jiēdài [动] receive

接二连三 jiē èr lián sān one after another ◇他接二连三来信叫我去他那里过圣诞节。He sent one letter after another asking me to spend Christmas at his place.

接风 jiēfēng [动] hold a welcoming dinner (*pt, pp* held)

接管 jiēguǎn [动] take over (*pt* took, *pp* taken)

接轨 jiēguǐ [动] be brought into line with

接火 jiēhuǒ [动] **1** (射击) exchange fire **2** (接电) connect ◇照明设备安装好了，就等接火。The lights have been installed. We're just waiting for them to be connected.

接济 jiējì [动] support

接见 jiējiàn [动] have an interview with

接近 jiējìn **I** [动] approach **II** [形] approachable

接口 jiēkǒu [名] (计算机的) interface

接力 jiēlì [动] relay◇接力赛跑 relay race

接连 jiēlián [副] in a row ◇雨接连下了3天。It rained for three days in a row.

接纳 jiēnà [动] **1** (接受) admit ◇我被俱乐部接纳为会员。I was admitted as a member of the club. **2** (采纳) accept ◇他的建议被大家所接

纳。His proposal was accepted by everyone.

接洽 jiēqià [动] take up a matter with (*pt* took, *pp* taken) ◇我们将与有关部门接洽。We are taking the matter up with the relevant department.

接任 jiērèn [动] take over (*pt* took, *pp* taken)

接生 jiēshēng [动] deliver

接收 jiēshōu [动] **1** (收受) receive **2** (接管) take over (*pt* took, *pp* taken) **3** (接纳) admit ◇我们俱乐部准备接收一批新会员。Our club is getting ready to admit a new group of members.

接手 jiēshǒu [动] take over (*pt* took, *pp* taken)

接受 jiēshòu [动] accept

接替 jiētì [动] replace ◇他将接替原来的大使。He's replacing the former ambassador.

接头 jiētóu [动] **1** (连接) link up ◇两颗卫星要在太空中接头了。The two satellites will link up with one another in space. **2** (联系) contact ◇我明天和他接头。I'll contact him tomorrow.

接吻 jiēwěn [动] kiss

接应 jiēyìng [动] **1** (配合) back … up ◇你们先干，随后我们接应。You go first, we'll act as backup. **2** (供应) supply ◇药品暂时接应不上。There's a temporary shortage of medical supplies.

接着 jiēzhe [动] **1** (用手接) catch (*pt, pp* caught) ◇给你一个桃子，接着！ Here's a peach for you – catch! **2** (紧跟着) follow

接踵而来 jiēzhǒng ér lái a constant stream of people ◇到这里旅游的人接踵而来。There's a constant stream of tourists here.

秸 jiē [名] straw

揭 jiē [动] **1** (取下) take … down (*pt* took, *pp* taken) ◇把墙上的画揭下来。Take the picture down from the wall. **2** (拿起) pick … up **3** (揭露) reveal

揭穿 jiēchuān [动] expose

揭发 jiēfā [动] expose

揭竿而起 jiē gān ér qǐ rise up in arms

揭露 jiēlù [动] reveal

揭幕 jiēmù [动] unveil

揭示 jiēshì [动] **1** (发布) announce **2** (使人领会) reveal

揭晓 jiēxiǎo [动] announce

嗟 jiē [动] (书) sigh

嗟来之食 jiē lái zhī shí handouts

街 jiē [名] **1** (街道) street **2** (方) (集市) market

街道 jiēdào [名] **1** (马路) street **2** (社区) neighbourhood (英), neighborhood (美)

街坊 jiēfang [名] (口) neighbour (英), neighbor (美)

街谈巷议 jiē tán xiàng yì the talk of the town

街头巷尾 jiē tóu xiàng wěi all over town

孑 jié [形] solitary

孑然 jiérán [形] alone ◇他孑然一身。He's all alone in the world.

节 jié **I** [名] **1** (连接处) joint **2** (段落) paragraph **3** (节日) festival ♦圣诞节 Christmas **4** (事项) item ♦细节 details (*pl*) **5** (节操) moral fibre (英) 或 fiber (美) ♦气节 integrity **II** [动] **1** (节约) save **2** (删节) abridge **III** [量] ◇3节课 three classes ◇一节管子 a length of pipe
▷另见 jiē

节哀 jié'āi [动] overcome one's grief (*pt* overcame, *pp* overcome)

节操 jiécāo [名] integrity

节俭 jiéjiǎn [形] frugal

节令 jiélìng [名] seasonal changes (*pl*) ◇吃穿跟着节令走。What we eat and wear depends on what festival it is.

节目 jiémù [名] programme (英), program (美)

节拍 jiépāi [名] beat

节气 jiéqi [名] solar term

节日 jiérì [名] festival

节省 jiéshěng [动] conserve

节外生枝 jié wài shēng zhī complicate matters ◇眼看问题就要解决了，没想到又节外生枝。We were just about to solve the problem. We hadn't imagined that there would be additional complications.

节衣缩食 jié yī suō shí scrimp and save

节余 jiéyú [名] saving

节育 jiéyù [动] practise (英) 或 practice (美) birth control

节约 jiéyuē [动] save

节制 jiézhì [动] 1 (控制) control 2 (指挥) command

节奏 jiézòu [名] rhythm

劫 jié [动] 1 (抢劫) rob ♦打劫 take ... by force 2 (胁迫) coerce ♦劫持 hijack

劫持 jiéchí [动] hijack

劫富济贫 jié fù jì pín rob the rich to give to the poor

劫后余生 jié hòu yúshēng have a close brush with death

劫机 jiéjī [动] hijack a plane

杰 jié I [名] hero (*pl* heroes) ♦豪杰 hero II [形] outstanding ♦杰作 masterpiece

诘 jié [动] question ... closely ♦反诘 refute

诘问 jiéwèn [动] interrogate

拮 jié 见下文

拮据 jiéjū [形] hard-up ◇他手头拮据。He's pretty hard-up.

洁 jié I [形] clean ♦整洁 clean and tidy II [动] clean

洁白 jiébái [形] pure white

洁净 jiéjìng [形] clean

洁具 jiéjù [名] cleaning materials (*pl*)

洁身自好 jié shēn zì hào maintain one's moral integrity

结 jié I [动] 1 (编织) tie ♦结网 weave a net 2 (结合) unite ◇两国结为联盟。The two countries formed an alliance. 3 (凝聚) freeze (*pt* froze, *pp* frozen) ♦结冰 ice up 4 (了结) settle up ♦结账 settle up II [名] 1 (绳扣) knot ♦活结 slip-knot 2 (字据) written undertaking 3 (生理) node ▷另见 jié

结案 jié'àn [动] close a case

结拜 jiébài [动] swear friendship (*pt* swore, *pp* sworn) ◇结拜兄弟 blood brothers

结伴 jiébàn [动] form groups ◇结伴而行 go in groups

结冰 jiébīng [动] ice over

结仇 jiéchóu [动] become enemies (*pt* became, *pp* become)

结党营私 jié dǎng yíng sī form a conspiracy

结发夫妻 jiéfà fūqī couple married for the first time

结构 jiégòu [名] composition ◇产品结构 composition of a product

结果 jiéguǒ I [名] result ◇结果出人预料。The result was unexpected. II [副] in the end ◇结果，他赢了比赛。In the end, he won the contest.

结合 jiéhé [动] 1 (联系) combine◇劳逸结合 strike a balance between work and play 2 (结为夫妇) become husband and wife (*pt* became, *pt* become)

结婚 jiéhūn [动] get married ◇她和一位富商结了婚。She married a rich businessman. ◇这对夫妇结婚30多年了。This couple have been married for over thirty years.

结交 jiéjiāo [动] associate with

结晶 jiéjīng I [动] crystallize II [名] 1 (晶体) crystal 2 (成果) crystallization

结局 jiéjú [名] outcome

结论 jiélùn [名] conclusion ◇得出结论 come to a conclusion

结盟 jiéméng [动] align◇不结盟政策 policy of non-alignment

结亲 jiéqīn [动] become related through marriage (*pt* became, *pp* become) ◇两家最近结亲了。The two families have recently become related through marriage.

结社 jiéshè [动] form an association

结识 jiéshí [动] become acquainted with (*pt* became, *pp* become)

结束 jiéshù [动] end

结算 jiésuàn [动] settle up ◇你先付账，事后我们再结算。You pay the bill, and we can settle up later.

结尾 jiéwěi [名] ending

结业 jiéyè [动] finish ◇两个月的学习班即将结业。The two-month course is about to finish.

结账 jiézhàng [动] settle up ◇饭菜我来结账。Let me pay for the meal.

桀 Jié 见下文

桀骜不驯 jié'ào bù xún stubborn and intractable

捷 jié **I** [形] quick ♦敏捷 nimble **II** [名] victory

捷报 jiébào [名] news of victory

捷径 jiéjìng [名] short cut ◇这是去公园的捷径。This is the short cut to the park. ◇他在工作上总想走捷径。He always tries to take short cuts in his work.

捷足先登 jié zú xiān dēng the early bird catches the worm

睫 jié [名] eyelash

截 jié **I** [动] **1** (切断) chop **2** (阻拦) block **II** [量] piece ◇一截木头 a piece of wood ◇半截粉笔 half a stick of chalk

截长补短 jié cháng bǔ duǎn use one's strengths to compensate for one's shortcomings

截断 jiéduàn [动] **1** (切断) cut … off (*pt, pp* cut) **2** (打断) interrupt

截获 jiéhuò [动] intercept

截流 jiéliú [动] dam

截取 jiéqǔ [动] cut … out (*pt, pp* cut)

截然 jiérán [副] completely ◇截然不同 completely different

截止 jiézhǐ [动] be over ◇报名已经截止了。Registration is already over.

竭 jié [动] use … up

竭诚 jiéchéng [副] wholeheartedly

竭尽 jiéjìn [动] exert ◇他们竭尽全力完成了这项任务。They really pulled out all the stops to get the task finished.

竭力 jiélì [动] do one's utmost

竭泽而渔 jié zé ér yú kill the goose that lays the golden eggs

姐 jiě [名] elder sister

姐妹 jiěmèi [名] sisters (*pl*)

解 jiě [动] **1** (分开) divide ♦解剖 dissect **2** (解开) untie ◇解鞋带 untie one's shoelaces **3** (解除) relieve ♦解热 allay a fever **4** (解答) answer♦解题 solve a problem **5** (理解) understand ◇令人不解 confusing
▷另见 jiè

解除 jiěchú [动] get rid of ◇解除痛苦 get rid of suffering ◇解除婚约 break off one's engagement

解答 jiědá [动] answer

解冻 jiědòng [动] **1** (融化) thaw **2** (解除冻结) unfreeze (*pt* unfroze, *pp* unfrozen) **3** (喻) (缓和关系) thaw

解放 jiěfàng [动] liberate◇妇女解放运动 the women's liberation movement

解雇 jiěgù [动] dismiss

解救 jiějiù [动] rescue

解决 jiějué [动] **1** (处理) resolve ◇解决问题 resolve a problem **2** (消灭) annihilate

解闷 jiěmèn [动] relieve the boredom

解囊相助 jiě náng xiāng zhù be generous to those in need ◇当他人遇到困难的时候，我们应该慷慨解囊。When others are in difficulties, we should be generous to them.

解聘 jiěpìn [动] dismiss ◇解聘某人的职务 dismiss someone from their job

解剖 jiěpōu [动] dissect

解气 jiěqì [动] let off steam (*pt, pp* let)

解散 jiěsàn [动] **1** (散开) disperse **2** (取消) dissolve

解释 jiěshì [动] explain

解手 jiěshǒu [动] relieve oneself

解说 jiěshuō [动] explain

解体 jiětǐ [动] disintegrate

解脱 jiětuō [动] 1 (摆脱) break away from (*pt* broke, *pp* broken) ◇他终于从逆境中解脱出来了。He finally extricated himself from the predicament. 2 (开脱) explain … away ◇不要为自己的过失解脱。Don't go explaining away your mistakes.

解围 jiěwéi [动] 1 (解除包围) break a siege (*pt* broke, *pp* broken) 2 (摆脱窘境) save … blushes ◇他们捉弄我，你该帮我解围。If they tease me you'll have to save my blushes.

介 jiè I [动] be situated between ◇这个湖介于两座山之间。The lake is situated between the two mountains. II [形] upstanding ♦耿介 principled

介词 jiècí [名] preposition

介入 jièrù [动] intervene ◇我们不该介入他们夫妻间的争吵。We really shouldn't intervene in their marital strife.

介绍 jièshào [动] 1 (使相识) introduce ◇自我介绍 introduce oneself ◇我把妻子介绍给了同事。I introduced my wife to my colleagues. 2 (推荐) sponsor 3 (使了解) give an introduction to (*pt* gave, *pt* given) ◇导游向我们介绍了当地的风土人情。The guide gave us an introduction to local customs and culture.

介意 jièyì [动] mind ◇我打开窗户你介意吗？ Do you mind if I open the window?

戒 jiè I [动] 1 (防备) guard against 2 (戒除) give up (*pt* gave, *pp* given) ♦戒烟 give up smoking II [名] 1 (警告) warning 2 (戒律) religious discipline 3 (戒指) ring

戒备 jièbèi [动] be on the alert

戒除 jièchú [动] give up (*pt* gave, *pp* given)

戒毒 jièdú [动] come off drugs (*pt* came, *pp* come)

戒律 jièlǜ [名] religious tenets (*pl*)

戒严 jièyán [动] impose martial law ◇宣布戒严 declare martial law

戒指 jièzhi [名] ring

芥 jiè 见下文

芥菜 jiècài [名] mustard leaf (*pl* leaves)

届 jiè I [动] fall due (*pt* fell, *pp* fallen) ♦届期 at the appointed time II [量] ◇82届毕业生 the class of '82 ◇第九届人代会 the Ninth People's Congress

届时 jièshí [动] ◇届时请您光临。When the time comes, do come and have a look around.

界 jiè [名] 1 (界限) boundary ◇国界 national boundaries (*pl*) 2 (阶层) circles (*pl*) ◇各界人士 people from all walks of life ◇新闻界 media circles 3 (范围) range ◇大开眼界 broaden one's horizons 4 (类别) category ◇动物界 the animal kingdom

界定 jièdìng [动] demarcate

界面 jièmiàn [名] interface

界限 jièxiàn [名] 1 (分界) dividing line 2 (限度) limits (*pl*)

界线 jièxiàn [名] 1 (边界) boundary 2 (分界线) dividing line

疥 jiè [名] scabies

诫 jiè I [动] warn ♦告诫 warn II [名] religious tenets (*pl*)

借 jiè [动] 1 (借入) borrow ◇我从图书馆借了几本书。I borrowed some books from the library. 2 (借出) lend (*pt, pp* lent) ◇请把词典借我用一下。Please can you lend me your dictionary a moment? 3 (假托) use … as a means of ◇这家公司借广告欺骗消费者。The company uses advertising as a means of cheating consumers. 4 (凭借) make use of ◇我借此机会向大家表示感谢。May I take this opportunity to express my thanks to all of you.

借词 jiècí [名] loan word

借贷 jièdài I [动] 1 (借入) borrow money 2 (借出) lend money (*pt, pp* lent) II [名] debtors and creditors (*pl*)

借刀杀人 jiè dāo shā rén get others to do one's dirty work

借端 jièduān [动] use … as a pretext

借故 jiègù [动] make an excuse

借光 jièguāng [动] (谦) excuse me

借鉴 jièjiàn [动] learn from ◇借鉴别人的经验 learn from other people's experiences

借酒浇愁 jiè jiǔ jiāo chóu drown one's sorrows

借据 jièjù [名] IOU

借口 jièkǒu I [动] use … as an excuse ◇他借口有事不来上班。He used the fact that he had things to do as an excuse not to go to work. II [名] excuse ◇他企图找借口为自己辩护。He tried to find an excuse to justify himself.

借尸还魂 jiè shī huán hún come back in a new form

借题发挥 jiè tí fāhuī use an excuse to hold forth

借助 jièzhù [动] enlist the help of

解 jiè [动] escort
▷另见 jiě

解送 jièsòng [动] escort

巾 jīn [名] cloth ♦毛巾 towel

巾帼 jīnguó [名] (书) women (*pl*)

斤 jīn [量] *unit of weight, equal to 500 grams*

斤斤计较 jīnjīn jìjiào quibble over every detail

今 jīn I [形] **1** (现在的) present **2** (当前的) current II [名] today ◇今明两天都可以来。Come today or tomorrow, as you wish.

今后 jīnhòu [副] from now on

今年 jīnnián [名] this year ◇今年年底我父亲就要退休了。My father will retire at the end of this year. ◇今年夏天他大学就要毕业了。He graduates from university this summer.

今日 jīnrì [名] today ◇今日气温偏高。It's pretty hot today.

今世 jīnshì [名] this life ◇今生今世我都不会忘记父母的恩情。I will remember my parents' kindness for the rest of my life.

今天 jīntiān [名] today ◇今天是我的生日。Today's my birthday. ◇今天我想去看场戏。I want to go and see a play today.

今朝 jīnzhāo [名] today

金 jīn I [名] **1** (化) gold **2** (金属) metal ♦五金 hardware **3** (钱) money ◇奖金 prize money II [形] golden ◇金发 blonde hair

金榜 jīnbǎng [名] roll of honour (英) 或 honor (美)

金碧辉煌 jīnbì-huīhuáng magnificent

金蝉脱壳 jīnchán tuō qiào make a cunning getaway

金额 jīn'é [名] sum

金刚石 jīngāngshí [名] diamond

金黄 jīnhuáng [形] golden

金婚 jīnhūn [名] golden wedding

金科玉律 jīn kē yù lǜ golden rule

金口玉言 jīnkǒu-yùyán pearls of wisdom

金牌 jīnpái [名] gold medal

金钱 jīnqián [名] money

金秋 jīnqiū [名] autumn (英), fall (美)

金融 jīnróng [名] finance ◇金融行业 the financial sector

金属 jīnshǔ [名] metal

金丝猴 jīnsīhóu [名] golden monkey

金玉良言 jīnyù liángyán words of wisdom

金枝玉叶 jīn zhī yù yè aristocrat

金子 jīnzi [名] gold

金字塔 jīnzìtǎ [名] pyramid

津 jīn [名] **1** (津液) saliva **2** (汗) sweat **3** (渡口) ferry

津津乐道 jīnjīn lè dào talk with great enthusiasm ◇不要对别人的隐私津津乐道。Don't talk about other people's private business with such enthusiasm.

津津有味 jīnjīn yǒu wèi with great enjoyment

津贴 jīntiē [名] subsidy

矜 jīn I [动] have pity on ♦矜恤 pity II [形] **1** (自大) egotistical ♦骄矜

self-important **2** (拘谨) reserved

矜持 jīnchí [形] reserved

筋 jīn [名] **1** (肌腱) tendon **2** (肌肉) muscle ♦筋骨 physique **3** (口) (静脉血管) vein ♦青筋 blue vein **4** (像筋的东西) ♦橡皮筋 rubber band

筋道 jīndao [形] (方) chewy

筋斗 jīndǒu [名] (方) somersault

筋骨 jīngǔ [名] physique

筋疲力尽 jīn pí lì jìn dog-tired

筋肉 jīnròu [名] muscle

禁 jīn [动] **1** (禁受) endure **2** (忍住) restrain **3** (耐) bear (*pt* bore, *pp* borne)
▷另见 jìn

禁受 jīnshòu [动] stand (*pt, pp* stood) ◇我们的友谊禁受了时间的考验。Our friendship has stood the test of time.

襟 jīn [名] **1** (上衣前面) front ♦衣襟 shirt front **2** (连襟) brother-in-law (*pl* brothers-in-law) **3** (胸怀) mind ◇胸襟广阔 broad-minded

襟怀 jīnhuái [名] mind

仅 jǐn [副] only ◇此书仅存一本。We only keep one copy of this book.

仅仅 jǐnjǐn [副] just ◇我们的工作才仅仅开始。Our work has only just begun.

尽 jǐn I [副] **1** (尽量) as far as possible ♦尽快 as early as possible **2** (最) most ◇尽东边 the most easterly point ◇尽底下 the very bottom **3** (表示继续) constantly ◇这些天尽下雨了。It's been raining non-stop for the last few days. II [动] **1** (不超过) take no more than (*pt* took, *pp* taken) ◇我们准备尽着4天把工作做完。We're planning to take no more than four days over this work. **2** (考虑在先) give priority to (*pt* gave, *pp* given) ◇他爱尽旧衣服穿。He likes wearing old clothes.
▷另见 jìn

尽管 jǐnguǎn I [副] without reserve ◇有话尽管说。If there's something you'd like to say please don't hold back. II [连] even though ◇尽管在下大雨，他还是要出去。Even though it was pouring with rain, he still wanted to go out.

尽量 jǐnliàng [副] to the best of one's ability ◇你尽量早点来。Do your best to come a bit earlier.

尽早 jǐnzǎo [副] as soon as possible ◇有消息，我会尽早通知你。As soon as I have news I will contact you.

紧 jǐn I [形] **1** (不松) tight **2** (牢固) secure **3** (接近) close **4** (急迫) pressing **5** (严格) strict **6** (拮据) short of money II [动] tighten

紧巴巴 jǐnbābā [形] **1** (不松) tight **2** (拮据) hard-up

紧凑 jǐncòu [形] tight ◇日程安排得很紧凑。We're on a very tight schedule.

紧急 jǐnjí [形] urgent

紧密 jǐnmì [形] **1** (密切的) close **2** (密集的) dense

紧迫 jǐnpò [形] pressing

紧俏 jǐnqiào [形] in demand ◇紧俏商品 products in demand

紧缩 jǐnsuō [动] cut down on (*pt, pp* cut)

紧要 jǐnyào [形] crucial

紧张 jǐnzhāng [形] **1** (激烈) intense **2** (不安) nervous **3** (不足) in short supply ◇最近药品比较紧张。Recently, the demand for medicines has exceeded the supply.

锦 jǐn I [名] brocade II [形] glorious

锦标 jǐnbiāo [名] prize ◇锦标赛 championship

锦缎 jǐnduàn [名] brocade

锦囊妙计 jǐnnáng miàojì a masterplan

锦上添花 jǐn shàng tiān huā improve on perfection

锦绣 jǐnxiù [形] splendid

谨 jǐn [副] **1** (谨慎地) warily **2** (郑重地) solemnly

谨慎 jǐnshèn [形] wary

谨小慎微 jǐn xiǎo shèn wēi over-cautious

谨严 jǐnyán [形] meticulous

尽 jìn I [动] 1 (完) exhaust ◇我已经想尽了办法。I've exhausted all my ideas. 2 (达到极限) go to extremes (*pt* went, *pp* gone) ◇山穷水尽 at the end of one's tether 3 (充分发挥) use … to the full ◇人尽其才 everyone uses their talents to the full 4 (努力完成) strive to accomplish (*pt* strove, *pp* striven) ◇尽职尽责 strive to fulfil one's professional responsibilities II [形] complete◇尽人皆知 be common knowledge◇尽收眼底 have a grandstand view
▷另见 jǐn

尽瘁 jìncuì [动] drive oneself to the brink of exhaustion (*pt* drove, *pp* driven)

尽力 jìnlì [动] try one's hardest ◇我们会尽力完成。We'll try our hardest to get the job done.

尽量 jìnliàng [动] do all one can ◇我尽量不麻烦别人。I do all I can to avoid annoying other people.

尽情 jìnqíng [副] to one's heart's content ◇尽情享受 enjoy oneself to one's heart's content

尽善尽美 jìn shàn jìn měi flawless

尽头 jìntóu [名] end

尽心 jìnxīn [动] put one's heart and soul into (*pt*, *pp* put) ◇医护人员要尽心尽力抢救病人。Medical workers should put their hearts and souls into saving their patients.

尽心竭力 jìnxīn-jiélì give one's all ◇在工作上，他尽心竭力。He gave his all to the job.

尽兴 jìnxìng [副] to one's heart's content ◇大家尽兴玩吧！ Have a wonderful time, everybody!

尽责 jìnzé [动] meet all one's obligations (*pt*, *pp* met)

尽职 jìnzhí [动] fulfil (英) 或 fulfill (美) one's duty

进 jìn [动] 1 (前进) advance 2 (进入) enter ♦进城 go to town 3 (接纳) bring … in (*pt*, *pp* brought) ♦进货 stock up 4 (吃食) eat (*pt* ate, *pp* eaten) ◇他滴水不进。Not even a drop of water passed his lips. 5 (呈上) submit 6 (攻进) enter ◇进球 score a goal

进逼 jìnbī [动] press on

进补 jìnbǔ [动] pep … up ◇喝鸡汤可进补。Drinking chicken soup can pep you up.

进步 jìnbù I [动] improve II [形] advanced

进程 jìnchéng [名] progression

进度 jìndù [名] 1 (进行速度) pace 2 (工作计划) schedule

进而 jìn'ér [连] then ◇首先我们得先测试产品，进而再推广。First we have to test the product, and then we have to promote it.

进发 jìnfā [动] set out for (*pt*, *pp* set)

进犯 jìnfàn [动] invade

进攻 jìngōng [动] attack

进贡 jìngòng [动] offer tribute

进化 jìnhuà [动] evolve ◇人类的进化 human evolution

进货 jìnhuò [动] stock up

进军 jìnjūn [动] advance ◇中国正在向现代化进军。China is advancing towards modernization.

进口 jìnkǒu [动] import

进取 jìnqǔ [动] forge ahead◇进取精神 ambition

进入 jìnrù [动] 1 (走进) enter 2 (到了) reach 3 (到位) get inside ◇进入角色 get inside a role

进退 jìntuì [动] advance and retreat

进退维谷 jìn tuì wéi gǔ on the horns of a dilemma

进项 jìnxiang [名] income

进行 jìnxíng [动] carry … out ◇我们正在进行改革。We're carrying out reforms. ◇会议正在进行。The meeting is in progress.

进行曲 jìnxíngqǔ [名] march

进修 jìnxiū [动] take a refresher course (*pt* took, *pp* taken)

进展 jìnzhǎn [动] make progress

近 jìn [形] 1 (不远) near ◇这两所大学离得很近。The two universities are very near one another. ♦近日 recently 2 (接近) close ◇平易近人

approachable **3** (亲近) close to ♦近邻 family and neighbours (英) 或 neighbors (美)

近代 jìndài [名] modern times (*pl*)

近乎 jìnhu **I** [动] be little short of ◊你不及格的可能性近乎为零。The chances of you failing this exam are little short of zero. **II** [形] intimate

近况 jìnkuàng [名] the latest ◊你知道史蒂芬的近况吗? Have you heard the latest about Stephen?

近来 jìnlái [副] recently

近亲 jìnqīn [动] be closely related ◊近亲不能结婚。Close relatives cannot marry.

近视 jìnshì [形] short-sighted (英), near-sighted (美)

近水楼台 jìn shuǐ lóu tái be favourably (英) 或 favorably (美) situated

近似 jìnsì [形] similar ◊两种物质很近似。The two types of material are very similar.

劲 jìn [名] **1** (力气) strength **2** (情绪) spirit **3** (态度) manner **4** (趣味) fun

劲头 jìntóu [名] energy

晋 jìn [动] call on

晋级 jìnjí [动] be promoted

晋见 jìnjiàn [动] have an audience with

晋升 jìnshēng [动] promote ◊学院将他晋升为教授。The college promoted him to a professorship.

烬 jìn [名] ash

浸 jìn [动] **1** (浸泡) soak **2** (渗入) soak through ◊汗水把她的衣服浸透了。Sweat soaked through her clothes.

浸礼 jìnlǐ [名] (基督教的) baptism

浸没 jìnmò [动] immerse

浸透 jìntòu [动] drench ◊他浑身被雨水浸透了。He got drenched to the bone.

禁 jìn **I** [动] **1** (禁止) forbid (*pt* forbade, *pp* forbidden) ◊严禁赌博。Gambling is forbidden. **2** (监禁) imprison ♦禁闭 lock … up **II** [名] taboo
▷另见 jīn

禁闭 jìnbì [动] lock … up

禁地 jìndì [名] restricted area

禁锢 jìngù [动] **1** (关押) imprison **2** (束缚) fetter

禁忌 jìnjì **I** [名] taboo **II** [动] avoid

禁令 jìnlìng [名] ban ◊政府已经解除了对这部电影的禁令。The government has lifted the ban on the film.

禁区 jìnqū [名] restricted area

禁止 jìnzhǐ [动] forbid (*pt* forbade, *pp* forbidden)

觐 jìn [动] have an audience with

觐见 jìnjiàn [动] have an audience with

噤 jìn [动] **1** (不说话) keep silent (*pt, pp* kept) **2** (哆嗦) shiver

噤若寒蝉 jìn ruò hán chán keep one's mouth shut

茎 jīng [名] **1** (指植物) stem **2** (茎状物) ◊刀茎 handle of a knife

京 jīng [名] **1** (首都) capital **2** (北京) Beijing

京城 jīngchéng [名] capital

京剧 jīngjù [名] Beijing opera

京腔 jīngqiāng [名] Beijing accent

泾 jīng 见下文

泾渭分明 Jīng Wèi fēnmíng entirely different

经 jīng **I** [名] **1** (经线) warp ♦经纱 warp **2** (指中医) channels (*pl*) **3** (经度) longitude **4** (经典) scripture ♦佛经 Buddhist sutra **II** [动] **1** (经营) run (*pt* ran, *pp* run) ♦经商 be in business **2** (经受) endure ◊她经得起折腾。She can endure suffering. **3** (经过) ◊这文章经老师一解释，我们都理解了。Once the article had been explained by the teacher, we all understood it. ◊途经西安 go via Xi'an **III** [形] regular ♦经常 often

经办 jīngbàn [动] handle

经常 jīngcháng **I** [形] day-to-day ◊经常开支 day-to-day costs **II** [副] often ◊我经常出差。I often go on business trips.

经典 jīngdiǎn [名] classics *(pl)* ◇经典著作 classical works

经度 jīngdù [名] longitude

经费 jīngfèi [名] funds *(pl)*

经管 jīngguǎn [动] be in charge of ◇他经管这个项目。He's in charge of this project. ◇招聘会计由我经管。Recruiting accountants is my responsibility.

经过 jīngguò **I** [动] **1** (通过) pass ◇这路公共汽车经过我家。This bus passes by my home. ◇我们将经过王子街。We'll go along Prince's Street. **2** (延续) ◇经过3年的恋爱，他们终于结婚了。Having been together for three years, they finally got married. **3** (经历) ◇企业经过裁员缩减了经费开支。Business expenditure was reduced through staff cutbacks. **II** [名] course ◇事情发生的经过 the course of events

经纪 jīngjì **I** [动] (管理) manage **II** [名] broker

经纪人 jīngjìrén [名] broker

经济 jīngjì **I** [名] **1** (社会生产关系) economy ◇国民经济 national economy ◇经济发展 economic development **2** (个人财政状况) financial situation ◇他家经济条件好。His family are well-off. ◇经济拮据 hard-up **II** [形] **1** (有关国民经济) economic ◇经济作物 cash crop **2** (实惠) economical ◇经济舱 economy-class cabin

经济危机 jīngjì wēijī [名] economic crisis

经济学 jīngjìxué [名] economics *(sg)*

经久 jīngjiǔ [形] **1** (时间长) prolonged **2** (耐久) durable

经理 jīnglǐ [名] manager

经历 jīnglì [动] experience ◇成长经历 the experience of growing up

经贸 jīngmào [名] economy and trade ◇经贸关系 economic and trade relations

经商 jīngshāng [动] be in business

经手 jīngshǒu [动] handle

经手人 jīngshǒurén [名] ◇她是这个案件的经手人。She's handling this case.

经受 jīngshòu [动] experience ◇经受折磨 experience suffering ◇经受打击 sustain an attack

经销 jīngxiāo [动] deal in (*pt, pp* dealt) ◇经销商 dealer

经验 jīngyàn [名] experience ◇丰富的教学经验 rich teaching experience ◇交流经验 exchange experiences

经营 jīngyíng [动] **1** (管理) run (*pt* ran, *pp* run) ◇经营一个小牧场 run a small farm ◇经营地产开发 manage a property business ◇企业经营管理 business management **2** (组织) organize an art exhibition **3** (销售) deal in (*pt, pp* dealt) ◇该店经营各类摄影器材。This shop deals in all sorts of photography equipment.

经传 jīngzhuàn [名] classics *(pl)*

荆 jīng 见下文

荆棘 jīngjí [名] **1** (字) brambles *(pl)* **2** (喻) difficulties *(pl)*

菁 jīng 见下文

菁华 jīnghuá [名] cream ◇社会的菁华 the cream of society

惊 jīng [动] **1** (紧张) start **2** (惊动) startle ◇打草惊蛇 alert the enemy

惊诧 jīngchà [动] be amazed ◇他工作效率之高让我惊诧。I was amazed at his efficiency. ◇她脸上现出惊诧的神色。A look of amazement appeared on her face.

惊动 jīngdòng [动] **1** (震动) alarm **2** (打扰) disturb

惊慌 jīnghuāng [形] scared ◇惊慌失措 be scared out of one's wits

惊厥 jīngjué [动] faint from fear

惊恐 jīngkǒng [形] terrified ◇惊恐失色 turn pale with terror

惊奇 jīngqí [形] surprised

惊人 jīngrén [形] amazing

惊世骇俗 jīng shì hài sú astounding

惊叹号 jīngtànhào [名] exclamation mark(英) 或 point (美)

惊涛骇浪 jīng tāo hài làng stormy seas *(pl)*

惊天动地 jīng tiān dòng dì earth-shattering

惊喜 jīngxǐ [动] be pleasantly surprised

惊险 jīngxiǎn [形] thrilling

惊心动魄 jīng xīn dòng pò horrifying

惊讶 jīngyà [形] astonished ◊听到这个消息后他感到很惊讶。He was astonished to hear the news.

晶 jīng I [形] sparkling II [名] crystal

晶体 jīngtǐ [名] crystal

晶莹 jīngyíng [形] sparkling and translucent

睛 jīng [名] eyeball ◊目不转睛 stare fixedly

兢 jīng 见下文

兢兢业业 jīngjīngyèyè meticulous ◊她工作兢兢业业。She works meticulously.

精 jīng I [形] **1** (经挑选的) refined ♦精兵 crack troops **2** (完美) excellent **3** (细密) precise ◊精打细算 careful budgeting **4** (心细) sharp ♦精明 shrewd **5** (精通) skilled ◊精于书法 be good at calligraphy II [名] **1** (精华) essence ♦酒精 alcohol **2** (精力) energy ◊聚精会神 focus all one's energies on **3** (精子) sperm **4** (妖) demon III [副] (方) extremely

精彩 jīngcǎi [形] wonderful

精粹 jīngcuì [形] succinct

精打细算 jīng dǎ xì suàn budget carefully

精当 jīngdàng [形] precise

精干 jīnggàn [形] competent

精光 jīngguāng [形] ◊她饿极了，把饭菜吃了个精光。She was so hungry, she cleaned her plate. ◊电影票卖得精光。Tickets for the film are all sold out.

精华 jīnghuá [名] cream

精力 jīnglì [名] energy

精练 jīngliàn [形] succinct

精炼 jīngliàn I [动] refine II [形] succinct

精良 jīngliáng [形] excellent

精灵 jīnglíng [名] **1** (鬼怪) spirit **2** (指人) clever thing

精美 jīngměi [形] exquisite

精密 jīngmì [形] accurate ◊精密仪器 precision instrument

精明 jīngmíng [形] shrewd

精疲力竭 jīng pí lì jié completely worn out

精辟 jīngpì [形] penetrating

精品 jīngpǐn [名] quality goods (*pl*) ◊精品书店 quality bookshop ◊民间艺术精品 fine pieces of folk art

精巧 jīngqiǎo [形] exquisite

精确 jīngquè [形] precise ◊这篇论文对海外市场作了精确的分析。This essay gives a thorough analysis of overseas markets.

精锐 jīngruì [形] crack ◊精锐部队 crack troops

精深 jīngshēn [形] profound

精神 jīngshén [名] **1** (主观世界) mind ◊精神负担 a load on one's mind ◊精神病 mental illness **2** (宗旨) gist ◊把握文件精神 get the gist of a document

精神 jīngshen I [名] energy II [形] energetic

精神文明 jīngshén wénmíng [名] intellectual and ideological development

精髓 jīngsuǐ [名] (喻) essence

精通 jīngtōng [动] be proficient in

精细 jīngxì [形] fine

精心 jīngxīn [形] meticulous ◊精心策划的阴谋 a meticulously planned plot

精选 jīngxuǎn [动] select … carefully

精益求精 jīng yì qiú jīng always striving to improve

精英 jīngyīng [名] elite ◊信息技术行业的精英 the elite of the IT industry

精湛 jīngzhàn [形] exquisite

精致 jīngzhì [形] delicate

精装 jīngzhuāng [形] (指书) hard-back

精子 jīngzǐ [名] sperm

鲸 jīng [名] whale

鲸吞 jīngtūn [动] swallow up

井 jǐng I [名] **1** (用于取水) well **2** (井状

物) ♦天井 skylight ♦矿井 mine shaft **II** [形] neat

井底之蛙 jǐng dǐ zhī wā person with limited vision

井井有条 jǐngjǐng yǒu tiáo in perfect order

井然 jǐngrán [形] orderly

阱 jǐng [名] trap

颈 jǐng [名] neck

景 jǐng **I** [名] **1** (风景) scenery **2** (情形) situation ♦背景 background **3** (布景) scene ♦外景 outdoor scene **II** [动] admire

景点 jǐngdiǎn [名] scenic spot

景观 jǐngguān [名] scenery

景况 jǐngkuàng [名] situation ◊他景况很不如意。His situation is not at all to his liking. ◊生活景况 living conditions

景气 jǐngqì **I** [名] boom **II** [形] booming

景色 jǐngsè [名] scenery

景物 jǐngwù [名] scenery

景象 jǐngxiàng [名] scene

景致 jǐngzhì [名] scenery

警 jǐng **I** [形] alert ♦警惕 on the alert **II** [动] **1** (使警觉) warn **2** (戒备) be on the alert **III** [名] **1** (危急) alarm ♦报警 raise the alarm **2** (警察) police ♦巡警 an officer on the beat

警报 jǐngbào [名] alarm

警备 jǐngbèi [动] guard

警察 jǐngchá [名] police ◊便衣警察 plain-clothes police

警告 jǐnggào [动] warn ◊警察鸣枪警告。The police fired a warning shot.

警戒 jǐngjiè [动] **1** (告戒) warn **2** (防备) guard ◊放松警戒 let one's guard down ◊采取警戒措施 take precautionary measures

警句 jǐngjù [名] epigram

警觉 jǐngjué [名] vigilance ◊保持警觉 maintain vigilance ◊一人出门在外必须提高警觉。Anyone going out alone should be extra vigilant.

警力 jǐnglì [名] police force ◊每天有4000警力上街巡逻。Every day 4,000 police patrol the streets.

警示 jǐngshì [名] warning

警惕 jǐngtì [动] watch out for

警卫 jǐngwèi [名] guard

警钟 jǐngzhōng [名] alarm bell

劲 jìng [形] powerful

劲敌 jìngdí [名] formidable opponent

径 jìng **I** [名] **1** (小路) path **2** (方法) way ♦捷径 short cut **3** (直径) diameter ♦半径 radius **II** [副] directly ♦径自 without letting anyone know

径赛 jìngsài [名] track event

径自 jìngzì [副] without consultation ◊我决定径自到她家走一趟。Without asking I decided to pay her a visit at home.

净 jìng **I** [形] **1** (干净) clean **2** (光) all gone ◊钱花净了。The money is all gone. **3** (纯) net **II** [副] only ◊啥都不干，净吹牛 all talk and no action

净化 jìnghuà [动] purify

净值 jìngzhí [名] net value

净重 jìngzhòng [名] net weight

胫 jìng [名] shin

痉 jìng 见下文

痉挛 jìngluán [动] convulse

竞 jìng [动] compete

竞技 jìngjì [名] sports (*pl*)

竞赛 jìngsài [名] competition

竞相 jìngxiāng [动] compete

竞选 jìngxuǎn [动] run for (*pt* ran, *pp* run) ◊竞选总统 run for president

竞争 jìngzhēng [动] compete ◊竞争上岗 compete for a job

竟 jìng **I** [动] finish ◊未竟之业 unfinished task **II** [副] **1** (终于) in the end ◊有志者事竟成。Where there's a will there's a way. **2** (竟然) actually ◊谁也没想到，他竟发这么大的火。Who would have thought he would actually get this angry.

竟然 jìngrán [副] unexpectedly ◇玛莉竟然放弃事业，甘当家庭妇女。Mary unexpectedly gave up her career and became a housewife. ◇走到半路上竟然下起雨来。They were halfway down the road when, to their surprise, it began to rain.

敬 jìng I [动] 1 (尊重) respect 2 (恭敬地给) offer II [形] respectful

敬爱 jìng'ài [动] revere

敬而远之 jìng ér yuǎn zhī keep away from

敬酒 jìngjiǔ [动] propose a toast ◇主席举杯向来宾们敬酒。The chairman proposed a toast to the guests.

敬礼 jìnglǐ [动] salute

敬佩 jìngpèi [动] admire

敬畏 jìngwèi [动] be in awe of

敬仰 jìngyǎng [动] revere ◇令人敬仰的作家 a revered author

敬业 jìngyè [动] be committed to one's work

敬意 jìngyì [名] tribute ◇我们对奋战在第一线的护士表示崇高的敬意。We paid tribute to the nurses who worked on the front line.

敬重 jìngzhòng [动] have high regard for ◇他深受同事敬重。He is highly regarded by those who have worked with him.

静 jìng [形] 1 (不动) still 2 (无声) quiet

静电 jìngdiàn [名] static electricity

静脉 jìngmài [名] vein

静悄悄 jìngqiāoqiāo [形] very quiet

静态 jìngtài [名] static state

静物 jìngwù [名] still life

静止 jìngzhǐ [动] be still

静坐 jìngzuò [动] 1 (指气功) meditate 2 (指抗议) stage a sit-in

境 jìng [名] 1 (边界) border ♦国境 border 2 (地方) place ♦仙境 fairyland 3 (景况) situation ♦困境 predicament

境地 jìngdì [名] (地步) situation

境界 jìngjiè [名] 1 (界限) boundary 2 (程度) level

境况 jìngkuàng [名] condition

境遇 jìngyù [名] circumstances (*pl*)

镜 jìng [名] 1 (镜子) mirror 2 (指光学器具) lens ♦眼镜 glasses ♦望远镜 telescope

镜头 jìngtóu [名] 1 (指装置) camera lens 2 (照相画面) shot 3 (指一系列画面) take

镜子 jìngzi [名] mirror

迥 jiǒng [形] (书) (相差大) completely different

迥然 jiǒngrán [形] completely different

炯 jiǒng 见下文

炯炯 jiǒngjiǒng [形] bright

窘 jiǒng [形] 1 (穷困) hard-up 2 (为难) embarrassed

窘况 jiǒngkuàng [名] difficult situation

窘迫 jiǒngpò [形] 1 (穷困) very poor 2 (为难) embarrassed

窘态 jiǒngtài [名] embarrassment ◇在记者的追问下，总统面露窘态。Under questioning from the journalist, the president looked embarrassed.

纠 jiū [动] 1 (缠绕) entangle 2 (集合) assemble 3 (督察) supervise 4 (改正) correct

纠察 jiūchá I [动] maintain order II [名] steward

纠缠 jiūchán [动] 1 (绕在一起) entangle ◇他们两人的关系纠缠不清。Their relationship is very complicated. 2 (找麻烦) hassle

纠纷 jiūfēn [名] dispute

纠葛 jiūgé [名] dispute

纠合 jiūhé [动] (贬) gang up ◇当地的毒贩纠合起来走私海洛因。The local drug traffickers worked together on a heroin smuggling operation.

纠正 jiūzhèng [动] correct

究 jiū I [动] investigate ♦深究 investigate thoroughly II [副] actually

究竟 jiūjìng **I** [名] outcome **II** [副] actually ◇究竟发生了什么事？ What actually happened?

赳 jiū 见下文

赳赳 jiūjiū [形] valiant

阄 jiū [名] lot ♦抓阄 draw lots

揪 jiū [动] seize

揪辫子 jiū biànzi (喻) have a hold over

揪心 jiūxīn [动] worry ◇用不着揪心，他会应付的。 No need to worry – he can cope.

九 jiǔ [数] **1** (指数字) nine **2** (表示多数或多次) ◇九死一生 have a narrow escape

九牛二虎之力 jiǔ niú èr hǔ zhī lì (喻) enormous effort ◇我费了九牛二虎之力将冰箱运回家。I bust a gut to get the fridge home.

九牛一毛 jiǔ niú yī máo a drop in the ocean

九泉 jiǔquán [名] the underworld ◇含笑九泉 rest happy in one's grave

九死一生 jiǔ sǐ yī shēng have a narrow escape

九霄云外 jiǔ xiāo yún wài far away ◇他早把誓言抛到了九霄云外。 He has long since forgotten his promise.

久 jiǔ [形] **1** (时间长) long ♦恒久 permanent ◇久别重逢 be reunited after a long time apart **2** (时间长短) long ◇回家住了多久？ How long did you go home for?

久而久之 jiǔ ér jiǔ zhī over time

久久 jiǔjiǔ [形] ◇精彩表演使观众久久不愿离去。The performance was so good that for a long time the audience didn't want to leave.

久违 jiǔwéi [动] (客套) ◇聚会上有许多久违的老友。There were loads of old friends at the party that we hadn't seen for ages. ◇久违了！近来还好吗？ Long time no see! Have you been well?

久仰 jiǔyǎng [动] (客套) ◇久仰大名，幸会幸会！ I'm delighted to have the opportunity to meet you at last!

久远 jiǔyuǎn [形] remote ◇久远的历史 remote history

玖 jiǔ [数] nine

韭 jiǔ 见下文

韭菜 jiǔcài [名] chive

酒 jiǔ [名] alcohol ♦葡萄酒 wine ♦敬酒 propose a toast ♦啤酒 beer ♦酒鬼 wino

酒店 jiǔdiàn [名] **1** (酒馆) bar **2** (宾馆) hotel

酒会 jiǔhuì [名] party ◇鸡尾酒会 cocktail party

酒家 jiǔjiā [名] (饭馆) restaurant

酒精 jiǔjīng [名] alcohol

酒量 jiǔliàng [名] alcohol tolerance ◇他酒量大，喝七八杯没问题。 He can hold his drink well – he drinks seven or eight glasses without a problem.

酒令 jiǔlìng [名] drinking game

酒楼 jiǔlóu [名] restaurant

酒肉朋友 jiǔròu péngyǒu [名] fair-weather friend

酒窝 jiǔwō [名] dimple

酒席 jiǔxí [名] feast

旧 jiù **I** [形] **1** (过时) old ◇旧观念 old-fashioned idea **2** (陈旧) used ◇旧衣服 used clothes **II** [名] old friend

旧地 jiùdì [名] familiar place

旧观 jiùguān [名] old look

旧交 jiùjiāo [名] old friend

旧居 jiùjū [名] former residence

旧历 jiùlì [名] lunar calendar

旧情 jiùqíng [名] old friendship

旧式 jiùshì [形] old-style

咎 jiù **I** [名] blame ◇引咎辞职 take the blame and resign **II** [动] blame ◇既往不咎 let bygones be bygones

咎由自取 jiù yóu zì qǔ only have oneself to blame

疚 jiù [动] (书) be remorseful ♦内疚 have a guilty conscience

厩 jiù [名] barn

救 jiù [动] save ♦呼救 cry for help ♦救灾 provide disaster relief

救国 jiùguó [动] save the nation

救护 jiùhù [动] give first-aid (*pt* gave, *pp* given) ◊救护伤员 give first-aid to the wounded

救护车 jiùhùchē [名] ambulance

救荒 jiùhuāng [动] send relief (*pt*, *pp* sent)

救济 jiùjì [动] provide relief ◊救济灾民 provide relief to disaster victims

救命 jiùmìng [动] save a life ◊他救了我的命。He saved my life. ◊救命啊！ Help!

救生 jiùshēng [动] save a life ♦救生员 lifeguard

救世主 jiùshìzhǔ [名] the Saviour

救死扶伤 jiù sǐ fú shāng save the dying and nurse the wounded

救亡 jiùwáng [动] save a nation

救星 jiùxīng [名] saviour

救援 jiùyuán [动] go to the rescue (*pt* went, *pp* gone) ◊救援小组 rescue team ◊救援灾区 bring relief to a disaster area

救灾 jiùzāi [动] **1** (救济灾民) provide disaster relief **2** (消除灾害) perform a clean-up operation

就 jiù **I** [动] **1** (靠近) move close to ◊避重就轻 evade serious issues and dwell on the trivial **2** (开始) take … up (*pt* took, *pp* taken) ◊就职 take up a position **3** (完成) accomplish **4** (趁) take the opportunity (*pt* took, *pp* taken) ◊等你看完了这本书，就手把读后感写完吧。You should write the review as soon as you've finished reading the book. **5** (搭配着吃) eat … with (*pt* ate, *pp* eaten) ◊泡菜就稀粥 eat pickles with rice congee **II** [副] **1** (强调时间短) shortly ◊请稍等，我这就做完。Wait a moment, I'll be finished shortly. **2** (早已) already ◊他清晨5点就起床了。He was already up at five in the morning. **3** (表示紧接着) as soon as ◊我一回家就打电话给你。I'll call you as soon as I get home. **4** (表示条件关系) then ◊用功点就能考出好成绩。If you put in a bit of work then you'll get good exam results. **5** (强调数量多) as much as ◊他一个月写两篇文章，我一星期就写3篇。He writes two articles a month. I write as many as three a week. ◊那么多行李他一人就拎走了。He carried all that luggage by himself. **6** (仅仅) only ◊就他一人没来。He was the only one who didn't come. **7** (原本) already ◊我就知道他喜欢撒谎。I already knew he liked to tell lies. ◊裤子本来就小，洗了后更小。The trousers were already small, and after washing them they got even smaller. **8** (表示坚决) simply ◊我就不信完成不了任务。I simply don't believe I can't finish the job. **9** (强调事实) exactly ◊这里就是我童年生活过的地方。This is exactly the place where I spent my childhood. **10** (表示容忍) even though ◊衬衫难看就难看些吧，因为便宜，我就买了。Even though the shirt wasn't that nice, I bought it because it was cheap. **III** [连] even if ◊你就不来，我也无所谓。Even if you don't come, I really don't care. **IV** [介] on ◊就贸易争端进行了会谈 hold talks on trade disputes

就便 jiùbiàn [副] in passing ◊你来学校时，请就便到我办公室来一下。When you come to school, please visit my office at your convenience.

就餐 jiùcān [动] dine

就此 jiùcǐ [副] at this point ◊今天的课就此结束。We'll conclude today's class here.

就地 jiùdì [副] on the spot

就读 jiùdú [动] study ◊就读于清华大学历史系 study at Qinghua University's history department

就范 jiùfàn [动] give in (*pt* gave, *pp* given)

就近 jiùjìn [副] nearby

就寝 jiùqǐn [动] go to bed (*pt* went, *pp* gone)

就任 jiùrèn [动] take up a post (*pt* took, *pp* taken) ◊就任市长一职 take up the post of mayor

就事论事 jiù shì lùn shì confine oneself to the facts

就是 jiùshì **I** [副] **1** (表示赞同) exactly

◇"他索价太高。" "就是！" "He's asking too much." – "Exactly!" **2** (表示坚决) still ◇无论大家怎么解释，他就是不相信。No matter what everyone said, he still didn't believe them. **3** (表示强调) really ◇东立就是聪明。Dong Li is really clever. **4** (确定范围) only ◇他挺聪明的，就是不够勤勉。He's very clever, only he doesn't work hard enough. **II** [助] ◇我一定准时到。你放心就是了。I will definitely arrive on time – just stop worrying! ◇你干就是了，没人说你。Just go ahead and do it – no one will blame you! **III** [连] even if ◇你就是再努力，也没人理你。Even if you try harder, people still won't pay attention to you.

就手 jiùshǒu [副] on the way ◇出门时就手关灯。Can you turn off the lights on your way out?

就算 jiùsuàn [连] even if ◇就算你不去参加会议也没关系。Even if you don't attend the conference, it is not a problem.

就位 jiùwèi [动] be in place

就绪 jiùxù [动] be in order ◇爆破准备就绪。Preparations for the demolition are all in order.

就业 jiùyè [动] get a job ◇就业指导 careers advice ◇就业服务中心 job centre (英) 或 center (美) ◇帮助下岗工人再就业 help those laid off to find a new job

就医 jiùyī [动] go to the doctor (*pt* went, *pp* gone)

就义 jiùyì [动] die a martyr

就诊 jiùzhěn [动] see a doctor (*pt* saw, *pp* seen)

就职 jiùzhí [动] take office (*pt* took, *pp* taken) ◇新总统宣誓就职。The new president was sworn into office.

就座 jiùzuò [动] take one's seat (*pt* took, *pp* taken) ◇双方就座后，谈判就开始了。After the two sides took their seats, the talks began. ◇大型会议室能容纳500余人就座。The large conference hall can seat more than 500 people.

舅 jiù [名] **1** (舅父) uncle **2** (妻的弟兄) brother-in-law (*pl* brothers-in-law)

舅舅 jiùjiu [名] uncle

舅子 jiùzi [名] brother-in-law (*pl* brothers-in-law)

拘 jū **I** [动] **1** (逮捕) arrest **2** (拘束) restrain ◇无拘无束 free and easy **3** (拘泥) be small-minded ◇王教授是个不拘小节的人。Professor Wang isn't the type to worry about little things.

拘捕 jūbǔ [动] arrest

拘谨 jūjǐn [形] overcautious

拘留 jūliú [动] detain

拘拿 jūná [动] arrest

拘泥 jūní [动] stick rigidly to (*pt, pp* stuck)

拘束 jūshù **I** [动] restrain ◇少一份拘束多一份积极 a little less restraint and a little more action **II** [形] restrained

拘押 jūyā [动] take … into custody (*pt* took, *pp* taken)

狙 jū [动] (书) watch for

狙击 jūjī [动] snipe ◇狙击手 sniper

居 jū **I** [动] **1** (住) live **2** (在) be (*pt* was, *pp* been) ◇居全国第一 be number one in the country **3** (任) claim ♦居功 claim the credit **4** (积蓄) store … up **II** [名] house

居安思危 jū ān sī wēi be prepared for danger in times of peace

居多 jūduō [动] be in the majority ◇这个商场里本地货居多。The majority of the goods in the store are local. ◇相册里黑白照片居多。Most of the photos in the album are black and white.

居高临下 jū gāo lín xià occupy a commanding position

居家 jūjiā [动] run a household (*pt* ran, *pp* run) ◇居家过日，以俭为本。In order to run an efficient household, you have to be thrifty. ◇居家生活 domestic life

居民 jūmín [名] resident

居然 jūrán [副] unexpectedly ◇他考试居然敢做弊！ No one would have expected him to cheat in his exam.

居室 jūshì [名] room

居心 jūxīn [动] ◇居心不良 harbour (英) 或 harbor (美) bad intentions

居心叵测 jū xīn pǒ cè have ulterior motives

居住 jūzhù [动] live

驹 jū [名] **1** (好马) fine horse **2** (驹子) foal

掬 jū [动] hold … in both hands (*pt, pp* held)

鞠 jū [动] (书) bow

鞠躬 jūgōng [动] bow

鞠躬尽瘁 jūgōng jìn cuì devote oneself entirely to

局 jú **I** [名] **1** (棋盘) chessboard **2** (次) game ♦平局 a draw **3** (形势) situation ♦时局 current political situation **4** (聚会) gathering ♦赌局 gambling party ♦饭局 dinner party **5** (圈套) ruse ♦骗局 fraud **6** (部分) part **7** (机关部门) department **8** (业务机构) office **9** (商店) shop **II** [量] ◇我赢了这局棋。I won the chess game. ◇下一局比赛明天进行。The next match is taking place tomorrow.

局部 júbù [名] part ◇局部麻醉 local anaesthetic (英) 或 anesthetic (美)

局促 júcù [形] **1** (拘谨) inhibited **2** (狭小) cramped

局面 júmiàn [名] situation ◇打破电信垄断局面 break the telecommunications monopoly

局势 júshì [名] situation

局限 júxiàn [动] limit

局限性 júxiànxìng [名] limitation

局域网 júyùwǎng [名] local area network

菊 jú [名] chrysanthemum

橘 jú [名] tangerine

咀 jǔ [动] chew

咀嚼 jǔjué [动] **1** (嚼) chew **2** (体会) mull … over

沮 jǔ [形] depressed

沮丧 jǔsàng [形] depressed

矩 jǔ [名] **1** (曲尺) square **2** (规则) regulation

矩形 jǔxíng [名] rectangle

举 jǔ **I** [动] **1** (往上托) raise ♦举重 weightlifting **2** (兴起) mobilize ♦举兵 dispatch troops **3** (选举) elect **4** (提出) cite ♦举例 cite an example **II** [名] act **III** [形] (书) whole

> 请勿混淆 **raise** 和 **rise**。**raise** 是及物动词，其后通常要跟宾语，而 **rise** 是不及物动词，其后通常不跟宾语。**rise** 不能用在被动语态中。*…the government's decision to raise prices… The number of people affected is likely to rise.* **raise** 和 **rise** 都能够用作名词，表示加薪；**raise** 用于美式英语中，而 **rise** 用在英式英语中。*Millions of Americans get a pay raise today… Last year she got a rise of 12 per cent.*

举办 jǔbàn [动] hold (*pt, pp* held)

举报 jǔbào [动] report

举措 jǔcuò [名] measure

举动 jǔdòng [名] action

举国 jǔguó [名] the whole country

举荐 jǔjiàn [动] recommend

举例 jǔlì [动] give an example (*pt* gave, *pp* given) ◇举例说明 illustrate with examples

举目无亲 jǔmù wú qīn be a stranger in a strange land

举棋不定 jǔ qí bù dìng dither

举世 jǔshì [名] the whole world ◇举世闻名 world-famous ◇举世无双 unrivalled

举手之劳 jǔ shǒu zhī láo no trouble at all ◇"谢谢你开车送我回家。""不客气。举手之劳。" "Thanks for driving me home." – "You're welcome – it was no trouble at all."

举行 jǔxíng [动] hold (*pt, pp* held) ◇举行会议 hold a meeting

举一反三 jǔ yī fǎn sān extrapolate information

举止 jǔzhǐ [名] conduct

举足轻重 jǔ zú qīng zhòng play a key role

龃 jǔ 见下文

龃龉 jǔyǔ [动] (书) (喻) disagree

巨 jù [形] huge ♦巨著 monumental work ♦艰巨 onerous

巨大 jùdà [形] huge

巨额 jù'é [名] enormous amounts (*pl*)

巨匠 jùjiàng [名] (书) giant

巨人 jùrén [名] giant

巨头 jùtóu [名] tycoon

巨子 jùzǐ [名] giant ◇媒体巨子 media giant

句 jù I [名] sentence II [量] ◇说几句话 say a few words ◇写两句诗 write two lines of verse

句法 jùfǎ [名] 1 (句子结构) sentence structure 2 (指语法学) syntax

句号 jùhào [名] full stop (英), period (美)

句型 jùxíng [名] sentence pattern

句子 jùzi [名] sentence

拒 jù [动] 1 (抵抗) resist 2 (拒绝) refuse

拒捕 jùbǔ [动] resist arrest

拒绝 jùjué [动] refuse ◇他拒绝签合同。He refused to sign the contract. ◇婉言拒绝邀请 turn down an invitation

具 jù I [动] have (*pt, pp* had) ◇初具规模 begin to take shape II [名] utensil ♦餐具 tableware ♦玩具 toy ♦文具 stationery III [量] ◇一具棺材 a coffin ◇一具尸体 a corpse

具备 jùbèi [动] have (*pt, pp* had) ◇这手机具备收发电子信件的功能。This mobile phone has the capacity to send and receive emails.

具体 jùtǐ [形] 1 (明确) detailed 2 (特定) particular

具有 jùyǒu [动] have (*pt, pp* had)

炬 jù [名] torch

俱 jù [副] ◇面面俱到 attend to each and every aspect

俱乐部 jùlèbù [名] club

剧 jù I [名] drama ♦喜剧 comedy ♦丑剧 farce ♦剧团 troupe II [形] severe ♦剧变 dramatic change

剧本 jùběn [名] script

剧毒 jùdú [名] deadly poison

剧烈 jùliè [形] severe

剧目 jùmù [名] repertoire

剧务 jùwù [名] 1 (指事务) stage management 2 (指人) stage manager

剧院 jùyuàn [名] 1 (剧场) theatre (英), theater (美) 2 (剧团) company

剧种 jùzhǒng [名] genre

剧组 jùzǔ [名] crew

据 jù I [动] 1 (占据) occupy ♦盘据 forcibly occupy ◇据为己有 appropriate 2 (凭借) rely on ♦据点 stronghold II [介] according to ◇据报道 according to reports III [名] evidence ♦收据 receipt ♦论据 grounds for argument ◇真凭实据 hard evidence

据点 jùdiǎn [名] stronghold

据理力争 jùlǐ lìzhēng put forward a strong and fair argument

据说 jùshuō [动] be said ◇据说他已定居美国。It is said that he's already settled in America.

距 jù [名] distance ◇这两个城市相距不远。The distance between these two cities is not great. ◇相距遥远 far apart from each other

距离 jùlí [动] be at a distance from ◇住宅距离办公室约有3英里。The house is about 3 miles from the office. ◇俩人的观点有距离。The two of them have quite different views.

惧 jù [动] be frightened

惧怕 jùpà [动] fear ◇人人都惧怕生病。Everyone fears getting ill.

飓 jù 见下文

飓风 jùfēng [名] hurricane

锯 jù I [名] saw II [动] saw (*pt* sawed, *pp* sawn)

聚 jù [动] 1 (集合) get together ♦团

聚 reunite **2** (积聚) amass ♦凝聚 condense ◇聚敛财富 amass a vast illegal fortune

聚宝盆 jùbǎopén [名] treasure trove

聚餐 jùcān [动] have a dinner party

聚合 jùhé [动] (聚集) get together

聚会 jùhuì [动] get together ◇周末有个同学聚会。At the weekend there's a get-together of classmates.

聚积 jùjī [动] accumulate ◇聚积一些钱 save a bit of money

聚集 jùjí [动] gather

聚焦 jùjiāo [动] focus ◇聚焦保险市场 focus on the insurance market

聚精会神 jù jīng huì shén focus all one's attention on

聚众 jùzhòng [动] mob

踞 jù [动] (占据) occupy

踞守 jùshǒu [动] guard

捐 juān **I** [动] **1** (舍弃) relinquish ◇捐躯 die for a cause **2** (捐助) donate ♦募捐 appeal for donations **II** [名] levy

捐款 juānkuǎn [动] donate money ◇收到一笔捐款 receive a donation

捐躯 juānqū [动] sacrifice one's life

捐献 juānxiàn [动] donate

捐助 juānzhù [动] contribute

涓 juān [名] (书) trickle

涓涓 juānjuān [形] (书) trickling

娟 juān [形] (书) beautiful

娟秀 juānxiù [形] (书) beautiful

圈 juān [动] pen … in ◇别总把孩子圈在家里。You shouldn't keep the children penned up in the house.
▷另见 juàn, quān

镌 juān [动] (书) engrave ♦镌刻 engrave

卷 juǎn **I** [动] **1** (裹成筒形) roll … up **2** (撮起) sweep … up (*pt, pp* swept) ◇飓风把房屋卷走了。The hurricane swept the house away. **3** (喻) (牵涉) be swept up in **II** [名] roll **III** [量] roll ◇一卷卫生纸 a roll of toilet paper
▷另见 juàn

卷逃 juǎntáo [动] run off with (*pt* ran, *pp* run)

卷土重来 juǎn tǔ chóng lái stage a comeback

卷 juàn **I** [名] **1** (书本) book **2** (试卷) exam paper **3** (文件) document **II** [量] volume
▷另见 juǎn

卷子 juànzi [名] exam paper ◇出卷子 set exam papers

卷宗 juànzōng [名] **1** (文件) file **2** (纸夹子) folder

隽 juàn [形] (书) meaningful ♦隽永 meaningful

倦 juàn **I** [形] tired **II** [动] be tired of

倦容 juànróng [名] tired look ◇满脸倦容 look completely tired out

倦色 juànsè [名] tired look

绢 juàn [名] silk

眷 juàn **I** [名] family member **II** [动] (书) care about

眷恋 juànliàn [动] (书) be sentimentally attached to

眷念 juànniàn [动] (书) feel nostalgic about (*pt, pp* felt)

眷属 juànshǔ [名] **1** (亲属) family member **2** (夫妻) husband and wife

圈 juàn [名] pen ♦猪圈 pigsty
▷另见 juān, quān

撅 juē [动] stick up (*pt, pp* stuck) ◇撅起嘴巴 pout

决 jué **I** [动] **1** (决定) decide ◇犹豫不决 be unable to make a decision **2** (执行死刑) execute **3** (决口) burst (*pt, pp* burst) **4** (定胜负) decide on a result ♦决战 decisive battle **II** [副] under any circumstances ◇无论多困难，我都决不放弃努力。No matter how difficult it is, I won't give up under any circumstances. **III** [形] decisive ♦果决 resolute

决策 juécè [动] make a strategic decision

决定 juédìng [动] **1** (打定主意) decide ◇决定远走高飞 decide to run away ◇这盘棋决定胜负。This game of chess will be the decider. ◇作出惊人的决定 make a startling decision **2** (表示条件关系) determine ◇他的个性决定了他对职业的选择。His character was the determining factor in his choice of career.

决斗 juédòu [动] **1** (字) duel **2** (殊死的斗争) engage in a decisive battle

决断 juéduàn **I** [动] make a decision **II** [名] **1** (决定) decision **2** (指作风) decisiveness

决计 juéjì **I** [动] have made up one's mind **II** [副] definitely

决口 juékǒu [动] burst (*pt, pp* burst)

决裂 juéliè [动] break with (*pt* broke, *pp* broken) ◇戒毒后，他与过去的生活彻底决裂了。After giving up drugs, he made a complete break with his past life. ◇夫妻俩争吵之后彻底决裂了。After their quarrel the couple completely broke it off.

决赛 juésài [名] final ◇半决赛 semi-final ◇四分之一决赛 quarter-final

决心 juéxīn [名] determination ◇我从未见过像他这样有决心的人。I've never seen anyone as determined as him.

决一雌雄 jué yī cí xióng fight it out

决议 juéyì [名] resolution

决意 juéyì [动] be determined ◇她决意要辞职。She was determined to resign.

决战 juézhàn [动] fight a decisive battle (*pt, pp* fought)

诀 jué **I** [名] **1** (指词句) mnemonic **2** (诀窍) knack **II** [动] part

诀别 juébié [动] bid farewell (*pt* bade, *pp* bidden)

诀窍 juéqiào [名] knack

抉 jué [动] (书) pick … out ♦抉择 choose

角 jué **I** [名] **1** (角色) role **2** (女演员) actress **3** (男演员) actor **II** [动] fight (*pt, pp* fought) ♦口角 quarrel ▷另见 jiǎo

角斗 juédòu [动] wrestle ◇角斗士 wrestler ◇角斗场 wrestling ring

角色 juésè [名] **1** (剧中人物) part ◇扮演主要角色 play the main part **2** (某类人) role ◇他在公司中是什么样的角色？ What role does he have in the company?

角逐 juézhú [动] compete ◇权力角逐 power struggle ◇角逐诺贝尔文学奖 compete for the Nobel Prize for Literature

觉 jué **I** [动] **1** (感觉) feel (*pt, pp* felt) ◇穿得太少，会觉得冷的。If you don't wear enough clothes you'll feel cold. **2** (睡醒) wake up (*pt* woke, *pp* woken) ◇大梦初觉 come to one's senses **3** (觉悟) become aware of (*pt* became, *pp* become) **II** [名] sense ♦触觉 sense of touch ♦知觉 consciousness ▷另见 jiào

觉察 juéchá [动] detect

觉得 juédé [动] **1** (感到) feel (*pt, pp* felt) ◇觉得有点冷 feel a bit cold **2** (认为) think (*pt, pp* thought) ◇他觉得我不适合做这项工作。He doesn't think I'm suited for this work. ◇我觉得应该亲自去一趟。I think I should go in person.

觉悟 juéwù [名] awareness ◇觉悟到改革的重要性 become aware of the importance of reform

觉醒 juéxǐng [动] awaken ◇民族意识的觉醒 the awakening of a national consciousness

绝 jué **I** [动] **1** (断绝) cut … off (*pt, pp* cut) ♦隔绝 isolate **2** (穷尽) exhaust **3** (无后代) have no descendants ◇断子绝孙 be the last in one's line **4** (死) die ◇悲痛欲绝 be torn apart with grief **II** [形] **1** (不通) hopeless ♦绝路 blind alley ♦绝地 impasse **2** (高超) superb **III** [副] **1** (最) extremely ♦绝密 top secret **2** (绝对) absolutely ◇绝无此意 have absolutely no such intentions

绝笔 juébǐ [名] **1** (最后的作品) last work **2** (最好的作品) masterpiece

绝处逢生 jué chù féng shēng make a miraculous recovery

绝代 juédài [形] (书) exceptional

绝顶 juédǐng **I** [副] extremely ◇绝顶聪明 extremely intelligent **II** [名] (书) summit

绝对 juéduì I [形] absolute ◇绝对真理 absolute truth II [副] absolutely

绝后 juéhòu [动] **1** (无后代) be childless **2** (不会再有) never to be seen again ◇空前绝后 unprecedented and unrepeatable

绝活 juéhuó [名] speciality (英), specialty (美)

绝技 juéjì [名] expertise

绝交 juéjiāo [动] **1** (指国家间) break ties (*pt* broke, *pp* broken) **2** (指个人) break up (*pt* broke, *pp* broken) ◇他背信弃义，我只好和他绝交。He was dishonest with me so I had no choice but to break up with him.

绝境 juéjìng [名] (绝望的境地) hopeless situation

绝口 juékǒu [动] **1** (住口) stop talking ◇骂不绝口 continuously insult **2** (回避不谈) not open one's mouth

绝妙 juémiào [形] brilliant

绝情 juéqíng [形] heartless

绝食 juéshí [动] go on hunger strike (*pt* went, *pp* gone)

绝望 juéwàng [动] feel desperate (*pt, pp* felt)

绝无仅有 jué wú jǐn yǒu unique

绝育 juéyù [动] sterilize

绝缘 juéyuán [动] (电子) insulate ◇绝缘材料 insulating materials ◇绝缘体 insulator

绝招 juézhāo [名] **1** (绝技) unique skill **2** (妙举) masterstroke

绝症 juézhèng [名] terminal illness

绝种 juézhǒng [动] become extinct (*pt* became, *pp* become) ◇保护濒临绝种的野生动物 protect wild animals on the verge of extinction

倔 jué 见下文
▷另见 juè

倔强 juéjiàng [动] be stubborn

掘 jué [动] dig (*pt, pp* dug) ♦挖掘 excavate

崛 jué 见下文

崛起 juéqǐ [动] (书) **1** (突起) soar **2** (兴起) spring up (*pt* sprang, *pp* sprung)

厥 jué [动] faint ♦晕厥 faint

橛 jué [名] peg

爵 jué [名] peerage ♦公爵 duke

爵士 juéshì [名] **1** (作为头衔，用于全名前) Sir ◇温斯顿·丘吉尔爵士 Sir Winston Churchill **2** (指级别) knight ◇他被封为爵士。He was awarded a knighthood.

爵士乐 juéshìyuè [名] jazz

蹶 jué [动] (喻) (失败) suffer a setback ◇一蹶不振 unable to recover from a setback

嚼 jué [动] chew
▷另见 jiáo

攫 jué [动] seize

攫取 juéqǔ [动] plunder

倔 juè [形] surly
▷另见 jué

军 jūn I [名] **1** (军队) army ♦参军 enlist ♦海军 navy **2** (指军队编制单位) regiment **3** (指集体) forces (*pl*) ◇革命的后备军 revolutionary reserve forces II [形] military ♦军费 military expenditure ♦军令 military order ♦军乐 military music

军备 jūnbèi [名] arms (*pl*)

军队 jūnduì [名] troops (*pl*)

军阀 jūnfá [名] warlord

军工 jūngōng [名] **1** (军事工业) arms industry **2** (军事工程) military project

军官 jūnguān [名] officer

军国主义 jūnguó zhǔyì [名] militarism

军火 jūnhuǒ [名] ammunitions (*pl*) ◇军火商 arms dealer

军界 jūnjiè [名] the military

军情 jūnqíng [名] military movement ◇刺探军情 gather military intelligence

军区 jūnqū [名] military region

军人 jūnrén [名] soldier ◇退伍军人 ex-serviceman

军事 jūnshì [名] military affairs (*pl*) ◇军事法庭 military tribunal

军属 jūnshǔ [名] soldier's family

军衔 jūnxián [名] military rank ◇他被赐予上校军衔。He was given the rank of colonel.

军心 jūnxīn [名] troop morale

军需 jūnxū [名] military supplies (*pl*)

军营 jūnyíng [名] barracks

军用 jūnyòng [形] military ◇军用物资 military supplies

军长 jūnzhǎng [名] military commander

军政 jūnzhèng [名] **1** (军事和政治) military affairs and politics (*pl*) **2** (指军中行政工作) military administration **3** (军队和政府) army and government

军职 jūnzhí [名] military post

军种 jūnzhǒng [名] armed services (*pl*)

军装 jūnzhuāng [名] army uniform

均 jūn **I** [动] divide ... equally ◇把钱均一下。Divide the money out equally. **II** [形] even ♦平均 average ◇分配不均 uneven distribution **III** [副] **1** (都) all ◇来作客的均是老同学。All the guests were old classmates. **2** (平均) equally ◇均分利润 divide the profits equally

均等 jūnděng [形] equal ◇机会均等 equal opportunities

均分 jūnfēn [动] divide ... equally

均衡 jūnhéng [形] balanced

均势 jūnshì [名] even balance

均摊 jūntān [动] share ... equally

均匀 jūnyún [形] even ◇将咖啡牛奶搅拌均匀。Mix the coffee and milk evenly.

均沾 jūnzhān [动] share ... equally ◇利益均沾 share the profits equally

龟 jūn 见下文
▷另见 guī

龟裂 jūnliè [动] **1** (指皮肤) chap ◇龟裂的嘴唇 chapped lips **2** (裂缝) crack

君 jūn [名] **1** (君主) monarch **2** (书) (指尊称) Mr. ◇李君 Mr. Li

君权 jūnquán [名] monarchical power

君王 jūnwáng [名] monarch

君主 jūnzhǔ [名] monarch

君子 jūnzǐ [名] gentleman (*pl* gentlemen)

君子协定 jūnzǐxiédìng [名] gentleman's agreement

菌 jūn [名] **1** (指植物) fungus ◇蘑菇是食用菌的一种。Mushrooms are a type of edible fungus. **2** (特指细菌) bacterium (*pl* bacteria)

皲 jūn 见下文

皲裂 jūnliè [动] chap ◇皲裂的皮肤 chapped skin

俊 jùn **I** [形] **1** (指女性) pretty **2** (指男性) handsome **II** [名] talented

俊杰 jùnjié [名] hero

俊美 jùnměi [形] beautiful

俊俏 jùnqiào [形] (口) charming

俊秀 jùnxiù [形] delicate

峻 jùn [形] **1** (高大) high **2** (严厉) harsh

峻峭 jùnqiào [形] precipitous

浚 jùn [动] dredge

骏 jùn [名] fine horse ♦骏马 steed

竣 jùn [动] complete

竣工 jùngōng [动] be complete ◇写字楼按时竣工。The office block has been completed to schedule.

Kk

咖 kā 见下文
▷另见 gā

咖啡 kāfēi [名] coffee ◊咖啡豆 coffee bean ◊速溶咖啡 instant coffee ◊我想喝杯咖啡。I'd like a cup of coffee. ◊请来3杯加奶的咖啡。Three white coffees, please.

卡 kǎ **I** [量] (物) calorie **II** [名] **1** (卡片) card ◊生日卡 birthday card **2** (指录音机) cassette
▷另见 qiǎ

卡车 kǎchē [名] lorry (英), truck (美)

卡拉OK kǎlā'ōukèi [名] karaoke

卡路里 kǎlùlǐ [量] calorie

卡片 kǎpiàn [名] card

卡通 kǎtōng [名] cartoon

开 kāi **I** [动] **1** (打开) open ♦开门 open the door **2** (开辟) open up **3** (绽放) bloom ◊菊花开了。The chrysanthemums are in bloom. **4** (松开) come undone (*pt* came, *pp* come) ◊信封开了。The envelope has come unstuck. ◊扣子开了。The buttons have come undone. **5** (驾驶) drive (*pt* drove, *pp* driven) ◊他喜欢开汽车。He likes driving. ◊我喜欢开飞机。I like flying planes. **6** (办) run (*pt* ran, *pp* run) **7** (开始) start **8** (举行) hold (*pt*, *pp* held) **9** (写出) write … out (*pt* wrote, *pp* written) ◊请医生开一张药方。Ask the doctor to write out a prescription. **10** (支付) pay (*pt*, *pp* paid) **11** (沸腾) boil **12** (摆出) serve ◊开饭了。Dinner is ready. **13** (指比例) be in a ratio of ◊三七开 be in a ratio of three to seven **II** [量] (出版) (开本) ◊这个本子是4开的。This book is in quarto format.

开办 kāibàn [动] set up (*pt*, *pp* set) ◊他们开办了一家药店。They set up a pharmacy.

开本 kāiběn [名] ◊这本杂志是8开本的。This magazine is in octavo format.

开场 kāichǎng [动] start

开场白 kāichǎngbái [名] **1** (指演出) prologue **2** (指话语) introduction

开诚布公 kāi chéng bù gōng frank ◊大家开诚布公地谈了自己的看法。Everyone spoke their mind.

开除 kāichú [动] dismiss ◊他被公司开除了。He was dismissed by the company.

开创 kāichuàng [动] initiate

开刀 kāidāo [动] **1** (做手术) operate on ◊她的背部开过刀。She had an operation on her back. **2** (喻) make an example of

开导 kāidǎo [动] talk round ◊经朋友们开导，她终于想通了。Her friends talked her round and finally she agreed.

开动 kāidòng [动] **1** (启动) start ◊请大家开动脑筋，想想办法。Please would everyone get their brains in gear, and think of a solution. **2** (前进) get going

开端 kāiduān [名] beginning

开发 kāifā [动] **1** (开采) exploit ◊开发自然资源 exploit natural resources **2** (开垦) reclaim **3** (发现) develop

开放 kāifàng [动] **1** (展开) bloom **2** (解禁) open ◊实行对外开放政策 implement a policy of openness **3** (开朗) be open-minded

开工 kāigōng [动] **1** (指工厂) go into operation (*pt* went, *pp* gone) **2** (指工程) start

开关 kāiguān [名] **1** (指电器) switch **2** (指管道) valve

开国 kāiguó [动] found a state

开户 kāihù [动] open an account ◊公司准备在另一家银行开户。The company is going to open an account with another bank.

开花 kāihuā [动] **1** (开放) flower ◊茉莉开了花。The jasmine is in flower. **2** (喻) (破裂) split (*pt*, *pp* split) **3** (喻) (高兴) ◊她心里乐开了花。She's bursting with joy. **4** (喻) (兴起) take off (*pt* took, *pp* taken) ◊这项新技术在农村已遍地开花。The new technology has already taken off in the countryside.

开化 kāihuà [动] **1** (文明) become civilized (*pt* became, *pp* become) **2**(方) (融化) thaw

开怀 kāihuái [形] happy ◇乐开怀 be extremely happy ◇宴会上, 大家开怀畅饮。At the dinner party everyone drank to their heart's content.

开会 kāihuì [动] have a meeting

开火 kāihuǒ [动] **1** (进攻) open fire **2** (喻) (抨击) attack

开价 kāijià [动] quote ◇这件古董开价5千美元。This antique is quoted at five thousand dollars.

开奖 kāijiǎng [动] announce the winner

开禁 kāijìn [动] lift a ban ◇那部电影终于开禁了。At last the ban on that film has been lifted.

开局 kāijú **I** [动] start **II** [名] opening

开卷有益 kāi juàn yǒu yì reading broadens the mind

开课 kāikè [动] **1** (开学) start **2** (授课) teach a course (*pt, pp* taught) ◇胡教授准备给研究生开课。Professor Hu will be teaching a postgraduate course.

开垦 kāikěn [动] reclaim

开口 kāikǒu [动] **1** (说话) open one's mouth ◇开会时她一直没开口。She didn't open her mouth during the meeting. **2** (开刃) sharpen **3** (裂开) split (*pt, pp* split)

开口子 kāi kǒuzi [动] **1** (指堤岸等) burst (*pt, pp* burst) ◇河堤开口子了! The dam has burst! **2** (指政策等) gain a concession ◇在这件事上不能给任何人开口子。We can't allow anyone any concessions.

开阔 kāikuò [形] **1** (指地域) wide **2** (指胸怀) broad ◇他心胸开阔。He's broad-minded. ◇旅游能开阔眼界。Travel broadens the horizons.

开朗 kāilǎng [形] **1** (指空间) open **2** (指性格) cheerful

开路 kāilù [动] **1** (开辟道路) open up a path ◇我们开了一条穿山路。We opened up a path through the mountains. **2** (引路) lead the way (*pt, pp* led) ◇村民在森林里开路。The villager led the way into the forest.

开门见山 kāi mén jiàn shān get straight to the point ◇我写文章喜欢开门见山。When I write essays I like to get straight to the point.

开明 kāimíng [形] enlightened

开幕 kāimù [动] **1** (指演出) start **2** (指会) open

开辟 kāipì [动] **1** (开通) open up **2** (开发) develop

开窍 kāiqiào [动] **1** (指思想) get it straight ◇无论我怎么说, 她就是不开窍。No matter how often I explained, she couldn't get it straight. **2** (指儿童) grow up (*pt* grew, *pp* grown) ◇他还没有开窍, 不知道生孩子是怎么一回事。He's not yet grown-up enough to understand the facts of life.

开设 kāishè [动] set up (*pt, pp* set) ◇开设工厂 set up a factory

开始 kāishǐ **I** [动] start, begin ◇他明天开始上班。He'll start work tomorrow. **II** [名] beginning

> **start, begin,** 和 **commence** 在语意上很相近, 不过 **commence** 更为正式, 通常不用于日常会话。*The meeting is ready to begin/start... He tore the list up and started/began a new one... the new school term commences in September...* 注意, **start, begin**, 和 **commence** 后面都可以跟名词或动词的 **-ing** 形式, 但是, 只有 **start** 和 begin 后面能够跟带 **'to'** 的动词不定式。可以说 *It's starting/beginning to rain.*, 但不能说 *'It's commencing to rain.'*

开水 kāishuǐ [名] boiling water

开庭 kāitíng [动] convene ◇明天法庭要开庭审理那宗杀人案。The court is convening tomorrow to hear the murder case.

开通 kāitōng [动] **1** (通畅) clear **2** (开始使用) start to use

开通 kāitong [形] broad-minded

开头 kāitóu **I** [动] begin (*pt* began, *pp* begun) **II** [名] beginning

开脱 kāituō [动] shake … off (*pt* shook, *pp* shaken) ◊他尽力为自己开脱罪责。He did everything he could to shake off the guilt.

开拓 kāituò [动] **1** (开辟) open up ◊开拓新市场 open up new markets **2** (开阔) broaden ◊开拓眼界 broaden one's horizons

开玩笑 kāi wánxiào [动] joke ◊我只是开玩笑。I was only joking. ◊别拿我开玩笑。Don't make fun of me.

开销 kāixiāo **I** [动] cover one's expenses ◊每月的工资不够他开销。His monthly salary is not enough to cover his expenses. **II** [名] expenses (*pl*) ◊旅游开销 travel expenses

开小差 kāi xiǎochāi [动] **1** (当逃兵) desert **2** (喻) (走神儿) be absent-minded

开心 kāixīn **I** [形] happy ◊他好像有点儿不开心。He looks a little unhappy. ◊他们玩得开心极了。They had a lot of fun. **II** [动] make fun of ◊他老拿别人开心。He's always making fun of people.

开眼 kāiyǎn [动] open one's eyes ◊这次旅游让我们对地方风情开了眼。The trip opened our eyes to local customs. ◊义务劳动可真叫人开眼。Voluntary work is a real eye-opener.

开业 kāiyè [动] start a business

开凿 kāizáo [动] cut (*pt, pp* cut)

开展 kāizhǎn [动] launch ◊他们为灾区开展募捐活动。They launched a campaign to get donations for the disaster area.

开张 kāizhāng [动] **1** (开业) open a business **2** (开门) open for business ◊这个小店每天上午9点开张。This shop opens for business at 9 a.m. every day. **3** (喻) (重新开始) start again ◊失败了不要紧，可以重打鼓另开张嘛！ Don t worry about losing – you can always have another go!

开支 kāizhī [动] **1** (支付) spend (*pt, pp* spent) ◊她从不乱开支。She never spends extravagantly. ◊我们要节约开支。We should cut down on expenses. **2** (方) (发工资) pay wages (*pt, pp* paid) ◊我公司月底开支。My firm pays us at the end of the month.

揩 kāi [动] wipe ◊揩干碟子 dry the dishes ◊他用手绢揩了揩汗。He wiped away the sweat with his handkerchief.

凯 kǎi [名] triumph

凯歌 kǎigē [名] victory song

凯旋 kǎixuán [动] return in triumph

铠 kǎi [名] armour (英), armor (美)

铠甲 kǎijiǎ [名] suit of armour (英) 或 armor (美)

慨 kǎi **I** [动] be indignant **II** [形] generous

慨叹 kǎitàn [动] sigh with regret

楷 kǎi [名] (典范) model

楷模 kǎimó [名] example

刊 kān **I** [动] **1** (出版) publish **2** (修改) correct ♦刊误 correct printing errors **II** [名] periodical ♦报刊 the press ♦月刊 monthly

刊登 kāndēng [动] publish

刊物 kānwù [名] periodical

刊载 kānzǎi [动] publish ◊这份报纸正在连续刊载她的小说。This newspaper is serializing her novel.

看 kān [动] **1** (照料) look after ◊她每天在家看孩子。She's at home every day looking after the children. ◊帮我看会儿行李吧。Please could you watch my luggage? **2** (看管) watch over ◊父母不应看着孩子学习。Parents shouldn't watch over their children while they study. ◊这些囚犯不易看。Guarding these prisoners isn't easy.
▷另见 kàn

看管 kānguǎn [动] **1** (看守) guard **2** (照管) look after ◊孩子需要好好看管。Children need a lot of looking after. ◊我不在时他会看管花园。He'll look after the garden while I'm away.

看护 kānhù [动] take care of (*pt* took, *pp* taken)

看家 kānjiā **I** [动] look after the house **II** [形] special ◇看家本领 special skill

看守 kānshǒu **I** [动] guard **II** [名] guard

勘 kān [动] **1** (校订) collate **2** (探测) survey ♦勘察 explore

勘测 kāncè [动] survey

勘探 kāntàn [动] explore

勘误 kānwù [动] correct printing errors

坎 kǎn [名] ridge

坎肩儿 kǎnjiānr [名] sleeveless jacket

坎坷 kǎnkě [形] **1** (字) (坑坑洼洼) bumpy **2** (喻) (不顺利) rough ◇他经历相当坎坷。He's had a really rough ride. ◇坎坷的人生之路 the rocky road of life

侃 kǎn [动] (口) chat

侃大山 kǎn dàshān [动](方) shoot the breeze (*pt, pp* shot)

侃侃而谈 kǎnkǎn'értán speak frankly and in measured tones

砍 kǎn [动] **1** (劈) chop **2** (减) cut (*pt, pp* cut)

砍伐 kǎnfá [动] fell

看 kàn **I** [动] **1** (观看) look at ◇看电视 watch TV ◇我昨天晚上去看京剧了。I went to see Beijing Opera last night. **2** (阅读) read (*pt, pp* read) **3** (认为) think (*pt, pp* thought) ◇你看这事儿怎么办? What do you think we should do about this? **4** (拜访) visit **5** (照料) look after **6** (预测) expect ◇英镑看涨。The pound is expected to rise. **7** (对待) treat ◇我把他当知己看。I treat him like a bosom friend. **8** (诊治) treat ◇昨天张医生给她看过病。Doctor Zhang treated her yesterday. ◇我要带孩子去看病。I am taking my child to see the doctor. **9** (取决于) depend on ◇"你明年买车吗?" "看情况吧。" Are you going to buy a car next year? – It depends. ◇下午踢不踢球得看天气。Whether we play football this afternoon depends on the weather. **II** [助] (表示尝试) ◇你试试看,衣服合适不? Why don't you try on the clothes and see if they fit? ◇"这果子好吃吗?" "尝尝看。" How is the fruit? – Have a taste. **III** [叹] (表示惊讶、责备) ◇你看你!怎么又迟到了! Goodness! How come you're late again! ◇看,你又忘了锁门吧! Look, you forgot to lock the door again! ▷另见 kān

> 📖 **look at** 或 **watch** 表示某人注意到某个可见的事物。通常, **look at** 表示观看静止不动的物体,而 **watch** 用于移动中或者变化中的事物。*He watched David run down the stairs… I stayed up late to watch the film… I asked him to look at the picture above his bed… It is polite to look at people when they are talking to you.* **look** 不能够直接跟宾语,其后必须加 **at** 或其他介词。*He looked at me for a long time before he spoke… I looked towards the plane.*

看不起 kàn bu qǐ [动] look down on

看待 kàndài [动] regard ◇他们把我当朋友看待。They regard me as a friend.

看法 kànfǎ [名] opinion

看好 kànhǎo [动] look good ◇今年的经济形势看好。The economic prospects look good this year.

看见 kànjiàn [动] see (*pt* saw, *pp* seen) ◇黑暗中我看见一个人影。I could make out a figure in the dark. ◇你看见过瀑布吗? Have you ever seen a waterfall?

看来 kànlái [动] seem ◇她看来好多了。She seems much better . ◇这看来是个好主意。That seems like a good idea. ◇看来他不想来了。It seems he didn't want to come.

看破红尘 kàn pò hóngchén be disillusioned with the world ◇他因看破红尘而出家了。He became a monk because he was disillusioned with the world.

看望 kànwàng [动] visit

看重 kànzhòng [动] value

康 kāng [形] **1** (健康) healthy **2** (书) (富裕) well off ◇小康生活 a relatively comfortable life

康复 kāngfù [动] recover ◇祝您早日康复！ I hope you get well soon.

康乐 kānglè [形] happy and peaceful

慷 kāng 见下文

慷慨 kāngkǎi [形] **1** (激昂) fervent **2** (大方) generous

扛 káng [动] shoulder ◇他能扛两百磅的袋子。He can shoulder a 200-pound bag. ◇他老板的过失由他扛着。He's shouldering the blame for the boss's mistake.

亢 kàng [形] **1** (高亢) high **2** (高傲) haughty

亢奋 kàngfèn [形] excited

伉 kàng [动] be equal

伉俪 kànglì [名](书) married couple

抗 kàng [动] **1** (抵抗) resist ◇抗衰老 anti-aging **2** (抗拒) refuse ♦违抗 defy **3** (对等) be a match for ♦抗衡 contend with

抗衡 kànghéng [动] match ◇我们的实力无法与他们抗衡。There's no way we can match them in strength.

抗拒 kàngjù [动] resist

抗议 kàngyì [动] protest ◇他们对虐待动物的行为提出了强烈抗议。They protested vehemently against cruelty to animals.

抗争 kàngzhēng [动] resist

考 kǎo [动] **1** (测试) have an exam ◇明天我们考数学。We have our maths exam tomorrow. **2** (检查) check **3** (研究) study ♦考古 archaeology

考查 kǎochá [动] check

考察 kǎochá [动] **1** (实地调查) investigate **2** (细致观察) analyse (英), analyze (美) ◇仔细考察后，他们终于发现了问题的所在。After careful analysis they finally understood what was wrong.

考古 kǎogǔ **I** [动] study archaeology (英) 或 archeology (美) **II** [名] archaeology (英), archeology (美)

考核 kǎohé [动] check

考究 kǎojiu **I** [动] **1** (考察) investigate **2** (讲究) be particular about ◇她在衣着方面非常考究。She's extremely particular about her clothes. **II** [形] exquisite

考虑 kǎolǜ [动] consider ◇这个问题需要慎重考虑。This problem needs to be considered carefully. ◇这事儿你考虑了吗？ Have you thought it over? ◇我已把一切都考虑在内。I've already taken everything into consideration.

考勤 kǎoqín [动] check attendance ◇学校开始对学生加强考勤。The school is stepping up attendance checks on its pupils.

考试 kǎoshì [动] sit an exam (*pt, pp* sat) ◇他英语考试没及格。He failed the English exam.

考研 kǎoyán [动] sit the entrance exam for postgraduate studies (*pt, pp* sat)

考验 kǎoyàn [动] test ◇她想考验一下我的诚实。She wants to test my honesty. ◇经受考验 undergo an ordeal

考证 kǎozhèng [动] confirm through research

拷 kǎo [动] **1** (打) beat (*pt* beat, *pp* beaten) ♦拷打 beat **2** (拷贝) copy ◇文件已拷到光盘上了。The file has been copied to CD-ROM.

拷贝 kǎobèi **I** [名] copy **II** [动] copy

拷打 kǎodǎ [动] torture

烤 kǎo [动] **1** (指东西) roast ◇烤牛肉 roast beef **2** (指人体) warm oneself ♦烤火 warm oneself by a fire

烤炉 kǎolú [名] oven

烤面包 kǎomiànbāo [名] toast

烤鸭 kǎoyā [名] roast duck

铐 kào **I** [名] handcuffs (*pl*) **II** [动] handcuff

犒 kào [动] reward

犒劳 kàoláo [动] reward with a feast

靠 kào [动] **1** (倚) lean ◇梯子靠在墙

上。The ladder was leaning against the wall. **2** (近) keep to (*pt, pp* kept) ◇请大家往这边靠一点。Could everyone keep this way please. **3** (依赖) ◇他靠自己的努力实现了梦想。He achieved his dreams through hard work. ◇不要指望别人, 要靠自己。There's no use in looking to anyone else – you have to do it yourself. **4** (信赖) trust ◇他的话靠不住。You can't trust what he says.

靠拢 kàolǒng [动] draw close (*pt* drew, *pp* drawn)

靠山 kàoshān [名](贬) patron

苛 kē [形] harsh

苛捐杂税 kējuān záshuì heavy taxation

苛刻 kēkè [形] harsh

苛求 kēqiú [动] be demanding ◇你对人不能太苛求。You shouldn't be so demanding of others.

科 kē [名] **1** (指学术) discipline ♦文科 humanities (*pl*) **2** (指部门) department ♦人事科 human resources (*pl*) **3** (生物) (指分类) family ♦猫科 cat family **4** (法律条文) law

科班 kēbān [名] professional training

科幻 kēhuàn [名] science fiction

科技 kējì [名] science and technology ◇他在科技战线工作了一辈子。He's spent a lifetime working at the forefront of science and technology.

科举 kējǔ [名] imperial examination

科目 kēmù [名] subject

科普 kēpǔ [名] popular science

科学 kēxué **I** [名] science **II** [形] scientific

科学家 kēxuéjiā [名] scientist

科研 kēyán [名] scientific research

棵 kē [量] ◇一棵稻草 a piece of straw ◇一棵水仙 a narcissus

窠 kē [名] nest

窠臼 kējiù [名](书) set pattern

颗 kē [量] ◇一颗种子 a seed ◇一颗汗珠 a bead of sweat

颗粒 kēlì [名] **1** (指药片等) ◇这些药物颗粒颜色不一。These pills are not uniform in colour (英) 或 color (美). **2** (指粮食等) grain

磕 kē [动] **1** (碰) bump ◇我的头磕在了门框上。My head bumped against the doorframe. **2** (敲) knock out ◇她把米粒从碗里磕了出来。She knocked the grains of rice out of the bowl.

磕碰 kēpèng **I** [动] knock ◇玻璃器皿禁不住磕碰。Glass objects cannot be knocked about. ◇碗上有个磕碰儿。There's a crack in the bowl. **II** [名] clash ◇同事之间出现磕碰是难免的。It's difficult to avoid clashes between colleagues.

瞌 kē 见下文

瞌睡 kēshuì [动] doze

蝌 kē 见下文

蝌蚪 kēdǒu [名] tadpole

壳 ké [名] shell
▷另见 qiào

咳 ké [动] cough
▷另见 hāi

咳嗽 késou [动] cough

可 kě **I** [动] **1** (同意) approve ♦认可 approve **2** (适合) suit ♦可心 satisfying **II** [助动] **1** (可以) can ◇对我来说, 房子可大可小。As far as I'm concerned, the house can be big or small. ◇参考书不可带出去。The reference sources can't be taken out. **2** (值得) ◇没什么可担心的。There's no need to worry. ◇没有什么可抱怨的。There's nothing to complain about. ◇展览的确可看。The exhibition is really worth seeing. **III** [连] but ◇不让他去, 可他还是去了。I didn't give him permission to go, but he went anyway. **IV** [副] **1** (表示强调) very **2** (加强反问) ◇可不是嘛! Absolutely! ◇这个建议好是好, 可谁愿意去做呢? The proposal is great but who's actually going to implement it? **3** (加强疑问) ◇这件事他可知道? Did he ever know about this? ◇这书你可看过? Have you read this book before?

可爱 kě'ài [形] adorable

可悲 kěbēi [形] lamentable

可鄙 kěbǐ [形] despicable

可耻 kěchǐ [形] disgraceful

可歌可泣 kě gē kě qì be deeply moving

可观 kěguān [形] 1 (值得看) worth seeing ◇展览馆的艺术品着实可观。The gallery's art collection is really worth seeing. 2 (程度高) considerable

可贵 kěguì [形] valuable

可恨 kěhèn [形] detestable

可见 kějiàn [连] so ◇玛丽苗条了，可见她减肥成功。Mary has slimmed down, so her diet has obviously been successful.

可见度 kějiàndù [名] visibility

可靠 kěkào [形] reliable

可可 kěkě [名] cocoa ◇可可豆 cocoa bean

可口 kěkǒu [形] tasty

可乐 kělè [名] Coke®

可怜 kělián I [形] pitiful ◇那位病人看上去很可怜。That patient looks pitiful. ◇我存的那点钱少得可怜。I've only managed to save a pitiful amount. II [动] pity

可能 kěnéng I [形] possible ◇我们实现目标是可能的。It's possible we'll realize our targets. II [副] maybe ◇他可能去重庆了。Maybe he went to Chongqing. III [名] possibility

可怕 kěpà [形] frightening

可气 kěqì [形] annoying

可巧 kěqiǎo [副] as luck would have it

可是 kěshì I [副] ◇他儿子可是真聪明。His son is really clever. ◇我可是不和他一起去。I'll definitely not be going with him. II [连] but ◇这个小镇不大，可是很热闹。This is a small town, but it's very lively.

可视电话 kěshì diànhuà [名] videophone

可塑性 kěsùxìng [名] 1 (指物) plasticity 2 (指人) flexibility

可望而不可即 kě wàng ér bù kě jí unattainable ◇登上月球，对古人来说是可望而不可即的幻想。Previous generations would never have believed that man could go to the moon.

可恶 kěwù [形] detestable

可惜 kěxī I [形] regrettable ◇错过了那个工作机会，真可惜！What a shame you missed out on that job opportunity! II [副] regrettably ◇可惜我不能参加你们的婚礼了。Unfortunately, I can't attend your wedding.

可喜 kěxǐ [形] heartening

可笑 kěxiào [形] 1 (令人耻笑) ridiculous 2 (引人发笑) funny

可行 kěxíng [形] workable

可疑 kěyí [形] suspicious

可以 kěyǐ I [助动] 1 (能够) can ◇别人能做到的，你也可以。If other people can do it, so can you. 2 (有权) may ◇这个俱乐部任何人都可以参加。Anyone may attend this club. II [形] 1 (不坏) not bad ◇他乒乓球打得还可以。He's not bad at table tennis. 2 (厉害) awful ◇今天我忙得够可以的。I'm awfully busy today.

渴 kě I [形] thirsty II [副] eagerly ♦渴慕 admire

渴求 kěqiú [动] hunger for ◇她渴求成功。She's hungry for success.

渴望 kěwàng [动] long ◇他渴望回到祖国的怀抱。He longs to return to his country.

克 kè I [动] 1 (克制) restrain ♦克己 restrain oneself 2 (战胜) overcome (*pt* overcame, *pp* overcome) ◇克敌制胜 win victory over the enemy II [量] gram

克服 kèfú [动] 1 (战胜) overcome (*pt* overcame, *pp* overcome) ◇克服困难 overcome difficulties 2 (克制) put up with (*pt, pp* put)

克己奉公 kè jǐ fèng gōng make sacrifices for the public good

克隆 kèlóng [动] clone

克制 kèzhì [动] restrain

刻 kè I [动] engrave II [名] 1 (雕刻物品) engraving ♦石刻 stone inscription 2 (指十五分钟) quarter ◇现在是十点一刻。It's now a quarter past ten. 3 (泛指时间)

moment ◇刻不容缓 be very urgent **III** [形] **1** (表示程度) extreme ♦刻苦 hardworking **2** (刻薄) harsh ♦刻毒 evil

刻板 kèbǎn **I** [动] cut printing blocks (*pt, pp* cut) **II** [形] rigid

刻薄 kèbó [形] harsh

刻骨铭心 kè gǔ míng xīn be engraved in one's memory ◇那件事给我留下了刻骨铭心的记忆。That event is engraved in my memory.

刻画 kèhuà [动] **1** (涂抹) scribble on **2** (描绘) portray

刻苦 kèkǔ [形] hardworking

刻意 kèyì [副] painstakingly

恪 kè [形](书) scrupulous

恪守 kèshǒu [动](书) keep scrupulously (*pt, pp* kept) ◇多年来，他一直恪守诺言。He's kept his promise scrupulously for many years now.

客 kè **I** [名] **1** (客人) visitor ♦送客 see off a visitor **2** (旅客) traveller (英), traveler (美) ♦客车 passenger train **3** (顾客) customer ♦客户 customer **4** (指某类人) ♦政客 politician ♦刺客 assassin **II** [动] settle down

客场 kèchǎng [名] ◇曼联队本周将客场作战。Manchester United are playing away this weekend.

客串 kèchuàn [动] be a guest performer

客观 kèguān [形] objective

客户 kèhù [名] customer ◇客户对这种新产品非常满意。The customers are very satisfied with this new product.

客气 kèqi **I** [形] polite ◇他对人总是那么客气。He's always polite to people. **II** [动] be polite ◇女主人请我们不要客气。The hostess asked us not to stand on ceremony.

客人 kèrén [名] guest

客套 kètào **I** [名] civility **II** [动] exchange greetings

客座 kèzuò [名] guest seat ◇这边是主人座位，那边是客座。These seats are for the hosts and those are for the guests. ◇他是这所大学的客座教授。He's a visiting professor at the university.

课 kè [名] **1** (学科) subject **2** (学时) class **3** (单元) lesson

课本 kèběn [名] textbook

课程 kèchéng [名] course

课程表 kèchéngbiǎo [名] timetable

课堂 kètáng [名] classroom

课题 kètí [名] **1** (论题) topic ◇研究课题 research topic **2** (难题) problem

课文 kèwén [名] text

肯 kěn [助动] be willing ◇他不肯帮我。He isn't willing to help me. ◇孩子肯接受老师的意见。The child is ready to take the teacher's advice.

肯定 kěndìng **I** [动] confirm ◇他是否同意，我不能肯定。I can't confirm whether he agrees or not. **II** [形] **1** (确定的) affirmative ◇老师的回答是肯定的。The teacher answered in the affirmative. **2** (明确的) clear ◇她没有给我肯定的答复。She didn't give me a clear reply. **III** [副] certainly

垦 kěn [动] cultivate

垦殖 kěnzhí [动] reclaim land

恳 kěn **I** [形] sincere **II** [动] request

恳切 kěnqiè [形] earnest

恳求 kěnqiú [动] beg ◇她恳求朋友陪她一起去。She begged her friend to go with her.

啃 kěn [动] **1** (咬) gnaw **2** (喻) pore over ◇他喜欢啃书本。He likes to pore over books.

坑 kēng **I** [名] **1** (洼) hole **2** (洞) tunnel **II** [动] cheat

坑害 kēnghài [动] entrap

坑坑洼洼 kēngkengwāwā bumpy

坑骗 kēngpiàn [动] cheat

吭 kēng [动] utter

吭哧 kēngchi **I** [拟] huff and puff ◇他搬箱子时，累得吭哧吭哧的。Moving the box left him huffing and puffing with exhaustion. **II** [动] toil ◇他吭哧了半天才把活儿干完。

He toiled for a long time to finish the work.

铿 kēng [拟] clang

铿锵 kēngqiāng [形] ringing

空 kōng I [形] empty ◇柜子里是空的。The cupboard is empty. II [名] sky III [副] for nothing ◇我们空欢喜了一场。Our happiness had no foundation.
▷另见 kòng

空荡荡 kōngdàngdàng [形] empty

空洞 kōngdòng I [名] cavity II [形] empty

空间 kōngjiān [名] space ◇实验室没有足够的空间放设备。There isn't enough space for the equipment in the laboratory. ◇这个故事给读者留下了想像的空间。This story gives the reader space to use their imagination.

空军 kōngjūn [名] air force

空旷 kōngkuàng [形] spacious

空难 kōngnàn [名] aircrash

空气 kōngqì [名] **1** (大气) air **2** (气氛) atmosphere

空前绝后 kōng qián jué hòu unmatched ◇恺撒大帝被称为罗马历史上空前绝后的军事领袖。Julius Caesar has been called the most unmatched military general in Roman history.

空谈 kōngtán [动] talk idly ◇他的许诺不过是一纸空谈。His promise is just idle talk.

空袭 kōngxí [动] attack from the air ◇这个城市又一次遭受了空袭。The city experienced another air raid.

空想 kōngxiǎng [动] fantasize ◇别再空想了。Stop fantasizing. ◇这种理论纯粹是一种空想。This theory is just pure fantasy.

空虚 kōngxū [形] empty ◇我感到精神空虚。I feel spiritually empty.

孔 kǒng [名] hole ♦鼻孔 nostril

孔穴 kǒngxué [名] hole

恐 kǒng I [动] fear ♦惶恐 be frightened II [副] probably ◇恐明天要变天。The weather will probably change tomorrow. ◇此人恐不可靠。I'm afraid he's unreliable.

恐怖 kǒngbù I [形] terrifying II [名] terror ◇恐怖主义 terrorism ◇恐怖小说 horror fiction

恐吓 kǒnghè [动] threaten

恐慌 kǒnghuāng [形] frightened

恐惧 kǒngjù [动] be frightened ◇突如其来的暴风雨使我恐惧万分。The sudden thunderstorm really frightened me. ◇这条新闻引起了人们的恐惧。This news created fear among the people.

恐龙 kǒnglóng [名] dinosaur

恐怕 kǒngpà [副] **1** (担心) fearfully ◇他恐怕考不好。He's afraid that he won't do well in the exam. **2** (大概) probably ◇火车恐怕要晚点了。The train will probably be late.

空 kòng I [动] leave ... empty (*pt, pp* left) ◇请你把书架的第一层空出来。Please empty out the first shelf of the bookcase. II [形] vacant ♦空位 vacant seats III [名] **1** (空间) space ◇储藏室里没空放你的行李了。There's no space left in the cupboard for your luggage. **2** (时间) free time ♦有空 have free time
▷另见 kōng

空白 kòngbái [名] blank ◇他们的研究成果填补了科学技术上的一项空白。The findings of their research filled a scientific and technological gap.

空缺 kòngquē [名] vacancy

空隙 kòngxì [名] **1** (指空间) gap **2** (指时间) interval **3** (指机会) opening ◇别给你的对手留下任何空隙。Don't give your opponent any kind of opening.

空闲 kòngxián [动] be free ◇等我空闲下来再去拜访你。I'll call on you when I'm free. ◇这个操场空闲两年了。This games area has been unused for two years. ◇他一有空闲就下棋。When he has free time he plays chess.

空子 kòngzi [名] **1** (空间) space ◇车里没空子了。There's no space left in the car. **2** (时间) time ◇咱们抽空

子去打篮球吧。Let's find time to go and play basketball. **3** (喻) (机会) opportunity ◊他这人爱钻空子。He's a bit of an opportunist.

控 kòng [动] **1** (控制) control ♦自控 self-control **2** (控告) charge ♦指控 charge **3** (指流体) drain ◊她把瓶子里的水控干了。She drained the water from the bottle.

控告 kònggào [动] accuse ◊员工们控告公司违反劳动法。The workers accused the company of violating the labour (英) 或 labor (美) laws.

控股公司 kònggǔ gōngsī [名] holding company

控诉 kòngsù [动] denounce

控制 kòngzhì [动] control

抠 kōu **I** [动] **1** (挖) pick ◊他把掉在洞里的东西抠了出来。He picked out the things that had fallen into the hole. **2** (雕刻) carve **3** (探明) work out ◊我非把这道题抠出来不可。I simply have to work the problem out. **II** [形](口) stingy

抠门儿 kōuménr [形] stingy

口 kǒu **I** [名] **1** (嘴) mouth **2** (丁) ♦家口 family member **3** (味) taste ♦口轻 not too salty **4** (指容器) rim ♦瓶口 the mouth of a bottle **5** (指端口) ♦出口 exit ♦入口 entrance ♦窗口 window **6** (缝) split **7** (刃) edge ♦刀口 the edge of a knife **8** (行) department ♦卫生口 public health department **II** [量] ◊两口猪 two pigs ◊一口井 one well ◊我家有五口人。There are five people in my family.

口岸 kǒu'àn [名] port

口碑 kǒubēi [名] opinion ◊他在同事中口碑很差。His colleagues have a poor opinion of him.

口才 kǒucái [名] eloquence ◊她的口才很好。She speaks eloquently.

口吃 kǒuchī [形] stammering ◊他有点儿口吃。He has a slight stammer.

口齿 kǒuchǐ [名] **1** (发音) enunciation ◊他口齿不清。He doesn't enunciate clearly. **2** (说话) ability to speak ◊这个小姑娘口齿伶俐。The little girl is very eloquent.

口供 kǒugòng [名] confession

口号 kǒuhào [名] slogan

口红 kǒuhóng [名] lipstick

口技 kǒujì [名] vocal mimicry

口角 kǒujiǎo [名] corner of the mouth

口角 kǒujué [动] quarrel

口口声声 kǒukoushēngshēng keep on saying ◊他口口声声说要参加比赛，却没报名。He kept on saying that he wanted to enter the competition but he never did enrol.

口令 kǒulìng [名] **1** (命令) verbal command **2** (暗语) password

口气 kǒuqì [名] **1** (语气) tone **2** (气势) spoken manner ◊他没什么本事，口气倒不小。He has no real ability, but his spoken manner is very imposing. **3** (含义) implication ◊听你的口气，你是不想给她道歉了？Are you implying that you don't want to apologize to her?

口腔 kǒuqiāng [名] the inside of the mouth

口舌 kǒushé [名] **1** (纠纷) dispute **2** (话语) persuasion ◊为了她俩和解，我费了不少口舌。I spent ages persuading them to make up.

口是心非 kǒu shì xīn fēi not say what one means ◊口是心非的人很令人厌恶。People hate it when you don't say what you mean.

口述 kǒushù [动] dictate

口头 kǒutóu [名] **1** (嘴) word ◊他只是口头上答应了。He agreed verbally. **2** (口语) ◊口头作文 oral composition

口头禅 kǒutóuchán [名] pet phrase

口味 kǒuwèi [名] taste ◊流行音乐不合我的口味。Pop music is not to my taste. ◊每个人欣赏艺术品的口味不同。Everyone has their own different taste in art. ◊她做菜口味不错。She cooks delicious food.

口吻 kǒuwěn [名] **1** (指动物) snout **2** (口气) tone

口信 kǒuxìn [名] message

口音 kǒuyin [名] **1** (声音) voice **2** (方音) accent

口语 kǒuyǔ [名] spoken language

口子 kǒuzi I [量] person (*pl* people) ◇他家有六口子。There are six people in his family. II [名] **1** (豁口) gap ◇院墙上出了个大口子。There's a big gap in the garden wall. **2** (喻) (指变通做法) exception

叩 kòu [动] **1** (敲) knock ♦叩门 knock at a door **2** (磕头) kowtow

叩拜 kòubài [动] kowtow

扣 kòu I [动] **1** (拉紧) fasten **2** (朝下) put ... upside down (*pt, pp* put) ◇孩子把碗扣在了桌子上。The child put the bowl upside down on the table. **3** (喻) (戴) frame **4** (抓) arrest **5** (击) smash **6** (减) deduct II [名] button

扣除 kòuchú [动] deduct

扣留 kòuliú [动] arrest

扣人心弦 kòu rén xīnxián be thrilling

扣押 kòuyā [动] detain

扣子 kòuzi [名] button

寇 kòu I [动] invade II [名] invader

枯 kū [形] **1** (枯萎) withered ♦枯草 withered grass **2** (干涸) dried-up **3** (指肌肉) emaciated ♦枯瘦 skinny **4** (乏味) dull ♦枯燥 uninteresting

枯竭 kūjié [形] **1** (干涸) dried-up **2** (用尽) exhausted

枯萎 kūwěi [形] withered

枯燥 kūzào [形] dull

哭 kū [动] cry

哭鼻子 kū bízi [动](口) snivel

哭哭啼啼 kūkutítí sob one's eyes out ◇一晚上她都哭哭啼啼的。She sobbed her eyes out the entire evening.

哭泣 kūqì [动] weep (*pt, pp* wept)

窟 kū [名] **1** (洞穴) cave **2** (聚居地) ♦匪窟 gangster hideout ♦贫民窟 slum

窟窿 kūlong [名] **1** (洞) hole **2** (亏空) deficit

骷 kū 见下文

骷髅 kūlóu [名] skeleton

苦 kǔ I [形] **1** (苦涩) bitter **2** (艰苦) hard II [动] **1** (苦害) be hard on ◇照顾6个孩子可苦了她。Looking after six children has taken its toll on her. **2** (遭受) suffer from ♦苦旱 suffer from drought III [副] painstakingly ♦苦练 train hard IV [名] suffering ♦吃苦 bear hardships

苦处 kǔchu [名] suffering

苦干 kǔgàn [动] work hard

苦功 kǔgōng [名] hard work

苦果 kǔguǒ [名] **1** (指果实) bitter fruit **2** (指结果) unfortunate consequences

苦口婆心 kǔ kǒu pó xīn do one's best to persuade ◇父母苦口婆心地劝他，他就是不听。His parents did their best to persuade him but he just didn't listen.

苦闷 kǔmèn [形] depressed

苦难 kǔnàn I [名] hardship II [形] hard

苦恼 kǔnǎo [形] distressed

苦涩 kǔsè [形] bitter

苦思冥想 kǔ sī míng xiǎng rack one's brains ◇他苦思冥想了一整天，仍然没有结果。He racked his brains for the whole day to no effect.

苦头 kǔtóu [名] suffering

苦笑 kǔxiào [动] give a wry smile (*pt* gave, *pp* given)

苦心 kǔxīn I [名] pains ◇煞费苦心 take great pains II [副] painstakingly ◇他曾苦心研究过这题目。He painstakingly researched the topic.

苦衷 kǔzhōng [名] predicament

库 kù [名] warehouse ♦国库 state treasury

库存 kùcún [名] stock

裤 kù [名] trousers (*pl*) (英), pants (*pl*) (美)

裤子 kùzi [名] trousers (*pl*)

酷 kù I [形] cruel II [副](书) extremely ♦酷热 extremely hot ♦酷爱 love passionately

夸 kuā [动] **1** (夸大) exaggerate **2** (夸奖) praise

夸大 kuādà [动] exaggerate

夸奖 kuājiǎng [动] praise

夸口 kuākǒu [动] boast ◇李太太总夸口说自己的女儿聪明。Mrs. Li is always boasting about how clever her daughter is. ◇他夸口说自己能得冠军。He boasted that he would become a champion.

夸夸其谈 kuākuā qí tán hype things up ◇我们提倡脚踏实地，反对夸夸其谈。We encourage a down-to-earth manner – we don't go in for hype.

夸张 kuāzhāng **I** [形] exaggerated **II** [名] hyperbole

垮 kuǎ [动] **1** (坍塌) collapse ◇大坝被水冲垮了。The dyke burst under the weight of the water. **2** (伤身) wear down (*pt* wore, *pp* worn) ◇她因繁重的工作而垮了下来。She was worn down by the heavy work.

垮台 kuǎtái [动] collapse

挎 kuà [动] carry

挎包 kuàbāo [名] satchel

胯 kuà [名] hip

胯骨 kuàgǔ [名] hipbone

跨 kuà [动] **1** (迈步) step **2** (骑) ride (*pt* rode, *pp* ridden) ◇跨上马 ride a horse **3** (架) span ◇独木桥横跨在山谷。The single-plank bridge spans the mountain valley. **4** (超越) surpass ♦跨国 transnational **5** (附着) adhere to

跨度 kuàdù [名] span

跨越 kuàyuè [动] surpass

会 kuài [名] accounting ♦财会 finance and accounting
▷另见 huì

会计 kuàijì [名] **1** (指工作) accounting **2** (指人员) accountant

块 kuài **I** [名] lump ♦土块 lump of earth **II** [量] piece ◇一块蛋糕 a piece of cake ◇一块烤面包 a slice of toast ◇一块方糖 a lump of sugar

块头 kuàitóu [名] build

快 kuài **I** [形] **1** (快速) fast **2** (赶快) ◇快点儿，要不我们就迟到了。Hurry up, or we'll be late. **3** (灵敏) quick ◇她反应特别快。She responds extremely quickly. ◇他脑子快，做事效率高。He's quick-witted and does things efficiently. **4** (锋利) sharp **5** (直爽) straightforward ♦爽快 frank **6** (愉快)(书) happy **II** [副] soon ◇学生快毕业了。The students will graduate soon.

快餐 kuàicān [名] fast food

快感 kuàigǎn [名] delight

快活 kuàihuo [形] delighted

快件 kuàijiàn [名] **1** (指货品) express delivery ◇这件行李用快件托运。The luggage will be sent express. **2** (指邮件) express mail

快乐 kuàilè [形] happy

快马加鞭 kuài mǎ jiā biān go at top speed

快速 kuàisù [形] quick ◇面对突发事件，当地政府做出了快速反应。Local government reacted quickly to the sudden turn of events.

快要 kuàiyào [副] soon ◇路快要修好了。The road will be repaired soon.

脍 kuài(书) **I** [名] sliced meat **II** [动] slice

脍炙人口 kuài zhì rén kǒu win universal acclaim ◇他的文章脍炙人口。His article won universal acclaim.

筷 kuài [名] chopsticks (*pl*)

宽 kuān **I** [形] **1** (距离大) wide **2** (范围广) broad **3** (宽大) lenient ♦宽容 tolerant **4** (宽裕) well-off ◇日子比原来宽点儿了。We are better-off than we were before. **II** [动] extend ◇我们的访问时间宽至本月底。Our visit is extended until the end of the month. **III** [名] width ◇这条路有20米宽。The road is twenty metres wide.

宽敞 kuānchang [形] spacious

宽大 kuāndà [形] **1** (指面积) spacious **2** (宽容) lenient

宽带 kuāndài [名] broadband

宽广 kuānguǎng [形] extensive

宽宏大量 kuānhóng dàliàng generous-minded

宽厚 kuānhòu [形] **1** (指人体) muscular **2** (指为人) generous

宽阔 kuānkuò [形] **1** (指范围) wide **2** (指心胸) broad ◇心胸宽阔 broad-minded

宽容 kuānróng [形] lenient

宽松 kuānsōng [形] **1** (不拥挤) ◇这条裤子很宽松。These trousers are quite loose. ◇电影院人不多, 很宽松。There aren't many people in the cinema – it's not crowded. **2** (宽畅) relieved **3** (宽裕) well-off **4** (宽舒) relaxed

宽裕 kuānyù [形] **1** (指生活) good **2** (指时间) ample ◇不用着急, 时间还很宽裕。Don't worry, there's still ample time.

宽窄 kuānzhǎi [名] width

款 kuǎn [名] **1** (项目) section ◇第1条第3款 article 1, section 3 **2** (钱) sum of money ♦现款 cash **3** (题名) signature ♦落款 inscribe **4** (样式) style

款待 kuǎndài [动] entertain

款式 kuǎnshì [名] style

款项 kuǎnxiàng [名] **1** (钱) sum of money **2** (项目) section

诓 kuāng [动] deceive

诓骗 kuāngpiàn [动] deceive

筐 kuāng **I** [名] basket **II** [量] basket ◇一筐土豆 a basket of potatoes

狂 kuáng **I** [形] **1** (疯狂) crazy ♦发狂 go crazy **2** (猛烈) violent ♦狂风 gale **3** (狂妄) arrogant **4** (狂热) wild ◇欣喜若狂 be wild with joy **II** [副] wildly

狂暴 kuángbào [形] violent

狂欢 kuánghuān [动] have a mad time of it

狂热 kuángrè [形] fanatical

狂妄 kuángwàng [形] arrogant

旷 kuàng **I** [形] **1** (空阔) spacious ♦旷野 wilderness **2** (开阔) free from worry ◇心旷神怡 carefree and happy **3** (松) loose **II** [动] neglect ♦旷课 play truant

旷达 kuàngdá [形](书) broad-minded

旷课 kuàngkè [动] play truant

旷日持久 kuàng rì chí jiǔ protracted ◇双方进行了旷日持久的谈判。The negotiations between the two sides were protracted.

况 kuàng **I** [名] situation ♦状况 condition **II** [连](书) besides ♦何况 moreover

况且 kuàngqiě [连] besides

矿 kuàng [名] **1** (矿场) mine **2** (矿石) ore

矿藏 kuàngcáng [名] mineral resources (*pl*)

矿产 kuàngchǎn [名] mineral

矿井 kuàngjǐng [名] mine

矿山 kuàngshān [名] mine

矿石 kuàngshí [名] ore

矿物 kuàngwù [名] mineral

矿业 kuàngyè [名] mining industry

框 kuàng **I** [名] **1** (框架) frame **2** (方框) box **II** [动] **1** (画圈) box ◇我用红笔把这句话框了起来。I put a red box around the sentence. **2**(口) (限制) limit ◇我们不能把市场只框在北京。We can't limit the market to Beijing.

框架 kuàngjià [名] **1** (指建筑) frame **2** (指文书) framework

眶 kuàng [名] socket ♦眼眶 eye socket

亏 kuī **I** [动] **1** (亏损) lose (*pt, pp* lost) **2** (欠缺) lack ♦理亏 be in the wrong **3** (亏负) allow ... to suffer losses ◇公司亏不了股东。The company can't allow its shareholders to suffer losses. **II** [副] **1** (幸亏) luckily ◇亏你把我叫醒, 要不我就迟到了。It's lucky you woke me up or I would have been late. **2** (表示讥讽) ◇这种烂主意, 亏你想得出来! How could you think up such a stupid idea? ◇亏他还是个经理, 连这点问题都解决不了! What a joy to have him as a manager - when he can't even solve a problem as small as this!

亏待 kuīdài [动] treat badly ◇公司不能亏待员工。The company can't treat its workers badly.

亏空 kuīkong **I** [动] be in debt **II** [名] deficit

亏欠 kuīqiàn [动] be in arrears

亏心 kuīxīn [动] feel guilty (*pt, pp* felt)

盔 kuī [名] helmet

盔甲 kuījiǎ [名] suit of armour (英) 或 armor (美)

窥 kuī [动] **1** (偷看) peep **2** (窥探) pry

窥测 kuīcè [动] seek out (*pt, pp* sought)

窥探 kuītàn [动] pry ◇不要窥探别人的隐私。You shouldn't pry into other people's private affairs. ◇字体专家能从字体中窥探人的性格。Handwriting specialists can tell people's character from their handwriting.

葵 kuí 见下文

葵花 kuíhuā [名] sunflower

魁 kuí I [名] head ♦夺魁 win first place II [形] well-built

魁梧 kuíwú [形] tall and sturdy

傀 kuǐ 见下文

傀儡 kuǐlěi [名] puppet

匮 kuì [动](书) be deficient

匮乏 kuìfá [形](书) deficient ◇灾区生活用品极为匮乏。The disaster area is very low in basic necessities.

馈 kuì [动](书) present

馈赠 kuìzèng [动](书) present

溃 kuì [动] **1** (指伤口) fester **2** (指军队) be defeated

溃败 kuìbài [动] be defeated

溃烂 kuìlàn [动] fester

愧 kuì I [形] ashamed II [名] shame ◇问心无愧 have nothing to be ashamed of

愧疚 kuìjiù [形](书) guilty

坤 kūn [形] female

坤表 kūnbiǎo [名] lady's watch

昆 kūn 见下文

昆虫 kūnchóng [名] insect

捆 kǔn I [动] tie up ◇请你把报纸捆一捆。Could you please tie up the newspapers. II [量] bundle ◇一捆书 a bundle of books

捆绑 kǔnbǎng [动] tie up

困 kùn I [动] **1** (困扰) be stricken ◇少女为情所困。The girl was stricken by love. **2** (限制) trap II [形] **1** (瞌睡) sleepy **2** (困难) difficult ♦困境 predicament

困乏 kùnfá [形] tired

困惑 kùnhuò [形] confused ◇我对下一步该怎么做感到困惑。I'm confused about what to do next.

困苦 kùnkǔ [形] hard

困难 kùnnan [形] **1** (指事情) difficult ◇克服困难 overcome difficulties **2** (指经济) poor ◇他家生活困难。His family lives in poverty.

困扰 kùnrǎo [动] trouble

扩 kuò [动] expand

扩充 kuòchōng [动] expand ◇实验室需要扩充设备。The laboratory needs additional equipment.

扩大 kuòdà [动] expand ◇扩大生产 expand production ◇扩大经济影响 extend economic influence

扩散 kuòsàn [动] spread (*pt, pp* spread)

扩展 kuòzhǎn [动] expand

扩张 kuòzhāng [动] **1** (医) (指血管等) dilate **2** (指领土等) expand

括 kuò [动] **1** (包括) include **2** (加括号) bracket (英), parenthesize (美)

括弧 kuòhú [名] bracket (英), parenthesis (美) (*pl* parentheses)

阔 kuò [形] **1** (宽广) wide **2** (阔气) wealthy

阔别 kuòbié [动] be separated for a long time ◇他阔别故乡已多年。He hasn't seen his home town for a long time. ◇阔别多年的朋友 long-lost friend

阔步 kuòbù [动] take great strides (*pt* took, *pp* taken)

阔绰 kuòchuò [形] ostentatious

阔气 kuòqi [形] extravagant ◇他爱摆阔气。He likes to throw his money about.

Ll

垃 lā 见下文

垃圾 lājī [名] rubbish (英), garbage (美) ◇垃圾邮件 junk mail ◇垃圾食品 junk food

> 📖 在英式英语中, 表示垃圾最常用的词汇是 **rubbish**。在美式英语中, **garbage** 和 **trash** 更为常用。*...the smell of rotten garbage... She threw the bottle into the trash.* **garbage** 和 **trash** 有时也用于英式英语中, 但语体仅限于非正式或者具有喻义。*I don't have to listen to this garbage... The book was trash.*

拉 lā [动] **1** (用力移动) pull ◇拉人力车 pull a rickshaw ♦拉纤 tow **2** (载运) transport ◇拉一车货 transport a truckload of goods ◇出租车司机拉我到了机场。The taxi driver took me to the airport. **3** (演奏) play ◇拉小提琴 play the violin **4** (拖长) extend ◇拉橡皮筋 stretch an elastic band ◇拉长声音 hold a note **5** (帮助) help ◇朋友遇到困难, 我就拉他一把。I would always help a friend in trouble. **6** (拉拢) draw ... in (*pt* drew, *pp* drawn) ◇不是我主动加入俱乐部的, 而是被拉入伙的。I didn't join the club of my own volition, I got drawn in. ♦拉关系 establish connections **7** (口) (排泄) excrete ♦拉肚子 have diarrhoea (英) 或 diarrhea (美)
▷另见 lá

拉扯 lāche [动] **1** (抚养) bring ... up (*pt, pp* brought) **2** (拽住) stop ◇你不要拉扯他, 否则他揍你。Don't stop him, or else he'll punch you. **3** (牵涉) drag ... in ◇一人做事一人当, 别把我拉扯进去。This has nothing to do with me – don't drag me into it.

拉锯 lājù [动] see-saw ♦拉锯战 stalemate

拉拉队 lālāduì [名] cheering squad

拉拢 lālǒng [动] draw ... in (*pt* drew, *pp* drawn)

拉平 lāpíng [动] draw level (*pt* drew, *pp* drawn)

拉纤 lāqiàn [动] tow

邋 lā 见下文

邋遢 lātā [形] (口) scruffy

拉 lá [动] tear (*pt* tore, *pp* torn) ◇我把大衣拉了个口子。I've torn a hole in my coat.
▷另见 lā

喇 lǎ 见下文

喇叭 lǎba [名] **1** (管乐器) trumpet ◇吹喇叭 play the trumpet **2** (扩音器) loudspeaker

落 là [动] **1** (遗漏) be missing ◇文章结尾落了个句号。There's a full stop missing at the end of the article. **2** (忘记) leave (*pt, pp* left) **3** (落后) fall behind (*pt* fell, *pp* fallen) ◇快点走, 别落下。You'd better walk a bit quicker – you don't want to fall behind.
▷另见 lào, luò

腊 là [名] **1** (农历12月) twelfth lunar month **2** (冬天腌制的) cured meat ♦腊肠 sausage

腊味 làwèi [名] cured meat

辣 là I [形] **1** (指味道) hot ♦辣酱 chilli sauce ♦辣椒 chilli **2** (指心肠) vicious II [动] sting (*pt, pp* stung) ◇我被洋葱辣得直流眼泪。The onion stung my eyes and made them water.

辣手 làshǒu I [名] vicious behaviour II [形] tricky

蜡 là [名] candle

蜡烛 làzhú [名] candle

啦 la [助] ◇你回来啦! Hey – you're back!

来 lái I [动] **1** (来到) come (*pt* came, *pp* come) ◇家里来了几个客人。Some guests came to the house. **2** (发生) happen ◇刚到家, 麻烦来了。As soon as I got home, the trouble started. **3** (泛指做事) ◇请来

碗面条。A bowl of noodles, please. ◊你累了，让我来。You're tired – let me do it. **4** (表示可能) can, be able to ◊她弹得来钢琴。She can play the piano. ◊芭蕾舞我跳不来。I can't do ballet. **5** (表示要做) ◊请你来帮个忙。Can you help me with this? ◊让我们大家一起来渡难关。Together we can get through this crisis. **6** (表示目的) ◊母亲买了些调料来腌肉。My mother bought some seasonings to cure the meat. ◊我要想个法子来对付他。I must think of a way to deal with him. **7** (表示朝向) ◊服务员很快就把饭菜端了上来。Soon the waiter had brought the food to the table. II [形] coming ♦来年 the coming year III [助] **1** (表示持续) ◊几年来 in the last few years ◊近来 lately **2** (表示概数) about ◊10来公斤重 about 10 kilos

来宾 láibīn [名] guest

来访 láifǎng [动] visit

来回 láihuí [动] **1** (去了再来) make a round trip ◊从住宅小区到市中心来回有多远？How far is it from the residential area to town and back? **2** (来来去去) move back and forth II [名] round trip ◊我从学校到家一天跑两个来回。I make the round trip from school to home twice a day.

来历 láilì [名] past

来临 láilín [动] come (*pt* came, *pp* come) ◊你会有好运来临。Good luck will come to you.

来龙去脉 lái lóng qù mài ins and outs

来路 láilù [名] **1** (道路) approach **2** (来历) origins (*pl*) ◊不要打开来路不明的下载文件。Don't open downloaded documents if it's not clear where they came from.

…来…去 …lái…qù [动] ◊跑来跑去 run back and forth ◊眉来眼去 make eyes at each other

来日方长 lái rì fāng cháng have plenty of time

来势 láishì [名] force

来头 láitou [名] **1** (来历) connections **2** (缘由) reason

来往 láiwang [动] have dealings with

来由 láiyóu [名] reason

来源 láiyuán I [名] origin II [动] originate ◊小说素材来源于生活。The material for the novel originates in real life.

来之不易 lái zhī bù yì be hard to come by

睐 lài [动] look at

赖 lài I [动] **1** (依靠) depend **2** (留) stay **3** (抵赖) deny **4** (诬赖) blame … wrongly ◊你自己做错了事不要赖别人。You shouldn't blame others for your mistakes. II [形] bad

赖皮 làipí [名] shameless behaviour (英) 或 behavior (美) ◊耍赖皮 act shamelessly

兰 lán [名] orchid

拦 lán [动] stop ◊你喜欢去就去，我不拦你。If you want to go, just go – I won't stop you.

拦劫 lánjié [动] rob

拦截 lánjié [动] intercept

拦路虎 lánlùhǔ a stumbling block

拦腰 lányāo [动] break in half (*pt* broke, *pp* broken) ◊狂风将大树拦腰斩断。The trees were snapped in half by the storm.

拦阻 lánzǔ [动] block

栏 lán [名] **1** (栏杆) fence **2** (圈) shed **3** (部分版面) column ◊备注栏 comments column

栏杆 lángān [名] fence

栏目 lánmù [名] column

阑 lán [形] (书) late

阑珊 lánshān [动] fade

蓝 lán [形] blue

蓝本 lánběn [名] original version

蓝领 lánlǐng [名] ◊蓝领工人 blue-collar worker

蓝图 lántú [名] blueprint

蓝牙 lányá [名] Bluetooth®

澜 lán [名] waves (*pl*)

褴 lán 见下文

褴褛 lánlǚ [形] shabby

篮 lán [名] **1** (篮子) basket **2** (球篮) hoop

篮球 lánqiú [名] basketball

览 lǎn [动] **1** (观看) see (*pt* saw, *pp* seen) ♦游览 go sightseeing **2** (阅读) read (*pt, pp* read) ♦阅览 read

揽 lǎn [动] **1** (搂) hug **2** (捆) tie **3** (包揽) take … on (*pt* took, *pp* taken) **4** (把持) monopolize

揽活 lǎnhuó [动] take on work (*pt* took, *pp* taken)

缆 lǎn **I** [名] **1** (粗绳) rope **2** (似缆之物) cable **II** [动] moor

缆车 lǎnchē [名] cable car

懒 lǎn [形] **1** (懒惰) lazy **2** (疲倦) lethargic

懒怠 lǎndai **I** [形] lazy **II** [动] be lazy

懒得 lǎnde [动] not feel like ◇天太热，我懒得出门。I don't feel like going out, it's too hot.

懒惰 lǎnduò [形] lazy

懒散 lǎnsǎn [形] lazy

懒洋洋 lǎnyāngyāng [形] lethargic

烂 làn **I** [形] **1** (松软) soft ◇土豆炖烂了。The potatoes are done. **2** (破烂) worn-out **3** (头绪乱) messy ♦烂摊子 a shambles **II** [动] be rotten ◇西瓜烂了。The watermelon has gone off.

烂漫 lànmàn [形] **1** (指颜色) brightly-coloured (英), brightly-colored (美) **2** (指性格) unaffected

烂熟 lànshú [形] **1** (煮得熟) well-cooked ◇牛肉炖得烂熟。The beef is overcooked. **2** (熟练) learn … by heart ◇他把这首诗背得烂熟。He learned the poem off by heart.

烂摊子 làntānzi [名] mess

滥 làn **I** [动] flood **II** [副] excessively ♦滥用 squander

滥调 làndiào [名] cliché

滥用 lànyòng [动] misuse

滥竽充数 làn yú chōng shù be a makeweight

郎 láng [名] ♦放牛郎 cowherd ♦女郎 young lady

狼 láng [名] wolf (*pl* wolves)

狼狈 lángbèi [形] in dire straits ◇他遭遇失败，处境狼狈。He failed, and is now in dire straits.

狼狈为奸 lángbèi wéi jiān join in a conspiracy

狼藉 lángjí [形] (书) messy ◇屋子久未整理，一片狼藉。This room hasn't been tidied for ages – it's a complete mess. ◇声名狼籍 have a bad name

狼吞虎咽 láng tūn hǔ yàn wolf … down ◇他狼吞虎咽地吃下了一大碗面。He wolfed down a big bowl of noodles.

廊 láng [名] corridor ♦走廊 corridor ♦画廊 gallery

榔 láng 见下文

榔头 lángtou [名] hammer

锒 láng 见下文

锒铛 lángdāng **I** [名] (书) iron chain **II** [拟] clink

朗 lǎng [形] **1** (明亮) bright **2** (响亮) clear

朗读 lǎngdú [动] read … aloud (*pt, pp* read)

朗诵 lǎngsòng [动] recite

浪 làng **I** [名] wave ♦浪花 foam ♦声浪 sound wave **II** [形] wasteful ♦浪费 squander

浪潮 làngcháo [名] tide

浪荡 làngdàng [动] loaf around

浪费 làngfèi [动] waste

浪迹 làngjì [动] wander ◇浪迹天涯 wander to the ends of the earth

浪漫 làngmàn [形] romantic

浪头 làngtou [名] **1** (口) (波浪) wave **2** (潮流) trend

浪子 làngzǐ [名] prodigal

捞 lāo [动] **1** (取) take (*pt* took, *pp* taken) ♦捕捞 fish for **2** (攫取) wangle ◇捞好处 wangle benefits

捞取 lāoqǔ [动] seek (*pt, pp* sought)

牢 láo **I** [名] **1** (牲畜圈) pen **2** (监狱) prison **II** [形] firm

牢固 láogù [形] firm

牢靠 láokào [形] 1 (坚固) firm 2 (可靠) reliable

牢笼 láolóng [名] shackles (*pl*)

牢骚 láosāo [名] grumble ◊他一肚子牢骚。He's full of complaints. ◊他牢骚了一整天。He grumbled for the entire day.

劳 láo I [动] 1 (劳动) work 2 (烦劳) trouble ◊劳您帮我看下行李。Would you mind keeping an eye on my luggage? 3 (慰劳) reward II [名] 1 (劳苦) toil ◊积劳成疾 collapse from overwork 2 (功劳) service

劳动 láodòng [名] labour (英), labor (美) ◊脑力劳动 brain work ◊他下地劳动去了。He's gone to work in the fields.

劳动力 láodònglì [名] 1 (劳动能力) labour (英), labor (美) 2 (人力) workforce

劳改 láogǎi [动] *reform through hard labour*

劳驾 láojià [动] (客套) excuse me ◊劳驾，把盐递过来。Excuse me, would you mind passing me the salt?

劳苦 láokǔ [形] hard-working

劳累 láolèi [形] exhausted

劳力 láolì [名] 1 (气力) labour (英), labor (美) 2 (劳动力) labour (英) 或 labor (美) force

劳碌 láolù [动] toil

劳民伤财 láo mín shāng cái waste of manpower and resources

劳务 láowù [名] labour (英) 或 labor (美) service

劳役 láoyì [名] hard labour (英) 或 labor (美)

劳资 láozī [名] labour (英) 或 labor (美) and capital

唠 láo 见下文

唠叨 láodao [动] be talkative

痨 láo [名] TB, tuberculosis

痨病 láobìng [名] TB, tuberculosis

老 lǎo I [形] 1 (年岁大的) old ◊老婆婆 old lady 2 (有经验的) experienced ♦老手 veteran 3 (旧的) old ◊老同学 old school friend 4 (火候大的) well-done ◊肉煮老了。The beef is well-done. II [名] old people ◊爱老携幼 care for and nurture the old and young III [副] 1 (经常) always ◊他老去父母家吃饭。He always eats dinner at his parent's house. 2 (长久) for a long time ◊电器老不用就会坏。If electrical equipment isn't used for a long time it can break down. 3 (非常) very ♦老远 very far

老百姓 lǎobǎixìng [名] ordinary people

老板 lǎobǎn [名] boss

老本 lǎoběn [名] capital ◊他失业后尽吃老本。After he lost his job, he had to use up all his savings.

老巢 lǎocháo [名] den

老成 lǎochéng [形] mature

老大 lǎodà I [名] head ◊他是我们小组的老大。He is the leader of our group. II [副] very ◊今天我心里老大不高兴。I'm feeling very upset today.

老大难 lǎodànán [名] long-standing problem ◊交通阻塞的确是北京的老大难。Congestion really is a long-standing problem in Beijing.

老底 lǎodǐ [名] dubious past

老调重弹 lǎo diào chóng tán it's the same old tune

老公 lǎogōng [名] (方) husband

老汉 lǎohàn [名] old man (*pl* men)

老虎 lǎohǔ [名] tiger

老化 lǎohuà [动] age ◊这些机器设备正在老化。These machines are getting old.

老话 lǎohuà [名] saying

老家 lǎojiā [名] home ◊回老家 return home ◊我老家在上海。Shanghai is my hometown.

老奸巨滑 lǎo jiān jù huá sly old devil

老练 lǎoliàn [形] experienced

老迈 lǎomài [形] aged

老谋深算 lǎo móu shēn suàn ◊我们教练老谋深算，善于利用对手的弱点。Our coach is a wise old bird

– he's good at using the opponents' weaknesses.

老年 lǎonián [名] old age

老牌 lǎopái [名] established brand

老婆 lǎopo [名] (口) **1** (老太太) old woman (*pl* women) **2** (妻子) wife (*pl* wives)

老气 lǎoqì [形] **1** (指人) mature **2** (指服装) old-fashioned

老生常谈 lǎo shēng cháng tán commonplace

老师 lǎoshī [名] teacher

老实 lǎoshi [形] **1** (诚实规矩) honest **2** (不聪明) naive ◇你怎么这样老实，居然把实情告诉他！ How can you be so naive? I can't believe you told him!

老手 lǎoshǒu [名] expert ◇修车老手 expert mechanic

老鼠 lǎoshǔ [名] mouse (*pl* mice)

老态龙钟 lǎotài lóngzhōng worn out with age ◇他变得老态龙钟，牙掉了，路也走不动。He has aged a great deal – he's lost his teeth and has become house-bound.

老外 lǎowài [名] foreigner

老乡 lǎoxiāng [名] fellow villager

老朽 lǎoxiǔ [形] decrepit

老爷 lǎoye [名] master

老于世故 lǎo yú shì gù worldly-wise

老账 lǎozhàng [名] old debts (*pl*)

老子 lǎozi [名] (口) **1** (父亲) father **2** (自称) I ◇老子才不怕老板呢。I'm not afraid of the boss.

老字号 lǎozìhào [名] established name

佬 lǎo [名] (贬) guy ♦乡巴佬 country bumpkin ♦阔佬 rich guy

姥 lǎo 见下文

姥姥 lǎolao [名] (口) granny

姥爷 lǎoye [名] (口) grandpa

涝 lào [名] waterlogging ♦洪涝 flood

烙 lào [动] **1** (物体) iron **2** (食品) bake

烙印 làoyìn [名] **1** (痕迹) brand **2** (印象) impression ◇童年生活在我心底留下了深刻烙印。My childhood has left a deep impression on me.

落 lào 见下文
▷另见 là, luò

落价 làojià [动] drop in price

乐 lè **I** [形] happy **II** [动] **1** (乐于) take pleasure in (*pt* took, *pp* taken) ◇幸灾乐祸 take pleasure in the misfortunes of others **2** (笑) laugh ◇漫画把大家逗乐了。The cartoon made everybody laugh.
▷另见 yuè

乐观 lèguān [形] optimistic ◇保持乐观情绪 adopt an optimistic attitude

乐呵呵 lèhēhē [形] joyful

乐极生悲 lè jí shēng bēi out of extreme joy comes extreme sorrow

乐趣 lèqù [名] delight

乐土 lètǔ [名] paradise

乐意 lèyì **I** [动] be willing to ◇他不乐意帮我们。He's unwilling to help us. **II** [形] happy

乐园 lèyuán [名] playground ◇迪斯尼乐园 Disneyland

乐滋滋 lèzīzī [形] contented

勒 lè [动] **1** (收住缰绳) rein … in **2** (强制) force ♦勒令 order ♦勒索 extort
▷另见 lēi

勒令 lèlìng [动] order

勒索 lèsuǒ [动] blackmail

勒 lēi [动] tie … tightly ◇勒紧绳子 tie a tight knot
▷另见 lè

累 léi 见下文
▷另见 lěi, lèi

累累 léiléi [形] (书) countless

累赘 léizhui [形] cumbersome

雷 léi [名] **1** (雷电) thunder ◇电闪雷鸣 thunder and lightning **2** (武器) mine ♦鱼雷 torpedo

雷电 léidiàn [名] thunder and lightning

雷厉风行 léi lì fēng xíng with the speed of lightning

雷同 léitóng **I** [动] echo **II** [形] duplicate

镭 léi [名] radium

垒 lěi I [动] build (*pt, pp* built) II [名] rampart

垒球 lěiqiú [名] softball

累 lěi I [动] 1 (积累) accumulate 2 (牵连) involve II [形] repeated ▷另见 léi, lèi

累次 lěicì [副] repeatedly ◇经过累次打击，走私得到遏制。After repeated attacks the smuggling was finally contained.

累积 lěijī [动] accumulate

累及 lěijí [动] involve

累计 lěijì [动] add up

累累 lěilěi [形] countless

磊 lěi 见下文

磊落 lěiluò [形] open and upright

蕾 lěi [名] bud

肋 lèi [名] rib

肋骨 lèigǔ [名] rib

泪 lèi [名] tear ♦眼泪 tears (*pl*) ♦流泪 shed tears

泪花 lèihuā [名] teardrop

泪汪汪 lèiwāngwāng [形] teary

类 lèi I [名] kind ♦分类 classify ♦另类 alternative II [动] be similar to ♦类似 similar to

类比 lèibǐ [名] analogy

类别 lèibié [名] category

类似 lèisì [形] similar

类型 lèixíng [名] type

累 lèi I [形] tired II [动] 1 (使劳累) tire ◇孩子身体弱，别累着他。The child isn't strong – be careful not to tire him out. 2 (操劳) work hard ▷另见 léi, lěi

累死累活 lèi sǐ lèi huó work oneself to death

擂 lèi I [动] beat (*pt* beat, *pp* beaten) II [名] competition

擂台 lèitái [名] 1 (指拳击) ring 2 (指竞技) arena

棱 léng [名] 1 (平面连接处) edge 2 (凸起处) ridge

棱角 léngjiǎo [名] 1 (字) edges and corners (*pl*) ◇一张棱角分明的脸 an angular face 2 (喻) sharp-wittedness

冷 lěng [形] 1 (温度低) cold ◇我觉得好冷。I feel really cold. 2 (不热情) frosty ◇他冷冷地对我说了声再见。He said goodbye to me very coldly. 3 (寂静) silent 4 (生僻) rare 5 (不受欢迎的) unpopular 6 (暗中的) hidden ♦冷枪 a shot from a sniper

冷冰冰 lěngbīngbīng [形] cold ◇那个老师对我们总是冷冰冰的。That teacher is always cold towards us. ◇孩子们的手和脚冻得冷冰冰的。The kids' hands and feet are frozen.

冷不防 lěngbufáng [副] suddenly

冷藏 lěngcáng [动] refrigerate

冷场 lěngchǎng [动] 1 (指演出) freeze up (*pt* froze, *pp* frozen) ◇请把台词再背几遍，以免上台时冷场。You should run through your lines a few more times, to avoid drying up on stage. 2 (指开会) go silent (*pt* went, *pp* gone) ◇我们最好事先多安排几个发言人，不要在开会时冷场。We'd better organise several people to speak at the meeting – we don't want any awkward silences.

冷嘲热讽 lěng cháo rè fěng have a dig at

冷处理 lěngchǔlǐ [动] shelve temporarily ◇专家认为此问题需冷处理。Experts think this problem should be shelved temporarily.

冷淡 lěngdàn I [形] cold II [动] cold-shoulder ◇多炒几个菜，别冷淡了客人。Make sure you do enough food – we don't want our guests to feel slighted.

冷冻 lěngdòng [动] freeze (*pt* froze, *pp* frozen) ◇冷冻食品 frozen produce

冷宫 lěnggōng [名] limbo

冷静 lěngjìng [形] 1 (方) (不热闹) quiet 2 (沉着) cool-headed

冷酷 lěngkù [形] cold-blooded

冷酷无情 lěngkù wúqíng ruthless

冷冷清清 lěnglěngqīngqīng [形] deserted

冷落 lěngluò **I** [形] isolated **II** [动] isolate ◇陪他聊聊，别冷落了他。Why don't you go chat to him – you shouldn't be leaving him out.

冷门 lěngmén [名] **1** (指专业) unpopular specialty ◇我弟弟选了个冷门专业。My brother has chosen an unusual specialty. **2** (指比赛) outsider

冷漠 lěngmò [形] indifferent

冷暖 lěngnuǎn [名] changes in temperature (*pl*) ◇冷暖空调设备 adjustable air-conditioning equipment

冷僻 lěngpì [形] **1** (冷落偏僻) deserted **2** (不常见的) rare

冷清 lěngqīng [形] deserted ◇没有你家里变得多么冷清。The house seems so deserted without you.

冷却 lěngquè [动] cool

冷若冰霜 lěng ruò bīng shuāng icy manner

冷色 lěngsè [名] cool colour (英) 或 color (美)

冷飕飕 lěngsōusōu [形] chilly

冷笑 lěngxiào [动] smile sarcastically

冷血动物 lěngxuè dòngwù [名] **1** (指动物) cold-blooded animal **2** (指人) cold fish

冷言冷语 lěng yán lěng yǔ make sarcastic comments

冷眼 lěngyǎn [名] **1** (冷静的态度) cool detachment **2** (冷淡的待遇) cold shoulder ◇冷眼相待 give sb the cold shoulder

冷饮 lěngyǐn [名] cold drink

冷遇 lěngyù [名] the cold shoulder ◇我遭到了她的冷遇。She gave me the cold shoulder.

冷战 lěngzhàn [名] cold war

愣 lèng **I** [形] staggered ◇听到这个消息，大家愣住了。Everyone was staggered at the news. **II** [副] bluntly

厘 lí 见下文

厘米 límǐ [量] centimetre (英), centimeter (美)

离 lí [动] **1** (分离) leave (*pt, pp* left) ◇离乡 leave the country **2** (距离) be far away from ◇我家离办公室不太远。My home is quite near to the office. **3** (缺少) do without ◇成功离不开奋斗和自信心。There can be no achievement without diligence and self-confidence.

离别 líbié [动] part

离间 líjiàn [动] sow dissent (*pt* sowed, *pp* sown)

离谱 lípǔ [形] unreasonable

离奇 líqí [形] odd

离散 lísàn [动] be separated

离休 líxiū [动] retire

离异 líyì [动] get divorced ◇离异后她独自生活。After the divorce, she lived alone.

离子 lízǐ [名] ion

梨 lí [名] pear

犁 lí **I** [名] plough (英), plow (美) **II** [动] plough (英), plow (美)

黎 lí 见下文

黎明 límíng [名] dawn

罹 lí [动] (书) suffer from ◇罹祸 suffer misfortune

罹难 línàn [动] (书) have a fatal accident

篱 lí [名] fence

篱笆 líba [名] bamboo fence

礼 lǐ [名] **1** (仪式) ceremony **2** (表示尊敬) courtesy **3** (礼物) present

礼拜 lǐbài [名] **1** (宗) religious service **2** (星期) week **3** (天) day of the week ◇礼拜六你来我家吃饭吧！ Come over for a meal on Saturday.

礼服 lǐfú [名] ceremonial robe

礼节 lǐjié [名] courtesy

礼貌 lǐmào [名] manners (*pl*)

礼品 lǐpǐn [名] gift

礼尚往来 lǐ shàng wǎng lái ◇朋友之间应该礼尚往来。Friends should treat each other the way they would like to be treated themselves.

礼堂 lǐtáng [名] hall

礼物 lǐwù [名] present

礼仪 lǐyí [名] etiquette

礼遇 lǐyù [动] receive special treatment

李 lǐ [名] plum

里 lǐ I [名] 1 (反面) inside ◇裤子里儿 trouser lining 2 (里边) inner ♦里屋 inner room 3 (街坊) neighbour (英), neighbor (美) ♦邻里 neighbourhood (英), neighborhood (美) 4 (家乡) hometown ♦故里 birthplace II [介] in ◇屋子里 in the room III [副] ♦这里 here ♦那里 there IV [量] *unit of length, equal to 500 metres*

里程 lǐchéng [名] 1 (路程) mileage 2 (发展过程) course

里程碑 lǐchéngbēi [名] milestone

里手 lǐshǒu [名] 1 (左边) left-hand side 2 (内行) expert

里应外合 lǐ yìng wài hé have inside help ◇我军与城里的部队里应外合攻下了这座城市。Our troops collaborated with troops inside the town to take the city.

俚 lǐ [名] vulgar

俚语 lǐyǔ [名] slang

理 lǐ I [名] 1 (条纹) texture 2 (道理) reason ♦合理 reasonable 3 (自然科学) natural science II [动] 1 (管理) manage ♦理财 manage the finances 2 (整理) tidy ♦理发 get one's hair cut 3 (表示态度) acknowledge ◇置之不理 ignore

理财 lǐcái [动] manage the finances

理睬 lǐcǎi [动] pay attention (*pt, pp* paid) ◇3个电话打了过来，他都不予理睬。Three phone calls came though, but he ignored them all.

理发 lǐfà [动] get a haircut

理会 lǐhuì [动] 1 (懂) understand (*pt, pp* understood) ◇我理会他的意思。I understand what he means. 2 (注意) notice ◇他下车之后，竟没有理会站在对面的我。He got out of the car, but didn't notice me standing opposite him.

理解 lǐjiě [动] understand (*pt, pp* understood)

理科 lǐkē [名] science

理疗 lǐliáo [名] physiotherapy

理论 lǐlùn [名] theory

理念 lǐniàn [名] principle

理事 lǐshì [名] 1 (负责人) director ◇常务理事 managing director ◇理事会 board of directors 2 (成员国) member ◇理事国 member of the UN Security Council

理所当然 lǐ suǒ dāng rán natural ◇他认为我给他礼物是理所当然的。He reckons it's entirely natural that I should give him a present.

理想 lǐxiǎng I [名] ideal II [形] ideal

理性 lǐxìng [名] reason

理由 lǐyóu [名] reason

理直气壮 lǐ zhí qì zhuàng with complete confidence

理智 lǐzhì I [名] intellect II [形] rational ◇我们一定要理智地去想想啊。We must think about this rationally.

鲤 lǐ [名] carp (*pl* carp) ♦鲤鱼 carp

力 lì I [名] 1 (物) force 2 (功能) strength ◇理解力 comprehension 3 (体力) physical strength ◇四肢无力 weak all over II [动] fight (*pt, pp* fought) ◇力争冠军 fight for the championship

力不从心 lì bù cóng xīn feel inadequate to the task

力度 lìdù [名] intensity

力量 lìliang [名] 1 (力气) strength ◇这一拳力量很大。That was a very powerful punch. 2 (能力) power ◇请尽一切力量按时完成任务。Please do everything in your power to complete the task on time. 3 (作用) strength ◇这种药的力量大。This medicine is very strong.

力排众议 lì pái zhòng yì override objections

力气 lìqi [名] strength ◇生病后我走路没力气。After the illness I didn't have enough strength to walk.

力所能及 lì suǒ néng jí do everything in one's power ◇红十字会将为战争受害者提供力所能及的援助。The Red Cross will do everything in their power to help the war victims. ◊让孩子去做一些自己力所能及的家务事。Let the child do his best with the housework.

力图 lìtú [动] strive (*pt* strove, *pp* striven) ◊新政府力图解决经济危机。The new government strove to solve the economic crisis.

力学 lìxué [名] mechanics (*pl*)

力争 lìzhēng [动] **1** (极力争取) strive (*pt* strove, *pp* striven) ◊力争上游 strive for progress **2** (极力争辩) argue ◊据理力争 argue on good grounds

力作 lìzuò [名] masterpiece

历 lì **I** [名] **1** (经历) experience **2** (历法) calendar **II** [形] previous

历程 lìchéng [名] course

历次 lìcì [名] all previous occasions ◊他在历次战斗中都立下了功勋。In all previous battles he has achieved glorious victories.

历代 lìdài [名] successive generations (*pl*)

历来 lìlái [副] always

历历在目 lìlì zài mù flood back

历史 lìshǐ [名] history ◊历史文物 historical relic

厉 lì [形] **1** (严格) strict **2** (严肃) stern

厉害 lìhai [形] terrible ◊他口渴得厉害。He was terribly thirsty.

立 lì **I** [动] **1** (站) stand (*pt, pp* stood) **2** (竖立) stand … up (*pt, pp* stood) ◊请把竹竿立在角落里。Please stand the bamboo pole in the corner. **3** (建立) ♦立功 make contributions **4** (制定) set … up (*pt, pp* set) ♦立法 legislate **5** (存在) exist ♦自立 stand on one's own two feet **II** [形] upright ♦立柜 wardrobe **III** [副] immediately

立场 lìchǎng [名] position

立春 lìchūn [名] the start of spring

立冬 lìdōng [名] the start of winter

立法 lìfǎ [动] legislate

立方 lìfāng **I** [名] cube ◊2的立方是8。2 cubed is 8. **II** [量] cubic ◊立方米 cubic metre (英) 或 meter (美)

立竿见影 lì gān jiàn yǐng produce instant results

立即 lìjí [副] immediately ◊家中有急事，我得立即回去。There's a crisis at home, I have to go back immediately. ◊听到留言后他立即回了电话。As soon as he got the message he returned the call.

立刻 lìkè [副] immediately ◊老师让我们立刻打扫教室卫生。The teacher told us to tidy up the classroom immediately. ◊回家后立刻给我打个电话。Give me a call as soon as you get home.

立论 lìlùn **I** [动] present one's argument **II** [名] argument

立秋 lìqiū [名] the start of autumn

立身处世 lì shēn chǔ shì social conduct

立体 lìtǐ [名] solid **II** [形] solid

立体声 lìtǐshēng [名] stereo

立夏 lìxià [名] the start of summer

立项 lìxiàng [动] officially set up a project

立意 lìyì [动] **1** (打定主意) be determined ◊他立意要走。He's determined to go. **2** (命意) approach ◊文章立意独特。The article has a unique approach.

立正 lìzhèng [动] stand to attention (*pt, pp* stood)

立志 lìzhì [动] be determined ◊他立志当一名海军。He is determined to become a naval captain.

立足 lìzú [动] **1** (站得住脚) be established ◊在海外立足对她来说不容易。It wasn't easy for her to establish herself overseas. **2** (处于某立场) be based in

吏 lì [名] official

沥 lì **I** [动] drip **II** [名] drop

沥青 lìqīng [名] asphalt

丽 lì [形] beautiful ♦壮丽 magnificent

丽人 lìrén [名] beauty

丽质 lìzhì [名] beauty

励 lì [动] encourage ♦奖励 reward

利 lì **I** [形] **1** (锋利) sharp **2** (顺利) advantageous **II** [名] **1** (利益) interest ♦利弊 pros and cons (*pl*) **2** (利润) profit and interest ♦暴利 staggering profits (*pl*) ◇高利贷 high-interest loan **III** [动] benefit ◇利国利民 benefit both people and country ◇互惠互利 mutually beneficial

利弊 lìbì [名] pros and cons (*pl*)

利害 lìhài [名] advantages and disadvantages (*pl*) ◇利害得失 gains and losses

利害 lìhai [形] terrible ◇这句话真利害。That's a terrible thing to say. ◇天冷得利害。It's terribly cold today.

利率 lìlǜ [名] interest rate

利落 lìluo [形] **1** (灵活的) nimble ◇说话利落 be quick with words **2** (有条理的) orderly **3** (完毕的) settled ◇事情办利落了。The matter has been settled.

利器 lìqì [名] **1** (兵器) sharp weapon **2** (工具) useful tool

利润 lìrùn [名] profit

利税 lìshuì [名] profits tax

利息 lìxī [名] interest

利益 lìyì [名] benefit

利用 lìyòng [动] **1** (物) use ◇合理利用自然资源 use natural resources appropriately **2** (人) exploit ◇你甭想利用我，我没那么幼稚。Don't even consider taking advantage of me – I'm not that naive.

利诱 lìyòu [动] entice

例 lì **I** [名] **1** (例子) example ♦举例 give an example **2** (依据) precedent ♦先例 precedent ◇史无前例 without precedent **3** (事例) case **4** (规则) rule **II** [形] regular

例假 lìjià [名] public holiday

例如 lìrú [动] give an example (*pt* gave, *pp* given) ◇大商场货物齐全，例如服装、家电、食品等应有尽有。The big shopping centre sells all kinds of goods, for example, clothes, household appliances and food.

例外 lìwài [动] be an exception ◇每个人都要加班加点，头儿也不例外。Everyone had to work overtime, and the boss was no exception. ◇所有人见到市长都点头哈腰，只有他是个例外。When everyone saw the mayor, they all bowed obsequiously – he was the only exception.

例行公事 lìxíng-gōngshì mere formality

例证 lìzhèng [名] instance

隶 lì **I** [动] be subordinate to **II** [名] slave

隶属 lìshǔ [动] be subordinate to

栎 lì [名] oak

荔 lì 见下文

荔枝 lìzhī [名] lychee

俪 lì **I** [形] parallel **II** [名] couple

莅 lì [动] (书) arrive

莅临 lìlín [动] (书) arrive

栗 lì **I** [名] chestnut **II** [动] tremble

砾 lì [名] debris (*sg*)

砾石 lìshí [名] gravel

粒 lì **I** [名] grain **II** [量] ◇一粒珍珠 a pearl ◇三粒入球 three goals

粒子 lìzi [名] **1** (颗粒) grain ◇米粒子 a grain of rice **2** (物) granule

痢 lì 见下文

痢疾 lìji [名] dysentery

俩 liǎ [数] (口) **1** (两个) two ◇我俩 the two of us **2** (几个) some ◇多赚俩钱 make some profit

连 lián **I** [动] connect ♦连接 link **II** [副] in succession ◇连年闹水灾 be flooded several years in succession ◇连看了几眼 glance at several times **III** [介] **1** (包括) including ◇连他4人 four people, including him **2** (甚至) even ◇连小伙都嫌冷。Even the young men thought it was too cold.

连词 liáncí [名] conjunction

连带 liándài [动] be related

连…带… lián…dài… and ◇连人

带车 people and cars ◇连滚带爬 roll and crawl ◇连蹦带跳 jump and skip

连贯 liánguàn [动] be coherent ◇她讲话简明、连贯、得体。She spoke concisely, coherently and appropriately.

连接 liánjiē [动] connect

连累 liánlěi [动] implicate ◇战争连累了旅游业。The war had negative implications for tourism. ◇自己做事不要连累别人。You should not involve other people in things you have done.

连忙 liánmáng [副] at once ◇孩子发烧，他连忙去请大夫。When he found out that the child had a fever, he went to call a doctor at once.

连绵 liánmián [形] continuous ◇阴雨连绵 rainy spell

连任 liánrèn [动] re-elect ◇他连任市长一职。He was re-elected as mayor for another term.

连锁 liánsuǒ [名] chain ◇连锁反应 chain reaction

连续 liánxù [动] go on without stopping (*pt* went, *pp* gone) ◇他连续干了3天，觉都没睡。He worked for three days in a row without sleeping.

连夜 liányè [副] **1** (当天夜里) that night ◇接到电话后，我连夜赶到他家去。After receiving the call, I went to his house that very night. **2** (连续几夜) nights on end ◇听说他生病了，我连夜不得安心。After hearing that he was ill, I couldn't stop worrying for nights on end.

连载 liánzǎi [动] serialize

帘 lián [名] curtain

怜 lián [动] **1** (怜悯) pity **2** (怜爱) love

怜悯 liánmǐn [动] pity

怜惜 liánxī [动] take pity on (*pt* took, *pp* taken)

涟 lián [名] **1** (波纹) waves (*pl*) **2** (泪痕) flow

涟漪 liányī [名] (书) ripple ◇感情涟漪 waves of emotion

莲 lián [名] lotus

莲花 liánhuā [名] lotus flower

联 lián **I** [动] unite ♦联赛 league match **II** [名] couplet

联邦 liánbāng [名] federation ◇英联邦 the British Commonwealth

联播 liánbō [动] broadcast (*pt, pp* broadcast) ◇新闻联播 news broadcast

联合 liánhé **I** [动] **1** (人) unite **2** (骨) rejoin **II** [形] joint ◇联合声明 joint statement

联合国 Liánhéguó [名] United Nations, UN

联欢 liánhuān [动] have a get-together ◇师生联欢 a student/teacher get-together

联结 liánjié [动] connect ◇全球由因特网连接起来了。The entire world is connected by the Internet.

联络 liánluò [动] contact ◇保持联络 maintain contact ◇联络方式 ways to maintain contact

联袂 liánmèi [副] (书) together ◇联袂出演 perform together ◇联袂提议 make a joint proposal

联盟 liánméng [名] alliance

联名 liánmíng [动] do … jointly

联网 liánwǎng [动] network

联系 liánxì [动] connect ◇他与恐怖分子有联系。He has connections with terrorists. ◇理论联系实际 apply theory to practise ◇和老同学失去了联系 lose touch with old schoolmates ◇和上层人物联系紧密 have close relations with one's superiors ◇促进经济贸易联系 encourage economic and trade relations

联想 liánxiǎng [动] associate

联谊 liányì [动] keep up a friendship (*pt, pp* kept) ◇联谊会 reunion

联姻 liányīn [动] be related by marriage

廉 lián [形] **1** (廉洁) honest **2** (便宜) cheap

廉耻 liánchǐ [名] integrity

廉价 liánjià [形] cheap ◇廉价日用品 cheap everyday goods

廉洁 liánjié [形] honest

廉政 liánzhèng [动] govern honestly

鲢 lián [名] silver carp（*pl* silver carp）

镰 lián [名] sickle ♦镰刀 sickle

敛 liǎn [动] **1** (收起) collect ♦敛容 assume a serious expression **2** (约束) restrain ♦敛迹 lie low **3** (收集) collect

敛财 liǎncái [动] accumulate wealth

敛迹 liǎnjì [动] lie low（*pt* lay, *pp* lain）◇刑满出狱后他有所敛迹。After he was released from jail he lay low for a while.

脸 liǎn [名] **1** (面部) face ◇洗脸 wash one's face **2** (前部) front ♦门脸 shop front (英), storefront (美) **3** (情面) face ◇脸皮厚 thick-skinned

脸蛋儿 liǎndànr [名] cheeks (*pl*)

脸面 liǎnmiàn [名] **1** (面部) face **2** (情面) feelings（*pl*）

脸皮 liǎnpí [名] **1** (情面) feelings（*pl*）**2** (羞耻心) skin ◇他脸皮厚，不知羞耻。He's very thick-skinned and has no sense of shame.

脸色 liǎnsè [名] **1** (气色) complexion **2** (表情) expression

练 liàn **I** [动] practise (英), practice (美) ♦练武 practise martial arts **II** [形] experienced ♦熟练 skilful (英), skillful (美)

练笔 liànbǐ [动] **1** (练习写作) practise (英) 或 practice (美) writing **2** (练习书法) practise (英) 或 practice (美) calligraphy

练兵 liànbīng [动] drill

练功 liàngōng [动] do exercises

练习 liànxí **I** [动] practise (英), practice (美) **II** [名] exercise ◇练习簿 exercise book

炼 liàn [动] **1** (锻炼) do exercise **2** (烧铸) smelt **3** (琢磨) consider

炼制 liànzhì [动] refine ◇石油炼制 petroleum refining

恋 liàn [动] **1** (恋爱) love ♦相恋 fall in love with each other **2** (想念) miss ◇恋家 be homesick

恋爱 liàn'ài [动] love ◇你和谁恋爱了？Who are you in love with? ◇谈恋爱 be in love

恋恋不舍 liànliànbùshě be reluctant to part

恋情 liànqíng [名] romantic love

恋人 liànrén [名] lover

殓 liàn [动] put … in a coffin（*pt, pp* put）

链 liàn [名] chain ♦项链 necklace

链条 liàntiáo [名] chain

良 liáng **I** [形] good **II** [副] much

良好 liánghǎo [形] good ◇考试成绩良好 good exam results

良师益友 liáng shī yì yǒu [名] ◇书籍是我们的良师益友。Books are our best teachers and most faithful friends.

良心 liángxīn [名] conscience ◇昧着良心做事 act against one's conscience

良性 liángxìng [形] benign ◇良性肿瘤 benign tumour

良知 liángzhī [名] intuition

凉 liáng [形] **1** (冷) cool **2** (灰心) disappointed
▷另见 liàng

凉快 liángkuai [形] cool ◇树阴下面挺凉快。It's nice and cool under the trees. ◇我去空调房里凉快凉快。I'm going into the air-conditioned room to cool off.

凉爽 liángshuǎng [形] cool

凉飕飕 liángsōusōu [形] chilly

梁 liáng [名] **1** (房梁) beam **2** (桥梁) bridge **3** (隆起物) ridge

量 liáng [动] **1** (衡量) measure ◇让我们量一量这张床的长宽高. Let's measure the bed. **2** (估量) appraise
▷另见 liàng

量度 liángdù [动] measure

量具 liángjù [名] measuring tool

粮 liáng [名] grain

粮食 liángshi [名] cereals (*pl*)

两 liǎng I [数] **1** (表示具体数目) two ◇两米 two metres (英) 或 meters (美) ◇两个小时 two hours **2** (表示不定数目) a few ◇说两句 say a few words ◇敲两下门 knock several times on the door II [名] both ◇两全其美 satisfy both sides ◇势不两立 be mutually exclusive III [量] *unit of weight, equal to 50 grams*

两败俱伤 liǎng bài jù shāng lose-lose situation

两便 liǎngbiàn [形] be convenient for all involved ◇你去拜会老友，我去喝茶，咱们两便。You go and visit old friends, and I'll go and drink tea – that way everyone will be happy.

两可 liǎngkě [动] be ambiguous

两口子 liǎngkǒuzi [名] couple

两难 liǎngnán [形] difficult ◇他面临两难选择。He's facing some difficult choices.

两栖 liǎngqī [动] be amphibious ◇两栖作战 an amphibious military operation

两全其美 liǎng quán qí měi satisfy both sides ◇我有个两全其美的方法。I have a solution that will please everybody.

两袖清风 liǎng xiù qīng fēng be incorruptible

亮 liàng I [形] **1** (光线) bright **2** (声音) clear **3** (心胸) tolerant ◇心明眼亮 see and think clearly II [动] **1** (发光) shine (*pt, pp* shone) ◇灯还亮着。The lights are still lit. **2** (显露) show (*pt* showed, *pp* shown) ♦亮底 come clean ◇亮身份 reveal one's identity

亮光 liàngguāng [名] light ◇屋子里透出一丝亮光。A ray of light shone through the room.

亮晶晶 liàngjīngjīng [形] sparkling ◇她的珠宝在烛光下显得亮晶晶的。All her jewels were sparkling in the candlelight.

亮堂 liàngtang [形] **1** (物体) bright **2** (胸怀) enlightened

亮相 liàngxiàng [动] appear on stage ◇香港歌星昨日亮相广州。Yesterday, pop stars from Hong Kong were playing Guangzhou.

凉 liàng [动] let … cool (*pt, pp* let) ◇夏天我喜欢把西瓜放冰箱里凉凉。In summer I like to put the watermelon in the fridge to cool.
▷另见 liáng

谅 liàng [动] understand (*pt, pp* understood)

谅解 liàngjiě [动] forgive (*pt* forgave, *pp* forgiven) ◇网站正在建设之中，不便之处，敬请谅解。This website is still under construction – please forgive us for any inconvenience.

辆 liàng [量] ◇一辆汽车 a car ◇两辆坦克 two tanks

靓 liàng [形] (方) **1** (指女性) beautiful **2** (指男性) handsome

靓女 liàngnǚ [名] pretty girl

靓仔 liàngzǎi [名] handsome man (*pl* men)

量 liàng I [名] **1** (限度) capacity **2** (数量) quantity II [动] estimate ♦量力 make an estimation of one's own abilities ◇量入为出 live within one's means
▷另见 liáng

量变 liàngbiàn [名] quantitative change

量力 liànglì [动] make an estimation of one's own abilities ◇凡事须量力而行。In all matters one should act according to one's abilities.

量入为出 liàng rù wéi chū live according to one's means

量刑 liàngxíng [动] determine a penalty

量子 liàngzǐ [名] quantum

晾 liàng [动] **1** (弄干) dry ◇晾干菜 dry out vegetables **2** (晒干) air

踉 liàng 见下文

踉跄 liàngqiàng [动] stagger

撩 liāo [动] **1** (掀) raise ◇撩起窗帘 raise the curtain ◇撩撩头发 put one's hair up **2** (水) sprinkle
▷另见 liáo

辽 liáo [形] distant

辽阔 liáokuò [形] vast ◇辽阔的土地 vast territory

疗 liáo [动] treat ◆治疗 treat

疗程 liáochéng [名] course of treatment

疗养 liáoyǎng [动] convalesce ◇疗养院 convalescent home

聊 liáo **I** [副] just ◇聊以自慰 just to console oneself **II** [动] (口) chat ◇我们经常聚在一起聊聊。We often get together for a chat.

聊赖 liáolài [名] interest ◇百无聊赖 bored stiff

聊天儿 liáotiānr [动] (口) chat

聊天室 liáotiānshì [名] chat room

寥 liáo [形] **1** (稀少) few ◇寥寥无几 very few **2** (静寂) silent

寥廓 liáokuò [形] (书) vast

寥寥 liáoliáo [形] few

僚 liáo [名] **1** (官吏) official ◆官僚 bureaucrat **2** (同僚) associate ◆同僚 colleague

撩 liáo [动] tease
▷另见 liāo

撩拨 liáobō [动] tease

嘹 liáo 见下文

嘹亮 liáoliàng [形] clear

潦 liáo 见下文

潦草 liáocǎo [形] **1** (字迹) illegible **2** (做事) sloppy ◇办事潦草 do things sloppily

潦倒 liáodǎo [形] down on one's luck

缭 liáo [动] **1** (缠绕) curl **2** (缝纫) sew (*pt* sewed, *pp* sewn) ◇缭贴边 hem

缭乱 liáoluàn [形] (书) confused ◇眼花缭乱 dazzled

缭绕 liáorào [动] float in the air ◇烟雾缭绕。The smoke floated into the air.

燎 liáo [动] burn ◇心急火燎 burning with impatience

了 liǎo **I** [动] **1** (完毕) finish ◇不了了之 finish without any concrete results ◇了账 settle a debt **2** (放在动词之后表示可能) ◇办不了 not be able to handle ◇受得了 be able to bear **3** (明白) understand (*pt, pp* understood) ◆明了 understand **II** [副] (书) ◇了无惧色 without a trace of fear ◇了无长进 no progress at all

了不得 liǎobude [形] **1** (惊异) amazing ◇能做这样的事情真是了不得。It's amazing to be able to do such a thing. **2** (非凡) extraordinary ◇高兴得了不得 extraordinarily happy **3** (严重) terrible

了不起 liǎobuqǐ [形] amazing

了得 liǎode [形] terrible

了结 liǎojié [动] put an end to (*pt, pp* put)

了解 liǎojiě [动] **1** (知道) understand (*pt, pp* understood) ◇我了解他的为人。I understand his behaviour. ◇政府应推动对艾滋病的了解。The government should promote understanding of the AIDS crisis. **2** (打听) find … out (*pt, pp* found) ◇你去了解一下事情的真相。You go and find out the truth behind this matter.

了然 liǎorán [形] clear ◇一目了然 in a flash of understanding

了如指掌 liǎo rú zhǐ zhǎng know like the back of one's hand

料 liào **I** [动] expect ◇我没料到你会来。I never expected that you would be able to come. ◇世事难料。 Human affairs are hard to predict. ◇不出所料 as expected **II** [名] **1** (材料) material ◆木料 timber ◆燃料 fuel ◆布料 cloth **2** (谷物) feed ◆草料 fodder

料理 liàolǐ [动] manage

料想 liàoxiǎng [动] expect

撂 liào [动] (口) **1** (放下) put … down (*pt, pp* put) ◇他把纸牌撂在桌上走出去了。He put the cards down on the table and left. **2** (弄倒) knock … down ◇他一下就把我撂倒了。He knocked me down with one blow. **3** (抛弃) abandon ◇孩子出生后被撂掉了。The baby was abandoned at birth.

瞭 liào 见下文

瞭望 liàowàng [动] keep a look-out (*pt, pp* kept)

镣 liào [名] fetters (*pl*)

镣铐 liàokào [名] shackles (*pl*)

咧 liē 见下文
▷另见 liě

咧咧 liēlie [动] (方) **1** (乱说) gossip **2** (哭啼) cry

咧 liě [动] grin
▷另见 liē

咧嘴 liězuǐ [动] grin

裂 liě [动] split (*pt, pp* split)
▷另见 liè

列 liè **I** [动] **1** (排列) set … out (*pt, pp* set) **2** (安排) list **II** [名] **1** (行列) rank **2** (类别) category

列兵 lièbīng [名] private

列车 lièchē [名] train

列岛 lièdǎo [名] archipelago

列举 lièjǔ [动] list

列席 lièxí [动] attend as an observer ◇列席会议 attend a meeting as an observer

劣 liè [形] bad ♦恶劣 bad ♦低劣 inferior

劣根性 liègēnxìng [名] inherent flaw

劣迹 lièjì [名] offence (英), offense (美)

劣势 lièshì [名] position of weakness

劣质 lièzhì [形] poor-quality

烈 liè **I** [形] **1** (强烈) strong ♦激烈 fierce ♦猛烈 violent **2** (刚正) upright ♦壮烈 heroic **II** [名] **1** (烈士) martyr **2** (功业) exploits (*pl*)

烈士 lièshì [名] martyr

烈性 lièxìng [形] **1** (指性情) fiery ◇烈性马 a spirited horse **2** (指浓度) strong ◇烈性酒 strong liquor

猎 liè [动] hunt ♦打猎 go hunting

猎奇 lièqí [动] seek novelty (*pt, pp* sought)

裂 liè [动] split (*pt, pp* split) ♦分裂 split ♦破裂 break
▷另见 liě

裂变 lièbiàn [动] split (*pt, pp* split)

裂痕 lièhén [名] crack

裂口 lièkǒu [名] split

拎 līn [动] carry

邻 lín **I** [名] neighbour (英), neighbor (美) ♦邻居 neighbour (英), neighbor (美) **II** [形] neighbouring (英), neighboring (美) ♦邻邦 neighbouring (英) 或neighboring (美) country

邻邦 línbāng [名] neighbouring (英) 或 neighboring (美) country

邻近 línjìn **I** [动] be close to **II** [名] vicinity ◇邻近就有一家超市。There's a supermarket in the vicinity.

邻居 línjū [名] neighbour (英), neighbor (美)

林 lín [名] **1** (树林) wood ◇风景林 scenic wood **2** (同类) ◇艺林 artistic circles ◇石林 the Stone Forest **3** (林业) forestry ♦林业 forestry

林立 línlì [动] cluster

林木 línmù [名] forest

林业 línyè [名] forestry

临 lín [动] **1** (靠近) face ♦临危 face danger **2** (到达) reach ♦光临 presence **3** (将要) be about to ♦临产 be in labour (英) 或 labor (美) **4** (临摹) copy

临场 línchǎng [动] enter a competition

临床 línchuáng [形] clinical

临近 línjìn [动] be close to ◇那家饭店临近机场。That restaurant is close to the airport. ◇考试临近了。The exams are approaching.

临摹 línmó [动] copy

临时 línshí [副] temporarily ◇临时措施 temporary measures

临头 líntóu [动] happen

临危 línwēi [动] **1** (即将死亡) be dying **2** (面临危险) be in mortal danger

临阵磨枪 lín zhèn mó qiāng leave things until the last moment ◇平时要努力，靠临阵磨枪不行。You should work hard all the time, not leave everything until the last moment.

临终 línzhōng [动] be on the point of death

淋 lín [动] drench
淋巴 línbā [名] lymph
淋漓尽致 línlí jìn zhì thorough
淋浴 línyù [动] take a shower (*pt*, took, *pp* taken)
琳 lín [名] precious jade
琳琅满目 línláng mǎn mù a feast for the eyes
粼 lín 见下文
粼粼 línlín [形] clear
嶙 lín 见下文
嶙峋 línxún [形] 1 (指山石) jagged 2 (指人体) bony
霖 lín [名] downpour
磷 lín [名] phosphorus
鳞 lín I [名] scale II [形] scaly
鳞次栉比 lín cì zhì bǐ row upon row ◊街道两旁的建筑物鳞次栉比。On either side of the road are row upon row of houses.
凛 lǐn [形] 1 (寒冷) cold ♦凛冽 bitterly cold 2 (严肃) strict ♦凛然 stern 3 (害怕) afraid
凛冽 lǐnliè [形] bitterly cold
凛然 lǐnrán [形] stern
吝 lìn [形] miserly
吝啬 lìnsè [形] stingy
吝惜 lìnxī [动] grudge
赁 lìn [动] rent ◊房屋出赁 room for rent
赁金 lìnjīn [名] rent
伶 líng [名] (旧) actor
伶仃 língdīng [形] lonely
伶俐 línglì [形] clever
伶牙俐齿 líng yá lì chǐ articulate
灵 líng I [形] 1 (灵活) nimble ♦灵敏 agile 2 (灵验) effective II [名] 1 (灵魂) soul 2 (神灵) deity ♦精灵 spirit 3 (灵柩) bier
灵便 língbiàn [形] 1 (指身体) nimble 2 (指工具) easy
灵丹妙药 líng dān miào yào panacea
灵魂 línghún [名] soul
灵活 línghuó [形] 1 (敏捷的) agile 2 (机动的) flexible
灵机一动 língjī yī dòng have a brainwave
灵柩 língjiù [名] bier
灵敏 língmǐn [形] sensitive
灵巧 língqiǎo [形] agile
灵堂 língtáng [名] mourning hall
灵通 língtōng [形] 1 (指信息) well-informed ◊他这个人信息灵通。He is well informed about current affairs. 2 (指效果) effective
灵性 língxìng [名] aptitude
灵验 língyàn [形] 1 (有效) effective 2 (应验) accurate
囹 líng 见下文
囹圄 língyǔ [名] prison
玲 líng 见下文
玲珑 línglóng [形] 1 (精巧细致) exquisite 2 (灵活敏捷) nimble
玲珑剔透 línglóng tītòu exquisitely made
凌 líng I [动] 1 (侵犯) insult ♦欺凌 bully 2 (升高) rise (*pt* rose, *pp* risen) 3 (逼近) approach ♦凌晨 before daybreak II [名] ice ♦冰凌 icicle
凌晨 língchén [名] before daybreak
凌驾 língjià [动] look down one's nose at ◊他总是凌驾于他人之上。He always looks down his nose at other people.
凌厉 línglì [形] quick and powerful
凌乱 língluàn [形] messy
凌辱 língrǔ [动] insult
铃 líng [名] 1 (响器) bell 2 (铃状物) ♦哑铃 dumb-bell
铃铛 língdang [名] small bell
陵 líng [名] 1 (小山) mound ♦丘陵 hill 2 (陵墓) tomb
陵墓 língmù [名] tomb
陵园 língyuán [名] cemetery
羚 líng [名] antelope
羚羊 língyáng [名] antelope

聆 líng [动] listen

聆听 língtīng [动] listen attentively

菱 líng [名] water chesnut

菱形 língxíng [名] rhombus

翎 líng [名] feather

翎毛 língmáo [名] plumage

零 líng **I** [名] **1** (零数) zero **2** (零头) odd ◇她年纪七十有零。She's seventy-odd years old. **II** [形] **1** (零碎的) odd ♦零活 odd jobs (*pl*) ♦零钱 small change **2** (部分的) spare ♦零件 spare parts (*pl*) **III** [动] wither ♦凋零 wither and fall **IV** [连] ◇两年零三个月 two years and three months ◇五元零二分 five yuan two fen

零部件 língbùjiàn [名] parts (*pl*)

零点 língdiǎn [名] midnight

零件 língjiàn [名] spare parts (*pl*)

零钱 língqián [名] small change

零敲碎打 língqiāosuìdǎ do things in bits and pieces ◇我建议你把作业一次做完，别零敲碎打。I suggest that you finish your homework in one go – don't do it in bits and pieces.

零散 língsǎn [形] scattered

零食 língshí [名] snack

零售 língshòu [动] retail ◇零售店 retail shop

零碎 língsuì **I** [形] trivial **II** [名] odds and ends (*pl*)

零头 língtóu [名] **1** (零碎部分) remnant **2** (零钱) small change

零星 língxīng [形] **1** (零碎的) fragmentary **2** (少量的) a little **3** (零散的) scattered

零用 língyòng [动] use … as spending money

零用钱 língyòngqián [名] pocket money (英), allowance (美)

龄 líng [名] **1** (年龄) age **2** (年限) duration

岭 lǐng [名] **1** (山) mountain ridge **2** (山脉) range

领 lǐng **I** [名] **1** (衣领) collar **2** (脖颈) neck **3** (大纲) outline **II** [动] **1** (带领) lead (*pt, pp* led) **2** (占有) possess ♦占领 occupy **3** (领取) get (*pt* got, *pp* got (英), gotten (美)) ♦招领 advertise lost property ♦冒领 falsely lay claim to **4** (接受) accept **5** (了解) understand (*pt, pp* understood) **6** (领养) adopt ◇这孩子有人领了。Someone has adopted this child. **III** [形] belonging to ♦领土 territory **IV** [量] ◇一领凉席 a summer mat ◇一领长袍 a long dress

领班 lǐngbān [名] supervisor

领导 lǐngdǎo **I** [动] lead (*pt, pp* led) ◇他领导有方。He's an effective leader. **II** [名] leader ◇好的领导总是承认自己的错误。A good leader always acknowledges his or her mistakes.

领地 lǐngdì [名] **1** (指私人土地) fief **2** (指国家领土) territory

领海 lǐnghǎi [名] territorial waters (*pl*)

领会 lǐnghuì [动] understand (*pt, pp* understood)

领教 lǐngjiào [动] **1** (表示客气) accept ◇你说得对，领教了！You're right, I take your point. **2** (表示请教) ask for advice ◇有几个问题要向您领教一下，好吗？Can I ask you for your advice about a few things? **3** (表示经历) experience

领空 lǐngkōng [名] air space

领略 lǐnglüè [动] appreciate

领情 lǐngqíng [动] be grateful ◇你的帮助，我十分领情。I am extremely grateful for your help.

领取 lǐngqǔ [动] get (*pt* got, *pp* got (英), gotten (美))

领事 lǐngshì [名] consul

领受 lǐngshòu [动] accept

领头儿 lǐngtóur [动] take the lead (*pt* took, *pp* taken)

领土 lǐngtǔ [名] territory

领悟 lǐngwù [动] comprehend

领先 lǐngxiān [动] lead (*pt, pp* led) ◇他在比赛中遥遥领先。He took a runaway lead in the competition.

领衔 lǐngxián [动] **1** (领头) head a list **2** (主演) star ◇他在一部新影片中领

衔主演。He's starring in a new film.

领袖 lǐngxiù [名] leader

领有 lǐngyǒu [动] possess

领域 lǐngyù [名] **1** (区域) district **2** (范围) field ◇社会科学领域 the field of social sciences

另 lìng **I** [代] another **II** [副] separately

另当别论 lìng dāng bié lùn treat … differently ◇他的问题应该另当别论。His problem should be treated differently.

另类 lìnglèi [名] something out of the ordinary

另起炉灶 lìng qǐ lú zào make a fresh start

另外 lìngwài **I** [代] other ◇我不喜欢这些衣服，我喜欢另外那些。I don't like these clothes – I like the others. **II** [副] in addition ◇我去了邮局，另外还去了果蔬店。In addition to going to the post office, I also went to the greengrocer.

另眼相看 lìng yǎn xiāng kàn look at … in a new light

令 lìng **I** [名] **1** (命令) order **2** (酒令) drinking game **3** (时节) season ◇时令菜 seasonal vegetables **II** [动] **1** (令) order **2** (使) make (*pt, pp* made) **III** [形] **1** (美好) excellent ♦令誉 good reputation **2** (表示尊敬) your

令行禁止 lìng xíng jìn zhǐ stick to the letter of the law

溜 liū **I** [动] **1** (滑行) slide (*pt, pp* slid) **2** (走开) sneak off **3** (加热) heat **4** (熘) quick fry **II** [形] smooth

溜达 liūda [动] go for a stroll (*pt* went, *pp* gone)

溜须拍马 liū xū pāi mǎ toady

刘 liú 见下文

刘海儿 liúhǎir [名] fringe

浏 liú [形] clear

浏览 liúlǎn [动] glance over

留 liú [动] **1** (不走) stay **2** (使留) keep … back (*pt, pp* kept) ♦挽留 persuade … to stay **3** (留意) be careful ♦留神 be careful **4** (保留) keep (*pt, pp* kept) **5** (积蓄) grow (*pt* grew, *pp* grown) ◇留胡子 grow a beard **6** (接受) accept **7** (遗留) leave … behind (*pt, pp* left) ◇他死后留下很多遗产。When he died he left behind a considerable legacy. **8** (留学) study abroad ◇留英 study in Britain

留步 liúbù [动] stop here

留后路 liúhòulù [动] leave a way out (*pt, pp* left)

留后手 liúhòushǒu [名] leave room for manoeuvre (英) 或 maneuver (美) (*pt, pp* left)

留恋 liúliàn [动] be reluctant to leave

留念 liúniàn [动] keep as a souvenir (*pt, pp* kept)

留情 liúqíng [动] show mercy (*pt* showed, *pp* shown)

留任 liúrèn [动] remain in office

留神 liúshén [动] be on the alert

留宿 liúsù [动] put … up for the night (*pt, pp* put)

留心 liúxīn [动] take note (*pt* took, *pp* taken)

留学 liúxué [动] study abroad ◇她要到国外去留学。She wants to go abroad to study.

留言 liúyán [动] leave a message (*pt, pp* left)

留意 liúyì [动] look … out

留影 liúyǐng [动] have a picture taken as a souvenir

流 liú **I** [动] **1** (流动) flow ♦漂流 drift **2** (传播) spread (*pt, pp* spread) **3** (转变) change for the worse **4** (发配) banish ♦流放 exile **II** [名] **1** (水流) current ♦洪流 torrent **2** (等级) grade

流弊 liúbì [名] abuse

流产 liúchǎn [动] **1** (医) have an abortion **2** (失败) fall through (*pt* fell, *pp* fallen)

流畅 liúchàng [形] graceful

流程 liúchéng [名] **1** (指水流) course **2** (指生产) flow

流传 liúchuán [动] spread (*pt, pp* spread)

流窜 liúcuàn [动] go on the run (*pt* went, *pp* gone)

流动 liúdòng [动] **1** (移动) flow **2** (流离) move about ◇流动演出队 travelling (英) 或 traveling (美) performing troupe

流毒 liúdú [动] spread evil influence (*pt, pp* spread)

流芳百世 liúfāng bǎishì be remembered for posterity

流放 liúfàng [动] exile

流感 liúgǎn [名] the flu

流浪 liúlàng [动] roam about

流离失所 liúlí shī suǒ destitute and homeless

流利 liúlì [形] fluent ◇他讲一口非常流利的英语。He speaks completely fluent English.

流里流气 liúlǐliúqì naughty

流连忘返 liúlián wàngfǎn enjoy oneself so much that one forgets to go home ◇这里的美景令我们流连忘返。The scenery here is so lovely that I don't want to go home.

流露 liúlù [动] reveal

流落 liúluò [动] drift about

流氓 liúmáng [名] **1** (下流) perversion **2** (歹徒) hooligan

流派 liúpài [名] school

流失 liúshī [动] erode

流水 liúshuǐ [名] **1** (流动水) running water **2** (销售额) turnover

流淌 liútǎng [动] flow

流体 liútǐ [名] fluid

流通 liútōng [动] circulate ◇货币流通 circulation of money

流线型 liúxiànxíng [形] streamlined

流星 liúxīng [名] meteor

流行 liúxíng [动] be fashionable ◇这种服装开始流行起来。These clothes are becoming fashionable. ◇流行音乐 pop music

流言 liúyán [名] gossip

流域 liúyù [名] basin

硫 liú [名] sulphur (英), sulfur (美)

硫酸 liúsuān [名] sulphuric (英) 或 sulfuric acid (美)

瘤 liú [名] tumour (英), tumor (美)

瘤子 liúzi [名] tumour (英), tumor (美)

柳 liǔ [名] willow

柳树 liǔshù [名] willow

柳絮 liǔxù [名] catkin

绺 liǔ [量] hank ◇一绺头发 a lock of hair

六 liù [数] six

陆 liù [数] *an elaborate form of "six" used in writing cheques etc to prevent mistakes and forgery*
▷另见 lù

遛 liù [动] **1** (指人) take a stroll (*pt* took, *pp* taken) **2** (指动物) walk ◇我要出去遛狗。I have to go out to walk the dog.

馏 liù [动] warm ... up

龙 lóng **I** [名] dragon **II** [形] imperial ◇龙袍 imperial robe

龙飞凤舞 lóng fēi fèng wǔ lively and elegant

龙卷风 lóngjuǎnfēng [名] tornado

龙腾虎跃 lóng téng hǔ yuè bustle about

龙头 lóngtóu [名] tap (英), faucet (美)

聋 lóng [形] deaf

聋子 lóngzi [名] ◇他是个聋子。He's deaf.

笼 lóng [名] **1** (笼子) basket **2** (笼屉) steamer
▷另见 lǒng

隆 lóng **I** [形] **1** (盛大) grand ♦隆重 solemn **2** (兴盛) prosperous **3** (深厚) deep **II** [动] bulge

隆冬 lóngdōng [名] midwinter

隆隆 lónglóng [拟] rumble

隆重 lóngzhòng [形] solemn

拢 lǒng [动] **1** (聚拢) hold (*pt, pp* held) **2** (靠近) get close to **3** (总合) add ... up **4** (梳理) comb **5** (合上) close

垄 lǒng [名] 1 (土埂) ridge 2 (小路) *raised path between fields*

垄断 lǒngduàn [动] monopolize

笼 lǒng [动] cover
▷另见 lóng

笼络 lǒngluò [动] win … over (*pt, pp* won)

笼统 lǒngtǒng [形] general ◇笼统地介绍 give a general introduction

笼罩 lǒngzhào [动] envelop

弄 lòng [名] (方) lane
▷另见 nòng

弄堂 lòngtáng [名] (方) alley

搂 lōu [动] 1 (聚集) rake … up 2 (提起) pull … up 3 (搜刮) extort 4 (方) (扳) pull 5 (方) (核算) check
▷另见 lǒu

娄 lóu I [形] (方) feeble II [动] (方) go bad (*pt* went, *pp* gone)

娄子 lóuzi [名] (口) blunder

楼 lóu [名] 1 (楼房) tall building ◇教学楼 teaching block 2 (楼层) floor ◇语音室在二楼。The language lab is on the second floor. 3 (城楼) city gate tower

楼房 lóufáng [名] multi-storey building

楼盘 lóupán [名] building

搂 lǒu [动] embrace
▷另见 lōu

搂抱 lǒubào [动] embrace

篓 lǒu [名] basket

陋 lòu [形] 1 (难看) ugly ♦丑陋 ugly 2 (狭小) narrow 3 (粗俗) common ♦陋习 bad habit 4 (肤浅) shallow ♦浅陋 superficial

陋习 lòuxí [名] bad habit

漏 lòu [动] 1 (雨、水) leak 2 (消息、风声) divulge 3 (词、句) leave … out (*pt, pp* left)

漏洞 lòudòng [名] 1 (空隙) leak 2 (破绽) loophole

漏斗 lòudǒu [名] funnel

漏网 lòuwǎng [动] slip through the net

镂 lòu I [动] engrave II [名] engraving plate

镂刻 lòukè [动] engrave

露 lòu [动] reveal
▷另见 lù

露富 lòufù [动] flaunt one's wealth

露脸 lòuliǎn [动] enjoy one's moment of fame

露马脚 lòumǎjiǎo [动] give oneself away (*pt* gave, *pp* given)

露头 lòutóu [动] 1 (露出头) show one's face (*pt* showed, *pp* shown) 2 (刚出现) appear

露馅儿 lòuxiànr [动] give the game away (*pt* gave, *pp* given)

芦 lú [名] reed

芦苇 lúwěi [名] reed

庐 lú [名] cottage

庐山真面目 lúshān zhēnmiànmù true character

炉 lú [名] stove ◇煤油炉 paraffin (英) 或 kerosene (美) stove ◇炼钢炉 steel-making furnace

炉火纯青 lú huǒ chún qīng reach perfection

炉灶 lúzào [名] kitchen range

颅 lú [名] skull

卤 lǔ I [名] 1 (盐卤) bittern 2 (卤汁) thick gravy II [动] stew … in soy sauce

卤肉 lǔròu [名] pot-stewed meat

虏 lǔ I [名] captive ♦俘虏 prisoner of war II [动] capture

掳 lǔ [动] carry … off

掳掠 lǔlüè [动] pillage

鲁 lǔ [形] 1 (迟钝) stupid ♦愚鲁 ignorant 2 (莽撞) impetuous ♦粗鲁 coarse

鲁莽 lǔmǎng [形] rash

陆 lù [名] land
▷另见 liù

陆地 lùdì [名] land

陆军 lùjūn [名] land forces (*pl*)

陆续 lùxù [副] one after another ◇代表团陆续抵达。The delegates arrived one after the other.

录 lù **I** [名] record **II** [动] **1** (记载) record ♦记录 take notes **2** (选取) choose (*pt* chose, *pp* chosen) ♦选录 select **3** (录音) tape-record

录取 lùqǔ [动] admit ◇她被剑桥大学录取了。She was given a place at the University of Cambridge.

录像 lùxiàng [动] video

录音 lùyīn [动] record

录用 lùyòng [动] recruit

鹿 lù [名] deer

鹿死谁手 lùsǐshuíshǒu who will win the prize ◇到底鹿死谁手, 一会儿就见分晓了。As to who will win the prize, we'll find out soon.

禄 lù [名] official pay ♦俸禄 official's salary

碌 lù [形] **1** (平凡) ordinary ♦庸碌 mediocre **2** (繁忙) busy ♦忙碌 busy

碌碌 lùlù [形] **1** (平庸) commonplace **2** (辛苦) busy

路 lù [名] **1** (道路) road ♦路标 signpost **2** (路程) journey ◇一路平安 have a safe journey **3** (门路) means ♦财路 a means of getting rich **4** (条理) sequence ♦思路 train of thought **5** (方面) sort ◇外路货 foreign goods **6** (路线) route ♦8路车 No. 8 bus **7** (种类) kind ◇他俩是一路的。They're two of a kind. ◇他们俩不是一路人。They're two very different people.

路标 lùbiāo [名] signpost

路程 lùchéng [名] journey

路过 lùguò [动] pass through

路径 lùjìng [名] **1** (道路) route **2** (门路) means (*sg*)

路况 lùkuàng [名] road conditions (*pl*)

路线 lùxiàn [名] **1** (指交通) route **2** (指思想) line

路子 lùzi [名] way

辘 lù 见下文

辘轳 lùlu [名] winch

辘辘 lùlù [拟] rumble

戮 lù [动] **1** (杀) kill ♦杀戮 slaughter **2** (合) unite

麓 lù [名] (书) foot of a mountain ♦山麓 foot of a mountain

露 lù **I** [名] **1** (水珠) dew **2** (饮品) juice **II** [动] reveal ♦暴露 expose ♦揭露 unmask
▷另见 lòu

露骨 lùgǔ [形] undisguised

露宿 lùsù [动] sleep outdoors (*pt*, *pp* slept)

露天 lùtiān [名] the open air ◇露天剧场 open-air theatre (英) 或 theater (美)

露头角 lù tóujiǎo [动] show promise (*pt* showed, *pp* shown)

露营 lùyíng [动] camp out

驴 lú [名] donkey

驴唇不对马嘴 lúchún bú duì mǎzuǐ incongruous

侣 lǚ [名] companion ♦情侣 lover ♦伴侣 partner

侣伴 lǚbàn [名] partner

捋 lǚ [动] stroke
▷另见 luō

旅 lǚ **I** [名] **1** (军队编制) brigade **2** (泛指军队) force **II** [动] travel **III** [副] together

旅伴 lǚbàn [名] travelling (英) 或 traveling (美) companion

旅差费 lǚchāifèi [名] travelling (英) 或 traveling (美) expenses (*pl*)

旅程 lǚchéng [名] itinerary

旅居 lǚjū [动] live away from home

旅客 lǚkè [名] passenger

旅途 lǚtú [名] journey ◇祝你旅途愉快! Have a good journey!

旅行 lǚxíng [动] travel

旅游 lǚyóu [名] tour ◇旅游业 tourism ◇去国外旅游 travel abroad

铝 lǚ [名] aluminium (英), aluminum (美)

屡 lǚ [副] repeatedly

屡次 lǚcì [副] repeatedly

屡见不鲜 lǚjiànbùxiān common occurrence

屡屡 lǚlǚ [副] time and again

缕 lǚ **I** [名] thread **II** [量] wisp ◇一缕烟 a wisp of smoke

缕缕 lǚlǚ [形] continuous

履 lǚ **I** [名] **1** (鞋子) shoe **2** (脚步) step **II** [动] **1** (踩踏) walk on ◇如履薄冰 treading on thin ice **2** (执行) carry … out

履历 lǚlì [名] personal details (*pl*) ◇履历表 CV (英), resumé (美)

履行 lǚxíng [动] carry … out

律 lǜ **I** [名] law ♦纪律 discipline ♦定律 law **II** [动] restrain ♦自律 self-disciplined

律师 lǜshī [名] lawyer

> 在英式英语和美式英语中, **lawyer** 是对律师的通称, 表示某人具有法律专业资格, 并能够为他人做司法代理。在美式英语中, **lawyer** 具有备案资格, 并且可以代表其当事人上庭辩护。美式英语中, **lawyer** 的同义词是 **attorney**。在英国, 由 **solicitor** 处理诸如遗嘱和合同之类的法律文件, 并且准备上庭所需要的各类文件; 由 **solicitor** 上庭为当事人辩护, 特别是在初级法院审理的案件。在高等法院中, 通常由 **barrister** 为控辩双方辩护。在苏格兰, **barrister** 被称为 **advocate**。

虑 lǜ **I** [动] think about (*pt, pp* thought) ♦考虑 consider **II** [名] concern ♦忧虑 worry

绿 lǜ [形] green

绿灯 lǜdēng [名] **1** (指交通信号) green light **2** (指方便条件) the go-ahead

绿化 lǜhuà [动] make … green ◇绿化荒山 plant trees on the mountains

绿卡 lǜkǎ [名] green card

绿油油 lǜyōuyōu [形] glossy green

绿洲 lǜzhōu [名] oasis (*pl* oases)

氯 lǜ [名] chlorine

滤 lǜ [动] filter ♦过滤 filter

孪 luán 见下文

孪生 luánshēng [动] be a twin ◇孪生兄弟 twin brothers

挛 luán [动] curl up ♦痉挛 convulse

卵 luǎn [名] ovum (*pl* ova)

卵巢 luǎncháo [名] ovary

卵子 luǎnzǐ [名] ovum (*pl* ova)

乱 luàn **I** [形] **1** (没有秩序的) disorderly ♦杂乱 muddled ♦混乱 confused **2** (心绪不宁的) disturbed **II** [名] **1** (指冲突) chaos ♦战乱 war chaos ♦骚乱 disturbance **2** (指男女) promiscuity ♦淫乱 licentiousness **III** [动] confuse ♦扰乱 disturb **IV** [副] carelessly

乱哄哄 luànhōnghōng [形] chaotic

乱七八糟 luànqībāzāo in a mess

乱世 luànshì [名] turbulent times (*pl*)

乱真 luànzhēn [动] pass … off as genuine ◇以假乱真 pass off a fake as genuine

乱子 luànzi [名] disturbance

掠 lüè [动] **1** (掠夺) ransack ♦抢掠 plunder **2** (拂过) speed past (*pt, pp* sped)

掠夺 lüèduó [动] plunder

掠取 lüèqǔ [动] grab

掠影 lüèyǐng [名] panorama

略 lüè **I** [名] **1** (简述) summary ♦要略 summary ♦节略 outline **2** (计谋) plan ♦策略 tactic ♦方略 general plan **II** [动] **1** (夺取) capture ♦侵略 invade **2** (简化) simplify ♦省略 omit **III** [形] simple **IV** [副] slightly

略微 lüèwēi [副] a little

略语 lüèyǔ [名] abbreviation

抡 lūn [动] swing (*pt, pp* swung)

伦 lún [名] **1** (人伦) human

relationships (*pl*) **2** (条理) order **3** (同类) match

伦比 lúnbǐ [动] rival

伦理 lúnlǐ [名] ethics (*sg*)

沦 lún [动] **1** (沉没) sink (*pt* sank, *pp* sunk) **2** (没落) be reduced to ◇这位前总统已沦为阶下囚。The former president was reduced to the status of a prisoner.

沦落 lúnluò [动] sink to (*pt* sank, *pp* sunk)

沦丧 lúnsàng [动] be ruined

沦陷 lúnxiàn [动] be occupied

轮 lún **I** [名] **1** (轮子) wheel **2** (轮状物) ◇年轮 growth ring **3** (轮船) steamship **II** [量] ◇一轮明月 a bright moon ◇他比我大一轮。He's a dozen years older than me.

轮船 lúnchuán [名] steamship

轮番 lúnfān [副] successively

轮换 lúnhuàn [动] take turns (*pt* took, *pp* taken) ◇他们轮换站岗。They took turns to stand guard.

轮回 lúnhuí [动] recur

轮廓 lúnkuò [名] outline

轮流 lúnliú [副] in turns ◇我们轮流辅导孩子学习。We take it in turns to coach the child.

轮椅 lúnyǐ [名] wheelchair

论 lùn **I** [名] **1** (文章) essay ♦立论 argument ♦社论 editorial **2** (学说) theory ◇相对论 theory of relativity **II** [动] **1** (分析) discuss ♦评论 comment on ♦争论 dispute **2** (看待) consider ◇不能一概而论。You can't consider everything at once. **3** (衡量) set (*pt*, *pp* set) ◇按质论价 determine price according to quality **III** [介] in terms of ◇论水平，他比我强。In terms of ability, he's better than I am.

论处 lùnchǔ [动] punish

论点 lùndiǎn [名] argument

论调 lùndiào [名] view

论断 lùnduàn [名] thesis (*pl* theses)

论据 lùnjù [名] argument

论述 lùnshù [动] set forth (*pt*, *pp* set) ◇精辟的论述 brilliant analysis

论坛 lùntán [名] forum ◇世界经济论坛 the World Economic Forum

论文 lùnwén [名] dissertation

论战 lùnzhàn [动] debate

论证 lùnzhèng **I** [名] proof **II** [动] expound

论著 lùnzhù [名] work

捋 luō [动] stroke
▷另见 lǚ

罗 luó **I** [名] **1** (网) net **2** (筛) sieve **3** (丝织品) silk gauze **II** [动] **1** (捕捉) catch … with a net (*pt*, *pp* caught) **2** (陈列) spread … out (*pt*, *pp* spread) **3** (搜集) collect

罗锅儿 luóguōr **I** [名] hunchback **II** [形] hunchbacked ◇罗锅桥 humpbacked bridge

罗列 luóliè [动] **1** (陈列) set … out (*pt*, *pp* set) **2** (列举) enumerate

罗马数字 Luómǎ shùzì [名] Roman numeral

罗盘 luópán [名] compass

罗网 luówǎng [名] net

罗织 luózhī [动] frame

萝 luó [名] trailing plant

萝卜 luóbo [名] turnip ♦胡萝卜 carrot

逻 luó [动] patrol

逻辑 luóji [名] logic ◇逻辑推理 logical reasoning

锣 luó [名] gong

箩 luó [名] bamboo basket

箩筐 luókuāng [名] large bamboo basket

骡 luó [名] mule

螺 luó [名] **1** (指动物) snail **2** (指指纹) whorl

螺钉 luódīng [名] screw

螺旋 luóxuán [名] **1** (曲线) spiral **2** (指简单机械) screw

裸 luǒ [动] expose

裸露 luǒlù [动] expose

裸体 luǒtǐ [形] naked

骆 luò 见下文

骆驼 luòtuo [名] camel

络 luò 见下文

络绎不绝 luòyì bù jué endless stream ◊参观的人络绎不绝。There was an endless stream of spectators.

落 luò I [动] **1** (掉下) fall (*pt* fell, *pp* fallen) ♦脱落 shed ♦坠落 drop **2** (下降) go down (*pt* went, *pp* gone) ♦降落 descend **3** (降下) lower **4** (衰败) decline ♦衰落 wane **5** (落后) fall behind (*pt* fell, *pp* fallen) ♦落榜 fail an examination **6** (停留) stay ♦落栈 stay at a hotel **7** (归属) fall to (*pt* fell, *pp* fallen) ◊家庭的重任落在了他的身上。The responsibilities of the household fell to him. **8** (得到) suffer ◊从政就意味着要落责难。Being a politician means laying oneself open to public censure. **9** (记录) record II [名] **1** (停留之地) whereabouts (*pl*) ♦着落 location ♦下落 whereabouts **2** (聚居之地) settlement ♦部落 tribe ♦村落 village
▷另见 là, lào

落榜 luòbǎng [动] fail the college entrance examination

落差 luòchā [名] drop

落成 luòchéng [动] complete

落地 luòdì [动] **1** (坠地) fall to the ground (*pt* fell, *pp* fallen) **2** (出生) be born

落后 luòhòu I [动] fall behind (*pt* fell, *pp* fallen) ◊落后于时代 fall behind the times II [形] backward

落户 luòhù [动] settle

落花流水 luò huā liú shuǐ in a sorry state

落脚 luòjiǎo [动] stay

落井下石 luò jǐng xià shí kick a man when he's down

落空 luòkōng [动] come to nothing (*pt* came, *pp* come)

落落大方 luòluò dàfāng elegant and graceful

落马 luòmǎ [动] be brought to justice

落难 luònàn [动] suffer misfortune

落魄 luòpò [形] (潦倒) (书) down-and-out

落实 luòshí I [形] workable II [动] implement

落网 luòwǎng [动] be caught

落伍 luòwǔ I [动] drop out II [形] outdated

落叶归根 luò yè guī gēn return to one's roots

落座 luòzuò [动] take one's seat (*pt* took, *pp* taken)

摞 luò I [动] pile ... up II [量] ◊一摞杂志 a stack of magazines ◊一摞碟子 a pile of plates

Mm

妈 mā [名] 1 (口) (母亲) mum (英), mom (美) 2 (长一辈妇女) ♦姑妈 aunt ♦舅妈 aunt

妈妈 māma [名] (口) mum (英), mom (美)

抹 mā [动] 1 (擦) wipe ◊我把桌子抹干净了。I wiped the table clean. 2 (拉) pull ◊他把帽檐儿往下一抹。He pulled the brim of his hat down. ▷另见 mǒ

抹布 mābù [名] cloth

麻 má I [名] 1 (指植物) hemp ♦大麻 marijuana ♦亚麻 flax 2 (指纤维) hemp 3 (芝麻) sesame 4 (麻将牌) mahjong II [形] 1 (麻木) numb ◊我的脚都站麻了。My foot has gone numb from standing for so long. 2 (粗糙) rough

麻痹 mábì I [名] paralysis ♦小儿麻痹症 polio II [动] lower one's guard ◊麻痹对手 throw one's opponent off guard

麻烦 máfan I [形] problematic ◊入学手续很麻烦。The enrolment process was problematic. ◊申请签证很麻烦。Applying for visas can be such a hassle. II [名] trouble III [动] trouble ◊不好意思，麻烦您了。Sorry to trouble you.

麻将 májiàng [名] mahjong

麻利 máli [形] dexterous

麻木 mámù [形] 1 (指知觉) numb ◊他冻得手脚麻木了。He was so cold that his hands and feet went numb. 2 (喻) (迟钝) insensitive ◊他对别人的批评很麻木。He's insensitive to the criticisms of others.

麻木不仁 mámù bù rén (贬) 1 (反应迟钝) be insensitive 2 (不关心) uncaring

麻酥酥 másūsū [形] tingly ◊蹲了一小会儿，脚就麻酥酥的。After squatting for a short while, I got pins and needles in my feet.

麻醉 mázuì [动] 1 (医) anaesthetize (英), anesthetize (美) ◊全身麻醉 a general anaesthetic (英) 或 anesthetic (美) 2 (喻) be lulled

马 mǎ [名] horse

马不停蹄 mǎ bù tíng tí non-stop

马达 mǎdá [名] motor

马大哈 mǎdàhā I [形] careless II [名] scatterbrain

马到成功 mǎ dào chénggōng achieve immediate success

马后炮 mǎhòupào [名] ◊他总是爱放马后炮。He's always too slow to act. ◊事后才提建议，这不是马后炮嘛！ Isn't it a bit late to be making suggestions after the event?

马虎 mǎhu [形] careless

马脚 mǎjiǎo [名] giveaway ◊走私者在海关露了马脚。The smugglers gave themselves away at customs.

马拉松 mǎlāsōng [名] marathon ◊马拉松式的研究 a marathon piece of research

马路 mǎlù [名] road

马匹 mǎpǐ [名] horse

马赛克 mǎsàikè [名] (建筑) mosaic

马上 mǎshàng [副] right away ◊他马上就到。He'll be here right away. ◊妈妈接到电话后，马上就走了。After getting the call, Mum left right away. ◊准备好了吗？我们马上就走。Are you ready? We're going right now.

马戏 mǎxì [名] circus

吗 mǎ 见下文

吗啡 mǎfēi [名] morphine ▷另见 ma

玛 mǎ 见下文

玛瑙 mǎnǎo [名] agate

码 mǎ I [名] numeral ♦数码 number ♦页码 page number II [量] ◊我们说的是两码事儿。We were talking about two different things. ◊这根本就是一码事儿嘛！These are basically the same thing after all! III [动] (口) stack … up

码头 mǎtou [名] pier

蚂 mǎ 见下文
▷另见 mà

蚂蚁 mǎyǐ [名] ant

蚂 mà 见下文
▷另见 mǎ

蚂蚱 màzha [名] locust

骂 mà [动] **1** (侮辱) insult **2** (斥责) tell … off (*pt, pp* told) ◇他因为没完成家庭作业而挨骂。He was told off for not doing his homework.

骂街 màjiē [动] shout and scream in public

骂名 màmíng [名] bad reputation

吗 ma [助] **1** (表示疑问) ◇你去银行吗？ Are you going to the bank? **2** (表示反问) ◇你不是去过她的家吗？ Haven't you been to her house before?
▷另见 mǎ

嘛 ma [助] **1** (表示显而易见) ◇事实就是这样嘛！ That's just the way things are! **2** (表示期望) ◇别不高兴嘛！ Please don't be unhappy. **3** (表示停顿) ◇那件事嘛，明天再说吧！ Oh that! Well, let's talk about it tomorrow.

埋 mái [动] **1** (盖住) bury **2** (隐藏) hide (*pt* hid, *pp* hidden) ◇隐姓埋名 go incognito

埋藏 máicáng [动] bury ◇埋藏在心中的秘密 a secret buried in one's heart

埋伏 máifú [动] **1** lie in ambush (*pt* lay, *pp* lain) **2** ambush

埋没 máimò [动] **1** (埋住) cover **2** (忽视) overlook

埋头 máitóu [动] bury oneself in ◇埋头苦读 bury oneself in serious reading

埋葬 máizàng [动] bury

买 mǎi [动] **1** (购买) buy (*pt, pp* bought) ◇她爱买贵的衣服。She liked to buy expensive clothes. ◇不是每个人都买得起房。Not everyone can afford to buy a flat. ◇我去市场买东西。I'm going shopping in the market. **2** (换取) win … over (*pt, pp* won) ◇收买民心 win people over ♦买通 buy … off

买单 mǎidān [动] (方) pay a bill (*pt, pp* paid) ◇买单！ The bill, please! ◇今天吃饭我来买单吧！ Today the meal's on me.

买空卖空 mǎi kōng mài kōng speculate on the stock market

买卖 mǎimai [名] **1** (生意) business ◇当地市场的买卖很兴隆。Business is brisk at the local market. **2** (商店) shop (英), store (美)

买通 mǎitōng [动] bribe ◇为了提前出狱，他买通了监狱长。In order to get out of prison early he bribed the prison governor.

买账 mǎizhàng [动] buy (*pt, pp* bought) ◇他喜欢对别人指手画脚，但没人买他的账。He likes to try and order people around, but no one buys it.

迈 mài I [动] step ♦迈步 stride II [形] elderly III [量] mile

迈进 màijìn [动] stride forward (*pt* strode, *pp* stridden) ◇我们正向我们的目标迈进。We are making great strides towards our objectives.

麦 mài [名] **1** (麦类粮食) wheat ♦燕麦 oats (*pl*) **2** (小麦) wheat

麦克风 màikèfēng [名] microphone, mike (口)

麦秋 màiqiū [名] wheat-harvesting season

卖 mài [动] **1** (出售) sell (*pt, pp* sold) ◇书都卖完了。The books are all sold out. **2** (出卖) betray **3** (尽量使出) do all one can ♦卖劲儿 spare no effort **4** (故意表现) make a show of ♦装疯卖傻 play the fool

卖点 màidiǎn [名] selling point

卖关子 mài guānzi [动] keep … guessing (*pt, pp* kept) ◇她说话爱卖关子。When she talks she likes to keep people guessing.

卖命 màimìng [动] work oneself to the bone ◇他每天卖命赚钱。He works himself to the bone every day.

卖弄 màinong [动] show off (*pt* showed, *pp* shown)

卖淫 màiyín [动] sell sex (*pt, pp* sold)

卖座 màizuò [动] attract customers ◇这个小咖啡馆儿很卖座。This small coffee house attracts a lot of customers.

脉 mài [名] **1** (血管) blood vessels (*pl*) ♦动脉 artery (*pl* arteries) ♦静脉 vein **2** (脉搏) pulse ♦号脉 feel a pulse **3** (脉状物) ♦山脉 mountain range ♦矿脉 mineral veins ♦叶脉 leaf veins ▷另见 mò

脉搏 màibó [名] pulse

脉络 màiluò [名] **1** (医) blood vessels (*pl*) **2** (喻) (条理) train of thought ◇写文章脉络要清楚。When writing essays, the sequence of ideas must be clear.

埋 mán 见下文

埋怨 mányuàn [动] **1** (指责) blame **2** (抱怨) complain

蛮 mán **I** [形] rough ♦野蛮 wild **II** [副] **1** (鲁莽) recklessly **2** (方) (很) very

蛮干 mángàn [动] act recklessly

蛮横 mánhèng [形] boorish

馒 mán 见下文

馒头 mántou [名] steamed bun

瞒 mán [动] hide the truth from (*pt* hid, *pp* hidden) ◇快告诉我们吧，别瞒着啦！ Hurry up and tell us – don't keep us in the dark!

瞒天过海 mán tiān guò hǎi act in an underhand way

满 mǎn **I** [形] **1** (充实) full **2** (全) complete ♦满分 full marks ◇她满眼泪花。Her eyes are full of tears. **II** [动] **1** (使充满) fill ◇快给客人满上酒。Hurry up and fill the guests' glasses with wine. **2** (满足) be satisfied ◇他对自己的生活心满意足。He is fully satisfied with his life. **III** [副] fully

满不在乎 mǎn bù zàihu be indifferent to

满城风雨 mǎn chéng fēng yǔ cause a sensation

满怀 mǎnhuái **I** [动] be filled with ◇她满怀着伤痛，离开了家乡。She left her hometown filled with sorrow. **II** [名] chest ◇他们在黑暗中撞了个满怀。They bumped right into each other in the darkness.

满面春风 mǎnmiàn chūnfēng beaming with joy

满腔 mǎnqiāng [动] be filled with ◇他对工作满腔热情。He is full of enthusiasm about his work.

满意 mǎnyì [动] be satisfied

满员 mǎnyuán [动] be full

满月 mǎnyuè **I** [动] ◇孩子马上就满月了。The child is almost a month old. **II** [名] full moon

满足 mǎnzú [动] **1** (感到满意) be satisfied ◇他对生活很满足。He is very satisfied with life. ◇满足现状 satisfied with the status quo **2** (使满足) satisfy ◇产量无法满足市场需求。Output cannot satisfy the demands of the market.

曼 màn [形] **1** (轻柔) graceful **2** (长) prolonged

曼延 mànyán [动] stretch

谩 màn [形] rude

谩骂 mànmà [动] hurl abuse at

蔓 màn 见下文

蔓延 mànyán [动] spread (*pt, pp* spread) ◇大火迅速蔓延到整个村落。The fire spread quickly to the whole village.

漫 màn **I** [动] overflow **II** [形] all over **III** [副] (随便) randomly

漫不经心 màn bù jīngxīn absent-mindedly

漫步 mànbù [动] stroll

漫长 màncháng [形] endless

漫画 mànhuà [名] comic strip

漫骂 mànmà [动] rant and rave

漫山遍野 màn shān biàn yě all over the place

漫谈 màntán [动] discuss … informally

漫天 màntiān [形] **1** (满天) filling the sky ◇云雾漫天。The sky was filled with clouds and mist. **2** (无限度) outrageous

漫延 mànyán [动] spread (*pt, pp* spread)

漫游 mànyóu [动] travel around ◇我希望将来能漫游全世界。I hope that in the future I will be able to travel the world.

慢 màn I [形] **1** (缓慢) slow **2** (冷漠) indifferent ♦傲慢 haughty II [动] hold on (*pt, pp* held) ◇且慢，我有话要说。Hold on – I have something to say.

慢慢腾腾 mànmantēngtēng sluggish

慢条斯理 màntiáo-sīlǐ in a leisurely way

慢悠悠 mànyōuyōu [形] leisurely

忙 máng I [形] busy II [动] be busy with ◇你这一段忙什么呢？ What's been keeping you busy recently?

忙乎 mánghu [动] be busy ◇我忙乎着搬家呢！ I'm busy moving house.

忙碌 mánglù [动] be busy ◇快考试了，同学们都很忙碌。The exams are approaching and the students are all very busy.

忙乱 mángluàn [形] rushed ◇早上总是很忙乱。Mornings are always rushed.

盲 máng [形] blind ♦文盲 illiterate

盲从 mángcóng [动] follow … blindly

盲打 mángdǎ [动] touch-type

盲点 mángdiǎn [名] blind spot ◇法律盲点 loopholes in the law

盲动 mángdòng [动] act rashly

盲目 mángmù [形] blind ◇盲目崇拜 blind worship

盲目性 mángmùxìng [名] blindness

盲人摸象 mángrén mō xiàng mistake a part for the whole

盲文 mángwén [名] braille

茫 máng [形] **1** (远而模糊) hazy **2** (迷惑) puzzling

茫茫 mángmáng [形] vast

茫然 mángrán [形] at a loss ◇给他解释了半天，他还是茫然地望着我。I took a long time explaining it to him but he still stared at me blankly.

莽 mǎng I [名] coarse grass II [形] rash

莽莽 mǎngmǎng [形] vast

莽撞 mǎngzhuàng [形] impetuous

蟒 mǎng [名] (动物) python

猫 māo [名] cat

猫儿腻 māornì [名] (方) trick

猫儿眼 māoryǎn [名] spyhole

毛 máo I [名] **1** (毛发) hair ♦羽毛 feather **2** (指食物上) mould (英), mold (美) ◇面包上长毛了。The bread is mouldy (英) 或 moldy (美). **3** (指墙上或衣物上) mildew **4** (指植物) ◇不毛之地 barren land ◇空气中飞着一些小毛毛。There are small bits of fluff floating in the air. II [形] **1** (粗糙) crude ♦毛坯 semi-finished product **2** (不纯) gross ♦毛重 gross weight **3** (粗率) careless **4** (小) little

毛笔 máobǐ [名] brush pen

毛病 máobìng [名] **1** (故障) problem **2** (缺点) shortcoming **3** (疾病) illness ◇他的腿有点毛病。He has something wrong with his leg.

毛糙 máocao [形] **1** (指物) crude **2** (指人) careless ◇他干活毛糙。He's careless about his work.

毛骨悚然 máo gǔ sǒngrán make sb's flesh creep

毛孔 máokǒng [名] pore

毛利 máolì [名] gross profit

毛皮 máopí [名] fur

毛茸茸 máorōngrōng [形] **1** (指人) hairy **2** (指有羽动物) feathered **3** (指有毛皮的动物) furry

毛手毛脚 máo shǒu máo jiǎo careless

毛遂自荐 Máo Suì zì jiàn volunteer one's services

毛重 máozhòng [名] gross weight

矛 máo [名] spear

矛盾 máodùn I [名] **1** (相抵之处) conflict **2** (哲) contradiction II [形] uncertain ◇对于选择哪个专业，她内心很矛盾。She's uncertain about which major to choose.

矛头 máotóu [名] (喻) target ◇会上，

大家把批评的矛头都指向了老赵。At the meeting, Lao Zhao was the target of everybody's criticism.

茅 máo [名] thatch

茅庐 máolú [名] thatched cottage

茅塞顿开 máo sè dùn kāi suddenly see the light

锚 máo [名] anchor ♦起锚 weigh anchor

茂 mào [形] 1 (茂盛) luxuriant 2 (丰富) abundant

茂密 màomì [形] dense

茂盛 màoshèng [形] flourishing

冒 mào I [动] 1 (往外) give … off (*pt* gave, *pp* given) ◇锅冒烟了。The wok is giving off smoke. 2 (不顾) risk ◇冒着生命危险 putting one's life at risk 3 (假充) pretend to be ◇冒牌 bogus ♦冒认 lay false claim to II [副] falsely ♦冒进 jump the gun

冒充 màochōng [动] pass … off as ◇这个店将商品冒充名牌出售。This store sells products which are passed off as brand names.

冒犯 màofàn [动] 1 (他人、尊严) offend 2 (纪律、规定) violate ◇无人敢冒犯军纪。No one dares to violate military discipline.

冒火 màohuǒ [动] fly into a rage (*pt* flew, *pp* flown)

冒尖儿 màojiānr [动] 1 (高出容器) brim over 2 (稍稍超出) be just over ◇他10岁冒点尖儿。He's just over ten years old. 3 (突出) be outstanding 4 (初显) emerge

冒进 màojìn [动] jump the gun

冒昧 màomèi [形] (谦) presumptuous ◇冒昧打断您一下。May I interrupt you a moment?

冒牌 màopái [动] pirate ◇冒牌商品 pirated goods

冒失 màoshi [形] abrupt

冒头 màotóu [动] emerge

冒险 màoxiǎn [动] take a risk (*pt* took, *pp* taken) ◇不要轻易去冒险。Don't take risks lightly.

贸 mào [动] trade ♦外贸 foreign trade

贸然 màorán [副] rashly

贸易 màoyì [名] trade ◇他在一家对外贸易公司工作。He works for a company that's engaged in foreign trade.

帽 mào [名] 1 (帽子) hat 2 (帽状物) ♦笔帽儿 pen cap ♦螺丝帽 screw cap

帽子 màozi [名] 1 (字) hat 2 (喻) (坏名义) label ◇他脱不掉捣蛋鬼的帽子。He can't shake off the label of troublemaker.

貌 mào [名] (相貌、外表) appearance

貌合神离 mào hé shén lí appear united on the outside but be troubled underneath

貌似 màosì [动] appear to be

没 méi I [动] not have ◇他们没孩子。They don't have any children. ◇屋子里没人。There's no one in the room. II [副] not ◇他没去美国。He did not go to America. ◇他没看过大海。He's never seen the sea before. ◇他没吃早餐就走了。He left before eating breakfast. ▷另见 mò

没大没小 méi dà méi xiǎo show no respect for one's elders

没劲 méijìn I [动] have no energy II [形] uninteresting

没精打采 méi jīng dǎ cǎi be out of sorts

没门儿 méiménr [动] (方) 1 (没门路) not have the right connections 2 (不可能) be impossible ◇不努力工作就想赚大钱？没门儿！ You want to earn big bucks without hard work? Not a chance!

没谱儿 méipǔr [动] 1 (心里没数) not have a clue ◇论文怎么写，他根本没谱儿。He doesn't have a clue how to write his thesis. 2 (没准儿) be unreliable ◇不要听他的，他说话没谱儿。Don't listen to him – he's a loose cannon.

没趣 méiqù [形] putout

没完 méiwán [动] 1 (没结束) be unfinished ◇活儿还没完，你怎么就走了？ The work isn't finished yet – how can you just leave? 2 (不罢休)

not let ... drop ◇你要是不还我钱，我跟你没完！ If you don't give me my money back, I won't let it drop!

没戏 méixì [动] (方) be a lost cause

没心没肺 méi xīn méi fèi **1** (没良心) heartless **2** (缺心眼) thoughtless **3** (过于单纯) simple-minded

没有 méiyǒu **I** [动] **1** (不具有) not have ◇我没有手机。I don't have a mobile phone. **2** (不存在) there is not ◇办公室里没有人。There's no one in the office. **3** (全都不) ◇放心吧，没有谁敢欺负你。Relax – no one's going to dare to bully you. ◇他们中没有谁敢说谎。None of them dares to lie. ◇没有一个答案是正确的。None of the answers are correct. **4** (不如) be not as ... as ... ◇他没有你努力。He's not as hard working as you. ◇我的房子没有你的大。My house isn't as big as yours. **5** (不到) be less than ◇他们干了没有两个小时就休息了。They had been working for less than two hours when they took a rest. **II** [副] **1** (尚未) not yet ◇庄稼还没有成熟。The crops haven't ripened yet. **2** (未曾) never before ◇我没有吃过西餐。I have never eaten Western food before.

没辙 méizhé [动] (方) not be able to do anything about ◇他不想去，我也没辙。He doesn't want to go, and I can't do anything about it.

玫 méi 见下文

玫瑰 méigui [名] rose

枚 méi [量] ◇一枚硬币 one coin ◇两枚炸弹 two bombs

眉 méi [名] **1** (眉毛) eyebrow **2** (书眉) top margin

眉飞色舞 méi fēi sè wǔ beam with joy ◇运动会上得了冠军，他高兴得眉飞色舞。His whole face lit up when he became champion at the athletics meeting.

眉开眼笑 méi kāi yǎn xiào beam with joy

眉目 méimù [名] **1** (容貌) features (*pl*) **2** (条理) order ◇这篇文章眉目不清。This article is badly ordered. **3** (头绪) light at the end of the tunnel

眉批 méipī [名] headnote

眉头 méitóu [名] brows (*pl*)

梅 méi [名] **1** (指树) plum tree **2** (指花) plum blossom **3** (指果) plum

梅毒 méidú [名] syphilis

梅花 méihuā [名] plum blossom

媒 méi [名] **1** (媒人) matchmaker ♦做媒 be a matchmaker **2** (媒介) intermediary

媒介 méijiè [名] intermediary

媒人 méiren [名] matchmaker

媒体 méitǐ [名] media

煤 méi [名] coal

煤气 méiqì [名] **1** (指燃料) gas **2** (指有毒气体) carbon monoxide ◇煤气中毒 carbon monoxide poisoning

煤油 méiyóu [名] kerosene

酶 méi [名] enzyme

霉 méi [动] **1** (指食物) mould (英), mold (美) **2** (指衣物) mildew

霉变 méibiàn [动] **1** (指衣物) become mildewy (*pt* became, *pp* become) **2** (指食物) go mouldy (英) 或 moldy (美) (*pt* went, *pp* gone)

霉烂 méilàn [动] go rotten (*pt* went, *pp* gone)

每 měi **I** [形] every, each ◇每个晚上他都要加班。He has to work overtime every evening. ◇他热爱这里的每一片土地。He loves every corner of this land. ◇她努力做好每一项工作。She worked hard on each piece of work. **II** [副] every time ◇每回答一个问题，他都增强一份信心。Every time he answers a question, he gains in confidence. ◇每逢周六他都去打工。He works every Saturday.

每况愈下 měi kuàng yù xià go from bad to worse

每每 měiměi [副] more often than not

美 měi **I** [形] **1** (美丽) beautiful ◇这幅画太美了。This painting is so beautiful. ◇京剧演员表演得真美。The Beijing Opera actress performed beautifully. **2** (好) good

◊这个店的商品物美价廉。The merchandise in this shop is good and reasonably priced. ◊我们的明天会更美。Our future will be even better. **II** [动] (方) be pleased with oneself ◊穿了身儿新衣服，看把你美的！ Don't you look pleased with yourself, all dressed up in your new clothes! **III** [名] **1** (好事) good deed ◊成人之美 do a good deed **2** (美洲) North and South America **3** (美国) the USA ◊中美关系 Sino-American relations

美不胜收 měi bù shèng shōu indescribably beautiful ◊黄山的风景美不胜收。The scenery at Huangshan is indescribably beautiful.

美感 měigǎn [名] beautiful impression

美观 měiguān [形] beautiful

美国 Měiguó [名] the US, the USA

> 美国被称为 **the US** 或 **the USA**，其相应的全称为 **the United States** 和 **the United States of America**。美国还可被称为 **America** 或 **the States**，后者的语体更加不正式。

美好 měihǎo [形] wonderful

美化 měihuà [动] beautify

美丽 měilì [形] beautiful ◊像花儿一样美丽 as beautiful as a flower ◊美丽的人生 beautiful life

> 描述某人的外貌时，通常使用 **beautiful** 和 **pretty** 形容漂亮的妇女、女孩或婴儿。**beautiful** 比 **pretty** 的程度强烈得多。*She was a pretty little girl who grew up to be a beautiful woman.* 表示男性英俊的词是 **handsome**。*David is a very handsome man and popular with women.* **good-looking** 和 **attractive** 既可以描述女性也可以描述男性。*Not all of the boys in the class were as good-looking as John… His wife isn't particularly attractive but she's nice and has a good sense of humour.*

美满 měimǎn [形] perfectly satisfactory

美妙 měimiào [动] splendid

美容 měiróng [动] make oneself more beautiful ◊美容店 beauty salon ◊她做了美容手术。She's had cosmetic surgery.

美食 měishí [名] delicacy

美术 měishù [名] **1** (造型艺术) fine arts (*pl*) **2** (绘画) painting

美谈 měitán [名] legend

美味 měiwèi [名] delicacy

美学 měixué [名] aesthetics (英), esthetics (美) (*pl*)

美言 měiyán [动] put in a good word for (*pt, pp* put)

美元 měiyuán [名] US dollar

美中不足 měi zhōng bù zú small imperfection ◊这汤美中不足的是不够咸。The only thing wrong with the soup is that it isn't salty enough.

美滋滋 měizīzī [形] (口) pleased with oneself

镁 měi [名] magnesium

妹 mèi [名] **1** (指同胞) younger sister **2** (指亲戚) ♦表妹 cousin **2** (方) (指年轻女子) young girl

妹妹 mèimei [名] **1** (指同胞) younger sister **2** (指亲戚) ◊她是我叔伯妹妹。She's my cousin.

昧 mèi **I** [形] hazy ♦愚昧 ignorant **II** [动] **1** (隐藏) conceal **2** (违背) go against (*pt* went, *pp* gone)

昧心 mèixīn [形] against one's principles ◊他从不说昧心话。He never says anything that goes against his principles. ◊他从不赚昧心钱。He'll never make money dishonestly.

媚 mèi **I** [动] flatter **II** [形] charming

媚俗 mèisú [动] pander to public opinion

媚态 mèitài [名] **1** (讨好姿态) obsequiousness **2** (妩媚姿态) feminine charms (*pl*)

魅 mèi [名] demon

魅力 mèilì [名] charm ◇他已经50岁了，却依然魅力十足。He's already 50 but he's still utterly charming.

闷 mēn I [形] stuffy II [动] 1 (盖) cover … tightly 2 (不出声) keep silent (*pt, pp* kept) 3 (呆) shut oneself in (*pt, pp* shut) ◇星期天他也闷在教室里学习。Even on Sundays he shuts himself in the classroom and studies.
▷另见 mèn

闷热 mēnrè [形] muggy

闷头儿 mēntóur [副] silently

门 mén I [名] 1 (指出入口) door ◇北门 north gate 2 (指开关装置) switch ♦电门 switch 3 (门状物) ◇橱门 cupboard door ◇球门 goal 4 (门路) knack ◇对于修电脑，他终于摸着点门儿了。He finally got the hang of repairing computers. 5 (派别) school of thought ♦佛门 Buddhism 6 (门类) category II [量] ◇我选了5门课。I chose five courses. ◇一门技术 a skill ◇一门大炮 a cannon

门当户对 mén dāng hù duì families of equal rank ◇门当户对的婚姻未必幸福。Marrying within your own class will not necessarily make you happy.

门道 méndao [名] know-how ◇他做生意很有门道。He has excellent business know-how.

门第 méndì [名] family status

门户 ménhù [名] 1 (门) door 2 (通路) gateway 3 (家) family 4 (派别) sect

门类 ménlèi [名] category

门路 ménlu [名] 1 (窍门) knack ◇多动脑筋，就能找出门路来。If you put your mind to it you'll get the knack of it. 2 (贬) (后门儿) connection ◇他家很有门路。His family is very well-connected.

门面 ménmian [名] 1 (门脸儿) shop front (英), storefront (美) 2 (喻) (外表) appearance

门徒 méntú [名] disciple

门外汉 ménwàihàn [名] layman

门卫 ménwèi [名] guard

门诊 ménzhěn [名] outpatient department

扪 mén [动] (书) touch

扪心自问 mén xīn zì wèn examine one's conscience

闷 mèn [形] 1 (烦) low 2 (无聊) bored 3 (密闭) tightly closed ◇闷罐子 a sealed jar
▷另见 mēn

闷棍 mèngùn [名] 1 (字) blow ◇一闷棍打得他眼冒金星儿。After one blow he saw stars. 2 (喻) (打击) bolt from the blue

闷闷不乐 mèn mèn bù lè be low ◇他这几天总是闷闷不乐的。These last few days he's been really low.

蒙 mēng [动] 1 (欺骗) deceive 2 (乱猜) make a wild guess
▷另见 méng, Měng

蒙蒙亮 mēngmēngliàng [形] just light ◇天刚蒙蒙亮，部队就出发了。Dawn was just breaking as the team set off.

蒙骗 mēngpiàn [动] deceive

萌 méng [动] sprout

萌动 méngdòng [动] 1 (指植物) sprout 2 (指事物) arise (*pt* arose, *pp* arisen) ◇对私家车的市场需求萌动。A demand for private cars has arisen.

萌发 méngfā [动] 1 (指种子) sprout 2 (指事物) come into being (*pt* came, *pp* come)

萌生 méngshēng [动] form ◇看到别人发了财，他就萌生了邪念。Seeing other people getting rich, wicked thoughts formed in his mind.

萌芽 méngyá [动] 1 (指植物) sprout 2 (指事物) emerge

蒙 méng I [动] 1 (遮盖) cover 2 (受到) receive II [形] ignorant ♦启蒙 enlighten
▷另见 mēng, Měng

蒙蔽 méngbì [动] deceive

蒙混 ménghùn [动] deceive ◇蒙混过关 muddle through

蒙眬 ménglóng [形] sleepy

蒙昧 méngmèi [形] 1 (未开化) uncivilized 2 (无知) ignorant ◇有些人因为蒙昧无知而犯罪。Some people commit crimes through ignorance.

蒙蒙 méngméng [形] **1** (指雨) drizzly **2** (指烟雾) misty

蒙受 méngshòu [动] **1** (耻辱，冤屈) suffer ◇蒙受了巨大损失 suffer a great loss **2** (恩惠) receive

蒙太奇 méngtàiqí [名] montage

盟 méng [名] **1** (同盟) alliance ♦二战盟国 the Allies **2** (指行政区) league

盟军 méngjūn [名] allied forces (*pl*)

盟誓 méngshì [动] swear an oath (*pt* swore, *pp* sworn)

盟约 méngyuē [名] treaty of alliance

朦 méng 见下文

朦胧 ménglóng [形] **1** (月光) hazy **2** (烟雾) misty

猛 měng **I** [形] **1** (凶猛) fierce **2** (勇猛) brave **II** [副] **1** (猛烈) fiercely **2** (忽然) suddenly

猛烈 měngliè [形] fierce

猛然 měngrán [副] suddenly

猛醒 měngxǐng [动] wake up to reality (*pt* woke, *pp* woken)

蒙 Měng [名] Mongolia
▷另见 mēng, méng

蒙古族 Měnggǔzú [名] Mongolian nationality

锰 měng [名] manganese

懵 měng [形] muddled

懵懵懂懂 měngmengdǒngdǒng muddled ◇听了他的解释，我还是懵懵懂懂。I was still muddled, even after he had explained.

孟 mèng [形] (指排行) eldest

孟子 Mèngzǐ [名] Mencius

梦 mèng **I** [名] **1** (睡梦) dream **2** (幻想) illusion **II** [动] dream ◇她梦到自己是电影明星。She dreamed she was a film star.

梦话 mènghuà [名] **1** (字) ◇我听见你晚上说梦话了。I heard you talk in your sleep. **2** (喻) nonsense

梦幻 mènghuàn [名] illusion ◇她仿佛来到了梦幻世界。She seemed to have entered a dreamworld.

梦境 mèngjìng [名] dreamworld

梦寐以求 mèngmèi yǐ qiú ◇他梦寐以求的愿望终于实现了。He finally realized his long-cherished dream.

梦想 mèngxiǎng [动] dream ◇不奋斗就能成功，简直是梦想！ You'd be dreaming to imagine that success can be achieved without a struggle. ◇他梦想着开一家自己的公司。He dreamed of opening his own company. ◇她实现了当一名作家的梦想。She fulfilled her dream of being a writer.

咪 mī 见下文

咪咪 mīmī [拟] miaow (英), meow (美)

眯 mī [动] **1** (眼皮微合) squint **2** (方) (小睡) take a nap (*pt* took, *pp* taken)
▷另见 mí

眯缝 mīfeng [动] squint

弥 mí **I** [形] full **II** [动] fill **III** [副] more

弥补 míbǔ [动] make … up ◇我们要想方设法弥补这一重大损失。We must think of a way to make up for this heavy loss.

弥合 míhé [动] patch … up ◇感情上的裂痕是不容易弥合的。It's hard to patch up emotional wounds.

弥留 míliú [动] (书) be on one's deathbed

弥漫 mímàn [动] pervade

弥撒 mísa [名] mass

弥散 mísàn [动] disperse

迷 mí **I** [动] **1** (迷失) be lost ♦迷路 lose one's way **2** (迷恋) become obsessed with (*pt* became, *pp* become) **3** (迷惑) be deluded **II** [名] fan ♦球迷 sports fan

迷彩服 mícǎifú [名] camouflage clothing

迷宫 mígōng [名] maze

迷糊 míhu [形] confused

迷惑 míhuò [动] **1** (不明白) be confused ◇听了他的话，我更迷惑了。After listening to him I was even more confused. **2** (使迷糊) baffle

迷恋 míliàn [动] be obsessed with

迷茫 mímáng [形] **1** (广阔而模糊) vast and hazy **2** (迷离) dazed ◊他神色迷茫地望着前方，仿佛周围的一切都不存在了。He stared ahead in a daze as if nothing around him existed.

迷你 mínǐ [形] mini ◊你的迷你裙真漂亮。Your mini-skirt is really lovely.

迷失 míshī [动] lose (*pt, pp* lost) ◊迷失方向 lose one's bearings ◊在诱惑面前，不要迷失了自己。You mustn't lose your head in the face of temptation.

迷途 mítú [动] lose one's way (*pt, pp* lost) ◊误入迷途 go astray

迷信 míxìn [动] **1** (鬼神) be superstitious about ◊他迷信鬼神。He has a superstitious belief in ghosts and spirits. **2** (人或事) have blind faith in ◊迷信可能会让人丧失理智。Superstition may cause people to behave irrationally.

眯 mí [动] get … into one's eye ◊沙子眯了我的眼。The sand got into my eye.
▷另见 mī

猕 mí 见下文

猕猴 míhóu [名] rhesus monkey

猕猴桃 míhóutáo [名] **1** (指植物) kiwi plant **2** (指果实) kiwi fruit

谜 mí [名] **1** (谜语) riddle **2** (神秘) mystery

谜语 míyǔ [名] riddle

糜 mí **I** [名] gruel ♦肉糜 mincemeat **II** [形] rotten **III** [动] waste

糜烂 mílàn [形] **1** (腐烂) rotten ◊他的伤口已经糜烂。His wound has already become infected. **2** (喻) (腐化) debauched

米 mǐ **I** [名] **1** (稻米) rice ◊米饭 cooked rice **2** (去壳种子) husked seeds (*pl*) ♦虾米 dried shrimp ◊一袋花生米 a bag of peanuts **II** [量] metre (英), meter (美)

米饭 mǐfàn [名] cooked rice

米色 mǐsè [名] beige

靡 mǐ [动] blow … down (*pt* blew, *pp* blown) ♦风靡 be fashionable

觅 mì [动] look for

觅取 mìqǔ [动] look for

泌 mì [动] secrete

泌尿 mìniào [动] urinate ◊泌尿系统疾病 disease of the urinary system

秘 mì **I** [形] secret **II** [动] keep … secret (*pt, pp* kept) **III** [名] secretary

秘方 mìfāng [名] secret recipe

秘诀 mìjué [名] secret ◊成功的秘诀 secret of success

秘密 mìmì [名] secret ◊一定要保守秘密！ You must keep this a secret!

秘书 mìshū [名] **1** (指人) secretary **2** (指工作) secretarial work

秘书处 mìshūchù [名] secretariat

密 mì [形] **1** (空隙小) dense **2** (关系近) close **3** (精致) meticulous ♦精密 precise **4** (秘密) secret

密布 mìbù [动] be full of

密度 mìdù [名] density ◊这个地区人口密度很大。This region has a high population density.

密封 mìfēng [动] seal … tightly ◊密封机舱 air-tight cabin

密集 mìjí [形] concentrated

密码 mìmǎ [名] **1** (口令) password **2** (符号系统) code

密密麻麻 mìmimámá crammed ◊他笔记上的字密密麻麻的。His notebook was crammed full of writing.

密谋 mìmóu [动] conspire

密切 mìqiè [形] close ◊他俩的关系一直很密切。They've always had a very close relationship. ◊密切与欧洲的关系是十分重要的。It is important to establish close links with Europe.

密探 mìtàn [名] spy

幂 mì [名] (数) power ◊2的3次幂得8。2 to the power of 3 is 8.

蜜 mì **I** [名] honey **II** [形] sweet

蜜蜂 mìfēng [名] bee

蜜饯 mìjiàn [名] preserved fruit

蜜月 mìyuè [名] honeymoon ◇新婚夫妇一起去度蜜月了。The newly married couple went on their honeymoon. ◇两个人的关系正处在蜜月期。The two of them are going through their honeymoon period.

眠 mián [动] **1** (睡) sleep (*pt, pp* slept) ♦失眠 suffer from insomnia **2** (冬眠) hibernate ♦休眠 be dormant

绵 mián **I** [名] silk thread **II** [形] **1** (连绵) continuous **2** (柔软) soft

绵薄 miánbó [名] (谦) meagre effort

绵长 miáncháng [形] long ◇绵长的岁月 many years

绵里藏针 mián lǐ cáng zhēn **1** (贬) soft on the outside but ruthless within **2** (褒) an iron fist in a velvet glove

绵绵 miánmián [形] continuous

绵软 miánruǎn [形] weak

绵延 miányán [动] go on and on (*pt* went, *pp* gone) ◇绵延不断的文化传统 unbroken cultural tradition

棉 mián [名] **1** (指植物) cotton ♦棉田 cotton field **2** (棉花) cotton ◇姑娘们正在纺棉织布。The girls are weaving cotton cloth. **3** (棉状物) fibre (英), fiber (美)

棉花 miánhua [名] **1** (指植物) cotton **2** (棉絮) cotton wadding

棉衣 miányī [名] cotton-padded clothing

免 miǎn [动] **1** (除去) exempt ♦免试 be exempt from an exam ♦免费 free ◇她被免职了。She was fired from her job. **2** (避免) avoid **3** (不要) not be allowed ◇闲人免进 staff only ◇此事免谈。This matter is non-negotiable.

免除 miǎnchú [动] **1** (避免) prevent ◇机器常检修，能免除大的故障。Frequent servicing can prevent machines from having major breakdowns. **2** (免去) discharge ◇他被免除了职务。He was discharged from his post. ◇他的债务被免除了。He was relieved of his debts.

免费 miǎnfèi [动] be free of charge ◇世上没有免费午餐。There's no such thing as a free lunch in this world. ◇这里的孩子可以免费入学。Children here can attend school free of charge. ◇送你一张免费参观券。I'll give you a free visitor's ticket. ◇实行免费医疗制度 implement a system of free medical care ◇注册一个免费电子邮箱 register for free email

免检 miǎnjiǎn [动] be exempt from inspection

免俗 miǎnsú [动] do one's own thing

免疫 miǎnyì [名] immunity ◇这位病人的免疫系统受到了破坏。This patient's immune system has been destroyed.

免罪 miǎnzuì [动] be exempt from punishment

勉 miǎn [动] **1** (努力) strive ♦勉力 exert oneself **2** (勉励) encourage **3** (勉强) force … to carry on

勉励 miǎnlì [动] encourage

勉强 miǎnqiǎng **I** [动] **1** (尽力) push oneself hard ◇身体不好，做事就不要太勉强。If your health is not good, don't push yourself too hard. **2** (强迫) force ◇孩子不想学钢琴，就不要勉强他。If the child does not want to study the piano, don't force him. **II** [形] **1** (不情愿) reluctant ◇我让他帮忙，他勉强答应了。I asked him to help, and he reluctantly agreed. **2** (凑合) barely enough ◇他挣的钱勉强够自己花。The money he earned was barely enough to support himself. **3** (牵强) far-fetched

勉为其难 miǎn wéi qí nán attempt the impossible ◇拿不到冠军也无所谓，不要勉为其难。It doesn't matter if you don't win first prize – don't be attempting the impossible.

娩 miǎn [动] give birth (*pt* gave, *pp* given)

冕 miǎn [名] crown

缅 miǎn I [形] (书) remote II [动] (方) roll … up

缅怀 miǎnhuái [动] cherish the memory of

腼 miǎn 见下文

腼腆 miǎntiǎn [形] bashful

面 miàn I [名] 1 (脸) face ♦面色 expression ◇面露难色 look reluctant ◇他面带笑容。He had a smile on his face. 2 (表面) surface ♦水面 surface of the water 3 (方位) aspect ♦前面 front ◇考虑问题要全面。We should examine every aspect of this problem. 4 (书) (当面) ♦面试 interview ◇法国签证得面签。You have to have an interview to get a French visa. 5 (情面) self-respect ♦面子 face 6 (粉末) powder ♦辣椒面 chilli powder 7 (磨成粉的粮食) flour ♦白面 wheat flour 8 (面条) noodles (*pl*) II [动] (朝) face ◇面墙而坐 sit facing the wall III [量] 1 (用于扁平物) ♦一面墙 a wall ♦两面镜子 two mirrors 2 (指见面的次数) ◇我曾见过他一面。I have met her once before.

面包房 miànbāofáng [名] bakery

面点 miàndiǎn [名] pastry

面对 miànduì [动] face ◇我们要勇于面对任何困难。We must face any difficulties head on. ◇面对失败，他毫不气馁。In the face of defeat he wasn't in the least disheartened.

面额 miàn'é [名] denomination

面红耳赤 miàn hóng ěr chì go red in the face

面积 miànjī [名] area

面颊 miànjiá [名] cheek

面孔 miànkǒng [名] face

面料 miànliào [名] 1 (布料) material 2 (表层材料) covering

面临 miànlín [动] face

面貌 miànmào [名] 1 (面容) features (*pl*) 2 (喻) appearance

面面俱到 miàn miàn jù dào cover every detail

面目 miànmù [名] 1 (相貌) appearance ◇他面目可憎。He looks repulsive. ◇车祸后，那辆车已经面目全非。After the accident, the car was totally unrecognizable. 2 (颜面) face

面前 miànqián [名] ◇当他出现在我面前时，我又惊又喜。When he appeared in front of me, I was surprised and pleased. ◇在困难面前，他们没有低头。They never admitted defeat in the face of difficulties.

面色 miànsè [名] 1 (气色) complexion 2 (神情) expression

面纱 miànshā [名] veil

面善 miànshàn [形] 1 (面熟) familiar ◇他看着面善。He looks familiar. 2 (面容和善) kind-faced ◇面善的老婆婆 kind-faced old lady

面生 miànshēng [形] unfamiliar

面世 miànshì [动] come out (*pt* came, *pp* come)

面试 miànshì [动] have an interview

面熟 miànshú [形] familiar

面值 miànzhí [名] denomination

面子 miànzi [名] 1 (表面) outside 2 (体面) face ◇丢面子 lose face 3 (情面) feelings (*pl*) ◇给我点面子，你就答应吧！ Show some respect for my feelings and say yes!

喵 miāo [拟] miaow (英), meow (美)

苗 miáo [名] 1 (指植物) seedling ♦树苗 sapling 2 (指动物) young ♦鱼苗 fry 3 (指人) descendant ◇他是他家的独苗儿。He's the only remaining descendant in his family.

苗条 miáotiao [形] slim

苗头 miáotou [名] premonition◇他早就看出了这件事的苗头。He had had a premonition about this a long time ago.

苗子 miáozi [名] 1 (农) seedling 2 (喻) (指人) ◇他是个当总经理的苗子。He's a managing director in the making. ◇她是个当记者的好苗子。She's a budding young journalist.

描 miáo [动] 1 (画) trace ◇描图纸 tracing paper 2 (涂抹) touch … up

描绘 miáohuì [动] depict

描摹 miáomó [动] 1 (照底样写画) trace 2 (文字描绘) portray

描述 miáoshù [动] describe

描写 miáoxiě [动] describe

瞄 miáo [动] fix one's eyes on ◇瞄靶子 aim at the target

瞄准 miáozhǔn [动] 1 (对准) take aim (*pt* took, *pp* taken) 2 (专注于) focus on

秒 miǎo [量] (指时间) second

秒表 miǎobiǎo [名] stopwatch

渺 miǎo [形] 1 (远而模糊) distant 2 (微小) tiny

渺茫 miǎománg [形] 1 (远而模糊) distant 2 (难料) uncertain

渺小 miǎoxiǎo [形] tiny

藐 miǎo I [形] small II [动] treat … with contempt

藐视 miǎoshì [动] treat … with contempt ◇对困难既不要藐视，也不要惧怕。You should neither belittle nor fear difficulties.

藐小 miǎoxiǎo [形] tiny

妙 miào [形] 1 (好) wonderful 2 (巧妙) ingenious ♦妙举 ingenious move

妙龄 miàolíng [名] youthfulness

妙趣横生 miàoqù héngshēng sparkling with wit

妙手回春 miào shǒu huí chūn achieve a miraculous cure

庙 miào [名] temple

庙宇 miàoyǔ [名] temple

灭 miè [动] 1 (熄灭) go out (*pt* went, *pp* gone) ◇炉子里的火灭了吗？Has the fire in the stove gone out? 2 (使熄灭) extinguish ♦灭火器 fire extinguisher 3 (淹没) submerge 4 (消亡) perish 5 (消灭) kill

灭迹 mièjì [动] destroy evidence

灭绝 mièjué [动] 1 (消亡) become extinct (*pt* became, *pp* become) 2 (完全失掉) ◇灭绝人性 inhuman

灭口 mièkǒu [动] dispose of a witness

灭亡 mièwáng [动] destroy

灭种 mièzhǒng [动] 1 (指人类) be exterminated 2 (指动植物) become extinct (*pt* became, *pp* become)

蔑 miè I [形] contemptuous II [动] slander

蔑视 mièshì [动] show contempt for (*pt* showed, *pp* shown)

民 mín [名] 1 (人民) the people 2 (人) person ♦网民 Internet user 3 (民间) folk 4 (非军方) civilian

民办 mínbàn [动] privately run ◇民办大学 private university

民兵 mínbīng [名] militia

民法 mínfǎ [名] civil law

民愤 mínfèn [名] public anger

民风 mínfēng [名] folklore

民歌 míngē [名] folk song

民间 mínjiān [名] 1 (百姓中间) folk ◇民间传说 folklore 2 (非官方) ◇民间交往 non-governmental exchanges ◇民间组织 non-governmental organization

民警 mínjǐng [名] civil police

民居 mínjū [名] private house

民情 mínqíng [名] 1 (风俗情况) conditions (*pl*) 2 (民意) public opinion

民权 mínquán [名] civil rights (*pl*)

民俗 mínsú [名] folklore

民谣 mínyáo [名] popular ballad

民营 mínyíng [动] run privately ◇民营企业 privately-run enterprise

民乐 mínyuè [名] folk music

民政 mínzhèng [名] civil administration

民众 mínzhòng [名] the common people (*pl*)

民主 mínzhǔ I [名] democracy II [形] democratic

民族 mínzú [名] nationality ◇少数民族 ethnic minority

抿 mǐn [动] 1 (轻轻合拢) close … lightly ◇抿嘴一笑 smile with one's lips closed 2 (用嘴轻沾) sip

泯 mǐn [动] (书) vanish

泯灭 mǐnmiè [动] disappear

敏 mǐn [形] **1** (快) quick ♦敏感 sensitive **2** (聪明) clever ♦机敏 quick-witted

敏感 mǐngǎn [形] sensitive

敏捷 mǐnjié [形] quick ◊反应敏捷 quick reactions ◊猴子的动作非常敏捷。Monkeys are extremely agile.

敏锐 mǐnruì [形] keen

名 míng **I** [名] **1** (名字) name ◊书名 book title **2** (名声) reputation ◊这部名著早已名扬四海。This famous work has long enjoyed a worldwide reputation. ◊名利双收 win fame and fortune **II** [形] famous ◊世界名校 world-famous school ◊她抄写了一整本名人名言。She copied out a whole book of well-known sayings of famous people. **III** [量] **1** (指人) ◊5名工人 five workers **2** (指名次) ◊期末考试她得了第一名。She came first in the end-of-term exams. **IV** [动] describe ◊她有一种不可名状的恐惧。She feels an indescribable fear.

名不副实 míng bù fù shí not live up to one's reputation

名不虚传 míng bù xū chuán live up to one's reputation

名称 míngchēng [名] name

名词 míngcí [名] noun

名次 míngcì [名] ranking

名存实亡 míng cún shí wáng exist in name only

名单 míngdān [名] list of names ◊他上了黑名单。He was blacklisted.

名额 míng'é [名] quota

名分 míngfèn [名] (书) status

名副其实 míng fù qí shí live up to the name of ◊他是一位名副其实的大科学家。He really lives up to his name as a great scientist.

名贵 míngguì [形] priceless

名家 míngjiā [名] master

名利 mínglì [名] fame and fortune

名列前茅 míng liè qiánmáo come out among the top ◊他在期末考试中名列前茅。He came out among the top candidates in the end-of-term exams.

名流 míngliú [名] celebrity

名落孙山 míng luò Sūn Shān fail to make the grade ◊这次考试他又名落孙山。Yet again he failed the exams.

名目 míngmù [名] items (*pl*) ◊名目众多的收费 all kinds of charges

名牌 míngpái [名] famous name ◊他从上到下穿的都是名牌。He was dressed in designer clothing from head to foot.

名片 míngpiàn [名] business card

名气 míngqi [名] fame ◊有名气 be famous

名人 míngrén [名] famous person

名声 míngshēng [名] reputation

名胜 míngshèng [名] tourist site ◊名胜古迹 sites of scenic and historical interest

名堂 míngtang [名] **1** (花样) variety **2** (花招) trick ◊你搞什么名堂！ What are you up to? **3** (道理) reason ◊他这么做一定有名堂。There must be a reason why he did this. **4** (结果) achievement

名望 míngwàng [名] fame ◊老先生在学术圈里很有名望。The old gentleman is very famous in academic circles.

名义 míngyì [名] name ◊以人民的名义 in the name of the people ◊他名义上是校长，其实很多事并不由他决定。He is the College Principal in name only – in fact many decisions are not taken by him.

名誉 míngyù [名] **1** (名声) reputation **2** (名义) ◊名誉校长 honorary principal

名正言顺 míng zhèng yán shùn legitimate

名字 míngzi [名] name ◊你叫什么名字？ What's your name?

明 míng **I** [形] **1** (亮) bright ◊明月 bright moon **2** (清楚) clear ◊讲明 clarify **3** (公开) open **4** (有眼力) perceptive **II** [名] **1** (视力) sight ◊他双目失明。He's lost his sight in both eyes. **2** (光明) light **III** [动] **1** (懂) understand (*pt, pp* understood) ◊他是个明理的人。

He's an understanding person. **2** (显示) show (*pt* showed, *pp* shown) ♦表明 indicate ◇以死明志 be willing to die for one's beliefs **IV** [副] openly ◇明知故犯 openly do wrong

明白 míngbai **I** [形] **1** (清楚) clear ◇他没讲明白。He didn't explain clearly. **2** (聪明) sensible **3** (公开) explicit ◇他已明白表示不会退出比赛。He explicitly said that he wouldn't be retiring from the match. **II** [动] understand (*pt, pp* understood)

明察秋毫 míng chá qiū háo not miss a trick

明晃晃 mínghuānghuāng [形] gleaming

明净 míngjìng [形] clear and bright

明快 míngkuài [形] **1** (明白顺畅) lucid and lively **2** (爽快) straightforward

明朗 mínglǎng [形] **1** (明亮) bright and clear **2** (明确) clear-cut **3** (明快) bright and cheerful

明亮 míngliàng [形] **1** (亮堂) bright **2** (发亮) shining **3** (明白) clear

明媚 míngmèi [形] bright and beautiful

明明 míngmíng [副] obviously

明目张胆 míng mù zhāng dǎn brazenly

明确 míngquè [形] clear-cut ◇大会明确了今后的奋斗目标。The congress clarified the future goals to strive for.

明文 míngwén [名] written document ◇教育部明文规定，一定要减轻学生负担。The Education Department has stipulated in writing that the burden on students must be reduced.

明显 míngxiǎn [形] obvious ◇他的进步非常明显。It's obvious that he's progressed. ◇人民的生活水平明显提高了。The people's standard of living has visibly improved.

明星 míngxīng [名] star

明哲保身 míng zhé bǎo shēn keep one's distance

明智 míngzhì [形] sensible

鸣 míng [动] **1** (叫) chirp **2** (响) sound ◇仪式开始了，首先鸣礼炮20响。The ceremony began, and first a 20-gun salute was sounded. ◇电闪雷鸣 a flash of lightning and the rumble of thunder ◇鸣枪警告 fire a warning shot **3** (表达) express

冥 míng **I** [形] (书) **1** (昏暗) dark **2** (深沉) deep **3** (糊涂) stupid ♦冥昧 ignorant **II** [名] the underworld

冥思苦想 míng sī kǔ xiǎng be deep in thought

冥想 míngxiǎng [动] be deep in thought

铭 míng **I** [名] inscription **II** [动] (书) engrave

瞑 míng [动] close one's eyes

瞑目 míngmù [动] die content

命 mìng **I** [名] **1** (性命) life **2** (命运) fate **3** (寿命) lifespan **4** (命令) order **II** [动] set (*pt, pp* set)

命案 mìng'àn [名] murder case

命根子 mìnggēnzi [名] lifeblood ◇经理说，顾客就是我们的命根子。The manager says that the customers are our lifeblood. ◇这孩子是全家人的命根子。This child is the very life of the family.

命令 mìnglìng [动] order ◇我们还没接到上级的命令。We still haven't received the order from above.

命脉 mìngmài [名] lifeblood

命名 mìngmíng [动] name ◇这座山被命名为"英雄山"。This mountain was named Heroes' Mountain.

命题 mìngtí [动] assign ... a topic

命运 mìngyùn [名] fate

命中 mìngzhòng [动] hit the target (*pt, pp* hit)

谬 miù [形] false

谬论 miùlùn [名] fallacy

谬误 miùwù [名] falsehood

摸 mō [动] **1** (触摸) stroke **2** (取) fish ... out ◇他从兜儿里摸出两块钱。He fished two yuan out of his pocket. **3** (偷) pilfer ◇小偷小摸 petty theft **4** (探索) find one's way (*pt, pp* found)◇别急，慢慢

就能摸出门道儿来。Don't worry – slowly does it and you'll find your way. **5** (摸黑行动) feel one's way (*pt, pp* felt)

摸底 mōdǐ [动] make a full assessment of a situation

摸索 mōsuǒ [动] **1** (试探) grope ◇黑暗中，他摸索着上楼。He groped his way upstairs in the dark. **2** (探索) try to find out

摹 mó [动] copy

摹拟 mónǐ [动] imitate

模 mó **I** [名] model ♦模型 model **II** [动] imitate
▷另见 mú

模范 mófàn [形] model ◇他是一位劳动模范。He's a model worker.

模仿 mófǎng [动] imitate

模糊 móhu [形] blurred ◇不要模糊事物之间的差别 Don't blur the distinctions between things.

模棱两可 móléng liǎngkě equivocal

模拟 mónǐ [动] imitate

模式 móshì [名] pattern ◇写文章没有固定的模式。There's no fixed pattern for essay-writing.

模特儿 mótèr [名] model

模型 móxíng [名] **1** (样品) model **2** (模具) mould (英), mold (美)

膜 mó [名] **1** (体内薄皮组织) membrane **2** (膜状物) film

膜拜 móbài [动] prostrate oneself

摩 mó [动] **1** (摩擦) rub … together **2** (轻抚) stroke ♦按摩 massage **3** (切磋) mull … over

摩擦 mócā **I** [动] rub ◇两个物体摩擦会生热。When two objects are rubbed together they will produce heat. **II** [名] **1** (阻力) friction **2** (冲突) conflict

摩登 módēng [形] modern

摩肩接踵 mó jiān jiē zhǒng jostle each other

摩拳擦掌 mó quán cā zhǎng itch to

摩托车 mótuōchē [名] motorbike

磨 mó [动] **1** (摩擦) rub **2** (指用磨料) grind (*pt, pp* ground) ♦打磨 polish ◇磨刀 sharpen a knife **3** (折磨) wear … down (*pt* wore, *pp* worn) **4** (纠缠) pester **4** (拖延) dawdle **5** (消亡) die out
▷另见 mò

磨擦 mócā [名] rub

磨蹭 móceng **I** [动] **1** (摩擦) rub … lightly **2** (纠缠) be in a tangle **II** [形] sluggish

磨合 móhé [动] **1** (指机器) run … in (*pt* ran, *pp* run) **2** (适应) adapt to each other **3** (协商) consult ◇经过多次磨合，双方签署了协议。After much consultation both parties signed the agreement.

磨炼 móliàn [动] steel

磨灭 mómiè [动] obliterate ◇他的伟大功绩不可磨灭。His huge achievements cannot be obliterated.

磨难 mónàn [名] hardship

磨损 mósǔn [动] wear … out (*pt* wore, *pp* worn)

磨洋工 mó yánggōng [动] dawdle over one's work

蘑 mó [名] mushroom

蘑菇 mógu **I** [名] mushroom **II** [动] **1** (纠缠) pester **2** (磨蹭) dawdle

魔 mó **I** [名] **1** (魔鬼) demon **2** (魔法) magic **II** [形] magic

魔法 mófǎ [名] magic

魔鬼 móguǐ [名] devil

魔力 mólì [名] charm

魔术 móshù [名] magic

魔术师 móshùshī [名] magician

魔王 mówáng [名] **1** (字) demon king **2** (喻) fiend

魔掌 mózhǎng [名] (喻) clutches (*pl*) ◇她终于逃出了歹徒的魔掌。She finally escaped from the clutches of the thugs.

魔爪 mózhǎo [名] (喻) claws (*pl*)

抹 mǒ [动] **1** (涂抹) apply **2** (擦) wipe **3** (去除) erase ◇我很难将这次经历从记忆中抹去。I'm finding it hard to erase the experience from my memory.
▷另见 mā

抹黑 mǒhēi [动] (喻) blacken sb's name ◇媒体企图抹黑他的形象。The media tried to blacken his name.

抹杀 mǒshā [动] write … off (*pt* wrote, *pp* written)

末 mò [名] **1** (尾) end ◆末梢 end ◇世纪末 the end of the century **2** (次要) minor details (*pl*) **3** (屑) powder ◇面包末 breadcrumbs

末端 mòduān [名] end

末了 mòliǎo [名] end

末流 mòliú [形] inferior

末日 mòrì [名] **1** (宗) Judgment Day **2** (灭亡日) end ◇侵略者的末日终于到来了。The end had finally come for the invaders.

末尾 mòwěi [名] end

没 mò [动] **1** (沉没) sink (*pt* sank, *pp* sunk) **2** (漫过) overflow **3** (隐没) disappear ◆出没 appear and disappear
▷另见 méi

没落 mòluò [动] decline

没收 mòshōu [动] confiscate

沫 mò [名] foam

茉 mò 见下文

茉莉 mòlì [名] jasmine

陌 mò [名] (书) footpath

陌生 mòshēng [形] unfamiliar

陌生人 mòshēngrén [名] stranger

脉 mò 见下文
▷另见 mài

脉脉 mòmò [形] affectionate

莫 mò **I** [代] (书) **1** (指人) nobody **2** (指物) nothing **II** [副] (书) **1** (不) not ◇望尘莫及 be too far behind to catch up **2** (别) ◇莫打岔 don't interrupt ◇莫生气 don't get angry

莫不 mòbù [副] ◇大家对他莫不啧啧称赞。There was no-one who did not sing his praises. ◇全家莫不为他感到骄傲。There is no-one in the family who is not proud of him.

莫大 mòdà [形] greatest

莫非 mòfēi [副] ◇莫非那对恋人分手了？ Can it be that the couple have split up? ◇莫非老板要给我加工资？Is it possible that the boss is going to give me a pay rise?

莫名其妙 mò míng qí miào baffling

莫须有 mòxūyǒu fabricated

蓦 mò [副] suddenly ◆蓦然 suddenly

漠 mò **I** [名] desert **II** [副] indifferently

漠不关心 mò bù guānxīn indifferent

漠然 mòrán [形] indifferent

漠视 mòshì [动] ignore

墨 mò **I** [名] **1** (墨汁) ink **2** (字画) calligraphy and painting **3** (喻) (学问) learning **II** [形] dark ◇一副墨镜 a pair of sunglasses

墨迹 mòjì [名] **1** (字) ink mark **2** (真迹) true work

墨绿 mòlǜ [形] dark green

墨守成规 Mò shǒu chéngguī (贬) be a stickler for routine

默 mò [动] **1** (不出声) do … silently **2** (默写) write … from memory (*pt* wrote, *pp* written) ◇默古诗 write classical poetry from memory ◇每个字默5遍。Write out every character five times.

默哀 mò'āi [动] pay … silent tribute (*pt, pp* paid)

默默 mòmò [形] silent

默契 mòqì **I** [形] ◇双方合作非常默契。The cooperation between the two sides is one of tacit agreement. **II** [名] tacit agreement ◇我们俩之间很有默契。There's a tacit agreement between us.

默认 mòrèn [动] tacitly agree

默写 mòxiě [动] write … from memory (*pt* wrote, *pp* written)

默许 mòxǔ [动] tacitly consent to

磨 mò **I** [名] mill **II** [动] grind (*pt, pp* ground) ◇磨咖啡豆 grind coffee beans
▷另见 mó

磨坊 mòfáng [名] mill

牟 móu [动] seek (*pt, pp* sought) ◇牟私利 seek personal gain

牟取 móuqǔ [动] seek (*pt, pp* sought)

◇牟取巨额利润 seek a vast profit

眸 móu [名] (书) eye

眸子 móuzǐ [名] pupil

谋 móu I [名] plan ◇他是个足智多谋的人。He is a resourceful person. II [动] **1** (谋求) seek (*pt, pp* sought) **2** (商议) consult ◇不谋而合 agree without prior consultation

谋反 móufǎn [动] plot a rebellion

谋害 móuhài [动] **1** (谋杀) plot a murder **2** (陷害) plot against

谋划 móuhuà [动] plan

谋略 móulüè [名] strategy ◇他是个有谋略、有才智的军事家。He is a resourceful and astute strategist.

谋求 móuqiú [动] seek (*pt, pp* sought)

谋取 móuqǔ [动] seek (*pt, pp* sought)

谋杀 móushā [动] murder ◇谋杀案 murder case

谋生 móushēng [动] make a living

谋私 móusī [动] seek personal advantage (*pt, pp* sought) ◇以权谋私 abuse power for personal gain

谋事 móushì [动] **1** (筹划事情) plan things **2** (找工作) look for a job

某 mǒu [代] **1** (指确定的人或事) ◇张某 a certain person called Zhang **2** (指不确定的人或事) ◇找出某种办法解决问题。Find some way to solve the problem. ◇一定有某人知道这件事。Someone must know about this.

某人 mǒurén [代] (指他人) somebody

模 mú [名] mould (英), mold (美) ▷另见 mó

模具 mújù [名] mould (英), mold (美)

模样 múyàng [名] **1** (相貌) looks (*pl*) ◇她模样不错。She is not bad-looking. **2** (表示大概) ◇这女人有40岁模样儿。This woman is about forty. ◇吃了一个小时模样，大家就结束了。After eating for about an hour everyone has finished.

母 mǔ I [名] **1** (母亲) mother **2** (指长辈女子) ♦祖母 grandmother **3** (喻) (基础) origin ◇失败乃成功之母。Failure is the mother of success. II [形] **1** (雌性) female ♦母牛 cow **2** (指能力或作用) ♦航空母舰 aircraft carrier ♦母体 matrix

母爱 mǔ'ài [名] maternal love

母带 mǔdài [名] master tape

母公司 mǔgōngsī [名] parent company

母亲 mǔqīn [名] mother

母系 mǔxì [形] **1** (母亲方面) maternal ◇他家母系亲属很多。He has a lot of relatives on his mother's side. **2** (母女相承) matriarchal ◇母系社会 matriarchal society

母校 mǔxiào [名] alma mater ◇我离开母校已经20年了。I left my old school twenty years ago.

母性 mǔxìng [名] maternal instinct

母语 mǔyǔ [名] (第一语言) mother tongue

牡 mǔ [形] (书) male

牡丹 mǔdan [名] peony

拇 mǔ [名] 见下文

拇指 mǔzhǐ [名] **1** (指手) thumb **2** (指脚) big toe

木 mù I [名] **1** (树) tree **2** (木材) wood II [形] **1** (僵) numb ◇天太冷，我的脚都冻木了。It's freezing, my feet are numb with cold. **2** (呆) stupid

木材 mùcái [名] timber

木工 mùgōng [名] **1** (指工作) woodwork **2** (指人) carpenter

木匠 mùjiang [名] carpenter

木刻 mùkè [名] woodcarving

木料 mùliào [名] timber

木马 mùmǎ [名] **1** (鞍马) vaulting horse **2** (跳马) vault **3** (指玩具) rocking horse

木乃伊 mùnǎiyī [名] mummy

木偶 mù'ǒu [名] puppet

木然 mùrán [形] stupefied

木头 mùtou [名] wood

木已成舟 mù yǐ chéng zhōu what's done is done

目 mù [名] **1** (眼睛) eye **2** (条目) item **3** (目录) catalogue (英), catalog (美) **4** (名) title **5** (指生物) order

目标 mùbiāo [名] **1** (对象) target ◇雾太大，看不清目标。The fog's too heavy – we can't see the target properly. ◇他们侦察了一个晚上，也没发现目标。They searched all evening, but didn't find what they were looking for. **2** (目的) goal ◇有目标的生活才有意义。Life only has meaning if you have goals.

目不识丁 mù bù shí dīng completely illiterate

目不暇接 mù bù xiá jiē too much for the eye to take in

目不转睛 mù bù zhuǎn jīng stare fixedly

目瞪口呆 mù dèng kǒu dāi be dumbstruck ◇听了那个消息，他惊得目瞪口呆。He was dumbstruck at the news.

目的 mùdì [名] **1** (指地点) destination ◇旅游目的国 tourist destination **2** (结果) aim ◇有明确的学习目的 have clear study aims ◇他终于达到了目的了。He finally achieved his goal. ◇学习的目的是为了增长知识。The purpose of study is to increase knowledge. **3** (企图) intention

目睹 mùdǔ [动] witness

目光 mùguāng [名] **1** (视线) gaze ◇大家的目光都聚集在老师身上。Everyone's gaze was focused on the teacher. **2** (眼神) look ◇他用奇怪的目光看着我。He gave me a strange look. **3** (见识) sight ◇目光敏锐 sharp-eyed

目击 mùjī [动] witness ◇目击者 eyewitness

目空一切 mù kōng yīqiè supercilious

目录 mùlù [名] **1** (指事物) catalogue (英), catalog (美) **2** (指书刊中) table of contents

目前 mùqián [名] present ◇目前，全国经济形势很好。At present the country's economic situation is very good. ◇我们目前的任务是什么？ What are our current duties? ◇到目前为止，公司已出售两万台电脑。To date the company has sold 20,000 computers.

目中无人 mù zhōng wú rén be condescending

沐 mù [动] (书) **1** (洗头) wash one's hair **2** (蒙受) receive

沐浴 mùyù [动] **1** (洗澡) take a bath (*pt* took, *pp* taken) **2** (喻) (沉浸) revel ◇沐浴在幸福和欢乐之中 revel in one's fortune and happiness

牧 mù [动] herd

牧民 mùmín [名] herdsman (*pl* herdsmen)

牧师 mùshi [名] priest

牧童 mùtóng [名] shepherd boy

牧业 mùyè [名] animal husbandry

募 mù [动] **1** (钱款) raise ◇募款 raise funds **2** (兵员) enlist

募集 mùjí [动] collect

募捐 mùjuān [动] collect donations

墓 mù [名] grave

墓碑 mùbēi [名] gravestone

墓地 mùdì [名] graveyard

幕 mù **I** [名] **1** (帐篷) tent **2** (帷幔) curtain ♦银幕 the silver screen **II** [量] act

幕后 mùhòu [名] (贬) behind the scenes ◇将军正在幕后策划一起叛乱。The General is plotting a rebellion behind the scenes.

睦 mù [动] get on ♦和睦 harmonious

睦邻 mùlín [动] get on with one's neighbours (英) 或 neighbors (美) ◇两国建立了睦邻友好关系。The two countries have built up good, neighbourly (英) 或 neighborly (美) relations.

慕 mù [动] admire

慕名 mùmíng [动] be impressed by a reputation

暮 mù [名] **1** (傍晚) dusk **2** (晚) ◇暮春时节 in late spring

暮年 mùnián [名] old age

暮气 mùqì [名] lethargy

穆 mù [形] solemn

穆斯林 mùsīlín [名] Muslim

Nn

拿 ná **I** [动] **1** (握) hold (*pt, pp* held) ◊他手里拿着一本书。He's holding a book in his hand. **2** (夺) capture ◊我们拿下了敌人的阵地。We captured the enemy position. **3** (有把握) be sure ◊我拿不准他到底来不来。I'm not sure whether he's coming or not. **4** (掌握) cope with ◊家里活他样样拿得起来。He can cope with all the housework. **5** (架子、样子) put on (*pt, pp* put) ◊我们老板总拿架子。Our boss always puts on airs. **6** (得) get (*pt* got, *pp* got (英), gotten (美))◊他拿了季军。He got third prize. **II** [介] **1** (用) with ◊她拿毛巾把头发擦干。She dried her hair with a towel. ◊少拿这个吓唬我! Stop trying to scare me with that stuff! **2** (把) ◊他不拿工作当回事。He doesn't take the job seriously.

拿手 náshǒu [动] be good at ◊做菜她很拿手。She's good at cooking.

哪 nǎ **I** [代] **1** (什么) which ◊哪是我的包裹? Which is my parcel? ◊你喜欢哪种音乐? What kind of music do you like? ◊哪个人是李先生? Which one is Mr Li? **2** (任何一个) any ◊你哪天来都行。You can come any day. **II** [副] how ◊不努力哪会成功? How can you be successful without hard work?

哪里 nǎli [代] **1** (用于问处所) ◊你住在哪里? Where do you live? **2** (指任何地方) ◊游牧民族总是哪里有水,就迁往哪里。Nomads always move to wherever there is water. **3** (指某一地方) ◊我们应该在哪里见过。I'm sure we've met somewhere before. **4** (用于反问) ◊我哪里去过美国? When was I supposed to have gone to America? ◊他哪里会弹钢琴? How is he supposed to be able to play the piano? **5** (谦) ◊哪里,哪里,你过奖了。No, no, it was nothing.

哪怕 nǎpà [连] no matter ◊哪怕有再多的困难,我也要坚持到底。No matter how many difficulties remain, I will hold fast till the end.

哪样 nǎyàng [代] **1** (表示提问) what kind **2** (表示任何一种) whatever

那 nà **I** [代] **1** (指远处) that (*pl* those) ◊那楼是去年建的。That block was built last year. **2** (表示不确指) ◊他这也想学,那也想学。He wants to study everything. **3** (表示复指) that ◊赚钱,那个才是商人真正关心的。Making money – that's all businessmen care about. **II** [连] then ◊你想买,那就买吧。If you want to buy it, then buy it. ◊小明不在家,那我们就走吧。Xiao Ming is out, so we should just go.

那个 nàge [代] **1** (指代人、事或物) that (*pl* those) ◊那个是主卧。That's the master bedroom. ◊那个房间是我妹妹的。That's my sister's room. **2** (表示婉转) ◊他说话挺那个的。What he said was too much.

那里 nàli [代] ◊我去过那里。I've been there. ◊我也要去那里吗? Shall I go over there as well?

那么 nàme [代] **1** (表示程度) ◊你不该那么相信他。You shouldn't trust him so much. **2** (表示数量) ◊再有那么七八个就够了。Another seven or so will be enough. **3** (表示方式) ◊你别那么想。Don't think in that way.

那些 nàxiē [代] those ◊那些书是我的。Those are my books.

那样 nàyàng [副] ◊我没有说过那样的话。I never said anything like that.

呐 nà 见下文

呐喊 nàhǎn [动] cheer

纳 nà [动] **1** (收) receive ♦出纳 cashier **2** (接受) accept ♦采纳 accept **3** (享受) enjoy **4** (放进去) put (*pt, pp* put) **5** (交付) pay (*pt, pp* paid) **6** (缝纫) sew (*pt* sewed, *pp* sewn)

纳粹 nàcuì [名] Nazi

纳凉 nàliáng [动] enjoy the shade

纳闷儿 nàmènr [动] (口) not see ◊我纳闷儿他为什么还没到。I don't understand why he hasn't arrived yet.

纳米技术 nàmǐ jìshù [名] nanotechnology

纳入 nàrù [动] be incorporated into ◇他的提议被纳入议事范围。His suggestion was incorporated into the agenda of the meeting.

纳税 nàshuì [动] pay taxes (*pt, pp* paid)

纳税人 nàshuìrén [名] taxpayer

钠 nà [名] sodium

捺 nà [动] control

乃 nǎi [动] (书) be (*pt* was, *pp* been) ◇失败乃成功之母。Failure is the mother of success.

乃至 nǎizhì [连] (书) even ◇他在国内乃至海外都很有影响。He's very influential, in his own country and even overseas.

奶 nǎi **I** [名] **1** (乳房) breast **2** (乳汁) milk **II** [动] breast-feed (*pt, pp* breast-fed)

奶酪 nǎilào [名] cheese

奶妈 nǎimā [名] wet nurse

奶名 nǎimíng [名] baby name

奶奶 nǎinai [名] granny

奶昔 nǎixī [名] milkshake

耐 nài [动] **1** (指人) endure **2** (指衣服) be durable **3** (指材料) be resistant ◇这种材料耐腐蚀。This material is corrosion-resistant.

耐烦 nàifán [形] patient ◇她有点不耐烦了。She's getting a bit impatient.

耐久 nàijiǔ [形] long-lasting

耐劳 nàiláo [动] not be afraid of hard work

耐力 nàilì [名] stamina

耐人寻味 nài rén xún wèi be thought-provoking

耐心 nàixīn [形] patient ◇她对孩子很有耐心。She's very patient with children.

耐性 nàixìng [名] patience

男 nán [名] **1** (男性) male **2** (儿子) son

男儿 nán'ér [名] man (*pl* men)

男女 nánnǚ [名] men and women (*pl*) ◇男女平等 equality between men and women

男人 nánrén [名] man (*pl* men)

男人 nánren [名] (方) husband

男士 nánshì [名] gentleman (*pl* gentlemen)

男性 nánxìng [名] male

男子汉 nánzǐhàn [名] man (*pl* men) ◇孩子已经长成了男子汉。The child has already become a man.

南 nán [名] south ♦东南 south-east ♦西南 south-west

南方 nánfāng [名] the South ◇南方风俗 a southern custom

南国 nánguó [名] (书) the South ◇南国风光 southern scenery

南腔北调 nán qiāng běi diào strong accent ◇他讲话南腔北调的。He speaks with a strong accent.

南辕北辙 nán yuán běi zhé at odds with ◇你的行为和你的承诺南辕北辙。Your actions are at odds with your words.

难 nán **I** [形] **1** (困难) hard **2** (不好) bad ◇难吃 unpalatable **II** [动] baffle ▷另见 nàn

难产 nánchǎn [动] **1** (医) have a difficult labour **2** (不易完成) be hard to carry out ◇我们的计划一再难产。Our plan was beset with difficulties.

难处 nánchǔ [动] be hard to get along with

难处 nánchu [名] trouble ◇各家有各家的难处。Every family has its own troubles.

难道 nándào [副] ◇你难道还不明白吗？How can you not understand? ◇难道你就不累？Aren't you tired?

难怪 nánguài **I** [副] ◇难怪一个人找不到，原来今天不上班。No wonder no one's here – it's not a working day! **II** [动] be understandable

难关 nánguān [名] crisis (*pl* crises)

难过 nánguò **I** [动] have a hard time ◇他挣得不多，日子难过。He doesn't earn much – he has a hard time of it. **II** [形] upset

难解难分 nán jiě nán fēn **1** (形容比赛) be locked in battle **2** (形容关系) be inseparable

难堪 nánkān [形] (尴尬) embarrassed ◇他因为没钱付小费而感到难堪。He felt embarrassed at not having enough money for a tip.

难看 nánkàn [形] **1** (丑) ugly **2** (不体面) ashamed

难免 nánmiǎn [动] be unavoidable ◇年轻人犯点错误是难免的，关键要从中吸取教训。It's unavoidable that young people will make mistakes. The important thing is that they learn from them.

难能可贵 nán néng kě guì highly commendable

难受 nánshòu [动] **1** (指身体) not feel well ◇我头疼得难受。I've got a bad headache. **2** (指心情) feel down (*pt, pp* felt)

难说 nánshuō [动] be hard to say ◇他来不来还难说。It's hard to say if he'll come or not.

难听 nántīng [动] **1** (不悦耳) sound awful **2** (粗俗) be crude **3** (不体面) be shameful

难为情 nánwéiqíng [形] **1** (难堪) embarrassed **2** (过意不去) awkward

难为 nánwei [动] **1** (使人为难) embarrass **2** (客套) (表示感谢) put … out (*pt, pp* put) ◇帮我打扫房间，真难为你了。Thank you for helping me with the cleaning – I know I've really put you out. **3** (指做难事) be tough ◇一个人把几个孩子拉扯大，真难为她了。It must have been very tough for her, bringing up all those children on her own.

难言之隐 nán yán zhī yǐn be reluctant to discuss ◇他似乎有难言之隐。He seemed reluctant to discuss the subject.

难以 nányǐ [副] hard ◇难以启齿 not know where to start ◇难以置信 hard to believe

难于 nányú [副] hard ◇没有本科学历，难于找工作。Without an undergraduate degree it can be hard to find work.

难 nàn **I** [名] trouble **II** [动] blame ♦非难 blame ▷另见 nán

难民 nànmín [名] refugee

难兄难弟 nànxiōng-nàndì fellow sufferers (*pl*) ◇大家都是难兄难弟，应该互相关照。Everyone's in the same boat – we should be looking after each other.

囊 náng [名] **1** (口袋) bag **2** (袋状物) pocket ♦胆囊 gall bladder

囊括 nángkuò [动] **1** (包罗) encompass **2** (指比赛) win (*pt, pp* won)

孬 nāo [形] (方) (怯懦) cowardly

孬种 nāozhǒng [名] coward

挠 náo [动] **1** (轻抓) scratch **2** (阻止) prevent ♦阻挠 hinder **3** (屈服) yield

挠头 náotóu [形] troublesome

恼 nǎo [形] **1** (生气) angry ♦气恼 get angry **2** (不痛快) unhappy ♦烦恼 worried

恼火 nǎohuǒ [形] annoyed

恼羞成怒 nǎo xiū chéng nù fly off the handle

脑 nǎo [名] **1** (生理) brain **2** (脑筋) brain ◇他不爱动脑。He's not in the habit of using his brain. **3** (头部) head **4** (头领) leader ♦首脑 head

脑袋 nǎodai [名] head

脑海 nǎohǎi [名] mind

脑筋 nǎojīn [名] **1** (指思考能力) brain **2** (指思想) mind ◇他脑筋灵活。He's got a quick mind.

脑力 nǎolì [名] brain power ◇脑力劳动 brain work

闹 nào **I** [形] noisy **II** [动] **1** (吵闹) have a row **2** (发泄) vent **3** (病、灾难) suffer from ◇他家乡闹了地震。His hometown suffered an earthquake. ◇前两天她闹胃炎。A couple of days ago she had a bout of gastritis. **4** (玩) go out (*pt* went, *pp* gone)

闹别扭 nào bièniu [动] **1** (吵架) fall out (*pt* fell, *pp* fallen) ◇夫妻俩闹别扭了。The couple have fallen out. **2** (合不来) be at loggerheads ◇两

国就贸易问题闹别扭。The two countries are at loggerheads over trading issues.

闹肚子 nào dùzi [动] have diarrhoea (英) 或 diarrhea (美)

闹鬼 nàoguǐ [动] be haunted

闹哄哄 nàohōnghōng [形] noisy

闹剧 nàojù [名] farce ◇你们的闹剧也该收场了。You should put a stop to this nonsense.

闹情绪 nào qíngxù [动] take things badly (*pt* took, *pp* taken)

闹市 nàoshì [名] busy commercial area

闹腾 nàoteng [动] **1** (吵闹) make a row **2** (大声说笑) make a din

闹钟 nàozhōng [名] alarm clock

呢 ne [助] **1** (表示疑问) ◇你们都走，我呢？ If you all go, what about me? ◇我到底错在哪儿呢？ What did I actually do wrong? **2** (表示陈述) ◇离北京还远着呢。Beijing is still quite far. ◇他导演的电影好看着呢。The film he directed is actually really good. **3** (表示持续) ◇老师还在办公室呢。The teacher is still in the office. ◇警察正在搜索逃犯呢。The police are hunting down the escaped convict. **4** (表示停顿) ◇如今呢，我们住上了大房子。Nowadays, we live in a big house. ▷另见 ní

馁 něi [形] disheartened

内 nèi [名] **1** (里头) inside ◇他躲在大楼内。He hid inside the building. ◇保龄球是室内运动。Bowling is an indoor sport. ◇他在一个月内完成了任务。He finished the task within a month. **2** (指妻子的亲属) in-laws (*pl*) ♦内弟 brother-in-law (*pl* brothers-in-law)

内部 nèibù [形] internal

内存 nèicún [名] memory

内地 nèidì [名] the interior ◇很多港澳台同胞到内地旅游参观。Many tourists from Hong Kong, Macao and Taiwan come to mainland China for sightseeing.

内定 nèidìng [动] be appointed internally

内分泌 nèifēnmì [名] endocrine system

内服 nèifú [动] take orally (*pt* took, *pp* taken) ◇此药可内服。This medicine is to be taken orally.

内阁 nèigé [名] cabinet

内涵 nèihán [名] connotation

内行 nèiháng **I** [名] expert **II** [形] expert

内河 nèihé [名] inland river

内讧 nèihòng [名] internal conflict

内疚 nèijiù [动] feel guilty (*pt, pp* felt) ◇我为失职而内疚。I felt guilty about my unprofessional behaviour. ◇他被内疚折磨着。He is tortured by guilt.

内科 nèikē [名] internal medicine ◇内科病房 medical ward ◇内科医生 physician

内陆 nèilù [形] inland

内乱 nèiluàn [名] civil conflict

内幕 nèimù [名] inside story

内勤 nèiqín [形] office-based **II** [名] office staff

内容 nèiróng [名] content

内务 nèiwù [名] (国内事务) internal affairs (*pl*)

内线 nèixiàn [名] **1** (指人) mole **2** (指电话) internal line ◇内线电话 internal phone call

内向 nèixiàng [形] introverted

内销 nèixiāo [动] sell on the domestic market (*pt, pp* sold)

内心 nèixīn [名] mind ◇谁知道他内心怎么想的？Who knows what he's thinking deep down?

内秀 nèixiù [形] quietly intelligent ◇我的男朋友长相平平，但很内秀。My boyfriend looks pretty ordinary, but he's intelligent in an understated way.

内应 nèiyìng [名] mole

内在 bèizài [形] internal ◇内在规律 intrinsic law

内脏 nèizàng [名] internal organs (*pl*)

内债 nèizhài [名] internal debt

内政 nèizhèng [名] domestic affairs (*pl*)

嫩 nèn [形] **1** (指皮肤) delicate **2** (指食品) tender **3** (指颜色) light **4** (口) (指阅历) green

能 néng **I** [名] **1** (能力) ability ◊无才无能 untalented and incapable **2** (物) (能量) energy ◊核能 nuclear energy **II** [形] capable **III** [助动] can ◊我能照顾好自己。I can take care of myself.

能动 néngdòng [形] active ◊我们能动地改造世界。We are working actively to change the world.

能够 nénggòu [动] be able to ◊飞机一个小时后能够起飞。The flight will be able to take off in an hour. ◊有谁能够帮我解决这个问题？Who can help me solve this problem?

> 📖 请勿混淆 **able** 和 **capable**。这两个词都可以表示某人能做某事。如果说某人 **able to do something**，表示他有能力做某事，因为他具做此事所需的知识或技能，或条件允许可以做此事。*He wondered if he would be able to climb over the rail… They were able to use their profits for new investments.* 注意，如果时态是过去时，则表示某人事实上已经做了某事。*We were able to reduce costs.* 如果某人 **capable of doing something**，表示他具备做某事的知识和技能，或者他有可能去做某事。*The workers are perfectly capable of running the organization themselves… She was quite capable of ruining the project if it didn't please her.* 可以说某人 **capable of** 某种感情或行为。*He's capable of loyalty… I don't believe he's capable of murder.* 也可以用 **capable of** 表示汽车或机器的性能。*The car was capable of 110 miles per hour.* 如果将某人描述为 **able** 或者 **capable**，说明他能力很强。*His father was an able golfer…She's certainly a capable gardener.*

能力 nénglì [名] ability

> 📖 请勿混淆 **ability, capability** 和 **capacity**。**ability** 表示某人有能力做好某事。*He had remarkable ability as a musician… the ability to bear hardship…* 某人的 **capability** 是指他所能完成的工作量及工作质量的好坏。*…a job that was beyond the capability of one man… the film director's ideas of the capability of the actor…* 如果某人具有某种特殊的 **capacity**，或 **a capacity for something**，或 **a capacity to do something**，说明他具备做该事所需的能力。**capacity** 比 **ability** 更为正式。*…their capacity for hard work… his capacity to see the other person's point of view…*

能量 néngliàng [名] (物) energy

能耐 néngnai [名] ability

能人 néngrén [名] ◊我们要让个能人来处理这件事。We should let somebody competent take care of this.

能手 néngshǒu [名] expert

能源 néngyuán [名] source of energy ◊能源短缺 energy shortage

呢 ní [名] woollen cloth ▷另见 ne

呢子 nízi [名] woollen cloth ◊呢子大衣 woollen overcoat

泥 ní [名] **1** (指土) mud **2** (泥状物) paste ◊土豆泥 mashed potato

泥泞 nínìng **I** [形] muddy **II** [名] mud

泥潭 nítán [名] marsh

霓 ní 见下文

霓虹灯 níhóngdēng [名] neon light

拟 nǐ [动] **1** (起草) draft **2** (打算) plan

拟订 nǐdìng [动] draft

拟人 nǐrén [名] personification

拟声词 nǐshēngcí [名] onomatopoeia

你 nǐ [代] **1** (称对方) you ◊你是我最好的朋友。You are my best friend. **2** (你的) ◊你家有几口人？How many people are there in your family?

你们 nǐmen [代] you (*pl*)

昵 nì [形] intimate ♦亲昵 affectionate

昵称 nìchēng [名] pet name

逆 nì **I** [形] adverse **II** [动] go against (*pt* went, *pp* gone)

逆差 nìchā [名] deficit

逆耳 nì'ěr [形] hard to take ◇忠言逆耳 the truth hurts

逆反心理 nìfǎn xīnlǐ [名] rebellious mentality

逆境 nìjìng [名] adversity

逆来顺受 nì lái shùn shòu resign oneself to

逆流 nìliú **I** [动] go against the trend (*pt* went, *pp* gone) **II** [名] (喻) unhealthy trend ◇我们一定要抵制这股社会逆流。We must fight this unhealthy social trend.

逆水行舟 nì shuǐ xíng zhōu go against the stream

逆子 nìzǐ [名] disobedient son

匿 nì [动] (书) conceal ♦隐匿 secrete

匿迹 nìjì [动] go into hiding (*pt* went, *pp* gone) ◇他怎么销声匿迹了？ Why has he vanished from the scene?

匿名 nìmíng [形] anonymous

腻 nì **I** [形] **1** (太油) oily **2** (厌烦) fed-up **3** (细致) meticulous ♦细腻 exquisite **II** [名] dirt

腻烦 nìfan [动] **1** (厌烦) be bored ◇这个电影我看了3遍也没有腻烦。I've seen this film three times and I'm still not bored of it. **2** (厌恶) loathe

腻味 nìwei [动] **1** (方) (厌烦) be bored ◇这纪录片真腻味人。This documentary is so boring. **2** (方) (厌恶) dislike

溺 nì [动] **2** (淹没) drown **2** (过分) indulge in ♦溺爱 overindulge

蔫 niān [形] **1** (枯萎) withered ◇花因为缺水都蔫了。The flowers withered from lack of water. **2** (萎靡不振) listless

年 nián **I** [名] **1** (时间单位) year ◇今年 this year **2** (元旦或春节) New Year ◇过年 celebrate Spring Festival **3** (岁数) age ◇年过半百 over fifty years old **4** (阶段) age ◇老年 old age ♦童年 childhood **5** (时代) era ◇明朝末年 the end of the Ming dynasty ◇近年来 in recent years **6** (年成) harvest **II** [形] annual ◇年薪 annual salary

年表 niánbiǎo [名] chronology

年成 niáncheng [名] harvest

年代 niándài [名] **1** (时代) period **2** (十年) decade

年度 niándù [名] year ◇年度预算 annual budget

年份 niánfèn [名] a particular year ◇这两笔支出不在一个年份。These two expenses were not incurred in the same year.

年富力强 nián fù lì qiáng in the prime of life

年关 niánguān [名] the end of the year

年华 niánhuá [名] (书) years (*pl*)

年会 niánhuì [名] annual meeting

年货 niánhuò [名] Spring Festival goods

年级 niánjí [名] year (英), grade (美)

年纪 niánjì [名] age ◇他年纪不大。He's quite young.

年鉴 niánjiàn [名] yearbook

年景 niánjǐng [名] **1** (年成) harvest **2** (过年景象) holiday atmosphere

年龄 niánlíng [名] age

年迈 niánmài [形] (书) old

年谱 niánpǔ [名] chronology

年青 niánqīng [形] young

年轻 niánqīng [形] young

年头 niántóu [名] **1** (年份) year **2** (多年时间) years (*pl*) ◇他从事翻译有年头了。He's been doing translation for years. **3** (时代) times (*pl*) ◇那年头，日子不好过。In those days, life was hard.

年限 niánxiàn [名] time limit ◇贷款偿还年限 mortgage repayment period

年月 niányue [名] (书) years (*pl*)

黏 nián [形] glutinous

黏糊 niánhu [形] 1 (指东西) sticky ◇这粥黏糊了。The rice porridge has thickened. 2 (指人) languid

黏着 niánzhuó [动] stick together (*pt, pp* stuck)

碾 niǎn I [名] roller II [动] 1 (使粉碎) grind (*pt, pp* ground) 2 (使平坦) flatten

撵 niǎn [动] drive ... away (*pt* drove, *pp* driven) ◇我们把他撵走了。We drove him away.

念 niàn I [动] 1 (读) read (*pt, pp* read) 2 (上学) study 3 (想念) miss II [名] idea

念叨 niàndao [动] 1 (唠叨) nag 2 (谈论) discuss ◇我有些事情想念叨念叨。There's something I want to discuss with you.

念旧 niànjiù [动] be nostalgic

念念不忘 niànniàn bù wàng always remember ◇他对老师的帮助念念不忘。He always remembered his teacher's help.

念头 niàntou [名] idea

娘 niáng [名] 1 (方) (母亲) mum 2 (指年长妇女) auntie

娘家 niángjia [名] *a married woman's parents' home* ◇她要带孩子回娘家。She wants to take her child back to her parents' home.

娘胎 niángtāi [名] womb

酿 niàng I [动] 1 (葡萄酒、蜜) make (*pt, pp* made) 2 (啤酒) brew 3 (祸事) lead to (*pt, pp* led) ◇酒后驾车会酿成大祸。Drink-driving can lead to disaster. II [名] alcohol

酿造 niàngzào [动] 1 (葡萄酒、醋、酱油) make (*pt, pp* made) 2 (啤酒) brew

鸟 niǎo [名] bird

鸟瞰 niǎokàn I [动] get a bird's-eye view ◇从山顶可以鸟瞰全城。From the mountain top you get a bird's-eye view of the whole city. II [名] (书) overview

鸟语花香 niǎo yǔ huā xiāng the sounds and scents of nature

袅 niǎo [形] (书) delicate

袅袅 niǎoniǎo [形] 1 (书) (指烟雾) curling 2 (书) (指声音) lingering

尿 niào I [名] urine ♦排尿 urinate II [动] urinate
▷另见 suī

捏 niē [动] 1 (拿) hold (*pt, pp* held) 2 (饺子) make (*pt, pp* made) 3 (泥人) mould (英), mold (美)

镊 niè I [名] tweezers (*pl*) II [动] pick ... up

镍 niè [名] nickel

蹑 niè [动] creep

蹑手蹑脚 niè shǒu niè jiǎo creep ◇他蹑手蹑脚地走进教室。He crept into the classroom.

孽 niè [名] sin

孽种 nièzhǒng [名] (旧) undutiful child (*pl* children)

您 nín [代] you ◇您慢走！ Mind how you go!

宁 níng [形] peaceful
▷另见 nìng

宁静 níngjìng [形] quiet

拧 níng [动] 1 (毛巾、衣服) wring (*pt, pp* wrung) ◇你洗完衣服后，把它们拧一下。When you've washed the clothes, wring them out. 2 (皮肤) pinch
▷另见 nìng

狞 níng [形] (书) ferocious ♦狰狞 savage

狞笑 níngxiào [名] evil laugh

柠 níng 见下文

柠檬 níngméng [名] lemon

凝 níng [动] 1 (凝结) congeal 2 (集中注意力) gaze

凝固 nínggù [动] solidify

凝结 níngjié [动] 1 (指气体) liquefy 2 (指液体) solidify

凝聚 níngjù [动] embody

凝练 níngliàn [形] (书) concise

凝视 níngshì [动] gaze

凝重 níngzhòng [形] (书) imposing

宁 nìng [副] ◇我们宁早勿晚。We'd rather be early than late.
▷另见 níng

宁可 nìngkě [副] ◇我宁可回家。I'd rather go home.

宁肯 nìngkěn [副] ◇我宁肯熬夜，也不要迟交作业。I'd rather work all night than hand my homework in late.

宁缺毋滥 nìng quē wù làn place quality over quantity ◇对于买衣服，我的原则是宁缺毋滥。When buying clothes, I go by the principle of quality over quantity.

宁死不屈 nìng sǐ bù qū rather die than surrender

宁愿 nìngyuàn [副] ◇我宁愿走也不乘公交车。I'd rather walk than take the bus.

拧 nìng [形] stubborn
▷另见 níng

牛 niú [名] **1** (指动物) cow ♦公牛 bull **2** (指肉) beef

牛犊 niúdú [名] calf (*pl* calves)

牛劲 niújìn [名] **1** (大力气) great strength ◇这小子还真有股牛劲。This child is really strong. **2** (牛脾气) obstinacy

牛皮 niúpí [名] **1** (牛的皮) leather **2** (大话) boast

牛脾气 niúpíqi [名] stubbornness

牛市 niúshì [名] bull market

牛头不对马嘴 niú tóu bù duì mǎ zuǐ incongruous

牛仔裤 niúzǎikù [名] jeans (*pl*)

扭 niǔ [动] **1** (掉转) turn around **2** (拧) twist **3** (崴) sprain **4** (指走路) sway **5** (指打架) wrestle

扭打 niǔdǎ [动] wrestle

扭捏 niǔnie [形] coy ◇他扭捏地说话。He spoke coyly.

扭曲 niǔqū [动] twist ◇扭曲事实 twist the facts ◇扭曲的灵魂 twisted soul

扭转 niǔzhuǎn [动] turn ... around ◇他扭转船头。He turned the boat around. ◇她突然扭转身子。Suddenly, she turned round. ◇最后的进球扭转了整个局面。The last goal turned the whole game around.

纽 niǔ [名] (扣子) button

纽带 niǔdài [名] tie ◇建立起友谊的纽带 establish ties of friendship

拗 niù [形] obstinate ◇他脾气拗得很。He's terribly obstinate. ◇我可拗不过他。I won't be able to persuade him.
▷另见 ào

农 nóng [名] **1** (农业) agriculture **2** (农民) farmer

农产品 nóngchǎnpǐn [名] agricultural produce

农场 nóngchǎng [名] farm

农村 nóngcūn [名] the countryside

农活 nónghuó [名] farm work

农具 nóngjù [名] farm tools (*pl*)

农历 nónglì [名] lunar calendar

农贸市场 nóngmào shìchǎng [名] farmer's market

农民 nóngmín [名] farmer

农药 nóngyào [名] pesticide

农业 nóngyè [名] agriculture ◇农业现代化 agricultural modernisation

农作物 nóngzuòwù [名] crops (*pl*)

浓 nóng [形] **1** (指气味、味道) strong **2** (指烟雾) thick ◇浓烟 thick smoke **3** (指兴趣) great ◇他对语言有很浓的兴趣。He has a great interest in languages.

浓度 nóngdù [名] **1** (化) concentration **2** (指酒) strength ◇威士忌酒浓度高。Whisky is strong.

浓厚 nónghòu [形] **1** (指烟雾、云层) thick **2** (指色彩、气氛、意识) strong **3** (指兴趣) great

浓烈 nóngliè [形] strong

浓缩 nóngsuō **I** [动] condense **II** [形] condensed

浓郁 nóngyù [形] strong

浓重 nóngzhòng [形] strong

脓 nóng [名] pus

脓包 nóngbāo [名] boil

弄 nòng [动] **1** (搞) make (*pt, pp* made) ◇我要把问题弄清楚。I'd like to clarify this issue. ◇别把衣服弄脏了。Don't get your clothes dirty. **2** (设法取得) get (*pt* got, *pp* got (英), gotten (美)) **3** (摆弄) play with ▷另见 lòng

弄巧成拙 nòng qiǎo chéng zhuō be too clever for one's own good

弄虚作假 nòng xū zuò jiǎ falsify

奴 nú [名] slave

奴才 núcai [名] flunkey

奴隶 núlì [名] slave

奴仆 núpú [名] servant

奴役 núyì [动] enslave

努 nǔ [动] **1** (劲儿) make an effort ◇我们再努把力。Let's make one last effort. **2** (嘴) pout ◇他努了下嘴，摆出不在乎的样子。He pouted, making a big show of not caring.

努力 nǔlì [动] try hard ◇他不努力工作。He doesn't work hard. ◇我会尽最大努力。I'll try my very best.

怒 nù **I** [形] **1** (生气) angry ♦恼怒 furious **2** (指气势) powerful ◇玫瑰在怒放。The roses are in full bloom. **II** [名] anger ◇发怒 lose one's temper

怒斥 nùchì [动] (书) reproach

怒吼 nùhǒu [动] roar

怒火 nùhuǒ [名] fury ◇强压怒火 curb one's fury

女 nǚ [名] **1** (女子) woman (*pl* women) ◇女科学家 female scientist ◇女演员 actress **2** (女儿) daughter ◇长女 eldest daughter ♦子女 children (*pl*)

女儿 nǚ'ér [名] daughter

女郎 nǚláng [名] girl ◇封面女郎 cover girl

女强人 nǚqiángrén [名] superwoman (*pl* superwomen)

女权 nǚquán [名] women's rights (*pl*) ◇女权运动 Women's Movement

女人 nǚrén [名] woman (*pl* women)

女人 nǚren [名] **1** (妻子) wife (*pl* wives) **2** (口) (情妇) mistress

女色 nǚsè [名] feminine charm ◇他贪图女色。He chases after women.

女士 nǚshì [名] **1** (指称呼) Ms. ◇王女士，你好！ Hello, Ms. Wang! **2** (对妇女的尊称) lady

女性 nǚxìng [名] **1** (指性别) the female sex **2** (指女人) woman (*pl* women)

女婿 nǚxu [名] son-in-law (*pl* sons-in-law)

女子 nǚzǐ [名] woman (*pl* women)

暖 nuǎn **I** [形] warm **II** [动] warm ◇天气暖起来了。The weather has become warmer.

暖和 nuǎnhuo **I** [形] warm **II** [动] warm up

暖流 nuǎnliú [名] **1** (地理) warm current **2** (喻) (指感觉) glow

暖色 nuǎnsè [名] warm colour (英) 或 color (美)

暖水瓶 nuǎnshuǐpíng [名] Thermos flask®

暖洋洋 nuǎnyángyáng [形] balmy

疟 nüè 见下文

疟疾 nüèji [名] malaria

虐 nüè [形] cruel ♦暴虐 brutality ◇虐政 tyranny

虐待 nüèdài [动] ill-treat

挪 nuó [动] move

挪动 nuódong [动] move

挪用 nuóyòng [动] **1** (移作别用) divert **2** (公款) misappropriate

诺 nuò [动] promise ♦承诺 undertake

诺言 nuòyán [名] promise

懦 nuò [形] weak ♦怯懦 timid

懦夫 nuòfū [名] coward

懦弱 nuòruò [形] cowardly

糯 nuò [形] glutinous

糯米 nuòmǐ [名] glutinous rice

Oo

哦 ó [叹] oh ◇哦，他也来了。Oh, he's come too.

噢 ǒ [叹] oh ◇噢，你竟然也在。Oh, you're actually in.

哦 ò [叹] oh ◇哦，我明白了。Oh, now I understand.

讴 ōu 见下文

讴歌 ōugē [动] (书) sing the praises of (*pt* sang, *pp* sung) ◇这篇报道讴歌了白衣天使。This report sings the praises of doctors and nurses.

欧 ōu [名] **1** (欧洲) Europe **2** (欧姆) ohm

欧元 ōuyuán [名] euro

殴 ōu [动] beat … up (*pt* beat, *pp* beaten) ♦斗殴 fight

殴打 ōudǎ [动] beat …up (*pt* beat, *pp* beaten)

鸥 ōu [名] gull

呕 ǒu [动] vomit

呕吐 ǒutù [动] vomit

呕心沥血 ǒu xīn lì xuè work one's heart out

偶 ǒu **I** [名] **1** (人像) image ♦木偶 puppet **2** (双数) even number **3** (配偶) mate **II** [形] chance ◇我们的相识是由于一次偶遇。We met through a chance encounter.

偶尔 ǒu'ěr [副] occasionally ◇我偶而去游泳。Occasionally I go swimming.

偶然 ǒurán [形] chance ◇我偶然发现了这则消息。I found out this piece of news by chance.

偶然性 ǒuránxìng [名] chance

偶数 ǒushù [名] even number

偶像 ǒuxiàng [名] idol

藕 ǒu [名] lotus root

藕断丝连 ǒu duàn sī lián separated but still together in spirit

怄 òu [动] (方) annoy

怄气 òuqì [动] (方) be annoyed

Pp

趴 pā [动] **1** (卧倒) lie prone (*pt* lay, *pp* lain) **2** (伏靠) bend over (*pt, pp* bent) ◇上课别趴在桌子上。Don't lean on the desk during class.

趴伏 pāfú [动] lie prone (*pt* lay, *pp* lain)

啪 pā [拟] bang ◇字典啪地一声掉在地上。The dictionary dropped to the floor with a bang.

扒 pá [动] **1** (拢) rake **2** (方) (挠) scratch ◆扒痒 scratch an itch **3** (偷) steal (*pt* stole, *pp* stolen) ◇我的钱包被扒走了。My wallet has been stolen.
▷另见 bā

扒窃 páqiè [动] steal (*pt* stole, *pp* stolen)

扒手 páshǒu [名] pickpocket

爬 pá [动] **1** (前移) crawl **2** (上移) climb ◆爬山 climb a mountain **3** (起床) get up **4** (升迁) be promoted ◇他靠巴结老板往上爬。He got promoted by sucking up to the boss.

爬格子 pá gézi [动] write (*pt* wrote, *pp* written)

爬升 páshēng [动] rise (*pt* rose, *pp* risen) ◇飞机爬升到万米高空。The plane rose to an altitude of 10,000 metres. ◇物价的不断爬升令人担忧。Continual price rises are worrying. ◇近两年，他爬升很快。He's risen very fast in the last two years.

爬行 páxíng [动] crawl

耙 pá [名] rake
▷另见 bà

耙子 pázi [名] rake

帕 pà [名] handkerchief

怕 pà [动] **1** (惧怕) fear **2** (担心) be afraid ◇我怕这么做不合适。I'm afraid it's not appropriate to do it this way. **3** (估计) may be ◇我们怕有3年没见面了。It might be three years since we last met.

怕生 pàshēng [动] be shy

怕羞 pàxiū [动] be shy ◇在生人面前，她很怕羞。She's very shy in front of strangers.

拍 pāi **I** [动] **1** (击打) beat (*pt* beat, *pp* beaten) ◇我拍掉了鞋上的泥。I knocked the mud off my shoes. **2** (拍摄) shoot (*pt, pp* shot) ◇他最近拍了一部电影。He's recently shot a film. **3** (发) send (*pt, pp* sent) **4** (拍马屁) flatter **II** [名] **1** (用具) bat (英), paddle (美) **2** (节奏) beat

拍板 pāibǎn **I** [名] **1** (指乐器) clappers (*pl*) **2** (决定) final say ◇没有老板的拍板，谁也不敢行动。No one will want to act without the go-ahead from the boss. **II** [动] **1** (字) (成交) clinch a deal ◇又一批生意拍板成交了。Another business deal has been clinched. **2** (喻) (同意) give the OK (*pt* gave, *pp* given) ◇这个方案老板还没拍板。The boss still hasn't given the proposal the OK.

拍击 pāijī [动] strike (*pt, pp* struck)

拍马屁 pāi mǎpì [动] suck up ◇他很善于拍马屁。He's very good at sucking up to people.

拍卖 pāimài [动] auction

拍摄 pāishè [动] shoot (*pt, pp* shot)

拍手称快 pāi shǒu chēng kuài applaud ◇犯罪分子落网，人人拍手称快。Everyone applauded when the criminals were caught.

拍照 pāizhào [动] take a photograph (*pt* took, *pp* taken)

拍子 pāizi [名] **1** (用具) bat (英), paddle (美) ◇网球拍子 tennis racket **2** (节奏) beat ◇打拍子 beat time

排 pái **I** [动] **1** (摆放) put … in order (*pt, pp* put) ◇请把椅子排好。Please arrange the chairs. **2** (排演) rehearse **3** (除去) drain **II** [名] **1** (行列) row ◇我坐在教室的前排。I sit in the front row in class. **2** (指军队) platoon **3** (指水运) raft **III** [量] row ◇两排桌子 two rows of tables

排比 páibǐ [名] parallelism

排场 páichǎng [名] ostentation ◊他们的婚宴办得真排场。Their wedding was very ostentatious.

排斥 páichì [动] exclude

排除 páichú [动] remove

排放 páifàng [动] discharge

排挤 páijǐ [动] squeeze … out ◊她被排挤出了决策层。She was squeezed out of policy-making.

排解 páijiě [动] 1 (调解) mediate ◊朋友排解了他们的纠纷。Friends mediated between them in the dispute. 2 (消除) dispel

排练 páiliàn [动] rehearse

排列 páiliè [动] arrange ◊人名按字母顺序排列。People's names have been put in alphabetical order.

排遣 páiqiǎn [动] shake … off (*pt* shook, *pp* shaken) ◊我无法排遣心中郁闷。I can't shake off these gloomy feelings.

排山倒海 pái shān dǎo hǎi overwhelming

排外 páiwài [动] be xenophobic ◊排外阻碍了这个国家的发展。Xenophobia hindered the country's development.

排泄 páixiè [动] 1 (指雨水、污水) discharge 2 (指新陈代谢) excrete

排演 páiyǎn [动] rehearse

排印 páiyìn [动] typeset and print (*pt, pp* typeset)

排忧解难 pái yōu jiě nàn sort out problems

牌 pái [名] 1 (标志板) board ♦广告牌 hoarding ♦门牌 house number ♦招牌 shop sign 2 (商标) brand

牌号 páihào [名] 1 (字号) store name 2 (商标) brand

牌价 páijià [名] list price

牌照 páizhào [名] 1 (指车辆) registration number 2 (指商业) licence (英), license (美)

牌子 páizi [名] 1 (标志板) board 2 (商标) brand

派 pài I [名] 1 (帮派) group ♦学派 school of thought 2 (风度) manner II [动] 1 (分配) set (*pt, pp* set) ◊他派给我一大堆活。He set me a huge pile of work. 2 (委派) send (*pt, pp* sent) 3 (安排) assign ◊他们派我去机场接客人。They assigned me to go to the airport to meet people. 4 (分摊) apportion 5 (指摘) expose III [形] stylish IV [量] 1 (帮) ◊两派学者 scholars of two schools ◊这两派总是意见不一。The two parties never agree. 2 (用于景色、语言等) ◊一派新气象 a new scene ◊一派胡言 a pack of lies

派别 pàibié [名] school of thought

派对 pàiduì [名] party

派遣 pàiqiǎn [动] dispatch

派生 pàishēng [动] derive ◊许多英语词汇是拉丁文的派生。Many English words are derived from Latin.

派头 pàitóu [名] style ◊你穿这件夹克很有派头。You look very stylish in this jacket.

派系 pàixì [名] faction

攀 pān [动] 1 (向上爬) climb ♦攀岩 rock-climbing 2 (指关系) seek friends in high places (*pt, pp* sought) ♦高攀 be a social climber 3 (拉扯) chat

攀比 pānbǐ [动] compete

攀登 pāndēng [动] scale

攀附 pānfù [动] 1 (指植物) climb 2 (指人) try to get in with

攀谈 pāntán [动] chat

盘 pán I [名] 1 (盘子) tray ♦茶盘 tea tray 2 (盘状物) ♦棋盘 chessboard 3 (行情) quotation II [动] 1 (绕) wind (*pt, pp* wound) ♦盘旋 wind 2 (核查) examine ♦盘问 interrogate 3 (清点) make an inventory ♦盘货 stocktake 4 (转让) transfer III [量] 1 (指物量) ◊一盘电线 a coil of wire ◊三盘录像带 three videotapes 2 (指动量) game ◊我再跟你下盘棋。I'll play another game of chess with you.

盘查 pánchá [动] interrogate

盘点 pándiǎn [动] stocktake

盘根错节 pán gēn cuò jié knotty

盘根究底 pán gēn jiū dǐ get to the

heart of the matter

盘踞 pánjù [动] occupy

盘绕 pánrào [动] wind … round (*pt, pp* wound)

盘算 pánsuàn [动] figure … out

盘问 pánwèn [动] interrogate

盘旋 pánxuán [动] **1** (环绕) circle ◇飞机在上空盘旋。The plane circled overhead. **2** (萦绕) linger ◇这个想法一直在他脑子里盘旋。The thought lingered in his mind.

盘子 pánzi [名] plate

磐 pán 见下文

磐石 pánshí [名] huge rock

蹒 pán 见下文

蹒跚 pánshān [形] limp

判 pàn **I** [动] **1** (分辨) distinguish ♦判明 ascertain **2** (评定) judge ◇判卷子 mark exams **3** (裁决) sentence ♦审判 try **II** [副] clearly

判别 pànbié [动] distinguish ◇判别是非 tell right from wrong

判处 pànchǔ [动] sentence

判定 pàndìng [动] judge ◇法院判定他无罪。The court found him not guilty.

判断 pànduàn [动] judge

判决 pànjué [动] **1** (裁定) come to a verdict (*pt* came, *pp* come) ◇法院的判决已经出来了。The court has already come to a verdict. **2** (判断) judge

判若两人 pàn ruò liǎng rén become a completely different person ◇他一工作起来简直判若两人。When he's working he's a completely different person.

盼 pàn [动] **1** (盼望) long ◇我盼着见到亲人。I long to see my loved ones. **2** (看) look ◇左顾右盼 look around

盼头 pàntou [名] good prospects (*pl*)

盼望 pànwàng [动] long ◇人们盼望战争早日结束。The people longed for the war to be over soon.

叛 pàn [动] betray

叛变 pànbiàn [动] betray

叛离 pànlí [动] betray

叛乱 pànluàn [名] revolt

叛逆 pànnì [动] rebel ◇他从小就是个叛逆的人。He has been a rebel ever since he was young.

畔 pàn [名] **1** (旁边) bank **2** (田边) boundary ♦田畔 edge of a field

乓 pāng [拟] bang ◇门乓地一声关上了。The door banged shut.

滂 pāng 见下文

滂沱 pāngtuó [形] torrential

彷 páng 见下文

彷徨 pánghuáng [动] hesitate

庞 páng **I** [形] **1** (体积大) huge **2** (多而杂) innumerable and disordered **II** [名] face ♦脸庞 face

庞大 pángdà [形] huge

庞然大物 pàngrán dà wù giant

庞杂 pángzá [形] jumbled up

旁 páng **I** [名] side ◇他站在了我身旁。He stood by my side. **II** [形] (口) other ◇我还有旁的事儿要做。I still have other things to do.

旁观 pángguān [动] look on

旁敲侧击 páng qiāo cè jī make oblique references

旁若无人 páng ruò wú rén oblivious of others

旁听 pángtīng [动] **1** (指开会) sit in on (*pt, pp* sat) ◇他旁听了昨天的董事会。He sat in on yesterday's board meeting. **2** (指上课) take (*pt* took, *pp* taken) ◇他旁听夜校的课。He's taking evening classes.

旁征博引 páng zhēng bó yǐn cite extensive sources

旁证 pángzhèng [名] circumstantial evidence

膀 páng 见下文
▷另见 bǎng

膀胱 pángguāng [名] bladder

磅 páng 见下文
▷另见 bàng

磅礴 pángbó [形] majestic

螃 páng 见下文

螃蟹 pángxiè [名] crab

胖 pàng [形] fat

胖墩儿 pàngdūnr [名] chubby little thing

胖乎乎 pànghūhū [形] fat

胖子 pàngzi [名] fatty

抛 pāo [动] **1** (投掷) throw (*pt* threw, *pp* thrown) **2** (丢下) leave … behind (*pt, pp* left) ◇他把别的车手远远抛在了后面。He left the other drivers far behind him. **3** (暴露) bare ◇抛头露面 appear in public **4** (脱手) dispose of

抛光 pāoguāng [动] polish

抛锚 pāomáo [动] **1** (指船) cast anchor (*pt, pp* cast) **2** (指车) break down (*pt* broke, *pp* broken) ◇我的车半路上抛锚了。My car broke down on the way.

抛弃 pāoqì [动] desert ◇抛弃妻子 desert one's wife ◇抛弃旧观念 give up on one's old ideas

抛售 pāoshòu [动] dispose of

抛头露面 pāo tóu lù miàn (贬) appear in public ◇他是个经常抛头露面的公众人物。He is a highly visible public figure.

抛砖引玉 pāo zhuān yǐn yù (谦) get the ball rolling

刨 páo [动] **1** (挖掘) dig (*pt, pp* dug) **2** (除去) exclude
▷另见 bào

刨除 páochú [动] deduct

刨根问底 páo gēn wèn dǐ get to the root of things

咆 páo 见下文

咆哮 páoxiào [动] roar

炮 páo 见下文
▷另见 bāo, pào

炮制 páozhì [动] concoct

袍 páo [名] gown ♦旗袍 cheongsam

跑 pǎo [动] **1** (奔) run (*pt* ran, *pp* run) ◇小男孩跑向妈妈。The little boy ran to his mother. **2** (逃) escape **3** (奔波) run around (*pt* ran, *pp* run) ◇我为这事跑了好几天。I've been running around trying to sort this out for several days. **4** (漏) leak ◇车胎跑气了。The tyre (英) 或 tire (美) is flat.

跑步 pǎobù [动] run (*pt* ran, *pp* run) ◇我每天跑步去学校。I run to school every day. ◇他喜欢跑步。He likes jogging.

跑买卖 pǎo mǎimai [动] travel on business

跑题 pǎotí [动] stray from the topic

跑腿 pǎotuǐ [动] do the legwork (*pt* did, *pp* done)

泡 pào **I** [名] **1** (指气体) bubble **2** (指泡状) ♦灯泡 light bulb ◇我的脚上磨起了泡。I've got blisters on my feet from the rubbing. **II** [动] **1** (浸) soak **2** (消磨) dawdle **3** (沏) infuse ♦泡茶 make tea

泡吧 pàobā [动] go clubbing (*pt* went, *pp* gone)

泡沫 pàomò [名] foam

泡影 pàoyǐng [名] lost hope ◇他的一切希望都化为泡影。All his hopes came to nothing.

炮 pào [名] **1** (武器) cannon **2** (爆竹) firecracker
▷另见 bāo, páo

炮火 pàohuǒ [名] gunfire

炮筒子 pàotǒngzi [名] **1** (指物) barrel **2** (指人) ◇他像个炮筒子。He's always shooting his mouth off.

疱 pào [名] blister

呸 pēi [叹] bah

胚 pēi 见下文

胚胎 pēitāi [名] **1** (生物) (指动物) embryo **2** (雏形) embryonic form ◇欧共体是欧盟的胚胎。The EEC was the EU in embryonic form.

陪 péi [动] **1** (相伴) go with (*pt* went, *pp* gone) ◇我要陪母亲去医院。I have to go to the hospital with my mother. ◇我不用你陪。You don't need to come with me. **2** (协助) assist ♦陪考 assistant examiner

陪伴 péibàn [动] keep … company (*pt, pp* kept) ◇她常常陪伴在奶奶身

边。She often keeps her grandma company.

陪衬 péichèn [动] set off (*pt, pp* set)

陪同 péitóng **I** [动] accompany ◇他陪同外宾参观了工厂。He accompanied the foreigners visiting the factory. **II** [名] guide

培 péi [动] foster

培训 péixùn [动] train ◇新教师需要培训。New teachers need training.

培养 péiyǎng [动] cultivate ◇培养细菌 cultivate bacteria

培育 péiyù [动] **1** (培植养育) cultivate ◇培育幼苗 cultivate seedlings **2** (培养教育) nurture

赔 péi [动] **1** (赔偿) make good ◇损失应该你来赔。You should make good the loss. **2** (亏本) make a loss ◇这次生意我们赔了。We've made a loss in this transaction.

赔本 péiběn [动] make a loss

赔偿 péicháng [动] compensate ◇他应该赔偿我们的损失。He should compensate us for the loss. ◇他们得到了及时的赔偿。They received prompt compensation.

赔了夫人又折兵 péile fūrén yòu zhé bīng pay a double penalty

赔罪 péizuì [动] apologize

佩 pèi [动] **1** (佩带) wear (*pt* wore, *pp* worn) ◇他腰佩一支手枪。He carries a pistol at his belt. **2** (佩服) admire ♦钦佩 esteem

佩带 pèidài [动] wear (*pt* wore, *pp* worn) ◇他胸前佩带着一枚勋章。He is wearing a medal on his chest.

佩服 pèifú [动] admire

配 pèi **I** [动] **1** (指两性) marry **2** (指动物) mate **3** (调和) mix ♦配药 make up a prescription **4** (分派) allocate ♦配售 ration **5** (补充) ◇配钥匙 have a key made ◇配货 replace goods **6** (衬托) match **7** (符合) fit ◇她的穿着和身份很相配。She dresses to fit her role. **II** [名] spouse

配备 pèibèi **I** [动] provide ◇公司给他配备了一辆轿车。The company provided him with a car. **II** [名] equipment

配餐 pèicān **I** [动] ◇配餐要讲究营养均衡。Planning meals demands particular attention to nutritional balance. **II** [名] meal

配方 pèifāng **I** [动] dispense prescriptions **II** [名] prescription

配合 pèihé [动] cooperate ◇他们善于相互配合。They are good at cooperating with each other.

配合 pèihe [形] complementary

配角 pèijué [名] supporting role

配偶 pèi'ǒu (书) [名] spouse

配套 pèitào **I** [动] be a set ◇所有的家具都要配套。The furniture should all be from the same range. **II** [形] coherent

配制 pèizhì [动] **1** (调制) make … up ◇他在酒吧里配制鸡尾酒。He mixes cocktails in a bar. **2** (附衬) add ◇他为这本书配制了插图。He added illustrations to the book.

配置 pèizhì [动] deploy

喷 pēn [动] gush ◇油井终于喷油了。Finally oil gushed from the well.
▷另见 pèn

喷发 pēnfā [动] erupt

喷泉 pēnquán [名] fountain

喷洒 pēnsǎ [动] spray

喷嚏 pēntì [名] sneeze

喷泻 pēnxiè [动] gush

喷嘴 pēnzuǐ [名] nozzle

盆 pén [名] **1** (盛具) basin ♦脸盆 washbasin **2** (盆状物) ♦骨盆 pelvis

盆地 péndì [名] basin

盆盆罐罐 pénpénguànguàn [名] household utensils (*pl*)

喷 pèn 见下文
▷另见 pēn

喷香 pènxiāng [形] delicious

抨 pēng 见下文

抨击 pēngjī [动] attack

怦 pēng [拟] thump ◇我吓得心怦怦直跳。My heart is thumping with fear.

砰 pēng [拟] bang

烹 pēng [动] cook

烹饪 pēngrèn [动] cook ◇他擅长烹饪。He's an excellent cook.

烹调 pēngtiáo [动] cook

朋 péng [名] friend

朋党 péngdǎng [名] clique

朋友 péngyǒu [名] **1** (指友谊) friend **2** (女友) girlfriend **3** (男友) boyfriend

棚 péng [名] awning ◇自行车棚 bicycle shed

蓬 péng **I** [形] dishevelled (英), disheveled (美) **II** [量] clump ◇一蓬草 a clump of grass

蓬勃 péngbó [形] vigorous

蓬松 péngsōng [形] fluffy

蓬头垢面 péng tóu gòu miàn unkempt appearance

鹏 péng 见下文

鹏程万里 péng chéng wàn lǐ go far ◇祝你鹏程万里，事业有成。I hope your undertaking succeeds and that you go far.

澎 péng 见下文

澎湃 péngpài [形] **1** (指波涛) surging **2** (指心情) racing

篷 péng [名] **1** (顶) covering ♦篷车 wagon **2** (帆) sail

膨 péng [动] expand

膨化 pénghuà [动] pop

膨胀 péngzhàng [动] **1** (指体积) expand **2** (指事物) inflate ◇政府有效地抑制了通货膨胀。The government controlled inflation effectively.

捧 pěng **I** [动] **1** (托) hold … in both hands (*pt, pp* held) ◇他手捧一束鲜花。He held a bouquet of flowers in both hands. **2** (奉承) flatter **II** [量] handful ◇一捧花生 a handful of peanuts

捧场 pěngchǎng [动] support ◇感谢各位的捧场。Thanks for everyone's support.

捧腹 pěngfù [动] split one's sides laughing (*pt, pp* split) ◇这段小品令人捧腹。This sketch is side-splittingly funny.

碰 pèng [动] **1** (撞击) hit (*pt, pp* hit) **2** (遇见) bump into ◇我在街上碰到了一位老同学。I bumped into an old classmate in the street. **3** (试探) take a chance (*pt* took, *pp* taken)

碰壁 pèngbì [动] hit a brick wall (*pt, pp* hit)

碰钉子 pèng dīngzi [动] be rebuffed

碰巧 pèngqiǎo [副] by chance ◇我碰巧遇见他。I met him by chance.

碰头 pèngtóu [动] meet (*pt, pp* met)

碰一鼻子灰 pèng yī bízi huī meet with a rebuff

碰撞 pèngzhuàng [动] **1** (撞击) collide **2** (冒犯) offend

批 pī **I** [动] **1** (批示) comment ♦批示 comment **2** (批评) criticize **II** [名] wholesale ◇我们将成批购进材料。We are going to buy the materials wholesale. **III** [量] ◇一批大学生 a group of university students ◇新到的一批货 a new batch of goods

批驳 pībó [动] rebut

批发 pīfā [动] **1** (成批出售) sell … wholesale (*pt, pp* sold) ◇他专门批发建筑材料。He specializes in selling building materials wholesale. **2** (批准转发) be authorized for dispatch

批复 pīfù [动] respond to ◇总经理批复了我们的申请。The managing director has responded to our request.

批改 pīgǎi [动] correct

批量 pīliàng [名] batch

批判 pīpàn [动] **1** (驳斥) repudiate **2** (批评) criticize

批评 pīpíng [动] criticize ◇接受批评 accept criticism

批示 pīshì [动] comment ◇文件上有校长的亲笔批示。The document contained comments from the principal himself.

批准 pīzhǔn [动] approve ◇没有我的批准，谁也不许离开。No one may leave without my approval.

纰 pī [动] unravel

纰漏 pīlòu [名] slip

披 pī [动] **1** (搭) drape … over one's shoulders ◇他披上了大衣。He draped the coat over his shoulders. ◇她披着白色披肩。She's wrapped in a white shawl. **2** (开裂) split (*pt, pp* split)

披风 pīfēng [名] cape

披肝沥胆 pī gān lì dǎn loyal and sincere

披肩 pījiān [名] **1** (指饰物) scarf **2** (指衣服) cape

披荆斩棘 pī jīng zhǎn jí clear away obstacles

披露 pīlù [动] **1** (公布) announce **2** (表露) reveal

披星戴月 pī xīng dài yuè day and night

砒 pī 见下文

砒霜 pīshuāng [名] arsenic

劈 pī **I** [动] **1** (砍) chop ◇他把木头劈成了两半。He chopped the wood in two. **2** (裂开) split (*pt, pp* split) **3** (雷击) strike (*pt, pp* struck) **II** [形] (方) hoarse ◇他嗓子喊劈了。He's shouted himself hoarse. **III** [介] right in ♦劈脸 in one's face ◇他一进门劈脸就问我干了什么。As soon as he came in he asked me straight out what I was doing.
▷另见 pǐ

劈波斩浪 pī bō zhǎn làng weather a storm

劈里啪啦 pīlipālā [拟] pitter-patter

劈头 pītóu [副] **1** (朝头上) right on the head **2** (迎面) in one's face ◇我一出门，劈头遇上了老王。As soon as I went out, I came face to face with Lao Wang. **3** (开头) at the very start ◇他劈头第一句话就问出了什么事。His first words were to ask what was up.

劈头盖脸 pī tóu gài liǎn in one's face

霹 pī 见下文

霹雳 pīlì [名] thunderbolt

皮 pí **I** [名] **1** (表皮) skin **2** (皮革) leather **3** (外皮) covering ♦漆皮 coat of paint **4** (表面) surface **5** (薄片) sheet ♦奶皮儿 skin on the milk **6** (指橡胶) rubber **II** [形] **1** (韧) thick-skinned **2** (变韧的) rubbery **3** (顽皮) naughty

皮尺 píchǐ [名] tape measure

皮肤 pífū [名] skin

皮革 pígé [名] leather

皮货 píhuò [名] fur

皮开肉绽 pí kāi ròu zhàn be horrifically beaten

皮毛 pímáo [名] **1** (指兽皮) fur **2** (指知识) superficial knowledge

皮实 píshi [形] **1** (结实) sturdy **2** (耐用) durable

皮试 píshì [动] have a skin test

皮笑肉不笑 pí xiào ròu bù xiào (贬) put on a false smile ◇他皮笑肉不笑的样子真可恶。His false smile is really unbearable.

皮子 pízi [名] hide

毗 pí 见下文

毗连 pílián [动] border on ◇美国的北部跟加拿大毗连。The United States borders on Canada to the north.

疲 pí [形] **1** (疲劳) tired ◇筋疲力尽 be exhausted **2** (厌倦) tired of

疲惫 píbèi [形] weary

疲乏 pífá [形] tired

疲倦 píjuàn [形] tired

疲劳 píláo [形] **1** (劳累) weary **2** (衰退) weakened

疲软 píruǎn [形] **1** (怠倦) weary **2** (不景气) weak

疲塌 píta [形] slack

疲于奔命 pí yú bēn mìng be constantly on the run

啤 pí 见下文

啤酒 píjiǔ [名] beer

琵 pí 见下文

琵琶 pípá [名] Chinese lute

脾 pí [名] spleen

脾气 píqi [名] **1** (怒气) temper **2** (性情) temperament

脾性 píxìng [名] (方) character

匹 pǐ **I** [动] match **II** [量] **1** (指动物) ◊三匹马 three horses ◊几匹骡子 some mules **2** (指布料) bolt ◊两匹绸缎 two bolts of silk **III** [形] single

匹敌 pǐdí [动] match

匹夫 pǐfū [名] the man on the street

匹配 pǐpèi [动] match

痞 pǐ 见下文

痞子 pǐzi [名] hooligan

劈 pǐ [动] **1** (分开) split (*pt, pp* split) ◊他把线劈成了两股。He split the thread into two strands. **2** (分裂) break off (*pt* broke, *pp* broken) **3** (叉开) open very wide
▷另见 pī

劈叉 pǐchà [动] do the splits

劈柴 pǐchái [动] chop firewood

癖 pǐ [名] addiction

癖好 pǐhào [名] favourite (英) 或 favorite (美) hobby

癖性 pǐxìng [名] inclination

屁 pì **I** [名] wind ♦放屁 fart **II** [形] meaningless ♦屁事 trivialities (*pl*)

屁股 pìgu [名] **1** (指人) bottom **2** (指后部) rear

屁滚尿流 pì gǔn niào liú (贬) scare the hell out of

屁话 pìhuà [名] (讳) rubbish

辟 pì **I** [动] **1** (开辟) open … up ◊这里将辟为工业园区。This will be opened up as industrial land. ◊新辟一块菜地 start a vegetable patch **2** (驳斥) repudiate ♦辟谣 deny a rumour (英) 或 rumor (美) **II** [形] incisive ♦透辟 penetrating
▷另见 bì

媲 pì 见下文

媲美 pìměi [动] rival

僻 pì [形] **1** (僻静) secluded ♦偏僻 out-of-the-way **2** (古怪) eccentric **3** (不常见) rare

僻静 pìjìng [形] secluded

譬 pì [名] analogy ♦譬如 for example ♦譬喻 metaphor

譬如 pìrú [动] take … for example (*pt* took, *pp* taken) ◊譬如饮食习惯，南北各不相同。Taking eating habits as an example, there are big differences between the north and the south.

譬喻 pìyù [名] analogy

片 piān 见下文
▷另见 piàn

片子 piānzi [名] **1** (电影) film (英), movie (美) **2** (X光) X-ray **3** (唱片) record

扁 piān 见下文
▷另见 biǎn

扁舟 piānzhōu [名] skiff

偏 piān [形] **1** (倾斜的) slanting **2** (不公的) biased

偏爱 piān'ài [动] show favouritism (英) 或 favoritism (美) to (*pt* showed, *pp* shown)

偏差 piānchā [名] **1** (指方向) deviation **2** (指工作) error

偏废 piānfèi [动] give unequal emphasis to (*pt* gave, *pp* given) ◊经济增长与环境保护，二者不可偏废。Economic growth and environmental protection should be given equal emphasis.

偏激 piānjī [形] extreme

偏见 piānjiàn [名] prejudice ◊你对他有偏见。You're prejudiced against him.

偏劳 piānláo [动] (敬) go to trouble (*pt* went, *pp* gone) ◊让您偏劳，谢谢了。Thanks for going to so much trouble.

偏离 piān lí [动] deviate from ◊飞机偏离了航线。The plane went off course.

偏僻 piānpì [形] remote

偏偏 piānpiān [副] **1** (表示主观) persistently ◊别人都同意，他偏偏唱反调。Everyone else agreed, but he was persistent in his disagreement. **2** (表示客观) contrary to expectation ◊我去找他，他偏偏离开了。I went to see him, but he happened to be out. **3** (表示范围) only ◇大家我都想到了，偏偏把他给漏了。I thought of everyone, but of all people I left him out.

偏颇 piānpō [形] (书) biased ◇您这种看法有点偏颇。You're a bit biased in your outlook.

偏巧 piānqiǎo [副] **1** (刚好) as luck would have it ◇我正要去找他，偏巧，他来了。I was just going to see him when, as luck would have it, he turned up. **2** (偏偏) as it happens ◇我找他有事，偏巧他不在。I went to see him about something, but as it happens he was out.

偏袒 piāntǎn [动] side with ◇爸爸总是偏袒弟弟。Dad always sides with my younger brother.

偏向 piānxiàng I [动] **1** (袒护) favour (英), favor (美) ◇你不能这么偏向他。You shouldn't favour him like this. **2** (倾向) prefer to II [名] deviation

偏心 piānxīn [动] be biased ◇经理的偏心引起了员工的不满。The manager's bias created dissatisfaction among the workers.

偏重 piānzhòng [动] emphasize

篇 piān I [名] **1** (文章) writing ♦篇章 sections (*pl*) **2** (单张纸) sheet ♦歌篇儿 song sheet II [量] ◇一篇作文 a composition ◇三篇文章 three essays

篇幅 piānfu [名] **1** (指文章长度) length ◇文章篇幅不要过长。The essay shouldn't be overlong. **2** (指篇页数量) space ◇报纸用整版篇幅登载了这条消息。The newspaper gave this story a whole page.

篇目 piānmù [名] **1** (标题) title **2** (目录) contents (*pl*)

篇章 piānzhāng [名] sections (*pl*) ◇篇章布局 structure of an article

便 pián 见下文
▷另见 biàn

便便 piánpián [形] fat ◇他大腹便便。He's got a pot-belly.

便宜 piányi I [形] cheap II [名] small gains (*pl*) III [动] let … off lightly (*pt, pp* let) ◇你不能这么便宜了他。You shouldn't let him off so lightly.

片 piàn I [名] **1** (指薄度) piece ♦纸片儿 scraps of paper **2** (指地区) area II [动] slice III [形] **1** (不全) incomplete ♦片面 one-sided **2** (简短) brief IV [量] **1** (指片状物) ◇两片药 two tablets ◇几片树叶 some leaves **2** (指水陆) stretch ◇一片沼泽地 a stretch of marsh **3** (指声音、心意等) ◇一片忠心 in all sincerity ◇一片掌声 a burst of applause
▷另见 piān

片段 piànduàn [名] extract

片断 piànduàn I [名] **1** (零碎) fragment **2** (片段) extract II [形] fragmentary

片刻 piànkè [名] instant ◇昨晚，我片刻也没离开房间。Last night I didn't leave my room for a moment.

片面 piàmiàn I [名] one side ◇不要听信他的片面之词。You shouldn't listen to his one-sided account. II [形] one-sided

片言只语 piàn yán zhī yǔ just a few words ◇你要经常给我发电邮，哪怕片言只语也好。You should email me often – just a few words will do.

片子 piànzi [名] **1** (薄片) piece ◇玻璃片子 pieces of glass **2** (名片) namecard

骗 piàn [动] **1** (欺骗) deceive **2** (骗得) swindle ♦骗钱 swindle

骗局 piànjú [名] swindle

骗取 piànqǔ [动] ◇他骗取了上级的信任。He wormed his way into his boss's confidence. ◇你骗取不了我的同情。You can't trick me into sympathizing with you.

骗术 piànshù [名] trick

骗子 piànzi [名] swindler

剽 piāo I [动] rob II [形] agile

剽悍 piāohàn [形] agile and brave

剽窃 piāoqiè [动] plagiarize

漂 piāo [动] **1** (浮) float **2** (流动) drift
▷另见 piǎo, piào

漂泊 piāobó [动] **1** (指船舶) float **2** (指生活) drift

漂浮 piāofú **I** [动] float **II** [形] superficial

漂流 piāoliú [动] drift

漂移 piāoyí [动] drift

漂游 piāoyóu [动] **1** (浮动) float **2** (漂泊) drift

缥 piāo 见下文

缥缈 piāomiǎo [形] indistinct

飘 piāo [动] **1** (飞扬) flutter **2** (指腿、脚) wobble

飘荡 piāodàng [动] **1** (浮动) float **2** (漂泊) drift

飘动 piāodòng [动] drift

飘零 piāolíng [动] **1** (坠落) fall (*pt* fell, *pp* fallen) **2** (流浪) wander

飘飘然 piāopiāorán [形] **1** (轻飘飘) floating **2** (很得意) smug

飘洒 piāosǎ [动] fall (*pt* fell, *pp* fallen)

飘洒 piāosa [形] graceful

飘扬 piāoyáng [动] flutter

飘摇 piāoyáo [动] sway

飘逸 piāoyì **I** [形] (书) graceful **II** [动] drift

嫖 piáo [动] visit prostitutes

嫖客 piáokè [名] client (*of a prostitute*)

瓢 piáo [名] ladle

瓢泼大雨 piáopōdàyǔ downpour

漂 piǎo [动] **1** (漂白) bleach **2** (冲洗) rinse
▷另见 piāo, piào

漂白 piǎobái [动] bleach

漂洗 piǎoxǐ [动] rinse

瞟 piǎo [动] give a sidelong look (*pt* gave, *pp* given)

票 piào [名] **1** (作凭证) ticket **2** (指钞票) note (英), bill (美) **3** (指戏曲) amateur performance

票房价值 piàofáng jiàzhí [名] box office takings (*pl*)

票据 piàojù [名] **1** (汇票) note (英), bill (美) **2** (凭证) voucher

票子 piàozi [名] (口) note (英), bill(美)

漂 piào 见下文
▷另见 piāo, piǎo

漂亮 piàoliang [形] **1** (好看) good-looking ◇过新年了，孩子们穿上了漂亮衣服。At New Year, the children wore beautiful clothes. ◇你女儿真漂亮。Your daughter is very pretty. **2** (精彩) wonderful ◇这场球踢得漂亮。It was a brilliant football match.

撇 piē [动] **1** (弃) cast … aside (*pt, pp* cast) ◇他撇下家庭，外出创业。He cast aside his family and went off to make a new career for himself. **2** (舀) skim
▷另见 piě

瞥 piē [动] shoot a glance at (*pt, pp* shot) ◇他瞥了我一眼。He shot me a glance.

瞥视 piēshì [动] glance at

撇 piě **I** [动] **1** (扔) throw (*pt* threw, *pp* thrown) **2** (扭) curl ♦撇嘴 curl one's lip **II** [量] tuft ◇两撇胡子 two tufts of facial hair
▷另见 piē

撇开 piěkāi [动] leave … aside (*pt, pp* left) ◇撇开成见 leave one's prejudices aside

撇嘴 piězuǐ [动] curl one's lip

拼 pīn [动] **1** (合) join together ◇我们把两张桌子拼了起来。We joined the two tables together. ◇拼图游戏 jigsaw puzzle **2** (竭尽全力) go all out (*pt* went, *pp* gone) ♦拼命 with all one's might **3** (字、词) spell ◇你能拼一下这个词吗？ Can you spell this word?

拼搏 pīnbó [动] go all out (*pt* went, *pp* gone) ◇经过90分钟的拼搏，我们终于赢得了那场足球赛。By going all out for ninety minutes, we finally won the football match.

拼凑 pīncòu [动] piece … together

拼命 pīnmìng [动] **1** (不要命) risk one's life ◇歹徒见她要拼命转身跑掉了。When the thugs saw that she was ready to fight to the death, they turned and fled. **2** (努力) go all out (*pt* went, *pp* gone) ◇他为了给父亲治病拼命挣钱。He went all out to earn the money to cure his father.

拼盘 pīnpán [名] cold platter

拼死 pīnsǐ [动] risk one's life

拼写 pīnxiě [动] spell

拼音 pīnyīn [名] Pinyin

姘 pīn [动] (贬) have an affair ♦姘妇 lover ♦姘夫 lover

姘头 pīntou [名] (贬) lover

贫 pín I [形] 1 (穷) poor ♦贫民 the poor 2 (少) deficient ♦贫血 anaemia (英), anemia (美) II [动] (方) be a chatterbox

贫乏 pínfá [形] lacking ◇自然资源贫乏 lacking in natural resources

贫寒 pínhán [形] (书) impoverished

贫瘠 pínjí [形] poor

贫苦 pínkǔ [形] poverty-stricken

贫困 pínkùn [形] impoverished

贫民 pínmín [名] the poor (*pl*)

贫民窟 pínmínkū [名] slums (*pl*)

贫穷 pínqióng [形] poor ◇贫穷是造成犯罪的原因之一。Poverty is one of the causes of crime.

贫嘴 pínzuǐ [形] (方) garrulous

频 pín [副] frequently ◇他频频旷课。He frequently plays truant.

频道 píndào [名] channel

频繁 pínfán [形] frequent

频率 pínlǜ [名] 1 (物) frequency 2 (指心脏) rate

频频 pínpín [副] frequently

品 pǐn I [名] 1 (物品) article ♦商品 merchandise 2 (等级) grade ♦精品 special product 3 (种类) type ♦品种 variety 4 (品质) character ♦品德 moral character II [动] taste

品尝 pǐncháng [动] savour (英), savor (美)

品德 pǐndé [名] moral character

品格 pǐngé [名] character

品级 pǐnjí [名] grade

品貌 pǐnmào [名] appearance

品牌 pǐnpái [名] brand

品评 pǐnpíng [动] (书) judge

品头论足 pǐn tóu lùn zú make personal remarks

品位 pǐnwèi [名] 1 (质量) quality 2 (喜好) taste

品味 pǐnwèi [动] 1 (尝) taste 2 (体会) appreciate ◇品味古典音乐 appreciate classical music

品行 pǐnxíng [名] character and conduct

品性 pǐnxìng [名] nature

品质 pǐnzhì [名] 1 (品德) character 2 (质量) quality ◇这些种子品质优良。These are top-quality seeds.

品种 pǐnzhǒng [名] 1 (动) breed 2 (植) species 3 (指产品) kind ◇超市里货物品种齐全。There are all kinds of products in the supermarket.

聘 pìn [动] engage

聘礼 pìnlǐ [名] betrothal gift

聘请 pìnqǐng [动] invite

聘任 pìnrèn [动] engage

聘用 pìnyòng [动] engage

乒 pīng I [拟] bang ◇乒的一声气球爆了。The balloon exploded with a bang. II [名] (乒乓球) table tennis ◇世乒赛 Table Tennis World Championships

乒乓 pīngpāng I [拟] bang ◇隔壁一天到晚的乒乓声不断。There was an incessant banging noise next door. II [名] ping-pong

平 píng I [形] 1 (平坦) flat ♦平原 plain 2 (安定) calm ◇心平气和 even-tempered 3 (普通) ordinary 4 (平均) even ♦平分 fifty-fifty 5 (指比分) ♦平局 a draw II [动] 1 (夷平) level 2 (指成绩) equal 3 (镇压) suppress

平安 píng'ān [形] safe and sound

平常 píngcháng I [形] common II [副] usually

平淡 píngdàn [形] 1 (语气、文章) flat 2 (谈话、生活) dull

平等 píngděng [形] equal

平定 píngdìng [动] 1 (叛乱、暴乱) put … down (*pt, pp* put) 2 (情绪) calm … down

平凡 píngfán [形] uneventful

平反 píngfǎn [动] overturn a sentence ◇他被平反了。His sentence was overturned.

平方 píngfāng [名] **1** (数) square **2** (平方米) square metre (英) 或 meter (美)

平房 píngfáng [名] single-storey house

平分 píngfēn [动] divide equally ◇咱们一起干，赚了钱平分。Let's do the work together, and go halves on the money we earn.

平和 pínghé [形] **1** (指人) placid **2** (指药物) mild

平衡 pínghéng [名] balance ◇保持平衡 maintain a balance ◇平衡收支 balance revenue and expenditure

平缓 pínghuǎn [形] gentle

平静 píngjìng [形] calm

平均 píngjūn [形] average

平米 píngmǐ [名] square metre (英) 或 meter (美)

平民 píngmín [名] the common people (*pl*)

平平 píngpíng [形] mediocre

平铺直叙 píng pū zhí xù pedestrian ◇这篇文章虽然平铺直叙，但十分感人。Although this essay is a little pedestrian, it's deeply moving all the same.

平起平坐 píng qǐ píng zuò be on an equal footing ◇他和总经理平起平坐。He's on an equal footing with the general manager.

平日 píngrì [名] the usual

平生 píngshēng [名] one's whole life ◇这是他平生最大的遗憾。This is the greatest regret of his whole life.

平时 píngshí [副] usually

平手 píngshǒu [名] draw ◇我看这场拳击会成平手。I think the fight will end in a draw.

平台 píngtái [名] platform

平坦 píngtǎn [形] flat

平稳 píngwěn [形] **1** (稳定) stable **2** (不摇晃) steady

平息 píngxī [动] quieten (英) 或 quiet (美) down

平心而论 píng xīn ér lùn in all fairness

平心静气 píng xīn jìng qì calmly

平行 píngxíng [形] parallel

平易 píngyì [形] amiable

平庸 píngyōng [形] mediocre

平原 píngyuán [名] plain

平整 píngzhěng I [动] level II [形] neat

评 píng [动] **1** (评论) criticize ♦批评 criticize ♦书评 book review ◇他的新书获得好评。His new book was well received. **2** (评判) judge ♦评分 mark **3** (选) select

评比 píngbǐ [动] appraise

评定 píngdìng [动] assess

评估 pínggū [动] evaluate

评价 píngjià [动] evaluate ◇后人对他的一生给予了高度的评价。He was very much revered by later generations.

评介 píngjiè [动] review

评论 pínglùn [动] review

评判 píngpàn [动] judge

评书 píngshū [名] storytelling

评述 píngshù [动] comment on

评说 píngshuō [动] evaluate

评头论足 píng tóu lùn zú make personal remarks

评选 píngxuǎn [动] select ◇印度小姐被大众评选为新一届世界小姐。The public selected Miss India as the new Miss World.

评议 píngyì [动] consult

评语 píngyǔ [名] comment

坪 píng [名] level ground ♦草坪 lawn

苹 píng 见下文

苹果 píngguǒ [名] apple

凭 píng I [动] rely on ◇他总是凭经验解决难题。He relies on experience to solve his problems. ◇他是凭能力当上市长的。He became mayor thanks to his own ability. II [介] ◇减价商品能凭礼券购买。Cut-price products can be paid for with gift vouchers. ◇你凭什么说我们的产品不合格？ On what basis are you saying that our products are not up to standard? **III** [名] evidence ♦凭据 credentials (*pl*) ◊真凭实据 hard evidence **IV** [连] no matter ◊凭他怎么叫，也没人答理他。No matter what he asked for, no one took any notice of him.

凭借 píngjiè [动] be based on ◊公司凭借高质量的产品占领市场。The company's domination of the market is based on the high quality of its products.

凭据 píngjù [名] credentials (*pl*)

凭空 píngkōng [副] out of thin air ◊小报凭空捏造最荒谬的新闻。The tabloids make up the most ridiculous stories out of thin air.

凭仗 píngzhàng [动] rely on

凭证 píngzhèng [名] evidence

屏 píng [名] (屏风) screen ▷另见 bǐng

屏蔽 píngbì [名] screen

屏风 píngfēng [名] screen

屏幕 píngmù [名] screen

屏障 píngzhàng [名] barrier

瓶 píng [名] bottle

萍 píng 见下文

萍水相逢 píng shuǐ xiāng féng have a chance encounter ◊我和他在巴黎萍水相逢。I had a chance encounter with him in Paris.

坡 pō [名] slope ♦山坡 slope

坡度 pōdù [名] gradient

泼 pō **I** [动] splash **II** [形] shrewish ♦泼妇 harridan

泼辣 pōla [形] bold

泼冷水 pō lěngshuǐ [动] ◊他有信心的时候，不要给他泼冷水。Don't dampen his spirits when he's feeling confident.

颇 pō [副] rather

婆 pó [名] **1** (老年妇女) old lady ♦老太婆 old lady **2** (丈夫的母亲) mother-in-law (*pl* mothers-in-law) ♦公婆 parents-in-law (*pl*)

婆家 pójia [名] husband's family

婆婆妈妈 pópomāmā fussy

迫 pò **I** [动] **1** (逼迫) force **2** (接近) approach **II** [形] urgent ◊迫不及待 cannot wait

迫不得已 pò bù dé yǐ have no alternative ◊市长迫不得已向市民道歉。The mayor had no alternative but to apologize to the townspeople.

迫不及待 pò bù jí dài be unable to wait ◊她迫不及待地把房子卖掉。She couldn't wait to sell the house.

迫害 pòhài [动] persecute

迫降 pòjiàng [动] crash-land

迫近 pòjìn [动] approach

迫切 pòqiè [形] pressing

迫使 pòshǐ [动] necessitate

迫在眉睫 pò zài méi jié be imminent ◊解决交通堵塞迫在眉睫。A solution to the traffic jam problem is imminent.

破 pò **I** [形] **1** (受损) broken ◊裤子都被穿破了。The trousers were completely worn out. **2** (烂) lousy ◊没人愿做那破工作。No one is willing to do that lousy job. **II** [动] **1** (受损) cut ◊他的膝盖破了。He's cut his knee. **2** (破除) break (*pt* broke, *pp* broken) ♦破例 make an exception ◊我不想把10镑钱破开。I don't want to have to break a ten pound note. ◊破世界记录 break a world record **3** (钱、工夫) spend (*pt, pp* spent) **4** (揭穿) expose ♦破案 solve a case **5** (打败) defeat

破败 pòbài [形] **1** (家族、经济) declining **2** (房子、城市建筑) run-down

破产 pòchǎn [动] go bankrupt (*pt* went, *pp* gone)

破除 pòchú [动] do away with

破费 pòfèi [动] spend money (*pt, pp* spent)

破釜沉舟 pò fǔ chén zhōu burn one's bridges

破格 pògé [动] break a rule (*pt* broke, *pp* broken)

破罐破摔 pò guàn pò shuāi not learn

from one's mistakes ◊他失业后破罐破摔。After he lost his job, he learned nothing from his mistakes.

破坏 pòhuài [动] **1** (建筑、环境、文物、公物) destroy **2** (团结、社会秩序) undermine **3** (协定、法规、规章) violate **4** (计划) bring … down (*pt, pp* brought) **5** (名誉) damage

破解 pòjiě [动] decipher

破镜重圆 pò jìng chóng yuán get back together

破旧 pòjiù [形] shabby

破烂 pòlàn **I** [形] ragged **II** [名] scrap

破例 pòlì [动] make an exception

破裂 pòliè [动] **1** (谈判) break down (*pt* broke, *pp* broken) **2** (感情) break up **3** (外交关系) break off

破落 pòluò [形] declining

破灭 pòmiè [动] destroy

破碎 pòsuì **I** [动] **1** (破成碎块) smash **2** (指梦想) break (*pt* broke, *pp* broken) **II** [形] broken

破天荒 pòtiānhuāng be unprecedented ◊他破天荒地给妻子买了一束玫瑰。In an unprecedented move, he bought his wife a bouquet of roses.

破译 pòyì [动] crack

破折号 pòzhéhào [名] dash

魄 pò [名] **1** (精神) spirit ♦魂魄 soul **2** (魄力) courage ♦气魄 verve

魄力 pòlì [名] courage

剖 pōu [动] **1** (破开) cut open (*pt, pp* cut) ♦解剖 dissect **2** (分析) analyse (英), analyze (美)

剖白 pōubái [动] explain oneself

剖面 pōumiàn [名] section

剖析 pōuxī [动] analyse (英), analyze (美)

扑 pū [动] **1** (冲向) rush at ◊狮子猛地向猎物扑过去。The lion rushed after its prey. **2** (专注于) devote ◊他一心扑在工作上。He's totally devoted to his work. **3** (扑打) swat ◊他用树枝扑蜻蜓。He used a branch to swat at dragonflies. **4** (翅膀) beat (*pt* beat, *pp* beaten)

扑鼻 pūbí [动] be pungent ◊香水味扑鼻。The smell of the perfume was pungent.

扑哧 pūchī [拟] **1** (指笑声) chuckle **2** (指撒气) hiss

扑打 pūdǎ [动] beat (*pt* beat, *pp* beaten)

扑救 pūjiù [动] put … out (*pt, pp* put)

扑克 pūkè [名] poker

扑空 pūkōng [动] come away empty-handed (*pt* came, *pp* come)

扑灭 pūmiè [动] put … out (*pt, pp* put)

扑朔迷离 pūshuò mílí complicated and confusing

扑簌 pūsù [形] streaming ◊听到那个消息，他的眼泪就扑簌簌地落了下来。When he heard the news, tears streamed from his eyes.

扑腾 pūtēng [拟] thud

扑腾 pūteng [动] **1** (打水) splash **2** (跳动) flop

扑通 pūtōng [拟] plop

铺 pū [动] **1** (摊开) spread (*pt, pp* spread) **2** (铺设) lay (*pt, pp* laid) ▷另见 pù

铺垫 pūdiàn [动] **1** (垫子) cushion **2** (指叙事) foreshadow

铺盖 pūgài [动] cover

铺盖 pūgai [名] bedroll

铺设 pūshè [动] lay (*pt, pp* laid)

铺天盖地 pū tiān gài dì all over the place

铺张 pūzhāng [形] extravagant

仆 pú [动] (旧) servant

仆人 púrén [名] servant

匍 pú 见下文

匍匐 púfú [动] grovel

菩 pú 见下文

菩萨 púsà [名] **1** (宗) bodhisattva **2** (善人) saint ◊老婆婆像菩萨一样善良。The old lady is as kind as a saint.

葡 pú 见下文

葡萄 pútáo [名] grape

朴 pǔ 见下文

朴实 pǔshí [形] **1** (简朴) simple **2** (诚实) honest

朴素 pǔsù [形] **1** (衣着) plain **2** (生活) simple **3** (语言) plain

圃 pǔ [名] garden

普 pǔ [形] general

普遍 pǔbiàn **I** [形] common **II** [副] commonly

普及 pǔjí [动] **1** (传布) spread (*pt, pp* spread) **2** (推广) popularize

普通 pǔtōng [形] common

谱 pǔ **I** [名] **1** (指烹饪) book **2** (指音乐) score **3** (指棋) manual **4** (指家族) family records (*pl*) **5** (口) (把握) confidence ◊这项工程需要多少钱他心里有谱儿。He is fairly confident about how much money this project will require. **II** [动] set to music (*pt, pp* set)

谱写 pǔxiě [动] compose

谱子 pǔzi [名] score

铺 pù [名] **1** (商店) shop ♦杂货铺 general store **2** (床) plank bed ♦卧铺 berth
▷另见 pū

铺面 pùmiàn [名] shop front

铺位 pùwèi [名] bunk

铺子 pùzi [名] (口) shop

瀑 pù [名] waterfall

瀑布 pùbù [名] waterfall

曝 pù [动] (书) expose … to the sun

曝露 pùlù [动] (书) expose

曝晒 pùshài [动] expose … to strong sunlight

Qq

七 qī [数] seven ◇七年 seven years

七零八落 qī líng bā luò scattered around ◇屋子里七零八落地放着一些书。Books were scattered around the room.

七上八下 qī shàng bā xià be agitated

七十二行 qīshí'èr háng [名] all sorts of occupations (*pl*)

七手八脚 qī shǒu bā jiǎo with great commotion

沏 qī [动] brew ◇她沏了壶茶。She made a pot of tea.

妻 qī [名] wife (*pl* wives) ♦未婚妻 fiancée

妻小 qīxiǎo [名] wife and children

妻子 qīzi [名] wife (*pl* wives)

柒 qī [数] *an elaborate form of "seven", used in writing cheques etc to prevent mistakes and forgery*

栖 qī [动] perch ♦两栖动物 amphibian

栖身 qīshēn [动] (书) inhabit

栖息 qīxī [动] roost

凄 qī [形] (书) **1** (寒冷) cold **2** (萧条) miserable ♦凄凉 desolate **3** (悲伤) sad

凄惨 qīcǎn [形] tragic

凄厉 qīlì [形] (书) **1** (风声) howling **2** (叫声) shrill

凄凉 qīliáng [形] dreary

萋 qī 见下文

萋萋 qīqī [形] (书) luxuriant

戚 qī [名] (亲人) relative ♦亲戚 relative

期 qī **I** [名] **1** (预定时间) time limit ♦到期 expire **2** (一段时间) period of time ♦假期 holiday **II** [量] **1** (指训练班) class **2** (指杂志、报纸) edition **III** [动] expect

期待 qīdài [动] await

期货 qīhuò [名] futures (*pl*)

期刊 qīkān [名] periodical

期盼 qīpàn [动] await

期望 qīwàng **I** [名] expectations (*pl*) **II** [动] expect

期限 qīxiàn [名] time limit

欺 qī [动] **1** (欺骗) deceive **2** (欺负) bully

欺负 qīfu [动] bully

欺行霸市 qī háng bà shì monopolize

欺凌 qīlíng [动] humiliate

欺骗 qīpiàn [动] deceive

欺生 qīshēng [动] take advantage of a fresh face (*pt* took, *pp* taken)

欺侮 qīwǔ [动] (书) bully

欺压 qīyā [动] tyrannize

欺诈 qīzhà [动] swindle ◇欺诈他人钱财 swindle people out of their money

漆 qī **I** [名] lacquer ♦油漆 paint **II** [动] paint

漆黑 qīhēi [形] pitch-black ◇房间里一片漆黑。The room was in complete darkness.

蹊 qī 见下文

蹊跷 qīqiāo [形] odd

齐 qí **I** [形] **1** (整齐) neat **2** (一致) joint **3** (完备) ready ◇人都到齐了。Everyone is present. **II** [动] **1** (达到) reach ◇水深齐腰。The water is waist deep. **2** (取齐) level **III** [副] at the same time

齐备 qíbèi [形] ready

齐全 qíquán [形] complete

齐心 qíxīn [动] be of one mind ◇大家齐心了，事情就好办了。With everyone working together, everything will be well managed.

齐心协力 qí xīn xié lì join forces

齐整 qízhěng [形] neat

其 qí [代] (书) **1** (他的) his ◇他是演员，其父也是演员。He's an actor, and his father is also an actor. **2** (她的) her **3** (它的) its **4** (他们的、她们的、它们的) their **5** (他) him **6** (她) her **7** (它) it ◇我们应尽量促其成功。We must make sure that it is successful. **8** (他们、她们、它们) them **9** (那个) that

其次 qícì [代] **1** (下一个) ◇其次要做的事是什么？ What are we going to do next? **2** (次要的) the second

其貌不扬 qí mào bù yáng plain

其实 qíshí [副] actually ◇其实不然。Actually, it wasn't like that. ◇他看起来很壮，其实身体不好。He looks very strong, but he's actually in poor health.

其它 qítā [代] other

其他 qítā [代] other ◇除了看书，他还有很多其他爱好。Apart from reading, he has a lot of other hobbies. ◇我不知道，你问其他人吧。I don't know, ask someone else. ◇还有其他事情没有？ Is there anything else?

其余 qíyú [代] the rest

其中 qízhōng [名] ◇他有六套西服，其中两套是黑色的。He has six suits, of which two are black. ◇学校有50位老师，其中10位是男老师。The school has 50 teachers, and ten of them are male.

奇 qí **I** [形] **1** (非常少见的) strange ♦奇闻 fantastic story ♦奇事 miracle **2** (出人意料的) unexpected ♦奇袭 surprise attack ♦奇遇 lucky encounter **II** [动] surprise ♦惊奇 surprise ◇不足为奇 be not at all surprising **III** [副] unusually ◇天气奇冷。The weather is unusually cold.
▷另见 jī

奇才 qícái [名] genius ◇足球奇才 footballing genius

奇耻大辱 qí chǐ dà rǔ a crying shame

奇怪 qíguài [形] strange

奇观 qíguān [名] wonder ◇世界七大奇观 the seven wonders of the world

奇迹 qíjì [名] miracle

奇妙 qímiào [形] wonderful

奇缺 qíquē [动] be very short of

奇特 qítè [形] peculiar

奇闻 qíwén [名] incredible story ◇简直是天下奇闻！ That really is the most incredible story!

奇形怪状 qí xíng guài zhuàng grotesque

奇异 qíyì [形] **1** (奇怪) strange **2** (惊异) astonished ◇他用奇异的目光看着我。He looked at me in astonishment.

奇遇 qíyù [名] chance encounter

祈 qí [动] (书) **1** (祈祷) pray **2** (希望) wish ♦祈求 invoke

歧 qí [形] **1** (途、路) forked **2** (不一致) different

歧路 qílù [名] (书) (喻) wrong turning ◇他走上了条人生歧路。He took a wrong turning in life.

歧视 qíshì [动] discriminate ◇种族歧视 racial discrimination ◇不要歧视残疾人。Don't discriminate against handicapped people.

歧途 qítú [名] wrong path ◇误入歧途 go astray

歧义 qíyì [名] ambiguity

脐 qí [名] navel

脐带 qídài [名] (生理) umbilical cord

崎 qí 见下文

崎岖 qíqū [形] rugged

骑 qí **I** [动] ride (*pt* rode, *pp* ridden) **II** [名] cavalry

棋 qí [名] chess ♦围棋 go (*board game*)

棋子 qízǐ [名] piece

旗 qí [名] flag ♦锦旗 silk banner

旗鼓相当 qí gǔ xiāngdāng be well-matched

旗开得胜 qí kāi dé shèng win in the first contest

旗袍 qípáo [名] cheongsam

旗帜 qízhì [名] **1** (旗子) banner **2** (立

场) stand **3** (榜样) model

鳍 qí [名] fin

乞 qǐ [动] beg ♦行乞 go begging

乞丐 qǐgài [名] beggar

乞求 qǐqiú [动] beg ◇乞求宽恕 beg for forgiveness

乞讨 qǐtǎo [动] beg

岂 qǐ [副] (书) how ◇工作很多，岂敢懈怠！ With so much on, how can you dare be so lazy?

岂敢 qǐgǎn [动] dare ◇我岂敢不承担责任？ Do I dare shirk the responsibility?

岂有此理 qǐ yǒu cǐ lǐ outrageous

企 qǐ [动] look forward to

企鹅 qǐ'é [名] penguin

企及 qǐjí [动] hope ◇这个目标无法企及。There's no hope for this cause.

企盼 qǐpàn [动] (书) wait in hope

企求 qǐqiú [动] (书) seek (*pt, pp* sought)

企图 qǐtú **I** [动] plan **II** [名] (贬) plan

企业 qǐyè [名] enterprise ◇国有企业 state-owned enterprise

启 qǐ [动] **1** (打开) open ♦开启 open **2** (开导) enlighten ♦启发 enlighten **3** (开始) start

启程 qǐchéng [动] set out (*pt, pp* set)

启迪 qǐdí [动] enlighten ◇他的话给了我们很多启迪。We found his words very enlightening.

启动 qǐdòng [动] start

启发 qǐfā **I** [动] inspire ◇我从这个故事里得到很大启发。I drew a lot of inspiration from this story. **II** [名] inspiration

启蒙 qǐméng [动] **1** (促使思想进步) enlighten **2** (传授基本知识) impart rudimentary knowledge ◇启蒙读物 early learning materials

启示 qǐshì [动] enlighten ◇她从这则寓言中得到了启示。She was very inspired by the parable.

启事 qǐshì [名] announcement ◇寻人启事 missing persons announcement

启用 qǐyòng [动] start using

启运 qǐyùn [动] begin shipping (*pt* began, *pp* begun)

起 qǐ **I** [动] **1** (起来) rise (*pt* rose, *pp* risen) ♦起立 stand up **2** (取出) remove ◇起瓶盖 remove a bottle top **3** (长出) form ◇脚上起泡 form a blister on one's foot **4** (产生) become (*pt* became, *pp* become) ◇起疑心 become suspicious **5** (拟订) sketch out ♦起草 draft **6** (建立) establish ◇白手起家 make a fortune from nothing **II** [量] ◇一起交通事故 a traffic accident ◇一起火灾 a fire

起步 qǐbù [动] get going ◇我们的事业才刚刚起步。Our careers have only just got going.

起草 qǐcǎo [动] draft

起程 qǐchéng [动] set out (*pt, pp* set) ◇我们起程前往巴黎。We set out in the direction of Paris.

起初 qǐchū [名] origin ◇他起初在班里排名第一。Originally he was top of the class.

起点 qǐdiǎn [名] starting point

起动 qǐdòng [动] start

起飞 qǐfēi [动] take off (*pt* took, *pp* taken) ◇飞机准时起飞。The plane took off on time. ◇中国经济起飞了。China's economy has taken off.

起伏 qǐfú [动] undulate

起哄 qǐhòng [动] **1** (捣乱) create a disturbance **2** (开玩笑) mock

起家 qǐjiā [动] build ... up (*pt, pp* built) ◇他靠卖服装起家。He built himself up by selling clothes.

起见 qǐjiàn [动] be for ◇为方便起见 for the sake of convenience ◇为安全起见 for safety's sake

起劲 qǐjìn [形] enthusiastic

起居 qǐjū [名] everyday life

起来 qǐlái [动] **1** (站起或坐起) get up ◇赶快起来，来客人了。Get up quick, there's a visitor. **2** (起床) get up ◇起来吧，天都亮了。Time to get up – it's already light.

起立 qǐlì [动] stand up (*pt, pp* stood)

起落 qǐluò [动] rise and fall (*pt* rose and fell, *pp* risen and fallen)

起码 qǐmǎ [形] minimum ◇起码的常识 the minimum of common sense ◇一本词典起码要50块。A dictionary should cost at least fifty yuan.

起色 qǐsè [名] improvement

起身 qǐshēn [动] set out (*pt, pp* set) ◇我明天天亮就起身。I am setting out at first light tomorrow.

起誓 qǐshì [动] swear (*pt, pp* sworn)

起死回生 qǐ sǐ huí shēng bring ... back from the dead

起诉 qǐsù [动] sue ◇向法院起诉 take a case to court

起头 qǐtóu **I** [动] start **II** [名] the beginning ◇我们起头遇到些困难，后来就好多了。We encountered some difficulties at the beginning, but later things got a lot better.

起先 qǐxiān [名] the beginning

起义 qǐyì [动] revolt ◇农民起义 peasant revolt

起因 qǐyīn [名] cause

起用 qǐyòng [动] employ

起源 qǐyuán **I** [动] originate ◇这种舞起源于亚洲。This type of dancing originated in Asia. **II** [名] origin ◇生命的起源 the origins of life

起早贪黑 qǐ zǎo tān hēi work from dawn until dusk

起子 qǐzi [名] **1** (开瓶盖) bottle opener **2** (螺丝刀) screwdriver

气 qì **I** [名] **1** (气体) gas ♦毒气 poison gas **2** (空气) air ◇这球没气了。This ball is deflated. **3** (气息) breath ◇上气不接下气 out of breath **4** (精神) mood ◇垂头丧气 be dejected **5** (气味) smell ♦臭气 stink **6** (习气) manner ♦孩子气 childishness ♦书生气 scholarly manner **7** (怒气) anger ◇忍下这口气 put up with someone's attitude **8** (医) qi **II** [动] **1** (生气) be angry **2** (使生气) provoke ◇别气我！ Don't provoke me!

气冲冲 qìchōngchōng [形] furious

气度 qìdù [名] bearing

气氛 qìfēn [名] atmosphere

气愤 qìfèn [形] angry ◇我们对这种恶劣行为十分气愤。We got extremely angry about this terrible behaviour.

气概 qìgài [名] spirit

气功 qìgōng [名] qigong

气候 qìhòu [名] climate

气急败坏 qìjí bàihuài exasperated

气力 qìlì [名] strength

气量 qìliàng [名] tolerance

气流 qìliú [名] air flow

气恼 qìnǎo [形] sulky

气派 qìpài [名] impressive manner

气魄 qìpò [名] imposing manner

气球 qìqiú [名] balloon

气色 qìsè [名] complexion

气势 qìshì [名] imposing manner

气体 qìtǐ [名] gas

气味 qìwèi [名] smell

气息 qìxī [名] **1** (呼吸) breath **2** (气味) smell ◇春天的气息 the smell of spring **3** (指时代、生活) sign ◇时代气息 a sign of the times

气象 qìxiàng [名] **1** (大气现象) weather **2** (气象学) meteorology **3** (情景) atmosphere

气压 qìyā [名] air pressure

气质 qìzhì [名] disposition

弃 qì [动] abandon

弃权 qìquán [动] abstain ♦弃权票 abstention

汽 qì [名] **1** (气体) vapour (英), vapor (美) **2** (蒸气) steam

汽车 qìchē [名] car ♦公共汽车 bus

汽化 qìhuà [动] (物) vaporize

汽水 qìshuǐ [名] fizzy drink

汽油 qìyóu [名] petrol (英), gasoline (美)

泣 qì [动] (书) weep (*pt, pp* wept)

泣不成声 qì bù chéng shēng choke with tears ◇她哭得泣不成声。She was crying so much that she couldn't get the words out.

契 qì **I** [动] agree ♦默契 tacit agreement **II** [名] deed

契合 qìhé [动] agree with

契约 qìyuē [名] contract

砌 qì [动] build (*pt, pp* built) ◇他在房子后面砌了堵墙。He has built a wall at the back of the house.

器 qì [名] **1** (器具) utensil ♦乐器 musical instrument ♦瓷器 china **2** (器官) organ

器材 qìcái [名] equipment

器官 qìguān [名] organ

器具 qìjù [名] utensil

器量 qìliàng [名] tolerance

器皿 qìmǐn [名] container

器械 qìxiè [名] instrument ◇手术器械 surgical instruments

器重 qìzhòng [动] think highly of (*pt, pp* thought) ◇上司很器重他。The boss thinks highly of him.

憩 qì [动] (书) rest

掐 qiā [动] **1** (截断) pinch **2** (按住) throttle

掐算 qiāsuàn [动] count … on one's fingers

卡 qiǎ **I** [动] **1** (不能动) get stuck **2** (脖子) wedge **3** (阻挡) block **II** [名] **1** (指夹东西) fastener ♦发卡 hairpin **2** (关卡) checkpoint ♦边卡 border checkpoint
▷另见 kǎ

卡壳 qiǎké [动] get stuck

洽 qià **I** [形] harmonious **II** [动] consult ♦洽谈 hold talks

洽谈 qiàtán [动] hold talks (*pt, pp* held)

恰 qià [副] **1** (适当) appropriately **2** (刚好) exactly

恰当 qiàdàng [形] appropriate

恰好 qiàhǎo [副] luckily ◇他恰好也在。Luckily he's here as well.

恰恰 qiàqià [副] exactly ◇这恰恰是我们不想看到的。This is exactly what we didn't want to see.

恰巧 qiàqiǎo [副] luckily ◇恰巧我带着这本书。Luckily I had the book with me.

恰如其分 qià rú qí fèn appropriate

千 qiān **I** [数] thousand **II** [形] many

千差万别 qiān chā wàn bié different in every possible way

千方百计 qiān fāng bǎi jì do everything in one's power ◇医护人员千方百计抢救病人。The hospital staff did everything in their power to save the patient.

千古 qiāngǔ [名] ◇千古名言 ancient wisdom ◇千古遗恨 eternal regret

千金 qiānjīn [名] (敬) daughter

千钧一发 qiān jūn yī fà at the crucial moment

千里迢迢 qiān lǐ tiáotiáo from far away

千篇一律 qiān piān yīlǜ follow the same pattern

千万 qiānwàn **I** [数] ten million **II** [副] ◇你千万要记住老师的话。Be sure to remember what the teacher said. ◇你千万别做傻事。You absolutely mustn't do anything stupid.

仟 qiān [数] *an elaborate form of "thousand", used in writing cheques etc to prevent mistakes and forgery*

迁 qiān [动] **1** (迁移) move **2** (转变) change

迁就 qiānjiù [动] make allowances ◇我们不能迁就这么多错误。We cannot make allowances for so many mistakes.

迁怒 qiānnù [动] ◇不要迁怒于他人。Don't take your anger out on others.

迁徙 qiānxǐ [动] migrate

迁移 qiānyí [动] move

牵 qiān [动] **1** (拉住) pull **2** (牵涉) involve

牵扯 qiānchě [动] involve ◇这起案件牵扯到许多人。This case has involved a lot of people.

牵动 qiāndòng [动] influence

牵挂 qiānguà [动] worry ◇她牵挂孩子。She worried about her children.

牵就 qiānjiù [动] yield to

牵累 qiānlěi [动] **1** (牵制) tie … down **2** (连累) implicate

牵连 qiānlián [动] **1** (连累) implicate **2** (联系) connect ◇不要把两件事故意牵连到一起。You shouldn't deliberately connect the two issues.

牵强 qiānqiǎng [形] far-fetched

牵涉 qiānshè [动] involve

牵引 qiānyǐn [动] draw (*pt* drew, *pp* drawn) ◇火车由内燃机牵引。Trains are drawn by internal combustion engines.

铅 qiān [名] (化) lead

铅笔 qiānbǐ [名] pencil

谦 qiān [形] modest

谦卑 qiānbēi [形] modest

谦恭 qiāngōng [形] courteous

谦和 qiānhé [形] modest and gentle

谦让 qiānràng [动] modestly decline

谦虚 qiānxū **I** [形] modest ◇谦虚是一种美德。Modesty is a virtue. **II** [动] speak modestly (*pt* spoke, *pp* spoken) ◇他谦虚了一下，最后接受了礼物。He was shy about it at first, but in the end he accepted the present.

谦逊 qiānxùn [形] unassuming

签 qiān **I** [动] **1** (名字) sign **2** (意见) endorse **II** [名] **1** (指占卜、赌博、比赛) lot ◇抽签决定 draw lots **2** (标志) label ♦书签 bookmark **3** (细棍子) stick ♦牙签 toothpick

签到 qiāndào [动] sign in

签名 qiānmíng [动] sign

签署 qiānshǔ [动] sign

签约 qiānyuē [动] sign

签证 qiānzhèng [名] visa

签字 qiānzì [动] sign one's name

前 qián **I** [形] **1** (正面的) front ◇前门 front door **2** (指次序) first ◇前几名 the front-runners **3** (从前的) former ◇前市长 the former mayor ♦前夫 ex-husband **4** (未来的) future **II** [动] advance ◇勇往直前 take the bull by the horns

前辈 qiánbèi [名] older generation

前程 qiánchéng [名] future

前方 qiánfāng [名] **1** (前面) front **2** (前线) the front

前锋 qiánfēng [名] (体育) forward

前功尽弃 qián gōng jìn qì a waste of effort

前后 qiánhòu [名] **1** (时间接近) ◇春节前后 around the time of the Spring Festival ◇暑假前后 summer holiday time **2** (自始至终) ◇创作这部小说，前后用了3年时间。Creating the story took three years from start to finish. **3** (总共) ◇他前后去过3次欧洲。He's been to Europe three times altogether. **4** (前面和后面) the front and the back

前进 qiánjìn [动] **1** (向前走) advance **2** (发展) make progress

前景 qiánjǐng [名] prospects (*pl*)

前科 qiánkē [名] criminal record

前列 qiánliè [名] **1** (指排、列) front row **2** (指带头) forefront

前驱 qiánqū [名] pioneer

前人 qiánrén [名] predecessor

前身 qiánshēn [名] previous existence ◇这所大学的前身是一所女子师范学校。In a previous existence, this university was a ladies' teaching college.

前提 qiántí [名] precondition

前途 qiántú [名] future

前往 qiánwǎng [动] be bound for

前卫 qiánwèi **I** [名] forward **II** [形] fashionable

前夕 qiánxī [名] eve ◇圣诞节前夕 Christmas Eve

前线 qiánxiàn [名] front line

前言 qiányán [名] foreword

前沿 qiányán [名] front line

前兆 qiánzhào [名] omen

前缀 qiánzhuì [名] (语言) prefix

前奏 qiánzòu [名] (音) prelude

虔 qián 见下文

虔诚 qiánchéng [形] devout

钱 qián [名] money ◇挣钱 make money

钱财 qiáncái [名] money

钳 qián [名] pliers (*pl*)

钳子 qiánzi [名] pliers (*pl*)

乾 qián 见下文

乾坤 qiánkūn [名] (书) the universe

潜 qián **I** [动] **1** (入水) dive **2** (隐藏) hide (*pt* hid, *pp* hidden) ♦潜伏 lurk **II** [形] latent ♦潜能 potential **III** [副] secretly ♦潜逃 abscond

潜藏 qiáncáng [动] hide (*pt* hid, *pp* hidden)

潜伏 qiánfú [形] hidden

潜力 qiánlì [名] potential

潜台词 qiántáicí [名] (喻) implication

潜移默化 qián yí mò huà exert a subtle influence over

潜意识 qiányìshí [名] the subconscious

潜在 qiánzài [形] latent

浅 qiǎn [形] **1** (指深度) shallow **2** (指难度) easy **3** (指学识) lacking **4** (指颜色) light ◇浅蓝色 light blue ◇浅绿色 pale green **5** (指时间) short

浅薄 qiǎnbó [形] superficial

浅近 qiǎnjìn [形] (书) simple

浅显 qiǎnxiǎn [形] obvious

遣 qiǎn [动] send (*pt*, *pp* sent) ♦派遣 dispatch

遣返 qiǎnfǎn [动] repatriate

遣送 qiǎnsòng [动] deport

谴 qiǎn [动] censure

谴责 qiǎnzé [动] condemn

欠 qiàn [动] **1** (钱、情) owe **2** (缺乏) lack **3** (移动) raise … slightly

欠缺 qiànquē [动] lack

欠身 qiànshēn [动] lift oneself up

纤 qiàn [名] towrope
▷另见 xiān

纤夫 qiànfū [名] tracker

堑 qiàn [名] **1** (沟) moat ♦堑壕 trench **2** (挫折) setback

嵌 qiàn [动] inlay

歉 qiàn **I** [形] poor ♦歉收 poor harvest **II** [名] apology ♦抱歉 apologize

歉疚 qiànjiù [动] regret

歉收 qiànshōu [动] have a poor harvest

歉意 qiànyì [名] apology

呛 qiāng [动] choke
▷另见 qiàng

枪 qiāng [名] **1** (旧兵器) spear **2** (兵器) gun ♦手枪 pistol

枪毙 qiāngbì [动] **1** (打死) execute (*by firing squad*) **2** (否定) turn down

枪手 qiāngshǒu [名] gunman (*pl* gunmen)

枪手 qiāngshou [名] *someone who sits in for someone else in an exam*

枪械 qiāngxiè [名] weapons (*pl*)

枪支 qiāngzhī [名] firearms (*pl*)

腔 qiāng [名] **1** (指身体) cavity **2** (曲调) tune **3** (指口音) accent

强 qiáng **I** [形] **1** (力量大) strong **2** (程度高) able **3** (好) better ◇现在的生活是一年比一年强。Life is getting better year by year. **4** (略多于) extra ◇三分之一强 a third extra **II** [动] force
▷另见 jiàng, qiǎng

强暴 qiángbào **I** [形] violent **II** [动] rape

强大 qiángdà [形] powerful

强盗 qiángdào [名] robber

强调 qiángdiào [动] stress ◇强调重点 stress the important points

强度 qiángdù [名] intensity

强固 qiánggù [形] solid

强悍 qiánghàn [形] valiant

强化 qiánghuà [动] strengthen ◇强化地板 reinforced floor

强奸 qiángjiān [动] rape

强健 qiángjiàn [形] strong

强劲 qiángjìng [形] powerful

强烈 qiángliè [形] intense ◇强烈地震 a powerful earthquake

强权 qiángquán [名] power

强身 qiángshēn [动] work out ◇强身健体 get fit by working out

强盛 qiángshèng [形] powerful and prosperous

强手 qiángshǒu [名] talent

强项 qiángxiàng [名] forte

强行 qiángxíng [动] force

强硬 qiángyìng [形] tough ◇采取强硬的态度 take a tough stance

强有力 qiángyǒulì [形] forceful

强制 qiángzhì [动] force ◇采取强制手段 adopt forceful measures

强壮 qiángzhuàng [形] strong

墙 qiáng [名] wall

蔷 qiáng 见下文

蔷薇 qiángwēi [名] rose

抢 qiǎng [动] **1** (抢劫) rob **2** (抢夺) grab **3** (抢先) forestall **4** (赶紧) rush

抢夺 qiǎngduó [动] loot ◇抢夺市场 seize a market

抢购 qiǎnggòu [动] panic-buy (*pt, pp* panic-bought)

抢劫 qiǎngjié [动] rob ◇抢劫银行 rob a bank

抢手 qiǎngshǒu [形] in great demand ◇这种商品在市场上很抢手。These products are in great demand on the market.

抢先 qiǎngxiān [动] be the first ◇抢先报道新闻 be the first to report the news

抢眼 qiǎngyǎn [形] striking

强 qiǎng [动] **1** (勉强) make an effort ◇强装笑脸 force a smile **2** (迫使) force
▷另见 jiàng, qiáng

强词夺理 qiǎng cí duó lǐ argue irrationally

强迫 qiǎngpò [动] force

强求 qiǎngqiú [动] insist on

襁 qiǎng [名] swaddling clothes (*pl*)

襁褓 qiǎngbǎo [名] swaddling clothes (*pl*)

呛 qiàng [动] irritate
▷另见 qiāng

悄 qiāo 见下文
▷另见 qiǎo

悄悄 qiāoqiāo [副] **1** (悄然无声) quietly ◇天黑了，到处静悄悄的。As darkness fell everything became very quiet. **2** (不让知道) stealthily

跷 qiāo [名] (高跷) stilt

跷跷板 qiāoqiāobǎn [名] seesaw

锹 qiāo [名] spade

敲 qiāo [动] **1** (击) knock ◇他使劲敲门。He knocked hard on the door. ◇这事给我们敲了警钟。This rang alarm bells with us. **2** (敲诈) blackmail ◇他想敲我一笔钱。He wants to blackmail some money out of me.

敲打 qiāodǎ [动] beat (*pt* beat, *pp* beaten)

敲定 qiāodìng [动] determine

敲诈 qiāozhà [动] extort ◇敲诈他人钱财 extort money

橇 qiāo [名] sledge

乔 qiáo [形] tall

乔木 qiáomù [名] (植) arbour (英), arbor (美)

乔迁 qiáoqiān [动] (书) move ◇乔迁新居 move to a new house

乔装 qiáozhuāng [动] disguise

侨 qiáo **I** [动] live abroad **II** [名] expatriate ♦华侨 overseas Chinese

侨胞 qiáobāo [名] *fellow countryman living abroad*

侨居 qiáojū [动] emigrate

侨眷 qiáojuàn [名] *relatives of nationals living abroad*

侨民 qiáomín [名] emigrant

荞 qiáo 见下文

荞麦 qiáomài [名] (农) buckwheat

桥 qiáo [名] bridge

桥梁 qiáoliáng [名] bridge

桥牌 qiáopái [名] bridge

翘 qiáo [动] raise
▷另见 qiào

翘盼 qiáopàn [动] long for

憔 qiáo 见下文

憔悴 qiáocuì [形] haggard

瞧 qiáo [动] look ♦瞧病 see a doctor

巧 qiǎo [形] **1** (手、口) nimble **2** (有技能的) skilful (英), skillful (美) **3** (恰好) coincidental **4** (虚浮的) false ◇花言巧语 falsehood

巧合 qiǎohé [名] coincidence

巧克力 qiǎokèlì [名] chocolate

巧妙 qiǎomiào [形] clever ◇巧妙地拒绝 cleverly deny

悄 qiǎo 见下文
▷另见 qiǎo

悄然 qiǎorán [副] (书) quietly

壳 qiào [名] shell ♦地壳 the earth's crust
▷另见 ké

俏 qiào [形] **1** (漂亮) pretty **2** (畅销) saleable

俏货 qiàohuò [名] saleable goods (*pl*)

俏丽 qiàolì [形] beautiful

俏皮 qiàopi [形] witty

峭 qiào [形] steep ♦陡峭 steep

峭壁 qiàobì [名] precipice

峭立 qiàolì [形] steep

窍 qiào [名] **1** (窟窿) hole **2** (关键) crux ♦开窍 enlighten ♦诀窍 knack

窍门 qiàomén [名] knack

翘 qiào [动] **1** (仰起) stick up (*pt, pp* stuck) **2** (腿、拇指) raise
▷另见 qiáo

撬 qiào [动] prise ◇她把门撬开了。She prised the door open.

鞘 qiào [名] scabbard

切 qiē [动] cut (*pt, pp* cut) ◇请把土豆切成块儿。Please cut the potatoes into pieces.

切除 qiēchú [动] excise

切磋 qiēcuō [动] compare notes

切割 qiēgē [动] cut (*pt, pp* cut)

切削 qiēxiāo [动] cut (*pt, pp* cut)

茄 qié [名] aubergine (英), eggplant (美)
▷另见 jiā

茄子 qiézi [名] aubergine (英), eggplant (美)

且 qiě **I** [副] for the time being ◇这件事且放放。Leave this for the time being. ◇先别急，且听我说。Stop worrying: listen to me a moment. **II** [连] **1** (尚且) even ◇既便宜且实用 cheap and useful **2** (而且) and

切 qiè **I** [动] correspond to ◇他的想法不切实际。His ideas don't correspond to reality. **II** [形] eager **III** [副] definitely

切合 qièhé [动] correspond to ◇切合实际 correspond to reality

切记 qièjì [动] bear … in mind (*pt* bore, *pp* borne)

切身 qièshēn [形] personal ◇切身利益 personal gain ◇切身经历 personal experience

切实 qièshí **I** [形] realistic **II** [副] conscientiously

切中 qièzhòng [动] hit (*pt, pp* hit)◇你的批评切中要害。Your criticism hits the mark.

妾 qiè [名] concubine

怯 qiè [形] timid ♦胆怯 timid

怯场 qièchǎng [动] get stage fright

怯懦 qiènuò [形] over-cautious

怯弱 qièruò [形] timid and weak-willed

怯生生 qièshēngshēng [形] shy

窃 qiè **I** [动] steal (*pt* stole, *pp* stolen) **II** [副] surreptitiously

窃取 qièqǔ [动] steal (*pt* stole, *pp* stolen)

窃听 qiètīng [动] eavesdrop

窃贼 qièzéi [名] thief (*pl* thieves)

惬 qiè 见下文

惬意 qièyì [形] pleased

锲 qiè [动] carve

锲而不舍 qiè ér bù shě persevering

钦 qīn 见下文

钦佩 qīnpèi [动] admire

侵 qīn [动] invade

侵犯 qīnfàn [动] infringe ◇侵犯著作权 infringe copyright

侵害 qīnhài [动] **1** (权利、利益) violate **2** (指自然) encroach on

侵略 qīnlüè [动] invade

侵权 qīnquán [动] violate rights

侵入 qīnrù [动] invade ◇侵入他国领空 violate another country's airspace

侵蚀 qīnshí [动] erode ◇土壤侵蚀 soil erosion

侵吞 qīntūn [动] **1** (非法占有) embezzle **2** (武力吞并) annex

侵袭 qīnxí [动] invade ◇台风侵袭东南沿海地区。The typhoon has struck the south-east coastal area.

侵占 qīnzhàn [动] seize

亲 qīn **I** [名] **1** (父母) parent **2** (亲戚) relative **3** (婚姻) marriage ♦定亲 engagement **4** (新娘) bride **II** [形] **1** (指血缘近) blood ◇亲兄弟 blood brothers **2** (指感情好) intimate **III** [副] personally **IV** [动] **1** (亲吻) kiss ◇她亲了一下孩子的脸。She gave the child a kiss on the cheek. **2** (亲近) be close to

亲爱 qīn'ài [形] dear

亲笔 qīnbǐ **I** [动] write ... personally (*pt* wrote, *pp* written) **II** [名] personal inscription

亲近 qīnjìn [形] close ◇大家都愿亲近她。Everyone wants to be close to her.

亲眷 qīnjuàn [名] relatives (*pl*)

亲密 qīnmì [形] close ◇亲密朋友 close friend ◇亲密无间 be as thick as thieves

亲昵 qīnnì [形] very intimate

亲戚 qīnqi [名] relative

亲切 qīnqiè [形] warm

亲热 qīnrè [形] affectionate

亲人 qīnrén [名] close relative

亲身 qīnshēn [形] personal

亲生 qīnshēng [形] one's own ◇亲生父母 one's own parents

亲事 qīnshi [名] marriage

亲属 qīnshǔ [名] relatives (*pl*)

亲吻 qīnwěn [动] kiss

亲眼 qīnyǎn [副] with one's own eyes ◇他亲眼看到了事情的经过。He witnessed the whole event.

亲自 qīnzì [副] personally

芹 qín 见下文

芹菜 qíncài [名] celery

琴 qín [名] ♦钢琴 piano ♦小提琴 violin

禽 qín [名] birds (*pl*)

禽兽 qínshòu [名] **1** (字) birds and animals (*pl*) **2** (喻) beast

勤 qín **I** [形] hard-working **II** [副] regularly **III** [名] **1** (勤务) duty ♦值勤 be on duty **2** (到场) attendance ♦考勤 check attendance

勤奋 qínfèn [形] diligent

勤俭 qínjiǎn [形] hard-working and thrifty

勤恳 qínkěn [形] hard-working and conscientious

勤快 qínkuai [形] hard-working

勤劳 qínláo [形] hard-working

勤勉 qínmiǎn [形] hard-working

擒 qín [动] capture

擒拿 qínná [动] **1** (格斗) immobilize **2** (捉拿) catch (*pt*, *pp* caught)

噙 qín [动] **1** (叼) hold ... in the mouth (*pt*, *pp* held) ◇老板总是噙着雪茄。The boss always has a cigar in his mouth. **2** (含) ◇她眼里噙着泪花。Her eyes are full of tears.

寝 qǐn **I** [动] sleep (*pt*, *pp* slept) **II** [名] **1** (指卧室) bedroom **2** (指陵墓) tomb

沁 qìn [动] ooze

沁人心脾 qìn rén xīn pí be refreshing

青 qīng **I** [形] **1** (指绿色) green **2** (指黑色) black **3** (指年纪) young ♦青年

youth **II** [名] **1** (指青草) grass **2** (指庄稼) unripe crops

青出于蓝而胜于蓝 qīng chū yú lán ér shèng yú lán the student surpasses the teacher

青春 qīngchūn [名] youth ◊充满青春活力 full of youthful energy

青春期 qīngchūnqī [名] youth

青红皂白 qīng hóng zào bái the rights and wrongs ◊他不分青红皂白就批评人。He just started to criticize people, without taking any interest in the rights and wrongs of the matter.

青黄不接 qīng huáng bù jiē temporary shortage ◊大学师资出现了青黄不接现象。There is a temporary shortage of university teachers.

青年 qīngnián [名] youth

青山绿水 qīngshān lǜshuǐ [名] beautiful landscape

青丝 qīngsī [名] black hair ◊她的青丝已成白发。Her black hair has gone grey.

青天 qīngtiān [名] **1** (蓝天) blue sky **2** (清官) unbiased judge

轻 qīng **I** [形] **1** (指重量) light **2** (指数量或程度) ◊他们年纪很轻。They are quite young. ◊他的病可不轻。His illness is very serious. **3** (指无足轻重) not important ◊任务轻 light task **4** (指轻松愉快) relaxed ◊轻音乐 light music **II** [副] **1** (指少用力) gently ◊这只箱子得轻拿轻放。This box should be handled with care. **2** (轻率) rashly ◊不要轻信他人。Don't trust people too readily. **III** [动] disparage

轻便 qīngbiàn [形] portable ◊轻便电视机 portable TV

轻薄 qīngbó [形] frivolous

轻车熟路 qīng chē shú lù a piece of cake ◊干这项工作，他是轻车熟路。This job is a piece of cake for him.

轻而易举 qīng ér yì jǔ without effort

轻浮 qīngfú [形] frivolous

轻举妄动 qīng jǔ wàng dòng act rashly

轻快 qīngkuài [形] **1** (轻捷) brisk **2** (轻松) light-hearted

轻慢 qīngmàn [动] treat … disrespectfully ◊不要轻慢客人。Be sure not to treat the guests disrespectfully.

轻描淡写 qīng miáo dàn xiě brush over

轻蔑 qīngmiè [形] disdainful ◊他轻蔑地瞪了我一眼。He stared disdainfully at me.

轻飘飘 qīngpiāopiāo [形] light

轻巧 qīngqiǎo [形] **1** (灵巧) handy **2** (灵活) dexterous **3** (容易) simple

轻柔 qīngróu [形] gentle ◊轻柔的音乐 gentle music

轻生 qīngshēng [动] commit suicide

轻声 qīngshēng [副] in a gentle voice

轻视 qīngshì [动] look down on ◊轻视他人 look down on others

轻率 qīngshuài [形] hasty

轻松 qīngsōng [形] relaxing

轻佻 qīngtiāo [形] frivolous

轻闲 qīngxián [形] free

轻信 qīngxìn [动] be credulous ◊不要轻信谣传。Don't believe rumours (英) 或 rumors (美) too readily.

轻易 qīngyì [副] **1** (容易) easily ◊这些资料不是轻易能得到的。These materials are not easily obtained. **2** (随便) rashly ◊不要轻易下结论。Don't jump to rash conclusions.

轻音乐 qīngyīnyuè [名] light music

轻盈 qīngyíng [形] graceful

氢 qīng [名] (化) hydrogen

氢弹 qīngdàn [名] hydrogen bomb

倾 qīng **I** [动] **1** (斜) lean ◊房子的墙有点往外倾。The walls of the house lean outwards slightly. **2** (塌) collapse **3** (倒出) empty out **4** (用尽) exhaust **II** [名] tendency

倾巢 qīngcháo [动] turn out in full force

倾倒 qīngdǎo [动] **1** (倒下) topple **2** (佩服) fall for (*pt* fell, *pp* fallen) ◊大家都为她的美貌而倾倒。Everyone fell for her good looks.

倾倒 qīngdào [动] empty ◇倾倒垃圾 empty the rubbish (英) 或 garbage (美)

倾覆 qīngfù [动] overturn

倾家荡产 qīng jiā dàng chǎn be ruined ◇赌博使他倾家荡产。Gambling ruined him.

倾慕 qīngmù [动] admire

倾盆大雨 qīngpén dàyǔ downpour ◇昨天下了场倾盆大雨。There was a downpour yesterday.

倾诉 qīngsù [动] pour … out ◇倾诉衷肠 pour out one's feelings

倾吐 qīngtǔ [动] pour out ◇倾吐心中的苦水 pour out one's pain

倾向 qīngxiàng **I** [动] incline to ◇这两种观点我倾向于前者。I incline to the first of these two views. **II** [名] tendency ◇他有发胖的倾向。He has a tendency to put on weight.

倾销 qīngxiāo [动] dump

倾斜 qīngxié [动] slant

倾泻 qīngxiè [动] come down in torrents (*pt* came, *pp* come)

倾心 qīngxīn [动] **1** (爱慕) have a soft spot for ◇她倾心于那个戴眼镜的老师。She likes that teacher with the glasses. **2** (尽心) be sincere ◇老师和学生在倾心交谈。The teacher is having a heart-to-heart talk with his student.

倾注 qīngzhù [动] **1** (流泻) pour ◇山洪向河里倾注。The mountain torrents poured into the river. **2** (集中) throw into (*pt* threw, *pp* thrown) ◇他把自己的精力都倾注在事业上。He threw all his energy into the undertaking.

清 qīng **I** [形] **1** (纯净) clear ◇清水 clear water **2** (寂静) quiet ◇你该享清福了。You ought to enjoy a quiet life. **3** (清楚) distinct ◆分清 distinguish **4** (完全) settled ◇把钱还清 settle the debt **5** (纯洁) pure ◇玉洁冰清 pure and virtuous **II** [动] **1** (清除) get rid of ◇清垃圾 get rid of the rubbish (英) 或 garbage (美) **2** (结清) settle ◇账都清了吗？Are the accounts all settled? **3** (清点) check **4** (清理) put in order (*pt, pp* put)

清白 qīngbái [形] clean ◇历史清白 clean record

清查 qīngchá [动] check

清场 qīngchǎng [动] clear the place ◇电影演完了，该清场了。The film's finished – the cinema should be cleared.

清除 qīngchú [动] get rid of

清楚 qīngchu **I** [形] clear ◇发音清楚 clear pronunciation ◇头脑清楚 clear-headed **II** [动] understand (*pt, pp* understood) ◇这个问题你清楚吗？Do you understand this question?

清脆 qīngcuì [形] melodious

清单 qīngdān [名] detailed list ◇货物清单 stock inventory

清淡 qīngdàn [形] **1** (不浓) light ◇清淡口味 delicate flavour **2** (不腻) non-oily **3** (萧条) slack ◇最近生意清淡。Business has been slack recently.

清点 qīngdiǎn [动] check ◇清点货物 do stock-taking

清高 qīnggāo [形] noble and virtuous

清规戒律 qīngguī jièlǜ excessive rules ◇我们不要受某些清规戒律的束缚。We don't want to be bound by any excessive rules.

清寒 qīnghán [形] **1** (清贫) impoverished **2** (清冷) clear and crisp

清洁 qīngjié [形] clean

清净 qīngjìng [形] quiet

清静 qīngjìng [形] quiet

清苦 qīngkǔ [形] poor and honest

清朗 qīnglǎng [形] clear ◇清朗的月夜 a clear moonlit night ◇清朗的声音 a clear sound

清冷 qīnglěng [形] **1** (凉) chilly **2** (冷清) deserted

清理 qīnglǐ [动] tidy … up ◇清理房间 tidy up a room

清廉 qīnglián [形] honest

清凉 qīngliáng [形] refreshing ◇清凉饮料 refreshing drink

清明 qīngmíng [形] **1** (清朗) clear and bright **2** (清醒) clear ◇神志清明 clear-headed

清贫 qīngpín [形] impoverished

清扫 qīngsǎo [动] sweep … clean (*pt, pp* swept)

清爽 qīngshuǎng [形] **1** (清凉) refreshing **2** (轻松) relaxed ◇听了他的话，我心里清爽多了。Hearing his words put me more at ease.

清算 qīngsuàn [动] **1** (账目) settle **2** (罪行) redress

清晰 qingxī [形] clear ◇口齿清晰 clear enunciation

清洗 qīngxǐ [动] **1** (洗净) wash ◇清洗衣物 wash clothes **2** (清除) purge

清闲 qīngxián [形] leisurely

清香 qīngxiāng [形] lightly scented

清心寡欲 qīng xīn guǎ yù be pure of heart and free from desire

清新 qīngxīn [形] refreshing

清醒 qīngxǐng **I** [形] clear-headed **II** [动] come to (*pt* came, *pp* come) ◇我们去看病人时，他还没有清醒。When we went to see him, he still hadn't come to.

清秀 qīngxiù [形] delicate

清一色 qīngyīsè [形] uniform

清真 qīngzhēn [形] Muslim

蜻 qīng 见下文

蜻蜓 qīngtíng [名] dragonfly

蜻蜓点水 qīngtíng diǎn shuǐ skim over

情 qíng [名] **1** (感情) feeling ♦热情 warmth **2** (情面) kindness ◇求情 plead for leniency **3** (爱情) love ◇一见钟情 love at first sight **4** (性欲) passion ♦情欲 passion **5** (情况) condition ♦病情 patient's condition ♦实情 true state of affairs ♦军情 military situation

情报 qíngbào [名] intelligence report ◇军事情报 military intelligence

情不自禁 qíng bù zì jīn be unable to refrain from ◇他们情不自禁地欢呼起来。They were unable to refrain from cheering. ◇我们情不自禁唱了起来。We couldn't help but start singing.

情操 qíngcāo [名] sentiment

情敌 qíngdí [名] rival (*in a love triangle*)

情调 qíngdiào [名] sentiment

情窦初开 qíngdòu chū kāi adolescent love

情分 qíngfèn [名] affection ◇夫妻情分 affection between husband and wife

情感 qínggǎn [名] feeling

情怀 qínghuái [名] feelings (*pl*)

情节 qíngjié [名] **1** (内容) plot **2** (事实) circumstances (*pl*)

情结 qíngjié [名] complex ◇自卑情结 inferiority complex

情景 qíngjǐng [名] sight ◇感人的情景 moving sight

情况 qíngkuàng [名] **1** (状况) situation ◇情况危急 desperate situation ◇我父母身体情况良好。My parents are in excellent health. **2** (变化) military development ◇前线有什么情况？What developments are there on the front line?

情理 qínglǐ [名] reason ◇合乎情理 reasonable

情侣 qínglǚ [名] lovers (*pl*)

情面 qíngmiàn [名] feelings (*pl*) ◇他一点不讲情面。He's completely ruthless.

情趣 qíngqù [名] interest ◇她的生活充满情趣。She's got an interesting life.

情人 qíngrén [名] sweetheart

情人节 qíngrénjié [名] Valentine's Day

情书 qíngshū [名] love letter

情投意合 qíng tóu yì hé have a lot in common

情形 qíngxing [名] situation

情绪 qíngxù [名] **1** (心理状态) mood ◇急躁情绪 irritable mood ◇情绪低落 depressed **2** (不很开心) moodiness ◇他有点情绪。He's a bit moody.

情义 qíngyì [名] affection

情谊 qíngyì [名] friendship

情意 qíngyì [名] affection

情由 qíngyóu [名] whys and wherefores (*pl*) ◇他不分情由就开始胡乱批评人。Without asking the whys and wherefores he started to criticize people indiscriminately.

情有可原 qíng yǒu kě yuán forgivable ◊他这样做情有可原。What he did is forgivable.

情愿 qíngyuàn [动] **1** (愿意) be willing to **2** (宁愿) prefer ◊天太热，我情愿留在家里。It's too hot. I would prefer to stay at home.

晴 qíng [形] fine ◊天晴了。It's cleared up.

晴好 qínghǎo [形] fine

晴朗 qínglǎng [形] sunny

晴天霹雳 qíngtiān pīlì a bolt from the blue ◊她父亲去世的消息对她来说是晴天霹雳。The news that her father had died came like a bolt from the blue.

顷 qǐng **I** [名] a little while **II** [副] just now

请 qǐng [动] **1** (请求) ask ◊请他进来。Ask him to come in. **2** (邀请) invite ◊我们将请一位知名学者来讲学。We will invite a well-known scholar to come and lecture. ◊这位教授是从国外请来的。This professor has been invited from abroad. **3** (敬) ◊请这边走。This way, please. ◊请大家安静一下。Everyone quiet, please.

请便 qǐngbiàn [动] go ahead ◊如果你现在就想吃午餐，那就请便吧。If you want to have your lunch now, do go ahead. ◊你若要退出这个项目，请便！If you want to quit this project, go ahead!

请假 qǐngjià [动] ask for leave ◊她请假10天去度假。She asked for ten days' holiday leave.

请教 qǐngjiào [动] consult

请客 qǐngkè [动] treat ◊昨晚伊芙请客吃晚餐。Last night Eve treated us to dinner. ◊今天我来请客。Today it's on me.

请命 qǐngmìng [动] plead on behalf of

请求 qǐngqiú [动] ask ◊请求谅解 ask for understanding

请示 qǐngshì [动] ask for instructions

请帖 qǐngtiě [名] invitation ◊发请帖 send out invitations

请问 qǐngwèn [动] ◊请问你几岁了？May I ask you how old you are? ◊请问怎么出去？Could you show me the way out, please?

请勿 qǐngwù [动] ◊请勿触摸。Please don't touch. ◊请勿吸烟。No smoking.

请愿 qǐngyuàn [动] petition

请罪 qǐngzuì [动] apologize

庆 qìng **I** [动] celebrate ◊庆新年 celebrate New Year **II** [名] festival ♦国庆 National Day

庆典 qìngdiǎn [名] celebration

庆贺 qìnghè [动] celebrate ◊值得庆贺的事 something worth celebrating

庆幸 qìngxìng [动] rejoice

庆祝 qìngzhù [动] celebrate ◊庆祝生日 celebrate a birthday

穷 qióng **I** [形] poor **II** [名] limit ◊无穷无尽 limitless **III** [副] **1** (彻底) thoroughly **2** (极端) extremely

穷苦 qióngkǔ [形] destitute

穷困 qióngkùn [形] poverty-stricken

穷年累月 qióng nián lěi yuè for years on end ◊他们穷年累月在这儿工作。They've worked here for years on end.

穷酸 qióngsuān [形] down at heel

穷乡僻壤 qióng xiāng pì rǎng remote and backward places

穷凶极恶 qióng xiōng jí è diabolical

丘 qiū [名] **1** (指土堆) mound ♦沙丘 sand dune **2** (指坟墓) grave ♦坟丘 grave

丘陵 qiūlíng [名] hill

秋 qiū [名] **1** (指季节) autumn (英), fall (美) **2** (指庄稼) harvest time **3** (指一年) year ◊千秋万代 thousands of years **4** (指厄运期) period

秋分 qiūfēn [名] autumnal equinox

秋高气爽 qiū gāo qì shuǎng crisp autumn weather

秋千 qiūqiān [名] swing

秋天 qiūtiān [名] autumn (英), fall (美)

蚯 qiū 见下文

蚯蚓 qiūyǐn [名] earthworm

囚 qiú I [动] imprison II [名] prisoner

囚犯 qiúfàn [名] prisoner

囚禁 qiújìn [动] imprison

求 qiú I [动] **1** (请求) request ◇求人帮助 request help ◇他求我办事。He asked me to handle things. **2** (追求) strive (*pt* strove, *pp* striven) ◇求和平 strive for peace ◇求进步 seek advancement II [名] demand ◇供不应求 supply doesn't meet demand ◇供大于求 supply outstrips demand

求爱 qiú'ài [动] woo

求和 qiúhé [动] **1** (指战争) sue for peace **2** (指下棋) claim a draw

求婚 qiúhūn [动] propose ◇他向她求婚。He proposed to her.

求教 qiújiào [动] seek advice (*pt, pp* sought)

求情 qiúqíng [动] beg for leniency ◇他为同学向老师求情。He interceded with the teacher on behalf of his classmate.

求饶 qiúráo [动] ask for forgiveness

求同存异 qiú tóng cún yì seek common ground while retaining independence

求证 qiúzhèng [动] seek verification (*pt, pp* sought)

求之不得 qiú zhī bù dé exactly what one's been looking for ◇你帮助我，真是求之不得啊！ Your help was exactly what I needed!

求知 qiúzhī [动] seek knowledge (*pt, pp* sought) ◇他把精力都放在求知上。He put all his energy into the pursuit of knowledge.

求助 qiúzhù [动] seek help (*pt, pp* sought)

酋 qiú [名] **1** (酋长) tribal chief **2** (头领) chief

酋长 qiúzhǎng [名] **1** (指部落首领) tribal chief **2** (指酋长国首领) sheikh

球 qiú [名] **1** (数) (球体) sphere **2** (指球状) ball ♦雪球 snowball **3** (指体育) ball ♦橡皮球 rubber ball ♦篮球 basketball ♦足球 football **4** (指比赛) ball game **5** (地球) the Earth ♦全球 the whole world ♦西半球 western hemisphere

球赛 qiúsài [名] ball game

球艺 qiúyì [名] ball skills (*pl*)

遒 qiú [形] powerful

遒劲 qiújìng [形] vigorous

区 qū I [动] distinguish ♦区别 distinguish II [名] **1** (地区) area ◇林区 wooded area ◇工业区 industrial area **2** (指行政单位) region ♦自治区 autonomous region ◇海淀区 Haidian District

区别 qūbié [动] distinguish ◇我看不出它们之间有什么区别。I can't see any distinction between them.

区分 qūfēn [动] differentiate ◇区分两种植物 differentiate between two kinds of plant

区区 qūqū [形] trivial

区域 qūyù [名] area ◇行政区域 administrative area

曲 qū I [形] **1** (弯曲) bent **2** (理亏) wrong ◇是非曲直 the rights and wrongs of a matter II [动] bend (*pt, pp* bent) III [名] **1** (弯曲处) bend ♦河曲 bend in a river **2** (发酵剂) leaven ▷另见 qǔ

曲解 qūjiě [动] distort ◇你曲解了我的本意。You've distorted my original meaning.

曲线 qūxiàn [名] curve

曲折 qūzhé [形] **1** (弯曲) winding **2** (复杂) complicated

曲直 qūzhí [名] right and wrong

驱 qū [动] **1** (赶) drive (*pt* drove, *pp* driven) **2** (奔) gallop **3** (赶) expel ♦驱散 disperse

驱除 qūchú [动] drive … away (*pt* drove, *pp* driven) ◇驱除侵略者 drive away invaders

驱动 qūdòng [动] drive (*pt* drove, *pp* driven)

驱赶 qūgǎn [动] drive … away (*pt* drove, *pp* driven)

驱使 qūshǐ [动] **1** (迫使) order … about **2** (推动) urge

驱逐 qūzhú [动] drive … out (*pt* drove, *pp* driven)

屈 qū **I** [动] **1** (弯) bend (*pt, pp* bent) **2** (服) submit ♦屈服 surrender **3** (冤) wrong ◊你这样说真屈他了。What you said really wronged him. **II** [形] wrong **III** [名] injustice

屈才 qūcái [动] do work beneath one's ability

屈从 qūcóng [动] give way (*pt* gave, *pp* given)

屈服 qūfú [动] give in (*pt* gave, *pp* given)

屈辱 qūrǔ [名] humiliation

屈膝 qūxī [动] kneel (*pt, pp* knelt)

屈指可数 qūzhǐ kě shǔ can be counted on the fingers ◊这样的好作家屈指可数。Good authors like this are few and far between.

屈尊 qūzūn [动] lower oneself

祛 qū [动] dispel

祛除 qūchú [动] get rid of

躯 qū [名] human body ◊为国捐躯 die for one's country

躯干 qūgàn [名] trunk

躯体 qūtǐ [名] body

趋 qū [动] **1** (走) hasten ◊疾趋而过 speed past **2** (趋向) tend to become ◊大家的观点趋于一致。All our opinions are tending to unanimity.

趋势 qūshì [名] trend

趋向 qūxiàng **I** [动] tend to **II** [名] trend

趋炎附势 qū yán fù shì ingratiate oneself with influential people

蛐 qū 见下文

蛐蛐儿 qūqur [名] cricket

渠 qú [名] ditch ◊排水渠 drainage ditch

渠道 qúdào [名] **1** (水道) irrigation ditch **2** (途径) channel ◊两国应通过外交渠道解决彼此间的分歧。The two countries need to resolve their differences through diplomatic channels.

曲 qǔ [名] **1** (指歌曲) song ◊让我们高歌一曲。Let's sing a song. **2** (指乐曲) music ◊钢琴曲 piano music
▷另见 qū

曲调 qǔdiào [名] melody

曲子 qǔzi [名] tune

取 qǔ **1** (拿到) take (*pt* took, *pp* taken) ◊取款 withdraw money ◊取包 collect a parcel **2** (得到) obtain ◊咎由自取 have only oneself to blame ◊取信于人 win the trust of others **3** (采取) adopt ◊取中立态度 adopt a neutral position ◊取赞成立场 give the seal of approval **4** (选取) choose (*pt* chose, *pp* chosen) ◊给孩子取个名 name a child

取材 qǔcái [动] draw material (*pt* drew, *pp* drawn) ◊这部小说取材于现实生活。This novel draws on real life.

取长补短 qǔ cháng bǔ duǎn learn from each other's strong points

取代 qǔdài [动] replace ◊许多人工劳动被计算机取代了。A lot of manual work has been replaced by computers.

取得 qǔdé [动] get (*pt* got, *pp* got (英), gotten (美)) ◊取得学位 get a degree ◊取得圆满成功 achieve complete success

取缔 qǔdì [动] ban

取而代之 qǔ ér dài zhī replace ◊老前锋受伤了，教练只能让替补球员取而代之。The original forward was injured – the coach had to replace him with a substitute player.

取经 qǔjīng [动] learn from the experience of others

取决 qǔjué [动] depend on

取名 qǔmíng [动] choose a name (*pt* chose, *pp* chosen)

取巧 qǔqiǎo [动] pull a fast one

取舍 qǔshě [动] make a choice

取消 qǔxiāo [动] cancel ◊取消比赛 cancel the competition ◊半决赛由于下雨取消了。The semi-final has been called off because of rain. ◊市政府取消了放鞭炮的禁令。The municipal government has lifted a ban on firecrackers.

取笑 qǔxiào [动] make fun of

取样 qǔyàng [动] take a sample (*pt* took, *pp* taken)

取悦 qǔyuè [动] please

取证 qǔzhèng [动] collect evidence

娶 qǔ [动] marry ◇我哥哥娶了位护士。My brother got married to a nurse.

娶亲 qǔqīn [动] get married

龋 qǔ 见下文

龋齿 qǔchǐ [名] tooth decay

去 qù **I** [动] **1** (到) go (*pt* went, *pp* gone) ◇从广州去北京 go from Guangzhou to Beijing ◇我们昨天去上海了。We went to Shanghai yesterday. **2** (除) get rid of **3** (距) be apart ◇相去不远 not far apart **4** (发) send (*pt, pp* sent) ◇去了一封信 send a letter **II** [形] past ♦去年 last year

去处 qùchù [名] site

去路 qùlù [名] way ◇挡住某人的去路 block someone's way

去世 qùshì [动] pass away

去向 qùxiàng [名] whereabouts (*pl*) ◇不知去向 nowhere to be found

趣 qù **I** [名] interest ♦志趣 interest ◇这个故事有趣。This is an interesting story. **II** [形] interesting

趣味 qùwèi [名] taste ◇低级趣味 vulgar taste

圈 quān **I** [名] **1** (环形物) circle ♦北极圈 Arctic Circle **2** (界) group **II** [动] circle ◇请圈出正确的答案。Please circle the right answer.
▷另见 juān, juàn

圈点 quāndiǎn [动] **1** (加标点) punctuate **2** (标出) mark

圈套 quāntào [名] trap ◇落入圈套 fall into a trap

圈子 quānzi [名] **1** (环形) circle ◇说话绕圈子 express oneself in a roundabout way **2** (范围) ◇学生的活动圈子很小。The students socialize within a small circle. ◇她到哪儿都搞小圈子。Wherever she goes she creates little networks.

权 quán **I** [名] **1** (权力) power ♦当权 be in power **2** (权利) right ♦表决权 the right to vote **3** (形势) ◇主动权 initiative ◇控制权 control **4** (权宜) expediency ◇通权达变 adapt to circumstances **II** [副] for the time being

权衡 quánhéng [动] weigh ... up ◇权衡利弊 weigh up the pros and cons

权力 quánlì [名] power ◇滥用权力 abuse power

权利 quánlì [名] right ◇受教育权利 right to education ◇民主权利 democratic rights (*pl*)

权且 quánqiě [副] for the time being

权势 quánshì [名] power and influence

权术 quánshù [名] political trickery ◇玩弄权术 play politics

权威 quánwēi [名] authority

权限 quánxiàn [名] jurisdiction ◇超越权限 go beyond one's jurisdiction

权宜 quányí [形] expedient

权益 quányì [名] rights and interests (*pl*) ◇保护消费者的权益 protect the rights and interests of consumers

全 quán **I** [形] **1** (齐全) complete ◇人都到全了吗？ Is everyone here? **2** (整个) whole ◇全世界 the whole world **II** [副] entirely ◇我们班同学全去了。Our entire class went. **III** [动] keep ... intact (*pt, pp* kept) ◇两全齐美 satisfy both sides

全部 quánbù [形] whole

全才 quáncái [名] all-rounder ◇他是个全才。He's an all-rounder.

全称 quánchēng [名] full name

全程 quánchéng [名] whole journey

全副 quánfù [形] complete ◇全副武装 fully armed

全国 quánguó [形] nationwide ◇全国人口普查 nationwide census ◇全国游泳冠军 national swimming champion

全会 quánhuì [名] plenary session

全集 quánjí [名] complete works ◇莎

士比亚全集 the complete works of Shakespeare

全家福 quánjiāfú [名] family photo

全局 quánjú [名] overall situation

全军覆没 quán jūn fùmò be wiped out

全力 quánlì [名] all one's strength ◇竭尽全力 spare no effort ◇全力以赴 go all out

全貌 quánmào [名] full view

全面 quánmiàn [形] comprehensive ◇全面发展 comprehensive development ◇全面出击 all-out attack

全民 quánmín [名] all the people

全能 quánnéng [形] all-round ◇全能运动员 all-round athlete

全盘 quánpán [形] overall ◇全盘否定 total denial

全球 quánqiú [名] the whole world

全权 quánquán [名] full powers (*pl*)

全神贯注 quán shén guàn zhù with undivided attention ◇学生们全神贯注地听老师讲课。The students listened to the teacher with undivided attention.

全速 quánsù [名] full speed ◇警车全速前进。The police car is driving at full speed.

全体 quántǐ [名] everyone

全心全意 quán xīn quán yì wholeheartedly

全自动 quánzìdòng [形] automatic ◇全自动洗衣机 automatic washing machine

诠 quán [动] (书) annotate

诠释 quánshì [动] annotate

泉 quán [名] spring ♦温泉 hot spring

泉水 quánshuǐ [名] spring water

泉源 quányuán [名] **1** (水源) spring **2** (来源) source ◇知识的泉源 source of knowledge

拳 quán [名] fist

拳打脚踢 quán dǎ jiǎo tī beat … up

拳击 quánjī [名] boxing

拳击手 quánjīshǒu [名] boxer

痊 quán 见下文

痊愈 quányù [动] recover

蜷 quán [动] coil ◇蛇把身子蜷成一团儿。The snake coiled itself up.

蜷曲 quánqū [动] curl ◇乞丐把身体蜷曲成一团儿。The beggar curled up.

鬈 quán [形] curly

鬈曲 quánqū [形] crinkled

颧 quán 见下文

颧骨 quángǔ [名] cheekbone

犬 quǎn [名] dog ◇嗅探犬 sniffer dog

犬牙交错 quǎnyá jiāocuò jigsaw pattern

劝 quàn [动] **1** (说服) advise ◇我劝他放弃这个计划。I advised him to abandon this plan. **2** (勉励) encourage

劝导 quàndǎo [动] persuade ◇在家人的劝导下，他想通了。Under the persuasive influence of his family, he came round.

劝告 quàngào [动] advise ◇我们劝告他不要这样做。We advised him not to do it.

> 注意 **advice** 是不可数名词。可以说 **a piece of advice** 或 **some advice**, 但不能说‘*an advice*’或‘*advices*’。请勿混淆 **advice** 和 **advise**。**advise** 是与 **advice** 同词根的动词。

劝架 quànjià [动] mediate

劝解 quànjiě [动] **1** (劝导) reassure ◇经他人劝解，他终于想通了。With others' reassurance, he finally came round. **2** (劝架) mediate

劝诫 quànjiè [动] admonish

劝说 quànshuō [动] persuade ◇他们劝说我们去青岛度假。They persuaded us to go on holiday to Qingdao.

劝阻 quànzǔ [动] dissuade

券 quàn [名] ticket ♦奖券 lottery

ticket ♦入场券 admission ticket

缺 quē I [动] 1 (缺乏) lack ◊这地方缺水。This place is short of water. 2 (残破) be incomplete ◊这本书缺两页。This book is missing two pages. 3 (缺席) be absent ◊人全到了，一个不缺。Everyone's here, no one's absent. II [名] vacancy ♦补缺 fill a vacancy

缺德 quēdé [形] wicked

缺点 quēdiǎn [名] shortcoming

缺乏 quēfá [动] lack ◊缺乏资源 lack the resources

缺憾 quēhàn [名] regret

缺口 quēkǒu [名] 1 (口子) gap 2 (缺额) shortfall ◊我们的资金还有很大缺口。There's still a huge shortfall in our funds.

缺门 quēmén [名] gap

缺欠 quēqiàn [名] defect

缺勤 quēqín [动] be absent ◊他最近常缺勤。He's been absent a lot recently.

缺少 quēshǎo [动] lack ◊我这里缺少人手。I'm shorthanded here.

缺席 quēxí [动] be absent

缺陷 quēxiàn [名] defect ◊生理缺陷 physical defect

瘸 qué [动] be lame

瘸子 quézi [名] ◊她是瘸子。She is lame.

却 què I [动] 1 (后退) step back 2 (使退却) drive … back (*pt* drove, *pp* driven) 3 (拒绝) decline ♦推却 decline ◊盛情难却。It's difficult to refuse such a kind offer. 4 (表示完成) ♦冷却 cool off ♦忘却 forget II [副] however ◊我有许多话要说，却不知从何说起。I have a lot to say, but don't know where to start.

却步 quèbù [动] shrink back (*pt* shrank, *pp* shrunk)

雀 què [名] sparrow

雀跃 quèyuè [动] jump for joy

确 què [副] 1 (确实地) really ◊确有其事。It really happened. 2 (坚定地) firmly ♦确信 firmly believe

确定 quèdìng I [动] determine II [形] definite ◊确定的证据 definite proof

确立 quèlì [动] establish

确切 quèqiè [形] precise

确认 quèrèn [动] confirm

确实 quèshí I [形] true II [副] really ◊他确实聪明。He's really clever.

确凿 quèzáo [形] irrefutable

确诊 quèzhěn [动] diagnose

鹊 què [名] magpie

裙 qún [名] skirt

裙子 qúnzi [名] skirt

群 qún I [名] crowd II [量] ◊一群绵羊 a flock of sheep ◊一群蜜蜂 a swarm of bees ◊一群奶牛 a herd of cows ◊一群学生 a group of students

群策群力 qún cè qún lì pull together

群岛 qúndǎo [名] archipelago

群起 qúnqǐ [动] rise together (*pt* rose, *pp* risen)

群情 qúnqíng [名] popular feeling

群体 qúntǐ [名] 1 (指生物) colony 2 (指社会) group

群众 qúnzhòng [名] the masses (*pl*)

Rr

然 rán I [形] correct II [代] so III [连] (书) however

然而 rán'ér [连] however ◇他发了财，然而生活依然俭朴。Even after he'd made it, he led a simple and thrifty life.

然后 ránhòu [连] afterwards ◇我先看新闻，然后吃晚饭。I'm watching the news first, and I'll have supper afterwards.

髯 rán [名] side whiskers (*pl*)

燃 rán [动] **1** (燃烧) burn ♦易燃物 flammable substance **2** (点燃) light (*pt, pp* lit)

燃点 rándiǎn I [动] light (*pt, pp* lit) II [名] ignition point

燃放 ránfàng [动] let … off (*pt, pp* let) ◇燃放烟花 let off fireworks

燃料 ránliào [名] fuel ◇炭是一种固体燃料。Coal is a form of solid fuel.

燃眉之急 rán méi zhī jí matter of extreme urgency

燃烧 ránshāo [动] burn

冉 rǎn 见下文

冉冉 rǎnrǎn [副] slowly ◇冉冉升起的太阳 the slowly rising sun

染 rǎn [动] **1** (着色) dye ◇她把头发染成了蓝色。She dyed her hair blue. **2** (感染) contract ◇他身染重病。He's contracted a serious illness. **3** (沾染) catch (*pt, pp* caught) ◇他染上了抽烟喝酒的习惯。He's acquired the habit of smoking and drinking.

染料 rǎnliào [名] dye

染指 rǎnzhǐ [动] take more than one's fair share (*pt* took, *pp* taken)

嚷 rāng 见下文
▷另见 rǎng

嚷嚷 rāngrang [动] **1** (喧哗) shout ◇小声点儿，别嚷嚷了！Quieten down a bit – don't shout! **2** (声张) make … widely known

瓤 ráng [名] **1** (指瓜果) flesh **2** (指物品) padding

壤 rǎng [名] **1** (土地) soil **2** (地域) region ◇穷乡僻壤 remote backwater

嚷 rǎng [动] **1** (喊叫) howl **2** (吵闹) make a racket
▷另见 rāng

嚷叫 rǎngjiào [动] shout

让 ràng I [动] **1** (退让) make allowances ◇孩子小，你就让着点吧。The child's only young – you should make allowances for him. **2** (谦让) invite ◇先把客人让进屋 invite guests to enter a room first **3** (允许) let (*pt, pp* let) ◇老板不让我休假。My boss won't let me take any holiday. **4** (避开) make way **5** (转让) transfer ◇这张演出票能让给我吗？Can the ticket for the performance be transferred to me? II [介] by ◇大树让风吹倒了。The big tree was blown down by the wind.

让步 ràngbù [动] make a concession

让利 rànglì [动] give up a share of the profits (*pt* gave, *pp* given)

让位 ràngwèi [动] **1** (指职位) step down ◇老领导主动让位给年轻人。The old leader stepped down in favour of someone younger. **2** (指座位) give up one's seat (*pt* gave, *pp* given)

让贤 ràngxián [动] step down in favour of a worthier candidate

饶 ráo I [形] rich II [动] **1** (宽恕) forgive (*pt* forgave, *pp* forgiven) **2** (添加) add

饶命 ráomìng [动] spare a life ◇皇帝饶了他一命。The emperor spared his life. ◇小偷被打得连喊饶命。They beat the thief until he begged for mercy.

饶舌 ráoshé [动] prattle ◇快点说，别再饶舌了。Tell me quickly – no more beating about the bush.

饶恕 ráoshù [动] let … off (*pt, pp* let)

◇他还年轻，就饶恕他这一次吧！ He's still young – can't you let him off just this once?

扰 rǎo **I** [动] (搅扰) disturb ♦打扰 disturb **II** [形] (书) (混乱) chaotic

扰乱 rǎoluàn [动] disrupt

绕 rào [动] **1** (缠绕) wind (*pt, pp* wound) **2** (围绕) go round (*pt* went, *pp* gone) ◇他每天绕着操场跑步。He runs several times round the sports ground every day. **3** (迂回) make a detour ◇前方修路，车辆绕行。There are road-works ahead – please make a detour.

绕口令 ràokǒulìng [名] tongue twister

绕圈子 rào quānzi [动] **1** (指走路) go round and round in circles (*pt* went, *pp* gone) **2** (喻) (指说话) beat about the bush (*pt* beat, *pp* beaten)

绕弯子 rào wānzi [动] (喻) beat about the bush (*pt* beat, *pp* beaten)

绕嘴 ràozuǐ [形] awkward ◇这篇文章读起来绕嘴。This essay doesn't read well.

惹 rě [动] **1** (引起) stir up ◇他在单位老惹麻烦。He's always stirring up trouble at work. **2** (触动) provoke ◇她爱生气，你不要惹她。She's got a quick temper – don't provoke her. **3** (招) make (*pt,pp* made) ◇他的话常常惹人发笑。He often makes people laugh when he talks.

惹祸 rěhuò [动] stir up trouble

惹事 rěshì [动] cause trouble

惹是生非 rě shì shēng fēi stir up trouble

惹眼 rěyǎn [形] showy ◇她那件粉色衣服很惹眼。That pink dress of hers is very showy.

热 rè **I** [名] **1** (物) heat **2** (高烧) fever ♦退热 dispel a fever **II** [形] **1** (温度高) hot ◇今天真热。It's so hot today. **2** (情谊深) warm ◇她是个热心肠。She's very warm-hearted. **3** (羡慕) envious **4** (走俏) popular **5** (热潮) ◇出国热开始降温了。The craze for going abroad is starting to wear off. ◇西方国家兴起了汉语热。Studying Chinese has become all the rage in Western countries. **III** [动] heat ◇把米饭热一热再吃。Heat up the rice before you eat it.

热爱 rè'ài [动] love ◇她非常热爱教育事业。She loves her work as a teacher.

热潮 rècháo [名] craze

热忱 rèchén [名] enthusiasm

热诚 rèchéng [形] warm and sincere

热带 rèdài [名] the tropics (*pl*) ◇这些都是热带植物。These are all tropical plants.

热点 rèdiǎn [名] **1** (指地区) prime site ◇这一地区已成为外商投资的热点。This region has become a prime site for foreign investment. **2** (指问题) sticking point

热度 rèdù [名] **1** (冷热程度) temperature **2** (高烧) fever **3** (热情) enthusiasm

热敷 rèfū [名] hot compress

热狗 règǒu [名] hot dog

热乎乎 rèhūhū [形] warm

热乎 rèhu [形] **1** (热) hot **2** (亲热) (指人际关系) affectionate

热火朝天 rè huǒ cháo tiān be in full swing ◇建筑工地上，大家干得热火朝天。On the construction site, the work was in full swing.

热辣辣 rèlālā [形] burning hot ◇他觉得脸上热辣辣的。He felt his face was burning. ◇阳光热辣辣地炙烤着大地。The land was roasting under the burning hot sun.

热浪 rèlàng [名] heat wave

热恋 rèliàn [动] be passionately in love ◇两人正处于热恋之中。They are having a passionate love affair.

热量 rèliàng [名] amount of heat

热烈 rèliè [形] heated ◇班会上，大家讨论得非常热烈。At the class meeting, everyone was having a heated discussion.

热流 rèliú [名] **1** (热气流) warm front **2** (指感受) warmth **3** (热潮) upsurge ◇移民的热流 a rise in emigration

热卖 rèmài [动] sell like hot cakes (*pt, pp* sold)

热门 rèmén [名] popularity ◊这些都属于热门专业。These are all very popular majors.

热闹 rènao I [形] lively II [动] liven up ◊我们准备在元旦热闹热闹。We're getting ready for a lively time at New Year's. III [名] spectacle

热启动 rèqǐdòng [动] reboot ◊电脑死机时，试试热启动。When the computer crashes, try rebooting it.

热切 rèqiè [形] eager ◊孩子们热切地盼望着儿童节的到来。The children were eagerly looking forward to Children's Day.

热情 rèqíng I [名] passion II [形] enthusiastic ◊招待客人要热情周到。When entertaining guests you should be enthusiastic and attentive. ◊她对顾客非常热情。She's very friendly to the clients.

热身 rèshēn [动] warm … up ♦热身赛 warm-up match

热腾腾 rètēngtēng [形] piping hot

热线 rèxiàn [名] **1** (指电话或电报) hotline ◊这个广播电台开通了观众热线。This radio station has opened an audience hotline. **2** (指交通) busy route ◊旅游热线 busy tourist route

热销 rèxiāo [动] sell like hot cakes (*pt, pp* sold)

热心 rèxīn [形] warm-hearted

热血 rèxuè [名] enthusiasm ◊20年前，他还是一个热血青年。Twenty years ago he was still an enthusiastic youth.

热饮 rèyǐn [名] hot drink

热战 rèzhàn [动] open war

热中 rèzhōng [动] **1** (渴望) be desperate for ◊他热中于权势和金钱。He's desperate for power and money. **2** (爱好) be keen on ◊他热中于集邮。He's keen on stamp collecting.

人 rén [名] **1** (人类) human being **2** (指某种人) person (*pl* people) ♦军人 soldier **3** (每人) everybody ◊这个孩子人见人爱。Everyone who sees this child likes him. **4** (成年人) adult **5** (别人) other people (*pl*) ◊我们要真诚待人。We must treat other people with honesty. **6** (为人) personality **7** (人手) manpower ◊我们这里活儿多，能不能派几个人？We've got so much to do here – can you send us some more manpower? ◊我们办公室缺人。Our office is short-staffed.

> **person** 的复数形式通常为 **people**。*At least fifty-four people have been killed.* **persons** 通常只用于非常正式的场合，或作为法律用语。

人才 réncái [名] **1** (指能人) talent ◊他是个难得的人才。He is an unusually talented person. **2** (指外貌) good looks (*pl*) ◊他长得一表人才。He's a good-looking man.

人称 rénchēng [名] person ◊"我"是第一人称。"I" is the first person.

人次 réncì [量] person time

人道 réndào [形] humane ♦人道主义 humanitarianism

人地生疏 rén dì shēngshū ◊我对这里人地生疏，请多多指教。I'm a stranger here – please give me as much advice as you can.

人多势众 rén duō shì zhòng safety in numbers

人浮于事 rén fú yú shì be overstaffed

人格 réngé [名] **1** (品质) character **2** (资格) dignity

人工 réngōng I [形] man-made II [名] manpower III [量] man-day

人和 rénhé [动] stand united (*pt, pp* stood)

人际 rénjì [名] ◊人际状况 personal situation ◊搞好人际关系非常重要。It's very important to have good personal relationships.

人家 rénjiā [名] **1** (住户) household **2** (家庭) family **3** (婆家) fiancé's family ◊姑娘大了，该找个人家了。The girl's grown up – should find her a husband.

人家 rénjia [代] **1** (别人) others ◊人家都去了，你怎么不去？Other people have gone, so why don't you go? **2** (他) he **3** (她) she **4** (他们) they **5** (指自己) I

人间 rénjiān [名] the world

人口 rénkǒu [名] **1** (地区人数) population ◊人口众多 large population ◊全国人口普查 national census **2** (家庭人数) ◊他家人口很多。There are a lot of people in his family. **3** (泛指人) people (*pl*)

人来疯 rénláifēng [动] ◊我儿子总是人来疯。My son always gets over-excited when we have guests.

人类 rénlèi [名] mankind, humankind ◊人类正面临着越来越多的挑战。Mankind is facing more and more challenges.

人力 rénlì [名] manpower

人马 rénmǎ [名] **1** (指军队) forces (*pl*) **2** (指机构) members (*pl*)

人面兽心 rén miàn shòu xīn a wolf in sheep's clothing

人民 rénmín [名] the people ◊为人民服务 serve the people ◊公务员是人民的公仆。Government officials are the servants of the people.

人命 rénmìng [名] life (*pl* lives)

人品 rénpǐn [名] **1** (品质) character **2** (仪表) appearance

人气 rénqì [名] popularity

人情 rénqíng [名] **1** (人的感情) human emotion **2** (情面) feelings (*pl*) ◊好朋友都不愿帮我，真不讲人情！None of my good friends were willing to help me – what an unfeeling bunch! **3** (礼俗) etiquette **4** (礼物) gift

人权 rénquán [名] human rights (*pl*)

人山人海 rén shān rén hǎi a sea of people ◊国庆节那天，天安门广场上人山人海。On National Day, Tiananmen Square was a sea of people.

人身 rénshēn [名] person (*pl* people)

人参 rénshēn [名] ginseng

人生 rénshēng [名] life (*pl* lives) ♦人生观 philosophy of life

人士 rénshì [名] figure ◊知名人士 famous figure

人世 rénshì [名] the world ◊他离开人世已经5年了。It's already five years since he passed away.

人事 rénshì [名] **1** (指人员安排) personnel **2** (指人际关系) personal relations (*pl*) **3** (指人情事理) the ways of the world ◊他这么大了，应该懂点人事了。At his age, he ought to know the ways of the world. **4** (指人的意识) consciousness ◊等我赶到时，他已人事不知。By the time I got there, he'd already lost consciousness.

人手 rénshǒu [名] manpower ◊缺人手 lack the manpower

人体 réntǐ [名] the human body ◊人体器官移植 human organ transplants

人头 réntóu [名] **1** (人的头) human head **2** (人数) people (*pl*) ◊按人头拨款 allocate money according to the number of people **3** (指人际关系) links (*pl*)

人为 rénwéi **I** [动] put in the effort (*pt, pp* put) ◊事在人为 human effort can achieve anything **II** [形] man-made

人文科学 rénwén kēxué [名] humanities (*pl*)

人物 rénwù [名] **1** (能人) figure ◊他是一位有世界影响的领袖人物。He is a figure of global stature. **2** (艺术形象) character ◊这部小说塑造了100多个人物。There are over a hundred characters in this novel.

人心 rénxīn [名] **1** (感情和愿望) popular feeling **2** (人性) conscience

人性 rénxìng [名] human nature ◊这是一种灭绝人性的行为。This is inhuman behaviour.

人选 rénxuǎn [名] candidate

人烟 rényān [名] signs of human habitation (*pl*)

人员 rényuán [名] **1** (雇员) staff **2** (指某类人) ◊退休人员 retirees ◊走私人员 smugglers

人缘儿 rényuánr [名] personal relations (*pl*) ◊她人缘儿很好。She gets on very well with people.

人云亦云 rén yún yì yún parrot

人造 rénzào [形] artificial ◊发射人造卫星 launch an artificial satellite

人证 rénzhèng [名] testimony

人质 rénzhì [名] hostage

人种 rénzhǒng [名] ethnic group

仁 rén [名] **1** (仁爱) benevolence **2** (果肉) kernel

仁爱 rén'ài [名] benevolence

仁慈 réncí [形] benevolent

仁义 rényì [名] benevolence and righteousness

仁至义尽 rén zhì yì jìn do everything one can ◊我对他已做到仁至义尽。I've already done all I can for him.

忍 rěn [动] **1** (忍受) endure ♦容忍 tolerate **2** (忍心) have the heart to ♦残忍 ruthless

忍耐 rěnnài [动] show restraint (*pt* showed, *pp* shown)

忍气吞声 rěn qì tūn shēng suffer in silence

忍让 rěnràng [动] hold back (*pt, pp* held) ◊大家都忍让一点儿。Everyone held back a bit.

忍辱负重 rěn rǔ fù zhòng ◊他忍辱负重30年，终于完成了使命。After enduring thirty years of humiliation, he finally accomplished his mission.

忍受 rěnshòu [动] bear (*pt* bore, *pp* borne)

忍无可忍 rěn wú kě rěn ◊对于他们的卑劣行为，大家已忍无可忍。Everyone is at the end of their tether with their appalling behaviour.

忍心 rěnxīn [动] bear (*pt* bore, *pp* borne) ◊看到孩子受罪，你忍心吗？ How can you bear to watch the children suffer?

荏 rěn [形] weak ◊色厉内荏 all bark no bite

荏苒 rěnrǎn [动] (书) slip by

刃 rèn **I** [名] **1** (锋) blade **2** (刀) knife (*pl* knives) **II** [动] (书) kill

认 rèn [动] **1** (识) know (*pt* knew, *pp* known) **2** (建立关系) establish a relationship **3** (承认) admit ◊认输 admit defeat **4** (接受吃亏) accept ◊这东西贵就贵吧，我认了。Never mind the expense – I can take it.

认错 rèncuò [动] **1** (承认错误) admit one's mistakes ◊你去向老师认个错吧。Go and tell the teacher you admit you were wrong. **2** (误认) mistake … for … (*pt* mistook, *pp* mistaken) ◊他不是你同学，你认错了人。He's not your classmate – you've got the wrong man.

认可 rènkě [动] **1** (许可) endorse ◊他的方案已得到上级认可。His project was endorsed by his superiors. **2** (承认) approve ◊他的能力得到了同事们的认可。His abilities won him the approval of his colleagues.

认生 rènshēng [动] be shy of strangers

认识 rènshi **I** [动] know (*pt* knew, *pp* known) ◊他们是在一次晚会上认识的。They got to know each other at a party. **II** [名] understanding ◊他对这件事的认识是不对的。His knowledge of this is incorrect.

认输 rènshū [动] concede defeat

认为 rènwéi [动] think (*pt, pp* thought) ◊你认为这篇文章怎么样？ What do you think of this essay? ◊我们认为，这个决定是错误的。We think that the decision is wrong.

认真 rènzhēn **I** [形] serious **II** [动] take … seriously (*pt* took, *pp* taken) ◊他开个玩笑，你就认真了。He was joking, but you took him seriously.

认证 rènzhèng [动] authenticate

认罪 rènzuì [动] plead guilty ◊证据确凿，他不得不低头认罪。The proof was incontestable – he had no choice but to admit defeat and plead guilty.

任 rèn **I** [动] **1** (聘) appoint ♦委任 appoint **2** (担当) take up (*pt* took, *pp* taken) **3** (听凭) let (*pt, pp* let) ◊各种款式，任你选择。There's a variety of different styles – I'll let you decide. **II** [名] (职责) responsibility **III** [量] ◊他是这个公司的第3任总裁。He's the third CEO of this company. ◊他当了两任总统。He's been president for two terms.

IV [连] no matter ◇任你去哪里，我也不管。No matter where you go, I won't care.

任何 rènhé [形] any ◇你们可以从中选择任何一个。You can choose any one of them. ◇任何人都不能迟到。No one can be late. ◇任何事物都有两面性。Every coin has two sides.

任劳任怨 rèn láo rèn yuàn work hard despite other people's criticism

任命 rènmìng [动] appoint ◇他被任命为部门经理。He was appointed branch manager.

任凭 rènpíng **I** [动] allow … to do as they please ◇这种情况下不能任凭你一人做主。Under these circumstances we can't let you take the decision alone. **II** [连] no matter ◇任凭你是谁，都不该违反规定。No matter who you are, you still can't break the rules.

任人唯贤 rèn rén wéi xián choose the best person for the job

任务 rènwu [名] task

任性 rènxìng [形] headstrong

任意 rènyì **I** [副] at will ◇你可以任意指派一个人做这件事。You can send anyone you like to do this job. **II** [形] unconditional

任用 rènyòng [动] appoint

任重道远 rèn zhòng dào yuǎn shoulder a heavy responsibility

纫 rèn [动] **1** (穿针) thread **2** (缝) sew (*pt* sewed, *pp* sewn)

韧 rèn [形] resilient ♦柔韧 pliant

韧劲 rènjìn [名] (口) tenacity

韧性 rènxìng [名] **1** (指物体) flexibility **2** (指精神) tenacity

妊 rèn 见下文

妊娠 rènshēn [动] be pregnant

扔 rēng [动] **1** (掷) throw (*pt* threw, *pp* thrown) **2** (丢) throw … away ◇他把垃圾扔了。He threw the rubbish away.

仍 réng (书) **I** [动] **1** (沿袭) remain **2** (频繁) occur frequently **II** [副] still ◇事故仍在调查中。The accident is still under investigation. ◇困难仍未克服。The difficulties have not yet been overcome.

仍旧 réngjiù **I** [动] continue as before ◇此项法规仍旧。This statute will remain as it was before. **II** [副] still ◇我劝了半天，她仍旧不同意。I spent ages trying to persuade her, but she still wouldn't agree.

仍然 réngrán [副] **1** (表示继续) still ◇他仍然保持着老习惯。He still sticks to his old habits. **2** (表示恢复) ◇回国后，他仍然到原公司工作。After his return from overseas he went back to work in his old company.

日 rì [名] **1** (太阳) sun ♦日出 sunrise ♦日落 sunset **2** (白天) daytime ◇他们日夜不停地赶路。They travelled onwards, not stopping during the day or at night. **3** (天) day ♦明日 tomorrow **4** (每天) every day ◇城市面貌日见改善。The city looks better and better every day. **5** (泛指一段时间) days (*pl*) ♦往日 the past **6** (指某一天) day ♦生日 birthday **7** (日本) Japan ◇日货 Japanese goods

日常 rìcháng [形] everyday ◇日常生活用语 everyday words and expressions

日程 rìchéng [名] agenda

日后 rìhòu [名] future ◇这个问题日后再解决。This problem can be resolved at some point in the future.

日积月累 rì jī yuè lěi accumulate …over a long period

日久天长 rì jiǔ tiān cháng year in, year out ◇只要坚持锻炼，日久天长就会有效果。You just have to keep on with the exercise – you'll see the results over time.

日理万机 rì lǐ wàn jī be occupied with important matters

日历 rìlì [名] calendar

日内 rìnèi [名] next few days (*pl*) ◇运动员将于日内回国。The athletes will return home within the next few days.

日期 rìqī [名] date ◇出生日期 date of birth ◇考试日期还没定下来。

The date of the exam hasn't been fixed yet.

日新月异 rì xīn yuè yì change rapidly and continuously

日以继夜 rì yǐ jì yè work round the clock

日益 rìyì [副] increasingly

日用 rìyòng I [形] everyday II [名] day-to-day expenses (*pl*)

日子 rìzi [名] **1** (日期) date **2** (时间) day ◇近些日子，你都忙什么呢？ What have you been up to these last few days? **3** (生活) life (*pl* lives) ◇老百姓的日子越来越好了。The lives of ordinary people are getting better and better.

戎 róng [名] army ◇戎装 military uniform

戎马 róngmǎ [名] **1** (字) war horse **2** (喻) military career

茸 róng I [形] downy II [名] young deer antlers (*pl*)

茸毛 róngmáo [名] down

茸茸 róngróng [形] downy

荣 róng [形] **1** (茂盛) flourishing **2** (兴旺) thriving **3** (光荣) glorious

荣华富贵 rónghuá fùguì glory and wealth

荣幸 róngxìng [形] honoured (英), honored (美) ◇认识您，我感到非常荣幸。I feel honoured to know you.

荣耀 róngyào [形] glorious

荣誉 róngyù [名] **1** (指名声) glory ◇这次比赛，他为学校赢得了荣誉。He won glory for the school in this competition. **2** (指名义上的) honour (英), honor (美) ◇荣誉市民 honoured (英) 或 honored (美) citizens

绒 róng [名] **1** (绒毛) down **2** (纺织品) ♦天鹅绒 velvet ♦灯芯绒 corduroy

绒线 róngxiàn [名] **1** (丝线) floss **2** (毛线) (方) wool ◇绒线背心 a woollen (英) 或 woolen (美) vest

容 róng I [动] **1** (容纳) fit ◇这个会议室容得下300人吗？ Can this meeting room fit three hundred people? **2** (容忍) tolerate ◇他容不得比他强的人。He can't tolerate anyone better than him. **3** (允许) allow ◇他根本不容别人发表观点。He just doesn't allow anyone else to express their views. II [名] **1** (神情) facial expression **2** (相貌) appearance **3** (喻) (外观) appearance ♦市容 appearance of a city

容光焕发 róngguāng huànfā glowing with health

容积 róngjī [名] volume

容量 róngliàng [名] capacity

容貌 róngmào [名] features (*pl*)

容纳 róngnà [动] **1** (盛下) hold (*pt, pp* held) ◇这个电影院能容纳近千人。This cinema can hold almost a thousand people. **2** (接受) tolerate ◇容纳异议 tolerate different opinions

容器 róngqì [名] container

容忍 róngrěn [动] tolerate ◇她不能容忍孩子的懒惰。She couldn't tolerate the child's laziness.

容许 róngxǔ [动] allow ◇老师不容许任何人缺课。The teacher didn't allow anyone to miss class.

容易 róngyì [形] **1** (简便) easy ◇学好一门外语不容易。Learning a foreign language isn't easy. ◇英文录入比中文录入容易。It's easier to type in English than it is to type in Chinese. **2** (较可能) likely ◇天冷容易感冒。When the weather's cold it's easy to catch a cold.

溶 róng [动] dissolve

溶化 rónghuà [动] **1** (溶解) dissolve **2** (融化) melt

溶解 róngjiě [动] dissolve

溶液 róngyè [名] solution

熔 róng [动] melt

熔点 róngdiǎn [名] melting point

熔化 rónghuà [动] melt

熔炼 róngliàn [动] **1** (指物质) smelt **2** (喻) steel oneself ◇熔炼意志 steel oneself

熔炉 rónglú [名] **1** (指炉子) furnace **2** (喻) forge

融 róng [动] **1** (融化) melt **2** (融合) blend **3** (流通) circulate

融合 rónghé [动] merge ◇两种文化正在互相融合。The two cultures are merging together.

融化 rónghuà [动] melt

融会贯通 róng huì guàn tōng thoroughly master

融洽 róngqià [形] harmonious ◇他们的关系一直很融洽。Their relationship has always been very harmonious.

融资 róngzī [动] pool funds ◇这个公司通过融资解决了资金问题。The company resolved its financial problems through a pooling of funds.

冗 rǒng [形] 1 (多余) superfluous ♦冗员 redundant personnel 2 (烦琐) trivial

冗长 rǒngcháng [形] long-winded

柔 róu [形] 1 (软) soft 2 (柔和) gentle

柔肠 róucháng [名] (喻) tender feelings (*pl*)

柔道 róudào [名] judo

柔和 róuhé [形] 1 (温和) gentle 2 (柔软) soft

柔滑 róuhuá [形] silky

柔美 róuměi [形] gentle and beautiful

柔情 róuqíng [名] tender feelings (*pl*)

柔软 róuruǎn [形] soft

柔顺 róushùn [形] meek

揉 róu [动] 1 (搓) rub ◇揉伤口 rub a wound 2 (团弄) knead

揉搓 róucuo [动] 1 (搓) rub ◇别老揉搓你的衣服。Don't keep rubbing at your clothes. 2 (方) (折磨) torment ◇别老揉搓我了。Stop tormenting me.

糅 róu [动] mix ♦糅杂 mix

糅合 róuhé [动] blend ◇糅合东西方文化 blend Eastern and Western cultures

蹂 róu [动] (书) tread on (*pt* trod, *pp* trodden)

蹂躏 róulìn [动] trample on ◇饱受战争蹂躏的城市 a city trampled on by war

肉 ròu **I** [名] **1** (指人) flesh **2** (指动物) meat ♦猪肉 pork **3** (指瓜果) flesh **II** [形] (不脆) spongy

肉搏 ròubó [动] fight hand to hand (*pt, pp* fought)

肉麻 ròumá [形] sickening ◇不要说那么肉麻的话。Don't say such sickening things.

肉体 ròutǐ [名] the human body ◇他的精神和肉体都受到了折磨。He endured both physical and mental torture.

肉刑 ròuxíng [名] corporal punishment

肉眼 ròuyǎn [名] **1** (指视力) the naked eye ◇肉眼看到的星星很有限。A limited number of stars can be seen with the naked eye. **2** (喻) lack of perceptiveness

肉欲 ròuyù [名] sexual desires (*pl*)

如 rú **I** [动] **1** (依从) comply with **2** (好似) be like ◇她俩亲如姐妹。The two of them are as close as sisters. ◇对她来说，这话如五雷轰顶。The words hit her like a thunderbolt. **3** (比得上) be as good as ♦不如 not as good as **4** (例如) ◇北京有很多名胜，如故宫、天坛等。Beijing has many tourist attractions, such as the Forbidden City, the Temple of Heaven and so on. **II** [介] as **III** [连] if ◇如一切顺利，我们会提前到达。If everything goes well, we'll be arriving early.

如出一辙 rú chū yī zhé be exactly the same

如此 rúcǐ [代] ◇人生如此美好！Life is so beautiful! ◇他的态度竟如此恶劣。His attitude was so unpleasant. ◇听说要放10天假。—但愿如此。I've heard we're getting ten days holiday – let's hope so.

如法炮制 rú fǎ páozhì follow a set pattern

如果 rúguǒ [连] if ◇如果我是你，就接受那份工作。If I were you, I'd accept that job. ◇我想周末去爬山，如果不下雨的话。I'd like to go mountain-climbing at the weekend, as long as it doesn't rain.

如何 rúhé [代] ◇此事如何解决？ How are we going to sort this out? ◇你今后如何打算？ What are your plans for the future?

如火如荼 rú huǒ rú tú magnificent

如获至宝 rú huò zhì bǎo like hitting the jackpot

如饥似渴 rú jī sì kě be hungry for ◇他如饥似渴地学习古代汉语。 He threw himself eagerly into the study of classical Chinese.

如箭在弦 rú jiàn zài xián have one's finger on the trigger

如胶似漆 rú jiāo sì qī joined at the hip ◇小两口新婚燕尔，如胶似漆。 That newly-wed couple are joined at the hip.

如今 rújīn [名] today

如雷贯耳 rú léi guàn ěr be a household name

如梦初醒 rú mèng chū xǐng as if woken from a dream ◇老师的一番话，使他如梦初醒。 It was as if the teacher's words had woken him from a dream.

如期 rúqī [副] on time ◇工人们如期完成了生产指标。 The workers achieved their production target on time.

如日中天 rú rì zhōng tiān be at the height of one's powers

如实 rúshí [副] accurately ◇如实讲述事情的经过 tell it like it is

如释重负 rú shì zhòng fù breathe a sigh of relief

如数家珍 rú shǔ jiā zhēn know … like the back of one's hand

如数 rúshù [副] exactly the right number

如同 rútóng [动] be like

如意 rúyì [动] be satisfied ◇大家对你这么好，还不如意？ Everyone's been so good to you – are you still not satisfied?

如意算盘 rúyì suànpán wishful thinking

如鱼得水 rú yú dé shuǐ (喻) like a duck to water ◇他在新公司如鱼得水。 He took to his new post like a duck to water.

如愿以偿 rúyuàn yǐ cháng have one's wish granted

如醉如痴 rú zuì rú chī be entranced

如坐针毡 rú zuò zhēn zhān be on edge ◇案情毫无进展，使他如坐针毡。 The case was making no progress at all, and he was completely on edge.

儒 rú [名] **1** (儒家) Confucianism **2** (旧) (读书人) scholar

儒家 Rújiā [名] Confucianism

孺 rú [名] child (*pl* children)

蠕 rú [动] 见下文

蠕动 rúdòng [动] wriggle

乳 rǔ **I** [名] **1** (乳房) breast **2** (乳汁) milk **3** (乳状物) milk ♦炼乳 condensed milk ♦豆乳 soya milk **II** [形] suckling ♦乳猪 suckling 或 sucking pig

乳儿 rǔ'ér [名] nursing baby

乳名 rǔmíng [名] pet name

乳臭未干 rǔxiù wèi gān wet behind the ears

乳制品 rǔzhìpǐn [名] milk products (*pl*)

辱 rǔ **I** [名] dishonour (英), dishonor (美) **II** [动] **1** (侮辱) insult **2** (玷污) disgrace

辱骂 rǔmà [动] call … names

辱没 rǔmò [动] disgrace

入 rù **I** [动] **1** (进入) enter ♦入场 enter **2** (参加) join ♦入学 enrol **3** (合乎) agree with **II** [名] (收入) income ♦岁入 yearly income

入不敷出 rù bù fū chū live beyond one's means

入超 rùchāo [名] import surplus

入耳 rù'ěr [形] pleasant-sounding

入股 rùgǔ [动] buy shares (*pt, pp* bought)

入骨 rùgǔ [动] cut to the bone (*pt, pp* cut)

入伙 rùhuǒ [动] **1** (参加) join **2** (搭伙) share a meal

入籍 rùjí [动] become a citizen (*pt* became, *pp* become) ◇他在美国居住10年后入籍。He was resident in America for ten years before becoming a citizen.

入境 rùjìng [动] enter a country ◇他去办理美国入境签证。He went to apply for a US visa.

入口 rùkǒu **I** [动] **1** (指嘴) put … in the mouth (*pt, pp* put) ◇入口的东西，要注意卫生。You should make sure that you only put clean things in your mouth. **2** (指货物) import **II** [名] (门) entrance

入流 rùliú [动] be up to standard ◇他写的小说不入流。His novel isn't up to standard.

入门 rùmén **I** [动] cross the threshold **II** [名] introduction ◇他正在读《电脑入门》。He's reading "*An Introduction to Computers*".

入迷 rùmí [动] be engrossed in ◇他下棋入了迷。He was engrossed in his chess game.

入魔 rùmó [动] be obsessed ◇他玩游戏像入了魔一样。He is obsessed with playing games.

入木三分 rù mù sān fēn (喻) incisive

入侵 rùqīn [动] invade

入情入理 rù qíng rù lǐ reasonable and logical

入神 rùshén **I** [动] be enthralled ◇她看小说看得入了神。She was enthralled by the novel. **II** [形] wonderful

入时 rùshí [形] fashionable

入手 rùshǒu [动] begin (*pt* began, *pp* begun) ◇教学应该从培养孩子兴趣入手。Education should begin with encouraging the child's interests.

入网 rùwǎng [动] **1** (手机、寻呼机) have a network connection **2** (计算机) connect to the Internet

入围 rùwéi [动] be short-listed

入味 rùwèi [形] **1** (有滋味) tasty **2** (有趣味) interesting

入伍 rùwǔ [动] join the army

入乡随俗 rù xiāng suí sú when in Rome, do as the Romans do

入选 rùxuǎn [动] be selected

入眼 rùyǎn [形] eye-catching ◇这衣服不怎么入眼。These clothes don't look good.

褥 rù [名] bedding

软 ruǎn [形] **1** (柔) soft **2** (温和) gentle **3** (柔弱) weak **4** (没主见) easily swayed

软包装 ruǎnbāozhuāng [名] **1** (指材料) soft packaging **2** (指包装) soft package

软刀子 ruǎndāozi [名] (喻) underhand tactics (*pl*)

软骨头 ruǎngǔtou [名] (喻) spineless person

软化 ruǎnhuà [动] soften

软和 ruǎnhuo [形] soft

软件 ruǎnjiàn [名] **1** (计算机) software ◇他们正在开发更先进的软件。They're developing more advanced software. **2** (指素质、服务、水平等) staff capacity

软禁 ruǎnjìn [动] put under house arrest (*pt, pp* put)

软绵绵 ruǎnmiānmiān [形] **1** (柔软) soft **2** (缠绵) sentimental **3** (软弱) feeble

软盘 ruǎnpán [名] floppy disk

软弱 ruǎnruò [形] weak ◇她大病初愈，身子还有些软弱。She's just getting over a serious illness, and she's still quite weak.

软水 ruǎnshuǐ [名] soft water

软卧 ruǎnwò [名] soft sleeper

软饮料 ruǎnyǐnliào [名] soft drink

软硬兼施 ruǎn yìng jiān shī (贬) use both hard and soft tactics

软着陆 ruǎnzhuólù [动] make a soft landing ◇这颗卫星安全地实现了软着陆。The satellite safely achieved a soft landing.

蕊 ruǐ [名] pistil

锐 ruì **I** [形] sharp **II** [名] vigour (英), vigor (美) **III** [副] sharply

锐不可当 ruì bù kě dāng unstoppable ◇这个球队锐不可当，一举拿下冠军。This team

is unstoppable – they won the championship with one bash at it.

锐角 ruìjiǎo [名] acute angle

锐利 ruìlì [形] **1** (锋利) sharp **2** (尖锐) astute ◊锐利的辞令 astute language

锐气 ruìqì [名] drive

锐意 ruìyì [形] determined

瑞 ruì [名] good luck

瑞雪 ruìxuě [名] timely fall of snow

睿 ruì [形] (书) far-sighted

睿智 ruìzhì [形] (书) far-sighted

闰 rùn [名] 见下文

闰年 rùnnián [名] leap year

闰日 rùnrì [名] February 29th

闰月 rùnyuè [名] leap month

润 rùn **I** [形] sleek **II** [动] **1** (加油或水) lubricate **2** (修饰) polish **III** [名] profit

润滑 rùnhuá [动] lubricate

润色 rùnsè [动] polish

润泽 rùnzé **I** [形] moist **II** [动] moisten

若 ruò **I** [动] be like ◊他一副若有所失的样子。He looked as if he had lost something. **II** [连] if ◊现在若不努力，将来会后悔的。If you don't work hard now you'll regret it in the future.

若非 ruòfēi [连] if not ◊若非众人相助，哪有他的今天？ If it wasn't for everybody's help, where would he be today?

若干 ruògān [数] several ◊若干人 several people

若是 ruòshì [连] if ◊若是你能参加，那就太好了。It would be great if you could join in.

若无其事 ruò wú qí shì act as if nothing is the matter ◊他心里很生气，表面上却装出若无其事的样子。Inside he was very angry, but on the outside he pretended that nothing was the matter.

若有所思 ruò yǒu suǒ sī as if lost in thought

偌 ruò 见下文

偌大 ruòdà [形] so big ◊偌大的公园，连个人影也没有。This park is so big, and yet there isn't a soul in sight.

弱 ruò [形] **1** (弱小) weak **2** (年幼) young **3** (软弱) weak

弱不禁风 ruò bù jīn fēng fragile

弱点 ruòdiǎn [名] weakness

弱化 ruòhuà [动] weaken

弱肉强食 ruò ròu qiáng shí the weak are food for the strong

弱视 ruòshì [名] lazy eye

弱项 ruòxiàng [名] Achilles' heel

弱小 ruòxiǎo [形] weak

弱智 ruòzhì [形] retarded ◊她女儿有点弱智。Her daughter has learning difficulties.

Ss

仨 sā [数] (口) three ♦哥仨 three brothers

撒 sā [动] **1** (手、网) let … go (*pt*, *pp* let) **2** (贬) (疯、野) lose control of oneself (*pt*, *pp* lost) ♦撒野 have a tantrum
▷另见 sǎ

撒欢儿 sāhuānr [动] (方) gambol

撒谎 sāhuǎng [动] (口) lie

撒娇 sājiāo [动] behave like a spoiled child

撒泼 sāpō [动] make a scene

撒气 sāqì [动] **1** (球、车胎) get a puncture **2** (发泄怒气) take one's anger out on (*pt* took, *pp* taken) ◇别拿我撒气！ Don't take your anger out on me!

撒手 sāshǒu [动] **1** (松手) let go (*pt*, *pp* let) **2** (不管) ignore ◇这么大的事你不能撒手不管。This matter is too important – you can't just ignore it. **3**(婉) (死) pass away

撒手锏 sāshǒujiǎn [名] trump card ◇不到紧急关头不要亮出撒手锏。Don't reveal your trump card before the crucial moment.

撒野 sāyě [动] throw a fit (*pt* threw, *pp* thrown) ◇一个醉汉在街上撒野。A man was throwing a drunken fit in the middle of the street. ◇这孩子没得到礼物，就在后院里撒野。Not having received a gift, the child had a tantrum in the back yard.

洒 sǎ [动] **1** (泼) sprinkle **2** (指不小心) spill

洒落 sǎluò [动] shower

洒脱 sǎtuo [形] carefree

撒 sǎ [动] **1** (散布) scatter ◇撒点酱油 sprinkle soy sauce **2** (散落) spill
▷另见 sā

撒播 sǎbō [动] sow (*pt* sowed, *pp* sown)

飒 sà 见下文

飒爽 sàshuǎng [形] valiant

腮 sāi [名] cheek

腮帮子 sāibāngzi [名] (口) cheek

塞 sāi **I** [动] stuff … into ◇我把零碎东西塞进了抽屉。I stuffed the bits and pieces into the drawer. **II** [名] cork
▷另见 sài

塞子 sāizi [名] cork

塞 sài [名] place of strategic importance
▷另见 sāi

塞翁失马 sài wēng shī mǎ blessing in disguise

赛 sài **I** [名] match ◇排球赛 volleyball match ◇演讲比赛 debating contest **II** [动] outdo (*pt* outdid, *pp* outdone)

赛车 sàichē **I** [动] race **II** [名] **1** (指汽车) racing car **2** (指自行车) racer

赛程 sàichéng [名] **1** (指距离) distance **2** (比赛日程) programme (英), program (美) **3** (比赛进度) schedule

赛季 sàijì [名] season

赛跑 sàipǎo [动] race

赛区 sàiqū [名] area

赛事 sàishì [名] competition

赛制 sàizhì [名] competition rules (*pl*)

三 sān [数] **1** (指数目) three ◇三本书 three books **2** (表示序数) third ◇我住三层。I live on the third floor. **3** (表示多数) several ♦三思 think twice ◇三番五次 over and over again **4** (表示少数) a few ◇三言两语 in a few words ◇三三两两 in twos and threes

三百六十行 sānbǎi liùshí háng [名] all walks of life

三长两短 sān cháng liǎng duǎn accident ◇孩子要有个三长两短，父母该怎么办呢？ If something happens and the child dies, what will his parents do then?

三番五次 sān fān wǔ cì over and over again

三伏 sānfú [名] the hottest days of summer (*pl*)

三更半夜 sāngēng-bànyè the middle of the night ◇你三更半夜不睡觉，跑出去干吗？ It's the middle of the night – why aren't you asleep and what are you doing outside?

三角 sānjiǎo [名] triangle ◇三角恋爱 love triangle

三九天 sānjiǔtiān [名] the coldest days of winter (*pl*)

三令五申 sān lìng wǔ shēn give repeated orders ◇政府三令五申司机不能在开车时打手机。The government has given repeated orders that drivers must not use mobile phones while driving.

三明治 sānmíngzhì [名] sandwich

三亲六故 sān qīn liù gù friends and relatives (*pl*)

三三两两 sānsānliǎngliǎng in twos and threes ◇大家三三两两地离开了办公室。Everyone left the office in twos and threes.

三生有幸 sān shēng yǒu xìng be extremely lucky

三思而行 sān sī ér xíng think twice ◇处理这个棘手的问题，望你三思而行，切莫鲁莽。I hope you'll think twice before you deal with this difficult issue, and not do anything rash.

三天打鱼，两天晒网 sān tiān dǎ yú, liǎng tiān shài wǎng work in fits and starts ◇你三天打鱼，两天晒网，根本练不好书法。You lack perseverance, so you'll never get anywhere with your calligraphy.

三天两头 sān tiān liǎng tóu (口) almost every day

三围 sānwéi [名] vital statistics (*pl*)

三维空间 sānwéi kōngjiān [名] three-dimensional space

三五成群 sān wǔ chéng qún (口) in little groups

三下五除二 sān xià wǔ chú èr efficiently ◇他三下五除二把我交给的任务完成了。He efficiently completed the task I gave him.

三心二意 sān xīn èr yì half-hearted ◇他工作三心二意的。He's half-hearted about his work.

三言两语 sān yán liǎng yǔ in a few words ◇三言两语解释不清。It's not possible to explain in a few words.

叁 sān [数] *an elaborate form of "three", used in writing cheques etc to prevent mistakes and forgery*

伞 sǎn [名] umbrella

伞兵 sǎnbīng [名] paratrooper

散 sǎn **I** [动] loosen **II** [形] loose
▷另见 sàn

散户 sǎnhù [名] small-scale investor

散乱 sǎnluàn [形] messy

散漫 sǎnmàn [形] slack

散文 sǎnwén [名] prose

散装 sǎnzhuāng [形] loose

散 sàn [动] **1** (分离) break up (*pt* broke, *pp* broken) ◇班会散了。The class meeting broke up. ◇乌云散了。The dark clouds scattered. **2** (散布) give ... out (*pt* gave, *pp* given) **3** (排除) dispel
▷另见 sǎn

散布 sànbù [动] **1** (传单) distribute **2** (谣言) spread (*pt, pp* spread)

散步 sànbù [动] go for a stroll (*pt* went, *pp* gone)

散发 sànfā [动] give ... off (*pt* gave, *pp* given) ◇她身上散发出一股香水味。She gives off a scent of perfume. ◇散发广告单 send out flyers

散会 sànhuì [动] end a meeting ◇散会之后请把会议室打扫一下。When the meeting is over, please tidy up the meeting room.

散伙 sànhuǒ [动] **1** (团体、组织) dissolve **2** (夫妻) split up (*pt, pp* split) ◇小夫妻散伙后，孩子怎么办？When the young couple split up, what will happen to the children?

散失 sànshī [动] **1** (物品) lose (*pt, pp* lost) ◇一些文物在战争中散失了。Some cultural relics were lost in the war. **2** (水分) evaporate

丧 sāng [名] funeral
▷另见 sàng

丧服 sāngfú [名] mourning suit

丧事 sāngshì [名] funeral arrangements (*pl*)

丧葬 sāngzàng [动] bury

丧钟 sāngzhōng [名] death knell

桑 sāng [名] mulberry

桑那浴 sāngnàyù [名] sauna

嗓 sǎng [名] **1** (嗓子) throat **2** (嗓音) voice

嗓门 sǎngmén [名] voice ◊他嗓门大。He's got a loud voice.

嗓音 sǎngyīn [名] voice

嗓子 sǎngzi [名] **1** (喉咙) throat **2** (嗓音) voice

丧 sàng [动] lose (*pt, pp* lost)
▷另见 sāng

丧胆 sàngdǎn [动] be terrified ◊敌军闻风丧胆。The enemy were terrified.

丧尽天良 sàng jìn tiān liáng heartless ◊她丧尽天良地为私利而贩卖奴隶。She heartlessly sold people into slavery for her own profit.

丧命 sàngmìng [动] die

丧偶 sàng'ǒu [动] be widowed

丧气 sàngqì [动] lose heart (*pt, pp* lost)

丧气 sàngqi [形] (口) unlucky ◊烧烤会碰上下雨，真丧气！ It rained on our barbecue – what bad luck!

丧失 sàngshī [动] lose (*pt, pp* lost) ◊丧失尊严 lose one's dignity

丧心病狂 sàng xīn bìng kuáng frenzied

搔 sāo [动] scratch

骚 sāo I [动] disturb II [形] (贬) flirty

骚动 sāodòng I [名] disturbance ◊总统被暗杀，在全国引起骚动。The assassination of the president led to disturbances all over the country. II [动] create an uproar ◊电影放到一半突然停电，观众骚动起来。Halfway through the film there was a power cut and the audience was in an uproar.

骚乱 sāoluàn [动] riot

骚扰 sāorǎo [动] harass ◊性骚扰 sexual harassment

臊 sāo [名] foul smell
▷另见 sào

扫 sǎo [动] **1** (打扫) sweep (*pt, pp* swept) **2** (除去) clear ... away ♦扫黄 anti-pornography campaign **3** (快速掠过) sweep (*pt, pp* swept) ◊演员向观众扫了一眼。The actor's gaze swept over the audience.
▷另见 sào

扫除 sǎochú [动] **1** (打扫) sweep ... up (*pt, pp* swept) **2** (除掉) eliminate ◊扫除文盲 eliminate illiteracy

扫地出门 sǎo dì chū mén be cast out into the world with nothing to one's name ◊父母死后，她被扫地出门。After her parents died, she was cast out into the world with nothing to her name.

扫黄 sǎohuáng [动] hold an anti-pornography campaign (*pt, pp* held)

扫盲 sǎománg [动] eliminate illiteracy

扫描 sǎomiáo [动] scan

扫描仪 sǎomiáoyí [名] scanner

扫墓 sǎomù [动] tend a grave

扫射 sǎoshè [动] strafe

扫视 sǎoshì [动] take a quick look (*pt* took, *pp* taken) ◊他向人群扫视了一遍，开始发表演讲。He took a quick look at the audience and then began his speech.

扫尾 sǎowěi [动] wind ... up (*pt, pp* wound) ◊工作大体做完了，明日谁来扫尾？ The work is pretty much finished. Who's going to come in tomorrow to wind things up?

扫兴 sǎoxìng [形] disappointed

嫂 sǎo [名] **1** (哥哥之妻) sister-in-law (*pl* sisters-in-law) **2** (泛称已婚妇女) auntie

嫂子 sǎozi [名] (口) sister-in-law (*pl* sisters-in-law)

扫 sào 见下文
▷另见 sǎo

扫帚 sàozhou [名] broom

瘙 sào 见下文

瘙痒 sàoyǎng [动] itch

臊 sào [形] shy
▷另见 sāo

色 sè [名] **1** (颜色) colour (英), color (美) **2** (脸色) expression **3** (种类) kind **4** (景象) scenery **5** (质量) quality **6** (美貌) good looks (*pl*)
▷另见 shǎi

色彩 sècǎi [名] **1** (颜色) colour (英), color (美) **2** (指情调) tone ◇小说笼罩着悲剧色彩。The novel is tragic in tone.

色调 sèdiào [名] **1** (指色彩) shade **2** (指思想) tone

色鬼 sèguǐ [名] lecher

色狼 sèláng [名] lecher

色盲 sèmáng [名] colour (英) 或 color (美) blindness

色眯眯 sèmīmī [形] lewd

色情 sèqíng [形] pornographic

色素 sèsù [名] pigment

色相 sèxiàng [名] charm

色泽 sèzé [名] lustre (英), luster (美)

涩 sè [形] **1** (味道) astringent **2** (文句) obscure

啬 sè [形] stingy

瑟 sè [名] Chinese harp

瑟缩 sèsuō [动] huddle ◇他瑟缩在角落里抽烟。He huddled in the corner to have a smoke.

森 sēn [形] **1** (形容树多) wooded **2** (阴暗) gloomy

森林 sēnlín [名] forest

森严 sēnyán [形] heavily guarded ◇军事重地戒备森严。The military area is heavily guarded.

僧 sēng [名] Buddhist monk

僧侣 sēnglǚ [名] Buddhist monk

杀 shā **I** [动] **1** (杀死) kill **2** (战斗) fight (*pt, pp* fought) **3** (削弱) reduce ◇杀威风 cut down to size **II** [助] ◇这个喜剧笑杀人。The comedy was utterly hilarious.

杀毒 shādú [动] get rid of a virus ◇杀毒软件 anti-virus software

杀风景 shā fēngjǐng spoil the mood ◇草坪上的垃圾真杀风景。The rubbish on the lawn really spoils the atmosphere.

杀害 shāhài [动] murder

杀机 shājī [名] murderous intent

杀价 shājià [动] bargain ◇我很会杀价。I'm a very good bargainer.

杀戒 shājiè [名] *Buddhist prohibition against taking life*

杀戮 shālù [动] massacre

杀气 shāqì [名] murderous look

杀青 shāqīng [动] be complete ◇电影杀青并进入发行阶段。The film is complete and ready for release.

杀生 shāshēng [动] kill

杀手 shāshǒu [名] killer

沙 shā **I** [名] **1** (石粒) sand **2** (指食品) paste **II** [形] hoarse

沙场 shāchǎng [名] (书) battlefield

沙尘 shāchén [名] dust

沙尘暴 shāchénbào [名] sandstorm

沙发 shāfā [名] sofa

沙锅 shāguō [名] casserole

沙化 shāhuà [动] desertify ◇草原逐渐沙化。The grasslands are gradually turning into desert. ◇沙化是自然环境的大患。Desertification is a disaster for the natural environment.

沙皇 shāhuáng [名] tsar

沙龙 shālóng [名] salon

沙漠 shāmò [名] desert

沙滩 shātān [名] beach

沙哑 shāyǎ [形] hoarse

沙眼 shāyǎn [名] trachoma

沙子 shāzi [名] sand

纱 shā [名] **1** (指材料) yarn **2** (指织品) gauze

纱布 shābù [名] gauze

刹 shā [动] brake
▷另见 chà

刹车 shāchē **I** [动] **1** (停止机器) brake ◇他没能刹住车，撞到了树上。He didn't brake in time, and crashed into the tree. **2** (喻) (制止) put a stop to (*pt, pp* put) ◇这个项目成了烂摊子。赶快刹车吧。This project is turning into a real shambles. We should put a stop to it at once. **II** [名] brake
▷另见 chà

砂 shā [名] grit (*pl* grit)

煞 shā **I** [动] **1** (结束) stop **2** (勒紧) tighten ◇煞车 brake **II** [副] (书) extremely
▷另见 shà

煞车 shāchē **I** [动] **1** (停止机器) brake **2** (喻) (制止) put a stop to (*pt, pp* put) **II** [名] brake

鲨 shā [名] shark

傻 shǎ [形] **1** (蠢) stupid **2** (死心眼) inflexible

傻瓜 shǎguā [名] fool

傻乎乎 shǎhūhū [形] simple-minded

傻气 shǎqì [形] foolish

傻笑 shǎxiào [动] giggle

傻眼 shǎyǎn [动] be stunned

傻子 shǎzi [名] fool

厦 shà [名] tall building ◇摩天大厦 skyscraper

煞 shà **I** [名] evil spirit **II** [副] extremely
▷另见 shā

煞白 shàbái [形] deathly pale

煞费苦心 shà fèi kǔxīn take great pains ◇父母对孩子的教育煞费苦心。Parents take great pains over their children's education.

霎 shà [名] instant

霎时间 shàshíjiān [名] instant

筛 shāi [动] sieve

筛选 shāixuǎn [动] **1** (指用筛子) sieve **2** (挑选) select ◇筛选运动员 select athletes

色 shǎi [名] colour (英), color (美)
▷另见 sè

色子 shǎizi [名] dice

晒 shài [动] **1** (阳光照射) ◇他被晒黑了。He's tanned. ◇我被晒伤了。I've got sunburn. ◇我被晒得直出汗。I was sweating constantly out in the sun. **2** (吸收光热) lie in the sun (*pt* lay, *pp* lain) ◇她躺在沙滩上晒太阳。She was lying on the beach, sunbathing. ◇我把衣服拿出去晒。I put the clothes out to dry in the sun.

晒台 shàitái [名] roof terrace

山 shān [名] **1** (地质) mountain ♦山峦 mountain range **2** (似山之物) ♦冰山 iceberg ◇人山人海 crowds of people

山崩 shānbēng [名] landslide

山川 shānchuān [名] landscape

山村 shāncūn [名] mountain village

山洞 shāndòng [名] cave

山峰 shānfēng [名] peak

山冈 shāngāng [名] hillock

山歌 shāngē [名] folk song

山沟 shāngōu [名] **1** (流水沟) gully **2** (山谷) valley **3** (偏僻山区) mountainous area

山谷 shāngǔ [名] valley

山河 shānhé [名] (书) lands (*pl*)

山货 shānhuò [名] mountain delicacies (*pl*)

山涧 shānjiàn [名] mountain stream

山脚 shānjiǎo [名] foothills (*pl*)

山林 shānlín [名] wooded hill

山峦 shānluán [名] mountain range

山脉 shānmài [名] mountain range

山盟海誓 shān méng hǎi shì make a pledge of everlasting love

山南海北 shān nán hǎi běi **1** (字) far and wide **2** (喻) (指说话) far-ranging

山坡 shānpō [名] mountainside

山清水秀 shān qīng shuǐ xiù beautiful natural scenery

山穷水尽 shān qióng shuǐ jìn reach the end of the road ◇股市还没到山

穷水尽的地步。The stock market still hasn't reached its lowest point.

山区 shānqū [名] mountainous area

山水 shānshuǐ [名] **1** (风景) scenery **2** (画) landscape painting

山头 shāntóu [名] mountaintop

山寨 shānzhài [名] mountain village

山珍海味 shān zhēn hǎi wèi [名] exotic delicacies (*pl*)

杉 shān [名] Chinese fir

删 shān [动] delete

删除 shānchú [动] delete

删改 shāngǎi [动] revise

删节 shānjié [动] abridge

衫 shān [名] shirt

姗 shān 见下文

姗姗来迟 shānshān lái chí arrive late

珊 shān 见下文

珊瑚 shānhú [名] coral

舢 shān 见下文

舢板 shānbǎn [名] sampan

扇 shān [动] **1** (扇子) fan **2** (耳光) slap ▷另见 shàn

扇动 shāndòng [动] flap

煽 shān [动] incite

煽动 shāndòng [动] incite ◇煽动民族仇恨 incite racial hatred

煽风点火 shān fēng diǎn huǒ (喻) stir up trouble

煽情 shānqíng **I** [动] stir up emotion **II** [形] **1** (褒) moving **2** (贬) sentimental

潸 shān [动] (书) shed tears (*pt*, *pp* shed)

潸然 shānrán [形] (书) tearful ◇潸然泪下 with tears rolling down one's cheeks

闪 shǎn **I** [动] **1** (闪避) dodge **2** (受伤) sprain **3** (突然出现) flash ◇流星一闪而过。The meteor flashed by. **4** (闪耀) shine (*pt*, *pp* shone) **II** [名] lightning

闪避 shǎnbì [动] dodge

闪电 shǎndiàn [名] lightning

闪动 shǎndòng [动] flash

闪念 shǎnniàn [动] be seized by a sudden thought

闪闪 shǎnshǎn [形] sparkling

闪身 shǎnshēn [动] sidestep

闪失 shǎnshī [名] accident

闪烁 shǎnshuò [动] **1** (忽明忽暗) twinkle ◇星星闪烁着。The stars were twinkling. **2** (吞吞吐吐) speak evasively (*pt* spoke, *pp* spoken)

闪烁其词 shǎnshuò qí cí speak evasively (*pt* spoke, *pp* spoken) ◇从他的闪烁其词能看出他分明是在掩饰什么。You can tell from his evasive language that he's got something to hide.

闪现 shǎnxiàn [动] flash

闪耀 shǎnyào [动] shine (*pt*, *pp* shone)

讪 shàn **I** [动] mock **II** [形] embarrassed

讪笑 shànxiào [动] mock

扇 shàn **I** [名] **1** (扇子) fan **2** (板状物) leaf (*pl* leaves) **II** [量] ◇一扇窗 a window ◇两扇门 two doors ▷另见 shān

善 shàn **I** [形] **1** (善良) kind **2** (良好) good ♦善事 good deeds **3** (友好) friendly **II** [动] **1** (办好) sort ... out ♦善后 deal with the aftermath **2** (擅长) be an expert at **3** (容易) be prone to ♦善忘 forgetful **III** [副] well

善罢甘休 shàn bà gān xiū ◇你就这样打发他走，他绝不会善罢甘休的。If you send him away like that, he won't take it lying down.

善待 shàndài [动] treat ... well ◇善待朋友 treat friends well

善后 shànhòu [动] deal with the aftermath (*pt*, *pp* dealt) ◇处理事故的善后问题 deal with the aftermath of an accident

善举 shànjǔ [名] charitable act

善良 shànliáng [形] kind-hearted

善始善终 shàn shǐ shàn zhōng start well and end well

善意 shànyì [名] good intention

◇善意的提醒 a well-intentioned warning

善于 shànyú [动] be good at ◇善于绘画 be good at painting

善终 shànzhōng [动] 1 (老死) die a natural death 2 (做好最后工作) end well

禅 shàn [动] abdicate ▷另见 chán

禅让 shànràng [动] abdicate

骟 shàn [动] neuter

缮 shàn [动] 1 (修补) repair 2 (书) (抄写) copy

缮写 shànxiě [动] copy ◇缮写文件 copy documents

擅 shàn I [动] be expert at ◇他擅辩。He's an expert debater. II [副] without leave ◇擅离职守 be absent without leave

擅长 shàncháng [动] be skilled in ◇擅长外交 be skilled in diplomacy ◇擅长武术 be skilled at martial arts

擅自 shànzì [动] take it upon oneself (*pt* took, *pp* taken) ◇上司不在，他擅自和客户签了协议。Since the boss was out, he took it upon himself to sign the agreement.

膳 shàn [名] (书) meal

膳食 shànshí [名] food

赡 shàn [动] support

赡养 shànyǎng [动] support ◇赡养父母 support one's parents

鳝 shàn [名] eel

伤 shāng I [动] 1 (身体部位) injure ♦扭伤 sprain ◇她伤了胳膊。She injured her arm. 2 (感情) hurt (*pt*, *pp* hurt) II [名] injury

伤残 shāngcán [名] the disabled (*pl*) ◇伤残军人 a disabled soldier

伤风 shāngfēng [动] catch a cold (*pt*, *pp* caught)

伤风败俗 shāng fēng bài sú offend public decency ◇这本小说被公认为伤风败俗。This novel was widely condemned as an offence to public decency.

伤感 shānggǎn [形] sentimental ◇一部伤感的电影 a sentimental film

伤害 shānghài [动] 1 (感情) hurt (*pt*, *pp* hurt) 2 (身体) damage ◇吸烟伤害身体。Smoking damages your health.

伤痕 shānghén [名] scar

伤口 shāngkǒu [名] wound

伤脑筋 shāng nǎojīn [动] be a headache ◇他让父母伤脑筋。He's a headache for his parents.

伤神 shāngshén [动] 1 (耗费精神) be stressful ◇你天天熬夜工作很伤神的。It's very stressful for you to stay up late working every night. 2 (伤心) be upset

伤天害理 shāng tiān hài lǐ do things that are against reason or nature

伤亡 shāngwáng [名] casualty

伤心 shāngxīn [形] sad

商 shāng I [动] discuss ♦磋商 consult ♦协商 negotiate II [名] 1 (商业) commerce ♦经商 trade 2 (商人) businessman (*pl* businessmen), businesswoman (*pl* businesswomen) ♦珠宝商 jeweller (英), jeweler (美) 3 (数) quotient ◇10被5除的商是2。Ten divided by five is two.

商标 shāngbiāo [名] trademark

商场 shāngchǎng [名] shopping centre (英) 或 mall (美)

商店 shāngdiàn [名] shop (英), store (美)

商定 shāngdìng [动] agree on ◇合同条款还未商定。The articles in the contract have not yet been agreed on.

商贩 shāngfàn [名] pedlar

商会 shānghuì [名] chamber of commerce

商机 shāngjī [名] business opportunity

商界 shāngjiè [名] business circles (*pl*)

商量 shāngliáng [动] discuss

商贸 shāngmào [名] commerce

商品 shāngpǐn [名] commodity ◇商

品交易会 trade fair ◇进出口商品 the import and export of goods

商品房 shāngpǐnfáng [名] commercial housing

商洽 shāngqià [动] discuss ◇我们需要与制造商商洽。We need to discuss matters with the manufacturer.

商情 shāngqíng [名] market conditions (*pl*)

商榷 shāngquè [动] discuss

商人 shāngrén [名] businessman (*pl* businessmen), businesswoman (*pl* businesswomen)

商谈 shāngtán [动] negotiate

商讨 shāngtǎo [动] discuss

商务 shāngwù [名] business ◇商务谈判 business negotiation ◇电子商务 e-commerce

商业 shāngyè [名] commerce ◇商业合作 commercial collaboration ◇商业银行 merchant bank ◇商业信息 commercial information

商酌 shāngzhuó [动] deliberate over ◇商酌反恐怖法案 deliberate over the anti-terrorism bill

晌 shǎng [名] **1** (一段时间) moment **2** (方) (晌午) noon

晌午 shǎngwu [名] (口) noon

赏 shǎng **I** [动] **1** (赏赐) award ◇因为他的出色表现，公司赏他一辆车。Because of his outstanding performance, the company awarded him a car. **2** (欣赏) admire ◇赏月 look at the moon **3** (赏识) appreciate **II** [名] reward

赏赐 shǎngcì **I** [动] grant **II** [名] reward

赏罚分明 shǎng fá fēn míng [动] be fair in meting out rewards and punishments

赏光 shǎngguāng [动] (敬) visit ◇本人非常感谢您能赏光我的个人主页。Thank you very much for visiting my website.

赏鉴 shǎngjiàn [动] appreciate

赏脸 shǎngliǎn [动] (敬) do ... the honour (英) 或 honor (美) ◇请您赏脸收下这份礼物。Please do me the honour of accepting this gift.

赏识 shǎngshí [动] think highly of (*pt*, *pp* thought)

赏析 shǎngxī [动] appreciate

赏心悦目 shǎng xīn yuè mù aesthetically pleasing ◇一幅赏心悦目的山水画 an aesthetically pleasing landscape painting

上 shàng **I** [名] **1** (指方位) upper part ♦上游 upper stream ◇上层 upper layer **2** (指等级、质量) ♦上级 higher authorities (*pl*) ♦上品 high-quality products **3** (指时间、次序) ◇上个月 last month ◇上半年 the first half of the year **II** [动] **1** (向上) go up (*pt* went, *pp* gone) ◇上楼 go upstairs **2** (按点前往) go (*pt* went, *pp* gone) ◇上学 go to school ♦上班 go to work **3** (去) go to (*pt* went, *pp* gone) ◇他上天津开会去了。He went to Tianjin to attend a meeting. **4** (出场) make an entrance ◇上场时，队长先上。When a team makes its entrance, the captain leads the way. **5** (添补) fill ♦上货 restock **6** (饭、菜) serve ◇上菜 serve food **7** (安装) fix ◇上螺丝 fix a screw **8** (涂) apply ◇上涂料 apply paint **9** (登载) appear ◇上杂志 appear in a magazine **10** (拧紧) tighten ◇我的表已上弦了。I've wound up my watch. **11** (达到) reach ◇上岁数 reach a great age ◇上百艘船停靠在岸边。Over a hundred boats were moored on the bank. **12** (楼、山) go up (*pt* went, *pp* gone) **13** (表示从低到高) ◇我跑上楼梯。I ran up the stairs. ◇演员走上舞台。The performer walked onto the stage. **14** (表示达到目的) ◇考上大学 pass the university entrance exams ◇当上老师 become a teacher **15**(表示开始) ◇喜欢上古典音乐 come to like classical music ◇他干上了导游。He's started work as a tour guide. **III** [介] **1** (在物体表面) on ◇椅子上 on the chair **2** (表示范围) in ◇报纸上 in the newspaper **3** (表示某方面) in ◇事实上 in fact

上班 shàngbān [动] go to work (*pt* went, *pp* gone)

上报 shàngbào [动] **1** (报告) report

◇这一急情况应及时上报。This urgent matter should be reported immediately. **2** (刊登) be in the newspaper

上辈 shàngbèi [名] **1** (祖先) ancestor **2** (上代) previous generation

上菜 shàngcài [动] serve food

上操 shàngcāo [动] do morning exercises

上策 shàngcè [名] the best plan

上层 shàngcéng [名] upper level ◇上层领导 upper echelons of leadership

上层建筑 shàngcéng jiànzhù [名] superstructure

上场 shàngchǎng [动] enter

上乘 shàngchéng [形] first-class ◇中国家具质量上乘。The quality of Chinese furniture is first class.

上蹿下跳 shàng cuàn xià tiào **1** (乱蹦) jump about ◇小丑上蹿下跳，把观众逗得哈哈大笑。The clown jumped about, and the audience burst into peals of laughter. **2** (贬) (指拉拢人) pull strings

上当 shàngdàng [动] be taken in ◇数次上当之后，我不再信他的话了。After I'd been taken in several times, I stopped believing what he said.

上等 shàngděng [形] first-class

上帝 Shàngdì [名] God

上吊 shàngdiào [动] hang oneself (*pt, pp* hanged)

上访 shàngfǎng [动] appeal to the higher authorities

上坟 shàngfén [动] pay one's respects at a grave (*pt, pp* paid)

上风 shàngfēng [名] **1** (指风) windward **2** (喻) (有利地位) advantage ◇占上风 get the upper hand

上浮 shàngfú [动] raise

上岗 shànggǎng [动] take up a post (*pt* took, *pp* taken) ◇企业员工竞争上岗。The workers are competing for jobs.

上告 shànggào [动] **1** (告状) appeal ◇上告法院 appeal to a higher court **2** (报告) report

上钩 shànggōu [动] rise to the bait (*pt* rose, *pp* risen)

上古 shànggǔ [名] ancient times (*pl*)

上轨道 shàng guǐdào [动] be on the right track

上好 shànghǎo [形] top-quality ◇上好的丝绸 top-quality silk

上火 shànghuǒ [动] (方) (发怒) get angry

上货 shànghuò [动] stock up ◇新品上货 stock up on new goods

上机 shàngjī [动] use a computer

上级 shàngjí [名] higher authorities (*pl*) ◇上级机关 higher level organization

上将 shàngjiàng [名] general

上交 shàngjiāo [动] hand … in

上缴 shàngjiǎo [动] hand … over

上进 shàngjìn [动] make progress

上空 shàngkōng [名] ◇直升机在上空盘旋。A helicopter is hovering overhead.

上口 shàngkǒu **I** [动] flow well **II** [形] flowing

上来 shànglái [动] **1** (指动作趋向) ◇饭菜端上来了。The meal was brought to the table. ◇他从坑里爬上来了。He climbed out of the pit. **2** (表示成功) ◇这个问题我答不上来。I can't answer this question. **3** (指等级提升) promote ◇这名干部是从基层提拔上来的。This official was promoted from the grass roots.

上梁不正下梁歪 shàngliáng bù zhèng xiàliáng wāi those in subordinate positions will follow the example set by their superiors

上流 shàngliú **I** [名] upper reaches (*pl*) **II** [形] upper-class

上马 shàngmǎ [动] begin (*pt* began, *pp* begun)

上门 shàngmén [动] **1** (到家里) call on ◇他亲自上门向他们道谢。He called on them in person to offer his thanks. ◇送货上门 delivery service **2** (锁门) lock the door

上面 shàngmian [名] **1** (指位置高) ◇书

桌上面挂着风铃。A windchime is hanging above the desk. ◊他住在我上面。He lives above me. **2** (物体表面) ◊墙上面挂着相片。Photographs were hanging on the walls. ◊袖子上面有墨迹。There are ink stains on the sleeve. **3** (以上的部分) ◊上面的例子很具说服力。The previous example is very persuasive. ◊上面我们分析了各种可能性。As can be seen above, we have made an analysis of all possibilities. **4** (方面) ◊他没时间花在看小说上面。He doesn't have time for reading novels. ◊他在音乐上面的造诣很深。His achievements in the field of music are considerable. **5** (上级) superior ◊上面来了指示。We have received instructions from our superiors.

上年纪 shàng niánji [动] get old ◊妈妈上了年纪，视力下降了。Mum's getting old – her eyesight is failing.

上品 shàngpǐn [名] top grade

上去 shàngqù [动] **1** (指由低到高) go up (*pt* went, *pp* gone) **2** (提高) improve

上任 shàngrèn [动] take up a new post (*pt* took, *pp* taken)

上色 shàngshǎi [动] colour (英), color (美)

上身 shàngshēn **I** [名] upper body **II** [动] put … on (*pt*, *pp* put)

上升 shàngshēng [动] **1** (往高处移) ascend **2** (增加) increase

上市 shàngshì [动] appear on the market ◊明日有新股上市。Tomorrow the new stock will appear on the market. ◊8月桃子大量上市。In August, peaches are in season.

上手 shàngshǒu [动] start

上书 shàngshū [动] submit a statement ◊工人联名上书揭发厂长贪污受贿。The workers submitted a statement revealing how the plant manager had accepted bribes.

上司 shàngsi [名] superior

上诉 shàngsù [动] appeal

上溯 shàngsù [动] trace … back

上算 shàngsuàn [形] worthwhile

上台 shàngtái [动] **1** (指舞台、讲台) appear on stage **2** (贬) (掌权) come to power (*pt* came, *pp* come) ◊新领导上台了。The new leader has come to power.

上天 shàngtiān **I** [动] **1** (升空) launch ◊人造卫星上天了。A man-made satellite was launched. **2** (死亡) (婉) pass away **II** [名] Heaven

上网 shàngwǎng [动] go online (*pt* went, *pp* gone) ◊上网查信 go online to check one's e-mail ◊上网聊天 go online to chat

上文 shàngwén [名] preceding paragraph ◊请见上文。Please see above.

上午 shàngwǔ [名] morning

上西天 shàng xītiān (口) (贬) kick the bucket

上限 shàngxiàn [名] upper limit

上相 shàngxiàng [形] photogenic

上演 shàngyǎn [动] perform

上瘾 shàngyǐn [动] be addicted to

上映 shàngyìng [动] show (*pt* showed, *pp* shown)

上游 shàngyóu [名] **1** (指河流) upper reaches (*pl*) **2** (先进) front rank

上涨 shàngzhǎng [动] rise (*pt* rose, *pp* risen)

上阵 shàngzhèn [动] pitch in ◊厂长亲自上阵抓生产。The boss pitched in personally in the struggle to increase production.

上座率 shàngzuòlǜ [名] box-office figures (*pl*)

尚 shàng **I** [动] esteem **II** [副] (书) still ◊现在下结论为还时尚早。It's still too early to jump to conclusions.

尚且 shàngqiě [连] ◊简单的对话他尚且都不懂，更何况难的了。He can't even understand simple conversations, let alone difficult ones. ◊宝宝尚且不会走路，更何况跑呢。The baby can't even walk, let alone run.

捎 shāo [动] deliver ◊捎口信 deliver a message

捎带 shāodài [副] in passing ◇每次出差我都捎带买些礼物。Every time I go away on business I always pick up presents.

烧 shāo [动] **1** (着火) burn ◇她把信烧掉了。She burned the letter. ◇房子烧了。The house was burned down. **2** (加热) heat ◇烧水 boil water **3** (烹) braise ◇红烧牛肉 beef braised in soy sauce **4** (烤) roast ♦烧鸡 roast chicken **5** (发烧) have a temperature ◇她烧到了39度。She has a temperature of 39 degrees.

烧毁 shāohuǐ [动] be burned down

烧烤 shāokǎo [动] barbecue

烧香 shāoxiāng [动] burn incense

烧灼 shāozhuó [动] burn

梢 shāo [名] top ♦树梢 treetop

稍 shāo [副] slightly ◇他比我稍矮点。He's slightly shorter than me. ▷另见 shào

稍稍 shāoshāo [副] a little

稍微 shāowēi [副] a little

稍纵即逝 shāo zòng jí shì fleeting ◇商人要善于抓住稍纵即逝的市场机遇。Business people must be good at taking advantage of every fleeting window of opportunity.

艄 shāo [名] **1** (船尾) stern **2** (舵) rudder ◇撑艄 be at the helm

艄公 shāogōng [名] helmsman

勺 sháo [名] ladle

少 shǎo **I** [形] few ◇你要少吃甜食。You should eat fewer sweet things. ◇屋里家具太少。There is very little furniture in the room. **II** [动] **1** (缺) lack ◇汤里少了葱。There is no onion in the soup. **2** (丢) be missing ◇她发现自行车少了。She discovered that a bike was missing. **III** [副] ◇少等一会儿 Please wait a moment. ▷另见 shào

少见多怪 shǎo jiàn duō guài ◇大千世界无奇不有，你用不着少见多怪。The world is full of miraculous things, you shouldn't be so easily impressed. ◇也许是我少见多怪，我觉得最美丽的地方莫过于桂林了。Perhaps I haven't seen much of the world, but I think nowhere is more beautiful than Guilin.

少量 shǎoliàng [名] a little ◇在汤里放少量盐。Put a little salt in the soup.

少陪 shǎopéi [动] (客套) ◇我得先走一步， 少陪了。I'm afraid I really have to go.

少时 shǎoshí [名] ◇他少时就回来了。He came back after a short while. ◇少时雷雨停了，探险队又继续赶路。Before long the storm stopped and the exploration team continued on its way.

少数 shǎoshù [名] minority

少许 shǎoxǔ [形] (书) a little

少 shào **I** [形] young ♦少女 young girl **II** [名] teenager ♦阔少 rich kid ▷另见 shǎo

少不更事 shàobùgēngshì green ◇新来的工人少不更事。The new workers are very green.

少妇 shàofù [名] young wife (*pl* wives)

少男少女 shàonán shàonǔ [名] teenagers (*pl*)

少年老成 shàonián lǎochéng mature beyond one's years

少女 shàonǔ [名] young girl

少相 shàoxiang [形] young-looking

少壮 shàozhuàng [形] young and strong

哨 shào [名] **1** (兵站) post ♦哨所 post **2** (哨子) whistle ◇吹哨 whistle

哨兵 shàobīng [名] sentry

哨卡 shàoqiǎ [名] sentry post

哨子 shàozi [名] whistle

稍 shào 见下文 ▷另见 shāo

稍息 shàoxī [动] stand at ease (*pt, pp* stood)

奢 shē [形] extravagant ♦奢靡 wasteful ♦奢望 high hopes (*pl*)

奢侈 shēchǐ [形] luxurious

奢华 shēhuá [形] sumptuous

奢求 shēqiú [动] make excessive demands

奢望 shēwàng [名] high hopes (*pl*)

赊 shē [动] buy … on credit (*pt, pp* bought) ♦赊购 buy … on credit

赊欠 shēqiàn [动] buy on credit (*pt, pp* bought)

赊账 shēzhàng [动] buy on credit (*pt, pp* bought)

舌 shé [名] tongue ♦火舌 flame

舌头 shétou [名] tongue

舌战 shézhàn [动] have a heated dispute

折 shé [动] **1** (折断) snap ◊树枝折了。The branch snapped. **2** (亏损) lose money (*pt, pp* lost)
▷另见 zhē, zhé

折本 shéběn [动] lose money (*pt, pp* lost) ◊他把那批货折本卖掉了。He sold all of those goods at a loss.

蛇 shé [名] snake

舍 shě [动] **1** (舍弃) abandon ◊舍己为人 be altruistic **2** (施舍) give (*pt* gave, *pp* given) ◊他时常舍些钱给乞丐。He frequently gives to beggars.
▷另见 shè

舍本逐末 shě běn zhú mò get one's priorities wrong ◊大学生过多参与社会活动其实是舍本逐末。Students who get too involved in social activities have got their priorities wrong.

舍己为人 shě jǐ wèi rén be altruistic ◊他舍己为人的精神令人感动。His sense of altruism is touching.

舍近求远 shě jìn qiú yuǎn go far afield ◊附近商店有各种装修材料，我们不必舍近求远。The local shops have all sorts of decorating materials – there's no need for us to go far afield.

舍命 shěmìng [动] risk one's life

舍弃 shěqì [动] give up (*pt* gave, *pp* given)

舍身 shěshēn [动] give one's life (*pt* gave, *pp* given) ◊舍身救人 give one's life for others

设 shè [动] **1** (摆) set … up (*pt, pp* set) ◊山顶设了个气象站。A weather station has been set up at the summit. ◊设宴 give a banquet **2** (想) plan ♦设计 work out a plan **3** (假定) suppose ♦设想 envisage

设备 shèbèi [名] equipment ◊办公设备 office equipment

设法 shèfǎ [动] try

设防 shèfáng [动] set up defences (英) 或 defenses (美) (*pt, pp* set)

设计 shèjì [动] design ◊服装设计 fashion design ◊这本词典的封面设计太美了。This dictionary has a great jacket design.

设立 shèlì [动] establish

设身处地 shè shēn chǔ dì put oneself in another person's shoes

设施 shèshī [名] facilities (*pl*)

设想 shèxiǎng [动] **1** (想像) imagine **2** (着想) consider

设置 shèzhì [动] **1** (设立) set … up (*pt, pp* set) ◊设置障碍 set up a barrier **2** (安装) install ◊起居室里设置了空调。Air conditioning has been installed in the living room.

社 shè [名] organization ♦报社 newspaper office ♦旅行社 travel agent

社会 shèhuì [名] society ◊国际社会 international community ◊社会福利 social welfare

社会主义 shèhuì zhǔyì [名] socialism

社交 shèjiāo [名] social contact ◊社交活动 social activity

社论 shèlùn [名] editorial

社区 shèqū [名] community ◊社区服务 community service

社团 shètuán [名] organization

舍 shè [名] house ♦宿舍 dormitory ♦猪舍 pigsty
▷另见 shě

射 shè [动] **1** (发) shoot (*pt, pp* shot) ◊射箭 shoot an arrow **2** (喷) spout

♦喷射 spurt **3** (放出) emit ♦照射 shine

射程 shèchéng [名] range

射击 shèjī **I** [动] fire **II** [名] shooting

射门 shèmén [动] shoot (*pt, pp* shot)

射线 shèxiàn [名] **1** (电磁波) ray **2** (数) straight line

射影 shèyǐng [名] projection

涉 shè [动] **1** (渡) cross ◇跋山涉水 cross mountains and rivers **2** (经历) go through (*pt* went, *pp* gone) ♦涉险 go through dangerous situations **3** (牵涉) involve ♦涉嫌 be a suspect

涉及 shèjí [动] involve ◇走私案涉及海关和警方。The smuggling case involves Customs and the police. ◇这个问题书里面没涉及到。The book does not touch on this question.

涉猎 shèliè [动] **1** (浏览) browse ◇这类书只需涉猎就行了。It's enough just to browse through a book like this. **2** (接触) touch

涉世 shèshì [动] have experience of life ◇他涉世不深，常常受骗。He has little experience of life and is always getting cheated.

涉嫌 shèxián [动] be a suspect

赦 shè [动] pardon

赦免 shèmiǎn [动] pardon

摄 shè [动] **1** (吸取) absorb **2** (摄影) take a photo (*pt* took, *pp* taken) **3** (代理) act for

摄取 shèqǔ [动] **1** (吸收) take in (*pt* took, *pp* taken) **2** (拍摄) take a photo of

摄像 shèxiàng [动] make a video

摄影 shèyǐng [动] **1** (照相) take a photo (*pt* took, *pp* taken) **2** (拍电影) shoot a film (英) 或 movie (美) (*pt, pp* shot)

摄制 shèzhì [动] produce ◇摄制电影 produce a film (英) 或 movie (美)

慑 shè [动] (书) fear

慑服 shèfú [动] **1** (屈服) submit **2** (使屈服) make … submit

申 shēn [动] express

申办 shēnbàn [动] **1** (申请举办) bid for (*pt, pp* bid) ◇申办奥运会 bid for the Olympics **2** (申请办理) apply for ◇申办寿险 apply for a pension

申报 shēnbào [动] declare

申辩 shēnbiàn [动] defend oneself

申斥 shēnchì [动] reprimand

申明 shēnmíng [动] declare

申请 shēnqǐng [动] apply ◇申请工作 apply for a job

申诉 shēnsù [动] appeal

申冤 shēnyuān [动] **1** (昭雪冤屈) get justice **2** (申诉冤屈) appeal for justice

伸 shēn [动] stretch ♦伸懒腰 stretch oneself

伸手 shēnshǒu [动] **1** (伸出手) hold out one's hand (*pt, pp* held) **2** (索要) ask for help

伸缩 shēnsuō [动] **1** (伸展和收缩) expand and contract **2** (变通) be flexible

伸展 shēnzhǎn [动] stretch

伸张 shēnzhāng [动] uphold (*pt, pp* upheld)

身 shēn **I** [名] **1** (身体) body ◇身强力壮 be strong and fit **2** (生命) life ◇舍身 lay down one's life **3** (自己) oneself ◇以身作则 set a good example (*with one's own conduct*) **4** (品德) moral character **5** (部分) body ♦车身 body (*of a car*) **II** [量] ◇一身新衣 a set of new clothes

身败名裂 shēn bài míng liè be utterly discredited

身不由己 shēn bù yóu jǐ not be able to help oneself ◇他社交活动太多，确实身不由己。He's got himself involved so many activities – he just can't help himself.

身材 shēncái [名] figure

身段 shēnduàn [名] figure

身份 shēnfen [名] **1** (地位) position **2** (尊严) dignity

身份证 shēnfènzhèng [名] identity card

身价 shēnjià [名] social status

身教 shēnjiào [动] teach by example (*pt, pp* taught)

身经百战 shēn jīng bǎi zhàn be seasoned ◇这位球星身经百战。This football star is a seasoned player.

身临其境 shēn lín qí jìng actually be there ◇这幅油画使人有身临其境之感。This painting makes you feel you are actually there.

身强力壮 shēn qiáng lì zhuàng tough

身躯 shēnqū [名] body

身世 shēnshì [名] life experience

身手 shēnshǒu [名] skill

身受 shēnshòu [动] experience ... personally

身体 shēntǐ [名] body

身体力行 shēn tǐ lì xíng practise (英) 或 practice (美) what one preaches ◇当领导身体力行非常重要。It's very important for a leader to practise what he preaches.

身外之物 shēn wài zhī wù worldly things ◇金钱和荣誉都是身外之物。Money and fame are worldly things.

身心 shēnxīn [名] body and mind ◇身心健康 physical and mental health

身孕 shēnyùn [名] pregnancy ◇她有了身孕。She is pregnant.

身子 shēnzi [名] (口) **1** (身体) body ◇她生病后身子很弱。Since she became ill she has been very weak. **2** (身孕) pregnancy ◇她已有了3个月的身子。She is three months pregnant.

呻 shēn 见下文

呻吟 shēnyín [动] groan

参 shēn [名] ginseng ▷另见 cān, cēn

绅 shēn [名] gentry

绅士 shēnshì [名] gentleman

深 shēn **I** [形] **1** (指深度) deep ♦深水 deep water **2** (指距离) remote ♦深山 remote mountain **3** (深奥) difficult ◇这本书对孩子来说太深了。This book is too difficult for children. **4** (深刻) deep ◇我对老经理的印象特别深。My old boss left a deep impression on me. **5** (密切) close ◇我和父母的感情都很深。I am very close to my parents. **6** (浓重) dark ♦深蓝 dark blue **7** (指时间久) late ♦深夜 late at night **II** [名] depth ◇这口井有10米深。This well is 10 metres (英) 或 meters (美) deep. **III** [副] very ♦深信不疑 firmly believe

深奥 shēn'ào [形] profound

深层 shēncéng [名] the depths (*pl*) ◇雨水渗到了土壤的深层。The rain has seeped deep into the soil. ◇深层原因 underlying reason

深沉 shēnchén [形] deep ◇暮色深沉。The dusk is deepening. ◇他的嗓音深沉。He has a deep voice. ◇我哥哥很深沉。My brother is a deep one.

深仇大恨 shēn chóu dà hèn deep hatred

深度 shēndù **I** [名] depth ◇测量油井的深度 gauge the depth of an oil well ◇这篇文章缺乏深度。This essay lacks depth. **II** [形] extreme ◇深度近视 extreme short-sightedness

深更半夜 shēngēng-bànyè in the dead of night

深广 shēnguǎng [形] broad

深厚 shēnhòu [形] **1** (浓厚) deep **2** (坚实) solid

深化 shēnhuà [动] deepen

深究 shēnjiū [动] get to the bottom of

深居简出 shēn jū jiǎn chū be a recluse

深刻 shēnkè [形] deep ◇首相的讲话给我留下深刻的印象。The prime minister's speech made a deep impression on me.

深明大义 shēn míng dàyì be principled ◇父亲深明大义，送儿子去投案自首。The father was very principled: he sent his son to give himself up.

深谋远虑 shēn móu yuǎn lǜ think ahead ◇决策者需要深谋远虑。Policy makers need to think ahead.

深浅 shēnqiǎn [名] **1** (深度) depth **2** (分寸) sense of propriety ◇他

说话没深浅。He often speaks inappropriately.

深切 shēnqiè [形] **1** (深厚) heartfelt ◇对朋友们深切的关怀我非常感谢。Many thanks to my friends for their heartfelt concern. **2** (切实) deep ◇我对这种事有深切的体会。I have a deep understanding of these things.

深情 shēnqíng [名] deep feeling

深情厚谊 shēn qíng hòu yì [名] deep friendship

深入 shēnrù **I** [动] penetrate **II** [形] thorough

深入浅出 shēn rù qiǎn chū explain difficult concepts simply

深山 shēnshān [名] remote mountains (*pl*)

深思 shēnsī [动] reflect on

深思熟虑 shēn sī shú lǜ careful consideration ◇购房时一定要深思熟虑。When buying a house you must give it careful consideration.

深邃 shēnsuì [形] **1** (距离远) deep **2** (深奥) profound

深恶痛绝 shēn wù tòng jué detest

深信 shēnxìn [动] believe deeply

深渊 shēnyuān [名] abyss

深远 shēnyuǎn [形] far-reaching

深造 shēnzào [动] pursue advanced studies

深湛 shēnzhàn [形] profound

深重 shēnzhòng [形] serious

什 shén 见下文
▷另见 shí

什么 shénme [代] **1** (表示疑问) what ◇你要什么？What do you want? **2** (表示虚指) something ◇他们在商量着什么。They are discussing something. **3** (表示任指) anything ◇我什么都不怕。I'm not afraid of anything. **4** (表示惊讶、不满) what ◇什么！他拒绝出席会议！What! He refused to attend the meeting! ◇这是什么菜！一点都不好吃。What sort of food is this? It's disgusting. **5** (表示责难) ◇你在胡说什么！What's that rubbish? **6** (表示不同意) ◇什么不好意思？她脸皮厚得很。What do you mean she's embarrassed? She's very thick-skinned. **7** (表示例举不尽) ◇什么水果、酸奶、糖果，她都爱吃。She likes eating things like fruit, yoghurt and sweets.

什么的 shénmede [代] ◇餐桌上摆满了香蕉、李子、苹果什么的。The dining table was loaded with bananas, plums, apples and so on.

神 shén **I** [名] **1** (宗) god ♦鬼神 supernatural beings (*pl*) **2** (精神) spirit ♦走神 be absent-minded **II** [形] **1** (高超) amazing ♦神奇 magical **2** (方) (聪明) clever ◇你可真神！ How clever you are!

神不守舍 shēn bù shǒu shè drift off ◇他在课堂上总是神不守舍。He's always drifting off in class.

神采 shéncǎi [名] demeanour

神出鬼没 shén chū guǐ mò come and go ◇那批人神出鬼没，居无定所。That bunch come and go – they don't live anywhere permanently.

神乎其神 shén hū qí shén so wonderful ◇这是一个神乎其神的传说。This is such a wonderful legend.

神化 shénhuà [动] deify

神话 shénhuà [名] myth

神魂颠倒 shén hún diān dǎo be infatuated ◇他被那女人弄得神魂颠倒。He's become infatuated with that woman.

神机妙算 shén jī miào suàn have foresight

神经 shénjīng [名] nerve ◇神经系统 nervous system

神灵 shénlíng [名] spirit

神秘 shénmì [形] mysterious

神明 shénmíng [名] god

神奇 shénqí [形] magical

神气 shénqì **I** [名] manner ◇他说话的神气很严肃。His manner as he spoke was serious. **II** [形] **1** (精神) impressive ◇他穿上西装显得很神气。He looks impressive in a suit. **2** (得意) cocky

神情 shénqíng [名] expression

神色 shénsè [名] look

神圣 shénshèng [形] sacred

神思 shénsī [名] state of mind

神似 shénsì [形] lifelike

神速 shénsù [形] incredibly fast

神态 shéntài [名] look

神通 shéntōng [名] remarkable ability

神往 shénwǎng [动] be amazed ◊桂林山水令人神往。The scenery around Guilin is amazing.

神仙 shénxiān [名] immortal

神学 shénxué [名] theology

神志 shénzhì [名] mind

审 shěn I [形] careful ♦审慎 cautious II [动] 1 (审查) go over (*pt* went, *pp* gone) ◊审稿 review 2 (审讯) try ◊审案 try a case

审查 shěnchá [动] examine

审订 shěndìng [动] revise

审定 shěndìng [动] examine and approve

审核 shěnhé [动] verify

审计 shěnjì [动] audit

审理 shěnlǐ [动] hear (*pt, pp* heard)

审美 shěnměi [动] appreciate

审判 shěnpàn [动] try

审批 shěnpī [动] examine and approve

审慎 shěnshèn [形] cautious

审时度势 shěn shí duó shì take stock of a situation

审视 shěnshì [动] examine … closely

审问 shěnwèn [动] interrogate

审讯 shěnxùn [动] interrogate

审议 shěnyì [动] consider

审阅 shěnyuè [动] check

婶 shěn [名] aunt

肾 shèn [名] kidney

甚 shèn I [形] extreme ◊欺人太甚 be too high-handed II [副] very ◊这家饭店的服务甚佳。The service at this restaurant is very good.

甚至 shènzhì I [副] even ◊父亲去世后，他痛苦得甚至无法工作。After his father passed away, he was so distressed he couldn't even work. II [连] ◊对职员们的相继辞职，老板感到遗憾甚至痛苦。The boss felt regret, even distress, about the spate of resignations. ◊在巴西，不但年轻人，甚至老年人都喜欢足球。In Brazil everybody loves football, not just the young, but older people too.

渗 shèn [动] seep

渗漏 shènlòu [动] leak

渗入 shènrù [动] 1 (液体) seep into 2 (势力等) penetrate

渗透 shèntòu [动] 1 (液体、气体) permeate 2 (抽象事物) infiltrate

蜃 shèn 见下文

蜃景 shènjǐng [名] mirage

慎 shèn [形] careful

慎重 shènzhòng [形] cautious

升 shēng I [动] 1 (由低往高) rise (*pt* rose, *pp* risen) 2 (提升) promote ♦升职 be promoted II [量] litre (英), liter (美) ◊1升牛奶 a litre of milk

升格 shēnggé [动] promote ◊他由系主任升格为校长。He was promoted from head of department to principal.

升华 shēnghuá [动] 1 (物) sublimate 2 (升级) distil (英), distill (美)

升级 shēngjí [动] 1 (升高年级) go up (*pt* went, *pp* gone) ◊我儿子将升到2年级。My son will go up into year two (英) 或 second grade (美). 2 (规模扩大) escalate ◊战争还在升级。The war continues to escalate.

升级换代 shēng jí huàn dài upgrade

升迁 shēngqiān [动] *get promoted and transferred to a different department*

升天 shēngtiān [动] die

升学 shēngxué [动] *move to a more advanced school*

升值 shēngzhí [动] appreciate

生 shēng I [动] 1 (生育) give birth to (*pt* gave, *pp* given) ◊生孩子 have a baby **2** (长) grow (*pt* grew, *pp* grown) ◇生根 take root **3** (活) live ◇生死 life and death **4** (患) get (*pt* got, *pp* got (英), gotten (美)) ♦生病 get ill **5** (点) light (*pt, pp* lit) ♦生火 light a fire **II** [名] **1** (生命) life (*pl* lives) ♦求生 eke out a living **2** (生平) life (*pl* lives) ♦今生 this life **3** (学生) student ♦新生 new student ♦小学生 primary school pupil (英), elementary school student (美) **III** [形] **1** (活的) living ♦生物 living things **2** (未熟的) unripe ◇生苹果 unripe apples **3** (未煮的) raw ◇生鱼片 slices of raw fish **4** (未加工的) crude ♦生铁 crude iron **5** (生疏) unfamiliar ♦生人 stranger **6** (生硬) stiff ◇这个句子是生凑的。This sentence is awkwardly put together. **IV** [副] very ♦生疼 very painful

生搬硬套 shēng bān yìng tào copy … mechanically ◇对别人的学习方法不能生搬硬套。One should not mechanically copy other students' study methods.

生产 shēngchǎn [动] **1** (制造) produce **2** (生孩子) give birth to (*pt* gave, *pp* given)

生产线 shēngchǎnxiàn [名] production line

生辰 shēngchén [名] birthday

生存 shēngcún [动] survive

生动 shēngdòng [形] lively

生还 shēnghuán [动] survive

生活 shēnghuó **I** [名] life ◇提高生活质量 improve quality of life ◇日常生活 daily life **II** [动] **1** (居住) live ◇他从小和祖母一起生活。He's lived with his grandmother since he was little. **2** (生存) survive ◇没有水，人就不能生活。Without water, human beings can't survive.

生机 shēngjī [名] **1** (生存机会) lease of life ◇一线生机 a chance of survival **2** (活力) life ◇春天来了，大地充满生机。It's spring and the earth is teeming with life.

生计 shēngjì [名] make a living

生就 shēngjiù [动] be born with

生来 shēnglái [副] ◇人生来都是平等的。All human beings are born equal.

生离死别 shēng lí sǐ bié part forever

生理 shēnglǐ [名] physiology

生力军 shēnglìjūn [名] **1** (指军队) new troops (*pl*) **2** (指人员) fresh blood

生灵 shēnglíng [名] (书) (生命) the people (*pl*)

生龙活虎 shēng lóng huó hǔ full of energy

生路 shēnglù [名] way out

生命 shēngmìng [名] life (*pl* lives) ◇挽救生命 save a life ◇生命科学 life science

生命力 shēngmìnglì [名] vitality

生命线 shēngmìngxiàn [名] lifeblood

生怕 shēngpà [副] ◇我生怕着凉，多盖了条毯子。So as not to get cold, I put on another blanket. ◇我睡觉时把钱放在枕头下，生怕贼偷了去。I slept with all my money under my pillow for fear of thieves.

生僻 shēngpì [形] obscure

生平 shēngpíng [名] one's life ◇我生平从未感到这么震惊过。I have never been so astonished in my whole life.

生气 shēngqì **I** [动] get angry **II** [名] vitality

生趣 shēngqù [名] life's pleasures

生人 shēngrén [名] stranger

生日 shēngri [名] birthday

生色 shēngsè [动] add colour (英) 或 color (美) to

生身父母 shēngshēn fùmǔ [名] natural parents (*pl*)

生事 shēngshì [动] make trouble

生手 shēngshǒu [名] ◇我刚来，是个生手。I've just arrived and am new to the job.

生疏 shēngshū [形] **1** (没接触过的) unfamiliar **2** (不熟练的) rusty **3** (疏远的) distant

生死存亡 shēng sǐ cún wáng of vital importance

生死攸关 shēng sǐ yōu guān a matter of life and death

生死与共 shēng sǐ yǔ gòng live and die side by side

生态 shēngtài [名] ecology

生吞活剥 shēng tūn huó bō adopt … wholesale ◇学习他国经验不能生吞活剥。When learning from the experience of other countries, it's no good adopting everything wholesale.

生物 shēngwù [名] living things (*pl*)

生物学 shēngwùxué [名] biology

生息 shēngxī [动] **1** (取得利息) bear interest (*pt* bore, *pp* borne) **2** (书) (生存) live

生肖 shēngxiào [名] animal of the Chinese zodiac

生效 shēngxiào [动] come into effect (*pt* came, *pp* come)

生性 shēngxìng [名] disposition

生涯 shēngyá [名] career

生意 shēngyi [名] business

生硬 shēngyìng [形] **1** (不自然) unnatural **2** (不柔和) rigid

生育 shēngyù [动] give birth to (*pt* gave, *pp* given)

生长 shēngzhǎng [动] **1** (植物) grow (*pt* grew, *pp* grown) **2** (生物) grow up (*pt* grew, *pp* grown)

生殖 shēngzhí [动] reproduce

生字 shēngzì [名] new word

声 shēng **I** [名] **1** (声音) sound ♦歌声 song **2** (名声) reputation ♦声誉 fame **II** [动] make a sound ◇不声不响 silent

声辩 shēngbiàn [动] argue

声波 shēngbō [名] sound wave

声称 shēngchēng [动] claim ◇他声称将把所有财产捐献给慈善机构。He claims he will give all his money to charity.

声带 shēngdài [名] vocal cords (*pl*)

声调 shēngdiào [名] tone

声东击西 shēng dōng jī xī decoy tactics ◇这位将军作战时善于声东击西。In war this general is excellent at decoy tactics.

声价 shēngjià [名] reputation

声明 shēngmíng [动] state ◇联合声明 joint statement

声色 shēngsè [名] voice and expression ◇不动声色 maintain one's composure

声势 shēngshì [名] power and influence

声嘶力竭 shēng sī lì jié hoarse

声讨 shēngtǎo [动] condemn

声望 shēngwàng [名] prestige

声息 shēngxī [名] **1** (声音) noise **2** (消息) information

声响 shēngxiǎng [名] noise

声言 shēngyán [动] declare

声音 shēngyīn [名] **1** (指人) voice **2** (指物) sound

声誉 shēngyù [名] reputation

声援 shēngyuán [动] publicly support

声乐 shēngyuè [名] (音) vocal music

声张 shēngzhāng [动] disclose

牲 shēng [名] **1** (家畜) domestic animal **2** (祭神的牲畜) animal sacrifice

牲畜 shēngchù [名] livestock

牲口 shēngkou [名] beast of burden

甥 shēng [名] nephew

甥女 shēngnǚ [名] niece

绳 shéng **I** [名] rope **II** [动] (书) restrain

绳子 shéngzi [名] rope

省 shěng **I** [动] **1** (节约) save ◇省钱 save money **2** (免掉) leave … out (*pt, pp* left) **II** [名] province ◇广东省 Guangdong Province
▷另见 xǐng

省城 shěngchéng [名] provincial capital

省吃俭用 shěng chī jiǎn yòng live frugally

省会 shěnghuì [名] provincial capital

省略 shěnglüè [动] leave … out (*pt, pp* left)

省事 shěngshì [动] save trouble ◇请人装修房子比自己动手省事很多。Having someone else decorate your house is much simpler than doing it yourself.

省心 shěngxīn [动] save worry ◊雇了个保姆，我省心多了。Hiring a nanny has saved me a lot of worry.

圣 shèng **I** [形] holy ♦神圣 sacred **II** [名] **1** (圣人) sage **2** (帝王) emperor

圣诞 shèngdàn [名] Christmas

圣地 shèngdì [名] **1** (宗) the Holy Land **2** (名胜) sacred place

圣洁 shèngjié [形] holy and pure

圣经 Shèngjīng [名] the Bible

圣人 shèngrén [名] sage

圣贤 shèngxián [名] saint

胜 shèng **I** [动] **1** (赢) win (*pt, pp* won) ◊这次竞赛我们胜了。We won the competition. **2** (打败) defeat ◊曼联又胜了对手。Manchester United again defeated their opponents. **3** (好于) be better than ◊实际行动胜过动人的言辞。Actions speak louder than words. **II** [形] superb ♦胜景 wonderful scenery

胜地 shèngdì [名] scenic area

胜迹 shèngjì [名] historical site

胜利 shènglì [动] **1** (打败对方) be victorious **2** (获得成功) be successful

胜券 shèngquàn [名] confidence in one's own success

胜任 shèngrèn [动] be qualified

胜诉 shèngsù [动] win a lawsuit (*pt, pp* won)

盛 shèng **I** [形] **1** (兴盛) flourishing ◊牡丹花开得盛极了。The peonies are in full bloom. **2** (强烈) intense ◊森林大火烧得很盛。The forest fire is intense. **3** (盛大) grand ♦盛宴 sumptuous dinner **4** (深厚) abundant ♦盛情 great kindness **5** (盛行) popular ◊这种款式今年很盛。This style is popular this year. **II** [副] deeply ♦盛赞 highly praise ▷另见 chéng

盛产 shèngchǎn [动] produce large quantities of ◊该地区盛产煤。This region produces large quantities of coal.

盛传 shèngchuán [动] spread (*pt, pp* spread)

盛大 shèngdà [形] magnificent

盛典 shèngdiǎn [名] grand ceremony

盛会 shènghuì [名] grand assembly

盛举 shèngjǔ [名] grand event

盛况 shèngkuàng [名] grand occasion

盛怒 shèngnù [动] be in a rage

盛气凌人 shèng qì líng rén overbearing

盛情 shèngqíng [名] great kindness

盛世 shèngshì [名] heyday

盛夏 shèngxià [名] midsummer

盛行 shèngxíng [动] be in fashion

盛誉 shèngyù [名] fame

盛装 shèngzhuāng [名] best clothes (*pl*)

剩 shèng [动] be left ◊买完东西后，我还剩10镑钱。After I'd been shopping, I still had ten pounds left.

剩余 shèngyú [动] be left

尸 shī [名] corpse

尸体 shītǐ [名] corpse

尸体解剖 shītǐ jiěpōu [名] post-mortem

失 shī **I** [动] **1** (丢失) lose (*pt, pp* lost) ◊他失血过多。He lost a lot of blood. **2** (改变) deviate ♦失色 turn pale **3** (未得到) fail ♦失望 be disappointed **4** (背弃) break (*pt* broke, *pp* broken) ◊失信 break a promise **II** [名] mistake ♦过失 error

失败 shībài [动] fail ◊卫星发射失败了。The satellite launch was unsuccessful. ◊他雅思考试又失败了。He failed IELTS again. ◊我军在那次战斗中遭到了失败。Our army was defeated in that battle.

失策 shīcè [动] be unwise ◊公司投资失策。The company invested unwisely.

失常 shīcháng [动] be odd ◊在学校, 他的表现失常。At school he behaves very oddly.

失传 shīchuán [动] be lost ◊造剑的手艺失传了。The art of swordmaking has been lost.

失聪 shīcōng [动] go deaf (*pt* went, *pp* gone)

失掉 shīdiào [动] 1 (失去) lose (*pt, pp* lost) ◇失掉职位 lose one's job 2 (错过) miss ◇失掉机会 miss a chance

失和 shīhé [动] become estranged (*pt* became, *pp* become)

失衡 shīhéng [动] become unbalanced (*pt* became, *pp* become) ◇因为不吃蔬菜, 他营养失衡。Because he's not eating vegetables his nutrition has become unbalanced.

失火 shīhuǒ [动] catch fire (*pt, pp* caught)

失控 shīkòng [动] be out of control ◇森林大火失控了。The forest fire is out of control.

失礼 shīlǐ [动] 1 (违背礼节) be rude ◇戴手套握手被认为是失礼。Wearing gloves to shake hands is considered rude. 2 (客套) (表示歉意) ◇让您久等了, 失礼! 失礼! I'm very sorry to have kept you waiting so long.

失利 shīlì [动] lose (*pt, pp* lost)

失恋 shīliàn [动] be jilted

失灵 shīlíng [动] not work

失落 shīluò [形] 1 (遗失的) lost ◇失落的文明 a lost civilization 2 (低沉) dejected ◇他找不到工作, 心里非常失落。He can't find a job and is feeling very dejected.

失眠 shīmián [动] be unable to sleep

失眠症 shīmiánzhèng [名] insomnia

失明 shīmíng [动] go blind (*pt* went, *pp* gone)

失陪 shīpéi [动] (客套) ◇我有事, 先失陪了。I have something to do, so please excuse me if I leave now.

失窃 shīqiè [动] be stolen

失散 shīsàn [动] be separated from ◇他终于找到了失散多年的女儿。He finally found the daughter he had been separated from for many years.

失声 shīshēng [动] 1 (指哭泣) be choked with tears 2 (指唱歌) ◇这位歌手在演唱时突然失声。When this singer was performing, his voice suddenly cracked.

失实 shīshí [动] be false

失事 shīshì [动] have an accident

失手 shīshǒu [动] let ... slip (*pt, pp* let) ◇我失手打破了花瓶。I let the vase slip and it broke. ◇上届奥运会冠军意外失手, 卫冕失败。The previous Olympic champion let the contest slip through his fingers and lost the title. ◇他失手打了哥哥。He lost control and hit his brother.

失守 shīshǒu [动] be taken

失算 shīsuàn [动] miscalculate

失态 shītài [动] forget oneself (*pt* forgot, *pp* forgotten)

失调 shītiáo [动] 1 (比例不均) lose balance (*pt, pp* lost) ◇大学生男女比例失调。There is a disproportionate ratio of men to women at university. 2 (调养不当) lack proper care

失望 shīwàng **I** [形] disappointed **II** [动] lose hope (*pt, pp* lost) ◇球迷对中国足球队永远失望了。The fans have lost all hope in the Chinese football team.

失误 shīwù [动] slip up

失效 shīxiào [动] 1 (不起作用) stop working ◇电池失效了。The battery has run out. 2 (没有法力) be no longer valid

失信 shīxìn [动] go back on one's word (*pt* went, *pp* gone)

失学 shīxué [动] drop out of school

失业 shīyè [动] be unemployed, be out of work ◇失业人口在增加。Unemployment is rising.

失意 shīyì [形] disappointed

失约 shīyuē [动] fail to show up ◇我们约好今早见面, 可她失约了。We had an arrangement to meet this morning, but she didn't show up.

失真 shīzhēn [动] be unclear ◇传真照片经常失真。Faxed photos are often unclear. ◇录音里的声音完全失真了。The recording was completely distorted.

失职 shīzhí [动] neglect one's duty

失主 shīzhǔ [名] owner (*of lost property*)

失踪 shīzōng [动] be missing

失足 shīzú [动] **1** (跌倒) slip **2** (犯法) go off the rails (*pt* went, *pp* gone)

师 shī [名] **1** (老师) teacher **2** (军) division

师范 shīfàn [名] (指学院) teacher training college

师父 shīfu [名] master

师傅 shīfu [名] (口) master

师长 shīzhǎng [名] teacher

师资 shīzī [名] teachers (*pl*)

诗 shī [名] poetry ◇自由诗 free verse

诗歌 shīgē [名] poetry ◇诗歌朗诵 poetry reading

诗篇 shīpiān [名] poem

诗人 shīrén [名] poet

诗坛 shītán [名] the poetry world

虱 shī [名] louse (*pl* lice)

狮 shī 见下文

狮子 shīzi [名] lion

施 shī [动] **1** (实行) carry … out ♦施工 construct **2** (给予) exert ♦施压 exert pressure **3** (肥料) apply ♦施肥 spread fertilizer

施工 shīgōng [动] construct ◇施工现场 construction site

施加 shījiā [动] exert

施舍 shīshě **I** [动] give (*pt* gave, *pp* given) **II** [名] charity

施行 shīxíng [动] (执行) implement

施展 shīzhǎn [动] put … to good use (*pt, pp* put) ◇施展本领 put one's abilities to good use

湿 shī [形] wet

湿度 shīdù [名] humidity

湿漉漉 shīlūlū [形] damp

湿润 shīrùn [形] moist

嘘 shī [叹] shush
▷另见 xū

十 shí [名] ten

十恶不赦 shí è bù shè irredeemably evil ◇十恶不赦的杀人犯 evil murderer

十二分 shí'èrfēn [形] a hundred per cent ◇我对赢得比赛有十二分的信心。I'm one hundred per cent confident of winning the competition.

十分 shífēn [副] extremely ◇我十分满意。I'm extremely satisfied.

十进制 shíjìnzhì [名] decimal system

十拿九稳 shí ná jiǔ wěn practically certain ◇这场球赛, 教练是十拿九稳。The coach is practically certain of winning the match.

十全十美 shí quán shí měi perfect in every way

十字架 shízìjià [名] cross

十足 shízú [形] complete ◇他是个十足的笨蛋。He's a complete idiot.

什 shí 见下文
▷另见 shén

什锦 shíjǐn [形] mixed

石 shí [名] stone

石沉大海 shí chén dà hǎi elicit no response ◇我写给他的信石沉大海。The letter I wrote him elicited no response.

石窟 shíkū [名] grotto

石器时代 shíqì shídài [名] the Stone Age

石油 shíyóu [名] oil ◇石油工业 the oil industry

时 shí [名] **1** (指时间单位) hour ◇钟表要报时了。The clock is about to strike the hour. ◇营业时间是从上午9时到下午5时。Business hours are from 9 a.m. to 5 p.m. **2** (指规定时间) time ♦准时 on time **3** (时常) ◇天气时冷时热。The weather fluctuates between hot and cold. **4** (时尚) fashion ♦入时 fashionable ♦过时 out-of-date **5** (时候) time ♦当时 at that time **6** (机会) opportunity ♦失时 miss an opportunity **7** (语法) tense ◇过去时 past tense

时差 shíchā [名] time difference

时常 shícháng [副] often

时代 shídài [名] **1** (指时期) age ◇信息时代 the information age **2** (指人生) period ◇青年时代 youth ◇少年时代 childhood

时代精神 shídài jīngshén [名] spirit of the age

时而 shí'ér [副] sometimes ◊电脑时而出故障。The computer sometimes plays up. ◊他精神失常了，时而大哭，时而大笑。He's psychologically unbalanced – one moment he's in floods of tears, the next he's laughing uncontrollably.

时光 shíguāng [名] (书) time ◊时光飞逝。Time flies.

时过境迁 shí guò jìng qiān things have changed

时候 shíhou [名] time ◊你什么时候上班? What time do you go to work? ◊时候不早了，我们该睡觉了。It's late, and we should go to bed.

时机 shíjī [名] opportunity

时间 shíjiān [名] time ◊时间到了。Time's up! ◊他不抓紧时间。He didn't make the best use of his time. ◊办公时间 working hours

时局 shíjú [名] political situation

时刻 shíkè **I** [名] moment ◊紧急时刻 critical moment **II** [副] constantly ◊士兵们时刻准备战斗。The soldiers are ready for combat at all times.

时刻表 shíkèbiǎo [名] timetable (英), schedule (美)

时来运转 shíláiyùnzhuǎn have a change of luck ◊她时来运转，当上了女主角。She's lucky enough to be playing the female lead.

时髦 shímáo [形] fashionable

时期 shíqī [名] period

时区 shíqū [名] time zone

时尚 shíshàng [名] fad

时时 shíshí [副] often

时势 shíshì [名] current trend

时事 shíshì [名] current affairs (*pl*)

时下 shíxià [名] current

时兴 shíxīng [动] be in fashion

时装 shízhuāng [名] fashion

识 shí **I** [动] know (*pt* knew, *pp* known) **II** [名] knowledge

识别 shíbié [动] distinguish

识货 shíhuò [动] have a discerning eye for goods

识趣 shíqù [形] tactful

实 shí **I** [形] **1** (实心) solid ◊这玻璃球里面是实的。This ball is solid glass. **2** (真实) true ♦实话 truth **II** [名] reality

实地 shídì [副] ◊记者在进行实地报道。The journalist is reporting on the spot.

实干 shígàn [动] get on with the job

实惠 shíhuì **I** [名] material benefit **II** [形] solid

实际 shíjì **I** [名] reality **II** [形] **1** (实有的) real **2** (合乎事实的) practical

实价 shíjià [名] actual price

实践 shíjiàn **I** [动] practise (英), practice (美) **II** [名] practice

实况 shíkuàng [名] ◊电视台将实况转播世界杯决赛。The TV station will broadcast the World Cup final live.

实力 shílì [名] strength

实情 shíqíng [名] actual state of affairs ◊他一点不了解实情。He doesn't understand the actual situation at all.

实施 shíshī [动] implement

实事求是 shí shì qiú shì based on solid evidence

实体 shítǐ [名] entity

实物 shíwù [名] material object

实习 shíxí [动] practise (英), practice (美)

实习生 shíxíshēng [名] trainee

实现 shíxiàn [动] realize

实效 shíxiào [名] actual effect ◊这种教学方法很有实效。This kind of teaching method is very effective.

实心 shíxīn [形] (指物体) solid

实行 shíxíng [动] put … into practice (*pt, pp* put)

实验 shíyàn **I** [动] test **II** [名] experiment

实验室 shíyànshì [名] laboratory

实业 shíyè [名] industry

实业家 shíyèjiā [名] industrialist

实用 shíyòng [形] practical

实在 shízài **I** [形] honest **II** [副] really ◇我实在不明白。I really don't understand.

实质 shízhì [名] essence ◇这两种现象实质不一样。These two phenomena are essentially different. ◇改革取得了实质的进展。The reforms have made substantial headway.

拾 shí **I** [动] pick … up **II** [数] *an elaborate form of "ten", used in writing cheques etc to prevent mistakes and forgery*

拾掇 shíduo [动] (整理) tidy … up

食 shí **I** [动] eat (*pt* ate, *pp* eaten) ♦食肉动物 carnivore **II** [名] **1** (食物) food ♦主食 staple ♦狗食 dog food **2** (指天体) eclipse ♦日食 solar eclipse

食粮 shíliáng [名] **1** (食物) grain **2** (喻) (指精神) food for the soul

食量 shíliàng [名] appetite

食品 shípǐn [名] food

食谱 shípǔ [名] recipe

食堂 shítáng [名] canteen

食物 shíwù [名] food

食言 shíyán [动] break a promise (*pt* broke, *pp* broken)

食用 shíyòng [形] edible

食欲 shíyù [名] appetite

蚀 shí [动] erode

蚀本 shíběn [动] lose one's capital (*pt, pp* lost)

史 shǐ [名] history

史册 shǐcè [名] (书) annals (*pl*)

史迹 shǐjì [名] historical remains (*pl*)

史料 shǐliào [名] historical data (*pl*)

史前 shǐqián [名] prehistory ◇史前文明 prehistoric civilization

史诗 shǐshī [名] epic

史实 shǐshí [名] historical fact

史书 shǐshū [名] historical record

史无前例 shǐ wú qián lì unprecedented

史学 shǐxué [名] history

矢 shǐ [名] (书) arrow

矢口否认 shǐkǒu fǒurèn flatly deny

使 shǐ **I** [动] **1** (使用) use ◇他不会使电脑。He can't use a computer. ◇电子词典很好使。Electronic dictionaries are very easy to use. **2** (让) make (*pt, pp* made) ◇服务员的恶劣态度使顾客很不满意。The assistants' appalling attitude made the customers quite upset. ◇他使父母失望了。He disappointed his parents. **II** [名] envoy ♦大使 ambassador

使馆 shǐguǎn [名] embassy ◇中国驻英国使馆 the Chinese embassy in the UK

使坏 shǐhuài [动] play tricks

使唤 shǐhuan [动] order … about

使节 shǐjié [名] envoy

使命 shǐmìng [名] mission

使用 shǐyòng [动] use ◇我使用宽带上网。I use broadband to go online. ◇使用说明 operating instructions (*pl*)

始 shǐ [动] start

始末 shǐmò [名] the whole story ◇报纸登载了"9. 11"事件始末。The newspaper covered the whole story of 9-11.

始终 shǐzhōng [副] all along ◇我始终没有勇气告诉他。All along I didn't have the courage to tell him.

始祖 shǐzǔ [名] earliest ancestor

驶 shǐ [动] **1** (车) drive (*pt* drove, *pp* driven) ◇疾驶 speed **2** (船) sail ◇驶离港口 sail out of the harbour (英) 或 harbor (美)

屎 shǐ [名] **1** (粪便) excrement **2** (眼、耳) wax ◇耳屎 ear wax

士 shì [名] **1** (军人) soldier **2** (军衔) non-commissioned officer ♦中士 sergeant **3** (专业人员) ♦护士 nurse ♦博士 doctor

士兵 shìbīng [名] private

士气 shìqì [名] morale

氏 shì [名] surname

氏族 shìzú [名] clan

示 shì [动] show (*pt* showed, *pp* shown)

示范 shìfàn [动] demonstrate

示例 shìlì [动] give a demonstration (*pt* gave, *pp* given)

示威 shìwēi [动] demonstrate ◇伦敦民众示威反对战争。People in London demonstrated against the war.

示意 shìyì [动] signal

示众 shìzhòng [动] parade

世 shì [名] **1** (生) life ◆来世 afterlife **2** (代) generation ◆世仇 family feud **3** (时期) age ◆世纪 century **4** (世界) world ◆世上 in this world

世仇 shìchóu [名] family feud

世代 shìdài [名] generation

世道 shìdào [名] attitudes (*pl*) ◇世道变了。人人都向"钱"看。Attitudes have changed. Everyone's just interested in money.

世风 shìfēng [名] (书) atmosphere

世故 shìgù [名] the ways of the world (*pl*)

世故 shìgu [形] (贬) worldly-wise

世纪 shìjì [名] century

世家 shìjiā [名] well-known family

世交 shìjiāo [名] family friend

世界 shìjiè [名] world

世贸组织 shìmào zǔzhī [名] WTO

世面 shìmiàn [名] facet of life

世人 shìrén [名] (书) the common people (*pl*)

世事 shìshì [名] (书) world affairs (*pl*)

世俗 shìsú **I** [名] custom **II** [形] secular

世态炎凉 shìtài yán liáng the hypocrisy of the world

世外桃源 shì wài Táoyuán utopia ◇世外桃源是不存在的。Utopia does not exist.

世袭 shìxí [动] inherit

仕 shì 见下文

仕途 shìtú [名] (书) official career

市 shì [名] **1** (城市) city **2** (市场) market

市场 shìchǎng [名] market

市价 shìjià [名] market price

市郊 shìjiāo [名] suburb

市侩 shìkuài [名] money-grubber

市面 shìmiàn [名] market

市民 shìmín [名] city residents (*pl*)

市区 shìqū [名] urban area

市容 shìróng [名] the city's appearance

市政 shìzhèng [名] municipal administration ◇市政工程 municipal projects (*pl*)

式 shì [名] **1** (样式) style ◇欧式家具 European-style furniture **2** (典礼) ceremony **3** (式子) formula ◆公式 formula

式样 shìyàng [名] style

式子 shìzi [名] formula (*pl* formulae)

似 shì 见下文
▷另见 sì

似的 shìde [助] ◇她的眼睛像天空似的那么蓝。Her eyes are as blue as the sky.

事 shì [名] **1** (事情) thing ◆私事 private matter ◇我想和你说几件事。I want to talk to you about a number of things. **2** (事故) accident ◆出事 have an accident **3** (事端) trouble ◆闹事 make trouble **4** (责任) responsibility ◇这没我的事。This is not my responsibility. **5** (工作) job ◇他刚下岗，正在找事做。He's just become unemployed and is looking for a job. **6** (用于问答) problem ◇有事吗？没事。Are you OK? – I'm fine.

事变 shìbiàn [名] **1** (事件) incident **2** (事故) emergency

事出有因 shì chū yǒu yīn ◇国家队换教练事出有因。There was a good reason for the national team to change their coach.

事端 shìduān [名] incident

事故 shìgù [名] accident

事迹 shìjì [名] achievement

事件 shìjiàn [名] event

事理 shìlǐ [名] reason

事例 shìlì [名] example

事情 shìqing [名] matter ◊他公司事情很多。He is very busy with business matters. ◊事情不会这么简单。Things can't be that simple.

事实 shìshí [名] fact ◊事实上 in fact

事态 shìtài [名] situation

事务 shìwù [名] work

事物 shìwù [名] thing

事项 shìxiàng [名] item

事业 shìyè [名] **1** (用于个人) undertaking **2** (用于社会) activity ◊她献身公益事业。She dedicated herself to welfare activities. **3** (指非企业) facilities (*pl*)

事业心 shìyèxīn [名] dedication

事宜 shìyí [名] (书) arrangements (*pl*)

事与愿违 shìyǔyuànwéi not go according to plan

势

势 shì [名] **1** (势力) force **2** (姿态) gesture **3** (地理) feature **4** (趋势) tendency

势必 shìbì [副] ◊人们对手机的需求势必会增长。People's demand for mobile phones (英) or cell phones (美) is bound to increase.

势不可挡 shì bù kě dǎng unstoppable ◊信息全球化势不可挡。The globalization of information is unstoppable.

势不两立 shì bù liǎng lì be irreconcilable ◊英格兰和苏格兰橄榄球队势不两立。The English and Scottish rugby teams are sworn enemies.

势均力敌 shì jūn lì dí equally matched

势力 shìli [名] power ◊势力范围 sphere of influence

势利 shìli [形] snobbish

势利眼 shìliyǎn [名] snob

势如破竹 shì rú pò zhú inexorable ◊数字媒体的发展势如破竹。The development of digital media is inexorable.

势头 shìtou [名] momentum

势在必行 shì zài bì xíng be imperative ◊保护知识产权势在必行。It is imperative that intellectual properties are protected.

侍

侍 shì [动] serve

侍奉 shìfèng [动] look after

侍候 shìhòu [动] serve

侍卫 shìwèi [名] bodyguard

侍者 shìzhě [名] (旧) servant

饰

饰 shì **I** [动] **1** (装饰) decorate **2** (扮演) play ◊她在歌剧中饰卡门。She plays Carmen in the opera. **II** [名] ornament ♦首饰 jewellery (英), jewelry (美)

饰物 shìwù [名] ornaments (*pl*)

饰演 shìyǎn [动] play ◊他饰演孙悟空。He plays the Monkey King.

试

试 shì **I** [动] try ◊你可以在网上试玩新游戏。You can try playing new games online. ◊我可以试一下这双鞋吗？ Can I try on this pair of shoes? **II** [名] examination

试点 shìdiǎn **I** [动] do a pilot project **II** [名] test site

试管 shìguǎn [名] test tube ◊试管婴儿 test-tube baby

试金石 shìjīnshí [名] touchstone

试卷 shìjuàn [名] exam paper

试探 shìtan [动] sound ... out ◊美国试探英国对美伊战争的态度。The United States sounded the British out about how they felt about the war with Iraq.

试题 shìtí [名] exam question

试行 shìxíng [动] try ... out

试验 shìyàn [动] test

试用 shìyòng [动] try ... out

试用期 shìyòngqī [名] probation ◊我还在试用期呢。I'm still on probation.

视

视 shì [动] **1** (看到) look at **2** (看待) look on ◊视为知己 look on as an intimate friend **3** (考察) inspect

视察 shìchá [动] inspect

视角 shìjiǎo [名] angle ◊他的研究视角很独特。He has a unique angle in his research.

视觉 shìjué [名] vision ◇DVD给人们带来全新的视觉享受。DVDs give people a brand new visual experience.

视力 shìlì [名] sight

视听 shìtīng [名] sight and hearing

视线 shìxiàn [名] **1** (指眼睛) line of vision **2** (注意力) attention

视野 shìyě [名] field of vision

柿 shì 见下文

柿子 shìzi [名] persimmon, sharon fruit

拭 shì [动] (书) wipe … away

拭目以待 shì mù yǐ dài eagerly await ◇人们对总统大选的结果拭目以待。People were eagerly awaiting the result of the presidential election.

是 shì **I** [动] be (*pt* was, were, *pp* been) ◇我是学生。I am a student. ◇遍地是雪。There's snow everywhere. ◇我们是3个孩子的家。We have three children. ◇他绝不是想省钱。It's certainly not that he's trying to save money. ◇是学生就要听老师话。Every student should listen to what their teacher says. **II** [名] right ♦是非 right and wrong **III** [副] yes ◇你要见他吗？－是，我现在就要见他。Are you going to see him? – Yes, I'm going to see him right now.

是非 shìfēi [名] **1** (对与错) right and wrong ◇他不辨是非。He can't tell the difference between right and wrong. **2** (麻烦) trouble ◇他老惹是非。He's always making trouble.

是否 shìfǒu [副] ◇我不知道他是否同意。I don't know whether he agrees or not.

适 shì [形] **1** (适合) suitable **2** (恰好) right **3** (舒服) well ◇他最近身体不适。He's not been well recently.

适当 shìdàng [形] appropriate

适得其反 shì dé qí fǎn lead to just the opposite ◇服药过量会适得其反。Taking more than the prescribed dose will produce the opposite effect.

适度 shìdù [形] moderate

适合 shìhé [形] suitable

适可而止 shì kě ér zhǐ not go too far

适量 shìliàng [形] of an appropriate amount ◇适量用药 take medicine in appropriate doses

适龄 shìlíng [形] appropriately aged ◇适龄青年可以参军。Young people of the appropriate age can enter the army.

适时 shìshí [形] timely ◇你要适时督促他一下。You need to give him a bit of timely encouragement.

适销 shìxiāo [动] sell well (*pt, pp* sold)

适宜 shìyí [形] advisable ◇吃止痛药后不适宜饮酒。After taking painkillers it's not advisable to drink alcohol.

适应 shìyìng [动] adapt

适中 shìzhōng [形] moderate

室 shì [名] room ♦办公室 office

室外 shìwài [形] outdoor

逝 shì [动] **1** (人) die **2** (书) (时间等) pass

逝世 shìshì [动] (书) pass away

释 shì [动] (解释) explain

释放 shìfàng [动] release

释疑 shìyí [动] clear up doubts

释义 shìyì [动] define ◇老师给出生词的释义。The teacher gave a definition of the new word.

嗜 shì [动] be addicted to ◇嗜酒 be an alcoholic

嗜好 shìhào [名] hobby ◇她的最大嗜好是购物。Her favourite (英) 或 favorite (美) hobby is shopping.

誓 shì **I** [动] swear (*pt* swore, *pp* sworn) **II** [名] vow

誓不罢休 shì bù bàxiū swear not to give up ◇他不打赢官司，誓不罢休。He swore not to give up until he had won the case.

誓词 shìcí [名] oath

誓死 shìsǐ [副] ◇他誓死报仇。He is ready to die in pursuit of revenge.

誓言 shìyán [名] oath

誓约 shìyuē [名] oath

收 shōu [动] 1 (归拢) put ... away (*pt, pp* put) ♦收拾 tidy ... up 2 (取回) take ... back (*pt* took, *pp* taken) ◇我把晾在外面的被单收了进来。I took in the sheet, which had been drying in the sun outside. 3 (收割) harvest 4 (接纳) accept 5 (约束) restrain 6 (逮捕) arrest 7 (结束) stop ♦收工 stop work 8 (获得) gain ♦收入 income

收编 shōubiān [动] incorporate

收兵 shōubīng [动] 1 (指战斗) retreat 2 (指工作) complete

收藏 shōucáng [动] collect

收场 shōuchǎng I [动] end up II [名] (贬) ending

收成 shōucheng [名] harvest

收复 shōufù [动] recapture

收割 shōugē [动] harvest

收购 shōugòu [动] 1 (买入) purchase 2 (并购) take ... over (*pt* took, *pp* taken) ◇由于市场竞争十分激烈，大部分小公司被收购。As the market is very competitive, the majority of small companies have been taken over.

收获 shōuhuò [动] 1 (指庄稼) harvest 2 (指成果) gain ◇这次出国考察，他的收获很大。He has gained a great deal from this trip overseas.

收集 shōují [动] collect

收据 shōujù [名] receipt

收敛 shōuliǎn [动] 1 (笑容) vanish 2 (指行为) restrain oneself

收留 shōuliú [动] take ... in (*pt* took, *pp* taken) ◇父母去世后，他的一个远方亲戚收留了他。After his parents died, a distant relative took him in.

收买 shōumǎi [动] 1 (收购) purchase 2 (笼络) buy ... off (*pt, pp* bought)

收盘 shōupán [动] close

收入 shōurù [名] income ◇近几年，人们的收入明显增加。In recent years, people's incomes have markedly increased.

收视率 shōushìlǜ [名] ratings (*pl*)

收拾 shōushi [动] 1 (整顿) tidy 2 (修理) repair 3 (口) (惩罚) punish ◇他被人收拾了。He's been punished.

收缩 shōusuō [动] 1 (指物理现象) contract 2 (紧缩) cut back (*pt* cut, *pp* cut) ◇公司资金紧张，需要收缩开支。The company's under financial pressure – we have to cut back on expenditure.

收听 shōutīng [动] listen to ◇他的收音机能收听BBC的节目。His radio can pick up BBC programmes (英) 或 programs (美).

收尾 shōuwěi [动] conclude ◇这篇文章收尾仓促了些。This article concludes in a hasty fashion.

收效 shōuxiào [动] yield results

收养 shōuyǎng [动] adopt

收益 shōuyì [名] profit

收音机 shōuyīnjī [名] radio

收支 shōuzhī [名] income and expenditure

手 shǒu I [名] 1 (指人体) hand ◇有问题的同学请举手。Will any student who has a question please raise their hand. 2 (指人) expert ♦选手 player II [量] ◇他这手可真厉害！He really made a good move there!

手笔 shǒubǐ [名] 1 (手迹) handwriting 2 (造诣) literary skill

手臂 shǒubì [名] arm

手表 shǒubiǎo [名] watch

手册 shǒucè [名] 1 (记录本) handbook 2 (参考书) reference book

手电筒 shǒudiàntǒng [名] torch (英), flashlight (美)

手段 shǒuduàn [名] 1 (方法) method 2 (贬) (花招) trick

手法 shǒufǎ [名] technique

手风琴 shǒufēngqín [名] accordion

手感 shǒugǎn [名] feel ◇真丝面料手感很好。This silk has a really nice feel.

手稿 shǒugǎo [名] manuscript

手工 shǒugōng I [名] craft ◇这个包全凭手工。The bag is completely hand-made. II [动] make ... by hand

手工业 shǒugōngyè [名] cottage industry

手工艺 shǒugōngyì [名] handicraft

手机 shǒujī [名] mobile phone (英), cell phone (美)

手疾眼快 shǒu jí yǎn kuài quick off the mark ◇幸亏他手疾眼快，一下子拔掉了电源。 Luckily he was quick off the mark, and took the plug out of the socket at once.

手迹 shǒujì [名] handwriting

手脚 shǒujiǎo [名] **1** (动作) movement ◇他手脚非常敏捷。 He is very agile. **2** (贬) (捣鬼) sleight of hand ◇他在账目上做了手脚。 He's used sleight of hand on the accounts.

手紧 shǒujǐn [形] **1** (指不随便花钱) stingy **2** (口) (缺钱) hard-up

手绢 shǒujuàn [名] handkerchief

手铐 shǒukào [名] handcuffs (*pl*)

手忙脚乱 shǒu máng jiǎo luàn in a mad rush ◇他做事从容冷静，从不手忙脚乱。 He does things calmly, never in a mad rush.

手气 shǒuqì [名] luck

手枪 shǒuqiāng [名] pistol

手软 shǒuruǎn [动] be soft ◇对待毒贩子决不能手软。 You can't be soft on drug smugglers.

手势 shǒushì [名] sign

手术 shǒushù **I** [名] operation **II** [动] operate

手套 shǒutào [名] glove ◇一副手套 a pair of gloves

手头 shǒutóu **I** [副] to hand ◇我手头没有你要的这本书。 I don't have the book you need to hand. **II** [名] financial situation ◇最近我手头比较紧。 Recently, my financial situation's been bad.

手腕 shǒuwàn [名] **1** (指人体) wrist **2** (喻) (手段) trick

手舞足蹈 shǒu wǔ zú dǎo dance for joy ◇听到这个好消息，他高兴得手舞足蹈。 When he heard the good news, he was so happy that he danced for joy.

手下 shǒuxià **I** [名] subordinate **II** [副] **1** (领导下) under ◇他一直在部长手下工作。 He works directly under the minister. **2** (手头) on one's hands ◇我们手下有个大项目。 I've got a big job on my hands.

手心 shǒuxīn [名] **1** (指手) palm **2** (喻) (控制范围) the palm of one's hand ◇她把他们控制在手心里。 She has them all in the palm of her hand.

手续 shǒuxù [名] procedure

手艺 shǒuyì [名] skill

手淫 shǒuyín **I** [动] masturbate **II** [名] masturbation

手语 shǒuyǔ [名] sign language

手掌 shǒuzhǎng [名] palm

手纸 shǒuzhǐ [名] toilet paper

手指 shǒuzhǐ [名] finger

手镯 shǒuzhuó [名] bracelet

手足 shǒuzú [名] **1** (指人体) hands and feet (*pl*) **2** (兄弟) brother

守 shǒu [动] **1** (防卫) guard **2** (遵循) observe ♦守法 observe the law **3** (看护) nurse

守备 shǒubèi [动] be on garrison duty

守候 shǒuhòu [动] **1** (等待) wait for **2** (看护) attend

守护 shǒuhù [动] guard

守岁 shǒusuì [动] stay up to see the new year in ◇中国人有守岁的习俗。 The Chinese have a tradition of staying up all night to see the new year in.

守旧 shǒujiù [动] be conservative

守口如瓶 shǒu kǒu rú píng keep one's mouth shut ◇他对此事守口如瓶。 He kept his mouth shut about it.

守望 shǒuwàng [动] keep watch (*pt, pp* kept)

守卫 shǒuwèi [动] guard

守业 shǒuyè [动] keep a business going (*pt, pp* kept) ◇创业难，守业更难。 It is difficult to start an enterprise, but even more difficult to keep it going.

守夜 shǒuyè [动] stay up all night

守则 shǒuzé [名] regulation

守株待兔 shǒu zhū dài tù wait for good things to drop into one's lap

◊没有人能靠守株待兔取得成功。 Nobody succeeds by sitting around waiting for things to happen.

首 shǒu I [名] **1** (脑袋) head **2** (头领) leader II [形] **1** (第一) first ♦首富 the richest person **2** (最早) first ◊首发车时间为5:30。 The first bus leaves at 5:30. III [量] ◊这是一首人们熟悉的古诗。 This is a well-known old poem.

首创 shǒuchuàng [动] pioneer

首当其冲 shǒu dāng qí chōng bear the brunt ◊出现险情时，这支部队总是首当其冲。 This unit always bears the brunt of any danger.

首都 shǒudū [名] capital

首犯 shǒufàn [名] ringleader

首富 shǒufù [名] the richest

首领 shǒulǐng [名] chief

首脑 shǒunǎo [名] head of state

首屈一指 shǒu qū yī zhǐ be second to none ◊这个大学对微生物领域的研究在全国首屈一指。 This university is second to none in this country in the field of micro-organic research.

首饰 shǒushi [名] jewellery (英), jewelry (美)

首尾 shǒuwěi [名] **1** (开始和结尾) the beginning and the end ◊这部电影首尾都很出人意料。 This film has an unexpected beginning and end. **2** (从头至尾) ◊整个项目，首尾经过了4年。 From start to finish, the whole project took four years.

首席 shǒuxí I [名] seat of honour (英) 或 honor (美) II [形] chief ◊他是该公司的首席顾问。 He's the company's chief advisor.

首先 shǒuxiān [副] **1** (最早) first ◊王教授在会上首先发言。 Professor Wang spoke first in the meeting. **2** (第一) first ◊首先，我们要找到问题的根源。 First, we need to find the root of the problem.

首相 shǒuxiàng [名] prime minister

首要 shǒuyào I [形] primary II [名] head

首长 shǒuzhǎng [名] commander-in-chief

寿 shòu I [名] **1** (敬) (岁数) longevity ◊您高寿？ How old are you? **2** (寿命) lifespan **3** (寿辰) birthday II [形] (婉) burial ♦寿衣 burial clothes (*pl*)

寿辰 shòuchén [名] birthday

寿命 shòumìng [名] life ◊随着生活水平的提高，人们的寿命越来越长。 Since living standards are higher, life expectancy is steadily increasing.

寿星 shòuxīng [名] **1** (神) *the god of longevity* **2** (指老人) very long-lived person

受 shòu [动] **1** (接受) receive ◊每个儿童都有受教育的权利。 Every child has the right to receive an education. **2** (遭受) suffer ◊他受了很多打击。 He suffered many setbacks. **3** (忍受) bear (*pt* bore, *pp* borne) ◊天气太热，她受不了了。 The weather's too hot. She can't bear it. ◊你能受得了住在这样艰苦的环境里吗？ Can you bear to live in this terrible environment?

受宠若惊 shòu chǒng ruò jīng be overwhelmed with gratitude ◊您的到来令我受宠若惊。 I'm so grateful you could come.

受挫 shòucuò [动] suffer a setback

受害 shòuhài [动] **1** (受伤害) suffer injury **2** (受损害) suffer loss

受贿 shòuhuì [动] accept bribes

受惊 shòujīng [动] be startled

受精 shòujīng [动] be fertilized

受累 shòulěi [动] involve

受理 shòulǐ [动] hear a case (*pt, pp* heard) ◊对于此案，法院拒绝受理。 The court has refused to hear the case.

受命 shòumìng [动] receive instructions

受权 shòuquán [动] be authorized

受审 shòushěn [动] stand trial (*pt, pp* stood)

受洗 shòuxǐ [动] be baptized

受刑 shòuxíng [动] be tortured

受益 shòuyì [动] reap the benefits of ◊她受益于英语好。 She is reaping the benefits of her good English.

受用 shòuyòng [动] reap the benefits of ◊保护环境，世代受用。 Future generations will reap the benefits of environmental protection.

受用 shòuyong [形] well ◊我近来身体不太受用。 I haven't been well recently.

受孕 shòuyùn [动] conceive

受制 shòuzhì [动] (书) **1** (受限) be constrained **2** (受迫害) be persecuted

受罪 shòuzuì [动] **1** (指苦难) suffer **2** (指不愉快的事) have a hard time

狩 shòu 见下文

狩猎 shòuliè [动] hunt

兽 shòu [名] beast

兽行 shòuxíng [名] **1** (凶残行为) brutal act **2** (秽乱行为) bestial behaviour

兽性 shòuxìng [名] barbarity

兽医 shòuyī [名] vet

授 shòu [动] **1** (奖) award **2** (传授) instruct

授奖 shòujiǎng [动] present awards

授命 shòumìng [动] give orders (*pt* gave, *pp* given)

授权 shòuquán [动] authorize

授勋 shòuxūn [动] decorate

授意 shòuyì [动] suggest

授予 shòuyǔ [动] award

售 shòu [动] sell (*pt, pp* sold)

售货 shòuhuò [动] sell goods (*pt, pp* sold)

瘦 shòu [形] **1** (指人) thin **2** (指食用肉) lean **3** (指衣服、鞋袜) tight

瘦骨嶙峋 shòu gǔ línxún bony

瘦弱 shòuruò [形] emaciated

瘦削 shòuxuē [形] gaunt

瘦子 shòuzi [名] thin person ◊他年轻时是个瘦子，现在发胖了。 When he was young he was thin, but now he's fat.

书 shū **I** [动] write (*pt* wrote, *pp* written) ♦书写 write **II** [名] **1** (字体) handwriting **2** (册子) book ♦精装书 hardback **3** (书) (信) letter ♦情书 love letter **4** (文件) document ♦申请书 application documents (*pl*)

书本 shūběn [名] book

书呆子 shūdāizi [名] bookworm

书店 shūdiàn [名] bookshop

书法 shūfǎ [名] calligraphy

书稿 shūgǎo [名] manuscript

书画 shūhuà [名] painting and calligraphy

书籍 shūjí [名] books (*pl*)

书记 shūjì [名] secretary

书刊 shūkān [名] books and periodicals (*pl*)

书面 shūmiàn [形] written

书面语 shūmiànyǔ [名] written language

书目 shūmù [名] catalogue ◊看书前我习惯先看书目。 Before reading a book, I normally look at the bibliography.

书生气 shūshēngqì [名] bookishness

书香门第 shūxiāng méndì [名] scholarly family

书写 shūxiě [动] write (*pt* wrote, *pp* written)

书信 shūxìn [名] letter

书展 shūzhǎn [名] book fair

抒 shū [动] express

抒发 shūfā [动] express

抒情 shūqíng [动] express emotion

抒写 shūxiě [动] express

枢 shū [名] **1** (指门) hinge **2** (中心) centre (英), center (美)

枢纽 shūniǔ [名] hub

叔 shū [名] (指父亲的弟弟) uncle

叔叔 shūshu [名] (口) **1** (指亲戚) uncle **2** (指父辈男性) uncle

殊 shū [形] **1** (不同) different **2** (特别) special

殊荣 shūróng [名] special honour (英) 或 honor (美)

殊死 shūsǐ [形] desperate

殊途同归 shū tú tóng guī independently reach the same

conclusion ◇我们俩的解题思路简直殊途同归。 We have handled this problem in different ways, but we have both reached the same conclusion.

梳 shū I [名] comb II [动] comb

梳理 shūlǐ [动] **1** (头发、胡须) comb **2** (思路) put ... in order (*pt, pp* put)

梳妆 shūzhuāng [动] get dressed up

淑 shū [形] ladylike

淑女 shūnǚ [名] lady

舒 shū I [动] **1** (指身体) stretch out **2** (指心情) relax II [形] (书) (缓慢) leisurely

舒畅 shūchàng [形] carefree

舒服 shūfu [形] comfortable

舒适 shūshì [形] cosy (英), cozy (美)

舒坦 shūtan [形] comfortable

舒心 shūxīn [形] content ◇老两口的日子越来越舒心。 The old couple are increasingly content with their lives.

舒展 shūzhǎn I [动] stretch out II [形] comfortable

疏 shū I [动] **1** (清理) dredge **2** (分散) scatter II [形] **1** (指距离) distant **2** (指关系) distant **3** (粗心) neglectful

疏导 shūdǎo [动] **1** (水道) dredge **2** (交通) direct **3** (思想) guide

疏忽 shūhu I [形] careless II [动] neglect III [名] carelessness

疏解 shūjiě [动] **1** (矛盾) resolve **2** (交通) clear

疏漏 shūlòu I [动] miss II [名] slip

疏散 shūsàn I [形] (书) scattered II [动] evacuate

疏松 shūsōng I [形] loose II [动] loosen

疏通 shūtōng [动] **1** (河道) dredge **2** (关系) mediate

疏远 shūyuǎn I [形] distant II [动] become estranged from (*pt* became, *pp* become) ◇尽管他犯了错，你也不该疏远他。 Although he's done wrong, you shouldn't become estranged from him.

输 shū [动] **1** (运送) transport **2** (失败) lose (*pt, pp* lost)

输出 shūchū [动] **1** (指从内到外) emit ◇报警器输出信号。 The alarm emits a signal. **2** (出口) export

输家 shūjiā [名] loser

输理 shūlǐ [动] lose the argument (*pt, pp* lost)

输入 shūrù [动] **1** (指从外到内) enter ◇把数据输入计算机 enter data into a computer **2** (进口) import

输送 shūsòng [动] **1** (物品) convey **2** (人员) transfer

蔬 shū [名] vegetable

蔬菜 shūcài [名] vegetable

赎 shú [动] **1** (换回) redeem ◇他们赎回了典当的项链。 They redeemed the necklace they had pawned. ◇绑匪声称100万美金才能赎出人质。 The kidnapper demanded a ransom of 1,000,000 dollars for the release of the hostage. **2** (弥补) atone for

赎金 shújīn [名] **1** (指抵押品) deposit **2** (指人质) ransom

赎买 shúmǎi [动] buy ... out (*pt, pp* bought)

赎罪 shúzuì [动] atone for one's crime ◇他得用一生来赎罪。 It will take him his whole life to atone for his crimes.

熟 shú [形] **1** (指果实) ripe **2** (指食物) cooked **3** (熟悉) familiar ◇他对北京很熟。 He knows Beijing well. **4** (熟练) skilled

熟练 shúliàn [形] skilled

熟门熟路 shú mén shú lù be on one's home ground ◇他对这儿熟门熟路。 He's on his home ground here.

熟能生巧 shú néng shēng qiǎo practice makes perfect ◇你要反复练习弹钢琴，毕竟熟能生巧嘛。 You need to constantly practice the piano. After all, practice makes perfect.

熟人 shúrén [名] old acquaintance

熟食 shúshí [名] cooked food

熟视无睹 shú shì wú dǔ turn a blind eye to ◇我们不能对不良社会行为熟视无睹。 We can't turn a blind eye to anti-social behaviour.

熟识 shúshi [动] get to know ◇两个小孩儿很快就熟识起来。 The two kids got to know each other really quickly.

熟悉 shúxī I [动] know well (*pt* knew, *pp* known) II [形] familiar

熟习 shúxí [动] be skilled at

熟语 shúyǔ [名] idiom

属 shǔ I [名] **1** (生物) genus **2** (家属) family member II [动] **1** (隶属) be under **2** (指属相) ◇你属什么？ What sign of the Chinese zodiac are you?

属地 shǔdì [名] dependency

属相 shǔxiang [名] (口) sign of the Chinese zodiac

属性 shǔxìng [名] attribute

属于 shǔyú [动] belong to

暑 shǔ [名] **1** (热) heat **2** (盛夏) midsummer

暑假 shǔjià [名] summer holidays (*pl*) (英) 或 vacation (美)

暑期 shǔqī [名] **1** (指暑假) summer holidays (*pl*) (英) 或 vacation (美) **2** (指夏季) summertime

署 shǔ I [名] department ◇审计署 auditing department I [动] **1** (布置) arrange **2** (名字) sign

署名 shǔmíng [动] sign

鼠 shǔ [名] **1** (指家鼠) mouse (*pl* mice) ◇米老鼠 Mickey Mouse **2** (比家鼠大，尾巴长) rat

鼠辈 shǔbèi [名] (贬) scoundrel

鼠标 shǔbiāo [名] mouse

鼠目寸光 shǔ mù cùn guāng short-sighted (英) 或 near-sighted (美)

数 shǔ [动] **1** (数目) count **2** (指名次) rank ◇他的学习成绩在班里数第一。 His marks are top of the class. **3** (列举) list
▷另见 shù

数不胜数 shǔ bù shèng shǔ innumerable ◇中国近几年的变化数不胜数。 In recent years, China has undergone innumerable changes.

数落 shǔluo [动] scold

数说 shǔshuō [动] **1** (列举) list **2** (责备) scold

数一数二 shǔ yī shǔ èr the top one or two ◇他一直是成绩数一数二的学生。 His grades are in the top one or two of his class.

薯 shǔ [名] potato (*pl* potatoes)

曙 shǔ (书) [名] dawn

曙光 shǔguāng [名] first light

术 shù [名] **1** (技艺) skill **2** (策略) tactic

术语 shùyǔ [名] terminology

戍 shù [动] defend

束 shù I [动] **1** (捆) tie **2** (约束) restrain II [量] bunch ◇他送给妻子一大束鲜花。 He gave his wife a big bunch of flowers. III [名] **1** (指花) bunch **2** (指光) cluster

束缚 shùfù [动] **1** (书) (捆绑) tie **2** (局限) restrain ◇他从不受传统思想的束缚。 He has never been restrained by traditional thinking.

束手无策 shù shǒu wú cè be at one's wits end ◇他什么都试过了，最后还是束手无策。 He'd tried everything, and in the end he was at his wits end.

束之高阁 shù zhī gāo gé let … gather dust ◇很多人买了书就束之高阁。 Many people buy books and just let them gather dust.

束装 shùzhuāng [动] pack up

述 shù [动] state

述评 shùpíng I [动] review II [名] review

述说 shùshuō [动] give an account (*pt* gave, *pp* given) ◇他述说着昨晚发生的事情。 He gave an account of yesterday evening's incident.

述职 shùzhí [动] report ◇述职报告 work report

树 shù I [名] tree II [动] **1** (书) (培育) cultivate **2** (建立) establish

树碑立传 shù bēi lì zhuàn (贬) seek the limelight ◇我做好事不为树碑

立传，而是为大家服务。 I do good things not to seek the limelight, but to serve everyone.

树敌 shùdí [动] antagonize

树立 shùlì [动] establish ◇树立信心 establish confidence

树林 shùlín [名] wood

树木 shùmù [名] trees (*pl*)

树阴 shùyīn [名] shade

竖 shù I [形] vertical II [动] erect III [名] vertical stroke

竖立 shùlì [动] erect

恕 shù [动] forgive (*pt* forgave, *pp* forgiven)

数 shù I [名] **1** (数目) number **2** (数) number **3** (语法) ♦单数 singular ♦复数 plural
▷另见 shǔ

数额 shù'é [名] amount

数据 shùjù [名] data (*pl*)

数据库 shùjùkù [名] database

数量 shùliàng [名] quantity

数码 shùmǎ I [名] numeral II [形] digital

数码相机 shùmǎ xiàngjī [名] digital camera

数目 shùmù [名] amount

数学 shùxué [名] mathematics (*sg*)

数字 shùzì [名] **1** (指系统) numeral **2** (数据) figure

数字化 shùzìhuà [动] digitize ◇我们生活在数字化时代。 We are living in the digital age.

漱 shù [动] gargle

漱口 shùkǒu [动] rinse one's mouth out

刷 shuā I [名] brush II [动] **1** (清除) scrub **2** (淘汰) eliminate III [拟] rustle
▷另见 shuà

刷卡 shuākǎ [动] swipe a card ◇购物付款可以刷卡。 Goods can be paid for by card.

刷洗 shuāxǐ [动] scrub

刷新 shuāxīn [动] **1** (字) refurbish **2** (喻) break (*pt* broke, *pp* broken) ◇他刷新了男子跳高世界记录。 He broke the men's high jump world record.

刷子 shuāzi [名] brush

耍 shuǎ [动] **1** (方) (玩) play **2** (戏弄) mess … around ◇你别想耍我们！ Don't think you can mess us around! **3** (贬) (施展) play ◇别再耍小聪明了。 Don't play those petty tricks again.

耍把戏 shuǎ bǎxì [动] play tricks

耍花招 shuǎ huāzhāo [动] play tricks

耍滑 shuǎhuá [动] slack off ◇我们不喜欢耍滑的人。 We don't like slackers.

耍赖 shuǎlài [动] act shamelessly

耍弄 shuǎnòng [动] take … for a ride (*pt* took, *pt* taken) ◇当心别让别人耍弄了。 Be careful not to let other people take you for a ride.

刷 shuà 见下文
▷另见 shuā

刷白 shuàbái [形] (方) pale

衰 shuāi I [形] declining II [动] decline

衰败 shuāibài [动] decline

衰变 shuāibiàn [动] decay

衰竭 shuāijié [形] exhausted

衰老 shuāilǎo [形] ageing ◇经常运动可以延缓衰老过程。 Regular exercise can delay the ageing process. ◇她非常害怕衰老。 She's really afraid of getting old.

衰落 shuāiluò [动] go downhill (*pt* went, *pp* gone)

衰弱 shuāiruò [形] weak

衰退 shuāituì [动] **1** (视力) fail **2** (经济) decline

衰亡 shuāiwáng [动] deteriorate ◇民族的衰亡关系到每个人。 The nation's deterioration affects everyone.

摔 shuāi [动] **1** (跌倒) fall (*pt* fell, *pp* fallen) **2** (下落) fall out (*pt* fell, *pp* fallen) ◇他从床上摔了下来。 He fell out of bed. **3** (跌坏) break (*pt* broke, *pp* broken) **4** (扔) throw (*pt* threw, *pp* thrown)

摔打 shuāidǎ [动] **1** (拍打) beat (*pt* beat, *pp* beaten) ◇他把鞋上的泥摔打掉。 He beat the mud off the shoes. **2** (锻炼) toughen oneself up ◇经过几年摔打，他坚强了很多。 After a few years of toughening himself up, he had become much stronger.

摔跤 shuāijiāo **I** [动] **1** (摔倒) fall over (*pt* fell, *pp* fallen) **2** (受挫) come to grief (*pt* came, *pp* come) ◇你这么不谦虚，会摔跤的。 If you show such lack of modesty, you'll come to grief. **II** [名] wrestling

甩 shuǎi [动] **1** (抡) swing (*pt, pp* swung) **2** (扔) fling (*pt, pp* flung) **3** (抛开) throw off (*pt* threw, *pp* thrown) ◇你要甩开包袱。 You need to throw off your burden.

甩卖 shuǎimài [动] sell at a reduced price (*pt, pp* sold)

甩手 shuǎishǒu [动] **1** (指运动) swing one's arms (*pt, pp* swung) **2** (指工作、事情) wash one's hands of ◇这件事做了一半，你不能甩手不管。 You're only halfway through. You can't wash your hands of the matter now.

帅 shuài **I** [名] commander-in-chief **II** [形] handsome

帅气 shuàiqi [形] handsome

率 shuài **I** [动] command **II** [形] **1** (不慎重) rash **2** (坦白) frank

率领 shuàilǐng [动] lead (*pt, pp* led)

率先 shuàixiān [副] ◇中国率先研制出了这种高效肥料。 China has taken the lead in developing this highly efficient fertilizer.

率真 shuàizhēn [形] sincere

率直 shuàizhí [形] forthright ◇他的率直赢得了大家的好评。 His forthrightness won everyone's approval.

闩 shuān **I** [名] bolt **II** [动] bolt

拴 shuān [动] tie

栓 shuān [名] **I** (开关机件) plug **2** (塞子) cork

涮 shuàn [动] **1** (清洗) rinse **2** (指吃法) dip-boil **3** (方) be tricked ◇这张票是假的，我们被涮了。 This ticket is a fake – we've been tricked.

双 shuāng **I** [形] **1** (两个) two **2** (偶数) even ♦双数 even number **3** (加倍) double **II** [量] pair

双胞胎 shuāngbāotāi [名] twins (*pl*)

双边 shuāngbiān [形] bilateral

双重 shuāngchóng [形] double

双方 shuāngfāng [名] both sides (*pl*)

双杠 shuānggàng [名] parallel bars

双关 shuāngguān [名] double entendre

双管齐下 shuāng guǎn qí xià work in parallel ◇治疗和锻炼双管齐下，他很快就会恢复健康。 With medical treatment and exercise working in parallel, he will quickly recover.

双料 shuāngliào [形] double ◇他是语言学和社会学双料博士。 He's got two PhDs – one in linguistics and the other in sociology.

双亲 shuāngqīn [名] parents (*pl*) ◇她小时候，双亲就去世了。 When she was young, both her parents died.

双全 shuāngquán [动] have both … and … ◇智勇双全 be both wise and brave

双休日 shuāngxiūrì [名] the weekend

霜 shuāng [名] frost

霜冻 shuāngdòng [名] frost

孀 shuāng [名] widow

孀居 shuāngjū [动] (书) be a widow ◇她已经孀居多年了。 She has been a widow for many years.

爽 shuǎng [形] **1** (指天气) clear **2** (指性格) frank **3** (指健康) well ◇他今天感觉身体不爽。 Today he doesn't feel well.

爽口 shuǎngkǒu [形] refreshing

爽快 shuǎngkuài [形] **1** (舒服) refreshed ◇喝一杯冰啤酒，感觉爽快极了！ After drinking a glass of cold beer, you feel very refreshed. **2** (直爽) frank

爽朗 shuǎnglǎng [形] **1** (指天气) clear **2** (指性格) open **3** (指笑声) cheerful

爽目 shuǎngmù [形] easy on the eye

爽直 shuǎngzhí [形] frank

水 shuǐ [名] **1** (物质) water **2** (指江河湖海) waters (*pl*) **3** (汁) liquid ♦消毒水 disinfectant ♦墨水 ink

水兵 shuǐbīng [名] sailor

水彩 shuǐcǎi [名] **1** (指颜料) watercolour (英), watercolor (美) **2** (指画) watercolour (英), watercolor (美)

水草 shuǐcǎo [名] **1** (植物) water weed **2** (资源) water and pasture

水产 shuǐchǎn [名] aquatic products (*pl*)

水到渠成 shuǐ dào qú chéng success comes naturally ◇他经验丰富，资金充足，开公司是水到渠成的事。 He has a lot of experience and enough capital, so when he starts up a company, success will come naturally.

水分 shuǐfèn [名] **1** (指物质) moisture content **2** (虚假成分) exaggeration

水果 shuǐguǒ [名] fruit

水火 shuǐhuǒ [名] **1** (形容对立物) opposites (*pl*) **2** (形容灾难) misery

水货 shuǐhuò [名] **1** (走私品) smuggled goods (*pl*) **2** (劣质品) inferior goods (*pl*)

水晶 shuǐjīng [名] crystal

水库 shuǐkù [名] reservoir

水力 shuǐlì [名] hydraulic power

水利 shuǐlì [名] (水利工程) irrigation project

水淋淋 shuǐlīnlīn [形] sopping wet

水灵 shuǐling [形] **1** (指水果) fresh and juicy **2** (指人、花) charming

水流 shuǐliú [名] **1** (江河统称) river **2** (流动的水) current

水陆 shuǐlù [名] land and water ◇这种交通工具是水陆两用的。 This is an amphibious vehicle.

水路 shuǐlù [名] waterway

水落石出 shuǐ luò shí chū get to the bottom of

水面 shuǐmiàn [名] the water's surface

水平 shuǐpíng **I** [名] standard ◇人们的生活水平越来越高。 People's living standards are getting higher and higher. **II** [形] horizontal ◇箱子要保持水平。 Ensure that the box is horizontal.

水禽 shuǐqín [名] aquatic birds (*pl*)

水渠 shuǐqú [名] ditch

水乳交融 shuǐ rǔ jiāo róng in complete harmony ◇这幅画人物和景物水乳交融，非常和谐。 The figure in this picture is in complete harmony with the scenery.

水势 shuǐshì [名] current

水手 shuǐshǒu [名] sailor

水土 shuǐtǔ [名] **1** (水和土) water and land **2** (环境气候) climate

水汪汪 shuǐwāngwāng [形] **1** (形容充满水) watery **2** (指眼睛) bright

水乡 shuǐxiāng [名] region of rivers and lakes

水泄不通 shuǐ xiè bù tōng completely packed ◇汽车把这条路堵得水泄不通。 The road was so packed with cars that nothing could get through at all.

水性 shuǐxìng [名] ability to swim ◇他水性很好。 He's a good swimmer.

水性杨花 shuǐxìng yánghuā flirtatious ◇她不是个水性杨花的女子。 She's not a flirtatious woman.

水银 shuǐyín [名] mercury

水域 shuǐyù [名] waters (*pl*)

水源 shuǐyuán [名] **1** (指河流) source of a river **2** (指民用水) water source

水灾 shuǐzāi [名] flood

水涨船高 shuǐ zhǎng chuán gāo ◇留学生越来越多，学费也水涨船高。 The number of overseas students is continually increasing, and there has been a corresponding increase in tuition fees. ◇足球运动员出了名，其身价也水涨船高。 Once a footballer has made a name for himself, his social status increases along with his fame.

水质 shuǐzhì [名] water quality

水中捞月 shuǐ zhōng lāo yuè impractical

水准 shuǐzhǔn [名] **1** (水平) standard **2** (水平面) water level

水族 shuǐzú [名] aquatic animals (*pl*)

说 shuì [动] persuade
▷另见 shuō

税 shuì [名] tax

税法 shuìfǎ [名] tax law

税率 shuìlǜ [名] tax rate

税收 shuìshōu [名] tax revenue

税务局 shuìwùjú [名] tax office

睡 shuì [动] sleep (*pt, pp* slept)

睡觉 shuìjiào [动] sleep (*pt, pp* slept) ◇睡觉是有效的休息方式。 Sleeping is an effective way of relaxing.

睡梦 shuìmèng [名] dream

睡眠 shuìmián [名] sleep

睡意 shuìyì [名] drowsiness

吮 shǔn [动] suck◇小男孩儿吮着拇指。 The little boy was sucking his thumb.

吮吸 shǔnxī [动] suck

顺 shùn **I** [介] **1** (指方向) with ♦顺时针 clockwise **2** (沿) along **3** (趁便) ♦顺便 on the way **II** [动] **1** (朝同一方向) follow **2** (使有条理) put … in order (*pt, pp* put) **3** (顺从) obey **4** (合意) be to one's liking ♦顺心 as one would wish **III** [形] successful◇他找工作很顺。His job hunt has been very successful.

顺便 shùnbiàn [副] **1** (指乘方便) on the way◇你去超市时顺便帮我到邮局寄封信吧。Would you mind going to the post office to post this letter for me on your way to the supermarket? **2** (说、问) by the way ◇顺便问一下，他给你回电话了吗？ By the way, did he call you back?

顺差 shùnchā [名] favourable (英) 或 favorable (美) balance

顺畅 shùnchàng [形] smooth ◇交通很少有顺畅的时候。There is seldom a smooth flow of traffic.

顺从 shùncóng [动] obey

顺当 shùndang [形] smooth

顺耳 shùn'ěr [形] pleasant to hear ◇这首歌听起来挺顺耳的。This tune is quite pleasant. ◇他一句不顺耳的话也听不进去。He won't listen to anything he doesn't want to hear.

顺风 shùnfēng [动] **1** (指风向) travel downwind **2** (指祝福) ◇祝你一路顺风。Have a safe journey! ◇一路顺风 Bon voyage!

顺境 shùnjìng [名] favourable (英) 或 favorable (美) circumstances (*pl*)

顺口 shùnkǒu **I** [形] flowing ◇这首诗念起来不太顺口。This poem doesn't flow too well. **II** [副] without thinking ◇他顺口把我们的秘密透露出去了。He revealed our secret without thinking.

顺理成章 shùn lǐ chéng zhāng logical and coherent

顺利 shùnlì [副] smoothly ◇你们的计划执行得顺利吗？ Did your plan go smoothly?

顺路 shùnlù [副] on the way ◇下班后你能顺路到医院去看他吗？ On your way home after work, would you mind going to see him in the hospital?

顺手 shùnshǒu **I** [形] **1** (顺利) smooth **2** (好使) easy to use ◇这些新工具都很顺手。These new tools are very easy to use. **II** [副] on the way◇我顺手把灯关上。I turned out the lights as I went past.

顺手牵羊 shùn shǒu qiān yáng walk off with

顺藤摸瓜 shùn téng mō guā trace … to its roots

顺心 shùnxīn [形] satisfactory ◇他现在日子过得很顺心。Life is going very well for him at the moment. ◇咱们出去走走，忘掉那些不顺心的事。Let's go out for a walk and try and forget this whole mess.

顺序 shùnxù [名] order

顺延 shùnyán [动] postpone

顺眼 shùnyǎn [形] attractive ◇这套家具看起来挺顺眼。This furniture is very attractive. ◇她对男朋友看不顺眼。She had a low opinion of her boyfriend.

顺应 shùnyìng [动] follow ◇顺应时代的变化 change with the times

瞬 shùn [名] flash ♦一瞬间 in a flash

瞬息万变 shùnxī wàn biàn fast-changing

说 shuō [动] **1** (用语言表达意思) say (*pt, pp* said) ◇他说他不来了。He said he wouldn't come. **2** (解释) explain **3** (责备) tell … off (*pt, pp* told) ◇衣服弄得这么脏，看你妈妈不说你。Your mum will give you such a telling-off for getting your clothes so dirty.
▷另见 shuì

> 表示"说"最常用的词汇是 **say**。请注意，在使用动词 **say** 时，如果想要表示说话的对象，应该使用介词 **to**。*'What did she say you?'* 是错误的用法。*'What did she say to you?'* 则是正确的表达。表示告知某人某事用 **tell**。*The manufacturer told me that the product did not contain corn.* 然而，动词 **tell** 通常带直接宾语，表示说话的对象。*He told Alison he was suffering from leukaemia… What did she tell you? 'What did she tell to you?'* 是错误的用法。**tell** 可以和带 **to** 的动词不定式连用，表示命令或指示。*My mother told me to shut up and eat my dinner.*

说长道短 shuō cháng dào duǎn criticize

说唱 shuōchàng [名] **1** (曲艺) *a form of popular entertainment consisting mostly of singing and comic dialogue* **2** (音) rap ◇说唱艺人 rapper

说法 shuōfa [名] **1** (措辞) version **2** (见解) opinion ◇大家对这件事说法不一。Everybody has different opinions on this matter. **3** (公道) justification

说服 shuōfú [动] persuade

说合 shuōhe [动] **1** (指亲事) bring … together (*pt, pp* brought) **2** (商量) discuss

说和 shuōhe [动] mediate

说话 shuōhuà I [动] **1** (用语言表达意思) talk **2** (闲谈) chat II [副] (马上) any minute

说教 shuōjiào [动] preach

说客 shuōkè [名] persuasive talker

说理 shuōlǐ [动] argue ◇这篇论文说理充分，论证严谨。This essay is well argued and precisely reasoned.

说媒 shuōméi [动] act as matchmaker

说明 shuōmíng I [动] **1** (解释明白) explain **2** (证明) prove II [名] explanation ◇产品使用说明 instruction manual

说情 shuōqíng [动] plead for

说三道四 shuō sān dào sì gossip

说书 shuōshū [动] *give a storytelling performance*

说闲话 shuō xiánhuà gossip

说笑 shuōxiào [动] joke around

说一不二 shuō yī bù èr be a man of one's word ◇我们的女老板说一不二。Our boss is a woman of her word.

烁 shuò [形] twinkling

硕 shuò [形] large

硕果 shuòguǒ [名] success

硕士 shuòshì [名] master's degree ◇文科硕士 MA ◇理科硕士 MSc

司 sī I [动] take charge of (*pt* took, *pp* taken) ♦司机 driver ◇各司其职 each attends to their own duties II [名] department

司法 sīfǎ [名] judiciary

司机 sījī [名] driver

司空见惯 sīkōng jiàn guàn be used to

司令 sīlìng [名] commander

司仪 sīyí [名] master of ceremonies, MC

丝 sī I [名] **1** (指蚕) silk **2** (指像丝) thread ♦铁丝 wire ◇把土豆切成丝。Shred the potato.

丝绸 sīchóu [名] silk

丝毫 sīháo [形] slightest ◇丝毫无损 not harmed in the slightest

私 sī [形] **1** (个人的) private ♦私事 private affairs **2** (自私的) selfish ♦无私 unselfish **3** (暗地里的) secret **4** (非法的) illegal

私奔 sībēn [动] elope

私产 sīchǎn [名] private property

私党 sīdǎng [名] clique

私邸 sīdǐ [名] private residence

私房 sīfang [形] 1 (指积蓄) personal savings (*pl*) 2 (指话) personal matters (*pl*)

私愤 sīfèn [名] grudge

私活 sīhuó [名] moonlighting ◇他因利用上班时间干私活被罚没全年奖金。He lost a whole year's bonuses for moonlighting during office hours.

私交 sījiāo [名] personal connections (*pl*)

私立 sīlì [形] private

私了 sīliǎo [动] settle … privately

私囊 sīnáng [名] one's own pocket ◇他用纳税人的钱中饱私囊。He was lining his own pockets with taxpayers' money.

私情 sīqíng [名] 1 (私人交情) personal considerations (*pl*) 2 (不正当的男女情爱) relationship

私人 sīrén [形] 1 (属于个人的) private 2 (人与人之间的) personal ◇你和老板的私人关系怎么样？ How do you get on with your boss?

私生活 sīshēnghuó [名] private life

私生子 sīshēngzǐ [名] illegitimate child (*pl* children)

私通 sītōng [动] 1 (私下勾结) have secret communication 2 (通奸) commit adultery

私下 sīxià [副] privately

私心 sīxīn [名] selfishness

私营 sīyíng [动] privately run ◇这家工厂顺利地完成了由国营到私营的转变。The factory smoothly carried out the transformation from state ownership to private ownership.

私有 sīyǒu [形] private ♦私有化 privatization

私语 sīyǔ [动] whisper

私欲 sīyù [名] selfish desires (*pl*)

私自 sīzì [副] without permission

思 sī I [动] 1 (思考) think (*pt, pp* thought) 2 (思念) miss 3 (希望) hope II [名] thought ♦思路 train of thought

思潮 sīcháo [名] 1 (指社会) trend 2 (指个人) thought ◇他思潮起伏，久久不能入睡。His head was full of restless thoughts, and for a long time he could not sleep.

思考 sīkǎo [动] think (*pt, pp* thought) ◇请给我时间思考一下你的建议。Please give me some time to think your suggestion over.

思量 sīliang [动] consider

思路 sīlù [名] reasoning ◇你这道题的思路是对的。Your reasoning in this question is correct. ◇敲门声打断了他的思路。The knock on the door interrupted his train of thought.

思念 sīniàn I [动] miss II [名] longing

思索 sīsuǒ [动] ponder

思维 sīwéi [名] thinking ◇动物有类似人的思维能力吗？ Do animals have mental abilities similar to those of humans?

思乡 sīxiāng [动] be homesick

思想 sīxiǎng [名] 1 (指有体系) thought 2 (念头) idea ◇这些学生都很有自己的思想。These students all have their own ideas.

思绪 sīxù [名] state of mind

斯 sī 见下文

斯文 sīwen [形] gentle

撕 sī [动] tear (*pt* tore, *pp* torn) ◇她把信撕得粉碎。She tore the letter into pieces.

撕毁 sīhuǐ [动] tear … up (*pt* tore, *pp* torn)

撕票 sīpiào [动] kill the hostage ◇绑架他女朋友的人威胁说不马上给钱他们就撕票。The people who had kidnapped his girlfriend threatened to kill her if he didn't immediately pay the ransom.

嘶 sī I [动] neigh II [形] hoarse

嘶哑 sīyǎ [形] hoarse

死 sǐ **I** [动] die **II** [形] **1** (死亡的) dead ♦死尸 corpse **2** (不可调和的) implacable ♦死敌 sworn enemy **3** (不能通过的) impassable ♦死胡同 dead end **4** (确切的) fixed ◇我们要把出发的时间定死。We should fix our departure time. **5** (脑筋) slow-witted **6** (规定) rigid **7** (水) still **III** [副] **1** (拼死) to the death ♦死战 fight to the death **2** (表示固执或坚决) stubbornly ◇死等 wait indefinitely **3** (表示到达极点) extremely ◇累死我了。I'm completely exhausted.

死板 sǐbǎn [形] **1** (不活泼的) stiff **2** (不灵活的) inflexible

死不瞑目 sǐ bù míngmù die discontented

死党 sǐdǎng [名] diehard supporters (*pl*)

死敌 sǐdí [名] sworn enemy

死灰复燃 sǐhuī fù rán revive

死活 sǐhuó **I** [名] safety ◇煤矿主不顾矿工的死活，让他们没日没夜地工作。The mine manager didn't care at all about his employees' safety and made them work day and night. **II** [副] simply ◇交通灯变绿了但车子死活打不着火。The lights had changed to green, but the car simply wouldn't start.

死机 sǐjī [动] crash

死角 sǐjiǎo [名] (喻) untouched area ◇知识产权法中的死角 areas untouched by intellectual property laws

死结 sǐjié [名] tight knot

死劲儿 sǐjìnr [副] with all one's strength

死里逃生 sǐ lǐ táo shēng have a narrow escape

死路 sǐlù [名] **1** (走不通的路) dead end **2** (喻) (引向毁灭的道路) road to ruin

死命 sǐmìng **I** [名] doom **II** [副] desperately

死难 sǐnàn [动] die in an accident ◇这家公司向死难者家属进行了赔付。The company gave compensation to the families of the victims of the accident.

死皮赖脸 sǐ pí lài liǎn brazen

死气沉沉 sǐqì chénchén dead

死去活来 sǐ qù huó lái devastated ◇她哭得死去活来。She was crying her eyes out. ◇他爱她爱得死去活来。He was madly in love with her.

死神 sǐshén [名] Death

死尸 sǐshī [名] corpse

死水 sǐshuǐ [名] **1** (指水) stagnant water **2** (指气氛、环境) lifelessness

死亡 sǐwáng [动] die

死心 sǐxīn [动] give up on (*pt* gave, *pp* given) ◇她对出国死心了。She's given up on the idea of going abroad.

死心塌地 sǐ xīn tā dì have one's heart set on

死刑 sǐxíng [名] death penalty

死硬 sǐyìng [形] **1** (形容硬) stiff **2** (顽固) stubborn

死有余辜 sǐ yǒu yú gū death is too good for ◇这种坏人死有余辜。Death's too good for people like that.

死于非命 sǐ yú fēi mìng die a violent death

死战 sǐzhàn **I** [名] life-and-death battle **II** [动] fight to the death (*pt*, *pp* fought)

死者 sǐzhě [名] the deceased

四 sì [数] four

四不像 sìbùxiàng (喻) (不伦不类) neither one thing nor the other

四处 sìchù [名] everywhere

四方 sìfāng [名] **1** (形状) square **2** (各处) all directions

四方步 sìfāngbù [名] leisurely pace

四分五裂 sì fēn wǔ liè be torn asunder

四海 sìhǎi [名] the world

四季 sìjì [名] the four seasons (*pl*)

四邻 sìlín [名] neighbours (英), neighbors (美) (*pl*)

四平八稳 sì píng bā wěn well-balanced

四舍五入 sì shě wǔ rù round off to the nearest number ◇5.61四舍五入后得5.6。5.61 can be rounded down to 5.6.

四声 sìshēng [名] *the four tones of Standard Chinese pronunciation*

四通八达 sì tōng bā dá extend in all directions ◇地铁线路四通八达。The different lines of the underground link everywhere up.

四肢 sìzhī [名] limbs (*pl*)

四周 sìzhōu [名] all sides ◇四周都是人。There are people everywhere. ◇餐馆四周都是写字楼。The restaurant is surrounded by office buildings.

寺 sì [名] **1** (指佛教) temple ♦喇嘛寺 Tibetan Buddhist temple **2** (指伊斯兰教) mosque ♦清真寺 mosque

寺院 sìyuàn [名] temple

似 sì **I** [动] (像) be like ◇他的脸似纸一样白。His face was as white as a sheet of paper. **II** [副] apparently ◇她看似单纯，其实很成熟。She appears to be naive, but actually she's very worldly-wise. **III** [介] than ◇赛马一匹快似一匹。Each racehorse is quicker than the last.
▷另见 shì

似曾相识 sì céng xiāngshí look familiar ◇他俩初次见面，但却都有似曾相识的感觉。It was the first time the two had met, and yet they felt strangely familiar.

似乎 sìhū [副] apparently

似是而非 sì shì ér fēi specious ◇他的推理似是而非。His reasoning is specious.

伺 sì [动] watch ♦窥伺 spy on
▷另见 cì

伺机 sìjī [动] wait for the opportunity to ◇伺机进攻 wait for an opportunity to attack

饲 sì [动] raise ♦饲养 raise

饲料 sìliào [名] fodder

饲养 sìyǎng [动] raise

肆 sì **I** [动] be unrestrained **II** [名] *an elaborate form of "four", used in writing cheques etc to prevent mistakes and forgery*

肆虐 sìnüè [动] wreak havoc ◇那年蝗虫肆虐。That year locusts wreaked havoc.

肆无忌惮 sì wú jì dàn unscrupulous

肆意 sìyì [副] wantonly

松 sōng **I** [名] **1** (树) pine tree **2** (食品) *a condiment made of finely shredded preserved meat* **II** [动] **1** (放开) relax ◇他松开了抓着绳子的手。He relaxed his grip on the rope. **2** (鞋带、腰带) loosen **III** [形] loose ◇他的腰带有点松。His belt is a bit loose. ◇你管学生不能太松了。You shouldn't be too soft on the students.

松绑 sōngbǎng [动] **1** (解开绳索) untie **2** (放宽限制) relax

松弛 sōngchí [形] **1** (肌肉) limp **2** (心情) relaxed **3** (纪律) lax

松动 sōngdòng [动] **1** (牙齿、岩石、螺丝) loosen **2** (口气) relax **3** (规定) relax

松劲 sōngjìn [动] relax one's efforts

松口 sōngkǒu [动] **1** (松嘴) let go (*pt, pp* let) **2** (不坚持) (主张、意见) relent

松快 sōngkuai [形] **1** (指精神) relieved ◇和老师谈话后，他心里松快了许多。After he talked to his teacher, he felt much relieved. **2** (指身体) relaxed **3** (指空间上) less crowded

松软 sōngruǎn [形] **1** (指物体) soft **2** (指肢体) weak

松散 sōngsǎn [形] **1** (指结构) loose **2** (指精神) lax

松松垮垮 sōngsōngkuǎkuǎ [形] **1** (指衣着) baggy **2** (指精神) sluggish

松懈 sōngxiè [形] **1** (放松) relaxed **2** (松散) lax

怂 sǒng 见下文

怂恿 sǒngyǒng [动] provoke

耸 sǒng [动] **1** (伸向高处) tower **2** (引起注意) alarm

耸动 sǒngdòng [动] (肩膀) shrug

耸立 sǒnglì [动] tower

耸人听闻 sǒng rén tīng wén sensationalize

悚 sǒng 见下文

悚然 sǒngrán [形] terrified

讼 sòng [动] take a case to court (*pt* took, *pp* taken) ♦诉讼 lawsuit

送 sòng [动] **1** (信、邮包、外卖) deliver **2** (礼物) give (*pt* gave, *pp* given) ◊你准备送他什么结婚礼物？ What are you going to give him as a wedding present? **3** (送行) see … off (*pt* saw, *pp* seen) ◊他把女朋友送到家。He saw his girlfriend home. **4** (陪着去) take (*pt* took, *pp* taken) ◊我把客人送到机场。I took the guests to the airport.

送别 sòngbié [动] see … off (*pt* saw, *pp* seen) ◊老师为毕业生举行了送别晚会。The teachers held a farewell banquet for the graduating students.

送命 sòngmìng [动] lose one's life (*pt, pp* lost)

送死 sòngsǐ [动] (口) court death

送行 sòngxíng [动] see … off (*pt* saw, *pp* seen) ◊她到机场给朋友送行。She went to the airport to see a friend off.

送葬 sòngzàng [动] be part of a funeral procession

送终 sòngzhōng [动] **1** (临终照料) be with … in his/her last moments **2** (安排丧事) make funeral arrangements

诵 sòng [动] **1** (大声读) read … aloud (*pt, pp* read) **2** (背诵) recite

诵读 sòngdú [动] read … aloud (*pt, pp* read)

颂 sòng **I** [动] praise **II** [名] ode

颂词 sòngcí [名] ode

颂歌 sònggē [名] hymn of praise

颂扬 sòngyáng [动] extol

搜 sōu [动] search

搜捕 sōubǔ [动] hunt for ◊他试图逃避警方的搜捕。He attempted to avoid the hunt organised by the police.

搜查 sōuchá [动] search ◊警察拦截住一辆可疑车辆进行搜查。The police stopped a suspicious vehicle and carried out a search.

搜刮 sōuguā [动] extort

搜集 sōují [动] gather

搜罗 sōuluó [动] recruit

搜索 sōusuǒ [动] search for

搜索引擎 sōusuǒ yǐnqíng [名] search engine

搜寻 sōuxún [动] hunt for

嗖 sōu [拟] whizz ◊一辆摩托车嗖的一声从他身边驶过。A motorbike whizzed past him.

馊 sōu [形] sour

馊主意 sōu zhǔyi [名] bad idea

艘 sōu [量] ◊3艘游艇 three yachts

嗽 sòu [动] cough ♦咳嗽 cough

苏 sū [动] revive ♦复苏 recover

苏打 sūdá [名] soda

苏醒 sūxǐng [动] come to (*pt* came, *pp* come)

酥 sū **I** [名] biscuit **II** [形] **1** (用于食物) crisp **2** (用于人体) limp

酥软 sūruǎn [形] weak ◊工作一天之后，他回到家累得浑身酥软。After a day's work, he returned home so tired that his whole body felt really weak .

酥松 sūsōng [形] loosened

酥油 sūyóu [名] butter

俗 sú **I** [名] **1** (风俗) custom ♦民俗 folk custom ◊入乡随俗 when in Rome, do as the Romans do **2** (没出家的人) laity ♦僧俗 clergy and laity **II** [形] **1** (大众的) popular **2** (庸俗) vulgar

俗不可耐 sú bù kě nài as common as muck

俗话 súhuà [名] proverb

俗气 súqi [形] vulgar

俗人 súrén [名] **1** (一般人) ordinary person (*pl* people) **2** (庸俗的人) vulgar person (*pl* people)

俗套 sútào [名] **1** (无聊的礼节) conventions (*pl*) **2** (陈旧的格调) cliché

俗语 súyǔ [名] common saying

夙 sù [形] (书) **1** (早) early **2** (旧有的) old ♦夙怨 old grudge

夙兴夜寐 sù xīng yè mèi work day and night

夙愿 sùyuàn [名] long-cherished ambition

诉 sù [动] 1 (说给人) tell (*pt, pp* told) ♦诉说 tell 2 (倾吐) pour ... out ♦诉苦 complain 3 (控告) accuse ♦上诉 appeal to a higher court

诉苦 sùkǔ [动] complain

诉说 sùshuō [动] tell (*pt, pp* told)

诉讼 sùsòng [名] legal proceedings (*pl*)

肃 sù [形] 1 (恭敬的) respectful ♦肃立 stand to attention 2 (严肃) serious

肃静 sùjìng [形] silent

肃立 sùlì [动] stand to attention (*pt, pp* stood)

肃然起敬 sùrán qǐ jìng filled with deep respect ◇老人的宽厚让我肃然起敬。The old people's generosity filled me with deep respect.

素 sù I [形] plain II [副] always ♦平素 usually III [名] 1 (蔬菜、瓜果等食物) vegetable ♦素食者 vegetarian 2 (有根本性质的) element ♦维生素 vitamin

素材 sùcái [名] material

素餐 sùcān [名] vegetarian meal

素净 sùjing [形] neat

素来 sùlái [副] usually ◇她素来很安静。She's usually very quiet. ◇他俩素来不和。Those two never get on.

素昧平生 sù mèi píng shēng never met ◇一位素昧平生的女孩子给她买了火车票。A girl she had never met before bought her a train ticket.

素描 sùmiáo [名] sketch

素食 sùshí [名] vegetarian food

素雅 sùyǎ [形] elegant

素养 sùyǎng [名] cultivation

素质 sùzhì [名] character

速 sù I [名] speed II [形] quick ♦速算 quick calculation

速成 sùchéng [动] take a crash course (*pt* took, *pp* taken) ◇计算机速成班 a crash course in computers

速递 sùdì [动] send by express delivery (*pt, pp* sent)

速度 sùdù [名] speed

速记 sùjì [动] take shorthand notes (*pt* took, *pp* taken) ◇我非常羡慕会速记的人。I really admire people who know shorthand.

速溶 sùróng [动] dissolve quickly ◇速溶咖啡 instant coffee

速效 sùxiào [名] fast action ◇用这种方法减肥有速效。You will see quick results with this diet. ◇速效止痛片 fast-acting pain killer

速写 sùxiě [名] sketch

宿 sù [动] stay ▷另见 xiǔ

宿敌 sùdí [名] old enemy

宿命论 sùmìnglùn [名] fatalism

宿舍 sùshè [名] dormitory

宿营 sùyíng [动] camp

宿愿 sùyuàn [名] long-cherished ambition

粟 sù [名] millet

塑 sù I [动] model II [名] mould (英), mold (美)

塑料 sùliào [名] plastic

塑像 sùxiàng [名] statue

塑造 sùzào [动] 1 (指用物质材料制造) shape 2 (指用艺术手段制造) model

溯 sù [动] 1 (逆水走) go upstream (*pt* went, *pp* gone) 2 (回想) recollect

溯源 sùyuán [动] trace ... back to its roots

簌 sù I [拟] rustle II [形] 1 (形容眼泪) streaming 2 (形容发抖) shivering

酸 suān I [形] 1 (指味道) sour 2 (伤心) sad 3 (迂腐) pedantic 4 (疼) sore II [名] acid

酸楚 suānchǔ [形] miserable

酸溜溜 suānliūliū [形] 1 (形容味道) sour 2 (形容嫉妒) envious 3 (形容言谈举止) pedantic

酸奶 suānnǎi [名] yoghurt

酸甜苦辣 suān tián kǔ là all the pains and pleasures of life

酸性 suānxìng [名] acidity

蒜 suàn [名] garlic

蒜头 suàntóu [名] bulb of garlic

算 suàn [动] **1** (计算) calculate **2** (计算进去) count **3** (谋划) plan ♦暗算 plot against **4** (当作) be considered as **5** (由某人负责) blame **6** (算数) count **7** (作罢) ◇算了吧，这些小事我们就不要再管了。Forget it, we needn't worry about these small details. ◇这工作今天做不完就算了，明天再说。Let's leave it for today and try again tomorrow. **8** (推测) suppose **9** (表示突出) ◇几个朋友中算他最有钱。He must be the richest of that group of friends. ◇全班算他最小。He has to be the youngest in the class.

算法 suànfǎ [名] algorithm

算计 suànji **I** [动] **1** (计算数目) calculate **2** (考虑) consider **3** (估计) guess **4** (暗中谋算) plot **II** [名] plan

算命 suànmìng [动] tell sb's fortune (*pt, pp* told) ♦算命先生 fortune teller

算盘 suànpán [名] **1** (计算用具) abacus **2** (喻) (打算) scheme

算术 suànshù [名] maths (*sg*) (英), math (美)

算数 suànshù [动] count

算账 suànzhàng [动] **1** (计算账目) work out accounts ◇年底一算账，他赚了1万多元。When he worked out his accounts at the end of the year, he had earned over ten thousand yuan. **2** (把事情扯平) get even with

尿 suī [名] piss (讳)
▷另见 niào

虽 suī [连] although ◇他个子虽小，力气却很大。Although he isn't big, he's very strong.

虽然 suīrán [连] although

随 suí [动] **1** (跟随) follow **2** (顺从) go along with (*pt* went, *pp* gone) **3** (任凭) let … do as they like (*pt, pp* let) ◇孩子大了，随他去吧。The child's grown up – let him do as he wishes. **4** (方) (像) take after (*pt* took, *pp* taken) ◇小女孩长得随她爸爸。The little girl takes after her father.

随便 suíbiàn **I** [动] do as one wishes ◇这件事怎样处理你随便吧。Deal with this matter as you wish. **II** [形] **1** (随意) casual **2** (欠考虑的) thoughtless **III** [副] ◇大家随便坐。Everyone can sit where they like. ◇她在商店里随便逛逛。She's wandering around the shops. **IV** [连] no matter

随波逐流 suí bō zhú liú go with the flow

随处 suíchù [副] anywhere

随从 suícóng **I** [名] entourage **II** [动] accompany

随大溜 suí dàliù follow the crowd

随地 suídì [副] anywhere

随风倒 suífēngdǎo be easily swayed

随风转舵 suí fēng zhuǎn duò (贬) follow the prevailing wind

随和 suíhe [形] easygoing

随后 suíhòu [副] soon after

随机应变 suí jī yìng biàn change with the times

随即 suíjí [副] immediately

随口 suíkǒu [副] carelessly

随身 suíshēn [副] ◇每个士兵要随身携带30多公斤物品。Every soldier must carry over 30 kilos on their back. ◇乘客的随身行李不能超过10公斤。Passengers may not bring more than ten kilograms of hand luggage on board.

随身听 suíshēntīng [名] Walkman®

随声附和 suí shēng fùhè echo sb's words ◇他的讲话真荒唐，但有很多人随声附和。What he says is ridiculous, yet many people echo his words.

随时 suíshí [副] at any time

随手 suíshǒu [副] on one's way ◇请随手关门。Please close the door on your way. ◇他随手把信放在抽屉里。He put the letter in a drawer on his way past.

随同 suítóng [动] accompany

随意 suíyì [动] do as one likes

随遇而安 suí yù ér ān adapt to changing circumstances

随着 suízhe [动] follow ◊他随着父母移民加拿大了。Following his parents, he emigrated to Canada.

髓 suǐ [名] marrow ♦骨髓 bone marrow

岁 suì I [名] year II [量] year ◊他20岁了。He's 20 years old.

岁数 suìshu [名] age ◊在他这个岁数，不应该再干重体力活了。He shouldn't be doing heavy manual work at his age.

岁月 suìyuè [名] years (*pl*)

遂 suì [动] **1** (如意) satisfy **2** (成功) succeed ◊杀人未遂 attempted murder

遂愿 suìyuàn [动] fulfil sb's wishes

碎 suì I [动] **1** (破碎) break (*pt* broke, *pp* broken) **2** (使粉碎) smash ♦碎纸机 shredder II [形] **1** (不完整) broken **2** (说话唠叨) garrulous

隧 suì [名] tunnel

隧道 suìdào [名] tunnel

燧 suì [名] flint

燧石 suìshí [名] flint

穗 suì [名] **1** (指植物) ear ♦麦穗 ear of wheat **2** (指装饰品) tassel

孙 sūn [名] grandchild (*pl* grandchildren) ◊祖孙三代 three generations

孙女 sūnnǚ [名] granddaughter

孙子 sūnzi [名] grandson

损 sǔn I [动] **1** (减少) decrease **2** (损害) harm **3** (损坏) damage **4** (方) (挖苦) make fun of II [形] (方) mean

损公肥私 sǔn gōng féi sī embezzle public funds

损害 sǔnhài [动] **1** (健康) damage **2** (利益) harm **3** (名誉) ruin **4** (关系) damage

损耗 sǔnhào [动] lose (*pt, pp* lost) ◊我们必须减少生产过程中的能源损耗。We must reduce loss of resources in the production process.

损坏 sǔnhuài [动] damage

损人利己 sǔn rén lì jǐ hurt others to benefit oneself

损失 sǔnshī I [动] lose (*pt, pp* lost) II [名] loss

笋 sǔn [名] bamboo shoot

唆 suō [动] instigate

唆使 suōshǐ [动] incite

梭 suō [名] shuttle

梭镖 suōbiāo [动] spear

梭巡 suōxún [动] patrol

梭子 suōzi [名] **1** (用于纺织) shuttle **2** (用于枪支) clip

缩 suō [动] **1** (收缩) contract **2** (收回去) withdraw (*pt* withdrew, *pp* withdrawn)

缩减 suōjiǎn [动] **1** (经费) cut (*pt, pp* cut) **2** (人员) reduce

缩略语 suōlüèyǔ [名] abbreviation

缩手缩脚 suō shǒu suō jiǎo **1** (指寒冷) shrink with cold (*pt* shrank, *pp* shrunk) **2** (形容顾虑多) be overcautious

缩水 suōshuǐ [动] shrink (*pt* shrank, *pp* shrunk) ◊这件T恤衫缩水吗？Will this T-shirt shrink in the wash?

缩写 suōxiě I [名] abbreviation ◊NATO是英文North Atlantic Treaty Organization的缩写。NATO is the abbreviation for the North Atlantic Treaty Organization. II [动] abridge

缩影 suōyǐng [名] epitome

所 suǒ I [名] **1** (处所) place **2** (用于机构名称) office ♦派出所 local police station ♦诊所 clinic II [量] ◊一所大学 a university III [助] **1** (表示被动) ◊她被我的真诚所感动。She was deeply moved by my sincerity. ◊他被金钱所迷惑。He's obsessed with money. **2** (表示强调) ◊我所看过的影片很少有大片。Out of all the films I've seen, hardly any have been blockbusters. ◊这正是大家所不理解的。This is the bit that no-one understands.

所得税 suǒdéshuì [名] income tax

所属 suǒshǔ [名] **1** (统属之下的) subordinate **2** (自己隶属的) affiliation

所谓 suǒwèi [形] **1** (通常说的) ◇中医所谓"上火"不止是指嗓子疼一种症状。What is known in Chinese medicine as 'excess internal heat' covers a lot more than sore throats and the like. ◇所谓"网虫"，就是上网上瘾的人。The people we refer to as 'Net Worms' are addicted to the Internet. **2** (形容不认可) so-called

所向披靡 suǒ xiàng pī mǐ invincible

所以 suǒyǐ [连] **1** (表示结果) so ◇路上堵车，所以我迟到了。There was a lot of traffic, so I am late. **2** (表示突出原因) the reason why ◇她之所以成功，是因为坚持不懈。The reason for her success is her unremitting effort.

所以然 suǒyǐrán [名] the reason why

所有 suǒyǒu **I** [动] own **II** [名] possession **III** [形] all

所有权 suǒyǒuquán [名] proprietary rights (*pl*)

所有制 suǒyǒuzhì [名] ownership

所在 suǒzài [名] ◇这便是问题的症结所在。This is the crux of the matter. ◇巨大的市场是中国的魅力所在。What gives China its appeal is its enormous markets.

索 suǒ **I** [名] **1** (绳子) rope **2** (链子) chain **II** [动] **1** (找) search ♦探索 explore **2** (要) request

索赔 suǒpéi [动] claim damages ◇他的车祸索赔要求迟迟未能得到保险公司的明确答复。His claim for damages after the car accident has still not been properly dealt with by the insurance company after all this time.

索取 suǒqǔ [动] demand ◇他来索取欠款。He's come to demand the money he's owed.

索性 suǒxìng [副] might as well ◇既然已经帮助他了，就索性帮到底。Since we've already helped him out, we might as well help until the job is done.

索引 suǒyǐn [名] index

琐 suǒ [形] petty

琐事 suǒshì [名] triviality

琐碎 suǒsuì [形] petty

锁 suǒ **I** [名] lock **II** [动] **1** (用锁锁住) lock **2** (眉) frown

锁链 suǒliàn [名] chain

Tt

他 tā [代] **1** (另一人) he ◇他是教师。He's a teacher. ◇他的包在书桌上。His bag is on the desk. **2** (其他) other ◇另有他故。There is another reason.

他们 tāmen [代] they ◇他们学习刻苦。They study hard. ◇学生应当尊敬他们的老师。Students should respect their teachers.

他人 tārén [名] others (*pl*)

他乡 tāxiāng [名] a place far from home

它 tā [代] it ◇把它扔掉。Throw it away. ◇它的牙锋利无比。Its teeth are razor sharp.

它们 tāmen [代] they ◇如果下周没人来认领这些东西，它们就会被销毁了。If no-one claims these items in the next week, they will be destroyed. ◇词典都在那里，把它们拿来。The dictionaries are over there, bring them here.

她 tā [代] she ◇她是个杰出的外交家。She's a distinguished diplomat. ◇她的裙子在衣柜里。Her skirt is in the wardrobe.

趿 tā 见下文

趿拉 tāla [动] shuffle along

塌 tā [动] **1** (倒塌) collapse **2** (凹下) sink (*pt* sank, *pp* sunk) ◇他瘦得连双颊都塌下去了。He's got so thin that even his cheeks are sunken. **3** (安定) settle down

塌方 tāfāng [动] collapse

塌实 tāshi [形] **1** (不浮躁) steady **2** (放心) at peace

塔 tǎ [名] **1** (指佛教建筑物) pagoda **2** (指塔形物) tower

塔楼 tǎlóu [名] tower block

獭 tǎ [名] otter

踏 tà [动] **1** (踩) step onto **2** (喻) start ◇我刚踏上工作岗位。I've just started working.

踏青 tàqīng [动] go on an outing in spring (*pt* went, *pp* gone)

胎 tāi [名] **1** (母体内的幼体) foetus (英), fetus (美) ♦怀胎 be pregnant **2** (生育次数) pregnancy **3** (轮胎) tyre (英), tire (美)

胎儿 tāi'ér [名] foetus (英), fetus (美)

胎记 tāijì [名] birthmark

胎盘 tāipán [名] placenta

胎生 tāishēng [形] viviparous ♦胎生动物 viviparous animal

台 tái **I** [名] **1** (指建筑) tower ♦观测台 observation tower **2** (指讲话、表演) stage ♦舞台 stage **3** (指作座子用) stand ♦蜡台 candlestick **4** (台形物) ♦窗台 window sill ♦站台 platform **5** (桌子或类似物) table ♦梳妆台 dressing table ♦写字台 desk **6** (指电话服务) telephone service ♦长途台 long-distance service ♦查号台 directory inquiries (*sg*) **7** (指广播电视) station ◇电视台 television station **8** (台湾) Taiwan **II** [量] **1** (指机器) ◇一台电脑 a computer **2** (指戏剧、戏曲) ◇两台京剧 two Beijing Opera performances

台布 táibù [名] tablecloth

台词 táicí [名] line

台风 táifēng [名] typhoon

台阶 táijiē [名] **1** (指建筑) step **2** (喻) way out ◇我赶快换了话题以便给他们找个台阶儿下。I hurriedly changed the subject to give them a way out.

台历 táilì [名] desk calendar

台球 táiqiú [名] **1** (指美式) pool **2** (指英式) billiards

台柱子 táizhùzi [名] leading figure

苔 tái [名] moss

苔藓 táixiǎn [名] moss

抬 tái [动] **1** (举) raise **2** (搬) carry **3** (抬杠) bicker

抬杠 táigàng [动] bicker

抬举 táiju [动] favour (英), favor (美)

◇别太抬举他了，他会骄傲的。Don't favour him too much or he'll get conceited. ◇你真不识抬举！You're so ungrateful!

抬头 táitóu [动] 1 (昂头) raise one's head 2 (喻) (势力、受压制的人) get a foothold ◇我们绝对不能让偷渡活动抬头。We must not let the people-smugglers get a foothold.

太 tài I [形] 1 (高或大) highest ♦太空 space 2 (指辈分高) senior ♦太爷爷 great-grandfather II [副] 1 (指程度过分) too ◇这部电影太长。This film is too long. 2 (指程度极高) so ◇我太高兴了。I am so happy. 3 (用于否定) that ◇她跑得不太快。She's not that fast a runner.

太极拳 tàijíquán [名] Tai-chi

太监 tàijiàn [名] eunuch

太空 tàikōng [名] space

太平 tàipíng [形] peaceful

太平间 tàipíngjiān [名] mortuary

太平无事 tàipíng wú shì all is well

太太 tàitai [名] 1 (妻子) wife (*pl* wives) 2 (指对老年妇女) lady 3 (对已婚妇女) Mrs ◇张太太 Mrs. Zhang

太阳 tàiyáng [名] sun ◇太阳系 solar system

太子 tàizǐ [名] crown prince

态 tài [名] 1 (状态) state ♦常态 normality ♦体态 posture 2 (语言) voice

态度 tàidu [名] 1 (举止神情) manner ◇这里的服务员态度好。The service is good here. 2 (看法) attitude ◇他对这件事表明了态度。He made his attitude to the affair clear.

泰 tài [形] (平安) peaceful

泰斗 tàidǒu [名] leading authority

泰然 tàirán [形] calm

坍 tān [动] collapse

坍塌 tāntā [动] fall down (*pt* fell, *pp* fallen)

贪 tān I [动] 1 (贪污) be corrupt 2 (不满足) crave ♦贪玩 be too fond of a good time ♦贪吃 be greedy 3 (好处、便宜) covet II [形] greedy

贪杯 tānbēi [动] be too fond of alcohol

贪得无厌 tān dé wú yàn insatiably greedy

贪官污吏 tān guān wū lì corrupt official

贪婪 tānlán [形] greedy

贪恋 tānliàn [动] overindulge in

贪生怕死 tān shēng pà sǐ do anything to save one's neck

贪图 tāntú [动] covet

贪污 tānwū [动] embezzle

贪心 tānxīn I [形] greedy II [名] greed

贪赃 tānzāng [动] take bribes (*pt* took, *pp* taken)

摊 tān I [动] 1 (摆开) spread … out (*pt, pp* spread) ◇摊开地图 spread out a map ◇我们把问题摊开来解决。In order to solve a problem we need to air it. 2 (指烹调) fry ◇他摊了个鸡蛋。He fried an egg. 3 (分担) share 4 (碰到) run into (*pt* ran, *pp* run) II [名] stall

摊点 tāndiǎn [名] stall

摊贩 tānfàn [名] street trader

摊牌 tānpái [动] put one's cards on the table (*pt, pp* put)

摊派 tānpài [动] apportion

摊位 tānwèi [名] stall

摊子 tānzi [名] 1 (摊位) stall 2 (喻) (规模) scale 3 (喻) (混乱) shambles (*sg*) ◇他被派来收拾烂摊子。He's been sent here to sort out this shambles.

滩 tān [名] 1 (指河、湖) bank 2 (指海) beach 3 (指水很急) rapids (*pl*)

瘫 tān I [名] paralysis II [形] paralysed (英), paralyzed (美)

瘫痪 tānhuàn I [名] paralysis II [动] be paralysed (英) 或 paralyzed (美)

坛 tán [名] 1 (祭坛) altar 2 (土台) raised plot ♦花坛 raised flower bed 3 (圈子) circles (*pl*) 4 (台子) platform ♦论坛 forum 5 (壶) jug

谈 tán I [动] talk ◇谈生意 discuss business II [名] talk ◇无稽之谈 nonsense

谈何容易 tán hé róngyì easier said than done

谈虎色变 tán hǔ sè biàn turn pale at the mention of

谈话 tánhuà [动] chat

谈论 tánlùn [动] discuss

谈判 tánpàn [动] negotiate ◇商业谈判 commercial negotiation

谈天 tántiān [动] chat

谈吐 tántǔ [名] way of talking

谈笑风生 tán xiào fēng shēng talk cheerfully

谈心 tánxīn [动] have a heart-to-heart talk

弹 tán I [动] **1** (指弹性) spring (*pt* sprang, *pp* sprung) ◇门弹了回来。The door sprang back. ◇球弹不起来了。The ball doesn't bounce. ◇香槟酒瓶盖弹上了天。The champagne cork shot into the air. **2** (棉花、羊毛) fluff ... up **3** (土、灰、球) flick **4** (乐器) play II [形] springy ▷另见dàn

弹劾 tánhé [动] impeach

弹簧 tánhuáng [名] spring ♦弹簧门 swing door

弹力 tánlì [名] elasticity ♦弹力裤 stretch trousers (英) 或 pants (美)

弹性 tánxìng [名] **1** (弹力) elasticity **2** (喻) flexibility ◇弹性工作制 flexible working system ◇法律是没有弹性的。The law is inflexible.

弹奏 tánzòu [动] play

痰 tán [名] phlegm

潭 tán [名] deep pool

檀 tán [名] sandalwood

忐 tǎn 见下文

忐忑 tǎntè [形] disturbed ◇忐忑不安 ill at ease

坦 tǎn [形] **1** (平整) flat **2** (直率) candid **3** (心里安定) calm ♦坦然 composed

坦白 tǎnbái I [形] candid II [动] confess

坦诚 tǎnchéng [形] frank

坦荡 tǎndàng [形] **1** (指道路) broad and smooth **2** (指心胸) magnanimous

坦然 tǎnrán [形] calm ◇他坦然面对死亡。He is facing death calmly.

坦率 tǎnshuài [形] frank ◇双方坦率地交换了意见。The two parties had a frank exchange of views.

坦途 tǎntú [名] smooth road

袒 tǎn [动] **1** (露出) expose **2** (偏心) be biased

袒护 tǎnhù [动] shield

袒露 tǎnlù [动] expose

毯 tǎn [名] **1** (指地上) carpet ♦地毯 carpet **2** (指床上) blanket ♦毛毯 wool blanket **3** (指墙上) tapestry ♦壁毯 tapestry

叹 tàn [动] **1** (叹气) sigh ♦哀叹 lament **2** (书) (吟哦) chant **3** (书) (赞美) extol ♦惊叹 marvel at

叹词 tàncí [名] exclamation

叹服 tànfú [动] gasp in admiration

叹气 tànqì [动] sigh

叹为观止 tàn wéi guān zhǐ take sb's breath away

叹息 tànxī [动] sigh

炭 tàn [名] charcoal

探 tàn I [动] **1** (试图发现) explore **2** (看望) visit **3** (伸出去) stick ... out (*pt*, *pp* stuck) **4** (过问) inquire ♦打探 scout II [名] scout ♦侦探 detective

探测 tàncè [动] survey

探查 tànchá [动] examine

探访 tànfǎng [动] **1** (搜寻) seek ... out (*pt*, *pp* sought) **2** (亲友) visit

探戈 tàngē [名] tango

探究 tànjiū [动] investigate

探亲 tànqīn [动] visit one's relatives

探求 tànqiú [动] seek (*pt*, *pp* sought)

探视 tànshì [动] visit

探索 tànsuǒ [动] probe ◇科学探索 scientific investigation

探讨 tàntǎo [动] investigate

探听 tàntīng [动] scout about

探望 tànwàng [动] **1** (看望) visit **2** (看) look around

探险 tànxiǎn [动] explore

碳 tàn [名] carbon

碳水化合物 tànshuǐ-huàhéwù [名] carbohydrate

汤 tāng [名] **1** (热水) hot water **2** (指食物) soup

汤剂 tāngjì [名] herbal medicine

汤料 tāngliào [名] stock

汤药 tāngyào [名] herbal medicine

趟 tāng [动] wade ◇我们趟过一条小河。We waded through a stream. ▷另见 tàng

唐 táng [名] (唐朝) the Tang Dynasty

唐突 tángtū [形] brusque

堂 táng **I** [名] **1** (房屋) hall ♦礼堂 auditorium ♦课堂 classroom ♦教堂 church **2** (厅) hall **II** [量] ◇两堂课 two lessons

堂皇 tánghuáng [形] imposing

堂堂 tángtáng [形] dignified

塘 táng [名] **1** (堤防) embankment ♦海塘 sea wall **2** (水池) pond **3** (浴池) public bathhouse

搪 táng [动] **1** (抵挡) keep … out (*pt*, *pp* kept) **2** (搪塞) prevaricate

搪瓷 tángcí [名] enamel

搪塞 tángsè [动] prevaricate

膛 táng [名] **1** (胸) chest **2** (中空部分) cavity ♦枪膛 bore

糖 táng [名] **1** (指做饭) sugar ◇糖醋鸡 sweet-and-sour chicken **2** (糖果) sweet

糖果 tángguǒ [名] sweet

糖衣 tángyī [名] sugar coating ◇糖衣片 sugar-coated tablet

螳 táng [名] mantis

倘 tǎng [连] if

倘若 tǎngruò [连] if

倘使 tǎngshǐ [连] if

淌 tǎng [动] drip ◇淌眼泪 shed tears

躺 tǎng [动] lie (*pt* lay, *pp* lain)

烫 tàng **I** [形] very hot ◇这汤真烫。This soup is boiling hot. ◇滚烫的水 boiling hot water **II** [动] **1** (人) scald ◇他被热水烫了。He was scalded by hot water. **2** (加热) heat … up ◇日本清酒要烫过后再喝。Japanese wine should be heated before drinking. ◇她每天都烫脚。She bathes her feet in warm water everyday. **3** (熨) iron **4** (头发) perm

烫手 tàngshǒu [形] scalding

趟 tàng **I** [量] ◇我已经去了好几趟。I've made several trips. **II** [名] ranks (*pl*) ▷另见 tāng

涛 tāo [名] wave

掏 tāo [动] **1** (拿出) take … out (*pt* took, *pp* taken) **2** (挖) dig (*pt*, *pp* dug) **3** (偷) steal (*pt* stole, *pp* stolen)

滔 tāo [形] torrential

滔滔 tāotāo [形] **1** (指水势) torrential **2** (指说话) verbose ◇他说起话来是滔滔不绝。When he starts talking, he just goes on and on.

滔天 tāotiān [形] **1** (指波浪) towering **2** (指灾祸或罪恶) heinous

韬 tāo **I** [名] (书) art of war **II** [动] conceal

韬略 tāolüè [名] military strategy

逃 táo [动] **1** (逃跑) run away (*pt* ran, *pp* run) **2** (逃避) flee (*pt*, *pp* fled)

逃避 táobì [动] escape ◇逃避责任 shirk responsibility ◇逃避关税 evade customs duties

逃窜 táocuàn [动] flee (*pt*, *pp* fled)

逃犯 táofàn [名] escaped criminal

逃荒 táohuāng [动] flee from famine (*pt*, *pp* fled)

逃命 táomìng [动] run for one's life (*pt* ran, *pp* run)

逃难 táonàn [动] flee from disaster (*pt*, *pp* fled)

逃跑 táopǎo [动] escape

逃生 táoshēng [动] run for one's life (*pt* ran, *pp* run) ◇他们真是死里逃生。They had a narrow escape from death.

逃亡 táowáng [动] go into exile (*pt* went, *pp* gone)

逃之夭夭 táo zhī yāoyāo make a getaway

桃 táo [名] peach

桃李 táolǐ [名] **1** (桃和李) peaches and plums **2** (喻) (学生) student

桃色 táosè **I** [名] (粉红色) peach ◇她穿着一件桃色的连衣裙。She was wearing a peach-coloured dress. **II** [形] sexual ◇桃色新闻 sexual scandal

陶 táo **I** [名] pottery **II** [动] **1** (制陶) make pottery **2** (教育培养) mould (英), mold (美) ♦熏陶 nurture **III** [形] happy ♦乐陶陶 happy and contented

陶瓷 táocí [名] ceramics (*sg*)

陶器 táoqì [名] pottery

陶然 táorán [形] carefree

陶冶 táoyě [动] mould (英), mold (美)

陶醉 táozuì [动] be intoxicated ◇他们陶醉于成功的喜悦中。They are intoxicated with the joys of success.

淘 táo **I** [动] **1** (米) wash **2** (金子) pan for ♦淘金 pan for gold **3** (厕所) clean ... out **II** [形] naughty

淘气 táoqì [形] naughty

淘汰 táotài [动] eliminate ◇意大利足球队在第一轮就被淘汰了。The Italian football team was eliminated in the first round.

讨 tǎo [动] **1** (债) demand **2** (饭、钱) beg **3** (帮助) ask for **4** (谴责) denounce ♦声讨 censure **5** (娶) marry **6** (招惹) provoke **7** (讨论) discuss ♦探讨 inquire into

讨伐 tǎofá [动] send troops against (*pt, pp* sent)

讨好 tǎohǎo [动] **1** (取得欢心) curry favour with **2** (得到好效果) get a good result

讨价还价 tǎo jià huán jià haggle ◇做分给你的工作，不要讨价还价。Do the job you've been given and don't make a fuss.

讨教 tǎojiào [动] ask for advice

讨论 tǎolùn [动] discuss ◇小组展开了一次讨论。The team held a discussion.

> 注意 **discuss** 绝不能用作不及物动词。例如，'They discussed.', 'I discussed with him.' 或 'They discussed about politics.' 都是不正确的用法。然而，可以说跟某人就某事 **have a discussion**。*I had a long discussion about all this with Stephen.* 或者，**discuss** 某事物 **with** 某人。*I discussed my essay with my teacher.* 若讨论不十分正式，可以只用动词 **talk**。*They come here and sit for hours talking about politics... We talked all night long.*

讨嫌 tǎoxián [形] annoying

讨厌 tǎoyàn **I** [形] **1** (可恶) disgusting **2** (指难办) nasty **II** [动] dislike

套 tào **I** [名] **1** (套子) cover ♦手套 glove ♦避孕套 condom **2** (应酬话) convention **3** (阴谋) trap **II** [动] **1** (罩在外面) slip ... on **2** (拴) harness **3** (引出) trick ... into ◇套口供 trick a suspect into making a confession **4** (模仿) copy **5** (拉拢) win ... over (*pt, pp* won) **III** [量] ◇一套西装 a suit ◇两套邮票 two sets of stamps

套餐 tàocān [名] set meal

套话 tàohuà [名] cliché

套袖 tàoxiù [名] oversleeve

套用 tàoyòng [动] apply ... indiscriminately

套语 tàoyǔ [名] polite formula

套装 tàozhuāng [名] suit

套子 tàozi [名] **1** (罩子) cover **2** (俗套) formula **3** (圈套) trap

特 tè **I** [形] special ♦特价 special price **II** [副] **1** (特地) especially **2** (非常) extremely **III** [名] secret agent

特别 tèbié **I** [形] peculiar ◇他的口音很特别。His accent is peculiar. **II** [副] **1** (格外) exceptionally ◇这种产品质量特别好。The quality of this product is exceptionally good. **2** (特地) specially ◇我们特别为你准备了你爱吃的东西。We've prepared the things you like to eat specially for you.

特别行政区 tèbié xíngzhèngqū [名] special administration region

特产 tèchǎn [名] speciality (英), specialty (美)

特长 tècháng [名] speciality (英), specialty (美)

特此 tècǐ [副] hereby ◇他是我公司职员，特此证明。I hereby declare that he is an employee of my company.

特地 tèdì [副] especially

特点 tèdiǎn [名] characteristic

特定 tèdìng [形] specific

特技 tèjì [名] **1** (指表演) stunt **2** (指电影) special effects (*pl*)

特价 tèjià [名] bargain price ◇特价商品 bargain

特例 tèlì [名] special case

特区 tèqū [名] special zone ◇经济特区 special economic zone

特权 tèquán [名] privilege

特色 tèsè [名] characteristic

特赦 tèshè [动] give a special pardon to (*pt* gave, *pp* given)

特使 tèshǐ [名] special envoy

特殊 tèshū [形] special ◇特殊情况 special circumstances

特务 tèwu [名] special agent

特写 tèxiě [名] **1** (指文学) feature **2** (指电影) close-up

特性 tèxìng [名] characteristic

特许 tèxǔ [名] special permission ◇特许出口证 special export permit

特邀 tèyāo [动] specially invite ◇特邀代表 specially invited representative

特异 tèyì [形] exceptional

特意 tèyì [副] deliberately

特征 tèzhēng [名] characteristic

特种 tèzhǒng [形] special ◇特种部队 special forces

疼 téng **I** [形] sore ◇我牙疼。I have toothache. **II** [动] love

疼爱 téng'ài [动] love … dearly

腾 téng [动] **1** (奔跑) gallop **2** (跳跃) jump **3** (升到空中) rise (*pt* rose, *pp* risen) **4** (空出) vacate ◇我腾出时间学习。I make time for study. **5** (激动) excite

腾达 téngdá [动] take … off (*pt* took, *pp* taken)

腾飞 téngfēi [动] boom

腾腾 téngténg [形] seething

誊 téng [动] copy

誊写 téngxiě [动] copy

藤 téng [名] vine ♦藤椅 cane chair

剔 tī [动] **1** (牙、指甲) pick **2** (除) pick … out **3** (肉) pick meat off a bone

剔除 tīchú [动] reject

梯 tī [名] ladder ♦电梯 lift (英), elevator (美) ♦楼梯 stairs (*pl*)

梯形 tīxíng [名] trapezoid

踢 tī [动] kick ◇踢足球 play football

提 tí [动] **1** (拿) carry ◇他提着个箱子。He's carrying a suitcase. **2** (升) raise ◇提嗓子 raise one's voice ◇他被提为大副。He was promoted to first mate. **3** (提前) bring forward (*pt, pp* brought) ◇会议向前提了。The meeting has been brought forward. **4** (提出) put … forward (*pt, pp* put) ◇他提了个建议。He put forward a proposal. **5** (提取) collect ♦提炼 extract **6** (谈起) mention ◇别再提那件事了。Don't mention that subject again.
▷另见 dī

提案 tí'àn [名] motion

提拔 tíbá [动] promote

提倡 tíchàng [名] promote

提成 tíchéng [名] commission

提出 tíchū [动] put … forward (*pt, pp* put) ◇提出改革方案 put forward a proposal for reform

提纲 tígāng [名] synopsis (*pl* synopses)

提纲挈领 tí gāng qiè lǐng bring out the essential points

提高 tígāo [动] raise ◇提高效率 increase efficiency ◇提高管理水平 raise the standard of management

提供 tígōng [动] provide ◇提供住宿 provide accommodation

提货 tíhuò [动] take delivery of goods (*pt* took, *pp* taken)

提交 tíjiāo [动] submit

提炼 tíliàn [动] refine

提名 tímíng [动] nominate

提前 tíqián I [动] bring … forward (*pt, pp* brought) II [副] early

提亲 tíqīn [动] propose marriage

提请 tíqǐng [动] put … forward (*pt, pp* put)

提取 tíqǔ [动] **1** (取出) collect ◇提取现金 withdraw cash **2** (提炼) extract

提神 tíshén [动] refresh oneself

提审 tíshěn [动] **1** (审讯) bring … to court (*pt, pp* brought) **2** (上一级法院审判) review

提升 tíshēng [动] **1** (指职位) promote **2** (指档次) upgrade **3** (温度、价格) raise

提示 tíshì [动] **1** (指出) point … out **2** (提醒) remind ◇你要忘了台词，我提示你。If you forget your lines, I'll prompt you.

提问 tíwèn [动] ask a question

提携 tíxié [动] give guidance and support (*pt* gave, *pp* given)

提心吊胆 tí xīn diào dǎn be on tenterhooks

提醒 tíxǐng [动] remind

提要 tíyào [名] synopsis (*pl* synopses)

提议 tíyì I [动] propose II [名] proposal

啼 tí [动] **1** (哭) cry **2** (叫) call

啼笑皆非 tí xiào jiē fēi not know whether to laugh or cry

题 tí I [名] subject ♦标题 title II [动] inscribe

题跋 tíbá [名] preface and postscript

题材 tícái [名] theme

题词 tící I [动] write a dedication (*pt* wrote, *pp* written) II [名] dedication

题库 tíkù [名] collection of past papers

题名 tímíng I [动] autograph II [名] title

题目 tímù [名] **1** (标题) title **2** (考题) question

题字 tízì I [动] inscribe II [名] inscription

蹄 tí [名] hoof (*pl* hooves)

体 tǐ I [名] **1** (身体) body ♦人体 human body **2** (物体) substance ♦液体 liquid **3** (指书法或文学) style **4** (语法) aspect ◇进行体 progressive aspect **5** (体制) system ♦政体 system of government II [动] **1** (亲自做) do … personally ◇身体力行 practice what you preach **2** (为人着想) be considerate

体裁 tǐcái [名] genre

体操 tǐcāo [名] gymnastics (*sg*)

体察 tǐchá [动] observe

体格 tǐgé [名] physique

体会 tǐhuì I [动] come to understand (*pt* came, *pt* come) II [名] understanding

体积 tǐjī [名] volume

体检 tǐjiǎn [名] physical examination

体力 tǐlì [名] physical strength

体例 tǐlì [名] style

体谅 tǐliàng [动] show understanding (*pt* showed, *pp* shown) ◇她体谅他人的难处。She shows understanding for others' difficulties.

体面 tǐmiàn I [名] dignity II [形] **1** (荣耀) respectable **2** (好看) good-looking

体魄 tǐpò [名] physique

体态 tǐtài [名] posture

体坛 tǐtán [名] the world of sport

体贴 tǐtiē [动] show consideration for (*pt* showed, *pp* shown) ◇体贴老人 show consideration for the elderly

体统 tǐtǒng [名] decency

体温 tǐwēn [名] temperature

体无完肤 tǐ wú wán fū **1** (指人) be beaten black and blue **2** (指论点、文章) be savaged by criticism

体系 tǐxì [名] system

体现 tǐxiàn [动] embody

体形 tǐxíng [名] physique

体型 tǐxíng [名] physique

体恤 tǐxù [动] show sympathy for (*pt* showed, *pp* shown)

体验 tǐyàn [动] learn from experience

体育 tǐyù [名] **1** (课程) P. E. **2** (运动) sport ◊体育比赛 sports event

体制 tǐzhì [名] system

体质 tǐzhì [名] physique

体重 tǐzhòng [名] weight

屉 tì [名] **1** (笼屉) steamer **2** (抽屉) drawer

剃 tì [动] shave

涕 tì [名] **1** (书) (眼泪) tear **2** (鼻涕) mucus

替 tì **I** [动] **1** (代) replace ◊我替你看孩子。I'll look after the children for you. **2** (衰败) decline **II** [介] for ◊别替他操心了。Don't worry about him.

替补 tìbǔ [形] substitute

替代 tìdài [动] replace

替换 tìhuàn [动] replace

替身 tìshēn [名] body double

替罪羊 tìzuìyáng [名] scapegoat

天 tiān **I** [名] **1** (天空) sky ◊鸽子在天上飞。Pigeons were flying in the sky. **2** (一昼夜) day ♦昨天 yesterday ◊他3天后回来。He'll come back in three days' time. **3** (一段时间) ◊五更天 before dawn ◊天还早呢。It's still so early. **4** (季节) season ♦秋天 autumn (英), fall (美) **5** (天气) weather ♦阴天 overcast weather ◊天很热。It's a very hot day. **6** (自然) nature ◊人定胜天。Man can conquer nature. **7** (造物主) God ◊天知道！ God knows! **8** (神的住所) Heaven ◊上西天 go to Heaven **II** [形] (指位于顶部的) overhead ♦天桥 overhead walkway

天才 tiāncái [名] **1** (才能) talent **2** (人) genius

天长地久 tiān cháng dì jiǔ eternal

天窗 tiānchuāng [名] skylight

天敌 tiāndí [名] natural enemy

天地 tiāndì [名] **1** (天和地) world ◊天地间 in this world **2** (境地) field ◊科学研究的新天地 a new field of scientific research

天鹅 tiān'é [名] swan

天翻地覆 tiān fān dì fù **1** (指变化) earth-shattering **2** (形容胡闹) upheaval

天方夜谭 tiānfāng yètán pie in the sky ◊你的想法简直就是天方夜谭。Your ideas are just pie in the sky.

天分 tiānfèn [名] talent

天赋 tiānfù **I** [动] be innate **II** [名] talent ◊他很有艺术天赋。He has a talent for art.

天高地厚 tiān gāo dì hòu **1** (恩情) profound **2** (复杂性) complex

天各一方 tiān gè yī fāng be far apart ◊夫妻俩现在是天各一方。The couple are currently far away from each other.

天寒地冻 tiān hán dì dòng freezing

天花乱坠 tiān huā luàn zhuì wild exaggeration

天昏地暗 tiān hūn dì àn **1** (指天气) a murky sky over a dark earth **2** (指政治) chaos and corruption

天机 tiānjī [名] **1** (字) mysteries of nature (*pl*) **2** (喻) important secret

天价 tiānjià [名] astronomical price

天经地义 tiān jīng dì yì unalterable truth

天空 tiānkōng [名] sky

天理 tiānlǐ [名] justice

天良 tiānliáng [名] conscience ◊他这样做是丧尽天良。He acted completely without conscience in this affair.

天伦 tiānlún [名] natural bonds (*pl*) ◊享受天伦之乐 enjoy the happiness of family life

天罗地网 tiān luó dì wǎng tight encirclement

天命 tiānmìng [名] fate

天南海北 tiān nán hǎi běi **1** (遥远) far away ◊即使身处天南海北，我

们也要互相关心。Even if we are far away from one another, we must still care for each other. **2** (不同的地区) different places ◇大家来自天南海北。We all come from very different places. **3** (指话题) far-reaching

天平 tiānpíng [名] scales (*pl*)

天气 tiānqì [名] weather ◇天气预报 weather forecast

天然 tiānrán [形] natural

天壤之别 tiānrǎng zhī bié poles apart ◇我们之间的信仰有着天壤之别。Our beliefs are poles apart.

天日 tiānrì [名] light

天色 tiānsè [名] time of day ◇天色已晚。It's getting late.

天生 tiānshēng [形] inherent ◇这孩子天生聋哑。This child was born deaf-mute.

天时 tiānshí [名] opportunity

天使 tiānshǐ [名] angel

天书 tiānshū [名] (喻) gobbledegook

天堂 tiāntáng [名] Heaven

天体 tiāntǐ [名] heavenly body

天文 tiānwén [名] astronomy ◇天文望远镜 astronomical telescope

天文数字 tiānwén shùzì [名] astronomical figure

天无绝人之路 tiān wú jué rén zhī lù there is always a way out

天下 tiānxià [名] the world

天仙 tiānxiān [名] **1** (男神仙) god **2** (女神仙) goddess **3** (美女) beauty

天险 tiānxiǎn [名] natural barrier

天线 tiānxiàn [名] aerial

天象 tiānxiàng [名] astronomical phenomena (*pl*)

天性 tiānxìng [名] nature

天旋地转 tiān xuán dì zhuàn feel dizzy ◇坐缆车使我觉得天旋地转。Sitting in the cable car, I felt as though the world was spinning.

天涯 tiānyá [名] the ends of the earth ◇浪迹天涯 wander to the ends of the earth

天衣无缝 tiān yī wú fèng flawless

天意 tiānyì [名] God's will

天有不测风云 tiān yǒu bùcè fēngyún something unexpected can always happen ◇天有不测风云，人有旦夕祸福。Life is as unpredictable as the weather.

天灾 tiānzāi [名] natural disaster

天造地设 tiān zào dì shè ideal

天真 tiānzhēn [形] innocent

天之骄子 tiān zhī jiāozǐ child of good fortune

天职 tiānzhí [名] bounden duty

天资 tiānzī [名] talent ◇天资聪颖 endowed with great intelligence

天子 tiānzǐ [名] the emperor of China

天字第一号 tiān zì dì yī hào greatest in the world ◇你是天字第一号傻瓜。You are the most stupid fool in the world.

添 tiān [动] **1** (增加) add ◇添衣服 put on more clothes **2** (生孩子) give birth to (*pt* gave, *pp* given)

添补 tiānbǔ [动] replenish

添加剂 tiānjiājì [名] additive

添枝加叶 tiān zhī jiā yè embellish the facts

添置 tiānzhì [动] acquire

田 tián [名] **1** (耕地) field **2** (开采地) field ◇油田 oilfield

田地 tiándì [名] **1** (指耕种) field **2** (地步) plight

田径 tiánjìng [名] track and field sports (*pl*)

田野 tiányě [名] open country

田园 tiányuán [名] countryside ◇田园风光 rural scenery

恬 tián [形] quiet ♦恬适 quiet and comfortable

恬不知耻 tián bù zhī chǐ have no sense of shame

恬静 tiánjìng [形] peaceful

甜 tián [形] **1** (指味道) sweet **2** (指睡觉) sound **3** (喻) (幸福) happy

甜点 tiándiǎn [名] dessert

甜蜜 tiánmì [形] happy ◇甜蜜的话语 honeyed words

甜食 tiánshí [名] sweet

甜丝丝 tiánsīsī [形] **1** (指味道) sweet **2** (指心情) happy

甜头 tiántou [名] **1** (指味) sweet taste **2** (指利益) benefit ◇他尝到了科学种田的甜头。He benefited from scientific farming.

甜言蜜语 tián yán mì yǔ honeyed words ◇不要为甜言蜜语所迷惑。Don't be taken in by honeyed words.

填 tián [动] **1** (塞满) fill **2** (补充) fill ◇填补空白 fill a gap **3** (填写) complete ◇填表格 fill in a form

填报 tiánbào [动] complete and submit

填充 tiánchōng [动] **1** (填上) stuff **2** (补足) fill ... in

填空 tiánkòng [动] **1** (指工作) fill a vacancy **2** (指考试) fill in the blanks

填写 tiánxiě [动] fill ... in

舔 tiǎn [动] lick

挑 tiāo [动] **1** (肩扛) carry ... on a carrying pole **2** (挑选) choose (*pt* chose, *pp* chosen) **3** (挑剔) nitpick ▷另见 tiǎo

挑刺儿 tiāocìr [动] be overcritical

挑肥拣瘦 tiāo féi jiǎn shòu be picky

挑拣 tiāojiǎn [动] be particular ◇挑拣饮食 be particular about one's food

挑三拣四 tiāo sān jiǎn sì be petty ◇不要挑三拣四了，哪个都不错的。Don't be so petty, they're all OK.

挑食 tiāoshí [动] be a fussy eater

挑剔 tiāotì [动] nitpick ◇他的工作无可挑剔。You can't find fault with his work.

挑选 tiāoxuǎn [动] select

条 tiáo **I** [名] **1** (细树枝) twig **2** (长条) strip **3** (层次) order ◇有条有理 well-ordered **4** (分项) item ◇逐条分析 analyse (英) 或 analyze (美) item by item **5** (律令) article **6** (短书信) note **II** [量] **1** (用于细长东西) ◇两条腿 two legs ◇一条烟 a multipack of cigarettes ◇两条肥皂 two bars of soap **2** (指分事项的) ◇一条新闻 an item of news **3** (指与人有关) ◇一条人命 a life

条幅 tiáofú [名] scroll

条件 tiáojiàn [名] **1** (客观因素) condition ◇自然条件 natural conditions **2** (要求) requirement ◇她符合入学条件。She fits the entry requirements for the school. ◇无条件接受 accept unconditionally **3** (状况) circumstances (*pl*)

条款 tiáokuǎn [名] provision

条理 tiáolǐ [名] order

条例 tiáolì [名] regulations (*pl*)

条令 tiáolìng [名] regulations (*pl*)

条目 tiáomù [名] **1** (指规章) clauses (*pl*) **1** (指词典) entry

条条框框 tiáo tiáo kuàng kuàng conventions and restrictions

条文 tiáowén [名] article

条形码 tiáoxíngmǎ [名] bar code

条约 tiáoyuē [名] treaty

迢 tiáo [形] remote

迢迢 tiáotiáo [形] far away ◇我的家乡在迢迢千里以外。My home town is far away. ◇千里迢迢 from afar

调 tiáo **I** [动] **1** (使和谐) harmonize ♦失调 imbalance **2** (使均匀) blend ◇把调料调均匀。Blend in the seasoning. ◇给钢琴调音 tune a piano **3** (调解) mediate **4** (挑逗) tease **5** (挑拨) provoke ▷另见 diào

调和 tiáohé **I** [形] harmonious **II** [动] **1** (调解) reconcile **2** (妥协) compromise

调剂 tiáojì [动] **1** (配药剂) make up a prescription **2** (调整) liven ... up ◇她累的时候，就去散步调剂一下。When she's tired, she livens herself up with a walk.

调教 tiáojiào [动] **1** (孩子) educate **2** (动物) train

调节 tiáojié [动] adjust

调解 tiáojiě [动] mediate ◇调解纠纷 mediate in a dispute ◇调解矛盾 resolve a conflict

调理 tiáolǐ [动] **1** (调养) recuperate **2** (管理) take care of (*pt* took, *pp* taken) ◇她身体不好，需要调理饮食。She's not in good health and has to take care with what she eats. **3** (管教) discipline

调料 tiáoliào [名] seasoning

调配 tiáopèi [动] mix

调皮 tiáopí [形] **1** (顽皮) naughty **2** (难对付) unruly

调情 tiáoqíng [动] flirt

调试 tiáoshì [动] debug

调停 tiáotíng [动] mediate

调戏 tiáoxì [动] molest

调养 tiáoyǎng [动] take care of oneself (*pt* took, *pp* taken) ◇调养身体 take care of one's health

调整 tiáozhěng [动] adjust

笤 tiáo 见下文

笤帚 tiáozhou [名] broom

挑 tiǎo [动] **1** (扯起一头) raise **2** (向上拨) prick ◇挑水泡 lance a blister **3** (挑拨) incite **4** (喻) (公开提出) bring … out into the open (*pt, pp* brought)
▷另见 tiāo

挑拨 tiǎobō [动] stir … up ◇他总是挑拨他们之间的关系。He's always stirring up trouble between them. ◇挑拨是非 sow discord

挑大梁 tiǎo dàliáng [动] be the mainstay

挑动 tiǎodòng [动] provoke ◇挑动内战 provoke a civil war

挑逗 tiǎodòu [动] tease

挑唆 tiǎosuō [动] instigate

挑衅 tiǎoxìn [动] provoke ◇武装挑衅 armed provocation

挑战 tiǎozhàn [动] challenge ◇挑战体能极限 challenge the limits of one's physical abilities ◇挑战自我 set oneself a challenge ◇面临新挑战 face a new challenge

眺 tiào [动] survey ♦远眺 look far into the distance

眺望 tiàowàng [动] survey from up high ◇眺望远方 look far into the distance

跳 tiào [动] **1** (跃) jump ◇从床上跳下来 leap out of bed ◇跳上马背 jump onto a horse **2** (弹起) bounce **3** (起伏地动) beat (*pt* beat, *pp* beaten) ◇他激动得心直跳。His heart is beating with excitement. **4** (越过) jump over ◇跳过几页 skip a few pages

跳槽 tiàocáo [动] change jobs

跳动 tiàodòng [动] beat (*pt* beat, *pp* beaten)

跳高 tiàogāo [名] high jump

跳水 tiàoshuǐ [名] diving

跳舞 tiàowǔ [动] dance

跳远 tiàoyuǎn [名] long jump

跳跃 tiàoyuè [动] jump

帖 tiē I [动] obey II [形] proper
▷另见 tiě

贴 tiē I [动] **1** (粘) stick (*pt, pp* stuck) **2** (紧挨) be close to ◇后背贴后背站着 stand back to back **3** (贴补) subsidize II [名] allowance

贴补 tiēbǔ [动] subsidize ◇挣钱贴补家用 earn money to help with the family expenses

贴金 tiējīn [动] **1** (贴金箔) gild **2** (吹捧) boast about ◇如果他不总往自己脸上贴金，他会有很多朋友。He'd make a lot more friends if he stopped blowing his own trumpet all the time.

贴切 tiēqiè [形] suitable ◇你对他的评价很贴切。Your appraisal of him is very apt.

贴身 tiēshēn [形] **1** (衣服) ◇贴身衣服 underclothes (*pl*) **2** (随从) personal ◇贴身侍卫 personal bodyguard

贴心 tiēxīn [形] intimate ◇贴心话 confidential talk

帖 tiě [名] **1** (请帖) invitation ◇发喜帖 send out wedding invitations **2** (小卡片) card
▷另见 tiē

帖子 tiězi [名] **1** (请帖) invitation **2** (招贴) poster

铁 tiě [名] **1** (金属) iron **2** (武器) weapon ◇手无寸铁 unarmed **3** (喻) (坚强) toughness ♦铁人 iron man ♦铁哥们 fast friends (*pl*) **4** (喻) (形容强暴) ferocity **5** (喻) (确

定) unshakable ◇铁的纪律 iron discipline ◇铁的事实 hard fact

铁窗 tiěchuāng [名] 1 (窗户) window with an iron grating 2 (监狱) prison

铁道 tiědào [名] railway (英), railroad (美)

铁饭碗 tiěfànwǎn [名] (喻) job for life ◇经济改革后，很多工人都失去了铁饭碗。After the economic reforms, a lot of workers lost their job security.

铁路 tiělù [名] railway (英), railroad (美)

铁面无私 tiě miàn wú sī strict and impartial

铁器 tiěqì [名] ironware ◇铁器时代 the Iron Age

铁青 tiěqīng [形] livid ◇她气得脸色铁青。Her face turned livid with rage.

铁石心肠 tiě shí xīncháng hard-hearted

铁丝 tiěsī [名] wire

铁腕 tiěwàn [名] iron fist ◇以铁腕统治 rule with an iron fist

铁心 tiěxīn [动] make up one's mind to

铁证 tiězhèng [名] irrefutable proof

帖 tiè [名] copybook

厅 tīng [名] 1 (大堂) hall ♦客厅 sitting room ♦餐厅 canteen 2 (机关) office 3 (省部门名称) provincial government department ◇省教育厅 Provincial Education Department

听 tīng I [动] 1 (收听) listen to ◇听广播 listen to a broadcast 2 (听从) obey ◇听老师的话 do as the teacher says 3 (判断) supervise ◇听政 administer affairs of state 4 (任凭) allow ◇听其自然 let things take their own course II [名] tin III [量] can ◇一听啤酒 a can of beer

听从 tīngcóng [动] obey

听而不闻 tīng ér bù wén turn a deaf ear

听候 tīnghòu [动] await

听话 tīnghuà I [动] obey II [形] obedient

听话儿 tīnghuàr [动] wait for a reply

听觉 tīngjué [名] hearing ◇听觉灵敏 acute hearing

听凭 tīngpíng [动] let (*pt, pp* let)

听其自然 tīng qí zìrán let things take their course

听取 tīngqǔ [动] listen to

听任 tīngrèn [动] (书) allow

听天由命 tīng tiān yóu mìng resign oneself to one's fate

听之任之 tīng zhī rèn zhī take a laissez-faire attitude ◇我们对毒品泛滥不能听之任之。We can't take a laissez-faire attitude to drug abuse.

听众 tīngzhòng [名] audience

廷 tíng [名] court

亭 tíng [名] 1 (亭子) pavilion 2 (小房子) kiosk ♦报亭 newspaper stand ♦电话亭 phone box (英), phone booth (美)

亭亭玉立 tíngtíng yù lì slender

庭 tíng [名] 1 (书) (厅堂) hall 2 (院子) courtyard 3 (法庭) law court

庭院 tíngyuàn [名] courtyard

停 tíng I [动] 1 (止) stop 2 (停留) stop off ◇我在德国停了两天。I stopped off in Germany for two days. ◇这列火车在武汉停多长时间？ How long does this train stop in Wuhan? 3 (停放) park ◇车就停在大门口。The car is parked at the main gate. ◇船停在港口。The boat is moored in the harbour. II [形] ready ♦停妥 settled

停泊 tíngbó [动] anchor

停车场 tíngchēchǎng [名] car park (英), car lot (美)

停当 tíngdang [形] ready ◇一切准备停当。Everything's ready.

停顿 tíngdùn I [动] 1 (中止) halt 2 (指说话) pause II [名] pause

停放 tíngfàng [动] park

停火 tínghuǒ [动] cease fire ◇签订停火协议 sign a cease-fire agreement

停靠 tíngkào [动] stop at ◇船停靠在码头。The ship is berthed at the quay.

停歇 tíngxiē [动] **1** (停止) stop **2** (歇息) rest

停薪留职 tíng xīn liú zhí [动] take unpaid leave (*pt* took, *pp* taken)

停业 tíngyè [动] close down ◇一批小饭店将停业整顿。Some small restaurants will be closed while being brought up to standard.

停职 tíngzhí [动] suspend

停止 tíngzhǐ [动] stop ◇停止营业 cease trading

停滞 tíngzhì [动] stagnate

挺 tǐng **I** [动] **1** (伸直) straighten **2** (凸出) stick out (*pt, pp* stuck) **3** (勉强支撑) endure ◇挺过了一场病 pull through an illness ◇如果头疼，别硬挺着。If you've got a headache, don't just grin and bear it. **II** [形] **1** (直) upright **2** (突出) distinguished **III** [副] very

挺拔 tǐngbá [形] **1** (直立突出) tall and straight **2** (坚强有力) forceful

挺进 tǐngjìn [动] press on ◇大军挺进前线。The army pressed on to the front line.

挺立 tǐnglì [动] stand upright (*pt, pp* stood)

铤 tǐng [形] (书) quick

铤而走险 tǐng ér zǒu xiǎn rush headlong into danger

艇 tǐng [名] boat ♦游艇 yacht ♦救生艇 lifeboat

通 tōng **I** [动] **1** (连接) connect with ♦通商 have trade relations with ◇这间办公室不通风。This office is poorly ventilated. ◇这条高速公路直通上海。This expressway leads directly to Shanghai. **2** (使不堵) clear … out ◇通下水道 clear out a drain **3** (传达) inform ◇通电报 send a telegram **4** (通晓) understand (*pt, pp* understood) ◇精通英语 have a good command of English **II** [名] expert **III** [形] **1** (没有障碍) open ◇电话打通了。The call has been put through. **2** (顺畅) workable ◇这个计划行不通。This plan is unworkable. ◇我怎么也想不通他为什么要这么做。I just don't understand why he would do something like that. **3** (通顺) coherent **4** (普通) common **5** (整个) overall ◇通盘规划 overall plan **IV** [副] **1** (全部) completely **2** (一般) normally
▷另见 tòng

通报 tōngbào **I** [动] **1** (指对下级) circulate a notice **2** (通知) inform **II** [名] **1** (文件) notice **2** (刊物) bulletin

通病 tōngbìng [名] common failing

通才 tōngcái [名] versatile person

通常 tōngcháng **I** [形] normal **II** [名] normal circumstances (*pl*) ◇我通常7点起床。Under normal circumstances, I get up at seven o'clock.

通畅 tōngchàng [形] **1** (指运行) unobstructed ◇道路通畅 the road is clear **2** (流畅) smooth

通车 tōngchē [动] open to traffic ◇环路已通车。The ring road has opened to traffic.

通称 tōngchēng **I** [名] common term **II** [动] be generally known as

通达 tōngdá [动] understand (*pt, pp* understood)

通道 tōngdào [名] **1** (大路) route **2** (指出入) passageway ◇剧院的通道上站满了人。The aisle of the theatre (英) 或 theater (美) was full of people. ◇地下通道 tunnel

通电 tōngdiàn [动] **1** (指电器) switch … on ◇给冰箱通电 switch on the refrigerator **2** (指用上电) be connected to the electricity grid **3** (打电报) send a telegram (*pt, pp* sent)

通牒 tōngdié [名] diplomatic note ◇最后通牒 ultimatum

通告 tōnggào **I** [动] announce **II** [名] announcement ◇张贴通告 put up a notice

通过 tōngguò **I** [动] **1** (经过) pass ◇通过边境线 cross the border ◇通过障碍物 pass through barriers **2** (同意) pass ◇国会议员一致通过了这个法案。The congressmen passed the bill unanimously. **II** [介] by means of ◇他通过不正当手段牟取暴利。

He made enormous profits by dishonest methods.

通红 tōnghóng [形] bright red

通婚 tōnghūn [动] intermarry

通货 tōnghuò [名] currency

通货膨胀 tōnghuò péngzhàng [动] inflate ◇战后出现了大面积的通货膨胀。After the war, there was widespread inflation.

通缉 tōngjī [动] list … as wanted ◇通缉令 wanted notice ◇毒品犯正被通缉。The drug dealers are listed as wanted.

通奸 tōngjiān [动] commit adultery

通力 tōnglì [动] make a concerted effort

通令 tōnglìng I [动] issue a general order ◇政府通令全国进入战争状态。The government issued a general order, declaring that the nation was at war. II [名] general order

通明 tōngmíng [形] brightly lit

通盘 tōngpán [形] overall

通气 tōngqì [动] **1** (指空气) ventilate **2** (指信息) keep in touch (*pt, pp* kept) ◇我们朋友之间要通气。We friends should keep in touch.

通融 tōngróng [动] **1** (给人方便) make an exception ◇请你帮助通融一下。Please help us by making an exception in this case. **2** (暂时借) make a short-term loan

通商 tōngshāng [动] have commercial relations

通顺 tōngshùn I [形] coherent II [动] polish

通俗 tōngsú [形] popular

通天 tōngtiān I [形] extremely high II [动] have direct access to the highest authorities

通通 tōngtōng [副] completely

通宵 tōngxiāo [名] all night

通晓 tōngxiǎo [动] have a good knowledge of

通信 tōngxìn [动] correspond

通行 tōngxíng [动] **1** (指交通) pass through **2** (普通适用) be in general use

通讯 tōngxùn I [名] dispatch ◇新华社通讯 Xinhua News Agency dispatch II [动] communicate

通用 tōngyòng [动] be in common use

通知 tōngzhī I [名] notification ◇发出通知 issue a notice II [动] inform

同 tóng I [动] **1** (一样) be the same ◇我们个性不同。Our personalities are different. **2** (共同) do … together ♦同居 cohabit ◇同甘苦 stick together through thick and thin II [介] **1** (跟) with ◇你最好同他谈谈这事。You had better talk about it with him. ◇他同朋友在一起吃饭。He is eating with friends. **2** (指比较) as ◇我同我哥哥一样高。I'm just as tall as my older brother.

同伴 tóngbàn [名] companion

同胞 tóngbāo [名] **1** (指同父母) brother and sister **2** (指同一国家或民族) compatriot

同病相怜 tóng bìng xiāng lián sympathize with each other

同步 tóngbù [形] **1** (字) synchronized **2** (喻) in step with ◇工业发展和环境保护要同步进行。Industrial development must be in step with environmental protection.

同窗 tóngchuāng I [动] study together II [名] fellow student

同等 tóngděng [形] of the same level ◇同等待遇 equal treatment

同犯 tóngfàn [名] accomplice

同房 tóngfáng [动] **1** (指住在一起) live together **2** (婉) have sex

同甘共苦 tóng gān gòng kǔ go through thick and thin together

同感 tónggǎn [名] sympathy

同归于尽 tóng guī yú jìn die together

同行 tóngháng [动] be in the same line of work ◇他的父母是同行，都是老师。His parents are in the same line of work – they are both teachers.

同化 tónghuà [动] assimilate

同伙 tónghuǒ I [名] accomplice II [动] conspire

同居 tóngjū [动] cohabit

同类 tónglèi I [形] of the same kind II [名] the same kind

同流合污 tóng liú hé wū associate with criminals

同盟 tóngméng [名] alliance

同谋 tóngmóu I [动] conspire II [名] conspirator

同年 tóngnián I [名] **1** (同一年) the same year **2** (同龄人) a person of the same age ◇我们同年，都属虎。We're the same age, we were both born in the Year of the Tiger. II [动] be a contemporary of ◇我们俩同年。We're the same age.

同情 tóngqíng [动] sympathize ◇我们同情那些受害者。We sympathize with the victims. ◇我们对遇难者家属表示同情。We expressed our sympathies to the families of the deceased.

同声传译 tóng shēng chuán yì [名] simultaneous interpretation

同时 tóngshí I [名] at the same time ◇同时发生 occur simultaneously II [连] besides ◇桌子太大了，同时也太贵了。Besides being expensive, the table was also too big. ◇该项目时间紧，同时工作量也很大。Time is tight on the project, and the workload is huge too.

同事 tóngshì I [动] work together II [名] colleague

同乡 tóngxiāng [名] fellow countryman ◇我们几个是同乡。We're all from the same place.

同行 tóngxíng [动] travel together

同性恋 tóngxìngliàn [名] homosexuality

同学 tóngxué [名] **1** (指同校) fellow student **2** (指同班) classmate **3** (学生) student

同样 tóngyàng [形] **1** (一样) same ◇同样的愿望 the same aspirations **2** (情况类似) similar

同一 tóngyī [形] **1** (一样) same **2** (统一的) unanimous

同义词 tóngyìcí [名] synonym

同意 tóngyì [动] agree ◇我们需要得到老板的同意。We have to obtain authorization from our boss.

同志 tóngzhì [名] comrade

同舟共济 tóng zhōu gòng jì be in the same boat

铜 tóng [名] copper

铜牌 tóngpái [名] bronze medal

铜器 tóngqì [名] bronzeware ◇铜器时代 the Bronze Age

铜墙铁壁 tóng qiáng tiě bì impassable barrier

童 tóng [名] **1** (小孩) child (*pl* children) ♦神童 child prodigy **2** (指未婚) virgin

童工 tónggōng [名] child worker

童话 tónghuà [名] fairy tale

童年 tóngnián [名] childhood

童声 tóngshēng [名] child's voice ◇童声合唱 children's choir

童心 tóngxīn [名] childlike innocence

童谣 tóngyáo [名] nursery rhyme

童贞 tóngzhēn [名] chastity

童真 tóngzhēn [名] innocence

瞳 tóng [名] pupil

瞳孔 tóngkǒng [名] pupil

统 tǒng I [名] ♦系统 system ♦血统 bloodline II [动] command III [副] all

统称 tǒngchēng I [动] be collectively known as II [名] general designation

统筹 tǒngchóu [动] make an overall plan ◇统筹全局 plan on the basis of the situation as a whole

统计 tǒngjì I [名] statistics (*pl*) ◇人口统计 census II [动] count ◇统计选票 count votes

统考 tǒngkǎo [名] unified examination ◇高考是全国统考。The university entrance exams are run on a nationwide system.

统属 tǒngshǔ [动] be subordinate to

统帅 tǒngshuài I [名] **1** (军) commander-in-chief **2** (喻) (主导) driving force II [动] command

统率 tǒngshuài [动] command

统统 tǒngtǒng [副] entirely

统辖 tǒngxiá [动] have jurisdiction over

统一 tǒngyī I [动] **1** (使成一体) unite **2** (使一致) unify ◇统一思想 reach a common understanding II [形] unified

统治 tǒngzhì [动] rule ◇推翻独裁统治 overthrow dictatorial rule

捅 tǒng [动] **1** (戳) stab ◇小心别让针捅了眼睛。Be careful not to stab yourself in the eye with that needle. ◇一次打架时他被捅了两刀。He was stabbed twice in a fight. **2** (揭穿) disclose

捅娄子 tǒnglóuzi cause trouble

捅马蜂窝 tǒng mǎfēngwō create pandemonium

桶 tǒng I [名] bucket ◇汽油桶 petrol (英) 或 gasoline (美) drum ◇啤酒桶 beer barrel II [量] barrel ◇一桶柴油 a barrel of diesel oil ◇两桶牛奶 two churns of milk

筒 tǒng [名] **1** (竹管) bamboo tube **2** (粗管状物) ♦笔筒 pen holder ♦邮筒 post box (英), mailbox (美) **3** (指衣服) ◇袖筒 sleeve ◇长筒袜 stockings (*pl*)

通 tòng [量] **1** (遍) ◇她一通一通地打电话。She made one phone call after another. ◇她跳了一通舞。She danced for a while. **2** (指言语) ◇老师说了他一通。The teacher gave him a telling-off.
▷另见 tōng

痛 tòng I [动] **1** (疼) ache ◇头痛 have a headache ◇胃痛 have a stomach ache **2** (悲伤) grieve ♦哀痛 sorrow II [副] deeply ◇痛饮 swig ◇痛打 give a sound beating to

痛不欲生 tòng bù yù shēng overwhelmed with grief

痛楚 tòngchǔ [名] anguish

痛定思痛 tòng dìng sī tòng learn from bitter experience

痛改前非 tòng gǎi qián fēi make a clean break with the past

痛恨 tònghèn [动] detest

痛苦 tòngkǔ [形] painful ◇医生的首要职责是减轻病人的痛苦。The first duty of the doctor is to reduce the patient's suffering.

痛快 tòngkuài [形] **1** (高兴) joyful **2** (尽兴) to one's heart's content ◇吃个痛快 eat one's fill ◇玩个痛快 play to one's heart's content **3** (爽快) straightforward

痛快淋漓 tòngkuài línlí with great eloquence

痛心 tòngxīn [动] be deeply distressed

痛心疾首 tòng xīn jí shǒu **1** (指痛恨) detest **2** (指伤心) be devastated

痛痒 tòngyǎng [名] **1** (疾苦) sufferings (*pl*) **2** (要紧事) importance ◇无关痛痒的事 a matter of no importance

偷 tōu I [动] **1** (窃) steal (*pt* stole, *pp* stolen) **2** (抽出) take time off (*pt* took, *pp* taken) ◇偷工夫干点私活儿 take time off to do private work **3** (苟且) muddle along II [名] thief (*pl* thieves) III [副] stealthily

偷盗 tōudào [动] steal (*pt* stole, *pp* stolen)

偷渡 tōudù [动] cross a border illegally ♦偷渡客 illegal immigrant

偷工减料 tōu gōng jiǎn liào produce inferior goods with shoddy materials

偷空 tōukòng [动] take time off (*pt* took, *pp* taken)

偷懒 tōulǎn [动] be lazy

偷窃 tōuqiè [动] steal (*pt* stole, *pp* stolen)

偷情 tōuqíng [动] have a secret affair

偷偷 tōutōu [副] secretly

偷偷摸摸 tōutōumōmō on the sly

偷闲 tōuxián [动] take a break (*pt* took, *pp* taken)

头 tóu I [名] **1** (脑袋) head ◇点头 nod one's head **2** (头发) hair ♦分头 parted hair ♦平头 crew cut ◇梳头 comb one's hair **3** (顶端) tip ◇笔头儿 pen tip ◇船头 bows **4** (开始) beginning ◇从头说起 tell the story from the beginning **5** (结尾) end **6** (剩余) remnant ◇布头儿 leftover cloth ◇烟头儿 cigarette end 7 (头目) head ♦工头 foreman ◇谁是你们的头儿？ Who's your boss? 8 (方面) aspect ◇复习英语时，只顾语法一头可不行。When you're revising English, it won't do just to concentrate on the grammar aspect of the subject. 9 (界限) boundary ◇老师批评学生过了头。The teacher overstepped the mark when he criticized the student. II [形] 1 (第一) first ♦头奖 first prize 2 (领头) leading 3 (时间在前) first ◇头几年 first few years III [量] 1 (指动物) ◇5头公牛和3头母牛 five bulls and three cows 2 (指蒜) bulb ◇一头蒜 a bulb of garlic

头等 tóuděng [形] first class

头发 tóufa [名] hair

头角 tóujiǎo [名] (喻) talent

头领 tóulǐng [名] leader

头颅 tóulú [名] skull

头面人物 tóumiàn rénwù [名] (贬) bigwig

头目 tóumù [名] leader

头脑 tóunǎo [名] brains (*pl*)

头破血流 tóu pò xuè liú be beaten black and blue

头饰 tóushì [名] headdress

头头是道 tóu tóu shì dào clear and logical

头衔 tóuxián [名] title

头绪 tóuxù [名] 1 (条理) clue 2 (心思) thoughts (*pl*)

头重脚轻 tóu zhòng jiǎo qīng top-heavy

投 tóu [动] 1 (扔) throw (*pt* threw, *pp* thrown) 2 (放进去) put … in (*pt*, *pp* put) 3 (跳下去) throw oneself (*pt* threw, *pp* thrown) ◇刚才有个男的投河自尽了。A man has just thrown himself into a river in an act of suicide. 4 (投射) cast (*pt*, *pp* cast) ◇投去羡慕的目光 cast an admiring glance 5 (寄) post 6 (奔向) seek … out (*pt*, *pp* sought) ◇弃暗投明 turn from evil to good

投案 tóu'àn [动] give oneself up (*pt* gave, *pp* given)

投保 tóubǎo [动] take out insurance (*pt* took, *pp* taken)

投奔 tóubèn [动] seek refuge (*pt*, *pp* sought) ◇他无家可归，只好去投奔老朋友。He was left homeless, and had to seek refuge with an old friend.

投币电话 tóu bì diànhuà [名] payphone

投标 tóubiāo [动] tender

投产 tóuchǎn [动] go into production (*pt* went, *pp* gone)

投递 tóudì [动] deliver

投放 tóufàng [动] 1 (食物、药物) throw … in (*pt* threw, *pp* thrown) 2 (人力、物力、财力) invest 3 (市场) supply

投合 tóuhé I [动] (融洽) get along 2 (迎合) cater to

投机 tóujī I [动] speculate II [形] agreeable

投靠 tóukào [动] 1 (依靠) depend on 2 (屈服) give oneself up (*pt* gave, *pp* given)

投其所好 tóuqísuǒhào cater to sb's tastes

投入 tóurù I [形] 1 (指专注) engrossed 2 (指逼真) realistic II [动] 1 (放入) put … in (*pt*, *pp* put) ◇把球投入球篮。Put the ball through the hoop. ◇开发新产品需要很大的投入。Developing new product lines requires a considerable investment. 2 (参加) throw oneself into (*pt* threw, *pp* thrown)

投身 tóushēn [动] throw oneself into (*pt* threw, *pp* thrown)

投诉 tóusù I [动] lodge a complaint II [名] appeal

投胎 tóutāi [动] be reincarnated

投降 tóuxiáng [动] surrender ◇无条件投降 unconditional surrender

投影 tóuyǐng I [动] project II [名] 1 (影子) projection 2 (喻) reflection

投缘 tóuyuán [形] congenial

投掷 tóuzhì [动] throw (*pt* threw, *pp* thrown)

投资 tóuzī I [动] invest II [名] investment

透 tòu I [动] 1 (渗透) penetrate ◇阳光从窗户透进来。The sunlight is coming in through the windows. 2 (泄露) leak out 3 (显露) appear II [形] 1 (透彻) thorough ◇他对植物学了解很透。He has a thorough knowledge of botany. 2 (程度深) complete ◇我浑身都湿透了。I'm soaked to the skin. ◇这些芒果熟透了。These mangoes are completely ripe.

透彻 tòuchè [形] incisive

透顶 tòudǐng [形] thorough

透风 tòufēng [动] 1 (透气) ventilate 2 (透露消息) divulge a secret

透露 tòulù [动] disclose

透明 tòumíng [形] transparent

透视 tòushì [动] 1 (表现立体空间) make … three-dimensional 2 (医) X-ray 3 (喻) (看清楚) grasp the essence of

透支 tòuzhī [动] overdraw (*pt* overdrew, *pp* overdrawn) ◇透支金额 overdraft

凸 tū [形] protuberant

秃 tū [形] 1 (指毛发) bald 2 (指山) barren 3 (指树) bare 4 (不锐利) blunt 5 (指文章) incomplete

秃顶 tūdǐng I [动] be bald II [名] 1 (指人) bald man (*pl* men) 2 (指头顶) bald patch

秃子 tūzi [名] (口) baldy

突 tū I [动] break out (*pt* broke, *pp* broken) ♦突围 escape from a siege II [形] protruding III [副] suddenly

突变 tūbiàn [动] 1 (突然变化) change suddenly 2 (生物) mutate ◇基因突变 genetic mutation

突出 tūchū I [动] give prominence to (*pt* gave, *pp* given) ◇他从不突出自己。He never pushes himself forward. II [形] 1 (明显) noticeable ◇突出的特点 prominent feature 2 (隆起) protruding

突飞猛进 tū fēi měng jìn advance by leaps and bounds

突击 tūjī I [动] 1 (突然袭击) assault 2 (加快完成) do a rush job II [副] from nowhere

突破 tūpò [动] 1 (防线、界线) break through (*pt* broke, *pp* broken) ◇突破敌人的封锁线 break through the enemy's blockade 2 (僵局、难关) make a breakthrough ◇癌症治疗上的新突破 a new breakthrough in cancer treatment 3 (限额) surpass ◇突破定额 overfulfil a quota ◇这位长跑运动员突破了他的体能极限。The long-distance runner has broken the limits of his physical endurance. 4 (记录) break (*pt* broke, *pp* broken)

突起 tūqǐ I [动] 1 (突然发生) erupt ◇家庭矛盾突起。A family conflict has erupted. 2 (高耸) tower II [名] bulge

突然 tūrán I [形] sudden II [副] suddenly

突如其来 tū rú qí lái unexpected

图 tú I [名] 1 (图画) picture ◇几何图 geometrical figure 2 (地图) map 3 (计划) plan ♦宏图 grand plan II [动] 1 (贪图) seek (*pt, pp* sought) ◇图一时痛快 seek momentary gratification 2 (谋划) scheme

图案 tú'àn [名] design

图表 túbiǎo [名] chart

图画 túhuà [名] picture

图解 tújiě I [名] diagram II [动] illustrate ◇图解词典 illustrated dictionary

图景 tújǐng [名] 1 (景物) image 2 (前景) prospect

图谋 túmóu I [动] 1 (阴谋策划) plot 2 (谋求) seek (*pt, pp* sought) ◇图谋私利 seek personal advantage II [名] plot

图书 túshū [名] books (*pl*)

图书馆 túshūguǎn [名] library

图腾 túténg [名] totem

图像 túxiàng [名] image

图章 túzhāng [名] seal

图纸 túzhǐ [名] drawing

徒 tú I [名] 1 (徒弟) apprentice ♦门徒 disciple 2 (指信教) believer 3 (贬) (同类人) clique ♦赌徒 gambler ♦匪徒 gangster II [动] walk ♦徒步 on foot III [形] empty ♦徒手 unarmed IV [副] 1 (仅仅) only 2 (白白地) in vain

徒弟 túdì [名] apprentice

徒劳 túláo [形] futile

徒然 túrán **I** [形] futile **II** [副] to no avail

徒手 túshǒu [形] unarmed

徒刑 túxíng [名] imprisonment ◇无期徒刑 life imprisonment

徒有虚名 tú yǒu xū míng have an undeserved reputation

途 tú [名] way ♦旅途 journey ♦前途 prospect ◇沿途 along the way

途径 tújìng [名] channel ◇通过合法途径解决 resolve through legal channels ◇通过外交途径寻求国际援助 seek international aid through diplomatic channels ◇经非法途径入境 enter a country by illegal means

涂 tú [动] **1** (抹) spread … on (*pt, pp* spread) ◇涂油漆 apply paint **2** (乱写乱画) scribble **3** (改动) cross … out

涂改 túgǎi [动] alter

涂料 túliào [名] paint

涂抹 túmǒ [动] **1** (随意写) scribble **2** (油漆、颜料) paint **3** (改动) alter

涂饰 túshì [动] **1** (上油漆) paint **2** (美化) do … up ◇涂饰墙壁 do up the walls

涂写 túxiě [动] scribble

涂鸦 túyā [动] scrawl

涂脂抹粉 tú zhī mǒ fěn (喻) whitewash

屠 tú **I** [动] **1** (动物) slaughter **2** (人) massacre **II** [名] butcher

屠夫 túfū [名] **1** (字) butcher **2** (喻) mass murderer

屠杀 túshā [动] massacre

屠宰 túzǎi [动] slaughter

土 tǔ **I** [名] **1** (泥) soil **2** (土地) land ♦故土 native land ♦领土 territory **3** (鸦片) opium **II** [形] **1** (地方) local **2** (民间) folk **3** (不时髦) unfashionable

土包子 tǔbāozi [名] yokel

土崩瓦解 tǔ bēng wǎ jiě disintegrate

土产 tǔchǎn [名] local product

土地 tǔdì [名] **1** (田地) land **2** (疆域) territory

土豆 tǔdòu [名] potato (*pl* potatoes)

土法 tǔfǎ [名] traditional method

土方 tǔfāng [名] folk remedy

土话 tǔhuà [名] local dialect

土皇帝 tǔhuángdì [名] local despot

土货 tǔhuò [名] local product

土木 tǔmù [名] (土木工程) civil engineering

土气 tǔqì [形] vulgar

土壤 tǔrǎng [名] soil

土特产 tǔtèchǎn [名] local speciality (英) 或 specialty (美)

土语 tǔyǔ [名] local dialect

土政策 tǔzhèngcè [名] local policies (*pl*)

土著 tǔzhù [名] indigenous peoples (*pl*)

吐 tǔ [动] **1** (排出口外) spit (*pt, pp* spat) **2** (露出) put … out (*pt, pp* put) ◇蚕吐丝。Silkworms spin silk. **3** (说出来) speak out (*pt* spoke, *pp* spoken) ▷另见 tù

吐口 tǔkǒu [动] **1** (讲实情) tell the truth (*pt, pp* told) **2** (同意) agree **3** (提出要求) come out with (*pt* came, *pp* come) ◇他吐口要1000元。He came out with a demand for 1000 Yuan.

吐露 tǔlù [动] reveal

吐气 tǔqì [动] let off steam (*pt, pp* let)

吐 tù [动] vomit ▷另见 tǔ

吐沫 tùmo [名] saliva

兔 tù [名] **1** (野兔) hare **2** (家兔) rabbit

湍 tuān **I** [形] (书) torrential **II** [名] rapids (*pl*)

湍急 tuānjí [形] fast-flowing

团 tuán **I** [名] **1** (球形物) ball ◇毛线团 ball of wool **2** (组织) group ♦剧团 drama company **3** (军) regiment **4** (政治组织) league **II** [动] **1** (聚合) unite ♦团聚 reunite **2** (揉成球状) roll into a ball **III** [形] round **IV** [量]

◇一团面 a lump of dough ◇一团毛线 a ball of wool

团队 tuánduì [名] team

团伙 tuánhuǒ [名] gang

团结 tuánjié [动] unite

团聚 tuánjù [动] reunite

团体 tuántǐ [名] organization

团圆 tuányuán [动] reunite

推 tuī [动] **1** (门、窗、车) push **2** (指用工具) scrape ♦推土机 bulldozer ◇他推了个光头。He's shaved his head. **3** (开展) push forward **4** (推断) deduce **5** (辞让) decline **6** (推诿) shift **7** (推迟) postpone **8** (举荐) elect

推波助澜 tuī bō zhù lán exacerbate

推测 tuīcè [动] infer

推崇 tuīchóng [动] esteem

推辞 tuīcí [动] decline

推出 tuīchū [动] bring … out (*pt, pp* brought) ◇HarperCollins出版社又推出了一本畅销书。HarperCollins Publishers have brought out yet another best-seller.

推导 tuīdǎo [动] derive

推动 tuīdòng [动] promote

推断 tuīduàn [动] deduce

推度 tuīduó [动] infer

推翻 tuīfān [动] **1** (推倒) overturn **2** (打垮) overthrow (*pt* overthrew, *pp* overthrown) **3** (根本否定) repudiate

推广 tuīguǎng [动] popularize

推荐 tuījiàn [动] recommend

推举 tuījǔ [动] elect

推理 tuīlǐ [动] infer

推论 tuīlùn [动] infer

推拿 tuīná [动] massage ◇用推拿疗法治疗疼痛 treat pain by massage

推敲 tuīqiāo [动] submit … to close scrutiny

推却 tuīquè [动] decline

推让 tuīràng [动] decline

推三阻四 tuī sān zǔ sì fob … off with excuses

推算 tuīsuàn [动] calculate

推托 tuītuō [动] make excuses

推脱 tuītuō [动] shirk

推诿 tuīwěi [动] pass the buck ◇要尽职尽责，不要互相推诿。You should do your duty and not pass the buck to each other.

推销 tuīxiāo [动] promote ◇推销新产品 promote new products

推卸 tuīxiè [动] shirk

推心置腹 tuī xīn zhì fù confide in ◇我们俩做了推心置腹的长谈。The two of us had a long, heart-to-heart talk.

推行 tuīxíng [动] implement

推选 tuīxuǎn [动] elect

推移 tuīyí [动] **1** (时间变迁) pass ◇随着时间的推移 with the passage of time **2** (发展) develop ◇随着政治时局的推移，经济情况稳定了。As the current political situation develops, the economy is stabilizing.

颓 tuí **I** [动] decline **II** dispirited ♦颓废 dejected

颓废 tuífèi [形] decadent

颓唐 tuítáng [形] dejected

腿 tuǐ [名] **1** (下肢) leg ♦大腿 thigh ♦小腿 calf (*pl* calves) **2** (支撑物) leg ◇桌子腿儿 table leg **3** (火腿) ham

腿脚 tuǐjiǎo [名] mobility ◇这位老人的腿脚不太利索。The old man isn't very mobile.

退 tuì [动] **1** (后移) retreat **2** (使后移) cause … to withdraw ◇他把刀从刀套里退出来。He drew the knife from its sheath. **3** (退出) quit (*pt, pp* quit) **4** (减退) recede **5** (减弱) fade **6** (退还) return **7** (撤销) cancel

退步 tuìbù **I** [动] **1** (落后) lag behind **2** (让步) give way (*pt* gave, *pp* given) **II** [名] leeway

退化 tuìhuà [动] degenerate

退路 tuìlù [名] **1** (道路) line of retreat **2** (余地) leeway

退却 tuìquè [动] **1** (军) retreat **2** (退缩) flinch

退让 tuìràng [动] make a concession ◇在原则问题上，我们不能退让。We can make no concessions on matters of principle.

退缩 tuìsuō [动] hold back (*pt, pp* held)

退位 tuìwèi [动] abdicate

退伍 tuìwǔ [动] demobilize ◇退伍军人 ex-serviceman

退休 tuìxiū [动] retire

退役 tuìyì [动] **1** (军人) demobilize ◇退役军官 retired officer **2** (运动员) retire

蜕 tuì [动] **1** (蛇、蝉) slough **2** (鸟) moult (英), molt (美)

蜕变 tuìbiàn [动] transform

蜕化 tuìhuà [动] **1** (脱皮) slough ... off **2** (喻) (腐化堕落) degenerate

褪 tuì [动] **1** (衣服) take ... off (*pt* took, *pp* taken) **2** (毛) shed (*pt, pp* shed) **3** (颜色) fade
▷另见 tùn

吞 tūn [动] **1** (整个咽下) swallow **2** (吞并) take over (*pt* took, *pp* taken)

吞并 tūnbìng [动] annex

吞没 tūnmò [动] **1** (据为己有) misappropriate **2** (淹没) engulf

吞噬 tūnshì [动] engulf

吞吐 tūntǔ **I** [动] handle ◇这个港口每年可吞吐8000万吨货物。This port can handle 80 milllion tons of cargo every year. **II** [形] hesitant

吞吞吐吐 tūntūntǔtǔ hum and haw

屯 tún **I** [动] **1** (储存) store ... up **2** (驻扎) station ◇屯兵 be stationed **II** [名] village

囤 tún [动] store

囤积 túnjī [动] hoard

臀 tún [名] buttock

褪 tùn [动] take ... off (*pt* took, *pp* taken)
▷另见 tuì

托 tuō **I** [动] **1** (撑) support **2** (委托) entrust **3** (依赖) rely on **II** [名] tray

托词 tuōcí **I** [动] make an excuse **II** [名] excuse

托福 tuōfú **I** [动] (客套) ◇托您的福，我们都好。We're fine, thanks to you. **II** [名] TOEFL, Test of English as a Foreign Language

托付 tuōfù [动] entrust

托管 tuōguǎn [动] entrust to

托人情 tuō rénqíng [动] pull strings

托运 tuōyùn [动] ship ◇托运行李 checked baggage

拖 tuō [动] **1** (拉) pull **2** (地板) mop **3** (下垂) trail ◇她的长裙拖地。Her long dress trailed along the ground. **4** (拖延) delay

拖拉 tuōlā **I** [动] delay **II** [形] dilatory

拖拉机 tuōlājī [名] tractor

拖累 tuōlěi [动] **1** (成为负担) be a burden **2** (使受牵连) implicate

拖泥带水 tuō ní dài shuǐ be slapdash ◇他工作总拖泥带水。He's always slapdash in his work. ◇说话要直接，别拖泥带水。Say what you've got to say, don't beat about the bush.

拖欠 tuōqiàn [动] be in arrears

拖沓 tuōtà [形] dilatory

拖延 tuōyán [动] delay

脱 tuō [动] **1** (皮肤、毛发) shed (*pt, pp* shed) **2** (衣服、鞋帽) take ... off (*pt* took, *pp* taken) **3** (摆脱) escape **4** (颜色) fade **5** (油脂) skim

脱产 tuōchǎn [动] be released from one's regular work

脱稿 tuōgǎo [动] complete

脱钩 tuōgōu [动] **1** (车厢) disconnect **2** (喻) cut ties (*pt, pp* cut) ◇他和原单位早就脱钩了。He cut his ties with his former unit long ago.

脱轨 tuōguǐ [动] derail

脱节 tuōjié [动] be separated

脱臼 tuōjiù [动] dislocate

脱口而出 tuō kǒu ér chū the words roll off one's tongue

脱离 tuōlí [动] **1** (关系) break off (*pt* broke, *pp* broken) ◇脱离关系 break off relations **2** (危险) get away from

脱落 tuōluò [动] **1** (毛发、牙齿) lose (*pt, pp* lost) **2** (油漆、墙皮) come off (*pt* came, *pp* come)

脱贫 tuōpín [动] escape from poverty

脱身 tuōshēn [动] get away (*pt, pp* come)

脱手 tuōshǒu [动] **1** (离开手) let … slip (*pt, pp* let) **2** (卖出) get rid of

脱水 tuōshuǐ [动] dehydrate

脱俗 tuōsú [形] refined

脱销 tuōxiāo [动] be sold out

脱颖而出 tuō yǐng ér chū come to the fore

驮 tuó [动] carry on one's back ◊马驮着米袋。The horse is carrying bags of rice.
▷另见 duò

驼 tuó **I** [名] camel **II** [形] hunchbacked

坨 tuó **I** [名] lump **II** [动] stick together (*pt, pp* stuck)

鸵 tuó 见下文

鸵鸟 tuóniǎo [名] ostrich

妥 tuǒ [形] **1** (适当) appropriate **2** (停当) ready

妥当 tuǒdang [形] appropriate

妥善 tuǒshàn [形] appropriate

妥帖 tuǒtiē [形] appropriate

妥协 tuǒxié [动] compromise

椭 tuǒ 见下文

椭圆 tuǒyuán [名] oval

拓 tuò [动] open … up

拓荒 tuòhuāng [动] open up virgin land

拓宽 tuòkuān [动] **1** (扩大) expand **2** (加宽) widen

拓展 tuòzhǎn [动] expand

唾 tuò **I** [名] saliva **II** [动] spit (*pt, pp* spat)

唾骂 tuòmà [动] revile

唾沫 tuòmo [名] (口) saliva

唾弃 tuòqì [动] spurn

唾手可得 tuò shǒu kě dé within easy reach ◊真是唾手可得的好机会。It really is a golden opportunity.

Ww

挖 wā [动] **1** (掘) dig (*pt, pp* dug) ◊挖洞 dig a hole ◊挖隧道 dig a tunnel **2** (耳朵、鼻子) pick

挖掘 wājué [动] excavate

挖空心思 wā kōng xīnsī (贬) rack one's brains ◊他挖空心思赚大钱。He racked his brains for ways to make a lot of money.

挖苦 wāku [动] have a dig at ◊他总挖苦成绩差的学生。He is always having a dig at underachieving students.

挖墙脚 wā qiángjiǎo (贬) undermine ◊两个党派经常互挖墙脚。The two parties are always undermining each other.

哇 wā [拟] **1** (指哭声) wail **2** (指呕吐声) vomit

洼 wā I [形] low-lying II [名] dip

洼陷 wāxiàn [动] dip ◊桥面洼陷。The bridge dips. ◊这儿的地面洼陷了。The ground dips here.

蛙 wā [名] frog

蛙泳 wāyǒng [名] breaststroke

娃 wá [名] (方) baby

娃娃 wáwa [名] **1** (小孩) baby **2** (玩具) doll

瓦 wǎ [名] tile

瓦解 wǎjiě [动] collapse ◊这个恐怖组织已经瓦解了。The terrorist network has already collapsed. ◊我们瓦解了敌人的阴谋。We smashed the enemy's plot.

瓦砾 wǎlì [名] rubble

瓦斯 wǎsī [名] gas

袜 wà [名] sock ♦长筒袜 stocking

袜子 wàzi [名] sock

歪 wāi I [形] **1** (倾斜) slanting ◊画挂歪了。The picture is crooked. **2** (坏) devious ◊他出了个歪点子。He came up with a devious suggestion. II [动] incline

歪打正着 wāi dǎ zhèng zháo have a stroke of good luck ◊他歪打正着中了彩票头彩。By a stroke of good luck, he won first prize in the lottery.

歪门邪道 wāi mén xié dào dishonest means

歪曲 wāiqū [动] distort

歪斜 wāixié [形] crooked

崴 wǎi [动] sprain

外 wài I [名] **1** (范围以外) ◊户外运动 outdoor sports ◊他把车停在门外。He parked the car outside the gate. **2** (外国) ♦外宾 foreign visitor II [形] **1** (非所属的) ♦外国 abroad **2** (疏远的) ♦外人 outsider **3** (非正式) informal ♦外号 nickname III [副] besides ♦外加 plus

外币 wàibì [名] foreign currency

外表 wàibiǎo [名] exterior ◊大楼外表很气派。The exterior of the building is very imposing. ◊人的外表不可信。Don't judge by appearances.

外宾 wàibīn [名] foreign visitor

外部 wàibù I [名] exterior II [形] external

外地 wàidì [名] other parts of the country ◊我们班有几个外地学生。Our class has several students from other parts of the country. ◊他去外地出差。He went away on business.

外地人 wàidìrén [名] person from another part of the country

外调 wàidiào [动] transfer ◊两位网络工程师从IT部外调到了纽约办事处。Two network engineers were transferred from the IT department to the New York office.

外敷 wàifū [动] apply externally

外公 wàigōng [名] maternal grandfather

外观 wàiguān [名] appearance

外行 wàiháng I [名] layman (*pl*

laymen) ◊对电脑编程，我是个外行。I'm a layman where computer programming is concerned. **II** [形] amateurish

外号 wàihào [名] nickname

外汇 wàihuì [名] **1** (外汇兑换) foreign exchange **2** (外币) foreign currency

外籍 wàijí [形] foreign

外交 wàijiāo [名] foreign affairs

外交部 wàijiāobù [名] Ministry of Foreign Affairs

外交部长 wàijiāo bùzhǎng [名] Minister of Foreign Affairs

外交官 wàijiāoguān [名] diplomat

外界 wàijiè [名] outside world ◊外界因素 external factors

外景 wàijǐng [名] scene shot on location

外科 wàikē [名] surgery

外科手术 wàikē shǒushù [名] surgical operation

外科医生 wàikē yīshēng [名] surgeon

外快 wàikuài [名] extra income ◊他在夜校教课赚外快。He earns some extra income by teaching evening classes.

外流 wàiliú [动] drain ◊中国的很多人才外流到国外。There is a major brain drain from China to other countries.

外露 wàilù [动] show (*pt* showed, *pp* *shown*) ◊我父亲的感情从不外露。My father never shows his feelings.

外卖 wàimài [名] takeaway (英), takeout (美) ◊中国餐馆提供外卖服务。Chinese restaurants provide a takeaway (英) 或 takeout (美) service.

外贸 wàimào [名] foreign trade

外貌 wàimào [名] appearance

外婆 wàipó [名] maternal grandmother

外企 wàiqǐ [名] foreign enterprise

外强中干 wài qiáng zhōng gān outwardly strong but inwardly weak

外侨 wàiqiáo [名] foreign resident

外人 wàirén [名] **1** (局外人) outsider **2** (外国人) foreigner

外伤 wàishāng [名] injury ◊他从马上摔了下来，只受了点外伤。He fell off his horse, but only had a slight injury.

外商 wàishāng [名] foreign businessman (*pl* businessmen)

外甥 wàisheng [名] nephew

外事 wàishì [名] foreign affairs

外孙 wàisūn [名] grandson

外套 wàitào [名] overcoat

外围 wàiwéi [名] periphery

外文 wàiwén [名] foreign language

外线 wàixiàn [名] outside line

外乡 wàixiāng [名] another part of the country ◊他在外乡遭了劫。He was robbed while away from home.

外向 wàixiàng [形] **1** (指性格) extrovert **2** (指经济) export-oriented

外销 wàixiāo [动] sell ... externally (*pt*, *pp* sold) ◊本厂产品外销到美国。The products from the factory are sold abroad to the United States.

外因 wàiyīn [名] external cause

外语 wàiyǔ [名] foreign language

外遇 wàiyù [名] extra-marital affair ◊她有外遇后，就想和丈夫离婚。After having an affair, she wanted to divorce her husband.

外援 wàiyuán [名] **1** (援助) foreign aid **2** (外国球员) foreign player

外在 wàizài [形] external

外债 wàizhài [名] foreign debt

外资 wàizī [名] foreign capital

外资企业 wàizī qǐyè [名] foreign-funded enterprise

弯 wān **I** [形] curved **II** [动] bend (*pt*, *pp* bent) ◊我弯着腰扫地。I bent down to sweep the floor. **III** [名] bend

弯路 wānlù [名] **1** (字) (弯曲的路) winding road **2** (喻) (曲折) tortuous route

弯曲 wānqū [形] **1** (头发) wavy **2** (小路、小河) winding

剜 wān [动] cut … out (*pt*, *pp* cut)

湾 wān [名] bay

蜿 wān 见下文

蜿蜒 wānyán [形] **1** (路、河) winding ◇蜿蜒的长城 the winding Great Wall **2** (指蛇) wriggling

豌 wān 见下文

豌豆 wāndòu [名] pea

丸 wán **I** [名] **1** (球形物) ball **2** (指药) pill **II** [量] pill ◇他服了一丸药。He took a pill.

丸药 wányào [名] pill

完 wán **I** [形] whole ♦完整 complete **II** [动] **1** (完成) complete **2** (耗尽) run out (*pt* ran, *pp* run)◇打印纸使完了。The printing paper has run out. **3** (了结) finish ◇他的书写完了。He's finished writing his book.

完备 wánbèi [形] complete

完毕 wánbì [动] finish

完成 wánchéng [动] complete

完蛋 wándàn [动] be finished

完好 wánhǎo [形] intact ◇这些文物保存完好。These cultural relics have been kept intact and in good condition.

完结 wánjié [动] finish

完满 wánmǎn [形] successful

完美 wánměi [形] perfect

完全 wánquán **I** [形] complete **II** [副] completely ◇我完全赞成你的观点。I completely endorse your point of view.

完善 wánshàn **I** [形] perfect **II** [动] perfect ◇法律体系需要完善。The legal system needs to be improved.

完整 wánzhěng [形] complete

玩 wán [动] **1** (玩耍) play **2** (游玩) have a good time ◇我去泰国玩了一个星期。I went to Thailand for a week's holiday. **3** (做客) visit ◇欢迎到我家来玩儿！ Please come and visit me at home. **4** (表示祝愿) enjoy ◇玩得好！ Enjoy yourself! **5** (耍弄) play ◇他爱对人玩花招。He likes to play tricks on people.

玩具 wánjù [名] toy

玩弄 wánnòng [动] **1** (贬) (调情) play games with ◇他老玩弄年轻女子。He is always playing games with young girls. **2** (贬) (使用) employ

玩儿命 wánrmìng [动] (口) bust a gut (*pt* bust, *pp* busted) ◇他玩儿命学英语。He put everything into learning English.

玩世不恭 wán shì bù gōng (贬) frivolous ◇他是个玩世不恭的花花公子。He is a frivolous playboy.

玩耍 wánshuǎ [动] play

玩物 wánwù [名] plaything

玩笑 wánxiào [名] joke ◇他喜欢跟人开玩笑。He likes to play jokes on people. ◇我把他的话当玩笑。I took what he said as a joke.

玩意儿 wányìr [名] (口) **1** (东西) thing **2** (人) ◇千万别和他交朋友。他不是什么好玩意儿。Whatever you do don't make friends with him. He's bad news. **3** (玩具) toy **4** (器械) gadget

顽 wán [形] **1** (难以摆脱的) stubborn **2** (淘气) naughty

顽固 wángù [形] **1** (贬) (指思想) obstinate **2** (指病) persistent **3** (指政治) diehard

顽抗 wánkàng [动] stubbornly resist

顽皮 wánpí [形] mischievous

顽强 wánqiáng [形] tenacious

顽症 wánzhèng [名] chronic illness

宛 wǎn 见下文

宛如 wǎnrú [动] (书) be just like ◇美丽的风景宛如仙境。The beautiful scenery is just like paradise.

挽 wǎn [动] **1** (拉) hold (*pt*, *pp* held) ◇他们俩经常手挽手去学校。They often go to school hand in hand. **2** (卷起) roll … up ◇卷起袖子 roll up one's sleeves

挽回 wǎnhuí [动] redeem ◇挽回局面 redeem the situation ◇挽回面子 save face

挽救 wǎnjiù [动] save

挽留 wǎnliú [动] press … to stay ◇老师挽留我与他共进晚餐。My teacher pressed me to stay for dinner.

晚 wǎn I [形] late ◆晚秋 late autumn ◇火车晚了10分钟。The train was ten minutes late. ◇我起晚了。I got up late. II [名] evening

晚安 wǎn'ān [形] ◇祝你晚安。Good night.

晚辈 wǎnbèi [名] younger generation

晚点 wǎndiǎn [动] be late

晚饭 wǎnfàn [名] dinner

晚会 wǎnhuì [名] party

晚年 wǎnnián [名] old age

晚期 wǎnqī [名] late period ◇他晚期的作品更优秀。His later works are even more outstanding.

晚上 wǎnsha [名] evening

晚熟 wǎnshú [动] develop late ◇这孩子晚熟。This child is a late developer.

惋 wǎn 见下文

惋惜 wǎnxī [动] regret ◇教练为队员受伤感到惋惜。The coach regretted the injury to the team member.

婉 wǎn [形] **1** (委婉) tactful ◆婉谢 decline **2** (柔顺) gracious ◆婉顺 docile

婉言 wǎnyán [名] tactful language ◇我婉言拒绝了他的邀请。I tactfully refused his invitation.

婉转 wǎnzhuǎn [形] **1** (温和) tactful ◇他婉转地批评了学生。He tactfully criticized the student. **2** (优美) melodious

碗 wǎn [名] bowl

碗柜 wǎnguì [名] sideboard

万 wàn I [数] ten thousand II [副] definitely ◇你万不可错失良机。You really mustn't let slip a good opportunity.

万不得已 wàn bù dé yǐ as a last resort

万分 wànfēn [副] extremely

万金油 wànjīnyóu [名] (贬) jack of all trades

万能 wànnéng [形] **1** (无所不能) omnipotent **2** (多用途的) all-purpose ◇万能钥匙 master key

万人空巷 wàn rén kōng xiàng the whole town turns out ◇这位奥斯卡得主访问上海时，万人空巷。When the Oscar winner visited Shanghai, the whole town turned out.

万世 wànshì [名] (书) the ages ◇他的发明会流传万世。His invention will be passed on through the ages.

万岁 wànsuì [叹] long live

万万 wànwàn I [副] absolutely ◇我万万没想到他这么无礼。I had absolutely no idea that he was so rude. II [数] hundred million

万无一失 wàn wú yī shī be sure of success ◇我们为这次登山活动做了精心准备，以确保万无一失。We made careful preparations for climbing the mountain, so as to be sure of success.

万物 wànwù [名] the whole of creation ◇春天到了，万物复苏。Spring has arrived – everything is coming back to life.

万象 wànxiàng [名] (书) everything under the sun

万幸 wànxìng [形] very lucky

万一 wànyī I [连] if by any chance ◇万一他不在，把信交给他的秘书。If by any chance he isn't there, give the letter to his secretary. II [名] contingency

万紫千红 wàn zǐ qiān hóng blaze of colour (英) 或 color (美)

腕 wàn [名] **1** (指手) wrist **2** (指脚) ankle

腕儿 wànr [名] (口) star

腕子 wànzi [名] **1** (指手) wrist **2** (指脚) ankle

汪 wāng I [动] collect II [拟] bark

汪汪 wāngwāng [形] tearful

汪洋 wāngyáng [名] expanse of water

亡 wáng I [动] die II [形] (书)

deceased ♦亡父 late father ♦亡友 deceased friend

亡故 wánggù [动] (书) pass away

亡命徒 wángmìngtú [名] desperate criminal

亡羊补牢 wáng yáng bǔ láo better late than never

王 wáng [名] king

王八 wángba [名] (动) tortoise

王八蛋 wángbadàn [名] (讳) bastard

王朝 wángcháo [名] dynasty

王储 wángchǔ [名] crown prince

王法 wángfǎ [名] (口) law of the land

王公 wánggōng [名] aristocracy

王国 wángguó [名] kingdom

王牌 wángpái [名] ace ◊他是王牌记者。He's an ace reporter.

王室 wángshì [名] royalty

王子 wángzǐ [名] prince

网 wǎng I [名] 1 (工具) net ♦渔网 fishing net 2 (网状物) web ♦蜘蛛网 spider's web 3 (系统) network ♦互联网 the Internet ♦信息网 information network ♦交通网 communication network II [动] net

网吧 wǎngbā [名] Internet café

网点 wǎngdiǎn [名] points (*pl*) ◊银行在各地设有服务网点。The bank has set up service points everywhere.

网罗 wǎngluó [动] headhunt

网络 wǎngluò [名] network ◊网络服务器 network server ◊经济网络 economic network ◊他建立了广泛的人际网络。He built up a wide network of relationships.

网迷 wǎngmí [名] Internet fan

网民 wǎngmín [名] Internet user

网球 wǎngqiú [名] tennis

网球场 wǎngqiúchǎng [名] tennis court

网页 wǎngyè [名] web page

网友 wǎngyǒu [名] chat buddy

网站 wǎngzhàn [名] website

网址 wǎngzhǐ [名] web address

枉 wǎng I [动] ♦枉法 pervert the course of justice II [副] (书) in vain

枉法 wǎngfǎ [动] (书) pervert the course of justice

枉费 wǎngfèi [动] (书) waste ◊他不会听你的，别枉费唇舌了。He won't listen, so don't waste your breath on him.

往 wǎng I [介] to ◊飞机正飞往柏林。The plane is flying to Berlin. II [形] past ♦往事 past events (*pl*)

往常 wángcháng [名] ◊他往常不吃早饭。He didn't use to eat breakfast.

往来 wǎnglái [动] 1 (去和来) come and go 2 (交往) ◊两国往来密切。Contacts between the two countries are close.

往往 wǎngwǎng [副] often

妄 wàng [形] 1 (不合理) unreasonable 2 (随意) presumptuous

妄图 wàngtú [动] try in vain (*pt, pp* tried)

妄想 wàngxiǎng I [动] (贬) have a pipe dream II [名] pipe dream

妄自菲薄 wàng zì fěibó underestimate oneself

妄自尊大 wàng zì zūn dà (贬) have a high opinion of oneself

忘 wàng [动] forget (*pt* forgot, *pp* forgotten) ◊我忘了带雨伞。I forgot my umbrella.

忘恩负义 wàng ēn fù yì (贬) be ungrateful ◊他是个忘恩负义的小人。He's an ungrateful rat.

忘乎所以 wàng hū suǒ yǐ (贬) get carried way ◊他高兴得忘乎所以。He was so happy he got quite carried away.

忘怀 wànghuái [动] (书) forget (*pt* forgot, *pp* forgotten)

忘记 wàngjì [动] forget (*pt* forgot, *pp* forgotten) ◊我忘记了他的样子。I've forgotten what he looks like. ◊我忘记了给朋友写信。I forgot to write a letter to my friend.

忘年交 wàngniánjiāo [名] friend (*who is significantly older or younger*) ◊这位学生和老教授成

了忘年交。The student and the elderly professor became friends despite their age difference.

忘却 wàngquè [动] (书) forget (*pt* forgot, *pp* forgotten)

忘我 wàngwǒ [形] selfless ◇他忘我地朝他的目标奋斗着。He worked selflessly towards his goal. ◇他忘我地研究诗歌。He lost himself in his study of poetry.

旺 wàng [形] **1** (火) roaring **2** (人、生意) flourishing **3** (花) blooming ◇十月菊花开得正旺。In October the chrysanthemums are in full bloom.

旺季 wàngjì [名] **1** (指生意) peak season ◇秋天是北京的旅游旺季。Autumn is the peak season for tourism in Beijing. **2** (指水果、蔬菜) season ◇夏天是西瓜旺季。Summer is the season for watermelons.

旺盛 wàngshèng [形] **1** (精力、生命力) full of energy **2** (植物) thriving ◇果园的桃树长得很旺盛。The peach trees in the orchard are thriving.

旺销 wàngxiāo [动] sell well (*pt, pp* sold)

望 wàng [动] **1** (向远处看) look into the distance **2** (察看) watch ♦望风 be on the lookout **3** (希望) hope ◇望一路顺风。I hope you have a safe journey.

望子成龙 wàng zǐ chéng lóng have high expectations of one's children ◇父母太望子成龙, 会给孩子很大压力。If parents' expectations are too high it will put a lot of pressure on the children.

危 wēi **I** [形] dangerous **II** [动] endanger

危害 wēihài [动] harm ◇抽烟危害健康。Smoking damages your health.

危机 wēijī [名] crisis (*pl* crises)

危急 wēijí [形] critical

危难 wēinàn [名] danger ◇他有危难时, 总能找朋友帮忙。When he was in danger, he could always look to his friends for help.

危险 wēixiǎn **I** [形] dangerous **II** [名] danger ◇消防员冒着生命危险扑灭森林大火。The firefighter put his life in danger to extinguish the forest fire.

危言耸听 wēi yán sǒng tīng scare story

危在旦夕 wēi zài dàn xī be in imminent danger

威 wēi [名] power

威风 wēifēng **I** [名] air of authority **II** [形] impressive

威力 wēilì [名] power

威猛 wēiměng [形] powerful

威名 wēimíng [名] renown ◇这位医生威名远扬。This doctor is renowned far and wide.

威慑 wēishè [动] terrorize

威士忌 wēishìjì [名] whisky

威望 wēiwàng [名] prestige

威武 wēiwǔ [形] powerful

威胁 wēixié [动] threaten

威信 wēixìn [名] prestige

威严 wēiyán **I** [形] dignified **II** [名] dignity

偎 wēi [动] snuggle up to

偎依 wēiyī [动] snuggle up to

微 wēi **I** [形] tiny ♦微米 micron ♦微秒 microsecond ◇门缝里射出一线微光。A ray of light shone through the crack in the door. **II** [副] slightly ◇她们姐妹俩的性格微有不同。The two sisters were slightly different in character.

微波 wēibō [名] **1** (涟漪) ripple **2** (电子) (超短波) microwave

微波炉 wēibōlú [名] microwave oven

微薄 wēibó [形] meagre (英), meager (美)

微不足道 wēi bù zú dào not worth mentioning ◇这是件微不足道的小事。This is a trivial matter.

微风 wēifēng [名] gentle breeze

微观 wēiguān [前缀] micro- ◇微观结构 microstructure

微观世界 wēiguān shìjiè [名] microcosm

微乎其微 wēi hū qí wēi very little ◇他夺冠的可能性微乎其微。There is very little possibility of his becoming the champion.

微粒 wēilì [名] particle

微量元素 wēiliàng yuánsù [名] trace element

微妙 wēimiào [形] delicate

微弱 wēiruò [形] faint

微生物 wēishēngwù [名] micro-organism

微小 wēixiǎo [形] tiny

微笑 wēixiào [动] smile ◇她的微笑很迷人。Her smile was enchanting.

微型 wēixíng [形] mini ◇微型唱片机 MiniDisc®

煨 wēi [动] (烹饪) stew

巍 wēi 见下文

巍峨 wēi'é [形] towering

为 wéi I [动] 1 (是) be ◇一公斤为两磅。A kilo is two pounds. 2 (变成) ◇他懂得如何变弊为利。He knows how to turn a disadvantage into an advantage. 3 (充当) act as ◇他选朋友为他的代言人。He chose his friend to act as his spokesman. II [介] ◇这部老电影为大家喜爱。Everyone loves this old film.
▷另见 wèi

为非作歹 wéi fēi zuò dǎi commit all kinds of crimes

为富不仁 wéi fù bù rén wealthy but uncharitable

为害 wéihài [动] cause harm

为难 wéinán I [形] embarrassed II [动] make things difficult for ◇考官出了些难题，故意为难学生。The examiner set tough questions, deliberately making things difficult for the students.

为期 wéiqī [动] be scheduled for ◇电影节为期一周。The film festival is scheduled to last a week.

为生 wéishēng [动] make a living

为数 wéishù [动] ◇抢手的房产为数不少。There is a lot of fast-selling property.

为所欲为 wéi suǒ yù wéi (贬) do just as one pleases

为伍 wéiwǔ [动] associate with

为止 wéizhǐ [动] ◇到上周末为止，我们收到了上千封求职信。By the end of last week, we had received over a thousand letters of application.

违 wéi [动] break (*pt* broke, *pp* broken) ♦违法 break the law

违背 wéibèi [动] go against (*pt* went, *pp* gone)

违法 wéifǎ I [动] break the law (*pt* broke, *pp* broken) II [形] illegal

违反 wéifǎn [动] go against (*pt* went, *pp* gone)

违犯 wéifàn [动] violate

违禁 wéijìn [形] banned

违抗 wéikàng [动] disobey

违心 wéixīn [形] ◇他违心地投了赞成票。He voted for the motion against his conscience.

违约 wéiyuē [动] break a contract (*pt* broke, *pp* broken) ◇这家公司被控违约。The company was accused of breach of contract.

违章 wéizhāng [动] break regulations (*pt* broke, *pp* broken)

围 wéi I [动] surround II [名] 1 (四周) all sides ♦外围 periphery 2 (周长) measurement ♦三围 vital statistics ♦胸围 chest measurement

围攻 wéigōng [动] 1 (用语言) attack … from all sides 2 (用武力) besiege

围观 wéiguān [动] look on ◇他从河里救孩子时，一群人在围观。A crowd of people looked on as he rescued the child from the river. ◇围观的人越来越多。There were more and more onlookers.

围困 wéikùn [动] strand

围拢 wéilǒng [动] crowd around

围棋 wéiqí [名] go (*board game*)

围绕 wéirào [动] 1 (物体) revolve around 2 (话题) centre (英) 或 center (美) on ◇大家围绕着此议题展开讨论。Everyone began a discussion centred on this subject.

桅 wéi [名] mast

桅杆 wéigān [名] mast

帷 wéi [名] curtain

帷幕 wéimù [名] **1** (指舞台) curtain **2**(指事件) ◇世界杯拉开了帷幕。The World Cup has begun.

惟 wéi [副] **1** (单单) only **2** (书) (只是) but ◇他各科成绩都不错, 惟数学不好。He achieved good results in all subjects but mathematics.

惟独 wéidú [副] only ◇客人都到了, 惟独她没来。She was the only guest who had not arrived.

惟恐 wéikǒng [动] be afraid

惟利是图 wéi lì shì tú only interested in profit

惟妙惟肖 wéi miào wéi xiào remarkably true to life

惟一 wéiyī [形] only ◇他是班里惟一的男生。He is the only male student in the class.

维 wéi **I** [动] **1** (连接) hold ... together (*pt, pp* held) **2** (保持) maintain **II** [名] dimension ◇三维空间 three-dimensional space

维持 wéichí [动] **1** (保持) maintain ◇维持交通秩序 direct the traffic **2**(资助) support ◇他靠卖画维持生活。He relies on selling paintings to support himself.

维护 wéihù [动] safeguard ◇维护和平 safeguard peace ◇维护消费者的利益 defend consumers' interests

维生素 wéishēngsù [名] vitamin

维系 wéixì [动] maintain

维修 wéixiū [动] maintain

伟 wěi [形] great

伟大 wěidà [形] great

伟哥 wěigē [名] (医) Viagra®

伟人 wěirén [名] great man (*pl* men)

伪 wěi [形] false ♦伪钞 counterfeit note (英) 或 bill (美)

伪君子 wěijūnzǐ [名] hypocrite

伪劣 wěiliè [形] fake and second-rate

伪善 wěishàn [形] hypocritical

伪造 wěizào [动] forge ◇他的护照是伪造的。His passport was forged.

伪装 wěizhuāng **I** [动] disguise ◇间谍伪装成农民, 混进了城里。The spy infiltrated the city disguised as a peasant. **II** [名] disguise

苇 wěi [名] reed

尾 wěi [名] **1** (尾巴) tail **2** (末端) end ♦排尾 the person at the end of a row ◇他喜欢坐大巴的车尾。He likes sitting at the back of the bus. **3** (残余) remainder ♦扫尾 finish off

尾巴 wěiba [名] **1** (尾部) tail **2** (残余) unfinished business ◇今天的会议留了个尾巴。Today's meeting left unfinished business. **3** (跟踪的人) ◇他发现他的车后有个尾巴。He discovered that his car was being tailed.

尾气 wěiqì [名] exhaust (英)

尾声 wěishēng [名] **1** (文学) epilogue **2** (指活动) end ◇国际艺术节已接近尾声。The International Arts Festival is already drawing to an end.

尾数 wěishù [名] (指小数点后) *digits after the decimal point*

尾随 wěisuí [动] tail

纬 wěi [名] **1** (地理) latitude **2** (指纺织) weft

纬度 wěidù [名] latitude

纬线 wěixiàn [名] **1** (地理) latitude **2** (指纺织) weft

委 wěi **I** [动] entrust **II** [名] **1** (委员) committee member **2** (委员会) committee

委派 wěipài [动] appoint

委培 wěipéi [动] send ... for training (*pt, pp* sent)

委屈 wěiqu **I** [名] unjust treatment **II** [形] aggrieved **III** [动] wrong

委任 wěirèn [动] appoint ◇董事长委任他当策划总监。The Chairman of the Board appointed him Chief Planning Inspector.

委托 wěituō [动] entrust ◇我委托姐姐看了几天孩子。I entrusted the children to my sister's care for a few days.

委婉 wěiwǎn [形] **1** (指言词) tactful

◇我委婉地拒绝了他的邀请。I tactfully refused his invitation. **2** (语气) mild

萎 wěi [形] withered

萎靡 wěimǐ [形] downhearted

萎缩 wěisuō [动] **1** (医) atrophy **2** (经济) shrink (*pt* shrank, *pp* shrunk)

唯 wěi 见下文

唯唯诺诺 wěiwěinuònuò obsequious

猥 wěi 见下文

猥亵 wěixiè **I** [形] (贬) obscene **II** [动] (贬, 书) act indecently towards

卫 wèi [动] protect

卫兵 wèibīng [名] guard

卫冕 wèimiǎn [动] defend a title

卫生 wèishēng **I** [名] **1** (干净) hygiene **2** (扫除) clean-up ◇我在打扫教室卫生。I am giving the classroom a clean-up. **II** [形] hygienic ◇饭前不洗手不卫生。It is unhygienic not to wash your hands before eating.

卫生间 wèishēngjiān [名] toilet (英), rest room (美)

卫生球 wèishēngqiú [名] mothball

卫生纸 wèishēngzhǐ [名] toilet paper (英) 或 tissue (美)

卫星 wèixīng [名] satellite

为 wèi [介] for ◇我真为你高兴！I am really happy for you! ◇为健康着想, 他每天去跑步。He went jogging every day for the sake of his health. ◇她在为孩子唱催眠曲。She is singing lullabies to the children. ▷另见 wéi

为了 wèile [介] in order to ◇为了买房子, 他把车卖了。He sold his car in order to buy a house. ◇为了联系方便, 他买了个手机。He bought a mobile phone to keep in contact more easily.

为什么 wèi shénme [副] why ◇你为什么迟到了？Why were you late?

未 wèi [副] not ◇她还未回信。She has still not written back.

未必 wèibì [副] not necessarily ◇他未必会接受邀请。He may not necessarily be able to accept the invitation.

未曾 wèicéng [副] not … before ◇我未曾见过他。I haven't seen him before.

未尝 wèicháng [副] not ◇他未尝不想取得好成绩。It wasn't that he didn't want good results.

未成年人 wèichéngniánrén [名] minor

未婚夫 wèihūnfū [名] fiancé

未婚妻 wèihūnqī [名] fiancée

未来 wèilái [名] future ◇他能预见未来。He can foresee the future. ◇未来的几天将有沙尘暴。In the next few days there will be a sandstorm.

未免 wèimiǎn [副] rather ◇他的讲话未免太长了。His speech went on rather too long. ◇他说的未免都是对的。What he says is not always correct.

未遂 wèisuì [动] fail ◇他自杀未遂。He attempted suicide.

未知数 wèizhīshù [名] **1** (数) unknown number **2** (未知事物) ◇他能否成名还是个未知数。It is uncertain whether he will become famous or not.

位 wèi **I** [名] **1** (位置) location **2** (地位) position ♦岗位 post **3** (数学) digit ◇两位数 two-digit number ◇他挣六位数的工资。He earns a six-figure salary. **II** [量] ◇主持人请来了两位嘉宾。The host invited two guests of honour (英) 或 honor (美).

位次 wèicì [名] position ◇歌曲排行榜的位次没变。The position of the songs in the charts has not changed.

位于 wèiyú [动] be located ◇格拉斯哥位于苏格兰。Glasgow is located in Scotland.

位置 wèizhi [名] **1** (地点) location ◇这房子的位置不好。This house is not well located. **2** (地位) place ◇他在人们心中的位置很高。He has an important place in peoples' hearts. ◇他在家里没有位置。He's a nobody at home. **3** (职位) position ◇人事部有5个空位置。The Human

Resources Department has five vacant positions.

位子 wèizi [名] **1** (座位) seat **2** (职位) position ◇市场部里没位子了。There are no vacancies in Marketing.

味 wèi [名] **1** (滋味) taste **2** (气味) smell ◇这花没香味。This flower has no scent.

味道 wèidao [名] **1** (滋味) taste ◇这家饭馆的菜味道不错。The food in this restaurant is delicious. **2** (感觉) ◇他越想越不是味道。The more he thinks about it, the less palatable it becomes.

味精 wèijīng [名] monosodium glutamate

畏 wèi [动] (害怕) be afraid of

畏惧 wèijù [动] be afraid of ◇他畏惧失败。He is afraid of losing.

畏缩 wèisuō [动] shrink in fear (*pt* shrank, *pp* shrunk)

畏罪 wèizuì [动] fear punishment for one's crimes

胃 wèi [名] stomach ◇我的胃不舒服。I have a stomach upset.

胃口 wèikǒu [名] **1** (食欲) appetite **2** (喜好) liking ◇这套家具不合我的胃口。This furniture is not to my liking.

谓 wèi [动] (书) call ◇此谓自食其果。This is called "reaping what you have sown".

谓语 wèiyǔ [名] predicate

喂 wèi **I** [动] feed (*pt, pp* fed) **II** [叹] **1** (指打电话) hello **2** (指招呼) hey

喂养 wèiyǎng [动] raise

蔚 wèi 见下文

蔚蓝 wèilán [形] azure

蔚然成风 wèirán chéng fēng become the trend

慰 wèi [动] comfort

慰劳 wèiláo [动] show appreciation (*pt* showed, *pp* shown)

慰问 wèiwèn [动] express appreciation ◇市长向医务人员表示了亲切慰问。The mayor expressed his sincere appreciation to the medical workers.

慰问信 wèiwènxìn [名] letter of support

温 wēn **I** [形] **1** (不冷不热) warm **2** (平和) mild **II** [动] **1** (加热) warm ... up ◇你最好把剩饭温一温再吃。You'd be best to warm up the leftovers before eating them again. **2** (复习) revise **3** (回忆) recall **III** [名] temperature

温饱 wēnbǎo [名] adequate food and clothing

温差 wēnchā [名] difference in temperature

温床 wēnchuáng [名] hotbed

温带 wēndài [名] temperate zone

温度 wēndù [名] temperature

温故知新 wēn gù zhī xīn gain new insights by studying the past

温和 wēnhé [形] **1** (指性情、态度) mild **2** (指气候) temperate

温暖 wēnnuǎn [形] warm ◇温暖的阳光 warm sunshine ◇在那些困难的日子里，家人给了她很多温暖。Her family gave her a lot of warmth during those difficult times.

温情 wēnqíng [名] tenderness

温泉 wēnquán [名] hot spring

温柔 wēnróu [形] gentle

温室 wēnshì [名] greenhouse ◇温室效应 the greenhouse effect

温顺 wēnshùn [形] docile

温文尔雅 wēn wén ěr yǎ cultured

温习 wēnxí [动] revise

温馨 wēnxīn [形] cosy (英), cozy (美)

瘟 wēn **I** [名] communicable disease **II** [形] infected

瘟疫 wēnyì [名] plague

文 wén **I** [名] **1** (字) writing ♦文盲 illiterate **2** (书面语) written language ♦中文 the Chinese language **3** (文章) essay **4** (指社会产物) culture ♦文明 civilization **5** (指自然现象) ♦天文 astronomy **6** (文科) humanities (*pl*) ◇他是学文的。He studied the humanities. **7** (非军事) civilian **II** [形] gentle **III** [动] tattoo

文本 wénběn [名] **1** (版本) version **2** (文件) text

文笔 wénbǐ [名] style ◇他的文笔很好。He has an excellent writing style.

文不对题 wén bù duì tí go off on a tangent

文才 wéncái [名] literary talent

文采 wéncǎi [名] **1** (指文艺) literary talent **2** (指词藻) flowery language

文法 wénfǎ [名] (语法) grammar

文风 wénfēng [名] **1** (指风气) atmosphere **2** (指语言) style

文工团 wéngōngtuán [名] song and dance ensemble

文豪 wénháo [名] great writer

文化 wénhuà [名] **1** (精神财富) culture ◇他对中国茶文化很有研究。He had researched Chinese tea culture in great detail. ◇他们的文化生活很丰富。They have a rich cultural life. **2** (知识) education

文火 wénhuǒ [名] gentle heat

文集 wénjí [名] collected works (*pl*)

文件 wénjiàn [名] **1** (公文) document ◇这是一份机密文件。This is a classified document. **2** (计算机) file ◇把文件存放在C盘。Save the file on the C drive.

文教 wénjiào [名] culture and education

文静 wénjìng [形] gentle

文具 wénjù [名] stationery

文科 wénkē [名] humanities (*pl*)

文盲 wénmáng [名] **1** (无知的人) illiterate **2** (无知) illiteracy

文明 wénmíng **I** [名] civilization **II** [形] civilized

文凭 wénpíng [名] diploma

文气 wénqi [形] reserved

文人 wénrén [名] scholar

文书 wénshū [名] **1** (公文) official document **2** (文职人员) secretary

文坛 wéntán [名] literary circles (*pl*)

文体 wéntǐ [名] **1** (体裁) genre **2** (文娱) recreation

文物 wénwù [名] cultural relic

文献 wénxiàn [名] document

文学 wénxué [名] literature

文雅 wényǎ [形] refined

文艺 wényì [名] **1** (文学艺术) art and literature **2** (文学) literature **3** (演艺) performing arts (*pl*)

文娱 wényú [名] recreation

文摘 wénzhāi [名] abstract ◇她对读过的文章做了文摘。She made abstracts of the articles she read.

文章 wénzhāng [名] **1** (著作) essay **2** (含义) implication

文质彬彬 wén zhì bīnbīn gentle and refined

文绉绉 wénzhōuzhōu [形] genteel

文字 wénzì [名] **1** (指符号) script **2** (指文章) writing

纹 wén [名] line

纹理 wénlǐ [名] grain

纹丝不动 wén sī bù dòng motionless ◇一丝风都没有，树枝纹丝不动。There wasn't a breath of wind – the branches were motionless. ◇接受检阅的士兵纹丝不动地立正站着。The soldiers under inspection stood to attention without moving a muscle.

闻 wén **I** [动] **1** (书) (听见) hear (*pt, pp* heard) **2** (嗅) smell **II** [名] **1** (消息) news **2** (声望) reputation

闻风而动 wén fēng ér dòng act at once on hearing the news ◇记者的"嗅觉"特别灵敏，总能闻风而动。The reporter had a particularly good journalistic nose and always acted quickly on a story.

闻风丧胆 wén fēng sàng dǎn tremble with fear on hearing the news ◇这批勇猛的缉毒警令毒品贩子闻风丧胆。The drug dealers trembled with fear when they heard about the courageous drugs squad.

闻名 wénmíng **I** [动] be famous **II** [形] famous

蚊 wén [名] mosquito (*pl* mosquitoes)

刎 wěn [动] cut one's throat (*pt, pp* cut) ◊他自刎身亡。He committed suicide by cutting his own throat.

吻 wěn **I** [名] **1** (动物的嘴) mouth **2** (口气) tone **II** [动] kiss

吻合 wěnhé [形] identical

紊 wěn [形] disorderly

紊乱 wěnluàn [形] chaotic

稳 wěn **I** [形] **1** (平稳) steady **2** (坚定) firm **3** (稳重) composed **4** (可靠) reliable **5** (肯定) sure ◊这场足球赛我们稳赢。We're sure to win this football match. **II** [动] keep calm (*pt, pp* kept)

稳操胜券 wěn cāo shèng quàn be sure to win ◊这场比赛，红队稳操胜券。The red team are sure to win this competition.

稳当 wěndang [形] **1** (牢稳) steady ◊她的孩子两岁时就走得很稳当了。At two years old her child was very steady on his legs. **2** (妥当) reliable

稳定 wěndìng **I** [形] steady ◊他有份十分稳定的工作。He's got a really steady job. ◊近期，市场物价稳定。Market prices have been stable recently. **II** [动] settle ◊新政策有助于稳定市场价格。The new policy will help to settle market prices.

稳固 wěngù **I** [形] stable **II** [动] firm ... up ◊他稳固了政权后，又推行了一系列改革措施。After firming up his political power, he carried out another series of reforms.

稳健 wěnjiàn [形] **1** (矫健) firm **2** (沉着) calm

稳妥 wěntuǒ [形] safe

稳重 wěnzhòng [形] steady

问 wèn **I** [动] **1** (提问) ask ◊他总是喜欢问各种问题。He likes to ask a lot of questions. **2** (问候) send regards to (*pt, pp* sent) ◊代我向你妈妈问好。Please send my regards to your mother. **3** (审讯) interrogate **4** (干预) ask about ◊她的父母从不过问她的工作。Her parents never asked about her work. **II** [介] from ◊我问他借了一支钢笔。I borrowed a pen from him. **III** [名] question ♦疑问 doubt

问寒问暖 wèn hán wèn nuǎn ask how things are going ◊老邻居之间总是问寒问暖。Old neighbours always ask each other how things are going.

问候 wènhòu [动] send regards to (*pt, pp* sent) ◊请代我问候你的爸妈。Please send my regards to your parents.

问津 wènjīn [动] (书) inquire about ◊退休人员的住房问题一直无人问津。Nobody ever inquires about the housing problems of retired people.

问世 wènshì [动] come out (*pt* came, *pp* come)

问题 wèntí [名] **1** (疑问) question ◊欢迎大家踊跃提问题。Everyone is invited to get up and ask questions. **2** (困难) problem ◊高校扩招造成了一定的就业问题。The expansion of higher education has created some employment problems. **3** (故障) fault ◊我的电脑出问题了。There's something wrong with my computer. **4** (关键) point ◊问题在于他还没意识到形势的严峻。The point is, he still hasn't realized how grim the situation is. **5** (分项) issue ◊今天开会主要讲两个问题。Today's meeting mainly concerns two issues.

问讯 wènxùn [动] **1** (打听) inquire ◊他到处问讯失散亲人的消息。He inquired all over the place about his lost relatives. **2** (审问) question

问罪 wènzuì [动] denounce

翁 wēng [名] **1** (配偶的父亲) father-in-law **2** (男性老人) old man (*pl* men)

嗡 wēng [拟] buzz

瓮 wèng [名] jar

莴 wō 见下文

莴笋 wōsǔn [名] asparagus lettuce

涡 wō [名] eddy

涡流 wōliú [名] whirlpool

窝 wō **I** [名] **1** (栖息地) nest **2** (小家)

home **3** (据点) den ◇这是一个贼窝。This is a den of thieves. **4** (凹陷处) depression ♦酒窝 dimple ◇当心，这里有个小水窝。Mind the puddle. **II** [动] **1** (藏匿) harbour (英), harbor (美) **2** (躲藏) hide (*pt* hid, *pp* hidden) **3** (停滞) halt **4** (郁积) contain ♦窝火 contain one's anger **5** (弯曲) bend (*pt, pp* bent) **III** [量] brood

窝藏 wōcáng [动] harbour (英), harbor (美)

窝火 wōhuǒ [动] seethe with anger

窝囊 wōnang [形] **1** (烦恼) annoyed **2** (软弱无能) hopeless

窝棚 wōpeng [名] shed

窝赃 wōzāng [动] conceal stolen goods

蜗 wō 见下文

蜗牛 wōniú [名] snail

我 wǒ [代] **1** (自己，作主语) I ◇我今天下午有事，不能开会了。I'm busy this afternoon so I can't go to the meeting. ◇她是我的同事。She's my colleague. **2** (自己，作宾语) me ◇请帮我一下。Please give me a hand. **3** (书) (我们) we ◇我公司最近更新了设备。Our company has recently updated its equipment. **4** (书) (我方) our side ◇敌我双方的力量悬殊较大。There's a big difference in strength between us and the enemy. **5** (自己) self ◇他的忘我精神令人佩服。Everyone admired his selflessness.

我们 wǒmen [代] **1** (作主语) we ◇我们去年去了希腊。Last year we went to Greece. ◇我们一起去公园吧。Let's go to the park. ◇我们的公寓非常干净。Our flat is very clean. **2** (作宾语) us ◇老师邀请我们去他家作客。Our teacher invited us to his house. **3** (我) I ◇我们孩子特别乖。My children are really good. ◇我们在论文中引用了大量的新数据。I've used a lot of new data in my thesis.

我行我素 wǒ xíng wǒ sù do things one's own way ◇她向来我行我素，不会因别人改变自己。She always does things her own way and doesn't change for anyone.

卧 wò **I** [动] **1** (躺) lie (*pt* lay, *pp* lain) ◇她睡觉时习惯侧卧。She tends to lie on her side when she sleeps. **2** (趴伏) sit (*pt, pp* sat) **II** [形] sleeping **III** [名] berth

卧病 wòbìng [动] be laid up

卧床 wòchuáng [动] stay in bed

卧底 wòdǐ [动] go undercover (*pt* went, *pp* gone)

卧铺 wòpù [名] berth

卧室 wòshì [名] bedroom

握 wò [动] **1** (抓) grasp **2** (掌握) master

握别 wòbié [动] part with a handshake

握手 wòshǒu [动] shake hands (*pt* shook, *pp* shaken)

斡 wò 见下文

斡旋 wòxuán [动] mediate ◇经过他的斡旋，两国签署了停战协议。Following his mediation, the two countries signed an armistice.

龌 wò 见下文

龌龊 wòchuò [形] **1** (肮脏) filthy **2** (喻) (指品质) dirty **3** (书) (指气量) narrow-minded

乌 wū **I** [名] crow **II** [形] black

乌龟 wūguī [名] tortoise

乌合之众 wū hé zhī zhòng (贬) mob

乌黑 wūhēi [形] jet-black

乌纱帽 wūshāmào [名] official post

乌烟瘴气 wū yān zhàng qì foul ◇别抽烟了，弄得房间里乌烟瘴气的。Don't smoke – it makes the room smell really foul.

乌有 wūyǒu [动] (书) not exist

乌云 wūyún [名] black cloud

污 wū **I** [名] dirt **II** [形] **1** (肮脏) dirty **2** (腐败) corrupt **III** [动] **1** (弄脏) dirty ◇当心，别污了新衣服。Careful not to dirty your new clothes. **2** (羞辱) smear

污点 wūdiǎn [名] stain ◇他的白衬衣上有好多污点。There were stains all over his white shirt. ◇这件事成了他终生洗不掉的污点。This affair became the stain that he was never able to wash away.

污垢 wūgòu [名] dirt

污秽 wūhuì **I** [名] filth **II** [形] filthy

污蔑 wūmiè [动] **1** (侮辱) slander **2** (玷污) tarnish

污染 wūrǎn [动] pollute ◇政府采取了一系列措施治理大气污染。The government has adopted a series of measures to combat air pollution.

污辱 wūrǔ [动] **1** (侮辱) insult **2** (玷污) sully

污浊 wūzhuó [形] filthy

巫 wū [名] sorcerer

巫师 wūshī [名] wizard

巫术 wūshù [名] witchcraft

呜 wū [拟] hoot

呜咽 wūyè [动] sob

诬 wū [动] falsely accuse

诬告 wūgào [动] falsely accuse

诬蔑 wūmiè [动] slander

诬陷 wūxiàn [动] frame

屋 wū [名] **1** (房子) house **2** (房间) room

屋顶 wūdǐng [名] roof

屋子 wūzi [名] room

无 wú **I** [动] **1** (没有) not have ♦无效 invalid ♦无形 invisible ◇他毫无常识。He has no common sense. ◇因发烧，我四肢无力。Because of the fever, my arms and legs were completely limp. **2** (无论) never mind ◇大家都在无日无夜地赶这个项目。Everyone worked day and night to get the project done. **II** [副] not ◇无论怎么解释，他也不肯原谅我。It doesn't matter how I explain it, he won't forgive me. ◇你无须多说，行动最有说服力。You don't need to say any more – actions speak louder than words.

无比 wúbǐ [形] incomparable

无边无际 wú biān wú jì boundless

无病呻吟 wú bìng shēnyín **1** (人) make a fuss about nothing **2** (文章) be excessively sentimental

无常 wúcháng [形] changeable

无偿 wúcháng [形] free

无耻 wúchǐ [形] shameless

无从 wúcóng [副] ◇这道题目很难，我感到无从入手。This question is so difficult – I don't know how I'm going to tackle it.

无敌 wúdí [动] invincible

无的放矢 wú dì fàng shǐ be aimless ◇复习时要目标明确，决不能无的放矢。When revising you need clear targets – never be aimless.

无地自容 wú dì zì róng feel too ashamed to show one's face

无动于衷 wú dòng yú zhōng be completely indifferent ◇他对妈妈的一番苦心无动于衷。He was completely indifferent to his mother's considerable efforts.

无独有偶 wú dú yǒu ǒu (贬) come in pairs ◇无独有偶，他丢了钥匙，钱包被偷了。These things come in pairs – just as he lost his keys, his wallet was stolen too.

无度 wúdù [形] excessive

无端 wúduān [副] for no reason ◇他无端受了批评，感到很委屈。He was upset at being criticized for no reason.

无恶不作 wú è bù zuò commit all kinds of atrocities

无法无天 wú fǎ wú tiān be completely lawless

无妨 wúfáng **I** [动] be harmless **II** [副] may as well ◇我有没讲清楚的地方，无妨提出来。If there's anything I haven't made clear, you may as well say so.

无非 wúfēi [副] simply

无辜 wúgū **I** [动] be innocent **II** [名] the innocent

无关 wúguān [动] have nothing to do with ◇这件事与你无关。This has nothing to do with you.

无稽 wújī [形] absurd

无几 wújǐ [形] very little

无济于事 wú jì yú shì be of no avail ◇我们怎么劝都无济于事，她还是哭个不停。However hard we tried to pacify her, it was to no avail – she still couldn't stop crying.

无精打采 wú jīng dǎ cǎi **1** (没有活力) be listless ◇夏天的午后，人们总是无精打采的。People are always listless on summer afternoons. **2** (情绪低落) be dispirited ◇他们比赛输了，个个无精打采地退了场。Having lost the game, they all left the pitch feeling very dispirited.

无拘无束 wú jū wú shù be free and easy ◇他向往无拘无束的生活。He longed for a free and easy life.

无可厚非 wú kě hòu fēi give no cause for criticism ◇她虽有点儿私心，但也无可厚非。Although she was a little selfish, that was no cause for criticism.

无可奈何 wú kě nàihé have no alternative ◇我一再坚持，妈妈终于无可奈何地同意让我出国读书。I persevered and persevered, and in the end my mother had no alternative but to agree to let me study abroad.

无可置疑 wú kě zhì yí be beyond doubt ◇他们夺冠的实力无可置疑。Their ability to win the championship was beyond doubt.

无孔不入 wú kǒng bù rù (贬) be everywhere ◇小偷无孔不入，大家要提高警惕。Thieves are everywhere and everybody should be on the lookout.

无愧 wúkuì [动] be worthy of ◇他无愧于"人民英雄"的称号。He was worthy of the title of "people's hero".

无赖 wúlài **I** [形] shameless **II** [名] rascal

无理取闹 wú lǐ qǔ nào be deliberately provocative

无量 wúliàng [动] be boundless

无论 wúlùn [连] no matter what ◇无论受到什么挫折，我们都不会退缩。No matter what setbacks we meet, we can't go back now.

无名 wúmíng [形] **1** (没名称的) unnamed **2** (不出名的) unknown **3** (匿名的) anonymous **4** (没来由的) indescribable

无奈 wúnài **I** [形] helpless **II** [连] but ◇我正想出门，无奈朋友来访，我只好作罢。I was just about to go out, but my friend came round so I had to drop my plans.

无能为力 wú néng wéi lì be powerless ◇这件事我实在无能为力。I'm powerless to do anything about this.

无奇不有 wú qí bù yǒu full of extraordinary things ◇他的科幻小说无奇不有，引人入胜。His science fiction novel was full of extraordinary things that people found fascinating.

无情 wúqíng [形] **1** (指感情) heartless **2** (不留情) ruthless

无穷 wúqióng [形] infinite

无伤大雅 wú shāng dàyǎ not matter much ◇这是朋友聚会，穿得随意些也无伤大雅。It's just a meeting of friends, so it doesn't matter much if you dress a bit casually.

无上 wúshàng [形] highest

无师自通 wú shī zì tōng self-taught ◇他对家电维修可谓无师自通。You could say he is self-taught when it comes to repairing electrical household goods.

无事生非 wú shì shēng fēi make a fuss about nothing

无数 wúshù **I** [形] countless **II** [动] be uncertain

无所事事 wú suǒ shì shì do nothing ◇失业后，他整天呆在家里无所事事。After he lost his job he stayed at home all day doing nothing.

无所适从 wú suǒ shì cóng be unsure what to do ◇大家都帮着出主意，他反而无所适从了。Everybody helped him to come up with ideas but he was unsure what to do.

无所谓 wúsuǒwèi [动] **1** (谈不上) never mind **2** (不在乎) be indifferent ◇她对别人的看法一向都持无所谓的态度。She was always indifferent to other people's views. ◇会议不重要，你来不来无所谓。The meeting isn't important so it doesn't matter if you're there or not.

无所作为 wú suǒ zuòwéi accomplish nothing

无微不至 wú wēi bù zhì meticulous ◊父母对子女的关爱无微不至。Parents are meticulous about caring for their children.

无谓 wúwèi [形] pointless

无限 wúxiàn [形] boundless

无线电 wúxiàndiàn [名] radio

无懈可击 wú xiè kě jī unassailable ◊他的回答无懈可击。His reply was unassailable.

无心 wúxīn **I** [动] not be in the mood for ◊儿子生病时，她根本无心工作。When her son was ill she wasn't in the mood to work. **II** [形] unintentional

无形 wúxíng **I** [形] imperceptible **II** [副] imperceptibly

无须 wúxū [副] needlessly ◊你无须多言，行动是最有力的证明。You needn't say much – actions speak a lot louder than words.

无意 wúyì **I** [动] have no intention of ◊我无意打断你们的谈话。I have no intention of interrupting you. **II** [形] inadvertent

无意识 wúyìshí [形] unconscious

无与伦比 wú yǔ lún bǐ unparalleled ◊金字塔是世界上无与伦比的建筑奇迹。The pyramids are marvels of construction that are unparalleled throughout the world.

无缘 wúyuán [动] have no luck with

无缘无故 wú yuán wú gù for no reason at all

无知 wúzhī [形] ignorant

无中生有 wú zhōng shēng yǒu make … up ◊你这是无中生有，造谣诬陷。You're just making it up and starting false rumours (英) 或 rumors (美).

无足轻重 wú zú qīng zhòng be insignificant

毋 wú [副] not

毋宁 wúnìng [副] rather

芜 wú **I** (书) [形] **1** (指草) overgrown with weeds **2** (指文辞) miscellaneous **II** [名] (书) grassland

芜杂 wúzá [形] disorderly

梧 wú 见下文

梧桐 wútóng [名] Chinese parasol tree

五 wǔ [名] five ◊他五岁时得了一场重病。When he was five, he contracted a serious illness. ◊今年的产量是去年的五倍。This year's output is five times last year's. ◊五分之一 one fifth

五大三粗 wǔ dà sān cū tall and well-built

五谷 wǔgǔ [名] crops (*pl*)

五官 wǔguān [名] the five sense organs

五光十色 wǔ guāng shí sè brilliantly-coloured (英) 或 colored (美)

五湖四海 wǔ hú sì hǎi all over the country ◊北京每天都迎来来自五湖四海的游客。Every day, people from all over the country come to Beijing.

五花八门 wǔ huā bā mén wide variety ◊五花八门的电视节目让我无从选择。I find it hard to select from such a wide variety of television programmes (英) 或 programs (美).

五金 wǔjīn [名] hardware

五体投地 wǔ tǐ tóu dì be lost in admiration

五味 wǔwèi [名] all sorts of flavours (英) 或 flavours (美)

五脏 wǔzàng [名] the five internal organs

午 wǔ [名] noon

午饭 wǔfàn [名] lunch

午夜 wǔyè [名] midnight

伍 wǔ [名] **1** (军队) army **2** (同辈) company ◊我不与虚伪的人为伍。I don't keep company with hypocrites. **3** (五) *an elaborate form of "five", used in writing cheques etc to prevent mistakes and forgery*

妩 wǔ 见下文

妩媚 wǔmèi [形] lovely

武 wǔ [形] **1** (军事的) military ♦武力 military force **2** (勇猛) valiant ♦威武 powerful

武打 wǔdǎ [名] *acrobatic fighting in Chinese opera*

武断 wǔduàn [动] be arbitrary

武功 wǔgōng [名] **1** (书) military exploits (*pl*) **2** (武术) martial arts (*pl*)

武官 wǔguān [名] **1** (指军队) officer **2** (指大使馆) attaché

武警 wǔjǐng [名] armed police

武力 wǔlì [名] **1** (军事力量) military strength **2** (暴力) force

武器 wǔqì [名] weapon

武士 wǔshì [名] warrior

武术 wǔshù [名] martial arts circles (*pl*)

武艺 wǔyì [名] skill in martial arts

武装 wǔzhuāng I [名] **1** (武装力量) armed forces (*pl*) **2** (武力) arms (*pl*) **3** (军备) armaments (*pl*) II [动] **1** (用武器) arm **2** (用精神、物质) equip

侮 wǔ [动] **1** (侮辱) insult **2** (外侵) foreign aggression

侮蔑 wǔmiè I [动] scorn II [形] scornful

侮辱 wǔrǔ [动] insult

捂 wǔ [动] cover

舞 wǔ I [名] dance II [动] **1** (跳舞) dance **2** (飞舞) flutter **3** (挥舞) brandish **4** (玩弄) play with

舞弊 wǔbì [动] embezzle

舞蹈 wǔdǎo [名] dance

舞剧 wǔjù [名] ballet

舞台 wǔtái [名] stage

勿 wù [副] not ◇请勿吸烟 no smoking ◇请勿入内 no entry

勿忘草 wùwàngcǎo [名] forget-me-not

务 wù I [名] business ◇我有要务在身。I've got urgent business. ◇他负责公司内务。He's in charge of the company's internal affairs. II [动] be engaged in III [副] without fail

务必 wùbì [副] without fail

务实 wùshí [动] be pragmatic

务虚 wùxū [动] discuss principles

坞 wù [名] **1** (指地形) depression ♦村坞 village settlement ♦山坞 col **2** (指建筑) ♦花坞 sunken flowerbed ♦船坞 dock

物 wù [名] **1** (东西) thing **2** (物产) produce **3** (动物) creature **4** (指哲学) matter **5** (指法律) property **6** (指环境) the outside world **7** (内容) content

物产 wùchǎn [名] produce

物极必反 wù jí bì fǎn things go into reverse when pushed to the extreme ◇不要总是批评学生，否则，物极必反。Don't criticize the students or it may backfire on you.

物价 wùjià [名] price

物件 wùjiàn [名] article

物理 wùlǐ [名] **1** (书) (常理) laws of nature (*pl*) **2** (指学科) physics (*sg*)

物力 wùlì [名] material resources (*pl*)

物品 wùpǐn [名] article

物色 wùsè [动] look for

物体 wùtǐ [名] body

物业 wùyè [名] property

物证 wùzhèng [名] material evidence

物质 wùzhì [名] **1** (哲) matter **2** (非精神) material things (*pl*)

物种 wùzhǒng [名] species

物资 wùzī [名] material

误 wù I [名] mistake II [形] **1** (不正确) erroneous ♦误会 misunderstand **2** (非故意) accidental ♦误伤 accidentally injure III [动] **1** (耽误) miss ◇快点儿，别误了火车！Hurry up – we don't want to miss the train! **2** (损害) harm

误差 wùchā [名] error

误导 wùdǎo [动] mislead (*pt, pp* misled)

误会 wùhuì [动] misunderstand (*pt, pp* misunderstood)

误解 wùjiě [动] misunderstand (*pt, pp* misunderstood)

误区 wùqū [名] long-standing misunderstanding

误人子弟 wùrénzǐdì lead young people astray

误事 wùshì [动] mess things up ◇不提前做好准备，就会误事。You'll mess things up if you don't prepare in advance.

恶 wù [动] loathe
▷另见 ě, è

悟 wù [动] realize

悟性 wùxing [名] intelligence ◇他学钢琴很有悟性。He has picked up the piano very quickly.

晤 wù 见下文

晤谈 wùtán (书) [动] discuss … face-to-face ◇他每周与导师晤谈一次。He has a face-to-face discussion with his supervisor once a week.

焐 wù [动] **1** (使变暖) warm … up ◇冬天，她用暖水袋焐脚。During winter she uses a hot water bottle to warm her feet up. **2** (保温) keep … warm (*pt, pp* kept) ◇把饭放在锅里焐着。You should keep the rice warm in the pot.

骛 wù [动] seek (*pt, pp* sought)

雾 wù [名] fog

雾里看花 wù lǐ kàn huā have blurred vision ◇摘了眼镜，她看什么都好像雾里看花。When she took her glasses off everything was blurred.

雾茫茫 wùmāngmāng [形] foggy

Xx

夕 xī [名] **1** (傍晚) sunset **2** (晚上) evening ♦除夕 New Year's Eve

夕阳 xīyáng [名] setting sun

西 xī [名] **1** (方向) west **2** (疆域) the West

西餐 xīcān [名] Western food

西方 Xīfāng [名] the West

西服 xīfú [名] Western clothes

西化 xīhuà [动] Westernize

西洋 Xīyáng [名] the West

西药 xīyào [名] Western medicine

西医 xīyī [名] **1** (药品) Western medicine **2** (医生) doctor

西乐 xīyuè [名] Western music

西装 xīzhuāng [名] Western clothes

吸 xī [动] **1** (气、水等) draw ... in (*pt* drew, *pp* drawn) ♦吸气 breathe ◊用吸管吸酸奶 drink yoghurt with a straw **2** (吸收) absorb ◊用海绵吸水 mop up water with a sponge **3** (吸引) attract ◊异性相吸 opposites attract

吸尘器 xīchénqì [名] vacuum cleaner

吸纳 xīnà [动] attract

吸取 xīqǔ [动] absorb ◊吸取热量 absorb heat ◊吸取教训 draw a lesson ◊吸取知识 acquire knowledge

吸收 xīshōu [动] **1** (摄取) absorb **2** (接纳) recruit ◊俱乐部吸收了一批海外球员。The club has recruited some foreign players.

吸引 xīyǐn [动] attract

汐 xī [名] evening tide ♦潮汐 morning and evening tides (*pl*)

希 xī I [动] hope II [形] 稀

希罕 xīhan I [形] rare II [动] cherish III [名] rarity

希奇 xīqí [形] strange

希望 xīwàng I [动] hope ◊她希望早点嫁人。She's hoping to get married soon. ◊我希望你成个大歌星。I hope you make it as a pop star. II [名] hope ◊他的病有希望了。There's hope he will recover. ◊这批小球员大有希望。These young footballers show a lot of promise.

昔 xī [名] the past

昔日 xīrì [名] former times (*pl*)

析 xī [动] **1** (分开) separate **2** (解释) analyse (英), analyze (美) ♦剖析 analyse

牺 xī 见下文

牺牲 xīshēng [动] **1** (献身) sacrifice oneself ◊他为救落水儿童牺牲了。He lost his life saving the drowning child. **2** (放弃) sacrifice ◊牺牲个人利益 sacrifice personal gain

息 xī I [名] **1** (呼吸) breath **2** (消息) news (*sg*) **3** (利息) interest II [动] **1** (休息) rest ♦歇息 have a rest **2** (停止) stop ♦息怒 calm down

息怒 xīnù [动] calm down

息事宁人 xī shì níng rén keep the peace

息息相关 xī xī xiāng guān be closely connected with ◊当今任何一个国家所发生的事情都和整个世界息息相关。Today, events in any individual country are closely connected with the rest of the world.

奚 xī 见下文

奚落 xīluò [动] mock

悉 xī I [形] ♦悉心 devote all one's attention to II [动] learn ♦获悉 learn of an event

淅 xī 见下文

淅沥 xīlì [拟] pitter-patter

惜 xī [动] **1** (珍惜) cherish ◊惜时如命 regard one's time as precious **2** (可惜) pity ♦惋惜 feel sorry for **3** (吝惜) spare ♦吝惜 stint ◊不惜一切代价 at any price

惜别 xībié [动] part reluctantly

惜力 xīlì [动] not give one's all ◇他工作时从不惜力。He always gives his all at work.

晰 xī [形] clear ♦清晰 distinct

稀 xī [形] 1 (稀有) rare 2 (稀疏) sparse ◇奶奶的头发太稀了。Granny's hair is very thin. 3 (水多的) watery ♦稀饭 rice porridge

稀薄 xībó [形] thin

稀客 xīkè [名] infrequent visitor

稀里糊涂 xīlihútú muddle-headed

稀少 xīshǎo [形] sparse

稀疏 xīshū [形] scattered

稀松 xīsōng [形] sloppy

稀稀拉拉 xīxilālā sparse

稀有 xīyǒu [形] rare

犀 xī [名] rhinoceros

犀利 xīlì [形] penetrating ◇犀利的评论 incisive comments ◇犀利的目光 sharp eyes

犀牛 xīniú [名] rhinoceros

锡 xī [名] tin

锡箔 xībó [名] tinfoil

溪 xī [名] brook

溪流 xīliú [名] brook

熙 xī 见下文

熙熙攘攘 xīxī rǎngrǎng bustling

熄 xī [动] put … out (*pt, pp* put) ♦熄灯 put out the light ◇他的车在半坡上熄火了。His car gave out halfway up the slope.

熄灭 xīmiè [动] put … out (*pt, pp* put)

嘻 xī I [叹] wow ◇嘻，魔术师太神了！ Wow! The magician is amazing! II [拟] ha ha

嘻嘻哈哈 xīxī hāhā laughing ◇一群年轻人坐在草地上嘻嘻哈哈地说笑。A crowd of young people sat on the grass laughing and chatting.

膝 xī [名] knee ♦屈膝 kneel

嬉 xī [动] (书) play ♦嬉戏 play

嬉皮士 xīpíshì [名] hippie

嬉皮笑脸 xī pí xiào liǎn grin cheekily

蹊 xī [名] (书) footpath ▷另见 qī

蹊径 xījìng [名] (书) path

曦 xī [名] (书) sunlight ♦晨曦 early morning sunlight

习 xí I [动] 1 (学习) practise (英), practice (美) ♦习武 study martial arts 2 (熟悉) be used to ◇习以为常 become used to II [名] custom ♦习俗 custom ♦习气 bad habit

习惯 xíguàn I [动] be used to ◇我习惯早起。I'm used to getting up early. II [名] habit

习气 xíqì [名] bad habit

习俗 xísú [名] custom

习题 xítí [名] exercises (*pl*)

习习 xíxí [形] gently blowing

习性 xíxìng [名] habits (*pl*)

习以为常 xí yǐ wéi cháng become used to ◇大熊猫对人山人海的参观者已经习以为常了。The panda has long become accustomed to the huge crowds of visitors.

习语 xíyǔ [名] idiom

习作 xízuò [名] sketch

席 xí I [名] 1 (编织物) mat ♦竹席 bamboo mat 2 (座位) seat ♦席位 seat ♦出席 be present 3 (宴席) feast ♦酒席 banquet II [量] ◇一席长谈 a long chat ◇一席佳肴 a table covered with delicacies

席地 xídì [动] sit on the ground (*pt, pp* sat)

席卷 xíjuǎn [动] engulf

席位 xíwèi [名] seat

袭 xí [动] 1 (攻击) make a surprise attack ♦空袭 air raid 2 (仿做) follow the pattern of ♦抄袭 plagiarize

袭击 xíjī [动] attack

袭用 xíyòng [动] follow

媳 xí [名] daughter-in-law (*pl* daughters-in-law)

媳妇 xífù [名] 1 (儿子的妻子) daughter-in-law (*pl* daughters-in-law) **2** (晚辈的妻子) wife (*pl* wives) ◊侄媳妇 nephew's wife

媳妇儿 xífur [名] **1** (方) (妻子) wife (*pl* wives) **2** (妇女) married woman (*pl* women)

洗 xǐ [动] **1** (衣、碗等) wash ♦洗衣店 Launderette® (英), Laundromat® (美) **2** (胶卷) develop **3** (录音、录像) wipe **4** (麻将、扑克) shuffle **5** (洗礼) baptize **6** (洗劫) loot **7** (洗雪) redress ♦洗冤 redress a wrong

洗尘 xǐchén [动] give a dinner of welcome (*pt* gave, *pp* given)

洗涤 xǐdí [动] wash

洗耳恭听 xǐ ěr gōng tīng listen in respectful silence

洗劫 xǐjié [动] loot

洗礼 xǐlǐ [名] **1** (宗) baptism **2** (喻) (考验) trial

洗钱 xǐqián [动] launder money

洗刷 xǐshuā [动] **1** (地板、厕所) scrub **2** (耻辱、污点) clear oneself of

洗心革面 xǐ xīn gé miàn turn over a new leaf

洗衣机 xǐyījī [名] washing machine

洗澡 xǐzǎo [动] have a bath

喜 xǐ **I** [形] **1** (高兴) happy ♦欢喜 happy **2** (可贺的) celebratory **II** [动] **1** (爱好) like ♦喜好 like **2** (适宜) suit **III** [名] (口) pregnancy ♦有喜 be pregnant

喜爱 xǐ'ài [动] like

喜出望外 xǐ chū wàng wài be overjoyed at unexpected news

喜好 xǐhào [动] like

喜欢 xǐhuan [动] like

喜剧 xǐjù [名] comedy

喜庆 xǐqìng [形] joyous

喜鹊 xǐque [名] magpie

喜事 xǐshì [名] **1** (开心事) happy event **2** (婚礼) wedding ◊他俩决定从简办喜事。The couple decided on a simple wedding.

喜闻乐见 xǐ wén lè jiàn love to be entertained by ◊说书是中国人喜闻乐见的民间艺术。Story-telling is a folk art much loved by the Chinese.

喜笑颜开 xǐ xiào yán kāi light up ◊老人一见到孙子就喜笑颜开的。As soon as the old man sees his grandchild his face lights up.

喜形于色 xǐ xíng yú sè beam with pleasure

喜洋洋 xǐyángyáng [形] beaming

喜悦 xǐyuè [形] happy ◊掩饰不住内心的喜悦 be unable to hide one's happiness

禧 xǐ [名] (书) happiness ♦福禧 good fortune

戏 xì **I** [动] **1** (玩耍) play ♦嬉戏 have fun **2** (嘲弄) joke ♦戏弄 tease **II** [名] show ♦京戏 Beijing Opera ♦马戏 circus

戏法 xìfǎ [名] magic

戏剧 xìjù [名] theatre (英), theater (美)

戏弄 xìnòng [动] tease ◊他没有发觉自己是在受人戏弄。He didn't realize he was being teased.

戏曲 xìqǔ [名] Chinese opera

戏院 xìyuàn [名] theatre (英), theater (美)

系 xì **I** [名] **1** (系统) system ♦星系 galaxy **2** (部门) department ♦法语系 French department **II** [动] **1** (拴) tie ◊把绳子系在树上 tie a rope to a tree **2** (在) relate to ◊战争胜败系此一役。Success or failure in the war comes down to the campaign. **3** (书) (是) be (*pt* was, were, *pp* been) ◊纯系捏造 be pure fabrication
▷另见 jì

系列 xìliè [名] series (*sg*)

系数 xìshù [名] coefficient

系统 xìtǒng [名] system

细 xì **I** [形] **1** (绳、线等) thin **2** (沙、粮等) fine **3** (声、语等) gentle **4** (节、则等) detailed ♦细节 details (*pl*) **II** [副] minutely ♦细看 scrutinize ◊细问 ask in detail ◊细想 consider carefully

细胞 xìbāo [名] cell

细节 xìjié [名] details (*pl*)

细菌 xìjūn [名] germ

细密 xìmì [形] **1** (精细) finely woven **2** (仔细) detailed

细腻 xìnì [形] exquisite

细微 xìwēi [形] subtle

细心 xìxīn [形] careful

细则 xìzé [名] detailed rules (*pl*)

细枝末节 xì zhī mò jié minor details (*pl*)

细致 xìzhì [副] meticulously

隙 xì [名] **1** (指物体) crack ◆岩隙 crevice **2** (指情感) rift ◇二人向来有隙。There's always been disagreement between them. **3** (漏洞) opportunity

呷 xiā [动] (方) sip ◇呷一口酒 take a sip of wine

虾 xiā [名] shrimp ◆龙虾 lobster

瞎 xiā **I** [形] **1** (失明) blind **2** (方) (糟蹋) wasted **II** [副] groundlessly

瞎扯 xiāchě [动] talk nonsense

瞎话 xiāhuà [名] lie

瞎子 xiāzi [名] blind man/woman ◇她是瞎子。She is blind.

匣 xiá [名] box ◆金属匣 metal box

匣子 xiázi [名] box

侠 xiá **I** [名] knight **II** [形] chivalrous ◆侠义 chivalrous

侠客 xiákè [名] knight

峡 xiá [名] gorge ◆海峡 strait ◇三峡工程 the Three Gorges Project

峡谷 xiágǔ [名] canyon

狭 xiá [形] narrow ◆狭窄 narrow

狭隘 xiá'ài [形] narrow ◇心胸狭隘 narrow-minded

狭路相逢 xiá lù xiāng féng come into unavoidable confrontation

狭小 xiáxiǎo [形] cramped ◇狭小的空间 cramped space ◇作为领导他的气量过于狭小。He was too narrow-minded a leader.

狭义 xiáyì [名] narrow sense

狭窄 xiázhǎi [形] narrow

遐 xiá 见下文

遐迩闻名 xiá ěr wén míng (书) be known far and wide

遐想 xiáxiǎng [动] daydream

瑕 xiá [名] flaw ◇洁白无瑕 spotlessly white

瑕不掩瑜 xiá bù yǎn yú small failings do not detract from overall excellence ◇她的缺点和优点相比可以说是瑕不掩瑜。On balance, her strong points more than make up for her weaknesses.

瑕疵 xiácī [名] blemish

暇 xiá [名] time

辖 xiá [动] have jurisdiction ◆直辖 under direct jurisdiction

辖区 xiáqū [名] area of jurisdiction

辖制 xiázhì [动] control

霞 xiá [名] red sky ◆彩霞 red sky

霞光 xiáguāng [名] rays of sunlight (*pl*)

下 xià **I** [动] **1** (走下) go down (*pt* went, *pp* gone) ◆下山 go down the mountain ◆下楼 go downstairs ◇下船 disembark from a boat ◇下床 get out of bed **2** (落下) fall (*pt* fell, *pp* fallen) ◆下雨 rain ◆下雪 snow **3** (传发) issue ◆下令 issue an order **4** (下锅煮) put … in (*pt, pp* put) ◇下面条 put the noodles into the boiling water **5** (给出) give (*pt* gave, *pp* given) **6** (开始) begin (*pt* began, *pp* begun) ◆下笔 start to write **7** (结束) finish ◆下班 finish work ◆下课 finish class **8** (生下) ◆下蛋 lay an egg ◇下猪崽 have a litter of piglets **9** (用于动词后，表示由高到低) ◇落下 fall down **10** (用于动词后，表示有些空间) ◇车里装不下这么多东西。We won't be able to fit so many things in the car. **11** (用于动词后，表示脱离物体) ◇拧下灯泡 unscrew a light bulb **12** (用于动词后，表示动作完成) ◇记录下会议内容 take the minutes at a meeting ◇他拿下了乒乓球比赛的第一局。He won the first set in table tennis. **II** [名] **1** (低) ◆下层 lower level ◆下品 inferior products (*pl*) **2** (另) ◇下次 next time **3** (指方位或时间) ◆眼下

at the moment ◊树下 under the tree ◊楼下 downstairs **4** (指范围、情况、条件) ◊在朋友的帮助下 with help from friends ◊在权威的压力下 under pressure from authority **III** [量] ◊我拍了他好几下才把他叫醒。Only after slapping him a few times did I wake him up.

下班 xiàbān [动] finish work

下辈子 xià bèizi [名] the next life

下笔 xiàbǐ [动] start to write

下不为例 xià bù wéi lì not to be repeated ◊这次的事就算了，下不为例。I'll forget about it this time, but it mustn't be repeated.

下策 xiàcè [名] bad move

下层 xiàcéng [名] lower level

下场 xiàchǎng [动] **1** (退场) leave the pitch (*pt, pp* left) ◊大卫只踢了不到10分钟就下场了。David had been playing for less than ten minutes when he left the pitch. **2** (下舞台) go off stage (*pt* went, *pp* gone)

下场 xiàchǎng [名] end ◊悲惨的下场 a tragic end ◊你这样做不会有好下场。If you do this, the result will be disastrous.

下达 xiàdá [动] issue

下跌 xiàdiē [动] fall (*pt* fell, *pp* fallen) ◊物价在下跌。Prices are falling.

下放 xiàfàng [动] (降职) be demoted

下岗 xiàgǎng [动] **1** (完工) leave one's post (*pt, pp* left) **2** (失业) be laid off

下海 xiàhǎi [动] **1** (指捕鱼) go out to sea (*pt* went, *pp* gone) **2** (指经商) go into business (*pt* went, *pp* gone)

下怀 xiàhuái [名] one's heart's desire ◊正中下怀 be exactly what one wants

下级 xiàjí [名] subordinate

下贱 xiàjiàn [形] (讳) contemptible

下课 xiàkè [动] finish class ◊下课了，大家可以走了。Class is over – everyone can go.

下款 xiàkuǎn [名] signature

下来 xiàlái **I** [动] **1** (指由高到低) come down (*pt* came, *pp* come) ◊我不上去了，你下来吧。I won't come up – you come down. **2** (指作物成熟) be harvested **3** (用于动词后，指脱离物体) ◊那孩子从床上摔了下来。The child fell off the bed. ◊他把眼睛摘了下来。He took off his glasses. ◊他把书中的一页撕了下来。He tore a page out of the book. **4** (用于动词后，指持续时间) ◊这条老规矩是祖上传下来的。This custom has been passed down by our predecessors. ◊学习非常艰难，但他坚持下来了。Studying was arduous, but he persisted. **5** (用于动词后，表示动作完成) ◊夫妇俩的争吵平息下来了。The couple's argument petered out. ◊这道难题我们一定要拿下来。We certainly need to sort out this problem. **6** (表示出现某种状态) ◊队伍的步伐慢了下来。The pace of the team began to slow. ◊灯光暗了下来。The light started to fade.

下流 xiàliú [形] dirty ◊下流的玩笑 dirty jokes

下落 xiàluò [名] whereabouts (*pl*)

下马 xiàmǎ [动] **1** (指骑马) dismount **2** (喻) (停工) abandon

下马威 xiàmǎwēi [名] initial show of strength

下面 xiàmian **I** [副] **1** (指位置) underneath **2** (指次序) next ◊这个问题我下面会谈到的。I will discuss this question next. **II** [名] lower levels (*pl*)

下去 xiàqù **I** [动] **1** (指由高到低) go down (*pt* went, *pp* gone) **2** (指时间的延续) continue **3** (用于动词后，指空间上) ◊从楼上跳下去 jump from a building ◊把部队从前线撤下去 withdraw troops from the frontline **4** (时间上的持续) ◊这口气他忍不下去。He won't be able to go on in that vein. **5** (指数量下降) ◊高烧已经退下去了。His temperature has already gone down. **6** (指程度深化) ◊天气有可能热下去。The weather will probably go on getting hotter. ◊他狠不下去心戒毒。He's unable to endure detox any longer.

下手 xiàshǒu **I** [名] assistant **II** [动] begin (*pt* began, *pp* begun)

下属 xiàshǔ [名] subordinate

下水 xiàshuǐ **I** [动] **1** (入水) launch **2** (入伙) get into trouble **II** [名] down river

下榻 xiàtà [动] (书) stay

下台 xiàtái [动] 1 (下舞台) step down 2 (交权) step down 3 (难堪) get out of an awkward situation ◇你这样做真让我下不来台。If you do this, you'll be putting me in an awkward situation.

下网 xiàwǎng [动] 1 (撒网) cast a net (*pt*, *pp* cast) 2 (计算机) go offline (*pt* went, *pp* gone)

下文 xiàwén [名] 1 (指文章) ◇一看下文他才知道是怎么回事。As soon as he read what followed, he understood what had happened. 2 (喻) (指结果) further development

下午 xiàwǔ [名] afternoon

下限 xiàxiàn [名] ◇我们的计划最好早一点儿完成，下限不得超过月底。It would be best to complete the scheme early – at the very latest we must be finished by the end of the month.

下意识 xiàyìshí [名] subconscious

下游 xiàyóu [名] 1 (指江河) lower reaches (*pl*) 2 (喻) (指地位) bottom

下载 xiàzǎi [动] download

吓 xià [动] frighten ♦惊吓 scare ◇那部电影真吓人。That film is quite frightening.
▷另见 hè

吓唬 xiàhu [动] frighten

夏 xià [名] summer ♦盛夏 the height of summer

夏历 xiàlì [名] lunar calendar

夏令营 xiàlìngyíng [名] summer camp

夏天 xiàtiān [名] summer

仙 xiān [名] immortal ♦成仙 become immortal

仙境 xiānjìng [名] fairyland

仙女 xiānnǚ [名] fairy

仙人 xiānrén [名] immortal

先 xiān [形] 1 (指时间) earlier ♦事先 beforehand 2 (敬) (指人) late ♦先父 one's late father

先辈 xiānbèi [名] ancestors (*pl*)

先导 xiāndǎo [名] guide

先锋 xiānfēng [名] vanguard

先河 xiānhé [名] start

先后 xiānhòu I [名] ◇公司晋升不分先后，只凭个人能力。The company makes no distinction as to seniority but promotes people on the basis of ability. II [副] successively

先进 xiānjìn [形] advanced

先决 xiānjué [形] prerequisite

先前 xiānqián [名] the past

先遣 xiānqiǎn [形] advance

先驱 xiānqū [名] pioneer

先人 xiānrén [名] ancestor

先声夺人 xiān shēng duó rén show of strength

先生 xiānsheng [名] 1 (指男士) Mr ◇吴先生 Mr Wu 2 (老师) teacher 3 (丈夫) husband 4 (医生) doctor

先天 xiāntiān [名] ◇你臂上的印记是先天的吗？ Is that a birth mark on your arm?

先行 xiānxíng [动] 1 (先走) go ahead (*pt* went, *pp* gone) 2 (优先) ◇本规定在部分城市先行实施。This regulation is being implemented ahead of time in just a few cities.

先兆 xiānzhào [名] omen

纤 xiān [形] fine ♦纤小 fine
▷另见 qiàn

纤巧 xiānqiǎo [形] delicate

纤维 xiānwéi [名] fibre

纤细 xiānxì [形] fine

掀 xiān [动] lift ◇大风掀了房顶。The gale blew the roof off.

掀起 xiānqǐ [动] 1 (揭起) lift 2 (涌起) surge 3 (兴起) start

锨 xiān [名] shovel ♦铁锨 shovel

鲜 xiān I [形] 1 (新鲜) fresh ♦鲜桃 fresh peaches 2 (鲜美) delicious II [名] delicacy ♦海鲜 seafood

鲜活 xiānhuó [形] live

鲜货 xiānhuò [名] fresh produce

鲜美 xiānměi [形] delicious

鲜明 xiānmíng [形] 1 (鲜艳) bright 2 (突显) distinct

鲜艳 xiānyàn [形] brightly-coloured (英), brightly-colored (美)

闲 xián I [形] 1 (不忙) idle ◇他直到退休后才闲下来。Only when he retired did he start to take it easy. 2 (安静) quiet 3 (闲置) unused ♦闲房 empty house ♦闲田 fallow fields (*pl*) II [名] leisure

闲话 xiánhuà [名] 1 (流言) gossip 2 (废话) digression

闲情逸致 xián qíng yì zhì be in a carefree mood ◇没想到您还有钓鱼这种闲情逸致。I never expected you to be in the mood for fishing.

闲人 xiánrén [名] layabout

闲散 xiánsǎn [形] free

闲事 xiánshì [名] other people's business

闲暇 xiánxiá [名] leisure

闲言碎语 xián yán suì yǔ gossip

闲杂 xiánzá [形] miscellaneous

闲置 xiánzhì [动] be unused ◇闲置资金 unused funds

贤 xián I [形] virtuous ♦贤达 worthy II [名] virtuous person

贤惠 xiánhuì [形] kind-hearted

贤明 xiánmíng [形] wise

贤妻良母 xián qī liáng mǔ good wife and loving mother

弦 xián [名] 1 (指乐器) string ♦小提琴弦 violin string 2 (指钟表) spring 3 (数) hypotenuse

弦外之音 xián wài zhī yīn implication

咸 xián [形] salted ♦咸菜 pickled vegetables (*pl*) ◇这汤稍有点咸。The soup's a little salty.

涎 xián [名] saliva ♦垂涎 drool

涎皮赖脸 xián pí lài liǎn be brazen

娴 xián [形] 1 (书) (文雅) refined ♦娴雅 elegant 2 (熟练) skilled ♦娴熟 skilled

娴静 xiánjìng [形] refined

娴雅 xiányǎ [形] elegant

衔 xián I [动] 1 (噙) hold … in the mouth (*pt, pp* held) ◇她嘴里衔着一支铅笔。She had a pencil in her mouth. 2 (连) link … up ♦衔接 link … up II [名] rank ♦军衔 military rank

衔接 xiánjiē [动] link up

舷 xián [名] side of a boat ♦左舷 port ♦右舷 starboard ♦舷梯 gangway

嫌 xián I [动] dislike ◇我们嫌老板太挑剔。We dislike our boss because he's too fussy. ◇我抽支烟你嫌不嫌？ Do you mind if I smoke? ◇他嫌这儿吵，搬走了。He found it too noisy here and moved away. II [名] 1 (嫌怨) grudge ◇二人捐弃了前嫌。The two of them buried old grudges. 2 (嫌疑) suspicion ◇他因涉嫌贪污被逮捕。He was arrested on suspicion of corruption.

嫌弃 xiánqì [动] cold-shoulder

嫌恶 xiánwù [动] detest

嫌疑 xiányí [名] suspicion

显 xiǎn I [动] 1 (表现) display ◇各显其能 each displaying their skill 2 (呈现) be apparent ◇她40多了，一点也不显老。She's over 40 but doesn't look it. II [形] illustrious ♦显赫 celebrated

显而易见 xiǎn ér yì jiàn obvious

显赫 xiǎnhè [形] illustrious

显露 xiǎnlù [动] appear

显然 xiǎnrán [副] obviously ◇他的成绩显然。His achievements are obvious.

显示 xiǎnshì [动] demonstrate

显眼 xiǎnyǎn [形] conspicuous ◇她的胸针很显眼。Her brooch is very showy.

显要 xiǎnyào I [形] influential II [名] influential figure

显著 xiǎnzhù [形] striking

险 xiǎn [形] 1 (险要) strategic ♦险地 strategic position 2 (危险) dangerous ♦险境 dangerous situation 3 (狠毒) vicious ♦阴险 sinister

险恶 xiǎn'è [形] **1** (阴险恶毒) sinister **2** (危险可怕) perilous

险峻 xiǎnjùn [形] precipitous

险情 xiǎnqíng [名] hazard

险胜 xiǎnshèng [动] narrowly win (*pt, pp* won) ◇英格兰队以1比0险胜阿根廷。England narrowly beat Argentina one-nil.

险要 xiǎnyào [名] strategic location

险阻 xiǎnzǔ [名] difficulty

县 xiàn [名] county

现 xiàn **I** [形] **1** (现在) present ♦现状 present situation **2** (现有) ready ♦现钱 ready money **II** [副] on the spot **III** [动] reveal ♦现形 give oneself away **IV** [名] ready money ♦兑现 cash a cheque (英) 或 check (美)

现场 xiànchǎng [名] scene ◇犯罪现场 scene of the crime ◇现场报道 live report

现成 xiànchéng [形] ready-made ◇现成的解决问题的方法 a ready-made solution to the problem

现代 xiàndài [名] modern times (*pl*) ◇现代通讯器材 modern communications equipment

现今 xiànjīn [名] today ◇现今的生产力远非50年前可比。Production today can't be compared with that of 50 years ago.

现金 xiànjīn [名] cash

现身说法 xiàn shēn shuō fǎ cite one's own experience

现实 xiànshí [名] reality ◇现实主义 realism

现象 xiànxiàng [名] phenomenon (*pl* phenomena)

现行 xiànxíng [形] current

现眼 xiànyǎn [动] make a fool of oneself

现役 xiànyì **I** [名] active service **II** [形] active

现在 xiànzài [名] now ◇他要我们现在就去。He wants us to go now. ◇你的笔记本电脑现在不在我手里。I don't have your laptop at the moment.

> 📖 **now** 和 **at present** 都可用来表示说话时存在或发生的事物。**now** 可以指一段时间或者某个具体时刻。*She gradually built up energy and is now back to normal… I'm feeling much better now… I'm going home now.* **at present** 指一段时间，并且暗示情况可能会发生改变。语体较为正式。*I don't want to get married at present… At present there is a world energy shortage.* **presently** 表示不久，是有些过时的用法。*The Prince of Wales will be here presently … I shall have more to say presently.* **presently** 有时跟 **at present** 的用法一样，但有人认为这种用法是不正确的。*We are presently looking at ways to cut costs.*

现状 xiànzhuàng [名] the current situation

限 xiàn **I** [动] limit ◇自愿捐赠，款数不限。There are no limits on voluntary contributions. ◇此项权利只限本地区居民享用。This right is limited to people resident in the area. **II** [名] limit ♦权限 the limits of power (*pl*)

限定 xiàndìng [动] restrict

限度 xiàndù [名] limit

限量 xiànliàng [动] limit

限令 xiànlìng [动] order

限期 xiànqī **I** [动] set a deadline (*pt, pp* set) **II** [名] deadline

限制 xiànzhì **I** [动] restrict ◇这种产品出口有限制。There are restrictions on the export of this kind of product.

线 xiàn **I** [名] **1** (指细长物品) thread ♦棉线 cotton thread ♦电线 electric wire **2** (交通干线) line ♦主线 main line **II** [量] ◇一线生机 a ray of hope

线路 xiànlù [名] **1** (指交通) route **2** (指电流等) circuit

线索 xiànsuǒ [名] clue

线条 xiàntiáo [名] (指绘画) line

宪 xiàn [名] constitution ♦立宪 constitutionalism

宪法 xiànfǎ [名] constitution

宪章 xiànzhāng [名] charter

陷 xiàn I [名] 1 (书) (陷阱) trap 2 (过失) fault ♦缺陷 defect II [动] 1 (沉入) get bogged down ◊小心别陷进沼泽里。Be careful not to get stuck in the marsh. 2 (凹进) sink (*pt* sank, *pp* sunk) ◊房子的地基陷下去了。The house's foundations have subsided somewhat. 3 (卷入) get involved ◊他陷在一场政治斗争中不能脱身。He's got involved in a political conflict he can't extricate himself from.

陷害 xiànhài [动] frame

陷阱 xiànjǐng [名] trap

陷落 xiànluò [动] 1 (下陷) sink (*pt* sank, *pp* sunk) 2 (被攻陷) be captured by the enemy

馅 xiàn [名] stuffing ◊饺子馅 jiaozi filling

馅儿饼 xiànrbǐng [名] pie

羡 xiàn [动] admire

羡慕 xiànmù [动] envy

献 xiàn [动] 1 (给) give (*pt* gave, *pp* given) ♦献花 give flowers ♦献血 donate blood 2 (表演) show (*pt* showed, *pp* shown) ♦献技 display one's skill

献丑 xiànchǒu [动] (谦) show oneself up (*pt* showed, *pp* shown)

献词 xiàncí [名] message of congratulation

献礼 xiànlǐ [动] present a gift

献身 xiànshēn [动] devote one's life to

献殷勤 xiàn yīnqín [动] be attentive ◊他拼命向姑娘献殷勤。He was very attentive to the young lady.

腺 xiàn [名] gland ♦泪腺 tear duct

乡 xiāng [名] 1 (乡村) countryside 2 (家乡) home town 3 (行政区划) township

乡村 xiāngcūn [名] village

乡亲 xiāngqīn [名] 1 (同乡) fellow townspeople 2 (当地群众) local people

乡土 xiāngtǔ [名] native soil

乡下 xiāngxia [名] countryside

相 xiāng I [动] evaluate ◊相对象 evaluate a prospective marriage partner ◊那种手机样式太旧，估计你相不上。That style of mobile phone is very old. I reckon you won't like it. II [副] 1 (互相) mutually ♦相差 differ 2 (对) ◊笑脸相迎 greet … with a smile ◊好言相劝 comfort …with kind words
▷另见 xiàng

相称 xiāngchèn [形] matching ◊他的举止和他的年龄不相称。His behaviour (英) 或 behavior (美) is not in keeping with his age.

相持 xiāngchí [动] lock … in stalemate ◊双方谈判已经相持了很久。Negotiations between the two sides have already been locked in stalemate for a long time.

相处 xiāngchǔ [动] get along ◊大家在一起相处很融洽。Everybody gets along very well together.

相传 xiāngchuán [动] 1 (传说) be traditionally said ◊相传，这个湖里有个水怪。Traditionally, there is said to be a monster in this lake. 2 (传递) hand … down ◊这项手工艺是一代代相传下来的。This handicraft has been handed down through the generations.

相当 xiāngdāng I [动] match ◊这几位棋手水平相当。These few chess experts are evenly matched. II [形] appropriate ◊他做这项工作正相当。This work is really appropriate for him. III [副] quite ◊昨天晚上的演出相当精彩。The performance yesterday evening was quite brilliant.

相对 xiāngduì I [动] be opposite II [形] 1 (非绝对的) relative 2 (比较的) comparative

相对论 xiāngduìlùn [名] theory of relativity

相反 xiāngfǎn I [形] opposite II [连] ◊她不但没生气，相反，显得特别高兴。Not only was she not angry; on the contrary she seemed very pleased.

相仿 xiāngfǎng [形] similar ◊他儿子和我女儿年龄相仿。His son and my daughter are of a similar age.

相辅相成 xiāng fǔ xiāng chéng complement each other

相干 xiānggān [动] have to do with ◊这事跟我不相干。This has nothing to do with me.

相关 xiāngguān [动] be related ◊新出台的政策与农民的利益密切相关。The new policy has a major bearing on the welfare of farmers.

相好 xiānghǎo I [动] **1** (亲密) be very close **2** (恋爱) be lovers II [名] **1** (朋友) close friend **2** (情人) lover

相互 xiānghù I [形] mutual II [副] ◊在这个问题上，希望大家能相互理解。As regards this question, hopefully everyone will understand each other.

相继 xiāngjì [副] in succession ◊去年，他的爷爷、奶奶相继去世了。Last year his grandfather and grandmother died one after the other.

相敬如宾 xiāng jìng rú bīn treat each other with respect ◊夫妻俩多年来相敬如宾，从没红过脸。The couple have treated each other with respect for many years and have never had a heated exchange.

相配 xiāngpèi [形] well-matched

相亲 xiāngqīn [动] evaluate a prospective marriage partner

相识 xiāngshí [动] be acquainted ◊我们俩是老相识了。The two of us are old acquaintances.

相思 xiāngsī [动] be lovesick

相似 xiāngsì [形] similar

相提并论 xiāng tí bìng lùn lump … together ◊这些概念之间没有任何联系，不能相提并论。There's no connection between these concepts – you can't lump them together.

相同 xiāngtóng [形] identical

相投 xiāngtóu [动] be compatible

相像 xiāngxiàng [动] be alike

相信 xiāngxìn [动] believe ◊他不相信任何人。He doesn't believe anyone. ◊我相信他们一定会准时到达。I'm quite sure they will arrive on time.

相形见绌 xiāng xíng jiàn chù pale into insignificance

相依为命 xiāngyī wéi mìng depend on each other for survival

相宜 xiāngyí [形] fitting

相应 xiāngyìng I [动] correspond II [形] corresponding ◊经济效益提高了，工厂的环境也得到了相应的改善。With the factory's profitability having increased, there was a corresponding improvement in the working environment.

相知 xiāngzhī [动] be well acquainted

相左 xiāngzuǒ [动] conflict ◊双方意见相左。The two parties held different views.

香 xiāng I [形] **1** (芬芳) fragrant **2** (美味) delicious **3** (胃口好的) ◊他病了，吃什么都不香。He's ill – he has no appetite at all. **4** (睡得熟的) sound ◊屋子里暖暖的，睡觉真香！The room was very warm so I slept very soundly. **5** (受欢迎的) popular II [名] **1** (香料) spice **2** (烧的香) incense

香波 xiāngbō [名] shampoo

香肠 xiāngcháng [名] sausage

香料 xiāngliào [名] spice

香喷喷 xiāngpēnpēn [形] delicious

香水 xiāngshuǐ [名] perfume

香甜 xiāngtián [形] **1** (指味道) fragrant **2** (指睡眠) sound

香烟 xiāngyān [名] **1** (卷烟) cigarette **2** (烧香的烟) incense smoke

厢 xiāng [名] **1** (厢房) wing **2** (像房子的空间) ♦车厢 railway carriage ♦包厢 box

厢房 xiāngfáng [名] wing

箱 xiāng [名] **1** (箱子) box **2** (箱状物) ♦信箱 postbox (英), mailbox (美)

箱子 xiāngzi [名] box

襄 xiāng 见下文

襄助 xiāngzhù [动] (书) assist

镶 xiāng [动] edge

镶嵌 xiāngqiàn [动] mount ◇这枚戒指上镶嵌着钻石。This ring is mounted with diamonds.

详 xiáng I [形] detailed II [动] 1 (细说) explain 2 (知道) know (*pt* knew, *pp* known)

详尽 xiángjìn [形] detailed

详情 xiángqíng [名] details (*pl*)

详实 xiángshí [形] full and accurate

详细 xiángxì [形] detailed ◇老板需要一份详细的报告。The boss requires a detailed report. ◇他详细叙述了事情发生的经过。He recounted in detail how the incident occurred.

降 xiáng [动] 1 (投降) surrender 2 (降伏) control ◇这孩子调皮捣蛋，谁也降不住他。This child is acting up – no-one can control him.
▷另见 jiàng

降伏 xiángfú [动] subdue ◇这匹马性子烈，很难降伏。This horse has a fierce temper and is very difficult to subdue.

降服 xiángfú [动] surrender

祥 xiáng [形] auspicious

祥和 xiánghé [形] auspicious and harmonious

翔 xiáng [动] circle in the air

翔实 xiángshí [形] full and accurate

享 xiǎng [动] enjoy

享乐 xiǎnglè [动] lead a life of pleasure (*pt, pp* led)

享受 xiǎngshòu [动] enjoy ◇听音乐是一种精神享受。Listening to music is a kind of spiritual enjoyment.

享有 xiǎngyǒu [动] enjoy ◇18岁以上的公民享有选举权。Citizens above the age of eighteen enjoy the right to vote.

响 xiǎng I [名] 1 (回声) echo 2 (声音) sound II [动] sound ◇下课铃响了。The bell for the end of class sounded. ◇响锣 sound a gong III [形] loud

响当当 xiǎngdāngdāng [形] 1 (响亮) loud 2 (喻) (出色) outstanding

响动 xiǎngdong [名] sound of movement

响亮 xiǎngliàng [形] loud and clear

响应 xiǎngyìng [动] respond ◇大家积极响应班长的倡议。Everyone responded enthusiastically to the class monitor's proposal.

想 xiǎng [动] 1 (思考) think (*pt, pp* thought) ◇你帮我想个办法吧！Help me think of a way to do it! 2 (推测) reckon ◇我想他会同意的。I reckon he'll agree. ◇我想今天可能会下雨。I reckon it might rain today. 3 (打算) want to ◇我想换个工作。I want to change jobs. 4 (想念) miss ◇孩子们很想妈妈。The children miss their mother. ◇刚到这里时，她特别想家。When she first arrived here she missed home terribly.

想必 xiǎngbì [副] presumably ◇他满脸不高兴，想必和老婆吵架了。He looked totally miserable – presumably he had had an argument with his wife.

想当然 xiǎngdāngrán [动] take … for granted (*pt* took, *pp* taken) ◇事情不是那么简单，不能想当然。The matter's not that simple; we can't take it for granted.

想法 xiǎngfǎ [名] opinion

想方设法 xiǎng fāng shè fǎ move heaven and earth ◇她遇到困难时，朋友们想方设法帮她解决。When she encountered a difficulty, her friends moved heaven and earth to help her.

想念 xiǎngniàn [动] miss

想入非非 xiǎng rù fēi fēi take off on a flight of fancy ◇读小说时，她经常想入非非，把自己当成书中的主人公。When reading novels, she often takes off on a flight of fancy where she becomes the protagonist in the book.

想头 xiǎngtou [名] (口) 1 (念头) idea 2 (希望) hope

想像 xiǎngxiàng I [动] imagine II [名] imagination

向 xiàng I [名] direction ♦风向 wind direction II [动] 1 (对着) face ◇我的

卧室向东。My bedroom faces east. **2** (偏袒) side with ◇妈妈老是向着妹妹。The mother always sides with her younger daughter. **III** [介] to ◇我向他表示了感谢。I expressed my thanks to him. **IV** [副] always ◇老先生对考古学向有研究。The old gentleman has always done research in archaeology.

向导 xiàngdǎo **I** [名] guide ◇山高路险，我们最好找一位向导。It's a tricky, high path; it's best we look for a guide. **II** [动] guide

向来 xiànglái [副] always

向往 xiàngwǎng [动] yearn ◇向往自由 yearn for freedom ◇山里的孩子向往着到外面的世界看一看。The children in the mountains yearn to have a look at the outside world.

项 xiàng **I** [名] **1** (颈后部) nape ♦颈项 nape **2** (款项) sum ♦用项 expenditure ♦进项 income **3** (项目) item ♦事项 item **II** [量] item ◇会议讨论内容共5项。There are altogether five items to be discussed at the meeting. ◇3项要求 three requirements

项链 xiàngliàn [名] necklace

项目 xiàngmù [名] item ◇出口项目去年增加了一倍。Export items doubled last year. ◇他将参加3个运动项目的比赛。He will take part in a competition of three sporting events.

巷 xiàng [名] lane
▷另见 hàng

相 xiàng **I** [动] **1** (判断) judge **2** (书) (辅助) assist **II** [名] **1** (相貌) appearance ◇狼狈相 sorry appearance **2** (姿势) posture ♦吃相 table manners **3** (官位) minister ♦外相 foreign minister ♦首相 prime minister **4** (相片) photograph ♦照相 take a photograph
▷另见 xiāng

相貌 xiàngmào [名] appearance

相片 xiàngpiàn [名] photograph

象 xiàng **I** [名] **1** (大象) elephant **2** (样子) appearance ♦景象 scene **II** [动] imitate

象棋 xiàngqí [名] Chinese chess

象牙 xiàngyá [名] ivory

象征 xiàngzhēng [动] symbolize ◇长城是中国的象征。The Great Wall is a symbol of China.

像 xiàng **I** [名] portrait ♦画像 paint portraits ♦雕像 statue **II** [动] **1** (相似) look like ◇他长得像妈妈。He looks like his mother. ◇这姐妹俩模样太像了。These two sisters are very similar in looks. **2** (比如) ◇像他这样的好孩子，谁不喜欢呢！ Who doesn't like good children like this one! ◇像洗衣机这种家用电器，在这里还不普遍。Domestic appliances such as washing machines are still not widespread here. **III** [副] as if ◇门外像有人说话。It sounds as if there are people talking outside. ◇像要下雪了。It looks as if it might snow.

像话 xiànghuà [动] be reasonable

像模像样 xiàng mú xiàng yàng presentable ◇他俩都想办一个像模像样的婚礼。They both want to have a decent wedding.

像样 xiàngyàng [动] be decent

橡 xiàng [名] **1** (橡树) oak **2** (橡胶树) rubber tree

橡胶 xiàngjiāo [名] rubber

橡皮 xiàngpí [名] rubber (英), eraser (美)

削 xiāo [动] peel ◇削苹果 peel an apple
▷另见 xuē

逍 xiāo 见下文

逍遥 xiāoyáo [形] carefree

逍遥法外 xiāoyáo fǎ wài evade capture ◇杀人犯逍遥法外10年，现在终于被抓获归案。The murderer evaded capture for ten years; now finally he's been caught and brought to justice.

消 xiāo [动] **1** (消失) disappear **2** (使消失) remove **3** (度过) spend (*pt, pp* spent) ♦消夏 pass a leisurely summer **4** (需要) take (*pt* took, *pp* taken) ◇只消一天，我们就到了。

It'll only take a day, then we'll be there.

消沉 xiāochén [形] depressed

消除 xiāochú [动] eliminate

消防 xiāofáng [名] fire fighting

消费 xiāofèi [动] consume

消耗 xiāohào [动] consume

消化 xiāohuà [动] digest ◇这种食品不易消化。This kind of food is not easy to digest. ◇学过的东西要消化、吸收。You must digest and absorb what you study.

消极 xiāojí [形] **1** (反面) negative **2** (消沉) demoralized

消解 xiāojiě [动] dispel

消灭 xiāomiè [动] **1** (消失) die out **2** (除掉) eradicate

消磨 xiāomó [动] **1** (逐渐消耗) wear ... down (*pt* wore, *pp* worn) ◇消磨意志 wear down one's willpower **2** (排遣) while away ◇消磨时光 while away time

消遣 xiāoqiǎn [动] while away time

消散 xiāosàn [动] dissipate

消失 xiāoshī [动] vanish

消逝 xiāoshì [动] elapse

消瘦 xiāoshòu [动] become thin (*pt* became, *pp* become) ◇几个月不见，她愈加消瘦了。In the several months since I last saw her she's become even thinner.

消亡 xiāowáng [动] wither away

消息 xiāoxi [名] news (*sg*) ◇电台报道了战争的最新消息。The radio reported the latest news of the war. ◇分别多年，他们一直没有互通消息。In the many years they've been apart they've had no news of each other.

消闲 xiāoxián **I** [动] spend one's free time (*pt, pp* spent) **II** [形] carefree

消夜 xiāoyè [名] night-time snack

宵 xiāo [名] night ♦通宵 all night

萧 xiāo [形] desolate

萧瑟 xiāosè **I** [拟] rustle **II** [形] desolate

萧条 xiāotiáo [形] **1** (寂寞冷落) bleak **2** (经济) depressed

销 xiāo [动] **1** (熔化) melt **2** (除去) cancel **3** (销售) market **4** (消费) spend (*pt, pp* spent)

销毁 xiāohuǐ [动] **1** (熔化毁掉) destroy **2** (烧掉) burn

销魂 xiāohún [动] overwhelm

销假 xiāojià [动] report back after being on holiday

销路 xiāolù [名] market

销声匿迹 xiāo shēng nì jì disappear from sight ◇到了冬天，某些动物停止了活动，销声匿迹了。When winter arrives, some animals cease being active and disappear from sight.

销售 xiāoshòu [动] sell (*pt, pp* sold) ◇家电部今天销售了50台空调。The household appliances division has sold fifty air-conditioning units today. ◇他负责公司的销售工作。He is responsible for the company's sales. ◇公司在国外也打开了销售市场。The company has also opened up sales markets abroad.

销赃 xiāozāng [动] **1** (销售赃物) dispose of stolen goods **2** (销毁赃物) destroy stolen goods

潇 xiāo [形] (书) deep and clear

潇洒 xiāosǎ [形] natural and unaffected

霄 xiāo [名] clouds (*pl*)

嚣 xiāo [动] clamour (英), clamor (美)

嚣张 xiāozhāng [形] arrogant

淆 xiáo [形] confused

小 xiǎo **I** [形] **1** (不大) small ◇小毛病 small problem ♦小床 single bed ◇年龄小 young **2** (排行最末的) youngest ◇他的小女儿才两岁。His youngest daughter is only two years old. **II** [副] **1** (短时间) ♦小憩 take a short rest **2** (稍微) a bit ◇小有名气 have something of a reputation **III** [名] young children

> 📖 可以用 **little** 形容小的事物。 *...a little house... little children...* 但是，**little** 通常不用于强调某事物的体积小。例如，不能说 'The town is little.' 或 'I have a very little car.'，但是可以说 **The town is small.** 或 **I have a very small car.**。 **little** 没有 **small** 那么精确，但通常暗示说话者对于所谈论的对象的态度。因此，**little** 通常用在其他形容词的后面。 *What a nice little house you've got here!... Shut up, you horrible little boy!*

小辈 xiǎobèi [名] younger member

小便 xiǎobiàn I [动] urinate II [名] urine

小菜 xiǎocài [名] **1** (下酒菜) pickled vegetables (*pl*) **2** (喻) easy job

小册子 xiǎocèzi [名] pamphlet

小产 xiǎochǎn [名] miscarriage

小吃 xiǎochī [名] **1** (非正餐) snack **2** (冷盘) cold dish

小丑 xiǎochǒu [名] **1** (滑稽演员) clown **2** (喻) scoundrel

小聪明 xiǎocōngming [名] petty trick

小道儿消息 xiǎodàor xiāoxi [名] hearsay

小动作 xiǎodòngzuò [名] little trick

小恩小惠 xiǎo ēn xiǎo huì [名] small favours (英) 或 favors (美) (*pl*)

小儿科 xiǎo'érkē [名] **1** (医) paediatrics (英) 或 pediatrics (美) department **2** (喻) kid's stuff

小费 xiǎofèi [名] tip

小鬼 xiǎoguǐ [名] little devil

小伙子 xiǎohuǒzi [名] lad

小节 xiǎojié [名] **1** (小事) trifle **2** (音) bar

小姐 xiǎojiě [名] **1** (称呼) Miss ◇李小姐 Miss Li **2** (女子) young lady ◇有位小姐找你。There's a young lady looking for you.

小金库 xiǎojīnkù [名] supplementary fund

小看 xiǎokàn [动] underestimate

小康 xiǎokāng [形] relatively well-off

小麦 xiǎomài [名] wheat

小名 xiǎomíng [名] pet name

小品 xiǎopǐn [名] short sketch

小气 xiǎoqi [形] **1** (气量小) petty **2** (吝啬) stingy

小巧玲珑 xiǎoqiǎo línglóng dainty

小区 xiǎoqū [名] housing estate

小人 xiǎorén [名] vile character

小商品 xiǎoshāngpǐn [名] small items (*pl*)

小时 xiǎoshí [名] hour ◇很多公司实行8小时工作制。Lots of companies have implemented an eight-hour working day.

小市民 xiǎoshìmín [名] philistine

小说 xiǎoshuō [名] novel

小算盘 xiǎosuànpan [名] (喻) calculation ◇打小算盘 be calculating

小题大做 xiǎo tí dà zuò make a mountain out of a molehill ◇他不过是迟到了几次，老板就把他开除了，真是小题大做。He was late no more than a few times, and the boss sacked him – that was making a mountain out of a molehill.

小提琴 xiǎotíqín [名] violin

小偷 xiǎotōu [名] thief (*pl* thieves)

小巫见大巫 xiǎo wū jiàn dà wū pale into insignificance

小鞋 xiǎoxié [名] (喻) ◇因为给公司提过意见，老板常常给他穿小鞋。Because he made some complaints to the company, the boss often gives him a hard time.

小写 xiǎoxiě [名] lower case

小心 xiǎoxīn I [动] be careful ◇过马路，一定要小心。You must be careful when crossing the road. II [形] careful

小型 xiǎoxíng [形] small-scale

小学 xiǎoxué [名] primary school (英), elementary school (美)

小学生 xiǎoxuéshēng [名] primary school pupil (英), elementary school student (美)

小意思 xiǎoyìsi [名] **1** (微薄心意) small token **2** (小事情) nothing significant

小子 xiǎozi [名] (口) **1** (男孩子) boy **2** (贬) (男性) guy

小字辈 xiǎozìbèi [名] youngster

小组 xiǎozǔ [名] group

晓 xiǎo **I** [名] dawn **II** [动] **1** (知道) know (*pt* knew, *pp* known) **2** (使人知道) tell (*pt, pp* told)

晓得 xiǎode [动] know (*pt* knew, *pp* known) ◊这件事你晓得不晓得? Do you know about this matter or not?

孝 xiào **I** [动] be dutiful ◊孝子 a filial son **II** [名] filial piety

孝敬 xiàojìng [动] **1** (孝顺尊敬) show filial respect for (*pt* showed, *pp* shown) ◊孝敬父母是中华民族的美德。Showing filial respect for one's parents is a virtue of Chinese people. **2** (献礼物) give as a present (*pt* gave, *pp* given) ◊过年了，他买了两瓶好酒孝敬爷爷。At New Year, he bought two bottles of good wine to give as a present to his grandfather.

孝顺 xiàoshùn **I** [动] show filial obedience (*pt* showed, *pp* shown) ◊孝顺父母 show filial obedience to one's parents **II** [形] filial

肖 xiào [动] resemble

肖像 xiàoxiàng [名] portrait

校 xiào [名] **1** (学校) school **2** (军) (校官) field officer
▷另见 jiào

校规 xiàoguī [名] school rules (*pl*)

校历 xiàolì [名] school calendar

校长 xiàozhǎng [名] principal

哮 xiào **I** [名] wheezing **II** [动] wheeze

哮喘 xiàochuǎn [名] asthma

笑 xiào [动] **1** (欢笑) laugh ◊孩子们笑得开心极了! The children laughed with great delight! **2** (嘲笑) laugh at ◊别担心，大家不会笑你的。Don't worry, nobody will laugh at you.

笑柄 xiàobǐng [名] laughing stock

笑话 xiàohua **I** [名] joke ◊他爱说笑话。He likes to tell jokes. **II** [动] laugh at

笑里藏刀 xiào lǐ cáng dāo be a wolf in sheep's clothing

笑料 xiàoliào [名] laughing stock

笑眯眯 xiàomīmī [形] smiley

笑面虎 xiàomiànhǔ [名] wolf in sheep's clothing

笑容 xiàoróng [名] smile

笑嘻嘻 xiàoxīxī [形] grinning

笑逐颜开 xiào zhú yán kāi beam with pleasure

效 xiào **I** [名] effect **II** [动] **1** (仿效) imitate **2** (献出) devote ... to

效法 xiàofǎ [动] **1** (模仿) model oneself on **2** (学习) learn from ◊我们应该效法先进的教育制度。We ought to learn from advanced educational systems.

效果 xiàoguǒ [名] **1** (结果) effect **2** (戏剧) effects (*pl*)

效劳 xiàoláo [动] serve

效力 xiàolì **I** [动] serve **II** [名] effectiveness ◊这种药很有效力。This medicine is very effective.

效率 xiàolǜ [名] efficiency

效益 xiàoyì [名] returns (*pl*)

效应 xiàoyìng [名] effect

啸 xiào [动] **1** (指人) whistle **2** (指禽兽) roar **3** (指自然界) roar

些 xiē [量] **1** (不定量) some ◊我要去超市买些食品。I have to go to the supermarket to buy some provisions. **2** (略微) a little ◊这条路近些。This street is a little nearer.

楔 xiē [名] wedge

楔子 xiēzi [名] **1** (木片) wedge **2** (木钉) peg **3** (引子) prologue (英), prolog (美)

歇 xiē [动] **1** (休息) rest ◊太累了，我们歇会儿吧! I'm too tired, let's rest for a while! **2** (停) stop

歇脚 xiējiǎo [动] stop for a rest

歇斯底里 xiēsīdǐlǐ [名] hysteria ◊昨天她和一个售货员歇斯底里地大吵了一顿。Yesterday she argued hysterically with a salesman.

歇息 xiēxi [动] **1** (休息) have a rest ◇忙了半天了，歇息一会儿吧。We've been busy for ages, let's have a rest for a while. **2** (睡觉) go to sleep (*pt* went, *pp* gone)

蝎 xiē [名] scorpion

协 xié **I** [动] assist **II** [副] jointly ♦协办 jointly run ♦协议 agree on

协定 xiédìng [名] agreement

协会 xiéhuì [名] association

协商 xiéshāng [动] consult

协调 xiétiáo **I** [动] coordinate **II** [形] coordinated

协同 xiétóng [动] coordinate ◇经理助理协同经理工作。The manager's assistant coordinates his work.

协议 xiéyì [名] agreement

协助 xiézhù [动] help ◇在各方的协助下，展览取得了成功。Thanks to the help of all concerned, the exhibition was a great success.

协作 xiézuò [动] collaborate

邪 xié **I** [形] **1** (不正当) evil **2** (不正常) abnormal **II** [名] misfortune

邪恶 xié'è [形] evil

邪教 xiéjiào [名] heresy

邪路 xiélù [名] evil ways (*pl*)

邪门儿 xiéménr [形] (方) abnormal

邪门歪道 xié mén wāi dào devious means (*pl*)

邪念 xiéniàn [名] evil thought

胁 xié **I** [名] side **II** [动] coerce

胁迫 xiépò [动] coerce

挟 xié [动] **1** (夹住) hold … under one's arm (*pt*, *pp* held) **2** (挟制) coerce **3** (心怀) harbour (英), harbor (美)

挟持 xiéchí [动] **1** (抓住) seize by the arms **2** (威胁) hold under duress (*pt*, *pp* held)

偕 xié [动] be together with

偕老 xiélǎo [动] grow old together (*pt* grew, *pp* grown)

偕同 xiétóng [动] be together with ◇总理偕同政府各部官员参加了仪式。The prime minister took part in the ceremony, together with officials from each government department.

斜 xié **I** [形] slanting **II** [动] slant

斜路 xiélù [名] (喻) wrong path

斜坡 xiépō [名] slope

谐 xié [形] **1** (和谐) harmonious **2** (诙谐) humorous

谐和 xiéhé [形] harmonious

谐音 xiéyīn [动] sound the same

携 xié [动] **1** (携带) carry **2** (拉着) hold (*pt*, *pp* held)

携带 xiédài [动] carry

携手 xiéshǒu [动] **1** (字) join hands **2** (喻) collaborate ◇中美双方决定携手建设这个项目。China and the US decided to collaborate on the establishment of this project.

鞋 xié [名] shoes (*pl*)

鞋匠 xiéjiang [名] cobbler

写 xiě [动] **1** (书写) write (*pt* wrote, *pp* written) **2** (写作) write (*pt* wrote, *pp* written) **3** (描写) describe **4** (绘画) draw (*pt* drew, *pp* drawn)

写生 xiěshēng [动] sketch from nature

写实 xiěshí [动] write realistically (*pt* wrote, *pp* written)

写意 xiěyì [名] freehand brushwork

写照 xiězhào [名] portrayal

写作 xiězuò [动] write (*pt* wrote, *pp* written) ◇他上小学时就开始写作了。He first started writing when he was at primary school (英) 或 elementary school (美).

血 xiě [名] (口) blood
▷另见 xuè

血淋淋 xiělínlín [形] blood-soaked

泄 xiè [动] **1** (排出) discharge **2** (泄露) let … out (*pt*, *pp* let) **3** (发泄) vent

泄劲 xièjìn [动] lose heart (*pt*, *pp* lost)

泄漏 xièlòu [动] **1** (逸出) leak ◇这起火灾是由于煤气泄漏引起的。This

fire was caused by a gas leak. **2** (泄露) let ... out (*pt, pp* let) ◇不要把这个消息泄漏出去。Don't let this news get out.

泄露 xièlòu [动] let ... out (*pt, pp* let) ◇公司机密被泄露出去了。The company secrets have been let out.

泄密 xièmì [动] divulge a secret

泄气 xièqì [动] lose heart (*pt, pp* lost)

泻 xiè [动] **1** (流) pour down **2** (腹泻) have diarrhoea (英) 或 diarrhea (美)

卸 xiè [动] **1** (搬下) unload ♦卸车 unload a vehicle **2** (除去) remove ♦卸装 disrobe **3** (拆卸) strip ◇卸下钟表的零件 strip the parts of a clock **4** (解除) be relieved of ♦卸任 step down

卸任 xièrèn [动] step down ◇总统卸任后，去一所大学当了校长。After the president stepped down, he became vice-chancellor of a university.

卸妆 xièzhuāng [动] remove one's makeup

屑 xiè **I** [名] bits (*pl*) **II** [形] trivial **III** [动] deign to

械 xiè [名] **1** (器械) tool **2** (武器) weapon

亵 xiè **I** [动] be disrespectful to **II** [形] indecent

亵渎 xièdú [动] profane

谢 xiè [动] **1** (感谢) thank ◇帮了我大忙，多谢了！Many thanks for helping me out so much! **2** (认错) apologize **3** (拒绝) decline **4** (脱落) wither

谢绝 xièjué [动] decline

谢客 xièkè [动] decline to receive visitors

谢幕 xièmù [动] take a curtain call (*pt* took, *pp* taken)

谢谢 xièxie [动] thank you, thanks (口)

谢罪 xièzuì [动] offer an apology

邂 xiè 见下文

邂逅 xièhòu [动] meet by chance (*pt, pp* met)

懈 xiè [动] be lax

懈怠 xièdài [形] slack

懈气 xièqì [动] stop trying ◇失败是常有的事，不要懈气。Failure is a common occurrence: don't stop trying.

蟹 xiè [名] crab

心 xīn [名] **1** (心脏) heart **2** (思想) mind ♦用心 attentively ♦谈心 heart-to-heart talk **3** (中心) centre (英), center (美) ♦圆心 centre (英) 或 center (美) of a circle

心爱 xīn'ài [形] treasured

心安理得 xīn ān lǐ dé have a clear conscience ◇他做错事，还能心安理得。He can do wrong and still have a clear conscience.

心病 xīnbìng [名] **1** (焦虑) anxiety **2** (隐痛) sore point

心不在焉 xīn bù zài yān be absent-minded ◇他做事心不在焉，经常出错。He does things absent-mindedly and often makes mistakes.

心肠 xīncháng [名] **1** (心地) heart ◇她心肠好。She has a good heart. **2** (兴致) mood ◇我现在没心肠听音乐。I'm not in the mood for listening to music at the moment.

心驰神往 xīn chí shén wǎng yearn for

心得 xīndé [名] what one has learned

心地 xīndì [名] character

心服口服 xīn fú kǒu fú be utterly convinced

心腹 xīnfù [名] **1** (指人) trusted subordinate **2** (指事) confidence

心肝 xīngān [名] **1** (良心) conscience **2** (心爱的人) darling

心广体胖 xīn guǎng tǐ pán healthy and happy

心寒 xīn hán [形] disappointed

心怀鬼胎 xīn huái guǐtāi harbour (英) 或 harbor (美) evil intentions

心慌意乱 xīn huāng yì luàn be nervous and flustered ◇遇到这种麻烦事，他心慌意乱，不知所措。

When he comes up against this kind of problem, he gets nervous and flustered and doesn't know what to do.

心灰意懒 xīn huī yì lǎn be disheartened

心机 xīnjī [名] thinking

心计 xīnjì [名] calculation

心惊胆战 xīn jīng dǎn zhàn terrified ◇回忆起大地震时的场景，她到现在还心惊胆战。When she remembers the scene at the time of the earthquake, she still feels terrified.

心境 xīnjìng [名] state of mind

心坎 xīnkǎn [名] the bottom of one's heart ◇我从心坎上感谢你。I thank you from the bottom of my heart.

心旷神怡 xīn kuàng shén yí feel relaxed and happy

心理 xīnlǐ [名] psychology

心灵 xīnlíng I [名] mind II [形] quick-witted

心领神会 xīn lǐng shén huì understand tacitly ◇看到母亲使了个眼色，她心领神会，马上就出去了。On seeing her mother's glance, she took the hint and immediately went out.

心平气和 xīn píng qì hé in a calm state of mind ◇只要双方心平气和地谈一谈，矛盾是能够解决的。It only needs the two sides to talk calmly, and the conflict can be resolved.

心情 xīnqíng [名] frame of mind ◇这几天我心情不好。In the last few days I've not been in a good frame of mind.

心神 xīnshén [名] **1** (心情) state of mind ◇这件事搞得他心神不定。This matter made him feel uncertain. **2** (精力) effort ◇写这部书费了他不少心神。He devoted a lot of energy to writing the book.

心事 xīnshì [名] preoccupation

心思 xīnsi [名] **1** (想法) thoughts (*pl*) ◇对这件事，不知道她是什么心思。I don't know what her thoughts are about this. **2** (脑筋) brains (*pl*) ◇为赚钱，他挖空了心思。He racked his brains to think of ways of making money. **3** (兴致) mood ◇她只想着度假，工作上根本没心思。She's only thinking of her holiday – she's not in the mood for work at all.

心态 xīntài [名] mentality

心心相印 xīn xīn xiāng yìn be a kindred spirit ◇她希望找一位心心相印的伴侣。She hopes to find a partner who is a kindred spirit.

心胸 xīnxiōng [名] **1** (胸怀) broadmindedness ◇他心胸狭隘。He is narrow-minded. **2** (志向) aspiration ◇他是个很有心胸的青年。He is a young man with great aspirations.

心绪 xīnxù [名] mood

心血 xīnxuè [名] painstaking care

心血来潮 xīnxuè lái cháo be seized by a whim

心眼儿 xīnyǎnr [名] **1** (内心) heart ◇听他这么说，她从心眼儿里不高兴。Hearing him speak in this way, she was deeply unhappy. **2** (心地) intention ◇她心眼儿好。Her intentions are good. **3** (机智) intelligence ◇这姑娘有心眼儿，样样能干。This girl is intelligent, and competent in every way. **4** (顾虑) unfounded misgivings (*pl*) ◇他心眼儿太多，很难打交道。He is oversensitive – it's difficult to establish a rapport with him. **5** (气量) tolerance ◇小心眼儿 intolerant

心意 xīnyì [名] **1** (情意) feelings (*pl*) **2** (意思) meaning

心有余悸 xīn yǒu yú jì have a lingering fear

心愿 xīnyuàn [名] one's heart's desire

心悦诚服 xīn yuè chéng fú wholeheartedly admire ◇对手的为人和能力，令他心悦诚服。He wholeheartedly admired his opponent's conduct and ability.

心脏 xīnzàng [名] heart

心照不宣 xīn zhào bù xuān have a tacit understanding

辛 xīn [形] **1** (辣) hot **2** (辛苦) laborious **3** (痛苦) bitter

辛苦 xīnkǔ I [形] laborious II [动] trouble ◇真不好意思，辛苦你了！

I'm really sorry to trouble you!

辛辣 xīnlà [形] biting ◇这篇文章对官僚主义作风进行了辛辣的讽刺。This piece is a biting satire on bureaucracy.

辛劳 xīnláo [动] toil

辛勤 xīnqín [形] hardworking

辛酸 xīnsuān [形] bitter

欣 xīn [形] glad

欣然 xīnrán [副] gladly ◇老板欣然同意了我的请求。The boss gladly agreed to my request.

欣赏 xīnshǎng [动] **1** (赏识) admire ◇朋友们都非常欣赏他的才学。His friends all greatly admired his learning. **2** (享受) enjoy

欣慰 xīnwèi [形] satisfied

欣喜 xīnxǐ [形] joyful

欣欣向荣 xīnxīn xiàng róng flourishing

新 xīn **I** [形] **1** (跟旧相对) new ◇新家具 new furniture **2** (刚结婚的) newly-wed ◇新媳妇 newly-wed wife **II** [副] newly ◇新买的衣服 newly bought clothes

新潮 xīncháo **I** [形] fashionable **II** [名] new trend

新陈代谢 xīn chén dàixiè the old gives way to the new ◇生命就是新陈代谢的过程。Life is a process of the old giving way to the new.

新村 xīncūn [名] new estate

新大陆 Xīn Dàlù [名] the New World

新房 xīnfáng [名] bridal chamber

新欢 xīnhuān [名] new sweetheart

新近 xīnjìn [名] ◇北京新近变化很大。Great changes have taken place recently in Beijing.

新郎 xīnláng [名] bridegroom

新年 xīnnián [名] **1** (指一段时间) New Year **2** (指元旦当天) New Year's Day

新娘 xīnniáng [名] bride

新奇 xīnqí [形] novel ◇他的想法很新奇，富有创造性。He has lots of novel ideas: he's bursting with creativity.

新人 xīnrén [名] **1** (新婚夫妇) newly married couple **2** (新型人才) new talent

新式 xīnshì [形] up-to-date

新手 xīnshǒu [名] beginner

新闻 xīnwén [名] news (*sg*) ◇新闻记者 news reporter ◇国际新闻 international news ◇国内新闻 domestic news ◇新闻节目 news programme (英) 或 program (美) ◇最近，我们公司的新闻还真不少呢！ Recently, there has been a lot of news in our company!

新鲜 xīnxiān [形] **1** (指食物) fresh ◇这些水果很新鲜。This fruit is very fresh. **2** (指植物) tender ◇新鲜的嫩芽 tender shoots **3** (清新) fresh ◇新鲜空气 fresh air **4** (新奇) novel ◇新鲜经验 novel experience

新兴 xīnxīng [形] newly emerging

新型 xīnxíng [形] new-style

新秀 xīnxiù [名] rising talent

新颖 xīnyǐng [形] original

薪 xīn [名] **1** (柴火) firewood **2** (薪水) salary

薪水 xīnshui [名] salary

馨 xīn [名] strong fragrance

馨香 xīnxiāng [名] (书) **1** (芳香) fragrance **2** (烧香的香味) smell of burning incense

信 xìn **I** [动] **1** (相信) believe ♦轻信 readily believe **2** (信奉) ◇信教 be religious ◇信佛教 be a Buddhist **II** [副] at will ◇信口开河 shoot one's mouth off **III** [名] **1** (书信) letter ♦信箱 letterbox (英), mailbox (美) ◇寄信 send a letter **2** (信息) information ♦口信 verbal message **3** (信用) trust ♦失信 lose trust **4** (凭据) proof ♦信物 evidence

信贷 xìndài [名] credit

信封 xìnfēng [名] envelope

信奉 xìnfèng [动] believe in ◇信奉基督教 be a Christian

信服 xìnfú [动] be convinced ◇他的话漏洞百出，不能让我信服。His speech was full of inconsistencies – he couldn't convince me.

信号 xìnhào [名] signal ◊接收信号 receive a signal

信件 xìnjiàn [名] letter

信口雌黄 xìn kǒu cíhuáng make irresponsible remarks ◊我们对那些记者的信口雌黄感到愤慨。We are outraged at the irresponsible comments made by the journalists.

信口开河 xìn kǒu kāi hé talk off the top of one's head

信赖 xìnlài [动] trust

信念 xìnniàn [名] belief

信任 xìnrèn [动] trust ◊他为人忠厚朴实，大家都信任他。He's loyal and honest – everybody trusts him.

信手 xìnshǒu [副] at one's fingertips

信守 xìnshǒu [动] stand by (*pt, pp* stood) ◊信守誓言 stand by one's word

信条 xìntiáo [名] tenet

信徒 xìntú [名] follower

信托 xìntuō [动] trust ◊信托公司 trust company

信息 xìnxī [名] information ◊传递信息 pass on information ◊信息时代 the information age

> 请注意, **information** 在任何情况下都只能用作不可数名词。不能说 'an information' 或 'informations'。*For further information contact the number below.* 但是, 在特指从他人处获知的某一具体信息时, 可以用 **a piece of information** 或 **an item of information**。*We will be looking at every piece of information we receive.*

信心 xìnxīn [名] faith ◊他对前途失去信心。He lost faith in his future.

信仰 xìnyǎng [动] believe in ◊他没有宗教信仰。He has no religious faith.

信用 xìnyòng [名] **1** (指信任) word ◊他一向守信用。He always keeps his word. **2** (指借贷) credit

信用卡 xìnyòngkǎ [名] credit card

信誉 xìnyù [名] reputation

衅 xìn [名] quarrel ♦挑衅 pick a quarrel

兴 xīng [动] **1** (旺盛) prosper ♦兴衰 rise and fall **2** (流行) be popular ♦时兴 fashionable **3** (使盛行) promote ◊大兴反腐败之风 heavily promote anti-corruption **4** (发动) begin (*pt* began, *pp* begun) ♦兴修 begin construction
▷另见 xìng

兴办 xīngbàn [动] set … up (*pt, pp* set) ◊兴办合资企业 set up a joint venture

兴奋 xīngfèn [动] be excited ◊他兴奋得跳了起来。He leaped with excitement.

兴风作浪 xīng fēng zuò làng create chaos ◊黑客兴风作浪攻击一些著名网站。Hackers have been creating chaos on some well-known websites.

兴建 xīngjiàn [动] build (*pt, pp* built)

兴起 xīngqǐ [动] rise up (*pt* rose, *pp* risen)

兴盛 xīngshèng [形] prosperous

兴师动众 xīng shī dòng zhòng drag in a lot of people ◊为这件小事不值得兴师动众。This little matter does not require a lot of people to be dragged in.

兴旺 xīngwàng [形] prosperous

兴许 xīngxǔ [副] (方) maybe ◊他这么晚还没到，兴许有事不来了。He's so late getting here – maybe something's come up and he can't come.

星 xīng [名] **1** (指天体) star ♦星空 a starry sky **2** (指名人) star ♦球星 football star **3** (细碎物) bit ♦火星 spark ◊星星点点 bits and pieces

星辰 xīngchén [名] star

星斗 xīngdǒu [名] stars (*pl*)

星火 xīnghuǒ [名] **1** (微小的火) spark **2** (流星之光) meteor

星罗棋布 xīng luó qí bù be dotted with ◊旅游区内名胜古迹星罗棋布。The tourist area is dotted with historic and scenic attractions.

星期 xīngqī [名] **1** (周) week **2** (指

某天) ♦星期天 Sunday ♦星期三 Wednesday

星球 xīngqiú [名] heavenly body

星体 xīngtǐ [名] heavenly body

星系 xīngxì [名] galaxy

星移斗转 xīng yí dǒu zhuǎn the passing of time ◊星移斗转，此塔何时建造已无史料可考。With the passing of time there are no longer any records as to when this tower was built.

星座 xīngzuò [名] constellation

猩 xīng [名] orang-utan ♦黑猩猩 chimpanzee

猩红 xīnghóng [形] blood-red

惺 xīng 见下文

惺忪 xīngsōng [形] bleary

腥 xīng I [名] raw meat II [形] fishy

刑 xíng [名] 1 (刑罚) punishment ♦死刑 the death penalty 2 (体罚) corporal punishment

刑罚 xíngfá [名] punishment

刑法 xíngfǎ [名] criminal law

刑事 xíngshì [形] criminal ◊刑事案件 criminal case

行 xíng I [动] 1 (走) walk ♦步行 go on foot 2 (流通) be current ♦发行 issue 3 (做) do (*pt* did, *pp* done) ♦行医 practise (英) 或 practice (美) medicine II [助动] ◊另行通知 issue another notice III [形] 1 (可以) OK ◊行，就这么说定了。OK, so that's settled. 2 (能干) capable IV [名] 1 (旅行) travel ♦行踪 track 2 (行为) conduct ♦暴行 act of cruelty ▷另见 háng

行程 xíngchéng [名] journey

行动 xíngdòng [动] 1 (行走) move about ◊奶奶年纪大了，行动不便。Grandma's getting old and finding it harder to move about. 2 (活动) take action (*pt* took, *pp* taken) ◊采取行动 take action

行贿 xínghuì [动] bribe

行进 xíngjìn [动] advance

行径 xíngjìng [名] conduct

行军 xíngjūn [动] march

行李 xíngli [名] luggage

> **luggage** 是不可数名词。可以说某人有 **a piece of luggage** 或 **some luggage**, 但不能说有 'a luggage' 或 'some luggages'。在英式英语中, 人们通常用 **luggage** 指旅行者所携带的行李。**baggage** 是比较专业的词汇, 例如在机场或谈论旅游保险时使用。在美式英语中, **luggage** 是指空的旅行袋或手提箱, **baggage** 是指装有物品的箱包。无论是英式还是美式英语, 旅行者所携带的行李都可称作 **bags**。美国人还将一个手提箱称为 **a bag**。

行人 xíngrén [名] pedestrian

行使 xíngshǐ [动] exercise

行驶 xíngshǐ [动] travel

行为 xíngwéi [名] behaviour (英), behavior (美) ◊行为不轨 improper behaviour ◊行为规范 standards of behaviour

行星 xíngxīng [名] planet

行云流水 xíng yún liú shuǐ natural and unforced

行政 xíngzhèng [名] administration

行装 xíngzhuāng [名] luggage

行踪 xíngzōng [名] whereabouts (*pl*) ◊他行踪不定，四海为家。His whereabouts are uncertain – he could be living anywhere.

行走 xíngzǒu [动] walk

形 xíng I [名] 1 (形状) shape 2 (形体) body II [动] 1 (显露) appear 2 (对照) compare

形成 xíngchéng [动] form ◊这种自然现象形成于几千年前。This natural phenomenon formed thousands of years ago. ◊二氧化碳形成温室效应。Carbon dioxide has caused the greenhouse effect. ◊火山的形成 volcanic formation

形骸 xínghái [名] (书) the human body

形迹 xíngjì [名] traces (*pl*)

形容 xíngróng [动] describe

形容词 xíngróngcí [名] adjective

形式 xíngshì [名] form

形势 xíngshì [名] situation ◇形势很严峻。The situation is grave.

形态 xíngtài [名] **1** (形状) form **2** (语言) morphology

形体 xíngtǐ [名] physique ◇形体美 physical beauty

形象 xíngxiàng [名] image

形形色色 xíngxíngsèsè of every description ◇小说描绘了形形色色的人物。The novel depicts characters of every description.

形状 xíngzhuàng [名] shape

型 xíng [名] type ♦体型 build ♦模型 model ♦血型 blood group ♦典型 typical ♦造型 mould (英), mold (美)

型号 xínghào [名] model ◇这种牌子的电脑有好几种型号。This make of computer comes in several different models.

省 xǐng [动] **1** (检查) examine oneself critically ♦反省 self-questioning **2** (探望) visit ♦省亲 visit one's relatives **3** (醒悟) be aware ◇发人深省 be enlightening
▷另见 shěng

省察 xǐngchá [动] examine one's conscience ◇你们要省察自己的行为。You must examine your behaviour (英) 或 behaviour (美).

醒 xǐng **I** [动] **1** (神志恢复) come to (*pt* came, *pp* come) ◇车祸后很久他才醒过来。After the car crash it took him a long time to come to. ◇她还酒醉未醒。She still hasn't sobered up. **2** (睡醒) wake up (*pt* woke, *pp* woken) ♦惊醒 wake up with a start **3** (醒悟) become aware (*pt* became, *pp* become) ♦提醒 remind **II** [形] eye-catching

醒目 xǐngmù [形] eye-catching

醒悟 xǐngwù [动] wake up to (*pt* woke, *pp* woken) ◇多年后我才醒悟，自己当时是错误的。It wasn't until years later that it dawned on me that I'd been wrong.

兴 xìng [名] excitement
▷另见 xīng

兴冲冲 xìngchōngchōng [形] excited

兴高采烈 xìng gāo cǎi liè be on top of the world ◇喜讯传来，全家兴高采烈。When the good news arrived, the family was on top of the world.

兴趣 xìngqù [名] interest ◇他对集邮有浓厚的兴趣。He has a deep interest in stamp-collecting.

兴致 xìngzhì [名] interest ◇他对打牌下棋兴致不高。He has no great interest in card games or chess.

杏 xìng [名] apricot

幸 xìng **I** [形] lucky **II** [动] rejoice **III** [副] fortunately

幸而 xìng'ér [副] fortunately

幸福 xìngfú **I** [名] happiness **II** [形] happy

幸好 xìnghǎo [副] luckily ◇我一人在家闷得慌，幸好你来串门。I was really bored at home by myself – lucky for me you came by!

幸会 xìnghuì [动] be honoured (英) 或 honored (美) ◇久仰大名，幸会幸会！ I've been looking forward to meeting you for a long time – I'm honoured!

幸亏 xìngkuī [副] fortunately

幸免 xìngmiǎn [动] survive

幸运 xìngyùn **I** [名] good luck **II** [形] lucky

幸灾乐祸 xìng zāi lè huò gloat at others' misfortunes ◇看到他家破人亡，她却幸灾乐祸地笑了。When she saw that the family was ruined, she gloated at his misfortune.

性 xìng [名] **1** (性格) character ♦品性 moral character ♦任性 stubborn **2** (性能) function ♦酸性 acidity **3** (性别) gender ♦男性 male **4** (情欲) sex ♦性关系 sexual intercourse **5** (性质) ♦可靠性 reliability ♦实用性 utility **6** (语法) gender ♦阳性 masculine

性别 xìngbié [名] sex

性感 xìnggǎn [形] sexy

性格 xìnggé [名] personality

性交 xìngjiāo [动] have sex

性命 xìngmìng [名] life (*pl* lives)

性能 xìngnéng [名] function

性情 xìngqíng [名] disposition ◊这女孩儿性情温和。This girl has a gentle disposition.

性骚扰 xìngsāorǎo [动] sexually harass ◊法律如何保护受到性骚扰的女性？ How does the law protect women from sexual harassment?

性欲 xìngyù [名] sexual desire

性质 xìngzhì [名] character

姓 xìng I [动] ◊我姓李。My surname is Li. II [名] surname

姓名 xìngmíng [名] full name

姓氏 xìngshì [名] surname

凶 xiōng I [形] **1** (不幸的) unlucky ♦凶兆 ill omen **2** (凶恶) ferocious ♦凶相 fierce look **3** (厉害) terrible ◊俩人吵得很凶。The two men had a terrible quarrel. II [名] act of violence

凶暴 xiōngbào [形] ferocious

凶残 xiōngcán [形] savage

凶恶 xiōng'è [形] fierce

凶狠 xiōnghěn [形] vicious

凶猛 xiōngměng [形] ferocious

凶器 xiōngqì [名] weapon

凶手 xiōngshǒu [名] murderer

凶险 xiōngxiǎn [形] **1** (危险可怕) perilous ◊这条山路极其凶险。This mountain road is perilous. ◊老人病情凶险。The old man's condition is critical. **2** (凶恶阴险) ruthless

兄 xiōng [名] brother

兄弟 xiōngdì [名] brother

兄长 xiōngzhǎng [名] elder brother

汹 xiōng [动] upsurge

汹汹 xiōngxiōng [形] turbulent

汹涌澎湃 xiōngyǒng péngpài tempestuous

胸 xiōng [名] **1** (胸部) chest **2** (心胸) heart ◊胸怀大志 have a big heart

胸怀 xiōnghuái [名] heart

胸襟 xiōngjīn [名] **1** (气量) broadmindedness ◊胸襟开阔 broadminded **2** (胸部衣襟) chest

胸脯 xiōngpú [名] chest

胸有成竹 xiōng yǒu chéng zhú have a well thought-out strategy

雄 xióng I [形] **1** (公的) male **2** (有气魄的) imposing **3** (强有力的) strong II [名] very powerful person

雄辩 xióngbiàn [名] convincing argument

雄厚 xiónghòu [形] abundant

雄赳赳 xióngjiūjiū [形] gallant

雄图 xióngtú [名] grand plan

雄伟 xióngwěi [形] imposing

雄心 xióngxīn [名] ambition

雄壮 xióngzhuàng [形] majestic

熊 xióng [名] bear

熊猫 xióngmāo [名] panda

熊熊 xióngxióng [形] blazing

休 xiū I [动] **1** (停止) stop **2** (休息) rest II [副] ◊你休想得逞。Don't imagine you can win.

休克 xiūkè [名] shock

休戚相关 xiūqī xiāng guān be interconnected

休息 xiūxi [动] rest

休闲 xiūxián [动] **1** (闲置) be unused **2** (悠闲) be at leisure ◊休闲服装 casual clothes

休养 xiūyǎng [动] recuperate

休养生息 xiūyǎng shēngxī recovery ◊本届政府实行了休养生息政策。This government has pursued policies for national recovery.

休整 xiūzhěng [动] rest and reorganize

休止 xiūzhǐ [动] cease ◊对环境的破坏何时才能休止？ When will the damage to the environment cease?

修 xiū [动] **1** (修饰) decorate **2** (修理) mend **3** (学习) study **4** (兴建) build (*pt, pp* built) **5** (剪) trim

修补 xiūbǔ [动] mend

修长 xiūcháng [形] slender

修辞 xiūcí [动] engage in rhetoric

修订 xiūdìng [动] revise ◊修订草案 revise a draft

修改 xiūgǎi [动] alter ◇修改计划 alter one's plans ◇修改文章 revise an essay

修建 xiūjiàn [动] build (*pt, pp* built)

修理 xiūlǐ [动] repair

修女 xiūnǚ [名] nun

修身 xiūshēn [动] improve oneself

修饰 xiūshì [动] **1** (修整装饰) decorate **2** (修改润饰) polish

修养 xiūyǎng [名] **1** (水平) accomplishments (*pl*) ◇文学修养 literary accomplishments **2** (指态度) gentility

修正 xiūzhèng [动] correct

羞 xiū **I** [形] shy **II** [动] disgrace **III** [名] shame

羞惭 xiūcán [形] ashamed

羞耻 xiūchǐ [形] ashamed

羞答答 xiūdādā [形] coy

羞愧 xiūkuì [形] ashamed

羞怯 xiūqiè [形] timid

羞辱 xiūrǔ **I** [名] humiliation **II** [动] humiliate

羞涩 xiūsè [形] shy

朽 xiǔ [动] **1** (腐烂) rot **2** (衰老) go senile (*pt* went, *pp* gone)

宿 xiǔ [量] night ◇他在旅店里住了两宿。He stayed at the guesthouse for two nights.
▷另见 sù

秀 xiù **I** [形] **1** (清秀) elegant **2** (优异) outstanding **II** [名] talent ♦新秀 new talent

秀才 xiùcai [名] scholar

秀丽 xiùlì [形] beautiful

秀美 xiùměi [形] elegant

秀气 xiùqi [形] **1** (清秀) delicate **2** (文雅) refined

臭 xiù [名] smell
▷另见 chòu

袖 xiù [名] sleeve

袖手旁观 xiù shǒu páng guān stand by and do nothing

袖珍 xiùzhēn [形] pocket-sized ◇袖珍收音机 pocket radio

绣 xiù **I** [动] embroider **II** [名] embroidery

绣花枕头 xiùhuā zhěntou pretty on the outside but lacking substance underneath

锈 xiù [名] rust ♦生锈 go rusty ◇刀锈了。The knife has rusted.

嗅 xiù [动] smell

嗅觉 xiùjué [名] sense of smell ◇狗的嗅觉很灵敏。Dogs have an acute sense of smell.

吁 xū [动] (书) sigh
▷另见 yù

吁吁 xūxū [拟] huff and puff

须 xū **I** [副] ♦必须 must **II** [名] beard

须要 xūyào [动] need

须知 xūzhī [名] essentials (*pl*)

虚 xū **I** [形] **1** (空着) empty **2** (胆怯) timid **3** (虚假) false **4** (虚心) modest **5** (弱) weak **II** [副] in vain

虚词 xūcí [名] function word

虚浮 xūfú [形] superficial

虚构 xūgòu [动] fabricate ◇故事情节纯属虚构。This story has been completely fabricated.

虚怀若谷 xū huái ruò gǔ be open-minded

虚幻 xūhuàn [形] illusory

虚假 xūjiǎ [形] false

虚惊 xūjīng [名] false alarm

虚名 xūmíng [名] undeserved reputation

虚情假意 xū qíng jiǎ yì ◇我看得出他对我只是虚情假意。I realized that his apparent friendliness to me was not genuine.

虚荣 xūróng [名] vanity

虚弱 xūruò [形] frail

虚伪 xūwěi [形] hypocritical

虚无 xūwú [形] non-existent

虚心 xūxīn [形] open-minded ◇我们要虚心向他人学习。We need to learn from others in an open-minded way.

虚张声势 xū zhāng shēngshì bluff and bluster ◇面对虚张声势的商家，如何讨个好价钱? How is it possible to bargain with shopkeepers who bluff and bluster?

墟 xū [名] ruins (*pl*)

需 xū **I** [动] need ◇去英国留学需一大笔经费。You'll need considerable funds if you want to go to Britain to study. **II** [名] needs (*pl*) ♦军需 military requirements (*pl*)

需求 xūqiú [名] demand ◇该地区对中药材的需求很旺盛。There is a thriving demand for Chinese medicinal herbs in this area.

需要 xūyào **I** [动] need ◇常人每天需要吃一定量的水果和蔬菜。Everyone needs to eat a certain amount of fruit and vegetables each day. **II** [名] needs (*pl*) ◇日常生活需要 necessities of life

嘘 xū [叹] (方) sh ◇嘘！别吵醒了他。Sh! Don't wake him!
▷另见 shī

徐 xú [副] slowly

徐徐 xúxú [副] slowly

许 xǔ **I** [动] **1** (称赞) praise **2** (答应) promise **3** (允许) allow ◇妻子不许他抽烟喝酒。His wife doesn't allow him to smoke or drink. **II** [副] maybe ◇他看上去脸色苍白，许是生病了。He looks a bit pale – maybe he's ill.

许多 xǔduō [形] many ◇这套家具用了许多年了。This furniture has been in use for many years. ◇他养了许多金鱼。He keeps a lot of goldfish.

许久 xǔjiǔ [名] ages (*pl*) ◇我等了许久才收到他的回信。I had to wait for ages before he replied to my letter.

许可 xǔkě [动] allow ◇如果条件许可，我就报名参赛。If circumstances allow, I'll sign up for the competition.

许诺 xǔnuò [动] promise ◇他曾许诺来看她，可是终究没来。He promised to visit her, but he never came.

许配 xǔpèi [动] marry ... off ◇父母将她许配给了一个有钱人。Her parents married her off to a rich man.

许愿 xǔyuàn [动] **1** (对神) vow **2** (对人) promise

诩 xǔ [动] (书) boast

栩 xǔ 见下文

栩栩 xǔxǔ [形] vivid

旭 xù [名] (书) sunrise

旭日 xùrì [名] the rising sun

序 xù **I** [名] **1** (次序) order **2** (序文) preface ◇我给这本书写了序。I wrote the preface to this book. **II** [形] preliminary

序列 xùliè [名] formation

序幕 xùmù [名] prologue

序曲 xùqǔ [名] overture

序数 xùshù [名] ordinal number

序言 xùyán [名] foreword

叙 xù [动] **1** (谈) chat **2** (记述) recount

叙别 xùbié [动] have a farewell talk

叙事 xùshì [动] narrate

叙述 xùshù [动] recount

恤 xù [动] **1** (怜悯) pity **2** (救济) give money (*pt* gave, *pp* given)

恤金 xùjīn [名] pension

畜 xù [动] raise
▷另见 chù

畜牧 xùmù [动] rear ◇畜牧业 animal husbandry

酗 xù 见下文

酗酒 xùjiǔ [动] get drunk ◇他因酗酒斗殴被警方拘留。He was arrested because he got drunk and was involved in a fight.

绪 xù [名] **1** (开端) beginning **2** (心情) feelings (*pl*)

绪论 xùlùn [名] preface

续 xù [动] **1** (接连) continue **2** (延长) extend **3** (添加) add

续聘 xùpìn [动] keep … on（*pt, pp* kept）◇合同期满后，公司续聘了他。When his contract expired, the company kept him on.

絮 xù **I** [名] **1** (棉絮) cotton wadding **2** (絮状物) ♦柳絮 willow catkin **II** [动] **1** (铺衬) pad with cotton **2** (啰唆) be long-winded

絮叨 xùdāo [动] go on（*pt* went, *pp* gone）◇她絮絮叨叨，我听得都厌烦了。How she went on! I was sick of the sound of it!

婿 xù [名] **1** (女婿) son-in-law（*pl* sons-in-law）**2** (丈夫) husband

蓄 xù [动] **1** (储存) store **2** (留着) grow（*pt* grew, *pp* grown）◇蓄胡子 grow a beard **3** (存有) harbour (英), harbor (美)

蓄积 xùjī [动] store

蓄谋 xùmóu [动] premeditate

蓄意 xùyì [动] premeditate

轩 xuān [形] (书) high

轩昂 xuān'áng [形] dignified

轩然大波 xuānrán dà bō complete crisis ◇球员罢赛掀起轩然大波。The footballers' strike caused a complete crisis.

宣 xuān [动] **1** (宣布) announce **2** (疏导) lead … off（*pt, pp* led）♦宣泄 get … off one's chest

宣布 xuānbù [动] announce

宣称 xuānchēng [动] announce

宣传 xuānchuán [动] disseminate ◇宣传工具 means of dissemination ◇宣传进步思想 promote progressive thought

宣告 xuāngào [动] proclaim

宣判 xuānpàn [动] pass judgment ◇法庭宣判被告无罪。The court declared the defendant not guilty.

宣誓 xuānshì [动] take an oath（*pt* took, *pp* taken）

宣泄 xuānxiè [动] get … off one's chest ◇明天的讨论是给大家一个宣泄的机会。Tomorrow's discussion will be an opportunity for everyone to get things off their chests.

宣言 xuānyán [名] declaration

宣扬 xuānyáng [动] advocate

宣战 xuānzhàn [动] declare war ◇珍珠港事件后，美国向日本宣战。After Pearl Harbor the United States declared war on Japan.

喧 xuān [动] make a noise

喧宾夺主 xuān bīn duó zhǔ get one's priorities wrong

喧哗 xuānhuá **I** [形] riotous **II** [动] create a disturbance

喧闹 xuānnào [形] rowdy

喧嚣 xuānxiāo **I** [形] noisy **II** [动] cause an uproar

玄 xuán [形] **1** (深奥) deep **2** (口) (玄乎) unreliable

玄乎 xuánhu [形] (口) unreliable

玄妙 xuánmiào [形] mysterious

玄虚 xuánxū [名] mystery

悬 xuán **I** [动] **1** (挂) hang（*pt, pp* hung）**2** (设想) imagine **3** (挂念) be concerned about **4** (未定) be unresolved ◇这件事还悬着呢。This matter is still unresolved. **II** [形] far apart

悬案 xuán'àn [名] unsolved case

悬挂 xuánguà [动] hang（*pt, pp* hung）

悬念 xuánniàn [名] suspense

悬赏 xuánshǎng [动] offer a reward ◇政府悬赏百万美金捉拿要犯。The government offered a reward of a million dollars for the arrest of the perpetrator.

悬殊 xuánshū [形] distant ◇大城市里贫富悬殊。In big cities there's a huge gap between the rich and the poor.

悬崖 xuányá [名] precipice

旋 xuán **I** [动] **1** (旋转) revolve **2** (返回) return **II** [名] spiral ▷另见 xuàn

旋律 xuánlǜ [名] melody

旋钮 xuánniǔ [名] knob

旋绕 xuánrào [动] circle ◇乐曲声在耳边旋绕不绝。The tune kept going round and round in my head.

旋涡 xuánwō [名] whirlpool

旋转 xuánzhuǎn [动] revolve ◊地球围绕太阳旋转。The earth revolves around the sun.

漩 xuán [名] whirlpool

漩涡 xuánwō [名] whirlpool

选 xuǎn I [动] **1** (挑选) choose (*pt* chose, *pp* chosen) **2** (选举) vote II [名] **1** (指人) selection ♦人选 selection of people **2** (作品集) collection ♦文选 collected works (*pl*)

选拔 xuǎnbá [动] select

选本 xuǎnběn [名] anthology

选材 xuǎncái [动] **1** (选人才) select talent **2** (选材料) select material

选集 xuǎnjí [名] anthology

选举 xuǎnjǔ [动] elect

选民 xuǎnmín [名] electorate

选派 xuǎnpài [动] select

选取 xuǎnqǔ [动] choose (*pt* chose, *pp* chosen)

选手 xuǎnshǒu [名] contestant

选修 xuǎnxiū [动] choose to study (*pt* chose, *pp* chosen) ◊这学期我选修了经济学。This term I've chosen to study economics. ◊选修课程 optional course

选择 xuǎnzé [动] choose (*pt* chose, *pp* chosen) ◊成千种商品供您自由选择。We have a thousand different products for you to choose from. ◊选择配偶 choose a partner ◊别无选择 have no choice ◊中文字体选择 a selection of Chinese fonts

炫 xuàn [动] **1** (晃眼) dazzle **2** (夸耀) show off (*pt* showed, *pp* shown)

炫耀 xuànyào [动] show off (*pt* showed, *pp* shown)

绚 xuàn [形] splendid

绚烂 xuànlàn [形] splendid

绚丽 xuànlì [形] gorgeous

眩 xuàn [形] (书) dizzy

眩目 xuànmù [动] dazzle

旋 xuàn [动] spin (*pt*, *pp* spun)
▷另见 xuán

旋风 xuànfēng [名] whirlwind

渲 xuàn 见下文

渲染 xuànrǎn [动] exaggerate

削 xuē 见下文
▷另见 xiāo

削减 xuējiǎn [动] cut (*pt*, *pp* cut) ◊削减财政开支 cut government expenditure

削弱 xuēruò [动] weaken

靴 xuē [名] boot

靴子 xuēzi [名] boot

穴 xué [名] **1** (洞) den **2** (穴位) acupuncture point

穴位 xuéwèi [名] acupuncture point

学 xué I [动] **1** (学习) study ◊学英语 learn English **2** (模仿) imitate ◊学鸟叫 imitate birdsong II [名] **1** (学问) learning ♦博学 erudition **2** (学科) science ♦数学 mathematics ♦生物学 biology ♦化学 chemistry **3** (学校) school ♦大学 university ♦中学 senior school (英), high school (美) ♦小学 primary school (英), elementary school (美)

学报 xuébào [名] academic journal

学潮 xuécháo [名] student movement

学风 xuéfēng [名] learning style

学府 xuéfǔ [名] institute of higher education

学籍 xuéjí [名] one's status as a student

学界 xuéjiè [名] educational circles (*pl*)

学究 xuéjiū [名] pedant

学科 xuékē [名] subject

学力 xuélì [名] level of academic attainment

学历 xuélì [名] educational background

学龄 xuélíng [名] school age ◊学龄前儿童 preschool children

学名 xuémíng [名] scientific name ◊食盐的学名是氯化钠。The scientific name for salt is sodium chloride.

学派 xuépài [名] school of thought

学生 xuésheng [名] student ◇学生会 student union

学识 xuéshí [名] knowledge

学士 xuéshì [名] 1 (读书人) scholar 2 (指学位) bachelor ◇文学学士 Bachelor of Arts, B.A.

学术 xuéshù [名] learning ◇学术论文 academic essay

学说 xuéshuō [名] theory

学位 xuéwèi [名] degree ◇硕士学位 master's degree

学问 xuéwen [名] learning

学习 xuéxí [动] study ◇学习英语语法 study English grammar ◇学习方法 study methods ◇学习发达国家的经验 learn from the experience of the developed countries

学校 xuéxiào [名] school ◇职业技术学校 vocational and technical school

学业 xuéyè [名] studies (*pl*) ◇你最好完成学业后再找工作。It would be best to look for work again after you've finished your studies.

学者 xuézhě [名] scholar

学子 xuézǐ [名] (书) student

雪 xuě **I** [名] snow **II** [形] bright **III** [动] avenge

雪白 xuěbái [形] snow-white

雪耻 xuěchǐ [动] avenge an insult

雪花 xuěhuā [名] snowflake

雪亮 xuěliàng [形] bright

雪中送炭 xuě zhōng sòng tàn give help when it is most needed

血 xuè [名] 1 (血液) blood 2 (刚强的气质) courage ◇血性男儿 courageous man
▷另见 xiě

血本 xuèběn [名] principal

血汗 xuèhàn [名] sweat and toil

血口喷人 xuè kǒu pēn rén vicious slander

血气方刚 xuèqì fāng gāng full of youthful vigour (英) 或 vigor (美)

血肉 xuèròu [名] flesh and blood

血统 xuètǒng [名] blood relationship

血型 xuèxíng [名] blood type

血压 xuèyā [名] blood pressure

血液 xuèyè [名] 1 (血) blood 2 (主要力量) lifeblood

血缘 xuèyuán [名] blood relationship

血债 xuèzhài [名] blood debt

血战 xuèzhàn [名] bloody battle

勋 xūn [名] merit

勋章 xūnzhāng [名] medal

熏 xūn [动] 1 (烟气接触物体) ◇烟把墙熏黑了。The smoke has blackened the wall. ◇一股怪味直熏鼻子。I'm aware of a strange smell. 2 (熏制) smoke ♦熏肉 smoked meat

熏染 xūnrǎn [动] influence ◇他深得古典艺术之熏染。He has been deeply influenced by classical art.

熏陶 xūntáo [动] influence ◇他从小受到古典音乐的熏陶。He had been influenced by classical music since he was small.

旬 xún [名] 1 (十日) ten days ♦上旬 the first ten days of the month 2 (指十岁) ◇他年过7旬。He's more than seventy years old.

寻 xún [动] search

寻常 xúncháng [形] usual ◇这件事很不寻常。This is a most unusual business.

寻访 xúnfǎng [动] search for

寻呼 xúnhū [动] put out a call for (*pt, pp* put) ♦寻呼机 pager

寻觅 xúnmì [动] search for ◇寻觅人生伴侣 search for a life partner

寻求 xúnqiú [动] seek (*pt, pp* sought) ◇寻求法律帮助 seek legal assistance

寻死 xúnsǐ [动] commit suicide

寻思 xúnsi [动] ponder ◇他在寻思如何才能把问题解决好。He is pondering how to solve the problem.

寻衅 xúnxìn [动] pick a fight

寻找 xúnzhǎo [动] look for ◇寻找丢失的钱包 look for a lost purse ◇寻找人生的真谛 seek the meaning of life

巡 xún [动] patrol

巡查 xúnchá [动] patrol

巡警 xúnjǐng [名] policeman

巡逻 xúnluó [动] patrol ◇这个住宅区24小时都有警卫巡逻。This residential area is patrolled by guards 24 hours a day.

巡视 xúnshì [动] make a tour of inspection

询 xún [动] inquire

询问 xúnwèn [动] ask ◇母亲在信中询问我的生活情况。In her letters Mother asked how I was doing.

循 xún [动] abide by

循规蹈矩 xún guī dǎo jǔ stick to the rules

循环 xúnhuán [动] circulate

循序渐进 xúnxù jiànjìn take a progressive approach ◇我主张循序渐进的学习方法。I'd advise a study method that takes a progressive approach.

循循善诱 xúnxún shàn yòu teach with skill and patience

训 xùn I [动] 1 (教导) teach (*pt, pp* taught) 2 (训练) train II [名] rule

训斥 xùnchì [动] reprimand

训导 xùndǎo [动] give … training and guidance (*pt* gave, *pp* given)

训话 xùnhuà [动] reprimand

训练 xùnliàn [动] training ◇ 职业训练 vocational training

讯 xùn I [动] interrogate ♦审讯 interrogate II [名] message ♦传讯 pass on a message ♦简讯 brief message ♦喜讯 good news (*sg*)

讯问 xùnwèn [动] 1 (问) ask ◇医生讯问了她的身体状况。The doctor asked about her physical condition. 2 (审问) question

汛 xùn [名] flood

汛期 xùnqī [名] flood season

汛情 xùnqíng [名] flood situation

迅 xùn [形] swift

迅猛 xùnměng [形] swift and violent

迅速 xùnsù [形] swift

驯 xùn I [形] tame II [动] tame

驯服 xùnfú I [形] tame II [动] tame ◇驯服野兽 tame wild animals

驯化 xùnhuà [动] domesticate

驯良 xùnliáng [形] docile

驯养 xùnyǎng [动] tame

徇 xùn [动] (书) give way to (*pt* gave, *pp* given)

徇情 xùnqíng [动] (书) be swayed by personal considerations

徇私 xùnsī [动] show favouritism (英) 或 favoritism (美) (*pt* showed, *pp* shown)

逊 xùn [形] 1 (谦虚) modest 2 (书) (差) inferior

逊色 xùnsè [动] be inferior to ◇你的工作成绩和他相比毫不逊色。Your achievements at work are not inferior to his.

殉 xùn [动] die for ♦殉情 die for love

殉难 xùnnàn [动] die ◇他在抗洪救灾中不幸殉难。Sadly, he died fighting the floods.

殉职 xùnzhí [动] die in the line of duty ◇3名消防队员在救火时殉职。Three members of the fire brigade died in the line of duty.

熏 xùn [动] (方) suffocate

Yy

丫 yā [名] **1** (分叉) fork **2** (方) (女孩子) girl

丫头 yātou [名] **1** (女孩子) girl **2** (旧) (丫鬟) maid

压 yā **I** [动] **1** (施力) press **2** (超越) outdo (*pt* outdid, *pp* outdone) **3** (使稳定) control **4** (压制) suppress **5** (积压) put … off (*pt, pp* put) ◇上访信要及时处理，不能压着。Appeals to the authorities should be dealt with promptly – you mustn't put them off. **6** (下注) bet (*pt, pp* bet) **II** [名] pressure
▷另见 yà

压价 yājià [动] force a price down

压力 yālì [名] **1** (物) pressure **2** (指对人) pressure ◇她承受着来自媒体的压力。She is coming under pressure from the media. **3** (负担) burden ◇沉重的生活压力 the heavy burden of existence

压迫 yāpò [动] **1** (压制) oppress **2** (挤压) put pressure on (*pt, pp* put) ◇囊肿压迫神经。Cysts put pressure on the nerves.

压岁钱 yāsuìqián [名] *traditional gifts of money given to children during the Spring Festival*

压缩 yāsuō [动] **1** (指体积) compress **2** (减少) reduce

压抑 yāyì [动] suppress

压制 yāzhì [动] **1** (抑制) suppress **2** (指制造方法) press

呀 yā **I** [叹] (表示惊异) oh ◇呀！已经12点了！ Oh! It's 12 o'clock already! **II** [拟] creak

押 yā **I** [动] **1** (抵押) leave … as a security (*pt, pp* left) **2** (拘留) detain ◇这所监狱押着几百名犯人。Several hundred convicts are held in this prison. **3** (看管) guard **II** [名] signature

押金 yājīn [名] deposit

押送 yāsòng [动] send … under escort (*pt, pp* sent)

押韵 yāyùn [动] rhyme

鸦 yā [名] crow

鸦片 yāpiàn [名] opium

鸦雀无声 yā què wú shēng so quiet you could hear a pin drop ◇教室里鸦雀无声。It was so quiet in the classroom that you could hear a pin drop.

鸭 yā [名] duck

牙 yá [名] **1** (牙齿) tooth (*pl* teeth) **2** (牙状物) ◆月牙 crescent moon

牙齿 yáchǐ [名] tooth (*pl* teeth)

牙床 yáchuáng [名] gum

牙膏 yágāo [名] toothpaste

牙关 yáguān [名] jaw ◇我们咬紧牙关渡过了难关。We gritted our teeth through the tough times.

牙科 yákē [名] dental department

牙签 yáqiān [名] toothpick

牙刷 yáshuā [名] toothbrush

牙痛 yátòng [名] toothache

牙医 yáyī [名] dentist

牙龈 yáyín [名] gum

芽 yá [名] **1** (指植物) sprout **2** (芽状物) spike

涯 yá [名] **1** (边际) end ◆天涯 the ends of the earth **2** (喻) (极限) limit

崖 yá [名] cliff

哑 yǎ [形] **1** (不能说话) mute **2** (不说话) speechless **3** (嘶哑) hoarse

哑巴 yǎba [名] mute

哑剧 yǎjù [名] mime

哑口无言 yǎ kǒu wú yán be reduced to silence ◇他被质问得哑口无言。He was reduced to silence by the interrogation.

哑铃 yǎlíng [名] dumbbell

哑谜 yǎmí [名] riddle ◇你就直说吧，别打哑谜了！ Tell me straight – don't talk in riddles!

哑语 yǎyǔ [名] sign language ◇第五频道可以收看哑语新闻。You can see the news in sign language on Channel Five.

雅 yǎ I [形] 1 (合乎规范) proper 2 (高尚) elegant II [名] (敬) you ♦雅意 your esteemed opinion

雅观 yǎguān [形] tasteful ◇这种动作很不雅观。Gestures like that are in really bad taste.

雅量 yǎliàng [名] 1 (大的气度) magnanimity 2 (大的酒量) tolerance for drink

雅皮士 yǎpíshì [名] yuppie

雅俗共赏 yǎ sú gòng shǎng suit all tastes

雅兴 yǎxìng [名] inspiration

雅致 yǎzhì [形] elegant

雅座 yǎzuò [名] private room

轧 yà I [动] 1 (碾) roll 2 (排挤) push out ♦倾轧 push out II [拟] creak ▷另见 zhá

亚 yà I [形] inferior ♦亚热带 sub-tropical belt ◇我们的产品质量不亚于其他工厂。The quality of our products is not inferior to any other factory's. II [名] Asia

亚军 yàjūn [名] runner-up (*pl* runners-up)

亚洲 yàzhōu [名] Asia ◇她是亚洲人。She's Asian.

压 yà 见下文 ▷另见 yā

压根儿 yàgēnr [副] at all ◇我压根儿就没见过这样的事。I've never seen anything like it.

揠 yà [动] (书) pull … up

揠苗助长 yà miáo zhù zhǎng do more harm than good

咽 yān [名] pharynx ▷另见 yàn

咽喉 yānhóu [名] 1 (字) throat 2 (喻) (险要处) strategic pass

烟 yān I [名] 1 (指气体) smoke 2 (烟状物) mist 3 (烟草) tobacco ♦香烟 cigarette 4 (鸦片) opium II [动] be irritated by smoke ◇厨房里的烟烟得人睁不开眼睛。The smoke in the kitchen irritated our eyes so badly that we couldn't keep them open.

烟草 yāncǎo [名] 1 tobacco plant 2 (烟草制品) tobacco

烟花 yānhuā [名] firework ◇孩子们爱放烟花。Kids like to set off fireworks.

烟灰缸 yānhuīgāng [名] ashtray

烟火 yānhuǒ [名] 1 (烟花) fireworks (*pl*) 2 (烟和火) smoke and fire

烟卷儿 yānjuǎnr [名] cigarette

烟民 yānmín [名] smokers (*pl*)

烟幕 yānmù [名] smokescreen ◇他的和平演说不过是一种烟幕。His peace talks are merely a smokescreen.

烟消云散 yān xiāo yún sàn vanish into thin air ◇得知真实情况后，人们的不满情绪烟消云散了。When they found out what was really going on, the people's feelings of discontent vanished into thin air.

殷 yān [形] (书) dark red ▷另见 yīn

殷红 yānhóng [形] dark red

胭 yān 见下文

胭脂 yānzhi [名] rouge

阉 yān I [动] castrate II [名] (书) eunuch

阉割 yāngē [动] castrate

淹 yān [动] 1 (淹没) flood 2 (浸渍) tingle

淹没 yānmò [动] 1 (漫过) submerge 2 (喻) drown … out ◇歌声被歌迷们尖叫声所淹没。The song was drowned out by the screeches of the fans. ◇她瘦小的身影很快淹没在人海中。Her slight form was soon drowned in the crowd.

腌 yān [动] pickle

腌制 yānzhì [动] pickle ◇腌制食品不宜多吃。Pickled foods should not be eaten in large quantities.

延 yán [动] 1 (延长) extend 2 (推迟) delay 3 (聘请) employ

延长 yáncháng [动] extend

延迟 yánchí [动] delay

延年益寿 yán nián yì shòu prolong life ◊据说少食多餐能够延年益寿。It is said that eating little but often can prolong your life.

延伸 yánshēn [动] stretch

延误 yánwù [动] delay

延续 yánxù [动] go on (*pt* went, *pp* gone)

严 yán [形] **1** (严密) tight ◊我把门关严了。I shut the door tightly. **2** (严格) strict **3** (形容程度深) severe

严惩 yánchéng [动] punish … severely

严打 yándǎ [动] crack down on ◊开展针对盗版的严打 launch a crackdown on pirating

严格 yángé [形] strict ◊大家要严格遵守规章制度。Everyone must strictly abide by the rules and regulations.

严谨 yánjǐn [形] **1** (严密谨慎) meticulous **2** (严密细致) compact

严峻 yánjùn [形] rigorous

严酷 yánkù [形] **1** (严厉) stern **2** (残酷) cruel

严厉 yánlì [形] severe ◊父亲严厉地批评了他。His father gave him a severe telling-off.

严密 yánmì [形] **1** (没有缝隙) tight ◊罐头封得很严密。The tin is closed very tightly. **2** (没有疏漏) close ◊人们严密关注着事态的发展。People kept a close watch on how the situation was developing.

严明 yánmíng **I** [形] firm but fair **II** [动] be firm but fair

严肃 yánsù **I** [形] **1** (庄重) solemn **2** (严格认真) severe ◊对于违章人员一定要严肃处理。People who break the rules must be dealt with severely. **II** [动] enforce

严正 yánzhèng [形] stern but fair

严重 yánzhòng [形] serious ◊这一工程存在着严重的质量问题。There are serious problems with the quality of this project. ◊他的病情非常严重。His illness is extremely serious.

言 yán **I** [动] speak (*pt* spoke, *pp* spoken) ◊言之有理 sound reasonable **II** [名] **1** (话) speech **2** (字) words (*pl*)

言不由衷 yán bù yóu zhōng not say what one means ◊他的回答言不由衷。He didn't say what he meant.

言辞 yáncí [名] wording

言归正传 yán guī zhèng zhuàn get back to business ◊刚才大家闲聊了半天，现在言归正传吧。We've been chatting for ages – now let's get back to business.

言简意赅 yán jiǎn yì gāi be brief and to the point

言论 yánlùn [名] speech ◊言论自由 freedom of speech

言情片 yánqíngpiān [名] romantic film (英) 或 movie (美)

言谈 yántán [名] what one says ◊从言谈中, 我了解了他的过去。From what he said, I learned a lot about his past.

言听计从 yán tīng jì cóng take people at their word ◊他对他妈妈言听计从。He took his mother at her word.

言语 yányǔ [名] language

岩 yán [名] **1** (岩石) rock **2** (山峰) crag

岩洞 yándòng [名] cave

炎 yán **I** [形] scorching **II** [名] **1** (炎症) inflammation **2** (权势) power

炎黄子孙 yánhuángzǐsūn [名] Chinese people (*pl*)

炎热 yánrè [形] scorching hot ◊他在北京度过了一个炎热的夏天。He spent a scorching hot summer in Beijing.

炎症 yánzhèng [名] inflammation

沿 yán **I** [介] along ◊沿着这条路往前走。Go straight along this road. **II** [动] **1** (依照) follow ♦沿袭 follow **2** (镶边) border **III** [名] edge

沿岸 yán'àn [名] bank

沿革 yángé [名] evolution

沿海 yánhǎi [名] coast ◊夏天，很多人到沿海城市度假。In summer, many people go to the coastal cities for their holidays.

沿袭 yánxí [动] follow

沿用 yányòng [动] continue to use

研 yán [动] **1** (细磨) grind (*pt, pp* ground) **2** (研究) research

研读 yándú [动] research ◊他正在研读语言学理论方面的书籍。He's researching linguistic theory from a series of books.

研究 yánjiū [动] **1** (探求) research ◊做生意首先要研究市场。When doing business, one must first research the market. ◊历史研究对今天很有借鉴意义。Much can be gained today from historical research. **2** (商讨) discuss ◊领导们正在研究职工提交的建议。The leaders are discussing the suggestions submitted by the workers. ◊这套方案有待于进一步研究。This scheme is awaiting further discussion.

研讨 yántǎo [动] discuss

研制 yánzhì [动] develop

盐 yán [名] salt

筵 yán [名] banquet

筵席 yánxí [名] banquet

颜 yán [名] **1** (字) face **2** (体面) face **3** (颜色) colour (英), color (美)

颜料 yánliào [名] colouring (英), coloring (美)

颜色 yánsè [名] **1** (色彩) colour (英), color (美) ◊她喜欢穿深颜色的衣服。She likes to wear dark colours. **2** (表情) expression **3** (指报复) revenge ◊给你点颜色看看！ I'll show you!

檐 yán [名] **1** (房檐) eaves (*pl*) **2** (檐状物) brim

奄 yǎn 见下文

奄奄 yǎnyǎn [形] feeble

俨 yǎn [形] (书) solemn

俨然 yǎnrán **I** [形] (书) solemn **II** [副] just like ◊她走上讲台，俨然是个老师。She walked up to the podium, just like a teacher.

衍 yǎn [动] **1** (书) develop **2** (多余) be redundant

衍变 yǎnbiàn [动] evolve

衍生 yǎnshēng [动] **1** (指化合物) derive **2** (产生) give rise to (*pt* gave, *pp* given) ◊这个地方衍生了很多美丽动人的传说。This place has given rise to many beautiful and touching legends.

掩 yǎn [动] **1** (遮盖) cover **2** (关) close

掩蔽 yǎnbì **I** [动] take shelter (*pt* took, *pp* taken) **II** [名] shelter

掩藏 yǎncáng [动] hide (*pt* hid, *pp* hidden)

掩耳盗铃 yǎn ěr dào líng bury one's head in the sand

掩盖 yǎngài [动] **1** (遮盖) cover **2** (隐藏) conceal ◊陷阱用树枝掩盖起来。The trap is covered with tree branches.

掩护 yǎnhù **I** [动] cover for **II** [名] cover

掩埋 yǎnmái [动] bury

掩饰 yǎnshì [动] conceal

眼 yǎn **I** [名] **1** (眼睛) eye **2** (小洞) small hole **3** (关键) crux **II** [量] ◊村里打了两眼井。Two wells were dug in the village.

眼巴巴 yǎnbābā [形] **1** (形容急切盼望) eager ◊孩子们眼巴巴地盼着过年。The children were eagerly awaiting the New Year. **2** (形容无可奈何) helpless ◊他眼巴巴地看着自己的家被大火吞噬。He watched helplessly as he saw his house being engulfed by flames.

眼馋 yǎnchán [动] covet

眼福 yǎnfú [名] a feast for the eyes

眼高手低 yǎn gāo shǒu dī have great ambition but little talent

眼光 yǎnguāng [名] **1** (视线) gaze **2** (观察能力) vision ◊在选拔人才方面，他非常有眼光。He has real vision when it comes to promoting talent. **3** (观点) perspective ◊你不能用老眼光来评价现在的年轻人。You can't apply outdated perspectives when criticizing today's youth.

眼红 yǎnhóng **I** [动] be jealous **II** [形] furious

眼睑 yǎnjiǎn [名] eyelid

眼界 yǎnjiè [名] horizons (*pl*) ◇读书能扩大眼界。Reading can broaden your horizons.

眼睛 yǎnjing [名] eye ◇她的眼睛里涌出了喜悦的泪花。Tears of joy welled up in her eyes.

眼看 yǎnkàn **I** [动] **1** (指正在发生) look on ◇她眼看着信被风吹跑了。She looked on as the letter got blown away by the wind. **2** (任凭) allow **II** [副] soon ◇眼看着就到秋天了。Soon it'll be autumn.

眼泪 yǎnlèi [名] tear

眼力 yǎnlì [名] **1** (视力) eyesight **2** (鉴别能力) judgement ◇你真有眼力，买了能升值的房子。You've obviously got good judgement, buying property that's likely to go up in value.

眼色 yǎnsè [名] look ◇怕我说漏了，她赶紧给我使眼色。She shot me a look, worried that I might give the game away.

眼神 yǎnshén [名] **1** (指神态) expression **2** (方) (视力) eyesight

眼生 yǎnshēng [形] unfamiliar ◇我看她有点眼生。She doesn't look particularly familiar.

眼熟 yǎnshú [形] familiar

眼下 yǎnxià [名] ◇眼下正是大学生毕业找工作的时候。Now is the time when university graduates start looking for work.

眼睁睁 yǎnzhēngzhēng [形] helpless ◇别眼睁睁地看着他受罪。Don't just stand there watching him suffer.

眼中钉 yǎnzhōngdīng [名] thorn in one's side

偃 yǎn [动] (书) lay ... down (*pt, pp* laid)

偃旗息鼓 yǎn qí xī gǔ lay down one's arms

演 yǎn [动] **1** (演变) evolve **2** (发挥) bring ... into play (*pt, pp* brought) **3** (依照程式) follow a routine **4** (表演) perform

演变 yǎnbiàn [动] evolve

演出 yǎnchū [动] perform

演化 yǎnhuà [动] evolve

演讲 yǎnjiǎng [动] make a speech

演示 yǎnshì [动] demonstrate

演说 yǎnshuō [动] make a speech

演算 yǎnsuàn [动] work ... out ◇数学课上，老师让我们演算了10道题。In the maths class the teacher made us work out ten problems.

演习 yǎnxí [动] manoeuvre (英), maneuver (美)

演义 yǎnyì [名] historical novel

演绎 yǎnyì [名] deduction

演员 yǎnyuán [名] performer

演奏 yǎnzòu [动] perform ◇这位音乐大师演奏得非常美妙。This great musician gave an exquisite performance.

鼹 yǎn [名] mole

鼹鼠 yǎnshǔ [名] mole

厌 yàn [动] **1** (满足) be satisfied **2** (厌烦) be fed up with **3** (厌恶) detest

厌烦 yànfán [动] be sick of ◇他老打扰我，很让人厌烦。He keeps disturbing me – I'm sick of it.

厌倦 yànjuàn [动] be weary of

厌世 yànshì [动] be world-weary

厌恶 yànwù [动] loathe

砚 yàn [名] ink stone

砚台 yàntai [名] ink stone

咽 yàn [动] **1** (吞咽) swallow ◇5片药他一口就咽了下去。He swallowed down five tablets in one go. **2** (憋住) hold back (*pt, pp* held)
▷另见 yān

咽气 yànqì [动] (死) die

宴 yàn [动] host a dinner

宴会 yànhuì [名] banquet ◇他们举行宴会欢迎国际友人。They held a banquet to welcome their friends from overseas.

宴请 yànqǐng [动] invite ... to dinner ◇公司宴请了10位贵宾。The company held a dinner for ten important guests.

艳 yàn **I** [形] **1** (华丽) gorgeous **2** (指

情爱) romantic II [动] (书) envy

艳福 yànfú [名] luck in love ◇公司最漂亮女孩儿爱上了他，真是艳福不浅呢！ The prettiest girl in the office has fallen for him: he's certainly not short of luck!

艳丽 yànlì [形] gorgeous

唁 yàn [动] extend condolences ♦ 吊唁 offer one's condolences

唁电 yàndiàn [名] condolences (*pl*)

验 yàn I [动] **1** (检查) test **2** (灵验) produce the expected result II [名] result

验光 yànguāng [动] have an eye test ◇配眼镜前要先验光。Before you get new glasses you should have your eyes tested.

验尸 yànshī [动] perform an autopsy

验收 yànshōu [动] accept … after checking

验算 yànsuàn [动] check one's calculations

验血 yànxiě [动] have a blood test

验证 yànzhèng [动] verify

谚 yàn [名] saying

谚语 yànyǔ [名] proverb

雁 yàn [名] wild goose (*pl* geese)

焰 yàn [名] **1** (火苗) flame **2** (喻) (气势) momentum

焰火 yànhuǒ [名] firework

燕 yàn [名] swallow

燕麦 yànmài [名] oats (*pl*)

燕尾服 yànwěifú [名] tailcoat

燕窝 yànwō [名] edible bird's nest

赝 yàn [形] (书) forged

赝本 yànběn [名] forgery

赝品 yànpǐn [名] fake

央 yāng I [动] plead ◇孩子央了半天，母亲才答应。The child pleaded with his mother for ages before she agreed. II [名] centre (英), center (美)

央告 yānggao [动] beg

央求 yāngqiú [动] plead

秧 yāng [名] **1** (幼苗) seedling **2** (茎) stem **3** (稻秧) rice seedling

扬 yáng I [动] **1** (高举) raise **2** (传播) spread (*pt*, *pp* spread) II [形] good-looking

扬长避短 yáng cháng bì duǎn play to one's strengths ◇在用人上要注意扬长避短。When managing people you should get them to play to their strengths.

扬长而去 yángcháng ér qù storm out ◇他把杯子摔在地上, 然后扬长而去。He threw his cup onto the floor, and stormed out.

扬帆 yángfān [动] (书) set sail (*pt*, *pp* set)

扬眉吐气 yáng méi tǔ qì hold one's head up high

扬名 yángmíng [动] become famous (*pt* became, *pp* become)

扬弃 yángqì [动] (抛弃) discard

扬言 yángyán [动] (贬) spread it about (*pt*, *pp* spread) ◇他扬言要打断陶陶的腿。He was spreading it about that he was going to break Taotao's legs.

扬扬 yángyáng [形] complacent

羊 yáng [名] sheep (*pl* sheep) ♦ 山羊 goat

羊肠小道 yángcháng xiǎodào [名] narrow, winding road

羊毛 yángmáo [名] wool

羊绒衫 yángróngshān [名] cashmere

阳 yáng I [名] **1** (阴的对立面) Yang (*of Yin and Yang*) **2** (太阳) sun II [形] **1** (突出) protruding **2** (外露) overt **3** (带正电) positive

阳春 yángchūn [名] springtime

阳奉阴违 yáng fèng yīn wéi pretend to obey orders ◇他阳奉阴违，最后被免了职。He pretended to obey orders without actually executing them, and in the end he was dismissed.

阳刚 yánggāng [形] masculine

阳历 yánglì [名] the Gregorian calendar

阳台 yángtái [名] balcony

阳性 yángxìng [名] **1** (医) positive **2** (语言) masculine

杨 yáng [名] poplar

杨柳 yángliǔ [名] **1** (杨树和柳树) poplars and willows (*pl*) **2** (柳树) willow

佯 yáng [动] feign

佯装 yángzhuāng [动] pretend

洋 yáng **I** [名] **1** (海洋) ocean **2** (洋钱) silver dollar **II** [形] **1** (盛大) vast **2** (外国的) foreign

洋白菜 yángbáicài [名] cabbage

洋葱 yángcōng [名] onion

洋货 yánghuò [名] foreign goods (*pl*)

洋气 yángqì [形] **1** (指有西方味的) Western **2** (贬) (时髦的) trendy

洋相 yángxiàng [名] spectacle ◇今天他在全班同学面前出了个大洋相。Today he made a real spectacle of himself in front of all his classmates.

洋洋 yángyáng [形] **1** (盛大) copious **2** (得意) smug

洋溢 yángyì [动] brim with

仰 yǎng [动] **1** (脸向上) look up **2** (敬慕) respect **3** (依赖) depend on

仰慕 yǎngmù [动] look up to

仰望 yǎngwàng [动] look up

仰仗 yǎngzhàng [动] depend on

养 yǎng **I** [动] **1** (供给) provide for **2** (饲养) keep (*pt, pp* kept) ◇她总爱养很多狗。She's always kept lots of dogs. ◇我爱养花。I like growing flowers. **3** (生育) give birth to (*pt* gave, *pp* given) **4** (培养) form ◇他养成了早睡早起的习惯。He had formed the habit of going to bed early and getting up early. **5** (调养) recuperate **6** (维修) maintain **7** (扶助) support **8** (保持) look after ◇你的头发太干，需要好好养养。Your hair's too dry – you need to look after it a bit. **II** [形] foster ♦养母 foster-mother ♦养子 adopted son **III** [名] cultivation

养分 yǎngfèn [名] nutrient

养护 yǎnghù [动] **1** (指物体) maintain **2** (指人体) build up one's strength (*pt, pp* built)

养活 yǎnghuo [动] (口) **1** (提供生活费用) support **2** (饲养) raise **3** (生育抚养) give birth to (*pt* gave, *pp* given)

养精蓄锐 yǎng jīng xù ruì conserve one's strength

养老 yǎnglǎo [动] **1** (奉养老人) care for the elderly **2** (年老休养) enjoy one's old age

养料 yǎngliào [名] nourishment

养生 yǎngshēng [动] keep fit (*pt, pp* kept)

养育 yǎngyù [动] bring up (*pt, pp* brought)

养殖 yǎngzhí [动] breed (*pt, pp* bred)

养尊处优 yǎng zūn chǔ yōu live a life of luxury

氧 yǎng [名] oxygen

氧化 yǎnghuà [动] oxidize

痒 yǎng [动] itch ◇他全身痒得难受。His whole body is horribly itchy. ◇见别人出国旅游，她心里也有点痒了。Seeing others travelling abroad gave her itchy feet. ◇他心里痒痒的，想马上就开始该项目。He's itching to get started on the project.

样 yàng **I** [名] **1** (模样) style **2** (标准物) sample **II** [量] type ◇她带了3样水果。She brought three types of fruit. ◇我每样菜都尝了尝。I've tasted every single dish.

样板 yàngbǎn [名] **1** (板状样品) sample **2** (板状工具) template **3** (榜样) model

样本 yàngběn [名] **1** (指商品图样) book of samples **2** (指出版物) proofs (*pl*)

样品 yàngpǐn [名] sample

样式 yàngshì [名] style

样子 yàngzi [名] **1** (模样) appearance ◇这个手机样子不错。This mobile phone looks good. **2** (神情) expression **3** (样板) pattern **4** (口) (情形) the look of things ◇看样子他不来了。By the look of things, he's not coming.

漾 yàng [动] **1** (水面微动) ripple **2** (向外流) overflow

幺 yāo **I** [数] one **II** [形] youngest

夭 yāo [动] die young

夭折 yāozhé [动] **1** (未成年而死) die young **2** (喻) (形容停止) come to an untimely end (*pt* came, *pp* come)

吆 yāo 见下文

吆喝 yāohe [动] call out

妖 yāo **I** [名] evil spirit **II** [形] **1** (邪恶) wicked **2** (书) (妖艳) bewitching

妖怪 yāoguài [名] monster

妖精 yāojing [名] **1** (妖怪) demon **2** (喻) scarlet woman (*pl* women)

妖媚 yāomèi [形] seductive

妖魔 yāomó [名] monster

妖艳 yāoyàn [形] coquettish

要 yāo [动] **1** (求) ask **2** (威胁) threaten **3** (邀请) invite
▷另见 yào

要求 yāoqiú **I** [动] demand ◇工人们要求改善工作环境。The workers demanded improvements to their working environment. ◇要求加薪 request a pay rise **II** [名] request ◇航空公司满足了乘客的要求。The airline company satisfied all the passengers' requests. ◇老师的要求非常严格。The teacher's demands are very severe. ◇这些要求很难达到。These requirements are going to be difficult to meet.

要挟 yāoxié [动] threaten

腰 yāo [名] **1** (身体中部) waist ◇她疼得直不起腰来。She was in so much pain that she couldn't stand up straight. **2** (裤腰) waist ◇这条裙子腰太肥。This skirt's too big at the waist. **3** (腰包) wallet **4** (事物中段) middle

腰板儿 yāobǎnr [名] **1** (腰和背) back **2** (口) (体格) health ◇她80岁了，腰板儿还挺硬朗。She's eighty years old, but still in excellent health.

腰包 yāobāo [名] wallet

腰带 yāodài [名] belt

腰杆子 yāogǎnzi [名] **1** (口) (腰部) back **2** (靠山) backing ◇他腰杆子硬，当然什么都不怕啦！ He's got very secure backing – of course he doesn't have much to fear!

腰果 yāoguǒ [名] cashew nut

腰围 yāowéi [名] waistline

腰子 yāozi [名] kidney

邀 yāo [动] **1** (邀请) invite **2** (书) (求得) seek (*pt, pp* sought)

邀功 yāogōng [动] take all the credit (*pt* took, *pp* taken)

邀集 yāojí [动] invite … to a get-together ◇他经常邀集一些朋友。He often invites friends to get-togethers.

邀请 yāoqǐng [动] invite ◇她愉快地接受了邀请。She accepted the invitation readily.

肴 yáo [名] meat dishes (*pl*) ◇美味佳肴 delectable dishes

窑 yáo [名] **1** (用于烧砖) kiln **2** (指煤矿) pit **3** (窑洞) cave dwelling **4** (指妓院) brothel

窑洞 yáodòng [名] cave dwelling

窑子 yáozi [名] brothel

谣 yáo [名] **1** (歌谣) folk song **2** (谣言) rumour (英), rumor (美)

谣传 yáochuán **I** [动] be rumoured (英) 或 rumored (美) ◇谣传罗素破产了。Rumour has it that Russell has gone bankrupt. **II** [名] rumour (英), rumor (美)

谣言 yáoyán [名] hearsay

摇 yáo [动] shake (*pt* shook, *pp* shaken)

摇摆 yáobǎi [动] wave

摇荡 yáodàng [动] sway

摇动 yáodòng [动] **1** (摇东西) wave **2** (晃) shake (*pt* shook, *pp* shaken)

摇滚乐 yáogǔnyuè [名] rock and roll

摇晃 yáohuàng [动] shake (*pt*, shook *pp* shaken) ◇他太醉了，走路都摇晃。He was so drunk that he was staggering around.

摇奖 yáojiǎng [动] hold a draw (*pt, pp* held)

摇篮 yáolán [名] cradle ◇尼罗河流域是古埃及文明的摇篮。The River

Nile was the cradle of ancient Egyptian civilization.

摇旗呐喊 yáo qí nàhǎn bang the drum ◊球迷为足球队摇旗呐喊。The football fans banged the drum for their team.

摇钱树 yáoqiánshù [名] source of easy money

摇摇欲坠 yáoyáo yù zhuì hang by a thread ◊他的明星地位摇摇欲坠。His celebrity status hung by a thread. ◊这座老桥摇摇欲坠。This old bridge is on the verge of collapse.

摇曳 yáoyè [动] sway

遥 yáo [形] distant

遥感 yáogǎn [名] remote sensing

遥控 yáokòng [动] operate by remote control

遥望 yáowàng [动] gaze into the distance

遥遥 yáoyáo [形] **1** (指距离) distant **2** (指时间) lengthy

遥远 yáoyuǎn [形] **1** (指距离) distant **2** (指时间) far-off ◊遥远的将来 the far-off future

杳 yǎo [形] (书) far away and out of sight

杳无音信 yǎo wú yīnxìn never heard from again ◊他20年前去了海外，至今杳无音信。He went overseas twenty years ago, and he hasn't been heard of since.

咬 yǎo [动] **1** (指用嘴) bite (*pt* bit, *pp* bitten) **2** (夹住) grip ◊这个钳子太小，咬不住。These pliers are too small – I can't get a grip. **3** (牵扯) incriminate **4** (过分钻研) nit-pick **5** (紧追) be neck and neck

咬耳朵 yǎo ěrduo [动] (口) whisper

咬文嚼字 yǎo wén jiáo zì pay excessive attention to wording ◊咬文嚼字未必能写出好文章。Paying excessive attention to wording doesn't necessarily produce a good essay.

咬牙 yǎoyá [动] **1** (咬紧牙关) clench one's teeth **2** (磨牙) grind one's teeth (*pt, pp* ground)

舀 yǎo [动] ladle

舀子 yǎozi [名] ladle

窈 yǎo 见下文

窈窕 yǎotiǎo [形] (书) gentle and beautiful

药 yào **I** [名] **1** (指治病) medicine **2** (指化学物品) chemical **II** [动] **1** (书) (治疗) cure **2** (毒死) poison

药补 yàobǔ [名] drug therapy ◊药补和食补相结合对她恢复健康有好处。A combination of drug therapy and diet will help her recovery.

药材 yàocái [名] herbal medicine

药方 yàofāng [名] prescription ◊医生给我开了一张药方。The doctor wrote me out a prescription.

药理 yàolǐ [名] pharmacology

药力 yàolì [名] effects (*pl*)

药品 yàopǐn [名] medicine

药物 yàowù [名] medicine

药性 yàoxìng [名] medicinal properties (*pl*)

药学 yàoxué [名] pharmacology

要 yào **I** [形] important **II** [名] main issue **III** [动] **1** (想得到) want ◊我女儿要一个新书包。My daughter wants a new schoolbag. **2** (要求) ask ◊老师要我们安静。The teacher asked us to be quiet. **IV** [助动] **1** (应该) should ◊饭前要洗手。You should wash your hands before you eat. **2** (需要) need ◊我要上厕所。I need the toilet. ◊这台风扇要多少钱？ How much is this fan? **3** (表示意志) want ◊我要学开车。I want to learn to drive. **4** (将要) be about to ◊我们要放暑假了。We're about to break for summer vacation. **5** (用于比较) ◊姐姐比妹妹要高些。The elder sister is taller than the younger. ◊她要挣得比你多点。She earns a bit more than you. **V** [连] **1** (如果) if ◊你要碰见他，替我问声好。If you meet him, say hello from me. **2** (要么) either … or ◊要就同意，要就不同意，别模棱两可。Either you agree or you disagree – don't sit on the fence.
▷另见 yāo

要案 yào'àn [名] major case

要不 yàobù [连] **1** (否则) otherwise ◊快点走，要不你要迟到了。Go quickly, otherwise you'll be late. **2** (表示选择) either … or ◊我们要不去看电影，要不去咖啡厅，你说呢？We can either go to see a film or go to a coffee shop – which would you prefer?

要点 yàodiǎn [名] rudiments (*pl*)

要犯 yàofàn [名] main offender

要害 yàohài [名] **1** (指身体) vulnerable spot **2** (军事要地) strategic point **3** (关键) key part

要好 yàohǎo [形] **1** (感情融洽) amicable **2** (上进) eager to improve ◊你的房间总是乱糟糟的，怎么一点也不要好？Your room's always such a tip – don't you care about making it any better?

要紧 yàojǐn [形] **1** (重要) important **2** (严重) serious

要领 yàolǐng [名] **1** (要点) gist **2** (基本要求) main points (*pl*)

要么 yàome [连] either … or ◊你要么学文，要么学理。You either study arts or science.

要命 yàomìng [动] **1** (使丧生) kill **2** (表示程度) be incredibly ◊这个人吝啬得要命。This man's incredibly stingy. **3** (表示抱怨) be dreadful ◊这个饭馆真要命，上菜得一个小时。This is a truly dreadful restaurant – it's taken them an hour to bring our food.

要强 yàoqiáng [形] competitive ◊她在工作上非常要强。She's very competitive at work.

要是 yàoshi [连] if ◊要是你不满意，可以随时退货。If you're not satisfied, you can return the goods at any time.

要死 yàosǐ [副] extremely ◊昨天我忙得要死。I was extremely busy yesterday.

要素 yàosù [名] key element

要职 yàozhí [名] important post

钥 yào 见下文

钥匙 yàoshi [名] key

耀 yào **I** [名] radiance **II** [动] **1** (照射) shine (*pt, pp* shone) **2** (炫耀) boast of **III** [形] brilliant

耀武扬威 yào wǔ yáng wēi flaunt one's power

耀眼 yàoyǎn [形] dazzling

耶 yē 见下文

耶稣 Yēsū [名] Jesus

掖 yē [动] tuck ◊他把信掖在了裤兜里。He tucked the letter into his trouser pocket.

椰 yē [名] coconut

椰子 yēzi [名] **1** (树) coconut tree **2** (果实) coconut

噎 yē [动] **1** (堵塞) choke ◊我吃鱼时噎住了。I choked on the fish. **2** (方) (话) reduce … to silence

爷 yé [名] **1** (祖父) grandfather **2** (方) (父亲) dad **3** (长辈) uncle **4** (旧) (显贵) master **5** (指神、佛) god

爷爷 yéye [名] **1** (口) (祖父) granddad **2** (祖父的同辈人) ◊李爷爷常来我家下棋。Old Mr Li often comes to my house to play chess.

也 yě [副] **1** (同样) also ◊我也是名律师。I'm also a lawyer. ◊他也去过中国。He's been to China too. **2** (表示对等) ◊这条街上有中餐馆，也有西餐馆。There are Chinese restaurants on this street as well as Western restaurants. ◊他特别聪明，也很能干。He's highly intelligent, and also very competent. **3** (表示结果) ◊这道题太难，怎么想也想不出来。This question is too difficult – I just can't figure it out. ◊他太固执，谁劝也不听。He's very stubborn – he never listens to anyone who tries to give him advice. **4** (表示转折) ◊即使他来了，也帮不上忙。Even if he comes, it still won't be of any use. ◊虽然她心里不高兴，也没说什么。Although she was unhappy, she didn't say anything. **5** (表示委婉) ◊这个电影倒也不错。This film really isn't at all bad. **6** (表示强调) ◊她病了，一口饭也不想吃。She's ill – she doesn't want to eat anything at all.

也罢 yěbà [助] **1** (表示容忍) ◊也罢，

我们就不等他了。All right then, we won't wait for him. **2** (表示条件) ◇你高兴也罢，不高兴也罢，反正就这样定了。We've settled the matter anyway, whether you like it or not.

也许 yěxǔ [副] perhaps ◇他还没到，也许是没赶上车。He's still not arrived – perhaps he missed the bus.

冶 yě [动] smelt ♦冶铁 smelt iron

冶炼 yěliàn [动] smelt

野 yě **I** [名] **1** (野外) open country ♦野餐 picnic **2** (界限) border ♦分野 dividing line **3** (民间) ♦在野 out of power **II** [形] **1** (野生) wild ♦野菜 wild herbs **2** (蛮横) rude ♦粗野 rough **3** (无约束) unruly

野餐 yěcān [动] have a picnic ◇周末我们去山上野餐吧！ Let's go for a picnic in the mountains this weekend!

野鸡 yějī [名] **1** (雉) pheasant **2** (妓女) prostitute

野蛮 yěmán [形] **1** (蒙昧) uncivilized **2** (残暴) brutal

野生 yěshēng [形] wild

野兽 yěshòu [名] wild animal

野外 yěwài [名] open country

野味 yěwèi [名] game

野心 yěxīn [名] ambition

野性 yěxìng [名] wild nature

野营 yěyíng [名] camp

业 yè **I** [名] **1** (行业) industry ◇饮食业 the food and drink industry **2** (职业) job ♦就业 obtain employment ♦失业 be unemployed **3** (学业) studies (*pl*) ♦结业 finish one's studies ♦毕业 graduate **4** (事业) enterprise ♦功业 achievement **5** (产业) property ♦家业 family property **II** [副] already ♦业已 already

业绩 yèjì [名] achievement

业务 yèwù [名] profession ◇这些年轻人业务能力很强。These young people are very professional. ◇公司经常组织业务学习活动。The company often organizes professional training sessions.

业余 yèyú **I** [名] spare time ◇业余爱好 hobby **II** [形] amateurish

业主 yèzhǔ [名] owner

叶 yè [名] **1** (叶子) leaf (*pl* leaves) ♦叶脉 vein **2** (时期) period ◇明朝中叶 the mid-Ming period

叶落归根 yè luò guī gēn return to one's roots

页 yè **I** [名] page ♦活页笔记本 loose-leaf notebook **II** [量] page ◇这本书被撕掉了一页。A page has been torn out of this book. ◇翻开了人生新的一页 turn over a new leaf

页码 yèmǎ [名] page number

曳 yè [动] drag ♦拖曳 haul

夜 yè [名] night

夜班 yèbān [名] night shift

夜半 yèbàn [名] midnight

夜不闭户 yè bù bì hù leave one's door unlocked at night

夜长梦多 yè cháng mèng duō long delays cause complications ◇我们争取尽早签合同，免得夜长梦多。We'll do our best to sign the contract as soon as possible, to avoid the problems that may be incurred by a delay.

夜景 yèjǐng [名] night view ◇西湖夜景，美丽迷人。The view of the West Lake by night is absolutely enchanting.

夜郎自大 Yèláng zìdà be foolishly conceited

夜猫子 yèmāozi [名] (方) **1** (猫头鹰) owl **2** (喻) (晚睡者) night owl

夜幕 yèmù [名] night

夜生活 yèshēnghuó [名] nightlife

夜市 yèshì [名] night market

夜宵 yèxiāo [名] late-night snack

夜以继日 yè yǐ jì rì day and night ◇加固堤坝的工程夜以继日地进行着。Work on reinforcing the dam continued day and night.

夜总会 yèzǒnghuì [名] nightclub

液 yè [名] liquid

液化 yèhuà [动] liquefy

液态 yètài [名] liquid

液体 yètǐ [名] liquid

腋 yè [名] (夹肢窝) armpit ♦腋毛 underarm hair

一 yī [数] **1** (指数目) one ◊一分钟 one minute **2** (相同) ◊他们是一类人。They are the same sort of people. ◊大家观点不一。Everyone has different opinions. **3** (另一) ◊传呼机一名寻呼机。Pager is another name for a beeper. **4** (全) ◊一屋子烟 full of smoke **5** (专) ◊一心一意 heart and soul **6** (表示短暂) ◊看一看 take a look **7** (与'就'连用) ◊我一碰杯子，它就掉地上了。I barely touched the glass, and it fell to the floor.

一把手 yī bǎ shǒu [名] **1** (一员) member **2** (能手) skilled worker **3** (负责人) boss

一败涂地 yī bài tú dì come a cropper

一般 yībān [形] **1** (一样) same ◊他们俩一般大。The two of them are the same age. **2** (普通) ordinary ◊他很不一般，工作非常出色。He is quite out of the ordinary, and his work is exceptional.

一板一眼 yī bǎn yī yǎn meticulous

一…半… yī…bàn… [数] ◊我看她的病一时半会儿好不了。It seems to me that she's not going to get well for a while. ◊这个问题不是一句半句能讲清楚的。This can't be explained in a few sentences.

一本正经 yī běn zhèng jīng be prim and proper

一边 yībiān **I** [名] **1** (一面) side ◊镜子的另一边是水银。There is mercury on the other side of this mirror. ◊今天的辩论，你认为哪一边更强？ Which do you think was the strongest side in today's debate? **2** (旁边) ◊你过来帮帮忙，别在一边呆着。Come over and help – don't just hang around on the sidelines. **II** [副] at the same time ◊她吃着晚饭，一边还看着电视。She was eating and watching television at the same time.

一边倒 yī biān dǎo [动] predominate

一并 yībìng [副] together

一…不… yī…bù… [副] **1** (用于两动词之间) ◊他离家出走后一去不返。He left home, never to return. **2** (用于一名一动之间) ◊大厅明亮宽敞，一尘不染。The great hall was bright and spacious – and spotless.

一不做，二不休 yī bù zuò, èr bù xiū go the whole hog

一步登天 yī bù dēng tiān have a meteoric rise

一刹那 yīchànà [名] instant

一唱一和 yī chàng yī hè sing the same tune

一成不变 yī chéng bù biàn immutable

一筹莫展 yī chóu mò zhǎn be at one's wits end

一锤定音 yī chuí dìng yīn settle … there and then

一蹴而就 yī cù ér jiù accomplish at one stroke

一带 yīdài [名] region

一旦 yīdàn **I** [名] single day ◊这座城堡竟然在一次大火中毁于一旦。The great fire destroyed this castle in a single day. **II** [副] ◊一旦发生核战争，整个地球将会陷入灾难。If atomic war were to break out, it would be disastrous for the whole world.

一刀切 yīdāoqiē [动] take a sweeping approach (*pt* took, *pp* taken)

一道 yīdào [副] together

一点 yīdiǎn [量] **1** (一些) some ◊你行李太多，我帮你提一点儿吧。You've got so much luggage – let me help you with some of it. **2** (很少) a little ◊我兜里就剩一点儿钱了。There's a little money left in my pocket. ◊这件事我一点儿都不知道。I know nothing about this.

一定 yīdìng **I** [形] **1** (规定的) definite **2** (固定的) fixed ◊她在城里做小时工，没有一定的收入和住所。She did casual work in the city, but had no fixed income or address. **3** (相当) certain ◊生活条件有了一定的改善。There has been a certain improvement in living conditions. **4** (特定) given ◊在一定条件下

under given circumstances II [副] definitely ◇放心，我一定去机场接你。Don't worry, I'll definitely pick you up at the airport.

一…而… yī…ér… [连] … in one … ◇满满一杯酒，他一饮而尽。The glass was full to overflowing, but he drank it down in one gulp. ◇看到警察来了，围观的人们一哄而散。On seeing the police arrive, the people who had gathered to watch scattered.

一发 yīfā [副] 1 (更加) even more ◇如不抓紧处理，局面将一发不可收拾。If we don't deal with the matter quickly, the situation will become even more unmanageable. 2 (一并) together ◇这件事情，明天会上和其他事情一发讨论。We'll deal with this matter together with other issues at the meeting tomorrow.

一发千钧 yī fà qiān jūn in imminent danger

一帆风顺 yī fān fēng shùn plain sailing

一概 yīgài [副] without exception

一共 yīgòng [副] altogether ◇参加晚会的一共有27个人。There were 27 people at the party altogether. ◇这套书一共多少本？ How many books are there in this set?

一鼓作气 yī gǔ zuò qì make a push for it

一贯 yīguàn [形] consistent

一挥而就 yīhuī'érjiù dash … off

一己 yījǐ [名] oneself

一见如故 yī jiàn rú gù hit it off at once

一见钟情 yī jiàn zhōng qíng love at first sight ◇爱情小说中，男女主人公常常是一见钟情。In romantic fiction, the hero and heroine often fall in love at first sight.

一箭双雕 yī jiàn shuāng diāo kill two birds with one stone

一经 yījīng [副] as soon as ◇决议一经通过，就立即执行。The resolution must be implemented as soon as it's passed.

一…就… yī…jiù… [副] as soon as ◇他一看书就打盹儿。As soon as he started reading he fell asleep.

一举 yījǔ I [名] one action II [副] at one stroke

一蹶不振 yī júe bù zhèn be unable to recover after a setback

一览 yīlǎn [名] overview

一劳永逸 yī láo yǒng yì get things right once and for all

一连 yīlián [副] on end ◇ 一连下了几个月的雨。It's been raining for months on end.

一了百了 yī liǎo bǎi liǎo find a single solution ◇事情错综复杂，很难找到一个一了百了的解决办法。Matters are very complex. It's very difficult to find a single solution to all problems.

一路 yīlù I [名] 1 (行程) journey ◇一路顺利吗？ Did you have a good journey? 2 (一类) a kind ◇他们俩一路货色。They are two of a kind. 3 (一起) the same way ◇明天出差，咱俩是一路。When we go on business tomorrow, we're going the same way. II [副] all the way ◇那辆红色赛车一路领先。That red racing car was in the lead all the way.

一律 yīlù I [形] same II [副] without exception

一马当先 yī mǎ dāng xiān take the lead

一脉相承 yī mài xiāng chéng share the same origins

一毛不拔 yī máo bù bá be very stingy ◇有些人腰缠万贯，对他人却一毛不拔。Some people have bags of money, but they're very stingy with other people.

一面 yī miàn I [名] side ◇这个规定也有合理的一面。This rule has its reasonable side. II [副] at the same time ◇她一面听音乐，一面看小说。She was listening to music and reading a novel at the same time.

一鸣惊人 yī míng jīng rén set the world on fire

一目了然 yī mù liǎo rán be clear at a glance

一诺千金 yī nuò qiān jīn one's word is one's bond

一瞥 yīpiē [动] glance

一齐 yīqí [副] simultaneously

一起 yīqǐ I [名] the same place II [副] together

一气呵成 yī qì hē chéng go without a hitch

一窍不通 yī qiào bù tōng not know the first thing about

一切 yīqiè [代] 1 (全部) all ◇承担一切责任 take full responsibility ◇消除一切困难 eliminate all difficulties 2 (全部事物) everything ◇那里的一切，她都记得很清楚。She remembers everything about the place very clearly.

一日千里 yī rì qiān lǐ at a tremendous pace ◇人类在科学技术方面的进步一日千里。Humanity has made tremendous progress in science and technology.

一日三秋 yīrì sān qiū days creep by like years

一如 yīrú [动] be just like ◇这里污染严重、环境恶劣，一如所闻。It's heavily polluted here – it's just like people say it is.

一身 yīshēn [名] 1 (全身) ◇水洒了他一身。The water splashed all over him. 2 (一人) ◇她独自一身去国外求学。She went abroad to study all on her own.

一时 yīshí I [名] 1 (一个时期) time 2 (短暂时间) moment II [副] 1 (临时) for the moment ◇书名我一时想不起来了。I can't think of the book title for the moment. 2 (时而) sometimes

一视同仁 yī shì tóng rén treat everyone the same

一手 yīshǒu I [名] 1 (本领) skill 2 (贬) (手段) trick ◇你这一手骗不了我。You can't fool me with that trick. II [副] single-handedly

一手遮天 yī shǒu zhē tiān engage in a cover-up

一丝不苟 yī sī bù gǒu be meticulous ◇她对教学工作一丝不苟。She's meticulous in her teaching work.

一体 yītǐ [名] whole ◇全球经济一体化 the unification of the global economy

一同 yītóng [副] together

一团和气 yī tuán héqì keep on good terms

一网打尽 yī wǎng dǎ jìn round … up in one fell swoop

一往情深 yī wǎng qíng shēn be devoted to

一味 yīwèi [副] blindly

一文不名 yī wén bù míng be penniless

一窝蜂 yīwōfēng [副] (口) ◇人们一窝蜂地跑过去看热闹。People came swarming over to see the fun.

一无所有 yī wú suǒ yǒu not have a penny to one's name

一五一十 yī wǔ yī shí every last detail ◇她把事情的经过一五一十地告诉了我。She told me every last detail of the events.

一下 yīxià I [量] ◇我去问一下儿。I'll just go and ask. ◇请大家自我介绍一下儿。I'd like everybody to introduce themselves. ◇这件事我们还得商量一下儿。We still need to discuss this. II [副] at once ◇天一下儿就冷了。All at once the weather turned cold.

一线 yīxiàn I [名] the front line ◇他一直在科研第一线工作。He's always worked on the front line of scientific research. II [形] ◇一线阳光 a ray of sunlight ◇一线希望 a ray of hope

一相情愿 yī xiāng qíngyuàn wishful thinking

一向 yīxiàng [副] always ◇他做事一向拖拖拉拉。Whatever he does he always drags his feet.

一些 yīxiē [量] 1 (部分) some ◇这项工作让他也分担一些吧。Let him take responsibility for some of this work. 2 (几个) a few ◇别的都卖了，只剩这一些了。All the others have been sold – there are only these few left. ◇他曾游历过一些名山大川。He has visited several famous scenic spots. 3 (略微) a little ◇她感觉好一些了。She feels a little better.

一心 yīxīn I [形] united II [副] wholeheartedly

一行 yīxíng [名] group

一言既出，驷马难追 yī yán jì chū, sì mǎ nán zhuī what's said can't be unsaid

一言以蔽之 yī yán yǐ bì zhī in short ◊一言以蔽之，任何一种改革都必须从实际出发。In short, any kind of reform must have a basis in reality.

一样 yīyàng [形] same ◊他俩爱好一样。They have the same hobbies. ◊两个人成绩一样好。Their results are equally good. ◊姐俩性格完全不一样。The sisters' personalities are completely different. ◊这位老人的头发像雪一样白。The old man's hair is as white as snow.

一叶知秋 yī yè zhī qiū a straw in the wind

一一 yīyī [副] in turn ◊对记者提出的问题，他一一做了回答。He replied to each of the journalist's questions in turn.

一…一… yī…yī… **1** (表示整个) ◊希望我们能一生一世在一起。I hope we will be able to spend our whole lives together. **2** (表示量少) ◊即使一分一秒她也舍不得浪费。She didn't want to waste even a second. **3** (表示对比) ◊这里多数家庭是一夫一妻，而不是一夫多妻。Most households here consist of one husband and one wife, and not one husband and several wives. **4** (表示连续) ◊他一瘸一拐地离开了足球场。He limped off the field. ◊小船一上一下地颠簸着。The little boat bobbed up and down. **5** (表示交替) ◊他俩一问一答, 配合密切。Their question and answering was very tight. ♦一张一弛 alternately tense and relaxed **6** (表示对应) ◊姐妹俩一左一右搀扶着母亲。The two sisters supported their mother, one on the right and one on the left.

一衣带水 yī yī dài shuǐ be separated by a narrow strip of water

一意孤行 yī yì gū xíng go one's own way

一应 yīyīng [代] everything

一再 yīzài [副] repeatedly ◊他们一再要求改善待遇。They repeatedly demanded an improvement in their treatment.

一朝一夕 yī zhāo yī xī overnight

一针见血 yī zhēn jiàn xiě be spot on

一知半解 yī zhī bàn jiě have a smattering of knowledge

一直 yīzhí [副] **1** (不变向) straight ◊一直走到十字路口, 再向右拐。Go straight ahead to the crossroads, then turn right. ◊顺着这条大街一直走500米就到了。Follow this avenue for five hundred metres and you'll be there. **2** (不间断) always ◊这个牌子的电视一直很受欢迎。This brand of TV has always been very popular. ◊大风一直刮了两天两夜。The gale blew for two days and two nights. **3** (指一定范围) all the way ◊从最北一直到最南，这股寒流袭击了整个国家。The cold current hit the country from the north all the way to the south. ◊他被雨淋得从头顶一直湿到脚底。The rain soaked him from head to foot.

一致 yīzhì **I** [形] unanimous ◊他们夫妻俩在很多方面意见不一致。The couple disagreed about quite a number of things. **II** [副] unanimously

一字千金 yī zì qiān jīn be full of pearls of wisdom

衣 yī [名] **1** (衣服) clothing **2** (表层) cover **3** (医) afterbirth

衣服 yīfu [名] clothes (*pl*)

衣冠 yīguān [名] clothing

衣裳 yīshang [名] clothes (*pl*)

衣着 yīzhuó [名] clothing

伊 yī 见下文

伊甸园 yīdiànyuán [名] the Garden of Eden

医 yī **I** [名] **1** (医生) doctor ♦牙医 dentist **2** (医) medicine ♦中医 Chinese traditional medicine **II** [动] treat

医疗 yīliáo [动] treat ◊免费医疗制度 system of free medical care ◊改善医疗卫生条件 improve medical hygiene

医生 yīshēng [名] doctor

医术 yīshù [名] medical skill

医务 yīwù [名] ◇医务工作者 medical worker

医学 yīxué [名] medicine

医药 yīyào [名] medicine

医院 yīyuàn [名] hospital

医治 yīzhì [动] cure

依 yī I [动] **1** (依靠) depend on **2** (依从) comply with II [介] according to

依从 yīcóng [动] comply with

依存 yīcún [动] depend on

依附 yīfù [动] rely on

依旧 yījiù [副] still ◇10年了，他依旧孑然一身。It's been ten years, and he's still all alone.

依据 yījù I [动] go by (*pt* went, *pp* gone) II [名] basis (*pl* bases) ◇做这种判断你有什么依据吗？Do you have any basis for this judgment?

依靠 yīkào I [动] rely on II [名] support

依赖 yīlài [动] depend on

依恋 yīliàn [动] be reluctant to leave

依然 yīrán I [副] still ◇她依然像10年前那么漂亮。She's still as beautiful as she was ten years ago.

依托 yītuō I [动] entrust II [名] support

依稀 yīxī [形] vague

依依 yīyī [形] **1** (摇摆) fluttering **2** (留恋) reluctant

依照 yīzhào [介] according to ◇依照规定，你是不能请假的。According to the regulations, you're not allowed to request leave. ◇我们就依照你的建议试一试吧。Let's try it your way.

咿 yī 见下文

咿呀 yīyā [拟] **1** (指物) squeak **2** (指人) prattle

壹 yī [数] *an elaborate form of "one", used in writing cheques etc to prevent mistakes and forgery*

仪 yí [名] **1** (外表) appearance **2** (礼节) ceremony **3** (礼物) gift **4** (仪器) meter

仪表 yíbiǎo [名] **1** (外表) appearance **2** (仪器) meter

仪器 yíqì [名] meter

仪式 yíshì [名] ceremony

仪仗队 yízhàngduì [名] guard of honour (英) 或 honor (美)

夷 yí I [形] (书) safe ◇化险为夷 head off disaster II [动] (书) **1** (破坏) raze ◇夷为平地 raze to the ground **2** (杀掉) exterminate ♦夷灭 destroy

怡 yí [形] (书) cheerful

怡然自得 yírán zìdé contented

宜 yí I [形] suitable II [副] ◇事不宜迟。Matters should not be delayed.

宜人 yírén [形] pleasant

贻 yí [动] (书) **1** (赠送) present **2** (遗留) bequeath

贻误 yíwù [动] affect … adversely

贻笑大方 yíxiào dàfāng expose oneself to ridicule

姨 yí [名] **1** (母亲的姐妹) aunt **2** (妻子的姐妹) sister-in-law (*pl* sisters-in-law)

姨表 yíbiǎo [名] cousin

移 yí [动] **1** (移动) move **2** (改变) change

移动 yídòng [动] move

移交 yíjiāo [动] hand … over

移民 yímín I [动] emigrate ◇去年我移民法国。Last year I emigrated to France. II [名] immigrant ◇他是来自西班牙的移民。He's a Spanish immigrant.

移植 yízhí [动] transplant

遗 yí I [名] lost item II [动] **1** (遗失) lose (*pt, pp* lost) **2** (遗漏) omit **3** (留下) leave … behind (*pt, pp* left) **4** (死者留下) bequeath **5** (排泄) discharge

遗产 yíchǎn [名] legacy

遗传 yíchuán [动] inherit ◇有些疾病可能会遗传。Some diseases can be hereditary.

遗存 yícún [动] survive

遗骸 yíhái [名] remains (*pl*)

遗憾 yíhàn **I** [名] regret ◇没上过大学是他终身的遗憾。It was his lifelong regret that he had not gone to university. **II** [动] be a pity ◇真遗憾，我没看到你的表演。It's such a pity that I didn't see your performance.

遗迹 yíjì [名] remains (*pl*)

遗精 yíjīng [动] emit

遗留 yíliú [动] leave (*pt, pp* left) ◇父亲去世后遗留了很多钱财。My father left a lot of money when he died.

遗漏 yílòu [动] omit

遗弃 yíqì [动] **1** (车、船等) abandon **2** (妻、子等) desert

遗容 yíróng [名] (死后容貌) remains (*pl*)

遗失 yíshī [动] lose (*pt, pp* lost)

遗书 yíshū [名] **1** (前人著作) posthumous papers **2** (书面遗言) last letter

遗孀 yíshuāng [名] widow

遗体 yítǐ [名] remains (*pl*)

遗忘 yíwàng [动] forget (*pt* forgot, *pp* forgotten)

遗址 yízhǐ [名] ruins (*pl*)

遗嘱 yízhǔ [名] will

颐 yí **I** [名] (书) cheek **II** [动] (书) take care of oneself (*pt* took, *pp* taken)

颐和园 Yíhéyuán [名] the Summer Palace

颐养 yíyǎng [动] (书) take care of one's health (*pt* took, *pp* taken)

疑 yí [动] doubt

疑案 yí'àn [名] **1** (疑难案件) difficult case **2** (神秘事件) mystery

疑惑 yíhuò [动] have doubts

疑难 yínán [形] knotty

疑神疑鬼 yí shén yí guǐ be extremely suspicious

疑团 yítuán [名] doubts and suspicions (*pl*)

疑问 yíwèn [名] question

疑心 yíxīn **I** [名] suspicion **II** [动] suspect ◇她疑心邻居偷了她的手表。She suspected that her neighbour (英) 或 neighbor (美) stole her watch.

乙 yǐ [名] second ◇乙等 second grade

已 yǐ **I** [动] stop ♦不已 endlessly ◇死而后已 to the end of one's days **II** [副] already ◇大会已于昨日闭幕。The convention ended yesterday. ◇前期工作已准备完毕。Preparations for the preliminary stage of the work are already complete.

已经 yǐjing [副] already ◇已经到深秋了。It's already late autumn.

已然 yǐrán **I** [动] already be a fact **II** [副] already

已往 yǐwǎng [名] the past ◇已往他好吃懒做，现在完全变了样。In the past he was greedy and lazy – now he's completely changed.

以 yǐ (书) **I** [动] use ◇以强凌弱 use one's strength to humiliate the weak **II** [介] **1** (依照) by ◇以新的标准衡量 judge by new standards **2** (因为) for ◇他以博学多才闻名于全校。He became well-known throughout the school for his wide-ranging academic achievements. **3** (表示界限) ♦以内 within ♦以南 to the south **III** [连] ◇我们要改进技术，以提高生产效率。We should improve the technology so as to increase production.

以便 yǐbiàn [连] in order that

以讹传讹 yǐ é chuán é Chinese whispers

以后 yǐhòu [名] ◇两年以后，他果然去周游世界了。Two years later, he did indeed go on a round-the-world tour. ◇以后我们去看电影。Afterwards we're going to see a film.

以及 yǐjí [连] as well as ◇夜校开设了英文班、法文班以及德文班。The night school has started up classes in English, French and German. ◇医学专家讲解了这一传染病的特点以及防治方法。The medical expert explained the peculiarities of this infectious disease, as well as the methods of prevention.

以来 yǐlái [名] ◇入冬以来，这里已经下了5场雪。There have been five snowfalls here since the beginning of the winter.

以免 yǐmiǎn [连] in case ◇做好准备，以免不必要的麻烦。Prepare yourself thoroughly in case of unnecessary trouble.

以前 yǐqián [名] ◇10年以前，这里还是一片废墟。Ten years ago this was still a complete ruin. ◇她以前是老师。She was a teacher before.

以身作则 yǐ shēn zuò zé set an example

以往 yǐwǎng [名] the past ◇他以往身体不好，现在非常健康。In the past his health wasn't too good, but he's very healthy now.

以为 yǐwéi [动] think (*pt, pp* thought) ◇我以为你不想来呢！ I thought you didn't want to come! ◇老李以为这件事跟他没关系。Old Li reckoned that this had nothing to do with him.

以…为… yǐ…wéi… [动] take … as (*pt* took, *pp* taken)

以下 yǐxià [名] **1** (低于某点) ◇这里的气温常年在20度以下。The temperature here is below twenty degrees all year round. ◇俱乐部成员多数在30岁以下。Most of the club members are under thirty. ◇这个店的玩具价格200元以下的占了80%。80% of the toys in the shop sell for less than two hundred yuan. **2** (接下来) ◇以下我来谈谈应该注意的问题。Next I will discuss the problems to which we must pay special attention. ◇以下请王先生给大家讲一讲。Now I would like to ask Mr. Wang to talk to us.

以眼还眼，以牙还牙 yǐ yǎn huán yǎn, yǐ yá huán yá an eye for an eye and a tooth for a tooth

以逸待劳 yǐ yì dài láo wait for the enemy to wear themselves out

以至 yǐzhì [连] **1** (表示延伸) ◇这项工程可能需要两年以至更长的时间。This project will perhaps require two years or even more. ◇这项政策会影响到整个国家、省以至县。This policy will effect the whole country, down to province and county level. **2** (表示结果) to such an extent that ◇他紧张得以至胃疼。He was so nervous that he got a stomachache.

以致 yǐzhì [连] so that ◇她操劳过度，以致累垮了身体。She worked so hard that she damaged her health.

蚁 yǐ [名] ant

倚 yǐ **I** [动] **1** (靠着) lean on **2** (仗恃) rely on **II** [形] biased

倚靠 yǐkào [动] **1** (斜躺) lean on **2** (依赖) depend on

倚老卖老 yǐ lǎo mài lǎo take advantage of one's seniority

倚仗 yǐzhàng [动] rely on

倚重 yǐzhòng [动] depend heavily on

椅 yǐ [名] chair

椅子 yǐzi [名] chair

旖 yǐ 见下文

旖旎 yǐnǐ [形] (书) charming

亿 yì [数] hundred million

义 yì **I** [名] **1** (正义) righteousness **2** (情谊) human ties (*pl*) **3** (意义) meaning **II** [形] **1** (正义的) just **2** (人工的) artificial **3** (拜认的) adopted ♦义父 adoptive father

义不容辞 yì bù róng cí be duty-bound

义愤 yìfèn [名] righteous indignation

义卖 yìmài [动] sell … for charity (*pt, pp* sold) ◇义卖所得钱款已全部寄往灾区。All money raised from this charity sale has already been sent to the disaster area.

义气 yìqi **I** [名] loyalty **II** [形] loyal

义无反顾 yì wú fǎn gù be duty-bound

义务 yìwù **I** [名] duty **II** [形] compulsory

义演 yìyǎn [名] charity gala

义正词严 yì zhèng cí yán speak sternly out of a sense of justice

艺 yì [名] **1** (技能) skill ♦手艺

craftsmanship **2** (艺术) art

艺名 yìmíng [名] stage name

艺人 yìrén [名] **1** (演员) performer **2** (工人) artisan

艺术 yìshù **I** [名] **1** (文艺) art **2** (方法) skill ◇管理艺术 management skills **II** [形] artistic ◇花园的布局很艺术。The layout of the garden is very artistic.

艺术家 yìshùjiā [名] artist

忆 yì [动] remember

议 yì **I** [名] opinion ♦建议 propose **II** [动] discuss ♦商议 discuss

议案 yì'àn [名] proposal

议程 yìchéng [名] agenda

议会 yìhuì [名] parliament

议决 yìjué [动] pass a resolution

议论 yìlùn **I** [动] discuss **II** [名] talk ◇对新一届领导，人们私下里有很多议论。Privately, there was a lot of talk about the new leadership.

议题 yìtí [名] topic

议员 yìyuán [名] MP (英), congressman, congresswoman (美)

议政 yìzhèng [动] discuss politics

屹 yì [形] towering

屹立 yìlì [动] stand (*pt, pp* stood)

屹然 yìrán [形] towering

亦 yì [副] also ◇反之亦然 vice versa

亦步亦趋 yì bù yì qū blindly follow suit

异 yì **I** [形] **1** (不同) different ♦差异 difference **2** (奇异) strange **3** (惊奇) surprising ♦诧异 be surprised **4** (另外) other ♦异国 foreign country **II** [动] separate ♦离异 separate

异邦 yìbāng [名] foreign country

异常 yìcháng [形] unusual

异端 yìduān [名] (书) heresy

异乎寻常 yìhū xúncháng exceptional ◇这个月，公司的销售情况异乎寻常地顺利。This month, the company's sales have been exceptionally good.

异化 yìhuà [动] **1** (哲) alienate **2** (语言) dissimilate

异己 yìjǐ [名] dissident

异口同声 yì kǒu tóng shēng speak with one voice ◇大家异口同声地称赞她是个热心人。Everyone unanimously agreed that she was a really warm-hearted person.

异曲同工 yì qǔ tóng gōng employ different methods with equal success ◇这两座桥的设计、造型异曲同工。These two bridges were planned and built equally successfully using different methods.

异物 yìwù [名] **1** (医) foreign body **2** (奇异物品) curiosity

异乡 yìxiāng [名] foreign parts (*pl*)

异想天开 yì xiǎng tiān kāi have one's head in the clouds

异性 yìxìng [名] **1** (指性别) the opposite sex **2** (指性质) opposite

异议 yìyì [名] objection ◇如果有异议，我们可以进一步讨论。If there are any objections, we can discuss this further.

译 yì [动] translate

译文 yìwén [名] translation

译者 yìzhě [名] translator

译制 yìzhì [动] dub ◇很多美国电影都被译制成了中文。A lot of American movies have been dubbed into Chinese.

抑 yì [动] repress

抑扬顿挫 yìyáng dùncuò speak with a lilt

抑郁 yìyù [形] depressed

抑制 yìzhì [动] **1** (生理) inhibit **2** (控制) control

呓 yì [名] **1** (梦话) ◇梦呓 talk in one's sleep **2** (胡话) ravings (*pl*)

呓语 yìyǔ [名] ◇他睡觉时常说呓语。He often talks in his sleep.

役 yì **I** [名] **1** (劳力) labour (英), labor (美) ♦劳役 forced labour **2** (兵役) military service ♦退役 retire from the army **3** (奴仆) servant **4** (战争) battle **II** [动] treat as a servant ♦奴役 enslave

易 yì I [形] **1** (容易) easy ◇不讲卫生，易得传染病。If you're not careful about hygiene, it's easy to get an infection. **2** (和气) amiable ◇平易近人 amiable and easy to get on with II [动] **1** (改变) change **2** (交换) exchange ◇以物易物 barter

易如反掌 yì rú fǎn zhǎng easy as falling off a log

轶 yì [形] **1** (超群) superior **2** (散失) lost

轶事 yìshì [名] anecdote

疫 yì [名] epidemic

疫苗 yìmiáo [名] inoculation

益 yì I [名] benefit II [形] beneficial III [动] increase IV [副] increasingly

益处 yìchù [名] benefit

谊 yì [名] friendship

逸 yì I [形] **1** (安乐) leisurely **2** (散失) lost II [动] **1** (逃跑) escape **2** (超越) surpass

逸事 yìshì [名] anecdote

逸闻 yìwén [名] anecdote

翌 yì [名] the next ♦翌日 the next day

肄 yì [动] study

肄业 yìyè [动] study

裔 yì [名] **1** (书) (后代) descendant ♦华裔 *foreign citizen of Chinese descent* **2** (书) (边疆) border region ♦四裔 the frontiers (*pl*)

意 yì I [名] **1** (意思) meaning ◇他词不达意。He couldn't express what he meant. **2** (心愿) wish ♦好意 good intention II [动] expect

意会 yìhuì [动] sense

意见 yìjiàn [名] **1** (看法) opinion ◇请你发表一下意见。Please give us your opinion. ◇大家互相交换了意见。Everyone exchanged ideas. ◇对这个计划大家还有什么意见？What does everyone think of this plan? **2** (不满) objection ◇工人们对这件事的处理意见很大。The workers greatly objected to the way this matter was dealt with. ◇有意见就提出来。If you have objections, raise them.

意境 yìjìng [名] artistic conception

意料 yìliào [名] expect

意念 yìniàn [名] thought

意气 yìqì [名] **1** (气概) spirit **2** (志趣) temperament **3** (情绪) emotions (*pl*)

意识 yìshi I [名] consciousness II [动] realize

意思 yìsi [名] **1** (意义) meaning **2** (意见) idea **3** (愿望) wish **4** (趣味) interest ◇这个连续剧太没意思。This series is so boring. **5** (心意) token ◇这是我们的一点小意思，请收下。This is a small token of our esteem – do accept it.

意图 yìtú [名] intention

意外 yìwài I [名] accident II [形] unexpected

意味 yìwèi [名] **1** (意思) significance **2** (情调) flavour (英), flavor (美)

意向 yìxiàng [名] intention

意义 yìyì [名] **1** (含义) meaning **2** (作用) significance

意译 yìyì [动] translate freely

意愿 yìyuàn [名] wish ◇作决定要符合大多数人的意愿。The decision must accord with the wishes of the majority.

意志 yìzhì [名] will

意中人 yìzhōngrén [名] the object of one's affections

溢 yì I [动] overflow II [副] excessively

溢出 yìchū [动] overflow

溢于言表 yì yú yán biǎo an outpouring of emotion

毅 yì [形] resolute

毅力 yìlì [名] perseverance

毅然 yìrán [形] resolute

臆 yì [副] subjectively

臆测 yìcè [动] conjecture

臆断 yìduàn [动] make assumptions

臆造 yìzào [动] fabricate

翼 yì [名] 1 (翅膀) wing ♦机翼 aircraft wing 2 (侧面) side

翼翼 yìyì [形] (书) cautious

因 yīn I [连] because ◊因交通阻塞，他们无法准时到达。Because there was a traffic jam, they were unable to arrive on time. ◊因天气恶劣，今天的郊游取消了。Today's outing has been cancelled due to bad weather. II [介] because of ◊昨天他因病缺课。He missed a class yesterday because of illness. III [名] cause ♦外因 external cause ♦病因 cause of the illness ◊事出有因 there are reasons why things happen

因材施教 yīn cái shī jiào teach according to one's student's ability ◊教师在教学时应尽量因材施教。Teachers, when teaching, ought as far as possible to teach students according to their abilities.

因此 yīncǐ [连] so ◊他迷恋于玩游戏，因此无心学习，成绩下降。He is obsessed with playing games, so he's not interested in studying and his achievements have dropped off. ◊这种病很容易复发，因此要格外注意。It's very easy to have a relapse with this kind of illness, so you have to be exceptionally careful. ◊由于引进了先进技术，生产效率因此大大提高。The production rate has increased hugely due to imported advanced technology.

因地制宜 yīn dì zhì yí act according to local conditions

因而 yīn'ér [连] therefore ◊由于工人们加强了安全意识，因而事故发生率大大减少了。Workers have become more safety conscious, and therefore the accident rate has fallen greatly.

因果 yīnguǒ [名] 1 (原因和结果) cause and effect 2 (宗) karma

因陋就简 yīn lòu jiù jiǎn make do with what's available ◊老师们因陋就简，给孩子们建了一个小活动室。The teachers made do with what was available and built a small activity room for the children.

因势利导 yīn shì lì dǎo give advice appropriate to the situation

因素 yīnsù [名] 1 (成分) element 2 (原因) factor ◊影响学生学习成绩的因素有很多。There are many factors that influence students' grades.

因特网 yīntèwǎng [名] the Internet

因为 yīnwèi [连] because ◊因为有暴风雨，所以他们取消了航海计划。They cancelled their plans to go sailing because of the stormy weather. ◊她昨天请了一天的假，是因为孩子生病了。Yesterday she requested a day off because her child was sick.

因袭 yīxí [动] follow traditional ways

因循 yīnxún [动] follow

因噎废食 yīn yē fèi shí give up eating for fear of choking

因缘 yīnyuán [名] 1 (宗) karma 2 (缘分) ◊他俩好像有前世因缘，一见面就坠入了情网。It seems that the two of them were destined for each other – they fell in love at first sight.

阴 yīn I [形] 1 (指天气) overcast ◊天阴得厉害。It's a very overcast day. 2 (隐蔽的) secret ◊阳奉阴违 support in public but undermine in secret 3 (阴险的) insidious ♦阴谋 plot 4 (物) negative ♦阴极 cathode II [名] 1 (阳的对立面) Yin (*of Yin and Yang*) 2 (指月亮) the moon ♦阴历 lunar calendar 3 (背面) back 4 (阴凉处) shade ♦树阴 the shade

阴暗 yīn'àn [形] gloomy

阴部 yīnbù [名] private parts (*pl*)

阴沉 yīnchén [形] gloomy

阴错阳差 yīn cuò yáng chā unexpected mishap

阴毒 yīndú [形] sinister

阴魂 yīnhún [名] spirits of the dead (*pl*)

阴极 yīnjí [名] (物) 1 (指电波) negative pole 2 (指电子) cathode

阴茎 yīnjīng [名] penis

阴冷 yīnlěng [形] 1 (指天气) chilly ◊今天天气阴冷阴冷的。It's really raw today. 2 (指脸色) gloomy

阴历 yīnlì [名] lunar calendar

阴凉 yīnliáng [形] shady and cool

阴谋 yīnmóu [动] plot ◇敌人的阴谋被识破了。The enemy's plot has been uncovered.

阴森 yīnsēn [形] gloomy

阴险 yīnxiǎn [形] sinister

阴性 yīnxìng [名] **1** (医) negative **2** (语言) feminine gender

阴阳 yīnyáng [名] Yin and Yang

阴阳怪气 yīn yáng guàiqì odd ◇他说话老是阴阳怪气的，让人听着别扭。He has such an odd way of speaking that it's irritating to listen to him.

阴郁 yīnyù [形] **1** (阴沉沉的) gloomy **2** (沮丧的) depressed

茵 yīn [名] mattress

音 yīn [名] **1** (声音) sound **2** (消息) news (*sg*) **3** (音节) syllable

音标 yīnbiāo [名] phonetic symbols (*pl*)

音调 yīndiào [名] pitch ◇他讲话时音调很高亢。He has a high-pitched voice.

音符 yīnfú [名] note

音节 yīnjié [名] syllable

音量 yīnliàng [名] volume ◇请把收音机的音量放大点儿。Turn up the volume on the radio a bit.

音容 yīnróng [名] face and voice

音色 yīnsè [名] timbre

音素 yīnsù [名] phoneme

音响 yīnxiǎng [名] **1** (声音) sound **2** (指设备) acoustics (*pl*)

音像 yīnxiàng [名] audio and video

音信 yīnxìn [名] news (*sg*) ◇最近几年，他音信全无。There's been no news of him for several years.

音译 yīnyì [名] transliteration

音乐 yīnyuè [名] music

音乐会 yīnyuèhuì [名] concert

洇 yīn [动] saturate ◇纸被墨水洇透了。This paper has been saturated with ink.

姻 yīn **I** [名] marriage **II** [形] related by marriage

姻亲 yīnqīn [名] in-law

殷 yīn [形] (书) **1** (丰富) prosperous **2** (深厚) earnest **3** (殷勤) courteous ▷另见 yān

殷切 yīnqiè [形] earnest

殷勤 yīnqín [形] courteous ◇她对待客人一向殷勤。She treats guests very courteously.

吟 yín [动] recite

吟诵 yínsòng [动] recite

银 yín **I** [名] **1** (指金属) silver **2** (指货币) money ♦收银台 cashier's desk **II** [形] silver

银行 yínháng [名] bank

银河 yínhé [名] the Milky Way

银灰 yínhuī [形] silvery grey (英) 或 gray (美)

银婚 yínhūn [名] silver wedding

银幕 yínmù [名] screen

银牌 yínpái [名] silver medal ◇他在长跑比赛中获得了银牌。He won a silver medal in the long-distance race.

银屏 yínpíng [名] (荧光屏) fluorescent screen

淫 yín [形] **1** (过多) excessive **2** (放纵) licentious **3** (淫秽) obscene

淫荡 yíndàng [形] lewd

淫秽 yínhuì [形] obscene

淫乱 yínluàn [形] debauched

龈 yín [名] gum

引 yǐn [动] **1** (牵引) draw (*pt* drew, *pp* drawn) **2** (引导) lead (*pt*, *pp* led) ♦引路 lead the way **3** (离开) leave (*pt*, *pp* left) **4** (引起) cause **5** (引用) cite

引导 yǐndǎo [动] **1** (带领) lead (*pt*, *pp* led) ◇校长引导我们参观了校园。The principal led us round the campus. **2** (启发诱导) guide

引渡 yǐndù [动] extradite

引发 yǐnfā [动] initiate

引见 yǐnjiàn [动] introduce

引进 yǐnjìn [动] **1** (人) recommend **2** (物) import

引经据典 yǐn jīng jù diǎn quote from the classics ◇这篇文章引经

据典，非常令人信服。This article quotes from the classics, which makes it more convincing.

引咎 yǐnjiù [动] take the blame (*pt* took, *pp* taken)

引狼入室 yǐn láng rù shì expose oneself to danger

引力 yǐnlì [名] gravitation

引起 yǐnqǐ [动] cause ◊人们担心，贫富不均可能会引起社会动荡。People are worried that inequalities in wealth might cause social unrest. ◊这一事件的发生马上引起了媒体的注意。As soon as it happened the event aroused media interest.

引擎 yǐnqíng [名] engine

引人入胜 yǐn rén rù shèng absorbing ◊这个故事悬念迭出，引人入胜。This story is full of suspense, and deeply absorbing.

引申 yǐnshēn [动] extend

引退 yǐntuì [动] retire ◊从官场引退之后，他感到无比轻松。When he retired from political life he felt incredibly relaxed.

引言 yǐnyán [名] foreword

引用 yǐnyòng [动] **1** (引述) quote **2** (任用) appoint

引诱 yǐnyòu [动] **1** (诱导) induce **2** (诱惑) tempt

引证 yǐnzhèng [动] cite

引子 yǐnzi [名] **1** (戏剧) prologue **2** (音) prelude **3** (开场白) prologue

饮 yǐn **I** [动] drink (*pt* drank, *pp* drunk) **II** [名] drink

饮料 yǐnliào [名] drink

饮食 yǐnshí [名] food and drink

饮食店 yǐnshídiàn [名] eatery

饮用水 yǐnyòngshuǐ [名] drinking water

隐 yǐn **I** [动] conceal **II** [形] hidden **III** [名] (书) secret

隐蔽 yǐnbì **I** [动] take cover (*pt* took, *pp* taken) ◊警察隐蔽在一堵墙的后面。The policeman took cover behind a wall. **II** [形] concealed

隐藏 yǐncáng [动] conceal

隐讳 yǐnhuì [动] hold back (*pt*, *pp* held)

隐晦 yǐnhuì [形] obscure

隐瞒 yǐnmán [动] cover … up

隐匿 yǐnnì [动] **1** (隐瞒) cover … up **2** (隐藏) hide (*pt* hid, *pp* hidden)

隐私 yǐnsī [名] private matters (*pl*)

隐退 yǐntuì [动] **1** (消失) disappear **2** (退职) retire

隐隐 yǐnyǐn [副] faintly

隐语 yǐnyǔ [名] **1** (暗示的话) riddle **2** (黑话) code words (*pl*)

隐约 yǐnyuē [形] faint

瘾 yǐn [名] **1** (嗜好) addiction **2** (兴趣) strong interest

印 yìn **I** [名] **1** (图章) stamp **2** (痕迹) print **II** [动] **1** (留下痕迹) print **2** (符合) be in line with

印发 yìnfā [动] print and distribute

印泥 yìnní [名] red ink paste

印刷 yìnshuā [动] print

印象 yìnxiàng [名] impression

印章 yìnzhāng [名] seal

印证 yìnzhèng [动] confirm ◊这些奖励是她努力工作最好的印证。All those prizes are the best confirmation of her hard work.

荫 yìn [形] shady

荫凉 yìnliáng [形] shady and cool

应 yīng **I** [动] **1** (答应) answer ◊我朝屋子里喊了两声，没人应。I shouted twice towards the room but no-one answered. ◊人家在叫你，你倒应一声儿啊！Someone's calling you, go on, answer! **2** (应允) agree ◊他们的要求，你应了吗？Have you agreed to their demands? **II** [助动] should ◊发现危险，应立即发出警报。If you discover danger, you should raise the alarm immediately. ◊应按照医嘱服药。You should take your medicine according to the doctor's orders.
▷另见 yìng

应当 yīngdāng [助动] should ◊天太热，应当洗个冷水澡。When it's

too hot you should take a cold shower.

应该 yīnggāi [助动] should ◇你不应该惹她生气。You shouldn't make her angry. ◇家长应该鼓励孩子。Parents should encourage their children.

应允 yīngyǔn [动] consent

英 yīng [名] **1** (书) (花) flower **2** (才能出众者) hero (*pl* heroes) **3** (英国) Britain

英镑 yīngbàng [名] pound sterling

英才 yīngcái [名] **1** (杰出才智) talent ◇他具有盖世英才。He possesses outstanding talent. **2** (杰出人才) talented person

英豪 yīngháo [名] hero (*pl* heroes)

英俊 yīngjùn [形] **1** (有才干的) very talented **2** (漂亮的) handsome

英明 yīngmíng [形] wise

英年 yīngnián [名] the flush of one's youth

英武 yīngwǔ [形] (书) valiant

英雄 yīngxióng **I** [名] hero (*pl* heroes) **II** [形] heroic

英勇 yīngyǒng [形] brave

英语 yīngyǔ [名] English

英姿 yīngzī [名] dashing appearance

婴 yīng [名] baby

婴儿 yīng'ér [名] baby

缨 yīng [名] **1** (带子) strap **2** (装饰物) tassel **3** (缨状物) tassel

樱 yīng [名] **1** (樱桃) cherry **2** (樱花) cherry blossom

樱桃 yīngtáo [名] **1** (指植物) (树) cherry tree ◇院子里种了几棵樱桃树。Several cherry trees have been planted in the yard. **2** (果实) cherry

鹦 yīng 见下文

鹦鹉 yīngwǔ [名] parrot

鹰 yīng [名] eagle

迎 yíng [动] **1** (迎接) welcome **2** (对着) meet (*pt, pp* met)

迎合 yínghé [动] cater to ◇这家餐馆迎合南方人的口味。This restaurant caters to the tastes of people from South China.

迎候 yínghòu [动] await

迎接 yíngjiē [动] welcome

迎刃而解 yíng rèn ér jiě be neatly solved

迎头 yíngtóu [动] be head-on ◇我刚进校门，迎头碰上了李教授。Just after I came in through the school gates, I bumped right into Professor Li.

迎战 yíngzhàn [动] meet head-on (*pt, pp* met) ◇中国队将迎战美国队。The Chinese team will meet the American team head-on.

荧 yíng [形] (书) luminous

荧光 yíngguāng [名] fluorescence ◇荧光灯比普通灯泡节能。Fluorescent lights are more energy-efficient than ordinary light bulbs.

荧屏 yíngpíng [名] **1** (电子) fluorescent screen **2** (电视) television

盈 yíng [动] **1** (充满) fill **2** (增长) increase **3** (多出来) have a surplus of

盈亏 yíngkuī **I** [动] wax and wane **II** [名] profit and loss

盈利 yínglì [名] profit

盈余 yíngyú [动] profit ◇这笔生意做下来有3万元的盈余。If we do this business then we'll make thirty thousand dollars profit.

萤 yíng [名] firefly

萤火虫 yínghuǒchóng [名] firefly

营 yíng **I** [动] **1** (谋求) seek (*pt, pp* sought) **2** (经营) operate **3** (建造) build (*pt, pp* built) **II** [名] **1** (军队驻地) barracks (*pl*) **2** (军队编制) battalion **3** (营地) camp

营地 yíngdì [名] camp

营房 yíngfáng [名] barracks (*pl*)

营火 yínghuǒ [名] campfire

营救 yíngjiù [动] rescue

营私 yíngsī [动] feather one's nest

营销 yíngxiāo [动] sell (*pt, pp* sold)

营养 yíngyǎng [名] nourishment ◇大病初愈，你要好好营养一下身体。When recovering from a serious illness, you have to nourish your body well. ◊水果中含有丰富的营养。Fruit contains a lot of nutrients.

营业 yíngyè [动] do business ◊这家商店明天开始正式营业。This shop will open for business tomorrow.

营造 yíngzào [动] **1** (建筑) build (*pt*, *pp* built) **2** (林木) plant **3** (气氛) create

萦 yíng [动] (书) entwine

萦怀 yínghuái [动] linger

萦绕 yíngrào [动] linger

蝇 yíng [名] fly

蝇头 yíngtóu [名] speck ◊蝇头小利 minuscule profit

赢 yíng [动] **1** (胜) win (*pt*, *pp* won) **2** (获利) gain

赢利 yínglì [名] gain

赢余 yíngyú [动] profit ◊这个月音像店盈余上万元。This month the record shop's profit is more than ten thousand yuan. ◊除去开支，我们只有几百元的赢余。After our expenses, we only have a few hundred yuan profit.

颖 yǐng **I** [名] intelligence **II** [形] intelligent

颖慧 yǐnghuì [形] (书) intelligent

影 yǐng **I** [名] **1** (影子) shadow **2** (照片) photograph **3** (电影) film (英), movie (美) **II** [动] copy

影片 yǐngpiàn [名] **1** (胶片) film **2** (电影) film (英), movie (美)

影射 yǐngshè [动] allude to

影视 yǐngshì [名] film and television

影坛 yǐngtán [名] the world of film

影响 yǐngxiǎng **I** [动] affect ◊一场大风严重影响了庄稼的长势。A large gale seriously affected the growth of the crops. ◊小声点，别影响他们的学习。Quiet! Don't disturb their studies. **II** [名] influence ◊有些书会使青少年受到不良影响。Some books have a bad influence on young people.

影印 yǐngyìn [动] photocopy ◊影印资料 photocopied material

应 yìng [动] **1** (回答) answer ♦回应 answer **2** (满足) respond to ◊应顾客需要，我们增开了两家分店。In response to the customers' needs, we opened two more branches. **3** (顺应) comply with **4** (应付) handle ♦应急 handle an emergency **5** (相符合) correspond to
▷另见 yīng

应变 yìngbiàn [动] take emergency measures (*pt* took, *pp* taken)

应标 yìngbiāo [动] bid (*pt*, *pp* bid)

应承 yìngchéng [动] agree ◊我请她帮忙，她满口应承。When I asked her to help, she readily agreed.

应酬 yìngchou **I** [动] socialize with ◊他去应酬客人了。He went to socialize with the guests. **II** [名] social engagement

应付 yìngfù [动] **1** (采取办法) handle **2** (敷衍) do half-heartedly **3** (将就) make do with ◊没有更好的衣服，就穿这件应付吧。I don't have any better clothes: I'll just make do with this.

应接不暇 yìngjiē bù xiá have more to do than one can cope with

应聘 yìngpìn [动] accept an offer

应时 yìngshí [形] seasonal

应试 yìngshì [动] **1** (应考) take exams (*pt* took, *pp* taken) **2** (适应考试) ◊应试教育不利于学生身心全面发展。Education that is geared towards exams has a bad effect on students' overall development.

应验 yìngyàn [动] come true (*pt* came, *pp* come) ◊他的很多预言都应验了。Many of his predictions have come true.

应邀 yìngyāo [动] be invited to ◊我应邀参加了昨天的宴会。I was invited to yesterday's banquet.

应用 yìngyòng **I** [动] apply ◊这项技术已经广泛应用于农业生产。This technology has already been widely applied to agricultural production. **II** [形] applied ◊应用科学 applied science

应战 yìngzhàn [动] **1** (作战) engage the enemy **2** (接受挑战) accept a challenge

映 yìng [动] reflect

映衬 yìngchèn [动] set … off (*pt, pp* set)

映射 yìngshè [动] shine (*pt, pp* shone)

映照 yìngzhào [动] shine upon (*pt, pp* shone) ◊柔和的灯光映照着她美丽的面庞。The soft lighting is shining upon her beautiful face.

硬 yìng **I** [形] **1** (坚固) hard **2** (刚强) firm **3** (能干的) strong **II** [副] obstinately

硬邦邦 yìngbāngbāng [形] rock hard

硬币 yìngbì [名] coin

硬度 yìngdù [名] hardness ◊这种木头硬度不高。This kind of wood is not hard enough. ◊这种水硬度太高，不适合饮用。This kind of water is too hard: it's not suitable for drinking.

硬化 yìnghuà [动] **1** (变硬) harden **2** (喻) stiffen

硬件 yìngjiàn [名] **1** (计算机) hardware **2** (设备) equipment

硬朗 yìnglang [形] (口) sturdy

硬盘 yìngpán [名] hard disk

硬性 yìngxìng [形] inflexible

哟 yō [叹] (表示轻微的惊异或赞叹) oh ◊哟，他怎么来了？ Oh, how did he get here?

佣 yōng **I** [动] hire **II** [名] servant ▷另见 yòng

佣工 yōnggōng [名] servant

拥 yōng [动] **1** (抱) embrace **2** (围着) gather round **3** (拥挤) swarm **4** (拥护) support

拥抱 yōngbào [动] embrace

拥戴 yōngdài [动] support

拥护 yōnghù [动] support ◊决议草案得到了大多数议员的拥护。The draft resolution obtained the support of most of the representatives.

拥挤 yōngjǐ **I** [形] crowded **II** [动] crowd

拥有 yōngyǒu [动] have (*pt, pp* had)

庸 yōng **I** [形] **1** (平凡) commonplace **2** (不高明) mediocre **II** [动] need

庸才 yōngcái [名] mediocrity

庸碌 yōnglù [形] mediocre

庸人 yōngrén [名] (书) nonentity

庸俗 yōngsú [形] vulgar

雍 yōng [形] (书) harmonious

雍容 yōngróng [形] graceful

壅 yōng [动] obstruct

壅塞 yōngsè [动] block … up

臃 yōng [形] (书) obese

臃肿 yōngzhǒng [形] **1** (指身体) obese **2** (指机构) overstaffed

永 yǒng **I** [形] (书) everlasting **II** [副] forever

永恒 yǒnghéng [形] everlasting

永久 yǒngjiǔ [形] eternal

永生 yǒngshēng **I** [动] live forever **II** [副] forever

永世 yǒngshì [副] forever ◊您的恩德，我永世不忘。I will remember your kindness forever.

永远 yǒngyuǎn [副] eternally ◊我们将永远怀念这位可敬的朋友。We will eternally cherish the memory of this respected friend. ◊他们希望一辈子生活在一起，永远不分离。They want to be together all their lives, and never part.

泳 yǒng [名] swim (*pt* swam, *pp* swum)

泳道 yǒngdào [名] lane

俑 yǒng [名] figurine

勇 yǒng [形] brave

勇敢 yǒnggǎn [形] brave

勇猛 yǒngměng [形] valiant

勇气 yǒngqì [名] courage

勇士 yǒngshì [名] warrior

勇往直前 yǒng wǎng zhí qián carry on bravely

勇于 yǒngyú [助动] have the courage to ◊勇于迎接挑战 have the courage to take on a challenge

涌 yǒng [动] 1 (冒出) gush 2 (喻) emerge

涌现 yǒngxiàn [动] emerge

踊 yǒng [动] leap

踊跃 yǒngyuè I [形] eager II [动] leap

用 yòng I [动] 1 (使用) use ◊你们可以用这个教室。You can use this classroom. 2 (需要) need ◊不用担心，他们很快就到了。There's no need to worry, they'll be here soon. ◊我自己去就行，不用你陪着。I'll go by myself; you don't have to come. 3 (消费) consume ♦用餐 have a meal ♦用茶 drink tea II [名] 1 (费用) expense ♦家用 household expenses (*pl*) 2 (用处) use ♦没用 useless

用场 yòngchǎng [名] use

用处 yòngchu [名] use

用功 yònggōng I [形] hardworking II [动] work hard

用户 yònghù [名] user ◊网络用户 internet user

用具 yòngjù [名] tool

用力 yònglì [动] exert oneself ◊他用力举起了大石头。He really exerted himself lifting the big stone.

用品 yòngpǐn [名] goods (*pl*) ◊办公用品 office goods ◊体育用品 sporting goods

用人 yòngrén [动] 1 (使用人) make the best use of staff 2 (需要人) be understaffed

用事 yòngshì [动] act

用途 yòngtú [名] use

用心 yòngxīn I [动] be careful II [形] careful ◊他做什么事都很用心。Whatever he does he's always very careful. III [名] intention

用意 yòngyì [名] intention

用语 yòngyǔ I [动] word II [名] term

佣 yòng 见下文
▷另见 yōng

佣金 yòngjīn [名] commission

优 yōu I [形] 1 (优良) excellent 2 (书) (充足) abundant II [动] give … preferential treatment (*pt* gave, *pp* given)

优待 yōudài [动] give preferential treatment (*pt* gave, *pp* given) ◊这个公司格外优待老客户。This company gives preferential treatment to old customers. ◊立功人员理应得到优待。Hardworking staff should receive preferential treatment.

优点 yōudiǎn [名] strong point

优厚 yōuhòu [形] generous

优化 yōuhuà [动] optimize

优惠 yōuhuì [形] preferential

优良 yōuliáng [形] fine

优美 yōuměi [形] elegant

优胜 yōushèng I [名] victory II [形] superior

优势 yōushì [名] advantage ◊我们要尽量发挥出自己的优势。We have to do our best to give play to our own advantages.

优先 yōuxiān [动] have priority

优秀 yōuxiù [形] outstanding

优雅 yōuyǎ [形] refined

优异 yōuyì [形] outstanding

优越 yōuyuè [形] superior

优质 yōuzhì [形] high-quality

忧 yōu I [形] anxious II [动] worry III [名] anxiety

忧愁 yōuchóu [形] depressed

忧患 yōuhuàn [名] suffering

忧虑 yōulǜ [动] worry ◊他为自己的前途感到忧虑。He was worried about his prospects.

忧伤 yōushāng [形] sad

忧郁 yōuyù [形] depressed

呦 yōu [叹] ooh!

幽 yōu I [形] 1 (暗) dim 2 (深) remote 3 (隐蔽的) hidden 4 (沉静) tranquil II [动] imprison III [名] the underworld

幽暗 yōu'àn [形] gloomy

幽会 yōuhuì [名] date ◊他们在电影院幽会。They went on a date to the cinema. ◊这对恋人经常去公园幽会。The couple often meet in the park.

幽禁 yōujìn [动] imprison

幽静 yōujìng [形] peaceful

幽灵 yōulíng [名] ghost

幽默 yōumò [形] humorous ◊他说话很幽默。He's got a very humorous way of talking.

幽情 yōuqíng [名] deep feelings (*pl*)

幽深 yōushēn [形] serene

幽雅 yōuyǎ [形] refined

悠 yōu **I** [形] **1** (久远) remote **2** (闲适) leisurely **II** [动] (口) swing (*pt, pp* swung)

悠长 yōucháng [形] drawn-out

悠久 yōujiǔ [形] long-standing

悠然 yōurán [形] carefree ◊他在乡下过着悠然的日子。He lives a carefree life in the country.

悠闲 yōuxián [形] leisurely

悠扬 yōuyáng [形] melodious

悠悠 yōuyōu [形] **1** (久远) remote **2** (从容不迫) unhurried

悠远 yōuyuǎn [形] **1** (指时间) distant **2** (指距离) far

尤 yóu [副] especially

尤其 yóuqí [副] especially ◊他爱好体育，尤其喜欢踢足球。He loves sport, especially football.

由 yóu **I** [动] **1** (听凭) give in to (*pt* gave, *pp* given) ◊不能什么事都由着孩子。You can't give in to children in everything. **2** (经过) go through (*pt* went, *pp* gone) ◊必由之路 the only way **II** [介] **1** (归) by ◊这件事由你去安排吧！ This business will be dealt with by you. **2** (根据) ◊这篇论文由三个部分构成。This essay is made up of three parts. ◊由此可见 from this we can see… **3** (从) ◊由简到繁 from simple to complex ◊由上海到深圳 from Shanghai to Shenzhen **4** (由于) due to ◊她头痛是由睡眠不足引起的。Her headache is due to lack of sleep. **III** [名] cause ♦理由 reason

由来 yóulái [名] origin ◊没人知道这个传说的由来。No-one knows the origins of this legend.

由于 yóuyú [介] as a result of ◊由于司机一时不慎，发生了一起重大交通事故。As a result of the driver's momentary carelessness, there was a serious accident. ◊由于不用功，他没能通过考试。Because he didn't work hard, he couldn't pass the exam.

由衷 yóuzhōng [形] heartfelt

邮 yóu **I** [动] post (英), mail (美) **II** [名] **1** (邮务) post (英), mail (美) **2** (邮票) stamp

邮递 yóudì [动] send … by post (英) 或 mail (美) (*pt, pp* sent) ◊邮递印刷品很便宜。It's very cheap to send printed matter by post.

邮电 yóudiàn [名] post and telecommunications

邮寄 yóujì [动] post (英), mail (美)

邮件 yóujiàn [名] post (英), mail (美) (美) ◊朋友之间用电子邮件联系非常方便。It's very convenient for friends to use email to keep in touch. ◊这个歌星在生日那天收到了大量邮件。The pop star received a lot of mail on his birthday.

邮局 yóujú [名] post office

邮票 yóupiào [名] stamp

邮政 yóuzhèng [名] postal service

邮资 yóuzī [名] postage

犹 yóu **I** [动] be like **II** [副] still

犹然 yóurán [副] still

犹如 yóurú [动] be like

犹豫 yóuyù [形] hesitant

油 yóu **I** [名] oil **II** [动] **1** (油漆) oil **2** (被油弄脏) stain with oil **III** [形] oily

油光 yóuguāng [形] shiny

油乎乎 yóuhūhū [形] oily

油滑 yóuhuá [形] slippery ◊这个人很油滑，待人没有一点诚意。This person is very slippery: he treats people completely insincerely.

油腻 yóunì **I** [形] greasy **II** [名] oily food

油漆 yóuqī **I** [名] varnish **II** [动] varnish

油腔滑调 yóu qiāng huá diào glib

油水 yóushui [名] **1** (脂肪) oil **2** (贬) (好处) profit

油头粉面 yóu tóu fěn miàn overdressed ◊他打扮得油头粉面，一看就让人不舒服。He was so overdressed that people felt uncomfortable looking at him.

油头滑脑 yóu tóu huá nǎo slick

油印 yóuyìn [动] mimeograph

油脂 yóuzhī [名] oil ◊这种小吃含油脂过多，少吃为好。This kind of snack is too oily, the less you eat the better.

鱿 yóu [名] squid

鱿鱼 yóuyú [名] squid

游 yóu **I** [动] **1** (游泳) swim (*pt* swam, *pp* swum) **2** (游览) tour **II** [名] reach **III** [形] roving

游程 yóuchéng [名] **1** (距离) distance ◊1, 000米的游程他很快就游完了。He swam the distance of 1000 metres very quickly. **2** (路程) journey **3** (日程) itinerary

游荡 yóudàng [动] **1** (闲逛) wander **2** (飘荡) float

游逛 yóuguàng [动] stroll

游记 yóujì [名] travel notes (*pl*)

游客 yóukè [名] tourist

游览 yóulǎn [动] tour

游民 yóumín [名] vagrant

游牧 yóumù [动] live a nomadic life ◊这个民族仍然过着游牧生活。This tribe still live a nomadic life.

游刃有余 yóu rèn yǒu yú be more than equal to ◊他经验丰富，做这项工作游刃有余。He has plenty of experience, so he is more than equal to this task.

游手好闲 yóu shǒu hào xián [形] loaf about ◊一个游手好闲、不愿工作的人，很难得到尊重。It's very difficult for people who are idle and unwilling to work to gain respect.

游说 yóushuì [动] lobby

游戏 yóuxì **I** [名] game ◊孩子们都喜欢玩电脑游戏。Children all like to play computer games. ◊做任何事，首先要弄清游戏规则。No matter what you do, first you have to clarify the rules of the game. **II** [动] play ◊年轻人要珍惜生活，不要游戏人生。Young people must cherish life and mustn't play at it.

游行 yóuxíng [动] march

游移 yóuyí [动] waver

游泳 yóuyǒng **I** [动] swim (*pt* swam, *pp* swum) **II** [名] swimming ◊游泳是很好的健身运动。Swimming is a very good way of keeping fit.

游泳池 yóuyǒngchí [名] swimming pool

游子 yóuzǐ [名] person far from home

友 yǒu **I** [名] friend ♦男友 boyfriend **II** [形] friendly ♦友邦 friendly nation

友爱 yǒu'ài [形] affectionate

友好 yǒuhǎo **I** [形] friendly **II** [名] friend

友情 yǒuqíng [名] friendship

友人 yǒurén [名] friend

友善 yǒushàn [形] (书) amicable

友谊 yǒuyì [名] friendship

有 yǒu [动] **1** (具有) have (*pt, pp* had) ◊我有一套《红楼梦》。I have a set of "Dream of Red Chamber". **2** (存在) ◊院子里有一棵大树。There's a big tree in the courtyard. **3** (表示估量) ◊她有我那么大。She is as old as me. **4** (发生) occur ◊我的生活有了一些变化。A few changes have occurred in my life. **5** (表示程度) have (*pt, pp* had) ◊她很有修养。She has many accomplishments. ◊他特别有学问。He's extremely knowledgeable. **6** (某) ◊有一次，他得了冠军。He won a prize once. ◊有人说，这个湖里有怪兽。Some people say that there's a monster in the lake. ◊有时候他去健身房锻炼。Sometimes he goes to the gym to work out. **7** (客套) ◊有劳您给我查一下地图好吗？Could I trouble you to help me look it up on the map?

有碍 yǒu'ài [动] (书) obstruct

有板有眼 yǒu bǎn yǒu yǎn orderly ◊这位经理讲起话来不紧不慢，有板有眼。This manager speaks in a calm, orderly manner.

有备无患 yǒu bèi wú huàn be prepared

有偿 yǒucháng [形] paid

有的 yǒude [名] some ◊展出的作品，有的来自本土，有的来自海外。Of the articles on display, some are local, others are from overseas. ◊他说这些论文写得都很好，我看有的很一般。He says that all the essays are good, but some of them look pretty mediocre to me.

有的放矢 yǒu dì fàng shǐ be to the point ◊会议发言不要漫无边际，要有的放矢。Conference speeches shouldn't be rambling – they should be to the point.

有方 yǒufāng [形] competent ◊新经理管理有方，受到一致拥护。The new manager is very competent and enjoys universal support.

有关 yǒuguān [动] **1** (有关系) be relevant ◊这个案子跟某个大公司有关。This case is relevant to a certain large company. **2** (涉及到) be about ◊他写了一本有关风水方面的书。He has written a book about feng shui. ◊国家出台了一项有关计划生育问题的政策。The government has issued a policy on family planning. ◊他们讨论了有关教育制度改革的若干问题。They discussed several questions relating to reform of the education system.

有过之无不及 yǒu guò zhī wú bù jí go even further than ◊跟我住的地方比，这里的环境污染程度有过之无不及。The environmental pollution here is even worse than where I live.

有机 yǒujī [形] (化) organic ◊传统理论与新思潮有机地结合。Traditional theory and new thinking are linked in one organic whole.

有口皆碑 yǒu kǒu jiē bēi be universally acclaimed

有口无心 yǒu kǒu wú xīn ◊她是个有口无心的人，你不要太计较。Don't take any of it to heart – her bark is worse than her bite.

有赖 yǒulài [动] depend on

有劳 yǒuláo [动] trouble ◊有劳您帮我咨询一下。Could I trouble you to help me make a few enquiries?

有利 yǒulì [形] favourable (英), favorable (美)

有门儿 yǒuménr [动] (口) be hopeful ◊我看李杨找工作的事有门儿。I reckon that Li Yang's search for a job is looking pretty hopeful.

有名无实 yǒu míng wú shí lack substance ◊畅销书未必都好，有些不过是有名无实。Not all bestsellers are good, some lack substance.

有目共睹 yǒu mù gòng dǔ be plain for all to see

有气无力 yǒu qì wú lì feeble ◊他有气无力地说："我想喝水。" He said feebly, "I want water."

有求必应 yǒu qiú bì yìng never refuse a request

有趣 yǒuqù [形] interesting

有如 yǒurú [动] be like ◊老太太的头发有如雪一样白。The old lady's hair is as white as snow.

有声有色 yǒu shēng yǒu sè vivid ◊文中对乡村的描写有声有色、情趣盎然。The description of the village is vivid and full of emotion.

有恃无恐 yǒu shì wú kǒng secure in the knowledge that one has backing ◊经理的秘书总是对我们指手画脚，因为她有恃无恐。The manager's secretary is always bossing us around, secure in the knowledge that she has backing.

有数 yǒushù **I** [动] know all about (*pt* knew, *pp* known)◊这件事怎么做，我心中有数。I know all about how to do this. **II** [形] just a few ◊我们的任务必须在有数的几天内完成。Our assignment has to be completed in just a few days.

有条不紊 yǒu tiáo bù wěn methodical

有头有脸 yǒu tóu yǒu liǎn command respect ◊他在单位里可是有头有脸的，大家都服他。He commands a lot of respect at work – everyone listens to him.

有为 yǒuwéi [形] promising

有喜 yǒuxǐ [动] (口) be pregnant

有戏 yǒuxì [动] (方) look hopeful

有限 yǒuxiàn [形] limited ◊旅馆床位数量有限，请提前预订。The guesthouse has a limited number of beds – please book in advance. ◊有限的几个电脑，满足不了学生的需要。This small number of computers are insufficient for the students' needs.

有限公司 yǒuxiàn gōngsī [名] limited company

有线电视 yǒuxiàn diànshì [名] cable TV

有心 yǒuxīn I [动] be determined to ◊我有心帮朋友一把，却不知怎么做。I am determined to help my friend, but I don't know what to do. II [副] deliberately

有形 yǒuxíng [形] tangible

有幸 yǒuxìng [形] fortunate ◊她有幸获得了世界名牌大学的奖学金。She was fortunate enough to receive a scholarship from a world-class university.

有眼无珠 yǒu yǎn wú zhū be totally lacking in perception

有意 yǒuyì I [动] (有兴趣) be interested in ◊姑娘好像对那个小伙子有意。It seems as if the girl is interested in that guy. II [副] on purpose ◊你这不是有意叫我为难嘛！You're just doing this on purpose to make me feel bad!

有意识 yǒu yìshí [形] conscious

有意思 yǒuyìsi I [形] **1** (有意义) significant **2** (有趣味) interesting II [动] be interested in ◊你没看出来他对你有意思吗？ Haven't you noticed he's interested in you?

有朝一日 yǒu zhāo yī rì one day ◊我希望有朝一日能到世界一流大学读书。I hope that one day I can go and study at one of the world's best universities.

黝 yǒu 见下文

黝黑 yǒuhēi [形] dark

又 yòu [副] **1** (重复) again ◊今天他又来了。He came again today. **2** (同时) ◊车开得又快又稳。The car drives fast and smoothly. ◊她是一个好教师，又是一个好妈妈。She's both a good teacher and a great mother. **3** (也) too ◊天黑了，路又滑，最好别出门。It's dark, and the roads are slippery too – you'd better not go out. **4** (另外) another ◊家里又买了一个书架。They bought another set of bookshelves for their home. ◊老师又布置了几项作业。The teacher set several more questions for homework. **5** (再加上) and ◊一又三分之二 one and two thirds ◊两个月又三天 two months and three days **6** (可是) but ◊她想去旅游，又怕累。She wants to go travelling but she's afraid it'll tire her out. **7** (根本) even ◊又不是我的错，你怪我干吗？It's not even my fault – why are you blaming me? ◊他又不知道，你问他干什么？ What are you asking him for? He has no idea.

又及 yòují [动] ◊信写完了，她在下面又添上一行字："又及…" At the end of her letter, she added another line: "PS …"

右 yòu [名] **1** (右边) right ◊请向右转。Please turn right. **2** (右翼) the Right

幼 yòu I [形] young II [名] child (*pl* children)

幼儿 yòu'ér [名] small child (*pl* children)

幼年 yòunián [名] infancy

幼小 yòuxiǎo [形] young

幼稚 yòuzhì [形] **1** (书) (年龄很小) young **2** (头脑简单) naive

囿 yòu I [名] (书) enclosure ◊鹿囿 deer park II [动] limit ◊囿于成见 be blinded by prejudice ◊囿于孤陋寡闻 be handicapped by ignorance

诱 yòu [动] **1** (诱导) guide **2** (引诱) entice

诱导 yòudǎo I [动] guide II [名] (生理) induce

诱饵 yòu'ěr [名] bait

诱发 yòufā [动] **1** (诱导启发) bring out (*pt, pp* brought) ◊他的鼓动大大诱发了人们的积极性。His encouragement did a lot to bring out people's initiative. **2** (导致发生) induce

诱惑 yòuhuò [动] **1** (引诱) entice **2** (吸引) attract

诱使 yòushǐ [动] lure ◇他经常诱使那几个少年去偷盗。He often lures those kids into stealing things.

诱因 yòuyīn [名] cause

迂 yū [形] **1** (指路) circuitous **2** (指人) pedantic

迂腐 yūfǔ [形] pedantic

迂回 yūhuí **I** [形] winding **II** [动] (军) outflank

淤 yū **I** [名] silt **II** [动] silt up

淤积 yūjī [动] silt up

淤泥 yūní [名] silt

淤塞 yūsè [动] silt up

于 yú **I** [介] **1** (在) in ◇这位老人生于1899年。This old man was born in 1899. ◇暑期班已于昨日开课。The summer-holiday class began lessons yesterday. **2** (向) from ◇问道于盲 ask the way from a blind person ◇求助于朋友 ask for help from friends **3** (对) to ◇印刷术的发明于人类非常有益。The invention of printing was of great benefit to humanity. **4** (从) from ◇很多成语来源于历史故事。Many Chinese idioms originate from historical stories. **5** (比) than ♦大于 bigger than **6** (在…方面) ◇乐于助人 delight in helping people ◇我从早到晚都忙于家务。I'm busy with household chores from morning till night.

于是 yúshì [连] so ◇同学们对学英语很感兴趣，于是成立了一个英语俱乐部。The students were very interested in English, so they started an English club.

余 yú **I** [动] remain ◇除去花销，尚余千元。With the costs deducted, more than a thousand yuan still remains. **II** [名] **1** (零头) ◇500余人 more than five hundred people ◇我导师40岁有余。My supervisor is over 40. **2** (指时间) ♦课余 extra-curricular

余波 yúbō [名] aftereffects (*pl*)

余地 yúdì [名] room ◇这件事已没有商量的余地。There is no longer any room for negotiation in this matter.

余悸 yújì [名] lingering fear

余力 yúlì [名] spare energy

余生 yúshēng [名] **1** (指晚年) remaining years (*pl*) **2** (指性命) survival

余味 yúwèi [名] aftertaste

余暇 yúxiá [名] free time

余兴 yúxìng [名] **1** (兴致) excitement **2** (文娱) entertainment

盂 yú [名] jar ♦痰盂 spittoon (英), cuspidor (美)

鱼 yú [名] fish (*pl* fish)

鱼贯 yúguàn [形] in single file ◇参加葬礼的人们鱼贯进入教堂。The mourners at the funeral entered the church in single file.

鱼雷 yúléi [名] torpedo (*pl* torpedoes)

鱼龙混杂 yú lóng hùnzá a mix of good and bad people ◇这个乐队鱼龙混杂。This band has a mixture of good and bad musicians.

鱼肉 yúròu **I** [名] fish **II** [动] (书) savagely oppress

鱼死网破 yú sǐ wǎng pò everyone is a loser

鱼跃 yúyuè [动] dive

娱 yú **I** [动] amuse **II** [名] amusement

娱乐 yúlè **I** [动] have fun ◇放假了，大家好好娱乐一下。The holidays are here – everyone should have some fun. **II** [名] entertainment

渔 yú [动] **1** (捕鱼) fish **2** (谋取) filch ♦渔利 profit

渔产 yúchǎn [名] aquatic products (*pl*)

渔利 yúlì **I** [动] profit ◇他名为帮忙，实际是想从中渔利。On the surface he was helping out, but in fact he was profiting from the situation. **II** [名] easy pickings (*pl*)

渔业 yúyè [名] fisheries (*pl*)

隅 yú [名] **1** (角落) corner **2** (边地) outlying area

逾 yú **I** [动] (书) exceed **II** [副] (书) even more

逾期 yúqī [动] be overdue

逾越 yúyuè [动] exceed ◇他认为自己与父母之间有不可逾越的鸿沟。He believed there was an unbridgeable gulf between him and his parents.

渝 yú [动] change ◇忠贞不渝 unswervingly loyal

愉 yú [形] happy

愉快 yúkuài [形] happy ◇祝你旅行愉快! Have a pleasant journey!

愉悦 yúyuè [形] cheerful

愚 yú **I** [形] foolish **II** [动] fool

愚笨 yúbèn [形] clumsy

愚蠢 yúchǔn [形] foolish

愚昧 yúmèi [形] ignorant

愚弄 yúnòng [动] make a fool of ◇明白自己被人愚弄之后,他决定报复。Once he realized he had been made a fool of, he resolved to get his revenge.

舆 yú **I** [形] popular **II** [名] (书) chariot

舆论 yúlùn [名] public opinion

与 yǔ **I** [动] give (*pt* gave, *pp* given) ♦赠与 present **II** [介] with ◇我永远不会与政客为友。I will never make friends with politicians. ◇与敌人决一死战 fight the enemy to the death **III** [连] and ◇春季与秋季 spring and autumn

与其 yǔqí [连] rather than ◇与其每天发牢骚,不如想办法改变现状。Rather than grumbling all the time, it would be better to find a way to change the situation.

与人为善 yǔ rén wéi shàn glad to help others ◇他一向与人为善,大家都很信任他。He's always glad to help people – everybody has great trust in him.

与日俱增 yǔ rì jù zēng grow day by day ◇随着经济的发展,这个国家的国力与日俱增。As the economy develops, the country is getting stronger day by day.

予 yǔ [动] give (*pt* gave, *pp* given) ♦授予 award

予以 yǔyǐ [动] give (*pt* gave, *pp* given)

屿 yǔ [名] islet ♦岛屿 islands (*pl*)

宇 yǔ [名] **1** (房屋) house **2** (四方) the universe **3** (风度) appearance

宇航 yǔháng **I** [动] travel through space **II** [名] space travel

宇航员 yǔhángyuán [名] astronaut

宇宙 yǔzhòu [名] universe

羽 yǔ [名] **1** (羽毛) feather **2** (翅膀) wing

羽毛 yǔmáo [名] feather

羽毛球 yǔmáoqiú [名] **1** (指运动) badminton **2** (指球体) shuttlecock

羽翼 yǔyì [名] **1** (翅膀) wing **2** (帮手) assistant

雨 yǔ [名] rain

雨后春笋 yǔ hòu chūnsǔn spring up like mushrooms

雨具 yǔjù [名] waterproofs (*pl*)

雨量 yǔliàng [名] rainfall

雨露 yǔlù [名] **1** (雨水和露水) rain and dew **2** (喻) (恩惠) favour (英), favor (美)

雨水 yǔshuǐ [名] (降水) rain

语 yǔ **I** [名] **1** (语言) language ◇他会说多种外国语。He can speak many foreign languages. ♦手语 sign language ♦旗语 semaphore **2** (谚语) saying **II** [动] talk

语病 yǔbìng [名] grammatical mistake

语词 yǔcí [名] words and phrases (*pl*)

语调 yǔdiào [名] tone

语法 yǔfǎ [名] grammar

语感 yǔgǎn [名] feel for language ◇他语感好,因此文章写得好。He has a good feel for language, and so he writes very good essays.

语境 yǔjìng [名] context

语句 yǔjù [名] sentence

语料 yǔliào [名] corpus

语气 yǔqì [名] **1** (口气) tone of voice **2** (语法) mood

语文 yǔwén [名] **1** (语言文字) language **2** (中文) Chinese **3** (语言与文学) language and literature

语无伦次 yǔ wú lúncì speak incoherently ◊他紧张得双腿发抖，说话语无伦次。He was so nervous that his legs were shaking and his speech was incoherent.

语系 yǔxì [名] language family

语序 yǔxù [名] word order

语言 yǔyán [名] language

语义 yǔyì [名] ◊这两个词语义相同，但使用场合不同。These two words are the same semantically, but they are used in different contexts.

语音 yǔyīn [名] pronunciation

语音信箱 yǔyīnxìnxiāng [名] voice mail

语种 yǔzhǒng [名] language

语重心长 yǔ zhòng xīn cháng sincere words

玉 yù [名] **1** (玉石) jade **2** (美丽) beauty **3** (敬) (指对方身体) ♦玉照 your photograph

玉米 yùmǐ [名] **1** (指植物) maize (英), corn (美) **2** (指子实) corn on the cob

玉器 yùqì [名] jadeware

玉石俱焚 yù shí jù fén destruction of both good and bad

玉照 yùzhào [名] your photograph

驭 yù [动] drive (*pt* drove, *pp* driven)

芋 yù [名] **1** (指植物) taro **2** (指块茎) tuber

芋头 yùtou [名] taro

吁 yù [动] plead
▷另见 xū

吁请 yùqǐng [动] request

吁求 yùqiú [动] plead with

郁 yù [形] **1** (香气浓) strong-smelling **2** (茂盛) lush **3** (烦闷) gloomy

郁积 yùjī [动] repress ◊郁积在他心中的委屈，终于倾诉出来了。He finally poured out all the grievances that he'd kept repressed.

郁结 yùjié [动] repress

郁闷 yùmèn [形] melancholy

郁郁 yùyù [形] **1** (茂密) lush **2** (苦闷) depressed ◊近来他有点儿郁郁不乐。He's been a bit depressed lately.

育 yù **I** [动] **1** (生育) give birth to (*pt* gave, *pp* given) **2** (养活) raise **II** [名] education

育龄 yùlíng [名] childbearing age

育种 yùzhǒng [动] breed (*pt, pp* bred)

狱 yù [名] **1** (监狱) prison **2** (官司) lawsuit

浴 yù [动] wash

浴场 yùchǎng [名] outdoor swimming pool

浴盆 yùpén [名] bath

浴室 yùshì [名] bathroom

预 yù **I** [副] in advance **II** [动] take part in (*pt* took, *pp* taken)

预报 yùbào [动] predict ◊天气预报说今晚有霜冻。The weather forecast is for frost this evening.

预备 yùbèi [动] prepare

预测 yùcè [动] predict ◊谈判结果与人们的预测很不一样。The result of the negotiations was completely different from everyone's predictions.

预防 yùfáng [动] prevent

预感 yùgǎn [动] have a premonition ◊他买彩票时预感会中大奖，果真应验了。As he bought the lottery ticket he had a premonition that he was going to win a big prize, and sure enough it came true.

预告 yùgào [动] give advance warning (*pt* gave, *pp* given) ◊下周的电影预告你看了吗？Have you seen the trailer for next week's film?

预计 yùjì [动] estimate

预见 yùjiàn [动] foresee (*pt* foresaw, *pp* foreseen) ◇那位人类学家的预见非常准确。That anthropologist's predictions were accurate.

预警 yùjǐng [动] give advance warning (*pt* gave, *pp* given)

预科 yùkē [名] foundation course

预料 yùliào [动] predict ◇不出我的预料，他果然当上了经理。As I predicted, he did become a manager.

预算 yùsuàn [名] budget

预习 yùxí [动] prepare for lessons ◇每天的功课，他都提前预习。He always prepares every day's lesson in advance.

预先 yùxiān [副] in advance ◇租用会议室，要预先提出申请。If you want to hire the meeting room you have to submit a request in advance.

预言 yùyán [动] predict ◇他的预言果然变成了现实。It turned out that his prophecy came true.

预兆 yùzhào [名] premonition ◇出车祸的那天早晨，他就有一种不祥的预兆。The morning before the car accident, he had a premonition of disaster.

域 yù [名] region ♦领域 realm

欲 yù **I** [名] desire **II** [动] (书) want ◇为所欲为 do what one wants **III** [副] (书) ◇喷薄欲出 about to burst forth

欲盖弥彰 yù gài mí zhāng protest too much

欲念 yùniàn [名] sexual desire

欲速则不达 yù sù zé bù dá try to run before one can walk ◇学习外语是一个循序渐进的过程，欲速则不达。Studying foreign languages is a progressive, gradual process – you can't run before you can walk.

欲望 yùwàng [名] desire

遇 yù **I** [动] meet (*pt, pp* met) **II** [名] **1** (待遇) treatment **2** (机会) opportunity

遇害 yùhài [动] be murdered

遇救 yùjiù [动] be rescued

遇难 yùnàn [动] **1** (意外死亡) be killed in an accident **2** (遭难) meet with misfortune (*pt, pp* met)

喻 yù [动] **1** (明白) understand (*pt, pp* understood) ◇知识就是力量，这个道理是不言而喻的。It goes without saying that knowledge is power. **2** (说明) explain **3** (比方) give an example (*pt* gave, *pp* given)

御 yù (书) [动] **1** (赶车) drive (*pt* drove, *pp* driven) **2** (抵挡) keep … out (*pt, pp* kept)

御寒 yùhán [动] keep out the cold (*pt, pp* kept)

寓 yù **I** [动] **1** (居住) live **2** (寄托) imply **II** [名] residence

寓所 yùsuǒ [名] residence

寓言 yùyán [名] fable

寓意 yùyì [名] moral

裕 yù [形] plentiful

愈 yù **I** [形] (书) recover **II** [副] (书) the more … the more … ◇士兵们愈战愈勇。The more the soldiers fought the braver they became.

愈合 yùhé [动] heal up

愈加 yùjiā [副] increasingly ◇年轻时他就我行我素，上了年纪愈加固执。He was set in his ways when he was young, and as he got older he became increasingly stubborn.

誉 yù **I** [名] reputation **II** [动] praise

誉满全球 yù mǎn quánqiú have a worldwide reputation ◇早在古代，中国丝绸就已誉满全球。Early in antiquity, Chinese silk already had a worldwide reputation.

鹬 yù [名] snipe

鸳 yuān [名] mandarin duck

鸳鸯 yuānyāng [名] **1** (指鸟) mandarin duck **2** (指人) lovebirds (*pl*)

冤 yuān **I** [名] **1** (冤枉) injustice **2** (冤仇) enmity **II** [形] ◇花这么多钱买了假货，太冤了！ What bad luck to spend so much money on a fake.

冤仇 yuānchóu [名] enmity

冤大头 yuāndàtóu [名] squanderer

冤家 yuānjia [名] **1** (仇人) enemy **2** (可气又可爱的人) ◇你这个小冤家，别再气我了！ Stop annoying me you little devil.

冤枉 yuānwang **I** [动] treat unfairly ◇他没什么责任，你别冤枉他。 He wasn't responsible – don't be unfair to him. **II** [名] wrongful treatment **III** [形] not worthwhile

渊 yuān **I** [名] ♦深渊 abyss **II** [形] deep

渊博 yuānbó [形] erudite

渊源 yuānyuán [名] origin

元 yuán **I** [名] **1** (始) first **2** (首) chief ♦元凶 chief culprit **3** (主) fundamental ♦元素 element **4** (整体) component ♦单元 unit **5** (圆形货币) coin ♦金元 gold coin **II** [量] yuan ◇5元钱 five yuan

元旦 Yuándàn [名] New Year's Day

元件 yuánjiàn [名] part

元老 yuánlǎo [名] founding member

元气 yuánqì [名] vitality

元首 yuánshǒu [名] head of state

元帅 yuánshuài [名] commander-in-chief

元宵 yuánxiāo [名] the Lantern Festival

元宵节 Yuánxiāo Jié [名] the Lantern Festival

元勋 yuánxūn [名] founding father

元音 yuányīn [名] vowel

园 yuán [名] **1** (指菜地或果林) garden **2** (指游乐场所) park

园地 yuándì [名] **1** (田园) garden **2** (活动范围) field

园丁 yuándīng [名] **1** (园艺工人) gardener **2** (老师) teacher

园林 yuánlín [名] garden

园艺 yuányì [名] gardening

员 yuán **I** [名] **1** (指工作或学习的人) ♦理发员 hairdresser ♦学员 student **2** (成员) member **II** [量] ◇一员大将 an able general

员工 yuángōng [名] staff (*pl*)

原 yuán **I** [形] **1** (本来的) original ◇原计划 original plan **2** (未加工的) raw ♦原油 crude oil **II** [动] forgive (*pt* forgave, *pp* forgiven) ♦原谅 forgive **III** [名] plain

原本 yuánběn **I** [名] **1** (原稿) original manuscript **2** (初本) first edition **3** (原书) original **II** [副] originally

原材料 yuáncáiliào [名] raw and processed materials (*pl*)

原稿 yuángǎo [名] manuscript

原告 yuángào [名] plaintiff

原籍 yuánjí [名] native home

原来 yuánlái **I** [形] original ◇几十年过去，这个小镇还是原来的样子。 Decades have passed, but this town is still as it always was. **II** [副] **1** (起初) originally ◇我原来并不知道他们两人之间的恩恩怨怨。 Originally I knew nothing about their complicated emotional history. **2** (其实) all along ◇我以为你出国了，原来你还在国内呢！ I thought you had gone abroad, and all along you were still in the country!

原理 yuánlǐ [名] principle

原谅 yuánliàng [动] forgive (*pt* forgave, *pp* forgiven) ◇我得早点走，请原谅。 I have to leave early, please excuse me. ◇我求她原谅我的过失。 I begged her pardon for my mistake.

原料 yuánliào [名] (指烹饪) ingredient

原始 yuánshǐ [形] **1** (古老) primitive **2** (最初) original

原委 yuánwěi [名] full details (*pl*)

原先 yuánxiān **I** [形] original **II** [副] originally

原形 yuánxíng [名] true colours (英) 或 colors (美)

原因 yuányīn [名] reason ◇这次没考好，主要原因是没重视。 The main reason I didn't do well in this exam is that I didn't take it very seriously. ◇医生们尚未查出得这种病的原因。 The doctors have never established the causes of this illness.

原原本本 yuányuánběnběn from start to finish ◇他把事情的经过原原本本地讲了一遍。 He gave us a full and detailed account of the affair.

原则 yuánzé [名] principle ◇我们原则上同意你的观点。We agree with you in principle.

原著 yuánzhù [名] the original

原子 yuánzǐ [名] atom

圆 yuán I [形] 1 (圆形的) round ♦圆圈 circle 2 (球形的) spherical 3 (圆满的) satisfactory II [动] justify III [名] 1 (数) (圆周) circle 2 (金属货币) coin ♦银圆 silver coin

圆场 yuánchǎng [动] mediate

圆规 yuánguī [名] compasses (*pl*)

圆滑 yuánhuá [形] sly

圆满 yuánmǎn [形] satisfactory

圆梦 yuánmèng [动] 1 (释梦) interpret dreams 2 (实现梦想) realize one's dream ◇他一直想出国，这次终于可以圆梦了。He's always wanted to go abroad. This time he can finally realize his dream.

圆舞曲 yuánwǔqǔ [名] waltz

援 yuán [动] 1 (牵引) pull ♦攀援 clamber 2 (引用) cite ♦援例 cite a precedent 3 (援助) help ♦支援 support

援救 yuánjiù [动] rescue

援引 yuányǐn [动] cite ◇他援引专家的结论来支持自己的观点。He cited the conclusions of the experts in support of his view.

援助 yuánzhù [动] help

缘 yuán [名] 1 (缘故) cause 2 (缘分) fate 3 (边缘) edge

缘分 yuánfèn [名] fate ◇恋爱婚姻，要看两个人的缘分。The success of love and marriage depends on predestination.

缘故 yuángù [名] cause

缘由 yuányóu [名] cause

猿 yuán [名] ape

猿猴 yuánhóu [名] apes and monkeys (*pl*)

猿人 yuánrén [名] ape-man (*pl* ape-men)

源 yuán [名] source ♦水源 source

源泉 yuánquán [名] source

源源 yuányuán [形] continuous

源远流长 yuán yuǎn liú cháng have a long history ◇中华文明源远流长。Chinese civilization has a long history.

远 yuǎn [形] 1 (指距离) far ◇两条河相距不远。The two rivers are not far from one other. 2 (指血统) distant 3 (指程度) far ◇这本词典远比其他词典好。This dictionary is far better than other dictionaries. ◇这本小说远不如我上星期读的那本有意思。This novel is nowhere near as interesting as the one I read last week.

远程 yuǎnchéng [名] long distance ◇远程导弹 long-range missile

远程会议 yuǎnchénghuìyì [名] teleconference

远大 yuǎndà [形] far-reaching

远方 yuǎnfāng [名] afar ◇客人们从远方来。The guests have come from afar.

远见 yuǎnjiàn [名] foresight

远近 yuǎnjìn [名] 1 (距离的长短) distance 2 (远处和近处) far and near ◇他可是远近闻名的大人物。He's known of far and wide.

远景 yuǎnjǐng [名] 1 (远处景物) distant view 2 (未来景象) future prospect

远亲 yuǎnqīn [名] distant relative

远视 yuǎnshì [名] (医) long sight ◇他是远视眼，近处的东西看不清。He's long-sighted – he can't see anything properly close to.

远洋 yuǎnyáng [名] ocean

远征 yuǎnzhēng [动] go on an expedition (*pt* went, *pp* gone)

远走高飞 yuǎnzǒugāofēi travel far away

远足 yuǎnzú [动] hike ◇他周末远足。At the weekends he goes hiking.

苑 yuàn [名] 1 (园林) garden 2 (书) (指文艺) circles (*pl*) ♦艺苑 artistic circles

怨 yuàn I [动] blame II [名] resentment

怨恨 yuànhèn [动] hold a grudge

against (*pt, pp* held) ◊他小时候没能上学，到现在还怨恨父母。He couldn't go to school when he was young, and to this day he still holds a grudge against his parents.

怨声载道 yuàn shēng zài dào ◊对于不合理的税收制度，人们怨声载道。There were many complaints about the unfair taxation system.

怨天尤人 yuàn tiān yóu rén blame everyone and everything except oneself

怨言 yuànyán [名] complaint

院 yuàn [名] **1** (院落) courtyard **2** (指机关和处所) ♦研究院 research institute ♦电影院 cinema (英), movie theater (美) **3** (学院) college **4** (医院) hospital

院落 yuànluò [名] yard

院士 yuànshì [名] fellow

愿 yuàn **I** [名] **1** (愿望) wish ♦愿望 desire **2** (愿心) promise **II** [情] ◊他愿出力，不愿出钱。He is volunteering work, not money.

愿望 yuànwàng [名] wish

愿意 yuànyì [动] **1** (同意) be willing to ◊你愿意负责这项工作吗？Are you willing to take on this project? **2** (希望) wish

约 yuē **I** [动] **1** (束缚) restrict **2** (商定) arrange **3** (邀请) invite **4** (节俭) economize **5** (数) (约分) reduce ◊十分之五可以约成二分之一。Five over ten can be reduced to one over two. **II** [形] brief ♦简约 brief **III** [副] about ◊这袋米约有20公斤。This sack of rice weighs about twenty kilograms.

约定俗成 yuē dìng sú chéng established by usage ◊对这种事我们有约定俗成的解决办法。We have established practice for dealing with this kind of thing.

约法三章 yuē fǎ sān zhāng establish a set of rules

约会 yuēhuì [动] make an appointment ◊今天的约会临时取消了。The appointment today has been put off.

约略 yuēlüè [副] approximately ◊参加示威的人数，约略有10万人。Approximately a hundred thousand people attended the demonstration.

约束 yuēshù [动] bind (*pt, pp* bound) ◊法律约束人，也保护人。The law binds people but also protects them.

月 yuè [名] **1** (月球) the moon ♦满月 full moon **2** (月份) month ♦3月 March **3** (每月) monthly ♦月薪 monthly salary **4** (月亮状) ♦月饼 mooncake

月份 yuèfèn [名] month

月光 yuèguāng [名] moonlight

月经 yuèjīng [名] **1** (例假) period **2** (经血) menses (*pl*)

月亮 yuèliang [名] the moon

月票 yuèpiào [名] monthly ticket

月食 yuèshí [名] lunar eclipse

月下老人 yuèxià lǎorén matchmaker

乐 yuè [名] music ♦器乐 instrumental music ♦民乐 folk music
▷另见 lè

乐队 yuèduì [名] band

乐理 yuèlǐ [名] musical theory

乐谱 yuèpǔ [名] score

乐器 yuèqì [名] musical instrument ◊他会演奏多种乐器。He can play a lot of different instruments.

乐曲 yuèqǔ [名] music

乐坛 yuètán [名] musical circles (*pl*)

乐团 yuètuán [名] philharmonic orchestra

乐章 yuèzhāng [名] movement

岳 yuè [名] **1** (高山) mountain **2** (妻子的父母) parents-in-law (*pl*)

岳父 yuèfù [名] father-in-law (*pl* fathers-in-law)

岳母 yuèmǔ [名] mother-in-law (*pl* mothers-in-law)

阅 yuè [动] **1** (看) read (*pt, pp* read) **2** (检阅) inspect **3** (经历) experience

阅读 yuèdú [动] read (*pt, pp* read)

阅览 yuèlǎn [动] read (*pt, pp* read)

阅历 yuèlì [动] experience

悦 yuè I [形] happy II [动] please

悦耳 yuè'ěr [形] beautiful ◇这男孩子嗓音清脆，唱起歌来悦耳动听。The boy has a clear voice – when he sings it's beautiful.

悦目 yuèmù [形] beautiful ◇这些女孩们的服装色彩悦目。These girls' clothes are a beautiful colour (英) 或 color (美).

跃 yuè [动] leap

跃跃欲试 yuèyuè yù shì itching to have a go ◇听完老师的介绍，同学们跃跃欲试。Having heard the teacher's introduction, the students were itching to have a go.

越 yuè I [动] 1 (跨过) jump over 2 (超过) exceed ♦越级 skip a grade 3 (昂扬) be in high spirits II [副] ◇这门课越学越有意思。The more you study this subject, the more interesting it gets. ◇这姑娘长得越来越漂亮了。This girl is becoming more and more beautiful.

越冬 yuèdōng [动] live through winter

越发 yuèfā [副] increasingly ◇到了晚年，他越发固执。Towards the end of his life, he became increasingly stubborn.

越轨 yuèguǐ [动] overstep the mark

越来越 yuèláiyuè [副] more and more ◇他的英语说得越来越流利了。His English is getting more and more fluent. ◇天气越来越暖和了。The weather is getting warmer and warmer.

越权 yuèquán [动] overstep one's authority

越野 yuèyě [动] go cross-country (*pt* went, *pp* gone)

越狱 yuèyù [动] escape from prison

越…越… yuè...yuè... [副] the more … the more … ◇你越说，那家伙越不听。The more you talk, the more that guy won't listen. ◇明天大家来得越早越好。The earlier everyone can come tomorrow the better.

越俎代庖 yuè zǔ dài páo meddle in other's affairs ◇这件事必须由他自己做，你不能越俎代庖。He has to do this himself – don't you go getting involved.

晕 yūn [动] 1 (晕眩) dizzy 2 (昏迷) faint
▷另见 yùn

晕厥 yūnjué [动] pass out

云 yún I [名] cloud II [动] say (*pt, pp* said)

云彩 yúncai [名] cloud

云集 yúnjí [动] converge

云雾 yúnwù [名] mist

云霄 yúnxiāo [名] the skies (*pl*)

匀 yún I [形] even II [动] 1 (使均匀) even … out 2 (分) apportion

匀称 yúnchèn [形] well-proportioned

匀整 yúnzhěng [形] regular

芸 yún 见下文

芸芸众生 yúnyún zhòng shēng all living things ◇他认为自己是旷世奇才，不同于芸芸众生。He thinks he's got some sort of unique talent – that he's a cut above all other mortals.

耘 yún [动] hoe

允 yǔn I [动] allow ♦应允 assent II [形] fair

允诺 yǔnnuò [动] promise

允许 yǔnxǔ [动] allow ◇儿童饮酒是绝对不允许的。Children aren't allowed to drink alcohol.

陨 yǔn [动] (书) fall from the sky (*pt* fell, *pp* fallen)

陨落 yǔnluò [动] 1 (坠落) fall from the sky (*pt* fell, *pp* fallen) 2 (喻) (去世) die

陨石 yǔnshí [名] meteorite

孕 yùn I [动] be pregnant II [名] pregnancy

孕育 yùnyù [动] be pregnant with ◇平静的表面下孕育着一场政治风暴。Beneath the calm exterior, a political hurricane was brewing.

运 yùn I [动] 1 (运动) move 2 (搬运) transport ♦货运 transport 3 (运用) use II [名] luck ♦好运 good luck

运筹帷幄 yùnchóu wéiwò plan ... from behind the scenes

运动 yùndòng I [动] (物) move II [名] **1** (体育活动) sport ◊适量运动有益健康。A degree of sporting activity is good for the health. **2** (大规模) movement

运动鞋 yùndòngxié [名] trainer

运动员 yùndòngyuán [名] athlete

运河 yùnhé [名] canal

运气 yùnqi [名] luck

运输 yùnshū [动] transport

运算 yùnsuàn [动] calculate

运行 yùnxíng [动] move

运用 yùnyòng [动] make use of ◊应尽量把书本知识运用到实践中去。You should make practical use of what you have learned in books.

运转 yùnzhuǎn [动] **1** (指星球) orbit ◊月亮绕着地球运转。The moon orbits the earth. **2** (指机器) run (*pt* ran, *pp* run)

运作 yùnzuò [动] operate

晕 yùn I [动] feel giddy (*pt, pp* felt) ♦晕机 be airsick II [名] **1** (指日、月) halo ♦月晕 lunar halo **2** (指光、色) glow ♦红晕 red glow ▷另见 yūn

晕场 yùnchǎng [动] get stage fright

晕车 yùnchē [动] be carsick

晕船 yùnchuán [动] be seasick

酝 yùn [动] (书) brew

酝酿 yùnniàng [动] brew ◊这件事已经酝酿好长时间了。This affair has been brewing for a long time.

韵 yùn [名] **1** (声音) music **2** (情趣) charm **3** (韵母) rhyme

韵味 yùnwèi [名] lasting appeal

蕴 yùn I [动] (书) contain II [名] (书) store

蕴藏 yùncáng [动] contain

蕴涵 yùnhán [动] contain

熨 yùn [动] iron

熨斗 yùndǒu [名] iron

Zz

扎 zā [动] tie
▷另见 zhā

咂 zā [动] **1** (吸入) sip **2** (咂嘴) make noises of appreciation **3** (品味) savour (英), savor (美)

咂嘴 zāzuǐ [动] make noises of appreciation

杂 zá **I** [形] miscellaneous ♦复杂 complicated **II** [动] mix ◇棉花中间杂进其他纤维。Other fibres (英) 或 fibers (美) are mixed into the cotton.

杂感 zágǎn [名] **1** (偶感) random thoughts (*pl*) **2** (杂记) notes (*pl*)

杂烩 záhuì [名] **1** (指菜) stew **2** (拼凑) mixture

杂货 záhuò [名] groceries (*pl*)

杂技 zájì [名] acrobatics (*pl*)

杂交 zájiāo [动] hybridize ◇杂交水稻 rice hybrid

杂乱 záluàn [形] jumbled up ◇冰箱里的东西很杂乱。The things in the fridge are all jumbled up.

杂念 zániàn [名] distracting thoughts (*pl*)

杂牌 zápái [名] inferior brand

杂耍 záshuǎ [名] variety show

杂碎 zásui [名] entrails (*pl*)

杂物 záwù [名] litter

杂音 záyīn [名] **1** (干扰) static **2** (噪声) noise **3** (医) murmur

杂志 zázhì [名] magazine ◇专业杂志 technical magazine ◇学术杂志 academic journal

杂质 zázhì [名] impurity ◇这种米杂质很多。This rice has a lot of impurities in it.

杂种 zázhǒng [名] **1** (生物) hybrid **2** (侮辱) bastard

砸 zá [动] **1** (撞击) pound **2** (打破) break (*pt* broke, *pp* broken) ◇杯子砸坏了。The cup was broken. **3** (方) (失败) fail ◇戏演砸了。The performance went badly.

咋 zǎ [代] **1** (为什么) ◇你咋不回家呢？ Why don't you go home? **2** (怎么) ◇那里咋样啊？ How are things going there?
▷另见 zhā

灾 zāi [名] **1** (灾害) disaster ♦水灾 flood **2** (不幸) misfortune

灾害 zāihài [名] disaster

灾荒 zāihuāng [名] famine

灾祸 zāihuò [名] calamity

灾难 zāinàn [名] disaster

灾区 zāiqū [名] disaster area

栽 zāi [动] **1** (种) plant ◇栽花 grow flowers **2** (插) stick … in (*pt*, *pp* stuck) **3** (强加) frame **4** (摔倒) tumble

栽培 zāipéi [动] **1** (种植) cultivate ◇水稻栽培 rice cultivation **2** (造就) nurture **3** (提拔) promote

栽赃 zāizāng [动] frame

栽种 zāizhòng [动] plant

载 zǎi **I** [名] year **II** [动] record ♦登载 publish
▷另见 zài

宰 zǎi [动] **1** (管) rule ♦主宰 dominate **2** (杀) slaughter

宰割 zǎigē [动] oppress

仔 zǎi [名] **1** (儿子) son **2** (指动物) young animal ◇下仔 drop a litter

再 zài [副] **1** (又) again ◇你再说一遍。Say that again. **2** (更) more ◇你再做得认真些就更好了。If you were a bit more serious about it, it would be better. ◇请把音量放得再大些。Please turn the volume up a bit. ◇再大的风雨我也不怕。Even if the storm were worse I wouldn't be afraid. **3** (继续) ◇我不能再等了。I can't wait any longer. ◇即使再给几天，任务也完不成。Even if we're given another few days, this job won't be done. **4** (接着) then ◇吃完饭再打电脑游戏。

Eat your dinner and then you can play your computer game. ◇你做完功课再看小说。You can read your book when you've finished your homework. **5** (另外) ♦再说 besides ◇再就是 and also

再次 zàicì [副] once again ◇再次相聚 get together again

再会 zàihuì [动] say goodbye (*pt, pp* said)

再见 zàijiàn [动] say goodbye (*pt, pp* said) ◇再见！Goodbye!

再接再厉 zài jiē zài lì persevere

再就业 zàijiùyè [动] re-employ

再三 zàisān [副] again and again ◇再三叮嘱 warn ... again and again ◇再三思考 on second thoughts

再生 zàishēng [动] **1** (复活) revive **2** (回收) recycle

再现 zàixiàn [动] reappear

再造 zàizào [动] rebuild (*pt, pp* rebuilt)

在 zài **I** [动] **1** (存在) live ◇精神永在。The spirit will live forever. **2** (处于) be (*pt* was, *pp* been) ◇你的书在桌子上。Your book is on the table. ◇我父母在纽约。My parents are in New York. **3** (在于) rest with ◇和解的关键在他们。The key to reconciliation rests with them. **II** [副] ◇情况在改变。Things are changing. ◇他们在看电视。They're watching TV. **III** [介] at ◇在机场等候 wait at the airport ◇在人类历史上 in human history

在岗 zàigǎng [形] employed

在行 zàiháng [形] expert ◇他对计算机很在行。He's a computer expert.

在乎 zàihu [动] care ◇他对别人的批评满不在乎。He doesn't care about criticism.

在劫难逃 zài jié nán táo ◇这次我看他是在劫难逃。This time I see him there will be no escape.

在世 zàishì [动] be alive

在逃 zàitáo [动] be on the run

在望 zàiwàng [动] **1** (可以看见) be visible **2** (即将到来) be in sight ◇胜利在望。Victory is in sight.

在位 zàiwèi [动] be in power

在押 zàiyā [动] be in prison

在业 zàiyè [形] employed

在意 zàiyì [动] care ◇你说什么我都不会在意的。Whatever you say, I just don't care.

在于 zàiyú [动] **1** (存在) lie in (*pt* lay, *pp* lain) **2** (取决于) depend on

在职 zàizhí [动] be employed ◇他是在职研究生。He's working and also doing a postgraduate degree.

在座 zàizuò [动] be present

载 zài [动] [动] **1** (装载) carry ♦载重 load **2** (充满) be full of ◇怨声载道 complaints on all sides ▷另见 zǎi

载歌载舞 zài gē zài wǔ sing and dance

载运 zàiyùn [动] transport

载重 zàizhòng [名] load ◇载重能力 loading capacity

簪 zān **I** [名] hairpin **II** [动] put ... in one's hair (*pt, pp* put) ◇簪花 put flowers in one's hair

咱 zán [代] **1** (咱们) we **2** (方) (我) I

咱们 zánmen [代] **1** (我们) we **2** (方) (我) I ◇咱们只是个普通劳动者。I'm just an ordinary labourer.

攒 zǎn [动] save ▷另见 cuán

暂 zàn **I** [形] brief **II** [副] temporarily ◇暂住朋友那里 stay at a friend's temporarily ◇暂停 suspend

暂且 zànqiě [副] for the moment

暂时 zànshí [名] ◇暂时的需要 temporary need ◇我们暂时休息一下。We'll rest for a moment.

暂行 zànxíng [形] provisional

錾 zàn **I** [动] engrave **II** [名] chisel

赞 zàn **I** [动] **1** (帮助) assist ♦赞助 assistance **2** (称颂) commend **II** [名] eulogy

赞成 zànchéng [动] approve ◇赞成政府的决策 approve of the

government's policy ◇投赞成票 cast a yes vote

赞歌 zàngē [名] paean

赞美 zànměi [动] praise

赞赏 zànshǎng [动] admire

赞颂 zànsòng [动] sing the praises of (*pt* sang, *pp* sung)

赞叹 zàntàn [动] marvel at

赞同 zàntóng [动] approve of

赞扬 zànyáng [动] pay tribute to (*pt*, *pp* paid) ◇学校赞扬学生们的勇敢行为。The school paid tribute to the students' bravery.

赞助 zànzhù [动] assist ◇为残疾人提供赞助 offer assistance to disabled people

赃 zāng [名] **1** (赃物) booty ♦分赃 share the booty **2** (贿赂) bribes (*pl*) ♦贪赃 take bribes

赃款 zāngkuǎn [名] dirty money

赃物 zāngwù [名] **1** (被盗物品) stolen goods (*pl*) **2** (受贿之物) bribe

脏 zāng [形] dirty ▷另见 zàng

脏话 zānghuà [名] dirty word

脏字 zāngzì [名] swear word

脏 zàng [名] internal organ ♦心脏 heart ♦肝脏 liver ♦肾脏 kidney ▷另见 zāng

脏器 zàngqì [名] organ

葬 zàng [动] bury ♦送葬 attend a funeral

葬身 zàngshēn [动] be buried

葬送 zàngsòng [动] ruin

藏 zàng [名] **1** (储存地) store **2** (经典) scriptures (*pl*) **3** (西藏) Tibet ▷另见 cáng

藏蓝 zànglán [形] purplish blue

藏青 zàngqīng [形] dark blue

遭 zāo **I** [动] meet with (*pt*, *pp* met) ♦遭殃 suffer **II** [量] time ◇头一遭 the first time

遭际 zāojì [名] encounter

遭受 zāoshòu [动] suffer ◇遭受水灾 be hit by floods

遭殃 zāoyāng [动] suffer

遭遇 zāoyù **I** [动] meet with (*pt*, *pp* met) **II** [名] experience

遭罪 zāozuì [动] suffer

糟 zāo **I** [名] dregs (*pl*) **II** [动] **1** (浪费) waste ♦糟蹋 spoil **2** (腌制) flavour (英) 或 flavor (美) with alcohol **III** [形] **1** (腐烂) rotten **2** (弄坏) messy

糟糕 zāogāo [形] ◇真糟糕, 我的钥匙丢了。Oh no, I've lost my key! ◇糟糕, 庄稼给毁了。How awful! The crops have been ruined.

糟践 zāojian [动] **1** (浪费) waste **2** (侮辱) insult

糟粕 zāopò [名] rubbish

糟蹋 zāota [动] **1** (浪费) waste **2** (损坏) abuse

凿 záo **I** [名] chisel **II** [动] cut (*pt*, *pp* cut)

早 zǎo **I** [名] morning **II** [副] a long time ago ◇这事我早就知道了。I knew about this a long time ago. **III** [形] early ♦早餐 breakfast ◇你早点来。Come early.

早安 zǎo'ān [名] ◇早安! Good morning!

早操 zǎocāo [名] morning exercises (*pl*)

早产 zǎochǎn [名] (医) premature birth

早晨 zǎochen [名] morning ◇他早晨9点上班。He goes to work at 9 o'clock in the morning.

早点 zǎodiǎn [名] breakfast

早年 zǎonián [名] youth ◇他早年当过兵。In his youth he was a soldier.

早期 zǎoqī [名] early stage ◇他的早期作品 his early works

早晚 zǎowǎn **I** [名] morning and evening **II** [副] **1** (迟早) sooner or later **2** (方) (将来) some day

枣 zǎo [名] date

枣红 zǎohóng [形] claret

澡 zǎo [动] bathe

澡盆 zǎopén [名] bathtub

澡堂 zǎotáng [名] public baths (*pl*)

皂 zào I [名] soap II [形] black

灶 zào [名] 1 (炊具) cooker (英), stove (美) 2 (厨房) kitchen ◇学生灶 students' canteen

灶具 zàojù [名] cooking utensil

造 zào I [动] 1 (制作) make (*pt, pp* made) ◇造船 build a ship 2 (瞎编) concoct ♦造谣 start a rumour (英) 或 rumor (美) 3 (书) (前往) arrive ♦造访 visit 4 (培养) train II [名] harvest

造成 zàochéng [动] cause

造反 zàofǎn [动] rebel

造访 zàofǎng [动] visit

造福 zàofú [动] benefit ◇这项新发明将造福于人类。This new invention will benefit humanity.

造化 zàohua [名] good fortune

造价 zàojià [名] cost

造就 zàojiù [动] train

造孽 zàoniè [动] do evil

造型 zàoxíng [名] model

造谣 zàoyáo [动] start a rumour (英) 或 rumor (美)

造诣 zàoyì [名] achievements (*pl*)

造作 zàozuò [动] make (*pt, pp* made)

造作 zàozuo [形] artificial

噪 zào [动] 1 (叫) chirp ◇蝉噪 noise of cicadas 2 (嚷) clamour (英), clamor (美) ♦鼓噪 create an uproar

噪音 zàoyīn [名] noise

燥 zào [形] dry ♦干燥 dry

燥热 zàorè [形] 1 (指天气) hot and dry 2 (医) dry

躁 zào [形] rash ♦烦躁 be agitated

躁动 zàodòng [动] fidget

则 zé I [名] 1 (榜样) standard ♦准则 standard 2 (规章) rule ♦总则 general principle II [量] piece ◇新闻三则 three items of news III [连] 1 (就) then ◇不战则已，战则必胜。If you don't fight, then fine. If you do fight, fight to win. 2 (却) but ◇他很虚荣，她则不然。He's very vain, but she's not. ◇南方湿润，北方则干燥。The south is humid, but the north is dry. IV [副] ◇不能让老人们干这种活儿，一则他们年纪大，二则身体差。You can't let elderly people do this kind of work. For one thing, they're too old, and for another, they're not up to it health-wise.

责 zé I [名] responsibility ♦负责 be responsible for II [动] 1 (要求) demand ♦责令 order 2 (质问) cross-examine ♦责问 call to account 3 (责备) blame ♦指责 censure

责备 zébèi [动] blame

责成 zéchéng [动] instruct ◇此事要责成人事部来办。We need to instruct the human resources department to handle this.

责怪 zéguài [动] accuse ◇他责怪孩子太粗心。He accused the child of being thoughtless.

责令 zélìng [动] order

责任 zérèn [名] responsibility ◇这件事也有你的责任。This is also your responsibility.

责无旁贷 zé wú páng dài be duty-bound

择 zé [动] choose (*pt* chose, *pp* chosen)
▷另见 zhái

择交 zéjiāo [动] choose one's friends (*pt* chose, *pp* chosen)

择偶 zé'ǒu [动] choose a partner (*pt* chose, *pp* chosen)

择优 zéyōu [动] choose the best (*pt* chose, *pp* chosen)

咋 zé 见下文

咋舌 zéshé [动] be speechless ◇他惊讶得直咋舌。He was left speechless with surprise.

泽 zé [名] 1 (聚水地) pool ♦沼泽 swamp 2 (潮湿) damp ♦润泽 moist 3 (光) sheen ♦色泽 colour (英) 或 color (美) and sheen ♦光泽 lustre (英), luster (美) 4 (恩惠) kindness

啧 zé [拟] click

啧啧称赞 zézé chēngzàn shout and cheer

贼 zéi I [名] 1 (小偷) thief (*pl*

thieves) ♦盗贼 robber **2** (叛徒) traitor **II** [形] **1** (邪恶) evil **2** (狡猾) cunning **III** [副] (方) especially ◇天贼冷。It's especially cold.

贼头贼脑 zéi tóu zéi nǎo behave furtively ◇瞧他贼头贼脑的样子就不像好人。Look at him going around so furtively – surely he's up to no good.

怎 zěn [代] (方) ◇你怎能相信他的话？ How can you believe him? ◇他怎这么小心眼？ Why is he being so petty?

怎么 zěnme **I** [代] ◇你看这事我该怎么办？ What do you think I should do about this? ◇你昨天怎么没来上课？ Why weren't you in class yesterday? ◇这到底是怎么一回事？ What on earth has happened here? **II** [副] **1** (泛指方式) ◇他愿意怎么办就让他怎么办。Let him do it however he wants. ◇我是怎么想就怎么说。I say whatever I think. ◇他最近怎样？ How has he been doing? **2** (表示程度) ◇他今天不怎么高兴。He's not that happy today. ◇这本书不怎么好看。This book isn't that interesting.

怎样 zěnyàng [副] how ◇这种情况怎样处理？ How is this to be dealt with? ◇你怎样批评都可以。Whatever criticisms you have are fine.

曾 zēng [形] ◇曾祖父母 great-grandparents
▷另见 céng

曾孙 zēngsūn [名] great-grandson

曾祖 zēngzǔ [名] great-grandfather

增 zēng [动] increase

增加 zēngjiā [动] increase ◇增加人民收入 increase people's income

增色 zēngsè [动] add to

增长 zēngzhǎng [动] increase ◇控制人口增长 control the increase in population

增值 zēngzhí [名] (经济) increase

增值税 zēngzhíshuì [名] VAT

增殖 zēngzhí **I** [名] proliferation **II** [动] multiply

憎 zēng [动] hate

憎恨 zēnghèn [动] detest

憎恶 zēngwù [动] loathe

锃 zèng [形] (方) shiny

锃亮 zèngliàng [形] shiny

赠 zèng [动] present ♦馈赠 present ♦捐赠 donate

赠品 zèngpǐn [名] gift

赠送 zèngsòng [动] present

赠言 zèngyán [名] advice

扎 zhā [动] **1** (刺) prick **2** (住下) set up camp (*pt, pp* set) ◇部队驻扎在村子里。The troops set up camp in the village. **3** (钻进) plunge into ◇他一下扎进水中。He plunged into the water.
▷另见 zā

扎根 zhāgēn [动] take root (*pt* took, *pp* taken)

扎实 zhāshi [形] **1** (结实) sturdy **2** (实在) solid ◇他英语基础比较扎实。He has a solid foundation in English.

扎眼 zhāyǎn [形] **1** (刺眼) dazzling **2** (惹人注意) loud

咋 zhā 见下文
▷另见 zǎ

咋呼 zhāhu [动] (方) **1** (吆喝) cry out **2** (炫耀) show off (*pt* showed, *pp* shown)

喳 zhā [拟] chatter
▷另见 chā

渣 zhā [名] **1** (渣滓) residue ♦残渣 dregs (*pl*) **2** (碎屑) crumbs (*pl*)

渣滓 zhāzǐ [名] dregs (*pl*) ◇那些人是社会的渣滓。Those people are the dregs of society.

札 zhá [名] **1** (木片) wooden writing tablets (*pl*) **2** (信件) letter

札记 zhájì [名] notes (*pl*)

轧 zhá [动] roll
▷另见 yà

轧制 zházhì [动] roll

闸 zhá **I** [名] **1** (水闸) sluice **2** (制动器) brake **3** (电闸) switch **II** [动] dam

闸门 zhámén [名] sluice

炸 zhá [动] fry
▷另见 zhà

铡 zhá I [名] cutter II [动] cut (*pt*, *pp* cut)

铡刀 zhádāo [名] cutter

眨 zhǎ [动] wink

眨眼 zhǎyǎn [动] blink ◇他一眨眼工夫就不见了。He disappeared in the blink of an eye.

乍 zhà I [副] **1** (起初) first ◇乍一看, 这东西不错。On first inspection this isn't bad. **2** (忽然) suddenly II [动] spread (*pt*, *pp* spread) ♦乍翅 spread one's wings

诈 zhà [动] **1** (骗) swindle **2** (装) pretend ♦诈降 pretend to surrender **3** (诱) draw ... out (*pt* drew, *pp* drawn) ◇其实他是在诈你。Actually he's trying to draw you out.

诈唬 zhàhu [动] trick

诈骗 zhàpiàn [动] swindle

栅 zhà [名] railing

栅栏 zhàlan [名] bar

炸 zhà [动] **1** (爆破) blow ... up (*pt* blew, *pp* blown) **2** (破裂) explode ◇暖水瓶炸了。The flask exploded. **3** (逃离) run scared (*pt* ran, *pp* run) ▷另见 zhá

炸弹 zhàdàn [名] bomb

炸药 zhàyào [名] explosive

榨 zhà [动] extract

榨取 zhàqǔ [动] squeeze

斋 zhāi [名] **1** (斋戒) fast **2** (素食) vegetarian diet **3** (屋子) room ♦书斋 study

斋戒 zhāijiè [动] fast

摘 zhāi [动] **1** (取) pick **2** (选) select ♦摘编 take extracts from **3** (借) borrow

摘录 zhāilù [动] take extracts (*pt* took, *pp* taken) ◇摘录新闻 take extracts from the news

摘取 zhāiqǔ [动] select

摘要 zhāiyào I [动] summarize II [名] abstract

宅 zhái [名] house ♦住宅 house

宅子 zháizi [名] house

择 zhái [动] select ▷另见 zé

窄 zhǎi [形] **1** (不宽敞) narrow **2** (气量小) narrow-minded **3** (不宽裕) hard up

窄小 zhǎixiǎo [形] narrow

债 zhài [名] debt

债权 zhàiquán [名] (法) creditor's rights (*pl*)

债券 zhàiquàn [名] bond

债务 zhàiwù [名] debt

寨 zhài [名] **1** (村寨) stockade **2** (山寨) mountain stronghold **3** (营寨) camp

占 zhān [动] divine ▷另见 zhàn

占卜 zhānbǔ [动] divine

占卦 zhānguà [动] divine

沾 zhān [动] **1** (浸) moisten **2** (被附上) stick (*pt*, *pp* stuck) ◇她身上沾的都是泥。She was covered with mud. **3** (碰) touch ◇他滴酒不沾。He doesn't touch alcohol. **4** (得) benefit from ◇他总想沾点便宜。He always wants to take advantage.

沾光 zhānguāng [动] benefit from association ◇他的提干显然是沾了他老领导的光。His promotion obviously came from his connection with his old boss.

沾染 zhānrǎn [动] be contaminated by ◇你要防止伤口沾染细菌。You must prevent the wound from becoming contaminated with germs.

沾沾自喜 zhānzhān zì xǐ pat oneself on the back

毡 zhān [名] felt

粘 zhān [动] stick (*pt*, *pp* stuck)

粘贴 zhāntiē [动] stick (*pt*, *pp* stuck)

瞻 zhān [动] look up

瞻前顾后 zhān qián gù hòu be indecisive ◇他做事总是瞻前顾后。Whatever he does he's always indecisive about it.

瞻仰 zhānyǎng [动] revere ◇瞻仰遗容 pay one's respects

斩 zhǎn [动] chop

斩草除根 zhǎn cǎo chú gēn destroy root and branch

斩钉截铁 zhǎn dīng jié tiě categorical ◇他斩钉截铁地回答对方的问题。He answered the other side's questions categorically.

盏 zhǎn I [名] small cup II [量] ◇一盏灯 an electric lamp

展 zhǎn I [动] **1** (进行) develop **2** (施展) give free rein to (*pt* gave, *pp* given) **3** (暂缓) postpone II [名] exhibition

展播 zhǎnbō [名] show

展开 zhǎnkāi [动] **1** (张开) spread (*pt*, *pp* spread) **2** (进行) develop

展览 zhǎnlǎn [名] exhibition

展品 zhǎnpǐn [名] exhibit

展示 zhǎnshì [动] reveal ◇展示个性 reveal one's personality

展望 zhǎnwàng [动] look into the distance

展现 zhǎnxiàn [动] emerge

展销 zhǎnxiāo [动] display ... for sale

崭 zhǎn 见下文

崭露头角 zhǎn lù tóujiǎo begin to make a name for oneself

崭新 zhǎnxīn [形] brand-new

辗 zhǎn [动] toss and turn

辗转 zhǎnzhuǎn [动] **1** (翻来覆去) toss and turn **2** (传来传去) pass through many different hands

占 zhàn [动] **1** (占用) occupy ◇非常抱歉，占了您很多时间。I apologize for taking up so much of your time. **2** (处于) ◇占上风 get the upper hand
▷另见 zhān

占据 zhànjù [动] occupy

占领 zhànlǐng [动] capture

占用 zhànyòng [动] occupy ◇会议室已被占用了。The meeting room is already occupied.

占有 zhànyǒu [动] own

战 zhàn I [名] war ◇枪战 exchange of fire II [动] **1** (战斗) fight (*pt*, *pp* fought) **2** (发抖) shiver

战败 zhànbài [动] **1** (打败) defeat **2** (失败) be defeated

战场 zhànchǎng [名] front

战斗 zhàndòu [动] fight (*pt*, *pp* fought)

战犯 zhànfàn [名] war criminal

战俘 zhànfú [名] prisoner of war

战绩 zhànjì [名] military successes (*pl*)

战乱 zhànluàn [名] ravages of war (*pl*)

战略 zhànlüè [名] strategy ◇战略反攻 plan a counter-attack

战胜 zhànshèng [动] overcome (*pt* overcame, *pp* overcome)

战士 zhànshì [名] soldier

战术 zhànshù [名] tactics (*pl*)

战役 zhànyì [名] battle

战战兢兢 zhànzhànjīngjīng ◇他们非常害怕，战战兢兢地往前走。They were scared out of their wits and walked on trembling with fear.

战争 zhànzhēng [名] war

站 zhàn I [动] **1** (站立) stand (*pt*, *pp* stood) ◇我在火车上站3个多小时了。I stood on the train for more than three hours. ◇我们站在你这边。We'll stand by you. **2** (停下) stop ◇等车站稳了乘客才可以下车。When the bus comes to a stop, the passengers can get off. II [名] **1** (停车地点) stop ◇公共汽车站 bus stop **2** (服务机构) centre (英), center (美) ◇医疗站 treatment centre

站立 zhànlì [动] stand (*pt*, *pp* stood)

站台 zhàntái [名] platform

站住 zhànzhù [动] **1** (站稳) stand firm (*pt*, *pp* stood) **2** (停步) halt **3** (停留) wait **4** (合理) hold up (*pt*, *pp* held) ◇你的解释站不住。Your explanation doesn't hold up.

绽 zhàn [名] split

绽放 zhànfàng [动] bloom

湛 zhàn [形] **1** (深邃) deep **2** (清澈) crystal clear

湛蓝 zhànlán [形] azure

颤 zhàn [动] tremble
▷另见 chàn

颤栗 zhànlì [动] tremble

蘸 zhàn [动] dip … in ◇我喜欢蘸点醋吃饺子。I like to eat dumplings dipped in vinegar.

张 zhāng I [动] 1 (打开) open ◇张大嘴巴 open one's mouth wide 2 (展开) extend ♦扩张 stretch 3 (夸大) exaggerate ♦夸张 exaggerate 4 (看) look ◇东张西望 look around 5 (开业) open for business ◇商店要开张了。The shop is about to open for business. 6 (陈设) lay … on (*pt, pp* laid) ◇他们结婚时不想大张筵席。When they get married, they don't want to lay on a big reception. II [量] ◇一张海报 a poster ◇一张书桌 a desk

张灯结彩 zhāng dēng jié cǎi be decorated with lanterns and streamers

张挂 zhāngguà [动] hang … up (*pt, pp* hung)

张冠李戴 Zhāng guān Lǐ dài confuse one thing with another ◇他不是我们经理，我看你是张冠李戴了。He's not our manager – you're confusing him with someone else.

张皇 zhānghuáng [形] alarmed

张口结舌 zhāng kǒu jié shé be at a loss for words

张罗 zhāngluo [动] 1 (料理) take care of (*pt* took, *pp* taken) 2 (筹划) raise ◇我得去张罗点儿钱。I need to raise some money. 3 (接待) attend to ◇赶快张罗客人吧！ Go and attend to the guests!

张望 zhāngwàng [动] look around

张牙舞爪 zhāng yá wǔ zhǎo make threatening gestures

张扬 zhāngyáng [动] spread … about (*pt, pp* spread) ◇这事不要到处张扬。You mustn't go spreading this about everywhere.

章 zhāng [名] 1 (作品) article ♦文章 article 2 (章节) chapter 3 (条理) order 4 (章程) regulation ♦宪章 charter 5 (图章) seal 6 (标志) badge (英), button (美)

章程 zhāngchéng [名] regulation

章法 zhāngfǎ [名] 1 (规则) regulation 2 (条理) orderliness ◇这篇文章很有章法。This essay is very well-organized.

彰 zhāng I [形] obvious ♦昭彰 evident II [动] praise ♦表彰 praise

樟 zhāng [名] camphor tree

樟脑 zhāngnǎo [名] camphor

蟑 zhāng 见下文

蟑螂 zhāngláng [名] cockroach

长 zhǎng I [形] 1 (大) older ◇他年长我3岁。He's three years older than me. 2 (排行第一) oldest ◇长兄 oldest brother II [名] 1 (年长者) ♦兄长 elder brother ♦师长 teacher 2 (头领) head ♦校长 head teacher ◇理事长 chairman of the board III [动] 1 (生) form ◇他身上长了疥疮。A sore formed on his body. 2 (发育) grow (*pt* grew, *pp* grown) ◇他长得像他爸爸。He looks like his father. 3 (增加) acquire ◇长知识 acquire knowledge
▷另见 cháng

长辈 zhǎngbèi [名] elder

长进 zhǎngjìn [名] progress

长势 zhǎngshì [名] crop growth

长相 zhǎngxiàng [名] features (*pl*)

涨 zhǎng [动] increase
▷另见 zhàng

涨幅 zhǎngfú [名] increase ◇物价涨幅平稳。Prices are increasing, but at a steady rate.

掌 zhǎng I [名] 1 (手掌) palm 2 (人的脚掌) sole 3 (动物的脚掌) foot (*pl* feet) ◇鸭掌 duck's foot ◇熊掌 bear's paw 4 (掌形物) ◇仙人掌 cactus 5 (U型铁) horseshoe 6 (鞋掌) sole II [动] 1 (打) slap ◇我掌了他一下。I gave him a slap. 2 (钉) sole ◇掌鞋 sole shoes 3 (主持) be in charge of ◇掌管家事 be in charge of household affairs

掌舵 zhǎngduò [动] be at the helm ◇有他掌舵我们放心。As long as he's at the helm, we feel at ease.

掌管 zhǎngguǎn [动] administer

掌柜 zhǎngguì [名] manager

掌上明珠 zhǎng shàng míngzhū be the apple of sb's eye ◇她可是父亲的掌上明珠啊！ She is the apple of her father's eye!

掌握 zhǎngwò [动] control ◇掌握一门新技术 master a new skill

丈 zhàng [名] 1 (敬) old man (*pl* men) ♦岳丈 father-in-law 2 (丈夫) husband ♦妹丈 brother-in-law

丈夫 zhàngfu [名] husband

丈量 zhàngliáng [动] measure

丈人 zhàngrén [名] father-in-law

仗 zhàng I [名] 1 (战斗) battle ♦打仗 fight 2 (兵器) weapons (*pl*) II [动] 1 (拿着) be armed ◇仗刀 armed with a knife 2 (依靠) rely on

仗恃 zhàngshì [动] rely on

仗义 zhàngyì [形] righteous

仗义执言 zhàng yì zhí yán speak out from a sense of justice

杖 zhàng [名] 1 (拐杖) walking stick 2 (棒子) ♦擀面杖 rolling pin

帐 zhàng [名] curtain ♦蚊帐 mosquito net ♦营帐 tent

帐篷 zhàngpeng [名] tent

账 zhàng [名] 1 (账目) accounts (*pl*) 2 (账簿) ledger 3 (债务) credit ♦赊账 buy on credit

账单 zhàngdān [名] bill

账号 zhànghào [名] account number

账面 zhàngmiàn [名] statement

胀 zhàng [动] 1 (膨胀) expand 2 (肿胀) swell (*pt* swelled, *pp* swollen)

涨 zhàng [动] 1 (涨大) expand 2 (充血) flush
▷另见 zhǎng

障 zhàng I [名] barrier ◇屏障 screen ◇路障 blockade II [动] hinder

障碍 zhàng'ài I [动] hinder II [名] obstacle

招 zhāo I [动] 1 (挥动) beckon ◇他招手让我进里面去。He beckoned me inside. 2 (招收) recruit 3 (引来) attract 4 (惹怒) provoke 5 (坦白) confess II [名] 1 (计谋) trick 2 (指下棋) move

招标 zhāobiāo [动] invite tenders

招待 zhāodài [动] entertain ◇招待宾客 entertain guests ◇招待会 reception

招供 zhāogòng [动] confess ◇他在法庭上全都招供了。He confessed everything in court.

招呼 zhāohu [动] 1 (呼唤) call 2 (问候) greet 3 (吩咐) tell (*pt, pp* told) ◇请招呼他进来坐一会儿。Please tell him to come in and sit down for a while.

招集 zhāojí [动] assemble

招架 zhāojià [动] hold one's own (*pt, pp* held)

招揽 zhāolǎn [动] solicit

招领 zhāolǐng [动] post a 'Found' notice

招牌 zhāopai [名] sign

招聘 zhāopìn [动] advertise for ◇这家饭店要招聘服务员。The hotel wants to advertise for waiters.

招惹 zhāorě [动] cause ◇他总招惹是非。He always causes trouble.

招商 zhāoshāng [动] attract business

招式 zhāoshì [名] body language

招收 zhāoshōu [动] enrol

招数 zhāoshù [名] strategic move

招贴 zhāotiē [名] poster

招摇 zhāoyáo [动] show off (*pt* showed, *pp* shown)

招展 zhāozhǎn [动] flutter

招致 zhāozhì [动] 1 (招收) recruit 2 (引起) lead to (*pt, pp* led)

昭 zhāo I [形] clear ♦昭然 obvious II [动] show (*pt* showed, *pp* shown)

昭然若揭 zhāorán ruò jiē clear as day

昭雪 zhāoxuě [动] exonerate

着 zhāo [名] 1 (步) move ◇他这着棋可走错了。This move of his has really gone wrong. 2 (法) tactic ◇这下他没着了。He has no tactics beyond this.
▷另见 zháo, zhuó

着数 zhāoshù [名] move

朝 zhāo [名] **1** (晨) morning **2** (天) day ▷另见 cháo

朝晖 zhāohuī [名] morning sunlight

朝令夕改 zhāo lìng xī gǎi keep chopping and changing

朝气 zhāoqì [名] youthful spirit

朝三暮四 zhāo sān mù sì blow hot and cold ◇交朋友不能朝三暮四。You shouldn't blow hot and cold with your friends.

朝夕 zhāoxī [名] **1** (每天) every day **2** (时间) a very short time

着 zháo [动] **1** (挨) touch ◇他说话总是不着边际。When he's talking he never sticks to the point. **2** (受到) be affected by ◇小心着凉。Be careful not to get cold. **3** (燃烧) be lit ◇木炭着了。The charcoal is lit. **4** (入睡) fall asleep (*pt* fell, *pp* fallen) ◇昨晚我一躺下就着了。Yesterday evening I fell asleep as soon as I lay down. ▷另见 zhāo, zhuó

着急 zháojí [形] worried ◇别着急，休息几天就好了。Don't worry, you'll be fine after a few days' rest.

着迷 zháomí [动] be fanatical ◇他对足球着迷。He's fanatical about football.

爪 zhǎo [名] claw ▷另见 zhuǎ

爪牙 zhǎoyá [名] flunkey

找 zhǎo [动] **1** (寻找) look for ◇他去电影院找女儿了。He went to the cinema to look for his daughter. **2** (退余额) give change (*pt* gave, *pp* given) ♦找钱 give change **3** (求见) call on ◇有事找他就行。If you encounter any problem it's fine to ask him.

找茬儿 zhǎochár [动] pick holes

找到 zhǎodào [动] find (*pt, pp* found)

找事 zhǎoshì [动] **1** (找工) look for a job **2** (滋事) make trouble

沼 zhǎo [名] pool

沼气 zhǎoqì [名] methane

沼泽 zhǎozé [名] marsh

召 zhào [动] summon

召唤 zhàohuàn [动] call

召集 zhàojí [动] convene

召见 zhàojiàn [动] summon

召开 zhàokāi [动] hold (*pt, pp* held)

兆 zhào **I** [名] (预兆) sign ◇病兆 the sign of an illness **II** [量] million ♦兆瓦 megawatt **III** [动] foretell (*pt, pp* foretold)

兆头 zhàotou [名] omen

照 zhào **I** [动] **1** (照射) light up (*pt, pp* lit) ◇阳光照得满屋亮堂堂的。The sunlight lit up the whole room. **2** (映现) reflect ◇照镜子 look at oneself in the mirror **3** (拍摄) take a photograph (*pt* took, *pp* taken) ◇这张照片照得不错。This photograph is excellent. **4** (照料) look after ◇请帮我关照一下孩子。Please can you help me and look after the children for a while. **5** (对照) contrast ♦比照 contrast **6** (遵照) refer to ♦参照 consult **7** (明白) understand (*pt, pp* understood) ◇心照不宣 have a tacit understanding **II** [名] **1** (照片) photograph **2** (执照) licence (英), license (美) **III** [介] **1** (按照) according to ◇照章办事 act according to the rules **2** (向着) in the direction of ◇照这个方向一直走就到了。Just keep walking in this direction and you'll find it.

照本宣科 zhào běn xuān kē go by the book

照常 zhàocháng [副] as usual ◇节日期间，商店照常营业。On holidays the shop will open for business as usual.

照顾 zhàogù [动] **1** (照料) look after **2** (考虑) consider

照会 zhàohuì **I** [动] deliver a note to **II** [名] note

照例 zhàolì [副] as a rule

照料 zhàoliào [动] take care of (*pt* took, *pp* taken)

照面儿 zhàomiànr **1** [动] put in an appearance (*pt, pp* put) ◇他打了个照面儿就走了。He put in an appearance and then left.

照明 zhàomíng [名] lighting

照片 zhàopiàn [名] photograph

照射 zhàoshè [动] light up (*pt, pp* lit)

照相 zhàoxiàng [动] take a picture (*pt* took, *pp* taken)

照相机 zhàoxiàngjī [名] camera

照样 zhàoyàng [副] **1** (依照样品) in the same style **2** (依然) still ◊没有他，我们照样能做好。Even without him, we'll still be able to do it.

照耀 zhàoyào [动] illuminate

照应 zhàoyìng [动] **1** (呼应) correlate **2** (照料) look after

罩 zhào I [名] **1** (罩子) cover ♦床罩 bedcover ♦口罩 face mask **2** (罩衣) overall ♦外罩 dustcoat II [动] cover

肇 zhào [动] **1** (开始) start **2** (发生) cause

肇事 zhàoshì [动] cause trouble

折 zhē [动] **1** (翻转) roll over ◊他在床上折来折去。In bed he rolled this way and that. **2** (倒) pour … back and forth ◊她拿两个杯子把水折几下就凉了。She poured the water from one cup to another to cool it. ▷另见 shé, zhé

折腾 zhēteng [动] **1** (翻来覆去) toss and turn **2** (反复做) do … over and over again **3** (折磨) cause suffering ◊头痛可真折腾人。Headaches can cause a lot of suffering.

蜇 zhē [动] sting (*pt, pp* stung) ◊他被马蜂蜇了一下。He was stung by a hornet.

遮 zhē [动] **1** (遮挡) hide … from view (*pt* hid, *pp* hidden) ◊乌云遮住了阳光。The sun was hidden by dark clouds. **2** (阻拦) obstruct ◊遮雨 keep out the rain **3** (遮盖) conceal

遮蔽 zhēbì [动] obstruct

遮挡 zhēdǎng I [动] keep … out (*pt, pp* kept) ◊请找个东西遮挡一下阳光。Please find something to protect us from the sun. II [名] cover

遮掩 zhēyǎn [动] **1** (遮蔽) obscure ◊屋子被门帘遮掩着。The room is obscured by a door curtain. **2** (掩饰) hide (*pt* hid, *pp* hidden)

折 zhé I [动] **1** (折断) break (*pt* broke, *pp* broken) **2** (损失) lose (*pt, pp* lost) **3** (弯曲) wind (*pt, pp* wound) **4** (回转) turn back **5** (使信服) convince ◊精湛的演出折服了观众。The audience were bowled over by the brilliant performance. **6** (折合) convert … into **7** (折叠) fold II [名] **1** (折子) notebook ♦存折 bank book **2** (折扣) discount ◊所有服装在打折销售。All clothes are reduced. ▷另见 shé, zhē

折叠 zhédié [动] fold

折服 zhéfú [动] **1** (说服) subdue **2** (佩服) be bowled over by

折合 zhéhé [动] convert … into ◊我把人民币都折合成了英镑。I've converted all my renminbi to pounds sterling.

折旧 zhéjiù [动] depreciate

折扣 zhékòu [名] discount ◊打折扣销售 sell at a discount

折磨 zhémó [动] torment ◊她身体虚弱，经常遭受疾病的折磨。She's in poor health and often tormented by illness.

折射 zhéshè [名] refraction

折算 zhésuàn [动] convert

折中 zhézhōng [动] compromise ◊折中方案 a compromise plan

哲 zhé I [形] wise II [名] sage

哲理 zhélǐ [名] philosophical theory

哲学 zhéxué [名] philosophy

辙 zhé [名] **1** (车痕) wheel track **2** (韵律) rhyme **3** (办法) way ◊这事我也没辙了。There's no way out of this.

者 zhě [名] **1** (人) ♦长者 elder ♦记者 journalist ♦作者 author ♦编者 editor ◊教育工作者 educationalist (英), educator (美) **2** (物) ♦前者 the former ♦后者 the latter

褶 zhě [名] crease

褶皱 zhězhòu [名] wrinkle

这 zhè [代] **1** (指人或事物) this (*pl* these) ◊这本书写得不错。This book is well-written. **2** (指时间) ◊他这才突然明白过来。He's just suddenly understood. ◊我这就过

去。I'm going right now.

这个 zhège I [代] this ◇这个可比那个好多了。This one is much better than that one. ◇为这个他耽误了好几天工作。He put off work for several days on account of this. II [副] ◇瞧他这个忙啊! Look how busy he is!

这里 zhèlǐ [代] ◇这里发生了一起交通事故。A traffic accident happened here.

这么 zhème [代] 1 (指程度) ◇今天这么热。It's so hot today. 2 (指方式) ◇我看就应该这么做。I think it should be done this way.

这些 zhèxiē [代] these (*pl*) ◇这些事情够他忙的。These things are enough to keep him busy.

这样 zhèyàng [代] 1 (指程度) ◇乡村的风景这样美。The scenery in the countryside is so beautiful. 2 (指状态) ◇再这样下去可不行。It really won't do to carry on like this. ◇他就这样死心眼。He is just so stubborn.

这种 zhèzhǒng [代] ◇这种菜好吃。This kind of vegetable is tasty.

蔗 zhè [名] sugarcane

蔗糖 zhètáng [名] sucrose

贞 zhēn I [形] 1 (坚定) loyal ♦坚贞 loyal 2 (贞洁) chaste II [名] chastity

贞操 zhēncāo [名] 1 (贞节) chastity 2 (忠贞) loyalty

贞节 zhēnjié [名] chastity

贞洁 zhēnjié [形] chaste

针 zhēn [名] 1 (工具) needle 2 (针状物) ♦表针 hand ♦别针 safety pin 3 (针剂) injection 4 (缝合) stitch

针对 zhēnduì [动] 1 (对准) be aimed at ◇他的话不是针对你。What he said was not aimed at you. 2 (按照) have … in mind ◇针对当前形势，我想谈谈自己的看法。With the current situation in mind, I would like to give my own views. ◇针对不同年龄用药。Vary the dose according to age.

针锋相对 zhēn fēng xiāng duì tit for tat

针灸 zhēnjiǔ [名] acupuncture

侦 zhēn [动] investigate

侦查 zhēnchá [动] investigate

侦察 zhēnchá [动] reconnoitre (英), reconnoiter (美)

侦缉 zhēnjī [动] track down and arrest

侦破 zhēnpò [动] crack

侦探 zhēntàn I [动] spy on II [名] detective ◇侦探小说 detective novel

珍 zhēn I [名] treasure ♦珍宝 jewellery (英), jewelry (美) II [动] value ♦珍惜 value III [形] valuable

珍爱 zhēn'ài [动] cherish

珍宝 zhēnbǎo [名] treasure

珍藏 zhēncáng [动] collect

珍贵 zhēnguì [形] precious

珍视 zhēnshì [动] value

珍惜 zhēnxī [动] value

珍稀 zhēnxī [形] rare

珍重 zhēnzhòng [动] value … highly

珍珠 zhēnzhū [名] pearl

真 zhēn I [形] true ♦真话 truth ◇真品 genuine product II [副] really ◇他真勇敢。He is really brave. ◇昨晚的电影真不错。Last night's film was really good.

真才实学 zhēn cái shí xué real knowledge and true ability

真诚 zhēnchéng [形] sincere

真谛 zhēndì [名] true meaning

真迹 zhēnjì [名] authentic work

真空 zhēnkōng [名] vacuum

真理 zhēnlǐ [名] truth

真切 zhēnqiè [形] vivid

真实 zhēnshí [形] true

真是 zhēnshi [副] really ◇我真是搞不懂，他到底想干什么。I really can't make out what on earth he's up to. ◇真是，她把雨伞忘在火车上了。She's gone and left her umbrella on the train.

真相 zhēnxiàng [名] true situation

真正 zhēnzhèng [形] true ◇他是我真正的朋友。He's a true friend of

mine. ◇我们要真正对工作负责。We have to be truly responsible for the work.

真挚 zhēnzhì [形] genuine

真主 Zhēnzhǔ [名] Allah

斟 zhēn [动] pour

斟酌 zhēnzhuó [动] consider

箴 zhēn [动] advise

箴言 zhēnyán [名] advice

臻 zhēn [动] become (*pt* became, *pp* become)

诊 zhěn [动] examine ♦就诊 see a doctor

诊断 zhěnduàn [动] diagnose ◇医生把他的这种症状诊断为胃溃疡。The doctor diagnosed his symptoms as a gastric ulcer.

诊所 zhěnsuǒ [名] clinic

枕 zhěn **I** [名] pillow **II** [动] rest one's head on ◇他枕着衣服睡着了。He fell asleep with his head resting on his clothes.

枕头 zhěntou [名] pillow

疹 zhěn [名] rash ♦湿疹 eczema ♦麻疹 measles (*sg*)

缜 zhěn 见下文

缜密 zhěnmì [形] meticulous

阵 zhèn **I** [名] **1** (军) (阵形) battle formation **2** (军) (阵地) position **3** (时间) a while **II** [量] ◇一阵暴雨 a burst of rain ◇一阵掌声 a burst of applause

阵地 zhèndì [名] position

阵脚 zhènjiǎo [名] position

阵容 zhènróng [名] battle formation

阵势 zhènshì [名] battle formation

阵亡 zhènwáng [动] be killed in action

阵线 zhènxiàn [名] frontline

阵营 zhènyíng [名] camp

振 zhèn [动] **1** (振动) vibrate **2** (振作) boost ◇最近我食欲不振。Recently my appetite has been poor.

振动 zhèndòng [动] vibrate

振奋 zhènfèn [动] rouse

振聋发聩 zhèn lóng fā kuì enlighten ◇这篇报道起了振聋发聩的作用。This report had an enlightening effect.

振兴 zhènxīng [动] revitalize

振振有辞 zhènzhèn yǒu cí speak convincingly

振作 zhènzuò [动] pull oneself together ◇受挫之后他又振作起来。After this setback he pulled himself together again.

赈 zhèn [动] relieve

赈济 zhènjì [动] relieve

震 zhèn **I** [动] **1** (震动) shake (*pt* shook, *pp* shaken) **2** (激动) be excited **II** [名] earthquake ◇余震 after-shock

震荡 zhèndàng [动] shake (*pt* shook, *pp* shaken)

震动 zhèndòng [动] shake (*pt* shook, *pp* shaken)

震耳欲聋 zhèn ěr yù lóng deafening

震撼 zhènhàn [动] shake (*pt* shook, *pp* shaken)

震惊 zhènjīng [动] amaze ◇得知这个消息，人们震惊了。People were amazed to hear this news.

震慑 zhènshè [动] frighten

镇 zhèn **I** [名] **1** (城镇) town **2** (重地) garrison **II** [动] **1** (抑制) suppress **2** (守卫) guard ♦镇守 guard **3** (安定) calm ♦镇抚 calm **4** (冷却) cool **III** [形] calm ♦镇静 calm

镇定 zhèndìng [形] calm

镇静 zhènjìng [形] calm

镇静剂 zhènjìngjì [形] sedative

镇压 zhènyā [动] suppress

正 zhēng 见下文
▷另见 zhèng

正月 zhēngyuè [名] *first month of the lunar year*

争 zhēng [动] **1** (争夺) contend **2** (争论) argue

争辩 zhēngbiàn [动] argue ◇她老为孩子的教育问题与丈夫争辩。

She's constantly arguing with her husband about the children's education.

争吵 zhēngchǎo [动] quarrel ◇这对夫妻经常为小事争吵。The couple often quarrel about trivial things.

争斗 zhèngdòu [动] fight (*pt, pp* fought)

争端 zhēngduān [名] dispute

争夺 zhēngduó [动] fight for (*pt, pp* fought)

争光 zhēngguāng [动] win honour (英) 或 honor (美) for (*pt, pp* won)

争论 zhēnglùn [动] argue ◇不管什么问题，他总爱与人争论。He'll argue over anything.

争鸣 zhēngmíng [动] contend

争气 zhēngqì [动] be a credit to

争取 zhēngqǔ [动] strive for (*pt* strove, *pp* striven) ◇争取机会 grasp the opportunity ◇争取主动 grasp the initiative

争先 zhēngxiān [动] try to be the first ◇昨天的讨论会上，个个都争先发言。At yesterday's conference everyone was vying to speak.

争议 zhēngyì [名] dispute ◇对这个方案大家有许多争议。Everyone is in hot dispute over this scheme.

争执 zhēngzhí [动] quarrel ◇他们两人为此事争执很久了。The two of them have been quarrelling for a long time over this.

征 zhēng **I** [动] **1** (征讨) mount a military expedition ♦征战 go on a military campaign **2** (召集) draft ♦征兵 conscript ◇应征入伍 enlist **3** (征收) levy ♦征税 levy taxes **4** (征求) solicit ♦征订 solicit subscriptions **II** [名] **1** (征程) journey ♦长征 the Long March **2** (迹象) sign ♦特征 feature

征调 zhēngdiào [动] draft

征服 zhēngfú [动] conquer

征购 zhēnggòu [动] procure

征集 zhēngjí [动] **1** (收集) collect **2** (征募) recruit

征求 zhēngqiú [动] solicit

征收 zhēngshōu [动] levy

征途 zhēngtú [名] journey

征用 zhēngyòng [动] requisition

征兆 zhēngzhào [名] sign

怔 zhēng [形] terror-stricken

挣 zhēng 见下文
▷另见 zhèng

挣扎 zhēngzhá [动] struggle

峥 zhēng 见下文

峥嵘 zhēngróng [形] **1** (高峻) soaring **2** (非凡) remarkable

狰 zhēng 见下文

狰狞 zhēngníng [形] sinister

症 zhēng 见下文
▷另见 zhèng

症结 zhēngjié [名] crux

睁 zhēng [动] open

睁眼瞎 zhēngyǎnxiā [名] illiterate

蒸 zhēng [动] **1** (指烹饪方法) steam **2** (蒸发) evaporate

蒸馏 zhēngliú [动] distil (英), distill (美)

蒸气 zhēngqì [名] vapour (英), vapor (美)

蒸汽 zhēngqì [名] steam

蒸蒸日上 zhēngzhēng rì shàng developing fast

整 zhěng **I** [形] **1** (完整) whole **2** (规整) tidy **II** [动] **1** (整理) sort … out **2** (修理) repair **3** (刁难) punish

整顿 zhěngdùn [动] reorganize ◇整顿工作作风 reorganize working methods ◇整顿纪律 consolidate discipline

整个 zhěnggè [形] whole ◇整个假期我全给浪费了。I wasted the whole holiday.

整合 zhěnghé [动] integrate

整洁 zhěngjié [形] tidy

整理 zhěnglǐ [动] sort … out

整齐 zhěngqí [形] **1** (有序的) orderly **2** (均匀的) even ◇整齐的步伐 march in step

整容 zhěngróng [动] have a make-over

整数 zhěngshù [名] whole number

整体 zhěngtǐ [名] whole

整形 zhěngxíng [动] carry out plastic surgery ◇面部整形手术 facial plastic surgery

整治 zhěngzhì [动] restore

整装 zhěngzhuāng [动] pack

正 zhèng I [形] 1 (不偏不斜) straight ◇这幅照片挂得不正。This photograph is not hung straight. ◇请坐端正。Please sit up straight. ◇他把靶子放在了正前方。He put the target directly ahead of him. 2 (居中的) main ◇正殿 main hall 3 (正面) right ◇纸张的正面 the right side of the paper 4 (正直) upright ♦公正 just 5 (正当) right ◇走上正轨 get on the right track 6 (纯正) pure ◇这道菜的味儿有点不正。This dish does not taste authentic. 7 (规范的) regular ◇这小伙子五官端正。This young man has regular features. 8 (主要的) principal ♦正餐 main meal 9 (指图形) regular ◇正八角形 regular octagon 10 (物) positive ◇正离子 positive ion 11 (数) (大于零的) positive ♦正数 positive number II [动] 1 (使不歪) straighten ◇他把帽子正了一正，出门了。He straightened his hat, and went out. 2 (改正) put ... right (*pt, pp* put) III [副] 1 (恰好) just ◇这双鞋大小正合适。This pair of shoes is just the right size. 2 (正在) right now ◇天正刮着风。It's windy right now. ◇他们正在酒店就餐。They're in the hotel eating right now. ▷另见 zhēng

正版 zhèngbǎn [形] original

正本 zhèngběn [名] original

正常 zhèngcháng [形] normal

正当 zhèngdāng [形] legitimate

正道 zhèngdào [名] the right way

正点 zhèngdiǎn [名] ◇火车将正点到达。The train will arrive on schedule.

正法 zhèngfǎ [动] execute

正规 zhèngguī [形] standard

正轨 zhèngguǐ [名] right track

正襟危坐 zhèng jīn wēi zuò sit upright and attentively

正经 zhèngjing I [形] 1 (正派) decent 2 (正当的) serious 3 (标准的) standard II [副] really ◇这件家具正经不错。This furniture is really not bad.

正面 zhèngmiàn I [名] 1 (指方位) front ◇正面进攻 frontal attack ◇正面交锋 head-on clash 2 (主要的一面) the right II [形] positive III [副] directly

正派 zhèngpài [形] honest

正品 zhèngpǐn [名] quality products (*pl*)

正确 zhèngquè [形] correct

正式 zhèngshì [形] official ◇正式报告 official report ◇他已被这所学校正式录取。He's been officially enrolled at this school.

正视 zhèngshì [动] face

正题 zhèngtí [名] topic

正统 zhèngtǒng I [名] orthodoxy II [形] orthodox

正文 zhèngwén [名] text

正义 zhèngyì I [名] justice II [形] just

正音 zhèngyīn I [动] correct one's pronunciation II [名] standard pronunciation

正在 zhèngzài [副] right now ◇会议正在进行。The meeting is taking place right now.

正直 zhèngzhí [形] upright

正中下怀 zhèng zhòng xià huái just what one wants ◇他父亲让他报考军校，对他来说真是正中下怀。His father let him take the entrance exam for the military academy, which is just what he wanted.

正宗 zhèngzōng I [名] orthodox school II [形] authentic

证 zhèng I [动] prove ♦证明 prove II [名] 1 (证据) evidence ♦物证 material evidence ◇出庭作证 give evidence in court 2 (证件) ♦身份证 identity card ◇驾驶证 driver's licence (英) 或 license (美)

证词 zhèngcí [名] testimony

证件 zhèngjiàn [名] certificate

证据 zhèngjù [名] evidence

证明 zhèngmíng **I** [动] prove ◊事实证明我的分析是对的。The facts prove my analysis is correct. **II** [名] certificate

证券 zhèngquàn [名] bond

证实 zhèngshí [动] confirm ◊这条消息有待于证实。This news remains to be confirmed.

证书 zhèngshū [名] certificate

证物 zhèngwù [名] exhibit

证言 zhèngyán [名] verbal evidence

郑 zhèng 见下文

郑重 zhèngzhòng [形] serious ◊对方郑重表示愿意与我们合作。The other party is expressing a serious desire to work with us.

政 zhèng [名] **1** (政治) politics (*sg*) **2** (事务) affairs (*pl*)

政变 zhèngbiàn [名] coup

政策 zhèngcè [名] policy

政党 zhèngdǎng [名] political party

政法 zhèngfǎ [名] politics and law

政府 zhèngfǔ [名] government

政绩 zhèngjì [名] political achievements (*pl*)

政见 zhèngjiàn [名] political view

政界 zhèngjiè [名] political circles (*pl*)

政局 zhèngjú [名] political situation

政客 zhèngkè [名] politician

政权 zhèngquán [名] political power

政治 zhèngzhì [名] politics (*sg*)

政治家 zhèngzhìjiā [名] statesman, stateswoman

挣 zhèng [动] **1** (赚得) earn ♦挣钱 earn money ◊挣口饭吃 earn a living **2** (摆脱) break free (*pt* broke, *pp* broken) ◊挣开枷锁 break free from one's shackles
▷另见 zhēng

症 zhèng [名] disease
▷另见 zhēng

症候 zhènghòu [名] **1** (症状) symptom **2** (疾病) disease

症状 zhèngzhuàng [名] symptom

之 zhī **I** [代] ◊他考上了重点大学，朋友们为之高兴。When he got into a top university, his friends were very happy for him. **II** [助] **1** (的) ◊爱国之心 patriotic feeling ◊父母之爱 parental love ◊自知之明 self-awareness **2** (用在主谓结构之间) ◊世界之大，无奇不有。There is nothing too strange in this vast world.

之一 zhīyī [代] one of ◊他是他们班最用功的学生之一。He is one of the hardest working students in their class. ◊沈阳是中国最大的城市之一。Shenyang is one of China's biggest cities.

支 zhī **I** [名] branch ◊支公司 branch of a company **II** [动] **1** (支撑) prop … up ◊这棚子该用东西支一下。This shed needs something to prop it up. ◊把雨伞支开 put up an umbrella **2** (伸出) raise ◊小兔子支起了耳朵。The rabbit pricked up its ears. ◊他的门牙有些往外支。His front teeth stick out a bit. **3** (支持) bear (*pt* bore, *pp* borne) ◊她牙疼得有点支不住了。She could hardly bear her toothache. **4** (调度) send (*pt, pp* sent) ◊她借故支走了他。She found an excuse to send him away. **5** (付出) pay … out (*pt, pp* paid) ◊上个月家里开支很大。Last month household expenses were very high. **6** (领取) get (*pt* got, *pp* got (英), gotten (美)) ◊出差前，我们从财务处支了些钱。Before going on the business trip, we got some money from the finance department. **III** [量] **1** (指乐曲) ◊一支钢琴曲 a piano tune **2** (指细长物) ◊一支钢笔 a pen **3** (指队伍) ◊一支部队 an army unit **4** (指灯) ◊60支光的灯泡 60 watt bulb

支部 zhībù [名] branch

支撑 zhīchēng [动] **1** (抵挡) support **2** (维持) maintain

支持 zhīchí [动] **1** (鼓励) support ◊他们夫妻俩在事业上互相支持。Husband and wife support each other in their work. **2** (支撑) hold out (*pt, pp* held) ◊他走了3个小时，实在支持不住了。After he had walked for three hours, he really couldn't last anymore.

支出 zhīchū **I** [动] spend (*pt, pp*

spent) **II** [名] expenditure

支付 zhīfù [动] pay (*pt, pp* paid)

支解 zhījiě [动] dismember

支离破碎 zhīlí pòsuì break into fragments

支流 zhīliú [名] **1** (指江河) tributary **2** (指事物) minor aspect

支配 zhīpèi [动] **1** (安排) allocate **2** (控制) control

支票 zhīpiào [名] cheque (英), check (美) ◊把支票兑付成现金 cash a cheque

支使 zhīshi [动] **1** (使唤) order ... about ◊她爱支使人。She likes to order people about. **2** (打发走) send ... away (*pt, pp* sent) ◊他让我把孩子们支使走。He asked me to send the children away.

支线 zhīxiàn [名] feeder

支援 zhīyuán [动] help

支柱 zhīzhù [名] pillar

只 zhī **I** [形] single ◊只言片语 a few words ◊形单影只 solitary **II** [量] ◊一只拖鞋 a slipper ◊两只小船 two boats ◊3只小鸟 three birds ▷另见 zhǐ

只身 zhīshēn [副] by oneself ◊他只身去了国外。He went abroad by himself.

只言片语 zhī yán piàn yǔ a few words

汁 zhī [名] juice ♦果汁 fruit juice ♦椰子汁 coconut milk ♦肉汁 beef extract ♦胆汁 bile

芝 zhī 见下文

芝麻 zhīma [名] sesame

枝 zhī [名] branch

枝节 zhījié [名] **1** (次要的事) minor issue **2** (麻烦的事) unexpected difficulty

知 zhī **I** [动] **1** (知道) know (*pt* knew, *pp* known) ◊此事我全然不知。I'm completely in the dark about this. **2** (使知道) inform ◊通知学生下午2点开会。Tell the students the meeting will start at 2 p.m. **II** [名] knowledge

知道 zhīdào [动] know (*pt* knew, *pp* known) ◊这事我可不知道。I really know nothing about this. ◊谁知道他想要干什么。Who knows what he wants to do?

知根知底 zhī gēn zhī dǐ know ... through and through ◊对于他我是知根知底的。I know him through and through.

知己 zhījǐ **I** [形] intimate **II** [名] bosom friend

知交 zhījiāo [名] intimate friend

知觉 zhījué [名] perception

知名 zhīmíng [形] famous

知趣 zhīqù [动] behave tactfully

知识 zhīshi [名] knowledge

知识分子 zhīshi fènzǐ [名] intellectual

知心 zhīxīn [形] intimate

知音 zhīyīn [名] bosom friend

肢 zhī [名] limb

肢解 zhījiě [动] dismember

肢体 zhītǐ [名] limbs (*pl*)

织 zhī [动] knit

脂 zhī [名] **1** (油脂) grease **2** (胭脂) rouge ◊唇脂 lipstick

脂肪 zhīfáng [名] fat

蜘 zhī 见下文

蜘蛛 zhīzhū [名] spider

执 zhí **I** [动] **1** (拿着) hold (*pt, pp* held) **2** (执掌) take charge of (*pt* took, *pp* taken) ♦执教 be a teacher **3** (坚持) stick to (*pt, pp* stuck) **4** (执行) carry out **II** [名] written acknowledgment ♦回执 receipt

执法 zhífǎ [动] enforce the law

执教 zhíjiào [动] teach (*pt, pp* taught)

执迷不悟 zhí mí bù wù stick to one's bad old ways

执拗 zhíniù [形] obstinate

执勤 zhíqín [动] be on duty

执行 zhíxíng [动] carry out

执意 zhíyì [副] ◊他执意要请我们吃

饭。He insisted on treating us to a meal.

执照 zhízhào [名] licence (英), license (美)

执政 zhízhèng [动] be in power

执著 zhízhuó [形] persevering

直 zhí I [形] 1 (不弯曲) straight ◊笔直的道路 dead straight road 2 (竖的) vertical ◊房间直里有5米。The room is 5 metres (英) 或 meters (美) long. 3 (公正) upstanding ◊他为人正直。He's an upstanding person. 4 (直爽) candid ◊她说话很直。She speaks very candidly. II [动] straighten ◊请把身子直起来。Straighten up. III [副] 1 (直接) straight ◊有话请直说吧。If you have something to say, come straight out with it! 2 (不断地) continuously ◊她直说个没完。She talked non-stop. 3 (简直) simply ◊我疼得直想死。I was simply in agony.

直观 zhíguān [形] audio-visual

直角 zhíjiǎo [名] right angle

直接 zhíjiē [形] direct ◊他将直接飞往伦敦。He will fly direct to London.

直截了当 zhíjié-liǎodàng bluntly

直径 zhíjìng [名] diameter

直觉 zhíjué [名] intuition

直升机 zhíshēngjī [名] helicopter

直属 zhíshǔ I [动] be directly under ◊该市直属中央政府管辖。That town is directly under the jurisdiction of central government. II [形] subordinate to

直率 zhíshuài [形] frank

直爽 zhíshuǎng [形] forthright

直系亲属 zhíxì qīnshǔ [名] directly related family members

直辖 zhíxiá [形] directly under

直线 zhíxiàn I [名] straight line II [形] sharp ◊经济直线增长 sharp economic growth

直言 zhíyán [动] speak bluntly (*pt* spoke, *pp* spoken) ◊直言不讳 call a spade a spade

直译 zhíyì [名] literal translation

侄 zhí [名] nephew

侄女 zhínǚ [名] niece

值 zhí I [名] 1 (价值) value 2 (数) value II [动] 1 (值得) be worth ◊这事不值一提。It's not worth mentioning. 2 (碰上) just happen to be ◊我访问伦敦时，正值圣诞节。It just happened to be Christmas when I visited London. 3 (轮到) be on duty ◊值夜班 be on night duty

值班 zhíbān [动] be on duty

值得 zhídé [动] be worth ◊这书值得买。This book is worth buying.

值勤 zhíqín [动] be on duty

值日 zhírì [动] be on duty for the day ◊今天该我值日。Today it's my turn to be on duty.

职 zhí [名] 1 (职位) post 2 (职责) duty

职称 zhíchēng [名] professional title

职工 zhígōng [名] 1 (员工) staff 2 (工人) blue-collar worker

职能 zhínéng [名] function

职权 zhíquán [名] authority

职位 zhíwèi [名] post

职务 zhíwù [名] post

职业 zhíyè [名] occupation ◊职业律师 professional lawyer

职员 zhíyuán [名] member of staff

职责 zhízé [名] responsibility

植 zhí [动] 1 (栽种) plant 2 (树立) establish

植被 zhíbèi [名] vegetation

植物 zhíwù [名] plant ◊草本植物 herbs

殖 zhí [动] breed (*pt, pp* bred) ♦生殖 reproduce

殖民 zhímín [动] colonize ◊殖民政策 colonial policy

殖民地 zhímíndì [名] colony

止 zhǐ I [动] 1 (停止) stop ◊止住伤口流血 staunch a wound ◊终止合同 suspend a contract 2 (截止) end II [副] only ◊他不止一次欺骗我。He's deceived me on more than one occasion.

止境 zhǐjìng [名] limit

只 zhǐ [副] only ◇我只在周末有时间。I only have time at the weekend.
▷另见 zhī

只顾 zhǐgù [动] 1 (专心) be absorbed in ◇他只顾看电视，连饭都没吃。He's so absorbed in watching television he's not even eating. 2 (只顾及) only care for ◇你只顾自己的眼前利益是不对的。It's bad that you only care for your own immediate interests.

只管 zhǐguǎn [副] by all means ◇有什么问题大家只管问。If anyone has a question by all means ask.

只是 zhǐshì I [副] merely ◇他只是在找托词。He's merely looking for a pretext. ◇问题肯定会解决，只是时间而已。The problem will certainly be resolved, it's merely a question of time. II [连] but ◇大家纷纷出钱，只是数额有多有少。One after another everyone offered money, but the amounts were varied.

只要 zhǐyào [连] so long as ◇只要我们有信心，就会战胜困难。As long as we have confidence, we can overcome difficulties.

只有 zhǐyǒu [副] only ◇只有发展经济才能振兴国家。The country can only be revitalized if the economy is developed.

旨 zhǐ I [名] 1 (用意) purpose ♦要旨 main point 2 (意旨) decree ♦圣旨 imperial decree II [形] tasty

旨趣 zhǐqù [名] intent

纸 zhǐ [名] paper

纸币 zhǐbì [名] note (英), bill (美)

纸巾 zhǐjīn [名] paper towel

纸上谈兵 zhǐ shàng tán bīng all talk and no action

纸张 zhǐzhāng [名] paper

纸醉金迷 zhǐ zuì jīn mí live a life of debauchery

指 zhǐ I [名] finger ♦中指 middle finger ♦无名指 ring finger II [动] 1 (对着) point to 2 (点明) point … out 3 (针对) refer to ◇我没指他。I wasn't referring to him. 4 (依靠) rely on

指标 zhǐbiāo [名] target

指出 zhǐchū [动] point … out

指导 zhǐdǎo [动] instruct ◇英语老师在指导学生写作。The English teacher is instructing the students in essay writing.

指点 zhǐdiǎn [动] show … how (*pt* showed, *pp* shown)

指定 zhǐdìng [动] appoint ◇老板指定王小姐当秘书。The boss appointed Miss Wang as his secretary. ◇指定赞助商 official sponsor

指挥 zhǐhuī I [动] command II [名] 1 (指挥官) commander 2 (乐队指挥) conductor

指教 zhǐjiào [动] give advice (*pt* gave, *pp* given)

指控 zhǐkòng [动] charge ◇他被指控犯杀人罪。He was charged with murder.

指令 zhǐlìng I [动] instruct II [名] instruction

指鹿为马 zhǐ lù wéi mǎ distort the facts

指名 zhǐmíng [动] name

指南 zhǐnán [名] guide

指南针 zhǐnánzhēn [名] compass

指派 zhǐpài [动] assign ◇上司指派我做这项工作。The boss assigned me to this work.

指日可待 zhǐ rì kě dài be just round the corner

指桑骂槐 zhǐ sāng mà huái attack by innuendo

指使 zhǐshǐ [动] incite ◇他经常指使年幼无知的孩子做坏事。He often incites the young to mischief.

指示 zhǐshì [动] instruct ◇我们接到了上级的指示。We have received instructions from high up.

指手画脚 zhǐ shǒu huà jiǎo 1 (用手势示意) gesticulate 2 (轻率地批评) pick fault with

指数 zhǐshù [名] index

指望 zhǐwang I [动] count on ◇我们指望孩子将来有出息。We count on our children being successful in the future. II [名] hope

指纹 zhǐwén [名] fingerprint

指引 zhǐyǐn [动] point the way

指责 zhǐzé [动] criticize

指正 zhǐzhèng [动] **1** (纠正错误) correct mistakes **2** (客套) make comments

咫 zhǐ 见下文

咫尺 zhǐchǐ [名] (书) (喻) the immediate vicinity

咫尺天涯 zhǐchǐ tiānyá so near and yet so far

趾 zhǐ [名] **1** (脚指头) toe **2** (脚) foot (*pl* feet)

趾高气扬 zhǐ gāo qì yáng high and mighty

至 zhì **I** [动] arrive ◊我于明日至沪。I'll arrive in Shanghai tomorrow. **II** [介] to ◊从古至今 from ancient times to the present ◊从东至西 from east to west **III** [副] **1** (至于) ◊至于他什么时候回来，我不知道。As to what time he's due back, I'm just not sure. ♦甚至 even **2** (最) extremely ♦至少 at least ◊兴奋之至 extreme excitement

至高无上 zhì gāo wú shàng paramount

至交 zhìjiāo [名] best friend

至理名言 zhìlǐ-míngyán [名] maxim

至亲 zhìqīn [名] close relative

至上 zhìshàng [形] highest

至少 zhìshǎo [副] at least

至于 zhìyú [介] as to ◊我已经尽了力，至于行不行，就全凭运气了。I've done what I can, so as to whether or not it will work, all I can rely on is luck.

志 zhì **I** [名] **1** (志向) will **2** (记录) record **3** (记号) sign **II** [动] remember

志大才疏 zhì dà cái shū have ideas above one's station

志气 zhìqì [名] will

志趣 zhìqù [名] aspiration

志士 zhìshì [名] strong-willed person

志同道合 zhì tóng dào hé share one's ambitions and outlook on life ◊我喜欢结交志同道合的朋友。I'd like to make friends with someone who shares my ambitions and outlook on life.

志向 zhìxiàng [名] ambition

志愿 zhìyuàn **I** [名] aspiration **II** [动] volunteer

帜 zhì [名] flag

制 zhì **I** [动] **1** (制造) make (*pt, pp* made) **2** (拟订) work … out **3** (约束) restrict **II** [名] system

制裁 zhìcái [动] impose sanctions ◊法律制裁 legal sanctions (*pl*)

制订 zhìdìng [动] work … out

制定 zhìdìng [动] draw … up (*pt* drew, *pp* drawn)

制度 zhìdù [名] system

制服 zhìfú **I** [名] uniform **II** [动] subdue

制剂 zhìjì [名] preparation

制品 zhìpǐn [名] product

制胜 zhìshèng [动] win (*pt, pp* won)

制约 zhìyuē [动] restrict

制造 zhìzào [动] **1** (物品) manufacture **2** (气氛、局势) create

制止 zhìzhǐ [动] prevent

制作 zhìzuò [动] make (*pt, pp* made) ◊制作工艺品 make handicrafts ◊制作网页 create a web page ◊制作商 manufacturer

质 zhì **I** [名] **1** (性质) nature ♦本质 nature **2** (质量) quality ◊高质产品 high-quality goods **3** (物质) matter ♦流质 fluid **4** (抵押品) pledge ♦人质 hostage **II** [形] simple ♦质朴 plain **III** [动] question ♦质疑 cast doubt on

质变 zhìbiàn [名] fundamental change

质地 zhìdì [名] texture

质感 zhìgǎn [名] sense of reality

质量 zhìliàng [名] **1** (物) mass **2** (优劣) quality

质问 zhìwèn [动] inquire

质疑 zhìyí [动] query

治 zhì [动] **1** (治理) control **2** (医治) cure **3** (消灭) exterminate **4** (惩办) punish **5** (研究) research

治安 zhì'ān [名] security ♦社会治安 public order

治理 zhìlǐ [动] 1 (统治管理) administer 2 (处理) manage

治疗 zhìliáo [动] cure

治学 zhìxué [动] (书) study

桎 zhì [名] (书) shackles (*pl*)

桎梏 zhìgù [名] (书) shackles (*pl*)

挚 zhì [形] (书) sincere

挚友 zhìyǒu [名] close friend

致 zhì I [动] 1 (给与) send (*pt, pp* sent) 2 (集中) concentrate 3 (招致) cause 4 (以致) result in II [名] appeal III [形] fine

致力 zhìlì [动] dedicate oneself to

致命 zhìmìng [动] cause death ◇这种药可能致命。This medicine can cause death. ◇致命的打击 a fatal blow

致使 zhìshǐ [连] so that ◇航空人员违反规章制度，致使发生重大飞行事故。Flouting of the rules by airline staff led to a serious plane crash.

致意 zhìyì [动] greet

秩 zhì [名] order

秩序 zhìxù [名] sequence

掷 zhì [动] throw (*pt* threw, *pp* thrown)

痔 zhì 见下文

痔疮 zhìchuāng [名] piles (*pl*)

窒 zhì [动] obstruct

窒息 zhìxī [动] suffocate

智 zhì I [形] wise II [名] wisdom

智慧 zhìhuì [名] intelligence

智力 zhìlì [名] intelligence

智囊 zhìnáng [名] brain ◇智囊团 think-tank

智能 zhìnéng I [名] intelligence and ability II [形] smart

智商 zhìshāng [名] IQ

智育 zhìyù [名] intellectual education

痣 zhì [名] mole

滞 zhì [动] come to a stop (*pt* came, *pp* come)

滞后 zhìhòu [形] lagging behind ◇这个城市的服务业发展滞后。This city's service industry is lagging behind.

滞留 zhìliú [动] stay behind

滞销 zhìxiāo [动] not sell well

置 zhì [动] 1 (搁) put (*pt, pp* put) 2 (设立) set up (*pt, pp* set) 3 (购置) buy (*pt, pp* bought)

置换 zhìhuàn [动] exchange

置若罔闻 zhì ruò wǎng wén shut one's eyes to ◇地方官员对中央政府下文置若罔闻。Local officials shut their eyes to memos from the central government.

置身 zhìshēn [动] take up a position (*pt* took, *pp* taken)

置疑 zhìyí [动] doubt

置之度外 zhì zhī dù wài give no thought to ◇为了追求理想他将金钱置之度外。In pursuit of his dreams, he gave money no thought.

雉 zhì [名] pheasant

稚 zhì [形] young

稚嫩 zhìnèn [形] 1 (娇嫩) tender 2 (幼稚) naive

稚气 zhìqì [形] childish

中 zhōng I [名] 1 (中心) centre (英), center (美) ♦中央 central 2 (中国) China ♦中餐 Chinese food 3 (范围内) ◇人海中 amid the crowd ◇在我的印象中，他很有才华。To my mind, he's very talented. 4 (两端之间的) the middle ♦中层 mid-level 5 (不偏不倚) impartial ♦适中 moderate 6 (在过程里的) course ◇在改革中 in the course of reform ◇会议在进行中。The meeting is in progress. II [动] be suitable for ◇这套家具中看不中用。This furniture looks great, but it's no use. III [形] (方) OK ◇这件事情中不中？ Is this OK?
▷另见 zhòng

中饱 zhōngbǎo [动] misappropriate

中断 zhōngduàn [动] break ... off (*pt* broke, *pp* broken)

中国 Zhōngguó [名] China

中华 Zhōnghuá [名] China ◇中华民族 the Chinese nation

中坚 zhōngjiān [形] core

中间 zhōngjiān [名] **1** (中心) middle **2** (之间) ◇我站在他俩中间。I was standing in between the both of them. ◇他是我们中间最刻苦的一个。He is the most hard-working of all of us.

中介 zhōngjiè [名] agency ♦房产中介 estate agent

中立 zhōnglì [动] be neutral ♦中立国 neutral country◇我方保持中立。We will remain neutral.

中流 zhōngliú **I** [名] (指河流) the middle reaches *(of a river)* **II** [形] mediocre

中流砥柱 zhōngliú Dǐzhù tower of strength

中年 zhōngnián [名] middle age

中世纪 zhōngshìjì [名] the Middle Ages (*pl*)

中枢 zhōngshū [名] centre (英), center (美)

中途 zhōngtú [名] ◇他中途辍学了。He abandoned his studies halfway through.

中文 Zhōngwén [名] Chinese ◇学中文 study Chinese

中午 zhōngwǔ [名] noon

中心 zhōngxīn [名] centre (英), center (美) ◇广场中心有一座雕塑。There's a statue in the centre of the square. ◇国际会议中心 international conference centre ◇北京是中国的政治文化中心。Beijing is the political and cultural heart of China.

中学 zhōngxué [名] high school (英), senior school (美)

中旬 zhōngxún [名] *the middle ten days of a month* ◇我们学校9月中旬开学。Our school term starts in mid-September.

中央 zhōngyāng [名] **1** (中心地) centre (英), center (美) **2** (最高机构) central government

中药 zhōngyào [名] Chinese medicine

中医 zhōngyī [名] **1** (医学) traditional Chinese medicine **2** (医生) doctor of traditional Chinese medicine

中庸 zhōngyōng [形] mediocre

中用 zhōngyòng [形] useful

中游 zhōngyóu [名] **1** (河流) the middle reaches (*of a river*) **2** (水平) ordinariness

中原 Zhōngyuán [名] the central Chinese plains (*pl*)

中止 zhōngzhǐ [动] cease

中转 zhōngzhuǎn [动] transfer

忠 zhōng [形] faithful

忠诚 zhōngchéng [形] loyal

忠厚 zhōnghòu [形] loyal and sincere

忠实 zhōngshí [形] **1** (忠诚可靠) loyal **2** (真实) true ◇译文必须忠实于原文的主旨。A translated text should be true to the purpose of the original.

忠贞 zhōngzhēn [形] faithful

终 zhōng **I** [动] die **II** [副] in the end **III** [形] all ♦终身 all one's life

终点 zhōngdiǎn [名] **1** (尽头) terminus (*pl* termini) **2** (体育) finish

终端 zhōngduān [名] terminal

终归 zhōngguī [副] in the end

终结 zhōngjié [动] end

终究 zhōngjiū [副] in the end ◇自然资源终究会枯竭。Natural resources will run out in the end.

终了 zhōngliǎo [动] end

终年 zhōngnián [名] **1** (全年) the whole year **2** (去世年龄) ◇他于1970年去世，终年85岁。He died in 1970, at the age of 85.

终日 zhōngrì [名] the whole day ◇他当了总经理后终日不得闲。After taking up the post of general manager he was busy the whole day long.

终身 zhōngshēn [名] one's whole life

终审 zhōngshěn [名] final verdict

终生 zhōngshēng [名] one's whole life

终于 zhōngyú [副] finally ◇他终于答应了我的要求。He finally agreed to

my request. ◇暴雨终于停了。The storm's over at last.

终止 zhōngzhǐ [动] stop

钟 zhōng [名] **1** (响器) bell **2** (记时器) clock **3** (指时间) ◇5点钟 five o'clock

钟爱 zhōng'ài [动] adore

钟情 zhōngqíng [动] be in love ◇一见钟情 fall in love at first sight

衷 zhōng [名] heart

衷肠 zhōngcháng [名] innermost feelings (*pl*)

衷情 zhōngqíng [名] emotion

衷心 zhōngxīn [形] heartfelt

肿 zhǒng [动] swell (*pt* swelled, *pp* swollen)

肿瘤 zhǒngliú [名] tumour (英), tumor (美)

种 zhǒng **I** [名] **1** (物种) species (*pl* species) ◇灭种 become extinct as a species **2** (人种) race **3** (种子) seed ◇播种 sow seeds **4** (胆量) courage ◇有种 be brave **II** [量] ◇各种商品 all kinds of commodities ◇3种选择 three choices
▷另见 zhòng

种类 zhǒnglèi [名] type

种子 zhǒngzi [名] seed ◇小麦种子 wheat seeds ◇种子选手 seeded player

种族 zhǒngzú [名] race ◇种族歧视 racial discrimination

中 zhòng [动] **1** (对准) hit (*pt*, *pp* hit) ◇子弹打中了靶子。The bullet hit the target. ◇彩票中了头奖。The lottery ticket won first prize. ◇他猜中了谜语。He guessed the riddle correctly. **2** (受到) be hit by ♦中毒 be poisoned ♦中暑 heatstroke◇胸口中了颗子弹。He was hit in the chest by a bullet.
▷另见 zhōng

中标 zhòngbiāo [动] make a successful bid for

中彩 zhòngcǎi [动] win the lottery (*pt*, *pp* won)

中毒 zhòngdú [动] be poisoned

中肯 zhòngkěn [形] relevant

中伤 zhòngshāng [动] slander

中意 zhòngyì [动] be ideal ◇这台洗衣机我中意。This washing machine is ideal for me.

仲 zhòng [形] intermediary

仲裁 zhòngcái [动] arbitrate

众 zhòng **I** [形] many ♦众人 everyone **II** [名] crowd ♦公众 the public

众多 zhòngduō [形] numerous

众口难调 zhòng kǒu nán tiáo tastes differ

众目睽睽 zhòng mù kuíkuí in full view of everybody ◇劫匪在众目睽睽下持刀杀人。The bandit stabbed a man to death in full view of everybody.

众叛亲离 zhòng pàn qīn lí outcast

众人 zhòngrén [名] everybody

众矢之的 zhòng shǐ zhī dì target of public criticism

众志成城 zhòng zhì chéng chéng unity is strength

种 zhòng [动] sow (*pt* sowed, *pp* sown) ♦耕种 cultivate ♦种田 farm ♦种痘 vaccinate ◇种果树 plant fruit trees
▷另见 zhǒng

种瓜得瓜，种豆得豆 zhòng guā dé guā, zhòng dòu dé dòu reap what one sows

种植 zhòngzhí [动] plant

重 zhòng **I** [名] weight ◇这袋面粉有多重? How much does this bag of flour weigh? **II** [形] **1** (重量大) heavy ◇水比油重。Water is heavier than oil. **2** (程度深) strong ◇情深意重 deep affection **3** (重要) important ♦重任 important task **4** (不轻率) serious ♦稳重 staid **III** [动] stress ♦注重 pay attention to
▷另见 chóng

重创 zhòngchuàng [动] be seriously injured

重大 zhòngdà [形] major ◇重大转变 a major change

重点 zhòngdiǎn [名] key point ◇重点政策 key policy

重工业 zhònggōngyè [名] heavy industry

重力 zhònglì [名] gravity

重量 zhòngliàng [名] weight

重任 zhòngrèn [名] important task

重视 zhòngshì [动] attach importance to

重武器 zhòngwǔqì [名] heavy weapons

重心 zhòngxīn [名] **1** (物) centre (英) 或 center (美) of gravity **2** (主要部分) core

重要 zhòngyào [形] important ◇重要文献 important document ◇发表重要讲话 give an important speech

重音 zhòngyīn [名] **1** (重读的音) stress **2** (音) accent

重镇 zhòngzhèn [名] strategic town

舟 zhōu [名] (书) boat

州 zhōu [名] **1** (自治州) autonomous prefecture **2** (美国的行政区) state ◇加利福尼亚州 the State of California

周 zhōu I [名] **1** (圈子) circle **2** (星期) week II [动] **1** (环绕) circle **2** (接济) give … financial help (*pt* gave, *pp* given) III [形] **1** (普遍) widespread **2** (完备) thorough

周边 zhōubiān [名] periphery

周长 zhōucháng [名] perimeter

周到 zhōudào [形] thorough

周而复始 zhōu ér fù shǐ come full circle

周济 zhōujì [动] give … financial help (*pt* gave, *pp* given)

周密 zhōumì [形] meticulous

周期 zhōuqī [名] period

周全 zhōuquán I [形] thorough II [动] bring about (*pt, pp* brought)

周围 zhōuwéi [名] the vicinity ◇房子周围种了很多树。A number of trees were planted in the vicinity of the house. ◇周围的人都睁大眼睛看着他。The people around him stared at him in astonishment.

周旋 zhōuxuán [动] **1** (回旋) circle **2** (交际) socialize **3** (较量) compete with

周游 zhōuyóu [动] travel ◇周游世界 travel all over the world

周折 zhōuzhé [名] twists and turns (*pl*) ◇他费尽周折终于找到了亲生父母。After various twists and turns, he finally found his birth parents.

周转 zhōuzhuǎn [动] **1** (经济) have a turnover of ◇公司有3千万英镑供周转。The company has a turnover of thirty million pounds. **2** (调度) have enough

洲 zhōu [名] **1** (大陆) continent **2** (沙洲) island

洲际 zhōujì [名] continent

粥 zhōu [名] porridge

粥少僧多 zhōu shǎo sēng duō not enough to go round ◇毕业生到处寻找工作机会，但粥少僧多。Recent graduates are looking everywhere for work, but there aren't enough jobs to go round.

轴 zhóu I [名] **1** (零件) axle **2** (直线) axis (*pl* axes) **3** (器物) spool II [量] scroll ◇一轴国画 a Chinese watercolour painting

轴承 zhóuchéng [名] bearing

轴心 zhóuxīn [名] **1** (轮轴) axle **2** (联合阵线) axis (*pl* axes)

肘 zhǒu [名] elbow

帚 zhǒu [名] broom

咒 zhòu [动] curse

咒骂 zhòumà [动] swear at (*pt* swore, *pp* sworn)

昼 zhòu [名] daylight

昼夜 zhòuyè [名] day and night

皱 zhòu [动] wrinkle ◇丝绸易皱。Silk fabrics crease easily.

皱纹 zhòuwén [名] wrinkle

骤 zhòu I [动] gallop II [形] sudden

骤然 zhòurán [副] suddenly

朱 zhū [形] bright red

朱红 zhūhóng [名] vermilion

侏 zhū 见下文

侏儒 zhūrú [名] dwarf (*pl* dwarves)

珠 zhū [名] **1** (珍珠) pearl **2** (球型物) bead ♦汗珠 a bead of sweat ♦泪珠 a teardrop

珠宝 zhūbǎo [名] jewels (*pl*)

珠联璧合 zhū lián bì hé a good combination

株 zhū **I** [名] **1** (树根) stem **2** (植株) plant **II** [量] ◇一株幼苗 a seedling ◇三株桃树 three peach trees

株连 zhūlián [动] implicate ◇在封建社会里，一人犯罪，株连九族。In feudal times, when a man committed a crime, the whole clan was implicated.

诸 zhū [代] all

诸多 zhūduō [形] large numbers of ◇新政府面临诸多挑战。The new government is facing a number of challenges.

诸如此类 zhū rú cǐ lèi and so forth ◇我喜欢看动画、漫画诸如此类的东西。I like cartoons, caricatures, and so forth.

诸位 zhūwèi [代] you (*pl*)

猪 zhū [名] pig

蛛 zhū [名] spider

蛛丝马迹 zhū sī mǎ jì clues ◇大劫案的蛛丝马迹渐渐浮出水面。Clues were gradually starting to surface in the big robbery case.

竹 zhú [名] bamboo

逐 zhú **I** [动] **1** (追赶) chase **2** (驱逐) drive … away (*pt* drove, *pp* driven) **II** [副] one after another ♦逐年 year in year out◇大家逐个发言。The people gave one speech after another.

逐步 zhúbù [副] step by step

逐渐 zhújiàn [副] gradually

逐一 zhúyī [副] one after another

烛 zhú **I** [名] candle **II** [动] (书) illuminate

烛台 zhútái [名] candlestick

主 zhǔ **I** [名] **1** (接待者) host ♦东道主 host **2** (所有者) owner ♦房主 home-owner **3** (当事人) person concerned ♦事主 crime victim **4** (主见) idea ◇他慌张得心里没了主。He was in such a state that he had no idea what to do next. **5** (上帝) God **II** [形] main ◇主干道 main road **III** [动] **1** (主持) take charge (*pt* took, *pp* taken) ♦主办 take charge of **2** (主张) be in favour (英) 或 favor (美) of ♦主战 be in favour of war **3** (从自身出发) look at … subjectively ♦主观 subjective

主持 zhǔchí [动] **1** (负责掌握) take charge of (*pt* took, *pp* taken) **2** (主张) support

主导 zhǔdǎo [动] direct

主动 zhǔdòng [形] voluntary

主犯 zhǔfàn [名] main culprit

主妇 zhǔfù [名] housewife (*pl* housewives)

主观 zhǔguān [形] subjective

主见 zhǔjiàn [名] opinion

主教 zhǔjiào [名] bishop

主角 zhǔjué [名] lead role ◇谁在剧中担任主角？ Who's got the lead in the play?

主力 zhǔlì [名] leading player

主流 zhǔliú [名] **1** (指河流) main current **2** (指事物) general trend

主谋 zhǔmóu **I** [动] conspire **II** [名] ringleader

主权 zhǔquán [名] sovereignty

主人 zhǔrén [名] **1** (接待者) host **2** (雇佣者) master ♦女主人 mistress **3** (所有者) owner

主食 zhǔshí [名] staple food

主题 zhǔtí [名] subject

主体 zhǔtǐ [名] main part

主席 zhǔxí [名] chairman, chairwoman

主旋律 zhǔxuánlǜ [名] theme

主演 zhǔyǎn [动] play the lead

主要 zhǔyào [形] major ◇主要问题 major issue ◇主要原因 major cause

主页 zhǔyè [名] home page

主义 zhǔyì [名] doctrine ♦社会主义 socialism ♦浪漫主义 romanticism

主意 zhǔyi [名] **1** (办法) idea ◇他给我们出了个好主意。He gave us a

good idea. **2** (主见) opinion ◇你自己拿主意吧。You make up your own mind.

主语 zhǔyǔ [名] subject

主宰 zhǔzǎi [动] dominate

主张 zhǔzhāng **I** [动] advocate **II** [名] standpoint

主旨 zhǔzhǐ [名] main point

主子 zhǔzi [名] master

煮 zhǔ [动] boil

嘱 zhǔ [动] admonish

嘱咐 zhǔfù [动] urge ◇他嘱咐儿子要好好学习。He urged his son to study hard.

嘱托 zhǔtuō [动] entrust … with ◇上司把这项重任嘱托给了我。My boss entrusted me with this important task.

瞩 zhǔ [动] look closely

瞩目 zhǔmù [动] watch with interest

伫 zhù 见下文

伫立 zhùlì [动] (书) stand for a long time (*pt, pp* stood)

助 zhù [动] help

助词 zhùcí [名] auxiliary word

助动词 zhùdòngcí [名] auxiliary verb

助人为乐 zhù rén wéi lè take pleasure in helping others

助手 zhùshǒu [名] assistant

助兴 zhùxìng [动] liven things up

住 zhù [动] **1** (居住) live ◇他和父母住在一起。He lives with his parents. **2** (停住) stop ◇住口！Shut up! **3** (用作动词补语) ◇卡车停住了。The truck stopped. ◇听到这消息，她一下愣住了。She was struck dumb by the news.

住户 zhùhù [名] household

住宿 zhùsù [动] stay

住宅 zhùzhái [名] house

住址 zhùzhǐ [名] address

贮 zhù [动] store

贮藏 zhùcáng [动] store

注 zhù **I** [动] **1** (灌入) pour ♦注射 inject **2** (集中) concentrate **3** (解释) explain ♦批注 comment on **II** [名] **1** (记载) record ♦注册 enrol (英), enroll (美) **2** (赌注) bet

注册 zhùcè [动] enrol (英), enroll (美) ◇新生明天开始注册。The new students will begin enrolling tomorrow. ◇注册表 register ◇注册会计师 chartered (英) 或 certified (美) accountant

注定 zhùdìng [动] be destined ◇他注定要失败。He was destined to lose.

注解 zhùjiě [动] annotate

注目 zhùmù [动] focus

注射 zhùshè [动] inject

注视 zhùshì [动] stare ◇她注视着窗台上的一束鲜花。She's staring at the bunch of fresh flowers on the windowsill.

注释 zhùshì [动] annotate

注销 zhùxiāo [动] cancel

注意 zhùyì [动] be careful ◇请注意交通安全。Please be careful on the roads. ◇登山前特别要注意服装和鞋子。Before you climb the mountain, be careful to kit yourself out correctly.

注音 zhùyīn [动] give a phonetic notation (*pt* gave, *pp* given)

注重 zhùzhòng [动] stress

驻 zhù [动] **1** (停留) stop **2** (设立) stay ◇中国驻伦敦大使馆 the Chinese embassy in London

驻地 zhùdì [名] camp

驻守 zhùshǒu [动] garrison

驻扎 zhùzhā [动] be stationed

祝 zhù [动] wish ◇祝你成功！Wishing you every success! ◇祝你生日快乐！Happy birthday!

祝福 zhùfú [动] wish … luck ◇我们祝福你！We wish you good luck! ◇祝福你万事如意！May all your wishes come true!

祝贺 zhùhè [动] congratulate ◇祝贺你考上了名牌大学。Congratulations on getting into such a prestigious university.

祝愿 zhùyuàn [动] wish ◇祝愿你

早日康复。I wish you a speedy recovery.

著 zhù **I** [形] marked **II** [动] **1** (显出) show (*pt* showed, *pp* shown) **2** (写作) write (*pt* wrote, *pp* written) **III** [名] work

著称 zhùchēng [动] be famous ◇埃及以金字塔著称。Egypt is famous for its pyramids.

著名 zhùmíng [形] famous ◇长江三峡是中国著名的风景区。The Three Gorges are one of China's famous beauty spots.

著述 zhùshù **I** [动] write (*pt* wrote, *pp* written) **II** [名] writings (*pl*)

著作 zhùzuò [名] writings (*pl*)

蛀 zhù **I** [动] bore **II** [名] moth

蛀虫 zhùchóng [名] moth

铸 zhù [动] smelt

铸造 zhùzào [动] smelt

筑 zhù [动] build (*pt, pp* built)

抓 zhuā [动] **1** (拿住) grab **2** (划过) scratch **3** (捉拿) catch (*pt, pp* caught) **4** (着重) take control of (*pt* took, *pp* taken) **5** (吸引) attract **6** (把握住) seize

抓耳挠腮 zhuā ěr náo sāi scratch one's head

抓获 zhuāhuò [动] capture

抓紧 zhuājǐn [动] make the most of ◇我们时间不多了，你得抓紧。We don't have much time, you'd better make the most of it.

抓阄儿 zhuājiūr [动] draw lots (*pt* drew, *pp* drawn)

爪 zhuǎ [名] claw
▷另见 zhǎo

拽 zhuài [动] pull

专 zhuān [动] **1** (集中) concentrate **2** (独占) dominate ♦专卖 monopoly

专长 zhuāncháng [名] speciality (英), specialty (美)

专诚 zhuānchéng [副] specially

专程 zhuānchéng [副] specially ◇他专程来到桂林拍摄记录片。He made the journey to Guilin specially to shoot a documentary.

专断 zhuānduàn [形] arbitrary

专攻 zhuāngōng [动] specialize in

专横 zhuānhèng [形] domineering

专家 zhuānjiā [名] expert ◇专家门诊 specialist clinic

专利 zhuānlì [名] patent

专门 zhuānmén **I** [形] specialized **II** [副] especially

专权 zhuānquán [动] monopolize

专任 zhuānrèn [动] work full-time ◇他专任舞蹈教师。He's a full-time dancing teacher.

专题 zhuāntí [名] special subject ◇新闻专题 special report

专心 zhuānxīn [形] single-minded

专业 zhuānyè [名] special field of study ◇英语专业 English major ◇专业人才 professionals

专一 zhuānyī [形] single-minded

专职 zhuānzhí [名] full-time work

专制 zhuānzhì [形] despotic

专注 zhuānzhù [形] concentrated on

砖 zhuān [名] brick

砖头 zhuāntou [名] brick

转 zhuǎn [动] **1** (改换) turn ♦转弯 turn a corner ♦转学 change schools **2** (传送) pass ... on ♦转送 deliver ◇请把文件转给他。Please pass this document on to him.
▷另见 zhuàn

转变 zhuǎnbiàn [动] transform

转播 zhuǎnbō [动] relay

转达 zhuǎndá [动] pass ... on ◇请转达我对他的问候。Please give him my regards.

转轨 zhuǎnguǐ [动] be in transition

转化 zhuǎnhuà [动] change

转换 zhuǎnhuàn [动] convert

转机 zhuǎnjī **I** [名] a turn for the better ◇生意已有转机。Business has taken a turn for the better. **II** [动] change planes

转嫁 zhuǎnjià [动] **1** (改嫁) remarry **2** (转移) transfer

转交 zhuǎnjiāo [动] pass ... on

转让 zhuǎnràng [动] transfer

转手 zhuǎnshǒu [动] resell (*pt, pp* resold)

转瞬 zhuǎnshùn [副] in an instant

转型 zhuǎnxíng [动] transform

转眼 zhuǎnyǎn [副] in an instant

转业 zhuǎnyè [动] change jobs

转移 zhuǎnyí [动] change

转账 zhuǎnzhàng [动] transfer accounts

转折 zhuǎnzhé [动] change dramatically ♦转折点 turning point

转正 zhuǎnzhèng [动] become a permanent member (*pt* became, *pp* become)

传 zhuàn [名] **1** (传记) biography **2** (历史故事) tale
▷另见 chuán

传记 zhuànjì [名] biography

转 zhuàn [动] turn ◇电风扇被摔坏，不转了。The fan's broken – it's not turning round. ◇月亮围着地球转。The Moon orbits the Earth.
▷另见 zhuǎn

转动 zhuàndòng [动] revolve

转向 zhuànxiàng [动] lose one's way (*pt, pp* lost)

转悠 zhuànyou [动] (口) **1** (转动) roll **2** (漫步) stroll

赚 zhuàn [动] **1** (获得利润) make a profit **2** (挣钱) earn

赚头 zhuàntou [名] (口) profit

撰 zhuàn [动] write (*pt* wrote, *pp* written)

撰述 zhuànshù [动] compose

妆 zhuāng **I** [动] put on make-up (*pt, pp* put) ♦梳妆 do one's hair and put on make-up **II** [名] adornments (*pl*)

庄 zhuāng [名] **1** (指村庄) village ♦农庄 village **2** (指土地) manor ♦庄园 manor **3** (指商店) ♦茶庄 teahouse ♦饭庄 restaurant

庄稼 zhuāngjia [名] crops (*pl*)

庄严 zhuāngyán [形] solemn

庄园 zhuāngyuán [名] manor

庄重 zhuāngzhòng [形] solemn ◇首相讲话时声音庄重。When the prime minister spoke, his tone was solemn.

桩 zhuāng **I** [名] pile ♦打桩 drive in a pile **II** [量] ◇一桩事 an issue

装 zhuāng **I** [动] **1** (修饰) dress up ♦装饰 decorate **2** (假装) pretend ◇装疯卖傻 play the fool **3** (装载) load ◇装车 load a truck with goods **4** (装配) install ◇我们家里装了空调。We've had air-conditioning installed. **II** [名] (服装) clothing ♦套装 matching outfit

装扮 zhuāngbàn [动] **1** (打扮) dress up **2** (假装) disguise

装备 zhuāngbèi **I** [名] equipment **II** [动] equip

装点 zhuāngdiǎn [动] decorate

装订 zhuāngdìng [动] bind (*pt, pp* bound)

装潢 zhuānghuáng [动] decorate

装甲 zhuāngjiǎ [形] armoured (英), armored (美)

装聋作哑 zhuāng lóng zuò yǎ feign ignorance

装门面 zhuāng ménmian [动] keep up appearances (*pt, pp* kept)

装束 zhuāngshù [名] outfit

装修 zhuāngxiū [动] fit … out

装置 zhuāngzhì **I** [动] install **II** [名] equipment

壮 zhuàng **I** [形] **1** (强壮) strong ♦健壮 robust **2** (雄壮) grand ♦壮阔 grand **II** [动] bolster ♦壮胆 embolden

壮大 zhuàngdà **I** [形] well-built **II** [动] expand

壮观 zhuàngguān [形] magnificent

壮举 zhuàngjǔ [名] brave feat

壮丽 zhuànglì [形] majestic

壮烈 zhuàngliè [形] heroic

壮年 zhuàngnián [名] prime of life

壮士 zhuàngshì [名] hero (*pl* heroes)

壮实 zhuàngshi [形] sturdy

壮志 zhuàngzhì [名] high ideals (*pl*)

状 zhuàng [名] **1** (形状) shape ◇奇

形怪状 weirdly-shaped **2** (情况) state ♦症状 symptom **3** (诉状) complaint ♦告状 bring a case **4** (证书) certificate ♦奖状 certificate

状况 zhuàngkuàng [名] condition

状态 zhuàngtài [名] condition

状元 zhuàngyuán [名] the best ◊三百六十行，行行出状元。No matter what career you choose, you can be the best.

撞 zhuàng [动] **1** (碰撞) collide ◊小男孩被车撞了。The little boy was knocked down by a car. **2** (碰见) bump into ◊逛街时我撞上了老同学。While window shopping I bumped into an old classmate. **3** (试探) try ◊撞运气 try one's luck **4** (闯) dash

撞车 zhuàngchē [动] **1** (车辆相撞) collide **2** (发生分歧) clash

撞击 zhuàngjī [动] collide

撞骗 zhuàngpiàn [动] swindle

幢 zhuàng [量] ◊一幢别墅 a villa ◊两幢楼房 two blocks of flats (英) 或 apartments (美)

追 zhuī [动] **1** (追赶) chase ♦追随 follow **2** (追究) investigate ♦追查 investigate **3** (追求) seek (*pt, pp* sought) ◊追名逐利 seek fame and fortune **4** (回溯) reminisce ♦追思 reminisce **5** (补办) ♦追加 supplement

追捕 zhuībǔ [动] pursue and capture

追悼 zhuīdào [动] mourn

追赶 zhuīgǎn [动] chase

追悔 zhuīhuǐ [动] regret

追击 zhuījī [动] pursue

追加 zhuījiā [动] supplement

追究 zhuījiū [动] investigate

追求 zhuīqiú [动] **1** (争取) seek (*pt, pp* sought) **2** (求爱) chase after

追溯 zhuīsù [动] trace

追随 zhuīsuí [动] follow

追忆 zhuīyì [动] recollect

追逐 zhuīzhú [动] **1** (追赶) chase **2** (追求) seek (*pt, pp* sought)

追踪 zhuīzōng [动] track

锥 zhuī [名] **1** (锥子) awl **2** (锥状物) cone

坠 zhuì I [动] **1** (书) (落) fall (*pt* fell, *pp* fallen) ♦坠落 drop **2** (垂) droop ♦下坠 droop II [名] pendant ♦耳坠 earring

坠落 zhuìluò [动] fall (*pt* fell, *pp* fallen)

惴 zhuì [形] (书) anxious

惴惴不安 zhuìzhuì bù'ān ill at ease ◊他暴虐的脾气让每个人都惴惴不安。His brutal temper made everyone feel very ill at ease.

赘 zhuì [形] superfluous

赘词 zhuìcí [名] superfluous words (*pl*)

谆 zhūn [形] earnest

谆谆 zhūnzhūn [形] earnest

准 zhǔn I [动] **1** (准许) allow ♦批准 ratify ◊不准随地吐痰。Spitting is prohibited. **2** (依据) be in accord with II [名] standard ◊以此为准 take this as the standard III [形] **1** (准确) accurate ♦准时 punctual **2** (类似) quasi ♦准科学 quasi-science

准备 zhǔnbèi [动] **1** (筹划) prepare ◊心理准备 psychological preparation **2** (打算) plan

准确 zhǔnquè [形] accurate

准绳 zhǔnshéng [名] benchmark

准头 zhǔntou [名] (口) accuracy

准许 zhǔnxǔ [动] permit

准予 zhǔnyǔ [动] allow

准则 zhǔnzé [名] norms (*pl*)

拙 zhuō [形] **1** (笨) clumsy ♦拙劣 poor **2** (谦) (自己的) ♦拙著 my writing

拙劣 zhuōliè [形] poor

捉 zhuō [动] **1** (握住) clutch **2** (捕捉) catch (*pt, pp* caught)

捉襟见肘 zhuō jīn jiàn zhǒu have more problems than one can cope with

捉摸 zhuōmō [动] predict

捉弄 zhuōnòng [动] play with

桌 zhuō I [名] table ♦书桌 desk

II [量] table ◇一桌菜 a table covered in dishes

灼 zhuó I [动] burn ♦烧灼 burn II [形] bright

灼见 zhuójiàn [名] penetrating insight

灼热 zhuórè [形] scorching

茁 zhuó [形] thriving

茁壮 zhuózhuàng [形] sturdy

卓 zhuó [形] **1** (高而直) upright **2** (高明) eminent ♦卓越 outstanding

卓识 zhuóshí [名] good judgement

卓有成效 zhuó yǒu chéngxiào highly effective

卓越 zhuóyuè [形] outstanding

卓著 zhuózhù [形] distinguished

浊 zhuó [形] **1** (浑浊) muddy **2** (粗重) deep

酌 zhuó [动] **1** (斟酒) pour out wine **2** (饮酒) drink (*pt* drank, *pp* drunk) **3** (斟酌) consider

酌量 zhuóliàng [动] consider

酌情 zhuóqíng [动] use one's discretion

啄 zhuó [动] peck

啄木鸟 zhuómùniǎo [名] woodpecker

着 zhuó I [动] **1** (穿) wear (*pt* wore, *pp* worn) ♦着装 clothing **2** (接触) come into contact with (*pt* came, *pp* come) ♦着陆 land **3** (使接触) apply ♦着手 set about ♦着眼 keep … in mind **4** (派遣) send (*pt, pp* sent) ◇着人去调查 send someone to investigate II [名] whereabouts (*pl*) ◇衣食无着 without food or clothing ▷另见 zhāo, zháo

着力 zhuólì [动] put effort into (*pt, pp* put)

着陆 zhuólù [动] land

着落 zhuóluò I [名] **1** (下落) whereabouts (*pl*) **2** (来源) source II [动] rest with ◇这些任务着落在我们身上。The responsibility rests with us.

着实 zhuóshí [副] **1** (实在) really **2** (狠狠) severely

着手 zhuóshǒu [动] set about (*pt, pp* set)

着想 zhuóxiǎng [动] consider

着眼 zhuóyǎn [动] keep … in mind (*pt, pp* kept) ◇大处着眼 keep the big picture in mind

着意 zhuóyì [动] take pains (*pt* took, *pp* taken)

着重 zhuózhòng [动] stress

琢 zhuó [动] carve ♦雕琢 carve ▷另见 zuó

琢磨 zhuómó [动] polish

镯 zhuó [名] bracelet

吱 zī [拟] squeak

吱声 zīshēng [动] (方) say the word (*pt, pp* said)

孜 zī 见下文

孜孜不倦 zīzī bù juàn diligently

咨 zī [动] consult ♦咨询 seek advice from

咨询 zīxún [动] seek advice from (*pt, pp* sought)

姿 zī [名] **1** (容貌) looks (*pl*) ♦姿色 good looks (*pl*) **2** (姿势) posture ♦舞姿 dancer's movement

姿色 zīsè [名] good looks (*pl*)

姿势 zīshì [名] posture

姿态 zītài [名] **1** (姿势) posture **2** (态度) attitude

资 zī I [名] **1** (钱财) money ♦外资 foreign capital ♦邮资 postage **2** (资质) ability ♦天资 natural ability **3** (资格) qualifications (*pl*) ♦资历 record of service II [动] **1** (资助) aid … financially ♦资敌 aid the enemy **2** (提供) provide

资本 zīběn [名] **1** (本钱) capital **2** (优势) ◇他把贵族的出身作为取得事业成功的资本。He capitalized on his aristocratic origins to advance his career.

资本主义 zīběn zhǔyì [名] capitalism

资产 zīchǎn [名] property

资产阶级 zīchǎn jiējí [名] bourgeoisie

资格 zīgé [名] **1** (条件) qualifications (*pl*) **2** (身份) seniority

资金 zījīn [名] funds ◇募集资金 raise funds

资历 zīlì [名] record of service

资料 zīliào [名] 1 (必需品) means (*pl*) ◇生产资料 means of production 2 (材料) material

资讯 zīxùn [名] data (*pl*) ◇商业资讯 trade data

资源 zīyuán [名] resources (*pl*) ◇自然资源 natural resources ◇资源丰富 rich in natural resources

资助 zīzhù [动] aid ... financially

孳 zī [动] multiply

孳生 zīshēng [动] multiply

滋 zī [动] 1 (滋生) grow (*pt* grew, *pp* grown) ♦滋长 grow 2 (增添) increase ♦滋养 nourish

滋补 zībǔ [动] nourish

滋润 zīrùn I [形] 1 (水份多) moist 2 (方) (舒服) comfortable ◇日子过得挺滋润。The days pass very comfortably. II [动] moisten

滋生 zīshēng [动] 1 (繁殖) multiply 2 (引起) cause

滋事 zīshì [动] cause trouble

滋味 zīwèi [名] 1 (味道) flavour (英), flavor (美) 2 (感受) feeling ◇听了他的冷言冷语，我心里不是滋味。After hearing his cold words, I felt very upset.

滋长 zīzhǎng [动] grow (*pt* grew, *pp* grown)

龇 zī [动] ◇龇着牙 bare one's teeth

龇牙咧嘴 zī yá liě zuǐ look fierce

子 zǐ I [名] 1 (儿子) son ♦母子 mother and son 2 (人) person ♦男子 man 3 (种子) seed ♦瓜子 melon seed 4 (卵) egg ♦鱼子 fish roe 5 (粒状物) ♦棋子 chess piece 6 (铜子) coin ◇我身上一个子儿都没有。I haven't got a penny on me. II [形] 1 (幼小) young ♦子鸡 chick 2 (附属) affiliated ◇子公司 subsidiary company

子弟 zǐdì [名] children

子公司 zǐgōngsī [名] subsidiary company

子女 zǐnǚ [名] children

子孙 zǐsūn [名] descendants (*pl*)

子午线 zǐwǔxiàn [名] meridian

子夜 zǐyè [名] midnight

仔 zǐ [形] young

仔细 zǐxì [形] 1 (细心) thorough 2 (小心) careful

姊 zǐ [名] sister

姊妹 zǐmèi [名] sisters (*pl*)

籽 zǐ [名] seed ♦菜籽 vegetable seed

紫 zǐ [形] purple

紫外线 zǐwàixiàn [名] ultraviolet ray

自 zì I [代] oneself ◇自讨苦吃 bring trouble on oneself II [副] certainly ◇他这样做自有一番用意。In doing this he certainly has some motive. III [介] from ◇他自小就聪明能干。From an early age he has been clever and capable.

自爱 zì'ài [名] self-respect

自拔 zìbá [动] free oneself

自白 zìbái [动] vindicate oneself

自不量力 zì bù liàng lì overestimate one's abilities

自成一家 zì chéng yī jiā have one's own style

自持 zìchí [动] control oneself

自从 zìcóng [介] since

自大 zìdà [形] arrogant

自得 zìdé [形] self-satisfied

自动 zìdòng [形] 1 (主动的) voluntary ◇自动让出座位 voluntarily give up one's seat 2 (机械的) automatic ◇按下电钮，门会自动打开。When you press the button, the door will open automatically.

自动化 zìdònghuà [动] automate

自动取款机 zìdòng qǔkuǎnjī [动] cashpoint (英), ATM (美)

自发 zìfā [形] spontaneous

自负 zìfù I [形] conceited II [动] take responsibility (*pt* took, *pp* taken)

自高自大 zì gāo zì dà self-important

自告奋勇 zì gào fènyǒng volunteer ◇他自告奋勇地要为她出庭辩护。

He volunteered to appear in court in her defence.

自顾不暇 zì gù bù xiá be unable to take care of oneself

自豪 zìháo [形] proud ◇我们为你获得冠军感到自豪。We are very proud that you won the championship.

自己 zìjǐ I [代] oneself ◇你要相信自己的能力。You must have faith in your own ability. ◇炮弹自己不会爆炸。The shell won't detonate by itself. ◇我能够照顾好自己。I can take care of myself. II [形] our ◇自己人 our people

自给 zìjǐ [动] be self-sufficient

自尽 zìjìn [动] commit suicide

自觉 zìjué I [动] be aware of II [形] conscientious

自绝 zìjué [动] isolate oneself

自理 zìlǐ [动] take care of oneself (*pt* took, *pp* taken)

自力更生 zì lì gēng shēng self-reliant

自立 zìlì [动] support oneself ◇自立门户 become independent

自流 zìliú [动] 1 (指水) flow freely 2 (指事) develop freely 3 (指人) do as one pleases

自律 zìlǜ [动] be self-disciplined

自满 zìmǎn [形] self-satisfied

自鸣得意 zì míng déyì be very pleased with oneself

自命 zìmìng [动] consider oneself ◇自命不凡 consider oneself exceptional

自欺欺人 zì qī qī rén deceive oneself and others

自然 zìrán I [名] nature II [形] natural ◇自然免疫 natural immunity ◇表情自然 natural expression III [副] naturally ◇你对他那么冷淡，他自然不会再来了。Since you were so cold to him, he naturally won't want to come again.

自杀 zìshā [动] commit suicide

自食其果 zì shí qí guǒ reap what one has sown

自首 zìshǒu [动] give oneself up (*pt* gave, *pp* given)

自私 zìsī [形] selfish

自卫 zìwèi [动] defend oneself

自我 zìwǒ [代] self ◇自我介绍 introduce oneself

自相矛盾 zìxiāng máodùn contradictory

自信 zìxìn [形] self-confident

自修 zìxiū [动] 1 (自习) study by oneself 2 (自学) teach oneself (*pt, pp* taught) ◇他自修了企业管理课程。He taught himself business management.

自选 zìxuǎn [形] optional ◇自选商场 supermarket

自以为是 zì yǐ wéi shì believe oneself to be infallible

自缢 zìyì [动] hang oneself (*pt, pp* hanged)

自由 zìyóu I [名] freedom II [形] free

自由职业者 zìyóu zhíyèzhě [名] freelancer

自圆其说 zì yuán qí shuō justify oneself

自怨自艾 zì yuàn zì yì repent

自愿 zìyuàn [动] volunteer

自在 zìzài [形] 1 (自由) free 2 (舒适) comfortable

自知之明 zì zhī zhī míng self-knowledge

自治 zìzhì [动] be autonomous

自重 zìzhòng I [形] self-possessed ◇请你自重。Please behave yourself. II [名] weight

自主 zìzhǔ [动] make decisions by oneself

自助餐 zìzhùcān [名] self-service buffet

自传 zìzhuàn [名] autobiography

自转 zìzhuàn [动] rotate

自尊 zìzūn [名] self-respect

自作自受 zī zuò zì shòu suffer as a result of one's own actions

字 zì [名] 1 (文字) character 2 (字音) pronunciation ◇字正腔圆 have perfect enunciation 3 (书法作品) calligraphy ◆字画 painting and calligraphy 4 (字体) script ◇黑体字

bold face **5** (字据) written pledge

字典 zìdiǎn [名] dictionary

字节 zìjié [名] byte

字据 zìjù [名] ◊别人向我借钱时一般都会请求立字据。When someone borrows money from me, I usually ask for an IOU. ◊我们有字据为证。We have it in writing.

字里行间 zì lǐ háng jiān between the lines

字母 zìmǔ [名] letter

字眼 zìyǎn [名] wording

恣 zì [动] act freely

恣意 zìyì [副] wantonly

宗 zōng **I** [名] **1** (祖宗) ancestor **2** (家族) clan ♦同宗 of the same clan **3** (宗派) school ♦正宗 orthodox school **4** (宗旨) purpose **II** [量] ◊一宗心事 a worrying matter

宗教 zōngjiào [名] religion

宗派 zōngpài [名] faction

宗师 zōngshī [名] master

宗旨 zōngzhǐ [名] purpose

宗族 zōngzú [名] clan

综 zōng [动] summarize ♦综述 sum ... up

综合 zōnghé **I** [动] synthesize **II** [形] comprehensive ◊综合大学 university

棕 zōng [名] **1** (棕榈) palm **2** (棕毛) palm fibre (英) 或 fiber (美)

棕榈 zōnglú [名] palm

踪 zōng [名] tracks *(pl)* ♦行踪 tracks *(pl)*

踪迹 zōngjì [名] trace

鬃 zōng [名] ♦马鬃 mane ♦猪鬃 bristles *(pl)*

总 zǒng **I** [动] gather ♦总括 sum ... up **II** [形] **1** (全部的) total ◊总金额 total amount of money **2** (为首的) chief ♦总部 headquarters *(pl)* **III** [副] **1** (一直) always ◊他总迟到。He's always late. **2** (毕竟) after all ◊发生这么大的事, 我总得告诉他。After all, I couldn't not tell him about an event of this importance.

总裁 zǒngcái [名] director

总得 zǒngděi [副] ◊我们也总得有个地方坐坐呀。There must be somewhere for us to sit.

总督 zǒngdū [名] governor

总而言之 zǒng ér yán zhī in brief

总纲 zǒnggāng [名] general principles *(pl)*

总共 zǒnggòng [副] altogether

总归 zǒngguī [副] after all

总和 zǒnghé [名] total

总计 zǒngjì [动] total

总结 zǒngjié **I** [动] summarize **II** [名] summary

总括 zǒngkuò [动] sum ... up

总理 zǒnglǐ [名] premier

总数 zǒngshù [名] total

总算 zǒngsuàn [副] **1** (最终) finally ◊多年的心血总算没有白费。All those years of struggle have finally paid off. **2** (大体上) all things considered ◊他能这样待你总算可以了。All things considered, the way he treats you isn't bad.

总体 zǒngtǐ [名] ◊总体评估 overall evaluation ◊总体战略思路 overall strategy

总统 zǒngtǒng [名] president

总务 zǒngwù [名] **1** (指事务) general affairs *(pl)* **2** (指官员) general manager

总之 zǒngzhī [连] ◊你需要找好的管理人才, 财务人才, 总之你一个人是不够的。You need to find a good manager and accountant – in short you can't do it all on your own.

纵 zòng **I** [形] **1** (从南向北的) north-south ◊运河纵贯两省。The canal runs north-south through two provinces. **2** (从前到后的) ♦纵深 depth ♦纵向 forward direction **II** [动] **1** (释放) release **2** (放任) indulge ♦纵酒 drink too much **3** (纵身) jump **III** [副] (书) ◊纵有千辛万苦, 我也毫不畏惧。Even if there are a lot of difficulties, I will not be at all afraid.

纵横 zònghéng **I** [动] move freely **II** [形] **1** (竖的和横的) vertical and horizontal **2** (奔放自如的) easy ◊笔意纵横 write with ease

纵火 zònghuǒ [动] set fire to (*pt, pp* set) ◇有人故意纵火烧毁了房屋。Someone deliberately set fire to the house.

纵情 zòngqíng [副] to one's heart content ◇纵情歌唱 sing to one's heart's content

纵然 zòngrán [连] even though

纵容 zòngróng [动] connive

纵深 zòngshēn [名] depth

走 zǒu [动] **1** (行走) walk ♦走路 walk ◇出去走走 go out for a walk **2** (跑动) run (*pt* ran, *pp* run) ♦奔走 run around **3** (运行) move ◇钟不走了。The clock's stopped. **4** (离开) leave (*pt, pp* left) ◇我先走。I'll be off. **5** (来往) visit ◇走亲戚 visit relatives **6** (通过) go through (*pt* went, *pp* gone) ◇走这条街比较近。If we go through this street it's quicker. **7** (漏出) leak ◇走气了。There's a gas leak. **8** (改变) depart from ◇走样 deviate from **9** (去世) die ◇他聪明能干，却早早地走了。He was clever and able, but died very young.

走动 zǒudòng [动] **1** (行走) walk about **2** (来往) visit each other

走访 zǒufǎng [动] interview

走过场 zǒu guòchǎng go through the motions

走后门 zǒu hòumén use one's connections

走火 zǒuhuǒ [动] **1** (枪支) go off accidentally (*pt* gone, *pp* went) **2** (失火) be on fire ◇房子走火了。The house is on fire.

走江湖 zǒu jiānghú lead a nomadic life

走廊 zǒuláng [名] corridor

走漏 zǒulòu [动] **1** (泄露) leak **2** (走私漏税) smuggle and evade taxes

走马看花 zǒu mǎ kàn huā have a superficial understanding

走南闯北 zǒu nán chuǎng běi travel extensively

走俏 zǒuqiào [动] sell well (*pt, pp* sold)

走人 zǒurén [动] leave (*pt, pp* left)

走神 zǒushén [动] lose concentration (*pt, pp* lost)

走兽 zǒushòu [名] beasts (*pl*)

走私 zǒusī [动] smuggle

走投无路 zǒu tóu wú lù have no way out

走向 zǒuxiàng **I** [名] alignment **II** [动] move towards

走穴 zǒuxué [动] moonlight

走样 zǒuyàng [动] deviate from

走运 zǒuyùn [动] (口) be lucky

走嘴 zǒuzuǐ [动] let something slip (*pt, pp* let)

奏 zòu [动] **1** (演奏) play ♦奏乐 play music **2** (发生) produce ♦奏效 have effect

奏鸣曲 zòumíngqǔ [名] sonata

奏效 zòuxiào [动] have effect ◇这感冒药吃下去立即奏效。As soon as you take this flu medicine it will have the desired effect.

揍 zòu [动] (口) beat (*pt* beat, *pp* beaten)

租 zū **I** [动] **1** (租用) (房屋) rent **2** (租用) (汽车, 自行车, 录像带) hire (英), rent (美) **3** (出租) rent out **II** [名] rent ♦房租 rent

> 📖 请勿混淆 **rent**, **hire**, 和 **let**。在英式英语中, **hire** 表示通过支付一笔费用从而能够暂时使用某物。在美式英语中, 同样情况下**rent** 更为常用。*He was unable to hire another car... He rented a car for the weekend.* 以连续付款的方式而长期使用某物, 应使用 **rent**。*...the apartment he had rented... He rented a TV.* **rent** 还可以表示以收取租金的方式将房屋出租给他人。*We rented our house to an American professor.* 英式英语中，也可以使用单词 **let**。*They were letting a room to a school teacher.*

租借 zūjiè [动] rent

租赁 zūlìn [动] rent

租用 zūyòng [动] rent

足 zú **I** [名] foot (*pl* feet) ♦足迹

footprint **II** [形] ample ♦充足 adequate **III** [副] **1** (达到某种程度) as much as ◇一顿酒席足足可以花上1000块钱。You can spend as much as a thousand yuan on a banquet. ◇他足足用了两年时间写这本书。It took him a whole two years to write this book. **2** (足以) enough

足够 zúgòu [动] be enough

足金 zújīn [名] solid gold

足球 zúqiú [名] football

足坛 zútán [名] footballing world

足以 zúyǐ [动] be enough

足智多谋 zú zhì duō móu wise and resourceful

族 zú [名] **1** (家族) clan ♦族人 clan member **2** (种族) nationality **3** (类别) group

诅 zǔ 见下文

诅咒 zǔzhòu [动] curse

阻 zǔ [动] block ♦劝阻 dissuade from

阻碍 zǔ'ài [动] obstruct

阻挡 zǔdǎng [动] stop

阻击 zǔjī [动] block

阻拦 zǔlán [动] block

阻力 zǔlì [名] **1** (物) resistance **2** (障碍) obstruction

阻挠 zǔnáo [动] obstruct

阻塞 zǔsè [动] block ◇交通阻塞 traffic jam

阻止 zǔzhǐ [动] stop

组 zǔ **I** [动] form ♦组建 set … up **II** [名] group ◇兴趣小组 interest group **III** [量] ◇几组电池 some batteries

组成 zǔchéng [动] form

组阁 zǔgé [动] form a cabinet

组合 zǔhé **I** [动] constitute **II** [名] combination

组建 zǔjiàn [动] set … up (*pt, pp* set)

组织 zǔzhī **I** [动] organize **II** [名] **1** (集体) organization **2** (指器官) tissue **3** (指纱线) weave

组装 zǔzhuāng [动] assemble

祖 zǔ [名] **1** (祖辈) grandparent ♦祖母 grandmother **2** (祖宗) ancestor **3** (首创者) founder

祖传 zǔchuán [动] hand … down

祖父 zǔfù [名] grandfather

祖国 zǔguó [名] motherland

祖籍 zǔjí [名] ancestral home

祖母 zǔmǔ [名] grandmother

祖师 zǔshī [名] founder

祖先 zǔxiān [名] ancestors (*pl*)

祖宗 zǔzong [名] ancestors (*pl*)

钻 zuān [动] **1** (打洞) drill ♦钻探 drilling **2** (穿过) go through (*pt* went, *pp* gone) **3** (钻研) bury one's head in
▷另见 zuàn

钻空子 zuān kòngzi exploit loopholes

钻探 zuāntàn [动] drill

钻研 zuānyán [动] study … intensively

钻营 zuānyíng [动] further one's own interests

钻 zuàn [名] **1** (工具) drill ♦电钻 electric drill **2** (钻石) diamond ♦钻戒 diamond ring
▷另见 zuān

钻石 zuànshí [名] **1** (金刚石) diamond **2** (宝石) jewel

嘴 zuǐ [名] **1** (口) mouth **2** (嘴状物) ◇茶壶嘴 spout of a teapot **3** (话) words (*pl*) ♦插嘴 interrupt

嘴尖 zuǐ jiān [形] sharp-tongued ◇他不但嘴尖，脸皮也厚。He's not just sharp-tongued but also very thick-skinned.

嘴紧 zuǐ jǐn [形] tight-lipped

嘴脸 zuǐliǎn [名] features (*pl*)

嘴碎 zuǐ suì [形] talkative

嘴甜 zuǐ tián [形] ingratiating

嘴硬 zuǐ yìng [形] stubborn

最 zuì [副] most ◇最难忘的海外之旅 the most unforgettable trip abroad ◇这家饭店服务最好。The service at this restaurant is the best. ◇3人中他薪水最高。He's got the highest salary of the three.

最惠国 zuìhuìguó [名] most-favoured (英) 或 most-favored (美) nation

最近 zuìjìn [形] recent ◇最近的一期杂志 a recent edition of the magazine ◇他最近发表了几篇文章。He's recently published several essays.

罪 zuì I [名] 1 (恶行) crime ♦犯罪 commit a crime 2 (过失) blame ♦归罪 lay the blame on others 3 (苦难) hardship ♦遭罪 encounter hardship 4 (刑罚) punishment ♦死罪 death sentence II [动] blame ♦怪罪 blame

罪恶 zuì'è [名] crime

罪犯 zuìfàn [名] criminal

罪过 zuìguo [名] fault

罪魁 zuìkuí [名] chief culprit

罪名 zuìmíng [名] charge

罪孽 zuìniè [名] sin

罪行 zuìxíng [名] crime

罪证 zuìzhèng [名] evidence of a crime

罪状 zuìzhuàng [名] crime

醉 zuì I [形] 1 (饮酒过量的) drunk ♦醉鬼 drunk 2 (用酒泡制的) steeped in wine II [动] drink too much (*pt* drank, *pp* drunk) ♦陶醉 revel in

醉生梦死 zuì shēng mèng sǐ drunken haze

醉翁之意不在酒 zuì wēng zhī yì bù zài jiǔ have an ulterior motive

醉心 zuìxīn [动] be engrossed in

醉醺醺 zuìxūnxūn [形] drunk

尊 zūn I [形] senior II [动] respect III [量] ◇一尊神像 an image of a deity

尊称 zūnchēng I [名] term of address II [动] address

尊崇 zūnchóng [动] revere

尊贵 zūnguì [形] respected

尊敬 zūnjìng [动] respect

尊严 zūnyán I [形] dignified II [名] dignity

尊重 zūnzhòng I [动] respect II [形] serious ◇放尊重些！ Behave yourself!

遵 zūn [动] follow

遵从 zūncóng [动] follow

遵守 zūnshǒu [动] observe ◇遵守纪律 observe discipline ◇遵守命令 comply with orders ◇遵守法律 abide by the law

遵循 zūnxún [动] follow

遵照 zūnzhào [动] obey

作 zuō [名] workshop ▷另见 zuò

作坊 zuōfang [名] workshop

昨 zuó [名] 1 (昨天) yesterday ♦昨日 yesterday 2 (过去) the past ◇今是昨非 repent of past actions

昨天 zuótiān [名] yesterday

琢 zuó 见下文 ▷另见 zhuó

琢磨 zuómo [动] ponder

左 zuǒ I [名] left ♦左边 the left II [形] 1 (相反的) conflicting ◇观点相左 conflicting opinions 2 (进步的) leftist ♦左派 left-wing

左顾右盼 zuǒ gù yòu pàn look around

左撇子 zuǒpiězi [名] ◇她是左撇子。She is left-handed.

左右 zuǒyòu I [名] 1 (左和右) left and right ◇他左右各站一名保镖。Bodyguards stood to his left and right. 2 (跟随者) attendants (*pl*) 3 (上下) ◇他身高1点75米左右。He is about 1.75 metres (英) 或 meters (美) tall. II [动] control ◇左右政局 control the political situation

左…右… zuǒ…yòu… again and again ◇我左一句右一句地劝他别辞职。I tried again and again to persuade him not to give up his job.

左右逢源 zuǒ yòu féng yuán succeed regardless

左右开弓 zuǒ yòu kāi gōng use each hand alternately ◇他左右开弓凌空射门。He shot first with his right foot and then with his left.

左右手 zuǒyòushǒu [名] (喻) right-hand man

左右为难 zuǒ yòu wéi nán be in a dilemma ◇去也不好，不去也不好，真让我左右为难。It's a problem if I go, but also a problem if I don't – I'm in a real dilemma.

佐 zuǒ **I** [动] assist **II** [名] assistant

佐料 zuǒliào [名] seasoning

佐证 zuǒzhèng [名] evidence

作 zuò **I** [动] **1** (起) rise (*pt* rose, *pp* risen) ◇鞭炮声大作。There was a sudden loud noise of firecrackers. **2** (写) write (*pt* wrote, *pp* written) ◆作家 writer ◆作曲 compose music **3** (装) pretend ◆造作 affected **4** (犯) do (*pt* did, *pp* done) ◆作案 commit a crime **5** (当) take … as (*pt* took, *pp* taken) ◆作废 become invalid **6** (发作) feel (*pt, pp* felt) ◆作呕 feel sick **II** [名] work ◆杰作 masterpiece ▷另见 zuō

作罢 zuòbà [动] drop

作弊 zuòbì [动] cheat

作壁上观 zuò bì shàng guān be an onlooker

作对 zuòduì [动] **1** (为敌) oppose **2** (成对) partner

作法 zuòfǎ [名] **1** (写法) writing technique **2** (做法) method

作风 zuòfēng [名] style

作家 zuòjiā [名] writer

作假 zuòjiǎ [动] **1** (冒充) fake **2** (耍花招) play tricks **3** (故作客套) stand on ceremony (*pt, pp* stood)

作茧自缚 zuò jiǎn zì fù make things difficult for oneself

作践 zuòjian [动] (口) run … down (*pt* ran, *pp* run)

作乐 zuòlè [动] enjoy oneself

作美 zuòměi [动] make things easy

作难 zuònán [动] be in a quandary

作孽 zuòniè [动] commit a sin

作弄 zuònòng [动] tease

作呕 zuò'ǒu [动] feel sick (*pt, pp* felt)

作陪 zuòpéi [动] help entertain

作品 zuòpǐn [名] work ◇文学作品 literary work

作曲 zuòqǔ [动] compose music

作威作福 zuò wēi zuò fú act like a tyrant

作为 zuòwéi **I** [名] **1** (行为) action ◇我们要根据一个人的作为来评判他。We should judge a person by their actions. **2** (成绩) accomplishment ◇有所作为 considerable accomplishment **3** (干头儿) scope **II** [动] **1** (当作) regard … as ◇我把种花作为一种休闲方式。I regard gardening as a form of relaxation. **2** (身为) ◇作为一名母亲，抚育儿女是她的责任。As a mother, looking after one's children is one's responsibility.

作文 zuòwén [动] write an essay (*pt* wrote, *pp* written)

作物 zuòwù [名] crop

作秀 zuòxiù [动] (贬) put a positive spin on things (*pt, pp* put)

作业 zuòyè **I** [名] work ◇野外作业 fieldwork **II** [动] do work

作用 zuòyòng **I** [动] affect **II** [名] **1** (影响) effect **2** (活动) action

作者 zuòzhě [名] author

坐 zuò [动] **1** (坐下) sit (*pt, pp* sat) ◇坐在窗口 sit by the window **2** (乘坐) travel by ◇坐飞机 travel by plane

坐班 zuòbān [动] work nine to five

坐标 zuòbiāo [名] coordination

坐吃山空 zuò chī shān kōng fritter away a fortune

坐次 zuòcì [名] seating plan

坐而论道 zuò ér lùn dào sit and pontificate

坐井观天 zuò jǐng guān tiān have a restricted outlook

坐牢 zuòláo [动] be in prison

坐冷板凳 zuò lěngbǎndèng be sidelined

坐立不安 zuò lì bù ān be on tenterhooks

坐落 zuòluò [动] be located

坐位 zuòwèi [名] seat

坐享其成 zuò xiǎng qí chéng benefit from others' efforts

坐以待毙 zuò yǐ dài bì sit and await one's fate

坐镇 zuòzhèn [动] take personal command (*pt* took, *pp* taken)

座 zuò **I** [名] **1** (坐位) seat ♦座号 seat number **2** (垫子) stand ◇茶杯座 coaster **3** (星座) constellation ◇双子座 Gemini **II** [量] ◇一座山 a mountain

座上客 zuòshàngkè [名] guest of honour (英) 或 honor (美)

座谈 zuòtán [动] discuss

座位 zuòwèi [名] seat

座无虚席 zuò wú xū xí have no empty seats ◇这部影片首映的时候，电影院里座无虚席。There was a full house at the film premier.

座右铭 zuòyòumíng [名] motto (*pl* mottoes)

做 zuò [动] **1** (制造) make (*pt*, *pp* made) ◇做个布娃娃 make a cloth doll **2** (写作) write (*pt* wrote, *pp* written) ◇做文章 write an essay **3** (从事) do (*pt* did, *pp* done) ◇做生意 do business **4** (举行) hold (*pt*, *pp* held) ◇做寿 hold a birthday party **5** (充当) be (*pt* was, were, *pp* been) ◇做大会主席 chair a meeting **6** (用作) be used as (*pt* was, were, *pp* been) ◇这块布可以做窗帘。This piece of cloth can be used as a curtain. **7** (结成) become (*pt* became, *pp* become) ◇做朋友 become friends

做爱 zuò'ài [动] make love

做伴 zuòbàn [动] keep … company (*pt*, *pp* kept)

做东 zuòdōng [动] be host ◇今天聚餐我做东。The meal today is my treat.

做法 zuòfǎ [名] method

做工 zuògōng **I** [动] work **II** [名] workmanship

做活儿 zuòhuór [动] work

做客 zuòkè [动] be a guest

做媒 zuòméi [动] be a matchmaker

做梦 zuòmèng [动] dream ◇你想当市长？别做梦了！ You want to be mayor? Dream on!

做人 zuòrén [动] **1** (待人接物) know how to behave (*pt* knew, *pp* known) **2** (当正派人) be an upright person

做声 zuòshēng [动] make a sound

做事 zuòshì [动] **1** (办事) deal with matters (*pt*, *pp* dealt) **2** (工作) work

做手脚 zuò shǒujiǎo [动] use underhand methods

做文章 zuò wénzhāng [动] (喻) make an issue of

做戏 zuòxì [动] **1** (演戏) put on a play (*pt*, *pp* put) **2** (假装) pretend

做贼心虚 zuò zéi xīn xū have a guilty conscience

做主 zuòzhǔ [动] decide

做作 zuòzuo [形] affected

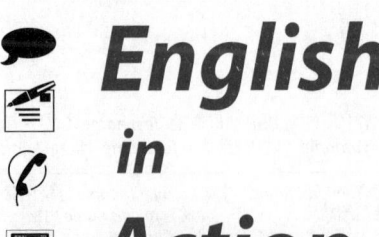

English in Action

▼ 姓名和称谓

姓名

在说英语的国家中，姓名是由父母取的 *first name*（名字）和父母双方或一方的 *surname*（姓氏）组成。*forename* 即 *first name*。

> **i** 许多人还有 *middle name*（中名）。*middle name* 也是由父母取的，通常用缩略形式，而不用全称。*middle name* 用缩略形式在美国尤为常见：*John F Kennedy*。*Christian name*（教名）是指基督徒给孩子取的名字。

姓名缩写

initials（姓名缩写）是由某人的 *first name, middle name* 和 *surname* 的第一个字母的大写形式组成。例如，如果某人的全名是 *Elizabeth Margaret White*，她的姓名缩写即为 *EMW*。在某些商务和银行业环境中，她可以自称或被称为：*E.M. White*。
作者的姓名通常用 *initials*：*J.K. Rowling, E.M. Forster*。

先生、夫人等

如果某人不是你的朋友，你可以用头衔加姓氏礼貌地称呼他。*Mr*（先生）用于男士的姓氏前。已婚女士被称为 *Mrs*（夫人），未婚女士使用 *Miss*（小姐）或 *Ms*（女士）。

Mr Nichols can see you now.（用于办公室会话）

人们有时也用这种比较礼貌的方式称呼比自己年长的人。

We'd better let Mrs Townsend know.
Perhaps you should invite Mr Thomson as well.

> **i** 过去，已婚的女性总是改用夫姓。如今，一些女性婚后仍延用自己的姓氏。如果不清楚一位女士是否已婚，可使用称呼 *Ms*。一些较年轻的女性更倾向于使用 *Ms*，而不是 *Mrs* 或 *Miss*，但是较年长的女性则不喜欢使用 *Ms* 这一称呼。

知名人士

一般只用姓氏来称呼作家、作曲家、艺术家和其他知名人士。

the works of Shakespeare
the paintings of Van Gogh

昵称

人们常用 *nickname*，名字的非正式形式，来称呼他人，在会话中是如此。许多名字都有约定俗成的简短形式。例如，如果某人字是 *James*，人们可以称他为 *Jamie*，*Jim* 或 *Jimmy*。

日常交流

▼ 称呼他人

称呼不认识的人

- 如果你想引起某个不认识的人的注意 —— 比如，在大街上或在商店里 —— 通常说 *Excuse me*。

  Excuse me. You've dropped your scarf.
  Excuse me. I think I'm next.

- 在现代英语中，*Mr*，*Mrs*，*Miss* 和 *Ms* 作为头衔，只用在姓氏前，而不能单独使用。*gentleman* 或 *lady*，*sir* 或 *madam* 也都不能单独用来称呼不认识的人。*sir* 或 *madam* 通常是商店中的工作人员用于招呼顾客时才用的礼貌性称呼。

> **i** 在正式的场合称呼一群人 —— 例如，开会时 —— 可用 *ladies and gentlemen*。如果是性别单一的一群人，可以只称呼 *ladies* 或 *gentlemen*。
> *Good evening, ladies and gentlemen.*

称呼认识的人

- 如果你知道对方的姓氏，你可用头衔（通常是 *Mr*，*Mrs* 或 *Miss*）加姓氏称呼他们。这种用法相当正式。初次见面，或在电话中与你不认识的人交谈时，你会使用这种称呼方式。

  Thank you, Mr Jones.
  Goodbye, Dr Kirk

- 在英国、美国、澳大利亚等国的工作场所中，人们通常直呼名字，甚至对老板也是如此。在学校里，学生通常用 *Mr*，*Mrs* 或 *Miss* 加上姓氏称呼老师。在许多日常会话中，除非你想特别指明说话的对象，否则根本不用提及对方的姓名。

  What do you think, John?
  Are you going to the meeting with the new Finance Director?

> ⚠ 在 *Mr*，*Mrs* 和 *Miss* 后，只能加姓氏，而绝对不能加名。

▼ 问候

与人打招呼

- 与人打招呼通常用 *hello*。这个词既非太正式，又不会太随便，适用于大多数场合。在 *hello* 的后面，通常加上对方的名字或寒暄的话。

  'Hello, Tina.' — 'Hello. How are you today?'
  Hello, John. Had a good day?

- *hi* 或 *hiya*是更为随便的问候方式，在年轻人中以及美式英语中尤为常用。

  Hiya, Tommy. How are you doing?

- 若要以正式方式问候他人，所用的词要视一天里的具体时间而定。

  中午12点钟之前说 *good morning*。

  Good morning, Mr Wright. How are you today?

  中午12点钟和6点钟之间说 *good afternoon*，6点之后人们说 *good evening*。

  Good afternoon. Could I speak to Ms Duff, please?
  Good evening. I'd like a table for four, please.

在拨打正式电话，以及与政府官员、商界人士等会面时，通常使用这些问候形式。

> ⚠ 只有晚间与人告别，或当自己或他人上床睡觉之前，才能说 *good night*。它不能用来问候别人。
> *good day* 在英式英语中是一种已经过时，并且相当正式的说法，但在美式英语和澳大利亚英语中仍较为常见。

- 如果某人说 *How are you?*，你可以简单地回答 *Very well, thank you.* 或 *Fine, thanks.*。你也可以礼貌地反问一声 *How are you?*，或更随便些 *And you?*。

  'Hello, John. How are you?' — 'Fine, thanks, Mark. And you?'

- 在见面问候或告别时显得热情而有礼貌，人们有时说 *Nice to see you.*。

  'Hello, it's nice to see you again. How are you?' – 'Nice to see you too, Mr Bates.'

日常交流

特别的日子

- 在某人的生日见到其人时，可以说 *Happy Birthday!* 或 *Many happy returns!*。
- 在圣诞节见到别人时，可以说 *Merry Christmas!* 或 *Happy Christmas!*。
- 在新年，你可以祝愿人们 *Happy New Year!*。

分别

- 与人分别时，说 *goodbye*。这种表达方式有点正式。

  'Goodbye, John,' Miss Saunders said.

- *bye* 是更常用的告别方式，而且比较随便。

  See you about seven. Bye.

- *bye-bye* 的语气更加随便，它用于关系密切的亲戚和朋友之间，以及向小孩子道别时。

  Bye-bye, dear. See you tomorrow.

> **i** 道晚安时，可以用 *goodnight* 或 *night*。
> *Well, I must be going. Night, John.*
> *I'm off to bed. Goodnight, everyone.*

- 如果你认为很快能再次见到对方，可以说 *See you later.*。

  'See you later.' – 'Okay, bye.'
  See you on Monday.

- 许多讲美式英语的人会用 *have a nice day* 向他们不太熟识的人道别。例如，在商店或酒店中工作的人员会对顾客这样说。

> ⚠ 在现代英语中，*good morning*，*good afternoon* 和 *good evening* 不用于告别。

> **i** 在正式场合，比如商务会议，人们通常用握手以示问候或道别。在不太正式的场合下表示问候或道别，男士们也会握手，或者，互相轻拍后背或肩膀，而女士们则常常亲吻女性或男性亲友。在问候或道别时，你也可以只用上述表达方式而不使用任何肢体动作，如握手、拍肩或是亲吻。

▼ 自我介绍和介绍他人

自我介绍

- 与陌生人初次见面，在自我介绍时，可以告诉对方你的姓名或介绍你是谁。你需要先说 *hello* 或其他客套的话。

  'Hello. I'm Harry,' said the boy.
  'I don't think we've met, have we? Are you visiting?' – 'Yes, I'm Peter Taylor.'

- 如果想显得正式些，则说 *May I introduce myself?*。

  May I introduce myself? I'm Dr Anderson.

> *i* 初次见面说 *How do you do?*，是一种极为正式，并且已经过时的表达方式。正确的回答也应是 *How do you do?*。
>
> *'I'm Nigel Jessop. How do you do?' – 'How do you do? I'm Alison Vere.'*

介绍他人

- 在介绍从未谋面的人相互认识时，说 *This is ...*。介绍时，使用何种姓名形式可以视场合的正式程度而定（见第2页）。

  This is Shirley , Mr McKay. Shirley, this is Mr McKay.

- 如果需要正式些，则说 *I'd like to introduce ...*。

  Mr Anderson, I'd like to introduce my wife.

- 比较随意的介绍某人的方式是 *I don't think you know ..., do you?*。

  'I don't think you know Ann, do you?' – ' No, I don't think we've met. How are you?'

> ⚠ 用手指指着别人介绍是很无礼的行为。但是，可以用手指指着物品或指示方向。

对介绍的应答

- 当你被介绍给对方后，你们双方都互道 *hello*。

  'Francis, this is James.' – 'Hello, Francis. How are you?'

- 如果双方都很年轻，而且不是在很正式的场合，可以说 *hi*。

  'Jan, this is my boyfriend Jeff.' – 'Hi, Jeff.'

日常交流

▼ 邀请

邀请某人做某事

- 通常，礼貌地邀请某人做某事，应说 *Would you like to ...?*。

  Would you like to come to my party on Saturday?
  Well, would you like to comment on that, Tessa? (在会议或讨论中)

- 另一种礼貌的邀请形式是，祈使句与 *please* 连用。这种形式多由处于主导位置的一方使用。

  Please help yourself to a drink.
  Sit down, please.

- 也可用 *How would you like to ...?* 或 *Why don't you ...?* 间接地邀请某人，或用以 *how about* 开头的问句邀请。

  How would you like to come and work for me?
  Why don't you come to the States with us in November?
  How about coming to stay for a few days?
  How about some lunch?

> ***i*** 如果应邀到某人家中做客，通常要带小礼物，比如鲜花或蛋糕。如被邀请就餐，大多数人会顺便带一瓶酒。主人通常会当面打开礼物。

回应邀请

- 如果接受邀请，就说 *thank you*。如果更加随便的话，就说声 *thanks*。

  'You could borrow our tent if you'd like.' – 'Thank you. I'll come round and pick it up some time.'

  也可加一句 *Yes, I'd love to.* 或 *I'd like that very much.*。

  'Won't you join me for lunch?' – 'Thanks, I'd like that very much.'

- 如果拒绝邀请，不愿拜访某人或随某人去某地，则说 *I'm sorry, I can't.*。如果想解释原因，则用 *I'm afraid ...* 或 *I'd like to but ...*，再加上原因。

  'Can you come and spend the day with me on Sunday?' – 'Oh, I'm sorry. I can't.'
  'We're having a party on Saturday. Can you come?' – 'I'm afraid I'm busy.'
  'Would you like to stay for dinner?' – 'I'd like to but I can't tonight.'

▼ 感谢他人

表示感谢

- 如果别人刚刚为你做了某事，或送给你某物，表示感谢的常用方式是说 *thank you*，或更随意地说声 *thanks*。

  'Don't worry. I've given you a good reference.' – 'Thank you, Mr Dillon.'
  'There's your receipt.' – 'Thanks.' (在商店)

- 人们常常加上 *very much* 以加强语气。

  'Here you are.' – 'Thank you very much.'

  你也可以说 *Thanks a lot.*（但不能说 *Thank you a lot.* 或 *Thanks lots.*）。

  'I'll ring you tomorrow morning.' – 'OK. Thanks a lot.'

- 如果需要解释为何感谢对方，则说 *Thank you for ...* 或 *Thanks for ...*。

  Thank you for the earrings, Dad.
  Thanks for helping out.

  在信中感谢某人（见第19页），一般都说 *Thank you for ...*。

  Dear Madam, Thank you for your letter of 5 June.

  在正式的商务信函中，可以用 *I am grateful for ...*。

  I am grateful for your prompt reply to my request.

  如果是给朋友的信，则用 *Thanks for ...*。

  Thanks for writing.

> **i** 你会听到一些讲英式英语的人说 *cheers* 或 *ta* 表示感谢，这是非正式的表达方式。

如果某人请你吃东西，表示拒绝时，可以说 *No, thank you.* 或 *No, thanks.*（不能只说 *Thank you.*）。

'Would you like a coffee?' – 'No, thank you.'

如何回答感谢

- 如果某人因你帮忙而表示感谢，则应回答 *That's all right.* 或 *That's OK.*。

  'Thank you, Charles.' – 'That's all right, David.'

  如果想显得既礼貌又友好，可以说 *It's a pleasure.* 或 *Pleasure.*。

  'Thank you very much for talking to us about your research.' – 'It's a pleasure.'

▼道歉

致歉

- 如果打扰了某人或麻烦了某人，有多种道歉方式。最常用的是 *sorry* 或 *I'm sorry*。

  'Stop that, you're giving me a headache.' – 'Sorry.'
  Sorry I'm late.

  可以在 *I'm sorry* 中加上副词 *very*，*so*，*terribly* 或 *extremely*，加强语势。

  I'm very sorry if I worried you.
  I'm terribly sorry but I have to leave.

> *i* 当不小心做了某事，例如踩了某人的脚，可以说 *sorry* 或 *I'm sorry*。讲美式英语的人则说 *excuse me*。

- 当打搅了某人或打断了某人的工作时，用 *Excuse me, I'm sorry to disturb you.*。这是礼貌的道歉方式。

  Excuse me for disturbing you at home.
  I'm sorry to disturb you but I need your signature.

- 如果想请某人让一下路，或想同陌生人讲话时，可以用 *excuse me*。一些说美式英语的人则会说 *pardon me*。

  Excuse me, but is there a good restaurant near here?
  Excuse me, do you mind if I squeeze past you?
  Pardon me, Sergeant. I wonder if you'd do me a favor? (美)

- 如果因需要做某事而不得不离开片刻，例如在商务环境中，或与不太熟识的人在一起时，也可以说 *Excuse me*。

  Excuse me for a moment. I have to make a telephone call.

> *i* 如果做了令人尴尬或失礼的事时，譬如打饱嗝、打嗝、打喷嚏或吃东西时发出声音，应该道歉。人们通常会说 *excuse me* 或 *I beg your pardon*。

接受道歉

- 接受道歉通常有固定的表达形式，例如 *That's okay.*，*Don't worry about it.*，或 *It doesn't matter.*。

  'I'm sorry.' – 'That's okay.'
  'I apologize for what I said.' – 'Don't worry about it.'
  'I'm sorry to ring so late.' – 'I'm still up. It doesn't matter.'

▼ 请某人重复所说过的话

- 让某人重复所说的话时，通常用固定的简短表达方式，例如 *Sorry?*，*I'm sorry?*，或 *Pardon?*。这些都是非正式的说法。

  'Have you seen the guide book anywhere?'
  'Sorry?'
  'The guide book.' (英)

  在美式英语中，通常用 *Excuse me?* 或 *Pardon me?*。

  'How old is she?'
  'Pardon me?'
  'I said how old is she?' (美)

- 也可用 *wh-* 开头的特殊疑问词，核对对方所说过的部分内容。

  'Can I speak to Nick, please?'
  'Who?'
  'Nick.'
  'We're going to Spain in April.'
  'Where?'
  'Spain.'

⚠ 当与不太熟识的人说话时 —— 例如，在电话中 —— 使用稍长一些的表达形式，譬如 *I'm sorry, I didn't quite catch that.* 或 *I'm sorry, would you mind repeating that, please?*。

'What about tomorrow at three?'
'I'm sorry, would you mind repeating that, please?'
'I said, what about meeting tomorrow at three?'

▼ 许可

请求许可

- *Can I …?* 用于请求许可做某事。

  Can I put the heating on? I'm cold.

  Could I …? 更礼貌些。若要显得愈加礼貌，例如在电话中或在商务环境中，则加上 *please*。

  Could I stay at your place for a bit, Rob?
  Good afternoon. Could I speak to Mr Duff, please?

- 用 *Would it be all right if I …?* 或 *Would it be all right to …?* 一类的表达形式，比较间接地请求许可。

  Would it be all right if I used your phone?
  Would it be all right to take one of these brochures?

  在不太正式的情况下，可以说 *Is it okay if I …?*

  Is it okay if I smoke?

  更加礼貌的方式是说 *Do you mind if I …?* 或 *Would you mind if I …?*。

  Do you mind if we speak English?
  Would you mind if I just asked you a few questions?

> **i** 在英国和美国，许多人不喜欢别人抽烟，所以当在某人家中做客或与他人外出时，在抽烟前先征求对方许可是非常礼貌的做法。

准许某人的请求

- 在非正式的场合，可以只说 *OK* 或 *all right*。

  'Could I have a word with you, please?' – 'OK.'

- *sure* 语气稍微强些，且用于美式英语。

  'Can I go with you?' – 'Sure.'

- *of course* 和 *by all means* 比较正式，语气也较强。

  'Could I make a telephone call?' – 'Of course.'
  'Can I come too?' – 'By all means.'

拒绝请求

- 拒绝某人请求最常用的方式是用 *Sorry*，*I'm sorry* 或 *I'm afraid not* 等，然后解释原因。

  'Could I see him for a few minutes?' – 'I'm sorry, you can't. He's very ill.'

▼ 同意和不同意

寻求赞同

- 反问句可以用来询问某人是否同意自己的说法。使用反问句，通常是期望他人同意自己的观点。

That's an extremely interesting point, isn't it?
The film was really good, wasn't it, Andy?
Property in London is quite expensive, isn't it?

- 在表示喜欢或不喜欢某事，或认为某事是对是错后，可以用反问句 *don't you?* 寻求对方的赞同。代词 *you* 重读。

I love these shoes, don't YOU?
I think it would be best if I left, don't YOU?

表示同意

- 表明赞同某人或某事最简单的方式，是说 *yes*。人们常常用 *mm* 来代替 *yes*。

'You like jazz, don't you?' – 'Yes.'
'She's a bit strange, isn't she?' – 'Mm.'

可以在 *yes* 后面加上适当的动词形式。

'I was really rude to you at the party.' – 'Yes, you were.'

也可以在 *yes* 后面跟一个反问句。

'That car's fantastic!' – 'Yes, it is, isn't it?'

⚠ 如果对某个带有否定词的陈述表示同意，应说 *no* 而不是 *yes*。
'She's not a very nice person.'- 'No.'

- 在表示同意某事是事实时，可以用以下表达方式 *That's right.*，*That's true.* 或 *True.*。

'I'll have more to spend then.' – 'Yes, that's true.'

i *I agree* 是相当正式的表达方式。
'The whole thing's a disaster.' – 'I agree.'

- 当某人说出他所喜欢的事物或他的想法时，可以用 *So do I.* 或 *I do too.* 来表明自己同意他的观点。

'I find that amazing.' – 'So do I.'
'I love champagne.' – 'Yes, I do too.'

如果对某人带有否定的观点表示同意时，则可以说 *Neither do I.* 或 *I don't either.*。

'I don't like him.' – 'Neither do I.'

- 可以用 *absolutely* 这样的表达方式来表示完全同意，语气强烈。

'I thought her performance was brilliant.' '– Absolutely.'

如果表示同意，但并不完全同意某人的观点时，可以说 *I suppose so.* 或 *I suppose not.*。美式英语用 *I guess so.*。

'Some of these places haven't changed a bit.' – 'I suppose not.' (英)

> **i** 你会发现，说英语国家的人们常运用面部表情、手势或其他肢体动作，来强调同意或不同意，或发表看法。其中最常见的是，上下点头表示同意或允许某人做某事，左右摇头表示不同意或不允许做某事。

表示不同意

- 人们通常避免说 *no*，不直接表示完全不赞同，以此显得比较礼貌。人们用 *I don't think so.* 和 *Not really.* 等表达方式使不赞同的话听上去柔和些。

'You'll change your mind one day.' – 'Well, I don't think so.'
'That sort of holiday must be really expensive.' – 'Well, not really.'

- 人们常常先说 *yes* 或 *I see what you mean*，然后再用 *but* 引出表示反对的观点。

'It's a very clever book.' – 'Yes, perhaps, but I didn't like it.'

- 在正式场合，可以使用以下任何一种表达方式：

'She was a brilliant prime minister.' – 'I totally disagree.'
'University education can divide families.' – 'I can't go along with that.'
'We ought to be asking the teachers what they think.' – 'With respect, shouldn't you be asking the students too?'

▼ 反应

有几种对听到和看到的事作出反应的方式表达。

感叹句

- 感叹句常用来表达对某事的反应。

Wonderful!
Oh dear!
That's awful!

- 有时用 *how* 和 *what* 引出感叹句。*how* 一般与形容词连用，并且形容词后没有其他句子成分。

'He never rang, even though he said he would.' – 'How strange!'

what 用于名词前。如果用单数可数名词，则必须在 *what* 后面加不定冠词 *a*（或 *an*）。

'I can't come on Saturday. I've got to work.' – 'What a shame!'
What an awful thing to say!

表示惊奇或感兴趣

- 表示惊奇可以用 *Really?*，或其他简短的固定表达方式，譬如 *good heavens*。

'It only takes 35 minutes to get into town from my house.'
– 'Really?'
Good heavens, is that the time?

> ⚠ *Good God* 和 *My God* 是相当常见的表达方式，语气强烈。因为这可能会冒犯信仰宗教的人，所以应该慎用。

- 反问句可用于表示惊奇或感兴趣。

'He goes swimming every day.' – 'Does he?'

- *that's* … 或 *how* … 可与形容词连用，例如 *strange* 或 *interesting*，用于表示惊奇或感兴趣。

'He said he hated the place.' – 'How strange! I wonder why.'
'They both say they saw a light in the sky.' – 'How interesting.'

表示愉快

- 可以用 *That's great.* 或 *That's wonderful.* 等表示对某个情形或某人所说的话感到高兴。

'I've booked the flights.' – 'Oh, that's great.'

- 你也可单独使用形容词，例如 *Wonderful.*。

'We can give you an idea of what the final price would be.'
– 'Wonderful.'

表示如释重负

- *Oh good.* 或 *That's all right then.* 用于表达听到某事感到松了口气。

'I think he'll understand.' – 'Oh good.'
'Are the earrings all right?' – 'They're perfect.' – 'Good, that's all right then.'

- 也可以说 *That's a relief.* 或 *What a relief!*。

He didn't seem to notice.' – 'Well, that's a relief.'

- *thank God* 或 *thank goodness* 之类的表达方式可用于表示如释重负。

Thank God you're safe!
'I've found your passport.' – 'Thank goodness for that.'

表示恼怒

- 可以用 *Oh no!* 来表示恼怒。也可以说 *That's a nuisance.* 或 *What a nuisance.*。

  'I don't know if we'll make it to the airport in time.' – 'Oh no!'
  'I'm sorry. He's just left.' – 'What a nuisance!'

⚠ 你可能会听到有人用骂人的话表示恼怒，但你不能这么说，因为，听上去特别粗鲁无礼。

表示失望或忧虑

- 可以用 *Oh dear.*，*That's/What a pity.* 或 *That's/What a shame.* 来表达失望、烦乱之情。

  Oh dear. I wonder where they are.
  'I'm leaving New York tomorrow.' – 'That's a shame.'

- 如果非常心烦，则说 *Oh no!*。

  'John's had a nasty accident.' – 'Oh no! What happened?'

表示同情

- 当某人告诉你发生在他们身上不好的事情时，可以说 *Oh dear.*。

  'It was pouring with rain.' – 'Oh dear.'

  也可以用 *how* 加一个恰当的形容词。

  'We couldn't even see the stage.' – 'Oh, how annoying.'

  也可以说 *What a pity.* 或 *What a shame.*。

  'The journey took us four hours.' – 'What a shame.'

- *I'm sorry to hear that.* 显得比较正式。

  'I was ill last week.' – 'I'm sorry to hear that.'

- 如果所发生的事情非常严重，可以说 *I'm so sorry.* 或 *That's terrible.*。

  'You remember my sister? Well, she died last month.' – 'I'm so sorry.'
  'I've just lost my job.' – 'That's terrible.'

  如果某人未能做成某事，你可以说 *Bad luck.* 或 *Hard luck.*，暗示失败并非他们的过错。

  'I failed my driving test again.' – 'Oh, bad luck.'

▼ 写信该如何开头和结尾

给公司或组织机构的信件

称谓	结束语
Dear Sir *Dear Madam* *Dear Sir or Madam* *Dear Sirs* (英)/*Gentlemen* (美)	*Yours faithfully* (英) *Yours truly* (美)

如果是非常正式的信件，或不知道收信人的姓名，对男士用 *Dear Sir*，对女士则用 *Dear Madam*。如果不确定收信人的性别，写 *Dear Sir or Madam* 是最保险的。如果是写给公司而不是个人时，在英式英语中用 *Dear Sirs*，在美式英语中用 *Gentlemen*。

写给已知姓名的个人正式信件

称谓	结束语
Dear Ms Roberts *Dear Dr Jones* *Dear Professor Honeyford*	*Yours sincerely* (英) *Sincerely yours/Yours truly* (美)

结尾可用下列表达方式，显得不那么正式：

Yours
Kind regards
(With) best wishes

给朋友或熟人的信件

称谓	结束语
Dear Jeremy *Dear Aunt Jane* *Dear Granny* *Hi Josh*	*All the best* *Love (from)* *Lots of love (from)* *All my love*

男士给男士写信时，不常用 *Love*，*All my love* 和 *Lots of love*，而多用 *Yours*，*Best wishes* 或 *All the best* 一类的表达方式。

电子邮件

尽管有时也需要用电子邮件发送正式信函，但是，当人们写电子邮件时，普遍比写信要随意。信件的开头和结尾方式同样适用于电子邮件。

信件和电话

> **i** 人们在给关系亲密的朋友或男/女朋友写信或电子邮件时，往往在落款后加几个X。X代表吻。

▼ 英国地址

> **i** 邮政编码写在城市名称或地区名称的下面。

▼ 美国地址

> **i** 邮政编码写在城市名称和州名之后，州名用缩略形式。

- 寄往海外的信件通常要写发件人的地址。发件人的地址写在信封的背面，并在地址前加注 sender 或 from。
- 称呼通常由收信人的头衔、名字的首字母及姓氏组成：

Ms S Wilkins
Dr. P Smith

- 如果是非正式书信，可以只写收信人的名和姓：

Sarah Wilkins

- 如果收信人是已婚的夫妇，通常只写男方名字的首字母：

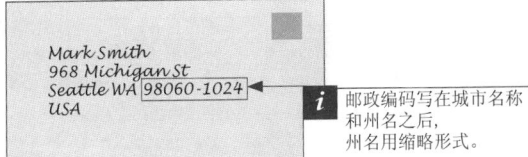

Mr and Mrs G T Black

信件和电话

▼给朋友的电子邮件

reply forward compose inbox get mail

To: gemma@net.co.uk
From: gordon@onemo.net
Subject: Concert next week
cc:
bcc:

> **i** 电子邮件（gemma@net.co.uk）的英文读法为：gemma **at** net **dot** co **dot** uk

Hi Gemma

I've just bought the new album by 'The Roads', and it's brilliant! I've got a spare ticket to a concert they're giving in Edinburgh next Wednesday evening, so I hope you can make it.

See you soon!

Gordon

▼商业电子信函

reply forward compose inbox get mail

To:kevin.morrison@unt.com
From:charles.stimpson@unt.com
Subject:Budget meeting
cc:
bcc:

Following on from our phone conversation this morning, the Budget meeting will now be held on Wednesday at 10 a.m. in the South Meeting Room. I hope that you can attend.

Charles

重点词组

To	收件人	Send	发送
From	发件人	Forward	转发
Subject	主题	Reply	答复发件人
Cc	抄送	Compose	撰写
Bcc	密件抄送	Delete	删除
Attachment	附件		

▼ 感谢信（英式）

41 Mallard Crescent
Leeds
LS6 9BR

i 在非正式信件中，地址和日期写在右上角，或只写日期。参见第45页日期的写法。

2 January 2003

Dear Tom and Lucy

Thank you for the lovely Christmas presents you sent me. The scarf is beautiful and the book is just what I wanted. As you know, J K Rowling is my favourite author.

I hear you're off to Spain soon. I'm so envious! I haven't got any holidays planned, but I'm going to London next weekend to see my aunt and uncle.

Thanks again for the presents, and have a great time in Spain. Don't forget to send me a postcard!

Lots of love

Carolyn

重点词组

可以用下列方式开头：
It was lovely to hear from you.
Thanks for your letter.
Sorry I haven't written sooner.
It was great to see you last weekend/week/Monday.

可以用下列方式结尾：
Write soon.
Look forward to seeing you soon.
Give my regards to Sally.
Julia sends you a big hug.

▼给笔友的信

14 Glebe Avenue
Bristol
BR6 7AL

14 August 2003

Dear Xiao Ming

I'm so excited to have a Chinese pen pal! I'm hoping to learn lots about your country and the way you live from your letters.

I thought I would start by telling you a few things about myself. I'm 14 years old and live with my mum and dad and my little sister, Jenny, in a city in the south of England. Our house has three bedrooms and a big garden. We have two cats who are quite old now and sleep all the time. My best friend, Jack, lives next door.

My school isn't far from the house, so I can walk there when it isn't raining. My favourite subjects are languages and geography. I'd like to learn to speak a few words in Chinese. Can you teach me something?

What sorts of things do you like doing in your spare time? I like playing on the computer and watching football. Mum says I should get more exercise!

Please write back soon and tell me all about yourself and your family. I can't wait to hear from you!

All the best

Nick

• 重点词组

I'm hoping to …
… a few things about myself/you …
What sorts of things … ?
I can't wait to hear from you

1386 Pine Boulevard
Los Angeles, California
20015

May 25, 2003

> *i* 以英式风格写信的人，在*Dear* ... 后面加逗号或不加任何标点。以美式风格写信的人，则在*Dear* ... 后面加冒号。参见第2页有关姓名和头衔的内容。

Dear Julia:
How are things? I'm sorry I haven't written earlier but I've been so busy moving into my new apartment.

It's my birthday on June 14 and I'm having a party to celebrate. Can you come? It starts at 7 p.m. and will probably end around midnight. There'll be food but please bring a bottle! If you'd like to stay the night, I have plenty of room and it will give us a chance to catch up on each other's news.

I hope you'll be able to come and look forward to hearing from you soon.

Love

Marie

▼酒店预订函(英式)

26 Guanghua Road
Chaoyang District
Beijing 100027
China

Mrs Elaine Hudson
Manager
Poppywell Cottage
Devon
DV3 9SP

23rd June 2003

Dear Mrs Hudson

> *i* 在商务信函的右上角，写上发信人自己的地址，但不要写发信人的姓名。日期紧跟在收信人地址的下一行。在信纸的左上角，通常在日期的下一行，写上收信人的姓名和/或职务头衔。如果使用带信头的信纸，日期写在收信人地址的上一行上或下一行，或写在信纸的右上角。参见第45页有关日期的写法。

My sister stayed with you last year and has recommended your guest house very highly.

I would like to reserve a room for one week from 18th–24th August. I would be very grateful if you would let me know how much this would be for two adults and two children and whether you have a room free between these dates.

Yours sincerely
Ming Li

ENGLISH IN ACTION

▼投诉信（美式）

323 Florida Grove Rd
Hopelawn
New Jersey
NJ 08851

Railroad Inc.
43 Abbeyhill Drive
Hopelawn
New Jersey
NJ 08952

November 27, 2003

Dear Sir or Madam:

I traveled from Atlantic City to New York on one of your trains last Thursday November 20 and am writing to let you know that I am very dissatisfied with the service you are providing.

The train was not only one hour late leaving Atlantic City it lost a further 30 minutes en route. The heating did not appear to be working and there was no restaurant car. I feel that your customers are paying very high prices for tickets to travel on your trains but are receiving a very unsatisfactory level of service. I have been very reluctant to take my car into the city and have no wish to add to the general congestion and pollution but you can be sure that I will be driving from now on.

Yours truly

Michael Pentangeli

▼英式工作申请函

CURRICULUM VITAE

Name: **Sarah Williamson**
Address:11 North Street, Barnton, NE6 2BT
Telephone: 01294 476230
E-mail: sarah@metalcomp.co.uk
Date of birth: 2 February 1970
Nationality: British

Qualifications

BA (Hons) in Business Studies (2.1), University of Newby,1991–1995
3 A-levels: Economics (A), German (B), Mathematics (C)
7 GCSEs: English Language, Mathematics, Physics, Biology, French, German, Geography

Employment

1997–present:	*Sales and Marketing Executive*, Metal Company plc, Barnton
1995–1997:	*Marketing Assistant*, Metal Company plc

Other skills

- Computer literate (Word for Windows, Excel)
- Good working knowledge of German
- Full, clean driving licence

Interests

- Travel (have travelled extensively throughout Europe and North America)
- Sailing
- Running marathons (New York 1999, Glasgow 2002)

Referees

Mrs Susan Beattie
Sales and Marketing Director
Metal Company plc
Barnton
NE4 3KL

Dr John Findlay
Department of Business Studies
University of Newby
Newby
NE13 2RR

▼工作申请书(英式)

11 North Street
Barnton
NE6 2BT

Director of Human Resources
Clifton Manufacturing Ltd
Firebrick House
Clifton
MK45 6RB

17 January 2003

Dear Sir or Madam

Re: Job Reference 685Z

With reference to your advertisement in the Guardian of 16 January, I wish to apply for the position of Marketing Manager in your company.

I am currently employed as a Sales and Marketing Executive for the Metal Company in Barnton, where my role is maintaining and developing links with our customers within the UK and producing material for marketing purposes.

I am interested in this position as it offers an opportunity to apply my sales and marketing skills in a new and challenging direction. I enclose my curriculum vitae for your consideration. Please do not hesitate to contact me if you require any further details.

Yours faithfully

Sarah Williamson

▼美式工作申请函

RÉSUMÉ

Name: Lisa Brown
Address: 110 West 92nd Street
New York
New York 10025
Telephone: 1-212-873-4150
E-mail: lisa.brown@skynet.com

Education
University of Pennsylvania, 1992-1994
Master of Arts in Business

Cornell University, 1987-1991
Bachelor of Arts in History, Magna Cum Laude

Employment
1997-present: General Sportswear Company, New York, New York: *Export Sales Co-ordinator:*
Sell the entire range of sportswear products to all key German accounts. Negotiate terms with all German customers, and conduct regular sales trips to Germany.

1994-1997: Brooklyn Candy Company, Brooklyn, New York: *Sales Representative:*
Sold the entire range of products to all key national and French accounts. Increased domestic sales by 24% in the fiscal year 1997.

Skills
- Fluent German. Working knowledge of French, Spanish, and Italian.
- Negotiating.
- Selling.
- Familiarity with many computer programs.
- Typing at 65 words per minute.

References
References available upon request.

▼工作申请书(美式)

110 West 92nd Street
New York, New York
10025

Mr. John Smith
Personnel Director
Thomas International Corporation
53 Madison Avenue
New York, New York
10016

January 17, 2003

Dear Mr. Smith

With reference to your advertisement in the New York Times of January 25, I wish to apply for the position of Export Sales Manager in your company.

I am currently employed as an Export Sales Co-ordinator with General Sportswear Company, have almost ten years of experience in sales and marketing, and am responsible for all sales to the German market. I speak fluent German, and have a working knowledge of French, Spanish, and Italian. I feel that my skills and experience would be great assets for your company in this position.

I enclose my résumé for your reference, and am available for an interview at any time. Please feel free to contact me if you require any further information.

Thank you for your time and consideration.

Sincerely

Lisa Brown

▼ 打电话

接通

- 下列表达可以帮助你找到正确的电话号码：

  What is the dialling code for Liverpool? (英式)
  What is the area code for Los Angeles? (美式)
  What is the number for directory enquiries? (英式)
  What is the number for directory assistance? (美式)
  I want to make a reverse-charge call to London. (英式)
  I want to make a collect call to London. (美式)
  How do I get an outside line?

开始通话

接听电话

- 接听电话时，通常先说 *hello*，或使用比较正式的问候方式（参见第4页）。如果当时你在工作，可以给出自己的姓名，所在部门或公司的名称，或给出电话号码或分机号码。参见第41页，如何报电话号码。

  Hello?
  Hello, Li Xin speaking.
  Good morning, Lotus Blossom Hotel. Can I help you?
  Eight six nine two three five seven. Hello?

如何问候接听电话的人

- 当对方接听电话并致以问候后，打电话的人通常也要问候对方，然后说 *It's ...* 或 *This is ...* 以表明自己的身份。

  Oh, hello. It's Mei Rong here.
  Hello. This is Rong.

结束通话

- 可以用第5页中任何一种告别方式结束通话。也可以说 *Speak to you soon.* 或 *Thanks for ringing.*。

在办公室

要求接通某人

- 如果你知道联络对方的姓名或分机号码，或想转接到某个特定部门，可以使用下列的短语。

  Hello. Could I speak to Susan, please?
  Hello. Is Paul there, please?
  Could you put me through to Dr Henderson, please?
  Can I have extension 5443, please?

- 如果你认为自己知道接听电话的人是谁，则可以问 *Is that ...?*。

如果正是其人，对方则回答 *Speaking.*。

'Hello. Is that Emma?' – 'Speaking.'

<u>接线员或秘书可能会说</u>…

- 如果是与接线员或秘书通话，他们可能会使用以下表达方式：

Who shall I say is calling?
Hold the line, please.
Hold on, I'll see if she's in.
I'll just get him.
One moment, please.
I'm putting you through now.
Dr Jackson is on another line. Do you want to hold?
There's no reply.
I'm sorry. Mr Green isn't here at the moment.
Would you like to leave a message?

<u>留言</u>

- 如果想找的人不在，你可以留言，告知晚些时候会再打，或者让别人转告，请他回电话。

Could I leave a message, please?
I'll call back in half an hour.
Would you ask him to call me when he gets back?

通话故障

- 如果无法接通想拨打的号码，可以用下列惯用语解释问题所在：

I can't get through.
Their phone is out of order.
I can't get a signal here.
I must have dialled the wrong number.
We were cut off.

- 也有可能无法听清对方的话：

We've got a crossed line.
This is a very bad line.
The line is breaking up.

<u>录音留言</u>

- 录音留言在英国和美国非常普遍，在大型公司或组织里就更加常见。无人接听电话时就会听到：

Your call is in a queue and will be answered shortly.
All our operatives (美) are busy at the moment. Please hold the line.
Please replace the handset and try again.
The number you are calling is engaged (英)/busy (美). Please try

ENGLISH IN ACTION

again later.
The number you have dialled has not been recognized.
Please hold the line while we try to connect you.

- 人们通常也会在家中的电话答录机上录下个人留言，以下是告知拨打电话的人何时开始录音的标准方式：

  Please speak after the tone (英)/*beep* (美).

▼ 手机短信

随着手机的出现, 一种新的短信"语言"诞生了, 并且因其迅捷、有趣, 尤其受到年轻人的青睐。它的特点是, 根据类似的发音, 采用简短的拼写方式: 例如, *U* 代表 *you*, *R* 代表 *are*, *d8* 代表 *date* 以及 *2nite* 代表 *tonight*。新的表达方式总是不断地出现。

2 = to
2DAY = today
2MORO = tomorrow
2NITE = tonight
2U = to you
4 = for
B = be
B4 = before
COZ = because
CU = see you
D8 = date
EZ = easy
GR8 = great
H8 = hate
L8R = later
LOL = laugh out loud/lots of love
LV = love
M8 = mate
MSG = message
NE = any
NE1 = anyone
OIC = oh I see
PLS = please
PPL = people
R = are
RN = right now
RU = are you
RUOK = are you OK?
S/O = someone
S/TH = something
SUM1 = someone
THX = thanks
TTFN = ta ta *or* by for now
TTYL = talk to you later
TXT = text
U = you
V = very
WAN2 = want to
WIV = with
XLNT = excellent
WKND = weekend
W/O = without
WUD = what are you doing?
Y = why
YR = your

THX 4 THE MSG.
XLNT NEWS! CU AT
THE WKND THEN.
LOL JAMES

ENGLISH IN ACTION

▼大写字母

- 大写字母用于句子的第一个单词，或某人所说的原话的第一个单词：

  We went to the theatre yesterday.
  Then our friends said, "We're going."

- 下列单词的第一个字母也必须大写：

  – 人名或机构名：

  Miss Helen Perkins from Price Waterhouse

  – 书名、电影名和戏剧名（但其间常用短词不用大写，比如 *of*, *the* 和 *and*）：

  Johnny Depp's new film, Pirates of the Caribbean

  – 地名：

  He was born in India in 1941.
  I'm going to Edinburgh tomorrow.

  – 日期、月份和节日名称：

  The trial continues on Monday.
  It was mid-December and she was going home for Christmas.

  – 表示来自或在某个特定国家或地方的人、物、事件的名词和形容词：

  the Germans and the British　*a French poet*
  the Californian earthquake

  – 作为商标的产品的名称：

  a secondhand Volkswagen
  a new Hoover

  – 用于某人名字前的头衔：

  President Bush
  King Henry II

  – 代词I：

  I thought I was alone.

- 下列大写字母和小写字母均可：

  – 表示方向的单词，例如 *north* 和 *southeast*：

  I'm from the north/North of England.

  – 表示年代的单词：

  music from the seventies/Seventies

  – 不带人名的头衔：

  a great prime minister/Prime Minister

拼写和标点

▼ 表示所属关系的撇号

- 撇号(')用于表示某物属于某人。它加在单数名词、代词或人名后，其后跟s。

my friend's house *someone's house* *Helen's house*

⚠
- 在以s结尾的名词的复数形式后加撇号。

  our friends' houses (= the houses of our friends)

- 撇号不用于构成物主代词：*yours, hers, ours* 和 *theirs*。也不用于构成名词复数：*apples, cars*。
- 以英语为母语的人也会被这些规则弄糊涂。在果蔬店或市场小摊上，你经常可以看到诸如"*tomatoe's*"或"*orange's*"这样的拼写，而不是 *tomatoes* 或 *oranges*。有时这种错误的用法被幽默地称为"果蔬店老板的撇号"。

▼ 动词缩写形式中的撇号

- 撇号用于单词的缩写形式中，表示一个或多个字母已经被省略。它常用于 *be, have, shall, will* 和 *would* 等词的缩写形式前：

  I'm terribly sorry. (= I am)
  I'll come round about seven. (= I will)
  It's really hot today. (= It is)

- 当 *not* 与前面的动词连写时，撇号也用于 *n* 和 *t* 之间：

  I can't see a thing. (= I cannot)
  I don't like him very much. (= I do not)
  I wouldn't do that if I were you. (= I would not)

- 你有时会发现撇号用在表示年份或年代的两个数字前：

  souvenirs from the '68 campaign (= 1968)
  the clothes we used to wear in the '60s and '70s (= 1960s and 1970s)

▼ 何时用连字符

- 连字符(-)用于连接构成一个形容词的两个或多个单词之间。只有当形容词位于被它所形容的名词前时，才使用连字符。当形容词位于名词之后时，连字符省略。

  a twentieth-century painter
  a step-by-step guide to giving up smoking
  a stained-glass window
  a painter from the twentieth century
  the stained glass above the door

- 一些表示家庭成员的常用名词，书写时使用连字符：

  mother-in-law father-in-law parents-in-law
  sister-in-law brother-in-law

如果一个名词是由多个词构成，而且第一部分只有一个字母，也应使用连字符：

  X-ray T-shirt

- 从21到99的数字，书写时通常带有连字符，不以 a 开头的分数也用连字符：

  sixty-two people
  one-third of those interviewed
  three-quarters of the company's senior management

- 前缀用于以大写字母开头的单词前时，往往后加连字符：

  a wave of anti-British feeling
  anti-American protesters

- 连字符用于表示有关联的两个国家或团体的形容词之间，或表示往返于两地之间：

  Swedish-Norwegian relations
  the New York-Montreal train

> *i* 在印刷文本中，当一个完整的单词在一行中写不下，而得断开写到下一行时，在断词的行末使用连字符，表示该单词转至下一行。

> ⚠ 许多由多个词构成的名词、动词和形容词，书写时使用连字符。为确定单词的拼写，你应该查阅字典英语部分的相关词条：
>
> *non-smoker push-up self-confidence*
> *absent-minded short-lived*

▼ 基本拼写规则

这些基本拼写规则旨在帮助你拼写新词或难词。

双写辅音字

- 以元音开头的词尾，例如 *-ance*, *-ence*, *-ing*, *-er* 或 *-ed*，加在以单元音加一个辅音结尾的词后时，如果重音落在单词的最后一个音节上，或单词只有一个音节时，双写辅音。（在下列例子中，重读音节用横线标出）

  *ad<u>mit</u> + ance = admi**tt**ance*

*be<u>gin</u> + ing = begi**nn**ing*
*stop + ed = sto**pp**ed*
*run + er = ru**nn**er*

- 以元音开头的词尾加在以一个元音 +l 或 +p 结尾的词后，不论重音落在哪个音节，通常双写 l 或 p。

*<u>can</u>cel + ation = cance**ll**ation*
*dial + ing = dia**ll**ing*
*ful<u>fil</u> + ed = fulfi**ll**ed*
*<u>kid</u>nap + er = kidna**pp**er*
*slip + ing = sli**pp**ing*

⚠ 词尾 *-ful* 总是拼写成一个 l，而词尾 *-fully* 则总是拼写成两个 l。

grateful – gratefully
careful – carefully
beautiful – beautifully

以不发音的 e 结尾的词

- 当以元音开头的词尾，例如 *-ible*, *-able*, *-ing*, *-ed*, *-er* 或 *-ity*，加在以不发音的 e 结尾的词后时，省略 e。

response + ible = responsible
value + able = valuable
fascinate + ing = fascinating
secure + ity = security
fame + ous = famous
nice + est = nicest

⚠ 当以元音开头的词尾加在以 *-ce* 或 *-ge* 结尾的词后时，保留 e。这是为了保持 c 或 g 仍发清音。

*notice + able = noti**cea**ble*
*change + able = chan**gea**ble*
*outrage + ous = outra**geo**us*

- 在英语中，许多副词以 *-ly* 结尾。如果 *-ly* 加在以辅音字母加 *-le* 结尾的形容词后，形容词词末的 *-e* 省略。

gentle + ly = gently
idle + ly = idly
subtle + ly = subtly

在以 -y 结尾的词后加词尾

- 当词尾加在以辅音 *-y* 结尾的词后时，y 通常变成 i：

*carry + es = carr**ie**s*

*early + er = earl**i**er*
*lovely + est = lovel**i**est*
*beauty + ful = beaut**i**ful*
*crazy + ly = craz**i**ly*

⚠ 但是, 加 *-ing* 时, y 不变成 i 。

carry + ing = carrying
try + ing = trying

像 *dry* 和 *shy* 这样的单音节形容词, 结尾的 y 通常不变。

dry + ness = dryness
shy + ly = shyly

以 -y 结尾的名词复数

- 以辅音 + y 结尾的单词的复数, 先变 y 为 i 再加 *-es* :

*story + es = stor**ie**s*
*quality + es = qualit**ie**s*
*spy + es = sp**ie**s*

- 以一个元音 + y 结尾的单词, 其复数通过加 *-s* 构成:

donkey + s = donkeys
holiday + s = holidays
boy + s = boys

以 -s, -x, -z, -sh 或 -ch 结尾的单词

以 *-s*, *-x*, *-z*, *-sh*, 或 *-ch* 结尾的名词, 其复数通过加 *-es* 构成。以这些字母或字母组合结尾的动词, 其第三人称单数形式也同样由加 *-es* 构成。

名 词	动 词
bus + es = buses	*fuss + es = fusses*
mass + es = masses	*pass + es = passes*
fox + es = foxes	*mix + es = mixes*
buzz + es = buzzes	*buzz + es = buzzes*
rash + es = rashes	*diminish + es = diminishes*
match + es = matches	*reach + es = reaches*

以 -c 结尾的单词

- 当以 e 或 i 开头的词尾加在以 c 结尾的单词后时, c 后加一个 k, 以保持 c 仍发浊音:

mimic + k + ed = mimicked
picnic + k + ing = picnicking

- 以 *-ic* 结尾的形容词，其副词形式是加 *-ally* 而不是 *-ly*：

  artistic – artistically
  automatic – automatically
  specific – specifically

i	词尾 *-ally* 的发音同 *-ly*。

以 -ous/-ary 结尾的形容词

- 英语中，许多形容词以 *-ous* 或 *-ary* 结尾。在英式英语中，当 *-ous* 或 *-ary* 加在以 *-our* 结尾的单词后时，*-our* 变成 *-or*。

  glamour + ous = glamorous
  honour + ary = honorary
  humour + ous = humorous

-ie- 或 -ei-?

- 有时很难记住发音 /i:/ 的字母排列顺序。基本规则是，"i 在 e 之前，但当 i 和 e 的组合在 c 之后时，i 在 e 之后"，但也有一些例外：

  i 在 e 之前

  believe field piece relief thief

  e 在 i 之前

  ceiling conceited deceive receipt receive

▼ 难拼写的单词

下面是许多人认为很难拼写的单词列表：

accommodation（英）/*accommodations*（美）
address
alcohol
autumn
awkward
beautiful
committee
confident
disappointment
doubt
embarrass
foreign

government
handkerchief
independent
island
lightning
necessary
occasion
opportunity
precede
proceed
professor
pronunciation
psychiatrist
recommend
sandwich
science
sign
succeed
suspicious
tomorrow
vegetable
vehicle
Wednesday

▼ 英式英语和美式英语的拼写差异

英式英语和美式英语的拼写，有一些非常常见的区别，多数情况下可以通过规则掌握。最重要的规则列出如下：

-our 和 -or

英式英语中以 *-our* 结尾的单词在美式英语中拼作 *-or*。

英式英语	美式英语
behaviour	*behavior*
flavour	*flavor*
neighbour	*neighbor*

-re 和 -er

英式英语中以 *-re* 结尾的单词在美式英语中拼作 *-er*。

英式英语	美式英语
centre	*center*
litre	*liter*
theatre	*theater*

-ae-/-oe- 和 -e-

某些英式英语中含有 *-ae-* 或 *-oe-* 的单词在美式英语中只拼作一个 e。

英式英语	美式英语
anaesthetic	*anesthetic*
diarrhoea	*diarrhea*
manoeuvre	*maneuver*

-oul- 和 -ol-

- 英式英语中带有 *-oul* 拼写的单词在美式英语中拼作 *-ol*。

英式英语	美式英语
mould	*mold*
moult	*molt*
smoulder	*smolder*

双写辅音

- 在美式英语中，当一个词尾加在双音节单词后，而该双音节单词的最后一个音节不重读时，不双写 l。

	英式英语	美式英语
cancel + ed	*cancelled*	*canceled*
jewel + er	*jeweller*	*jeweler*
travel + ing	*travelling*	*traveling*

- 一些单词在英式英语中含有双辅音但在美式英语中是单辅音。

英式英语	美式英语
carburettor	*carburetor*
jewellery	*jewelry*
programme	*program*
tranquillize	*tranquilize*
woollen	*woolen*

⚠ 若最后一个音节重读，不论在英国英语还是美国英语中，最后的辅音都要双写。

	英式英语	美式英语
admit + ed	*admitted*	*admitted*
admit + ing	*admitting*	*admitting*

有些动词，例如 *appal, distil, enrol* 和 *fulfil*，在英式英语中，其基本形式和带 *-s* 的形式只有一个单辅音，但在美式英语中是双辅音。

英式英语	美式英语
appal	*appall*
appals	*appalls*

-iz- 和 –is-

- 英语中的许多动词，例如 *criticize – criticise* 和 *organize – organise*，以及由它们派生的名词，例如 *organization – organisation*，可以拼写成 *-iz-* 或 *-is-*。英式英语中，两种拼法都是正确的，但在美式英语中，*-iz-* 是惟一正确的拼写形式。

英式英语	美式英语
apologize apologise	*apologize*
emphasize emphasise	*emphasize*
recognize recognise	*recognize*

- 在英式英语中以 *-yse* 结尾的动词，在美式英语中拼作 *-yze*。

英式英语	美式英语
analyse	*analyze*
paralyse	*paralyze*

i 为避免麻烦，你可以全部使用 *-ze-* 形式，但下列单词是例外，它们必须拼作 *-is-*。

advertise	*disguise*	*revise*
advise	*exercise*	*supervise*
comprise	*franchise*	*surprise*
despise	*improvise*	*televise*
devise	*promise*	

重要单词的不同拼写形式

英式英语	美式英语
analogue	*analog*
axe	*ax*
catalogue	*catalog*
cheque	*check*
defence	*defense*
dialogue	*dialog*
disk	*disc*
grey	*gray*

英式英语	美式英语
licence（名词）（动词都拼作 *license*）	*license*（名词）
offence	*offense*
practise（动词）（名词都拼作 *practice*）	*practice*（动词）
pretence	*pretense*
pyjamas	*pajamas*
sceptical	*skeptical*
speciality	*specialty*
storey	*story*
tyre	*tire*

数字

▼基数

下列的数字称作基数。根据此表，你可以知道如何构成其他数字。数字可用作形容词（用于名词前，有时也称作限定词）或代词（用于代替名词）。

0	nought (英)/naught (美), zero, nothing, oh
1	one
2	two
3	three
4	four
5	five
6	six
7	seven
8	eight
9	nine
10	ten
11	eleven
12	twelve
13	thirteen
14	fourteen
15	fifteen
16	sixteen
17	seventeen
18	eighteen
19	nineteen
20	twenty
21	twenty-one
22	twenty-two
23	twenty-three
24	twenty-four
25	twenty-five
26	twenty-six
27	twenty-seven
28	twenty-eight
29	twenty-nine
30	thirty
40	forty
50	fifty
60	sixty
70	seventy
80	eighty
90	ninety
100	one hundred/a hundred
101	one hundred and one/ a hundred and one
102	one hundred and two/ a hundred and two
110	one hundred and ten/ a hundred and ten
120	one hundred and twenty/ a hundred and twenty
200	two hundred
300	three hundred
400	four hundred
500	five hundred
1000	one thousand/ a thousand
1001	one thousand and one/ a thousand and one
1010	one thousand and ten/ a thousand and ten
1100	one thousand one hundred
1200	one thousand two hundred
1500	one thousand five hundred
2000	two thousand
5000	five thousand
10,000	ten thousand
20,000	twenty thousand
100,000	one hundred thousand/ a hundred thousand
150,000	one hundred and fifty thousand/a hundred and fifty thousand
1,000,000	one million/a million
2,000,000	two million
1,000,000,000	one billion/a billion

▼重点短语

She's fifteen (years old).
on page two hundred and fifty-six
two plus seven are nine
eight minus two are six
hundreds of years
the two women
all five candidates
two small children
Fifteen people were missing.
Five of the children came with their father.
in fives
They sold the house for £150 000.

数字

- one 作为数字用在名词前，强调只有一个事物，或用于表示表达的精确性。当谈论一个团体中的特定一员时也用 one。否则，就用 a。

    There was only one gate into the palace.
    One member said that he would never vote for such a proposal.
    A car came slowly up the road.

- 数字0有如下几种表达方式

  在温度、税率、利率中，用 *zero*
    It was fourteen below zero when they woke up.
  在小数点前，用 *nought* (英式)/*naught* (美式)
    nought point eight nine (0.89)
  表示计算，在口语中用 *nothing*
    five minus five is nothing
  当一个一个地报数字，或在小数点后时，用 oh 或字母 0
    point oh eight nine (.089)
  在体育比分中，用 *nil*
    England beat Germany one-nil.

- 介于999和100的数字通常用阿拉伯数字表示。当朗读或写成单词时，在英式英语中，百位数和十位数之间用 *and* 连接，而在美式英语中，省略 *and*。

    261 → *two hundred and sixty-one* (英)
    two hundred sixty-one (美)

- 介于 1000 和 9999 之间的数字，逗号通常放在第1个数字后：*1,526*

- 有时以空格代替逗号：*15 000*　*1 986 000*

- 当大于 9999 的数字写成阿拉伯数字时，通常在右起第3位数字前加逗号，在右起第6位数字前加逗号，依次类推，从而把数字分成3个数字一组的几组：*15,000*　*1,986,000*

欲知更多?

报电话号码时，要单独报出每个数字

0171 447 3352
oh one seven one four four seven three three five two

当重复数字时，英国人用单词 “double”，美国人直接重复数字

0171 447 3352
oh one seven one double four seven double three five two (英)
zero one seven one four four seven there three five two (美)

ENGLISH IN ACTION

▼ 序数词

序数词用于表明某物在一个系列或序列中所处的位置，可以用作形容词（用于名词前，*the* 或 *her* 一类的限定词之后）、代词（代替名词），或副词（在谈论赛跑或其他比赛时，与某些动词连用，比如 *come* 或 *finish*）。大多数分数的分母用序数词表示。

1st	first	26th	twenty-sixth
2nd	second	27th	twenty-seventh
3rd	third	28th	twenty-eighth
4th	fourth	29th	twenty-ninth
5th	fifth	30th	thirtieth
6th	sixth	31st	thirty-first
7th	seventh	32nd	thirty-second
8th	eighth	40th	fortieth
9th	ninth	41st	forty-first
10th	tenth	42nd	forty-second
11th	eleventh	50th	fiftieth
12th	twelfth	60th	sixtieth
13th	thirteenth	70th	seventieth
14th	fourteenth	80th	eightieth
15th	fifteenth	90th	ninetieth
16th	sixteenth	100th	hundredth
17th	seventeenth	101st	hundred and first
18th	eighteenth	102nd	hundred and second
19th	nineteenth	103rd	hundred and third
20th	twentieth	110th	hundred and tenth
21st	twenty-first	200th	two hundredth
22nd	twenty-second	1000th	thousandth
23rd	twenty-third	2000th	two thousandth
24th	twenty-fourth	10,000th	ten thousandth
25th	twenty-fifth	1,000,000th	millionth

1,000,000,000th billionth

We live on the fourth floor.
in the twelfth century
on her twenty-first birthday
The first two years have been very successful.
An Italian came second.
I was the first to arrive.
the third of a series of documentaries

- 如上表所示，序数词常用缩略形式表示，1加 *st* 为 *first*，2加 *nd* 为 *second*，3加 rd 为 *third*，*fourth* 到 *ninth* 分别用相应的基数词加 *th* 表示 —— 例如，*6th*。这些缩写形式在日期中尤为常用。

- *10* 以上不是 *10* 的倍数的序数词, 由基数词加序数词构成, 之间用连字符分开。

  my thirty-third birthday
  on the fifty-sixth floor
  our forty-fifth wedding anniversary

> **i** 楼房的第一层, 在英式英语中被称为 ground floor, 在美式英语中则被称为 first floor。在英式英语中, 再往上的一层为first floor, 在美式英语中则为 second floor。

▼ 分数、小数和百分数

1/2	a half
1/3	a third
1/4	a quarter
1/5	a fifth
1/6	a sixth
1/10	a tenth
2/3	two-thirds
5/8	five-eighths
0.5	(nought) point five (英)/(naught) point five (美)
3.5	three point five
6.89	six point eight nine
10%	ten per cent (英)/ten percent (美)
100%	one hundred per cent (英)/one hundred percent (美)

- 除了half (一半)和 quarter (四分之一)以外, 分数的分母用序数词表示。

  four and a half centuries
  a mile and a half below the surface
  The state produces a third of the nation's oil.
  More than two-thirds of the Earth is water.

- 分数的分子通常可以用不定冠词 a。

  The country spends over a fifth of its budget on education.

  正式用语和书面语中, 或需要强调数量时, 用 one。

  one quarter of the total population

- 分子大于1时, 通常要加连字符。

  the first two-thirds of this century
  He's due at the office in three-quarters of an hour.

星期和日期

▼ 星期

Monday	星期一	Saturday	星期六
Tuesday	星期二	Sunday	星期日
Wednesday	星期三		
Thursday	星期四		
Friday	星期五		

What day is it today? It's Thursday.
Why didn't you come to the meeting on Wednesday?
I'm usually here on Mondays and Fridays.
Deliveries usually arrive on a Thursday.
The attack took place last Thursday.
Talks are likely to start next Tuesday.
We meet here every Saturday morning.
I'll be away from Monday to Friday.
I'll need an answer by Monday.
We're having a party on the last Sunday in May.

▼ 月份

January	一月	July	七月
February	二月	August	八月
March	三月	September	九月
April	四月	October	十月
May	五月	November	十一月
June	六月	December	十二月

- 月份前用介词 in。

It always snows in January.
I flew to London in early March.
It happened in late May, and the apple trees were in bloom.
He spent two weeks with us in July 1993.

⚠ next（下一个）或 last（上一个）加月份，前面不用介词 in。
Staff were on strike last June.
I don't know where I'll be next November.

- 某月中的具体日子前用介词 on。

His exhibition opens on 5 February (英)*/February 5* (美).
The trial will begin on August the twenty-second.

i 在英国，一学年分为三个 terms（学期），夏季有长假期，圣诞节和复活节各有一个较短的假期。在美国，一学年分为两个 semesters（学期），十月、四月以及圣诞节和复活节都会放假。

ENGLISH IN ACTION

星期和日期

▼ 季节

Spring	春季	Autumn (英)/Fall (美)	秋季
Summer	夏季	Winter	冬季

- 季节前的介词用 in。

  In winter the nights are extremely cold.
  It's nice to get away in the spring.
  We met again in the spring of 1977.

⚠ next(下一个)或 last(上一个)加上季节，前面不用介词 in。
The final report is due out next autumn (英)/fall (美).
I was supposed to go last summer.

▼ 日期的写法

- 书写日期有几种不同的方式:

  13 September *September 13*
  13th September *September 13th*

- 上面的例子是书信中日期的书写方式。美国人通常把月份放在最前面。
- 若想给出年份，则将年份放在最后。如果将日放在月后，则用逗号将年份与日期分开。

  13th September 2004 (in a letter)
  My date of birth is 13 September 1957.
  I was born on September 13th, 1957.

- 也可按如下所示的方式，将日期完全用数字表达。数字形式常常用于信或表格的上部。在英国，日放在最前面。

  13/9/57 或 13.9.57

- 在美国，月份放在日之前。

  9/13/57 或 9.13.57

▼ 日期的读法

- 即使日期是用基数词表示，也要读作序数词。

  September 13 读作 *September the thirteenth* (英)

- 若月放在表示日的数字之后，月份前要加介词 of。

13 September 读作 *the thirteenth of September*

i 在以上两种情况下，美国人通常都读作 September thirteenth。

ENGLISH IN ACTION

- 若所指的月份很明确，就可省略月份。

  'What's the date today?' – 'It's the twelfth.'

▼ 年的读法

- 读年份时一般分成两部分。例如：

  1957 读作 *nineteen fifty-seven*
  1860 读作 *eighteen sixty*。

以"20-"开头的年份 —— 例如，*2003* 和 *2010* —— 可以读作 *two thousand and ...*。例如：

  2003 读作 *two thousand and three*
  2010 读作 *two thousand and ten*。

以"20-"开头的年份也可以分成两部分读，例如：

  2020 可读作 *twenty twenty*
  2004 可读作 *twenty oh four*。

- 以"-00"结尾的年份，可将第二部分读作 *hundred*。例如：

  1900 读作 *nineteen hundred*。

人们常常写 *the year 2000*，而不是仅仅写成 *2000*。人们通常将其读作 *the year two thousand*。

- 以"01–09"结尾的年份有两种读法。例如：

  1807 可以读作 *eighteen oh seven* 或 *eighteen hundred and seven*。

▼ 年代和世纪

- *1970 –1979* 可以读作 *the nineteen seventies*，或非正式的读法为 *the seventies*。

  the 1960s 读作 *the (nineteen) sixties*
  the 1970s 读作 *the (nineteen) seventies*

- 说到 20 世纪的年代时，不必指出世纪。例如，1920s 可以读作 the twenties。它可以写作 the '20s, the 20s 或 the Twenties。

> ⚠ 1400 – 1499 称作 the fifteenth century (15世纪)而不是 "the fourteenth century" (14世纪)。这非常合逻辑，因为1世纪是指从1年 —— 公元纪年的开始 —— 到99年。我们现在正处于 21 世纪 (2000–2099)。

- 世纪还可以写作序数词，例如，the 20th century。

时间

▼几点了?

It's one o'clock

It's a quarter past one (英)
It's a quarter after one (美)
It's one fifteen

It's half past one (英)
It's half after one (美)
It's one thirty

It's a quarter to two (英)
It's a quarter of two (美)
It's one forty-five

Its twenty-five past one (英)
It's twenty-five after one (美)
It's one twenty-five

It's ten to two (英)
It's ten of two (美)
It's one fifty

It's 13 minutes to two (英)
It's 13 minutes of two (美)
It's one forty-seven

⚠ o'clock 只用在表示整点的时间后。例如,可以说 five o'clock,但不能说“ten past five o'clock ”或“ a quarter past five o'clock”。

- 可以用 minutes 表示5分钟以内的时间,或精确地表示时间。

  It was twenty-four minutes past ten.
  We left home at exactly five minutes to ten.

- 从以上例子可知,可以用小时加过了多少分钟来表示时间。

  7.35 可以读作 *seven thirty-five* 或 *twenty-five minutes to eight*。

- 在整点后未必一定用 o'clock。人们常常只用数字。

  I used to get up every morning at six.

时间

- 如果过整点的分钟数小于10，许多人在分钟数前用 0，读作 oh。例如：

  10.07 可以读作 *ten oh seven* 或 *ten seven*。

  注意，在写时间时，英国人在小时后加圆点，譬如：10.07。而美国人多用冒号：7:35。

- 若所指的钟点很明确，在介词 past 或 to 之后不必加钟点。

  'What time is it?' – 'Twenty-five past.'
  'What time does the train leave?' – 'I think it's at quarter to.'

问时间	回答
What time is it?	*It's nearly ten past twelve.* (英) *It's nearly ten after twelve.* (美)
What's the time now?	*It's three o'clock exactly.*
What time do you make it?	*I make it four twenty-seven.*
Do you have the time (on you)?	*Yes, it's half past nine.*
Can you tell me the time?	*Yes, it's nearly quarter to eight.*

相关用语
Mary left at three and caught the bus.
The students must leave their rooms by nine o'clock this morning.
He was home by six for dinner.
She was busy until three o'clock, when she had to meet her parents.
I've been awake since four.
Did you see the eleven o'clock news?

04:00
four in the morning
4 a.m.

16:00
four in the afternoon
4 p.m.

09:00
nine in the morning
9 a.m.

21:00
nine in the evening
9 p.m.

12:00
twelve in the morning
12 a.m.

midday
noon

- 可以加 a.m.（代表 ante meridiem，拉丁语，表示"中午之前"）表示午夜到中午之间的时间。同样，p.m.（代表 post meridiem，表示"中午之后"）表示中午到午夜之间的时间。这些缩写通常不用于对话中，而且从不与 o'clock 连用。

  The doors will be opened at 10 a.m.
  He finally got home at 11.30 p.m., having set out at 6 a.m.

▾ 与时间有关的惯用语

- 时间表达法中经常用到名词词组

yesterday
today
tomorrow

yesterday { *morning* / *afternoon* / *evening* }

last night

tomorrow { *morning* / *afternoon* / *evening* / *night* }

last { *Friday* / *week* / *month* / *year* }

next { *Friday* / *week* / *month* / *year* }

the day before yesterday
the day after tomorrow
the previous day
the day before
the next day
the following day
the day after
the week before last
the week after next
a week on Thursday (下周二起的一个星期)

⚠ 表示时间的词或短语不与介词at, in 或 on连用。
One of my friends wrote to me today.
So, you're coming back next week?

- 表示时间的词或短语常常与动词的一般现在时或现在进行时连用，表示将来会发生的事情。

The plane leaves tomorrow morning.
They're coming next week.

时间

▼ 定期发生的事

every { *hour / day / Saturday / week / month / year etc* }

on { *Saturdays / Tuesdays and Fridays etc* }

every other { *day / week / month / year etc* }

every { *two / three / etc* } { *hours / days / weeks etc* }

once { *an hour / a day etc* }

once every { *week / month / 2 weeks etc* }

twice / three times / four times / etc { *an hour / a day / week / month / etc* }

The nurse comes in to see him every day.
He has driving lessons on Mondays and Fridays.
We wrote to each other every other day.
The Olympics are held every four years.
The group meets once a week.
It only rains here once every five or ten years.
The medicine should be taken three times a day.

▼ 与时间连用的介词

AT

- at 用于:
  - ▸ 表示钟点的时间:at eight o'clock, at three fifteen
  - ▸ 宗教节日:at Christmas, at Easter
  - ▸ 用餐时间:at breakfast, at lunchtimes
  - ▸ 具体的较短的一段时间:at night, at the weekend, at weekends, at half-term

IN

- in 用于:
  - ▸ 季节:in winter, in the spring
  - ▸ 年份、年代和世纪:in 1985, in the year 2000, in the thirties, in the nineteenth century
  - ▸ 月份:in July, in December
  - ▸ 一天中的各时段:in the morning, in the evenings

▸ 较长的一段时间: in wartime, in the holidays

- in 也可用于表示某事将要发生在将来的某个时间段期间或之后。

  I think we'll find out in the next few days.

ON

- on 用于:

▸ 星期: on Monday, on Tuesday morning, on Sunday evenings
▸ 特殊的日子: on Christmas Day, on my birthday
▸ 具体日期: on the twentieth of July, on June 21st, on the twelfth

DURING/OVER

- during 和 over 表示某事发生在某个特定的时间段中的某个时候或贯穿于整个时间段。

  I saw him twice during the holidays.
  Will you stay here over Christmas?

FROM ...TO ...

- from ... to ... 表示某段时间从开始到结束的整段时间。

  The building is closed from April to June.
  We had no rain from March to October.

  也可用 till 或 until 代替 to。

  The ticket office will be open from 10 a.m. until 1 p.m.
  They were working from dawn till dusk.

BY

- by 表示“不迟于”。

  By eleven o'clock, Brody was back in his office.
  Can we get this finished by tomorrow?

SINCE/FOR/AGO

- for 可与任何时态的动词连用, 表示某事持续发生或不发生了多长时间, 具体指一段时间时也用 for。

  He didn't speak for a long time.
  I will be in London for three weeks.
  I've lived here for nine years.

- since 用于现在完成时或过去完成时, 表示某事从何时开始发生。

  Marilyn has lived in Paris since 1984.
  I had eaten nothing since breakfast.

- ago 用于一般过去时, 表示某事是在距离说话时间多久前发生的。

  We saw him about a month ago.
  John's wife died five years ago.

⚠ ago常与时间段连用。ago不与现在完成时连用。不能说 "We have seen him about a month ago."。

度量衡

> **i** 英国沿用两种度量系统:“公制”系统,如中国所使用的,和“英制”(非公制)系统。公制系统是官方系统,用途广泛。但英制系统仍用于度量人的身高和体重、酒吧饮品,显示在路标上的距离和某些体育运动,譬如板球、足球和马术等。在美国,公制系统除了在军事、医学和科学领域外,并不太常用。

- 每种系统都有自己的度量单位名词,如下所示。缩写形式在括号中给出。若用公制单位,就用十进制数字表示: 1.69 metres (读作 one point six nine metres), 4.8 kilograms (读作 four point eight kilograms)。
- 对于非公制单位,常用分数形式: 6 ¾ inches (读作 six and three quarter inches),1 ½ tons of wheat (one and a half tons of wheat)。

长度

公制

1 kilometre (km)	=	1000 metres	=	0.6214 miles
1 metre (m)	=	100 centimetres	=	1.094 yards
1 centimetre (cm)	=	10 millimetres	=	0.394 inches

非公制

1 mile	=	1760 yards	=	1.609 kilometres
1 yard (yd)	=	3 feet	=	0.914 metres
1 foot (ft)	=	12 inches	=	30.48 centimetres
1 inch (in)	=	25.4 millimetres		

> **i** 符号 ′ 有时用于表示英尺;符号 ″ 表示英寸。例如,3′6″ 表示3英尺6英寸。
>
> - 单数形式 foot 和复数形式 feet 都可与数字连用。
>   *The room is almost 20 foot long.*

面积

公制

1 square kilometre (km^2)	=	100 hectares	=	0.386 square miles
1 hectare (ha)	=	100 ares	=	2.471 acres
1 are (a)	=	100 square metres	=	119.6 square yards
1 square metre (m^2)	=	1.196 square yards		

非公制

1 square mile	=	640 acres	=	2.59 square kilometres
1 acre	=	4840 square yards	=	0.405 hectares
1 square yard	=	9 square feet	=	0.836 square metres
1 square foot	=	144 square inches	=	929.03 square centimetres
1 square inch			=	6.452 square centimetres

度量衡

重量

公制

1 tonne	=	1000 kilograms	=	19.688 hundredweight
1 kilogram (kg)	=	1000 grams	=	2.205 pounds
1 gram (g)	=	1000 milligrams		

非公制

1 ton	=	20 hundredweight	=	1.016 tonnes
1 hundredweight (cwt)	=	8 stone	=	50.8 kilograms
1 stone (st)	=	14 pounds	=	6.356 kilograms
1 pound (lb)	=	16 ounces	=	454 grams
1 ounce (oz)	=	28.35 grams		

i 有时 kilo（公斤）可以代替 kilogram, metric ton（公吨）代替 tonne。

容量

公制

1 decalitre (dal)	=	10 litres	=	2.2 gallons (2.63 US gallons)
1 litre (l)	=	100 centilitres	=	1.76 pints (2.1 US pints)
1 centilitre (cl)	=	10 millilitres	=	0.018 pints (0.021 US pints)

非公制

1 gallon (gal)	=	4 quarts	=	4.546 litres
1 quart (qt)	=	2 pints	=	1.136 litres
1 pint (pt)	=	20 fluid ounces	=	56.8 centilitres
1 fluid ounce (fl oz)	=	28.4 millilitres		

i 在美式英语中, metre 和 litre 拼写为 meter（米）和 liter（公升）。

- 美国非公制容量度量单位不同于英国。一美制品脱等于 0.833 英制品脱, 相当于16美制液量盎司。

提问	回答
How tall is he?	*He's about six feet/ foot tall.*
How high is the Shanghai TV Tower?	*It's 468 metres* (英)*/meters* (美) *high.*
How far is it to Glasgow from here?	*It's about fifteen miles.*
How much do you weigh? / *What weight are you?*	*I'm/I weigh twelve stone four* (英), *I'm/I weigh 68 pounds* (美).
You're about ten and a half stone, aren't you? (英)	*I'm a little heavier than that.*

ENGLISH IN ACTION

度量衡

- 下列形容词和相应的介词短语可用于表示尺寸的度量单位名词后。
    - *long/in length*
    - *deep/in depth*
    - *high/in height*
    - *tall*
    - *thick/in thickness*
    - *wide/in width*

The room is almost 20 foot long.
I need a piece of wood two foot six long.
The water was 2 metres deep.
Each layer is 6 metres thick.
He was five foot seven tall.
The island is about 25 miles long by 12 miles wide.

> *i* 在英国, a pint 单独使用时, 常指一品脱啤酒。a half 也可以单独使用, 指酒吧里的半品脱饮品。a quarter 单独使用时, 指四分之一磅的物品, 譬如蔬菜等。
> *He's gone out to the pub for a pint.*
> *I'll have a half of lager.*
> *A quarter of mushrooms, please.*

货币

▼英国货币

- 英国的货币单位为英镑，1英镑等于100便士。
- 英镑的符号为 £，写在数字之前。字母 p 代表便士，写在数字之后。

  £40 读作 *forty pounds*
  60p 读作 *sixty pence or sixty p (pronounced /pi:/)*
  £2.50 读作 *two pounds fifty or two fifty*

> ***i*** 在日常生活中，人们常用一些非正式的说法，表示不同面值的纸币和硬币。

美式英语		**英式英语**	
penny	1 cent	*quid*	£1
nickel	5 cents	*fiver*	£5
dime	10 cents	*tenner*	£10
quarter	25 cents	*ton*	£100
Buck	$1	*grand*	£1000

- 美国的货币单位为美元，1美元等于100美分。
- 美元的符号为 $，写在数字之前。字母 c 代表美分，写在数字之后。

  $40 读作 *forty dollars*
  60c 读作 *sixty cents*
  $2.50 读作 *two dollars fifty cents*

提问	**回答**
How much is that?	*That's four seventy-eight, please.*
How much is it to park?	*Two dollars twenty cents.*
How much will it cost?	*It'll cost you about a hundred pounds.*
Do you have any change?	*I'm sorry, I don't.*
Do you have change for five pounds?	*Yes, I can give you five pound coins.*

- 下表列出了世界上人口超过 750,000 的大多数国家的名称。
- 形容词 (ADJ) 一列的词条，表示来自某国或与某国有关的事物。人民 (people) 一列的词条，表示某个国家或来自某个国家的人。人民 (people) 的表示方法通常与表示国籍的 形容词 (ADJ) 是一样的，故不重复列出。例如，Belgian (比利时的) 首都为布鲁塞尔，来自比利时的人称为 Belgian (比利时人)。
- 人民 (people) 一列中，前面有定冠词 the 的词条只能用作复数。以 -man 结尾的词条只能用来指男性；以 -woman 结尾的词条只能指女性。

> *i* 当心别冒犯了别人！Great Britain，或 Britain是一个地理名词，指包括英格兰、威尔士和苏格兰在内的英伦岛。the United Kingdom是一个政治名词，包括英格兰、威尔士、苏格兰和北爱尔兰。尽管苏格兰、威尔士和北爱尔兰分别有自己的议会，但他们和英格兰一起，都从属于伦敦议会。苏格兰人、爱尔兰人和威尔士人都不是英格兰人，如果称他们为“英格兰人”或来自英格兰，对他们是一种冒犯。不列颠群岛 (the British Isles) 也是一个地理名词，指包括英伦岛、爱尔兰岛及其附近小岛在内的所有岛屿。但是，爱尔兰共和国是一个独立的国家，首都是都柏林。
> the United States of America,America, the USA 和 the US都用于指同一个国家。然而，必须得谨用America，因为它实际上是指整个美洲大陆，加拿大、墨西哥等国家的人会认为他们也是America的一部分。

国家		形容词	人民	语言	货币
Afghanistan	阿富汗	Afghan, Afghani		Pashto, Dari	afghani
Albania	阿尔巴尼亚	Albanian		Albanian	lek
Algeria	阿尔及利亚	Algerian		Arabic, French	Algerian dinar
America	美国	American		English	US dollar
Angola	安哥拉	Angolan		Portuguese	new kwanza
Argentina	阿根廷	Argentine, Argentinian		Spanish	Argentinian Peso

国家		形容词	人民	语言	货币
Armenia	亚美尼亚	Armenian		Armenian	dram
Australia	澳大利亚	Australian		English	Australian dollar
Austria	奥地利	Austrian		German	euro (previously schilling)
Azerbaijan	阿塞拜疆	Azeri, Azerbaijani		Azeri	manat
Bangladesh	孟加拉国	Bangladeshi		Bengali	taka
Belarus	白俄罗斯	Belarussian		Belorussian, Russian	Belarussian rouble
Belgium	比利时	Belgian		Flemish, French	euro (previously franc)
Benin	贝宁	Beninese, Beninois		French, Fon	CFA franc
Bhutan	不丹	Bhutanese		Dzongkha, Nepali	ngultrum
Bolivia	玻利维亚	Bolivian		Spanish, Quechua, Aymara	boliviano
Bosnia and Herzegovina	波斯尼亚和黑塞哥维那	Bosnian, Herzegovinian		Bosnian, Croatian, Serbian	convertible marka
Botswana	博茨瓦纳	Botswanan		English, Setswana	pula
Brazil	巴西	Brazilian		Portuguese	real
Britain	英国	British	Briton, the British	English	pound sterling
Bulgaria	保加利亚	Bulgarian		Bulgarian	lev
Burkina Faso	布基纳法索	Burkinabé		French, Mossi	CFA franc
Burundi	布隆迪	Burundi	Burundian	Kirundi, French	Burundi franc
Cambodia	柬埔寨	Cambodian		Khmer	new riel
Cameroon	喀麦隆	Cameroonian		French, English	CFA franc
Canada	加拿大	Canadian		English, French	Canadian dollar
Central African Republic	中非共和国	Central African		French, Sango	CFA franc
Chad	乍得	Chadian		French, Arabic, Sara, Sango	CFA franc

国家		形容词	人民	语言	货币
Chile	智利	Chilean		Spanish	Chilean peso
China	中国	Chinese	the Chinese	Chinese	yuan
Colombia	哥伦比亚	Colombian		Spanish	Colombian peso
Congo, Democratic Republic of	刚果民主共和国	Congolese		French	Congolsese franc
Congo, Republic of	刚果共和国	Congolese		French	CFA franc
Costa Rica	哥斯达黎加	Costa Rican		Spanish	colón
Côte d'Ivoire	科特迪瓦	Ivorian		French	CFA franc
Croatia	克罗地亚	Croat, Croatian		Croatian	Croatian kuna
Cuba	古巴	Cuban		Spanish	Cuban peso
Cyprus	塞浦路斯	Greek Cypriot, Turkish Cypriot		Greek, Turkish	Cypriot pound, Turkish lira
Czech Republic	捷克共和国	Czech		Czech, Slovak	koruna
Denmark	丹麦	Danish	Dane	Danish	Danish krone
Dominican Republic	多米尼加共和国	Dominican		Spanish	Dominican peso
East Timor	东帝汶	East Timorese		Tetum	US dollar
Ecuador	厄瓜多尔	Ecuadorean		Spanish, Quechua	US dollar
Egypt	埃及	Egyptian		Arabic	Egyptian pound
El Salvador	萨尔瓦多	Salvadoran, Salvadorean		Spanish	Salvadoran colón
Eritrea	厄立特里亚	Eritrean		Tigre, Kunama	nakfa
Estonia	爱沙尼亚	Estonian		Estonian	kroon
Ethiopia	埃塞俄比亚	Ethiopian		Amharic	birr
Finland	芬兰	Finnish	Finn	Finnish, Swedish	euro (previously markka)

国家		形容词	人民	语言	货币
France	法国	French	Frenchman, Frenchwoman, the French	French	euro (previously franc)
Gabon	加蓬	Gabonese		French, Fang	CFA franc
Gambia, The	冈比亚	Gambian		English	dalasi
Georgia	格鲁吉亚	Georgian		Georgian, Russian	lari
Germany	德国	German		German	euro (previously Deutschmark)
Ghana	加纳	Ghanaian		English, Akan	new cedi
Great Britain	大不列颠及北爱尔兰联合王国	British	Briton, the British	English	pound sterling
Greece	希腊	Greek		Greek	euro (previously drachma)
Guatemala	危地马拉	Guatemalan		Spanish	quetzal
Guinea	几内亚	Guinean		French	Guinean franc
Guinea-Bissau	几内亚比绍	Guinea Bissauan		Portuguese, Creole	CFA franc
Guyana	圭亚那	Guyanese, Guyanan	the Guyanese	English	Guyanese dollar
Haiti	海地	Haitian		French, Creole	gourde
Honduras	洪都拉斯	Honduran		Spanish	lempira
Hungary	匈牙利	Hungarian		Hungarian	forint
Iceland	冰岛	Icelandic	Icelander	Icelandic	krona
India	印度	Indian		Hindi, English	Indian rupee
Indonesia	印度尼西亚	Indonesian		Bahasa Indonesia	Indonesian rupiah
Iran	伊朗	Iranian		Farsi	Iranian rial
Iraq	伊拉克	Iraqi		Arabic, Kurdish	Iraqi dinar

国家		形容词	人民	语言	货币
Ireland, Republic of	爱尔兰共和国	Irish	Irishman, Irishwoman, the Irish	Irish, English	euro (previously punt)
Israel	以色列	Israeli		Hebrew, Arabic	new Israeli shekel
Italy	意大利	Italian		Italian	euro (previously lira)
Jamaica	牙买加	Jamaican		English	Jamaican dollar
Japan	日本	Japanese	the Japanese	Japanese	yen
Jordan	约旦	Jordanian		Arabic	Jordanian dinar
Kazakhstan	哈萨克斯坦	Kazakh, Kazakhstani		Kazakh, Russian	tenge
Kenya	肯尼亚	Kenyan		Kiswahili, English	Kenyan shilling
Kuwait	科威特	Kuwaiti		Arabic	Kuwaiti dinar
Kyrgyzstan	吉尔吉斯斯坦	Kyrgyzstani, Kyrgyz		Kyrgyz	som
Laos	老挝	Lao, Laotian		Lao, Laotian	new kip
Latvia	拉脱维亚	Latvian		Latvian	lat
Lebanon	黎巴嫩	Lebanese	the Lebanese	Arabic, French	Lebanese pound
Lesotho	莱索托	Lesothan, Basotho	Mosotho, Basotho	Sesotho, English	loti
Liberia	利比里亚	Liberian		English	Liberian dollar
Libya	利比亚	Libyan		Arabic	Libyan dinar
Lithuania	立陶宛	Lithuanian		Lithuanian	litas
Luxembourg	卢森堡	Luxembourg	Luxembourger	French, German, Luxemburgian	euro (previously Luxembourg franc, Belgian franc)
Macedonia	马其顿	Macedonian		Macedonian	denar
Madagascar	马达加斯加	Malagasy		French, Malagasy	Malagasy franc
Malawi	马拉维	Malawian		English, Chichewa	Malawian kwacha

国家		形容词	人民	语言	货币
Malaysia	马来西亚	Malaysian		Malay	ringgit
Maldives	马尔代夫	Maldivian		Divehi	rufiyaa
Mali	马里	Malian		French, Bambara	CFA franc
Malta	马耳他	Maltese	the Maltese	Maltese, English	Maltese lira
Mauritania	毛里塔尼亚	Mauritanian		French, Arabic	ouguiya
Mauritius	毛里求斯	Mauritian		English, Creole	Mauritian rupee
Mexico	墨西哥	Mexican		Spanish	New Mexican peso
Moldova	摩尔瓦多	Moldovan		Moldovan, Romanian, Russian	leu
Mongolia	蒙古共和国	Mongol, Mongolian		Khalkha, Mongolian	tugrik
Morocco	摩洛哥	Moroccan		Arabic, Berber	Moroccan dirham
Mozambique	莫桑比克	Mozambican		Portuguese	metical
Myanmar	缅甸	Myanmar		Burmese	kyat
Namibia	纳米比亚	Namibian		Afrikaans, English	Namibian dollar
Nepal	尼泊尔	Nepalese	the Nepalese	Nepali	Nepalese rupee
Netherlands, The	荷兰	Dutch	Dutchman, Dutchwoman, the Dutch	Dutch	euro (previously guilder)
New Zealand	新西兰	New Zealand	New Zealander	English, Maori	New Zealand dollar
Nicaragua	尼加拉瓜	Nicaraguan		Spanish	gold cordoba
Niger	尼日尔	Nigerien		French	CFA franc
Nigeria	尼日利亚	Nigerian		English, Hausa, Yoruba, Ibo	naira
North Korea	朝鲜	North Korean		Korean	North Korean won
Norway	挪威	Norwegian		Norwegian	Norwegian krone

国家		形容词	人民	语言	货币
Oman	阿曼	Omani		Arabic	Omani rial
Pakistan	巴基斯坦	Pakistani		Urdu, English, Punjabi	Pakistani rupee
Panama	巴拿马	Panamanian		Spanish	balboa
Papua New Guinea	巴布亚新几内亚	Papua New Guinea		Pidgin, English, Motu	kina
Paraguay	巴拉圭	Paraguayan		Spanish, Guaraní	guaraní
Peru	秘鲁	Peruvian		Spanish, Quechua	nuevo sol
Philippines, The	菲律宾	Filipino, Philippine	Filipino, Filipina (women only), Philippine	Filipino, English	Philippine peso
Poland	波兰	Polish	Pole	Polish	zloty
Portugal	葡萄牙	Portuguese	the Portuguese	Portuguese	euro (previously escudo)
Puerto Rico (US)	波多黎各 (美)	Puerto Rican		Spanish, English	US dollar
Romania	罗马尼亚	Romanian		Romanian	leu
Russia	俄罗斯	Russian		Russian	rouble
Rwanda	卢旺达	Rwandan		Kinyarwanda, French, English	Rwandan franc
Saudi Arabia	沙特阿拉伯	Saudi, Saudi Arabian		Arabic	Saudi riyal
Senegal	塞内加尔	Senegalese	the Senegalese	French	CFA franc
Serbia and Montenegro	塞尔维亚和黑山	Serb, Serbian or Montenegrin	Serb, Montenegrin	Serbo-Croation	new dinar
Sierra Leone	塞拉利昂	Sierra Leonean		English	leone
Singapore	新加坡	Singapore, Singaporean	Singaporean	Malay, Chinese, Tamil, English	Singapore dollar
Slovakia	斯洛伐克	Slovak		Slovak	koruna
Slovenia	斯洛文尼亚	Slovenian, Slovene		Slovenian	tolar

国家		形容词	人民	语言	货币
Somalia	索马里	Somali		Somali, Arabic	Somali shilling
South Africa	南非	South African		Afrikaans, English, Bantu	rand
South Korea	韩国	South Korean		Korean	South Korean won
Spain	西班牙	Spanish	Spaniard, the Spanish	Castilian Spanish	euro (previously peseta)
Sri Lanka	斯里兰卡	Sri Lankan		Singhalese, Tamil, English	Sri Lankan rupee
Sudan	苏丹	Sudanese	the Sudanese	Arabic	Sudanese dinar
Swaziland	斯威士兰	Swazi		English, Siswati	lilangeni
Sweden	瑞典	Swedish	Swede	Swedish	Swedish krona
Switzerland	瑞士	Swiss	the Swiss	German, French, Italian	Swiss franc
Syria	叙利亚	Syrian		Arabic	Syrian pound
Tajikistan	塔吉克斯坦	Tajik		Tajik, Uzbek, Russian	somoni
Tanzania	坦桑尼亚	Tanzanian		Swahili, English	Tanzanian shilling
Thailand	泰国	Thai		Thai	baht
Togo	多哥	Togolese		French, Ewe	CFA franc
Trinidad and Tobago	特立尼达和多巴哥	Trinidadian, Tobagoan		English	Trinidad and Tobago dollar
Tunisia	突尼斯	Tunisian		Arabic, French	Tunisian dinar
Turkey	土耳其	Turkish	Turk	Turkish, Kurdish, Arabic	Turkish lira
Turkmenistan	土库曼斯坦	Turkmen		Turkmen, Russian	manat
Uganda	乌干达	Ugandan		English, Luganda, Swahili, Luo	Ugandan shilling
Ukraine	乌克兰	Ukrainian		Ukrainian, Russian	hryvni
United Arab Emirates	阿联酋	Emirian		Arabic	Emirian dirham

国家		形容词	人民	语言	货币
United Kingdom	大不列颠及北爱尔兰联合王国	British	Briton, the British	English	pound sterling
United States of America	美利坚合众国	American		English	US dollar
Uruguay	乌拉圭	Uruguayan		Spanish	Uruguayan peso
Uzbekistan	乌兹别克斯坦	Uzbek		Uzbek, Russian	sum
Venezuela	委内瑞拉	Venezuelan		Spanish	bolívar
Vietnam	越南	Vietnamese	the Vietnamese	Vietnamese	new dông
Yemen	也门	Yemeni		Arabic	yemeni rial
Zambia	赞比亚	Zambian		English	Zambian kwacha
Zimbabwe	津巴布韦	Zimbabwean		English, Shona	Zimbabwean dollar

Chinese in Action

GREETINGS

▼ MEETING PEOPLE

- It is very important to use the appropriate form of greeting in China. As with other cultures, the way that you greet somebody will depend on whether you know them or whether they are a stranger. The most common greeting is:

  你好 (nǐ hǎo), *or*
  您好 (nín hǎo)

- The form 您好 (nín hǎo) is more formal and should be used when you want to show particular respect.

- Chinese people show great respect for the wisdom and experience of their elders. The senior people present will usually initiate the greetings, and you should greet the oldest, most senior person before any others.

▼ SOME TYPICAL GREETINGS

你好！(nǐ hǎo) *Hello!*
嗨！(hāi) *Hi!*
喂！(wèi) *Hello! (usually on the phone)*
早上好! (zǎoshang hǎo) *Good morning!*
早！(zǎo) *Morning!*
最近身体怎么样? (zuìjìn shēntǐ zěnmeyàng)
How have you been?
还不错，谢谢 (hái bùcuò, xièxie)
Fine, thanks.
好久不见! 最近还好吗？(hǎojiǔ bù jiàn! zuìjìn hái hǎo ma?)
Long time no see! How are you doing?
很好，谢谢，你怎么样？(hěn hǎo, xièxie, nǐ zěnmeyàng)
Very well, thank you, and you?
挺好的，多谢。(tǐng hǎo de, duōxiè)
Fine, thanks.
棒极了！(bàng jí le) *Great!*
一般。(yībān) *So-so.*

▼ CHINESE NAMES

- Chinese family names are placed first, followed by the given name. For instance, in the name "Zhao Li," "Zhao" is the family name, "Li" the given name. Family names usually consist of one syllable, whereas given names can have either one or two syllables.

- Chinese people call their close friends and family members by their given names. For example, "Ma Wenli" may be addressed by close friends as "Wenli."

GREETINGS

- In formal situations you should address Chinese people by their family name or full name and the appropriate courtesy title. Unlike English, professional, social, and family titles always follow the name:

  Mr. Liu would be 刘先生 (Liú xiānsheng)
  Mr. Li Nan 李楠先生 (Lǐ Nán xiānsheng)
  Mrs. Liu 刘夫人 (Liú fūrén)
  Miss Liu 刘小姐 (Liú xiǎojiě)
  Ms. Liu 刘女士 (Liú nǚshì)
  Dr. Ma would be 马医生 (Mǎ yīshēng)
  Professor Xu would be 徐教授 (Xú jiàoshòu)

- Chinese people will often address people by their surname followed by their job title, for example

  叶主任 (Yè zhǔrèn) Director Ye
  林老师 (Lín lǎoshī) Teacher Lin

- Most Chinese women continue using their maiden names even after marriage, but they may indicate their marital status by using 太太 (tàitai) or 夫人 (fūrén) with their maiden name.

- 小姐 (xiǎojiě) is a polite and common form of address for a woman. An older woman can be addressed as 大姐 (dàjiě)

- If you want to address a group of people formally – for example, at a meeting – you say 女士们先生们 (nǚshìmen xiānshengmen) meaning 'Ladies and Gentlemen' (or just 女士们 ('Ladies') or 先生们 ('Gentlemen') if the group is not mixed).

- When you are not sure about someone's name or title, you should address him or her as 先生 (xiānsheng) (Sir) or 女士(nǚshì) (Madam) or 小姐 (xiǎojiě) (Miss).

▼ INTRODUCTIONS

让我把你介绍给我的朋友们。(ràng wǒ bǎ nǐ jièshào gěi wǒ de péngyoumen) *Let me introduce you to my friends.*
我想让你认识一下我的丈夫。(wǒ xiǎng ràng nǐ rènshi yīxià wǒ de zhàngfu) *I'd like you to meet my husband.*
请允许我介绍一下到场的嘉宾。(qǐng yǔnxǔ wǒ jièshào yīxià dàochǎng de jiābīn) *Please allow me to introduce the present distinguished guests.*
这是珍妮特。(zhè shì Zhēnnítè) *This is Janet.*

In response:

很高兴见到您。(hěn gāoxìng jiàndào nín) *Pleased to meet you.*

嗨，你好。(hāi, nǐ hǎo) *Hi, how are you doing?*
您好。(nín hǎo) *How do you do?*

- If you want to attract the attention of someone you do not know – for example, in the street or in a shop – you say 劳驾 (láojià).

▼ PARTING

- The most common way to say goodbye to someone is 再见 (zàijiàn). Other alternatives are 回见 (huíjiàn) and 再会 (zàihuì).

再见！(zàijiàn) *Goodbye!*
再会！(zàihuì) *Bye!*
7点见。(qīdiǎn jiàn) *See you about seven.*
晚安！(wǎn'ān) *Good night!*
明天见！(míngtiān jiàn) *See you tomorrow!*
星期一见！(xīngqīyī jiàn) *See you on Monday!*
"回见!" "好，再会" (huíjiàn – hǎo, zàihuì) *'See you later.' – 'Okay, bye.'*

▼ BUSINESS CARDS

- Business/name cards are universally used in Chinese business and will almost always be exchanged when meeting someone for the first time on business.

- Cards should be held in both hands when you are offering or receiving one. When receiving another person's card, you should take the time to look at it attentively before putting it away.

- Business cards are often printed in English on one side and Chinese on the other.

寰宇进出口有限责任公司

王长海 总经理

地址:北京市和平路15号
邮编:100082
电话:+8610 64446666
传真:+8610 64446688
E-mail: wangchanghai@huanyu.com

Huan Yu Import & Export Co. Ltd.

Wang Changhai General Manager

Address: No. 15 Heping Road, Beijing, China
Zip Code: 100082
Tel.: +8610 64446666
Fax: +8610 64446688
E-mail: wangchanghai@huanyu.com

TELEPHONE

▼ MAKING A PHONE CALL

- When Chinese people make a phone call, they ask for the person they wish to speak to by name. It is not the Chinese caller's habit to give their own name first when making or receiving a call.

- When answering the telephone the standard response upon picking up the receiver is 喂 (wèi).

- When giving telephone numbers, Chinese speakers normally read out the numbers one by one so that:

  020 7900 0283 would be read:

  零二零 七九零零 零二八三
  líng'èrlíng qījiǔlínglíng líng'èrbāsān

- When making a phone call, you might want to say:

喂？(wèi) *Hello?*
请问…在吗？(qǐngwèn...zài ma) *Could I speak to ... please?*
是…吗？(shì...ma) *Is that ...?*
我怎么拨外线电话？(wǒ zěnme bō wàixiàn diànhuà) *How do I make an outside call?*
…的区号是多少？(...de qūhào shì duōshao) *What is the code for ... ?*
我5分钟后打回来。(wǒ wǔ fēnzhōng hòu dǎ huílái) *I'll call back in 5 minutes.*
他回来时，可否让他给我回电话？(tā huílái shí, kěfǒu ràng tā gěi wǒ huí diànhuà) *Could you ask him to call me when he gets back?*
对不起，我拨错号了。(duìbuqǐ,wǒ bōcuò hào le) *Sorry, I must have dialled the wrong number.*
电话掉线了。(diànhuà diàoxiàn le) *We were cut off.*
线路很不清楚。(xiànlù hěn bù qīngchu) *This is a very bad line.*

- You might hear:

请讲。(qǐng jiǎng) *Speaking.*
请问您是哪位？(qǐngwèn nín shì nǎ wèi) *Who's speaking?*
请问您找哪位？(qǐngwèn nín zhǎo nǎ wèi) *Who would you like to speak to?*
请别挂断。(qǐng bié guàduàn) *Please hold (the line).*
没人接听。(méi rén jiētīng) *There's no reply.*
电话占线。(diànhuà zhànxiàn) *The line is engaged (Brit) or busy (US).*
请问您是哪位？(qǐngwèn nín shì nǎ wèi) *Who shall I say is calling?*
您要留言吗？(nín yào liúyán ma) *Would you like to leave a message?*

TELEPHONE

▼ AN EXAMPLE CONVERSATION

您好，这里是北京饭店。
Hello, Beijing Hotel.

请转二零一六房间分机，我找张先生。
Please could you put me through to room number 2016? I'd like to speak to Mr. Zhang.

好的，请稍等。
Hold on one moment, please.

他不在，您能帮我给他捎个话吗？
He doesn't seem to be in at the moment. Can I leave a message?

当然可以。
Of course.

请让他给约翰・史密斯回电话，电话号码是零零四四二零七三零六三八九二。
Could you ask him to call John Smith back? The phone number is 00442073063892.

好的。
Okay.

▼ USEFUL TELEPHONE VOCABULARY

打电话 (dǎ diànhuà) *make a phone call*
电话号码 (diànhuà hàomǎ) *phone number*
分机号码 (fēnjī hàomǎ) *extension number*
市话 (shìhuà) *local call*
长途电话 (chángtú diànhuà) *national call*
国际长途电话 (guójì chángtú diànhuà) *international call*

CORRESPONDENCE

▼ PERSONAL LETTERS

● Starting and ending a personal letter

Opening lines:
亲爱的妈妈: *Dear Mum*
小强: *Dear Xiao Qiang*

Closing lines:
祝身体健康! *Take care!*
祝万事如意! *All the best*

● Sample letter

> **i** Note the use of a colon after the recipient's name.

婷婷:

好久没给你写信了。近来还好吗？最近工作忙吗？你是否还在上夜校？

我工作还很忙，天天加班。但老板对我很好，晚上经常开车顺路送我回家。过两天公司放假，准备和同事一起去旅游。

先写到这儿吧，有空给你打电话。

祝
万事如意!

毛毛
2004年2月4日

> **i** The date should be written after your signature.

● Useful expressions

真高兴收到你的来信。*It was lovely to hear from you.*
对不起，没能及时给你回信，只因… *Sorry I didn't reply sooner but …*
代我向…问好。*Give my regards to …*
东东谨祝一切安好。*Dong Dong sends his best wishes.*
盼早日回信。*Looking forward to hearing from you.*

CHINESE IN ACTION

CORRESPONDENCE

▼ FORMAL LETTERS

● Starting and ending a formal letter

Opening lines:
致启者: *Dear Sir or Madam*
致有关人: *To whom it may concern*

Closing lines:
敬上 *Regards*
此致 敬礼! *Yours sincerely*

● Sample letter

长江商贸公司
山东省青岛市市南区香港中路16号 （250920）

王先生:

不胜感激您在10月14日的来信中确认收到旅游费的定金。

可否告知余款的到期日? 根据贵方提供信息，全部款项应于本月定付讫，我将尽早支付其余款项。

此致
敬礼!

苏眉莉
2003年10月5日

i Note that the closing line is split over two lines.

● Useful expressions

现答复您…的来信。*In reply to your letter of…*
有关… *With reference to…*
收到您…来信不胜感激。*Thank you for your letter of…*
我们荣幸地通知您… *We are pleased to inform you that…*
我们很遗憾地通知您… *We regret to inform you that…*
为…致信给您。*I am writing to you to…*
如需详情，尽请与我联系。*If you require any further information, please do not hesitate to contact me.*
切盼回复。*I look forward to hearing from you.*

▼ ADDRESSING AN ENVELOPE IN CHINESE

- You should start in the upper left hand corner with the addressee's post code. The address is written in the middle of the envelope, followed by the name of the addressee.

- Note that the address is written in the order:
  province, city
  street, house number
  addressee's name

- The sender's address and name, followed by their postcode, should be written in the lower right hand corner of the envelope.

- **Sample envelope**

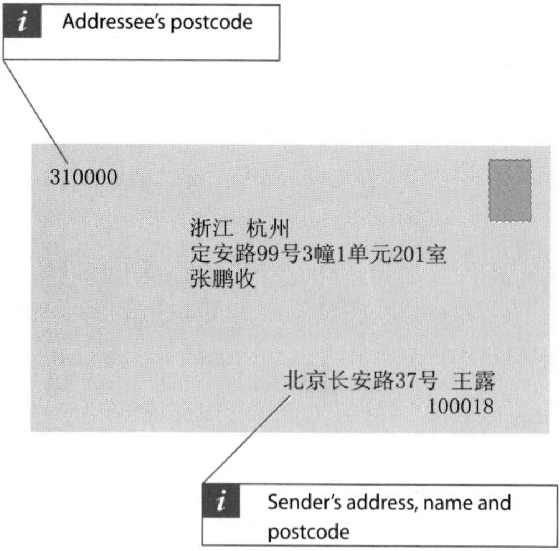

▼ E-MAIL

- E-mail is becoming very popular in China, but it is important to check that the person you are writing to actually uses it. Many Chinese executives and officials have an e-mail address but do not check their mail very regularly.

- Business e-mails should be brief but not too familiar or chatty.

Sample e-mail

回复 转发 写信 收件箱 收信

收件人: lili@cmail.com.cn

抄送:

主题: 拓展产品系列讨论会

王经理:

根据近期的市场调研，我公司的彩电产品系列目前有些滞后于市场的发展需要，为提高企业竞争力，建议召开一次讨论会，共同商讨、制定相应措施。

会议时间暂定为2004年6月2日星期三下午2:00，地点在公司二楼小会议室。请通知相关人员准时参加。

如有问题，请尽早回复。

此致

敬礼!

张 力

收件人:	To:
抄送:	Cc:
主题:	Subject:

CVS AND COVERING LETTERS

▼ APPLYING FOR A JOB

- When applying for a job in China, the general principles of covering letters, CVs and interview etiquette should be followed.

- Your CV should be no longer than three pages.

▼ SAMPLE COVERING LETTER

尊敬的人事部经理：

从2004年5月22日的《中国青年报》招聘版上获悉贵公司国际部需要一名英语专业应届毕业生。我深感自己符合招聘广告上的各项要求，特申请这一职位。

我将于2004年6月获得北京技术大学文科硕士学位，并于7月份毕业，所学专业为商务英语。我本科阶段的专业为科技英语。多年对英语的专门研究使自己具有扎实的英语基本功，顺利通过了英语专业四级和八级考试，并且在TOEFL和GRE考试中也获得了较高的分数。

在校期间，除了认真完成学业外还积极参加各种实践、实习活动。我分别在惠普（中国）公司和中国技术进出口公司进行了实习，在工作过程中学以致用，进一步提高了英语水平，锻炼了处理实际问题的能力，增强了团队配合的意识。

读研究生之前，我在青岛贸促会全职工作的一年中，参加了多次贸易谈判，并参与组织了两届大型国际贸易洽商会，工作得到了领导和同事的一致肯定。

贵公司在外贸界很有声誉，欣闻你们的招聘信息，我郑重地递交简历一份（随信附上），如蒙给予面试机会，将不胜感激。

联系地址：北京技术大学外贸英语系 （100008）
手机：13503321245

此致

敬礼!

李 明
2004年5月23日

CHINESE IN ACTION

▼ SAMPLE CV

个人简历

求职意向:	外贸公司、外企、国家机关及其他能发挥个人潜力的机构		
姓名:	李明	性别:	男
出生年月:	1979年9月1日	健康状况:	良好
毕业院校:	北京技术大学	专业:	外贸英语
电子邮件:	liming@yahoo.com.cn	联系电话:	010-87656666, 13503321245
通信地址:	北京技术大学外贸英语系		
邮编:	100008		

教育背景:

2001年9月—2004年7月 北京技术大学 外贸英语专业 文科硕士学位
1997年9月—2000年7月 北京技术大学 科技英语专业 文科学士学位

外语水平:

英语
* 基本技能: 听、说、读、写、口笔译能力
* 标准测试: 国家英语专业四、八级;TOEFL;GRE
法语
* 基本技能: 听、说、读、写、翻译能力

计算机水平:

编程、操作应用系统、网络、数据库

获奖情况:

1999年 北京市"优秀大学生"称号
1997年9月—2000年7月 一等奖学金

实践与实习:

2001年7月—2001年8月 惠普(中国)公司口、笔译工作
2003年5月—2004年5月 中国技术进出口公司

工作经历:

2000年7月—2001年8月 山东省青岛市贸易促进委员会

个性特点:

性格开朗，脚踏实地，乐于助人，善与人沟通

最喜欢的话:

有志者，事竟成

> *i* CVs often include a proverb as an expression of a salient feature of the applicant's personality.

证明人:

王成 硕士论文导师 010-68997543
田刚 山东省青岛市贸易促进委员会主任 0532-6789432

NUMBERS

▼ CARDINAL NUMBERS

0	零 (líng)
1	一 (yī)
2	二 (èr)
3	三 (sān)
4	四 (sì)
5	五 (wǔ)
6	六 (liù)
7	七 (qī)
8	八 (bā)
9	九 (jiǔ)
10	十 (shí)
11	十一 (shíyī)
12	十二 (shí'èr)
13	十三 (shísān)
14	十四 (shísì)
15	十五 (shíwǔ)
16	十六 (shíliù)
17	十七 (shíqī)
18	十八 (shíbā)
19	十九 (shíjiǔ)
20	二十 (èrshí)
21	二十一 (èrshíyī)
22	二十二 (èrshí'èr)
23	二十三 (èrshísān)
24	二十四 (èrshísì)
25	二十五 (èrshíwǔ)
30	三十 (sānshí)
31	三十一 (sānshíyī)
40	四十 (sìshí)
50	五十 (wǔshí)
60	六十 (liùshí)
70	七十 (qīshí)
80	八十 (bāshí)
90	九十 (jiǔshí)
100	一百 (yībǎi)
101	一百零一 (yībǎi líng yī)
212	二百一十二 (èrbǎi yīshí'èr)
1,000	一千 (yīqiān)
1,001	一千零一 (yīqiān líng yī)
2,500	二千五百 (èrqiān wǔbǎi)
100,000	十万 (shíwàn)
1,000,000	一百万 (yībǎi wàn)
1,000,000,000	十亿 (shíyì)

▼ ORDINAL NUMBERS

1st	第一 (dì-yī)
2nd	第二 (dì-èr)
3rd	第三 (dì-sān)
4th	第四 (dì-sì)
5th	第五 (dì-wǔ)
6th	第六 (dì-liù)
7th	第七 (dì-qī)
8th	第八 (dì-bā)
9th	第九 (dì-jiǔ)
10th	第十 (dì-shí)
15th	第十五 (dì-shíwǔ)
20th	第二十 (dì-èrshí)
50th	第五十 (dì-wǔshí)
100th	第一百 (dì-yībǎi)
101st	第一百零一 (dì-yībǎi líng yī)
110th	第一百一十 (dì yībǎi yīshí)
1,000th	第一千 (dì-yīqián)

▼ FRACTIONS AND PERCENTAGES

$\frac{1}{2}$	二分之一 (èr fēn zh īyī)
$\frac{1}{3}$	三分之一 (sān fēn zhī yī)
$\frac{1}{4}$	四分之一 (sì fēn zhī yī)
$\frac{2}{3}$	三分之二 (sān fēn zhī èr)
0.5	零点五 (líng diǎn wǔ)
3.5	三点五 (sān diǎn wǔ)
6.89	六点八九 (liù diǎn bājiǔ)
10%	百分之十 (bǎi fēn zhī shí)
100%	百分之百 (bǎi fēn zhī bǎi)